November 4–8, 2013
Berlin, Germany

Association for
Computing Machinery

Advancing Computing as a Science & Profession

CCS'13 VOL 1 of 2

The Proceedings of the 2013 ACM SIGSAC Conference on Computer and Communications Security

Sponsored by:

ACM SIGSAC

Supported by:

HGS, Army Research Office, BOSCH, SAP, NSF, Indiana University, CISCO, Intel, Google, Fraunhofer SIT, Heise Security, Microsoft Research, NXP, Kobil, Sirrix AG, Certgate, and IBM Research

Association for
Computing Machinery

Advancing Computing as a Science & Profession

The Association for Computing Machinery
2 Penn Plaza, Suite 701
New York, New York 10121-0701

ISBN: 978-1-4503-2477-9 (Digital)

ISBN: 978-1-4503-2688-9 (Print)

Additional copies may be ordered prepaid from:

ACM Order Department
PO Box 30777
New York, NY 10087-0777, USA

Phone: 1-800-342-6626 (USA and Canada)
+1-212-626-0500 (Global)
Fax: +1-212-944-1318
E-mail: acmhelp@acm.org
Hours of Operation: 8:30 am – 4:30 pm ET

Printed in the USA

CCS 2013 General Chair's Welcome

Information and communications security has become a fundamental element in our highly and globally computerized life. To tackle current and future security and privacy challenges adequately and globally, we need not only to advance research but also to bring together, from all over the world, researchers, developers and academics, as well as professionals from government agencies, research labs and corporate sectors.

The ACM Conference on Computer and Communications Security (CCS) is a leading forum, providing a highly suitable environment to conduct intellectual discussions and to exchange ideas. CCS is, in fact, the flagship annual conference of the Special Interest Group on Security, Audit and Control (SIGSAC) of the Association of Computing Machinery (ACM) and the oldest ACM conference in this field. Its reputation continues to grow and is reflected in its highly selective and prestigious technical program.

From 2002-2012, the number of paper submissions increased from about 150 to about 430. This year (2013), after more than a decade, CCS has moved to Europe/Germany. With 530 submissions we have witnessed the highest submission record in the history of CCS. Further, on the sponsorship side, CCS 2013 received over $125,000 funding support from various high-profile sources: The Army Research Office (ARO), The National Science Foundation (NSF), Bosch, Horst Görtz Stiftung (HGS), Fraunhofer SIT, SAP, Certgate, Google, Heise Security, Intel, Microsoft Research, NXP Semiconductors, IBM Research, Kobil and Sirrix AG. The Organizing Committee of CCS 2013 has put together an outstanding program that includes 105 papers (a new record), several keynote as well as invited speakers from academia, industry and government, 9 specialized pre- and post-conference workshops, 3 tutorials, 39 posters and demos, and one social event.

Given the above submission records causing an increased conference scale, organizing and setting up the program of CCS 2013 required a highly dedicated, committed and professional organizing committee, a strong technical program committee, and sponsoring decision makers who appreciate the high standards and impact of this flagship conference.

We are most grateful to the authors of the submitted papers (both to the main conference and to the workshops). We thank the technical program committee members and the program chairs as well as the external reviewers, who enabled a high quality review process. We thank the CCS 2013 Organizing Committee for selecting the workshops and tutorials on timely topics and cutting-edge technologies, and for the website design and maintenance, publications, publicity, local arrangements and registrations. Special acknowledgements go to the CCS Steering Committee, particularly to Prof. Elisa Bertino who strongly supported us with her advice. We thank the staff of the ACM for assisting us throughout the organization and publication process, the Center for Advanced Security Research Darmstadt (CASED) and the Fraunhofer SIT for providing their infrastructure and public relations. Last but not least, we would like to express our gratitude to our generous sponsors.

We wish you a pleasant stay in Berlin, a productive and highly utilized conference, and an exciting week at CCS 2013!

Ahmad-Reza Sadeghi
CCS 2013 General Chair
Technische Universität Darmstadt, Germany

CCS 2013 Program Chairs' Welcome

We are pleased to present to you the proceedings of the 2013 ACM Conference on Computer and Communications Security (CCS 2013), held in Berlin, Germany, November 4-8, 2013.

This year we received 530 submissions from 38 countries. This represents a record on at least two counts: it is both the largest number of submissions received by a computer security conference and the largest year-over-year submission increase (over 25%) to date. Remarkably, nearly half of the authors have professional affiliations in countries outside North America, with most in Europe and Asia-Pacific regions. A Program Committee comprising 82 experts from 16 countries as well as 310 external reviewers evaluated these submissions in the customary double-blind manner. At the end of the review process, 105 papers were selected for inclusion in the program, representing an acceptance rate of about 20%.

The review process was organized into three phases. After a first review phase, the authors of each paper were sent at least two preliminary reviews and were given an opportunity to respond to the comments received. During the second phase, reviews were updated as necessary, and in some cases additional reviews were solicited. At the end of the second phase, 403 papers received at least 3 reviews, 120 received 4, and 7 received 5. The third phase included discussion of papers that remained under consideration at that stage, and after intensive debate, the final acceptance decisions were made.

As is typically the case with very competitive conferences, many of the papers that could not be included in the program contained interesting ideas. Some also included new research results worth reporting to the security community. For these reasons, we encouraged the authors of these papers to consider submitting their work to the specialized workshops associated with CCS, as appropriate. Other works that could not be accepted for the program, will surely see the light of day in other leading venues after suitable improvement. We hope that all authors benefitted from the feedback received from the CCS reviewers and that the review process has helped them improve their papers.

We are very grateful to the members of the Program Committee for their hard work, professionalism, and responsiveness under very tight deadlines. On average, each individual reviewed 21 papers, and nearly a third of the members volunteered to help shepherd accepted papers towards improved presentations. Most engaged in lively discussions on both submissions and author responses, and updated their reviews to reflect valuable insights derived from those discussions. We are also indebted to the external reviewers whose focused expertise added substantial value to the feedback for authors. Moreover, we want to thank the CCS 2013 conference committee: the general chair, workshop co-chairs, tutorial co-chair, and other chairs and organizers, as well as the steering committee, for numerous discussions on how to produce an exceptional program and for their hard work on the production of these proceedings.

Lastly, we thank all authors for submitting their work to CCS 2013 and to all attendees for their participation in technical discussion and debate. We hope that you find the program stimulating and enjoyable, and that your contributions will help further computer and communication security.

Virgil Gligor
ACM CCS '13 Program Chair
Carnegie Mellon University, USA

Moti Yung
ACM CCS '13 Program Chair
Google, USA

Table of Contents

Session 3-C: Protocol Analysis & Synthesis

Keynote Talk 1

Session 4-A: Network Security

Session 4-B: Critical Infrastructures

Session 4-C: Attribute-based Encryption

Session 5-A: Programming Securely

Session 5-B: Secure Multiparty Computation

Session 5-C: Formal Methods

Session 6-A: Mobile Security Issues

Session 6-B: Randomness

Session 6-C: Hardware Security

Session 8-C: Be Aware & Beware

Keynote Talk 2

Session 9-A: Crypto Tools

Session 9-B: Audit & Code Randomization

Session 9-C: Mobile Privacy

Workshop Summaries

Tutorial Overviews

ACM CCS 2013 – Organization

General Chair:	Ahmad-Reza Sadeghi *(TU Darmstadt, CASED, Intel ICRI-SC, Germany)*
Program Chairs:	Virgil Gligor *(Carnegie Mellon University, USA)* Moti Yung *(Columbia University, USA)*
Workshop Co-Chairs:	Stefan Katzenbeisser *(TU Darmstadt, CASED, Intel ICRI-SC, Germany)* Christopher Kruegel *(University of California at Santa Barbara, USA)*
Tutorial Co-Chairs:	Thorsten Holz *(Ruhr-Universität Bochum, Germany)* Gregory Neven *(IBM Research, Zurich Research Laboratory, Switzerland)*
Poster/Demo Chairs:	Fabian Monrose *(University of North Carolina at Chapel Hill, USA)* Thomas Schneider *(TU Darmstadt, EC SPRIDE, Germany)* Carmela Troncoso *(Gradiant, Spain)*
Publicity Co-Chairs:	Thomas Gross *(University of Newcastle upon Tyne, UK)* Matthias Hollick *(TU Darmstadt, Germany)* Jun Li *(University of Oregon, USA)* Ivan Martinovic *(University of Oxford, UK)* Matthew Smith *(Leibnitz Universität Hannover, Germany)*
Event Management:	Wiebke Kronz *(TU Darmstadt, CASED, Intel ICRI-SC, Germany)* Anette Mittenhuber *(TU Darmstadt, CASED, Germany)*
Public Relations:	Oliver Küch *(Fraunhofer SIT, CASED, Germany)*
Website:	Lucas Davi *(TU Darmstadt, CASED, Intel ICRI-SC, Germany)*
Local Organization:	Stephan Heuser *(TU Darmstadt, CASED, Intel ICRI-SC, Germany)* Christian Wachsmann, *(TU Darmstadt, CASED, Intel ICRI-SC, Germany)* Christoph Busold *(TU Darmstadt, CASED, Intel ICRI-SC, Germany)* Alexandra Dmitrienko *(Fraunhofer SIT, Germany)* Sven Wohlgemuth *(TU Darmstadt, CASED, Germany)* Mihai Bucicoiu *(TU Darmstadt, CASED, Intel ICRI-SC, Germany)*
Steering Committee:	Elisa Bertino *(Purdue University, USA)* George Danezis *(Microsoft Research Cambridge, UK)* Trent Jaeger *(Pennsylvania State University, USA)* Carl Landwehr *(University of Maryland, USA)* John Mitchell *(Stanford University, USA)* Giovanni Vigna *(University of California at Santa Barbara, USA)* Marianne Winslet *(University of California at Urbana Champaign, USA)*

Program Committee: Gail-Joon Ahn *(Institute of North Carolina at Charlotte, USA)*
Bill Arbaugh *(University of Maryland, USA)*
Mikhail Atallah *(Purdue University, USA)*
Giuseppe Ateniese *(University of Rome, Italy)*
David Basin *(ETH Zurich, Swizerland)*
Lujo Bauer *(Carnegie Mellon University, USA)*
Konstantin Beznosov *(University of British Columbia, Canada)*
Matt Bishop *(University of California at Davis, USA)*
David Brumley *(Carnegie Mellon University, USA)*
Kevin Butler *(University of Oregon, USA)*
Jan Camenisch *(IBM Research, Zurich Research Laboratory, Swizerland)*
Srdjan Capkun *(ETH Zurich, Swizerland)*
Alvaro Cardenas *(University of Texas at Dallas, USA)*
Liqun Chen *(Hewlett-Packard Laboratories, UK)*
Stephen Chong *(Harvard University, USA)*
Nicolas Christin *(Carnegie Mellon University, USA)*
Veronique Cortier *(CNRS, Loria, France)*
Weidong Cui *(Microsoft Research, USA)*
Reza Curtmola *(New Jersey Institute of Technology, USA)*
Anupam Datta *(Carnegie Mellon University, USA)*
Roberto Di Pietro *(Università di Roma Tre, Italy)*
Wenliang Du *(Syracuse University,USA)*
David Evans *(University of Virginia, USA)*
Peter Gutmann *(University of Auckland, New Zealand)*
J. Alex Halderman *(University of Michigan, USA)*
Cormac Herley *(Microsoft Research, USA)*
Thorsten Holz *(Ruhr-Universität Bochum, Germany)*
Nicholas Hopper *(University of Minnesota, USA)*
Yih-Chun Hu *(University of Illinois at Urbana Champaign, USA)*
Sotiris Ioannidis *(FORTH-ICS, Greece)*
Trent Jaeger *(Pennsylvania State University, USA)*
Sushil Jajodia *(George Mason University, USA)*
Rob Johnson *(Stony Brook University, USA)*
Ari Juels *(RSA Laboratories, USA)*
Apu Kapadia *(Indiana University, USA)*
Jonathan Katz *(University of Maryland, USA)*
Stefan Katzenbeisser *(TU Darmstadt, CASED, Intel ICRI-SC, Germany)*
Angelos Keromytis *(Columbia University, USA)*
Florian Kerschbaum *(SAP Research, Germany)*
Yongdae Kim *(KAIST, Korea)*
Engin Kirda *(Northeastern University, USA)*
Farinaz Koushanfar *(Rice University, USA)*
Wenke Lee *(Georgia Institute of Technology, USA)*
Brian N. Levine *(UMass Amherst, USA)*
Yingjiu Li *(Singapore Management University, Singapore)*

Program Committee (continued):	Z. Morley Mao *(Columbia University, USA)* Jonathan McCune *(Google, USA)* Catherine Meadows *(Naval Research Laboratory, USA)* Refik Molva *(EURECOM, France)* Fabian Monrose *(University of North Carolina at Chapel Hill, USA)* Andrew Myers *(Cornell University, USA)* David Naccache *(Ecole Normale Supérieure, France)* Cristina Nita-Rotaru *(Purdue University, USA)* Alina Oprea *(RSA Security, USA)* Panos Papadimitratos (*KTH Stockholm, Sweden)* Bryan Parno *(Microsoft Research, USA)* Benny Pinkas *(Bar-Ilan University, Israel)* Mike Reiter *(University of North Carolina at Chapel Hill, USA)* Volker Roth *(Freie Universität Berlin, Germany)* Ravi Sandhu *(University of Texas at San Antonio, USA)* Vyas Sekar *(Stony Brook University, USA)* Simha Sethumadhavan *(Columbia University, USA*) Shiuhpyng Shieh *(National Chiao Tung University, Taiwan)* Clay Shields *(Georgetown University, USA)* Radu Sion *(Stony Brook University, USA)* Sean Smith *(Dartmouth College, USA)* Sal Stolfo *(Columbia University, USA)* Patrick Tague *(Carnegie Mellon University, USA)* Roberto Tamassia *(Brown University, USA)* George Theodorakopoulos *(Cardiff University, UK)* Wade Trappe *(Rutgers University, USA)* Patrick Traynor *(Georgia Institute of Technology, USA*) Carmela Troncoso *(Gradiant, Spain)* Vijay Varadharajan *(Macquarie University, Australia)* Michael Waidner *(Fraunhofer SIT, Germany)* Jesse Walker *(Intel, USA)* Bogdan Warinschi *(University of Bristol, UK)* Brent Waters *(University of Texas at Austin, USA)* Robert Watson *(Cambridge University, UK)* Nicholas Weaver *(ICSI, USA)* Dongyan Xu *(Purdue University, USA)*
Poster/Demo Program Committee:	Juan Caballero *(IMDEA Madrid, Spain)* Emiliano De Cristofaro *(PARC, USA)* William Enck *(North Carolina State University, USA)* Damon McCoy *(George Mason University, USA)* Prateek Mittal *(University of California at Berkeley, USA)* Thomas Ristenpart *(University of Wisconsin, USA)* Julie Thorpe *(University of Ontario Institute of Technology, Canada)* Ingrid Verbauwhede *(KU Leuven, Belgium)*

Additional Reviewers:

Amit Ahlawat
Massimiliano Albanese
Mohammed Almeshekah
Chaitrali Amrutkar
Elli Androulaki
Spyros Antonatos
Owen Arden
George Argyros
Aslan Askarov
Elias Athanasopoulos
Man Ho Au
Thanassis Avgerinos
Adam Aviv
Monir Azraoui
Basim Baig
Sumeet Bajaj
Ero Balsa
Davide Balzarotti
Boaz Barak
Adam Bates
Andrew Baumann
Alessandra De Benedictis
Emery Berger
David Bernhard
Sebastian Biedermann
Marina Blanton
Jeremiah Blocki
Nathaniel Boggs
Joseph Bonneau
Yazan Boshmaf
Kevin Bowers
Dan Brown
Christina Brzuska
Xiang Cai
Henry Carter
Sang Kil Cha
Rohit Chadha
Sambuddho Chakravarty
Sang-Yoon Chang
Peter Chapman
Chong-Kuan Chen
Pokai Chen
Vincent Cheval
Jerry Chiang
Michael Cheng Yi Cho
Hyunwoo Choi
Jaeyoung Choi
Kai-Min Chung
Michael Clarkson
Robert Cochran
Alessandro Colantonio
Cas Cremers
Emiliano De Cristofaro
Özgür Dagdelen
George Danezis
Mohammad Torabi Dashti
Lucas Davi
Zhui Deng
Alexandra Dmitrienko
Yevgeniy Dodis
Adam Doupe
Maria Dubovitskaya
Manuel Egele
Kaoutar Elkhiyaoui
William Enck
Robert Enderlein
Santiago Escobar
Antonio Faonio
Dario Fiore
Aurélien Francillon
Mario Frank
Sara Foresti
David Galindo
Deepak Garg
Paolo Gasti
Robert Gawlik
Xinyang Ge
John Geddes
Marco Ghiglieri
Ian Goldberg
Samantha Gottlieb
Robert Griffin
Oren Halvani
Kevin Hamlen
Kristiyan Haralambiev
Eiji Hayashi
Carmit Hazay
Nadia Heninger
Ryan Henry
Victor Heorhiadi
Michael Herrmann
Martin Hirt
Johannes Hoffmann
Owen Hofmann
Peter Honeyman
Byeongdo Hong
Hyunwook Hong
Endadul Hoque
Chia-Wei Hsu
Hongxin Hu
Yan Huang
Markus Huber
Sungjae Hwang
Qatrunnada Ismail
Malika Izabachene
Asim Jamshed
Kangkook Jee
Limin Jia
Xing Jin
Yiming Jing
Andrew Johnson
Lukas Kalabis
Seny Kamara
Nikos Karapanos
Nikolaos Karvelas
Michael Kasper
James Kelley
Vasileios P Kemerlis
Peter Kieseberg
Dongkwan Kim
Eunsoo Kim
Hongil Kim
Yu Seung Kim
Markulf Kohlweiss
Saranga Komanduri
Joonho Kong
Divyan Konidala
Georgios Kontaxis
Kari Kostiainen

Steve Kremer
Stephan Krenn
Christopher Kruegel
Marc Kuehrer
Anil KurmusChinawat Isradisaikul
Divya Kurthakoti
Cheolhyun Kwak
Minhee Kwon
Alptekin Küpçü
Tanja Lange
Adam Langley
Meixing Le
Hyojeong Lee
Youjin Lee
Anja Lehmann
Iraklis Leontiadis
Chaz Lever
Bing-Han Li
Ninghui Li
Peng Li
Shuai Li
Alana Libonati
Jed Liu
Giovanni Livraga
Andreas Lochbihler
Flavio Lombardi
Long Lu
Giuseppe Antonio Di Luna
Tongbo Luo
Tom Magrino
Ahmad Mahmoody
Ken Mai
Claudio Marforio
Matthew Maurer
Michelle Mazurek
Breno De Medeiros
Carlos Medrano
Byungho Min
Kazuhiro Minami
Bruno Conchina Montalto
Benjamin Mood
Scott Moore
Collin Mulliner
Arslan Munir
Divya Muthukumaran
Ryan Riley
Thomas Ristenpart
Shishir Nagaraja
Gregory Neven
Andrew Newell
Rishab Nithyanand
Adam O'Neill
Olga Ohrimenko
Melek Önen
Simon Oya
Omkant Pandey
Antonis Papadogiannakis
Charalampos Papamanthou
Vasilis Pappas
Ravi Pappu
Chunsung Park
Kenneth Paterson
Kenny Paterson
Sameer Patil
Arpita Patra
Mathias Payer
Marcus Peinado
Andreas Peter
Theofilos Petsios
Patrick Longa Pierola
Jérémy Planul
Joe Pletcher
Iasonas Polakis
Michalis Polychronakis
Marios Pomonis
Miodrag Potkonjak
Franz-Stefan Preiss
Pasquale Puzio
Sasa Radomirovic
Carla Rafols
Himanshu Raj
Kim Ramchen
Paul Ratazzi
Sasa Rdomirovic
Joel Reardon
Brad Reaves
Alexandre Rebert
Tazchy Reinman
Junghwan Rhee
Alfredo Rial
Ben Riva
Jean-Marc Robert
Masoud Rostami
Yves Roudier
Yannis Rouselakis
Arnab Roy
Carlos Rubio
Sandra Rueda
Malek Ben Salem
Brendan Saltaformaggio
Ralf Sasse
Guillaume Scerri
Thomas Schneider
Sebastian Schrittwieser
Max Schuchard
Steffen Schulz
Matthias Schunter
Edward Schwartz
Elaine Shi
Dongwan Shin
Hocheol Shin
Reza Shokri
Matteo Signorini
Hervais Simo
Dimitrios Simos
Arunesh Sinha
Karsten Sohr
Yingbo Song
Ebrahim Songhori
Claudio Soriente
Kyle Soska
Angelo Spognardi
Christoph Sprenger
Dannie Stanley
Emil Stefanov
Martin Stopczynski
William Sumner
Kun Sun
Yuqiong Sun
Gelareh Taban
Nirupama Talele
Rob Templeman
Stefano Tessaro
Abhradeep Guha Thakurta
Nikos Triandopoulos

Mahesh Tripunitara
Jonathan Trostle
Michael Carl Tschantz
Uday Tupakula
Mathieu Turuani
Yavgeniy Vahlis
Giorgos Vasiliadis
Amit Vasudevan
Daniele Venturi
Nino Vincenzo Verde
Giovanni Vigna
Hayawardh Vijayakumar
Antonio Villani
Sabrina De Capitani Di Vimercati
Jonathan Voris
Adam Waksman

Robert Walls
Chi-Wei Wang
Chiawei Wang
Lingyu Wang
Shumiao Wang
Yang Wang
Zhan Wang
Gaven J Watson
Lei Wei
Zachary Weinberg
Cyrille Wiedling
Peter Williams
Maverick Woo
Eric Wustrow
Qiang Yan
Dejun Yang

York Yannikos
Ting-Fang Yen
Yung Yi
Jun Yuan
Angeliki Zavou
Danfeng Zhang
Yinqian Zhang
Yizhou Zhang
Zhi-Kai Zhang
Hang Zhao
Ziming Zhao
Lan Zhou
Zhibin Zhou
Sebastian Zimmeck

CCS 2013 Sponsor & Supporters

Sponsor:

acm SIGSAC

Supporters:

HGS Horst Görtz Stiftung

Army Research Office

BOSCH Technik fürs Leben

SAP®

National Science Foundation

School of Informatics and Computing, Indiana University Bloomington

cisco™

intel®

Google™

Fraunhofer SIT

Supporters (continued):

A Security Framework for the Analysis and Design of Software Attestation

Frederik Armknecht
Universität Mannheim, Germany
armknecht@uni-mannheim.de

Ahmad-Reza Sadeghi
Technische Universität Darmstadt (CASED), Germany
ahmad.sadeghi@cased.de

Steffen Schulz*
Intel Corporation
steffen.schulz@intel.com

Christian Wachsmann
Intel CRI-SC at TU Darmstadt, Germany
christian.wachsmann@cased.de

ABSTRACT

Software attestation has become a popular and challenging research topic at many established security conferences with an expected strong impact in practice. It aims at verifying the software integrity of (typically) resource-constrained embedded devices. However, for practical reasons, software attestation cannot rely on stored cryptographic secrets or dedicated trusted hardware. Instead, it exploits side-channel information, such as the time that the underlying device needs for a specific computation. As traditional cryptographic solutions and arguments are not applicable, novel approaches for the design and analysis are necessary. This is certainly one of the main reasons why the security goals, properties and underlying assumptions of existing software attestation schemes have been only vaguely discussed so far, limiting the confidence in their security claims. Thus, putting software attestation on a solid ground and having a founded approach for designing secure software attestation schemes is still an important open problem.

We provide the first steps towards closing this gap. Our first contribution is a security framework that formally captures security goals, attacker models and various system and design parameters. Moreover, we present a generic software attestation scheme that covers most existing schemes in the literature. Finally, we analyze its security within our framework, yielding sufficient conditions for provably secure software attestation schemes. We expect that such a consolidating work allows for a meaningful security analysis of existing schemes, supports the design of secure software attestation schemes and will inspire new research in this area.

*At the time of writing this author was affiliated with Ruhr-University Bochum, Germany, Macquarie University, Australia as well as the Intel Collaborative Research Institute for Secure Computing at TU Darmstadt, Germany.

CCS'13, November 4–8, 2013, Berlin, Germany.

ACM 978-1-4503-2477-9/13/11 ...$15.00.
http://dx.doi.org/10.1145/2508859.2516650.

Categories and Subject Descriptors

D.4.6 [**Operating Systems**]: Security and Protection

Keywords

software attestation; security framework; keyless crypto

1. INTRODUCTION

Embedded systems are increasingly permeating our information society, being more and more used also in security- and safety-critical applications. This generates an increasing need for enabling technologies that can validate and verify the integrity of a system's software state against malicious code. In this context, *software attestation* has become a popular research topic at many established security conferences with a large body of literature [15, 24, 26, 11, 23, 25, 22, 9, 21, 20, 3, 10, 14, 17, 19, 16, 29].

Software attestation is a trust establishment mechanism that allows a system, the *verifier*, to check the integrity of the program memory content of another system, the *prover*, against modification, e.g., by malicious code. As it mainly targets resource-constrained embedded systems (such as Atmel tinyAVR [2] microcontrollers), software attestation aims to work without any security hardware at the prover. Software attestation deploys the common approach of challenge-response protocols, where the verifier challenges the prover with respect to the expected memory content. However, cryptographic challenge-response protocols typically rely on secret values that should be unknown to malicious provers. This cannot be assumed for software attestation, where the provers are resource-constrained embedded systems that typically cannot afford secure hardware (such as a TPM) [28, 18, 27, 5, 16]. Hence, the adversary may get full control of the prover and its cryptographic secrets, rendering classical cryptographic primitives and protocols useless, a fact that demands for keyless security solutions.

Therefore software attestation follows a radically different approach than most conventional security mechanisms: It exploits the intrinsic physical constraints of the underlying hardware and side-channel information, typically the *computation time* required by the prover to complete the attestation protocol. More detailed, software attestation schemes are typically designed to temporarily utilize all the computing and memory resources of the prover, aiming at ensuring that the prover can only give the correct responses *in time* if the memory state is genuine. Of course this requires that the verifier can authenticate the device characteristics of the prover using an out-of-band channel, such as visual authentication, which clearly distinguishes software attestation from other approaches like remote attestation.

Without question, this requires completely different forms of security reasoning and likewise demands for other security assumptions on the underlying core functionalities and system properties, representing a highly challenging task. This may be the main reason that, despite its popularity and practical relevance, software attestation has not received any formal treatment yet but is still subject to ambiguities. To start with, there exist no common adversary model and no precise formalization of the security goals so far, hindering a founded security analysis and making it difficult or even impossible to compare existing schemes.

Likewise the underlying security properties and assumptions have been only vaguely discussed, limiting the confidence in the security claims. In fact, current proposals often combine weak PRNGs and ad-hoc checksum function designs with unclear and possibly insufficient security properties. As a result, checksum collisions have been exploited directly to hide code modifications [24] and indirectly to manipulate the location of the measured code in the memory (memory copy attack [3]). Some works even propose to simply XOR consecutive memory blocks [32], leading to obvious collision attacks that were only indirectly considered in subsequent work [1]. Likewise, although several works consider the problem of free memory, i.e., unused sections of the memory, code compression attacks [3] have been ignored in recent works [17, 31] and considered as impractical [16] without giving any arguments.

Contribution.

In this paper, we make a first step towards putting software attestation on a solid ground. Our contributions are:

Security framework: We describe the first formal security framework for software attestation. This includes an adversary model that, interestingly, fundamentally deviates from classical cryptographic adversary models. Typically, the adversary is modelled by a *polynomially bounded* algorithm that aims to achieve a certain goal *without having certain knowledge* (e.g., cryptographic keys). In contrast, an adversary against a software attestation scheme can be *unbounded* in principle and has *complete knowledge* of the prover device configuration and state. However, during the attack it has to specify (or program) a malicious prover device with tight resource constraints. The goal is that this malicious prover can cheat in the attestation protocol within the *strict time bound* with *reasonable success probability* but *without* any interaction with the adversary. In other words, the adversary has unbound resources for *preparing* the attack but only a tight time-bound and limited computational and memory resources for *executing* the attack. Moreover we provide precise definitions for the security and the correctness of software attestation schemes and propose a formal system model that aims to balance between expressiveness and applicability. This allows a founded and comparable treatment of current and coming schemes and should help to avoid ambiguities in the future.

Generic software attestation scheme: We present a *generic* software attestation scheme that covers most existing software attestation protocols in the literature. Moreover, we identify and formalize several system parameters of software attestation and provide an upper bound of the success probability of a malicious prover against the generic scheme as a function of these parameters. The derived upper bound of the success probability implies *sufficient* conditions on the system parameters. Although some of these aspects have been implicitly assumed and informally discussed in the literature, we present their first formal treatment. Moreover, our approach provides new insights on how these parameters impact the security of the underlying software attestation scheme, which has never been analyzed before. This result allows to argue on the security of software attestation schemes by mapping the generic scheme and properties to the concrete scheme and by examining whether the properties are fulfilled. Moreover the generic scheme may serve as a blueprint for future schemes.

Argumentation techniques: The security treatment of the generic scheme required to use novel types of arguments. Since the common cryptographic proof technique of reducing the security of the scheme to a hard problem is not possible anymore, we had to argue *directly* that any attack strategy that is possible within the given time-bound fails with a certain probability. We conjecture that our approach may be of independent interest. For example, we expect that the security of concrete schemes that are not directly covered by the generic scheme may be argued using similar techniques.

New insights: Furthermore, our investigations yield new insights with respect to the cryptographic properties of the underlying primitives. Our work shows that cryptographic primitives can be used that are similar to established primitives, such as pseudo-random number generators or hash functions, but that differ in subtleties: Some cryptographic assumptions can be relaxed while others need to be strengthened. Such observations are relevant with respect to concrete realizations of secure software attestation schemes.

We see our work as a first step paving the way for a founded treatment of secure software attestation schemes. We expect that such a consolidating work allows for a meaningful security analysis of existing schemes and supports the design of arguably secure software attestation schemes and will inspire new research in this area.

Outline.

We give an overview of the related work in Section 2 and introduce our system model in Section 3. We present the formal framework for software attestation in Section 4, describe the generic software attestation scheme and its requirements in Section 5 and formally analyze its security in Section 6. Finally, we discuss our results and conclude in Section 7.

2. RELATED WORK

The existing literature on software attestation focuses on the design of checksum functions for different platform architectures and countering platform-specific attacks [24, 23, 9, 22, 17]. Several works consider the strengthening of checksum algorithms and their implementations against unintended modifications by either limiting the memory available to the prover during attestation [10, 29] or by using self-modifying and/or obfuscated attestation algorithms [25, 11]. Many works investigate the suitability and extension of software attestation to a variety of computing platforms, including sensors, peripherals and voting machines [21, 17, 9, 23, 16]. Furthermore, software attestation has been proposed as a key establishment mechanism [21].

Software attestation is different from *remote attestation* which has the goal to verify the integrity of remote provers, e.g., over a network. Specifically, remote attestation usually relies on secrets shared between the verifier and the honest prover, which is fundamentally different from software attestation that cannot rely on cryptographic secrets and instead typically assumes that the verifier can authenticate the prover using an out-of-band channel, such as visual authentication. Several works consider how to combine software attestation with hardware trust anchors such as TPMs and SIM-cards [20, 16, 14] or intrinsic hardware characteristics such as code execution side-effects [15, 24, 26] and Physically Unclonable Functions [19]. Interestingly, most proposed implementations employ hash functions and PRNGs that are not cryptographically secure. Further, works that use cryptographically secure algorithms do not consider whether these algorithms maintain their security properties in the "keyless" software attestation scenario where the underlying secrets, such as the PRNG states, are known to the adversary. This is the reason why existing analysis papers on remote attestation, such as [4, 8], cannot be applied to software-based attestation, as they assume trusted hardware or software components. In this respect, our formal analysis provides a fundamental first step towards a deeper and more comprehensive understanding of software attestation.

An approach [13, 12] related to software attestation uses *Quines*. The basic idea is that the device outputs the whole content of its memory such that the verifier can compare it to the expected memory content. In contrast, software attestation aims to use short outputs only for practical reasons. In that sense, both approaches can be seen as special instantiations of proof-of-knowledge schemes where the proof either includes the knowledge itself (Quines) or responses depending on the knowledge (software attestation). A further difference is that, to reduce the impact of network jitter, software attestation typically minimizes the interaction between the prover and the verifier. In contrast the Quine-schemes in [13, 12] require significant interaction between the verifier and the device.

Similar to software attestation protocols, *proofs of work* schemes challenge the prover with computationally expensive or memory-bound tasks [6, 7]. However, while the goal of these schemes is to mitigate denial-of-service attacks and Spam by imposing artificial load on the service requester, the goal of software attestation schemes is using all of the prover's resources to prevent it from executing malicious code within a certain time frame. Hence, proofs of work are in general not suitable for software attestation since they are usually less efficient and not designed to achieve the optimality requirements of software attestation algorithms.

3. PRELIMINARIES

Notation. Let X, Y be two sets and $x \in X$ and $y \in Y$ be an element of each set. We denote with $f : X \to Y$ a function f that maps the set X to set Y. Further $f : x \mapsto y$ means that function f maps an element x to an element y. Let A and B be arbitrary algorithms. Then $y \leftarrow \mathsf{A}(x)$ means that on input x, A assigns its output to y. The expression A^{B} means that A has black-box access to B. We denote with $\mathsf{A}^{\hat{\mathsf{B}}}$ an algorithm A that does *not* access an algorithm B. Let $\mathbb{D}$ be a probability distribution over the set X, then the term $x \overset{\mathbb{D}}{\leftarrow} X$ means the event of assigning an element of X to variable x that has been chosen according to $\mathbb{D}$. Further, we define $\mathbb{D}(x) := \Pr\left[x | x \overset{\mathbb{D}}{\leftarrow} X\right]$ for each $x \in X$ and denote with $\mathbb{U}$ the uniform distribution.

System Model. Software attestation is a protocol between a verifier $\mathcal{V}$ and a (potentially malicious) prover $\mathcal{P}$ where the latter belongs to a class of devices with clearly specified characteristics. That is, whenever we speak about a prover $\mathcal{P}$, we refer to a device that belongs to this class. Typically a prover $\mathcal{P}$ is a low-end embedded system that consists of memory and a computing engine (CE). The memory is composed of *primary memory* (PM), such as CPU registers and cache, and *secondary memory* (SM), such as RAM and Flash memory. We assume that the memory is divided into *memory words* and denote by $\Sigma := \{0,1\}^{l_s}$ the set of all possible memory words (e.g., $l_s = 8$ if words are bytes). Let $\mathfrak{s}$ and $\mathfrak{p}$ be the number of memory words that can be stored in SM and PM, respectively. An important notion is the state of a prover:

Definition 1 (State). *Let $\mathcal{P}$ be a prover, i.e., a device that belongs to the specified class of devices. The* state $\mathsf{State}(\mathcal{P}) = S$ *of $\mathcal{P}$ are the memory words stored in the secondary memory (SM) of $\mathcal{P}$.*

Note that S includes the program code of $\mathcal{P}$ and hence specifies the algorithms executed by $\mathcal{P}$.

The computing engine (CE) comprises an arithmetics and logic unit that can perform computations on the data in primary memory (PM) and alter the program flow. For performance reasons, PM is typically fast but also expensive. Hence, the size of PM is usually much smaller than the size of SM. To make use of SM, CE includes the Read instruction to transfer data from SM to PM and the Write instruction to write data from PM to SM. More precisely, $\mathsf{Read}(S, a, b)$ takes as input a memory address a of SM and a memory address b of PM and copies the data word x stored at address a in SM to the data word at address b in PM. For convenience, we write $\mathsf{Read}(S, a)$ instead of $\mathsf{Read}(S, a, b)$ whenever the address b of PM is not relevant. Note that $\mathsf{Read}(S, a, b)$ overwrites the content y of PM at address b. Hence, in case y should not be lost, it must be first copied to SM using Write or copied to another location in PM before Read is performed. It is important to stress that, whenever CE should perform some computation on some value x stored in SM, it is mandatory that x is copied to PM before CE can perform the computation. Further, since SM is typically much slower than PM, Read and Write incur a certain time overhead and delay computations on x. We denote the time required by CE to perform some instruction or algorithm Ins with $\mathsf{Time}(\mathsf{Ins})$. Note that we only consider provers as described above while the verifier $\mathcal{V}$ can be an arbitrary computing platform that may interact with $\mathcal{P}$.

Remark 1: Platform Architecture. Note that we focus on embedded microcontrollers since these are commonly targeted by software attestation. We explicitly exclude provers that are high-end computing platforms with multiple CPUs and/or Direct Memory Access (DMA) since these are typically equipped with secure hardware (such as TPMs) and hence could support common cryptographic solutions based on secrets. Further, their memory architectures are usually more complex than in our system model. In particular, such platforms usually feature additional hardware to predict and fetch memory blocks in advance, making the time-bounded approach much more difficult and its realization highly dependent on the concrete system.

4. SECURE SOFTWARE ATTESTATION

Secure software attestation enables the verifier $\mathcal{V}$ to gain assurance that the state of a prover $\mathcal{P}$ is equal to a particular state S. If this is the case, we say that $\mathcal{P}$ is in state S, i.e., formally $\mathsf{State}(\mathcal{P}) = S$. Consequently, a prover $\mathcal{P}$ is called *honest* (with respect to some state S) if $\mathsf{State}(\mathcal{P}) = S$, otherwise it is considered to be *malicious*.

Remark 2: Distance between Honest and Malicious Prover State. Observe that a prover $\widetilde{\mathcal{P}}$ is already considered to be malicious even if its state differs by only one state entry (memory word) from S. This is a necessary consequence of the goal of having a definition of honest and malicious provers that is as generic as possible.

The common approach of software attestation is to validate the prover's state by requesting N random samples of the prover memory content. Hence, the Hamming distance λ between the state S of an honest prover and the state $\widetilde{S}$ of a malicious prover $\widetilde{\mathcal{P}}$ directly affects a malicious prover's success probability. As far as we know, we are the first to formally take into account the impact of λ on the security of software attestation schemes (cf. λ in Theorem 1).

Ideal Approach. Ideally, $\mathcal{V}$ could disable the computing engine (CE) of $\mathcal{P}$ and directly read and verify the state S stored in the secondary memory (SM) of $\mathcal{P}$. However, exposing CE and SM of $\mathcal{P}$ to $\mathcal{V}$ in such a way requires hardware extensions[1] on $\mathcal{P}$, which contradicts the goal of software attestation to work with no hardware modifications.

Practical Approach. As the ideal approach is not feasible in practice, the common approach in the literature is that $\mathcal{V}$ and $\mathcal{P}$ engage in a *challenge-response protocol* Attest where $\mathcal{P}$ must answer to a challenge of $\mathcal{V}$ with a response that depends on S. In the following, whenever we refer to a software attestation scheme we actually mean the corresponding challenge-response protocol Attest. Observe that Attest needs to include a description of the algorithm that processes the verifier's challenge and computes the prover's response.

In general, software attestation aims to figure out whether the original state S of a device has been replaced by the adversary with a malicious state $\widetilde{S} \neq S$. Observe that although $\widetilde{S}$ is different from S, we cannot exclude that $\widetilde{S}$ may depend on S. This implies an important difference to common cryptographic scenarios: Software attestation cannot rely on any secrets since the adversary has access to the same information as the honest prover $\mathcal{P}$. Therefore software attestation follows a fundamentally different approach and leverages side-channel information, typically the time δ the prover takes to compute the response. A basic requirement of this approach is that S specifies a practically optimal implementation of the algorithm that processes the challenge according to Attest. This means that it should be hard to find any other implementation of this algorithm that can be executed by a prover $\mathcal{P}$ in significantly less time than δ. Otherwise, a malicious prover could use a faster implementation and exploit the time difference to perform additional computations, e.g., to lie about its state.

Furthermore, the communication time jitter between $\mathcal{V}$ and $\mathcal{P}$ is typically much higher than the time needed by the computing engine of $\mathcal{P}$ to perform a few instructions. Hence, to ensure that $\mathcal{V}$ can measure also slight changes to the prover's code (that could be exploited by a malicious prover to lie about its state), $\mathcal{V}$ needs to amplify the effect of such changes. The most promising approach to realize this in practice is designing the attestation protocol as an iterative algorithm with a large number of rounds.

Further, since showing the optimality of complex implementations is a hard problem and since $\mathcal{P}$ must compute the response in a reasonable amount of time, it is paramount that the individual rounds are simple and efficient. As a result, cryptographically secure hash functions and complex Pseudo-Random Number Generators (PRNGs) are not a viable option. Hence, several previous works deployed lightweight ad-hoc designs of compression functions and PRNGs, however, without analyzing the underlying requirements on these components and their interaction. In contrast, we identify concrete sufficient requirements.

Adversary Model and Security Definition.

In the following, we provide the first formal specification of the adversary model and the security of a software attestation scheme Attest based on a security experiment $\mathbf{Exp}^{\mathcal{A}}_{\mathsf{Attest}}$ that involves an adversary $\mathcal{A}$. The experiment is divided into two phases and works as follows:

Preparation Phase: At the beginning, the adversary $\mathcal{A}$ receives as input a state S and a time-bound δ. It outputs a (possibly) malicious prover $\widetilde{\mathcal{P}}$ by specifying its state $\widetilde{S}$, i.e., $\mathsf{State}(\widetilde{\mathcal{P}}) = \widetilde{S}$.

Execution Phase: The prover $\widetilde{\mathcal{P}}$ specified in the previous phase receives a challenge c and returns a "guess" $\widetilde{r}$ for the correct response r.

The result of the experiment is ACCEPT if $\widetilde{\mathcal{P}}$ responded within time δ and $\widetilde{r} = r$, and REJECT otherwise.

Based on this experiment we define *correctness* and *soundness*. Correctness is defined analogously to the common meaning of correctness of challenge-response protocols: In case $\mathsf{State}(\widetilde{\mathcal{P}}) = S$, that is $\widetilde{\mathcal{P}}$ is in the state expected by $\mathcal{V}$, the prover $\widetilde{\mathcal{P}}$ should always succeed, i.e., the result of the experiment should always be ACCEPT. Soundness means that in case $\mathsf{State}(\widetilde{\mathcal{P}}) \neq S$, the probability that the result of the experiment is ACCEPT should be below a certain threshold.

Definition 2 (Correctness and Soundness). *Consider a software attestation scheme* Attest *and a state* S*. For a given adversary* $\mathcal{A}$ *we denote by* `EqualState` *the event that the output of* $\mathcal{A}$ *during the experiment is a prover* $\widetilde{\mathcal{P}}$ *with* $\mathsf{State}(\widetilde{\mathcal{P}}) = S$.

[1] Note that existing testing interfaces such as JTAG cannot be used since they are typically disabled on consumer devices to prevent damage to the device and unintended reverse-engineering.

The software attestation scheme Attest *is* correct *if for all adversaries $\mathcal{A}$ it holds that*

$$\Pr\left[\mathbf{Exp}^{\mathcal{A}}_{\mathsf{Attest}}(S) = \text{ACCEPT}|\mathtt{EqualState}\right] = 1.$$

Attest *is* ε-secure *if for all adversaries $\mathcal{A}$ it holds that*

$$\Pr\left[\mathbf{Exp}^{\mathcal{A}}_{\mathsf{Attest}}(S) = \text{ACCEPT}|\neg\mathtt{EqualState}\right] \leq \varepsilon.$$

Remark 3: Power of $\mathcal{A}$. The security of software attention significantly differs from common cryptographic models, where the time effort of the adversary is typically bounded (often polynomially bounded in some security parameter). More detailed, in the preparation phase, $\mathcal{A}$ can be any *unrestricted* probabilistic algorithm. However, $\mathcal{A}$ has no influence anymore once Attest is executed between $\widetilde{\mathcal{P}}$ and $\mathcal{V}$ in the execution phase. As $\widetilde{\mathcal{P}}$ is a device with the same characteristics as an honest prover, $\widetilde{\mathcal{P}}$ has to comply to the same restrictions as $\mathcal{P}$. In other words, the adversary has unbounded resources for *preparing* the attack but only a tight time-bound and limited resources for *executing* the attack.

Observe that this reflects the strongest possible adversary model, which in principle could be relaxed by imposing bounds during the preparation phase.

Remark 4: Difference to Remote Attestation. The goal of *remote attestation* is to verify the integrity of remote provers, e.g., over a network. In particular, in practice a verifier $\mathcal{V}$ usually cannot exclude that a malicous prover may have more computational power than the honest prover. Therefore, remote attestation schemes usually rely on secrets shared between the verifier and the honest prover.

This is fundamentally different from software attestation which cannot rely on cryptographic secrets to authenticate the prover device to $\mathcal{V}$. Hence, as already elaborated, existing works on software attestation typically assume that $\mathcal{V}$ can authenticate the prover hardware using an out-of-band channel, such as visual authentication.

5. GENERIC SOFTWARE ATTESTATION

In this section, we formalize a generic software attestation scheme that captures most existing schemes in the literature. In particular, we formally define several aspects and assumptions, most of them being only informally discussed or implicitly defined so far.

5.1 Protocol Specification

The main components of our generic attestation scheme (cf. Figure 1) are two deterministic algorithms:

- Memory address generator:
  $\mathsf{Gen}: \{0,1\}^{l_g} \to \{0,1\}^{l_g} \times \{0,1\}^{l_a}$, $g \mapsto (g', a')$
- Compression function:
  $\mathsf{Chk}: \{0,1\}^{l_r} \times \Sigma \to \{0,1\}^{l_r}$, $(r,s) \mapsto r'$

Here l_g, l_a and l_r are the bit length of the state g of Gen, the memory addresses a and the attestation response r', respectively, and Σ is the set of possible state entries (memory words). Both algorithms are iteratively applied within the scheme over $N \in \mathbb{N}$ rounds. For the sake of readability, we provide an iterative definition of Chk^N: For some $r_0 \in \{0,1\}^{l_r}$ and $\vec{s} := (s_1, \ldots, s_N)$, we define $r_N \leftarrow \mathsf{Chk}^N(c, \vec{s})$ as $r_i := \mathsf{Chk}(r_{i-1}, s_i)$ for $i = 1, \ldots, N$.

Prover $\mathcal{P}$		**Verifier $\mathcal{V}$**
S		S
		$(g_0, r_0) \xleftarrow{\mathbb{U}} \{0,1\}^{l_g+l_r}$
	$\xleftarrow{g_0, r_0}$	Store current time t
$r'_0 \leftarrow r_0$		
for $i = 1, \ldots, N$ **do**		**for** $i = 1, \ldots, N$ **do**
$(g_i, a_i) \leftarrow \mathtt{Gen}(g_{i-1})$		$(g_i, a_i) \leftarrow \mathtt{Gen}(g_{i-1})$
$s_i \leftarrow \mathtt{Read}(S, a_i)$		$s_i \leftarrow \mathtt{Read}(S, a_i)$
$r'_i \leftarrow \mathtt{CHK}(r_{i-1}, s_i)$		$r_i \leftarrow \mathtt{CHK}(r_{i-1}, s_i)$
endfor		**endfor**
	$\xrightarrow{r'_N}$	Store current time t'
		Accept iff $r'_N = r_N \wedge t' - t \leq \delta$

Figure 1: The Generic Attestation Scheme Attest

The protocol works as follows: The verifier $\mathcal{V}$ sends a random attestation challenge (g_0, r_0) to the prover $\mathcal{P}$, which is used as seed for Gen and Chk. Specifically, $\mathcal{P}$ iteratively generates a sequence of memory addresses $(a_1, \ldots, a_N)$ based on g_0 using Gen. For each $i \in \{1, \ldots, N\}$, $\mathcal{P}$ reads the state entry $s_i = \mathsf{Read}(S, a_i)$ at address a_i and iteratively computes $r'_i = \mathsf{Chk}(r'_{i-1}, s_i)$ using $r'_0 = r_0$. Finally, $\mathcal{P}$ sends r'_N to $\mathcal{V}$, which executes exactly the same computations[2] as $\mathcal{P}$ using the state S and compares the final result with the response r'_N from $\mathcal{P}$. Eventually, $\mathcal{V}$ accepts iff $r'_N = r_N$ and $\mathcal{P}$ responded in time $\leq \delta := N(\delta_{\mathsf{Gen}} + \delta_{\mathsf{Read}} + \delta_{\mathsf{Chk}})$, where δ_{Gen}, δ_{Read} and δ_{Chk} are upper time-bounds for running Gen, Read and Chk, respectively, on a genuine and honest prover.

In practice the delay for submitting and receiving messages needs to be considered. The common approach is to choose N, the number of rounds, big enough such that this delay is small compared to the runtime of the protocol. For simplicity, we assume that this is the case in the following and hence ignore the time for sending messages.

Remark 5: Correctness. Observe that an honest prover $\mathcal{P}$ always makes an honest verifier $\mathcal{V}$ accept since both perform exactly the same computations on the same inputs and the honest prover by assumption requires at most time δ.

Remark 6: Generality of the Protocol. Note that the basic concept of our generic scheme and several instantiations of this concept for specific platforms can be found in the literature on software attestation (cf. Section 2). However, we aim at abstracting from the particularities of individual platforms and instead design and analyze a construction that is as generic as possible. Further, some existing software attestation schemes also use the memory addresses a_i and/or the index i as input to the checksum function Chk. However, since there is a clear dependence between the index i, the memory address a_i and the memory block $s_i = \mathsf{Read}(S, a_i)$ and since the use of simple components is a primary goal of software attestation, we restrict to the case where only the memory blocks are used as input to the checksum function.

5.2 Design Criteria and Properties

Next, we discuss the design criteria of the underlying algorithms and formally define their properties required later in the security analysis. Note that, although some of these

[2]Note that the verifier could also compute the expected result before, after or in parallel to the protocol.

properties have been informally discussed or implicitly made in prior work, they have never been formally specified and analyzed before.

5.2.1 Implementation of the Core Functionalities

The generic protocol deploys three core functionalities: Read, Gen and Chk, which of the execution time is of paramount importance for the security of software attestation. Hence, we make the following assumptions that are strongly dependent on the concrete implementation and prover hardware and are hard to cover in a generic formal framework:

1. **Optimality:** There is no implementation of Read, Gen and Chk (or their combination) that is more efficient (with respect to time and/or memory) than the implementation used by the honest prover in state S.
2. **Atomicity:** It is not possible to execute Read, Gen and Chk only partially, e.g., by omitting some of the underlying instructions.

We formally cover these assumptions by modelling Read, Gen and Chk as oracles. That is, whenever $\mathcal{P}$ wants, e.g., to execute $\mathsf{Read}(\mathsf{State}(\mathcal{P}), a)$, $\mathcal{P}$ sends a to the Read-oracle and receives the corresponding result s. While sending and receiving messages between $\mathcal{P}$ and the oracles are modelled to take no time, the *determination* of the response does. More precisely when $\mathcal{P}$ invokes one of these oracles, it takes a certain amount of time before $\mathcal{P}$ gets the result. Within this time period $\mathcal{P}$ is inactive and cannot perform any computations. We denote the response time of the Read, Gen and Chk-oracle by δ_{Read}, δ_{Gen} and δ_{Chk}, respectively. Moreover the inputs to and the outputs of the oracles need to be stored in the primary memory of $\mathcal{P}$.

Remark 7: Order of Computations. A consequence of this modelling approach is that a malicious prover $\widetilde{\mathcal{P}}$ can compute the outputs of Gen and Chk only in the correct order. For instance, before $\widetilde{\mathcal{P}}$ can determine s_i it must first determine s_{i-1}. Given that concrete instantiations of the generic scheme are iteratively executed, the limited size of the primary memory (PM) (see below) and the fact that accessing the secondary memory requires significantly more time than accessing PM, we consider this assumption to be reasonable for most practical instantiations.

5.2.2 System-Level Properties

The size and utilization of the primary memory (PM) plays a fundamental role for assessing the optimality of a software attestation scheme with regard to the resources used by a prover $\widetilde{\mathcal{P}}$. Therefore, a common assumption is that PM is just big enough to honestly execute Attest, i.e., there is no free PM that could be used otherwise.[3]

Another crucial assumption of any software attestation scheme not explicitly made in most previous works is that the state S should not be compressible into PM. For instance, consider the extreme case where all entries of S contain the same value s. In this case a malicious prover $\widetilde{\mathcal{P}}$ could easily determine the correct attestation response by simply storing s in PM while having a different state $\mathsf{State}(\widetilde{\mathcal{P}}) \neq S$. Hence, we require that $\widetilde{\mathcal{P}}$ should not be able to determine a randomly selected state entry s_i of S without accessing the secondary memory with better probability than guessing:

Definition 3 (State Incompressibility). *For a state S, let $\mathbb{D}_S$ denote the probability distribution of S in the following sense: For any state entry $x \in \Sigma$ it holds that*

$$\mathbb{D}_S(x) := \Pr\left[x = s | a \xleftarrow{U} \{0,1\}^{l_a} \wedge s := \mathsf{Read}(S, a)\right].$$

S is called incompressible *if for any algorithm $\mathsf{Alg}^{\widehat{\mathsf{Read}}}$ that can be executed by the prover $\mathcal{P}$ and that does not invoke* Read, *it holds that*

$$\Pr\left[\widetilde{s} = s | a \xleftarrow{U} \{0,1\}^{l_a} \wedge s = \mathsf{Read}(S, a) \wedge \widetilde{s} \leftarrow \mathsf{Alg}^{\widehat{\mathsf{Read}}}(a) \wedge \mathsf{Time}_{\mathcal{P}}(\mathsf{Alg}^{\widehat{\mathsf{Read}}}) \leq \delta_{\mathsf{Read}}\right] \leq \gamma = \max_{x \in \Sigma} \mathbb{D}_S(x).$$

5.2.3 Cryptographic Properties

Although it is quite obvious that the security of the software attestation scheme depends on the cryptographic properties of Gen and Chk, these requirements have not been systematically analyzed and formally specified before. While it would be straightforward to model these functions as pseudo-random number generators (PRNGs) and hash functions (or even random oracles), respectively, there are some subtle differences to the common cryptographic scenario which must be carefully considered. As we elaborate below, Gen needs to meet a property which is *stronger* than the common security definition of cryptographic PRNGs while for Chk a significantly *weaker* condition than the classical security properties of hash functions is sufficient.

Pseudo-Randomness of the Outputs of Gen. To prevent a malicious prover $\widetilde{\mathcal{P}}$ from using pre-computed attestation responses, the memory addresses a_i generated by Gen should be "sufficiently random". Ideally, all combinations should be possible for $(a_1, \ldots, a_N)$. While this is impossible from an information-theoretic point of view, the best one may ask for is that the memory addresses a_i generated by Gen should be computationally indistinguishable from uniformly random values within a certain time-bound t:

Definition 4 (Time-Bounded Pseudo-Randomness of Gen). $\mathsf{Gen} : \{0,1\}^{l_g} \to \{0,1\}^{l_g + l_a}$ *is called (t, ϱ)-*pseudo-random *if for any algorithm* Alg *that can be executed by $\mathcal{P}$ in $\mathsf{Time}(\mathsf{Alg}) \leq t$ it holds that*

$$\Big| \Pr\left[b = 1 | g_0 \xleftarrow{U} \{0,1\}^{l_g} \wedge (g_i, a_i) \leftarrow \mathsf{Gen}(g_{i-1}) : i \in \{1, \ldots, N\} \wedge b \leftarrow \mathsf{Alg}(a_1, \ldots, a_N)\right] - \Pr\left[b = 1 | a_i \xleftarrow{U} \{0,1\}^{l_a} : i \in \{1, \ldots, N\} \wedge b \leftarrow \mathsf{Alg}(a_1, \ldots, a_N)\right] \Big| \leq \varrho.$$

Observe that this definition requires that Alg does not know the seed g_0 of Gen, which is *not* given in the generic software attestation scheme. In principle nothing prevents a malicious prover $\widetilde{\mathcal{P}}$ from using g_0 to compute the addresses $(a_1, \ldots, a_N)$ on its own, making them easily distinguishable from random values. The best we can do is to require that $\widetilde{\mathcal{P}}$

[3] Possible measures to achieve this are either to choose Gen and/or Chk accordingly or to execute Gen and/or Chk several times per round on different inputs to occupy more primary memory.

cannot derive any meaningful information about a_{i+1} from g_i without investing a certain minimum amount of time. Specifically, we assume that an algorithm with input g that does *not* execute Gen cannot distinguish $(g', a') = \mathsf{Gen}(g)$ from uniformly random values. Formally:

Definition 5 (Time-Bounded Unpredictability of Gen). $\mathsf{Gen} : \{0,1\}^{l_g} \to \{0,1\}^{l_g} \times \{0,1\}^{l_a}$ *is* ν_{Gen}-unpredictable *if for any algorithm* $\mathsf{Alg}^{\widehat{\mathsf{Gen}}}$ *that can be executed by* $\mathcal{P}$ *and that does not execute* Gen, *it holds that*

$$\Big| \Pr\Big[b = 1 | g \xleftarrow{\mathbb{U}} \{0,1\}^{l_g} \wedge (g', a') \leftarrow \mathsf{Gen}(g) \wedge b \leftarrow \mathsf{Alg}^{\widehat{\mathsf{Gen}}}(g, g', a')\Big] - \Pr\Big[b = 1 | g \xleftarrow{\mathbb{U}} \{0,1\}^{l_g} \wedge (g', a') \xleftarrow{\mathbb{U}} \{0,1\}^{l_g} \times \{0,1\}^{l_a} \wedge b \leftarrow \mathsf{Alg}^{\widehat{\mathsf{Gen}}}(g, g', a')\Big] \Big| \leq \nu_{\mathsf{Gen}}.$$

Weakened Pre-image Resistance of Chk. The purpose of the compression function Chk^N is to map the state S of the prover $\mathcal{P}$ to a smaller attestation response r_N, which reduces the amount of data to be sent from $\mathcal{P}$ to the verifier $\mathcal{V}$. Observe that the output of Chk^N depends also on the challenge sent by the verifier to avoid simple replay attacks and the pre-computation of attestation responses. A necessary security requirement on Chk is that it should be hard for a malicious prover $\widetilde{\mathcal{P}}$ to replace the correct input $\vec{s} = (s_1, \ldots, s_N)$ to Chk with some other value $\widetilde{\vec{s}} \neq \vec{s}$ that yields the same attestation response r_N as $\vec{s}$. This is similar to the common notion of *second pre-image resistance* of cryptographic hash functions. However, due to the time-bound of the software attestation scheme it is sufficient that Chk^N fulfills only a much weaker form of second pre-image resistance since we need to consider only "blind" adversaries who (in contrast to the classical definition of second pre-image resistance) do not know the correct response r_N to the verifier's challenge (g_0, r_0). The reason is that, as soon as $\mathcal{P}$ knows the correct response r_N, he could send it to $\mathcal{V}$ and would not bother to determine a second pre-image. Hence, we introduce the definition of blind second pre-image resistance which concerns algorithms that are given only part of the input $\vec{s}$ of Chk^N and that have to determine the correct output of $\mathsf{Chk}^N(r_0, \vec{s})$:

Definition 6 (Blind Second Pre-image Resistance). $\mathsf{Chk} : \{0,1\}^{l_r} \times \Sigma \to \{0,1\}^{l_r}$ *is* ω-blind second pre-image resistant *with respect to the distribution* $\mathbb{D}_S$ *(cf. Definition 3) if for any* $N \in \mathbb{N}$, *any subset of indices* $J \subsetneq \{1, \ldots, N\}$ *and for any algorithm* Alg *that can be executed by* $\mathcal{P}$, *it holds that*

$$\Pr\Big[\widetilde{r} = r | r_0 \xleftarrow{\mathbb{U}} \{0,1\}^{l_r} \wedge s_i \xleftarrow{\mathbb{D}_S} \Sigma : i \in \{1, \ldots, N\} \wedge \widetilde{r} \leftarrow \mathsf{Alg}(r_0, (s_j)_{j \in J}) \wedge r \leftarrow \mathsf{Chk}^N(r_0, s_1, \ldots, s_N)\Big] \leq \omega.$$

In addition we require (similar to Definition 5) that $\widetilde{\mathcal{P}}$ cannot determine any information on $r_N = \mathsf{Chk}^N(r_0, s_1, \ldots, s_N)$ without executing Chk^N:

Definition 7 (Unpredictability of Chk^N). $\mathsf{Chk} : \{0,1\}^{l_r} \times \Sigma \to \{0,1\}^{l_r}$ *is* ν_{Chk}-unpredictable *with respect to the distribution* $\mathbb{D}_S$ *(cf. Definition 3) if for any algorithm* $\mathsf{Alg}^{\widehat{\mathsf{Chk}^N}}$ *that can be executed by* $\mathcal{P}$ *and that does not execute* Chk^N, *it holds that*

$$\Big| \Pr\Big[b = 1 | r_0 \xleftarrow{\mathbb{U}} \{0,1\}^{l_r} \wedge s_i \xleftarrow{\mathbb{D}_S} \Sigma : i \in \{1, \ldots, N\} \wedge r = \mathsf{Chk}^N(r_0, s_1, \ldots, s_N) \wedge b \leftarrow \mathsf{Alg}^{\widehat{\mathsf{Chk}^N}}(r_0, s_1, \ldots, s_N, r)\Big] - \Pr\Big[b = 1 | r_0 \xleftarrow{\mathbb{U}} \{0,1\}^{l_r} \wedge s_i \xleftarrow{\mathbb{D}_S} \Sigma : i \in \{1, \ldots, N\} \wedge r \xleftarrow{\mathbb{U}} \{0,1\}^{l_r} \wedge b \leftarrow \mathsf{Alg}^{\widehat{\mathsf{Chk}^N}}(r_0, s_1, \ldots, s_N, r)\Big] \Big| \leq \nu_{\mathsf{Chk}}.$$

6. SECURITY OF THE SCHEME

In this section we derive an upper bound for the success probability of a malicious prover $\widetilde{\mathcal{P}}$ to make the verifier $\mathcal{V}$ accept. This bound depends on the parameters defined in Section 5.2 which provide a sufficient condition to prove the generic attestation scheme secure. The bound is as follows:

Theorem 1 (Generic Upper Bound). *Let* S *be an incompressible state (Definition 3). Consider the generic attestation scheme in Figure 1 with the components* Read, Gen *and* Chk *such that*

1. Gen *is* $(N(\delta_{\mathsf{Gen}} + \delta_{\mathsf{Read}}), \varrho)$*-pseudo-random (Definition 4) and* ν_{Gen}*-unpredictable (Definition 5),*
2. Chk *is* ω*-blind second pre-image resistant (Definition 6) and* ν_{Chk}*-unpredictable (Definition 7).*

Consider an arbitrary prover $\widetilde{\mathcal{P}}$ *as in Section 3 with state* $\mathsf{State}(\widetilde{\mathcal{P}}) = \widetilde{S}$ *that can store* $\mathfrak{p}$ *memory words in its primary memory and* $\mathfrak{s}$ *memory words in its secondary memory (cf. Section 3). Let*

$$\lambda := \left| \left\{ a \in \{0,1\}^{l_a} | \mathsf{Read}(\widetilde{S}, a) = \mathsf{Read}(S, a) \right\} \right| \cdot 2^{-l_a},$$

denote the fraction of state entries that are different in S *and* $\widetilde{S}$. *Then the probability of* $\widetilde{\mathcal{P}}$ *to win the security experiment* $\mathbf{Exp}^{\mathcal{A}}_{\mathsf{Attest}}$ *(Definition 2) is upper bounded by*

$$\frac{\mathfrak{p}+\mathfrak{s}}{l_s/l_r} \cdot 2^{-(l_g+l_r)} + \max\{\omega, \nu_{\mathsf{Chk}}\} + \max_{0 \leq M \leq N} \left\{ (\pi(M, \mathsf{ops}) + \varrho) \cdot \gamma^{N-M} + \nu_{\mathsf{Gen}} \cdot (N - M) \right\} \quad (1)$$

where

$$\pi(n, x) := \sum_{j=\max\{0, n-2^{l_a}\}}^{n-1} \left(\max\{\lambda^{x+1}, \gamma\}\right)^{\frac{n}{x+1} - j} \cdot \binom{n}{j} \cdot \left(\prod_{i=0}^{n-j} \frac{2^{l_a} - i}{2^{l_a}} \right) \cdot \left(\frac{n-j}{2^{l_a}} \right)^j \quad (2)$$

and ops *denotes the number of instructions* $\widetilde{\mathcal{P}}$ *can execute in time* $\delta_{\mathsf{Read}} + \delta_{\mathsf{Gen}}$.

This result implies that a software attestation scheme is ε-secure if the expression in Equation 1 is $\leq \varepsilon$, yielding a sufficient condition for security. For example if a user aims for ε-security for a prover device with fixed system parameters, he may choose the number of rounds N in dependence of an expected value of λ accordingly (cf. Appendix B).

Note that the bound given in Equation 1 gives new insights on the impact of the distribution of the state entries in S (expressed by γ) and the similarity between the expected prover state S and the actual state $\widetilde{S}$ of the prover (expressed by λ) on the security of the scheme. Both aspects have been either neglected or have been considered only informally in previous work (cf. Section 7). To provide a better intuition and to show the general applicability of Theorem 1, we compute and discuss the bound for several concrete parameters that are typical for the systems considered in the literature on software attestation in Appendix B.

Proof of Theorem 1. Let $\mathtt{Win}$ denote the event that a malicious prover $\widetilde{\mathcal{P}}$ wins the security experiment $\mathbf{Exp}^{\mathcal{A}}_{\mathsf{Attest}}$, i.e., $\mathtt{Win}$ means that $\mathbf{Exp}^{\mathcal{A}}_{\mathsf{Attest}}(S,l) = \text{ACCEPT}$. We are interested in an upper bound for $\Pr[\mathtt{Win}]$. To this end we consider several sub-cases. Let $\mathtt{Precomp}$ denote the event that the verifier $\mathcal{V}$ sends a challenge (g_0, r_0) to $\widetilde{\mathcal{P}}$ for which $\widetilde{\mathcal{P}}$ has precomputed and stored the correct response r_N in its memory (primary and/or secondary).[4] Then we have

$$\begin{aligned}\Pr[\mathtt{Win}] =& \Pr[\mathtt{Win}|\mathtt{Precomp}] \cdot \Pr[\mathtt{Precomp}] \\ &+ \Pr[\mathtt{Win}|\neg\mathtt{Precomp}] \cdot \Pr[\neg\mathtt{Precomp}] \\ \leq& \Pr[\mathtt{Precomp}] + \Pr[\mathtt{Win}|\neg\mathtt{Precomp}].\end{aligned}$$

The maximum number of responses $\widetilde{\mathcal{P}}$ can store is $\frac{\mathfrak{p}+\mathfrak{s}}{l_s/l_r}$. Since the challenge $(g_0, r_0) \in \{0,1\}^{l_g+l_r}$ is uniformly sampled, it follows that $\Pr[\mathtt{Precomp}] = \frac{\mathfrak{p}+\mathfrak{s}}{l_s/l_r} \cdot 2^{-(l_g+l_r)}$.

We now estimate the term $\Pr[\mathtt{Win}|\neg\mathtt{Precomp}]$, which we abbreviate to $\overline{\Pr}[\mathtt{Win}]$. Let $\mathtt{Correct}$ denote the event that $\widetilde{\mathcal{P}}$ determined all state entries $(s_1, \ldots, s_N)$, i.e., $s_i = \mathsf{Read}(S, a_i)$ and $(g_i, a_i) = \mathsf{Gen}(g_{i-1})$ for $i \in \{1, \ldots, N\}$ *and* that $\widetilde{\mathcal{P}}$ has executed Chk^N. Then we have

$$\overline{\Pr}[\mathtt{Win}] \leq \overline{\Pr}[\mathtt{Correct}] + \overline{\Pr}[\mathtt{Win}|\neg\mathtt{Correct}].$$

It follows from the fact that Chk^N is ω-blind second preimage resistant (Definition 6) and ν_{Chk}-unpredictable (Definition 7) that $\overline{\Pr}[\mathtt{Win}|\neg\mathtt{Correct}] \leq \max\{\omega, \nu_{\mathsf{Chk}}\}$.

For the final term $\overline{\Pr}[\mathtt{Correct}]$, we use the following claim, which we prove afterwards.

Claim 1. *The probability $\overline{\Pr}[\mathtt{Correct}]$ that $\widetilde{\mathcal{P}}$ determines all $(s_1, \ldots, s_N)$ and $r_N = \mathsf{Chk}^N(r_0, s_1, \ldots, s_N)$ in the security experiment $\mathbf{Exp}^{\mathcal{A}}_{\mathsf{Attest}}$ under the assumption that the response to the requested challenge has not been precomputed is upper bounded by*

$$\max_{0 \leq M \leq N} \left\{ (\pi(M, \mathsf{ops}) + \varrho) \cdot \gamma^{N-M} + \nu_{\mathsf{Gen}} \cdot (N - M) \right\}$$

where $\pi(N, x)$ and ops are as in Theorem 1.

Taking these bounds together concludes the proof. □

Proof of Claim 1

We now prove Claim 1 used in the proof of Theorem 1. That is we show the claimed upper bound of $\overline{\Pr}[\mathtt{Correct}]$, which is the probability that a malicious prover $\widetilde{\mathcal{P}}$ with state $\widetilde{S} := \mathsf{State}(\widetilde{\mathcal{P}}) \neq S$ correctly determines all state entries $(s_1, \ldots, s_N)$ in the security experiment $\mathbf{Exp}^{\mathcal{A}}_{\mathsf{Attest}}$ (Definition 2) under the assumption that the response for the requested challenge has not been precomputed.

[4]More precisely, $\mathcal{A}$ has precomputed this value during the preparation phase and stored the response as part of $\widetilde{S}$.

Observe that $\widetilde{\mathcal{P}}$ may decide to deviate from the protocol specification, e.g., skipping some instructions with respect to one round i (probably accepting a lower success probability for determining s_i) to save some time that could be spent on the determination of another state entry s_j with $i \neq j$ (probably aiming for a higher probability to determine s_j). Hence the challenge is to show that for *any* of these approaches the success probability does not exceed a certain (non-trivial) bound, which cannot be done by a reduction to a single assumption.

We base our proof on a sequence of games played by $\widetilde{\mathcal{P}}$ and an oracle $\mathcal{O}$ that has access to S. All these games are divided into two phases: A *setup phase* and a *challenge phase*. In the setup phase $\mathcal{O}$ generates all addresses $(a_1, \ldots, a_N)$ and determines the corresponding state entries $s_i = \mathsf{Read}(S, a_i)$. Afterwards, in the challenge phase, $\widetilde{\mathcal{P}}$ and $\mathcal{O}$ exchange several messages. In particular $\widetilde{\mathcal{P}}$ must submit its guesses $\widetilde{x}_i$ for the state entries s_i to $\mathcal{O}$. $\widetilde{\mathcal{P}}$ wins the game only if all guesses are correct, i.e., $\widetilde{x}_i = s_i$ for all $i = 1, \ldots, N$.

The differences between the games lie in the possibilities of $\widetilde{\mathcal{P}}$ to deviate from the protocol specification. While these possibilities are quite limited in the first game (Game 0), $\widetilde{\mathcal{P}}$ gets more and more control with each subsequent game and thus can to perform more powerful attacks. For each transformation between two consecutive games, we show how the success probability of $\widetilde{\mathcal{P}}$ changes. In most cases it turns out that the previous game represents a subset of the possible attack strategies of the current game. Note that $\mathcal{O}$ formally represents the honest execution of certain parts of the protocol and should not be confused with a real party. Consequently, we assume that transferring messages between $\widetilde{\mathcal{P}}$ and $\mathcal{O}$ takes no time.

Observe that the intention of $\mathcal{O}$ is to have an elegant method for ignoring all computations of $\widetilde{\mathcal{P}}$ which are honestly executed by assumption. Hence to exclude artificial attacks where $\widetilde{\mathcal{P}}$ uses the time and/or memory gained by outsourcing the computation to $\mathcal{O}$, we restrict the time-bound and the size of the primary memory of $\widetilde{\mathcal{P}}$ to what is necessary for honestly executing those computations that are outsourced to $\mathcal{O}$.

Game 0: Randomly Sampling Addresses in Regular Time Intervals.

Game Description. The purpose of this game is to investigate provers $\widetilde{\mathcal{P}}$ which (1) do not exploit any aspects related to the execution of Gen and (2) that are forced to use exactly time δ_{Read} for the determination of each state entry s_i. This is captured by modelling the game as follows: Within the setup phase, $\mathcal{O}$ samples pairwise independent and uniform addresses $(a_1, \ldots, a_N)$ and sets $s_i := \mathsf{Read}(S, a_i)$ for all $i \in \{1, \ldots, N\}$. In the challenge phase, $\mathcal{O}$ iteratively queries $\widetilde{\mathcal{P}}$ with a_i and $\widetilde{\mathcal{P}}$ returns some response $\widetilde{x}_i$.

Hereby, $\widetilde{\mathcal{P}}$ can access the Read oracle, which on input a returns $s = \mathsf{Read}(\widetilde{S}, a)$ after time δ_{Read}. Since this is the only operation expected from an honest prover, the size of the primary memory only allows to store an address a and a state entry s. Moreover the total time-bound is limited to $N \cdot \delta_{\mathsf{Read}}$, meaning that $\widetilde{\mathcal{P}}$ automatically fails if it needs more time in total than this bound.

Observe that $\mathcal{O}$ ensures that $\widetilde{\mathcal{P}}$ cannot change the order of the memory addresses, i.e., $\mathcal{O}$ only sends a_i to $\widetilde{\mathcal{P}}$ after a_{i-1}

has been sent.[5] We denote with *round* i the time-frame between the point in time where $\widetilde{\mathcal{P}}$ receives a_i and the point in time where $\widetilde{\mathcal{P}}$ receives a_{i+1} for $i \in \{1, \ldots, N-1\}$. With *round* N we denote the time-frame between the point in time where $\widetilde{\mathcal{P}}$ receives a_N and the point in time where $\widetilde{\mathcal{P}}$ sends the last response $\widetilde{x}_N$ to $\mathcal{O}$. $\widetilde{\mathcal{P}}$ wins the game if (1) $\widetilde{x}_i = s_i$ for all $i \in \{1, \ldots, N\}$ and (2) each round took at most time δ_{Read}. Otherwise $\widetilde{\mathcal{P}}$ looses the game.

Success Probability. We are interested in an upper bound for the probability $\Pr[\mathtt{Win}_0]$ that $\widetilde{\mathcal{P}}$ wins Game 0. Since $\widetilde{\mathcal{P}}$ looses for sure when he uses more time than δ_{Read} to respond to a_i in at least one round i, it is sufficient to restrict to provers that take at most time δ_{Read} in each round. To this end, we derive an upper bound which allows to treat the individual rounds separately. We start with the final round N and distinguish between two cases.

In Case 1 the response $\widetilde{x}_N$ is the direct result of a query to the Read oracle, i.e., $\widetilde{x}_N = \mathsf{Read}(\widetilde{S}, a)$ for some address a. If $a = a_N$ the probability of $\widetilde{x}_N := \mathsf{Read}(\widetilde{S}, a_N) = s_N := \mathsf{Read}(S, a_N)$ is λ (cf. Theorem 1) since a_N is sampled uniformly and independently from the previous addresses. Now consider that $a \neq a_N$. Since $\widetilde{x}_N = \mathsf{Read}(\widetilde{S}, a)$ and due to the fact that $\widetilde{\mathcal{P}}$ must respond with $\widetilde{x}_N$ in time δ_{Read} after receiving a_N, $\widetilde{\mathcal{P}}$ has no time left to perform any other instructions than Read during round N. In particular a could not be chosen in dependence of a_N, hence being independent of a_N. Then $\widetilde{x}_N = s_N$ happens with probability of at most γ (cf. Definition 3). It follows that in Case 1 the probability $\Pr[\mathtt{Win}_0]$ is upper bounded by $\max\{\lambda, \gamma\} \cdot \Pr[\widetilde{x}_1 = \mathsf{Read}(S, a_1) \wedge \ldots \wedge \widetilde{x}_{N-1} = \mathsf{Read}(S, a_{N-1})]$.

Next we consider Case 2, where $\widetilde{x}_N$ is not the result of a query to the Read oracle. It follows from the incompressibility of S (Definition 3) and the fact that a_N has been sampled uniformly and independent of all previous addresses a_i with $i < N$, that the probability of $\widetilde{x}_N = \mathsf{Read}(S, a_N)$ is upper bounded by γ. Hence,

$$\gamma \cdot \Pr[\widetilde{x}_1 = \mathsf{Read}(S, a_1) \wedge \ldots \wedge \widetilde{x}_{N-1} = \mathsf{Read}(S, a_{N-1})]$$

is an upper bound of $\Pr[\mathtt{Win}_0]$ in Case 2. It follows from Cases 1 and 2 that

$$\Pr[\mathtt{Win}_0] \leq \max\{\lambda, \gamma\} \cdot \Pr[\widetilde{x}_1 = \mathsf{Read}(S, a_1) \wedge \ldots \wedge \widetilde{x}_{N-1} = \mathsf{Read}(S, a_{N-1})]$$

and by induction $\Pr[\mathtt{Win}_0] \leq \pi_0 = \pi_0(N) := (\max\{\lambda, \gamma\})^N$.

Game 1: Prover Controls the Address Generation Time.

Game Description. In this game we increase the power of the malicious prover $\widetilde{\mathcal{P}}$ and allow him to freely choose how much time he devotes to determine each value s_i, as long as the total time for determining $(s_1, \ldots, s_N)$ does not exceed $N \cdot \delta_{\mathsf{Read}}$. This reflects the fact that in the attestation protocol, a malicious prover $\widetilde{\mathcal{P}}$ may generate the memory addresses $(a_1, \ldots, a_N)$ on its own whenever it wants to.

Formally, this is captured by introducing a *req* protocol message which $\widetilde{\mathcal{P}}$ needs to send to $\mathcal{O}$ for receiving the next address a_i during the challenge phase. More precisely, $\mathcal{O}$ sends a_i to $\widetilde{\mathcal{P}}$ only when $\widetilde{\mathcal{P}}$ sent the i-th request *req* to $\mathcal{O}$.

[5]This is a consequence of Remark 7.

Since each round may take a different time period, the winning conditions are relaxed by replacing the time restriction on the individual rounds by an overall time-bound for the entire challenge phase. This means that $\widetilde{\mathcal{P}}$ wins Game 1 if (1) $\widetilde{x}_i = s_i$ for all $i \in \{1, \ldots, N\}$ and (2) the duration of the challenge phase does not exceed the time $N \cdot \delta_{\mathsf{Read}}$. The size of the primary memory remains as in Game 0.

Success Probability. We now upper bound the probability $\Pr[\mathtt{Win}_1]$ that $\widetilde{\mathcal{P}}$ wins Game 1. To this end, we divide the number of rounds into four distinct sets. Let N_{coll} denote the number of rounds where the address sampled by $\mathcal{O}$ is equal to an address of some previous round by coincidence, i.e., $N_{\text{coll}} := |\{i \in \{2, \ldots, N\} | \exists j \in \{1, \ldots, i-1\} : a_i = a_j\}|$.

With respect to the remaining $N - N_{\text{coll}}$ rounds, let N_{equal} (resp. N_{more}, resp. N_{less}) be the number of rounds where $\widetilde{\mathcal{P}}$ responds in time equal (resp. more, resp. less) than δ_{Read}. Thus we have $N = N_{\text{coll}} + N_{\text{equal}} + N_{\text{less}} + N_{\text{more}}$.

Let $\mathtt{Coll}(N_{\text{coll}})$ denote the event that exactly N_{coll} of the N addresses are equal to some previous addresses. This implies that in $N - N_{\text{coll}}$ rounds pairwise different addresses are sampled. Moreover, since there are only 2^{l_a} different addresses, $N - N_{\text{coll}}$ is upper bound by 2^{l_a}. It follows that $N - N_{\text{coll}} \leq 2^{l_a} \Leftrightarrow N_{\text{coll}} \geq N - 2^{l_a}$. Thus it must hold that $N_{\text{coll}} \geq \max\{0, N - 2^{l_a}\}$. Hence, $\Pr[\mathtt{Win}_1]$ is equal to

$$\sum_{N_{\text{coll}}=\max\{0, N-2^{l_a}\}}^{N-1} \Pr[\mathtt{Win}_1 | \mathtt{Coll}(N_{\text{coll}})] \cdot \Pr[\mathtt{Coll}(N_{\text{coll}})].$$

We now derive upper bounds for $\Pr[\mathtt{Win}_1 | \mathtt{Coll}(N_{\text{coll}})]$ and $\Pr[\mathtt{Coll}(N_{\text{coll}})]$.

In general, $\Pr[\mathtt{Coll}(N_{\text{coll}})]$ can be expressed by (number combinations of rounds with equal addresses) $\times$ (probability that addresses in $N - N_{\text{coll}}$ rounds are pairwise different) $\times$ (probability that addresses in the remaining rounds are equal to some previous address). The first term is at most $\binom{N}{N_{\text{coll}}}$ while an upper bound for the last term is $\left(\frac{N-N_{\text{coll}}}{2^{l_a}}\right)^{N_{\text{coll}}}$. This gives an upper bound

$$\binom{N}{N_{\text{coll}}} \cdot \left(\prod_{i=0}^{N-N_{\text{coll}}} \frac{2^{l_a} - i}{2^{l_a}}\right) \cdot \left(\frac{N - N_{\text{coll}}}{2^{l_a}}\right)^{N_{\text{coll}}} \quad (3)$$

for $\Pr[\mathtt{Coll}(N_{\text{coll}})]$ if $\max\{0, N - 2^{l_a}\} \leq N_{\text{coll}} \leq N - 1$. We now fix a value for N_{coll} and aim for an upper bound for the probability $\Pr[\mathtt{Win}_1 | \mathtt{Coll}(N_{\text{coll}})]$. We do so by giving separate upper bounds on the success probability for the four different types of rounds. Let $\mathtt{ops} = \mathtt{ops}(\delta_{\mathsf{Read}})$ be the number of instructions that can be executed by the computing engine of $\widetilde{\mathcal{P}}$ in time δ_{Read}. Since we are interested in an *upper bound* of $\widetilde{\mathcal{P}}$'s success probability, we make several assumptions in favor of $\widetilde{\mathcal{P}}$: (1) For rounds where $\widetilde{\mathcal{P}}$ invested more time than δ_{Read}, we use the trivial upper bound of 1 even if the time period exceeded δ_{Read} only by the time required to execute one single instruction. (2) For rounds where the requested address coincides with an address previously asked, we likewise use the bound of 1. Moreover we assume that these rounds take *no* time at all and the ops instructions saved can be used in ops other rounds. (3) In rounds that take less time than δ_{Read}, it follows from the incompressibility of S (Definition 3) and the fact that all addresses are pairwise distinct that $\widetilde{x}_i = s_i$ with probability $\leq \gamma$. Again, we assume that these rounds take *no* time at all and that the $\texttt{ops}$ instructions saved can be used in $\texttt{ops}$ other rounds. (4) In a round that takes exactly time δ_{Read} $\widetilde{\mathcal{P}}$ succeeds at most with probability $\max\{\lambda, \gamma\}$ (cf. Game 0).

While these assumptions strongly exaggerate the possibilities of $\widetilde{\mathcal{P}}$, they allow to identify optimum strategies. More precisely for each round where $\widetilde{\mathcal{P}}$ uses less time than δ_{Read} or where a previously asked address is requested again, the best approach is to spend the $\texttt{ops}$ saved instructions in $\texttt{ops}$ other rounds such that for each of these rounds the probability of correctly determining s_i is equal to 1. It follows that $N_{\text{more}} = \texttt{ops} \cdot (N_{\text{coll}} + N_{\text{less}})$ and hence $N = N_{\text{coll}} + N_{\text{equal}} + N_{\text{less}} + N_{\text{more}} = N_{\text{equal}} + (\texttt{ops} + 1) \cdot (N_{\text{coll}} + N_{\text{less}})$. Hence, we have

$$\Pr[\texttt{Win}_1 | \texttt{Coll}(N_{\text{coll}})] \leq \pi_0(N_{\text{equal}}) \cdot \gamma^{N_{\text{less}}} \cdot 1^{N_{\text{coll}}+N_{\text{more}}} =$$
$$\max_{N_{\text{less}}} \left\{ \lambda^{N-(\texttt{ops}+1)\cdot(N_{\text{coll}}+N_{\text{less}})} \cdot \gamma^{N_{\text{less}}}, \gamma^{N-(\texttt{ops}+1)\cdot N_{\text{coll}} - \texttt{ops}\cdot N_{\text{less}}} \right\}$$
$$\overset{\text{cf. Apx. A}}{=} \left(\max \left\{ \lambda^{\texttt{ops}(\delta_{\mathsf{Read}})+1}, \gamma \right\} \right)^{\frac{N}{\texttt{ops}(\delta_{\mathsf{Read}})+1} - N_{\text{coll}}}, \quad (4)$$

where the last equation is shown in Appendix A. This shows that $\pi(N, \texttt{ops}(\delta_{\mathsf{Read}}))$ is an upper bound for the probability $\Pr[\texttt{Win}_1]$, where $\pi(n, x)$ is defined as in Equation 2. Observe that for any fixed value of N_{coll}, the probability of having N_{coll} collisions (Equation 3) increases with N (as long as $N_{\text{coll}} \geq \max\{0, N - 2^{l_a}\}$) while the probability to determine the values $(s_1, \ldots, s_N)$ (Equation 4) decreases for N.

Game 2: Skipping Address Generation.

Game Description. So far we covered only provers $\widetilde{\mathcal{P}}$ that honestly generate all addresses $(a_1, \ldots, a_N)$. Now we change the game such that $\widetilde{\mathcal{P}}$ may decide in each round i to skip the generation of address a_i. This allows $\widetilde{\mathcal{P}}$ to "buy" more time for determining the values s_i but at the "cost" of not knowing a_i. Formally this is captured by defining a second message *skip* besides *req*. Specifically, in each round i of the challenge phase, $\widetilde{\mathcal{P}}$ either sends *req* or *skip*. In case of *req*, $\mathcal{O}$ behaves as in Game 1 and sends the next a_i to $\widetilde{\mathcal{P}}$. However, when $\widetilde{\mathcal{P}}$ sends *skip* then $\mathcal{O}$ does *not* send a_i to $\widetilde{\mathcal{P}}$ and extends the time-bound by δ_{Gen}. That is, at the beginning of the challenge phase, the winning conditions are that (1) all responses $(\widetilde{x}_1, \ldots, \widetilde{x}_N)$ of $\widetilde{\mathcal{P}}$ are correct, i.e., $\widetilde{x}_i = s_i \; \forall i \in \{1, \ldots, N\}$ and (2) the challenge phase does not take more time than $N \cdot \delta_{\mathsf{Read}}$. However each time $\widetilde{\mathcal{P}}$ sends a *skip* message to $\mathcal{O}$, the time-bound is extended by δ_{Gen}.

Success Probability. We now determine the probability $\Pr[\texttt{Win}_2]$ that $\widetilde{\mathcal{P}}$ wins Game 2. To this end we follow the same line of arguments as in Game 1. The only difference is that rounds where collisions in the addresses took place or where either Read or Gen have been skipped take no time at all and free $\texttt{ops}(\delta_{\mathsf{Read}} + \delta_{\mathsf{Gen}})$ instructions for other rounds. That is we get a bound with the same structure as in Game 1 but where $\texttt{ops}(\delta_{\mathsf{Read}})$ is replaced by $\texttt{ops}(\delta_{\mathsf{Read}} + \delta_{\mathsf{Gen}})$, i.e., $\Pr[\texttt{Win}_2] \leq \pi(N, \texttt{ops}(\delta_{\mathsf{Read}} + \delta_{\mathsf{Gen}}))$.

Game 3: Replacing the Random Sampling with Gen .

Game Description. Now we consider a variant of Game 2 with the only difference being that the addresses $(a_1, \ldots, a_N)$ are generated by Gen instead of being randomly sampled by $\mathcal{O}$. That is, during the setup phase $\mathcal{O}$ randomly samples g_0 and generates $(a_1, \ldots, a_N)$ using Gen.

Success Probability. Let $\Pr[\texttt{Win}_3]$ be the probability that $\widetilde{\mathcal{P}}$ wins Game 3. Using a standard argument, it follows from the pseudo-randomness of the outputs of Gen (Definition 4) that $|\Pr[\texttt{Win}_3] - \Pr[\texttt{Win}_2]| \leq \varrho$ and hence $\Pr[\texttt{Win}_3] \leq \Pr[\texttt{Win}_2] + \varrho \leq \pi(N, \texttt{ops}(\delta_{\mathsf{Read}} + \delta_{\mathsf{Gen}})) + \varrho$.

Game 4: Giving Access to Gen.

Game Description. In the final game $\mathcal{O}$ no longer generates $(a_1, \ldots, a_N)$ for $\widetilde{\mathcal{P}}$. Instead $\widetilde{\mathcal{P}}$ now queries the Gen oracle, which on input g_i returns $(g_i, a_i) = \mathsf{Gen}(g_{i-1})$ after time δ_{Gen}. To this end, $\mathcal{O}$ samples g_0 in the setup phase and gives this value to $\widetilde{\mathcal{P}}$.

Observe that the size of the primary memory of $\widetilde{\mathcal{P}}$ is increased to additionally store a value g. Further, the time-bound of the challenge phase is increased to $N \cdot (\delta_{\mathsf{Gen}} + \delta_{\mathsf{Read}})$.

Success Probability. The only difference between Game 4 and Game 3 is that $\widetilde{\mathcal{P}}$ now knows g_0 and can query the Gen oracle. Recall that g_0 is used by Gen for computing $(a_1, \ldots, a_N)$. Hence $\widetilde{\mathcal{P}}$ may decide to skip the generation of one or more addresses and save the time and memory for other computations. However, since Gen is assumed to be ν_{Gen}-unpredictable (Definition 5), $\widetilde{\mathcal{P}}$ cannot derive any information on a_{i+1} or g_{i+1} from g_i without querying Gen. Thus if $\widetilde{\mathcal{P}}$ never queries Gen with some value g_i it cannot distinguish the subsequent values $(g_{i+1}, \ldots, g_N)$ with a probability better than $(N - i) \cdot \nu_{\mathsf{Gen}}$. Therefore we can restrict to provers that compute $(a_1, g_1), \ldots, (a_M, g_M)$ and that skip $(a_{M+1}, g_{M+1}), \ldots, (a_N, g_N)$.

Let $\Pr[\texttt{Win}_4]$ be the probability to win Game 4 and let $\Pr[\texttt{Win}_4(M)]$ be the probability to win Game 4 for a fixed M. That is we have $\Pr[\texttt{Win}_4] \leq \max_M \{\Pr[\texttt{Win}_4(M)]\}$. Now consider a variation of Game 4 where $\mathcal{O}$ replaces the values $(a_{M+1}, g_{M+1}), \ldots, (a_N, g_N)$ by independent and uniformly sampled values and we denote with $\Pr[\texttt{Win}_4'(M)]$ the probability that $\widetilde{\mathcal{P}}$ wins this game. Since Gen is assumed to be ν_{Gen}-unpredictable (cf. Definition 5), it holds that $\Pr[\texttt{Win}_4(M)] \leq \Pr[\texttt{Win}_4'(M)] + \nu_{\mathsf{Gen}} \cdot (N - M)$.

With respect to $\Pr[\texttt{Win}_4(M)]$, observe that for the first M rounds the situation is as in Game 3. Hence the success probability for the first M rounds is upper bounded by $\pi(M, \texttt{ops}(\delta_{\mathsf{Read}} + \delta_{\mathsf{Gen}})) + \varrho$. For the remaining $N - M$ rounds, $\mathcal{O}$ uses uniformly sampled values $(a_{M+1}, \ldots, a_N)$ that are unknown to $\widetilde{\mathcal{P}}$. Hence the probability of $\widetilde{\mathcal{P}}$ deriving $(s_{M+1}, \ldots, s_N)$ correctly is upper bounded by γ^{N-M}. This yields $\Pr[\texttt{Win}_4'(M)] \leq (\pi(M, \texttt{ops}(\delta_{\mathsf{Read}} + \delta_{\mathsf{Gen}})) + \varrho) \cdot \gamma^{N-M}$ and hence $\overline{\Pr}[\texttt{Correct}]$ is at most

$$\max_{0 \leq M \leq N} \{(\pi(M, \texttt{ops}(\delta_{\mathsf{Read}} + \delta_{\mathsf{Gen}})) + \varrho) \cdot \gamma^{N-M} + \nu_{\mathsf{Gen}} \cdot (N - M)\}.$$

7. DISCUSSION AND CONCLUSION

We presented the first formal security framework for software attestation and precisely defined various of the underlying system and design parameters. Moreover we presented a generic software attestation protocol that encompasses most existing schemes in the literature. For this generic scheme we derived an upper bound on the success probability of a malicious prover that depends on the formalized parameters. We see the generic scheme and its proof as blueprints that can be adapted to concrete instantiations.

One lesson learned is the impact of these parameters on the security of the generic scheme. For example, it has been observed before that free memory should be filled with pseudo-random data [24] and a later code-compression attack [3] indicated that code redundancy also impacts security. However, the attack was dismissed as impractical [16] and ignored in later works [17, 29]. In contrast, we consider the general probability distribution of the state (code and data) in Definition 3 and directly connect it to the adversary advantage. As a result, one can directly evaluate the honest prover state and determine whether additional measures to achieve state incompressibility, such as filling free memory with pseudo-random data, are required to prevent memory copy and code compression attacks.

Our results also show that traditional cryptographic assumptions are partially too strong (second pre-image resistance) and partially too weak (pseudo-randomness). Further, we identified new (sufficient) conditions on the core functionalities of software attestation. Most previous works require the software attestation algorithm to iterate over all memory words of the secondary memory without giving any formal justification. Our bound allows to identify lower values for N (if the other parameters are known), enabling more efficient solutions that provide a tradeoff between the number of iterations N and the success probability of a malicious prover. Thus our work represents the first step towards efficient and provably secure software attestation schemes.

Still, several open questions remain for future work. One being to relax the presented conditions or to derive necessary conditions. A further task is to determine concrete instantiations. While Gen and Chk could be easily realized on devices that provide hardware-assisted cryptographic functions, such as block cipher implementations in hardware similar to the AES instructions in modern CPUs [30], this becomes more challenging on other platforms.

We are currently working on the following aspects: (1) a practical instantiation of the generic software attestation scheme and its evaluation and (2) the evaluation of existing software attestation schemes in our framework.

8. REFERENCES

[1] T. AbuHmed, N. Nyamaa, and D. Nyang. Software-based remote code attestation in wireless sensor network. In *Global Telecommunications (GLOBECOM)*. IEEE, 2009.

[2] Atmel. tinyAVR homepage. `http://www.atmel.com/tinyavr/`, 2013.

[3] C. Castelluccia, A. Francillon, D. Perito, and C. Soriente. On the difficulty of software-based attestation of embedded devices. In *Computer and Communications Security (CCS)*. ACM, 2009.

[4] A. Datta, J. Franklin, D. Garg, and D. Kaynar. A logic of secure systems and its application to trusted computing. In *Security and Privacy, 2009 30th IEEE Symposium on*, 2009.

[5] K. E. Defrawy, A. Francillon, D. Perito, and G. Tsudik. SMART: Secure and minimal architecture for (establishing a dynamic) root of trust. In *Network and Distributed System Security Symposium (NDSS)*. Internet Society, 2012.

[6] C. Dwork and M. Naor. Pricing via processing or combatting junk mail. In *Advances in Cryptology – CRYPTO*. Springer, 1993.

[7] C. Dwork, M. Naor, and H. Wee. Pebbling and proofs of work. In *Advances in Cryptology – CRYPTO*. Springer, 2005.

[8] A. Francillon, Q. Nguyen, K. B. Rasmussen, and G. Tsudik. Systematic treatment of remote attestation. Cryptology ePrint Archive, Report 2012/713, 2012. `http://eprint.iacr.org/`.

[9] J. Franklin, M. Luk, A. Seshadri, and A. Perrig. PRISM: Human-verifieable code execution. Technical report, Carnegie Mellon University, 2007.

[10] R. W. Gardner, S. Garera, and A. D. Rubin. Detecting code alteration by creating a temporary memory bottleneck. *Trans. Info. For. Sec.*, 4(4):638–650, 2009.

[11] J. T. Giffin, M. Christodorescu, and L. Kruger. Strengthening software self-checksumming via self-modifying code. In *Annual Computer Security Applications Conference (ACSAC)*. IEEE, 2005.

[12] V. Graizer and D. Naccache. Alien vs. Quine. *Security Privacy, IEEE*, 5(2):26 –31, 2007.

[13] V. Gratzer and D. Naccache. Alien vs. Quine, the vanishing circuit and other tales from the industry's crypt. In *Advances in Cryptology – EUROCRYPT*. Springer, 2007. Invited Talk.

[14] M. Jakobsson and K.-A. Johansson. Retroactive Detection of Malware With Applications to Mobile Platforms. In *Workshop on Hot Topics in Security (HotSec)*. USENIX, 2010.

[15] R. Kennell and L. H. Jamieson. Establishing the genuinity of remote computer systems. In *USENIX Security Symposium*. USENIX, 2003.

[16] X. Kovah, C. Kallenberg, C. Weathers, A. Herzog, M. Albin, and J. Butterworth. New results for Timing-Based attestation. In *Security and Privacy (S&P)*. IEEE, 2012.

[17] Y. Li, J. M. McCune, and A. Perrig. VIPER: verifying the integrity of PERipherals' firmware. In *Computer and Communications Security (CCS)*. ACM, 2011.

[18] B. Parno, J. M. McCune, and A. Perrig. Bootstrapping Trust in Commodity Computers. In *Security and Privacy (S&P)*. IEEE, 2010.

[19] A.-R. Sadeghi, S. Schulz, and C. Wachsmann. Lightweight remote attestation using physical functions. In *Wireless Network Security (WiSec)*. ACM, 2011.

[20] D. Schellekens, B. Wyseur, and B. Preneel. Remote attestation on legacy operating systems with Trusted Platform Modules. *Sci. Comput. Program.*, 74(1-2):13–22, 2008.

[21] A. Seshadri, M. Luk, and A. Perrig. SAKE: Software attestation for key establishment in sensor networks. *Distributed Computing in Sensor Systems*, pages 372–385, 2008.

[22] A. Seshadri, M. Luk, A. Perrig, L. van Doorn, and P. Khosla. SCUBA: Secure code update by attestation in sensor networks. In *Workshop on Wireless security (WiSe)*. ACM, 2006.

[23] A. Seshadri, M. Luk, E. Shi, A. Perrig, L. van Doorn, and P. Khosla. Pioneer: Verifying integrity and guaranteeing execution of code on legacy platforms. In *Symposium on Operating Systems Principles (SOSP)*. ACM, 2005.

[24] A. Seshadri, A. Perrig, L. van Doorn, and P. K. Khosla. SWATT: SoftWare-based ATTestation for embedded devices. In *Security and Privacy (S&P)*. IEEE, 2004.

[25] M. Shaneck, K. Mahadevan, V. Kher, and Y. Kim. Remote software-based attestation for wireless sensors. In *Security and Privacy in Ad-hoc and Sensor Networks*. Springer, 2005.

[26] U. Shankar, M. Chew, and J. D. Tygar. Side effects are not sufficient to authenticate software. In *USENIX Security Symposium*. USENIX, 2004.

[27] R. Strackx, F. Piessens, and B. Preneel. Efficient isolation of trusted subsystems in embedded systems. In *Security and Privacy in Communication Networks (SecureComm)*. Springer, 2010.

[28] Trusted Computing Group (TCG). *TPM Main Specification, Version 1.2*, 2011.

[29] A. Vasudevan, J. Mccune, J. Newsome, A. Perrig, and L. V. Doorn. CARMA: A hardware tamper-resistant isolated execution environment on commodity x86 platforms. In *ACM Symposium on Information, Computer and Communications Security (AsiaCCS)*. ACM, 2012.

[30] Wikipedia. AES instruction set. `http://en.wikipedia.org/wiki/AES_instruction_set`, 2013.

[31] Q. Yan, J. Han, Y. Li, R. H. Deng, and T. Li. A software-based root-of-trust primitive on multicore platforms. In *ACM Symposium on Information, Computer and Communications Security (AsiaCCS)*. ACM, 2011.

[32] Y. Yang, X. Wang, S. Zhu, and G. Cao. Distributed software-based attestation for node compromise detection in sensor networks. In *Symposium on Reliable Distributed Systems (SRDS)*. IEEE, 2007.

APPENDIX

A. DETAILS OF THE PROOF

We prove the upper bound of $\Pr[\texttt{Win}_1|\texttt{Coll}(N_{\text{coll}})]$ used in Game 1 of the proof of Theorem 1. Observe that $0 \le N_{\text{less}}$ and $0 \le N_{\text{equal}} = N - (\texttt{ops}+1)\cdot(N_{\text{coll}} + N_{\text{less}}) \Leftrightarrow N_{\text{less}} \le \frac{N}{\texttt{ops}+1} - N_{\text{coll}}$, i.e., $0 \le N_{\text{less}} \le \frac{N}{\texttt{ops}+1} - N_{\text{coll}}$. To simplify the first term $\lambda^{N-(\texttt{ops}+1)\cdot(N_{\text{coll}}+N_{\text{less}})} \cdot \gamma^{N_{\text{less}}}$, we define $e := \log_\lambda(\gamma)$ and rephrase it as $\lambda^{N-(\texttt{ops}+1)\cdot N_{\text{coll}}-(\texttt{ops}+1-e)\cdot N_{\text{less}}}$.

When $\texttt{ops}+1-e < 0$, the maximum is achieved for $N_{\text{less}} = 0$, hence in this case the upper bound is $\lambda^{N-(\texttt{ops}+1)\cdot N_{\text{coll}}}$. In the other case we get an upper bound for $N_{\text{less}} = \frac{N}{\texttt{ops}+1} - N_{\text{coll}}$, yielding

$$\lambda^{N-(\texttt{ops}+1)\cdot N_{\text{coll}}-(\texttt{ops}+1-e)\cdot\left(\frac{N}{\texttt{ops}+1}-N_{\text{coll}}\right)} = \gamma^{\frac{N}{\texttt{ops}+1}-N_{\text{coll}}}.$$

With respect to the second term, i.e., $\gamma^{N-(\texttt{ops}+1)\cdot N_{\text{coll}}-\texttt{ops}\cdot N_{\text{less}}}$, the maximum value is achieved if N_{less} is as big as possible, i.e., $N_{\text{less}} = \frac{N}{\texttt{ops}+1} - N_{\text{coll}}$. This gives an upper bound of

$$\gamma^{N-(\texttt{ops}+1)\cdot N_{\text{coll}}-\texttt{ops}\cdot N_{\text{less}}} = \gamma^{\frac{N}{\texttt{ops}+1}-N_{\text{coll}}}.$$

Altogether, it follows that

$$\Pr[\texttt{Win}_1|\texttt{Coll}(N_{\text{coll}})] \le \left(\max\left\{\lambda^{\texttt{ops}(\delta_{\text{Read}})+1}, \gamma\right\}\right)^{\frac{N}{\texttt{ops}(\delta_{\text{Read}})+1}-N_{\text{coll}}}.$$

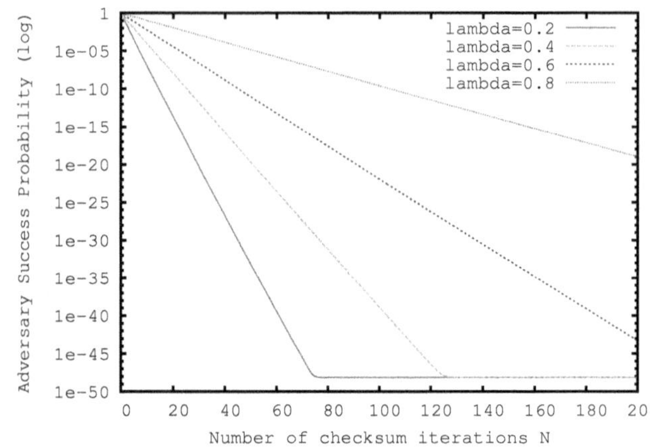

Figure 2: Upper Bound (Equation 1) for different values of N and λ.

B. EXAMPLE FOR UPPER BOUND

To get a better intuition of the upper bound (Equation 1) given in Theorem 1, especially on the impact of the similarity of the malicious prover's state to the honest prover's state expressed by λ and the number of rounds N, we provide some concrete examples in this section.

At first we have to fix various parameters. To this end, we consider typical parameters for l_g and l_r that can be found in the literature on software attestation. Moreover, we assume that all cryptographic primitives are *perfectly secure* and that the values in S are uniformly distributed:

$$\omega := 2^{-l_r},\ \nu_{\text{Chk}} = 0,\ \varrho := 0,\ \gamma := 2^{-l_s},\ \nu_{\text{Gen}} := 0.$$

The bound in Equation 1 then simplifies to

$$\frac{\mathfrak{p}+\mathfrak{s}}{l_s/l_r \cdot 2^{(l_g+l_r)}} + 2^{-l_r} + \max_{0\le M\le N}\left\{(\pi(M,\texttt{ops}))\cdot 2^{-l_s\cdot(N-M)}\right\}.$$

Recall that the value $\texttt{ops}$ has been defined as the number of operations a prover can perform in time $\delta_{\text{Read}} + \delta_{\text{Gen}}$. It was used in the proof to tackle the following question: *If an attacker decides to skip one round, for how many other rounds can he increase his probability of success?* While $\texttt{ops}$ certainly expresses an upper bound on this number (the adversary has to spend at least one instruction per round), it certainly is an overestimation of the adversary's capabilities. Hence, we set $\texttt{ops} = 2$ to get more meaningful results. This represents an adversary who can win two rounds if he skips another round.

Recall that λ expresses the fraction of state entries where the state of the malicious prover matches with the state S of the honest prover. We exemplarily use $\lambda \in \{0.2, \ldots, 0.8\}$. As shown in Figure 2, for small values of λ (i.e., for malicious provers with a state that is quite different from the honest prover's state), a relatively low number of rounds is sufficient to achieve a reasonably low adversary advantage. However, for large values of λ more rounds are required. Further, for the chosen system parameters, the advantage seems to converge to a minimal adversary advantage of 10^{-48}.

Observe that in the literature, it is often suggested to use $N = \log(\mathfrak{s})\cdot\mathfrak{s}$ rounds. Interestingly, our experiments indicate that significantly less rounds can be sufficient.

OASIS: On Achieving a Sanctuary for Integrity and Secrecy on Untrusted Platforms*

Emmanuel Owusu† Jorge Guajardo‡ Jonathan McCune† Jim Newsome† Adrian Perrig† Amit Vasudevan†

†CyLab, Carnegie Mellon University – {eowusu, jonmccune, jnewsome, perrig, amitvasudevan}@cmu.edu
‡Bosch Research and Technology Center, Robert Bosch LLC – jorge.guajardomerchan@us.bosch.com

ABSTRACT

We present OASIS, a CPU instruction set extension for externally verifiable initiation, execution, and termination of an isolated execution environment with a trusted computing base consisting solely of the CPU. OASIS leverages the hardware components available on commodity CPUs to achieve a low-cost, low-overhead design.

Categories and Subject Descriptors

C.0 [**General**]: Miscellaneous—*Hardware/Software Interfaces, Instruction Set Design*; K.6.5 [**Management of Computing and Information Systems**]: Security and Protection—*Physical Security, Unauthorized Access*

General Terms

Design, Security

Keywords

Secure Execution, Remote Attestation, Instruction Set Extension

1. INTRODUCTION

Despite numerous attacks against a wide spectrum of organizations [6, 29], secure execution environments protected by TCG have not seen widespread application – even in cloud computing, where customers want to verify execution [2, 41]. Perhaps this lack of application is due, in part, to the lack of end-to-end application software that benefit from TCG properties, lack of trust in the TPM vendors, lack of protection against local adversaries, and concerns over poor performance.

Many designs for an isolated execution environment (IEE) have been proposed, but an interesting question remains: What minimal additions do we need to add to a modern CPU to achieve a highly efficient isolated execution environment with remote attestation properties? This work investigates what minimal architectural changes are required to obtain the essential Trusted Computing Base (TCB) – an isolated execution environment completely contained inside a modern CPU – providing resilience against several classes of hardware attacks. In addition, we design this architecture such that minimal changes to a modern commodity CPU are required for deployment. In keeping with minimalist design, we provide a simple programming interface consisting of few instructions.

Contributions

- We present an instruction set for remotely verifiable, efficient code execution requiring a minimal TCB.
- We propose an API where the CPU provides unique cryptographic keys to security-sensitive applications.
- Our deployment model precludes the need for a distributor or manufacturer to protect platform secrets on behalf of the end-user or their customers.
- Our system is designed for deployment on existing commodity CPUs with minimal modifications.
- Contrary to prior approaches, our solution does not require on-chip non-volatile memory to store secrets. Thus, in addition to avoiding the strong assumption of *secure* non-volatile memory, our solution is cheaper to implement in practice as it leverages semiconductor processes already used in modern CPUs.

2. PROBLEM DEFINITION

2.1 Model and Assumptions

Deployment Model. Our use case defines outsourced computation in the sense advocated by public cloud computing. Thus, we identify three key parties; and their different roles and levels of trust as a device moves from production to use:

(i) The processor *hardware manufacturer* (HWM). The HWM is trusted to manufacture the CPU to initialize a cryptographic device key with a Physically Unclonable Function.

(ii) The *service provider* (or device owner) that offers the device as a platform to customers who wish to lease them for a certain amount of time or computation.

*This research was supported in part by CyLab at Carnegie Mellon under grants DAAD19-02-1-0389 from the Army Research Office, and by a gift from Robert Bosch LLC. The views and conclusions contained here are those of the authors and should not be interpreted as necessarily representing the official policies or endorsements, either expressed or implied, of ARO, Robert Bosch LLC, CMU, CyLab, or the U.S. Government or any of its agencies.

CCS'13, November 4–8, 2013, Berlin, Germany.

ACM 978-1-4503-2477-9/13/11 ...$15.00..

Finally, (iii) the *user* (or cloud customer) who wishes to lease computing resources. Users are interested in verifying the trustworthiness of devices leased to them, guaranteeing the integrity and confidentiality of their computations and data.

In the remainder of this paper, we refer to the service provider's device simply as the *platform* or P and to the user's device as the *verifier* or V.

Adversary Model. We assume a sophisticated adversary with physical access to the computing platform. In particular, the adversary can introduce malware into the computing platform (e.g., to compromise an application, the OS, or firmware), has access to the external ports of the platform to physically attach malicious peripherals to P. Similarly, the adversary can probe and tamper with low-speed and high-speed buses (e.g., to eavesdrop on a memory or PCI bus), and/or inject code and/or modify data. However, the adversary cannot perform attacks that require complete unscrutinized access to the CPU for extended periods of time. In particular, this implies that the service provider has organizational procedures in place to prevent attacks, but cannot guarantee the absence of a small set of rogue employees.[1] We consider denial-of-service, side-channel, and fault injection attacks beyond the scope of this paper.

Assumptions. With respect to the service provider, we assume that the CPU on the untrusted platform P is not malicious (i.e., we trust the processor). We assume that this CPU contains a Physically Unclonable Function that can only be accessed through the specified APIs. Additionally, we assume that the CPU has a true random number generator. We assume that the CPU is tamper-resistant. Thus, physical security is not a requirement. Finally, we assume that the verifier V has the correct public key of the provider's platform P.

2.2 Desired Properties

The following list contains the desired properties for OASIS.

- $P1$ **Secure.** We would like the following security objectives to be satisfied:
  - $P1.1$ *Externally Verifiable.* Attestable code execution that guarantees platform integrity, code integrity, launch point integrity, and unmodified code execution on the untrusted platform.
  - $P1.2$ *Key Code Binding.* Ensure that a unique cryptographic key is available to each distinct code module that executes in the isolated environment.
  - $P1.3$ *Program State Binding.* The ability to bind data to code.
  - $P1.4$ *Device Transferability.* The ability to transfer ownership of a chip without exposing the secrets of the previous owner.
  - $P1.5$ *Limited Trust.* The HWM should not have access to any device secrets.
- $P2$ **Economical.** We would like the following economic objectives to be satisfied:
  - $P2.1$ *Low-cost.* No substantial increase of manufacturing cost or complexity (e.g., by requiring non-volatile memory within the CPU).
  - $P2.2$ *Self-contained.* No requirement for additional hardware support such as secure co-processors or TPMs.
- $P3$ **Essential.** We aim for a balanced and simple design:
  - $P3.1$ *Minimal TCB.* On-die isolated execution environment with trustworthy computing primitives entirely within the CPU package.
  - $P3.2$ *Minimal Interface.* Minimal interface with minimal controls, which presents a usable programming abstraction.
  - $P3.3$ *Minimal Setup.* Efficient environment setup where expensive operations are bypassed during repeated invocation.

3. HARDWARE BUILDING BLOCKS

3.1 PUFs, Fuzzy Extractors, and TRNGs

Pappu et al. introduce the concept of Physical Unclonable Functions (PUFs), which are functions where the relationship between input (or *challenge*) C and output (or *response*) p_e is defined via a physical system [15, 35]. The physical system has the additional properties of being random and unclonable. The system's unclonability originates from random variations in a device's manufacturing process, which even the manufacturer cannot control. In their most general form, PUFs can accept a large number challenge-response pairs. Examples of PUF constructions include: optical PUFs [35], silicon PUFs [15, 14], coating PUFs [45], SRAM PUFs [16, 17], reconfigurable PUFs [23], and Flash memory-based PUFs [48].

Because of PUF variability across different environmental conditions (voltage, temperature, humidity, etc.), when a PUF is challenged with C_i, a response p'_e (a noisy version of p_e) is obtained. In applications where the PUF response is used as a cryptographic key this noisy response p'_e is not acceptable. To solve this problem, algorithms known as *fuzzy extractors* leverage non-secret helper data to work around the noisy nature of physical measurements typical of PUF applications [21, 27, 10]. We assume that the fuzzy extractor is implemented in a silicon block and is accessible as a function that is used (in combination with the PUF interface) to realize our instructions.

While stability is fundamental for PUFs, variation in unstable bits can be leveraged for random number generation [17, 44, 48]. For the purposes of this paper, we focus on PUFs based on memory arrays, such as SRAM commonly used in CPU caches. SRAM memory can be used as the raw source for a PUF as well as the entropy source for a True Random Number Generator (TRNG).[2]

[1]For example, a cloud service provider may unintentionally grant datacenter access to malicious [20] or negligent [43] employees.

[2]The new Intel random number generator is based on the instability of a couple of cross-coupled inverters, which are the basic building block of an SRAM cell [44].

3.2 Cache-as-RAM (CAR) Mode

Cache memory is ubiquitous across CPU architectures. Traditionally, SRAM is used to implement a cache. Modern CPUs often include several megabytes of memory on-die which can be leveraged to create a *Cache-as-RAM* (CAR) execution environment [28]. Typically, CAR mode is used to perform system boot-up tasks while DRAM (external to the CPU) is initialized. Prior work has demonstrated that the CPU cache subsystem can be repurposed as a general-purpose memory area for isolated code execution and data read/write operations [46]. The CPU CAR environment offers an isolated execution environment using exclusively on-die hardware.

4. OASIS CPU INSTRUCTION SET

We first provide a high-level overview of the design, describing the requirements, execution model, and implementation rationale for the instruction set extension (ISE) proposed in the paper. The notation used in the remainder of the paper is summarized in Table 1.

Requirements. OASIS is a set of new CPU instructions that aim to enable an isolated execution environment contained entirely on chip by leveraging CAR mode execution, and by creating a secret key only available to the CPU (e.g., derived from an SRAM PUF). OASIS is designed for ease of adoption and deployment with respect to existing computing systems.

A central feature of OASIS is the PUF-derived secret key K_p only available within the CPU and which is used as the root of trust of the whole environment. OASIS is based on SRAM-PUFs [16, 17]. This has several advantages: (i) SRAM is already available on modern CPUs in the form of the cache, (ii) SRAM PUFs need to be powered to create the secret key material, thus, they cannot be read offline making them resistant against scanning electron microscope based attacks, (iii) because of their properties, PUFs are tamper-evident (and in some cases tamper-resistant), a property which other technologies do not offer [16], and (iv) SRAM is manufactured using the standard semiconductor process, which leads to decreased costs when compared to non-volatile memory.

OASIS assumes the availability of external non-secure non-volatile memory. This memory is used to store public helper data as well as state and/or programs. External storage is plentiful and does not further complicate the OASIS design since no special security guarantees are assumed. In particular, alterations to the public helper data can be easily detected through the use of robust fuzzy extractors [5, 9].

Root-of-Trust Instantiation. The SRAM-PUF response, p_e, serves as a unique cryptographic secret which is used to bootstrap a unique device identity, per-application encryption and authentication keys, and random number generation. The resulting key material is unique not just per physical device, but per device owner. The SRAM-PUF response is used to derive the secret root key, K_p, which never leaves the processor and is never directly accessible by any party (including any software running on the processor).

The PUF-derived secret root key, K_p, enables the derivation of a key hierarchy as follows. The device owner derives a key (K_{po}) unique to themselves and the device via a key derivation function (KDF), which accepts as inputs an owner supplied seed, S_o, and the PUF-derived secret root key, K_p. This master processor secret, K_{po}, can then be used, in turn, to derive symmetric keys for bulk encryption, authentication, and asymmetric operations. The details are provided in Section 4.1.

Table 1: Notation used in Instruction Set and Protocol

Notation	
`hw_inst[]`	hardware instructions that make up the OASIS programming interface are denoted using a fixed-width font
`f_hw_func[]`	hardware functions are only accessible by OASIS hardware instructions and are denoted using a fixed-width font identifier starting with the letter `f`
$y \leftarrow x$	the value of x is assigned to variable y
$\perp$	this symbol is used to denote a failed platform operation
$x\|\|y$	concatenation of x and y
$x.param$	returns parameter $param$ of variable x
$x.*$	data element formed by concatenating all parameters of variable x
$A \rightarrow B : \langle m \rangle$	A sends message $\langle m \rangle$ to B
$r \xleftarrow{R} \{0,1\}^\ell$	assigns a random integer of ℓ bits to r
K_X	party X's symmetric key
K_X^+, K_X^{-1}	party X's public and private asymmetric key pair
$\{P\}_K$	the resulting ciphertext of plaintext P encrypted using key K
$H(x)$	cryptographic hash function with input x
$\mathsf{Enc}_K(P)$	encrypt plaintext P using key K
$\mathsf{Dec}_K(C)$	decrypt ciphertext C using key K
$\mathrm{KDF}_K(x)$	key derivation function of key K and non-secret parameter x
$\mathrm{MAC}_K(x)$	message authentication code of x under key K
$\mathtt{Sign}_{K_X^{-1}}(m)$	sign message m with party X's private key K_X^-
$\mathtt{Verify}_{K_X^+}(m,\sigma)$	verify signature σ on message m using party X's public key K_X^+
$\mathtt{Cert}_y(x, K_X^+)$	certificate issued by y that binds the identity x to the public key K_X^+

All keys are stored inside the CPU in a set of special purpose cache registers ($CR.*$) which are only available within the OASIS environment and only accessible by the OASIS instructions. Table 2 lists the keys stored in $CR.*$. Observe that the root key, K_p, is only used for the derivation of the master processor secret. More importantly, the entire key hierarchy is based on an owner seed (S_o), enabling personalization and device transferability.

ISE Overview and Flow. Next, we describe how the PUF-based root-of-trust is used to enable the desired security objectives of Section 2.2 by defining five new instructions: `init[]`, `create[]`, `launch[]`, `unbind[]`, and `bind[]`.

We distinguish between three stages in the life cycle of the CPU. The first stage is performed by the hardware manufacturer (Figure 1(a)). After manufacture, the HWM initializes the master processor key K_p by calling `init[]`. The output of this operation is helper data h_e and a hash $H(p_e, h_e)$,

Table 2: **Variables used in Instruction Set and Protocol.**

Hidden Variables: values accessible by processor	
p_e	Raw PUF response
K_p	Root key generated from PUF
S_o	Secret seed value set by platform owner
p^*, q^*	Primes corresponding to an RSA private key
$CR.K_{po}$	Master platform secret for a specific owner seed
$CR.K_{po\_auth}$	Platform key for authenticating data from untrusted storage
$CR.K_{po\_encr}$	Platform key for encrypting data before transfer to untrusted storage
$CR.K_{po\_code}$	Platform key used to derive code specific keys
$CR.S_{po\_bind}$	Platform binding secret used to derive asymmetric binding keys
$CR.K^{-1}_{po\_bind}$	Platform private binding key, derived deterministically from $CR.S_{po\_bind}$
$CR.PCR$	Platform configuration registers
$CR.K_C$	Unique cryptographic key for code $\mathbf{C}'$
Visible Variables: values accessible by software	
$K^{+}_{po\_bind}$	Platform public binding key, derived deterministically from $CR.S_{po\_bind}$
h_e	Helper data used for noise reduction of p_e
h_{PK}	Helper data used for generating asymmetric keys

which is published and available to anyone using the device. We assume that the function `init[]` can be called only once or a limited number of times to prevent attacks that exploit repeated invocations of the generator function `f_init_PUF[]` (described below) to learn p_e [9]. Given that the HWM does not have control of the PUF response p_e (or by extension K_p as it is derived from p_e), the `init[]` instruction enables the limited trust ($P1.5$), low cost ($P2.1$), self contained ($P2.2$), and the minimal TCB ($P3.1$) properties of Section 2.2.

The second stage corresponds to the set-up of the key hierarchy for OASIS, performed by the device owner (Figure 1(b)). This is accomplished by calling the `create[]` instruction, whose main purpose is to derive symmetric and asymmetric keys. These keys will be used to exchange confidential and authenticated messages between the prover (device owner) and the verifier (user) and to guarantee external verifiability ($P1.1$). The main output of the instruction is a public key, which has been derived from the PUF-based root key K_p and a seed S_o known only to the device owner. This allows for transferability of the platform ($P1.4$) as a new device owner can create his/her own public/private keypair ($K^{+}_{po\_bind}, K^{-1}_{po\_bind}$) by choosing a different seed S'_o. Furthermore, even though the device owner initiates generation of the public/private keypair, only the CPU can access the private key and thus decrypt messages encrypted with the public key.

The third and last stage corresponds to the execution of code on the device by the user (Figure 1(c)). Users will launch the code to be executed by issuing the `launch[]` instruction. This instruction populates the $CR.*$ registers with the symmetric keys derived from the PUF helper data h_e, the device owner's seed S_o, and the public key information generated using `create[]` in the previous stage. Then, the `unbind[]` instruction can be called to check the input's integrity with respect to a code-specific key and decrypt any input whose confidentiality is preserved by the verifier. The instruction provides two options, one using public-key and one using symmetric-key primitives. The asymmetric option is used the first time the application is called to transmit a secret symmetric key, K_{VP}, only known to the verifier (user) of the platform P. After this initial set-up, the verifier can use fast symmetric-key operations to verify integrity and confidentiality of its data ($P3.3$). At this point the code C can be executed in the isolated execution environment, state is saved (and encrypted if desired), and integrity information is computed on the state using `bind[]` ($P1.3$). Finally, all OASIS memory and internal registers are cleared out, and control is returned to the OS. Observe that any program can in principle be executed in a secure environment using these last three instructions, providing for a minimal and simple programming interface ($P3.2$). Furthermore, the `bind[]` and `unbind[]` instructions, together with the key hierarchy derived with the help of `create[]`, enable external verifiability ($P1.1$) and program state binding ($P1.2$), not only to a particular program but also to a specific CPU, a property unique to OASIS.

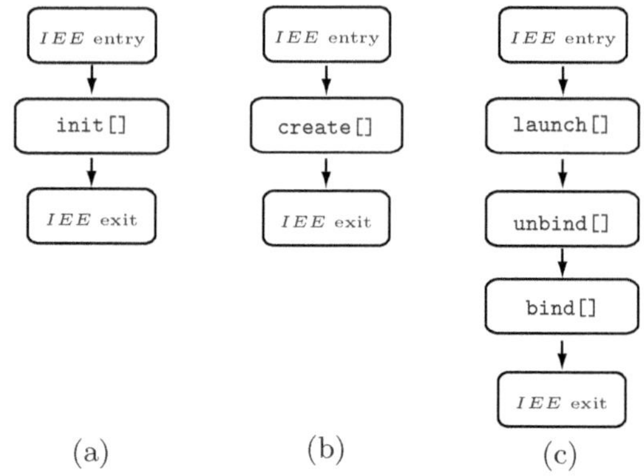

Figure 1: OASIS session during (a) initialization by the manufacturer, (b) setup by the device owner, and (c) code execution by the user.

4.1 OASIS Functions and Instructions

We describe the functions and instructions used in the design of OASIS. We make a distinction between functions (which are only *internally available* to instructions) and instructions, (which are *externally available* for call by executing software).[3] In practice, functions and instructions might be implemented as digital logic, integrity-checked firmware, microcode, or another process-specific mechanism.

4.1.1 Function Descriptions

We have omitted *explicit* pseudocode definitions for several functions where the specific implementation is left to the hardware manufacturer. Table 3 lists these functions. The functionality of `f_read_PUF[]`, `f_init_PUF[]` and `f_fuzzy_extract_PUF[]` is briefly discussed next.

[3]Instructions and functions are denoted using a fixed-width identifier. Functions begin with '`f_`'. See Table 1.

Table 3: Hardware Manufacturer Implemented Functions

p_e	$\leftarrow$ `f_read_PUF[]`
$h_e, H(p_e, h_e)$	$\leftarrow$ `f_init_PUF[`$p_e, rand$`]`
K_p	$\leftarrow$ `f_fuzzy_extract_PUF[`$p_e, h_e, H(p_e, h_e)$`]`
p, q	$\leftarrow$ `f_find_primes[`S_{po_bind}`, RSAParam.size]`
$K^{+}_{po\_bind}$, $K^{-1}_{po\_bind}$	$\leftarrow$ `f_rsa_key_gen[`p, q`, `e`]`

The function `f_read_PUF[]` does not accept any inputs; it simply outputs the raw PUF response p_e. We provide two functions to interact with a (robust) fuzzy extractor [5, 9] as is common in the literature: (1) The function `f_init_PUF[`$p_e, rand$`]` accepts a raw PUF response p_e and a random value $rand$ and outputs helper data h_e and a hash $H(p_e, h_e)$. The helper data h_e can be used to reconstruct a uniformly random value K_p from a noisy raw PUF response p'_e. The hash is used to guarantee that only values of K_p constructed with the original helper data h_e are used for further processing in OASIS. (2) The function `f_fuzzy_extract_PUF[`$p'_e, h_e, H(p_e, h_e)$`]` accepts a (noisy) raw PUF response p'_e and helper data h_e and outputs a uniformly random value K_p which can be used as a cryptographic key. The function `f_fuzzy_extract_PUF[]` checks for correctness in the value of $H(p_e, h_e)$ and outputs a special symbol $\perp$ if the input does not correspond to the computed value. If the output is $\perp$, the instruction calling `f_fuzzy_extract_PUF[]` should take appropriate action. In the case of OASIS, we clear all key registers and abort execution.

We assume the use of existing hardware-supported fuzzy extractor implementations [4, 30]. The functions `f_read_PUF[]`, `f_init_PUF[]` and `f_fuzzy_extract_PUF[]` are only available to the OASIS hardware instructions defined in Section 4 and they cannot be accessed by *any* software directly.

Func 1 $S_{po\_bind} \leftarrow$ `f_create_sym_keys[`$S_o, h_e, H(p_e, h_e)$`]`

$p'_e \leftarrow$ `f_read_PUF[]`
$K_p \leftarrow$ `f_fuzzy_extract_PUF[`$p'_e, h_e, H(p_e, h_e)$`]`
Clear p'_e
$CR.K_{po} \leftarrow KDF_{K_p}(S_o)$
$S_{po\_bind} \leftarrow KDF_{CR.K_{po}}(\text{“bind”})$
$CR.K_{po\_auth} \leftarrow KDF_{CR.K_{po}}(\text{“auth”})$
$CR.K_{po\_encr} \leftarrow KDF_{CR.K_{po}}(\text{“encr”})$
$CR.K_{po\_code} \leftarrow KDF_{CR.K_{po}}(\text{“code”})$
if $K_p = \perp$ **then**
  Clear $CR.*$
  $S_{po\_bind} \leftarrow \perp$
Clear K_p
return S_{po_bind}

Function 1. This function loads the helper parameter h'_e and the hash $H(p_e, h_e)$ into memory. Next, the PUF is read and the fuzzy extractor is invoked to generate the platform symmetric secret key, K_p. Internally, the fuzzy extractor checks whether the inputs $H(p_e, h_e)$ and h_e correspond with the reconstructed value. A special symbol $\perp$ is output should the values be different.

The key K_p and the (device owner) supplied seed S_o are used to derive the master processor secret, $CR.K_{po}$. The seed value S_o allows the device owner to personalize the processor keys. The symmetric key $CR.K_{po}$ is used for the derivation of four symmetric platform keys: (i) $CR.S_{po\_bind}$, the platform binding secret, (ii) $CR.K_{po\_auth}$, the platform key used for authenticating data residing in untrusted storage from prior invocations (iii) $CR.K_{po\_encr}$, the platform key used for encrypting data and (iv) $CR.K_{po\_code}$, the platform key used to derive code-specific keys. In all cases, keys are derived via a KDF, which in turn may use pseudo-random functions (e.g., HMAC, CMAC) as building blocks. Constructions of key derivation functions accepting secret and public parameters are well-known [7, 22]. At the end of the process, the function checks if the fuzzy extractor returned the special symbol $\perp$, which would indicate that either the PUF response was too noisy and therefore it was not possible to reconstruct K_p or $H(p_e, h_e) \neq H(p'_e, h'_e)$. In either case, all OASIS registers are cleared and the function returns the special symbol $\perp$ indicating failure. After the check, K_p is cleared and S_{po_bind} is returned.

Func 2a $h_{PK} \leftarrow$ `f_create_asym_keys[`S_{po_bind}`]`

$p, q, \leftarrow$ `f_find_primes[`S_{po_bind}`, RSAParam.size]`
$\left\{ \begin{matrix} K^{+}_{po\_bind}, \\ CR.K^{-1}_{po\_bind} \end{matrix} \right\} \leftarrow$ `f_rsa_key_gen[`p, q, e`]`
$\{K^{-1}_{po\_bind}\}_{CR.K_{po\_encr}} \leftarrow \mathsf{Enc}_{CR.K_{po\_encr}}(CR.K^{-1}_{po\_bind})$
$\tau \leftarrow \mathrm{MAC}_{CR.K_{po\_auth}}(\{K^{-1}_{po\_bind}\}_{CR.K_{po\_encr}}, K^{+}_{po\_bind})$
$h_{PK} \leftarrow \left\{ \{K^{-1}_{po\_bind}\}_{CR.K_{po\_encr}}, K^{+}_{po\_bind}, \tau \right\}$
if $S_{po\_bind} = \perp$ **then**
  Clear $CR.*$
  Clear h_{PK}
return h_{PK}

Function 2*a*. This function generates the processor asymmetric keys. The `f_find_primes[]` function picks a random seed value of size `RSAParam.size` and begins search until the first prime is found. The process is repeated for the second prime using a new seed value. `f_find_primes[]` returns secret primes, p and q. The function `f_rsa_key_gen[]` takes the primes and a public exponent as inputs and generates the keypair $K^{+}_{po\_bind}, K^{-1}_{po\_bind}$. Notice that the RSA private key $K^{-1}_{po\_bind}$ is composed of p, q, and the inverse of the RSA public exponent mod$\phi(N)$, where $N = p \cdot q$. Methodologies to generate primes are well-understood and standardized [18]. The RSA private key $K^{-1}_{po\_bind}$ is encrypted using $CR.K_{po\_encr}$, and a message authentication code τ is computed over this value and the corresponding public key $K^{+}_{po\_bind}$. Finally, a data store h_{PK}, containing the asymmetric keys and τ, is returned.

Func 2b $h_{PK} \leftarrow$ `f_create_asym_keys[`S_{po_bind}`]`

$\left\{ \begin{matrix} K^{+}_{po\_bind}, \\ CR.K^{-1}_{po\_bind} \end{matrix} \right\} \leftarrow$ `f_ecc_key_gen[`S_{po_bind}`, ECCParam]`
$\{K^{-1}_{po\_bind}\}_{CR.K_{po\_encr}} \leftarrow \mathsf{Enc}_{CR.K_{po\_encr}}(CR.K^{-1}_{po\_bind})$
$\tau \leftarrow \mathrm{MAC}_{CR.K_{po\_auth}}(\{K^{-1}_{po\_bind}\}_{CR.K_{po\_encr}}, K^{+}_{po\_bind})$
$h_{PK} \leftarrow \left\{ \{K^{-1}_{po\_bind}\}_{CR.K_{po\_encr}}, K^{+}_{po\_bind}, \tau \right\}$
if $S_{po\_bind} = \perp$ **then**
  Clear $CR.*$
  Clear h_{PK}
return h_{PK}

Function 2*b*. We describe an alternative implementation of the `f_create_asym_keys[]` (Function 2*a*) using elliptic curves in Function 2*b*. The implementation of this function is analogous but much more efficient than its RSA counterpart, since there is no prime search step. Key generation is a single elliptic curve multiplication, which in general is efficient. In addition, this version has the advantage of small area overhead, if support for asymmetric operations is implemented at the hardware level. These advantages come at the cost of a significant increase in the time required to perform a signature verification operation (when compared to RSA). It is up to the HWM to decide which implementation is more appropriate based on its own requirements and constraints.

Func 3 $K^{+}_{po\_bind} \leftarrow$ `f_read_asym_keys[`h_{PK}`]`

$\tau' \leftarrow \text{MAC}_{CR.K_{po\_auth}}\left(h_{PK}.\left\{\{K^{-1}_{po\_bind}\}_{CR.K_{po\_encr}}, K^{+}_{po\_bind}\right\}\right)$

if $h_{PK}.\tau \neq \tau'$ **then**
  Clear $CR.*$
  Clear $h_{PK}.K^{+}_{po\_bind}$
else
  $CR.K^{-1}_{po\_bind} \leftarrow \text{Dec}_{CR.K_{po\_encr}}(h_{PK}.\{K^{-1}_{po\_bind}\}_{CR.K_{po\_encr}})$
return $h_{PK}.K^{+}_{po\_bind}$

Function 3. This function is very efficient as it only requires symmetric cryptographic operations. In particular, `f_read_asym_keys[]` checks tag $h_{PK}.\tau$ to ensure that input data has not been tampered with. If this verification passes, the function decrypts the private binding key to $CR.K^{-1}_{po\_bind}$, using the symmetric key $CR.K_{po\_encr}$. Note that the corresponding read functions, for create functions $2a$ and $2b$, are the same except for the sizes of the operands, outputs, and registers required to store private and public keys.

4.1.2 Instruction Descriptions

Inst 1 $\{h_e, H(p_e, h_e)\} \leftarrow$ `init[]`

$p_e \leftarrow$ `f_read_PUF[]`
$rand \xleftarrow{R} \{0,1\}^{\ell}$
$\{h_e, H(p_e, h_e)\} \leftarrow$ `f_init_PUF[`$p_e, rand$`]`
Clear $p_e, rand$
return $\{h_e, H(p_e, h_e)\}$

Instruction 1. This instruction initializes the helper data h_e used to de-noise the raw SRAM PUF value p_e. The functions `f_read_PUF[]` and `f_init_PUF[]` read the raw PUF value and instantiate the helper data, as described in Section 4.1.1. The hash value $H(p_e, h_e)$ will be used by later instructions to prevent modified helper data from being used in attempts to learn information about the PUF. Observe that a hardware-generated random number, *rand*, is used to introduce entropy in the resulting helper data's value.

The variable *rand* needs to remain secret and exposed only inside the processor. It is also assumed that h_e can only be set once (or a limited number of times) to prevent exposing the output of the fuzzy extractor. This can be achieved during the initialization, which is performed by the HWM. Because of our use of *robust* fuzzy extractors [5, 9], we do not require *any secure* non-volatile memory. All data is stored outside the chip, either locally or externally published on a website. An additional step, not shown and not performed as part of Instruction 1 is the signing of $h_e||H(p_e, h_e)$ by the HWM or a TTP with output $\sigma_{h_e} \leftarrow \texttt{Sign}_{K^{-1}_{TTP}}(h_e||H(p_e, h_e))$. This guarantees to any third party (users, system integrators, device owners, etc.) that the helper data was created by the HWM and not some other (untrusted) party. Notice this is done only once during the lifetime of the device.

Inst 2 $h_{PK} \leftarrow$ `create[`$S_o, h_e, H(p_e, h_e), \sigma_{h_e}, K^{+}_{TTP}$`]`

if $\texttt{Verify}_{K^{+}_{TTP}}(h_e||H(p_e, h_e), \sigma_{h_e}) = \texttt{accept}$ **then**
  $S_{po\_bind} \leftarrow$ `f_create_sym_keys[`$S_o, h_e, H(p_e, h_e)$`]`
  $h_{PK} \leftarrow$ `f_create_asym_keys[`S_{po_bind}`]`
  Clear S_{po_bind}
  return h_{PK}
else
  ABORT

Instruction 2. This instruction generates a hierarchy of cryptographic keys from the raw PUF response p_e. Symmetric and asymmetric keys are generated by `f_create_sym_keys[]` (Function 1) and `f_create_asym_keys[]` (Function $2a$ or $2b$), respectively.

The h_{PK} variable is assigned the $\{K^{+}_{po\_bind}, K^{-1}_{po\_bind}\}$ key-pair generated by `f_create_asym_keys[]`. Observe that h_{PK} is encrypted and contains authentication information, which is verified internally by OASIS using a key derived from the internal PUF key and the seed S_o. Lastly, note that verification of the signature σ_{h_e} is most efficient if the signature algorithm is based on RSA using a small exponent (e.g., 3, 17, or $2^{16}+1$). Regardless of the latency due to signature verification, we expect that this step is performed rarely – e.g., whenever the device changes ownership or if a user desires to setup the environment for future use.

Inst 3 `launch[`$\mathbf{C}, \mathbf{C}.inputs, S_o, h_e, H(p_e, h_e), h_{PK}$`]`

Configure CPU into CAR Mode
Load **C** into the CPU cache
$S_{po\_bind} \leftarrow$ `f_create_sym_keys[`$S_o, h_e, H(p_e, h_e)$`]`
$K^{+}_{po\_bind} \leftarrow$ `f_read_asym_keys[`h_{PK}`]`
$CR.PCR \leftarrow H(\mathbf{C})$
$CR.K_C \leftarrow KDF_{CR.K_{po\_code}}(H(\mathbf{C}))$
if $(S_{po\_bind} = \perp)$ **then**
  Clear $CR.*$
  ABORT
Clear S_{po_bind}
Transfer control to **C**'s entry point

Instruction 3. The `launch[]` instruction is designed to setup the OASIS environment for code **C** and populate all necessary registers. It begins by setting up a clean-slate CAR environment, including disabling interrupts and hardware debugging access. It then reads and loads $CR.*$ registers with cryptographic key material for further processing by other instructions.[4]

[4]A possible optimization is to conditionally invoke `f_create_sym_keys[]` and `f_read_asym_keys[]`. For example, `launch[]` can be modified to only invoke `f_create_sym_keys[]` once after the processor reboots and maintain the resulting keys in CR.* during successive OASIS sessions. This optimization must be carefully considered and constructed by the implementer to manage the security trade-off (PUF-derived secrets persisting between invocations). Addition-

To avoid the expensive operations performed in `create[]` for asymmetric key generation (e.g., prime generation), an encrypted data store h_{PK} is returned by `f_create_asym_keys[]` and `f_read_asym_keys[`h_{PK}`]` is used on subsequent invocations. This function's overhead is equivalent to a few efficient *symmetric-key* operations.

Observe that if we want to make the public binding key available outside the environment, Instruction 2 must be called first. Also note that Instruction 2 verifies the signature σ_{h_e} every time it executes, whereas Instruction 3 does not. We expect that signature verification will be performed at most once *per session*, where each session might call the `launch[]` instruction multiple times. Notice that even if the signature verification function is performed every time, the overhead should be minimal, assuming RSA signatures. Refer to Figure 1 for details on when instructions are called.

Next, `launch[]` stores a hash of the target code **C** to the platform configuration register $CR.PCR$. Finally, a symmetric key K_C is generated using a key derivation function based on $CR.K_{po\_code}$ and a hash of target code **C**. K_C is used for encrypting and authenticating the executing code's *state* for local storage to untrusted memory.

At the end of `launch[]`, the following registers have been populated: $CR.K_{po}$, $CR.K_{po\_auth}$, $CR.K_{po\_encr}$, $CR.K_{po\_code}$, $CR.K^{-1}_{po\_bind}$, $CR.PCR$, and $CR.K_C$.

Inst 4 $X \leftarrow$ `unbind[`$\{X_1, PCR\_ver\}_{K^+_{po\_bind}}, \{X_2, PCR\_ver\}_{K_C}$`]`

---

if $\{X_1, PCR\_ver\}_{K^+_{po\_bind}} \neq NULL$ **then**
  $X, PCR\_ver \leftarrow \mathsf{Dec}_{CR.K^{-1}_{po\_bind}}(\{X_1, PCR\_ver\}_{K^+_{po\_bind}})$
else if $\{X_2, PCR\_ver\}_{K_C} \neq NULL$ **then**
  $X, PCR\_ver \leftarrow \mathsf{AuthDec}_{CR.K_C}(\{X_2, PCR\_ver\}_{K_C})$
else
  $X \leftarrow \perp$

if $CR.PCR \neq PCR\_ver$ **then**
  $X \leftarrow \perp$
return X

Instruction 4. Inputs X_1 and X_2 contain data values that should only be released to the code that generated the data. The unbind instruction provides assurance to the verifier that the inputs will only be released to the code with measurement PCR_ver. Note that `unbind[]` can decrypt data encrypted under either of the binding key $K^+_{po\_bind}$ or the application secret key K_C.

In the protocol described in Section 5, included in X_2 is a symmetric key K_{VP}, which is generated by the verifier V for bulk encryption of data to be transferred between V and the platform P. Notice that we do not suggest using the public binding key, $K^+_{po\_bind}$, for bulk encryption. Instead, symmetric keys should be used for bulk encryption operations and the public binding key for storing bulk encryption keys. This is a common practice used to avoid the performance cost of public key cryptography.

In choosing the asymmetric encryption scheme, some care must be taken to prevent an attacker from using the ciphertext $\{X, PCR\_ver\}_{K^+_{po\_bind}}$, which is intended to be decrypted only by the code with measurement PCR_ver, to generate a related ciphertext $\{X, PCR\_ver'\}_{K^+_{po\_bind}}$, which the device would be willing to decrypt for different code with measurement PCR_ver'. To prevent this, the encryption scheme must be *non-malleable* – i.e., an attacker cannot use one ciphertext to generate a second ciphertext that decrypts to a plaintext related to the original plaintext. The formal definition of non-malleable is known as Chosen Ciphertex Attack of type 2 or CCA2. Examples of CCA2 (non-malleable) asymmetric encryption schemes include RSA-OAEP and RSA-OAEP+ [39].[5] An alternative strategy to using a non-malleable public-key encryption scheme is to use the secret encrypted with the asymmetric primitive to derive two keys: an encryption key and a MAC key. The MAC key should be used to compute a MAC over the bulk-encrypted ciphertext, and the receiver should reject ciphertexts with an inconsistent MAC. This is the strategy used in the Integrated Encryption Scheme [38]. In this work, we simply assume that we are using a CCA2 public-key encryption scheme regardless of its particular implementation.

Inst 5 $out \leftarrow$ `bind[`$K_{VP}, stateOS, hashInputs, resultV, update$`]`

---

if $update \neq NULL$ **then**
  $\mathbf{C}' \leftarrow \mathsf{AuthDec}_{K_{VP}}(update)$
  if $\mathbf{C}' \neq \perp$ **then**
    $CR.PCR \leftarrow H(\mathbf{C}')$
    $CR.K_C \leftarrow KDF_{CR.K_{po\_code}}(CR.PCR)$
$out.OS \leftarrow \mathsf{AuthEnc}_{CR.K_C}(stateOS, CR.PCR)$
$V.hosstate \leftarrow H(stateOS)$
$V.hinp \leftarrow hashInputs$
$V.encK \leftarrow \mathsf{AuthEnc}_{CR.K_C}(K_{VP}, CR.PCR)$
$V.res \leftarrow resultV$
$out.V \leftarrow \mathsf{AuthEnc}_{K_{VP}}(V)$
Clear $CR.*$
Clear all state
return out

Instruction 5. The `bind[]` instruction prepares data for transfer to the untrusted code. This instruction should be called by the executing code right before returning. Inputs to this instruction include a shared secret K_{VP}, the application state $stateOS$, a hash of application input $hashInputs$, and the application results $results$. The variables $out.OS$ and $out.V$ are ciphertext to be stored in local memory and sent to the verifier, respectively. Please note that $out.OS$ and $V.encK$ bind $stateOS$ and K_{VP} to the launch point measurement of executing code C. Finally, observe that `bind[]` enables program code **C** updates. This is enabled by checking whether the update has been encrypted and authenticated with the shared secret K_{VP} and upon successful verification, updating $CR.PCR$ and $CR.K_C$, accordingly.

---

ally, the call to `f_read_asym_keys[]` may be skipped for sessions that only require symmetric keys.

[5]Note that it is possible for an encryption scheme to be semantically secure while still being malleable [11]. For example, in a hybrid scheme where RSA is used to encrypt a symmetric key, which is in turn used in a block cipher to encrypt the bulk data, then clearly the last block of the bulk-encrypted data can be modified without changing the decryption of the preceding plaintext blocks. This could allow the attacker to change the specified PCR if it appears at the end of bulk encrypted data. Even if the authorized PCR is at the beginning, the attacker would still be able to modify the end of the bulk data without changing the value of the preceding ciphertext.

5. SECURE REMOTE EXECUTION

Figure 2 shows the protocol for the initial and subsequent executions of security sensitive application $foo()$. We assume that the remote verifier V has a copy of the public platform binding key, $K^{+}_{po\_bind}$. Similarly, the verifier can keep a certificate that is used to confirm the authenticity of the public key it receives from the platform. We also assume that the verifier has access to the plaintext code.

In Step 1, the verifier V initiates an isolated execution session with the platform. V generates an encryption key K_{VP}, and binds the hash of the code $foo()$ with K_{VP}. Bind allows the verifier to encrypt data using the public part of the platform key while ensuring that only the correct code running in a correctly setup execution environment can access the data. The inputs along with the code are sent to the platform.

In Step 2, the OS calls the hardware instruction `launch[]` using the plaintext code $foo()$, the verifier inputs $V.inp$, and the previously stored state $OS.inp$ as inputs. If it is the first code execution $OS.inp$ is empty.

In Step 3, the isolated execution environment IEE first checks inputs received from the verifier. If a "setup" command was received from the verifier the IEE attempts to unbind the encrypted inputs from V as follows. The IEE releases shared encryption key K_{VP}, using the `unbind[]` instruction, and decrypts any private inputs, aborting execution if either operation fails. These checks prevent unauthorized code from proceeding. After the checks, the application logic is executed. For example, if the application is a secure counter, during the first iteration the counter is set to zero. In the case of an encrypted database, the first records could be stored in the database or all records could be initialized to zero.

Steps 4 and 5 show the parameters returned to the OS and the verifier, respectively. Step 5 is critical as it provides evidence to the verifier that the computation has been performed on the correct inputs and, in particular, that the inputs have not been manipulated prior to entering OASIS.

6. DISCUSSION

6.1 Linkable Code Blocks

So far, we have presented how an application C that is fully contained within the CPU cache is executed in OASIS. Recall that the `unbind[]` instruction guarantees that only C can access its protected state during future invocations by verifying that the loaded application has measurement $H(C)$ before decrypting.

Now we consider the case of an application that has size greater than the cache (e.g., application $C = C_0|C_1|\dots|C_n$ where C_i refers to the ith application code block). Execution of more complex applications is achieved by computing a Merkle hash tree over the entire program, and binding the resulting tree's root value to the application state. The loaded code block C_i is accepted if and only if the hash tree validation succeeds.

The hash tree construction provides several nice properties. First, it extends state protection and load-time integrity checking to applications of arbitrary size. Second, it maintains a small TCB. Third, it enables efficient execution because code block C_i may be safely executed before the entire application C has been hashed.

Setup Session

1. V	: $V.inp.cmd \leftarrow$ `command`
	: $V.inp.pubdata \leftarrow pubInputs$
	: **if** ($V.inp.cmd =$ "setup")
	: $K_{VP} \xleftarrow{R} \{0,1\}^{\ell}$
	: $V.inp.privdata \leftarrow \mathsf{AuthEnc}_{K_{VP}}(privInputs)$
	: $V.inp.encsym \leftarrow \mathsf{Enc}_{K^{+}_{po\_bind}}(\{K_{VP}, H(\mathbf{foo}())\})$
	: **else if** ($V.inp.cmd =$ "compute")
	: $V.inp.privdata \leftarrow$
	: $\mathsf{AuthEnc}_{K_{VP}}(privInputs, outV.hosstate)$
	: $V.inp.encsym \leftarrow outV.encK$
$V \rightarrow OS$	: $\langle \mathbf{foo}(), V.inp \rangle$
	: **else** /* other functionality */...

Launch Code[a]

2. OS	: $OS.inp \leftarrow out.OS$
	: `launch`$[\mathbf{foo}(), \{V.inp, OS.inp\}]$

Execute Code

3. IEE	: **if** ($V.inp.cmd =$ "setup") **then**
	: $ksym \leftarrow$ `unbind`$[V.inp.encsym, NULL]$
	: **if** ($ksym = \perp$) **then** ABORT
	: $data_1 \leftarrow V.inp.pubdata$
	: **if** ($V.inp.privdata \neq NULL$) **then**
	: $data_2 \leftarrow \mathsf{AuthDec}_{ksym}(V.inp.privdata)$
	: **if** ($data_2 = \perp$) **then** ABORT
	: **else**
	: $data_2 \leftarrow NULL$
	: $state \leftarrow \mathbf{doWork1}(data_1, data_2)$
	: $out \leftarrow$ `bind`$[ksym, state, H(V.inp), NULL]$
	: **else if** ($V.inp.cmd =$ "compute")**then**
	: $ksym \leftarrow$ `unbind`$[NULL, V.inp.encsym]$
	: **if** ($ksym = \perp$) **then** ABORT
	: $data_1 \leftarrow V.inp.pubdata$
	: **if** ($V.inp.privdata \neq NULL$) **then**
	: $data_2 \leftarrow \mathsf{AuthDec}_{ksym}(V.inp.privdata)$
	: **if** ($data_2 = \perp$) **then** ABORT
	: $state_{old} \leftarrow$ `unbind`$[NULL, OS.inp]$
	: **if** ($data_2.Vhosstate \neq H(state_{old})$) **then** ABORT
	: $\{state_{new}, res\} \leftarrow \mathbf{doWork2}(state_{old},$
	: $data_1, data_2)$
	: $out \leftarrow$ `bind`$[ksym, state_{new}, H(V.inp), res]$
	: **else** /* other functionality */...

Save State

4. $IEE \rightarrow OS$	: $\langle out.OS, out.V \rangle$
OS	: store $\langle \mathbf{foo}(), out.OS \rangle$

Verify Execution

5. $OS \rightarrow V$	: $\langle out.V \rangle$
V	: $outV \leftarrow \mathsf{AuthDec}_{K_{VP}}(out.V)$
	: **if** ($outV = \perp$) **then**
	: reject: invalid computation
	: **if** ($outV.hinp \neq H(V.inp)$) **then**
	: reject: invalid inputs

[a]Please note that $OS.inp$ is assigned $NULL$ during the first launch.

Figure 2: *OASIS Execution Protocol:* This protocol shows the interaction between the verifier V and untrusted system OS during the initial invocation (*setup*) and repeated invocations (*compute*) of code foo() within isolated execution environment IEE. During the initial invocation the verifier V uses the public platform key $K^{+}_{po\_bind}$ to establish shared secret K_{VP} which is used for repeat invocations.

6.2 Rollback Prevention

A *rollback attack* occurs when old state is presented to the isolated execution environment. Since the stale state is cryptographically consistent, an isolated execution environment implemented without rollback prevention will incorrectly accept it – potentially bypassing stateful protection mechanisms to, for example, undo the append-only property of an audit log. Thus, rollback resistance is needed to guarantee state continuity of the executing application.

One technique for ensuring state continuity is to include a protected monotonic counter as part of the state [33]. Another technique for rollback prevention is to keep a trusted summary (e.g., a hash) of the expected state. Parno et al. include a summary of the state *history* to permit reverting to a safe state in the case of an unexpected crash [36]. These methods can be achieved by using protected non-volatile memory for persistent storage of data describing the expected state. However, we seek a rollback prevention mechanism that enables OASIS to remain stateless between invocations. Additionally, we rule out using a trusted third party for state management.

What follows is a description of how the verifier can confirm state continuity using the OASIS instruction set. During the execution protocol, the `unbind[]` instruction is invoked to decrypt any state belonging to code C (Figure 2 step 3). After executing code C, the `bind[]` instruction is invoked to protect state destined for the OS as well as output destined for the verifier. Included in the output for the verifier is a summary of the current state, $H(stateOS)$. The verifier output is encrypted under key K_{VP} before transferring control to untrusted OS code for delivery to the verifier. The verifier includes this state summary as an input during the next invocation. If the state presented by the untrusted OS matches the expected state, the code executes and the new state summary is communicated to the verifier as acknowledgment. Otherwise, the protocol aborts. In this fashion, we achieve rollback prevention without requiring persistent application state in the OASIS TCB.

6.3 Distributed Deployment

We have presented cryptographic techniques for data secrecy, authenticity, and freshness. Still, the rollback prevention mechanism described thus far is insufficient if we consider the distributed deployment model where multiple verifiers collaborate through a remote service provider. In this asynchronous context, even if cryptographic techniques prevent forged responses and data snooping, a compromised OS can launch *forking attacks* by concealing the operations of one verifier from another. For example, a compromised server may simply omit the current state and replay an old state to the other verifiers.

Fork consistency ensures that all verifiers see the same operations log before an omission but no verifier can see any other verifier's operations after an omission fault (fork). Furthermore, the fork consistency condition enables the verifiers to detect a misbehaving service provider after a single omission.

Li et al. present a protocol for achieving fork consistency where each verifier maintains a signed version structure list [25]. Each verifier signs increasing version numbers and appends these to their respective lists, allowing them to compare lists and detect a fork attack.

6.4 Version Updating

To support version updating (i.e., updating code $\mathbf{C}$ to legitimate new code $\mathbf{C}'$), the application must implement an update command which calls `bind[]` with parameter *update* set (where the *update* parameter contains the new code version $\mathbf{C}'$ encrypted under key K_{VP}). The `bind[]` instruction first checks parameter *update* for authenticity and then updates $CR.PCR$ and $CR.K_C$ using the new code version $\mathbf{C}'$ (refer to Table 2 for definitions of variables and Instruction 5 for details on `bind[]`). In this way the application state of the current software version $\mathbf{C}$ is bound to the new software version $\mathbf{C}'$. Accordingly, the next invocation of `unbind[]` will release the application state to $\mathbf{C}'$.

The decryption and authentication operations prove to OASIS that the software originated from the verifier V as she is the only one in possession of the key K_{VP}. It is possible to design an alternative update mechanism based on asymmetric operations which has the advantage that an entity different from V can provide an update $\mathbf{C}'$, thus granting it access to the current OASIS state. However, this comes at the cost of requiring certification which would add complexity and computational overhead.

6.5 Device Transferability

Recall that the device owner selects seed value S_o during key generation (refer to Function 1 for details). The seed value S_o enables derivation of owner-specific processor keys. Customization, via the owner-generated seed S_o, precludes previous device owners, including the manufacturer, from generating the same platform secret as the current owner. Thus, the device can be safely transferred. This protects the owners of new devices by limiting the ability of malicious parties (e.g., along the supply chain) to learn the platform secrets of the end user. This allows, for example, a device to be repurposed at a new business unit or sold to a new owner.

Please note that the owner-generated seed S_o effectively disassociates any resulting key material from the device manufacturer. Nevertheless, the owner needs a mechanism to prove the authenticity of their processor to a third party. A default seed value that is fixed for the life of the device may be included to support secure device transfer while still providing a mechanism for proving the authenticity of the executing platform. We refer to this default seed value as the *identity* seed value or $S_o{}^*$. Next, a master signing key is derived from root secret K_p and identity seed $S_o{}^*$. Certification can be handled by a third party for further unlinkability. In this way, secrets linked to the hardware are derived from the fixed identity seed $S_o{}^*$ whereas secrets exclusive to the owner are derived from the custom owner seed S_o.

Allowing the owner to choose any S_o as often as they like may allow an attacker to leak the root platform key K_p through cryptanalysis. This can be mitigated by rate-limiting requests for a fresh S_o. Upon request, the device generates a fresh seed value S_o and computes a MAC over it using a key derived from the root secret K_p and the identity seed value $S_o{}^*$. This ensures that chosen values of S_o cannot be correlated with a response, during device initialization, to learn the root platform key K_p.

7. PERFORMANCE EVALUATION

7.1 System Configuration

We model our proposed processor instruction set using Simics, a full-system simulator [31]. We build a prototype system by adding our new instructions to the x86-hammer model.[6] We model a 2 GHz processor with non-unified L1 cache (64 KB data and instruction caches). We use a modified Linux 2.6.32 kernel as our target operating system.

7.2 Microbenchmark Results

To evaluate micro- and macro-level benchmarks, we measure the performance of our implementation against TCG-style implementations of common security-sensitive code operations. We use a pessimistic benchmark for the OASIS isolated execution environment and compare it to an optimistic benchmark for TCG 1.2. See Table 4 for a list of the platform primitives and their associated costs. See Table 5 for a comparison of performance overheads for OASIS and DRTM-based implementations.[7]

We base the median performance costs associated with the cryptographic primitives by leveraging open source libraries LibTomCrypt and OpenSSL.[8] It is likely that these functions further increase in performance with a hardware implementation.

7.3 Performance Advantages

We now present the performance advantages of our architecture as compared to a TPM implementation.

In terms of processor speed, cryptographic applications benefit from running on a processor core instead of a TPM. For example, the Infineon TPM co-processor operates at 33 MHz, which pales in comparison to even mid and low-end commodity processor speeds.

In terms of communication overhead, we avoid costly communication overheads by implementing cryptographic functions on chip instead of on a co-processor. For example, the TPM interfaces using the Low Pin Count (LPC) bus. The LPC is used to connect low-bandwidth devices to the CPU (4-bit-bus on a 33 MHz clock).

8. RELATED WORK

Architecture Extensions. Hardware-based security mechanisms have been proposed and implemented by both commercial and academic groups. In terms of commercial hardware-based IEE technologies, the main components are the Trusted Execution Environment (TEE) which provides capabilities for isolated execution and ensuring software is in a known good state before launch, and the Trusted Platform Module (TPM) which provides remote attestation, binding, and sealing capabilities. Popular TEE implementations include ARM Trust Zone [1], and Intel TXT [3]. More recently, Intel has improved on the TXT architecture with the development of Intel SGX [19]. These techniques can be combined with the OASIS API. For example, Enclaves from SGX would

[6] *x86-hammer* is a hardware model representing a generic 64-bit AMD Operteron processor sans on-chip devices [47].

[7] We have based performance overheads in Table 5 on TPM benchmarks from [37] where the reference DRTM implementation does not provide performance numbers for 2048-bit RSA operations.

[8] LibTom: `www.libtom.org`. OpenSSL: `www.openssl.org`.

Table 4: Performance overheads for platform operations used to instrument the OASIS isolated execution environment hardware simulation. Times are based on a 2 GHz processor clock.

	avg (of 2^{10} executions)	
	cycles	*time(ms)*
Platform Support		
$rand \xleftarrow{R} \{0,1\}^{\ell}$	1.6 K	$7.91 \cdot 10^{-4}$
`f_read_PUF`	~	$2.55 \cdot 10^{-5}$
`f_init_PUF`	~	$2.40 \cdot 10^{-5}$
`f_fuzzy_extract_PUF`	~	$3.30 \cdot 10^{-5}$
Crypto		
$H(p_e)$	4.9 K	$2.49 \cdot 10^{-3}$
$KDF_{CR.K_{po}}$	20.9 K	$1.04 \cdot 10^{-2}$
`f_sym_encrypt`	1.2 K	$6.02 \cdot 10^{-4}$
`f_sym_decrypt`	1.2 K	$6.12 \cdot 10^{-4}$
`f_rsa_key_gen`	3.2 B	$1.61 \cdot 10^{+3}$
`f_rsa_encrypt`	3.08 M	$1.54 \cdot 10^{+0}$
`f_rsa_decrypt`	65.7 M	$3.29 \cdot 10^{+1}$
$\texttt{Sign}_{K_X^{-1}}(m)$	65.9 M	$3.30 \cdot 10^{+1}$
$\texttt{Verify}_{K_X^{+}}(m, \sigma)$	3.1 M	$1.53 \cdot 10^{+0}$
OASIS Functions		
`f_create_sym_keys`	104 K	$5.21 \cdot 10^{-2}$
`f_create_asym_keys`	3.7 B	$1.84 \cdot 10^{+3}$
`f_read_asym_keys`	18.5 K	$9.26 \cdot 10^{-3}$
OASIS Instructions		
`init`	7.2 K	$3.58 \cdot 10^{-3}$
`create`	4.3 B	$2.16 \cdot 10^{+3}$
`launch`	137 K	$6.84 \cdot 10^{-2}$
`unbind with asym`	68.1 M	$3.40 \cdot 10^{+1}$
`unbind with sym`	17.9 M	$8.95 \cdot 10^{+0}$
`bind`	3.12 M	$1.56 \cdot 10^{+0}$

replace CAR mode based memory isolation to support applications of much larger size.

Similar to our work, Defrawy et al. propose SMART, an architecture for establishing a dynamic root of trust in remote devices [13]. SMART focuses on remote embedded devices (in particular, low-end microcontroller units (MCUs)) whereas we are applicable to high-end processors. Additionally, SMART investigates the usage of secret key material to establish a root of trust, assuming the existence of *secure* non-volatile memory to store the secret. In contrast, OASIS is based on the use of SRAM memory–based PUFs [16, 17].

Previous work has explored hardware extensions designed for an adversary model where software and physical attacks are possible. Lie et al. present XOM, a hardware implementation of eXecute-only-memory [26]. Similar to our adversary model, XOM assumes a completely untrusted OS. Unlike OASIS, XOM assumes a secure manufacturing process, allows secure XOM applications to access the platform secret, and requires secure non-volatile memory. Lee et al. present SP, a processor architecture for isolated execution [24, 12]. Similar to OASIS, SP does not require a secure manufacturing process; however, SP includes no immutable device secret which makes it a challenge to prove the authenticity of the executing platform to a third party.

Memory cloaking provides secrecy and integrity of application data while allowing the OS to carry on most of its memory management tasks by limiting the OS's data access to ciphertext. More recently, Williams et al. (Secure Exe-

Table 5: Comparison of performance overheads by invocation scenario.

Scenario	OASIS		DRTM		
	operation(s)	*time*	*operation(s)*	*time*	*ref.*
One Time	`init[]`	3.6 μsec	NV Write, TPM 2048 Root Key Generation	> 25 sec	[37]
One Time per Owner	`create[]`	2.6 sec	TrustVisor-modeled AIK Generation: TPM and μTPM 2048 AIK Generation	> 25 sec	[37]
Per Module Launch (First Time)	`launch[]` and `unbind[]` with $K^{+}_{po\_bind}$ encrypted input	34.1 msec	TrustVisor-modeled DRTM: Transfer SLB over LPC, Unseal μTPM keys, quote SLB, μTPM HV_Quote of PAL	> 1.8 sec	[32]
Per Module Launch (Repeated Invocation)	`launch[]` and `unbind[]` with K_C encrypted input	9.0 msec	TrustVisor-modeled DRTM: Set-up and HV_Quote of PAL	22 msec	[32]

cutables [49]) and Chhabra et al. (SecureMe [8]) propose an isolated execution environment using hardware-based memory cloaking. Secure Executables uses CPU-protected memory regions to store the register set (e.g., while a Secure Executable is suspended during a system call). This solution has the advantage of avoiding cryptographic operations; however, direct memory attacks may be possible (e.g., by a DMA-enabled hardware component). The root of trust in Secure Executables is based on a public/private keypair that is installed in the CPU during manufacturing. In our design, the manufacturer and the device owner (or system integrator) both contribute to initializing a root of trust. This reduces the possibility of any large-scale data breaches and also facilities repurposing the device for new owners. SecureMe improves upon previous cloaking methods by ensuring that the entire address space of the application remains protected at all times. OASIS differs from SecureMe in its usage model. Unlike SecureMe, OASIS enforces isolation in the strictest sense by suspending the OS for the duration of its sessions.

PUF-Based Secrets. Similar to our work, Suh et al. propose a secure processing architecture, AEGIS, that makes use of Physical Unclonable Functions for creating and protecting secrets [42]. AEGIS consigns security-sensitive OS functionality (e.g., context switching and virtual memory management) to a security kernel. However, this approach faces the same problem as the trusted OS model – the resulting TCB can be quite large.

Alternate Deployment Models. Our ISE is inspired by the recommendations of McCune et al. [34] but in contrast to previous approaches that use a TPM as the root of trust, we use a PUF-derived key, integrated within the processor. This integration increases performance and diminishes the possibility of attacks on the buses connecting the platform to the TPM.

We use hardware instructions to ensure strong isolation properties during the execution of self-contained security-sensitive code. Another alternative is to use a special-purpose hypervisor instead of additional hardware instructions. The hypervisor provides a less expensive alternative to hardware instruction set extensions and is significantly smaller than a full OS. Nonetheless, a disadvantage of this approach is that the hypervisor is trusted to enforce memory isolation and DMA protection for executing code and, accordingly, must be included in the TCB.

An alternative to extending functionality to the CPU is to use a secure co-processor [40]. A dedicated TPM is the approach endorsed by the TCG. In terms of manufacturing, this approach has the advantage of decoupling system security from the production of traditional processors. A drawback of using co-processors, however, is a reduction of physical security due to the exposed bus. Additionally, the performance hit due to communicating over the bus is not suitable for minimal TCB execution where sessions are repeatedly setup and torn down.

Alternatively, a co-processor could be included as an IP on a SoC which would provide speed, tighter control, and enhanced security. The motivation for extending the processor ISA rather than a SoC TPM implementation is cost savings.

9. CONCLUSION

Currently, TPM-based solutions have not reached widespread application in security-sensitive contexts, perhaps because TCG solutions lack protection against a more resourceful adversary, lack sufficient properties for end-to-end application protection, lack architectural safeguards against supply-chain compromises, or concerns over poor performance. OASIS offers a stronger degree of protection through highly efficient isolated execution with no hardware dependencies outside the CPU.

We have explored the extent to which minimal modifications to commodity CPUs can support isolated code execution. The ISA extensions explored in this research enable compute service providers and application developers to provide high-security assurance at low cost in terms of platform and software complexity.

10. ACKNOWLEDGMENTS

We are thankful to Olatunji Ruwase, Chen Chen, Yanlin Li, and Siddhartha Chhabra for their insightful discussions and for making valuable suggestions for completing this work, and to the anonymous reviewers for their detailed comments and valuable feedback.

11. REFERENCES

[1] ARM Security Technology - Building a Secure System using TrustZone Technology, 2009. Available at http://infocenter.arm.com/.

[2] The CDW 2011 Cloud Computing Tracking Poll, 2011. Available at www.cdw.com.

[3] Intel Trusted Execution Technology (Intel TXT) - Software Development Guide, 2013. Document Number: 315168-009 Available at www.intel.com.

[4] Bösch, C., Guajardo, J., Sadeghi, A.-R., Shokrollahi, J., and Tuyls, P. Efficient Helper Data Key Extractor on FPGAs. In *Cryptographic Hardware and Embedded Systems (CHES)* (2008).

[5] Boyen, X., Dodis, Y., Katz, J., Ostrovsky, R., and Smith, A. Secure Remote Authentication Using Biometric Data. In *Advances in Cryptology (EUROCRYPT)* (2005).

[6] Brian Krebs. Coordinated ATM Heist Nets Thieves $13M, 2011. Available at http://krebsonsecurity.com.

[7] Chen, L. Recommendation for Key Derivation Using Pseudorandom Functions (Revised). NIST Special Publication 800-108, 2009.

[8] Chhabra, S., Rogers, B., Solihin, Y., and Prvulovic, M. SecureME: A Hardware-Software Approach to Full System Security. In *ACM International conference on Supercomputing (ICS)* (2011).

[9] Dodis, Y., Katz, J., Reyzin, L., and Smith, A. Robust Fuzzy Extractors and Authenticated Key Agreement from Close Secrets. In *Advances in Cryptology (CRYPTO)* (2006).

[10] Dodis, Y., Reyzin, M., and Smith, A. Fuzzy Extractors: How to Generate Strong Keys from Biometrics and Other Noisy Data. In *Advances in Cryptology (EUROCRYPT)* (2004).

[11] Dolev, D., Dwork, C., and Naor, M. Non-Malleable Cryptography. In *SIAM Journal on Computing* (2000).

[12] Dwoskin, J. S., and Lee, R. B. Hardware-rooted trust for secure key management and transient trust. In *ACM conference on Computer and communications security (CCS)* (2007).

[13] El Defrawy, K., Francillon, A., Perito, D., and Tsudik, G. SMART: Secure and Minimal Architecture for (Establishing a Dynamic) Root of Trust. In *Network and Distributed System Security Symposium (NDSS)* (2012).

[14] Gassend, B., Clarke, D., van Dijk, M., and Devadas, S. Controlled Physical Random Functions. In *Proceedings of Annual Computer Security Applications Conference (ACSAC)* (2002).

[15] Gassend, B., Clarke, D., van Dijk, M., and Devadas, S. Silicon Physical Random Functions. In *ACM conference on Computer and Communications Security (CCS)* (2002).

[16] Guajardo, J., Kumar, S. S., Schrijen, G.-J., and Tuyls, P. FPGA Intrinsic PUFs and Their Use for IP Protection. In *Cryptographic Hardware and Embedded Systems (CHES)* (2007).

[17] Holcomb, D. E., Burleson, W. P., and Fu, K. Power-Up SRAM State as an Identifying Fingerprint and Source of True Random Numbers. *IEEE Trans. Computers* (2009).

[18] IEEE. IEEE Standard Specifications for Public-Key Cryptography — IEEE Std 1363^{TM}-2000, 2000. Available at www.ieee.org.

[19] Ittai Anati, Shay Gueron, S. P. J. Innovative Technology for CPU Attestation and Sealing. In *Workshop on Hardware Architecture for Security and Privacy* (2013).

[20] Jason Kincaid. Google Confirms That It Fired Engineer For Breaking Internal Privacy Policies, 2010. Available at http://techcrunch.com.

[21] Juels, A., and Wattenberg, M. A Fuzzy Commitment Scheme. In *ACM conference on Computer and Communications Security (CCS)* (1999).

[22] Krawczyk, H. Cryptographic Extraction and Key Derivation: The HKDF Scheme. In *Advances in Cryptology* (2010), CRYPTO.

[23] Kursawe, K., Sadeghi, A.-R., Schellekens, D., Skoric, B., and Tuyls, P. Reconfigurable Physical Unclonable Functions – Enabling Technology for Tamper-Resistant Storage. In *IEEE International Workshop on Hardware-Oriented Security and Trust (HOST)* (2009).

[24] Lee, R., Kwan, P., McGregor, J., Dwoskin, J., and Wang, Z. Architecture for Protecting Critical Secrets in Microprocessors. In *Proceedings of the International Symposium on Computer Architecture (ISCA)* (2005).

[25] Li, J., Krohn, M., Mazières, D., and Shasha, D. Secure Untrusted Data Depository (SUNDR). In *USENIX Symposium on Operating Systems Design & Implementation (OSDI)* (2004).

[26] Lie, D., Thekkath, C., Mitchell, M., Lincoln, P., Boneh, D., Mitchell, J., and Horowitz, M. Architectural Support for Copy and Tamper Resistant Software. *ACM SIGPLAN Notices* (2000).

[27] Linnartz, J.-P., and Tuyls, P. New Shielding Functions to Enhance Privacy and Prevent Misuse of Biometric Templates. In *International conference on Audio and Video Based Biometric Person Authentication (AVBPA)* (2003).

[28] Lu, Y., Lo, L.-T., Watson, G., and Minnich, R. CAR: Using Cache as RAM in LinuxBIOS, 2012. Available at http://rere.qmqm.pl/ mirq.

[29] Lucian Constantin. One year after DigiNotar breach, Fox-IT details extent of compromise, 2012. Available at www.wired.com.

[30] Maes, R., Tuyls, P., and Verbauwhede, I. Low-Overhead Implementation of a Soft Decision Helper Data Algorithm for SRAM PUFs. In *Cryptographic Hardware and Embedded Systems (CHES)* (2009).

[31] Magnusson, P., Christensson, M., Eskilson, J., Forsgren, D., Hallberg, G., Hogberg, J., Larsson, F., Moestedt, A., and Werner, B. Simics: A full system simulation platform. *Computer* (2002).

[32] McCune, J. M., Li, Y., Qu, N., Zhou, Z., Datta, A., Gligor, V. D., and Perrig, A. TrustVisor: Efficient TCB Reduction and Attestation. In *IEEE Symposium on Security and Privacy (S&P)* (2010).

[33] McCune, J. M., Parno, B., Perrig, A., Reiter, M. K., and Isozaki, H. Flicker: An Execution Infrastructure for TCB Minimization. In *ACM European Conference in Computer Systems (EuroSys)* (2008).

[34] McCune, J. M., Parno, B., Perrig, A., Reiter, M. K., and Seshadri, A. How Low Can You Go? Recommendations for Hardware-Supported Minimal TCB Code Execution. In *ACM Conference on Architectural Support for Programming Languages and Operating Systems (ASPLOS)* (2008).

[35] Pappu, R. S., Recht, B., Taylor, J., and Gershenfeld, N. Physical One-way Functions. *Science* (2002). Available at web.media.mit.edu.

[36] Parno, B., Lorch, J. R., Douceur, J. R., Mickens, J. W., and McCune, J. M. Memoir: Practical state continuity for protected modules. In *IEEE Symposium on Security and Privacy (S&P)* (2011).

[37] Schmitz, J., Loew, J., Elwell, J., Ponomarev, D., and Abu-Ghazaleh, N. B. TPM-SIM: A Framework for Performance Evaluation of Trusted Platform Modules. In *ACM Design Automation Conference (DAC)* (2011).

[38] Shoup, V. A Proposal for an ISO Standard for Public Key Encryption. Version 2.1, 2001. Available at www.shoup.net.

[39] Shoup, V. OAEP Reconsidered. In *Advances in Cryptology (CRYPTO)* (2001). Available at www.shoup.net.

[40] Smith, S. W., and Weingart, S. "building a high-performance, programmable secure coprocessor". *Computer Networks* (1999).

[41] Song, D., Shi, E., Fischer, I., and Shankar, U. Cloud data protection for the masses. *IEEE Computer* (2012).

[42] Suh, G. E., O'Donnell, C. W., and Devadas, S. AEGIS: A Single-Chip Secure Processor. *Information Security Technical Report* (2005).

[43] Symantec. Symantec-Sponsored Ponemon Report Finds Negligent Employees Top Cause of Data Breaches in the U.S. While Malicious Attacks Most Costly, 2012. Available at www.symantec.com.

[44] Taylor, G., and Cox, G. Behind Intel's New Random-Number Generator. *IEEE Spectrum* (2011). Available at http://spectrum.ieee.org.

[45] Tuyls, P., Schrijen, G.-J., Skoric, B., van Geloven, J., Verhaegh, N., and Wolters, R. Read-Proof Hardware from Protective Coatings. In *Cryptographic Hardware and Embedded Systems (CHES)* (2006).

[46] Vasudevan, A., McCune, J., Newsome, J., Perrig, A., and van Doorn, L. CARMA: A Hardware Tamper-Resistant Isolated Execution Environment on Commodity x86 Platforms. In *ACM Symposium on Information, Computer and Communications Security (ASIACCS)* (2012).

[47] Virtutech. Simics x86-440BX Target Guide, 2010.

[48] Wang, Y., kei Yu, W., Wu, S., Malysa, G., Suh, G. E., and Kan, E. C. Flash Memory for Ubiquitous Hardware Security Functions: True Random Number Generation and Device Fingerprints. In *IEEE Symposium on Security and Privacy (S&P)* (2012).

[49] Williams, P., and Boivie, R. CPU Support for Secure Executables. In *Trust and Trustworthy Computing* (2011).

BIOS Chronomancy: Fixing the Core Root of Trust for Measurement

John Butterworth
jbutterworth@mitre.org

Corey Kallenberg
ckallenberg@mitre.org

Xeno Kovah
xkovah@mitre.org

Amy Herzog
aherzog@mitre.org

The MITRE Corporation

ABSTRACT

In this paper we look at the implementation of the Core Root of Trust for Measurement (CRTM) from a Dell Latitude E6400 laptop. We describe how the implementation of the CRTM on this system doesn't meet the requirements set forth by either the Trusted Platform Module (TPM) PC client specification[12] or NIST 800-155[20] guidance. We show how novel *tick* malware, a 51 byte patch to the CRTM, can replay a forged measurement to the TPM, falsely indicating that the BIOS is pristine. This attack is broadly applicable, because all CRTMs we have seen to date are rooted in mutable firmware. We also show how *flea* malware can survive attempts to reflash infected firmware with a clean image. To fix the untrustworthy CRTM we ported an open source "TPM-timing-based attestation" implementation[17] from running in the Windows kernel, to running in an OEM's BIOS and SMRAM. This created a new, stronger CRTM that detects *tick*, *flea*, and other malware embedded in the BIOS. We call our system "BIOS Chronomancy", and we show that it works in a real vendor BIOS, with all the associated complexity, rather than in a simplified research environment.

Categories and Subject Descriptors

D.4.6 [**Software**]: Operating Systems-Security and Protection

Keywords

Trusted Computing, Firmware, BIOS, TPM, Malware, Timing-based Attestation

1. INTRODUCTION

The Trusted Computing Platform Alliance began work on the Trusted Platform Module (TPM) specification in 2000. In 2003 the Trusted Computing Group (TCG) was founded, and adopted the initial TPM 1.1 specification, before announcing the 1.2 specification in 2004[12]. Today, most enterprise-grade laptops and desktops contain a version 1.2 TPM, and the TPM 2.0 specification is under active development, with Windows 8 supporting draft compliant commands.

The TPM is a passive chip that relies on code running on the main CPU to direct its actions. In this paper we do not focus on the roots of trust for storage and reporting that reside physically within the TPM. Instead we examine the Static Root of Trust for Measurement (SRTM) that is rooted within the BIOS.[1] The SRTM is not used for on-demand runtime measurements, but rather to achieve a trusted boot. Per the TPM PC client spec, when the system boots the SRTM will measure itself as well as other parts of the BIOS, the master boot record, etc. and store the measurements in the TPM. The component that specifically performs self-measurement is considered the *Core* Root of Trust for Measurement (CRTM). If the CRTM can be modified without the self-measurement detecting the change, the chain of trust is fundamentally broken, and all subsequent elements in the chain can be corrupted without detection. In order to be reported in a trustworthy way, the SRTM stores measurements into the TPM Platform Configuration Registers (PCRs). Measurement appraisers that want to evaluate the boot measurements can ask the TPM for a copy of the PCRs signed by a key only the TPM has access to.

The flexibility with which the TPM PC client spec is written at times leads to ambiguity. This has lead to implementations inadvertently not measuring components that require change detection to be adequately secure. In some respect, the NIST 800-155[20] special publication (which is entirely advisory, and not associated with the official TCG specs) can be seen as an attempt to decrease ambiguity of the TCG specs by providing specific areas that should be measured to ensure a secure boot. However, in the case of the particular SRTM code we analyzed in this paper, we found it does not even adhere to some of the clear recommendations found in every revision of the TPM PC client spec. Therefore we hope this paper will serve as a cautionary tale of why today's SRTM implementations need to not

CCS'13, November 4–8, 2013, Berlin, Germany.

ACM 978-1-4503-2477-9/13/11 ...$15.00.
http://dx.doi.org/10.1145/2508859.2516714.

[1]The SRTM is in contrast to the Dynamic RTM (DRTM), a mechanism that can instantiate a trusted environment at some later time, even if the system booted in an untrusted state. An example implementation of a DRTM is Intel's Trusted Execution Technology[8].

be blindly trusted, and why future implementations should closely follow the more detailed NIST guidance.

While the NIST 800-155 guidance is an excellent starting point, in our opinion it is insufficient because it relies too heavily on access control to keep the attacker out of the BIOS. We believe attackers will always find a way to achieve the same privileges as the defender. The history of exploits is the history of access control being bypassed, even to the point of subverting requirements for signed BIOS updates[31][14][15].

We therefore believe it is necessary to apply techniques explicitly designed to combat attackers at the same privilege level[17, 18, 24, 25, 26, 27]. We call our implementation BIOS Chronomancy because our additional trust is *divined from timing*. The application of this technique to the BIOS provides many advantages over higher level implementations, because the environment in which both the attacker and defender are working is more constrained. This dramatically improves the likelihood of the CRTM detecting an unauthorized modification of itself. In this paper we will show a proof-of-concept custom BIOS that detects our CRTM-targetting malware, as well as other stronger attacks. We have run this custom BIOS on 17 Dell Latitude E6400 laptops for months without issue.

This paper makes the following contributions:

1. We analyze the implementation of the existing Latitude E6400 SRTM, how it measures itself, and how it deviates from the TPM PC client spec.
2. We describe the implementation of a *tick*, a CRTM-subverting BIOS parasite.
3. We describe the implementation of a *flea*, a CRTM-subverting, reflash-hopping, BIOS parasite that shows why enforcing signed updates is insufficient to protect currently deployed systems.
4. We discuss our design for the application of TPM timing-based attestation at the BIOS level. We also evaluate this implementation's performance against a worst case attacker, who is adding only the minimal timing overhead necessary to hide from detection, but not achieve any other goal.
5. We found and fixed a problem with the existing TPM timing-based timing attestation systems[24][17] that would allow an attacker to always forge his runtime to be within acceptable limits.

This paper is organized as follows. In the next section we discuss related work in the area of BIOS security and trusted computing. In Section 3 we describe how we have extracted information about the SRTM implementation, and in Section 4 we analyze how the Latitude E6400's SRTM implementation was found lacking. In Section 5 we discuss implementation details of our timing-based attestation system, and in Section 6 we evaluate it against various attacks. We detail our conclusions in Section 7.

2. RELATED WORK

There have been a number of papers and proof of concept attacks that took advantage of deficient access control on the BIOS reflashing procedure to introduce malicious code into the BIOS. One of the first attacks claiming to be a "BIOS Rootkit" was described by Heasman[13]. This attack did not target the BIOS code itself, but rather modified the ACPI tables set up by the BIOS. Subsequent ACPI table interpretation caused beneficial effects for the attacker, like arbitrary kernel memory writes. Later attacks by both Core Security[22], and Brossard[5] relied on the open source CoreBoot[1] project. This project was meant to serve as an open source BIOS alternative, although at the time of writing the newest Intel chipset (ICH7) supported by CoreBoot is approximately 6 years old. For in-the-wild attacks, there is the famous example of the CIH or Chernobyl virus[32] that would render a machine unbootable by writing zeros to the BIOS flash chip. In a much more recent attack, the Mebromi malware[11] rewrote the BIOS of a machine with code that would then write a typical Master Boot Record infection routine to the first sector of the disk. This allowed the malware to persist even if the hard drive was replaced or reformatted. Both of these attacks were limited in their spread because they supported only one chipset configuration.

All of the preceding attacks on the BIOS relied on the BIOS being unprotected and easily writeable, and only having security through the obscurity of the knowledge needed to reflash a BIOS. The most noteworthy exception to this assumption of an unprotected BIOS is the attack by Invisible Things Lab (ITL) which reflashed an Intel BIOS despite a configuration requiring all updates be signed[31]. They achieved this by exploiting a buffer overflow in the processing of the BIOS splash screen image. Given the prevalence of legacy, presumably un-audited, code in BIOSes, we expect there are many other similar vulnerabilities lurking. This is a key reason why we advocate for designing under the assumption that access control mechanisms protecting the SRTM will fail.

In 2007 Kauer[16] reported that there were no mechanisms preventing the direct reflashing of the BIOS of a HP nx6325, and he specifically targeted manipulation of the SRTM. He decided to simply replace the SRTM with an AMD-V-based DRTM to "remove the BIOS, OptionROMs and Bootloaders from the trust chain."[2] While the intent of a DRTM is to not depend on the SRTM, as was acknowledged by Kauer, the DRTM can in fact depend on the SRTM for its security. ITL has shown this through multiple attacks. In [29] ITL described an attack where manipulation of the ACPI tables generated by the BIOS and parsed by the DRTM could lead to arbitrary code execution within the context of the DRTM; the SRTM was part of the root of trust for the DRTM. In [30] ITL showed how an attacker with SMM access could execute in the context of a TXT DRTM thanks to the lack of a System Management Mode (SMM) Transfer Monitor (STM). Given the BIOS's control over the code in SMM, and the longstanding lack of a published Intel STM specification, it is expected that most systems attempting to use TXT will be vulnerable to attacks originating from SMM for quite some time.

Because the BIOS sets the SMM code, it is worth pointing out that the lack of a trustworthy SRTM undermines security systems relying solely on SMM's access control to achieve their security, such as HyperGuard[21], HyperCheck

[2]We believe that the security community should either attempt to create a truly secure CRTM, as we are trying to do in this paper, or should push for its removal everywhere so that no one falsely believes it to be providing trust it cannot actually provide.

[28], HyperSentry[4],and SICE[3]. If such systems were using timing-based attestation to detect changes to their SMM code, they would be much harder to subvert even by a malicious BIOS flash. Similarly, a subverted SRTM undercuts load-time attestation systems such as IMA[23] and DynIMA[9]. It also subverts systems like BitLocker[2] that rely on sealing a key against PCRs that are *expected to change* in the presence of an attacker[6].

While the timing-based attestation presented in this paper is adapted from the open source reference implementation provided by Checkmate[17], which is derived from Pioneer[26], in spirit this work is much more closely tied to earlier application of software-based attestation to embedded systems such as SWATT[27] or SBAP[18]. This is because the environment in which a BIOS executes is more constrained, allowing for better coverage. While PioneerNG[25] also ran in SMM, it did not work in conjunction with a real world BIOS, but instead was implemented within CoreBoot. Further, it derived timing-based trust from attestation to a USB device. As our work uses the TPM for trusted timing, it serves as a more stand-alone trusted computing system, allowing for easier adoption.

Our system is therefore the first which has been shown to work within a real environment; which takes into account which portions of the SRTM should remain with Original Equipment Manufacturer (OEM) code; and which shows how existing SRTM code's self-protection is lacking and in need of timing-based attestation. Our system does currently lack a countermeasure for malicious code running on peripheral processors parallel to the BIOS execution. We believe that the use of a system like VIPER[19] to verify peripherals' firmware would mesh well with ours in the future.

3. JOURNEY TO THE CORE ROOT OF TRUST FOR MEASUREMENT

To analyze a system SRTM, a BIOS firmware image from that system must be obtained to identify both where and how the SRTM is instantiated. There are three primary ways to obtain a BIOS image for analysis. One is to desolder the flash chip from the mainboard and dump the image to a binary file using an EEPROM flash device. The EEPROM device is invaluable when having to recover a "bricked" system resulting from an experiment to modify a BIOS gone awry. The second way to get the BIOS is to use a custom kernel driver that reads the firmware image from the flash chip and writes it to a binary file. The third is to extract and decode the information from vendor-provided BIOS update files. In all cases, the binary in the obtained file can be statically analyzed using software such as IDA Pro. However in situations where you want to investigate "live" BIOS/SMM code, e.g. a routine that reads an unknown value from an unknown peripheral, a hardware debugger such as the Arium ECM-XDP3 is very useful.

NIST 800-155 uses the term "golden measurement", to refer to a PCR value provided by a trusted source (such as the OEM) indicating the value that should exist on an un-tampered system. The intention is that an organization should investigate any PCR change that does not result in an expected golden measurement value. However, currently no SRTM golden measurements are provided by OEMs. This leads to a situation where organizations must simply measure a presumed-clean system, and treat the values as golden measurements. Table 1 displays the "presumed-good" PCR hashes for our E6400.

We discovered that the SRTM measurement in PCR0 in Table 1 is derived from a hash provided to the TPM from a function which is executed during the early BIOS POST process. The function is called from within a table of function pointers. Each pointer is part of a structure which includes a 4-byte ASCII name. The name of the function that initially serves to instantiate PCR0 is "TCGm", presumably for "Trusted Computing Group measure".

This function uses a software SHA1 computation (as opposed to the TPM's built in SHA1 function) to hash slices of the BIOS and then presents that hash to the TPM for extension to PCR0. A hash is constructed from the first 64 bytes of each compressed module contained within the BIOS ROM (there are 42 of these modules in total); two small slices of memory; and the final byte of the BIOS firmware image. Within the first 64 bytes is a data structure containing the size, and therefore the SRTM developers most likely are assuming that measurement of the first 64 bytes will be sufficient to detect any changes within the compressed module. After all of these locations have been hashed and combined, the final hash is extended into PCR0 of the TPM. But we also found that a second extend is done on PCR0 with the single last byte of the BIOS, similar to what was done with the other PCRs as described in section 4.2.

4. SRTM IMPLEMENTATION WEAKNESSES

While the weaknesses described below are in terms of the Dell Latitude E6400, it is believed that due to known BIOS code reuse[14], that the same problems occur in 22 Dell models. The E6400 was released prior to NIST 800-147 and 800-155 publication, and was only designed with the TPM PC client specification as a a guide. We picked the E6400 for analysis in 2010 only because it was readily available and it fit our Arium debugging hardware. This system is still supported as the latest BIOS update was released in July 2013. We acknowledge that there have been subsequent changes in BIOS implementation by vendors, most notably adoption of the Unified Extensible Firmware Interface (UEFI). However, we have analyzed newer machines in less depth, and universally the SRTM and CRTM are still implemented in mutable firmware. The problems of open BIOSes and inadequate SRTM coverage we discuss in this paper are not automatically solved in newer UEFI systems, as has also been shown by Bulygin[6].

4.1 Overwritability

As pointed out by [16], being able to freely modify the SRTM completely undercuts its function as the root of trust for measurement. Indeed, the TPM PC client spec [12] says: "The Core Root of Trust for Measurement (CRTM) MUST be an **immutable** portion of the Host Platform's initialization code that executes upon a Host Platform Reset." (Emphasis ours.) Unfortunately this immutability is not per the dictionary definition. Instead, "In this specification, immutable means that to maintain trust in the Host Platform, the replacement or modification of code or data MUST be performed by a Host Platform manufacturer-approved agent and method." There are therefore a number of reasons why the CRTM may in practice be quite mutable.

Table 1: **Dell Latitude E6400 presumed-good PCR's (BIOS revision A29)**

hexadecimal value	index	TCG-provided description
5e078afa88ab65d0194d429c43e0761d93ad2f97	0	S-CRTM, BIOS, Host Platform Extensions, and Embedded Option ROMs
a89fb8f88caa9590e6129b633b144a68514490d5	1	Host Platform Configuration
a89fb8f88caa9590e6129b633b144a68514490d5	2	Option ROM Code
a89fb8f88caa9590e6129b633b144a68514490d5	3	Option ROM Configuration and Data
5df3d741116ba76217926bfabebbd4eb6de9fecb	4	IPL Code (usually the MBR) and Boot Attempts
2ad94cd3935698d6572ba4715e946d6dfecb2d55	5	IPL Code Configuration and Data

Unlike NIST 800-155, NIST 800-147[7]provides BIOS configuration guidelines for end users to minimize exposure to malicious changes; most importantly setting a BIOS password and requiring signed BIOS updates.This signed update process would thereby provide the immutability specified by the TPM PC client spec. Like many other legacy systems, ours shipped without signed updates being required, leaving the SRTM vulnerable. But beyond this, we found that the revision A29 BIOS original on our system was not only unsigned, it did not even have an option to turn on signed updates! Only beginning in revision A30 was the BIOS signed, and a configuration option requiring signed updates available. But signed updates are not a panacea. Methods to bypass signed updates have been shown by ITL[31], Bulygin[6], and ourselves[14][15]. Although [6] did not give specifics of the misconfigurations checked for, we can infer that it was similar to the below.

On systems with Intel IO Controller Hub 9, like the E6400, the BIOS flash chip can be directly overwritten by a kernel module unless provisions are implemented by the BIOS manufacturer to prevent this from occurring. The mechanism to prevent direct overwrite has two components: proper configuration of the BIOS_CNTL register's BIOSWE and BLE bits, and a routine in SMM to properly field the System Management Interrupts (SMI) that subsequently occur.

When properly configured, the BIOS_CNTL register causes an SMI to be triggered whenever an application attempts to enable write-permission to the BIOS flash. This provides SMM the opportunity to determine whether this is a sanctioned write to the flash chip or not and, in the latter case, reconfigure the BIOS_CNTL register to permit read-only access to the BIOS flash. All this occurs prior to the application having any opportunity to perform any writes to the flash chip. This security mechanism was missing from the E6400 in revision A29, but fixed in A30. Misconfigurations like this that can generically undercut signed BIOS updates could be common across all vendors, but no one has the data on this yet. We are currently working to collect this data across large deployed populations.

4.2 Inaccuracy

PCR0 is the primary PCR value that we are concerned with as it captures the measurement of the CRTM. However, it is worth noting the duplication of values among PCRs 1, 2, 3 in Table 1. Projects attempting to implement TPM-supported trusted boot capabilities are often puzzled by what is actually being measured by the SRTM to set those values. We determined the origin of such PCRs as we had previously noted similar duplicate PCR values among many of our enterprise systems. After observing the BIOS's interaction with the TPM it was determined that the oft seen duplicate value in our PCR values was simply an extend of the single last byte of the BIOS![3] This complete failure to measure the important parts of the system associated with these PCR values contravenes the TPM PC client spec.

As shown in Figure 1, the OEM SRTM excludes the overwhelming majority of the BIOS memory from measurement. To generate PCR0, it only measures the dark gray portion of the BIOS, which amounts to only 0xA90 out of 0x1A_0000 bytes (.2%) in the BIOS range! The bulk of the measurements consist of measuring the first 64 bytes of each of the 42 compressed modules. There are also two slices of 8 bytes, at 0xDF45_13C0 and 0xDF45_13C7 that we have been unable to determine the purpose of measuring.

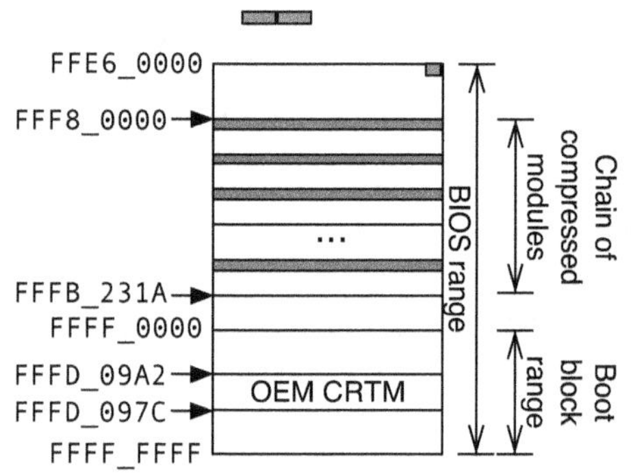

Figure 1: Some components found in the BIOS range (not to scale). Dark grey is memory measured by the SRTM, white is unmeasured.

The intent of the SRTM is to provide trust that no critical BIOS contents have been modified; something this implementation cannot do. This is an important discovery, and we are not aware of any related work validating the functioning of an SRTM, rather than blindly trusting it. We have conducted cursory examinations of other SRTMs and observed similar problems with incomplete coverage. This suggests the need for more validation going forward to ensure SRTMs are properly implementing NIST 800-155 guidance.

4.3 Proof of Concept Attacks

4.3.1 Naive

We describe a naive attack as one that reflashes the BIOS but which can be trivially detected by PCR0 changing. We would call this naive even in the presence of an SRTM which

[3]Specifically, $PCR_{1,2,3} \leftarrow SHA1(0x00_{20}||SHA1(0x00))$; a fact that is trivially independently verifiable.

had more complete coverage. In this paper we are primarily concerned with advanced attackers who are seeking to bypass existing trusted computing technologies that are assumed to be provisioned correctly.

4.3.2 The Tick

We define a *tick* to be a piece of parasitic stealth malware that attaches itself to the BIOS to persist, while hiding its presence by forging the PCR0 hash. A tick has to exist in the same space as the SRTM. Regardless of whether the entirety of the BIOS is hashed to generate PCR0, a tick can perform the same process on a clean copy of data, or simply replay expected SHA1 hash values to the TPM for PCR0 extension. On the E6400 this later strategy is easily performed at the end of the "TCGm" function just before the hash is passed to the TPM. For example, to forge the known-good PCR0 hash shown in Table 1 for BIOS revision A29 running on a Dell E6400, a hardcoded hash value of "F1 A6 22 BB 99 BC 13 C2 35 DF FA 5A 15 72 04 30 BE 58 39 21" is passed to the TPM's PCRExtend function.[4] So even though the BIOS has been tampered with in a way that would normally change PCR0, the change goes undetected since the dynamic calculation of the hash to extend PCR0 with has been substituted with a hardcoded constant of the known-good hash. It is worth pointing out that the BIOS modifications made by Kauer in [16] did not constitute a tick, because there was no forgery of PCR0, only disabling TPM commands (which leads to trivially detection). Our tick implementation is only a 51 byte patch to the BIOS. After a tick is attached to the BIOS, it can make other changes go undetected by traditional trusted boot systems.

4.3.3 The Flea

We define a *flea* as parasitic stealth malware that, like a tick, forges PCR0 but is additionally capable of transferring itself ("hopping") into a new BIOS image when an update is being performed. By controlling the BIOS update process, a flea is able to persist where a tick would be exterminated. On the E6400 it achieves this by hooking the SMRAM runtime executable code that performs the BIOS update process. The flea can then detect when an update is occurring, identify what revision of BIOS is being flashed, and, based on that revision, appropriately patch itself into the prospective update image. At a minimum the flea must modify the update candidate with the following patches: a patch to enable the new image to forge PCR0; the compressed module that defines SMRAM containing the flea SMM runtime portion that controls the update process; and the necessary hooks required to force control flow to the flea's execution.

Our flea residing on an E6400 with BIOS Revision A29, forges the known-good PCR0 value as described in the previous section. A BIOS update is about to occur which the flea has determined will be to BIOS revision A30. The flea retrieves and applies the A30 patches, among which will be one that provides the necessary constant so that PCR0 will provide the known-good value for BIOS revision A30.

One challenge for the flea is that it must find storage for its patches. We ultimately chose to use unused portions of the flash chip. In our current implementation these patches can consume upwards of 153KB per revision and there can be many BIOS revisions to support across the lifetime of a system. However our current implementation inefficiently stores the data uncompressed, because we did not have time to utilize a compression method that could use the BIOS's built in decompression routine. Our flea code implementation absent the patches is only 514 bytes. An open question is what a flea should do if it is not able to identify the incoming BIOS revision. We preface this discussion by asserting that in practice we believe this will be an uncommon situation. Any attacker that cares to persist in a system's BIOS will likely have the resources to analyze BIOS updates and deploy updates for the flea's patch database well before a compromised organization can deploy BIOS updates. However, as a stalling strategy, our flea will begin to act as if it is updating the BIOS, but then display an error and not make any changes if it cannot identify the pending update.

The key takeaway about our creation of a flea is that it mean to underscore the point that simply following the NIST 800-147 guidance to lock down a system and enable signed updates on existing deployed systems *is not enough to protect them.* Once a system is compromised, the presence of a flea means it will stay compromised. This is why we advocate for confronting the problem head-on with BIOS Chronomancy.

[4]For independent verification purposes, Table 1's $PCR_0 \leftarrow SHA1(SHA1(0x00_{20}||SHA1(0xF1A6...21))||SHA1(0x00))$

5. BUILDING A BETTER CRTM WITH BIOS CHRONOMANCY

We want to make it clear that we are not completely replacing or re-implementing all the functionality of existing SRTM code. Given our proof of concept attacks' ability to subvert CRTM self-measurement, we outline a mechanism that can be added to commercial CRTMs to provide trustworthy evidence that the CRTM specifically has not been tampered with.

5.1 Timing-based Attestation

As described in Section 2, there has been much work in the area of timing-based attestation. In [17] the phrase "timing-based attestation" was coined to be a superset of software-based attestation, including techniques that require dedicated hardware such as the TPM to perform trustworthy timing measurement. In all such systems, the general principle is to use a specialized software construction that has an explicit timing side-channel built into it. The side-channel is meant to allow the software to have a consistent runtime in the absence of an attacker, and an increased runtime in the presence of an attacker who is manipulating its operation. The crux of such software construction is to create a looping system that checks itself, and any other security/measurement code the defender wishes to protect. If the attacker would like to manipulate the behavior of the security code, he must do so in a way that still generates a correct self-checksum. Doing this requires modifying the looping code that generates the checksum. Each additional instruction of logic added to the loop code to help the attacker subvert security code will increase the runtime of a single loop. This time increase is multiplied by the number of loops, leading to a detectable timing change when compared to the expected baseline runtime. As described in previous work, baseline runtimes will be specific to a CPU and its frequency.

We have adapted the open source TPM tickstamp-based attestation code from [17] to run within a customized E6400

BIOS and serve as an improved CRTM. Unlike other CRTMs, ours is actually capable of detecting an attacker at the same privilege level who is explicitly attempting to subvert our measurement. Our timing is specifically derived from the timing delta between two TPM "tickstamp" requests. A tickstamp can be thought of as just a signed value of the TPM microprocessor's clock tick count. The TPM 1.2 specification provides a TPM_TickStampBlob command which takes a nonce, data blob, and a TPM signing key as arguments. The TPM then returns a structure containing a signature, the current TPM ticks value, and the current Tick Session Nonce (TSN), denoted as $(signature, ticks, TSN) \leftarrow TickStamp_{key}(data, nonce)$. The *signature* is given by $Sign_{key}(data, nonce, ticks, TSN)$. On TPM reset (typically a reboot), a new 20 byte TSN is generated by the TPM hardware random number generator and the TPM tick counter is reset to zero, beginning a new timing session. The TPM 2.0 specification has moved the tickstamp functionality to the new TPM2_GetTime command and we anticipate our attestation model will work with 2.0 compliant TPMs.

Our self-check protocol was inspired by the Schellekens et al. protocol and begins in the first stage of system boot. BIOS Chronomancy operates as follows:

1. The current TSN is read using the TPM_GetTicks operation. $TSN_{curr} \leftarrow GetTicks()$
2. The tickstamp 1 (TS1) structure is generated by requesting a tickstamp with the TSN_{curr} from above used as both the data and the nonce. The AIK key is discussed in the next section.
   $TS1 \leftarrow TickStamp_{AIK}(TSN_{curr}, TSN_{curr})$
3. Data from the signature of TS1 is used as a nonce to generate the self-check function checksum (CS).
   $CS \leftarrow SelfCheck(TS1.signature)$
   The self-check function is broken down into the following stages:
   (a) The self-check function measures *the self-check code proper* by performing a pseudorandom traversal over its own memory.
   (b) The self-check function performs linear sweeps over static portions of SMRAM, the BIOS, and Interrupt Vector Table.
4. The result of the checksum is then tickstamped.
   $TS2 \leftarrow TickStamp_{AIK}(CS, CS)$
5. TS1, TS2, and checksum are then stored to SMRAM to report back to an external appraiser upon request.

One key difference between the BIOS Chronomancy protocol and the Schellekens protocol is that our nonce has to be derived internally, as opposed to being received from an outside appraiser. Because of this requirement, our protocol differs slightly in both the attestation and the appraisal process. We chose to perform BIOS Chronomancy as early as possible in the boot process so that the system state has changed as little as possible, and therefore is more easily verified. Our appraisal process is detailed in Section 5.3.

5.1.1 Tickstamp Forgery Attack

While implementing our BIOS attestation code we discovered and implemented an attack on the Schellekens et al. protocol implemented by Kovah et al. Both groups describe using a TPM signing key in the tickstamp operations in their protocols. However, the use of a TPM signing key in this way allows the TPM to behave as a signing oracle on behalf of an attacker. An attacker can abuse this signing oracle to request that the TPM sign artificially crafted tickstamp structures with a TPM_Sign operation. This allows the attacker to forge a tickstamp with an arbitrary tick value. Thus an attacker can beat the existing systems by forging tickstamp structures with either ticks added to TS1 or subtracted from TS2. The delta between the two tickstamps will then always fall within the acceptable timing limits. We have implemented this attack and verified that it works. We utilize the following improvement to the protocol in order to fix this vulnerability. According to the TPM specification it is possible to use an *Attestation Identity Key* (AIK) as opposed to a signing key to perform the TPM Tickstamp operation. AIKs are restricted by the TPM to be used only with specific operations like TPM_TickStampBlob or TPM_Quote. They can not be used to sign arbitrary data with the TPM_Sign operation, and thus can not be abused to forge tickstamps. We have implemented this improved version of the protocol in BIOS Chronomancy and confirmed it to be safe against the tickstamp forging attack.

5.2 What to Measure?

To build a proper self-check, we must provide evidence that neither our code, operating as the CRTM, nor the OEM SRTM that will be handed off to has been subverted. The high-level measurement process is as follows. As shown in Figure 2 (a), BIOS code (1) instantiates SMRAM (2), which contains the BIOS Chronomancy code (3)-(6). Immediately after instantiating SMRAM, the BIOS sends a signal to the SMI handler requesting that a measurement take place. The SMI handler fields this request and begins executing the BIOS Chronomancy (BC) code. First, the BC code requests a TPM tickstamp. Then the BC self-measurement code measures the entire BC range (Section 5.2.1). Next it measures the entire SMRAM ((4) - Section 5.2.2) and the BIOS ((5) - Section 5.2.3).

5.2.1 Self Measurement

The self-measurement portion of the attestation code is logically divided into 8 blocks. The self-measurement traverses pseudorandomly through these blocks as it measures its own code. Each block incorporates the following components into the checksum:

1. EIP_DST - This is the address of the block being transferred *to*. This provides evidence of the self-check's location in memory, so that if the code *executes* from an unexpected address, it cause a different checksum.
2. DP - The data pointer for the self-check's own memory being read. This provides additional evidence of the code's location in memory so that if it is *read* from an unexpected address (such as an attacker copy), it causes a different checksum result. A 32 bit pointer.
3. *DP - This is the 4 bytes of data read from memory by dereferencing DP. This causes the final checksum to change if there are any code integrity attacks on the self-check.
4. PRN - A pseudorandom number that is seeded from the TPM tick session nonce, and updated after every use per the below pseudocode. It determines such choices as what the next DP and EIP_DST should be.

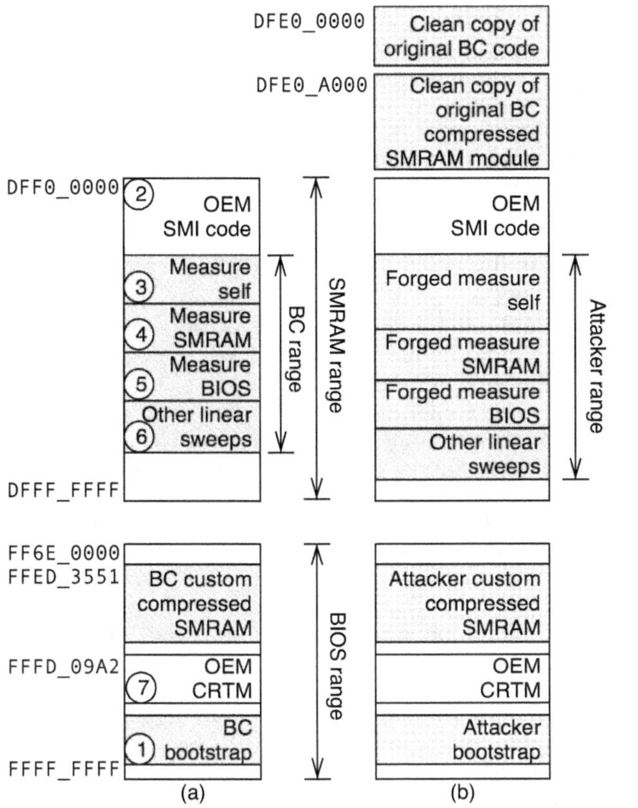

Figure 2: BIOS Chronomancy (BC) memory layout by default (a), and when an attacker is present (b)

The following presents the general construction of one of the blocks composing our self-measurement code.

```
blockOne:
  PRN += (PRN*PRN | 5);
  accumulator ^= PRN;
  accumulator += DP;
  accumulator ^= *DP;
  DP = codeStart + (PRN % codeSize);
  DiffuseIntoChecksum(accumulator);
  iterations--;
  if (iterations == 0)
    goto linearSweeps;
  //start of inter-block-transfer
  EIP_DST = blockAddressTable[PRN & 7];
  accumulator ^= EIP_DST;
  goto EIP_DST;
```

In the above C-style pseudocode, *codeStart* is the address of the start of the self-checksum code and *codeSize* defines the total size of the BIOS Chronomancy code. Each of the 8 self-checksum blocks follows the general layout presented above, but differ in both the order and logical operators used to incorporate the self-checksum components into the *accumulator* value. This is so that an attacker must follow the exact same series of pseudorandomly chosen blocks in order to compute the same checksum. The *accumulator* value is then diffused into the bits of the checksum at the end of each block with an add and rotate in order to counter the attack described in [26]. Our implementation of the self-checksum blocks were programmed by hand in x86 assembly to ensure maximum optimization. The lack of a proof of optimality of a given assembly sequence is a well known caveat of work in this field. At the end of each block, the PRN is used to determine which block should be executed next. This area is referred to as the *inter-block transfer*. A description of how an attacker can attempt to produce the correct self-checksum by modifying the block construction to forge the checksum components is given in Section 5.4.

5.2.2 SMRAM Measurement

After the BC code checks itself, in order to cede minimal space in which an attacker can hide, the entirety of SMRAM must be measured. This provides a measurement of the OEM SMM code which could have been modified by attacks such as [10]. It also provides another measurement of the self-check code, which resides in SMRAM. We use a simple linear sweep snippet of code to incorporate 4 bytes at a time from the SMRAM into the self-checksum. We also note that it is important to find and measure the SMBASE register, as this tells the processor what the base address for SMRAM should be the next time SMM is entered.

Because there is a single SMM entry point, it is required that an attacker (like a flea) residing in SMRAM will have to modify existing code or data. The entry point to SMM always has a series of conditional checks to determine the reason SMM was invoked. To gain control flow, the attacker would have to insert inline code hooks, or find a function pointer in data that could be pointed at his own code.

Immediately upon being decompressed from the BIOS firmware image, the E6400's SMRAM has a lot of "placeholder" values that get overwritten. For example, the base address of SMRAM is calculated dynamically for the given system, and this base value is then added to locations within the decompressed SMRAM executable. This is analogous to "relocations" in normal executables. A large portion of the SMRAM memory range is uninitialized and unused. Initializing this space with a pseudorandom sequence is necessary to effectively measuring SMRAM. If a static value were used, an attacker could hardcode that value into his code while residing in and forging the contents of this region. That would lead to an attacker speed up.

At the time our attestation code is invoked, SMRAM has its EBP pointing to address 0x20E and its ESP pointing to 0xDFF0_421E. Our code is compiled to expect the stack frame to point to 0xDFFF_FF00, so we have to relocate EBP for the duration of our measurements. Our local variables are large enough that, if we didn't, we would end up underflowing EBP and writing data to read-only high memory. To help optimize cache accesses, the stack pointer was modified so that our data was located on a 64-byte aligned boundary, 0xDFF0_3A80.

5.2.3 BIOS Measurement

The BIOS range is measured after the SMRAM. Because the BIOS sets up SMRAM, measuring the BIOS range will cover the compressed version of the SMRAM module. This further raises the bar for the attacker to provide consistent lies. The BIOS is mapped to high memory at 0xFFFF_FFFF minus the size of the BIOS, in bytes. So for a BIOS image of size 0x1A_0000 bytes, its measurable range in RAM would be 0xFFE6_0000 to 0xFFFF_FFFF. We use a simple linear sweep snippet of code to incorporate 4 bytes at a time from the BIOS into the self-checksum.

It has been observed on the Latitude E6400 that the entire flash chip remains static for a given BIOS revision. Therefore, the entire contents of the chip could also be incorporated into the self-check. This would include the management engine, platform data, gigabit ethernet, and flash descriptor regions in addition to the BIOS region which is mapped to memory. Some of these regions could be used by malware for the storage of malicious data and/or code. Strictly speaking, any security relevant portions should already be measured by the OEM SRTM, therefore we would be duplicating functionality, while unnecessarily increasing runtime. However, we intend to experiment with inclusion of the entire flash chip data in the future, to understand the full performance implications.

5.3 Attestation Appraisal

Appraisal of the BIOS timing based attestation proceeds similarly to the original Schellekens et al. paper. An appraiser is for instance code running on a separate server that verifies the provided attestation, and a reporting agent can be an OS application or kernel driver.

1. The appraiser sends an attestation request that includes a nonce to the reporting agent.
2. The reporting agent requests attestation results by invoking an SMI with an appropriate input and the appraiser's nonce.
3. The reporting agent generates the current tick stamp (CTS) by performing $CTS \leftarrow TickStamp_{AIK}(nonce, nonce)$.
4. The reporting agent presents to the external appraiser: CTS, TS1, TS2 and the checksum (CS).
5. The appraiser verifies the signature on TS1, TS2, and CTS to confirm that they were produced by an authentic TPM.
6. The appraiser verifies $TS1.TSN = TS2.TSN$ to confirm that the TPM tick counter was not reset during the attestation.
7. The appraiser verifies that $TS1.TSN = TS2.TSN = CTS.TSN$ to ensure that the current attestation reflects the most recent reboot of the system and a replay attack is not taking place.
8. The appraiser confirms that the nonce used to generate the checksum is a function of the signature on TS1.TSN. This enforces the requirement that TS1.TSN was calculated before the checksum calculation started.
9. The appraiser confirms that the data signed by TS1 is equal to the current tick session nonce. This precludes precalculation attacks because the attacker can not know what a future TSN will be.
10. The appraiser confirms that the data signed by TS2 is equal to the checksum returned by the agent. This enforces the requirement that TS2 was calculated after the checksum calculation was complete.
11. The appraiser extracts $\Delta = TS2.ticks - TS1.ticks$, (the time needed to perform the attestation) and confirms it is within acceptable limits.
12. The appraiser confirms that the checksum received from the agent is equal to the checksum it has calculated based on the same nonce.

If all of the above steps are completed successfully the appraisal is considered successful. To facilitate the above appraisal, a method to retrieve the measurement data is required. In our proof-of-concept implementation, the timing-based attestation code copies the measurement data from its storage address at physical address 0xA_0000 to 0x9_0000. This destination address was chosen for the proof-of-concept because it is accessible by the Windows kernel.

5.4 Attestation Forgery Attack

In this section we discuss our reference attacker under the best-case scenario for the attacker, and worst-case scenario for the defender. The attacker has full knowledge of the BIOS Chronomancy technique, and coexists in SMM alongside the measurement code. The attacker is assumed to have the minimum timing overhead because he is not trying to achieve any objective beyond forging the self-checksum to hide the fact that he is resident in the BIOS. Also, we assume the attacker knows what ranges we are measuring and has stored his copies of original binaries in locations we are not measuring, eliminating the added step of concealing them. Additionally, we ensure that the attackers code, like the original measurement code, is cache-optimized to minimize the frequency of cache collisions. The goal was to grant the attacker every advantage possible to minimize the overhead incurred from performing the forgery attack.

To hide his modifications to the self-check code, the attacker must forge the *DP values measured in each block. This can be performed by adding additional arithmetic instructions that apply an offset to DP before dereferencing it, to point it to a clean copy of the self-check code. These additional arithmetic instructions cause the block addresses of the attackers code to become misaligned with the block addresses of the original measurement code. Since these block addresses influence the EIP_DST values and are incorporated into the checksum, these too must also be forged by the attacker, adding additional timing overhead.

The original measurement code incorporates the EIP_DST component during the inter-block transfer process, requiring just a single table containing each of the measurement-block base addresses. Forging EIP_DST, however, requires the attacker to use two tables. One table stores the locations of the attacker's blocks, while an additional table is required to keep track of what the original block locations were in the un-modified code. The use of two tables instead of one introduces extra instructions and therefore extra timing overhead for the attacker. Alternatively, the attacker could use the block sizes in the unmodified code in combination with the location of the first block in the unmodified code to calculate the original EIP_DST during each inter-block transfer. However, we determined that table lookup was more efficient than on the fly calculation. The general construction of an attacker self-checksum block is presented here:

```
forgeryBlockOne:
  PRN += (PRN*PRN | 5);
  accumulator ^= PRN;
  //apply an offset "offToClean" to DP
  //to ensure it reads clean data
  accumulator += DP
  accumulator ^= *(DP-offToClean);
  DP = codeStart + (PRN % codeSize);
  iterations--;
  if (iterations == 0)
    goto forgeryLinearSweeps;
```

```
tmp = PRN & 7;
//attacker forges EIP_DST incorporation
//but incurs an additional table lookup
accumulator ^= originalAddressTable[tmp];
EIP_DST = forgeryAddressTable[tmp];
DiffuseIntoChecksum(accumulator);
goto EIP_DST;
```

In total, our original self checksum blocks were comprised of 43 x86 assembly instructions, 11 of which were memory accesses. Our most optimized attacker self checksum blocks were comprised of 47 instructions, 12 of which were memory accesses. This yields an attacker overhead of 4 instructions and 1 memory access. This overhead is incurred when the attacker attempts to maintain the correct checksum during the self-checksum's measurement of itself. However, our attestation code is designed to measure other parts of the BIOS as well during the linear sweeps that occur during Section 5.3's phase 3.b of the self-checksum algorithm. The attacker incurs additional overhead while attempting to forge the checksum during these linear sweep phases. Since this malware has achieved persistence by modifying the BIOS firmware, the attacker must hide the changes in the BIOS range from detection. Also, the attacker must hide its active runtime presence in SMRAM. To hide modifications to these regions, the attacker must provide an alternate version of the linear sweeps measurement code. The attacker's linear sweep code substitutes original good values wherever the attacker has modified code or data. We implemented a simple if/then statement to check whether the DP falls within a range where the malicious code is stored. If DP does fall within this range, then it is modified to point to the equivalent known-good *DP stored in the clean copy.

When we went to optimize for our 3rd revision of the attack, we found from performance testing that the forgery of linear sweeps accounted for a negligible amount of the total attacker overhead, as described in the next section. So we did not make a variant attacker that has code to sweep the original measurement area for known good ranges, and then switches to alternate code reading from a different DP when reading known bad ranges. But we do expect such an attacker would have slightly lower overhead and we will test that in a future revision.

6. EVALUATION

For our first experiment, we wanted to see if it was possible to have a single baseline for the expected number of TPM ticks that a good measurement should take. It was observed in [17] that different instances of the same TPM model had different baseline tick count times. The experiment outlined in that paper used STMicro TPMs, and we wanted to see if our Broadcom TPMs would behave similarly.

This experiment was performed on 17 Latitude E6400 laptops running Windows 7 32 bit on a 2.80 GHz Core 2 Duo CPU with a Broadcom BCM5880KFBG TPM. Two versions of our BC code were created: an unmodified (hereafter referred to as "clean") version and a version containing hide-only malware (hereafter referred to as the "forged" version). Both the clean and forged version of the code were run twenty times at each of 625K, 1.25M, and 2.5M iterations of the BC measurements. Each measurement recorded 8 separate timing data points that will be discussed later. To support the experiments, additional code was added to both the clean and forged versions to record the timing data points to SMRAM memory. To collect the stored data, a kernel driver was written to signal the SMI handler to make the data available for reading and outputting to file. Additionally, a windows batch file was written to execute on Windows startup to load and execute the kernel driver and then reboot the machine. The batch file repeats this process 20 times.

We found that the Broadcom TPMs did provide an equivalent baseline for the runtimes across multiple hosts for the clean and forged code. The results are shown in Table 2.

Table 2: Clean and forged BIOS Chronomancy runtimes for different numbers of iterations. 1 Broadcom TPM tick is about 64μs.

Iterations	Clean average TPM ticks	Clean std. dev. TPM ticks	Forged average TPM ticks	Forged std. dev. TPM ticks
625K	16723	15.98	16771	29.13
1.25M	21069	16.42	21793	156.75
2.5M	29756	16.90	31817	207.78

Additionally, if this technique is to be used in commercial BIOSes, we need to set a fixed number of iterations for the BC code that show a clear difference between the attacker runtime and defender runtime. This means setting some range relative to the average runtime which if exceeded indicates that an attacker has influenced the runtime. We have chosen to set the baseline range to $avg. \pm 3 * std.dev.$, ensuring a less than .3% chance that a normal measurement will fall outside of the expected range. In Figure 3 we have taken the attacker runtimes and normalized them against the upper bound of the acceptable range by subtracting it from each attacker measurement; displaying the difference in time the attackers code took to execute. This figure shows that a few of the 625K iteration attacker measurements are negative, indicating that they fall within the acceptable range. However, even the machine which had the best results for an attacker only had 6 of 20 measurements fall into the acceptable range; therefore in practice the attacker would be detected. But for all measurements with 1.25M and 2.5M iterations, the attacker data is well into positive territory, and therefore can clearly be distinguished. To guard against possible future optimization by the attacker, it would make sense to use a number of iterations of 1.25M or 2.5M in practice.

For experimental purposes we collected eight more-granular measurement time points to show what subcomponents of measurement or forgery dominate runtime.

1. RDTSC_OUT - Time stamp obtained from the RDTSC time stamp counter; referred to as "out" because it occurs "outside" of the TPM tickstamp.
2. TPM Tickstamp 1(TS1) - Tickstamp used for reporting run start
3. RDTSC_IN start - Time stamp obtained from the RDTSC time stamp counter; referred to as "in" because it falls "inside" the TPM tickstamp measurement and the actual measurement code.
4. Linear Sweeps start - Measured with an RDTSC
5. Linear Sweeps end - Measured with an RDTSC
6. RDTSC_IN end

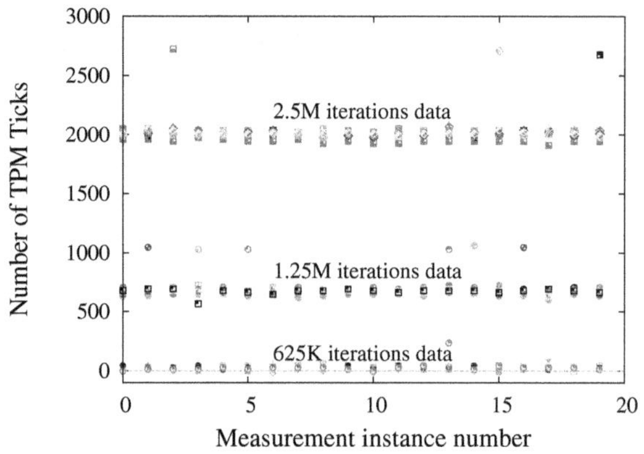

Figure 3: Attacker overhead runtimes, normalized against upper bound of acceptable clean runtime. Positive values indicate that the attacker failed to hide runtime overhead. Negative values indicate the attacker succeeded in running in an acceptable amount of time. 1 tick is about 64μs.

7. TPM Tickstamp 2 (TS2)
8. RDTSC_Out End

We will refer to these times by their number. So for instance time 3 minus time 1 is the time it takes to receive the tickstamp result from the TPM. Time 4 minus 3 is dominated by the self-check code running. Time 5 minus 4 is the time for all the linear sweeps over SMRAM, BIOS, and IVT. The total runtime, time 8 minus 1 gives us the total runtime for BIOS Chronomancy in CPU cycles, which can then be converted to an absolute runtime, as shown in Table 3. Note that runtimes do not double as the number of iterations double, in part because of overhead such as the 2 TPM tickstamp operations taking about 166ms each. The difference on top of the baseline runtime *is* seen to double as the number of iterations doubles.

Table 3: Average total runtime for BIOS Chronomancy on a single host for a 20 runs, for a given number of iterations, in milliseconds.

Iterations	Runtime (ms)
625K	1376
1.25M	1646
2.5M	2188

When we examined the runtime for clean code within the time range given by times 3 to 6, we found that 72.9 % of the time is spent between time 3 and 4, and only 6.9% of the time is spent between time 4 and 5. When we examine the hide-only adversary's 20 run average time overhead on a single host at 1.25M iterations, we see that he takes 47.1ms more than the clean code, for a total of 2.9% overhead. By comparing the RDTSC measurements again from times 3 to 6 we found that 98.6% of the overhead occurs between time 3 and time 4. Only .02% of his overhead occurs between times 4 and 5 (where even a hide-only adversary must forge the sweep of SMRAM and BIOS.) This same comparison can be seen in Table 4. Ultimately, this tells us that even for more complicated malware like a flea, the overwhelming majority of differences in timing are caused by forging the self-checksum itself, not by any other miscellaneous cleanup the attacker must do.

Table 4: Percentage overhead for a sub-section of runtime, as a portion of total overhead for the given attacker. Data taken from average of 20 runs using 1.25M iterations.

Attack Type	Percentage of total overhead incurred from time 3 to 4	Percentage of total overhead incurred from time 4 to 5
Hide-only	98.6	.02
Tick	73.55	6.73
Flea	73.80	6.75

7. CONCLUSION

As the *core* root of trust for measurement, proper implementation of the CRTM is critical. However, this work is the first detailed examination of a real implementation of a CRTM & SRTM and finds that implementation to be untrustworthy.

We believe that both NIST 800-147 and 800-155 are important guidelines which should be followed by their respective audiences. To demonstrate the danger of putting false trust in opaque SRTM implementations, we implemented a proof of concept attack that we called a *tick*, that modified the BIOS on our Dell Latitude E6400 while not causing a change to any of the PCRs. A common remediation that might be employed to try to remove a tick is to reflash the BIOS with a known-clean version. However this is not sufficient to protect against existing BIOS malware maintaining a foothold on the system. To show this we implemented a *flea*, which can jump into and compromise the new BIOS image during the update process.

Because all CRTMs, including those on the latest UEFI systems, are rooted in mutable firmware, the applicability of these attacks is very broad. PC vendors seem unwilling to root their trust in truly immutable ROM, likely because modern firmware is large and complex (as multiple BIOS updates attest to). Therefore, in the absence of immutable roots of trust, we have found and fixed problems with existing work on TPM tickstamp timing-based attestation, and adapted it to run in BIOS and SMM. Our BIOS Chronomancy system provides robust protection under the demonstrably real assumption that an attacker can be operating at the same privilege level as the CRTM in the BIOS. Although BIOS vendors place a premium on speed of boot time, some customers such as governments require much higher assurance that their firmware is not modified. We believe our evaluation has shown that BC is a practical technique and can be incorporated into existing OEM BIOS codebases as an optional configurable option for those customers who need trustworthy detection of BIOS infection.

8. ACKNOWLEDGEMENTS

Special thanks to Jonathan McCune for helpful feedback on an early version of this paper. And to Rafal Wojtczuk and Yuriy Bulygin for detailed ideas on future attacks.

9. REFERENCES

[1] Coreboot. http://www.coreboot.org/. Accessed: 5/01/2013.

[2] Microsoft bitlocker drive encryption. http://windows.microsoft.com/en-US/windows-vista/BitLocker-Drive-Encryption-Overview. Accessed: 2/01/2013.

[3] A. Azab, P. Ning, and X. Zhang. SICE: A hardware-level strongly isolated computing environment for x86 multi-core platforms. In *Proceedings of 2011 ACM Conference on Computer and Communications Security.*

[4] A. M. Azab, P. Ning, Z. Wang, X. Jiang, X. Zhang, and N. C. Skalsky. HyperSentry: enabling stealthy in-context measurement of hypervisor integrity. In *Proceedings of the 2010 ACM conference on Computer and Communications Security.*

[5] J. Brossard. Hardware backdooring is practical. In *BlackHat*, Las Vegas, USA, 2012. Accessed: 5/01/2013.

[6] Y. Bulygin. Evil maid just got angrier: Why full-disk encryption with TPM is insecure on many systems. In *CanSecWest*, Vancouver, Canada, 2013. Accessed: 5/01/2013.

[7] D. Cooper, W. Polk, A. Regenscheid, and M. Souppaya. BIOS Protection Guidelines). NIST Special Publication 800-147, Apr. 2011.

[8] I. Corporation. Intel 64 and IA-32 Architectures Software Developer Manual, Vol. 3b, Part 2. http://www.intel.com/content/dam/doc/manual/64-ia-32-architectures-software-developer-vol-3b-part-2-manual.pdf. Accessed: 5/01/2013.

[9] L. Davi, A.-R. Sadeghi, and M. Winandy. Dynamic integrity measurement and attestation: towards defense against return-oriented programming attacks. In *Proceedings of the 2009 ACM workshop on Scalable trusted computing.*

[10] L. Duflot, O. Levillain, B. Morin, and O. Grumelard. Getting into the SMRAM: SMM Reloaded. Presented at CanSec West 2009, http://www.ssi.gouv.fr/IMG/pdf/Cansec_final.pdf. Accessed: 02/01/2011.

[11] M. Giuliani. Mebromi: the first BIOS rootkit in the wild. http://blog.webroot.com/2011/09/13/mebromi-the-first-bios-rootkit-in-the-wild/. Accessed: 5/01/2013.

[12] T. C. Group. TPM PC Client Specific Implementation Specification for Conventional BIOS. Version 1.21 Errata version 1.0, Feb. 24 2012.

[13] J. Heasman. Implementing and detecting a ACPI BIOS rootkit. In *BlackHat Europe*, Amsterdam, Netherlands, 2006. Accessed: 5/01/2013.

[14] C. Kallenberg, J. Butterworth, and X. Kovah. Dell BIOS in some Latitude laptops and Precision Mobile Workstations vulnerable to buffer overflow. http://www.kb.cert.org/vuls/id/912156. Accessed: 08/01/2013.

[15] C. Kallenberg, J. Butterworth, and X. Kovah. Under submission. http://www.kb.cert.org/vuls/id/255726. Accessed: 08/01/2013.

[16] B. Kauer. OSLO: improving the security of trusted computing. In *Proceedings of 2007 USENIX Security Symposium on USENIX Security Symposium.*

[17] X. Kovah, C. Kallenberg, C. Weathers, A. Herzog, M. Albin, and J. Butterworth. New results for timing-based attestation. In *Proceedings of the 2012 IEEE Symposium on Security and Privacy.*

[18] Y. Li, J. M. McCune, and A. Perrig. SBAP: Software-Based Attestation for Peripherals. In *Proceedings of the 2010 International Conference on Trust and Trustworthy Computing (Trust).*

[19] Y. Li, J. M. McCune, and A. Perrig. VIPER: Verifying the integrity of peripherals' firmware. In *Proceedings of the 2011 ACM Conference on Computer and Communications Security (CCS).*

[20] A. Regenscheid and K. Scarfone. BIOS Integrity Measurement Guidelines (Draft). NIST Special Publication 800-155 (Draft), Dec. 2011.

[21] J. Rutkowska and R. Wojtczuk. Preventing and detecting Xen hypervisor subversions. In *BlackHat*, Las Vegas, USA, 2008. Accessed: 5/01/2013.

[22] A. Sacco and A. Ortega. Persistent BIOS infection. In *CanSecWest*, Vancouver, Canada, 2009. Accessed: 5/01/2013.

[23] R. Sailer, X. Zhang, T. Jaeger, and L. van Doorn. Design and implementation of a TCG-based integrity measurement architecture. In *Proceedings of the 2004 conference on USENIX Security Symposium - Volume 13.*

[24] D. Schellekens, B. Wyseur, and B. Preneel. Remote attestation on legacy operating systems with trusted platform modules. *Electron. Notes Theor. Comput. Sci.*, 197:59–72, February 2008.

[25] A. Seshadri. *A Software Primitive for Externally-verifiable Untampered Execution and its Applications to Securing Computing Systems.* PhD thesis, Carnegie Mellon University, 2009.

[26] A. Seshadri, M. Luk, E. Shi, A. Perrig, L. van Doorn, and P. Khosla. Pioneer: verifying code integrity and enforcing untampered code execution on legacy systems. In *Proceedings of the ACM symposium on Operating systems principles*, SOSP, pages 1–16, 2005.

[27] A. Seshadri, A. Perrig, L. van Doorn, and P. Khosla. SWATT: Software-based attestation for embedded devices. In *Proceedings of the 2004 IEEE Symposium on Security and Privacy.*

[28] J. Wang, A. Stavrou, and A. Ghosh. HyperCheck: a hardware-assisted integrity monitor. In *Proceedings of the 2010 international conference on Recent advances in intrusion detection.*

[29] R. Wojtczuk and J. Rutkowska. Attacking Intel TXT via SINIT code execution hijacking. http://invisiblethingslab.com/resources/2011/Attacking_Intel_TXT_via_SINIT_hijacking.pdf. Accessed: 5/01/2013.

[30] R. Wojtczuk and J. Rutkowska. Attacking Intel TXT. In *BlackHat Federal*, Washington D.C., USA, 2009. Accessed: 5/01/2013.

[31] R. Wojtczuk and A. Tereshkin. Attacking Intel BIOS. In *BlackHat*, Las Vegas, USA, 2009. Accessed: 5/01/2013.

[32] M. Yamamura. W95.CIH - Symantec. http://www.symantec.com/security_response/writeup.jsp ?docid=2000-122010-2655-99. Accessed: 5/01/2013.

APPENDIX

A. TERMINOLOGY REFERENCE

There are numerous acronyms related to low level firmware, trusted computing, and timing-based attestation technologies. Although all terms are defined when first used in the paper, this appendix can serve as an easier reference.

AIK - Attestation Identity Key - A TPM key with more restricted capabilities than a general signing key.
BIOS - Basic Input Output System - The firmware that executes at system reboot on an x86 PC.
BC - BIOS Chronomancy - The name of our timing-based attestation system hosted in the BIOS.
CS - (BC-specific) CheckSum
CTS - (BC-specific) Current TickStamp
CRTM - Core Root of Trust for Measurement - The initial component of the SRTM that must be trusted implicitly, and that must measure itself.
DP - (BC-specific) Data Pointer
***DP** - (BC-specific) A pseudo-C language style indication of dereferencing the DP
DRTM - Dynamic Root of Trust for Measurement - A root of trust that is instantiated on demand. While technically BC is a DTRM, we use this term only to refer to the more commonly understood implementations such as Intel TXT or AMD SVM.
EEPROM - Electronically Erasable Programmable Read Only Memory - The storage type often used for BIOS.
EIP_DST - (BC-specific) The x86 extended instruction pointer (EIP) that is the destination for the next BC block jump.
flash chip - Synonym of EEPROM for our purposes.
ICH - I/O Controller Hub - Responsible for mediating access to slow peripherals
LPC Bus - Low Pin Count Bus - The bus the TPM is on.
MCH - Memory Controller Hub - Responsible for mediating access to RAM and fast peripherals
OEM - Original Equipment Manufacturer
PCR - Platform Configuration Register - A storage area on a TPM that can only be set by SHA1 hashing the current value concatenated with the input value.
PRN - (BC-specific)Pseudo-Random Number - Updated in every BC block, and seeded by the TSN.
SMI - System Management Interrupt - Dedicated x86 interrupt to invoke SMM code
SMM - System Management Mode - The most privileged general execution domain on x86 systems
SMRAM - System Management RAM - The memory where SMM code and data is stored
SPI Bus - Serial Peripheral Interface Bus - The bus the BIOS EEPROM is located on.
SRTM - Static Root of Trust for Measurement - A root of trust that indicates the configuration that the system booted into.
TCG - Trusted Computing Group - Responsible for the TPM specification.
Tickstamp - A tick count *according to the TPM's internal clock*, that has been signed by a TPM key.
TPM - Trusted Platform Module - A dedicated chip that provides some cryptographic capabilities.
TS1,TS2 - (BC-specific) TickStamp1,2
TSN - Tick Session Nonce - A part of a TPM TickStamp data that is pseudo-randomly generated on each TPM reset.
UEFI - Unified Extensible Firmware Interface - A specification for firmware design.

B. ADDITIONAL FIGURES

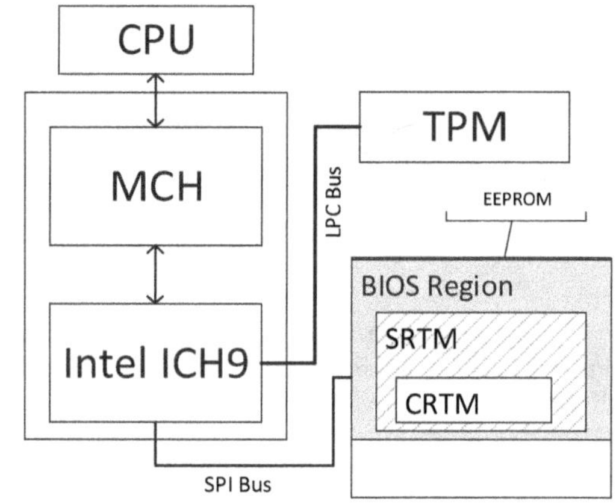

Figure 4: Relation of major components discussed in this paper

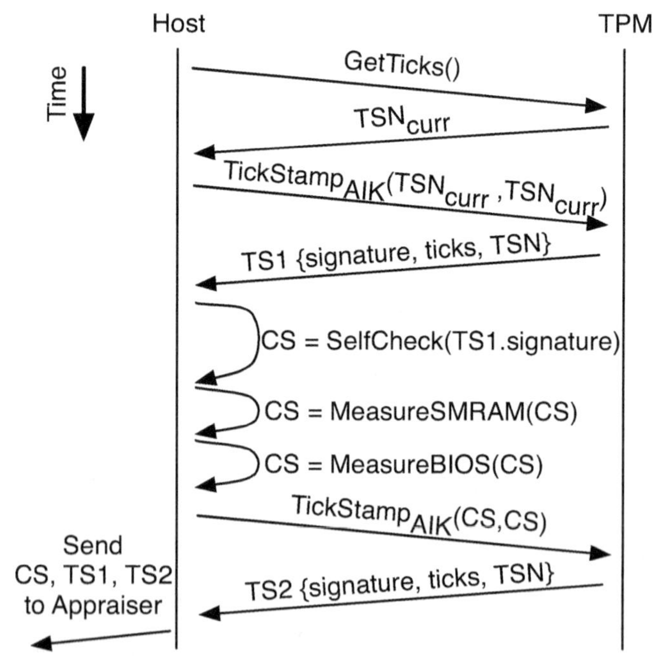

Figure 5: Graphical representation of protocol described in section 5.1

Flexible and Scalable Digital Signatures in TPM 2.0

Liqun Chen
HP Laboratories
Bristol, UK
liqun.chen@hp.com

Jiangtao Li
Intel Corporation
Portland, Oregon, USA
jiangtao.li@intel.com

ABSTRACT

Trusted Platform Modules (TPM) are multipurpose hardware chips, which provide support for various cryptographic functions. Flexibility, scalability and high performance are critical features for a TPM. In this paper, we present the new method for implementing digital signatures that has been included in TPM version 2.0. The core part of this method is a single TPM signature primitive, which can be called by different software programmes, in order to implement signature schemes and cryptographic protocols with different security and privacy features. We prove security of the TPM signature primitive under the static Diffie-Hellman assumption and the random oracle model. We demonstrate how to call this TPM signature primitive to implement anonymous signatures (Direct Anonymous Attestation), pseudonym systems (U-Prove), and conventional signatures (the Schnorr signature). To the best of our knowledge, this is the first signature primitive implemented in a limited hardware environment capable of supporting various signature schemes without adding additional hardware complexity compared to a hardware implementation of a conventional signature scheme.

Categories and Subject Descriptors

K.6.5 [**Management of Computing and Information Systems**]: Security and Protection

Keywords

TPM; Digital Signatures; Direct Anonymous Attestation

1. INTRODUCTION

A Trusted Platform Module (TPM) is a hardware chip used to provide verifiable attestation and integrity for a computer platform and to also provide support for multiple cryptographic functions necessary to implement data protection in the platform. The implementation of these functions in hardware has an advantage that it provides much better tamper resistance than any software. But the disadvantage of hardware implementation is that it usually costs more and is less flexible than software implementation. Therefore, it is essential to find a good balance between hardware and software implementation, in order to achieve high security using the minimum hardware resources.

TPMs can be made by any chip manufacturer, but to be useful they must all obey standard protocols and use a common interface. The specification of these protocols and interfaces has been developed by an industrial standards body, namely the Trusted Computing Group (TCG). The current version of the TPM specification is 1.2 [30]. This specification is also available as the international standard ISO/IEC 11889 [1]. TPMs implementing version 1.2 of the standard have been embedded in hundreds of millions of computing platforms.

TPM 1.2 only requires support for a small number of cryptographic algorithms: SHA-1, HMAC, RSA signature and encryption, AES[1], one-time-pad with XOR for symmetric encryption, and Direct Anonymous Attestation (DAA). As the TPM becomes widely used, there is a need for more flexible cryptographic algorithms being supported, because different countries and regions around the world have their own standard cryptographic algorithms and therefore their own differing requirements for a cryptographic processor. With a target of providing support for algorithm agility, the TCG has developed a new version of TPM specifications (TPM 2.0), which is now available for public review [31].

One critical challenge when designing the new TPM specification is including multiple cryptographic functionalities and flexibly selective cryptographic algorithms but ensuring that the chip can be made cheaply and still have high performance. In this paper, we describe how the digital signature primitive in TPM 2.0 was developed.

This work is based on two observations: (1) In a complex signature scheme, like DAA [5] and U-Prove [24], which we aim to implement using TPM 2.0, the computation directly using a private key is only a small part of the computation of the signature; (2) the computation using the private key is a self-contained signature operation that can be used by different pieces of software to create different/multiple complicated signatures. Based on these two observations, we designed a small signature primitive, which is implemented within a TPM and can be called by a number of other schemes and protocols. The starting point for this work was the requirement that a TPM be able to support three different types of signature: conventional signatures,

CCS'13, November 4–8, 2013, Berlin, Germany.

http://dx.doi.org/10.1145/2508859.2516729.

[1]AES is optional for TPM 1.2 according on revision 116 of the TPM 1.2 specification, published on March 3, 2011.

DAA signatures, and U-Prove signatures. All of them can be based on Elliptic Curve Cryptography (ECC). Our goal was to implement these signature schemes without more overhead in hardware than implementing a conventional signature scheme, such as the Schnorr signature scheme [28].

In our scheme the signing functionality is protected by the TPM, but the verification function exists external to the TPM. This is acceptable, because verification does not involve the private key and anybody is able to verify the integrity of a signature for themselves. We transfer a major part of the computation of the signing process to external software and only keep a small core operation in the TPM. The assurance of the scheme is not reduced by moving these computations outside the TPM. The TPM is a principal signer who holds the private key, the external software only plays the role of a helper that does not have the key, and it cannot forge a signature without the aid of the TPM.

The contributions of this paper are summarized as follows:

- We design a new TPM signature primitive, denoted by tpm.sign. It can be seen as a Schnorr type of signature scheme [28]. The special feature is that it has two generators of a group - one is conventional and the other is derived from a hash of an arbitrary integer. Each generator is associated with a Schnorr signature. The signing algorithm combines the two separated signatures into one. We demonstrate how to implement tpm.sign using a few simple TPM 2.0 commands. Most of these commands are also used for other TPM functions; as a result tpm.sign requires very little additional TPM resources.
- We conduct rigorous security analysis of tpm.sign. We prove that tpm.sign is secure under the static Diffie-Hallmen assumption in the random oracle model.
- We present how to use tpm.sign to implement DAA in TPM 2.0. Our implementation supports two different pairing-based DAA schemes using a single interface. The DAA implementation no longer requires any heavy, expensive and single purpose TPM commands as used in TPM 1.2.
- We present how to use tpm.sign to implement U-Prove 1.1 protocol in TPM 2.0. The U-Prove implementation does not require any extra TPM resources, as it simply reuses the TPM commands existing for DAA.

Although the proposed scheme was designed for TPM 2.0, the central idea of the scheme, i.e. using a single hardware-based signature to enable a variety of cryptographic protocols, is not just useful for TPM, but can also benefit other applications; for example, DAA can be used to provide an anonymous announcement system in vehicular networks [15], and U-Prove can use a smartcard or mobile phone for different applications [24].

In the remainder of the paper, we will first introduce the TPM signature primitive, tpm.sign, in §2, including the security proof of this algorithm, which will be followed by implementation details in TPM 2.0 in §3. After that we will present the first application of tpm.sign, which is DAA, in §4; our implementation supports two different pairing-based DAA schemes. We will further demonstrate that tpm.sign can be used as the protected hardware device for Microsoft U-Prove in §5. We will conclude our paper and discuss the future work in §6.

2. THE TPM SIGNATURE PRIMITIVE

2.1 Functional Description

We first describe the TPM signature primitive in TPM 2.0, denoted by tpm.sign. This is a Schnorr type of signature scheme, and has the following three procedures: key generation, signing, and verification. Only the key generation and signing procedures are implemented in TPM. In the rest of the paper, we use the following notation: Let $\mathbb{G} = \langle g \rangle$ be a cyclic group of prime order p and g be a generator. Let $H : \{0,1\}^* \to \mathbb{Z}_p$ and $H_{\mathbb{G}} : \{0,1\}^* \to \mathbb{G}$ be two collision-resistent hash functions.

Key Generation This procedure selects a random $x \leftarrow \mathbb{Z}_p^*$ and computes $y := g^x$. The secret key is x while the public key is y.

Signing This procedure takes a message $m \in \{0,1\}^*$, a string $str \in \{0,1\}^*$, and a group element $P_1 \in \mathbb{G}$, and calls the following two sub-procedures:

Commit Oracle ($\mathcal{O}_C$) Given P_1, str as input:

1. Verify that $P_1 \in \mathbb{G}$.
2. If $str = \emptyset$, set $P_2 := 1$ (the identity element of $\mathbb{G}$), otherwise, compute $P_2 := H_{\mathbb{G}}(str)$.
3. Choose a random integer $r \leftarrow \mathbb{Z}_p$.
4. Compute $R_1 := P_1^r$, $R_2 := P_2^r$, and $K_2 := P_2^x$ where x is the private key.
5. Output R_1, R_2, and K_2.

Sign Oracle ($\mathcal{O}_S$) Given $c_h, m \in \{0,1\}^*$ as input, where $c_h = (R_1, R_2)$ for simplicity:[2]

1. Compute $c := H(c_h, m)$.
2. Compute $s := r + cx \mod p$ using r from the commit oracle and delete r.
3. Output (c, s).

The signature on m is $(P_1, P_2, R_1, R_2, K_2, c, s)$. It is a signature of knowledge

$$SPK\{(x) : K_1 = P_1^x \wedge K_2 = P_2^x\}(m).$$

Verification This procedure takes the message m, the signature $(P_1, P_2, R_1, R_2, K_2, c, s)$, and $K_1 \in \mathbb{G}$ as input, such that $K_1 = P_1^x$ and $K_2 = P_2^x$. It performs the following steps:

1. If $P_1 = 1$ and $P_2 = 1$, return 0 (invalid).
2. Verify that $H(R_1, R_2, m) = c$.
3. Verify that $R_1 = P_1^s \cdot K_1^{-c}$ and $R_2 = P_2^s \cdot K_2^{-c}$.
4. If any of the verification steps fails, return 0 (invalid), otherwise return 1 (valid).

The verification procedure relies on $K_1 = P_1^x$ and $K_2 = P_2^x$. If they are not guaranteed, then the signature can be easily forged. In the TPM 2.0 implementation of U-Prove and Schnorr signature, K_1 is the public key y. In DAA, the discrete log between P_1 and K_1 can be verified by the verifier through other means. Note that K_2 is a pseudonym

[2]In the TPM implementation of this oracle, c_h could be a hash of R_1, R_2, and other information.

of TPM in the DAA and U-Prove schemes. If the same P_2 is used, K_2 is always the same for a private key x.

Observe that a special case of this signature algorithm is the Schnorr signature. In the signing procedure, choose $P_1 = g$ and $str = \emptyset$ such that $R_1 = g^r$ and $R_2 = K_2 = 1$. In the verification procedure, set $P_1 = g$, $K_1 = y$, and $P_2 = K_2 = 1$. It is easy to see that $R_1 = g^r = g^s \cdot y^{-c} = P_1^s \cdot K_1^{-c}$ holds and the Schnorr signature can be verified successfully.

2.2 Security Notions and Proof

To prove security of tpm.sign, we use the standard security notion for digital signature schemes. We consider *existential forgery* where the goal of the adversary is to produce a valid signature on a message that he chooses. We consider the *chosen-message attack* where the adversary is given adaptive access to signatures on messages of his choice while attempting to forge a signature. In the TPM 2.0 implementation, the signing procedure is implemented using two separate TPM commands, one for each sub-procedure. Besides allowing the adversary to obtain signatures on the messages of his choice, we allow him to directly query the commit oracle $\mathcal{O}_C$ and the sign oracle $\mathcal{O}_S$ of his choice. For example, the adversary can query $\mathcal{O}_C$ a few times before querying $\mathcal{O}_S$, or the adversary can modify c_h to a different value before querying $\mathcal{O}_S$.

Definition 1 (Security Definition). *The* tpm.sign *scheme is secure if an existential forgery is computationally impossible, if the adversary is given adaptive access to signature on messages of his choice and given adaptive access to oracles $\mathcal{O}_C$ and $\mathcal{O}_S$.*

The security of our TPM 2.0 signature scheme depends on the following static Diffie-Hellman (DH) problem.

Definition 2 (Static DH Oracle). *Let $\mathbb{G}$ be a cyclic group of prime order p. Let x be a value in $\mathbb{Z}_p^*$. Given any $P \in \mathbb{G}$, the static DH oracle on x computes and outputs P^x.*

Definition 3 (Static DH Problem). *Let $\mathbb{G}$ be a cyclic group of prime order p. Given $g, h \in \mathbb{G}$ such that $h = g^x$, the static DH problem is to compute x given access to a static DH oracle on x.*

The static DH assumption is that it is computationally infeasible to solve the static DH problem. The static DH assumption is a stronger assumption than the discrete log assumption, as if one can solve the discrete log problem, then he can solve the static DH problem as well. It is believed in the cryptography community that the static DH problem is a computationally hard problem. Several cryptographic protocols rely on the static DH assumption, such as the basic El Gamal encryption [19], Ford-Kaliski server-assisted key generation protocol [21], and Chaum and van Antwerpen's Undeniable Signatures [12]. These protocols provide a static DH oracle on the secret key to the adversary.

To prove security of the tpm.sign scheme, we first review the well-known forking lemma from Pointcheval and Stern [26]. For a signature scheme based on three-pass honest-verifier zero-knowledge identification protocol using the Fiat and Shamir transformation [20], such as the Schnorr signature [28], a signature of a message m is a triple (σ_1, h, σ_2), where σ_1 represents all successive "commitment" of the protocol, $h = H(\sigma_1, m)$ where H is a hash function, and σ_2 represents all successive "answers" of the protocol.

Lemma 1 (The Forking Lemma). *Let $\mathcal{A}$ be a probabilistic polynomial time turning machine. Let Q and R be the number of queries that $\mathcal{A}$ can ask to the random oracle and the number of queries $\mathcal{A}$ can ask to the signer, respectively. Assume that within a time bound T, $\mathcal{A}$ produces a valid signature $(m, \sigma_1, h, \sigma_2)$ with probability $\epsilon \geq 10(R+1)(R+Q)/2^k$. If the triples (σ_1, h, σ_2) can be simulated without knowing the secret key, with an indistinguishable distribution probability, then there is another machine which has control over the machine obtained from $\mathcal{A}$ replacing interaction with the signer by simulation and produces two valid signatures $(m, \sigma_1, h, \sigma_2)$ and $(m, \sigma_1, h', \sigma_2')$ such that $h \neq h'$ in expected time $T' \leq 120686QT/\epsilon$.*

Theorem 2. *The* tpm.sign *scheme is secure under the security definition in Definition 1 in the random oracle model under the static DH assumption.*

Proof. Suppose there is an adversary $\mathcal{A}$ that breaks the tpm.sign scheme above, i.e., $\mathcal{A}$ outputs a forged signature $(m, P_1, P_2, R_1, R_2, K_2, c, s)$ after given access to signatures on messages of its choices and access to oracles $\mathcal{O}_C$ and $\mathcal{O}_S$. We can construct an algorithm $\mathcal{B}$ which makes use of $\mathcal{A}$ to solve the static DH assumption. $\mathcal{B}$ is given a pair $(g, h = g^x)$, where $\mathcal{B}$ can access the static DH oracle on x in polynomial time. That is, $\mathcal{B}$ can sends any $P \in \mathbb{G}$ to the static DH oracle and obtains P^x back. The goal is for $\mathcal{B}$ to compute the private key x. Algorithm $\mathcal{B}$ works as follows.

Key generation: $\mathcal{B}$ sets h as the public key and outputs it to $\mathcal{A}$ and sets $\log_g h$ as the corresponding private key x, although $\mathcal{B}$ does not know x.

Signature Query: If $\mathcal{A}$ makes a signature query on m with P_1 and str as input, $\mathcal{B}$ computes $P_2 := H_{\mathbb{G}}(str)$ and queries the static DH oracle with P_1 and P_2 and obtains $K_1 = P_1^x$ and $K_2 = P_2^x$ back. $\mathcal{B}$ chooses at random c and s and computes $R_1 := P_1^s \cdot K_1^{-c}$ and $R_2 := P_2^s \cdot K_2^{-c}$. $\mathcal{B}$ patches the random oracle such that $c := H(R_1, R_2, m)$. $\mathcal{B}$ outputs $(m, P_1, P_2, R_1, R_2, K_2, c, s)$ as the signature. Observe that the distribution of this simulated signature by $\mathcal{B}$ is the same as the distribution of a real tpm.sign signature.

Query on $\mathcal{O}_C$: If $\mathcal{A}$ makes a commit query on $\mathcal{O}_C$ to $\mathcal{B}$ with P_1 and str as input, $\mathcal{B}$ computes $P_2 := H_{\mathbb{G}}(str)$ and queries the static DH oracle with P_1 and P_2 and obtains $K_1 = P_1^x$ and $K_2 = P_2^x$, respectively. $\mathcal{B}$ chooses at random c and s, and computes $R_1 = P_1^s \cdot K_1^{-c}$ and $R_2 = P_2^s \cdot K_2^{-c}$. $\mathcal{B}$ outputs (R_1, R_2, K_2). It is easy to see that that this simulation of (R_1, R_2, K_2) is perfect.

Query on $\mathcal{O}_S$: If $\mathcal{A}$ makes a signing query on $\mathcal{O}_S$ to $\mathcal{B}$ with c_h and m as input. $\mathcal{B}$ checks whether (c_h, m) has been queries before. If not, $\mathcal{B}$ sets $c := H_2(c_h, m)$ and outputs (c, s) where c and s were chosen in the commit oracle query. If (c_h, m) has been queried before and $H_2(c_h, m)$ is different from c in the corresponding commitment query, $\mathcal{B}$ returns failure. Clearly, the signature $(m, P_1, P_2, R_1, R_2, K_2, c, s)$ generated from $\mathcal{O}_C$ and $\mathcal{O}_S$ queries can be verified correctly by $\mathcal{A}$. Furthermore, the distribution of this simulated signature by $\mathcal{B}$ is computationally indistinguishable with a real tpm.sign signature.

Forgery: After $\mathcal{A}$ makes the above queries, $\mathcal{A}$ outputs a forged signature $(m, P_1, P_2, R_1, R_2, K_2, c, s)$ that can be successfully verified. Using the forking lemma above (Lemma 1), we can build another simulator $\mathcal{B}$' such that $\mathcal{A}$ outputs two valid tpm.sign signatures $\sigma_1 = (m, P_1, P_2, R_1, R_2, K_2, m, c, s)$ and $\sigma_2 = (m, P_1, P_2, R_1, R_2, K_2, c', s')$. Let $K_1 = P_1^x$. Since both signatures can be verified, we have

$$R_1 \cdot K_1^c = P_1^s, \qquad R_1 \cdot K_1^{c'} = P_1^{s'},$$
$$R_2 \cdot K_2^c = P_2^s, \qquad R_2 \cdot K_2^{c'} = P_2^{s'}.$$

Let $\Delta c = c - c'$ and $\Delta s = s - s'$, we have $K_1^{\Delta c} = P_1^{\Delta s}$ and $K_2^{\Delta c} = P_2^{\Delta s}$, where at least one of P_1 and P_2 is not the identity element. The algorithm $\mathcal{B}$' can compute $x := \Delta s / \Delta c$ where $x = \log_{P_1} K_1 = \log_{P_2} K_2$. In other words, $\mathcal{B}$' can compute the secret key x of the static DH and break the static DH problem.

Observe that there is a loss of efficiency in the reduction, due to possible failure in the query on $\mathcal{O}_S$. Since $c_h = (R_1, R_2)$, if $\mathcal{A}$ follows the signing procedure, the chance of (c_h, m) being queried before is negligible. Therefore, under the static DH assumption, the tpm.sign scheme is secure. □

Although security of the tpm.sign scheme is proved under the static DH assumption, in its implementation of TPM 2.0 there is no obvious way that an adversary can use the TPM as a static DH oracle via$\mathcal{O}_C$. This is because TPM computes $P_2 = H_{\mathbb{G}}(str)$ rather than accepting any P_2 value chosen by the adversary. Whether security of tpm.sign can be proved without the static DH assumption is an open question.

3. IMPLEMENTATION OF tpm.sign

In this section, we present how the tpm.sign scheme is implemented in TPM 2.0. We start with some relevant terms and notation and then explain the commands that are used to implement tpm.sign.

3.1 Terms and Notation

Throughout the paper, we use the notation shown in Table 1. We now introduce a few terms, which will be used to implement tpm.sign.

- Key handle: If a key is associated with multiple commands, the connection between these commands is presented as a key handle that uniquely identifies the key. A key handle is a 32-bit random value. The TPM assigns a key handle when a key is loaded into the TPM. When the key is subsequently used in another command (or multiple commands), the handle is taken as input for this command (or these commands). If more than one key are involved in a command, all handles of these keys are taken as input for the command.

- Key name: The name of an asymmetric key is used for identifying the key externally. It is a message digest of the public portion of the key. It is usually used for computing and verifying the integrity value of the key.

- Key blob: For the reason of limiting TPM resources, most TPM keys are not stored inside of the TPM. Each key is stored outside of the TPM in a format called a key blob, and it is associated with a parent key, say parentK, for the purpose of safe storage and integrity check. For an asymmetric key pair, written as tk = (tpk, tsk), the key blob includes the following information: the private part of the key tsk encrypted under the parent key, the public part of the key tpk, and an integrity tag. The tag allows the TPM to verify integrity and authenticity of the key and is achieved by using a message authentication code (MAC). Both the encryption key SK and MAC key MK are derived from parentK by using a key derivation function (KDF). In the rest of this paper, a key blob of tk is denoted as $(\mathsf{tk})^*$ if we do not specify which key the parent key is. The following is an example of a key blob of tk under the parent key parentK:

$$(\text{SK}, \text{MK}) := \text{KDF}(\mathsf{parentK}),$$
$$(\mathsf{tk})^* := (\mathsf{tsk})_{\text{SK}} \| \mathsf{tpk} \| \text{MAC}_{\text{MK}}((\mathsf{tsk})_{\text{SK}} \| \mathsf{tpk}.\text{name}).$$

- Encryption blob: Let k_1 and k_2 be two asymmetric public keys of a TPM. To send a message m to the TPM such that only the TPM possessing k_1 and k_2 can release m to the host platform, we use the following encryption blob which encrypts m. The encryption blob has the following format

$$\text{ENC}_{k_1}(k_2, m) = (seed)_{k_1} \| (m)_{\text{SK}} \| \text{MAC}_{\text{MK}}((m)_{\text{SK}} \| k_2.\text{name}),$$

where *seed* is a random secret seed value, SK is a symmetric encryption key and MK is a message authentication key, both derived from *seed*. The encryption blob is a KEM-DEM type of encryption over m. To release the value m to the caller, the TPM must be satisfied that both k_1 and k_2 have been loaded in the TPM.

Notation	*Descriptions*
ek	TPM endorsement key pair
epk/esk	public/private portion of ek
tk	asymmetric key created by TPM
tpk/tsk	public/private portion of tk
k.handle	handle of k used for identifying the key internally by a TPM
k.name	name of k used for identifying the key externally
KDF(s)	key derivation function using s as seed
MAC$_k(m)$	message authentication code of m computed using key k
ENC$_k(m)$	encryption of m under public key k
DEC$_k(c)$	decryption of c under private key k
SIG$_k(m)$	signature of m signed under key k
$(m)_k$	encryption of m under symmetric key k
$(c)_k^{-1}$	decryption of c under symmetric key k
$(k)^*$	key blob of k wrapped by another key
ENC$_{k_1}(k_2, m)$	encryption blob of m under key k_1 associated with key k_2
$x \| y$	concatenation of x and y
$x \leftarrow S$	x chosen equally at random from a set S
$\|x\|$	bit size of x

Table 1: Notation used in this paper

3.2 The Relevant TPM Commands

All TPM functions are served by using a set of TPM commands. Each command is specified by its input and output, and an operation between the input and output. Most of the TPM commands have multiple options, regarding to different types of keys and applications. For simplicity, we only explain these options which are related to the tpm.sign implementation and its applications that will be discussed in the later part of the paper. For the same reason, we may also omit some input and output information if they are not relevant to our purposes. The following TPM 2.0 commands are used to implement the tpm.sign scheme.

3.2.1 *Key Generation:* TPM2_Create()

This command is used to generate a TPM asymmetric key pair tk for tpm.sign. The command takes a handle of a parent key (say parentK) and public parameters as input, creates a fresh asymmetric key pair $\mathsf{tk} = (\mathsf{tpk}, \mathsf{tsk})$, and outputs a wrapped key blob, denoted as $(\mathsf{tk})^*$ as described before. In the remaining of the paper, we use

$$(\mathsf{tk})^* \leftarrow \mathsf{TPM2\_Create}() \quad \text{or} \quad (\mathsf{tk})^* \leftarrow \mathsf{Create}()$$

to denote this command and omit the information on how tsk was encrypted by the parent key or which key is the parent key. In the context of tpm.sign, to respond to this command, the TPM performs the following steps:

1. TPM picks a random $x \leftarrow \mathbb{Z}_p$ and computes $y = g^x$, where the values p and g are a part of the public parameters as described in Section 2.
2. TPM sets $\mathsf{tpk} := y$, $\mathsf{tsk} := x$, and $\mathsf{tk} := (\mathsf{tpk}, \mathsf{tsk})$.
3. TPM wraps tk with the parent key and outputs a key blob $(\mathsf{tk})^*$.

A variation of this command is TPM2_CreatePrimary(), in which the private key tsk is derived from a primary seed of the TPM using a key derivation function (KDF). A primary seed is a secret key stored inside of the TPM. As a result, the key tk is an alternative version of the primary seed. The same primary seed can be used to create multiple keys. In order to make each created key unique, some index value(s) shall be used. For simplicity, in the remaining of this paper, we will keep using TPM2_Create() only.

3.2.2 *Load a Key into TPM:* TPM2_Load()

When the TPM creates tk in TPM2_Create(), it does not store a copy of this key internally. In order to use tk, the key has to be loaded into the TPM using the command TPM2_Load(). This command takes as input a parent key handle and a key blob $(\mathsf{tk})^*$, which was created under $(\mathsf{tk})^* \leftarrow \mathsf{TPM2\_Create}()$. The TPM verifies integrity of the key. If the verification succeeds, the TPM outputs a handle (tk.handle) and the name (tk.name) for the key. In the remaining part of the paper, we use

$$(\mathsf{tk.handle}, \mathsf{tk.name}) \leftarrow \mathsf{TPM2\_Load}((\mathsf{tk})^*)$$
$$\text{or } \mathsf{tk.handle} \leftarrow \mathsf{Load}((\mathsf{tk})^*)$$

to denote this command. After TPM2_Load() has been called, tk is now stored inside the TPM and can be used for future operations.

3.2.3 *Certify a TPM Key:* TPM2_ActivateCredential()

To provision a certificate to the TPM key tk, the command TPM2_ActivateCredential() is used. Suppose that the TPM has an asymmetric endorsement key pair ek, and an authentic copy of the public portion of this key, epk, is accessible to a Certificate Authority (CA). The TPM associated computer platform sends tpk along with epk to the CA for certification. The CA checks that epk is a valid TPM endorsement key, and then computes a certificate (say *cert*) associated with tpk, generates a fresh symmetric encryption key k, computes the encryption blob $\text{ENC}_{\mathsf{epk}}(\mathsf{tpk}, k)$ along with the encrypted certificate $(cert)_k$, and sends the encryption blob and encrypted certificate back to the platform.

The platform uses the TPM2_ActivateCredential() command to let the TPM decrypt and release the symmetric key k, but the TPM will only respond to this command if the TPM has the corresponding esk and the loaded tk. The command has following input: a handle of ek, a handle of tk, and an encryption blob $\text{ENC}_{\mathsf{epk}}(\mathsf{tpk}, k)$ of a secret key k. The encryption blob has the following format

$$\text{ENC}_{\mathsf{epk}}(\mathsf{tpk}, k) = (seed)_{\mathsf{epk}} \| (k)_{\text{SK}} \| \text{MAC}_{\text{MK}}((k)_{\text{SK}} \| \mathsf{tk}.\text{name}).$$

In the remaining part of the paper, we use

$$m \leftarrow \mathsf{TPM2\_ActivateCredential}(k_1.\text{handle}, k_2.\text{handle}, c)$$
$$\text{or } m \leftarrow \mathsf{ActivateCredential}(k_1, k_2, c)$$

to denote this command. In the content of tpm.sign m is the symmetric key k, k_1 is ek, k_2 is tk and c is $\text{ENC}_{\mathsf{epk}}(\mathsf{tpk}, k)$. Suppose that the TPM has both keys internally. To respond to this command the TPM performs the following steps:

1. Decrypt $(seed)_{k_1}$ using k_1 to obtain *seed*.
2. Derive SK and MK from *seed*, i.e., $\text{SK}\|\text{MK} := \text{KDF}(seed)$.
3. Retrieve k_2.name and compute $\text{MAC}_{\text{MK}}((k)_{\text{SK}} \| k_2.\text{name})$.
4. Check whether the computed MAC value matches the MAC value in c.
5. If mismatch, return failure; otherwise, decrypt $(k)_{\text{SK}}$ and output k.

3.2.4 *Committing Process:* TPM2_Commit()

As mentioned in Section 2, the signing procedure in tpm.sign includes two phases: committing and signing. The committing process is achieved using the command TPM2_Commit().

This command is specially designed for a number of applications, including DAA (See Section 4) and U-Prove (See Section 5). It causes the TPM to compute the first part of the tpm.sign signature operation. It takes as input a key handle of a signing key tk, a point P_1 in $\mathbb{G}$, a string $\hat{s}$, and an integer $\hat{y}$, where $\hat{s}$ and $\hat{y}$ are used to construct another point P_2 in $\mathbb{G}$, see below for details. The TPM outputs three points R_1, R_2, K_2, and a counter *ctr* to the host, where *ctr* is used for identifying the random value r created by this command. In the remaining part of the paper, we use

$$(R_1, R_2, K_2, ctr) \leftarrow \mathsf{TPM2\_Commit}()$$
$$\text{or } (R_1, R_2, K_2) \leftarrow \mathsf{Commit}()$$

to denote this command. To respond this command the TPM performs the following steps:

1. TPM computes $\hat{x} := H(\hat{s})$ where H is a collision-resistant hash function, and sets $P_2 := (\hat{x}, \hat{y})$.
2. TPM verifies P_1 and P_2 are elements in $\mathbb{G}$.
3. TPM chooses a random integer $r \leftarrow \mathbb{Z}_p$.

4. TPM computes $R_1 := P_1^r$, $R_2 := P_2^r$, and $K_2 := P_2^x$.
5. TPM outputs R_1, R_2, K_2 and ctr while keeping r internally.

Note that some input to this command can be empty. If P_1 is an empty field, then R_1 is not computed. If s and $\hat{y}$ are empty, then R_2 and K_2 are not computed.

Note also that this command is slightly different from the description of tpm.sign in Section 2. In the command, the value P_2 is computed as $P_2 := (H(\hat{s}), \hat{y})$, whereas in the tpm.sign scheme, $P_2 := H_{\mathbb{G}}(str)$. This is because it is expensive for TPM to implement a new hash function $H_{\mathbb{G}}$. Given str, the host will compute $\hat{s}$ an $\hat{y}$ such that $H_{\mathbb{G}}(str) = (H(\hat{s}), \hat{y})$, therefore the TPM does not need to implement $H_{\mathbb{G}}$. Details can be found in Appendix A.

3.2.5 *Signing Process:* TPM2_Sign()

This command causes a TPM to sign a digest of a given message, which is a hash output of the message. The command takes as input a handle of the signing key tk, a message digest c_h, and optionally a counter value ctr, and outputs a signature σ on the message. The counter value ctr is only needed when the sign command is called after executing a commit command Commit(). Standard digital signature algorithms can be used, such as RSA, EC-DSA, or EC-Schnorr signatures. If a conventional signature scheme is used, then there is no need to call the commit command. In the remaining part of the paper, we use

$$\sigma \leftarrow \mathsf{TPM2\_Sign}() \quad \text{or} \quad \sigma \leftarrow \mathsf{Sign}()$$

to denote this command. In the context of tpm.sign, the TPM responds this comment by performing the following steps:

1. TPM computes $c := H(c_h, m)$, where m is the data required to be signed.
2. TPM retrieves r from the commit command based on the ctr value.
3. TPM computes $s := r + c \cdot x \bmod p$ where x is the private key tsk, and deletes r.
4. TPM outputs $\sigma = (c, s)$.

In the description of Commit() and Sign(), we assume an ideal implementation where the random value r created in the commit command is stored inside the TPM. The value r is deleted after the corresponding sign command has been executed. However, for the resource-constrained TPM, such implementation is too expensive. In the TPM 2.0 specification, as suggested by David Wooten [32], the following alternative method is used.

- During each boot of TPM, a random seed value $seed$ is generated and stored. The TPM maintains a maximum counter value $mctr$ (with initial value 0) and a bit table T of $N = 2^n$ entries.
- In each execution of the commit command, the TPM increments $mctr$ and sets $ctr := mctr$. The TPM derives r from $seed$ and ctr, i.e., $r := \text{KDF}(seed, ctr)$. Let i be the least significant n bits of ctr. The TPM sets $T[i] = 1$. In the end of this command, the TPM outputs ctr.
- In the sign command with ctr as input, the TPM first verifies that $mctr - N < ctr \leq mctr$. Let i be the least significant n bits of ctr. The TPM then checks that $T[i] = 1$. If all the verification succeed, the TPM uses the $seed$ and ctr to re-generate r. The TPM then sets $T[i] = 0$.

Using the above method, TPM does not need to save r for each commit command. Observe that the TPM checks $ctr \leq mctr$ and makes sure the same ctr has not been used by the sign command before, an attacker cannot query the future ctr or re-use an old ctr value. In the rest of this paper, we assume r is generated randomly instead of being derived for the purpose of security analysis.

4. APPLICATION 1: DAA IN TPM 2.0

Direct anonymous attestation (DAA) is an anonymous digital signature primitive, providing a balance between user privacy and signer authentication in a reasonable way. In a DAA scheme, there are issuers, signers and verifiers. The role of an issuer is to verify legitimacy of signers and to issue a unique DAA credential to each legitimate signer. A signer proves possession of her credential to a verifier by providing a DAA signature, which reveals neither of the DAA credential nor the signer's identity but allows the verifier to authenticate the signer.

The concept and first concrete scheme of DAA were proposed by Brickell, Camenisch, and Chen [5] for the purposes of remote anonymous attestation of a trusted computing platform. Security of their DAA scheme is based on the Strong RSA problem. In this paper, we call this scheme RSA-DAA for short. This DAA scheme was designed as a TPM function for the TCG and specified in the TPM specification version 1.2 [30]. Since the first introduction of DAA, it has attracted lots of attention from both industry and cryptographic researchers, e.g., [2, 3, 6, 7, 8, 9, 10, 13, 14, 16, 17, 22, 23, 27, 29].

Although the RSA-DAA scheme was adopted by the TCG and included in the TPM 1.2 specification ten years ago, TPM vendors have never been happy with it. The major reason is that the scheme is very expensive. In TPM 1.2 there are two expensive and single purpose commands used to implement the RSA-DAA scheme, namely DAA_Join() and DAA_Sign(). The description of these two commands takes about 10% space of the entire specification of TPM 1.2. Following IBM software TPM 1.2 implementation, DAA takes 6.9% of total code space (see Section 4.6 for the details). In the development of TPM 2.0, the functionality of DAA is still required, as addressing privacy concerns is important in a trusted computing environment. However, both TPM users and vendors want a new DAA implementation with minimum overhead and much higher efficiency than the RSA-DAA scheme. This is one of the motivations of the work described in this paper.

In this section, we demonstrate how to use the tpm.sign scheme to implement DAA, which no longer requires any heavy commands. We first give a general description of DAA, and then show that two existing pairing-based EC-DAA schemes ([16, 10]) can be interpreted following this description. After that, we demonstrate that the DAA Join process and Sign process can be implemented using tpm.sign. This application was the main motivation why we designed tpm.sign, and the result provides evidence that tpm.sign is a flexible and scalable signature algorithm.

4.1 A General Description of DAA

As described in many DAA papers [5, 22, 9, 6, 17, 16, 10, 8], a DAA scheme involves a set of DAA issuers $\mathfrak{I}$, a set of signers $\mathfrak{S}$ and a set of verifiers $\mathfrak{V}$. Each signer comprises a host platform and its associated TPM. A DAA scheme $\mathcal{DAA}$ = (Setup, Join, Sign, Verify, Link) consists of the following five polynomial-time algorithms and protocols:

- Setup: On input of a security parameter 1^t, an issuer $\mathfrak{i} \in \mathfrak{I}$ uses this randomized algorithm to produce its secret key isk, public key ipk and the global public parameters param. param includes a list called RogueList that contains rogue signers' secret keys. RogueList is set as an empty list in Setup and will be updated every time a rogue signer is discovered. Note that how to find a rogue signer is out the scope of a DAA scheme. We will assume that param are publicly known so that we do not need to explicitly provide them as input to other algorithms.
- Join: This protocol is run between an issuer $\mathfrak{i} \in \mathfrak{I}$ and a signer $(\mathfrak{t}, \mathfrak{h}) \in \mathfrak{S}$, where $\mathfrak{t}$ is a TPM and $\mathfrak{h}$ is the corresponding host. The protocol creates the TPM's secret key tsk and its DAA credential cre. The value cre is a signature on tsk under isk and can be verified under ipk. In this paper, we denote this signing and verification algorithms by i.sign and i.verify. The value cre is given to both $\mathfrak{t}$ and $\mathfrak{h}$, but the value tsk is known to $\mathfrak{t}$ only.
- Sign: On input of tsk, cre, a basename bsn (the name string of a verifier $\mathfrak{v} \in \mathfrak{V}$ or a special symbol $\perp$), a message msg to be signed and optionally the verifier's nonce n_V for freshness, $\mathfrak{t}$ and $\mathfrak{h}$ run this protocol to produce a DAA signature σ. More specifically, $\mathfrak{t}$ creates a signature σ_t under tsk and $\mathfrak{h}$ converts σ_t to σ using cre. In this paper, we denote the TPM's signing algorithm and its corresponding verification algorithm by t.sign and t.verify.
- Verify: On input of msg, bsn, and a candidate signature σ for msg and bsn. $\mathfrak{v} \in \mathfrak{V}$ uses this deterministic algorithm to return either **true** (accept) or **false** (reject). Note that if σ was created under a key listed in RogueList, it will be rejected.
- Link: On input of two signatures σ_0 and σ_1, $\mathfrak{v}$ uses this deterministic algorithm to return **linked** (linked), **unlinked** (not linked) or $\perp$ (invalid signatures). Note that, unlike Verify, the result of Link is not relied on RogueList.

We now give a new interpretation of DAA, which will lead us to implement two DAA schemes with the same TPM algorithm, tpm.sign. In our interpretation, a DAA scheme contains the following two underlying signature schemes that intercommunicate to each other:

- i.sign & i.verify: the DAA issuer's signature and verification algorithms. We use cre$\leftarrow$i.sign(isk, tsk) to indicate that a DAA credential cre is a signature on the signed message tsk under the signing key isk. The correction of cre can be verified via **accept**$\leftarrow$i.verify(ipk, cre, tsk). This signature algorithm has the properties of blinded signing and randomization. By these two properties we mean the following:
  - Given a commit value of tsk rather than tsk, the issuer can create cre. This allows the issuer to sign tsk without knowing this value.
  - Given cre, one can randomize it to obtain another signature cre$'$ satisfying **accept**$\leftarrow$i.verify(ipk, cre$'$, tsk).
  - The issuer cannot tell whether cre$'$ and cre are signatures on the same tsk value or not.
- t.sign & t.verify: the TPM's signature and verification algorithms. We use $\sigma_t \leftarrow$t.sign(tsk, bsn, (msg, n_V)) to indicate that a TPM part of the DAA signature is a signature on bsn, msg and n_V under the TPM signing key tsk. This signature has a property of user-controlled-linkability, which has the following meanings:
  - σ_t includes two parts $\sigma_t = (\sigma_{t,\alpha}, \sigma_{t,\beta})$.
  - $\sigma_{t,\alpha}$ is a deterministic signature on bsn under tsk. If two signatures contains the same bsn and $\sigma_{t,\alpha}$ values, they show that these two signatures are signed under the same tsk by the same TPM.
  - $\sigma_{t,\beta}$ is a "conventional" signature on (msg, n_V) under tsk. Depending on a DAA scheme, $\sigma_{t,\beta}$ may only available to the host $\mathfrak{h}$, not the Verifier $\mathfrak{v}$.

A DAA signature is a proof of knowledge of two underlying signatures, cre$'$ and $\sigma_{t,\alpha}$, in a signature format, denoted by:

$$SPK\{(\mathsf{tsk}, \mathsf{cre}) : \mathsf{cre}' \wedge \sigma_{t,\alpha}\}(\mathsf{msg}, \mathsf{bsn}, n_V).$$

Given the value cre and accessing to the TPM for t.sign, the host is able to compute such a proof. However, without accessing the TPM for t.sign, the host is not able to do so. The tpm.sign algorithm described in Section 2 is an implementation example of t.sign. In the next two subsections, we will explain how the LRSW-DAA scheme [16] and SDH-DAA scheme [10] can be interpreted using the two underlying signatures, i.sign and t.sign. As security of these two DAA schemes have been analyzed in their original work and we only suggest a new way to implement them, we do not repeat the security proof of these two DAA schemes in this paper. Our security analysis of tpm.sign in Section 2.2 proves that the host is not able to forge a tpm.sign signature; this proof indicates that the new implementation does not reduce security level of these two DAA schemes. This follows from the argument that except the host, from the view point of any other entities of the DAA scheme (a DAA Issuer or a DAA Verifier), a DAA signature created following the TPM 2.0 implementation is identical to the one created following the original schemes.

4.2 The LRSW-DAA Scheme

The above general description fits with the LRSW-DAA scheme as follows (we keep the names of parameters as used in [16]):

- tsk $= f$ and tpk $= (P_1, F)$, where $F = P_1^f$.
- cre $= (A, B, C, D, u, v)$: as shown in the join protocol of the DAA scheme in [8]; (A, B, C) is the CL signature [11] on f; (u, v) is a Schnorr signature by the

issuer; as a result, cre is a variety of the CL signature on tpk, that allows the host to verifies it without aid of the TPM.

- $\mathsf{cre}' = (R, S, T, W, h, s)$: as shown in the sign/verify protocol of the DAA scheme in [16]; (h, s) is a Schnorr signature by the TPM. cre′ is a blinded CL signature on tsk.
- $\sigma_{t,\alpha} = (J, K)$, where J is equivalent to P_2 and $K = J^f$ equivalent to K_2 in tpm.sign.
- $\sigma_{t,\beta} = (h, s)$.
- $SPK\{(\mathsf{tsk}, \mathsf{cre}) : \mathsf{cre}' \wedge \sigma_{t,\alpha}\}(\mathsf{msg}, \mathsf{bsn}, n_V) = (R, S, T, W, J, K, h, s)$.

4.3 The SDH-DAA Scheme

The above general description fits with the SDH-DAA scheme as follows (again we keep the names of parameters as used in [10]):

- $\mathsf{tsk} = f$ and $\mathsf{tpk} = (h_1, F)$, where $F = h_1^f$.
- $\mathsf{cre} = (A, x)$: cre is a signature on tpk (therefore on tsk) that can be verified by, $e(A, wg_2^x) = e(g_1F, g_2)$.
- $\mathsf{cre}' = T = Ah_2^a$: cre′ is a blind signature on tsk that holds $e(T^{-x}h_1^f h_2^{ax}, g_2)e(h_2, w)^a = e(T, w)/e(g_1, g_2)$.
- $\sigma_{t,\alpha} = (J, K)$, where, similar to the LRSW-DAA scheme, J is equivalent to P_2 and $K = J^f$ equivalent to K_2 in tpm.sign.
- $\sigma_{t,\beta}$ is only available to the host.
- $SPK\{(\mathsf{tsk}, \mathsf{cre}) : \mathsf{cre}' \wedge \sigma_{t,\alpha}\}(\mathsf{msg}, \mathsf{bsn}, n_V) = (J, K, T, c, s_f, s_x, s_a, s_b)$.

4.4 The TPM 2.0 DAA Join Process

There are two options for the TPM 2.0 join process. In the first option, the process is performed in the platform manufacturing line, e.g., the DAA issuer is the Original Equipment Manufacturer (OEM) of the platform. In this case, the issuer knows that it is talking to a genuine TPM. The issuer uses Create() to generate a DAA key, and then creates the corresponding DAA credential for the TPM.

In the second option, the DAA join process is after the platform has been shipped to an end user and the platform has a certified manufacturing endorsement key, ek, which is an asymmetric encryption key and its certificate is available to the DAA issuer. This is a common situation. The Join protocol, as shown in Figure 1, is run among a TPM $\mathfrak{t}$, the corresponding host $\mathfrak{h}$ and a DAA Issuer $\mathfrak{i}$. Suppose that the host and the TPM know which key is a parent key and this key is already available to the TPM. In our description, we assume that this may be the TPM endorsement key ek. The Join protocol has the following four steps. We refer each step to its corresponding line numbers in Figure 1.

1. *Create a DAA key (1-2).* The host asks the TPM to create a DAA key tk, by invoking Create(). The result is a key blob denoted by $(\mathsf{tk})^*$ wrapped by the parent key.
2. *Request a credential (2-7).* The host contacts the issuer to request for a DAA credential by sending public keys epk and tpk. The issuer validates epk and returns back with an encryption blob a of a nonce c using epk and tpk. The host loads the DAA key tk to the TPM by using Load(). The host then asks the TPM to release the nonce c by using ActivateCredential(ek, tk, a), in which the TPM verifies the integrity of the ciphertext a and returns the nonce c.
3. *Prove key possession (8-11).* The host asks the TPM to sign the nonce c from the previous step by using Sign(tk, c) on a conventional signature scheme. The host then sends the signature σ and nonce c back to the issuer. The issuer verifies the nonce c from the previous step and verifies the signature. The issuer creates the corresponding DAA credential $\mathsf{cre} = \mathrm{SIG}_{\mathsf{isk}}(\mathsf{tpk})$ using its secret key isk and the TPM public key tpk. The issuer then creates a session key k, an authentication encryption of cre using k denoted as b, and creates an encryption blob of k denoted as d. The issuer returns back b and d.
4. *Release the credential (11-12).* In order to ask the TPM to release the session key k that was used to encrypt the credential cre, the host uses ActivateCredential once again with input (ek, tk, d). After the host obtains k from the TPM, it decrypts the credential cre and verifies its integrity.

4.5 The TPM 2.0 DAA Sign/Verify Process

The DAA Sign/Verify process involves three entities: a TPM $\mathfrak{t}$, the TPM's host $\mathfrak{h}$ and a verifier $\mathfrak{v}$. Suppose that when the Sign/Verify protocol starts, these entities have already obtained the following necessary key materials and other parameters. The TPM has a private storage key internally and this key is called a parent key, denoted by parentK. The host has access to the DAA issuer's public key ipk and a copy of the TPM's DAA key blob $(\mathsf{tk})^*$ together with the associated credential cre. The verifier has access to the DAA issuer's public key ipk and a list of rogue TPM's private keys RogueList. A DAA scheme allows the verifier to detect whether or not a given DAA signature was created by a key in RogueList. Any signature signed by a key in RogueList will be rejected. We assume that in advance the verifier and host have agreed a basename value bsn, a message msg and a verifier's nonce n_V, all of which will be signed in the protocol. As shown in Figure 2, the Sign/Verify protocol has the following three steps. We refer each step to its corresponding line numbers in Figure 2.

1. *Pre-signing process (1).* The host randomizes the credential cre to obtain cre'. As mentioned in Section 4.1, given an arbitrary pair of cre and cre' values, finding whether or not they are associated to each other is computationally infeasible. The host can make this operation as pre-computation, since it is independent to bsn, msg and n_V.
2. *Signing process (1-6).* The host first loads the key blob $(\mathsf{tk})^*$ into the TPM. The TPM decrypts the blob using the parent key parentK and checks whether the key is valid. If the check passes, the TPM creates a key handle tk.handle and returns it to the host. The

	TPM ($\mathfrak{t}$)		Host ($\mathfrak{h}$)		Issuer ($\mathfrak{i}$)
Entities	TPM ($\mathfrak{t}$)		Host ($\mathfrak{h}$)		Issuer ($\mathfrak{i}$)
Keys	esk		epk, ipk		isk, ipk, epk
1:	$(\mathsf{tk})^* \leftarrow \mathsf{Create}()$	← request key			
2:		$(\mathsf{tk})^*$ →		tpk, epk →	If epk $\notin$ Valid, return **reject**
3:					Else $c \leftarrow \{0,1\}^{\lvert c \rvert}$
4:	$\mathsf{tk.handle} \leftarrow \mathsf{Load}((\mathsf{tk})^*)$	← $(\mathsf{tk})^*$		← a	$a = \text{ENC}_{\mathsf{epk}}(\mathsf{tpk}, c)$
5:		tk.handle →			
6:	$c \leftarrow \mathsf{ActivateCredential}(\mathsf{ek}, \mathsf{tk}, a)$	← a			
7:		c →			
8:	$w \leftarrow \mathsf{Sign}(\mathsf{tk}, c)$	← c			
9:		w →		c, w →	If c or $w \notin$ Valid, return **reject**
10:					Else $k \leftarrow \{0,1\}^{\lvert k \rvert}$, $d = \text{ENC}_{\mathsf{epk}}(\mathsf{tpk}, k)$
11:	$k \leftarrow \mathsf{ActivateCredential}(\mathsf{ek}, \mathsf{tk}, d)$	← d		← d, b	$\mathsf{cre} = \text{SIG}_{\mathsf{isk}}(\mathsf{tpk})$, $b = (\mathsf{cre})_k$
12:		k →	$\mathsf{cre} = (b)_k^{-1}$		

Figure 1: The TPM 2.0 DAA Join protocol.

	TPM ($\mathfrak{t}$)		Host ($\mathfrak{h}$)		Verifier ($\mathfrak{v}$)
Entities	TPM ($\mathfrak{t}$)		Host ($\mathfrak{h}$)		Verifier ($\mathfrak{v}$)
Keys	parentK		$(\mathsf{tk})^*$, cre, ipk		ipk
Be signed			msg, bsn, n_V		msg, bsn, n_V
1:	$\mathsf{tk.handle} \leftarrow \mathsf{Load}((\mathsf{tk})^*)$	← $(\mathsf{tk})^*$	$\mathsf{cre}' \leftarrow \mathsf{Randomize}(\mathsf{cre})$		
2:		tk.handle →	Compute $\hat{s}, \hat{y}$		
3:	$(R_1, R_2, K_2) \leftarrow \mathsf{Commit}(P_1, \hat{s}, \hat{y})$	← $P_1, \hat{s}, \hat{y}$			
4:		R_1, R_2, K_2 →	Compute c_h		
5:	$\sigma_{\mathfrak{t}} \leftarrow \mathsf{Sign}(\mathsf{tk}, c_h)$	← c_h			
6:		$\sigma_{\mathfrak{t}}$ →	$\sigma \leftarrow (\mathsf{cre}', \sigma_{\mathfrak{t}})$	σ →	If $\sigma \notin$ Valid, return **false**
7:					$\forall f' \in$ RogueList
8:					if $(\sigma, f', \mathsf{bsn}) \in$ Valid
9:					return **false**
10:					return **true**

Figure 2: The TPM 2.0 DAA Sign/Verify protocol.

host then computes the values $\hat{s}$ and $\hat{y}$ from bsn and calls the Commit() command with the values $\hat{s}$, $\hat{y}$ and P_1, where P_1 is a part of ipk. The TPM responses the command as Commit Oracle of tpm.sign described in Section 2, and returns the values R_1, R_2 and K_2. The host then computes the value c_h and calls the Sign() command with this value as input. The TPM responses the command as Sign Oracle of tpm.sign described again in Section 2, and returns the value σ_t. The host packs the DAA signature σ from cre′ and σ_t and sends the signature to the verifier.

3. *Verifying process (6-10).* The verifier first verifies the validation of the signature σ, and then checks whether the signature was created by any key in RogueList. If both of the verifications given an appropriate answer, the TPM accepts the signature; otherwise rejects it.

4.6 Comparison with DAA in TPM 1.2

We compare our DAA schemes in TPM 2.0 with the DAA scheme in TPM 1.2 with two aspects: code size and performance. We shall show that our signature primitive achieves significant code and performance savings.

For code size, IBM software TPM 1.2 implementation[3] takes 3.28MB code space, in which 225KB code is used for DAA. In other words, DAA takes 6.9% of total code space. On TPM 2.0 v0.98 software reference implementation released by Microsoft, TPM 2.0 takes 1.61MB code space, in which only 7KB code is used for DAA. This is less than 0.5% of the total code space.

As for performance, DAA join protocol in TPM 1.2 takes 9 modular exponentiations, where modulus is either 1632-bit or 2048-bit, and exponents are more than 200-bit, with two exponents larger than 2048-bit. DAA sign protocol in TPM 1.2 takes 6 modular exponentiations and one of them has exponent more than 2048-bit. In TPM 2.0, the most expensive operation in the DAA join protocol is a conventional signature, including one scalar multiplication on an elliptic curve. The DAA sign operations takes 3 scalar multiplications on an elliptic curve. According to [18], on an Infineon TPM 1.2 chip (revision 1.2.3.16), DAA join takes 56.7 seconds and DAA sign takes 37.7 seconds. We do not have concrete DAA performance numbers on TPM 2.0, as TPM 2.0 chips are not publicly available yet. Based on prelimi-

[3]http://ibmswtpm.sourceforge.net/

nary performance figures from Nationz Technologies[4] on a discrete 40MHz TPM 2.0 chip, a scalar multiplication operation takes only 125ms on a 256-bit prime curve. We estimate that DAA join or sign in TPM 2.0 takes less than 0.5 second.

5. APPLICATION 2: U-PROVE WITH TPM AS A PROTECTED DEVICE

Microsoft U-Prove technology [24] is based on the Stefan Brands pseudonym system [4] and uses the blind signatures and zero-knowledge proofs as the fundamental building blocks. Stefan Brands provided the first description of the U-Prove technology in 2000 [4]. Later Microsoft acquired the technology and published U-Prove 1.1 protocol specification, which were updated to the current revision of U-Prove 1.1 protocol specification (the 2nd version) that was published in April 2013 [24].

In the U-Prove scheme, a U-Prove token is served as a pseudonym for a prover. This token contains a number of attributes of the prover certified by an issuer; and the attributes can be selectively disclosed to a verifier.

The U-Prove 1.1 specification [24] suggests that a U-Prove token can be optionally protected by a trusted hardware device such as a smartcard or a mobile phone. In that case, the U-Prove token cannot be used by the prover without the assistant of this device. The device can protect multiple tokens issued by multiple issuers, but it is too costly to implement all the prover algorithms in the trusted device. U-Prove 1.1 specifies how to split the prover functionality between a trusted device and a prover platform.

U-Prove is not supported by TPM 1.2. Another motivation of this paper is to enable the U-Prove technology in TPM 2.0 such that the TPM can be a trusted device for U-Prove, using the same TPM signature primitive for DAA without any additional overhead. In other words, U-Prove is supported by TPM 2.0 with zero extra cost of the TPM resources. In this section, we briefly review the Microsoft U-Prove technology [24] and describe how to use TPM 2.0 as a protected device for U-Prove 1.1.

5.1 Brief Review of U-Prove 1.1

In U-Prove, there is a U-Prove token served as a pseudonym for the prover. This token contains a number of attributes of the prover certified by the issuer which can be selectively disclosed to a verifier. The prover can decide which attributes to show and which attributes to hide. For each token, there is a public key which aggregates all the information of the token and a signature from the issuer over the public key to certify the token. Let $\mathbb{G} = \langle g \rangle$ be a cyclic group of prime order p. The issuer public key is $(g_0, g_1, \ldots, g_n, g_t) \in \mathbb{G}$ and the corresponding private key is y_0 such that $g_0 = g^{y_0}$. Let $(A_1, \ldots, A_n) \in \{0,1\}^*$ be n attributes of the prover, encoded into the U-Prove token. The public key $h \in \mathbb{G}$ of a U-Prove token has the following form

$$h = (g_0 g_1^{x_1} \cdots g_n^{x_n} g_t^{x_t})^{\alpha}$$

where $(x_1, \ldots, x_n) \in \mathbb{Z}_p$ are the corresponding hash values of attributes $(A_1, \ldots, A_n)$ respectively, x_t is a hash value of the issuer parameters, and $\alpha \in \mathbb{Z}_p$ is the secret key of the prover. A U-Prove token is (h, σ), where σ is a blind signature on the prover public key h issued by the issuer. There are two protocols in U-Prove: issuing token and presenting token.

[4]Private communication with Nationz Technologies.

In the issuing token protocol, both the prover and the issuer agree on the attributes $(A_1, \ldots, A_n)$ of the prover, thus they agree on $\gamma = (g_0 g_1^{x_1} \cdots g_n^{x_n} g_t^{x_t})$. In the end of the issuing token protocol, the prover obtains a blind signature σ on $h = \gamma^{\alpha}$ such that the issuer does not know the secret α. The signature $\sigma = (\sigma_z, \sigma_c, \sigma_r)$ is a signature of knowledge of the following form

$$SPK\{(y_0) : g_0 = g^{y_0} \ \wedge \ \sigma_z = h^{y_0}\}.$$

In the presenting token protocol, the prover selectively discloses a set of her attributes encoded in the public key to a verifier. The goal of this protocol is to prove the integrity and authenticity of the disclosed attribute values. In addition, the prover may commit to the values encoded in some attributes and prove that the commitments are computed correctly. Let $D \subset \{1, \ldots, n\}$ be the indices of disclosed attributes, $U = \{1, \ldots, n\} - D$ to the indices of undisclosed attributes, and $C \subset U$ be indices of committed attributes. In this protocol, for each $i \in C$, the prover chooses o_i randomly from $\mathbb{Z}_p$ and computes a Pedersen commitment [25] of x_i as $c_i = g^{x_i} g_1^{o_i}$. Then the prover computes the following zero-knowledge proof of knowledge

$$SPK\{(\alpha, \{x_i\}_{i\in U}, \{o_i\}_{i\in C}) : \{c_i = g^{x_i} g_1^{o_i}\}_{i\in C} \\ \wedge \ h = (g_0 g_1^{x_1} \cdots g_n^{x_n} g_t^{x_t})^{\alpha}\}(m).$$

The prover sends the U-Prove token (h, σ), disclosed attributes $\{A_i\}_{i\in D}$, commitments of attributes $\{c_i\}_{i\in C}$, and the signature of knowledge to the verifier. The verifier verifies the blind signature σ on h, computes $\{x_i\}_{i\in D}$ from attributes $\{A_i\}_{i\in D}$, and verifies the above signature of knowledge.

5.2 Protocol Details of U-Prove 1.1

In U-Prove 1.1, a U-Prove token can be optionally protected by a hardware device such as a smart card. The presenting token protocol requires both the token secret key α and the presence of the hardware device. Therefore, even if the U-Prove token is stolen by an attacker, it cannot be used unless the device is also physically captured by the attacker. Let $g_d \in \mathbb{G}$ be the public device generator. Let $x_d \in \mathbb{Z}_p$ be the device private key and $h_d = g_d^{x_d}$ be the device public key. The public key h of U-Prove token with device protection has the following form:

$$h = (g_0 g_1^{x_1} \cdots g_n^{x_n} g_t^{x_t} g_d^{x_d})^{\alpha}.$$

The issuing token protocol requires no additional computation from the device as long as the device outputs the device public key h_d to the prover. The prover and the issuer can run the issuing token protocol based on the following agreed value: $\gamma = (g_0 g_1^{x_1} \cdots g_n^{x_n} g_t^{x_t} h_d) = (g_0 g_1^{x_1} \cdots g_n^{x_n} g_t^{x_t} g_d^{x_d})$. The presenting token protocol requires interaction of the device as follows: The device optionally computes $g_s = H_{\mathbb{G}}(str)$ where $H_{\mathbb{G}} : \{0,1\}^* \to \mathbb{G}$ is a collision-resistent hash function outputting elements in $\mathbb{G}$ and $P_s = g_s^{x_d}$. The value P_s is a pseudonym of the U-Prove token with regard to a specific scope str. The purpose of the (g_s, P_s) pair is similar to (J, K) pair in DAA: used for checking linkability between different U-Prove tokens. For a verifier with a specific scope str, she can link two presenting token protocols from a device, even if two different tokens are used. The device and the prover then jointly compute the signature of knowledge:

$$SPK\{(\alpha, x_d, \{x_i\}_{i\in U}, \{o_i\}_{i\in C}) : \{c_i = g^{x_i} g_1^{o_i}\}_{i\in C} \wedge h = (g_0 g_1^{x_1} \cdots g_n^{x_n} g_t^{x_t} g_d^{x_d})^\alpha \wedge P_s = g_s^{x_d}\}(m, m_d).$$

The device and the prover can compute the presenting token protocol as follows:

1. The prover computes x_i from A_i for $i \in \{1, \ldots, n\}$, and generates $w_0, w_d \leftarrow \mathbb{Z}_p$ at random and $w_i \leftarrow \mathbb{Z}_p$ at random for $i \in U$.
2. The prover sends str to the device.
3. The device computes $w'_d \leftarrow \mathbb{Z}_p$ and $a_d := g_d^{w'_d}$. If $s \neq \emptyset$, the device computes $g_s := H_{\mathbb{G}}(str)$, $a'_p := g_s^{w'_d}$, and $P_s := g_s^{x_d}$. The device returns a_d, a'_p, and P_s.
4. The prover computes

$$SPK\{(\alpha, \{x_i\}_{i\in U}, \{o_i\}_{i\in C}) : \{c_i = g^{x_i} g_1^{o_i}\}_{i\in C} \wedge h = (g_0 g_1^{x_1} \cdots g_n^{x_n} g_t^{x_t} h_d)^\alpha\}(m, m_d).$$

   as follows: Compute $a = H(h^{w_0}(\prod_{i\in U} g_i^{w_i}) g_d^{w_d} a_d)$ and $a_p = H(g_s^{w_d}\ a'_p)$. For each $i \in C$, choose $o_i, w'_i \leftarrow \mathbb{Z}_p$ and compute $c_i := g^{x_i} g_1^{o_i}$ and $a_i := H(g^{w_i} g_1^{w'_i})$. Compute $m'_d := H(a, D, \{x_i\}_{i\in D}, C, \{c_i, a_i\}_{i\in C}, a_p, P_s, m)$, $c := H(m_d, m'_d)$ and $r_0 := w_0 + c\alpha^{-1} \bmod p$. For each $i \in U$, compute $r_i := w_i - cx_i \bmod p$. For each $i \in C$, compute $r'_i := w'_i - co_i \bmod p$.
5. The prover sends m_d, m'_d to the device.
6. The device computes $c := H(m_d, m'_d)$, and $r'_d := w_d - cx_d \bmod p$, and then outputs r'_d to the prover.
7. The prover computes $r_d := r'_d + w_d \bmod p$.

The signature of the presenting token protocol is: $(\{A_i\}_{i\in D}, a, (a_p, P_s), r_0, \{r_i\}_{i\in U}, r_d, \{c_i, a_i, r'_i\}_{i\in C})$. In the next subsection, we will discuss how to make use of a TPM implementing the TPM 2.0 specification as such a device.

5.3 Using TPM 2.0 as Protected Device

To enable TPM 2.0 as protected device for U-Prove, the prover can compute the presenting token protocol as follows:

1. The prover runs the first step of the presenting token protocol in Section 5.2.
2. The prover loads the device key blob into the TPM and calls the TPM2_Commit() command with $(g_d, \hat{s}, \hat{y})$ as input where $H_{\mathbb{G}}(str) = (H(\hat{s}), \hat{y})$. The prover obtains $(a_d = R_1, a'_p = R_2, P_s = K_2)$.
3. The prover runs Step 4 of the presenting token protocol in Section 5.2.
4. The prover calls the TPM2_Sign() command with (m_d, m'_d) as input and obtains $(c, r'_d = s)$.
5. The prover computes $r_d := r'_d + w_d \bmod p$ and outputs the signature of the protocol $(\{A_i\}_{i\in D}, a, (a_p, P_s), r_0, \{r_i\}_{i\in U}, r_d, \{c_i, a_i, r'_i\}_{i\in C})$.

Since both the TPM2_Commit() and TPM2_Sign() commands have already been used to implement the two DAA schemes as described in Section 4, the implementation of U-Prove in TPM 2.0 does not require any extra TPM resources.

6. CONCLUSION AND FUTURE WORK

We have presented a new digital signature primitive in TPM 2.0 with provable security. The interesting and unique property of this TPM signature primitive is that it can be called by different software programmes, in order to implement different cryptographic schemes and protocols, such as DAA, U-Prove, and Schnorr signatures.

Future work includes: (1) Explore other usages of this TPM signature primitive. (2) Provide a more tight security proof of the TPM signature primitive. In particular we would like to see an answer of the question whether security of this primitive can be proved without the static DH assumption or without the random oracle model. (3) Construct a new tpm.sign scheme which can be proved secure under a weaker assumption but without adding much cost.

Acknowledgement

We thank Ernie Brickell, Chris Newton, Graeme Proudler, Claire Vishik, Monty Wiseman and David Wooten for their useful inputs and discussions. We also thank the TCG TPM working group for their support to this work. We thank Fan Qin and Liu Xin from Nationz Technologies for providing the TPM 2.0 performance data. We appreciate Kevin Butler and anonymous CCS reviewers for their helpful comments.

7. REFERENCES

[1] ISO/IEC 11889:2009 Information technology – Security techniques – Trusted platform module.

[2] Michael Backes, Matteo Maffei, and Dominique Unruh. Zero-knowledge in the applied pi-calculus and automated verification of the direct anonymous attestation protocol. In *Proceedings of IEEE Symposium on Security and Privacy*, pages 202–215. IEEE Computer Society, 2008.

[3] D. Bernhard, G. Fuchsbauer, E. Ghadafi, N. P. Smart, and B. Warinschi. Anonymous attestation with user-controlled linkability. *International Journal of Information Security*, 12(3):219–249, 2013.

[4] Stefan A. Brands. *Rethinking Public Key Infrastructures and Digital Certificates: Building in Privacy.* MIT Press, August 2000.

[5] Ernie Brickell, Jan Camenisch, and Liqun Chen. Direct anonymous attestation. In *Proceedings of the 11th ACM Conference on Computer and Communications Security*, pages 132–145. ACM Press, 2004.

[6] Ernie Brickell, Liqun Chen, and Jiangtao Li. A new direct anonymous attestation scheme from bilinear maps. In *Proceedings of 1st International Conference on Trusted Computing*, volume 4968 of *LNCS*, pages 166–178. Springer, 2008.

[7] Ernie Brickell, Liqun Chen, and Jiangtao Li. Simplified security notions of direct anonymous attestation and a concrete scheme from pairings. *International Journal of Information Security*, 8(5):315–330, 2009.

[8] Ernie Brickell, Liqun Chen, and Jiangtao Li. A (corrected) DAA scheme using batch proof and verification. In *Proceedings of 3rd International Conference on Trusted Systems*, volume 7222 of *LNCS*, pages 304–337. Springer, 2011.

[9] Ernie Brickell and Jiangtao Li. Enhanced Privacy ID: A direct anonymous attestation scheme with enhanced revocation capabilities. In *Proceedings of the 6th ACM Workshop on Privacy in the Electronic Society*, pages 21–30, October 2007.

[10] Ernie Brickell and Jiangtao Li. A pairing-based DAA scheme further reducing TPM resources. In *Proceedings of 3rd International Conference on Trust and Trustworthy Computing*, volume 6101 of *LNCS*, pages 181–195. Springer, 2010.

[11] Jan Camenisch and Anna Lysyanskaya. Signature schemes and anonymous credentials from bilinear maps. In *Advances in Cryptology — CRYPTO '04*, volume 3152 of *LNCS*, pages 56–72. Springer, 2004.

[12] David Chaum and Hans Van Antwerpen. Undeniable signatures. In *Advances in Cryptology — CRYPTO '89*, volume 435 of *LNCS*, pages 212–216. Springer, 1989.

[13] Liqun Chen. A DAA scheme using batch proof and verification. In *Proceedings of the 3rd International Conference on Trust and Trustworthy Computing*, volume 6101 of *LNCS*, pages 166–180. Springer, 2010.

[14] Liqun Chen, Paul Morrissey, and Nigel P. Smart. Pairings in trusted computing. In *Proceedings of the 2nd International Conference on Pairing-Based Cryptography*, volume 5209 of *LNCS*, pages 1–17. Springer, 2008.

[15] Liqun Chen, Siaw-Lynn Ng, and Guilin Wang. Threshold anonymous announcement in VANETs. *IEEE Journal on Selected Areas in Communications, Special Issue on Vehicular Communications and Networks*, 2010.

[16] Liqun Chen, Dan Page, and Nigel P. Smart. On the design and implementation of an efficient DAA scheme. In *Proceedings of the 9th Smart Card Research and Advanced Application IFIP Conference*. Springer, 2010.

[17] Xiaofeng Chen and Dengguo Feng. Direct anonymous attestation for next generation TPM. *Journal of Computers*, 3(12):43–50, 2008.

[18] Kurt Dietrich. Anonymous client authentication for transport layer security. In *Communications and Multimedia Security*, volume 6109 of *LNCS*, pages 268–280, 2010.

[19] Taher El Gamal. A public key cryptosystem and a signature scheme based on discrete logarithms. In *Advances in Cryptology — CRYPTO '84*, volume 196 of *LNCS*, pages 10–18. Springer, 1985.

[20] Amos Fiat and Adi Shamir. How to prove yourself: Practical solutions to identification and signature problems. In *Advances in Cryptology — CRYPTO '86*, volume 263 of *LNCS*, pages 186–194. Springer, 1987.

[21] Warwick Ford and Burton S. Kaliski. Server-assisted generation of a strong secret from a password. In *Proceedings of the IEEE 9th International Workshops on Enabling Technologies: Infrastructure for Collaborative Enterprises*, pages 176–180, 2000.

[22] He Ge and Stephen R. Tate. A direct anonymous attestation scheme for embedded devices. In *Proceeding of 10th International Conference on Practice and Theory in Public Key Cryptography*, volume 4450 of *LNCS*, pages 16–30. Springer, 2007.

[23] Adrian Leung and Chris J. Mitchell. Ninja: Non identity based, privacy preserving authentication for ubiquitous environments. In *Proceedings of 9th International Conference on Ubiquitous Computing*, volume 4717 of *LNCS*, pages 73–90. Springer, 2007.

[24] Microsoft U-Prove Community Technology. U-Prove cryptographic specification version 1.1, 2013. `http://www.microsoft.com/u-prove`.

[25] Torben P. Pedersen. Non-interactive and information-theoretic secure verifiable secret sharing. In *Advances in Cryptology — CRYPTO '91*, volume 576 of *LNCS*, pages 129–140. Springer, 1991.

[26] David Pointcheval and Jacques Stern. Security arguments for digital signatures and blind signatures. *Journal of Cryptology*, 13(3):361–396, 2000.

[27] Carsten Rudolph. Covert identity information in direct anonymous attestation (DAA). In *Proceedings of the IFIP TC-11 22nd International Information Security Conference (SEC)*, pages 443–448. Springer, 2007.

[28] Claus P. Schnorr. Efficient identification and signatures for smart cards. *Journal of Cryptology*, 4(3):161–174, 1991.

[29] Ben Smyth, Mark Ryan, and Liqun Chen. Direct anonymous attestation (DAA): Ensuring privacy with corrupt administrators. In *Proceedings of 4th European Workshop on Security and Privacy in Ad-hoc and Sensor Networks*, volume 4572 of *LNCS*, pages 218–231. Springer, 2007.

[30] Trusted Computing Group. TCG TPM specification 1.2, 2003. `http://www.trustedcomputinggroup.org`.

[31] Trusted Computing Group. TCG TPM specification 2.0, 2013. `http://www.trustedcomputinggroup.org/resources/trusted_platform_module_specifications_in_public_review`.

[32] David Wooten. Private communications.

APPENDIX

A. COMPUTATION OF $H_{\mathbb{G}}$

We first describe a method of constructing $H_{\mathbb{G}} : \{0,1\}^* \rightarrow \mathbb{G}$, where $\mathbb{G}$ is an elliptic curve group $E : y^2 = x^3 + ax + b$ over $\mathbb{F}_q$ with cofactor $= 1$. Given a message $m \in \{0,1\}^*$, $H_{\mathbb{G}}(m)$ can be computed as follows:

1. Set $i := 0$ be a 32-bit unsigned integer.
2. Compute $x := H(i, m)$.
3. Compute $z := x^3 + ax + b \bmod q$.
4. Compute $y := \sqrt{z} \bmod q$. If y does not exist, set $i := i + 1$, repeat step 2 if $i < 2^{32}$, otherwise, report failure.
5. Set $y := \min(y, q - y)$.
6. Output the result as (x, y).

The host platform can help the TPM compute $H_{\mathbb{G}}(m)$, yet the TPM can verify the computation as follows. Given m, the host runs the above algorithm. For a successful execution, let $\hat{s} := (i, m)$ and $\hat{y}$ be the y value in the last step. The host sends $\hat{s}$ and $\hat{y}$ to the TPM. The TPM computes $H_{\mathbb{G}}(m) := (H(\hat{s}), \hat{y})$. This is the first step of the TPM 2.0 commit command.

Rethinking SSL Development in an Appified World

Sascha Fahl, Marian Harbach, Henning Perl, Markus Koetter, Matthew Smith
Distributed Computing & Security Group
Leibniz University Hannover, Germany
Hannover, Germany
{fahl,harbach,perl,koetter,smith}@dcsec.uni-hannover.de

ABSTRACT

The Secure Sockets Layer (SSL) is widely used to secure data transfers on the Internet. Previous studies have shown that the state of non-browser SSL code is catastrophic across a large variety of desktop applications and libraries as well as a large selection of Android apps, leaving users vulnerable to Man-in-the-Middle attacks (MITMAs). To determine possible causes of SSL problems on all major appified platforms, we extended the analysis to the walled-garden ecosystem of iOS, analyzed software developer forums and conducted interviews with developers of vulnerable apps. Our results show that the root causes are not simply careless developers, but also limitations and issues of the current SSL development paradigm. Based on our findings, we derive a proposal to rethink the handling of SSL in the appified world and present a set of countermeasures to improve the handling of SSL using Android as a blueprint for other platforms. Our countermeasures prevent developers from willfully or accidentally breaking SSL certificate validation, offer support for extended features such as SSL Pinning and different SSL validation infrastructures, and protect users. We evaluated our solution against 13,500 popular Android apps and conducted developer interviews to judge the acceptance of our approach and found that our solution works well for all investigated apps and developers.

Categories and Subject Descriptors

D.4.4 [**Software**]: Communications Management—*Network communication*; H.3.5 [**Information Storage and Retrieval**]: Online Information Services—*Data Sharing*

General Terms

Security, Human Factors

Keywords

Android, Apps, iOS, MITMA, Security, SSL

CCS'13, November 4–8, 2013, Berlin, Germany.
Copyright 2013 ACM 978-1-4503-2477-9/13/11 ...$15.00.
http://dx.doi.org/10.1145/2508859.2516655.

1. INTRODUCTION

The proliferation of smartphones and tablet devices is changing the way software is being developed. Both the Android Play Market and the Apple App Store offer over half a million apps and more than one billion apps are installed from these markets every year. The *"There is an app for that"* attitude and the possibility to quickly reach a huge global market has inspired thousands of small software companies and hobby developers to create software on an unprecedented scale. These join big businesses in vying for the lucrative app market. One issue issue many developers seem to have in common is that they often have problems when working with SSL. In previous work, we conducted an in-depth study of 13,500 Android apps which showed that a large number of apps did not use SSL correctly [5], thus making them vulnerable to Man-In-The-Middle attacks. The affected applications ranged from home-brew and open source apps to those developed by large corporations and security specialists, suggesting that SSL problems are not just a matter of untrained developers getting it wrong.

While our previous work and a related study by Georgiev et al. [8] discuss possible reasons for why so many apps across such a wide range of developers are affected and make recommendations on how to prevent these problems in the future, the actual causes of the problems have not yet been identified nor have the potential countermeasures been evaluated. In this paper, we continue where this work left off and evaluate the root causes of SSL coding problems. Based on these findings, we argue that the way developers work with SSL needs to be changed significantly. We designed a framework for SSL development to demonstrate our proposal, implemented it for Android, evaluated it against the set of 13,500 popular apps we analyzed in our previous study and conducted developer interviews to show its functionality and feasibility.

Our solution makes several changes to the status quo: First, it removes the need for developers to write actual SSL code. Instead an app developer can turn on and configure SSL using only configuration options in case they intend to deviate from the standard use case. Second, unlike in the current system, all use-cases we found in apps and those described by developers are supported securely, removing the need for dangerous customization. Third, the framework can make a distinction between developer devices and end-user devices. This allows developers to rapidly prototype applications and tinker without much effort, but it also automatically and properly protects end-users. Fourth, in the remaining rare cases that there is a problem with SSL, the end-user is reliably informed about the nature of the problem which means that apps can no longer silently ignore these warnings and invisibly make users vulnerable to MITM attacks. Finally, our approach allows for new SSL validation strategies and infrastructures, such as Certificate Transparency [11], Convergence [13], and AKI [10], to be deployed centrally instead of potentially requiring tens of thousands of app developers to make adjustments to their code, thus significantly easing the deployment of new SSL validation strategies[1].

Our contributions can be summarized as follows:

- We conducted the first analysis of iOS SSL security to ascertain whether the walled garden approach and stricter code auditing process of Apple could prevent the kind of problems previously seen on Android. We manually examined 1,009 iOS apps. The results show that, similar to Android, 14 % of apps using SSL do not implement SSL validation correctly and are thus vulnerable to active MITMAs.

- We conducted the first in-depth study of the reasons behind the widespread problems with SSL on the two major app platforms Android and iOS, including both technical aspects as well as an in-depth study with affected developers.

- Based on the above research, we designed and implemented countermeasures for handling SSL on Android. This solution can also serve as a blueprint for SSL handling on other appified platforms.

- We conducted an extensive evaluation of our approach by auditing 13,500 apps and showing that our solution covers all use-cases present in these apps. We also conducted a follow-up developer study to ensure our approach does not break any development needs and would find acceptance within the target community.

2. RELATED WORK

2.1 SSL Validation

The main body of work on SSL has centered around finding a replacement for the current weakest link, the CA-based validation of certificates. Many new proposals have been made that promise to strengthen the security of certificate validation, including Perspectives [18], Convergence [13], Certificate Transparency [11], Sovereign Keys [3], TACK [12], and DANE [9]. However, none of these systems has achieved widespread adoption yet. While this is certainly at least in part due to the fact that some have only recently been proposed, a major issue faced by all systems is that they require modification of client code handling SSL connections. While on desktop systems updating the handful of browsers would already cover a large amount of SSL real estate, the situation on appified platforms is bleak. Here thousands of apps contain their own SSL validation implementation and thus must potentially update their code to support a new certificate validation strategy.

[1]We believe this last feature could be useful in the light of the many new solutions suggested in this domain that are currently facing adoption/deployment problems.

2.2 SSL on Appified Platforms

Research has shown that the appification and app market trend has caused new security and privacy challenges for users, developers and researchers [15, 2, 4, 19, 5, 1, 17, 7, 6]. This research focused mainly on the threats posed by malicious entities and their apps. The problems with SSL we [5] and Georgiev et al. [8] discovered are different in that they are not caused by malicious intent, but nonetheless pose a serious threat.

While the bulk of SSL connections on desktop systems occurs in browsers which validate SSL certificates correctly, there are also applications that use SSL to protect their communication. Georgiev et al. [8] analyzed the security of SSL certificate validation in a wide range of SSL libraries and programming frameworks. They conclude that many popular libraries fail when it comes to SSL certificate validation and thus endanger the applications which are based on these libraries.

In [5] we examined the state of SSL on Android. We analyzed the SSL security of 13,500 popular free apps from Google's Play Market. The results showed that 1,074 apps contained SSL code that either accepted all certificates or all hostnames for a certificate and thus leaves the users potentially vulnerable to MITMAs. The cumulative install base of the apps with confirmed vulnerabilities against MITMAs ranged between 40 and 185 million users.

Georgiev et al. [8] make recommendations for what could be done to alleviate these widespread problems. They recommend that app developers should use fuzzing and adversarial testing. Developers should not modify application code and disable certificate validation for testing with self-signed and/or untrusted certificates, but create a temporary keystore with the untrusted CA's public key in it. They also recommend that app developers should not rely on SSL libraries to do things correctly for them. Instead they should set all necessary security parameters themselves explicitly. For library developers, they recommend that SSL libraries be made more explicit about the semantics of their APIs. They also recommend that libraries use safe defaults as much as possible. Furthermore, they should not silently skip important functionalities such as hostname verification and should remain consistent in using return values or flags for reporting purposes.

Our central suggestion was to drastically limit custom SSL handling in apps. In an alternative approach we suggested that a static code analysis be performed by the app store or the app installer to then inform developers/users about potentially unsafe code.

Both papers only briefly describe their potential countermeasures as part of their recommendations for future work. No implementations or evaluations were presented. Interestingly, the countermeasures suggested by the two parties diverge somewhat in their direction. Georgiev et al. call for better APIs for developers, emphasize that developers need to check their apps themselves instead of relying on libraries to do things correctly and to work around API restrictions using custom keystores instead of modifying validation for development purposes, while we suggest almost the opposite approach by recommending to limit the developers' capabilities for customizing SSL and adding checks to prevent broken apps from entering the market or the device. In the next two sections of this paper, we will examine the root causes of the problems facing developers when using SSL to better judge which countermeasures are likely to achieve the best results.

2.3 SSL Development Paradigm

There are countless SSL libraries and TrustManagers that aim to make the integration of SSL into apps easier. However, as the studies by Georgiev et al. [8] and us [5] have shown, many of these are either broken or so error-prone that developers break their apps using them. To the best of the authors' knowledge there is no related work evaluating the root causes of these SSL coding problems nor any work suggesting changes to the development paradigm. Our paper makes important contributions to both these areas.

3. SSL ON IOS

To examine whether or not the widespread SSL problems of apps and libraries introduced above are endemic to the Android and open source ecosystems, we conducted the first in-depth analysis of iOS apps to see if the more restrictive and curated Apple App Store would prevent apps with broken SSL code from entering the iOS ecosystem. While iOS does not offer developers as many options as Android, it still offers similar freedom concerning the implementation and use of SSL. Developers can decide if they want to use SSL or not and just like on Android they can use SSL but can turn SSL certificate validation off. They are also left alone with the challenge to find an appropriate way to handle certification validation errors and inform the user: In terms of SSL APIs, Android and iOS are fairly similar. However, Apple performs a code analysis on all apps, in order to prevent apps that do not conform to their policies from entering the store.

We did not have the means to automatically crawl Apple's app store and use static code analysis on tens of thousands of apps as we did with Android, so we opted for a manual approach. Initially, we downloaded 150 cherry-picked apps for analysis. Based on the findings in these apps we conducted developer interviews as described in section 4.2. We then extended our study to include 1,009 apps for a more robust evaluation. We downloaded the 1,009 apps by selecting the most popular free apps. Since iOS does not work with permissions the way Android does, it was not possible to see which apps have access to sensitive information and can connect to the Internet before installation. We therefore installed all of the apps on an iPhone 4S running iOS 5 to study them in action. We then mounted active Man-In-The-Middle attacks against SSL connections using a transparent proxy to see how the apps react and what kind of sensitive information we could gather.

We captured network traffic from 884 apps and SSL-protected network traffic from 697 of these 884 apps. Of these 697 apps, 98 (14 %, 9.7 % of all 1,009 apps) were vulnerable to our MITMA and leaked sensitive information. Of the remaining 599 apps that were not vulnerable to our active MITMA, 312 apps presented the user with a warning message; 58 apps presented a warning message indicating that there were problems with the SSL certificate. 254 presented warning messages that did not give an appropriate description of what was going on, for instance stating that the login credentials were wrong or that there was no Internet connection available. Finally, 287 apps simply did not connect to the attacked host either doing nothing, hanging indefinitely or crashing. Additionally, 82 (9.27 %) of the 884 apps used plain HTTP connections to transfer sensitive information. Two apps were vulnerable to SSL stripping attacks. One of these was an online banking app that loaded the bank's website via plain HTTP, while the other app connected to the HTTP version of Facebook. Thus we were able to gather sensitive information from 182 apps, i.e. 20.5 % of apps from which we captured network traffic. The information included the usual suspects of login credentials, banking accounts, data stored on cloud storage services, emails, or chat messages.

This shows that the SSL problems on iOS are similar to those on Android and that Apple's more restrictive and curated app development model and App Store do not prevent SSL-related security issues. Just like on Android, app developers turn off SSL certificate validation, write apps that are vulnerable to SSL stripping and even in cases where apps apply SSL certificate validation correctly, they often do not present sensible feedback when validation fails.

While there are many more details worth discussing in the context of iOS, for the purpose of this work, the fact that iOS apps suffer from a similar number of SSL problems shows that these problems must have underlying causes which are not specific to a platform or app store model. For more details on the iOS analysis the reader is referred to AppendixA.

4. CAUSE ANALYSIS

The iOS study shows that the trouble developers have using SSL correctly is common to the major platforms and across all applications and platform paradigms. To develop an effective countermeasure, we wanted to identify the root causes of these problems. Therefore, we studied entries about SSL development for both Android and iOS in online forums and conducted interviews with developers who had produced broken SSL code.

4.1 Online Forums

We used `stackoverflow.com`, a popular online forum for software developers, to search for results that contained text such as *"android/ios allow all certificates"* and *"android/ios trust all certificates"* first. These kinds of results were found in threads where developers asked how they could *"work with self-signed certificates"* or *"make 'javax.net.ssl.SSLException' go away"*. Answers to these and similar questions mainly contained explanations on how to turn off SSL certificate validation or hostname verification without mentioning that this would create serious security issues. Studying these discussions confirmed our impression that many developers on both platforms – iOS as well as Android – lack an adequate understanding of how SSL works and were frustrated with the complexity of customizing SSL code and thus willing to use the quick fixes offered by the forums – potentially without understanding the consequences. These threads had more than 30,000 views. To put this number into perspective, searching for *"android ssl pinning"* or *"ios ssl pinning"* returns only one result for Android and two results for iOS with less than 600 views in total.

4.2 Interviews

While online forums give a good indication of potential issues, a more reliable way to confirm whether or not these issues are the actual reasons causing the problems in the thousands of real world apps is to talk to developers. We contacted 78 developers of the 82 vulnerable apps[2] from the 100 Android and 150 iOS apps we studied in detail. We informed the developers of the discovered vulnerabilities via email and kindly asked them to contact us for further information and assistance in fixing their problems. We received responses from 39 of the 78 developers. We disclosed the respective vulnerability, offered further assistance and asked whether the developers were willing to discuss the details of the security bug either via telephone or email. We promised the developers to anonymize all information they provided and to make neither their names nor the apps' names publicly available. 14 developers agreed to an interview while the rest was not willing to discuss the topic in further detail – often with regard to "constraints" dictated by their legal departments. The interviews were conducted in German or English, depending on the developer's origin. However, not all developers were native speakers. Statements were translated by the authors, grammatical errors were not corrected.

4.2.1 Results

One of the main causes for the problems we found, was that developers wanted to use self-signed certificates during development. 5 of the 14 developers reported that they needed to turn off SSL certificate validation during development because they were working with test servers that used self-signed SSL certificates. To avoid certificate validation exceptions, they implemented their own SSL certificate validation strategies that accept all certificates, or copied code from the online forums mentioned above that promised to help with getting out of the *"self-signed certificate dilemma"*. While it is understandable that developers turn off SSL certificate validation in the development phase, these developers basically forgot to remove their accept-all code when they released their apps. Three of these five developers realized that this was a serious security threat and stated that they should fix this security issue as soon as possible. The other two did not see the problem and even after our explanations stated the following:

> *"You said that an attacker with access to the network traffic can see the data in cleartext. I tried that and I connected my phone to a Wi-Fi hotspot on my laptop. When I used Wireshark to look at the traffic, Wireshark said that this is a proper SSL protected data stream and I could not see any cleartext information when I manually inspected the packets. So I really cannot see what the problem is here."*

This supports the hypothesis stated by Georgiev et al. [8] that too little adversarial testing is conducted by app developers. However, it also raises the issue that there are developers, who, while being technically adept enough to use Wireshark to check if their app's traffic is really encrypted, do not understand the nature of the threat and thus take no precautions to counter it.

Apart from developers wanting to use self-signed certificates during development, we also talked to developers who actually wanted to use them in their production environment but were unaware of the security implications of accepting any certificate:

> *"I was using a self-signed certificate for my app because it is free and CA-signed certificates cost a lot. But, actually, I had no idea that working with self-signed certificates could have resulted in such a security issue. I think the online forum where I found the code snippet only said that it makes self-signed certificates work."*

> *"We added this piece of code because our client uses an SSL certificate for his web-service which was signed by a certificate authority that is not pre-installed on Android and actually we did not realize that this would cause such trouble."*

Sometimes, the broken SSL code was added because developers had difficulties understanding the problem and just went for the first solution that seemingly made the problem disappear:

> *"This app was one of our first mobile apps and when we noticed that there were problems with the SSL certificate, we just implemented the first working solution we found on the Internet. [...] We usually build Java backend software for large-scale web services."*

However, there were also developers who even after being informed about the problems and the threat scenario did not properly understand the problem and their countermeasures did not address the threat arising from a MITMA:

> *"We hadn't realized that it would cause such an issue by using self-signed certificates in the past time, and we just verified if the certificate was expired. But after noticing this issue, we strengthened the security check like verifying host name. We believe this improvement can ensure users' security. So we still stick to trust self-signed certificates right now for its smaller size and lower bandwidth cost."*

So while they added hostname verification after we informed them about the issue, they still accept all self-signed certificates thus defeating hostname verification entirely. In another case, a development company of a vulnerable online banking app needed two iterations to fix their app correctly, even though we had sent them the necessary code snippets. There were also cases where developers thought using broken SSL was adequate to protect information that they deemed to be not that valuable:

> *"We checked into this. Only the [...] feature is using a weak SSL certificate and that connection only sends the device models and IMEI, but that's not a security concern."*

Some developers knew that their code could cause security problems but saw no other option but to work with self-signed certificates by turning off certificate validation entirely, since their customers wanted to use self-signed certificates.

> *"This issue exists because many of our customers use self-signed certificates for SSO (single sign on). Some time back, a **fix** was implemented to allow this to work."*

One of those developers raised the interesting point that Android does not offer any default warning, forcing developers to provide one for themselves if they wish to inform users about failed certificate validations:

> *"The app accepts all SSL certificates because some users wanted to connect to their blogs with self-signed certs*

[2] Some developers were responsible for both an Android and an iOS app; thus there were only 78 developers for 82 apps.

and [...] because Android does not provide an easy-to-use SSL certificate warning message, it was a lot easier to simply accept all self-signed certificates."

The consequence of this design decision was that all users of this app were at risk because some wanted to use self-signed certificates.

The iOS developers in our study tended to rely on frameworks and libraries during development and were understandably startled and upset when told that their apps were endangered because of faulty code generated by the framework (cf. Appendix A):

> *"I am using the MKNetworkToolkit as a network wrapping library and its SSL features for HTTPS. After you informed me of the issue I checked the library's code and found that by default SSL certificate validation is off. But, when I used the library in my app, I trusted it and did not check for the SSL MITMA vulnerability because it is a widely used library."*

> *"When I was starting to build apps for iOS, I had a strong background in coding web applications. When I came up with the Titanium framework that allows developers to build native mobile apps by writing HTML and Javascript, I decided to use this framework just because it was easier for me. [...] I never thought that the framework would produce broken code for SSL encryption and [...], although we conduct security audits for our apps, we did not include SSL certificate validation checks into the audit process."*

The feedback from app developers confirms that developers struggle to implement SSL correctly when they have a need to deviate from the standard use-case. They also rely on the implementations of frameworks and libraries to protect their apps without thoroughly testing either the frameworks' or their app's security. However, our investigation also provides some new insights: developers modified certificate validation code for internal testing purposes, e. g. working with arbitrary self-signed certificates on test servers, but forgot about that and thus did not remove the code for the production environment. So even those developers who understood the current need for signed and trusted certificates put their customers at risk. Also, the developers' problems did not only lie in the complexity of the code, but were based on a lack of understanding of how SSL works. There were also some cases where developers turned SSL validation off because of a customer's request, either accepting or not realizing the implications. Even when we explained what could go wrong and how to correct it, developers struggled when trying to fix their app (cf. Section 4.4). Altogether, our results imply that code-level customization of SSL-handling is an overwhelming problem for many developers and that there is a fairly high level of frustration with the complexity of adapting code to their use-cases.

4.3 Summary

After studying code snippets and advice in developer forums, as well as talking to app developers that use broken SSL certificate validation, we believe that in most cases when Android and iOS developers deviate from default SSL certificate validation strategies – that are secure on both platforms by default – they apply customization features in a way that weakens security significantly (c.f. Section 6.2 for a quantitative confirmation). Many developers of affected apps seem to have only a partial understanding of what SSL does and how it works. Yet, there are also developers who complain about the bad support for self-signed certificates and the lack of easy-to-use SSL warning messages.

One interesting aspect we found in the interviews was that developers in general seem to be interested in providing a high level of security for their users. We offered all developers to help them with their SSL problems and most of them took the offer. After giving background information on the security model of SSL and certificate validation, 10 of the 14 interviewed developers accepted our assitance. 7 of these 10 developers decided to strengthen their app's security by implementing SSL pinning. They did this because it gave them full control over the SSL certificates trusted by their app and they found that this was the most secure, flexible and cheapest way to provide a high level of security. We provided the developers with code to integrate SSL pinning based on Moxie Marlinspike's github page[3]. All developers agreed that being able to control exactly which certificates their apps trust is a great way to increase security, but that they would not have known how to do this without our help.

Our results imply that allowing app developers to customize SSL handling on source-code level overburdens many developers and leads to insecure apps. While it is easy to weaken app security by removing the default SSL certificate validation code, it is hard to strengthen it by implementing pinning or other security-strengthening strategies. Only one developer stated that using insecure SSL should not be taken too seriously, which makes us believe that in most cases insecure SSL connections are unintentional and that users must be protected against careless developers and developers who usually are no security experts.

4.4 Follow-up Analysis

Our developer study showed that many developers were unaware of the dangers facing their SSL connections and interested in fixing the issues. Some of the developers who accepted our help were capable of fixing the SSL problems in their apps. To analyze how developers cope with this situation without direct help, we ran a follow-up analysis. All affected developers (iOS & Android) were informed about the vulnerabilities and the possible security consequences for their users at the time of discovery of the vulnerability. They were given the recommendation that they should fix the identified issues as soon as possible. Three months after the respective notifications, we downloaded the apps again to check if they had fixed the SSL vulnerabilities. We found that 51 of the 78 developers did not fix the SSL issues. Six apps were not available any more which means we could not test them a second time. Only 21 (26.9 %) apps were fixed and implemented correct SSL certificate validation in their current versions. Of these 21 apps, 9 belonged to developers we had helped directly during the interview process. However, 5 of the 14 developers we interviewed did not fix the SSL issues in their apps. Furthermore, developers of an app that included vulnerable SSL certificate validation on both Android and iOS only fixed it for Android while the iOS app was still vulnerable in the second test.

The results of this follow-up analysis indicate that even after informing and educating developers about vulnerabilities in their SSL code, problems in correcting these mistakes and

[3]`https://github.com/moxie0/AndroidPinning`

deploying a safe solution still remain. Finding that 73.1 % of all informed developers did not fix the reported SSL issues demonstrates even more that the current SSL mechanisms on appified platforms need rethinking.

5. A NEW APPROACH TO SSL SECURITY ON APPIFIED PLATFORMS

In the previous sections, we showed that incorrect SSL validation is a widespread problem on appified platforms and analyzed the causes of these issues. In a follow-up study, we found that only a small part of previously vulnerable apps had fixed their app's SSL vulnerabilities, even after we informed the developers about the problems. In the following, we propose a major change in how app developers use SSL to address these issues. While we implemented our ideas for the Android platform, they can serve as a blueprint for increasing SSL security on other platforms such as iOS, but also OS X and Windows 8 which are moving towards the app paradigm as well.

Based on our analysis described above, we believe that simplifying SSL libraries or trying to educate developers in the context of SSL security will not solve the problem. For most developers, network security is not a primary concern and they just want to "make it work". An ideal solution would enable developers to use SSL correctly without coding effort and prevent them from breaking SSL validation through customization. However, it is also important not to restrict their capabilities to produce functional (and secure) applications: If our solution does not offer the needed functionality, developers will be tempted to break it just like they are breaking the built-in SSL code at the moment.

Before going into detail, we summarize the desired features for SSL validation identified during analysis:

Self-Signed Certificates – Development. Developers commonly wish to use self-signed certificates for testing purposes and hence want to turn off certificate validation during testing.

Self-Signed Certificates – Production. A few developers wanted to use self-signed certificates in their production app for cost and effort reasons.

Certificate Pinning / Trusted Roots. Developers liked the idea of having an easy way to limit the number of trusted certificates and/or certificate authorities.

Global Warning Message. Developers requested global SSL warning messages since they described building their own warning messages as too challenging.

Code Complexity. Developers described the code-level customization features of SSL as too complex and requiring too much effort.

In addition to these developer requirements, we add a user requirement to our list of desired changes on how SSL is handled in apps. We base this goal on the related area of SSL handling in browsers. While a website can choose not to offer SSL at all, it cannot prevent the browser from warning the user about an unsafe connection. The website also cannot turn off SSL validation for the user. In the world of apps, developers currently have the power to define SSL policies for an app without those being transparent for the user. While there are well known usability problems with SSL warning messages in browsers [16], we believe that allowing developers to for instance silently ignore SSL errors and put the user at risk is worse. We thus define an additional goal:

User Protection. The capabilities of a developer should be limited in a way that prevents them from invisibly putting user information at risk.

To achieve all these features, several changes to the way SSL is used on appified platforms are necessary. First and foremost, we propose the following paradigm-shift: instead of letting all developers implement their own SSL code (and potentially break SSL in the process, with no chance for the user to notice), the main SSL usage patterns should be provided by the OS as a service that can be added to apps via configuration instead of implementation. This is a fairly radical shift in responsibility, however, we believe there now is enough evidence to warrant this move. Furthermore, the evaluation of our system presented in Section 6 shows that it is both technically possible and acceptable from the developer's standpoint. Configuration instead of implementation also lends itself well to offer other requested features, such as allowing developers to turn off SSL certificate validation for their app on their device in the settings during development. This would allow the use of self-signed certificates during development, but would not affect the installation of an app on a user's device. Surprisingly, none of the major mobile or desktop operating systems provide this feature, although we believe it would offer significant benefits to all parties.

The platform should offer configurable options for the new SSL service so that developers cannot and need not circumvent security features on the code level. The simple removal of the need to tinker with SSL security aspects for testing purposes will already reduce the amount of vulnerable apps significantly. It will also protect users from developers who do not understand how SSL works and who therefore make honest mistakes during implementation.

Table 1 gives an overview of our proposed modifications compared to the traditional code-level approach.

5.1 Implementation on Android

Figure 1 gives a high-level overview of the modifications we implemented to create the proposed SSL service on Android. The white boxes contain classes we modified or created for our solution. The dashed lines show Android components that are now circumvented since they proved to be insecure. The grey boxes are comments on what the different components do. The start arrow shows the entry point where app code passes control over to the central SSL system. The features offered by our solution are presented in the following sections.

5.2 Features

5.2.1 Mandatory SSL Validation

As stated above, we propose that the capability and need to customize SSL certificate validation and hostname verification on source code-level is removed. Instead, SSL certificate validation should be enforced for every SSL handshake automatically, while taking into account the different usage scenarios such as development vs. production.

	CA Validation	CA Pinning	Certificate Pinning	Development Mode	Logging	Validation Strategies
Standard	✓	—	—	—	—	—
Our approach	✓	✓	✓	✓	✓	P

Table 1: A comparison between the status quo and our approach concerning validation features.
✓ = supported out of the box;
– = custom code required;
P = pluggable.

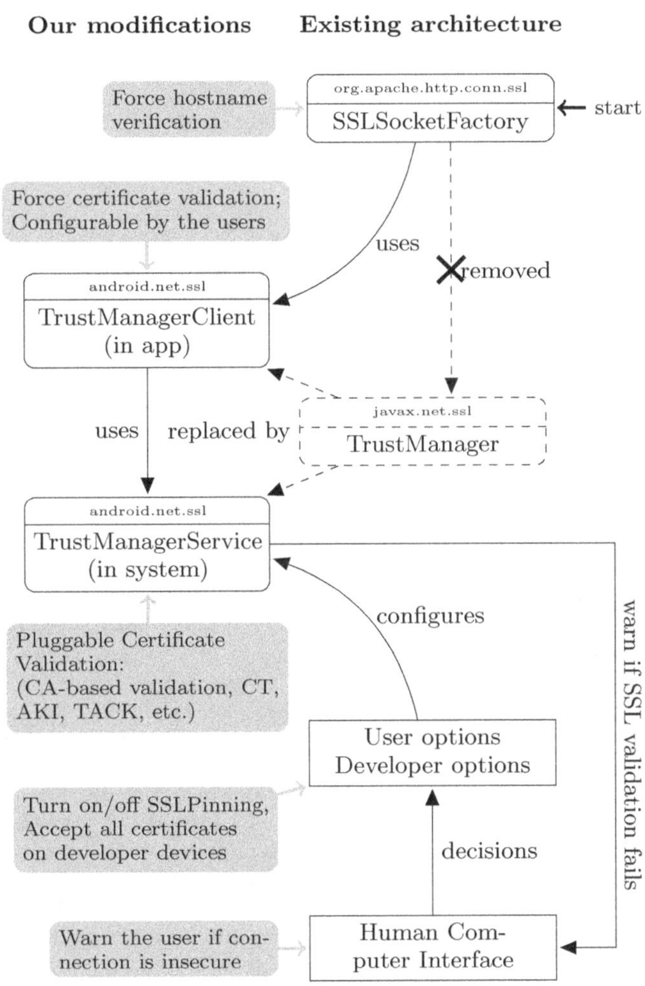

Figure 1: This figure illustrates the process of creating an SSL protected network connection. The grey boxes comment on our contributions.

To this end, we provide the `TrustManagerClient` and `TrustManagerService` that replace the capabilities of Android's default TrustManager (cf. Figure 1). We only modify methods which are private and final, thus binary compatibility is given and we do not break modularity. More information on the compatibility of our approach can be found in Section 6.2 and Appendix B. Both the client and service part of our SSL validation implementation prevent Android apps from using broken certificate validation. Upon creation of a socket, the newly developed `TrustManagerClient` automatically requests SSL certificate validation from the service counterpart. App developers cannot circumvent secure validation anymore, since customized TrustManager implementations are prevented by our modification. The `TrustManagerService` enforces SSL certificate validation against the trusted root CAs and can drop the connection or present the user with a warning message in case validation fails (more on this in Section 5.2.4).

To mandate secure hostname verification, we patched all stock hostname verifiers to enforce browser compatible hostname verification. We also added hostname verification to the central `SSLSocketFactory` (cf. Figure 1). Hostname verification is conventionally delegated to the application layer: With HTTPS for example, the hostname for verification is extracted from the requested URL. In contrast, Android's SSLSocketConnection implementation does not check the hostname, even though it may have been provided in the method call. Our patch improves this behavior by verifying hostnames with the parameters provided during connection establishment for any SSL connection.

This strict enforcement could cause developer issues in some usage scenarios described by our study participants, so several configuration options are described in the following in order to adapt our solution to different situations. Additionally, we discuss potential pathological cases in the appendix (see App. B.1).

5.2.2 Self-Signed Certificates

To allow developers to use self-signed certificates for testing purposes, we add a new option (cf. Figure 2) to the *Developer* settings, allowing app developers to turn off SSL certificate validation for specific apps installed on their device without needing to modify the code of their app. This option is monitored by the `TrustManagerService` and skips certificate validation for this app only. These settings only affect the specific app on the developer device, not the apps deployed onto users' devices or other apps on the developer's device. Thus, even if developers forget to turn on certificate validation again, this has no effect on apps on user devices. This feature effectively protects users from forgetful developers and solves many of the problems we discovered during code analysis and interviews.

We only allow this option on devices that have developer settings enabled. Thus, app developers have a simple way to work with self-signed certificates during development while preventing careless users from turning off SSL certificate validation for their apps.[4] Nonetheless, we show a warning message using strong wording that advises against abuse (cf. Fig. 2(b)) when this option is toggled.

[4]While it is conceivable that users annoyed by warning messages could find information online on how to activate developer options and then turn off certificate validation for a specific app, we believe this risk is fairly low compared to the huge benefit this option brings. Additionally, we recommend limiting this option to devices that are registered with Google developer accounts to prevent normal users from

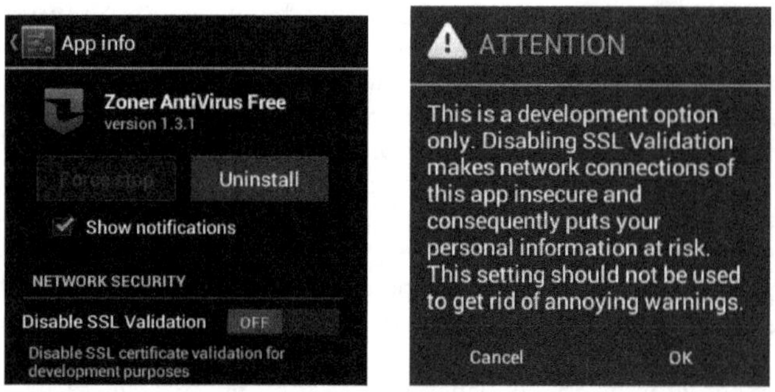

(a) Developer settings to turn off certificate validation for an app. This option is not displayed for normal users.

(b) On disabling validation, a message warns against security threats.

Figure 2: Instead of writing code, SSL parameters can be changed with via Developer settings options.

5.2.3 SSL Pinning

SSL public key pinning can be configured by app developers to limit the number of certificates an app trusts. It can either be used to specify exactly which CA certificates are trusted to sign SSL certificates for this app or directly specify which individual SSL certificates are to be used. The standard Android approach to use certificate pinning requires developers to implement it individually in their source code, resulting in only very few apps implementing pinning at all.[5] The standard approach for limiting the number of trusted issuers is using a custom keystore, which is also complex and requires custom code to load the keystore. Using our extension, it is possible to configure SSL certificate pinning in an Android app's `Manifest.xml` file. This allows developers who know which endpoints their app connects to (this should be most apps) to easily and securely add SSL pinning without having to write any code. Figure 3 shows the `Manifest.xml` for an Android app with SSL pinning.

Pinning individual leaf certificates also allows developers to use self-signed certificates in a production environment in a secure way, which is a requirement several app developers articulated (cf. Section 4). In case developers wish to restrict the number of trusted issuers instead of pinning individual leaf certificates, pins for certificate issuers can be added to the `Manifest.xml` file in the same way. The app then accepts only certificates issued by the pinned certificate issuers. To simplify the process of creating certificate pins and adding them to the `Manifest.xml` file, we extended Eclipse's Android Development Tools. This way pins for given certificates can be generated and added to an app's `Manifest.xml` file automatically.

Since SSL public key pinning can be problematic in some rare cases, for instance if a company mandates the use of an SSL proxy[6], we allow for SSL pinning to be disabled globally using the (enterprise) Device Administration API policies. While careless users cannot unintentionally turn off SSL pinning since they do not have access to the Device Administration API, enterprises can configure devices to respect company policies.

```
<!-- SSLConfiguration for my App -->
<ssl>
 <pinning>
  <!-- Only trust my self-signed certificate. -->
  <pin type="leaf" val="18:DA:D1:9E:26:7D..."/>
  <!-- And certificates signed by Verisign. -->
  <pin type="issuer" val="8F:57:5A:C8:5B..."/>
 </pinning>
 <logging level="INFO"/>
 <handle-validation-fails action="Do-Not-Connect"/>
</ssl>
```

Figure 3: The new SSL configuration options for an Android app's Manifest.xml file allow developers to easily configure different options for handling SSL. Developers can pin either leaf or issuer certificates, determine if their app should log SSL-relevant information and observe how their apps react to failed SSL certificate validations. By default no pin is set, logging is turned off and apps refuse to connect to hosts for which certificate validation failed.

5.2.4 User Protection

Currently it is entirely up to the developers to implement the UI to interact with the user when something goes wrong with SSL. This has led to a large number of apps silently accepting invalid certificates, crashing or displaying unintelligible warning messages such as: *"Reset your local time to the current time"* when faced with a certificate validation error. The lack of a ready-to-use warning message was also an issue criticized by developers in our study. It should also be impossible for app developers to invisibly accept untrusted certificates without the users' consent. We offer a system-triggered, standardized warning that gives app users the chance to recognize security threats originating from insecure SSL connections, thus preventing app developers from silently accepting invalid certificates. This capability is needed for apps that connect to endpoints outside of the control of developers and thus might not have trusted certificates, such as mobile browsers, news readers, blog aggregators, etc.[7]. In these cases, the users are allowed to decide if they want to connect anyway after being shown a warning message.

Usability studies on SSL warning messages for browsers [16] show that designing meaningful and effective SSL warning messages is a challenging task. Designing such a system is outside the scope of this paper which is why we use Android's stock browser warning message for now. Still, we think that having a standardized warning message that app developers can use to let the user decide what to do with untrusted certificates is a good starting point for such future work. Issues such as habituation need to be taken into account at that point, but showing any warning message is better than allowing apps to silently accept all invalid certificates due to developers' negligence.

carelessly breaking their apps' SSL security.

[5]One of these apps is the Twitter app by Twitter Inc., for whom Moxie Marlinspike developed the SSL pinning code.

[6]Some companies use SSL proxy servers to monitor the network traffic of their employees.

[7]One of the developers we interviewed explicitly stated he turned off certificate validation for his app entirely because his customers wanted to connect to blogs with self-signed certificates.

While we no longer allow developers to silently accept connections for which validation fails, we do allow developers to be more restrictive and drop connections for which validation fails without allowing the user to override. This is the correct (and default) behavior for most apps where the developer knows which endpoints the app communicates with and these endpoints have valid certificates, such as online banking, social networking and most other single purpose apps. As long as developers exercise due diligence with their server certificates, the only validation errors would be in the presence of a real MITMA.[8] In these cases, users would be effectively protected from themselves.

The decision of whether a warning message should be displayed or connections should be dropped was added as a configuration parameter to an app's manifest (cf. Fig. 3).

Thus, our framework can protect users of multi-purpose apps from developers who would hide warnings and accept untrusted certificates as well as enabling developers to protect their users from accidentally accepting connections from MITMAs for apps where the endpoints are known in advance.

5.2.5 *Alternate SSL Validation Strategies*

One feature which offers promising future potential is the capability of our system to plug new validation strategies into the system and thus protect both new and existing apps without requiring a large number of app developers to update their code. This could significantly speed up the adoption of alternatives to the current weakest-link CA based system. We have created a plugin infrastructure for this purpose and are in the process of evaluating Certificate Transparency (CT) [11] and AKI [10] as new approaches to validate certificates. This feature is still in the experimental phase and is currently configured into an app's manifest. It is a matter for future work to research how and by whom this feature should be configured and of course to create plugins to improve certificate validation.

6. EVALUATION

As Section 4 showed, all broken SSL implementations on Android and iOS came about because developers wanted to customize the way their app uses SSL and failed to do so safely. While our new approach to SSL-development in apps closes all the security holes we found, it will only be adopted by developers if all their needs are met and they feel comfortable with configuration instead of coding. To evaluate our approach, we conducted two evaluation studies.

We ran interviews with the 14 developers of our previous developer study to discuss how they perceived our proposed solution and if they would be comfortable using it. Since the number of developers available for interview was fairly small, we also did an extensive code analysis of all custom SSL-handling code in the set of 13,500 Android apps to ensure that all use-cases could be covered by our solutions and thus remove the need for dangerous code-level customization.

6.1 Developer Evaluation

We conducted a pre-test study in which novice developers added SSL to their apps and used pinning and self-signed certificates. Since our framework made all these tasks trivial, we decided not to deploy this study on a large scale, since it would not have led to any valuable insights. Instead, we focused on whether the proposed paradigm shift would find the developers' approval and make them feel comfortable with configuring SSL instead of implementing it. We presented our approach to the 14 developers from Section 4.2 and queried them if these features would fulfill their requirements and remove the need to customize the way their app uses SSL. We also asked if they would feel comfortable using configuration instead of coding to add advanced features such as SSL pinning to their apps.

All use-cases of these developers were met with our new design and the reaction of the developers was very positive. They confirmed their previous statements – that SSL development is too complex – and that they very much appreciated anything which would ease the burden. They were particularly positive about the option to use self-signed certificates during development and to use pinning in such an easy way for their production apps. None of the interviewed developers were concerned that they could not fulfill their certificate validation tasks with the provided configuration options. Due to the small number of developers willing to discuss the problems they have with SSL development, we decided to follow up this qualitative study with a quantitative study.

6.2 Compatibility Evaluation

To evaluate whether our proposed solution really covers all relevant use-cases, we ran another static code analysis on the set of 13,500 Android apps [5]. We extracted all customized TrustManager implementations and manually analyzed the semantics of the `checkServerTrusted` methods. Unlike in the previous study, we also analyzed the 2.04 % of implementations that customized SSL handling without breaking SSL. While there are not many apps in this category, it is still imperative that these good apps also continue to work as expected with our new approach. In total, we found 3,464 classes that implement customized TrustManagers. We categorized them based on their handling of SSL validation compared to the default procedure. Table 2 gives an overview of the customizations we found. We denote a customization that weakens certificate validation with a "−", a customization that strengthens validation with a "+" and customizations that do not affect validation security with a "=".

Customized Implementations	3,464	**Security Impact**
Accept All Certificates	3,098	−
Expiry-Only Check	263	−
Leaf-Cert Pinning	47	+
Add Logging to Default Validation	32	=
Add Hostname Pinning to Default Validation	16	+
Limit Trusted Issuers	8	+

Table 2: Distribution of Customized TrustManager Implementations in Android Apps

[8]We realize not all developers practice due diligence with their certificates, however we still believe this to be the right default setting. With this setting developers would quickly realize that there is a problem with their certificate and would be forced to update it.

In the 97.02 % of cases where TrustManagers accept all certificates or only check certificates' expiry dates, our approach protects app users from careless developers by enforcing secure certificate validation. As we previously showed [5], 97.1 % of the endpoints in the 1,074 vulnerable apps had valid certificates. In these cases, our modification fixes the apps without any development effort or negative side-effects for the developer or the user. In the remaining 2.9 % of cases, the endpoints used by the apps do not have valid certificates. In these cases, our system would prevent the connection, unless the developer installs a valid certificate, updates their application to pin the current certificate or sets the **`handle-validation-fails`** option in the manifest (cf. Fig. 3) to show warning messages. Since all three modifications a developer would have to perform are very easy in our framework, we believe this to be a good trade-off for the broken apps.

While the majority of all implementations turns effective SSL certificate validation off entirely, a small number of developers created beneficial customizations. 0.9 % of TrustManagers add logging to the default certificate validation process. While this does not strengthen certificate validation itself, it still is a potentially positive feature that should not be made impossible. We therefore added a configuration option (cf. Fig. 3) that allows developers to get log output from the framework's validation process.

0.5 % of implementations add hostname verification directly to the certificate validation process. This strengthens an app's security since default SSL certificate validation does not cover checking the hostname during the SSL handshake outside of an HTTPSUrlConnection. This feature is covered in our framework (cf. Section 5.2.1 above).

In the 1.6 % of cases where TrustManagers were used to improve SSL validation (i. e. through pinning a leaf certificate or a CA), the functionality added by the custom code is available as a configurable option in our solution. Thus, we found no custom SSL code which implements a use-case that is not covered by our solution with significantly less effort. We conducted field trials that confirmed this analysis.

6.3 Deployability

All our modifications are implemented as part of Android's Java Framework. A system update would thus be the most convenient way to make the new features of our system available to developers and users. All apps built from then on would use this update by default and would benefit from our framework's features. Existing apps' binaries do not need to be modified to benefit. However, it is possible for power users with root access to their device to install our modifications on their devices without having to wait for an official update or having to make major changes to their device, such as flashing the device.

A noteworthy feature of our solution is that it does not break binary compatibility and could in theory be used to protect existing apps as well. Our modifications only affect private final methods of the Java Framework and thus do not break modularity or collide with developer code. This would instantly fix all the vulnerable apps we discovered in our studies. However there are some rare pathological cases which would need to be considered if our system were to be applied to all apps blindly. We discuss these issues and the possible trade-offs in Appendix B.1.

7. LIMITATIONS

We contacted 78 developers and asked them to participate in interviews about the identified SSL issues in their apps. Only 14 developers agreed to participate in an interview while all others either did not respond at all or turned down our request with reference to company guidelines forbidding them to talk about confidential information. Despite the relatively small number of participants, we were still able to identify a wide range of causes which lead to serious security issues in the context of app development and SSL. After the developer study, we conducted a large scale code analysis and did not find any indication that there were further issues that would warrant more interviews.

8. CONCLUSION

In this paper, we argue for a new way of handling SSL connections on appified platforms, since previous work discovered severe problems in this area. To discover the root causes of these problems, we conducted a study of 1,009 iOS apps to ascertain whether iOS suffers from the same problems as Android. We also surveyed developer forums and conducted a developer study. Based on our findings, we proposed to rethink how developers interact with SSL: instead of requiring developers to work with SSL on the code level, we designed and implemented a framework that allows them to protect their network connections via configuration. Our solution prevents developers from willfully or accidentally breaking SSL, while at the same time giving them easy access to additional features, such as pinning and the secure use of self-signed certificates. We evaluated our proposal with existing Android apps and showed that all use-cases we found can be implemented more easily and securely with our approach. The feedback we gathered from developers was also very positive.

There are several important areas of future work: Our framework offers all necessary features to include alternative certificate validation strategies such as Certificate Transparency and AKI just to name two. We are currently working on plugins for these proposals to implement these promising solutions. Since currently there is a great amount of research being conducted on these alternative validation approaches, we believe our framework can make a valuable contribution by enabling this research to be deployed with greater ease and thus not only to be studied better but also hopefully to help with real world adoption.

Furthermore, while we currently recommend our solution to be adopted by new or updated apps, it is in theory possible to apply our changes to all existing apps, thus fixing all broken apps with one update. In future work, we will investigate how to discover and avoid possible side-effects in apps that applied benign code modifications to the SSL validation process. For more on this avenue of research, the reader is referred to Appendix B.

Acknowledgments

We would like to thank all the developers that agreed to support our research, openly discussed security issues in their apps and provided us with the background needed to design our solution.

References

[1] P. P. F. Chan, L. C. K. Hui, and S. M. Yiu. DroidChecker: Analyzing Android Applications for Capability Leaks. In *WISEC '12: Proceedings of the Fifth ACM Conference on Security and Privacy in Wireless and Mobile Networks*. ACM Press, Apr. 2012.

[2] L. Davi, A. Dmitrienko, A. Sadeghi, and M. Winandy. Privilege Escalation Attacks on Android. In *Proceedings of the 13th International Conference on Information Security*, pages 346–360, 2011.

[3] P. Eckersley. Sovereign Key Cryptography for Internet Domains. `https://git.eff.org/?p=sovereign-keys.git;a=blob;f=sovereign-key-design.txt;hb=master`.

[4] A. Egners, B. Marschollek, and U. Meyer. Messing with Android's Permission Model. In *Proceedings of the IEEE TrustCom*, pages 1–22, Apr. 2012.

[5] S. Fahl, M. Harbach, T. Muders, L. Baumgärtner, B. Freisleben, and M. Smith. Why Eve and Mallory Love Android: An Analysis of Android SSL (In)Security. In *Proceedings of the 19th ACM Conference on Computer and Communications Security*. ACM Press, Oct. 2012.

[6] A. Felt, E. Ha, S. Egelman, A. Haney, E. Chin, and D. Wagner. Android Permissions: User Attention, Comprehension, and Behavior. In *Proceedings of the Eighth Symposium on Usable Privacy and Security*. ACM Press, 2012.

[7] A. P. Felt, E. Chin, S. Hanna, D. Song, and D. Wagner. Android permissions Demystified. In *Proceedings of the 18th ACM Conference on Computer and Communications Security*. ACM Press, Oct. 2011.

[8] M. Georgiev, S. Iyengar, S. Jana, R. Anubhai, D. Boneh, and V. Shmatikov. The Most Dangerous Code in the World: Validating SSL Certificates in Non-Browser Software. In *Proceedings of the 2012 ACM Conference on Computer and Communications security*. ACM Press, Oct. 2012.

[9] P. Hoffman and J. Schlyter. The DNS-Based Authentication of Named Entities (DANE) Protocol for Transport Layer Security (TLS): TLSA . `https://tools.ietf.org/html/rfc6698`, Aug. 2012.

[10] T. Hyun-Jin Kim, L.-S. Huang, A. Perrig, C. Jackson, and V. Gligor. Accountable Key Infrastructure (AKI): A Proposal for a Public-Key Validation Infrastructure. In *Proceedings of the 2013 Conference on World Wide Web, to appear*, 2013.

[11] B. Laurie, A. Langley, and E. Kasper. Certificate Transparency. Network Working Group Internet-Draft, v12, work in progress. `http://tools.ietf.org/html/draft-laurie-pki-sunlight-12`, Apr. 2013.

[12] M. Marlinspike. TACK: Trust Assertions for Certificate Keys. `http://tack.io/draft.html`.

[13] M. Marlinspike. SSL And The Future Of Authenticity. In *BlackHat USA 2011*, 2011.

[14] P. Saint-Andre and J. Hodges. RFC 6125, Mar. 2011.

[15] R. Schlegel, K. Zhang, X. Zhou, M. Intwala, and e. al. Soundcomber: A Stealthy and Context-aware Sound Trojan for Smartphones. *Proceedings of the Network and Distributed System Security Symposium*, 2011.

[16] J. Sunshine, S. Egelman, H. Almuhimedi, N. Atri, and L. Cranor. Crying Wolf: An Empirical Study of SSL Warning Effectiveness. In *Proceedings of the 18th USENIX Security Symposium*, pages 399–416, 2009.

[17] T. Vidas, D. Votipka, and N. Christin. All Your Droid Are Belong To Us: A Survey Of Current Android Attacks. In *Proceedings of the 5th USENIX Workshop on Offensive Technologies*, pages 10–10, 2011.

[18] D. Wendlandt, D. G. Andersen, and A. Perrig. Perspectives: improving ssh-style host authentication with multi-path probing. In *USENIX 2008 Annual Technical Conference on Annual Technical Conference*, ATC'08, pages 321–334, Berkeley, CA, USA, 2008. USENIX Association.

[19] Y. Zhou and X. Jiang. Dissecting android malware: Characterization and evolution. In *Security and Privacy (SP), 2012 IEEE Symposium on*, pages 95–109, 2012.

APPENDIX

A. IOS SURVEY DETAILS

Several of the vulnerable apps we found were created using popular programming frameworks. Since any bug introduced by such a framework could potentially affect a large number of apps, we decided to take a closer look at these frameworks. During our analysis, we identified two cross-platform mobile application SDKs and an iOS networking wrapper library that all create code that contains vulnerable SSL certificate validation.

MKNetworkKit.

The MKNetworkKit[9] is a networking wrapper library for iOS with the aim to be easy to use and to simplify the iOS default networking stack. In online forums, such as `stackoverflow.com`, developers often complain about problems with iOS's built-in networking APIs, accounting for the popularity of libraries such as MKNetworkKit, which provides lightweight methods for standard networking tasks. The library can also handle HTTPS requests, but fails when it comes to SSL server certificate validation.

Titanium Framework.

The Titanium cross platform mobile application SDK[10] is a JavaScript-based platform which enables developers to write mobile apps in JavaScript and automatically translates them into native mobile apps. Titanium targets iOS, Android and HTML5, making it particularly attractive for web developers who want to create mobile apps. While the

[9] `http://blog.mugunthkumar.com/products/ios-framework-introducing-mknetworkkit/`

[10] `http://www.appcelerator.com/platform/titanium-sdk/`

Titanium framework generates secure SSL code for Android, SSL certificate validation for iOS apps is turned off. Based on app creation statistics posted on their website, this could affect more than 30,000 apps built with the framework.

PhoneGap.

PhoneGap[11] is a free open source framework for developing mobile apps for seven platforms including Android and iOS, using HTML, CSS and JavaScript. It contains dedicated classes for data transfer that include customized SSL verification code. For Android and iOS, the framework produces code that effectively turns SSL certificate validation off. If developers do not manually check the generated code, they will not see the comment and thus not be aware of the problem. According to PhoneGap[12], more than 23,000 apps could be affected.

B. TRANSITION PERIOD/COLD-TURKEY UPDATE

With such a high number of users at risk and such a slow/non-existent response time by developers when fixing the vulnerabilities, it might be worth considering activating our framework not only for new apps but for all existing apps as well. This would instantly fix all instances of apps with broken SSL we could find. There are two ways in which our framework could be deployed in such a case. The first approach would simply override custom SSL code. This would work fine for 98 % of the 13,500 apps we analyzed and fix all the broken ones. However, the remaining 2 % would lose important functionality (such as custom pinning) until the developers update their apps. They would still have standard certificate validation but their custom improvements would be disabled. So while applying our framework for all apps in this way is simple and helps most apps, it would be good to avoide this undesirable side-effect. A second approach could combine our framework's validation code with the app's custom SSL validation code. In this case, the simple rule would be only if both validation methods accept a certificate, then the connection is established. If one of the two validation processes rejects a certificate, a warning message is shown to the user by our framework.[13] The main issue with this is that users could potentially see two warning messages for the same connection: In those cases where validation legitimately fails and the developers of the app followed best practices and warns the user and the users accepts the invalid certificate, our framework would also warn the user and the user would have to accept again. While this is not a security threat per se, it is a highly undesirable characteristic to have in a system. However, our code analysis has shown that these cases should be very rare when no MITM attacker is present. Thus this could be considered an acceptable trade-off to fix the many vulnerabilities which otherwise will remain unfixed for an unknown amount of time. It might also be possible to get the developers of the "good" apps to update their apps for the greater good by contacting them before the cold-turkey roll-out. Ironically getting the few "good" developers to react is probably easier than getting all the developers with vulnerable apps to react. However, evaluating and discussing the ramifications of this kind of roll-out is beyond the scope of this paper and would need to be discussed in the community.

B.1 Pathological Cases

There are some pathological cases that need to be considered when activating our framework for existing apps:

B.1.1 IP Addresses Instead of Hostnames

The current Android API allows URLs and socket connections to be established with IP addresses instead of hostnames. Using an IP address has the drawback that hostname verification might not work properly. The concept of virtual hosts for HTTP(S) servers hinders effective hostname verification when an IP address is used to establish a connection instead of a hostname, since common names for SSL certificates typically are fully qualified domain names [14]. Yet, there are certificate authorities[14] that issue certificates with IP addresses as the common name. So, while creating a secure connection using an IP address can cause problems because hostname verification fails, there is also a valid use-case for this practice. Our SSL API treats IP addresses as normal hostnames during hostname verification.

We analyzed the set of Android 13,500 apps to find those that include URLs using IP addresses instead of hostnames to estimate the scope of this practice in Android apps. In all 13,500 apps, we found 163 apps (1.21 %) that include IP address-based URLs, pointing to 118 different hosts. 88 of these IP addresses did not support SSL. Of the 30 which supported SSL, only one of the remaining used a certificate for which hostname verification did not fail. However, this certificate was self-signed, so none of the IP address-based apps used SSL correctly.

B.1.2 Custom Sockets

If an app implements a custom application layer socket that resolves hostnames by itself, it may rely on the SSLSocketFactory to create an SSL-secured socket based on only an IP, but cater for hostname verification itself at a later stage. Given the modifications of our framework, this implementation would break, as our modified SSLSocketFactory would attempt to verify the hostname (in this case the IP address) during the handshake and fail because the hostname in the certificate presented by the server is unknown to the SSLSocketFactory. While it is uncommon to not delegate hostname resolution to the operating system, we acknowledge that such implementations would need to be updated to work with our modifications.

---

[11] `http://phonegap.com/`

[12] `http://www.slideshare.net/AndreCharland/phone-gap-stats-growth`

[13] For the cold-turkey approach, the default warning mechanism would be switched from "drop connection" to "warning" since we cannot automatically tell in advance if the app has a legitimate reason to connect to untrusted hosts.

[14] e. g. `https://www.globalsign.com/`

Protocol Misidentification Made Easy with Format-Transforming Encryption

Kevin P. Dyer
Portland State University

Scott E. Coull
RedJack, LLC.

Thomas Ristenpart
University of Wisconsin

Thomas Shrimpton
Portland State University

ABSTRACT

Deep packet inspection (DPI) technologies provide much-needed visibility and control of network traffic using port-independent protocol identification, where a network flow is labeled with its application-layer protocol based on packet contents. In this paper, we provide the first comprehensive evaluation of a large set of DPI systems from the point of view of protocol misidentification attacks, in which adversaries on the network attempt to force the DPI to mislabel connections. Our approach uses a new cryptographic primitive called format-transforming encryption (FTE), which extends conventional symmetric encryption with the ability to transform the ciphertext into a format of our choosing. We design an FTE-based record layer that can encrypt arbitrary application-layer traffic, and we experimentally show that this forces misidentification for all of the evaluated DPI systems. This set includes a proprietary, enterprise-class DPI system used by large corporations and nation-states. We also show that using FTE as a proxy system incurs no latency overhead and as little as 16% bandwidth overhead compared to standard SSH tunnels. Finally, we integrate our FTE proxy into the Tor anonymity network and demonstrate that it evades real-world censorship by the Great Firewall of China.

Categories and Subject Descriptors

D.4.6 [**Security and Protection**]: Invasive software; C.2.0 [**Computer-Communication Networks**]: Security and protection

Keywords

deep packet inspection; protocol classification; regular expressions; censorship circumvention; applied cryptography

CCS'13, November 4–8, 2013, Berlin, Germany.

ACM 978-1-4503-2477-9/13/11 ...$15.00.
http://dx.doi.org/10.1145/2508859.2516657.

1. INTRODUCTION

Network operators increasingly deploy deep packet inspection (DPI) to improve visibility into network activities and control those activities based on identified application-layer protocols and content. The most advanced in-use DPI systems use regular expressions to encode fingerprints for, in particular, the protocols of interest, and whether packet contents match against these expressions informs what is often called port-independent protocol identification [3, 10, 12, 25, 36]. This may be followed by other, potentially more sophisticated, traffic and content analysis methods, or may lead to filtering or other discriminatory behavior. For example, corporations use DPI to block file-sharing protocols that often cause accidental data leakage, while ISPs often use DPI to throttle bandwidth-heavy BitTorrent traffic [23, 54]. More controversially, nation-states use DPI to censor their citizens' use of the Internet, in part by blocking privacy tools like Tor [14].

Despite their growing roles in many security-critical settings, we are unaware of any work that specifically studies the robustness of state-of-the-art DPI protocol-identification tools in the face of dedicated attacks. Thus, we address the following question: *are there practical attacks that will force* any *regular-expression-based DPI into misclassifying connections as protocols of the attacker's choosing?* And, if such attacks do exist, can these misclassified connections carry practically useful amounts of information?

The results of our work conclude that, indeed, misclassification attacks exist against enterprise-grade DPI, and that these attacks can be mounted while carrying sufficient information to surf the web, transfer files, and use Tor. Rather than building an array of ad-hoc schemes to trick specific DPI systems, we instead target the implicit premise underlying modern DPI: that regular expressions (regexes) are sufficient for identifying network protocols. To that end, we develop a generic approach for controlling the format of encrypted data, so that it will match whatever regex we desire to specify. With this ability, we can force protocol misidentification across a broad range of DPI systems.

The development of a generic approach to evasion of regex-based DPI implies that, for settings with adversarial network users, future protocol-identification systems will have to move to more expensive techniques based on machine learning [27, 34, 35, 56], active probing [29], or something else entirely. At the same time, the approach also suggests a promising way forward for tools aiming to circumvent network censors.

Format-Transforming Encryption. The foundation of our approach is a new cryptographic primitive called format-transforming encryption (FTE). It allows the user to input a regex of their choosing and output ciphertexts that are guaranteed to match it. This gives FTE a built-in mechanism for forcing misidentification by regex-based DPI. It will additionally achieve more traditional privacy and authenticity goals.

We consider a variety of methods to specify the regular expressions that are input to the FTE scheme. In those scenarios where we know which DPI systems are being used, the simplest method is lifting them directly from systems themselves, or manually creating them using knowledge of RFCs and the DPI code. When we do not have information about the DPI system, we provide a simple procedure for learning regexes from network traces of the application-protocols that we wish our traffic to match.

Under the hood, our FTE scheme relies heavily on well-known algorithms for ranking strings in a given regular language [18]. The algorithms were previously suggested for use in the related context of format-preserving encryption [5], however, as far as we are aware, our work gives the first implementation and performance analysis of the algorithms. To realize a working FTE proxy system capable of tunneling arbitrary network traffic, we specify and implement a full, FTE-powered record layer. By this we mean that we build, around the FTE core, logic to manage buffering and fragmentation of incoming plaintext streams on the sender's side, and ciphertext stream buffering, parsing and fragment reassembly on the receiver's side.

We use this FTE proxy system to explore the resistance of six state-of-the-art DPI systems to protocol misclassification attacks. We show that even expensive, proprietary systems can be forced to mistakenly identify FTE-protected traffic as any of a number of target protocols chosen by the user, including HTTP, SMB, and SSH. We stress that our approach works no matter what the underlying FTE-encapsulated application-layer protocol actually is. To the best of our knowledge, this is the first comprehensive analysis exposing how ineffectual modern DPI systems can be rendered.

One immediate implication is that our proxy system provides a ready-made mechanism for circumventing actual, deployed DPI tools. When used to surf the web, FTE imposes as little as 16% bandwidth overhead and no latency overhead compared to conventional encryption of traffic. By comparison, FTE is both more flexible and efficient than existing circumvention tools that also attempt to prevent proper protocol identification [21, 31, 53] As a practical matter, our FTE system works as a drop-in pluggable transport [43] for Tor, and we are working to include FTE in the official Tor Browser Bundle. Furthermore, the FTE library source code has been released under the GNU General Public License, and is available on GitHub[1]. Initial tests from servers within the Great Firewall of China (GFC) using an FTE-powered Tor Browser Bundle have been successful, and enabled us to browse a variety of censored websites.

2. MODERN DPI SYSTEMS

In our evaluation, we focus on port-independent protocol identification as used by six modern DPI systems. These systems span a wide range of complexity, cost, and expected deployment environments. Here, we discuss details of the systems we evaluate, and present a summary in Figure 1. Unless otherwise mentioned, our discussion and later evaluations will use default configurations.

System	DPI Type	Multi-stage Pipeline	Classifier Complexity HTTP	SSH	SMB
			DFA States		
appid	regex-only	✗	15	8	104
l7-filter	regex-only	✗	55	8	6
YAF	regex-only	✓	29	10	5
			Lines of C/C++ Code		
bro	hybrid	✓	1593	30	1188
nProbe	hybrid	✓	807	89	24
DPI-X	?	?	?	?	?

Figure 1: Summary of evaluated DPI systems. *Type* indicates the kind of DPI engine used. *Multi-stage pipelines* chain together several passes over packet contents. *Classifier complexity* is the number of DFA states used for regular expressions or total lines non-whitespace/non-comment C/C++ code.

appid. The appid [3] library uses port-based pre-filtering to determine a set of protocol-identifying regexes, against which each TCP stream should be evaluated. It applies each regular expression in the set against the stream, and returns the first match as the protocol label. A match is attempted for bi-directional (i.e., client-server and server-client) streams. In our evaluation we used the latest available version of appid (as of April 2013), and instantiated it via its included Python module.

L7-filter. The l7-filter [10] software also performs regex-only matching. However, it differs from appid in that it does not pre-filter based on port numbers. Moreover, l7-filter specifies only regexes to identify uni-directional server-to-client streams. In our evaluation we used version 2009-05-28 of the l7-filter userspace classification engine, and invoked it with its included test suite.

Yet Another Flowmeter. YAF [25] is a network monitor that performs application labeling. The YAF protocol-classification engine is predominantly regex-only, although in a few cases (e.g., the classification of TLS) it employs C-based logic. We classify YAF as regex-only because the majority of protocols are classified using a regex-only strategy. Additionally, for some protocols, YAF performs its regex analysis in two stages; HTTP is one example. A first-pass match for HTTP (caused, say, by matching the string `HTTP/`) triggers a second-pass to extract message contents, such as the User-Agent field of the HTTP request. In our evaluation we used the latest stable version of YAF (2.3.3, January 2013) compiled with application identification support.

Bro Network Security Monitor. bro's [36] Dynamic Protocol Detection (DPD) is implemented as a set of regexes and associated C/C++ based parsers, where a parser is triggered in the event that its partnering regular expression(s) match the input stream. The parser is used to extract additional information from the stream, when possible, and to determine when the regular expression match was actually a false positive. In its default configuration, bro parses in-

[1]`https://github.com/redjack/FTE`

dividual messages and extracts per-message attributes, such as the URI of an HTTP request, or the version number of the SSH protocol being used. In our evaluation, we used the latest, stable version (2.1, Aug. 2012) of bro, and extracted the assigned stream label from the `service` field of the `conn.log` file.

For classification of SMB streams, which is not supported in version 2.1, we used an alpha-release SMB parser available in the bro git repository. We bootstrapped this parser into an SMB-classifier by labeling a flow as SMB only if the parser did not encounter parse errors, which is consistent with the strategy of other classifiers present in bro.

nProbe Pro. nProbe [12] is an open-source network monitoring utility that costs €299.95 for commercial use. nProbe includes the ability to identify the encapsulated data within a protocol. As an example, it can identify a web request to YouTube or FaceBook. This means that nProbe can reassemble TCP streams, identify the contents of a flow, and then parse individual message within a flow. nProbe uses hard-coded C-based logic, for the sake of efficiency, to identify attributes that could be captured by a regular expression. As an example, for HTTP it searches for a finite list of values (i.e. GET, POST, HTTP, etc.), in order to identify an HTTP stream. When such a match occurs, a C-based second-pass parser is triggered. In our evaluation we used version 6.9.5 of nProbe Pro, and the NetFlow output value `%L7_PROTO_NAME` to determine nProbe's stream label.

DPI-X. We obtained access to an enterprise-grade security gateway device sold by a well-known network equipment manufacturer. The DPI capabilities of this device, as advertised, enable classifying over 900 applications and protocols, including nested and tunneled applications (e.g., Facebook over HTTP). We disclosed our results to the equipment manufacturer, but did not receive approval to release details about the device. Hence, we refer to this system as DPI-X. This device belongs to a class of commercial systems, ranging from lower-end systems capable of handling a maximum throughput of 90 Mbps ($600), up to carrier-grade products capable of 100 Gbps (over $25,000). The system used in our testing has a maximum throughput of 1.5 Gbps and a cost of $8,000. We believe DPI-X is representative of the DPI products employed in many enterprise and carrier networks. In fact, the maker of this product has been identified as one of the suppliers of censorship equipment for Iran [37].

Threat model. A primary goal in this work is to experimentally ascertain the extent to which these representative DPI systems are vulnerable to *protocol-misidentification attacks*. (We will use misidentification and misclassification interchangeably.) To define this term, consider a setting in which a DPI system monitors all connections traversing a network. Two parties want to communicate via an application-layer protocol that uses connection(s) traversing the DPI-protected network. We will refer to these two parties as the "attacker" to emphasize that the DPI faces adversarially generated traffic. In a *white-box DPI* attack, the attacker knows the DPI classification algorithms that are used, while in a *black-box DPI* setting the attacker does not. The latter may be because the particular DPI being used is not known (even if the set of possible DPIs is known), or simply because the algorithms are proprietary.

We call the application-layer protocol used for communicating data the *source protocol*. In a misidentification attack, the attacker's goal is to have its connections, which use the source protocol, be (mis)identified by the DPI as a *target protocol* of the attacker's choosing. An example would be to have SSH as the source protocol, and HTTP as the target protocol. In a successful attack, the DPI will incorrectly label the actual (encrypted) SSH connections as (unencrypted) HTTP connections. To declare a practical success, we also require that the attack does not significantly degrade performance of the source protocol.

Despite the clear importance of protocol misidentification attacks, we are unaware of any prior work that evaluate the DPI systems in our test set (or other similar systems). See Section 7 for discussion of related settings and other potential approaches for forcing protocol misidentification that are different from ours.

3. FORMAT-TRANSFORMING ENCRYPTION

All of the open-source DPI systems in our evaluation set use membership in a regular language — either explicitly with regexes or implicitly by logic coded in languages such as C/C++ — to inform application-layer protocol classification. We therefore target mechanisms which enable an attacker to force protocol misidentification against any DPI that relies on regex checks. Note that this goal is more aggressive than merely defeating the systems in our corpus (but we will do that as well!), and we expect our approach will work against any currently deployed regex-based DPI system.

Our main idea is to build DPI resistance into encryption schemes. The key technological enabler, which we explain in the remainder of this section, is augmenting the normal encryption interface to take a regex as an input. The purpose of this regex is to specify the format of ciphertexts: this means that ciphertexts, when taken as a string over the appropriate alphabet, are guaranteed to match against the specified regex. We call the resulting primitive format-transforming encryption (FTE). In turn, we show how to use FTE as a component within a record layer that handles streams of messages from an arbitrary source protocol. Through proper choice of regex, ciphertexts produced by this record layer -which are actually carrying the source protocol- will be classified as messages from another protocol (of our choosing) by the DPI.

Our FTE record layer will be used for two purposes. First, we will build an FTE (single-hop) proxy system by combining the FTE record layer with SOCKS in a straightforward way. We will then use it to support our hypothesis that the regex-based DPI used in practice is fundamentally vulnerable to misclassifcation attacks. We do this by showing how to use the FTE proxy to force protocol misidentification by the entire set of DPI systems and with respect to a variety of target protocols. We also show that doing so has essentially negligible overhead for most relevant regular languages. We believe these results suggest that DPI systems must move to more advanced mechanisms (discussed in Section 7) in settings with adversarial users.

Our second purpose, empowered by the ease with which it forces protocol misidentification and the high performance it obtains, will be to incorporate the FTE record layer into

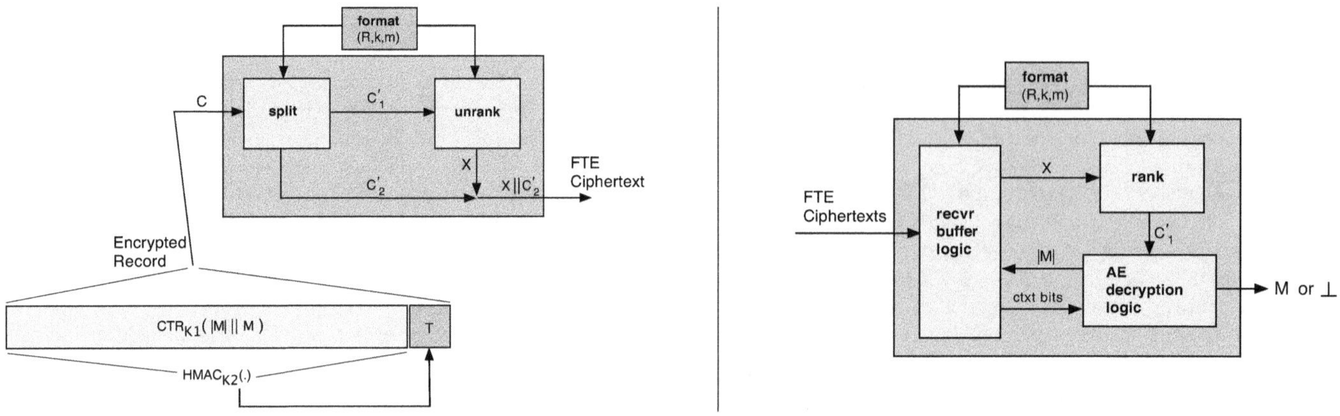

Figure 2: Sender-side (left) and receiver-side (right) record-layer flow. We discuss the various modules in the text.

Tor for use in circumventing censorship. We discuss this more in Section 6.

3.1 FTE via Encrypt-then-Unrank

An FTE scheme is a triple of algorithms: key generation, encryption and decryption. Key generation works as in conventional encryption, outputting a randomly chosen symmetric key K. Encryption Enc takes inputs of a key K, a format $\mathcal{F}$, and a message M. It can be randomized, stateful, or deterministic, and always outputs a ciphertext C or a distinguished error symbol $\perp$. Decryption Dec takes inputs of a key K, a format $\mathcal{F}$, and a ciphertext C. It outputs a message or $\perp$. The format $\mathcal{F}$ specifies a set $L(\mathcal{F})$ called the language of $\mathcal{F}$. The requirement is that any C output by Enc must be a member of $L(\mathcal{F})$.

FTE is a related to format-preserving encryption (FPE), first formalized by Bellare, Ristenpart, Rogaway, and Stegers (BRRS) [5]. FPE is used in the context of in-place encryption of credit-card numbers (or other records) within databases. It likewise uses formats, but requires that both plaintext messages and ciphertexts be members of the same format-specified language.

We desire FTE schemes that support formats described by regexes. This will allow easy "programming" of formats and endows FTE with the same expressive power as regex-based DPI. To do so, we start by following an approach similar to one used by BRRS. Loosely speaking, to implement $\mathsf{Enc}(K, \mathcal{F}, M)$ for a regular expression $\mathcal{F}$ we: (1) encrypt M using a standard authenticated encryption scheme to obtain an intermediate ciphertext Y; (2) treat Y as an integer in $\mathbb{Z}_{|L(\mathcal{F})|}$ (the set of integers from 0 to the size of the language minus one); and (3) apply an encoding function $\mathsf{unrank}\colon \mathbb{Z}_{|L(\mathcal{F})|} \to L(\mathcal{F})$. To be able to decrypt, we require that unrank is in fact a bijection with efficiently computable inverse $\mathsf{rank}\colon L(\mathcal{F}) \to \mathbb{Z}_{|L(\mathcal{F})|}$.

The key algorithmic challenge is implementing rank and unrank efficiently. These associate to each string in the language its rank, i.e., its position in a total ordering of the language. The notion of ranking was first explored by Goldberg and Sipser [18] in the context of language compression. Goldberg and Sipser also gave an efficient way to rank a regular language when that language is represented by a deterministic finite automaton (DFA). BRRS used this for an (unimplemented) FPE scheme for arbitrary regular languages encoded as DFAs, but they also emphasize that, asymptotically speaking, there is provably no way to give efficient rank and unrank functions starting just from a regex. Standard tools exist for converting from a regex to an nondeterministic finite automaton (NFA) and from there to a DFA (see Section 5), but the second step potentially incurs an exponential blow-up in state size. We observe that this worst-case behavior is not an issue for FTE, in part because the kinds of regexes used by DPIs are themselves designed explicitly to avoid the worst-case blowup.

Our implementation uses the time-space tradeoff of Goldberg and Sipser to support more efficient runtime performance by precomputing tables that allow (un)ranking of all strings $x \in L$ with $|x| \le n$. (These algorithms appear in the full version [15] of this paper.) The complexity of this precomputation is $\mathcal{O}(n{\cdot}|\Sigma|{\cdot}|Q|)$, where Σ is the underlying alphabet and Q is the state set for the DFA implementing the FTE regular expression. Given these tables, the complexity of rank_L and unrank_L are $\Omega(n)$ and $\mathcal{O}(n{\cdot}|\Sigma|)$, where n is the length of the output of rank_L or input of unrank_L, respectively. We can also formalize all of the above and prove that the Encrypt-then-Unrank approach preserves the message confidentiality and authenticity security of the underlying authenticated encryption scheme. Due to space constraints, we omit details of the optimizations and formal treatment, and instead move on to discuss how we build a full FTE record layer.

3.2 FTE Record Layer

In order to transform arbitrary TCP streams, we need additional "record layer" machinery to buffer, encode, unambiguously parse, and decode streams of FTE messages. In Figure 2 we give an overview of the processes by which plaintexts are transformed into FTE ciphertexts, and vice versa. We assume that sender and receiver share a pre-established set of keys, possibly derived from a single shared master key. Our record layer also assumes an underlying, reliable network transport protocol, e.g. TCP.

Implementing FTE formats. We will find it useful to specify in our formats more than just a regular expression. Thus a format $\mathcal{F}$ for the record layer is as a tuple (R, k, m): a regular expression R, a number $k > 0$ that specifies the length of strings to use from the language $L(R)$, and an integer $m \ge 0$ that controls the number of unformatted ciphertext bits to append to the end of the FTE-encoded message. The reason to use a specific length k is that it is an expedient way of rendering easy-to-parse FTE ciphertexts, while the value m is used to cheaply enable more capacity in cases where the desired language is, in fact, any string with a prefix in $L(R)$. All told, for $\mathcal{F} = (R, k, m)$ the language becomes $L(\mathcal{F}) = (L(R) \cap \Sigma^k) \,\|\, \Sigma^{\leq m}$ where Σ is the alphabet underlying R. For simplicity we assume $\Sigma = \{0, 1\}$ in what follows, but in implementations one will typically use larger alphabets. In our implementation we use values $m = 2^{18}$ and $k = 2^{10}$, unless otherwise specified.

FTE Sender. See the left diagram in Figure 2 and consider a format $\mathcal{F} = (R, k, M)$. Let $L_k(R) = L(R) \cap \{0,1\}^k$ be the k-bit slice of $L(R)$ we will use and $t = \lfloor \log_2(|L_k(R)|) \rfloor$ be that slice's capacity (the number of bits one can encode using the slice). The first action on the sender's side is to prepare an encrypted record using a secret key K. From a plaintext message buffer, grab a plaintext message M of length at most $|M| < m$. Then form a plaintext record, containing an encoding of $|M|$ followed by M. The record is then encrypted using a standard, stateful authenticated-encryption (AE) scheme with K to produce a ciphertext C. We assume that $|C|$ is defined solely by $|M|$, which is true for AE schemes used in practice. We also pad M, if required, to ensure that $|C| \geq t$. Our implementation uses CTR mode over AES and then authenticates the resulting ciphertext with HMAC-SHA256.

The encrypted record C is passed to the split module, and appended to an internal buffer maintained by split. The job of split is to produce two strings: one to be passed to unrank for formatting, and one that will be passed along as-is. In particular, split takes up to $t + m$ bits (and at least t bits) from the front of the buffer, which we refer to as C'. Note that C' may be a full AE ciphertext, part of one, or include bits from multiple ciphertexts. Then split partitions C' into C'_1 and C'_2 with $|C'_1| = t$ and $|C'_2| \leq m$. The first portion C'_1 is forwarded to unrank, which produces a formatted string $X \in L_k(R)$. Finally, the concatenation $X \,\|\, C'_2$ becomes the sender's FTE ciphertext which can then be transmitted.

FTE Receiver. Referring to the right-hand diagram in Figure 2, the receiver buffer logic is responsible for managing the stream of incoming FTE ciphertexts. One issue here, is that there are no explicit markers to demarcate FTE-encoded ciphertext boundaries. We therefore must take care to ensure that the receiver can correctly decrypt given that its buffer may contain multiple contiguous ciphertexts. To do so, the receiver takes advantage of the fact that the sender used a fixed[2] slice $L_k(R)$. As soon as it has the first k FTE ciphertext bits in its buffer, it treats these as a string $X \in L_k(R)$ and applies rank(X) to recover C'_1. (Should $X \notin L_k(R)$ decryption should abort.) It then feeds C'_1 to the AE decryption algorithm in order to retrieve $\ell = |M|$ and possibly some initial bits of a message M. (Those latter message bits should not yet be released to higher layers.) Note that this means that the AE scheme must be able to perform incremental decryption and that it should not be vulnerable to attacks (c.f., [1]) that abuse use of the length field before ensuring integrity. CTR mode plus HMAC provides these properties.

[2]One could instead rely on $L(R)$ being prefix-free, but we found using fixed slices simpler and sufficient.

Given ℓ the receiver now knows how many more bits of AE ciphertext are expected. From here it can remove the next up to m bits of ciphertext from the input buffer, and then go back into a state where it treats the subsequent k bits in the buffer as a string in $L_k(R)$, applying rank as above, and so on. When it retrieves a full AE ciphertext, it finishes decryption, verifies integrity of the ciphertext, and only now releases the buffered message bits up to the application.

Regex negotiation. One unique feature of FTE is the ability to quickly change regexes on the fly. We would like to be able to provide in-band negotiation of formats, but since all data sent on the wire must be formatted to pass DPI checks, it is not possible to negotiate regexes in the clear. We address this limitation by allowing the client/server to agree upon regexes for the duration of a TCP connection assuming they support some initial large set of possible regexes.

In more detail, we assume the client and server have a shared, ordered list of FTE formats $(\mathcal{F}_1, \ldots, \mathcal{F}_n)$, and still assume the client and server have negotiated cryptographic keys out-of-band. For each TCP connection, the client determines the FTE format $\mathcal{F}_i$ it wishes to use for client-to-server messages, and the $\mathcal{F}_j$ it wishes to use for server-to-client message. Then, the client constructs the message $M \leftarrow \langle i \rangle \,\|\, \langle j \rangle$, encrypts M as a distinguished `negotiate` message-type, designated by the value of a first (reserved) byte of the plaintext, encodes it with $\mathcal{F}_i$, then sends it to the server.

When the server receives an initial message from the client it iterates through its list of formats, attempting to decode the message with each of the FTE formats. Once it encounters a successful decryption, it evaluates the message and then uses for the session $\mathcal{F}_i$ for client-server messages and $\mathcal{F}_j$ for server-client messages. The server finalizes the negotiation by responding to the client with a distinguished `negotiate_acknowledge` message.

We can improve on the naïve receiver-side implementation of this procedure by having an implementation of rank that contains special checks that short-circuit evaluation to terminate early in cases when the string being ranked is not accepted by the DFA. This enables the server to quickly exclude certain formats, thereby making it possible to support dozens of formats.

4. PROTOCOL MISCLASSIFICATION

In this section, we experiment with three strategies for providing regexes used with our FTE record layer: regexes extracted from open-source DPI systems (4.1); regexes programmed manually (4.2); and regexes automatically learned from samples of target protocol traffic (4.3). We will always use a pair of formats: one for upstream (client-to-server) and one for downstream (server-to-client) communications. We will then use our FTE record layer to assess the vulnerability of the DPI systems in our evaluation to protocol-misidentification attacks.

Recall that a source protocol is the application-layer protocol whose connections the attacker wants to have misclassified. We explored HTTP [17], HTTPS [13], secure copy (SCP) [55], and Tor [14] as source protocols, and found that the choice of source protocol does not influence our results. We therefore focus our discussion primarily on HTTP(S).

For each regex generation strategy we explore three target protocols: HTTP [17], SSH [55], and SMB [30]. The latter is a proprietary protocol designed by Microsoft to support sharing of resources, such as files and printers, over networks. We also explored other target protocols, including SIP [38] and RTSP [39], but limit our discussion here to the prior three as the results for the others were the same. Indeed, we suspect FTE can be successfully used for almost any target protocol.

Experimental testbed. We implemented our FTE record layer as a library that can be used to relay arbitrary data streams. More implementation details appear in Section 5. In our evaluation we use it in the following configuration. The FTE client listens for incoming TCP connections on a local client-side port. Upon receipt of an incoming connection the FTE record layer encrypts the messages using the upstream format and relays them to a remote FTE server. The FTE server receives these FTE ciphertexts, decrypts them, and then relays the recovered plaintexts to a preconfigured destination TCP port. Downstream, the process is reversed, with the FTE server encrypting returned messages using the downstream format.

We use Mozilla Firefox version 17.0.3, controlled by version 2.28.0 of the Selenium browser automation framework to request the Alexa Top 50 (US) websites over the FTE record layer; this is repeated five times for each upstream-downstream format pair tested. The testing framework generates a mixture of HTTP, HTTPS and DNS source traffic and a total of roughly 12,000 TCP connections. On the server-side we relayed all HTTP(S) messages via a SOCKS proxy. We used the default Firefox configuration, with the following exceptions: we tunneled all DNS requests through the SOCKS connection, specified our start page as blank, and disabled caching to disk.

4.1 DPI-Extracted Regular Expressions

As our first method of programming the FTE record layer, we build FTE formats by extracting them directly from the source code of open-source regex-based DPI systems. This models a white-box DPI attack setting for the DPI systems from which we extract regexes, and a black-box DPI attack for others (e.g., DPI-X).

Extracting regular expressions. Using regexes from DPI systems within our FTE record layer is straightforward. Given a regular expression R from the DPI, we specify a format $\mathcal{F} = (R', k, m)$ where R' is exactly R except without a ".*" (match any) prefix, should there be one. This makes $L(R') \subseteq L(R)$, while ensuring that FTE ciphertexts will include the formatting information found in R after the prefix. We set $k = 128$ and $m = 2^{15}$ for good performance (the misclassification results do not change with other reasonable settings).

We use the naming convention of ⟨DPI system⟩-⟨target protocol⟩ to reference a pair of upstream-downstream regexes extracted from the given DPI system. (Some systems only have a regex for a single direction, in which case we use ".*" for the other direction.) YAF contains at least two regexes for each target protocol, and we indicate that using a 1 or 2 in the format name. The result is 12 different formats.

Misclassification evaluation. The misclassification rates for all 12 formats against the 6 classifiers appears in Figure 3. Here (and throughout this section) the rate is calculated as the number of TCP connections labeled as the target protocol by the classifier, divided by the total number of TCP

Format	Misclassification Rate					
	appid	l7-filter	YAF	bro	nProbe	DPI-X
appid-http	1.0	0.0	1.0	0.0	0.0	1.0
l7-http	0.0	1.0	0.16	0.0	0.0	1.0
yaf-http1	0.0	0.0	1.0	0.0	0.0	1.0
yaf-http2	0.0	0.0	1.0	0.57	0.0	1.0
appid-ssh	1.0	0.32	1.0	1.0	0.0	1.0
l7-ssh	0.16	1.0	0.16	0.13	0.0	1.0
yaf-ssh1	1.0	0.31	1.0	1.0	0.0	1.0
yaf-ssh2	1.0	0.21	1.0	1.0	0.0	1.0
appid-smb	1.0	1.0	1.0	0.08	0.0	1.0
l7-smb	0.0	1.0	0.38	0.0	0.0	1.0
yaf-smb1	0.0	0.04	1.0	0.0	0.0	1.0
yaf-smb2	0.0	0.04	1.0	0.0	0.0	1.0

Figure 3: Misclassification rates for the twelve DPI-Extracted FTE formats against the six classifiers in our evaluation testbed.

connections generated when using that FTE format. Thus a rate of 1.0 means complete misclassification success, and 0.0 is complete failure. Throughout our evaluations, a connection that failed to be misclassified as the target protocol by a DPI system was always marked as an unknown protocol, regardless of the DPI system.

What Figure 3 reveals is that DPI-extracted regexes always succeed against the DPI system from which they were extracted, and can even force misclassification by different DPI systems. As an example of the latter, we need only look at DPI-X, which is by far the easiest system to force misclassification against despite having no information about its operation. We confirmed the proper operation of the device by running a variety of control traffic, such as Facebook, Gmail, and SSH, through the device, and found that our results were indeed correct. While we still do not know the exact DPI strategy used, our best guess is that DPI-X performs minimalistic analyses, favoring performance and optimistic labeling of protocols. These regexes were not effective against nProbe, and had varied success against bro. This can be attributed to the latter DPI systems requiring slightly more stringent protocol conformance.

Intersection formats. We also consider formats whose regex R is the explicit intersection of multiple DPI regexes. FTE based on such an intersection format will produce ciphertexts matching all of the individual regexes used to form R. Using the intersection of the four DPI-extracted formats for each target protocol resulted in formats with perfect 1.0 misclassification rates for appid, l7-filter, YAF, and DPI-X. The rates against bro and nProbe are comparable to those for the individual regexes.

4.2 Manually-Generated Regular Expressions

As our next strategy for producing regexes, we will code them manually. Our FTE record layer makes this easy since most developers are already familiar with regexes due to their use in other programming contexts. Moreover, it turns out to be very simple to build fast, simple regexes that achieve perfect misclassification for *all* classifier/target protocol combinations in our evaluation set.

Coding regexes for FTE. We started by inspecting the open-source DPI systems, in particular for cases from the last section where the extracted regexes failed, in order to educate regex design. For HTTP regular expressions, we observed the following requirements. l7-filter requires that responses have an HTTP version of 0.9, 1.0, or 1.1; an HTTP status code in the range of 100-599; and Connection, Content-Type, Content-Length, or Date fields. appid requires that responses have a string of length greater than zero following the status code, and that the status line is terminated with `\r\n`. YAF requires that we have a valid HTTP method verb for requests (i.e. GET, POST, etc.). nProbe requires that we terminate HTTP messages with `\r\n\r\n`. Finally, bro require that we have no payload for HTTP requests, or a payload and a valid Content-Length field — we accommodate this requirement by not allowing a payload for requests and specifying an FTE format parameter of $m = 0$. (Section 3.1)

For SSH all classifiers require that the first downstream, and in some cases upstream, messages start with `SSH-`. Next, l7-filter demands that the first two messages in a stream start with `SSH-1.x` or `SSH-1.y`. nProbe requires the first messages in an SSH stream to be less than or equal to 99 bytes long, and we achieve this by setting our FTE format parameter to $k = 99$ for both directions of traffic, which constricts message lengths.

All classifiers in our evaluation require that SMB messages have a valid SMB fingerprint, which is the byte `\xFF`, followed by `SMB` encoded in ASCII. In addition, nProbe requires that message have a valid length that matches the length of the message payload, that the length field is located as the first 32-bit word in the message, and that `SMB` is encoded as ASCII in the second 32-bit word. Here we encounter a check that is not easily encoded as a regular language (or avoided as above for nProbe's checking of HTTP Content-Length fields), at least if one wants to support all 2^{32} possible lengths. However, we can simply use a specific value for the length field and provide an equivalently sized payload. For the regexes in our experiments, we set the FTE format parameter m to zero, meaning that we do not append any raw AE ciphertext bytes.

Misclassification evaluation. We specified regexes that met the above requirements for each of the target protocols. It took less than 30 minutes for one of the authors to specify each regex and debug it by testing it against known DPI engines. The resulting regexes achieved perfect misclassification for all classifier/target protocol combinations, as shown in Figure 4. Every TCP connection was tagged as the target protocol of our choosing.

4.3 Automatically-Generated Regular Expressions

When we know the DPI systems and their classification methods, the DPI-extracted and manually-generated regexes provide guaranteed evasion and optimal capacity. Unfortunately, there are many cases where it is not possible to know this information, like when the DPI classification strategy abruptly changes or when proprietary systems are used. In these situations, we can use a simple but effective process to automatically generate regexes from network traffic samples using widely-available protocol parsers. This allows us to implicitly learn FTE formats from data that is assumed (or known) to pass DPI scrutiny without raising alerts. Although other, more complex, methods of format discovery are available [7, 8, 42, 51], we focus on well-known network message formats to avoid unnecessary complexity while still providing robust regex generation capabilities. The regex generation process proceeds as follows.

1. Collect packet trace data for target protocol message.
2. Apply a parser to label message fields.
3. Create a set containing observed values for each field, called a *dictionary*.
4. Create a *template* for each message type by replacing the values with placeholders for the associated dictionaries.
5. Convert each dictionary into a regex by concatenating the values with an "or" operator between them.
6. For each template, replace the placeholders with the associated dictionary regexes.
7. Choose one or more of the resultant template regexes as the language(s) used by the FTE system.

Format	Misclassification Rate					
	appid	l7-filter	YAF	bro	nProbe	DPI-X
manual-http	1.0	1.0	1.0	1.0	1.0	1.0
manual-ssh	1.0	1.0	1.0	1.0	1.0	1.0
manual-smb	1.0	1.0	1.0	1.0	1.0	1.0
auto-http	1.0	1.0	1.0	1.0	1.0	1.0
auto-ssh	1.0	1.0	1.0	1.0	0.0	1.0
auto-smb	1.0	1.0	1.0	1.0	1.0	1.0

Figure 4: Misclassification rates for the manually-generated and automatically-generated FTE formats against all six classifiers.

There are a number of ways this method can be tuned to adjust the quality and capacity of the resultant language(s). First, we can control the properties of the messages that are collected in the packet trace data, such as their message types or payload lengths. Data containing a single, consistent message type will produce more coherent regexes at the cost of smaller dictionaries, while a mix of message types will produce much larger dictionaries with more capacity but with potentially inconsistent, low-quality regexes. We can also control the regexes through the granularity of the parsers used to break the data into fields. Fine-grained parsing produces a greater number of dictionaries within each template and, consequently, an increase in the number of possible combinations among their values. Conversely, coarse parsers will create templates that are more likely to produce valid outputs, but with less overall capacity.

Regex generation. The packet trace data used to evaluate the security of the generated regexes was produced by agents that randomly logged into and crawled HTTP, SMB, and SSH servers. For HTTP, we used the *wget* utility to download the front page of a random selection of web sites on the Alexa Top 1000. SMB and SSH data was generated by scripts that logged into local Linux and Windows servers, randomly crawled the directory structure, accessed files, and logged out several times over the course of a one-hour period. We partitioned the captured data into groups based on their message types and payload lengths. From these partitions, we extracted client headers for HTTP POST requests, SMB transaction requests, and SSH handshake banner messages. The server messages that we use include HTTP 200 OK responses, SMB transaction responses, and SSH handshake banner messages. Each of these message types was parsed using their respective Wireshark dissectors, and the highest-capacity template regular expression was chosen for the FTE format. Any remaining payload bytes not included in the

FTE format	DFA states	avg. unrank (ms)	avg. rank (ms)
intersection-http-downstream	70	0.52	0.48
intersection-smb-downstream	104	0.55	0.54
intersection-ssh-downstream	11	0.55	0.52
manual-http-downstream	38	0.43	0.43
manual-smb-downstream	130	0.53	0.5
manual-ssh-downstream	9	0.42	0.42
auto-http-downstream	13,815	1.6	1.5
auto-smb-downstream	222	0.82	0.79
auto-ssh-downstream	237	0.52	0.49

Figure 5: Average rank and unrank performance for our downstream FTE formats.

parsed message header were automatically replaced with a regular expression that produced the appropriate number of random bytes.

Misclassification evaluation. Figure 4 presents the results of our evaluation, and illustrates that the generated regexes achieved perfect misclassification rates except for the nProbe SSH classifier, which had a misclassification rate of zero. The nProbe SSH classifier requires that the first message in each direction be an appropriately formatted banner message with an arbitrary length limitation of 100 bytes. Since our regex generation method is limited to only using what it observes (in this case a single client banner and less than five server banners), the generated regex would have only two bits of capacity. To enhance the capacity, we artificially generated RFC-compliant banner messages with the optional comment field used to carry random bytes up to the specified maximum length of 255 bytes, which provided sufficient capacity and the ability to evade all classifiers but nProbe. This highlights a natural limitation of the simple generation process, though avenues for improvement are possible through more advanced generalization procedures or the use of multiple FTE formats within a single connection (e.g., zero-capacity banner messages followed by high-capacity key exchange messages).

5. PERFORMANCE

Our FTE prototype was developed in C/C++ and Python. Performance-critical algorithms such as rank, unrank, and BuildTable are implemented in C/C++. We use a customized version of the re2 library for regular expression to DFA conversion, and OpenFST for DFA minimization. Cryptographic algorithms are implemented using PyCrypto. Multiple precision arithmetic is performed using GMP. Logic for the record layer and networking is multi-threaded and implemented in Python.

For performance benchmarks our client machine was an AMD Opteron 8220 SE @ 2.80GHz running CentOS 6.4 and server was an Intel Core i5-2400 @ 3.4GHz running Ubuntu 12.04. Each machine was connected to the Internet at an academic institution.

Rank/Unrank. Recall that for FTE we must perform unranking starting from regexes, which can require exponential time in the worst case (see Section 3.1). In practice, however, the regexes we require for misidentification attacks admit fast (un)ranking. In Figure 5, we present the DFA size and average time to perform ranking and unranking for our intersection, manual, and automated formats over 100k trials using random integers as input. We present performance results for downstream formats only. In all cases the upstream formats perform better than their downstream counterpart in (un)ranking benchmarks and have smaller DFA state-spaces. The FTE format parameters used in these benchmarks are described in Section 3.2. The DPI-extracted intersection formats and manual formats resulted in very compact DFAs, with no more than 130 states. We note that the automatically generated regexes resulted in the largest DFAs, but were still very fast even for $>10,000$ state DFAs. This all evidences that the worst-case blow-up in state sizes when converting from an NFA to DFA does not greatly impede performance.

Web-browsing performance. We setup our FTE record layer to proxy HTTP(S) traffic as described in Section 4. As a baseline for comparison, we use a conventional encrypted tunnel. Using OpenSSH's integrated functionality we established a SOCKS proxy which listened client-side, such that all connections were routed through the SSH connection to the remote server, and then ultimately on to the destination IP address. We call this our *socks-over-ssh* configuration.

We download the Alexa Top 50 websites five times each using the socks-over-ssh setup. We do the same with the FTE proxy for each of the intersection, manual, and automatically generated regexes. Each of the four separate runs (inclusive of socks-over-ssh) therefore resulted in 250 data points. In our socks-over-ssh configuration, websites in the Alexa Top 50 took an average of 5.5 seconds to render the webpage and all dependencies, and required an average of 1,164KB of data transfer including all TCP/IP overhead. In Figure 6, we show the cumulative distribution of the latency and bandwidth data points for the four different runs.

The lowest average download time of the FTE formats was the intersection-ssh format, which incurred no increase (5.5s avg.) in latency compared to socks-over-ssh, and 1,348KB (16%) increase in data transfer overhead. The highest average download time of all the formats was the automatic-http format, with an average page-render time of 7.1s (29%) and an average of 3,279KB (181%) transferred per website. The increase in data transferred is due to (1) ciphertext expansion and (2) Firefox generating persistent TCP connections that cause FTE/SOCKS negotiation, but do not result in data transfer. These latter empty connections do not use much bandwidth in the socks-over-ssh case.

In our testing we note that engineering issues often overshadow the overheads of FTE. For example, the socks-over-ssh system performed better on sites with low bandwidth requirements and a small number of TCP connections, while our FTE prototype actually performs *better* than socks-over-ssh for websites that use a large number of TCP connections. This is because our FTE implementation uses multi-threading more aggressively than OpenSSH, and this is better aligned with the Firefox's use of multiple TCP connections in parallel.

Goodput. As a goodput baseline, we performed a direct copy of a 100MB file with SCP from our server to our client and achieved 58Mbps on average over 100 trials. Average round-trip latency between the client and server was 70ms. When using SCP with the FTE record layer, our best performing format was intersection-ssh and it achieved 42Mbps.

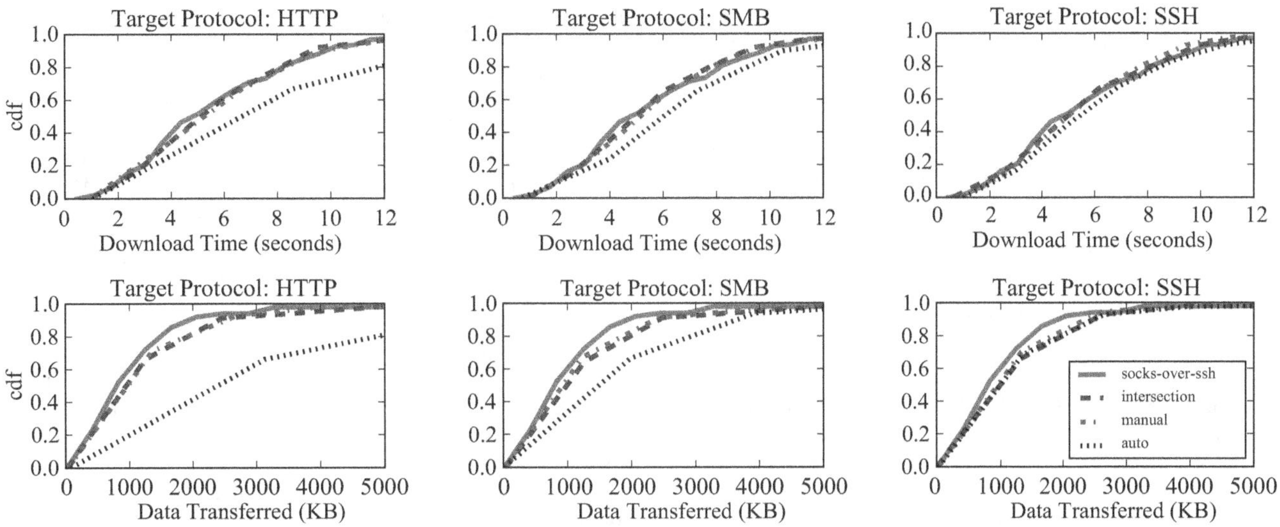

Figure 6: Distribution of webpage (Alexa top fifty) download times (top row) and data transferred (bottom row) for our intersection, manually-generated and automatically-generated FTE formats, compared to using our socks-over-ssh configuration.

All other FTE formats with $m > 0$ exhibited similar performance. For our worst performing format, automated-http, we achieved 1.9Mbps and other formats with $m = 0$ had similar goodput. The slower performance for the latter formats stems from their not allowing raw AE ciphertext bytes to follow unrank output.

In our goodput tests, the FTE implementation was never CPU bound. Hence, the performance of our (un)ranking algorithms was not the bottleneck. Profiling of our FTE prototype indicates that future performance gains could be had by optimizing the buffer management and networking logic.

Memory utilization. To determine the memory utilization of our FTE prototype, we first measured the memory requirements of the BuildTable algorithm, which is the largest consumer of memory in our prototype. For all formats, except auto-http, the BuildTable algorithm required at most 2 MB of memory. The auto-http upstream format requires 15 MB and the auto-http downstream format requires 184 MB. As expected, memory utilization increases linearly with respect to DFA state space.

As an additional test we profiled the maximum heap usage, inclusive of the Python interpreter and all dependent libraries, when browsing the web with our FTE prototype. For all formats, except auto-http, peak heap usage never exceed 13 MB, while auto-http used roughly 383 MB at its peak. We can attribute this nearly two-fold increase in memory usage, compared to its BuildTable requirement, to an inefficient copy of BuildTable's output — this will be resolved in the next release of our prototype.

6. CENSORSHIP CIRCUMVENTION

In the previous sections, we focused on using FTE to evaluate the efficacy of modern enterprise-grade DPI. We showed that not only can our FTE record layer easily force DPI misclassification, but it can do so while incurring negligible performance impact. This suggests that FTE can be a useful tool for settings where one wants to circumvent DPI-enabled censorship. Here, we experimentally investigate integrating our FTE record layer into the Tor anonymity network as a as a pluggable transport [2].

Integration. A pluggable transport is a record-layer mechanism that processes Tor messages before being transmitted on the wire. The only currently deployed transport is obfsproxy [43], which applies a stream cipher to every bit output by Tor using a shared key. Originally, this shared key was a hard-coded, but a newer version (not yet deployed) replaces this with an in-band, anonymous Diffie-Hellman key exchange [44]. The result of this latter approach is a cryptographic guarantee that all the bitstrings seen by a (passive) DPI are indistinguishable from random strings, so that the obfuscated Tor messages will not have fixed fingerprints. This does not, however, force protocol misclassification, and therefore would fail to bypass DPI that use a whitelist of allowed protocols.

We can do better using our FTE record layer as the pluggable transport. Integrating it into Tor with a hard-coded key is immediate, and it is straightforward to add key exchange to our record layer. Specifically, one could just initiate sessions using the existing obfs3 [44] Diffie-Hellman key exchange, but running the key-exchange messages through our unranking mechanisms before being sent on the wire, since the messages in this exchange are indistinguishable from uniformly random bit strings, they behave like the AE ciphertext bits in our record layer. Together with our existing library of regex formats, we arrive at a version of Tor that can easily force misclassification for the DPI systems currently used in practice. Indeed we verified that misclassification rates for all the six systems in our corpus are as seen in Section 4, but now using Tor with FTE as the pluggable transport. We believe that FTE is an attractive pluggable transport option for several reasons:

- *Flexibility*: The FTE record layer already supports a variety of target protocols, and adding new ones requires only specifying new regexes. Extending prior steganographic systems to support many targets (see Section 7), on the other hand, would be very labor intensive.

- *Sufficiency*: The FTE record layer forces misclassification by all evaluated DPIs, even DPI-X whose proprietary classification strategy is unknown to us and is similar to systems used in censorship settings [37].
- *Speed*: The FTE record layer has essentially negligible overhead and, when used with Tor, its overhead is lost in the noise of the Tor network's performance variability.

FTE through the GFC. We set up an FTE client on a Virtual Private Server (VPS) located within China and an FTE server in the United States. The server was configured to accept incoming connections on port 80. To set a censorship baseline, we first attempted to browse several websites that are known to be censored, including YouTube and Facebook, *without* using FTE to tunnel the traffic, and found that these sites were blocked. We then attempted to browse the same websites through the FTE tunnel, using our intersection, manual, and automatic HTTP formats. In every case, the FTE tunneled traffic successfully traversed the GFC, and we were able to browse the censored websites.

Next, we considered using FTE to tunnel Tor traffic. Again, to set a baseline, we attempted to connect to a private Tor bridge listening on port 443 of our server, using the default Tor distribution. We observed behavior consistent with the recent analysis of the Great Firewall of China (GFC) by Winter et al. [50]: initial Tor connections to our private bridge were successful, and they were followed by an active probe from a Chinese IP address after roughly 15 minutes. The probe performed a handshake with the bridge, then blacklisted the (IP,port)-combination used by the bridge. We validated the blacklisting by observing that subsequent attempts to connect to our Tor bridge (IP,port)-combinations resulted in a successful SYN packet from the VPS to our bridge, followed by spoofed TCP RSTs transmitted to the client and bridge to terminate the TCP connection.

Having established that Tor was indeed being censored, we then attempted the same tasks through our FTE tunnel, again using each of our intersection, manual, and automatic HTTP formats. Despite port 443 being blacklisted from our previous Tor tests, using FTE on port 80 was successful, and we were able to circumvent the GFC with this FTE-tunneled Tor circuit. After these initial tests we established a persistent FTE tunnel between our FTE client and server. Every five minutes we selected a censored URL and downloaded it through our FTE-powered tunnel. This tunnel remained active for one month, and successfully subverted the GFC until the termination of our VPS account.

On detecting FTE. Censors have been aggressive at rolling out new DPI-based mechanisms for detecting and blocking circumvention tools. How will FTE fare in this kind of arms race? The first idea would be for DPI systems to obtain the FTE regex formats and then use them to mark any traffic exactly matching the regex as FTE. For most of the regexes we consider, this would lead to prohibitively high false positive rates (e.g., 100% of HTTP traffic). The one exception is the automatically generated regexes, which may not match against other traffic, because of (for example) time stamps or unique hash values that were learned from collected traffic traces.

A second approach might be for DPI to perform more non-regular checks, such as verifying correctness of length fields for protocols that include them, e.g., the Content-Length field of HTTP responses. Note that actually this example would not work for DPI in practice, as one-third of the response messages generated when downloading the Alexa Top 50 did not include a valid Content-Length field despite it being strongly recommended in the HTTP RFC. Elsewhere this kind of check can be addressed by, for example, developing formats that encode a large number of lengths that are frequently observed in legitimate traffic, and for each length ensuring appropriate length of ciphertexts. In theory, one could also use FTE for more powerful language classes (i.e., an algorithm for ranking unambiguous CFGs appears in [18]).

More generally, DPI is faced with finding checks for protocol semantics or formatting with fidelity beyond what is captured by the FTE record layer. Since the latter takes a minimalist approach, there are innumerable ways in which FTE communications differ from real target protocol runs. The recent work of Houmansadr et al. [20], for example, shows how to exploit discrepancies in other circumvention systems that do much more than FTE in terms of attempting to mimic a target protocol [31,46,47]. However, finding such discrepancies is easy, and the hard open question (not addressed in [20]) is how to make such checks effective—fast, scalable, and with negligible errors—in the messy deployment environments faced by DPI and for all of the essentially arbitrary target protocols FTE supports.

The GFC, as discussed above, also engages in active probing. For example, attempting to connect to destination systems suspected of undesirable behavior. Determining how to resist such active attacks in practice is an ongoing research topic (c.f., [40]). Use of FTE, however, can hope to force active probing for all legitimate connections using the target protocol, vastly increasing the complexity of such censorship techniques.

7. RELATED WORK

Steganography/censorship circumvention. Steganographic systems seek to hide the existence of messages from all observers by way of embedding the message in real cover traffic such as TCP/IP connections [33], HTTP [16], email [46], VoIP [22], or social media [9,26]. FTE does not embed data in real cover traffic, but instead ensures that ciphertexts are formatted to include the telltale protocol fingerprints that DPI systems look for.

Other recent work targets censorship circumvention via so-called protocol mimicking [21,31,32,46,47,53]. In these systems, data is embedded within specific application-layer headers and content so that it appears to be a specific unblocked target protocol. These systems target DPI misclassification, but (to the best of our knowledge) their efficacy against production DPI systems has not been systematically measured. FTE, when used as a circumvention mechanism, can be thought of as new lightweight protocol mimicking tool that targets a certain class of adversary, those being the regex-based (or similarly powerful) DPI used in practice. We note that FTE is more efficient than prior protocol mimicing systems, yet already forces misclassification against enterprise-grade DPI.

Tunneling traffic over another protocol (e.g., SSH) does not usually lead to protocol misclassification because the protocol used for the tunnel will be correctly identified by the DPI. Tunneling may suffice for DPI circumvention in some settings, but is more expensive and less flexible than using an FTE record layer. For instance, tunneling can have high overheads for certain source protocol/tunnel protocol pairs (e.g., HTTP over DNS [28]) and FTE can easily switch between target protocols in a fine-grained manner.

The Dust [49] protocol and Tor's recent obfsproxy [43] systems strive to ensure that no application-layer bits are left unencrypted in order to remove any identifiable fingerprint. FTE also encrypt all bits sent, but additionally allows one to selectively add back into ciphertexts the formatting needed to force protocol misclassification.

DPI. Performance and scalability of regex-based traffic classification has been extensively studied [4, 19, 45]. Alternative protocol identification strategies that have been explored include using packet sizes and timings [6, 52], the types and number connections initiated by a host (its "social behavior") [24, 27], and various machine learning techniques [34,35,56]. However, the feasibility of deploying more sophisticated classification strategies for DPI at scale remains unclear [11, 34, 41].

Recent work uses fast small-sample hypothesis tests to identify and discard compressed or encrypted packets [48]. Such tests might flag FTE packets from our simpler formats as compressed/encrypted due to their use of unformatted AE ciphertext bits, thereby preventing protocol misclassification. However, these tests are easy to defeat by simply changing the format so that the hypothesis test fails on the first few packets in a flow.

Acknowledgements

We thank the anonymous reviewers and Juniper Networks for their constructive feedback on earlier versions of this paper. Kevin Dyer and Thomas Shrimpton were supported by NSF CAREER grant CNS-0845610. Thomas Ristenpart was supported in part by generous gifts from Microsoft, as well as NSF grant CNS-1065134.

8. REFERENCES

[1] M. R. Albrecht, K. G. Paterson, and G. J. Watson. Plaintext recovery attacks against ssh. In *Security and Privacy, 2009 30th IEEE Symposium on*, pages 16–26. IEEE, 2009.

[2] J. Appelbaum and N. Mathewson. Pluggable transports for circumvention. Available at: `https://gitweb.torproject.org/torspec.git/HEAD:/proposals/180-pluggable-transport.txt`, 2010.

[3] Arbor Networks, Inc. appid. Available at: `https://code.google.com/p/appid/`.

[4] M. Becchi, M. Franklin, and P. Crowley. A workload for evaluating deep packet inspection architectures. In *IEEE International Symposium on Workload Characterization, 2008.*, pages 79–89, 2008.

[5] M. Bellare, T. Ristenpart, P. Rogaway, and T. Stegers. Format-preserving encryption. In M. Jacobson, V. Rijmen, and R. Safavi-Naini, editors, *Selected Areas in Cryptography*, volume 5867 of *Lecture Notes in Computer Science*. 2009.

[6] L. Bernaille and R. Teixeira. Early recognition of encrypted applications. In S. Uhlig, K. Papagiannaki, and O. Bonaventure, editors, *Passive and Active Network Measurement*, volume 4427 of *Lecture Notes in Computer Science*. 2007.

[7] D. Brumley, J. Newsome, D. Song, H. Wang, and S. Jha. Towards automatic generation of vulnerability-based signatures. In *Security and Privacy, 2006 IEEE Symposium on*, pages 15–pp. IEEE, 2006.

[8] D. Brumley, J. Newsome, D. Song, H. Wang, and S. Jha. Theory and techniques for automatic generation of vulnerability-based signatures. *Dependable and Secure Computing, IEEE Transactions on*, 5(4):224–241, 2008.

[9] S. Burnett, N. Feamster, and S. Vempala. Chipping away at censorship firewalls with user-generated content. In *Proceedings of the 19th USENIX conference on Security*, USENIX Security'10, 2010.

[10] Clear Foundation. l7-filter. Available at: `http://l7-filter.clearfoundation.com/`.

[11] A. Dainotti, A. Pescapè, and K. C. Claffy. Issues and future directions in traffic classification. *Network, IEEE*, 26(1):35–40, 2012.

[12] L. Deri. nprobe: an open source netflow probe for gigabit networks. In *In Proc. of Terena TNC 2003*, 2003.

[13] T. Dierks and E. Rescorla. The Transport Layer Security (TLS) Protocol Version 1.2. RFC 5246 (Proposed Standard), Aug. 2008.

[14] R. Dingledine, N. Mathewson, and P. Syverson. Tor: The second-generation onion router. In *In Proceedings of the 13th USENIX Security Symposium*, 2004.

[15] K. P. Dyer, S. E. Coull, T. Ristenpart, and T. Shrimpton. Protocol misidentification made easy with format-transforming encryption. Cryptology ePrint Archive, Report 2012/494, 2012. `http://eprint.iacr.org/`.

[16] N. Feamster, M. Balazinska, G. Harfst, H. Balakrishnan, and D. Karger. Infranet: Circumventing Web Censorship and Surveillance. In *Proceedings of the 11th USENIX Security Symposium*, 2002.

[17] R. Fielding, J. Gettys, J. Mogul, H. Frystyk, L. Masinter, P. Leach, and T. Berners-Lee. Hypertext Transfer Protocol – HTTP/1.1. RFC 2616 (Draft Standard), June.

[18] A. Goldberg and M. Sipser. Compression and ranking. In *Proceedings of the 17th Annual ACM symposium on Theory of computing*, STOC '85, 1985.

[19] D. Guo, G. Liao, L. N. Bhuyan, B. Liu, and J. J. Ding. A scalable multithreaded l7-filter design for multi-core servers. In *Proceedings of the 4th ACM/IEEE Symposium on Architectures for Networking and Communications Systems*, ANCS '08, 2008.

[20] A. Houmansadr, C. Brubaker, and V. Shmatikov. The Parrot is Dead: Observing Unobservable Network Communications. In *The 34th IEEE Symposium on Security and Privacy (Oakland)*, 2013.

[21] A. Houmansadr, G. T. Nguyen, M. Caesar, and N. Borisov. Cirripede: circumvention infrastructure using router redirection with plausible deniability. In *Proceedings of the 18th ACM conference on Computer and communications security*, CCS '11, 2011.

[22] A. Houmansadr, T. Riedl, N. Borisov, and A. Singer. I Want my Voice to be Heard: IP over Voice-over-IP for Unobservable Censorship Circumvention. In *The 20th Annual Network and Distributed System Security Symposium (NDSS)*, 2013.

[23] M. Iliofotou, H.-c. Kim, M. Faloutsos, M. Mitzenmacher, P. Pappu, and G. Varghese. Graph-based p2p traffic classification at the internet backbone. In *INFOCOM Workshops 2009, IEEE*, pages 1–6. IEEE, 2009.

[24] M. Iliofotou, P. Pappu, M. Faloutsos, M. Mitzenmacher, S. Singh, and G. Varghese. Network monitoring using traffic dispersion graphs (tdgs). In *Proceedings of the 7th ACM SIGCOMM conference on Internet measurement*, IMC '07, 2007.

[25] C. M. Inacio and B. Trammell. Yaf: yet another flowmeter. In *Proceedings of the 24th international conference on Large installation system administration*, LISA'10, 2010.

[26] L. Invernizzi, C. Kruegel, and G. Vigna. Message In A Bottle: Sailing Past Censorship. In *Hot Topics in Privacy Enhancing Technologies – PETS*, 2012.

[27] T. Karagiannis, K. Papagiannaki, and M. Faloutsos. Blinc: Multilevel traffic classification in the dark. In *In Proceedings of ACM SIGCOMM*, 2005.

[28] Kryo. iodine DNS Tunnel. Available at: `http://code.kryo.se/iodine/`, 2010.

[29] E. Menahem, G. Nakibly, and Y. Elovici. Network-based intrusion detection systems go active! In *Proceedings of the 2012 ACM conference on Computer and communications security*, pages 1004–1006. ACM, 2012.

[30] Microsoft. [MS-SMB2]: Server Message Block (SMB) Protocol Versions 2 and 3. Available at: `http://msdn.microsoft.com/en-us/library/cc246482.aspx`, 2013.

[31] H. Mohajeri Moghaddam, B. Li, M. Derakhshani, and I. Goldberg. Skypemorph: protocol obfuscation for tor bridges. In *Proceedings of the 2012 ACM conference on Computer and communications security*, CCS '12, 2012.

[32] S. J. Murdoch. Proof of concept transport plugin: http headers. Available at: `https://trac.torproject.org/projects/tor/ticket/2759`, 2011.

[33] S. J. Murdoch and S. Lewis. Embedding covert channels into TCP/IP. In *Proceedings of the 7th International Workshop on Information Hiding*, 2005.

[34] T. T. Nguyen and G. Armitage. A survey of techniques for internet traffic classification using machine learning. *Communications Surveys & Tutorials, IEEE*, 10(4):56–76, 2008.

[35] T. T. T. Nguyen, G. Armitage, P. Branch, and S. Zander. Timely and continuous machine-learning-based classification for interactive IP traffic. *IEEE/ACM Trans. Netw.*, 20(6), Dec. 2012.

[36] V. Paxson. Bro: a system for detecting network intruders in real-time. In *Proceedings of the 7th conference on USENIX Security Symposium - Volume 7*, SSYM'98, 1998.

[37] C. Rhoads and F. Fassihi. Iran vows to unplug internet. Available at: `http://online.wsj.com/article/SB10001424052748704889404576277391449002016.html`, December 2011.

[38] J. Rosenberg, H. Schulzrinne, G. Camarillo, A. Johnston, J. Peterson, R. Sparks, M. Handley, and E. Schooler. SIP: Session Initiation Protocol. RFC 3261 (Proposed Standard), June 2002.

[39] H. Schulzrinne, A. Rao, and R. Lanphier. Real Time Streaming Protocol (RTSP). RFC 2326 (Proposed Standard), Apr. 1998.

[40] R. Smits, D. Jain, S. Pidcock, I. Goldberg, and U. Hengartner. Bridgespa: improving tor bridges with single packet authorization. In *Proceedings of the 10th annual ACM workshop on Privacy in the electronic society*. ACM, 2011.

[41] R. Sommer and V. Paxson. Outside the closed world: On using machine learning for network intrusion detection. In *Security and Privacy (SP), 2010 IEEE Symposium on*, 2010.

[42] G. Szabó, Z. Turányi, L. Toka, S. Molnár, and A. Santos. Automatic protocol signature generation framework for deep packet inspection. In *Proceedings of the 5th International ICST Conference on Performance Evaluation Methodologies and Tools*, pages 291–299. ICST (Institute for Computer Sciences, Social-Informatics and Telecommunications Engineering), 2011.

[43] Tor Project. Obfsproxy. Available at: `https://www.torproject.org/projects/obfsproxy.html.en`, 2013.

[44] Tor Project. Obfsproxy3. Available at: `https://gitweb.torproject.org/pluggable-transports/obfsproxy.git/blob/HEAD:/doc/obfs3/obfs3-protocol-spec.txt`, 2013.

[45] M. Vallentin, R. Sommer, J. Lee, C. Leres, V. Paxson, and B. Tierney. The nids cluster: Scalable, stateful network intrusion detection on commodity hardware. In C. Kruegel, R. Lippmann, and A. Clark, editors, *Recent Advances in Intrusion Detection*, volume 4637 of *Lecture Notes in Computer Science*. 2007.

[46] Q. Wang, X. Gong, G. Nguyen, A. Houmansadr, and N. Borisov. CensorSpoofer: Asymmetric Communication using IP Spoofing for Censorship-Resistant Web Browsing. In *The 19th ACM Conference on Computer and Communications Security (CCS)*, 2012.

[47] Z. Weinberg, J. Wang, V. Yegneswaran, L. Briesemeister, S. Cheung, F. Wang, and D. Boneh. Stegotorus: a camouflage proxy for the tor anonymity system. In *ACM Conference on Computer and Communications Security*, 2012.

[48] A. M. White, S. Krishnan, M. Bailey, F. Monrose, and P. Porras. *Clear and Present Data: Opaque Traffic and its Security Implications for the Future*. NDSS, 2013.

[49] B. Wiley. Dust: A blocking-resistant internet transport protocol. Technical report, School of Information, University of Texas at Austin, 2011.

[50] P. Winter and S. Lindskog. How the Great Firewall of China is Blocking Tor. In *Free and Open Communications on the Internet*, 2012.

[51] G. Wondracek, P. M. Comparetti, C. Kruegel, E. Kirda, and S. S. S. Anna. Automatic network protocol analysis. In *15th Symposium on Network and Distributed System Security (NDSS)*, 2008.

[52] C. V. Wright, F. Monrose, and G. M. Masson. On inferring application protocol behaviors in encrypted network traffic. *Journal on Machine Learning Research*, 7, Dec. 2006.

[53] E. Wustrow, S. Wolchok, I. Goldberg, and J. A. Halderman. Telex: Anticensorship in the network infrastructure. In *Proceedings of the 20th USENIX Security Symposium*, Aug. 2011.

[54] A.-m. Yang, S.-y. Jiang, and H. Deng. A p2p network traffic classification method using svm. In *Young Computer Scientists, 2008. ICYCS 2008. The 9th International Conference for*, pages 398–403. IEEE, 2008.

[55] T. Ylonen and C. Lonvick. The Secure Shell (SSH) Transport Layer Protocol. RFC 4253 (Proposed Standard), Jan. 2006.

[56] S. Zander, T. Nguyen, and G. Armitage. Automated traffic classification and application identification using machine learning. In *Local Computer Networks, 2005. 30th Anniversary. The IEEE Conference on*, pages 250–257. IEEE, 2005.

An Empirical Study of Cryptographic Misuse in Android Applications

Manuel Egele, David Brumley
Carnegie Mellon University
{megele,dbrumley}@cmu.edu

Yanick Fratantonio, Christopher Kruegel
University of California, Santa Barbara
{yanick,chris}@cs.ucsb.edu

ABSTRACT

Developers use cryptographic APIs in Android with the intent of securing data such as passwords and personal information on mobile devices. In this paper, we ask whether developers use the cryptographic APIs in a fashion that provides typical cryptographic notions of security, e.g., IND-CPA security. We develop program analysis techniques to automatically check programs on the Google Play marketplace, and find that 10,327 out of 11,748 applications that use cryptographic APIs – 88% overall – make at least one mistake. These numbers show that applications do not use cryptographic APIs in a fashion that maximizes overall security. We then suggest specific remediations based on our analysis toward improving overall cryptographic security in Android applications.

Categories and Subject Descriptors

D.2.7 [**Software Engineering**]: Distribution, Maintenance, and Enhancement—*Restructuring, reverse engineering, and reengineering*

Keywords

Software Security, Program Analysis

1 Introduction

Developers use cryptographic primitives like block ciphers and message authenticate codes (MACs) to secure data and communications. Cryptographers know there is a right way and a wrong way to use these primitives, where the right way provides strong security guarantees and the wrong way invariably leads to trouble.

In this paper, we ask whether developers know how to use cryptographic APIs in a cryptographically correct fashion. In particular, given code that type-checks and compiles, does the implemented code use cryptographic primitives correctly to achieve typical definitions of security? We assume that developers who use cryptography in their applications make this choice consciously. After all, a developer would not likely try to protect data that they did not believe needed securing.

CCS'13, November 4–8, 2013, Berlin, Germany.
Copyright 2013 ACM 978-1-4503-2477-9/13/11 ...$15.00
http://dx.doi.org/10.1145/2508859.2516693.

We focus on two well-known security standards: security against chosen plaintext attacks (IND-CPA) and cracking resistance. For each definition of security, there is a generally accepted right and wrong way to do things. For example, electronic code book (ECB) mode should only be used by cryptographic experts. This is because identical plaintext blocks encrypt to identical ciphertext blocks, thus rendering ECB non-IND-CPA secure. When creating a password hash, a unique salt should be chosen to make password cracking more computationally expensive.

We focus on the Android platform, which is attractive for three reasons. First, Android applications run on smart phones, and smart phones manage a tremendous amount of personal information such as passwords, location, and social network data. Second, Android is closely related to Java, and Java's cryptographic API is stable. For example, the `Cipher` API, which provides access to various encryption schemes has been unmodified since Java 1.4 was released in 2002. Third, the large number of available Android applications allows us to perform our analysis on a large dataset, thus gaining insight into how developers use cryptographic primitives.

One approach for checking cryptographic implementations would be to adapt verification-based tools like the Microsoft Crypto Verification Kit [7], Murφ [22], and others. The main advantage of verification-based approaches is that they provide strong guarantees. However, they are also heavy-weight, require significant expertise, and require manual effort. The sum of these three limitations make the tools inappropriate for large-scale experiments, or for use by day-to-day developers who are not cryptographers.

Instead, we adopt a light-weight static analysis approach that checks for common flaws. Our tool, called CryptoLint, is based upon the Androguard Android program analysis framework [12]. The main new idea in CryptoLint is to use static program slicing to identify flows between cryptographic keys, initialization vectors, and similar cryptographic material and the cryptographic operations themselves. CryptoLint takes a raw Android binary, disassembles it, and checks for typical cryptographic misuses quickly and accurately. These characteristics make CryptoLint appropriate for use by developers, app store operators, and security-conscious users.

Using CryptoLint, we performed a study on cryptographic implementations in 11,748 Android applications. Overall we find that 10,327 programs – 88% in total – use cryptography inappropriately. The raw scale of misuse indicates a widespread misunderstanding of how to properly use cryptography in Android development.

We find there are exacerbating factors, and suggest remediations. First, while current developer tools can check a number of security properties, using cryptography correctly is not one of them. Adding light-weight checks, such as in CryptoLint, would improve security. Second, implementations abstract away semantic assumptions about the correct use of cryptographic primitives. For example, the documentation for CBC encryption does not state that the initialization vector should not be a constant. Adding a security discussion to cryptographic API documentation would address this problem. Third, the default behavior in cryptographic libraries is often not a recommended practice. For example, the predominant Android Java security provider API defaults to using the ECB block cipher mode for AES encryption. To remedy this problem, we suggest changing the default behavior to a more secure variant.

Contributions: Overall, our contributions are:

- We propose light-weight static analysis techniques and tools that can catch common cryptographic misuses (§5). Application developers and app store maintainers can use the tools to identify likely misuses in cryptography before an end-user uses the application.
- We perform a large-scale experiment to measure cryptographic misuse in Android (§6). To the best of our knowledge, we are the first to perform such a study at scale, demonstrate a widespread problem, and identify the likely culprits.
- We suggest remediation measures to help address the widespread issues identified (§7).

2 Definitions

This section presents common cryptographic definitions for symmetric encryption, password-based encryption, and the respective notions of security. We adopt the notation used by Bellare and Rogaway [6].

Block Ciphers and Symmetric Encryption Schemes A block cipher is a function:

$$E : \{0,1\}^k \times \{0,1\}^n \rightarrow \{0,1\}^n$$

where k is the key size and n is the block size. We call the input the plaintext, and the output the ciphertext. For each $K \in \{0,1\}^k$, let $E_K : \{0,1\}^n \rightarrow \{0,1\}^n$ be defined as $E_K(M) = E(K, M)$. A block cipher $E_k(\cdot)$ is a permutation, with E_k^{-1} as its inverse. Thus, $E_K^{-1}(E_K(M)) = M$ and $E_K(E_K^{-1}(C)) = C$ for all $M, C \in \{0,1\}^n$.

While block ciphers encrypt fixed-length messages, an encryption scheme encrypts messages of arbitrary length. A symmetric encryption scheme $\mathcal{SE}$ is a triple of algorithms $\mathcal{SE} = (\mathcal{K}, \mathcal{E}, \mathcal{D})$, where:

- $\mathcal{K}$ is a key generation algorithm producing a key K. We denote picking a key uniformly at random from the key space $KEYS(\mathcal{SE})$ as $K \stackrel{\$}{\leftarrow} \mathcal{K}$.
- An encryption algorithm $\mathcal{E}$, which might be randomized or stateful, takes a plaintext $\{0,1\}^*$, a key K returned by the key generation algorithm, and outputs a ciphertext $C \in \{0,1\}^* \cup \{\perp\}$.
- A deterministic decryption algorithm $\mathcal{D}$, which takes a ciphertext $C \in \{0,1\}^*$, a key K, and outputs $M \in \{0,1\}^* \cup \{\perp\}$. That is, $M \leftarrow \mathcal{D}_K(C)$.
- For correctness, we should be able to decrypt messages:

$$D_k(\mathcal{E}_k(M)) = M$$

We give two examples of encryption schemes built from block ciphers: ECB mode and CBC mode encryption.

Electronic codebook (ECB) mode is a stateless, deterministic encryption scheme defined over a block cipher. The encryption function (ECB) is:

```
ECB_K(M)
    M[1]...M[m] ← M
    for i ← 1 to m do
        C[i] ← E_K(M[i])
    C ← C[1]...C[m]
    return C
```

Algorithm 1: ECB Mode

Ciphertext Block Chaining (CBC) is an encryption algorithm built from a block cipher where each block of plaintext is XORed with the previous block of ciphertext. The first block of plaintext is XORed with an initialization vector (IV). As we will see, one insecure way to initialize the IV is by using a constant. A secure version, called CBC\$, initializes the IV with a random number upon each invocation of the algorithm, as shown below:

```
CBC$_K(M)
    M[1]...M[m] ← M
    C[0] ←$ {0,1}^n
    for i ← 1 to m do
        C[i] ← E_K(M[i] ⊕ C[i − 1])
    C ← C[0]...C[m]
    return C
```

Algorithm 2: CBC\$ Mode

Encryption and IND-CPA Security The goal of an encryption scheme is to provide privacy. Informally, privacy means that an adversary should have a hard time discerning even a single bit of information about the plaintext given the ciphertext. This intuition is formalized in the notion of indistinguishability under a chosen plaintext attack (IND-CPA). We should only consider an encryption scheme to be secure if and only if it is IND-CPA secure.

IND-CPA security can be formalized in a game where:

1. An oracle flips a fair coin $b = \{0,1\}$.
2. The adversary picks a pair of messages of equal length (M_0, M_1). The adversary, who does not have access to the secret key, gives the pair to the encryption oracle
3. The oracle for all encryption calls returns $C_b = \mathcal{E}_K(M_b)$ to the attacker.
4. The attacker executes steps 2 and 3 q times.
5. The attacker outputs a guess b'. The attacker wins if $b' = b$, else the attacker looses.

An encryption scheme is considered IND-CPA secure if the probability that the attacker, after seeing the encryption of q messages, cannot do better than guessing b.

We state as fact a well-known theorem (proven in [6]):

Theorem 1. *An encryption scheme must be either probabilistic or stateful to be indistinguishable under chosen plaintext attacks (IND-CPA).*

For instance, by Theorem 1 ECB mode cannot be IND-CPA secure. In particular, the attacker can learn b using only two queries to the oracle. Let the underlying block cipher length be n. The attacker constructs $M_1 = 0^{2n}$ and $M_0 = 0^n 1^n$. The attacker receives back a $2n$-bit ciphertext consisting of blocks $C[0]$ and $C[1]$. If $C[0] = C[1]$, then message M_1 was encrypted, else message M_0 was encrypted. Thus, the attacker can tell whether $b = 1$ or $b = 0$. CBC\$, on the other hand, can be proven IND-CPA secure [6].

Password-based Encryption User-chosen passwords are often vulnerable to dictionary brute-force attacks. Password-based encryption schemes make such brute force attacks more expensive. RFC 2898 (PKCS#5) [19] defines PBE, where encrypting a message M using a password pw and salt sa is defined as (as described in [5]):

PBE(pw, M)
  $sa \xleftarrow{\$} \{0,1\}^s$
  $L \leftarrow \texttt{KD}(pw||sa)$
  return $\mathcal{E}_k(L, M)||sa$

Algorithm 3: Password-based encryption

In PBE, $\mathcal{E}$ should be a IND-CPA secure encryption scheme, and KD is the key derivation algorithm. The key derivation algorithm is a c-fold iteration of a cryptographically secure hash function H.

While the c-fold iteration makes brute force attacks more expensive a random salt sa effectively thwarts brute force attacks that rely on pre-computed information, such as rainbow tables. Without any salt, a brute force attack with a dictionary of size N using PBE takes at least an additional cN iterations of H. Assuming $s = |sa|$ is sufficiently large that salts are unique, the complexity rises to scN. RFC 2898 recommends using no less than 1,000 iterations and a 64-bit salt. For example, Apple's iOS Data Protection Layer choses an iteration count so that generating a single key from a password takes roughly 80ms [3]. This delay is hardly noticeable by the user, but significantly slows down brute-forcing attacks.

Abadi and Warinschi [2] provide a computational analysis of password based encryption schemes. Bellare et al. [5] propose a theory of multi-instance security, where they show the key-derivation functions proposed in PKCS#5 and prove that per password salts amplify multi-instance security.

3 Common Rules in Cryptography

While cryptographic security is precisely defined, this paper asks the question whether developers who use cryptographic APIs achieve this notion of security. Using cryptographic primitives correctly can be challenging. In particular, any application that violates one of the following six rules cannot be secure.

Rule 1: Do not use ECB mode for encryption. [6]
Rule 2: Do not use a non-random IV for CBC encryption. [6, 23]
Rule 3: Do not use constant encryption keys.
Rule 4: Do not use constant salts for PBE. [2, 5]
Rule 5: Do not use fewer than 1,000 iterations for PBE. [2, 5]
Rule 6: Do not use static seeds to seed `SecureRandom(·)`.

Rule 1 forbids the use of ECB mode because a symmetric encryption scheme in ECB mode does not provide a general notion of privacy (i.e., it is not IND-CPA secure). Recall that ECB mode is deterministic and not stateful, thus cannot be IND-CPA secure by Theorem 1. A significant problem with ECB mode is that identical messages encrypt to identical ciphertexts. Such a leak of information is often intolerable. One commonly stated exception is that ECB mode is secure if the message is smaller than the underlying block cipher block size *and* all messages are unique. However, even in such cases an IND-CPA secure scheme would also work while providing greater theoretic security, and would thus be a more robust choice.

Rule 2 states that the CBC-mode construction (in Alg. 2) should always use a random IV. In essence, CBC\$ should always be used. Unfortunately, it is common to initialize the IV with a constant, e.g., all zeros (i.e., setting line 3 of Algorithm 2 to a constant). A constant IV results in a deterministic, stateless cipher, which by Theorem 1 cannot be IND-CPA secure. One can fix the situation by requiring that the first message block is a random number (essentially taking on the role of a randomized IV). We note that such exceptions to CBC\$ are often historically a band-aide patch for implementations that do not follow Rule 2 initially, e.g., as in TLS [23] and SSH [4].

Rule 3 states that an encryption scheme should not use a constant key. Intuitively, a constant key hard-coded in publicly available software is not a secret key, thus the resulting encryption does not provide privacy. Symmetric encryption schemes commonly include a notion of a randomized key generation algorithm $\mathcal{K}$ (see Section 2).

Rule 4 and Rule 5 are both recommended best practices for PBE schemes. Recall from §2 that the iteration count and salt entail a multiplicative increase in work for a brute force dictionary attack. An application that does not follow Rule 4 and uses a constant salt reduces to a program, for cryptographic purposes, with no salt at all. We chose the threshold for the iteration count at 1,000 because this minimum value is suggested in PKCS#5.

Finally, Rule 6 states that the Android `SecureRandom(·)` function should not be seeded with a constant. Android's `SecureRandom` is a *pseudo*-random number generator (PRNG) that is seeded. A PRNG seeded with a constant seed will produce a constant, known output across all implementations. Since PRNG's are often used to create key material, the resulting keys are not random thus not secure. As the name of the API – `SecureRandom` – suggests its use for security relevant tasks, we flag applications that seed the `SecureRandom` PRNG with static values.

4 Crypto in Android

Android applications are authored as Java source code and then compiled to Dalvik bytecode. This bytecode is packaged with additional resources, such as images and configuration files into an application package (apk) file. When the user installs an application from Google Play, the apk file is downloaded and installed on the device. Although, the application's source is Java, the Dalvik virtual machine (DVM) considerably differs from the Java virtual machine. For example, while the Oracle Java virtual machine is stack-based, the DVM is register based. Furthermore, Android provides a rich execution framework. This framework offers access to a variety of subsystems such as graphical user interfaces, networking, or the telephony and messaging sub-systems.

The sub-system relevant to this paper is the Java Cryptography Architecture (JCA). This architecture standardizes how application developers can make use of cryptographic algorithms. To this end, so-called cryptographic service providers (CSP) are registered with the JCA. A CSP is a package providing implementations of cryptographic algorithms, such as message authentication codes, encryption schemes, or key generation algorithms. This modularized architecture enables distributors and developers to seamlessly install and use different CSPs in parallel, or substitute one for the other, as long as they provide implementations for the same algorithms. For example, while Oracle Java contains the SunJCE as the default CSP, Android (since version 2.1) uses BouncyCastle [1] as its default cryptographic service provider.

Block ciphers, symmetric, and asymmetric encryption schemes are accessible to an application through the `Cipher` API. To obtain an instance of a specific encryption scheme, the developer calls the `Cipher.getInstance` factory method and provides a *transformation* as the argument. A transformation is a string that specifies the name of the algorithm, the cipher mode, and padding scheme to use. For example, to obtain a cipher object that uses AES in CBC mode with PKCS5 padding the developer would specify the transformation as: `AES/CBC/PKCS5Padding`. Only the algorithm part is mandatory. The security provider maintains default values for the cipher mode as well as the padding scheme should the developer choose to omit these values. Unfortunately, Java as well as Android chose ECB and PKCS7Padding as default values in case only the AES encryption algorithm is specified. Thus, a developer who only specifies the arguably secure AES block cipher ends up in a potentially insecure situation where the ECB block cipher mode is used.

5 System Design and Implementation

At a high level we observe that the rules specified in Section 3 are temporal properties. We have built an automated analysis tool to evaluate these rules on real-world Android applications. More precisely, we compute static program slices that terminate in calls to cryptographic APIs, and then extract the necessary information from these slices.

In this section we first discuss how we extract the control flow and super control flow graphs from real-world Android applications. We then detail our static program slicing approach, and how we evaluate the rules from Section 3 based on a program slice.

Control flow graphs Our approach targets the Dalvik bytecode of Android applications directly. We build our analysis on top of the Androguard [12] Android application analysis platform. Androguard disassembles an application into classes, methods, basic blocks, and individual instructions.

CryptoLint then first translates this low-level representation into an intermediate representation (IR). In this IR we combine the more than 200 Dalvik instructions into 19 semantically similar *instruction groups* (e.g., arithmetic instructions, invoke instructions). CryptoLint also extracts the intra-procedural control flow graphs for all methods in the application.

An application's use of cryptographic functionality might not be limited to a single method. For example, a cipher object could be instantiated in an object constructor and then used in two different methods (e.g., `encrypt` and `decrypt`) to encrypt or decrypt data respectively. If these two methods are analyzed in isolation, we would not be able to extract the encryption scheme that was used when the cipher object was instantiated. Thus, our approach implements inter-procedural analysis based on the application's super control flow graph to correlate the use of the cipher object for encryption and decryption with the cipher's instantiation. However, before CryptoLint reconstructs the super control flow graph two additional steps are performed.

First, CryptoLint translates all methods into single static assignment (SSA) form as described in [10]. Second, CryptoLint also extracts the class hierarchy of all classes implemented in the Application. Because in Android it is common and often necessary to extend classes that are defined in the Android framework, we also include all classes that are defined by the Android framework into this analysis. For example, any class implementing a user interface component has to extend the class `View`, which is defined in the Android framework. This analysis yields the class hierarchy tree rooted at the `Object` class, and contains all inheritance relationships between classes in the application and the Android framework. Furthermore, this data structure also contains information pertaining to Java interfaces and the classes that implement them. In our current implementation CryptoLint targets API version 16 of the Android framework (i.e., Android Jelly Bean). Of course, CryptoLint can be used with any other version of the framework too.

5.1 Extracting the super control flow graph

A super control flow graph (sCFG) consists of the call graph of an application superimposed over the control flow graphs of the individual functions. Call edges are added between call instructions and function entry points, and function exit points are connected with exit edges back to the call site. CryptoLint reconstructs an over-approximation the sCFG of an application by executing the following steps.

First, CryptoLint computes the possible types each register can hold at each program point. Initially, CryptoLint assumes that each register can hold values of any type. CryptoLint then analyzes how registers are used and refines the set of possible types of values accordingly. CryptoLint leverages the static type information that is present in the application's byte code. For example, the types of arguments and return values are listed in the datastructures that describe methods. CryptoLint propagates types to registers that receive arguments or return values from method calls. CryptoLint also leverages additional type information, such as `check-cast` instructions that assure that a register contains (a subtype of) the specified static type. The `new-instance` instruction is used to instantiate a new objects of the given type.

Dalvik bytecode only contains information regarding the static type of the objects used. However, the dynamic type of an object at runtime can be any subtype of the static type. An exception to this rule is the `new-instance` instruction, the dynamic and static type for operands used with a `new-instance` instruction are always identical. Thus, a `new-instance` instruction precisely defines what type of object the operand register contains. This refinement is performed until a fixed-point is reached.

Second, CryptoLint leverages the information from the type refinement step to resolve targets of the `invoke` family of instructions. These instructions consist of `invoke-virtual`, `-super`, `-direct`, `-static`, `-interface`, and their respective `-range` variants. To this end, we follow the approach presented by Dean et al. [11], and combine the information from the class hierarchy analysis with the possible types of the registers to identify the possible targets of invoke instructions.

5.2 Static program slicing

Static program slicing [27] is specified with respect to a slicing criterion. A slicing criterion is defined as a program point p and a variable x. The slicing algorithm then determines all program instructions that might affect the value of x at point p.

The slicing algorithm iteratively traverses the program backward starting at program point p. During execution, the algorithm keeps a working set of registers whose definitions need to be determined. Initially, this working set contains the registers from the slicing criterion (i.e., x). A register is removed from the working set if the algorithm encounters an instruction that statically defines that register. For an instruction that defines a register in the working set but uses other registers, the algorithm performs the following two steps: First, the defined register is removed from the working set. Second, all registers used by the instruction are added to the working set.

The slicing algorithm terminates successfully, once the working set is empty. This means that all operands in the working set were statically defined. The slicing algorithm terminates unsuccessfully, if it reaches the beginning of a method, but the sCFG does not contain any incoming edges to the currently analyzed method.

Additionally, our implementation of the slicing algorithm is also field sensitive. To this end, we keep a list of fields that are accessed by instructions in the `get` family of instructions (i.e., `iget`, `aget`, `sget`) during the execution of the slicing algorithm. The slicing algorithm is then recursively applied at each program location where the corresponding fields are defined, with the slicing criterion set to the location and the register that defines the field.

5.3 Evaluating security properties

We now describe how CryptoLint evaluates the security rules outlined above on real-world Android applications.

Rule 1: Do not use ECB mode for encryption. An application will use the ECB block cipher mode under one of two conditions. First, if the developer explicitly specifies that she wants to use ECB this is reflected in the transformation string (e.g., `AES/ECB`). The second, and arguably more subtle instance of using ECB, occurs if the developer only specifies a block cipher to use in the transformation. For example, if the developer only specifies `AES` as the transformation, BouncyCastle will automatically choose ECB as the default block cipher mode.

Thus, to identify applications that make use of the ECB block cipher mode, CryptoLint resolves for each call to the `Cipher.getInstance` factory method what transformation string is specified by the developer. To this end, CryptoLint calculates the backward slice for the slicing criterion consisting of the invoke statement to the factory method and the register that specifies the encryption scheme to be used. CryptoLint raises a warning if either only a block cipher is used as the transformation string or, the transformation explicitly lists a block cipher and the ECB mode.

Rule 2: Do not use a non-random IV for CBC encryption. Block ciphers in feedback mode (e.g., AES/CBC) require an initialization vector. While the CBC$ algorithm (see Algorithm 2) specifies the random selection of a fresh IV for each invocation of the algorithm, the Java API allows the developer to override this random selection and specify an IV herself. If the developer does not specify an IV, the BouncyCastle implementation of CBC will follow the CBC$ algorithm and generate an IV at random using the `SecureRandom` API.

To evaluate this property CryptoLint computes the backward slice for all calls to the `Cipher.init` method and uses as the slicing criterion the `ParameterSpec` argument of the method call. CryptoLint will flag an application as using constant initialization vectors if the following two conditions hold: (1) The slice includes an object of type `IvParameterSpec`, and (2) all values that are used for the constructor for that `IvParameterSpec` are static. The first condition is necessary because the `ParameterSpec` argument can hold types other than `IvParameterSpec`, such as `PBEParameterSpec` or `DSAParameterSpec`.

The second requirement allows us to identify whether the used IV consists of constant values. That is, if the slice does only depend on constant values, this implies that the IV is constant too.

Although the security prerequisites for IVs in block cipher modes require non-predictable and unique IVs, CryptoLint only identifies the use of static IV values. Static IVs are a subset of predictable IVs (i.e., they are trivially predictable). More precisely, for IVs that are not static, CryptoLint cannot distinguish between predictable and unpredictable IVs. The reason is that a non-static IV might still be predictable due to information that is not available to our analysis.

Rule 3: Do not use constant encryption keys. To identify the use of static symmetric encryption keys, CryptoLint calculates backward slices for the *key* argument to all invocations of the `SecretKeySpec` constructors. Because the Java security provider API is generic for symmetric and asymmetric encryption, CryptoLint only reports the violation of this property if a static key is used in a symmetric encryption scheme. In an asymmetric encryption scheme it is perfectly legitimate that an encryption key (e.g., the public key of a keypair) is statically included in the application.

Rule 4: Do not use constant salts for PBE. CryptoLint identifies applications that use static salt values for password based encryption by computing the backward slice for all calls to constructors of the `PBEParameterSpec` and `PBEKeySpec` APIs. The slicing criterion is specified as the call-site of the API call and the register that specifies the salt. If all instructions in the slice exclusively depend on static values, the salt has to be static too, and CryptoLint alerts respectively.

Rule 5: Do not use fewer than 1,000 iterations for PBE. To identify applications that violate this rule, CryptoLint computes a backward slice for the register that specifies the iteration count at each call to the `PBEParameterSpec` and `PBEKeySpec` constructors. If CryptoLint identifies that the iteration count is below 1,000 this use of password-based encryption is flagged as insecure. We chose this threshold value of 1,000 because RFC 2898 recommends using at least an iteration count of 1,000.

Rule 6: Do not use static seeds to seed `SecureRandom(·)`. CryptoLint flags applications that do seed `SecureRandom` with static values. To this end, CryptoLint computes a backward slice from all call-sites to the constructor of `SecureRandom` for the seed value specified. We were positively surprised to see that the documentation on `SecureRandom` does include a discussion about its secure usage[1] and possible pitfalls when seeding `SecureRandom`. This is the only crypto related API investigated in this work whose documentation contains such useful security relevant discussions.

To identify applications that do seed `SecureRandom` with static values, CryptoLint computes a backward slice from all constructors of `SecureRandom` that accept a seed argument. If all instructions in the slice depend exclusively on static values, the seed is considered to be static too.

6 Evaluation

Dataset The goal of this evaluation is twofold. First, we want to demonstrate that CryptoLint is indeed useful to identify violations of the specified rules. Second, by applying CryptoLint on a large number of real-world applications, we gain an insight into the prevalence of the misuse of cryptographic functionality in Android applications.

For this evaluation we downloaded 145,095 applications from the official Google Play marketplace. This dataset was collected between May and July 2012. The security rules that CryptoLint evaluates are related to functionality that resides in the `javax/crypto` and `java/security` namespaces. Thus, CryptoLint first assesses whether an application makes use of functionality in these name-spaces. 15,134 or 10.4% of all applications in our dataset use crypto functionality.

Name	Description
scoreloop	Cross platform social gaming
vending	Google License verification library
urbanairship	Mobile marketing solutions
openfeint	Social gaming platform
google/ads	Google Advertising
phonegap	Cross platform application development
vpon	Mobile advertising
unity3d	Mobile game engine
apache/james	Internet messaging
microad	Advertising
amazonaws	Libraries for Amazon AWS

Table 1: White-listed libraries

Similar to existing research (e.g., [25]), we observed the pervasive use of third-party libraries for advertisement and statistics purposes. In order to prevent over-counting, we whitelisted common libraries that use cryptography, as listed in Table 1. CryptoLint discards applications if their only use of cryptographic functionality is confined to these libraries. We assume that the applications we analyze do not actively try to disguise the use of these libraries, and thus, identify these libraries by matching their package names.

6.1 Results

In total, CryptoLint successfully analyzed 11,748 applications. The analysis of the remaining applications was unsuccessful for one of two reasons. First, the analysis of 2,614 applications did not terminate within a timeout of 30 minutes. Second, the analysis infrastructure ran out of memory during the analysis of 765 applications. All numbers reported from here on are in reference to the 11,748 successfully analyzed applications.

[1]Seeding SecureRandom may be insecure at `http://developer.android.com/reference/java/security/SecureRandom.html`

# apps	violated rule
5,656	Uses ECB (BouncyCastle default) (R1)
3,644	Uses constant symmetric key (R3)
2,000	Uses ECB (Explicit use) (R1)
1,932	Uses constant IV (R2)
1,636	Used iteration count $<$ 1,000 for PBE(R5)
1,629	Seeds SecureRandom with static (R6)
1,574	Uses static salt for PBE (R4)
1,421	No violation

Table 2: Violations of cryptographic security rules

Table 2 lists the number of distinct applications that violated the rules from §3. Only 1,421 applications in our data set did not violate any of the rules. We discuss the remaining rule violations in order of prevalence below.

Rule 1: Do not use ECB mode for encryption. This was the most frequent rule violated, with 7,656 total apps violating this rule at least once. The primary cause of ECB mode was developers using the default values in the BouncyCastle security provider. More precisely, in 5,656 applications the developer only specifies a block cipher (e.g., `AES`, `DES`, `DESede`) and the BouncyCastle provider configures the resulting cipher in ECB mode. These results indicate that developers are not aware that the API default does not provide the IND-CPA strong notion of privacy.

Additionally, 2,000 applications explicitly request a block cipher in ECB mode from the security provider. While there are legitimate uses for ECB mode (see §3), we manually inspected several applications and verified that they a) were trying to achieve privacy, and b) were using ECB mode on data that was over a block length or non-random. Examples of misuse of ECB mode include:

- One game uses DES/ECB to encrypt personal identifiers. The identifiers exceed the DES block size, thus an adversary can learn which parts of the encrypted ID are the same.
- One anti-virus product encrypts the MD5 hash of viruses found in DES3/ECB mode. An adversary can learn if multiple instances of the same virus are found on the device.
- One password manager stores passwords encrypted using AES in ECB mode. A more detailed discussion of this application will be presented in the case studies (below).

Rule 3: Do not use constant encryption keys. The second most violated cryptographic security property in our dataset is the use of a constant symmetric encryption key. As mentioned in Section 2, the security of symmetric encryption schemes depends on the secrecy of the shared key. Thus, embedding such secret keys into an application negates the security benefits of symmetric encryption. For example, AdMob encrypts the phone's location data using a constant key and sends it over the network. Another example is an application that stores the user's Google credentials on disk encrypted using a static key.

Rule 2: Do not use a non-random IV for CBC encryption. CryptoLint identified 1,932 applications that make

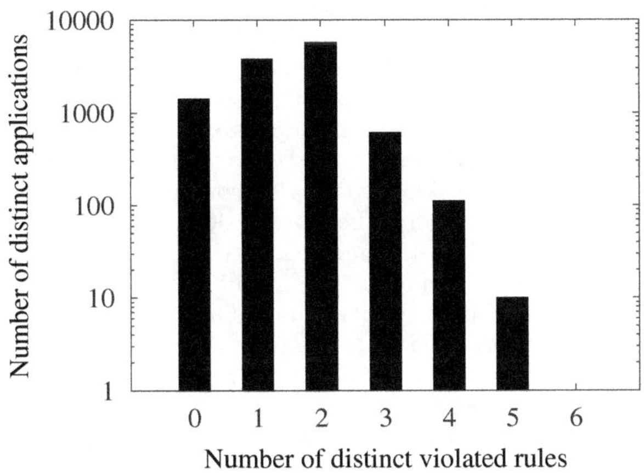

Figure 1: Number of applications violating 0, 1, 2, . . . 6 rules.

use of constant initialization vectors in CBC mode encryption.

Rule 4: Do not use constant salts for PBE. CRYPTOLINT identified 1,574 applications that use a static value for the salt used with the key derivation function in PBE. Using a static salt allows an attacker to pre-compute a dictionary based on the known salt, negating much of the benefit of using a salt at all. While the use of a static salt is better than using the password directly as encryption key, this choice negates the advantages in multi-instance security [5].

Rule 5: Do not use fewer than 1,000 iterations for PBE. The Java `PBEKeySpec` API implements password based encryption based on the PKCS#5 standard. The RFC for PKCS#5 recommends an iteration count of at least 1,000. CRYPTOLINT identified 1,636 applications that use fewer iterations. Applications that use a low iteration count and a static salt for password-based encryption are exposed to trivial dictionary-based off-line attacks, exactly the type of attacks that password-based encryption schemes were designed to protect against.

Applications violating multiple rules We next investigated the number of applications that violate multiple rules. These results are illustrated in Figure 1. Interestingly, it was more common for applications to violate two rules than only violating a single rule. Of the applications violating a single rule, rule 1 was violated the most (3,033 times). 511 applications violated rule 2 and used constant IVs. For 246 applications CRYPTOLINT identified the use of a static symmetric encryption key (violation of rule 3). 29 applications were flagged for using a low iteration count, and 13 applications use static salt values for password-based encryption schemes. CRYPTOLINT identified 6 applications that only violated rule 6 by seeding `SecureRandom` with a static seed.

The numbers of applications that violated exactly two rules are listed in Table 3. Additionally, our dataset contained exactly one application that violated all six rules that CRYPTOLINT evaluates.

# apps	rules violated
1,905	Rule 1 & Rule 3
1,588	Rule 1 & Rule 6
1,247	Rule 4 & Rule 5
866	Rule 2 & Rule 3
109	Rule 1 & Rule 2
24	Rule 1 & Rule 5
11	Rule 3 & Rule 5
5	Rule 2 & Rule 5
2	Rule 1 & Rule 4
2	Rule 3 & Rule 4

Table 3: Applications violating two rules

6.2 Case Studies

Social gaming platform To estimate the impact of applying cryptographic primitives incorrectly, we manually examined a popular game that CRYPTOLINT reported as misusing crypto. This game is from a development studio that released a series of popular games, all containing a social platform for connecting and interacting with friends. This social platform is used to track high-scores on a leader board. According to Google play, the application we analyzed has between 50,000,000 and 100,000,000 installations. The application communicates with the back-end servers of the social components over http. However, data that is transmitted between the server and the client is encrypted. This application got flagged by CRYPTOLINT for two reasons. First, it uses the DES blockcipher in ECB mode. The developers explicitly specified the ECB block cipher mode as the used transformation string is `DES/ECB`). Furthermore, CRYPTOLINT also complains that the application uses a static key with this encryption scheme. We evaluated the correctness of these results by interacting with the game and exercising the social network functionality while at the same time recording all network traffic sent by the application. With the key material retrieved by CRYPTOLINT, it was trivially possible to decrypt the encrypted network traffic.

Bookmark Manager We also investigated a bookmark manager application in more detail (install base between 1,000,000 and 5,000,000). This application allows the user to synchronize bookmarks between different browsers installed on the mobile device. Furthermore, it provides the functionality to synchronize browser bookmarks with Google's web services. To make use of this functionality, the user has to provide her Google credentials. The application stores these credentials in a regular Java property file. While the Google user-name is stored in the clear, the password is encrypted. CRYPTOLINT flagged this application because it uses the DES blockcipher in ECB mode to store that information in the property file. Furthermore, the application also uses a constant key for the encryption. Again we verified that decryption of the password is trivially possible. We agree that safe storage of access credentials is challenging to get right. To this end, Android provides a `KeyStore` facility that is designed for exactly the purpose of storing access credentials and is accessible through the API.

Password management application Users entrust their passwords to password manager applications for safe keeping and easy management. Because password information is important to protect securely, we investigated one application in this category closer. Although this application only has between 100,000 and 500,000 installations, the fact that the application is open source with a publicly available GIT repository warrants a closer analysis. In the earliest versions of the application the developer used the AES block cipher in ECB mode. However, before encryption, the application prepends two bytes of random data to the password. After decryption the initial two bytes are discarded. Furthermore, the application derives the key by calculating an HMAC over the master password the user supplies.

Several design decisions reduce the security of this implementation and render it non IND-CPA secure. Although prepending the password with two random bytes prevents two identical passwords from being encrypted to identical ciphertexts, this measure only protects the first 14 bytes of a password. Because individual blocks are encrypted independently, all plaintext blocks after the initial 14 bytes would be encrypted to the same ciphertext blocks. Furthermore, the developer chose to use a single HMAC operation with a static key to derive key material from the master password. Instead, the author should have used existing password-based encryption schemes to protect the key database against dictionary attacks.

In a subsequent version the author substituted the ECB mode for an encryption scheme based on AES/CBC. However, the author also hard-coded a static IV into the application. Similar to before, the author prepended the password to store in the database with two random bytes of data before performing the encryption. While the use of CBC and the two random bytes constitute a significant security improvement over earlier versions of the application, the application is still not IND-CPA secure. The reason is that two random bytes at the beginning of the plain text is not enough to preserve the IND-CPA security of the CBC$ algorithm. More precisely, two passwords are encrypted into the same cipher texts with probability of $1/2^{16} = 1/65536$, which is considered non-negligible.

Finally, in more recent versions of the app the author relies on AES/CBC and generates IVs at random. However, the author uses the regular random number generator instead of the `SecureRandom` API, which should be used in cryptographic contexts.

This development history spans two years of development on a system that is arguably designed to keep personal data secure. Our analysis shows that it is non-trivial even for well-intended developers to apply cryptographic primitives correctly. Thus, we propose a series of mitigations in Section 7 to make it easier for developers to use cryptographic algorithms correctly.

Popular libraries In the following we discuss our findings regarding how popular libraries apply cryptographic algorithms.

AdMob[2]. Google's AdMob advertising library is one of the most popular libraries included in Android applications. In fact we found that 36 % of the applications in our dataset make use of this library. AdMob uses the AES block cipher in CBC$ mode to encrypt device location and identifiers before transmitting that information to the ad-server. This library correctly uses the default behavior of the BouncyCastle provider to generate a random IV through the `SecureRandom` API. Thus, AdMob makes correct use of the cryptographic functionality provided in Android. However, AdMob also uses a constant encryption key for this operation. Thus, the security provided by the symmetric encryption scheme is undermined.

[2]`http://www.google.com/ads/admob/`

Scoreloop[3]. The Scoreloop library provides functionality to integrate social capabilities to mobile applications. The platform allows the developer to add virtual currencies and game items to her application and supports multiple payment options. When analyzing an example application that makes use of the Scoreloop library, CryptoLint correctly alerts that the library is using AES/CBC with constant initialization vectors. More precisely, the library derives the used IVs deterministically from the hard-coded URL endpoints of the Scoreloop backend servers. This result illustrates that not all developers of high profile libraries are capable of using cryptography correctly.

Android License Verification Library[4]. The LVL provides the developer with the necessary functionality to enforce a licensing policy on her applications. The documentation states that to keep licensing information persistent, this information has to be stored in an obfuscated manner on the device. To this end, the LVL provides an obfuscation scheme that is based on the AES block cipher in CBC mode. This default implementation however uses a constant initialization vector[5]. As the name of this API (i.e., **`AESObfuscator`**) suggests, the intended purpose here is to obfuscate instead of achieving IND-CPA security. However, modifying the source code to at least choose an IV at random would be straight forward, as the AdMob library illustrates.

6.3 Limitations

Our current system has a number of limitations. For example, Android applications can make use of native code. However, CryptoLint currently only targets Dalvik bytecode. Therefore, applications that invoke cryptographic primitives from native code cannot be analyzed. Furthermore, the property that initialization vectors have to be unique is not globally valid. For example, the Kerberos protocol uses a static initialization vector with the CBC block cipher mode. However, the protocol also specifies that the first block of a message is filled with random data and discarded at decryption. This basically transforms the first block into fulfilling the role of the initialization vector instead. Thus, the IV does not need to be transmitted along with cipher-text message. Inferring this valid use of a static IV in CBC mode would require CryptoLint to infer the implicit knowledge of the protocol designer, which is clearly beyond the scope of this work.

CryptoLint only detects the use and misuse of cryptographic primitives if they are properly exposed through the intended interfaces (e.g., security providers, ciphers, and MACs). CryptoLint cannot reason about applications that implement cryptographic primitives ad-hoc. To do so, CryptoLint would have to infer whether a particular piece of code implements cryptographic functionality. This is outside the scope of this work. Furthermore, history has shown that developers are rarely better off rolling their own cryptographic implementations as opposed to using well-tested library functionality. Thus, any such implementation is most likely less secure than the OS provided cryptographic algorithms.

[3]`http://www.scoreloop.com/`

[4]`http://developer.android.com/google/play/licensing/index.html`

[5]The source for the LVL and the AESObfuscator can be obtained at: `http://code.google.com/p/marketlicensing/source/browse/library/src/com/android/vending/licensing/AESObfuscator.java`

#Occurences	Symmetric encryption scheme
5,878	AES/CBC/PKCS5Padding
4,803	AES *
1,151	DES/ECB/NoPadding
741	DES *
501	DESede *
473	DESede/ECB/PKCS5Padding
468	AES/CBC/NoPadding
443	AES/ECB/PKCS5Padding
235	AES/CBC/PKCS7Padding
221	DES/ECB/PKCS5Padding
220	AES/ECB/NoPadding
205	DES/CBC/PKCS5Padding
155	AES/ECB/PKCS7Padding
104	AES/CFB8/NoPadding

Table 4: Distribution of frequently used symmetric encryption schemes. Schemes marked with * are used in ECB mode by default.

Recent events demonstrated that the assumption that cryptographic primitives are implemented correctly can be violated [20]. However, CryptoLint's focus is to identify applications that use these primitives incorrectly and not the identification of flawed implementations of the primitives themselves.

7 Mitigations

We now discuss a set of possible countermeasures that would likely reduce the prevalence of misused cryptographic primitives in Android applications. As explained in the introduction three main issues cause the problems we see with applying cryptography in Android applications. (1) APIs are not expressive enough to enforce semantic contracts (e.g., IVs should be unique and non-predictable). (2) APIs ship with poor default configurations, and (3) the documentation insufficiently describes the APIs.

Semantic contracts in APIs . One approach is to use tools such as CryptoLint to vet software, e.g., as part of the Google Play marketplace. Additionally, compilers can provide safety warnings on typically insecure method calls to the crypto API. For example, a call to the ECB encryption mode could raise a warning similar to the way that the `strcpy` function is flagged by the Microsoft C compiler.

Poor default configurations in APIs . Switching default configurations in APIs is challenging, especially in the light of backward compatibility. However, because of the negative characteristics of today's default values, we believe that choosing better defaults would mitigate many problems that lead to misused cryptography.

Table 4 lists the symmetric encryption schemes used by at least 100 applications in our dataset. The most popular API call is to CBC mode encryption, where CBC mode is explicitly picked in the name. The second (AES), fourth (DES), and fifth most popular (DESede) do not indicate which mode is being used. One possibility is to ban APIs that do not make the encryption mode explicit. Such an approach would require developers to investigate an appropriate encryption mode. Paired with appropriate documentation, this change would potentially make more developers aware of the cryptographic issues associated with block cipher encryption modes.

API documentation. The Java and Android API documentation contains a disclaimer that it is not designed to teach a developer the prerequisites of cryptography. However, the documentation could suggest sane defaults, e.g., CBC mode with a random IV because it is secure. Furthermore, we strongly advocate that the documentation for the cryptographic security provider explicitly state the default values. In some cases the default value is not mentioned at all. For example, the `Cipher` class states that a block cipher mode can be requested. However, it fails to mention if no mode is requested, ECB mode will be used by default. As it stands, the only way for a developer to determine default values, and whether they are secure, is via trial and error, Internet searches, or the inspection of the source code of the security provider.

Although Google regularly pulls up-to-date BouncyCastle revisions into the Android source tree, not all enhancements within the security provider are exposed to applications via the SDK. For example, BouncyCastle has supported Galois counter mode (GCM [6]) for authenticated encryption with associated data since 2008. Oracle Java has supported this mode and the necessary APIs since version 1.7, which was released in 2011. However, the latest Android version (at the time of writing Jelly Bean 4.3) does not expose the necessary APIs to use associated data with any authenticated encryption modes. Furthermore, the Android documentation does not mention authenticated encryption at all. Thus, developers who want to use these encryption modes have to gather their knowledge from other resources.

8 Related Work

The popularity of the Android operating system has attracted the attention of many researchers in the past. With TaintDroid, Enck et al. [13] track the propagation of sensitive information through Android applications. Hoffmann et al. [17] present SAAF, a static analysis framework that helps a human analyst to examine Android applications. Furthermore, the Android permission system has been at the core of many scientific publications [14, 16, 24]. While the permission system is the first line of defense in the Android security landscape, cryptographic primitives allow developers to add another line of defense by encrypting data before storing or transmitting it. Thus, to the best of our knowledge, CryptoLint is the first approach that investigates whether application developers make correct (i.e., secure) use of cryptographic primitives.

Zhou [29] and Vidas [26] investigate malicious applications in the Android ecosystem. The focus of CryptoLint, however, is to identify benign applications that employ cryptographic primitives incorrectly.

Our work is similar to the Lint program checker [18]. That is, we identify a series of common programming mistakes and automatically identify applications that contain such mistakes. Similarly, LCLint [21] uses source-code analysis and manual annotations to identify likely buffer overflows in C programs. The main difference between these approaches and CryptoLint is, however that CryptoLint does not have access to source code and operates on compiled Android applications instead. To ensure wide applicability of CryptoLint, we have to operate on compiled Android applications

[6] Within the Android documentation GCM is used to refer to the Google Cloud Messaging API.

instead. Chen and Wagner presented MOPS [8] to examine security properties of software at compile time. CRYPTOLINT is similar to MOPS as its goal is also to evaluate security properties. However, CRYPTOLINT operates on compiled applications. Furthermore, a major contribution of this work is the broad overview that we gained about the prevalence of misused cryptographic functionality in Android applications. Fahl et al. [15] presented MaloDroid, a system that identifies Android applications that do not perform the necessary validation on SSL certificates. MaloDroid is similar to CRYPTOLINT as it targets Android applications. However, the single property that is evaluated by MaloDroid is whether applications adequately verify SSL certificates. CRYPTOLINT checks for properties that are generally applicable to a cryptographic context, such as the proper use of initialization vectors, or random salt values for password based encryption schemes.

Mitchell et al. [22] present Murφ a tool that allows them to detect vulnerabilities in cryptographic and security-relevant protocols through state enumeration. Bhargavan et al. [7] illustrate how verification tools can be used to show the security of cryptographic protocol implementations. The verification of the TLS1.0 protocol required the authors to write an implementation from scratch that makes itself amenable to the suggested verification techniques. While such an approach is desirable, it seems unreasonable to require the large population of Android application developers to adapt such programming standards. Similar to these two approaches, we treat encryption primitives as black boxes. That is, we trust their security and implementations. However, developers using cryptographic primitives rarely implement well known protocols themselves.

Similar to Whitten et al. [28] and Clark and Goodspeed [9] we analyze the usability of cryptography. However, while the mentioned works analyze the usability for end-users, CRYPTOLINT focuses on the usability of cryptographic APIs, and functionality for application developers. However, our findings are somewhat comparable in that end-users as well as developers seem to lack the proper knowledge or support to make correct decisions when applying cryptography.

9 Conclusions and Future work

CRYPTOLINT checks real-world Android applications for the violation of the six security rules outlined in Section 3. With this automated approach we identified 10,327 applications (88% of our dataset) that violate at least one of these rules. We identified one of the contributing factors to be the undocumented insecure default configuration of the BouncyCastle cryptographic security provider used on the Android platform. Based on the insights we gained from the large-scale analysis of real-world Android applications, we also illustrated different mitigation approaches, we believe would be beneficial to the overall security of the Android ecosystem.

We are currently working on making CRYPTOLINT a publicly accessible online service where developers and curious users can submit Android applications and have them evaluated with respect to the cryptographic security rules described herein. In the future we also plan to extend CRYPTOLINT with security rules that capture the misuse of asymmetric cryptography.

Acknowledgements

This material is based on research sponsored by DARPA under CSSP #23143.2.1080246 and agreement number FA8750-12-2-0101. The U.S. Government is authorized to reproduce and distribute reprints for Governmental purposes notwithstanding any copyright notation thereon.

References

[1] The legion of the bouncy castle. `http://bouncycastle.org/`, 2013.

[2] M. Abadi and B. Warinschi. Password-Based Encryption Analyzed. In *Proceedings of the international colloquium of Automata, Languages and Programming*, pages 664–676. Springer, 2005.

[3] I. Apple. iOS Security Contents, 2012.

[4] M. Bellare, T. Kohno, and C. Namprempre. Authenticated encryption in SSH: Provably Fixing the SSH Binary Packet Protocol. In *Proceedings of the 9th ACM conference on Computer and communications security*, pages 1–11, 2002.

[5] M. Bellare, T. Ristenpart, and S. Tessaro. Multi-instance Security and Its Application to Password-Based Cryptography. In *Proceedings of the 32nd Annual Cryptology Conference*, pages 312–329. Springer, 2012.

[6] M. Bellare and P. Rogaway. Course notes for introduction to modern cryptography. `cseweb.ucsd.edu/users/mihir/cse207/classnotes.html`.

[7] K. Bhargavan, C. Fournet, R. Corin, and E. Zalinescu. Cryptographically verified implementations for TLS. In *Proceedings of the 15th ACM conference on computer and Communications security*, pages 459–468, 2008.

[8] H. Chen and D. Wagner. MOPS: An Infrastructure for Examining Security Properties of Software. In *Proceedings of the 9th ACM conference on Computer and communications security*, pages 235–244, 2002.

[9] S. Clark and T. Goodspeed. Why (special agent) Johnny (still) can't encrypt: a security analysis of the APCO project 25 two-way radio system. In *Proceedings of the 20th USENIX Security Symposium*, 2011.

[10] R. Cytron, J. Ferrante, B. K. Rosen, M. N. Wegman, and F. K. Zadeck. Efficiently Computing Static Single Assignment Form and the Control Dependence Graph. *ACM Transactions on Programming Languages and Systems*, 13(4):451–490, Oct. 1991.

[11] J. Dean, D. Grove, and C. Chambers. Optimization of object-oriented programs using static class hierarchy analysis. In *Proceedings of the 9th European Conference on Object-Oriented Programming*, pages 77–101. Springer, 1995.

[12] A. Desnos. Androguard: Reverse engineering, malware and goodware analysis of android applications ... and more (ninja !). `http://code.google.com/p/androguard/`.

[13] W. Enck, P. Gilbert, B.-G. Chun, L. P. Cox, J. Jung, P. McDaniel, and A. N. Sheth. TaintDroid: an information-flow tracking system for realtime privacy monitoring on smartphones. In *Proceedings of the 9th*

USENIX Symposium on Operating Systems Design and Implementation, 2010.

[14] W. Enck, M. Ongtang, and P. McDaniel. On lightweight mobile phone application certification. In *Proceedings of the 16th ACM conference on computer and Communications security*, pages 235–245, 2009.

[15] S. Fahl, M. Harbach, T. Muders, M. Smith, L. Baumgärtner, and B. Freisleben. Why Eve and Mallory Love Android: An Analysis of Android SSL (In)Security. In *Proceedings of the 19th ACM conference on Computer and communications security*, pages 50–61, 2012.

[16] A. P. Felt, E. Chin, S. Hanna, D. Song, and D. Wagner. Android permissions demystified. In *Proceedings of the 18th ACM conference on Computer and communications security*, pages 627–638, 2011.

[17] J. Hoffmann, M. Ussath, T. Holz, and M. Spreitzenbarth. Slicing droids: program slicing for smali code. In *In Proceedings of the 28th ACM Symposium on Applied Computing*, 2013.

[18] S. C. Johnson. Lint , a C Program Checker. Technical report, 1978.

[19] B. Kaliski. PKCS #5: Password-based cryptography specification version 2.0. `http://tools.ietf.org/html/rfc2898`.

[20] A. Klyubin. Some SecureRandom thoughts. `http://android-developers.blogspot.co.uk/2013/08/some-securerandom-thoughts.html`, 2013.

[21] D. Larochelle and D. Evans. Statically Detecting Likely Buffer Overflow Vulnerabilities. In *Proceedings of the 10th USENIX Security Symposium*, pages 177–190, 2001.

[22] J. C. Mitchell, M. Mitchell, and U. Stern. Automated Analysis of Cryptographic Protocols Using Murphi. In *Proceedings of the IEEE Symposium on Security and Privacy*, pages 141–151, 1997.

[23] B. Moeller. TLS insecurity (attack on CBC). `http://www.openssl.org/~bodo/tls-cbc.txt`, 2001.

[24] M. Nauman, S. Khan, and X. Zhang. Apex: extending android permission model and enforcement with user-defined runtime constraints. In *Proceedings of the 5th ACM Symposium on Information, Computer and Communications Security*, pages 328–332, 2010.

[25] P. Pearce, A. P. Felt, G. Nunez, and D. Wagner. AdDroid: Privilege separation for applications and advertisers in android. In *Proceedings of the 7th ACM Symposium on Information, Computer and Communications Security*, 2012.

[26] T. Vidas, D. Votipka, and N. Christin. All Your Droid Are Belong To Us: A Survey of Current Android Attacks. In *Proceedings of the 5th USENIX Workshop on Offensive Technologies*, 2011.

[27] M. Weiser. Program Slicing. In *Proceedings of the 5th international conference on Software engineering*, pages 439–449, 1981.

[28] A. Whitten and J. Tygar. Why Johnny Can't Encrypt : A Usability Evaluation of PGP 5.0. In *Proceedings of the 8th USENIX Security Symposium*, 1999.

[29] Y. Zhou, Z. Wang, W. Zhou, and X. Jiang. Hey, you, get off of my market: Detecting malicious apps in official and alternative android markets. In *Proceedings of the 19th Annual Network and Distributed System Security Symposium*, 2012.

Detecting Stealthy, Distributed SSH Brute-Forcing

Mobin Javed[†] and Vern Paxson[†◇]

[†]University of California, Berkeley [◇]International Computer Science Institute

Abstract

In this work we propose a general approach for detecting distributed malicious activity in which individual attack sources each operate in a stealthy, low-profile manner. We base our approach on observing statistically significant changes in a parameter that summarizes *aggregate* activity, bracketing a distributed attack in time, and then determining which sources present during that interval appear to have coordinated their activity. We apply this approach to the problem of detecting stealthy distributed SSH bruteforcing activity, showing that we can model the process of legitimate users failing to authenticate using a beta-binomial distribution, which enables us to tune a detector that trades off an expected level of false positives versus time-to-detection. Using the detector we study the prevalence of distributed bruteforcing, finding dozens of instances in an extensive 8-year dataset collected from a site with several thousand SSH users. Many of the attacks—some of which last months—would be quite difficult to detect individually. While a number of the attacks reflect indiscriminant global probing, we also find attacks that targeted only the local site, as well as occasional attacks that succeeded.

Categories and Subject Descriptors

K.6.5 [**Computing Milieux**]: MANAGEMENT OF COMPUTING AND INFORMATION SYSTEMS—*Security and Protection*

Keywords

Scanning; SSH; Brute-forcing; Distributed

1. INTRODUCTION

A longstanding challenge for detecting malicious activity has been the problem of how to identify attacks spread across numerous sources, such that the individual activity of any given source remains modest, and thus potentially not particularly out of the ordinary. These scenarios can arise whenever a detector employs a *threshold* used to flag that a given candidate attack source has exhibited a suspiciously high level of activity (e.g., when conducting scanning or DoS flooding). Attackers can respond to such detection procedures by employing multiple sources in order to thin out their activity to prevent any single source from exceeding the threshold; their attack becomes *distributed* and therefore potentially *stealthy*, i.e., hard to detect based on any individualized analysis.

In this work we present a general strategy for potentially detecting such stealthy activity, which consists of two basic steps. First, we employ the statistical technique of *change-point detection* to identify times during which a global property has shifted—indicating that, *in aggregate*, a site's activity reflects the presence of problematic activity. We then determine the range of time over which this activity occurred and, within that interval, identify which sources appear to have contributed to the activity.

In particular, we apply this approach to the problem of detecting *distributed SSH brute-forcing*: attackers employing a number of systems that each try different username/password combinations against a site's SSH login servers, hoping that one of them will stumble across a working combination made possible by a careless user. The threat of SSH brute-forcing is well-known: indeed, any SSH server open to general Internet access receives incessant probing by hostile remote systems that energetically attempt to locate instances of weak authentication [5]. The degree to which such attempts also occur in a stealthy slow-but-steady fashion, however, has attracted little study. The difference between single energetic probes and stealthy distributed ones is significant: defenders can easily detect the former, and therefore either block the activity or investigate it (to ensure none of the attempts succeeded). The latter, however, poses a much more difficult detection problem. If each host in a distributed brute-forcing attack itself only attempts username/password logins at a low rate, then distinguishing hostile activity from the inevitable login failures made by legitimate user errors becomes much more difficult. Yet the distinction is vital: a pattern of *attempt/attempt/attempt/success* made by a legitimate user simply reflects a set of typos, or a password that took a few stabs to remember; but by a distributed SSH brute-forcer, it provides the only slender indication of success amongst a mass of probing that in aggregate predominantly failed.

We aim to both provide an exemplar of our general strategy in terms of detecting distributed (but *coordinated*) SSH brute-forcing attacks, as well as developing an assessment of the prevalence of such attacks as seen over years of data. In terms of our two-step approach, we first identify *attack epochs* during which in aggregate we can with statistical confidence determine that some sort of SSH brute-forcing event occurred. Here, we employ change-point detection framed in terms of a parameter that summarizes the network/server activity of groups of remote hosts—in particular, the *aggregate login failure rate*. Our second step classifies the hosts appearing during the detected epochs as either *participants* or *non-participants* in the activity, based on both individual past his-

CCS'13, November 4–8, 2013, Berlin, Germany.
Copyright 2013 ACM 978-1-4503-2477-9/13/11 ...$15.00.
http://dx.doi.org/10.1145/2508859.2516719.

tory and "coordination glue", i.e., the degree to which a given host manifests patterns of probing similar to that of other hosts during the epoch.

We develop and evaluate our detector on 8 years of SSH login records collected via central syslogging at the Lawrence Berkeley National Laboratory, a large ($\approx$ 4,000 employees and visitors) research facility. We measure and quantify the duration, intensity and behavior of the detected attacks. We find multiple large-scale coordinated attacks from botnets, the longest one spanning about 1.5 months. All the attacks we detect would have been completely missed by a point-wise host-based detector. We correlate these attacks with data from several other sources, finding that half of the large-scale incidents at the site are part of global attacks, with a significant average overlap of $\approx$ 70% attack hosts appearing at multiple sites in the same time span.

We organize the rest of the paper as follows. We begin with related work in § 2. § 3 details the characteristics of the dataset we use in developing and evaluating our detector. § 4 frames our detection approach. In § 5 we develop a model of the process by which legitimate users make authentication errors when attempting to log in, which serves as the basis for parameterizing our SSH password brute-force detector. We discuss our evaluation results and findings in § 6, and summarize in § 7.

2. RELATED WORK

The literature relevant to our work lies in three domains: (i) coordinated attack detection, (ii) SSH brute-force attack detection, and (iii) studies of the prevalence of SSH brute-forcing activity.

The detection of coordinated attacks has received little treatment in the literature. The earliest work of which we are aware is that of Staniford et al., who correlate anomalous events using simulated annealing for clustering [17]. Gate's work on coordinated scan detection is the most prominent subsequent effort in this domain [8]. Given an input set of scan sources, Gate's algorithm extracts the subset of hosts that appear coordinated by using a set-covering approach; the premise is that the attacker divides the work among the coordinating scanning hosts in a manner that maximizes information gain while minimizing work overlap. For our purposes this work has two limitations: (i) the individual attack hosts require pointwise identification, and thus the approach will not find stealthy attacks, and (ii) the algorithm lacks a procedure for determining when a site is under attack. Other work has addressed the somewhat similar problem of detecting DDoS attacks, but these detection approaches face a difficult problem of how to differentiate attack participants from legitimate users [19, 16].

With regard to SSH brute-forcing, host-based detection techniques such as DenyHosts [2], BlockHosts [1], BruteForceBlocker [9], fail2ban [12], and sshguard [3] block hosts that cross a threshold for failed attempts in a specified amount of time. Other work has developed network-based approaches. Kumagai et al. propose an increase in the number of DNS PTR record queries to detect SSH dictionary attacks [13]. This increase results from the SSH server logging the fully qualified domain names of the SSH clients attempting access. This work does not discuss how to establish detection thresholds, nor does it present an evaluation of the system's accuracy. Vykopal et al. develop flow signatures for SSH dictionary attacks [18]. They show that a large number of short flows having a few bytes transferred in both directions and appearing together in a short duration of time are indicative of failed login attempts, providing the means to then detect brute-force attacks from flow data. Hellemons also studied the possibility of using only flow data to detect SSH brute-force attacks, modeling the brute-force attacks as consisting of three phases: scanning, brute-force and die-off (in case of successful compromise) [11]. They monitor the ranges of three parameters—flows-per-second, packets-per-flow and bytes-per-packet—to identify these phases. Both of these works test their detectors only on simulated dictionary attacks, and do not address how to distinguish instances of forgotten usernames/passwords from brute-forcers. More generally, none of these brute-force detection approaches have the ability to detect stealthy coordinated attacks.

Malecot et al. use information visualization techniques to detect distributed SSH brute-force attacks [14]. For each local host, the remote IP addresses that attempt to log in are displayed using a quadtree—a tree data structure formed by recursively subdividing two dimensional space into four quadrants. The procedure performs 16 iterations to map 32-bit IP addresses onto a quadtree, each time deciding the next sub-quadrant by looking at the next two bits of the IP address. The analyst then visually compares quadtrees for different local hosts to identify as coordinated attackers remote IP address(es) that appear in quadtrees of multiple local hosts.

Finally, regarding the prevalence of SSH brute-force attacks, Bezut et al. studied four months of SSH brute-force data collected using three honeypot machines [6]. They find recurring brute-forcing activity, sometimes with several weeks in between, indicating that the attacks target a wide range of IP address space. Owens et al. performed a measurement study of SSH brute-force attacks by analyzing data from honeypots on three networks—a small business network, a residential network, and a university network—for eleven weeks during 2007–2008 [15]. They find that the number of login attempts during different attacks varied from 1 or 2 to thousands. More than a third of the attacks consisted of ten or fewer login attempts. They find instances of both slow and distributed attacks designed to evade detection. They also find that precompiled lists of usernames and passwords are shared across different attackers, identifying five such dictionaries. Their study reveals that only 11% of the attempted passwords are dictionary words.

3. DATASETS AND DATA FILTERING

We evaluate our detector on eight years of SSH login data collected at the Lawrence Berkeley National Laboratory (LBNL), a US national research laboratory. The temporal breadth of this dataset allows us to study attack patterns at the site across the years. We also draw upon SSH datasets from four other sites spread across the IP address space (and several geographic locations) to assess whether attacks we detect at LBNL reflect targeted behavior or indiscriminant probing. We refer to these sites as HONEY, RSRCHLAB, HOMEOFF, and CAMPOFF, and describe them below. In this section we present these datasets and discuss ways in which we filtered the data for our subsequent analysis.

3.1 Main dataset

Table 1 provides summary statistics for our main dataset, LBNL. This site's systems primarily reside in two /16 address blocks (from two separate /8's). Only a small fraction of the address space runs externally accessible SSH servers, providing access to both individual user machines and compute clusters. The benign SSH activity in this data consists of interactive as well as scripted logins.

For this site we have datasets collected at two vantage points: (i) logs collected by a central syslog server that records information about login attempts reported by (most of) the SSH servers, and (ii) flow data for SSH port 22 collected by border monitoring. For each login attempt, the syslog data provides the time, client

Time span	Jan 2005–Dec 2012
SSH servers	2,243
Valid users	4,364
Distinct valid user/server pairs	10,809
Login attempts	12,917,223
Login successes	8,935,298
Remote clients	154,318
Attempts using passwords	5,354,833
successes	1,416,590
remote clients	119,826
SSH border flows	215,244,481
remote clients seen in flows	140,164
High-rate brute-forcers	7,476
Mean attempts per high-rate brute-forcer	382.84
Mean daily password login attempts	486.13 ($\sigma = 182.95$)
Mean daily users	116.44 ($\sigma = 32.41$)

Table 1: Summary of LBNL syslog and flow data.

and server[1] IP addresses, username on the server, whether the login succeeded, and the authentication type used. The flow data supplements this perspective by providing contact information (but no details) for attempts to access IP addresses that do not run an SSH server, or that run an SSH server that does not log via the central syslog server. This data thus enables us to establish the complete[2] set of machines targeted by an attack.

Filtering. For the central syslog data, we work with the subset of SSH authentication types vulnerable to brute-forcing (i.e., we omit those using public key authentication), about half of the attempts. We perform all of the characterizations and analyses in the remainder of the paper in terms of this subset.

In addition, we filter this dataset to remove individual brute-forcers that we can readily detect using a per-host threshold for the number of failed login attempts per remote host within a window of time. Given the ease of detecting these brute-forcers, they do not reflect an interesting problem for our detector, though they would heavily dominate the data by sheer volume if we kept them as part of our analysis.

To identify and remove such brute-forcers, we need to empirically establish reasonable thresholds for such a per-host detector. We do so by analyzing the process by which legitimate users make password authentication failures, as follows. We assume that any user who makes repeated failed login attempts followed by a successful attempt reflects a legitimate user. (This assumption may allow consideration of a few successful SSH brute-forcers as "legitimate", but these are very rare and thus will not skew the results.)

Figure 1 plots the number of failed attempts such users make prior to finally succeeding. We see that instances exceeding 10 failed attempts are quite rare, but do happen occasionally. Accordingly, we consider 20 failed attempts as constituting a conservative threshold. We manually analyzed the instances of legitimate users falling after this cutoff (the upper right tail in the figure) and found they all reflect apparent misconfigurations where the user evidently set up automation but misconfigured the associated password. Thus, we deem any client exhibiting 20 or more failures logging into a single server (with no success) over a one-hour period with as a *high-rate brute-forcer*, and remove the client's entire

[1] Some of the syslog records log the server's hostname rather than its IP address. For these we correlated the records against the site's DNS and DHCP logs to resolve to IP addresses.

[2] The flow data has some gaps, though we have it in full for each attack we identified. These gaps are the source of observing fewer "remote clients seen in flows" than "Remote clients" in Table 1.

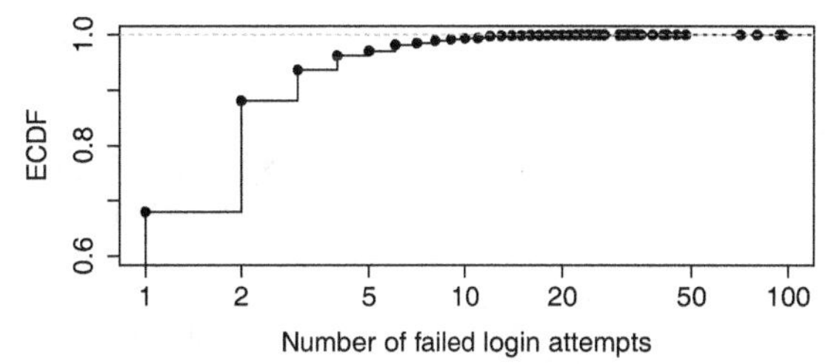

Figure 1: Empirical CDF of the number of failed login attempts per hour until a success for legitimate user login efforts with forgotten or mistyped usernames/passwords.

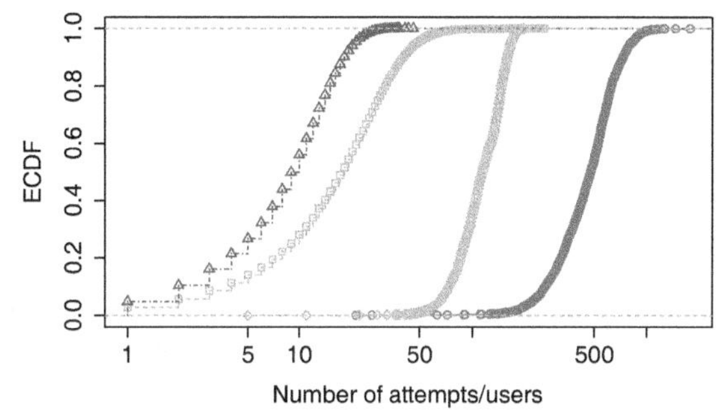

Figure 2: Empirical CDFs for benign password-based SSH usage in LBNL data. Left to right: (i) valid users per hour, (ii) successful logins per hour, (iii) valid users per day, (iv) successful attempts per day.

activity from our dataset. Table 1 summarizes the brute-forcers removed using this definition.

Finally, to give a sense of the volume of activity that remains after these filtering steps, Figure 2 shows the empirical CDF of the hourly and daily numbers of successful logins. A typical day sees 500 successful logins (maximum seen: 1,200) involving 117 distinct users (maximum: 197).

3.2 Correlation datasets

The HONEY dataset reflects five manually identified SSH brute-forcing "campaigns" (our term for ongoing instances, as discussed later) as captured by 2 SSH honeypot servers in Norway [4]. Table 2 summarizes these campaigns, which for the most part we characterize as large-scale, persistent, and stealthy. For all but the last campaign, many of the remote clients would evade detection by our simple per-host detector.

The RSRCHLAB dataset reflects flow data from the International Computer Science Institute, a research organization in Berkeley, CA, with a /23 address block. The dataset spans the same time as that of LBNL, though due to the limitations of flow data, we cannot

Attack Episode	Days	Remote clients	Login attempts	Avg. attempts per remote client
Oct 2009–Jan 2010	78	4,158	44,513	10 (σ=24)
Jun 2010–Aug 2010	56	5,568	23,009	4 (σ=7)
Oct 2011	6	338	4,773	14 (σ=16)
Nov 2011	13	252	4,903	20 (σ=24)
Apr 2012	6	23	4,757	206 (σ=760)

Table 2: Summary of attacks in the HONEY data.

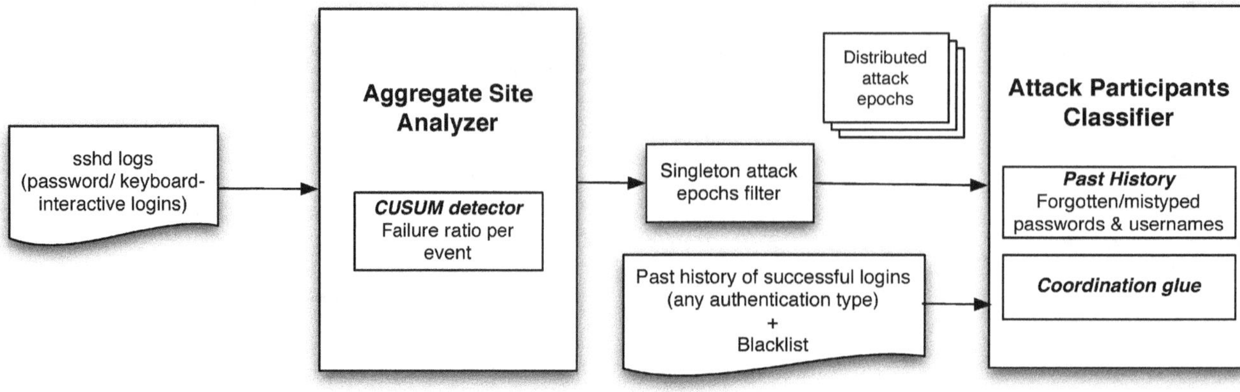

Figure 3: System diagram of our distributed SSH brute-forcing detector

establish how many coordinated attacks exist in it. We discuss our correlation strategy for this dataset in § 6.

HOMEOFF and CAMPOFF capture inbound SSH flow data for a home office (HOMEOFF) and a campus office (CAMPOFF), both in Cleveland, OH (but in separate netblocks). The data likewise spans Jan 2005–Dec 2012, and again due to its limitation to flow data, we cannot identify coordinated attacks in these datasets.

4. DETECTION

We structure our detection approach as the sequential application of two components. In general terms, the *Aggregate Site Analyzer* first monitors the site's activity to detect *when* an attack of some sort occurs. Upon detection, the *Attack Participants Classifier* analyzes the activity to identify *who* participated in the attack (which remote systems). In this section we develop both the general detection framework and our particular implementation of it for detecting and analyzing distributed SSH brute-forcing attacks. Figure 3 presents a system diagram for this latter specific context.

4.1 Aggregate Site Analyzer

This component detects the general presence of a coordinated, distributed attack based on complete view of a site's activity. We based the approach on devising a *site-wide* parameter that aggregates information from individual users/machines/events at the site. The *Aggregate Site Analyzer* monitors the probability distribution of this parameter for excessive change and flags the deviations as attacks. Often a single party can by itself induce significant change in the parameter. In this case (which arises for detecting SSH brute-forcing) we need to employ a filtering step to omit *singleton* attacks from the alarms, if our overall goal is focused on detecting distributed activity.

One important design question concerns the *accumulation granularity* of the site-wide parameter, i.e., over what sort of collection of activity do we compute it. For example, if the parameter relates to arrival rates, then windows of time will often be natural choices. In other scenarios, we might achieve better results by defining a normalized parameter amenable to longitudinal comparison. To illustrate, consider the scenario where the two consecutive time windows have 50 and 4 attempts, respectively. If these also have 25 and 2 problematic attempts, then we would equate them as having equivalent failure rates; but if we expect failures to appear somewhat rarely, we would like to treat the first instance as much more striking than the second, as the latter only needs some modest degree of stochastic fluctuation to occur. Thus, comparing *ratios* across time can prove misleading.

Given that, for detectors that monitor failure ratios we can benefit from a different accumulation granularity: if we compute the site-wide parameter in terms of *events*—defined as the occurrence of n attempts—then we needn't worry about the effects of stochastic fluctuation that can manifest when using windows of time. In addition, such time-variant events have the property that they allow for faster detection of high-rate attacks, as the detector does not need to wait a fixed amount of time before detecting the attack.

In the case of detecting distributed SSH brute-force attacks, we can define an apt *site-wide* parameter, Global Failure Indicator (GFI) as:

$$\text{GFI} = \text{Number of failed login attempts per event}$$

where an event occurs every n login attempts to the site. These n attempts represent a collection of users authenticating to the site, where the number of users will generally vary across events. (Note, while we could normalize GFI by dividing by n, we leave it as a count rather than a ratio, since our subsequent modeling benefits from using discrete variables.) We show in § 5 that in the absence of an attack (i.e., when failures only occur due to mistakes by legitimate users), this distribution is well-modeled as beta-binomial.

Brute-force activity perturbs the GFI distribution, shifting its mean to a higher value. We use sequential change-point detection to detect significant increases in the mean GFI. In comparison to threshold-based detection, sequential change-point schemes can detect small incremental effects that cumulatively lead to an eventual change of mean. This property enables the detector to detect stealthy attacks. Specifically, we use a Cumulative Sum (CUSUM) change-detection algorithm, as prior work has shown its sensitivity to small shifts in the mean [10].

CUSUM Algorithm. CUSUM models significant changes as shifts in the mean of a random variable from negative to positive. To use it requires transforming an original random variable Y to an associated value Z that has a negative mean under normal operation. One achieves this by subtracting the empirical mean μ of Y plus a small reference value k, i.e., $Z_n = Y_n - \mu - k$. To do so we need to compute μ based on data that describes normal operation (no attack underway); see § 5 for how we identify such activity. Finally, note that with little modification to the general framework we can for convenience select k so that Z_n is integer-valued rather than real-valued. We do so for our subsequent development of the detector.

We then accumulate Z_n over time using the following (again discrete) test statistic: $S_n = \max(0, S_{n-1} + Z_n)$, where $S_0 = 0$. In the case of no change, the value of S_n hovers around zero, but in the face of a change (increase), S_n starts to accumulate in the positive direction.

By convention, one terms the situation of the mean corresponding to normality as *in-control*. When the mean shifts by an amount $\Delta\mu$, one terms the situation *out-of-control*, which corresponds to an attack in our problem domain. Note that the choice of $\Delta\mu$ is specific to the problem we design the detector to detect. In some situations, we might desire a small $\Delta\mu$, while in others we might only have interest in detecting changes corresponding to a large value of $\Delta\mu$. In practical terms, we achieve a given target $\Delta\mu$ by setting two detector parameters, k and H, as discussed below.

The algorithm flags an *out-of-control* situation when S_n crosses an operator-set threshold, H. The subsequent appearance of an event with normal mean marks the return of the situation to *in-control*, and we reset the test statistic S_n to zero at this point. Thus, the CUSUM detector decides whether the mean has shifted or not according to the decision function D_n:

$$D_n = \begin{cases} 1, & \text{if } S_n > S_{n-1} \text{ and } S_n > H \\ 0, & \text{otherwise.} \end{cases}$$

Determining CUSUM parameters and span of change. One tunes the parameters k and H of CUSUM based on: the amount of change $\Delta\mu$ to detect, the desired false alarm rate, and the desired time to detection. First, a general rule of thumb when designing a CUSUM detector to detect a mean shift of $\Delta\mu$ is to set k equal to half the change in shift [10]. The other parameter, H, controls both the false alarm rate and the detection speed. A lower H means faster detection but a higher false alarm rate.

To assess the balance between these two, we consider the effects of H on the average number of steps the CUSUM detector takes to raise an alarm under in-control and out-of-control distributions. (Note that the first of these corresponds to alarms reflecting false positives, while the latter corresponds to true positives.) We refer to these as *in-control ARL* (Average Run Length) and *out-of-control ARL*, respectively, and choose the value of H that results in the closest match with the desired ARLs.

To determine these ARLs, we can model the CUSUM process as a Markov chain with finite states $X_0, X_1, \ldots, X_H$, corresponding to the test statistic values $S_n \leq 0, S_n = 1, S_n = 2, \ldots, S_n \geq H$ respectively. (Recall that we constrain Z and thus S to discrete integer values.) Note that X_H is the absorbing state. The transition probabilities of this Markov chain depend only on the underlying distribution of the random variable Z:

$$P[X_i \to X_0] = P[Z \leq -i]$$
$$P[X_i \to X_j] = P[Z = j - i]$$
$$P[X_i \to X_H] = P[Z \geq H - i]$$

For the intuition behind this formulation, consider the first equation. If the cumulative sum has reached i (i.e., $S_n = i$, corresponding to the state X_i) then the possible ways for progressing from it to the state X_0 (i.e., $S_n \leq 0$) are to add a value of Z less than or equal to $-i$. A similar perspective holds for the other two equations. Given the complete transition probability matrix $\mathbf{R}$ of the Markov chain, we can compute the above probabilities and the *in-control ARL* as:

$$\textit{in-control ARL} = (\mathbf{I} - \mathbf{R})^{-1}\mathbf{1}$$

where $\mathbf{R}$ is the transition probability matrix, $\mathbf{I}$ is the $(H+1) \times (H+1)$ identity matrix, and $\mathbf{1}$ the $(H+1) \times 1$ matrix of ones [7].

We can likewise compute the *out-of-control ARL* of the detector using the same formulation but substituting $k' = k - \Delta\mu$ [10]. We can then estimate the point of the true start of a change by subtracting the value of *out-of-control ARL* (detection delay) from the time of detection.

Finally, the *Aggregate Site Analyzer* reports the information from CUSUM in the form of *attack epochs*. An attack epoch constitutes of: (i) the set of consecutive *out-of-control* events (i.e., $i = 1 \ldots n$ where $D_i = 1$), and (ii) the set of previous events also incorporated into the epoch based on stepping back through the number of events given by the *out-of-control ARL*.

Each attack epoch can reflect instances of either *singleton* or *coordinated* attacks. The first of these corresponds to a global perturbation of the site-wide variable Y induced by a single source. The second refers to the perturbation arising due to the combined action of multiple sources. Since in this work we focus on distributed attack epochs, we need at this point to exclude singleton attacks.[3] We do so by checking whether CUSUM still flags any events in the epoch as reflecting an attack even if we remove the remote host with the highest number of failed login attempts. If so, we mark the attack epoch as a coordinated attack epoch, and proceed to the second component of our analysis. Otherwise, we discard the epoch as uninteresting (which occurred about 3/4s of the time).

4.2 Attack Participants Classifier

The second component of our general detection approach addresses how to go from the global site-wide view to that of individual entities. Here we employ a set of heuristics to analyze activity in the attack epochs flagged by the *Aggregate Site Analyzer* to identify *who* participated in the attack. (The need for heuristics rather than more principled identification arises almost fundamentally from the problem domain: if we could directly identify participants with confidence, we could very likely use the same approach to develop an effective pointwise detector and not have to employ a separate approach for detecting stealthy distributed activity in the first place.)

For our particular problem of detecting distributed SSH brute-force attacks, the individual entities we wish to identify are remote hosts (clients). In addition to the problem of including remote hosts corresponding to legitimate users within it, a distributed attack epoch—particularly if spanning a long period of time—can capture multiple brute-forcers, some of whom might operate in a coordinated fashion, while others might function independently. For example, an attack epoch we detect that includes activity from five remote hosts might in fact be composed of four coordinating remote hosts and one singleton brute-forcer that happens to probe the site at the same time.

For each remote host that appears during the attack epoch, we make a decision about whether to classify it as a legitimate remote host, a singleton brute-forcer (operating alone), or a brute-forcer working with other hosts as part of a coordinated attack. This decision might require manual analysis, as sometimes the categories have significant overlap. To illustrate, Figure 4 diagrams the characteristics that remote hosts in each of these categories can manifest. Legitimate users that fail due to forgotten or mistyped usernames/passwords generally exhibit only a modest number of attempts, similar to low-rate distributed brute-forcers. A remote

[3] Note that such single sources can arise even though we previously filtered out high-rate brute-forcers (per § 3.1) because these singletons might spread their activity across multiple servers, or probe at a rate lower than the 20 failures/hour threshold.

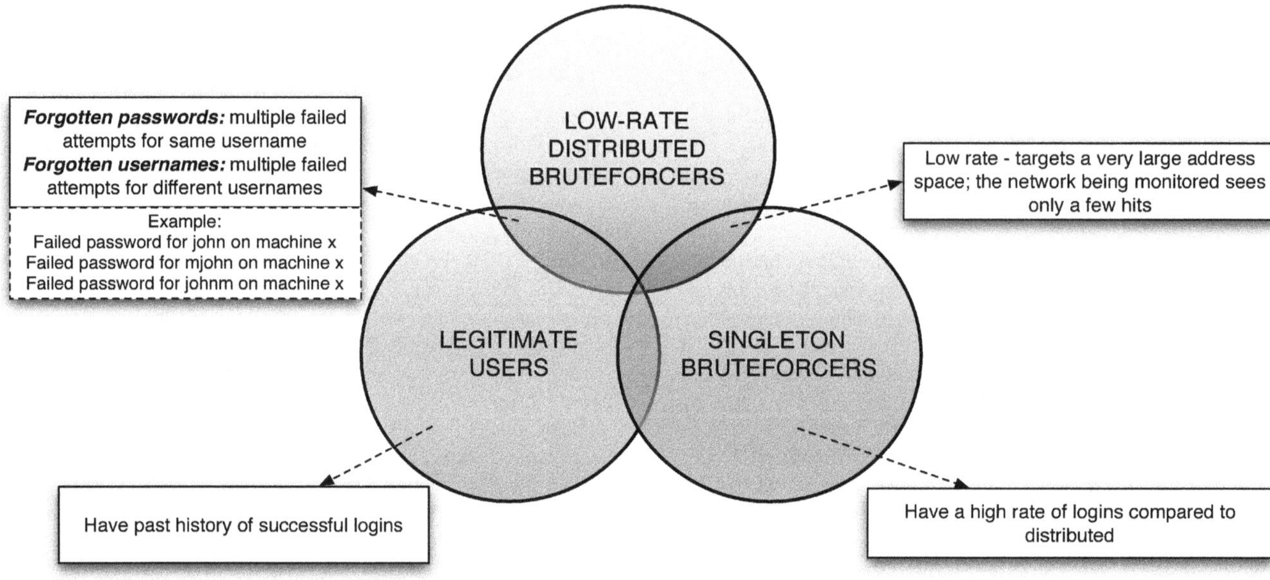

Figure 4: Possible characteristics of remote hosts that fail.

client with no past history of successful logins (see below) provides us with little indication as to whether it reflects a legitimate user or a distributed brute-forcer. Likewise, while we can readily identify singleton brute-forcers that probe at rates higher than distributed brute-forcers, ones that probe at low rates fall into a grey area that we find difficult to automatically classify.

Our classification procedure has two parts. First, we make a set of decisions based on past history. Second, for the remaining hosts during an attack epoch we assess the degree to which they evince the same *coordination glue*: that is, commonality in the set of servers and/or usernames that the hosts probe. The premise behind this second step comes from assuming that attack hosts in a distributed attack aim to work together to achieve a particular task: attackers achieve little utility if their multiple attack hosts do not effectively focus their work. We might also expect that coordinated attack hosts probe at similar levels (number of attempts) due to use of common automation software.

Classifying activity based on past history. To facilitate our discussion of this step, we use the following notation: L refers to a *Local host*; R to a *Remote host*; and U to a *Username*. Given that, we classify activity by analyzing past history as follows:

(1) *Forgotten/mistyped passwords:* we identify ⟨R, U⟩ pairs that have authenticated successfully in the past to any local machine at the site, and consider such activity benign, removing it from the attack epoch. (We filter ⟨R, U⟩ pairs instead of only remote hosts because multiple users might be behind a NAT.) We can safely filter out this set because the remote client has already established its ability to successfully authenticate as the given user, and thus has no need to try to guess that user's password. While the current activity is not necessarily benign (due to the possibility of a malicious login using stolen/compromised credentials), that scenario lies outside the scope of what we try to detect here.

(2) *Forgotten/mistyped usernames:* the previous step of filtering ⟨R, U⟩ pairs will miss instances of benign failures when the user mistypes or fails to recall their username. To identify such failures, for each remote host we determine whether it produced a successful login in the past to *any* internal host using a username *closely related* (edit distance = 1) to a username present in the event. If so, we again mark the ⟨R, U⟩ pair as benign. (Note that we skip this step if we have previously identified R as a singleton brute-forcer.)

Identifying coordination glue. After filtering out some activity on the basis of past history, we then turn to making decisions about attack participation amongst the remaining activity on the basis of evidence of "coordination glue", as discussed above. We expect to find either a common set-of-local-servers or set-of-usernames as the coordination glue in most of attacks.

We identify such glue using an approach based on bi-clustering. We construct a bipartite graph with the remote clients as the first node set A and either usernames or local servers as the second node set B. We create an edge between remote client r in node set A and a username u (local server l) in node set B if r made a login attempt as u (to l). For each graph we then look for partitions of the graph that maximize the edges within the partitions and exhibit very few edges across partitions. We mark nodes belonging to very small partitions as either legitimate users or coincidental singleton brute-forcers, and remove them.

Presently we proceed with the above as a manual process, which we find tractable since the number of attack epochs that emerge from our various filtering steps is quite manageable. In addition, we observe that a distributed attack that targets many hosts on the Internet might lead to activity at the site that exhibits little in the way of apparent coordination glue. In these scenarios, we also take into account timing patterns, number of attempts per remote host, and the presence of an alphabetical progression of usernames as alternate forms of coordination glue.

5. MODELING USER AUTHENTICATION FAILURES

To apply the approach developed in the previous section, we need to model the process by which legitimate users make authentication errors when attempting to log in. We want to achieve this modeling not simply in a highly aggregated fashion (e.g., by determining a global benign-user failure rate), but distributionally, as the latter will allow us to form well-grounded estimates of the expected false positives and time-to-detection behavior of our detection procedure. In particular, capturing the distribution will allow us to model GFI (number of failures per event of n login attempts), and thus to determine the Markov chain probabilities required to compute average-run-lengths.

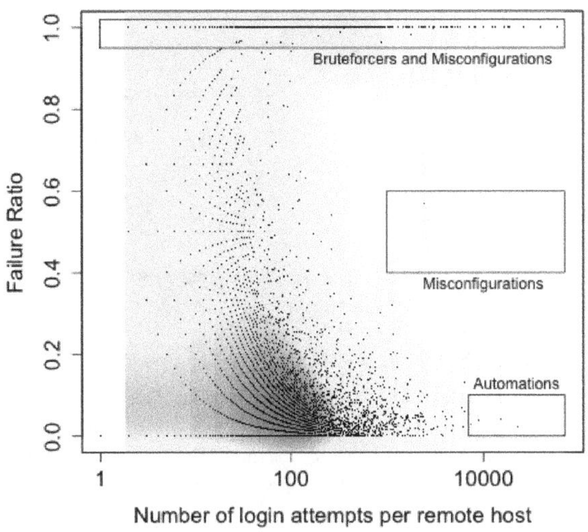

Figure 5: Number of logins and failure ratio of remote hosts over the complete dataset. Note that the dataset has been filtered to remove high-rate brute-forcers that can be detected pointwise using per host detection.

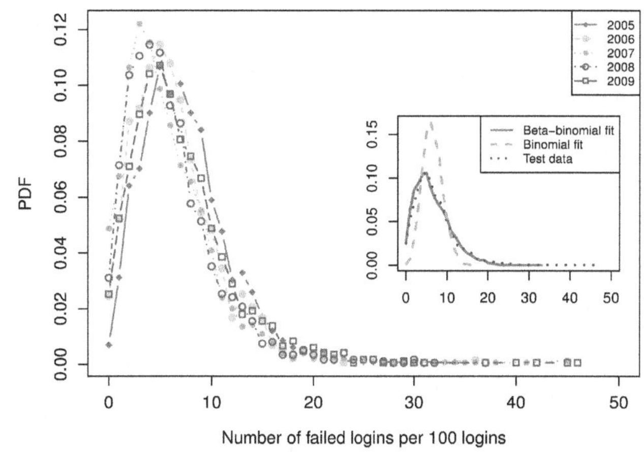

Figure 6: Probability distribution of GFI with n=100 logins.

In order to extract a characterization of legitimate login failures from the LBNL syslog data, we need to first identify clients within it that do *not* reflect legitimate users. Figure 5 shows a heat map of the number of login attempts vs. failure ratio per remote host computed over the complete data for password-based authentication (except with high-rate brute-forcers already filtered out, per § 3). The major density of remote clients resides in the lower left and middle areas of the plot; these mainly depict benign activity. The top region of the plot is highly dominated by brute-forcers (those that went slowly or broadly enough to survive the high-rate filtering), with a few legitimate users in the top-left corner, and some possible misconfigurations throughout. The mid-right region, with a high number of login attempts and a failure ratio in the range 0.4–0.6, very likely consists of misconfigured automations. Finally, the lower-right region captures well-configured automations; these use scripts that log in repeatedly with the correct password, and thus no chance of failure, except for intervening interactive access.

We now discuss our techniques to clean the data to remove both brute-forcers and automations (both well-configured and misconfigured) in the data. After doing so, we illustrate a distribution that fits the cleaned data quite well, providing us with the means to then model GFI.

Removing brute-forcers. Accurately identifying low-rate brute-forcers poses a circular problem, as that is exactly what we ultimately set out to detect in this work. Instead we develop an *approximate* procedure to remove the brute-forcers, as follows. We remove from the dataset all remote hosts that never achieve a successful login attempt. The chance that this removes legitimate hosts is low, because it should be rare that a legitimate user repeatedly attempts to log in and never succeeds.

This heuristic removes all of the brute-forcers except the successful ones. In order to cull them, we remove remote hosts with failure ratio ≥ 0.95 and ≥ 20 login attempts. We choose these thresholds based on our earlier finding that legitimate users extremely rarely have 20 failed login attempts before success (Figure 1). We find 13 remote hosts whose activity falls within these thresholds. Our manual investigation of these determined that six of them reflect misconfigurations (established due to periodicity in the attempts), six eluded classification (activity low enough that they could reflect either legitimate users or participants in coordinated attacks), and one brute-forcer that succeeded in breaking in (clearly an attacker due to employment of a dictionary of generic usernames).

Removing automations and misconfigurations. To find candidates for automated activity, we used Zhang's χ^2-based detection [20], which tests for uniformity of when activity occurs in terms of seconds-of-the-minute and minutes-of-the-hour. The premise of this approach is that human-initiated activity should be well-modeled as uniform in terms of these fine-grained timing elements, but automation will generally sharply deviate due to the use of periodic execution.

We applied the test on 3-day windows of activity, requiring each remote client to have at least 50 logins during the window. (We chose the parameters as reflecting clear automation even if spread out over a good amount of time). We used a significance level of 0.001 and a two-sided test in order to detect both non-uniform and extremely-uniform distributions, as both of these likely correspond to automated activity.

The test flagged 363 instances of remote hosts. We manually assessed the 79 of these that triggered detection in multiple windows, since these present instances of long-term automations that can skew our modeling. Doing so found 9 remote hosts that engaged in well-configured long-term automation, and 5 instances of misconfigured automations that frequently failed.[4] As examples, the well-configured automations included jobs that ran: (i) every six minutes for a year, (ii) every ten minutes for two months, (iii) every half hour for two months.

Deriving the model. Given the cleaned data, Figure 6 then presents the distribution of GFI (using $n = 100$ logins) for five different years. We see a possible trend towards overall less failure from 2005–2008, but 2009 reverses this drift, so we do not attempt to model the prevalence of failure as a function of time.

The figure inset shows the empirical density for 2010 along with two synthetic datasets. First, we fitted a binomial distribution to the 2010 data and randomly generated a new dataset of equal size from that distribution. Second, we applied the same process but

[4] We found it interesting that in some of these cases, when contacted the local administrators were unaware or had forgotten about the existence of this automation.

instead used a beta-binomial distribution. We see from the inset that the actual data exhibits more variance than we can capture using a binomial model. The beta-binomial model provides a significantly better fit as it allows for an extra variance factor termed *over-dispersion*. Beta-binomial is the predictive distribution of a binomial random variable with a beta distribution prior on the success probability, i.e., $k \sim \text{Binomial}(p, n)$ where $p \sim \text{Beta}(\alpha, \beta)$. Then for a given n, α and β, we have:

$$k \sim \binom{n}{k} \frac{\text{Beta}(k+\alpha, n-k+\beta)}{\text{Beta}(\alpha, \beta)}$$

We can interpret the success of this fitting in terms of lack of independence. If all login attempts were IID, then we would expect to capture GFI effectively using a binomial distribution. The need to resort to a beta-binomial distribution indicates that the random variables lack independence or come from different distributions, such that the probability of success has a beta-prior instead of being constant. This makes sense intuitively because (i) different users will have different probabilities of success, and (ii) the login attempts from a single user are not independent: one failed login attempt affects the probability of success of the next login attempt (negatively if the user has forgotten their password, positively if they simply mistyped it).

6. EVALUATION

In this section we apply our detection procedure to the extensive LBNL dataset. We discuss parameterizing the detector, assess its accuracy, and characterize the attacks it finds, including whether the attacks appear targeted or indiscriminant.

6.1 Parameterization

Our procedure first requires selecting a mean shift $\Delta\mu$ that we wish to detect. We set this to 10 failed logins per event of 100 logins, basing our choice on the stealthiest attack we wish to detect without overburdening the analyst. On average this site sees 500 logins per day, so a threshold of $\Delta\mu = 10$ bounds the number of attempts a brute-forcer can on average make without detection to 45 (9 attempts $\times$ 5 events) spread over a day. Fitting our beta-binomial distribution (§ 5) to the 2005–2008 data yields the parameters $\mu = 7$ and $\sigma = 4.24$, and so our chosen value corresponds to a shift in mean of approximately 2σ. (Note that this is *different* from stating that we detect a "two sigma" event, because due to the cumulative nature of the detection process, it takes significantly more perturbation to the site's activity than simple stochastic fluctuations to reach this level.)

We choose the other parameter, the decision threshold H, based on computing ARLs using the Markov chain analysis sketched in § 4.1. Table 3 shows the *in-control* and *out-of-control* ARLs for $k = 5$ and varying values of H. (We use $k = 5$ based on the rule-of-thumb of setting $k = \frac{\Delta\mu}{2}$ [10].) Given these results, we choose $H = 20$, as this gives a quite manageable expected false alarm rate of one-per-3,720 events, which, given that the site produces about 5 events per day, translates to an average of two alarms per year, and thus an expected 16 false alarms for the complete dataset. This level detects actual stealthy attacks after 5 events (50 brute-forcer login attempts, since the computation is for a shift in the mean of $\Delta\mu = 10$). In a practical setting, $H = 10$ (one false alarm per month) could work effectively.

To validate the assumptions underlying our detection model, we ran the CUSUM detector on the "cleaned" data (per § 5) to compare the expected false alarms with empirical false alarms. The detector

H	In-control ARL	Out-of-control ARL
1	9	1
10	144	3
20	3,720	5
30	99,548	7
40	2,643,440	9

Table 3: In-control and out-of-control ARLs for $k = 5$ and varying values of H.

flagged a total of 12 false alarms, reflecting cases where the failure of benign users lead to the alarm.

6.2 Assessment of Detection

The two components of our detector can each exhibit false alarms: *false coordinated attack epochs* and *false attack participants*. We can readily identify the former by inspection, as incorrect attack epochs can manifest in one of three ways: (i) the epoch consists of a singleton brute-forcer and a collection of legitimate users who had failures, (ii) the epoch consists of non-coordinating brute-forcers having no apparent coordination glue, and (iii) bad luck: the epoch consists of just legitimate users who failed. The latter kind of false alarms (false attack participants) pose a harder challenge to classify, given we lack ground truth. Since LBNL didn't itself detect and assess the majority of the attacks we detect, we use the following heuristic to gauge whether our procedure correctly classified a remote host as a brute-forcer. We inspect the the host's login activity in the attack epoch along with its future activity. If none of this succeeded, we can with high confidence deem that host as a brute-forcer. For hosts that ultimately succeed, we confirm whether the success reflected a break-in by checking whether LBNL's incident database eventually noted the activity.

Running the procedure over 8 years of data, the *Aggregate Site Analyzer* detected a total of 99 attack epochs. After then processing these with the *Attack Participants Classifier*, we find nine[5] represent false alarms. We detect a total of 9,306 unique attack hosts participating in the distributed attack epochs, two of which succeed in breaking-in. The procedure classified only 37 benign hosts as attack hosts, reflecting a very low false alarm rate. On days that include an attack epoch, we find on average about 100 benign $\langle R, U \rangle$ pairs filtered out using our past-history assessment, but on average only about 1.7 "forgotten username" instances detected and removed.

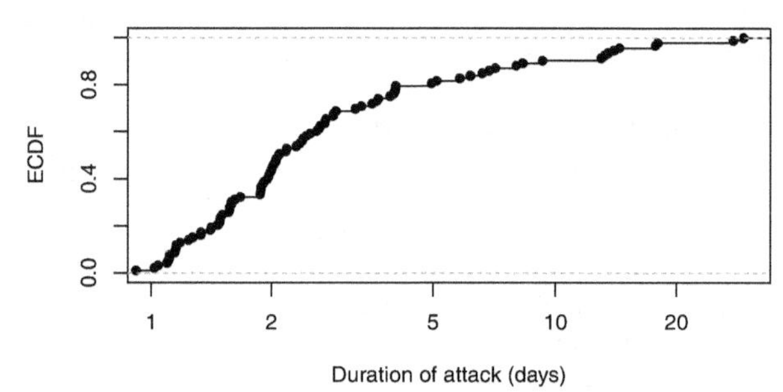

Figure 7: Empirical CDF of the duration of attacks (number of days)

[5]Note that this number differs from that found earlier on "cleaned" data because some of those false alarms coincided with actual attack epochs, and the *Attack Participants Classifier* then removed them due to a mismatch of coordination glue.

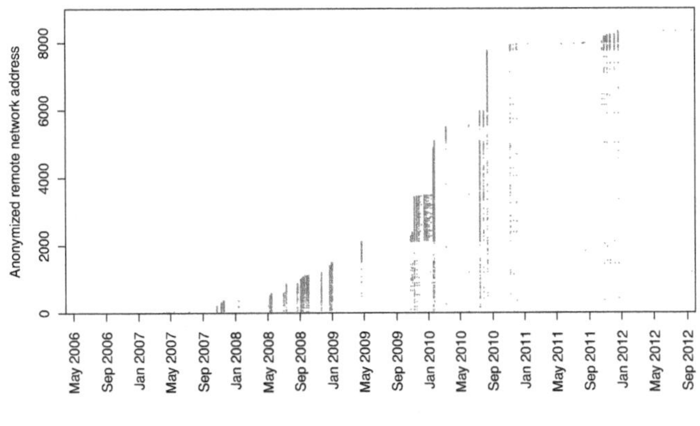

Figure 8: Participating attack hosts in the distributed attacks detected from 2005 to 2012 at LBNL.

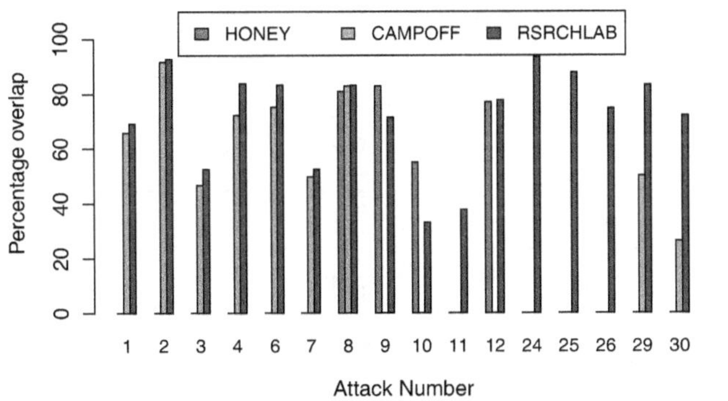

Figure 9: Percentage overlap of attack hosts seen at LBNL with that at sites HONEY, CAMPOFF and RSRCHLAB. The figure displays only the subset of attacks that appear in at least one of the three sites. (Note that none of the attacks appear in HOMEOFF).

Figure 7 shows the empirical CDF of the span of detected attack epochs. These coordinated attacks often span multiple days, and sometimes multiple weeks. The majority of the attacks exhibit strong coordination glue in terms of either the set of local machines probed or the usernames targeted for brute-forcing. Of the 90 true attack epochs, 62 have common-set-of-local-machines glue and 25 have username-"root" glue. Only 3 epochs did not manifest any glue we could identify; these epochs probed machines across a wide range of addresses and using a dictionary of generic usernames, such as *mysql* and *admin*.

Figure 8 shows the attack hosts participating in the various distributed attack epochs over time, where we number distinct hosts consecutively starting at 1 for the first one observed. The significant overlap of attack hosts across attack episodes shows that many of these attacks employ the same botnet. We then analyzed the coordination glue in these attack epochs to consolidate the set of epochs into *attack campaigns*. We use the following rules to group epochs into campaigns based on observing evidence that the same attacker conducting different attack epochs that work towards the same goal: (i) epochs with the same common-set-of-local-machines coordination glue, and (ii) epochs appearing on the same day with username-*root* coordination glue. Our detector considers these as multiple attack epochs rather than a single attack because this is indeed how the campaign proceeds, stopping for a few hours/days and then reappearing. Using these rules, we group the 62 attacks with common-set-of-local-machines glue into 12 distinct attack campaigns. Only a few of the 25 epochs group using heuristic (ii), condensing the root-set to 20 campaigns. This leaves us with a total of 35 attack campaigns.

Table 4 summarizes the magnitude, scope and stealthiness of the attacks we detect. All of these attacks were stealthy when observed from the viewpoint of individual hosts; on average the attack hosts made ≈ 2 attempts per local machine per hour. We can however detect a large fraction of these attack campaigns using a point-wise network-based detector that looks for high-rate hourly activity in terms of either the total number of failed attempts or the number of local hosts contacted. Note that we also detect attacks that a site cannot detect using either host-based or network-based point-wise detection (campaigns 5, 7 and 8 in Table 4). Finally, two of the campaigns succeeded, the first of which (campaign 1) as best as we can tell went undetected by the site.

We also find a difference in the characteristics between attacks that have set-of-local-machines coordination glue versus the ones that only have username-*root* glue. The latter tend to target a wide range of the site's address space and often involve just a few attack hosts brute-forcing at a high rate. Attacks having set-of-local-machines coordination glue often exhibit the pattern of the attackers stopping and coming back. We did not find any sequential pattern in any of these campaigns; rather, the attackers targeted servers spread across the address space, often including addresses in both of LBNL's distinct address blocks. We also did not find any pattern among the local servers in terms of belonging to the same research group or compute cluster.

6.3 Establishing the scope of attacks

Next, we attempt to establish which attacks specifically targeted the LBNL site versus global attacks that indiscriminantly probed the site. To do so we look for whether the attack hosts of a given campaign appeared in any of our four correlation datasets, HONEY, RSRCHLAB, HOMEOFF, and CAMPOFF.

We find that 16 campaigns appear in at least one of these four datasets. These include five username-root coordination glue attacks and all but one of the attacks with set-of-local-machines coordination. Figure 9 plots the percentage overlap of the attack hosts detected in the global attacks at LBNL with that at other sites, showing a high overlap in most cases. We investigated campaign 5, which does not appear at any of the other sites, and found that it indeed targeted LBNL, as the attack hosts all probed a set of six usernames each valid at the site. As shown by the hourly rates in Table 4, this targeted attack also proceeded in a stealthy fashion, with each remote host on average making only 9 attempts and contacting 3 local servers per hour. It's possible that some of the other campaigns also specifically targeted LBNL, though for them we lack a "smoking gun" that betrays clear knowledge of the site.

Finally, to give a sense of the nature of global attacks, Figure 10 shows the timing patterns of login attempts at the LBNL and HONEY sites during part of campaign 8. From the clear correlation (though with a lag in time), we see that the activity at both reflects the same rate (which varies) and, for the most part, the same active and inactive periods.

7. CONCLUSION

In this work we propose a general approach for detecting distributed, potentially stealthy activity at a site. The foundation of the method lies in detecting change in a *site-wide* parameter that summarizes *aggregate* activity at the site. We explored this approach in concrete terms in the context of detecting stealthy distributed SSH brute-forcing activity, showing that the process of legitimate users

ID	Appearances	Attrs.	Aggregate statistics		Per remote avg. hourly characteristics		
			Attack machines	Local machines	Attempts	Locals contacted	Per-Local attempts
1	2007: [Jul 7-9], [Oct 20-23], [Nov 5-9](2), [Nov 13-18](2)	**L,!!**	431	133	74.68	56.10	1.33
2	2008: [Apr 30 - May 7],[May 8-14](3)	**L**	286	140	98.50	54.80	1.79
3	2008: [Jun 28-29], [Jun 30 - Jul 1] [Jul 7-9], [Aug 17-21], [Sep 1-8] (5)	**L**	969	113	293.30	41.70	7.00
4	2008: [Sep 8-13](3)	**L**	378	257	52.50	40.70	1.28
5	2008: [Sep 16-18]	**L,S,T**	88	12	9.00	2.53	3.57
6	2008: [Sep 23-26](2), [Sep 29 - Oct 2](2)	**L**	185	109	48.50	38.38	1.26
7	2008: [Nov 18-19], [Nov 20 - Dec 29](5) 2009: [Apr 7-9]	**L,S**	1,097	22	16.01	8.04	1.99
8	2009: [Oct 22-23], [Oct 27 - Nov 24](5)	**L,S**	1,734	5	5.60	3.70	1.50
9	2010: [Dec 6 - Jan 10](6), [Jan 11-18], [Jan 20-22], [Mar 4-8]	**L**	3,496	44	38.80	21.50	1.80
10	2010: [Jun 16 - Jul 27](2), [Jul 29 - Aug 11]	**L**	7,445	1,494	90.80	34.50	2.70
11	2010: [Nov 1-6] (2), [Nov 7-8], [Nov 27 - Dec 1], [Dec 15-17]	**L,!**	581	98	140.60	45.47	3.09
12	2011: [Oct 11-19], [Oct 25-29](2), [Nov 4-7], [Nov 17-20]	**L**	377	158	33.93	25.25	1.34
13	2010: [Mar 30 - Apr 1]	**R,t**	78	18,815	999.70	118.91	1.33
14	2010: [Apr 23-26]	**R,t**	130	29,924	2325.57	117.97	1.22
15	2010: [May 7-10]	**R,t**	72	9,300	713.05	67.47	1.36
16	2010: [Sep 20-22]	**R,t**	33	5,380	69.05	60.72	1.14
17	2010: [Dec 27-30]	**R,t**	32	3,881	260.59	43.11	1.34
18	2011: [Feb 10-14](2)	**R,t**	108	7,520	40.45	27.21	1.48
19	2011: [May 16-18]	**R,t**	30	1,621	153.23	19.70	2.02
20	2011: [Jul 21-22]	**R,t**	20	2,556	388.25	38.13	1.18
21	2011: [Aug 2-6]	**R,t**	45	9,465	315.12	21.66	2.41
22	2011: [Aug 7-9]	**R,t**	48	6,516	444.16	17.60	2.18
23	2011: [Aug 17-21](2)	**R,t**	22	3,279	33.07	16.40	2.02
24	2011: [Nov 2-4]	**R**	31	3,446	273.80	20.08	1.02
25	2011: [Nov 30 - Dec 5]	**R**	181	10,467	829.68	18.31	1.03
26	2011: [Dec 18-20]	**R**	258	961	1099.85	14.00	1.02
27	2012: [Jul 20-21]	**R,t**	2	53,219	20,844	11,749	1.06
28	2012: [Aug 27 - Sep 2]	**R,t**	10	1,912	20.84	14.38	1.23
29	2012: [Sep 26-29]	**R**	6	1,971	72.30	13.05	1.59
30	2012: [Oct 8 - Nov 1](4)	**R,S**	190	19,639	5.27	4.97	1.06
31	2012: [Nov 16-18]	**R,t**	3	493	38.36	12.22	2.99
32	2012: [Nov 30 - Dec 2]	**R,t**	3	344	133.00	68.80	1.93
33	2008: [Jan 9-12]	**X,t**	17	63,015	2,846.44	1,761.69	1.61
34	2011: [Apr 8-26]	**X,t**	67	19,158	591.34	87.41	6.76
35	2012: [Dec 14-17]	**X,t**	13	45,738	1,490.26	1,430.67	1.04

Table 4: Characteristics of the detected coordinated *attack campaigns*. In *Appearances*, numbers in parentheses reflect how many attack epochs occurred during the given interval. *Attrs.* summarizes different attributes of the activity: **L** = coordination glue was set of local machines, **R** = coordination glue was username "root", **X** = no discernible coordination glue, **S** = stealthy, **T** = targeted, **t** = possibly targeted but no corroborating evidence, **!** = successful, **!!** = successful and apparently undetected by the site.

failing to authenticate is well-described using a beta-binomial distribution. This model enables us tune the detector to trade off an expected level of false positives versus time-to-detection.

Using the detector we studied the prevalence of distributed brute-forcing, which we find occurs fairly often: for eight years of data

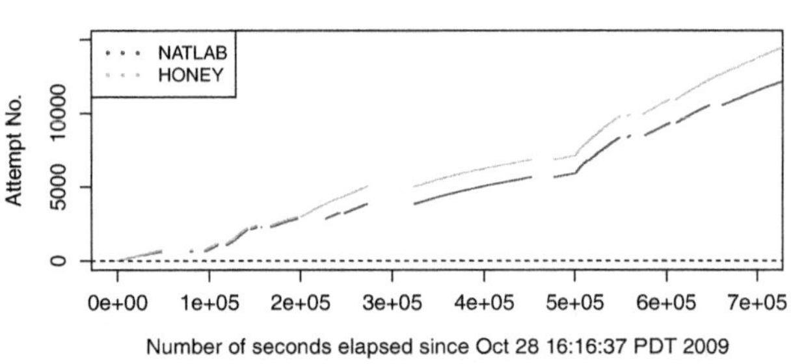

Figure 10: Timing of login attempts at HONEY machine and LBNL sites during part of attack number 8 (Oct 2009 - Nov 2009). The plot is based on data for only one of the machines targeted during the attack at LBNL.

collected at a US National Lab, we identify 35 attack *campaigns* in which the participating attack hosts would have evaded detection by a pointwise host detector. Many of these campaigns targeted a wide range of machines and could possibly have been detected using a detector with a site-wide view, but we also find instances of stealthy attacks that would have proven very difficult to detect other than in aggregate. We correlated attacks found at the site with data from other sites and found many of them appear at multiple sites simultaneously, indicating indiscriminant global probing. However, we also find a number of attacks that lack such global corroboration, at least one of which clearly targeted only the local site. Some campaigns in addition have extensive persistence, lasting multiple months. Finally, we also find that such detection can have significant positive benefits: users indeed sometimes choose weak passwords, enabling brute-forcers to occasionally succeed.

Acknowledgments

Our thanks to Mark Allman, Peter Hansteen, and Robin Sommer for facilitating access to the different datasets required for this work. Our special thanks to Aashish Sharma for running down various puzzles and to Partha Bannerjee and James Welcher for providing crucial support for the processing of the LBNL dataset.

This work was supported by the U.S. Army Research Office under MURI grant W911NF-09-1-0553, and by the National Science Foundation under grants 0831535, 1161799, and 1237265. Any opinions, findings, and conclusions or recommendations expressed in this material are those of the authors and do not necessarily reflect the views of the sponsors.

8. REFERENCES

[1] BlockHosts. `http://www.aczoom.com/blockhosts/`.

[2] DenyHosts. `http://denyhosts.sourceforge.net/`.

[3] sshguard. `http://www.sshguard.net/`.

[4] The Hail Mary Cloud Data - Data collected by Peter N. M. Hansteen (peter@bsdly.net). `http://www.bsdly.net/~peter/hailmary/`.

[5] ICS-ALERT-12-034-01 — SSH Scanning Activity Targets Control Systems. `http://www.us-cert.gov/control_systems/pdf/ICS-ALERT-12-034-01.pdf`, Feburary, 2012.

[6] R. Bezut and V. Bernet-Rollande. Study of Dictionary Attacks on SSH. Technical report, University of Technology of Compiegne, `http://files.xdec.net/TX_EN_Bezut_Bernet-Rollande_BruteForce_SSH.pdf`, 2010.

[7] D. Brook and D. A. Evans. An approach to the probability distribution of CUSUM run length. In *Biometrika*, volume 59, pages 539–549, 1972.

[8] C. Gates. Coordinated scan detection. In *16th Annual Network and Distributed System Security Symposium*, 2009.

[9] D. Gerzo. BruteForceBlocker. `http://danger.rulez.sk/projects/bruteforceblocker`.

[10] D. M. Hawkins and D. H. Olwell. Cumulative sum charts and charting for quality improvement. Springer, 1998.

[11] L. Hellemons. Flow-based Detection of SSH Intrusion Attempts. In *16th Twente Student Conference on IT*. University of Twente, January 2012.

[12] C. Jacquier. Fail2Ban. `http://www.fail2ban.org`.

[13] M. Kumagai, Y. Musashi, D. Arturo, L. Romana, K. Takemori, S. Kubota, and K. Sugitani. SSH Dictionary Attack and DNS Reverse Resolution Traffic in Campus Network. In *3rd International Conference on Intelligent Networks and Intelligent Systems*, pages 645–648, 2010.

[14] E. L. Malecot, Y. Hori, K. Sakurai, J. Ryou, and H. Lee. (Visually) Tracking Distributed SSH BruteForce Attacks? In *3rd International Joint Workshop on Information Security and Its Applications*, pages 1–8, Feburary, 2008.

[15] J. Owens and J. Matthews. A Study of Passwords and Methods Used in Brute-Force SSH Attacks. In *USENIX Workshop on Large-Scale Exploits and Emergent Threats (LEET)*, 2008.

[16] A. V. Siris and F. Papagalou. Application of anomaly detection algorithms for detecting SYN flooding attacks. In *IEEE GLOBECOM*, pages 2050–2054. IEEE, 2004.

[17] S. Staniford, J. A. Hoagland, and J. M. McAlerney. Practical automated detection of stealthy portscans. In *7th ACM Conference on Computer and Communications Security*, Athens, Greece, 2000.

[18] J. Vykopal, T. Plesnik, and P. Minarik. Network-based Dictionary Attack Detection. In *International Conference on Future Networks*, 2009.

[19] H. Wang, D. Zhang, and S. K. Detecting SYN flooding attacks. In *21st Joint Conference IEEE Computer and Communication Societies (IEEE INFOCOM)*, pages 1530–1539, 2002.

[20] C. M. Zhang and V. Paxson. Detecting and Analyzing Automated Activity on Twitter. In *Passive and Active Measurement*. Springer, 2011.

A Clinical Study of Risk Factors Related to Malware Infections

Fanny Lalonde Lévesque
École Polytechnique de Montréal
Montréal, Canada

Jude Nsiempba
École Polytechnique de Montréal
Montréal, Canada

José M. Fernandez
École Polytechnique de Montréal
Montréal, Canada

Sonia Chiasson
Carleton University
Ottawa, Canada

Anil Somayaji
Carleton University
Ottawa, Canada

ABSTRACT

The success of malicious software (malware) depends upon both technical and human factors. The most security conscious users are vulnerable to zero-day exploits; the best security mechanisms can be circumvented by poor user choices. While there has been significant research addressing the technical aspects of malware attack and defense, there has been much less research reporting on how human behavior interacts with both malware and current malware defenses.

In this paper we describe a proof-of-concept field study designed to examine the interactions between users, antivirus (anti-malware) software, and malware as they occur on deployed systems. The 4-month study, conducted in a fashion similar to the clinical trials used to evaluate medical interventions, involved 50 subjects whose laptops were instrumented to monitor possible infections and gather data on user behavior. Although the population size was limited, this initial study produced some intriguing, non-intuitive insights into the efficacy of current defenses, particularly with regards to the technical sophistication of end users. We assert that this work shows the feasibility and utility of testing security software through long-term field studies with greater ecological validity than can be achieved through other means.

Categories and Subject Descriptors

K.6.5 [**Management of computing and information systems**]: Security and Protection—*Invasive software*; K.4.2 [**Computers and Society**]: Social Issues—*Abuse and crime involving computers*

CCS'13, November 4–8, 2013, Berlin, Germany.
Copyright 2013 ACM 978-1-4503-2477-9/13/11 ...$15.00.
http://dx.doi.org/10.1145/2508859.2516747.

Keywords

anti-virus evaluation; malware infection; field study; user behavior; clinical trial; risk factors

1. INTRODUCTION

The growth of malicious activity on the Internet is unabated. Beyond sheer numbers of different samples, what has made the problem of malware detection and prevention more complex is the variety of threats and attack vectors that modern malware authors deploy to infect their victim's computers. In the early 2000's massive computer worms infected large swaths of the Internet in a few hours through open network ports with almost no human intervention. Today, however, we have a situation closer to that of an earlier era where threats were propagated through diskettes, email attachments, and innocuous-looking Trojans. Malware infections now occur largely because users are enticed to take an action that leads to their computers being infected. Today, this could be opening an email attachment (still a popular classic), visiting a malicious Web site, or even willingly installing a piece of software whose true intention they ignore (move over cuteware, here comes the codec).

Meanwhile, anti-virus (AV) products have had to evolve as well. The signature-based file-scanning engines that used to be the core technology of AV products have been complemented by multiple layers of protection, including identification of hazardous URLs, reputation-based software classification, system behaviour monitoring, etc. Computers are no longer stand-alone machines that need to be protected as such, and what used to be a security problem —their connectedness— is increasingly being leveraged by AV vendors to better protect their customers. Periodic signature file updates are being replaced by on-demand resource lookups on databases in cloud infrastructures, who are in turn fed by the continuous reporting of millions of AV client installations. AV products have thus evolved into complex pieces of "anti-malware" software, or rather complex software systems involving several semi-independent components with which, in some cases, the user must interact. While many AV vendors try to make the installation and operation of their product as transparent to the user as possible (or rather as "user-proof" as possible), the truth is that how well the AV operates depends on its user. This dependence is not only due to user configuration of the many features of AV products, but also to other user-driven factors such as how often the machine is connected to the Internet, how often its software and signatures are updated, but most importantly, how the humans in front of the machine are interacting with the computer and the Internet when confronted with situations where their actions could lead to infection.

In other words, the operating environment of both malware and AV products not only includes the machine it is trying to penetrate/protect, but also the network that connects it to the rest of the world and the *user* that sits in front of it. Indeed, the human is part of the operating environment of the machine, including the software that attempts to execute on it or protect it. It thus seems natural to adopt a *Homo in machina* (human in the machine) approach to evaluate not only the performance of AV products but also the susceptibility of users to getting their machines infected.

This change of paradigm is fundamental if we want to better understand what role user actions really play in the process of infection. In particular, it becomes paramount to understand how user characteristics, such as demographics, perception of threat, computer literacy, and user actions may affect the risk of infection by malware. For instance, while we might hypothesise that users who spend a lot of time browsing less reputable Web sites are more prone to malware infections based on the fact that they are often used by criminals to spread malware, it is important to be able to quantitatively confirm such hypotheses. This question goes beyond the performance evaluation of the AV alone, but of the AV *with* the human or of the human by itself.

This philosophy of *Homo in machina* is also in sharp contrast with current AV evaluation methods, largely based on automated tests in controlled environments, where machines installed with an AV product are subject to various infecting stimuli. In order to better assess the effectiveness of the multi-layered protection of modern AV, traditional file-scanning tests (also called "static" or "on-demand" tests in the AV industry) have largely fallen out of favour and are being replaced with tests involving known bad URLs (also called "dynamic" or "real-world"). While this latter type of tests does evaluate the performance of AV products as a whole (and not that of individual features), the truth is that they are not "real world" in that the effect of the main contributing factor in infections, i.e. the human factor, is not being measured. In addition, the results of these tests are often biased because the stimuli chosen by the tester could very well not be representative of what is typically experienced by the average user; this is often refereed to as the *sample selection problem.* Furthermore, such test do not measure the effectiveness of AV products at communicating risk effectively to the user and how they can affect user behaviour.

What we need then is to test using a methodology that can evaluate the interactions between humans, malware, and AV products (and other security software) with much greater ecological validity. Any testing methodology will have some impact on the phenomena being tested; to minimise this impact, testing needs to be done in an environment as close as possible to that of normal usage. One potential way to achieve such ecological validity is through conducting clinical trials of software as we proposed in 2009 [24]. With clinical trials, security software is installed and monitored on systems in regular use by regular users. Data is then gathered on the performance of the security software in protecting the system and on how the user interacted with the system during this time period. By correlating user behaviour, application use, and security software activity, we can gain insights into the interactions between all three in an ecologically valid context.

Thus, in order to address both the question of how to better evaluate AV and how to understand the influence of the human factor in infections, we decided to conduct such a clinical trial of anti-virus. In this paper we report on the first study of this kind, conducted at the École Polytechnique de Montréal from October 2011 to April 2012, involving 50 participants that used their own computers in everyday life during a 4-month period. The data collected during the study attempted to take into consideration many of the reasonable factors that could influence infection such as user profiling, user behaviour, host configuration and environment. In addition, the study collected data that would allow us to evaluate the performance of the AV and in some cases determine the causes of infections. In this paper, however, while we do present results on AV performance, we concentrate on finding and understanding the correlations between these factors and occurrences of infection, in order to determine which ones could be identified as risk factors. Detailed performance analysis of the various AV protection mechanisms through the determination of the causal mechanisms of infection is out of scope of this paper and will be the object of future research based on further analysis of the data produced by this experiment.

We should note that other methodologies, such as bench tests, cognitive walkthroughs, and lab-based user testing can give finer-grained insight into user and system behaviour than is possible in clinical trials, and can do so at lower cost. As we show here, though, clinical trials can gain insight into how systems perform and how users interact with them in practise, something that cannot be addressed with these other methodologies.

The remainder of the paper is organised as follows. Section 2 presents the related work. Section 3 describes the study and provides a summary of its methodology, a detailed description of which is also given in a previous methodology publication [14]. In Section 4, we describe and discuss in detail the results of the study in terms of threat detections by AV, missed detections, and identification of potential risk factors related to user characteristics and behaviour. While the study itself and a few of the preliminary results, especially on AV performance, were already presented at a industry conference shortly after the conclusion of the study [15], Section 4 contains a more in-depth and complete statistical analysis and interpretation of the study results, with an emphasis on risk factors. We discuss limitations, applications, and future work in Section 5 and conclude in Section 6.

2. RELATED WORK

Numerous studies evaluating the performance of AV products and the influence of user interactions factors on IT security have been conducted in recent years. There are currently several methods for evaluating anti-malware products used in the AV industry [4, 7, 8], but they do not reflect the performance of products in real life. Typical evaluation methods conducted by commercial testing labs (e.g. [2, 19]) are based on scanning collected or synthesised malware samples along with legitimate programmes. While such approaches can measure raw detector accuracy, they cannot take into account factors such as user interactions, evolving threats, and different environments. One major issue is that the sample collection is often too small, inappropriate, and not validated [9, 12]. Even with a well-maintained malware collection, testing against such data sets has become unreliable due to the increasingly dynamic nature of malware. To partially address this issue, Vrabec and Harley [27] proposed emulating user interaction with the system and creating user-specific testing scenarios. Another alternate method for evaluating the performance of desktop AV is through the use of on-demand detection tools, that in addition to detecting installed threats can detect whether an AV was installed and which one. For example, the security company SurfRight made public a report [25] describing a 55-day study conducted at the end of 2009 involving more than 100,000 machines that used their product. This repport included statistics of detections missed by the installed desktop AV products. Finally, infection statistics based on self-reporting of (perceived) security incidents by users, can be obtained from user surveys and be used to estimate AV performance, such as in the report published by Eurostat —the statistical office of the European Union— based on the 12-month reporting period in 2010 [6]. Unfortunately, self-reported rates of infection are probably quite inaccurate. Finally, the experiment proposed in [24] eliminates many of these problems and potential inaccuracies by adapting the concept of clinical trials to the computer security domain. The initial proposal was to evaluate security products using methods and controls similar to those used in clinical trials of medical products.

Other field studies in computer security have been conducted following an ethnographic approach. This type of approach explores the impacts of the manners, the customs, and the social, physical, and fiscal environment of users when they are facing computer security decisions. It primarily uses qualitative methods such as surveys and observations to understand how and why participants interact with computer systems. For example, Botta *et al.* [3] conducted an ethnographic study of security professionals. Rode [20] used this approach to examine parental behaviour in protecting children's on-line safety. The study showed that there are a host of security threats of which the children are not aware and provides an overview of parental rules and strategies for keeping children safe. Wash [28] used interviews to understand users' mental models of security. He identified eight 'folk models' of security threats that are used by home computer users to decide what security software to use, and which expert security advice to follow. De Luca *et al.* conducted a field observation of ATM users to evaluate PIN usage [5]. This study shows that contextual factors on security such as distractions, physical hindrance, trust relationships, and memorability have a big influence on PIN-based ATM use. Lastly, Sheng *et al.* focus on susceptibility of users against phishing attacks [21]. They conclude from the results of an on-line study with 1001 users that prior exposure to phishing education is associated with less susceptibility to phishing, suggesting that phishing education may be an effective tool. They also found that age is a contributing risk factor. Indeed, young people aged 18 to 25 are also more susceptible to phishing. This last assertion is confirmed by a study conducted by Milne *et al.* [16] that concluded, through a survey of 449 on-line buyers (also students), that age affected the behaviour of subjects when faced with a potential computer threat. Ngo and Paternoster [17] used the results of a survey based on the self-assessment of 295 students, to deduct that age is a significant risk factor of infection, with older respondents being less likely to get infected.

Another methodological approach is that based on the concepts and methods of Epidemiology. This approach, similarly as the ethnographic approach, uses statistical methods. However, it refers to the threat and how it spreads, while ethnography refers to environmental and demographic factors that influence the user when faced with this threat. By analogy to the field of health, the concepts that underlie this approach are: infection, detection, disinfection, quarantine, epidemics, environment control, etc. [22]. Its methods are borrowed from the biological sciences in order to determine the likely causes and risk factors for infection, understanding the spread of malware and, where appropriate, the methods to remedy it. This approach has been used in many studies. We summarise three of them here. First of all, Carlinet *et al.* used it to analyse the behaviour of ADSL customers and identify customer characteristics that are risk factors for malware infection. The study showed that using the Windows operating system and heavy usage of Web applications and streaming are major risk factors of malware infection. Unfortunately, the study does not say anything about the type of Web sites as a risk factor. Secondly, Kephart and White [10] attempted to adapt the epidemiological approach to determine the conditions under which virus epidemics are likely to occur, and in cases where they do, they explore the dynamics of the expected number of infected individuals as a function of time. They concluded that there is a threshold of rate of infection from which we can speak of an epidemic. Thirdly, Kondakci [11] used a stochastic model to analyse the epidemic states of infected computers and determine the state probabilities of susceptible populations. He shows that there is more than one state transition. A healthy but susceptible computer can become infected by a virus, can then become a transmitter, and can also return to a healthy state.

Regarding the impact of a user's domain of expertise on risk of infection, Solic and Ilakovac [23] conducted studies with two groups of participants: one group consisting of 19 doctors and another of 20 professors from an engineering school, who anonymously answered a questionnaire on their behaviour when faced with threats to their computer and the consequences that ensue. This study concluded that the domain of expertise does not have a major impact on user behaviour when it comes to threats and security risk.

On the other hand, the level of expertise or non-expertise in computer security does influence users' perception of security risk, as demonstrated by Ashgarpour *et al.* [1]. Two experiments were conducted: a quantitative study used to approximate the mental models of computer users with regards to common security risks, and qualitative interviews with experts and non-experts. The results of these two experiments suggest that the mental models of people concerned with security risks are strongly correlated to their computer security level of expertise.

In summary, we note that all studies reviewed cover separately one or a few of the factors described above. However, none of these studies cover all of these factors or study the relationship between them. Thus, one of our main contribution is to use the clinical trial method to analyse the impacts of all these individual factors on infection by malware to gain a better understanding of the causes of these infections.

3. STUDY DESCRIPTION

This first study of its kind was conducted as a 4-month proof-of-concept study involving only 50 participants in order to prove its feasibility as an alternative experimental performance evaluation approach in computer security. The details of the methodology have been published elsewhere [14], but we nonetheless provide a brief summary here. The study monitored real-world computer usage through diagnostics and logging tools, monthly interviews and questionnaires, and in-depth investigation of any potential infections. The study had the following goals:

1. Develop an effective methodology to evaluate anti-virus products in real-world environment;
2. Determine how malware infects computer systems and identify source of malware infections;
3. Determine how phenomena such as the configuration of the system, the environment in which the system is used, and user behaviour affect the probability of infection of a system;

The 50 participants were recruited through posters and newspaper advertisements on the Université de Montréal campus (where the École Polytechnique is located). A short on-line questionnaire was used to collect initial demographic information. Using these profiles, we categorised interested volunteers based on their gender, age group, status and field of work/study. We randomly chose a sample from each category in order to have a diverse and representative sample of users that included students and employees from various fields.

3.1 Ethical and Privacy Considerations

Since the study involved human subjects, the entire project had to undergo strict review by the *Comité d'évaluation des risques informatiques* (CÉRI) and the Ethics Review Board of the university. The Board imposed certain restrictions on the study such as limits to the type of (potentially) personal information kept, the length of time data could be kept, the purpose of the research, and adequate remuneration for participation in the study.

All raw data and statistics generated during the experiment were anonymised, as they were only identifiable through a unique number attributed to the laptop. Only the project leader knew what subject corresponded to which number, and this only for administrative purposes. This personal information was destroyed three months after the end of the study. It is therefore not possible to associate collected information with the identity of the subject.

All data collected was kept in a locked cabinet in a high-security zone, which was protected with three-factor authentication (biometrics, PIN and ID card). This work zone is completely isolated from the Internet and the university network, and only personnel authorised within the context of this project had access to the data. The security policy of the laboratory was also applied to the deletion of all personal data related to the experiment. This policy applies to all information whether on paper or electronic media, and conforms with Government of Canada standards.

The use of collected data during this experiment was bound to the stated research objectives of the project. Nonetheless, in circumstance where the law imposes it, such as the inadvertent discovery of information leading a reasonable person to believe that a (serious) crime has been committed or is about to be committed, we would have had to report this information to the appropriate authorities (law enforcement agencies, etc.).

Furthermore, given that the experiment required the handling of malware files, special precautions were taken in order to protect the university's IT infrastructure. For example, all files identified as potentially malicious were encrypted before being stored in the high security zone of the lab.

3.2 Equipment

The laptops that were provided to the subjects all had identical configurations, with the following software installed: Windows 7 Home Premium; Trend Micro's Titanium Maximum Security (Trend Micro's premium AV product for home users); monitoring and diagnostic tools including HijackThis, ProcessExplorer, Autoruns, SpyBHORemover, SpyDLLRemover, tshark, WinPrefetchView, WhatChanged; and custom Perl scripts developed for this experiment.

These scripts automated the execution of the tools and compiled statistical data about system configuration, the environments in which the system is used, and the manner in which the system is used. The data compiled by our scripts included: the list of applications installed and the list of applications for which updates are available; the number and the type of web sites visited; the number and the type of files downloaded; the list of browser plug-ins installed; the number of different hosts to which the laptop communicates per day; the list of the different locations from which the laptop establishes connection to the Internet; the average number of hours per day the laptop is connected to the Internet; and the average number of hours per day the laptop is on.

The AV product was centrally managed on our own server, in a manner similar as is usually done for corporate installations to centralise distribution of signature file updates. All the AV clients installed on the laptops were thus sending relevant information to our server about any malware detected or suspected infections as they occured.

Before deployment, we benchmarked the laptops by running tools and recording the output. The recorded information included: a hash of all files plus information about whether the files were signed; a list of auto-start programs; a list of processes; a list of registry keys; a list of browser helper objects (BHO); a list of the files loaded during the booting process; and a list of the pre-fetch files.

In order to avoid biases in user behaviour and at the same time limit the liability of the university, the laptops were sold to the participants at an advantageous, below retail-market price, with laptops staying in their possession at the end of the study.

3.3 Experimental Protocol

The study consisted of 5 in-person sessions: an initial session where participants received their laptop and instructions, followed by monthly 1-2 hour sessions where we performed analysis to determine if the laptop was infected.

To encourage the participants to remain in the study until its end, we paid them to attend the monthly in-person sessions. If participants completed all required sessions, the entire cost of the laptop would be reimbursed, along with an additional compensation. We encouraged participants to configure their laptop as they desired and use it as they would normally use their own computer. The only restrictions applied during the experiment were that the participants not format the hard drive, not replace the operating system, not create a disk partition, not install any other AV product on the laptop, and not delete our software and tools.

Each month, participants booked an appointment via an on-line calendar system hosted on our server. During these monthly sessions, participants completed an on-line questionnaire about their computer usage and experience. The questionnaire was intended to assess the participant's experience with the AV product and gain insights about how the laptop was used. Meanwhile, the experimenter collected the local data compiled by the automated scripts. Diagnostics tools were also executed on the laptop to determine if an infection was suspected. If the AV product detected any malware over the course of the month, or if our diagnostics tools indicated that the laptop may be infected, we requested additional written consent from the participant to collect specific data, such as the browser history, the tshark log files (i.e. network traffic data), and the suspected file(s), in order to help us identify the means and the source of the infection.

In the last visit, participants completed an on-line exit survey about their experience during the study. The aim of this final survey was to identify activities or mindsets that may have unduly influenced the experimental results. We requested that participants keep the experiment data stored on their laptops for an additional three months, so that if we discovered that further analysis was necessary, we could contact them and seek their permission to collect and analyse additional relevant data. Finally, we provided them with a procedure for deleting the diagnostic tools and the scripts, as well as the experiment data stored on their laptop.

4. RESULTS AND DISCUSSION

Our analysis focuses on several aspects, first examining the number and type of detections found during the study, and secondly by exploring how user characteristics and behavioural patterns may have affected the likelihood of getting infected.

4.1 Threats Detected by AV

During the 4-month study, 380 files were detected on 19 different user machines by the AV product being evaluated. However, some of these files were detected twice or more on the same user machine. Removing these repetitions, we obtain a total of 95 detections.

In terms of overall virulence, this indicates that over a period of 4 months, 38% of our population was exposed to malware. In truth, this figure far exceeded the expectations of the members of the research team, largely based on their own experience (e.g. number of AV warnings over an equivalent period of time). More importantly, however, these results would indicate that, if they are representative of the whole user population, almost 1 out of 2 newly installed machine would be infected within 4 months if they had not had an AV installed! This figure might seem at first alarming and surprising, but in fact the Eurostat report mentioned earlier [6] indicates that over a period of 12-months in 2010, 31% of users reported a virus infection on their home computers, while 84% of these users reported having some kind of security software installed (AV, anti-spam, firewall, etc.). Thus, if these figures are to be trusted a theoretical 38% exposure rate should not be surprising.

In terms of the evolution of the number of infections over time, we can see that the level of detections is very similar for each month, contradicting the hypothesis that users are most at-risk when they first start using their machines. This is shown in Figure 1 where the distribution of the detections without repetition for each month is depicted.

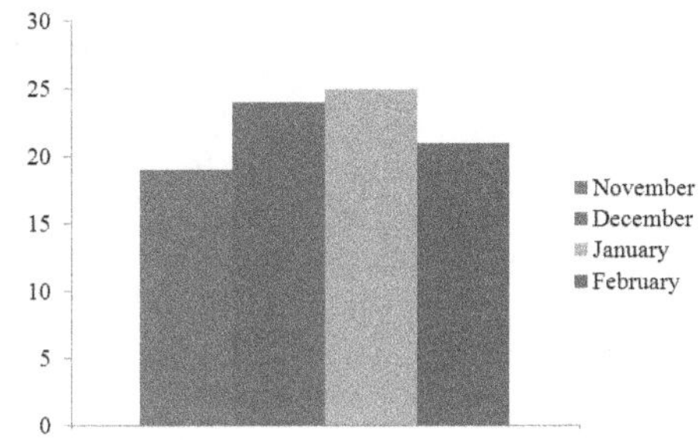

Figure 1: Unique malware detections by month

Finally, in terms of type of malware each of these detections was classified based on the information provided by the AV product. Figure 2 shows the distribution of malware detections by type. As we can see, almost all detections were classified as trojans, while viruses and adware have a relatively weak representation.

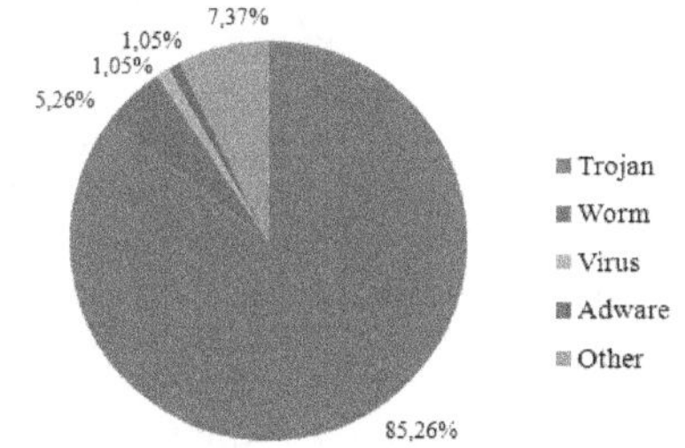

Figure 2: Malware detections by type

These figures are somewhat similar to those reported for overall infections by other AV vendors. For example, the first 2012 quarterly report from Panda Security [18], indicates that trojans account for most detections with a ratio of 63.30%, while worm, virus, adware and other have respectively ratios of 8.39%, 7.90%, 7.81% and 9.60%. Nonetheless, the differences with our results could be partially attributed to differences in the classification methods. For example, a file can be classified as a trojan by the AV product being evaluated and as a virus by another product. Furthermore, statistical error could be significant since our results are only based on a collection of 95 malware samples, while those of Panda Security are probably based on thousands of different samples.

While a detailed analysis of the causes and means by which these threats ended up on the computers still remains to be done in future work, we already know that 17 of these malware propagated through portable storage devices.

4.2 Missed Detections

Our experimental protocol [14, 13] describes in detail the monthly procedure for identifying and classifying suspicious files that were not detected by the AV. This process of identification and classification is based on user reporting of suspicious machine behaviour, the analysis of logs from the monitoring tools, the results of automated queries to on-line sources with respect to processes found on the machine, file and start-up programme databases (obtained automatically by scripts that we wrote), and any other relevant piece of information that the technician conducting the review might deem relevant.

Suspicious files found on the computer were classified into four categories: dangerous, suspicious, safe and unrated. All files marked as dangerous, suspicious and unrated were subjected to a more in-depth analysis. When we suspected that a file might be dangerous, additional data were collected with the consent of the user, including the actual browsing history, the suspicious file, and other related files present on the computer.

Our analysis identified 20 possible infections on 12 different machines. The most useful detection tool was HijackThis, which was involved in identifying 18 of the suspected infections. SpyBHORemover helped us find one additional infection. The last suspected infection was reported by the user, who called the project manager using the provided contact number when he suspected that his machine had been infected. All suspicious files were captured during the monthly visits, except for the user-reported suspected infection. While the logs show the location and filename, the file could not be retrieved as it seems that the suspected malware uninstalled itself between the time the user called in and the following lab visit. All captured files (19 out of 20) were later scanned with the evaluated AV product to see if they would be detected *a posteriori*. Even several months after the end of the experiment, none were detected by the AV product or identified as a potential threat. We scanned the captured files *a posteriori* with the VirusTotal service to compare the results obtained by several AV products and to compare these later results with those obtained a few months earlier. Additionally, we searched the Internet to find as much detail as we could for each of these 20 detections. As a result of this analysis, we classified two of the samples as clean, seven as unwanted software, nine as adware, one as definite malware, and one as suspected (but unconfirmed) malware.

The detected adware samples were either BHO or toolbars. In all cases, they were unknowingly installed by the users. Their effects included changing the web browser home page, redirecting web searches, or displaying advertisements. Further analysis will be required to determine if these adware are indeed malicious, in that they show additional behaviour that might have further consequences for the user than those described (e.g. theft of personal/private information). While we have not yet analysed in detail the two suspected malware samples, we have confirmed that one of them is rogueware. As previously mentioned, the corresponding user contacted us to inform us that his laptop was probably infected. It turned out that the laptop was infected with the fake "AV Security Scanner". Windows were regularly appearing to inform the user that harmful software was on his computer and every application started was killed except for web browsers. In order to get rid of these infections, the user was invited to register and provide his contact and payment information. At that moment, the user suspected that he may be infected and contacted us. As explained before, since the files disappeared from the computer before it was brought in for inspection, it was not possible for us to verify if the AV product detected this threat *a posteriori*.

Overall, 18 threats have been detected on 10 machines, which represents 20% of the users. One first point of comparison is the above-mentioned Eurostat report. Unfortunately, that report does not provide separate infection statistics for the population with and without AV installed. However, if we assume a theoretical comparison population with the same ratio of with/without AV (84% and 16%, respectively) and the same infection rates as we observed or inferred (20% and 38%), this would give a combined infection rate of 23%, in comparison with the self-reported 31% combined infection ratio of the Eurostat report. It has been said that the Eurostat report might have been an underestimation due to users only being able to notice a fraction of the actual infections, but it can be equally argued that they might be exaggerated due to users being paranoid and attributing performance problems to "viruses". Closer examination of the Eurostat results indicate a strong variance of reported infection percentage by EU countries, e.g. low twenties for Germany, Netherlands, Finland, and 40% and higher for many Eastern European countries. Thus, it would appear the lower infection ratio observed for our Canadian users might be related to geographical factors (whether location or cultural).

Another point of comparison is the SurfRight report [25]. Over a period of 55 days, 107,435 users used the Scan Cloud product, 73% of which were found to have an up-to-date AV product installed. Of those, Scan Cloud found that 32% were infected, while 46% of unprotected machines were infected. In comparison with our 20% and 38% ratio, it would appear that our sample population was less at risk than those using SurfRight's Scan Cloud. One possible explanation is simply that one of the motivations for using such a product is that the user already suspects that his machine is infected, probably a good indicator that it already is.

In all cases, it is important to point that straight comparison of these numbers is not significant given the fact that the definition and classification methods for threats in these studies are quite different. In our case we depend on a classification given by the Trend Micro AV product and our own investigations, similarly as for the SurfRight date, while the Eurostat results totally depend on user's self-assessment.

4.3 User Profiling and Behaviour

We examined whether an increase in certain types of user behaviour leads to a higher probability of the users' system being infected with malware. We also investigated whether user demographic factors and characteristics had any bearing on incidences of infection.

4.3.1 *Characteristics and demographic factors*

We examined whether gender, age, employment/student status, and work/study domain, and computer expertise had any relationship with likelihood of getting infected. To test the impact of these characteristic and demographic factors, we divided the users in two groups. The first group contains *at-risk* users, which are those who received at least one detection, and the second group contains *low-risk* users who received no detections during the experiment. Table 1 shows the users distribution between the total population and the at-risk group based on user characteristics and demographic factors.

Table 1: Proportion of users for each factor

Factor		Total population	At-risk population
Gender	Male	60%	61%
	Female	40%	39%
Age	18-24	38%	35%
	25-35	38%	48%
	36+	24%	17%
Status	Student	64%	70%
	Worker	30%	26%
	Unemployed	6%	4%
Field	Computer Science	26%	22%
	Natural Sciences	52%	48%
	Arts/Humanities	22%	30%
Computer Expertise	High	18%	31%
	Low	82%	69%

The results in Table 1 suggest that age and computer expertise could potentially be risk factors for increased incidence of infection. We therefore conducted statistical analysis to determine whether this was the case.

Prior to our analysis, we performed a residual analysis in order to find the presence of outliers among the data with respect to the number of detections. The normal probability plot of raw residuals, as shown in Figure 3, allowed us to identify the presence of one outlier (who had 28 unique detections), reducing the sample to 49 users.

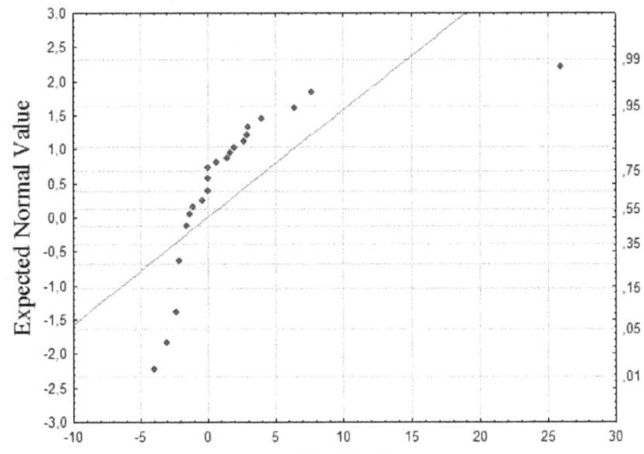

Figure 3: Normal probability plot of raw residuals

We conducted a logistic regression analysis to assess if particular characteristic and demographic factors may increase the infection risk. The dependent variable was the level of risk (at-risk vs. low-risk groups). It was indicated by either 1 or 0, depending on whether the user was exposed to any threats during the experiment. Results of the logistic regression analysis are summarised in Table 2. Items in bold are statistically significant.

We also used one-way ANOVA tests to assess whether the number of unique detections was affected by the characteristics and demographic factors. Results of the ANOVAs are presented in Table 3. In all cases, we consider $p < 0.05$ as statistically significant.

Table 2: Logistic regression analysis comparing risk of exposure

Factor	χ^2	p-value
Gender	0.098	0.75
Age	2.220	0.34
Status	0.465	0.80
Field	0.307	0.86
Computer expertise	**0.299**	**0.042**

Table 3: One-Way ANOVA comparing the number of unique detections

Factor	SS	MS	F	p
Gender	10.36	10.36	1.69	0.20
Age	19.25	9.62	1.58	0.22
Status	5.10	2.55	0.40	0.67
Field	21.56	10.78	1.79	0.18
Computer Expertise	4.41	4.41	0.70	0.41

Gender.

The total population included 30 males and 20 females which gives a proportion of 60% and 40% respectively. Table 1 shows that the gender distribution among the 23 at-risk users is 61% for the males and 39% for the females. The logistic regression analysis revealed no statistically significant differences between males and females (Table 2) with respect to exposure to threats.

We next examined the number of detections to determine whether there were any differences between the two groups. Figure 4 suggests that there is a minor difference in the average number of unique detections between males and females. However, statistical analysis reveals no statistically significant difference between males and females for number of unique detections (Table 3). While previous studies [15, 16] have addressed gender difference in computer security, to the best of our knowledge, no empirical experiment has evaluated gender differences in risk of infection. Our statistical tests suggest that gender is not a risk factor.

Age.

We divided our users into three age groups as evenly as possible (although we note that the older age group has fewer users due to our sample). Table 1 shows that the proportion of 18 to 24-year-olds who are at-risk is almost the same as for the total population. For those 25 to 35, the proportion in the at-risk group (48%) is higher than for the total population (38%). And for the group 36+ age group, we observe a slight decrease of 7% in the proportion between the total population and the at-risk group. Our logistic regression re-

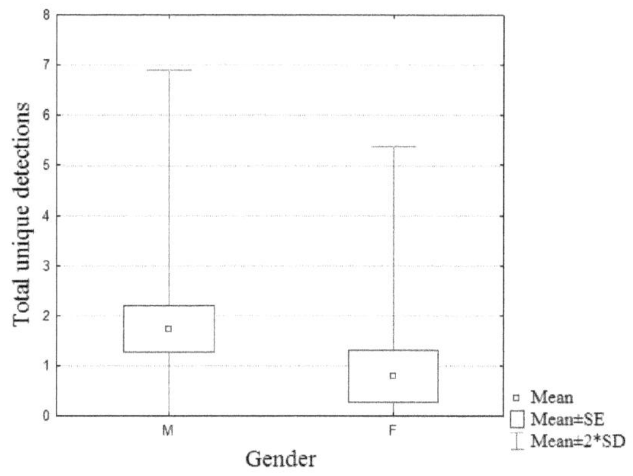

Figure 4: Box plot of unique detections by gender

sults (Table 2) show no statistically significant difference for the impact of the age on exposure to threats.

We further investigated whether the number of detections was impacted by age of the participant. Figure 5 mildly suggests differences between age groups, however these results were not statistically significant (Table 5).

Unlike the previous studies mentioned in Section 2 [16, 21, 17] that concluded that younger users are more at-risk, our statistical results suggest that age is not a significant risk factor. This discrepancy can be explained first because the experimental methods are quite different: all of them involve surveys of users where susceptibility levels are evaluated either through a theoretical model or from user self-declarations of previous incidents, and not from actual observation. Second, these results are not (all) specific to malware infections. Finally, the granularity of the age data recorded is different (coarse in our case) so it is hard to compare precisely these discrepancies, especially since the age distributions are quite different.

In any case, what is clear is that none of these studies, including ours, can be used to make categorical statements about risk and age, as all of these studies were based on biased samples of the population, i.e. students and other persons recruited on campus. Large scale studies with more uniform population sampling will be required to settle the issue of age as a risk factor for malware infections.

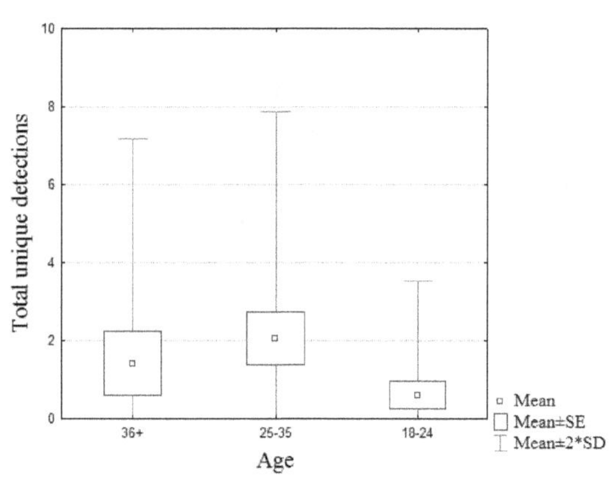

Figure 5: Box plot of unique detections by age

Status.

Participants were classified in three categories: students, workers, or unemployed. Table 1 indicates that the proportion between the total population and the at-risk group is quite similar for each category. Logistic regression confirms that no statistically significant differences exist.

Similarly, Figure 6 illustrates the relationship between these categories and the number of detections. Results of the ANOVA show no statistically significant differences (Table 3), further supporting that student/employment status is not a risk factor.

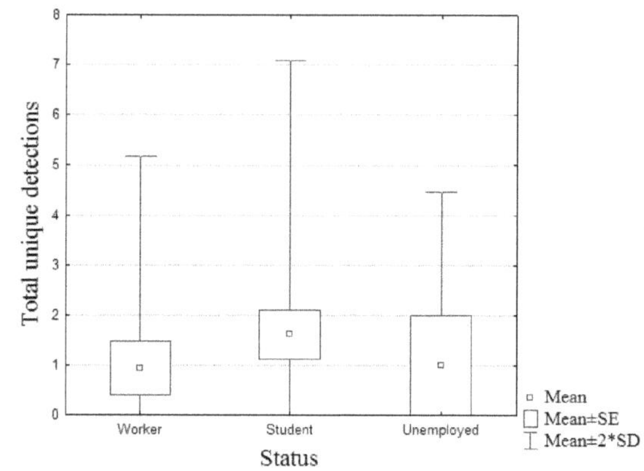

Figure 6: Box plot of unique detections by student/employment status

Work/study domain.

We recruited participants based on their domain of work or study in order to have a representative sample. As shown in Table 1, 26.5% of participants self-identified as being in computer science/information technology fields, 47% in natural sciences and 26.5% in arts and humanities. Although the table suggests that those in the Arts/Humanities might be slightly more at-risk, results of the Logistic Regression (Table 2) show no statistically significant differences between the three groups.

Figure 7 presents the average number of unique detections per domain. Interestingly, it appears that participants in the Arts/Humanities have fewer detections. However, these differences were not statistically significant (Table 3). Our statistical tests provide no support indicating that domain of work or study is a risk factor.

Computer expertise.

We assessed computer expertise by asking users about their proficiency with certain technical tasks. Users were considered to have a high level of computer expertise if they had previously completed all of the following tasks: configured a home network, created a web page, and installed or re-installed an operating system on a computer. Overall, 18% of users were classified as computer experts for the purposes of our analysis. As observed in Table 1, those with high expertise were nearly twice as likely to be in the high-risk group when compared to the total population. This may indicate that a high level of expertise increases the risk of exposure to threats. This was confirmed by the logistic

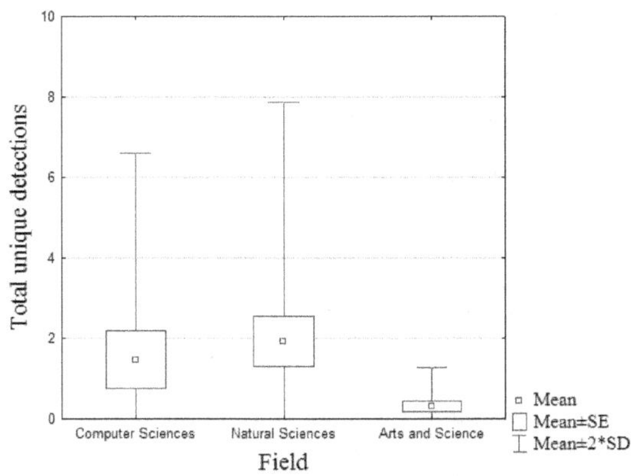

Figure 7: Box plot of unique detections by domain expertise

regression which shows that those with high computer expertise were statistically more likely to be exposed to threats.

As illustrated in Figure 8, we further compared the number of detections between the high and low computer expertise groups. Higher variance is apparent for the high-expertise group, but the differences are not statistically significant (Table 3). Our results suggest that while computer experts are more likely to have at least one exposure to threats, overall they do not see a higher number of detections.

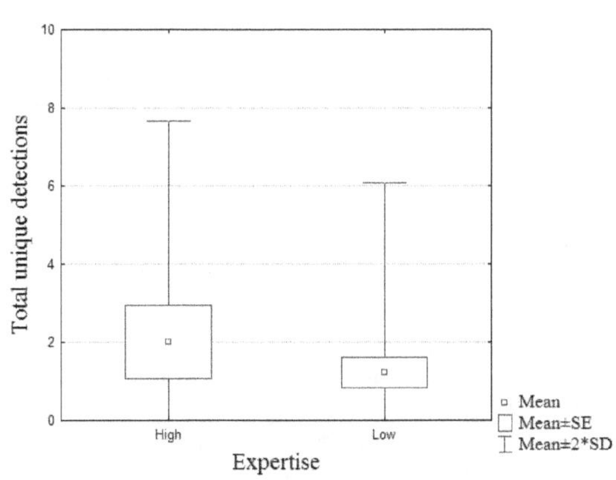

Figure 8: Box plot of unique detections by computer expertise

Summary of user characteristics.

In summary, we found little evidence linking user characteristics to increased risk of threat exposure. Gender, age, student/employment status, and domain of expertise showed no statistically significant differences. However, we did find partial support linking high computer expertise to increased risk of exposure.

4.3.2 Behavioural factors

To assess if specific user behaviours led to a higher risk of infection, we focused our analysis on 4 variables: most used browser, total number of applications installed, total number of websites visited, and categories of websites visited.

Using a similar approach to that described in section 4.3.1, we first conducted a logistic regression analysis where users were divided in two groups: at-risk and low-risk users. Secondly, we performed a general regression analysis to assess if there was a relationship between the behavioural factors analysed and the number of unique detections. General regression analysis was chosen instead of ANOVA because some of the independent variables represent continuous values (e.g. the number of gambling websites visited) rather than categorical data. Table 4 summarises the statistical results. Items in bold are statistically significant.

Browser.

Each month, users were asked which web browser they used most. We compiled these results in order to obtain for each user the most frequently used browser for the entire duration of the study. Table 5 summarises the proportion of users who utilised each web browser for the total population and the at-risk population. Even though a small increase is observed between the two populations for Chrome, our logistic regression analysis revealed no statistically significant differences between the two groups with respect to the type of browser used.

Table 5: Most frequently used browser

Browser	Total population	At-risk population
Internet Explorer	30%	17.4%
Firefox	30%	26.1%
Chrome	40%	56.5%

We also studied whether the use of a specific browser may influence the number of unique detections per user. To this end, the results obtained from our general regression analysis in Table 4 confirm our previous findings. The usage of a specific web browser is not related to the risk of infection.

Applications installed.

We monitored the number of applications installed by each user. To assess the potential effect of number of applications on the risk of infection, we performed a logistic regression, as shown in Table 4, which suggests that installing many applications may increase the exposure to malware and thus the probability of being infected.

This finding is also supported by our general regression analysis which shows that number of applications installed significantly impacts the number of detections (Table 4). The more a user installs applications, the more he is likely to get infections, as illustrated in Figure 9. Our analysis supports the idea that number of applications is a risk factor for infection.

Websites visited.

The number of websites visited was also recorded for the entire duration of the study to evaluate the impact on the risk of infection. Figure 10 shows that at-risk users visited many more websites than low-risk users, suggesting that visiting many websites could potentially increase exposure to threats. Logistic regression analysis confirms this finding (Table 4), showing that the number of websites significantly impacts the risk of exposure.

Table 4: Statistical analysis results of user behaviour factors

	Logistic Regression		General Regression	
Factor	χ^2	p-value	t-value	p-value
Type of browser	2.563	0.278	0.75	0.50
Number of applications installed	**4.709**	**0.030**	**2.29**	**0.03**
Total number of websites visited	**6.247**	**0.012**	1.71	0.09
Number of streaming media/MP3 sites visited	**11.999**	**0.001**	**3.372**	**0.001**
Number of peer-to-peer sites visited	**6.864**	**0.009**	1.942	0.064
Number of Internet Infrastructure sites visited	**7.469**	**0.006**	**5.466**	**0.000**
Number of Software download sites visited	**14.326**	**0.000**	**4.012**	**0.000**
Number of Sports sites visited	**4.194**	**0.041**	**2.601**	**0.013**
Number of Social Networking sites visited	**6.260**	**0.012**	1.965	0.056
Number of Computers/Internet sites visited	**7.357**	**0.007**	**2.292**	**0.026**
Number of Gambling sites visited	**4.998**	**0.025**	**3.601**	**0.001**
Number of Pornography sites visited	2.930	0.087	**6.425**	**0.000**
Number of Illegal/Questionable sites visited	0.022	0.881	**2.697**	**0.025**
Number of Translator/Cached sites visited	1.689	0.194	**5.799**	**0.000**

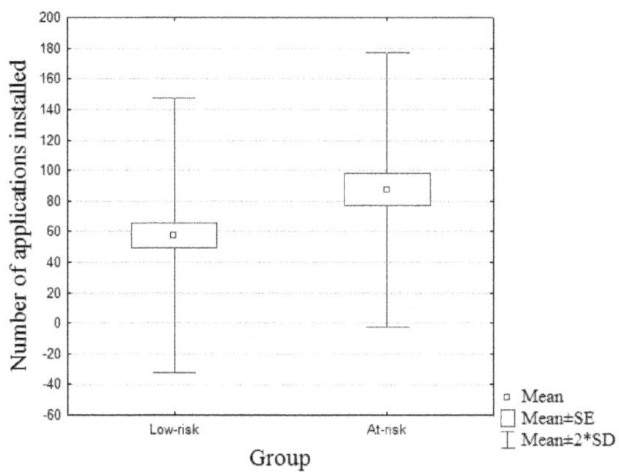

Figure 9: Box plot of applications installed by group

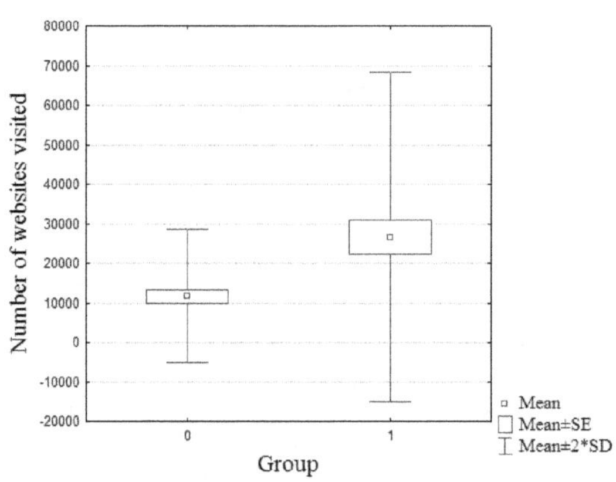

Figure 10: Box plot of websites visited by group

However, our general regression analysis did not confirm that the number of websites visited is a significant risk factor. The associated p-value (0.09) is under 0.1, which could suggest that the effect may be a potential risk factor that would need to be validated in a larger-scale study.

Type of websites visited.

We further wanted to analyse if particular types of websites were more prone to causing malware exposure. To this end, we classified each website visited using the Site Safety Center of Trend Micro [26]. We then performed a logistic regression using the number of websites visited for each category to determine if some categories were riskier. As shown in Table 4, our results allowed us to identify eight risky categories: streaming media/MP3, peer-to-peer, Internet infrastructure, software downloads, sports, social networking, and computers/Internet and gambling.

The general regression analysis showed quite similar results (Table 4) with nine categories showing that more frequent visits led to higher number of detections. Statistically significant results were found for the following categories: streaming media/MP3, infrastructure sites, software download, sports, computers/Internet, gambling, pornography, illegal/questionable and translator/cached. Our results indicate that type of website visited is a risk factor for infection.

Summary of user behaviour.

We have been able to identify three different risk factors related to user behaviour. We found that users who install many applications are more prone to install infected applications, thus increasing his risk of being infected. Also, visiting many websites could be considered as a risk factor as some pages have malicious code that is automatically executed. Finally, we have also confirmed that certain categories of websites place users at a greater risk of getting infected.

5. DISCUSSION

The results we have obtained and discussed here are subject to certain limitations. For one, the AV performance evaluation is limited to only 113 detected threats, a very small number compared to the numerous threats in the wild, especially considering that some of these may be false positives. In addition, the false negative number might also be underestimated due to the fact that we cannot guarantee that our protocol caught all malware missed by the AV. In other words, we do not have absolute ground truth.

One obvious limitations of the study concerns potential biases in selection of the population. First of all, subjects were located in the Greater Montréal area. Second, their age distribution is different from that of Canadian Internet users. However, unlike some of the studies discussed, ours is not restricted to undergraduate students in the 18-24 group; in our study, they represent only 38% of our subjects.

Another potential source of bias might have been the fact the users knew that they were part of a computer security experiment. This knowledge might have caused them to alter their usage of their laptop. We asked that question in the exit survey and 43 users claimed that they did not modify their behaviour. Of the other 7 users, 2 admitted having modified their behaviour to fulfil experiment constraints (no OS reinstallation, creation of partitions, etc.), 2 others admitted voluntarily not performing potentially embarrassing activities on the computer, 1 mentioned refraining from visiting secure Internet banking sites, 1 admitted forcing himself to use the computer more frequently, and the last one explained that he controlled access to his computer in order to ensure being its only user. All in all, and considering the usage statistics we gathered show normal to high levels of computer and web activity, and given the fact that the laptops were sold to and were to be kept by the subjects, we are confident this potential experimental bias did not significantly affect our results.

Finally, even though we were able to determine several factors correlated with risk of infection, these factors in themselves are not sufficient to explain the causal link leading to infection. To this effect, a more detailed analysis of the collected data is required in order to determine the sources and means of infection for each of the 113 detected threats. Only then will we be able to determine which of these of these factors are causes of infection, and which are consequences of other causal common factors that were not considered in this study, e.g. risk averseness or risk propensity of users, etc.

In terms of applications, we believe the single product field study methodology described in this paper is of potential utility in at least two contexts. One is that it should be suitable for AV vendors seeking to understand how their products perform in real-world usage and might help identify which aspects of the product (user interface, detection, remediation, etc.) could be further improved. The other is to help understand what characteristics of user behaviour lead to higher risks of infection. These characteristics could be used to improve the content and targeting of user education and training; they could also be used by insurance companies to assess relative risk in IT insurance policies.

Today most AV tests are lab-based and designed to identify which AV products perform better than others, whether the purpose is to allow users to make a more educated choice of product or to help AV vendors determine R&D and marketing strategies. Given the advantages in term or ecological validity and availability of user data of field tests such as the one described here, a natural question is whether it is feasible to conduct a comparative field study of AV products to complement the results of lab-based comparative testing.

One of the major issues in lab-based comparative AV testing is ensuring that all AV products are evaluated under exactly the same conditions. Not only should they be tested in the same environment, but they should also be exposed to the same threats at the same time. While it is relatively easy to guarantee consistent conditions when tests are performed within a controlled environment, such consistency cannot be guaranteed in field studies. The exposition of the product to threats cannot be controlled as it is user driven. On the other hand, field studies are inherently unbiased in that threats applied to each AV are independently "chosen" by users who have no vested interest in the test results. Furthermore, the law of large numbers guarantees that for sufficiently large populations, each product will be exposed to a large enough sampling of threats to make the results statistically significant. In order words, and to eliminate bias in user-driven threat selection, comparative field studies should be conducted with a large enough population and over a large enough period of time to guarantee a statistically significant sample of user and malware behaviour. Based on our experiences documented here, we postulate that such a study should include at least 200 participants per AV tested and last at least four months to accomplish that aim.

Thus, if we are to compare multiple AV products, we can easily be looking at a study with a thousand or more subjects. Increasing to this scale will likely require increased use of automation to gather user feedback. Such automation, however, is potentially beneficial as well because it allows for feedback to be obtained in context, i.e. just after a user has interacted with the AV software. Care must be taken, though, to make sure the automated questions do not themselves overly influence the results.

It would also be nice to gather more detailed information about user behaviour and computer state. Any such efforts will require very careful ethical review. We note that medical clinical trials involve people revealing intimate life details and subjecting themselves sometimes to interventions that can potentially kill them. As such, it should be possible to create protocols that provide sufficient care for end users and their computers while providing greater insight into malware attacks and defences as they happen in the field.

6. CONCLUSION

We have presented the results from the first field study of anti-virus software performed with real users in non-laboratory conditions. While the population studied was small compared to medical clinical trials, it is comparable to that of other usability studies and was sufficient to obtain some interesting results with respect to infection risk factors.

In terms of AV performance, our results indicate that 38% of users got exposed to a threat caught by the AV, indicating that at least 38% of the population would have got infected had they had no AV installed. In addition, 20% of our users were found to have been infected by some form of undesirable software that was not detected by the AV. These figures are indeed alarming, but they are comparable with figures reported by other studies conducted by other methods (user self-reporting and on-line scanning of machines).

In terms of risk factors, our results show that user behaviour is indeed significant, thus confirming previous work in the area. However, our results show that user characteristics such as age or gender are not significant risk factors, contradicting related research. We observed some surprising patterns in web browsing risk, with seemingly innocuous categories of sites such as sports and Internet infrastructure being associated with a higher rate of infection while more "shady" sites such those containing pornography and illegal/questionable content were less so. And somewhat non-intuitively, we found that computer expertise is a weak factor *increasing* the risk of infection.

Beyond the contribution of these results, this work demonstrates that field studies are a viable alternative to lab-based

AV evaluation. The methodological issues are comparable to that of other computer science user studies, particularly those in usable security. While studies comparing multiple AV or other security products will require larger populations to get statistically significant results, increasing use of automation should allow such studies to be performed at relatively modest cost. We thus believe the work presented here illustrates the merits of future larger scale clinical trials of AV and other security software.

7. ACKNOWLEDGMENTS

This project was funded by Trend Micro and Canada's Natural Sciences and Engineering Research Council (NSERC), through the Inter-networked Systems Security Network (ISSNet) Strategic Research Network, the Discovery Grant programme, and a Canada Research Chair (fourth author).

8. REFERENCES

[1] F. Asgharpour, D. Liu, and L. J. Camp. Mental models of computer security risks. In *Workshop on the Economics of Information Security (WEIS)*, 2007.

[2] AV Comparatives. File detection test of malicious software. Technical report, AV Comparatives, 2013.

[3] D. Botta, R. Werlinger, A. Gagne, K. Beznosov, L. Iverson, S. Fels, and B. Fisher. Towards understanding IT security professionals and their tools. In *ACM Symposium on Usable Privacy and Security (SOUPS)*, pages 100–111, 2007.

[4] J. Canto, M. Dacier, E. Kirda, and C. Leita. Large scale malware collection: lessons learned. In *IEEE SRDS Workshop on Sharing Field Data and Experiment Measurements on Resilience of Distributed Computing Systems*, 2008.

[5] A. De Luca, M. Langheinrich, and H. Hussmann. Towards understanding ATM security: a field study of real world ATM use. In *ACM Symposium on Usable Privacy and Security (SOUPS)*, 2010.

[6] Eurostat. Nearly one third of internet users in the EU27 caught a computer virus. `http://epp.eurostat.ec.europa.eu/cache/ITY_PUBLIC/4-07022011-AP/EN/4-07022011-AP-EN.PDF`, February 2011.

[7] I. Gashi, V. Stankovic, C. Leita, and O. Thonnard. An experimental study of diversity with off-the-shelf antivirus engines. In *IEEE International Symposium on Network Computing and Applications (NCA)*, 2009.

[8] S. Gordon and R. Ford. Real world anti-virus product reviews and evaluations: the current state of affairs. In *National Information Systems Security Conference*, 1996.

[9] D. Harley and A. Lee. Who will test the testers. In *18th Virus Bulletin International Conference*, pages 199–207, 2008.

[10] J. Kephart and S. White. Directed-graph epidemiological models of computer viruses. In *IEEE Symposium on Security and Privacy*, 1991.

[11] S. Kondakci. Epidemic state analysis of computers under malware attacks. *Modelling Practice and Theory*, 16:571–584, 2008.

[12] P. Kosinar, J. Malcho, R. Marko, , and D. Harley. AV testing exposed. In *20th Virus Bulletin International Conference*, 2010.

[13] F. Lalonde-Levesque. Évaluation d'un produit de sécurité par essai clinique. Master's thesis, École Polytechnique de Montréal, August 2013.

[14] F. Lalonde-Levesque, C. Davis, J. Fernandez, S. Chiasson, and A. Somayaji. Methodology for a field study of anti-malware software. In *Workshop on Usable Security (USEC)*, pages 80–85. LNCS, 2012.

[15] F. Lalonde-Levesque, C. Davis, J. Fernandez, and A. Somayaji. Evaluating antivirus products with field studies. In *22th Virus Bulletin International Conference*, pages 87–94, September 2012.

[16] G. R. Milne, L. I. Labrecque, and C. Cromer. Toward an understanding of the online consumer's risky behavior and protection practices. *Journal of Consumer Affairs*, 43:449–473, 2009.

[17] F. T. Ngo and R. Paternoster. Cybercrime victimization: An examination of individual and situational level factors. *International Journal of Cyber Criminology*, 5(1):773–793, 2011.

[18] Panda Security Labs. Panda Labs quarterly report January - March 2012. `http://press.pandasecurity.com/wp-content/uploads/2012/05/Quarterly-Report-PandaLabs-January-March-2012.pdf`, 2012.

[19] PC Security Labs. Security solution review on Windows 8 platform. Technical report, PC Security Labs, 2013.

[20] J. A. Rode. Digital parenting: designing children's safety. In *British Human Computer Interaction Conference (British HCI)*, pages 244–251, 2009.

[21] S. Sheng, M. Holbrook, P. Kumaraguru, L. F. Cranor, and J. Downs. Who falls for phish? A demographic analysis of phishing susceptibility and effectiveness of interventions. In *ACM Conference on Human Factors in Computing Systems (CHI)*, pages 373–382, 2010.

[22] R. Shyamasundar, H. Shah, and N. Kumar. Malware: from modelling to practical detection. *Distributed Computing and Internet Technology*, pages 21–39, 2010.

[23] K. Solic and V. Ilakovac. Security perception of a portable PC user (the difference between medical doctors and engineers): A pilot study. In *Medicinski Glasnik*, volume 6, pages 261–264, 2009.

[24] A. Somayaji, Y. Li, H. Inoue, J. Fernandez, and R. Ford. Evaluating security products with clinical trials. In *USENIX Workshop on Cyber Security Experimentation and Test (CSET)*, 2009.

[25] SurfRight. 32% of computers still infected, despite presence of antivirus program. `http://www.surfright.nl/en/home/press/32-percent-infected-despite-antivirus`, 2009.

[26] Trend Micro. Website classification. `http://solutionfile.trendmicro.com/solutionfile/Consumer/new-web-classification.html`, 2012.

[27] J. Vrabec and D. Harley. Real performance? In *EICAR Annual Conference*, 2010.

[28] R. Wash. Folk models of home computer security. In *ACM Symposium on Usable Privacy and Security (SOUPS)*, page 11, 2010.

Delta: Automatic Identification of Unknown Web-based Infection Campaigns

Kevin Borgolte, Christopher Kruegel, Giovanni Vigna
Department of Computer Science
University of California, Santa Barbara
Santa Barbara, California, United States of America
kevinbo,chris,vigna@cs.ucsb.edu

ABSTRACT

Identifying malicious web sites has become a major challenge in today's Internet. Previous work focused on detecting if a web site is malicious by dynamically executing JavaScript in instrumented environments or by rendering web sites in client honeypots. Both techniques bear a significant evaluation overhead, since the analysis can take up to tens of seconds or even minutes per sample.

In this paper, we introduce a novel, purely static analysis approach, the Δ-system, that (i) extracts change-related features between two versions of the same website, (ii) uses a machine-learning algorithm to derive a model of web site changes, (iii) detects if a change was malicious or benign, (iv) identifies the underlying infection vector campaign based on clustering, and (iv) generates an identifying signature.

We demonstrate the effectiveness of the Δ-system by evaluating it on a dataset of over 26 million pairs of web sites by running next to a web crawler for a period of four months. Over this time span, the Δ-system successfully identified previously unknown infection campaigns. Including a campaign that targeted installations of the Discuz!X Internet forum software by injecting infection vectors into these forums and redirecting forum readers to an installation of the Cool Exploit Kit.

Categories and Subject Descriptors

C.2.0 [**Computer-Communication Networks**]: General—*Security and protection*; D.4.6 [**Software Engineering**]: Security and Protection—*Invasive software (malware)*; H.3.3 [**Information Storage and Retrieval**]: Information Search and Retrieval—*Clustering, Information filtering, Selection process*

Keywords

computer security; web-based malware; malware detection; infection vector identification; infection campaigns; clustering; trend detection; web dynamics

CCS'13, November 4–8, 2013, Berlin, Germany.

ACM 978-1-4503-2477-9/13/11 ...$15.00.
http://dx.doi.org/10.1145/2508859.2516725.

1 INTRODUCTION

The rapid growth and widespread access to the Internet, and the ubiquity of web-based services make it easy to communicate and interact globally. However, the software used to implement the functionality of web sites is often vulnerable to different attack vectors, such as cross-site scripting or SQL injections, and access policies might not be properly implemented. An attacker can exploit these server-side vulnerabilities to inject malicious code snippets, called *infection vectors*, which, in turn, attack visitors through drive-by install or download attacks. Drive-by install and download attacks try to exploit client-side vulnerabilities to download or install malware, or lure the user into installing malware. If an attacker finds a server-side vulnerability that affects multiple web sites (possibly thousands), he can automate the exploitation, search for other vulnerable web sites, and launch a carefully crafted infection campaign in order to maximize the number of potential victims.

Recent reports by the security company Sophos [1, 2] show that in 2012 over 80% of all web sites attacking users were infected legitimate web sites, such as those of trade associations, nightclubs, television companies or elementary schools. All of these web sites had been altered, in one way or another, to attack visitors. In another case, in early 2013, web sites hosting documentation for software developers were modified to serve carefully crafted infection vectors that exploited client-side vulnerabilities, which were then leveraged as the first stepping stone in sophisticated attacks against Twitter [3], Facebook's engineering team [4], and Apple [5].

Major challenges in detecting infection vectors are that web sites become more and more dynamic and that their static content changes regularly, i.e., the underlying infection vector might not be clearly visible to analysis tools, or even to well-trained human security analysts. Adding new content to the web site, showing different, personalized advertisements, or even comments left by visitors are legitimate modifications. Yet, these modifications force the user to reevaluate the maliciousness of the web site, either through an automatic detection system or by manually inspecting any new content prior to its inclusion into the web site. Unwanted modifications to a web site on the other hand, i.e., changes from which a user might want himself to be protected, include defacements or the insertion of exploit code to infect visitors of the web site with malware. Previous work in the area of web evolution [6–10] suggests that web sites do not change randomly, but that they evolve constantly through small changes, and, if one takes into account personalized advertisements, a change might happen at every visit, which, in turn, makes it necessary to analyze the web sites on each visit.

The current state of the art in protecting a user from malicious content is mainly realized through blacklists, which are queried before the web site is rendered or retrieved by the web browser. The *Google Safe Browsing* list [11] is likely the most prominent example. By definition, blacklists are reactive, which is an undesirable property for any protection mechanism because a malicious web site can potentially stay undetected for an extended period of time. Once a web site is blacklisted, its operator must go to great lengths to remove his/her web site from the blacklist, although it might have become benign. Such a removal process can take a frustrating amount of time since it is often subject to some form of verification that the web site is now benign, a process that might not happen immediately. More important, however, is that each web site infected as part as an infection campaign needs to be identified and added to the blacklist even though the web sites attack visitors in the same, well-known way. Clearly, a proactive approach is preferable for both unknown and known infection vectors. On the other hand, scanning a web site proactively with online analyzer systems [12–14] is computationally very expensive, and would introduce delays up to multiple seconds per web site. Since such a delay is undesirable, it is unlikely that such a proactive approach would be deployed in a general setting, or that it would find its way into current browsers as a protection mechanism.

It is important to mention that, generally, the same infection vector is reused by an attacker and spread among a multitude of different web sites to maximize its impact; however, some parts of the infection vector might be randomized. Often, the infected web sites are from a single community, e.g., in a targeted attack on this community, they employ the same underlying software stack, or they share a web server that was attacked. Recent examples include attacks targeting installations of the Apache web server to replace the web server's executable with the backdoor "Linux/Cdorked.A" [15, 16], which injects code to redirect visitors of the web site to exploit pages. These compromised web sites are not necessarily targeted, they usually follow a simple pattern: the infection vector was inserted in the same or in a very similar way. Be it, as previously mentioned, through improper access control, exploited vulnerabilities in a web framework or application used by all web sites. Being able to identify an infection vector, instead of just detecting that the web site is malicious, can provide important feedback since the initial cause of the infection vector can be investigated much more easily due to additional information, such as commonalities in different observations of the same infection vector.

To overcome the limitations of current approaches mainly based on dynamic analysis of web sites, we introduce the Δ-system to identify malicious activity in a web site based on static analysis of the differences between the current and previous versions of the web site. We cluster these differences, determine if the introduced or removed elements are associated with malicious behavior, we identify the infection campaign it belongs to, pinpoint the actual infection vector, and automatically generate an identifying signature that can be leveraged for content-based protection.

The main contributions of this paper are the following:

- We introduce the Δ-system, which is based on a novel approach to statically analyze and detect web-based infection vectors, and which identifies infection campaigns based on features associated with modifications observed between two versions of a web site.
- We develop a tree difference algorithm that is resistant to tiny changes, such as typographical corrections or the small evolutionary modifications a web site undergoes.
- We develop a set of modification-motivated similarity measures to model the concepts of inserting and removing malicious behavior into and from a web site.
- We evaluate the Δ-system on a large scale dataset, containing 26 million unique pairs of web sites, to show its applicability in real-world scenarios in terms of infection campaign detection and identification capabilities.

2 Δ-SYSTEM DESIGN

The Δ-system, instead of trying to solve the problem of deciding if a web site is malicious or benign provides a solution to the search problem of finding new infection campaigns and identifying similar, known infection campaigns. Nonetheless we are still interested in deciding if a web site's current behavior is malicious or benign. Instead of analyzing web sites in their entirety, the Δ-system investigates only the difference between two versions of the same web site.

The main idea of the Δ-system is to identify if the change made to a web site altered the behavior of the web site, i.e., if we can be certain that the new version of the web site is malicious or benign, by investigating if the modifications are similar to already observed ones, such as modifications associated with an ongoing infection campaign. In order to identify the changes that were made to a web site, we need a base version, i.e., an older version of the same web site.

The analysis process of our system is described hereinafter, followed by a discussion on potential uses of our system, and the impact of deploying the Δ-system.

2.1 Analysis Process

The Δ-system's analysis process follows a simple four-step process, which is shown in Figure 1, and whose steps are:

1. Retrieval and normalization of the web site.
2. Similarity measurement with respect to a base version.
3. Cluster assignment of the similarity vector.
4. Generation of the identifying signature.

Evidently, a base version of a web site has to be available. In the case that a local base version does not exist, however, we might still be able to retrieve an older version through web archives, such as the Internet Archive[1] or a web cache provided by a search engine. This makes our approach applicable for web sites that are visited rarely and were no local base version is kept, if we accept the overhead to retrieve the base version from a remote archive. While this might seem counter-intuitive because of the potentially large time difference between the archived and current version, we show in our evaluation that this is indeed a possible alternative.

Following this brief overview, we discuss the important steps of the analysis process in more detail. First, normalization of a web site; second, how the similarity to the base version is measured; third, how the identifying signature is generated.

2.1.1 Retrieval and Normalization

First, we retrieve the current version of a web site, for instance the web site a user requested. Then, after we have retrieved the source code of that web site, excluding all external references, such as included scripts or frames, we perform multiple normalization steps: we normalize capitalization of all tags, we reorder attributes of each tag and discard invalid attributes, and we normalize the quotation of an attribute's value. We perform this normalization step to ensure that functional equivalent tags are treated equally during our evaluation, and that changes such as changing the capitalization of a tag or switching from single to double quotes do not affect our final results.

[1]Internet Archive, `http://www.archive.org`

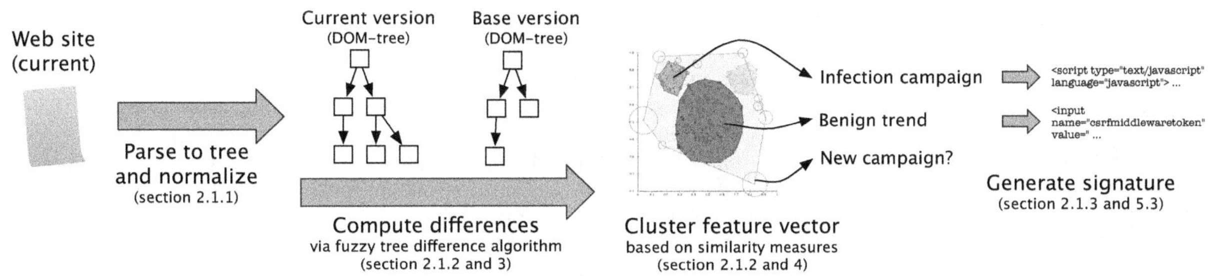

Figure 1: Analysis pipeline of the Δ-system.

2.1.2 *Similarity Measurement and Clustering*

Following these normalization steps, we measure the similarity to an already known (and normalized) base version. Measuring the similarity between two versions of the same web site in a meaningful way is non-trivial. The Δ-system first performs unordered tree-to-tree comparison via a novel algorithm that we introduce in Section 3. The algorithm extracts the nodes (or tags; subsequently, we use both terms interchangeably) from the Domain Object Model (DOM) tree of a web site that are different between base and current version. Second, based on the extracted nodes, we leverage a variety of different features to extract meaningful information from the two versions (described in detail in Section 4). The system then tries assigning these feature vectors to a cluster, or detects them as outliers, if they are not similar to any previously-observed modifications. Each different tag type, e.g., <input> or <script>, is treated separately, i.e., each type is assigned its own feature space; we do not project two tags of a different type into the same feature space. Additionally, due to the different nature of our features, where different distance metrics are essential for accurate cluster assignment, we perform consensus clustering for different groups: binary features, absolute and relative features are all treated as separate clustering instances. The cluster assignment and outlier detection process then distinguishes between three different cases:

- Assignment to an existing cluster:
  - Insertion or removal of an infection vector, if the cluster corresponds to a known infection campaign.
  - Legitimate modification, e.g., a version update of a library or the insertion of Facebook's like button, if the cluster does not correspond to an infection campaign.
- Detection as an outlier:
  - Potentially the start of a new infection campaign, if malicious behavior was inserted.
  - Potentially the end of a running infection campaign, if malicious behavior was removed.
  - A modification that is not of primary interest to us, such as a new article, template modifications, or a redesign of the web site.
- Formation of a new cluster (the similarity vector we are clustering and other vectors that are close, which were outliers before, put the number of total vectors in this area of the feature space above the threshold to form a new cluster, i.e., we observed the number of the same modification in the wild that we require to constitute a trend, c.f. Section 5.1):
  - New infection campaign, if the node was inserted and is associated with malicious behavior.
  - End of an infection campaign, if the node was removed and is associated with malicious behavior.
  - Legitimate modification, e.g., an update to a new, bleeding-edge version of a library or the content-management system used, such as Wordpress.

Upon cluster assignment of the similarity vector, we output the associated cluster, i.e., the corresponding trend (subsequently, we use these terms interchangeably). For instance, an infection campaign if the corresponding modification inserted or removed a known infection vector. Here, it is important to note that the detected clusters do not discriminate between removed and inserted nodes but treat them equally because we do not leverage the notion of removal or insertion in the feature computation, but attach it to the vector as "external" meta information that is not used during clustering. This supports the detection of removal and insertion of the same trend with the exact same cluster in both cases and, therefore, increases robustness of our system.

The Δ-system does not provide detection capabilities for malicious behavior on its own, but rather relies on an external detection system. This detection system is queried once a new cluster is formed to identify if this observed trend constitutes a malicious or a benign cluster. In order to guarantee a high likelihood, we "bootstrap" each cluster by querying for 10 random samples, and acquire a consensus decision for the returned labels. For instance, a new cluster is observed and 9 out of 10 of the random samples from this cluster have been assigned the label malicious, then the Δ-system will assign the label malicious to any new observation in this cluster.

2.1.3 *Signature Generation*

For each of the identified trends, we generate a signature that matches the textual representation of all of the nodes assigned to a cluster (e.g., a cluster describing "<script src='http://$random-url/exploit.js'>"). This signature is generated by simply interpreting the textual representation of each node as a deterministic finite automaton, merging them together, and calculating the minimal version, which can be done in polynomial time. The resulting DFA can then be translated into a regular expression that can be used by intrusion detection/prevention systems[2].

Such an identifying signature is, generally, an under-approximation of the actual (unknown) signature. For instance, in the above example the URL is randomized. Here, the generated signature only describes the observed samples, i.e., where $random-url might be "a.com" or "b.org", while the trend could be more general and also include "c.net". Leveraging only the identifying signature would miss web sites that follow the same trend, i.e., web sites who might serve the same infection vector. While this is of no concern in the case of

[2]Although generated signatures match normalized tags by default, it is trivial to normalize incoming data in the same way and match arbitrary tags that follow the same trend.

leveraging the Δ-system for every request (here, we would assign a similar, but unobserved, tag to the same cluster), it can be an issue if the generated signature is used as input to other tools. A possible remedy is to generalize the signature and to introduce a widening operator to describe the different parts of the nodes following this trend. For instance, one could simply widen 5 different characters at the same position in 5 different random samples picked from a cluster to an over-approximating wildcard. An over-approximation, however, is also likely to introduce incorrect matches, which is why we recommend using the Δ-system if no exact signature matched.

2.2 Use Cases

We see the Δ-system to be deployed in two main scenarios: next to a web crawler to actively search for new infection campaigns, and next to a proxy to identify infection campaigns (passive) or to improve user-protection (active). Additionally, there is a third, minor scenario: providing feedback on evasions of detection systems. Subsequently, we describe all three use cases in more detail, however, in the remaining of the paper, we focus on the first use case: paired with a web crawler.

The most interesting use case, in our opinion, is the active identification of new infection campaigns. In this case, one deploys the system side-by-side to a web crawler. While the web crawler retrieves potentially interesting web sites multiple times over a given period of time, our system analyzes the differences. When our system detects a new cluster, i.e., a significant number of very similar modifications, an external detection system then decides if this change is associated with malicious behavior or not. If malicious behavior was introduced then we found a new infection campaign and we can generate the identifying signature for this cluster. Based on the elements of the cluster, we can then pinpoint the infection vector (e.g., identify parts of the tag that are common among all web sites in that cluster) and investigate other similarities manually (e.g., only online stores running a specific version of the PHP application osCommerce were infected). Starting from those similarities, it is then possible to: generate a more precise fingerprint for the campaign, find other infections via search engines, and estimate the scope of an infection campaign.

The second envisioned deployment of the Δ-system is the extension of a web browser or a proxy. In most cases, the browser or proxy already caches visited web sites for performance reasons. Moreover, in security-sensitive environments, it is very likely that a detection system (e.g., an anti-malware engine) is already in place to ensure that only benign web sites can be accessed by the user. Such a detection system can be leveraged by the Δ-system to analyze inserted tags. The system can complement these tools to prevent repetitive scanning of web sites, to improve user experience by increasing analysis performance, and to provide insight into targeted attacks. For example, small changes a user might encounter include automatic page impressions counter, updated weather or date information, or the output of the processing time to render the web site on the server's side. While previous work requires the reevaluation of the entire web site, the Δ-system can identify these changes as benign much more easily. It is even possible to obtain more accurate results with our system than with the detection system, e.g., if it is based upon simple detection methods, such as fingerprinting of known malicious scripts, or if the detection system is being evaded. Additionally, once a malicious web site is identified, the Δ-system can verify that a malicious modification was removed and that the web site is now benign. Particularly, if an infection campaign is dormant or the exploit page is offline, dynamic analysis systems detect that the web site is benign because it does not detect any malicious behavior. Since the Δ-system is purely static and verifies that the malicious content was removed, it does not have this disadvantage.

Lastly, the Δ-system can also be leveraged to detect evasions and bugs in detection systems and online analyzers. For example, if the analyzer is dynamic, but behaves differently than a standard browser in even a single case, then malware can fingerprint the detection system. Such a fingerprinting method allows the attacker to thwart detection much more easily, for instance, without having to utilize a blacklist of the IP addresses used by the online analyzer. Leveraging our system, we can detect these evasions when they are introduced. The system can pinpoint the changed content precisely and, by doing this, support the developer in identifying the reason why the analyzer is behaving differently, correcting the corresponding bug, and preventing further evasions leveraging the same bug.

3 FUZZY TREE DIFFERENCE

First, to be able to measure the similarity between two web sites in a meaningful way, we need to define the notion of difference. We are primarily concerned if a web site behaves in a benign or malicious way. To this end, we need to understand what modifications to the content can result in behavioral changes, and how we can isolate the modifications from other parts of the web site that have no effect on the overall behavior. We identify these interesting parts by leveraging the hierarchical structure of a web site and interpreting a web site through its DOM tree.

Previous work introduced various algorithms to detect the semantic change in hierarchical structured data. The main idea behind HTML, i.e., describing how to display data instead of describing the semantics of the data itself, renders nearly all introduced XML-centered approaches unsuitable to extract meaningful information about the modifications. An often made assumption is that the underlying tree structure has a significant semantic relationship with the content, which is not necessarily the case for HTML. Moreover, leveraging standard maximum cardinality matching on cryptographic hashes and simple edge weights of 1 (based in the nature of cryptographic hash functions), any change would be visible, including very small changes that are uninteresting to us, such as single character or word changes and legitimate evolutions. We denote such a tree-to-tree comparison as *not tiny change resistant* or *not fuzzy*. To solve this problem, and to identify interesting modifications made to a web site more precisely and more efficiently, we generalize the previous notion of tree difference algorithms and introduce a similarity weight. We refer to our algorithm as the *fuzzy tree difference algorithm*, which is heavily influenced by the unordered tree-to-tree comparison algorithms by Chawathe et al. [17] and Wang et al. [18]. Such a fuzzy algorithm is necessary when comparing web sites that have evolved over an extended period of time, e.g., have been edited constantly over a two week period. Otherwise, the sheer number of remaining nodes to analyze makes it infeasible to leverage computationally expensive features with reasonable performance overhead.

While we provide a formal description of the algorithm in Algorithm 1, we give a brief informal description first: the algorithm expects three parameters, T_1, T_2 and t_r. T_1 and T_2 are normalized DOM trees, i.e., all tags are capitalized in the same way, all attributes occur in the same order and their values are enclosed in the same way (quote-wise). t_r is the threshold value for the similarity measurement, and can range from 0 to 1. Starting from the trees T_1 and T_2, we create a temporary graph to match pairs of similar nodes through maximum weighted bipartite graph matching (Hungarian algorithm [19]). This graph is constructed by inserting every node of T_1, then inserting every node of T_2. For each node from T_2, we connect it with an edge to every node from T_1 that has a similar fuzzy hash value (i.e., the Jaro distance of both hashes must be greater or equal to t_r) and that takes the exact same path (in the sense of unordered tree-traversal) as the node from T_2. The edge's weight is equal to the similarity measured through the Jaro distance between both hashes (i.e., at least t_r). Additionally, we color all matched nodes blue. In the last step, we remove the corresponding matched nodes from the trees T_1 and T_2 and output a list of removed (remaining in T_1) and inserted (remaining in T_2) nodes.

While the reason for coloring nodes might not be obvious, later on, we leverage the color of a node in the remaining nodes of T_1 and T_2 in our similarity measures to detect a matching asymmetry, i.e., if a tag with a very similar hash and the same path from the root node was matched, such as a template that was used more often in T_2 than in T_1.

The implementation of the Δ-system under evaluation leverages *ssdeep* [20] as the fuzzy hash function and a threshold of 0.99 for the Jaro distance [21] (which is normalized to 0 to 1, i.e., we require very similar tags). Similar to cryptographic hash functions like MD5 or SHA, a fuzzy hash function, such as *ssdeep*, maps arbitrary long values to a short hash. In contrast to cryptographic hash function, however, a fuzzy hash function maps similar values to similar hashes that can be then used to measure their similarity. This property allows us to efficiently compare nodes of the DOM tree or their content regardless of their actual length, which otherwise might be computational too expensive when using standard string similarity measures for longer tags or content. We selected the Jaro distance function to compare two hash values because it is a simple string similarity measure originally introduced for duplicate detection by Jaro [21] and best suited for short strings while accounting for exactly matched characters as well as transpositions, therefore it quantifies the similarity of fuzzy hashes for similar data accurately.

In general, a threshold value of 1 when used with a cryptographic hash function is equivalent to standard unordered tree-to-tree algorithms. On the other hand, a threshold value of 0 regardless of the hash function is equivalent to comparing every element to every other element and impractical for any modern web site due to the sheer number of possible combinations, which is why a reduction of potential matches is essential.

3.1 Example

An example of the tree difference algorithm is shown in Figure 2. The source code of a simple base version and current version of a web site are shown in Listing 1 and Listing 2 respectively. Two modifications to the source code were made: first, a head tag including a script tag with an external source URL was inserted, and, second, a typographical mistake in the class of the p tag was fixed and one word in its content was changed: "foo" was replaced by "bar". Figure 2 illustrates that for a standard tree difference algorithm the modified p tag would, correctly, constitute a modified p tag (the removed p tag is marked with a red chessboard pattern, while the inserted p tag is marked with a green diagonal pattern). However, since we are interested in severe changes and modifications associated with behavioral changes, these tiny changes are uninteresting to us, and, like the example shows, they are discarded by our algorithm.

Algorithm 1 Fuzzy Tree Difference

```
function FuzzyTreeDifference(T1, T2, tr)
    G ← Graph
    for all n ∈ T1.nodes do
        G ← G.insert_node(n)
    for all n ∈ T2.nodes do
        for all m ∈ T1.nodes do
            if path(m) = path(n) then
                d(m,n) ← jaro(hash(m), hash(n))
                if d(m,n) ≥ tr then
                    G.insert_node(n)
                    m.color ← blue
                    n.color ← blue
                    G.insert_edge(m, n, d(m,n))
    M ← max_weight_matching(G)
    for all (m, n) ∈ M do
        T1.remove_node(m)
        T2.remove_node(n)
    return T1, T2
```

4 SIMILARITY MEASURES / FEATURES

The most interesting part of web sites from a malicious code point of view is described by the HTML markup language: JavaScript, inline frames, or the use of plugins. Most research on document similarity, however, assumes that markup language is not of major interest and that it can be removed without substantial loss of information. For detecting infection vectors, this assumption does not hold. Essentially, this violation makes applying existing work in document similarity for identifying infection vectors impractical, because core elements are discarded.

Therefore, we introduce our own similarity measures. Once we have extracted the different tags between two versions of a web site, we can map each tag into the feature space in which we cluster similar changes together. In this section, we describe the features we are using and the intuition behind them. Each of our features we apply on multiple levels (where applicable): the whole tag and for every value of its attributes.

4.1 Template Propagation

First, we introduce the template propagation measure, a binary feature that simply models what content was introduced or removed from the web site in terms of their similarity to previous DOM tree nodes, i.e., it captures the concept of reused templates by checking if a node exist already in the base version, but are unmatched, e.g., because there are more matching candidates than actual matches are possible. Since all matched nodes in the output T_1 and T_2 of our tree difference algorithm are colored blue, we can simply set the value of this feature to 1 if the node is blue and 0 if it is not.

The motivation for this measure is that many web sites, for example blogs, use templates when publishing a new article or when showing a new comment, classified, or advertisement. Detecting that a template is repeated allows us to model the degree to which a web site has drifted away from expected changes, e.g., in terms of character count distributions for a blog with articles written in English.

4.2 Shannon Entropy

Second, we leverage the Shannon entropy as a feature of information in a tag or an attribute's value. Two different features are derived from the Shannon entropy: (a) the absolute Shannon entropy, which is dependent on the length of the string, (b) the normalized Shannon entropy, i.e., the absolute Shannon

```
<html>
  <body>
    <p class="sumamry">
      [...] foo [...]
    </p>
  </body>
</html>
```

Listing 1: Base version, source code.

```
<html>
  <head><script
    src="http://url/malicious.js">
  </script></head>
  <body><p class="summary">
      [...] bar [...]
  </p></body>
</html>
```

Listing 2: Current version, source code.

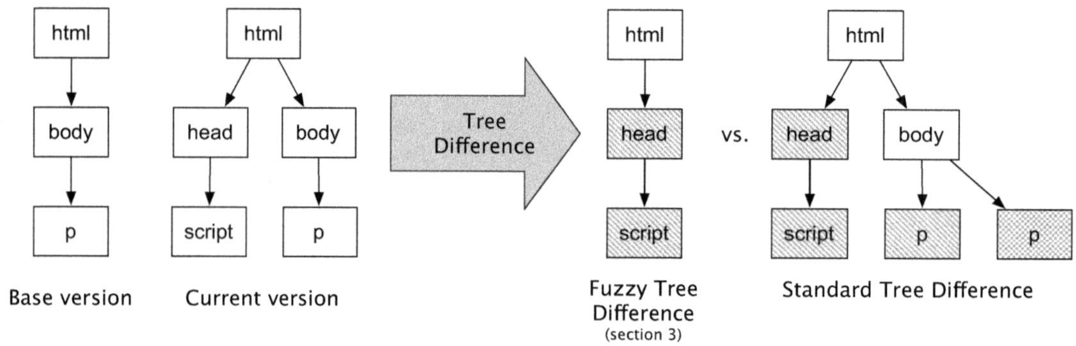

Figure 2: Comparison between a general tree difference algorithm and the fuzzy tree difference algorithm (section 3). Nodes with a green diagonal stripes pattern denote nodes that were detected as inserted, while nodes with a red chessboard pattern were detected as being removed.

entropy divided by the ideal Shannon entropy of a string of the same length (i.e., it is normalized to the interval from 0 to 1).

Our intuition behind the Shannon entropy is to measure the distance on how far the tag or attribute is away from a random source. For instance, to model that the URL in a "src" attribute of a <script> tag was generated by a random source.

4.3 Character Count

In the third set of features we employ a character count. The first feature in this set simply measures how often a single character occurs in the tag or the attribute's value and discriminates between upper- and lower-case characters. The second feature also measures how often a single character occurs, however, it ignores capitalization and counts an "A" as an "a". The third feature follows in simplicity and is the count of each digit. A fourth, fifth and sixth feature are taking advantage of the same method, but are performed on the fuzzy hash value (ssdeep in our implementation) of the tag or attribute instead.

Beyond these six features, we are also computing relative features for both of those two sets, as we did already in case of the Shannon entropy. Alike to the Shannon entropy features, the motivation behind these features is to model the character and digit distribution in a string.

4.4 Kolmogorov Complexity

The third set of measures we introduce is based on an approximation of the upper-bound on the Kolmogorov complexity [22]. Kolmogorov complexity denotes a complexity measure specifying the lower-bound of text necessary to describe another piece of text in an algorithmic way. One of the most important properties of the complexity is its incomputability. An upper-bound on the other hand is easy to compute by taking the length of the text compressed by any lossless compression algorithm. Since these features are based on a second information theoretical measure, next to the Shannon entropy, it is necessary to emphasize that they are complementary in our scenario: on the one hand, Kolmogorov complexity is conceptually different from the Shannon entropy, and on the other hand, we approximate the Kolmogorov complexity up to (at best) an additive constant.

These measures exploit the upper-bound and the fact that compressing already packed data results in nearly no benefit, in order to measure a change that introduces packed or encrypted data, such as malicious data trying to evade detection.

We introduce, again, two different features based on computing an upper-bound of the Kolmogorov complexity. First, the absolute upper-bound on the tag extracted by our tree difference algorithm; second, the ratio of the upper-bound over the length of the string. In case of very short strings, the upper-bound might even take up more space than the actual string.

4.5 Script Inclusion

Scripts included in web sites are the most prominent way to infect a user with malware, but they are also used legitimately. Differences exist between how malicious scripts and legitimate ones are used and included. For instance, malicious scripts are rarely including local files; instead, they usually include from an external source or provide the source code directly. The following two binary features model these differences.

4.5.1 Absolute Source URL

The enduring rise of content-delivery networks, which are often heavily relying on load-balancing based on the domain name system (DNS), lead to scripts being included much more often with an absolute and external source address in legitimate cases than it was the case prior to the predominance of these networks (due to potential compatibility issues if scripts are included differently). It is important to understand if a web site is hosted on a content-delivery network since it bears the reasoning that these web sites are generally much more optimized than personal web sites, to save on bandwidth on account of the smaller size. This then has an impact on the importance of other features. This feature is also binary; it is 1 for an absolute non-external source URL and 0 otherwise.

The many legitimate use cases of including scripts from an absolute URL suggest that this feature will not have a discriminatory impact on its own; rather, it supports other features by modeling the inclusion-style in a web site. The notion of a single inclusion-style roots in previous work by Nikiforakis et al. [23], which suggests that web sites follow the same inclusion patterns, i.e., the distribution of how scripts are included is biased toward either relative or absolute inclusions, and only rarely uniform.

4.5.2 External Source URL

While the last feature is a bias function to judge the use of scripts with an absolute source, the next feature is a bias function for the concept of external source URLs. It is important to mention that, if an external script is included, assuming the external domain is maintained by a third party, then the web site operator has to trust that the third party providing the external script will not insert any malicious code.

4.6 Inline Frames

Similar to the features to model the use of script tags, the following three binary features try to model the inclusion of malicious inline frames, by looking into properties that are uncommon for benign inclusions.

4.6.1 Absolute and External Source URL

Likewise to the nature of the source URL features for scripts, these features give an intuition on the use of inline frames. Both features are identical to their script sibling, but they examine <iframe> tags instead of <script> tags.

Their motivation follows closely the motivation for the script features: i.e., the feature for absolute source URLs is supporting other inline frame measures as a bias function. In the past, inline frames with an external source address were often used to include either advertisements or third party widgets. Recently, those moved to inline JavaScript or embedding plugins directly. Adversaries, on the other hand, still use these frames because they allow for easier fingerprinting and support delivering different infection vectors per user, for example depending on the browser's patch-level, installed plugins, or by obfuscating each reply differently. This fine-grained control helps the adversary to maximize the attack efficacy while reducing the likelihood of detection.

4.6.2 Hidden Frame

Beyond absolute and external frames, another indicator for malicious content being included exists: hidden frames. Legitimate frames are generally made visible to the user. Adversaries on the other hand prefer that the included web site is invisible, which is why they often resort to setting width and height of the frame to a low value, so that the frame is visually hard to spot for a human. We investigated a random sample of 10,000 inline frame tags that we extracted from our dataset and found that legitimate inline frames are often set to a width and height of larger than 100 and rarely hidden (the style attribute "display: none" is rarely used). We model this phenomenon, assuming that a majority of malicious inline frames uses a much smaller area of screen space, by restricting width and height of our feature to a maximum of 15 pixels. The feature is simply 1 for hidden frames and 0 otherwise.

5 EVALUATION

Generally, the problem we are trying to solve is an instance of *knowledge discovery in databases* [24, 25]. More precisely, when searching actively for infection campaigns next to a web crawler, we are interested in detecting outliers, i.e., novel changes, and the appearance of clusters, i.e., when a new trend is observed, for instance an infection campaign. While various clustering algorithms can be employed, the design of our system encourages the use of an algorithm that detects local outliers. Additionally, the distribution of a cluster can differ from the distribution of any other cluster, particularly for clusters with a low member count, i.e., it is not reasonable to assume that all changes follow a very similar distribution in the feature space. Since we are primarily interested in the formation of new clusters, when it is even less likely that this assumption will hold, centroid- or distribution-based clustering algorithms such as k-means (which will give spherically shaped clusters) or expectation-maximization (e.g., Gaussian mixture models) are unlikely to provide any valuable insight on new infection campaigns early enough. To counter this issue, we adopt a variant of the density-based clustering algorithm OPTICS (Ordering Points To Identify the Clustering Structure, by Ankerst et al. [26]), namely OPTICS-OF (OPTICS with Outlier Factors) by Breunig et al. [27].

5.1 OPTICS-OF

The OPTICS-OF algorithm takes two parameters: the maximum distance for a cluster and the minimal number of vectors necessary to form a cluster. In the scenario of trend analysis, the maximum distance corresponds to the similarity of a change, while the minimal number of vectors necessary describes the number of instances of a change we want to observe before we consider it a trend, i.e., before we want to verify that we found a previously-unknown infection campaign.

The algorithm works, in essence, as follows: if two vectors in the feature space are closer than the maximum distance, then they are directly density-reachable. If at least the minimal number of vectors are directly density-reachable from a vector, then this vector is a core object and forms a cluster. A cluster does not only contain directly density-reachable vectors from this core object, but is defined transitively, i.e., it contains all vectors that are directly and transitively density-reachable from the core objects. Therefore, an outlier is either not density-reachable to any other vector at all, or only density-reachable to a number of vectors, where none of the vectors is a core object, i.e., none of the vectors forms a cluster. In our experiments, we require 10 similarity vectors that are directly density-reachable to form a cluster.

5.2 Dataset

First, in this section, we describe in detail what constraints we imposed on our dataset, why these constraints were imposed, and how we obtained our dataset. In general, it is a challenging problem to obtain a representative sample of different and distinct malicious web sites. Invernizzi et al. [28] have shown that this is even the case when only mediocre toxicity[3] is required, i.e., it is even difficult for a dataset with a small but non-negligible percentage of malicious web sites. This poses a problem for collecting our dataset because we desire moderate toxicity and diversity among malicious infection vectors to verify that we can correctly, and without bias, identify similar trends, and by this, similar infection campaigns. Moreover, to discard trivial cases, the requirements on the web sites in our dataset are even more restrictive:

- Web sites must have been set-up for a legitimate reason, i.e., we are interested in landing pages and not interested

[3]Toxicity measures the maliciousness of dataset and simply corresponds to the fraction of malicious samples in a dataset over all the samples of the dataset.

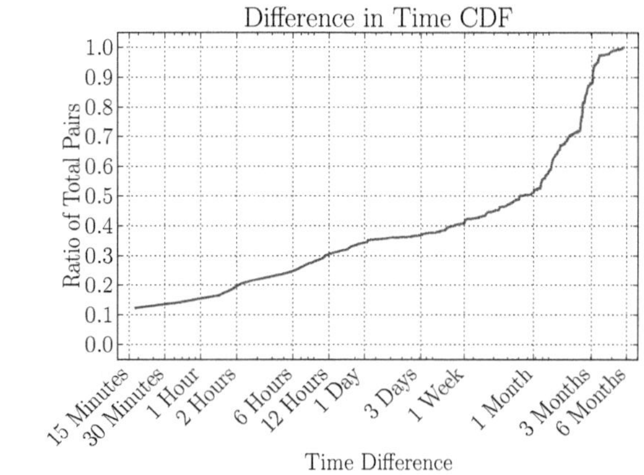

Figure 3: Overview of the difference in time between base and current version of a pair in the final dataset.

in exploit pages. Exploit pages denote web sites that are set up by an adversary to exclusively deliver malicious code, while landing pages denote the infected legitimate page. We enforce this restriction because recent work establishes that legitimate web sites are nowadays the primary target and because other approaches by Provos et al. [11, 14], Ratanaworabhan et al. [29], Curtsinger et al. [30] or Seifert et al. [31] are already able to detect purely malicious web sites with outstanding accuracy.

- Two distinct versions of a web site are required, i.e., a web sites must have been modified (legitimately or maliciously) to constitute a realistic sample.

We obtained our dataset by crawling the web from January 2013 to May 2013 via a 10-node cluster of custom crawlers running an adaptive fetch schedule with a recrawl delay of at least 15 minutes and an exponential back-off delay (multiplied by a constant factor of 10 if no change was observed in a recrawl and with a strict maximum of one week). The hourly seed of URLs for our crawler contained web sites that were already present in our dataset and also Yandex's search engines results for Twitter's trending topics. Additionally, to counter the problem of low toxicity and prevent a bias toward benign web sites, we injected a total of 2,979,942 URLs of web sites into our crawl seed that the Wepawet online analyzer [12] had analyzed previously, starting with samples observed in the beginning of January 2013 and ending with samples observed at the end of April 2013. In total, after removing exact duplicates and restricting the number of pairs per unique URL to a maximum of 10, our dataset spans a size of 700GiB and 26,459,103 distinct web site pairs from 12,464,920 unique URLs. A distinct pair denotes a pair where both versions are different from each other in respect to the SHA256 checksum of their normalized DOM tree.

The time difference, before a change between base and current version of a web site was observed, is shown in Figure 3. The average time difference of our pairs is 4 weeks, with 80% of all pairs being 2 hours or more apart, 70% being 12 hours or more apart, 60% being 7 days or more apart, and 50% being 20 days or more apart (median). Since not all web sites have been recrawled after exactly 15 minutes, we can only observe that a change happens in at least 16% of the web sites in a 15 minute interval after a visit.

5.3 Case Studies: Identified Trends/Clusters

In our experiments, we identified a total of 67,038 different clusters, with the majority of clusters having 30 or less elements.

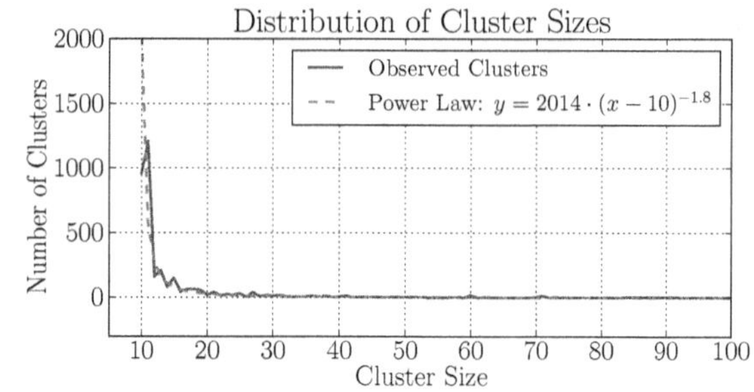

Figure 4: Overview of the number of different elements that are in each cluster.

Figure 4 depicts the final distribution of cluster sizes we observed in our experiments. Evidently, the observed distribution follows closely the power law function: $y = 2014 \cdot (x - 10)^{-1.8}$. In addition, we observe that the total sum over all cluster sizes is less than the number of distinct tags that we have analyzed. This is the case because any remaining tags are still considered to be outliers and do not constitute a trend yet. As a matter of fact, both the close resemblance to a power law function and a non-negligible amount of outliers are expected, because some changes are only made to a limited number of web sites, e.g., very similar articles might be posted to less web sites than we require as a lower-bound to constitute a trend, and also because our view of changes is limited by the seed and link expansion of the web crawler, i.e., it is possible that we only observed a subset of the true instances of each unique trend.

We feel that it is important to understand what a single cluster is actually describing, and we provide different examples about what tags have been clustered together. Therefore, we investigate two clusters in more detail. Although both clusters are low-count clusters, i.e., relatively small, their small size actually illustrates that the Δ-system does detect when a trend reaches a significant distribution and that it does not rely on an unreasonable large number of observations of a single trend.

The first example we discuss is an actual infection campaign that we have observed in the wild, an instance of a redirection to a Cool Exploit Kit installation. In contrast, the second example we discuss corresponds to a cluster describing the change in cross-site request forgery tokens.

We selected these two clusters manually by filtering clusters based on the generated signature with simple heuristics that suggest malicious behavior, such as external scripts that are included with a random component or JavaScript with a non-negligible ratio of digits over characters (suggesting obfuscation). Clearly, these and other heuristics can also be leveraged to order clusters according to "levels of interest" or to remove clusters that are likely uninteresting and should not be analyzed manually by an analyst.

Other trends we observed, but will not discuss in detail, include the modification of Facebook Like buttons (the backlink URL changes), a version update for the JQuery library served for blogs hosted on Wordpress.com, or the insertion of user-tracking tokens.

5.3.1 *Cool Exploit Kit Infections of Discuz!X*

One of the most interesting clusters, which shows the applicability of the Δ-system in practice, describes an infection vector used to redirect to a specific infection campaign that uses the Cool Exploit Kit to distribute malware. This in-the-wild infection campaign was found at the beginning of April 2013 in a set of 15 different web sites from the following 10 unique URLs:

- http://att.kafan.cn

- http://frozen-fs.net
- http://jses40813.ibbt.tw
- http://ppin888.com
- http://www.dv3.com.cn
- http://www.kxxwg.com
- http://www.ruadapalma.com
- http://www.sdchina.cn
- http://www.wlanwifi.net
- http://www.yysyuan.com

Once we verified that the cluster was indeed malicious, we investigated the underlying commonalities between them. We found that all web sites were using the discussion platform "Discuz!X" [32]. Discuz!X is an Internet forum software written in PHP and, according to the Chinese National Radio [33], the most popular Internet forum software used in China. Clearly, these infections are part of the same infection campaign. Additionally, such a strong common ground suggests that the infection is likely to be rooted in a security vulnerability in the Discuz!X software, and it provides support identifying the cause and a removal method.

Listing 3 shows the respective generated signature of the infection. For this infection campaign, we did not observe any differences in the tags that were clustered together.

```
<script type
    ="text/javascript" language="javascript">
  p=parseInt;
  ss=(123) ? String.fromCharCode : 0;
  asgq=" [4036 character obfuscated string] "
       .replace(/@/g,"9").split("!");
  try { document.body&=0.1 } catch(gdsgsdg) {
    zz=3; dbshre=79;
    if(dbshre) { vfvwe=0;
      try { document; }
      catch(agdsg) { vfvwe=1; }
      if(!vfvwe) { e=eval; }
      s="";
      if(zz) for(i=0;i-1374!=0;i++) {
        if(window.document)
          s+=ss(p(asgq[i],16)); }
      if(window.document) e(s); }}</script>
```

Listing 3: Cool Exploit Kit infection vector.

Beyond the inclusions of infection vectors pointing to an installation of the Cool Exploit Kit observed in all pairs, one web site (http://frozen-fs.net) also included an infection vector that tried to infect visitors via an installation of the Blackhole exploit kit.

The domain that included the Cool Exploit Kit and the Blackhole exploit kit, "frozen-fs.net", was not cleaned up, and we observed that it was suspended by the provider 27 days after we detected the infection.

5.3.2 *Cross-Site Request Forgery Tokens*

A second interesting low-count cluster we found during our evaluation models variations in cross-site request forgery tokens in deployments of the Django web application framework. In total, we identified a similar modification among 17 different pairs of web sites. Each web site used form-based cross-site request forgery tokens and used the same identifier for a hidden form field, namely "csrfmiddlewaretoken". For every pair, the attribute features did not diverge for the name attribute, while all were different for the value attribute. Nonetheless, the Δ-system clustered them together, since the random entropy was nearly constant for the value attribute among all observed removed and inserted instances. The entropy was nearly constant for the normalized case as well as for the absolute entropy features. The exact identifying signature for that cluster is shown in Listing 4.

```
<input
 name="csrfmiddlewaretoken"
 value="(JhD3IwCXcnnpRtvE42MN6r8d0B0WRoxG
        |hH4f6e0MC0TEYF0RYoXFRDaTLzym6102
        [...]
        |DNczoWjeN1nK6nq3whXYpSSnZGdxx00g
        |F9yLS0jNUXIURsXDRqxS5NVW7qXfWsgf)"/>
```

Listing 4: Cross-site request forgery token; | denotes an or.

We feel that this observed trend constitutes a perfect example in which the limitations of the signature generation stick out and where the Δ-system shows its robustness by clustering these changes correctly together. While the signature can detect all observed instances correctly, it is clear that when trying to match new versions of a web site with the signature we would fail to identify the changed token value correctly since the value will change to a new, unobserved random value.

5.4 Performance

In order to judge the actual applicability of our system in practice, a performance analysis is necessary. We show in Figure 5 that the performance of the Δ-system allows for deployments in real-world scenarios. However, corner cases exist that could impact an actual deployment, if the difference between the base and current version of a web site is particularly large. We performed a manual in-depth analysis of the system that highlighted the actual performance bottleneck of our system: close to 80% of the time when analyzing the two versions was spent by the Python library BeautifulSoup to parse the HTML structure of a page. Although, the number of changes made to a web site plays the most important role in analyzing the changes, pairs that took longer than 3 seconds to analyze were exclusively web sites that sent data in an encoding different than specified. BeautifulSoup tries to take care of this and follows a code path that can get multiple thousand function calls deep, and easily hits the recursion limit of CPython. While we increased this limit in our evaluation to keep these pairs and prevent a dataset bias, the particular functions are actually tail-recursive and, therefore, can be expressed iteratively (thus, removing the necessity of allocating stackframes). However, the abstruseness of the involved functions prevented us from doing the very same in a reasonable amount of time. Regardless of these (still outstanding) engineering challenges for a general deployment, we could analyze a single pair in a median time of 0.340 seconds and in an average time of in 2.232 seconds. It is also evident that we finished each analysis in at most 20 seconds, regardless of the aforementioned problems encountered in BeautifulSoup.

These results, when taking into account that 60% of our data is 7 days or more apart (c.f. Figure 5), support our claim that the Δ-system does not necessarily need to keep a base version locally, but could rely on public archives like the Internet Archive or a web cache by a search engine. Nonetheless, we strongly recommend keeping a local version to prevent an additional delay in fetching the web site and to prevent running into the problem of a potentially outdated or even non-existing version on the side of the public archive.

6 LIMITATIONS

Similar to other static analysis approaches leveraging machine learning, our approach has some limitations, which can be used to evade detection. This section discusses these limitations and how they could be managed in a real-world deployment of the Δ-system. First, we introduce a limitation called

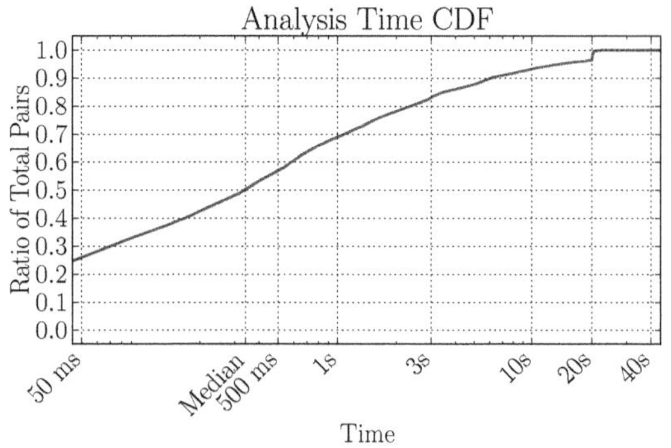

Figure 5: Overview of the ratio of web site pairs that have been completely analyzed in our experiments in less than x seconds.

Step-by-step Injection. Second, we will briefly discuss the *Evolution of Infection Vectors* as a major fundamental problem in detecting malicious code. Lastly, we discuss the trade-off between dynamic and static analysis and the limitations of either approach.

6.1 Step-by-step Injection

It is possible to circumvent the Δ-system by adding malicious code in small steps, i.e., in a series of modifications where each step on its own gets detected as being benign, while the aggregation is malicious. For example, an attacker could build an infection vector that delivers these small steps depending on a cookie or the visitor's IP address to keep track of the client's previous version. However, we argue that the scope of such an attack is heavily limited because: (a) it requires an attacker to be able to inject code that is executed on the server-side, otherwise detection is possible because it has to be done client-side, and the attack can also be impeded or even avoided by keeping the first version instead of updating the stored base version with every visit; or (b) the DOM tree will be modified online, for example through JavaScript. In the first case, an important and drastically scope-reducing factor is that the vulnerability needs to support such an iterative process, where, e.g., memory regions are shared among browser tabs or between multiple visits to the same web site, which is highly unlikely given the strict separation current browser sandboxes enforce. In the latter case, on the other hand, we suggest to analyze the web site on every mutation event[4], i.e., by considering the web site that was modified online as a new current version and comparing it to the stored base version.

6.2 Evolution of Infection Vectors

Detecting malicious code is an arms race and malicious web sites are no exception. Malware developers are trying to evade detection systems to gain the upper hand, while detection system developers are trying to catch and prevent these evasions. Previous work on evasions motivated the search for better and different detection systems [34]. More advanced obfuscation [35], encryption, poly- and metamorphic code [36] and virtualized environments have become more common in response to these improvements and impeded detection systems. With more approaches being able to handle these cases, it is to be expected that malware and infection vectors will evolve and successfully circumvent available detection systems. While retraining the machine learning algorithm on a more recent dataset is often a possible approach to counter the evasion problem, it is only a near-sighted solution to counter the dataset shift, as malware will deviate more severely, up to the point where the features will not model the underlying problem anymore. Even in cases where the features are not publicly known to an adversary, it is possible to partially derive these by probing the system carefully, which then will either allow for successful evasion of the system or (on re-training) increase the false positive and false negative rate because of misclassification due to minuscule differences between legitimate and malicious code in the feature space. Both cases are obviously not desired for a detection system, however, it is a general problem of all approaches employing machine learning [10,11,13,14,31,37–39], and it is generally only countered reliably by adapting to a new feature space, which we leave for future work.

6.3 Dynamic vs. Static Analysis

The Δ-system in its current form is a purely static analysis system, while, at the same time, the Internet is becoming more and more dynamic. While one might think that static analysis is inferior to dynamic analysis here, this is not the case. Instead, our system complements dynamic analysis systems: it detects trends/infections statically and can forward the interesting trends/infections to dynamic analysis systems that extract further information.

Our motivation to rely on a purely static analysis is based on multiple reasons. First, dynamic analysis is not necessarily useful at the early stage in which our system operates, i.e., trends that change the behavior and are interesting to us show themselves first with static content changes, rendering dynamic analysis (currently) unnecessary. A second argument against dynamic analysis for the Δ-system is that it, for instance by instrumenting embedded or included JavaScript to modify the DOM tree to retrieve a "final" version of the web site, under-approximates the behavior of the web site to this specific execution environment and might yield a potentially incomplete or untrue representation of the DOM tree. It also poses the questions of when to consider the DOM tree "final", i.e., when to take a snapshot. Consequently, it might then be possible to evade the trend detection step in the first place. Additionally, we might also miss infection campaigns that are statically present in the web site, but are removed dynamically or are inactive (for us). For example, servers could be unavailable (for us) or code might not be loaded (for us), we could be fingerprinted, the IP address of our analysis system might be in a region of the world that is not affected or simply because the user-agent of our browser does not match a (unknown) regular expression. The third argument in favor of static analysis is that it can be considerably faster than dynamic analysis, which, in turn, allows us to leverage more computationally-expensive features to increase trend detection accuracy.

Lastly, while the trend detection step is purely static, to detect malicious behavior, the Δ-system relies on an external analysis system that might very well use dynamic analysis. Generally, we do not impose any limitations on this detection engine but that it can detect malicious behavior.

7 RELATED WORK

In the following we discuss related work in areas tangent to our research, such as web dynamics and the detection of malicious code. To the best of our knowledge, no prior work exists that actively searches and finds previously unknown infection campaigns.

[4]JavaScript events are called mutation events if they modify the DOM tree, e.g., by changing attributes of a node, such as the *src* attribute of a *script* tag, or inserting or removing elements from the DOM tree.

7.1 Detection of Malicious Code

Numerous papers have been published on detecting malicious activity in web sites. The majority of them focus on dynamic analysis of JavaScript in instrumented environments or on rendering web sites in high-interaction client honeypots. Generally, it is important to recall that our system provides additional information: the infection campaign and the responsible node of the DOM tree.

Eshete et al. [40] discuss the effectiveness and efficacy issues of malicious web site detection techniques. Approaches from blacklists, to static heuristics, to dynamic analysis are compared in their detection accuracy and time spent analyzing the web site. A major argument in short-comings of previous work is the missing discussion on the necessity of episodic re-training or online learning capabilities, to keep up with the ongoing evolution of web-based malware, and to prevent the evasion of deployed detection systems.

Cova et al. [12] introduce the system *JSAND* to detect and analyze drive-by download attacks and malicious JavaScript in an instrumented environment. The system leverages a comprehensive dynamic analysis approach by instrumenting JavaScript to extract a variety of different features from redirection and cloaking, to deobfuscation, to observing heap exploitation. The system is compared to client honeypots, such as Capture-HPC and PhoneyC, as well as the anti-virus engine ClamAV. It shows a much lower false positive (0%) and false negative rate (0.2%) than all other approaches (5.2% to 80.6% respectively), while taking an average of 16.05 seconds to analyze a web site. CaptureHPC, the closest system in terms of accuracy takes 20 seconds per sample.

Canali et al. [13] extend the dynamic analysis system *JSAND*, by implementing a faster pre-filtering step. The main goal is to prevent the submission of certainly-benign web sites to the dynamic analysis system and hereby to reduce the time spent on analyzing benign samples, i.e., the system assigns to a false negative a much higher cost than it does to a false positive. The filter method leverages a C4.5 (J48) decision tree and a diverse set of features spanning from the HTML content, to the JavaScript code, to information about the host, to uniform resource location (URL) patterns. The filter is evaluated on a dataset of 15,000 web sites and compared to similar methods by Seifert et al. [31] and Ma et al. [39]. Both other methods yield more false positives and false negatives, but process up to 10 times more samples in the same time.

Provos et al. [11, 14] introduce a system to detect URLs to malicious web sites. However, they are not considering legitimate, infected web sites in general, as their approach is restricted to detecting the inclusion of exploit pages, and hence their approach is complementary to our system's capabilities. Their system uses a proprietary machine learning algorithm to classify URLs based on features like use in "out of place" inline frames, obfuscated JavaScript, or links to known malware distribution sites. Besides detecting 90% of all malicious landing pages with 0.1% false positives, they validate previous work by Moshchuk et al. [41] that infection vectors are inserted into legitimate web sites through exploiting vulnerabilities, advertisement networks, and third party widgets.

7.2 Web Dynamics in Security

Maggi et al. [10] introduce a web application intrusion detection system, which is able to learn about changes made to the web application. The problem of web application concept drift is addressed by learning how the web application is accessed by a legitimate user and employing an unsupervised classification algorithm. Features include, for example, a sequence corresponding to the order in which web sites are accessed or how web page parameters are distributed. However, the presented technique is orthogonal to our approach. The main goal is not to find new infection campaigns or to protect the visitor of a web site, but rather to protect the integrity of the web application. Protecting a normal, wandering user would require intrusion detection and protection of all web sites the user visits, since the access pattern, on which the system is based on, depend on the underlying architecture of the web site. Although possible theoretically, it is practically impossible.

Davanzi et al. [42] studied a similar approach for detecting the impact of web dynamics. They introduce a system to detect if changes made to a web site are defacements, which might cause serious harm to the organization, money- or reputation-wise, or are legitimate, "officially approved" content changes. However, they explicitly point out that their approach does not work with malicious modifications because their approach detects changes that are visible to the end-user, which is the exact opposite of how malicious infection vectors are placed in practice. In detail, they employ anomaly detection to regularly visit and monitor a set of 300 web sites actively and detect if changes made to the web site constitute a defacement or not.

8 CONCLUSION

In this paper, we introduced the Δ-system, a novel, lightweight system to identify changes associated with malicious and benign behavior in web sites. The system leverages clustering of modification-motivated features, which are extracted based on two versions of a web site, rather than analyzing the web site in its entirety. To extract the important modifications accurately, we introduced a fuzzy tree difference algorithm that extracts DOM tree nodes that were more heavily modified, discarding changes in single characters or words, or legitimate evolutions. Beyond detecting if a change made to a web site is associated with malicious behavior or not, we showed that the Δ-system supports the detection of previously-unknown infection campaigns by analyzing, unknown trends and measuring the similarity to previous, known infection campaigns. Furthermore, we showed that the system can generate an identifying signature of observed infection campaigns, which can then be leveraged to protect users via content-based detection systems or as test-cases for online analyzer systems. Ultimately, the system's ability to identify specific infections is helpful in identifying the reason why the web site was infected by a specific campaign in the first place, such as a distinct version of the web application among all infections; additionally, it facilitates the removal of malicious code and the mitigation of additional infections in the future.

Acknowledgment

We want to express our gratitude toward our shepherd Matt Bishop and the reviewers for their helpful feedback, valuable comments and suggestions to improve the quality of the paper.

This work was supported by the Office of Naval Research (ONR) under grant N000140911042, the Army Research Office (ARO) under grant W911NF0910553, the National Science Foundation (NSF) under grants CNS-0845559 and CNS-0905537, and Secure Business Austria.

9 REFERENCES

[1] SOPHOS Security Team, "SOPHOS Security Threat Report 2013," SOPHOS, Tech. Rep., 2013. [Online]. Available: http://goo.gl/YuW65

[2] P. Baccas, "Malware injected into legitimate JavaScript code on legitimate websites," Article, 2013. [Online]. Available: http://goo.gl/rDFZ4

[3] D. Goodin, "Twitter detects and shuts down password data hack in progress," February 2013. [Online]. Available: http://goo.gl/YwfMd

[4] Facebook Security Team, "Protecting People On Facebook," Article, February 2013. [Online]. Available: http://goo.gl/OUPtk

[5] J. Finke and J. Menn, "Exclusive: Apple, Macs hit by hackers who targeted Facebook," *Reuters*, February 2013. [Online]. Available: http://goo.gl/fzhIo

[6] D. Fetterly, M. Manasse, M. Najork, and J. Wiener, "A large-scale study of the evolution of web pages," in *Proceedings of the 12th International Conference on World Wide Web*, ser. WWW '03. ACM, 2003, pp. 669–678.

[7] B. A. Huberman and L. A. Adamic, "Evolutionary Dynamics of the world wide web," *Condensed Matter*, January 1999.

[8] F. Douglis, A. Feldmann, B. Krishnamurthy, and J. Mogul, "Rate of Change and other Metrics: a Live Study of the World Wide Web." in *Proceedings of the USENIX Symposium on Internet Technologies and Systems*, vol. 119. USENIX Association, 1997.

[9] R. Baeza-Yates, C. Castillo, and F. Saint-Jean, "Web Dynamics, Structure, and Page Quality," in *Web Dynamics*. Springer-Verlag, 2004, pp. 93–109.

[10] F. Maggi, W. Robertson, C. Kruegel, and G. Vigna, "Protecting a Moving Target: Addressing Web Application Concept Drift," in *Proceedings of the 12th International Symposium on Recent Advances in Intrusion Detection*, ser. RAID '09. Springer-Verlag, 2009, pp. 21–40.

[11] N. Provos, D. McNamee, P. Mavrommatis, K. Wang, and N. Modadugu, "The ghost in the browser analysis of web-based malware," in *First Workshop on Hot Topics in Understanding Botnets*, ser. HOTBOTS '07. USENIX Association, 2007, pp. 4–4.

[12] M. Cova, C. Kruegel, and G. Vigna, "Detection and analysis of drive-by-download attacks and malicious JavaScript code," in *Proceedings of the 19th International Conference on World Wide Web*, ser. WWW'10. ACM, 2010, pp. 281–290.

[13] D. Canali, M. Cova, G. Vigna, and C. Kruegel, "Prophiler: a fast filter for the large-scale detection of malicious web pages," in *Proceedings of the 20th International Conference on World Wide Web (WWW '11)*, ser. WWW '11. ACM, 2011, pp. 197–206.

[14] N. Provos, P. Mavrommatis, M. A. Rajab, and F. Monrose, "All your iFRAMEs point to Us," in *Proceedings of the 17th USENIX Security Symposium*, ser. SEC'08. USENIX Association, 2008, pp. 1–15.

[15] P.-M. Bureau, "Linux/Cdorked.A: New Apache backdoor being used in the wild to serve Blackhole," April 2013. [Online]. Available: http://goo.gl/g2Vfl

[16] D. Cid, "Apache Binary Backdoors on Cpanel-based servers," April 2013. [Online]. Available: http://goo.gl/BXq8Q

[17] S. S. Chawathe and H. Garcia-Molina, "Meaningful Change Detection in Structured Data," in *Proceedings of the ACM SIGMOD International Conference on Management of Data*, ser. MOD'97. ACM, 1997.

[18] Y. Wang, D. J. DeWitt, and J.-Y. Cai, "X-Diff: An effective change detection algorithm for XML documents," in *Proceedings of the 19th International Conference on Data Engineering*, ser. ICDE '03. IEEE, 2003, pp. 519–530.

[19] H. W. Kuhn, "The Hungarian method for the assignment problem," *Naval Research Logistics Quarterly*, vol. 2, no. 1-2, pp. 83–97, 1955.

[20] J. Kornblum, "Identifying almost identical files using context triggered piecewise hashing," *Digital Investigation*, vol. 3, no. 0, pp. 91 – 97, 2006, the Proceedings of the 6th Annual Digital Forensic Research Workshop (DFRWS '06).

[21] M. A. Jaro, "Advances in Record-Linkage Methodology as Applied to Matching the 1985 Census of Tampa, Florida," *Journal of the American Statistical Association*, vol. 84, no. 406, pp. 414–420, 1989.

[22] A. N. Kolmogorov, "Three approaches to the quantitative definition of information," *International Journal of Computer Mathematics*, vol. 2, no. 1-4, pp. 157–168, 1968.

[23] N. Nikiforakis, L. Invernizzi, A. Kapravelos, S. Van Acker, W. Joosen, C. Kruegel, F. Piessens, and G. Vigna, "You Are What You Include: Large-scale Evaluation of Remote JavaScript Inclusions," in *Proceedings of the 19th ACM Conference on Computer and Communications Security*, ser. CCS '12. ACM, 2012.

[24] U. Fayyad, G. Piatetsky-Shapiro, P. Smyth *et al.*, "Knowledge Discovery and Data Mining: Towards a Unifying Framework." *Knowledge Discovery and Data Mining*, vol. 96, pp. 82–88, 1996.

[25] U. M. Fayyad, G. Piatetsky-Shapiro, P. Smyth, and R. Uthurusamy, "Advances in knowledge discovery and data mining," 1996.

[26] M. Ankerst, M. M. Breunig, H.-P. Kriegel, and J. Sander, "OPTICS: Ordering Points To Identify the Clustering Structure," in *Proceedings of the ACM SIGMOD International Conference on Management of Data*, ser. MOD'99. ACM, 1999, pp. 49–60.

[27] M. Breunig, H.-P. Kriegel, R. T. Ng, and J. Sander, "OPTICS-OF: Identifying Local Outliers," in *Lecture Notes in Computer Science*. Springer-Verlag, 1999.

[28] L. Invernizzi, P. Milani Comparetti, S. Benvenuti, M. Cova, C. Kruegel, and G. Vigna, "EvilSeed: A Guided Approach to Finding Malicious Web Pages," *Security and Privacy (SP), 2012 IEEE Symposium on*, vol. 0, pp. 428–442, 2012.

[29] P. Ratanaworabhan, B. Livshits, and B. Zorn, "Nozzle: A defense against heap-spraying code injection attacks," in *Proceedings of the 18th USENIX Security Symposium*, ser. SEC'09. USENIX Association, 2009, pp. 169–186.

[30] C. Curtsinger, B. Livshits, B. Zorn, and C. Seifert, "ZOZZLE: fast and precise in-browser JavaScript malware detection," in *Proceedings of the 20th USENIX Security Symposium*, ser. SEC'11. USENIX Association, 2011, pp. 3–3.

[31] C. Seifert, I. Welch, and P. Komisarczuk, "Identification of Malicious Web Pages with Static Heuristics," in *Telecommunication Networks and Applications Conference*, ser. ATNAC '08, 2008, pp. 91–96.

[32] "Discuz!" Retrieved, May 2013. [Online]. Available: http://goo.gl/e8nCD

[33] X. Yang, "Report on the success of the Discuz! software," Chinese National Radio Report, August 2010, in Chinese. [Online]. Available: http://goo.gl/beq4O

[34] M. Rajab, L. Ballard, N. Jagpal, P. Mavrommatis, D. Nojiri, N. Provos, and L. Schmidt, "Trends in Circumventing Web-Malware Detection," 2011.

[35] J. Mason, S. Small, F. Monrose, and G. MacManus, "English shellcode," in *Proceedings of the 16th ACM Conference on Computer and Communications Security*, ser. CCS '09. ACM, 2009, pp. 524–533.

[36] M. Polychronakis, K. Anagnostakis, and E. Markatos, "Network-level polymorphic shellcode detection using emulation," *Journal in Computer Virology*, vol. 2, pp. 257–274, 2007, 10.1007/s11416-006-0031-z.

[37] J. Choi, G. Kim, T. Kim, and S. Kim, "An Efficient Filtering Method for Detecting Malicious Web Pages," in *Proceedings of the 13th International Workshop on Information Security Applications*, 2012.

[38] Y.-T. Hou, Y. Chang, T. Chen, C.-S. Laih, and C.-M. Chen, "Malicious web content detection by machine learning," *Expert Systems with Applications*, vol. 37, no. 1, pp. 55 – 60, 2010.

[39] J. Ma, L. K. Saul, S. Savage, and G. M. Voelker, "Beyond blacklists: learning to detect malicious web sites from suspicious URLs," in *Proceedings of the 15th ACM SIGKDD Conference on Knowledge Discovery and Data Mining*, ser. KDD '09. ACM, 2009, pp. 1245–1254.

[40] B. Eshete, A. Villafiorita, and K. Weldemariam, "Malicious website detection: Effectiveness and efficiency issues," in *First SysSec Workshop*, ser. SysSec. IEEE, 2011, pp. 123 –126.

[41] A. Moshchuk, T. Bragin, S. D. Gribble, and H. M. Levy, "A Crawler-based Study of Spyware in the Web," in *Network and Distributed System Security Symposium*, ser. NDSS '06, 2006.

[42] G. Davanzo, E. Medvet, and A. Bartoli, "Anomaly detection techniques for a web defacement monitoring service," *Expert Systems with Applications*, vol. 38, no. 10, pp. 12 521–12 530, Sep. 2011.

Beheading Hydras: Performing Effective Botnet Takedowns

Yacin Nadji
College of Computing
Georgia Institute of Technology
Atlanta, GA
yacin.nadji@cc.gatech.edu

Manos Antonakakis
Damballa, Inc.
Atlanta, GA
manos@damballa.com

Roberto Perdisci
Department of Computer Science
University of Georgia
Athens, GA
perdisci@cs.uga.edu

David Dagon
College of Computing
Georgia Institute of Technology
Atlanta, GA
dagon@sudo.sh

Wenke Lee
College of Computing
Georgia Institute of Technology
Atlanta, GA
wenke@cc.gatech.edu

ABSTRACT

Devices infected with malicious software typically form botnet armies under the influence of one or more command and control (C&C) servers. The botnet problem reached such levels where federal law enforcement agencies have to step in and take actions against botnets by disrupting (or "taking down") their C&Cs, and thus their illicit operations. Lately, more and more private companies have started to independently take action against botnet armies, primarily focusing on their DNS-based C&Cs. While well-intentioned, their C&C takedown methodology is in most cases ad-hoc, and limited by the breadth of knowledge available around the malware that facilitates the botnet.

With this paper, we aim to bring order, measure, and reason to the botnet takedown problem. We propose a takedown analysis and recommendation system, called *rza*, that allows researchers to perform two tasks: 1) a postmortem analysis of past botnet takedowns, and 2) provide recommendations on how to successfully execute future botnet takedowns. As part of our system evaluation, we perform a postmortem analysis of the recent Kelihos, Zeus and 3322.org takedowns. We show that while some of these takedowns were effective, others did not appear to have a significant long-term impact on the targeted botnet. In addition to the postmortem analyses, we provide takedown recommendation metrics for 45 currently active botnets, where we find that 42 of them can likely be disabled entirely by using a DNS-based takedown strategy only.

CCS'13, November 4–8, 2013, Berlin, Germany.

ACM 978-1-4503-2477-9/13/11
http://dx.doi.org/10.1145/2508859.2516749.

Categories and Subject Descriptors

K.6.m [**Management of Computing and Information Systems**]: Security; K.5.m [**Legal Aspects of Computing**]: Contracts

General Terms

Botnets

Keywords

botnet takedowns; takedown analysis; takedown policy

1. INTRODUCTION

Botnets represent a persistent threat to Internet security. To effectively counter botnets, security researchers and law enforcement organizations have been recently relying more and more on *botnet takedown* operations. Essentially, a botnet takedown consists of identifying and disrupting the botnet's command-and-control (C&C) infrastructure. For example, in 2009 law enforcement and security operators were able to takedown the Mariposa botnet, which at that time consisted of approximately 600,000 bots. The takedown operation was accomplished by first identifying the set of domain names through which bots would locate their C&C network infrastructure. By seizing this set of domains via a collaboration with domain registrars, security operators effectively "sinkholed" the botnet, thus shunting the C&C traffic away from the botmaster and avoiding any further commands to be issued to the bots.

While sophisticated botnet developers have attempted, in some cases successfully, to build peer-to-peer (P2P) botnets that avoid entirely the use of C&C domains [18], most modern botnets make frequent use of the domain name system (DNS) to support their C&C infrastructure. This is likely due to the fact that DNS-based botnets are much easier to develop and manage compared to their P2P-based counterparts, and yet provide a remarkable level of *agility* that makes a takedown challenging. For example, the Mariposa case required a coordinated effort involving law enforcement, security operators, and domain registrars across several different countries. In addition, some recent takedown efforts [13] have caused some level of collateral damage, thus raising both technical issues and policy-related questions regarding the efficacy of botnet takedowns.

In this paper, we propose a novel *takedown analysis and recommendation system*, which we call *rza*. Our main goals are: (1) to provide a way to "go back in time" and *quantitatively analyze past takedown efforts* to highlight incomplete takedowns and identify what worked and what could have been done better; (2) to build a *takedown recommendation engine* that aims to automatically enumerate a botnet's C&C infrastructure, and suggest appropriate domain sets to disable to maximize the chance of success. Specifically, *rza* identifies additional domains that are likely part of a botnet's C&C infrastructure by examining historical relationships in the DNS and analyzing the botnet's malware samples. This aids the takedown process by identifying domains that may have been missed by hand, both from the network-level and the malware-level, aggregating this information, and automatically labeling the domains with evidence of their maliciousness. While *rza* focuses on disrupting botnets that use DNS-based C&C infrastructure, it can also assist in cases where botnets are more advanced and use domain name generation algorithms (DGA) or communicate using a peer-to-peer structure (P2P). In particular, *rza* provides the first few steps for remediating advanced C&C infrastructure: (i) identifying DNS-based primary C&C infrastructure, if it exists; (ii) automatically identifying if the botnet has DGA or P2P capabilities; and (iii) automatically identifying the malware samples that exhibit these behaviors to triage binaries for reverse engineering. To successfully takedown DGA/P2P botnets we must fully understand their non-deterministic portions, such as the randomness seed for DGAs [3] or the peer enumeration and selection algorithms for P2P [18]. If we disable a botnet's primary infrastructure but do not account for the DGA-based backup mechanism, our efforts will be futile.

We show that in cases of past takedowns, likely malicious domain names were left unperturbed. Worst yet, in some cases malicious domains were unintentionally given enterprise-level domain name resolution services. We show that *rza* can identify additional sets of domain names that ought to be considered in a future takedown, as well as automatically identify malware contingency plans when their primary C&C infrastructure is disabled.

In summary, we make the following contributions:

- We propose *rza*, a takedown analysis and recommendation system that allows us to measure and reason about the success of past and future takedown efforts. To the best of our knowledge, we are the first to propose such a botnet takedown analysis system.

- We apply *rza* to analyze three recent botnet takedown operations. We show that while some takedowns were effective, others did not appear to actually disrupt the entire targeted botnet.

- We use *rza*'s recommendation engine to analyze 45 live botnets, and discuss in which cases a DNS-based takedown operation is likely to succeed and what steps would be necessary to accomplish the takedown in practice. Of these, 42 could be straightforwardly eliminated using only DNS sinkholing.

The remainder of the paper is structured as follows: Section 2 provides the necessary background on the DNS, botnet takedowns, and our datasets. Section 3 describes *rza* in detail. Section 4 presents our postmortem experiments and analyses of three recent, high-profile takedown attempts. Section 5 presents the output of *rza* when applied to 45 recently identified, distinct botnet C&C infrastructures. In Appendix A we discuss non-technical difficulties associated with performing takedowns that would make takedowns more complete if alleviated.

2. BACKGROUND

In this section, we first provide an historical explanation of some past takedowns and explain why takedowns deserve to be studied in detail. Then, we describe the datasets used by *rza* to perform takedown analysis and to build the takedown recommendation system.

2.1 Botnets and Takedowns

Botnet takedowns are not uncommon, and may take many different forms. Considering the heterogeneous nature of client machines and the difficulty in keeping individual machines clean from infection, taking down the botnet C&C is an attractive alternative. A successful takedown eliminates most external negative impacts of the botnet, effectively foiling further attacks (e.g., spam, DDoS, etc.) by the infected hosts, which can number in the millions. In the past, takedowns have been performed by revoking sets of C&C IP addresses from hosting providers, de-peering entire Autonomous Systems (AS), or, more recently, sinkholing or revoking C&C domains.

Conficker is an Internet worm that infected millions of computers and remains one of the most nefarious threats seen on the Internet to date [3]. Conficker's latter variants employed a DGA that would generate 50,000 pseudo-random domain names every day to communicate with its C&C server. The takedown of Confiker required immense coordination across hundreds of countries and top-level domains (TLDs), and numerous domain registrars and registries. The takedown efforts were coordinated by the Conficker Working Group (CWG) [3]. The takedown required reverse-engineering the malware binaries, and reconstructing the DGA. Then, the CWG pre-registered all 50,000 domains per day that could potentially be used for C&C purposes, thus preventing the botmaster from regaining control of the bots. The success of CWG's efforts highlight the importance of participation and support from key governing and regulatory bodies, such as ICANN, and the need of cooperation between the private sector and governments around the world.

Mariposa, a 600,000-strong botnet of Spanish origin, provides another example of a takedown operation initiated by a working group that relied on sinkholing known malicious domains. Interestingly, Mariposa's botmasters were able to evade a full takedown by bribing a registrar to return domain control to the malicious operators [10], underscoring the fact that barriers to successful takedowns are not only technical ones.

The DNSChanger [19] "click-jacking" botnet was also taken down through a working group. DNSChanger altered upwards of 300,000 clients' DNS configurations to point to rogue DNS resolvers under the control of the attackers. This allowed the attackers to direct infected hosts to illegitimate websites, often replacing advertisements with their own to generate revenue. DNSChanger had to be taken down by physically seizing the botnet's rogue DNS servers. The takedown was accomplished in late 2011. Largely considered successful, the DNSChanger once again shows the importance of collaboration when performing comprehensive takedowns.

Not all takedowns are performed at the DNS-level, however, as shown in the takedowns of McColo [8], AS Troyak [11], and other "bulletproof hosting providers," or networks known to willingly support malicious activities. These are extreme cases where the networks in question essentially hosted only malicious content, and removing the entire network would disable large swaths of botnets and related malicious network infrastructure. The effect of these takedowns were indirectly measured by witnessing drops in spam levels, for example, upwards of two-thirds decrease after McColo's shutdown [9]. Unfortunately, if a particular botnet relied on the DNS to perform C&C resolutions into these bulletproof networks, once a new host was provisioned the threat would continue. Sure enough, we saw spam levels rise back to normal levels as botnets moved to other hosting providers [5].

2.2 Datasets

rza relies on two primary data sources: a large passive DNS database and a malware database that ties malicious binaries to the domain names the query during execution.

Passive DNS.

A passive DNS (pDNS) database stores historic mappings between domain names and IP addresses based on successful resolutions seen on a live network over time. pDNS databases allow us to reconstruct the historical structure of DNS-based infrastructure based on how it was used by clients. Our pDNS is constructed from real-world DNS resolutions seen in a large North American ISP. This allows us to identify the *related historic domain names* (RHDN) for a given IP, namely all domains that resolved to that IP in the past. Also, pDNS allows us to find the *related historic IP addresses* (RHIP) for a given domain name, i.e., all the IPs to which the domain resolved to in the past. Furthermore, the RHIP/RHDNs can be limited to domain-to-IP mappings that occurred during a particular time frame of interest, thus allowing us to focus on the crucial days before and after a takedown took place.

To enable our takedown analysis we define the following functions over the pDNS database:

- RHIP(`domain`, `start_date`, `end_date`): returns all domains historically related to the `domain` argument over the period between the desired start and end dates. For example, RHIP(`foo.com`, 2012/01/01, 2012/01/05) would return the set of all IP addresses `foo.com` successfully resolved to between January 1st, 2012 and January 5th, 2012, inclusive.
- RHDN(`IP`, `start_date`, `end_date`): similarly, RHDN returns all domains historically related to the IP argument over the period between the start and end dates.
- Volume(`domain` and/or `IP`, `date`): the total successful lookup volume to the argument domain, IP, or domain and IP tuple on the argument date.

It is important to note that our use of private pDNS data was dictated mainly by convenience and cost issues. To demonstrate that *rza* can properly function using different sources of passive DNS data, we obtained temporary access to the ISC-SIE passive DNS database [4], which is available to other researchers and offers an arguably more global perspective.

Malware Domains.

We also make use of a separate malware database that contains mappings between a malware sample's MD5 sum and binary and the domain names and IP addresses it has queried during dynamic malware analysis. Each entry in the database is a 4-tuple that includes the MD5 of the malware sample, the queried domain name, the resolved IP address, and the date and time of the analysis. These data are collected from a combination of internal malware analysis output as well as the output from a commercial malware feed.

3. RZA SYSTEM

In this section, we detail the internals of *rza*, our takedown analysis and recommendation system.

3.1 Overview

Figure 1 shows the overall process implemented by *rza*. Given a set of known seed botnet domains D_S, *rza* can be asked to generate either a "Postmortem Report" or a "Takedown Recommendation".

In the "Postmortem Report" mode, the input domains represent the domains known to have been targeted by an historic takedown. This produces a report that shows the effectiveness of the takedown of the domain names (Figure 1, step 5a) with respect to the expanded infrastructure *rza* identifies.

In the "Takedown Recommendation" mode, the input domains represent the currently known malicious domains used for C&C infrastructure. Furthermore, the takedown recommendation engine explores possible network resources that may be used by the botnet as a C&C backup mechanism, and suggests any additional measures that must be taken after the primary C&C is disabled to fully eliminate the threat (Figure 1, step 5b).

At a high level, the processing steps executed by *rza* are similar when producing both the "Postmortem Report" and "Takedown Recommendation", despite the difference in inputs and the meaning of the results. The steps are:

1. Expand the initial domain seed set D_S using the pDNS database to identify other domains that are likely related to the botnet's C&C infrastructure. Intuitively, domains are cheap but IP addresses are relatively more expensive. By identifying additional domains that resolve to the same hosts as malicious domains, we can identify other potentially malicious domains related to the botnet.
2. Identify the subset of the expanded domains that are queried by known malware samples. If a domain both points to a host known to facilitate a C&C and is also used by known malware, it increases the likelihood of that domain itself being malicious as well.
3. Identify the subset of the expanded domains with low domain name reputation. Similar to the intuition of

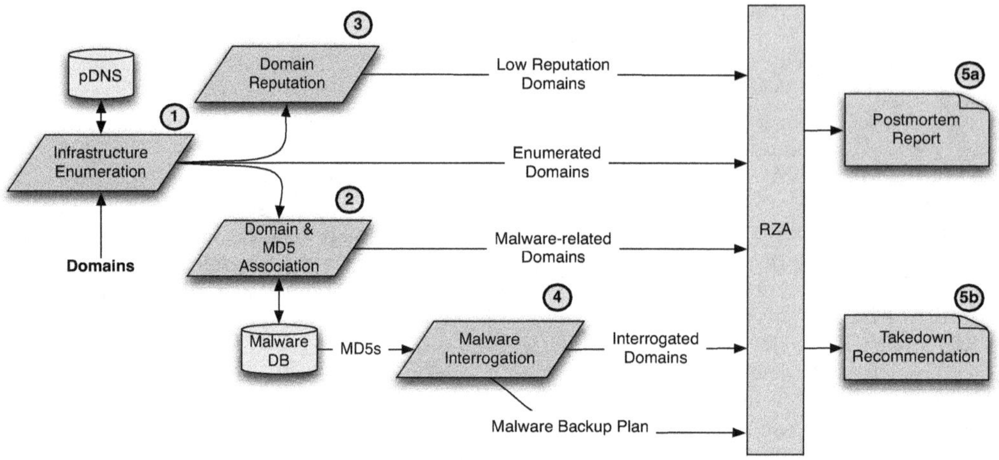

Figure 1: Overview of *rza*.

Step 2, a domain that points to a known malicious host and also has low domain reputation is more likely to itself be malicious.

4. Analyze the malware samples identified in Step 2. In addition to straightforward dynamic malware analysis, we trick executing malware samples into believing that their primary C&C infrastructure is unavailable using a custom malware analysis system [17] to extract additional C&C domain names. Intuitively, domains used by malware related to the infrastructure we are studying are likely to be related and malicious. Furthermore, we use the results of the analysis to identify malware contingency plans that would allow the botnet to continue to function after its primary C&C infrastructure has been disabled (e.g., a DGA-based or P2P C&C).

5. Output either the "Postmortem Report" or "Takedown Recommendation" depending on the mode of operation selected at the beginning.

The guiding principle we follow with *rza* is to push our understanding of malicious C&C infrastructure towards completeness. Only once we have fully enumerated the C&C infrastructure can we successfully disable it. We can begin to enumerate C&Cs from the network-level by identifying historic relationships between domain names and hosts using pDNS evidence, and from the host-level by interrogating malware samples. Since the pDNS may contain additional domains not necessarily related to the botnet in question, we identify subsets of domains so we can focus our investigative efforts on those that are most likely to be malicious and not inundate ourselves with information. Each subset serves a different purpose: the low reputation subset holds the domain names from the network-level that are most likely to be malicious. The subset of domains queried by malware represents a reasonable baseline to expect from prior takedowns, as much of this information is readily available to the security community. The subset gleaned from malware analysis contains the domains from the host-level that are the most likely to be malicious. We can use these sets to measure the effectiveness of past takedowns and recommend domains for future takedowns.

In the remainder of this section we describe each of these high-level tasks in detail, and discuss how they work together to suggest a takedown response.

3.2 Infrastructure Enumeration

Botnets often make use of the DNS to increase the reliability of their C&C infrastructure, for example using domain name fluxing or simply replacing retired or blacklisted domains with new domains. This cycling of domains, however, leaves a trail in the pDNS database and can be used to enumerate the infrastructure. For example, consider a malware sample m that on day t_1 uses domain d_1 as its primary C&C domain, but on day t_2 switches to domain d_2 to evade the blacklisting of d_1. Assume d_1 and d_2 resolve to the same IP address. Analysis during either t_1 or t_2 yields only one of the possible domains, but the relationship between d_1 and d_2 can be identified in a pDNS database because both resolved to the same IP address.

Using the passive DNS database and the seed domain set D_S, we compute the enumerated infrastructure domain set D_e using Algorithm 1. First, the related-historic IPs (RHIP) of D_S are retrieved and known sinkhole, parking, and private IP addresses are removed. The related-historic domain names (RHDN) for the remaining IPs are retrieved, and any benign domain names are removed, yielding the enumerated infrastructure of D_S: D_e. The relationships retrieved from the pDNS database are within a range of dates to ignore historic relationships that are no longer relevant. This constant is customizable but we empirically chose seven days based on the trend in domain name activations and deactivations to the domain names contained in D_e as described in Appendix C.

To understand why we filter out benign domains consider an attacker that, in an attempt to mislead our analysis, temporarily has their malicious domains resolve into benign IP space (e.g., Google's) or uses a popular hosting provider (e.g., Amazon AWS). If either of these occur, the D_e domain set may include unrelated, benign domain names. To handle this, we filter domains if they are a member, or are a subdomain of a member, of the set of the Alexa top 10,000 domain names. These domains are unlikely to be persistently malicious and should not be considered for takedown. IP

Input: D_S, startdate, enddate: seed domain set, and bounding dates
Output: D_e: enumerated domain set

$I_b \leftarrow$ set of known sinkhole, private, parking IPs
$W_d \leftarrow$ set of Alexa top 10,000 domain names
$I \leftarrow RHIP(D_S, \text{startdate}, \text{enddate})$
$I \leftarrow I \setminus I_b$
$D_e \leftarrow RHDN(I, \text{startdate}, \text{enddate})$
$D_e \leftarrow D_e \setminus W_d$
return D_e

Algorithm 1: Infrastructure enumeration procedure.

addresses that are non-informative (private, sinkhole, etc.) are also removed, as the domains that resolve to them are unlikely to be related. For example, malware domains sometimes point to private IP addresses (e.g., `127.0.0.1`) when they are not in use, which if not removed would link otherwise unrelated domain names. We use the Alexa top 10,000 in Section 3.3, and for consistency we use it here as well. In future work we intend to explore the effect of using smaller and larger whitelists on the generated sets and their accuracy.

3.3 Malware Interrogation

We can interrogate a single malware sample under different environmental conditions to learn additional domains it may use to reach its C&C, as well as any contingency plans for C&C infrastructure failure. We identify the set of malware samples M that communicate with domains in D_e for interrogation. To accomplish this, we can use our existing system that studies malware's behavior under primary C&C failure [17] to automatically determine malware backup plans. We run an individual malware sample under five execution scenarios, extract the network endpoints the malware sample used to "phoned home", and based on the differences observed during executions, we identify likely backup plans.

Behaviorally, most malware when presented with unavailable centralized infrastructure resort to one of the following backup plans:

1. The malware simply retries connecting to hardcoded domains and/or IP addresses.
2. The malware attempts to connect to a *finite* set of additional domains and/or additional IP addresses.
3. The malware attempts to connect to an "*infinite*" set of domains and/or IPs. This occurs when a malware uses a DGA- or P2P-based backup system.

We can isolate and detect these behaviors by running each sample and applying various packet manipulation scenarios to simulate infrastructure takedown. As a control, we manipulate *none* of the packets during execution. To show that a domain name has been revoked, we rewrite all DNS response packets that resolve non-whitelisted domain names to say the domain no longer exists (NXDomain). We run a sample under this scenario twice for durations t and $2t$. To feign IP address takedowns, we interrupt TCP streams with TCP reset (RST) packets when the destination is to a non-whitelisted IP address. We also run this scenario for durations t and $2t$. Intuitively, if the number of endpoints (domains or IPs) remains consistent across all runs, the malware sample does not include a contingency plan for C&C failure. If the number of endpoints is greater when the DNS or TCP rewriting is enabled, but remains similar between the two runs with different durations, we expect the malware contains a finite set of additional endpoints as a backup mechanism. However, if we see many more endpoints in the $2t$ duration run than in the t run, this suggests the malware is capable of constantly generating additional candidate domains or IPs to connect to, which indicates DGA or P2P behavior, respectively. In the event that the primary C&C infrastructure is already disabled as we would expect in the postmortem studies, the interrogation results still hold. If the botnet employs a backup DGA/P2P mechanism, we will still detect this as the t and $2t$ duration runs will still differ. The system may misclassify a sample as having no backup plan if its infrastructure is already disabled, but this is unlikely to effect *rza* from functioning properly. Consider a sample m that has a finite number of backup domains, but all of the primary domains have already expired and return NXDomain. The control run and DNS rewriting run will be identical and the sample will be misclassified as having no backup behavior, however, we will still identify all the backup domains so the results will still hold.

We empirically design heuristics using the above intuition and by analyzing 595 malware samples from 10 malware families with known contingency plans and catering our rules to perform the identification. Of the samples analyzed, 433 had no contingency plan, 55 used a DGA, 81 used P2P communications, and 22 employed a finite set of backup domains. None of the analyzed malware used a finite number of additional IP addresses. Our heuristics successfully classified 97% of the samples' contingency plans correctly.

3.4 Categorizing the Expanded Infrastructure

Not all domains identified during the infrastructure enumeration process are guaranteed to be malicious, but we can identify subsets that are more likely to be malicious. For example, a domain that resolves to an IP address in a virtual web hosting provider is likely to have many benign and unrelated domains that resolve to the same infrastructure as well. To account for this, we focus on domains with known (often public) malware associations, and domains that have low domain name reputation.

Using the passive DNS, we expand the initial seed domain set, D_S, into the expanded set D_e. Next, we identify $D_m \subseteq D_e$ and $D_r \subseteq D_e$, the subset of domain names in D_e with known malware associations and low domain name reputation, respectively. Malware associations are retrieved from our domain name to malware MD5 database and are commonly available in the security community [20]. To determine if a domain name has low reputation, we use a system similar in spirit to [1, 2] which scores domain reputation between 0.0 and 1.0, where 1.0 denotes a low reputation (i.e., likely malicious) domain name. Any domains with > 0.5 reputation are considered malicious and are added to D_r. Unlike D_r and D_m, the set D_i is not necessarily a subset of D_e. Any domains that are used by malware during malware interrogation are added to D_i. These domains expand our coverage as they may unearth domain names that were not previously included in D_e. During our postmortem analysis, we compare these sets to the domains that were actually involved in the takedown (D_S).

Figure 2 shows a Venn diagram representation of a possible configuration of enumerated infrastructure sets. All sets, excluding D_i, are subsets of D_e. D_i is the most likely to include domains outside of the scope of D_e, but suffers the most from the problem of completeness as it relies on dynamic malware analysis.

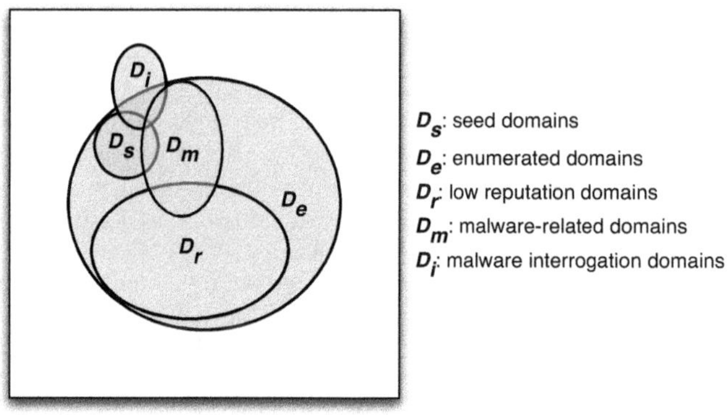

Figure 2: Venn diagram of identified infrastructure sets.

3.5 Takedown Recommendation Engine

Using the four aforementioned techniques, we can run our takedown protocol as shown by the decision tree in Figure 3. Suppose we are interested in taking down a hypothetical botnet where the current known infrastructure is D_S = {`01.hans.gruber.com`}. After enumerating the infrastructure, we identify the additional domain name `02.hans.gruber.com` that resolves to the same IP as the `01` child domain. We identify and retrieve the malware samples that have queried the `01...` and `02...` domain names and interrogate them. We identify an additional domain name, `03.hans.gruber.com`, when the first two domain names fail to resolve. Since we identified a finite number of new domain names, we re-run the process with the expanded set of three domain names and this time the malware analysis yields no behavioral changes from what we have already identified. In the event a DGA or a P2P backup scheme is present, the DGA must be reverse-engineered or the P2P network must be subverted as described in [18] after disabling the main C&C infrastructure, respectively.

The question remains which sets of domains should be revoked or sinkholed in order to terminate the botnet's C&C infrastructure, which ultimately must be decided by human operators. In the case where eliminating the botnet is more important than any possible collateral damage that may be incurred, the set of domains in $D_e \cup D_i$ should be targeted, which we consider to be the "nuclear" option. This contains any domain name associated with the C&C infrastructure as well as domains queried by the related malware. In other scenarios, however, this may incur too much collateral damage. We recommend revoking $D_r \cup D_i$ instead in these cases, as these domains are very likely to be malicious. These decisions should be made by threat researchers based on the potential risks associated with deactivating these domain names. Another, less extreme option is to simply block these domains at the network's egress point. This allows enterprise-sized networks to protect themselves while lessening the negative impact incurred by collateral damage.

Ground truth for C&C infrastructure is difficult to come by, which makes evaluating true positives and false positives exceedingly difficult. To roughly estimate this, we present the precision and recall of each set against the "correct" set of $D_r \cup D_i$. If we assume that domains flagged as low reputation or used by malware known to be affiliated with a given botnet are malicious, we can use this union to roughly correspond to ground truth. In our case, the precision of a set D is the fraction of the number of domain names d that are $d \in D \wedge d \in D_r \cup D_i$ over the size of D or $|D|$ and the recall is the fraction between the same number of domain names as in the precision but over the size of the "correct" set, or $|D_r \cup D_i|$.

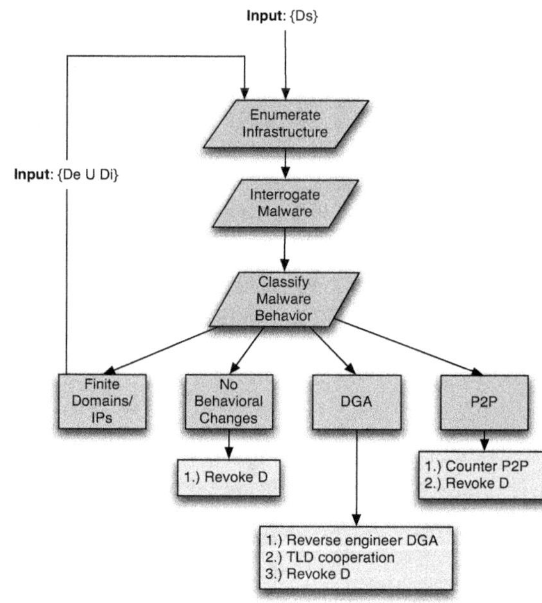

Figure 3: Takedown recommendation engine shown as a decision tree. D in this case represents either $D_r \cup D_i$, which only targets C&C domains that are very likely to be malicious or $D_e \cup D_i$, or the "nuclear" option that should only be used when the threat of the botnet outweighs potential collateral damage.

3.6 Use of Other Sources of pDNS Data

Out of both financial and analysis convenience, we ran our experiments using Damballa's internal passive DNS database. To show that our results are not tied to private data and can be replicated by other researchers, we run a subset of our experiments using the Internet System Consortium/Security Information Exchange's (ISC/SIE) passive DNS database [4][1]. While the database is not exactly public, it is generally available to practicing researchers and professionals in the security community (possibly for a fee). As pDNS data becomes more popular, we expect the number of these databases to increase and become more easily accessible by researchers.

[1]Since the additional experiments were run, the ISC/SIE's pDNS database has been acquired by a private company, Farsight Security Inc. The website suggests database access will continue to be made available to qualified security researchers and practitioners.

Using ISC/SIE's pDNS database and *rza*'s process outlined in this section, we generate the D_e, D_m, and D_r domain sets of one postmortem takedown and five current botnets. As before, we compute the respective TIR values of each set. We chose the five botnets with the largest C&C infrastructure that Damballa began tracking in April, 2013. Our results from the SIE dataset are presented in Appendix B.

4. POSTMORTEM STUDIES

In this section, we describe how we use *rza* to evaluate historical takedowns. We introduce the takedowns we study and describe the measurements we use to understand the effectiveness of the takedown. We end the section with our experimental results on the postmortem studies. We briefly describe how we identified the initial seed domain sets (D_S) for prior takedowns in Section ??.

4.1 Postmortem Analysis

For our postmortem analysis, we chose to study the takedowns of Kelihos [12] (aka Operation b79), a Zeus botnet instance [14] (aka Operation b71), and the 3322.org NS takedown that targeted the Nitol botnet [13] (aka Operation b70). We chose these takedowns because they are both recent and high profile. For each takedown, we collect the domains described in the temporary restraining orders (TRO) and use these as our seed domains (D_S).

Measuring Takedown Improvement.

Prior studies of botnet takedowns relied on secondary measurements, such as global spam volumes, to determine the success of a takedown. Instead, we directly measure the successful domain name resolutions to the identified infrastructure to proxy for the victim population. By comparing the lookup volume to the seed domains (D_S) with the lookup volume to the sets of domains identified by *rza*, we can determine if a takedown was successful and what domains it missed. For example, if all domain sets are equivalent, their lookup volumes will be identical and the takedown would be considered successful.

More formally, for each takedown, t, and its collected seed domains, D_S^t, we generate the enumerated infrastructure sets D_e^t, D_m^t, D_r^t and D_i^t using *rza*. D_e^t is generated using *only* successful DNS resolutions that were issued during the seven days *before* the takedown of t was performed according to the court documents[2]. This allows us to compare what was actually disabled and/or sinkholed during the takedown with what *rza* would have recommended.

For a period of 14 days surrounding the takedown, we plot the successful aggregate daily lookup volume to each of the previously identified sets. To quantify the gains in takedown effectiveness, we calculate the *takedown improvement ratio* as defined by Equation 1.

$$TIR(D_1, D_2) = \frac{MDLV(D_1)}{MDLV(D_2)} \quad (1)$$

Where D_1 and D_2 are two domain name sets and $MDLV$ is a function on domain name sets that computes the median daily successful lookup volume. We use the median, rather than the mean, since we are interested in preserving long-term lookup volume trends, which are not captured by outliers. If $TIR(D_m^t, D_S^t) > 1$, this means the subset of D_e of malware-related domain names D_m^t had a stronger lookup volume and accounts for domain names missed by the takedown domains D_S^t. Conversely, if the $TIR \leq 1$, the takedown deactivated related malware domains already and was successful. We also identify malware backup behaviors.

Estimating Risk.

To provide a different perspective, we also quantify the potential risk of *collateral damage*, or the negative effect of mistakenly taking down benign domains. Ideally, we would represent this by the number of distinct clients that would be denied access to benign services, however, we can once again turn to the lookup volumes to proxy for this.

If we assume all infected botnet hosts behave identically, the aggregate lookup volume on a given day is proportional to the number of infected clients. At most, a single lookup corresponds to a distinct client reaching that domain, however, due to DNS caching effects, differences in malware variant and human behaviors, and network address translation (NAT), this is likely an overestimation of the actual client population. We assume that these behaviors are consistent with respect to queries towards a given botnet.

We quantify the potential risk of collateral damage for a takedown as the difference in the median lookup volume between an enumerated set and the initial seed domain set as defined by Equation 2.

$$Risk(D_1, D_2) = MDLV(D_1) - MDLV(D_2) \quad (2)$$

Using similar notation as seen in Equation 1. Intuitively, the difference between these two quantities is proportional to the number of individuals that would be inconvenienced by this takedown if *all* the domains in D_1 that are not in D_2 *are not malicious*. This provides an upper bound on the potential risk involved. The "nuclear option" of taking down all the domains in D_e, or sinkholing all domains that resolve to hosts known to provide C&C for a botnet, is the only way to ensure the C&C communication line is severed, however, this should be weighed against the potential risks.

An analyst wishing to perform a takedown can use the risk values to weigh whether to employ the "nuclear" option or the more reserved options as described in Section 3.5. In future work, we hope to improve the risk measure in two ways. First, we can correlate the risk value with the identified true and false positive rates during a real, or simulated, takedown. Furthermore, we wish to more accurately estimate the true population of visitors to infrastructure, malicious or otherwise. This can further help analysts by allowing them to weigh the likelihood of maliciousness against the population that would be affected by a takedown.

For each of the following takedown postmortem analysis, the dashed red line on each plot indicates the date the takedown was performed according to the court proceedings. Each line plot represents the aggregate daily lookup volume to a subset of domains that are either directed to a sinkhole or contained within the enumerated infrastructure sets generated by *rza*. In all cases the D_e lookup volume represents an upper bound of malicious lookups.

[2]These are September 11th, 2012; March 25th, 2012 and September 26th, 2011 for the 3322.org, Zeus and Kelihos takedowns, respectively.

Sets	TIR value	Risk
D_m, D_S	0.913	-399.5
D_r, D_S	5.690	21,555
D_i, D_S	0.022	-4,492.5
D_e, D_S	10.230	42,415.5

Table 1: TIR and *Risk* values for Kelihos takedown. These values represent the improvement to a takedown based on *rza*'s output and the potential risk of collateral damage, respectively.

4.2 Kelihos

The Kelihos botnet was a spam botnet that sent approximately four billion spam messages[15] a day in its first iteration and was targeted for takedown in late 2011. We show the daily volumes for the sets D_S, D_e and D_m for Kelihos in Figure 4. The day Kelihos was taken down, we see lookups to the seed domains completely stop, showing that these domains were effectively remediated. The court order did not specify sinkholes to be used, which explains why the domains simply cease to resolve. The set of malware-related domains, D_m, and interrogated domains, D_i, also cut off sharply at this point, with a handful of successful resolutions occurring for D_m a few days after the takedown date and ceasing to resolve afterwards. This suggests the initial takedown missed some domains, but these were quickly remediated as well. D_r has a spike similar to D_e, and upon further investigation the spike was revealed to be a malicious domain that resolved into Kelihos' infrastructure but could not be confirmed to be a Kelihos C&C. This domain stopped resolving after the peak date (September 24th).

The computed TIR values are shown in Table 1. Much like the daily volumes figure, the TIR values suggest this takedown was successful. We see large TIR values for D_e and D_r, which indicate additional malicious domains were left unperturbed that resolved into Kelihos' hosting infrastructure. The similar trend between D_e and D_r suggests that many of the extended infrastructure domains are in fact malicious and could have been removed during the Kelihos takedown effort.

For the D_e and D_m sets, we have precision and recall of 0.22/0.67 and 0.25/0.03, respectively. The recall for D_e is quite low as this means upwards of 30% of the domain names that are likely malicious were harvested from malware interrogation. This stresses the importance of labeling both from network information from pDNS, as well as information gathered from malware.

According to the analysis by *rza*, this takedown was largely a success, however, we know that new variants of Kelihos emerged soon after. Analyzing its 168 malware samples from before the takedown shows that a P2P C&C mechanism existed as a backup plan in the malware, which may have helped bootstrap its resurgence. This stresses the importance of being prepared to counter malware behavior after its primary infrastructure has been disabled.

4.3 Zeus

The Zeus takedown targeted a large botnet that used the popular malware kit Zeus to create its malware. This takedown relied on sinkholing the seed domains. We show the daily volumes for the sets D_S, D_e, D_m, D_r, as well the volumes for *domains in* D_e that resolve into sinkholes operated by Microsoft and the other sinkholing party, in Figure 5. Of

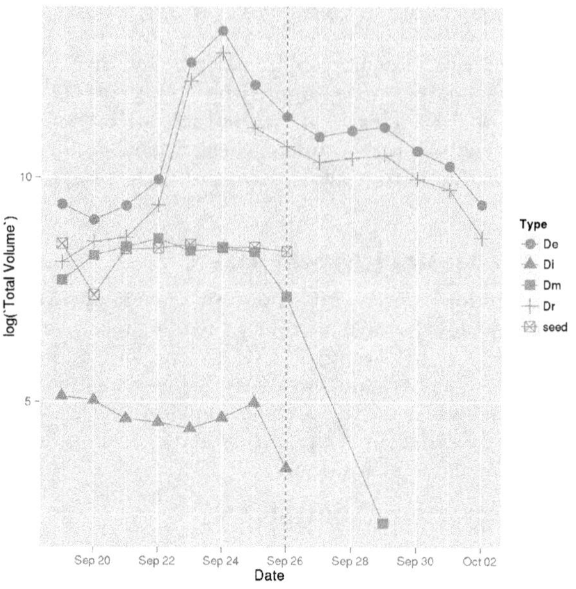

Figure 4: Kelihos aggregate daily lookup volume (log-scale).

the 2,825 malware samples analyzed, none of them included a P2P- or DGA-based contingency plan.

The first observation is that unlike in the case of Kelihos, Microsoft began sinkholing domains *before* the date specified in the court order as evidenced by the non-zero query volume resolving into Microsoft's sinkholes before the takedown date. To reiterate, domains that resolved only to the sinkhole before the takedown date were not included to prevent prior uses of the sinkhole from interfering with our results. Furthermore, the volume of lookups that resolve into the sinkhole are orders of magnitude larger than the lookups only to the seed domains, suggesting that domains *not* specified in the court order were also sinkholed. We see a spike in lookup traffic directed towards the seed domains and domains that resolve to Microsoft's sinkhole, indicating increased sinkholing action at the time of takedown. *rza*'s D_m set captured fewer domains than those sunk by Microsoft's sinkhole, however, there is a large discrepancy in lookups to domains flagged as malicious by our reputation system, i.e., lookups to the domains in set D_r. We see a drop in lookups to D_r that corresponds to the Microsoft sunk domains, which indicates D_r subsumes the set of sunk domains. The other sinkhole operation experienced a similar drop after the Microsoft takedown, which suggests there was contention over which domains belonged to which sinkhole.

In this takedown, the ad-hoc nature of takedowns made coordination between companies difficult and the lack of oversight allowed the court order to not be followed exactly. While Microsoft was clearly sinkholing more domain names, the takedown interfered with an existing takedown. Without a centralized method of communicating who is sinkholing what, this pattern of stepping on other researchers' toes is likely to continue.

The computed TIR values are shown in Table 2. We compare against both the seed domain set, and the set of domains resolving into Microsoft's sinkhole. With respect to the seed domain set, we nearly tie considering malware-related domains and capture many more lookups to poten-

Sets	TIR value	Risk
D_m, D_S	0.979	-11,357.5
D_r, D_S	3.921	1,641,580
D_i, D_S	0.148	-478,874
D_e, D_S	14.321	7,486,221
D_m, D_{mssink}	0.553	-444,265.5
D_r, D_{mssink}	2.215	1,208,672
D_i, D_{mssink}	0.084	-911,782
D_e, D_{mssink}	8.091	7,053,313

Table 2: *TIR* and *Risk* values for Zeus takedown.

tially malicious domains when considering the dataset derived from reputation, D_r. The story is similar when compared to domains that resolve into the Microsoft sinkhole, but to a lesser extent. Recall the volumes for Microsoft sinkhole resolutions *only* include domains we identified in D_e. This suggests that not only were these deemed malicious by a 3rd party, but they were added by Microsoft independent of the domains listed in the court order.

For the D_e and D_m sets, we have precision and recall of 0.03/0.98 and 0.30/0.01, respectively. Most of these values are quite low, with the exception of D_e's recall, which is unsurprising. This indicates most of the malicious domains could be identified through passive DNS. The low precision value for D_e indicates that many of these domains should probably not be targeted in a takedown and the low precision for D_m suggests that while many have low reputation and are likely malicious there are no known malware associations, reinforcing the motivation for using domain name reputation.

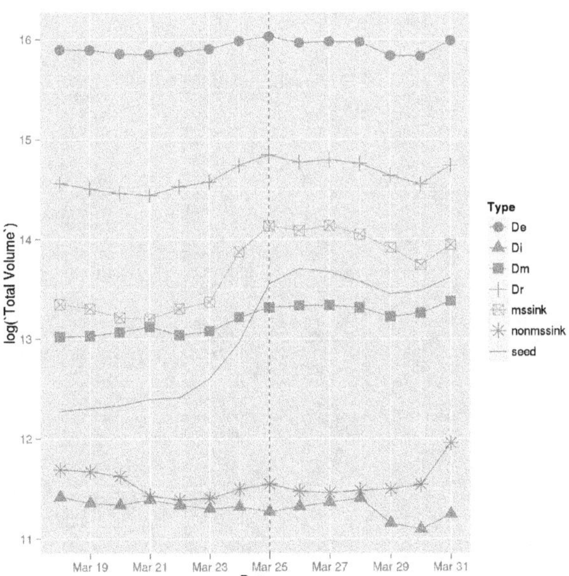

Figure 5: Zeus aggregate daily lookup volume (log-scale).

4.4 3322.org

The 3322.org takedown represents the most extreme case where *rza* would have improved a takedown's effectiveness. This takedown was accomplished by transferring the entire 3322.org Name Server's (NS) authority to Microsoft and domains deemed malicious resolved to a set of known sinkhole IP addresses. The daily volume plot for 3322.org is shown in Figure 6. Unlike the Zeus takedown, domains were sunk on the day of the takedown and were limited to *.3322.org domain names. Unfortunately, this only accounted for a fraction of the lookups to domains with known malware associations, D_m, and domains with low reputation, D_r that resolved to hosts known to support malicious activity. We notice a drop in lookups to D_m and D_r when the takedown is performed, showing that most of the domains targeted by the takedown were likely malicious, however, the lookups to remaining infrastructure identified by *rza* are still frequent. We see D_i closely matches the sinkholed domain names, suggesting this is the primary method that was used to identify the takedown domains. Unlike the previous two cases, all enumerated sets have *TIR* values greater than one. This agreement suggests that malicious domains were almost certainly missed during the 3322.org takedown effort. Of the 10,135 malware samples we analyzed, none of them had a P2P- or DGA-based contingency plan.

Sets	TIR value	Risk
D_m, D_{mssink}	13.821	409,593.5
D_r, D_{mssink}	18.956	573,627.5
D_i, D_{mssink}	1.049	1,560
D_e, D_{mssink}	654.940	20,890,774

Table 3: *TIR* and *Risk* values for 3322.org takedown.

This case shows the importance of using multiple sources to determine related malicious infrastructure before performing a takedown. Simply identifying domains with known malware associations offers a substantial improvement on the effectiveness of the takedown. Further, the similarity between the D_m and D_r trends shows most of the domains overlap between the two, which only further bolsters the likelihood that they are indeed malicious. To make matters worse, all the domains that were not sinkholed were given enterprise-level domain name resolution services, despite the high probability they were involved in malicious activities. The computed *TIR* values for the 3322.org takedown are shown in Table 3. Unlike the previous two postmortems, *rza* identified numerous additional malicious domains that were left undisturbed by the takedown on 3322.org.

For the D_e and D_m sets, we have precision and recall of 0.06/0.95 and 0.38/0.03, respectively. These results are similar to those for Zeus and further reinforce the need to include domain reputation as a measure in *rza*. Simply relying on passive DNS (for D_e) and malware associations (for D_m) overestimate and underestimate the malicious domain names, respectively.

5. TAKEDOWN RECOMMENDATION ANALYSIS

In this section, we run *rza*'s takedown protocol on 45 botnet C&Cs being tracked by Damballa, Inc. during the month of April, 2013 and present the results. We chose to use the C&Cs already tracked by Damballa out of convenience and it is important to stress that they could be substituted by any set of domain names known to correspond to a botnet's C&C infrastructure. There are many publicly available sources of this information that allow similar experiments to be repeated. The calculated TIR values and

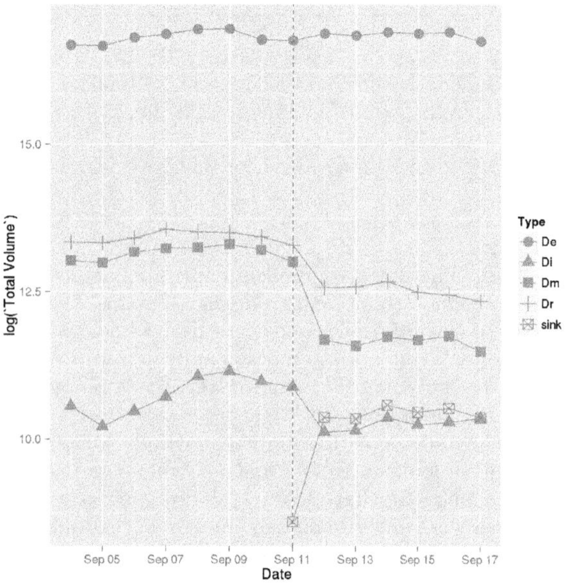

Figure 6: 3322.org aggregate daily lookup volume (log-scale).

predicated backup plans for the 45 botnets are shown in Table 4 and the associated Risk values are shown in Table 5.

Overall, the TIR values indicate we are gaining additional infrastructure information as we did in the postmortem cases. Similarly, we see very large TIRs for the expanded infrastructure set, D_e, further evidence that infrastructure related by the passive DNS includes additional domains that need to be narrowed down by categorizing the domain sets. These TIR values were smaller, as we saw with the postmortems, with the malware-related and reputation-based sets—D_m and D_r, respectively—contributing the bulk of the newly observed lookup volumes.

In addition to describing the enumerated infrastructure sets, we also identify the backup mechanisms, if any, present in the botnet. If a botnet's malware has no backup plan, it is a prime candidate for a smooth, DNS-only takedown, otherwise we have identified the necessary conditions for performing an effective takedown. The most important finding, however, is that of the 45 botnets we studied 42 of them had no contingency plan for central C&C failure, suggesting the bulk of these botnets can be successfully taken down *without* requiring additional measures, such as reverse engineering a DGA or combating a P2P-based C&C. This suggests that while performing a takedown is difficult, we are likely to succeed in many cases.

6. CONCLUSION

We presented *rza*, a takedown analysis and recommendation system that performs postmortem analyses of past takedowns, as well as making recommendations for performing more effective takedowns in the future. *rza* would be useful in helping to both expedite the takedown process, as well as ensuring future takedowns are more complete.

Acknowledgments

The authors thank the anonymous reviewers for their helpful comments and insightful questions, and our shepherd

ID	D_e	D_m	D_r	D_i	Backup Plan
1	7.229	2.719	6.815	1.446	finite-domain
2	13.669	0.000	23.891	275.751	p2p
3	0.856	0.000	0.764	0.142	none
4	2.808	1.158	2.602	0.554	dga
5	12.005	10.117	11.612	0.023	none
6	20.632	1.448	15.665	0.044	none
7	2.130	0.015	0.798	11.917	none
8	289.387	154.932	233.521	0.000	none
9	42.570	0.000	23.522	1.395	finite-domain
10	0.746	0.000	0.597	0.241	finite-domain
11	3.783	1.068	3.208	0.255	none
12	13.115	3.809	11.896	0.246	none
13	10.139	1.698	8.726	0.697	none
14	8.266	0.000	8.259	3.190	none
15	2.028	0.189	0.131	0.094	finite-domain
16	471.226	76.176	392.788	1.045	finite-domain
17	87.004	33.807	72.759	4.052	none
18	27.036	1.810	14.952	1.021	none
19	8715.005	816.740	8696.197	8.520	none
20	170.752	0.743	10.210	0.405	finite-domain
21	7.260	2.012	5.828	0.056	none
22	13.492	1.364	12.011	0.000	none
23	14.146	0.000	12.891	7.449	none
24	52.593	0.000	52.174	0.967	finite-domain
25	223.201	6.869	21.504	0.000	none
26	1067.604	0.000	1062.696	0.001	finite-domain
27	293.466	46.070	232.437	0.005	none
28	1.251	0.311	0.923	0.082	dga
29	13.589	0.547	4.886	1.100	finite-domain
30	380.568	27.986	350.686	0.082	none
31	17.700	0.000	16.837	0.500	finite-domain
32	5.857	4.679	5.724	0.575	finite-domain
33	25.042	4.085	21.460	3.094	none
34	0.156	0.139	0.152	0.014	finite-domain
35	25.048	1.272	15.638	0.000	none
36	12.121	7.364	11.183	0.336	finite-domain
37	11.698	10.329	11.544	2.321	none
38	91.364	0.457	9.618	0.000	none
39	4.640	1.085	3.694	0.599	finite-domain
40	7.491	0.303	6.865	257.059	finite-domain
41	3.161	0.485	2.700	0.187	finite-domain
42	2.378	0.487	2.372	1.288	finite-domain
43	33.227	12.958	31.650	3.014	none
44	21.761	2.219	3.061	1.108	none
45	2.217	0.101	2.150	0.103	none

Table 4: Recent botnet TIR values (compared against D_S) and backup plan classification.

ID	D_e	D_m	D_r	D_i
1	376,591	103,904	351,529	26,974
2	6260	−494	11,312	135,766
3	−7425	−51,681	−12,205	−44,352
4	694,233	60,473	614,941	−171,099
5	485,427	402,158	468,070	−44,110
6	362,341	8262	270,663	−18,457
7	6103	−5320	−1088	58,936
8	1,249,414	666,902	1,007,383	−4332
9	255,237	−6140	138,285	2427
10	−5122	−20,195	−8131	−15,320
11	3,024,316	73,348	2,399,494	−1,086,629
12	89,727	20,801	80,695	−7406
13	9,150,880	698,974	7,735,834	−1,001,304
14	17,959	−2472	17,942	5412
15	585	−461	−494	−515
16	4,106,017	656,434	3,421,089	−8732
17	80,537	30,721	67,197	−936
18	3128	97	1676	−120
19	277,603	25,987	277,004	−32
20	5,719,294	−8674	310,317	−33,692
21	1,061,289	171,489	818,507	−169,516
22	5,586,161	162,678	4,923,961	−447,172
23	478,741	−36,417	433,040	234,848
24	204,816	−3970	203,153	−130
25	9,034,976	238,626	833,715	−40,652
26	31,892,669	−29,901	31,745,933	−29,860
27	2,023,910	311,893	1,601,580	−6889
28	692	−1897	−212	−2528
29	26,164,386	−942,098	8,075,579	−2,078,370
30	341,286	24,265	314,418	−825
31	23,614	−1414	22,393	−707
32	392,925	297,607	382,154	−34,345
33	3,798,382	487,342	3,232,483	−157,989
34	−6385	−6519	−6416	−7466
35	468,361	5289	285,099	−19,476
36	741,041	424,070	678,530	−44,278
37	452,686	394,741	446,180	−42,314
38	6,688,344	−40,216	637,882	−74,015
39	1,676,605	39,173	1,240,928	−184,676
40	5,515,527	−592,194	4,983,178	217,562,247
41	160,793	−38,321	126,529	−60,522
42	224,265	−83,469	223,419	46,946
43	243,983	90,534	232,045	−7571
44	3,648,885	214,216	362,154	−175,760
45	498,000	−367,626	470,334	−409,148

Table 5: Recent botnet *Risk* values (compared against D_S).

Dr. Shiuhpyng Shieh for his guidance in improving our paper. We also thank RZA for reinventing rap production and bringing us the Wu-Tang Clan.

This material is based upon work supported in part by the National Science Foundation under Grants No. CNS-1017265, CNS-0831300, and CNS-1149051, by the Office of Naval Research under Grant No. N000140911042, and by the Department of Homeland Security under contract No. N66001-12-C-0133. Any opinions, findings, and conclusions or recommendations expressed in this material are those of the authors and do not necessarily reflect the views of the National Science Foundation, the Office of Naval Research, or the Department of Homeland Security.

APPENDIX

A. POLICY DISCUSSION

Takedowns are currently performed in an ad-hoc manner with little oversight, which makes it difficult for the security community at large to assist by contributing intelligence. Furthermore, there is no standard policy for enacting a takedown at the DNS-level forcing companies to coordinate with multiple registrars, pay for expensive court proceedings, or both to disable botnets. Existing measures for handling domain name issues exist, however, in the form of handling trademark disputes.

Our postmortem studies illustrated several drawbacks to the current ad-hoc manner in which takedowns are performed, namely: a lack of coordination, little to no oversight, and an environment that discourages collaboration. Without an effective form of coordination, we will continue to see instances in where two or more security companies, with good intentions, will step on each others toes as we saw in the Zeus takedown case. We also saw oversight issues in the Zeus takedown where domains were clearly being sinkholed *before* the date presented in the court order. Yet another, but more subtle, oversight issue deals with the method of instigating these takedowns: court orders. Each of the court orders for the presented takedowns were filed under seal, meaning they are not open to the public and require either the claimant to release the record under their discretion, or other legal action to unseal the record. Even more worrisome is language explicitly allowing further unverified action. In the 3322.org takedown temporary restraining order it was specified that "the authoritative name server ... [is] to respond to requests for the IP addresses of the sub-domains of 3322.org may respond to requests for the IP address of any domain listed in Appendix A *or later determined to be associated with malware activity...*" [13] (emphasis ours). While an authoritative name server takeover technically grants this ability, if the purpose of the court order is to prevent collateral damage or unlawful takedown this clause effectively negates any future protection. It also suggests that the full scope of the threat was not clear at the time of the takedown by specifically permitting further cleanup actions.

Trademark and intellectual property interests were involved very early on in during the formation of the Internet Corporation for Assigned Names and Numbers (ICANN), which is responsible for coordinating, among other critical Internet infrastructure, the DNS. Through the World Intellectual Property Organization (WIPO), trademark interests were arguing for procedures to protect trademarks in the DNS as early as December 1998 [16], and successfully forced ICANN to require a dispute resolution procedure dubbed the "Uniform Dispute Resolution Policy" or URDP.

URDP is an ICANN policy that specifies independent arbitrators to oversee the process of dispute resolution. These "[i]ndependent arbitrators make a decision quickly and (relative to courts) inexpensively" [16] and are built in to the accreditation contracts to registrars. The UDRP requires three conditions to be met to file a complaint:

i. your domain name is identical or confusingly similar to a trademark or service mark in which the complainant has rights; and

ii. you have no rights or legitimate interests in respect of the domain name; and

iii. your domain name has been registered and is being used in bad faith.

[6]. In its first year, UDRP successfully "handled over 2,500 cases involving nearly 4,000 names" [16] and has expanded since. In fact, ICANN is introducing The Uniform Rapid Suspension System (URS) [7] as a more expedited form of the URDP and is requiring new generic top-level domains (gTLDs) to follow URS in their contracts.

We suggest a similar procedure ought to be available to provide the security community a point of coordination and a formal process to follow when performing takedowns. It would reduce exorbitant fees paid to courts, would likely be faster, and would mandate oversight from arbitrators. The procedure could be applied to future TLDs as a test, much like URS. Automated systems like *rza* could serve an invaluable place in this process to reduce the burden on human operators and further expedite the takedown process.

B. RZA WITH ISC/SIE PDNS DATA

We replicated part of our evaluation using only ISC-SIE data. Specifically, we generated the D_e, D_m, and D_r domain sets and computed the respective TIR values of Zeus and five of the current botnets with the most domains we tracked in our paper. D_i sets were excluded due to time limitations. Our results from the SIE dataset are shown in Table 6 and are largely consistent and show that the process employed by RZA can be done with other sources of pDNS data. The important detail to glean is that the process *rza* uses is independent of our private dataset and can be performed using public sources of passive DNS data. Due to regional variations, the TIR values are unlikely to be identical between the two datasets; however, the process and generated sets are the important factors.

Takedown	$\mathbf{D_e}$	$\mathbf{D_m}$	$\mathbf{D_r}$
Zeus	4.843	0.000	1.014
#1	1.108	1.012	1.082
#2	0.969	0.969	0.459
#3	0.787	0.787	0.718
#4	0.680	0.680	0.613
#5	1.944	1.451	1.122

Table 6: SIE-computed TIR values.

C. WINDOW JUSTIFICATION

We consider the activation of a domain name $d \in D_e$ to occur when d first begins to resolve to a global IP address in the observation period and a deactivation to be the day when $d \in D_e$ no longer resolves to a global IP address. Figure 7 shows the number of new domain activations and deactivations for the domains in D_e for one of the takedowns analyzed in Section 4, as well as the net change for each day. We see that around seven days prior to the takedown the number of activations/deactivations has achieved an equilibrium motivating the choice of a 14 day observation window around the time of the takedown. Other takedowns exhibited similar behavior, but the details are not reported due to space limitations.

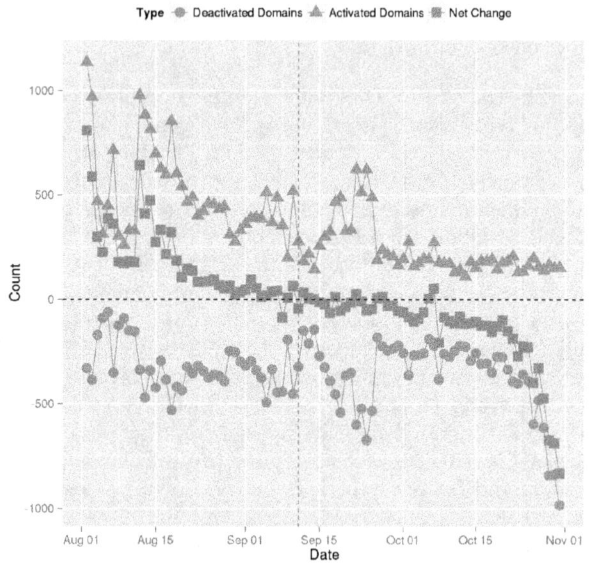

Figure 7: Domain name activations and deactivations in 3322.org takedown's D_e set.

D. REFERENCES

[1] M. Antonakakis, R. Perdisci, D. Dagon, and W. Lee. Building a Dynamic Reputation System for DNS. In *Proceedings of the USENIX Security Symposium*, 2010.

[2] L. Bilge, E. Kirda, C. Kruegel, and M. Balduzzi. EXPOSURE: Finding Malicious Domains Using Passive DNS Analysis. In *Network and Distributed System Security Symposium (NDSS)*, 2011.

[3] Conficker Working Group. Conficker Working Group: Lessons Learned, 2011. `http://www.confickerworkinggroup.org/wiki/uploads/Conficker_Working_Group_Lessons_Learned_17_June_2010_final.pdf`.

[4] Farsight Security, Inc. SIE/Farsight Security's DNSDB, 2013. `https://www.dnsdb.info/`.

[5] M. Harris. Spammers recovering from McColo shutdown, 2009. `http://www.techradar.com/news/internet/spammers-recovering-from-mccolo-shutdown-591118`.

[6] Internet Corporation for Assigned Names and Numbers. Uniform Domain Name Dispute Resolution Policy. Technical report, 1999.

[7] Internet Corporation for Assigned Names and Numbers. Uniform Rapid Suspension System. Technical report, 2012.

[8] B. Krebs. Major Source of Online Scams and Spams Knocked Offline, 2008. `http://voices.washingtonpost.com/securityfix/2008/11/major_source_of_online_scams_a.html`.

[9] B. Krebs. Spam Volumes Drop by Two-Thirds After Firm Goes Offline, 2008. `http://voices.washingtonpost.com/securityfix/2008/11/spam_volumes_drop_by_23_after.html`.

[10] B. Krebs. Mariposa Botnet Authors May Avoid Jail Time, 2010. `http://krebsonsecurity.com/2010/03/mariposa-botnet-authors-may-avoid-jail-time/`.

[11] R. McMillan. After takedown, botnet-linked ISP Troyak resurfaces, 2010. `http://www.computerworld.com/s/article/9169118/After_takedown_botnet_linked_ISP_Troyak_resurfaces`.

[12] Microsoft Corporation. Microsoft Corporation v. Dominique Alexander Piatti; Jone Does 1-22. 2011. Virginia Eastern District Court.

[13] Microsoft Corporation. Microsoft Corporation v. Peng Yong et. al. 2012. Virginia Eastern District Court.

[14] Microsoft Corporation. Microsoft v. John Does 1-39. 2012. New York Eastern District Court.

[15] E. Mills. Microsoft halts another botnet: Kelihos, 2011. `http://news.cnet.com/8301-1009_3-20112289-83/microsoft-halts-another-botnet-kelihos/`.

[16] M. Mueller. *Ruling the root*. The MIT Press, 2004.

[17] Y. Nadji, M. Antonakakis, R. Perdisci, and W. Lee. Understanding the prevalence and use of alternative plans in malware with network games. In *Proceedings of the 27th Annual Computer Security Applications Conference (ACSAC '11)*, 2011.

[18] C. Rossow, D. Andriesse, and T. Werner. P2PWNED: Modeling and Evaluating the Resilience of Peer-to-Peer Botnets. In *Proceedings of the 34th IEEE Symposium on Security and Privacy (S&P 2013)*, 2013.

[19] U.S. Attorney's Office - Southern District of New York. Manhattan U.S. Attorney Charges Seven Individuals for Engineering Sophisticated Internet Fraud Scheme, 2011. `http://www.fbi.gov/newyork/press-releases/2011/manhattan-u.s.-attorney-charges-seven-individuals-for-engineering-sophisticated-internet-fraud-scheme-that-infected-millions-of-computers-worldwide-and-manipulated-internet-advertising-business`.

[20] VirusTotal. VirusTotal Intelligence. `https://www.virustotal.com/en/documentation/private-api/`.

Shady Paths: Leveraging Surfing Crowds to Detect Malicious Web Pages

Gianluca Stringhini, Christopher Kruegel, and Giovanni Vigna
University of California, Santa Barbara
{gianluca, chris, vigna}@cs.ucsb.edu

ABSTRACT

The web is one of the most popular vectors to spread malware. Attackers lure victims to visit compromised web pages or entice them to click on malicious links. These victims are redirected to sites that exploit their browsers or trick them into installing malicious software using social engineering.

In this paper, we tackle the problem of detecting malicious web pages from a novel angle. Instead of looking at particular features of a (malicious) web page, we analyze how a large and diverse set of web browsers reach these pages. That is, we use the browsers of a collection of web users to record their interactions with websites, as well as the redirections they go through to reach their final destinations. We then aggregate the different redirection chains that lead to a specific web page and analyze the characteristics of the resulting redirection graph. As we will show, these characteristics can be used to detect malicious pages.

We argue that our approach is less prone to evasion than previous systems, allows us to also detect scam pages that rely on social engineering rather than only those that exploit browser vulnerabilities, and can be implemented efficiently. We developed a system, called SpiderWeb, which implements our proposed approach. We show that this system works well in detecting web pages that deliver malware.

Categories and Subject Descriptors

K.6.5 [**Security and Protection**]: Invasive software; H.3.5 [**Online Information Services**]: Web-based services

General Terms

Security

Keywords

HTTP redirections, detection, malware

CCS'13, November 4–8, 2013, Berlin, Germany.
Copyright 2013 ACM 978-1-4503-2477-9/13/11 ...$15.00.
http://dx.doi.org/10.1145/2508859.2516682.

1. INTRODUCTION

The world-wide web is one of the main vectors used to spread malware. The most common way of infecting victims with malware is to present them with a web page that performs a *drive-by download attack* [18]. In a drive-by download attack, the malicious web page tries to exploit a vulnerability in the victim's browser or in a browser plugin. If successful, the injected code instructs the victim's computer to download and install malicious software. In other cases, attackers rely on simple social engineering scams to infect victims. That is, the web page tricks users into downloading and installing malicious software without exploiting any client-side vulnerability; an example of this are *fake antivirus scams* [23]. In this paper, we refer to the pages used to deliver both types of attacks as *malicious web pages.*

Existing systems to identify malicious web pages fall into two main categories. The first category uses techniques to statically analyze web pages and embedded code (such as JavaScript or Flash), looking for features that are typical of malicious activity. Such features can be patterns in the Uniform Resource Locators (URLs) of web pages [14,31], the presence of words or other information that are associated with malicious content [16,25,26], or the presence of malicious JavaScript snippets that are typical for exploits [2,3]. The second category leverages dynamic techniques; these approaches rely on visiting websites with an instrumented browser (often referred to as a *honeyclient*), and monitoring the activity of the machine for signs that are typical of a successful exploitation (e.g., the creation of a new process) [15,20,21,28].

Although existing systems help in making users safer, they suffer from a number of limitations. First, attackers can obfuscate their pages to make detection harder and, in many cases, they are able to successfully evade feature-based systems [8]. Second, attackers frequently hide their exploits by leveraging a technique called *cloaking* [27,30]. This technique works by fingerprinting the victim's web browser, and revealing the malicious content only in case the victim is using a specific version of the browser and a vulnerable plugin. Additionally, miscreants check the IP address of their visitors, and display a benign page to those IP addresses that belong to security companies or research institutions. Cloaking makes the work of dynamic analysis approaches much harder, because defenders need to run every combination of web browsers and plugins to ensure complete coverage (or use special techniques to work around this requirement [9]). Also, defenders require elaborate routing infrastructures to hide the source of their traffic. A third limitation is that many techniques, in particular honeyclients, can only detect malicious pages that exploit vulnerabilities — they cannot identify scams that target users with social engineering. Fourth, most dynamic techniques introduce a considerable amount of overhead into the instrumented browser, making these approaches difficult to deploy as online detectors.

In this paper, we propose a novel approach to detect malicious web pages. To this end, we leverage a large population of web surfers as diverse, distributed "sensors" that collect their interactions with the web pages that they visit. The interactions we are interested in are *HTTP redirection chains* that are followed by clients before reaching web pages. Redirections are widely used by attackers, because they make detection harder, and they give the flexibility of changing any intermediate step in the chain, without having to update all the entry points (i.e., the pages containing the links that start the redirection process). Redirection chains are an important part of the malware delivery infrastructure and, unlike the web page contents, they are not easy to obfuscate. Of course, HTTP redirections have many legitimate uses too. For example, advertising networks make extensive use of redirections to make sure that a suitable ad is displayed to the right user. The key difficulty is distinguishing between chains that correspond to malicious activity and those that are legitimate.

A few previous systems, SURF and WARNINGBIRD [10, 13], have incorporated redirection chain information into their detection approaches. To make the distinction between malicious and benign redirects, however, these systems all require additional information for their analysis. For example, WARNINGBIRD [10] analyzes features of the Twitter profile that posted a malicious URL. Unfortunately, attackers can easily modify the characteristics of those Twitter profiles, and make their detection ineffective.

In our approach, we aggregate the redirection chains from a collection of different users, and we build *redirection graphs*, where each redirection graph shows how a number of users have reached a specific target web page. By analyzing both the properties of the set of visitors of a page and its corresponding redirection graph, we can accurately distinguish between legitimate and malicious pages. In particular, we show that malicious web pages have redirection graphs with very different characteristics than the ones shown by legitimate ones. No information about the destination page is required. It is important to note that our approach can only detect malicious web pages that make use of redirection chains. However, this is not a severe limitation, because, as previous work pointed out, the use of redirection chains is pervasive in the malware delivery process [10, 13, 23, 29].

Our approach overcomes the limitations listed previously. We do not look at the content of web pages at all, and therefore, we are not affected by attempts to obfuscate the elements on a page or the scripts that are executed. Moreover, we do not check for exploits, so the system can cover a broader class of malicious pages. Also, the effect of cloaking is mitigated, because of the diverse population of web surfers involved in the data collection. As a last aspect, the data collection from the user browsers is lightweight, because data is collected as users browse the web, without any additional computation. Therefore, the performance penalty experienced by the users is negligible.

We implemented our approach in a tool called SPIDERWEB. We ran our system on a dataset representative of the browsing history of a large population of users, and we show that SPIDERWEB is able to detect malicious web pages that evade state-of-the-art systems.

In summary, this paper makes the following contributions:

- We propose a new way of detecting malicious web pages by collecting HTTP redirection data from a large and diverse collection of web users. The individual redirection chains are combined into redirection graphs that allow for the distinction between legitimate and malicious pages.
- We developed a system, called SPIDERWEB, which is able to detect malicious web pages by looking at their redirection graphs, and we show that the system works well in practice, by running it on a dataset collected from the users of a popular anti-virus tool.
- We show that SPIDERWEB is a useful tool to improve the detection provided by state-of-the-art systems, and that a redirection-graph based detection is hard to evade by attackers.

2. HTTP REDIRECTIONS

HTTP redirections are used by web developers to redirect the user to a different URL than the one originally accessed. Typically, this happens by sending a specific HTTP response to the user's browser, followed by the new page that the client should access. The URL of this new page is sent in the `location` header field of the HTTP response. When the browser receives a redirection response, it automatically redirects the user to the target page. Modern browsers transparently redirect their users when they receive a `301`, `302`, `303`, `304`, or `307` HTTP response [4]. Although each code has a different meaning, browsers behave in the same way upon receiving any of them, so we do not treat them differently either. Other types of redirections include HTML-based redirections (triggered by the `META` tag in a web page), JavaScript-based redirections, or Flash-based redirections. In our analysis, we do not differentiate between these classes of redirections.

2.1 HTTP Redirection Graphs

In this section, we describe how we build redirection graphs. We start with introducing HTTP redirection chains, as they represent the building blocks of redirection graphs.

Formalizing HTTP redirection chains. To define HTTP redirection chains, we start by defining two types of entities: *users* and *web pages*. A *user* is represented by a tuple

$$\mathbf{U} = < I, O, B, C >,$$

where I is the IP address of the user, O is a string that identifies her operating system, B is a string that identifies her browser's configuration (the browser type, version, and the different plugins that are installed), and C is the country corresponding to I. A *web page* is represented by a tuple

$$\mathbf{W} = < URL, D, L, TLD, Pg, Pa, I, C >,$$

where URL is the URL to the web page, D is the domain of the URL (including the Top-Level domain), L is the length of the domain name (in characters), TLD is the Top-Level domain of the URL (notice that we take care of special cases such as `.co.uk`), Pg is the name of the page in the URL (more precisely, the sub-string of the URL that goes from the last "/" character to either the "?" character or the end of the URL, whichever comes first), Pa is a set of strings that holds the names of the parameters in the URL, I is the IP address that hosts the web page, and C is the country in which the web page is hosted. For example, consider the URL `http://evil.com/a/search.php?q=foo&id=bar`. For this page, the full URL is U, D is `evil.com`, L is 4, TLD is `.com`, Pg is `search.php`, Pa is `(q,id)`, and the IP address returned by the DNS server for `evil.com` is I. C is calculated by performing geolocation on I.

Given our notion of users and web pages, we define a redirection chain as a tuple

$$\mathbf{RC} =< \mathbf{U}_{rc}, \mathbf{G}, \mathbf{Ref}, \mathbf{Lan}, \mathbf{Fin} >,$$

where $\mathbf{U}_{rc}$ is the user visiting the redirection chain and $\mathbf{G}$ is a graph $< \mathbf{V}, \mathbf{E} >$ where $\mathbf{V}$ is the set of web pages that are accessed in the redirection chain and $\mathbf{E}$ is a set of edges that specifies the order in which the web pages in $\mathbf{V}$ are accessed. Each edge is a tuple $< \mathbf{v}_1, \mathbf{v}_2 >$ containing the starting web page instance $\mathbf{v}_1$ and the destination web page instance $\mathbf{v}_2$. **Ref**, **Lan**, and **Fin**, are three "special" web pages in the redirection chain:

- **Ref** represents the *referrer*, which is the URL the user was coming from when she entered the redirection chain. The referrer could be the URL of the web page that contains the link that the user clicked on. Alternatively, it could be the URL of the web page that hosts an iframe. If the user inserted the URL manually into the browser address bar, the referrer will be empty. In this paper, we consider the referrer to be the first node of a redirection chain.
- **Lan** is the *landing page*, which is the web page on which the first redirection happens.
- **Fin** is the *final page*, which is the last web page in the redirection chain. The final page is the web page in **G** that has no outgoing edges, except for self-loops.

As we will see later, referrer, landing, and final page carry important information about the redirection chain that is useful to assess the maliciousness of a web page.

Building a redirection graph. As mentioned previously, we want to combine the redirection chains directed to the same destination into a redirection graph. A redirection graph is defined as:

$$\mathbf{RedGraph} =< \mathbf{R}, \mathbf{C}_{rg}, \mathbf{U}_{rg}, \mathbf{G}_{rg}, \mathbf{Ref}_{rg}, \mathbf{Lan}_{rg}, \mathbf{Fin}_{rg} >,$$

where $\mathbf{R}$ is the target node where all the chains in the graph end. In the basic case, $\mathbf{R}$ will be a single web page with a specific URL. However, in other cases, it might be useful to group together web pages that have different URLs, but share common characteristics. For example, in the case of a malicious campaign that infects websites using always the same web page name, the domain names of the infected pages will be different for different URLs. However, other parts of these URLs will be the same.

To support graphs that point to pages with different URLs, we allow groups in which $\mathbf{R}$ has certain fields that are marked with a *wildcard*. We consider a web page $\mathbf{W}$ to match $\mathbf{R}$ if, for each field of $\mathbf{R}$ that is not a wildcard, $\mathbf{W}$ and $\mathbf{R}$ contain the same value. In Section 3.2 we describe different ways for specifying $\mathbf{R}$ and, hence, for aggregating redirection chains into a redirection graph.

In our definition of redirection graphs, $\mathbf{C}_{rg}$ is a set that contains all the individual redirection chains that make up the graph **RedGraph**. $\mathbf{U}_{rg}$ is a set that contains all users in the redirection chains $\mathbf{C}_{rg}$. $\mathbf{G}_{rg} =< \mathbf{V}_{rg}, \mathbf{E}_{rg} >$ is a graph composed of the union of all the redirection chains in $\mathbf{C}_{rg}$. $\mathbf{Ref}_{rg}$, $\mathbf{Lan}_{rg}$, and $\mathbf{Fin}_{rg}$ are sets that contain all the referrers, the landing pages, and the final pages, respectively, of the redirection chains in $\mathbf{C}_{rg}$.

Given a set of redirection chains, and an instance of $\mathbf{R}$, we build the redirection graph **RedGraph** as follows:

Step 1: Initially, $\mathbf{U}_{rg}$, $\mathbf{G}_{rg}$, $\mathbf{R}_{rg}$, $\mathbf{Lan}_{rg}$, and $\mathbf{Fin}_{rg}$ are empty.

Step 2: We compare each redirection chain to $\mathbf{R}$. For each redirection chain, we compare its final page **Fin** to $\mathbf{R}$. If **Fin** matches $\mathbf{R}$, we will use the chain to build the redirection graph. Otherwise, the redirection chain is discarded.

Step 3: For each redirection chain that matches $\mathbf{R}$, we add the user $\mathbf{U}$ to $\mathbf{U}_{rg}$, the referrer **Ref** to $\mathbf{Ref}_{rg}$, the landing page **Lan** to $\mathbf{Lan}_{rg}$, and the final page **Fin** to $\mathbf{Fin}_{rg}$.

Step 4: For each redirection chain that matches $\mathbf{R}$, we compare the graph $\mathbf{G} =< \mathbf{V}, \mathbf{E} >$ to the graph $\mathbf{G}_{rg} =< \mathbf{V}_{rg}, \mathbf{E}_{rg} >$. For each vertex $\mathbf{v}$ in $\mathbf{V}$, if $\mathbf{V}_{rg}$ does not have a vertex with the same exact values as $\mathbf{v}$, we add $\mathbf{v}$ to $\mathbf{V}_{rg}$. For each edge $\mathbf{e} =< \mathbf{v}_1, \mathbf{v}_2 >$ in $\mathbf{E}$, if $\mathbf{E}_{rg}$ does not contain an edge starting at $\mathbf{v}_1$ and ending at $\mathbf{v}_2$,we add the edge $\mathbf{e}$ to $\mathbf{E}_{rg}$.

2.2 Legitimate Uses of HTTP Redirections

HTTP redirections have many legitimate uses. The most straightforward one is to inform a visitor that a certain website has moved. For example, if a user accesses a web page under an old domain, she will be automatically redirected to the new one. As another example, HTTP redirections are used to perform logins on websites. If a user accesses a page without being logged in, she is redirected to a login page. After providing her credentials, the web page will check them and, in case they are correct, redirect the user back to the page she originally tried to access. Advertising networks (ad networks) are another example for legitimate uses of HTTP redirections. Typically, advertisements undergo a series of redirections, to allow the advertiser to find the ad that is the right match for a user [24].

Since redirection chains are so pervasive, we cannot simply flag all of them as malicious. In certain ways, malicious and benign redirection graphs look very similar. Fortunately, there are some features that are characteristic of malicious redirection graphs, and these are the ones that we can use for detection. We describe them in detail in the next section.

2.3 Malicious Redirection Graphs

To build our system, we are interested in the characteristics that distinguish malicious redirection graphs from the ones generated by legitimate uses.

Uniform software configuration. The exploits and/or malicious code used by cyber-criminals target a specific (set of) browser, plugin, or operating system versions. To avoid giving away their exploit code, or triggering content-aware detection systems when not needed, attackers typically use cloaking, and serve the malicious JavaScript only when the exploit has a chance of successfully compromising the user's machine. Cloaking can be performed by the malicious page itself, by fingerprinting the user's browser on the client side. Alternatively, it can be performed during an intermediate step of the redirection chain on the server side [29]. In the latter case, the victim will be redirected to the exploit page only in case her operating system and/or browser are vulnerable to the exploits that the malicious web page is serving.

From the point of view of our system, cloaking performed during the redirection process will lead to the situation where only victims with a uniform software configuration visit the malicious web page. Users who do not run a browser that matches a vulnerable software configuration will be redirected to a different page, possibly on a different domain. Note that modern exploit kits target multiple browsers and plugins versions. For this reason, in some cases, we do not observe a single browser version accessing a malicious web page, but a few of them. However, the diversity of browser configurations visiting the attack page will still be lower than the one visiting a popular legitimate web page.

Cross-domain redirections. Malicious redirection chains typically span over multiple domains. This happens mostly because it makes the malicious infrastructure resilient to take-down efforts. It also makes it modular, in the sense that a redirection step can be replaced without having to modify all the web pages in the redirection chain. On the other hand, benign redirection chains typically contain one or more pages on the same domain. An example of this behavior is the login process on a website; a user who is not authenticated is first redirected to a login page, and, after providing valid credentials, back to the original page.

Hubs to aggregate and distribute traffic. It is common for victims who click on malicious links to be first redirected to an aggregating page, which forwards them to one of several backend pages [28]. This behavior is similar to the one seen with legitimate advertising networks, where the user is first redirected to a central distribution point. From this point, the user will then be forwarded to one of the many different ads. Attackers use this type of infrastructure for robustness. By having a hub, it is easy for them to redirect their victims to a new, malicious web page in case the current one is taken down. Since the aggregation point does not serve the actual attack, it is more difficult to shut it down.

Commodity exploit kits. The underground economy has evolved to the point that exploit kits are sold to customers like any other software, and even offered as software as a service [5]. An exploit kit is a software package that takes care of exploiting the victims' browsers and infecting their computers with malware. After buying an exploit kit, a cyber-criminal can customize it to suit his needs, and install it on a number of servers. Typically, this customization includes the selection of a specific template that is used to generate one-time URLs on the fly. Previous work showed that detecting such templates is important, and can be leveraged for malicious URL detection [31]. We assume that different groups of attackers might use the same URL-generation templates for each server they control.

Geographically distributed victims. Cyber-criminals often try to reach as many victims as possible, irrespective of the country they live in. As a result, the victims of a campaign will come from a diverse set of countries and regions. On the other hand, many legitimate sites have a less diverse user population, since a large fraction of their users come from the country in which the website is located.

3. SYSTEM DESIGN

We leveraged the observations described in the previous section to build a system, called SpiderWeb, which determines the maliciousness of a web page by looking at its redirection graph. Our approach operates in three steps: First, we need to obtain input data for SpiderWeb. To this end, we collect redirection chains from a large set of diverse web users. In the second step, SpiderWeb aggregates the redirection chains leading to the same (or similar) page(s) into redirection graphs. As a last step, SpiderWeb analyzes each redirection graph, and decides whether it is malicious.

3.1 Collecting Input Data

SpiderWeb requires a set of redirection chains as input. For this work, we obtained a dataset from a large anti-virus (AV) vendor. This dataset contains redirection chain information from a large number of their global users. The data was generated by the users who installed a browser security product, and voluntarily shared their data with the company for research purposes. This data was collected according to the company's privacy policy. In particular, the data did not contain any personal identifiable information: The source IP of the clients was replaced with a unique identifier and the country of origin. Moreover, the parameter values in URLs along the redirection chains were obfuscated. Thus, the data contained only the domain, path and parameter name information of the URLs, which is sufficient for our approach. We will discuss the dataset in more detail in Section 4.

Note that SpiderWeb is not limited to this particular dataset. Any collection of redirection data from a crowd of diverse users would represent a suitable input.

3.2 Creating Redirection Graphs

Given a set of redirection chains, the second step is to aggregate them into redirection graphs. To this end, the system leverages the algorithm described in Section 2.1.

A key challenge is to determine which pages should be considered "the same" by this algorithm. The most straightforward approach is to consider pages to be the same only when their URLs (domain, path, parameter names) match exactly. However, certain malware campaigns change their URLs frequently to avoid detection. This can be done by changing the domain or by varying the path and parameter values. If SpiderWeb would only aggregate redirection chains that lead to the same exact URL, it might miss campaigns that obfuscate their URLs. To overcome this problem, we propose five different ways to recognize variations of destination pages, where all chains that lead to one of these pages should be aggregated. In other words, there are five different ways to specify page similarity via $\mathbf{R}$.

Domain + page name + parameters: This grouping is the most specific one. Pages are considered the same only when all parts of the URL (domain, path and name of the page, and parameter names) match.

Top-level domain + page name: With this grouping, two pages will be considered the same when they share the same top-level domain and page name. Cyber-criminals frequently register their domains in bulk, using less popular and less vigilant domain registrars (e.g., `.co.cc` or `.am`) [7]. However, they use an automated setup for their exploit infrastructure, and hence, the page names remain unchanged.

Top-level domain + page name + parameters: This grouping is similar to the previous one, but also takes into

Domain+Page+Parameters:	evil.com,index.php,id
TLD+Page:	com,index.php
TLD+Page+Parameters:	com,index.php,id
Domain length+TLD+Page+Param.:	4,com,index.php,id
IP:	IP address for evil.com

Table 1: Different fields used for grouping for the URL `http://evil.com/dir/index.php?id=victim`.

account the name of the parameters in the URL. This grouping works well for campaigns that use specific URL parameters. It is also useful to detect malicious campaigns in cases where the previous grouping would be too general (according to our popularity filter, described below).

Domain name length + Top Level Domain + page name + parameters: For this grouping, we consider the length of the domain name instead of the concrete name itself. This grouping is useful to detect campaigns that create domains based on a specific template, such as random strings of a specific length.

IP address: This grouping leverages the observation that even if attackers completely vary their URLs (and hence, could bypass the previous groupings), they only use a small set of servers to host their malicious web pages (typically, on bulletproof hosting providers). In such cases, the IP address grouping will allow SpiderWeb to aggregate all chains that end at the same IP address.

To see an example of the different parts of the URL that are considered for each grouping, consider Table 1. In addition to groupings, SpiderWeb leverages two thresholds during its operation. The first threshold discards those groupings that are too general, while the second one discards redirection graphs that have low complexity, and do not allow an accurate decision.

Popularity filter. Intuitively, certain ways of grouping similar pages might be too generic and result in the combination of chains that do not belong together. For example, grouping all chains that end in URLs that have *.com* as their top-level domain and *index.html* as their page name would not produce a meaningful redirection graph. The reason is that most of the landing pages in $\mathbf{Fin}_{rg}$ will not be controlled by the same entity, and, thus, will not share similar properties. To exclude unwanted redirection graphs from further analysis, we introduce a *popularity metric.* More precisely, for each redirection graph, we look at its redirection chains and extract all domains that belong to the chains' final pages. If any domain has been accessed more than a threshold t_p times in the *entire* dataset, the graph is discarded. The intuition is that one (or more) domain(s) included in the graph are so popular that it is very unlikely that this graph captures truly malicious activity. In Section 4.2, we describe how we determined a suitable value for threshold t_p for our dataset.

Complexity filter. On the other side of the spectrum (opposite of too generic graphs) are graphs that are too small. That is, these graphs contain too few chains to extract meaningful features. Typically, these graphs belong to legitimate sites where one landing page redirects to one specific destination. Intuitively, this makes sense: A malicious website is likely to be composed of redirections that start at many different web sites (e.g., infected web pages). For this reason, SpiderWeb discards any redirection graph that contains less than t_c distinct redirection chains. Again, we discuss our choice for the value of t_c in Section 4.2.

3.3 Classification Component

In the third step, SpiderWeb takes a redirection graph as input and produces a verdict on whether the final web page(s) of this graph are malicious or not. This step represents the core of our detection technique. We developed a set of 28 features that describe the characteristics of a redirection graph. These features fall into five main categories: *client features*, *referrer features*, *landing page features*, *final page features*, and *redirection graph features.* Their purpose is to capture the typical characteristics of malicious redirection graphs as reflected in the discussion in Section 2.3.

An overview of our features is given in Table 2. It can be seen that most features (21 out of 28) have not been used before. The reason is that many features rely on the fact that we collect data from a distributed crowd of diverse users. Specifically, these include *client features* and *redirection graph features.* In the following, we describe our features in more detail. Then, we discuss how the features are leveraged to build a classifier.

Client features. These features analyze characteristics of the user population $\mathbf{U}_{rg}$ that followed the redirection chains in the graph **RedGraph**. The *Country Diversity* feature is computed by counting the number of different countries for the users in $\mathbf{U}_{rg}$ and dividing this value by the size of $\mathbf{C}_{rg}$ (which is the number of redirection chains in **RedGraph**). As discussed previously, many legitimate web pages are visited by users in a small number of countries. The *Browser Diversity* and *Operating Systems Diversity* features reflect the diversity in the software configurations of the clients that access a certain web page. Similarly to the *Country Diversity* feature, these two features are computed by taking the number of distinct browsers and operating systems in $\mathbf{U}_{rg}$ and dividing it by the size of $\mathbf{C}_{rg}$. If all clients that visit a page share a similar software configuration, this is often the result of profiling their browsers to deliver effective exploits.

Referrer features. These features capture characteristics of the referrers that lead users into redirection chains. Referrers provide information about the locations of the links on which users click to reach the actual final web page, or information about the locations of iframes, in case iframes are used to trigger redirections.

The *Distinct Referrer URLs* counts the number of different referrer URLs in $\mathbf{Ref}_{rg}$, divided by the size of $\mathbf{C}_{rg}$. Malicious redirection chains are typically accessed by a smaller number of referrers than legitimate ones. For example, a malicious campaign that spreads through social networks will show only referrers from such sites (e.g., Twitter of Facebook), while a legitimate news site will be pointed to by a higher variety of web pages (e.g., blogs or other news sites). The *Referrer Country Ratio* feature is computed similarly to the *Country Diversity* described in the previous section. This ratio characterizes how geographically distributed the various starting points (referrers) that lead to a certain web page are. Certain types of legitimate web pages (e.g., news sites), are accessed mostly through links posted in specific countries. On the other hand, malicious web pages are often linked by websites that reside in different countries. The *Referrer Parameter Ratio* feature is computed by taking the number of distinct parameters Pa in $\mathbf{Ref}_{rg}$, divided by the size of $\mathbf{C}_{rg}$. This feature provides information about the di-

Feature Category	Feature Name	Feature Domain	Novel
Client Features	Country Diversity	Real	✔
	Browser Diversity	Real	✔
	Operating System Diversity	Real	✔
Referrer Features	Distinct Referrer URLs	Integer	✔
	Referrer Country Ratio	Real	✔
	Referrer Parameter Ratio	Real	✔
	Referrer Has Parameters	Real	✔
Landing Page Features	Distinct Landing Page URLs	Integer	[10]
	Landing Country Ratio	Real	✔
	Landing Parameter Ratio	Real	✔
	Landing Has Parameters	Real	✔
Final Page Features	Distinct Final Page URLs	Integer	[10]
	Final Parameter Ratio	Real	✔
	Top-Level Domain	String	[25]
	Page	String	[25]
	Domain is an IP	Boolean	[13]
Redirection Graph Features	Maximum Chain Length	Integer	[10, 13]
	Minimum Chain Length	Integer	[10, 13]
	Maximum Same Country of IP and Referrer	Boolean	✔
	Maximum Same Country Referrer and Landing Page	Boolean	✔
	Maximum Same Country Referrer and Final Page	Boolean	✔
	Minimum Same Country of IP and Referrer	Boolean	✔
	Minimum Same Country Referrer and Landing Page	Boolean	✔
	Minimum Same Country Referrer and Final Page	Boolean	✔
	Intra-domain Step	Boolean	✔
	Graph has Hub 30%	Boolean	✔
	Graph has Hub 80%	Boolean	✔
	Self-loop on the Final Page	Boolean	✔

Table 2: Features used by SpiderWeb to detect malicious domains. It can be seen that most features used by our system are novel. For those that have been used in the past, we included a reference to the works that used such features.

versity of the pages that lead to the redirection chain. The *Referrer Has Parameters* feature measures how many of the web page entities in $\mathbf{Ref}_{rg}$ have a value for Pa, divided by the size of $\mathbf{C}_{rg}$. The last two features help in understanding how a web page is accessed. For example, in the case of a malicious web page that is promoted through Search Engine Optimization (SEO), one expects to see a high number of distinct search engine queries that lead to a malicious page. This is not the case for legitimate pages, which will be found with a limited number of search keywords.

Landing page features. Analyzing the landing pages of a redirection graph provides interesting insights into the diversity of the URLs that are used as landing pages. The four features in this category (*Distinct Landing Page URLs*, *Landing Country Ratio*, *Landing Parameter Ratio*, and *Landing Has Parameters*) are calculated in the same way as for the referrer features, by dividing the distinct value of URLs, countries, parameters, and the number of non-empty parameters in $\mathbf{Lan}_{rg}$ by the size of $\mathbf{C}_{rg}$. Legitimate and malicious landing pages differ in a similar way to the referrer.

Final page features. Similar to the referrer and the landing page analysis, examining the characteristics of the final pages helps us in distinguishing between legitimate and malicious redirection graphs.

The *Distinct Final Page URLs* feature value is calculated in the same way as the value for *Distinct Referrer URLs*. Having a large number of distinct URLs for the final page is suspicious – it indicates that attackers are generating one-time URLs. The *Final Parameter Ratio* is calculated in the same way as for the referrer and the landing pages. Based on our observations, benign redirection graphs exhibit a higher variety of GET parameters than malicious ones. One reason for this is that legitimate web pages often use single pages that provide multiple services, and each different service is selected by a set of specific GET parameters. The *Top-Level Domain* feature identifies the set of top-level domain(s). Some top-level domains are more likely to host malicious web pages than others, because of the cost of registering a new domain that contains such a top-level domain [12]. The *Page* feature represents the page names, if any (e.g., `index.html`). As explained previously, many exploit kits use recognizable URL patterns. The *Domain is an IP* feature indicates if, for any destination web page, the domain value is the same as the IP. Many malicious web pages are accessed through their IP addresses directly, as previous work noted [13].

Redirection graph features. These features characterize the redirection graph as a whole. In Section 4.3, we show that this category of features is critical for malicious web page detection, because it allows us to flag as malicious a large number of malicious web pages that would look legitimate otherwise.

The *Maximum* and *Minimum Chain Length* features capture the maximum and minimum number of redirection steps observed for a single redirection chain in $\mathbf{C}_{rg}$. Previous work showed that a long redirection chain can be a sign of malicious activity [10, 13]. We then introduce six Boolean features that model the country distributions for important nodes that are involved in the redirection process. The calculation of these six features works as follows: For all redirection chains in $\mathbf{C}_{rg}$, we examine pairs of important elements s_1 and s_2. The elements s_1 and s_2 can be either the user and the referrer, the referrer and the landing page, or the referrer and the final page. For each pair s_1 and s_2, we check whether the corresponding entities are located in the same country. If this is true, we set the value V for this chain to *true*, otherwise we set it to *false*. In the next step, for each of the three pairs, we compute the logic **AND** as well as the logic **OR** for the values V. We expect legitimate redirection chains to have more geographic consistency across the different steps of the chain (i.e., having multiple steps located in the same country). On the other hand, malicious redirection chains, which are often made by compromised servers, tend to have multiple steps located in different countries. A similar observation was made by Lu et al. [13]. Notice that, for the features in this category, we only considered the minimum and maximum values, and not the average. The reason for this is that the average values turned out not to be discriminative at all. We perform a more detailed analysis of the features that we decided to use in Section 4.3.

The *Intra-domain Step* feature captures whether, along any of the redirection chains in $\mathbf{C}_{rg}$, there is at least one step where a page redirects to another page on the same domain. If this holds, the feature is set to *true*, otherwise, it is set to *false*. Legitimate redirection chains often contain intra-domain steps, while malicious chains typically contain domains that are all different.

Two *Graph has Hub* features (30% and 80%) characterize the shape of the redirection graph. More precisely, they capture the fact that a hub is present in a redirection graph. To locate a hub, we look for a page (other than any final page in $\mathbf{Fin}_{rg}$) that is present in at least 30% (or 80%) of the redirection chains, respectively. These features are based on the assumption that malicious redirection graphs are much more likely to contain hubs.

The *Self-loop on Final Page* is true when any of the redirection chains in $\mathbf{C}_{rg}$ has a self-loop for the final page. A self-loop is a redirection that forwards a user to the same page from where she started. This behavior is often present in benign redirection graphs, where users are redirected to the same page but with different parameters. On the other hand, malicious redirection graphs typically send the victim from a compromised (legitimate) page to a page that has been prepared by the attacker. This is the page that serves the actual exploit, and there is no self-loop present.

Building and using a classifier. We use the features described previously (and a labeled training set) to build a classifier. This classifier takes a redirection graph as input. If the graph does not contain at least t_c distinct redirection chains, we discard it as benign (because of the complexity filter). If any of its domains has been visited by more than t_p distinct IP addresses, we also mark the graph as benign (because of the popularity filter). Otherwise, we compute values for our features and submit the resulting feature vector to a classifier based on Support Vector Machines (SVM) trained with Sequential Minimal Optimization (SMO) [17]. We used the implementation provided by the Weka machine-learning tool to this end [6][1]. When the SVM determines that the redirection graph should be considered as malicious, SPIDERWEB marks all final page(s) that belong to this graph as malicious.

4. EVALUATION

In this section, we describe how we evaluated the ability of SPIDERWEB to detect malicious web pages. For our evaluation, we leveraged a dataset **S** that contains redirection chains collected over a period of two months, from February 1, 2012 to March 31, 2012 from the customers of a browser security tool developed by a large AV vendor.

[1]We deal with features of different types as follows: we convert strings to integers, by substituting each string with an index, and we treat boolean values as 0 and 1.

The users that generated this traffic are representative of the users of this security product: they are distributed across the globe, and they use a variety of different software configurations. For each HTTP redirection chain, the company logged a time stamp, the obfuscated IP address and country of origin of the client, the initial URL that is requested, the referrer of this request, the final destination URL, all the steps along the chain, and the operating system and browser of the user. In addition, some records are labeled as malicious or benign, a verdict made by the AV tool running on the client. This was done by applying heuristics to identify malicious content in the final pages. If the final page triggered a heuristics, the record is flagged as malicious. On the other hand, the AV vendor employs a whitelist of known, good websites to flag records as benign. If a page is neither detected as bad nor good, that record remains unlabeled.

The entire dataset **S** was composed of 388,098 redirection chains, which lead to 34,011 distinct URLs. To estimate the total number of users in the dataset, we calculated the average number of distinct (obfuscated) IP addresses observed during periods of one week (over all weeks in our dataset). Although this number does not give us a precise number of users, it gives us an idea of their magnitude. The average number of distinct IP addresses per week is 13,780. The users that generated the dataset were located in 145 countries, and therefore the produced dataset is representative of the surfing behavior of different people across the globe.

4.1 Building a Labeled Dataset

To train the classifier needed by SPIDERWEB to detect malicious web pages, we need a labeled dataset of benign and malicious redirection graphs. To this end, we look at redirection graphs built based on the data collected during the first month by the AV vendor (February 2012). As a preliminary filter, we set t_c to 2, which means that we considered only redirection graphs that were composed of at least two distinct redirection chains.

For labeling purposes, if the AV vendor flagged the domain of **Fin** as malicious, we manually assessed the maliciousness of the URL. For example, we considered domains that did not exist anymore at the time of our experiment as clearly malicious. Also, we checked the verdict given by the AV vendor to all the redirection chains leading to the same URL. If not all the verdicts agreed in considering the page as malicious, we did not consider that redirection graph for our ground truth. The detection techniques used by the AV vendor are conservative. That is, when they flag a page as malicious, it is very likely that the page is indeed bad. The opposite, however, is not true and, as we will show later, they miss a non-trivial fraction of malicious pages. In total, we picked 2,533 redirection chains flagged as malicious by the AV vendor, leading to 1,854 unique URLs.

We then selected, among the redirection chains in **S** whose domain was flagged explicitly as benign by the AV vendor, those redirection chains relative to domains that we consider reputable and legitimate. In particular, we picked both popular websites, such as Google and Facebook, as well as less popular sites that appeared legitimate after careful manual inspection (e.g., local news sites). In the end, we picked 2,466 redirection chains, redirecting to 510 legitimate URLs. More precisely, the final pages of the legitimate redirection chains include all the top 10 Alexa domains [1], and 48 of the top 100. In the remaining of the paper, we refer to the ground truth set, composed of the manually labeled malicious and legitimate redirection chains, as **Tr**.

4.2 Selecting Thresholds

As discussed in Section 3, SPIDERWEB relies on two thresholds: a complexity threshold t_c, to discard any redirection graph that is not complex enough to guarantee an accurate classification, and a popularity threshold t_p, to discard those groupings that are too general. In this section, we discuss how we selected the optimal value for these thresholds.

Calculation of the complexity threshold. We needed to understand what is the "complexity" that allows for a reliable classification for a redirection graph. With complexity, we mean the number of distinct redirection chains in $\mathbf{C}_{rg}$. Ideally, having graphs of a certain complexity would allow SPIDERWEB to detect all malicious redirection graphs with no false positives.

We set up our experiment as follows. First, we built the *Domain + page + parameters* groupings from **Tr**. Then, for each threshold value i between 2 and 10, we removed any redirection graph that had complexity lower than i. We call the remaining set of groupings $\mathbf{Gr}_i$. We then performed a ten-fold cross validation on each of the $\mathbf{Gr}_i$ sets, by using Support Vector Machines with SMO, and analyzed the performance of the classifier for each threshold value. As we increase the threshold, the number of false positives decreases. With a threshold of 6, the number of false positives flagged by SPIDERWEB is zero. At this threshold, the number of false negatives also reaches zero. This gives us confidence that, by being able to observe enough people surfing the web, SPIDERWEB could reliably detect any malicious redirection graph.

Unfortunately, as the threshold value increases, the number of possible detections decreases. This happens because the dataset **S** is limited, and the number of graphs that have high complexity is low. For example, with a threshold t_c of 6, $\mathbf{Gr}_6$ is composed by only 131 redirection graphs, of which only 3 are malicious. Thus, to detect a reasonable number of malicious web pages in our dataset, we have to use a lower t_c, and accept a certain rate of false positives. We decided to set t_c to 4. At this threshold, the number of redirection graphs in $\mathbf{Gr}_4$ is 196, of which 25 are malicious. A 10-fold cross-validation on $\mathbf{Gr}_4$ results in a 1.2% false positive rate, and in a true positive rate of 83%.

Calculation of the popularity threshold. To derive a suitable value for t_p, we analyzed the *Top-Level Domain + page* groupings calculated from **Tr**. We then ran a *precision versus recall* analysis. The reason we did not use the same grouping as for the evaluation of t_c is that, as we said previously, t_p aims at detecting those groupings that are too general for our approach to perform an accurate detection. For this reason, we used *Top-Level Domain + page* groupings, which are the most general among the ones used by SPIDERWEB. For each value of t_p, we discarded any grouping that had at least one domain that had been visited by more than t_p distinct IP addresses. For the remaining groupings, we analyzed the URLs contained in it. If all the domains that the URLs belonged to ever got marked as malicious by the security company, we flagged the grouping as a true positive. Otherwise, we flagged the grouping as too general (i.e., a false positive). Note that, in this experiment, a single domain flagged as benign by the AV vendor is sufficient to flag the whole grouping as too general. Figure 1 shows the

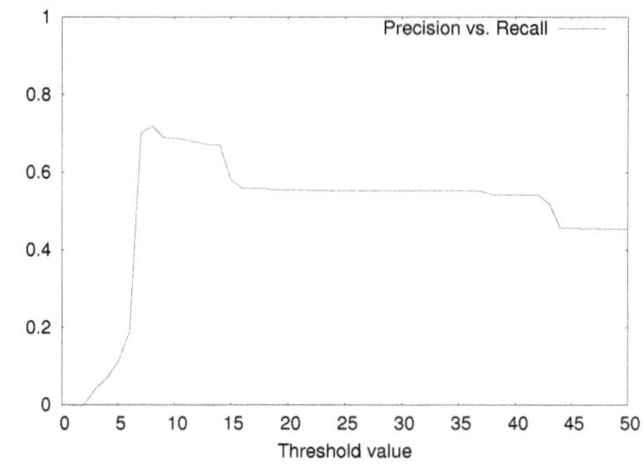

Figure 1: Precision vs. Recall analysis of the popularity threshold value.

outcome of the precision versus recall analysis. In the case of our dataset, the optimal value for t_p turned out to be 8. Notice that this analysis is specific to the dataset **S**. In case SPIDERWEB would be run on a different dataset, an additional analysis of t_c should be performed, and the optimal value of the threshold might be different.

4.3 Analysis of the Classifier

Given the labeled ground truth set **Tr** and suitable threshold values for t_c and t_p, we wanted to understand how well our classifier works in finding malicious pages. We performed this analysis for different choices for **R** (which determines how redirection chains are grouped into graphs). More precisely, using the dataset **Tr**, we first generated the redirection graphs leading to the *Top-Level Domain + Page*, the *Top-Level Domain + Page + Parameters*, the *Length + Top-Level Domain + Page + Parameters*, and the *Domain + Page + Parameters* groupings, respectively[2]. We then removed any redirection graph that exceeded the popularity threshold t_p, or that did not have at least complexity equal to t_c. Each set of redirection graphs (one set of graphs for each choice of R) was used in a 10-fold cross validation experiment. The results of these experiments are shown in Table 3. As it can be seen, the false positive rate for the different groupings is generally low. On the other hand, the number of false negatives could appear high. However, as we discussed previously, being able to observe a higher number of connections would allow SPIDERWEB to use a higher value for t_c, and lower both false positives and false negatives. Table 3 also shows how our system compares to two classifiers based on previous work (SURF and WARNINGBIRD). We describe these experiments in Section 4.5.

We then analyzed the expressiveness of our features. From our experiments, the most effective features that characterize a malicious redirection graph are, in order, the "Referrer Country Ratio," the "Graph has Hub 80%," and the "Final Page Domain is an IP" features. On the other hand, the most expressive features that characterize benign redirection graphs are the "Landing Page Country Ratio," the "Intra-domain Step," and the "Top-Level Domain" feature.

[2]Note that we did not use the *IP address* grouping. The reason is that when we obtained the dataset, it was already a few weeks old. Unfortunately, many of the malicious domains did no longer resolve. In those cases, it was impossible for us to determine the IP addresses that corresponded to malicious domains.

System	# of chains	# of URLs	False Positive rate	False Negative rate	F-Measure
TLD + Page	112	1,945	2.5%	16.1%	0.881
TLD + Page + Parameters	112	1,642	0%	21.4%	0.88
Length + TLD + Page + Parameters	139	1,233	3.4%	20.4%	0.857
Domain + Page + Parameters	196	815	1.2%	17%	0.863
No graph-specific features	196	815	1.2%	67%	0.43
No client-specific features	196	815	1.2%	21%	0.844
No client and graph-specific features	196	815	1.5%	84.78%	0.113
SURF-based classifier	196	815	0%	81%	0.319
WarningBird-based classifier	196	815	2.9%	62%	0.492

Table 3: Summary of the classification performance for different groupings and systems.

Interestingly, features that would intuitively make sense turned out not to be the most discriminating. For example, it is commonly believed that a long redirection chain is indicative of a malicious web page [10, 13]. As it turns out, the redirection chain length is not among the most important features. In particular, having a short redirection chain is the 8th most important characterizing feature for a malicious web page, while having a long redirection chain is the 9th most characterizing feature for a benign chain.

As an additional experiment, we also wanted to evaluate how much the features that can only be collected by a crowd of users, and not by a centralized collector, contribute to the detection of malicious web pages. First, we disabled the twelve graph-specific features in the classifier, and we performed another 10-fold cross validation using this feature set. We used the *Domain + Page + Parameters* groupings for this experiment. Surprisingly, the ten-fold cross validation returned the same false positive rate as the one for the full classifier (1.2%). However, the true positive rate dropped to only 33%, compared to the 83% of the full classifier. Then, we ran the 10-fold cross validation with the three client-specific features disabled. Again, we obtained the same false positive rate than for the full classifier, but the true positive rate dropped to 79%. By disabling both the graph-specific and the client-specific features, the true positive rate drops to 15.2%. This means that the features that can only be collected by observing a crowd of users are important to achieve a successful classification. Comparative results with the full classifier are shown in Table 3. These results give us confidence that SpiderWeb indeed improves the state of the art of malicious web page detection, allowing us to perform detection based on features that are specific of the malicious web page ecosystem's structure, rather than on the web page content. Since the redirection-specific features are harder to obfuscate than the content-specific ones, we believe that our technique can help in performing a more reliable malicious web page detection. To underline this, we performed an experiment that shows that SpiderWeb outperforms previous systems (assuming that attackers perfectly succeed in evading the context-specific features). We discuss this experiment in Section 4.5.

4.4 Detection Results on Entire Dataset

In the next experiment, we evaluated SpiderWeb on the redirection graphs built from the entire dataset **S** collected by the security company. After checking for complexity and popularity, SpiderWeb generated 3,549 redirection graphs from this dataset, obtained with the *Top-Level Domain + page* (700 graphs), the *Top-Level Domain + page + parameters* (825 graphs), the *Domain Length + Top-Level Domain + page + parameters* (957 graphs), and the *Domain + page + parameters* (1,067 graphs) groupings.

Of the 3,549 redirection graphs built from **S** (using the four groupings), 562 graphs were flagged as malicious by our detection algorithm. In total, these graphs led to 3,368 URLs. We manually identified seven large-scale campaigns, composed of URLs that were sharing common traits.

To check how accurate the results produced by SpiderWeb are, we compared our detections with the ones performed by the AV vendor on the same dataset. To this end, we built a set $\mathbf{Fin}_a$ of analyzed URLs. For each redirection graph in **S**, we added the final URLs in $\mathbf{Fin}_{rg}$ to $\mathbf{Fin}_a$. In total, the AV vendor flagged 3,156 URLs in $\mathbf{Fin}_a$ as malicious. For 2,590 URLs, SpiderWeb and the defenses deployed by the AV vendor agreed. We then manually analyzed the remaining 556 URLs that the AV vendor detected, but SpiderWeb did not. 59 of them turned out to be legitimate web sites that hosted malicious JavaScript, probably because of a cross-site scripting (XSS) vulnerability. SpiderWeb was not designed to detect this kind of web pages, whose redirection graphs, as it turns out, do not show the characteristics that are typical of malicious redirection graphs. The redirection graphs leading to the remaining 497 URLs had low complexity (on average, they were accessed by five distinct redirection chains). As we show in Section 4.2, SpiderWeb needs to observe six or more distinct redirection chains to form a graph that leads to no false positives or false negatives. We are confident that, if more data were available to us, SpiderWeb would have been able to detect also these URLs as malicious.

On the other hand, SpiderWeb detected 778 URLs as malicious that went undetected by the AV vendor. We manually analyzed them, to assess false positives. The vast majority of URLs returned non-existing domain errors when we tried to resolve them. Others showed clear patterns in their URLs typical of exploit kits. For 51 (out of 778) URLs, we could not confirm the maliciousness of the page. We consider all of them as false positives of SpiderWeb. This accounts for 1.5% of the total.

Even if our system has false positives, we think that these false positives are so low in number that it would be possible to whitelist such domains, and use SpiderWeb to detect and blacklist previously-unknown malicious web pages. In addition, SpiderWeb is able to perform more comprehensive detections than existing techniques. Interestingly, in several cases, the software deployed by the AV vendor identified only a few of the malicious web pages that belong to a certain campaign, because only those pages triggered their signature-based detection. The detection of the other pages was successfully evaded by the attackers. On the other hand, once SpiderWeb detects a redirection graph as malicious, it flags each URL in $\mathbf{Fin}_{rg}$ as malicious. Because of the nature of the redirection graphs, and their importance for the attacker, evading detection by SpiderWeb is more difficult.

4.5 Comparison with Other Systems

To the best of our knowledge, SPIDERWEB is the first system that is able to detect whether a web page is malicious or not just by looking at the redirection chains that lead to it, and at the characteristics of the clients that access it.

However, there are a few recent systems that do make use of redirection information to detect malicious web pages. Unlike SPIDERWEB, these systems also leverage "context" (domain-specific) information associated with the redirection chain itself, such as information about the page on which links are posted. In this section, we show that previous systems depend on such contextual information, and that their detection capability suffers significantly if this information is not present. The first problem with these approaches is that attackers can easily modify such context information, for example by changing the way in which they disseminate malicious links. A second problem is that the context information leveraged by previous systems is only available in specific situations, like in the case of a URL posted on Twitter or of a SEO campaign. SPIDERWEB, on the other hand, can operate regardless of where the initial URL has been posted. To show this, we compared how SPIDERWEB performs compared to two classifiers based on SURF [13] and WARNINGBIRD [10].

WARNINGBIRD is a system that aims at detecting malicious web pages, such as spam and malware pages, whose links have been posted on Twitter. It takes advantage of redirection graphs, as well as information about the accounts that posted the URLs on Twitter. SURF, on the other hand, is a system that analyzes redirection chains to detect malicious pages that use Search Engine Optimization (SEO) to attract victims. To aid its detection, SURF looks at the search words that attackers poisoned to make their malicious pages appear as results on search engines. Although both systems, to some extent, leverage redirection graphs (SURF visits links twice to evaluate the consistency of a redirection, and WARNINGBIRD has a notion of hubs), the analysis performed by SPIDERWEB is more comprehensive, and allows one to make decisions just by looking at the graph. Both SURF and WARNINGBIRD work very well in detecting malicious web pages that use redirection chains, in the context that they were designed to operate. For instance, SURF is very effective in detecting malicious webpages advertised by SEO, while WARNINGBIRD is effective in detecting malicious URLs on Twitter. However, attackers can evade detection by these systems by modifying the way in which they post their links, or they can leverage different methods to spread their malicious content (other than Twitter and SEO). We show that, in the presence of an attacker evading the context information leveraged by previous systems, SPIDERWEB performs a better detection.

We developed two classifiers based on the redirection-chain features of WARNINGBIRD [10] and SURF [13]. In the case of SURF, we used the *Total redirection hops*, the *Cross-site redirection hops*, the *Landing to terminal distance*, and the *IP-to-name ratio*. In particular, we re-implemented the *Landing to terminal distance* as follows: For each redirection chain, we considered the country of the landing and the terminal domain. If the countries resulted being the same, we set this feature to 1. Otherwise, we set it to 0. Note that we could not re-implement the *Redirection consistency* and the *Page to load/render errors* features, since this information was not available in **S**. In fairness, this could have impacted the performance of our SURF-based classifier in our experiment, since the authors mention that these are among the most discriminative features in their classifier.

In the case of WARNINGBIRD, we used the *Redirection chain length*, the *Frequency of entry point URL*, the *Number of different initial URLs*, and the *Number of different landing URL* features. Note that, in WARNINGBIRD's terminology, an entry point is what we call a hub. Also, notice that we did not use the *Position of entry point URL* feature. The reason is that WARNINGBIRD had a uniform set of referrers (`twitter.com` pages), while we do not. For this reason, it was impossible for us to calculate this feature.

We then applied a ten-fold cross validation using SMO for the two classifiers, using *Domain + Page + Parameter* groupings built from **Tr** as a training dataset. The results are reported in Table 3. As it can be seen, SPIDERWEB has by far a better recall than both other classifiers, and a comparable precision to the SURF-based classifier, which is the system that generated the least false positives. To be fair, both SURF and WARNINGBIRD achieve better detection rates by leveraging contextual information, which our system does not consider by design. Of course, our system could include contextual information to enhance its detection capabilities, but this is out of the scope of this paper.

Interestingly, the SURF-based and WARNINGBIRD-based classifiers detect redirection graphs as malicious that SPIDERWEB misses, and vice versa. In particular, SPIDERWEB fails in detecting five redirection graphs in $\mathbf{Tr}_4$ as malicious. However, the SURF-based classifier can detect three of those as malicious, and the WARNINGBIRD-based classifier can detect the other two. This means that, by using the three systems together, one could reach a complete recall.

4.6 Possible Use Cases for SPIDERWEB

We envision two possible deployments for our tool: as an offline detection system, and as an online protection system.

Offline detection. SPIDERWEB can be used offline, to analyze a dataset of historic redirection chains (similar to the one we used for our evaluation). This allows the system to identify a set of malicious URLs. The knowledge of these URLs is useful in several scenarios. For example, it can help to reveal blind spots in alternative detection tools.

Online prevention. The problem with the offline approach is that it introduces a possibly significant delay between the appearance of a malicious page and its detection. A better way is to deploy SPIDERWEB online, so that it receives a real-time feed of redirection chains from users. Note that the AV vendor already receives such a feed from its users; hence, deployment would be relatively straightforward. Whenever a new redirection chain is received, SPIDERWEB adds it to the current set of redirection graphs. Once a graph has reached a sufficient complexity, the classifier is executed. When a page is detected as malicious, this information can be immediately pushed out to the clients, blocking any subsequent access to this page.

Of course, this approach has the limitation that users are potentially exploited until the system observes enough distinct redirection chains to identify a malicious page. To evaluate the extent of this problem, we set up the following experiment: First, we took the 562 redirection graphs in our dataset that SPIDERWEB detected as malicious (as discussed in Section 4.4). We then looked at each redirection chain in **S**, in chronological order (based on the time stamp when

the redirection chain was entered by the user). The goal was to simulate an online deployment, checking how many users would get compromised before SpiderWeb recognized and blocked a malicious page. We proceeded as follows:
Step 1: We keep a list of occurrences $\mathbf{O}$. Each element in $\mathbf{O}$ is a tuple $< \mathbf{R}_i, \mathbf{C}_i >$, where $\mathbf{R}_i$ is a grouping that identifies a malicious redirection graph, and $\mathbf{C}_i$ is a set that contains the distinct redirection chains that previously lead to URLs in $\mathbf{R}_i$. At the beginning, we have an entry in $\mathbf{O}$ for each of the 562 malicious redirection graphs. The set $\mathbf{C}_i$ for each of these graphs is empty. We also keep a value u_c of users who have possibly been compromised, and a value u_p of users who have been protected by SpiderWeb. At the beginning, both these values are set to zero.
Step 2: For each redirection graph $\mathbf{G}$ in $\mathbf{S}$, we check its final page $\mathbf{Fin}$ against each grouping $\mathbf{R}_i$ in $\mathbf{O}$. If $\mathbf{G}$ matches $\mathbf{R}_i$, we add the redirection chain $\mathbf{C}$ to $\mathbf{C}_i$.
Step 3: If the size of $\mathbf{C}_i$ is lower than 6, it means that the user visiting the page could have potentially been compromised[3]. Therefore, we increase u_c by one. Otherwise, we consider the user as safe, because SpiderWeb would have already blocked the page, and we increase u_p by one.

Running this simulation, we find that the number of compromised users u_c is 723, while the number of protected users u_p is 10,191. This means that out of 10,914 visits of malicious web pages, SpiderWeb would have successfully blocked 93% of them. Note that this is a lower bound, because in many cases less than 6 distinct redirection chains are enough to make a successful detection. Clearly, SpiderWeb cannot provide perfect protection, but its coverage compares favorably to existing blacklists [5]. Also, after identifying a page as malicious, the system knows which users have been potentially infected. These observations could be used to inform the host-based components (e.g., anti-virus scanners) that are already running on those machines.

4.7 Limitations and Evasion

Although SpiderWeb is a useful tool for detecting malicious web pages, it has some limitations. The first limitation is that SpiderWeb requires redirection graphs of a certain complexity to perform an accurate classification. We acknowledge that this might be an issue in some cases. The second limitation is that the groupings currently used by SpiderWeb might miss some advanced ways of generating URLs, such as creating a different domain, as well as a different web page name, for each request. As a result, SpiderWeb might fail grouping such URLs together. Although this is a problem, as we discussed in Section 3.2, we picked such groupings because they were the only ones available to us, given the dataset $\mathbf{S}$. In a real scenario, other groupings, such as the IP address at which a domain is hosted, could be used. A grouping by IP addresses would be non-trivial to evade. A third limitation is that, in principle, the attacker might redirect its victim to a popular, legitimate page after having infected her. By doing this, this particular redirection chain would be merged with the others going to the popular site, and SpiderWeb would likely not detect the threat. This is a potential concern, although we did not observe such practice in the wild. A solution to this problem is that SpiderWeb could be modified to build redirection graphs ending at pages other than the final page.

[3]As shown in Section 4.2, with redirection graphs of complexity 6 or higher, SpiderWeb reaches complete coverage.

Attackers could also evade detection by making their redirection graphs look similar to the legitimate ones. However, in case miscreants successfully evaded detection by our system, this would make them easier to detect by previous work. For example, attackers could stop using cloaking. By doing this, their websites would look like regular web pages, accessed by a diverse population of browsers and plugins. However, this evasion would leak their malicious JavaScript in all cases, making it easier for researchers to analyze and block the malicious code. As another example, attackers could stop using hubs. By doing this, they would need to redirect their victims to multiple servers under their control (or compromised servers). The effort of setting up this type of infrastructure raises the bar for attackers. As an alternative, miscreants could redirect their users to the final page directly. However, this would make their redirection chains less complicated, and easier to be flagged by previous work.

5. RELATED WORK

Detecting malicious web pages is an important problem, and a wealth of research has been conducted on this topic. Typically, proposed systems aim at detecting a particular type of "malicious" page (e.g., spam or malware). Existing approaches fall in three main categories: *honeypots*, *intra-page feature-* and *inter-page feature*-based detection systems.
Honeypots. Systems based on honeypots typically visit web pages with a virtual machine, and monitor the system for changes that are typical of a compromise (e.g., a registry change). HoneyC, capture-hpc, and PhoneyC are examples of such systems [15, 20, 21]. Wang et al. presented a system that runs virtual machines with multiple combinations of browsers and plugins [28]. Although this approach has a higher chance of detecting malicious web pages than the ones using a single browser version, it does not scale, as the number of configurations is constantly increasing.
Intra-page features. The second category of systems looks at features that are typical of malicious web pages in order to detect them. Some systems leverage the observation that the URLs used by certain cyber-criminals to point to malicious web pages have recognizable patterns [14,31]. Other systems analyze the actual web page content, looking for words that are indicative of the content to be malicious (e.g., typical of spam or SEO pages) [16, 25, 26]. Another approach is to analyze the JavaScript code in the web page looking for features that are typical of malicious code. This can be done statically [3], or dynamically, by either visiting the page with an emulated browser [2] or a real one [19]. In general, a handful of commercial products leverage data collected in a distributed fashion to detect malicious web pages. However, such products look at the reputation of the pages, or at their content. Systems based on intra-page features are prone to evasion by obfuscation. For example, attackers might obfuscate their malicious JavaScript, making it impossible for an analyzer to detect it.
Inter-page features. The third category of systems looks at features of the different pages that are involved in the malicious process, rather than just of the final malicious page. Zhang et al. developed a system to generate signatures that identify URLs that deliver malware, by looking at the redirection chains followed by honeypots as they are directed to the malicious domains [32]. Stokes et al. proposed WebCop, a system that, starting from known malicious domains, traverses the web graph to find malware landing pages [22].

Similarly to SPIDERWEB, other systems leverage HTTP redirection chains to detect malicious domains. SURF is designed to detect malicious SEO sites [13], while WARNINGBIRD detects malicious web pages posted on Twitter [10]. However, both systems use contextual information to make their detection accurate. In particular, SURF looks at the search engine results that attackers poison, while WARNINGBIRD looks at the characteristics of the social network account that posted the link. While they make detection easier, these features are relatively easy to evade by the cyber-criminals. MADTRACER [11] is a system that aims at detecting malicious web advertisements by looking at the redirection chains that the users follow. Unlike SPIDERWEB, this system uses contextual information about the web advertisement process. Since SPIDERWEB does not use any contextual information about the purpose of malicious web pages, it is more generic, and it can detect multiple types of malicious campaigns. To the best of our knowledge, we are the first ones to develop a system that is able to make a decision about the maliciousness of a domain by looking at HTTP redirections only.

6. CONCLUSIONS

We presented SPIDERWEB, a system that is able to detect malicious web pages by looking at the redirection chains that lead to them. We showed that SPIDERWEB can detect malicious web pages in a reliable way. We believe that SPIDERWEB complements nicely previous work on detecting malicious web pages, since it leverages features that are harder to evade.

7. ACKNOWLEDGMENTS

This work was supported by the Office of Naval Research (ONR) under grant N000140911042, the Army Research Office (ARO) under grant W911NF0910553, the National Science Foundation (NSF) under grants CNS-0845559 and CNS-0905537, and Secure Business Austria. We would like to thank TrendMicro for their support in the project, as well as the anonymous reviewers for their insightful comments.

8. REFERENCES

[1] Alexa, the Web Information Company. `http://www.alexa.com`.

[2] M. Cova, C. Kruegel, and G. Vigna. Detection and Analysis of Drive-by-Download Attacks and Malicious JavaScript code. In *International Conference on World Wide Web*, 2010.

[3] C. Curtsinger, B. Livshits, B. Zorn, and C. Seifert. Zozzle: Low-overhead mostly static javascript malware detection. In *USENIX Security Symposium*, 2011.

[4] A. Doupè, B. Boe, C. Kruegel, and G. Vigna. Fear the EAR: discovering and mitigating execution after redirect vulnerabilities. In *ACM Conference on Computer and Communications Security (CCS)*, 2011.

[5] Chris Grier, Lucas Ballard, Juan Caballero, Neha Chachra, Christian J. Dietrich, Kirill Levchenko, Panayiotis Mavrommatis, Damon McCoy, Antonio Nappa, Andreas Pitsillidis, et al. Manufacturing compromise: The emergence of exploit-as-a-service. In *ACM Conference on Computer and Communications Security (CCS)*, 2012.

[6] Hall, M. and Frank, E. and Holmes, G. and Pfahringer, B. and Reutemann, P. and Witten, I.H. The WEKA Data Mining Software: An Update. In *SIGKDD Explorations*, 2009.

[7] McAfee Inc. Mapping the Mal Web. Technical report, 2010.

[8] A. Kapravelos, Y. Shoshitaishvili, M. Cova, C. Kruegel, and G. Vigna. Revolver: An Automated Approach to the Detection of Evasive Web-based Malware. In *USENIX Security Symposium*, 2013.

[9] C. Kolbitsch, B. Livshits, B. Zorn, and C. Seifert. Rozzle: De-Cloaking Internet Malware. In *IEEE Symposium on Security and Privacy*, 2012.

[10] S. Lee and J. Kim. WARNINGBIRD: Detecting Suspicious URLs in Twitter Stream. In *Symposium on Network and Distributed System Security (NDSS)*, 2012.

[11] Z. Li, K. Zhang, Y. Xie, F. Yu, and X.F. Wang. Knowing Your Enemy: Understanding and Detecting Malicious Web Advertising. In *ACM Conference on Computer and Communications Security (CCS)*, 2012.

[12] H. Liu, K. Levchenko, M. Félegyházi, C. Kreibich, G. Maier, G.M. Voelker, and S. Savage. On the effects of registrarlevel intervention. In *USENIX Workshop on Large-Scale Exploits and Emergent Threats (LEET)*, 2011.

[13] L. Lu, R. Perdisci, and W. Lee. SURF: Detecting and Measuring Search Poisoning. In *ACM Conference on Computer and Communications Security (CCS)*, 2011.

[14] J. Ma, L.K. Saul, S. Savage, and G.M. Voelker. Beyond Blacklists: Learning to Detect Malicious Web Sites from Suspicious URLs. In *ACM SIGKDD international conference on Knowledge discovery and data mining*, 2009.

[15] J. Nazario. PhoneyC: a Virtual Client Honeypot. In *USENIX Workshop on Large-Scale Exploits and Emergent Threats (LEET)*, 2009.

[16] A. Ntoulas, M. Najork, M. Manasse, and D. Fetterly. Detecting Spam Web Pages Through Content Analysis. In *International Conference on World Wide Web*, 2006.

[17] J. Platt et al. Sequential minimal optimization: A fast algorithm for training support vector machines. Technical report, 1998.

[18] N. Provos, P. Mavrommatis, M.A. Rajab, and F. Monrose. All Your Iframes Point to Us. In *USENIX Security Symposium*, 2008.

[19] P. Ratanaworabhan, B. Livshits, and B. Zorn. Nozzle: A defense against heap-spraying code injection attacks. In *USENIX Security Symposium*, 2009.

[20] C. Seifert and R. Steenson. Capture-honeypot Client (capture-hpc), 2006.

[21] C. Seifert, I. Welch, P. Komisarczuk, et al. Honeyc: the Low-interaction Client Honeypot. *Proceedings of the 2007 NZCSRCS*, 2007.

[22] J.W. Stokes, R. Andersen, C. Seifert, and K. Chellapilla. Webcop: Locating Neighborhoods of Malware on the Web. In *USENIX Workshop on Large-Scale Exploits and Emergent Threats (LEET)*, 2010.

[23] B. Stone-Gross, R. Abman, R. Kemmerer, C. Kruegel, D. Steigerwald, and G. Vigna. The Underground Economy of Fake Antivirus Software. In *Workshop on the Economics of Information Security (WEIS)*, 2011.

[24] B. Stone-Gross, R. Stevens, A. Zarras, R. Kemmerer, C. Kruegel, and G. Vigna. Understanding fraudulent activities in online ad exchanges. In *ACM SIGCOMM Conference on Internet Measurement*, 2011.

[25] K. Thomas, C. Grier, J. Ma, V. Paxson, and D. Song. Design and Evaluation of a Real-time URL Spam Filtering Service. In *IEEE Symposium on Security and Privacy*, 2011.

[26] T. Urvoy, E. Chauveau, P. Filoche, and T. Lavergne. Tracking Web Spam with HTML Style Similarities. *ACM Transactions on the Web (TWEB)*, 2008.

[27] D.Y. Wang, S. Savage, and G.M. Voelker. Cloak and Dagger: Dynamics of Web Search Cloaking. In *ACM Conference on Computer and Communications Security (CCS)*, 2011.

[28] Y.M. Wang, D. Beck, X. Jiang, R. Roussev, C. Verbowski, S. Chen, and S. King. Automated Web Patrol with Strider Honeymonkeys. In *Symposium on Network and Distributed System Security (NDSS)*, 2006.

[29] Y.M. Wang and M. Ma. Detecting Stealth Web Pages That Use Click-Through Cloaking. Technical report, Microsoft Research Technical Report, MSR-TR-2006-178, 2006.

[30] B. Wu and B.D. Davison. Detecting Semantic Cloaking on the Web. In *International Conference on World Wide Web*, 2006.

[31] Y. Xie, F. Yu, K. Achan, R. Panigrahy, G. Hulten, and I. Osipkov. Spamming Botnets: Signatures and Characteristics. In *ACM SIGCOMM Computer Communication Review*, 2008.

[32] J. Zhang, C. Seifert, J.W. Stokes, and W. Lee. ARROW: Generating Signatures to Detect Drive-By Downloads. In *International Conference on World Wide Web*, 2011.

Honeywords: Making Password-Cracking Detectable

Ari Juels
RSA Laboratories
Cambridge, MA, USA
ari.juels@rsa.com

Ronald L. Rivest
MIT CSAIL
Cambridge, MA, USA
rivest@mit.edu

ABSTRACT

We propose a simple method for improving the security of hashed passwords: the maintenance of additional "honeywords" (false passwords) associated with each user's account. An adversary who steals a file of hashed passwords and inverts the hash function cannot tell if he has found the password or a honeyword. The attempted use of a honeyword for login sets off an alarm. An auxiliary server (the "honeychecker") can distinguish the user password from honeywords for the login routine, and will set off an alarm if a honeyword is submitted.

Categories and Subject Descriptors

D.4.6 [**OPERATING SYSTEMS**]: Security and Protection—*Authentication*

General Terms

Security

Keywords

passwords; password hashes; password cracking; honeywords; chaffing; login; authentication

1. INTRODUCTION

Passwords are a notoriously weak authentication mechanism. Users frequently choose poor passwords. An adversary who has stolen a file of hashed passwords can often use brute-force search to find a password p whose hash value $H(p)$ equals the hash value stored for a given user's password, thus allowing the adversary to impersonate the user.

A recent report by Mandiant[1] illustrates the significance of cracking hashed passwords in the current threat environment. Password cracking was instrumental, for instance, in a recent cyberespionage campaign against the *New York Times* [32]. The past year has also seen numerous high-profile thefts of files containing consumers' passwords; the hashed passwords of Evernote's 50 million users were exposed [20] as were those of users at Yahoo, LinkedIn, and eHarmony, among others [19].

One approach to improving the situation is to make password hashing more complex and time-consuming. This is the idea behind the "Password Hashing Competition."[2] This approach can help, but also slows down the authentication process for legitimate users, and doesn't make successful password cracking easier to detect.

Sometimes administrators set up fake user accounts ("honeypot accounts"), so that an alarm can be raised when an adversary who has solved for a password for such an account by inverting a hash from a stolen password file attempts to login. Since there is really no such legitimate user, the adversary's attempt is reliably detected when this occurs. However, the adversary may be able to distinguish real usernames from fake usernames, and thus avoid detection.

Our suggested approach may be viewed as extending this basic idea to *all* users (i.e., including the legitimate accounts), by having *multiple possible passwords* for each account, only one of which is genuine. The others we refer to as "*honeywords.*" The attempted use of a honeyword to log in sets off an alarm, as an adversarial attack has been reliably detected.

This approach is not terribly deep, but it should be quite effective, as it puts the adversary at risk of being detected with *every* attempted login using a password obtained by brute-force solving a hashed password.

Consequently, honeywords can provide a very useful layer of defense.

Some similar ideas have arisen in the literature. The closest related work we're aware of is the Kamouflage system of Bojinov et al. [6]. To the best of our belief, the term "honeyword" first appeared in that work. Also closely related to our proposal is the anecdotally reported practice of placing whole, bogus password files ("honeyfiles") on systems and watching for submission of any password they contain as signalling an intrusion. Finally, a patent application by Rao [34] describes the use of per-account decoy passwords called "failwords" used to trick an adversary into believing he has logged into successfully, when he hasn't. We give an overview of related work in Section 8.

In any case, our hope is that this paper will help to encourage the use of honeywords.

[1] `http://intelreport.mandiant.com/`

[2] `https://password-hashing.net/index.html`

CCS'13, November 4–8, 2013, Berlin, Germany.

ACM 978-1-4503-2477-9/13/11 ...$15.00.
http://dx.doi.org/10.1145/2508859.2516671.

2. TECHNICAL DESCRIPTION

We assume a computer system with n users $u_1, u_2, \ldots, u_n$; here u_i is the username for the ith user. By "computer system" (or just "system" for short) we mean any system that allows a user to "log in" after she has provided a username and a password; this includes multi-user computer systems, web sites, smart phones, applications, etc.

We let p_i denote the password for user u_i. This is the correct, legitimate, password; it is what user u_i uses to log in to the system.

In current practice, the system uses a cryptographic hash function H and stores hashes of passwords rather than raw passwords. That is, the system maintains a file F listing username / password-hash pairs of the form

$$(u_i, H(p_i))$$

for $i = 1, 2, \ldots, n$. On Unix systems the file F might be `/etc/passwd` or `/etc/shadow`.

The system stores password hashes rather than raw passwords so that an adversary with access to F does not find out the passwords directly; he must invert the hash function (compute p_i from $H(p_i)$) to find out the password for user u_i (see Evans et al. [1] and Purdy [33]).

The computation of the hash function H may (should!) involve the use of system-specific or user-specific parameters ("salts"); these details don't matter to us here. When a user attempts to log in, the file F is checked for the presence of the hash of the proffered password in the user's entry (see Morris and Thompson [26]).

2.1 Attack scenarios

There are many attack scenarios relating to passwords, including the following six:

- **Stolen files of password hashes:** An adversary is somehow able to steal the file of password hashes, and solve for many passwords using offline brute-force computation. He may more generally be able to steal the password hash files on many systems, or on one system at various times.
- **Easily guessable passwords:** A substantial fraction of users choose passwords so poorly that an adversary can successfully impersonate at least some users of a system by attempting logins with common passwords. (See Bonneau [7, 8].) Schecter et al. [37] suggest addressing this threat by requiring users to use uncommon passwords.
- **Visible passwords:** A user's password is compromised when an adversary views it being entered (shoulder-surfing), or an adversary sees it on a yellow stickie on a monitor. A *one-time password generator*[3] such as RSA's SecurID token provides good protection against this threat.
- **Same password for many systems or services:** A user may use the same password on many systems, so that if his password is broken on one system, it is also thereby broken on others.
- **Passwords stolen from users:** An adversary may learn user passwords by compromising endpoint devices, such as phones or laptops, using malware or by perpetrating phishing attacks against users.
- **Password change compromised:** The mechanism for allowing users to change or recover their passwords is defective or compromised, so an adversary can learn a user's password, or set it to a known value.

We focus on the first attack scenario where an adversary has obtained a copy of the file F of usernames and associated hashed passwords, and has obtained the values of the salt or other parameters required to compute the hash function H.

In this scenario, the adversary can perform a brute-force search over short or likely passwords, hashing each one (with salting if necessary) until the adversary determines the passwords for one or more users. (See for example Weir et al. [41].) If passwords are the only authentication mechanism in place, the adversary can then log in to the accounts of those users in a reliable and undetected manner.

In this paper, we assume that the adversary can invert most or many of the password hashes in F.

We assume that the adversary does not compromise the system on a persistent basis, directly observing and capturing newly created passwords and honeywords. (Certainly, the adversary risks detection the *first* time he tries logging in using a cracked password, since he may be using a honeyword; after that, the ability of the system to detect further attempts to login using cracked passwords may be compromised if the adversary is able to modify the login routine and its checks, or the password-change routine.)

Although our methods are directed to the first attack scenario, some of our approaches (e.g., the take-a-tail method) also have beneficial effects on password strength, thus helping to defeat the other attacks as well.

2.2 Honeychecker

We assume that the system may incorporate an auxiliary secure server called the "*honeychecker*" to assist with the use of honeywords.

Since we are assuming that the computer system is vulnerable to having the file F of password hashes stolen, one must also assume that salts and other hashing parameters can also be stolen. Thus, there is likely no place on the computer system where one can safely store additional secret information with which to defeat the adversary.

The honeychecker is thus a separate hardened computer system where such secret information can be stored. We assume that the computer system can communicate with the honeychecker when a login attempt is made on the computer system, or when a user changes her password. We assume that this communication is over dedicated lines and/or encrypted and authenticated. The honeychecker should have extensive instrumentation to detect anomalies of various sorts.

We also assume that the honeychecker is capable of raising an alarm when an irregularity is detected. The alarm signal may be sent to an administrator or other party different than the computer system itself.

Depending on the policy chosen, the honeychecker may or may not reply to the computer system when a login is attempted. When it detects that something is amiss with the login attempt, it could signal to the computer system that login should be denied. On the other hand it may merely

[3] `http://en.wikipedia.org/wiki/One-time_password`

signal a "silent alarm" to an administrator, and let the login on the computer system proceed. In the latter case, we could perhaps call the honeychecker a "login monitor" rather than a "honeychecker."

Our honeychecker maintains a single database value $c(i)$ for each user u_i; the values are small integers in the range 1 to k, for some small integer parameter k (e.g. $k = 20$). The honeychecker accepts commands of exactly two types:

- **Set:** i, j
  Sets $c(i)$ to have value j.
- **Check:** i, j
  Checks that $c(i) = j$. May return result of check to requesting computer system. May raise an alarm if check fails.

Key security and design principles. The computer system and honeychecker together provide a basic form of *distributed security.* A distributed security system aims to protect secrets even when an adversary compromises some of its systems or software. Diversifying the resources in the system—for example, placing the computer system and honeychecker in separate administrative domains or running their software on different operating systems—makes it harder to compromise the system as a whole.

We have designed the protocol so that compromise of the honeychecker database by itself does not allow an adversary to impersonate a user. In fact, the honeychecker only stores randomly selected integers (the index c(i) for each u_i).

Indeed, one of our design principles is that *compromise (i.e. disclosure) of the honeychecker database at worst only reduces security to the level it was at before the introduction of honeywords and the honeychecker.* Disclosure of the file F then means that an adversary will now no longer be fooled by the honeywords; he will just need to crack the users' actual passwords, since he now knows which hash values are for real passwords, and which hash values are for honeywords.

We also design the honeychecker interface to be extremely simple, so that building a hardened honeychecker should be realistic. Importantly, the honeychecker need not interact with the computer system. If configured to send "silent alarms" to administrators or trigger defenses such as we consider in Section 2.4, it need not even provide input to user authentication decisions. Additionally, the honeychecker can be configured to manage a only minimal amount of secret state. The index $c(i)$ for each u_i can, for instance, be stored in a table that is encrypted and authenticated under keys stored by the honeychecker.

As we discuss in Section 8, other distributed approaches to password protection are possible. Distributed cryptographic protocols, for instance, can entirely prevent disclosure of passwords or password hashes against compromise of the computer system. Unlike such schemes, though, honeywords can be incorporated into existing password systems with few system changes and little overhead in computation or communication.

The honeychecker could be a product, using a standardized interface. The honeychecker could serve a number of computer systems.

2.3 Approach – Setup

This subsection describes how honeywords work, in simplest form.

For each user u_i, a list W_i of distinct words (called "potential passwords" or more briefly, "sweetwords") is represented:

$$W_i = (w_{i,1}, w_{i,2}, \ldots, w_{i,k}) \ .$$

Here k is a small integer, such as our recommended value of $k = 20$. For simplicity we assume that k is a fixed system-wide parameter, although k could be chosen in a per-user manner—for example, $k_i = 200$ for the system administrator(s). Values as low as $k = 2$ or as large as $k = 1000$ might be reasonable choices in some circumstances.

Exactly one of these sweetwords $w_{i,j}$ is equal to the password p_i known to user u_i. Let $c(i)$ denote the "correct" index of user u_i's password in the list W_i, so that

$$w_{i,c(i)} = p_i .$$

Although we call the $w_{i,j}$ entries "potential passwords," they could be phrases or other strings; a potential password could be a "potential passphrase" or a "sweetphrase."

The correct password is also called the "sugarword."

The other $(k - 1)$ words $w_{i,j}$ are called "honeywords," "chaff," "decoys," or just "incorrect passwords."

The list W_i of sweetwords thus contains one sugarword (the password) and $(k - 1)$ honeywords (the chaff).

We also allow a sweetword to be what we call a "*tough nut*"—that is, a very strong password whose hash the adversary is unable to invert. We represent a tough nut by the symbol '$\boxed{?}$'. A honeyword, or the password itself, may be a tough nut.

The definition of the file F is changed so that it now contains an extended entry for each user u_i, of the form:

$$(u_i, H_i) \ ,$$

where

$$v_{i,j} = H(w_{i,j})$$

is the value of the hash of the user's jth sweetword $w_{i,j}$, and

$$H_i = (v_{i,1}, v_{i,2}, \ldots, v_{i,k})$$

is the list of all these hash values.

The file F is now larger by a factor of roughly k. Given the rapidly decreasing cost of storage this expansion should not cause any problems on a typical computer system, even for k as large as our recommended value of $k = 20$. Many systems already store hashes of ten or more old passwords per user to limit password reuse [17].

The user only needs (as usual) to remember her password p_i; she does not need to know the values of the honeywords or even know about their existence.

We let **Gen**(k) denote the procedure used to generate both a list W_i of length k of sweetwords for user u_i and an index $c(i)$ of the correct password p_i within W_i:

$$(W_i, c(i)) = \mathbf{Gen}(k)$$

Here **Gen** is typically randomized and must involve interaction with the user (otherwise the user cannot create or know the password). We may represent this user interaction in some cases by allowing an additional argument in the form of a user-supplied password p_i to **Gen**, so that **Gen**$(k; p_i)$ ensures that p_i is the password in W_i; that is, $p_i = w_{i,c(i)}$.

The table c is maintained in a secure manner; in the proposal of this paper it is stored on the honeychecker.

Salt. Again, we omit discussion of per-system or per-user salts or other parameters that may be included in the hash computation. We do, however, strongly urge the use of per-user salts.

We also recommend that hashing of $w_{i,j}$ now also take j as an additional parameter. Such distinct per-sweetword salting prevents an adversary from hashing a password guess once (with the per-user salt) and then checking the result simultaneously against all of the user's hashed sweetwords.

2.4 Approach – Login

The system login routine needs to determine whether a proffered password g is equal to the user's password or not. (Here mnemonics for g are "given" or "guess.") If g is not the user's password, the login routine needs to determine whether g is a honeyword or not.

If the user—or perhaps the adversary—has submitted the correct password for the user, then login proceeds successfully as usual.

If the adversary has entered one of the user's honeywords, obtained for example by brute-forcing the password file F, then an appropriate action takes place (determined by policy), such as

- setting off an alarm or notifying a system administrator,
- letting login proceed as usual,
- letting the login proceed, but on a honeypot system,
- tracing the source of the login carefully,
- turning on additional logging of the user's activities,
- shutting down that user's account until the user establishes a new password (e.g. by meeting with the sysadmin),
- shutting down the computer system and requiring all users to establish new passwords.

How does the login routine determine whether $g = p_i$ (that is, that the given word is the password)?

If the hash $H(g)$ of g does not occur in the file F in the user u_i's entry H_i, then word g is neither the user's password nor one of the user's honeywords, so login is denied.

Otherwise the login routine needs to determine whether g is the user's password, or it is merely one of the user's honeywords. The login routine can determine the index j such that $H(g) = v_{i,j}$, but the login routine doesn't know whether $j = c(i)$, in which case g is indeed the password, or not, in which case g is just a honeyword.

The table c is maintained securely in the separate secure "*honeychecker*" server described in Section 2.2. The computer system sends the honeychecker a message of the form:

Check: i, j

meaning: "Someone has requested to login as user u_i and has supplied sweetword j (that is, $w_{i,j}$) in response to the login password prompt. Please determine if $j = c(i)$, and take the appropriate action according to policy."

The honeychecker determines whether $j = c(i)$; if not, an alarm is raised and other actions may be taken. The honeychecker may then respond with a (signed) message indicating whether login should be allowed. (As mentioned above, however, some policy choices may cause honeychecker not respond to the computer system, but instead to permit login and activate special monitoring and/or a honeypot.)

It may be desirable for a "**Check**" message to be sent to the honeychecker, even when the proffered password g is not on the list W_i of sweetwords; in this case the check message could specify $j = 0$. In this variant the honeychecker is notified of *every* login attempt, and can observe when a password guessing attack is in progress.

It might also be desirable for a "**Check**" message to include additional information that might be forensically useful, such as the IP address of the user who attempted to log in. We don't pursue such ideas further here.

Many systems suspend an account if (say) five or more unsuccessful login attempts are made. With our approach, this limit is likely to be reached even if the adversary has access to the sweetword list W_i: The chance that the user's password does not appear in the first five elements of a random ordering of a list W_i of length 20 containing the user's password is exactly 75%. However, when the system detects failed attempts made with honeywords rather than arbitrary non-sweetwords, it may be appropriate for a reduced limit to trigger an account lockout and/or additional investigation.

2.5 Approach – Change of password

When user u_i changes her password, or sets it up when her account is first initialized, the system needs to:

- use procedure **Gen**(k) to obtain a new list W_i of k sweetwords, the list H_i of their hashes, and the value $c(i)$ of the index of the correct password p_i in W_i.
- securely notify the honeychecker of the new value of $c(i)$, and
- update the user's entry in the file F to (u_i, H_i).

We emphasize that the honeychecker does not learn the new password or any of the new honeywords. All it learns is the position $c(i)$ of the hash $v_{i,c(i)}$ of user u_i's new password in the user's list H_i in F. To accomplish this, the computer system sends the honeychecker a message of the form:

Set: i, j

meaning: "User u_i has changed or initialized her password; the new value of $c(i)$ is now j." (This message should of course be authenticated by the system to the honeychecker.)

3. SECURITY DEFINITIONS

We define the security of a honeyword generation algorithm **Gen**, using an *adversarial game*, an algorithm or thought experiment that models the capabilities of the adversary.

For simplicity, we consider a honeyword generation scheme of the form **Gen**$(k; p_i)$, with user input p_i. (The definition may be adapted to other forms of **Gen**.)

The game proceeds as follows:

- **Gen**(k, p_i) is run, using a user-provided input consisting of a proposed password p_i chosen according to a probability distribution U over passwords that meet a specified password-composition policy.

  The output of **Gen**$(k; p_i)$ is a list W_i of sweetwords and an index $c(i)$ such that the password p_i is in the $c(i)$-th position of W_i.

- The adversary is given W_i, with the exception that some randomly chosen honeywords output by $\mathbf{Gen}(k; p_i)$ may be "tough nuts"; for those honeywords the adversary only sees the symbol $\boxed{?}$ and not the underlying (hard) honeyword.
- The adversary must now either "pass" (refuse to play further) or else submit a guess $j \in \{1, 2, \ldots, k\}$ for the index $c(i)$.

The outcome is three-way:

- The adversary "wins" the game (or "succeeds") if he guesses and his guess is correct ($j = c(i)$).
- The adversary is "caught" if he guesses but his guess is a honeyword.
- The adversary "passes" if he doesn't play.

Flatness. Let z denote the adversary's expected probability of winning the game, given that the adversary does not pass. This probability is taken over the user's choice of password p_i, the generation procedure $\mathbf{Gen}(k; p_i)$, and any randomization used by the adversary to produce its guess j. Observe that $z \geq 1/k$, since an adversary can win with probability $1/k$ merely by guessing j at random.

We say a honeyword generation method is "ϵ-flat" ("epsilon-flat") for a parameter ϵ if the maximum value *over all adversaries* of the adversary's winning probability z is ϵ.

If the generation procedure is as flat as possible (i.e., $1/k$-flat), we say it is "perfectly flat" (for a given distribution U). If it is ϵ-flat for ϵ not much greater than $1/k$, we say that it is "approximately flat."

Our recommended value of $k = 20$ means that an adversary who has compromised F and inverted H successfully k times to obtain all 20 sweetwords has a chance of at most 5% of picking the correct password p_i from this list, if **Gen** is perfectly flat. In this ideal case, $\epsilon = 1/20$.

Note that if honeyword-generation is ϵ-flat, then an adversary who plays has at least a $(1 - \epsilon)$ chance of picking a honeyword, being caught, and setting off an alarm. So a method that is perfectly flat ensures that an adversary who plays has a chance of least $(k - 1)/k$ of being caught.

In some cases, even a modest chance of catching an adversary, e.g., $1 - \epsilon = 1/4$ (a 25% chance of detecting sweetword guessing), would be sufficient to detect systemic exploitation by the adversary of a compromised password file—and perhaps even deter the adversary from attacking the system altogether. So while a flat **Gen** is ideal, **Gen** *may be effective even if not flat.*

4. HONEYWORD GENERATION

This section proposes several flat (or approximately flat) generation procedures **Gen** for constructing a list W_i of sweetwords and for choosing an index $c(i)$ of the actual password within this list.

The procedures split according to whether there is an impact on the user interface (UI) for password change. (The login procedure is always unchanged.) We distinguish the two cases:

- With *legacy-UI* procedures, the password-change UI is unchanged. This is arguably the more important case. We propose two legacy-UI procedures: *chaffing-by-tweaking* (which includes *chaffing-by-tail-tweaking* and *chaffing-by-tweaking-digits* as special cases), and *chaffing-with-a-password-model.*
- With *modified-UI* procedures, the password-change UI is modified to allow for better password/honeyword generation. We propose a modified-UI procedure called *take-a-tail.* With take-a-tail, the UI change is really very simple: the user's new password is modified to end with a given, randomly-chosen three-digit value. Otherwise take-a-tail is the same as chaffing-by-tail-tweaking.

We explain the legacy-UI scenario and associated methods in Section 4.1, and the modified-UI scenario and the take-a-tail method in Section 4.2.

Many other approaches are possible, and we consider it an interesting problem to devise other practical methods under various assumptions about the knowledge of the adversary and the password-selection behavior of users.

4.1 Legacy-UI password changes

With a legacy-UI method, the password-change procedure asks the user for the new password (and perhaps asks her to type it again, for confirmation). The UI does not tell the user about the use of honeywords, nor interact with her to influence her password choice.

A nice aspect of legacy-UI methods is that one can change the honeyword generation procedure without needing to notify anyone or to change the UI.

We start with a password p_i supplied by user u_i.

The system then generates a set of $k-1$ honeywords "similar in style" to the password p_i, or at least plausible as legitimate passwords, so that an adversary will have difficulty in identifying p_i in the list W_i of all sweetwords for user u_i.

- **Chaffing:** The password p_i is picked, and then the honeyword generation procedure $\mathbf{Gen}(k; p_i)$ or "cha ff procedure" generates a set of $k - 1$ additional distinct honeywords ("chaff"). Note that the honeywords may depend upon the password p_i. The password and the honeywords are placed into a list W_i, in random order. The value $c(i)$ is set equal to the index of p_i in this list.

The success of chaffing depends on the quality of the chaff generator; the method fails if an adversary can easily distinguish the password from the honeywords.

We propose two basic methods for chaffing (and one method for embellishing chaff). They are somewhat heuristic; the chaffing approach in general offers no provable guarantee that the honeyword generation procedure **Gen** is flat. This particularly true if the user chooses her password in a recognizable manner.

We note (but do not discuss further) the obvious fact that if there are syntax or other restrictions on what is allowed as a password (see Section 6.1), then honeywords should also satisfy the same restrictions.

4.1.1 Chaffing by tweaking

Our first method is to "tweak" selected character positions of the password to obtain the honeywords. Let t denote the desired number of positions to tweak (such as $t = 2$ or $t = 3$). For example, with "*chaffing-by-tail-tweaking*" the *last* t positions of the password are chosen.

The honeywords are then obtained by tweaking the characters in the selected t positions: each character in a selected position is replaced by a randomly-chosen character of the same type: digits are replaced by digits, letters by letters, and special characters (anything other than a letter of a digit) by special characters.

For example, if the user-supplied password is "`BG+7y45`", then the list W_i might be (for tail-tweaking with $t = 3$ and $k = 4$):

```
BG+7q03, BG+7m55, BG+7y45, BG+7o92.
```

We call the password-tail the "sugar", while the honeyword tails we call "honey" (of course).

Other tweaking patterns could also be used, such as choosing the last digit position and the last special-character position. With "*chaffing-by-tweaking-digits*" the last t positions containing digits are chosen. (If there are less than t digits in the password, then positions with non-digits could also be selected as needed.) Here is an example of chaffing-by-tweaking-digits for $t = 2$:

```
42*flavors, 57*flavors, 18*flavors        (1)
```

Chaffing-by-tweaking-digits is typical of the "tweaks" users often use to derive new passwords from old ones; see Zhang et al. [43] for extended discussion of password tweaks and a model of tweaks used by users in practice when they change their passwords.

The positions to be tweaked should be chosen solely on the pattern of character types in the password, and not on the specific characters in the password, otherwise the password might be easily determined as the only sweetword capable of giving rise to the given list W_i.

For chaffing-by-tail-tweaking we consider each word w_{ij} to consist of a *head* h_{ij} followed by a t-character *tail* t_{ij}. For example, "`Hungry3741`" has head "`Hungry3`" and tail "`741`". The value of t need not be the same for all users. There does not need to be any separating character between the head and the tail; the parsing of a password into password-head and password-tail need not be obvious.

If the user picks the last three characters of her password randomly, then tail-tweaking is impossible to reverse-engineer—an adversary cannot tell the password from its tweaked versions, as all tails are random. Otherwise, an adversary may be able to tell the password from the honeywords: in the following list, which is the likely password?

```
57*flavors, 57*flavrbn, 57*flavctz        (2)
```

The *take-a-tail* method of the next section fixes the problem of poorly-chosen password tails by requiring new passwords to have system-chosen random password tails.

Chaffing-by-tweaking works pretty well as a legacy-UI honeyword generation method: it doesn't require users to follow any password syntax requirements, other than having enough characters in the password.

We now give another view of tweaking. Let $T(p)$ denote the class of sweetwords obtainable by tweaking p for the selected character positions.

Clearly p is in $T(p)$, since the randomly-chosen characters may be the same as the originals—in general p is always in $T(p)$. Note that $T()$ should have the property that tweaks don't change the class of a password: For any $p^* \in T(p)$, $T(p^*) = T(p)$. The classes $T(p)$ form a partition of the set of all passwords into disjoint sets of "similar" passwords.

We then define **Gen** to start with the singleton set $\{p\}$, and to repeatedly add elements chosen randomly from $T(p)$ to it until k distinct elements have been chosen. (Of course, the class $T(p)$ needs to contain at least k elements for this to work.)

The list W is then just a randomly chosen ordering of the elements in this set, and $c(i)$ is the position of p in this list.

Tweaking is perfectly flat in the case that each word in $T(p)$ was equally likely to be chosen as the password by the user—that is, $U(p^*)$ is constant for each word p^* in $T(p)$. In practice, users tend to favor some character strings more than others. (For instance, it's observed in [41] that for one-digit numbers in passwords, users choose '1' about half the time.) So perfect flatness may be difficult to achieve, and it may be helpful to bias selection of honeywords from $T(p)$ toward those most likely to be chosen by users.

4.1.2 Chaffing-with-a-password-model

Our second method generates honeywords using a probabilistic model of real passwords; this model might be based on a given list L of thousands or millions of passwords and perhaps some other parameters. (Note that generating honeywords solely from a *published* list L as honeywords is not in general a good idea: such a list may also be available to the adversary, who could use it to help identify honeywords.) Unlike the previous chaffing methods, this method does not necessarily need the password in order to generate the honeywords, and it can generate honeywords of widely varying strength.

Here is a list of 19 honeywords generated by one simple model (see Appendix for details):

```
kebrton1          02123dia
a71ger            forlinux
1erapc            sbgo864959
aiwkme523         aj1aob12
9,50PEe]KV.0?RI0tc&L-:IJ"b+Wol<*[!NWT/pb
xyqi3tbato        a3915
#NDYRODD_!!       venlorhan
pizzhemix01       dfdhusZ2
sveniresly        'Sb123
mobopy            WORFmgthness
```

Note the presence of one "tough nut," a very hard (length 40) password that the adversary will be unable to crack.

See Weir et al. [41] for a presentation of an interesting alternative model for passwords, based on probabilistic context-free grammars.

Modeling syntax. Bojinov et al. [6] propose an interesting approach (based on [41]) to chaffing-with-a-password-model in which honeywords are generated using the same syntax as the password. (Note that with this method, unlike the one above, honeywords *do* depend on the password.) In their scheme, the password is parsed into a sequence of "tokens," each representing a distinct syntactic element—a word, number, or set of special characters. For example, the password

```
mice3blind
```

might be decomposed into the token sequence $\mathbf{W}_4 \,|\, \mathbf{D}_1 \,|\, \mathbf{W}_5$, meaning a 4-letter word followed by a 1-digit number and then a 5-letter word. Honeywords are then generated by replacing tokens with randomly selected values that match the tokens. For example, the choice $\mathbf{W}_4 \leftarrow$ "gold," $\mathbf{D}_1 \leftarrow$ '5', $\mathbf{W}_5 \leftarrow$ "rings" would yield the honeyword

`gold5rings`.

Replacements for word tokens are selected from a dictionary provided as input to the generation algorithm. Further details are given in [6].

4.1.3 Chaffing with "tough nuts"

One might also like to have some honeywords that are *much harder* to crack than the average—so much so that they would probably never be cracked by an adversary. (These "honeywords" might not even be passwords; these "honeyword hashes" might just be long, e.g., 256-bit, random bit-strings.) So, the adversary would not then (as we have been assuming) be faced with a completely broken list of sweetwords, but rather only a partial list. There may possibly be some uncracked hashes (represented by '[?]' here) still to work on, with the correct password possibly among them. For example, what should the adversary do with the following list?

`gt79, tom@yahoo,` [?]`, g*7rn45, rabid/30frogs!,` [?]

Having some "tough nuts" among the honeywords might give the adversary additional reason to pause before diving in and trying to log in with one of the cracked ones. "Tough nuts" represent potentially correct passwords whose plausibility the adversary cannot evaluate. Thus, in the presence of "tough nuts," the adversary cannot fully evaluate the likelihood of being detected during login, even if the adversary has cracked all other sweetwords. To ensure that the adversary cannot tell whether the password itself lies among the set of "tough nuts," both the *positions* and the *number* of "tough nuts" added as honeywords should be random.

4.2 Modified-UI password changes

We now propose another method, "*take-a-tail*," which utilizes a modified UI for password-changes; the password-change UI is just a slight variant of the standard one.

The take-a-tail method is identical to the chaffing-by-tail-tweaking method, except that the tail of the new password is now *randomly chosen by the system*, and required in the user-entered new password.

That is, the password-change UI is changed from:

```
Enter a new password:
```

to something like:

```
Propose a password: •••••••
Append '413' to make your new password.
Enter your new password: ••••••••••
```

Thus, if the user proposes "`RedEye2`," his new password is "`RedEye2413`." This is a *very* simple change to the UI, and shouldn't require any user training. The required tail ("`413`" in this example) is randomly and freshly generated for each password change session. It could even be by chance the same as the tail of the user's previous password. (The login routine will normally prevent the user from trying to use his old password as his new password; the system might generate a new, different tail in this case.)

Once the password has been determined, the system can generate honeywords in same manner as chaffing-by-tail-tweaking.

With take-a-tail the head of the password is chosen by the user, thus increasing memorability, while the password tail is picked randomly to ensure that the password and honeyword generation procedure is perfectly flat.

A user might try to reset her password repeatedly to obtain a preferred tail, undermining the property of flatness. Most systems, however, prohibit frequent password changes (to prevent users from cycling through passwords and thus bypassing policies on old-password reuse).

4.3 Comparison of methods

Our proposed methods for generating honeywords have various benefits and drawbacks, as shown in Table 4.3. The hybrid method is described in Section 5.5.

5. VARIATIONS AND EXTENSIONS

We now consider a few other ways of generating honeywords and some practical deployment considerations.

5.1 "Random pick" honeyword generation

We now present a modified-UI procedure that is perfectly flat. At a high level, a good way of generating a password and honeywords is to first generate the list W_i of k distinct sweetwords in some arbitrary manner (which may involve interaction with the user) and then pick an element of this list uniformly at random to be the new password; the other elements become honeywords. As an example of user involvement, we might just ask the user for k potential passwords. The value $c(i)$ is set equal to the index of (randomly chosen) password p_i in this list.

For example, the user may supply $k = 6$ sweetwords:

```
4Tniners    all41&14all   i8apickle
sin(pi/2)   \{1,2,3\}     AB12:YZ90
```

and the system could then inform the user that password $c(i) = 6$ (the last one) is her password.

The random pick method is perfectly flat, no matter how the list W_i of sweetwords was generated, since the given procedure is equivalent to choosing $c(i)$ uniformly at random from $\{1, 2, \ldots, k\}$ independent of the actual sweetwords; there is thus no information in W_i that can aid in determining $c(i)$.

It is probably a bad idea, however, to ask the user for k sweetwords. Not only is this burdensome on the user, but the user may remember and mistakenly enter a sweetword supplied by her and used by the system as a honeyword.

Instead, the random pick method is probably better applied to a set of k sweetwords output by an algorithmic password generator.

5.2 Typo-safety

We would also like it to be rare for a legitimate user to set off an alarm by accidentally entering a honeyword. Typos are one possible cause of such accidents, especially for tweaking methods.

With tail-tweaking, it could thus be helpful if the password tail were quite different from the honeyword tails, so a typing error won't turn the password into a honeyword. (The honeyword tails should also be quite different from each other, so the password doesn't stand out as the sweetword that is the "most different" from the others.)

One can use an error-detection code to detect typos (as for ISBN book codes). Let q denote a small prime greater than

Honeyword method	Flatness (§3)	DoS resistance (§7.5)	Storage cost (# of hashes) (§5.4)	Legacy -UI? (§4)	Multiple-system protection (§7.6)
Tweaking (§4.1.1)	$(1/k)$ if U constant over $T(p)$	weak	1	yes	no
Password-model (§4.1.2)	$(1/k)$ if $U \approx G$	strong	k	yes	no
*Tough nuts** (§4.1.3)	N/A	strong	k	yes	no
Take-a-tail (§4.2)	$(1/k)$ unconditionally	weak	k	no	yes
Hybrid (§5.5)	$(1/k)$ if $U \approx G$ and U constant over $T(p)$	strong	$\sqrt{k}$	yes	no

Table 1: Comparison of honeyword-generation methods. All methods can achieve excellent $(1/k)$-flatness under some conditions. By "weak" DoS (denial of service) resistance, we mean that an adversary can with non-negligible probability submit a honeyword given knowledge of the password; by "strong" DoS resistance we mean that such attack is improbable. Multiple-system protection is the property that compromise of the same user's account in different systems will not immediately reveal p_i. Finally, G denotes the probability distribution of honeywords generated by chaffing-with-a-password-model. (Thus $U \approx G$ means that these honeywords are distributed like user passwords in the view of the adversary.) The * means "tough nuts" are not useful on their own; they are best used together with other methods. The storage costs assume generation of $k-1$ honeywords. For further details, see the indicated sections.

10, such as $q = 13$. Suppose tails are three-digit numbers; let t_{ij} denote the tail of w_{ij}. Then we just require that the difference $(t_{ij} - t_{ij'})$ between any two sweetword tails is a multiple of q. This property is easy to arrange, even if (at most) one of the words is chosen arbitrarily by the user. This property allows detection of a substitution of any single digit for another, or of a transposition of two adjacent digits, in the tail.

5.3 Managing old passwords

Many password systems, particularly for government and industry users, store hashes of users' old passwords—usually the last 10, as stipulated in, e.g., [17]. When a user changes her password, she is prohibited in such systems from reusing any stored ones.

We feel strongly that a system should *not* store old passwords or their hashes. The motivation of this paper is that the hashes are frequently inadequate protection for the passwords themselves; hash functions can be inverted on weak passwords, and most passwords are pretty weak. Moreover, the reason a user may have decided to change her password is that she decided it was indeed weak, and moreover she is using it on several systems. If the system keeps around her old password, it may be placing her account on the other system(s) at risk.

A better option is to not store old passwords on a per-user basis and instead record previously used passwords across the full user population. A newly created password that conflicts with *any* password in this list may then be rejected. The list should not consist of explicitly hashed passwords, but should be represented in a more compact, efficiently checkable data structure, such as a Bloom filter, that does not reveal passwords directly [38]. The related proposal by Schechter, Herley, and Mitzenmacher [37], which relies on a similar data structure called a "count-min sketch," allows one to reject new passwords that are already in common use within a user population.

When storing old passwords is required, however, we recommend storing them in a protected module strongly isolated from the basic functionality of the computer system—perhaps in a special server. A weaker alternative helpful for achieving legacy compatability might reside in the computer system itself. In this case, the set O_i of old passwords for user u_i should be encrypted, when not in use, under a user-specific key κ_i. When the system must access O_i for a password change, it decrypts O_i. The key κ_i should not, of course, be stored in the computer system itself, but might be stored in the honeychecker, which releases κ_i to the computer system only after successful authentication by the user using current password p_i. After reading and updating O_i, the computer system then re-encrypts it and immediately erases κ_i.

Alternatively, of course, old passwords could themselves be stored with honeywords.

5.4 Storage optimization

Some honeyword generation methods, such as tweaking and take-a-tail, can be optimized to reduce their storage to little more than a single password hash. Consider tail-tweaking where the tails are t-digit numbers.

Suppose that $T(p_i)$ is of reasonable size—for example, with $t = 2$ digit tails we have $|T(p_i)| = 100$. Let $k = |T(p)|$ and let $W_i = T(p_i) = \{w_{i,1}, \ldots, w_{i,k}\}$, sorted into increasing order lexicographically.

We select a random element $w_{i,r}$ of $T(p_i)$ and store $H(w_{i,r})$ on the computer system. (We pick this element by selecting the index $r \in \{0, 1, \ldots, k-1\}$ uniformly at random.) To verify a proffered password g, the computer system computes the hash of each sweetword in $T(g)$; if one is found equal to $H(w_{i,r})$ then $w_{i,r}$ is known, so W_i can be computed, as can the position j of g in W_i. The honeychecker operates as usual: The computer system sends j to the honeychecker to check whether $j = c(i)$.

We can also handle cases where $k < |T(p_i)|$. To do so, we restrict the set of sweetwords W_i to a subset of k passwords from $T(p_i)$. Suppose here that $T(p_i)$ is sorted into increasing lexicographical order as above. Then we might choose $W_i = \{w_{i,1}, \ldots, w_{i,k}\}$ to be a set of k consecutive elements (with wraparound) from $T(p_i)$ that includes p_i. Randomly selecting $c(i) \in \{1, \ldots, k\}$ and setting $w_{i,c(i)} = p_i$ yields such a set W_i with p_i in a random position. In this case the computer system should store both $w_{i,1}$ and the index of $w_{i,1}$ in the list $T(p_i)$, so it knows exactly what the relevant segment of $T(p_i)$ is.

5.5 Hybrid generation methods

It is possible to combine the benefits of different honeyword generation strategies by composing them into a "*hybrid*" scheme.

As an example, we show how to construct a hybrid legacy-UI scheme that combines chaffing-by-tweaking-digits with chaffing-with-a-password-model. We assume a password-composition policy that requires at least one digit, so that tweaking digits is always possible.

Here is a simple hybrid scheme:

1. Use *chaffing-with-a-password-model* on user-supplied password p to generate a set of a (≥ 2) seed sweetwords W', one of which is the password. Some seeds may be "tough nuts."
2. Apply *chaffing-by-tweaking-digits* to each seed sweetword in W' to generate b (≥ 2) tweaks (including the seed sweetword itself). This yields a full set W of $k = a \times b$ sweetwords.
3. Randomly permute W. Let $c(i)$ be the index of p such that $p = w_{c(i)}$, as usual.

Note the importance of the ordering of steps 1 and 2. The alternative approach of tweaking first and then chaffing-with-a-password-model would likely reveal p to an adversary as the sole tweaked password.

As an example, suppose we have $a = 3$, $b = 4$, and $k = 12$. The list W_i might look as follows:

```
abacad513    snurfle672    zinja750
abacad941    snurfle806    zinja802
abacad004    snurfle772    zinja116
abacad752    snurfle091    zinja649
```

A convenient choice of parameters is $a = b = \sqrt{k}$. We assume this choice in describing the properties of the hybrid scheme; concretely, $a = b = 10$ is a possible choice, given that $T(p) \geq 10$.

To detect a DoS (denial of service) attack against this scheme (see Section 7.5) we might disregard submission of honeywords in $T(p)$, and raise an alarm for all other $k - b$ honeywords. DoS attacks, then, are very unlikely to succeed. An adversary that has stolen F and guesses a honeyword, though, will still be caught with probability $1 - 1/a = 1 - 1/\sqrt{k}$. (For $a = b = 10$, this is 90%.)

The storage costs can be optimized along the lines of Section 5.4 if desired, storing only a hashes.

Table 4.3 illustrates how this hybrid honeyword scheme inherits desirable characteristics from both component methods. Note that the scheme is flat only if both flatness conditions given in the table hold. But if *either* condition is met, the scheme is still reasonably secure: it is ϵ-secure for $\epsilon = 1/\min(a, b) = 1/\sqrt{k}$. (For $a = b = 10$, an adversary is caught with 90% probability.)

Because the hybrid method is legacy-UI, achieves excellent flatness under reasonable assumptions, and provides resistance to DoS attacks, it is our recommended honeyword generation method.

6. POLICY CHOICES

6.1 Password Eligibility

Some words may be ineligible as passwords because they violate one or more policies regarding eligibility, such as:

- **Password syntax:** A password may be required to have a minimum length, a minimum number of letters, a minimum number of digits, and a minimum number of special characters. The initial character may be restricted. See [25] for an example of a common password-syntax (or "password complexity") policy. Cheswick [13] calls such rules "eye-of-newt" rules, because they are promulgated as if they had magical properties. We agree that today such rules seem to be more trouble than they are worth.
- **Dictionary words:** A password may not be a word in the dictionary, or a simple variant thereof.
- **Password re-use:** A password may be required to be different than any of the last r passwords of the same user, for some policy parameter r (e.g. r=10).
- **Most common passwords:** A password may not be chosen if it appears on a list of the 500 most common passwords in widespread use (to prevent online guessing attacks).
- **Popular passwords:** A password may not be chosen if m or more other users in a large population of users are currently using this password.

6.2 Failover

The computer system can be designed to have a "failover" mode so that logins can proceed more-or-less as usual even if the honeychecker has failed or become unreachable. In failover mode, honeywords are temporarily promoted to become acceptable passwords; this prevents denial-of-service attacks resulting from attack on the honeychecker or the communications between the system and the honeychecker. The cost in terms of increased password guessability is small. Temporary communication failures can be addressed by buffering messages on the computer system for later delivery to and processing by the honeychecker.

6.3 Per-user policies

We can have policies that vary per-user; this is not uncommon already.

- *Honeypot accounts:* The use of honeypot accounts, as mentioned in the introduction, is a useful addition to honeywords. Such accounts can help identify theft of F and distinguish over a DoS attack (see Section 7.5). Which accounts are honeypot accounts would be known only to the honeychecker.
- *Selective alarms:* It may be helpful raise an alarm if there are honeyword hits against administrator accounts or other particularly sensitive accounts, even at the risk of extra sensitivity to DoS attacks. Policies needn't (and perhaps shouldn't) be uniform across a user population.

6.4 Per-sweetword policies

The "**Set:** i, j" command to the honeychecker could have an optional third argument $a_{i,j}$, which says what action to take if a "**Check:** i, j" command is later issued. The actions might be of the form "Raise silent alarm," "Allow login," "Allow for single login only," etc... There could be k different entries for a given user, with potentially k different policies, one per sweetword. This feature could be used, for example, with the take-a-tail strategy to note which honeywords have small edit distance to the password (e.g., a single transposition or change of character), so that user typos invoke a less severe reaction. This gives added flexibility to the policies enabled by the use of the honeychecker.

7. ATTACKS

This section reviews more carefully various attacks possible against the methods proposed here.

7.1 General password guessing

Legacy-UI methods don't affect how users choose passwords, so they have no beneficial effect against adversaries who try common passwords in an online guessing attack.

We do favor methods such as those proposed by Schecter et al. [37] requiring users to choose uncommon passwords.

Modified-UI methods like take-a-tail also affect the choice of password—appending a three-digit random tail to a user-chosen password effectively reduces the probability of the password by a factor of 1000.

7.2 Targeted password guessing

Personal information about a user could help an adversary distinguish the user's password from her honeywords. It is often feasible to deanonymize users, that is, ascertain their real-world identities, based on their social network graphs [27] or just their usernames [31]. Given a user's identity, there are then many ways to find demographic or biographical data about her online—by exploiting information published on social networks, for example [5].

Knowing a user's basic demographic information, specifically his/her gender, age, or nationality, is known to enable slightly more effective cracking of the user's hashed password [7, 8]. Similarly, attackers often successfully exploit biographical knowledge to guess answers to personal questions in password recovery systems and compromise victims' accounts [36]. (The hacking of Governor Sarah Palin's Yahoo! account is a well known example.) As chaffing-with-a-password-model creates honeywords independently of user's password, this method of honeyword generation may enable adversaries to target data-mining attacks against users and gain some advantage in distinguishing their passwords from their honeywords.

7.3 Attacking the Honeychecker

The adversary may decide to attack the honeychecker or its communications with the computer system.

The updates ("**Set**" commands) sent to the honeychecker need to be authenticated, so that the honeychecker doesn't incorrectly update its database.

The requests ("**Check**" commands) sent to the honeychecker also need to be authenticated, so that the adversary cannot query the honeychecker so as to cause an alarm to be raised.

The replies from the honeychecker should be authenticated, so that the computer system doesn't improperly allow the adversary to login.

By disabling communications between the computer system and the honeychecker, the adversary can cause a failover (see Section 6.2. The computer system then either has to disallow login or take the risk of temporarily allowing login based on a honeyword and buffering messages for later processing by the honeychecker.

While our intention is that the honeychecker should be hardened and of minimalist design, the deployment of the computer system and the honeychecker as two distinct systems itself brings the usual benefits of separation of duties in enhancing security. The two systems may be placed in different administrative domains, run different operating systems, and so forth.

7.4 Likelihood Attack

If the adversary has stolen F and wishes to maximize his chance of picking p_i from W_i, he can proceed with a "likelihood attack" as follows.

We assume here that we are dealing with an approach based on generating honeywords using a probabilistic model. Let $G(x)$ denote the probability that the honeyword generator generates the honeyword x.

Similarly, let $U(x)$ denote the probability that the user picks x to be her password. (This may not be mathematically well-defined; it can be interpreted as a Bayesian prior for the adversary on such probabilities, and may or may not be user-specific.)

Let $W_i = \{w_{i,1}, \dots, w_{i,k}\}$. The likelihood that $c(i) = j$, given W_i, is equal to

$$U(w_{i,j}) \prod_{j' \neq j} G(w_{i,j'}) = C\,R(w_{ij})$$

where

$$C = \prod_{j'} G(w_{i,j'})$$

and where

$$R(x) = U(x)/G(x)$$

is the *relative likelihood* that the user picks x compared to the honeyword generator picking x. Note that it is desirable that for all eligible x, $G(x) > 0$ (that is, the honeyword generator is capable of generating all possible words); otherwise the password may be recognizable as one the honeyword generator could not possibly have produced.

The adversary wants to maximize his likelihood of picking the password, so he will pick the one maximizing $R(w_{ij})$. This is the password that is maximally more likely to be picked by the user than to be generated by the honeyword generator. As an example, a password like

```
NewtonSaid:F=ma
```

is not very likely to be generated by a honeyword generator, but is plausibly generated by a (physics-knowledgeable) user. An adversary might easily notice this password in a set of honeywords.

In this context, a user might be well advised either to (a) choose a very strong password that the adversary will never crack, or (b) choose a password of the sort that the honeyword generator might generate. That is, don't pick a password that has "obvious structure" to a human of a sort that an automatic generator might not use. Alternatively, a generator might take as input a private, handcrafted list of such distinctive passwords for (one-time) use as honeywords; "obvious structure," then, wouldn't always signal a true password to an adversary.

The above theory about relative likelihood is incomplete: it doesn't tell an adversary what to do when only some of the sweetword hashes are solved, as happens when "tough nuts" are used.

7.5 Denial-of-service

We briefly discuss denial-of-service (DoS) attacks—a potential problem for methods such as chaffing-by-tweaking that generate honeywords by predictably modifying user-supplied passwords. (In contrast, chaffing-with-a-password-model as well as the hybrid scheme of Section 5.5 offer strong DoS resistance.)

The concern is that an adversary who has not compromised the password file F, but who nonetheless knows a user's password—e.g., a malicious user or an adversary mounting phishing attacks—can feasibly submit one of the user's honeywords. For example, with chaffing-by-tweaking-digits, with $t = 2$, such an adversary can guess a valid honeyword with probability $(k-1)/99$. A *false appearance* of theft of the password file F results.

An overly sensitive system can turn such honeyword hits into a DoS vulnerability. One (drastic) example is a policy that forces a global password reset in response to a single honeyword hit. Conversely, in a system inadequately sensitive to DoS attacks, an adversary that has stolen F can guess passwords while simulating a DoS attack to avoid triggering a strong response. A policy of appropriately calibrated response is important and can reduce DoS attacks' potency.

Mitigating DoS attacks. To limit the impact of a DoS attacks against chaffing-by-tweaking, one possible approach is to select a relatively small set of honeywords randomly from a larger class of possible sweetwords. For example, we might use take-a-tail with a three-digit tail ($t = 3$), yielding $|T(p_i)| = 1000$. Setting $k = 20$, then, means randomly picking $k - 1 = 19$ honeywords from $T(p_i)$. Knowing the correct password p_i only gives an adversary (or malicious user) a chance of $(k-1)/1000 \approx 0.02$ of hitting a honeyword in this case, greatly reducing her ability to trigger an alarm. The vast majority ($\approx 98\%$) of her attempts will be passwords in $T(p_i)$, but *not* in W_i.

7.6 Multiple systems

As users commonly employ the same password across different systems, an adversary might seek an advantage in password guessing by attacking two distinct systems, system A and system B—or multiple systems, for that matter. We consider two such forms of attack, an "intersection" attack and a "sweetword-submission" attack.

Intersection attack. If a user has the *same* password but *distinct* sets of honeywords on systems A and B, then an adversary that compromises the two password files learns the user's password from their intersection. (Of course, without honeywords, an attacker learns the password by compromising *either* system.) We would aim instead that an intersection attack against systems using honeywords offer an adversary no advantage in identifying the password on either system.

Our favored approach, in the case where management of multiple systems is of concern, would be the take-a-tail generation approach of Section 4.2 on each system. Although the compromise of the password-hash file F would reveal the password-head to an adversary, the user's sugar would be independently and randomly generated on each system.

A significant advantage for system-chosen tails is that it becomes very likely that the user's password will be different on different systems, even if the user chooses the same password-head. This should increase overall security, as users will generally no longer use the exact same password on each system. The burden on memory is increased, but in our judgment this increase is well worth the cost—too many systems are compromised by having user passwords cracked on other systems.

Note that this ability to ensure that a user has different passwords on different systems is achieved *without* coordination between the systems: It is a statistical guarantee. An adversary who discovers a user's password on system A may still be detected trying to log in with a honeyword on system B.

The definition of flatness for a generation procedure **Gen** can be extended to handle this case: An adversary gets the outputs $(W_i, c(i))$ from multiple invocations of **Gen**, and then has to guess $c(i)$ for an additional, last invocation of **Gen** in which the adversary sees W_i (but not $c(i)$). Even with this additional information, the adversary's chance of guessing $c(i)$ should be at most $1/k$.

The take-a-tail method also protects users against an adversary who monitors changes in the password-hash file F *over time.* (In contrast, chaffing-with-a-password-model does not help much if the password is changed only slightly, but entirely new chaff is chosen.)

We note too that if system A and B make use of the same tweaking method, they will automatically generate identical sweetwords for a given password. For example, if both systems employ chaffing-by-tweaking-digits with $t = 1$ digit, they will both output the same ten tweaks (including the original password) as sweetwords. Under a suitable parameterization, our recommended hybrid scheme, which includes tweaking, may generate partially intersecting honeyword sets across systems.

Emerging laws in the United States, such as the Cyber Intelligence Sharing and Protection Act (CISPA)[28], encourage the exchange of cybersecurity intelligence across organizations. Honeyword generation methods might be shared in this context to help prevent intersection attacks.

Sweetword-submission attack. It is possible, as above, that the user has the same password on systems A and B, but distinct corresponding sets of honeywords; alternatively, system B may not use honeywords at all. In either case, an adversary that compromises the password file on system A can submit the user's sweetwords as password guesses to system B without special risk of detection: To system B, system A's honeywords will be indistinguishable from any other incorrect passwords. We refer to this as a "sweetword-submission" attack.

If system B uses honeywords, then, the same countermeasures to intersection attacks—particularly take-a-tail—can also provide resistance to sweetword-submission attacks.

Even if system B doesn't use honeywords, though, it still benefits somewhat from the presence of honeywords on system A in a sweetword-submission attack: The adversary will have to submit more than $k/2$ sweetwords on average before successfully guessing the password (assuming system A uses a flat **Gen**).

If the adversary compromises a system B that doesn't use honeywords, he can of course learn the user's password and impersonate her on system A, even if system A does in fact use honeywords.

8. RELATED WORK

Password strength. The current, state-of-the-art heuristic password cracking algorithm, due to Weir et al. is based on probabilistic, context-free grammars [41]. In a recent study, Kelley et al. [23] characterize the vulnerability of user-generated passwords to Weir-style cracking attacks under various password-composition policies. One such policy is a common, weak one dubbed "basic8," in which users are instructed, "Password must have at least 8 characters." One billion guesses suffice to crack 40.3% of such passwords. Recent work shows that cracking speeds for some hash functions (e.g., MD5) can approach three-billion guesses per second on a single graphical-processing unit (GPU); see, e.g., Table 15 of [3]. Also in recent work, Bonneau develops a framework to assess the strength of passwords (and other user secrets). Based on study of published password corpora, including one for 70 million Yahoo! users, he estimates that a majority of passwords have little more than 20 bits of effective entropy against an optimal attacker [7, 8].

Together, these results underscore the weakness of current password protections even with the use of sound practices, such as salting. There is good reason to believe that many systems don't even make use of salt [29]. While the reason for this lapse is unclear, we emphasize that honeywords may be used with or without salt (and even in principle with or without hashing).

Bonneau and Preibusch [9] offer an excellent survey of current password management practices on popular web sites, including password composition requirements and advice to users, account lockout policies, and update and recovery procedures. Herley and van Oorschot [21] argue that use of passwords will persist for many years, and highlight key research questions on how to create strong passwords and manage them effectively.

Password strengthening. The take-a-tail method may be viewed as a variant on previously proposed password strengthening schemes. Forget et al. [18], randomly interleave system-generated characters into a password. The user may request a reshuffling of these characters until she obtains a password she regards as memorable. The extra characters here are essentially sugar. (Rejected or unpresented interleavings could serve as honeywords.) Houshmand and Aggarwal [22] propose a related system that applies small tweaks to user-supplied passwords to preserve memorability while adding strength against cracking, specifically via [41]. Various proposed schemes, e.g., PwdHash [35], also aim to strengthen passwords within password managers.

Password storage and verification. There are stronger approaches than honeywords for splitting password-related secrets across servers. Some proposed and commercialized methods employ distributed cryptography to conceal passwords fully in the event of a server breach [11, 12, 15]. While such methods are perferrable to honeywords where practical, they require substantial changes to password verification systems and, ideally, client-side support as well. Honeywords may be seen as a stepping stone to such approaches.

Password-authenticated key-exchange methods, such as the Secure Remote Password Protocol (SRP)[4], provide another approach towards verifying that a remote party knows a correct password. However, the remote party must have a trusted computer to perform the necessary mathematical operations. If successful, both parties end up with the same secret key, which they may use to encrypt and/or authenticate further communications.

Decoys. The use of decoy resources to detect security breaches is an age-old practice in the intelligence community. Similarly, honeypots are a stock-in-trade of computer security. A survey of the use of honeypots and related decoys and of pertinent history and theory may be found in [14]. It is a common industry practice today to deploy "honeytokens," bogus credentials such as credit card numbers [39], to detect information leakage and degrade the value of stolen credentials. (Honeywords could likewise reduce the value of stolen passwords.) Similarly, fabricated or decoy files have been proposed as traps to detect intrusion [42] and insider attacks [10].

Honeywords also bear some resemblance to duress codes, plausible-looking but invalid secrets that users may submit to trigger a silent alarm.[5] A related idea are "collisionful" hash functions [2, 4]; these yield hash values with multiple, feasibly computed pre-images, thus creating ambiguity as to which pre-image is correct.

Most closely related to our proposed use of honeywords is the Kamouflage system of Bojinov et al. [6]. The setting in that work differs from ours, though. Kamouflage aims to protect a user's list of passwords in a client-side password manager against misuse should the user's device (e.g., laptop or tablet) be stolen or otherwise compromised. Kamouflage conceals the correct password list within a set of decoy lists, which contain honeywords created using the scheme described in Section 4.1.2. Password-consuming servers need not be aware of Kamouflage deployment. (The authors do note, though, that servers might store some honeywords to facilitate detection of compromise.)

9. OPEN PROBLEMS

This paper is just an initial stab at the issues surrounding the use of honeywords to protect password hash files; many open questions remain, such as:

- How can a honeyword system best be designed to withstand *active* attacks, e.g., malicious messages issued by a compromised computer system or code modification of the computer system (or the honeychecker)?
- Can a honeyword system be designed to protect at all against *persistent* attacks, in which an adversary observes passwords submitted to the computer system?
- How well can targeted attacks help identify users' passwords for particular honeyword-generation methods?

[4] http://en.wikipedia.org/wiki/Secure_Remote_Password_prot

[5] http://en.wikipedia.org/wiki/Duress_code

- Can the password models underlying cracking algorithms (e.g., [41]) be easily adapted for use in chaffing-with-a-password-model?
- Are there good experimental methods for quantifying the flatness of honeyword-generation methods?
- How should an adversary act optimally when some "tough nuts" are included among the honeywords?
- What is the best way to enforce password-reuse policies?
- How user-friendly in practice is take-a-tail?

10. DISCUSSION AND CONCLUSION

Someone who has stolen a password file can brute-force to search for passwords, even if honeywords are used.

However, the big difference when honeywords are used is that a successful brute-force password break does *not* give the adversary confidence that he can log in successfully without detection.

The use of an honeychecker thus forces an adversary to either risk logging in with a large chance of causing the detection of the compromise of the password-hash file F, or else to attempt compromising the honeychecker as well. Since the honeychecker's interface is extremely simple, one can more readily secure the honeychecker.

The use of honeywords may be very helpful in the current environment, and is easy to implement. The fact that it works for *every* user account is its big advantage over the related technique of honeypot accounts.

One could imagine other uses of an auxiliary server to support of password-based authentication. However, the architecture proposed here is clean and simple, reverts to current practice if auxiliary server files are compromised, and is even robust against auxiliary server failure (if one allows logins with honeywords).

Honeywords also provide another benefit. Published password files (e.g., one stolen from LinkedIn [30]) provide attackers with insight into how users compose their passwords. Attackers can then refine their models of user password selection and design faster password cracking algorithms [23]. Thus every breach of a password server has the potential to improve future attacks. Some honeyword generation strategies, particularly chaffing ones, obscure actual user password choices, and thus complicate model building for would-be hash crackers. It may even be useful to muddy attackers' knowledge of users' composition choices intentionally by drawing some honeywords from slightly perturbed probability distributions.

Despite their benefits over common methods for password management, honeywords aren't a wholly satisfactory approach to user authentication. They inherit many of the well known drawbacks of passwords and something-you-know authentication more generally. Eventually, passwords should be supplemented with stronger and more convenient authentication methods, e.g., [16], or give way to better authentication methods completely, as recently predicted by the media [24, 40].

In the meantime, honeywords are a simple-to-deploy and powerful new line of defense for existing password systems. We hope that the security community will benefit from their use. (See our note below on IP.) Additional materials may be found on the Honeyword Project webpage at `http://people.csail.mit.edu/rivest/honeywords`.

Acknowledgments

The second author thanks Andrew and Erna Viterbi for their support. The authors also thank Ben Adida, Sudhir Aggarwal, Ross Anderson, Mihir Bellare, Jeremiah Blocki, Dan Boneh, Joe Bonneau, Bill Cheswick, Burt Kaliski, Silvio Micali, Mike Mitzenmacher, Benny Pinkas, Raluca Ada Popa, Tom Ristenpart, Phil Rogaway, Tomas Sander, Stuart Schechter, Bruce Schneier, Eugene Spafford, Matt Weir, Nickolai Zeldovich, Yinqian Zhang, and their colleagues in RSA Labs for numerous helpful comments and suggestions regarding this paper.

Note on Intellectual Property (IP)

We do not know of any patent or other restrictions on the use of the ideas proposed here. We have not filed for any such patents (and will not). The authors place into the public domain any and all rights they have on the use of the ideas, methods or systems proposed here. As far as we are concerned, others may freely make, use, sell, offer for sale, import, embed, modify, or improve the ideas, methods, or systems described in this paper. There is no need to contact us or ask our permission in order to do so. We ask only that this paper be cited as appropriate.

11. REFERENCES

[1] A. Evans, Jr., W. Kantrowitz, and E. Weiss. A user authentication scheme not requiring secrecy in the computer. *Commun. ACM*, 17(8):437–442, August 1974.

[2] R. J. Anderson and T.M.A. Lomas. On fortifying key negotiation schemes with poorly chosen passwords. *Electronics Letters*, 30(13):1040–1041, 1994.

[3] M. Bakker and R. van der Jagt. GPU-based password cracking. Technical report, Univ. of Amsterdam, 2010.

[4] T. A. Berson, L. Gong, and T.M.A. Lomas. Secure, keyed, and collisionful hash functions. Technical Report SRI-CSL-94-08, SRI International Laboratory, 1993 (revised 2 Sept. 1994).

[5] L. Bilge, T. Strufe, D. Balzarotti, and E. Kirda. All your contacts are belong to us: automated identity theft attacks on social networks. In *WWW*, pages 551–560, 2009.

[6] H. Bojinov, E. Bursztein, X. Boyen, and D. Boneh. Kamouflage: loss-resistant password management. In *ESORICS*, pages 286–302, 2010.

[7] J. Bonneau. *Guessing human-chosen secrets.* PhD thesis, University of Cambridge, May 2012.

[8] J. Bonneau. The science of guessing: analyzing an anonymized corpus of 70 million passwords. In *IEEE Symposium on Security and Privacy*, pages 538–552, 2012.

[9] J. Bonneau and S. Preibusch. The password thicket: technical and market failures in human authentication on the web. In *Workshop on the Economics of Information Security (WEIS)*, 2010.

[10] B. M. Bowen, S. Hershkop, A. D. Keromytis, and S. J. Stolfo. Baiting inside attackers using decoy documents. In *SecureComm*, pages 51–70, 2009.

[11] J. Brainard, A. Juels, B. Kaliski, and M. Szydlo. A new two-server approach for authentication with short secrets. In *USENIX Security*, pages 201–214, 2003.

[12] J. Camenisch, A. Lysyanskaya, and G. Neven. Practical yet universally composable two-server password-authenticated secret sharing. In *ACM CCS*, pages 525–536, 2012.

[13] William Cheswick. Rethinking passwords. *Comm. ACM*, 56(2):40–44, Feb. 2013.

[14] F. Cohen. The use of deception techniques: Honeypots and decoys. In H. Bidgoli, editor, *Handbook of Information Security*, volume 3, pages 646–655. Wiley and Sons, 2006.

[15] EMC Corp. RSA Distributed Credential Protection. http://www.emc.com/security/rsa-distributed-credential-protection.htm, 2013.

[16] A. Czeskis, M. Dietz, T. Kohno, D. Wallach, and D. Balfanz. Strengthening user authentication through opportunistic cryptographic identity assertions. In *ACM CCS*, pages 404–414, 2012.

[17] Defense Information Systems Agency (DISA) for the Department of Defense (DoD). Application security and development: Security technical implementation guide (STIG), version 3 release 4, 28 October 2011.

[18] A. Forget, S. Chiasson, P. C. van Oorschot, and R. Biddle. Improving text passwords through persuasion. In *SOUPS*, pages 1–12, 2008.

[19] C. Gaylord. LinkedIn, Last.fm, now Yahoo? don't ignore news of a password breach. *Christian Science Monitor*, 13 July 2012.

[20] D. Gross. 50 million compromised in Evernote hack. *CNN*, 4 March 2013.

[21] C. Herley and P. Van Oorschot. A research agenda acknowledging the persistence of passwords. *IEEE Security & Privacy*, 10(1):28–36, 2012.

[22] S. Houshmand and S. Aggarwal. Building better passwords using probabilistic techniques. In *ACSAC*, pages 109–118, 2012.

[23] P.G. Kelley, S. Komanduri, M.L. Mazurek, R. Shay, T. Vidas, L. Bauer, N. Christin, L.F. Cranor, and J. Lopez. Guess again (and again and again): Measuring password strength by simulating password-cracking algorithms. In *IEEE Symposium on Security and Privacy (SP)*, pages 523–537, 2012.

[24] O. Kharif. Innovator: Ramesh Kesanupalli's biometric passwords stored on devices. *Bloomberg Businessweek*, 28 March 2013.

[25] Microsoft TechNet Library. Password must meet complexity requirements. Referenced March 2012 at http://bit.ly/YAsGiZ.

[26] R. Morris and K. Thompson. Password security: a case history. *Commun. ACM*, 22(11):594–597, November 1979.

[27] A. Narayanan and V. Shmatikov. De-anonymizing social networks. In *IEEE Symposium on Security and Privacy (SP)*, pages 173–187, 2009.

[28] U.S. House of Representatives. H.R. 624: The Cyber Intelligence Sharing and Protection Act of 2013. 113th Cong., 2013.

[29] B.-A. Parnell. LinkedIn admits site hack, adds pinch of salt to passwords. *The Register*, 7 June 2012.

[30] I. Paul. Update: LinkedIn confirms account passwords hacked. *PC World*, 6 June 2012.

[31] D. Perito, C. Castelluccia, M. A. Kaafar, and P. Manils. How unique and traceable are usernames? In *Privacy Enhancing Technologies*, pages 1–17, 2011.

[32] N. Perlroth. Hackers in China attacked The Times for last 4 months. *New York Times*, page A1, 31 January 2013.

[33] G. B. Purdy. A high security log-in procedure. *Commun. ACM*, 17(8):442–445, August 1974.

[34] Shrisha Rao. Data and system security with failwords. U.S. Patent Application US2006/0161786A1, U.S. Patent Office, July 20, 2006. `http://www.google.com/patents/US20060161786`.

[35] B. Ross, C. Jackson, N. Miyake, D. Boneh, and J.C. Mitchell. Stronger password authentication using browser extensions. In *USENIX Security*, 2005.

[36] S. Schechter, A. J. B. Brush, and S. Egelman. It's no secret. measuring the security and reliability of authentication "secret" questions. In *IEEE Symposium on Security and Privacy (SP)*, pages 375–390, 2009.

[37] S. Schechter, C. Herley, and M. Mitzenmacher. Popularity is everything: a new approach to protecting passwords from statistical-guessing attacks. In *USENIX HotSec*, pages 1–8, 2010.

[38] E. Spafford. Observations on reusable password choices. In *USENIX Security*, 1992.

[39] L. Spitzner. Honeytokens: The other honeypot. Symantec SecurityFocus, July 2003.

[40] T. Wadhwa. Why your next phone will include fingerprint, facial, and voice recognition. *Forbes*, 29 March 2013.

[41] M. Weir, S. Aggarwal, B. de Medeiros, and B. Glodek. Password cracking using probabilistic context-free grammars. In *IEEE Symposium on Security and Privacy (SP)*, pages 162–175, 2009.

[42] J. Yuill, M. Zappe, D. Denning, and F. Feer. Honeyfiles: deceptive files for intrusion detection. In *Information Assurance Workshop*, pages 116–122, 2004.

[43] Y. Zhang, F. Monrose, and M. K. Reiter. The security of modern password expiration: an algorithmic framework and empirical analysis. In *ACM CCS*, pages 176–186, 2010.

Appendix. Chaffing with a password model

This appendix describes a simple way to generate honeywords; this method is one way to implement *chaffing-with-a-password-model*. It is just a simple example of such a probabilistic model; better models certainly exist.

This method uses a list L of sample passwords. Honeywords are not taken from this file; rather, this list is used as an aid to generate plausible-looking honeywords. This list is intended to contain what look like plausible passwords users might generate; it is not intended to be a list of "high-strength" passwords.

Thus, this honeyword generation scheme is qualitatively different than the process of tweaking a password to generate a new password: it is OK for a honeyword to be much weaker than the true password in an attempt to trick the adversary. However, it should not be so weak that high-probability (i.e. very common) passwords are generated, as this would cause an online guessing attack to hit honeywords.

A simple model for generating a single honeyword. The password list L is initialized to a list of many thousands of real passwords, as well as some truly random passwords of varying lengths.

A "tough nut" is generated with some fixed probability (e.g. 8%).

Otherwise a honeyword is generated as follows. A target length d is first determined by picking a random password w from L and measuring its length.

Let the characters of the new password be denoted c_1, c_2, ..., c_d. These are determined sequentially. The first character c_1 is just the first character w_1 of w. Let $w = w_1 w_2 \ldots, w_d$.

To determine the jth character of c, for $j = 2, 3, \ldots, d$:

- With probability 0.1, replace w by a randomly chosen password in L of length t. Then let $c_j = w_j$.
- Else with probability 0.4, replace w by a randomly chosen password in L of length t that has $w_{j-1} = c_{j-1}$. Then let $c_j = w_j$.
- Else with probability 0.5, let $c_j = w_j$.

If the honeyword c is ineligible (§6.1), then begin again to generate c (excluding the tough-nut option this time).

Quantifying the Security of Graphical Passwords: The Case of Android Unlock Patterns

Sebastian Uellenbeck, Markus Dürmuth, Christopher Wolf, and Thorsten Holz
Horst Görtz Institute for IT-Security, Ruhr-University Bochum, Germany
{firstname.lastname}@rub.de

ABSTRACT

Graphical passwords were proposed as an alternative to overcome the inherent limitations of text-based passwords, inspired by research that shows that the graphical memory of humans is particularly well developed. A graphical password scheme that has been widely adopted is the *Android Unlock Pattern*, a special case of the Pass-Go scheme with grid size restricted to 3×3 points and restricted stroke count.

In this paper, we study the security of Android unlock patterns. By performing a large-scale user study, we measure actual user choices of patterns instead of theoretical considerations on password spaces. From this data we construct a model based on Markov chains that enables us to quantify the strength of Android unlock patterns. We found empirically that there is a high bias in the pattern selection process, e. g., the upper left corner and three-point long straight lines are very typical selection strategies. Consequently, the entropy of patterns is rather low, and our results indicate that the security offered by the scheme is less than the security of only three digit randomly-assigned PINs for guessing 20% of all passwords (i. e., we estimate a partial guessing entropy $G_{0.2}$ of 9.10 bit).

Based on these insights, we systematically improve the scheme by finding a small, but still effective change in the pattern layout that makes graphical user logins substantially more secure. By means of another user study, we show that some changes improve the security by more than doubling the space of actually used passwords (i. e., increasing the partial guessing entropy $G_{0.2}$ to 10.81 bit).

Categories and Subject Descriptors

K.6.5 [**Security and Protection**]: Authentication; D.4.6 [**Operating Systems**]: Security and Protection

General Terms

Security; Human Factors

CCS'13, November 4–8, 2013, Berlin, Germany.

ACM 978-1-4503-2477-9/13/11 ... $15.00.
http://dx.doi.org/10.1145/2508859.2516700.

Keywords

Passwords; Mobile Security; Android

1. INTRODUCTION

Authenticating a user is one of the central tasks in computer security, and it forms the basis for several other tasks as well. Text-based passwords are a common approach for authentication, but it is well-known (see for example [7]) that users typically choose weak passwords, and have problems to recall strong ones. As an alternative to text-based passwords, *graphical passwords* [4] have been proposed. These schemes are motivated by psychology research results suggesting that the human brain is particularly well-suited to remember graphical information [33].

In practice, very few graphical password schemes have been adopted and presumably the most widely deployed one is used in Android systems. Main reason is that Android is the most popular OS for modern smartphones. In the so called *Android Unlock Pattern scheme*, the user is presented a 3×3 grid and the secret (password) of a user is a drawing on that grid (i. e., a sequence of lines connecting the dots). During enrollment, a user has to choose a pattern and during the authentication phase, he has to recall his pattern and draw it on the screen. Android's Unlock Pattern is a modified version of Pass-Go [35] with minor adoptions to accommodate for the size of typical mobile devices. In general, the usability of graphical password schemes is well understood [4]. However, security aspects of such schemes are hardly studied, with only a few exceptions (e. g., [18,20,23,36]). As such, the question remains how secure graphical passwords are *in practice* in comparison to a theoretical analysis of password spaces. The latter is usually the far more impressive number, but not that meaningful as a metric for the strength of the corresponding scheme.

In this paper, we conduct the first (to the best of our knowledge) large-scale user study on Android Unlock Patterns, with a total of 584 participants and approximately 2,900 patterns. By means of a pen-and-paper study, we interviewed 105 people to find out their strategy to chose patterns on an Android phone. Furthermore, we performed a study with 113 participants as part of a game in which people were asked to chose a pattern for a phone provided by us, and also to guess patterns used by other participants of the study. The collected data enables us to analyze how people pick patterns and to attack them in order to evaluate their strength. We performed an analysis based on Markov chains to quantify their security and found that Android Unlock Patterns offer less security than a three digit (decimal) PIN. As our study only provides an *upper* limit on the entropy, the situation should be slightly worse in practice.

During our study, we found several typical strategies used by the participants for the pattern generation process (e. g., people often picked the top left corner as a starting point and prefer straight lines in their pattern). Drawing from this knowledge, we strive to improve the security of the scheme: by systematically changing the pattern layout in such a way that these typical strategies are thwarted, we encourage users to chose patterns in a more diverse way. However, we concentrate on small modifications that allow us to keep the overall design of the patterns to foster the roll-out of a potentially better graphical password scheme. Specifically, we experimented with different arrangements of the patterns, such as removing the top left point, arranging them in form of a circle, or a (seemingly) random pattern. We performed another user study with 366 participants to empirically verify which effect such changes in the pattern layout have in practice, and found that the entropy estimate for some patterns increases significantly. In one modified pattern, we removed the upper left corner as it is the source for most of the bias. However, it turned out that people simply started from the point to the right of it, so this modification did actually *worsen* the security and the entropy estimate decreased. We got a slightly better result by switching to a 4×3 grid and removing the left upper and right lower corner. We pursued a different approach with the two new patterns *Random* and *Circle*. In the first, a (seemingly) random pattern was presented that excluded straight lines between any 3-points, a clear top/left position, and also allowed easy transition from all 9 points to any of the remaining 8 points. In the second, we arranged the nine points in a circle instead of a grid. While the initial bias was in the same range as for Android Unlock Patterns, it turned out that the following *transitions* were more diverse: we found that people prefer the directly neighboring point, but also include a point slightly further away. In addition, the *Circle* pattern does not allow to stay "on one line" as opposed to a quadrangle. In particular, for the circle patterns this increased the overall entropy estimate.

In summary, we make the following contributions:

- We performed a user study on Android Unlock Patterns to find out how users typically chose patterns. While it is not surprising that Android Unlock Patterns fall short of reaching their theoretical strength, we are the first to actually quantify the strength of user chosen patterns on the Android platform.
- Based on the insights obtained during this study, we systematically change the pattern layout to remove bias in the pattern selection process to improve the security of the scheme. In another user study, we found that this simple re-ordering can greatly improve the entropy estimate of the patterns at basically no cost.
- Overall, we collected more than 2,800 patterns chosen by users. In total, more than 580 people participated in our study. On a broader scale, this work teaches us valuable lessons about user choice in selecting graphical passwords.

Paper Outline

The rest of this paper is structured as follows. In Section 2, we discuss related work, in particular on graphical password schemes. In Section 3 we consider the unmodified Android Unlock Patterns and provide details on the user study we used to collect a large number of patterns. We describe an attack based on Markov models in Section 4 and quantify the security given by those patterns. In Section 5, we identify several weak points of the original patterns, test a number of alternative (but similar) constructions, and quantify their security. We conclude this paper with a discussion of the results and an overview of future work in Section 6.

2. RELATED WORK

The security of (text-based) passwords has been studied as early as 1979 [27], and it has been realized early that passwords are susceptible to so called *dictionary attacks* as many users choose passwords from a small subset of all possible passwords that can be collected in a dictionary. Popular password guessers that perform dictionary attacks are *John the Ripper* [32] and *HashCat* [1], advanced password guessers are based on Markov models [28]. Several approaches have been tested to prevent users from choosing weak passwords. Best known are so-called *password rules*, which are deployed by most websites today, but have been shown to have limited effect [25]. More recent techniques use Markov models to measure password strength [13]. A good overview of passwords is given by Bonneau [7].

Numerous alternatives to text-based passwords have been proposed. One particularly interesting class is *graphical passwords*, which have the potential to offer better usability because the human brain is particularly well-suited to remember graphical information [33]. Graphical passwords are typically classified as *recall-based*, *recognition-based*, or *cued recall-based*, where Android Unlock Patterns fall into the first category. In the following we review some of the work on graphical passwords, and refer to the recent survey by Biddle, Chiasson, and van Oorschot [4] for more details.

Recall-based schemes.

The first recall-based graphical password scheme *Draw-A-Secret* (DAS) was proposed in 1999 by Jermyn et al. [24]. Users select one or more strokes on a 2D grid, and need to reproduce these strokes when logging in. BDAS [21] augments this scheme by adding a background image, which helps the user to choose more complex and in particular longer patterns. Robustness to small errors is improved with YAGP [22] and Passdoodles [38].

Most relevant for our work is the Pass-Go scheme [35], which uses the intersections of a 2D grid instead of the cells. To evaluate the strength and usability, the authors conducted an informal user study with 167 participants which showed that users chose passwords with an average length of approximately 17, which leads to an estimation for the size of the password space of 2^{109}. The participants attending to the study were students from two university courses. Therefore, the authors had chosen a very homogeneous set for their study. In contrast to this, we asked people from all faculties (engineering, humanities, medicine, and science) of the university to participate. As a result, we belief that our results better model reality. Furthermore, we asked more than two times as much people to participate in our study.

Variants of the Pass-Go scheme are PassShape [41], which use a different input interface and coding of the patterns, and a variant that additionally uses haptic input [29] in an attempt to counter shoulder-surfing attacks. GrIDsure employed patterns on a grid to implement one-time PINs (see [6, 10]). The Android Unlock Patterns are a special case of the Pass-Go scheme with restricted grid size and restricted stroke count, see Section 3.1 for more details.

An attack specific to implementations on devices with touch screen are so-called smudge attacks [2], where residue from using the touchscreen reveals information about the pattern. While this was originally studied for the Android Unlock Patterns, similar problems should arise for most authentication schemes on touch-screens.

Recognition-based schemes.

The classical example for recognition-based schemes are PassFaces [30]. Users choose a set of (images of) faces, and need to select those among a number of decoy images for login. Their usability is well studied [11]. However, [18] found that the PassFaces scheme with user-chosen faces, which is the proposed standard, is quite insecure: user's choices of faces are very biased, basically towards the user's race and towards female faces.

The scheme Story [18] is similar to PassFaces, but users learn images of more general persons and objects. The scheme Deja Vu [19] uses images displaying "random art". A further interesting concept was proposed by Weinshall [39], where the user learns a (relatively large) set of images, and for login he solves a "graphical puzzle" based on these images, in an attempt to counter shoulder-surfing attacks. Unfortunately, the resistance to shoulder-surfing was proven false [23].

Cued-recall based schemes.

Cued-recall systems are based on the idea that pictorial help can simplify the task of recall for a user. The prime example is the PassPoint scheme, which goes back to a patent of Blonder [5]. Wiedenbeck et al. [43], [44], [42] and Chiasson et al. [14] studied mostly the usability of the PassPoint scheme. However, a number of later papers showed [20, 31, 36] that the click points are far from being uniformly distributed which substantially weakens the security of the PassPoint scheme. An attempt to point users to more secure passwords can be found in a paper by Chiasson et al. [15].

Suo et al. [34] proposed a variant which is somewhat resistant to shoulder-surfing, further variants include *cued click points* (CCP) [17], where images are changed after each click based on that click, and *persuasive CCP* (PCCP) [15], where while initially selecting the click points the system suggests a specific image region. Estimations for the effective key sizes for PassPoints, CCP, and PCCP are given by Chiasson et al. [16]. Frequent passwords in graphical password schemes have been identified by van Oorschot and Thorpe [37] and we complement this kind of analysis via our user studies.

Under the name Windows 8 Picture Passwords (W8PP), a cued-recall scheme is used in Windows 8 for graphical login. Here, the user can use gestures, a mouse, a stylus, or an alternative input device to enter some password based on his picture. All in all, this gives a wider variety than Android unlock patterns. As Windows 8 is marketed as "one OS for all platforms", we can expect to see W8PP at a variety of systems: For desktops, laptops and tablets, the security of W8PP is clearly higher than any Android login scheme could achieve. Even correlation attacks between the picture and the password drawn [31] do not change this evaluation. Here we exploit that people simply follow the most prominent features of a picture (a.k.a. *points* in Android Unlock Patterns) when drawing their password on the screen. On smartphones, things become different as the display becomes smaller so people cannot draw too many different patterns on the space provided. In a sense, the prominent features attacks make W8PP degenerate to Pass-Go on devices with a very small screen.

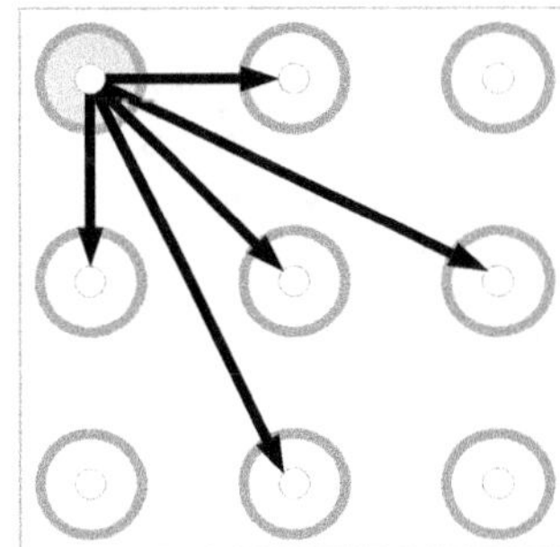

Figure 1: Android's graphical login mechanism and it's reachable points starting from the upper left point.

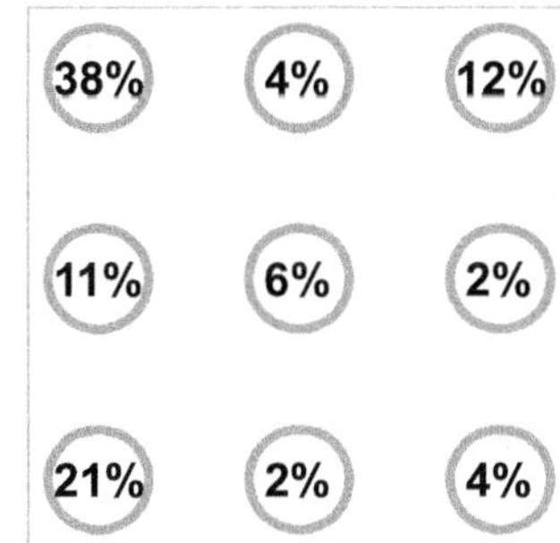

Figure 2: Bias of the initial point in Android Unlock Patterns from the pen-and-paper survey.

3. ANDROID UNLOCK PATTERNS

The unlock patterns used in Android are a simplified version of the Pass-Go scheme. We review the Pass-Go scheme in the following, describe the user study we performed to collect these patterns, and provide basic statistics about the collected data.

3.1 Pass-Go and Android Unlock Patterns

Pass-Go [35] is a graphical password scheme proposed by Tao and Adams in 2008 that can be seen as a successor of the Draw-a-Secret (DAS) scheme [24]. Pass-Go displays a grid of, say, 9×9 dots (similar to a Go board, hence the name). The secret (password) of a user is a drawing on that grid, i. e., a sequence of lines connecting the dots. These lines do not need to be connected, i. e., multiple strokes can be used, and a user may select different colors for each stroke. In order to log in, a user needs to reproduce the secret on a blank grid.

The Android OS uses a simplified variant of the Pass-Go scheme to increase usability and to adapt for the small screens found on typical devices running Android. It uses 9 points arranged in a 3×3 grid, typically on a touchscreen. The user can select a path through these points according to the following rules:

(i) At least four points must be chosen,
(ii) No point can be used twice,
(iii) Only straight lines are allowed, and
(iv) One cannot jump over points not visited before.

The first rule ensure a certain minimal strength of the resulting patterns, albeit little is known about the exact implications on pattern strength. The second and third rules resolve ambiguities from graphical representations of the patterns, which possibly increases usability.

Figure 1 shows the grid and the points that can be reached when starting at the upper left point. One can see that it is not possible to reach the upper right point directly because the straight line contains the upper middle point. Albeit, the connection between upper left and upper right point is possible, if the upper middle point is chosen previously. There is no easy way to directly calculate the number of possible patterns that follow these rules, but one can easily enumerate all possible patterns and finds that there are $389.112 \approx 2^{19}$ possible patterns, which would be sufficient if users chose their patterns uniformly from this set. It is expected that users do not choose patterns uniformly, and we will quantify this in the remainder of this work.

In addition to use these unlock patterns, Android offers the user the choice of a *personal identification number* (PIN) with four to 16 digits (resulting in a total space of $\sum_{i=4}^{16} 10^i \approx 2^{53}$ PINs) or passwords with four to 16 characters (resulting in a total space of about 2^{107}). For both cases it is well-known that users typically pick PINs and passwords with a distribution that is far from being uniform [9, 28, 40].

3.2 Study Design and Data Collection

As noted previously, there has been substantial work on the usability of graphical password schemes like Pass-Go. However, there is a lack of work in their (practical) security and we aim at closing this gap. One of the main challenges of the work on graphical passwords is collecting reliable user-generated data. In contrast to text-based passwords, where several leaked password lists are available, this is unlikely to happen for Android Unlock Patterns, as they are not stored in a centralized database.

All in all, our aim was to find frequently used passwords. This has to be seen as an initial study on the frequency and security of user passwords in Android Unlock Patterns. When designing this study, we opted for a large amount of data from different people. This is in line with our goal to perform an initial study of the real-world security of Android Unlock Pattern. Hence, usability concerns were *not* the primary focus of our work.

To evaluate the validity of the collected patterns, we additionally conducted a pen-and-paper survey, asking people for basic statistics about their Android Unlock Patterns. Both the user study and the survey were conducted at a large university. For the pen-and-paper survey, we went to different departments on campus and recruited randomly selected people. For all other parts of the study, we recruited university members at the (by far) largest university restaurant. This had the advantage that members of all faculties were represented and that the people were spending 20+ minutes there anyway. The drawback is that we had little to no control over the actual participants.

User study.

For the user study, our main concern was that users choose patterns that are weaker than the ones they would choose on their own mobile phone; note that this is a common concern in user studies. Therefore, we gave each user a "virtual sweet" (i. e., the *promise* that he will receive a real sweet such as for example a chocolate bar *after* the experiment). The task was to "lock" this sweet with a self-chosen, graphical password; we call this a *defensive pattern.*

If the user was able to remember this password after a 20-minute-time-period (in which they typically went for lunch), he could collect his sweet. There was a side-condition, though: No other user participating in our study was supposed to "unlock" this sweet within this 20-minute period. To try to unlock other sweets, each user could (in addition) try up to 5 other patterns (we call these *offensive patterns*).

In summary, the user performs the following tasks:

(i) Chooses a password (defensive pattern),

(i) Attacks up to 5 other passwords (offensive patterns),

(i) Waits 20 minutes (while other users attack this specific sweet), and

(i) Collects his sweet.

By offering users to "attack" other user's sweets we tried to offer an incentive to choose strong passwords. The results of the study (see below) seem to indicate that we achieved this goal, and probably slightly overdid it. A possible explanation is that the chance of losing the sweets was so present when we explained the experiment; for example, all types of sweets were on display as a mean to attract participants.

Giving a full explanation of the psychological background is clearly out of scope for this paper, but based on random, non-structured user feedback there are some explanations.

Looming attack: Interestingly, many people regarded our study as "highly unrealistic" as we assumed that "some random guy has access to my phone for full 20 minutes". So consequently, they chose more robust passwords for their sweets than for their phones as an attack on the first was regarded as far more likely than on the latter.

Environment: Asked by security people in a security study to choose a secure password, people tend to overcompensate and choose rather complicated password. This behavior is well-known in psychology under the name "priming" and documented in several studies [3].

All in all, this leads to the conclusion that the passwords chosen by participants of the study are stronger than the ones we would expect "in the wild".

Pen-and-paper survey.

To check the validity of the results, we conducted a simple pen & paper survey where we asked users for some statistical information about their *real* Android Unlock Pattern. In order to protect the user's patterns we only collected very limited information about those patterns, such as length (number of connected points) and starting point. Furthermore, all collected data was anonymized.

Ethical considerations.

As part of our work, we interviewed 584 people in a user study about their strategies to choose patterns. This user study was performed both as a traditional pen-and-paper survey and also as part of a game. Users were informed before participating in the study that they were to take part in a scientific study and that their data was used to evaluate the strength of Android Unlock Patterns. All data collected during our study was used in an anonymized way (i. e., there was no link between the collected data and an individual user). Furthermore, statistical data was only collected to verify that the overall user sample was not biased.

Our institute does not fall under the jurisdiction of an IRB or similar ethics committee. We did, however, get feedback from peers inside and outside our faculty to validate the ethical perspective of our research.

3.3 Basic Statistics

The pen-and-paper survey was conducted in November 2012. 105 participants helped us by disclosing the starting point and the length of their *real* Android Unlock Pattern.

Table 1: Basic statistic for our first study.

	Male	Female	Total
Engineering Students	35	3	38
Humanities Students	18	8	26
Medicine Students	-	1	1
Science Students	14	5	19
Students (other)	3	-	3
University Employees	15	1	16
Other	8	2	10
Age < 20	23	4	27
Age 21 – 30	61	15	76
Age 31 – 40	5	1	6
Age 41 – 50	-	-	-
Age > 51	4	-	4
Total	93	20	113

Figure 2 shows the bias of the initial point. One can see, that there is a strong bias of the starting point towards the corners. While the probability for all four corners should be 44% in total, we get 75% instead. In contrast to this, the center point, the right, the upper, and the lower center points get only 14% in total. We got 5.63 as average pattern length with a standard deviation of 1.50.

The user study was conducted in the end of 2012 until the beginning of 2013. 113 participants took part in the study. Table 1 summarizes the statistical data on the users we collected while conducting the study. The largest group (38, resp. 34%) of all participants are students of engineering. In addition, 82% of all participants are male and 91% are younger than 31. This data is in line with the overall population of the university, although there is a slight bias towards engineering and male students. The defensive pattern had an average length of 6.59 with a standard deviation of 1.74. For the offensive pattern we obtained 6.33 as average length with 1.68 as standard deviation.

All in all, there is statistical fluctuation between the data of the survey and the study. For example, the bias for the left upper corner is 38% vs. 43%. On the other hand, these statistical differences are in line with the sample sizes of 105 and 113, respectively. However, they do support our claim that the users "in the wild" choose less secure passwords than in our study, e. g., expressed in absolute password length. So the entropies computed in the remainder of this article is more an upper bound than an exact number on the entropy present in Android Unlock Patterns.

We discuss the results at the end of the next section.

4. STRENGTH EVALUATION

In the following, we give a framework to analyze the collected data about Android Unlock patterns regarding their strength. In particular, we need to establish a formal notion of "password strength".

4.1 Brief Introduction to Markov models

The basic idea of Markov models is that subsequent tokens, such as letters in normal text or nodes in the Pass-Go scheme, are rarely independently chosen by humans. For example, in English texts, the letter following a `t` is more likely to be an `h` than a `q`, and for the Pass-Go scheme nodes with distance one are more frequently chosen than distant ones. Based on this observation, in an n-gram Markov model one models the probability of the next token in a string based on a prefix of length $n-1$. Hence, for a given sequence of tokens $c_1, \ldots, c_m$, an n-gram Markov model estimates its probability as

$$\begin{aligned} &P(c_1, \ldots, c_m) \qquad (1) \\ &= P(c_1, \ldots, c_{n-1}) \cdot \prod_{i=n}^{m} P(c_i | c_{i-n+1}, \ldots, c_{i-1}). \end{aligned}$$

In order to use a Markov model we have to determine the *initial probabilities* $P(c_1, \ldots, c_{n-1})$ and the *transition probabilities* $P(c_n | c_1, \ldots, c_{n-1})$, where we get best results when learning these probabilities from data which is as close as possible to the set we are attacking. One can use the relative frequencies of the n-grams to compute the probabilities in the obvious way, but a number of problems arise, e. g., a probability of 0 would be assigned to n-grams that are not part of the training set. Preprocessing of the n-gram counts, so-called *smoothing*, can remedy these problems to a certain extent. We will discuss several design choices regarding Markov models in Section 4.3 and show several experiments that justify our choice of parameters.

4.2 Implementation

When guessing Android Unlock Patterns, or any other authentication strings such as traditional passwords, it is beneficial to guess the candidates in descending order of likelihood. While this is hard for passwords in general due to the large password space, we are in the fortunate position that we can solve this problem in this instance. On a high level, our implementation is structured as follows. The algorithm has access to a *training set* and a *test set*.

(i) We select the *frequent patterns* from the training set, as these are (with high probability) the frequent ones in the test set, too,
(ii) We *learn the n-gram probabilities* from the training set,
(iii) We *estimate probabilities* for all remaining patterns based on the Markov model,
(iv) We sort all patterns in decreasing (estimated) probability,
(v) We evaluate these guesses against the test set.

We perform 5-fold cross-validation on our dataset: we split our dataset into $K = 5$ disjoint subsets $S_1, \ldots, S_5$ of (roughly) equal size; all data points were distributed at random in one of the 5 sets. We select a testing set S_{i_0}, and use the union of the remaining sets as training set. We repeat this process for every set S_i as test set and average the final results over all 10 runs. Our samples have size around 100, so the training sets have size around 80 and the test sets have size about 20.

We use the training set in two different ways: First, we select all patterns that appear more than four times in the training set. While our sample size is too small to guarantee a small approximation error of the relative frequencies, it still provides a hint that it is more frequent than the others. As guessing a few infrequent passwords upfront does less harm than not guessing a frequent one upfront, we use a small threshold of 4. (In preliminary tests we found the results to be insensitive to reasonable parameter choices.)

In order to estimate the frequencies of the remaining patterns, we learn the n-gram frequencies for the Markov model.

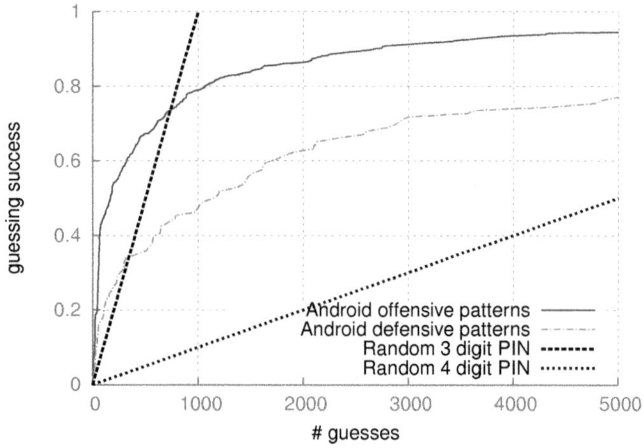

Figure 3: Guessing entropy estimate for plain Android Unlock Patterns.

We use a 3-gram model with a simple Laplace smoothing, see Section 4.3 for experiments justifying these parameter choices. In addition, we use a fixed additional set of patterns which is independent from both the test set and the training set to increase the training material.

Next, we enumerate all valid patterns (i. e., those that fulfill the requirements described in Section 3.1), using a straightforward recursive algorithm. For each pattern, we used both the initial probabilities and the transition probabilities learned before to utility by decreasing probability, overall running time is about five seconds on a standard PC.

Finally, we match the guesses against the test set, recording after how many (simulated) guesses what fraction of the test set was covered.

4.3 Model and Parameter Selection

In this section we discuss some of the design choices we made for the experiments, and discuss the results presented in this section.

3-grams vs. 2-grams.

The choice of the parameter n, i. e., the length of the n-gram, is of crucial importance. In general, longer n-grams yield better results, provided there is a sufficient amount of training data to estimate the occurring probabilities with high enough probability. For $n = 2$ we need to learn (slightly less than) $9 \cdot 8 = 72$ values, for $n = 3$ we need to learn (slightly less than) $9 \cdot 8 \cdot 7 = 504$ values. Each dataset has about 100 patterns at an average length of 6.6. For 2-grams, this yields about 560 data-points or 7.8 data-points per value to learn, for 3-grams, this yields about 460 data-points or 0.9 data-points per value to learn, and for 4-grams, this drops to about 360 data-points or 0.1 data-points per value to learn. This gives a strong indication that we do not have enough data to learn 4-gram probabilities, thus we concentrated on 2 and 3 grams. The results are shown in Figure 4, and clearly 3-grams show better performance. In addition, we believe that the nature of the Android Unlock Pattern scheme suggests the use of 3-grams instead of 2-grams: we found that many users choose points in a straight line, which is not modeled by 2-grams.

Additional information vs. no information.

When collecting data we obtained what we called defensive and offensive datasets (c.f. Section 3.2). We choose the training and test set as subsets of the defensive set. The offensive set is presumably drawn from a weaker distribution, so we can use the offensive set as additional training data. Two contradicting effects come into play: more training data typically means better approximation, but as the additional data is drawn from a (presumably) different distribution, it might actually worsen the results. We tested a number of sizes of the additional dataset, the results are shown in Figure 6. We can see that more data means better results, up to the maximum size of data we have. This is interesting because it seems to hint at the fact that the offensive and defensive patterns have very similar statistical properties.

Smoothing.

When there is not enough data to learn all n-grams, one can use *smoothing* to improve the approximation of n-grams, in particular for the rare n-grams. We tested two different smoothing techniques, simple *Laplace smoothing* (increasing each count by 1) and *Interpolation smoothing* (weighted average between between 2-gram and 3-gram probabilities). We found that the smoothing had very little influence on the success of guessing, which is shown in Figure 5.

4.4 Pattern Strength

A variety of measures for the strength of passwords has been proposed. On a high level, we can distinguish approaches that study *resistance against a specific password cracker* (either by directly attacking them, or by using mathematical models to estimate their effectiveness), and approaches that consider the *distribution of passwords.* While the former are motivated by practice and model real-world attacks pretty well, they highly depend on the specific attack and are usually not generalizable. The latter are based on mathematical models and thus have a clear meaning and are (in some sense) optimal; and usually still provide a reasonable approximation to practical security. See the survey by Bonneau et al. [8] for a review of a number of possible measures.

Partial guessing entropy estimate.

Guessing entropy [12,26] is one metric that can be used to measure the strength of a (password) distribution; it measures the average number of guesses that the optimal attack needs in order to find the correct password. However, an attacker is usually satisfied with breaking a certain fraction of accounts already, which guessing entropy does not take into account. *Partial guessing entropy* [8] (or *α-guesswork*) improves on this.

For $0 \leq \alpha \leq 1$ let $\mu_\alpha = \min\{i_0 \mid \sum_{i=1}^{i_0} p_i \geq \alpha\}$ the minimal number so that the guesses cover at least a fraction α of the passwords, and let $\lambda_\alpha = \lambda_{\mu_\alpha} = \sum_{i=1}^{\mu_\alpha} p_i$ the actual fraction covered (which is greater or equal to α). With these, partial guessing entropy is defined as

$$G_\alpha(X) = (1 - \lambda_\alpha) \cdot \mu_\alpha + \sum_{i=1}^{\mu_\alpha} i \cdot p_i \qquad (2)$$

Here the first term is contributed by those values that weren't guessed in the alloted time, and the second term is contributed by those that were guessed.

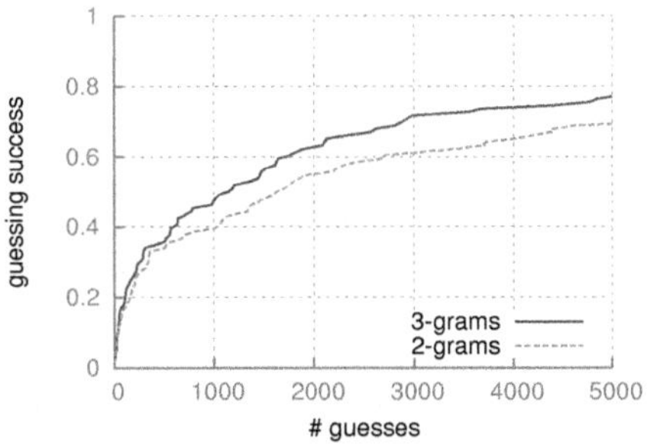

Figure 4: Android (defensive) patterns: Guessing entropy estimate with 3-grams and 2-grams.

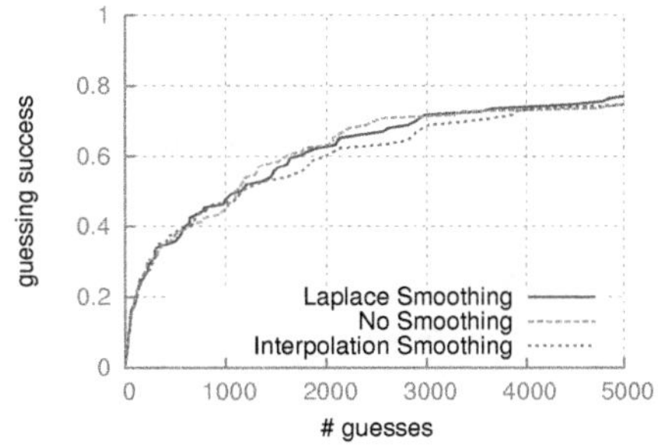

Figure 5: Android (defensive) patterns: Guessing entropy estimate for different smoothing.

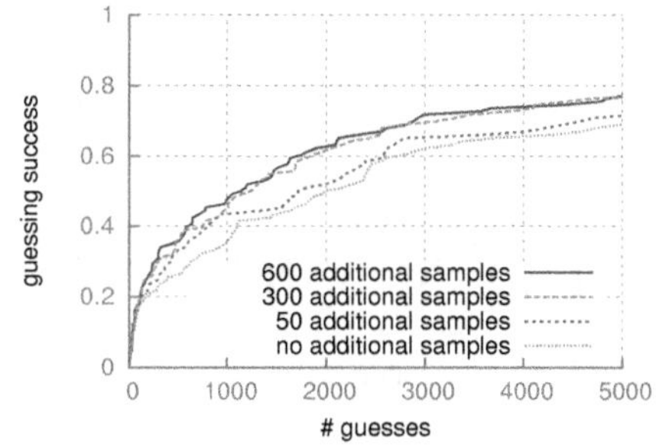

Figure 6: Android (defensive) patterns: Guessing entropy estimate with and without additional information.

Table 2: Comparing partial entropy estimate of several distributions and different values for the target fractions α.

Distribution	$\alpha = 0.1$	$\alpha = 0.2$	$\alpha = 0.5$
Android Unlock Patterns (Def, Markov)	8.72	9.10	10.90
Android Unlock Patterns (Off, Markov)	7.56	7.74	8.19
Random Android Unlock Pattern ($U_{389\,112}$)	18.57	18.57	18.57
Random 6-digit PINs ($U_{1\,000\,000}$)	19.93	19.93	19.93
Random 5-digit PINs ($U_{100\,000}$)	16.61	16.61	16.61
Random 4-digit PINs ($U_{10\,000}$)	13.29	13.29	13.29
Random 3-digit PINs ($U_{1\,000}$)	9.97	9.97	9.97
Random 2-digit PINs (U_{100})	6.64	6.64	6.64

We want to express this in "bits of information" to be able to compare it with other measures more easily. This is done as follows:

$$\tilde{G}_\alpha(X) = \log\left(\frac{2 \cdot G_\alpha(X)}{\lambda_\alpha} - 1\right) + \log\frac{1}{2-\lambda_\alpha} \quad (3)$$

where the term $\log\frac{1}{2-\lambda_\alpha}$ is used to make the metric constant for the uniform distribution (see [8] for a more detailed explanation).

We have two reasons to deviate from this approach. First, to approximate the distribution of X (i. e., the probabilities p_i) requires a certain *size of the sample set* which is beyond the data we collected; second, one can be interested in getting a more *comparable metric for a specific attack*. We are using a combined approach, where we replace the probabilities p_i that are in *optimal order* (as for guessing entropy), with probabilities whose order is given by the actual attack we are considering, i. e., p_i gives the fraction of passwords from the test set that was cracked by the i-th guess. We will refer to this modified guessing entropy estimate simply as *entropy* from here on.

Measuring entropy.

Our entropy estimates are shown in Table 2. We computed (partial) entropy estimates for three levels 10%, 20%, and 50%. We find that these three values span a reasonable range, where breaking half the logins is clearly bad, and even breaking 10% of all accounts is worrisome. As usual for non-uniform distributions, higher values for α give higher entropy estimates. Note that these values are computed on the basis of the attack outlined above, and thus give an upper bound only and the true entropy could be lower. However, in order to exploit such a lower entropy in practice one would need to find an attack that exploits this.

4.5 Evaluation

Results.

The results of our guessing attack is shown in Figure 3, which shows both the success against the defensive and the offensive pattern set. For comparison, we show the respective guessing curves for (randomly-assigned) PINs of three and four (decimal) digits. (4-digit PINs are typically used to protect the SIM-card; user-generated PIN numbers are known to be weaker [9]).

Typically, devices such as mobile phones try to protect against guessing attacks by locking the devices after a number of failed attempts, often requiring a master-PIN to unlock the device. This implies a trade-off between security and usability, which prevents manufacturers from picking too small a number of guesses. With 10 guesses, our data shows that we guess approximately 4% of the accounts correctly for the defensive patterns and approximately 7% for the offensive patterns; with 30 guesses this increases to approximately 9% for the defensive patterns and approximately 19% for the offensive patterns.

Discussion.

The results of our study reveal a lot of shortcomings of the plain Android Unlock Pattern approach. While they provide nearly 400,000 possibilities and are, from a theoretical point of view, therefore more secure than 5-digit randomly-assigned PINs, our evaluations shows that the collected patterns only have an estimated entropy slightly lower than 3-digit randomly-assigned PINs (1.4 bit lower for $\alpha = 0.1$, 1 bit higher for $\alpha = 0.5$). We believe that the collected patterns present an upper bound on the actual strength most Android users lock their smartphone with. This assumption is based on two facts: First, engineers are over-represented in our study and the faculty has a substantial number of students in computer security. Second, the imminent threat of having taken his sweet away, combined with the short timeframe for recall, might have biased the choice of a participant towards a more secure pattern. Furthermore, our evaluation reveals that the "offensive pattern" have a substantially lower estimated entropy, close to the entropy of 2-digit randomly-assigned PINs. We argue that patterns used in the wild have a lower entropy than the collected "defensive pattern" and are more like "offensive pattern" because people without a strong IT security background do not regard a weak pattern as threat for their valuable data on the smartphone. This is also in line with our initial survey on Android Unlock Patterns "in the wild".

5. FINDING MORE SECURE PATTERNS

User choices for the Android unlock patterns are highly biased, yielding security roughly comparable to three digit PINs. We evaluate the influence of several factors on the user choices, in particular we will see that small re-arrangements of the points can yield higher entropy estimates. Secondly, these alternative patterns provide us with insides on the rationals behind user choices.

5.1 Bias Found in the Android Patterns

The design of the Android Unlock Patterns imposes several biases to the patterns chosen by users, that we were able to identify in the collected data. We identified these sources for bias in order to systematically search for better patterns. Here we concentrate on relatively small modifications, in particular re-ordering of the points, because the design of the Android Unlock Patterns is well-known now and has quite good usability. As we will see, relatively small changes are sufficient to substantially improve the security of the scheme, without harming usability.

A basic and obvious weakness is a strong *bias of the starting point* towards the top-left corner, as is shown in Figure 7. While for a uniformly chosen pattern the probability for the top-left corner should be 11%, it is nearly four times higher (44%). Also, we can see a bias towards the corners and away from the center, which is heavily under-represented with 2% probability (less than a fifth from the average). These results are consistent with findings for the PassPoints system [16], which also found a bias to the top-left corner, even though the system is quite different. A plausible explanation is that in the Western hemisphere writing is from left to right and top to bottom.

We see a strong bias towards choosing *adjacent points* (i. e., points with Euclidean distance of 1), and to a lesser extent to *diagonally adjacent points* (i. e., points with a Euclidean distance of 1.4). The first 3-gram that connects two point that are *not* adjacent is the 14-th most frequent 3-gram, and the first 3-gram connecting two points that are not even diagonally adjacent is the 40-th most frequent 3-gram. This is probably caused by problems in usability, as adjacent points are the easiest to draw a connection, and points that are not even diagonally adjacent are very hard to connect without accidentally touching intermediate points. Furthermore, the resulting drawings become quite complicated and probably harder to recall.

There is also a tendency to *stay on the border*, i. e., avoiding the point in the middle. The first 3-gram to touch the middle point is the 12-th most frequent one. Also, there is a tendency for *straight lines* and right angles (the first non-rectangular corner is formed by the 14-th most likely 3-gram). Again, this is similar to the findings for PassPoints [16], where straight lines often can be found.

5.2 Alternative Patterns

We explored four approaches that systematically change the arrangement of the points in the grid without modifying the basic method.

For the first alternative, the *Leftout Small Pattern* (cf. Figure 9), we omitted the upper left point, as it had by far the strongest bias. Our hope was that this would spread the initial point to a larger set of three or four points, thus potentially increasing the entropy of chosen patterns. However, reducing the number of points has the potential to reduce both length and complexity of patterns, thus decreasing entropy.

The second alternative, the *Leftout Large Pattern* (cf. Figure 10), is similar to the previous one, but we added two points in the bottom row to increase the overall point count. We added symmetry by leaving out the bottom right point as well. Most mobile devices use a screen which is larger in one direction, so fitting a 3×4 grid of points should not be problematic.

The third alternative, the *Circle Pattern* (cf. Figure 11), targets another form of bias: For the plain Android Unlock Pattern, there are a many straight lines (horizontal, vertical and diagonal) that users prefer to follow, as we have seen in the previous section. In addition, by removing corner points (which were chosen as starting point in 78% of all patterns, see Figure 7), we hoped to increase entropy. A potential weak point of the *Circle* is that it might be tempting to just "follow the circle" to create a pattern.

The fourth and last alternative, the *Random Pattern* (cf. Figure 12), aims to break all symmetry and thus forcing the user to choose strong patterns. The arrangement of points looks fairly random, with the side condition that no three points should be on a straight line, and no point should be a clear upper-left corner point.

All these patterns were tested in a user study similar to the one before, with 366 participants approximately evenly spread over the four approaches, collecting 2,196 patterns in total.

5.3 Study Setup and Data Collection

We conducted a user study identical to the one described for Android Unlock Patterns in Section 3.2. This allows for a fair comparison of the data we collected.

The user study was conducted over several weeks between the end of 2012 and the beginning of 2013. In total, 366 people participated, some statistics about their affiliation with the university, gender, and age is given in Table 3. The data from the plain Android user study is given to facilitate comparison, it indicates that the population participating in the study should be comparable.

Combining both studies, 479 people supported our work by participating, at least 80 for each approach. The majority of participants are male students of engineering. One explanation is that they have a higher interest in mobile phone security and were therefore easier attracted to participate in our study.

5.4 Evaluation

We used the same methods as explained in Section 4 to test the strength of the collected patterns. The results are shown in Figure 15, and the resulting entropy estimates are given in Table 4.

For the *Leftout Small* patterns, we can indeed observe a more uniform distribution of the first point. However, overall the entropy is lower, most likely due to the smaller number of points and, as a consequence, the lower number of possible patterns.

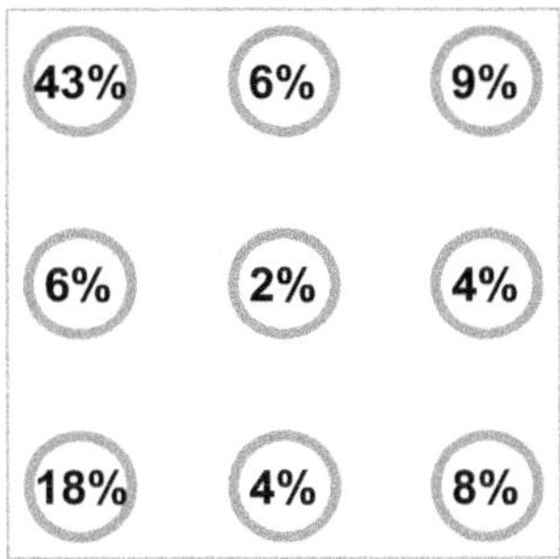

Figure 7: Bias of the initial point.

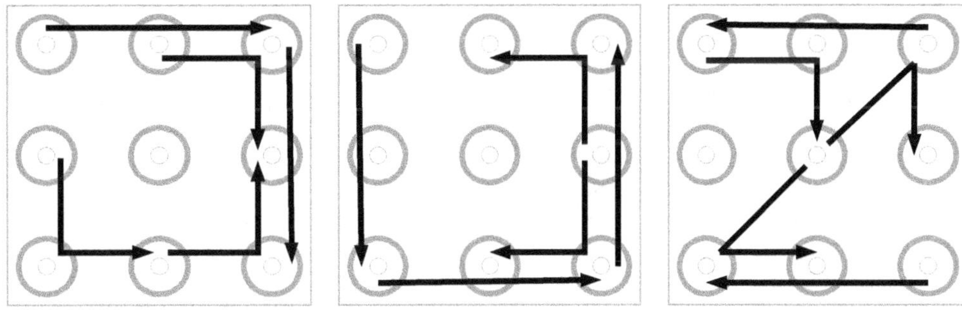

Figure 8: The most frequent 3-grams, from most frequent (left) to less frequent (right).

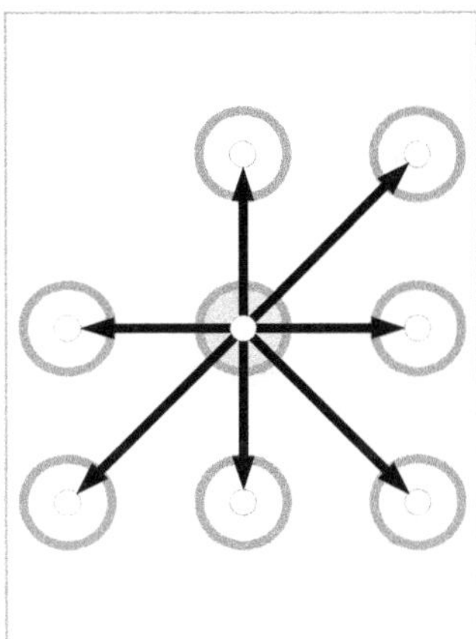

Figure 9: The Leftout Small approach and its reachable point starting from the center.

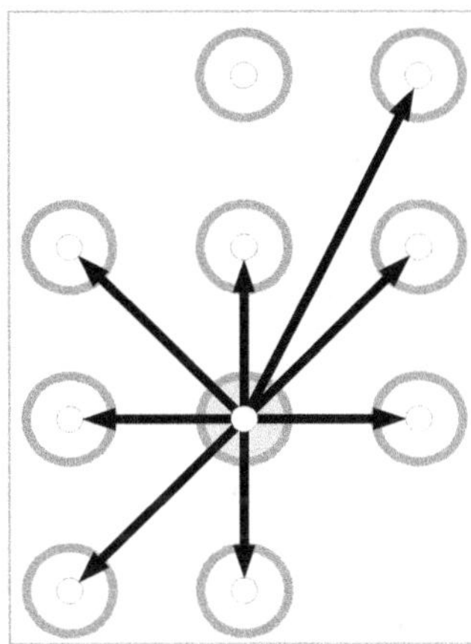

Figure 10: The Leftout Large approach and its reachable points starting from the lower center.

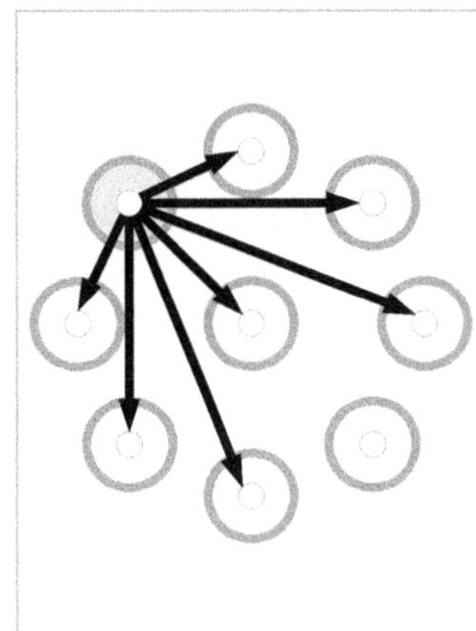

Figure 11: The Circle approach with the upper left corner as starting point and its reachable points.

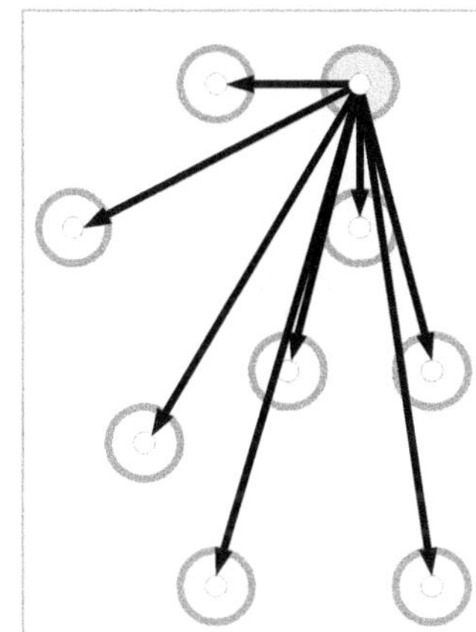

Figure 12: The Random approach with the upper right corner as starting point and its reachable points.

Figure 13: Bias of the initial point for Leftout Small, Leftout Large, Circle, and Random.

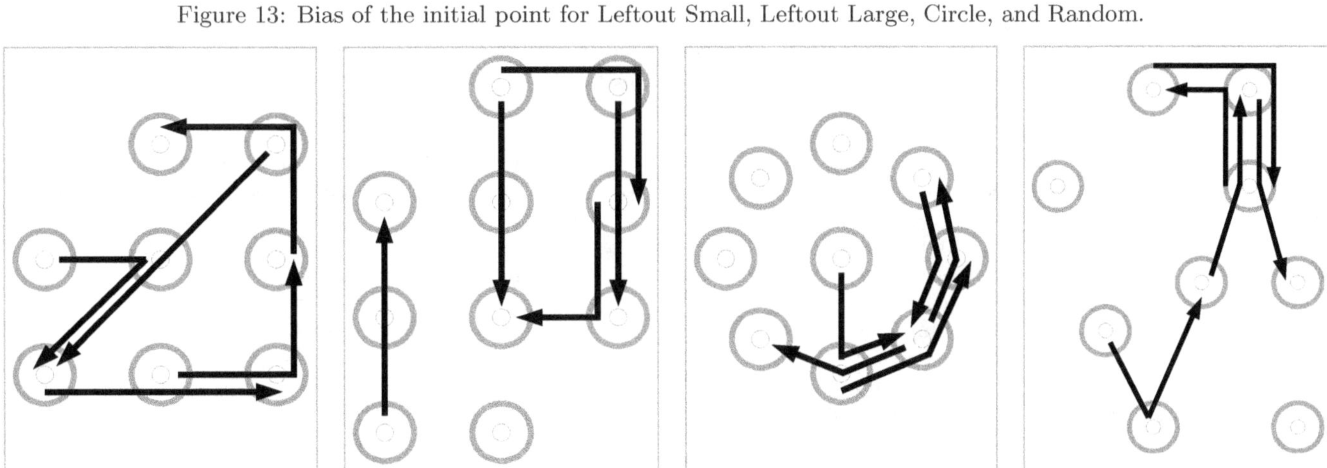

Figure 14: The most frequent 3-grams for Leftout Small, Leftout Large, Circle, and Random.

Table 3: Basic statistics for the plain Android and the alternative pattern user study.

	Plain Android Study	Alternative Pattern Study				
	Total	Total	Lefto. S.	Lefto. L.	Circ.	Rand.
Engineering students	38	133	39	37	31	26
Humanities students	26	74	20	21	18	15
Medicine students	1	39	17	9	4	9
Science students	19	40	9	13	7	11
Students (other)	3	8	6	2	-	-
University Employees	16	64	12	15	19	18
Other	10	8	2	2	3	1
Male	93	264	68	78	61	57
Female	20	102	37	21	21	23
Age $<$ 20	27	65	21	15	20	9
Age $21-30$	76	267	75	76	56	60
Age $31-40$	6	27	5	6	6	10
Age $41-50$	-	3	1	2	-	-
Age $>$ 51	4	4	3	-	-	1
Participants						
w/ successful recall	61	189	59	55	44	31
wo/ successful recall	1	41	8	5	9	19
Recall attempts						
Average	1.28	1.42	1.15	1.49	1.59	1.59
Standard Deviation	0.66	0.79	0.40	0.83	1.10	1.04
Total	113	366	105	99	82	80

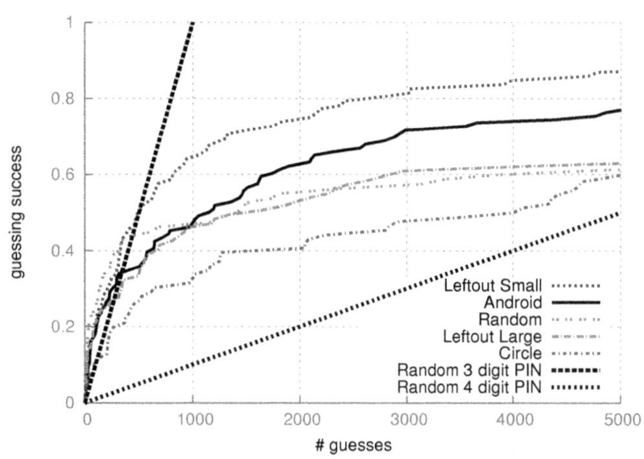

Figure 15: Comparison of the guessing entropy estimates for alternative constructions

For the *Leftout Large* patterns, somewhat surprisingly the bias of the first point is comparable to the original scheme. We do not have a definite explanation, but we believe that the rectangular form of the Leftout Small pattern leads the user to more uniform choices, and the rectangular shape of the Leftout Large patterns emphasizes the asymmetry of the shape. This highlights the importance of user study to understand the actual user choices. Due to the larger number of points, the entropy estimate is larger, and from Figure 15 we can see that the advantage over the original Android scheme is mostly for larger number of guesses.

To our surprise, the *Circle* patterns performed best in our experiments, even though the bias of the initial point is similar to the original patterns. While we had expected that more users would choose to draw a (partial) circle, we saw that many people were aware that simply drawing a circle is very insecure, and resorted to a number of other patterns, like drawing a square or a triangle into the circle. The guessing rate is smaller over the entire range of guesses, and the entropy estimate is about 1.5 bits higher.

The *Random* patterns were surprisingly weak. As expected, the initial point is closer to a uniform distribution. However, even though the points are spread randomly, many users chose a pattern loosely resembling a δ, the reason might be that human try to find patterns even in random data. It is noteworthy that *Random* patterns are particularly weak for very small number of guesses, even weaker than for the original patterns, and get only better for larger numbers of guesses.

Memorability is a clear lack in the above user study: We do not have any data on the long-term development for any given pattern. However, our main focus was to learn about frequently chosen passwords and the rationals behind it, so this question was simply not in focus.

On statistical significance.

The number of samples available for our study is substantially limited by the time requirement for the user study, which raises questions about statistical significance of the results. Unfortunately, guessing entropy does not allow directly computing confidence intervals, therefor we resort to techniques that were previously used by Bonneau [8].

We subsample samples of size 50 from the original dataset of 114 samples, and empirically determined sizes for the confidence intervals from those. We obtain confidence intervals of 8.72 ± 0.38, 9.10 ± 0.65, and 10.90 ± 0.45 for $G_{0.1}$, $G_{0.2}$, and $G_{0.5}$, respectively (for a confidence level of 90%). This indicates that the differences for circle and random are indeed significant even for 50 samples only.

However, this analysis is somewhat problematic, as the sampled subsets are (almost certainly) not disjoint (as 114 samples is not sufficient). But we still believe that it is indicative for the significance of the results, in particular because the above intervals were obtained from 50 samples only, and the larger number of samples should give even smaller intervals.

5.5 Usability Considerations

The main goal of our study was to measure the *security* of the Android Unlock Pattern scheme, as already pointed out in Section 3.2. Furthermore, we introduced small changes in the graphical layout of the scheme to learn about the rationals behind actual user choices for Android Unlock Patterns. Hence, the overall design of the study did *not* take usability into its main focus, but we have collected some data that allows us to argue about the usability of the resulting scheme. First, we recorded the number of attempts people needed to (correctly) enter their passwords. Second, we know how many attempts people needed to enter their password (or fail to do so) after the 20-minute-period. Both give us some indication on the memorability and usability of the scheme. Table 3 compares the usability of all approaches by this metric. The plain Android Unlock Pattern performs slightly better in relation to the *Leftout Large*, *Circle* and *Random* approaches. Only for *Leftout Small*, participants needed less attempts to recall the pattern on average.

A possible explanation is that many participants have already used Android Unlock Patterns before. This is supported by (informal) inquiries during our study. Consequently, they found it easier to choose (and remember) a password in this arrangement of nodes. This is in line with

Table 4: Comparing partial entropy estimate of several distributions and different values for the target fractions α.

Distribution	$\alpha = 0.1$	$\alpha = 0.2$	$\alpha = 0.5$
Android Unlock Patterns (Def, Markov)	8.72	9.10	10.90
Android Unlock Patterns (Off, Markov)	7.56	7.74	8.19
Leftout Large (Def, Markov)	7.56	8.73	11.40
Leftout Small (Def, Markov)	8.00	8.93	9.81
Circle (Def, Markov)	9.76	10.81	12.69
Random (Def, Markov)	7.76	7.43	11.10

the fact that *Leftout Small* performed better than all other approaches as has the biggest similarity to the plain approach. In addition, it has the smallest number of nodes. Consequently, the other approaches performed slightly worse as the arrangement of the points was new to the participants. This is particularly true for *Random*. As expected, it performed worst: only 62% of participants could recall their secret within five attempts.

Concluding, our new arrangements are not superior to the plain Android Pattern Login regarding usability. However, we think that this is based in the novelty of the approaches and cannot be seen as shortcoming. It is out of scope of this article to investigate deeper if the usability could be improved, for example by giving the users sufficient training on recalling patterns on the new arrangements.

6. CONCLUSIONS AND FUTURE WORK

To the best of our knowledge, this is the first large-scale user study of Android Unlock Patterns. In particular, we have focused on the *actual* entropy, in contrast to theoretical values such as the size of the key space, that do not provide a reasonable estimate for the strength. Interestingly, around 10% of all users use less than 190 patterns while less than 300 patterns capture around 50% of the whole test popluation (7.56 and 8.19 bit entropy, respectively for offensive patterns, cf. Table 2). Our findings are based on a study with a total of 584 participants. All in all, recruiting these 584 people was rather time consuming and the clear bottleneck of this approach. The dataset is large enough to create Markov models of transitions between points in the 3×3 grid (Android Unlock Patterns) and derive a very efficient attack, yielding a good approximation the exact strength, cf. Table 2 for a detailed comparison of the results for different unlock patterns. However, as explained in Section 3.2, they are most likely upper bounds on the strength we expect to see in real world systems.

To deepen these insights, we tested four simple modifications of Android Unlock Patterns. Interestingly, *Circle* was both a very simple but also a rather secure modification—pointing towards the fact that people like to follow lines (plain Android Unlock Patterns, but also *Leftout Small* and *Large*: As soon as we removed these lines, the overall entropy increased. Apparently, the *Random* pattern was too difficult for users to recognize so they were not able to choose good passwords on the short term. Probably this picture were to change if they were given more time to familiarize themselves with this specific pattern. However, this is out of scope for this article.

We believe some of the ideas presented in our work are worth exploring further. First, it might be possible to choose other patterns (that we did not test) that might offer even better security, at the same level of usability. Our work indicates a couple of potential directions. Clearly, we need to put a strong emphasis on usability here. Second, the system could provide some form of visual feedback to the user about the strength of the pattern he is about to choose: (*red:* weak password, *green:* strong password). While this certainly has the potential to increase the security of the patterns, this must be done more accurately than the prevalent "password rules" that are frequently used for text-based passwords, and it poses questions about usability. Third, we could prevent the attacker from building an attack dictionary (as we did) by having different (challenge) patterns for different smartphones/users.

Acknowledgments.

This work has been supported by the DFG (Emmy Noether grant *Long Term Security* and GRK 187 *UbiCrypt*). We also thank the anonymous reviewers for their valuable insights and comments.

7. REFERENCES

[1] atom. HashCat. Online at `http://hashcat.net/oclhashcat-plus/`.

[2] A. J. Aviv, K. Gibson, E. Mossop, M. Blaze, and J. M. Smith. Smudge Attacks on Smartphone Touch Screens. In *USENIX Workshop on Offensive Technologies (WOOT)*, 2010.

[3] J. A. Bargh, M. Chen, and L. Burrows. Automaticity of Social Behavior: Direct Effects of Trait Construct and Stereotype Priming on Action. *Journal of Personality and Social Psychology*, 71:230–244, 1996.

[4] R. Biddle, S. Chiasson, and P. Van Oorschot. Graphical Passwords: Learning From the First Twelve Years. *ACM Computing Surveys*, 44(4):19:1–19:41, Sept. 2012.

[5] G. Blonder. Graphical Passwords. US Patent 5559961, 1996.

[6] M. Bond. Comments on gridsure authentication. Online at `http://www.cl.cam.ac.uk/~mkb23/research/GridsureComments.pdf`.

[7] J. Bonneau. *Guessing Human-chosen Secrets.* PhD thesis, University of Cambridge, May 2012.

[8] J. Bonneau. The Science of Guessing: Analyzing an Anonymized Corpus of 70 Million Passwords. In *IEEE Symposium on Security and Privacy*, 2012.

[9] J. Bonneau, S. Preibusch, and R. Anderson. A Birthday Present Every Eleven Wallets? The Security of Customer-chosen Banking PINs. In *Financial Cryptography and Data Security (FC)*, 2012.

[10] S. Brostoff, P. Inglesant, and M. A. Sasse. Evaluating the Usability and Security of a Graphical One-time PIN System. In *BCS Interaction Specialist Group Conference (BCS)*, 2010.

[11] S. Brostoff and A. Sasse. Are Passfaces More Usable Than Passwords? A Field Trial Investigation. In *Conference on Human-Computer Interaction (HCI)*, 2000.

[12] C. Cachin. *Entropy Measures and Unconditional Security in Cryptography.* PhD thesis, ETH Zürich, 1997.

[13] C. Castelluccia, M. Dürmuth, and D. Perito. Adaptive Password-Strength Meters from Markov Models. In

Symposium on Network and Distributed System Security (NDSS), 2012.

[14] S. Chiasson, R. Biddle, and P. van Oorschot. A Second Look at the Usability of Click-based Graphical Passwords. In *Symposium on Usable Privacy and Security (SOUPS)*, 2007.

[15] S. Chiasson, A. Forget, R. Biddle, and P. C. van Oorschot. Influencing Users Towards Better Passwords: Persuasive Cued Click-points. In *British HCI Group Annual Conference on People and Computers: Celebrating People and Technology (BCS HCI)*, 2008.

[16] S. Chiasson, A. Forget, R. Biddle, and P. C. van Oorschot. User Interface Design Affects Security: Patterns in Click-based Graphical Passwords. *International Journal of Information Security*, 8(6):387–398, 2009.

[17] S. Chiasson, P. Oorschot, and R. Biddle. Graphical Password Authentication Using Cued Click Points. In *European Symposium on Research in Computer Security (ESORICS)*, 2007.

[18] D. Davis, F. Monrose, and M. K. Reiter. On User Choice in Graphical Password Schemes. In *USENIX Security Symposium*, 2004.

[19] R. Dhamija and A. Perrig. Deja Vu: A User Study Using Images for Authentication. In *USENIX Security Symposium*, 2000.

[20] A. E. Dirik, N. Memon, and J.-C. Birget. Modeling User Choice in the PassPoints Graphical Password Scheme. In *Symposium on Usable Privacy and Security (SOUPS)*, 2007.

[21] P. Dunphy and J. Yan. Do Background Images Improve "Draw a Secret" Graphical Passwords? In *ACM Conference on Computer and Communications Security (CCS)*, 2007.

[22] H. Gao, X. Guo, X. Chen, L. Wang, and X. Liu. YAGP: Yet Another Graphical Password Strategy. In *Annual Computer Security Applications Conference (ACSAC)*, 2008.

[23] P. Golle and D. Wagner. Cryptanalysis of a Cognitive Authentication Scheme (Extended Abstract). In *IEEE Symposium on Security and Privacy*, 2007.

[24] I. Jermyn, A. Mayer, F. Monrose, M. K. Reiter, and A. D. Rubin. The Design and Analysis of Graphical Passwords. In *USENIX Security Symposium*, 1999.

[25] S. Komanduri, R. Shay, P. G. Kelley, M. L. Mazurek, L. Bauer, N. Christin, L. F. Cranor, and S. Egelman. Of Passwords and People: Measuring the Effect of Password-Composition Policies. In *ACM Conference on Human Factors in Computing Systems (CHI)*, 2011.

[26] J. Massey. Guessing and Entropy. In *IEEE International Symposium on Information Theory (ISIT)*, 1994.

[27] R. Morris and K. Thompson. Password Security: A Case History. *Communications of the ACM*, 22(11):594–597, 1979.

[28] A. Narayanan and V. Shmatikov. Fast Dictionary Attacks on Passwords Using Time-space Tradeoff. In *ACM Conference on Computer and Communications Security (CCS)*, 2005.

[29] M. Orozco, B. Malek, M. Eid, and A. El Saddik. Haptic-based Sensible Graphical Password. *Proceedings of Virtual Concept*, 2006.

[30] Passfaces Corporation. The Science Behind Passfaces. White paper, available at `http://www.passfaces.com/enterprise/resources/white_papers.htm`.

[31] A. Salehi-Abari, J. Thorpe, and P. van Oorschot. On Purely Automated Attacks and Click-Based Graphical Passwords. In *Annual Computer Security Applications Conference (ACSAC)*, 2008.

[32] Solar Designer. John the Ripper. Online at `http://www.openwall.com/john/`.

[33] L. Standing, J. Conezio, and R. N. Haber. Perception and Memory for Pictures: Single-trial Learning of 2500 Visual Stimuli. *Psychonomic Science*, 19(2):73–74, 1970.

[34] X. Suo. A Design and Analysis of Graphical Password. Master's thesis, College of Arts and Science, Georgia State University, 2006.

[35] H. Tao and C. Adams. Pass-Go: A Proposal to Improve the Usability of Graphical Passwords. *International Journal of Network Security*, 7(2):273–292, 2008.

[36] J. Thorpe and P. C. van Oorschot. Human-seeded Attacks and Exploiting Hot-spots in Graphical Passwords. In *USENIX Security Symposium*, 2007.

[37] P. C. van Oorschot and J. Thorpe. Exploiting Predictability in Click-based Graphical Passwords. *Journal of Computer Security*, 19(4):669–702, 2011.

[38] C. Varenhorst, M. V. Kleek, and L. Rudolph. Passdoodles: A Lightweight Authentication Method. Online at `http://people.csail.mit.edu/emax/public_html/papers/varenhorst.pdf`, 2004.

[39] D. Weinshall. Cognitive Authentication Schemes Safe Against Spyware. In *IEEE Symposium on Security and Privacy*, 2006.

[40] M. Weir, S. Aggarwal, B. de Medeiros, and B. Glodek. Password Cracking Using Probabilistic Context-Free Grammars. In *IEEE Symposium on Security and Privacy*, 2009.

[41] R. Weiss and A. De Luca. PassShapes: Utilizing Stroke Based Authentication to Increase Password Memorability. In *Nordic Conference on Human-Computer Interaction (NordiCHI)*, 2008.

[42] S. Wiedenbeck, J. Waters, J.-C. Birget, A. Brodskiy, and N. Memon. Authentication Using Graphical Passwords: Basic Results. In *Conference on Human-Computer Interaction (HCI)*, 2005.

[43] S. Wiedenbeck, J. Waters, J.-C. Birget, A. Brodskiy, and N. Memon. Authentication Using Graphical Passwords: Effects of Tolerance and Image Choice. In *Symposium on Usable Privacy and Security (SOUPS)*, 2005.

[44] S. Wiedenbeck, J. Waters, J.-C. Birget, A. Brodskiy, and N. Memon. PassPoints: Design and Longitudinal Evaluation of a Graphical Password System. *International Journal of Human-Computer Studies*, 63(1-2):102–127, July 2005.

Measuring Password Guessability for an Entire University

Michelle L. Mazurek, Saranga Komanduri, Timothy Vidas, Lujo Bauer,
Nicolas Christin, Lorrie Faith Cranor, Patrick Gage Kelley*, Richard Shay, and Blase Ur

Carnegie Mellon University
Pittsburgh, PA
{mmazurek, sarangak, tvidas, lbauer,
nicolasc, lorrie, rshay, bur}@cmu.edu

*University of New Mexico
Albequerque, NM
pgk@cs.unm.edu

ABSTRACT

Despite considerable research on passwords, empirical studies of password strength have been limited by lack of access to plaintext passwords, small data sets, and password sets specifically collected for a research study or from low-value accounts. Properties of passwords used for high-value accounts thus remain poorly understood.

We fill this gap by studying the single-sign-on passwords used by over 25,000 faculty, staff, and students at a research university with a complex password policy. Key aspects of our contributions rest on our (indirect) access to plaintext passwords. We describe our data collection methodology, particularly the many precautions we took to minimize risks to users. We then analyze how guessable the collected passwords would be during an offline attack by subjecting them to a state-of-the-art password cracking algorithm. We discover significant correlations between a number of demographic and behavioral factors and password strength. For example, we find that users associated with the computer science school make passwords more than 1.5 times as strong as those of users associated with the business school. while users associated with computer science make strong ones. In addition, we find that stronger passwords are correlated with a higher rate of errors entering them.

We also compare the guessability and other characteristics of the passwords we analyzed to sets previously collected in controlled experiments or leaked from low-value accounts. We find more consistent similarities between the university passwords and passwords collected for research studies under similar composition policies than we do between the university passwords and subsets of passwords leaked from low-value accounts that happen to comply with the same policies.

Categories and Subject Descriptors

D.4.6 [**Management Of Computing and Information Systems**]: Security and Protection—*Authentication*

Keywords

Passwords; authentication; password security

CCS'13, November 4–8, 2013, Berlin, Germany.
ACM 978-1-4503-2477-9/13/11.
http://dx.doi.org/10.1145/2508859.2516726.

1. INTRODUCTION

Researchers have documented the numerous problems of text passwords for decades — passwords are easy to guess, hard to remember, easily stolen, and vulnerable to observation and replay attacks (e.g., [28, 38]). The research community has invested significant effort in alternatives including biometrics, graphical passwords, hardware tokens, and federated identity; however, text passwords remain the dominant mechanism for authenticating people to computers, and seem likely to remain that way for the foreseeable future [5,23]. Better understanding of text passwords therefore remains important.

Considerable effort has been spent studying the usage and characteristics of passwords (e.g., [13, 17, 34, 35, 45]), but password research is consistently hampered by the difficulty in collecting realistic data to analyze. Prior password studies all have one or more of the following drawbacks: very small data sets [36], data from experimental studies rather than from deployed authentication systems [31], no access to plaintext passwords [3], self-reported password information [47], leaked data of questionable validity, or accounts of minimal value [26, 53]. As a result, the important question of whether the results apply to real, high-value passwords has remained open.

In this paper, we study more than 25,000 passwords making up the entire user base of Carnegie Mellon University (CMU). Notably, these passwords are the high-value gatekeeper to most end-user (i.e., non-administrative) online functions within the university, including email, grading systems, transcripts, financial data, health data, payroll, and course content. Furthermore, these passwords were created under a password-composition policy among the stricter of those in common use [18], requiring a minimum of eight characters and four different character classes. Using indirect access to the plaintext of these passwords, we measure their strength. In addition, we obtain contextual information from personnel databases, authentication logs, and a survey about password creation and management, and correlate these factors with password strength. To acquire this data, we established a partnership with the CMU information technology division; the research was also vetted by our Institutional Review Board (IRB). Our approach to analyzing this sensitive data securely provides a blueprint for future research involving security-sensitive data in the wild.

Using this data, we make two important and novel contributions to the field of password research. First, we identify interesting trends in password strength, measured as resistance to offline guessing attacks, in which an attacker attempts to recover plaintext passwords from their hashes [2, 6, 44]. Using statistical methods adopted from survival analysis, we find that users associated with science and technology colleges within the university make passwords more than 1.5 times as strong as those of users associated with the business school. Perhaps unsurprisingly, strong passwords are correlated with higher rates of failed login attempts due to password errors. Users who report annoyance with CMU's complex password-composition policy made weaker passwords. For the first time, we are also able to directly investigate whether insights from work based on lower-value passwords also apply to high-value passwords. For example, we confirm Bonneau's finding that men's passwords are slightly stronger than women's [3]. We also confirm that passwords with more digits, symbols, and uppercase letters are stronger, and that digits and symbols are least effective when placed at the end of a password, while uppercase letters are least effective placed at the beginning.

Our second major contribution is a comparison of our real, high-value password data with password sets more typically used in password research. We compare the CMU passwords to passwords collected in an online study simulating CMU's password-creation process, as well as to data from online studies and a self-reported survey of CMU users discussed in prior work [30,47]. We also consider plaintext and cracked leaked passwords from low-value accounts [2,19,32,43,52]. We show that simulated password sets designed to closely mirror real authentication conditions consistently provide reasonably accurate substitutes for high-value real-world passwords, while leaked passwords vary widely in their effectiveness. This has important implications for passwords research, as most researchers must choose between leaked sets and experimental data. In the past, many researchers have chosen leaked sets; our results show this may be the wrong choice. Taken together, our approach and results provide a unique understanding of frequently used, high-value passwords as well as insight for improving future password research.

2. RELATED WORK

In this section, we review background in two key areas: the types of password corpora that have been analyzed previously, and efforts to define metrics for password strength.

2.1 Password corpora

Due to the sensitive nature of passwords, acquiring high-quality password corpora for analysis can be difficult. Data sets that have been used in previous work on passwords have all been non-ideal in at least one dimension.

Many researchers use password corpora collected from various security leaks [14,24,26,35,53,55]. These corpora tend to be very large (tens of thousands to millions), and they represent in-use passwords selected by users. While this approach has many benefits, these passwords come with no contextual information about how they were made or used, and the released lists are difficult to verify. Furthermore, the largest leaks thus far have come from low-value accounts with weak password-composition policies, such as the RockYou gaming website. In addition, if the password file is encrypted or hashed, only those passwords that have been successfully cracked can be analyzed, biasing the data toward the more guessable. Other researchers obtain an organization's hashed or encrypted password file with permission and attempt to crack it [10, 57]. As with leaked password sets, the results are biased toward more guessable passwords.

Researchers who want to control the circumstances under which passwords are created often use lab studies. Some of these studies are small and focus on targeted populations, such as undergraduates [9,41,54]. Others are larger online studies with a more diverse population [30,51]. In some cases, users are asked to create passwords for a low-value account associated with the study [9,31]. Others studies have asked students to create passwords for accounts tied to a class [21,29]. In contrast to these studies, the passwords used in our paper are created for high-value accounts, and are used frequently over a longer period of time.

Rather than collect passwords expressly for an experiment, some researchers ask users to self-report password information, including both password composition details and user sentiment information [7,33,37,47,49,58]. While self-reported data can be very useful and can provide a lot of context, it cannot always be considered reliable, particularly with regard to a sensitive topic like passwords.

Finally, a small number of researchers have been able to work with large organizations to collect authentic data. Florêncio and Herley used an opt-in component of the Windows Live toolbar to collect information when users log into websites [17]. Bonneau worked with Yahoo! to analyze plaintext passwords entered by their users [3]. Both studies include very large, reliable samples, as well as good contextual information. Due to security concerns, however, in both studies researchers were able to record only extremely limited information about the content of the passwords, precluding many types of interesting analyses. In contrast, our paper connects information about each user with analysis of that user's plaintext password. Perhaps closest to our work, Fahl et al. use a within-subjects study to manually compare passwords users made in lab and online studies with their actual passwords; they found that while study passwords do have some problems, they can provide a reasonable approximation for real passwords if used carefully [16]. While Fahl et al. compare real password data with online and lab studies, we also compare real password data with commonly used leaked password sets.

In this paper, we overcome many limitations of past studies. Our password corpus includes more than 25,000 real passwords, created by users for frequently used, high-value accounts unrelated to our research context. We have indirect, yet extensive, access to plaintext passwords, allowing us to perform more complex and thorough analyses than was possible for other similarly authentic corpora. We also collect a significant amount of contextual information, including demographics, behavioral data, and user sentiment.

2.2 Password cracking and strength metrics

Accurately judging the strength of a password is crucial to understanding how to improve security. Historically, information entropy has been used to measure password strength, but it may insufficiently capture resistance to intelligent guessing attacks [17,55]. More recently, researchers have suggested using password *guessability*, or ability to withstand guessing by a particular password cracker with particular training data, as a security metric [55]. This metric has the advantages of modeling knowledge a real-world adversary might have, as well as of bounding the attempts an adversary might make to guess a password, but its results are dependent on the chosen setup. *Guess numbers*, as defined by Kelley et al., measure how many guesses it would take a particular cracking algorithm and training setup to reach a given password [30]. Working without access to plaintext passwords, Bonneau suggests a guessing metric that reflects how many passwords an optimal attacker, who knows exactly which passwords to guess and what order to guess them in, will successfully break before guessing the password under consideration [4]. Several researchers have also used machine-learning techniques to classify passwords as weak or strong, based on labeled training data, but these techniques are only as good as the original classification [1,27,50].

The guessability metric of password strength dovetails with recent advances in password cracking. In contrast to prior brute-force or dictionary-based approaches [48], researchers have begun to use deeper insights about the structure of passwords in cracking. For instance, Narayanan and Shmatikov substantially reduce the search space for attacks by modeling passwords as a character-level Markov chain using the probabilities of letters in natural language [39]. Using passwords leaked from websites like RockYou and others as training data, Weir creates a probabilistic context-free grammar for password cracking [56]. In this approach, guesses are ordered according to their likelihood, based on the frequency of their character-class structures in the training data, as well as the frequency of their digit and symbol substrings. This approach has been shown to be efficient in password cracking [30,57]. In this paper, we primarily use the guessability metric, simulating cracking using a modified version of Weir's algorithm [30].

3. DATA COLLECTION

In this section, we discuss our data sources. First, we review the university data collected for this study. Second, we discuss our procedures for ensuring security while working with real data, as well as the challenges these procedures create for analysis. Third, we briefly review other data sets that we use as supplemental data in our analysis. Fourth, we discuss the composition of our sample and the generalizability of our results.

3.1 University data

We study the passwords used by all of the more than 25,000 faculty, staff, and students of Carnegie Mellon University. These passwords are used as part of a single-sign-on system that allows users to access resources like email, tax and payroll statements, personnel directories, health information, grades and transcripts, course information, and other restricted university resources.

CMU's password-composition policy is a complex one, requiring at least one each of upper- and lowercase letters, digits, and symbols, as well as forbidding a dictionary word. All non-letter characters are removed and the password is lowercased before it is checked against a 241,497-word dictionary, unless the password is greater than 19 characters. The minimum length is eight characters, and no character can appear more than four times unless the password is greater than 19 characters in length.

We collect data from four sources: logs from the university's single-sign-on web authentication service, demographic data from the university's two personnel databases, responses to a survey advertised to users immediately after changing their passwords, and the plaintext passwords themselves. The web logs represent the period from January 1, 2012 through July 27, 2012. On July 28, the university's authentication infrastructure was replaced, and the logs from the two systems are incomparable. The personnel databases, as with most large organizations, are subject to bureaucratic errors that may cause some data to be incorrect.

Data from all four sources can be correlated using hashed user IDs (salted with a salt unknown to us, as described below). Plaintext passwords are divided into two groups: 25,459 passwords belonging to users with active CMU accounts, and 17,104 passwords belonging to users whose accounts were deactivated after they left the university, but which have not yet been deleted. Hereafter we refer to these as the CMUactive and CMUinactive sets respectively. Some of the CMUinactive accounts were created under an earlier composition policy that required only that passwords contain at least one character; as result, 1,635 CMUinactive passwords do not conform to the strict policy described above.

3.2 Working with real data securely

To get access to this hard-to-acquire real data, we spent months negotiating a process, vetted by both our IRB and information security office, that would allow the university to remain comfortable about security while also allowing us to perform useful analyses.

Plaintext passwords were made indirectly available to us through fortunate circumstances, which may not be reproducible in the future. The university was using a legacy credential management system (since abandoned), which, to meet certain functional requirements, reversibly encrypted user passwords, rather than using salted, hashed records. Researchers were never given access to the decryption key.

We were required to submit all the analysis software needed to parse, aggregate, and analyze data from the various data sources for rigorous code review. Upon approval, the code was transferred to a physically and digitally isolated computer accessible only to trusted members of the university's information security team. Throughout the process, users were identified only by a cryptographic hash of the user ID, created with a secret salt known only to one information technology manager.

We were able to consult remotely and sanity-check limited output, but we were never given direct access to passwords or their guess numbers. We did not have access to the machine on which the passwords resided — information security personnel ran code on our behalf. Decrypted plaintext passwords were never stored in non-volatile memory at any point in the process, and the swap file on the target machine was disabled. All analysis results were personally reviewed by the director of information security to ensure they contained no private data. We received only the results of aggregate analyses, and no information specific to single accounts. After final analysis, the source data was securely destroyed. The information security staff, who are not authors of the paper, represented an independent check on the risks of our analysis.

There was also concern that analyses might open up small segments of the population to risk of targeted attack. To address this, categories for demographic factors were combined so that the intersection of any two groups from different factors always contained more than 50 users. In some cases, this required the creation of an "other" group to combine several small, unrelated categories.

This approach helped to ensure that users were not put at risk, but it did create some challenges for analysis. We were never allowed to explore the data directly. For the most part, decisions about what data to collect and how to analyze it were made far in advance, without benefit of exploratory data analysis to guide our choices. To compensate for this, we selected a large set of possibly useful statistical comparisons; the correspondingly high chance of false positives forced us to apply strong statistical correction, somewhat reducing the statistical power of our analysis. To avoid wasting the time of the information security team members who performed the analysis, we automated as much of it as possible. The combination of complex calculations with long automation scripts unsurprisingly led to many bugs; the inevitable differences between anonymized sample data provided by the information technology division and the real data led to many more. The result was many iterations of remote debugging and subsequent code re-audit.

Further, our inability to examine the passwords directly masks some aspects of the data. We rely on an algorithm to learn and exploit common strings and structures within the CMU passwords, but we cannot know which patterns it exploits. It is possible that the data contains commonalities a determined attacker could exploit, but which the algorithm is not sophisticated enough to recognize.

3.3 Supplemental data sets

We use guess numbers generated using a modified version of the Weir algorithm to measure password strength, applying the approach of Kelley et al. [30]. Guess numbers depend on the amount and quality of training data available to the guessing algorithm. We use training data that includes publicly available dictionaries (including the Google web corpus and the Openwall cracking dictionary); leaked password sets that were previously made public (including MySpace and RockYou), and data from online studies (using Amazon's Mechanical Turk service, or MTurk) in which participants created passwords under various conditions. For some tests, the algorithm is also trained on a subset of the CMU passwords (training and test sets are always kept disjoint for a given experiment).

We also compare the CMU passwords with 11 other data sets from various sources, as follows:

MTsim. 1,000 passwords collected from an MTurk experiment designed to simulate CMU password creation as closely as possible, both in policy requirements and in the website design.

MTbasic8. 1,000 passwords collected from MTurk [30]. The only requirement is a minimum length of 8 characters.

MTbasic16. 1,000 passwords collected from MTurk [30]. The only requirement is a minimum length of 16 characters.

MTdictionary8. 1,000 passwords collected from MTurk [30]. Minimum length 8. Discarding non-alphabetic characters, the password cannot be found in the 2.9-million-word free Openwall dictionary,[1] an order of magnitude larger than the dictionary used by CMU.

MTcomp8. 1,000 passwords collected from MTurk [30]. Same as MTdictionary8, but also requiring at least one lowercase letter, one uppercase letter, one digit, and one symbol.

SVcomp8. 470 self-reported responses to a previously published survey of CMU users [47].

We also compared our results with data from five real websites. In each case, we use a subset of the website passwords that meet CMU's requirements. Where more then enough conforming passwords were available, we draw the test set at random. Three of these leaked sets were leaked in plaintext; the other two come from the subset of the original leak that was successfully cracked.

RYcomp8. 1,000 plaintext passwords from RockYou (42,496 conforming, 32,603,144 total).

Ycomp8. 1,000 plaintext passwords from Yahoo! Voices (2,693 conforming, 453,488 total).

CSDNcomp8. 1,000 plaintext passwords from the Chinese Developer Network (12,455 conforming, 6,428,285 total).

SFcomp8. 1,000 cracked passwords from Strategic Forecasting, Inc., also known as *Stratfor*. (8,357 conforming, 804,034 total).

Gcomp8. 896 cracked passwords from Gawker (896 conforming, 694,064 total). All eight characters long.

Hereafter, we refer to all the leaked password sets, MTcomp8, MTsim, SVcomp8, and the real university passwords (CMUactive and CMUinactive) collectively as the *comprehensive-policy* passwords, as each includes four character classes and a dictionary check.

3.4 Experimental validity

CMU's complex password policy meets guidelines established by the InCommon Federation, which provides "a common framework for trusted shared management of access to on-line resources"[2] for educational and research institutions across the United States. As such, it is representative of similarly complex policies at other institutions. InCommon relies on NIST guidelines, which influence security standards at organizations across the United States [8].

We believe our results are reasonably representative of medium-sized research universities in the United States, and may be applicable to universities of other sizes or to other organizations with similar demographic profiles. CMU personnel represent a broad cross-section of ages, ethnic backgrounds, and nationalities, as well as a broad spectrum of geographic regions of origin within the United States. Although the sample is broad, its proportions do not match the general population.

Overall, the sample is considerably wealthier and more educated than the general American population. Most members of the sample currently live and work in or near Pittsburgh, where the main campus is located, but a fraction do live and work at other locations around the United States and internationally. We include some demographic factors as covariates, but many were not available from the university's personnel databases.

Compared to existing password research, we have significantly more knowledge of demographic factors than is available for most sets collected in the wild, and the CMU population overall is more diverse than the typical group of undergraduates used in lab studies. As a result, we believe that our results, if considered judiciously, can be applied to broader populations.

The guessing algorithm we use to measure password strength may not be optimal. While the algorithm has been used successfully in the past [30, 55], a more sophisticated algorithm might guess passwords more efficiently and produce different results.

4. UNDERSTANDING CMU PASSWORDS

In this section, we correlate the password strength of subsets of the CMU passwords with various demographic, password-composition, behavioral, and sentiment factors.

4.1 Analysis approach

For our correlation analysis in this section, we use guess numbers as our metric of password strength. We use a guess calculator for a modified version of Weir's guessing algorithm (see Section 2). We separate the CMUactive passwords into three folds for cross-validation, with each fold used once as a test set. The guess calculator is trained on the other two folds of CMUactive, all of CMUinactive, and a *Public* training set consisting of public and leaked password data. The *Public* set is composed of passwords from the MySpace, RockYou, Yahoo, CSDN, Stratfor, Gawker, and paid Openwall sets, as well as strings from the standard Unix dictionary and an inflection list[3] that includes various grammatical transformations. The set of alphabetic strings also includes unigrams from the Google Web N-Gram corpus.[4] The *Public* set was pruned so that only passwords containing at least eight characters and four character classes would be guessed.

Because of limitations in processing power, guess numbers can only be computed up to a given threshold. For each password, we either calculate a specific guess number, conclude that the password would have a guess number greater than the threshold n, or conclude that the password cannot be guessed given the current training data. The guessing threshold depends on the content of the training data as well as the experimental setup; experiments with higher guessing thresholds take longer to process. For this analysis, the guessing threshold is approximately 3.8 E14, or more than 380 trillion guesses; on our hardware, calculating guess numbers for each fold (about 8,000 passwords) takes about a day.

Once guess numbers are calculated for all CMUactive passwords, they are joined with data from the other university sources by matching hashed user IDs. Regressions are then performed on the re-

[1] http://download.openwall.net/pub/wordlists/

[2] http://www.incommon.org

[3] http://wordlist.sourceforge.net

[4] http://www.ldc.upenn.edu/Catalog/CatalogEntry.jsp?catalogId=LDC2006T13

sulting table to find correlations between guess numbers and other factors. Some of the factors we measure do not have useful values for all users, so we perform three separate regression analyses on appropriate subsets of users. These subsets are described in Sections 4.1.1-4.1.4.

The main regression technique we use is Cox regression, a technique adapted from the survival analysis literature, which typically studies factors that affect mortality [11]. The outcome variable is a pair of values: an observed state and the time of observation. If a password is guessed before the threshold, we mark the observed state as "dead" and the guess number as the "time of death." Otherwise, the observed state is "alive," and the guess threshold is the last time of observation. In the parlance of survival analysis, this is called right-censored data.

Using Cox regression, we are able to incorporate all the available data, over the range of guess numbers. This is an improvement over prior work, in which guessing success is examined at arbitrary points, such as the percentage guessed after a certain number of guesses [30,56] or the amount of effort required to crack some percentage of passwords [3]. As with ordinary linear regression models, Cox regression estimates a linear term for each factor. This assumes that factors affecting the probability of survival have a linear effect over the guessing range; this is a common simplification often used to represent factors which might, in reality, have nonlinear effects.

To counteract overfitting, we use the standard backward elimination technique, removing one factor from the model at a time, until we minimize the Bayesian information criterion (BIC) [42]. We only report the final model. Before the analysis, we centered all the quantitative variables around zero by subtracting the mean from each value; this standard technique makes the regression output easier to interpret [15].

In addition to the main analysis, we check for interactions between factors — that is, factors whose effects are not independent — by performing the above survival analysis with all two-way interaction terms, again using the BIC for model selection. Since this project required all code to be reviewed before the passwords were analyzed, and survival analysis is a novel approach to measuring password strength, we supplemented the Cox regressions with logistic regressions on a binary outcome: guessed before the cutoff threshold (success) or not (failure). We found that both regression approaches generally agreed.

We next describe the subsets of data used in this analysis and the factors included in the corresponding regressions.

4.1.1 Model 1: All personnel

This data set contains all current users with complete demographic information (17,088). We consider the following factors:

Gender. Male or female.

Age. Birth year as recorded in the personnel database.

Status. Undergraduate, graduate student, non-degree-seeking student, faculty, or staff. As with all regression techniques, categorical factors are represented as a set of binary factors, with only the appropriate category (e.g., "undergraduate" for an undergraduate student) coded as true for each user. One arbitrarily selected category, known as the baseline, is left out: users belonging to that category are coded false for every binary factor. For this factor, faculty is the baseline.

College. Personnel are divided into eight colleges within the university, including a catch-all "other" category.

Location. Because the vast majority of university personnel are based at the main campus, we use only two groups: main campus and other location. This unfortunately groups locations from several different areas of the world (e.g., Silicon Valley, Qatar, Australia) together, despite possibly important cultural and organizational differences.

4.1.2 Model 2: All personnel plus composition

This data set contains the 17,088 users from Model 1. We consider Models 1 and 2 separately because all the factors in Model 1 are included in each subsequent model, providing a baseline. For Model 2, we add the following factors related to the composition of passwords:

Number of digits, lowercase, uppercase, and symbols. Four separate factors that measure the number of occurrences of each type of character in the user's password.

Location of digits, uppercase, and symbols. For each of the three special character classes, we identified the location of characters of this type in the user's password. This location is categorized as either all at the beginning; all at the end; all in a single group in the middle of the password; or spread out in some other pattern.

4.1.3 Model 3: Personnel with stable passwords

This data set includes the 12,175 users who did not change their passwords throughout the log measurement period. This allows us to conclude that the password for which we calculate a guess number was in use during all behavioral measurements. Factors include everything from Model 1, plus the following factors extracted from the authentication service logs:

Login count. The number of times this user successfully logged in during the measurement period. We hypothesized that users who log in more often might use stronger passwords, either because they are confident that repetition will allow them to remember, or because they simply value the account more highly.

Median interlogin time. The median time elapsed between each pair of this user's successive web logins. We hypothesized that users who go a shorter time between logins might be able to choose and remember more complex (stronger) passwords.

Password and username failures. The number of login failures attributable to an incorrect password or username (treated separately), normalized by login count. To avoid counting potentially malicious guessing, we count only failures during what was eventually a successful login session. We hypothesized that users with passwords might find them more difficult to type, leading to more errors; alternatively, users who know they have difficulty typing might choose weaker passwords as a mitigation.

Median time elapsed during authentication. The median time elapsed between when the user arrives at the login page and when she successfully logs in, taken from server log data. This measure is imperfect; long elapsed times may represent users who open an authentication session in their browser and then ignore it for a long time before logging in, and different authentication servers may not have globally consistent timestamps. We hypothesized that users who take longer to log in might have passwords that are more difficult to remember or type in.

Wired login rate. The number of successful logins originating from an IP address associated with the main campus wired network, normalized by login count. This excludes logins made on the university's wireless network and those made from other campuses, as well as remote logins (such as from a user's home). We hypothesized that users who access their accounts only from organizational infrastructure on the main campus might think about passwords differently from those who frequently connect remotely or via wireless, since they are connecting over a more trusted medium. Unfortunately, we were unable to distinguish mobile devices like phones or tablets from other wireless devices like laptops using the available log data.

Non-web authentication rate. The number of successful logins that do not correspond to web authentication events, normalized by login count. Because of incomplete log data, this value is only an approximation. We hypothesized that users who routinely access their accounts via an email program or other tools that store passwords might choose stronger passwords.

Personnel who did not log in at least twice are excluded, as they have no interlogin time.

4.1.4 *Model 4: Survey participants*

This data set includes 694 users who completed the survey after changing their passwords. This group is disjoint from the *stable passwords* group, as all members of this group have changed their passwords at least once since the start of the logging period.

The survey sample is a subset of the overall university population. New users, who must all change their system-assigned starter passwords, made up 22% of the sample (164). The sample is of course also biased toward people who are willing to take a survey in exchange for an entry in a drawing for an Amazon.com gift card. All data is self-reported.

We include all the factors from Model 1, plus the following:

Method of creation. Each user's selections from a list including: reused a password from another account; added or substituted numbers or symbols within a dictionary word; used the name of someone or something; and other choices. Participants were asked to choose all that apply; each possible answer was represented as a factor and coded true if the user selected it or false otherwise.

Reason for change. Each user's choice from among changing the default starter password, feeling the password was too old, resetting a forgotten password, and suspicion of a security breach. Participants were allowed to choose only one option. We hypothesized that those who forget their passwords might select simpler passwords to reduce cognitive load.

Storage. True if the user indicated she stores her password, either electronically or on paper; otherwise false. Prior work suggests that users who are asked to make more complex passwords are more likely to write them down [25]. Self-reporting for this category may be an undercount, as users who write down passwords are contravening common (although not necessarily correct [46]) advice and may be embarrassed to admit to it.

Sentiment during creation. Three factors, coded as true for users who agree or strongly agree (on a five-point Likert scale) that it was difficult, annoying, or fun to create a password conforming to the university's policy. Users who indicated disagreement or neutrality were coded false for that factor. We hypothesized that users who struggle to create a conforming password might be more likely to give up and choose something simple out of frustration.

4.2 Results

We find interesting correlations between password strength and other factors across each of the subpopulations we investigate. We describe the results for each model separately. Note that while we interpret the results for the reader, this was not a controlled experiment with random assignment, so we make no formal attempt at a causal analysis — any observed effect may involve confounds, and many independent variables in our data set are correlated with other independent variables.

4.2.1 *Model 1: All personnel*

For these users, we find password strength to be correlated with gender and college. Men have slightly stronger passwords than women: men's passwords are only 92% as likely as women's to be guessed at any point. Among colleges, users from the business school are associated with the weakest passwords: 24% more likely to be guessed than users in the arts school (the baseline in the regression). Computer science users have the strongest passwords, 68% as likely as the arts school and 55% as likely as the business school to be guessed. Every college except public policy is significantly different from the baseline. The full regression results, after backward elimination, are shown in Table 1. No significant interactions between factors were found in the final model, meaning the effects of the various factors are independent.

Pairwise comparisons reveal science, engineering, and computer science to be associated with stronger passwords than humanities, business, and public policy; computer science is also associated with stronger passwords than arts (all Holm-corrected Wilcoxon test, $p < 0.05$). Figure 1 illustrates these relationships. Figure 2 shows guess number results by gender. Our findings agree with Bonneau's result that men's passwords are slightly more resistant to offline guessing [3].

It is perhaps equally interesting to note the factors that do not appear in the final regression, including age, primary campus, and status as faculty, staff, or student. While we cannot positively con-

Factor	Coef.	Exp(coef)	SE	p-value
gender (male)	-0.085	0.918	0.023	**<0.001**
engineering	-0.218	0.804	0.042	**<0.001**
humanities	-0.106	0.899	0.048	**0.028**
public policy	0.081	1.084	0.051	0.112†
science	-0.286	0.751	0.055	**<.001**
other	-0.102	0.903	0.045	**.025**
computer science	-0.393	0.675	0.047	**<.001**
business	0.211	1.235	0.049	**<.001**

Table 1: Final Cox regression results for all personnel. Negative coefficients indicate stronger passwords. The exponential of the coefficient (exp(coef)) indicates how strongly that factor being true affects the probability of being guessed over a constant guessing range, compared to the baseline category. The baseline category for gender is female and for college is fine arts. For example, the second line indicates that engineering personnel are 80.4% as likely to have their passwords guessed as fine arts personnel. Results that are not statistically significant with $p < 0.05$ are grayed out and indicated by †.

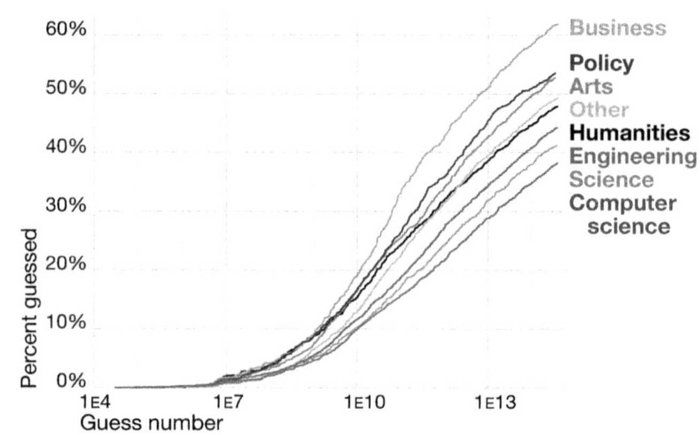

Figure 1: The percentage of passwords guessed after a given number of guesses (shown in log scale), by college within the university.

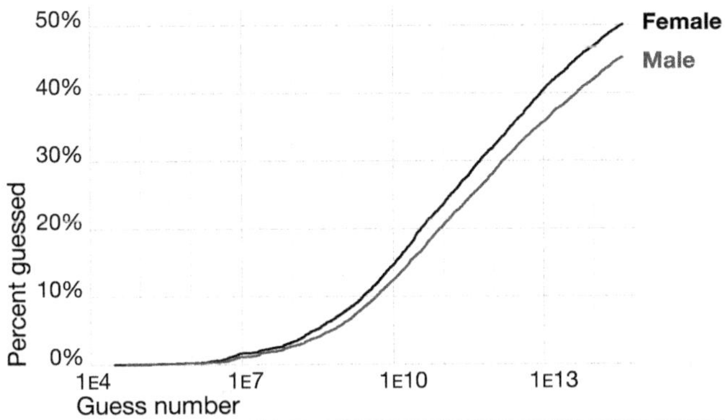

Figure 2: The percentage of passwords guessed after a given number of guesses (shown in log scale), by user gender.

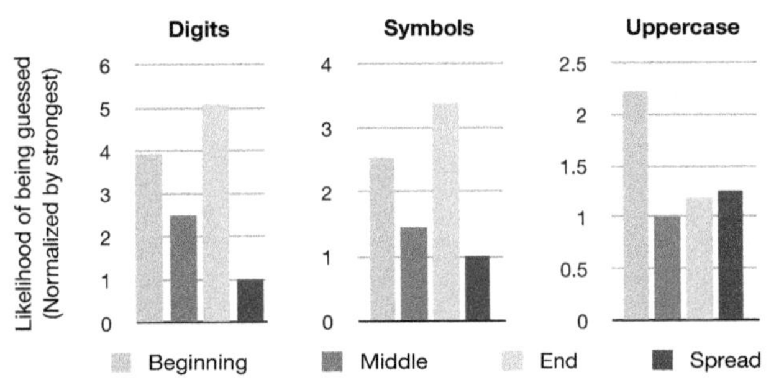

Figure 3: The relative likelihoods of passwords with digits, symbols, or uppercase letters in a given location being cracked. For example, a password with all its digits at the end is five times as likely to be cracked as a password with its digits spread throughout, other things being equal. The values are derived from the exponent of the regression coefficient, for the non-interaction model (Table 2). Each character class is normalized independently.

clude that these factors have no association with password strength, given our large sample size it seems likely that any effect is either a small one or is accounted for by the other factors in the regression.

4.2.2 Model 2: All personnel plus composition

In this section, we find that password composition is strongly correlated with password strength. In the non-interaction model, increasing the number of characters of any type is correlated with stronger passwords (Table 2). With the addition of each lowercase character or digit, a password becomes an estimated 70% as likely to be guessed. Additional symbols and uppercase characters have a stronger effect, reducing the likelihood of guessing to 56% and 46% per added character respectively. Placing digits and symbols anywhere but at the end, which is the baseline for the regression, is also correlated with stronger passwords. Multiple characters spread out in more than one location are associated with the strongest passwords — only 20% and 30% as likely to be guessed as passwords with digits and symbols, respectively, at the end. Placing uppercase characters at the beginning instead of at the end of a password is associated with much weaker passwords: 88% more likely to be guessed. Figure 3 illustrates the relative likelihood of being guessed based on placement for each character class.

Factor	Coef.	Exp(coef)	SE	p-value
number of digits	-0.343	0.709	0.009	**<0.001**
number of lowercase	-0.355	0.701	0.008	**<0.001**
number of uppercase	-0.783	0.457	0.028	**<0.001**
number of symbols	-0.582	0.559	0.037	**<0.001**
digits in middle	-0.714	0.490	0.040	**<0.001**
digits spread out	-1.624	0.197	0.051	**<0.001**
digits at beginning	-0.256	0.774	0.066	**<0.001**
uppercase in middle	-0.168	0.845	0.105	0.108†
uppercase spread out	0.055	1.057	0.114	0.629†
uppercase at beginning	0.631	1.879	0.105	**<0.001**
symbols in middle	-0.844	0.430	0.038	**<0.001**
symbols spread out	-1.217	0.296	0.085	**<0.001**
symbols at beginning	-0.287	0.751	0.070	**<0.001**
gender (male)	-4.4E-4	1.000	0.023	0.985†
birth year	0.005	1.005	0.001	**<0.001**
engineering	-0.140	0.870	0.042	**<0.001**
humanities	-0.078	0.925	0.049	0.108†
public policy	0.029	1.029	0.051	0.576†
science	-0.161	0.851	0.055	**0.003**
other	-0.066	0.936	0.046	0.154†
computer science	-0.195	0.823	0.047	**<0.001**
business	0.167	1.182	0.049	**<0.001**

Table 2: Final Cox regression results for all participants, including composition factors. For an explanation, see Table 1.

Adding composition factors seems to account for some of the results from Model 1. Gender is no longer a significant factor, and the effects of all colleges are reduced. This indicates that simple password features such as length and the number and location of special characters might partially explain differences in guessability between these populations. In this model, younger users are associated with weaker passwords. This result agrees with that of Bonneau [3], and is also fairly small: each additional year is estimated to increase the likelihood of guessing by 0.5%.

We find several significant terms in the model with interactions (Table 3). In most cases, these are superadditive interactions, where two factors that were correlated with stronger passwords in the no-interactions model are associated with a stronger-than-expected effect when combined. For example, having both digits and symbols in the middle of a password has a much stronger impact on reducing guessability than one would expect given a model with no interactions — 35% as likely to be guessed. In contrast, two significant interactions are subadditive. First, adding lowercase when uppercase characters are spread out is 25% less effective than one would expect. While we do not have the data to investigate this particular result, one possible explanation is that users are adding capitalized words in predictable ways. Second, although additional digits and lowercase letters are correlated with stronger passwords, the benefit of adding a letter decreases with each digit already present, and vice versa. Passwords with more digits than average receive 3% less benefit than expected, per extra digit, from adding lowercase letters. For example, if a password has three more digits than average, adding lowercase letters is 9% less effective than expected.

4.2.3 Model 3: Personnel with stable passwords

We next consider users who kept the same password throughout the analysis period, for whom we have additional behavioral data. In addition to college and gender, several behavioral factors correlate with password strength for these users. In the model without interaction, we find that users who make more password errors have stronger passwords than other users, and users who log in more often have slightly weaker passwords (Table 4). An additional password error per login attempt is associated with a password only

Factor	Coef.	Exp(coef)	SE	p-value
number of digits	-0.309	0.734	0.011	**<0.001**
number of lowercase	-0.349	0.705	0.085	**<0.001**
number of uppercase	-0.391	0.676	0.099	**<0.001**
number of symbols	-0.632	0.531	0.037	**<0.001**
digits in middle	-0.130	0.878	0.296	0.660†
digits spread out	-1.569	0.208	0.294	**<0.001**
digits at beginning	0.419	1.520	0.304	0.168†
uppercase in middle	-0.006	0.994	0.158	0.970†
uppercase spread out	0.540	1.717	0.175	**0.002**
uppercase at beginning	0.854	2.349	0.160	**<0.001**
symbols in middle	-0.319	0.727	0.296	0.281†
symbols spread out	-1.403	0.246	0.339	**<0.001**
symbols at beginning	0.425	1.530	0.296	0.151†
gender (male)	0.007	1.007	0.023	0.773†
birth year	0.007	1.007	0.001	**<0.001**
engineering	-0.137	0.872	0.042	**0.001**
humanities	-0.071	0.931	0.049	0.144†
public policy	0.032	1.033	0.051	0.530†
science	-0.170	0.844	0.055	**0.002**
other	-0.081	0.922	0.046	0.079†
computer science	-0.193	0.825	0.048	**<0.001**
business	0.167	1.182	0.049	**<0.001**
(# dig.:# lower.)	0.032	1.032	0.004	**<0.001**
(# lower.:dig. middle)	-0.110	0.896	0.027	**<0.001**
(# lower.:dig. spread)	-0.237	0.789	0.035	**<0.001**
(# lower.:dig. begin.)	0.045	1.046	0.036	0.216†
(# lower.:upper. middle)	0.029	1.030	0.073	0.688†
(# lower.:upper. spread)	0.222	1.249	0.076	**0.004**
(# lower.:upper. begin.)	0.134	1.143	0.074	0.071†
(# lower.:sym. middle)	-0.146	0.864	0.026	**<0.001**
(# lower.:sym. spread)	-0.164	0.849	0.051	**0.001**
(# lower.:sym. begin.)	0.019	1.019	0.041	0.638†
(# lower.:birth year)	0.002	1.002	<0.001	**<0.001**
(# upper.:upper. middle)	-0.310	0.733	0.111	**0.005**
(# upper.:upper. spread)	-0.613	0.542	0.134	**<0.001**
(# upper.:upper. begin.)	-0.528	0.590	0.106	**<0.001**
(dig. middle:sym. middle)	-1.042	0.353	0.300	**<0.001**
(dig. spread:sym. middle)	-0.137	0.872	0.293	0.640†
(dig. begin.:sym. middle)	-0.314	0.730	0.307	0.306†
(dig. middle:sym. spread)	0.207	1.230	0.341	0.545†
(dig. spread:sym. spread)	0.225	1.253	0.379	0.552†
(dig. begin.:sym. spread)	-0.602	0.548	0.559	0.282†
(dig. middle:sym. begin.)	-0.604	0.547	0.306	**0.048**

Table 3: Final Cox regression results for all participants, including composition factors, with interactions. Interaction effects, shown in parentheses, indicate that combination of two factors is associated with stronger (negative coefficient) or weaker (positive coefficient) passwords than would be expected simply from adding the individual effects of the two factors.

58% as likely to be guessed. Each additional login during the measurement period is associated with an estimated increase in the likelihood of guessing of 0.026%. Though this effect is statistically significant, we consider the effect size to be negligible. No significant interactions between factors were found in the final model.

Notable behavioral factors that do not appear in the final regression include median time between login events, wired login rate (as opposed to wireless), and non-web authentication rate (e.g., using an email client to retrieve email without using the web interface).

4.2.4 *Model 4: Survey participants*

Among survey participants, we find correlations between password strength and responses to questions about compliance strategies and the user sentiment during creation. As before, college also appears in the final model.

Factor	Coef.	Exp(coef)	SE	p-value
login count	<0.001	1.000	<0.001	**<0.001**
password fail rate	-0.543	0.581	0.116	**<0.001**
gender (male)	0.078	0.925	0.027	**0.005**
engineering	-0.273	0.761	0.048	**<0.001**
humanities	-0.107	0.898	0.054	**0.048**
public policy	0.079	1.082	0.058	0.176†
science	-0.325	0.722	0.062	**<0.001**
other	-0.103	0.902	0.053	0.051†
computer science	-0.459	0.632	0.055	**<0.001**
business	0.185	1.203	0.054	**<0.001**

Table 4: Final Cox regression results for personnel with consistent passwords, using a model with no interactions. For an explanation, see Table 1.

Factor	Coef.	Exp(coef)	SE	p-value
annoying	0.375	1.455	0.116	**0.001**
substituted numbers	-0.624	0.536	0.198	**0.002**
gender (male)	-0.199	0.820	0.120	0.098†
engineering	0.523	1.693	0.342	0.124†
humanities	0.435	1.545	0.367	0.235†
public policy	1.000	2.719	0.394	**0.011**
science	0.432	1.541	0.416	0.299†
other	0.654	1.922	0.334	0.051†
computer science	0.681	1.976	0.351	0.052†
business	1.039	2.826	0.376	**0.006**

Table 5: Final Cox regression results for survey participants. For an explanation, see Table 1.

Perhaps unsurprisingly, users who report that complying with the university's password policy was annoying have weaker passwords, 46% more likely to be guessed than those who do not report annoyance. This suggests that password policies that annoy users may be counterproductive. Users who substitute numbers for some of the letters in a word or name, by contrast, make passwords only 54% as likely to be guessed. We do not know whether or not these are typical "l33t" substitutions. Figures 4-5 illustrate these findings and full details appear in Table 5. For this subpopulation, there are not enough data points for a model with interaction to be valid.

Factors that do not appear in the final model include responses that complying with the password policy was difficult or fun; about twice as many users (302) agreed that it was annoying as agreed that it was difficult (162), and only 74 users found it fun. In addition, self-reported storage and the reason why the password was changed are not significant factors.

5. COMPARING REAL AND SIMULATED PASSWORD SETS

Acquiring high-quality password data for research is difficult, and may come with significant limitations on analyses. As a result, it is important to understand to what extent passwords collected in other settings — e.g., from data breaches or online studies — resemble high-value passwords in the wild. In this section, we examine in detail similarities and differences between the various password sets to which we have access. We first compare guessability, then examine other properties related to password composition. Overall, across several measures, passwords from online studies are consistently similar to the real, high-value CMU passwords. In contrast, passwords leaked from other sources prove to be close matches in some cases and by some metrics but highly dissimilar in others.

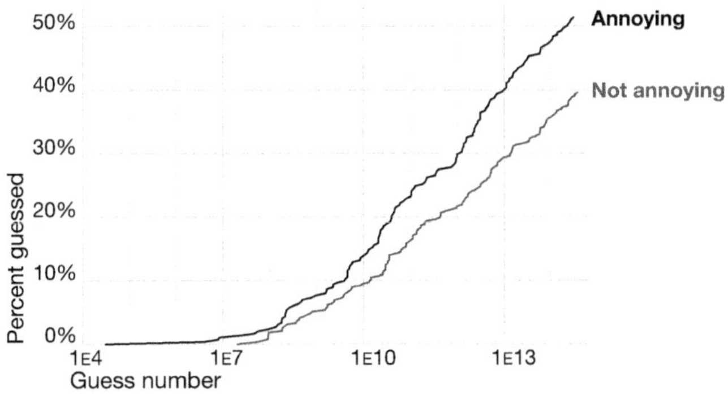

Figure 4: The percentage of passwords guessed after a given number of guesses (shown in log scale), by whether the user found password-creation annoying.

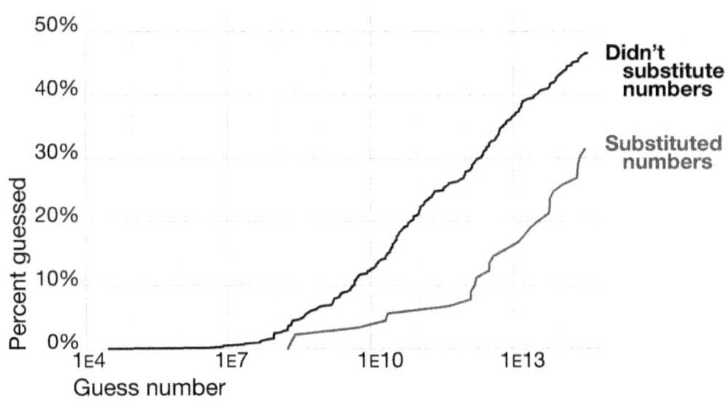

Figure 5: The percentage of passwords guessed after a given number of guesses (shown in log scale), by whether the user created the password by substituting numbers into a word.

5.1 Comparing guessability

We compare password sets primarily using guessability results. First, we calculate guess numbers for two attackers. The *limited-knowledge* attacker trains on publicly available data: the *Public* set described in Section 4.1. The *extensive-knowledge* attacker trains on the same public data, plus 20,000 CMUactive and 15,000 CMUinactive passwords. In each case, all data sources are weighted equally during training. Because these trainings are optimized for guessing passwords under the comprehensive policy, we cannot use this approach to compare university passwords to MTbasic8, MTbasic16, or MTdictionary8. We do compare CMUactive passwords to the other comprehensive-policy conditions: MTsim and MTcomp8 (online studies), RYcomp8, Ycomp8, and CSDNcomp8 (leaked plaintext sets), and Gcomp8 and SFcomp8 (leaked cracked sets). In all cases, we calculate and compare guess numbers only for passwords that are not used in training.

After calculating guess numbers, we compare guessability across password sets using another technique from the survival analysis literature: the Peto-Peto generalization of the Wilcoxon test [40], also known as a G^ρ test with $\rho = 1$ [20]. This test is designed to compare two survival data sets under the null hypothesis that both data sets were drawn from the same distribution. It has the additional property of weighting differences in early parts of the curve more heavily than later parts. As passwords are guessed and the population dwindles, the power of the test decreases. Unlike Cox regression, it does not assume that differences should occur at a constant rate across the entire curve. Table 6 shows percentages guessed at several guessing thresholds, as well as results of the G^1 significance test. In this table, differences in p-values indicate relative similarity to CMUactive; smaller p-values indicate greater divergence. Figure 6 shows guessability results for both attackers.

Online studies. Overall, the online studies provide more consistently similar matches to the CMU passwords than the leaked sets do. For both attackers, the CMUactive passwords are weaker than MTcomp8 and stronger than MTsim, but closer to MTcomp8. While the MTsim passwords were restricted to exactly match CMU policy, the MTcomp8 passwords were collected under a policy that, while similar, includes a notably harder dictionary check. As a result, it is unsurprising that MTcomp8 might produce more guess-resistant passwords. In fact, instrumentation from the MTurk studies shows that more than twice as many MTcomp8 participants as MTsim participants failed the dictionary check at least once during password creation (35% to 14%), suggesting the harder dictionary check did make an important difference.

The real CMUactive passwords were produced under the easier dictionary check, but they more closely resemble MTcomp8 than MTsim. We hypothesize that deployed passwords are harder to guess than the simulated version because online studies can only partially reproduce the effort users make to create strong passwords for high-value accounts.

Cracked password sets. As might be expected, cracked password sets provide especially poor points of comparison. Because they consist of a subset of the original data that was easiest to crack, they are guessed much more quickly than the CMU passwords, with 62% (SFcomp8) and 79% (Gcomp8) guessed before the cutoff.

Plaintext leaked password sets. The three plaintext leaked password sets are a more complicated case. Although the RYcomp8 subset appears highly similar to the CMU passwords under both attackers, CSDNcomp8 is only similar for the public attacker, and Ycomp8 is far off under both. Subsetted passwords from Ycomp8 and CSDNcomp8 are harder to guess than CMU passwords created under the same policy, which agrees with a previous finding [30]. Although this pattern does not hold for RYcomp8, it is important to note that there is much more RockYou data than data for any other set available in the training data. This advantage may partially compensate for subsets otherwise tending to be harder to guess.

To further examine our hypothesis that online studies provide a reasonably good proxy for real passwords, we obtain CMUactive guess numbers for two additional attackers: one trained on *Public* plus 3,000 CMUactive passwords, and another trained on *Public* plus 3,000 MTsim passwords. The distribution of guess numbers in the two data sets is not significantly different (G^1, uncorrected $p = 0.583$). This suggests that using MTsim passwords for cracking CMUactive passwords is a viable strategy. These results are shown in Figure 7.

5.2 Comparing other password properties

In addition to guessability, we compare several other properties of our data sets, including mean password length and quantity of characters per password from various character classes. We also consider estimated entropy, calculated as described in prior work [31]. For length, composition, and entropy, we can also compute confidence intervals using the statistical technique known as bootstrapping. Specifically, we use the "basic" bootstrap technique as identified by Davison and Hinkley [12].

We also compare the diversity of password structures, which correspond to high-level representations of passwords in the Weir grammar [56]. For example, the structure of "PassW0rd!" is "UL-

Attacker	Password set	N	1 E6	1 E9	1 E12	Cutoff	G^1 p-value compared to CMUactive
public	CMUactive	25,459	0.1	4.4	27.0	44.0	–
	MTsim†	1,000	0.2	6.3	30.5	47.5	0.005
	MTcomp8†	1,000	0.0	3.7	26.3	42.8	0.453
	RYcomp8†	1,000	0.1	3.6	26.6	47.3	0.250
	Ycomp8	1,000	0.0	2.7	20.8	37.7	**9.02 E-6**
	CSDNcomp8†	1,000	0.4	2.3	20.9	42.5	0.007
	SFcomp8	1,000	0.0	8.4	41.9	62.0	**0**
	Gcomp8	896	0.3	8.3	44.1	79.1	**0**
knowledgeable	CMUactive	5,459	0.4	6.4	30.7	48.7	–
	MTsim	1,000	0.1	11.5	34.7	54.1	**5.26 E-5**
	MTcomp8 †	1,000	0.0	7.7	27.9	43.1	0.008
	RYcomp8 †	1,000	0.0	5.0	29.4	49.4	0.573
	Ycomp8	1,000	0.0	4.9	23.3	39.7	**4.08 E-8**
	CSDNcomp8	1,000	0.4	2.9	24.1	42.2	**8.66 E-7**
	SFcomp8	1,000	0.2	10.4	44.2	63.0	**0**
	Gcomp8	896	0.2	10.7	49.4	73.3	**0**

Table 6: Guessing results for comprehensive-policy password sets. The columns provide the number of passwords in the set (N), the percentage of passwords guessed at various guessing points, and the results of the G^1 test comparing the guessing distributions. Rows in bold have guessing distributions that are statistically significantly different from CMUactive, with Bonferroni-corrected $p < 0.00139$; rows that are not significantly different are marked with †. The guessing cutoff is 3.6 E14 for the limited-knowledge attacker and 3.8 E14 for the extensive-knowledge attacker.

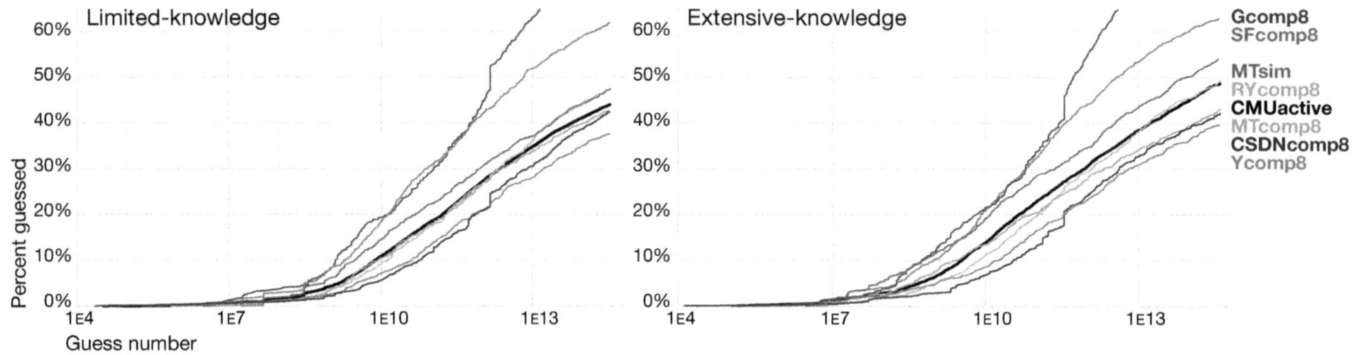

Figure 6: The percentage of passwords guessed after a given number of guesses (shown in log scale), by password set. The guessability results on the left are for the *limited-knowledge* attacker, who has only publicly available data. The guessability results on the right are for the *extensive-knowledge* attacker, who has access to some data from the same password sets for training.

LLUDLLS" (U = uppercase, L = lowercase, D = digit, and S = symbol). We measure diversity by randomly sampling 1,000 passwords from a data set, identifying their structures, and counting the number of distinct structures in the sample; we repeat this sampling process 100 times and use the average structure count. The choice of 1,000 for sample size is arbitrary and any reasonable sample size might be used.

Finally, we compare password sets using their probability distributions, an essential component of many password-strength metrics [3]. We use empirical probabilities as observed in each data set. We can only consider the most popular passwords, since almost all passwords are unique in sets as small as many of our sources.

For each of these measurements, we use all conforming passwords from each original data set, rather than the 1,000-password samples that were used for consistency in the guessability results.

Results for length, composition, entropy, and structural diversity are given in Table 7, and a subset are also shown in Figure 8. For the most part, using these metrics, comprehensive-policy passwords more closely resemble each other than passwords from other policies. As expected, passwords from policies that did not require them have fewer symbols and uppercase letters.

Perhaps more interesting is to consider how the other password sets within the comprehensive-policy group relate to CMU passwords, which protect high-value accounts. In length and composition, the passwords from online studies are consistently similar to the real CMU passwords, while passwords from leaked sets show more variance, sometimes appearing very similar and other times very different. It is particularly interesting to note that although RYcomp8 appeared very similar to CMUactive in guessability, its composition features are highly dissimilar, suggesting that it may not make a good proxy for real high-value passwords.

Self-reported survey responses from comprehensive-policy users are perhaps surprisingly similar in length and composition to other comprehensive-policy responses; the small sample size makes it difficult to ascertain precisely how similar.

Using entropy as a metric, passwords taken from Yahoo! are most similar to CMU passwords, while RYcomp8 and CSDNcomp8 passwords are most different. In structural diversity MTsim and MTcomp8 are closest, while Ycomp8 and SFcomp8 are farthest; perhaps unsurprisingly, the cracked SFcomp8 set shows by far the least structural diversity of any comprehensive-policy set.

	N	Length	# Digits	# Symbols	# Uppercase	Entropy	# Structures
CMUactive	25,459	10.7 [10.67–10.74]	2.8 [2.77–2.81]	1.2 [1.20–1.21]	1.5 [1.44–1.47]	36.8 [36.20–37.40]	689
MTsim	3,000	10.7 [10.54–10.77]	2.6 [2.56–2.67]	1.2 [1.17–1.22]	1.5 [1.41–1.50]	35.1 [34.50–35.60]	624
MTcomp8	3,000	10.7 [10.60–10.77]	2.2 [2.15–2.25]	1.2 [1.14–1.17]	1.5 [1.48–1.56]	34.2 [33.75–34.67]	630
RYcomp8	42,496	12.6 [12.35–12.80]	2.6 [2.56–2.61]	1.9 [1.89–1.99]	1.8 [1.79–1.82]	40.3 [38.55–42.31	769
Ycomp8	2,693	10.4 [10.27–10.44]	2.5 [2.41–2.50]	1.6 [1.52–1.58]	1.8 [1.76–1.84]	36.7 [36.29–37.19]	811
CSDNcomp8	12,455	11.1 [11.01–11.11]	3.8 [3.78–3.86]	1.5 [1.44–1.47]	2.0 [1.96–2.00]	41.2 [40.47–41.91]	782
SFcomp8	8,357	11.0 [10.88–11.05]	2.4 [2.39–2.45]	1.3 [1.26–1.29]	1.5 [1.51–1.57]	34.7 [34.13–35.18]	585
Gcomp8	896	8.0	1.9 [1.80–1.93]	1.2 [1.13–1.18]	1.3 [1.29–1.38]	†	†
SVcomp8	470	10.5 [10.18–10.78]	2.7 [2.39–2.98]	1.4 [1.23–1.53]	1.5 [1.35–1.72]	†	†
MTbasic8	1,000	9.7 [9.52–9.82]	2.4 [2.23–2.56]	0.1 [0.09–0.25]	0.4 [0.33–0.52]	29.6	322
MTdictionary8	1,000	9.7 [9.57–9.83]	2.6 [2.39–2.77]	0.2 [0.11–0.20]	0.4 [0.30–0.46]	29.1	317
MTbasic16	1,000	17.9 [17.76–18.11]	3.8 [3.46–4.05]	0.2 [0.12–0.20]	0.5 [0.41–0.67]	44.7	391

Table 7: Comparing password properties. Shown are mean values with 95% confidence intervals for various password properties. The Structures column gives the number of unique structures found in 1,000 passwords (average of 100 samples). † Because fewer than 1,000 passwords were available for Gcomp8 and SVcomp8, comparable entropy values and structure counts could not be calculated.

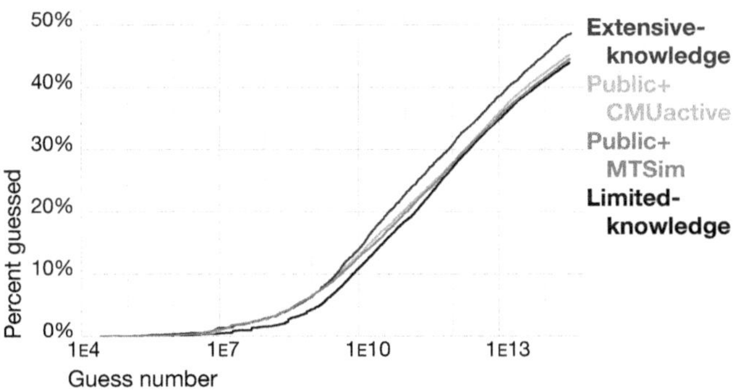

Figure 7: Results from a simulated attack from four different attackers, each with different training data, against CMUactive. *Public + 3K CMUactive* is trained on *Public* plus 3,000 CMUactive passwords. *Public + 3K MTsim* is trained on *Public* plus 3,000 MTsim passwords. The distributions of guess numbers for these two attackers do not differ significantly. *limited-knowledge* and *extensive-knowledge* are discussed in Figure 6.

Results from comparing probability distributions are given in Table 8. Based on the empirical probability of just the most popular password, CMUactive is the strongest policy, and RYcomp8, Ycomp8, CSDNcomp8, Gcomp8, MTbasic8, and MTdictionary8 are all significantly weaker. Among all sets considered, only the empirical probabilities of MTsim and MTcomp8 are not significantly different from CMUactive for passwords of any rank (Bonferroni-corrected χ^2, $p < 0.05$), though this could be attributed to small sample size. Surprisingly, SFcomp8 is not significantly different from CMUactive at first, but it becomes significantly different when comparing passwords of rank greater than one. In addition, the empirical probabilities of SFcomp8 do not drop off from ranks one to four, unlike every other set. If this is a byproduct of how the set was cracked, this provides further evidence against the use of cracked password sets in research.

6. CONCLUSIONS

The CMU information technology division agreed to work with us on this research in part to gain improved understanding of the current state of password security at CMU. We expect that future updates to the university's password policies and procedures will take our results into account. Beyond that, we believe our results provide guidance to users, system administrators, and information security personnel, as well as informing future password research.

We find that some elements of the university population create more vulnerable passwords than others. It is possible that some of these users, such as personnel in the business and arts schools, would create stronger passwords if they received instruction about how to do so. On the other hand, if these users are creating weak passwords because they don't feel that creating a strong password is in their interest [22], an education campaign could focus on password strength as a community issue.

In line with prior work, we find that male users, older users, and users who log in less frequently are correlated with slightly stronger passwords; however, in each case the effect size is small, and using different models we find that other factors may partially account for the effects. We also confirm patterns previously held as folk wisdom: passwords with more digits, symbols, and uppercase letters are harder to crack, but adding them in predictable places is less effective.

Using personnel databases, server logs, and surveys, we extend our analysis to include user behavior, sentiment, and additional demographic factors. We find that users who expressed annoyance with CMU's complex password policy were associated with weaker passwords; again, targeted education about the rationale for the policy requirements might help. Our findings also suggest further research into the usability and security implications of password managers as an aid to these users.

It is important to note that our analysis centers on passwords created under CMU's comprehensive password policy. While our results suggest that users who go beyond the minimum requirements of this policy have stronger passwords, our analysis does not allow us to draw conclusions about how the various requirements of the policy contribute to password strength. Our analysis suggests it would be useful to find policies that would be less annoying to users and that would discourage users from complying with the policy in predictable ways. Further work is needed to determine whether the CMU policy might be improved by relaxing some requirements and replacing them with others; for example, reducing the number of required character classes but requiring longer passwords, prohibiting special characters at the beginning or end of the password, or changing the dictionary check to permit dictionary words with symbols or digits in the middle.

Our research also provides guidance for future password studies. For researchers who may have an opportunity to gain limited access

	Observed probability of nth most popular password										%
	1	2	3	4	5	6	7	8	9	10	Unique
CMUactive	0.094%	0.051%	0.043%	0.039%	0.035%	0.035%	0.031%	0.027%	0.024%	0.024%	97.910%
MTsim	0.200%†	0.100%†	0.100%†	0.100%†	0.100%†	0.067%†	0.067%†	0.067%†	0.067%†	0.067%†	99.067%
MTcomp8	0.233%†	0.100%†	0.067%†	0.067%†	0.067%†	0.067%†	0.067%†	0.067%†	0.067%†	0.067%†	99.133%
RYcomp8	0.513%	0.304%	0.242%	0.214%	0.134%	0.115%	0.101%†	0.099%†	0.068%†	0.066%†	87.877%
Ycomp8	0.520%	0.149%†	0.149%†	0.149%†	0.111%†	0.111%†	0.111%†	0.111%†	0.111%†	0.111%†	93.427%
CSDNcomp8	2.529%	1.429%	0.715%	0.426%	0.241%	0.233%	0.225%	0.217%	0.161%	0.128%	78.667%
SFcomp8	0.191%†	0.191%	0.191%	0.191%	0.179%	0.168%	0.096%†	0.096%†	0.084%†	0.084%†	95.058%
Gcomp8	4.911%	0.893%	0.893%	0.893%	0.670%	0.670%	0.670%	0.558%	0.558%	0.558%	79.464%
MTbasic8	1.300%	0.700%	0.600%	0.200%†	0.200%†	0.200%†	0.200%†	0.200%†	0.100%†	0.100%†	96.400%
MTdictionary8	2.300%	0.800%	0.400%	0.300%	0.200%†	0.200%†	0.200%†	0.200%†	0.200%†	0.200%†	94.600%
MTbasic16	0.600%	0.500%	0.500%	0.400%	0.300%	0.300%	0.300%	0.200%†	0.200%†	0.200%†	95.700%

Table 8: Empirical probabilities for the 10 most popular passwords and the total probability mass of unique passwords in each set. Probabilities that are not significantly different from CMUactive for a given password rank are grayed out and marked with a † (Bonferroni-corrected χ^2 test, $p < 0.05$).

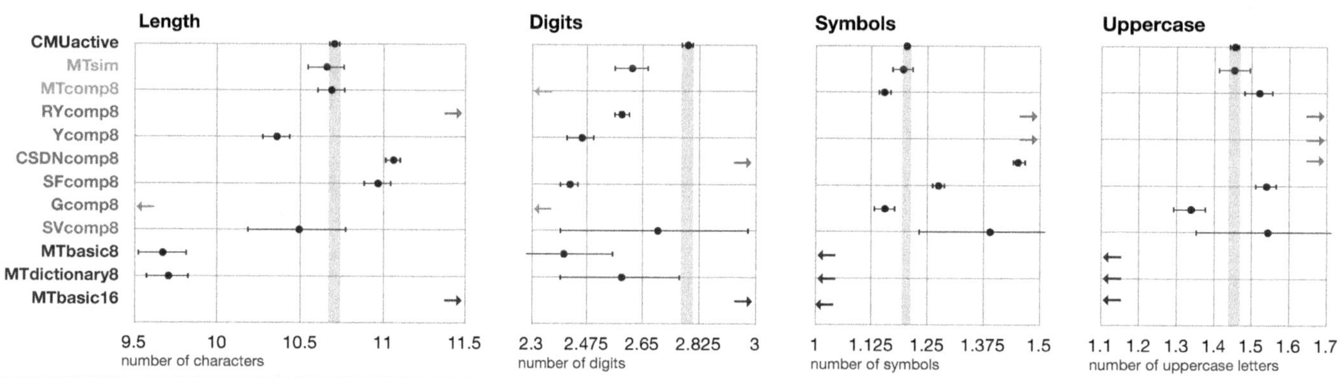

Figure 8: Password-composition characteristics, by password set, with 95% confidence intervals. The confidence interval for CMUactive is shaded. By these metrics, MTsim is generally the closest match for CMUactive.

to genuine passwords, we discuss our procedure for analyzing those passwords while respecting users' privacy and security.

For researchers restricted to more traditional mechanisms of password collection — such as lab or online studies and subsetting from leaked password data — we provide insight into similarities and differences between those passwords sets and frequently used passwords protecting real-world, high-value accounts. Consistent with previous work [30], we find that subsetting passwords from those created under one policy to approximate passwords created under another policy is not an optimal solution to gathering good password data for analysis. While these passwords are sometimes similar to the targeted passwords on some metrics, their high variance makes them unreliable as proxies.

We find that passwords created on MTurk are not a perfect substitute for high-value passwords either; the simulated passwords we collected were slightly weaker than the genuine ones. However, the simulated passwords do seem to be reasonably close in several respects, including length and character composition. Further, when used as training data for guessing genuine passwords, passwords from MTurk were just as effective as genuine passwords. These results indicate that passwords gathered from carefully controlled experimental studies may be an acceptable approximation of real-world, high-value passwords, while being much easier to collect.

7. ACKNOWLEDGMENTS

We gratefully acknowledge the many people at CMU who made this work possible, especially the identity services team and information security office. This research was supported by CyLab at Carnegie Mellon under grants DAAD19-02-1-0389 and W911NF-09-1-0273 from the Army Research Office, by NSF grants DGE-0903659 and CNS-1116776, by Air Force Research Lab Award No. FA87501220139, by the DoD through the NDSEG Fellowship Program, by the Facebook graduate fellowship program, and by a gift from Microsoft Research.

8. REFERENCES

[1] F. Bergadano, B. Crispo, and G. Ruffo. Proactive password checking with decision trees. In *Proc. CCS*, 1997.

[2] J. Bonneau. The Gawker hack: how a million passwords were lost. *Light Blue Touchpaper* blog, December 2010. `http://www.lightbluetouchpaper.org/2010/12/15/the-gawker-hack-how-a-million-passwords-were-lost/`.

[3] J. Bonneau. The science of guessing: Analyzing an anonymized corpus of 70 million passwords. In *Proc. IEEE Symposium on Security and Privacy*, 2012.

[4] J. Bonneau. Statistical metrics for individual password strength. In *Proc. SPW*, 2012.

[5] J. Bonneau, C. Herley, P. C. v. Oorschot, and F. Stajano. The quest to replace passwords: A framework for comparative evaluation of web authentication schemes. In *Proc. IEEE Symposium on Security and Privacy*, 2012.

[6] P. Bright. Sony hacked yet again, plaintext passwords, e-mails, DOB posted. *Ars Technica*, June 2011. `http:`

//arstechnica.com/tech-policy/2011/06/sony-hacked-yet-again-plaintext-passwords-posted/.

[7] K. Bryant and J. Campbell. User behaviours associated with password security and management. *Australasian Journal of Information Systems*, 14(1):81–100, 2006.

[8] W. E. Burr, D. F. Dodson, and W. T. Polk. Electronic authentication guideline. Technical report, NIST, 2006.

[9] D. S. Carstens, L. C. Malone, and P. McCauley-Bell. Applying chunking theory in organizational password guidelines. *Journal of Information, Information Technology, and Organizations*, 1:97–113, 2006.

[10] J. A. Cazier and B. D. Medlin. Password security: An empirical investigation into e-commerce passwords and their crack times. *Information Systems Security*, 15(6):45–55, 2006.

[11] D. R. Cox. Regression models and life-tables. *Journal of the Royal Statistical Society. Series B (Methodological)*, 34(2):187–220, 1972.

[12] A. C. Davison and D. V. Hinkley. *Bootstrap methods and their application*. Cambridge University Press, 1997.

[13] M. Dell'Amico, P. Michiardi, and Y. Roudier. Password strength: An empirical analysis. In *Proc. INFOCOM*, 2010.

[14] M. M. A. Devillers. *Analyzing password strength*. PhD thesis, Radboud University Nijmegen, 2010.

[15] J. L. Devore. *Probability and Statistics for Engineering and the Sciences*. Thomson Learning Brooks/Cole, 2004.

[16] S. Fahl, M. Harbach, Y. Acar, and M. Smith. On the ecological validity of a password study. In *Proc. SOUPS*, 2013.

[17] D. Florêncio and C. Herley. A large-scale study of web password habits. In *Proc. WWW*, 2007.

[18] D. Florêncio and C. Herley. Where do security policies come from? In *Proc. SOUPS*, 2010.

[19] D. Goodin. Hackers expose 453,000 credentials allegedly taken from Yahoo service. *Ars Technica*, July 2012. http://arstechnica.com/security/2012/07/yahoo-service-hacked/.

[20] D. P. Harrington and T. R. Fleming. A class of rank test procedures for censored survival data. *Biometrika*, 69(3):553–566, 1982.

[21] K. Helkala and N. Svendsen. The security and memorability of passwords generated by using an association element and a personal factor. In *Proc. NordSec*, 2011.

[22] C. Herley. So long, and no thanks for the externalities: the rational rejection of security advice by users. In *Proc. NSPW*, 2009.

[23] C. Herley and P. Van Oorschot. A research agenda acknowledging the persistence of passwords. *IEEE Security and Privacy*, 10(1):28–36, 2012.

[24] T. Hunt. The science of password selection. *TroyHunt.com* blog, July 2011. http://www.troyhunt.com/2011/07/science-of-password-selection.html.

[25] P. Inglesant and M. A. Sasse. The true cost of unusable password policies: Password use in the wild. In *Proc. CHI*, 2010.

[26] M. Jakobsson and M. Dhiman. The benefits of understanding passwords. In *Proc. HotSec*, 2012.

[27] K. S. Jamuna, S. Karpagavalli, and M. S. Vijaya. A novel approach for password strength analysis through support vector machine. *International Journal on Recent Trends in Engineering*, 2(1):79–82, 2009.

[28] D. L. Jobusch and A. Oldehoeft. A Survey of Password Mechanisms. *Computers and Security*, 8(8):675–689, 1989.

[29] M. Keith, B. Shao, and P. Steinbart. A behavioral analysis of passphrase design and effectiveness. *Journal of the Association for Information Systems*, 10(2):63–89, 2009.

[30] P. G. Kelley, S. Komanduri, M. L. Mazurek, R. Shay, T. Vidas, L. Bauer, N. Christin, L. F. Cranor, and J. Lopez. Guess again (and again and again): Measuring password strength by simulating password-cracking algorithms. In *Proc. IEEE Symposium on Security and Privacy*, 2012.

[31] S. Komanduri, R. Shay, P. G. Kelley, M. L. Mazurek, L. Bauer, N. Christin, L. F. Cranor, and S. Egelman. Of passwords and people: Measuring the effect of password-composition policies. In *Proc. CHI*, 2011.

[32] M. Kumar. China Software Developer Network (CSDN) 6 million user data leaked. *The Hacker News*, December 2011. http://thehackernews.com/2011/12/china-software-developer-network-csdn-6.html.

[33] N. Kumar. Password in practice: An usability survey. *Journal of Global Research in Computer Science*, 2(5):107–112, 2011.

[34] C. Kuo, S. Romanosky, and L. F. Cranor. Human selection of mnemonic phrase-based passwords. In *Proc. SOUPS*, 2006.

[35] D. Malone and K. Maher. Investigating the distribution of password choices. In *Proc. WWW*, 2012.

[36] B. D. Medlin and J. A. Cazier. An empirical investigation: Health care employee passwords and their crack times in relationship to hipaa security standards. *International Journal of Healthcare Information Systems and Informatics*, 2(3):39–48, 2007.

[37] B. D. Medlin, J. A. Cazier, and D. P. Foulk. Analyzing the vulnerability of US hospitals to social engineering attacks: how many of your employees would share their password? *International Journal of Information Security and Privacy*, 2(3):71–83, 2008.

[38] R. Morris and K. Thompson. Password security: a case history. *Communications of the ACM*, 22(11):594–597, 1979.

[39] A. Narayanan and V. Shmatikov. Fast dictionary attacks on passwords using time-space tradeoff. In *Proc. CCS*, 2005.

[40] R. Peto and J. Peto. Asymptotically efficient rank invariant test procedures. *Journal of the Royal Statistical Society. Series A (General)*, pages 185–207, 1972.

[41] R. W. Proctor, M.-C. Lien, K.-P. L. Vu, E. E. Schultz, and G. Salvendy. Improving computer security for authentication of users: Influence of proactive password restrictions. *Behavior Research Methods, Instruments & Computers*, 34(2):163–169, 2002.

[42] A. E. Raftery. Bayesian model selection in social research. *Sociological methodology*, 25:111–164, 1995.

[43] S. Ragan. Report: Analysis of the Stratfor password list. *The Tech Herald*, January 2012. http://www.thetechherald.com/articles/Report-Analysis-of-the-Stratfor-Password-List.

[44] Rapid7. LinkedIn passwords lifted. http://www.rapid7.com/resources/infographics/linkedIn-passwords-lifted.html, retrieved September 2012.

[45] D. A. Sawyer. *The Characteristics of User-Generated Passwords*. PhD thesis, Naval Postgraduate School, 1990.

[46] B. Schneier. Write down your password. *Schneier on Security* blog, 2005. http://www.schneier.com/blog/archives/2005/06/write_down_your.html.

[47] R. Shay, S. Komanduri, P. G. Kelley, P. G. Leon, M. L. Mazurek, L. Bauer, N. Christin, and L. F. Cranor. Encountering stronger password requirements: user attitudes and behaviors. In *Proc. SOUPS*, 2010.

[48] Solar Designer. John the Ripper, 1996-present. `http://www.openwall.com/john/`.

[49] J. M. Stanton, K. R. Stam, P. Mastrangelo, and J. Jolton. Analysis of end user security behaviors. *Computers and Security*, 24(2):124–133, 2005.

[50] G. Suganya, S. Karpgavalli, and V. Christina. Proactive password strength analyzer using filters and machine learning techniques. *International Journal of Computer Applications*, 7(14):1–5, 2010.

[51] B. Ur, P. G. Kelley, S. Komanduri, J. Lee, M. Maass, M. Mazurek, T. Passaro, R. Shay, T. Vidas, L. Bauer, N. Christin, and L. F. Cranor. How does your password measure up? The effect of strength meters on password creation. In *Proc. USENIX Security*, 2012.

[52] A. Vance. If your password is 123456, just make it hackme. *New York Times*, January 2010. `http://www.nytimes.com/2010/01/21/technology/21password.html`.

[53] R. Veras, J. Thorpe, and C. Collins. Visualizing semantics in passwords: The role of dates. In *Proc. VizSec*, 2012.

[54] K.-P. L. Vu, R. W. Proctor, A. Bhargav-Spantzel, B.-L. B. Tai, and J. Cook. Improving password security and memorability to protect personal and organizational information. *International Journal of Human-Computer Studies*, 65(8):744–757, 2007.

[55] M. Weir, S. Aggarwal, M. Collins, and H. Stern. Testing metrics for password creation policies by attacking large sets of revealed passwords. In *Proc. CCS*, 2010.

[56] M. Weir, S. Aggarwal, B. de Medeiros, and B. Glodek. Password cracking using probabilistic context-free grammars. In *Proc. IEEE Symposium on Security and Privacy*, 2009.

[57] Y. Zhang, F. Monrose, and M. K. Reiter. The security of modern password expiration: An algorithmic framework and empirical analysis. In *Proc. CCS*, 2010.

[58] M. Zviran and W. J. Haga. Password security: an empirical study. *Journal of Management Information Systems*, 15(4):161–185, 1999.

SAuth: Protecting User Accounts from Password Database Leaks

Georgios Kontaxis
Columbia University
kontaxis@cs.columbia.edu

Elias Athanasopoulos
Columbia University
elathan@cs.columbia.edu

Georgios Portokalidis
Stevens Inst. of Technology
gportoka@stevens.edu

Angelos D. Keromytis
Columbia University
angelos@cs.columbia.edu

ABSTRACT

Password-based authentication is the dominant form of access control in web services. Unfortunately, it proves to be more and more inadequate every year. Even if users choose long and complex passwords, vulnerabilities in the way they are managed by a service may leak them to an attacker. Recent incidents in popular services such as LinkedIn and Twitter demonstrate the impact that such an event could have. The use of one-way hash functions to mitigate the problem is countered by the evolution of hardware which enables powerful password-cracking platforms.

In this paper we propose SAuth, a protocol which employs authentication synergy among different services. Users wishing to access their account on service S will also have to authenticate for their account on service V, which acts as a vouching party. Both services S and V are regular sites visited by the user everyday (e.g., Twitter, Facebook, Gmail). Should an attacker acquire the password for service S he will be unable to log in unless he also compromises the password for service V and possibly more vouching services. SAuth is an extension and not a replacement of existing authentication methods. It operates one layer above without ties to a specific method, thus enabling different services to employ heterogeneous systems. Finally we employ password decoys to protect users that share a password across services.

Categories and Subject Descriptors

K.6.5 [**Management of Computing and Information Systems**]: Security and Protection—*Authentication*

General Terms

Security

Keywords

Authentication; Synergy; Password Leak; Decoys

CCS'13, November 4–8, 2013, Berlin, Germany.

ACM 978-1-4503-2477-9/13/11 ...$15.00.
http://dx.doi.org/10.1145/2508859.2516746.

1. INTRODUCTION

Password theft can cause annoyance, financial damages, data loss, and loss of privacy [5, 9]. Services employing passwords urge their users to choose complex combinations, never write them down, change them frequently, select a different password on each service they use and verify the authenticity of the site before logging in. However, even users that manage to follow all these rules risk having their passwords stolen. Security pitfalls in a series of popular services have resulted in frequent and massive password leaks [4, 8, 16, 20]. Even though services usually store a digest or hash of the password (excluding rare incidents [12]), the emergence of powerful password-cracking platforms [14, 44] has enabled attackers to recover the original passwords in an efficient manner [13]. What is more, password-reuse practices by the users have enabled domino-like attacks [17, 34].

We propose Synergetic Authentication (SAuth), an authentication mechanism based on the synergy between different services that complements their individual procedures for verifying the identity of a given user. To successfully log into service S one is required to successfully authenticate both with S and a cooperating vouching service V. For example, a user logging into his Gmail account, after successfully submitting his password to the Gmail server, he will be required to also submit his Facebook password to the Facebook server. Once Gmail receives notice from Facebook that the same user has managed to authenticate successfully it will have an additional assurance that the user is the actual owner of those accounts. Our approach is founded upon the way most users access the web. In particular, users remain concurrently and constantly authenticated with many services such as e-mail and social networks [24, 42] unless they explicitly log out. A service the user is already logged on can transparently vouch for him, e.g., through client-side cookies. In the above example, had the user been already logged in to Facebook, he would just be required to enter his Gmail password to access his e-mails. Facebook would use his user agent cookies to transparently authenticate him and subsequently vouch for him to Gmail. At the same time, an attacker that has compromised the user's password for S is unable to access that account as he is lacking the password for vouching service V and thus cannot complete the authentication process. In other words, for an attacker to compromise one account, he must acquire multiple account passwords for that user located in different databases of distinct services.

Password-based authentication has received a lot of criticism lately with many large services like Google and PayPal looking for alternative means to authenticate users [7,15,35]. Some alternatives that have been proposed in the past include public-key mechanisms, such as TLS client certificates [19], graphical passwords [25,38], and many more. Unfortunately, none of the proposed alternatives has proven sufficiently enticing [29]. Passwords have been the de facto method for authenticating users for many decades, and have proven to be resilient to change.

Two-factor authentication [22] has probably been the most successful proposal to complement password-based systems by requiring that an additional password is provided, acquired through a second independent channel. Unfortunately the overhead both in cost and effort to deploy and maintain such system has led to adoption only by high-value services such as banking sites and e-mail providers. Moreover, it scales poorly when users are required to manage multiple secondary factors for distinct services. Finally, a study has shown that it can push users to weaker passwords [57].

Single-sign-on services like OpenID, as well as the OAuth-based interfaces of social networking services [6,46], offer the alternative of maintaining a single online identity, protected by one, hopefully strong, password. Users of such services, instead of creating separate, new accounts and passwords with third-party services, authenticate with a trusted identity provider (e.g., Facebook), that vouches for them. However, these identity providers present a single point of failure, may carry privacy-related risks, and can also suffer vulnerabilities themselves [55]. A recent study [54] attributes the limited adoption of such services to concerns regarding their availability and relinquishing control of the user base as part of outsourcing authentication.

SAuth does not suffer from any of the above problems, as it complements, rather than substitutes, existing authentication procedures at each site. Therefore, it does not degrade the security of a service, but allows heterogeneous authentication systems to operate at each site, while preserving each party's user accounting system. Finally, it encourages symmetric relations between services as it enables all participating sites to operate both as relying and vouching parties if they wish to.

To address the issue of password reuse [41,53], which can render vouching ineffective if a user recycles the same password across all vouching services, we employ decoy passwords. Each service automatically generates multiple decoy passwords that are similar to the one chosen by the user. Furthermore, for the decoys to blend in, they receive no special treatment by the service and are thus considered as legitimate credentials for user authentication. Note however that the user is never aware of them. Enabling decoy passwords requires no changes in the database schema, can be implemented with wrappers to existing password management functions and introduces multiple password entries per user instead of a single one. An attacker cracking the passwords will be unable to identify the actual one and resort to online guessing against the vouching services [1].

Overall, this work makes the following contributions:

- We design, implement, and evaluate SAuth, a framework employing synergy between sites for stronger authentication.
- SAuth builds on widely used technologies and is orthogonal to the underlying authentication framework. Beyond providing stronger authentication, SAuth can be used as an alert system for password breaches.
- We leverage decoy passwords to tackle password reuse practices among the cooperating sites participating in an SAuth session.

The rest of the paper is organized as follows. We provide background information in §2. We present the design of SAuth in §3 and its implementation in §4. We discuss decoy passwords in §5 and evaluate their use in §6. Related work is presented in §7 and conclusions are in §8.

2. BACKGROUND

Password-based authentication has changed little in the many decades it is in use and today it is more popular than ever, with countless web applications using passwords to authenticate their users. In brief, when a user first registers with a service, he selects a username and password with which he will authenticate. The application stores the username in plain-text form, attaches a random prefix called salt to the password, gets the digest of this prefixed password using a cryptographic hash function such as MD5 or SHA1, stores the hash output along with the salt in the database and discards the plain-text password. Note that recently these general-purpose hash functions have received criticism [10] and alternatives such as bcrypt [48] have been proposed. The salt prefix ensures that even if a password is shared by multiple users, a different hash will be generated and stored in the database, and identical passwords cannot be inferred by their hash product. What is more, it defeats rainbow tables where the hashes for a large set of dictionary words and password-space permutations are precomputed and then compared against a password hash in real time. Upon login, users transmit their username and password to the service in plain text, hopefully through a secure communication protocol such as TLS. Subsequently the web service uses the stored salt and the provided password to compute their digest and compare it to the stored digest in the database. Note that unfortunately there are cases where passwords are simply stored verbatim in the database [3].

2.1 Password Leaks

In recent years we have witnessed an increasing amount of password leaks [8, 12, 16, 20] from major Internet sites. Between early 2012 and now these incidents have been occurring at an alarming rate of roughly one every couple of months. We use the term password leak to describe the exfiltration of user passwords stored by some service's accounting system. This can be due to malicious insiders or front-end bug exploitation, e.g., through SQL injection.

It is important to stress that password leaks are different in nature from phishing or social engineering attacks which may also be used to compromise user passwords. Leaks happen on the server side and usually lead to large-scale password exfiltration. As they don't involve the client side, in

[1] In this paper we model an on-line guessing attack according to the NIST specification [32] (see Section 6.1).

contrast to phishing attacks, even diligent users may have their password compromised.

2.2 Password Cracking

Following a successful database leak the attacker has in his possession all the elements necessary to attempt to crack the stolen passwords; he holds their digests, the corresponding salt values and has knowledge of the hashing function used.

Subsequently he can employ various cracking methodologies [44] ranging from brute-force attacks to dictionary attacks and a combination of the two. In the first case he can simply compute the salted hashes for all possible permutations in the given password space, e.g., passwords 1 to 8 characters in length involving upper and lower case English letters, numbers and symbols. Whenever a computed hash, for which the attacker knows the input, matches one of the hashes in the stolen set, that user's password is revealed. Clearly this approach requires abundant processing power and a lot of time. Alternatively, the attacker can compute the salted hashes for a pre-constructed dictionary of potential passwords. As users tend to choose passwords that are easy to remember [28], more often than not they select words such as "password" or phrases such as "letmein" or people's names. Therefore a dictionary-based attack can be very fast and efficient. Finally, a hybrid approach involving permutations of dictionary words can crack passwords that meet the bare minimum of otherwise complex password policies. "password1" or "letmein!" and "s3cur3" are such examples.

Even if an attacker designs his password cracking process in such an elaborate manner he still requires ample processing power to achieve high success rates in a reasonably short amount of time. The parallel architectures of modern GPUs can greatly shorten the password cracking process. Recently, GPU-based architectures were able to crack eight-character-long NTLM passwords for Microsoft Windows in just about five hours [14]. At the same time, cracking platforms utilizing the resources and scalability of the cloud have emerged [1]. Overall the sophistication of password cracking methodologies, along with the availability of increasingly more powerful hardware, significantly extends an attacker's capability to reveal complex passwords.

To mitigate the increase in the processing power of cracking platforms, alternatives to the standard cryptographic hash functions have been proposed. As general purpose functions like MD5 or SHA1 were designed to be fast and efficient, they serve in favor of the attacker who wants to compute a large number of digests in a short amount of time. On the other hand, adaptive hash functions, such as bcrypt [48] and scrypt [47], can be configured in terms of the work factor they introduce. In other words, as processing power increases over time these functions can be tuned to take constant amount of time. Therefore it is possible to slow down the cracking process significantly. Note however that these functions have a much lesser impact on dictionary attacks compared to brute-force attacks.

Our proposal does not make any assumptions about the way the password is stored in the database or the particular hash function employed. Nevertheless we assume that, as the way users select passwords favors password-cracking, leaked password hashes, or at least a significant portion of them, will eventually be cracked.

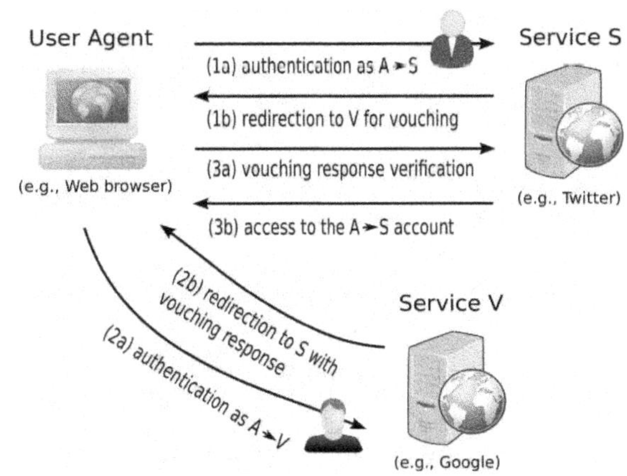

Figure 1: Overview of synergy-enhanced authentication. A user, with accounts in services S and V (e.g., Twitter and Google) tries to log in S. A standard authentication process takes place which involves the user's password for S (step 1a). Subsequently service S initiates our proposed protocol which involves service V vouching for the user (step 1b). The user is redirected to V with which he also engages in a standard authentication process (step 2a) at the end of which service V generates a vouching token for the user to return to S (step 2b). Finally, service S allows the user to access his account if and only if the vouching token from V is verified (step 3a) and optionally returns a persistent authentication token (e.g., cookie) that will bypass this authentication process for subsequent interactions (e.g., HTTP requests) with S.

2.3 Out of Scope Threats

We do not attempt to address password compromise due to social engineering, phishing, or man-in-the-middle attacks. Social engineering exploits the human psychology and we argue that technical means may not be able to offer adequate protection on their own. As far as phishing, malware, and man-in-the-middle attacks are concerned we stress that there are already sufficient protection mechanisms that can be employed independently to our proposal. For example, researchers have proposed PwdHash [50], BeamAuth [22] and Visual Skins [39] against phishing. They employ something unique to the original site, such as a URL or its appearance, to alert the user or safeguard against transmitting his password to the wrong site. Nevertheless, they do not have any effect on the server side nor do they present any benefit once the user's password has been leaked.

3. SAuth ARCHITECTURE

Alice has registered and maintains accounts with web sites S and V like she does today. We consider the case where Alice tries to authenticate to S using SAuth, while V is acting as a vouching party for Alice. We use the terms $A_{\rightarrow S}$ and $A_{\rightarrow V}$ for indicating Alice as announced to S and V, respectively. We use this notation for stressing that Alice has a different identity with each party. Below, we provide the steps executed for Alice to successfully authenticate with service S in the presence of service V, which is trusted by S and has agreed to vouch for its own users to S. The process is also depicted in Figure 1.

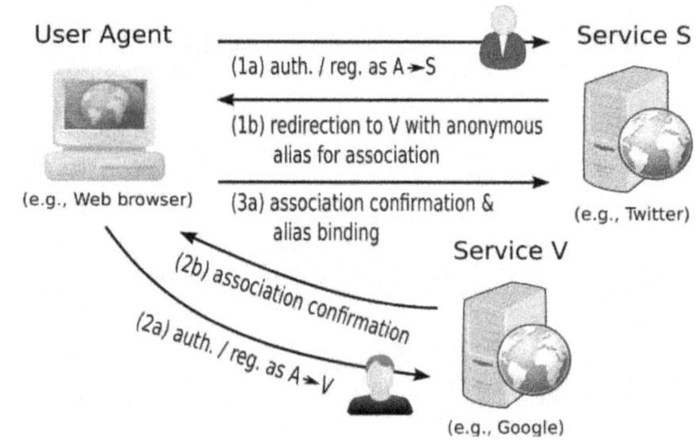

Figure 2: Overview of the association process to enable synergy-enhanced authentication. A user tries to register for a new account in service S (e.g., Twitter). Alternatively he logs in to an existing account with S for which he wants to enable SAuth (step 1a). S generates a unique anonymous alias for the user and redirects him to vouching service V (e.g., Google) (step 1b). The user is expected to authenticate to V or create a new account (step 2a). Note that the user may have already enabled SAuth in his V account. Upon authentication or registration, the anonymous alias from S is associated with the current account on V and user is redirected back to S with a confirmation message (step 2b). Finally, S binds that alias to the user's account and enables SAuth (step 3) so that subsequent authentication attempts can involve V as a vouching service and, if so, will require the receipt of that alias from V.

1. Alice visits service S and is challenged for her authentication credentials (e.g., an HTML form asking for her name and password or a cookie storing an authentication token). Note that these authentication credentials were established when Alice created her account, $A_{\rightarrow S}$, on service S. This is currently a standard method for authentication employed by web services. This step is depicted as (1a) in Figure 1. After providing the correct credentials for $A_{\rightarrow S}$, the synergy-based authentication protocol is initiated (step (1b) in Figure 1) and Alice is prompted to choose from a list of trusted vouching services, including service V, to complete the enhanced authentication process. Notice, that Alice has specified her vouching services in S when she registered or enabled SAuth. Alice chooses service V and a vouching request is issued towards V by S, while the user is being redirected to service V.

2. Service V receives the vouching request from S and challenges the current user for her authentication credentials (step (2a) in Figure 1). Note that these authentication credentials were established when Alice created her account, $A_{\rightarrow V}$, on service V. After successful authentication of user $A_{\rightarrow V}$, a verification response is returned and the user is redirected back to service S (step (2b) in Figure 1).

3. Service S receives a verification response from V signaling that current user, $A_{\rightarrow S}$, has managed to prove ownership of an account, $A_{\rightarrow V}$, on service V (step (3a) in Figure 1). As any user can prove ownership of two accounts on two distinct services, we require that accounts $A_{\rightarrow S}$ and $A_{\rightarrow V}$ have been associated in the past when user Alice opted in this enhanced authentication process. This association means that if some user manages to authenticate as $A_{\rightarrow S}$ but then authenticates as $B_{\rightarrow V}$, the enhanced authentication process will be terminated by service S as unsuccessful. The only way for the process to succeed is for the current user to authenticate as both $A_{\rightarrow S}$, on service S, and $A_{\rightarrow V}$, on service V. Once the enhanced authentication process concludes with a positive result on service S the current user is given an authentication token (e.g., HTTP cookie), which replaces the need for challenging her authentication credentials for every subsequent request, currently a common practice in the web and elsewhere. Note that at this point the current user has authenticated fully on S and V in case both services are vouching for each other. If a different service is selected to vouch for V then, as expected, the user has to follow a similar process for authenticating with V.

SAuth is proposed as an opt-in feature, designed to complement existing authentication methods. Sites providing SAuth can let users enable the mechanism at registration or at any later time. We now discuss the protocol details. We assume that SAuth operates above SSL.

3.1 Protocol Details

Security and Trust. When service S receives a vouching token from service V about some user, S trusts that V has indeed authenticated the user and its security practices do not allow some other user to generate the same vouching token while interacting with V. If V fails to meet those expectations, the security of the process followed by S is as if SAuth was not in place at all and S was operating alone. In other words, as S does not nullify its own authentication system, even if V implicitly or explicitly misbehaves, S will not be negatively impacted. As the first step in the SAuth protocol involves correctly authenticating with the target service, the security procedures of S take precedence over the ones by vouching parties. Note that including more than one vouching service reduces the dependence on a single external party and increases the redundancy in the face of vouching unavailability.

Activation. Registering for a new account in a synergy-supporting service or enabling synergy-enabled authentication for an existing account entails an association step between the target service S and potential vouching services V. When registering for a new account, the traditional registration process is carried out and then followed by the association step. Note that activation of SAuth can be deferred for a later time to limit the workload for new users as it is not strongly tied to the registration process. For existing accounts, only the association step needs to take place. The association step is necessary so that a link is established between the current account in the target service S and an account the user controls in a vouching service V. As mentioned earlier, a vouching party produces proof that the current user has managed to successfully authenticate. This alone is not useful to the target service as it is not necessary for the owner of the account in S to be the owner of the account in V. In other words, an attacker who manages to steal the password for an account in S could authenticate with his own account in V and have service V return that as proof of authentication. For that matter, upon registration of a new account or enabling of SAuth, service S generates an anonymous alias for the user. The user is then expected to provide that alias to a vouching service and associate it with an account there. Once this association is made, the vouching service will return this alias as part of the authentication proof to service S. Service S will check the returned alias against the one bound to the account of the current user and enable him to access the account if and only if the two are a match (Fig. 2).

Authenticity. As the user agent, i.e., web browser, is tasked to facilitate the communication between the target site and vouching parties, special measures are necessary to ensure the authenticity of protocol messages exchanged. The reason is that the user agent is both untrusted and motivated to misbehave when challenged to prove his identity. Secrecy is also important but, since the user is privy to all exchanged information, it can be achieved through secure layer, e.g., SSL, connections between the user and the sites. To safeguard authenticity, each protocol message is required to carry the `service`, `signature` and `signed_fields` parameters. The first one is the identifier of the sender service and could be the service's domain, a URI under that domain or an alias. The second one is a cryptographic signature, such as RSA-SHA1, computed over the rest of the parameters using the private key of the service sending the message. The final parameter is a list with the names of parameters and the order in which they have been signed. As soon as the user-agent relays a protocol message to the receiving service, it will parse the `signed_fields` parameter, verify the signature based on those fields and accept the values of those fields while discarding all other fields. Verifying the signature entails looking up the public key for the service, specified by the `service` parameter. To do so efficiently we employ the X.509 certificate it has for HTTP over SSL.

Password reset. In the general case, without SAuth present, users have the ability to be reminded of their password or better yet reset it and choose a new one. For this to happen, users may be asked some security questions, such as the name of their pet, that they chose during account registration and subsequently receive an e-mail, to an address they also chose during registration, with either their current password or a secure URL to select a new password. Note that this current practice is already one form of synergy-based authentication, since the service places trust in the e-mail provider and expects only the owner of that address to be able to read the password-reset message. Unfortunately, this model fails when an attacker manages to get access to the e-mail address and then proceeds to initiate password-reset procedures for the victim's online accounts. Enhancing the current model with SAuth means that the service will proceed as detailed above only after the current user proves ownership of an account in a vouching service. Assuming the user hasn't forgotten all of his passwords in all the vouching services, he is first prompted by target service S to authenticate with vouching service V before S proceeds with the steps to reset the user's password for S. Note that this process is not meant to replace the current security-question model, whose security has been questioned by researchers [51], but to precede it and thereby couple it.

3.2 Usability

SAuth is built on standard technologies and is founded upon the existing browsing habits of users. Thereby it does not affect their perceived web experience. We are taking advantage of the fact that users prefer to maintain concurrently many browser tabs open [58] and spend at least 57.4% of their time in switching tabs [42]. This suggests the use of multiple web applications in one session. Furthermore, researchers have observed long-lived sessions in online social networks [24], which is another indicator suggesting that users are concurrently active in multiple sites.

What is more, in favor of users' convenience, current web applications maintain authentication state, usually in the form of HTTP cookies, for each established session, which can be destroyed only if the user is explicitly logged off or decides to erase the browser cache. In other words, like the user is not prompted for his password for every HTTP request the browser makes when rendering a site, he won't be interrupted when a service he is already logged in is involved as a vouching party in SAuth. In addition, browsers implement auto-completion features for filling out password forms. Therefore, even if the user is not currently authenticated with one or more of the services involved in a SAuth session, this feature will alleviate his inconvenience.

Finally, one may be concerned with the involvement of multiple accounts in different services if a user needs to register for all of them at once to activate SAuth. We expect that such cases will be rare in practice as vouching services will be selected due to their popularity and dependability. As such we expect that users will almost always have an account with one of the supported vouching services so, when registering with an SAuth-enabled service, they will not need to additionally register with one of the vouching services. Our use case is aligned with the existing "sign in with Google" and "sign in with Facebook" single-sign-on mechanisms; users most probably will hold an account with one of those services. Moreover, SAuth's design enables users to include a vouching service of their choosing by supplying its domain name to the target service (Sec. 4). This clearly increases the flexibility of SAuth. Nevertheless, in the unlikely case that the user is unable to provide an account with an existing, or introduce a new, vouching party to the target service, activating SAuth could also be deferred to the future.

3.3 Availability

The synergistic nature of SAuth creates dependencies between sites during their user authentication process. The unavailability of a vouching site V means the target service S will have to rely solely on its own authentication procedure which, as mentioned earlier, is the first step in an SAuth session and takes precedence over any vouching responses. In other words, should a vouching site be unavailable, the target service will still be able to function and operate, as it would do without the use of SAuth. Administrators can make a policy decision on whether they want to operate without enhanced authentication, admit the user into his account on a provisional basis with limited functionality, or engage additional checks such as security questions. Note that once a user is authenticated and receives back a token, for instance an HTTP cookie, he is not affected by any changes in the availability of the vouching sites. He will not have to initiate SAuth unless he relinquishes that token.

3.4 Password Compromise Alerts

The multi-party authentication process of SAuth enables a warning system for when passwords from one or more parties are compromised. In a password leakage an attacker would gain access to all password hashes stored by a target site. We assume that he will eventually recover the plain-text passwords using any of the techniques described in Sec. 2.2. As he will still be lacking the corresponding passwords for the vouching sites he will resort to online guessing attempts which will result in failed SAuth sessions. Even if the user has chosen the same password for both the target and vouching site, as described in Section 5, the attacker will still end up guessing online. Note that for a vouching site to receive a request from a target site, the user must have already successfully authenticated with the latter. Therefore, a vouching site dealing with a user repeatedly failing to authenticate with it can suspect that the user is trying to log in to an account he doesn't own. Considering some leniency for typing errors, this creates a reliable system for triggering alerts. The vouching site is in a position to notify the target site that a specific user is failing to authenticate even through he has managed to do so at the target site. At the same time, the target site will notice repeated SAuth sessions failing at the vouching parties even though local authentication goes through. Overall, the nature of the SAuth design offers indications of anomalous activity that would otherwise go unnoticed.

4. IMPLEMENTATION

We define the SAuth protocol messages as a set of URIs [21] which makes it easier to project them on a URI-oriented application-level protocol such as HTTP [11]. We assume that the user is represented by an agent program, e.g., a web browser. Although we focus on HTTP, as it is employed by web services, our design can be applied to any other application-level protocol provided it supports the concept of end-point redirection. We group our messages into two categories; registration and authentication messages defined as registration and authentication URIs respectively.

For a target service and a vouching service to engage in an SAuth session, they need to be aware of each other's end-points. Registration and authentication end-points may be explicitly exchanged offline upon prior agreement, or they may be retrieved automatically from an XML file, named `sauth.xml` by convention, hosted under the domain of each service and served over a secure network layer such as SSL, e.g., `https://www.example.org/sauth.xml`. This enables users of a target service to include a vouching service of their choosing by supplying the voucher's domain name in the target service's SAuth activation page. Alternatively, users can select one of the pre-configured vouching services.

To realize the technical issues from the adoption of our protocol by a web application we have implemented it in its entirety in PHP and subsequently developed adopting sample applications including both a front and back end. We argue that once SAuth is offered as a module or library it requires effort comparable to the use of OAuth and similar authorization protocols, something which a plethora of sites today uses. Our implementation is less than 1000 LoC.

Registration. A user who registers with S selects a vouching party from a list of cooperating services or may specify one of his choosing by specifying its domain name as described earlier (Listing 1, line 1). Note that selection of a vouching service or introduction of a new one is only

```
1  schema://TARGET_SERVICE_S/registration
2          [username, password, vouching_service]
3
4  schema://TARGET_SERVICE_S/registration
5          [action="commit",service=
               VOUCHING_SERVICE_V,alias=
               FOREIGN_ALIAS,nonce=NONCE,signature,
               signed_fields="action,service,alias,
               nonce"]
```

Listing 1: SAuth registration messages as URIs.

```
1  schema://VOUCHING_SERVICE_V/authentication
2          [action="register_alias", alias=
               FOREIGN_ALIAS, service=
               TARGET_SERVICE_S, nonce=NONCE,
               signature, signed_fields="action,
               alias,service,nonce"]
3
4  schema://TARGET_SERVICE_S/authentication
5          [username, password, vouching_service]
6
7  schema://VOUCHING_SERVICE_V/authentication
8          [action="vouch",service=TARGET_SERVICE_S,
               nonce=NONCE,signature,signed_fields="
               action,service,nonce"]
9
10 schema://TARGET_SERVICE_S/authentication
11         [action="verify", alias=FOREIGN_ALIAS,
               service=VOUCHING_SERVICE_S, nonce=
               NONCE, signature, signed_fields="
               action,alias,service,nonce"]
```

Listing 2: SAuth authentication messages as URIs.

possible upon registering a new account with the target service or after successfully authenticating to an existing one, through SAuth if enabled. The response of service S to the user-agent's registration request is a redirection towards the authentication end-point of the selected vouching service V (Listing 2, line 1) with the parameter `action` set to instruct the vouching service to first authenticate the user and then associate the resulting account with an anonymous alias that has been just generated. Service S also binds that alias with the newly registered account once it receives confirmation from V. Assuming the current user has an account with service V, he provides his credentials to authenticate. If the current user has enabled SAuth on service V, a synergy-enhanced authentication process will follow. Note that if the user does not have an account with V, he can optionally create one at this point, but even if he does not, such cases can be handled in the manner discussed in Sec. 3.2. Eventually the user successfully authenticates or creates a new account with V. Service V then redirects the user's agent back to service S while setting parameter `action` to signal service S that it should bind the generated alias to the current user's account. This conveys to S that the alias has been associated with the user's account on V and it will be part of a future vouching authentication process (Listing 1, line 4). This completes the registration process under SAuth. Note that activating SAuth is not strongly tied to creating a user account on S and can take place independently.

Authentication. To authenticate under the enhanced process of SAuth a user initially visits the service he wants to access, labeled as target service S. He is prompted for his name and password. He is also asked to select a vouching service V (Listing 2, line 4). This selection may either

```
[Authentication Request to example.com (S)]
POST /login HTTP/1.1
Host: www.example.com

username=bob&password=password&vouching_service=
    example.org

[Authentication Response from example.com]
HTTP/1.1 303 See other
Location: https://www.example.org/login?action=
    vouch&service=example.com&nonce=...&signature
    =...&signed_fields=action%2Cservice%2Cnonce

[Authentication Request to example.org (V)]
GET /login HTTP/1.1
Host: www.example.org?action=vouch&service=example
    .com&nonce=...&signature=...&signed_fields=
    action%2Cservice%2Cnonce

...
```

Listing 3: Example use of HTTP redirection to relay the first message of the SAuth protocol between the target and vouching service through the user agent.

take place in the same screen as the log-in form or after his credentials are authenticated by S. In the first case he is given the option of selecting any of the vouching services S supports. This is to avoid revealing to attackers the vouching service(s) a given user employs. In the second case, he is given the option of selecting only from the vouching services that have already been associated with his account through a foreign alias. Note that if the user specified a vouching party of his choosing through its domain name that party will be available as an option at this point. Target service S then redirects the user's agent to V while setting the parameter `action` to signal that a vouching for current user is expected from the remote service (Listing 2, line 7).

The user then presents his credentials in an authentication request towards service V for his respective account. On successful local authentication with V, the service's response to the user agent redirects it to the target service S while setting parameter `action` to signal that current user has successfully authenticated with some account, that the associated foreign alias is included in the response, and that service S should verify this vouching response and decide whether the returned foreign alias matches the alias bound to the user's account on S. On match, service S has successfully authenticated the user using SAuth and can optionally return a persistent authentication token, such as an HTTP cookie, to the user's agent so that future interactions with service S can skip the enhanced authentication in a manner similar to the way users don't have to type their password for each HTTP request their web browser makes.

HTTP User-agent redirection. To facilitate message relaying through the user agent in HTTP we employ 3xx redirection messages [11]. For service S to redirect the user agent to service V, it responds to the user agent's request with the 303 "See other" status code. It also includes the `Location` header with its value being that of a URI under the service V domain that targets the desired end-point and carries the information it wants to communicate to V in the form of parameters. Listing 3 presents an example where the user agent is redirected to service V with a vouching request after successfully authenticating to service S.

Cryptographic Signatures. As the user agent is responsible for relaying messages between the target service and vouching services, it is necessary to ensure the integrity of those messages. We assume that the secrecy of the messages is preserved as long as the user agent maintains SSL connections with the two services and that there is no need for the messages to be hidden from the user agent. We implement cryptographic signatures using 1024-bit RSA key pairs and the SHA-1 digest algorithm. Each protocol message must contain the parameters **`service`**, **`signature`** and **`signed_fields`**. The first parameter identifies the sender and is used to retrieve the necessary information for verifying the signature. The last parameter specifies which parameters are contained in the signature.

Web services use the same private key that supports their HTTPS connections with clients and thus the corresponding public key is protected under an X.509 public key certificate. For a service to verify a signature in SAuth, it uses the **`service`** identifier to locate the corresponding URL for the sender. If the hostname of the sender service is used as the identifier, the service connects to the sender and downloads its public-key certificate. There are other ways to resolve an identifier to a hostname or URL but they are outside the scope of this paper. After retrieving the certificate, the service tries to verify the signature over the parameters specified by the **`signed_fields`** parameter. On success, the parameters are committed to the current user session. HTTP parameters not covered by the signature are discarded. If a parameter is specified twice, only the instance carrying a value which causes the signature verification to succeed is kept. Finally, if a signature fails the request is terminated immediately and no processing takes place.

Apart from the integrity of protocol messages, it is very important to ensure their freshness and avoid replay attacks. For that matter, a nonce is generated per message and per user and is bound to the current user's session state that a service maintains. That nonce is included as a parameter to the protocol message sent to a remote service and the respective response is expected to carry the same nonce. Nonces do not survive the termination of a user session.

5. PASSWORD REUSE

SAuth is rendered moot when a user is sharing the same password across web sites acting as vouching services. Unfortunately this is quite common in practice where a password is reused across six different web sites [40] on average. In essence reuse intensifies the problem of password leakage [17,34]. Password managing software, nowadays offered natively by web browsers, could remedy the situation but usability issues are presently obstructing wide adoption.

5.1 Decoys

In the spirit of recent research [27, 43], we propose placing decoy passwords in databases to introduce uncertainty about the actual passwords chosen by users. In other words, anyone examining the password database, including an attacker who has compromised it, will discover that every user account has N passwords instead of one. Any of those passwords can successfully authenticate the user to the service and that is a key difference between our proposal and Kamouflage [27] as well as Honeywords [43]. That is because decoy passwords carry no marks and receive no special treat-

	(a) normal login	(b) normal login (pwd reuse)	(c) leaked	(d) leaked (pwd reuse)
(1) Single-site authentication	PS^{-1}	PS^{-1}	1 ✗	1 ✗
(2) Two-site authentication without decoys	$(PS^2)^{-1}$	PS^{-1}	PS^{-1} ✓	1 ✗
(3) Two-site authentication with decoys	$K1 \cdot K2 \cdot (PS^2)^{-1}$	PS^{-1}	$K2 \cdot PS^{-1}$ ✓	$K1^{-1}$ ✓

Table 1: Probabilities of different log-in events under current and our proposed authentication systems. Case (a) refers to the normal scenario where someone without any prior knowledge of the password attempts to log in to a service while case (b) is a special sub-case where the user of the target account is reusing his password in more than one services. Cases (c) and (d) refer to the scenario where a service has been compromised and the user's password for that service leaked. Our approach (2) offers a significant increase in the security of cases (a), (b) and (c) but not (d). For that matter we couple our proposed system with decoys which overall decreases the probability of an attacker logging in all four cases.

ment from the service to eliminate heuristics that could distinguish them from the actual user-set passwords.

Decoy Generation. Generating decoys indistinguishable from actual data is an interesting research area. Bowen et al. have worked on providing believable decoys at the network and host level [30, 31]. Researchers have already proposed techniques for generating sets of similar tokens in an automated manner and applied them towards decoy passwords. In Honeywords [43] a tweaking algorithm with variations is used. The authors propose various transformations, such as chaffing-by-tail-tweaking, which basically produce new words similar to a core word, which is the original user's password. In Kamouflage [27] they extend the context free grammar rules proposed by Weir et al. [56] for generating similar passwords.

We consider the above works to be towards the right direction and extend them in our approach. The key idea is to identify the context of the password and randomly produce tokens that match it. However, it is important to keep two requirements in mind. First, there should be no single mask describing the set of decoy passwords. In other words, it should not be possible to determine the structure or the properties of all decoy passwords, including the actual password, by looking at any small subset of them. Therefore, we introduce variations in the structure and properties of the actual password to achieve diversity. Second, random generation might produce passwords that are unlikely to be chosen by actual humans. For instance, analysis of the leaked passwords from the RockYou service revealed that just 4% of passwords begin with a digit as opposed to a character. Randomly producing decoys with mixed characters and digits would produce a roughly equal amount of tokens starting with a character and a digit. The attacker could subsequently ignore any password starting with a digit without risking discarding the actual password. Therefore, we place weights on the generation process to favor human norms.

The process of generating decoys begins by analyzing the user-selected password. It is grammatically decomposed [56] and new passwords are generated by applying transformations to the core parts of the initial password. Transformations can be applied in the same fashion that users change their own password [59], like for example certain substitutions such as leetspeak [26]. We can also generate the corresponding parts of speech tags [45], and use them to produce random permutations that are still grammatically similar and valid. For example, "she runs fast" is written as "pronoun verb adverb" and could generate "she plays carefully" or "he speaks loudly". In the case where natural language processing fails to identify the presence of human language, we treat the password as a random string with certain statistical properties. For example, "6rZ" can be written as "digit lowercase uppercase" and generate "0xB" or "5cM" but not "5cm".

5.2 Incorporating Decoys

A site can transition gracefully into the use of decoy passwords. We have implemented generic wrappers of existing hash functions. Currently sites need to have a function that creates a password hash and one that validates it. Password decoys do not interfere with existing hashing schemes nor do they dictate any changes in the database schema. Instead, a site needs to enable `create(password, N)` and `validate(hash)` wrappers. The former takes as input a plaintext password and a positive integer `N`, produces `N` similar passwords and hashes each of them using the existing hashing functionality of the site. The function returns a password vector encapsulating `N` hashes per user and which is subsequently inserted into the database. The latter function looks up a given hash key in the user's password vector.

6. SECURITY EVALUATION

Here we evaluate the security of SAuth and compare it with the current practice of single-site authentication. We account for SAuth coupled with and without decoys and discuss the trade-offs. As already mentioned, there is no special marking for the service to distinguish the actual password from the decoys; any decoy password will successfully authenticate the user although the user is never made aware of them. Therefore if the number of generated decoys is too large in relation to the password space, typing a random password will result with good probability in authentication.

We consider the probability of two events, G_b and G_s, for someone guessing both passwords in a two-entity enhanced authentication process and someone guessing just the second password provided the first one is stolen. Considering the above, we wish the size of the decoy set to be as small as possible for event G_b and as large as possible for the second event, G_s. For a given password space, PS, and assuming $D(s)$ is the distribution of users that do share the same password with both services:

$$P(G_b) = \begin{cases} \frac{1}{PS} \cdot \frac{1}{PS-1} \approx \frac{1}{PS} \cdot \frac{1}{PS}, & \text{for all users,} \\ \frac{1}{PS} \cdot 1 & \text{for } D(s) \text{ of the users.} \end{cases}$$

In other words, for all users the probability of successful authentication is the probability of authenticating to the first service and the probability of authenticating to the second. However, for $D(s)$ of the users, after successfully authenticating to the first service, just trying the same password in the second will grant access to that user's account (we assume $D(s) = 70\%$ [40]). Similarly, the probability when the first password is known becomes:

$$P(G_s) = \begin{cases} 1 \cdot \frac{1}{PS-1} \approx 1 \cdot \frac{1}{PS} & \text{for all users,} \\ 1 \cdot 1 & \text{for } D(s) \text{ of the users.} \end{cases}$$

This means that the original design of synergy-based authentication will not be able to improve the security of accounts that reuse the password in the vouching service against a password-leak incident. It will however be able to significantly improve the security in the case where different passwords are employed and also when no site has been compromised.[2] By introducing $K1$ and $K2$ decoys in each service, respectively, the event probabilities become:

$$P(G_b) = \begin{cases} \frac{K1}{PS} \cdot \frac{K2}{PS-1} \approx \frac{K1}{PS} \cdot \frac{K2}{PS} & \text{for all users,} \\ \frac{K1}{PS} \cdot \frac{1}{K1} = \frac{1}{PS} & \text{for } D(s) \text{ of the users.} \end{cases}$$

We assume no overlap between decoy sets $K1$ and $K2$. As decoy sets are chosen at random without cooperation between the different services there may be some overlap. However, this is small and there is no hint for the attacker to determine the existence of overlap or its size. Finally, the probability of a successful login when the first password has been leaked becomes:

$$P(G_b) = \begin{cases} 1 \cdot \frac{K2}{PS-1} \approx 1 \cdot \frac{K2}{PS} & \text{for all users,} \\ 1 \cdot \frac{1}{K1} & \text{for } D(s) \text{ of the users.} \end{cases}$$

Table 1 summarizes and compares the probabilities of different events, with SAuth in place or not. Rows marked (1)-(3) characterize three different approaches, each one containing four cases marked as columns (a)-(d). Our initial approach (2) significantly improves the security of the authentication system when someone is trying to guess both passwords (column (a) in Table 1) unless the password is being reused in which case our approach offers the same security guarantees as current systems (column (b)). Moreover, while the original system would allow anyone with probability 1 to access the accounts of a service using leaked credentials, SAuth significantly reduces the probability to $1/PS$ (column (c)). Unfortunately, if the user of the target account has chosen to reuse his password in the vouching service, our method is rendered ineffective. For that matter we propose the decoy-enhanced approach (3) in which we can see that we maintain the same order of security in cases (a) through (b) and reduce probability 1 in case (c) to $1/K$ where K is the size of the decoy password set.

6.1 Decoy Set Size

[2]Consider an attacker that performs non-targeted online dictionary attack, where a single password is tried against all users of a particular web site.

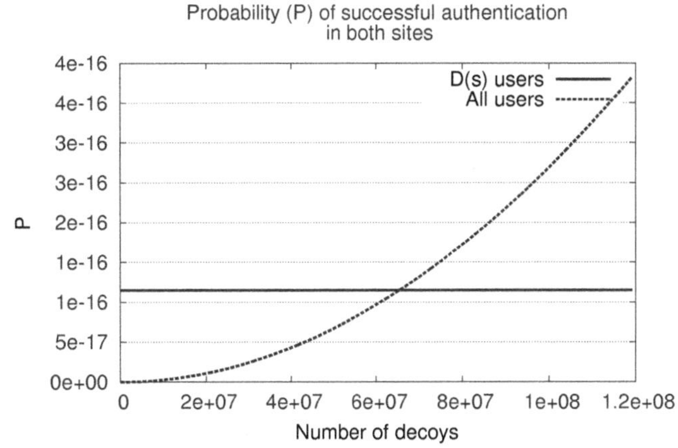

Figure 3: Probability of successful authentication in target site S and vouching site V when decoy passwords are used. As we do not distinguish between actual and decoy passwords, we require their number to be small over the password space.

In Honeywords [43] the authors suggest a typical set of 20 decoys and note that some sensitive accounts, such as the administrator's, may be associated with a larger set of 200 honey tokens. One could argue that adding more decoys increases the level of protection for the actual password as it creates more noise around it. In SAuth, where password decoys can actually be used for user authentication, reasoning about the size of the decoy set is not as straightforward. Here we theorize about the ideal size but then proceed to propose a more practical approach.

Based on Table 1 one observes in Figure 3 that in the absence of a security leak, and provided passwords are not recycled, expanding the decoy set actually makes guessing easier for an attacker (case (a)) as he can now figure out any one of the decoys as opposed to finding the actual user password. Case (b) is independent of the number of decoys and case (c), where the target site's passwords have been leaked, also requires a small number of decoys in relation to the password space. To justify the need for decoys we examine case (d) where users share the same password in both the target service and the vouching service. Since the attacker's probability of success is reduced to $1/K$ we want as many decoys as possible. Figure 4 presents this trade-off between the security of users with unique and shared passwords following a password database leak. Note that the password space drawn is $2 \cdot 10^{-6}\%$ of the entire space and has been selected as such to focus on the trade-off point between the two cases. Ideally, the size of the decoy set should result in an equal probability of success in both cases (c) and (d). In other words, there should be no incentive for the attacker to concentrate on either category of users. For example, given 70% probability that a user will reuse a certain password and a password space in the order of 94^8 ([a-zA-Z0-9] and symbols) we find that the decoy set should contain $O(94^4)$ decoys per user. For anything below that point, an attacker would prefer to guess among the already leaked decoy set, for a chance to attack 70% of the users of a service, rather than attempting a completely random password in hopes of falling within the decoy set of the second service. Note

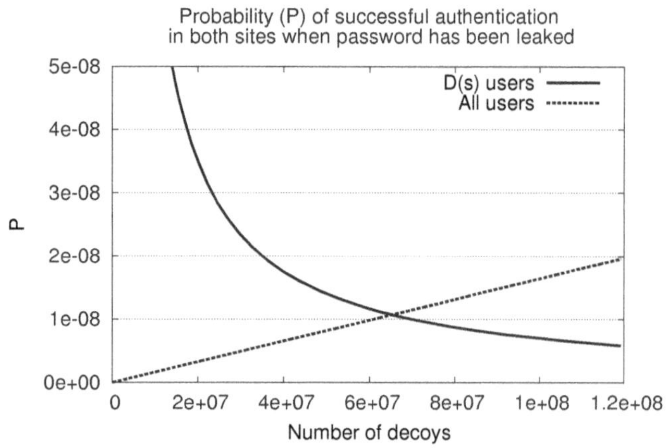

Figure 4: Probability of successful authentication in target service S following a password leak. Vouching site V and decoy passwords are employed. As the size of the decoy set for each user increases, the probability of attacking users who reuse their password across services is reduced. However, the probability of guessing a random password which falls within the decoy set increases in relation to the size of the password space. These conflicting requirements define the ideal size for the decoy set.

that this is a theoretical approximation which could however become practical as storage technology advances.

In practice, according to NIST [32], an online guessing attack for Level 1 should succeed with a probability of 1 in 1,024 and for Level 2 with a probability of 1 in 16,384. Thus, a site that meets the specification for Level 1 under case (d) should maintain at least 1,024 decoy passwords per user, while a site that meets the specification for Level 2 should maintain at least 16,384 decoy passwords per user. At the same time, the probabilities for case (c) are $\approx 10^{-12}$ and $\approx 10^{-11}$ respectively. Notice that even in the case of Level 2, the site needs to store an additional megabyte of information per user which we consider reasonable given that it is less than the size of some photos that users might upload online. [3]

6.2 Network Overhead

SAuth introduces additional network messages during the authentication process (see Fig. 1). During a traditional authentication the network time required is $t_{auth} = RTT_S$ where RTT_S is the round-trip time from browser to service S. With SAuth in place this time is $t_{sauth} = 2RTT_S + RTT_V$, where RTT_V is the round-trip time from browser to the vouching service V. Note that a single SAuth session can result in the user logging in to both the target site and the vouching site, something which in the traditional case requires $t = RTT_S + RTT_V$ if done in succession. In other words, SAuth introduces $RTT_S + RTT_V$ which can be just RTT if logging in to both services. Moreover, this overhead is incurred only in the absence of a persistent authentication token, e.g., a cookie, something which we expect to happen rarely.

[3]We assume a hash key of 512 bits.

7. RELATED WORK

Decoy Passwords. In Kamouflage [27] the authors propose injecting dummy passwords in password managers to protect the actual passwords if the master secret that unlocks the database is compromised. Similarly, honeywords [43] are fake passwords that are stored on the server together with the authentic password. Honeywords require a trusted third party for making sure, each time the user logs in, that the password entered is the authentic one and not a decoy.

k-Secret Sharing. Shamir et al. [52] proposed splitting up a secret into k pieces and distributing them to distinct parties in such a way at any given moment if $m < k$ pieces are present the original secret can be reconstructed. The same primitive has been applied to distributed user authentication by splitting up the stored password into multiple tokens [23,33]. Our proposal, SAuth, can be seen as a manifestation of this technique. In our terminology, the process of verifying each piece of the original password is called vouching. Instead of generating a password and splitting it up, we combine passwords the user already has to benefit from the security of a long and distributed secret.

Bounded Retrieval. Crescenzo et al. [36] propose making the authentication database too big for the attacker to retrieve. The server maintains a set of very large random files and each password is mapped to locations within them. The sum of those locations represents the password's digest requiring the full database to brute-force leaked hashes.

Authentication/Authorization. OAuth 2.0 [18] enables a third party to request access to a credential-restricted resource from its owner and receive that access without knowledge of the owner's credentials. OpenID 2.0 [49] provides a way for an end user to prove ownership of a claimed identity to a third party without a separate account. Facebook Connect [46] builds on top of both OAuth and OpenID to produce an authentication and authorization framework combined with the social information and graph its users form. BrowserID [2] or Mozilla Persona is a single-sign-on mechanism which uses e-mail addresses to represent user identities. PseudoID [37] employs blind cryptographic signatures to eliminate this privacy concern.

In this paper we propose a federated login system which may additionally facilitate the following use case; passwordless logins for a plethora of web services, much like Facebook Connect works today, but instead of using a single sign-on service, like Facebook, our system enables the use of a federated sign-on service which could include Facebook, Google and Twitter all vouching during log-in and thus making it harder for an attacker to exploit the single sign-on system.

8. CONCLUSION

We have presented SAuth, a novel protocol for synergy-based enhanced authentication in the face a password database leak. Users wishing to access their account on service S also have to authenticate for their account on service V, which acts as a vouching party. Both services can be regular sites already visited by the user every day, such as e-mail providers or social networks. The vouching process implicitly takes place through the user's browser and remains transparent to a large degree. With SAuth, should an attacker acquire the password for service S he will be unable to log in unless he also compromises the password for V. To mitigate password reuse habits we employ decoy passwords to introduce uncertainty regarding the actual one. SAuth is an extension and not a replacement of existing authentication methods, operates one layer above them and thus enables services to employ heterogeneous systems.

We make SAuth publicly available at `http://www.cs.columbia.edu/~kontaxis/sauth/`.

9. ACKNOWLEDGMENTS

We thank the anonymous reviewers and our shepherd, Anupam Datta, for the preparation of the final paper. We also thank Mariana Raykova and Michalis Polychronakis for early discussions. This work was supported by DARPA through contract FA8650-11-C-7190. Any opinions, findings, conclusions or recommendations expressed herein are those of the authors, and do not necessarily reflect those of the US Government or DARPA. It was also supported in part by the FP7-PEOPLE-2010-IOF project XHUNTER, No. 273765, and SysSec, funded by the European Commission under Grant Agreement No. 257007.

10. REFERENCES

[1] CloudCracker :: Online Hash Cracker. https://www.cloudcracker.com.

[2] BrowserID. https://github.com/mozilla/id-specs/blob/prod/browserid/index.md.

[3] Directory of web sites storing passwords in plain text. http://plaintextoffenders.com.

[4] E-mail discussion at Debian about the wiki.debian.org security breach. https://lwn.net/Articles/531727/.

[5] Gmail account security in Iran. http://googleonlinesecurity.blogspot.com/2011/09/gmail-account-security-in-iran.html.

[6] Google Accounts Authentication and Authorization. https://developers.google.com/accounts/docs/GettingStarted.

[7] Google Declares War on the Password. http://www.wired.com/wiredenterprise/2013/01/google-password/all/.

[8] Hacker Posts 6.4 Million LinkedIn Passwords. http://www.technewsdaily.com/7839-linked-passwords-hack.html.

[9] How apple and amazon security flaws led to my epic hacking. http://www.wired.com/gadgetlab/2012/08/apple-amazon-mat-honan-hacking/.

[10] How to Safely Store a Password. http://codahale.com/how-to-safely-store-a-password/.

[11] HTTP 1.1. http://tools.ietf.org/html/rfc2616.

[12] IEEE data breach: 100K passwords leak in plain text. http://www.neowin.net/news/ieee-data-breach-100k-passwords-leak-in-plain-text.

[13] LinkedIn cleartext passwords. http://dazzlepod.com/linkedin/.

[14] New 25 GPU Monster Devours Passwords In Seconds. http://securityledger.com/new-25-gpu-monster-devours-passwords-in-seconds/.

[15] PayPal Leads Industry Effort to Move Beyond Passwords. https://www.thepaypalblog.com/2013/02/paypal-leads-industry-effort-to-move-beyond-passwords/.

[16] Sony Hacked Again, 1 Million Passwords Exposed. http://www.informationweek.com/security/attacks/sony-hacked-again-1-million-passwords-ex/229900111.

[17] The Domino Effect of the Password Leak at Gawker. http://voices.yahoo.com/the-domino-effect-password-leak-gawker-10566853.html.

[18] The OAuth 2.0 Authorization Framework. http://www.ietf.org/rfc/rfc6749.txt.

[19] TLS 1.2. https://tools.ietf.org/html/rfc5246.

[20] Twitter detects and shuts down password data hack in progress. http://arstechnica.com/security/2013/02/twitter-detects-and-shuts-down-password-data-hack-in-progress/.

[21] URI. http://www.ietf.org/rfc/rfc2396.txt.

[22] B. Adida. Beamauth: Two-factor web authentication with a bookmark. In *Proceedings of the 14th ACM conference on Computer and Communications Security*, 2007.

[23] A. Bagherzandi, S. Jarecki, N. Saxena, and Y. Lu. Password-protected secret sharing. In *Proceedings of the 18th ACM conference on Computer and Communications Security*, 2011.

[24] F. Benevenuto, T. Rodrigues, M. Cha, and V. Almeida. Characterizing user behavior in online social networks. In *Proceedings of the 9th ACM SIGCOMM conference on Internet measurement conference*, 2009.

[25] R. Biddle, S. Chiasson, and P. Van Oorschot. Graphical passwords: Learning from the first twelve years. *ACM Computing Surveys*, 44(4), Sept. 2012.

[26] K. Blashki and S. Nichol. Game geek's goss: Linguistic creativity in young males within an online university forum (94//3 933k'5 9055oneone). *Australian Journal of Emerging Technologies and Society*, 3(2), 2005.

[27] H. Bojinov, E. Bursztein, D. Boneh, and X. Boyen. Kamouflage: Loss-resistant password management. In *Proceedings of the 15th European Symposium On Research In Computer Security*, September 2010.

[28] J. Bonneau. Statistical metrics for individual password strength. In *Proceedings of the 20th international conference on Security Protocols*. Springer, 2012.

[29] J. Bonneau, C. Herley, P. C. v. Oorschot, and F. Stajano. The quest to replace passwords: A framework for comparative evaluation of web authentication schemes. In *Proceedings of the 33rd IEEE Symposium on Security and Privacy*, 2012.

[30] B. M. Bowen, V. P. Kemerlis, P. V. Prabhu, A. D. Keromytis, and S. J. Stolfo. A system for generating and injecting indistinguishable network decoys. *Journal of Computer Security*, 20(2-3), 2012.

[31] B. M. Bowen, P. Prabhu, V. P. Kemerlis, S. Sidiroglou, A. D. Keromytis, and S. J. Stolfo. BotSwindler: tamper resistant injection of believable decoys in VM-based hosts for crimeware detection. In *Proceedings of the 13th international conference on Recent Advances in Intrusion Detection*, 2010.

[32] W. E. Burr, D. F. Dodson, and W. T. Polk. *Electronic authentication guideline.* US Department of Commerce, Technology Administration, National Institute of Standards and Technology, 2004.

[33] J. Camenisch, A. Lysyanskaya, and G. Neven. Practical yet universally composable two-server

password-authenticated secret sharing. In *Proceedings of the 2012 ACM conference on Computer and Communications Security*. ACM, 2012.

[34] W. Cheswick. Rethinking passwords. *Communications of the ACM*, 56(2), 2013.

[35] L. S. Clair, L. Johansen, W. Enck, M. Pirretti, P. Traynor, P. McDaniel, and T. Jaeger. Password exhaustion: predicting the end of password usefulness. In *Proceedings of the 2nd international conference on Information Systems Security*. Springer-Verlag, 2006.

[36] G. D. Crescenzo, R. J. Lipton, and S. Walfish. Perfectly secure password protocols in the bounded retrieval model. In *Theory of Cryptography Conference*. Springer, 2006.

[37] A. Dey and S. Weis. Pseudoid: Enhancing privacy in federated login. In *Hot Topics in Privacy Enhancing Technologies*, 2010.

[38] R. Dhamija and A. Perrig. Deja vu: a user study using images for authentication. In *Proceedings of the 9th USENIX Security Symposium*, 2000.

[39] R. Dhamija and J. D. Tygar. The battle against phishing: Dynamic security skins. In *Proceedings of the Symposium on Usable Privacy and Security*, 2005.

[40] D. Florencio and C. Herley. A large-scale study of web password habits. In *Proceedings of the international conference on World Wide Web*. ACM, 2007.

[41] S. Gaw and E. W. Felten. Password management strategies for online accounts. In *Proceedings of the Symposium on Usable Privacy and Security*, 2006.

[42] J. Huang and R. W. White. Parallel browsing behavior on the web. In *Proceedings of the 21st ACM conference on Hypertext and Hypermedia*, 2010.

[43] A. Juels and R. L. Rivest. Honeywords: Making password-cracking detectable, 2013.

[44] P. G. Kelley, S. Komanduri, M. L. Mazurek, R. Shay, T. Vidas, L. Bauer, N. Christin, L. F. Cranor, and J. Lopez. Guess again (and again and again): Measuring password strength by simulating password-cracking algorithms. In *Proceedings of the 33rd IEEE Symposium on Security and Privacy*, 2012.

[45] C. D. Manning and H. Schütze. *Foundations of statistical natural language processing*. MIT, 1999.

[46] M. Miculan and C. Urban. Formal analysis of facebook connect single sign-on authentication protocol. In *Proceedings of the 37th International Conference on Current Trends in Theory and Practice of Computer Science*. Springer, 2011.

[47] C. Percival. Stronger key derivation via sequential memory-hard functions. `http://tools.ietf.org/html/draft-josefsson-scrypt-kdf-00`.

[48] N. Provos and D. Mazières. A future-adaptive password scheme. In *Proceedings of the USENIX Annual Technical Conference*, 1999.

[49] D. Recordon and D. Reed. Openid 2.0: a platform for user-centric identity management. In *Proceedings of the ACM workshop on Digital Identity Management*, 2006.

[50] B. Ross, C. Jackson, N. Miyake, D. Boneh, and J. C. Mitchell. Stronger password authentication using browser extensions. In *Proceedings of the 14th USENIX Security Symposium*, 2005.

[51] S. Schechter, A. J. B. Brush, and S. Egelman. It's no secret. Measuring the security and reliability of authentication via secret questions. In *Proceedings of the 30th IEEE Symposium on Security and Privacy*, 2009.

[52] A. Shamir. How to share a secret. *Communications of the ACM*, 22(11), 1979.

[53] R. Shay, S. Komanduri, P. G. Kelley, P. G. Leon, M. L. Mazurek, L. Bauer, N. Christin, and L. F. Cranor. Encountering stronger password requirements: user attitudes and behaviors. In *Proceedings of the Symposium on Usable Privacy and Security*, 2010.

[54] S.-T. Sun, Y. Boshmaf, K. Hawkey, and K. Beznosov. A billion keys, but few locks: the crisis of web single sign-on. In *Proceedings of the New Security Paradigms Workshop*. ACM, 2010.

[55] R. Wang, S. Chen, and X. Wang. Signing me onto your accounts through facebook and google: A traffic-guided security study of commercially deployed single-sign-on web services. In *Proceedings of the 33rd IEEE Symposium on Security and Privacy*, 2012.

[56] M. Weir, S. Aggarwal, B. d. Medeiros, and B. Glodek. Password cracking using probabilistic context-free grammars. In *Proceedings of the 30th IEEE Symposium on Security and Privacy*, 2009.

[57] H. Wimberly and L. M. Liebrock. Using fingerprint authentication to reduce system security: An empirical study. In *Proceedings of the 32nd IEEE Symposium on Security and Privacy*, 2011.

[58] M. Wu, R. C. Miller, and S. L. Garfinkel. Do security toolbars actually prevent phishing attacks? In *Proceedings of the SIGCHI Conference on Human Factors in Computing Systems*. ACM, 2006.

[59] Y. Zhang, F. Monrose, and M. K. Reiter. The security of modern password expiration: an algorithmic framework and empirical analysis. In *Proceedings of the 17th ACM conference on Computer and Communications Security*.

Monitor Integrity Protection with Space Efficiency and Separate Compilation

Ben Niu
Lehigh University
19 Memorial Drive West
Bethlehem, PA, 18015
ben210@lehigh.edu

Gang Tan
Lehigh University
19 Memorial Drive West
Bethlehem, PA, 18015
gtan@cse.lehigh.edu

ABSTRACT

Low-level inlined reference monitors weave monitor code into a program for security. To ensure that monitor code cannot be bypassed by branching instructions, some form of control-flow integrity must be guaranteed. Past approaches to protecting monitor code either have high space overhead or do not support separate compilation. We present *Monitor Integrity Protection* (MIP), a form of coarse-grained control-flow integrity. The key idea of MIP is to arrange instructions in variable-sized chunks and dynamically restrict indirect branches to target only chunk beginnings. We show that this simple idea is effective in protecting monitor code integrity, enjoys low space and execution-time overhead, supports separate compilation, and is largely compatible with an existing compiler toolchain. We also show that MIP enables a separate verifier that completely disassembles a binary and verifies its security.

MIP is designed to support inlined reference monitors. As a case study, we have implemented MIP-based Software-based Fault Isolation (SFI) on both x86-32 and x86-64. The evaluation shows that MIP-based SFI has competitive performance with other SFI implementations, while enjoying low space overhead.

Categories and Subject Descriptors

D.2.4 [**Software Engineering**]: [Software/Program Verification]; D.4.6 [**Operating Systems**]: [Security and Protection]

Keywords

Control-Flow Integrity; Inlined Reference Monitors; Separate Compilation

1. INTRODUCTION

Inlined Reference Monitors (IRM [10, 9, 11]) are effective in enhancing software security. Low-level IRMs inline monitor code into low-level code such as assembly or binary code so that unsafe operations are checked before their execution. They have become popular in recent years thanks to their efficiency and broad applicability. A number of low-level IRMs have been described in the literature, including software-based fault isolation (SFI [20]), XFI [8], data flow integrity [5], fine-grained memory access control [2], and many others.

CCS'13, November 4–8, 2013, Berlin, Germany.

ACM 978-1-4503-2477-9/13/11 ...$15.00.
http://dx.doi.org/10.1145/2508859.2516649.

A basic requirement of a reference monitor is that the monitor mechanism must be tamper-proof. In the case of IRMs, we must have *monitor code integrity*: monitor code before unsafe operations cannot be bypassed by direct or indirect branches. In the presence of attacks that modify the control flow of a program, some form of Control-Flow Integrity (CFI) must be guaranteed to avoid the bypassing of checks including via jumping into the middle of an instruction, exploited in Return-Oriented Programming (ROP [18]) attacks on x86. Monitor code integrity is easy to enforce on direct branches, whose targets can be statically determined. The difficulty is how to restrict indirect branches, including indirect calls (e.g., function calls via registers), indirect jumps, and return instructions.

One way for monitor code integrity is through *aligned-chunk CFI* [14], which provides coarse yet sufficient granularity. In this approach, the code region is divided into chunks of the same size such as 16 bytes. Branch targets are aligned at chunk beginnings. All branches are restricted to target beginnings of chunks. For indirect branches, this is achieved by dynamic checks. Thanks to the restriction on branches, monitor code before unsafe operations cannot be bypassed as long as they stay in the same chunk. This form of CFI is coarse-grained in that indirect branches are allowed to target all chunk beginnings. It is easy to implement, efficient, and sufficient to guarantee that monitor code is always invoked. It has been adopted by PittSFIeld [14] and NaCl [22, 17].

However, for alignment of branch targets, aligned-chunk CFI requires the insertion of no-op instructions. For instance, the address after a function call must be an aligned address since it is the target of the return instruction in the callee function. If the address is not aligned, no-ops are inserted before the function call so that it becomes aligned after instrumentation. The extra no-ops slow down program execution. NaCl-JIT [4], a NaCl version that supports just-in-time compilation, reports no-ops account for half of the sandboxing cost (about 37% slowdown because of no-ops on x86-64). More importantly, the no-ops cause significant code-size blow up. For example, the code size after instrumentation in NaCl-x86-64 [17] is roughly 60% larger than the original program. Since NaCl applications are downloaded into a client browser on the fly, large code size implies long delay in starting up the application. Serious concerns were raised by developers about the large code-size increase on NaCl's mailing list [12].

Another way for monitor code integrity is through *fine-grained CFI*, in which the program is instrumented to enforce a given control flow graph (CFG). Once the CFG is enforced, static analysis can be performed based on the CFG to check whether monitor code can be bypassed. Various instrumentation techniques for fine-grained CFI have been proposed in the literature [1, 21, 2]. The classic CFI instrumentation [1] inserts IDs before branch targets and inserts ID checks before indirect branches to ensure that they jump to targets specified in the CFG.

The fine-grained CFI provides stronger security, but also comes with higher runtime overhead. Furthermore, unlike aligned-chunk CFI, none of the instrumentation techniques for fine-grained CFI supports *separate compilation*. The term separate compilation traditionally refers to the ability of a compiler to compile modules separately and link the compiled modules. In the context of IRMs, it refers to the ability to perform instrumentation of modules separately, without considering other modules, and to link instrumented modules into a working program. The instrumentation of fine-grained CFI techniques requires all modules of an application, including libraries, to be available during instrumentation time. For instance, the IDs in the classic CFI instrumentation cannot overlap with numbers already in the program. This property cannot be guaranteed without inspecting the whole program. The loss of separate compilation means it is impossible to instrument libraries once and reuse those instrumented libraries for all programs. This is especially cumbersome for dynamically linked libraries (DLLs), which are built for reuse across programs. It implies that each program has to come with its own instrumented version of libraries. We believe this is the major obstacle that prevents fine-grained CFI from being adopted in practice.

Therefore, the challenge is to design some form of CFI that is strong enough to ensure monitor code integrity, is space efficient, and supports separate compilation so that libraries can be reused across programs. We propose a simple yet effective approach we call *Monitor Integrity Protection* (MIP). The basic idea is to divide the code region of a program into variable-sized chunks and use a chunk table to record boundaries of chunks. Inter-chunk control flow with direct or indirect branches is restricted to target only chunk beginnings. The restriction is enforced on indirect branches by dynamic checks that look up information from a runtime representation of the chunk table. Compared to aligned-chunk CFI, MIP is more flexible in that chunks have variable sizes; as a result, there is no need to insert no-ops for alignment. Compared to fine-grained CFI, MIP supports separate compilation. We highlight our main contributions below:

- We show how the chunk-table approach can be made efficient and compatible with separate compilation. In particular, MIP encodes each entry in the chunk table as a single bit and uses a bitmap to store all bits. The bitmap representation enables efficient checks before indirect branches and yields a small memory footprint for the table representation during runtime. To support separate compilation, each module in a program is instrumented separately and a module-specific chunk table is produced. When modules are combined statically or dynamically, their chunk tables are merged.
- We have implemented a complete toolchain including a MIP rewriter, verifier, and dynamic linker. Using the toolchain and SPECCPU2006 programs, we have performed a careful evaluation of MIP's performance and code-size increase, as well as its support for separate compilation.
- On top of MIP, we have implemented SFI for both x86-32 and x86-64 platforms. We show in experiments that our MIP-based SFI has competitive performance relative to an industrial-strength SFI system [17], but with a much lower code-size increase.

The remainder of the paper is organized as follows. Sec. 2 discusses related work. Sec. 3 gives an overview of MIP. Sec. 4 presents MIP's major design choices and Sec. 5 elaborates on the implementation details. In Sec. 6, we present a case study in which MIP is used as the basis of an SFI implementation. Evaluation results are discussed in Sec. 7 and we conclude in Sec. 8.

2. RELATED WORK

In essence, MIP is a special form of CFI so that IRMs can build on top of it for monitor code integrity. It is inspired by many previous systems, including a large body of work on CFI and IRMs.

2.1 Control Flow Integrity (CFI)

In the introduction, we have motivated MIP by comparing briefly between MIP and some CFI systems. Next we present a more detailed discussion of CFI techniques and their comparison with MIP. In general, past CFI instrumentation techniques can be put into two broad groups: coarse-grained CFI and fine-grained CFI.

Coarse-grained CFI. In this group, an imprecise CFG is enforced on indirect branches. In the simplest case, all indirect branches share a common set of possible targets. In a slight refinement, targets are classified into several categories and each class of indirect branches is allowed to jump to a particular category; for instance, all indirect calls can jump to function entries (but not other targets). An example coarse-grained CFI is the aligned-chunk CFI, discussed in the introduction. Another example is CCFIR [25], which rewrites code to redirect all indirect branches into a new springboard code region. In the springboard region, roughly each direct and indirect branch target has an aligned entry that contains instructions that transfer the control flow. Indirect branches are checked to ensure they target springboard entries at runtime. binCFI [26] also enforces coarse-grained CFI on a binary program by replacing indirect branches with direct jumps that target an external routine, which consults an address translation map. The map's keys record all possible indirect branch targets in the binary and its values are direct jumps whose execution transfers the control to the actual target. Only if a target is within the map can the corresponding jump be triggered to perform the control transfer. The advantages of coarse-grained CFI are threefold: (1) its execution-time overhead is low; (2) its implementation is straightforward, because the building of its CFG does not require a sophisticated analysis; (3) it supports separate compilation. Aligned-chunk CFI has been extended to support just-in-time compilation [4], which generates code on the fly. Similarly, CCFIR allows each module to have its own springboard region and springboard regions of multiple modules can be combined during runtime. Moreover, binCFI supports separate compilation, since the address translation maps can be dynamically glued together. Our MIP is also a form of coarse-grained CFI and therefore enjoys the above benefits.

In contrast to past coarse-grained CFI systems, MIP is space efficient. Aligned-chunk CFI has a 60% space overhead [17] due to the extra no-op instructions inserted for chunk alignment. CCFIR does not require chunk alignment, but entries in its springboard region must start at aligned addresses (8-byte or 16-byte aligned). Its space overhead is about 33%, which is also on the high side. binCFI instruments the binary code and preserves a copy of the original code for referencing embedded data, thus its space overhead is nearly 139%. MIP's space overhead is around 15% thanks to its space-efficient encoding of the chunk table.

In addition to space overhead, MIP differs from previous coarse-grained CFI in its assumptions and instrumentation techniques. MIP requires compiler cooperation to produce a chunk table for every module. The chunk table ensures that a module can be completely disassembled. By contrast, CCFIR and binCFI work directly on binaries by first disassembling the code. Specifically, CCFIR disassembles Windows binaries aided by the attached relocation information. However, such information is not generally available on programs running on other OSes such as Linux; therefore CCFIR's disassembly would probably fail on such systems. binCFI adopts heuristics for disassembly and conservatively preserves the original code copy for unexpected data references. Although the CFI policy is enforced, the program's semantics might be changed. In addition, CCFIR's instrumentation is also much more involved than MIP, which requires instrumentation before only indirect branches. CCFIR further requires replacing all function addresses with corresponding addresses in the springboard region and requires instrumenting even direct function calls. Runtime performance comparison among MIP, CCFIR and binCFI will be discussed in the evaluation section.

Fine-grained CFI. In fine-grained CFI, each indirect branch has its own allowed jump targets, specified in a CFG. Fine-grained CFI provides stronger security and can prevent most attacks that induce illegal control-flow transfers. In addition, fine-grained CFI enables advanced static analysis for optimization and verification [24].

Different instrumentation techniques have been proposed for fine-grained CFI on x86 [1, 21, 2] and ARM [7]. As discussed before, the classic CFI [1] inserts a check instruction with an embedded ID before an indirect branch and inserts the same ID before all allowed targets of that instruction. HyperSafe [21] constructs a target table for every indirect branch. The table is statically constructed and contains all the entries that the indirect branch can jump to. The program is changed so that table indexes are passed in the program. Before an indirect branch, the index is converted into a target address based on entries in the table. WIT's CFI enforcement [2] uses a color table to record colors of control-flow targets. The color table is built by static analysis on the compiler IR code. Each indirect call is statically assigned a color, and functions that the call can target are assigned the same color. The color table is represented during runtime and dynamic checks consult the table before an indirect call.

The fine-grained CFI provides strong security and the space overhead is small. On the other hand, they are more difficult to implement because precise CFG generation requires program analysis. More importantly, none of the techniques support separate compilation. In the classic CFI [1], IDs have to be unique so that they do not appear in the rest of the code. This requires the availability of all code at the instrumentation time. Similarly, HyperSafe and WIT use a whole-program analysis to construct their CFI tables. As a result, it is impossible to instrument libraries once and reuse them, which severely limits fine-grained CFI's adoption in practice.

2.2 Inlined Reference Monitors (IRMs)

CFI is a special IRM. There are many other kinds of IRMs. SFI has been studied extensively [20, 14, 22]. It rewrites untrusted code to prevent it from accessing memory outside of a designated data region and executing instructions outside of a designated code region. It isolates untrusted code in a separate fault domain, but does not provide fine-grained memory-access control. XFI [8] and a series of papers [2, 6, 3] by Microsoft Research at Cambridge study how to enforce fine-grained memory access control, which allows different access permissions for small buffers in the data region. In addition, Data Flow Integrity (DFI [5]) can prevent some non-control data attacks.

As a case study, we demonstrate how SFI can build upon MIP for monitor code integrity. It is clear that MIP is a general approach: all IRMs can build upon MIP, which enforces sufficient CFI for protecting the monitor.

2.3 Dynamic instrumentation

IRMs statically rewrite binaries to embed checks that enforce a security policy. In contrast, program shepherding [13] and software dynamic translation [16] dynamically modify and monitor untrusted applications to enforce a policy such as CFI. These systems can be viewed as interpreters with embedded reference-monitor checks (together with a set of techniques for fast dynamic translation and for removing unnecessary checks). Compared to IRMs, the downside is that the whole dynamic optimization and monitoring framework is in the TCB. The performance overhead of program shepherding is also higher.

3. OVERVIEW

Before a detailed discussion of MIP's design and implementation, we present the main ideas and benefits of MIP. At a high level, MIP moves from equal-sized chunks in aligned-chunk CFI to variable-sized chunks. As a result, the beginnings of chunks have to be remembered in a chunk table. For reliable disassembly and separate compilation, each *MIP module* (e.g., a DLL library) contains a chunk table as well as its code and data. Multiple such modules compose an application. In addition, control flow has to respect chunks in the following way:

1. Inter-chunk control flow edges must target chunk beginnings or a known safe exit. This property is enforced on direct branches statically and on indirect branches through instrumentation code that validates the target by consulting the chunk table before the control transfer.
2. Within each chunk, intra-chunk control flow because of direct branches is allowed, but indirect branches are not allowed to produce intra-chunk control flow.

This approach yields several benefits. First, it supports reliable whole-module disassembly, because a module's chunk table tells exactly all possible indirect-branch targets. Intra-chunk control flow can also be completely determined statically as it can only be the result of direct branches. Consequently, a standard recursive-traversal disassembly algorithm [15] can be performed on each chunk to extract the intra-chunk CFG. Monitor code before an unsafe operation cannot be bypassed as long as the monitor code and the unsafe operation stay in the same chunk and the monitor code dominates the unsafe operation according to the chunk's intra-chunk CFG. Thanks to reliable disassembly, a MIP module can be statically verified to determine whether it is safe according to an IRM policy. Further, reliable disassembly allows MIP to support mixed code and data. On x86, read-only data, such as jump tables and alignment bytes, are sometimes embedded in the code region, and the data must not be recognized as code to avoid instrumentation that might change the program semantics.

Second, MIP is space efficient. Because chunks can have variable lengths, MIP does not need to insert extra no-op instructions for chunk alignment, the main reason for the large space overhead in aligned-chunk CFI. MIP needs space to represent the chunk table and checks are inserted before indirect branches to enforce chunk boundaries. MIP's implementation chooses a space-efficient data structure (a bitmap) to represent the chunk table. As we will see in the evaluation section, MIP's space overhead and execution-time overhead are low.

Finally, MIP supports separate compilation. Each module is separately compiled and instrumented according to a specific IRM. The instrumentation process produces the module's chunk table, which must be respected for the IRM's monitor code integrity. When modules are statically or dynamically linked, the MIP toolchain merges their chunk tables in addition to their code and data.

On the flip side, MIP asks for the cooperation of code producers to attach chunk tables to modules. Consequently, MIP is not designed to work on off-the-shelf stripped binaries, but provides support to code producers who intend to harden their applications using IRMs. The requirement of chunk tables is not an onerous task for a code producer. As we will show, chunk tables can be produced by information in standard assembly files generated by an unmodified compiler such as GCC. By contrast, fine-grained CFI requires much more cooperation to produce a CFG.

4. MIP DESIGN

MIP's design will be discussed in several steps. We will first have a brief discussion about its threat model. We then present MIP's instrumentation, including how the chunk table is implemented and the instrumentation before indirect branches. Discussion about the support for separate compilation is presented next, followed by description about MIP's verification process, which statically verifies code before running it.

Before proceeding, we stress that MIP's goal is to support other IRMs: preventing IRM instrumentation from being bypassed. Therefore, some MIP components are parametrized by an IRM. For instance, MIP's verification should invoke an IRM-specific verifier, in addition to the verification about MIP's own instrumentation.

4.1 Threat model

MIP adopts a concurrent-attacker model originated in CFI [1]. It is realistic and conceptually simple. Specifically, it models the attacker as a separate thread, which runs in parallel with the user program. The attacker thread can read and write any memory (subject to memory page protection). Therefore, the attacker can corrupt data memory between any two instructions in the user program. However, it is assumed that machine registers cannot be directly modified by the attacker thread and they provide a safe place for storing values.

In addition, MIP's runtime enforces the invariant that no memory regions are both writable and executable at the same time and all code in executable regions has been statically verified to obey the IRM policy. Without the invariant, MIP cannot prevent arbitrary code execution. The invariant is enforced when an application is initially loaded by the runtime. The runtime sets up a separate code and data region. After verification, code is loaded into the code region, which is executable and readable but not writable. Note that the code region can include some read-only data such as jump tables. The data region is readable and certain parts are writable, but not executable. The invariant is also enforced when loading DLLs. Libraries, after verification, are loaded into unoccupied parts in the code region. Sec. 4.3 will discuss more about the support for libraries.

4.2 Instrumentation

MIP uses a chunk table to remember boundaries of chunks and queries the chunk table to ensure that branches respect chunks. Next, we discuss a few design choices such as how the chunk table is represented.

Chunk table representation. The representation should meet two needs: (1) it is space efficient; (2) it supports time-efficient queries about whether an address is the beginning of a chunk. One candidate would be a balanced binary tree where tree nodes are chunk beginnings. This data structure would have low space overhead. However, the query time is logarithmically dependent on the number of chunks. Another representation choice would be a hash table that remembers the set of chunk beginnings. For instance, hash tables were used by an early SFI implementation for checking jump targets [19]. Although the query time of a hash table is usually constant, calculating the hash function may involve dozens of instructions and the collision cost is even higher.

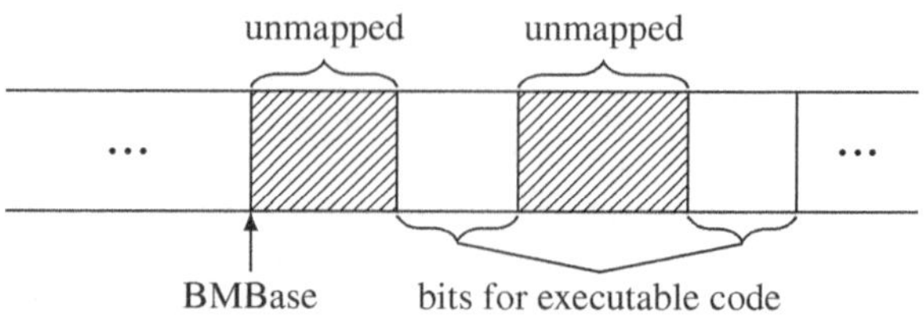

Figure 1: Bitmap memory layout.

MIP instead uses a bitmap to represent the chunk table. Conceptually, for every possible address, there is a corresponding bit in the bitmap. The bit is one if and only if the address is the beginning of a chunk. This representation clearly supports efficient queries. To check whether an address is the beginning of a chunk, just extract and test the bit based on the address and the start address of the bitmap (which can be achieved by a few machine instructions).

One worry about the bitmap representation is its space overhead. If every address has a bit in the bitmap, then its size is one eighth of the address-space size. However, notice that only those addresses belonging to executable code need to be represented by the bitmap. So one optimization is to represent bits for those addresses only in the code. Since the size of code is small compared to the address-space size, this optimization makes the bitmap compact. On the other hand, the code-address-only bitmap seems to require bounds checks. That is, given an address, we have to check that the address falls into the code region because otherwise we would retrieve a bit outside the code-address-only bitmap.

To avoid bounds checks, our solution is to reserve one eighth of the virtual address space for the complete bitmap, but leave those memory pages that do not correspond to the code region unmapped. This is depicted in Fig. 1. The bitmap has a start address `BMBase` (BitMap Base), which is the start address of the complete bitmap. Only those memory pages in the bitmap corresponding to code are mapped. Therefore, when an address is used to query the bitmap, we can omit the bounds checks because an address outside of the code region will be safely trapped by OS's page protection.

This solution results in low impact on the memory footprint because the physical memory for the bitmap is one eighth of the code-region size (not one eighth of the address space size). Furthermore, it supports separate compilation (discussed later). Note the code region is not required to be contiguous. When a new DLL library is loaded, MIP's runtime just needs to populate the bits corresponding its part of the bitmap. Finally, we note the bitmap is made read only for the user program so that untrusted code cannot tamper with the bitmap. On the other hand, MIP's trusted runtime can extend the bitmap when loading DLLs.

Checks before indirect branches. Dynamic checks to query the bitmap are inlined before indirect branches. For now, we use an abstract instruction "`CheckDest Reg`", which checks if the target in `Reg` is a valid chunk beginning according to the bitmap; if not, it jumps to the exit. The implementation section will discuss how the abstract instruction is lowered into machine instructions. The check is inlined before indirect branches straightforwardly. For instance, an indirect jump through register `eax` in "`jmp %eax`" becomes "`CheckDest %eax; jmp %eax`". An indirect branch through a memory location is first translated into an indirect branch through a register by reading the destination in a register and then instrumented. Return instructions are translated into an equivalent pop and indirect jump-through-register sequence and instrumented.

Chunk granularity. We have not discussed what constitutes a chunk. There is actually a spectrum of choices. In the simplest case, we can have *instruction chunks*. Many IRMs classify instructions into safe and unsafe instructions and insert checks immediately before unsafe instructions. We define a pseudo instruction to be either a safe instruction, or an unsafe instruction preceded by its check. In instruction chunks, a chunk is a single pseudo instruction. Although coarse-grained, enforcing instruction chunks prevents jumps into the middle of an instruction, and prevents checks before unsafe instruction from being bypassed.

Another choice is to have *basic-block chunks*, in which a chunk is a basic block with sequential intra-chunk control flow. A basic block can have multiple instructions, creating opportunities for intra-chunk check optimizations (e.g., redundant check elimination). One step further is to have *leaf-function chunks*, in which a chunk can be a leaf function or a basic block. A leaf function is one that does not call other functions; it can have complex intra-chunk control flow. Non-leaf function chunks are not allowed because function return addresses are targets of return instructions and so new chunks have to be formed at function return addresses.

Chunk granularity does not affect monitor code integrity as long as checks dominate unsafe instructions in chunks. On the other hand, bigger chunks have better security because it limits the space of indirect jump targets. We have implemented all three kinds of chunks and will discuss them more in Sec. 7.1.

4.3 Separate compilation support

In MIP, each module can be separately compiled and instrumented. It is important to note that the instrumentation code for one module does not need to be adjusted when it is combined with other modules. A module's instrumentation code is independent from the contents in its bitmap; its only assumption is that there is a bitmap that starts at `BMBase` and that bitmap is conceptually a complete bitmap that contains bits for all addresses (even though some parts are unmapped). When modules are combined, only their bitmaps need to be combined. We next discuss this step for both static linking and dynamic linking.

Support for static linking is straightforward. MIP's static linker first uses the standard static linker to link code and data of modules. Then it merges modules' bitmaps according to the relative positions of their code sections.

Support for dynamic linking is more complicated. MIP's dynamic loader augments a standard dynamic loader and performs dynamic linking in several steps. In the first step, memory pages for a new module are allocated and code is copied into memory. In this step, the newly allocated code pages are not executable so that the new code cannot be executed before verification. This step also allocates and populates memory pages in the bitmap memory area for the new module; the new bitmap memory pages are made read only. The second step is the standard dynamic-linking step, in which modules' data such as the global offset table (GOT) are adjusted for linking. In the final step, MIP verifies that the new code satisfies the IRM policy and, if verification succeeds, changes the new code pages to be executable. More about MIP's support for dynamic linking will be in Sec. 5.2.

One might worry about the bitmap's thread safety as one thread may query the bitmap and another thread may concurrently modify the bitmap when it loads a DLL library. However, since loading a DLL library only modifies part of the bitmap that is disjoint from the old parts of the bitmap, the bitmap is thread safe even without synchronization between threads.

4.4 Verification

MIP's verification takes a MIP module's code and bitmap as input and checks whether chunk boundaries are respected by the code. In addition, for each chunk the verification builds an intra-chunk CFG and invokes a custom IRMCheck procedure on the CFG. That is, the verification is parametrized by an IRM's check procedure, which validates that there is sufficient instrumentation in the chunk according to the IRM's policy. At a high level, MIP's verification checks the following two properties on a module:

P_1*: An inter-chunk control flow edge targets a chunk beginning or a safe exit.*

P_2*: Within a chunk, there is sufficient instrumentation before unsafe instructions according to a custom IRM, and the instrumentation cannot be bypassed because of intra-chunk control flow.*

With the bitmap, both P_1 and P_2 are local properties that can be checked on a per-chunk basis. If all chunks satisfy P_1 and P_2, the whole module obeys the IRM policy based on the following inductive argument. We assume that the module is initially entered at a chunk beginning. According to P_2, within the initial chunk, any unsafe instruction will be checked by sufficient instrumentation at runtime. When the control transfers outside the chunk, the destination can be only another chunk's beginning or a known safe exit according to P_1. In the former case, the execution in the next chunk obeys the IRM policy because of P_2; in the latter case, the module terminates safely.

Algorithm 1 presents the MIPVerify algorithm, which shows how the two properties are checked. The algorithm takes a module's $code$ and $bitmap$ as input and raises error if the verification fails. $code$ is an array of bytes and $bitmap$ is an array of bits. For ease of presentation, we assume that the code starts at address zero. We use notation $|code|$ for the size of the code and similarly for $|bitmap|$.

The MIPVerify procedure scans the bitmap and identifies chunk boundaries. It then disassembles a chunk to produce an intra-chunk CFG. The intra-chunk CFG is then examined by MIPCheck.

The Disassemble procedure performs two tasks on the chunk with beginning address i and end address j: (1) build an intra-chunk CFG, whose nodes are instructions and edges represent control flow between instructions; (2) check that chunk boundaries are respected by instructions in the chunk. It is a worklist algorithm that performs a recursive-traversal disassembly. It assumes an external procedure decodeOneInstr($code, n$), which performs the decoding of one instruction at address n and raises error if the decoding fails. A few data structures are used in Disassemble: cfg stores a partial CFG, whose nodes are pairs of addresses and instructions that have been decoded and whose edges represent control flow between instructions; $worklist$ contains a list of addresses to be decoded; and $occupied$ is an array for remembering what addresses have been occupied by decoded instructions. The $occupied$ array is used to prevent a direct branch from jumping into the middle of an instruction. At line 19, if the address range of a new instruction overlaps with a previous instruction, an error is raised. Variable $succ$ is used to hold the direct successor addresses of the current instruction. If the instruction is not a control-flow instruction, $succ$ is a singleton set with the fall-through address (that is, n' in the code); if the instruction is a direct branch, $succ$ contains all possible target addresses of the branch (two addresses if it is a conditional jump); if the instruction is an indirect branch, $succ$ is the empty set. For each address in $succ$, at line 23 the code checks whether it is an address in the chunk (intra-chunk control flow) or outside (inter-chunk control flow). For intra-chunk control flow, the edge is added to the CFG; if the destination address has not been processed (checked at line 25) and not in the middle of a previous instruction (checked at line 26), then it is added to the worklist. For

Algorithm 1: MIP's Verification Algorithm

1 **procedure** MIPVerify $(code, bitmap)$
2 **if** $|code| \neq |bitmap|$ **then** raise Error;
3 **foreach** $0 \leq i < |bitmap|$ **do**
4 **if** $bitmap[i] = 1$ **then**
5 $j :=$ the first index after i so that
6 $bitmap[j] = 1$ or $j = |bitmap|$;
7 $cfg := \text{Disassemble}(code, bitmap, i, j)$;
8 $\text{MIPCheck}(cfg)$
9 **procedure** $\text{Disassemble}(code, bitmap, i, j)$
10 $cfg.\text{nodes} := cfg.\text{edges} := \emptyset$;
11 $worklist := \{i\}$;
12 **foreach** $k \in [i..(j-1)]$ **do** $occupied[k] := 0$;
13 **while** $worklist \neq \emptyset$ **do**
14 Remove an address n from $worklist$;
15 $r := \text{decodeOneInstr}(code, n)$;
16 $cfg.\text{nodes} := cfg.\text{nodes} \cup \{(n, r)\}$;
17 $n' := n + \text{size}(r)$
18 **if** $n' > j$ **then** raise Error;
19 **if** $occupied[n..(n'-1)]$ *is not all 0* **then** raise Error;
20 **foreach** $k \in [n..(n'-1)]$ **do** $occupied[k] := 1$;
21 $succ :=$ the set of direct successor addresses for r;
22 **foreach** $s \in succ$ **do**
23 **if** $i \leq s < j$ **then**
24 $cfg.\text{edges} := cfg.\text{edges} \cup \{(n, s)\}$;
25 **if** $s \notin cfg.\text{nodes}$ **then**
26 **if** $occupied[s] = 1$ **then** raise Error
27 **else** $worklist := worklist \cup \{s\}$
28 **else if** $bitmap[s] \neq 1$ *and* $s \notin$ SafeExit **then**
29 raise Error
30 **procedure** $\text{MIPCheck}(cfg)$
31 **foreach** *instr* $r \in cfg.\text{nodes}$ **do**
32 **if** $r \in$ ForbiddenInstr **then** raise Error
33 **else if** $r \in$ IndirectBranch **then**
34 **if** r is not dominated by `CheckDest` on r's destination **then** raise Error
35 $\text{IRMCheck}(cfg)$

inter-chunk control flow, the code checks whether the destination is a chunk beginning or a safe exit (at line 28).

The MIPCheck performs several checks. First, it rules out forbidden instructions. For example, a `ret` instruction should have been translated into a pop followed by an indirect jump, so it is forbidden. Direct system calls through `int` or `syscall` are also forbidden. Second, indirect branch instructions must be preceded by a `CheckDest` instruction so that targets are chunk beginnings. Finally, IRMCheck is invoked to enforce the IRM policy on the chunk.

A few points are worth discussion about the verification. First, it performs modular verification. Each module is verified separately. The modular verification enables MIP to verify DLL libraries during dynamic linking. Second, the intra-chunk CFG for a chunk may not contain all bytes in the chunk. If some bytes are not reachable during recursive traversal, then they must be data and are not reachable during runtime. This is how MIP supports mixed code and read-only data. Finally, the verification trusts neither the code nor the bitmap. If a module's bitmap is modified by an attacker to change the chunk boundaries in a way so that the IRM's policy is violated, then the verification fails. This is because the verification checks that code follows the chunks specified in the bitmap and each chunk is validated in a modular way. In other words, if the attacker-provided code and bitmap pass the verification, then the IRM's policy is guaranteed to hold.

5. IMPLEMENTATION

We next describe MIP's implementation on Linux for x86-32 and x86-64 platforms. We first discuss how `CheckDest` is lowered into machine instructions. We next present MIP's toolchain including the rewriting tool, the verifier, the runtime, and the DLL support.

5.1 Check lowering

Conceptually "`CheckDest Reg`" extracts the bit corresponding to address `Reg` from the bitmap, tests if the bit is one, and jumps to an exit label when the bit is zero. This task can be accomplished by two simple machine instructions:

```
bt Reg, BMBase
jnc exit
```

"`bt Reg, BMBase`" is an x86 instruction called bit test. It selects the bit in a bit string in memory with base `BMBase` at the bit position `Reg` and stores the value of the bit in the CF flag. Recall that `BMBase` is the base address of the in-memory representation of the bitmap. Since this bit-test instruction has a base operand that specifies a memory location, the offset operand in `Reg` can be a 32/64-bit value. Therefore, it extracts the `Reg`-th bit from the bitmap to the CF flag. After that, a simple "`jnc exit`" instruction is used to test the bit and jump to an exit label when the bit is zero. We call this sequence `btm` (bit test on memory).

The `btm` sequence is simple and space efficient, but its execution time varies with different x86 micro-architectures. We tested it on x86 micro-architectures from Intel Core 2 to Nehalem to Sandy-Bridge, the cost ratio of "`bt Reg, BMBase`" to a single-clock-cycle instruction varies between 3 and 8 (after isolating the memory cache effect). Therefore, its execution-time overhead may be a concern for applications with heavy use of indirect branches.

An alternative but longer sequence is presented as follow (with comments after #).

```
mov Reg, SR1       # SR1 = Reg
mov Reg, SR2       # SR2 = Reg
shr $3, SR1        # SR1 = Reg / 8
mov BMBase(SR1), SR1 # SR1 = BMBase[SR1]
and $7, Reg        # Reg = Reg % 8
bt  Reg, SR1       # test whether the bit is one
mov SR2, Reg       # Reg = SR2; restore Reg
jnc exit
```

In the sequence, `SR1` and `SR2` are scratch registers. It moves the byte where the bit is into `SR1` and performs a bit test on `SR1`. Different from the previous sequence, the bit-test instruction operates on a bit string in a register. Therefore we call this sequence `btr` (bit test on register). The `btr` sequence is longer, but its execution time is shorter than `btm` based on our testing. The reason is that the `bt` instruction in `btm` causes the instruction decoder to stall several cycles. In contrast, although `btr` contains multiple instructions, each of them almost never stalls the instruction decoder.

The `btr` sequence requires two scratch registers `SR1` and `SR2`. Our implementation tries to find dead general purpose registers for them. If no general registers are available, we use dead SSE registers instead.[1]

[1]SSE registers are usually used only in specialized vector and multimedia routines, but not elsewhere. In our experiments, we found

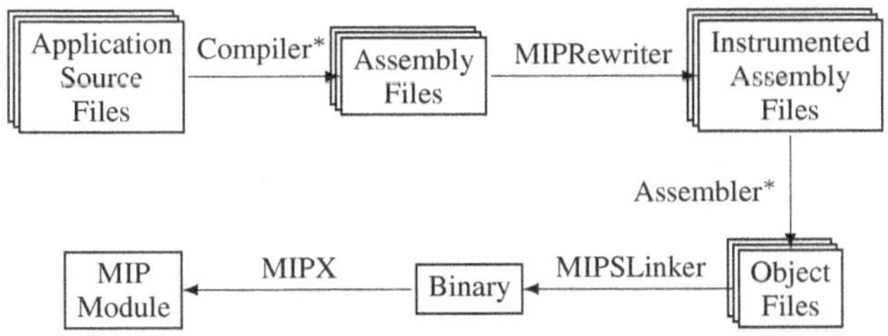

Figure 2: The MIP toolchain for creating a MIP module. Standard Linux tools are marked with *; the rest are MIP added tools.

5.2 MIP toolchain

We have built a MIP toolchain for rewriting and running x86 Linux applications. It operates at assembly level and takes advantage of symbolic information in assembly code for rewriting and for building the chunk table. As a result, it is compatible with any compiler such as GCC.

Fig. 2 visualizes the work flow of MIP's toolchain. Application source code is compiled into assembly code by a compiler such as GCC. The compiler produces meta information including labels and assembly directives that are embedded in assembly files. Afterwards, MIPRewriter performs assembly-level rewriting by extending the assembly code streamer of LLVM-MC, LLVM's assembling and disassembling component. MIPRewriter first transforms the assembly file's content into a stream of instructions, assembly labels and strings. On the stream, multiple rounds of rewriting according to different IRM instrumentation rules can be performed, with MIP's instrumentation being the last round. MIPRewriter provides a general interface for easily adding new IRM instrumentation. After instrumentation, MIPRewriter analyzes the stream for identifying the chunks of different kinds: instruction chunks, basic-block chunks, and leaf-function chunks. After MIPRewriter identifies a chunk, it inserts a unique label (called a MIP label) containing a special name before the first instruction of the chunk. In total, MIPRewriter's implementation includes around 2,800 lines of new C++ code on top of LLVM-MC.

Instrumented assembly files are then assembled by a native Linux assembler such as GNU AS into object files. The MIP labels inserted by MIPRewriter are transformed and stored in the symbol table and string table of the resulting ELF file, which effectively remembers the chunk beginnings.

The assembled object files are then fed to MIPSLinker for object linking. Modified from GNU LD, MIPSLinker emits an instrumented Procedure Linkage Table (PLT) for the symbol name resolution. The PLT contains indirect jumps whose targets depend on the runtime adjustable GOT entries. However, such indirect jumps may potentially violate chunk boundaries and need to be instrumented as well. Therefore, we changed around 60 lines of the LD's PLT entry template to emit instrumented indirect jumps. Note that each PLT entry is also a chunk with a fixed size. Except for this change, MIPSLinker performs exactly the same job as LD.

The binary created in the previous linking step essentially contains the module's chunk table—encoded as MIP labels and stored in the symbol table, string table and PLT section. Such information is extracted by a 120-line Python script MIPX to build the bitmap. Then a MIP module is assembled by composing the binary with the bitmap. We note that the process of creating an application's executable MIP module is the same as the process of creating a library MIP module.

Given an application's executable MIP module, MIPRunner loads the module into memory, invokes MIPVerify for verification, and executes the application. Thanks to the verification step, all the previous steps are outside of the TCB, including compilation, rewriting, assembling, and bitmap extraction. MIPVerify implements the algorithm presented in Section 4.4 and uses LLVM-MC's instruction decoding engine. MIPVerify's implementation has around 1,000 lines of C++ code.

MIPRunner is implemented on top of the NaCl runtime. We changed its application loading procedure so that it not only loads code, but also populates the bitmap. On x86-32, the application's code, data and bitmap stay in different segments from MIPRunner for isolation. On x86-64, MIPRunner allocates the lower 6GB with [4GB, 6GB) unmapped (described in detail in Section 6). In addition, since MIPRunner and application code run in the same address space on x86-64, for isolation MIPRunner unmaps the bitmap pages for its own code. Therefore, on both platforms, the application code is sandboxed and cannot directly jump to the MIPRunner code. In total, around 800 lines of C code were changed or added to the NaCl runtime code base.

The application's system call invocations must be intercepted. For example, if `mprotect` could be called without restriction, the application's code could arbitrarily change its memory protection. For monitoring system calls, we can either adopt an IRM or an external reference monitor. Since the NaCl runtime already provides a set of wrappers for security-sensitive system calls, we reuse that part for monitoring system calls. Therefore, application code is forbidden to invoke any system calls directly through `int` or `syscall` instructions. Instead, the relevant system calls are replaced by MIPRunner's system-call wrappers. For porting existing programs (especially the SPECCPU2006 benchmarks) to MIPRunner, we use a modified version of MUSL[2] standard C library, whose native system call invocation is replaced by MIPRunner's wrapper invocation. The MUSL library is also instrumented using the same IRM instrumentation as the application. Currently, C++ programs are not supported, since we have not ported any C++ libraries yet.

When the application is running, it may dynamically link and load DLLs. For dynamic linking, MIP provides a MIPDLinker, which is implemented by modifying MUSL's dynamic linker (for less than 100 lines of code). Our system could put MIPDLinker into MIPRunner and dynamically intercept `dlopen` and `dlsym` requests from the application. Instead, we put MIPDLinker into the application sandbox so that it is untrusted. The next three steps explain how MIPDLinker itself is loaded and how MIPDLinker loads a DLL library:

1. **Loading**. Before MIPRunner loads any application or library modules, it verifies and loads the dynamic linker MIPDLinker, which is also instrumented by the same IRMs as the application and libraries. Then, MIPRunner transfers control to MIPDLinker to further load other modules. When a module is loaded in memory, its memory pages are not executable.
2. **Linking**. When MIPDLinker finishes loading a module, it links that module with already installed modules that might be running. During the linking process, the already installed modules' code pages remain unchanged because MIPRunner restricts their protection to be not executable but writeable. However, all modules' GOT entries are subject to changes.
3. **Installation**. After linking, MIPDLinker invokes a MIPRunner provided API `InstallCode` for module installation.

that spilling general purpose registers into SSE registers imposed less overhead than spilling them into the stack.

[2]www.musl-libc.org

`InstallCode` first sets the new module code and bitmap to be read-only, forbidding MIPDLinker to further change the content. It then invokes MIPVerify for verifying the code and the bitmap. Once the verification succeeds, MIPRunner changes the protection of the new module's code pages to be executable.

6. MIP-BASED SFI

MIP provides control-flow support for an IRM to guarantee monitor code integrity. We next present a case study in which we implement Software-based Fault Isolation (SFI) on top of MIP. The SFI policy is to restrict control flow within a code region and restrict memory access within a data region. The control-flow part of the SFI policy is already enforced by MIP. Therefore, only memory accesses need to be restricted for the SFI policy. Direct memory accesses can be statically verified; indirect memory accesses should be restricted by dynamic checks. On x86-32, since the CPU supports memory segmentation that isolates memory access at the hardware level, our implementation allocates a data segment for holding application data (similar to NaCl-x86-32). On x86-64, since segmentation is not supported, we apply the following data-sandboxing scheme to control memory writes[3]:

- The sandbox range is [0, 4GB) with an unmapped guard zone [4GB, 6GB). The code and data region both reside in the sandbox with different memory protection.
- The stack pointer, `rsp`, is only used as an address reference register. Instructions changing `rsp` are replaced with equivalent ones changing `esp`. For example, `add $3, %rsp` is replaced by `add $3, %esp`. Because modifying `esp` automatically clears the upper 32 bits in `rsp`, the value of `rsp` is guaranteed to be within [0, 4GB).
- Memory writes to addresses `disp(%rsp)`/`disp(%rip)`, where `disp` is an immediate displacement and `rip` is the program counter, are not checked. The CPU accepts only a 32-bit signed integer displacement with a range of [-2GB, 2GB). Since `rsp` is dynamically restricted to be within [0, 4GB) and `rip` always points to the code region within [0, 4GB), memory references based on such forms could address [0, 6GB)∪[16EB-2GB, 16EB)[4]. This is safe because accesses to [16EB-2GB, 16EB) are trapped as it is used by the Linux kernel; accesses to [4GB, 6GB) are also trapped since it is the unmapped guard zone.
- Other memory writes are instrumented by dynamic checks to ensure the addresses are within [0, 4GB). Take instruction "`mov $3, (%rax)`" as an example. It writes constant 3 to the memory address stored in `rax`. This instruction is changed to "`lea (%rax), %ebx`", followed by "`mov $3, (%rbx)`". It uses `rbx` as a scratch register. The `lea` instruction automatically clearly the upper 32 bits of `rbx`, ensuring the target address is within [0, 4GB). Other memory writes are instrumented in the same way.

With the help of MIP, the SFI implementation is minimal. The implementation adds an SFI rewriting pass (about 200 lines of code) to MIPRewriter and adds an SFI check procedure (also about 200 lines of code) to MIPVerify.

[3]Similar to NaCl-x86-64, our implementation does not confine memory reads since they are considered less harmful than writes; this also enables a straightforward comparison between our SFI implementation and NaCl-x86-64.

[4]16EB = 2^{64}.

7. EVALUATION

We evaluated the space and time efficiency, and the support for separate compilation of MIP and MIP-based SFI. The experiments were conducted on both x86-32 and x86-64 platforms. In SPEC-CPU2006, only C benchmarks were included[5], with nine integer performance testing programs and three floating-point performance testing programs. All programs were compiled with the O3 optimization level. Experiments were performed on a system with 64-bit Ubuntu 12.10, an Intel Core i7-3770 CPU at 3.8 GHz, and 8GB physical memory.

7.1 Chunk granularity

We have discussed three kinds of chunks: instruction chunks, basic-block chunks and leaf-function chunks. We experimented with the three kinds of chunks on benchmark programs and measured the number of chunks in each case. Table 1 lists the numbers.

As seen in the table, the number of basic-block chunks is about an order of magnitude less than the number of instruction chunks, because a basic block contains multiple instructions. The number in the case of leaf-function chunks is less than the case of basic-block chunks, but the difference is small. As discussed before, a non-leaf function still needs to be split into basic blocks because of return targets in the middle of the function. Therefore, the number of basic blocks dominates the number of chunks even in the leaf-function chunk case. Nevertheless, there are still many leaf functions in a typical program. Table 1 includes columns that present the percentage of leaf functions among functions.

The coarse-grained CFI enforced by MIP is good for security because it disallows ROP gadgets that start in the middle of a chunk. We experimented with a ROP gadget finding tool called ROPgadget[6] to search for gadgets in benchmark programs. Table 2 lists the unique gadgets found in original and MIP-instrumented benchmarks (with the `btm` instrumentation) for the case of instruction chunks. In MIP instrumented programs, although ROPgadget can still find gadgets, none of them can be exploited, because they all start in the middle of instruction chunks. This rather surprising finding suggests even extremely coarse-grained CFI can significantly limit ROP attacks. Nevertheless, we believe basic-block and leaf-function chunks provide better security because any single gadget-finding tool cannot claim completeness and other kinds of attacks may be possible within the limit of a CFG.

Basic block and leaf-function chunks also lead to sparser bitmaps. Although our implementation does not take advantage of this, a MIP module could have a compressed bitmap, which could decrease the binary size. Experiments showed that basic-block/leaf-function chunk bitmaps have a compression ratio (by `gzip`) of about 80% while the instruction-chunk bitmaps have around only 40%.

Since our implementation uses uncompressed bitmaps, the space overhead and execution-time overhead of a program running under MIP are independent of which kind of chunks is used. For a given program and a given data set, the same execution path will be executed no matter which bitmap is used (assuming no control-flow violation happens during runtime). Consequently, the same instru-

[5]MIP's basic idea of using variable-sized chunks to restrict indirect branches clearly applies to C++ code. However, a code-sandboxing framework needs a system-call interposition mechanism to prevent/restrict dangerous system calls such as `mprotect`. Our system implements user-space system-call interposition, which replaces libraries' system calls by their wrappers. Therefore, the only part in our implementation that does not support C++ is the library support, as discussed in Sec 5.2.

[6]http://shell-storm.org/project/ROPgadget/

SPECCPU2006	x86-32 Instruction chunks	x86-32 Basic-block chunks	x86-32 Leaf func chunks	x86-32 Leaf function proportion	x86-64 Instruction chunks	x86-64 Basic-block chunks	x86-64 Leaf-func chunks	x86-64 Leaf function proportion
400.perlbench	251256	43732	43574	8.0%	237917	43974	43787	10.8%
401.bzip2	16936	1697	1684	14.5%	15352	1670	1657	14.5%
403.gcc	726919	125363	123599	10.3%	653678	122879	121248	11.9%
429.mcf	2898	435	353	41.7%	2567	436	351	41.7%
445.gobmk	197921	29310	28987	6.6%	188784	28828	28527	9.6%
456.hmmer	69328	10120	9808	15.9%	63757	10055	9736	16.3%
458.sjeng	26454	3984	3728	34.3%	24863	3964	3705	36.6%
462.libquantum	9359	1098	1082	18.9%	7927	1075	1061	18.9%
464.h264ref	197092	14976	13135	24.3%	177489	14992	12969	24.9%
433.milc*	38276	4998	4916	32.1%	32748	5138	5060	31.7%
470.lbm*	2263	166	119	23.5%	1901	165	119	23.5%
482.sphinx3*	41532	6333	6062	20.0%	38055	6305	6042	21.3%

Table 1: Numbers of chunks in SPECCPU2006 benchmarks. Floating-point benchmarks are marked by *.

SPECCPU2006	Original	After MIP	Exploitable
400.perlbench	242	148	0
401.bzip2	73	53	0
403.gcc	415	285	0
429.mcf	73	36	0
445.gobmk	195	119	0
456.hmmer	124	83	0
458.sjeng	106	73	0
462.libquantum	77	50	0
464.h264ref	169	107	0
433.milc*	103	67	0
470.lbm*	68	38	0
482.sphinx3*	123	80	0

Table 2: ROP gadgets removal by MIP on x86-32 benchmarks.

SPECCPU2006	MIP/SFI-32 btm	MIP/SFI-32 btr	MIP-64 btm	MIP-64 btr	SFI-64 btm	SFI-64 btr
400.perlbench	14.2	18.9	13.7	16.5	15.5	18.4
401.bzip2	13.3	15.4	13.6	15.1	19.6	21.1
403.gcc	13.0	16.9	12.0	14.5	13.1	15.6
429.mcf	15.4	20.9	15.4	19.7	21.7	26.0
445.gobmk	3.9	5.8	3.7	4.9	4.0	5.1
456.hmmer	13.8	17.8	13.7	16.3	16.2	18.7
458.sjeng	11.9	14.7	12.1	14.3	14.0	16.2
462.libquantum	15.3	20.7	15.9	20.1	17.2	21.1
464.h264ref	12.8	14.2	12.9	13.8	16.5	17.5
433.milc*	13.6	17.0	13.7	16.2	15.5	18.0
470.lbm*	12.8	15.8	13.3	14.6	15.9	18.0
482.sphinx3*	13.1	17.1	13.0	16.4	14.8	17.4
GM	12.7	16.2	12.7	15.1	15.1	17.7

Table 3: Static binary-size increase by MIP and MIP-based SFI in percentage (%).

mentation code is run and the same bits are retrieved. We tested all three kinds of chunks and confirmed that the results were similar. Therefore, in the following sections, we report overhead numbers only for the case of instruction chunks.

7.2 Space overhead

In general, MIP's space overhead is caused by the bitmap and also the instrumentation code inserted before indirect branches and unsafe instructions. For each benchmark program, we measured its space overhead in terms of both the static binary-size increase and the impact on dynamic memory footprint.

Table 3 presents the static binary-size increase for MIP and MIP-based SFI. It presents the cases for both sequences of bit tests discussed in Sec. 5.1: `btm` and `btr`. On x86-32, since MIP-based SFI uses hardware segmentation to constrain memory access, the SFI instrumentation is the same as the MIP instrumentation. Therefore, we use a single column in the table for MIP and MIP-based SFI-32. The MIP-64 column shows the overhead of MIP on x86-64, and the SFI-64 column shows the overhead of MIP-based SFI on x86-64. The GM row shows the geometric mean of columns.

The table shows that on x86-32 and x86-64 MIP incurs an average of around 13% and 16% binary-size increase, using `btm` and `btr`, respectively. Most binary-size increase is caused by the size of the bitmap (about 11%). The `btr` sequence adds an extra 2-5% increase than `btm`. Furthermore, the SFI-64 instrumentation increases the size for about 3% because of memory-write sandboxing. Thanks to variable-sized chunks, MIP's binary-size increase is much smaller than previous SFI systems. For instance, the binary-size increase of NaCl-x86-64 [17] is roughly 60%. We measured NaCl-x86-32's binary-size increase on SPECCPU2006 programs and its increase is also around 60%. PittSFIeld [14], another SFI system, has a binary-size increase of around 75% on SPECCPU2000 programs. Compared to CCFIR [25] and binCFI [26], MIP's binary-size increase is less: CCFIR incurs around 33% due to the inserted code and the springboard section; binCFI imposes around 139% due to the instrumentation, its address translation map, and a copy of the original code.

We also measured the impact of MIP on the memory footprint. The memory-footprint increase for the benchmark programs was negligible. The majority of physical memory used by a running program is occupied by its runtime data. MIP adds a bitmap, whose physical-memory size is one eighth of the code, and causes slight increase to the code region. As a result, it has a negligible impact on the memory footprint.

7.3 Execution-time overhead

Table 4 lists the execution-time overhead for MIP and MIP-based SFI. The GM (INT) row computes the geometric mean of all integer benchmarks, and the GM (ALL) row computes the geometric mean of integer and floating-point benchmarks.

MIP's performance overhead is around 5% for the `btr` sequence. It is lower than a typical fine-grained CFI implementation: the classic CFI [1] reports 15% and an improved implementation reports around 6–8% [23]. CCFIR [25] also enforces coarse-grained CFI. Its performance overhead on SPECCPU2006 programs is around 4.2%; however, CCFIR optimizes its treatment of return instructions (using a stack-based "ret" rather than a register based jump) in a way that improves performance but is unsafe under MIP's attacker model, because return addresses suffer from a time-of-check-to-time-of-use race condition. As another coarse-grained CFI instrumentation technique, binCFI [26] imposes around 4.3% overhead on SPECCPU2000 C benchmarks, comparable to MIP.

On top of MIP, SFI-64 data sandboxing adds only 1–2% more execution-time overhead. The reason is twofold: first, the memory-write sandboxing instruction `lea` is lightweight; second, many memory writes do not need to be instrumented because the targets are computed by adding a constant to `rip` or `rsp` (discussed in Section 6). In comparison, NaCl-x86-64 has an overhead of 14.7% on SPECCPU2000 programs. NaCl-x86-32 has an average overhead of 5%. Therefore, our SFI implementation achieves competitive performance, and a much less space overhead than previous SFI systems.

In general, the `btr` sequence incurs less execution-time overhead than `btm`. We did further micro-benchmark analysis, which showed that the `btr` sequence stalls the instruction decoder less, and therefore enables more instruction-level parallelism. When combining the results of space and execution-time increase, we can see that `btr` is more time efficient, at the expense of extra binary-size increase.

Some benchmarks in the table have much higher performance overheads than others. Further experiments showed that the performance overhead correlates with the frequency of indirect branches. For example, `perlbench`, a Perl script interpreter, has high overhead because its implementation first translates Perl scripts into its internally defined instructions and then interprets an instruction by executing its corresponding function through an indirect call. Therefore indirect calls and returns are executed frequently. In contrast, `bzip2`'s computation mostly executes arithmetic instructions for compression; its overhead is low. Some benchmarks report slight performance improvement, possibly because of alignment benefits after instrumentation.

We note that the performance numbers are for the case of statically linking benchmark programs with the MUSL library, which was rewritten with the same instrumentation. Further, we used MIPDLinker to dynamically load and link the benchmark programs and the MUSL library, and we found that the execution-time overhead was almost the same as the case of static linking.

We also measured the MIPVerify's SFI verification time of all SPEC programs. On average, MIPVerify can verify 10-megabyte code per second. The instruction decoding engine of LLVM-MC consumes about 60% of the verification time.

SPECCPU2006	MIP/SFI-32		MIP-64		SFI-64	
	`btm`	`btr`	`btm`	`btr`	`btm`	`btr`
400.perlbench	27.4	17.4	26.3	15.0	31.3	14.9
401.bzip2	-0.1	-0.1	1.2	1.5	4.6	4.6
403.gcc	6.1	4.8	11.7	7.5	14.5	8.9
429.mcf	1.0	0.5	-2.2	-1.0	0.3	-1.4
445.gobmk	11.8	11.4	13.3	11.1	14.2	13.2
456.hmmer	0.0	-0.3	0.2	0.0	4.6	4.0
458.sjeng	11.1	9.7	12.3	7.8	7.8	7.6
462.libquantum	1.1	-0.2	-0.1	-2.3	-0.7	-1.4
464.h264ref	11.7	7.3	25.5	16.0	24.6	14.7
433.milc*	2.5	1.4	1.5	0.4	1.7	0.4
470.lbm*	0.6	0.6	0.0	0.2	1.0	1.0
482.sphinx3*	2.3	0.4	1.9	0.2	2.4	-0.2
GM (ALL)	6.0	4.2	7.2	4.5	8.9	5.3
GM (INT)	7.4	5.4	9.3	6.0	11.3	7.1

Table 4: Execution-time overhead imposed by MIP/SFI in percentage (%).

8. CONCLUSIONS AND FUTURE WORK

This paper proposes MIP, an efficient instrumentation technique for monitor code integrity in low-level IRMs. To achieve this, MIP partitions the code into variable-sized chunks, maintains a bitmap for recording chunk beginnings, and instruments indirect branches so that they target chunk beginnings. Compared to other forms of CFI, MIP's coarse-grained CFI is sufficient for monitor code integrity, causes low space overhead, and requires only small changes to a compiler toolchain to support separate compilation. We believe MIP provides an IRM designer a sweet spot that combines efficiency, security, and convenience of reusing instrumented libraries.

As future work, we plan to extend MIP to support dynamically generated code, common in modern language interpreters such as JavaScript interpreters. When code is dynamically generated, the bitmap needs to be extended, similar to the case of DLLs.

Acknowledgments

We thank Stephen McCamant and anonymous reviewers for their valuable comments. This research is supported by US NSF grants CCF-0915157, CCF-1149211, CCF-1217710, and two research awards from Google.

9. REFERENCES

[1] ABADI, M., BUDIU, M., ERLINGSSON, Ú., AND LIGATTI, J. Control-flow integrity. In *12th ACM Conference on Computer and Communications Security (CCS)* (2005), pp. 340–353.

[2] AKRITIDIS, P., CADAR, C., RAICIU, C., COSTA, M., AND CASTRO, M. Preventing memory error exploits with WIT. In *IEEE Symposium on Security and Privacy (S&P)* (2008), pp. 263–277.

[3] AKRITIDIS, P., COSTA, M., CASTRO, M., AND HAND, S. Baggy bounds checking: An efficient and backwards-compatible defense against out-of-bounds errors. In *18th Usenix Security Symposium* (2009), pp. 51–66.

[4] ANSEL, J., MARCHENKO, P., ERLINGSSON, Ú., TAYLOR, E., CHEN, B., SCHUFF, D., SEHR, D., BIFFLE, C., AND YEE, B. Language-independent sandboxing of just-in-time compilation and self-modifying code. In *ACM Conference on Programming Language Design and Implementation (PLDI)* (2011), pp. 355–366.

[5] CASTRO, M., COSTA, M., AND HARRIS, T. Securing software by enforcing data-flow integrity. In *USENIX Symposium on Operating Systems Design and Implementation (OSDI)* (2006), pp. 147–160.

[6] CASTRO, M., COSTA, M., MARTIN, J.-P., PEINADO, M., AKRITIDIS, P., DONNELLY, A., BARHAM, P., AND BLACK, R. Fast byte-granularity software fault isolation. In

ACM SIGOPS Symposium on Operating Systems Principles (SOSP) (2009), pp. 45–58.

[7] DAVI, L., DMITRIENKO, R., EGELE, M., FISCHER, T., HOLZ, T., HUND, R., NURNBERGER, S., AND SADEGHI, A.-R. Mocfi: A framework to mitigate control-flow attacks on smartphones. In *Network and Distributed System Security Symposium(NDSS)* (2012).

[8] ERLINGSSON, Ú., ABADI, M., VRABLE, M., BUDIU, M., AND NECULA, G. XFI: Software guards for system address spaces. In *USENIX Symposium on Operating Systems Design and Implementation (OSDI)* (2006), pp. 75–88.

[9] ERLINGSSON, Ú., AND SCHNEIDER, F. SASI enforcement of security policies: A retrospective. In *Proceedings of the New Security Paradigms Workshop (NSPW)* (1999), ACM Press, pp. 87–95.

[10] ERLINGSSON, Ú., AND SCHNEIDER, F. IRM enforcement of Java stack inspection. In *IEEE Symposium on Security and Privacy (S&P)* (2000), pp. 246–255.

[11] EVANS, D., AND TWYMAN, A. Flexible policy-directed code safety. In *IEEE Symposium on Security and Privacy (S&P)* (1999), pp. 32–45.

[12] JIM, KHALYAVIN, A., MCCUTCHAN, J., AND CHEN, B. Some thoughts on NaCl binary size. Sent to the Native Client mailing list. URL: `https://groups.google.com/forum/#!topic/native-client-discuss/M9Jv5uCS3BA`, Aug. 2012.

[13] KIRIANSKY, V., BRUENING, D., AND AMARASINGHE, S. Secure execution via program shepherding. In *11th Usenix Security Symposium* (2002), pp. 191–206.

[14] MCCAMANT, S., AND MORRISETT, G. Evaluating SFI for a CISC architecture. In *15th Usenix Security Symposium* (2006).

[15] SCHWARZ, B., DEBRAY, S., AND ANDREWS, G. Disassembly of executable code revisited. In *In Proc. IEEE 2002 Working Conference on Reverse Engineering (WCRE* (2002), IEEE Computer Society, pp. 45–54.

[16] SCOTT, K., AND DAVIDSON, J. Safe virtual execution using software dynamic translation. In *Proceedings of the 18th Annual Computer Security Applications Conference* (2002), ACSAC '02, pp. 209–218.

[17] SEHR, D., MUTH, R., BIFFLE, C., KHIMENKO, V., PASKO, E., SCHIMPF, K., YEE, B., AND CHEN, B. Adapting software fault isolation to contemporary CPU architectures. In *19th Usenix Security Symposium* (2010), pp. 1–12.

[18] SHACHAM, H. The geometry of innocent flesh on the bone: return-into-libc without function calls (on the x86). In *14th ACM Conference on Computer and Communications Security (CCS)* (2007), pp. 552–561.

[19] SMALL, C., AND SELTZER, M. A tool for constructing safe extensible C++ systems. In *Proceedings of the Third Usenix Conference on Object-Oriented Technologies* (1997), pp. 13–23.

[20] WAHBE, R., LUCCO, S., ANDERSON, T., AND GRAHAM, S. Efficient software-based fault isolation. In *ACM SIGOPS Symposium on Operating Systems Principles (SOSP)* (New York, 1993), ACM Press, pp. 203–216.

[21] WANG, Z., AND JIANG, X. Hypersafe: A lightweight approach to provide lifetime hypervisor control-flow integrity. In *IEEE Symposium on Security and Privacy (S&P)* (2010), pp. 380–395.

[22] YEE, B., SEHR, D., DARDYK, G., CHEN, B., MUTH, R., ORMANDY, T., OKASAKA, S., NARULA, N., AND FULLAGAR, N. Native client: A sandbox for portable, untrusted x86 native code. In *IEEE Symposium on Security and Privacy (S&P)* (May 2009).

[23] ZENG, B., TAN, G., AND ERLINGSSON, Ú. Strato: A retargetable framework for low-level inlined-reference monitors. In *22nd Usenix Security Symposium* (2013).

[24] ZENG, B., TAN, G., AND MORRISETT, G. Combining control-flow integrity and static analysis for efficient and validated data sandboxing. In *18th ACM Conference on Computer and Communications Security (CCS)* (2011), pp. 29–40.

[25] ZHANG, C., WEI, T., CHEN, Z., DUAN, L., SZEKERES, L., MCCAMANT, S., SONG, D., AND ZOU, W. Practical control flow integrity and randomization for binary executables. *2013 IEEE Symposium on Security and Privacy 0* (2013), 559–573.

[26] ZHANG, M., AND SEKAR, R. Control flow integrity for COTS binaries. In *22nd Usenix Security Symposium* (2013).

Relational Abstract Interpretation for the Verification of 2-Hypersafety Properties

Máté Kovács
Technische Universität München, Germany
kovacsm@in.tum.de

Helmut Seidl
Technische Universität München, Germany
seidl@in.tum.de

Bernd Finkbeiner
Universität des Saarlandes, Germany
finkbeiner@cs.uni-sb.de

ABSTRACT

Information flow properties of programs can be formalized as *hyperproperties* specifying the relation of multiple executions. In this paper, we therefore introduce a framework for proving 2-hypersafety properties by means of abstract interpretation. The main idea is to apply abstract interpretation on the self-compositions of the control flow graphs of programs. As a result, our method is inherently capable of analyzing relational properties of even dissimilar programs.

Constructing self-compositions of control flow graphs is nontrivial. Therefore, we present an algorithm for constructing quality self-compositions driven by a tree distance measure between the abstract syntax trees of subprograms. Finally, we demonstrate the applicability of the approach by proving intricate information flow properties of programs written in a simple language for tree manipulation motivated by the Web Services Business Process Execution Language.

Categories and Subject Descriptors

F.3.1 [**Logics and Meanings of Programs**]: Specifying and Verifying and Reasoning about Programs—*Mechanical verification*

Keywords

abstract interpretation; hyperproperties; information flow control; semi-structured data

1. INTRODUCTION

Abstract interpretation [12] is a well established approach for proving safety properties of programs. However, an interesting class of properties, namely information flow properties, are best formalized not as safety properties, but as *safety hyperproperties* [10]. Safety hyperproperties are not invariants maintained by individual runs of systems but are properties of multiple runs.

In [10] it has been observed that the verification of k-hypersafety properties can be reduced to the verification of ordinary safety properties of the k-fold self-composition of the program. In this paper we apply this idea to control flow graphs (CFG), and present a method for proving 2-hypersafety properties. We apply the general approach for proving noninterference of programs written in an XML manipulating language.

CCS'13, November 4–8, 2013, Berlin, Germany.

ACM 978-1-4503-2477-9/13/11 ...$15.00.
http://dx.doi.org/10.1145/2508859.2516721.

Listing 1: A BPEL fragment updating the health status of patients based on the variable test

```
<if name="If">
 <condition> <![CDATA[$test < 0.5]]>
 </condition>
  <assign name="EvalGood">
   <copy> <from>"good"</from>
    <to> $pList/patientRecord[id=$patientId]
              /health/text()
    </to> </copy>
  </assign>
 <else>
  <assign name="EvalPoor">
   <copy> <from>"poor"</from>
    <to> $pList/patientRecord[id=$patientId]
              /health/text()
    </to> </copy>
  </assign>
 </else>
</if>
```

Noninterference means that two executions are indistinguishable based on public observations if their initial states only differ in secret data [19]. Consider, e.g., the code fragment in Listing 1 written in the Web Services Business Process Execution Language [3] (BPEL). The fragment is meant to update the health status of patients stored in the data structure of variable `pList`. The actual patient is identified by the value in the variable `patientId`, while the update depends on the value of `test`. Our goal is to prove that the value of `test` only interferes with the health status in the description of the patient, but neither with his name nor with the size of the data structure etc. It is challenging, because data manipulation is carried out in different branches depending on the secret. By comparing two executions corresponding to the two branches, we notice, however, that only the health status of the patient with the given id can be different in the results, while all public data remain equal. In this paper we show a method to prove properties like this automatically using static analysis.

We regard the execution of a program as the sequence of assignments and condition evaluations that take place during the computation. We take advantage of the fact that inserting `skip` instructions into arbitrary places of an execution does not change the result. Therefore, different *alignments* of a pair of executions can be achieved by the insertion of `skip` instructions. Knowing an initial abstract value describing the potential set of pairs of initial states, we are interested in computing the final abstract value describing the possible set of pairs of states that can result from any pairs of executions. For that we require a relational abstract domain describing *pairs* of concrete states, together with abstract transformers for *pairs* of instructions set in alignment within the two executions. The abstract effect of a given pair of executions w.r.t. a fixed alignment of instructions is obtained by applying the composition of the occurring transformers to the initial abstract value. Since the abstract effect of any alignment results in a safe over-approximation of the desired outcome, we can approximate it by the greatest lower bound over all alignments. In order to obtain a safe approximation for all pairs of executions reaching a given pair of program points, we then take the least upper bound of the values provided for each pair of executions individually. We refer to this value as the *merge over all twin computations* (MTC) solution, and consider it as the ideal solution of the analysis problem.

In general, it might be difficult to compute the MTC solution directly. Instead, we propose to select one promising static alignment of instructions for each pair of executions resulting in a *self-composition* of the CFG of the program. Here, the key problem is to find decent self-compositions of CFGs, which is nontrivial. Therefore, we present an algorithm to construct them recursively based on the abstract syntax trees of programs. In order to achieve maximal precision, the structural similarities of two subprograms are taken into account using a tree distance measure during the construction. Once a particular self-composition of the CFG is ready, an over-approximation of the MTC solution is obtained as a solution to a constraint system formulated based on the self-composition.

Our goal is to apply the general approach described above to verify the security of web service orchestrations implemented e.g., in BPEL. Web service orchestrations may implement workflows within organizations having access to sensitive data, while communicating with external partners over the Internet. Therefore, the security of these processes and the information they maintain should be granted. On the other hand, the central concept of the web service technologies is that data is stored in XML documents. Accordingly, the BPEL language is optimized for XML manipulation using XPath [8] expressions and XSLT [22] transformations. The extra challenge here is that information flow policies may not only refer to values of variables but to parts of the documents stored in variables too. Accordingly, information flow policies are composed in terms of public views of document trees specifying the potential positions of secrets. Therefore, we introduce an abstract domain based on regular sets of public views of documents together with abstract transformers modeling operations on document trees using Horn clauses. During the analysis implications are generated to specify the relations of abstract values corresponding to the nodes of the self-composition of the CFG. These implications fall into a special category, which can be solved e.g., using $\mathcal{H}_1$-normalization [31,37].

In order to simplify the presentation and concentrate on the key issues of information flow, we restricted ourselves to a minimalistic "assembly" language for tree manipulation.

To summarize, this paper has the following contributions:

- We introduce the ideal solution of the analysis problem of pairs of executions of a program, and propose to overapproximate it by applying abstract interpretation on a particular self-composition of the corresponding CFG.
- A concrete algorithm for the construction of self-compositions of CFGs is proposed, which is driven by a tree distance measure in order to take into account the similarities of subprograms.
- We demonstrate the applicability of the general framework using a complex abstract domain for semi-structured data. Based on the self-composition, a translation is proposed into Horn clauses, which can be solved, e.g., by means of $\mathcal{H}_1$-normalization [31,37].
- The approach is evaluated on case studies found in the literature [2,5,16].

The rest of the paper is structured as follows. In Section 2 the theoretical framework is elaborated. In Section 3 we show a method to construct the necessary self-compositions of CFGs based on structured programs, while in Section 4 we instantiate our approach for the case of a tree-manipulating programming language. In Section 5 we validate the presented analysis using practical experiments on case studies found in the literature. In Section 6 we relate our work to others, and in Section 7 we conclude.

2. MERGE OVER ALL TWIN COMPUTATIONS

In this section we establish the formal groundwork for proving 2-hypersafety properties using relational abstract interpretation.

We define the semantics of programs by means of control-flow graphs (CFG). A CFG is a tuple $G = (N, E, n_{in}, n_{fi})$ consisting of a set of nodes N including the unique initial and final nodes n_{in} and n_{fi}, and a set of directed and labeled edges E. Members of the set E are of the form (n_1, f, n_2), where the nodes n_1 and n_2 are the initial and final nodes of the edge and the label is f. Labels f of edges represent state transformers $[\![f]\!] : S \nrightarrow S$, i.e., partial mappings on the set of states S. We presume the existence of a special label `skip` with $[\![\texttt{skip}]\!]s = s$ for all $s \in S$. A run or execution of a program is defined by a path from the initial node to the final node. The effect of the sequence of labels $\pi = f_1...f_n$ of edges in a run is given by the composition of the effects of the individual labels: $[\![\pi]\!]s_0 = [\![f_1...f_n]\!]s_0 = [\![f_n]\!] \circ ... \circ [\![f_1]\!]s_0$. In the rest, we denote the set of sequences of labels of paths from node n_1 to node n_2 by $n_1 \rightsquigarrow n_2$.

Properties we aim to verify in this paper are defined below:

DEFINITION 1. *We define a 2-hypersafety property by an initial and a final relation of program states $\rho_{in}, \rho_{fi} \subseteq S \times S$. A program given by CFG $G = (N, E, n_{in}, n_{fi})$ satisfies the 2-hypersafety property specified by ρ_{in} and ρ_{fi}, if for all pairs of initial states $(s_0, t_0) \in \rho_{in}$ and all pairs of final states $s = [\![\pi_1]\!]s_0$ and $t = [\![\pi_2]\!]t_0$ reachable by arbitrary computations $\pi_1, \pi_2 \in n_{in} \rightsquigarrow n_{fi}$, it holds that $(s, t) \in \rho_{fi}$.*

When applying abstract interpretation to this problem, we may choose a *Cartesian* abstraction of pairs of states. This means that each program state in the pairs is abstracted separately. Let us briefly argue why this approach may often return unsatisfactory results. Consider, e.g., the program `p =if h>5 then l:=l+2 else l:=l+2`, with integer variables `h` and `l`. Assume that ρ_{in} and ρ_{fi} consist of all pairs of states where the values of variable `l` are equal. Since the precise initial values for `l` are unknown, the final values for `l` will also be unknown, implying that their equality cannot be inferred. Therefore, better results can be obtained by using a *relational* abstraction of pairs of program states. A relational abstraction of pairs of program states may record the fact that the variables `l` in the two program states tracked in parallel are equal, and that this equality is preserved by all possible pairs of program executions.

In general, let $(\mathbb{D}, \sqsubseteq)$ be a complete lattice forming a Galois connection $(\mathcal{P}(S\times S), \alpha, \gamma, \mathbb{D})$ with the powerset of pairs of states $\mathcal{P}(S \times S)$, where $\alpha : \mathcal{P}(S \times S) \to \mathbb{D}$ is an abstraction function and $\gamma : \mathbb{D} \to \mathcal{P}(S \times S)$ is a concretization function. The only requirement for abstract transformers $[\![f, g]\!]^\sharp$ of pairs of labels (f, g) (otherwise called *twin steps*) is that they must satisfy the following property:

$$\gamma([\![f,g]\!]^\sharp d) \supseteq \{ (s',t') \mid \exists (s,t) \in \gamma(d) : [\![f]\!]s = s' \wedge [\![g]\!]t = t' \} \tag{1}$$

Given two sequences[1], π_1 and π_2, the set of all possible *alignments* $A(\pi_1, \pi_2)$ is recursively defined by:

$$\begin{array}{lcl} A(\varepsilon,\varepsilon) & = & \varepsilon \cup \{(\mathtt{skip},\mathtt{skip})\omega \mid \omega \in A(\varepsilon,\varepsilon)\} \\ A(\varepsilon, g\pi) & = & \{(\mathtt{skip}, g)\omega \mid \omega \in A(\varepsilon,\pi)\} \cup \\ & & \{(\mathtt{skip},\mathtt{skip})\omega \mid \omega \in A(\varepsilon, g\pi)\} \\ A(f\pi,\varepsilon) & = & \{(f,\mathtt{skip})\omega \mid \omega \in A(\pi,\varepsilon)\} \cup \\ & & \{(\mathtt{skip},\mathtt{skip})\omega \mid \omega \in A(f\pi,\varepsilon)\} \\ A(f\pi_1, g\pi_2) & = & \{(f,g)\omega \mid \omega \in A(\pi_1,\pi_2)\} \cup \\ & & \{(\mathtt{skip},g)\omega \mid \omega \in A(f\pi_1,\pi_2)\} \cup \\ & & \{(f,\mathtt{skip})\omega \mid \omega \in A(\pi_1,g\pi_2)\} \cup \\ & & \{(\mathtt{skip},\mathtt{skip})\omega \mid \omega \in A(f\pi_1,g\pi_2)\} \end{array} \tag{2}$$

According to (2), an alignment of two sequences of labels of a CFG, π_1 and π_2, is a sequence of twin steps ω representing both of the original runs. The insertion of `skip` labels does not change the result of a run. Therefore, if $[\![\pi_1]\!]s_0 = s$, $[\![\pi_2]\!]t_0 = t$, $\omega \in A(\pi_1, \pi_2)$ and $\omega = (f_1, g_1)...(f_n, g_n)$, then we can write that $(s,t) = [\![\omega]\!](s_0, t_0) = [\![(f_1, g_1)... (f_n, g_n)]\!](s_0, t_0) = [\![f_n, g_n]\!] \circ ... \circ [\![f_1, g_1]\!](s_0, t_0)$, where for each i, $(s_i, t_i) = [\![f_i, g_i]\!](s_{i-1}, t_{i-1})$ if $s_i = [\![f_i]\!]s_{i-1}$ and $t_i = [\![g_i]\!]t_{i-1}$ so that $s = s_n$ and $t = t_n$.

Given two runs π_1, π_2 and an abstract value d_0, we are interested in the most precise abstract value d that can be computed using the abstract semantics of twin steps:

$$d = \bigsqcap_{\omega \in A(\pi_1,\pi_2)} [\![\omega]\!]^\sharp d_0$$

Since there can be multiple pairs of paths executed on the members of the concretization of an initial abstract value, we obtain a sound overapproximation for the abstract value at any pair of nodes by computing the least upper bound of the abstract effects for all possible pairs of paths of the CFG reaching these nodes.

[1]In this paper we apply the alignment construction to sequences of labels of CFGs, and in later sections to programs, i.e., sequences of commands as well.

DEFINITION 2. *Given a CFG $G = (N, E, n_{in}, n_{fi})$ and the initial abstract value d_0, the* merge over all twin computations solution *is defined by:*

$$MTC(G, d_0) = \bigsqcup_{\substack{\pi_1 \in n_{in} \rightsquigarrow n_{fi} \\ \pi_2 \in n_{in} \rightsquigarrow n_{fi}}} \bigsqcap_{\omega \in A(\pi_1,\pi_2)} [\![\omega]\!]^\sharp d_0$$

The MTC solution can be considered as the extension of the *meet over all paths* (MOP) solution of Kam and Ullman [21] to pairs of paths on the CFG.

THEOREM 1. *Consider a pair of sequences of labels $\pi_1, \pi_2 \in n_{in} \rightsquigarrow n_{fi}$ on the CFG $G = (N, E, n_{in}, n_{fi})$, and states $s_0, s, t_0, t \in S$, where $s = [\![\pi_1]\!]s_0$, $t = [\![\pi_2]\!]t_0$ and $(s_0, t_0) \in \gamma(d_0)$. In this case $d \sqsupseteq MTC(G, d_0)$ implies $(s, t) \in \gamma(d)$.*

The proof can be found in [23].

According to Theorem 1, the MTC solution is an abstraction of all possible pairs of states resulting from any pair of executions of the program. This result can be used to infer how relations of initial states are translated into relations of final states and thus prove 2-hypersafety properties. In general it might be difficult, though, to compute the MTC solution directly. A perhaps less precise, but still sound solution is obtained by restricting the set of alignments $A(\pi_1, \pi_2)$ for which the greatest lower bound is computed in the MTC solution. In particular, we may even fix a single alignment for each pair of paths. Such a fixed alignment can be obtained by constructing a self-composition GG of the CFG G. For later use, we define more generally, when is a graph a composition of two CFGs.

DEFINITION 3. *Given the CFGs $G = (N^G, E^G, n^G_{in}, n^G_{fi})$ and $H = (N^H, E^H, n^H_{in}, n^H_{fi})$, $GH = (N', E', n'_{in}, n'_{fi})$ is a composition of G and H, if each edge in E' has a label (f, g) where f and g are labels of G and H, respectively, or* `skip`, *and furthermore for all $\pi_G \in n^G_{in} \rightsquigarrow n^G_{fi}$ and $\pi_H \in n^H_{in} \rightsquigarrow n^H_{fi}$ there is an $\omega_{\pi_G,\pi_H} \in n'_{in} \rightsquigarrow n'_{fi}$ so that $\omega_{\pi_G,\pi_H} \in A(\pi_G, \pi_H)$.*

According to Definition 3, a CFG GG is considered to be a self-composition of G, if for all pairs of paths on G there is a path on GG so that the latter is an alignment of the former two paths. Note that due to the insertion of `skip` operations, a self-composition may be quite different from the Cartesian product of the two graphs, where every two aligned paths have exactly the same length.

THEOREM 2. *Given the CFG $G = (N, E, n_{in}, n_{fi})$ and a self-composition of it $GG = (N', E', n'_{in}, n'_{fi})$, the following holds for all d_0:*

$$\bigsqcup_{\omega \in n'_{in} \rightsquigarrow n'_{fi}} [\![\omega]\!]^\sharp d_0 \sqsupseteq MTC(G, d_0)$$

For the proof, please, refer to [23].

By Theorem 2, any solution of the analysis problem [21] corresponding to the self composition GG of G is a safe overapproximation of $\text{MTC}(G, d_0)$.

Proving a 2-hypersafety property by means of our methods succeeds in two steps. First, a self-composition GG of the CFG is constructed. The graph GG gives rise to a constraint system over a suitable relational abstract domain, which describes how relations of states are transformed by pairs of edges. A solution to this constraint system then provides the analysis result. Accordingly, the two key practical problems consist in finding a *decent* self-composition and a *decent* abstract domain, which achieve reasonable precision at an acceptable price. Note that different analysis results can be obtained if different self-compositions are chosen. Theorem 2 guarantees that all results are sound, and therefore allow to increase the precision of the analysis.

3. SELF-COMPOSITIONS OF CONTROL FLOW GRAPHS

When an appropriate alignment of computations is chosen, we assume that abstract transformers $[\![f, f']\!]^\sharp$ for pairs of identical or similar actions f, f' are more precise than abstract transformers for arbitrary pairs. Therefore, the goal is to maximize the number of edges labeled (f, f') in a self-composition of a CFG. If the program in question has been specified by means of a structured programming language, a quality self-composition can be obtained by means of syntactically matching abstract syntax trees (ASTs) of program fragments.

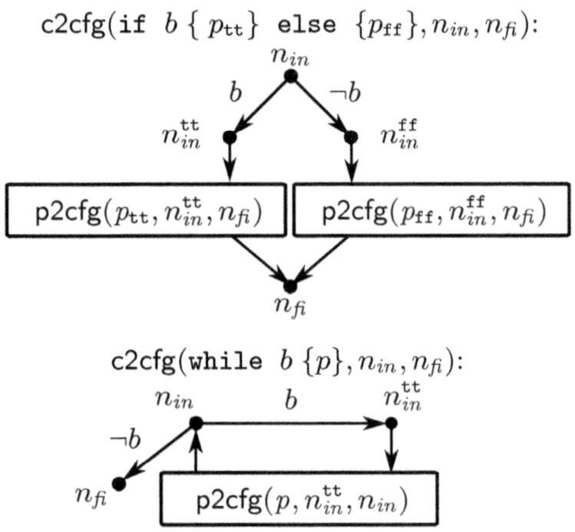

Figure 1: CFGs corresponding to branching constructs

In order to illustrate the approach, assume that programs are generated by the nonterminal p of the grammar below:

$$\begin{array}{llll} \text{(program)} & p & ::= & c; \mid c;p \\ \text{(command)} & c & ::= & \mathtt{skip} \mid x \mathrel{\mathtt{:=}} e \mid \mathtt{while}\ b\ \{p\} \mid \\ & & & \mathtt{if}\ b\ \{p_{\mathtt{tt}}\}\ \mathtt{else}\ \{p_{\mathtt{ff}}\} \end{array} \quad (3)$$

The grammar (3) defines a structured programming language, where the state of execution and the syntax of expressions e and b will be instantiated for our tree-manipulating language in Section 4.

CFGs of programs are constructed by two mutually recursive functions "program to CFG" (p2cfg) and "command to CFG" (c2cfg). The CFG corresponding to the program p can be obtained by means of the function p2cfg(p, n_{in}, n_{fi}), where the initial and final nodes of the resulting graph are n_{in} and n_{fi}, respectively. In case $p = c_1;...;c_m$, then $m-1$ fresh nodes are instantiated, and c2cfg(c_i, n_{i-1}, n_i) is called for each i to construct the CFG fragment corresponding to the command c_i so that $n_0 = n_{in}$ and $n_m = n_{fi}$. c2cfg(skip, n_i, n_{i+1}) = (n_i, skip, n_{i+1}) and c2cfg(x:=e, n_i, n_{i+1}) = (n_i, x:=e, n_{i+1}), furthermore, the CFG fragments corresponding to branching constructs are shown in Figure 1.

A self-composition of the CFG corresponding to a program can be constructed by two mutually recursive functions "pair of programs to CFG" (pp2cfg) and "pair of commands to CFG" (pc2cfg). The function pp2cfg(p_1, p_2, n_{in}, n_{fi}) can also be called for two different programs, p_1 and p_2, in order to align the two alternatives in a conditional. The function makes use of a distance measure for trees as introduced, e.g., in [34]. The evaluation of pp2cfg(p_1, p_2, n_{in}, n_{fi}) proceeds in two steps:

Step 1: Computing a Best Alignment of Two Programs.

Here, we adapt the definition of sets of alignments (2) to two sequences of commands. An optimal alignment of two sequences of commands, $c_1;...;c_k$ and $d_1;...;d_l$, with respect to a tree distance measure td is the sequence of pairs of commands ω_{opt}, where the distances td($c_i^{\omega_{\text{opt}}}, d_i^{\omega_{\text{opt}}}$) of the ASTs of the aligned pairs of commands ($c_i^{\omega_{\text{opt}}}, d_i^{\omega_{\text{opt}}}$) is minimal. Formally, an optimal alignment ω_{opt} of $p_1 = c_1;...;c_k$ and $p_2 = d_1;...;d_l$ is defined as:

$$\omega_{\text{opt}} = \underset{\omega \in A(p_1,p_2)}{\arg\min} \sum_{1 \le i \le |\omega|} \mathsf{td}(\omega[i].1, \omega[i].2) \quad (4)$$

In (4), $\omega[i]$ stands for the pair of commands number i in the sequence ω, and $\omega[i].1$ and $\omega[i].2$ denote the first and second components of the pair respectively. In our implementation we use the *Robust Tree Edit Distance* described in [32] as tree distance measure.

Step 2: Computing the Compositions of CFGs of Pairs of Commands.

If the alignment is ready, the compositions of the CFGs corresponding to the aligned pairs of commands need to be constructed. Assume that the chosen alignment of the two programs is $\omega = (c_1, d_1)...(c_k, d_k)$. In this case we instantiate a fresh node for each $1 \le i \le k-1$, and call pc2cfg(c_i, d_i, n_{i-1}, n_i) so that $n_0 = n_{in}$ and $n_k = n_{fi}$.

Now we discuss how the subgraphs corresponding to pairs of commands are constructed. First, the roots of the abstract syntax trees corresponding to the commands are compared. The roots of the ASTs corresponding to c and d are considered *composable* in the following cases:

- $c = d = x$:= e or $c = d =$ skip, i.e., in case of assignments the commands need to be identical including the variable on the left and the expression on the right.
- $c =$ if b_1 { $p_{\mathtt{tt}}^1$ } else { $p_{\mathtt{ff}}^1$ } and $d =$ if b_2 { $p_{\mathtt{tt}}^2$ } else { $p_{\mathtt{ff}}^2$ }.
- $c =$ while b_1 { p_1 } and $d =$ while b_2 { p_2 }.

In case the roots of the ASTs of the commands c and d are not composable, then we put them in sequence. This is achieved by means of two additional functions. The function skip1(G) replaces each label f of the edges of the graph G with (skip, f), and similarly, skip2(G) replaces these labels with (f, skip). In order to compute pc2cfg(c, d, n_{in}, n_{fi}) in this case, we instantiate a fresh node n' and compute skip2(c2cfg(c, n_{in}, n')) and skip1(c2cfg(d, n', n_{fi})).

It remains to consider a pair of commands c and d where the roots of the corresponding ASTs are composable. If they are not branching constructs, then pc2cfg(c, d, n_{in}, n_{fi}) = (n_{in}, (c, d), n_{fi}).

Now consider a pair of branching constructs. The corresponding self-compositions are illustrated in Figure 2. Here,

The resulting CFG of $\mathsf{pc2cfg}(p_1, p_2, n_{in}, n_{fi})$, where $p_1 = \texttt{if } b_1 \{ p^1_{\texttt{tt}} \} \texttt{ else } \{ p^1_{\texttt{ff}} \}$, and $p_2 = \texttt{if } b_2 \{ p^2_{\texttt{tt}} \} \texttt{ else } \{ p^2_{\texttt{ff}} \}$:

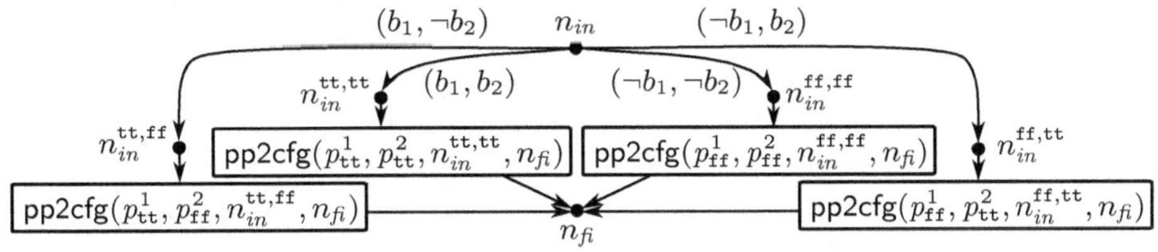

The resulting CFG of $\mathsf{pc2cfg}(\texttt{while } b_1 \{ p_1 \}, \texttt{while } b_2 \{ p_2 \}, n_{in}, n_{fi})$:

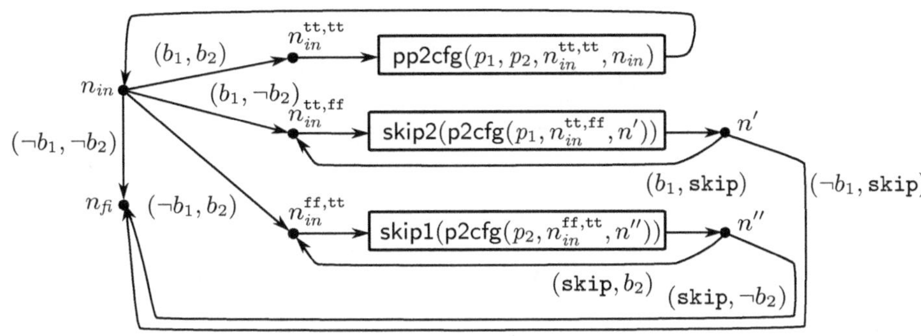

Figure 2: The compositions of CFGs corresponding to branching constructs

the idea is to compose the CFGs of the bodies of the branching constructs according to all possible valuations of the conditional expressions, and then connect them with edges so that they become compositions of the branching constructs according to Definition 3. In particular, the composition of two loops results in three. One loop handles the case when the bodies are executed simultaneously, the other two execute the body of only one original loop. This way we handle the situation, when the two original loops execute a different number of times.

Note that the functions pp2cfg and pc2cfg are mutually recursive. Accordingly, subprograms at each level of the ASTs are aligned separately.

The following theorem states the correctness of the construction of self-compositions of CFGs introduced above.

THEOREM 3. *Consider a program p together with its CFG G constructed by the function* $\mathsf{p2cfg}(p, n_{in}, n_{fi})$. *In this case, the resulting CFG of the function* $\mathsf{pp2cfg}(p, p, n'_{in}, n'_{fi})$ *is a self-composition of G according to Definition 3.*

The proof is by induction on the abstract syntax tree of p. Please, refer to [23] for the details.

4. PROVING NONINTERFERENCE

In this section we show how to apply the developments of Sections 2 and 3 in order to verify information flow properties of tree-manipulating programs. In Section 4.1 the programming language (3) is instantiated with an expression language optimized for tree manipulation, and in Section 4.2 an abstract interpretation is introduced. In Section 4.3 a case study is presented, where we model the BPEL fragment of Listing 1 with a program implemented in our language, and prove an information flow property on it.

4.1 A Language for Tree Manipulation

XML documents are unranked ordered trees, where there is no bound on the number of children of nodes. For the

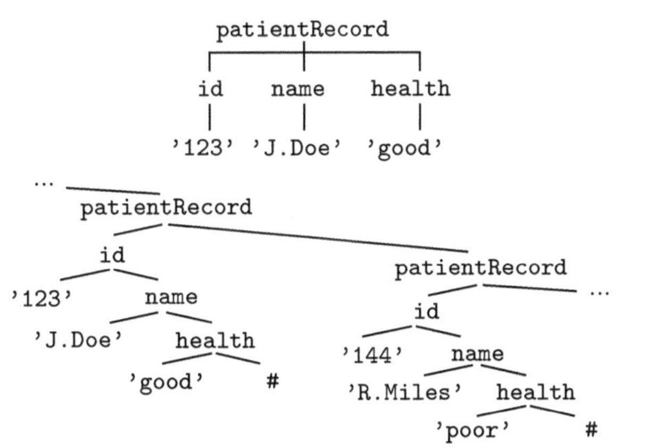

Figure 3: A document tree describing a patient (top), and the corresponding binary representation as member of a list (bottom)

sake of simplicity, here we represent tree-shaped data using binary trees by means of the first-child-next-sibling (FCNS) encoding [11]. Figure 3 illustrates an unranked tree-shaped record corresponding to a patient in a database on the top, and on the bottom its binary representation as a member of a list. As Figure 3 shows, the FCNS encoding maps the first child of a node in an unranked tree to its first child, and its sibling to the right to its second child. The set of binary trees over the alphabet Σ_2 of symbols for binary nodes and Σ_0 for nullary nodes is denoted by $\mathcal{T}_{\Sigma_2,\Sigma_0}$. Binary nodes labeled with the elements of Σ_2 model XML tags, while nullary nodes labeled with the elements of Σ_0 model textual entities of XML documents. Therefore, we identify the latter by putting their values between ' characters. One can think of the labels of nullary nodes as untyped values represented as strings. The extra label $\# \in \Sigma_0$ denotes the empty forest.

$$
\begin{array}{llll}
\text{(tree expressions)} & e & ::= & \texttt{\#} \mid x \mid x\texttt{/1} \mid x\texttt{/2} \mid \\
 & & & \sigma_2\texttt{(}x\texttt{,}y\texttt{)} \mid \\
 & & & \lambda_t\texttt{(}x_1\texttt{,}x_2\texttt{,...)} \\
\text{(Boolean expressions)} & b & ::= & \texttt{top(}x\texttt{)=}\sigma \mid \\
 & & & \lambda_b\texttt{(}x_1\texttt{,}x_2\texttt{,...)}
\end{array} \quad (5)
$$

In (5), the expression language of the programming language of (3) is defined. Tree expressions e evaluate to new tree-shaped values based on already existing ones, and Boolean expressions b compute Boolean values. The values of x/1 and x/2 are the first and second subtrees of the value stored in x, respectively, given that the root of x is binary. Otherwise, if x is a leaf, they result in the error state $\lightning$. The result of σ_2(x,y) is a tree having root labeled $\sigma_2 \in \Sigma_2$ with the content of x as its first and the content of y as its second child. In order to allow for arbitrary computations, we have introduced the interpreted functions λ_t and λ_b returning textual (otherwise called basic) and Boolean values respectively. In the following examples we will use infix operators like less or equal to =< or equivalence = as instances for interpreted function symbols with the intuitive semantics.

$$
\begin{array}{rcl}
[\![\texttt{top(}x\texttt{)=}\sigma]\!]s & = & s \text{ if } \sigma \in \Sigma_2 \cup \{\texttt{\#}\} \text{ and} \\
 & & s(x) \text{ has root labeled with } \sigma \\
[\![\neg\texttt{top(}x\texttt{)=}\sigma]\!]s & = & s \text{ if } \sigma \in \Sigma_2 \cup \{\texttt{\#}\} \text{ and} \\
 & & s(x) \text{ has root labeled with } \sigma' \neq \sigma \\
[\![\lambda_b\texttt{(}x_1\texttt{,}x_2\texttt{,...)}]\!]s & = & s \text{ if } [\![\lambda_b]\!](s(x_1), s(x_2), ...) \text{ holds}
\end{array}
$$

$$
[\![x\texttt{:=}y]\!]s = s[x \mapsto s(y)] \qquad [\![x\texttt{:=\#}]\!]s = s[x \mapsto \texttt{\#}]
$$

$$
[\![x\texttt{:=}\sigma_2\texttt{(}x_1\texttt{,}x_2\texttt{)}]\!]s = s[x \mapsto \sigma_2(s(x_1), s(x_2))]
$$

$$
[\![x\texttt{:=}y\texttt{/1}]\!]s = \begin{cases} s[x \mapsto t_1] & \text{if } s(y) = \sigma_2\texttt{(}t_1\texttt{,}t_2\texttt{)} \text{ for some label } \sigma_2, \text{ and trees } t_1 \text{ and } t_2 \\ \lightning & \text{otherwise} \end{cases}
$$

$$
[\![x\texttt{:=}y\texttt{/2}]\!]s = \begin{cases} s[x \mapsto t_2] & \text{if } s(y) = \sigma_2\texttt{(}t_1\texttt{,}t_2\texttt{)} \text{ for some label } \sigma_2, \text{ and trees } t_1 \text{ and } t_2 \\ \lightning & \text{otherwise} \end{cases}
$$

$$
[\![x\texttt{:=}\lambda_t\texttt{(}x_1\texttt{,}x_2\texttt{,...)}]\!]s = s[x \mapsto [\![\lambda_t]\!](s(x_1), s(x_2), ...)] \text{ or } \lightning
$$

$$
[\![f]\!]\lightning = \lightning \text{ for all edges } f
$$

Figure 4: State transformers of edges

The semantics of a program is given by means of the corresponding CFG according to Section 2. Here, a program state s is a mapping $(Var \to \mathcal{T}_{\Sigma_2,\Sigma_0}) \cup \{\lightning\}$ from the set of variables to binary trees, or the error state $\lightning$. The state transformers of edges are defined in Figure 4, where $s[x \mapsto v]$ denotes a state with each variable $y \neq x$ having value $s(y)$, and $s(x) = v$. In particular, we define $[\![f]\!]\lightning = \lightning$ for all edges.

4.2 Proving Noninterference Using Relational Abstract Interpretation

By the specification of information flow policies [15] we distinguish between two secrecy levels, namely *public* or *low* (L) and *secret* or *high* (H). The meaning is that the principals not entitled to learn information classified H, should not be able to make inferences on them based on observing data classified L. We are only concerned with termination *insensitive* noninterference, i.e., we neglect the amount of secret that can be learned by observing the non-termination of executions. A program is deemed secure only if for all pairs of states s_0 and t_0 the following holds. If the public parts of s_0 and t_0 are equal, i.e., $s_0|_L = t_0|_L$, then for all pairs of executions starting at the initial node of the CFG of the program in states s_0 and t_0, and reaching the final node in states s and t, respectively, the public parts of the two resulting states are equal as well, i.e., $s|_L = t|_L$.

In order to verify an information flow policy, our analysis maintains abstract states $d : Var \to \mathcal{P}(\mathcal{T}_{\Sigma_2,\{\#,bv,\star\}})$, which are mappings from variables to sets of trees possibly containing occurrences of dedicated leaves bv and $\star$. A pair of states (s,t) is in the concretization[2] $(s,t) \in \gamma(d)$ of d, if for all variables x, $(s(x), t(x)) \in \gamma(d(x))$ holds. A pair of trees τ_1, τ_2 is in the concretization of a set Λ of abstract trees, if Λ contains a tree τ such that both τ_1 and τ_2 can be obtained from τ by replacing the occurrences of bv with identical basic values, and the occurrences of $\star$ with any, possibly different subtrees. Consider, e.g., the language $\Lambda = \{\texttt{a(}\star\texttt{,}bv\texttt{)}, \texttt{b(}bv\texttt{,}\star\texttt{)}\}$. Then $(\tau_1, \tau_2) \in \gamma(\Lambda)$ for $\tau_1 =$ `a('Top secret!','42')`, and $\tau_2 =$ `a('Top secret, too!', '42')`. Accordingly, if $(\tau_1, \tau_2) \in \gamma(\Lambda)$, then the elements of Λ can be considered as potential public views of the trees τ_1 and τ_2, where the occurrences of $\star$ identify the positions of secrets. A public view is a piece of relational information on two trees in the sense that it determines their common upper part and the locations of potential secrets. Therefore, an information flow policy that can be verified by our method needs to be given in the form of a set of public views for each variable in the initial abstract value of the analysis. Abstract values do not record precise information on basic values. Leaves labeled bv only mark the positions of basic values having secrecy level L.

In order to deal with program errors as well, we extend this basic approach by recording in the abstract state for a program point not only public views of variables, but additionally provide Boolean values $B_\lightning$ and $B_\star$. If $B_\lightning$ holds, then $(\lightning, \lightning)$ can also be a member of the concretization. If $B_\star$ holds, then either of the two components of a pair of concrete states may be $\lightning$ meaning that the occurrence of an error may depend on the secret.

Given an initial abstract value d_0 describing the set of public views of pairs of potential initial states, we are interested in computing the sets of potential public views for every pair of jointly reachable program points. In our analysis, sets of public views for variables x occurring at a node n are described by means of unary predicates $\texttt{var}_{x,n}$, which are defined by means of Horn clauses. Formally, $\tau \in d(x)$ at node n if $\texttt{var}_{x,n}(\tau)$ holds. The values of $B_\lightning$ and $B_\star$ at node n are represented by means of the nullary predicates $\texttt{public\_error}_n$ and $\texttt{secret\_error}_n$ respectively.

There are two kinds of Horn clauses. A first group is used for specifying the information flow policy in terms of a set of initial public views for each variable at the initial node n_{in}. A second group describes how the views at different program points are related to each other. These clauses are obtained from the self-composition of the CFG.

For our analysis, we assume that information flow policies are defined by regular sets of public views, and thus can be described by finite tree automata. We will not define finite

[2] We overload the notation γ by applying it to the concretization of abstract states as well as to the concretization of abstract sets of trees.

tree automata here, but note that their languages can be defined by means of clauses of the form:

$$\texttt{p}(\sigma_0)\texttt{.} \quad \text{or} \quad \texttt{p}(\sigma_2(X_1,X_2)) \Leftarrow \texttt{p}_1(X_1)\texttt{,}\texttt{p}_2(X_2)\texttt{.}$$

Above, $\texttt{p}$, $\texttt{p}_1$ and $\texttt{p}_2$ are unary predicates corresponding to the states of the automaton, and σ_0 and σ_2 are nullary and binary constructors respectively.

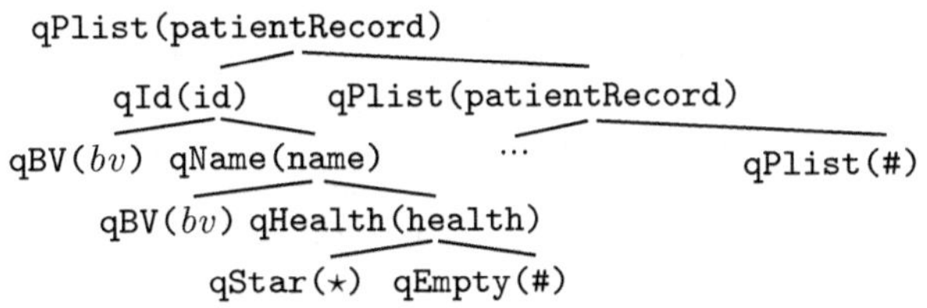

Figure 5: A run of the automaton specified in (6) accepting the public view of a list of records like that on the bottom of Figure 3 with state qPlist

In our running example, the health status of patients in the list of records seen in Figure 3 is confidential. Thus, the information flow policy, the set of public views of all possible databases is given by the predicate `qPlist` defined by the implications in (6):

$$\begin{array}{rcl} \texttt{qPlist(patientRecord(L,R))} & \Leftarrow & \texttt{qId(L),qPlist(R)}. \\ & \texttt{qPlist(\#)}. & \\ \texttt{qId(id(L,R))} & \Leftarrow & \texttt{qBV(L),qName(R)}. \\ \texttt{qName(name(L,R))} & \Leftarrow & \texttt{qBV(L),qHealth(R)}. \\ \texttt{qHealth(health(L,R))} & \Leftarrow & \texttt{qStar(L),qEmpty(R)}. \\ & \texttt{qBV}(bv)\texttt{.} \quad \texttt{qStar(}\star\texttt{).} \quad \texttt{qEmpty(\#).} & \end{array} \quad (6)$$

As Figure 5 illustrates, a list accepted by the predicate `qPlist` is either a tree with root labeled `patientRecord` having a first child accepted by `qId` and a second child accepted by `qPlist`, or it is a nullary node with label `#`. The other predicates can be understood similarly. In particular, the predicate `qHealth` accepts only trees, the first child of which is a leaf labeled $\star$ specifying that the corresponding value is confidential. Supposing that the variable `pList` contains the database in the initial state of our program, the corresponding information for the initial node n_{in} and for this variable is defined by: $\texttt{var}_{\texttt{pList},n_{in}}\texttt{(X)} \Leftarrow \texttt{qPlist(X)}$.

In the following, we describe how the abstract state transformers $[\![f,g]\!]^\sharp$ of edges $(n,(f,g),n')$ are formalized by means of Horn clauses. In order to do so we need that the set of binary elements Σ_2 potentially occurring in the program is finite and a priori known. This information can be extracted, e.g., from the interface descriptions of web services. Recall that due to our alignment procedure edges either refer to assignments or to Boolean expressions, but never to both.

4.2.1 *Assignments as Horn Clauses*

First, we discuss the case of assignments, i.e., transformers of the form $[\![x\texttt{:=}e_1(x_1,\ldots,x_n),y\texttt{:=}e_2(y_1,\ldots,y_m)]\!]^\sharp$. If no error occurs, then x and y are updated, the values of other variables remain unchanged. Error propagation is discussed later in Section 4.2.3. Accordingly, for all variables $z \neq x$ and $z \neq y$ the following clauses are defined, which propagate their values unmodified:

$$\texttt{var}_{z,n'}\texttt{(X)} \Leftarrow \texttt{var}_{z,n}\texttt{(X)}.$$

Values of variables on the left hand sides of the assignments are defined by the following clauses.

- For edges with label $(x\texttt{:=\#},x\texttt{:=\#})$ we have $\texttt{var}_{x,n'}\texttt{(\#)} \Leftarrow \texttt{var}_{y,n}\texttt{(\_)}$ for all variables y occurring in the program, where '_' denotes an anonymous logic variable. The implication is required to ensure that `#` is added to the predicate $\texttt{var}_{x,n'}$ only if n may be reachable. We consider a node n as unreachable, if there is no variable x and tree τ so that $\texttt{var}_{x,n}(\tau)$ holds.

- For edges with $(x\texttt{:=}y,x\texttt{:=}y)$ we have: $\texttt{var}_{x,n'}\texttt{(X)} \Leftarrow \texttt{var}_{y,n}\texttt{(X)}$.

- For edges with $(x\texttt{:=}\sigma_2(y,z),x\texttt{:=}\sigma_2(y,z))$ we have:

$$\texttt{var}_{x,n'}(\sigma_2\texttt{(L,R))} \Leftarrow \texttt{var}_{y,n}\texttt{(L)},\texttt{var}_{z,n}\texttt{(R)}.$$

- For edges with $(x\texttt{:=}y\texttt{/1},x\texttt{:=}y\texttt{/1})$ we have $\texttt{var}_{x,n'}\texttt{(L)} \Leftarrow \texttt{var}_{y,n}(\sigma_2\texttt{(L,\_))}$ for all $\sigma_2 \in \Sigma_2$. As an example, let us suppose that the abstract value of variable `pList` at node n is a model of the predicate `qPlist` according to implications in (6). Using the command `id := pList/1` we can assign the head of the list into variable `id`. The implication defining the abstract value of variable `id` after the assignment is $\texttt{var}_{\texttt{id},n'}\texttt{(L)} \Leftarrow \texttt{var}_{\texttt{pList},n}\texttt{(patientRecord(L,\_))}$. However, during the analysis the label of the root of the tree in a variable needs to be treated as unknown. Therefore, the implication is repeated for all possible binary alphabet elements $\sigma_2 \in \Sigma_2$.

An error is caused by an expression of the form x`/1`, if the content of x does not have children, i.e., it is a leaf. Therefore, in addition the following is defined:

$$\begin{array}{rcl} \texttt{public\_error}_{n'} & \Leftarrow & \texttt{var}_{y,n}\texttt{(\#)}. \\ \texttt{public\_error}_{n'} & \Leftarrow & \texttt{var}_{y,n}(bv)\texttt{.} \\ \texttt{secret\_error}_{n'} & \Leftarrow & \texttt{var}_{y,n}\texttt{(}\star\texttt{)}. \end{array} \quad (7)$$

- For edges with $(x\texttt{:=}y\texttt{/2},x\texttt{:=}y\texttt{/2})$ we have $\texttt{var}_{x,n'}\texttt{(R)} \Leftarrow \texttt{var}_{y,n}(\sigma_2\texttt{(\_,R))}$ for all $\sigma_2 \in \Sigma_2$. The implications handling errors are identical to those in (7).

- By edges with (f,f) where $f = x\texttt{:=}\lambda_t(x_1,\ldots,x_k)$, it needs to be examined whether the arguments of the function λ_t contain secret. The implications below are used for the purpose, where the second and third lines are defined for all $\sigma_2 \in \Sigma_2$:

$$\begin{array}{rcl} & \texttt{secret(}\star\texttt{).} & \\ \texttt{secret(}\sigma_2\texttt{(L,\_))} & \Leftarrow & \texttt{secret(L)}. \\ \texttt{secret(}\sigma_2\texttt{(\_,R))} & \Leftarrow & \texttt{secret(R)}. \end{array}$$

Concerning the resulting value of x we have:

$$\texttt{var}_{x,n'}(bv) \Leftarrow \texttt{var}_{x_1,n}\texttt{(\_)},\texttt{var}_{x_2,n}\texttt{(\_)}, \ldots,\texttt{var}_{x_k,n}\texttt{(\_)}. \quad (8)$$

$$\texttt{var}_{x,n'}\texttt{(}\star\texttt{)} \Leftarrow \texttt{var}_{x_i,n}\texttt{(X)},\texttt{secret(X)}, \texttt{var}_{x_1,n}\texttt{(\_)},\ldots, \texttt{var}_{x_k,n}\texttt{(\_)}. \quad (9)$$

According to implication (8), the value of x at node n' will potentially be bv if all of the arguments $x_1,...,x_k$ of λ_t are defined. Furthermore, according to implication (9), if any of the input variables depends on the secret, then the resulting abstract value will also contain $\star$. There is an implication of the form (9) defined for all arguments x_i of λ_t.

- By edges of the form $(x\texttt{:=}e(x_1,\ldots,x_k),\texttt{skip})$ and $(\texttt{skip},x\texttt{:=}e(x_1,\ldots,x_k))$ we have:

$$\texttt{var}_{x,n'}\texttt{(}\star\texttt{)} \Leftarrow \texttt{var}_{x_1,n}\texttt{(\_)},\ldots,\texttt{var}_{x_k,n}\texttt{(\_)}.$$

If the effect of an edge consists of an assignment and a `skip` command, then in the resulting abstract state the value of the variable on the left hand side becomes $\star$ indicating that its value might be different in the corresponding two concrete states. This happens independently of the values of arguments of expressions on the right hand side. If the expression is of the form x`/1` or x`/2`, then we have in addition $\texttt{secret\_error}_{n'} \Leftarrow \texttt{var}_{x,n}\texttt{(\_)}$ in order to indicate that an error may occur only in one member of the pair of corresponding concrete states.

4.2.2 Boolean Expressions as Horn Clauses

Now we discuss abstract transformers with Boolean expressions. In our implementation we treat two branching constructs composable only if their conditional expressions are syntactically equivalent in addition to the conditions discussed in Section 3.

- By edges labeled (b,b), $(b,\texttt{skip})$ or $(\texttt{skip},b)$, where $b = \lambda_b(x_1,\ x_2,\ldots,x_k)$, the values of all variables y occurring in the program are propagated the following way:

$$\texttt{var}_{y,n'}\texttt{(X)} \Leftarrow \texttt{var}_{y,n}\texttt{(X)},\texttt{var}_{x_1,n}\texttt{(\_)},\ldots,\texttt{var}_{x_k,n}\texttt{(\_)}.$$

In other words, it is checked whether the input variables of the conditional expression have been defined, in order to ensure that the node n is reachable. The actual values of variables are propagated without modification.

- In case the label of the root of a tree is tested using an edge having label of the form $(\texttt{top}(x)\texttt{=}\sigma,\texttt{top}(x)\texttt{=}\sigma)$, then the following clauses are defined to propagate the values of variables $y \neq x$ if $\sigma \in \Sigma_2$:

$$\begin{array}{lll}\texttt{var}_{y,n'}\texttt{(X)} & \Leftarrow & \texttt{var}_{y,n}\texttt{(X)},\\ & & \texttt{var}_{x,n}\texttt{(}\sigma\texttt{(\_,\_))}.\\ \texttt{var}_{y,n'}\texttt{(X)} & \Leftarrow & \texttt{var}_{y,n}\texttt{(X)},\texttt{var}_{x,n}\texttt{(}\star\texttt{)}.\end{array} \tag{10}$$

The value of the variable x is propagated as well:

$$\texttt{var}_{x,n'}\texttt{(}\sigma\texttt{(L,R))} \Leftarrow \texttt{var}_{x,n}\texttt{(}\sigma\texttt{(L,R))}. \tag{11}$$

$$\texttt{var}_{x,n'}\texttt{(}\sigma\texttt{(}\star\texttt{,}\star\texttt{))} \Leftarrow \texttt{var}_{x,n}\texttt{(}\star\texttt{)}. \tag{12}$$

If $\sigma = \texttt{\#}$ then $\sigma\texttt{(}X\texttt{,}Y\texttt{)}$ is exchanged with `#` (10), (11) and (12).

- For edges with $(\texttt{top}(x)\texttt{=}\sigma,\texttt{skip})$ or $(\texttt{skip},\texttt{top}(x)\texttt{=}\sigma)$ (10) and (11) need to be repeated, and in addition $\texttt{var}_{x,n'}\texttt{(}\star\texttt{)} \Leftarrow \texttt{var}_{x,n}\texttt{(}\star\texttt{)}$ defined.

- By edges with $(\neg\texttt{top}(x)\texttt{=}\sigma,\neg\texttt{top}(x)\texttt{=}\sigma)$, $(\neg\texttt{top}(x)\texttt{=}\sigma,$ $\texttt{skip})$ or $(\texttt{skip},\neg\texttt{top}(x)\texttt{=}\sigma)$, the values of the variables are propagated only in the case, when the root of the value of x is labeled with some $\delta \neq \sigma$. Therefore, the following implication is defined for all variables y other than x and for all alphabet elements $\delta \in \Sigma_2 \setminus \{\sigma\}$:

$$\texttt{var}_{y,n'}\texttt{(X)} \Leftarrow \texttt{var}_{y,n}\texttt{(X)},\texttt{var}_{x,n}\texttt{(}\delta\texttt{(\_,\_))}. \tag{13}$$

In order to handle the value of x as well, the following implication is defined for all $\delta \in \Sigma_2 \setminus \{\sigma\}$:

$$\texttt{var}_{x,n'}\texttt{(}\delta\texttt{(L,R))} \Leftarrow \texttt{var}_{x,n}\texttt{(}\delta\texttt{(L,R))}. \tag{14}$$

Additionally, we need to define (13) and (14) so that $\delta\texttt{(}X\texttt{,}Y\texttt{)}$ is replaced by $\star$, and if $\sigma \neq \texttt{\#}$ then by `#` too.

- In case the two components of the label of an edge are the negations of each other, e.g., $(\neg b(x_1, x_2, ..., x_k),$ $b(x_1, x_2, ..., x_k))$, then the values of variables need to be propagated only in the case, when at least one of the variables in the argument depends on the secret. Assuming that b is a function, the simultaneous execution of the two steps cannot take place otherwise. Accordingly, the following is defined for all variables y occurring in the program and for all variables $x_i \in \{x_1, ..., x_k\}$:

$$\begin{array}{lll}\texttt{var}_{y,n'}\texttt{(X)} & \Leftarrow & \texttt{var}_{y,n}\texttt{(X)},\texttt{var}_{x_i,n}\texttt{(X}i\texttt{)},\\ & & \texttt{secret(X}i\texttt{)}.\end{array} \tag{15}$$

4.2.3 Propagating the Error

Finally, in order to propagate the error state, for all edges we define:

$$\begin{array}{lll}\texttt{public\_error}_{n'} & \Leftarrow & \texttt{public\_error}_{n}.\\ \texttt{secret\_error}_{n'} & \Leftarrow & \texttt{secret\_error}_{n}.\end{array}$$

4.2.4 Discussion

THEOREM 4. *The abstract transformer* $[\![f,g]\!]^\sharp$ *for a pair* (f,g) *as defined by Horn clauses is a correct abstract transformer, i.e., it satisfies the conditions of (1). In other words, if* $[\![f]\!](s_0) = s$ *and* $[\![g]\!]t_0 = t$ *where* $(s_0,t_0) \in \gamma(d_0)$ *and* $[\![f,g]\!]^\sharp d_0 = d$, *then* $(s,t) \in \gamma(d)$ *holds.*

PROOF. The statement follows by a comparison of the concrete transformers in Section 4.1 and the implications defined for pairs of labels of edges. □

Because of Theorem 4, the least solution of the set of Horn clauses defined for a program over-approximates the MTC solution. Therefore, for example, noninterference for a particular output variable x holds at program exit n_{fi}, if the predicate $\texttt{var}_{x,n_{fi}}$ does not accept trees containing $\star$.

Algorithmically, therefore, the analysis boils down to computing (or approximating) the model of the set of Horn clauses defined for the program. The head of each clause possibly generated by our analysis is of one of the forms

$$h \;::=\; \texttt{p} \mid \texttt{p(}X\texttt{)} \mid \texttt{p(}\sigma_0\texttt{)} \mid \texttt{p(}\sigma_2\texttt{(}X_1\texttt{,}X_2\texttt{))},$$

where X_1, X_2 are distinct. Therefore, all of them belong to the class of Horn clauses $\mathcal{H}_1$ [31, 37]. Finite sets of clauses of this class are known to have least models consisting of regular sets. Moreover, finite automata characterizing these regular sets can be effectively computed.

4.3 Case Study

Let us come back to our running example, the routine manipulating the hospital database, which processes the list of records of patients. An implementation of the BPEL code of Listing 1 in our tree-manipulating core language is given by Listing 2:

Listing 2: A routine updating the health status of patients based on blood tests. Subroutines are syntactic sugar, and they are inlined before analysis or execution. Some analysis results are displayed in comments, where nodes of the self-composition of the corresponding CFG are identified by pairs of numbers of lines in the code.

```
subroutine query {
 found := 'ff';  // var_found,(3,3)(bv).
 while found = 'ff' {
  id := pList/1; // var_id,(5,5)(X) ⇐ qId(X).
5 idVal := id/1; // var_idVal,(6,6)(X) ⇐ qBV(X).
  if idVal = patientId {
   found := 'tt' // var_found,(8,8)(X) ⇐ qBV(X).
   name := id/2; // var_name,(9,9)(X) ⇐ qName(X).
   nameVal := name/1;
10          // var_nameVal,(11,11)(X) ⇐ qBV(X).
   pList := pList/2;
            // var_pList,(3,3)(X) ⇐ qPlist(X).
  } else {
   pListRev := patientRecord(id,pListRev);
15          // var_pListRev,(16,16)(X) ⇐ qPlist(X).
   pList := pList/2;
            // var_pList,(3,3)(X) ⇐ qPlist(X).
}}}
subroutine restore {
20 health := health(healthVal,empty);
 name := name(nameVal,health);
            // var_name,(23,23)(X) ⇐ qName(X).
 id := id(idVal,name);
            // var_id,(25,25)(X) ⇐ qId(X).
25 pList := patientRecord(id,pList);
            // var_pList,(27,27)(X) ⇐ qPlist(X).
 while top(pListRev) = patientRecord {
  id := pListRev/1;
            // var_id,(30,30)(X) ⇐ qId(X).
30 pList := patientRecord(id,pList);
  pListRev := pListRev/2;
            // var_pListRev,(27,27)(X) ⇐ qPlist(X).
}}
// Entry point:
35 empty := #;              // var_empty,(36,36)(#).
pListRev := empty;         // var_pListRev,(37,37)(#).
if test =< '0.5' {
 call query;
 healthVal := 'good'; // var_healthVal,(40,44)(*).
40 call restore;
} else {
 call query;
 healthVal := 'poor'; // var_healthVal,(40,44)(*).
 call restore;
45 }
```

Subroutines, which are not part of the core language, can be considered as abbreviations. Their definitions are meant to be inlined at their call sites before execution or analysis. In the initial state the variable **pList** contains the database, a list of records in the form of a binary tree as illustrated in Figure 3. The result of the blood test is in variable **test** and the patient's identifier to whom the test belongs is provided in **patientId**. The updated list is again stored in the variable **pList** at the end of the execution. The entry point of the program is at line 35. At line 37, a branch is selected based on the blood test. In both branches, the record of the patient is searched for in the database, and the corresponding health status is updated. Finally, the list representing the database is restored. The database is queried in a loop running as long as the record for the patient with identifier **patientId** is not found. If the actual record at the head of the list in variable **pList** is not the one we are looking for, then it is appended to the list in **pListRev**, which stores a prefix of the list of **pList** in reverse order. On the other hand, if the head of **pList** is the record we seek, then the name of the patient is stored in the variable **nameVal**. The restoration of the database succeeds in two steps. First, beginning with line 20 the binary tree representing the record of the actual patient is reconstructed, and appended to the database in **pList** at line 25. In the second step, the records stored in **pListRev** are appended to **pList** using the loop at line 27.

In the self-composition of the CFG corresponding to the program at Listing 2 after subroutines have been inlined, the **query** and **restore** routines of the two branches of the **if** construct at line 37 are aligned with each other. Therefore, the self-composition simulates the simultaneous query and database restoration in both branches. Listing 2 illustrates the result of the analysis on selected places with predicates of the form $\mathtt{var}_{x,(l_1,l_2)}$ in comments, where x is the variable the value of which the predicate describes, and (l_1, l_2) identifies a node in the self-composition corresponding to the pair of nodes l_1 and l_2 of the original CFG of the program. For the sake of clarity, the identifiers of the initial nodes of subgraphs (e.g., those in Figure 1) corresponding to commands coincide with the line numbers of the commands in the program text.

The initial values of variables are given by:

$$\begin{array}{c} \mathtt{var}_{\mathtt{pList},(35,35)}(\mathtt{X}) \Leftarrow \mathtt{qPlist}(\mathtt{X}). \\ \mathtt{var}_{\mathtt{test},(35,35)}(\star). \qquad \mathtt{var}_{\mathtt{patientId},(35,35)}(bv). \end{array} \tag{16}$$

Accordingly, after executing the instruction at line 4, the content of the variable **id** will be overapproximated by the set accepted by the predicate **qId**. The reason is that the first child of a tree accepted by predicate **qPlist** is accepted by predicate **qId** according to the implications in (6). The sets abstracting the values of variables at any pair of program points can be established with a similar reasoning. In particular, the abstract value of variable **healthVal** at the node corresponding to lines 40 and 44 is $\star$, indicating that it carries confidential information.

The result of the analysis reveals that the final abstract value of the variable **pList** equals to the initial one defined by the predicate **qPlist** in (16). In other words, the secret remains in the variable **test** and in the health status of the records in the list, but does not interfere with other values.

5. PRACTICAL EXPERIMENTS

We have implemented a prototype to carry out the analysis described in this paper. We have implemented the function $\mathsf{pp2cfg}(p_1, p_2, n_{in}, n_{fi})$ in OCaml, where the *Robust Tree Edit Distance* algorithm [32] is used to compute the distance between the ASTs of commands. The set of Horn clauses generated from the self-compositions of CFGs is solved using the $\mathcal{H}_1$ solver of [31]. We have carried out the analysis on four examples. *a)* **Blood Test.** This program is our example described in Section 4. *b)* **Joining Tables.** This program implements the join of two tables as published in [16] and in [5]. *c)* **Bayes Classifier.** This program is an implementation of the second example in [16], which demonstrates how to prove the noninterference of a data-mining algorithm, the *Naive Bayes classifier*. *d)* **Medical Records.** This ex-

Experiment	# of lines	$\|G\|$	$\|GG\|$	# of implications	running time	peak memory usage
Joining Tables	26	45	237	3510	2.791 sec	19.17 MiB
Blood Test	86	136	1102	23971	11.152 sec	26.71 MiB
Medical Records	97	163	859	22532	11.794 sec	21.82 MiB
Bayes Classifier	133	241	1561	89720	44.470 sec	89.85 MiB

Table 1: Summary of the runtime behavior of the analysis

ample implements the benchmark of [2], with four different operations on patient data.

For all four examples, our algorithm succeeded to infer noninterference automatically. Table 1 summarizes some quantitative details of our experiments. The experiments have been carried out in a 32 bit virtual machine on a laptop having a 2 GHz Intel® Core™ i7 processor. To each experiment we list the following information: a) Number of lines of the code without comment and empty lines. b) Size of the CFG $|G|$ as the sum of the number of nodes and number of edges. c) Size of the self-composition of the CFG $|GG|$. d) Number of implications generated. e) The complete running time of the analysis including the construction of the self-composition of the CFG, and the computation of models of predicates. f) The peak memory consumption during the verification process involving the computation of the self-composition of the CFG and models of predicates.

For all examples, the self-composition increases the size of the CFG by a factor significantly less then 10. The number of Horn clauses, on the other hand, does not only depend on the size of the corresponding self-composed graph, but additionally also on the number of variables to be tracked. As expected, the running times typically grow with the number of generated clauses.

6. RELATED WORK

This paper relies on the observation [7, 10, 14] that the verification of k-hypersafety properties of programs can be reduced to the verification of safety properties on the k-fold self-compositions of the programs.

Several authors have used self-compositions of programs for the analysis of hyperproperties, i.e., [7,14,30,35]. In [35] a type-system based transformation is presented to construct the self-composition. The self-composition of branching constructs results in one branching construct with the same condition expression. In [30] the same idea is applied for object-oriented languages. Differently from our approach, these solutions cannot take advantage of similarities in the code of different branches. Their motivation is to apply already existing techniques of proving safety properties for the purpose of proving hypersafety properties.

Barthe et al. [5] offer a variety of possibly conditional rewritings of the original program to achieve appropriate alignments. Such conditions may enforce, e.g., that two loops are iterated equally often. These conditions later must be discarded by the theorem prover or remain and then restrict the admissible input values. Furthermore, no algorithm or heuristics is provided how these rules should be applied. In our solution no extra conditions are imposed. Instead, `skip` instructions are inserted where needed. In case the conditions of two different loops are equal, we are still able to infer equal numbers of iterations and thus achieve a perfect alignment. In [6] notions of compositions of CFGs similar to ours are applied for proving relational properties of potentially dissimilar programs with the help of theorem provers. However, no algorithm is provided for the construction of the self-compositions. Furthermore, similarly to [6], our approach can also to deal with dissimilar programs, this capability is taken advantage of when different branches of a branching construct are analyzed.

While our method is based on self-compositions of control flow graphs, other people apply type systems for the verification of noninterference properties, e.g., [9, 27, 28, 36]. An other alternative is to use program dependency graphs [20]. Generally, though, the above solutions consider the program counter to have a security level implying that all data possibly manipulated in secret-dependent branches are secret. Accordingly, they would have difficulties with our running example, the data-base of patients.

In [18] a non-relational abstract interpretation has been presented, where the security of programs is investigated depending on the observational capabilities of attackers. If the public input values are handled as constants in the initial state, then no information leaks to public variables in the final state, if the property that the attackers can observe can be proved to be constant. A similar idea is applied in the runtime information flow monitor described in [24], where constant propagation is used to compute public values for the final states of branching constructs. A different way of applying abstract interpretation for proving the information flow security of programs is presented in [39] and in [4], where the security labels [15] are treated as abstractions of values, and a consistent labeling is computed according to the abstract semantics. The approaches of [4, 15, 18, 24, 39] do not consider self-compositions of the programs, and therefore cannot take advantage of similarities in different branches of branching constructs.

Abstract interpretation of tree-manipulating programs is described, e.g., in [25], where Møller et al. summarize their experiences using XML Graphs as an abstract domain. Our analysis is similar to that, in the sense that the trees generated by the grammars or automata correspond to public views. Each public view, though, represents a relational piece of information, namely, the common part of two tree-structured values.

There are also papers focusing on proving hyperproperties of programs manipulating complex data structures. In [24, 33] runtime monitors have been introduced for the enforcement of information flow properties on programs manipulating tree-structured data. In [5, 6, 29] the authors present potentially interactive approaches using theorem provers, which are also capable of dealing with our examples. In contrast to these techniques, our static analysis based on abstract interpretation is fully automatic.

Since XML is a standard format for hierarchically organizing and communicating data, security here is a major concern. Several authors therefore, have investigated how to enforce access control policies on XML documents by computing "user views", i.e., fragments of the documents accessible for certain users [1, 13, 17, 26]. These approaches however, do not consider self-compositions. Still, it remains for future work to clarify the precise relationship between our methods for verifying noninterference and such enforcement of access control.

7. CONCLUSION AND FUTURE WORK

We have presented a general approach for analyzing 2-hypersafety properties using relational abstract interpretation on self-compositions of control flow graphs. Properties like that naturally occur in information flow security analyses. Our approach is based on appropriate self-compositions of control flow graphs. Here, we presented an algorithm to construct quality self-compositions, which is completely deterministic and well tailored for the application of relational abstract interpretation. In particular, our solution uses the Robust Tree Edit Distance [32] measure in order to align similar program fragments with each other. We have applied the approach to analyze information flow properties of programs manipulating semi-structured data.

As the general idea of self-compositions of CFGs is independent of the programming language and semantics, our framework can be applied to other programming languages as well. Our results open many directions for further research, e.g.: a) In our analysis, different program variables are treated separately. Extra precision, perhaps may be obtained by using predicates that relate the contents of different variables in states. The resulting clauses then may no longer be members of the class $\mathcal{H}_1$. Still, one may apply a Horn clause based approach, but use a first order theorem prover such as, e.g., SPASS [38] as a back-end, instead of an $\mathcal{H}_1$ solver. b) The language we have considered in this paper does not support procedure calls. It still remains an open question how the Horn clause formulation of the analysis can be optimally extended also to recursive procedures.

Acknowledgments

This work was partially supported by the German Research Foundation (DFG) under the project SpAGAT in the priority program 1496 "Reliably Secure Software Systems – RS3".

8. REFERENCES

[1] R. Abassi, F. Jacquemard, M. Rusinowitch, and S. G. El Fatmi. XML access control: from XACML to annotated schemas. In *Second International Conference on Communications and Networking (ComNet)*, pages 1–8, Tozeur, Tunisie, 2010. IEEE Computer Society Press.

[2] R. Accorsi and A. Lehmann. Automatic information flow analysis of business process models. In A. P. Barros, A. Gal, and E. Kindler, editors, *Business Process Management - 10th International Conference, BPM 2012*, volume 7481 of *Lecture Notes in Computer Science*, pages 172–187. Springer, 2012.

[3] A. Alves, A. Arkin, S. Askary, C. Barreto, B. Bloch, F. Curbera, M. Ford, Y. Goland, A. Guízar, N. Kartha, C. K. Liu, R. Khalaf, D. Koenig, M. Marin, V. Mehta, S. Thatte, D. Rijn, P. Yendluri, and A. Yiu. Web services business process execution language version 2.0 (OASIS standard). WS-BPEL TC OASIS, `http://docs.oasis-open.org/wsbpel/2.0/wsbpel-v2.0.html`, 2007.

[4] R. Barbuti, C. Bernardeschi, and N. D. Francesco. Checking security of Java bytecode by abstract interpretation. In *Proceedings of the 2002 ACM Symposium on Applied Computing (SAC)*, pages 229–236. ACM, 2002.

[5] G. Barthe, J. M. Crespo, and C. Kunz. Relational verification using product programs. In M. Butler and W. Schulte, editors, *17th International Symposium on Formal Methods (FM 2011)*, volume 6664 of *Lecture Notes in Computer Science*, pages 200–214. Springer, 2011.

[6] G. Barthe, J. M. Crespo, and C. Kunz. Beyond 2-safety: Asymmetric product programs for relational program verification. In S. N. Artëmov and A. Nerode, editors, *Logical Foundations of Computer Science, International Symposium, LFCS 2013*, volume 7734 of *Lecture Notes in Computer Science*, pages 29–43. Springer, 2013.

[7] G. Barthe, P. R. D'Argenio, and T. Rezk. Secure information flow by self-composition. In *17th IEEE Computer Security Foundations Workshop, (CSFW-17 2004)*, pages 100–114. IEEE Computer Society, 2004.

[8] A. Berglund, S. Boag, D. Chamberlin, M. F. Fernández, M. Kay, J. Robie, and J. Siméon. XML path language (XPath) 2.0 (second edition). World Wide Web Consortium, Recommendation REC-xpath20-20101214, 14 December 2010.

[9] N. Broberg and D. Sands. Paralocks: role-based information flow control and beyond. In M. V. Hermenegildo and J. Palsberg, editors, *Proceedings of the 37th ACM SIGPLAN-SIGACT Symposium on Principles of Programming Languages, POPL 2010*, pages 431–444. ACM, 2010.

[10] M. R. Clarkson and F. B. Schneider. Hyperproperties. *Journal of Computer Security*, 18(6):1157–1210, 2010.

[11] H. Comon, M. Dauchet, R. Gilleron, C. Löding, F. Jacquemard, D. Lugiez, S. Tison, and M. Tommasi. Tree automata techniques and applications. Available on: `http://www.grappa.univ-lille3.fr/tata`, 2007. release October, 12th 2007.

[12] P. Cousot and R. Cousot. Abstract interpretation: A unified lattice model for static analysis of programs by construction or approximation of fixpoints. In R. M. Graham, M. A. Harrison, and R. Sethi, editors, *Conference Record of the Fourth ACM Symposium on Principles of Programming Languages (POPL)*, pages 238–252. ACM, 1977.

[13] E. Damiani, S. D. C. di Vimercati, S. Paraboschi, and P. Samarati. A fine-grained access control system for XML documents. *ACM Trans. Inf. Syst. Secur.*, 5(2):169–202, 2002.

[14] Á. Darvas, R. Hähnle, and D. Sands. A theorem proving approach to analysis of secure information flow. In D. Hutter and M. Ullmann, editors, *Security in Pervasive Computing, Second International Conference, SPC 2005*, volume 3450 of *Lecture Notes in Computer Science*, pages 193–209. Springer, 2005.

[15] D. E. Denning. A lattice model of secure information flow. *Commun. ACM*, 19(5):236–243, 1976.

[16] G. Dufay, A. P. Felty, and S. Matwin. Privacy-sensitive information flow with JML. In R. Nieuwenhuis, editor, *CADE-20, 20th International Conference on Automated Deduction*, volume 3632 of *Lecture Notes in Computer Science*, pages 116–130. Springer, 2005.

[17] I. Fundulaki and M. Marx. Specifying access control policies for XML documents with XPath. In T. Jaeger and E. Ferrari, editors, *SACMAT 2004, 9th ACM Symposium on Access Control Models and Technologies*, pages 61–69. ACM, 2004.

[18] R. Giacobazzi and I. Mastroeni. Abstract non-interference: parameterizing non-interference by abstract interpretation. In N. D. Jones and X. Leroy, editors, *Proceedings of the 31st ACM SIGPLAN-SIGACT Symposium on Principles of Programming Languages, POPL 2004*, pages 186–197. ACM, 2004.

[19] J. A. Goguen and J. Meseguer. Security policies and security models. In *IEEE Symposium on Security and Privacy*, pages 11–20, 1982.

[20] C. Hammer and G. Snelting. Flow-sensitive, context-sensitive, and object-sensitive information flow control based on program dependence graphs. *Int. J. Inf. Sec.*, 8(6):399–422, 2009.

[21] J. B. Kam and J. D. Ullman. Monotone data flow analysis frameworks. *Acta Informatica*, 7(3):305–317, September 1977.

[22] M. Kay. XSL transformations (XSLT) version 2.0. World Wide Web Consortium, Recommendation REC-xslt20-20070123, 23 January 2007.

[23] M. Kovács. Relational abstract interpretation for the verification of 2-hypersafety properties (proofs). Technical Report TUM-I1340, Technische Universität München, Institut für Informatik, Aug. 2013.

[24] M. Kovács and H. Seidl. Runtime enforcement of information flow security in tree manipulating processes. In G. Barthe, B. Livshits, and R. Scandariato, editors, *Engineering Secure Software and Systems - 4th International Symposium, ESSoS 2012*, volume 7159 of *Lecture Notes in Computer Science*, pages 46–59. Springer, 2012.

[25] A. Møller and M. I. Schwartzbach. XML graphs in program analysis. *Sci. Comput. Program.*, 76(6):492–515, 2011.

[26] M. Murata, A. Tozawa, M. Kudo, and S. Hada. XML access control using static analysis. *ACM Trans. Inf. Syst. Secur.*, 9(3):292–324, 2006.

[27] A. C. Myers. JFlow: Practical mostly-static information flow control. In A. W. Appel and A. Aiken, editors, *POPL '99, Proceedings of the 26th ACM SIGPLAN-SIGACT Symposium on Principles of Programming Languages*, pages 228–241. ACM, 1999.

[28] A. C. Myers and B. Liskov. A decentralized model for information flow control. In *SOSP '97: Proceedings of the Sixteenth ACM Symposium on Operating Systems Principles*, pages 129–142, New York, NY, USA, 1997. ACM Press.

[29] A. Nanevski, A. Banerjee, and D. Garg. Verification of information flow and access control policies with dependent types. In *IEEE Symposium on Security and Privacy*, pages 165–179. IEEE Computer Society, 2011.

[30] D. A. Naumann. From coupling relations to mated invariants for checking information flow. In D. Gollmann, J. Meier, and A. Sabelfeld, editors, *ESORICS 2006, 11th European Symposium on Research in Computer Security*, volume 4189 of *Lecture Notes in Computer Science*, pages 279–296. Springer, 2006.

[31] F. Nielson, H. R. Nielson, and H. Seidl. Normalizable Horn clauses, strongly recognizable relations, and Spi. In M. V. Hermenegildo and G. Puebla, editors, *Static Analysis, 9th International Symposium, SAS 2002*, volume 2477 of *Lecture Notes in Computer Science*, pages 20–35. Springer, 2002.

[32] M. Pawlik and N. Augsten. RTED: A robust algorithm for the tree edit distance. *PVLDB*, 5(4):334–345, 2011.

[33] A. Russo, A. Sabelfeld, and A. Chudnov. Tracking information flow in dynamic tree structures. In M. Backes and P. Ning, editors, *ESORICS 2009, 14th European Symposium on Research in Computer Security*, volume 5789 of *Lecture Notes in Computer Science*, pages 86–103. Springer, 2009.

[34] K.-C. Tai. The tree-to-tree correction problem. *Journal of the ACM*, 26(3):422–433, 1979.

[35] T. Terauchi and A. Aiken. Secure information flow as a safety problem. In C. Hankin and I. Siveroni, editors, *Static Analysis, 12th International Symposium, SAS 2005*, volume 3672 of *Lecture Notes in Computer Science*, pages 352–367. Springer, 2005.

[36] D. M. Volpano, C. E. Irvine, and G. Smith. A sound type system for secure flow analysis. *Journal of Computer Security*, 4(2/3):167–188, 1996.

[37] C. Weidenbach. Towards an automatic analysis of security protocols in first-order logic. In H. Ganzinger, editor, *CADE-16, 16th International Conference on Automated Deduction*, volume 1632 of *Lecture Notes in Computer Science*, pages 314–328. Springer, 1999.

[38] C. Weidenbach, D. Dimova, A. Fietzke, R. Kumar, M. Suda, and P. Wischnewski. SPASS version 3.5. In R. A. Schmidt, editor, *CADE-22, 22nd International Conference on Automated Deduction*, volume 5663 of *Lecture Notes in Computer Science*, pages 140–145. Springer, 2009.

[39] M. Zanotti. Security typings by abstract interpretation. In M. V. Hermenegildo and G. Puebla, editors, *Static Analysis, 9th International Symposium, SAS 2002*, volume 2477 of *Lecture Notes in Computer Science*, pages 360–375. Springer, 2002.

Formal Verification of Information Flow Security for a Simple ARM-Based Separation Kernel

Mads Dam, Roberto Guanciale,
Narges Khakpour, Hamed Nemati
KTH Royal Institute of Technology
SE-100 44, Stockholm, Sweden
{mfd, robertog, nargeskh,
hnnemati}@kth.se

Oliver Schwarz
SICS Swedish ICT
Box 1263
SE-164 29
Kista, Sweden
oliver@sics.se

ABSTRACT

A separation kernel simulates a distributed environment using a single physical machine by executing partitions in isolation and appropriately controlling communication among them. We present a formal verification of information flow security for a simple separation kernel for ARMv7. Previous work on information flow kernel security leaves communication to be handled by model-external means, and cannot be used to draw conclusions when there is explicit interaction between partitions. We propose a different approach where communication between partitions is made explicit and the information flow is analyzed in the presence of such a channel. Limiting the kernel functionality as much as meaningfully possible, we accomplish a detailed analysis and verification of the system, proving its correctness at the level of the ARMv7 assembly. As a sanity check we show how the security condition is reduced to noninterference in the special case where no communication takes place. The verification is done in HOL4 taking the Cambridge model of ARM as basis, transferring verification tasks on the actual assembly code to an adaptation of the BAP binary analysis tool developed at CMU.

Categories and Subject Descriptors

D4.6 [**Operating Systems**]: Security and Protection; D.2.4 [**Software Engineering**]: Software/Program Verification—*formal methods, correctness proofs*

Keywords

Formal verification; Information Flow Security; Separation Kernel; Hypervisor

1. INTRODUCTION

The design of secure systems needs to ensure that software components belonging to different security domains are adequately isolated from each other, such that only authorized communication can take place between them. One way of achieving this is by dedicated hardware, e.g. TPM's or SIM's. This, however, carries significant overhead, in terms of the hardware itself, and the associated infrastructure. An alternative is to execute the components in isolated partitions on shared hardware, using low-level software execution platforms such as separation kernels [25, 12] or secure hypervisors [10, 27, 17]. A key requirement of this solution is the verification of the tamper resistant trusted computing base, preferably by use of formal methods. Significant progress has been made recently in this direction, cf. the seL4 project [14], Microsoft's Hyper-V project [16], and Green Hills' CC certified INTEGRITY-178B separation kernel [23].

Our focusing scenario consists of an "untrusted" component (e.g. a smartphone software stack) that interacts with a set of trusted services, such as a virtual SIM card, or a virtual TPM. A shared execution platform for this scenario needs to provide the following minimal functionality:

1. Isolation of component resources

2. A communication mechanism that plays the role of external communication lines in a physically distributed system

3. A scheduling mechanism to commit shared resources (e.g. processors) among the components.

In this paper we present a proof-of-concept design and machine level verification of the PROSPER separation kernel for ARMv7 [3], which supports the above functionality. The kernel allows the execution of two component systems, such as a smartphone OS with a virtualized SIM application, on top of a single physical machine. The interesting feature of this set-up is that explicit, kernel-supported communication between partitions is essential, and a critical aspect of the security analysis is to ensure that this communication does not introduce (deliberate or accidental) side channels that can be exploited by an attacker.

This security analysis is far from trivial. The objective of a separation kernel[1], following Rushby [25], is first to make

[1]We use the label "separation kernel" in this paper mainly since no support for user/kernel space virtualization is provided to the component systems, but the borderline between separation kernels and secure hypervisors, and our use of the associated terminology, is admittedly fuzzy.

CCS'13, November 4–8, 2013, Berlin, Germany.
ACM 978-1-4503-2477-9/13/11.
http://dx.doi.org/10.1145/2508859.2516702.

it appear that each component system is executed on a separate, isolated, machine, and second to ensure that communication can only flow as authorized along known external channels. However, there are several problems in delegating communication to an external agent. First, it entails an extension of the trusted computing base to include the external channel itself. Second, virtualizing the component systems without also virtualizing the channel connecting them is hardly a reasonable design. Third, potential side channels are ignored. In a case such as this, where a partition must be able to access the virtualized SIM application at will, communication can convey critical timing information that an attacker can exploit to extract key material, as is well known [15].

We propose instead an approach where communication between partitions is made explicit in the top level specification (TLS), and information flow is analyzed in the presence of such an intended communication channel. We formulate the TLS such that it directly formalizes, in sufficient detail, the set of computation paths both allowed and required at the implementation level, and then we check that the implementation indeed satisfies this specification. The question is how to do this, if it can be done while maintaining a satisfactory account of isolation, and if it can be done at a satisfactory level of abstraction (such that the TLS does not conflate to become identical to the implementation itself). In this paper we present a proof-of-concept solution in the sense that functionality is limited as much as meaningfully possible, but such that the specification, implementation and correctness proof is carried through in complete detail from TLS to realization for ARMv7, and proved correct at the instruction reference semantics level using the HOL4 model of ARM developed at Cambridge [7].

In our case, the goal of verification is to show that there is no way for the partitions to affect each other, directly or indirectly, *except* through the intended channel. In particular, there should be no way for a partition to access the memory or register contents, by reading or writing, of the other partition, other than when the communication is realized by explicit usage of the intended channel, by both partitions in collaboration. This is not an easy property to reconcile with the standard information flow tools such as noninterference (NI) or intransitive noninterference:

- NI is problematic since the very purpose of the kernel is to *allow* rather than prevent information flow (through the intended channel). For the sake of illustration consider the recent NI-based verification of the seL4 kernel [20, 19]: A critical step in that work boils down to a proof of the *absence* of information flow from the previously scheduled partition to the scheduler itself, in order to prevent the scheduler being used as a communication channel. This type of approach is not applicable in our setting since communication must be allowed to affect the partitions in ways that are outside our control, as the partitions are not statically known. Moreover, for the same reason we have no control over what, where, or how the channel is intended to be used, and thus the various NI-based declassification schemes (cf. [26]) do not help.

- Intransitive noninterference [24] relaxes NI with the possibility to add unknown, but trusted, intermediary agents through which information flows can be required to pass. In our case that agent is the kernel, which is known, and not a priori trusted. This makes intransitive noninterference difficult to make use of in the present context.

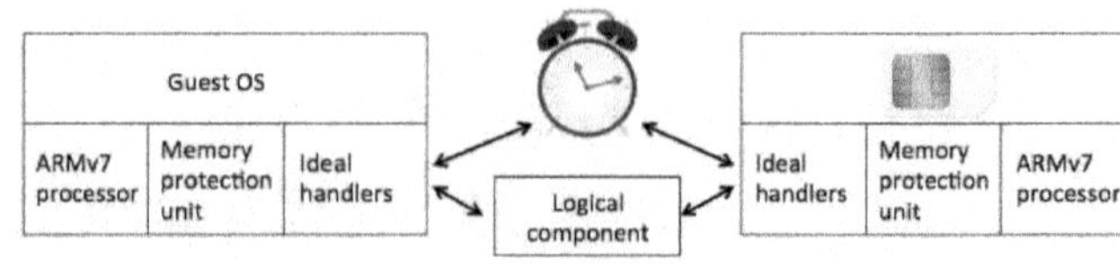

Figure 1: Ideal model

We thus take a different approach. We formulate the TLS as an "ideal model" which satisfies the required separation properties by construction, and then reduce correctness to trace equivalence w.r.t. a "real model", reflecting actual systems behaviour. The key idea is to execute the partitions on physically separate, ideal processors, connected by an explicit, ideal communication channel, and equipped with a little extra paraphernalia, as shown in Fig. 1. The ideal processors need to accurately mimick the execution of user space partitions on a real processor. This is done by augmenting the TLS processors by idealized functionality, the "ideal handlers" of Fig. 1, which is invoked whenever the actual processors would transition to privileged mode by an exception (e.g. a hardware interrupt, or an exception). This construction allows userland code to execute as desired (with the exception of fine grained timing differences we currently do not take into account), but the idealized processors are physically prevented from directly affecting their sibling machine, with the exception of explicit communication using the message delivery service.

The task is thus to show that, properly set up, the user observable traces of the ideal model are the same as those of a "real model", obtained by executing the software in different partitions on top of our separation kernel, on top of a real ARMv7-A processor, including a Memory Management Unit (MMU) for physical protection of memory regions belonging to different partitions. We prove this using the bisimulation proof method [28], by exhibiting a concrete bisimulation relation, a *candidate relation*, relating the state spaces of ideal and real models. The proof that the candidate relation is actually a bisimulation relation of the appropriate type is in turn reduced to subsidiary properties, several of which have natural correspondences in previous kernel verification literature, cf. [12, 23], namely that:

i The initial states of the ideal and the real models are in the candidate relation. This is ensured by the correctness of the bootstrap code.

ii A partition does not perform any isolation-violating operation while it is executing. Due to our use of memory protection, this is really a noninterference-like property of the ARMv7-A architecture rather than a property of the separation kernel. This property is similar to the partition management result reported in [30].

iii The processor state switches correctly upon transition to privileged mode. Again this is a processor architecture rather than a kernel dependent result.

iv Execution of ideal exception handlers vs the real separation kernel exception handlers preserve the candidate relation.

v Several invariants are preserved while partitions and /or kernel handlers are running.

For the actual verification we have used a combination of theorem proving and binary code analysis. The real and ideal models are built on top of the Cambridge ARM HOL4 model, extended with a simple MMU unit. The isolation lemmas of ARM, items (ii) and (iii), are proved using a tool, ARM-prover, developed for the purpose in HOL4. The proofs are costly and involve traversing the full ARM instruction sets. The ARM-prover allows the proofs to be automated to a large extent. This frees us from the onerous task of verifying the two theorems on each element of the large ARM instruction set. The ARM-prover tool is developed on top of the monadic ARM semantics reported in [7]. Handlers (item (iv)) are verified using pre/post conditions. Manual generation of these handlers is an error-prone process, and for this reason we generate the pre/post conditions automatically based on the specification of the ideal model, the candidate relation, and the ARM isolation Lemmas. We transfer the pre/post conditions to the binary code analysis tool BAP [6], and use BAP to verify the bootstrap code and the kernel handlers at the assembly code level. Several tools have been developed for lifting the ARM code to the input format of BAP and manipulating the code. Space prevents us from more than outlining the ARM isolation lemmas and the BAP extensions here; these will be reported in separate publications.

The paper is organized as follows: In section 2 we present the ARMv7 processor, MMU, and timing model. In section 3, the PROSPER kernel is presented, and the the ideal model is described in section 4. We then proceed to give an overview of the proof strategy, including the decomposition of the TLS into the ARM lemmas, and the handler verification tasks. In section 6 we partially validate our verification approach by proving a "monotonicity of release" property as suggested by Sabelfeld and Sands [26], that a corollary of our proof is an NI property in the special case where partitions do not actually communicate. In section 7 we present the proof implementation, and in section 8 information is given on the status of the kernel and some performance figures regarding the proof itself. In section 9 related work is discussed, and finally in section 10, we conclude and discuss some unresolved issues.

2. ARMv7

An ARMv7 CPU has execution mode $m \in \mathcal{M}$ where $\mathcal{M} = \{usr, svc, abort, undef, irq, fiq, sys\}$. The non-privileged usr mode is used by the user partitions, while the privileged modes $\mathcal{M}_p = \mathcal{M} \backslash \{usr\}$ are used to execute kernel activities. A machine state is a record $\sigma = \langle regs, psrs, mem, coregs\rangle$ where $regs$, $psrs$, mem and $coregs$, respectively represent the registers, program status registers ($psrs$), memory and coprocessors of the machine. The register set $regs$ consists of the sixteen user registers that are accessible in all modes as well as the banked-registers of each privileged mode that are available only in that mode. The program status registers is a record

$$\langle cpsr, psr_{svc}, psr_{abort}, psr_{undef}, psr_{irq}, psr_{fiq}, psr_{sys}\rangle$$

where $cpsr$ is the current psr and each psr_m is the banked psr in mode $m \in \mathcal{M}_p$. A psr encodes the arithmetical flags, the executing mode, the interrupt mask, and the instruction decoding. The functions $I(\sigma)$ and $M(\sigma)$ return the hardware interrupt mask and the current mode in state σ, respectively. Moreover, the memory is the function $mem \in word32 \rightarrow word8$.

The tuple $coregs = \langle c_1, c_2, c_3\rangle$ contains the three 32-bit registers of coprocessor CP15, used mainly to control the Memory Management Unit (MMU). The register c_1 represents whether the MMU is enabled or not, and c_2 gives the base address of the page table. In ARMv7, there are sixteen domains, each representing a security role. The coprocessor register c_3 holds the current status of the domains. An entry of the page table determines the owner domain of the corresponding page and its access permission.

In our setting, a "real' system" is an ARM machine connected to a timer device. A real system is modeled by the record $s = \langle \sigma, t\rangle \in \mathcal{S}$, where σ is an ARM machine state and t represents the clock cycles elapsed since system start. The behavior of a system is defined by the state transition relation $\rightarrow \subseteq \mathcal{S} \times \mathcal{S}$ where a transition is performed due to either the execution of an ARM instruction or a timer signal. We assume a simple time model that constrains all transitions to consume one clock cycle, i.e. if $\langle \sigma, t\rangle \rightarrow \langle \sigma', t'\rangle$ then $t' = t + 1$.

If the real system switches from the mode usr to a privileged mode, then an exception has occurred. The privileged mode svc is activated by a software interrupt (SWI). If the current instruction is undefined, then the system switches to the mode $undef$. The mode irq is activated by a hardware interrupt. In our setting, the timer triggers a hardware interrupt every fixed amount of clock (actually, instruction) cycles. If the MMU prevents an access to the memory, then the mode $abort$ is enabled. In our setting, no exception can activate the modes sys and fiq. In fact, sys mode can only be explicitly entered from a privileged mode. Moreover, in our model there is only one device (the timer) which delivers standard hardware interrupts. For this reason the fast interrupt mode fiq is never activated. Whenever an exception occurs, the CPU backs up the program counter and the cpsr into the banked registers and into the psr of the activated mode, disables hardware interrupts and jumps to a predefined address in the vector table to transfer the control to the corresponding exception handler.

Figure 2 (A) depicts an example computation of a real system. White and grey circles represent states in user mode and black circles represent states in privileged modes. The circle labels represent the system clocks and the solid arrows represent the transition relation. Transitions between two states in user mode (e.g. $1 \rightarrow 2$) do not cause any exceptions. The timer tick of this example is six clock cycles, then an interrupt is delivered in the states 6 and 12, switching the system to mode irq. The transition between the states 2 and 3 is caused by a different exception, for example the execution of a software interrupt. Finally, transitions from privileged modes to user mode (e.g. $4 \rightarrow 5$) are caused by instructions that explicitly change $cpsr$.

3. THE PROSPER KERNEL

The PROSPER kernel has four minimal functionalities: execution of two user partitions on one physical machine, protection of the partition resources, partition scheduling,

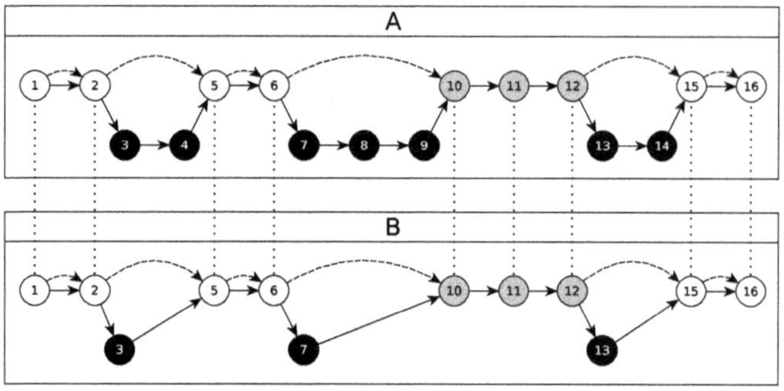

Figure 2: (A) The real world and (B) the Top Level Specification

and inter-partition communication. All low-level tasks of the kernel that depend on the architecture (e.g. accessing special registers and coprocessors, context saving and restoring) are implemented in assembly ($\sim$ 150 lines of codes), while all high-level tasks (e.g., hypercall, scheduling, page table setup) are implemented in C ($\sim$ 600 lines of code). The current implementation can host OSs (e.g. μClinux [18], FreeRTOS[8]) that do not require intra-partition memory protection.

The machine memory is partitioned into three separate regions: the region in the range of $[min_g, max_g]$ for the partition $g \in \{1, 2\}$, and a kernel memory region. The accesses to the partitions are controlled by the MMU where three ARMv7 domains 0,1, and 2 are used to represent the kernel, the first partition and the second partition, respectively. When the kernel resumes a partition, it updates the coprocessor c_3 to set the partition domain to the value *client* and to disable the domain of the other partition. The MMU is configured to enforce the following properties: (i) if a partition is running, then only its memory can be accessed, (ii) whenever the kernel is activated (e.g. a partition performs a software interrupt), it is able to read and write its memory and the memory of the "interrupted" partition. We have no concurrency inside the kernel, i.e. an exception can not interrupt while another exception is being handled.

The partitions communicate through asynchronous message passing. Each partition has two executing status variables: *message status* is intended to process the incoming messages while the *task status* is used for other activities. To each status is associated a context that contains a set of user registers and the cpsr. For the active partition, the context corresponding to the active status is the current user registers and the cpsr and the context of the non-active status is stored in the kernel memory. For the inactive partition, both contexts are stored in kernel memory. The hypercalls are used by the partitions to invoke the kernel by executing the software interrupt instruction. The kernel provides two types of hypercalls: *message sending hypercall* and *status switching hypercall*. To send a message, the partition executes the instruction "SWI 1". The software interrupt handler stores the message into the message-box of the receiver and restores the sender. The status switching hypercall changes the executing status of the partition by executing "SWI 0". The kernel backs up the CPU state into its own memory and reactivates the interrupted partition.

The irq-handler implements a static round-robin scheduler, that suspends the active partition and resumes the other one. It is also in charge of delivering the pending messages to the resuming (receiver) partition; if the message-box of the resuming partition is full, (i) its status is changed to "message", (ii) the context of its message status is updated with the content of the pending message, and (iii) the program counter of the resumed partition is updated to point to its message handler code. The reception of a message causes the resumed partition to enter into a local critical section, i.e. no other message can be received while the partition is running in the message status. To exist from the critical section, the receiver partition performs a status switch hypercall.

To start the system, a memory image of the system must be prepared by the linker. Let $mem_1 : [min_1, max_1] \rightarrow word8$ and $mem_2 : [min_2, max_2] \rightarrow word8$ be two initial partition memories in our setting. Then, the linker loads the initial partition memories and the kernel memory into the system memory, and activates the kernel bootstrap code. The *initial state* of the real system is the first reachable state in user mode obtained after the execution of the bootstrap code of the kernel. Clearly, this initial state of the system depends on the partitions memories. We denote the behavior of a real system starting from an initial state s_0 with initial partition memories mem_1 and mem_2 by the transition system $T_r(mem_1, mem_2) = \langle \mathcal{S}, s_0, \rightarrow \rangle$.

4. THE IDEAL SYSTEM

The *ideal system* formalizes the top level specification which satisfies the required separation properties by construction. The ideal system is composed of two separate special ARMv7 machines communicating via asynchronous message passing, a logical component and a shared timer (see Fig. 1). Each machine of the ideal system is used to execute one of the two partitions in a physically isolated environment. Intuitively, the logical component can be considered as an external device. Our special ARMv7 machine allows a partition to execute without the runtime support of the kernel. This machine executes the user-mode computations as a regular ARMv7 processor, but if the processor switches to a privileged mode, an abstract kernel functionality is atomically executed and the user mode is restored.

An ideal state is a record $q = \langle \sigma_1, \sigma_2, c_1, c_2, t, id \rangle \in \mathcal{Q}$ where t represents the clock cycles elapsed from the system start. At each instant, only one of the machines can perform computations, and $id \in \{1, 2\}$ identifies the active machine. The logical component consists of the records $c_i = \langle rdy, ctx, msg \rangle$, $i \in \{1, 2\}$. The flag rdy represents if the machine is ready to handle the incoming messages and the banked context ctx (set of registers and cpsr) is used to back up the machine state whenever a message is received. A message box $msg \in word32 \cup \{\perp\}$ can either contain a pending message or be empty ($\perp$). Henceforth, we say that an ideal system is in mode m if the active machine is in mode m and the inactive one is in the mode usr.

The initial state of the ideal system, similar to the real system, depends on the initial partition memories. We denote the behavior of a ideal system starting from an initial state q_0 with initial partition memories mem_1 and mem_2 by the transition system $T_i(mem_1, mem_2) = \langle \mathcal{Q}, q_0, \rightarrow \rangle$. In the initial state, all the components are initialized such that the partitions memories and the page tables are loaded into their corresponding machine memory, the program counter

$$\frac{M(\sigma_1) = usr \wedge \langle \sigma_1, t\rangle \rightarrow \langle \sigma_1', t'\rangle}{\langle \sigma_1, \sigma_2, c_1, c_2, t, 1\rangle \rightarrow \langle \sigma_1', \sigma_2, c_1, c_2, t', 1\rangle}\ UserR \qquad \frac{M(\sigma_1) = irq \wedge (c_2.msg = \perp \vee \neg c_2.rdy)}{\langle \sigma_1, \sigma_2, c_1, c_2, t, 1\rangle \rightarrow \langle RestoreUser(\sigma_1), \sigma_2, c_1, c_2, t + t_{sh}, 2\rangle}\ SchR$$

$$\frac{\begin{array}{c} M(\sigma_1) = svc \wedge curr(\sigma_1) = SWI\ 0 \\ (\sigma_1', c_1') = Switch(RestoreUsr(\sigma_1), c_1)\end{array}}{\langle \sigma_1, \sigma_2, c_1, c_2, t, 1\rangle \rightarrow \langle \sigma_1', \sigma_2, c_1', c_2, t + t_{switch}, 1\rangle}\ SwitchR \qquad \frac{\begin{array}{c} M(\sigma_1) = irq \wedge c_2.rdy \wedge c_2.msg \neq \perp \\ (\sigma_2', c_2') = Receive(\sigma_2, c_2)\end{array}}{\langle \sigma_1, \sigma_2, c_1, c_2, t, 1\rangle \rightarrow \langle RestoreUsr(\sigma_1), \sigma_2', c_1, c_2', t + t_{rcv}, 2\rangle}\ RcvR$$

$$\frac{\begin{array}{c} M(\sigma_1) = svc \wedge curr(\sigma_1) = SWI\ 1 \\ c_2' = \langle c_2.rdy, c_2.ctx, Out(\sigma_1)\rangle\end{array}}{\langle \sigma_1, \sigma_2, c_1, c_2, t, 1\rangle \rightarrow \langle IncPC(RestoreUsr(\sigma_1)), \sigma_2, c_1, c_2', t + t_{snd}, 1\rangle}\ SendR$$

Figure 3: Semantics of the Ideal System

of each machine points to the entry point of the corresponding partition, and both machines are in the mode *usr*.

Figure 3 shows the semantics of the ideal system when machine 1 is active. Due to lack of space, we only present the semantics of hypercalls and scheduling. In all cases, the ideal transitions yield the two machines in user mode. The rules for machine 2 active are similar. Each kernel functionality f comes with a fixed time budget t_f for its execution.

The rule *UserR* states that if the processor is in user mode, execution of an instruction does not affect the state of the logical component and the inactive machine, and it behaves as if it is executed on a regular ARMv7 machine. Instructions consume the same amount of cycles in the real and ideal systems.

A machine is rescheduled whenever a hardware interrupt is triggered by the timer. The function *RestoreUser* restores user mode and the corresponding banked registers. The rule *SchR* describes that if there is no message for the resumed machine or the resumed machine is not ready to handle a message, the active partition is changed to the current suspended one. The rule *RcvR* expresses the reception of a pending message by the resumed machine in which the function $receive(\sigma_2, c_2)$ disables the *rdy* flag for entering into a critical section, moves the pending message into the input buffer of the receiver, and sets the program counter to point to the message handler of the receiver.

The rule *SendR* describes the semantics of message sending (activated due to the execution of "SWI 1" in the previous state) that copies the message into the message box of the inactive machine. If the status switch hypercall is invoked, the rule *SwitchR* toggles the *rdy* flag and restores the banked context.

Figure 2 (B) depicts an example computation of an ideal system. In the states 2, 6 and 12 the system traps an exception raised on the active machine and atomically applies an ideal kernel functionality.

5. PROOF STRATEGY

To prove that the real model does not introduce information channels not already present in the ideal model it suffices to show that the observable traces for each partition are the same in both cases. In order to pin down this concept we need to define when each partition system is in control of the system, and what its observations are.

Top Level Proof Goal.

Intuitively, for the real system, partition g is in control when its program counter points to a location in mem_g. However, this is not entirely accurate. Instead we say that partition g is *active* in state s, $act_g(s)$, if the processor is in user mode and the status of the domain g, held by coprocessor register c_3 is client. For the ideal system, partition g is *active*, $act_g(q)$, if the *id* field of the ideal state is g and the corresponding machine is in the user mode.

The observations of partition g in real state s, assuming that g is active, are the CPU and memory resources observable by g in state s. This is the structure $O_g(s) = \langle uregs, cpsr, mem_g\rangle$ of user registers, cpsr and partition memory in state s. If g is inactive in s, g's observations are the user registers and cpsr of the saved context of g along with its partition memory. For the ideal system, $O_g(q)$ is the user registers, cpsr and the memory allocated to g of the corresponding machine in q.

Consider now an infinite execution $\pi_r = s_0 \rightarrow s_1 \rightarrow \cdots$ of the real system. The g-trace of π_r is the sequence $\omega(\pi_r, g)$ of observations obtained by first projecting out those states for which g is not active, and secondly extracting g's observations, or in other words, $\omega(\pi_r, g) = map(O_g, prj(\pi_r, act_g))$ where *prj* and *map* are the obvious projection/filtering functions. Similarly, if π_i is an ideal execution, the g-trace of π_i is $\omega(\pi_i, g) = map(O_g, prj(\pi_i, act_g))$.

Let now $tr_{g,r}(mem_1, mem_2)$ and $tr_{g,i}(mem_1, mem_2)$ be the set of g-traces of the real system and the ideal system with the initial partition memories of mem_1 and mem_2, respectively, and for arbitrary states s, q, let $tr_g(s)$ and $tr_g(q)$ be the sets of g-traces of executions starting in s, q, respectively. The top level proof goal is thus to prove that the sets of g-traces of the real and the ideal systems are identical, for $g \in \{1, 2\}$ and any arbitrary mem_1 and mem_2, or, more precisely, that

$$tr_{g,r}(mem_1, mem_2) = tr_{g,i}(mem_1, mem_2) \qquad (1)$$

for all initial partition memories mem_1, mem_2. If (1) holds we say that the PROSPER kernel guarantees isolation.

In order to prove (1), we first present three general lemmas concerning the safe executions of an ARM machine in user mode and its safe mode switching from user mode to privileged mode. Given the general ARM Lemmas, we prove lemmas for the real and the ideal systems to ensure correct initialization, correct userland execution, and isolation-guaranteed execution of the kernel handlers. We then proceed to present the proof of (1).

ARM Lemmas.

Our proof strategy identifies three lemmas concerning the ARM instruction set architecture that may have significance beyond the verification exercise reported here. The first is a general noninterference lemma stating that if an ARM machine executes in user mode in a memory protected configuration as studied here, the behavior of the active partition is influenced only by those resources allowed to do so. The predicate $sim_g(s_1, s_2)$ indicates that the status of the domain g held by coprocessor register c_3 is client in the user mode states s_1 and s_2, and they have the same user registers, cpsr, MMU configurations and the memory allocated to the domain g.

LEMMA 1. *If $sim_g(s_1, s_2)$ and $s_1 \rightarrow s_1'$, there exists s_2' s.t. $s_2 \rightarrow s_2'$ and $sim_g(s_1', s_2')$, and vice versa.*

The second lemma establishes $unmodified_g(s, s')$ stating that the non-accessible resources for a state s in user mode, including the privileged psrs/registers, coprocessor registers, interrupt flags and the memory regions not allocated to the active partition g, are not modified in a transition from s to another user mode state s'. If s' is in privileged mode m, the privileged registers, psr_m and the interrupt flags, are excluded from the non-modifiable resources. We obtain:

LEMMA 2. *If $s \rightarrow s'$ and $act_g(s)$ then $unmodified_g(s, s')$.*

The predicate $priv\_const_g(s, s')$ asserts that if an ARM machine switches from s in user mode to s' in privileged mode m then the conditions for the execution of the handler are prepared properly, e.g., the program counter points to the correct entry of the vector table, the link register of m contains the correct return address of the partition, and the flags of $cpsr$ and psr_m are set correctly.

LEMMA 3. *Suppose $s \rightarrow s'$, $act_g(s)$ and $M(s') \neq usr$. Then $priv\_const_g(s, s')$.*

(g, m)*-Compatible States.*

We then turn to the conditions needed to ensure that the partition observations are the same in the real and the ideal systems. These conditions depend on many aspects of the machine states and we are only able to outline the conditions here.

These conditions are complex because several elements can directly or indirectly influence the behavior of a partition. We briefly define the conditions for the user mode states (i.e. when all machines are in the user mode) and the switched mode states (i.e. the inactive machine of ideal machine is in the user mode but the real system and the active machine of ideal system have recently switched to the privileged mode).

Say that two states s and q are *(g, m)-compatible* if (i) s and q are in the mode m, (ii) g is the last active partition in s and q, i.e. the status of the domain g, held by coprocessor register c_3 is client in s, and the *id* field of the ideal state is g, (iii) the partitions have the same observations in s and q, $O_{g'}(s) = O_{g'}(q)$ for $g' \in \{1, 2\}$, (iv) the values of data-structures in the logical component of state q agree with the values of corresponding data structures in the kernel of state s, e.g. the message box of a partition in the kernel and the logical component contain the same values, (v) the MMU and coprocessors are configured correctly in all three machines, (vi) a set of invariants are held by the kernel data-structure in s, (vii) the interrupt flags are set correctly, e.g. the fast interrupt flag F of all machines are disabled, (viii) if m is a privileged mode then psr_m and the link register of the mode m must be identical in the active machine of q and s, to make sure that g is restored properly, (ix) s and q have the same system clock.

User/Handler Lemmas.

The relation of (g,m)-compatibility is our candidate unwinding relation, i.e. it is in some suitable sense which we go on to make precise preserved under computation. This involves showing the following two key properties:

- User Lemma: Each user mode transition in the real system is matched (in the sense of (g,m)-compatibility) by a corresponding user mode transition in the ideal system without interfering with the resources that are not intended to be accessible by the partition, and vice versa.
- Handler Lemma: Each complete handler execution in the real system is matched (as (g,m)-compatibility) by a corresponding execution of a kernel functionality in the ideal model, and vice versa.

Similar to the $unmodified_g$ predicate for the real system above, $unmodified_g(q, q')$ holds if the logical component, the inactive machine, and the non-accessible resources of the active machine are unmodified by an ideal transition from q to q' when g is active in q. The User Lemma then follows from the first and second ARM Lemmas as follows:

LEMMA 4 (USER). *For all (g, usr)-compatible states s and q, if $q \rightarrow q'$ then there exist s' and m such that*

(i) $s \rightarrow s'$,

(ii) the states s' and q' are (g, m)-compatible,

(iii) $unmodified_g(s, s')$, and (iv) $unmodified_g(q, q')$.

Vice versa, if $s \rightarrow s'$ then q' and m exists such that $q \rightarrow q'$ and the above properties (ii) and (iii) hold.

For the Handler Lemma we need to ensure that execution of the kernel handlers terminates, and that the compatibility conditions are satisfied when the control returns back to the partitions. Let $s_0 \rightsquigarrow s_n$ if there is a finite execution $s_0 \rightarrow \cdots \rightarrow s_n$ such that $M(s_n) = usr$ and $M(s_j) \neq usr$ for $0 < j < n$. Similarly, we define $\rightsquigarrow$ for the ideal system. These state relations are represented in Fig. 2 by the dashed arrows. The additional black states in the real world are internal kernel steps that can not be observed by the partitions.

LEMMA 5 (HANDLER). *Suppose that s and q are two (g, m)-compatible states, $m \neq usr$. Assume s and q are respectively reached by a transition from the states s' and q', and $priv\_const_g(q, q')$ and $priv\_const_g(s, s')$ hold. If $q' \rightsquigarrow q''$ then there exist s'' and $g' \in \{1, 2\}$ such that $s' \rightsquigarrow s''$, and the states s'' and q'' are (g', usr)-compatible, and vice versa.*

Furthermore, it is to be guaranteed that the initial states of the real and the ideal systems are compatible. That is, we must verify that the MMU is set up according to our model requirements, the kernel invariants are satisfied, the partitions memory and the interrupt flags are configured correctly. In addition, we must make sure that the kernel code is loaded in the right part of the memory.

PROPOSITION 1. *For all initial partition memories mem_1, mem_2, the kernel boot terminates in the state s_0, and there exists $g \in \{1, 2\}$ s.t. s_0 and q_0 are (g, usr)-compatible*

Proof of Main Theorem.

We can now proceed to prove (1). This is almost done once we show that the initial states are related by a bisimulation relation of a suitable form. To this end say that a relation R on pairs (s, q) of user mode states is a *candidate relation*, if whenever sRq then for some $g \in \{1, 2\}$, (i) $act_g(s)$, (ii) $act_g(q)$, (iii) $O_g(s) = O_g(q)$, and (iv) if $q \rightsquigarrow q'$, then there exists s' such that $s \rightsquigarrow s'$ and $s'Rq'$, and (v) vice versa, if $s \rightsquigarrow s'$, then there exists q' such that $q \rightsquigarrow q'$ and $s'Rq'$.

Note that for the user mode states s and s', if $s \rightarrow s'$ then $s \rightsquigarrow s'$. In Fig. 2, dotted lines exemplify a bisimulation relation. It is easy to check that the existence of a candidate relation is sufficient to ensure (1). In particular:

PROPOSITION 2. *Suppose that sRq for some candidate relation R. Then $tr_g(s) = tr_g(q)$.*

THEOREM 1. *The PROSPER separation kernel guarantees isolation.*

The proof of 1 obviously relies on the proofs of the above lemmas, which in turn, for Handler Lemma and the Lemma 1, relies on verification of the handler and the bootstrap code, as outlined in Section 7. But, it may be illustrative to explain how these lemma come together to allow the main Theorem 1 to be proved.

By Theorem 1 it suffices to find a candidate relation relating the initial states s_0 and q_0. Define the candidate relation as follows:

$$R = \{(s, q) | (g, usr)\text{-}compatible(s, q) \wedge g \in \{1, 2\}\}$$

We get $s_0 R q_0$ by prop. 1.

To prove that R is a candidate relation, assume that sRq. Then s and q are (g, usr)-*compatible.* Thus, $act_g(s)$, $act_g(q)$ and $O_g(s) = O_g(q)$ hold.

Suppose now that $q \rightsquigarrow q'$. There are two cases:

Case 1: If the ideal transition does not involve mode switching it follows from the User Lemma that s' exists such that $s \rightsquigarrow s'$ and q' and s' are (g, usr)-*compatible*, whence $s'Rq'$ as desired.

Case 2: If the ideal transition involves a switch to privileged mode m, it follows from the User Lemma that the real and ideal system evolve to the (g, m)-*compatible* states s'' and q''. According to the Third ARM Lemma, these transitions are performed safely, i.e. $priv\_const_g(s, s'')$ and $priv\_const_g(q, q'')$ hold. From the Handler Lemma, we can conclude that there exist (g', usr)-*compatible* states s' and q' where $s'' \rightsquigarrow s'$, $q'' \rightsquigarrow q'$ and $g' \in \{1, 2\}$. But then $s'Rq'$, as desired.

The converse direction, that $s \rightsquigarrow s'$ implies $q \rightsquigarrow q'$ and $s'Rq'$ for some q follows by a symmetric argument (or, in this simple case, by determinacy of the $\rightsquigarrow$ relation). This concludes the proof of Theorem 1.

6. ISOLATION PROPERTIES

The main theorem shows that the real system does not leak more information than the ideal system, under the caveats we have imposed. However, it may not be clear what information is leaked by the ideal system itself. Neither may it be clear how leakage properties of the ideal system can be transferred to the real system. In this section we throw light on these two issues.

Data Separation.

Concerning the ideal system itself we use the approach of [12] to analyze kernel data separation properties. Let $\mathcal{Q}_c = \{q | \exists s.\ sRq\}$ be the image of the candidate relation.

The *No-Exfiltration* property guarantees that a transition with the partition g active in its target, does not modify the resources of the other partition, except its communication channel, i.e. the message box:

LEMMA 6. *Let $g, g' \in \{1, 2\}$, $g' \neq g$ and $q \in \mathcal{Q}_c$. If $q \rightsquigarrow q'$ and $q'.id = g$, then $O_{g'}(q) = O_{g'}(q')$, $q.c_{g'}.rdy = q'.c_{g'}.rdy$ and $q.c_{g'}.ctx = q'.c_{g'}.ctx$.*

The *No-Infiltration* property is a noninterference property guaranteeing that a transition for which g is active in its target state, depends only on the partition observations, its logical component and the MMU configuration. In particular, a transition ending in a state with the partition g active, is not influenced by data owned by the other partition.

LEMMA 7. *Let $q_1, q_2 \in \mathcal{Q}_c$ such that $q_1.c_g = q_2.c_g$, $q_1.t = q_2.t$, $q_1.id = q_2.id$ and $O_g(q_1) = O_g(q_2)$. If $q_1 \rightsquigarrow q_1'$, $q_2 \rightsquigarrow q_2'$, $act_g(q_1')$ and $act_g(q_2')$ then $q_1'.c_g = q_2'.c_g$, $q_1'.t = q_2'.t$ and $O_g(q_1') = O_g(q_2')$*

Similar properties can be proven for the real system using the candidate relation and the properties of the ideal system. Let $\mathcal{S}_c = \{s | \exists q.\ sRq\}$ be the preimage of the candidate relation, and the function $lc_g(s)$ extracts from the kernel memory the content of the data-structure that corresponds to c_g in the logical component. The following corollary states the no-infiltration and no-exfiltration for the real system.

COROLLARY 1. *Let $s_1, s_2 \in \mathcal{S}_c$, $s_1.t = s_2.t$, $act_g(s_1) \Leftrightarrow act_g(s_2)$.*

- *Suppose if $g' \neq g$, $s_1 \rightsquigarrow s_1'$ and $act_g(s_1')$ then $O_{g'}(s_1) = O_{g'}(s_1')$, $lc_{g'}(s_1).rdy = lc_{g'}(s_1').rdy$ and $lc_{g'}(s_1).ctx = lc_{g'}(s_1').ctx$.*
- *Suppose if $lc_g(s_1) = lc_g(s_2)$, $O_g(s_1) = O_g(s_2)$, $s_1 \rightsquigarrow s_1'$ and $s_2 \rightsquigarrow s_2'$, $act_g(s_1')$ and $act_g(s_2')$ then $lc_g(s_1') = lc_g(s_2')$ and $O_g(s_1') = O_g(s_2')$*

We sketch the proof of the second statement. Since s_1 and s_2 are in $\mathcal{S}_c$, then there exist q_1 and q_2 s.t. $s_1 R q_1$ and $s_2 R q_2$. We follow from the assumptions and the definition of R that $q_1.c_g = q_2.c_g$, $q_1.t = q_2.t$, $O_g(q_1) = O_g(q_2)$ and $q_1.idx = q_2.idx$. Since the candidate relation is a bisimulation, then for $j = 1, 2$, there exists q_j' s.t. $q_j \rightsquigarrow q_j'$ and $s_j' R q_j'$. Thus, $act_g(q_j')$, $lc_g(s_j') = q_j'.c_g$ and $O_g(s_j') = O_g(q_j')$. We conclude the proof by showing that $O_g(q_1') = O_g(q_2')$ and $q_1'.c_g = q_2'.c_g$ according to the Lemma 7.

Noninterference.

The no-exfiltration/no-infiltration properties give limited data separation properties at the level of single transitions. They do not, however, lift to executions, because messages may be passed between partitions which can introduce explicit data dependencies. As a sanity check, we therefore show how the security condition is reduced to noninterference in the special case where no exception except timer signal takes place. This property formalizes the intuition that if the partition g does not communicate, then the execution of the other partition is completely independent of activities of g.

A partition with the initial memory mem is called non-communicating, if for all arbitrary mem' and all states q that are reachable from the initial state of $T_i(mem, mem')$, $M(q.\sigma_1) = \{usr, irq\}$ holds.

THEOREM 2. *For any two non-communicating partitions with the initial memories mem_1 and mem'_1, and an arbitrary partition with the initial memory mem_2,*

$$tr_{1,i}(mem_1, mem_2) = tr_{1,i}(mem'_1, mem_2)$$

The symmetric theorem is proved when the non- communicating partition is deployed on the second machine. The state of a machine can be externally changed only by the reception of a message. Since the non-communicating partition never raises an exception, it can not execute the software interrupt and it can not send a message. Moreover, the system clock, shared between the two machines, must be independent of the activity performed by the non-communicating machine. This is possible because we assume that all transitions, with the exception of the ideal functionalities, require one clock cycle. Note that the candidate relation allows Theorem 2 to be directly transferred to the real system. The details are left out.

7. PROOF IMPLEMENTATION

The overall proof is carried out in the HOL4 theorem prover, following the proof strategy presented in Section 5. For those parts (the Handler Lemma and Proposition 1) that depend on kernel code we generate contracts and transfer the verification to BAP. To realize this we have produced a number of helper tools of which the main ones are: (i) an ARMv7 prover tool implemented in SML/HOL4, (ii) various tools and tool components interfacing HOL4 with BAP, (iii) a lifter tool to convert ARM assembly to BAP's input language. Space prevents us from more than outlining the BAP extensions and the proof of the ARM Lemmas here; these will be reported in separate publications.

7.1 Verification in HOL4

Overview of the ARM Model.

We use Fox et al's monadic HOL4 model of the ARMv7 instruction set architecture. The model has been validated against a development board, giving some credence to its accuracy [7].

A *computation* in the monadic HOL4 ARM model is a term of type

$$\alpha\ M = \texttt{arm\_state} \mapsto (\alpha \times \texttt{arm\_state})\texttt{error\_option}.$$

Computations act on a state `arm_state` and return either `ValueState` a s, a new state s of type `arm_state` along with a return value a of type α, or an error `Error` e. Errors represent all unpredictable computations, i.e., those that are underspecified by the ARM specification. The monad unit injects a value into a computation, while binding is a sequential composition operation which passes the return value of the first computation to the input parameters of the second one as follows:

```
f >>= g = (λs.  case f s of Error e ↦ Error e
                || ValueState y t ↦ g y t )
```

The execution of an ARM instruction is defined by the computation `arm_next` modeling the entire processing of an instruction, from fetching the instruction pointed to by the program counter to the actual instruction execution.

The MMU Extension.

We extend the ARM model to support the MMU functionality in our setting. Given the complexity of memory management, the model is restricted to support only those parts of the MMU functionality used by the PROSPER kernel.[2] We also proved that the MMU configurations of all reachable states are supported by the extended model and not underspecified. The original ARM model tracks the history of memory accesses, allowing to compute the set of memory pages accessed by an instruction. To be accurate, it is necessary to check the access list after each primitive computation. To this end, the monadic structure is modified so that access history checks are introduced at every sequential composition of two computations. In case of an access violation within the first computation, the second one is simply disregarded, returning the unspecified value ARB along with the first state where an access violation has been recorded.

```
f >>= g = (λs.  case f s of Error e ↦ Error e
                || ValueState y t ↦
                (if (access_violation t)
                then (ValueState ARB t)
                else (g y t)) )
```

Proof of the ARM Lemmas.

We use a relational Hoare logic framework to prove the ARM Lemmas. For technical reasons we formulate the three ARM Lemmas as a single statement. For any computation `f` and predicates p_1, p_2, we define a relational predicate `preserving(f,`p_1`,`p_2`)` stating that, when starting from two states in the relation sim_g and satisfying p_1, then the states returned by `f` (i) are in the relation sim_g, (ii) satisfy the non-modification and mode-switching constraints, as presented in Section 5, and (iii) satisfy p_2. The state predicates p_1 and p_2 allow processor mode specific reasoning. The final goal is to show that the MMU-enabled variant of `arm_next` satisfies `preserving` when starting from user mode.

A set of sound inference rules have been implemented in a semi-automatic HOL4 helper tool. An example is the rule for sequential composition:

$$\frac{\texttt{preserving}(f_1, p_1, p_1) \quad \texttt{preserving}(f_2, p_1, p_2)}{\texttt{preserving}(f_1 \gg= (\lambda x.f_2), p_1, (p_1 \vee p_2))}$$

[2]Only section-based one-level page tables without address translation are supported so far.

The tool recognizes the structure of a computation, decomposes the verification goal in a set of sub-goals, proves the sub-goals recursively and applies the suitable inference rule to infer the initial goal. Moreover, it searches in the HOL4 database and the user-provided theorems to find a suitable theorem that can prove the goal. We prove `preserving` for the write primitive computations manually, but the tool can handle some read computations automatically, allowing to prove a large share of the workload automatically.

Generation of Pre- and Postconditions.

HOL4 is also used to generate pre- and postconditions for the kernel handlers, for subsequent verification with BAP. Consider a handler with the starting state s_1 in mode m such that $s_1 \rightsquigarrow s_2$. Suppose that s_1 and q_1 are (g, m)-compatible such that q_1 is the starting state of the corresponding ideal handler functionality. Let q_2 be a state such that $q_1 \rightsquigarrow q_2$. These conditions allow to automatically generate the precondition of the handler under which the final state s_2 will be (g, usr)-compatible with q_2. The preconditions are generated by the hypotheses of the Handler Lemma: the starting state of the kernel handler s_1 is (g, m)-*compatible* with q_1, and there are s_0 and q_0, such that $\mathit{priv\_const}_g(q_0, q_1)$, $\mathit{priv\_const}_g(s_0, s_1)$, and s_0 and q_0 are in the candidate relation.

7.2 Binary Code Verification

The kernel code verification relies on Hoare logic. To prove the Handler Lemma and Proposition 1, we are required to verify several Hoare triples $\{P\}C\{Q\}$ for the exception handlers and the bootstrap code, that is we check that if the precondition P holds in the starting state of C, then the postcondition Q is guaranteed by C. When possible, we adopt a standard semi-automatic strategy, i.e. firstly, we compute the weakest liberal precondition $wlp(C, Q)$ on the starting state, then prove that the precondition P implies the weakest precondition. This task can be fully automated if the predicate $P \implies wlp(C, Q)$ is equivalent to a predicate of the form $\forall x.A$ where A is quantifier free. The validity of A can then be checked using a Satisfiability Modulo Theory (SMT) solver that supports bitvectors to handle operations on words. In this work, we used STP [9].

Weakest preconditions can be computed directly in HOL4 using the ARMv7 model. However, this task requires a significant engineering effort. We adopted a more practical approach, by using (BAP) [6]. The BAP toolset provides platform-independent utilities to extract control flow graphs and program dependence graphs, to perform symbolic execution and to perform wp calculations. These utilities reason on the BAP Intermediate Language (BIL), a small and formally specified language that models instruction evaluation as compositions of variable reads and writes in a functional style.

We found the existing BAP front-end to translate ARM programs to BIL inadequate for our purpose: It supports only ARMv4, it does not manage the processor status registers, and it does not handle banked registers for the privileged modes and coprocessor management. To this end, we developed a new front-end for ARMv7 programs using the ARM model available in HOL4. This tool allows us to translate the code of the kernel handlers and the bootstrap into BIL.

The HOL4 ARM model provides the function `arm_steps` to compute the set of pairs $\langle c_1, t_1\rangle, \ldots \langle c_n, t_n\rangle$ for an instruction where the function t_i transforms a state provided that the condition c_i holds on that state. In other words, $\forall$`s:arm_state arm_next s` = `ValueState ()` t_i(`s`) if c_i(`s`). In order to use `arm_steps`, the execution mode and the instruction set type (e.g. Thumb, ARM) must be known. Our handlers preconditions set the value of these parameters. The translation from ARM to BIL is performed by translating the HOL4 conditions c_i and functions t_i to BIL fragments.

Verifying the Hoare triples using weakest preconditions requires us to handle some common issues. Algorithms to compute weakest preconditions rely on the absence of indirect jumps, i.e. the jumps whose target address is a variable. We used the SMT solver to automatically compute jump targets, depending on the instruction precondition. Weakest preconditions can grow exponentially in the number of instructions. We extended BAP to simplify the weakest precondition during its backward propagation using ARM specific simplification patterns. Finally, our verification task has been simplified by the structure of the kernel code. All loops of the kernel have a single control flow node that represents both the entry point and the exit point of the loop. In the general case, we defined a loop invariant and a loop variant and applied the standard Hoare logic rules to prove the contract. Verification has been simplified by the absence of loops in the kernel handlers and the fact that the boot code contains only for-loops that iterate over integer sets.

8. EVALUATION

We tested the kernel implementation using OVP [21] as main execution environment, which provides a simulation infrastructure convenient to evaluate our kernel. Slightly different versions of the kernel have been deployed on Beagleboard, Beagleboard-XM, Beaglebone, NovaThor and the Integrator development board. The size of kernel code, internal data-structures and page table are respectively less than 4 kB, 2 kB and 16 kB. The main functionality of the kernel is provided by the software and hardware interrupt handlers. In the worst case, the hardware interrupt handler executes 112 instructions, including 48 reading and 22 writing accesses to the memory. Similarly, the software interrupt handler executes at most 46 instructions, including 20 reading and 8 writing accesses to the memory. All the memory locations accessed by the kernel handlers belong to the internal kernel data-structures. To minimize the system overhead and avoid accesses to system memory during kernel tasks, we can use scratchpad memory or cache locking due to the size of the run-time footprint.

We identified and fixed several bugs in the kernel implementation during the verification process: (i) the registers were not sanitized after the bootstrap, (ii) some of the execution flags were not correctly restored during the context switch, (iii) the procedure to decode the hypercall identifier did not consider the case that the partition is running in thumb execution mode.

The model of the ideal system, the formalization of the verification procedure and the proofs of the theorems consist of 21k lines of HOL4 code. The tools developed to support the verification of the kernel contracts required 2k lines of HOL4 and python code. The kernel binary code is verified with respect to sixteen contracts, each of them consisting of $\sim$ 400 lines of assertions that are automatically generated from HOL4. In the worst case, the verification of one contract required $\sim$ 30 minutes using one Intel(R) Xeon(R) X3470 core; the contract is generated in $\sim$ 5 minutes, the indirect jumps are solved in $\sim$ 2 minutes, the weakest precondition is computed in $\sim$ 10 minutes and the SMT solver verifies the validity of the resulting condition in $\sim$ 15 minutes.

9. RELATED WORKS

Past work on formal verification of kernel information flow properties [12, 19, 23, 4] are based on variants of noninterference [11]. Typically, the goal is to allow a number of component systems, partitions, or guest systems, depending on terminology, to share a computing platform without any interaction, leaving possible communication between the partitions to be managed by mechanisms outside the model. In Heitmeyer et al [12], for instance, partitions have explicit input and output buffers, but communication is delegated to external agents, in this way allowing properties like absence of infiltration (roughly: direct flows) and exfiltration (indirect flows) to be proved. Similar results are reported in [23, 4] and in [30] at the firmware level. Murray et al [20] considers noninterference in presence of a dynamic scheduler and uses a version of intransitive noninterference [24] (actually, NI) to allow a scheduler to influence which partition is scheduled, without permitting the scheduler to be used as a covert channel, as discussed briefly in the introduction.

Several recent works address hypervisor/microkernel verification, although without taking information flow into account. In [14] a simulation property of an entire microkernel down to a C implementation was verified using the Isabelle theorem prover. This work was recently extended to ARM assembly using decompilation techniques [29]. Alkassar et al [2] proposed an automatic approach to verify a hypervisor for a (simplified) MIPS machine by annotating the C code with contracts and checking them using VCC. They establish a reachability property: at any time the state of a partition can be reached by executing the same partition on a completely isolated machine. This is sufficient to establish simulation when the specification is deterministic (but not otherwise). To allow VCC to reason about statically unknown partitions/guests, a C emulator of the MIPS machine has been implemented and annotated. The C emulator has been adopted also to verify parts of the hypervisor that mix C and assembly code [22].

Most kernel security analyses address the kernel routines one at a time, using suitable relational specifications. Without verifying the correct interaction between the kernel routines and the processor (e.g. mode switching and memory protection), these specifications are not sufficient to guarantee security at system level, i.e. at the level of "full" executions that interleave kernel routines with userland execution of the partitions. Performing such a systems-level, integrated analysis (kernel and processor) has not been done before for realistic processor architectures. For instance [30, 19] address kernel routines but not the processor interaction. Analysing each kernel routine in isolation can be done using existing versions of conditional non-interference (as discussed in [19]). However, this does not guarantee information flow security at system level. Our approach to formulating the TLS using idealized userland processors solves this problem, simply by showing that the full executions for the ideal and the real model are the same.

Barthe et al. [4] formalized a hypervisor model using the Coq proof assistant. They focus on establishing that the hypervisor ensures isolation properties between the guests, abstracting away from actual hypervisor implementation.

10. DISCUSSION

We have presented a separation kernel, the PROSPER kernel, for ARMv7-A and a machine-assisted proof of information flow correctness using a combination of tools (HOL4 [13] and BAP [6]). Our analysis has a number of distinguishing features:

- Our top-level specification (TLS) and verification approach is deliberately designed to take inter-component communication into account, an ever present challenge in the verification of information flow properties for real systems.
- We introduce a new technique for building a TLS for this type of application, based on communicating idealized userland processors.
- The security analysis is performed at systems level, modeling both the MMU-constrained user space execution of arbitrary partitions, the kernel handlers, and the interaction of the two.
- We validate the "monotonicity or release" property, as suggested by Sabelfeld and Sands [26], by showing that the security proof reduces to standard noninterference for the special case of non-communicating partitions.
- The entire analysis is performed at machine code level for a commodity processor architecture.

A number of subsidiary contributions include several tools for managing and executing the proofs, including the ARM prover tool for verifying critical partition correctness properties of the ARMv7 machine architecture based on an extension of Fox and Myreen's monadic ARM semantics [7], and several extensions to the BAP toolset.

By verifying the entire kernel at machine code level we avoid reliance on a C compiler, and we can transparently verify code that mix C and assembly. Generally speaking, verification at machine code level is time consuming, however we were supported by the fact that the code was mostly compiler produced and loops were used in only a few places.

Since our TLS specifies the exact set of traces allowed by an implementation, a worry might be that the TLS becomes overly detailed and unwieldy. We did not find this to be the case. Rather, the development of the ideal model, as we progressed to understand the various issues involved, was a great help in organizing the thinking. It is true that our approach (as in other work, cf. [12]) precludes an abstract treatment of scheduling, but this is to be expected when information flow is to be taken into account.

On two counts our model is not yet satisfactory. The first concerns timing. Our model counts instruction cycles [3], instead of real clock cycles. In our implementation the former is used. It is non-trivial to extend our analysis to a more

[3]This is the element of our "real system" that is not really real.

realistic time representation, as in this case well-known phenomena such as cache delays and instruction pipelining come into play. Cache leakage has been considered in the context of virtualization by Barthe et al [5]. Zhang et al [31] demonstrated an access-driven side-channel attack targeting the Xen hypervisor. The authors (i) use interprocess interrupts to affect the Xen scheduler and to reduce the time slot available to the victim and (ii) indirectly monitor the usage of the instruction cache, which is shared among partitions. Extending our approach to handle access-driven attacks requires a more refined analysis of timing behaviour, which is part of our ongoing research efforts.

The second count is unpredictable states. According to the ARM Architecture Reference Manual [3], unpredictable behaviour is not allowed to "perform any function that cannot be performed at the current or lower level of privilege using instructions that are not unpredictable". This definition is difficult to accommodate in our framework. An interpretation of allowed behaviour which is adequate for our purpose is "compliant with the ARM Lemmas". This enables our proofs to go through, and in fact we posit that this may be a more helpful and less prescriptive definition than that of [3]. Practically, the ARM Lemmas can be used to certify if a specific ARMv7-A implementation can be used to host our kernel. In the proof implementation we have used the error states introduced in the monadic ARM HOL4 model. This is not really satisfactory, though, as this allows partitions to exit the scope of our model at will, by entering an unpredictable state. We leave a better treatment of unpredictable behaviour, in addition to more realistic hardware models and kernel functionality, to future work.

Finally we emphasize that virtualization and/or separation kernels are not the only tools available for secure partitioning. The ARM-proprietary TrustZone solution [1] adds to the standard ARMv7 architecture a secure partition that can be used to split the CPU resources between an untrusted and a trusted OS. Our results show that the kernel can be protected using standard, less expensive hardware, and a smaller TCB. Moreover, extending the proposed verification strategy can be straightforwardly extended to manage a different number (>2) of partitions.

11. ACKNOWLEDGMENTS

Work supported by framework grant "IT 2010" from the Swedish Foundation for Strategic Research.

12. REFERENCES

[1] ARM TrustZone. `http://www.arm.com/products/processors/technologies/trustzone.php`.

[2] E. Alkassar, M. A. Hillebrand, W. J. Paul, and E. Petrova. Automated verification of a small hypervisor. In *Proc. VSTTE*, volume 6217 of *Lecture Notes in Computer Science*, pages 40–54. Springer, 2010.

[3] ARMv7-A architecture reference manual. `http://infocenter.arm.com/help/index.jsp?topic=/com.arm.doc.ddi0406c`.

[4] G. Barthe, G. Betarte, J. D. Campo, and C. Luna. Formally verifying isolation and availability in an idealized model of virtualization. In *Proc. FM'11*, volume 6664 of *Lecture Notes in Computer Science*, pages 231–245. Springer, 2011.

[5] G. Barthe, G. Betarte, J. D. Campo, and C. Luna. Cache-leakage resilient os isolation in an idealized model of virtualization. In *Proc. CSF'12*, pages 186–197, Washington, DC, USA, 2012. IEEE Computer Society.

[6] D. Brumley, I. Jager, T. Avgerinos, and E. J. Schwartz. BAP: A binary analysis platform. In *Proc. CAV'11*, volume 6806 of *Lecture Notes in Computer Science*, pages 463–469. Springer, 2011.

[7] A. C. J. Fox and M. O. Myreen. A trustworthy monadic formalization of the ARMv7 instruction set architecture. In *proc. ITP'10*, volume 6172 of *Lecture Notes in Computer Science*, pages 243–258. Springer, 2010.

[8] FreeRTOS. `http://www.freertos.org/`.

[9] V. Ganesh and D. L. Dill. A decision procedure for bit-vectors and arrays. In *Proc. CAV'07*, volume 4590 of *Lecture Notes in Computer Science*, pages 519–531. Springer, 2007.

[10] C. Gehrmann, H. Douglas, and D. Nilsson. Are there good reasons for protecting mobile phones with hypervisors? In *Consumer Communications and Networking Conference (CCNC), 2011 IEEE*, pages 906 –911, jan. 2011.

[11] J. A. Goguen and J. Meseguer. Security policies and security models. In *IEEE Symposium on Security and Privacy*, pages 11–20, 1982.

[12] C. Heitmeyer, M. Archer, E. Leonard, and J. McLean. Applying formal methods to a certifiably secure software system. *IEEE Trans. Softw. Eng.*, 34(1):82–98, Jan. 2008.

[13] HOL4. `http://hol.sourceforge.net/`.

[14] G. Klein, K. Elphinstone, G. Heiser, J. Andronick, D. Cock, P. Derrin, D. Elkaduwe, K. Engelhardt, R. Kolanski, M. Norrish, T. Sewell, H. Tuch, and S. Winwood. seL4: formal verification of an OS kernel. In *Proc. SOSP'09*, pages 207–220. ACM, 2009.

[15] P. C. Kocher. Timing attacks on implementations of Diffie-Hellman, RSA, DSS, and other systems. In *Proceedings of the 16th Annual International Cryptology Conference on Advances in Cryptology*, CRYPTO '96, pages 104–113, London, UK, 1996. Springer-Verlag.

[16] D. Leinenbach and T. Santen. Verifying the Microsoft Hyper-V hypervisor with VCC. In *Proc. FM'09*, volume 5850 of *Lecture Notes in Computer Science*, pages 806–809. Springer Berlin Heidelberg, 2009.

[17] J. McDermott, B. Montrose, M. Li, J. Kirby, and M. Kang. Separation virtual machine monitors. In *Proceedings of the 28th Annual Computer Security Applications Conference*, ACSAC '12, pages 419–428, New York, NY, USA, 2012. ACM.

[18] μClinux. `http://www.uclinux.org/`.

[19] T. C. Murray, D. Matichuk, M. Brassil, P. Gammie, T. Bourke, S. Seefried, C. Lewis, X. Gao, and G. Klein. seL4: From general purpose to a proof of information flow enforcement. In *IEEE Symposium on Security and Privacy*, pages 415–429. IEEE Computer Society, 2013.

[20] T. C. Murray, D. Matichuk, M. Brassil, P. Gammie, and G. Klein. Noninterference for operating system kernels. In *CPP*, volume 7679 of *Lecture Notes in Computer Science*, pages 126–142. Springer, 2012.

[21] Open Virtual Platforms. http://www.ovpworld.org/.

[22] W. J. Paul, S. Schmaltz, and A. Shadrin. Completing the automated verification of a small hypervisor - assembler code verification. In *SEFM*, volume 7504 of *Lecture Notes in Computer Science*, pages 188–202. Springer, 2012.

[23] R. Richards. Modeling and security analysis of a commercial real-time operating system kernel. In D. S. Hardin, editor, *Design and Verification of Microprocessor Systems for High-Assurance Applications*, pages 301–322. Springer US, 2010.

[24] J. Rushby. *Noninterference, transitivity, and channel-control security policies.* SRI International, Computer Science Laboratory, 1992.

[25] J. M. Rushby. Design and verification of secure systems. In *Proc. SOSP'81*, pages 12–21, 1981.

[26] A. Sabelfeld and D. Sands. Declassification: Dimensions and principles. *J. Comput. Secur.*, 17(5):517–548, Oct. 2009.

[27] R. Sailer, E. Valdez, T. Jaeger, R. Perez, L. V. Doorn, J. L. Griffin, S. Berger, R. Sailer, E. Valdez, T. Jaeger, R. Perez, L. Doorn, J. Linwood, and G. S. Berger. sHype: Secure hypervisor approach to trusted virtualized systems. In *IBM Research Report RC23511*, 2005.

[28] D. Sangiorgi. *Introduction to Bisimulation and Coinduction.* Cambridge University Press, 2012.

[29] T. A. L. Sewell, M. O. Myreen, and G. Klein. Translation validation for a verified os kernel. In *Proc. PLDI'13*, pages 471–482, 2013.

[30] M. M. Wilding, D. A. Greve, R. J. Richards, and D. S. Hardin. Formal verification of partition management for the AAMP7G microprocessor. In *Design and Verification of Microprocessor Systems for High-Assurance Applications*, pages 175–191. Springer US, 2010.

[31] Y. Zhang, A. Juels, M. K. Reiter, and T. Ristenpart. Cross-VM side channels and their use to extract private keys. In *Proc. CCS'12*, pages 305–316. ACM, 2012.

ShadowReplica: Efficient Parallelization of Dynamic Data Flow Tracking

Kangkook Jee
Columbia University
jikk@cs.columbia.edu

Vasileios P. Kemerlis
Columbia University
vpk@cs.columbia.edu

Angelos D. Keromytis
Columbia University
angelos@cs.columbia.edu

Georgios Portokalidis
Stevens Institute of Technology
gportoka@stevens.edu

ABSTRACT

Dynamic data flow tracking (DFT) is a technique broadly used in a variety of security applications that, unfortunately, exhibits poor performance, preventing its adoption in production systems. We present ShadowReplica, a new and efficient approach for accelerating DFT and other shadow memory-based analyses, by *decoupling analysis from execution and utilizing spare CPU cores to run them in parallel.* Our approach enables us to run a heavyweight technique, like dynamic taint analysis (DTA), *twice as fast*, while concurrently consuming *fewer* CPU cycles than when applying it in-line. DFT is run in parallel by a second shadow thread that is spawned for each application thread, and the two communicate using a shared data structure. We avoid the problems suffered by previous approaches, by introducing an off-line application analysis phase that utilizes both static and dynamic analysis methodologies to generate optimized code for decoupling execution and implementing DFT, while it also minimizes the amount of information that needs to be communicated between the two threads. Furthermore, we use a lock-free ring buffer structure and an N-way buffering scheme to efficiently exchange data between threads and maintain high cache-hit rates on multi-core CPUs. Our evaluation shows that ShadowReplica is on average ∼2.3× faster than in-line DFT (∼2.75× slowdown over native execution) when running the SPEC CPU2006 benchmark, while similar speed ups were observed with command-line utilities and popular server software. Astoundingly, ShadowReplica also reduces the CPU cycles used up to 30%.

Categories and Subject Descriptors

D.4.5 [**Operating Systems**]: Reliability; D.4.6 [**Information flow controls**]: Security and Protection; D.4.7 [**Parallelization**]: Organization and Design; D.4.8 [**Optimization**]: Performance

Keywords

Security, Information flow tracking, Optimization, Parallelization

CCS'13, November 4–8, 2013, Berlin, Germany.

http://dx.doi.org/10.1145/2508859.2516704.

1. INTRODUCTION

Dynamic data flow tracking (DFT) is being used extensively in security research for protecting software [24, 11], analyzing malware [32, 21], discovering bugs [23, 7], reverse engineering [29], information flow control [34], etc. However, dynamically applying DFT tends to significantly slow down the target application, specially when a virtualization framework [22, 5] is used to apply it on binary-only software. Overheads can range from a significant percentage over native execution to several orders of magnitude, depending on the framework used and particular traits of the implementation [19]. When performance is not an issue, the overhead can still be problematic: (a) if it changes the behavior of the application (e.g., when network connections timeout or the analysis is no longer transparent), or (b) when computational cycles are scarce or CPU energy consumption needs to be kept to a minimum, like in mobile devices.

We present ShadowReplica, a new and efficient approach for accelerating DFT and other shadow memory-based analyses [23], by *decoupling analysis from execution and utilizing spare CPU cores to run them in parallel.* Our approach enables us to run a heavyweight technique like dynamic taint analysis (DTA) *twice as fast*, while concurrently consuming *fewer* CPU cycles than when applying it in-line. The main motivation behind ShadowReplica has been to accelerate security techniques with well established benefits, such as DFT, but it can also host other types of analyses. We demonstrate this by also implementing a control-flow integrity (CFI) [1] tool over ShadowReplica, however, the greater benefits can be reaped by techniques based on memory shadowing [23, 4].

Decoupling analysis from execution to run it in parallel is by no means a novel concept [14, 8, 31, 25, 33, 6, 26]. Previous work can be classified into three categories. The first is based on recording execution and replaying it along with the analysis on a remote host, or simply a different CPU [8, 26, 6]. These are geared toward off-line analyses and can greatly reduce the overhead imposed on the application. However, the speed of the analysis itself is *not* improved, since execution needs to be replayed and augmented with the analysis code. These solutions essentially hide the overhead from the application, by sacrificing computational resources at the replica. Due to their design, they are not a good fit for applying preventive security measures, even though they can be used for post-fact identification of an intrusion.

The second category uses speculative execution to run application code including any in-lined analysis in multiple threads running in parallel [25, 31]. While strictly speaking the analysis is not decoupled, it is parallelized. These approaches sacrifice significant *processing power* to achieve speed up, as at least two additional threads need to be used for any performance gain, and the results of some of the threads may be discarded. Furthermore, handling multi-threaded applications without hardware support remains a challenge.

The third category aims at offloading the analysis code alone to another execution thread [14, 33]. These instrument the application to collect all the information required to run the analysis independently, and communicate the information to a thread running the analysis logic alone. In principle, these approaches are more efficient, since the application code only runs once. However, in practice, they have not been able to deliver the expected performance gains, due to *inefficiently* collecting information from the application and the high overhead of communicating it to the analysis thread.

ShadowReplica belongs to the third category of systems. Our main contribution is an off-line application analysis phase that utilizes both static and dynamic analysis approaches to generate optimized code for collecting information from the application, greatly reducing the amount of data that we need to communicate. For running DFT independently from the application, such data include dynamically computed information like memory addresses used by the program, control flow decisions, and certain operating system (OS) events like system calls and signals. We focus on the first two that consist the bulk of information. For addresses, we exploit memory locality to only communicate a smaller set of them, and have the DFT code reconstruct the rest based on information extracted by the off-line analysis. For control flow decisions, we exploit the fact that most branches have a binary outcome and introduce an intelligent encoding of the information sent to DFT to skip the most frequent ones.

DFT is run in parallel by a second shadow thread that is spawned for each application thread, and the two communicate using a shared data structure. The design of this structure is crucial to avoid the poor cache performance issues suffered by previous work. We adopt a lock-free ring buffer structure, consisting of multiple buffers (N-way buffering scheme [33]). After experimentation, we identified the optimal size for the sub-buffers of the structure, so that when two threads are scheduled on different cores on the same CPU die, we achieve a high cache-hit rate for the shared L3 cache and a low-eviction rate on each core's L1 and L2 caches. The latter is caused when two cores are concurrently read/write in memory that occupies the same cache line in their L1/L2 caches.

The code implementing DFT is generated during off-line analysis as a C program, and includes a series of compiler-inspired optimizations that accelerate DFT by ignoring dependencies that have no effect or cancel out each other [18]. Besides the tag propagation logic, this code also includes per-basic block functionality to receive all data required (e.g., dynamic addresses and branch decisions). Note that even though the code is in C, it is generated based on the analysis of the binary without the need for application source code. The implementation is also generic, meaning that it can accommodate different tag sizes in shadow memory, and it can be easily extended to different architectures (e.g., x86-64). Such flexibility is partly allowed by decoupling DFT from execution.

We implemented ShadowReplica using Intel's Pin dynamic binary instrumentation (DBI) framework [22] to instrument the application and collect the data required to decouple DFT. Shadow threads running the DFT code run natively (without Pin), but in the same address space, also implementing dynamic taint analysis [24] protection from memory corruption exploits. Our evaluation shows that compared with an already optimized in-lined DFT framework [18], it is extremely effective in accelerating *both* the application and DFT, but also using less CPU cycles. In other words, we do not sacrifice the spare cores to accelerate DFT, but exploit parallelization to improve the efficiency of DFT in all fronts. ShadowReplica is on average $\sim$2.3$\times$ faster than in-lined DTA when running the SPEC2006 benchmark ($\sim$2.75$\times$ slowdown over native execution). We observed similar speed ups with command-line utilities, like `bzip2` and `tar`, and the Apache and MySQL servers. We also discovered that with ShadowReplica applying DFT requires less CPU cycles than the in-lined case, reaching a 30% reduction in the 401.bzip2 benchmark.

The contributions of this paper can be summarized as follows:

- We propose a novel approach to efficiently parallelize in-line analysis by implementing low-cost communication between the primary original process and the secondary analyzer process.
- Our approach does not require a hardware component at runtime, but instead it is based on static and dynamic program analysis performed in advance.
- ShadowReplica preserves the functionality of both the original program being monitored, and the analysis logic that would be otherwise applied in-line.
- We implement a DFT analysis prototype, but our approach can be also applied to other analyses based on memory shadowing.
- We evaluate our prototype with the SPEC2006 CPU benchmark suite and various real-world applications, and our results confirm both the efficiency and effectiveness of our approach. Furthermore, we show that through ShadowReplica DFT uses less CPU cycles and energy, than when applied in-line.

The rest of this paper is organized as follows. Section 2 presents an overview of our approach. Section 3 describes the off-line analysis stage, which includes most of our optimizations. Section 4 explains the dynamic runtime. In Sec. 5, we provide implementation details, and the evaluation of our framework is presented in Sec. 6. After discussing related work in Sec. 7, we conclude the paper in Sec. 8.

2. OVERVIEW

2.1 In-line vs. Decoupled DFT

Dynamically applying DFT on binaries usually involves the use of a dynamic binary instrumentation (DBI) framework or a virtual machine monitor (VMM) that will transparently extend the program being analyzed. Such frameworks enable us to inject code implementing DFT in binaries, by interleaving framework and DFT code with application code, as shown in Fig.1 (*in-line*).

ShadowReplica proposes an efficient approach for accelerating dynamic DFT and similar analyses by decoupling them from execution and utilizing spare CPU cores to run the instrumented application and DFT code in parallel. We replace the in-line DFT logic in the application with a stub that *extracts* the minimal information required to independently perform the analysis in another thread, and *enqueues* the information in a shared data structure. The DFT code, which is running on a different CPU core, is prefixed with a consumer stub that *pulls out* the information and then *performs* the analysis.

Decoupling the analysis from execution enables us to run it completely independently and without involving the instrumentation framework, as illustrated in Fig. 1 (*decoupled*). Depending on the cost of the analysis (e.g., tracking implicit information flows is more costly than explicit flows), it can accelerate both application and analysis. In short, if I_i, A_i, and P_i are the instrumentation,

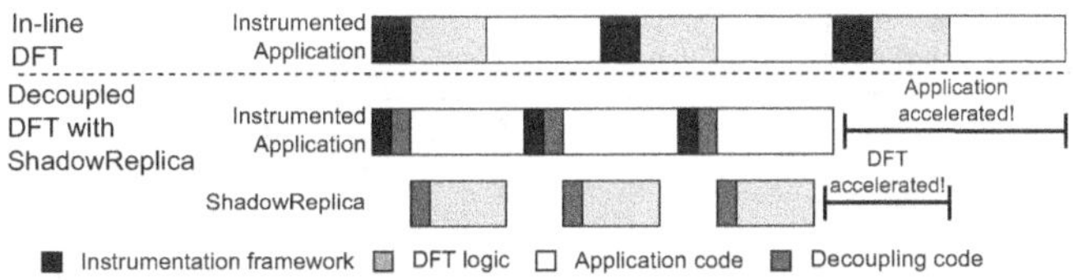

Figure 1: In-line vs. decoupled application of DFT with ShadowReplica and binary instrumentation.

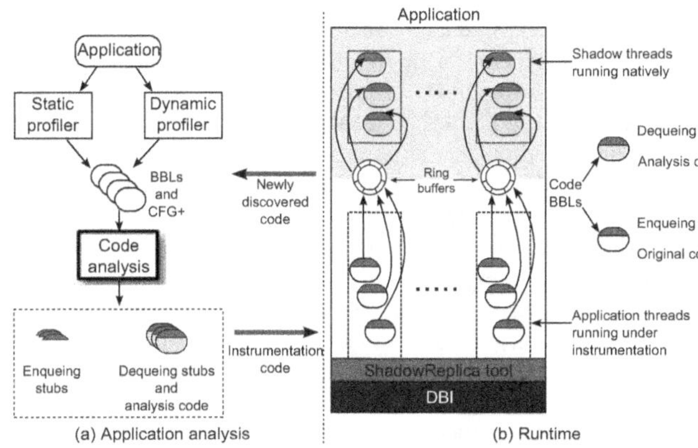

Figure 2: The architecture of ShadowReplica.

analysis, and application code costs with in-line analysis, and I_d, A_d, P_d, E_d and D_d are the costs of instrumentation, analysis, application, enqueueing and dequeueing code (as defined in the above paragraph), then decoupling is efficient when:

$$I_i + A_i + P_i > max(I_d + P_d + E_d, A_d + D_d) \quad (1)$$

Essentially, decoupling is more efficient when the following two conditions are met: *(a)* if the cost of the in-line analysis is higher than the cost of extracting the information and enqueueing, and *(b)* if the cost of program execution combined with instrumentation interference is higher than dequeueing cost. Ha et al. [14] provide a more extensive model of the costs and benefits involved with decoupling analysis.

Analyses that are bulky code-wise can experience even larger benefits because replacing them with more compact code, as decoupling does, exerts less pressure to the instrumentation framework, due to the smaller number of instructions that need to be interleaved with application code. For instance, when implementing DFT using binary instrumentation, the developer needs to take extra care to avoid large chunks of analysis code and conditional statements to achieve good performance [19]. When decoupling DFT, we no longer have the same limitations, we could even use utility libraries and generally be more flexible.

We need to emphasize that ShadowReplica does *not* rely on complete execution replay [8, 26] or duplicating execution in other cores through speculative execution [25, 31]. So even though other cores may be utilized,[1] it does not waste processing cycles. Application code runs exactly once, and the same stands for the analysis code that runs in parallel. The performance and energy conservation benefits gained are solely due to exploiting the true parallelism offered by multi-cores, and being very efficient in collecting and communicating all the data required for the analysis to proceed independently.

2.2 Decoupling DFT

DFT involves accurately tracking selected data of interest as they propagate during program execution, and has many uses in the security domain [12, 9, 3, 27, 32, 24, 34]. In ShadowReplica, we implemented DFT along with its most popular incarnation, DTA [24], where input data (e.g., network data) are deemed "tainted" and their use is prohibited in certain program locations (e.g., in instructions manipulating the control flow of programs, such as indirect branch instructions and function calls).

We created a code analysis module for ShadowReplica that implements DFT by generating optimized C code for performing data tracking for all the BBLs discovered during profiling, and generic code for newly discovered code. We follow the methodology we introduced in prior work for optimizing in-lined DFT code [18].

[1] We do not demand the kernel to schedule the replica on a different core, but we do enforce each replica to be on the same package/die with the process to benefit from L3 cache sharing.

To correctly and independently track data and propagate tags, the analysis code has two sources of information: the code itself and the application executing in parallel. For example, an x86 instruction like `mov eax, ebx` indicates that a tag should be propagated between registers, so no runtime information is required. However, for instructions that reference memory using dynamically calculated addresses, e.g., `mov eax, (ecx, ebp,4)`, we need to obtain the effective address used by the instruction during execution. Remember, that the analysis code does *not* execute application code, nor does it have access to data contained in the registers because it is executing in parallel. The application needs to also supply information regarding control-flow decisions, as well as any other data required by DFT, like when to tag (taint) an address range that is only available at runtime. *This is all the information required to accurately perform DFT in parallel.*

Security checks are normally performed in parallel with the application. However, it is necessary that we have the ability to synchronize with the analysis code, by waiting for it to complete. This is important because in the case of DTA we want to ensure that program control flow has not been compromised, and in the case of information flow control that no sensitive data has been leaked. This is achieved by injecting code in the application that checks whether the analysis has completed. For instance, to protect from leaking sensitive information, our prototype implementation synchronizes before system calls used to transmit data, like `write()` and `send()`.

Changing characteristics of DFT, like the size of tags it supports that affect the number of different data classes or labels it can track, only affects the analysis code. The application is only delayed when synchronization is required and, as our evaluation shows, currently this is not an issue because DFT executes as fast (if not faster) as the application.

2.3 Architecture

Figure 2 depicts the architecture of ShadowReplica, which comprises of two stages. The first stage, shown in the left of the figure and discussed thoroughly in Sec. 3, involves profiling an application both statically and dynamically to extract code blocks, or basic blocks (BBLs), and control-flow information (CFG+). The latter includes a partial control-flow graph showing how the extracted BBLs are connected, and frequency data indicating which branches are taken more frequently than others.

This data is processed to generate optimized code to be injected in the application, and code for running the analysis in parallel. The first contains code stubs that enqueue the information required to decouple DFT in a shared data structure. Note that ShadowReplica does not naively generate code for enqueueing everything, but ensures that only information that has potentially changed since the previous executed block are enqueued. This is one of our main contributions, and problems of previous work [25, 33] that failed to satisfy equation (1). The second includes code stubs that dequeue information along with the analysis code.

The generated code is passed to the runtime component of ShadowReplica, shown in Fig. 2(b) and discussed in Sec. 4. We utilize a DBI framework that allows us to inject the enqueueing stubs in the application in an efficient manner and with flexibility (i.e., on arbitrary instructions of a binary). Our motivation for using a DBI is that it allows us to apply ShadowReplica on unmodified binary applications, and it enables different analyses, security related or others, by offering the ability to "interfere" with the application at the lowest possible level.

Application threads are executing over the DBI and our tool, which inject the enqueueing stubs. We will refer to an application thread as the *primary*. For each primary, we spawn a shadow thread that will run the analysis code, which we will refer to as the *secondary*. While both threads are in the same address space, applications threads are running over the DBI's VMM, but shadow threads are executing *natively*, since the code generated in the first phase includes everything required to run the analysis. Our current design spawns secondary threads in the same process used by the DBI and the application. In the future, we are considering hosting the secondary threads in a different process for increased isolation.

Communication between primary and secondary threads is done through a ring-buffer structure optimized for multi-core architectures (Sec. 4.2). The ring buffer is also used for the primary thread to synchronize with the secondary, when it is required that the analysis is complete before proceeding with execution. For instance, ensuring that integrity has not been compromised before allowing a certain system call or performing a computed branch.

Multi-threaded applications accessing shared data within a critical area protected by locks (e.g., mutexes) are handled by using an additional ring buffer structure for every critical area. When a primary enters such an area by acquiring a lock, it first synchronizes with the secondary, and then they both switch to the new ring buffer, which now receives all the information generated by the enqueueing stubs. Before exiting the critical area, the primary synchronizes again with the secondary, and then both switch to the original buffer.

Finally, we export any new BBLs and CFG edges that are discovered at runtime, which can be passed back for code analysis. Extending the coverage of our analysis means that we can generate optimal code for a larger part of the application. Note that our analysis also generates generic code for handling application code not discovered during profiling. This "default" code performs all necessary functionality, albeit slower than the optimized code generated for known BBLs and control-flow edges.

2.4 Other Applicable Analyses

The main motivation behind ShadowReplica has been to accelerate security techniques with well established benefits, by providing a methodology and framework that can utilize the parallelism offered by multi-core CPUs. Besides DFT and DTA, we also implemented a control-flow integrity [1] tool to demonstrate the flexibility of our approach. We argue that many other analyses can benefit from it.

Control-flow Integrity. CFI [1], similarly to DTA, aims at preventing attackers from compromising applications by hijacking their control flow. Programs normally follow predetermined execution paths. CFI enforces program flow to follow one of these predetermined paths. Determining a complete CFG of a program is a challenging task in itself, but assuming such a CFG is available, CFI operates as follows. Run-time checks are injected in the application to ensure that control flow remains within the CFG. These checks are placed before every indirect control flow transfer in the application and check that the destination is one of the intended ones. Basically, all possible destinations of a particular control flow instruction are assigned the same id, which is validated before transferring control. While this can be overly permissive, because multiple instructions may have the same targets assigning the same id to the super-set of destinations, this approach allows for fast checks. We implemented CFI with ShadowReplica by using the CFG information extracted during the application profiling, and by generating analysis code that checks whether a control-flow transfer is allowable, using the same control flow enqueueing stubs we used for DFT.

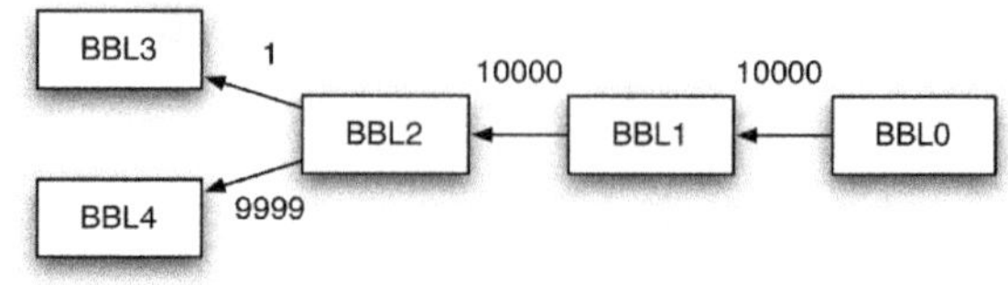

Figure 3: Example CFG. Nodes represent basic blocks and edges are control transfers. During dynamic profiling, we count how many times each edge is followed (edge labels).

Other Analyses. Dynamic analyses that use DBI frameworks [22, 5, 23] can also readily make use of ShadowReplica (e.g., techniques that focus on memory integrity detection). Valgrind's Memcheck [23] uses shadow memory to keep track of uninitialized values in memory and identify their (dangerous) use; Memcheck is an ideal candidate for accelerating through ShadowReplica. Dr. Memory [4] discovers similar types of programming errors including memory leaks, heap overflows, etc. Software-based fault isolation [30] mechanisms can also be easily supported through our framework by using the existing code analysis for the primary and small modifications to the secondary. Approaches that do not depend on shadow memory can also be supported with moderate engineering effort. Examples include call graph profiling, method counting, and path profiling. Finally, ShadowReplica can be extended to work for analyses that refer to memory contents such as integer overflow detection. Note that analyses of this type are less common for binaries, as they require access to source code.

Limitations. There are problem areas where ShadowReplica is not a good fit, exactly because analysis code is decoupled from execution. For instance, cache simulation [16] requires that the ordering of memory accesses can be reconstructed accurately. This task is challenging, even when using in-lined analysis code. It is even more so, when the analysis code runs in parallel.

3. OFF-LINE APPLICATION ANALYSIS

We analyze the application off-line to generate optimized instrumentation code to be injected in primary threads, as well as a new program in C that implements the analysis in the secondary (based on the execution trace recorded by the primary). This section describes our methodology for doing so.

3.1 Application Profiling

The first step of application analysis involves profiling (Fig. 2(a)) to gather code and control-flow information. ShadowReplica uses both static and dynamic profiling. Currently, we perform static profiling using the IDA Pro [15] disassembler, using its scripting API. To complement our data, we built a tool over the Pin [22] DBI framework that dynamically collects information about a binary by executing it with various inputs (e.g., test inputs and benchmarks). New methodologies that improve code and CFG identification are orthogonal to our design and could be included alongside our toolkit with little effort.

Every BBL identified during profiling is assigned a unique id (BBID). BBIDs are calculated by combining the block's offset from the beginning of the executable image it belongs to with a hash of the image's text section to produce a 32-bit value. An example control-flow graph collected during profiling is shown in Fig. 3. During dynamic profiling, we also keep a counter of how many times each control-flow transfer is observed. In the example in Fig. 3, when executing BBL2, BBL4 was followed 9999 times while BBL3 only once.

3.2 Primary Code Generation

During code analysis we generate optimized code for the primary thread to enqueue information necessary for performing DFT in the secondary. The most frequently enqueued data are effective addresses used in memory accesses and control-flow transfers. This section discusses our approach for minimizing the amount of data we need to send to the secondary.

3.2.1 Effective Address Recording

A naive approach would transfer all addresses involved in memory operations to the secondary, leading to excessive overhead. We developed a series of optimizations to reduce the number of addresses needed to be enqueued without compromising the soundness of the analysis. Fig. 4 will assist us in presenting our methods.

We begin by transforming the BBL in Fig. 4 (a) into the DFT-specific representation in Fig. 4 (b), which captures data dependencies and data tracking semantics, as defined in an intermediate representation called Taint Flow Algebra (TFA) [18]. Each register used in the BBL is treated like a variable. Whenever a register variable is updated, a new version of the variable is created (e.g., `eax1` in line 1 of Fig. 4(b)) that is valid within the BBL. For example, in lines 1 to 4 and 6, of Fig. 4(b), a tag is copied, while in line 5 two tags are combined, denoted by the OR ('|') operator.

Intra-block Optimization. We search for effective addresses within a BBL that correlate with each other to identify the minimum set required that would correctly restore all of them in the secondary. For instance, we only need to enqueue one of `[esp0]` or `[esp0 + 4]` from Fig. 4 (b), as one can be derived from the other by adding/subtracting a constant offset. This search is greatly facilitated by the DFT transformation and register variables versioning, but it is applicable to all shadow memory analyses, as it only tries to eliminate related addresses.

DFT Optimization. This optimization identifies instructions, and consequently memory operands, which are not going to be used by the analysis in the secondary, by applying compiler optimizations, such as dead code elimination and data-flow analysis, against our DFT-specific representation of the BBL [18]. For instance, in Fig. 4(b) we determine that the propagation in line 1 is redundant, as its destination operand (`eax1`) is overwritten later in line 3, before being referred by any other instruction. This allows us to ignore its memory operand `[esp0]`.

Inter-block Optimization. We extend the scope of the intra-block optimization to cover multiple blocks connected by control transfers. This implements backward data-flow analysis [2] with the partial CFG gathered during profiling. We begin by defining the input and output variables for each BBL. We then produce a list of input and output memory operands which are live before entering and when leaving a BBL. Using our representation, input memory operands are the ones with all of its constituent register variables in version 0, and output memory operands are the ones that have all of its constituent register variables at their maximum version. In our example in Fig. 4, the inputs list comprises of `[esp0]`, and the outputs list includes `[esp0]`, `[ebx1]`, `[eax2 + ebx1]`, and `[eax2 + 2 × ebx1 + 200]`. If all predecessors for the BBL contain `[esp0]` in their outputs list, the block can harmlessly exclude this from logging because the secondary still has a valid reference to the value. The optimization has greater effect as more inputs are found on the outputs lists of a block's predecessors.

Since we only have a partial CFG of the application, it is possible that at runtime we identify new execution paths that invalidate the backwards data-flow analysis. We tackle this issue by introducing two heuristics that make inter-block optimization more conservative. First, if we find any indirect jumps to a known BBL, we assume that others may also exist and exclude these blocks from optimization. Second, we assume that function entry point BBLs, may be reachable by other, unknown indirect calls, and we also exclude them. We consider these measures to be enough to cover most legitimate executions, but they are not formally complete, and as such may not cover applications that are buggy or malicious. Note that with the latter, we are not referring to vulnerable applications that may be compromised, an event that can be prevented by DTA, but malicious software that one may wish to analyze. In the case of malware, this optimization can be disabled with negligible impact on performance (see Sec. 6).

Linear Lower Bound. To enhance the intra- and inter-block optimizations, we introduce the concept of *Linear Lower bound*, which interprets memory operands as a series of linear equations:

$$b_{reg} + s \times i_{reg} + d \tag{2}$$

Memory addressing in x86 architectures can be expressed as a linear equation (2). It contains two variables for base and index registers (b_{reg} and i_{reg}), a coefficient s for scale, and a constant d for displacement.[2] Thus, we can say each BBL is associated with a group of linear equations, where each equation represents a distinct memory operand (Fig. 4(c)). For every BBL, we solve their group of linear equations, which results in reducing the number of memory operands that need to be enqueued and decreasing the size of a BBL's inputs and outputs lists for the inter-block optimization. For example, in line 5 of Fig. 4(c), `[ebx1]` is no longer required, as it can be calculated from `[eax2 + ebx1]` and `[eax2 + 2 × ebx1 + 200]` in lines 4 and 6. It also helps inter-block analysis by adding `[eax2]` to the BBL's outputs list.

Having applied all, except the inter-block optimization, the number of effective addresses that need to be transferred for our example is reduced from six to three (from Fig. 4(c) to (d)). The effects of individual optimizations are discussed in Sec. 6.1.

3.2.2 Control Flow Recording

As in the previous section, a naive approach to ensure control flow replication would involve the primary enqueueing the BBID of every BBL being executed. However, simply doing this for all BBLs is *too* costly.

After examining how control-flow transitions are performed in x86 architectures, we identify three different types of instructions:

[2]Segmentation registers see limited use today, mostly for referring to thread local storage (TLS). We ignore segmentation-based addressing for the Linear Lower Bound optimization.

```
1: pop eax
2: pop ebx
3: mov eax ← [eax + ebx + 100]
4: mov [eax + ebx ] ← ebx
5: add edi ← [ebx]
6: mov ecx ← [ecx + 2 × ebx + 200]
```

(a) x86 instruction

```
1: T(eax1) = T([esp0])
2: T(ebx1) = T([esp0 + 4])
3: T(eax2) = T([eax1 + ebx1 + 100] )
4: T( [eax2 + ebx1] ) = T(ebx1)
5: T(edi1) |= T([ebx1])
6: T(ecx1) = T([eax2 + 2 × ebx1 + 200])
```

(b) DFT representation

```
1: ea0 := esp0
2: ea1 := esp0 + 4
3: ea2 :=eax1 + ebx1 + 100
4: ea3 := eax2 + ebx1
5: ea4 := ebx1
6: ea5 := eax2 + 2 × ebx1 + 200
```

(c) Distinct EAs

```
1: void PROP(ea0, ea3, ea5) {
2:    REG(EBX) = MEM_E(ea0 + 4);
3:    ...
4:    REG(EDI) |= MEM_E(ea5 - ea3 -200);
5:    REG(ECX) = MEM_E(ea5);
6: }
```

(d) Propagation body

Figure 4: Example of how a BBL is transformed during code analysis.

(a) direct jumps, (b) direct branches, and (c) indirect jumps. For direct jumps, BBIDs for successor BBLs can be excluded from logging, since there is only a single, fixed exit once execution enters into BBL0. For example, the transitions from BBL0 to BBL1, and then to BBL2 in Fig. 3 can be excluded. Direct branches can have two outcomes. They are either taken, or fall through where execution continues at the next instruction. We exploit this property to only enqueue a BBID, when the least frequent outcome, according to our dynamic profiling, occurs. For instance, when BBL3 follows BBL2 in Fig. 3. We use the *absence* of BBL3's id to signify that BBL4 followed as expected. Note that if a BBL has two predecessors and it is the most frequent path for only one of them, we log its BBID. Last, for indirect jumps we always record the BBID following them, since they are hard to predict. Fortunately, the number of such jumps are less compared to direct transfers.

Applying our approach on the example CFG from Fig. 3, we would only need to enqueue the id of BBL3 once. Obviously, this approach offers greater benefits when the profiling covers the segments of the application that are to run more frequently in practice. It does not require that it covers all code, but unknown code paths will not perform as well. We evaluate the effects of this optimization for various applications in Sec. 6.

3.2.3 Ring Buffer Fast Checking

For every enqueueing operation from the primary, we should check whether there is available space in the ring buffer to avoid an overflow. However, performing this check within the DBI is very costly, as it requires backing up the `eflags` register. We attempt to reduce the frequency of this operation by performing it selectively. For instance, every 100 BBLs. However, to correctly placing the checks in the presence of CFG loops, so that they are actually performed every 100 executed blocks, is challenging. We mitigated this problem by introducing an algorithm, which finds basic blocks that program execution is ensured to visit at most every k block executions. The problem formally stated is as follows.

We are given a CFG defined as $C = (V, E)$. C is a weighted directed graph where V represents a set of basic blocks and E represents a set of edges that correspond to control transfers among blocks. We also have a weight function $w(v)$ that returns execution counts for $v \in V$. Given that we want to find a subset of vertices S such that:

- For a given parameter k, we can assure that the program execution will visit a node from S at most every k block executions.
- $\sum_{v \in S} w(v)$ is close to the minimum.

The above problem is identical to *the feedback vertex set problem* [13], which is NP-complete when any non-cyclic paths from C is smaller than k. Thus, we can easily reduce our problem to this one and use one of its approximation approaches. Additionally, to take into consideration new execution paths not discovered during profiling, the secondary monitors the ring buffer and signals the primary, when it exceeds a safety threshold. Finally, we also allocate a write-protected memory page at the end of the available space in the ring buffer that will generate a page fault, which can be intercepted and handled, in the case that all other checks fails.

3.3 Secondary Code Generation

During the off-line analysis we generate C code that implements a program to dequeue information from the shared ring-buffer and implement DFT. Listing 1 contains a secondary code block generated for the example in Fig. 4.

3.3.1 Control Flow Restoration

Each code segment begins with a goto label (line 2), which is used with the `goto` statement to transfer control to the segment. Control transfers are made by code appended to the segments. In this example, lines 21 $\sim$ 31 implement a direct branch. First, we check whether the ring buffer contains a valid effective address. The presence of an address instead of BBID (i.e., the *absence* of a BBID) indicates that the primary followed the more frequent path (BBID 0xef13a598), as we determined during code analysis (Sec. 3.2.2). Otherwise, the code most likely did not take the branch and continued to the BBL we previously identified (in this case 0xef13a5ba). We do not blindly assume this, but rather check that this is indeed the case (line 25). We do this to accommodate unexpected control-flow transfers, such as the ones caused by signal delivery (Linux) or an exception (Windows). If an unexpected BBID is found, we perform a look up in a hash table that contains all BBLs identified during the analysis, and the result of the search becomes the target of the transfer in line 29. Note that unknown BBIDs point to a block handling the slow path. While a look up is costly, this path is visited rarely. We also use macros `likely()` and `unlikely()` (lines 5, 21, and 25) to hint the compiler to favor the likely part of the condition.

3.3.2 Optimized DFT

Each code segment generated performs tag propagation for the BBL it is associated with. Effective addresses are referenced directly within the ring buffer, and shadow memory is updated as required by code semantics. For each BBL, optimized tag propagation logic is generated based on the methodology introduced in our previous work [18]. Briefly, this involves extracting tag propagation semantics and representing them in a DFT-specific form, which is susceptible to multiple compiler-inspired optimizations that aim at removing propagation instructions that have no practical effect or cancel out each other, as well as reducing the number of instructions required for propagation by grouping them together.

The propagation code in lines 6 $\sim$ 12 is generated based on the example in Fig. 4. `rbuf()` is a macro that returns a value in the ring buffer relative to the current reading index. Ring buffer accesses correspond to `ea0`, `ea3` and `ea5` in Fig. 4(d). The `MEM_E()` macro in lines 8 $\sim$ 11 translates memory addresses from the real execution context to shadow memory locations, while `REG()` does the same for registers.

```
1  /* BBL label */
2  BB_0xef13a586:
3
4  /* LIFT's FastPath(FP) optimization */
5  if (unlikely( REG(EBX) || MEM_E(rbuf(0) + 4) || REG(EDI) || . . . ))
6  {
7      /* propagation body */
8      REG(EBX) = MEM_E(rbuf(0) + 4);
9      . . .
10     REG(EDI) |= MEM_E(rbuf(2) − rbuf(1) −200);
11     REG(ECX) = MEM_E(rbuf(2));
12 }
13
14 /* update the global address array */
15 garg(0) = rbuf(1);
16
17 /* increase index */
18 INC_IDX(3) ;
19
20 /* control transfer */
21 if (likely(IS_VALID_EA(rbuf(0) )) {
22     /* direct jump */
23     goto BB_0xef13a598;
24 } else {
25     if (likely(rbuf(0) == 0xef13a5ba))
26         goto BB_0xef13a5ba;
27     } else {
28         /* hash lookup for computed goto */
29         goto locateBbIdLabel();
30     }
31 }
```

Listing 1: Example of secondary code for a BBL.

We exploit the fact that we can now run conditional statement fast, since we are running the analysis outside the DBI, to implement a simplified version of the FastPath (FP) optimization proposed by LIFT [28]. This is done in line 8, where we first check whether any of the input and output variables involved in this block are tagged, before propagating empty tags.

Last, in line 15 we save the EA that the inter-block optimization determined it is also used by successor BBLs in the global arguments array `garg`, and progress the increasing index of the ring buffer in line 18.

4. RUNTIME

The off-line application analysis produces the enqueueing stubs for the primary and the analysis body for the secondary. These are compiled into a single dynamic shared object (DSO) and loaded by ShadowReplica at start up. In this section, we describe various aspects of the runtime environment.

4.1 DFT

4.1.1 Shadow Memory Management

The shadow memory structure plays a crucial role in the performance of the secondary. Avoiding conditional statements in in-line DFT systems, frequently restricts them to flat memory structures like bitmaps, where reading and updating can be done directly. An approach that does not scale on 64-bit architectures, because the bitmap becomes excessively large. Due to our design, conditional statements do not have such negative performance effects.

The approach we adopted is borrowed from libdft [19] that implements byte-per-byte allocation, with a low-cost shadow address translation, and dynamic allocation to achieve a small memory footprint. Shadow memory is maintained in sync with the memory used by the application by intercepting system calls that manage memory (e.g., `mmap()`, `munmap()`, `brk()`) and enqueueing special control commands that allocate and deallocate shadow memory areas. The information sent includes the command code and an address range tuple *(offset, length)*.

To access shadow memory, we first consult a page table like data structure, which points to a per-page flat structure. The mechanism does not require a check for page validity because intercepting the memory management calls ensures it. Accesses to unallocated space are trapped to detect invalid memory addresses.

4.1.2 DFT Sources and Sinks for Taint Analysis

Tagging memory areas, when data are read from a file or the network, is performed by generating code that enqueues another control command in the ring buffer. The data sent to the secondary include the command code, an address range tuple *(offset, length)*, and the tag value (or label). The value with which to tag the address range in shadow memory depends on the particular DFT-logic. For instance, DTA uses binary tags, data can tainted or clean. In this case, we can simply omit the tag value.

Checking for tagged data can be either done by enqueueing a control command, or it can be done entirely by the secondary, as it is in the case of DTA. For instance, whenever a BBL ends with a `ret` instruction, the secondary checks the location of the return address in the stack to ensure it is clean. If we wanted to check for sensitive information leaks, we would have to issue a command from the primary whenever a `write()` or `send()` system call is made. Note that all checks are applied on the secondary, which can take action depending on their outcome. For DTA, if a check fails, we immediately terminate the application, as it signifies that the application's control flow has been compromised. Other actions could involve logging memory contents to analyze the attack [32], or allowing the attack to continue for forensics purposes [27].

Moreover, the primary synchronizes with the secondary before potentially sensitive system calls (e.g., `write()` and `send()`) that may leak sensitive information from the system. This ensures that the secondary does not fall behind, allowing an attack to go undetected for a long time, or at least not before leaking information. This granularity of synchronization does leave a small but, nevertheless, existing time window that the attacker can leverage to suppress the secondary and our checks. We have complemented our implementation to also require synchronization whenever a new BBL (i.e., a new execution path) is identified at run time to guard against such an event.

4.1.3 Generic Block Handler

BBLs that were not identified during profiling are processed by the Generic Block Handler (GBH), our slow-path implementation of DFT. In this case, the primary on-the-fly transforms instructions and their operands into their DFT-specific representation of TFA. Then, it implements a stack-based interpreter that enqueues the DFT operations (i.e., `AND`, `OR`, `ASSIGN`), which need to be performed by the secondary, in the ring buffer.

4.2 Ring Buffer

We implemented the ring buffer, as a lock-free, ring buffer structure for a single producer (primary), single consumer (secondary) model. Lamport et al. [20] initially proposed a lock-free design for the model, however, the design suffers from severe performance overheads on multi-core CPUs due to poor cache performance [14]. The most serious problem we observed was *forced* L1 eviction that occurs as the secondary attempts to read the page that was just modified by the primary, while it is still in the primary's L1 cache and before it is committed to RAM. In certain cases, the overhead due to ring-buffer communication increased to the point that our framework became unusable. To mitigate the problem, we switched to a N-way buffering scheme [33], where the ring-buffer is divided into N separate sub-buffers, and primary and secondary threads work on different sub-buffers at any point of time, maintaining a distance of least as much as the size of a single sub-buffer.

Synchronizing between primary and secondary is also performed through the shared data structure. We extended the typical N-way buffering implementation, by adding a control entry for each sub-buffer. When the primary finishes updating a sub-buffer, it records the number of entries it enqueued in the control entry and moves the next sub-buffer. If the next sub-buffer's control entry is zero, the secondary already finished its work, so the primary can proceed to fill that up as well. Otherwise, the primary waits, periodically polling the control entry. Likewise, the secondary polls the control entry to check whether there are data for it to process. When primary and secondary need to be synchronized (e.g., before the execution of sensitive system calls), the primary retires early from its current sub-buffer and waits until the secondary clears up all entries and updates the control entry with zero, thus synchronizing.

Data Encoding. Data enqueued in the ring buffer belong to one of the following three groups: (a) effective addresses (EAs), (b) BBIDs, and (c) control commands. We exploit the fact that valid EAs point to user-space ranges (0G $\sim$ 3G range on x86 Linux) to quickly differentiate them from other entries without using additional bits. We map BBIDs and control commands to address ranges that correspond to kernel space (3G $\sim$ 4G range on x86 Linux), which immediately differentiates them from EAs that are always in lower address ranges. This design is easily applicable on 64-bit architectures and other operating systems.

4.3 Support for Multi-threaded Applications

Multi-threaded applications are composed by *critical regions*, where they access shared data in a safe manner by acquiring a lock. To ensure that secondary threads operate on shadow memory in the same order that the primary threads operated on real data, we need to identify when a thread enters such a critical region. We accomplish this by intercepting mutex related calls in the POSIX threads library, namely `pthread_mutex_lock()` and `pthread_mutex_unlock()`. Our approach can be easily extended to also support other locking schemes, but currently does not guarantee shadow memory consistency for shared-data accesses where no locking is performed.

Lock-protected critical regions are handled as follows. When one of the primary threads acquires a lock, it waits until its secondary clears all entries from the ring buffer, essentially synchronizing with the secondary. Every lock in the primary is associated with a separate ring buffer structure and another secondary thread attached to it, when it is created. The primary proceeds to switch its ring-buffer pointer to the one that belongs to the particular lock and resumes execution. Similarly, when releasing the lock, the primary synchronizes with the current secondary and resumes using its original ring buffer. This process ensures that the order of shadow memory operations is consistent with the order of operations in the application. In the future, we plan to explore additional optimizations targeting multi-threaded applications.

5. IMPLEMENTATION

We implemented the dynamic profiler as tool for the Pin DBI framework in $\sim$ 3,800 lines of C++. The runtime environment, responsible for injecting the enqueueing stubs in the application and hosting the secondary threads, was also build as a tool for Pin in $\sim$4,000 lines of C++ code. The code analysis and generation represents the majority of our effort. It consists of $\sim$12,000 lines of Python code.

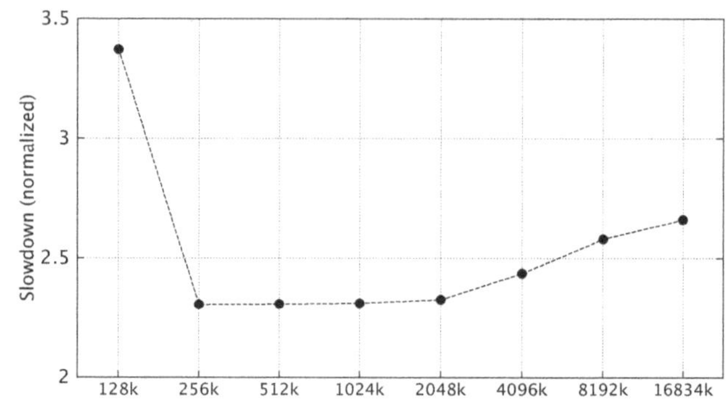

Figure 5: Choosing right ring-buffer size.

Currently, all of the secondary's functionality is implemented as a single function with labels for each BBL segment. This design choice was made to exploit the compiler's intra-procedure optimizations that can better organize the code and improve locality. An alternate design adopting a function abstraction per BBL cannot enjoy these optimizations, and would suffer higher function call/return overheads. We discovered that a large number of labels caused the GCC compiler to fail due to resource exhaustion when running CFG related optimizations.[3] This currently prevents us from building a single-function program for applications with more than $\sim$ 50K BBLs. As a workaround, we divide the analysis program into multiple sub-functions, where each represents a clustered subgraph from the CFG.

Fig. 5 shows how ShadowReplica's communication cost varies, as we set the size of the ring-buffer with different values. In this experiment, we ran `bzip2` compression against Linux kernel source (v3.7.10; $\sim$476MB) using a ring buffer comprising of 8 sub-buffers, and having the secondary only consume data. When the size of the whole structure is too small (128k), performance suffers due to L1 cache eviction, as each sub-buffer of 16KB is smaller than the size of L1 cache (32KB). When it becomes larger performance improves, until it becomes larger than 4096KB, where performance starts to suffer due to increased L3 cache misses. In our prototype implementation, we set the ring buffer size to 512KB and configured it with 8 sub-buffers. The size of each sub-buffer is 64KB, twice as large as our test system's L1 cache size.

6. EVALUATION

We evaluated ShadowReplica using common command-line utilities, the SPEC CPU2006 benchmark suite, and a popular web and database (DB) server. Our aim is to quantify the performance gains of our system, and analyze the effectiveness of the various optimizations and design decisions we took. We close this section with a security evaluation of the DTA and CFI tools we built over ShadowReplica.

The results presented throughout this section are mean values, calculated after running 5 repetitions of each experiment. Our testbed consisted of an 8-core host, equipped with two 2.66 GHz quad-core Intel Xeon X5500 CPUs and 48GB of RAM, running Linux (Ubuntu 12.04LTS with kernel v3.2). Note that ShadowReplica can run on commodity multi-core CPUs, such as the ones found on portable PCs. We used a relatively strong server for the evaluation because it was available at the time. The only crucial resource is the L3 cache, 32MB in our case, as the communication overhead

[3]Note that we have filed a bug for this issue [17], but it has not been completely resolved yet.

Category	Application	# BBLs	# Ins.	Unopt	Optimization				Rbuf	# DFT operands	Time (sec.)
					Intra	DFT	Inter	Exec			
Utilities	bzip2	6175	8.59	4.97	2.93	2.62	2.21	1.40	39.70 %	2.69	156.66
	tar	8615	5.20	2.31	1.82	1.70	1.53	0.69	33.49 %	4.52	141.79
SPEC2006	473.astar	5069	7.38	4.09	2.48	2.15	2.05	1.40	22.11 %	3.30	89.78
	403.gcc	78009	4.37	2.54	1.93	1.84	1.42	0.55	56.87 %	5.57	8341.53
	401.bzip2	4588	7.85	4.12	2.75	2.28	2.10	1.27	32.96 %	2.77	109.60
	445.gobmk	25939	5.97	3.04	2.11	1.90	1.72	0.95	27.09 %	3.56	674.74
	464.h264	11303	5.76	4.88	3.12	3.04	1.72	0.84	74.78 %	3.57	242.67
	456.hmmer	7212	19.14	12.62	6.99	6.66	6.34	5.95	59.62 %	6.64	115.81
	462.libquantum	3522	9.16	4.66	2.61	2.27	2.04	1.09	56.69 %	3.88	58.09
	429.mcf	3752	5.96	3.21	2.12	1.83	1.76	1.06	26.38 %	3.19	57.62
	471.omnetpp	15209	5.36	2.88	2.11	1.95	1.80	1.05	6.59 %	3.31	234.35
	400.perl	27391	5.71	2.86	1.89	1.82	1.64	0.84	7.79 %	4.47	421.10
	458.sjeng	5535	5.29	2.49	1.74	1.65	1.54	0.82	21.51 %	4.07	81.51
	483.xalanc	34881	4.79	2.02	1.54	1.44	1.34	0.50	21.40 %	5.97	1189.45
Server application	Apache	23079	8.39	3.17	1.91	1.84	1.6	1.05	28.08 %	5.57	706.63
	MySQL	40393	6.87	4.21	2.19	2.08	1.80	1.10	11.00 %	5.42	1486.60
Average		18792	7.24	4.17	2.52	2.32	2.04	1.29	32.88 %	4.28	881.74

Table 1: Results from static analysis. *Unopt* indicates the number of enqueue operations that a naive implementation requires. The *Intra*, *DFT*, *Inter*, and *Exec* columns correspond to the number of enqueue operations after progressively applying our intra-block, DFT, inter-block, and control flow optimizations. *Rbuf* shows the percentage of BBLs that need to be instrumented with analysis code that checks for ring buffer overflows. *# DFT operands* shows the operands from the secondary's analysis body. The last column, *Time*, shows the time for offline analysis.

heavily depends on its size. The version of Pin used during the evaluation was 2.11 (build 49306). While conducting our experiments hyper-threading was disabled and the host was idle.

6.1 Effectiveness of Optimizations

Table 1 summarizes the effects our optimizations had on reducing the amount of information that needs to be communicated to the secondary, and the effectiveness of the ring buffer fast checking optimization. The *# BBLs* column indicates the number of distinct BBLs discovered for each application, using the profiling process outlined in Sec. 3.1. *# Ins.* gives the average number of instructions per BBL. The *Unopt* column shows the average number of enqueue operations to the ring buffer that a naive implementation would require per BBL. The *Intra*, *DFT*, *Inter*, and *Exec* columns correspond to the number of enqueue operations after progressively applying the intra-block, DFT, and inter-block optimizations presented in Sec. 3.2.1, as well as the optimizations related to control flow recording (Sec. 3.2.2). *Rbuf* shows the percentage of BBLs that need to be instrumented with checks for testing if the ring buffer is full, according to the fast checking algorithm (Sec. 3.2.3). *# DFT operands*, shows *per BBL* average number of register and memory operands appeared from the secondary's analysis body. The last column, *Time* shows the time for offline analysis to generate codes for the primary and the secondary.

On average, a naive implementation would require 4.17 enqueue operations per BBL, for communicating EAs and control flow information to the secondary, and instrument 100% of the BBLs with code that checks for ring buffer overflows. Our optimizations reduce the number of enqueueing operations to a mere 1.29 per BBL, while only 32.88% of BBLs are instrumented to check for ring buffer overflows. A reduction of 67.12%.

While offline analysis requires a small amount of time (on average 881 sec.) for most programs, 403.gcc takes exceptionally long (8341 sec.) to complete. This is due to the program structure, which has a particularly dense CFG, thus making the *Rbuf* optimization wasting a long time ($\sim$ 6500 sec.) only to enumerate all available

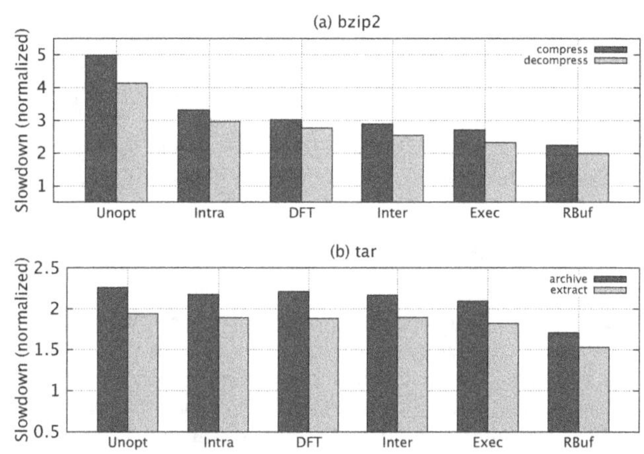

Figure 6: The slowdown of the primary process imposed by ShadowReplica, and the effects of our optimizations, when running `bzip2` and `tar`.

cycles to perform the analysis described in Sec. 3.2.3. We believe that this can be alleviated by parallelizing the algorithm.

To evaluate the impact of our various optimizations on the primary's performance, we used two commonly used Unix utilities, `tar` and `bzip2`. We selected these two because they represent different workloads. `tar` performs mostly I/O, while `bzip2` is CPU-bound. We run the GNU versions of the utilities natively and over ShadowReplica, progressively enabling our optimizations against a Linux kernel source "tarball" (v3.7.10; ~476MB).

We measured their execution time with the Unix `time` utility and draw the obtained results in Fig. 6. *Unopt* corresponds to the runtime performance of an unoptimized, naive, implementation, whereas *Intra*, *DFT*, *Inter*, *Exec*, and *RBuf* demonstrate the benefits of each optimization scheme, when applied cumulatively. With

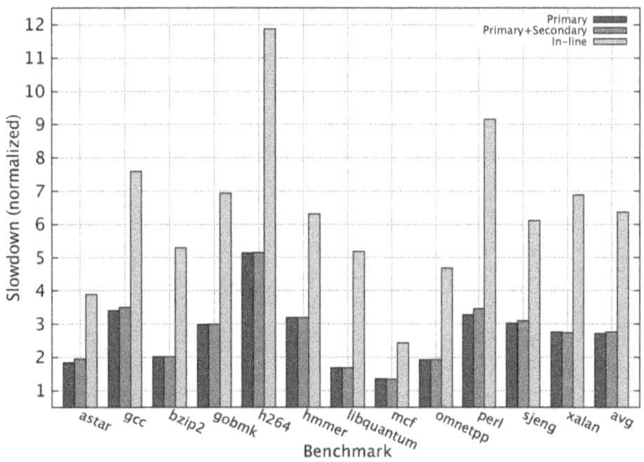

Figure 7: Running the SPEC CPU2006 benchmark suite with all optimizations enabled. *Primary* denotes the slowdown of the primary thread alone. *Primary+Secondary* is the overhead of ShadowReplica when it performs full-fledged DFT. *In-line* corresponds to the slowdown imposed when the DFT process executes in-line with the application.

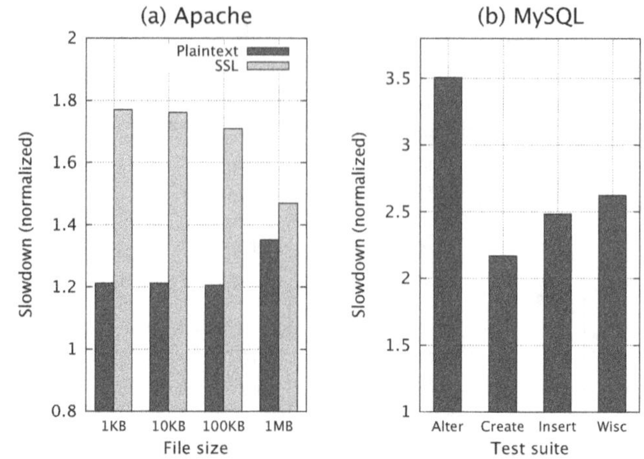

Figure 8: The slowdown incurred by ShadowReplica on the Apache web server and MySQL DB server.

all optimizations enabled, the slowdown imposed to `bzip2` drops from 5×/4.13× down to 2.23×/1.99× for compress/decompress (55%/51.82% reduction). Similarly, `tar` goes from 2.26×/1.94× down to 1.71×/1.53× for archive/extract (24.33%/ 21.13% reduction). It comes as no surprise that I/O bound workloads, which generally also suffer smaller overheads when running with in-lined DFT, benefit less from ShadowReplica. We also notice that *Intra* and *RBuf* optimizations have larger impact on performance.

6.2 Performance

SPEC CPU2006. Fig. 7 shows the overhead of running the SPEC CPU2006 benchmark suite under ShadowReplica, when *all* optimizations are enabled. *Primary* corresponds to the slowdown imposed by the primary thread alone. *Primary+Secondary* is the overhead of ShadowReplica when both the primary and secondary threads and running, and the secondary performs full-fledged DFT. Finally, *In-line* denotes the slowdown imposed when the DFT process executes in-line with the application, under our accelerated DFT implementation [18]. On average, *Primary* imposes a 2.72× slowdown on the suite, while the overhead of the full scheme (*Primary+Secondary*) is 2.75×. *In-line* exhibits a 6.37× slowdown, indicating the benefits from the decoupled and parallelized execution of the DFT code (56.82% reduction on the performance penalty).

During our evaluation, we noticed that for some benchmarks (astar, perlbmk, gcc, sjeng) the slowdown was not bound to the primary, but to the secondary. These programs generally required a high number of DFT operands to be sent to the secondary (*# DFT operands* from Table 1) compared to the number of enqueued entries.

The significant slowdown with the *h264ref* benchmark was due to the way Pin handles `rep`-prefixed string instructions (i.e., `rep movs`, `rep cmps`), heavily used in this benchmark. Pin assumes that the tool developer wants to instrument each one of these repetitions and transforms these instructions into explicit loops, introducing additional overhead. However, our DFT-specific representation [18], which captures source, destination, and offset from these instructions, does not require such a transformation. We used one of Pin's command-line options to disable this feature, which reduced our slowdown in this benchmark from 5× to 3.05×.

Apache and MySQL. We proceed to evaluate ShadowReplica with larger and more complex software. Specifically, we investigate how ShadowReplica behaves when instrumenting the commonly used Apache web server. We used Apache v2.2.24 and let all options to their default setting. We measured Apache's performance using its own utility `ab` and static HTML files of different size. In particular, we chose files with sizes of 1KB, 10KB, 100KB, and 1MB, and run the server natively and with ShadowReplica with all optimizations enabled. We also tested Apache with and without SSL/TLS encryption (i.e., *SSL* and *Plaintext*, respectively). Fig. 8 (a) illustrates our results. Overall, ShadowReplica has a 24% performance impact, on average, when Apache is serving files in plaintext. Unsurprisingly, the slowdown is larger when running on top of SSL (62%). The reason behind this behavior is that the intensive cryptographic operations performed by SSL make the server CPU-bound. In Fig. 8 (b), we present similar results from evaluating with the MySQL DB server, a multi-threaded application which spawned 10 $\sim$ 20 threads during its evaluation. We used MySQL v5.0.51b and its own benchmark suite (`sql-bench`), which consists of four different tests that assess the completion time of various DB operations like table creation and modification, data selection and insertion, etc. The average slowdown measured was 3.02× (2.17× – 3.5×).

6.3 Computational Efficiency

One of the goals of ShadowReplica was to also make DFT more efficient computation-wise. In other words, we not only desired to accelerate DFT, but also do it using less CPU resources. To evaluate this aspect of our approach, we chose two benchmarks from the SPEC CPU2006 suite; 401.bzip2 and 400.perl. Our choice was was not arbitrary. During our performance evaluation, we observed that in the first benchmark, DFT was running faster than the application. Performance is, hence, bound by the primary thread. On the other hand, in the second benchmark the secondary thread, performing DFT, was slower, hence its performance is bound by the secondary thread.

We run ShadowReplica and our accelerated in-line DFT implementation with these two benchmarks, and measured their CPU usage using the `perf` tool. Fig. 9 presents the results of our experiment. We run ShadowReplica with both primary and secondary

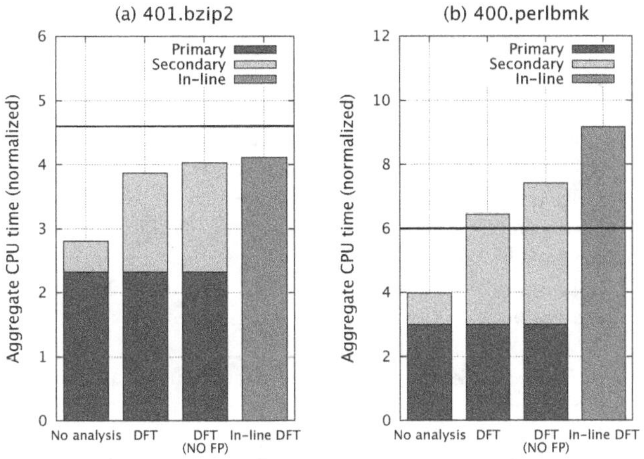

Figure 9: Aggregated CPU time consumed by two SPEC CPU2006 benchmarks when run under different configurations of ShadowReplica, and under in-line DFT. For ShadowReplica, we draw the CPU time taken by the primary and secondary threads separately. A darker horizontal line shows the threshold above which the secondary dominates CPU usage.

Application	Vulnerability	CVE-ID
exim-4.69	Format string	CVE-2010-4344
proftpd-1.3.3a	Stack overflow	CVE-2010-4221
nginx-0.6.32	Buffer underflow	CVE-2009-2629
memcached 1.1.12	Integer overflow	CVE-2009-2415
htget-0.93	Stack overflow	CVE-2004-0852
WsMp3-0.0.8	Heap overflow	CVE-2003-0338
athttpd-0.4b	Buffer overflow	CVE-2002-1816

Table 2: ShadowReplica-{DTA, CFI} successfully prevented the listed attacks.

threads running, having the secondary perform no analysis (*No analysis*), implementing DFT using all optimizations (*DFT*), and without the FastPath optimization from LIFT [28] (*DFT (NO FP)*). The last column (*in-line DFT*) shows the result for a DFT implementation that in-lines the analysis to the application process [18]. CPU usage is partitioned to show the amount of CPU cycles taken from the primary and secondary threads separately. The darker horizontal line visualizes the tipping point where the secondary thread starts dominating performance (i.e., it is slower than the primary), when we are running ShadowReplica with DFT and all optimizations enabled.

A take-out from these results is that the aggregated CPU usage of ShadowReplica is less or equal than that of in-line DFT analysis. In other words, we manage to satisfy equation 1 from Sec. 2.1. Astoundingly, in the case of 401.bzip2, we are so much more efficient that we require ~30% less CPU cycles to apply DFT.

6.4 Security

The purpose of developing the DTA and CFI tools over ShadowReplica was not to provide solid solutions, but to demonstrate that our system can indeed facilitate otherwise complex security tools. Nevertheless, we tested their effectiveness using the set of exploits listed in Table 2. In all cases, we were able to successfully prevent the exploitation of the corresponding application.

During the evaluation, DTA did not generate any false positives, achieving the same level of correctness guarantees to our previous DFT implementation [19, 18]. However, CFI suffered from some false positives due to the inability to obtain an accurate CFG by static and dynamic profiling. We leave the task of improving the soundness of CFG as a future work.

Having DTA and CFI implemented mostly from the secondary, performance overhead was negligible by having $\sim 5\%$ slowdown.

7. RELATED WORK

The idea of decoupling dynamic program analyses from execution, to run them in parallel, has been studied in past in various contexts [31, 8, 25, 33, 14, 26, 6]. Aftersight [8], ReEmu [6], and Paranoid Android [26] leverage record and replay for recording execution and replaying it, along with the analysis, on a remote host or a different CPU (replica). They are mostly geared toward offline analyses and can greatly reduce the overhead imposed on the application. However, the speed of the analysis itself is not improved, since execution needs to be replayed and augmented with the analysis code on the replica.

SuperPin [31] and Speck [25] use speculative execution to run application and (in-lined) analysis code in multiple threads that execute in parallel. These systems sacrifice significant processing power to achieve speed up. Furthermore, handling multi-threaded applications without hardware support remains a challenging issue for this approach.

CAB [14] and PiPA [33] aim at offloading the analysis code alone to another execution thread, and they are the closest to ShadowReplica. However, neither of the two has been able to deliver the expected performance gains, due to (a) naively collecting information from the application, and (b) the high overhead of communicating it to the analysis thread(s). This paper demonstrated how to tackle these problems.

DFT has been broadly used in the security domain but also elsewhere. TaintCheck [24] utilizes DTA for protecting binary-only software against buffer overflows and other types of memory corruption attacks. It applies DTA, using Valgrind [23], to detect illegitimate uses of network data that could enable attackers to seize control of vulnerable programs. Panorama [32] makes use of DTA for analyzing malware samples similarly to Argos [27]. TaintBochs [9] utilizes a whole system emulator for studying the lifetime of sensitive data, whereas TaintEraser [34] relies on DTA for preventing sensitive information leaks. ConfAid [3] leverages DFT for discovering software misconfigurations. Dytan [10] is a flexible DFT tool, allowing users to customize its data sources and sinks, as well as the propagation policy, while it can also track data based on control-flow dependencies.

8. CONCLUSION

We presented ShadowReplica, a new and efficient approach for accelerating DFT and other shadow memory-based analyses, by decoupling analysis from execution and utilizing spare CPU cores to run them in parallel. We perform a combined off-line dynamic and static analysis of the application to minimize the data that need to be communicated for decoupling the analysis, and optimize the code used to perform it. Furthermore, we design and tune a shared ring buffer data structure for efficiently sharing data between threads on multi-core CPUs. Our evaluation shows that performing DFT using ShadowReplica is more than $2\times$ faster and uses up to 30% less CPU cycles than in-line DFT. Although the overall performance impact of DFT remains significant, we hope that our optimizations will bring it closer to becoming practical for certain environments.

9. ACKNOWLEDGEMENT

We want to express our thanks to the anonymous reviewers for their valuable comments and to Rob Johnson, our shepherd, for his guidance. This work was supported by the US Air Force, the Office of Naval Research, DARPA, and the National Science Foundation through Contracts AFRL-FA8650-10-C-7024, N00014-12-1-0166, FA8750-10-2-0253, and Grant CNS-12-22748, respectively, with additional support by Intel Corp. Any opinions, findings, conclusions, or recommendations expressed herein are those of the authors, and do not necessarily reflect those of the US Government, the Air Force, ONR, DARPA, NSF, or Intel.

10. REFERENCES

[1] M. Abadi, M. Budiu, U. Erlingsson, and J. Ligatti. Control-flow integrity. In *Proc. of CCS*, 2005.

[2] A. V. Aho, M. S. Lam, R. Sethi, and J. D. Ullman. *Compilers: Principles, Techniques, and Tools (2nd Edition)*. Addison-Wesley Longman Publishing Co., Inc., 2006.

[3] M. Attariyan and J. Flinn. Automating configuration troubleshooting with dynamic information flow analysis. In *Proc. of OSDI*, 2010.

[4] D. Bruening and Q. Zhao. Practical memory checking with dr. memory. In *Proc. of CGO*, 2011.

[5] D. Bruening, Q. Zhao, and S. Amarasinghe. Transparent dynamic instrumentation. In *Proc. of VEE*, 2012.

[6] Y. Chen and H. Chen. Scalable deterministic replay in a parallel full-system emulator. In *Proc. of PPoPP*, 2013.

[7] V. Chipounov, V. Kuznetsov, and G. Candea. S2E: a platform for in-vivo multi-path analysis of software systems. In *Proc. of ASPLOS*, 2011.

[8] J. Chow, T. Garfinkel, and P. Chen. Decoupling dynamic program analysis from execution in virtual environments. In *Proc. of USENIX ATC*, 2008.

[9] J. Chow, B. Pfaff, T. Garfinkel, K. Christopher, and M. Rosenblum. Understanding data lifetime via whole system simulation. In *Proc. of USENIX Security*, 2004.

[10] J. Clause, W. Li, and A. Orso. Dytan: A generic dynamic taint analysis framework. In *Proc. of ISSTA*, 2007.

[11] M. Costa, J. Crowcroft, M. Castro, A. Rowstron, L. Zhou, L. Zhang, and P. Barham. Vigilante: End-to-end containment of internet worms. In *Proc. of SOSP*, 2005.

[12] W. Enck, P. Gilbert, B.-G. Chun, L. P. Cox, J. Jung, P. McDaniel, and A. N. Sheth. TaintDroid: An information-flow tracking system for realtime privacy monitoring on smartphones. In *Proc. of OSDI*, 2010.

[13] P. Festa, P. M. Pardalos, and M. G. Resende. Feedback set problems. *Handbook of Combinatorial Optimization*, 4:209–258, 1999.

[14] J. Ha, M. Arnold, S. M. Blackburn, and K. S. McKinley. A concurrent dynamic analysis framework for multicore hardware. In *Proc. of OOPSLA*, 2009.

[15] Hex-Rays. The IDA Pro Disassembler and Debugger, cited Aug. 2013. http://www.hex-rays.com/products/ida/.

[16] A. Jaleel, R. S. Cohn, C.-K. Luk, and B. Jacob. Cmp$im: A pin-based on-the-fly multi-core cache simulator. In *Proc. of MoBS*, 2008.

[17] K. Jee. Bug 56113. GCC Bugzilla, cited Aug. 2013. http://gcc.gnu.org/bugzilla/show_bug.cgi?id=56113.

[18] K. Jee, G. Portokalidis, V. P. Kemerlis, S. Ghosh, D. I. August, and A. D. Keromytis. A general approach for efficiently accelerating software-based dynamic data flow tracking on commodity hardware. In *Proc. of NDSS*, 2012.

[19] V. P. Kemerlis, G. Portokalidis, K. Jee, and A. D. Keromytis. libdft: practical dynamic data flow tracking for commodity systems. In *Proc. of VEE*, 2012.

[20] L. Lamport. Specifying Concurrent Program Modules. *ACM Transactions on Programming Languages and Systems (TOPLAS)*, 1983.

[21] K. H. Lee, X. Zhang, and D. Xu. High accuracy attack provenance via binary-based execution partition. In *Proc. of NDSS*, 2013.

[22] C. Luk, R. Cohn, R. Muth, H. Patil, A. Klauser, G. Lowney, S. Wallace, V. Reddi, and K. Hazelwood. Pin: building customized program analysis tools with dynamic instrumentation. In *Proc. of PLDI*, 2005.

[23] N. Nethercote and J. Seward. Valgrind: a framework for heavyweight dynamic binary instrumentation. In *Proc. of PLDI*, 2007.

[24] J. Newsome and D. Song. Dynamic taint analysis for automatic detection, analysis, and signature generation of exploits on commodity software. In *Proc. of NDSS*, 2005.

[25] E. B. Nightingale, D. Peek, P. M. Chen, and J. Flinn. Parallelizing security checks on commodity hardware. In *Proc. of ASPLOS*, 2008.

[26] G. Portokalidis, P. Homburg, K. Anagnostakis, and H. Bos. Paranoid Android: Versatile protection for smartphones. In *Proc. of ACSAC*, 2010.

[27] G. Portokalidis, A. Slowinska, and H. Bos. Argos: an Emulator for Fingerprinting Zero-Day Attacks. In *Proc. of EuroSys*, 2006.

[28] F. Qin, C. Wang, Z. Li, H.-s. Kim, Y. Zhou, and Y. Wu. LIFT: A low-overhead practical information flow tracking system for detecting security attacks. In *Proc. of MICRO*, 2006.

[29] A. Slowinska, T. Stancescu, and H. Bos. Howard: a dynamic excavator for reverse engineering data structures. In *Proc. of NDSS*, 2011.

[30] R. Wahbe, S. Lucco, T. E. Anderson, and S. L. Graham. Efficient software-based fault isolation. In *Proc. of SOSP*, 1993.

[31] S. Wallace and K. Hazelwood. Superpin: Parallelizing dynamic instrumentation for real-time performance. In *Proc. of CGO*, 2007.

[32] H. Yin, D. Song, M. Egele, C. Kruegel, and E. Kirda. Panorama: capturing system-wide information flow for malware detection and analysis. In *Proc. of CCS*, 2007.

[33] Q. Zhao, I. Cutcutache, and W. Wong. PiPA: pipelined profiling and analysis on multi-core systems. In *Proc. of CGO*, 2008.

[34] D. Zhu, J. Jung, D. Song, T. Kohno, and D. Wetherall. TaintEraser: Protecting sensitive data leaks using application-level taint tracking. In *SIGOPS Oper. Syst. Rev.*, 2011.

Multi-Cloud Oblivious Storage

Emil Stefanov
UC Berkeley
emil@cs.berkeley.edu

Elaine Shi
University of Maryland
elaine@cs.umd.edu

ABSTRACT

We present a 2-cloud oblivious storage (ORAM) system that achieves 2.6X bandwidth cost between the client and the cloud. Splitting an ORAM across 2 or more non-colluding clouds allows us to reduce the client-cloud bandwidth cost by at least one order of magnitude, shifting the higher-bandwidth communication to in-between the clouds where bandwidth provisioning is abundant. Our approach makes ORAM practical for bandwidth-constrained clients such as home or mobile Internet connections. We provide a full-fledged implementation of our 2-cloud ORAM system, and report results from a real-world deployment over Amazon EC2 and Microsoft Azure.

Categories and Subject Descriptors

K.6.5 [**Management of Computing and Information Systems**]: Security and Protection

General Terms

Algorithms; Security

Keywords

Oblivious RAM; outsourced storage; multi-cloud; privacy

1. INTRODUCTION

Storage outsourcing is a growing industry that shields storage users from the burden of in-house infrastructure maintenance, and offers economies of scale. However, due to concerns over data privacy, "many potential cloud users have yet to join the cloud, and many are for the most part putting only their less sensitive data in the cloud" [8]. Encryption alone is insufficient for ensuring data privacy, since access patterns can also leak a considerable amount of sensitive information. For example, Islam *et al.* demonstrate statistical attacks that leverage access patterns to successfully infer about 80% of the search queries made to an encrypted email repository [18].

CCS'13, November 4–8, 2013, Berlin, Germany.

ACM 978-1-4503-2477-9/13/11 ...$15.00.
http://dx.doi.org/10.1145/2508859.2516673.

Oblivious RAM (ORAM) [7, 9–11, 13, 14, 16, 19, 22, 23, 25, 30–32, 34, 35], first proposed by Goldreich and Ostrovsky [11], is a cryptographic construct that allows a client to access encrypted data residing on an untrusted storage provider, while completely hiding data access patterns. ORAM guarantees that the sequence of physical addresses accessed is independent of the actual data requested – in other words, the *physical* access patterns do not reveal information about the *logical* access patterns. To achieve this, the client continuously re-encrypts and reshuffles data blocks on the storage server, to cryptographically conceal the *logical* access pattern.

Due to the attractive security guarantees ORAM provides, several recent works have investigated how to make ORAM practical in an outsourced storage setting [20, 30, 31, 34, 35]. These works suggest that a primary hurdle for real-world ORAM deployment stems from its high bandwidth cost. Under realistic parameterizations (e.g., gigabytes to terabytes of outsourced storage), the best known ORAM schemes incur about 20X – 35X bandwidth cost, i.e., for every data block accessed, on average 20 to 35 blocks need to be transferred. This makes ORAM unsuitable especially for bandwidth constrained clients, e.g., home Internet connections or mobile devices.

In some cases, shipping computation to the cloud can alleviate the client-cloud bandwidth consumption. When the client does not trust the cloud provider, however, one immediate challenge is how to securely compute in the cloud without leaking data to the cloud provider. To this end, researchers have suggested combining trusted hardware and ORAM to securely delegate both computation and storage to the cloud [2, 3, 6, 17, 20, 26]. While this approach is promising, trusted hardware is not widely deployed on today's cloud platforms. Instead, we seek a solution that is *readily deployable* on today's cloud service providers.

1.1 Two-Cloud ORAM

We observe the following asymmetry in bandwidth resource provisioning: while client-cloud bandwidth is scarce in many settings such as cellular networks or slower home Internet connections; network bandwidth in between major cloud providers (e.g., Amazon Web Services and Microsoft Azure) is ample.

We show that by spreading data across multiple *non-colluding* cloud providers, we can shift the 20X – 35X bandwidth cost to inter-cloud communication, while keeping the client-cloud bandwidth cost minimal — about **2.6X** under typical parametrization, and out of which 2X is necessary to hide whether each access is a read or write. While a general k-cloud scheme exists as described in the full online version [29], we focus on designing a highly optimized two-cloud solution which we believe to be the more likely deployment scenario. We provide a full-fledged two-cloud ORAM implementation, and have successfully deployed it on two major cloud providers, Amazon Web Services (AWS) and Microsoft Azure.

While the idea of using multiple non-colluding clouds is natural, how to design a provably secure and practically efficient scheme is challenging. The main challenge is how to *avoid passing data through the client during data shuffling, and still ensuring security against a potentially malicious cloud that can arbitrarily deviate from the prescribed behavior.* Multi-server ORAM has been considered in a theoretic setting by Lu and Ostrovsky [21]. Their construction, however, focuses on asymptotic performance, and still requires passing data through the client during shuffling. Consequently, their construction would result in at least 20X-35X client-cloud bandwidth cost under typical parametrization.

Technical highlights. Our main technique is to let the two clouds shuffle the data amongst themselves. Particularly, one cloud shuffles the data blocks, adds an "onion" layer of encryption, and send them to the other cloud. In this way, one cloud observes the permutation while the other observes the accesses to these blocks — and neither cloud observes both. In the next round, the two clouds switch roles.

To enforce honest behavior when one of the clouds may be malicious, we design a novel *commutative checksum-encryption construction.* At a very high level, the client shares a secret checksum function with each cloud, such that the clouds can monitor each other's actions. After every shuffle, about 4λ checksum bits per block are transferred between the client and the clouds such that the client can verify the correctness of the shuffle. In the above, $\lambda = 128$ is the security parameter. The typical block size is much larger than λ, e.g., 4KB (size of a memory page) or higher. While transferring entire blocks to the client during shuffling would have incurred 20X-35X cost, by transferring 4λ bits per block we bring this part of the cost down to 0.1X to 0.2X (out of a total of 2.6X) as shown in Section 5. We also show that a similar technique may be employed to avoid reading a logarithmic number of blocks for each data access, which is necessary in most existing ORAM schemes.

Similar to the SSS construction [31], our 2-cloud ORAM scheme requires the client to store less than 1.5GB of data for an ORAM of 1TB in capacity (i.e., less than 0.15% of the ORAM capacity). Particularly, in addition to caching about $O(\sqrt{N})$ data blocks where N is the total number of blocks, the client also stores about 4 bytes of metadata per block. While the metadata size is linear in theory; its size in practice is typically comparable to or smaller than the $O(\sqrt{N})$ data blocks cached. Out of theoretic interest, with suitable modifications to our scheme, it is possible to achieve sublinear client storage by applying the recursion technique described in earlier works [27,31], such that we could (recursively) outsource the linear metadata to the cloud as well. In practice, however, this is rarely necessary – and even if one does apply the recursion, the recursion depth rarely exceeds 2 to 3 in practical settings [20,27].

In addition to minimizing the client-cloud bandwidth consumption, our 2-cloud ORAM scheme also roughly halves the total bandwidth consumption (including inter-cloud and client-cloud communication) in comparison with single-cloud counterparts [31].

Threat model. We assume that at least 1 cloud provider is honest, i.e., faithfully executes the prescribed protocol. The other cloud may be malicious and arbitrarily deviate from the protocol. We do not know ahead of time which cloud is malicious. It is not within our goal to prevent the malicious cloud from launching Denial-of-Service (DoS) style attacks — DoS defense is orthogonal to and outside the scope of this work. We also cannot prevent a malicious cloud from voluntarily divulging its local states and views to the honest cloud, which can potentially allow the honest cloud to learn additional information. For example, a malicious cloud can simply publish its states and protocol views on a public website.

However, we do guarantee that as long as there exists at least one honest cloud, *a malicious cloud cannot learn any information about the client's logical access patterns. In fact, any deviation from the prescribed protocol is immediately detectable by the client.* In other words, by deviating from the prescribed protocol, a malicious cloud can only help an honest cloud gain information, but cannot learn anything itself. Moreover, it will be caught immediately if it ever deviates.

The above intuitive security model is generalized to the k-cloud setting (when only 1 out of k clouds needs to be honest), and defined formally using a simulation-based definition in the full online version [29]. We prove that our constructions are secure under this simulation-based definition in the full online version [29].

2. PRELIMINARIES

Our algorithm depends on the partitioning framework and the partition ORAM construction proposed by Stefanov, Shi, and Song [31], referred to as the SSS construction. We give a brief background of the SSS construction.

It is important to note that partitions do not represent clouds. In fact, as will be later explained in our construction, each partition is split across multiple clouds.

2.1 Partitioning Framework

The SSS partitioning framework [31] allows us to securely break-up ORAM read/write operations into read/write operations over smaller partitions, where each partition is an ORAM itself.

The framework consists of two main techniques, *partitioning* and *eviction.* Through partitioning, a bigger ORAM instance of capacity N is divided into $O(\sqrt{N})$ smaller ORAM instances (called partitions), each with capacity $O(\sqrt{N})$. While naive partitioning can break security, Stefanov *et al.* [31] propose a novel approach to allow partitioning without compromising security, as outlined below.

Figure 1 illustrates the partitioning framework. At any point of time, a block resides in a random partition. The client stores a *position map* to keep track of which partition each block resides in. To access a block whose identifier is u, the client first looks up the position map and determine block u's current partition p. Then the client issues an ORAM read operation to partition p and looks up block u. On fetching the block from the server, the client logically assigns it to a freshly chosen random partition – without writing the block to the server immediately. Instead, this block is temporarily cached in the client's local *eviction cache.*

The partitioning framework [31]

// Divide the ORAM into $\sqrt{N}$ partitions of size $O(\sqrt{N})$.

Read(u):

- Look up position map and determine that u is assigned to partition p.
- If u is not found in eviction caches:
  - **ReadPartition**(p, u)

  Else if u is found in local eviction caches:
  - **ReadPartition**$(p, \perp)$ `//read dummy`
- Pick a random partition p', add the block identified by u to the eviction caches, and logically assign u to partition p'.
- Call **Evict** ν times where $\nu > 1$ is the eviction rate.

Write(u, B):

Same as **Read**(u), except that the block written to the eviction cache is replaced with the new block.

Evict:

- Pick a random partition p.
- If a block B exists in the eviction cache assigned to partition p, call **WritePartition**(p, B).
- Else, call **WritePartition**$(p, \perp)$, where $\perp$ represents a dummy block.

Figure 1: The SSS partitioning framework [31]. Our construction uses this framework to express ORAM **Read** and **Write** operations in terms of the **ReadPartition** and **WritePartition** operations of our multi-clouds construction.

A background eviction process evicts blocks from the eviction cache back to the server in an oblivious manner. With every data access, randomly select 2 partitions for eviction. If a block exists in the eviction cache assigned to the chosen partition, evict a real block; otherwise, evict a dummy block to prevent leakage.

2.2 Partition ORAM

Each partition is a fully functional ORAM in itself. Our partition ORAM construction is based on the partition ORAM of the SSS construction [31], which is a variant of the original hierarchical construction [11], but with various optimizations geared towards maximal practical performance.

Each partition consists of $L := \frac{1}{2}\log N + 1$ levels, where level $i \in \{0, 1, \ldots, L-1\}$ can store at more 2^i real blocks, and 2^i or more dummy blocks. We refer to the largest level, i.e., level $L-1$, as the *top level.*

We extend the client's position map to store the position tuple $(p, \ell, \mathit{offset})$ for each block, where p is the partition, ℓ is the level, and *offset* denotes the offset within the level.

Read. To read a block, the client first reads its position map and find out the position $(p^*, \ell^*, \mathit{offset}^*)$ of the block. Then, the client reads one block from each level of partition p. For level $\ell = \ell^*$, the client reads the block at offset^*. For other levels, the client reads a random unread dummy block. If the block is found in the client's eviction cache, one dummy block is read from each level.

Write. Writing back a block to a partition causes a reshuffling operation. Specifically, let $0, 1, \ldots, \ell$ denote consecutively filled levels such that level $\ell+1$ is empty. Writing back a block B causes levels $0, 1, \ldots, \ell$ to be reshuffled into level $\ell+1$. In the single-cloud SSS construction, the reshuffling is done by having the client download all blocks, permute them, re-encrypt them, and then write them back to the server.

3. BASIC TWO-CLOUD CONSTRUCTION IN THE SEMI-HONEST MODEL

We first explain a scheme that is secure when both clouds are semi-honest. Then, in Section 4, we explain how to use our commutative checksum-encryption construction to achieve security against one malicious cloud (without knowing which one might be malicious).

3.1 Intuition

Reducing ORAM shuffling overhead. In existing single-cloud ORAM schemes [30–32, 35], a major source of the client bandwidth overhead stems from shuffling. Periodically, the client has to download a subset of data blocks from the cloud, permute them, re-encrypt them locally, and write them back.

In our multi-cloud ORAM construction, we delegate the shuffling work to the two clouds to minimize client-cloud bandwidth usage. For example, cloud S_1 shuffles a subset of blocks, adds a layer of encryption (i.e., an "onion layer"), and sends them to S_2. Later when the client needs to read from that subset of blocks, it fetches them from S_2. In this way, while cloud S_1 knows the permutation used in the shuffling, it does not see which blocks the client requests from S_2 later. In contrast, while S_2 sees which shuffled blocks the client requests later, it has no knowledge of the permutation applied by S_1. As a result, neither cloud learns any information about the client's logical (i.e., "unshuffled") access pattern. The details of inter-cloud shuffling are described in Section 3.5.2.

Note that it is necessary for security to add onion encryption layers after every shuffle: if a block B gets shuffled from S_1 to S_2 and then back to S_1, we do not want S_1 to be able to link the two occurrences of the same block B based on the block's data. In the full online version [29], we introduce a background onion removal process to avoid adding an unbounded number of onion layers to a block.

Reducing ORAM read overhead. Existing single-cloud ORAM schemes can also incur significant bandwidth overhead for reading a data block in-between shufflings [30–32, 35]. For example, the client may need to read one or more blocks from $O(\log N)$ levels in a hierarchy.

In our multi-cloud construction, we are able to significantly reduce the bandwidth overhead for reading a block by doing the following. The client requests a set of (already shuffled) blocks from S_1. S_1 then randomly permutes them with a permutation known only by S_1 and the client, and then S_1 sends them to S_2. Finally, the client requests and downloads only a single block from S_2 by providing S_2 with the permuted index of the requested block. The details of reading a block from multiple clouds are described in Section 3.5.1.

3.2 Data Layout on Clouds

Our scheme leverages the partitioning framework as described in Section 2.1. We divide our ORAM into $O(\sqrt{N})$ partitions each of capacity $O(\sqrt{N})$. Each partition is divided into $L = O(\log N)$ levels, and each level resides on one of the two clouds. Which level resides on which cloud changes as partitions are shuffled. Each level can be filled (i.e., it contains blocks) or empty.

In practice, each cloud can distribute the data across multiple servers. For simplicity, we will first regard each cloud as a single logical entity; then in the full online version [29], we explain how to distribute the data and workload across multiple servers within each cloud.

New use of partitioning framework. We use partitioning for a somewhat different motivation than described in the SSS paper [31]. Particularly, the SSS construction relies on partitioning mainly to get rid of oblivious sorting [11,12], thus achieving a constant factor saving in bandwidth.

Like in ObliviStore [30], we use partitioning to achieve parallelism, and to greatly improve response time. We shuffle and read from multiple partitions in parallel as described in the full online version [29], and such parallelism is especially useful if each cloud has multiple servers each serving a subset of the partitions. If a read request happens on a partition not currently being shuffled, the read does not block on shuffling. In our system, the contention (probability of a read occurring on a partition involved in a large shuffle) is very small — since (1) each read happens to a uniformly random partition (regardless of the access pattern), (2) there are thousands of partitions, and (3) large shuffles happen very infrequently, i.e., with exponentially decreasing frequency. It's also important to note that as the amount of parallelism increases, the contention increases. However, in practice, for large enough ORAMs with many partitions, the amount of parallelism necessary to saturate the server bandwidth does not cause significant contention.

In our multi-cloud ORAM, we can still achieve about 2X-3X client-cloud bandwidth cost even with a single partition. However, with a single partition, reads would have to block waiting for reshuffling operations of up to N blocks to finish (e.g., gigabytes or terabytes of data transfered between the two clouds), resulting in prolonged response times. Williams and Sion [35] describe an algorithm for simultaneously reading and shuffling a single-partition ORAM, but we observe that this technique about doubles the cloud-to-cloud bandwidth used because the single partition has twice as many levels than our $O(\sqrt{N})$ sized partitions.

As studied in [31], a larger number of partitions requires a larger amount of client-side cache. Therefore, the number of partitions can be used as a knob to tune the tradeoff between the client-side storage and the response time.

3.3 Client Metadata

The client stores the following metadata. Note that even though the client storage is asymptotically linear, it has a very small constant and is quite small in practice. For example, all of the client storage combined is less than 1.5 GB for a 1 TB ORAM with 4KB blocks (i.e., less than 0.15% of the ORAM capacity). The amount of client storage used is similar to several existing single-cloud ORAM systems [30, 31, 35].

- The position tuple (p, ℓ, offset) denoting the block's current partition, level, and offset within the level.
- A bit vector for every partition and every filled level, indicating which blocks in the level have been read and (logically) removed.
- A time value for every partition, i.e., the total number of operations that have occurred so far for each partition.
- A next dummy block counter for each partition and each level. The counter is set to 0 when a level is being rebuilt; and incremented when a next dummy element is read. This counter is sufficient to implement the GetNextDummy function mentioned in Figure 4.

It is possible to even further reduce the client storage to $O(\sqrt{N})$ by recursing on the position map as was proposed in [31].

3.4 Initializing

Each partition is initially placed in a random cloud (S_1 or S_2). Each block is assigned to a random partition, and a random offset in the top level (the largest level) of the partition. The client's position map is initialized accordingly.

We assume initially, all blocks have the value zero. This can be done by initializing all blocks on the server to be encryptions of the zero block with appropriate metadata attached. Initialization can be optimized to consume much less bandwidth using a similar technique described in [31].

3.5 ORAM Read and Write Operations

A standard ORAM includes two operations: **Read** and **Write**. As previously mentioned in Section 2 and Section 3.2, our construction uses the SSS partitioning framework [31]. The SSS framework specifies how **Read** and **Write** operations can be securely expressed in terms of *partition ORAM* read/write operations called **ReadPartition** and **WritePartition**. Section 2 explains how this can be achieved. Since we rely on this framework we only need to describe how to implement **ReadPartition** and **WritePartition**.

ReadPartition and **WritePartition** operations are performed in parallel across all partitions but in serial for each individual partition to ensure consistency.

3.5.1 Reading from a Partition

In a typical single-cloud ORAM scheme [31], the client needs to download one block for each of the $O(\log N)$ levels in a partition to hide which level it wants to read from. In our construction, we rely on the inter-cloud shuffling technique such that the client only needs to download a single block.

Our **ReadPartition** protocol is illustrated in Figure 2(a) and described in detail in Figure 4. To read a block u, the client first looks up its position map to get the tuple $(p^*, \ell^*, \mathit{offset}^*)$ indicating the position (partition p^*, level ℓ^*, offset offset^*) for block u. The client then generates one offset for each filled level ℓ in partition p. For level $\ell = \ell^*$, the offset $\mathit{offset}_\ell = \mathit{offset}^*$. For all other levels, its offset_ℓ corresponds to a random unread dummy (obtained via GetNextDummy) determined by computing the permuted offset of the $\mathit{nextDummy}[p^*, \ell]$ counter of each level. The client now divides these offsets based on which cloud contains each level, and sends the corresponding offsets to each cloud. *It is important for security that the client sends to each cloud only the offsets of the levels contained within the cloud.*

Now, each cloud reads one block from each of its filled level, at the offsets indicated by the client. The cloud with fewer filled levels onion-encrypts the fetched blocks, and

Figure 2: Two-cloud ORAM protocol. Actions are performed in nondecreasing order specified by the circled numbers. If two actions have the same number within a diagram, it means that they can happen in parallel.

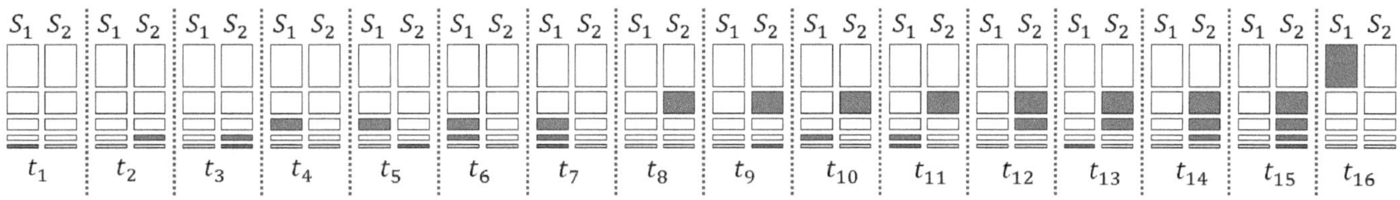

Figure 3: Layout of an ORAM partition across two clouds over time. This figure shows for a specific partition which levels are filled in each cloud (S_1 and S_2) over time ($t_i \in \{t_1, \ldots, t_{16}\}$). When the bottom-most level is empty, our algorithm automatically decides to which cloud to write the next block to preserve the invariant that all consequentially filled levels (from the bottom upwards) are always located on the same cloud.

sends them to the other cloud. Without loss of generality, assume S_2 sends its onion-encrypted blocks to S_1. S_1 now merges the blocks from S_2 with its own fetched set, onion-encrypts them, and reshuffles them using a PRP key shared with the client. The reshuffled set is sent to S_2.

The client now reveals the desired index within the reshuffled array to S_2, and S_2 returns the block at that index. In the full online version [29], we explain how the client decrypts the fetched block. Decrypting involves removing multiple onion layers of encryption as described in the full online version [29].

3.5.2 Writing to a Partition

Our **WritePartition** protocol is illustrated in Figure 2(b) and described in detail in Figure 4. Whenever a block is written to a partition p, it is shuffled with all consecutively filled levels $0, 1, 2, \ldots, \ell$ of the partition into level $\ell + 1$. If $\ell = L - 1$ is the top level, all levels will be shuffled into the top level.

Note that there are 2^L possible ways to divide L levels between two clouds. Our assignment algorithm is designed to best facilitate inter-cloud shuffling by enforcing the following invariant.

Invariant. *Any time when consecutive levels $0..i$ are filled and need to be shuffled into level $i+1$, levels $0..i$ all reside within the same cloud.*

This minimizes the cloud-cloud bandwidth because shuffles always involve consequentially filled levels (i.e., $0..i$). Suppose that, without loss of generality, cloud S_1 holds levels $0..i$ to be shuffled into level $i+1$ of cloud S_2. By ensuring that the above invariant holds, at the start of shuffling, S_1 already has all of levels being shuffled $(0..i)$ and does not have to fetch additional levels from S_2 before starting the shuffle. Figure 3 demonstrates how the levels of a partition are divided amongst the two clouds over time.

These shuffled blocks now form level $\ell + 1$ of the same partition, and reside on S_2. Levels $0, \ldots, \ell$ on S_1 of partition p are deleted and future requests for level ℓ of partition p are directed to S_2.

Shuffling the top level. The only exception is when all levels $0..L-1$ are shuffled, i.e., when the top level is involved in the shuffle. In this case, some dummy or obsolete blocks need to be discarded during the shuffle. Therefore, a top-level shuffle needs to be treated slightly differently, where the client tells S_1 (i.e., source of the shuffle) a subset of blocks to keep for each level — without leaking any information. The detailed protocol is described in Figure 4.

Note that almost all of the bandwidth consumed happens when the two clouds exchange blocks, and the client's bandwidth is conserved.

3.6 Onion Encryption Layers

Key generation. The client shares a master secret key msk_1 with cloud S_1; and msk_2 with cloud S_2.

Onion encryption. Whenever a cloud, say S_1, needs to onion encrypt a block, it generates a pseudo-random one-time encryption key based on msk_1, the time value for the partition under consideration, and the block's position tuple pos' after the shuffle[1].

[1]For read-phase shuffles, we use the block's position prior to shuffle.

ReadPartition(p^*, u):

C :	$(p^*, \ell^*, \mathit{offset}^*) \leftarrow \mathsf{pos}(\mathsf{u})$ *// find out where block* u *resides.*
C :	Let $\mathit{offset}_{\ell^*} := \mathit{offset}^*$. For $\ell \neq \ell^*$, let $\mathit{offset}_\ell = \mathsf{GetNextDummy}(p^*, \ell)$
	// The GetNextDummy *function returns the position of a random unread dummy in the level*
For $j \in \{1,2\} : C \to S_j$:	$\{\mathit{offset}_\ell$: for each filled level ℓ in partition $p^* \in S_j\}$
For $j \in \{1,2\} : S_j$:	$\mathbf{B}_i \leftarrow \{\mathsf{BlockAt}[p^*, \ell, \mathit{offset}_\ell] : \forall$ filled level ℓ in partition p^* on $S_j\}$
S_2 :	$\forall i \in \lvert\mathbf{B}_2\rvert : \mathbf{B}'_2[i] := E_{ek[i]}(\mathbf{B}_2[i])$ where $ek[i] := \mathsf{PRF}_{msk_2}(i, p^*, t,$ "read-enc-A")
$S_2 \to S_1$:	$\mathbf{B}'_2$ *// Without loss of generality, assume S_2 has fewer filled levels.*
S_1 :	$\mathbf{B} := \mathbf{B}_1 \cup \mathbf{B}'_2$
S_1 :	$\forall i \in \lvert\mathbf{B}\rvert : \mathbf{B}'[\mathsf{PRP}_{sk}(i)] := E_{ek[i]}(\mathbf{B}[i])$
	where $sk := \mathsf{PRF}_{msk_1}(p^*, t,$ "read-shuffle"), $ek[i] := \mathsf{PRF}_{msk_1}(i, p^*, t,$ "read-enc-B")
$S_1 \to S_2$:	$\mathbf{B}'$
$C \to S_2$:	$i =$ (offset of block u in $\mathbf{B}'$) *// C can compute this with msk_1 and msk_2*
$S_2 \to C$:	$\mathbf{B}'[i]$
For $j \in \{1,2\} : S_j \to C$:	*"Done"*

WritePartition(p^*, B):

/ Without loss of generality, assume that cloud 1 needs to shuffle ℓ consecutive levels and send to cloud 2. Assume that the block to be written B has been encrypted by the client using a secret key known only to itself. */*

Case 1: $\ell < L - 1$

$C \to S_1$:	*"Write partition"*, p^*, B
S_1:	$\mathbf{B} \leftarrow \mathsf{BlocksAt}[p^*, 0..\ell] \cup \{B\}$
S_1:	$\forall i \in \lvert\mathbf{B}\rvert$: **do**
	Let $i' = \mathsf{PRP}_{sk}(i)$, $\mathbf{B}'[i'] := E_{ek[i]}(\mathbf{B}[i])$
	where $sk := \mathsf{PRF}_{msk_1}(p^*, t,$ "write-shuffle"),
	$ek[i] := \mathsf{PRF}_{msk_1}(\mathsf{pos}', t,$ "write-enc")
	// pos′ *is $\mathbf{B}[i]$'s position after the shuffle*
	// pos′ *can be computed given i'*
	done
$S_1 \to S_2$:	$\mathbf{B}'$
S_2:	$\mathsf{BlocksAt}[p^*, \ell + 1] \leftarrow \mathbf{B}'$
$S_1 \to C$:	*"Done."*
$S_2 \to C$:	*"Done."*
C:	Update local metadata appropriately.

Case 2: $\ell = L - 1$

$C \to S_1$:	*"Write partition"*, p^*, B
C:	$I \leftarrow \emptyset$
	For each level $i = 0$ to $L - 1$:
	let $I_r :=$ {positions of all unread real blocks},
	let $I_d :=$ {positions of $2^i - \lvert I_r\rvert$ randomly chosen unread dummy blocks},
	$I \leftarrow I \cup (I_r \cup I_d)$
$C \to S_1$:	$\mathsf{sorted}(I)$
S_1 :	$\mathbf{B} \leftarrow \mathsf{BlocksAt}[I] \cup \{B\}$
S_1:	$\forall i \in \lvert\mathbf{B}\rvert$: **do**
	Let $i' = \mathsf{PRP}_{sk}(i)$, $\mathbf{B}'[i'] := E_{ek[i]}(\mathbf{B}[i])$
	where $sk := \mathsf{PRF}_{msk_1}(p^*, t,$ "write-shuffle"),
	$ek[i] := \mathsf{PRF}_{msk_1}(\mathsf{pos}', t,$ "write-enc")
	// pos′ *is $\mathbf{B}[i]$'s position after the shuffle*
	// pos′ *can be computed given i'*
	done
$S_1 \to S_2$:	$\mathbf{B}'$
S_2:	$\mathsf{BlocksAt}[p^*, L - 1] \leftarrow \mathbf{B}'$
$S_1 \to C$:	*"Done."*
$S_2 \to C$:	*"Done."*
C:	Update local metadata appropriately.

Figure 4: Partition read and write algorithms for the honest-but-curious model.

Whenever a cloud, say S_1, needs to shuffle a set of blocks, it generates a pseudo-random one-time shuffling key based on msk_1, the current partition, and its the time value.

Onion decryption and background onion removal. The client can recover all encryption keys and decrypt any onion-encrypted block. The details of this is deferred to the full online version [29] for our full construction — which is based on the basic construction described in this section, but augmented to provide security when one of the two clouds is malicious.

4. SECURITY AGAINST ONE MALICIOUS CLOUD

Informally, a malicious server can 1) corrupt data in storage; and 2) deviate from the prescribed protocol, particularly, not performing shuffling correctly.

Corrupted data blocks can be detected through standard techniques such as message authentication codes (MAC), as described in several earlier works [11, 31]. Therefore, we focus our attention on how to detect deviations from the prescribed protocol behavior.

High-level idea. The high-level idea is as follows. The client has two secret checksum functions σ_1 and σ_2. σ_1 is shared with cloud S_1, and σ_2 is shared with cloud S_2. *The client attaches encrypted and authenticated version of the two checksums, denoted $\tilde{\sigma}_1(B)$ and $\tilde{\sigma}_2(B)$ to each block B and stored on the servers along with the block.* The checksums are encrypted and authenticated with a private key that only the client knows.

The client treats the checksums the analogously to the way the clouds treats the blocks. For example, whenever a cloud permutes a set of blocks, the client will permute the corresponding checksums. Whenever a cloud adds an onion layer of encryption to a block, the client will compute the

S_1:	$\mathbf{B}' \leftarrow$ onion-encrypt and shuffle $\mathbf{B}$. *// Let π denote the shuffling permutation.*
$S_1 \rightarrow S_2$:	$\mathbf{B}'$
$S_1 \rightarrow C$:	$\{\tilde{\sigma}_1(B)$ and $\tilde{\sigma}_2(B) : \forall B \in \mathbf{B}\}$
$S_2 \rightarrow C$:	$\{\sigma_2(B')$: $\forall B' \in \mathbf{B}'\}$
C:	$\forall B \in \mathbf{B}$: $\sigma_1(B) :=$ Decrypt $\tilde{\sigma}_1(B)$ $\sigma_2(B) :=$ Decrypt $\tilde{\sigma}_2(B)$
C:	Verify that $g_{ek_i}(\sigma_2(B_i)) = \sigma_2(B'_{\pi(i)})$ for $0 \leq i < \|\mathbf{B}\| = \|\mathbf{B}'\|$ where ek_i is the time and position dependent one-time encryption key (for block B_i known only to C and S_1).
C:	Compute $\sigma_1(B')$ from $\sigma_1(B)$ for all blocks.
C:	$\forall B' \in \mathbf{B}' : \tilde{\sigma}_1(B') :=$ Encrypt & authenticate $\sigma_1(B')$
$C \rightarrow S_2$:	$\{\tilde{\sigma}_1(B') : \forall B' \in \mathbf{B}'\}$

Figure 5: Verifying shuffling and onion-encryption performed by cloud S_1. The protocol is symmetric and the same verification can be done with for S_2 by swapping the roles of S_1 and S_2. The verification is bandwidth efficient in that the client only needs to transfer checksums and not the blocks themselves. Encryption and authentication of the checksums is performed using a secret key known only to the client.

checksum for the onion-encrypted block from its old checksum. After updating a checksum and before uploading it back to the clouds, the client always re-encrypts it and re-authenticates it using authenticated encryption.

Suppose Cloud S_1 onion encrypts and shuffles a set of blocks and sends them to S_2. The client can verify that S_1 did this correctly by asking S_2 to compute and send the checksums of the shuffled and onion-encrypted blocks it received from S_1. The client can then verify the checksums it received from S_2 against the ones it computed directly from the checksums of the old blocks (before shuffling and onion encryption).

Detailed algorithm. Figure 5 describes in more detail how the client can verify that a set of blocks have been correctly shuffled and onion-encrypted by cloud S_1. The same protocol can be run with S_1 and S_2 interchanged to verify shuffling and onion encryption performed by S_2. We prove the security of this verification algorithm in the full online version [29].

In order make the verification in Figure 5 possible, our checksum construction is designed to have the following properties.

Commutative checksum/encryption construction. The client can compute the new checksum of a block (after onion encryption by S_1) from an old checksum (before onion encryption by S_1), *without having to download the block itself.* In other words, for $j \in \{1, 2\}$, there is an efficiently computable function g_{ek} taking the encryption key ek as the key, such that

$$g_{ek}(\sigma_j(B)) = \sigma_j(E_{ek}(B)) \qquad (1)$$

Unforgeability of checksum function. For the above construction to be secure, the checksum function σ needs to satisfy the following unforgeability property: when the checksum function σ is kept secret from an adversary (i.e., one of the clouds), and the adversary has *not* observed any input-output pairs, then, the adversary cannot find a pair $B \neq B'$ such that $\sigma(B) = \sigma(B')$ except with negligible probability. Note that our checksum function is *not* a hash function in the traditional sense, since for a traditional hash function, the description of the function is public.

Intuitively, this property ensures that S_1 cannot deviate from the shuffling protocol: suppose that after a shuffle from S_1 to S_2, the correct block at permuted index i' should be B'. If S_1 sent to S_2 some other $B^* \neq B'$ for index i', then $\sigma_2(B') \neq \sigma_2(B^*)$ except with negligible probability. Hence, the client can immediately detect such deviation.

This property can be formalized as below, and is used as a building block in our full proof in the full online version [29].

DEFINITION 1 (UNFORGEABILITY). *We say that a checksum function family Σ has our special collision resistance property if for all adversaries $\mathcal{A}$ (even when $\mathcal{A}$ is computationally unbounded),*

$$\Pr\left[\begin{array}{l}\textit{Pick random } \sigma \textit{ from } \Sigma; \\ (B_0, B_1) \leftarrow \mathcal{A}(1^\lambda)\end{array} : \begin{array}{l}\sigma(B_0) = \sigma(B_1) \\ \wedge\ B_0 \neq B_1\end{array}\right] = \mathsf{negl}(\lambda)$$

4.1 Commutative Checksum-Encryption Construction

Counter mode of AES encryption. We use counter mode of AES encryption. To encrypt a block $B \in \{0,1\}^\beta$, with a *one-time* key $ek \in \{0,1\}^\kappa$ where κ is 128 bits or 256 bits, compute the ciphertext $R \oplus B$ where R is defined as

$$R := \textit{prefix}\,(\mathsf{AES}_{ek}(0)||\mathsf{AES}_{ek}(1)||\mathsf{AES}_{ek}(2)\ldots) \qquad (2)$$

In the above *prefix* denotes the function that takes the first β bits of the string input. This is a secure one-time encryption scheme, since *each ek is used to encrypt only one message.*

Checksum construction. Let $\sigma : \{0,1\}^\beta \rightarrow \{0,1\}^\lambda$ denote our specially constructed checksum function, where β is the block size, and λ is the security parameter with a typical choice of 128. Our checksum function σ is defined by a $\lambda \times \beta$ matrix $M \in \{0,1\}^{\lambda\beta}$, where λ is the number of rows, and β is the number of columns. Each entry in the matrix is a bit picked at random from $\{0,1\}$. Checksuming a block is simply a matrix multiplication operation:

$$\sigma(B) := M \cdot B \pmod 2$$

Commutative property of checksum-encryption combination. Given an encryption key ek, and a previous checksum σ, we define a verification function g taking ek and σ as inputs:

$$g_{ek}(\sigma) := \sigma \oplus (M \cdot R) \qquad (3)$$

where the vector R is defined as in Equation (2) — taking ek as input.

LEMMA 1. *The above encryption and checksum combination satisfy Equation (1) for any $ek \in \{0,1\}^\kappa$, and any block $B \in \{0,1\}^\beta$,*

PROOF. Note that XOR denoted $\oplus$ is simply addition mod 2. Let $R \in \{0,1\}^\beta$ be a function of ek as defined by Equation (2). Therefore,

$$g_{ek}(\sigma(B)) = \sigma(B) \oplus (M \cdot R)$$
$$=(M \cdot B) \oplus (M \cdot R) = M \cdot (B \oplus R) = \sigma(E_{ek}(B))$$

□

Lemma 2 (Security of checksum function). *Our checksum function is secure by Definition 1.*

The proof of this lemma is deferred to the full online version [29].

Authenticated encryption of checksums. As mentioned earlier, our checksum function is secure only when an adversary has not seen any checksum value. Furthermore, we also need to ensure that a malicious cloud cannot modify the checksum and claim a different checksum. We therefore need to ensure the confidentiality and authenticity (implies freshness) of the checksums. To do this, the client will rely on authenticated encryption to encrypt these checksums before attaching them to the blocks and uploading them to a cloud. To ensure freshness, the authenticated encryption incorporate the *time* of write and the *position* as well. One way to do this is the following: for each block shuffled at time t and shuffled to position pos on cloud S_j, generate a one-time authenticated encryption key ak based off a master secret key ck known only to the client:

$$ak := \mathsf{PRF}_{ck}(\mathsf{pos}, t, j, \text{“AE-Write-Shuffle”})$$
$$\tilde{\sigma} := \mathsf{AE}_{ak}(\sigma)$$

where AE is an authenticated encryption scheme. For shuffles that occur in the **ReadPartition** algorithm (see Figure 4), a different tag “AE-Read-Shuffle” may be used.

Optimization. In description so far, S_2 sends the client a new checksum $\sigma_2(B')$ for each block B' after shuffling, and the client verifies them one-by-one. A simple optimization is for S_2 to use a collision-resistant hash function (e.g., SHA-256), and hash all of the $\sigma_2(B)$'s, and send a single hash to the client C — who can then verify the hash by reconstructing all the $\sigma_2(B)$'s.

4.2 Verifying Fetched Blocks

Whenever the client reads any data block using the **ReadPartition** algorithm, it needs to verify the authenticity and freshness of the fetched block. Our encrypted and authenticated checksums $\tilde{\sigma}_1(B)$ and $\tilde{\sigma}_2(B)$ allow the client to verify the authenticity and freshness for the block B. Particularly, the freshness property is due to the fact the authenticated encryption uses a time and position dependent key.

In the **ReadPartition** algorithm, we simply use the aforementioned algorithm to verify the shuffles associated with read operations. Finally, after fetching a block B, the client verifies its authenticity and freshness using $\tilde{\sigma}_1(B)$ or $\tilde{\sigma}_2(B)$.

5. EXPERIMENTAL RESULTS

5.1 Overview and Experimental Setup

We have implemented a full-fledged multi-cloud ORAM implementation, consisting of 12,000 lines of code. Our implementation uses hardware-accelerated AES-NI whenever available (it is available on most modern Intel processors).

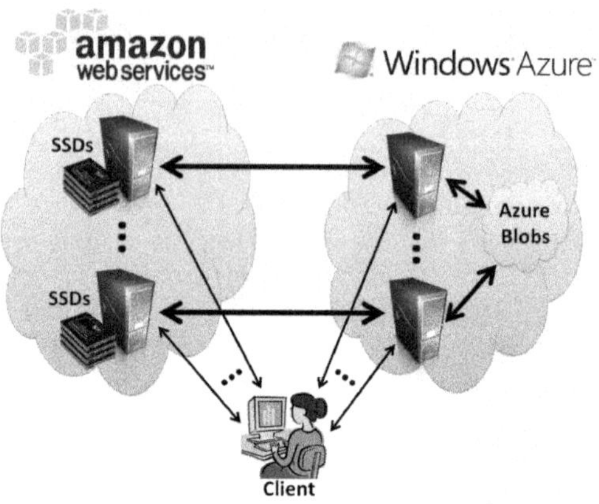

Figure 6: Our deployment. The workload is distributed across multiple servers per cloud communicating in pairs. We use this deployment for the experiments.

Our ORAM implementation uses asynchronous I/O operations to increase throughput. As Stefanov and Shi point out in their recent work [30], in an asynchronous ORAM, to avoid information leakage through timing of I/O events, we need to make sure that the scheduling module does not use any information related to the logical access pattern. We therefore follow this guideline in our multi-cloud ORAM design, to ensure security in the asynchronous ORAM model.

Deployment. We deployed our multi-cloud ORAM implementation running on top of two real-world major cloud providers: Amazon Web Services (AWS) [1] and Microsoft Azure [4]. We rented up to 5 servers per cloud. The AWS servers were High I/O Quadruple Extra Large Instances, each with 2 SSD-based volumes (1 TB each). The Azure servers were Extra Large instances, with the Azure blob storage as the storage backend (SSDs were not available on Azure). Figure 6 illustrates our deployment.

Although these VM instances have large memory and fast CPUs, we chose them only because they are provisioned by the cloud providers with higher disk I/O and network I/O than other instances. As explained in Section 5.4 and Section 5.5, CPU and memory were never the bottlenecks in our experiments.

Latency. Unless otherwise specified, we simulate a 50ms (round-trip) latency between the client and the closest cloud by asynchronously delaying the client's requests and responses. Since our two clouds are in fact two different clouds (Amazon and Azure), we do not simulate additional latency between the clouds.

Scaling. We scale our experiments up to 5 servers per cloud, because our experiments suggest that by this time, the client-cloud bandwidth would already have been saturated in most typical settings – hence, further scaling up inside the clouds would not have increased the overall ORAM throughput. We consider a single client as in most existing ORAM work.

Warming up. All of our experimental results represent the performance of a warmed-up ORAM with N blocks. We use the same technique for warming-up the ORAM as in previous work [30, 31]. As explained in the full online version [29], the client initializes the internal data structures of our construction so that the ORAM immediately starts-off in a warmed-up state (i.e., with multiple filled levels in each partition) without having to pre-initialize or zero-out the server-side storage. This ensures that our performance measurements are steady-state measurements, not burst or best-case performance.

Access pattern. Because our ORAM construction protects the privacy of the access pattern, the access pattern will have no distinguishable effect on the performance of the clouds. However, the access pattern can affect the size of the client's internal data structures (up to a certain point). In order to fairly evaluate our construction, we used a round-robin access pattern as in previous work [30, 31], which turns out to maximize the client storage by reducing the possibility of reusing data already stored by the client.

For ORAM, reads and writes are also indistinguishable. In our construction, they each involve invoking **ReadPartition** and then **WritePartition**, except that during write operation, the client locally updates the block's value in between the **ReadPartition** and **WritePartition** operations. Our access pattern hence consisted of writes.

System load. All of our experiments represent the performance of our system under full load. In other words, data is continuously being written to the ORAM as fast as the ORAM can handle it. For each trial of each data point, we started measuring the performance after 200 MB of data had been written to the ORAM and we stopped measuring after 400 MB of data had been written (committed to disk by the cloud). Although the client memory is up to 1.5 GB for a 1 TB ORAM, most of it is used for the position map, and semaphores in our implementation ensure that only at most 70 MB of it is used to temporarily store data blocks before they are evicted to the clouds. Therefore by starting our measurements after 200 MB of data is written, we eliminate the effect of data buffering by the client.

Number of trails. Except for Figure 15, which provides exact values calculated for our construction, each data point in each figure represents the average over 20 trials. The error bars represent one standard deviation.

5.2 Results: Single Server Per Cloud

We first experimented with a single server per cloud, and report our experimental results below.

Throughput to a large extent depends on the bandwidth of the bottleneck resource. If the client-cloud link is the bottleneck, then our throughput would be roughly $BW/2.6$ where BW denotes the available bandwidth on the client-cloud link. We refer to the number 2.6 as the client-cloud bandwidth cost, i.e., to access a block, roughly 2.6 blocks need to be transferred across the client-cloud link. A breakdown of the client-cloud bandwidth cost is shown in Figure 12.

In Figures 7, we measure maximum ORAM throughput that our multi-cloud system can handle with with 1 server per cloud when the client-to-cloud bandwidth is ample. A 300 GB ORAM of 4 KB blocks with a client over a 50ms latency connection to the clouds can handle up to about 0.8 to 1.0 MB/s throughput. If the block size is increased to 8 KB or 16 KB, the ORAM can sustain 1.2 to 1.6 MB/s of throughput. The graph shows that for ORAMs of sizes between 50 and 300 GB, the throughput is about the same. Theoretically it should decrease by about 15% because an ORAM of size 300 GB has about 14 levels per partition whereas an ORAM with size 50 GB has about 12 levels per partition and the cost I/O cost of the ORAM is proportional to the number of levels in the partitions. This slight decrease in performance is somewhat noticeable but it's mostly masked by variance due to external factors such as fluctuation in cloud network performance.

Figures 8,9, and 10 show the response time of our system under different parameterizations and the effect that the client-to-cloud latency has on the system throughput and response time. In Figure 10 the dotted line is the ideal $y = x$ curve, and represents the case when the request can be handled in exactly the client-to-cloud latency. The response-time of our system is about 200ms to 300ms higher than the client-to-cloud latency due to the cloud-to-cloud latency and the network congestion created by the fact that our system is under full load.

In these figures, the actual client-cloud bandwidth consumption is about 2.6 times the ORAM throughput.

5.3 Scaling to Multiple Servers per Cloud

Figure 11 shows the scaling effect when we use multiple servers per cloud as described in the full online version [29]. Each server handles roughly 300GB of ORAM capacity, and the load distribution scheme is described in the full online version [29]. The total ORAM capacity is therefore 300GB times the number of servers per cloud. We can see that the throughput roughly scales linearly as the number of servers grow (when the client-cloud link is not the bottleneck). The variations are due mostly to varying network performance between specific servers in the clouds. Our experiments also suggest that the response time grows very slightly as the number of servers per cloud grows (Figure 15).

We did not further scale up our experiments beyond 5 servers per cloud, since in the real-world settings we consider, the client-cloud bandwidth would already have been saturated at this scale.

5.4 Bottleneck Analysis

Client-cloud link is the bottleneck. As mentioned earlier, if the client-cloud link is the bottleneck, the ORAM throughput would just be $BW/2.6$, where BW is the client-cloud bandwidth.

Storage performance is the bottleneck. When the client-cloud link has ample bandwidth, the next immediate bottleneck is storage performance. In our deployment, since Azure did not offer SSD-capable instances, Azure's blob storage becomes the bottleneck. Figures 7, 8, 9, 10, and 11, reported above focus on this case.

Inter-cloud networking is the bottleneck. Figures 14 and 15 report the throughput and response time we could potentially obtain had the storage performance not been the bottleneck – e.g., if Azure could provide SSD as their storage; or if in the future, RAM-based persistent storage becomes available (e.g., RAMClouds [24]). In our deployment scenario, the cloud-cloud network bandwidth varied from 30–60MB/s between a pair of servers, which is slower than typical SSD performance (about 150MB/s). Therefore, to extrapolate the performance we could obtain had Azure provided SSD-based storage, in Figures 14 and 15 we emulate the storage back-end using `/dev/zero` (or its equivalent on Windows) – such that the cloud-cloud network is the bottleneck.

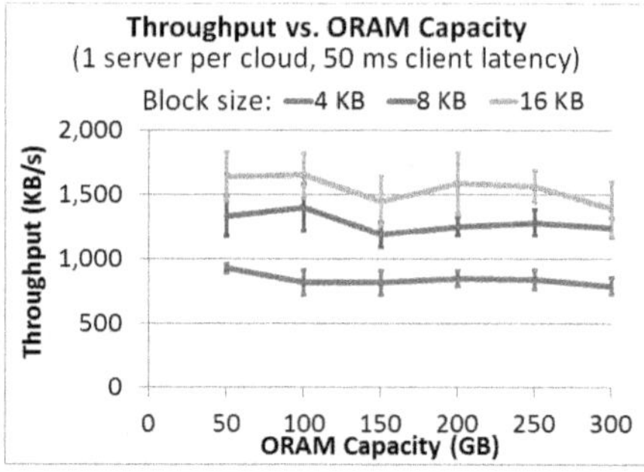

Figure 7: ORAM throughput vs. capacity. With 1 server per cloud, and a simulated 50ms latency client-cloud network link.

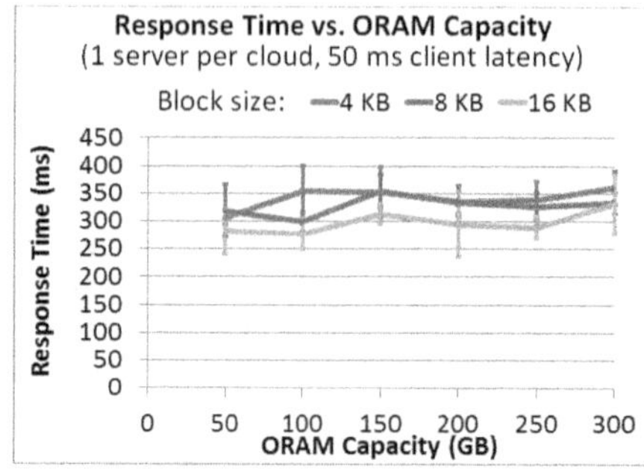

Figure 8: ORAM response time vs. capacity. With 1 server per cloud, and a simulated 50ms latency client-cloud network link.

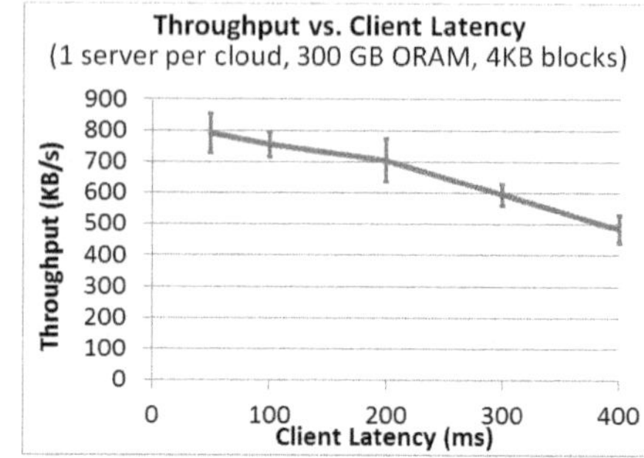

Figure 9: Effect of client-cloud network latency on throughput. With 1 server per cloud, and an ORAM of 300GB capacity.

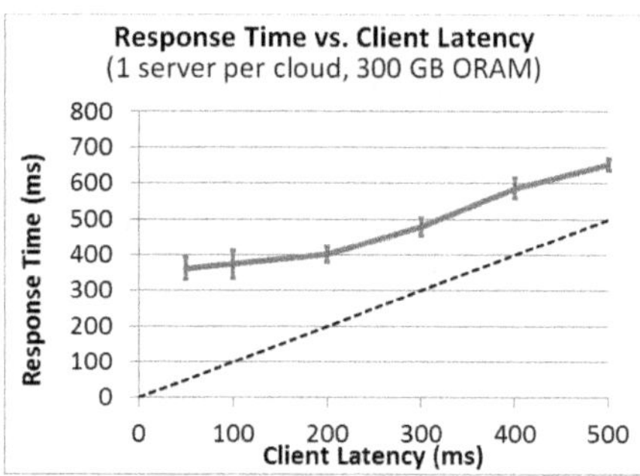

Figure 10: Effect of client-cloud network latency on response time. With 1 server per cloud, and an ORAM of 300GB capacity. The dotted line represents the network roundtrip latency – this is the lower bound on response time.

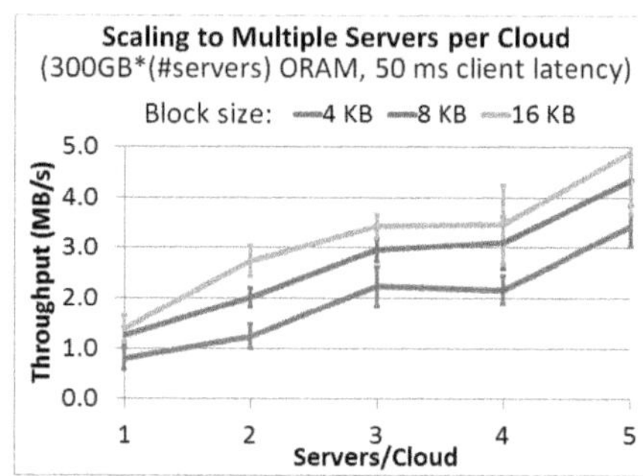

Figure 11: Scaling to multiple servers per cloud: Throughput. With a simulated 50ms latency client-cloud network link. The total ORAM capacity is 300GB times the number of servers. The workload distribution scheme across servers is explained in the full online version [29].

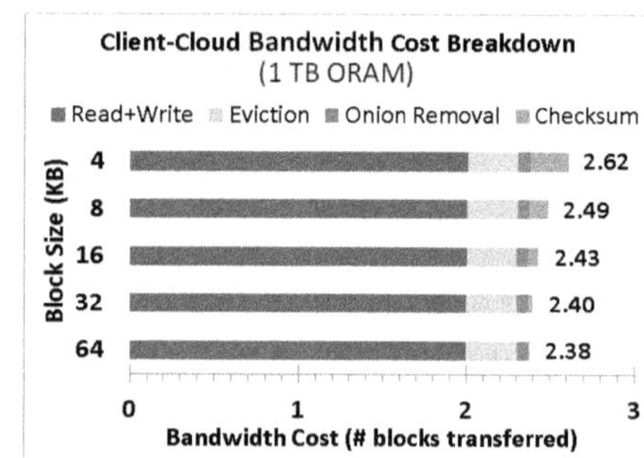

Figure 12: Breakdown of client-cloud bandwidth cost. Measured between the client and all clouds combined for a single ORAM read/write. The number of servers per cloud does not affect the client-cloud bandwidth cost.

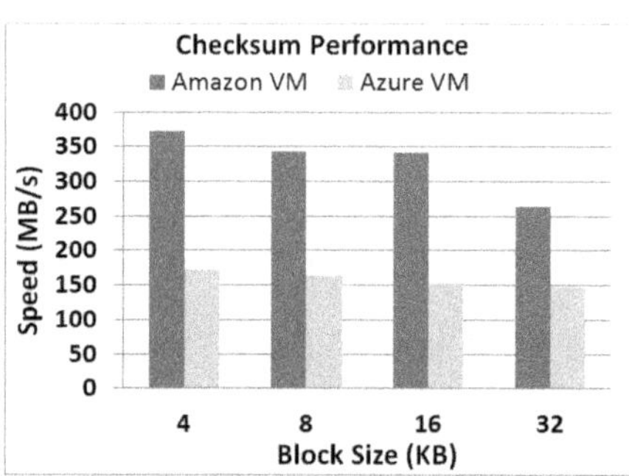

Figure 13: Microbenchmarks for checksum computation. Rate at which each VM in our experiments is able to perform the commutative checksum computation (parallelizing across all cores). Checksum performance slightly decreases with the block size due to a decrease in memory locality as the checksum matrix increases proportionally to the block size.

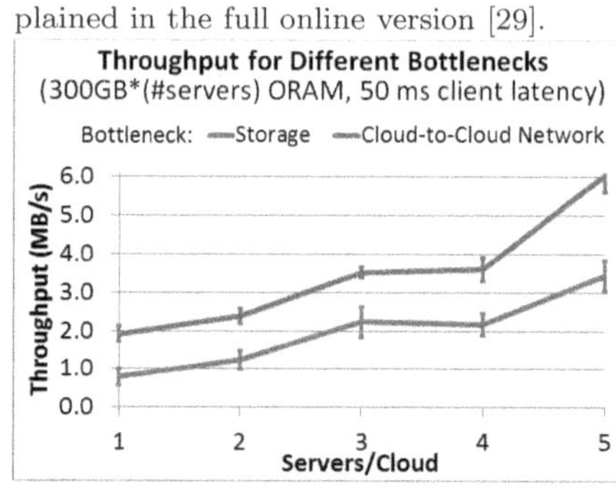

Figure 14: Potential improvement in throughput if storage were fast enough (for 4 KB blocks). The "Storage" curve represents the real-world case where the storage performance is the bottleneck. The "Cloud-cloud network" curve emulates the storage with `/dev/zero` such that the cloud-cloud network link is the bottleneck.

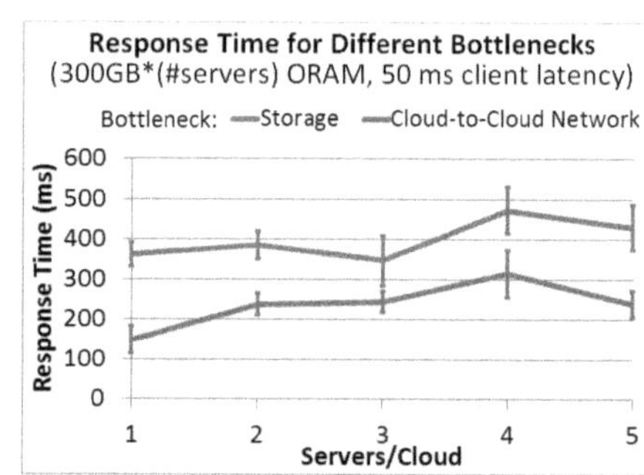

Figure 15: Potential improvement in response time if storage were fast enough (for 4 KB blocks). The "Storage" curve represents the real-world case where the storage performance is the bottleneck. The "Cloud-cloud network" curve emulates the storage with `/dev/zero` such that the cloud-cloud network link is the bottleneck.

5.5 Breakdown of Costs

Bandwidth baseline. Our baseline for bandwidth is a simple cloud storage system that just reads and writes unencrypted blocks to storage. For example, reading or writing a 4 KB block from the baseline system will incur 4 KB of bandwidth. When we say that there is kX ORAM bandwidth cost, we mean that it takes k times as much bandwidth to perform an ORAM read or a write operation.

Client-to-cloud bandwidth. Our construction achieves about 2.6X bandwidth cost which means it takes about 10,647 bytes to read or write 4096 bytes from our multi-cloud ORAM. Figure 12 shows the breakdown of the client-cloud bandwidth cost. Particularly, about 2X (out of a total of $\sim$ 2.6X) of the bandwidth cost is due to hiding whether the block is being read or written (i.e., fetching one block of data with 1X cost and writing one block of data with 1X cost).

For the SSS partitioning framework (Section 2), we use a background eviction rate at 0.3 times rate of data access (in addition to the piggybacked write-back with each operation). Therefore, background evictions account for 0.3X client-cloud bandwidth cost. Due to space limitations, the reader is encouraged to refer to [31] for details about the background eviction process.

The remaining 0.3X or so bandwidth cost is due to the background onion removal process and the transfer of (encrypted and authenticated) checksums between the client and cloud – as mentioned in Section 4, these checksums are necessary to ensure security against one malicious cloud. The checksum size is independent of the block size therefore when the block size increases, the checksum fraction of the bandwidth cost decreases.

Cloud-to-cloud bandwidth. The bandwidth cost of the entire system, which mostly consists of the cloud-to-cloud bandwidth is a constant factor smaller than that for the best known single-cloud construction [30] using the same amount of client memory. The intuition behind why that is the case is as follows. In the single-cloud ORAM by Stefanov *et al.* [30], when blocks need to be shuffled, the client downloads the blocks, shuffles them locally, and uploads them back to the cloud in order to avoid increasing the the client's storage. However, in our multi-cloud construction, one of the clouds just shuffles the blocks and sends them to the other cloud and the other cloud simply stores them and does not need to send the blocks back to the first cloud.

Cryptographic microbenchmarks. We report microbenchmarks for our new checksum function described in Section 4.1. Figure 13 shows that our checksum function can be computed at roughly 250-350 MB/s on our Amazon VM, and at 150 MB/s on our Azure VM. Using hardware-accelerated AES-NI in modern processors, decryption can be performed at 2.5 GB/s per onion layer.

Client computation. The client computation for a 1 TB ORAM mainly consists of: (1) encrypting and computing the initial checksum of a block when it is written to the ORAM, (2) encrypting about 15 checksums (16 bytes each) per block written using the commutative checksum-encryption technique described in Section 4.1, and (3) decrypting using AES about 5-15 onion layers of a fetched block that were added by the clouds during shuffling.

Even without hardware AES available on the client, a modern laptop or desktop computer can easily perform these cryptographic operations to sustain several megabytes per second of ORAM throughput, and most likely saturate its Internet connection (depending on the connection available to the client).

Server computation. In order for a server to sustain about 1 MB/s per sever of bandwidth for a 1 TB ORAM, the the server needs to be able to sustain about 30 MB/s of AES computation and 30 MB/s checksum computation over 4 KB blocks. As we just mentioned, our cryptographic microbenchmarks show that the Amazon and Azure servers we rented can sustain at least 5 to 10 times that rate for checksums and over 80 times that rate for AES.

Client memory and storage. Our client-side storage (memory) is less than 1.5 GB for an ORAM of up to 1 TB capacity (i.e., less than 0.15% of the entire ORAM capacity).

Monetary cost. The monetary cost of our system depends on several factors such as (1) the desired throughput and response time, (2) the size of the ORAM, (3) idle time, and (4) other factors such as geographic location. At the time the experiment was run, under full load, it's cost was about \$3.10/hour + \$2.50/GB data transfer for 1-server per cloud. By using Amazon S3 and cheaper VMs instead of high I/O VM instances, the hourly cost can likely be reduced significantly.

6. RELATED WORK

Oblivious RAM was first proposed by Goldreich and Ostrovsky [11] in the context of protecting software from piracy. They propose a seminal hierarchical construction with $O((\log N)^3)$ amortized bandwidth cost, where N denotes the storage capacity of the ORAM. Since then, a line of research in the theory community has been dedicated to ORAM [7, 9–11, 13–16, 19, 22, 23, 25, 32–34].

Several works have suggested the use of ORAM in cloud computing applications [13, 15, 16, 30, 32, 34, 35]. Williams, Sion *et al.* have significantly bridged the theory and practice of ORAM [32, 34, 35]. Goodrich, Mitzenmacher, Ohrimenko, Tamassia *et al.* [15, 16] have also made significant contributions in this space. Backes *et al.* [6] use a combination of the binary-tree ORAM [27] and trusted hardware to build privacy-preserving behavioral advertising applications.

Several recent efforts have made further progress towards making ORAM practical, including PrivateFS [35], Shroud [20], and ObliviStore [30]. PrivateFS and ObliviStore show how to build parallel or asynchronous ORAM schemes that achieve throughput in the range of hundreds of kilobytes per second on a single disk-bound server — assuming the client-cloud bandwidth is not the bottleneck. Unless trusted hardware is deployed in the cloud, these schemes result in 20X-35X client-cloud bandwidth cost, and is unsuitable for bandwidth constrained clients. Our multi-cloud ORAM is able to achieve a lower overall bandwidth cost than both ObliviStore [30] and PrivateFS [35], and an even lower client-cloud bandwidth cost. Shroud shows how to implement ORAM with trusted co-processors such as IBM 4764 [2], and scale it up in a distributed data center setting, but its performance is severely limited by the trusted co-processors. In comparison, our goal is to provide an implementation that is readily deployable today (i.e., not relying on trusted hardware), and that addresses the client-cloud bandwidth bottleneck.

As mentioned earlier, Lu and Ostrovsky study multi-server oblivious RAM from a theoretic perspective [21]. They show that if there exists two non-colluding servers, the total bandwidth cost of oblivious RAM (including messages sent between the client and the servers, as well as amongst the servers themselves) may be reduced to $O(\log N)$ under the constant client local storage setting. Their work is mostly theory-minded, and results in a high client-server bandwidth in practice. Lu and Ostrovsky's non-collusion model is stronger than ours, since their two non-colluding servers do not communicate with each other.

7. CONCLUSION

In this paper, we described a practical two-cloud Oblivious RAM protocol that *reduces the client-server bandwidth cost to about* 2.6 *times that of simply reading or writing the block from non-oblivious cloud storage.* In comparison, for the same amount of client memory available to the client, the best-known existing (single-cloud) ORAM constructions have a bandwidth cost of about 20X–35X.

We proposed a novel commutative checksum-encryption construction that allows our multi-cloud ORAM protocol to to efficiently protect the privacy of the access pattern against one malicious cloud (without necessarily knowing which one).

We implemented a complete end-to-end systemdeployed on multiple servers across two clouds (Amazon EC2 and Windows Azure) and demonstrated that it can scale and achieve several megabytes of throughput, saturating the available bandwidth of most typical client Internet connections.

Acknowledgments

This work is partially supported[2] by an NSF Graduate Research Fellowship under Grant No. DGE-0946797, by a DoD National Defense Science and Engineering Graduate Fellowship, NSF grant CNS-1314857, a Google Research Award, and a grant from Amazon Web Services. We would like to thank Matthew Green for helpful discussions and the anonymous reviewers for their insightful feedback.

8. REFERENCES

[1] Amazon web services. http://aws.amazon.com/.

[2] IBM 4764 PCI-X cryptographic coprocessor (PCIXCC). http://www-03.ibm.com/security/cryptocards/pcixcc/overview.shtml.

[3] Trusted computing group. http://www.trustedcomputinggroup.org/.

[4] Windows azure. http://www.windowsazure.com/.

[5] D. Asonov and J.-C. Freytag. Almost optimal private information retrieval. In *PET*, 2003.

[6] M. Backes, A. Kate, M. Maffe, and K. Pecina. Obliviad: Provably secure and practical online behavioral advertising. In *S & P*, 2012.

[7] D. Boneh, D. Mazieres, and R. A. Popa. Remote oblivious storage: Making oblivious RAM practical. Manuscript, 2011.

[8] R. Chow, P. Golle, M. Jakobsson, E. Shi, J. Staddon, R. Masuoka, and J. Molina. Controlling data in the cloud: outsourcing computation without outsourcing control. In *CCSW*, 2009.

[9] I. Damgård, S. Meldgaard, and J. B. Nielsen. Perfectly secure oblivious RAM without random oracles. In *TCC*, 2011.

[10] O. Goldreich. Towards a theory of software protection and simulation by oblivious RAMs. In *STOC*, 1987.

[2]Any opinions, findings, and conclusions or recommendations expressed in this material are those of the author(s) and do not necessarily reflect the views of the funding agencies.

[11] O. Goldreich and R. Ostrovsky. Software protection and simulation on oblivious RAMs. *J. ACM*, 1996.

[12] M. T. Goodrich. Randomized shellsort: A simple data-oblivious sorting algorithm. *J. ACM*, 58(6):27:1–27:26, Dec. 2011.

[13] M. T. Goodrich and M. Mitzenmacher. Privacy-preserving access of outsourced data via oblivious RAM simulation. In *ICALP*, 2011.

[14] M. T. Goodrich, M. Mitzenmacher, O. Ohrimenko, and R. Tamassia. Oblivious RAM simulation with efficient worst-case access overhead. In *ACM Cloud Computing Security Workshop (CCSW)*, 2011.

[15] M. T. Goodrich, M. Mitzenmacher, O. Ohrimenko, and R. Tamassia. Practical oblivious storage. In *CODASPY*, 2012.

[16] M. T. Goodrich, M. Mitzenmacher, O. Ohrimenko, and R. Tamassia. Privacy-preserving group data access via stateless oblivious RAM simulation. In *SODA*, 2012.

[17] A. Iliev and S. W. Smith. Protecting client privacy with trusted computing at the server. *IEEE Security and Privacy*, 3(2):20–28, Mar. 2005.

[18] M. Islam, M. Kuzu, and M. Kantarcioglu. Access pattern disclosure on searchable encryption: Ramification, attack and mitigation. In *Network and Distributed System Security Symposium (NDSS)*, 2012.

[19] E. Kushilevitz, S. Lu, and R. Ostrovsky. On the (in)security of hash-based oblivious RAM and a new balancing scheme. In *SODA*, 2012.

[20] J. R. Lorch, J. W. Mickens, B. Parno, M. Raykova, and J. Schiffman. Shroud: Enabling private access to large-scale data in the data center. In *FAST*, 2013.

[21] S. Lu and R. Ostrovsky. Distributed oblivious ram for secure two-party computation. Cryptology ePrint Archive, Report 2011/384, 2011. http://eprint.iacr.org/.

[22] R. Ostrovsky. Efficient computation on oblivious RAMs. In *ACM Symposium on Theory of Computing (STOC)*, 1990.

[23] R. Ostrovsky and V. Shoup. Private information storage (extended abstract). In *STOC*, pages 294–303, 1997.

[24] J. Ousterhout, P. Agrawal, D. Erickson, C. Kozyrakis, J. Leverich, D. Mazières, S. Mitra, A. Narayanan, G. Parulkar, M. Rosenblum, S. M. Rumble, E. Stratmann, and R. Stutsman. The case for ramclouds: scalable high-performance storage entirely in dram. *SIGOPS Oper. Syst. Rev.*, 43(4):92–105, Jan. 2010.

[25] B. Pinkas and T. Reinman. Oblivious RAM revisited. In *CRYPTO*, 2010.

[26] J. Schiffman, T. Moyer, H. Vijayakumar, T. Jaeger, and P. McDaniel. Seeding clouds with trust anchors. In *CCSW*, pages 43–46, 2010.

[27] E. Shi, T.-H. H. Chan, E. Stefanov, and M. Li. Oblivious RAM with $O((\log N)^3)$ worst-case cost. In *ASIACRYPT*, pages 197–214, 2011.

[28] S. W. Smith and D. Safford. Practical server privacy with secure coprocessors. *IBM Syst. J.*, 40(3):683–695, Mar. 2001.

[29] E. Stefanov and E. Shi. Multi-cloud oblivious storage. Technical report.

[30] E. Stefanov and E. Shi. ObliviStore: High performance oblivious cloud storage. In *IEEE Symposium on Security and Privacy*, 2013.

[31] E. Stefanov, E. Shi, and D. Song. Towards practical oblivious RAM. In *NDSS*, 2012.

[32] P. Williams and R. Sion. Usable PIR. In *NDSS*, 2008.

[33] P. Williams and R. Sion. Round-optimal access privacy on outsourced storage. In *CCS*, 2012.

[34] P. Williams, R. Sion, and B. Carbunar. Building castles out of mud: practical access pattern privacy and correctness on untrusted storage. In *CCS*, 2008.

[35] P. Williams, R. Sion, and A. Tomescu. Privatefs: A parallel oblivious file system. In *CCS*, 2012.

Policy-based Secure Deletion

Christian Cachin
IBM Research - Zurich
cca@zurich.ibm.com

Kristiyan Haralambiev
IBM Research - Zurich
kha@zurich.ibm.com

Hsu-Chun Hsiao
CyLab / CMU
hchsiao@cmu.edu

Alessandro Sorniotti
IBM Research - Zurich
aso@zurich.ibm.com

ABSTRACT

Securely deleting data from storage systems has become difficult today. Most storage space is provided as a virtual resource and traverses many layers between the user and the actual physical storage medium. Operations to properly erase data and wipe out all its traces are typically not foreseen, particularly not in networked and cloud-storage systems. This paper introduces a general cryptographic model for policy-based secure deletion of data in storage systems, whose security relies on the proper erasure of cryptographic keys. Deletion operations are expressed in terms of a policy that describes data destruction through deletion attributes and protection classes. The policy links attributes as specified in deletion operations to the protection class(es) that must be erased accordingly. A cryptographic construction is presented for deletion policies given by directed acyclic graphs; it is built in a modular way from exploiting that secure deletion schemes may be composed with each other. The model and the construction unify and generalize all previous encryption-based techniques for secure deletion. Finally, the paper describes a prototype implementation of a Linux filesystem with policy-based secure deletion.

Categories and Subject Descriptors

D.4.3 [**File Systems Management**]: Access methods; D.4.3 [**File Systems Management**]: File organization; D.4.6 [**Security and Protection**]: Cryptographic controls

Keywords

Secure deletion; security policy; filesystem security

1. INTRODUCTION

Modern storage systems do not include operations to reliably destroy stored information. Common deletion operations simply mark the occupied space as free and remove an entry from the directory, but some of the stored data may remain accessible for much longer. A technically knowledgeable user with low-level access to the storage system can still obtain the data. This description applies to simple magnetic storage devices like disks or tapes, but holds as well for networked storage services, such as storage controllers in a data center, file servers, or cloud storage. Storage systems nowadays contain many layers of virtualization and perform aggressive caching for increased performance. They leave around traces of stored data beyond the control of the users, because such data cannot be securely wiped out through the usual service interface.

However, users would like to control the deletion of their information because supposedly deleted data that reappears later may have undesirable consequences. Many companies have installed detailed polices for retaining data and for deleting expired data; also the Electronic Frontier Foundation recommends controlled deletion of data as a means to maintaining user privacy [9]. The European Data Protection Directive mandates that personal data must be erased upon request of the data subject [11].

With the advent of cloud computing, many clients who outsource storage want to take control over the shredding of their data themselves. They would like to retain an element of control that lets them erase their outsourced data from the cloud, without relying on the cooperation of the storage service. At the same time, providers of storage services are also interested to offer guaranteed destruction as a feature to their customers. For instance, providers would like to erase data so that no trace of it reappears later, not even during a forensic investigation.

In this paper, we explore the use of *encryption* and *key management* for securely deleting data. When data is stored encrypted, only the corresponding key has to be destroyed for erasing the data. Deleting (remote) data becomes a problem of managing and deleting (local) keys. We introduce the concept of *policy-based secure deletion*, where the stored data is grouped into *protection classes*, and *attributes* control the selective erasure of data through a *policy*. The design relies on a master key stored in a controlled and erasable memory, so that operations to delete data manipulate the master key, e.g., by updating it or erasing parts of it. No bulk data is ever re-encrypted.

This paper makes the following contributions.

- We introduce the notion of a *secure deletion scheme* and provide first formal model and a security definition for encryption-based secure deletion. It uses a coercive adversary that obtains the master key at the time of attack. The notion is formulated in the secret-key setting, but it can be extended to a public-key model.
- We construct a secure deletion scheme from encryption and threshold secret sharing; it supports arbitrary policies that are modeled as a circuit with AND, OR, and threshold gates.
- We show how secure deletion schemes can be composed in a modular way. Our approach unifies and generalizes all existing constructions for cryptographic secure deletion.

CCS'13, November 4–8, 2013, Berlin, Germany.
Copyright 2013 ACM 978-1-4503-2477-9/13/11 ...$15.00.
http://dx.doi.org/10.1145/2508859.2516690.

- We present a prototype implementation of a Linux filesystem with policy-based secure deletion.

Our encryption-based deletion methods apply to all kinds of storage systems, regardless of their physical storage media, and they can be integrated into existing systems with minimal effort. In contrast, solutions based on overwriting at the physical level [16, 23] only work in close connection with the media properties. This work aims at erasing data from large networked storage systems and assumes a small, controlled, and erasable keystore. Thus, it leverages physical (local) deletion to achieve secure deletion on (remote) large-scale data stores.

1.1 Related work

Secure deletion. Many systems have been proposed which essentially overwrite the data in order to delete it [16, 23]. Some methods are very flexible and can be integrated with arbitrary filesystems [17], provided their source code is available. Recent work has addressed solid-state storage, which requires completely different approaches than magnetic disks for destroying data [28, 22]. However, all solutions using overwriting depend heavily on the properties of the underlying physical storage. With cloud computing and the virtualized storage models that are widely used today, physical control over data-storage locations is no longer feasible. Therefore we do not further consider secure deletion mechanisms based on overwriting or other physical properties.

Employing encryption for the explicit goal of erasing information goes back to the work of Boneh and Lipton [4]. Di Crescenzo et al. [8] introduce a tree construction for efficient secure deletion of arbitrary files among a group of files. The master key at the root of the tree is kept in erasable memory, and every key in the tree encrypts several keys below, until the keys at the leaves encrypt the files themselves.

Mitra and Winslett [19] describe a method for creating an inverted index of keywords found in stored data records. The method uses encryption and allows to selectively delete a data record and the corresponding keywords in the index by assuming the encryption keys can be destroyed.

Perlman's Ephemerizer [20] employs a temporal sequence of keys modeling different expiration times for encrypted data. The FADE system [27] uses public-key cryptography and introduces some simple policies with Boolean operators governing deletion. FADE comes closest to our approach among the existing work. The policies of FADE are restricted to one- or two-level Boolean expressions, though, and its policies are intertwined with an implementation from a particular public-key cryptosystem. In contrast, our work permits general policies using Boolean expressions with threshold operators, may use generic cryptosystems, including secret-key systems, and supplies security proofs for all constructions.

Peterson et al. [21] use all-or-nothing transforms (AONT) at the block level for secure deletion, in combination with overwriting. The idea is to store every block through an AONT and then to overwrite only a part of it, which will render the whole block inaccessible.

Vanish [13] is a practical system for publishing content online with an expiration date, e.g., providing secure deletion for user data published in social networks. It encrypts the content and splits the key using secret sharing. The shares are then maintained by a peer-to-peer distributed system that gradually forgets the stored items unless they are refreshed. This gives the user some control over the expiration of his content.

Key-assignment schemes. Our approach to secure deletion is related to monotone secret sharing schemes and to key-assignment schemes for hierarchical access control. The survey by Crampton et al. [6] presents a summary of the literature on key assignment. Key assignment considers a publisher and multiple users. The publisher distributes one key to each user; every user can later derive suitable keys that allow the user to access information according to a hierarchical policy. The constructions may use public storage as well [1, 7]. Many constructions and improvements are available in the literature [6, 1, 2, 5]; they may be applied to the policy formulation and to the implementation of secure deletion schemes described here.

Attribute-based encryption. Our work also relates to the attribute-based encryption (ABE) schemes developed in the last few years [24], especially to ciphertext-policy ABE (CP-ABE) schemes [3]. Similar to CP-ABE, our policy-based secure deletion construction maintains keys for different attributes and the deletion policy is linked to the protected files. Many existing CP-ABE constructions suffer from creating large ciphertexts, though this deficiency has been removed recently [15]. While conceptually related to secure deletion in the sense that data is encrypted in a policy-specific way, CP-ABE does not already yield secure deletion. CP-ABE maintains a master key from which it produces attribute-specific decryption keys. Without knowing the attributes relevant in future decryption operations, either all such possible decryption keys must be generated in advance so the master key can be deleted or it must be kept around for generating decryption keys. However, this either is not efficient or contradicts the goal of secure deletion under coercion, when the master key must be revealed.

1.2 Organization

Section 2 introduces our notion of policy-based secure deletion. Multiple implementations of secure deletion schemes and the composition operation appear in Section 3, and Section 4 discusses their efficiency and other properties. Finally, Section 5 presents a filesystem with policy-based secure deletion.

2. MODEL

This section defines policy-based secure deletion schemes using a deletion policy represented by a graph.

2.1 Selective secure deletion

The goal of a policy-based secure deletion scheme is to maintain, on a permanent storage medium, a collection of *files* and to selectively delete some of them. Each file consists of a bit string of arbitrary length and is protected under a *protection class* from a set $\mathcal{P}$, as specified by a *deletion policy*; the formal definition of a deletion policy will be presented in the next section. A protection class is a logical grouping of files governed by an identical deletion rule. The universe of protection classes is denoted by $\mathcal{P} = \{p_1, p_2, \dots\}$.

The scheme provides operations for *protecting* a file, for *accessing* a file, and for *securely deleting* files. Secure deletion schemes in our model represent specialized encryption schemes and provide cryptographic security. We model only a secret-key secure deletion scheme, where the same key serves for protection of files and access to files; our model applies also to public-key schemes that may be defined analogously.

At the beginning, files of all protection classes are protected under an initial *master key*. The master key is stored in a closely guarded *erasable memory*, which is kept secret from an adversary. The master key will be changed later as a result of deletion operations. In contrast, all other data produced by the scheme is called *ciphertext* and stored in immutable *non-erasable memory*, which is public and exposed to the adversary at all times.

Each protection class is defined by means of *attributes* from a set $\mathcal{A}$ of strings over a fixed alphabet. *Secure deletion* operates on a subset of attributes, by ensuring that protection classes subject to those attributes become inaccessible. When a secure deletion operation is executed, a new master key is computed and stored in the erasable memory; the master key stored there previously is erased. Secure deletion may also change the ciphertext, i.e., add new ciphertext to the non-erasable memory.

2.2 Policy graph

A *deletion policy graph* G suitable for a secure deletion scheme is given by a pair (V, E) with $V = \mathcal{A} \cup \mathcal{P}$ such that (V, E) is a *directed acyclic graph (DAG)*. It has two kinds of nodes, sources and interior nodes. Nodes with no incoming edges (indegree zero) are *sources* and correspond one-to-one to the attributes in $\mathcal{A}$. All other nodes are called *interior nodes*; each of them is associated with a *threshold parameter* m, which is a positive integer less than or equal to the indegree of the node. Every interior node is labeled by a distinct protection class in $\mathcal{P}$. A policy graph must contain at least one source and one interior node, hence, the minimum policy graph has two nodes and one edge from the source node to the interior node.

Every node and every edge of the graph is associated to a Boolean value. All outgoing edges from a node take the same value as the node. The source nodes are assigned a value through the secure deletion scheme. An interior node with threshold m and n incoming edges corresponds to a Boolean threshold gate with threshold m: the node is TRUE whenever at least m among the n incoming edges are TRUE. Notice that G has a natural interpretation as a Boolean circuit whose sources correspond to $\mathcal{A}$. Threshold nodes subsume AND and OR gates as special cases.

2.3 Operation

Intuitively, deletion operations can be triggered by setting a subset of attributes to TRUE. The corresponding source nodes in G are then set to TRUE, which may cause some protection classes of G to become TRUE. This means that all files protected under these classes are deleted. Multiple secure deletion steps may follow each other.

More precisely, secure deletion works as follows. All protection classes are initially accessible, i.e., all source nodes and all their outgoing edges are FALSE at the start. As the circuit is monotone, this means that also all other nodes initially evaluate to FALSE according to G. Hence, none of the protection classes specified has been deleted and all files are accessible in the sense that their plaintext can be obtained from the ciphertext with the master key. A secure deletion operation takes a subset of the attributes as parameter and changes the associated source nodes, and, consequently, some edges in G to TRUE. Those files governed by protection classes that change their value to TRUE are no longer accessible after the master key has been updated. This model allows secure deletion of many files according to the policy and the given attributes. The attributes to delete can be specified independently of each other in arbitrary order.

Example 1. The policy graph of Figure 1 has six attributes (resp., source nodes) named *Alice, Bob, Project_X, Exp_2014, Exp_2015*, and *Audit* and six protection classes (resp., interior nodes) named $p_1, \ldots, p_6$. The latter are threshold nodes that implement binary AND and OR gates. The attributes model users that own files with different protection needs, a project category, expiration dates for stored data, and a special audit need for deleting stored data.

For example, protection class p_3 is governed by a policy *Alice* OR *Exp_2015*; thus data in p_3 becomes inaccessible as soon as a delete operation for protection classes owned by *Alice* is executed or a delete operation for the files with expiration *Exp_2015* takes place.

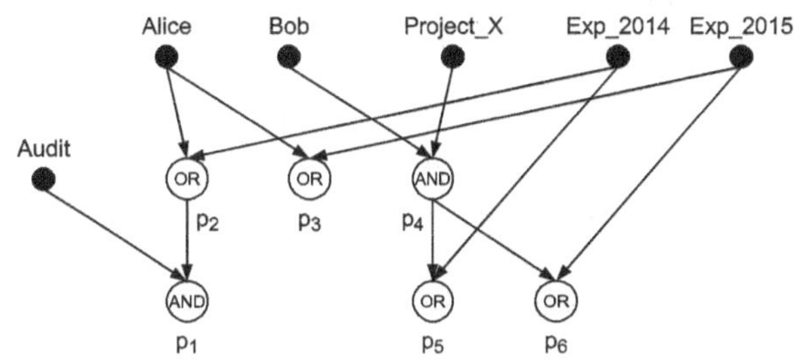

Figure 1: A sample policy graph.

Protection class p_1 has policy (*Alice* OR *Exp_2014*) AND *Audit*. Data protected under this class only disappears after the attribute *Alice* or the attribute *Exp_2014* has been deleted, and, furthermore, after a secure deletion operation for *Audit* has been executed. This might apply when data protected under p_1 is more important for retention than data under p_2, as data in class p_1 can be destroyed only after an auditor has given consent to its erasure.

User *Bob* owns the data protected under p_4, p_5, and p_6. The policy dictates that classes p_5 and p_6 become inaccessible after securely deleting the attributes *Exp_2014* or *Exp_2015*, respectively, or when data owned by *Bob* and data labeled by *Project_X* is securely deleted. For instance, *Bob* might be a temporary user working on project X, and regardless of whether *Bob* leaves the organization, his data must be retained until the end of the project, i.e., until it is erased explicitly by specifying *Project_X* for secure deletion.

Consider the initial state and suppose a secure deletion operation with attribute *Exp_2014* is invoked. Then p_2 and p_5 become inaccessible, but p_1 remains present as *Audit* has not been specified for deletion. If data protected with owner *Alice* securely deleted later, then p_3 becomes inaccessible but p_1 can still be retrieved.

2.4 System model

In a practical system supporting policy-based secure deletion, there are two distinct kinds of storage space: erasable and permanent memory. A small *erasable memory* forms the root of trust and must be under close control of the system operators. It is provided, for instance, by key-management systems, hardware-security modules (HSM), or local filesystems which support physical secure deletion. Content that has been deleted from the erasable memory is impossible to retrieve for both legitimate and malicious parties. On the other hand, *permanent memory* is readily available with large capacity, but its content can neither be erased nor hidden from an adversary. Many forms of storage encountered in practice fall in this category, ranging from the complex storage hierarchies of a data center to the mobile end-user devices attached to storage back-ends in the cloud.

In this work, we consider a user with access to erasable memory and permanent memory. Her goal is to store a potentially large number of files and to selectively delete files according to a deletion policy. Information to be stored is protected, resulting in ciphertext being written to permanent memory. The ciphertext is available later for accessing non-deleted files. Secure deletion operations make it impossible for an adversary to retrieve the deleted files, even if the adversary uses coercion and obtains all keys in the erasable memory. The constructions exploit the capability to remove data from erasable memory. (In other words, we assume a "bounded peek-a-boo adversary" according to Reardon et al. [23].)

We assume the adversary is passive and cannot modify data stored on either type of memory. In practice, one can ensure this easily through orthogonal data-authentication methods.

2.5 Secure deletion schemes

We now introduce the formal notion of a policy-based secure deletion scheme. The model is cryptographic and formulated as a secret-key scheme for simplicity.

We define a predicate $\mathsf{deleted}(G, D, p)$ for a deletion policy with attributes $\mathcal{A}$, policy graph G, and protection classes $\mathcal{P}$ that denotes whether deleting all attributes in a set $D \subseteq \mathcal{A}$ implies that the protection class $p \in \mathcal{P}$ should become inaccessible. In terms of the Boolean circuit interpretation of G, suppose those source nodes of G corresponding to the attributes in D are set to TRUE; then $\mathsf{deleted}(G, D, p)$ denotes the value of node p in G. The notation $[a, b]$ for two integers a and b denotes the set of integers $\{a, \ldots, b\}$; the expression $[a]$ is short for $[1, a]$.

Definition 1. A *policy-based deletion scheme* $\mathcal{E}$ is a tuple (Init, Protect, Access, Delete), consisting of four probabilistic polynomial-time algorithms (in terms of a security parameter κ) with the following properties:

- $\mathsf{Init}(\kappa, G) \to (M_0, S_0)$
  The *initialization* algorithm takes as inputs the security parameter κ and a policy graph G. It outputs an initial master key M_0 and initial auxiliary state S_0.
- $\mathsf{Delete}(M_t, S_t, A_t) \to (M_{t+1}, S_{t+1})$
  The *secure deletion* algorithm takes as inputs a master key M_t, auxiliary state S_t, and a set of attributes $A_t \subseteq \mathcal{A}$, and outputs a new master key/auxiliary state pair reflecting the deletion of the supplied attributes.
  Throughout the operation of the scheme, a set $D \subseteq \mathcal{A}$ that contains the union of all attributes deleted so far is implicitly maintained. That is, after $t+1$ calls to Delete, it holds $D = \cup_{i=0}^{t} A_i$.
- $\mathsf{Protect}(M_t, S_t, p, f) \to c$
  The *protect* algorithm takes as inputs a master key M_t, auxiliary state S_t, a protection class $p \in \mathcal{P}$, and a file f which is a binary string of any length, and outputs a ciphertext c. If $\mathsf{deleted}(G, D, p) = \text{TRUE}$, i.e., the protection class has already been deleted, then $c = \perp$. Otherwise, the protection class is still accessible and $c \in \{0,1\}^*$ is a protected version of the file f.
- $\mathsf{Access}(M_t, S_t, p, c) \to f$
  The *access* algorithm takes as inputs a master key M_t, auxiliary state S_t, a protection class p, and a ciphertext c, and outputs a string $f \in \{0,1\}^*$ or $\perp$.

Whenever a master key/auxiliary state tuple (M_t, S_t) appears here, we assume that M_t and S_t are *well-formed* and result from a call to Init and a number of subsequent repeated calls to Delete. In other words, for some $\mathsf{Init}(\kappa, G) = (M_0, S_0)$ and a sequence $A_0, A_1, \ldots, A_{t-1}$ of subsets of $\mathcal{A}$, it holds $\mathsf{Delete}(M_i, S_i, A_i) = (M_{i+1}, S_{i+1})$, for $i \in [t-1]$. Note that this assumption incurs no loss of generality in the adversarial model considered here.

All four algorithms except for Access are usually probabilistic; they output a random variable induced by their internal random choices. In statements about particular output values of an algorithm, such as in the preceding paragraphs, it is implied that these outputs may occur with non-zero probability.

Next, we discuss the completeness and security properties of a policy-based deletion scheme $\mathcal{E}$.

Definition 2. A policy-based deletion scheme defined as above is said to be *complete* if any protected file can be accessed at a later time unless it has been deleted. That is, for any t and $j \leq t$, for all $p \in \mathcal{P}$, for all $f \in \{0,1\}^*$, for all $\{A_i\}_{i=0}^{t-1}$, where $A_i \subseteq \mathcal{A}$, and all key/state tuples (M_i, S_i), for $i \in [t-1]$, such that $\mathsf{Init}(\kappa, G) = (M_0, S_0)$ and $\mathsf{Delete}(M_i, S_i, A_i) = (M_{i+1}, S_{i+1})$, it holds that

$$\mathsf{Access}(M_t, S_t, p, \mathsf{Protect}(M_j, S_j, p, f)) = f.$$

conditioned on $\mathsf{deleted}(G, \cup_{i=0}^{t-1} A_i, p) = \text{FALSE}$.

The security of a policy-based deletion scheme is defined using the following experiment for an adversary A and a security parameter κ.

Secure deletion experiment $\mathsf{Secdel}_{\mathsf{A},\mathcal{E}}(\kappa)$:

1. The adversary A is given κ and outputs a policy graph G with corresponding sets $\mathcal{A}$ and $\mathcal{P}$ for the attributes and the protection classes, respectively. Also, the adversary outputs a set $\mathcal{D} \subseteq \mathcal{A}$ of all attributes to be deleted at the end.
   Then, algorithm $\mathsf{Init}(\kappa, G) \to (M_0, S_0)$ is executed and S_0 is given to A.
2. A is given oracle access to protection and deletion operations. In particular, the set D of deleted attributes, the index t, and the current master key/auxiliary state pair (M_t, S_t) are maintained; A may choose inputs (p, f) for protection and receives the output of $\mathsf{Protect}(M_t, S_t, p, f)$; A may also specify $A_t \subseteq \mathcal{D}$, which causes algorithm $\mathsf{Delete}(M_t, S_t, A_t) \to (M_{t+1}, S_{t+1})$ to be invoked, then A receives S_{t+1}.
3. The adversary A outputs some $p^* \in \mathcal{P}$ such that $\mathsf{deleted}(G, D, p^*) = \text{FALSE}$ and two strings $f_0, f_1 \in \{0,1\}^*$ of the same length.
4. After a random bit $b \leftarrow \{0,1\}$ is chosen, a ciphertext $c^* \leftarrow \mathsf{Protect}(M_t, S_t, p^*, f_b)$ is computed and given to A.
5. The adversary is given further oracle access to protection and deletion operations, continued from step 2, until A stops under the condition that $\mathsf{deleted}(G, D, p^*) = \text{TRUE}$ and $D = \mathcal{D}$, i.e., p^* is inaccessible for the current set D of deleted attributes and that set is the same as the one defined in step 1.
6. A receives the current value of M_t and outputs a bit $\hat{b}$. The experiment returns 1 if $\hat{b} = b$ and 0 otherwise.

Definition 3. A *policy-based deletion scheme* $\mathcal{E}$ is called *secure* when for all probabilistic polynomial-time adversaries A, there exists a negligible function ε such that

$$\Pr\Big[\mathsf{Secdel}_{\mathsf{A},\mathcal{E}}(\kappa) = 1\Big] \leq \frac{1}{2} + \varepsilon(\kappa).$$

Remark. A secure deletion scheme maintains the secrecy of the protected and deleted content. According to the security definition, in the last step of Secdel, the adversary receives the master key. At this point, the files protected under all classes that have not yet been deleted are obviously exposed to A. However, any protected file that has already been deleted is guaranteed to remain confidential, even after the master key has been leaked.

Note that the security model requires the adversary to declare the attributes to delete upfront, before it can observe any output produced by the scheme and adaptively choose in what order to delete these attributes. Our security notion is similar to "selective security" for attribute-based encryption [24, 14].

The security notion may readily be extended to cover adversarial modifications to permanent memory, analogous to chosen-ciphertext attacks against encryption schemes. As storage systems typically protect data integrity through different means (that additionally prevent replay attacks), we omit this extension for clarity.

2.6 Measuring efficiency

We will characterize implementations of secure deletion schemes in terms of the cost incurred for executing their operations. We define the *deletion cost*, *protection cost*, and *access cost* as the complexities of running the deletion, protection, and access algorithms, respectively. Complexities are expressed in terms of computation steps or, more usually, through the number of calls to an encryption primitive made by the algorithm.

We consider deletion schemes with *constant* deletion cost, independent of the number of protected files, to be the most interesting. For the constructions considered in this work, protection and access cost do not differ, hence we are mainly interested in access cost.

Furthermore, the size of the erasable memory for storing the master key and the permanent memory for storing the auxiliary state are important parameters. We quantify them as the *master-key size* and *auxiliary-state size*, respectively. Note the protected files must be maintained outside the secure deletion scheme.

3. CONSTRUCTIONS

3.1 Prerequisites

In the constructions described below, we assume for simplicity that master keys and auxiliary state values M_t and S_t, returned by Init and Delete operations, are associative arrays indexed by nodes and edges of G. Thus, the values $S_t[v]$ and $S_t[e]$ denote the auxiliary data, if any, associated to $v \in V$ and $e \in E$, respectively. The notation $S_t|^{V',E'}$ denotes only the collection of entries of S_t restricted to $v \in V' \subseteq V$ and $e \in E' \subseteq E$; of course, we require $E' \subseteq V' \times V'$ for such restrictions.

Secret-key encryption schemes. A *secret-key encryption scheme* $\mathcal{S}$ consists of three algorithms Keygen, Encrypt, and Decrypt. The probabilistic key generation algorithm Keygen(κ) outputs a key K; algorithm Encrypt(K, m) takes a key K and a plaintext m as inputs and returns a ciphertext c; algorithm Decrypt(K, c) takes a key K and a ciphertext c as inputs and returns a plaintext m. We assume $\mathcal{S}$ is complete and IND-CPA secure according to the standard notions.

Secret-sharing schemes. A $(m+1)$-out-of-n secret-sharing scheme denotes a method to split a *secret* s into n *shares* $s_1, \ldots, s_n$ such that $m+1$ or more shares are sufficient to recover s, but m or fewer shares give away no statistical information about s. The operation of sharing s is expressed by $(s_1, \ldots, s_n) \leftarrow \mathsf{Share}^n_{m+1}(s)$, and the algorithm to recover s from shares $\bar{s}_1, \ldots, \bar{s}_{m+1}$ is written as $s \leftarrow \mathsf{Recover}(\bar{s}_1, \ldots, \bar{s}_{m+1})$. We use, for instance, the well-known implementation based on polynomial interpolation [25].

3.2 Direct secure deletion schemes

We now introduce a class of secure deletion schemes with a particularly simple implementation of the deletion operation. We call them *direct* because their deletion operation merely erases parts of the master key that corresponds directly to the deleted attributes.

More precisely, a *direct secure deletion scheme* always generates a master key M_t in the form of a tuple with exactly one component for every attribute in $\mathcal{A}$. The deletion operation for a set of attributes $A_t \subseteq \mathcal{A}$ erases those components of M_t that correspond to A_t. In other words, every master key M_t is an associative array indexed by $a \in \mathcal{A}$, where $M_t[a]$ denotes the component corresponding to a. The deletion operation for A_t computes M_{t+1} as

$$M_{t+1}[a] \leftarrow \begin{cases} \bot & \text{if } a \in A_t \\ M_t[a] & \text{otherwise.} \end{cases}$$

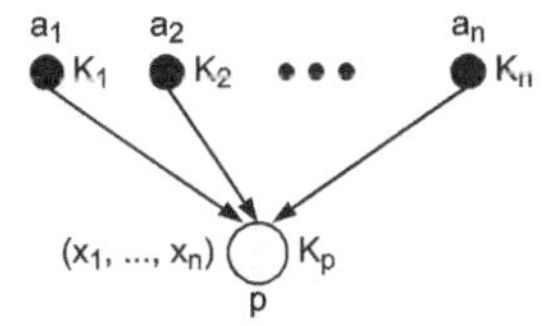

Figure 2: Basic secure deletion scheme, implemented from encryption and secret sharing.

Stronger security for direct schemes. Recall from Definition 3 that in the last step of its experiment, the adversary is given the current value of the master key. Given that $\mathcal{D}$ is supplied by A, the set of all attributes to be deleted eventually, in the first step, it is clear that the master key given to the adversary at the end is $M_0|^{\mathcal{A}\setminus\mathcal{D}}$. As a consequence, A can receive it in the first rather than last step, hence providing the adversary with more information earlier in the experiment. We use this stronger security definition when showing the security of direct policy-based deletion schemes.

3.3 Basic scheme

A secure deletion scheme with a very basic policy can be implemented directly from a secret-key encryption scheme $\mathcal{S}$ and a secret-sharing scheme.

Let $G = (V, E)$ be a policy graph with $n \geq 1$ source nodes, connected to a single interior node that is also the only protection class. In other words, as shown in Figure 2, the nodes $V = \mathcal{A} \cup \mathcal{P}$ are given by a set of attributes $\mathcal{A} = \{a_1, \ldots, a_n\}$ and a set $\mathcal{P} = \{p\}$ composed of a single protection class, and the edges are $E = \{e_1, \ldots, e_n\}$, where $e_i = (a_i, p)$ for $i \in [n]$. The interior node p has a threshold parameter m.

We construct $\mathcal{E}$ = (Init, Protect, Access, Delete) as follows:

- Init(κ, G)
  - For each attribute $a_i \in \mathcal{A}$ select a random key $K_i \leftarrow \mathcal{S}$.Keygen($\kappa$) and set $M_0[a_i] \leftarrow K_i$;
  - Select a random key $K_p \leftarrow \mathcal{S}$.Keygen($\kappa$) and construct a $(n-m+1)$-out-of-n secret sharing for the key, i.e., $(s_1, \ldots, s_n) \leftarrow \mathsf{Share}^n_{n-m+1}(K_p)$; then, compute $x_i \leftarrow \mathcal{S}$.Encrypt($K_i, s_i$) for $i \in [n]$ and set the initial auxiliary state to be $S_0[p] \leftarrow (x_1, \ldots, x_n)$;
  - Output (M_0, S_0).
- Delete(M_t, S_t, A_t)
  As this is a direct secure deletion scheme, proceed as defined in Section 3.2.
- Protect(M_t, S_t, p, f)
  If deleted(G, D, p) = TRUE, set $c \leftarrow \bot$. Otherwise, let $(x_1, \ldots, x_n) \leftarrow S_t[p]$; for each $i \in [n]$ such that $a_i \notin D$ compute the share $s_i \leftarrow \mathcal{S}$.Decrypt($M_t[a_i], x_i$) and reconstruct the key K_p from the shares; finally, compute $c \leftarrow \mathcal{S}$.Encrypt(K_p, f). Output c as a protected version of the file f.
- Access(M_t, S_t, p, c)
  If deleted(G, D, p) = FALSE, reconstruct K_p as above and output $f \leftarrow \mathcal{S}$.Decrypt(K_p, c). Otherwise, when the protection class is inaccessible, return $f \leftarrow \bot$.

The auxiliary state S_t contains data only for the interior node p, i.e., the shares of the key K_p encrypted under the keys representing the n attributes. Note that the Protect and Access methods obtain at least $n - m + 1$ shares for reconstructing K_p whenever deleted(G, D, p) = FALSE; this is shown in the next theorem.

Theorem 1. *The direct secure deletion scheme $\mathcal{E}$ with a policy graph G defined above is complete and secure.*

Proof. Given the structure of G with p being an interior node with threshold m, it follows that the predicate $\mathsf{deleted}(G, D, p)$ is TRUE if and only if $|D| \geq m$.

It is easy to check that the scheme is complete because as long as $\mathsf{deleted}(G, D, p) = $ FALSE, fewer than m attribute keys have been deleted; in other words, *more than* $n - m$ of the keys K_1, ..., K_n are present in the master key. Using the auxiliary data $S_t[p]$, this allows to recover more than $n - m$ of the secret shares $s_1, \ldots, s_n$. Then the key K_p can be obtained by running algorithm Recover of the secret-sharing scheme. Hence, Protect and Access can operate on all files protected under p.

The proof that the scheme is secure proceeds in a sequence of games [26]:

Game 0. This is the original game and its experiment is defined according to the security definition. Note that in the first step of the experiment, A is required to specify the set of attributes $\mathcal{D}$ which satisfies $\mathsf{deleted}(G, \mathcal{D}, p) = $ TRUE. As mentioned above, this happens if and only if $|\mathcal{D}| \geq m$.

Game 1. We proceed as in the previous game except that for each $i \in [n]$ such that $a_i \in \mathcal{D}$, the Init algorithm sets $x_i \leftarrow \mathcal{S}.\mathsf{Encrypt}(K_i, r_i)$, for a randomly chosen $r_i \in \{0,1\}^{|s_i|}$, and stores these in the auxiliary state value $S_0[p] = (x_1, \ldots, x_n)$. By the security of the encryption scheme $\mathcal{S}$ and the fact that all K_i with $a_i \in \mathcal{D}$ are removed from the master key before it is revealed to A, it holds that the adversary's advantage changes by at most negligible probability from the previous game.

Game 2. This game is initially the same as the previous game, in which Init chooses a random key $K_p \leftarrow \mathcal{S}.\mathsf{Keygen}(\kappa)$, secret-shares it to obtain the shares $s_1, \ldots, s_n$, and uses these for computing the auxiliary state. However, we also choose a different random key $K'_p \leftarrow \mathcal{S}.\mathsf{Keygen}(\kappa)$ and use this key rather than K_p to protect and access any files under p in responses to queries of A.

Recall that A will ask for at least m attributes to be deleted before it obtains the master key. Then, by the security of the secret-sharing scheme, the adversary cannot tell which key is secret-shared, hence behaves like in the previous game except for a negligible difference. Also, note that the key K'_p is completely independent from the master key and the auxiliary state.

Game 3. In this last game, when the adversary presents files f_0 and f_1 with the same length, the challenger computes $c^* \leftarrow \mathcal{S}.\mathsf{Encrypt}(K'_p, r)$ for a randomly chosen $r \in \{0,1\}^*$ of the same length as the files. By the security of the encryption scheme $\mathcal{S}$, the advantage of A changes at most by a negligible amount from the previous game. Moreover, as r is independent of f_1 and f_2, the adversary cannot do better than guess the bit b at random, hence $\Pr[\hat{b} = b] = \frac{1}{2}$.

As the adversary A can guess b exactly with probability $\frac{1}{2}$ in the last game and her advantage changes only negligibly between every two consecutive games, it follows that $\mathcal{E}$ is secure. □

Note that the auxiliary state contains values neither for the attributes nor for the edges incident with them. We use this property when constructing more complex secure deletion schemes and maintain this invariant for all *direct* schemes.

3.4 Composition

Two secure deletion schemes can be composed into a more elaborate scheme whose policy graph results from combining the two basic policy graphs. We consider first the case when both schemes are *direct* and relax this requirement later on.

Suppose the two secure deletion schemes are arranged in a hierarchy as a *higher* and a *lower* scheme. The key step of the composition uses the higher secure deletion scheme to protect the master key of the lower scheme. The protection classes applied to particular components of the lower scheme's master key will determine the policy graph of the resulting scheme. Importantly, the lower master key needs no longer be stored in the erasable memory. In this way, secure deletion operations of the higher scheme extend to files protected with the lower scheme.

Let $\mathcal{E}_h$ and $\mathcal{E}_l$ be secure deletion schemes with policy graphs $G_h = (V_h, E_h)$ and $G_l = (V_l, E_l)$, protection classes $\mathcal{P}_h$ and $\mathcal{P}_l$, and potentially overlapping attribute sets $\mathcal{A}_h$ and $\mathcal{A}_l$, respectively. Apart from $\mathcal{A}_h$ and $\mathcal{A}_l$, the nodes V_h and V_l in the two graphs are mutually exclusive. Then, a secure deletion scheme $\mathcal{E}$ with policy graph G, attributes $\mathcal{A}$, and protection classes $\mathcal{P}$ is constructed as follows.

The composition specifies two sets $\mathcal{P}_J$ and $\mathcal{A}_J$, where $\mathcal{P}_J \subseteq \mathcal{P}_h$ and $\mathcal{A}_J \subseteq \mathcal{A}_l$, as well as a map $J : \mathcal{A}_J \to \mathcal{P}_J$. The map J determines to which protection class in $\mathcal{P}_J$ each attribute of $\mathcal{A}_J$ is joined. Also, we require that $\mathcal{A}_J \cap \mathcal{A}_h = \emptyset$, i.e., the attributes to be joined contain no attributes of G_h, so that the new policy graph will not contain cycles. The policy graph $G = (V, E)$ is defined as:

- $V = V_h \cup V_l \setminus \mathcal{A}_J$, i.e., G contains all nodes from G_h and G_l except those attributes of G_l which are being joined to a protection class in G_h;
- $E = E_h \cup \{(u, v) \mid (u, v) \in E_l \wedge u \notin \mathcal{A}_J\} \cup \{(w, v) \mid (u, v) \in E_l \wedge u \in \mathcal{A}_J \wedge w = J(u)\}$; this denotes (1) all edges of G_h, (2) the edges of G_l not incident to nodes in $\mathcal{A}_J$, and (3) one edge (w, v) for every edge $(u, v) \in E_l$ with $u \in \mathcal{A}_J$, where $w = J(u)$ is the protection class to which u is joined according to the composition. Note that $|E| = |E_h| + |E_l|$ and there is a one-to-one mapping between E and $E_h \cup E_l$ determined by J and the original graph.

The attributes of $\mathcal{E}$ are all attributes of G_h and G_l except for those involved in the composition, i.e., $\mathcal{A} = \mathcal{A}_h \cup \mathcal{A}_l \setminus \mathcal{A}_J$, and the set of protection classes is the union of the present protection classes, $\mathcal{P} = \mathcal{P}_h \cup \mathcal{P}_l$. An illustration of how two policy graphs are composed is shown in Figure 3.

The algorithms (Init, Protect, Access, Delete) of $\mathcal{E}$ are composed from those of $\mathcal{E}_h$ and $\mathcal{E}_l$:

- $\mathcal{E}.\mathsf{Init}(\kappa, G)$

  Compute $(M_{h,0}, S_{h,0}) \leftarrow \mathcal{E}_h.\mathsf{Init}(\kappa, G_h)$ and $(M_{l,0}, S_{l,0}) \leftarrow \mathcal{E}_l.\mathsf{Init}(\kappa, G_l)$, and for every $a \in \mathcal{A}$ set

$$M_0[a] = \begin{cases} M_{h,0}[a] & \text{if } a \in \mathcal{A}_h \text{ and } a \notin \mathcal{A}_l, \\ M_{l,0}[a] & \text{if } a \notin \mathcal{A}_h \text{ and } a \in \mathcal{A}_l, \\ M_{h,0}[a] \parallel M_{l,0}[a] & \text{if } a \in \mathcal{A}_h \cap \mathcal{A}_l, \end{cases}$$

  where $\parallel$ denotes the concatenation of two entries or tuples into one tuple. Note that $M_0[a]$ may contain more than one entry; in general, $M_0[a]$ is a tuple with one entry for every edge incident to node a. For notational convenience, we write $M_0[a][v]$ for the entry in $M_0[a]$ that corresponds to the specific edge from a to v.

  The initial auxiliary state stores no data for the attributes in our constructions.[1] For every protection class $p \in V$, the

[1] This may not necessarily be true for other constructions; should that be the case, auxiliary data for $\mathcal{A}_J$ specified by the composition map can be stored either in the auxiliary data of the nodes to which

auxiliary data $S_0[p]$ is simply $S_{h,0}[p]$ or $S_{l,0}[p]$ respective to whether $p \in V_h$ or $p \in V_l$.

As there is one-to-one mapping between E and $E_h \cup E_l$, we consider every edge $e = (u, v) \in E_h \cup E_l$ and define the initial auxiliary state of its corresponding edge in E as follows:

- $S_0[(u,v)] = S_{h,0}[(u,v)]$, if $(u,v) \in E_h$;
- $S_0[(u,v)] = S_{l,0}[(u,v)]$, if $(u,v) \in E_l \wedge u \notin \mathcal{A}_J$;
- $S_0[(w,v)] = S_{l,0}[(u,v)] \parallel$ $\mathcal{E}_h$.Protect$(M_{h,0}, S_{h,0}, w, M_{l,0}[u][v])$, if $(u,v) \in E_l$ for $u \in \mathcal{A}_J$ and $w = J(u)$,

where $w \in \mathcal{P}_J$ is the protection class to which $u \in \mathcal{A}_J$ is joined. That is, all edges in E which are also present in E_h or E_l keep their initial auxiliary state unchanged. The edges from a node $w \in V_h$ to a node $v \in V_l$ store the auxiliary data of (u, v) and the master-key component from $\mathcal{E}_l$ related to (u, v) protected under w with $\mathcal{E}_h$; here, $u \in V_l$ is the attribute which was joined to w such that the edge $(u, v) \in E_l$ corresponds to $(w, v) \in E$. Note that in our construction, edges adjacent to the attributes have no auxiliary data; thus, in the last case, $S_0[(w,v)] = \mathcal{E}_h$.Protect$(M_{h,0}, S_{h,0}, w, M_{l,0}[u][v])$.

Protecting the components of the master key from the lower scheme with the higher scheme represents the main mechanism of the composition. It is also the building block for the hierarchical implementation of secure deletion schemes with arbitrary policy graphs, as explained in Section 3.5.

- $\mathcal{E}$.Delete(M_t, S_t, A_t)
  Execute $\mathcal{E}_h$.Delete$(M_t|^{V_h,E_h}, S_t|^{V_h,E_h}, A_t \cap \mathcal{A}_h)$ and $\mathcal{E}_l$.Delete$(M_t|^{V_l,E_l}, S_t|^{V_l,E_l}, A_t \cap \mathcal{A}_l)$, and update the master key and auxiliary state accordingly. Recall that when a scheme is direct, the deletion operation does not change the auxiliary state but only deletes part of the master key; hence, the deletion operations are trivial.
- $\mathcal{E}$.Protect(M_t, S_t, p, f)
  If $p \in \mathcal{P}_h$, then $c \leftarrow \mathcal{E}_h$.Protect$(M_t|^{V_h,E_h}, S_t|^{V_h,E_h}, p, f)$. Otherwise, when $p \in \mathcal{P}_l$, we reconstruct $M_{l,t}$ by computing for $a \in \mathcal{A}_l$:
  - If $a \notin \mathcal{A}_J$, then $M_{l,t}[a] = M_t[a]$;
  - If $a \in \mathcal{A}_J$, then $M_{l,t}[a]$ is computed as the concatenation of all $\mathcal{E}_h$.Access$(M_t|^{V_h,E_h}, S_t|^{V_h,E_h}, w, S_t[(w,v)])$ for $(a, v) \in E_l$,

  where $w = J(a)$. Then, compute $c \leftarrow \mathcal{E}_l$.Protect$(M_{l,t}, S_t|^{V_l,E_l}, p, f)$. Note that any node $u \in V_l$ and any edge $(u, v) \in E_l$, where $u \in \mathcal{A}_J$, are not present in G; hence, they are not defined in S_t and its restriction $S_t|^{V_l,E_l}$. This agrees with the invariant defined in the last section that a *direct* secure deletion scheme stores no data in the auxiliary state for attributes and edges incident with them.[2] Return c.
- $\mathcal{E}$.Access(M_t, S_t, p, c):
  This operation proceeds analogously to Protect:
  - If $p \in \mathcal{P}_h$, then compute $f \leftarrow$ $\mathcal{E}_h$.Access$(M_t|^{V_h,E_h}, S_t|^{V_h,E_h}, p, c)$;
  - If $p \in \mathcal{P}_l$, then reconstruct the master key $M_{l,t}$ of $\mathcal{E}_l$ as described in the $\mathcal{E}$.Protect algorithm and compute $f \leftarrow \mathcal{E}_l$.Access$(M_{l,t}, S_t|^{V_l,E_l}, p, c)$.

  Finally, return f.

they are joined or in the new edges created in the composition, i.e., those in case (3) described above.

[2]In the general case, when there is auxiliary data associated with attributes or their adjacent edges, we adjust the reconstruction of $M_{l,t}$ and $S_{l,t}$ easily to match the modification needed in that case as described in the Init algorithm.

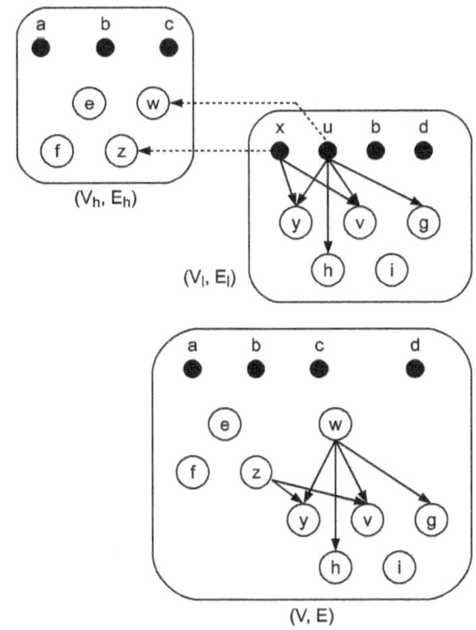

Figure 3: Two policy graphs (V_h, E_h) and (V_l, E_l) on the top are combined to (V, E), shown below. Note that $\mathcal{A}_J = \{x, u\}$ and $\mathcal{P}_J = \{w, z\}$, and the composition map specifies $J(x) = z$ and $J(u) = w$. Only the edges of case (3) in $\mathcal{E}$.Init are drawn here; the remaining edges are omitted and not affected by the composition.

Theorem 2. *The above policy-based secure deletion scheme $\mathcal{E}$ is* direct, *complete, and secure if $\mathcal{E}_h$ and $\mathcal{E}_l$ are* direct *policy-based secure deletion schemes,*

Proof. It is easy to show that $\mathcal{E}$ is complete from the fact that $\mathcal{E}_h$ and $\mathcal{E}_l$ are complete and from the way they are composed.

The proof of security proceeds in a sequence of games. In each game, we modify slightly further $\mathcal{E}$ when an algorithm B plays the role of a challenger in the experiment $\mathsf{Secdel}_{\mathsf{A},\mathcal{E}}(\kappa)$ against an adversary A attacking $\mathcal{E}$ by running the experiments $\mathsf{Secdel}_{\mathsf{B},\mathcal{E}_h}(\kappa)$ and/or $\mathsf{Secdel}_{\mathsf{B},\mathcal{E}_l}(\kappa)$; note that B plays the role of a challenger against A for $\mathcal{E}$ and the role of an adversary for $\mathcal{E}_h$ and/or $\mathcal{E}_l$.

Game 0. The experiment $\mathsf{Secdel}_{\mathsf{A},\mathcal{E}}(\kappa)$ proceeds according to its definition for the $\mathcal{E}$ defined above.

Game 1. The simulator B performs the experiment $\mathsf{Secdel}_{\mathsf{B},\mathcal{E}_h}(\kappa)$ in the role of the adversary, while simulating $\mathsf{Secdel}_{\mathsf{A},\mathcal{E}}(\kappa)$ for A. The scheme $\mathcal{E}$ is modified to use oracle access to protection and deletion operations for $\mathcal{E}_h$, and every time A moves from one step to the next in her experiment $\mathsf{Secdel}_{\mathsf{A},\mathcal{E}}(\kappa)$, so does B in $\mathsf{Secdel}_{\mathsf{B},\mathcal{E}_h}(\kappa)$.

In particular, for a set $\mathcal{D}$ given by A in the first step of her experiment, B outputs $\mathcal{D}_h \leftarrow \mathcal{D}|^{V_h,E_h}$ in the first step of his experiment. The $\mathcal{E}$.Init algorithm computes the auxiliary state as defined with the exception that B runs only $(M_{l,0}, S_{l,0}) \leftarrow \mathcal{E}_l$.Init$(\kappa, G_l)$, whereas $S_{h,0}$ is obtained from the challenger in his experiment; at any time, the respective induced calls to $\mathcal{E}_h$.Delete, $\mathcal{E}_h$.Protect, and $\mathcal{E}_h$.Access are replaced by oracle calls provided to B by the challenger of $\mathsf{Secdel}_{\mathsf{B},\mathcal{E}_h}(\kappa)$.

This game is indistinguishable to A from the previous one as the only difference is the way B handles the recursive calls to $\mathcal{E}_h$

which are perfectly simulated from the experiment B runs against his challenger.

Game 2. This game is identical to the previous one except for computing the auxiliary state for edges in case (3) in the $\mathcal{E}$.Init algorithm (see Figure 3). Previously, the auxiliary value for the edge in G corresponding to $(u, v) \in E_h \cup E_l$, for $u \in \mathcal{A}_J$, was computed as $S_0[(w, v)] = \mathcal{E}_h.\mathsf{Protect}(M_{h,0}, S_{h,0}, w, M_{l,0}[u][v])$, where $(u, v) \in E_l$ for $u \in \mathcal{A}_J$ and $w = J(u)$.

For the same $u \in \mathcal{A}_J$ and $w = J(u)$, if $\mathsf{deleted}(G, \mathcal{D}, w) =$ TRUE, this is modified to:

$$S_0[(w, v)] = \mathcal{E}_h.\mathsf{Protect}(M_{h,0}, S_{h,0}, w, r),$$

for a randomly chosen $r \leftarrow \{0,1\}^*$ of the same length as the corresponding key component.

This game is indistinguishable to A from the previous one except for a negligible probability due to the security of $\mathcal{E}_h$; in particular, for protection classes which are deleted before the master key is revealed, A cannot distinguish between a chosen value or a random value being protected under such a class.

Game 3. The simulator B performs the experiments $\mathsf{Secdel}_{\mathsf{B},\mathcal{E}_h}(\kappa)$ and $\mathsf{Secdel}_{\mathsf{B},\mathcal{E}_l}(\kappa)$ while simulating $\mathsf{Secdel}_{\mathsf{A},\mathcal{E}}(\kappa)$ for A. In the first step of the main experiment, A returns a set $\mathcal{D}$, from which B derives his set $\mathcal{D}_h \leftarrow \mathcal{D}|^{V_h, E_h}$ for the $\mathsf{Secdel}_{\mathsf{B},\mathcal{E}_h}(\kappa)$ experiment as before; for the experiment $\mathsf{Secdel}_{\mathsf{B},\mathcal{E}_l}(\kappa)$, $\mathcal{D}_l$ is computed as the union of all attributes $a \in \mathcal{A}_l$ such that:

- $a \notin \mathcal{A}_J \wedge a \in \mathcal{D}$; or
- $a \in \mathcal{A}_J \wedge \mathsf{deleted}(G, \mathcal{D}, J(a)) =$ TRUE.

That is, all attributes of $\mathcal{A}_l$ which are present in G and belong to $\mathcal{D}$ *or* which are attributes joined in the composition and whose protection classes from G_h become inaccessible when all attributes from $\mathcal{D}$ are deleted. Once B returns $\mathcal{D}_h$ and $\mathcal{D}_l$ in the first step of the respective experiments against his challengers, he is able to compute M_0, S_0 for $\mathcal{E}$ as defined in the previous game. As before, every time A moves from one step to the next in her experiment so does B for his.

This game is indistinguishable to A from the previous one as the only difference is the way B handles the respective induced calls to $\mathcal{E}_l$ which are perfectly simulated from experiment that B runs against his challengers.

Note that in the last game B simulates $\mathsf{Secdel}_{\mathsf{A},\mathcal{E}}(\kappa)$ perfectly without the knowledge of $M_{h,0}$ and $M_{l,0}$ using only oracle access provided by $\mathsf{Secdel}_{\mathsf{B},\mathcal{E}_h}(\kappa)$ and $\mathsf{Secdel}_{\mathsf{B},\mathcal{E}_l}(\kappa)$. Hence, any adversary A winning $\mathsf{Secdel}_{\mathsf{A},\mathcal{E}}(\kappa)$ with non-negligible advantage implies an adversary B which can break the security of $\mathcal{E}_h$ or $\mathcal{E}_l$. Therefore, if $\mathcal{E}_h$ and $\mathcal{E}_l$ are secure, so is the composed $\mathcal{E}$. □

Next, we observe that we can relax the requirement that $\mathcal{E}_h$ is a direct scheme if $\mathcal{E}_h$ and $\mathcal{E}_l$ share no attributes; note this implies $V_h \cap V_l = \emptyset$ as the composition requires that the nodes of both graphs are disjoint except for the attributes. Hence, one may compose an arbitrary policy-based secure deletion scheme $\mathcal{E}_h$ with a *direct* scheme $\mathcal{E}_l$.

Theorem 3. *Let $\mathcal{E}_h$ and $\mathcal{E}_l$ be policy-based secure deletion schemes, where $\mathcal{E}_l$ is* direct. *If $V_h \cap V_l = \emptyset$, the two schemes can be composed as described above and the resulting scheme $\mathcal{E}$ is complete and secure.*

Proof. The construction above and proof do not utilize the fact that $\mathcal{E}_h$ is direct except for the possibility that $\mathcal{E}_h$ and $\mathcal{E}_l$ share attributes. Thus, if $\mathcal{A}_h \cap \mathcal{A}_l = \emptyset$, the result follows analogously. □

3.5 Direct policy-graph construction

One may use the basic secure deletion scheme of Section 3.3 and the composition operation to implement *direct* secure deletion schemes for arbitrary policy graphs. Recall that every DAG $G = (V, E)$ has a topological order, computable in time $O(|V| + |E|)$, which arranges the nodes of G in a sequence that respects the direction of all edges.

We traverse G in the topological order and gradually build up a secure deletion scheme for G. Initially we take the first encountered interior node v_0 and implement a secure deletion scheme for v_0 according to the basic scheme of Section 3.3. Subsequently, whenever we encounter the next interior node v, we take the subgraph G_v induced by v and its incoming edges, implement a basic secure deletion scheme for G_v according to Section 3.3, and compose it with the secure deletion scheme realized so far.

The resulting secure deletion scheme for G implicitly contains a key for every node and a key for certain edges. More precisely, for a source node (attribute) a, the key K_a is explicitly stored in the master key and has one entry for every outgoing edge; for any interior node (protection class) p with n incoming edges and threshold m, the key K_p is stored encrypted as follows. For every incoming edge (v, p), except for those incident to an attribute, the auxiliary state contains an encryption of a key $K_{v,p}$ under the key K_v, which corresponds to node v. In turn, the auxiliary state associated to p contains a vector $(x_{p,1}, \ldots, x_{p,n})$, where some $x_{p,j}$ is associated to v and represents an encryption of $s_{p,j}$ under $K_{v,p}$. The value $s_{p,j}$ is a share of K_p in a $(m+1)$-out-of-n secret sharing scheme.

Thus, every node in G is associated with one encryption key and every edge in G not incident to a source is also associated with one encryption key. The resulting structure is an iterative key-encrypting key-assignment scheme (IKEKAS) according to Crampton et al. [6].

The access cost is proportional to the size of G. More precisely, accessing a node p needs a maximum of two secret-key cryptographic operations for every edge that must be traversed (i.e., set to TRUE), in order to derive p (i.e., set p to TRUE). The master key contains one component for every attribute and the total size of the auxiliary state is in $O(|V| + |E|)$.

Observe that one may eliminate the encryption keys associated to the edges and encrypt the share of a child node directly with the key of the parent node. This reduces the number of cryptographic operations without impacting the security of the construction. However, the resulting scheme cannot obtained from the modular composition operation in Section 3.4, and a detailed security proof is left for future work.

Furthermore, the master key component for an attribute a, the key K_a, is a tuple of keys with one entry for every outgoing edge. This is done so that the resulting secure deletion scheme is the same, regardless of which topological order is used during composition, as the edges adjacent to attributes are used in a special way in the composition. However, once constructed, one can replace the tuple K_a with a single key K'_a, and for every edge (a, p) store the key $K_{a,p}$ protected with K'_a in the auxiliary state of the edge (a, p), as done for all other edges; this reduces the master-key size.

3.6 Tree construction

In early work on secure deletion, Di Crescenzo et al. [8] introduce a tree construction that protects data in an arbitrary number of emulated memory locations. The scheme is realized from persistent storage exposed to an adversary and allows to overwrite individual memory locations. Only a small erasable memory of constant size is needed for maintaining a master key.

Using our terminology, their scheme permits n protection classes $p_1, \ldots, p_n$ and each one can be specified for deletion independently of the others. The deletion policy graph consists of n attributes $a_1, \ldots, a_n$, the n protection classes $p_1, \ldots, p_n$, and n edges (a_i, p_i) for $i \in [n]$.

A balanced tree with n leaves, labeled by $p_1, \ldots, p_n$, is constructed as follows. First, a key K_v of a secret-key encryption scheme is generated, ranging over all nodes v in the tree. Next, for every node v, the keys of all children of v are encrypted with K_v and the resulting ciphertext is added to the auxiliary state associated to v. The key of the root node represents the master key; is not stored in the auxiliary state.

For protecting or for accessing a file under protection class p_i, all keys along the path from the root to p_i are decrypted, starting from the root, and K_{p_i} is used to encrypt or decrypt the file, respectively.

Deletion for attribute a_i makes all data protected under p_i inaccessible. This operation is implemented by generating fresh keys for all nodes on the path from the root to p_i in the tree. More precisely, the keys of all nodes and their siblings along this path are first decrypted, then a fresh key is generated for every node on the path except for p_i, and finally all fresh keys are encrypted under the fresh key of the respective parent node and stored in the auxiliary state. The fresh root key is written to the master key and the previous root key is deleted in the erasable memory.

Clearly, this construction represents a secure deletion scheme, which can be proved secure assuming a secret-key cryptosystem along the lines of the existing proof [8]. The access cost of the scheme as well as its deletion cost are $O(\log n)$ secret-key operations. The erasable memory contains only one key of the secret-key encryption scheme as the master key and the auxiliary state is of size $O(n)$.

3.7 Time-tree construction

Our model and the tree construction above make no assumption about the order in which attributes are deleted. However, one may sometimes exploit such restrictions. Consider a sequence of attributes $a_1, \ldots, a_n$ modeling expiration time such that any a_i can only be deleted if $a_1, \ldots, a_{i-1}$ have been deleted beforehand. This property gives way to build a more efficient scheme.

More precisely, consider a deletion policy graph consisting of attributes $a_1, \ldots, a_n$, protection classes $p_1, \ldots, p_n$, and edges (a_i, p_i) for $i \in [n]$, which represent an ordered sequence of time units from $[n]$. We want to support deletion only as ordered by time, and we want to support an efficient operation that deletes multiple subsequent units at once. To this end, we construct a balanced tree over the leaves $p_1, \ldots, p_n$, design a master key of size $O(\log n)$, but use no auxiliary storage. The leaves of the tree represent the time units in a left-to-right order. The key of a node is computed from its parent's key using a pseudo-random function (PRF), where the parent's key serves as the PRF key and the input denotes whether the node is a left or right child. The root node's key is chosen uniformly at random. The master key consists of the key of the leaf corresponding to the earliest non-deleted time unit and the keys of all right siblings on the path from the root to that leaf. This way, only the keys for time units following the last deleted one can be derived. Storing only right-siblings like this is a well-known technique [18] to achieve forward-secure cryptosystems without changing the public key of an encryption scheme.

The deletion for the attribute a_t updates the master key to contain the key for the leaf p_{t+1} and the keys of all right siblings on the path from the root to that leaf; keys for all time periods greater than t can be derived from the master key in time $O(\log n)$ from the stored right-siblings. Deleting an arbitrary attribute a_t and all attributes preceding it takes $O(\log n)$ cryptographic operations, though the amortized cost is only $O(1)$ if the attributes are deleted one by one.

Hence, this tree construction is superior to the previous one both for deleting time units in order and for deleting in arbitrary increments.

3.8 Combined construction

Recall that for composing two secure deletion schemes with Theorem 2, only the lower scheme must be direct. Therefore, we can combine the tree construction of Section 3.6 with the direct scheme of Section 3.5 to obtain a secure deletion scheme with some attributes organized in a tree, as described above, whereas the rest are organized using a direct scheme. This is useful for modeling a case where many attributes are values from a large set or interval, such as user identities or dates.

One can further combine two or more such tree constructions trivially through logical expressions if the attributes in the trees are all distinct. In this way, we can compose many separate tree schemes with a direct scheme to obtain an elaborate and practical secure deletion scheme. The prototype implementation described later follows this approach.

4. PROPERTIES

4.1 Efficiency of the schemes

In Table 1, we present a comparison of the direct graph and tree schemes described, respectively, in Section 3.5 and Section 3.6; as well as two obvious "trivial" constructions, discussed next. As mentioned earlier, the protection cost is the same for all schemes considered in this paper.

The first trivial scheme uses a separate key for each protection class. This results in a large master secret key but achieves fast deletion operations. The Ephemerizer [20], for instance, encrypts all files with a particular expiration time with the same time-specific key, and Vanish [13] encrypts every user-data object with an independent key. Likewise, the Data Node Encrypted Filesystem (DNEFS) [22] uses this approach for protecting every data node of the flash filesystem independently.

The second trivial scheme implements a tree of depth one: it uses a single encryption key as a master key and one encryption key for each protection class; the master key is used to encrypt the keys of the protection classes and the ciphertexts are stored in the auxiliary state. Deletion requires the re-encryption of all remaining protection-class keys with a new master key. This scheme appears, e.g., in the extension of DNEFS to an encrypted filesystem [22]. Note that removing this level of indirection, and using the master key to protect the files directly, would result in much worse deletion performance, as the number of files is typically much greater than the number of protection classes.

The operational cost of our direct policy-graph secure deletion scheme is determined by the parameters of its graph, namely, the maximum in-degree d of a node and the longest path ℓ. The main advantages of this scheme are its fast deletion operation coupled with its high expressibility. Unlike the other schemes, which consider only protection classes mapped one-to-one to attributes, the policy-graph scheme allows flexible policies formulated through logical expressions over attributes. In practice, d and ℓ will often be small numbers, though in $O(|\mathcal{A}|)$ and $O(|\mathcal{P}|)$, respectively.

4.2 Relation to secret-key encryption

Every secure deletion scheme is also a secret-key cryptosystem with security against chosen-plaintext attacks. We only sketch this relation here; adding the formal details is straightforward.

Scheme	*Deletion cost*	*Access cost*	*Master-key size*
Trivial direct	$O(1)$	$O(1)$	$O(\|\mathcal{P}\|)$
Trivial tree	$O(\|\mathcal{P}\|)$	$O(1)$	$O(1)$
Direct graph	$O(1)$	$O(d \cdot \ell)$	$O(\|\mathcal{A}\|)$
Tree	$O(\log \|\mathcal{P}\|)$	$O(\log \|\mathcal{P}\|)$	$O(1)$
Time-tree*	$O(1)$	$O(\log \|\mathcal{P}\|)$	$O(\log \|\mathcal{P}\|)$

Table 1: Efficiency comparison. $|\mathcal{A}|$ and $|\mathcal{P}|$ denote the number of attributes and protection classes in the policy graph, d is the maximum in-degree of a node, and ℓ is the longest path in the graph. * The time-tree supports only deletion going forward in time; its amortized deletion cost is $O(1)$ and $O(\log |\mathcal{P}|)$ in the worst case.

Recall that a secret-key cryptosystem $\mathcal{S}$ consists of three algorithms for key generation, encryption, and decryption, respectively. The following steps emulate $\mathcal{S}$ from a secure deletion scheme $\mathcal{E}$:

1. Let G_1 be the minimal policy graph with one attribute a, one protection class p, and one edge from a to p. For key generation in $\mathcal{S}$, run the initialization algorithm of $\mathcal{E}$ with G_1 and use its output as the secret key.
2. For encryption of a plaintext m with $\mathcal{S}$, invoke the protection algorithm of $\mathcal{E}$ on p and m, obtain a ciphertext c, and output (p, c).
3. For decrypting a ciphertext (p, c) of $\mathcal{S}$, invoke the access algorithm of $\mathcal{E}$, and output the response.

We claim that $\mathcal{S}$ is a secret-key cryptosystem with indistinguishable ciphertexts under chosen-plaintext attacks (IND-CPA security). To see this, suppose $\mathcal{S}$ is not secure. Then we construct a simulator SIM that contradicts the security of $\mathcal{E}$ in experiment Secdel, by interacting with an adversary $\mathsf{A}_{\mathcal{S}}$ that breaks the security of $\mathcal{S}$.

The simulator executes the operations of $\mathcal{S}$ according the described emulation of $\mathcal{S}$ from $\mathcal{E}$; note that SIM does not call Delete. When $\mathsf{A}_{\mathcal{S}}$ outputs two plaintexts m_0 and m_1 such that one is to be encrypted as challenge, the simulator outputs p, m_0, and m_1. Then Secdel responds with a ciphertext c^* that contains a representation of m_b, where $b \in \{0, 1\}$. According to the emulation of $\mathcal{S}$, the simulator gives (p, c^*) to $\mathsf{A}_{\mathcal{S}}$. When $\mathsf{A}_{\mathcal{S}}$ outputs a bit $\hat{b}_{\mathcal{S}}$ as its guess for the challenge plaintext, then SIM queries its oracle for the deletion operation with attribute set $\{a\}$, ignores the master key that it receives, and outputs $\hat{b}_{\mathcal{S}}$. Note that SIM emulates the IND-CPA security experiment perfectly. By the assumption that $\mathsf{A}_{\mathcal{S}}$ breaks the indistinguishability of ciphertexts of $\mathcal{S}$, it follows that $\Pr[\mathsf{Secdel}_{\mathsf{SIM},\mathcal{E}}(\kappa) = 1] - \frac{1}{2}$ is not negligible. Hence, $\mathcal{E}$ is not a secure policy-based deletion scheme.

5. PROTOTYPE IMPLEMENTATION

Here we describe a filesystem prototype of a policy-based secure deletion scheme according to Sections 2 and 3. The *secure-deletion filesystem (delfs)* is implemented as an extension to EncFS [10], a virtual cryptographic filesystem in Linux based on FUSE [12]. As a virtual filesystem, *delfs* does not handle space allocation itself, just like EncFS, but acts as a transparent protection layer and projects the stored directories and files with the same structure onto a lower-layer (physical) filesystem.

5.1 Overview

Data stored in *delfs* seamlessly benefits from secure deletion. Together with every instance of a *delfs*-mounted directory tree, the user specifies a deletion policy in the format described later. Every file maintained by *delfs* is associated with a protection class and

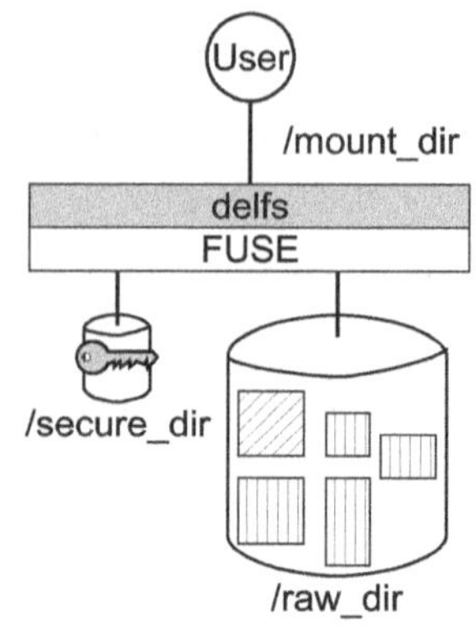

Figure 4: *delfs* architecture.

protected accordingly. A file can be accessed as long as its protection class is accessible according to the deletion policy.

As shown in Figure 4, three directories are involved in operating a *delfs* filesystem. First, *secure_dir* contains the master key of *delfs* and must be backed by erasable memory. It should be accessible only to the process running *delfs* and protected against exposure to any other entity during operation. In practice, it may be a POSIX-compatible local filesystem that supports physical secure deletion and that is never backed up. The *delfs* prototype uses a small ext2-formatted partition on a magnetic disk that supports secure deletion through in-place updates and free-space filling [23]. Second, bulk storage is provided by *raw_dir*, which represents the non-erasable memory such as a NAS server or cloud storage; only protected versions of files and auxiliary data reside here. Finally, the user stores and accesses protected files through *mount_dir*.

When a *delfs* directory is mounted for the first time, an initialization file has to be provided as well, which specifies the initial deletion policy and its attributes. All files written to *mount_dir* benefit from secure deletion. Files can be securely deleted by running a dedicated *delfsctl* utility and specifying attributes to delete. This securely deletes files according to the deletion policy such that an adversary can no longer recover them later. The adversary might obtain the contents of *secure_dir* afterwards and see all data that has ever been written to *raw_dir*, but can no longer infer anything about the data in the deleted files.

5.2 Attributes and policy specification

In order not to burden the user with specifying a deletion policy graph that may contain hundreds or thousands of possible attributes, *delfs* implements only restricted deletion policies compared to the model of Section 2. We argue below that these are sufficient for practical purposes.

All attributes in *delfs* are partitioned into *attribute types* such that every attribute occurs in one type. Types represent the categories relevant for secure deletion, such as owners, projects, organizations, or expiration dates. For each attribute type, many different attribute values can be specified through enumeration of strings or by giving a range for numeric attributes. A range is expanded into an enumeration. A sample *delfs* attribute specification in the initialization file might look like this (written in `libConfig++` syntax):

```
types = (
  {
      name = "user";
      attributes = ["Alice", "Bob", "Charlie"];
      implementation = "simple";                    },
  {
      name = "project";
```

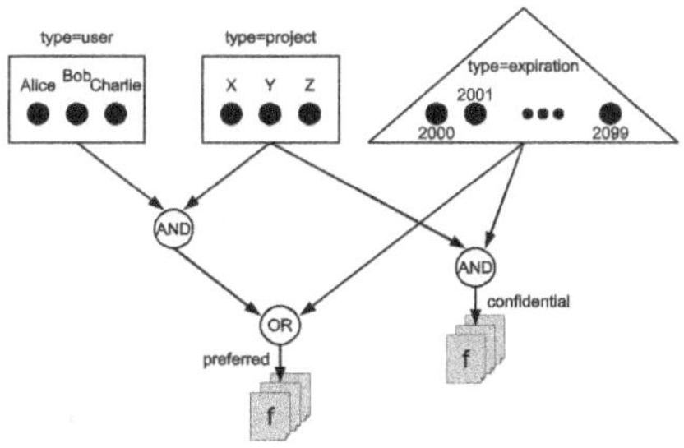

Figure 5: An illustration of the two *delfs* policies *preferred* and *confidential* as described in the text. The attribute type *expiration* uses the *tree* implementation, indicated by the triangle.

```
        attributes = ["X", "Y", "Z"];
        implementation = "simple";                      },
    {
        name = "expiration";
        attributes = ["2000", "2099"];
        specification = "range",
        implementation = "tree";                        } );
```

Here, attribute type *expiration* is specified as a range, and this simply maps to an enumeration of the 100 different attributes. The meaning of *implementation* is explained in the next section. The attribute types in *delfs* model the familiar convention that objects have typed attributes and that every attribute can have only one value (for example, attributes of a POSIX file in the *stat* structure or attributes in a tuple of a relational database).

The deletion policy is given as a collection of *policies*, where each policy has a name and is represented by a logical expression over the attribute types, using AND and OR operators. By instantiating every attribute type with all of its possible values, each policy maps to many different multiple protection classes. Hence, the exact protection class is defined by the policy and the attribute values associated to a file. Below is a sample *delfs* deletion policy from the initialization file, as shown in Figure 5:

```
policies = (
    {
        name = "preferred";
        expr = "((user AND project) OR expiration)"; },
    {
        name = "confidential";
        expr = "(expiration AND project)";          } );
```

When a file stored with policy *preferred* has attributes $user = Bob$, $project = X$, and $expiration = 2014$, this corresponds to protection class p_5 in the graph of Figure 1. Compared to the deletion policy graph in Section 2, *delfs* policies support only AND and OR gates. We discuss how attribute values are associated to files below.

5.3 Implementation

delfs implements the constructions of Section 3, with the exception of threshold gates and the time-tree scheme. The master key structure M is stored in *secure_dir*, whereas the auxiliary state S and all protected data reside in permanent memory under *raw_dir*. Every file stored in *delfs* is associated to one policy. If more flexibility is required, the policy graph should be extended.

A *delfs* attribute type with *simple* implementation corresponds to a direct secure deletion scheme with one protection class for every *delfs*-attribute value according to Section 3.3. For *delfs* attribute types with *tree* implementation, which are typically those with a large number of attribute values, the construction of Section 3.6 is invoked. These are further combined according to the *delfs* policies through the policy-graph construction in Section 3.5. The resulting scheme implements the combined model of Section 3.8.

When *delfs* is invoked for the first time on a particular mount point, the initial policy must be given. The current policy, some defaults, and auxiliary state are then stored in a system-wide state file in the root of *raw_dir*. Information specific to a file, such as its attribute values, the applicable policy, and the encrypted file-encryption key, are stored together with the file itself in its *extended attributes*.

Once the filesystem is mounted, every new file created inside *mount_dir* is protected according to the policy. The file takes its initial attribute values and policy from a special *defaults file*, located inside the directory where the file will reside; note that FUSE makes it possible to obtain the pathname when creating a file. If the defaults file is not present, parent directories in the path to *mount_dir* are searched; if no file defaults file is found, the system-wide initial policy stored in *raw_dir* is applied. An example *delfs* defaults file may contain:

```
attributes = ["project=X", "expiration=2013"];
policy = "confidential";
```

The user can perform regular filesystem operations on the files under *delfs* without affecting their deletion policy, as long as these operations leave the extended attributes intact.

Deletion-specific operations are done through a *delfsctl* administrative tool. In particular, (1) it performs secure deletion operations according to one or more given attributes and may update *secure_dir* during this operation; (2) it can reclaim space in *raw_dir* for files that have been deleted according to the policy and therefore have become inaccessible; and (3) it can manipulate the *delfs* policy and modify the attributes of existing files. However, the policy graph can only be extended. As this is, strictly speaking, not captured in our cryptographic model, we note that by allowing only extensions, each subsequent policy contains also the previous ones; hence, the security analysis for the latest policy captures also the previous states.

When *delfs* starts, it reads the master key from a file in *secure_dir* and buffers it in the daemon during operation. For every secure deletion operation, *delfs* first updates the auxiliary state and writes it back to *raw_dir*; then it updates the master key and overwrites the file in *secure_dir* with the changed contents.

Note that the design so far has no provision for securely deleting a directory and all its subdirectories. This can be achieved as follows. A predefined attribute named *PARENT* exists and can be used to formulate policies. The attribute may occur directly in a deletion policy. It represents the presence, in the filesystem, of the parent directory of a file, such that deleting that directory through a filesystem command triggers a secure deletion operation for the attribute *PARENT* on the children of the directory. Its implementation uses the tree construction of Section 3.6 with the topology of the filesystem tree and metadata maintained in per-directory state files. All *delfs* operations that modify the directory tree may thus implicitly modify the auxiliary state.

5.4 Evaluation

The prototype uses AES-256 for secret-key encryption in the *delfs*-specific code and the "standard configuration" of EncFS with AES-192 encryption. For the policy described in Figure 5, *delfs* has a master key composed of 7 encryption keys. The auxiliary state stores one ciphertext per edge and two ciphertexts per interior node plus the auxiliary data for the expiration tree, i.e., 201 ciphertexts in total with a binary tree of depth 7; all ciphertexts are encryptions of 256-bit AES keys. Every read and write operation has an overhead of 8 AES operations for the *confidential* protection class and of 12 AES operations for the *preferred* protection class, whereby all paths leading to the protection class' node are evaluated in the straightforward manner. In principle, the key-derivation could be optimized only for the necessary nodes; however, *delfs* resorts to caching and evaluates the whole graph only once at mount time. Every delete operation merely removes entries from the master key for the direct policies, performs the re-encryptions (in the auxiliary storage) for each of the 7 levels of the policy tree, and updates the root key stored in the *delfs* master key. The master key file is overwritten with the master key from the cached representation to complete the deletion operation.

The actual time incurred for secure deletion mainly depends on the choice of storage medium for the master key. When using a small ext2-formatted partition, one should also fill the filesystem with arbitrary data, in order to overwrite any potentially freed blocks from the master-key file. Measuring the performance of reading and writing files protected with EncFS and *delfs* shows that *delfs* introduces only a negligible overhead, as the encryption and decryption of the payload dominates the read and write operations.

Acknowledgments

We thank Robert Haas, Alexis Hafner, and Anıl Kurmuş for interesting suggestions and discussions about this topic.

This work has been supported in part by the European Union's Seventh Framework Programme (FP7/2007–2013), grant number ICT-257243 TCLOUDS.

6. REFERENCES

[1] M. J. Atallah, M. Blanton, N. Fazio, and K. B. Frikken. Dynamic and efficient key management for access hierarchies. *ACM Transactions on Information and System Security*, 12(3), 2009.

[2] M. J. Atallah, M. Blanton, and K. B. Frikken. Incorporating temporal capabilities in existing key management schemes. In *Proc. 12th European Symposium On Research In Computer Security (ESORICS)*, volume 4734 of *Lecture Notes in Computer Science*, pages 515–530. Springer, 2007.

[3] J. Bethencourt, A. Sahai, and B. Waters. Ciphertext-policy attribute-based encryption. In *Proc. 28th IEEE Symposium on Security & Privacy*, pages 321–334, 2007.

[4] D. Boneh and R. Lipton. A revocable backup system. In *Proc. 6th USENIX Security Symposium*, 1996.

[5] J. Crampton. Practical and efficient cryptographic enforcement of interval-based access control policies. *ACM Transactions on Information and System Security*, 14(1), 2011.

[6] J. Crampton, K. M. Martin, and P. R. Wild. On key assignment for hierarchical access control. In *Proc. 19th IEEE Computer Security Foundations Symposium (CSF)*, pages 98–111, 2006.

[7] A. De Santis, A. L. Ferrara, and B. Masucci. Efficient provably-secure hierarchical key assignment schemes. *Theoretical Computer Science*, 412:5684–5699, 2011.

[8] G. Di Crescenzo, N. Ferguson, R. Impagliazzo, and M. Jakobsson. How to forget a secret. In *Proc. 16th Symposium on Theoretical Aspects of Computer Science (STACS)*, volume 1563 of *Lecture Notes in Computer Science*, pages 500–509. Springer, 1999.

[9] Electronic Frontier Foundation. Surveillance self-defense project. `https://ssd.eff.org/`, 2013.

[10] EncFS. EncFS encrypted filesystem. `http://www.arg0.net/encfs`.

[11] European Parliament and Council. Protection of individuals with regard to the processing of personal data and on the free movement of such data. Directive 95/46/EC, 1995.

[12] FUSE. Filesystem in userspace. `http://fuse.sourceforge.net/`.

[13] R. Geambasu, T. Kohno, A. A. Levy, and H. M. Levy. Vanish: Increasing data privacy with self-destructing data. In *Proc. 18th USENIX Security Symposium*, 2009.

[14] V. Goyal, O. Pandey, A. Sahai, and B. Waters. Attribute-based encryption for fine-grained access control of encrypted data. In *Proc. 13th ACM Conference on Computer and Communications Security (CCS)*, pages 89–98, 2006.

[15] S. Hohenberger and B. Waters. Attribute-based encryption with fast decryption. In *Public Key Cryptography*, pages 162–179, 2013.

[16] N. Joukov, H. Papaxenopoulos, and E. Zadok. Secure deletion myths, issues, and solutions. In *Proc. 3rd International IEEE Security in Storage Workshop (SISW)*, 2005.

[17] N. Joukov and E. Zadok. Adding secure deletion to your favorite file system. In *Proc. 3rd International IEEE Security in Storage Workshop (SISW)*, 2005.

[18] H. Krawczyk. Perfect forward secrecy. In *Encyclopedia of Cryptography and Security*. 2005.

[19] S. Mitra and M. Winslett. Secure deletion from inverted indexes on compliance storage. In *Proc. Workshop on Storage Security and Survivability (StorageSS)*, pages 67–72, 2006.

[20] R. Perlman. File system design with assured delete. In *Proc. Network and Distributed Systems Security Symposium (NDSS)*, 2007.

[21] Z. N. J. Peterson, R. Burns, J. Herring, A. Stubblefield, and A. D. Rubin. Secure deletion for a versioning file system. In *Proc. 4th USENIX Conference on File and Storage Technologies (FAST)*, pages 143–154, 2005.

[22] J. Reardon, S. Capkun, and D. Basin. Data node encrypted file system: Efficient secure deletion for flash memory. In *Proc. 21st USENIX Security Symposium*, 2012.

[23] J. Reardon, S. Capkun, and D. Basin. SoK: Secure data deletion. In *Proc. 34th IEEE Symposium on Security & Privacy*, 2013.

[24] A. Sahai and B. Waters. Fuzzy identity-based encryption. In *Proc. EUROCRYPT*, volume 3494 of *Lecture Notes in Computer Science*, pages 457–473. Springer, 2005.

[25] A. Shamir. How to share a secret. *Communications of the ACM*, 22(11):612–613, Nov. 1979.

[26] V. Shoup. Sequences of games: A tool for taming complexity in security proofs. Cryptology ePrint Archive, Report 2004/332, 2004. `http://eprint.iacr.org/`.

[27] Y. Tang, P. P. C. Lee, J. C. S. Lui, and R. Perlman. FADE: Secure overlay cloud storage with file assured deletion. In *Proc. Securecomm*, 2010.

[28] M. Wei, L. M. Grupp, F. E. Spada, and S. Swanson. Reliably erasing data from flash-based solid state drives. In *Proc. 9th USENIX Conference on File and Storage Technologies (FAST)*, 2011.

Secure Data Deletion from Persistent Media

Joel Reardon
ETH Zurich, Switzerland
reardonj@inf.ethz.ch

Hubert Ritzdorf
ETH Zurich, Switzerland
rihubert@inf.ethz.ch

David Basin
ETH Zurich, Switzerland
basin@inf.ethz.ch

Srdjan Capkun
ETH Zurich, Switzerland
srdjan.capkun@inf.ethz.ch

ABSTRACT

Secure deletion is the task of deleting data irrecoverably from a physical medium. In this work, we present a general approach to the design and analysis of secure deletion for persistent storage that relies on encryption and key wrapping. We define a key disclosure graph that models the adversarial knowledge of the history of key generation and wrapping. We introduce a generic update function and prove that it achieves secure deletion of data against a coercive attacker; instances of the update function implement the update behaviour of all arborescent data structures including B-Trees, extendible hash tables, linked lists, and others. We implement a B-Tree instance of our solution. Our implementation is at the block-device layer, allowing any block-based file system to be used on top of it. Using different workloads, we find that the storage and communication overhead required for storing and retrieving B-Tree nodes is small and that this therefore constitutes a viable solution for many applications requiring secure deletion from persistent media.

Categories and Subject Descriptors

D.4.6 [**Operating Systems**]: Security and Protection; D.4.2 [**Operating Systems**]: Storage Management

Keywords

Secure deletion; privacy; persistent storage; B-Tree

1. INTRODUCTION

Secure data deletion is the task of deleting data irrecoverably from a physical medium. Persistent media, however, are not amenable to secure deletion. Such media include off-line tape archives, storage media under adversarial control, or media that leave analog remnants [11]. Encryption is a well-known technique to make data irrecoverable to those unauthorized to access it. However, long-term encryption keys are vulnerable to disclosure by coercive adversaries [3].

CCS'13, November 4–8, 2013, Berlin, Germany.

ACM 978-1-4503-2477-9/13/11 ...$15.00.
http://dx.doi.org/10.1145/2508859.2516699.

Consequently, encrypted data is only securely deleted when the *user* is unable to recover it [17]. To securely delete data, it is therefore necessary to securely delete the key, a technique first used by Boneh and Lipton to securely delete data written onto magnetic tape for off-line archiving [2].

Di Crescenzo et al. [6] first explicitly considered secure deletion on a storage medium consisting of two parts: a large *persistent medium* (such as a tape archive) and a small *securely-deleting medium* (such as local storage). In the related work section we describe a variety of other schemes that also securely delete from such mixed media. While the specific media targeted by these solutions vary radically, they all share the common premise that the securely deleting storage is orders of magnitude *smaller* than the persistent storage. Were this not the case, the user could eschew the use of persistent storage altogether. Consequently, data is stored on the persistent storage with the encryption keys required to access it stored on the securely-deleting medium.

Storing all the data keys on the securely-deleting medium is not always possible. In order to efficiently delete one data item while retaining all others, the system must provide an appropriate *deletion granularity* [17]. A high deletion granularity implies storing many keys—a different key for each data unit. In the case of tape archives, the number of keys required to achieve the appropriate deletion granularity may easily overwhelm the capacity of the securely-deleting medium. For instance, the securely-deleting medium may be an expensive trusted platform module for added security, or a portable smartcard so that a user can easily access their data anywhere; in both cases we can expect to store only a limited amount of data on the securely-deleting medium. In Boneh and Lipton's approach, all data keys are encrypted with a single master key; while storing the master key requires a fixed amount of data on the securely-deleting medium, the deletion operation involves generating a new master key and re-encrypting all data that was not deleted.

To overcome the limitations of Boneh and Lipton's approach, Di Crescenzo et al. designed a tree-based approach that also requires storing a fixed amount of data on the securely-deleting medium but can delete with logarithmic cost. Their approach arranges the persistent storage into blocks that are indexed by a static binary tree: the tree always retains its size and shape; only the values associated with the nodes can change. Both the data and the tree nodes are stored (encrypted) on the persistent medium, such that each internal node contains the decryption keys for its children, and the leaf nodes for the data. The root key is then stored on the securely-deleting medium.

This static key structure prevents both adding and removing nodes. To effect such a change, the user must construct a new data structure and re-encrypt all the data into it. An alternative, however, is to employ one of many dynamic data structures, such as a B-Tree [5]. These data structures, ubiquitously deployed in storage systems such as file systems and databases, change their internal structure based on current storage requirements. However, ensuring secure deletion with dynamic structures becomes less straightforward.

In this work, we describe a B-Tree-based dynamic structure that securely deletes data using a combination of a small securely-deleting storage medium and a large persistent storage medium. We prove the security of our solution by proving the security for a broad class of dynamic data structures: those whose underlying structure forms a directed tree (henceforth called an arborescence [21]). This includes self-balancing binary search trees and B-Trees [5], but also linked lists and extendible hash tables [8]. We develop a new approach to reasoning about this problem by modeling adversarial knowledge as a directed graph of keys and verifying the conditions that result in the secure deletion of data. We define a generic shadowing graph mutation that models how the adversary's knowledge grows and prove that after arbitrary sequences of such mutations one can still securely delete data in a simple and straightforward way. We prove that when using such mutations, data is securely deleted against an adversary given full access to the history of the persistent medium as well as access to all data stored on the securely-deleting medium outside of the data's lifetime. This strong adversary subsumes all weaker ones, who may only use coercive attacks once or obtain only recent history of the persistent storage. The generic shadowing mutation can express the update behaviour of any arborescent data structure; in the related work section we illustrate the resulting key disclosure graph's shape for existing approaches. Consequently, when deploying a secure-deletion system that uses an arborescent data structure to index data, the security guarantees proved in this work extend to that data structure, provided that all its update behaviours are instances of our generic shadowing graph mutation.

We implement our B-Tree-based instance of the secure deletion solution and test it in practice. Our implementation offers a virtual block device interface, i.e., it mimics the behaviour of a typical hard drive. This permits any block-based file system to use the device as a virtual medium, and so any medium capable of storing and retrieving data blocks can therefore be used as the persistent storage. We show that our solution achieves secure deletion from persistent media without imposing substantial overhead through increased storage space or communication. We validate this claim by implementing our solution and analyzing its resulting overhead and performance. We examine our design's overhead and B-Tree properties for different caching strategies, block sizes, and file system workloads generated by `filebench` [12]. We show that the caching strategy approximates the theoretical optimal (i.e., Bélády's "clairvoyant" strategy [1]) for many workloads and that the storage and communication costs are typically only a small percentage of the cost to store and retrieve the data itself.

To summarize, our contributions are the following:

- We propose an intuitive model that captures the growth of adversarial knowledge in secure deletion systems.
- We define a generic shadowing graph mutation that adheres to this model and can implement the update behaviour of any arborescent data structure.
- We prove that secure deletion of data is easily accomplished with a single, simple mutation.
- We design a caching B-Tree whose update mechanism is an instance of our generic mutation.
- We analyze different caching strategies and measure the communication and storage overhead of our B-Tree approach for different workloads; we show that caching is quite effective and that the overhead is typically negligible.

The remainder of this paper is organized as follows: Section 2 presents the adversarial model. Section 3 describes an example instantiation of a securely-deleting data structure in the form of a B-Tree. Section 4 presents the graph theoretic details and proves the security of such schemes in general. Section 5 provides implementation details for the B-Tree. Section 6 then experimentally evaluates the B-Tree approach. Finally, Section 7 discusses related work and Section 8 draws conclusions.

2. SYSTEM AND ADVERSARIAL MODEL

Our system model consists of a user who stores data on storage media such that the data can be retrieved during the data's lifetime but cannot be retrieved outside its lifetime. A data's *lifetime* is the time inclusively between two events: the data's initial creation and its subsequent secure deletion. We assume that the user divides the data to store into discrete *data units* that share a lifetime. These can be binary data objects, files, or individual blocks of a block-based file system. The user retains a sortable *handle* to recall these objects (e.g., an object name or a block address). These handles may also be stored on the persistent storage (e.g., a master list of all objects, or by using a file system on top of the block-based storage.)

The user has access to two storage media: a small securely-deleting medium and a large persistent medium. We assume that the securely-deleting medium automatically securely deletes any data that is removed and correctly handles analog remnants and other nuances of secure deletion. We also assume that the persistent medium does not securely delete any data; once (encrypted) data is written onto it, the data cannot be removed. In practice, the persistent medium can correspond to a wide range of use cases, such as sending data over a channel with an eavesdropper, giving another entity access to the storage medium through outsourced archiving or remote storage, storing data on media that do not facilitate secure deletion, or simply neglecting to take appropriate measures to ensure secure deletion. We assume that the securely-deleting medium is orders of magnitude smaller than the persistent storage; in particular, the data being stored does not fit onto the securely-deleting medium. It may even be the case that both media are the same physical device—it is only because ensuring secure deletion is sufficiently expensive (e.g., on flash memory) that it must be done at a smaller scale than the stored data.

We consider a computationally-bounded coercive adversary who can compromise both the securely-deleting medium and the persistent medium. The adversary has access to the history of all data previously written onto the persistent medium. The adversary has full knowledge of the algorithms and implementation of the system and both the persistent and securely-deleting media. The adversary, being coercive, may perform multiple compromises of the user's current secret keys (those keys that the user holds at the time of compromise) as well as the contents of both storage media. As the adversary is computationally bounded, it cannot recover the plain-text message from a cipher-text message without the corresponding encryption key. This strong attacker subsumes all weaker ones, who may be able to coercively attack a single time or may be given a limited amount of data from the persistent storage.

Our environment models many different types of persistent storage, which may vary greatly in what kind of data and how much of it is ultimately stored *persistently* and becomes available to the adversary. Since we do not want the security of our solution to rely on the chance that some persistent data was not disclosed to the adversary, we instead assume that all data written onto persistent storage is given to the adversary. This obviates the need for any assumptions about the storage medium's behaviour other than its ability to store and retrieve data. Moreover, while an adversary that coercively attacks the user at all times outside a data's lifetime is hard to conceive in the real world, the additional effort to prove the security against such an adversary is negligibly more than is required to defend against the adversary who coercively attacks only once after some data is deleted. Therefore, in this work we consider a very powerful attacker, but our solution is not significantly more complicated than would be necessary against a much weaker attacker.

For clarity in our presentation, we assume that all keys k have a name $\phi(k) \in \mathbb{Z}^+$, where ϕ is an injective one-way function mapping keys to their name. The key's name $\phi(k)$ reveals no information about the key k—even to an information-theoretic adversary. For example, the key's name could be the current count of the number of random keys generated by the user. We further assume that the adversary can identify the key used to encrypt data through the use of a *name function*, which maps an encrypted block to the corresponding key's name. Hence, given $E_k(\cdot)$, the adversary can compute a name $\phi(k)$. This permits the adversary to organize blocks by their unknown encryption key and recognize if these keys are later known. We do not concern ourselves with the implementation of such a function, but simply empower the adversary to use it.

Our security goal is to securely delete data, thus preventing the adversary from obtaining it. We want to achieve this goal for all data; though if the adversary coercively attacks the user during the data's lifetime, then the adversary obtains the data, preventing its subsequent secure deletion. Therefore, we aim to securely delete all data that was not compromised during its lifetime. Figure 1 shows example data lifetimes along with an adversarial coercive attack event. Data numbered 1 and 5 are compromised by this event but the remaining data lifetimes (i.e., data numbered 2–4 and 6) are unaffected by it. Hence, our security goal is to prevent the adversary from recovering any of the data items unaffected by the attack.

Note that in our work we also describe the integrity properties of our solution's design and implementation. This is done to consistently describe the actual data format and behaviour of our approach, but the used data integrity scheme is not a novel contribution of this work.

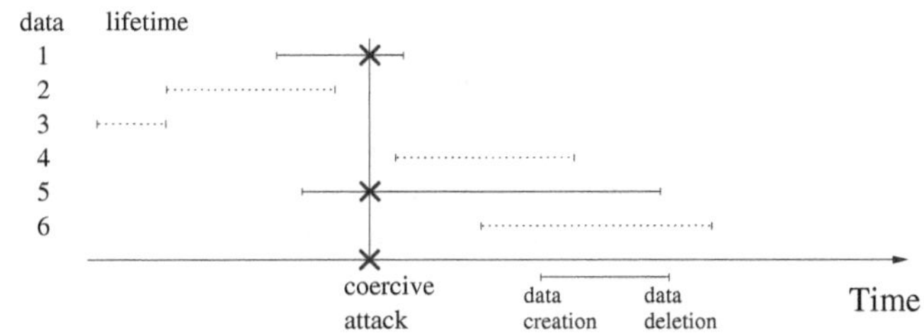

Figure 1: Secure deletion timeline for different data items. $\times$ marks data compromised by coercive adversarial attacks. Data with lifetimes in dotted lines are not affected by the coercive attack, while data with lifetimes in solid lines are disclosed by the attack.

3. B-TREE SECURE DELETION

This section details a B-Tree-based design to securely delete data stored on a persistent medium as described in Section 2. It is an example instance from the space of dynamic data structures whose general security we prove in Section 4. The B-Tree implements a securely-deleting key-value map that maps data handles to data units; new pairs can be inserted, existing pairs can be removed, and any stored data unit can be updated. Our map is securely deleting in that data units removed from the map are irrecoverable to an adversary, including old data units that are updated to a new value.

3.1 B-Trees

A B-Tree is a self-balancing search tree [5] that implements a key-value map interface. B-Trees are ubiquitously deployed in databases and file systems as they are well-suited to accessing data stored on block devices—devices that impose some non-trivial minimum I/O size.

A B-Tree of order N is a tree where each node has between $\lceil \frac{N}{2} \rceil$ and N child nodes, and every leaf has equal depth [5]. (The root is exceptional as it may have fewer than $\lceil \frac{N}{2} \rceil$ nodes.) The order of a B-Tree node is chosen to fit perfectly into a disk block, which maximizes the benefit of high-latency disk operations that return at minimum a full block of data. B-Trees typically store search keys whose corresponding values are stored elsewhere; leaf nodes store the location where the data can be found. The basic mutating operations `add`, `modify`, and `remove` keys from the tree. Because adding and removing children may violate the balance of children in a node, `rebalance`, `fuse`, and `split` are used to maintain the tree balance property.

B-Tree Storage Operations.

The `add`, `modify`, and `remove` functions begin with a `lookup` function, which takes a search key and follows a path in the tree from the root node to the leaf node where the search key should be stored. `Add` stores the search key and a reference to the data in the leaf node. `Modify` finds where the data is stored and replaces it with new data; alternatively it can store the new version out-of-place and update the reference. `Remove` removes the reference to data in the leaf node. Both add and remove change the number of children in a leaf node, which can violate the balance property.

B-Tree Balance Operations.

A B-Tree of order N is balanced when the number of children of each non-root node is inclusively between $\lceil \frac{N}{2} \rceil$ and N and the number of children in each root node is less than or equal to N. When there are more or fewer children than these thresholds, the node is overfull or underfull respectively and must be balanced.

Overfull nodes are `split` into two halves and become siblings. This requires an additional index in their parent, which may in turn cause the parent to become overfull. If the root becomes overfull, then a new root is created; this is the only way the height of a B-Tree increases.

Underfull nodes can be either `rebalanced` or `fused` to restore the tree balance property. Rebalancing takes excess children from one of the underfull node's siblings; this causes the parent to reindex the underfull node and its generous sibling and afterwards neither node violates the balance properties. If both the node's siblings have no excess children, then the node is fused with one of its siblings. This means that the sibling is removed and its children are given to the underfull node. This removes one child from their parent, which can cause the parent to become underfull—possibly propagating up to the root. The root node is uniquely allowed to be underfull. If, however, after a fuse operation the root has only one child, then the root is removed and its sole child becomes the new root. This is the only way the height of a B-Tree decreases.

3.2 Solution design

We use a B-Tree to organize, access, and securely delete data. We assume that the size of the B-Tree nodes is sufficiently large that the nodes cannot all be stored on the securely-deleting storage—otherwise the client can simply maintain a local list of keys, securely deleting them when the corresponding data should be deleted. Consequently, both data and B-Tree nodes are stored on the persistent storage medium, and they are first encrypted before being stored.

Data blocks are encrypted with a random key. The index for the data block, along with its encryption key, is then stored as a leaf node in the B-Tree. The nodes themselves are encrypted with a random key and stored on the persistent medium. Inner nodes of the B-Tree therefore store the encryption keys required to decrypt their children. The key that decrypts the root node of the B-Tree, however, is never stored on the persistent medium; the root key is only stored on the securely-deleting medium. Only one such key is stored at any time. Old keys are securely deleted and replaced with a new key.

In addition to encryption, each node also stores the *cryptographic digest* (henceforth called *hash*) of its children for integrity in a straightforward application of a Merkle tree [13]. An authentic parent node guarantees the authenticity of its children. The root hash is stored with the key.

To improve efficiency, we keep a cache of nodes available in memory to perform all B-Tree operations, which we call the *skeleton tree*. Figure 2 illustrates an example skeleton tree. The skeleton tree's nodes are loaded lazily from persistent storage and added to the skeleton tree after decryption and verification. To store local changes on the persistent storage, the skeleton tree is periodically *committed*, where all *dirty* nodes (i.e., those that have local modifications) are re-hashed for integrity and re-encrypted with a new key for security, and written onto persistent storage.

To prevent data loss between commit operations, a mechanism must be used for crash safety. Our approach simply keeps a local record of changes on the securely-deleting medium that can be replayed after a crash and is securely deleted once committed. Another option, which does not require using the securely-deleting medium, is DNEFS's approach of writing fresh encryption keys to the persistent storage ahead of time [18]. In particular, a block of fresh keys is directly wrapped with the new root key and stored during the commit operation; these keys are then sequentially used to encrypt data written in the next commit interval.

Cryptographic Details.

All encrypted data—both the B-Tree's node data and the user's actual data—are encrypted with AES keys in counter mode with a zero IV. All keys are randomly generated using a cryptographically-suitable entropy source. We use each key only once to encrypt data. Therefore, an encryption key's lifetime is the following: it is generated randomly, it is used once to encrypt data, and then it is used arbitrarily many times to decrypt that data until it is securely deleted.

In addition to encryption, we also hash data to ensure its integrity from the persistent storage. We use a cryptographic hash to ensure that even an adversary who directly controls the persistent storage cannot violate the data's integrity. Mykletun et al. [15] propose a variation of Merkle Hash Trees [13] designed specifically for B-Trees. We use a variant of their approach in our scheme: each node is hashed but the hashes of the children are independently stored in their parent (alongside their decryption key). This increases the space required to store each node; however, it allows us to perform B-Tree updates without loading all of a node's siblings from persistent storage.

Skeleton Tree.

All the B-Tree nodes are stored on the persistent storage. To improve efficiency, however, the actual B-Tree operations are performed on a smaller subset of the B-Tree cached in memory, which is called the *skeleton tree*. The skeleton tree reduces the cost of computing decryption keys for data when the relevant B-Tree nodes are available in memory; this strongly benefits, in particular, sequential data access. It also permits multiple updates to the B-Tree to be batched and committed together, which reduces the total number of B-Tree nodes to update. Finally, it allows the user to control the frequency that the root secret changes on the securely deleting medium; this is useful if updating the securely-deleting medium has a non-trivial cost in latency, wear, or human effort.

Initially, the skeleton tree only stores the root of the B-Tree; other node references are loaded lazily. Figure 2 gives an example of this configuration, where the persistent storage has a stale B-Tree and the skeleton tree reflects some combination of addition, removal, and rebalance operations. When a B-Tree operation requires accessing a node missing from the skeleton tree, the corresponding B-Tree node is read from persistent storage and decrypted. Its integrity is checked by using its hash value stored at the parent; if the check passes, then the missing reference is added to the skeleton tree. This new reference now stores the decryption keys and integrity hashes corresponding to all its (missing) chil-

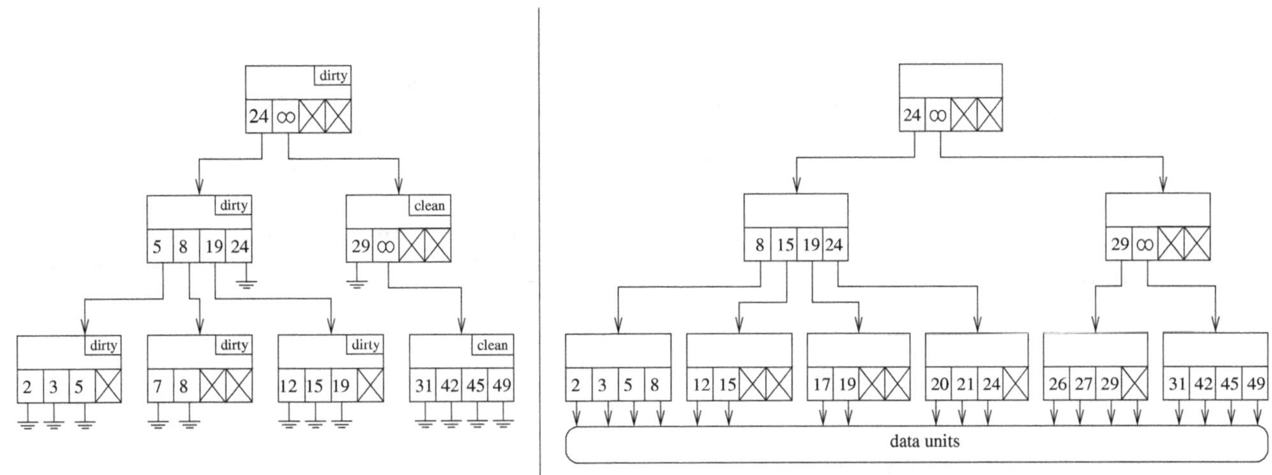

(a) Skeleton Tree

(b) Persistent Medium

Figure 2: Example of a B-Tree stored on the persistent medium along with an in-memory skeleton tree. (a) shows the skeleton tree of B-Tree nodes, where node 42 was read and local changes were made: the node 7 was added and the node 17 was deleted, causing a split operation and a fuse operation respectively. (b) shows the persistent medium which stores all the nodes in the tree, some of which are stale. Only the nodes that have been needed are loaded into the skeleton tree.

dren, allowing the skeleton tree to grow further on request. The size of the skeleton tree is limited: when it reaches its capacity then nodes are evicted from the tree. In Section 6 we present our experimental results with eviction strategies.

All modifications to the B-Tree—e.g., deleting data and rebalancing—are performed on the skeleton tree and periodically committed in batch to persistent storage. A *dirty* marker is kept with the skeleton nodes to indicate which of them have local changes that need committing. Whenever a tree node is mutated—i.e., adding, removing, or modifying a child reference—it is marked as dirty. This includes modifications made due to rebalance operations. B-Tree nodes that are created or deleted—due to splitting or fusing nodes—are also marked as dirty. Finally, dirtiness is propagated up the skeleton tree to the current root.

Commitment.

The B-Tree commit operation writes new versions of all the dirty nodes to persistent storage, thus achieving secure deletion of deleted and overwritten data. Modifications to the B-Tree are first cached and aggregated in the skeleton tree, and then they are simultaneously committed. Therefore, the time that deleted data remains available to the user (and thus the adversary) is based on the frequency that commit operations are performed. Depending on the crash-safety mechanism, an encrypted block of fresh unused encryption keys is written to the persistent storage medium for use in the next commit period. Therefore, the data's lifetime effectively grows in both directions to the nearest commit event; a compromise at one time point in a commit interval is equivalent to a compromise at all time points in that interval. The period between commit events is therefore a trade-off between system performance and deletion latency [17]. Figure 3 builds on Figure 1 by including commit operations.

The commit operation handles two kinds of dirty nodes: *deleted* ones that have been deleted from the B-Tree through

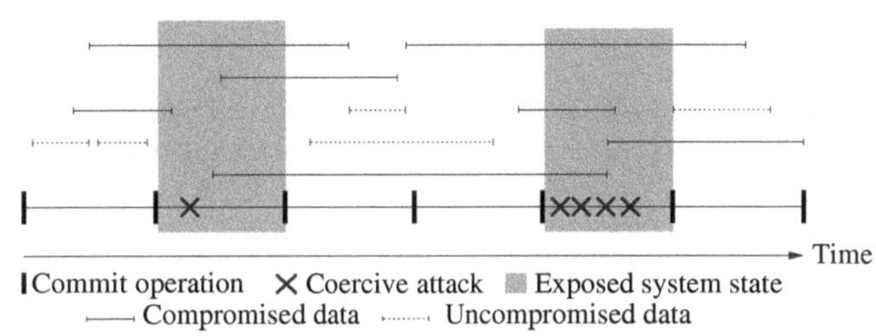

Figure 3: Secure deletion timeline with commit operations. $\times$ marks coercive attacks. Data with lifetimes in dotted lines are not affected by coercive attacks, while data with lifetimes in solid lines are disclosed by the attacks.

the fuse operation, and *valid* ones that are still part of the tree. Each valid dirty node is first associated with a fresh randomly-generated encryption key. Because parent nodes store the keys of their children, all parents of dirty valid nodes are updated to store the new keys associated with each child. After this, the sub-tree of valid dirty nodes is traversed in post order to compute each dirty valid node's integrity hash, which is then stored in the parent. The root node's key and integrity hash are stored outside the tree local to the user. The data for each valid dirty node (i.e., the keys, hashes, and search values for its children) is then encrypted with its newly-generated key and stored on persistent storage.

4. GRAPH-THEORETIC MODEL OF KEY DISCLOSURE

This section describes the security of a broad class of mutable data structures when used to retrieve and securely delete data stored on persistent storage. It relies heavily on graph theory, which we first briefly review. Afterwards, we present our three theoretical contributions. First, we define a key disclosure graph and show how it models adversarial knowledge. We then prove graph-theoretic conditions under which data is securely deleted against our worst-case adversary. Finally, we define a generic shadowing graph mutation and prove that all instances of it preserve a graph property that simplifies secure deletion.

4.1 Graph Theory Background

For completeness, and to commit to a particular nomenclature, we first briefly review the relevant aspects of graph theory. A more detailed treatment can be found elsewhere [21].

Directed Graphs.

A *directed graph* (henceforth called a *digraph*) is a pair of finite sets (V, E), where $E \subseteq V \times V$. Elements of V are called *vertices* and elements of E are called *edges*. If G is a digraph, then we write $V(G)$ for its vertices and $E(G)$ for its edges.

A digraph's edges are directed. If $(u, v) \in E(G)$, we say the edge goes *from* the *source* u and *to* the *destination* v. The edge is called *outgoing* for u and *incoming* for v. The *indegree* and *outdegree* of a vertex is the number of all incoming and outgoing edges for that vertex.

Paths.

A *non-degenerate walk* W of a graph G is a sequence of elements of $E(G)$: $(v_1, u_1), \ldots, (v_n, u_n)$ such that $n \geq 1$ and $\forall i : 1 < i \leq n,\ u_{i-1} = v_i$. The *origin* of W is v_1 and the *terminus* is u_n. We say W *visits* a vertex v (or equivalently, v is on W) if W contains an edge (v, u) or v is the terminus. A *non-degenerate path* P is a non-degenerate walk such that no vertex is visited more than once. Additionally, a graph with n vertices has n *degenerate paths*—zero-length paths that visit no edges and whose origin and terminus are $v \in V(G)$. A *cycle* is a non-degenerate walk C whose origin equals its terminus and all other vertices on the walk are visited once. A directed *acyclic* graph is one with no cycles.

A vertex v is *reachable* from vertex u if there is a directed path from u to v. If there is only one such path then we say that v is uniquely reachable from u and use P^u_v to denote this path. The *ancestors* of a vertex v, called $\text{anc}_G(v)$, is the largest subset of $V(G)$ such that v is reachable from each element. The *descendants* of a vertex u, called $\text{desc}_G(u)$, is the largest subset of $V(G)$ such that each element is reachable from u. If P^u_v is a directed path from u to v, then u is an *ancestor* of v and v is a *descendant* of u. Because of degenerate paths, all vertices are their own ancestors and descendants.

Subdigraphs.

A *subdigraph* S of a digraph G is a digraph whose vertices are a subset of G and whose edges are a subset of the edges of G with endpoints in S. Formally, a subdigraph has vertices $V(S) \subseteq V(G)$ and edges $E(S) \subseteq E(G)|_{V(S)\times V(S)}$. A subdigraph is called *full* if $E(S) = E(G)|_{V(S)\times V(S)}$. A *subdigraph induced by a vertex* v, denoted G_v, is a full subdigraph whose vertices are v and all vertices reachable from v in G. Formally, $V(G_v) = \text{desc}_G(v)$ and $E(G_v) = E(G)|_{V(G_v)\times V(G_v)}$.

Arborescences and Mangroves.

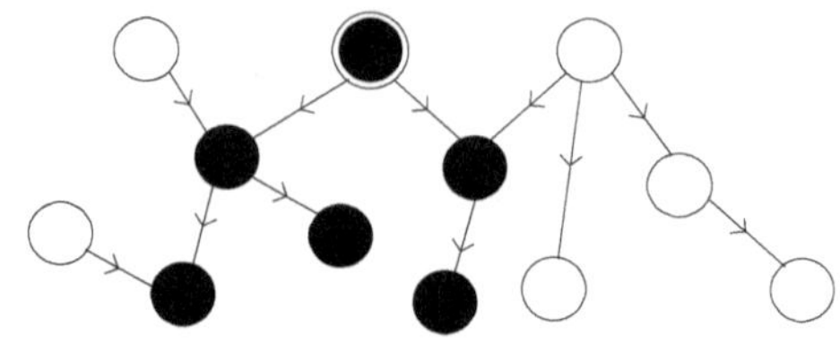

Figure 4: An example mangrove. Shaded vertices belong to the arborescent subdigraph induced by the circled vertex.

An *arborescence diverging from a vertex* $r \in V(A)$ (henceforth called arborescence) is a directed acyclic graph A whose edges are all directed away from r and whose underlying graph (i.e., the undirected graph generated by removing the direction of A's edges) is a (graph-theoretic) tree [21]. The vertex r is called the *root* and it is the only vertex in A that has no incoming edges; all other vertices have exactly one incoming edge (Theorem VI.1 [21]). There is no non-degenerate path in A with r as the terminus, and for all other vertices $v \in V(A)$ there is a unique path P^r_v (Theorem VI.8 [21]). To show that a graph A is an arborescence, it is necessary and sufficient to show that A has the following three properties (Theorem VI.26 [21]): (i) A is acyclic (ii) r has indegree 0 (iii) $\forall v \in V(A), v \neq r \Rightarrow v$ has indegree 1.

A directed graph is a *mangrove* if and only if the subdigraph induced by every vertex is an arborescence. This means that, for every pair of vertices, either one is uniquely and unreciprocatedly reachable from the other or neither one is reachable from the other. Observe that an arborescence is also a mangrove, as all its vertices induce arborescences. Figure 4 shows an example mangrove as well as an arborescent subdigraph induced by a vertex.

4.2 Key Disclosure Graph

In this section, we characterize the information obtained by the adversary and describe a way to structure it. We begin by limiting the functions the user computes on encryption keys to *wrapping* and *hashing*. Wrapping means that a key k is encrypted with another key k' to create $E_{k'}(k)$. With k' and $E_{k'}(k)$ one can compute k, while $E_{k'}(k)$ alone reveals no information about k to a computationally-bounded entity. Hashing means that a key k can be used to compute a one-way digest function $H(k)$ such that $H(k)$ reveals no information about k to a computationally-bounded entity. Furthermore, we require that no plain-text data is ever written onto the persistent medium.

The process of generating keys and using keys to wrap other keys induces a directed graph: nodes correspond to encryption keys and directed edges correspond to the destination key being wrapped by the source key. Knowledge of one key gives access to the data encrypted with it as well as any keys corresponding to its vertex's destinations. Recursively, all keys corresponding to descendants of a vertex are computable when the key corresponding to the ancestor vertex is known. We call this graph the *key disclosure graph*, whose definition follows.

Definition 1. Given a set K of encryption keys generated by the user, an injective one-way vertex naming function $\phi : K \rightarrow \mathbb{Z}^+$, and a set of wrapped keys C, then the *key disclosure graph* is a directed graph G constructed as follows: $\phi(k) \in V(G) \Leftrightarrow k \in K$ and $(\phi(k), \phi(k')) \in E(G) \Leftrightarrow E_k(k') \in C$.

The user can construct and maintain such a key disclosure graph by adding nodes and edges when performing key generation and wrapping operations respectively. The adversary can also construct this graph using its name function: whenever ciphertext is given to the adversary, the name corresponding to its encryption key is computed and added as a vertex to the graph with the ciphertext stored alongside. The adversary may only learn some parts of the key disclosure graph; we use $G^{adv} \subseteq G$ to represent the subgraph known to the adversary. For instance, the client may not write all the wrapped key values it computes to the persistent storage, or the adversary may not be able to read all data in the persistent storage. In the worst case, however, the adversary gets all wrapped keys and so $G^{adv} = G$; it is this worst case for which we prove our security.

If the adversary later learns an encryption key (e.g., through compromise), then the key's corresponding ciphertext can be decrypted. If the plaintext contains other encryption keys, then the adversary can determine the names of these keys to determine the edges directed away from this vertex. Therefore, the adversary can follow paths in G^{adv} starting from any vertex whose corresponding key it knows, thus deriving unknown keys.

The adversary's ability to follow paths in the key disclosure graph is independent of the age of the nodes and edges. In our scenario and adversarial model, every time data is stored on the persistent medium, the key disclosure graph G—and possibly the adversary's key disclosure graph G^{adv}—grows. After learning a key, the adversary learns all paths originating from the corresponding vertex in G^{adv}. The keys corresponding to vertices descendant to that origin are then known to the adversary along with the data they encrypt. Therefore, the user must perform secure deletion while reasoning about the adversary's key disclosure graph. Moreover, if the user is unaware of the exact value of $G^{adv} \subseteq G$, then they must reason about $G^{adv} = G$.

4.3 Secure Deletion

Secure data deletion against a coercive attacker requires that the user who securely deletes data is thereafter unable to recover the deleted data [17]. If the adversary already has an encrypted copy of the data being deleted, then the user must ensure that the corresponding decryption key is securely deleted. The decryption key must be securely deleted even with access to all secret keys managed by the user and all data ever sent to persistent storage. The user must not only securely delete the data's encryption key, but also any encryption key that decrypts any ancestor of the data's corresponding vertex in the adversary's key disclosure graph. This is because a vertex v is reachable from another vertex u in the key disclosure graph if and only if $\phi^{-1}(v)$ is computable from $\phi^{-1}(u)$. Definition 2 now defines secure deletion in terms of paths in the key disclosure graph.

Definition 2. Let $G = (V, E)$ be the key disclosure graph for a vertex naming function ϕ, a set of keys K, and a set of ciphertexts C, and let $G^{adv} \subseteq G$ be the adversary's subdigraph of the key disclosure graph. Let $R = \{r_1, \ldots, r_n\} \subseteq K$ be the set of keys stored by the user in the securely-deleting medium. Let D be data stored on the persistent medium encrypted with a key $k \in K$. Let $R_{\text{live}} \subseteq R$ be the set of keys stored in the securely-deleting medium at all times when D is alive (i.e., the times between the data's creation and deletion events).

Then D is *securely-deleted against a computationally-bounded coercive adversary* provided that no compromise of the securely-deleting medium occurs when it stores an element of R_{live} and for all $r \in R \setminus R_{\text{live}}$, there is no path in G^{adv} from $\phi(r)$ to $\phi(k)$.

This definition reflects the following facts: (i) a computationally-bounded adversary cannot recover the data D without the key k, (ii) the only way to obtain k is through compromise or through key unwrapping, (iii) an adversary that compromises at all permissible times can only obtain $R \setminus R_{live}$ directly and $\bigcup_{r \in R \setminus R_{live}} \text{desc}(\phi(r))$ through unwrapping, and (iv) k is not within this set.

Observe that this definition requires that no compromise occurs during which time the securely-deleting medium stores an element of R_{live}—the set of keys stored in the secure-deleting storage medium during the lifetime of the data being securely deleted. This is larger than or equal to the data's lifetime, e.g., by extending in both directions to the nearest commit event.

We have shown that to securely delete the data corresponding to a vertex v, we must securely delete data corresponding to all ancestors of v that are not already securely deleted. This is burdensome if it requires a full graph traversal, because the adversary's key disclosure graph perpetually grows. We make this efficient by establishing an invariant of the adversary's key disclosure graph: there is at most one path between every pair of vertices (i.e., it is a mangrove). We now define a family of graph mutations that preserves this invariant.

4.4 Shadowing Graph Mutations

Shadowing is a concept in data structures where updates to elements do not occur in-place. Instead, a new copy of the element is made and references in its parent are updated to reflect this [19]. This results in a new copy of the parent, propagating shadowing to the head of the data structure. We now define a generalized graph mutation, called a *shadowing graph mutation*, and show that if any shadowing graph mutation is applied to a mangrove, then the resulting *mutated graph* is also a mangrove. The mangrove property is therefore maintained throughout all possible histories of shadowing graph mutations.

Mangroves have at most one possible path between every pair of vertices. This simplifies secure deletion of data, as illustrated in Figure 5. Computing the set of all ancestors of a vertex—those vertices that must be also securely deleted—is done by taking the union of the unique paths to that vertex from each of the vertices whose corresponding keys are locally stored by the user. Determining the *unique* path to follow to find data is trivial by overlaying a search-tree data structure (e.g., a B-Tree). Moreover, if the user only stores one local key at any time, taking care to securely delete old keys, then data can be securely deleted by just securely deleting the vertices on a single path in the key disclosure graph.

Figure 5 shows an example mutation, where the old key disclosure graph G is combined with G_S and the edges $\hat{e}_1, \hat{e}_2$ to form the new key disclosure graph G'. The new nodes and edges correspond to the user generating new random keys and sending wrapped keys to the adversary, respectively.

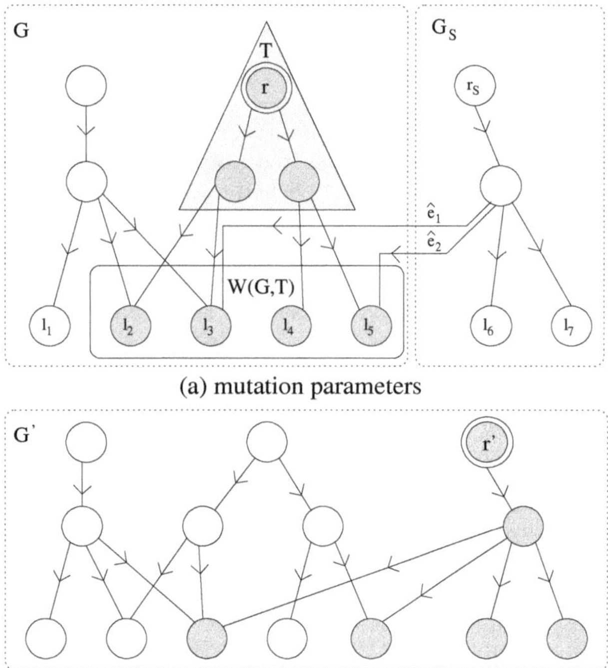

(a) mutation parameters

(b) post–mutated graph

Figure 5: An example shadowing mutation. (a) shows the parameters of a shadowing graph mutation and (b) shows the resulting graph. The pre-mutated graph G is combined with the shadowing graph G_S and connecting edges $\hat{E} = \{\hat{e}_1, \hat{e}_2\}$ to form G'. Shaded vertices are the vertices reachable from the circled vertex.

The node r represents the user's current stored secret key; the shaded nodes are r's descendants—those nodes whose corresponding keys are computable by the user. In the resulting graph G', we see that r' corresponds to the new user secret, resulting in a different set of shaded descendant vertices. In particular, the mutation securely deleted the leaves l_2 and l_4 while adding new leaves l_6 and l_7.

To perform the mutation, the user prepares T—a graph that contains the vertices to shadow. In the post-mutated graph G', no vertex in T is reachable from any vertex in G_S. The only vertices in G that are given a new incoming edge from a vertex in G_S are those in the set $W(G,T)$: vertices outside T but that have an incoming edge from a vertex in T. Formally, if G is a mangrove, $r \in V(G)$, and T is an arborescent subdigraph of G_r diverging from r, then $W(G,T) = \{v \in V(G) \setminus V(T) | \exists\, x \in V(T) \,.\, (x,v) \in E(G)\}$.

To ensure that G' is a mangrove, we must constrain the edges that connect G_S to G. We require that any connecting edge $\hat{e}$ goes from G_S to $W(G,T)$ and that each vertex in $W(G,T)$ receives at most one such incoming edge.

Formally, a tuple $(G, r, G_S, T, \hat{E})$ is a *shadowing graph mutation* if it has the following properties:

— G is a mangrove, called the *pre-mutated graph*.

— r is a vertex of G.

— G_S is an arborescence diverging from r_S such that $V(G) \cap V(G_S) = \emptyset$. It is called the *shadow graph*.

— T is a subdigraph of G_r such that T is an arborescence diverging from r. It is called the *shadowed graph*.

— $\hat{E}$ is a set of directed edges such that
(i) $\forall (i,j) \in \hat{E} \,.\, i \in V(G_S) \wedge j \in W(G,T)$ and
(ii) $\forall (i,j)(i',j') \in \hat{E} \,.\, i \neq i' \Rightarrow j \neq j'$ (i.e., $\hat{E}$ is injective).

A graph mutation contains the initial graph along with the parameters of the mutation. We assume there exists a function μ that takes as input a graph mutation $(G, r, G_S, T, \hat{E})$ and outputs the mutated graph G', defined by $V(G') \leftarrow V(G) \cup V(G_S)$ and $E(G') \leftarrow E(G) \cup E(G_S) \cup \hat{E}$. Observe that the sets in the unions are all disjoint. Moreover, every resulting path in G' has one of the following forms: P, P_S, or $(P_S, \hat{e}, P)$, where P is a path visiting only vertices in $V(G)$, P_S is a path visiting only vertices in $V(G_S)$, and $\hat{e} \in \hat{E}$.

Mangrove Preservation.

To simplify the enumeration of a vertex's ancestors in the key disclosure graph, which must be securely deleted in order to delete that vertex, we require as an invariant that the key disclosure graph is always a mangrove. We establish this by showing that, given a shadowing graph mutation, the mutated graph is always a mangrove. Since the graph with a single vertex is a mangrove, all sequences of shadowing mutations beginning from this mangrove preserve this property.

LEMMA 1. *Let G be a mangrove, $r \in V(G)$, and T an arborescent subdigraph of G_r diverging from r. Then $\forall i,j \in W(G,T), i \neq j \Rightarrow desc_G(i) \cap desc_G(j) = \emptyset$.*

PROOF. We prove the contrapositive. Suppose that $v \in \text{desc}_G(i) \cap \text{desc}_G(j)$. Then there exist distinct paths P^i_v and P^j_v. Since $i,j \in V(G_r)$, there exist distinct paths P^r_i and P^r_j. Consequently, $P^r_i P^i_v$ and $P^r_j P^j_v$ are two paths from r to v in G_r. Since G_r is an arborescence, these two paths must be equal and so (without loss of generality) $P^r_v = P^r_i P^i_j P^j_v$ and $P^r_j = P^r_i P^i_j$. However, by definition of $W(G,T)$, all edges except the final one in P^r_i and P^r_j are in $E(T)$. If P^i_j is non-degenerate, then $P^r_i P^i_j \neq P^r_j$ as P^r_i has an edge outside of T followed by more than one edge. Therefore, P^i_j is degenerate and $i = j$, as needed. □

LEMMA 2. *If $(G, r, G_S, T, \hat{E})$ is a valid shadowing mutation and $G' \leftarrow \mu(G, r, G_S, T, \hat{E})$, then G' is acyclic.*

PROOF. Since the mutation is valid, G is a mangrove. Suppose to the contrary that G' has a cycle C. By construction of $V(G')$, there are three cases:
(i) All of C's vertices are in $V(G)$. Then C is a cycle in G, which contradicts G being a mangrove.
(ii) All of C's vertices are in $V(G_S)$. Then C is a cycle in G_S, which contradicts G_S being an arborescence.
(iii) C's vertices are a mixture of vertices from $V(G)$ and $V(G_S)$. Suppose C visits $v \in V(G)$ and $u \in V(G_S)$. Then C can be divided into two paths $C = P^v_u P^u_v$, but no such path P^v_u exists. □

THEOREM 1. *If $(G, r, G_S, T, \hat{E})$ is a valid shadowing mutation and $G' \leftarrow \mu(G, r, G_S, T, \hat{E})$, then G' is a mangrove.*

PROOF. By the definition of a mangrove, we must show that all vertices in G' induce arborescences. Suppose to the contrary that there is some $r \in V(G')$ such that G'_r is not an arborescence. Then (at least) one of the three necessary and sufficient conditions of an arborescent graph is violated: (i) G'_r is not acyclic. This implies that G' is not acyclic,

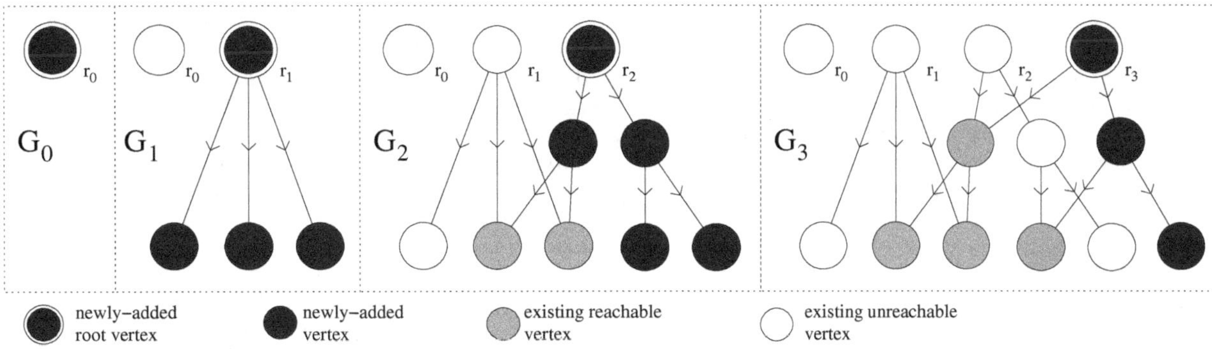

Figure 6: Example key disclosure graph evolving due to a shadowing graph mutation chain. All graphs except G_0 result from applying a shadowing graph mutation on the previous graph. Black nodes are ones added by the most recent mutation with the root node circled; grey nodes are ones from the previous graph that are still reachable from the new root; white nodes are ones from the previous graph that are no longer reachable.

which contradicts Lemma 2.
(ii) The indegree of $r \neq 0$. Then r must have at least one incoming edge, from a vertex v. This results in a cycle, since v is reachable from r by construction of the induced graph G'_r, also contradicting Lemma 2.
(iii) There is some $v \in V(G'_r)$ such that $v \neq r$ and indegree of $v \neq 1$.

As the first two conditions lead to immediate contradictions, we assume that the final condition is violated. Moreover, since v is a vertex on an induced graph, there is a path from r to v and thus v must have at least one incoming edge and therefore the indegree of $v \geq 2$. By the induced graph G'_v's construction, both parents of v are reachable from r, and so there are two distinct paths P^r_v and Q^r_v in G' from r to v. We have two cases: either $r \in V(G)$ or $r \in V(G_S)$.

Suppose that $r \in V(G)$, and so all vertices of P^r_v and Q^r_v are elements of $V(G)$. Also, by construction, $E(G')|_{V(G)\times V(G)} = E(G)$, and thus all edges of P^r_v and Q^r_v are elements of $E(G)$. Therefore, P^r_v and Q^r_v are distinct paths from r to v in G, contradicting G being a mangrove.

Now suppose that $r \in V(G_S)$. If $v \in V(G_S)$, then P^r_v and Q^r_v are distinct paths entirely in G_S, which contradicts G_S being an arborescence. So $r \in V(G_S)$ and $v \in V(G)$. We decompose the paths as follows: $P^r_v = P^r_u, (u, w), P^w_v$ and $Q^r_x, (x, y), Q^y_v$, where (u, w) and (x, y) are elements of $\hat{E}$. We know that $P^r_v \neq Q^r_v$, and so there are four different cases based on the edge in $\hat{E}$:
(i) If $(u, w) = (x, y)$, i.e., both paths cross from G_S to G over the same edge in $\hat{E}$, then the two paths must differ elsewhere. Either $P^r_u \neq Q^r_x$ or $P^w_v \neq Q^w_v$. As we have seen before, however, this contradicts either G_S being an arborescence or G being a mangrove respectively.
(ii) If $u \neq x$ and $w = y$, then (u, w) and (x, w) are distinct edges in $\hat{E}$, a violation of its construction. This contradicts $(G, r, G_S, T, \hat{E})$ being a valid shadowing mutation.
(iii), (iv) If $w \neq y$ then we have distinct paths P^w_v and Q^y_v in G. Since both paths terminate at the same vertex, either w or y is the ancestor of one of the other's descendants. This contradicts Lemma 1.

In conclusion, such distinct paths P^r_v and Q^r_v cannot exist. Therefore, for all $r \in V(G')$, G'_r is an arborescence and so G' is a mangrove. □

Shadowing Graph Mutation Chains.

Definition 2 tells us that we can achieve secure deletion with appropriate constraints on the shape of the key disclosure graph. We now show that performing a natural sequence of shadowing graph mutations satisfies these constraints, effecting simple secure deletion.

Definition 3. A *shadowing graph mutation chain* is a sequence of shadowing graph mutations $\mathcal{M} = (M_0, \ldots, M_p)$ such that: (i) $M_i = (G_i, r_i, G_{S,i}, T_i, \hat{E}_i)$, (ii) $G_0 = (\{\phi(0)\}, \emptyset)$, (iii) $r_0 = \phi(0)$, (iv) $\forall i > 0 \;.\; G_i = \mu(M_{i-1})$, and (v) $\forall i > 0 \;.\; r_i = r_{S,i-1}$.

A shadowing graph mutation chain describes a sequence of mutations applied on a key disclosure graph. Figure 6 shows an example key disclosure graph evolution as the result of three mutations. Each mutation in the chain is applied on the graph that results from the previous mutation, except for the base case. Observe that r_i—the root vertex in T_i—is always $r_{S,i-1}$ the root vertex added by the shadowing graph in the previous mutation (or the 'zero' key for the base of recursion).

We now prove our main result about the interplay of secure deletion and shadowing graph mutation chains. For convenience, given $M = (G, r, G_S, T, \hat{E})$, we say that a vertex $v \in V(G)$ is reachable in M if there exists a path from r to v in G.

LEMMA 3. *Given a shadowing graph mutation chain $\mathcal{M} = (M_0, \ldots, M_p)$, any vertex v first reachable in M_i and last reachable in M_{i+k} $(k \geq 0)$ is reachable in all intermediate mutations $M_{i+1}, \ldots, M_{i+k-1}$.*

PROOF. Suppose to the contrary that there exists a j, $i < j < i + k$, such that v is not reachable in M_j. By construction of shadowing graph mutations, $v \in V(G_i) \Rightarrow v \in V(G_j) \Rightarrow v \notin V(G_{S,j})$. Select the largest such j, so that v is reachable in M_{j+1}, and so there exists a path $P^{r_{j+1}}_v$ in G_{j+1}. Since $r_{j+1} \in V(G_{S,i})$ and $v \notin V(G_{S,i})$, such a path has the form $P^{r_{j+1}}_{\hat{e}}(\hat{e}, \hat{e}')P^{\hat{e}'}_v$ where $(\hat{e}, \hat{e}') \in \hat{E}_j$ and $P^{\hat{e}'}_v$ is a path in G_j. Then $\hat{e}' \in W(G_j, T_j)$ and so $P^{r_j}_{\hat{e}'}$ is a path in G_j, implying that $P^{r_j}_{\hat{e}'}P^{\hat{e}'}_v$ is a path from r_j to v in G_j, a contradiction. □

Lemma 3 tells us that, when building shadowing graph mutation chains as described, once some reachable vertex becomes unreachable then it remains permanently unreachable. Secure data deletion is achieved by a single mutation that makes the corresponding vertex unreachable from the new root. We now prove our final result on achieving secure deletion with shadowing graph mutation chains.

THEOREM 2. *Let $\mathcal{M} = (M_0, \ldots, M_p)$ be a shadowing graph mutation chain with resulting key disclosure graph $G = \mu(M_p)$. Let $T = (t_0, \ldots, t_p)$ be the (strictly-increasing) sequence of timestamps such that at time t_i*
(i) $\mu(M_i)$ is performed,
(ii) the value $k_{i+1} = \phi^{-1}(r_{i+1})$ is stored in the securely-deleting memory, and
(iii) all previous values stored are securely deleted.
Let D be data encrypted with the key k whose corresponding vertex $v = \phi(k)$ is reachable only in $M_i, \ldots, M_{i+l}$. Then D's lifetime is bounded by t_i and t_{i+l}, and D is securely deleted provided no compromise occurs during this time.

PROOF. The proof is by establishing the premises required for Definition 2. First, $R = \{k_0, \ldots, k_p\}$ and $R_{\text{live}} = \{k_i, \ldots, k_{i+l}\}$ which means that $R_{\text{dead}} = \{k_0, \ldots, k_{i-1}\} \cup \{k_{i+l+1}, \ldots, k_p\}$. Because no compromise occurs from time t_i until t_{i+l}, to apply Definition 2 we must only show that for all $k_j \in R_{\text{dead}}$, there is no path from $\phi(k_j)$ to v in $G = \mu(M_p)$.

Assume to the contrary that there is a $k_j = \phi^{-1}(r_j) \in R_{\text{dead}}$ such that there is a path $P_v^{r_j}$ in $G = \mu(M_p)$. Since v is unreachable in M_j, $P_v^{r_j}$ is not a path in G_j. So there must be an edge (u, v) on $P_v^{r_j}$ such that $u \in V(G_j), (u, v) \in E(G)$, and $(u, v) \notin E(G_j)$. Then $\exists m \geq 0 : (u, v) \notin E(G_{j+m}) \wedge (u, v) \in E(\mu(M_{j+m}))$, that is, some mutation adds (u, v) to the key disclosure graph. By construction, $E(\mu(M_{j+m})) = E(G_{j+m}) \cup E(G_{S,j+m}) \cup \hat{E}_{j+m}$, and since $u \notin V(G_{S,j+m}) \Rightarrow (u, v) \in E(G_{j+m})$, a contradiction. Definition 2 therefore tells us that D is securely deleted. □

5. IMPLEMENTATION DETAILS

We have implemented our B-Tree-based solution. We use Linux's network block device (**nbd**), which allows a listening TCP socket to receive and reply to block device I/O requests. In our case, we have our implementation listening on that TCP socket. The **nbd-client** program and **nbd** kernel module—required to connect a device to our implementation and format/mount the resulting device—remain unchanged, ensuring that no modifications to the operating system are required to use our solution. Our implementation includes the encrypted B-Tree as described in Section 3 and interacts with a variety of user-configurable storage backends. Our implementation is written in C++11 and is freely available with a GPL version 2 license.

Data Storage.

Our solution assumes the user somehow divides the data into data units indexed by a handle for storage. There are different ways this can be implemented. Trivially, a key-value storage system can be built where values are binary large objects (blobs) of data, and keys reference this data. The blobs can be entire files, components of files, etc. This allows our solution to implement a simple object storage device (OSD) [14]. If each blob is uniquely indexed by the B-Tree, then modifying the blob requires re-encrypting it entirely with a new key and updating its reference in the B-Tree. This inhibits the ability to efficiently securely delete data from large files such as databases.

Alternatively, data can be divided into fixed-size blocks indexed by the B-Tree. This facilitates random updates as only a fixed-size block must be updated to make any change to data. This is the construction we use in our implementation: a virtual array of data is indexed by offsets of fixed-size blocks and exposed as a block-device interface. This block-device can then be formatted as any block-based file system, which is then overlaid on the B-Tree. Sparse areas of the file system then do not appear as keys in the B-Tree; if written to, the corresponding keys are added to the B-Tree.

Network Block Device.

The network block device is a block device offered by Linux. It behaves as a normal block device that can be formatted with any block-based file system and mounted for use. However, it is actually a virtual block device that forwards all block operations over TCP (i.e., reading and writing blocks, as well as trim and flush commands). The listening user-space program is responsible for actually implementing the block device.

Virtual Storage Device.

While the default **nbd-server** program simply serves a local file as a block device, we wrote our own implementation of a virtual block device that interfaces with a variety of back-end storage media. The reading and writing of blocks pass through our shadowing B-Tree implementation. It uses block addresses as indices in the B-Tree; the data's remote storage location in that block address is kept in the leaves of the B-Tree. The user selects how the resulting data is stored, including data blocks for nodes and data (persistent medium) as well as the master key and integrity hash (securely-deleting medium).

6. EXPERIMENTAL EVALUATION

In this section, we evaluate the performance of the B-Tree under different workloads and investigate how the performance can be improved through different caching strategies.

Workloads.

We test our implementation's performance on a variety of different file system workloads. We used the **filebench** utility [12] to generate three workloads and we also created our own workload by replaying our research group's version control history. We used filebench's **directio** mode to ensure that all reads and writes are sent directly to the block device and not served by any file system page cache; similarly, we synchronized the file system and flushed all file system buffers after each version update in our version control workload. The workloads we use are summarized as follows:
—**sequential** writes a 25 GiB file and then reads it contiguously. This tests the behaviour when copying very large files to and from storage.
—**random_1KiB** performs random 1 KiB reads and writes on a pre-written 25 GiB file. This tests the performance for a near-worst-case scenario: reads and writes without any temporal or spatial locality.
—**random_1MiB** performs random 1 MiB reads and writes on a pre-written 25 GiB file. This tests the performance for

Workload	block size	Cache size: 5			Cache size: 10			Cache size: 20			Cache size: 50		
		LRU	LFU	Belady	LRU	LFU	Belady	LRU	LFU	Belady	LRU	LFU	Belady
sequential	1 KiB	0.06	47.3	81.4	98.1	60.8	97.9	98.3	70.1	98.1	99.1	74.7	99
	16 KiB	99.6	43.2	99.7	99.7	56.6	99.8	99.7	83.3	99.8	99.8	99.5	99.8
random (1KiB)	1 KiB	0.0023	12.2	15.9	11.8	15.3	19.8	15.6	21.3	25	26.4	26.3	33.5
	16 KiB	47.3	32.2	52.2	49.3	40.1	58.2	53.6	56	64.5	63.4	67.2	70.3
random (1MiB)	1 KiB	0.0068	21.5	82.1	97.5	25.4	97.7	97.7	31.6	97.8	97.9	38	98
	16 KiB	98.1	50.5	98.5	98.6	62.6	98.7	98.7	85.2	99	98.9	98.3	99.1
svn	1 KiB	95	35	95.6	96	47.2	96.1	96.5	57.1	96.9	97.1	75.9	97.4
	16 KiB	97.2	68.7	97.7	97.8	81.2	97.8	98.2	88	98.2	98.6	96.2	99

Table 1: Caching Hit Ratio (%) for B-Tree Nodes

random access patterns with a larger block size that provides some spatial locality in accessed data.

—`svn` replays 25 GiB of our research group's version control history by iteratively checking out each version. This test provides an example of a realistic usage scenario for data being stored on a shared persistent storage medium.

We run our implementation behind an `nbd` virtual block device, formatted with the `ext2` file system. We mount the file system with the `discard` option to ensure that the file system identifies deleted blocks through TRIM commands.

Caching.

We experimentally determine the effect of the skeleton tree's cache size and eviction strategy. Using the sequence of block requests characteristic of each workload, we use our B-Tree implementation to output a sequence of B-Tree node requests. A B-Tree node request occurs whenever the skeleton tree visits a node; missing nodes must be fetched from the persistent medium and correspond to cache misses. Observe that for the same workload, the sequence of node requests will vary depending on the B-Tree's block size. We output one B-Tree node request sequence for each block size that we test. With this sequence of node requests, we then simulate various cache sizes and caching behaviours.

We test three different strategies: Bélády's optimal "clairvoyant" strategy [1], least recently used (LRU), and least frequently used (LFU). Bélády's strategy is included as an objective reference point to compare caching strategies. We only maintain cache usage statistics for items currently in the cache.

The results of our experiment are shown in Table 1. We observe that caching nodes is generally quite successful; many of the workloads and configurations have very high hit ratios. This is because contiguous ranges of block address tend to share paths in the B-Tree. Consequently, the cache size itself is not so important; provided it is sufficiently large to hold a complete path then sequential access occurs rapidly.

LRU is generally preferable to LFU. The only exception is very small random writes with a small block size. This is because such writes have no temporal locality and so the frequency-based metric better captures which nodes contain useful data. For random-access patterns, the cache size is far more important than the eviction strategy, a feature also observable from Bélády's optimal strategy. For any form of sequential access, LRU outperforms LFU because LFU unfairly evicts newly cached nodes, which may currently have few visits but are visited frequently after their first caching. We see that LRU often approaches Bélády's optimal strategy, implying that more complicated strategies offer limited potential for improvement.

		B-Tree block size			
		4 KiB	16 KiB	64 KiB	256 KiB
general	total data blocks	6553600	1638400	409600	102400
	tree height	5	3	2	2
	cache size (nodes)	2048	512	128	32
	MiBs sharing path	0.16	2.65	42.6	682.5
sequent.	cache hits (%)	99.3	99.7	99.9	1
	storage overhead (%)	2.4	0.6	0.1	0.03
	comm overhead (%)	2.4	0.6	0.1	0.03
	block size ovrhd (%)	0	5.3	26.3	58.1
rand 1k	cache hits (%)	64.7	59	43.2	73.8
	storage overhead (%)	2.4	0.6	0.1	0.03
	comm overhead (%)	1308.5	3129	8623.5	20671.4
	block size ovrhd (%)	497.9	2293.2	9473	38191.8
rand 1m	cache hits (%)	99.2	98.9	96.5	95.5
	storage overhead (%)	2.47	0.59	0.14	0.03
	comm overhead (%)	4.9	3.7	7.8	17.7
	block size ovrhd (%)	1	7.7	34.6	82.1
svn	cache hits (%)	99.2	98.9	96.5	95.5
	storage overhead (%)	1.74	0.42	0.1	0.02
	comm overhead (%)	4.4	4.9	5.4	2.6
	block size ovrhd (%)	0	63.4	247.9	750.2

Table 2: B-Tree Secure Deletion Overhead

B-Tree Properties.

We investigate our system's overhead with regards to the fetching and storing of nodes that index the data. We now characterize this with regards to different workloads and parameters, expressing the results with the following metrics:

—Cache hits: percentage of B-Tree node visits that do not require fetching.

—Storage overhead: ratio of node storage size to data storage expressed as a percentage.

—Communication overhead: ratio of the persistent medium's communication for fetching and storing nodes compared to the sum of useful data read and written, expressed as a percentage.

—Block size overhead: ratio of additional network traffic (beyond the I/O) for fetching and storing data compared to the sum of data read and written by the file system, expressed as a percentage. (This is based only on the block size / workload and is independent of the use of the secure deletion B-Tree.)

Additionally, we characterize the following B-Tree properties common to all workloads:

—Total data blocks: 25 GiB divided by the block size.

—Tree height: the height of the B-Tree that indexes the number of data blocks.

—Cache size (nodes): the fixed cache size of 8 MiB expressed as nodes that fit into that capacity.

—MiBs sharing path: the size of contiguous data whose blocks all share a unique path, that is, how much data is indexed by a single leaf node.

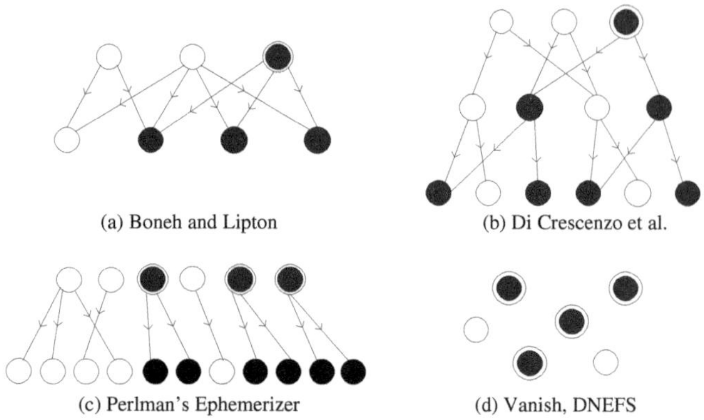

(a) Boneh and Lipton (b) Di Crescenzo et al.

(c) Perlman's Ephemerizer (d) Vanish, DNEFS

Figure 7: Mangrove key disclosure graphs for related work. Circled nodes represent the current key(s) stored in the securely-deleting medium, and shaded nodes represent the keys the adversary would gain with a coercive attack.

Table 2 shows the results of our experiments. We see that in all cases the storage overhead of the B-Tree nodes is a few percent and decreases with the block size. In all workloads except `random_1KiB`, the communication overhead is also reasonable. Large block sizes most benefit sequential access patterns, because a large block size means more sequential data can be accessed without fetching new nodes (e.g., using a block size of 256 KiB results in half a GiB of data indexed by the same path in the B-Tree). Degenerate performance is observed for our worst-case workload: where data blocks are accessed in a completely random fashion without any spatial or temporal locality. Even the block size overhead resulting from fetching unnecessary data shows a large amount of waste, and we conclude that further engineering effort is needed to optimize this use case.

7. RELATED WORK

Secure deletion has been studied in a variety of contexts and has also been extensively surveyed [7, 9, 17]. Moreover, a variety of work considers secure deletion in the context of mixed-media storage devices consisting of a small securely-deleting medium and a large persistent medium [2, 6, 10, 16, 18]. In this section we discuss these works and, when relevant, describe their corresponding key disclosure graphs. For these cases, the update mechanism is a shadowing graph mutation and the resulting key disclosure graph is a mangrove. Hence, we can apply our secure deletion proof to these works as well as our own. Figure 7 shows an example key disclosure graph for each of these works and shows which vertices would be revealed if a coercive attack occurred.

Boneh and Lipton's original use of cryptography to securely delete data considered an off-line large-capacity tape archive and a local low-capacity computer. Data for archiving is encrypted with a random key and the key is added to a list of valid keys. Each key on the list is encrypted with a master key that is periodically randomly regenerated; the new master key is used to re-encrypt the list of valid keys. The master key is then stored locally and securely—the authors propose floppy disks or writing the master key down on paper—such that it can be securely deleted. Data is deleted by removing its corresponding key from the key list and waiting until the next time the master key is regenerated. This scheme's corresponding key disclosure graph is illustrated in Figure 7 (a); it is a mangrove with a maximum path length of one.

Di Crescenzo et al.'s work explicitly assumes a large persistent medium and a small securely-deleting medium. They divide a fixed-size persistent medium into numbered blocks, which are indexed by a pre-allocated binary tree. The keys to decrypt data are stored in the leaves and the tree's internal nodes store the keys to decrypt the children. The root key is stored in a securely-deleting medium. Each change to a data block indexed by the binary tree results in a new key stored in a leaf node and all nodes on the path to the root are rekeyed. This scheme's corresponding key disclosure graph is also a mangrove and is illustrated in Figure 7 (b).

Perlman's Ephemerizer aims to make communication reliably unrecoverable after an expiration time [16]. Exchanged messages are encrypted using ephemeral keys with a predetermined lifetime. Secure deletion is used to ensure keys are irrecoverable after they expire. Perlman's scheme uses a trusted third party—the Ephemerizer—to manage the ephemeral keys and ensure their irrecoverability after expiration. Each message is encrypted with a random key, which is then blinded and sent to the Ephemerizer along with the desired message lifetime. The Ephemerizer encrypts the message key with a corresponding ephemeral key based on the desired lifetime. The message encrypted with the random key, along with the random key encrypted with the ephemeral key, are sent as the message. The recipient uses the Ephemerizer, with blinding, to determine the message key. Once the ephemeral key expires, the Ephemerizer no longer possesses it and is therefore unable to decrypt any keys wrapped with it. In this scheme, the Ephemerizer acts as the securely-deleting medium and the communication channel, being vulnerable to eavesdroppers, is the persistent storage. The resulting key disclosure graph, illustrated in Figure 7 (c) is a mangrove similar to Figure 7 (a) except that there are multiple keys stored in the securely-deleting medium, one key for each future expiration time.

Tang et al.'s Fade extends Perlman's Ephemerizer [20] by explicitly considering cloud storage as the persistent medium and by offering more expressive deletion policies than expiration dates. An Ephemerizer-like entity acts as the securely-deleting medium, but each key that it manages reflects a specific policy that can expire or be revoked. Policies are defined as boolean expressions of attributes.

Cachin et al.'s work also offers policy-based secure deletion with a more expressive policy language [4]. Their system builds a policy graph mapping attributes to policies. Each node is a configurable threshold cryptographic operator; logical 'or' and 'and' are then just special cases. Cachin et al.'s approach assumes a securely-deleting medium to store master keys, and can be implemented in a variety of ways with different retrieval complexities and storage costs.

In both Tang et al. and Cachin et al., data is deleted at the *granularity* of an entire policy, defined as boolean expressions. For instance, one policy may say that *data is not securely deleted* if *its expiration time has not elapsed* and *it has not been specifically redacted.* Each conjunct is associated with a key, both of which are needed to decrypt the message. To achieve this, Tang et al. uses nested key wrapping while Cachin et al. uses threshold cryptography. Consequently, we cannot directly apply our work to these schemes and leave the characterization of the key disclosure graph for these cryptographic concepts as future work.

Geambasu et al.'s Vanish is designed for erasable communication on the Internet [10]. Messages are encrypted with a unique key and published on the Internet (i.e., the persistent medium). Encryption keys are split into shares that are also stored on the Internet in a distributed hash table. The security of their scheme relies on the nodes in the distributed hash table implementing the securely-deleting medium: it requires—albeit contentiously [22]—that the nodes periodically delete the data and that the adversary is overwhelmed by the scale of the distributed hash table to effectively copy all the data therein. As their scheme does not use key wrapping, the corresponding key disclosure graph is trivially a mangrove as it lacks edges (Figure 7 (d)).

Reardon et al.'s data node encrypted file system [18] is designed for flash memory, for which data deletion is an expensive deletion operation. They divide the memory into two areas: a small securely-deleting key storage area and a large main storage which they assume to be persistent. Each atomic unit of data in main storage is encrypted with a unique key from the key storage area. The efficiency of this approach comes from colocating and compressing the key storage area thereby reducing secure deletion's cost. Like Vanish, their scheme does not use key wrapping and so the key disclosure graph is also a mangrove.

8. CONCLUSIONS

We developed a general approach to the design and analysis of secure deletion from persistent media. We used graph theory to reason about adversarial knowledge and developed a graph mutation that maintains properties on adversarial knowledge that allows straightforward provable secure deletion. Our mutation subsumes the update behaviour of all arborescent data structures. We designed and implemented a securely-deleting B-Tree based on this mutation. Our analysis showed that the communication and storage overhead is typically negligible and the skeleton tree's caching of B-Tree nodes is very effective.

9. ACKNOWLEDGMENTS

This work was partially supported by the Zurich Information Security Center and by the SNF grant Sinergia Project No. CRSII2_136318/1. It represents the views of the authors. We would like to thank our anonymous reviewers as well as Roberto Di Pietro, Thomas Themel, and Nils Ole Tippenhauer for their helpful comments.

10. REFERENCES

[1] Laszlo A. Bélády. A study of replacement algorithms for virtual-storage computer. *IBM Systems Journal*, 5(2):78–101, 1966.

[2] Dan Boneh and Richard J. Lipton. A Revocable Backup System. In *USENIX Security Symposium*, pages 91–96, 1996.

[3] Nikita Borisov, Ian Goldberg, and Eric Brewer. Off-the-record communication, or, why not to use PGP. In *ACM workshop on Privacy in the electronic society*, pages 77–84, 2004.

[4] Christian Cachin, Kristiyan Haralambiev, Hsu-Chun Hsiao, and Alessandro Sorniotti. Policy-based Secure Deletion. Cryptology ePrint Archive, Report 152, 2013.

[5] Douglas Comer. The ubiquitous B-tree. *ACM Computing Surveys*, 11:121–137, 1979.

[6] Giovanni Di Crescenzo, Niels Ferguson, Russell Impagliazzo, and Markus Jakobsson. How to Forget a Secret. In *STACS*, Lecture Notes in Computer Science, pages 500–509. Springer, 1999.

[7] Sarah M. Diesburg and An-I Andy Wang. A survey of confidential data storage and deletion methods. *ACM Computing Surveys*, 43(1):1–37, 2010.

[8] Ronald Fagin, Jurg Nievergelt, Nicholas Pippenger, and H. Raymond Strong. Extendible hashing—a fast access method for dynamic files. *ACM Trans. Database Syst.*, 4(3):315–344, 1979.

[9] Simson Garfinkel and Abhi Shelat. Remembrance of Data Passed: A Study of Disk Sanitization Practices. *IEEE Security & Privacy*, pages 17–27, January 2003.

[10] Roxana Geambasu, Tadayoshi Kohno, Amit A. Levy, and Henry M. Levy. Vanish: increasing data privacy with self-destructing data. In *USENIX Security Symposium*, pages 299–316, 2009.

[11] Peter Gutmann. Secure Deletion of Data from Magnetic and Solid-State Memory. In *USENIX Security Symposium*, pages 77–89, 1996.

[12] McDougall, R. and Mauro, J. FileBench. www.solarisinternals.com/si/tools/filebench/, 2005.

[13] Ralph C. Merkle. A certified digital signature. In *Proceedings on Advances in Cryptology*, CRYPTO '89, pages 218–238. Springer-Verlag New York, Inc., 1989.

[14] Mike Mesnier, Gregory R. Ganger, and Erik Riedel. Object-Based Storage. *Communications Magazine, IEEE*, 41(8):84–90, 2003.

[15] Einar Mykletun, Maithili Narasimha, and Gene Tsudik. Providing authentication and integrity in outsourced databases using Merkle hash trees. Technical report, University of California Irvine, 2003.

[16] Radia Perlman. The Ephemerizer: Making Data Disappear. Technical report, Sun Microsystems, 2005.

[17] Joel Reardon, David Basin, and Srdjan Capkun. SoK: Secure Data Deletion. In *IEEE Symposium on Security and Privacy*, 2013.

[18] Joel Reardon, Srdjan Capkun, and David Basin. Data Node Encrypted File System: Efficient Secure Deletion for Flash Memory. In *USENIX Security Symposium*, pages 333–348, 2012.

[19] Ohad Rodeh. B-trees, shadowing, and clones. *Trans. Storage*, 3(4):2:1–2:27, 2008.

[20] Yang Tang, Patrick P. C. Lee, John C. S. Lui, and Radia Perlman. FADE: Secure Overlay Cloud Storage with File Assured Deletion. In *SecureComm*, pages 380–397, 2010.

[21] W. T. Tutte. *Graph Theory*. Encyclopedia of Mathematics and its Applications. Addison-Wesley Publishing Company, 1984.

[22] Scott Wolchok, Owen S. Hoffman, Nadia Henninger, Edward W. Felten, J. Alex Haldermann, Christopher J. Rossback, Brent Waters, and Emmet Witchel. Defeating Vanish with Low-Cost Sybil Attacks Against Large DHTs. In *Proc. 17th Network and Distributed System Security Symposium*, 2010.

PoWerStore: Proofs of Writing for Efficient and Robust Storage

Dan Dobre[1] Ghassan O. Karame[1] Wenting Li[1] Matthias Majuntke[2] Neeraj Suri[3] Marko Vukolić[4]

[1]NEC Laboratories Europe
Heidelberg, 69115, Germany
{dan.dobre, ghassan.karame, wenting.li}@neclab.eu

[2]Capgemini Deutschland
Berlin, 10785, Germany
matthias.majuntke@capgemini.com

[3]TU Darmstadt
Darmstadt, 64289, Germany
suri@cs.tu-darmstadt.de

[4]EURECOM
Biot, 06410, France
vukolic@eurecom.fr

ABSTRACT

Existing Byzantine fault tolerant (BFT) storage solutions that achieve strong consistency and high availability, are costly compared to solutions that tolerate simple crashes. This cost is one of the main obstacles in deploying BFT storage in practice.

In this paper, we present PoWerStore, a robust and efficient data storage protocol. PoWerStore's robustness comprises tolerating network outages, maximum number of Byzantine storage servers, any number of Byzantine readers and crash-faulty writers, and guaranteeing high availability (wait-freedom) and strong consistency (linearizability) of read-/write operations. PoWerStore's efficiency stems from combining lightweight cryptography, erasure coding and metadata write-backs, where readers write-back only metadata to achieve strong consistency. Central to PoWerStore is the concept of "Proofs of Writing" (PoW), a novel data storage technique inspired by commitment schemes. PoW rely on a 2-round write procedure, in which the first round writes the actual data and the second round only serves to "prove" the occurrence of the first round. PoW enable efficient implementations of strongly consistent BFT storage through metadata write-backs and low latency reads.

We implemented PoWerStore and show its improved performance when compared to existing robust storage protocols, including protocols that tolerate only crash faults.

Categories and Subject Descriptors

D.4.5 [**Operating Systems**]: Reliability – Fault tolerance.

Keywords

Byzantine-Fault Tolerance; Secure Distributed Storage; Strong Consistency.

CCS'13, November 4–8, 2013, Berlin, Germany.

http://dx.doi.org/10.1145/2508859.2516750.

1. INTRODUCTION

Byzantine fault-tolerant (BFT) distributed protocols have attracted considerable research attention, due to their appealing promise of masking various system issues ranging from simple crashes, through software bugs and misconfigurations, all the way to intrusions and malware. However, the use of existing BFT protocols is questionable in practice due to, e.g., weak guarantees under failures [41] or high cost in performance and deployment compared to *crash-tolerant* protocols [27]. This can help us derive the following requirements for the design of future BFT protocols:

- A BFT protocol should be *robust*, i.e., it should tolerate Byzantine faults and *asynchrony* (modeling network outages) while maintaining correctness (data consistency) and providing sustainable progress (availability) even under *worst-case* conditions that still meet the protocol assumptions. This requirement has often been neglected in BFT protocols that focus primarily on *common*, failure-free operation modes (e.g., [22]).

- Such a *robust* protocol should be *efficient*. For example, virtually all BFT protocols resort to *data write-backs*, in which a reader must ensure that a value it is about to return is propagated to a sufficient number of servers before a read completes—effectively, this entails repeating a write after a read [5] and results in performance deterioration. We believe that the efficiency of a robust BFT protocol is best compared to the efficiency of its crash-tolerant counterpart. Ideally, a robust protocol should not incur significant performance and resource cost penalty with respect to a crash-tolerant implementation, hence making the replacement of a crash-tolerant protocol a viable option.

In this paper, we present PoWerStore, a *robust* and *efficient* asynchronous BFT distributed read/write storage protocol. The notion of *robustness* subsumes [5]: *(i) high availability*, or *wait-freedom* [23], where read/write operations invoked by correct *clients* always complete, and *(ii) strong consistency*, or *linearizability* [24] of read/write operations.

At the heart of PoWerStore is a novel data storage technique we call *Proofs of Writing* (PoW). PoW are inspired by commitment schemes; PoW incorporate a 2-round write procedure, where the second round of write effectively serves to "prove" that the first round has actually been completed before it is exposed to a reader. The second write round in PoW is lightweight and writes only metadata; however, it is powerful enough to spare readers of writing back the data allowing them to only write metadata to achieve strong consistency.[1] We construct PoW using cryptographic hash functions and efficient message authentication codes (MACs); in addition, we also propose an instantiation of PoW based on polynomial evaluation.

PoWerStore's efficiency is reflected in *(i) metadata write-backs* where readers write-back only metadata, avoiding expensive data write-backs, *(ii)* use of lightweight cryptographic primitives (such as hashes and MACs), *(iii) optimal resilience*, i.e., ensuring correctness despite the largest possible number t of Byzantine server failures; this mandates using $3t+1$ servers [35]. Moreover, PoWerStore achieves these desirable properties with *optimal latency*: namely, we show that no robust protocol, including crash-tolerant ones, that uses a bounded number of servers and avoids data write-backs can achieve better latency than PoWerStore. More specifically, in the single writer (SW) variant of PoWerStore, this latency is two *rounds* of communication between a client and servers for both reads and writes.

In addition, PoWerStore employs *erasure coding* at the client side to offload the storage servers and to reduce network traffic. Furthermore, PoWerStore tolerates an unbounded number of Byzantine readers and unbounded number of writers that can crash.

Finally, while our SW variant of PoWerStore demonstrates the efficiency of PoW, for practical applications we propose a multi-writer (MW) variant of PoWerStore (referred to as M-PoWerStore). M-PoWerStore features 3-round writes and reads, where the third read round is invoked only under active attacks. M-PoWerStore also resists attacks specific to multi-writer setting that exhaust the timestamp domain [6]. We evaluate M-PoWerStore and demonstrate its superiority even with respect to existing crash-tolerant robust atomic storage implementations. Our results show that in typical settings, the peak throughput achieved by M-PoWerStore improves over existing robust crash-tolerant [5] and Byzantine-tolerant [34] atomic storage implementations, by 50% and 100%, respectively.

The remainder of the paper is organized as follows. In Section 2, we outline our system and threat model. Section 3 outlines the main intuition behind Proofs of Writing. In Section 4, we introduce PoWerStore and we analyze its correctness. In Section 5, we present the multi-writer variant of PoWerStore, M-PoWerStore. In Section 6, we evaluate an implementation of M-PoWerStore. In Section 7, we overview related work and we conclude the paper in Section 8.

2. MODEL

We consider a distributed system that consists of three *disjoint* sets of processes: a set *servers* of size $S = 3t+1$, where t is the failure threshold parameter, containing processes $\{s_1, ..., s_S\}$; a set *writers* $w_1, w_2, ...$ and a set *readers* r_1, r_2, etc. The set *clients* is the union of writers and readers. We assume the *data-centric* model [12,40] with bi-directional point-to-point channels between each client and each server. Servers do not communicate among each other, nor send messages other than in reply to clients' messages. In fact, servers do not even need to be aware of each other.

2.1 Threat Model

We model processes as probabilistic I/O automata [43] where a distributed algorithm is a set of such processes. Processes that follow the algorithm are called *correct*. Similar to [3,4,16,34], we assume that any number of *honest* writers that may fail by crashing while allowing any number of readers and up to t servers to exhibit *Byzantine* [29] (or *arbitrary* [25]) faults.

We assume a strong adversary that can coordinate the Byzantine servers and readers to compromise the system. We further assume that the adversary controls the network and as such controls the scheduling of all transmitted messages in the network, resulting in *asynchronous* communication. However, we assume that the adversary cannot prevent the eventual delivery of messages between correct processes.

We opt not to focus on Byzantine writers because they can always obliterate the storage by constantly overwriting data with garbage, even in spite of (expensive) techniques that ensure that each individual write leaves a consistent state (e.g., [10,19,22,31]. As a consequence, with Byzantine writers and asynchronous message schedule, the adversary can make a correct reader return arbitrary data at will. Therefore, we assume appropriate access control mechanisms to prevent untrusted writers from having appropriate credentials to modify data.

Finally, we assume that the adversary is computationally bounded and cannot break cryptographic hash functions or forge message authentication codes. In this context, we assume the existence of a cryptographic (i.e., one way and collision resistant) hash function $H(\cdot)$, and a secure message authentication function $MAC_k(\cdot)$, where k is a λ-bit symmetric key. We further assume that each server s_i pre-shares one symmetric group key with each writer in W; in the following, we denote this key by k_i.[2] Note that, in this paper, we do not address the confidentiality of the outsourced data.

2.2 Atomic Storage

We focus on a read/write storage abstraction [28] which exports two operations: WRITE(v), which stores value v and READ(), which returns the stored value. We assume that the initial value of a storage is a special value $\perp$, which is not a valid input value for a write operation. While every client may invoke the READ operation, we assume that WRITEs are invoked only by writers.

We say that an operation (invocation) *op* is *complete* if the client receives the *response*, i.e., if the client returns from the invocation. In any execution of an algorithm, we say that a complete operation op_2 *follows* op_1 if the invocation of op_2 follows the response of $op1$ in that execution. We further assume that each correct client invokes at most one operation at a time (i.e., does not invoke the next operation until it receives the response for the current operation).

We focus on *robust* storage with the strongest storage progress consistency and availability semantics, namely *linearizability* [24] (or *atomicity* [28]) and *wait-freedom* [23].

[1]As proved in [17], in any robust storage readers must "write", i.e., modify the state of storage servers.

[2]Sharing group keys is not a requirement for the main functionality of the single-writer nor the multi-writer versions of PoWerStore. As we show in Section 5, this requirement is only needed to prevent a specific type of DoS attack where malicious readers exhaust the timestamp space.

	Construction costs	Verification costs
Hash-based PoW	1 hash	1 hash
Polynomial-based PoW	$O(\|t^3\|)$ modular exponentiations	$O(\|t^2\|)$ modular exponentiations
RSA signatures	$O(\|M\|)$ modular exponentiations	$O(\|M\|)$ modular exponentiations

Table 1: Construction and verification costs of our PoW instantiations. Here, t is the failure threshold, $M \gg t$ is the modulus used in RSA signatures.

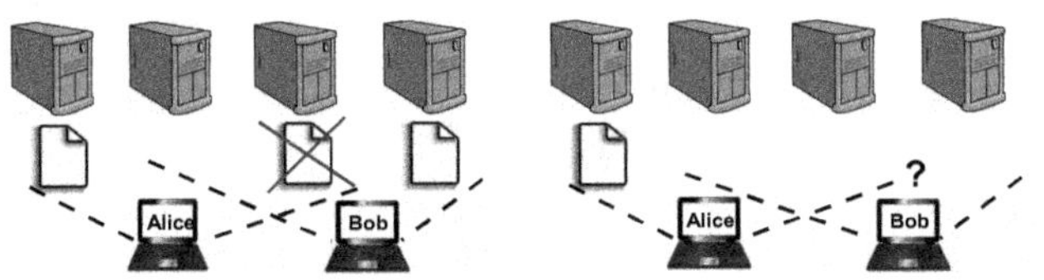

(a) Complete Write (b) Incomplete Write

Figure 1: Complete vs. Incomplete writes ($t = 1$, $S = 4$).

Wait-freedom states that if a correct client invokes an operation *op*, then *op* eventually completes. Linearizability provides the illusion that a complete operation *op* is executed instantly at some point in time between its invocation and response, whereas the operations invoked by faulty clients appear either as complete or not invoked at all.

Finally, we measure the time-complexity of an atomic storage implementation in terms of number of *communication round-trips* (or simply *rounds*) between a client and servers. Intuitively, a *round* consists of a client sending the message to (a subset of) servers and receiving replies. A formal definition can be found in, e.g., [18].

3. PROOFS OF WRITING

In this section, we give the main intuition behind Proofs of Writing (PoW) and describe two possible instantiations of PoW: *(i)* a hash-based variant of PoW that offers computation security, and *(ii)* a polynomial evaluation-based PoW variant that provides information theoretic guarantees.

3.1 Intuition behind PoW

A distributed storage that tolerates failures and asynchrony must prevent clients from blocking while waiting for t possibly faulty servers to reply. As depicted in Figure 1(a), this implies that operations by clients must return after probing a quorum of $S - t$ servers. Intuitively, by looking at a strict subset of the servers, a reader cannot obtain a global view of the system state and in particular, differentiate a complete write from an incomplete write.

For example, in Figure 1, reader Alice cannot tell apart a complete write (Fig. 1(a)) where one Byzantine server deletes the data, from an incomplete write without Byzantine servers (Fig. 1(b)). To ensure strong consistency, i.e., that a subsequent read by Bob does not observe stale data (Fig. 1(b)), Alice must ensure that the data she is about to read is propagated to a sufficient number of servers before her read completes. Essentially, Alice must complete the write herself by performing a *data write-back*, involving a full write of the data she reads [5] in both executions. However, if she somehow knew that the write in Figure 1(a) was in fact complete, Alice could safely skip data writeback, since Bob would anyway observe recent data.

In the context of BFT storage, data write-backs by readers are undesirable for two reasons: *(i)* the overhead of cryptographic schemes related to preventing malicious readers from exploiting such write-backs to jeopardize the storage by overwriting data with garbage, and *(ii)* the inherent bandwidth and latency cost associated with writing-back data. In addition, when combined with erasure coded storage, data write-backs are computationally expensive since readers may need to erasure code data.

Essentially, since the data write-back technique is driven by readers' uncertainty in differentiating between a complete write and an incomplete write, we aim at an efficient technique that would allow readers to tell incomplete and complete writes apart. Such a technique would allow readers to safely discard incomplete writes altogether, obviating the need for writing-back data. Currently, the most widespread technique to achieve this differentiation would be to have writers send an authenticated acknowledgement (e.g., by using digital signatures) upon completion of the write.

At the heart of PoWerStore is a novel storage technique we call Proofs of Writing (PoW) which enables to achieve this differentiation more efficiently. PoW are inspired by commitment schemes [21]; similar to commitment schemes, PoW consist of two rounds: *(i)* in the first round, the writer commits to a random value of its choice, whereas *(ii)* in the second round, the writer "opens" his commitment. Unlike commitment schemes, PoW are constructed by honest writers and stored along with the data in a set of servers, enabling them to collectively convince a reader that the requested data has been stored in sufficiently many correct servers. Furthermore, we show that PoW can be constructed without relying on any public-key infrastructure while incurring little cost when compared to digital signatures (Table 1).

PoW obviate the need for writing-back data, allowing readers to write-back metadata. Metadata write-backs *(i)* help to prevent malicious readers from compromising the storage, and *(ii)* feature low communication latency and bandwidth usage even in worst-case conditions. By doing so, PoW provide an efficient alternative to digital signatures in BFT storage protocols. In what follows, we describe two efficient instantiations of PoW using cryptographic hashes, and polynomial evaluation; we also outline their relative performance gains when compared to digital signatures.

3.2 PoW based on Cryptographic Hashes

We start by outlining a PoW implementation that is based on the use of one-way collision-resistant functions seeded with pseudo-random input.

In the first WRITE round, the writer generates a pseudorandom nonce and writes the hash of the nonce together with the data in a quorum of servers. In the second WRITE round, the writer discloses the nonce and stores it in a quorum. During the first round of a READ operation, the client collects the nonce from a quorum and sends (writes-back) the nonce to a quorum of servers in the second round. The server verifies the nonce by checking that the received nonce matches the hash of the stored nonce. If so, the server confirms the validity of the nonce by exposing the corresponding stored data to the client. The client obtains a PoW after receiving $t+1$ confirmations pertaining to a nonce.

Since the writer keeps the nonce secret until the start of the second round, it is computationally infeasible for the adversary to fabricate the nonce unless the first round of WRITE has completed, and hence the data is written. Thus, if the nonce received in the first READ round hashes to the stored hash at $t+1$ servers (one of which is necessarily correct), then this provides sufficient *proof* that the nonce has been disclosed by the writer, which implies that the data has been written.

3.3 PoW based on Polynomial Evaluation

In what follows, we propose an alternative construction of PoW based on polynomial evaluation. Here, at the start of every WRITE operation, the writer constructs a polynomial $P(\cdot)$ of degree t with coefficients $\{\alpha_t, \ldots, \alpha_0\}$ chosen at random from $\mathcal{Z}_q$, where q is a public parameter. That is, $P(x) = \sum_{j=0}^{j=t} \alpha_j x^j$.

The writer then constructs the PoW as follows: for each server s_i, the writer picks a random point x_i on $P(\cdot)$, and constructs the share (x_i, P_i), where $P_i = P(x_i)$. As such, the writer constructs S different shares, one for each server, and sends them to each server s_i over a *confidential channel.* Note that since there are at most t Byzantine servers, these servers cannot reconstruct the polynomial $P(\cdot)$ from their shares, even if they collude. In the second WRITE round, the writer reveals the polynomial $P(\cdot)$ to all servers. This enables a correct server s_i to establish that the first WRITE round has been completed by checking that the share (x_i, P_i) is indeed a point of $P(\cdot)$.

The argument of PoW relies on the assumption that the correct servers holding shares *agree* on the validity of the polynomial. Therefore, it is crucial to ensure that even after the disclosure $P(\cdot)$, the adversary cannot fabricate a polynomial $\hat{P}(\cdot) \neq P(\cdot)$ that intersects with $P(\cdot)$ in the share of a correct server. By relying on randomly chosen x_i, and the fact that correct servers never divulge their share, our construction prevents an adversary from fabricating $\hat{P}(\cdot)$.

Note that there exist other variant implementations for PoW that do not leak the polynomial to the servers [26]. We point that, unlike our prior solution based on cryptographic hash functions, this PoW construction provides information-theoretic guarantees [4,30]. Table 1 illustrates the PoW construction and verification costs incurred in our PoW constructs. Owing to its reduced costs, we focus in this paper on hash-based PoWs (Sec. 3.2).

4. PoWerStore

In this section, we provide a detailed description of the PoWerStore protocol and we analyze its correctness. In Appendix A, we show that PoWerStore exhibits optimal worst-case latency.

4.1 Overview of PoWerStore

In PoWerStore, the WRITE operation performs in two consecutive rounds, called STORE and COMPLETE. Likewise, the READ performs in two rounds, called COLLECT and FILTER. For the sake of convenience, each round $rnd \in$ {STORE, COMPLETE, COLLECT, FILTER} is wrapped by a procedure *rnd*. In each round *rnd*, the client sends a message of type *rnd* to all servers. A round completes at the latest when the client receives messages of type *rnd*_ACK from $S-t$ correct servers. The server maintains a variable lc to store the metadata of the last completed WRITE, consisting of a timestamp-nonce pair, and a variable LC that stores a set of such tuples written-back by clients. In addition, the server keeps a variable $Hist$ storing the history, i.e., a log consisting of the data written by the writer[3] in the STORE round, indexed by timestamp.

Algorithm 1 Algorithm of the writer in PoWerStore.

```
Definitions:
    ts : structure num, initially ts_0 ≜ 0

operation WRITE(V)
    ts ← ts + 1
    N ← {0,1}^λ
    N̄ ← H(N)
    STORE(ts, N̄, V)
    COMPLETE(ts, N)
    return OK

procedure STORE(ts, V, N̄)
    {fr_1, ..., fr_S} ← encode(V, t+1, S)
    cc ← [H(fr_1), ..., H(fr_S)]
    for 1 ≤ i ≤ S do send STORE⟨ts, fr_i, cc, N̄⟩ to s_i
    wait for STORE_ACK⟨ts⟩ from S − t servers

procedure COMPLETE(ts, N)
    send COMPLETE⟨ts, N⟩ to all servers
    wait for COMPLETE_ACK⟨ts⟩ from S − t servers
```

4.2 Write Implementation

The WRITE implementation is given in Algorithm 1. To write a value V, the writer increases its timestamp ts, generates a nonce N and computes its hash $\overline{N} = H(N)$, and invokes STORE with ts, V and $\overline{N}$. When the STORE procedure returns, the writer invokes COMPLETE with ts and N. After COMPLETE returns, the WRITE completes.

In STORE, the writer encodes V into S fragments fr_i $(1 \leq i \leq S)$, such that V can be recovered from any subset of $t+1$ fragments. Furthermore, the writer computes a cross-checksum cc consisting of the hashes of each fragment. For each server s_i $(1 \leq i \leq S)$, the writer sends a STORE$\langle ts, fr_i, cc, \overline{N}\rangle$ message to s_i. On reception of such a message, the server writes $(fr_i, cc, \overline{N})$ into the history entry $Hist[ts]$ and replies to the writer. After the writer receives $S-t$ replies from different servers, the STORE procedure returns, and the writer proceeds to COMPLETE.

In COMPLETE, the writer sends a COMPLETE$\langle ts, N\rangle$ message to all servers. Upon reception of such a message, the server changes the value of lc to (ts, N) if $ts > lc.ts$ and replies to the writer. After the writer receives replies from $S-t$ different servers, the COMPLETE procedure returns.

4.3 Read Implementation

The READ implementation is given in Algorithm 3; it consists of the COLLECT procedure followed by the FILTER procedure. In COLLECT, the client reads the tuples (ts, N) in-

[3] Recall that PoWerStore is a single-writer storage protocol.

Algorithm 2 Algorithm of server s_i in PoWerStore.

```
18: Definitions:
19:     lc : structure (ts, N), initially c0 ≜ (ts0, NULL)                              //last completed write
20:     LC : set of structure (ts, N), initially ∅                                   //set of written-back candidates
21:     Hist[...] : vector of (fr, cc, N̄) indexed by ts, with all entries initialized to (NULL, NULL, NULL)

22: upon receiving STORE⟨ts, fr, cc, N̄⟩ from the writer
23:     Hist[ts] ← (fr, cc, N̄)
24:     send STORE_ACK⟨ts⟩ to the writer

25: upon receiving COMPLETE⟨ts, N⟩ from the writer
26:     if ts > lc.ts then lc ← (ts, N)
27:     send COMPLETE_ACK⟨ts⟩ to the writer

28: procedure GC()
29:     c_hv ← max({c ∈ LC : valid(c)} ∪ {c0})
30:     if c_hv.ts > lc.ts then lc ← c_hv
31:     LC ← LC \ {c ∈ LC : c.ts ≤ lc.ts}

32: upon receiving COLLECT⟨tsr⟩ from client r
33:     GC()
34:     send COLLECT_ACK⟨tsr, LC ∪ {lc}⟩ to client r

35: upon receiving FILTER⟨tsr, C⟩ from client r
36:     LC ← LC ∪ C                                                                  //write-back
37:     c_hv ← max({c ∈ C : valid(c)} ∪ {c0})
38:     (fr, cc) ← π_{fr,cc}(Hist[c_hv.ts])
39:     send FILTER_ACK⟨tsr, c_hv.ts, fr, cc⟩ to client r

40: Predicates:
41:     valid(c) ≜ (H(c.N) = Hist[c.ts].N̄)
```

cluded in the set $LC \cup \{lc\}$ at the server, and accumulates these tuples in a set C together with the tuples read from other servers. We call such a tuple a *candidate* and C a *candidate set.* Before responding to the client, the server removes obsolete tuples from LC using the GC procedure. After the client receives candidates from $S-t$ different servers, COLLECT returns.

In FILTER, the client submits C to each server. Upon reception of C, the server performs a write-back of the candidates in C (*metadata write-back*). In addition, the server picks c_{hv} as the candidate in C with the highest timestamp such that $\mathsf{valid}(c_{hv})$ holds, or c_0 if no such candidate exists. The predicate $\mathsf{valid}(c)$ holds if the server, based on the history, is able to verify the integrity of c by checking that $H(c.N)$ equals $Hist[c.ts].\overline{N}$. The server then responds to the client with a message including the timestamp $c_{hv}.ts$, the fragment $Hist[c_{hv}.ts].fr$ and the cross-checksum $Hist[c_{hv}.ts].cc$. The client waits until $S-t$ different servers responded and either *(i)* $\mathsf{safe}(c)$ holds for the candidate with the highest timestamp in C, or *(ii)* all candidates have been excluded from C, after which COLLECT returns. The predicate $\mathsf{safe}(c)$ holds if at least $t+1$ different servers s_i have responded with timestamp $c.ts$, fragment fr_i and cross-checksum cc such that $H(fr_i) = cc[i]$. If $C \neq \emptyset$, the client selects the candidate with the highest timestamp $c \in C$ and restores value V by decoding V from the $t+1$ correct fragments received for c. Otherwise, the client sets V to the initial value $\perp$. Finally, the READ returns V.

4.4 Analysis

In what follows, we show that PoWerStore is robust, guaranteeing that READ/WRITE operations are linearizable and wait-free. We start by proving a number of core lemmas, to which we will refer to throughout the analysis.

DEFINITION 4.1 (VALID CANDIDATE). *A candidate c is* valid *if* $\mathsf{valid}(c)$ *holds at some correct server.*

LEMMA 4.2 (PROOFS OF WRITING). *If c is a valid candidate, then there exists a set Q of $t+1$ correct servers such that for each server $s_i \in Q$, $H(c.N) = Hist_i[c.ts].\overline{N}$.*

Proof: If c is valid, then by Definition 4.1, $H(c.N) = Hist_j[c.ts].\overline{N}$ holds at some correct server s_j. By the preimage resistance of H, no computationally bounded adversary can acquire $c.N$ from the sole knowledge of $H(c.N)$. Hence, $c.N$ stems from the writer in a WRITE operation wr with timestamp $c.ts$. By Algorithm 1, line 8, the value of $c.N$ is revealed only after the completion of the STORE round in wr. Hence, by the time $c.N$ is revealed, there is a set Q of $t+1$ correct servers such that each server $s_i \in Q$ assigned $Hist_i[c.ts].\overline{N}$ to $H(c.N)$. □

LEMMA 4.3 (NO EXCLUSION). *Let c be a valid candidate and let rd be a* READ *by a correct reader that includes c in C during* COLLECT. *Then c is never excluded from C.*

Proof: As c is valid, by Lemma 4.2 there is a set Q of $t+1$ correct servers such that each server $s_i \in Q$, $H(c.N) = Hist_i[c.ts]$. Hence, $\mathsf{valid}(c)$ is true at every server in Q. Thus, no server in Q replies with a timestamp $ts < c.ts$ in line 39. Therefore, at most $S-(t+1) = 2t$ timestamps received by the reader in the FILTER round are lower than $c.ts$, and so c is never excluded from C. □

We now explain why linearizability is satisfied by arguing that if a READ follows after a WRITE(V) (resp. after a READ that returns V) then the READ does not return a value older than V.

Read/Write Linearizability.

Suppose a READ rd by a correct client follows after a completed WRITE(V). If ts is the timestamp of WRITE(V), we argue that rd does not select a candidate with a timestamp lower than ts. Since a correct server never changes lc to a candidate with a lower timestamp, after WRITE(V) completed, $t+1$ correct servers hold a valid candidate with timestamp ts or greater in lc. During COLLECT in rd, the client awaits to receive the value of lc from $S-t$ different servers. Hence, a valid candidate c with timestamp ts or greater is received from at least one of these $t+1$ correct servers and included in C. By Lemma 4.3 (no exclusion), c is never excluded from C and by Algorithm 3, rd does not select a candidate with timestamp lower than $c.ts \geq ts$.

Read Linearizability.

Suppose a READ rd' by a correct client follows after rd. If c is the candidate selected in rd, we argue that rd' does not select a candidate with a timestamp lower than $c.ts$. By the time rd completes, $t+1$ correct servers hold c in LC. According to Algorithm 2, if a correct server removes c from

Algorithm 3 Algorithm of client r in PoWerStore.

```
42: Definitions:
43:    tsr: num, initially 0
44:    Q, R: set of pid, initially ∅
45:    C: set of (ts, N), initially ∅
46:    W[1...S]: vector of (ts, fr, cc), initially []

47: operation READ()
48:    C, Q, R ← ∅
49:    tsr ← tsr + 1
50:    C ← COLLECT(tsr)
51:    C ← FILTER(tsr, C)
52:    if C ≠ ∅ then
53:       c ← c' ∈ C : highcand(c') ∧ safe(c')
54:       V ← RESTORE(c.ts)
55:    else V ← ⊥
56:    return V

57: procedure COLLECT(tsr)
58:    send COLLECT⟨tsr⟩ to all servers
59:    wait until |Q| ≥ S − t
60:    return C

61: upon receiving COLLECT_ACK⟨tsr, C_i⟩ from server s_i
62:    Q ← Q ∪ {i}
63:    C ← C ∪ {c ∈ C_i : c.ts > ts_0}

64: procedure FILTER(tsr, C)
65:    send FILTER⟨tsr, C⟩ to all servers
66:    wait until |R| ≥ S − t ∧
       ((∃c ∈ C : highcand(c) ∧ safe(c)) ∨ C = ∅)
67:    return C

68: upon receiving FILTER_ACK⟨tsr, ts, fr, cc⟩ from server s_i
69:    R ← R ∪ {i}; W[i] ← (ts, fr, cc)
70:    C ← C \ {c ∈ C : invalid(c)}

71: procedure RESTORE(ts)
72:    cc ← cc' s.t. ∃R' ⊆ R : |R'| ≥ t + 1 ⋀
       (∀i ∈ R' : W[i].ts = ts ∧ W[i].cc = cc')
73:    F ← {W[i].fr : i∈R ∧ W[i].ts=ts ∧ H(W[i].fr)=cc[i]}
74:    V ← decode(F, t + 1, S)
75:    return V

76: Predicates:
77:    safe(c) ≜ ∃R' ⊆ R : |R'| ≥ t + 1 ⋀
       (∀i ∈ R' : W[i].ts = c.ts) ⋀
       (∀i, j ∈ R' : W[i].cc=W[j].cc ∧ H(W[i].fr)=W[j].cc[i])
78:    highcand(c) ≜ (c.ts = max({c'.ts : c' ∈ C}))
79:    invalid(c) ≜ |{i ∈ R : W[i].ts < c.ts}| ≥ S − t
```

LC, then the server changed lc to a valid candidate with timestamp $c.ts$ or greater. As such, $t+1$ correct servers hold in $LC \cup \{lc\}$ a valid candidate with timestamp $c.ts$ or greater. During COLLECT in rd', the client awaits to receive the value of $LC \cup \{lc\}$ from $S-t$ different servers. As such, it includes a valid candidate c' with timestamp $c.ts$ or greater from at least one correct server. By Lemma 4.3 (no exclusion), c' is never excluded from C and by Algorithm 3, rd' does not select a candidate with timestamp lower than $c'.ts \geq c.ts$.

In the following, we argue that READ does not block in FILTER (line 66) while waiting for the candidate c with the highest timestamp in C to become $\mathsf{safe}(c)$ or C to become empty, which is the most sophisticated waiting condition.

Wait-freedom.

Suppose by contradiction that rd blocks during FILTER after receiving FILTER_ACK messages from all correct servers. We distinguish two cases: (Case 1) C contains a valid candidate and (Case 2) C contains no valid candidate.

- **Case 1:** Let c be the valid candidate with the highest timestamp in C. As c is valid, by Lemma 4.2, at least $t+1$ *correct* servers hold history entries matching c. Since no valid candidate in C has a higher timestamp than $c.ts$, these $t+1$ correct servers responded with timestamp $c.ts$, corresponding erasure coded fragment fr_i and cross-checksum cc such that $H(fr_i) = cc[i]$. Therefore, c is $\mathsf{safe}(c)$. Furthermore, all correct servers (at least $S-t$) responded with timestamps at most $c.ts$. Hence, every candidate $c' \in C$ such that $c'.ts > c.ts$ becomes $\mathsf{invalid}(c')$ and is excluded from C. As such, c is also $\mathsf{highcand}(c)$ and rd does not block.

- **Case 2:** Since no candidate in C is valid, all correct servers (at least $S-t$) responded with timestamp ts_0, which is lower than any candidate timestamp. As such, every candidate $c \in C$ becomes $\mathsf{invalid}(c)$ is excluded from C. Therefore, rd does not block.

5. M-PoWerStore

In what follows, we present the multi-writer variant of our protocol, dubbed M-PoWerStore. M-PoWerStore resists attacks specific to multi-writer setting that exhaust the timestamp domain [6]. Besides its support for multiple writers, M-PoWerStore protects against denial of service attacks specific to PoWerStore, in which the adversary swamps the system with bogus candidates. While this attack can be contained in PoWerStore by a robust implementation of the point-to-point channel assumption using, e.g., a separate pair of network cards for each channel (in the vein of [13]), this may impact practicality.

5.1 Overview

M-PoWerStore supports an unbounded number of clients. In addition, M-PoWerStore features optimal READ latency of two rounds in the *common case*, where no process is Byzantine. Under malicious attacks, M-PoWerStore gracefully degrades to guarantee reading in at most three rounds. The WRITE has a latency of three rounds, featuring non-skipping timestamps [6], which prevents the adversary from exhausting the timestamp domain.

The main difference between M-PoWerStore and PoWerStore is that, here, servers store and transmit a single candidate instead of a (possibly unbounded) set. To this end, it is crucial that servers are able to determine the validity of a written-back candidate without consulting the history. For this purpose, we enhance our original PoW scheme by extending the candidate with message authentication codes (MACs) on the timestamp and the nonce's hash, one for each server, using the corresponding group key. As such, a valid MAC proves to a server that the written-back candidate stems from a writer, and thus, constitutes a PoW that a server can obtain even without the corresponding history entry. Note that in case of a candidate incorporating corrupted MACs, servers might disagree about the validity of a written-back candidate. Hence, a correct client might not be able to write-back a candidate to $t+1$ *correct* servers as needed. To solve this issue, M-PoWerStore "pre-writes" the MACs, enabling clients to recover corrupted candidates from the pre-written MACs.

To support multiple-writers, WRITE in M-PoWerStore comprises an additional distributed synchronization round, called

CLOCK, which is prepended to STORE. The READ performs an additional round called REPAIR, which is appended to COLLECT. The purpose of REPAIR is to recover broken candidates prior to writing them back, and is invoked only under attack by a malicious adversary that actually corrupts candidates.

Similarly to PoWerStore, the server maintains the variable *Hist* to store the history of the data written by the writer in the STORE round, indexed by timestamp. In addition, the server keeps the variable lc to store the metadata of the last completed write consisting of the timestamp, the nonce and a vector of MACs (with one entry per server) authenticating the timestamp and the nonce's hash.

The full WRITE implementation is given in Algorithm 4. The implementation of the server and the READ operation are given in Algorithm 5 and 6. In the following, we simply highlight the differences to PoWerStore.

5.2 Write Implementation

As outlined before, M-PoWerStore is resilient to the adversary skipping timestamps. This is achieved by having the writer authenticate the timestamp of a WRITE with a key k_W shared among the writers. Note that such a shared key can be obtained by combining the different group keys; for instance, $k_W \leftarrow H(k_1||k_2||\ldots)$.

To obtain a timestamp, in the CLOCK procedure, the writer retrieves the timestamp (held in variable lc) from a quorum of $S-t$ servers and picks the highest timestamp ts with a valid MAC. Then, the writer increases ts and computes a MAC for ts using k_W. Finally, CLOCK returns ts.

To write a value V, the writer, *(i)* obtains a timestamp ts from the CLOCK procedure, *(ii)* authenticates ts and the nonce's hash $\overline{N}$ by a vector of MACs vec, with one entry for each server s_i using group key k_i, and *(iii)* stores vec both in STORE and COMPLETE. Upon reception of a STORE$\langle fr_i, cc, \overline{N}, vec\rangle$ message, the server writes the tuple $(fr_i, cc, \overline{N}, vec)$ into the history entry $Hist[ts]$. Upon reception of a COMPLETE$\langle ts, N, vec\rangle$ message, the server changes the value of lc to (ts, N, vec) if $ts > lc.ts$.

5.3 Read Implementation

The READ consists of three consecutive rounds, COLLECT, FILTER and REPAIR. In COLLECT, a client reads the candidate triple (ts, N, vec) stored in variable lc in the server, and inserts it into the candidate set C together with the candidates read from other servers. After the client receives $S-t$ candidates from different servers, COLLECT returns.

In FILTER, the client submits C to each server. Upon reception of C, the server chooses c_{hv} as the candidate in C with the highest timestamp such that $\mathsf{valid}(c_{hv})$ is satisfied, or c_0 if no such candidate exists, and performs a write-back by setting lc to c_{hv} if $c_{hv}.ts > lc.ts$. Roughly speaking, the predicate $\mathsf{valid}(c)$ holds if the server verifies the integrity of the timestamp $c.ts$ and nonce $c.N$ either by the MAC, or by the corresponding history entry. The server then responds to the client with the timestamp $c_{hv}.ts$, the fragment $Hist[c_{hv}.ts].fr$, the cross-checksum $Hist[c_{hv}.ts].cc$ and the vector of MACs $Hist[c_{hv}.ts].vec$.

The client awaits responses from $S-t$ servers and waits until there is a candidate c with the highest timestamp in C such that $\mathsf{safe}(c)$ holds, or until C is empty, after which FILTER returns. The predicate $\mathsf{safe}(c)$ holds if at least $t+1$ different servers s_i have responded with timestamp $c.ts$, fragment fr_i, cross-checksum cc such that $H(fr_i) = cc[i]$, and vector vec. If C is empty, the client sets V to the initial value $\perp$. Otherwise, the client selects the highest candidate $c \in C$ and restores value V by decoding V from the $t+1$ correct fragments received for c.

In REPAIR, the client verifies the integrity of $c.vec$ by matching it against the vector vec received from $t+1$ different servers. If $c.vec$ and vec match then REPAIR returns. Otherwise, the client repairs c by setting $c.vec$ to vec and invokes a round of write-back by sending a REPAIR$\langle tsr, c\rangle$ message to all servers. Upon reception of such a message, if $\mathsf{valid}(c)$ holds then the server sets lc to c provided that $c.ts > lc.ts$ and responds with an REPAIR_ACK message to the client. Once the client receives acknowledgements from $S-t$ different servers, REPAIR returns. After REPAIR returns, the READ returns V.

Algorithm 4 Algorithm of writer w in M-PoWerStore.

Definitions:
  Q: set of *pid*, (process id) initially $\emptyset$
  ts: structure $(num, pid, MAC_{\{k_W\}}(num||pid))$,
  initially $ts_0 \triangleq (0, 0, \text{NULL})$

operation WRITE(V)
  $Q \leftarrow \emptyset$
  $ts \leftarrow$ CLOCK()
  $N \leftarrow \{0,1\}^\lambda$
  $\overline{N} \leftarrow H(N)$
  $vec \leftarrow [MAC_{\{k_i\}}(ts||\overline{N})_{1\le i\le S}]$
  STORE($ts, V, \overline{N}, vec$)
  COMPLETE(ts, N, vec)
  return OK

procedure CLOCK()
  send CLOCK$\langle ts\rangle$ to all servers
  wait until $|Q| \geq S-t$
  $ts.num \leftarrow ts.num + 1$
  $ts \leftarrow (ts.num, w, MAC_{\{k_W\}}(ts.num||w))$
  return ts

upon receiving CLOCK_ACK$\langle ts, ts_i\rangle$ from server s_i
  $Q \leftarrow Q \cup \{i\}$
  if $ts_i > ts \wedge \text{verify}(ts_i, k_W)$ **then** $ts \leftarrow ts_i$

procedure STORE($ts, V, \overline{N}, vec$)
  $\{fr_1, \ldots, fr_S\} \leftarrow \text{encode}(V, t+1, S)$
  $cc \leftarrow [H(fr_1), \ldots, H(fr_S)]$
  foreach server s_i send STORE$\langle ts, fr_i, cc, \overline{N}, vec\rangle$ to s_i
  wait for STORE_ACK$\langle ts\rangle$ from $S-t$ servers

procedure COMPLETE(ts, N, vec)
  send COMPLETE$\langle ts, N, vec\rangle$ to all servers
  wait for COMPLETE_ACK$\langle ts\rangle$ from $S-t$ servers

5.4 Analysis

We argue that M-PoWerStore satisfies linearizability by showing that if a completed READ rd by a correct client returns V then a subsequent READ rd' by a correct client does not return a value older than V. The residual correctness arguments are similar to those of PoWerStore (Section 4.4), and therefore omitted.

Suppose rd' follows after rd. If c is the candidate selected in rd, we argue that rd' does not select a candidate with a lower timestamp. By assumption c is selected in rd by a correct client that checks the integrity of $c.vec$ (during REPAIR). If $c.vec$ passes the check, then each of the correct servers (at least $S-2t \geq t+1$) that received c during FILTER

Algorithm 5 Algorithm of server s_i in M-PoWerStore.

```
Definitions:
    lc: structure (ts, N, vec), initially c0 ≜ (ts0, NULL, NULL)
    Hist[...]: vector of (fr, cc, N̄, vec) indexed by ts, with all
      entries initialized to (NULL, NULL, NULL, NULL)

upon receiving CLOCK⟨ts⟩ from writer w
    send CLOCK_ACK⟨ts, lc.ts⟩ to writer w

upon receiving STORE⟨ts, fr, cc, N̄, vec⟩ from writer w
    Hist[ts] ← (fr, cc, N̄, vec)
    send STORE_ACK⟨ts⟩ to writer w

upon receiving COMPLETE⟨ts, N, vec⟩ from writer w
    if ts > lc.ts then lc ← (ts, N, vec)
    send COMPLETE_ACK⟨ts⟩ to writer w

upon receiving COLLECT⟨tsr⟩ from client r
    send COLLECT_ACK⟨tsr, lc⟩ to client r

upon receiving FILTER⟨tsr, C⟩ from client r
    c_hv ← max({c ∈ C : valid(c)} ∪ {c0})
    if c_hv.ts > lc.ts then lc ← c_hv                //write-back
    (fr, cc, vec) ← π_{fr,cc,vec}(Hist[c_hv.ts])
    send FILTER_ACK⟨tsr, c_hv.ts, fr, cc, vec⟩ to client r

upon receiving REPAIR⟨tsr, c⟩ from client r
    if c.ts > lc.ts ∧ valid(c) then lc ← c           //write-back
    send REPAIR_ACK⟨tsr⟩ to client r

Predicates:
valid(c) ≜ (H(c.N) = Hist[c.ts].N̄) ∨
              verify(c.vec[i], c.ts, H(c.N), k_i)
```

Algorithm 6 Algorithm of client r in M-PoWerStore.

```
Definitions:
    tsr: num, initially 0
    Q, R: set of pid, initially ∅
    C: set of (ts, N, vec), initially ∅
    W[1...S]: vector of (ts, fr, cc, vec), initially []

operation READ()
    C, Q, R ← ∅
    tsr ← tsr + 1
    C ← COLLECT(tsr)
    C ← FILTER(tsr, C)
    if C ≠ ∅ then
        c ← c' ∈ C : highcand(c') ∧ safe(c')
        V ← RESTORE(c.ts)
        REPAIR(c)
    else V ← ⊥
    return V
  ...
upon receiving COLLECT_ACK⟨tsr, c_i⟩ from server s_i
    Q ← Q ∪ {i}
    if c_i.ts > ts0 then C ← C ∪ {c_i}
  ...
upon receiving FILTER_ACK⟨tsr,ts,fr,cc,vec⟩ from server s_i
    R ← R ∪ {i}; W[i] ← (ts, fr, cc, vec)
    C ← C \ {c ∈ C : invalid(c)}
  ...
procedure REPAIR(c)
    vec ← vec' s.t. ∃R' ⊆ R : |R'| ≥ t + 1 ⋀
      (∀i ∈ R' : W[i].ts = c.ts ∧ W[i].vec = vec')
    if c.vec ≠ vec then
        c.vec ← vec                                   //repair
        send REPAIR⟨tsr, c⟩ to all servers
        wait for REPAIR_ACK⟨tsr⟩ from S − t servers
Predicates:
    safe(c) ≜ ∃R' ⊆ R : |R'| ≥ t + 1 ⋀
      (∀i ∈ R' : W[i].ts = c.ts) ⋀
      (∀i, j ∈ R': W[i].cc=W[j].cc ∧ H(W[i].fr)=W[j].cc[i]) ⋀
      (∀i, j ∈ R' : W[i].vec = W[j].vec)
  ...
```

validates c (by verifying its own entry of $c.vec$) and sets lc to c unless it has already changed lc to a higher timestamped candidate. Otherwise, if $c.vec$ fails the integrity check, then the client in rd repairs $c.vec$ and subsequently writes-back c to $t+1$ correct servers or more. Hence, by the time rd completes, at least $t+1$ correct servers have set lc to c or to a valid candidate with a higher timestamp. Since during COLLECT in rd' the client receives the value of lc from $S-t$ different servers, a valid candidate c' such that $c'.ts \geq c.ts$ is included in C. By Lemma 4.3 (no exclusion), c' is never excluded from C and by Algorithm 6, rd' does not select a candidate with timestamp lower than $c'.ts \geq c.ts$.

6. IMPLEMENTATION & EVALUATION

In this section, we describe an implementation modeling a Key-Value Store (KVS) based on M-PoWerStore. To model a KVS, we use multiple instances of M-PoWerStore referenced by keys. We then evaluate the performance of our implementation and we compare it to: *(i)* M-ABD, the multi-writer variant of the crash-only atomic storage protocol of [5], and *(ii)* Phalanx, the multi-writer robust atomic protocol of [34] that relies on digital signatures.

6.1 Implementation Setup

Our KVS implementation is based on the JAVA-based framework Neko [2] that provides support for inter-process communication, and on the Jerasure [1] library for constructing the dispersal codes. To evaluate the performance of our M-PoWerStore we additionally implemented two KVSs based on M-ABD and Phalanx.

In our implementation, we relied on 160-bit SHA1 for hashing purposes, 160-bit keyed HMACs to implement MACs, and 1024-bit DSA to generate signatures[4]. For simplicity, we abstract away the effect of message authentication in our implementations; we argue that this does not affect our performance evaluation since data origin authentication is typically handled as part of the access control layer in all three implementations, when deployed in realistic settings (e.g., in Wide Area Networks).

We deployed our implementations on a private network consisting of a 4-core Intel Xeon E5443 with 4GB of RAM, a 4 core Intel i5-3470 with 8 GB of RAM, an 8 Intel-Core i7-37708 with 8 GB of RAM, and a 64-core Intel Xeon E5606 equipped with 32GB of RAM. In our network, the communication between various machines was bridged using a 1 Gbps switch. All the servers were running in separate processes on the Xeon E5606 machine, whereas the clients were distributed among the Xeon E5443, i7, and the i5 machines. Each client invokes operation in a closed loop, i.e., a client may have at most one pending operation. In all KVS implementations, all WRITE and READ operations are served by a local database stored on disk.

We evaluate the peak throughput incurred in M-PoWerStore in WRITE and READ operations, when compared to M-ABD and Phalanx with respect to: *(i)* the file size (64 KB, 128

[4]Note that our benchmarks feature balanced reads/writes in which case balanced sign/verify DSA performance seems more appropriate for Phalanx than RSA [14].

Parameter	Default Value
Failure threshold t	1
File size	256 KB
Probability of Concurrency	1%
Workload Distribution	100% READ 100% WRITE

Table 2: Default parameters used in evaluation.

KB, 256 KB, 512 KB, and 1024 KB), and *(ii)* to the server failure threshold t (1, 2, and 3, respectively). For better evaluation purposes, we vary each variable separately and we fix the remaining parameters to a default configuration (Table 2). We also evaluate the latency incurred in M-PoWerStore with respect to the attained throughput.

We measure peak throughput as follows. We require that each writer performs back to back WRITE operations; we then increase the number of writers in the system until the aggregated throughput attained by all writers is saturated. The peak throughput is then computed as the maximum aggregated amount of data (in bytes) that can be written/read to the servers per second.

Each data point in our plots is averaged over 5 independent measurements; where appropriate, we include the corresponding 95% confidence intervals. as data objects. On the other hand, READ operations request the data pertaining to randomly-chosen keys. For completeness, we performed our evaluation *(i)* in the Local Area Network (LAN) setting comprising our aforementioned network (Section 6.2) and *(ii)* in a simulated Wide Area Network (WAN) setting (Section 6.3). Our results are presented in Figure 2.

6.2 Evaluation Results within a LAN Setting

Figure 2(a) depicts the latency incurred in M-PoWerStore when compared to M-ABD and Phalanx, with respect to the achieved throughput (measured in the number of operations per second). Our results show that, by combining metadata write-backs with erasure coding, M-PoWerStore achieves lower latencies than M-ABD and Phalanx for both READ and WRITE operations. As expected, READ latencies incurred in PoWerStore are lower than those of WRITE operations since a WRITE requires an extra communication round corresponding to the CLOCK round. Furthermore, due to PoW and the use of lightweight cryptographic primitives, the READ performance of PoWerStore considerably outperforms M-ABD and Phalanx. On the other hand, writing in M-PoWerStore compares similarly to the writing in M-ABD.

Figure 2(b) depicts the peak throughput achieved in M-PoWerStore with respect to the number of Byzantine servers t. As t increases, the gain in peak throughput achieved in M-PoWerStore's READ and WRITE increases compared to M-ABD and Phalanx. This mainly stems from the reliance on erasure coding, which ensures that the overhead of file replication among the servers is minimized when compared to M-ABD and Phalanx. In typical settings, featuring $t = 1$ and the default parameters of Table 2, the peak throughput achieved in M-PoWerStore's READ operation is almost twice as large as that in M-ABD and Phalanx.

In Figure 2(c), we measure the peak throughput achieved in M-PoWerStore with respect to the file size. Our findings clearly show that as the file size increases, the performance gain of M-PoWerStore compared to M-ABD and Phalanx becomes considerable. For example, when the file size is 1 MB, the peak throughput of READ and WRITE operations in M-PoWerStore approaches the (network-limited) bounds of 50 MB/s[5] and 45 MB/s, respectively.

6.3 Evaluation Results within a Simulated WAN Setting

We now proceed to evaluate the performance (latency, in particular) of M-PoWerStore when deployed in WAN settings. For that purpose, we rely on a 100 Mbps switch to bridge the network outlined in Section 6.1 and we rely on NetEm [37] to emulate the packet delay variance specific to WANs. More specifically, we add a Pareto distribution to our links, with a mean of 20 ms and a variance of 4 ms.

Our measurement results (Figure 2(d)) confirm our previous analysis conducted in the LAN scenario and demonstrate the superior performance of M-PoWerStore compared to M-ABD and Phalanx in realistic settings. Here, we point out that the performance of M-PoWerStore incurred in both READ and WRITE operations does not deteriorate as the number of Byzantine servers in the system increases. This is mainly due to the reliance on erasure coding. In fact, the overhead of transmitting an erasure-coded file F to the $3t+1$ servers, with a reconstruction threshold of $t + 1$ is given by $\frac{3t+1}{t+1}|F|$. It is easy to see that, as t increases, this overhead asymptotically increases towards $3|F|$.

7. RELATED WORK

HAIL [8] is a distributed cryptographic storage system that implements a multi-server variant of Proofs of Retrievability (PoR) [9] to ensure integrity protection and availability (retrievability) of files dispersed across several storage servers. Like PoWerStore, HAIL assumes Byzantine failure model for storage servers, yet the two protocols largely cover different design space. Namely, HAIL considers a mobile adversary and a single client interacting with the storage in a synchronous fashion. In contrast, PoWerStore assumes static adversary, yet assumes a distributed client setting in which clients share data in an asynchronous fashion. Multiple clients are also supported by IRIS [42], a PoR-based distributed file system designed with enterprise users in mind that stores data in the clouds and is resilient against potentially untrustworthy service providers. However, in IRIS, all clients are pre-serialized by a logically centralized, trusted portal which acts as a fault-free gateway for communication with untrusted clouds. In contrast, PoWerStore relies on the highly available distributed PoW technique, which eliminates the need for any trusted and/or fault-free component. Notice that data confidentiality is orthogonal to all of HAIL, IRIS and PoWerStore protocols.

In the context of distributed storage asynchronously shared among multiple fault-prone clients across multiple servers without any fault-free component, a seminal crash-tolerant storage implementation (called ABD) was presented in [5]. ABD assumes a majority of correct storage servers, and achieves strong consistency by having readers write back the data they read. As shown in [17], server state modifications by readers introduced in ABD are unavoidable in *robust* storage such as ABD, where robustness is characterized by both strong consistency and high availability. However,

[5]Note that an effective peak throughput of 50MB/s in M-PoWerStore reflects an actual throughput of almost 820 Mbps when $t = 1$.

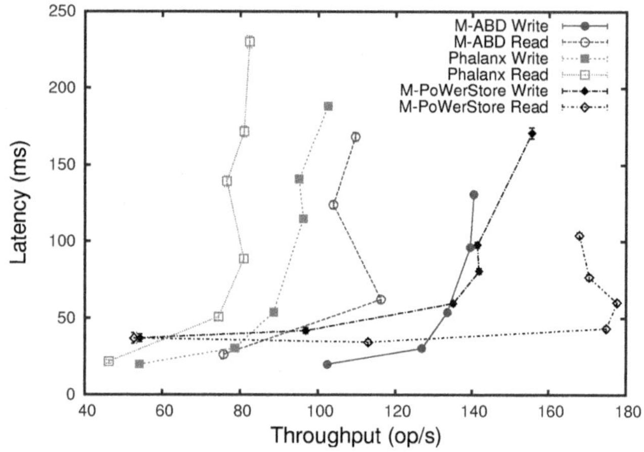

(a) Throughput vs. latency in a LAN setting.

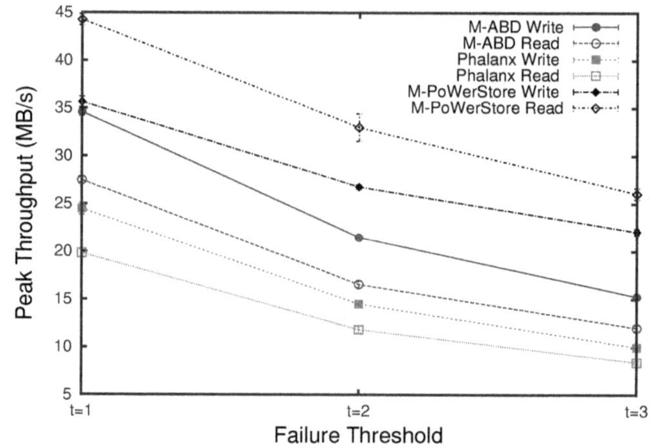

(b) Peak throughput with respect to the failure threshold in a LAN setting.

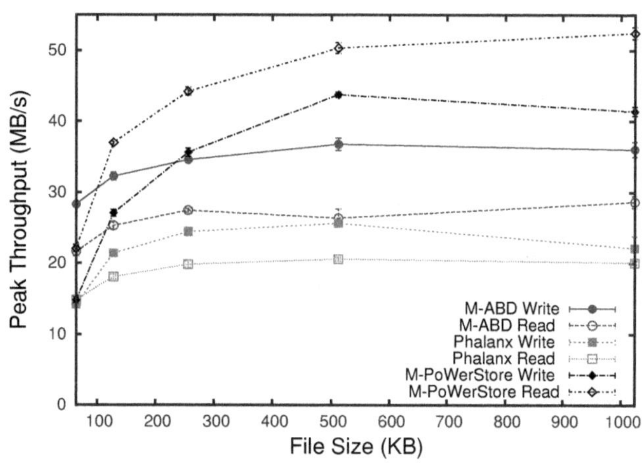

(c) Peak throughput with respect to the file size in a LAN setting.

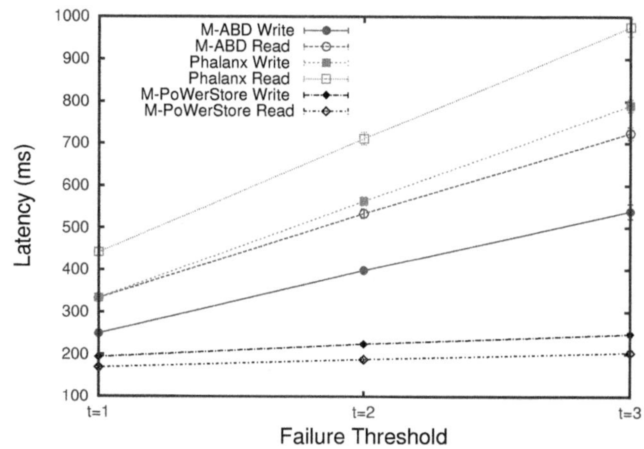

(d) Latency vs the failure threshold in a simulated WAN setting.

Figure 2: Evaluation Results. Data points are averaged over 5 independent runs; where appropriate, we include the corresponding 95% confidence intervals.

robust storage implementations differ in the writing strategy employed by readers: in some protocols readers write-back data (e.g., [4,5,15,18,20,34]) whereas in others readers only write metadata to servers (e.g., [11,16,17]).

Existing robust storage protocols in which readers write only metadata, either do not tolerate Byzantine faults [11, 17], or require a total number of servers linear in number of readers to tolerate t Byzantine servers [16], and hence are prohibitively expensive. PoWerStore is hence the first robust BFT protocol that uses a bounded number of storage servers and has readers write only metadata to servers.

Clearly, most distributed BFT storage implementations have been focusing on using as few servers as possible, ideally $3t+1$, which defines optimal resilience in the asynchronous model [35]. This was first achieved by Phalanx [34], a BFT variant of ABD [5]. Phalanx uses digital signatures, i.e., *self-verifying data*, to port ABD to the Byzantine model, maintaining the latency of ABD, as well as its data write-backs. However, since digital signatures introduce considerable overhead [33, 38], protocols that feature lightweight authentication, or no data authentication at all (unauthenticated model) have been designed. Unfortunately, in the unauthenticated model, optimal resilience in BFT storage incurs considerable latency penalties: at least two rounds of communication between clients and servers for writes [3] and at least four rounds[6] for reads [15], even in the single writer case. To avoid such a considerable overhead, some robust BFT storage protocols (e.g., PASIS [19]) store unauthenticated data across $4t+1$ servers.

Clearly, there is a big gap in efficiency (and, in particular, communication latency and the number of servers) between storage protocols that use self-verifying data and those that assume no authentication. Loft [22] aims at bridging this gap and implements erasure-coded optimally resilient linearizable storage while optimizing the failure-free case. Loft uses homomorphic fingerprints and MACs; it features 3-round wait-free writes, but reads are based on data write-backs and data might be unavailable in case of heavy read/write concurrency. Similarly, our *Proofs of Writing*

[6]Under constant number of write rounds.

Protocol	Data Authentication	Data Dispersal	Read/Write Latency	no. of readers/writers	no. of messages	Byz. clients
Phalanx [34]	signatures	replication	2D/(D+d)	any/any	$O(t)$	readers
[31]	signatures	replication	2D/(D+2d)	any/any	$O(t)$	all
[15]	none	replication	(2D+2d)/(D+d)	any/1	$O(t)$	no
[10]	signatures	erasure coding	>(D+2d) / >(3D+d)	any/any	$O(t^2)$	all
Loft [22]	hash/MAC	erasure-coding	∞/D+2d	any/any	$O(t^2)$	all
PoWerStore	hash/MAC	erasure-coding	(D+d)/(D+d)	any/1	$O(t)$	readers
M-PoWerStore	hash/MAC	erasure-coding	(D+2d)/(D+2d)	any/any	$O(t)$	readers

Table 3: Comparison of properties of existing strongly consistent optimally resilient BFT storage protocols. Shown latency is worst case and distinguishes between data rounds (D) and metadata rounds (d), where typically $D >> d$.

(PoW) incorporate lightweight authentication that is, however, sufficient to achieve optimal latency and to facilitate metadata write-backs while guaranteeing optimal resilience, high-availability and strong consistency. We find PoW to be a fundamental improvement in the light of BFT storage implementations that explicitly renounce strong consistency in favor of weaker consistency notions due to the high cost of data write-backs (e.g., [7]). A summary of the key properties of existing BFT storage protocols when compared to our protocols is shown in Table 3.

A separate line of research aims at a family of so-called forking semantics (e.g., [36]), which relax atomic semantics, yet require no trusted components whatsoever. Systems guaranteeing forking semantics guarantee that after a single atomicity violation by the service, the views seen by two inconsistent clients can never again converge. PoWerStore avoids the drawbacks of fork-consistent systems (reflected in, e.g., difficulties in understanding forking semantics and exploiting them in practice [39]), by offering easily understandable, fully linearizable, (i.e., atomic) semantics.

8. CONCLUSION

In this paper, we presented PoWerStore, an efficient robust storage protocol that achieves optimal latency, measured in maximum (worst-case) number of communication rounds between a client and storage servers. We also separately presented a multi-writer variant of our protocol called M-PoWerStore. The *efficiency* of our proposals stems from combining *lightweight cryptography*, *erasure coding* and *metadata writebacks*, where readers write-back only metadata to achieve linearizability. While robust BFTs have been often criticized for being prohibitively inefficient, our findings suggest that efficient and robust BFTs can be realized in practice by relying on lightweight cryptographic primitives without compromising *worst-case* performance.

At the heart of both PoWerStore and M-PoWerStore protocols are *Proofs of Writing (PoW)*: a novel storage technique inspired by commitment schemes in the flavor of [21], that enables single-writer PoWerStore to write and read in 2 rounds which we show optimal. Similarly, by relying on PoW, multi-writer M-PoWerStore features 3-round writes/reads where the third read round is only invoked under active attacks. Finally, we demonstrated M-PoWerStore's superior performance compared to existing crash and Byzantine-tolerant atomic storage implementations.

9. ACKNOWLEDGEMENTS

This work is supported in part by the EU CLOUDSPACES (FP7-317555) and SECCRIT (FP7-312758) projects and by LOEWE TUD CASED.

10. REFERENCES

[1] Jerasure. `https://github.com/tsuraan/Jerasure`, 2008.

[2] The Neko Project. `http://ddsg.jaist.ac.jp/neko/`, 2009.

[3] Ittai Abraham, Gregory Chockler, Idit Keidar, and Dahlia Malkhi. Byzantine Disk Paxos: Optimal Resilience with Byzantine Shared Memory. *Distributed Computing*, 18(5):387–408, 2006.

[4] Amitanand S. Aiyer, Lorenzo Alvisi, and Rida A. Bazzi. Bounded Wait-free Implementation of Optimally Resilient Byzantine Storage Without (Unproven) Cryptographic Assumptions. In *Proceedings of DISC*, 2007.

[5] Hagit Attiya, Amotz Bar-Noy, and Danny Dolev. Sharing Memory Robustly in Message-Passing Systems. *J. ACM*, 42:124–142, January 1995.

[6] Rida A. Bazzi and Yin Ding. Non-skipping Timestamps for Byzantine Data Storage Systems. In *Proceedings of DISC*, pages 405–419, 2004.

[7] Alysson Neves Bessani, Miguel P. Correia, Bruno Quaresma, Fernando André, and Paulo Sousa. Depsky: dependable and secure storage in a cloud-of-clouds. In *Proceedings of EuroSys*, pages 31–46, 2011.

[8] Kevin D. Bowers, Ari Juels, and Alina Oprea. Hail: a high-availability and integrity layer for cloud storage. In *CCS*, pages 187–198, 2009.

[9] Kevin D. Bowers, Ari Juels, and Alina Oprea. Proofs of retrievability: theory and implementation. In *CCSW*, pages 43–54, 2009.

[10] Christian Cachin and Stefano Tessaro. Optimal Resilience for Erasure-Coded Byzantine Distributed Storage. In *Proceedings of DSN*, pages 115–124, 2006.

[11] Brian Cho and Marcos K. Aguilera. Surviving congestion in geo-distributed storage systems. In *Proceedings of USENIX ATC*, pages 40–40, 2012.

[12] Gregory Chockler, Dahlia Malkhi, and Danny Dolev. Future directions in distributed computing. chapter A data-centric approach for scalable state machine replication, pages 159–163. 2003.

[13] Allen Clement, Edmund L. Wong, Lorenzo Alvisi, Michael Dahlin, and Mirco Marchetti. Making byzantine fault tolerant systems tolerate byzantine faults. In *Proceedings of NSDI*, pages 153–168, 2009.

[14] Wei Dai. Crypto++ 5.6.0 benchmarks. Website, 2009. Available online at `http://www.cryptopp.com/benchmarks.html`.

[15] Dan Dobre, Rachid Guerraoui, Matthias Majuntke, Neeraj Suri, and Marko Vukolić. The Complexity of

Robust Atomic Storage. In *Proceedings of PODC*, pages 59–68, 2011.

[16] Partha Dutta, Rachid Guerraoui, Ron R. Levy, and Marko Vukolić. Fast Access to Distributed Atomic Memory. *SIAM J. Comput.*, 39:3752–3783, December 2010.

[17] Rui Fan and Nancy Lynch. Efficient Replication of Large Data Objects. In *Proceedings of DISC*, pages 75–91, 2003.

[18] Chryssis Georgiou, Nicolas C. Nicolaou, and Alexander A. Shvartsman. Fault-tolerant Semifast Implementations of Atomic Read/Write Registers. *J. Parallel Distrib. Comput.*, 69(1):62–79, January 2009.

[19] Garth R. Goodson, Jay J. Wylie, Gregory R. Ganger, and Michael K. Reiter. Efficient Byzantine-Tolerant Erasure-Coded Storage. In *Proceedings of DSN*, 2004.

[20] Rachid Guerraoui and Marko Vukolić. Refined quorum systems. *Distributed Computing*, 23(1):1–42, 2010.

[21] Shai Halevi and Silvio Micali. Practical and provably-secure commitment schemes from collision-free hashing. In *Proceedings of CRYPTO*, pages 201–215, 1996.

[22] James Hendricks, Gregory R. Ganger, and Michael K. Reiter. Low-overhead Byzantine fault-tolerant storage. In *Proceedings of SOSP*, pages 73–86, 2007.

[23] Maurice Herlihy. Wait-Free Synchronization. *ACM Trans. Program. Lang. Syst.*, 13(1), 1991.

[24] Maurice P. Herlihy and Jeannette M. Wing. Linearizability: A Correctness Condition for Concurrent Objects. *ACM Trans. Program. Lang. Syst.*, 12(3), 1990.

[25] Prasad Jayanti, Tushar Deepak Chandra, and Sam Toueg. Fault-tolerant Wait-free Shared Objects. *J. ACM*, 45(3), 1998.

[26] Aniket Kate, Gregory M. Zaverucha, and Ian Goldberg. Constant-size commitments to polynomials and their applications. In *Proceedings of ASIACRYPT*, volume 6477, pages 177–194, 2010.

[27] Petr Kuznetsov and Rodrigo Rodrigues. Bftw^3: Why? When? Where? workshop on the theory and practice of Byzantine fault tolerance. *SIGACT News*, 40(4):82–86, 2009.

[28] Leslie Lamport. On Interprocess Communication. *Distributed Computing*, 1(2):77–101, 1986.

[29] Leslie Lamport, Robert E. Shostak, and Marshall C. Pease. The byzantine generals problem. *ACM Trans. Program. Lang. Syst.*, 4(3):382–401, 1982.

[30] Harry C. Li, Allen Clement, Amitanand S. Aiyer, and Lorenzo Alvisi. The Paxos Register. In *Proceedings of SRDS*, pages 114–126, 2007.

[31] Barbara Liskov and Rodrigo Rodrigues. Tolerating Byzantine Faulty Clients in a Quorum System. In *Proceedings of ICDCS*, 2006.

[32] Nancy A. Lynch and Mark R. Tuttle. An introduction to input/output automata. *CWI Quarterly*, 2:219–246, 1989.

[33] Dahlia Malkhi and Michael K. Reiter. A High-Throughput Secure Reliable Multicast Protocol. *J. Comput. Secur.*, 5(2):113–127, March 1997.

[34] Dahlia Malkhi and Michael K. Reiter. Secure and Scalable Replication in Phalanx. In *Proceedings of SRDS*, pages 51–58, 1998.

[35] Jean-Philippe Martin, Lorenzo Alvisi, and Michael Dahlin. Minimal Byzantine Storage. In *Proceedings of DISC*, pages 311–325, 2002.

[36] David Mazières and Dennis Shasha. Building secure file systems out of byantine storage. In *PODC*, pages 108–117, 2002.

[37] NetEm. NetEm, the Linux Foundation. Website, 2009. Available online at `http://www.linuxfoundation.org/collaborate/workgroups/networking/netem`.

[38] Michael K. Reiter. Secure Agreement Protocols: Reliable and Atomic Group Multicast in Rampart. In *Proceedings of CCS*, pages 68–80, 1994.

[39] Alexander Shraer, Christian Cachin, Asaf Cidon, Idit Keidar, Yan Michalevsky, and Dani Shaket. Venus: verification for untrusted cloud storage. In *CCSW*, pages 19–30, 2010.

[40] Alexander Shraer, Jean-Philippe Martin, Dahlia Malkhi, and Idit Keidar. Data-centric reconfiguration with network-attached disks. In *Proceedings of LADIS*, pages 22–26, 2010.

[41] Atul Singh, Tathagata Das, Petros Maniatis, Peter Druschel, and Timothy Roscoe. Bft protocols under fire. In *Proceedings of NSDI*, pages 189–204, 2008.

[42] Emil Stefanov, Marten van Dijk, Ari Juels, and Alina Oprea. Iris: a scalable cloud file system with efficient integrity checks. In *ACSAC*, pages 229–238, 2012.

[43] Sue-Hwey Wu, Scott A. Smolka, and Eugene W. Stark. Composition and behaviors of probabilistic i/o automata. In *Proceedings of CONCUR*, pages 513–528, 1994.

APPENDIX

A. OPTIMALITY OF PoWerStore

In this section, we prove that PoWerStore features optimal latency, by showing that writing in two rounds is necessary and we refer the reader to [16] for the necessity of reading in two rounds. We start by giving some informal definitions.

A distributed algorithm A is a set of automata [32], where automaton A_p is assigned to process p. Computation proceeds in steps of A and a *run* is an infinite sequence of steps of A. A *partial run* is a finite prefix of some run. We say that a (partial) run r *extends* some partial run pr if pr is a *prefix* of r. We say that an implementation is *selfish*, if clients write-back metadata to achieve linearizability (instead of the full value) [17]. Furthermore, we say that an operation is *fast* if it completes in a single round.

THEOREM A.1. *There is no* fast WRITE *implementation I of a multi-reader* selfish *robust storage that makes use of less than $4t+1$ servers.*

Preliminaries. We prove Theorem A.1 by contradiction assuming at most $4t$ servers. An illustration of the proof is given in Figure 3. We partition the set of servers into four distinct subsets (we call *blocks*), denoted by T_1, T_2, T_3 each of size exactly t, and T_4 of size at least 1 and at most t. Without loss of generality we assume that each block contains at least one server. We say that an operation *op* *skips* a block T_i, $(1 \leq i \leq 4)$ when all messages by *op* to

T_i are delayed indefinitely (due to asynchrony) and all other blocks T_j receive all messages by op and reply.

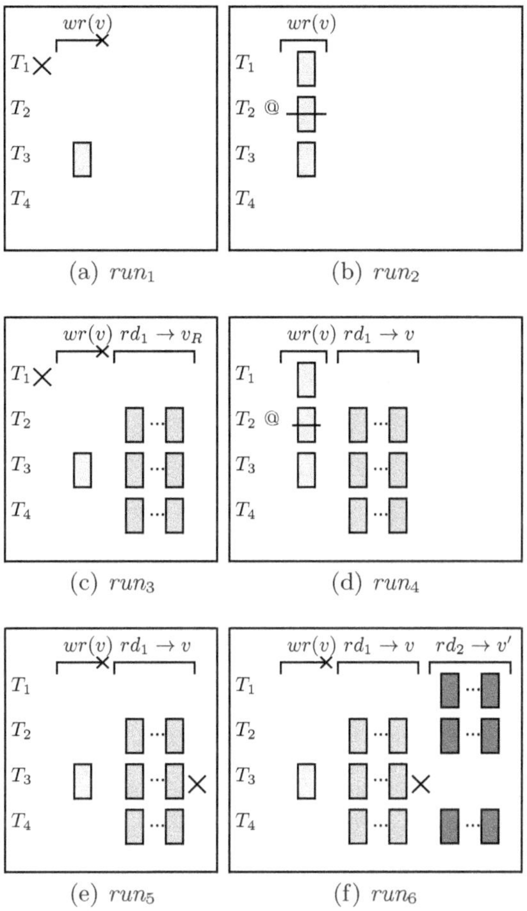

Figure 3: Sketch of the runs used in the proof of Theorem A.1.

Proof: We construct a series of runs of a linearizable implementation I towards a partial run that violates linearizability, i.e., that features two consecutive READ operations by distinct readers that return different values.

- Let run_1 be the partial run in which all servers are correct except T_1 which crashed at the beginning of run_1. Let wr be the operation invoked by the writer w to write a value $v \neq \perp$ in the storage. The WRITE wr is the only operation invoked in run_1 and w crashes after writing v to T_3. Hence, wr skips blocks T_1, T_2 and T_4.
- Let run_1' be the partial run in which all servers are correct except T_4, which crashed at the beginning of run_1'. In run_1', w is correct and wr completes by writing v to all blocks except T_4, which it skips.
- Let run_2 be the partial run similar to run_1', in which all servers except T_2 are correct, but due to asynchrony, all messages from w to T_4 are delayed. Like in run_1', wr completes by writing v to all servers except T_4, which it skips. To see why, note that wr cannot distinguish run_2 from run_1'. After wr completes, T_2 fails Byzantine by reverting its memory to the initial state.
- Let run_3 extend run_1 by appending a complete READ rd_1 invoked by r_1. By our assumption, I is wait-free. As such, rd_1 completes by skipping T_1 (because T_1 crashed) and returns (after a finite number of rounds) a value v_R.
- Let run_4 extend run_2 by appending rd_1. In run_4, all servers except T_2 are correct, but due to asynchrony all messages from r_1 to T_1 are delayed indefinitely. Moreover, since T_2 reverted its memory to the initial state, v is held only by T_3. Note that r_1 cannot distinguish run_4 from run_3 in which T_1 has crashed. As such, rd_1 completes by skipping T_1 and returns v_R. By linearizability, $v_R = v$.
- Let run_5 be similar to run_3 in which all servers except T_3 are correct but, due to asynchrony, all messages from r_1 to T_1 are delayed. Note that r_1 cannot distinguish run_5 from run_3. As such, rd_1 returns v_R in run_5, and by run_4, $v_R = v$. After rd_1 completes, T_3 fails by crashing.
- Let run_6 extend run_5 by appending a READ rd_2 invoked by r_2 that completes by returning v'. Note that in run_5, *(i)* T_3 is the only server to which v was written, *(ii)* rd_1 did not write-back v (to any other server) before returning v, and *(iii)* T_3 crashed before rd_2 is invoked. As such, rd_2 does not find v in any server and hence $v' \neq v$, violating linearizability.

□

It is important to note that Theorem A.1 allows for self-verifying data and assumes clients that may fail only by crashing. Furthermore, the impossibility extends to crash-tolerant storage using less than $3t + 1$ servers when deleting the Byzantine block T_2 in the above proof.

Path ORAM:
An Extremely Simple Oblivious RAM Protocol

Emil Stefanov[†], Marten van Dijk[‡], Elaine Shi[*], Christopher Fletcher[°], Ling Ren[°], Xiangyao Yu[°], Srinivas Devadas[°]

[†] UC Berkeley [‡] UConn [*] UMD [°] MIT CSAIL

ABSTRACT

We present Path ORAM, an extremely simple Oblivious RAM protocol with a small amount of client storage. Partly due to its simplicity, Path ORAM is the most practical ORAM scheme for small client storage known to date. We formally prove that Path ORAM requires $O(\log^2 N/\log\chi)$ bandwidth overhead for block size $B = \chi\log N$. For block sizes bigger than $\omega(\log^2 N)$, Path ORAM is asymptotically better than the best known ORAM scheme with small client storage. Due to its practicality, Path ORAM has been adopted in the design of secure processors since its proposal.

Categories and Subject Descriptors

K.6.5 [**Management of Computing and Information Systems**]: Security and Protection

General Terms

Algorithms, Security

Keywords

Oblivious RAM; ORAM; Path ORAM; access pattern

1. INTRODUCTION

It is well-known that data encryption alone is often not enough to protect users' privacy in outsourced storage applications. The sequence of storage locations accessed by the client (i.e., access pattern) can leak a significant amount of sensitive information about the unencrypted data through statistical inference. For example, Islam et. al. demonstrated that by observing accesses to an encrypted email repository, an adversary can infer as much as 80% of the search queries [21].

Oblivious RAM (ORAM) algorithms, first proposed by Goldreich and Ostrovsky [13], allow a client to conceal its access pattern to the remote storage by continuously shuffling and re-encrypting data as they are accessed. An adversary can observe the physical storage locations accessed, but the ORAM algorithm ensures that the adversary has negligible probability of learning anything about the true (logical) access pattern. Since its proposal, the research community has strived to find an ORAM scheme that is not only theoretically interesting, also practical [4, 7, 12, 14–17, 22, 23, 25–27, 30, 33–38].

In this paper, we propose a novel ORAM algorithm called *Path ORAM*[1]. This is to date the most practical ORAM construction under small client storage. We prove theoretical bounds on its performance and also present matching experimental results.

Path ORAM makes the following contributions:

Simplicity and practical efficiency. In comparison to other ORAM algorithms, our construction is arguably much simpler. Although we have no formal way of measuring its simplicity, the core of the Path ORAM algorithm can be described in just 16 lines of pseudocode (see Figure 1) and our construction does not require performing sophisticated deamortized oblivious sorting and oblivious cuckoo hash table construction like many existing ORAM algorithms [4, 7, 12–17, 22, 25–27, 35–37]. Instead, each ORAM access can be expressed as simply fetching and storing a single path in a tree stored remotely on the server. Path ORAM's simplicity makes it more practical than any existing ORAM construction with small (i.e., constant or poly-logarithmic) local storage.

Asymptotic efficiency. We prove that for a reasonably large block size $B = \chi\cdot\log N$ bits where N is the total number of blocks, Path ORAM with recursion (where recursion is proposed in Shi *et al.* [30]; see Section 3.7) achieves an asymptotic bandwidth cost of $O(\log^2 N/\log\chi)$ blocks, and consumes $O(\log^2 N/\log\chi)\omega(1)$ block client-side storage[2]. In other words, to access a single block, the client needs to in reality access $O(\log^2 N/\log\chi)$ physical blocks to hide its access patterns from the storage server. The above result achieves a failure probability of $N^{-\omega(1)}$, negligible in N.

As pointed out later in Section 1.1, our result outperforms the best known ORAM for small client storage [22], both in terms of asymptotics and practicality, for reasonably large block sizes, i.e., block sizes typically encountered in practical applications.

Practical and theoretic impact of Path ORAM. Since we first proposed Path ORAM [32] in February 2012, it

CCS'13, November 4–8, 2013, Berlin, Germany.

ACM 978-1-4503-2477-9/13/11 ...$15.00.
http://dx.doi.org/10.1145/2508859.2516660.

[1]Our construction is called Path ORAM because data on the server is always accessed in the form of tree paths.

[2]Throughout this paper, when we write the notation $g(n) = O(f(n))\cdot\omega(1)$, we mean that for any function $h(n) = \omega(1)$, it holds that $g(n) = O(f(n)h(n))$.

ORAM Scheme	Client Storage (# blocks)	Read & Write Bandwidth (# blocks)
Kushilevitz *et al.* [22]	$O(1)$	$O(\log^2 N/\log\log N)$
Gentry *et al.* [11] ($B=\chi\log N$)	$O(\log^2 N)\cdot\omega(1)$	$O(\log^3 N/(\log\log N\log\chi))\cdot\omega(1)$
Recursive Path ORAM ($B=\chi\cdot\log N$) (store stash on client)	$O(\log^2 N/\log\chi)\cdot\omega(1)$	$O(\log^2 N/\log\chi)$
Recursive Path ORAM ($B=\chi\cdot\log N$) (store stash on server)	$O(\log N)\cdot\omega(1)$	$O(\log^2 N/\log\chi)\cdot\omega(1)$

Table 1: Comparison to other ORAM schemes: Asymptotic bandwidth cost. B is the block size (in terms of # bits), N is the total number of blocks. The Path ORAM Stash is defined in Section 3. The failure probability is set to $N^{-\omega(1)}$ in this table, i.e., negligible in N.

has made both a practical and a theoretic impact in the community.

On the practical side, Path ORAM is the most suitable known algorithm for hardware ORAM implementations due to its conceptual simplicity, small client storage, and practical efficiency. Ren *et al.* built a simulator for an ORAM-enabled secure processor based on the Path ORAM algorithm [29] and the Ascend processor architecture [9,10] uses Path ORAM as a primitive. Maas *et al.* [24] implemented Path ORAM on a secure processor using FPGAs and the Convey platform.

On the theoretic side, subsequent to the proposal of Path ORAM, several theoretic works adopted the same idea of path eviction in their ORAM constructions — notably the works by Gentry *et al.* [11] and Chung *et al.* [6]. These two works also try to improve ORAM bounds based on the binary tree construction by Shi *et al.* [30]; however, as pointed out in Section 1.1 our bound is asymptotically better than those by Gentry *et al.* [11] and Chung *et al.* [6]. Gentry's Path ORAM variant construction has also been applied to secure multiparty computation [11].

Novel proof techniques. Although our construction is simple, the proof for upper bounding the client storage is quite intricate and interesting. Our proof relies on the creation of a second ORAM construction and a reduction from Path ORAM to the second ORAM construction. We provide *concrete* bounds showing that for M load/store operations on N data blocks, recursive Path ORAM with client storage $\leq R\log N/\log\chi$ blocks, server storage $28N$ blocks and bandwidth $14(\log N)^2/\log\chi$ blocks per load/store operation, fails during one of the M load/store operations with probability $\leq 14\cdot 0.625^{-R}M\log N/\log\chi$. Our empirical results in Section 5 indicate that the constants in practice are even lower than our theoretic bounds.

1.1 Related Work

Oblivious RAM was first investigated by Goldreich and Ostrovsky [12,13,25] in the context of protecting software from piracy, and efficient simulation of programs on oblivious RAMs. Since then, there has been much subsequent work [4,6,7,11–15,17,22,25–27,35,37] devoted to improving ORAM constructions. Path ORAM is based upon the binary-tree ORAM framework proposed by Shi *et al.* [30].

Optimality of Path ORAM. Under small (i.e., constant or poly-logarithmic) client storage, the best known ORAM was proposed by Kushilevitz *et al.*, and has $O(\log^2 N/\log\log N)$ blocks bandwidth cost [22].

Our Path ORAM algorithm with recursion as in Shi *et al.* [30] is competitive with Kushilevitz *et al.* [22] in terms of bandwidth cost, when the block size is at least $\Omega(\log^2 N)$ bits; and can asymptotically outperform Kushilevitz *et al.* [22] for larger block sizes. For example, for block size $B=\Omega(\log^2 N)$ bits, our bandwidth cost is $O(\log^2 N/\log\log N)$ blocks, matching the best known bound of Kushilevitz *et al.* [22], under small client storage.

Of particular interest is the case when block size is at least $\Omega(\lambda)$ bits, where λ is the security parameter (e.g., $\lambda=128$ or $\lambda=256$) and $N=poly(\lambda)$ — since this is what one typically encounters in practical applications. In this case, recursive Path ORAM's bandwidth cost is only $O(\log N)$ blocks; moreover it has $O(1)$ round-trips since the depth of recursion would be constant. Goldreich and Ostrovsky show that under $O(1)$ client storage, any ORAM algorithm must have bandwidth overhead $\Omega(\log N)$ (regardless of the block size). Since then, a long-standing open question is whether it is possible to have an ORAM construction that has $O(1)$ or $poly\log(N)$ client-side storage and $O(\log N)$ blocks bandwidth cost [13,14,22]. Our bound partially addresses this open question for reasonably large block sizes.

Comparison with Gentry *et al.* and Chung *et al.*. Gentry *et al.* [11] improve on the binary tree ORAM scheme proposed by Shi *et al.* [30]. To achieve $2^{-\lambda}$ failure probability, their scheme achieves $O(\lambda(\log N)^2/(\log\lambda\log\chi))$ blocks bandwidth cost, for block size $B=\chi\cdot\log N$ bits. Assuming that $N=poly(\lambda)$, their bandwidth cost is $O(\lambda\log N/\log\chi)$ blocks. In comparison, recursive Path ORAM achieves $O(\log^2 N/\log\chi)$ blocks bandwidth cost. Note that typically $\lambda\gg\log N$ since $N=poly(\lambda)$. Therefore, recursive Path ORAM is much more efficient than the scheme by Gentry *et al.*. Table 1 presents this comparison, assuming a failure probability of $N^{-\omega(1)}$, i.e., negligible in N. Since $N=poly(\lambda)$, the failure probability can also equivalently be written as $\lambda^{-\omega(1)}$. We choose to use $N^{-\omega(1)}$ to simplify the notation in the asymptotic bounds.

Chung and Pass [6] proved a similar (in fact slightly worse) bound as Gentry *et al.* [11]. As mentioned earlier, our bound is asymptotically better than Gentry *et al.* [11] or Chung and Pass [6].

Very recently, Chung *et al.* proposed another statistically secure binary-tree ORAM algorithm [5] based on Path ORAM. Their theoretical bandwidth bound is $\log\log n$ factor worse than ours. Their simulation results suggest an empirical bucket size of 4 [1] — which means that their practical bandwidth cost is a constant factor worse than Path ORAM, since they require operating on 3 paths in expectation for each data access, while Path ORAM requires reading and writing only 1 path.

Statistical security. We note that Path ORAM is also statistically secure (not counting the encryption). Statistically secure ORAMs have been studied in several prior works [2,8]. All known binary-tree based ORAM schemes and variants are also statistically secure [6, 11, 30] (assuming each bucket is a trivial ORAM).

2. PROBLEM DEFINITION

We consider a client that wishes to store data at a remote untrusted server while preserving its privacy. While traditional encryption schemes can provide confidentiality, they do not hide the data access pattern which can reveal very sensitive information to the untrusted server. In other words, the blocks accessed on the server and the order in which they were accessed is revealed. We assume that the server is untrusted, and the client is trusted, including the client's processor, memory, and disk.

The goal of ORAM is to completely hide the data access pattern (which blocks were read/written) from the server. From the server's perspective, read/write operations are indistinguishable from random requests.

Notations. We assume that the client fetches/stores data on the server in atomic units, referred to as *blocks*, of size B bits each. For example, a typical value for B for cloud storage is $64 - 256$ KB while for secure processors smaller blocks (128 B to 4 KB) are preferable. Throughout the paper, let N be the working set, i.e., the number of distinct data blocks that are stored in ORAM.

Simplicity. We aim to provide an extremely simple ORAM construction in contrast with previous work. Our scheme consists of only 16 lines of pseudo-code as shown in Figure 1.

Security definitions. We adopt the standard security definition for ORAMs from [34]. Intuitively, the security definition requires that the server learns nothing about the access pattern. In other words, no information should be leaked about: 1) which data is being accessed; 2) how old it is (when it was last accessed); 3) whether the same data is being accessed (linkability); 4) access pattern (sequential, random, etc); or 5) whether the access is a read or a write.

DEFINITION 1 (SECURITY DEFINITION). *Let*

$$\vec{y} := ((\mathsf{op}_M, \mathsf{a}_M, \mathsf{data}_M), \ldots, (\mathsf{op}_1, \mathsf{a}_1, \mathsf{data}_1))$$

denote a data request sequence of length M, where each op_i denotes a $\mathsf{read}(\mathsf{a}_i)$ or a $\mathsf{write}(\mathsf{a}_i, \mathsf{data})$ operation. Specifically, a_i denotes the identifier of the block being read or written, and data_i denotes the data being written. In our notation, index 1 corresponds to the most recent load/store and index M corresponds to the oldest load/store operation.

Let $A(\vec{y})$ denote the (possibly randomized) sequence of accesses to the remote storage given the sequence of data requests $\vec{y}$. An ORAM construction is said to be secure if (1) for any two data request sequences $\vec{y}$ and $\vec{z}$ of the same length, their access patterns $A(\vec{y})$ and $A(\vec{z})$ are computationally indistinguishable by anyone but the client, and (2) the ORAM construction is correct in that it returns on input $\vec{y}$ data that is consistent with $\vec{y}$ with probability $\geq 1 - negl(|\vec{y}|)$, i.e., the ORAM may fail with probability $negl(|\vec{y}|)$.

Like all other related work, our ORAM constructions do not consider information leakage through the timing channel, such as when or how frequently the client makes data requests. Achieving integrity against a potentially malicious server is discussed in Section 3.8. We do not focus on integrity in our main presentation.

3. THE PATH ORAM PROTOCOL

We first describe the Path ORAM protocol with $N/\chi + O(\log N) \cdot \omega(1)$ blocks of client storage, and then later in Section 3.7 we explain how the client storage can be reduced to $O(\log^2 N / \log \chi) \cdot \omega(1)$ blocks via recursion.

3.1 Overview

We now give an informal overview of the Path ORAM protocol. The client stores a small amount of local data in a stash. The server-side storage is treated as a binary tree where each node is a bucket that can hold up to a fixed number of blocks.

Main invariant. We maintain the invariant that at any time, each block is mapped to a uniformly random leaf bucket in the tree, and unstashed blocks are always placed in some bucket along the path to the mapped leaf.

Whenever a block is read from the server, the entire path to the mapped leaf is read into the stash, the requested block is remapped to another leaf, and then the path that was just read is written back to the server. When the path is written back to the server, additional blocks in the stash may be evicted into the path as long as the invariant is preserved and there is remaining space in the buckets.

3.2 Server Storage

Data on the server is stored in a tree consisting of buckets as nodes. The tree does not have to necessarily be a binary tree, but we use a binary tree in our description for simplicity.

Binary tree. The server stores a binary tree data structure of height $L = \lceil \log_2(N) \rceil - 1$ and 2^L leafs. The tree can easily be laid out as a flat array when stored on disk. The levels of the tree are numbered 0 to L where level 0 denotes the root of the tree and level L denotes the leafs.

Bucket. Each node in the tree is called a bucket. Each bucket can contain up to Z real blocks. If a bucket has less than Z real blocks, it is padded with dummy blocks to always be of size Z. It suffices to choose the bucket size Z to be a small constant such as $Z = 4$ (see Section 5.1).

Path. Let $x \in \{0, 1, \ldots, 2^L - 1\}$ denote the x-th leaf node in the tree. Any leaf node x defines a unique path from leaf x to the root of the tree. We use $\mathcal{P}(x)$ to denote set of buckets along the path from leaf x to the root. Additionally, $\mathcal{P}(x, \ell)$ denotes the bucket in $\mathcal{P}(x)$ at level ℓ in the tree.

Server storage size. Since there are about N buckets in the tree, the total server storage used is about $Z \cdot N$ blocks.

3.3 Client Storage and Bandwidth

The storage on the client consists of 2 data structures, a stash and a position map:

Stash. During the course of the algorithm, the client locally stores a small number of blocks in a local data structure S called the stash. In Section 6, we prove that the stash has a worst-case size of $O(\log N) \cdot \omega(1)$ blocks with high

N	Total # blocks outsourced to server
$L = \lceil \log_2 N \rceil - 1$	Height of binary tree
B	Block size (in bits)
Z	Capacity of each bucket (in blocks)
$\mathcal{P}(x)$	path from leaf node x to the root
$\mathcal{P}(x, \ell)$	the bucket at level ℓ along the path $\mathcal{P}(x)$
S	client's local stash
position	client's local position map
$x :=$ position[a]	block a is currently associated with leaf node x, i.e., block a resides somewhere along $\mathcal{P}(x)$ or in the stash.

Table 2: Notations.

probability. In fact, in Section 5.2, we show that the stash is usually empty after each ORAM read/write operation completes.

Position map. The client stores a position map, such that $x :=$ position[a] means that block a is currently mapped to the x-th leaf node — this means that block a resides in some bucket in path $\mathcal{P}(x)$, or in the stash. The position map changes over time as blocks are accessed and remapped.

Bandwidth. For each load or store operation, the client reads a path of $Z \log N$ blocks from the server and then writes them back, resulting in a total of $2Z \log N$ blocks bandwidth used per access. Since Z is a constant, the bandwidth usage is $O(\log(N))$ blocks.

Client storage size. Note that the position map is of size $NL = N \log N$ bits, or equivalently, N/χ blocks with block size $B = \chi \cdot \log N$. In Section 3.7, we use this property to recursively store the position map in $\log N / \log \chi$ separate Path ORAMs. This reduces the client storage to $O(\log^2 N / \log \chi) \cdot \omega(1)$ at the cost of increasing the bandwidth to $O(\log^2 N / \log \chi)$.

If the client stores its storage at the server, then at every load/store operation the client needs to retrieve this storage from the server. Since the client accesses the $\log N / \log \chi$ separate ORAMs one after another, the client only needs sufficient storage for reading in a single path and stash of each ORAM separately: This leads to a client storage of $O(\log N) \cdot \omega(1)$ and bandwidth $O(\log^2 N / \log \chi) \cdot \omega(1)$.

3.4 Path ORAM Initialization

The client stash S is initially empty. The server buckets are intialized to contain random encryptions of the dummy block (i.e., initially no block is stored on the server). The client's position map is filled with independent random numbers between 0 and $2^L - 1$. The position map initially contains null for the position of every block. The position null is a special value indicating that the corresponding block has never been accessed and the client should assume it has a default value of zero.

3.5 Path ORAM Reads and Writes

In our construction, reading and writing a block to ORAM is done via a single protocol called Access described in Figure 1. Specifically, to read block a, the client performs data $\leftarrow$ Access(read, a, None) and to write data* to block a, the client performs Access(write, a, data*). The Access protocol can be summarized in 4 simple steps:

Access(op, a, data*):

1: $x \leftarrow$ position[a]
2: position[a] $\leftarrow$ UniformRandom$(0 \ldots 2^L - 1)$

3: **for** $\ell \in \{0, 1, \ldots, L\}$ **do**
4: $\quad S \leftarrow S \cup \mathsf{ReadBucket}(\mathcal{P}(x, \ell))$
5: **end for**

6: data $\leftarrow$ Read block a from S
7: **if** op = write **then**
8: $\quad S \leftarrow (S - \{(\mathsf{a}, \mathsf{data})\}) \cup \{(\mathsf{a}, \mathsf{data}^*)\}$
9: **end if**

10: **for** $\ell \in \{L, L-1, \ldots, 0\}$ **do**
11: $\quad S' \leftarrow \{(\mathsf{a}', \mathsf{data}') \in S : \mathcal{P}(x, \ell) = \mathcal{P}(\mathsf{position}[\mathsf{a}'], \ell)\}$
12: $\quad S' \leftarrow$ Select $\min(|S'|, Z)$ blocks from S'.
13: $\quad S \leftarrow S - S'$
14: $\quad \mathsf{WriteBucket}(\mathcal{P}(x, \ell), S')$
15: **end for**

16: **return** data

Figure 1: Protocol for data access. Read or write a data block identified by a. If op = read, the input parameter data* = None, and the Access operation reads block a from the ORAM. If op = write, the Access operation writes the specified data* to the block identified by a and returns the block's old data.

1. **Remap block** (Lines 1 to 2): Randomly remap the position of block a to a new random position. Let x denote the block's old position.
2. **Read path** (Lines 3 to 5): Read the path $\mathcal{P}(x)$ containing block a.
3. **Update block** (Lines 6 to 9): If the access is a write, update the data stored for block a.
4. **Write path** (Lines 10 to 15): Write the path back and possibly include some additional blocks from the stash if they can be placed into the path. Buckets are greedily filled with blocks in the stash in the order of leaf to root, ensuring that blocks get pushed as deep down into the tree as possible. A block a′ can be placed in the bucket at level ℓ only if the path $\mathcal{P}(\mathsf{position}[\mathsf{a}'])$ to the leaf of block a′ intersects the path accessed $\mathcal{P}(x)$ at level ℓ. In other words, if $\mathcal{P}(x, \ell) = \mathcal{P}(\mathsf{position}[\mathsf{a}'], \ell)$.

Subroutines. We now explain the ReadBucket and the WriteBucket subroutine. For ReadBucket(bucket), the client reads all Z blocks (including any dummy blocks) from the bucket stored on the server. Blocks are decrypted as they are read.

For WriteBucket(bucket, blocks), the client writes the blocks blocks into the specified bucket on the server. When writing, the client pads blocks with dummy blocks to make it of size Z — note that this is important for security. All blocks (including dummy blocks) are re-encrypted, using a randomized encryption scheme, as they are written.

Computation. Client's computation is $O(\log N) \cdot \omega(1)$ per data access. In practice, the majority of this time is spent decrypting and encrypting $O(\log N)$ blocks per data access. We treat the server as a network storage device, so it only needs to do the computation necessary to retrieve and store $O(\log N)$ blocks per data access.

3.6 Security Analysis

To prove the security of Path-ORAM, let $\vec{y}$ be a data request sequence of size M. By the definition of Path-ORAM, the server sees $A(\vec{y})$ which is a sequence

$$\mathbf{p} = (\mathsf{position}_M[\mathsf{a}_M], \mathsf{position}_{M-1}[\mathsf{a}_{M-1}], \ldots, \mathsf{position}_1[\mathsf{a}_1]),$$

where $\mathsf{position}_j[\mathsf{a}_j]$ is the position of address a_j indicated by the position map for the j-th load/store operation, together with a sequence of encrypted paths $\mathcal{P}(\mathsf{position}_j(\mathsf{a}_j))$, $1 \leq j \leq M$, each encrypted using randomized encryption. The sequence of encrypted paths is computationally indistinguishable from a random sequence of bit strings by the definition of randomized encryption (note that ciphertexts that correspond to the same plaintext use different randomness and are therefore indistinguishable from one another). The order of accesses from M to 1 follows the notation from Definition 1.

Notice that once $\mathsf{position}_i(\mathsf{a}_i)$ is revealed to the server, it is remapped to a completely new random label, hence, $\mathsf{position}_i(\mathsf{a}_i)$ is statistically independent of $\mathsf{position}_j(\mathsf{a}_j)$ for $j < i$ with $\mathsf{a}_j = \mathsf{a}_i$. Since the positions of different addresses do not affect one another in Path ORAM, $\mathsf{position}_i(\mathsf{a}_i)$ is statistically independent of $\mathsf{position}_j(\mathsf{a}_j)$ for $j < i$ with $\mathsf{a}_j \neq \mathsf{a}_i$. This shows that $\mathsf{position}_i(\mathsf{a}_i)$ is statistically independent of $\mathsf{position}_j(\mathsf{a}_j)$ for $j < i$, therefore, (by using Bayes rule) $Prob(\mathbf{p}) = \prod_{j=1}^{M} Prob(\mathsf{position}_j(\mathsf{a}_j)) = (2^l)^{-M}$. This proves that $A(\vec{y})$ is computationally indistinguishable from a random sequence of bit strings.

Now the security follows from Theorem 1 in Section 6: For a stash size $O(\log N) \cdot \omega(1)$ Path ORAM fails (in that it exceeds the stash size) with at most negligible probability.

3.7 Recursion to Reduce Client Storage

For $\chi \geq 2$, we now explain how to reduce the client storage from N/χ blocks to $O((\log N)^2/\log\chi) \cdot \omega(1)$ blocks using an approach similar to the one introduced in [34]. The reduction of client storage comes at the cost of increasing the bandwidth from $O(\log N)$ to $O(\log^2 N/\log\chi)$. Notice that assuming that the block size $B = \chi \cdot \log(N)$ bits with $\chi \geq 2$ is a reasonable assumption that has been made by Stefanov *et al.* [33, 34] and Shi *et al.* [30]. For example, a standard 4KB block consists of 32768 bits and this assumption holds for all $N \leq 2^{16382}$.

The main idea is to recursively store the position map in a smaller Path ORAM with $N' = N/\chi$ blocks of size B bits. After $\log N/\log\chi$ recursions, this leads to a constant sized position map of the final Path ORAM. The position map stored on the client is only the one $O(1)$ sized position map for the last level of recursion. The client still needs to store the an $O(\log N) \cdot \omega(1)$ stash for each of the $O(\log N/\log\chi)$ levels of recursion, resulting in a total of $O((\log N)^2/\log\chi) \cdot \omega(1)$ blocks for the total client storage.

Path ORAM access with recursion. Consider a recursive Path ORAM made up of a series of ORAMs called $\mathsf{ORam}_0, \mathsf{ORam}_1, \mathsf{ORam}_2, \ldots, \mathsf{ORam}_X$ where ORam_0 contains the data blocks, the position map of ORam_i is stored in ORam_{i+1}, and the client stores the position map for ORam_X. To access a block in ORam_0, the client looks up its position in ORam_1, which triggers a recursive call to look up the position of the position in ORam_2, and so on until finally a position of ORam_X is looked up in the client storage. Essentially, we can replace lines 1–2 in Figure 1 with a recursive call to Access.

3.8 Integrity

Our protocol can be easily extended to provide integrity (with freshness) for every access to the untrusted server storage. Because data from untrusted storage is always fetched and stored in the form of a tree paths, we can achieve integrity by simply treating the Path ORAM tree as a Merkle tree where data is stored in all nodes of the tree (not just the leaf nodes). In other words, each node (bucket) of the Path ORAM tree is tagged with a hash of the following form

$$H(b_1 \parallel b_2 \parallel \ldots \parallel b_Z \parallel h_1 \parallel h_2)$$

where b_i for $i \in \{1, 2, \ldots, Z\}$ are the blocks in the bucket (some of which could be dummy blocks) and h_1 and h_2 are the hashes of the left and right child. For leaf nodes, $h_1 = h_2 = 0$. Hence only two hashes (for the node and its sibling) needs to be read or written for each ReadBucket or WriteBucket operation.

In [28], Ren *et al.* further optimize the integrity verification overhead for the recursive Path ORAM construction.

4. APPLICATIONS

4.1 Oblivious Binary Search Tree

Based on a class of recursive, binary tree based ORAM constructions, Gentry *et al.* propose a novel method for performing an entire binary search using a single ORAM lookup [11]. Their method is immediately applicable to Path ORAM. As a result, Path ORAM can be used to perform search on an oblivious binary search tree, using $O(\log^2 N/\log\chi)$ bandwidth. Note that since a binary search requires navigating a path of $O(\log N)$ nodes, using existing generic ORAM techniques would lead to bandwidth cost of $O((\log N)^3/\log\log N)$.

4.2 Stateless ORAM

Oblivious RAM is often considered in a single-client model, but it is sometimes useful to have multiple clients accessing the same ORAM. In that case, in order to avoid complicated (and possibly expensive) oblivious state synchronization between the clients, Goodrich *et al.* introduce the concept of *stateless* ORAM [18] where the client state is small enough so that any client accessing the ORAM can download it before each data access and upload it afterwards. Then, the only thing clients need to store is the private key for the ORAM (which does not change as the data in the ORAM changes).

In our recursive Path ORAM construction, we can download and upload the client state before and after each access. Since the client state is only $O(\log^2 N/\log\chi) \cdot \omega(1)$ and the bandwidth is $O(\log^2 N/\log\chi)$, we can reduce the permanent client state to $O(1)$ and achieve a bandwidth of $O(\log^2 N/\log\chi) \cdot \omega(1)$. Note that *during* an access the client still needs about $O(\log N) \cdot \omega(1)$ *transient* memory to perform the Access operation, but after the Access operation completes, the client only needs to store the private key.

4.3 Secure Processors

In a secure processor setting, private computation is done inside a tamper-resistant processor (or board) and main memory (e.g., DRAM) accesses are vulnerable to eavesdropping and tampering. As mentioned earlier, Path ORAM is particularly amenable to hardware design because of its simplicity and low on-chip storage requirements.

Fletcher *et al.* [9, 10] and Ren *et al.* [29] built a simulator for a secure processor based on Path ORAM. They optimize the bandwidth cost and stash size of the recursive construction by using a smaller $Z = 3$ in combination with a background eviction process that does not break the Path ORAM invariant.

Maas *et al.* [24] built a hardware implementation of a Path ORAM based secure processor using FPGAs and the Convey platform.

Ren *et al.* [29] and Maas *et al.* [24] report about 1.2X to 5X performance overhead for many benchmarks such as SPEC traces and SQLite queries. To achieve this high performance, these hardware Path ORAM designs rely on on-chip caches while making Path ORAM requests only when last-level cache misses occur.

5. EVALUATION

5.1 Stash Occupancy Distribution

Stash occupancy. *In both the experimental results and the theoretical analysis, we define the stash occupancy to be the number of overflowing blocks (i.e., the number of blocks that remain in the stash) after the write-back phase of each ORAM access.* This represents the *persistent* local storage required on the client-side. In addition, the client also requires under $Z \log_2 N$ *transient* storage for temporarily caching a path fetched from the server during each ORAM access.

Our main theorem in Section 6 shows the probability of stash overflow decreases exponentially with the stash size, given that the bucket size Z is large enough. This theorem is verified by experimental results as shown in Figure 3 and Figure 2. In each experiment, the ORAM is initially empty. We first load N blocks into ORAM and then access each block in a round-robin pattern. I.e., the access sequence is $\{1, 2, \ldots, N, 1, 2, \ldots, N, 1, 2, \ldots\}$. Section 6.3 shows this is a worst-case access pattern in terms of stash occupancy for Path ORAM. We simulate our Path ORAM for a single run for about 250 billion accesses after doing 1 billion accesses for warming-up the ORAM. It is well-known that if a stochastic process is regenerative (empirically verified to be the case for Path ORAM), the time average over a single run is equivalent to the ensemble average over multiple runs (see Chapter 5 of [19]).

Figure 2 shows the minimum stash size to get a failure probability less than $2^{-\lambda}$ with λ being the security parameter on the x-axis. In Table 3, we extrapolate those results for realistic values of λ. The experiments show that the required stash size grows linearly with the security parameter, which is in accordance with the Main Theorem in Section 6 that the failure probability decreases exponentially with the stash size. Figure 3 shows the required stash size for a low failure probability ($2^{-\lambda}$) does not depend on N. This shows Path ORAM has good scalability.

Though we can only prove the theorem for $Z \geq 6$, in practice, $Z = 4$ and $Z = 5$ also work well. $Z = 3$ behaves relatively worse in terms of stash occupancy, and it is unclear whether $Z = 3$ works.

We only provide experimental results for small security parameters to show that the required stash size is $O(\lambda)$ and does not depend on N. Note that it is by definition infeasible to simulate for practically adopted security parameters (e.g., $\lambda = 128$), since if we can simulate a failure in any reasonable amount of time with such values, they would not be considered secure.

A similar empirical analysis of the stash size (but with the path included in the stash) was done by Maas *et al.* [24].

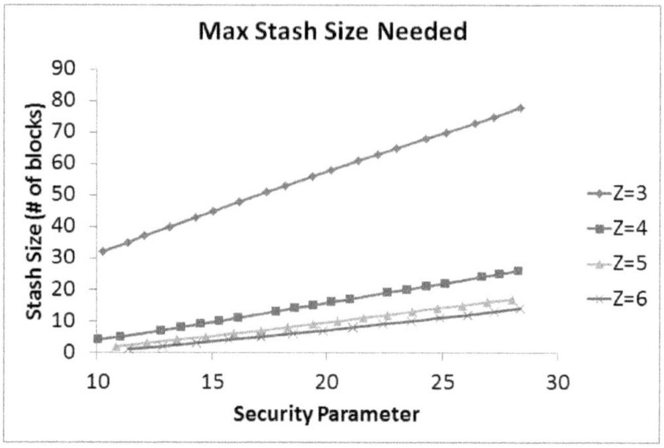

Figure 2: Empirical estimation of the required stash size to achieve failure probability less than $2^{-\lambda}$ where λ is the security parameter. Measured for $N = 2^{16}$, but as Figure 3 shows, the stash size does not depend on N (at least for $Z = 4$). The measurements represent a worst-case (in terms of stash size) access pattern. The stash size does not include the temporarily fetched path during Access.

Security Parameter (λ)	Bucket Size (Z)		
	4	5	6
	Max Stash Size		
80	89	63	53
128	147	105	89
256	303	218	186

Table 3: Required max stash size for large security parameters. Shows the maximum stash size required such that the probability of exceeding the stash size is less than $2^{-\lambda}$ for a worst-case (in terms of stash size) access pattern. Extrapolated based on empirical results for $\lambda \leq 26$. The stash size does not include the temporarily fetched path during Access.

5.2 Bucket Load

Figure 4 gives the bucket load per level for $Z \in \{3, 4, 5\}$. We prove in Section 6.3 that for $Z \geq 6$, the expected usage of a subtree T is close to the number of buckets in it. And Figure 4 shows this also holds for $4 \leq Z \leq 5$. For the levels close to the root, the expected bucket load is indeed 1 block (about 25% for $Z = 4$ and 20% for $Z = 5$). The fact that the root bucket is seldom full indicates the stash is empty after a path write-back most of the time. Leaves have slightly heavier loads as blocks accumulate at the leaves of the tree. $Z = 3$, however, exhibits a different distribution of bucket load (as mentioned in Section 5.1 and shown in Figure 2, $Z = 3$ produces much larger stash sizes in practice).

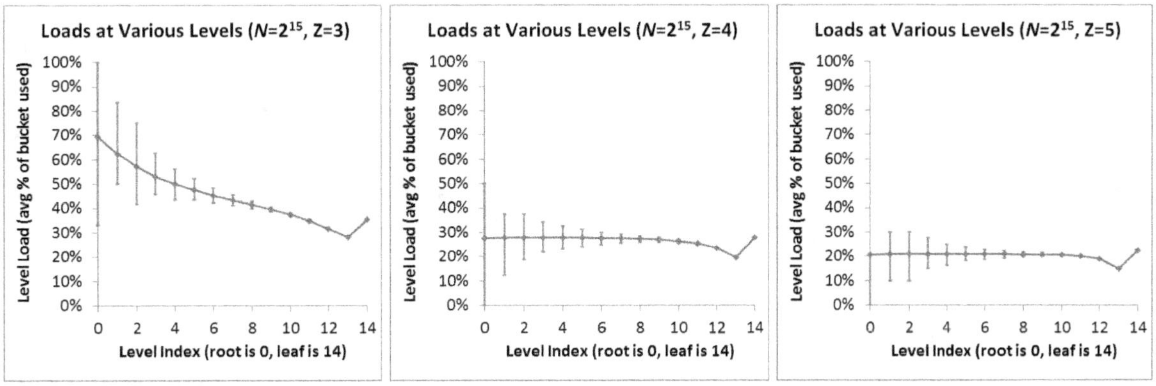

(a) Z=3 (b) Z=4 (c) Z=5

Figure 4: Average bucket load of each level for different bucket sizes. The error bars represent the 1/4 and 3/4 quartiles. Measured for a worst-case (in terms of stash size) access pattern.

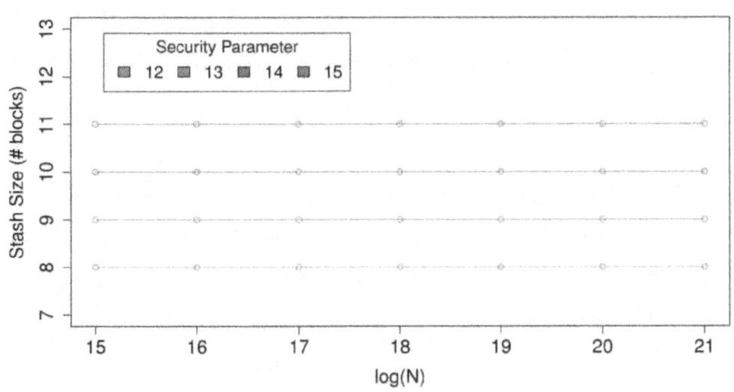

Figure 3: The stash size to achieve failure probability less than $2^{-\lambda}$ does not depend on N ($Z = 4$). Measured for a worst-case (in terms of stash size) access pattern. The stash size does not include the temporarily fetched path during Access.

6. THEORETIC BOUNDS

In this section we will bound the probability that, after a sequence of load/store operations, non-recursive Path-ORAM exceeds its stash size: We will show that this probability decreases exponentially in the size of the stash for a *constant* bucket size.

By $\mathcal{T}_L(Z)$ we denote a non-recursive Path-ORAM with $L+1$ levels in which each bucket stores Z real/dummy blocks; the root is at level 0 and the leafs are at level L.

We define a *sequence of load/store operations* $\mathbf{s}$ as a triple $(\mathbf{a}, \mathbf{x}, \mathbf{y})$ that contains (1) the sequence $\mathbf{a} = (a_j)_{j=1}^s$ of block addresses of blocks that are loaded/stored, (2) the sequence of labels $\mathbf{x} = (X_j)_{j=1}^s$ as seen by the server, and (3) the sequence $\mathbf{y} = (Y_j)_{j=1}^s$ of remapped leaf labels. (a_1, Y_1, X_1) corresponds to the most recent load/store operation, (a_2, Y_2, X_2) corresponds to the next most recent load/store operation, etc. The number of load/store operations is denoted by $s = |\mathbf{s}|$. The *working set* corresponding to $\mathbf{a}$ is defined as the number of distinct block addresses a_j in $\mathbf{a}$. We write $a(\mathbf{s}) = \mathbf{a}$.

By $\mathcal{T}_L(Z)[\mathbf{s}]$ we denote the distribution of real blocks in $\mathcal{T}_L(z)$ after a sequence $\mathbf{s}$ of load/store operations starting with an empty ORAM; $\mathbf{s}$ completely defines all the randomness needed to determine, for each block address a, its leaf label and which bucket/stash stores the block that corresponds to a. In particular the *number* of real blocks stored in the buckets/stash can be reconstructed.

We assume an infinite stash and in our analysis we investigate the usage $u(\mathcal{T}_L(Z)[\mathbf{s}])$ of the stash defined as the number of real blocks that are stored in the stash after a sequence $\mathbf{s}$ of load/store operations. In practice the stash is limited to some size R and Path-ORAM fails after a sequence $\mathbf{s}$ of load/store operations if the stash needs more space: this happens if and only if the usage of the infinite stash is at least $u(\mathcal{T}_L(Z)[\mathbf{s}]) > R$.

THEOREM 1 (MAIN). *Let* $\mathbf{a}$ *be any sequence of block addresses with a working set of size at most* N. *For a bucket size* $Z = 7$, *tree depth* $L \geq \lceil \log N \rceil + 1$ *and stash size* R, *the probability of a Path ORAM failure after a sequence of load/store operations corresponding to* $\mathbf{a}$, *is at most*

$$Prob(u(\mathcal{T}_L(Z)[\mathbf{s}]) > R | a(\mathbf{s}) = \mathbf{a}) \leq 14 \cdot 0.625^R,$$

where the probability is over the coin flips that determine $\mathbf{x}$ *and* $\mathbf{y}$ *in* $\mathbf{s} = (\mathbf{a}, \mathbf{x}, \mathbf{y})$.

For $Z = 6$ *and* $L \geq \lceil \log N \rceil + 3$ *we obtain the bound* $370 \cdot 0.667^R$.

As a corollary, for s load/store operations on N data blocks, Path ORAM with client storage $\leq R$ blocks, server storage $28N$ blocks and bandwidth $14 \log N$ blocks per load/store operation, fails during one of the s load/store operations with probability $\leq s \cdot 14 \cdot 0.625^R$. So, if we assume the number of load/stores is equal to $s = poly(N)$, then, for a stash of size $O(\log N)\omega(1)$, the probability of Path ORAM failure during one of the load/store operations is negligible in N.

Proof outline. The proof of the main theorem consists of several steps: First, we introduce a second ORAM, called ∞-ORAM, together with an algorithm that post-processes the stash and buckets of ∞-ORAM in such a way that if ∞-ORAM gets accessed by a sequence $\mathbf{s}$ of load/store operations, then post-processing leads to a distribution of real blocks over buckets that is exactly the same as the distribution as in Path ORAM after being accessed by $\mathbf{s}$.

Second, we characterize the distributions of real blocks over buckets in (a not post-processed) ∞-ORAM for which post-processing leads to a stash usage $> R$. We show that the stash usage after post-processing is $> R$ if and only if there exists a subtree T for which its "usage" in ∞-ORAM is more than its "capacity". This means that we can use the union bound to upper bound $Prob(\mathcal{T}_L(Z)[u(\mathbf{s})] > R | a(\mathbf{s}) = \mathbf{a})$ as a sum of probabilities over subtrees.

Third, we analyze the usage of subtrees T. We show how a mixture of a binomial and a geometric probability distribution expresses the probability of the number of real blocks that do not get evicted from T after a sequence $\mathbf{s}$ of load/store operations. By using the Chernoff bounding technique we prove the main theorem.

6.1 ∞-ORAM

We define ∞-ORAM, denoted by $\mathcal{R}_L(Z)$, as an ORAM that exhibits the same tree structure as Path-ORAM with $L+1$ levels but where each bucket has an *infinite* size. The interface of $\mathcal{R}_L(Z)$ operates as the interface of $\mathcal{T}_L(\infty)$ with the following distinguishing exception: Each bucket in $\mathcal{R}_L(Z)$ is partially stored in server storage and partially stored in the ORAM stash at the client; Z indicates the maximum number of blocks in a bucket that can be stored in server storage. If a bucket has more than Z real blocks, then the additional blocks are stored in the ∞-ORAM stash.

We define *post-processing*[3] $G(\mathcal{R}_L(Z)[\mathbf{s}])$ as a Greedy algorithm G that takes as input the state of $\mathcal{R}_L(Z)$ after a sequence $\mathbf{s}$ of load/store operations and repeats the following strategy:

1. Select a block in the stash that was not selected before. Suppose it has leaf label L and is stored in the bucket at level h on the path from the root to leaf L.
2. Find the highest level $i \leq h$ such that the bucket at level i on the path to leaf L stores $< Z$ blocks. If such a bucket exists, then use it to store the block. If it does not exist, then leave the block in the stash.

LEMMA 1. *The stash usage in a post-processed ∞-ORAM is exactly the same as the stash usage in Path-ORAM:*

$$u(G(\mathcal{R}_L(Z)[\mathbf{s}])) = u(\mathcal{T}_L(Z)[\mathbf{s}]).$$

Proof: We first notice that the order in which the Greedy strategy G processes blocks from the stash does not affect the number of real blocks in each bucket that are stored in server storage after post-processing: Suppose the Greedy strategy first processes a stash block b_1 with label X_1 stored in a bucket at level h_1 and suppose it finds empty space in server storage at level i_1; the Greedy strategy up to block b_1 has used up all the empty space in server storage allocated to the buckets along the path to the leaf with label X_1 at levels $i_1 < i \leq h_1$. Suppose next a stash block b_2 with label X_2 stored in a bucket at level h_2 finds empty space in server storage at level i_2; the Greedy strategy up to block b_2, which includes the post-processing of b_1, has used up all the empty space in server storage allocated to the buckets along the path to the leaf with label X_2 at levels $i_2 < i \leq h_2$. If we swap the post-processing of b_1 and b_2, then b_2 is able to find empty space in the bucket at level i_2, but may find empty space at a higher level since b_1 has not yet been processed. In this case, $i_2 < i_1$ and paths X_1 and X_2 intersect at least up to and including level i_1. This means that b_2 is stored at level i_1 and b_1 will use the empty space in server storage at level i_2. This means that the number of blocks that are stored in the different buckets after post-processing b_1 and b_2 is the same if b_1 is processed before or after b_2.

Now, we are able to show, by using induction in $|\mathbf{s}|$, that for each bucket b in a post-processed ∞-ORAM after a sequence $\mathbf{s}$ of load/store operations, the number of real blocks stored in b that are in server storage is equal to the number of blocks stored in the equivalent bucket in Path-ORAM after applying the same sequence $\mathbf{s}$ of load/store operations: The statement clearly holds for $|\mathbf{s}| = 0$ when both ORAMs are empty. Suppose it holds for $|\mathbf{s}| \geq 0$. Consider the next load/store operation to some leaf L'. After reading the path to leaf L' into the cache, Path-ORAM moves blocks from its cache/stash into the path from root to leaf L' according to algorithm $G(.)$. Therefore, postprocessing after the first $|\mathbf{s}|$ operations followed by the Greedy approach of Path ORAM that processes the $(|\mathbf{s}|+1)$-th operation is equivalent to post-processing after $|\mathbf{s}|+1$ operations where some blocks may be post-processed twice. Since the order in which blocks are post-processed does not matter, we may group together the multiple times a block b is being post-processed and this is equivalent to post-processing b exactly once as in $G(.)$. The number of real blocks in the stash is the same and this proves the lemma.

6.2 Usage/Capacity Bounds

To investigate which distributions of real blocks over buckets in a not post-processed ∞-ORAM $\mathcal{R}_L(Z)$ lead to a stash usage of $> R$ after post-processing, we start by analyzing distributions of blocks over subtrees: When we talk about a subtree T, we always implicitly assume that it is rooted at the root of the ORAM tree, i.e., T contains the root of the ORAM tree and all its nodes are connected to this root. We define $n(T)$ to be the total number of nodes in T. For ∞-ORAM we define the usage $u(\mathcal{R}_L(Z)[\mathbf{s}]; T)$ of T after a sequence $\mathbf{s}$ of load/store operations as the actual number of real blocks that are stored in the buckets of T (in ∞-ORAM blocks in a bucket are either in server storage or in the stash).

The following lemma characterizes the stash usage:

LEMMA 2. *The stash usage $u(G(\mathcal{R}_L(Z)[\mathbf{s}]))$ in post-processed ∞-ORAM is $> R$ if and only if there exists a subtree T in $\mathcal{R}_L(Z)$ such that $u(\mathcal{R}_L(Z)[\mathbf{s}]; T) > n(T)Z + R$.*

Proof: For a stash of size R, since post-processing can at most store $n(T)Z$ real blocks in T in server storage, we may interpret $n(T)Z + R$ as the *capacity* of T. Clearly, if the usage of T is more than the capacity of T, then post-processing leads to a stash usage of $> R$.

Suppose that $u(G(\mathcal{R}_L(Z)[\mathbf{s}])) > R$. Define T as the union of all paths from the root to a bucket b for which the buckets along the path in $G(\mathcal{R}_L(Z)[\mathbf{s}])$ each have Z real blocks stored in server storage. Then, $u(G(\mathcal{R}_L(Z)[\mathbf{s}]); T) > n(T)Z + R$. Also, if a real block in T or in the stash originated from a bucket b, then the Greedy approach of post-processing implies that the buckets on the path from where the block is stored in T to bucket b each store Z real blocks, therefore, $b \in T$. This shows that $u(\mathcal{R}_L(Z)[\mathbf{s}]; T) \geq u(G(\mathcal{R}_L(Z)[\mathbf{s}]); T)$, which finishes the proof of the lemma.

[3]Notice that the post-processing allows us to reason about Path-ORAM's stash size. It does not hide memory access patterns: ∞-ORAM + post-processing is only a tool for analysis, it is not an ORAM algorithm in itself.

Let $\mathbf{a}$ be a sequence of block addresses. As a corollary to Lemmas 1 and 2, we obtain

$$\begin{aligned} & Prob(u(\mathcal{T}_L(Z)[\mathbf{s}]) > R|a(\mathbf{s}) = \mathbf{a}) \\ = \; & Prob(u(G(\mathcal{R}_L(Z)[\mathbf{s}])) > R|a(\mathbf{s}) = \mathbf{a}) \\ = \; & Prob(\exists_T \; u(\mathcal{R}_L(Z)[\mathbf{s}];T) > n(T)Z + R|a(\mathbf{s}) = \mathbf{a}) \\ \leq \; & \sum_T Prob(u(\mathcal{R}_L(Z)[\mathbf{s}];T) > n(T)Z + R|a(\mathbf{s}) = \mathbf{a}), \end{aligned}$$

where the inequality follows from the union bound. The probabilities are over the coin flips that determines $\mathbf{s}$ given $a(\mathbf{s}) = \mathbf{a}$.

Since the number of ordered binary trees of size n is equal to the Catalan number C_n, which is $\leq 4^n$,

$$\begin{aligned} & Prob(u(\mathcal{T}_L(Z)[\mathbf{s}]) > R|a(\mathbf{s}) = \mathbf{a}) \leq \qquad (1) \\ & \sum_{n \geq 1} 4^n \max_{T:n(T)=n} Prob(u(\mathcal{R}_L(Z)[\mathbf{s}];T) > nZ + R|a(\mathbf{s}) = \mathbf{a}). \end{aligned}$$

6.3 Chernoff Bound

We will upper bound the probability in the sum of the right-hand side of (1) for T with $n(T) = n$. To this purpose let $\mathbf{a} = (a_j)_{j=1}^s$ be a sequence of block addresses with working set size N, i.e., $\mathbf{a}$ has N different block addresses. Let $\mathbf{s} = (\mathbf{a}, \mathbf{y} = (Y_j)_{j=1}^s, \mathbf{x} = (X_j)_{j=1}^s)$ be a sequence of load/store operations. In this section we only provide a proof sketch, precise arguments are in Section 6.4.

For each block Y_j we wish to determine the probability that Y_j gets evicted from T. We first observe that Y_j never gets evicted if $Y_j \in V$, the set of leafs in T that are also leafs in the ORAM tree. Therefore, the expectation of the usage of T is at most

$$\begin{aligned} & E[u(\mathcal{R}_L(Z)[\mathbf{s}];T)|a(\mathbf{s}) = \mathbf{a}] \leq \\ & E[\#Y_j \in V] + E[u(\mathcal{R}_L(Z)[\mathbf{s}];T)|a(\mathbf{s}) = \mathbf{a}, \forall_j Y_j \notin V]. \end{aligned}$$

Since the probability that $Y_j \in V$ is equal to $|V|/2^L$,

$$E[\#Y_j \in V] = N|V|/2^L. \qquad (2)$$

Next we observe that Y_j can only get evicted over paths to leafs with labels $X_j, X_{j-1}, \ldots, X_1$ (which correspond to the more recent load/store operations). Let u_j, as a function of the label values for $X_j, X_{j-1}, \ldots, X_1$, be the probability that Y_j is evicted from T given $Y_j \notin V$. In ∞-ORAM the worst-case address pattern $\mathbf{a}$ for a fixed working set size N does not duplicate block addresses, i.e., $s = N$ and as a consequence the labels in $(X_j)_{j=1}^N$ and $(Y_j)_{j=1}^N$ are all statistically independent of one another: Assuming non-duplicated block addresses, $u_1 \leq u_2 \leq u_3 \leq \ldots$, hence, there exist segments $U_1 = \{1, 2, \ldots, q_1\} \neq \emptyset$, $U_2 = \{q_1 + 1, \ldots, q_1 + q_2\} \neq \emptyset$, …, such that within each segment U_k the probabilities u_j, $j \in U_k$, are all equal to one another. I.e, there exists a probability h_k such that $h_k = u_j$, $j \in U_k$. We notice that the number of segments U_k with $h_k < 1$ equals $n - 2|V|$, the number of buckets that are one edge away from T, minus 1. By the definition of h_k,

$$E[\#Y_j, j \in U_k, \text{ not evicted from } T \mid |U_k|] = (1 - h_k)|U_k|. \qquad (3)$$

We notice that $u_{j+1} \neq u_j$ if and only if X_{j+1} matters in the calculation of u_{j+1}, i.e., there exists a block that can get evicted from T over the path to the leaf with label X_{j+1} while it cannot get evicted over a path to a leaf with label X_i, $1 \leq i \leq j$. This means that $X_{j+1} \notin V$ and, for each

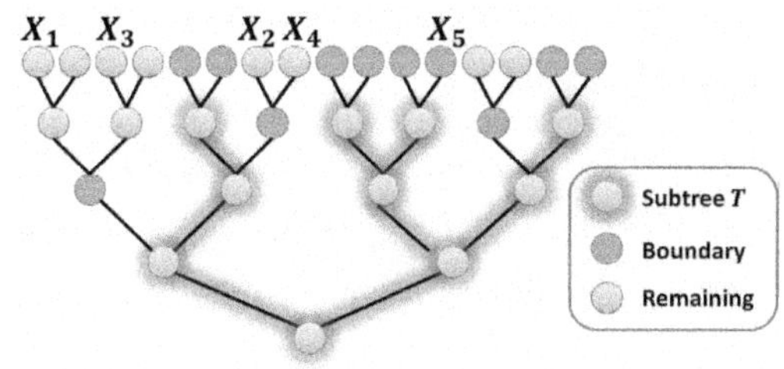

Figure 5: Subtree T for proof in Section 6.4.

$1 \leq i \leq j$, the intersection of the path to X_{j+1} and the path to X_i lies inside T, i.e., a block with label X_{j+1} cannot get evicted from T over a path to leaf X_i. This proves

$$\begin{aligned} & Prob(X_{j+1} \text{ such that } u_{j+1} = u_j) \\ = \; & Prob(X_{j+1} \in V \text{ or} \\ & \quad X_{j+1} \text{ can be evicted from } T \text{ over } (X_i)_{i=1}^j) \\ = \; & Prob(X_{j+1} \text{ evicted from } T|X_{j+1} \notin V)Prob(X_{j+1} \notin V) \\ & +Prob(X_{j+1} \in V) \\ = \; & u_j(1 - |V|/2^L) + |V|/2^L \\ = \; & 1 - (1 - u_j)(1 - |V|/2^L). \end{aligned}$$

This shows that $|U_k|$ has a geometric distribution with expectation $E[|U_k|]$ equal to

$$\begin{aligned} & \sum_{q \geq 1} (1 - (1 - h_k)(1 - |V|/2^L))^{q-1}(1 - h_k)(1 - |V|/2^L)q \\ = \; & \frac{1}{(1 - h_k)(1 - |V|/2^L)}. \qquad (4) \end{aligned}$$

Combining (3) and (4) yields

$$\begin{aligned} & E[u(\mathcal{R}_L(Z)[\mathbf{s}];T)|a(\mathbf{s}) = \mathbf{a}, \forall_j Y_j \notin V] \\ \leq \; & \sum_{k=1}^{n-2|V|} \frac{1 - h_k}{(1 - h_k)(1 - |V|/2^L)} = \frac{n - 2|V|}{1 - |V|/2^L}. \end{aligned}$$

Together with (2), the expectation of the usage of T is at most $N|V|/2^L + (n - 2|V|)/(1 - |V|/2^L)$.

In (1) we are only interested in a non-zero probability that T's usage is $> nZ + R$. Therefore, since $|V| \leq n$ and T's usage is at most N, we may constrain $|V| \leq N/Z$. For $N/2^L \leq 2$ and $Z \geq 4$, the expectation is at most $n/(1-|V|/2^L) \leq 2n$. In the sum of the right-hand side of (1) we bound the probability that T's usage is $> nZ + R$, which is a multiple larger than the expectation of the usage in T. This means that we are able to apply a Chernoff bounding technique to prove the main theorem: For bucket size Z large enough, we are able to compensate the 4^n term in (1).

6.4 Details of Chernoff Bound

Before getting into proof details, we start by giving some intuition on how blocks get evicted from a subtree T in ∞-ORAM. For simplicity we assume T has no leafs with the ORAM tree in common. Figure 5 gives an example of a subtree T; the figure also shows the boundary nodes that are at one edge distance from T. When blocks get evicted from T, they will pass through one of these boundary nodes to a higher level outside T. X_1 is the most recent label of a block that was read from ORAM and written back with a new random label Y_1. X_2 is the next older label of a block that was read from ORAM and written back with a new random label Y_2, etc.

We define S_j as the set of leafs of the ORAM tree that can be reached through a path that has a boundary node in common with one of the paths to X_1, X_2, ..., or X_j. In the example: $|S_1| < |S_2|$, since X_1 and X_2 have no boundary point in common; $S_2 = S_3$, since X_3 and X_1 have a boundary point in common; $S_3 = S_4$, since X_4 and X_2 have a boundary point in common; $|S_4| < |S_5|$, since X_5 has no boundary point in common with S_4.

Notice that the block with label Y_j only gets evicted if it is in S_j, i.e., one of the more recent load/stores of a path toX_i, $1 \leq i \leq j$, has a boundary node in common with the path to Y_j over which the corresponding block will get evicted from T. We introduce the following notation: $w_1 = |S_1| < w_2 = |S_2| = |S_3| = |S_4| < w_3 = |S_5| \ldots$ and $q_1 = 1$ denoting the number of sets S_j with size equal to w_1, $q_2 = 3$ denoting the number of sets S_j with size equal to w_2 etc. Let $m_1 = I(Y_1 \notin S_1)$, $m_2 = I(Y_2 \notin S_2)+I(Y_3 \notin S_3)+I(Y_4 \notin S_4)$, where $I(.)$ is the indicator function outputting 1 if the input is true and 0 if the input is false. We are interested in the sum $M = \sum_j m_j$, which is the number of blocks not evicted from T, in other words it equals the usage of T.

The probability distribution of q_i is a geometric distribution with its parameter a function of w_i. The probability distribution of m_i is a binomial distribution with its parameters characterized by q_i and w_i. The probability distribution of w_i is not correlated with q_i and m_i. These dependencies allow us to use Bayes rule to compute the probability distribution on M. The proof now proceeds by only considering the worst case sequence $(w_i)_{i\geq 1}$ and use probability generating functions to upper bound the tail distribution of M by using Chernoff bounding techniques.

We will now prove in detail an upper bound on the probability in the sum of the right-hand side of (1) for general T with $n(T) = n$. To this purpose let $\mathbf{a} = (a_j)_{j=1}^{s}$ be a sequence of block addresses with working set size N, i.e., $\mathbf{a}$ has N different block addresses.

Worst-case address pattern. In ∞-ORAM a worst-case address pattern $\mathbf{a}$ for a fixed working set size N does not duplicate block addresses, i.e., $s = N$ and as a consequence the labels in $(X_j)_{j=1}^N$ and $(Y_j)_{j=1}^N$ (that define $\mathbf{s}$ given $a(\mathbf{s}) = \mathbf{a}$) are all statistically independent of one another:

Suppose that there exists an address in $\mathbf{a}$ that has been loaded/stored twice in ∞-ORAM. Then, there exist indices i and j, $i < j$, with $a_i = a_j$. Without the j-th load/store, the working set remains the same and it is more likely for older blocks corresponding to a_k, $k > j$ to *not* have been evicted from T (since there is one less load/store that could have evicted an older block to a higher level outside T; also notice that buckets in ∞-ORAM are infinitely sized, so, removing the j-th load/store does not generate extra space that can be used for storage of older blocks that otherwise would not have found space). So, to maximize the probability of the right-hand side of (1), we may assume that $\mathbf{a} = (a_j)_{j=1}^{s}$ is a sequence of block addresses without duplicates.

Blocks that remain in T with probability 1. Let V be the set of leafs in T that are also leafs in the ORAM tree. Notice that if a block corresponds to a $Y_j \in V$, then it never gets evicted from T since the whole path to the leaf with label Y_j is part of T. The probability that m_0 out of the N labels Y_j are in V is equal to the binomial

$$p_0 = Prob(m_0) = \binom{N}{m_0}(\frac{|V|}{2^L})^{m_0}(1-\frac{|V|}{2^L})^{N-m_0}. \quad (5)$$

T's usage in (1) is *upper bounded* by the number m_0 of Y_j's that are in V added to T's usage after an *infinite* sequence of load/store operations, where (1) all $Y_j \notin V$ (those Y_j that were in V are replaced by labels not in V and the sequence is extended with labels not in V) and (2) labels X_j and Y_j are uniformly distributed and statistically independent.

In (1) we are only interested in a non-zero probability that T's usage is $> nZ + R$. Therefore, without loss of generality, we may constrain $|V|$ to lead to such a non-zero probability. Since $|V| \leq n$ and T's usage is at most the number N of different blocks, we may assume $|V|Z \leq nZ + R \leq N$, hence,

$$|V| \leq N/Z. \quad (6)$$

Block eviction from T. Consider the infinite sequence of load/store operations. For each leaf label X we define $X(T)$ as the set of leafs that can be reached from a bucket $b \notin T$ that is on the path from the root to X. Notice that $X(T) = \emptyset$ if and only if $X \in V$. Furthermore, the number of different non-empty sets $X(T)$ is equal to the number of nodes in the ORAM tree that are one edge away from T:

$$\#\text{ distinct non-empty sets } X(T) = 1 + n - 2|V|. \quad (7)$$

The non-empty sets $X(T)$ do not intersect with V.

By the definition of $X_i(T)$, if ∞-ORAM reads/writes a path to X_i and $Y_j \in X_i(T)$ for $j \geq i$, then Y_j gets written to a bucket outside T: The block corresponding to Y_j is counted in T's usage if and only if $Y_j \notin S_j = \cup_{i=1}^{j} X_i(T)$.

Eviction probability as a function of the sizes $|S_j|$. The sizes of sets S_j are uniquely determined by the sequence

$$w_1 = |S_1| = \ldots = |S_{q_1}|,\ w_2 = |S_{q_1+1}| = \ldots = |S_{q_1+q_2}|,\ \text{etc.}$$

By (7), the number of w_j is at most $1 + n - 2|V|$ and if $w_{1+n-2|V|}$ exists, then its is equal to $2^L - |V|$.

Let m_k be equal to the number of blocks in the subsequence $(Y_{(\sum_{t=1}^{k-1} q_t)+1}, \ldots, Y_{\sum_{t=1}^{k} q_t})$ that are $\notin S_{\sum_{t=1}^{k-1} q_t+1} = \ldots = S_{\sum_{t=1}^{k} q_t}$, in other words, they do not get evicted from T. Since leaf labels Y_j are $\notin V$, the probability that $Y_j \notin S_j$ is equal to $1 - |S_j|/(2^L - |V|)$, hence,

$$Prob(m_k|(w_t, q_t, m_t)_{t=1}^{k-1}, w_k, q_k) = Prob(m_k|w_k, q_k)$$
$$= \binom{q_k}{m_k}(1 - \frac{w_k}{2^L - |V|})^{m_k}(\frac{w_k}{2^L - |V|})^{q_k - m_k}. \quad (8)$$

Probability (8) is zero for $k \geq 1+n-2|V|$, so we may restrict k to $\leq n - 2|V|$.

Since leaf labels X_j are not constrained, the probability that S_j has size $|S_j| = |S_{j-1}|$ is equal to $(|S_{j-1}| + |V|)/2^L$, the probability that $X_j \in S_{j-1} \cup V$. Hence,

$$Prob(q_k|(w_t, q_t, m_t)_{t=1}^{k-1}, w_k) = Prob(q_k|w_k)$$
$$= (\frac{w_k + |V|}{2^L})^{q_k - 1}(1 - \frac{w_k + |V|}{2^L}). \quad (9)$$

The probability that w_k takes on a certain value only depends on the previous values w_t, $t < k$, since they determine the sizes of previously added $X_j(T)$s and therefore determine the sizes of sets $X_j(T)$ that can still be added to S_{k-1}:

$$Prob(w_k|(w_t, q_t, m_t)_{t=1}^{k-1}) = Prob(w_k|(w_t)_{t=1}^{k-1}). \quad (10)$$

We combine (8), (9) and (10) by using Bayes rule twice:

$$\begin{aligned} &Prob((w_t, q_t, m_t)_{t\geq 1}) \\ &= \prod_{k\geq 1} Prob(m_k|w_k, q_k)Prob(q_k|w_k)Prob(w_k|(w_t)_{t=1}^{k-1}) \\ &= Prob((w_t)_{t\geq 1}) \prod_{k\geq 1} Prob(m_k|w_k, q_k)Prob(q_k|w_k). \end{aligned}$$

If we sum over all possible sequences $(w_t, q_t)_{t\geq 1}$ we obtain

$$\begin{aligned} &Prob((m_t)_{t\geq 1}) \\ &= \sum_{(w_t,q_t)_{t\geq 1}} Prob((w_t)_{t\geq 1}) \cdot \\ &\quad \cdot \prod_{k\geq 1} Prob(m_k|w_k, q_k)Prob(q_k|w_k) \\ &= \sum_{(w_t)_{t\geq 1}} Prob((w_t)_{t\geq 1}) \cdot \\ &\quad \cdot \prod_{k\geq 1} \sum_{q\geq 1} Prob(m_k|w_k, q_k = q)Prob(q_k = q|w_k). \end{aligned}$$

Substituting (8) and (9) yields

$$Prob((m_t)_{t\geq 1}) = \sum_{(w_t)_{t\geq 1}} Prob((w_t)_{t\geq 1}) \prod_{k\geq 1} p_k \text{ where}$$

$$p_k = \sum_{q\geq 1} (\frac{w_k + |V|}{2^L})^{q-1}(1 - \frac{w_k + |V|}{2^L}) \cdot \binom{q}{m_k}(1 - \frac{w_k}{2^L - |V|})^{m_k}(\frac{w_k}{2^L - |V|})^{q-m_k}. \quad (11)$$

Expected number of blocks in T. Notice that the expectation $E[m_k|(w_t)_{t\geq 1}]$ is equal to

$$\begin{aligned} &\sum_{q\geq 1} (\frac{w_k + |V|}{2^L})^{q-1}(1 - \frac{w_k + |V|}{2^L})q(1 - \frac{w_k}{2^L - |V|}) \\ &= \frac{1 - w_k/(2^L - |V|)}{1 - (w_k + |V|)/2^L} = 1/(1 - |V|/2^l). \end{aligned}$$

This is proved in a different way in Section 6.3, where we use (6) to show that the expectation of the usage of T is at most $2n$ for utilization $N/2^L \leq 2$ and for bucket size $Z \geq 4$. For this reason we expect to be able to use a Chernoff bound to prove that with negligible probability T's usage is more than T's capacity:

Probability generating functions. From (5) and (11):

$$Prob(\sum_{t=0}^{n-2|V|} m_t > nZ + R) \leq \max_{(w_t)_{t\geq 1}} p, \text{ where}$$

$$p = \sum_{(m_t)_{t=0}^{n-2|V|} \text{ with } \sum_{t=0}^{n-2|V|} m_t > nZ+R} p_0 \cdot \prod_{k\geq 1} p_k.$$

The probability generating function corresponding to p_0 is

$$\begin{aligned} &\sum_{m=0}^{N} \binom{N}{m} (\frac{|V|}{2^L})^m (1 - \frac{|V|}{2^L})^{N-m} X^m \\ &= (1 + (|V|/2^L)(X-1))^N \leq exp((|V|/2^L)(X-1)N) \end{aligned}$$

and the probability generating function corresponding to p_k is equal to

$$\sum_{q\geq 1} \alpha^{q-1}(1-\alpha)[1 + \beta(X-1)]^q. \quad (12)$$

where

$$\alpha = \frac{w_k + |V|}{2^L} \leq 1 \text{ and } \beta = 1 - \frac{w_k}{2^L - |V|}.$$

By the binomial theorem, (12) is equal to

$$\begin{aligned} &\sum_{q\geq 1} \alpha^{q-1}(1-\alpha) \sum_{m=0}^{q} \binom{q}{m} (\beta(X-1))^m \\ &= 1 + \sum_{m\geq 1} \sum_{q\geq m} \binom{q}{m} \alpha^{q-1}(1-\alpha)(\beta(X-1))^m \\ &= 1 + \sum_{m\geq 1} \frac{\alpha^{m-1}}{(1-\alpha)^m} (\beta(X-1))^m. \end{aligned}$$

Notice that $\alpha \leq 1$ and $\beta/(1-\alpha) = 1/(1 - |V|/2^L) \leq 1/(1 - N/(Z2^L))$ by (6).[4] This proves that (12) is at most

$$\begin{aligned} &1 + \sum_{m\geq 1} \left[\frac{(X-1)}{1 - N/(Z2^L)}\right]^m \\ &= 1 + \frac{(X-1)}{(1 - N/(Z2^L)) - (X-1)} \\ &\leq exp(\frac{(X-1)}{(1 - N/(Z2^L)) - (X-1)}) \end{aligned}$$

for $1 \leq X < 2 - N/(Z2^L)$.

The probability generating function (corresponding to p) of the total number of blocks $M = \sum_k m_k$ in T (T's usage) given $(w_t)_{t\geq 1}$ is equal to the product of the probability generating functions of p_j, $0 \leq j \leq n - 2|V|$, which is at most

$$exp(\frac{(X-1)}{(1 - N/(Z2^L)) - (X-1)}(n - 2|V|) + (X-1)|V|\frac{N}{2^L}).$$

Let

$$L \geq \lceil \log N \rceil - 1. \quad (13)$$

Then $N/2^L \leq 2$, hence, the contribution to $(X-1)|V|$ in the exponential is negative and we obtain the upper bound

$$exp(\frac{(X-1)}{(1 - N/(Z2^L)) - (X-1)} n).$$

Let $M[X]$ denote this function.

Markov's inequality. By Markov's inequality, $\forall z$ with

$$1 < e^z < 2 - N/(Z2^L), \quad (14)$$

the tail distribution of the total number of blocks M in T given $(w_t)_{t\geq 1}$ is upper bounded by

$$\begin{aligned} Prob(M \geq nZ + R) &= Prob(e^{zM} \geq e^{z(nZ+R)}) \\ &\leq \frac{E[e^{zM}]}{e^{z(nZ+R)}} = \frac{M[e^z]}{e^{z(nZ+R)}}. \end{aligned}$$

[4]If we do not use the bound $\alpha \leq 1$ but explicitly maximize over all possible sequences $(w_t)_{t\geq 1}$ that may correspond to a subtree T of size n, then we may be able to prove the main theorem for even smaller bucket sizes $Z = 4$ or $Z = 5$.

Since the upper bound is independent of $(w_t)_{t\geq 1}$, it holds for the total number of blocks in T without a condition on $(w_t)_{t\geq 1}$, i.e.,

$$Prob(u(\mathcal{R}_L(Z)[\mathbf{s}]; T) > nZ + R | a(\mathbf{s}) = \mathbf{a}) \leq \frac{M[e^z]}{e^{z(nZ+R)}}$$
$$= exp(n\left[\frac{e^z - 1}{2 - N/(Z2^L) - e^z} - zZ\right] - zR).$$

Main theorem. The first part of the main theorem follows by substituting $Z = 7$, $e^z = 1.6$ and bounding $L \geq \lceil \log N \rceil + 1$ (notice that both (13) and (14) hold), which gives $0.625^R/4.3^n$ as an upper bound on the tail distribution. Plugging this into the union bound (1) yields

$$Prob(u(\mathcal{T}_L(Z)[\mathbf{s}]) > R | a(\mathbf{s}) = \mathbf{a})$$
$$\leq \sum_{n\geq 1} 4^n 0.625^R/4.3^n \leq 14 \cdot 0.625^R. \quad (15)$$

By substituting $Z = 6$, $e^z = 1.5$ and bounding $L \geq \lceil \log N \rceil + 3$ we obtain the bound $370 \cdot 0.667^R$, the second part of the main theorem.

Acknowledgments

This work is partially supported[5] by the NSF Graduate Research Fellowship grants DGE-0946797 and DGE-1122374, the DoD NFSEG Fellowship, NSF grant CNS-1314857, DARPA CRASH program N66001-10-2-4089, and a grant from the Amazon Web Services in Education program. We would like to thank Kai-Min Chung and Jonathan Katz for helpful discussions, Hubert Chan for his generous and unconditional help, and Kai-Min Chung for pointing out that our algorithm is statistically secure.

7. REFERENCES

[1] Personal communication with Kai-Min Chung, 2013.

[2] M. Ajtai. Oblivious rams without cryptogrpahic assumptions. In *Proceedings of the 42nd ACM symposium on Theory of computing*, STOC '10, pages 181–190, 2010.

[3] D. Asonov and J.-C. Freytag. Almost optimal private information retrieval. In *PET*, 2003.

[4] D. Boneh, D. Mazieres, and R. A. Popa. Remote oblivious storage: Making oblivious RAM practical. Manuscript, `http://dspace.mit.edu/bitstream/handle/1721.1/62006/MIT-CSAIL-TR-2011-018.pdf`, 2011.

[5] K.-M. Chung, Z. Liu, and R. Pass. Statistically-secure oram with $\tilde{O}(\log^2 n)$ overhead. `http://arxiv.org/abs/1307.3699`, 2013.

[6] K.-M. Chung and R. Pass. A simple oram. `https://eprint.iacr.org/2013/243.pdf`, 2013.

[7] I. Damgård, S. Meldgaard, and J. B. Nielsen. Perfectly secure oblivious RAM without random oracles. In *TCC*, 2011.

[8] I. Damgård, S. Meldgaard, and J. B. Nielsen. Perfectly secure oblivious ram without random oracles. In *TCC*, pages 144–163, 2011.

[9] C. Fletcher, M. van Dijk, and S. Devadas. Secure Processor Architecture for Encrypted Computation on Untrusted Programs. In *Proceedings of the 7th ACM CCS Workshop on Scalable Trusted Computing*, pages 3–8, Oct. 2012.

[10] C. W. Fletcher. Ascend: An architecture for performing secure computation on encrypted data. In *MIT CSAIL CSG Technical Memo 508*, April 2013.

[11] C. Gentry, K. Goldman, S. Halevi, C. Julta, M. Raykova, and D. Wichs. Optimizing oram and using it efficiently for secure computation. In *PETS*, 2013.

[12] O. Goldreich. Towards a theory of software protection and simulation by oblivious rams. In *STOC*, 1987.

[5]Any opinions, findings, and conclusions or recommendations expressed in this material are those of the author(s) and do not necessarily reflect the views of the funding agencies.

[13] O. Goldreich and R. Ostrovsky. Software protection and simulation on oblivious rams. *J. ACM*, 1996.

[14] M. T. Goodrich and M. Mitzenmacher. Privacy-preserving access of outsourced data via oblivious RAM simulation. In *ICALP*, 2011.

[15] M. T. Goodrich, M. Mitzenmacher, O. Ohrimenko, and R. Tamassia. Oblivious ram simulation with efficient worst-case access overhead. In *Proceedings of the 3rd ACM workshop on Cloud computing security workshop*, CCSW '11, pages 95–100, New York, NY, USA, 2011. ACM.

[16] M. T. Goodrich, M. Mitzenmacher, O. Ohrimenko, and R. Tamassia. Practical oblivious storage. In *CODASPY*, 2012.

[17] M. T. Goodrich, M. Mitzenmacher, O. Ohrimenko, and R. Tamassia. Privacy-preserving group data access via stateless oblivious RAM simulation. In *SODA*, 2012.

[18] M. T. Goodrich, M. Mitzenmacher, O. Ohrimenko, and R. Tamassia. Privacy-preserving group data access via stateless oblivious ram simulation. In *Proceedings of the Twenty-Third Annual ACM-SIAM Symposium on Discrete Algorithms*, SODA '12, pages 157–167. SIAM, 2012.

[19] M. Harchol-Balter. *Performance Modeling and Design of Computer Systems: Queueing Theory in Action.* Performance Modeling and Design of Computer Systems: Queueing Theory in Action. Cambridge University Press, 2013.

[20] A. Iliev and S. W. Smith. Protecting client privacy with trusted computing at the server. *IEEE Security and Privacy*, 3(2):20–28, Mar. 2005.

[21] M. Islam, M. Kuzu, and M. Kantarcioglu. Access pattern disclosure on searchable encryption: Ramification, attack and mitigation. In *Network and Distributed System Security Symposium (NDSS)*, 2012.

[22] E. Kushilevitz, S. Lu, and R. Ostrovsky. On the (in)security of hash-based oblivious RAM and a new balancing scheme. In *SODA*, 2012.

[23] J. R. Lorch, B. Parno, J. W. Mickens, M. Raykova, and J. Schiffman. Shroud: Ensuring private access to large-scale data in the data center. *FAST*, 2013:199–213, 2013.

[24] M. Maas, E. Love, E. Stefanov, M. Tiwari, E. Shi, K. Asanovic, J. Kubiatowicz, and D. Song. Phantom: Practical oblivious computation in a secure processor. ACM CCS, 2013.

[25] R. Ostrovsky. Efficient computation on oblivious rams. In *STOC*, 1990.

[26] R. Ostrovsky and V. Shoup. Private information storage (extended abstract). In *STOC*, pages 294–303, 1997.

[27] B. Pinkas and T. Reinman. Oblivious RAM revisited. In *CRYPTO*, 2010.

[28] L. Ren, C. Fletcher, X. Yu, M. van Dijk, and S. Devadas. Integrity verification for path oblivious-ram. In *Proceedings of the 17th IEEE High Performance Extreme Computing Conference*, September 2013.

[29] L. Ren, X. Yu, C. Fletcher, M. van Dijk, and S. Devadas. Design space exploration and optimization of path oblivious ram in secure processors. In *Proceedings of the Int'l Symposium on Computer Architecture*, pages 571–582, June 2013. Available at Cryptology ePrint Archive, Report 2012/76.

[30] E. Shi, T.-H. H. Chan, E. Stefanov, and M. Li. Oblivious RAM with $O((\log N)^3)$ worst-case cost. In *ASIACRYPT*, pages 197–214, 2011.

[31] S. W. Smith and D. Safford. Practical server privacy with secure coprocessors. *IBM Syst. J.*, 40(3):683–695, Mar. 2001.

[32] E. Stefanov and E. Shi. Path o-ram: An extremely simple oblivious ram protocol. *CoRR*, abs/1202.5150, 2012.

[33] E. Stefanov and E. Shi. ObliviStore: High performance oblivious cloud storage. In *IEEE Symposium on Security and Privacy*, 2013.

[34] E. Stefanov, E. Shi, and D. Song. Towards practical oblivious RAM. In *NDSS*, 2012.

[35] P. Williams and R. Sion. Usable PIR. In *NDSS*, 2008.

[36] P. Williams and R. Sion. Round-optimal access privacy on outsourced storage. In *CCS*, 2012.

[37] P. Williams, R. Sion, and B. Carbunar. Building castles out of mud: practical access pattern privacy and correctness on untrusted storage. In *CCS*, 2008.

[38] P. Williams, R. Sion, and A. Tomescu. Privatefs: A parallel oblivious file system. In *CCS*, 2012.

PHANTOM: Practical Oblivious Computation in a Secure Processor

Martin Maas, Eric Love, Emil Stefanov, Mohit Tiwari[‡], Elaine Shi[†], Krste Asanović, John Kubiatowicz, Dawn Song

University of California, Berkeley [‡] University of Texas, Austin [†] University of Maryland, College Park

ABSTRACT

We introduce PHANTOM[1], a new secure processor that obfuscates its memory access trace. To an adversary who can observe the processor's output pins, all memory access traces are computationally indistinguishable (a property known as obliviousness). We achieve obliviousness through a cryptographic construct known as Oblivious RAM or ORAM. We first improve an existing ORAM algorithm and construct an empirical model for its trusted storage requirement. We then present PHANTOM, an oblivious processor whose novel memory controller aggressively exploits DRAM bank parallelism to reduce ORAM access latency and scales well to a large number of memory channels. Finally, we build a complete hardware implementation of PHANTOM on a commercially available FPGA-based server, and through detailed experiments show that PHANTOM is efficient in both area and performance. Accessing 4KB of data from a 1GB ORAM takes 26.2us (13.5us for the data to be available), a 32× slowdown over accessing 4KB from regular memory, while SQLite queries on a population database see $1.2 - 6\times$ slowdown. PHANTOM is the first demonstration of a practical, oblivious processor and can provide strong confidentiality guarantees when offloading computation to the cloud.

Categories and Subject Descriptors

C.1 [**Processor Architectures**]: Miscellaneous

Keywords

Secure Processors; Oblivious RAM; FPGAs; Path ORAM

1. INTRODUCTION

Confidentiality of data is a major concern for enterprises and individuals who wish to offload computation to the cloud. In particular, cloud operators have physical access to machines and can observe sensitive information (data and code) as it moves between a CPU and physical memory [17, 19, 42]. In response to such attacks, commercial interest in protecting off-chip data has begun to grow [1].

[1]PHANTOM stands for **P**arallel **H**ardware to make **A**pplications **N**on-leaky **T**hrough **O**blivious **M**emory.

CCS'13, November 4–8, 2013, Berlin, Germany.

ACM 978-1-4503-2477-9/13/11 ...$15.00.
http://dx.doi.org/10.1145/2508859.2516692.

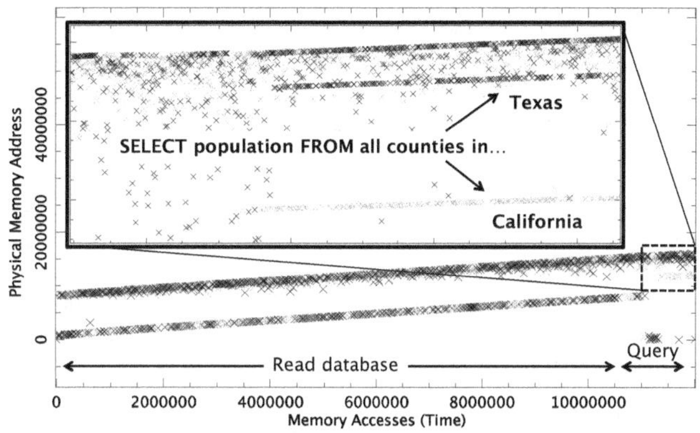

Figure 1: Visible information leakage in memory address traces from SQLite, running on a RISC-V processor model with caches. Two queries running on the same SQLite database yield clearly discernible memory accesses.

To protect against such attacks, prior work has proposed secure processors [27, 29, 33, 34] that automatically encrypt and integrity-check all data outside the processor – whether in DRAM or non-volatile storage.

Although secure processors encrypt memory contents, off-the-shelf DRAMs require that *memory addresses* be transmitted over the memory bus in cleartext. An attacker with physical access can snoop the memory bus and observe the locations of RAM accessed [19] and in turn learn sensitive data such as encryption keys or information about user-level programs [42] and guest VMs in a virtualized server [15].

As an example, we demonstrate how a program is susceptible to information leaks through the address bus. Figure 1 plots memory accesses over time for a simulated processor running two different SQLite queries – to select Californian citizens v. Texas citizens – on a population census database. The two queries generate a *visually* distinct address trace, even when the effects of on-chip caches and SQLite instruction fetches are accounted for.

Preventing such information leakage requires making memory address traces computationally indistinguishable, or *oblivious.* In this paper, we propose a new hardware architecture for efficient oblivious computation that ensures both *data confidentiality* and *memory trace obliviousness.* In other words, an attacker capable of snooping the memory bus and the DRAM contents cannot learn anything about the secret program memory – not even the DRAM locations accessed.

Oblivious RAM: We rely on an algorithmic construct called Oblivious RAM (ORAM), initially proposed by Goldreich and Ostrovsky [11], and later improved in numerous subsequent works [12, 14, 38]. Intuitively, ORAM techniques obfuscate memory access patterns through random permutation, reshuffling, and reencryption of memory contents, and require varying amounts of *trusted memory* that the adversary cannot observe. To develop a practical ORAM in hardware, we adopt Path ORAM proposed by Stefanov *et al.* [32] – a simple algorithm with a high degree of memory access parallelism. Path ORAM builds on the new binary-tree ORAM framework recently proposed by Shi *et al.* [28].

Other recent work has also used Path ORAM to propose a secure processor (ASCEND [9, 26]); this work focused on optimizing the basic Path ORAM *algorithm* and on a design-space exploration of algorithm parameters using a simple model of a CPU and ORAM controller. In contrast, we focus on building a practical oblivious system – complete with a CPU, an ORAM controller, and running non-trivial programs like SQLite running obliviously on the CPU. The high-level algorithmic optimizations in ASCEND are complementary to our algorithmic improvements targeted at Path ORAM's microarchitecture and to our work in designing and building a practical oblivious system.

Challenges: Making oblivious processors practical poses several challenges. The first is Path ORAM's significant memory bandwidth overhead – more than 100× over a non-secure access. Second, Path ORAM's irregular, data-driven nature makes it difficult to simply add more memory channels and build a deterministic yet efficient ORAM controller. Finally, we do not propose a custom chip but rely on an off-the-shelf FPGA platform that, on the one hand, can provide high memory bandwidth but on the other hand restricts us to use a slow FPGA for the ORAM controller logic. The ratio of slow logic to high memory bandwidth makes the problem of scaling to more memory channels even harder.

Contributions: In this paper, we present PHANTOM, a processor that exploits a highly parallel memory system in combination with a novel ORAM controller to implement an efficient oblivious system. Specifically, we make the following technical contributions:

1. Empirical Model for Path ORAM. We determine Path ORAM's trusted memory requirements by simulating both synthetic, worst-case memory access traces and SPEC benchmark traces. We develop an empirical model for Path ORAM's trusted memory size v. size of the ORAM, and show that SPEC benchmarks' high degree of memory locality means that they require considerably less trusted memory than the worst-case access traces.

2. Efficient ORAM Microarchitecture. We introduce an ORAM controller architecture that is very effective at utilizing high-bandwidth DRAM – even when implemented on slow FPGA logic. We propose critical improvements of the Path ORAM algorithm, and a deeply pipelined microarchitecture that utilizes 93% of the maximum DRAM bandwidth from 8 parallel memory controllers, while only fetching the minimum amount of data that Path ORAM requires. As a result, PHANTOM achieves close to the optimal 8× speedup over a baseline design with 1 memory controller.

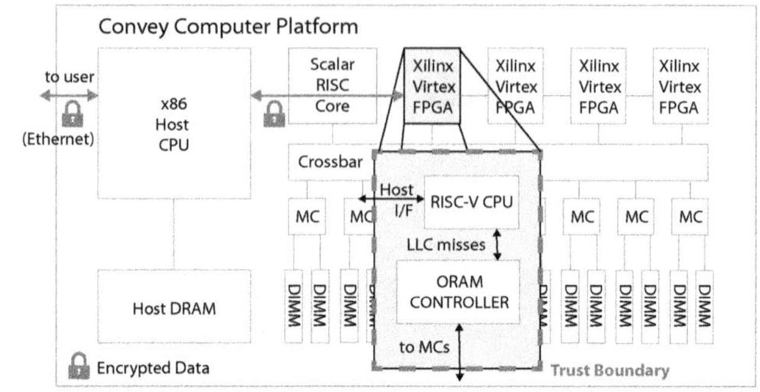

Figure 2: Phantom prototype on a Convey HC-2ex Computing Platform. PHANTOM comprises a CPU, non-volatile memory, and an ORAM controller implemented on a single chip (here, an FPGA). All *digital* signals outside the PHANTOM chip are assumed to be visible to the adversary.

3. Real-world evaluation. We build and evaluate PHANTOM's oblivious memory controller on an FPGA-based computing platform running SQLite workloads, and simulate its performance for different cache sizes. Using several ORAM configurations, we show that PHANTOM logic requires only 2% of the logic on a Xilinx Virtex 6 FPGA and a single FPGA is sufficient to support an ORAM of 1GB effective size. The PHANTOM prototype sustains 38,191 full 4KB ORAM accesses per second to a 1GB ORAM – which translates to 0.2× to 5× slowdown for SQLite queries.

To the best of our knowledge, this is the first practical demonstration of an oblivious processor.

2. PLATFORM OVERVIEW

2.1 Usage Model

We consider a setting where a *user* wants to offload sensitive data and computation to the cloud, a *cloud provider* sells infrastructure as a service, and a *hardware manufacturer* creates secure FPGAs.

We envision a secure processor that has non-volatile memory on-chip to store a unique private key. A remote client can establish a session key with a *loader* program on the secure processor and then transfer an encrypted ORAM image with sensitive data and code to the processors physical memory (i.e. DRAM). The loader then executes the code obliviously and stores results back into ORAM. The remote client can collect the encrypted results once the time allocated for the computation is complete.

PHANTOM is our take at this secure processor. It supports two usage scenarios: 1) The remote client stores all sensitive computation, including both code and data, into PHANTOM's ORAM. PHANTOM, which comprises a general purpose RISC core and an ORAM controller on a trusted chip (an FPGA in our prototype), then executes this program obliviously. 2) The remote user runs a trusted program on a standard processor (after establishing a dynamic root of trust), and does her best to keep sensitive data in confidential on-chip memory [1]. When sensitive data must be spilled off-chip, the trusted program makes encrypted ORAM reads/writes through the PHANTOM coprocessor. The second scenario is harder to make verifiably secure because preventing plain-text data from going off-chip on a commercial microprocessor is complicated, but has the benefit that existing applications can be ported easily and can run faster than on the FPGA.

2.2 Attack Model

We aim to protect against untrusted cloud providers. We trust users and hardware manufacturers (malicious hardware attacks [36] are out of scope) and focus on digital attacks where the cloud provider probes board-level interconnect and chip pins to learn confidential data. While existing secure processors prevent explicit data leakage with encryption, we prevent *implicit* information leakage through the address bus. Specifically, we provide the property that "for any two data request sequences of the same length, their access patterns are computationally indistinguishable by anyone but the client" (from definition of ORAM security [31]).

Note that the *total* execution time (i.e. a termination channel) is out of scope for ORAM. However, information leaks through this channel can be countered by computing the worst case execution time for a program, or through offline program analysis to set execution times that are independent of classified data. Further, the timing of *individual* ORAM accesses does not leak information if PHANTOM is deployed such that a non-stop stream of DRAM traffic is maintained. Cache hits inside the CPU or the ORAM controller would not alter the pattern of DRAM accesses observable by an adversary and only reduce the execution time (i.e. timing channels are reduced to a termination channel).

Our current implementation does not ensure *integrity* of data, but the Path ORAM tree can be treated as a Merkle tree to efficiently provide integrity with freshness [25, 32]. We do not consider software-level digital attacks where malicious software relies on covert channels through the processor or operating system. Such attacks can be addressed using architectural and OS support for strong isolation [20,35], obfuscation [23], and deterministic execution [4,8].

Analog attacks that exploit the physical side-effects of computation – such as temperature, EM radiation, or even power draw – are orthogonal to our proposal as well. These can be addressed through techniques that normalize or randomize the potential physical side-effects of computation. Further, timing and termination channels can be eliminated by normalizing the program execution time and rate of memory access by the secure CPU. Alternate obfuscation approaches [23] exist as well.

2.3 FPGAs: Opportunities & Challenges

We implemented our ORAM system on a Convey HC-2ex server (Figure 2). The HC2-ex is a heterogeneous computing platform with a server-grade Intel Xeon CPU connected to a custom board that features four large FPGAs (Xilinx Virtex-6 LX760) and 16 independent memory channels, each with 64 DRAM banks, for a combined memory of 64GB. Convey's combination of reconfigurable logic and high bandwidth memory system presents an opportunity to make the memory bandwidth-hungry ORAM algorithm practical.

Designing high performance logic on an FPGA, however, is challenging. FPGAs operate at much lower frequencies than custom chips – for instance, a simple RISC CPU runs at only 75MHz, and the PHANTOM controller runs at 150MHz – because logic is implemented as a network of interconnected look-up tables. Our task thus is to map Path ORAM, an irregular data-driven algorithm, onto slow FPGA logic and yet ensure that 1) PHANTOM maximizes memory bandwidth utilization, and 2) execution time of an ORAM access is independent of the access pattern. Sections 4 and 5 describe how we achieve these requirements.

3. THE PATH ORAM ALGORITHM

Intuitively, the Path ORAM algorithm prevents information leakage through memory addresses by reshuffling contents of untrusted memory after each access, such that accesses to the same location cannot be linked (while also encrypting the accessed content with a different nonce at every access). Furthermore, we assume the secure processor has a small amount of trusted memory, which the ORAM controller can access without revealing any information to the attacker. This memory is used to keep track of where data resides in untrusted memory. Path ORAM ensures that all that is visible to an attacker is a series of random-looking accesses to untrusted memory.

Path ORAM allows data to be read and written in units called *blocks*. All data stored by an ORAM instance is arranged in untrusted memory as a binary tree structure, each node of which contains space to store a few blocks. When a request is made to the ORAM for a particular block, the controller looks up the block's current location in a table in trusted memory called the *position map*. In the position map, every block is assigned to a particular *leaf node* of the ORAM tree, and the Path ORAM algorithm guarantees an invariant that each block will be resident in one of the nodes along the path from the tree's root to the block's designated leaf node. Reading this entire path into the *stash* – a data structure that stores data blocks in trusted memory – will thus necessarily retrieve the desired block along with other blocks on the path to the same leaf node.

After the requested block is found and its data returned to the requester (e.g. a CPU), the ORAM controller writes the same path back to memory. Since a requested block is reassigned to a random leaf node before it is written back to untrusted memory, it may belong to a different path from that on which it was read. Since all paths emanate from the root, they will have at least the root node in common, but there is a 50% chance they will not share any others, in which case the reassigned block will have to stay in the root node. If no additional steps were taken, the upper levels of the tree would thus quickly become full. A Path ORAM implementation therefore has to move blocks in the stash as deep as possible towards the leaf of the current path as it is written back – this is called *reordering*. At the same time, blocks may stay behind in the stash if there is no space for them in the path.

The obliviousness of Path ORAM stems from the fact that blocks are reassigned to random leaf nodes every time they are accessed. Repeated accesses to the same block will appear as accesses to a random sequence of paths through the tree (each of which consists of a full read followed by a full write of the same path). Algorithm 1 summarizes the Path ORAM algorithm, and Figure 3 illustrates its execution.

3.1 Algorithmic Details

Path ORAM represents the full binary tree as a set of partitions in untrusted memory that each represent a node of the tree and are called *buckets*. Buckets are themselves divided into a fixed number of *slots* (usually four) that can each hold a single block and its associated *header*.

All data stored in untrusted memory has to be encrypted at all times, and is reencrypted with a different nonce during every ORAM operation that touches it (otherwise it would be possible to correlate accesses to the same data). Each block's header therefore contains a nonce that changes every

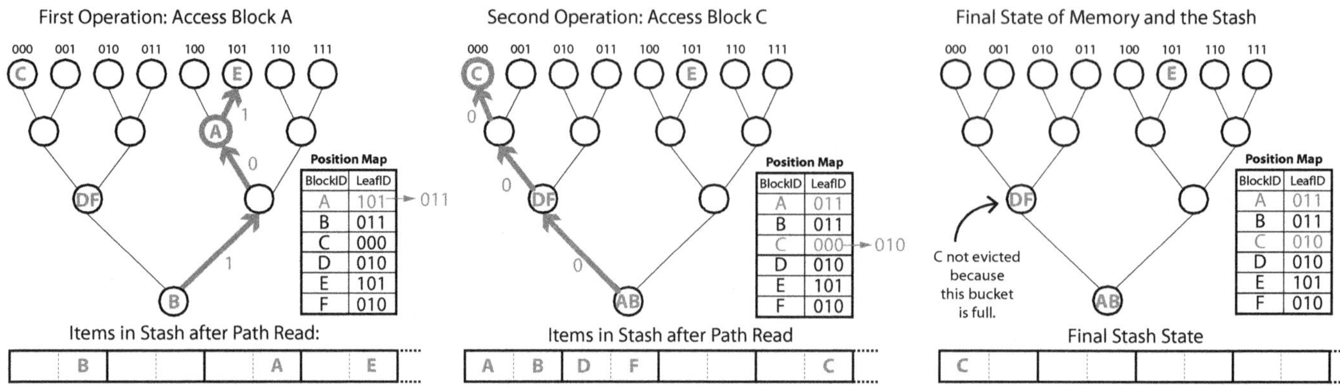

Figure 3: The Path ORAM Algorithm from [32]. The algorithm's operation is demonstrated for two path reads on a small ORAM tree. The first is a read of Block A, which the position map shows must be located somewhere on the path to leaf 101. Reading this path results in blocks B and E also being read into the stash. Block A is then randomly reassigned to leaf 011, and is therefore moved to the root of the path as it is being written back, since this is as far as it can now be inserted on the path to 101. Next, block C is read. Since the position map indicates that it is on the path to leaf bucket 000, that path is read, bringing blocks A, B, D, and F into the Stash as well. C is reassigned to leaf 010 and the bucket containing D and F is already full, so it can only be in the root of the path being written back. However, A and B must also be in the root as they cannot be moved any deeper, so C cannot be inserted. It therefore remains in the stash beyond the ORAM access.

time the block is accessed, and affects the encryption of the entire block.

All slots of the tree that do not contain a block are filled with *dummies*, which contain no actual data but are encrypted in the same way as blocks so that their cipher text is indistinguishable from that of a block. Dummies are ignored for reordering and are not written into the stash.

Even with reordering, there can be cases where not all blocks in the stash can be written back to the current path (Figure 3). This is addressed by making the stash larger than a path worth of blocks. Blocks that cannot be written back remain in the stash and are carried over into the next ORAM access and handled the same as if they had been read during that operation. At the start of an ORAM operation, it therefore has to be checked whether the block is in the stash already. If it is, a random path can be accessed to not leak this information.

Stash overflows: It is important to note that the stash may *overflow* (i.e. no more blocks can be fit into the stash). Path ORAM can recover from overflows by reading and writing random paths and try to evict blocks from the stash during those path reads and writes. While this does not leak information (the random path accesses are indistinguishable from regular ORAM accesses), it increases execution time and may hence cause execution to not finish in the allotted time. It is therefore desirable to size the stash in such a way that these accesses occur rarely. In Section 3.2 we present an empirical analysis to determine a stash size that makes these overflows extremely unlikely.

Access timing: To avoid information leakage through memory access timing, Path ORAM can perform a non-stop sequence of path reads and writes, accessing a random path if there is no outstanding ORAM request from the CPU. Stash hits can be hidden by performing a fake path access as well, and multiple stash hits can be hidden behind the same access. As described in Section 2.2, this is orthogonal to our microarchitecture (and hence not implemented) but would be required in a real deployment.

Algorithm 1 Pseudo-code of Path ORAM [32]

```
procedure ACCESS (block_id, read_write)
  if block_id in stash, access block there and exit
  leaf_id ← position_map [block_id]
  position_map [block_id] ← new random position
  path[] ← read path from root to leaf_id
  add all blocks found in path to stash
  if read_write = READ then
    return block with id block_id in stash
  else
    overwrite block with id block_id in stash
  end if
  write path from leaf_id to root (evicting as many blocks
    as possible and filling up with dummies)
```

Fundamental Overheads: Path ORAM's obliviousness has both space and bandwidth costs.

The capacity N of the ORAM is defined as the number of logical blocks it can store. We set the number of leaf nodes in the tree to $N/4$, and the number of blocks in each bucket to 4. As a result, 50% of the physical memory is available as oblivious memory (including data and 0.4% for block headers) and the rest is reserved for dummy blocks.

Since each block access results in an entire path read and write, Path ORAM's bandwidth overheads range from 104× for a 13-level ORAM tree (16MB capacity with 4KB blocks) to 192× for a 24-level tree (32GB capacity with a 4KB blocks). Consequently, the task of building a real, well-performing ORAM system becomes quite challenging: in particular, such a system will have to read two orders of magnitude more data per memory access.

3.2 Empirical Stash Size Analysis

To implement Path ORAM, we first had to determine a suitable stash size that makes stash overflows unlikely.

Our goal was to find a stash size such that the overflow probability is $2^{-\lambda}$ for a suitable value of λ, e.g. $\lambda = 128$. One way to do this is to rely on a recent theoretic bound [32]

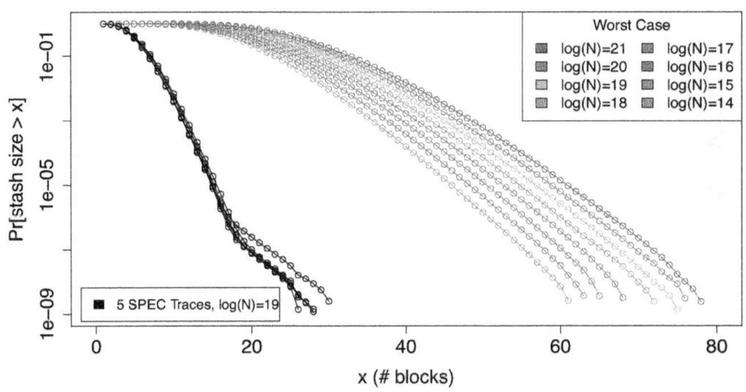

Figure 4: Distribution of stash sizes for SPEC and worst-case traces. N is the size of the ORAM in blocks. Unlike in the Path ORAM paper [32], the stash size measured includes the temporarily fetched path during Access.

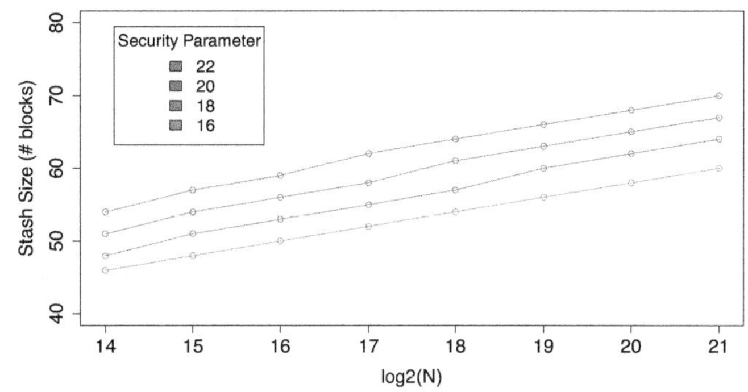

Figure 5: Empirical measurements of minimum stash size such that the probability of the stash overflowing is bounded by $2^{-\lambda}$ where λ is the security parameter. Unlike in the Path ORAM paper [32], the stash size measured includes the temporarily fetched path during Access.

on Path ORAM. However, this theoretic bound is only tight up to a constant factor.

We performed an empirical analysis that determines the required size of the stash with high confidence. Our analysis is based on a number of long simulation runs of the ORAM algorithm (reassigning ORAM blocks to random leaf nodes at every access)[2].

We run the algorithm for billions of time steps, and measure the fraction of time the stash has size at most x, for varying values of x. The purpose is to determine the stash size for a given overflow probability of $2^{-\lambda}$. We should set λ to be a large enough (say, 80). However, we cannot simulate far enough to $\lambda = 80$, since such negligible overflow probabilities are computationally infeasible to directly measure. We therefore simulate for smaller λ values and extrapolate the stash size for large λs based on the theoretic analysis of Path ORAM [32].

We used two different kind of memory access traces as input for this simulation. 1) *Worst-case traces* that exhibit no locality (i.e. blocks $1, 2, \ldots$ are accessed sequentially, wrapping around after the last block): this represents the worst-case input for the stash size [32] since accessing a block that is not already in the stash will cause more blocks to be read into the stash; and 2) *SPEC traces*: real-world memory access traces that exhibit high locality. We therefore expect to see lower stash consumption compared to worst-case traces. The benchmarks we ran were *mcf*, *cactus*, *gemsfdtd*, *lesli3d* and *soplex* with an ORAM block size of 4KB. We chose these benchmarks as they had a large number of cache misses and would thus stress the stash. While we choose our implementation's stash size conservatively based on the worst-case traces, the SPEC traces also shed light on how differently real-world traces behave in comparison with the worst-case.

We start with an initially empty ORAM and first perform N accesses to place all N blocks within the Path ORAM tree. Then we perform another 100 million round-robin (worst-case) memory accesses to warm up the ORAM. For the worst-case traces, we then simulate 5 billion memory accesses and record the stash size each time the stash content changes. The SPEC traces have 1.6 billion to 11 billion memory accesses.

[2]It is well-known that for regenerative stochastic processes, time average is equal to ensemble average — therefore, a single long run is as good as many shorter runs.

For each trace, Figure 4 plots the fraction of accesses during which the stash size exceeded a particular value. Each of the values on the y-axis corresponds to a particular probability $2^{-\lambda}$ that the stash will overflow at any given access, where we call λ the *security parameter*. In practice, a good value for λ may be 128. For large enough values of λ, we should not expect to see any stash overflows in any reasonable amount of time (just like encryption cannot be broken in any reasonable amount of time).

Using the data from Figure 4, we derived the minimum stash size that makes the probability of overflowing $2^{-\lambda}$ for a fixed λ, varying the size of the ORAM (N). The results are shown in Figure 5. The figure suggests that for a given security parameter, the stash size grows linearly in $\log N$.

Based on the findings in Figures 4 and 5, and the closed form theoretic bound in [32], using least square fitting, we determined the following minimum stash size (here the stash counts both the temporarily fetched path during access and the overflowing blocks):

$$2.19498 \log_2(N) + 1.56669\lambda - 10.98615$$

with an R^2 value of 0.9973.

From the known theoretic bound on Path ORAM [32], we know that the above stash size includes two parts: 1) a $O(\log N)$ part for storing the path fetched from the server; and 2) a $O(\lambda)$ part for storing overflowing blocks after the write-back phase of each ORAM access. Based on the above formula, we designed the PHANTOM prototype with a stash size of 128 or 256 for $\log N = 13$ to 19, to achieve corresponding security parameter values from $\lambda = 65$ to $\lambda = 143$.

4. THE ORAM CONTROLLER

In this section, we discuss how PHANTOM achieves high performance compared to a naïve Path ORAM implementation without breaking its security guarantees.

Recalling Section 2, PHANTOM receives an encrypted program and data as input, and produces encrypted data as output. PHANTOM's CPU runs the program and generates an address to access from the ORAM on each last-level cache miss. The ORAM controller then translates this address into a leaf node, reads and decrypts the path to the leaf, and returns a value to the CPU or updates the appropriate block. It then encrypts and writes back the entire path.

Levels (N)	17	19	17
Block size	4096	4096	1024
Stash size O(C)	128	256	128
1 MC (baseline)	34816	38912	8704
8 MCs, pick from stash	10880	21888	9248
8 MCs, non-overlapped sort	5248	6912	1984
8 MCs, overlapped sort (ours)	4352	4864	1088

Table 1: Potential improvement from optimizations in cycles (or time) per ORAM access. Baseline is an ORAM processor with one memory controller (MC). PHANTOM uses 8 MCs and adds novel sorting stage to Path ORAM; we expect it to be 8× better than the baseline.

4.1 Achieving High Performance

Like all ORAM schemes, Path ORAM has a fundamental overhead in the amount of data that needs to be accessed per memory request (e.g. 136× for a 1GB ORAM with 4KB block size). Path ORAM's bandwidth requirement thus motivates the use of platforms such as Convey HC-2ex that have wide memory systems: by employing a 1,024b-wide memory system rather than a conventional 128b-wide one, we can achieve a potential speed-up of 8× over a naïve implementation. However, exploiting the higher memory bandwidth is non-trivial: it is necessary to co-optimize the hardware implementation and the Path ORAM algorithm itself.

We now present the key design decisions of our implementation. Table 1 summarizes the potential performance gains over a naïve implementation. We call these numbers 'potential' because the analysis assumes a perfect PHANTOM implementation without DRAM stalls. We demonstrate experimentally in Section 6 that PHANTOM comes close to this ideal on an actual FPGA implementation.

Table 1 presents three different ORAM configurations and a baseline design that uses a standard, 128 bit wide memory controller (MC) operating at 150MHz. The baseline assumes that all ORAM logic is free and accesses are limited only by the bandwidth of a single MC, namely 34,816 cycles to access a 17-level ORAM with 4kB block. Our potential performance-gains are therefore conservative estimates.

Memory layout to improve utilization: Simply using a wide memory bus does not yield maximum DRAM utilization. Concurrent accesses to addresses in the same bank – bank conflicts – lead to stalls and decrease DRAM bandwidth utlilization. To resolve such bank conflicts, we present a precise layout of the Path ORAM tree in memory (DRAM) where data is striped across memory banks, ensuring that *all* DRAM controllers can return a value almost every cycle following an initial setup phase. Fully using eight memory controllers in parallel thus reduces the 136× bandwidth overhead to a 17×, making ORAM controller logic on the FPGA the main implementation bottleneck.

Picking Blocks for Writeback: Bringing 1,024b per cycle into PHANTOM raises acute performance problems: the operation of the Path ORAM algorithm now has to complete much faster than it did before, to keep up with the memory system (e.g. PHANTOM needs to decrypt and encrypt 1,024 bits per cycle in parallel). While encryption can be parallelized by using multiple AES units in counter mode, the Path ORAM algorithm still has to manage its stash and decide which blocks from the stash to write back after each ORAM access (the reordering step from Section 3).

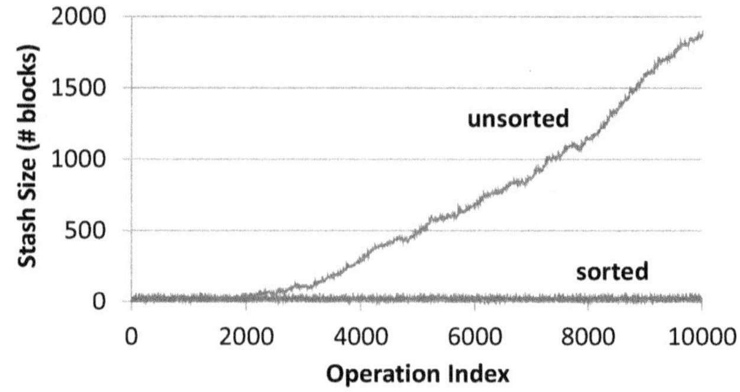

Figure 6: Benefits of sorting the stash contents before each write phase (N=2^{19}). Our heap-based reordering data structure ensures that we can sort the stash efficiently without stalling the ORAM. If we instead tried to use an efficient (O(1)) stash eviction strategy that doesn't perform sorting, the stash size will grow uncontrollably. Note: unlike in the Path ORAM paper [32], the stash size measured here includes the temporarily fetched path.

The latter is of particular importance: The ORAM controller has to find the block that can be placed deepest into the current path, and do so while the memory controllers push in data at 1,024b per cycle . One approach would be to scan the entire stash and pick a possible block for every position on the path (starting from the bottom), in parallel with writing to memory. However, with Convey's high memory bandwidth, scanning through the stash takes longer than writing out an ORAM block, causing this approach to achieve less than 2× the potential performance improvement with stash size $C = 128$ (Table 1).

At the same time, in order to keep the stash small, it is crucial to select each block from the *entire* stash – including both the current path blocks and old blocks. To verify whether a simpler alternative would suffice, we analyze an $O(1)$ option: choosing from the top 4 entries in a list of ORAM blocks to be written back, instead of considering the entire stash to find the block that can be pushed the furthest down the current path. Our analysis – in Figure 6 – shows that this simple scheme to choose blocks for write-back causes the stash to grow uncontrollably.

We hence propose a different approach – to split the task of picking the next block to write to the current path into two phases: a *sorting phase* that sorts blocks by how far they can be moved down the current path, and a *selection stage* that (during writeback) looks at the last block in the sorted list and checks in one cycle whether it can be written back into the current position or not – if not, no other block can, and we have to write a dummy.

We further improve on this approach by replacing the sorting and selection stages by a min-heap This replaces an $O(C \log C)$ operation by two $O(\log C)$ operations, where C is the size of the stash. This makes it now possible to overlap sorting completely with the path read and selecting with the path write phase.

Treetop Caching inside the Stash: While the stash is required by Path ORAM as a temporary store for ORAM blocks while they wait to be written out, it can also be used to improve performance by securely caching ORAM blocks on-chip. We propose to cache k levels of the ORAM tree inside the stash – we call this *treetop caching* – which saves PHANTOM from fetching these parts of the path from

DRAM. Since the number of nodes is low at levels close to the root, caching a few levels improves ORAM latency and throughput significantly while using only modest amounts of trusted memory. Our results demonstrate this insight experimentally (Figure 12).

We designed PHANTOM's stash management to support treetop caching with minimal effort (as well as other methods, such as LRU caching). To do so, we use a content-addressable memory (CAM) that serves as lookup-table for entries in the stash, but is also used as directory for caching and as free-list to find empty slots in the stash. This avoids placing caches separate from the stash – one of our previous prototypes showed that this leads to performance delays from checking the cache and moving ORAM blocks between the cache and the stash (and additionally complicates PHANTOM's logic, which makes obliviousness harder to ensure).

Meeting FPGA Constraints: Each on-chip memory module on an FPGA (i.e a Block RAM or BRAM) is limited to 2 read/write ports. However, BRAMs in PHANTOM that constitute the stash have to be multiplexed among four functional units (encryption, decryption and reads/writes by the secure CPU). We designed PHANTOM such that all the units that read from or write to the stash are carefully scheduled such that only a single read port and a single write port on the BRAM is in use at any particular clock cycle. Implementing the heap to reorder stash entries also requires similar tricks which we describe in Section 5.6.

FPGAs also impose strict timing constraints on our design. Convey's DRAM controllers operate at 150MHz which makes this frequency the minimum target for PHANTOM. We modified a baseline PHANTOM implementation extensively to replicate and pipeline critical paths, and implemented PHANTOM's RISC CPU on a separate clock domain (75MHz) from the ORAM controller to meet timing constraints.

4.2 Preserving Security

Design principles for obliviousness: We use two simple design principles to ensure that PHANTOM's design does not break Path ORAM's obliviousness guarantees. Any operation – checking the position map, reordering, caching etc – that depends on ORAM data is either a) statically fixed to take the worst-case time or b) is overlapped with another operation that takes strictly longer time. PHANTOM's decrypt operation could, for example, be optimized by not decrypting dummy ORAM blocks – but this leaks information since it would cause an operation to finish earlier depending on whether the last block was a dummy or not. Instead, PHANTOM pushes dummy blocks through the decryption units just the same as actual data blocks. These two design principles yield a completely deterministic PHANTOM pipeline. Figure 7 shows how the different operations in PHANTOM overlap with reading and writing a path.

Terminating timing channels at the periphery: The DRAM interface requires further attention to ensure security. PHANTOM sends path addresses to all DRAM controllers in parallel, but these controllers do not always return values in sync with each other. Although DRAM stalls do not compromise obliviousness (DRAM activity is not confidential), propagating these timing variations into PHANTOM's design can make PHANTOM's timing analysis complicated. To keep PHANTOM's internal behavior deterministic

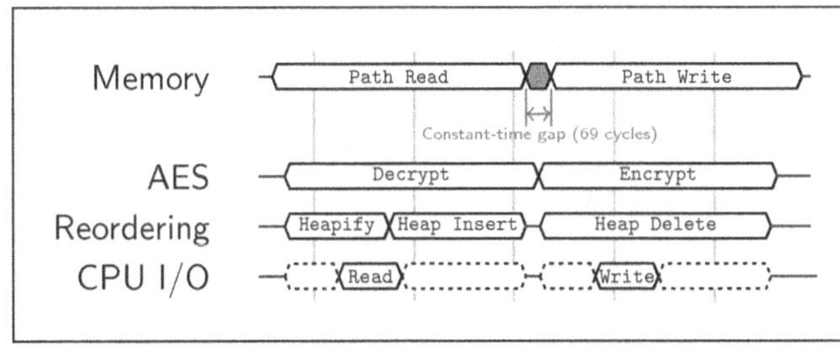

Figure 7: Overlapping the different steps of the Path ORAM algorithm with the memory accesses.

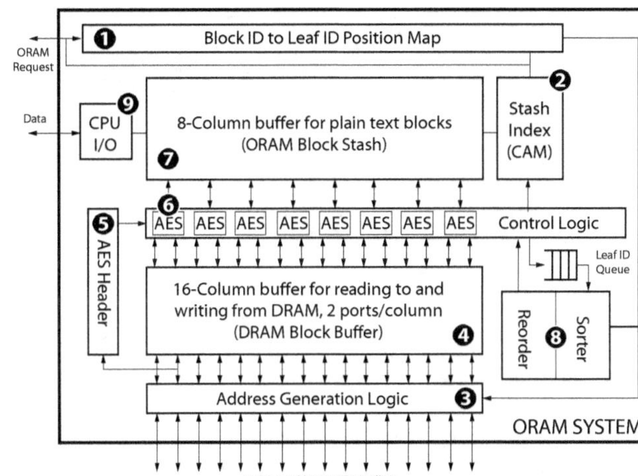

Figure 8: Overview of the ORAM system.

and simple to analyze, we introduce DRAM buffers at the interface with external DRAMs to isolate the rest of PHANTOM's ORAM controller from timing variations in the memory system. At the same time, all inputs to the DRAM interface and their timing are public (a leaf id and 1,024b of encrypted data per cycle during writeback), so that no information can be leaked out of PHANTOM.

5. DETAILED MICROARCHITECTURE

The goal of PHANTOM's microarchitecture is to make maximum use of the available DRAM bandwidth (e.g. up to 1,024b/cycle on the Convey HC-2ex). This involves accelerating all computation related to Path ORAM such that it can be completely overlapped with the memory accesses.

Figure 8 shows how the microarchitecture components fit together and Figure 9 illustrates PHANTOM's data path in further detail. First, ORAM blocks are read from memory, decrypted, and written to the stash – we call this the *read phase*. After the read phase, blocks are read from the stash, encrypted, and written back to memory using the *same functional units* as in the read phase. This is the *write phase*. Concurrently to the read and write phases, PHANTOM reorders the blocks in the stash and returns a value to the secure CPU (or writes a value into an ORAM block).

5.1 Data Structures

The *Position Map* (❶ in Figure 9) is the central data structure for making memory accesses oblivious, and stores a mapping from ORAM blocks to the leaf node in the ORAM tree that the block is assigned to.

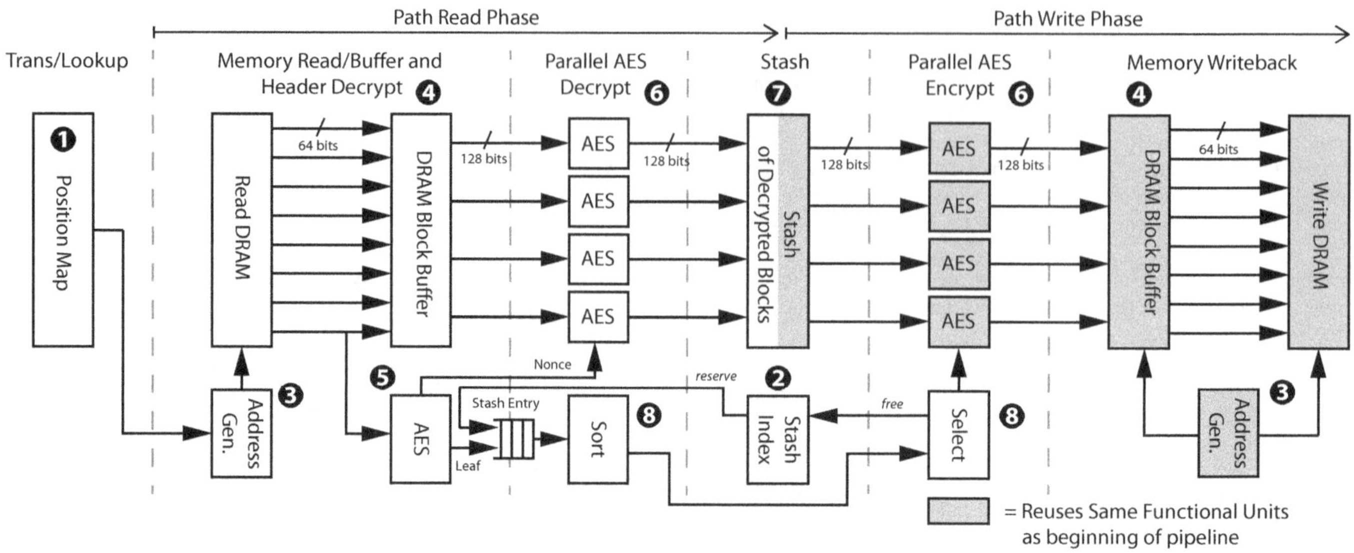

Figure 9: The data path in Phantom resembles a boomerang: Data is read, decrypted and written to the stash. It is then read from the stash, encrypted and written back to memory, using the same functional units.

The *Stash* ❼ buffers ORAM blocks in plaintext. Its size is chosen to make the overflow probability small (Section 3.2). Any block that is decrypted in the read phase is put into the stash, and blocks are removed from the stash when they are encrypted in the write phase. All blocks stored in the stash are striped across 8 independent *columns* (i.e. memories), each accessed by an AES unit (Section 5.3). This is necessary to reduce the critical path (and achieve the clock frequencies required for the Convey platform).

The *Stash Index* ❷ is a content-addressable memory (CAM) that stores the address of the block contained in each entry of the stash, including a bit to indicate whether a stash entry is occupied. Before decrypting a block, the stash index is queried to find a free slot. During a path write, once encryption of a block finishes, the corresponding entry of the Stash Index is set to free.

The Stash Index is queried before starting each ORAM access, in parallel with the position map. If the requested block is present, the ORAM controller will read or write to the stash directly, rather than initiating a Path ORAM access . Querying the Stash Index and the Position Map adds a single cycle latency to each request. Position Maps grow linearly with ORAM sizes and may have to be pipelined to keep the critical timing path low (up to 4-deep for the position map of a 17-level tree, representing an additional 4 cycles of latency). Updating the stash index requires 2 cycles, but these are overlapped with the path reads/writes.

5.2 DRAM Interface

PHANTOM's DRAM Interface takes a leaf ID and fetches an entire path from the untrusted DRAM into the trusted memory on the FPGA.

Memory Request Generation: The Convey platform features 1,024 DRAM banks (64 for each of its 16 memory channels). We cannot place ORAM blocks sequentially in the memory address space if we want to fetch data at (close to) peak bandwidth. Instead, we place each word such that the DRAM banks' latency can be hidden behind successive 64 bit words being read from different DRAM banks.

We stripe each ORAM block across the 1,024 banks such that every memory controller accesses all its banks in sequence, reading a 64 bit word from each bank, wrapping around after the last bank. Going round-robin across all DRAM banks allows each bank enough time to open a DRAM row and return its data to the memory controller without the controller having to stall.

DRAM Buffer: As encrypted data arrives from memory, it is put into the *DRAM Buffer* in order to be decrypted in subsequent stages. In practice, DRAM controllers often run ahead or fall behind, and the DRAM Buffer waits until it receives a complete row – the maximum number of bits received from DRAM each cycle (1,024 bits on the HC2-ex) – before forwarding it into AES decryption units. To account for worst case DRAM stalls, we provision the DRAM Buffer with space to store an entire path of ORAM blocks. During the write phase, the DRAM Buffer stores encrypted data from the AES units on its way to be written back to memory, absorbing DRAM stalls without stalling AES encryption.

The DRAM Buffer thus isolates the internals of PHANTOM from these timing variations. As long as it consumes 1,024 bits of data per cycle out of the DRAM buffer, and produces data at this rate during write-back, PHANTOM is completely shielded from any DRAM timing variations.

The DRAM Buffer is implemented using 16 independent columns. Each column serves one memory channel and keeps track of how much data it has received from the memory system – we use a feature of the HC-2ex that forces the memory controllers to buffer responses internally and deliver them in order, so that the DRAM Buffer only has to store how many words each column has received. As soon as all the words of a row are available, the buffer notifies the rest of the system that it is ready to be consumed.

5.3 Encryption of ORAM Blocks

Once data has arrived in the DRAM buffer, it is consumed by AES units to be decrypted into the stash. The same units also encrypt all data as it is written back from the stash into the DRAM buffer. PHANTOM uses eight AES-

128 units in counter mode (CTR). This approach was chosen since counter-mode allows to parallelize both encryption and decryption, which is crucial to maintain the required throughput of 1,024 bits per cycle.

Each ORAM block has an associated clear-text nonce for CTR stored in its first 128 bits. This is followed by the block's (encrypted) header which includes the block's address and whether or not it is a dummy. As an optimization, we store the block's leaf ID in the header as well – this reduces accesses to the position map.

Decryption is overlapped with the rest of the algorithm by adding a forwarding path ❺ from the first two memory channels. It buffers all words belonging to nonces in a way similar to the DRAM buffer, so that the nonces are available when the AES units start to decrypt the actual block.

Further, to avoid wasting oblivious storage, we store the nonce in the block header itself (since more than 80 out of 128 header bits are free—even for large configurations). The nonce now gets encrypted, since it is included in the header AES block. Thus, the forwarding path must be extended with an AES unit (❺) that pre-decrypts the header while the rest of the block is being fetched, and (due to overlapping and in-order memory fetch) is always finished by the time the rest of the block is available to be decrypted.

Decrypting the header in advance also allows PHANTOM to insert a block into its proper place in the reorder heap (Section 5.4) as the rest of the block is being read in. PHANTOM reserves an entry in the stash once the header is decrypted; subsequent outputs of the AES decrypt units can then be directly written to this entry without any stalls, thereby hiding the 2-cycle stall of the stash index lookup.

The choice AES implementation is a trade-off that is largely orthogonal to our architecture, as long as each AES unit is pipelined and provides 128 bit/cycle throughput. In our prototype, we model AES-128 units as 11-stage pipelines that take nonce, plain text and counter as input, and output the cipher text 11 cycles later. We also assume an on-chip pseudo-random number generator. While we do not include the size of AES and PRNG in our results, we show that PHANTOM's Oblivious RAM controller requires less than 2% of the logic on the FPGA, leaving ample space for AES and PRNG functionality (e.g. 9 instances of the AES unit from [18] would require 50% of the logic). Instead of generating truly random numbers, our prototype uses a linear feedback shift register to emulate the PRNG functionality (which is insecure but sufficient for prototyping purposes).

5.4 Heap-based Reordering

As described in Section 3, the blocks in the stash have to be reordered before being written back to memory, ensuring that each block is moved as far down the path as possible. A simple implementation would be to go through the entire stash to choose a candidate block for each slot. However, this search would take a larger number of cycles than the write-back of the block to memory would take, making PHANTOM computationally bound rather than memory bound (especially on an FPGA).

For this to be avoided, PHANTOM has $max\_time = (block\text{-}size / bits\_per\_cycle)$ cycles to pick a block to write back. In our prototype with 4KB block size, max_time is 32. With a stash of about 100 entries, a linear scan will not be hidden behind a 32-cycle ORAM block read, and will thus introduce a 68-cycle stall per block or $(68 \times path\_length \times blocks\_per\_bucket)$ cycles for each ORAM access – roughly 1,200 additional cycles for a 17-level ORAM. To avoid these stalls, we need a different approach to overlap reordering with memory accesses.

An alternative to scanning the entire stash is to pre-sort its entries based on their leaf IDs. PHANTOM reorders stash entries by performing a bit-wise XOR between the leaf IDs of entries in the stash and the leaf id of the current path (assuming the leaf id naming scheme from Figure 3), and then *sorting* (❽) them in increasing order. The resulting order reflects how deeply they can be placed in the tree, since the first bit where they disagree with the current leaf ID is at a later, lower-order bit.

Once entries have been sorted like this, PHANTOM determines which blocks to write back by going backwards through the path (starting from the leaf), always looking at the lowest element in the sorter and checking its leaf id to determine whether it can be placed in the currently examined slot in the tree. If yes, PHANTOM inserts the block, otherwise PHANTOM fills the slot with a dummy (dummies are generated directly by the AES units - instead of reading data from the stash, they simply encrypt some random data). We call this the *select* stage (❽) .

While this approach avoids going through the entire stash, the sorting step requires further attention. Algorithms like Merge sort cannot overlap the sorting with the memory reads and writes (because they require all entries to be present at the time the sort begins). On the other hand, algorithms like Insertion sort (which is simple to implement in hardware and can perform the insertion in parallel to the reads) would make the latency to insert each block to be linear in the stash size and larger than max_time (i.e. 32 cycles).

We therefore designed PHANTOM to use a min-heap instead. Rather than performing all the sorting either during the write phase or during the read phase, we insert the blocks into a heap as they are read in, and remove them from the heap as we write them back. This takes logarithmic time both during reading and write phases, but as a result, the phases can individually keep up with the speed at which blocks arrive from memory and have to be written back.

We also have to make sure that we *heapify* (re-sort) the current contents of the heap at the start of *each* ORAM operation, since the ordering changes with the leaf id of the path. We therefore added a queue (which holds as many entries as the stash) to buffer incoming blocks in case the heapify operation is not complete by the time the first blocks come out of the AES unit. We can show that the overall latency does not exceed the amount of time we have during the read phase, ensuring that we always finish sorting by the time the last block has finished reading (a proof can be found in Appendix A).

With these optimizations, we can overlap the reordering completely with the memory requests, making our system completely limited by the available memory bandwidth.

5.5 Control Logic

PHANTOM's control logic coordinates the movement of data through the ORAM controller, namely from the DRAM buffer through the AES units to the stash (and vice versa for the write-back), maintaining the invariant that data takes constant number of cycles to flow down the pipeline.

At its core, the control logic consists of a pipeline that runs in parallel to the pipelined AES units. Each stage of the

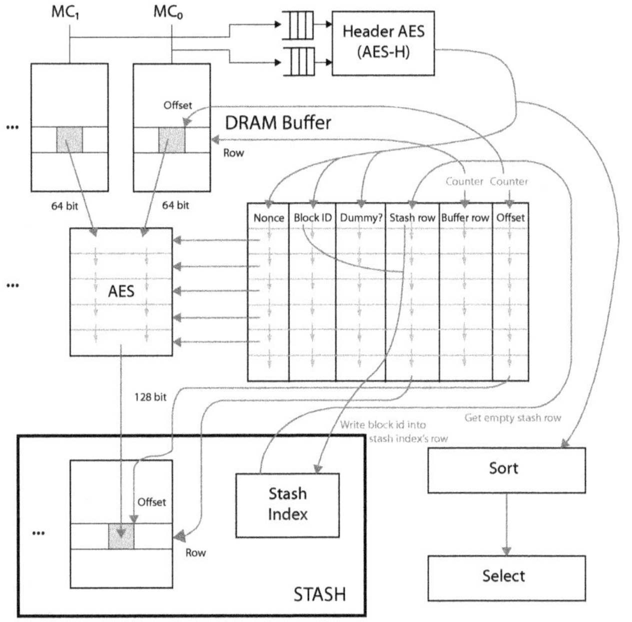

Figure 10: The Control Logic The arrows describe the flow of data through the logic.

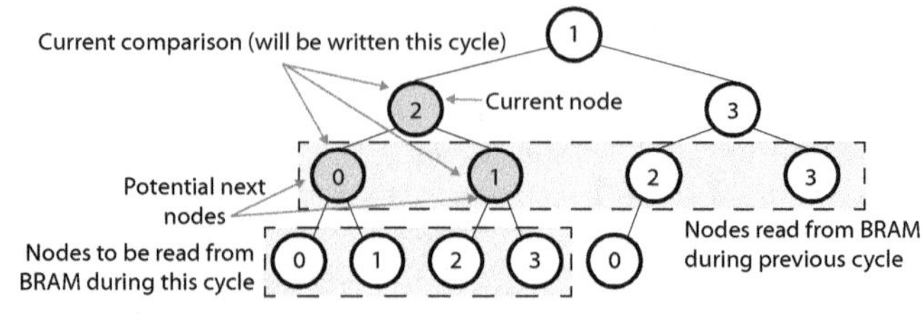

Figure 11: Min-heap on the FPGA's on-chip RAM. The numbers represent the RAM each node is stored in. The four second-degree children of each node are put into four separate RAMs in order to read them in parallel.

pipeline holds a *descriptor* for the data in the corresponding stage of the AES units (Figure 10), which is a tuple comprising an ORAM header, a row in the DRAM buffer, a stage in the AES pipeline, and an entry in the stash.

During the read phase, the control logic reads rows of data from the appropriate location in the DRAM buffer and feeds them into the AES units. It also directs the output of the AES units into the appropriate locations in the stash. In addition, the control logic checks each decrypted block header to see if it is the block the CPU has requested. Once the block is found, it is returned to the CPU and also remapped to a new, random leaf node in the ORAM tree (overwriting the block's header before writing it into the stash).

The write phase uses the same pipeline and AES units, but with different descriptors. As data is moved out from the stash to the DRAM buffer, the control logic queries the select stage (Section 5.4) to determine whether the next block to be written is a dummy, and if not, which entry from the stash to write back. Further, all block headers are updated with a new nonce.

If the ORAM access is a write, the CPU's block will be used to update the ORAM block in the stash in parallel to the write-back phase, so that the updated ORAM block is available for write-back at least one cycle ahead of the encryption unit. In the case of a dummy, no data is read from the stash and zeros are fed to the unit instead (since the nonce is randomly generated and affects the whole block, zero-valued dummies do not affect security).

The remainder of the write phase resembles the read phase: data is written to the DRAM Buffer in order from bottom to the top of the path and is guaranteed to arrive at 1,024 bits per cycle, so that the memory system can write at full pin bandwidth (1,024 bits/cycle).

5.6 FPGA-specific Challenges

PHANTOM has to overcome several challenges unique to an implementation on an FPGA:

The heap implementation requires some care to minimize the cost of each operation. For some heap operations, a node must be compared to both of its children, potentially doubling the access latency to the heap (from $\lceil \log k \rceil$ cycles to $2\lceil \log k \rceil$ cycles, where k is the number of nodes in the heap), since each of the FPGA's BRAM memories has only one read and one write port. We avoided this problem by splitting the heap into two separate memories, each with a read and a write port. One holds even memory locations, the other holds the odd memory locations. As a result, the two children of a node are always in different BRAMs and can be accessed in the same cycle. Furthermore, we perform reads and updates concurrently every cycle.

Though this approach is functionally correct, it results in a circuit with paths from one BRAM through multiple levels of logic to another BRAM, leading to a long critical path latency. We therefore split the memory even further: our final implementation uses 4 different BRAMs (Figure 11). At every cycle, we prefetch the four grandchildren of a node so that the two children we are interested in will be available in buffer registers at the point when they are required for comparison, whichever way the previous comparison goes.

The limit of one memory read and one write port also complicates the stash's design. While there are four units that access each stash column (read for encryption, write for decryption and reads/writes by the secure CPU), these operations are scheduled such that only two ports are required at the same time (reading the response data to the CPU is overlapped with decryption, writing with encryption).

5.7 Integrating ORAM with a CPU

Our ORAM controller is integrated with an in-order RISC processor implementing the RISC-V instruction set [37]. The processor (like our ORAM controller) is implemented using Chisel [5], a new hardware construction language embedded in Scala. The CPU features a full implementation of the RISC-V instruction set as well as an uncore with instruction, data and last-level cache (LLC). For our prototype, we use a version with very small caches (4KB instruction cache, 4KB data cache, 8KB LLC) and no floating-point unit. The reason for this choice is that our Convey platform requires the CPU to run at 75 Mhz on an FPGA, and supporting larger cache sizes at this frequency would have caused significant amounts of additional work (the CPU was optimized for an ASIC implementation before we adopted it for PHANTOM). Such work is orthogonal to our proposed ORAM controller (for our performance evaluation, we simulate a larger CPU with reasonable cache sizes to determine results for a realistic deployment).

The CPU is integrated with PHANTOM by translating memory requests from the LLC into ORAM requests, buffering 8 previously used ORAM blocks to reduce the miss rate. We use the CLOCK algorithm to determine which ORAM block to evict from the buffer. Furthermore, translating memory addresses into ORAM block addresses is non-trivial since it requires division by a non-power of two (due to the 128 bit used by the block header). Our current prototype uses a Xilinx divider IP core that takes an additional 36 cycles, but custom logic could eventually exploit the fact that this division is by a power-of-two multiple of 31 to reduce that latency to just a few cycles.

5.8 Utilizing Multiple FPGAs

The Convey HC-2ex features 4 FPGAs that provide additional logic and memory capacity which can be used for ORAM state. For example, we experimented with splitting the position map across the FPGAs adjacent to the one carrying the ORAM controller – this allows us to scale to larger ORAM sizes. When performing a position map access (which only happens at the start of an ORAM request), we send the (encrypted) address of the block we are looking for, as well as the new leaf ID to map it to, to both of the neighboring FPGAs. Both of them then send an encrypted reply at the same time. Since it is public knowledge that an ORAM request was initiated, this is secure.

6. EVALUATION

In this section, we experimentally determine the cost of obliviousness on PHANTOM, as well as its performance impact on real applications. Our evaluation demonstrates that: 1) ORAM latency to access a 4kB block is 22× over a non-secure access (30× for 128B blocks[3]) for a 64MB ORAM. ORAM access latencies vary from 18us to 30us for ORAMs of effective size 64MB to 4GB and a block size of 4kB. A non-ORAM access takes 812ns for a 4kB block and 592ns for a 128B block. 2) PHANTOM utilizes 93% of the theoretical peak bandwidth of the memory channel, validating our memory layout and micro-architectural optimizations. 3) PHANTOM requires less than 2% of the logic of the FPGA, leaving space to implement other accelerators or a CPU. PHANTOM's prototype implements ORAMs of up to 1GB on a single FPGA (before on-chip memory is exhausted) and 2GB or larger using multiple FPGAs. 4) The overall program performance depends upon access patterns and working set size. Different SQLite queries on a population census workload shows overheads from 20% to 5×.

6.1 ORAM Latency and Bandwidth

The primary metric of efficiency for an ORAM system is the time to service a single request to the ORAM. This approximates the amount of overhead per memory access (i.e. last-level cache miss).

We synthesized a set of different configurations of PHANTOM, with effective ORAM storage capacity ranging from 64MB to 4GB (13-19 tree levels with a 4KB block size). Each ORAM configuration includes a stash of 128 elements, which allows up to 3 levels of treetop caching. For 18 and 19-level ORAMs, PHANTOM's position map is stored on one and two adjacent FPGAs respectively.

[3]Since the granularity of ORAM accesses is much larger than a cache line, we compare to 128B reads to estimate the worst-case overhead where only a fraction of data is used.

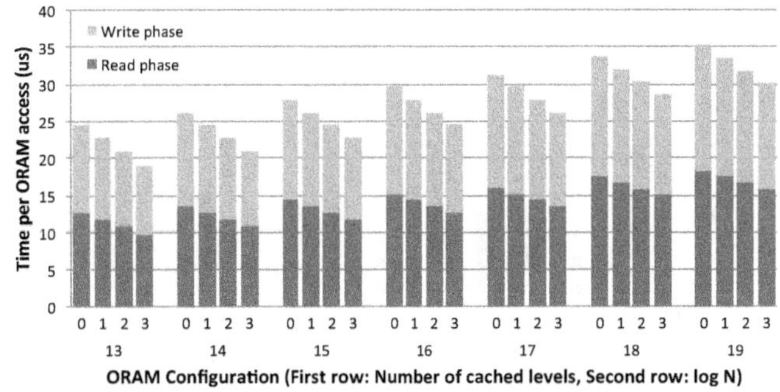

Figure 12: Average time per ORAM access for different configurations on hardware. 1M accesses each, block size 4KB, 18 & 19 levels are split across 3 FPGAs.

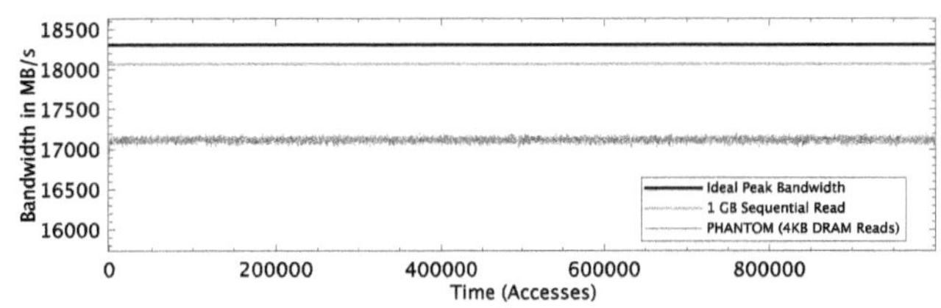

Figure 13: DRAM utilization over time.

Figure 12 shows the total time per ORAM access for these configurations. The experiments were conducted on the FPGAs of our Convey HC-2ex machine. We performed a sequence of 1 million random ORAM accesses (block reads and writes) for each experiment, and report the average times per access (note that times for accesses may vary without compromising security, but only due to timing variations in the DRAM system).

For each data point, we also report how long it takes until the data is available (for reads) – this is important since a client using the memory system can continue execution as soon as the data is returned from ORAM. For writes, execution can continue immediately.

We measured that PHANTOM's latency until ORAM data is available ranges from 10us for a 13-level (64MB) ORAM to 16 us for a 19-level (4GB) ORAM. Compared to sequentially reading a 4kB (812ns) or a 128B (592ns) block of data using all Convey memory controllers, this represents 12× to 27× overhead. An ORAM access that hits the stash takes 84 cycles (560ns) .

When considering full ORAM accesses, latencies range from 19us to 30us. Much of PHANTOM's real-world performance is therefore determined by how much of the write-back can be overlapped with computation, but is bounded above by 23× to 50× overhead.

Compared to the ideal numbers from Section 4, our prototype takes an average of 4,719 cycles per full ORAM access (for a 1GB ORAM without treetop caching), compared to the theoretical minimum of 4,352 cycles. The difference in performance is due to the additional overhead of encryption and the latencies in the DRAM system. This relatively small overhead over the theoretical numbers shows the effectiveness of PHANTOM.

DRAM Utilization. Figure 13 shows that PHANTOM utilizes 93% of the theoretical peak DRAM bandwidth, i.e. the actual number of cycles between receiving the first and last words from memory relative to the number of cycles

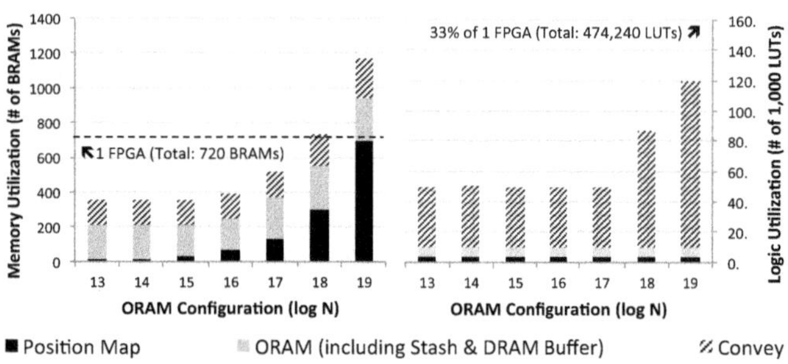

Figure 14: FPGA resource utilization. The design uses 30-52% (less than 2%) of available memory (logic); up to 74% (10%) including Convey's interface. It fits onto a single FPGA for up to 17 levels (1GB). For larger sizes, the position map is stored remotely on other FPGAs.

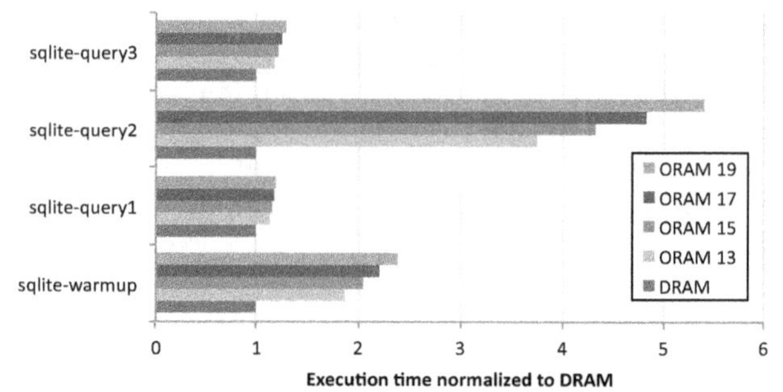

Figure 15: SQLite Performance Results. We simulated the performance of sqlite running with and without PHANTOM on a timing model of a processor on the same FPGA. We assume a 1MB L2 cache, 16KB icache, 32KB dcache and an extra buffer for 8 ORAM blocks (32KB).

that would be taken if each memory controller returned the maximum number of bits every cycle. For reference to a practical best-case – where an application reads memory sequentially from DRAM – PHANTOM achieves 94% of the read bandwidth[4]. Given that PHANTOM accesses no additional data beyond what is required by the Path ORAM algorithm, this shows that our goal of making high use of the available bandwidth has been achieved.

6.2 FPGA Resource Usage

Figure 14 reports PHANTOM's hardware resource consumption through the percentage of logic elements (LUTs) that are used by the different configurations, as well as the number of on-chip RAMs (BRAMs) used on the FPGA. The design itself uses 30-52% of memory and about 2% of logic – the other resources are used by Convey's interface logic that interacts with the memory and the x86 core.

This breakdown shows that the biggest contributors to memory usage are the position map and the stash. To support ORAM sizes larger than 1 GB, we therefore move the lookup table to another FPGA and communicate through (encrypted) messages over Convey's inter-FPGA communication facilities (Section 5.8).

These results do not include the resources that would be consumed by real AES crypto hardware. There exist optimized AES processor designs [18] that meet our bandwidth and frequency requirements while consuming about 22K logic elements and no BRAM – our nine required units would therefore fit onto our FPGA (as even large configurations of the ORAM controller leave almost 90% of the FPGA's logic elements available).

6.3 Impact on Application Performance

After evaluating PHANTOM's ORAM controller in isolation, we are now interested in how PHANTOM's ORAM latency translates into application slowdowns.

As an end-to-end example, we used our real RISC processor to run several SQLite queries on the 7.5MB census database from Figure 1 on our real hardware. Due to the processor's extremely small cache sizes, a very large percentage of memory accesses are cache misses (we ran the same workloads on a RISC-V simulator and found 7.7% dcache misses, and 55.5% LLC misses). As a result, we observed slow-downs of 6.5× to 14.7× for a set of different SQLite queries (which are described in more detail later in this section). This experiment shows how crucial caching is to achieve good ORAM performance: with high miss rates, the overhead of ORAM compared to regular memory accesses leads to order-of-magnitude slow-downs compared to a baseline without ORAM).

To investigate the effect on applications in the presence of realistic cache sizes (namely a 16KB cache, 32KB cache and 1MB LLC cache), we fed the same application traces into a timing model derived from our real processor to simulate how our system would perform with realistic cache sizes. The model assumes an in-order pipelined RISC-V processor with 1 cycle per instruction, 2 cycles for branch misses, 2 cycles to access the data cache, 14 cycles to access the LLC, and 89 cycles to access a 128B cache line from DRAM (using our measurement for the full Convey memory system) and our access latencies for different DRAM configurations. We also assumed that the processor waits for a full ORAM request to finish and additionally evict a previous block, essentially causing an up to 4× longer stall than a real execution. At the same time, we allow the baseline to use the full Convey memory system.

Despite these penalties, we see that a real-world workload, such as SQLite, can absorb a fair amount of our memory access overheads and make use of our relatively large block size of 4KB. Figure 15 shows our results for applying our timing model to several SQLite queries on the 7.5MB census database from Figure 1. `sqlite-warmup` and `sqlite-query1` are a `JOIN` operation between two large tables. The difference in execution times show the effect of caching: in the second query, much of the tables are already in the cache and the impact of ORAM accesses is much lower. `sqlite-query2` on the other hand shows fetching a single column of a relatively small table – here, PHANTOM performs poorer due to its large block size. `sqlite-query3` represents a full scan through all fields of a large table – this is an example where PHANTOM fares particularly well since it can make use of the locality (we would also like to point out that the baseline would also benefit from pipelining requests, which we do not account for).

In summary, our evaluation shows that the overheads exposed by PHANTOM are indeed reasonable for real-world workloads, especially given the fundamental cost of obliviousness is a bandwidth overhead of greater than 100×. Note

[4]Response data ordering was enabled for all experiments.

that these numbers depend upon the application's last level cache miss-rate and the overheads are small because most of the application's working set fits in the cache.

7. RELATED WORK

In the introduction, we highlighted representative prior work on secure processors. Here we focus on work on obliviousness, especially in the context of secure processors. Oblivious RAM (ORAM) is an algorithmic construct for hiding memory access patterns and was first proposed by Goldreich and Ostrovsky [12]. ORAM hides only memory access patterns, but does not hide the timing or the total number of memory accesses – complementary techniques can be used to secure timing and termination channels [2, 3, 7, 16, 41].

Recent research on ORAM [6, 10, 12–14, 21, 22, 24, 28, 31, 39, 40] shows that it is possible to achieve obliviousness with $O(\text{polylog}(N))$ overhead, i.e., every memory access translates into $O(\text{polylog}(N))$ seemingly random accesses.

The above algorithms have been demonstrated for disk accesses in datacenters [22, 30, 40], but are impractical to implement in a hardware memory controller since they are complex and have high constant factors. Some prior work (HIDE [42]) has looked at probabilistic solutions in hardware that do not provide complete obliviousness but have far lower overheads. Where strong obliviousness guarantees are not required, HIDE might be a better fit.

In this project, we build upon Path ORAM [32], an ORAM algorithm that is much simpler than prior ORAM algorithms. Path ORAM has also been adopted by ASCEND [9, 26], a proposed secure processor with an oblivious memory interface. While similar on the surface, we believe our work to be largely complementary to ASCEND. The authors apply optimizations such as hierarchical ORAM, background eviction, and integrity verification to Path ORAM. These optimizations can be applied on top of PHANTOM as well, while our optimizations are directed towards the hardware architecture for Path ORAM. Using simulations, they predict that a SPEC 2006 int benchmark subset can execute with a 3× (geometric mean) performance overhead over native. Note that with an ORAM latency of more than 2000 cycles, the low overhead can be attributed as much to the SPEC benchmarks' working set fitting in the cache (similar to our results for SQLite).

8. CONCLUSION

We present PHANTOM, a practical oblivious memory system that achieves high performance by exploiting memory parallelism and using an architecture that scales to wide memory channels. Importantly for adoption, implementing PHANTOM prototype on a Convey FPGA machine enables obliviousness to be available today. In the future, PHANTOM can expose a memory composed of DRAM, encrypted DRAM, and ORAM banks to software and thus open the door to compiler analyses that improve performance without compromising obliviousness.

Acknowledgements

We would like to thank John Lazzaro, John Wawrzynek and Brian Zimmer (for CS250 instruction, Fall'11), Yunsup Lee and Andrew Waterman (for RISC-V support), Derek Chiou and Walid Najjar (for Convey hardware), and Glen Edwards and George Vandegrift (for technical advice and support). Last but not least, we thank the anonymous reviewers for their comments.

This work partially supported by Microsoft (Award #024263), Intel (Award #024894) and matching U.C. Discovery funding (Award #DIG07-10227); by National Science Foundation (NSF) Grant #1136996 to the Computing Research Association for the CIFellows Project; by TerraSwarm, one of six centers of STARnet, a Semiconductor Research Corporation program sponsored by MARCO and DARPA; by the NSF Graduate Research Fellowship under Grant No. DGE-0946797; the DoD National Defense Science and Engineering Graduate Fellowship; a Google Research Award and a grant from the Amazon Web Services in Education program; the NSF under Grants No. CNS-1314857, CCF-0424422, 0311808, 0832943, 0448452, 0842694, 0627511, 0842695, 0808617, 0831501 CT-L, the Air Force Office of Scientific Research under MURI Award No. FA9550-09-1-0539, the Air Force Research Laboratory under grant No. P010071555, the Office of Naval Research under MURI Grant No. N000140911081, and by the MURI program under AFOSR Grant No. FA9550-08-1-0352. Any opinions, findings, and conclusions or recommendations expressed in this material are those of the author(s) and do not necessarily reflect the views of the funding agencies.

9. REFERENCES

[1] "PrivateCore," http://www.privatecore.com/.

[2] J. Agat, "Transforming out Timing Leaks," in *POPL*, 2000.

[3] A. Askarov, D. Zhang, and A. C. Myers, "Predictive black-box mitigation of timing channels," in *CCS*, 2010.

[4] A. Aviram, S. Hu, B. Ford, and R. Gummadi, "Determinating Timing Channels in Compute Clouds," in *CCSW*, 2010.

[5] J. Bachrach, H. Vo, B. Richards, Y. Lee, A. Waterman, R. Avizienis, J. Wawrzynek, and K. Asanovic, "Chisel: Constructing Hardware in a Scala Embedded Language," in *DAC*, 2012.

[6] K.-M. Chung, Z. Liu, and R. Pass, "Statistically-secure oram with $\tilde{O}(\log^2 n)$ overhead," http://arxiv.org/abs/1307.3699, 2013.

[7] B. Coppens, I. Verbauwhede, K. D. Bosschere, and B. D. Sutter, "Practical Mitigations for Timing-Based Side-Channel Attacks on Modern x86 Processors," in *SP*, 2009.

[8] J. Devietti, B. Lucia, L. Ceze, and M. Oskin, "DMP: Deterministic Shared Memory Multiprocessing," in *ASPLOS*, 2009.

[9] C. W. Fletcher, M. v. Dijk, and S. Devadas, "A Secure Processor Architecture for Encrypted Computation on Untrusted Programs," in *STC*, 2012.

[10] C. Gentry, K. Goldman, S. Halevi, C. Julta, M. Raykova, and D. Wichs, "Optimizing oram and using it efficiently for secure computation," in *PETS*, 2013.

[11] O. Goldreich, "Towards a Theory of Software Protection and Simulation by Oblivious RAMs," in *STOC*, 1987.

[12] O. Goldreich and R. Ostrovsky, "Software Protection and Simulation on Oblivious RAMs," *J. ACM*, 1996.

[13] M. T. Goodrich and M. Mitzenmacher, "Privacy-Preserving Access of Outsourced Data via Oblivious RAM Simulation," in *ICALP*, 2011.

[14] M. T. Goodrich, M. Mitzenmacher, O. Ohrimenko, and R. Tamassia, "Privacy-preserving Group Data Access via Stateless Oblivious RAM Simulation," in *SODA*, 2012.

[15] Y. Gu, Y. Fu, A. Prakash, Z. Lin, and H. Yin, "OS-Sommelier: Memory-only Operating System Fingerprinting in the Cloud," in *SoCC*, 2012.

[16] A. Haeberlen, B. C. Pierce, and A. Narayan, "Differential Privacy Under Fire," in *USENIX Security*, 2011.

[17] J. A. Halderman, S. D. Schoen, N. Heninger, W. Clarkson, W. Paul, J. A. Calandrino, A. J. Feldman, J. Appelbaum, and E. W. Felten, "Lest We Remember: Cold-boot Attacks on Encryption Keys," *Commun. ACM*, vol. 52, no. 5, 2009.

[18] A. Hodjat and I. Verbauwhede, "A 21.54 Gbits/s Fully Pipelined AES Processor on FPGA," in *FCCM*, 2004.

[19] A. Huang, "Keeping Secrets in Hardware: The Microsoft Xbox Case Study," in *CHES*, 2002.

[20] G. Klein, K. Elphinstone, G. Heiser, J. Andronick, D. Cock, P. Derrin, D. Elkaduwe, K. Engelhardt, R. Kolanski, M. Norrish, T. Sewell, H. Tuch, and S. Winwood, "seL4: Formal Verification of an OS Kernel," in *SOSP*, 2009.

[21] E. Kushilevitz, S. Lu, and R. Ostrovsky, "On the (In)security of Hash-based Oblivious RAM and a New Balancing Scheme," in *SODA*, 2012.

[22] J. R. Lorch and B. Parno, "Shroud: Ensuring Private Access to Large-Scale Data in the Data Center," in *FAST*, 2013.

[23] R. Martin, J. Demme, and S. Sethumadhavan, "TimeWarp: Rethinking Timekeeping and Performance Monitoring Mechanisms to Mitigate Side-channel Attacks," in *ISCA*, 2012.

[24] R. Ostrovsky and V. Shoup, "Private Information Storage (Extended Abstract)," in *STOC*, 1997.

[25] L. Ren, C. Fletcher, X. Yu, M. van Dijk, and S. Devadas, "Integrity verification for path oblivious-ram," in *HPEC*, 2013.

[26] L. Ren, X. Yu, C. W. Fletcher, M. van Dijk, and S. Devadas, "Design Space Exploration and Optimization of Path Oblivious RAM in Secure Processors," in *ISCA*, 2013.

[27] B. Rogers, S. Chhabra, M. Prvulovic, and Y. Solihin, "Using address independent seed encryption and bonsai merkle trees to make secure processors os- and performance-friendly," in *MICRO*, 2007.

[28] E. Shi, T.-H. H. Chan, E. Stefanov, and M. Li, "Oblivious RAM with $O((\log N)^3)$ Worst-Case Cost," in *ASIACRYPT*, 2011.

[29] S. W. Smith, "Outbound Authentication for Programmable Secure Coprocessors," in *ESORICS*, 2002.

[30] E. Stefanov and E. Shi, "Oblivistore: High performance oblivious cloud storage," in *S & P*, 2013.

[31] E. Stefanov, E. Shi, and D. Song, "Towards Practical Oblivious RAM," in *NDSS*, 2012.

[32] E. Stefanov, M. van Dijk, E. Shi, C. Fletcher, L. Ren, X. Yu, and S. Devadas, "Path O-RAM: An Extremely Simple Oblivious RAM Protocol," in *CCS*, 2013.

[33] G. E. Suh, D. Clarke, B. Gassend, M. van Dijk, and S. Devadas, "AEGIS: Architecture for Tamper-evident and Tamper-resistant Processing," in *ICS*, 2003.

[34] D. L. C. Thekkath, M. Mitchell, P. Lincoln, D. Boneh, J. Mitchell, and M. Horowitz, "Architectural Support for Copy and Tamper Resistant Software," *SIGOPS Oper. Syst. Rev.*, vol. 34, no. 5, pp. 168–177, 2000.

[35] M. Tiwari, H. M. Wassel, B. Mazloom, S. Mysore, F. T. Chong, and T. Sherwood, "Complete Information Flow Tracking from the Gates up," in *ASPLOS*, 2009.

[36] A. Waksman and S. Sethumadhavan, "Silencing Hardware Backdoors," in *SP*, 2011.

[37] A. Waterman, Y. Lee, D. A. Patterson, and K. Asanović, "The RISC-V Instruction Set Manual, Volume I: Base User-Level ISA," EECS Department, UC Berkeley, Tech. Rep. UCB/EECS-2011-62, May 2011.

[38] P. Williams and R. Sion, "Round-Optimal Access Privacy on Outsourced Storage," in *CCS*, 2012.

[39] P. Williams, R. Sion, and B. Carbunar, "Building castles out of mud: practical access pattern privacy and correctness on untrusted storage," in *CCS*, 2008.

[40] P. Williams, R. Sion, and A. Tomescu, "PrivateFS: A Parallel Oblivious File System," in *CCS*, 2012.

[41] D. Zhang, A. Askarov, and A. C. Myers, "Predictive Mitigation of Timing Channels in Interactive Systems," in *CCS*, 2011.

[42] X. Zhuang, T. Zhang, and S. Pande, "HIDE: An Infrastructure for Efficiently Protecting Information Leakage on the Address Bus," in *ASPLOS*, 2004.

APPENDIX

A. PROOF OF OVERLAPPING HEAPIFY.

For a heap with tree-depth d, *insert* and *extractMin* take $d+3$ cycles. For a stash size less than 256, $d \leq 8$ and hence the *extractMins* overlap with the (32 cycle) writes since $8+3 \leq 32$. To prove that the insertions overlap as well, we have to show that the *heapify* operation and all insertions always finish in the available time.

Heapify starts at the first cycle of the ORAM access, and incoming blocks from from AES decrypt are stored in a queue. Hence it is sufficient to show that the combined time for *heapify* and all *inserts* is smaller than the time the entire path read takes. Since *inserts* take $d+3$ cycles per block, for an ORAM tree with l levels and a bucket size of 4, we need to ensure that *heapify* takes at most $t_{max} = 4l(32-(d+3))$ cycles.

Heapify performs a $k+1$ cycle operation for each node in the heap but the ones on the last level, where k is the distance of the node to the leaves. Hence *heapify* takes

$$t_h = \sum_{i=1}^{d-1} 2^{i-1}(d-i+1) < \sum_{i=1}^{d-1} 2^{i-1}2^{d-i} = (d-1)2^{d-1}$$

cycles. Now if we set $d \leq 8$, $l \geq 13$, then $t_h < 7 \cdot 2^7 = 896$ while $t_{max} = 4 \cdot 13 \cdot (32-(8+3)) = 1,092$. Hence $t_h < t_{max}$ and therefore *heapify* and *inserts* overlap as described in Section 5.4. Note that this bound is not very tight (for $d \leq 8$, $t_h = 374$) and sorting can be further optimized.

Practical Dynamic Proofs of Retrievability

Elaine Shi
University of Maryland
elaine@cs.umd.edu

Emil Stefanov
UC Berkeley
emil@cs.berkeley.edu

Charalampos Papamanthou
University of Maryland
cpap@umd.edu

ABSTRACT

Proofs of Retrievability (PoR), proposed by Juels and Kaliski in 2007, enable a client to store n file blocks with a cloud server so that later the server can prove possession of all the data in a very efficient manner (i.e., with constant computation and bandwidth). Although many efficient PoR schemes for *static* data have been constructed, only two *dynamic* PoR schemes exist. The scheme by Stefanov *et al.* (ACSAC 2012) uses a large of amount of client storage and has a large audit cost. The scheme by Cash *et al.* (EUROCRYPT 2013) is mostly of theoretical interest, as it employs Oblivious RAM (ORAM) as a black box, leading to increased practical overhead (e.g., it requires about 300 times more bandwidth than our construction).

We propose a dynamic PoR scheme with constant client storage whose bandwidth cost is comparable to a Merkle hash tree, thus being very practical. Our construction outperforms the constructions of Stefanov *et al.* and Cash *et al.*, both in theory and in practice. Specifically, for n outsourced blocks of β bits each, writing a block requires $\beta + O(\lambda \log n)$ bandwidth and $O(\beta \log n)$ server computation (λ is the security parameter). Audits are also very efficient, requiring $\beta + O(\lambda^2 \log n)$ bandwidth. We also show how to make our scheme publicly verifiable, providing the first dynamic PoR scheme with such a property. We finally provide a very efficient implementation of our scheme.

Categories and Subject Descriptors

K.6.5 [**Management of Computing and Information Systems**]: Security and Protection

Keywords

dynamic proofs of retrievability; PoR; erasure code

1. INTRODUCTION

Storage outsourcing (e.g., Amazon S3, Google Drive) has become one of the most popular applications of cloud computing, offering various benefits such as economies of scale and flexible accessibility. When the cloud *storage provider* (also referred to as *server*) is untrusted, an important challenge is how to offer provable outsourced storage guarantees. In particular, a *data owner* (also referred to as *client*) wishes to obtain the following guarantees:

- **Authenticated storage.** The client wishes to verify that data fetched from the server is correct, where correctness is equivalent to *authenticity* and *freshness*;
- **Retrievability.** The client needs assurance that the server is indeed storing all of the client's data, and that no data loss has occurred.

Proofs of Retrievability (PoR), initially defined and proposed by Juels and Kalisky [14], are designed to offer the above guarantees for storage outsourcing applications, while requiring small client-side state.

Most existing PoR schemes [7–9, 20, 26] however, are impractical due to the prohibitive costs associated with data updates or client storage. A recent PoR construction by Cash *et al.* [8] shows how to achieve asymptotic efficiency in the presence of updates with constant client storage—however, their scheme relies on Oblivious RAM (ORAM), a rather heavy-weight cryptographic primitive. Recent works on ORAM [21,24,25,30,31] have shown that even the fastest known constructions incur a large bandwidth overhead in practice. In particular, under typical parametrizations, and with $O(1)$ amount of client storage, known ORAM constructions require **400+** blocks be transferred between a client and a server for a single data access. In contrast, **our construction requires transferring only about 1.05 to 1.35 blocks per data access**, which makes it both practical and orders of magnitudes more efficient than the scheme of Cash *et al.* [8].

This paper proposes a light-weight dynamic PoR construction that achieves *comparable bandwidth overhead and client-side computation with a standard Merkle hash tree*, reducing the above cost dramatically. Specifically, for each read and write, our construction requires transferring $O(\lambda \log n)$ bits of cryptographic information (independent of the block size) in addition to transferring the block itself, where λ is the security parameter, and n is the total number of outsourced blocks. To understand the implications of this, note that a Merkle hash tree offers authenticated storage, but does not offer retrievability guarantees. This paper essentially shows that under settings where the client-server bandwidth is the bottleneck (as is often the case in practice—e.g., Bitcoin and various file sharing applications [1]), we can make PoR almost as efficient as a Merkle hash tree, i.e., ready to be deployed in practical applications today.

CCS'13, November 4–8, 2013, Berlin, Germany.

ACM 978-1-4503-2477-9/13/11 ...$15.00.
http://dx.doi.org/10.1145/2508859.2516669.

Scheme	Client storage	Write cost		Audit cost		Verifiability
		Server cost	BW	Server cost	BW	
Iris [26]	$O(\beta\sqrt{n})$	$O(\beta)$	$O(\beta)$	$O(\beta\lambda\sqrt{n})$	$O(\beta\lambda\sqrt{n})$	secret
Cash *et al.* [8]	$O(\beta)$	$O(\beta\lambda(\log n)^2)$	$O(\beta\lambda(\log n)^2)$	$O(\beta\lambda(\log n)^2)$	$O(\beta\lambda(\log n)^2)$	secret
This paper (Section 5)	$O(\beta)$	$O(\beta \log n)$	$\beta + O(\lambda \log n)$	$O(\beta\lambda \log n)$	$\beta + O(\lambda^2 \log n)$	secret
This paper (Appendix)	$O(\beta\lambda)$	$O(\beta \log n)$	$\beta(1+\epsilon) + O(\lambda \log n)$ for any constant $\epsilon > 0$	$O(\beta\lambda \log n)$	$O(\beta\lambda \log n)$	public

β: block size (in terms of number of bits). λ: the security parameter. n: an upper bound on the number of blocks.
Server cost: includes the server-side disk I/O cost, and server computation.
BW: The client-server bandwidth cost.

Table 1: Comparison with existing dynamic PoR. All schemes have $O(\beta n)$ server side storage. Reads can be handled by keeping a separate, Merkle-hashed, up-to-date copy of the dataset; therefore each read costs $\beta + O(\lambda \log n)$. Numbers in this table are optimized for the typical case $\beta \geq \lambda$. We note that for the ORAM-based scheme of Cash *et al.*, we omit $\log \log n$ terms from the denominator.

In terms of disk I/O overhead on the server, our scheme also achieves asymptotic improvements for reads, writes, as well as audits, in comparison with the state-of-the-art scheme [8] (see Table 1). In our scheme, reads cost no more than a Merkle hash tree in terms of server disk I/O. Writes incur moderate server disk I/O: the server needs to read, write, and compute on $O(\log n)$ blocks for each write. However, our algorithms for writing access blocks *sequentially*, significantly reducing the disk seeks required for writes. We have a full-fledged, working implementation of our scheme and report detailed experimental results from a deployment. We also plan to open source our code in the near future.

We also point out that due to the blackbox application of ORAM, the scheme by Cash *et al.* [8] additionally offers access pattern privacy which we do not guarantee. In applications that demand access privacy, ORAM is necessary. We observe that the definition of PoR itself does not require access privacy, and when one requires only PoR guarantees (i.e., authenticated storage and retrievability) but not access privacy, a blackbox application of ORAM is impractical—in fact, as this paper shows, one can design truly practical PoR schemes when access privacy is not required. Table 1 summarizes the asymptotic performance of our scheme in comparison with related work.

1.1 Related Work

Comparison with proofs of data possession. A closely related line of research is called Proofs of Data Possession (PDP), initially proposed by Ateniese *et al.* [5]. We stress that PDP provides much weaker security guarantees than PoR. A successful PoR audit ensures that the server maintains knowledge of *all* outsourced data blocks; while a PDP audit only ensures that the server is storing *most* of the data. With PDP, a server that has lost a small number of data blocks can pass an audit with significant probability[1]. Erway *et al.* [10] recently demonstrated a dynamic PDP scheme with $\beta + O(\lambda \log n)$ cost for reads and writes, and $\beta + O(\lambda^2 \log n)$ cost for audits. *We stress that we provide the much stronger PoR guarantees,* roughly at the same practical and asymptotic overhead as dynamic PDP schemes.

[1]While some PDP schemes [6] achieve full security, *they require that the server read all of the client's data during an audit,* and thus is impractical.

Proofs of retrievability. Static proofs of retrievability were initially proposed by Juels and Kaliski [14], and later improved in a series of subsequent works [7–9, 17, 20, 26, 28, 32]. While some works [17, 28, 32] aim to achieve PoR, they essentially only achieve the weaker PDP guarantees when they wish to support dynamic updates efficiently.

The first dynamic proofs of retrievability construction was proposed by Stefanov, van Dijk, Juels, and Oprea as part of a cloud-based file system called Iris [26]. Although reads and writes in Iris are quite efficient, it requires $O(\lambda\beta\sqrt{n})$ bandwidth, server computation, and server I/O to perform an audit (it also requires $\beta\sqrt{n}$ local space). Cash *et al.* [8] proposed a dynamic POR scheme with constant client storage based on Oblivious RAM, but it requires $O(\beta\lambda(\log n)^2)$ bandwidth and server I/O to perform writes and audits. In contrast with these works, our scheme requires $\beta + O(\lambda \log n)$ write bandwidth, $\beta + O(\lambda^2 \log n)$ audit bandwidth, and constant storage.

2. INFORMAL TECHNICAL OVERVIEW

2.1 Previous Approaches

In this section we describe various approaches that could be used for the problem of dynamic proofs of retrievability and we highlight the problems of these approaches.

Strawman. We start from the most straightforward approach. Imagine that the client attaches a Message Authentication Code (MAC) to every block before uploading it to the server—to additionally ensure freshness under updates, one can use a Merkle hash tree instead of MACs. During the audit protocol, the client randomly samples a small number of blocks and ensures that the server possesses them by checking them against the MACs.

In fact, this approach illustrates the underlying idea of several Proof of Data Possession (PDP) schemes [10, 29]. The drawback of such an approach is that if the server has lost a small number of blocks (e.g., a $o(1)$ fraction), it can still pass the audit with significant probability.

Prior work: use of redundant encoding to boost detection probability. To address the aforementioned issue, prior PoR schemes [7, 9, 14, 20, 26] rely on erasure codes to boost the detection probability, and ensure that the server must possess all blocks to pass the audit test, which typically involves checking the authenticity of λ random code blocks, where λ is the security parameter. As a concrete example, suppose that the client outsources a total of n blocks, which are erasure coded into $m = (1+c)n$ blocks for some constant $0 < c \leq 1$, such that knowledge of any n blocks suffices to recover the entire dataset. In this way, the server has to delete at least cn blocks to actually incur data loss—however, if the server deletes that many blocks, it will fail the above audit protocol with overwhelming probability (specifically with probability at least $1 - 1/(1+c)^{\lambda}$).

Difficulty with updates. The issue with using erasure codes is that if the client wishes to update a single block, it has to additionally update cn parity blocks—this can be very expensive in practice.

One (failed) attempt to support updates (as described by Cash *et al.* [8]) is to use a *local* erasure coding scheme, i.e., each block only affects a small number of codeword blocks. For this approach to work, all the codeword blocks need to be randomly permuted, such that the server does not learn which codeword blocks correspond to one original data block—since otherwise, the server can selectively delete all codeword blocks corresponding to one block (say block i). Since the server has deleted only a small number of blocks, it can pass the audit with significant probability—however, in this case, block i would become irrecoverable.

The above approach fails to address the efficient update problem, since whenever the client updates a block, it reveals to the server which codeword blocks are related to this block—and this allows the server to launch the selective deletion attack as described above. To address this issue, Cash *et al.* [8] propose to employ ORAM to hide the access patterns from the server during updates. However, as mentioned in Section 1, known ORAM schemes incurs 400X or higher bandwidth overhead under typical parameterizations and constant client-side storage, and thus is impractical.

2.2 Our Idea

As before, suppose the client has n blocks, which are erasure-coded into $n + cn$ blocks for some small constant $c > 0$—we denote the erasure coded copy of data as $\mathbf{C}$. Now if the client needs to update a block, we encounter the issue that the client needs to update all of the cn parity blocks.

Our idea is to avoid the need to immediately update the cn parity blocks upon writes. Instead, the client will place the newly updated block into an erasure-coded log structure denoted $\mathbf{H}$, containing recently written blocks. During the audit, the client will sample blocks to check not only from the buffer $\mathbf{C}$, but also from the log structure $\mathbf{H}$. Note that since the buffer $\mathbf{C}$ does not get updated immediately upon writes, it may contain stale data—however, an up-to-date snapshot of all blocks is recoverable from the combination of $\mathbf{C}$ and $\mathbf{H}$, both of which are probabilistically checked during the audit. Two questions however remain:

1. How can reads be supported efficiently if the location of the up-to-date copy of a block is undetermined—since it can either exist in the buffer $\mathbf{C}$*, or in the log structure* $\mathbf{H}$*?*

The answer to this first question is relatively straightforward: one can always keep a separate, up-to-date, and memory-checked copy of all blocks just to support efficient reads. The client can verify the integrity (i.e., authenticity and fresheness) of the reads facilitated by the memory checking scheme (i.e., a Merkle hash tree). In our basic construction described in Section 4, this separate copy is denoted with $\mathbf{U}$. Section 5 describes further optimizations to reduce the server-side storage by a constant factor.

2. How can the log structure $\mathbf{H}$ *be efficiently updated upon writes?*

The answer to the latter question is much more involved, and turns out to be the main technical challenge we needed to overcome. Intuitively, when the log structure $\mathbf{H}$ is small, updating it upon writes should be relatively efficient. However, as $\mathbf{H}$ grows larger, updating it becomes slower. For example, in the extreme case, when $\mathbf{H}$ grows to as large as $\mathbf{C}$, updating $\mathbf{H}$ upon a write would cause an overhead roughly proportional to cn, as mentioned above.

Perhaps unsurprisingly, in order to achieve efficient amortized cost for updating $\mathbf{H}$ upon writes, we use a hierarchical log structure that is reminiscent of Oblivious RAM constructions [11]. In our construction, the log structure $\mathbf{H}$ consists of exactly $\lfloor \log n \rfloor + 1$ levels of exponentially growing capacity, where level i is an erasure coded copy of 2^i blocks. At a very high level, every 2^i write operations, level i will be rebuilt. Finally, the erasure-coded copy $\mathbf{C}$ can be informally (and a bit imprecisely) thought of as the top level of the hierarchical log, and is rebuilt every n write operations.

Despite the superficial resemblance to ORAM, our construction is *fundamentally different from using ORAM as a blackbox*, and thus orders of magnitude more efficient, since 1) we do not aim to achieve access privacy, or rely on access privacy to prove our PoR guarantees like in the scheme by Cash *et al.* [8]; and 2) each level of our hierarchical log structure $\mathbf{H}$ is erasure-coded. For this reason, we need a special erasure coding scheme that can be incrementally built over time (see Section 4 for details).

3. PRELIMINARIES

We begin with the definition of a dynamic PoR scheme, as given by Cash, Küpçü, and Wichs [8]. A dynamic POR scheme is a collection of the following four protocols between a stateful client $\mathcal{C}$ and a stateful server $\mathcal{S}$.

$(st, \bar{\mathcal{M}}) \leftarrow \mathsf{Init}(1^{\lambda}, n, \beta, \mathcal{M})$: On input the security parameter λ and the database $\mathcal{M}$ of n β-bit-size entries, it outputs the client state st and the server state $\bar{\mathcal{M}}$.

$\{B, \mathsf{reject}\} \leftarrow \mathsf{Read}(i, st, \bar{\mathcal{M}})$: On input an index $i \in [n]$, the client state st and the server state $\bar{\mathcal{M}}$, it outputs $B = \mathcal{M}[i]$ or reject.

$\{(st', \bar{\mathcal{M}}'), \mathsf{reject}\} \leftarrow \mathsf{Write}(i, B, st, \bar{\mathcal{M}})$: On input an index $i \in [n]$, data B, the client state st and the server state $\bar{\mathcal{M}}$, it sets $\mathcal{M}[i] = B$ and outputs a new client state st' and a new server state $\bar{\mathcal{M}}'$ or reject.

$\{\mathsf{accept}, \mathsf{reject}\} \leftarrow \mathsf{Audit}(st, \bar{\mathcal{M}})$: On input the client state st and the server state $\bar{\mathcal{M}}$, it outputs accept or reject.

Depending on whether the client state st in the above definition must be kept secret or not, we say that the dynamic PoR scheme is *secretly* or *publicly* verifiable.

3.1 Security Definitions

We define security, namely *authenticity* and *retrievability* in the same way as Cash *et al.* [8].

Authenticity. The authenticity requirement stipulates that the client can always detect (except with negligible probability) if any message sent by the server deviates from honest behavior. We use the following game between a challenger $\mathcal{C}$, a malicious server $\mathcal{S}^*$ and an honest server $\mathcal{S}$ for the adaptive version of authenticity, in the same way as Cash *et al.* [8].

- $\mathcal{S}^*$ chooses initial memory $\mathcal{M}$. $\mathcal{C}$ runs $\mathsf{Init}(1^\lambda, n, \beta, \mathcal{M})$ and sends the initial memory layout $\bar{\mathcal{M}}$ to $\mathcal{S}^*$. $\mathcal{C}$ also interacts with $\mathcal{S}$ and sends $\bar{\mathcal{M}}$ to $\mathcal{S}$.
- For polynomial number of steps $t = 1, 2, \ldots, \mathsf{poly}(\lambda)$, $\mathcal{S}^*$ picks an operation op_t where operation op_t is either $\mathsf{Read}(i, st, \bar{\mathcal{M}})$ or $\mathsf{Write}(i, B, st, \bar{\mathcal{M}})$ or $\mathsf{Audit}(st, \bar{\mathcal{M}})$. $\mathcal{C}$ executes the protocol with both $\mathcal{S}^*$ and $\mathcal{S}$.

$\mathcal{S}^*$ is said to win the game, if at any time, the message sent by $\mathcal{S}^*$ differs from that of $\mathcal{S}$, and $\mathcal{C}$ did not output reject.

Definition 1 (Authenticity). *A PoR scheme satisfies adaptive authenticity, if no polynomial-time adversary $\mathcal{S}^*$ has more than negligible probability in winning the above security game.*

Retrievability. Intuitively, the retrievability requirement stipulates that whenever a malicious server can pass the audit test with non-negligible probability, the server must know the entire memory contents $\mathcal{M}$; and moreover, one is able to extract $\mathcal{M}$ by repeatedly running the Audit protocol with the server. Formally, retrievability is defined with a security game as below, in the same way as Cash *et al.* [8].

- **Initialization phase.** The adversary $\mathcal{S}^*$ chooses the initial memory $\mathcal{M}$. The challenger runs $\mathsf{Init}(1^\lambda, n, \beta, \mathcal{M})$, and uploads the initial memory layout $\bar{\mathcal{M}}$ to $\mathcal{S}^*$.
- **Query phase.** For $t = 1, 2, \ldots, \mathsf{poly}(\lambda)$, the adversary $\mathcal{S}^*$ adaptively chooses an operation op_t where op_t is of the form $\mathsf{Read}(i, st, \bar{\mathcal{M}})$, $\mathsf{Write}(i, B, st, \bar{\mathcal{M}})$, or $\mathsf{Audit}(st, \bar{\mathcal{M}})$. The challenger executes the respective protocols with $\mathcal{S}^*$. At the end of the query phase, suppose the state of the challenger and the adversary is $state_C$ and $state_S$ respectively and the final state of the memory contents is $\mathcal{M}$.
- **Challenge phase.** The challenger now gets blackbox rewinding access in the configuration $state_S$. The challenger runs the Audit protocol repeatedly for a polynomial number of times with the server $\mathcal{S}^*$, starting from the configuration $(state_C, state_S)$. Denote with $\pi_1, \pi_2, \ldots, \pi_{\mathsf{poly}(\lambda)}$ the transcripts of all the successful Audit executions.

Definition 2 (Retrievability). *A PoR scheme satisfies retrievability, if there exists a polynomial-time extractor algorithm denoted $\mathcal{M}' \leftarrow \mathsf{Extract}(state_C, \{\pi_i\})$, such that for any polynomial-time $\mathcal{S}^*$, if $\mathcal{S}^*$ passes the* Audit *protocol with non-negligible probability, then after executing the* Audit *protocol with $\mathcal{S}^*$ for a polynomial number of times, the* Extract *algorithm can output the correct memory contents $\mathcal{M}' = \mathcal{M}$ except with negligible probability.*

We note here that in the above definition, "correct memory contents" are the contents of the memory $\mathcal{M}$ after the end of the query phase in the security game.

3.2 Building Blocks

Erasure codes. Our construction makes use of erasure codes [27] as defined below.

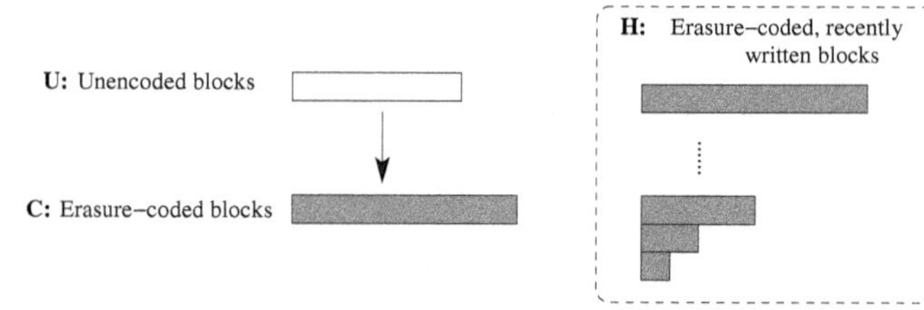

Figure 1: Server-side storage layout.

Definition 3 (Erasure codes). *Let Σ denote a finite alphabet. An $(m, n, d)_\Sigma$ erasure code is defined to be a pair of algorithms* $\mathsf{encode} : \Sigma^n \to \Sigma^m$, *and* $\mathsf{decode} : \Sigma^{m-d+1} \to \Sigma^n$, *such that as long as the number of erasures is bounded by $d - 1$,* decode *can always recover the original data. A code is* maximum distance separable *(MDS), if $n + d = m + 1$.*

Authenticated structures. For describing our basic construction, we can assume that we use a standard Merkle hash tree [16] to ensure the authenticity and freshness of all blocks (encoded or unencoded, stored across buffers **U**, **C** and **H**). However, later, we will show that in fact, only the raw buffer **U** needs to be verified with a Merkle hash tree; whereas the erasure-coded copy **C** and the hierarchical log structure **H** only require time/location-dependent MACs to ensure authenticity and freshness. This will lead to significant savings (specifically, by a multiplicative $\log n$ factor).

4. BASIC CONSTRUCTION

To begin with, assume the data to be outsourced contains n blocks, and each block is from an alphabet Σ. For simplicity, we will first assume that n is determined in advance—we will later explain in Section 6 how to expand or shrink the storage.

We first describe a basic construction that requires the client to perform $O(\beta \log n)$ computation for each block written (recall β is the size of the block). Later in Section 5 we will describe how to rely on homomorphic checksums to reduce this cost to $\beta + O(\log n)$.

4.1 Server-Side Storage Layout

The server-side storage is organized in three different buffers denoted with **U** (stands for *unencoded*), **C** (stands for *coded*) and **H** (stands for *hierarchical*). We now explain in detail the function of these buffers (see also Figure 1).

Raw buffer. All up-to-date blocks are stored in original, unencoded format in a buffer called **U**. Reads are performed by reading the corresponding location in **U**. Writes update the corresponding location in the buffer **U** immediately with the newly written block. However, unlike reads, writes also cause updates to a hierarchical log as explained later.

Erasure-coded copy. In addition, we store an (m, n, d) erasure-coded copy of the data in a buffer **C**, where $m = \Theta(n)$, and $d = m - n + 1 = \Theta(n)$, i.e., the code is maximum distance separable. The buffer **C** does not immediately get updated upon writes, and therefore may contain stale data.

Hierarchical log of recent writes. A hierarchical log structure denoted **H** stores recently overwritten blocks in erasure-coded format. **H** contains $k + 1$ levels, where $k = \lfloor \log n \rfloor$. We denote the levels of **H** as $(\mathbf{H}_0, \mathbf{H}_1, \ldots, \mathbf{H}_k)$.

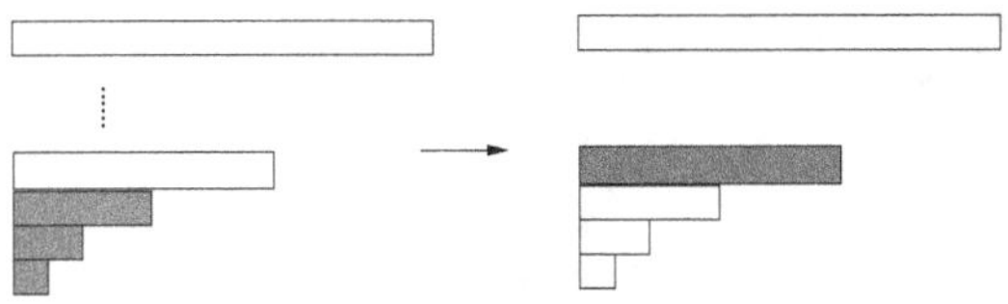

Figure 2: Rebuilding of level $\mathbf{H}_3$. When a newly written block is added to the hierarchical log structure $\mathbf{H}$, consecutive levels $\mathbf{H}_0, \mathbf{H}_1, \mathbf{H}_2$ are filled. A rebuild operation for $\mathbf{H}_3$ occurs as a result, at the end of which $\mathbf{H}_3$ is filled, and $\mathbf{H}_0, \mathbf{H}_1, \mathbf{H}_2$ are empty. Unlike ORAM schemes that employ oblivious sorting for the rebuilidng, our rebuilding algorithm involves computing linear combinations of blocks.

Each level $\ell \in \{0, 1, \ldots, k\}$ is an erasure code of some 2^ℓ blocks. For every block in $\mathbf{H}$, we define its age to be the time elapsed since when the block was written. Level $\mathbf{H}_0$ contains the most recently written block; and the age of the blocks contained in level $\mathbf{H}_\ell$ increases with ℓ. Particularly $\mathbf{H}_k$ (if filled) contains the oldest blocks.

Note that in practice, it is possible that the client keeps writing the same block, say B_i where $i \in [n]$. In this case, the hierarchical log structure $\mathbf{H}$ contains multiple copies of B_i. (as we will see later, duplicates are suppressed when the erasure-coded copy $\mathbf{C}$ is rebuilt.) Particularly, every time a block is written, the new value of the block along with its block identifier is added to the hierarchical log structure $\mathbf{H}$.

4.2 Operations

After describing the three types of buffers that we use to organize the original blocks, we are ready to give the high level intuition of the operations of our construction.

Reading blocks. In order to read a block, we read it directly from $\mathbf{U}$. Along with the block, the server returns the respective Merkle hash tree proof, allowing the client to verify the authenticity and the freshness of the block.

PoR audits. A PoR audit involves the following checks:

1. Checking the authenticity of $O(\lambda)$ random blocks from the erasure-coded copy $\mathbf{C}$;
2. Checking the authenticity of $O(\lambda)$ random blocks from each filled level $\mathbf{H}_\ell$, where $\ell \in [k]$.

Writing blocks and periodic rebuilding operations. Every write not only updates the raw buffer $\mathbf{U}$, but also causes the newly written block to be added to the hierarchical log structure $\mathbf{H}$ (specifically, the new block is always added into $\mathbf{H}_0$). Whenever a block is added, assume that levels $\mathbf{H}_0, \mathbf{H}_1, \ldots, \mathbf{H}_\ell$ are consecutively filled levels where $\ell < k$, and level $\ell + 1$ is the first empty level. This leads to the rebuilding of level $\mathbf{H}_{\ell+1}$. At the end of this rebuilding: 1) level $\mathbf{H}_{\ell+1}$ contains an erasure code of all blocks currently residing in levels $\mathbf{H}_0, \mathbf{H}_1, \ldots, \mathbf{H}_\ell$ and the newly added block; and 2) level $\mathbf{H}_0, \mathbf{H}_1, \ldots \mathbf{H}_\ell$ are emptied (see Figure 2).

This rebuilding technique has been previously used in various ORAM schemes (e.g., [25]). However, unlike ORAM schemes that require oblivious sorting for the rebuilding, our rebuilding process requires just computing an erasure code of the new level. This is a lot simpler since it just involves computing linear combinations of blocks (we employ a linear coding scheme). We will later show that it takes $O(\beta \cdot 2^\ell)$ time to rebuild level ℓ ($\ell = 0, 1 \ldots, \lfloor \log n \rfloor$), where β is the block size. Since each level ℓ is rebuilt every 2^ℓ write operations, the amortized rebuilding cost per write is $O(\beta \log n)$. In comparison, ORAM schemes [12, 13, 15] require roughly $O(\beta (\log n)^2 / \log\log n)$ or higher amortized cost for the rebuilding due to oblivious sorting.

For now, we assume that the client is performing the rebuilding for simplicity. Later in Section 5, we will show how to have the server perform the rebuilding computations, and the client instead simply verifies that the server adheres to the prescribed behavior. This will allow us to further reduce the bandwidth overhead from $O(\beta \log n)$ to $\beta + O(\lambda \log n)$.

Periodic rebuilding of the erasure coded copy. Finally, every n write operations, the erasure coded copy $\mathbf{C}$ is rebuilt, and all levels $\mathbf{H}_0, \mathbf{H}_1, \ldots, \mathbf{H}_k$ are emptied as a result. Recall that the log structure $\mathbf{H}$ may contain multiple copies of the same block, if that block is written multiple times. At the time $\mathbf{C}$ is rebuilt, all duplicates will be suppressed, and only the most recent copy of each block will be rebuilt into $\mathbf{C}$. As we later show, the cost of rebuilding $\mathbf{C}$ is $O(\beta n \log n)$ (see Figure 4). Since $\mathbf{C}$ is only rebuilt every n write operations, the amortized cost is $O(\beta \log n)$ per write.

4.3 Security

Before we introduce the rebuilding algorithm, which lies at the heart of our construction, we give an intuitive explanation of why the main security property of PoR, i.e., retrievability (see Definition 2), is satisfied by our construction. Our algorithm will maintain the following invariant:

INVARIANT 1. *Treat $\mathbf{C}$ as the $(k+1)$-th level $\mathbf{H}_{k+1}$. We will maintain the invariant that each level $\mathbf{H}_\ell$ where $\ell \in \{0, 1, \ldots, k+1\}$ is a $(m_\ell, 2^\ell, d_\ell)$ erasure coding of 2^ℓ blocks, where $m_\ell = \Theta(2^\ell)$. Furthermore, we will show that encoding is a maximum distance encoding scheme, such that $d_\ell = m_\ell - 2^\ell + 1 = \Theta(2^\ell)$, i.e., the encoding of level $\mathbf{H}_\ell$ can tolerate up to $d = \Theta(2^\ell)$ erasures.*

In our specific construction, each level is encoded into exactly twice as many blocks, i.e., $\mathbf{H}_\ell$ is a $(2^{\ell+1}, 2^\ell, 2^\ell)$ erasure coding of 2^ℓ recently written blocks. Similarly, $\mathbf{C}$ is also encoded into twice as many blocks.

Recall that our audit algorithm checks $O(\lambda)$ blocks for each level $\mathbf{H}_\ell$ and for $\mathbf{C}$. Intuitively, the server has to delete more than half of the blocks in any level $\mathbf{H}_\ell$ or $\mathbf{C}$ to incur any data loss. However, if the server deletes so many blocks, checking $O(\lambda)$ *random* blocks in level $\mathbf{H}_\ell$ or $\mathbf{C}$ will almost surely detect it (with probability at least $1 - 2^{-\lambda}$). Also, observe that the combination of the hierarchical structure $\mathbf{H}$ and the buffer $\mathbf{C}$ contains information about the up-to-date copy of all blocks. Therefore, we can intuitively conclude that as long as the above invariant is maintained, our audits can detect any data loss with overwhelming probability.

The formal proof requires showing that there exists an extractor which can extract the up-to-date copy of all blocks if the extractor can run the Audit algorithm a polynomial number of times, with blackbox rewinding access to the server. We defer the formal proof to the full online version [22].

4.4 Fast Incrementally Constructible Codes

To achieve the promised efficiency, our main technical challenge is to design a fast, incrementally constructible code. In our scheme, we employ a fast incrementally constructible code based on Fast Fourier Transform (FFT). At a very high level, each level $\mathbf{H}_\ell$ contains two size-2^ℓ FFT-based codes. As is well-known, FFT can be computed using a standard divide-and-conquer strategy [2,3], forming a butterfly network (see Figure 3). This means that $\mathbf{H}_\ell$ can be computed from two $\mathbf{H}_{\ell-1}$'s in time $O(\beta \cdot 2^\ell)$. Note that in comparison, the oblivious sorting in ORAM schemes take time $O(\beta \cdot \ell \cdot 2^\ell)$ time to rebuild level H_ℓ.

Other than our FFT-based encoding scheme, it is possible to employ known linear-time constructible codes [23], which take $O(c)$ time to encode c blocks. We choose to use our FFT-based codes because of the relative conceptual and implementation simplicity. Particularly, rebuilding a level $\mathbf{H}_\ell$ requires only taking $O(2^\ell)$ linear combinations of blocks—in fact, in Section 5, we will leverage this linearity property and a homomorphic checksum scheme to make the client-server the bandwidth cost per writes independent of the block size.

4.4.1 Detailed Code Construction

In our construction, level $\mathbf{H}_\ell$ contains 2^ℓ blocks, which are encoded into $2^{\ell+1}$ codeword blocks, such that knowledge of any 2^ℓ codeword blocks can recover the original 2^ℓ blocks.

Suppose the original blocks in level $\mathbf{H}_\ell$ are denoted as a vector $\mathbf{x}_\ell$, where each block in $\mathbf{x}_\ell$ arrived at time $t, t+1, t+2, \ldots, t+2^\ell-1 \pmod{n}$ respectively. For level $\mathbf{H}_\ell$, t is always a multiple of 2^ℓ. Note that the time t is only incremented for write requests since reads do not need to touch the hierarchical log.

Notation. For the description of our code, we define the partial bit-reversal function and permutation—this inherently results from the divide and conquer strategy of the FFT. Let $\psi_c(i)$ denote a partial *bit-reversal function* that reverses the least significant c bits of an integer i. For example, let $n = 8$, then $\psi_3(1) = 4$, $\psi_2(1) = 2$. Let $\pi_c(\mathbf{x})$ denote a partial *bit-reversal permutation*, where index i is permuted to index $\psi_c(i)$.

Let also w denote the $2n$-th primitive root of unity in an appropriate finite field defined explicitly in Figure 4.

Closed-form formula for each level. Level $\mathbf{H}_\ell$ contains code blocks output by the following linear encoding scheme:

$$\mathbf{H}_\ell := \pi_\ell(\mathbf{x}_\ell)\,[F_\ell,\ D_{\ell,t}F_\ell]\ , \tag{1}$$

where F_ℓ is the 2^ℓ by 2^ℓ Fourier Transform matrix from the finite field defined in Figure 4 and $D_{\ell,t}$ is an appropriate diagonal matrix defined as below.

$$D_{\ell,t} := \mathsf{diag}(w^{\psi_{k-\ell}(t)}, w^{\psi_{k-\ell}(t+1)}, \ldots, w^{\psi_{k-\ell}(t+2^\ell-1)})\,.$$

We now have the following lemma (its proof can be found in the full online version [22]):

LEMMA 1. *Any $2^\ell \times 2^\ell$ submatrix of the generator matrix $G_\ell := [F_\ell,\ D_{\ell,t}F_\ell]$ is full rank.*

Note that the above lemma means that if we have any 2^ℓ (out of $2^{\ell+1}$) code blocks for a level H_ℓ, we can recover all original blocks in that level. As mentioned earlier, using the divide-and-conquer strategy for computing FFT transforms, we can efficiently build our codes over time. The detailed algorithm is presented in the next subsection.

For a concrete small example when $n = 8$, please refer to the full online version [22].

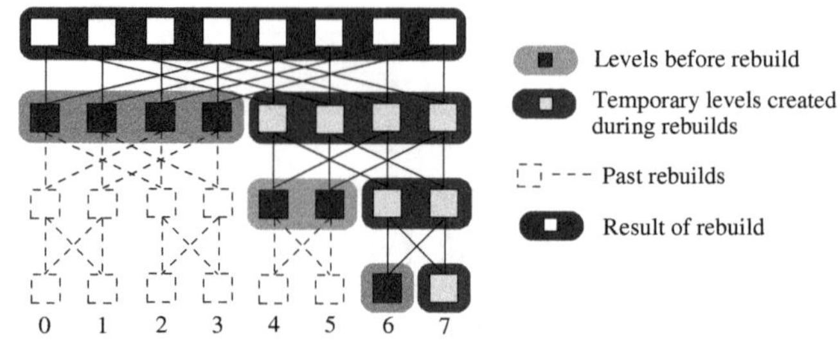

Figure 3: Butterfly network: the 8-th write operation encounters a full $\mathbf{H}_0$, $\mathbf{H}_1$, and $\mathbf{H}_2$. Blocks in $\mathbf{H}_0, \mathbf{H}_1, \mathbf{H}_2$ as well as the newly written block will be encoded and written to $\mathbf{H}_3$.

4.5 Detailed Protocol Description

The detailed protocol description is presented in Figure 4. The lemma below states that algorithm $\mathsf{mix}(\mathsf{A}_0, \mathsf{A}_1)$ specified in Figure 4 produces codes for the hierarchical log, satisfying Equation (1). Its proof can be found in the full online version [22].

LEMMA 2. *Algorithm $\mathsf{mix}(\mathsf{A}_0, \mathsf{A}_1)$ in Figure 4 ensures that each filled level $\mathbf{H}_\ell$ is a code of the form of Equation (1).*

4.6 Enhancements to Basic Construction

Segmenting blocks to avoid big integer operations. In the above description, each block is treated as a large integer during the encoding operations. We can avoid big integer arithmetic by dividing blocks into smaller segments. In our implementation, we choose a prime $p = \alpha n + 1$ for a small positive integer α, such that p can be represented with a basic integer type. We divide each block into $\beta_0 := \lceil \log p \rceil$ bits. and perform the mix algorithm described above on each smaller segment of the block. Note that using a smaller p does not affect the security of our scheme, since the parameter p is part of the erasure coding, and p is not related to the size of any cryptographic keys.

Ensuring authenticity and freshness. Since the last-write time of blocks in the buffers $\mathbf{H}$ and $\mathbf{C}$ are computable from the current time t, the client can simply use time and location encoded MACs to ensure authenticity and freshness of blocks in the buffers $\mathbf{H}$ and $\mathbf{C}$. Blocks in the buffer $\mathbf{U}$ need random access, therefore, we can use a standard Merkle hash tree (i.e., memory checking) to ensure freshness and authenticity of blocks in $\mathbf{U}$. We omit the details here since we will present an improved construction in Section 5 where we will revisit the authenticity and freshness issue.

THEOREM 1. *The basic dynamic PoR scheme of Figure 4 satisfies both authenticity (Definition 1) and retrievability (Definition 2).*

The authenticity and retrievability proofs of the above theorem can be found in the full online version [22].

5. IMPROVED CONSTRUCTION

In our basic construction (Section 4), every write incurs the reading and writing of $O(\log n)$ blocks, or $O(\beta \log n)$ bits on average, where β is the block size. In this section, we will describe an improved construction that achieves improved bandwidth and client computation overhead (however the server computation of the new construction remains

Main Dynamic PoR Construction

Let (encode, decode) *denote a maximum distance separable* (m, n, d) *erasure code, where* $m = O(n)$.

/* *Authenticity: Standard Merkle-hash tree techniques can be used to verify the authenticity/freshness of blocks retrieved from the server. For clarity, we omit such details from the scheme description. Section 5 presents more optimized techniques for achieving authenticity/freshness.* */

$\mathsf{Init}(1^\lambda, n, \beta, \mathcal{M})$:

$\mathbf{U} \leftarrow \mathcal{M}$; $\mathbf{C} \leftarrow \mathsf{encode}(\mathcal{M})$; $\mathbf{H} \leftarrow \emptyset$.

$\mathsf{Read}(i, st, \hat{\mathcal{M}})$: To read a block i, simply read $\mathbf{U}[i]$ and check its authenticity.

$\mathsf{Write}(i, B, st, \hat{\mathcal{M}})$: To overwrite block i with B, let $\mathbf{U}[i] \leftarrow B$. Call $\mathsf{HAdd}(B)$.

$\mathsf{Audit}(st, \hat{\mathcal{M}})$: Check the authenticity of $O(\lambda)$ number of blocks from the erasure coded copy $\mathbf{C}$ and $O(\lambda)$ number of blocks from each filled level $\mathbf{H}_\ell$.

Algorithm $\mathsf{HAdd}(B)$

Suppose each $\mathbf{H}_\ell$ *is of the form* $\mathbf{H}_\ell := (X_\ell, Y_\ell)$, *where* X_ℓ *and* Y_ℓ *each stores* 2^ℓ *blocks.*

Let the current write be the t*-th write operation* $(\bmod\ 2^k)$. *Let* $\psi(\cdot)$ *denote the bit reversal function, such that* $\psi(t)$ *outputs the value corresponding to reversing the bits of the binary representation of* t.

- If $\mathbf{H}_0$ is empty, let $X_0 = B$, $Y_0 = B \cdot w^{\psi(t)}$.
- Else, suppose levels $0, \ldots, \ell$ are consecutively full levels for some $\ell < k$, and level $\ell + 1$ is the first empty level.
  - Call $\mathsf{HRebuildX}(\ell + 1, B)$.
  - Call $\mathsf{HRebuildY}(\ell + 1, B \cdot w^{\psi(t)})$.
- Every 2^k time steps, call $\mathsf{CRebuild}()$.

Parameters: Let $p = \alpha \cdot (2n) + 1$ denote a prime for some $\alpha \in \mathbb{N}$. Suppose p is chosen to be large enough to encode blocks of β bits.
Let g denote a generator of $\mathbb{Z}_p^*$. Let $w = g^\alpha \bmod p$ be a $2n$-th primitive root of unity mod p.

Algorithms $\mathsf{HRebuildX}(\ell, B)$, $\mathsf{HRebuildY}(\ell, B)$

/* HRebuildY *is exactly the same as* HRebuildX, *except that all* X*'s are replaced with* Y*'s. Below we formally describe* HRebuildX *as an example.* */

Inputs: Consecutively filled levels $X_0 \ldots X_{\ell-1}$ (the X portion), and a new (possibly encoded) block B.

Output: A rebuilt X_ℓ. Levels $X_0, \ldots, X_{\ell-1}$ are emptied at the end of $\mathsf{HRebuildX}(\ell, B)$.

- $\widetilde{X}_1 \leftarrow \mathsf{mix}(X_0, B)$
- For $i = 1$ to $\ell - 1$: $\widetilde{X}_{i+1} \leftarrow \mathsf{mix}(X_i, \widetilde{X}_i)$
  // $\widetilde{X}_i$*'s are the red arrays in Figure 3.*
- Output $X_\ell := \widetilde{X}_\ell$.

Algorithm $\mathsf{mix}(\mathsf{A}_0, \mathsf{A}_1)$

Inputs: Two arrays $\mathsf{A}_0, \mathsf{A}_1 \in \mathbb{Z}_p^{2^\ell}$ each of length 2^ℓ.

Outputs: A new array A of length $2 \cdot 2^\ell$.

- Let $\nu = w^{n/2^\ell}$ be a $2^{\ell+1}$-th primitive root of unity.
- For $i = 0$ to $2^\ell - 1$:

$$\begin{aligned} \mathsf{A}[i] &:= \mathsf{A}_0[i] + \nu^i \mathsf{A}_1[i] \pmod p \\ \mathsf{A}[i + 2^\ell] &:= \mathsf{A}_0[i] - \nu^i \mathsf{A}_1[i] \pmod p \end{aligned}$$

- Output A.

Algorithm $\mathsf{CRebuild}()$

- $\mathbf{C} \leftarrow \mathsf{encode}(\mathbf{U})$.
- Empty $\mathbf{H}$.

Figure 4: Basic protocol description. We assume that blocks are tagged with their block identifier.

the same), by removing the dependence on the block size. In our improved construction, writing a block incurs only $\beta + O(\lambda \log n)$ cost, where λ is the security parameter; and the typical value for λ is 128 or 256 bits. This means that *the bandwidth overhead and the client computation for write operations of our PoR construction is analogous to that of a Merkle hash tree.* Recall that by the definition of PoR, PoR is a strictly stronger primitive than a Merkle hash tree since PoR not only needs to guarantee authenticity and freshness—which a standard Merkle hash tree ensures—but it needs to additionally guarantee that the server is storing all of the client's data. Our construction basically shows that we can obtain the additional PoR guarantee (on top of a Merkle hash tree) almost for free.

5.1 Intuition

Recall that in the basic construction, the $O(\beta \log n)$ cost arises from the periodical rebuilding of the hierarchical log structure $\mathbf{H}$ and the erasure-coded copy $\mathbf{C}$. In the basic construction, the server is conceptually treated as a passive remote storage device, and the client performs all the computation. Therefore, the client needs to download the blocks from the server to perform computation over these blocks, when rebuilding any level $\mathbf{H}_\ell$ in the hierarchical log structure, or when rebuilding $\mathbf{C}$.

Our idea is to have the server perform the computation on behalf of the client, thus significantly reducing the client computation and bandwidth. Observe that in our basic construction, the algorithms for rebuilding each $\mathbf{H}_\ell$ or $\mathbf{C}$ are publicly known to the server, and the server can perform the rebuilding on its own. The client simply needs to check that the server performed the rebuilding correctly.

To achieve this performance improvement and avoid downloading the blocks during a rebuilding, we will attach a *homomorphic checksum* along with each (encoded or unencoded) block in the hierarchical log structure $\mathbf{H}$ or $\mathbf{C}$. Each homomorphic checksum is a collision-resistant summary of a block. Now, instead of performing the rebuilding over real data blocks, the client simply downloads checksums, checks their authenticity and performs the rebuilding over these homomorphic checksums.

The homomorphic checksum for each block is then tagged with its position and time written, and stored on the server in encrypted and authenticated format. This ensures that 1) the server does not know the values of the homomorphic checksum which is necessary for security as explained later; and 2) the client can always verify the correctness and freshness of the homomorphic checksum retrieved.

We note here that we choose to use a special type of homomorphic checksums that are not publicly verifiable (though we later show that this is not a limitation for making our scheme publicly verifiable). The reason for that is that our homomorphic checksum construction is designed for performance. In comparison, publicly verifiable homomorphic checksums (e.g., lattice-based ones [19] or RSA-based ones [5]) are not as efficient practice.

5.2 Homomorphic Checksums: Definitions

We now give the definition of a homomorphic checksum scheme, along with its definition of security (unforgeability).

As mentioned in Section 4.6, we segment a block into segments of bit-length $\beta_0 = \lceil \log p \rceil$. Therefore, we can write a block B in the form $B \in \mathbb{Z}_p^{\lceil \beta/\beta_0 \rceil}$.

DEFINITION 4. *We define a homomorphic checksum scheme to consist of the following algorithms:*

$sk \leftarrow \mathbb{K}(1^\lambda)$. The key generation algorithm $\mathbb{K}$ takes in the security parameter 1^λ, the block size β, outputting a secret key sk.

$\sigma \leftarrow \mathbb{S}_{sk}(B)$. The authentication algorithm $\mathbb{S}$ takes in the secret key sk, a block $B \in \mathbb{Z}_p^{\lceil \beta/\beta_0 \rceil}$, and outputs a checksum σ. In our scheme σ has bit-length $O(\lambda)$.

DEFINITION 5 (UNFORGEABILITY OF CHECKSUM). *We say that a homomorphic checksum scheme is unforgeable, if for any (polynomial-time) adversary $\mathcal{A}$,*

$$\Pr\left[\begin{array}{l} sk \leftarrow \mathbb{K}(1^\lambda) \\ B_1, B_2 \leftarrow \mathcal{A}(1^\lambda) \end{array} : \begin{array}{l} B_1 \neq B_2 \\ \mathbb{S}_{sk}(B_1) = \mathbb{S}_{sk}(B_2) \end{array}\right] \leq \mathsf{negl}(\lambda) .$$

Namely, an adversary who has not seen the secret key sk or any checksum cannot produce two blocks B_1 and B_2 that result in the same checksum. In our scheme, the clients encrypts all checksums before storing them at the server, thus the server does not see the secret key or any checksums.

Additive homomorphism. We require our homomorphic checksum scheme to achieve additive homomorphism, i.e., for any $sk \leftarrow \mathbb{K}(1^\lambda)$, for any blocks $B_1, B_2 \in \mathbb{Z}_p^{\lceil \beta/\beta_0 \rceil}$, for any $a_1, a_2 \in \mathbb{Z}_p$, it is $a_1\mathbb{S}_{sk}(B_1) + a_2\mathbb{S}_{sk}(B_2) = \mathbb{S}_{sk}(a_1 B_1 + a_2 B_2)$.

5.3 Homomorphic Checksum Construction

We now present a simple homomorphic checksum scheme.

$\mathbb{K}(1^\lambda)$: The client picks a random matrix $\mathbf{M} \xleftarrow{\$} \mathbb{Z}_p^{\rho \times \lceil \beta/\beta_0 \rceil}$ and lets $sk := \mathbf{M}$. The number of rows ρ is chosen such that $\rho\beta_0 = O(\lambda)$, i.e., we would like the resulting checksum to have have about $O(\lambda)$ number of bits.

$\mathbb{S}_{sk}(B)$: On input a block $B \in \mathbb{Z}_p^{\lceil \beta/\beta_0 \rceil}$, compute checksum $\sigma := \mathbf{M} \cdot B$. Note that the checksum compresses the block from β bits to $O(\lambda)$ bits.

Additive homomorphism. It is not hard to see that the above homomorphic checksum scheme satisfies additive homomorphism, since $a_1\mathbf{M}B_1 + a_2\mathbf{M}B_2 = \mathbf{M}(a_1B_1 + a_2B_2)$.

Unforgeability. Inthe full online version [22] we show that the above construction satisfies unforgeability in an information theoretic sense (i.e., even for computationally unbounded adversaries).

THEOREM 2. *The above homomorphic checksum construction satisfies the unforgeability notion (Definition 5).*

Efficiency. As we saw in the definition of the homomorphic checksum, the blocks used are represented as vectors in $\mathbb{Z}_p^{\lceil \beta/\beta_0 \rceil}$. We use a very small p in our implementation—in fact we take $p = 3 \cdot 2^{30} + 1$ and therefore checksum operations do not need big integer operations and are highly efficient.

5.4 Using Homomorphic Checksums

Relying on homomorphic checksums, we can reduce the bandwidth cost and the client computation to $\beta + O(\lambda \log n)$ for write operations. To do this, we make the following modifications to the basic construction described in Section 4.

Store encrypted and authenticated checksums on server. First, for every (encoded or uncoded) block stored on the server, in the buffers $\mathbf{U}$, $\mathbf{C}$ and $\mathbf{H}$, the client attaches a homomorphic checksum, which is encrypted under an authenticated encryption scheme $\mathsf{AE} := (\mathbb{E}, \mathbb{D})$.

Let $sk := (\mathbf{M}, sk_0)$ denote the client's secret key (unknown to the server). Specifically $\mathbf{M} \in \mathbb{Z}_p^{\rho \times \lceil \beta/\beta_0 \rceil}$ is the random matrix used in the homomorphic checksum scheme, and sk_0 is a master secret key used to generate one-time keys for the authenticated encryption scheme AE.

For the buffers $\mathbf{C}$ and $\mathbf{H}$, suppose a block B is written to address addr on the server at time t. The client generates the following one-time key:

$$\kappa = \mathsf{PRF}_{sk_0}(0, \mathsf{addr}, t)$$

and attaches $\widetilde{\sigma}(B)$ with block B, where

$$\widetilde{\sigma}(B) := \mathsf{AE}.\mathbb{E}_\kappa(\mathbb{S}_M(B)) .$$

For buffer $\mathbf{U}$, the client uses a fixed encryption key $\kappa = \mathsf{PRF}_{sk_0}(1)$ as blocks in $\mathbf{U}$ have unpredictable last-write times.

Ensuring authenticity and freshness. For each block in buffers $\mathbf{H}$ and $\mathbf{C}$, its time and location dependent $\widetilde{\sigma}(B)$ allows the client to verify the authenticity and freshness of the block. The client need not separately MAC the blocks in $\mathbf{H}$ or $\mathbf{C}$.

For blocks in $\mathbf{U}$, a Merkle tree is built over these $\widetilde{\sigma}(B)$'s for the $\mathbf{U}$ buffer, and the client keeps track of the root digest. After fetching a block B from buffer $\mathbf{U}$, the client fetches its corresponding $\widetilde{\sigma}(B)$, verifies $\widetilde{\sigma}(B)$ with the Merkle tree, and verifies that the block B fetched agrees with $\widetilde{\sigma}(B)$.

Rebuilding H based on homomorphic checksum. In our improved scheme, the HRebuild algorithm is executed by the server. In order to enforce honest server behavior, the client performs the HRebuild algorithm, not directly over the blocks, but over $\widetilde{\sigma}(B)$'s. In other words, imagine the client were to execute the HRebuild algorithm on its own:

- Whenever the client needed to read a block B from the server, it now reads $\widetilde{\sigma}(B)$ instead, and decrypts $\sigma(B) \leftarrow \mathsf{AE}.\mathbb{D}_\kappa(\widetilde{\sigma}(B))$. In the above, $\kappa := \mathsf{PRF}_{sk_0}(0, \mathsf{addr}, t)$, where addr is the physical address of block B, and t is the last time B is written. Note that for any block in the hierarchical log structure $\mathbf{H}$ and in the erasure-coded copy $\mathbf{C}$, the client can compute exactly when the block was last written from the current time alone. The client rejects if the decryption fails, which means that the server is misbehaving.
- Whenever the client needed to perform computation over two blocks B_1 and B_2, the client now performs the same operation over the homomorphic checksums $\sigma(B_1)$ and $\sigma(B_2)$. Recall that in $\mathsf{HRebuild}$, we only have addition and multiplications by known constants—therefore, our additively homomorphic checksum would work.
- Whenever the client needed to write a block to the server, it now writes the new $\widetilde{\sigma}(B)$ instead.

Rebuilding C based on homomorphic checksum. Similar to the above, the server rebuilds $\mathbf{C}$ on behalf of the client, and the client only simulates the rebuilding of $\mathbf{C}$ operating on the $\widetilde{\sigma}(B)$'s instead of the full blocks. However, slightly differently from the rebuilding of $\mathbf{H}$, the buffer $\mathbf{C}$ is rebuilt by computing an erasure code of the fresh data in $\mathbf{U}$.

One way to do this is to use the same FFT-based code as described in Section 4. The server can compute the code using the butterfly diagram (Figure 3) in $O(\beta n \log n)$ time. The client simply has to simulate this encoding process using the $\widetilde{\sigma}(B)$'s rather than the data blocks—therefore the client-server bandwidth is $O(\lambda n \log n)$ for each rebuild of $\mathbf{C}$.

5.5 Reducing Client-Server Audit Bandwidth

In our basic construction in Section 4, audits require transferring $O(\lambda)$ random from each level $\mathbf{H}_\ell$ and from $\mathbf{C}$—therefore the audit cost is $O(\lambda\beta \log n)$. However this can be reduced by observing that audited blocks can be aggregated using a linear aggregation scheme, and the client can check the "aggregated block" using the homomorphic "aggregate checksum". This is similar to the technique used by Shacham and Waters [20]. The new audit protocol is as below:

- *Challenge.* Client picks $O(\lambda)$ random indices for each level $\mathbf{H}_\ell$ and for $\mathbf{C}$. Client picks a random challenge $\rho_i \in \mathbb{Z}_p$ for each selected index. The random indices are denoted $I := \{\mathsf{addr}_1, \mathsf{addr}_2, \ldots, \mathsf{addr}_r\}$, where $r = O(\lambda \log n)$. The random challenges are denoted $R := \{\rho_1, \rho_2, \ldots, \rho_r\}$. Client sends $I := \{\mathsf{addr}_1, \mathsf{addr}_2, \ldots, \mathsf{addr}_r\}$ and $R := \{\rho_1, \rho_2, \ldots, \rho_r\}$ to the server.
- *Response.* Let B_{addr} denote the block at addr. Server sends client the corresponding $\widetilde{\sigma}(B_{\mathsf{addr}})$ for each requested index $\mathsf{addr} \in I$. Server also computes $B^* = \sum_{i=1}^{r} \rho_i B_{\mathsf{addr}_i}$, and sends B^* to the client.
- *Verification.* The client decrypts all $\widetilde{\sigma}(B)$'s received and obtains $\sigma(B)$'s. Client computes $v = \sum_{i=1}^{r} \rho_i \sigma(B_{\mathsf{addr}_i})$, and the checksum $\sigma(B^*)$. The client checks if $v \stackrel{?}{=} \sigma(B^*)$.

This modification reduces the bandwidth for audits to $\beta + O(\lambda^2 \log n)$ since only checksums and *one* aggregate block need to be communicated from the server to the client.

THEOREM 3. *The improved dynamic PoR scheme that uses homomorphic checksums satisfies both authenticity (Definition 1) and retrievability (Definition 2).*

The proofs of the above theorem can be found in the full online version [22].

6. IMPLEMENTATION AND EVALUATION

We implemented a variant of our secretly-verifiable construction described in Section 5. The implementation is in C# and contains about 6,000 lines of code measured using SLOCCount [4].

6.1 Practical Considerations

Our implementation features several further optimizations in comparison with the theoretical construction in Section 5.

Reducing write cost. Our implementation is optimized for the common scenario where writes are frequent and audits are relatively infrequent. We apply a simple trick to reduce the client-server bandwidth for write operations; however, at slightly higher cost for audits.

To reduce the overhead of writing the log structure $\mathbf{H}$, the client can group about $O(\log n)$ blocks into a bigger block when writing to $\mathbf{H}$. The simplest instantiation is for the client to cache $O(\log n)$ blocks and write them in a batch as a single bigger block.

This optimization reduces the amortized cost of writing to $\mathbf{H}$ to $\beta + O(\lambda)$. Particularly, the client-server bandwidth overhead (in addition to transferring the block itself) can be broken down into two parts: 1) about $O(\lambda \log n)$ due to the Merkle hash tree for the buffer $\mathbf{U}$; and 2) $O(\lambda)$ for writing to the log structure $\mathbf{H}$—notice that this part is independent of n. This trick increases an audit's disk I/O cost to roughly $O(\lambda\beta \log^2 n)$ (but only $O(\lambda \log n)$ disk seeks), and increases an audit's client-server bandwidth to $\beta \log n + O(\lambda^2 \log n)$.

Deamortization. Our theoretic construction has low amortized cost per write, but high worst-case cost. We can perform a standard deamortization trick (introduced for similar multi-level hierarchical data structures used in several ORAM constructions [18,31]) to spread the hierarchical encoding work over time, such that we achieve good worst-case performance. We implemented deamortization, therefore it is reflected in the experimental results.

Reducing disk seeks. Our hierarchical log features sequential data accesses when rebuilding level $\mathbf{H}_\ell$ from two arrays of size $2^{\ell-1}$. (see Figure 3 and Algorithm mix of Figure 4). Due to such sequential access patterns, we can use a bigger chunk size to reduce the number of seeks. Every time, we read a chunk and cache it in memory while performing the linear combinations in Algorithm mix.

6.2 Experimental Results

We ran experiments on a single server node with an i7-930 2.8 Ghz CPU and 7 rotational WD1001FALS 1TB 7200 RPM HDDs with 12 ms random I/O latency. Since reads are not much different from a standard Merkle-tree, we focus on evaluating the performance overhead of writes and audits.

6.2.1 Write Cost

Client-server bandwidth. Figures 5 and 6 depict the client-server bandwidth cost for our scheme. Figure 5 plots the total client-server bandwidth consumed for writing a 4KB block, for various storage sizes. We compare the cost to a standard Merkle hash tree, and show that our POR scheme achieves comparable client-server bandwidth.

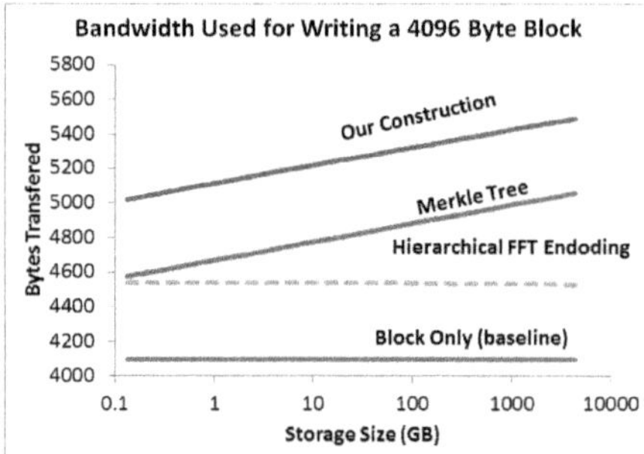

Figure 5: Client-server bandwidth for writing a 4KB block.

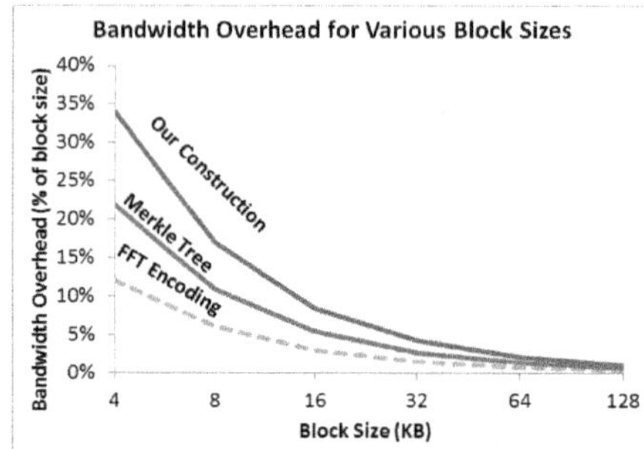

Figure 6: Percentage of bandwidth overhead for various block sizes. The total storage capacity is 1TB.

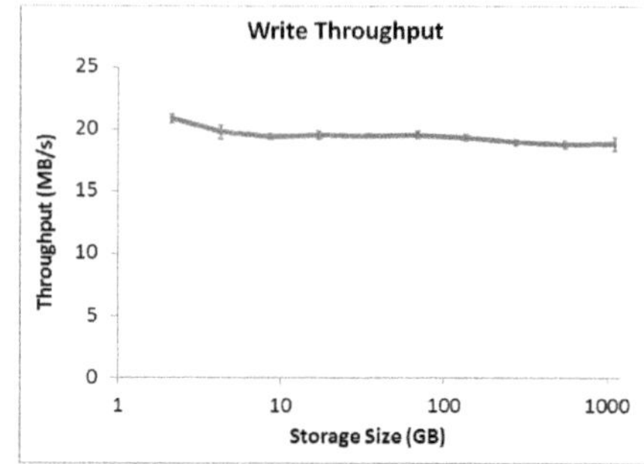

Figure 7: Throughput for write operations when client-server bandwidth is ample. The error bars indicate one standard deviation over 20 trials. A 4KB block size is used.

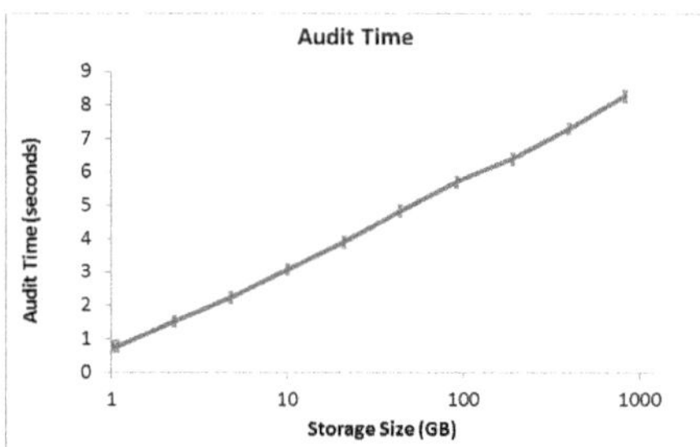

Figure 8: Time spent by server for performing an audit. Does not include network transfer time. Error bars denote 1 standard deviation from 20 trials. The majority of this time is disk I/O cost. A 4KB block size is chosen.

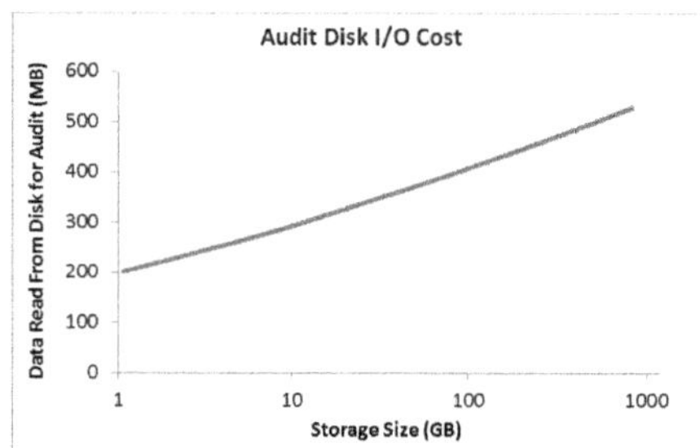

Figure 9: Disk I/O cost for each audit. Block size is chosen to be 4KB.

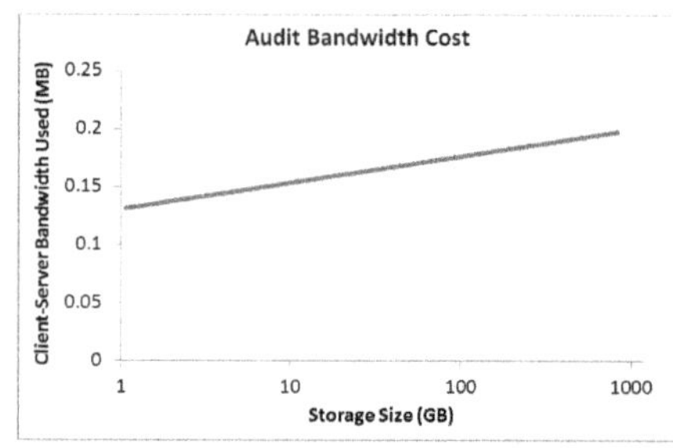

Figure 10: Client-server bandwidth for an audit. Block size is chosen to be 4KB.

We also plot the dotted "Hierarchical FFT encoding" curve, which represents the portion of our bandwidth cost dedicated to the rebuilding of the buffers **C** and **H**. As mentioned earlier in Section 6.1, our implementation features optimizations such that the client-server bandwidth overhead contains the sum of two parts 1) a $O(\lambda)$ part for rebuilding **H** and **C**. This is represented by the dotted line in Figure 5—note that it is independent of n, hence a straight-line; and 2) $O(\lambda \log n)$ bandwidth due to the Merkle tree for the up-to-date copy **U**.

Figure 6 shows the percentage of bandwidth overhead (not including transferring the block itself) for each write. In our scheme, the bandwidth overhead is indepedent of the block size. Therefore, the bigger the block size, the smaller the percentage of bandwidth overhead. We also compare against a standard Merkle-tree in the figure, and show the portion of the bandwidth overhead for the hierarchical encoding procedure.

Server disk I/O performance. Figure 7 shows the write throughput of our scheme. The server's disk I/O cost is about $O(\log n)$, i.e., it needs to read roughly $O(\log n)$ blocks for every write operation. Our experiments show that if server disk I/O were maxed out, the POR write throughput we can achieve would be roughly 20MB/s under our setup. We cache the smallest 10 levels of **H** in memory in this experiment. In practice, however, the client-server bandwidth is more likely to be the bottleneck, and the actual POR throughput achievable will be limited by the available client-server bandwidth.

While the server needs to read $O(\log n)$ blocks for each write, the number of seeks is very small. As mentioned earlier in Section 6.1, the hierarchical log structure **H** is mostly written in a sequential fashion, and since we choose a large chunk size (roughly 50MB), and cache chunks in memory, every write operation requires only 0.03 to 0.06 seeks on average. We cache the Merkle hash tree for **U** in memory in our experiments.

6.2.2 Audit Cost

We use a $\lambda = 128$ for these experiments, i.e., each audit samples 128 blocks from each level $\mathbf{H}_\ell$ and buffer **C**.

Figure 8 shows the time spent by the server for each audit operation—including time for reading disk and performing computation, but not including network transfer time between client and server (client-server network overhead is characterized separately in Figure 10). The majority of this time is spent on disk I/O, and is dominated by disk seeks. There are roughly $O(\lambda \log n)$ seeks per audit operation parallelized to 7 disks, and each seek takes roughly 12ms.

Figure 9 shows the disk I/O cost for an audit. As mentioned in Section 6.1, we optimize for writes at slightly higher audit cost, and the audit disk I/O cost is $O(\lambda\beta \log^2 n)$—this is why the line curves slightly, and is not linear.

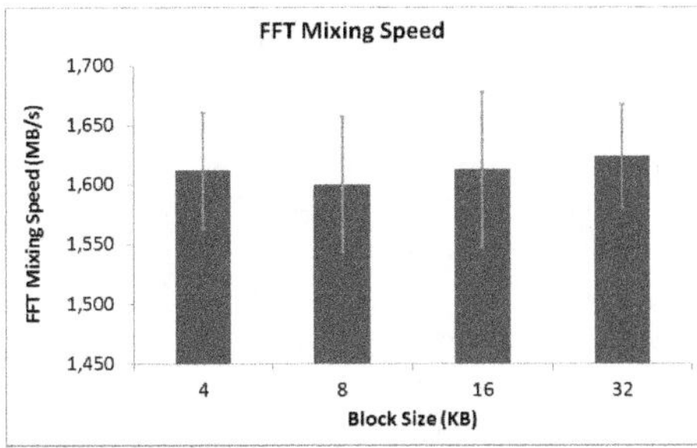

Figure 11: Computational throughput for hierarchical erasure coding. Error bars denote 1 standard deviation from 20 runs.

Figure 10 shows the client-server bandwidth consumed for an audit. As mentioned in Section 6.1, unlike our theoretic construction, our implementation chooses to speed up writes at slightly higher client-server bandwidth for audits, namely, $\beta \log n + O(\lambda \log n)$.

Computational overhead for hierarchical erasure coding. As shown in Figure 11, the hierarchical coding scheme can be computed at extremely fast speeds, i.e., >1600MB/s per level on a modern processor. To characterize the computational cost, we cached about 4GB of data in memory, and avoid performing disk fetches during this experiment.

7. REFERENCES

[1] https://en.wikipedia.org/wiki/Hash_tree.

[2] Fast fourier transform. http://math.berkeley.edu/~berlek/classes/CLASS.110/LECTURES/FFT.

[3] Fast fourier transform. http://en.wikipedia.org/wiki/Fast_Fourier_transform.

[4] Sloccount. http://www.dwheeler.com/sloccount/.

[5] G. Ateniese, R. Burns, R. Curtmola, J. Herring, L. Kissner, Z. Peterson, and D. Song. Provable data possession at untrusted stores. In *CCS*, 2007.

[6] S. Benabbas, R. Gennaro, and Y. Vahlis. Verifiable delegation of computation over large datasets. In *CRYPTO*, pages 111–131, 2011.

[7] K. D. Bowers, A. Juels, and A. Oprea. Proofs of retrievability: theory and implementation. In *CCSW*, pages 43–54, 2009.

[8] D. Cash, A. Küpçü, and D. Wichs. Dynamic proofs of retrievability via oblivious ram. In *Eurocrypt*, 2013.

[9] Y. Dodis, S. P. Vadhan, and D. Wichs. Proofs of retrievability via hardness amplification. In *TCC*, pages 109–127, 2009.

[10] C. Erway, A. Küpçü, C. Papamanthou, and R. Tamassia. Dynamic provable data possession. In *CCS*, 2009.

[11] O. Goldreich and R. Ostrovsky. Software protection and simulation on oblivious RAMs. *J. ACM*, 1996.

[12] M. T. Goodrich and M. Mitzenmacher. Privacy-preserving access of outsourced data via oblivious RAM simulation. In *ICALP*, 2011.

[13] M. T. Goodrich, M. Mitzenmacher, O. Ohrimenko, and R. Tamassia. Privacy-preserving group data access via stateless oblivious RAM simulation. In *SODA*, 2012.

[14] A. Juels and B. S. K. Jr. Pors: proofs of retrievability for large files. In *ACM Conference on Computer and Communications Security*, pages 584–597, 2007.

[15] E. Kushilevitz, S. Lu, and R. Ostrovsky. On the (in)security of hash-based oblivious RAM and a new balancing scheme. In *SODA*, 2012.

[16] R. C. Merkle. A certified digital signature. In *Proceedings on Advances in cryptology*, CRYPTO '89, 1989.

[17] Z. Mo, Y. Zhou, and S. Chen. A dynamic proof of retrievability (por) scheme with o(log n) complexity. In *ICC'12*, pages 912–916, 2012.

[18] R. Ostrovsky and V. Shoup. Private information storage (extended abstract). In *STOC*, pages 294–303, 1997.

[19] C. Papamanthou, E. Shi, R. Tamassia, and K. Yi. Streaming authenticated data structures. In *EUROCRYPT*, 2013.

[20] H. Shacham and B. Waters. Compact proofs of retrievability. In *ASIACRYPT*, pages 90–107, 2008.

[21] E. Shi, T.-H. H. Chan, E. Stefanov, and M. Li. Oblivious RAM with $O((\log N)^3)$ worst-case cost. In *ASIACRYPT*, pages 197–214, 2011.

[22] E. Shi, E. Stefanov, and C. Papamanthou. Practical dynamic proofs of retrievability. Technical report, 2013.

[23] D. A. Spielman. Linear-time encodable and decodable error-correcting codes. *IEEE Transactions on Information Theory*, 42(6):1723–1731, 1996.

[24] E. Stefanov and E. Shi. Oblivistore: High performance oblivious cloud storage. In *IEEE Symposium on Security and Privacy*, 2013.

[25] E. Stefanov, E. Shi, and D. Song. Towards practical oblivious RAM. In *NDSS*, 2012.

[26] E. Stefanov, M. van Dijk, A. Juels, and A. Oprea. Iris: a scalable cloud file system with efficient integrity checks. In *ACSAC*, pages 229–238, 2012.

[27] J. van Lint. *Introduction to Coding Theory.* Springer-Verlag, 1992.

[28] Q. Wang, C. Wang, J. Li, K. Ren, and W. Lou. Enabling public verifiability and data dynamics for storage security in cloud computing. In *ESORICS*, 2009.

[29] Q. Wang, C. Wang, K. Ren, W. Lou, and J. Li. Enabling public auditability and data dynamics for storage security in cloud computing. *IEEE Trans. Parallel Distrib. Syst.*, 22(5):847–859, 2011.

[30] P. Williams, R. Sion, and B. Carbunar. Building castles out of mud: practical access pattern privacy and correctness on untrusted storage. In *CCS*, 2008.

[31] P. Williams, R. Sion, and A. Tomescu. Privatefs: A parallel oblivious file system. In *CCS*, 2012.

[32] Q. Zheng and S. Xu. Fair and dynamic proofs of retrievability. In *CODASPY*, 2011.

APPENDIX

A. ACHIEVING PUBLIC VERIFIABILITY

Although our basic construction in Section 4 provides *public verifiability*, the more efficient scheme described in Section 5 does not, since the homomorphic checksum requires the client keep secret state. In this section we show how to turn the efficient scheme of Section 5 into publicly verifiable.

In a publicly verifiable setting, only a *trusted data source* can write data; however, anyone can perform *verifiable reads* and *PoR audits.*

Ensuring the public verifiability of reads comes for free, since a Merkle hash tree is maintained over the buffer $\mathbf{U}$. Therefore the trusted source can simply sign and publish the up-to-date root digest of this Merkle-hash tree and make it available to the public for verification of read operations.

We now focus on how to achieve public *auditability* so that to enable anyone challenge the server to prove that it possesses all data (owned by the source) and *still* maintain the bandwidth of the write operations to be low.

A.1 Public Auditability with Low Write Cost

To achieve public auditability, we build a separate Merkle hash tree over the blocks of each level $\mathbf{H}_\ell$, and one for $\mathbf{C}$.

The up-to-date root digests of all $O(\log n)$ hash trees will be publicized. During a public audit, a user with the root digests requests $O(\lambda)$ blocks at random for each level $\mathbf{H}_\ell$ and buffer $\mathbf{C}$, and checks them with the root digests.

One question remains: how does the trusted source keep track of these root digests without having to transfer original blocks during the rebuilding of the hierarchical levels? To address this question, we sketch our idea below, and leave the details and full proofs to the full online version [22].

Our idea is to have the server compute the new Merkle trees for a level (or the buffer $\mathbf{C}$) when it is being rebuilt. However, we need to protect against a malicious server that can potentially cheat and output the wrong digests. We apply a probabilistic checking idea again here.

When rebuilding a level $\mathbf{H}_\ell$ (or buffer $\mathbf{C}$), the following happens:

- As in the secretly-verifiable scheme (Section 5), the trusted source downloads the encrypted/authenticated homomorphic checksums and "simulates" the rebuilding over these $\widetilde{\sigma}(B)$'s.
- The server performs the rebuilding, computes the new digest h of $\mathbf{H}_\ell$, and commits h to the source.
- The source challenges $O(\lambda)$ random blocks in $\mathbf{H}_\ell$. For each challenged block B: the source downloads the block itself B, its $\widetilde{\sigma}(B)$, and the path in the Merkle tree necessary to verify block B. The client now checks that $\widetilde{\sigma}(B)$ verifies for B, and that the *already committed* root digest h verifies for B as well.

Proof intuition. At a high level, this idea works because if the server can pass the probabilistic check (of the committed root digest h), then at least a constant fraction of the rebuilt level $\mathbf{H}_\ell$ (or buffer $\mathbf{C}$) is correctly incorporated into the claimed digest h. Due to PoR's inherent erasure coding, it turns out that this suffices proving the retrievability of the publicly verifiable PoR scheme. The full proof is deferred to the full online version [22].

Write cost. Suppose the trusted source caches locally the smallest $\log\lambda+\log(2/\epsilon)$ levels consisting about $2\lambda/\epsilon$ number of blocks, for an arbitrarily small $0<\epsilon<1$. Note that these are the levels that are accessed more frequently during the write operations. We can then show that the source-server bandwidth for each write operation is $\beta(1+\epsilon)+O(\lambda\log n)$. The details of this analysis is elementary, and deferred to the full online version [22]. The above analysis assumes that exactly λ blocks are probabilistically checked for each Merkle tree hash tree of the remaining (uncached) levels.

A.2 Reducing Public Audit Cost

The publicly verifiable approach described above requires $O(\lambda\log n(\beta+\log n))$ overhead for public auditing. Particularly, for each of the $O(\log n)$ levels $\mathbf{H}_\ell$ as well as $\mathbf{C}$, $O(\lambda)$ blocks need to be checked; and to check a block involves downloading the block itself and $\log n$ hashes of the Merkle hash tree. With some additional tricks, in particular, by carefully aligning the Merkle tree structure with the hierarchical log structure $\mathbf{H}$, we can further improve the public audit overhead to $O(\lambda\beta\log n)$. We defer these details to the Appendix. The basic idea is as follows:

- Instead of building a separate Merkle tree per level $\mathbf{H}_\ell$, build a single Merkle tree over the entire hirarchical log structure $\mathbf{H}$, and another one for $\mathbf{C}$. Furthermore, the Merkle tree will be aligned on top of the hierarchical structure $\mathbf{H}$. Since $\mathbf{H}$ has exponentially growing levels, we can view $\mathbf{H}$ as a tree, where internal nodes are assigned values—in our case, the blocks are the values of internal nodes of the Merkle tree. The hash of each internal node in the Merkle tree is computed as $H(h_{\text{left}}, h_{\text{right}}, B)$, where h_{left} is the hash of the left child, h_{right} is the hash of the right child, and B is the block associated with that node. The client publishes the hash of the Merkle tree for $\mathbf{H}$ and the one for $\mathbf{C}$.
- During public audits, random checks for $\mathbf{C}$ are still done as before. To check $\mathbf{H}$, instead of randomly sample $O(\lambda)$ blocks from each level $\mathbf{H}_\ell$, the client randomly samples $O(\lambda)$ paths from the root to $O(\lambda)$ randomly selected leaf nodes, and sample the blocks on these paths. As a result $O(\lambda)$ blocks from each level gets sampled, and it is not hard to see that only $O(\lambda\log n)$ hashes needs to be transmitted to verify all the paths sampled – namely, hashes of all sibling nodes to the sampled paths need to be transmitted. This reduces the public audit overhead to $O(\lambda\beta\log n)$, assuming $\beta=O(\lambda)$.
- When a non-top level $\mathbf{H}_\ell$ gets rebuilt, the server rebuilds the Merkle hash tree, and the client performs the following probabilistic checking protocol.

  The client first retrieves all hashes at level $\mathbf{H}_{\ell+1}$, and makes sure that they are consistent with the old digest. The client then randomly samples $O(\lambda)$ blocks at level $\mathbf{H}_\ell$, to make sure that these blocks are correctly incorporated into the new root digest as claimed by the server.

  When the top level is rebuilt, the client simply checks $O(\lambda)$ random blocks in the top level, and ensures that they are correctly incorporated into the root digest.

THEOREM 4. *The dynamic PoR scheme with public verifiability satisfies both authenticity (Definition 1) and retrievability (Definition 2).* The proof is in the full online version [22].

A.3 Resizing the Storage

Our scheme can easily be modified to support insertions and deletions of blocks. Insertions can easily be supported by adding a level to the hierarchical log structure $\mathbf{H}$ whenever number of blocks doubles. Deletions can be supported by updating the deleted block with $\perp$. Further, whenever the number of deleted elements exceeds roughly half the size of the dataset, the client can rebuild and consilidate the hierarchical log by suppressing deleted items. We will provide more details in the online full version [22].

Acknowledgments

This work is partially supported by NSF grant CNS-1314857, a Google Research Award, the NSF Graduate Research Fellowship under Grant No. DGE-0946797, by a DoD National Defense Science and Engineering Graduate Fellowship, by Intel award through the ISTC for Secure Computing, and a grant from Amazon Web Services. Any opinions, findings, and conclusions or recommendations expressed in this material are those of the author(s) and do not necessarily reflect the views of the funding agencies. We would like to thank Hubert Chan, Jonathan Katz, and Hongsheng Zhou for helpful discussions, and the anonymous reviewers for their insightful feedback.

Users Get Routed: Traffic Correlation on Tor by Realistic Adversaries

Aaron Johnson[1] Chris Wacek[2] Rob Jansen[1] Micah Sherr[2] Paul Syverson[1]

[1]U.S. Naval Research Laboratory, Washington DC
{aaron.m.johnson, rob.g.jansen, paul.syverson}@nrl.navy.mil

[2]Georgetown University, Washington DC
{cwacek, msherr}@cs.georgetown.edu

ABSTRACT

We present the first analysis of the popular Tor anonymity network that indicates the security of typical users against reasonably realistic adversaries in the Tor network or in the underlying Internet. Our results show that Tor users are far more susceptible to compromise than indicated by prior work. Specific contributions of the paper include (1) a model of various typical kinds of users, (2) an adversary model that includes Tor network relays, autonomous systems (ASes), Internet exchange points (IXPs), and groups of IXPs drawn from empirical study, (3) metrics that indicate how secure users are over a period of time, (4) the most accurate topological model to date of ASes and IXPs as they relate to Tor usage and network configuration, (5) a novel realistic Tor path simulator (*TorPS*), and (6) analyses of security making use of all the above. To show that our approach is useful to explore alternatives and not just Tor as currently deployed, we also analyze a published alternative path selection algorithm, Congestion-Aware Tor. We create an empirical model of Tor congestion, identify novel attack vectors, and show that it too is more vulnerable than previously indicated.

Categories and Subject Descriptors

C.2.0 [**Computer-Communication Networks**]: General—*Security and protection*

Keywords

Anonymity; metrics; onion routing

1. INTRODUCTION

Tor is a volunteer-operated anonymity network that is estimated to protect the privacy of hundreds of thousands of daily users [13, 22]. However, Tor is known to be insecure against an adversary that can observe a user's traffic entering and exiting the anonymity network. Quite simple and efficient techniques can correlate traffic at these separate locations by taking advantage of identifying traffic patterns [29]. As a result, the user and his destination may be identified, completely subverting the protocol's security goals.

CCS'13, November 4–8, 2013, Berlin, Germany.

ACM 978-1-4503-2477-9/13/11 ...$15.00.
http://dx.doi.org/10.1145/2508859.2516651.

The traffic correlation problem in Tor has seen much attention in the literature. Prior Tor security analyses often consider entropy or similar statistical measures as metrics of the security provided by the system at a *static point in time*. In addition, while prior metrics of security may provide useful information about *overall* usage, they typically do not tell users how secure a *type of behavior* is. Further, similar previous work has thus far only considered adversaries that control either a subset of the members of the Tor network, a single autonomous system (AS), or a single Internet exchange point (IXP). These analyses have missed important characteristics of the network, such as that a single organization often controls several geographically diverse ASes or IXPs. That organization may have malicious intent or undergo coercion, threatening users of all network components under its control.

Given the severity of the traffic correlation problem and its security implications, we develop an analysis framework for evaluating the security of various user behaviors on the live Tor network and show how to concretely apply this framework by performing a comprehensive evaluation of the security of the Tor network [41] against the threat of complete deanonymization. To enable such an analysis, we develop a detailed model of a network adversary that includes (*i*) the largest and most accurate system for AS path inference yet applied to Tor and (*ii*) a thorough analysis of the threat of Internet exchange points and IXP coalitions. We also develop realistic metrics that inform this analysis, considering the network topology as it *evolves over time*, for example, as new relays are introduced and others go offline.

Our analysis shows that 80% of all types of users may be deanonymized by a relatively moderate Tor-relay adversary within six months. Our results also show that against a single AS adversary roughly 100% of users in some common locations are deanonymized within three months (95% in three months for a single IXP). Further, we find that an adversary controlling two ASes instead of one reduces the median time to the first client de-anonymization by an order of magnitude: from over three months to only 1 day for a typical web user; and from over three months to roughly one month for a BitTorrent user. This clearly shows the dramatic effect an adversary that controls multiple ASes can have on security.

We observe that since the relays that comprise Tor's egress points may independently specify IP and port-based access control policies, the set of relays available for anonymous circuits is dependent on the user's application (web browsing, IRC, BitTorrent, etc.). We examine how this choice of application affects the security of the user's anonymous connections. Our analysis shows that BitTorrent users not only degrade performance of the Tor network for everybody else, but against a Tor-relay adversary they get significantly less anonymity protection than typical users. They are bested for least anonymity among the uses we considered only by users of the collaborative-work real-time editor Gobby [1].

After describing background and related work, we next set out our adversary model and security metrics. We then describe our user models and the use of Monte Carlo simulation to sample how user traffic flows over the network, using our Tor Path Simulator (*TorPS*) to generate paths. We describe a newly-introduced Internet map that we use in the subsequent section to evaluate the security of circuits created via TorPS against a network adversary, after having analyzed security against a Tor-relay adversary. Finally we demonstrate the applicability of our approach beyond evaluation of the current Tor network by analyzing Congestion-Aware Tor [45], a system that attempts to improve Tor network performance by measuring relay congestion and avoiding the most congested parts of the network when sending application traffic.

2. BACKGROUND

The Tor network consists of roughly 3000 *relays* pushing over 2500 MiB/s in aggregate [40]. Tor clients select three of these relays to form a *circuit* through which they create TCP *streams* to communicate with external Internet destinations. Tor measures the real *bandwidth* (throughput over time) that each relay provides to the network, and assigns each relay a selection *weight* based on the bandwidth it provides. These weights are used to bias selection for circuits in order to distribute load toward relays with more available network resources. Relays may specify a bandwidth allowance over a desired time period: once the allowance is reached, the relay will hibernate until the end of the time period. Hibernating relays will neither participate in building new circuits nor transfer data for Tor.

Relays have status flags assigned to them by the *directory authority*, which clients consider when choosing relays for a circuit. The GUARD flag is assigned to relays whose uptime is at least the median for familiar relays, and if their bandwidth is at least the minimum of 250 KiB/s and the median relay bandwidth. Clients choose and maintain three active *guards* and use them as the entry relay for all of their circuits to reduce the chance of directly connecting to an adversary. Clients rotate each guard at a random time between 30 and 60 days. The EXIT flag is assigned to relays who allow direct connections with external Internet destinations. Exits set individual *exit policies* specifying the IP address ranges and port ranges to which they are willing to connect. Clients use these policies to determine which relay to choose for the final position in each circuit. Guards and exits are more-highly weighted for the entry and exit position in a circuit, respectively, as not all relays fulfill the requirements to obtain those flags. Additionally, a relay obtains the STABLE flag if its weighted mean time before failure is at least the median for known active relays. Clients building streams to a port in the *long-lived ports* list must choose stable relays in each position of the circuit. Finally, clients will never choose two relays from the same /16 subnet or *family* for the same circuit. A family is a set of relays that mutually indicate that they belong to a group together.

3. RELATED WORK

Anonymity systems have received significant study since Chaum's [11] seminal work on untraceable email in 1981. We highlight the most relevant methods for measuring anonymity and discuss many of the threats to anonymity systems.

Metrics and Methods for Evaluating Anonymity. Serjantov and Danezis [34] and Díaz *et al.* [12] independently propose evaluation frameworks that quantify anonymity using Shannon entropy computed over a set of potential senders (or receivers). Hamel *et al.* argue against entropy-based metrics and instead focus on how an adversary's actions can compromise anonymity [23]. They envision an adversary with a fixed bandwidth budget, and explore how the adversary can spend that budget to compromise anonymity. Syverson *et al.* also describe a bounded adversary and present a model in which the adversary can corrupt a fixed number of routers within a time period [38], using probabilistic analysis to quantify the resulting level of anonymity. Similar to this latter model, we assume the existence of a fixed adversary who either controls some relays ("Relay Adversary") or monitors a portion of the Internet such as an AS or IXP ("Network Adversary").

Elahi *et al.* [16] construct a simulation-based framework for measuring how well Tor's guard selection mechanism defends against profiling attacks [47]. Similar to our techniques, their *Changing of the Guards* simulator also uses data collected from the live Tor network [40] to repeatedly simulate the behavior a client. Their simulation study focuses on guard selection and adversarial relays. In contrast, this paper explores Tor's vulnerability to *traffic correlation attacks* (explained next) using various profiles of client behavior, adversary models, security metrics, and topological models of the Tor network.

Traffic Correlation Attacks. Onion routing is vulnerable to an adversary who can monitor a user's traffic as it enters and leaves the anonymity network; correlating that traffic using traffic analysis links the observed sender and receiver of the communication. Øverlier and Syverson first demonstrated the practicality of the attack in the context of discovering Tor Hidden Servers [32]. Later work by Murdoch and Danezis show that traffic correlation attacks can be done quite efficiently against Tor [29].

Given the potential severity of traffic correlation attacks, this paper explores in depth users' vulnerability to such attacks in the live Tor network. To quantify the anonymity offered by Tor, we examine path compromise rates and how *quickly* extended use of the anonymity network results in compromised paths.

Network Adversaries. Feamster and Dingledine first investigate the ability of AS-level adversaries to observe both sides of anonymous paths [19]. They argue that geographically diverse paths may adversely affect anonymity since paths that traverse many ASes are more likely than shorter paths to have the same AS on both sides of the path. Edman and Syverson also explore AS path diversity on Tor and introduce an AS-aware path selection algorithm that uses "snapshots" of Tor's AS graph to avoid AS-level traffic correlation attacks [15]. More recently, Akhoondi *et al.* propose a geographic-based relay selection method called LASTor [3] that ensures AS diversity in selected paths by relying on concise Internet atlases. A recent study by Wacek *et al.* indicates that the same AS may appear in both sides of as many as 18% of anonymous circuits [44].

Murdoch and Zieliński argue that ensuring AS diversity in anonymous circuits is insufficient to safeguard against traffic correlation attacks by network adversaries, since traffic is routed between ASes at IXPs (and hence a single IXP may observe traffic traversing multiple ASes) [30]. They apply a Bayesian approach to show that an adversary positioned at an IXP could sample traffic from multiple ASes and correlate flows. Juen proposes a refined relay selection algorithm that provides both AS and IXP diversity [28]. We remark that Tor does not currently implement any protection against adversaries who operate ASes or IXPs.

By considering how often *any* AS appears on both sides of circuits, these works implicitly assume that *all* ASes are malicious but are non-colluding. We also examine Tor's vulnerability to network adversaries, but improve upon existing work by modeling a more realistic adversary who monitors a fixed set of ASes or IXPs.

In this paper, we do not consider circuit clogging, network latency, or application[1] or other attacks against Tor (cf. [2, 5, 8, 14, 18, 24, 29]). A comprehensive evaluation of *all* potential threats against Tor is beyond the goals of this paper. Instead, we study in depth a particular and well-understood threat against Tor—traffic correlation attacks by either malicious relay operators or networks that monitor traffic as it enters and exits Tor.

4. SECURITY MODEL AND METRICS

We present here realistic and useful adversary models and security metrics for the threat of traffic correlation in onion routing. In particular, we consider the types and amounts of adversary resources, as well as how he may use them. We argue that security metrics should be defined in terms of such adversaries and should present the probabilities of compromise over time. By applying these methods, we will be able to obtain novel and realistic quantitative estimates of Tor security against traffic correlation.

4.1 Adversary Model

In general we consider it realistic that an adversary can observe, delay, alter, drop, or add communication in a variety of ways. As will become clear from our analysis, however, an adversary that merely passively observes can be significant and illuminating. We limit our description and attentions herein to a passive end-to-end correlating adversary: one that learns source or destination of communication when in position to observe either or both of these and that always links observations of the same communication flow anywhere in its path. This linking occurs regardless of how the flow's appearance may have changed en route. We do consider an adversary that may actively add network resources or corrupt existing resources. But we do not consider any addition, alteration, or disruption of network traffic directed over those added adversary resources. Nor do we consider adversarial removal or degradation of network resources in this paper.

Adversary Resources. Our adversary is assumed to have one or more types of resources at his disposal. Tor relays themselves are an obvious resource, although it is useful to further specify if the adversary observes guard, middle, or exit relays. Besides relays themselves the most obvious possible adversary resource is the destination server. At a somewhat more abstract level, an adversary may control an amount of bandwidth. This could represent either a portion of the existing network or a resource that the adversary can add to the network by contributing additional relays. In this paper we do not consider adversarial bridges [36].

Tor and other low-latency anonymous communications networks are overlays above the transport layer. The primary organizational unit for managing Internet routing below the overlay is the autonomous system (AS). An adversary may control one or several ASes and is assumed in that case to observe any traffic entering or leaving the AS. Another potential adversarial resource is Internet Exchange Points (IXes or IXPs), which are increasingly common facilities that allow exchange of traffic between ASes, usually at a cost savings or performance improvement vs. sending via an upstream traffic provider. An IXP is in a position to see all traffic flowing between its peered ASes. It is typically in a single geographic location while an AS is often geographically distributed, and thus it would seem only more likely to be under adversary control than an AS.

Resource Endowment. We give the adversary certain endowments of the resource types. We view adversarial institutions – such as corporations, intelligence agencies, or countries – as the endowment of the resources they control. For example, the adversary might control all of the ASes in a given country. If the source or destination ISP is under adversary control, this puts the ISP AS in the set of adversary assets. If the ISP controls multiple ASes, these could all be considered adversary assets depending on details of how the ISP is under adversary control. Similarly companies that are not end-user ISPs may control multiple ASes [7]. A single company could also run multiple IXPs. For example, Equinix has 19 IXPs in 17 metropolitan areas worldwide [17].

The fraction or number of individual relays has always been a measure of adversary endowment for onion routing systems and is the basis of the c^2/n^2 risk of individual path compromise (where c is the number out of n relays that are compromised) [20, 38]. But the Tor path selection protocol weights relay choice by the bandwidth relays offer. Bandwidth is thus a more accurate measure of adversary endowment for Tor [6]. Whether using number of relays or relay bandwidth, type of relay is also a factor. Of the approximately 3000 current Tor relays, roughly a third are flagged to be stable and fast enough to serve as entry guards and roughly a third are considered exits, where these amounts each include relays that are both exits and guards. For an end-to-end correlating adversary that controls Tor relays, guards and exits are of primary importance. Combining these leads to guard and/or exit bandwidth as a still more accurate measure of adversary endowment. Adding other routing criteria to Tor could affect the impact of adversarial relay endowment in other ways. For example, in latency-aware routing [35], an adversary with more compromised exits near popular destinations or likely destinations of a given target source will be more effective than one with the same exit endowment distributed differently.

We will consider adversary goals presently, however, we can note now that allocation of adversary endowment is important to adversary success. We will discuss in Section 6.1 advantageous allocation of adversary relay bandwidth among guards and exits. This allocation could be by chance or it could be that the adversary has the capability and knowledge to strategically allocate resources. Analysis of dynamic and responsive strategic allocation of adversary resources against onion routing communication predates Tor itself. Such responsive allocation might be in order to compromise existing circuits [38] or to increase the likelihood that future communication will be compromised [6]. Against Congestion-Aware Tor [45], an adversary might generally mask congestion at a controlled relay by variable padding of processing time, which would increase the overall fraction of circuits using adversary relays. But it is also possible to do more targeted attacks, for example, prioritizing service for circuits of detected targeted clients to reduce their experience of congestion. We leave to future work, however, analysis in the presence of a dynamic, responsive, strategic adversary.

Adversary Goals. Much prior analysis of onion routing security has been against an adversary with the primary goal of deanonymizing (linking source and destination) as many circuits as possible. It is likely, however, that real adversaries will be more focused. For example, an adversary may wish to compromise as many circuits as possible for a given user or a given class of user. Or the adversary may wish to identify as many destinations as possible for a given user or class of user. (Note that these need not be coextensive goals. For example, the user might make a large majority of

[1]We do, however, show how the choice of application may influence the user's susceptibility to traffic correlation attacks.

connections to a few destinations, and the adversary wishes to also know those destinations the user visits rarely.) Or the adversary may wish to compromise circuits connecting to a given destination or set of destinations. An adversary may simply wish to know if specific sources and destinations ever connect at all or ever connect during a critical time period.

4.2 Security Metrics

Security metrics in general, and for traffic security in particular, should be defined with respect to a specific adversary, should be usable for assessing security over human timescales, and should allow estimation of probability of all reasonably-likely relevant events [37]. Also, most metrics give information either about the system itself or summarize usage of the system. Examples of these are compromised fraction of a network resource, entropy, min-entropy, or compromised fraction of all circuits using the network. These are important but not ideal for a user who would like to know, "If I use the system in the following way, how secure am I?" or "How much can I do the following while maintaining security at least to level foo?" With this in mind, we use the following metrics in our analysis:

1. The probability distribution on number of path compromises for a given user (in a given period).
2. The probability distribution on time until first path compromise.

While there are many other interesting and valuable metrics along these lines, we believe that these are particularly pertinent to the typical user of Tor. We evaluate these with respect to the adversaries described in Section 4.1.

5. METHODOLOGY

We evaluate the security of the Tor network with respect to the adversaries and metrics that we have proposed. This requires estimation of the probabilities of security events. To do so, we use the Monte Carlo method to sample how user traffic flows over the network during various types and amounts of user activity. For each sample, we use a model of the Tor network, simulate the user behavior, and simulate the resulting Tor client software actions. We evaluate the user anonymity of these samples against relay and network adversaries.

5.1 Path Simulator

To enable our evaluation, we built the TorPS path selection simulator [42], which uses historical network data to recreate the conditions under which clients operated in the past and then executes path selection algorithms over those conditions given user actions. TorPS includes a model of the Tor relays and their past states, a model of user behavior, and a model of the Tor client[2]. For each sample simulation, it takes streams produced by the user model and network states from the network model and uses them as input to the client model, which chooses circuits and assign streams to them.

5.1.1 Tor Network Model

TorPS uses data from Tor Metrics [40] to model the past states of the Tor network. Tor Metrics provides archives of network consensuses and server descriptors, which TorPS uses to determine relay status over time, including flags, exit policies, hibernation state, and other parameters. Relays that do not appear in a consensus or do not have a descriptor are taken to be inactive.

[2]TorPS is based on the code in Tor version 0.2.3.25.

Rank	Port #	Exit BW %	Long-Lived
1	8300	19.8	Yes
2	6523	20.1	Yes
3	26	25.3	No
65312	993	89.8	No
65313	80	90.1	No
65314	443	93.0	No

Table 1: Default-accept ports by exit capacity.

Model	Streams/week	IPs	Ports (#s)
Typical	2632	205	2 (80, 443)
IRC	135	1	1 (6697)
BitTorrent	6768	171	118
WorstPort	2632	205	1 (6523)
BestPorst	2632	205	1 (443)

Table 2: User model stream activity.

5.1.2 User Model

In order to understand the security of real users, we develop five models of Tor network use, which each consist of a sequence of Tor streams and the times at which they occur. Streams here include DNS resolution requests in addition to TCP connections to specific destinations. We construct three of our models by using client applications on the live Tor network and tracing the behavior of our local Tor client. Each trace consists of 20 minutes of a prescribed activity. The five user models we evaluate are as follows:

Typical. This model is designed to represent average Tor use. It uses four traces consisting of (*i*) Gmail / Google Chat, (*ii*) Google Calendar / Docs, (*iii*) Facebook, and (*iv*) web search activity. These traces are played every day during the desired period, with one session of (*i*) at 9 a.m., one session of (*ii*) at 12 p.m., one session of (*iii*) at 3 p.m., and two sequential sessions of (*iv*) starting at 6 p.m.

IRC. This model represents the use of Tor for the repeated but exclusive purpose of IRC chat. It uses the trace of a single IRC session and plays the trace sequentially from 8 a.m. to 5 p.m., Monday through Friday, a total of 27 times each day.

BitTorrent. This model represents using BitTorrent over Tor. It consists of activity during the download of a single file. The model replays the trace sequentially from 12 a.m. to 6 a.m. on Saturday and Sunday, totaling 18 replays each day.

WorstPort. This model modifies the Typical model by replacing the port numbers with 6523, which is a port used by the "Gobby" collaborative real-time editor [1]. As Table 1 shows, 6523 is supported by the second-least amount of exit capacity, excluding ports that are rejected in the default Tor exit policy. Port 6523 is interesting because it was recently added to the "long-lived ports" by request [39], indicating that it is in active use. Connecting to ports designated by Tor as long-lived requires using `Stable` exit relays, which must have a higher minimum uptime.

BestPort. This model modifies the Typical model by replacing the port numbers with the HTTPS port 443, which, as shown in Table 1, is supported by the largest amount of exit capacity.

Table 2 shows the number of streams, unique IP addresses, and unique ports that appear in each of the user models. The Typical model contacted a large number of IP addresses relative to the number of streams, but many of these were from subnets used by Facebook or Google. The IRC trace only contacted `irc.oftc.net`. The BitTorrent trace used a large number of ports, as the client chose peer ports randomly.

While these models are limited and somewhat artificial, we believe that they actually allow for good estimates of our metrics for many users. The most relevant properties of user activities are their number, duration, and destinations. Our user models explore each of these parameters over a reasonable range, in particular exploring very good and very bad ports. Moreover, our use of traces exposes how some popular applications behave according to these parameters, which provides insight into how whole classes of activity are likely to act.

5.1.3 Tor Client Model

TorPS faithfully mimics the behavior of Tor client software for creating exit circuits, taking into account features significant to path selection, such as: bandwidth weighting; relay hibernation; guard selection and rotation; exit policies; family and /16-subnet conflicts; and DNS resolution. A Tor Metrics consensus and its corresponding descriptors are used as if they were retrieved by the client when the consensus was published. In a slight deviation from Tor's current operation, we use full server descriptor to evaluate a relay's exit policy rather than use the microdescriptor format. In addition, we do not consider hidden services or bridges, although our methods could easily be used to evaluate the security of both systems.

By default, TorPS does not account for any side effects stemming from underlying network performance. That is, when evaluating basic Tor path selection it behaves as if each circuit construction succeeds, each circuit experiences the same performance, and circuits do not fail while being used. Section 7 discusses an extension to the basic simulator in which network congestion and delays are taken into account.

5.1.4 Statistical Inference

We use the empirical distribution function that results from TorPS simulations to infer the probabilities of security events. Let n be the number of TorPS samples, and let $D(x)$ be the absolute difference between the empirical CDF and the true CDF at x. The Dvoretzky–Kiefer–Wolfowitz Inequality [46] gives that $Pr[\sup_x D(x) > \epsilon] \leq 2e^{-2n\epsilon^2}$.

With all of our simulations we use either $n = 100000$ or $n = 50000$. Thus the probability that the CDF of any of our simulations has error of more than 0.01 at any point is at most $2e^{-10} \approx 9.1 \times 10^{-5}$. We infer fewer than 50 distributions, and therefore the probability that any one of them has an error at any point of more than 0.01 is less than 0.0046 by the union bound.

5.2 Internet Map

We construct a detailed Internet map in order to evaluate the security of circuits produced by TorPS against a network adversary that can observe or control pieces of the network infrastructure, such as the network links, routers, and facilities that host this equipment. This map, combined with path inference algorithms, allows us to identify the autonomous systems and internet exchange points traversed by our simulated Tor users.

We construct the network map at the AS level from two sources. First, we consider links contained within BGP paths gathered during March 2013 from eight geographically distributed *RouteViews* routers [43]. We then supplement those links with additional ones identified from traceroutes in the CAIDA *IPv4 Routed /24 AS Links Dataset* from December 2012 [9]. This combined dataset produces a graph consisting of 44605 ASes connected by 305381 links.

We use a layered approach to obtain a near-complete set of relationship information for the AS links contained in our graph. First, we apply the heuristic algorithm originally suggested by Gao [21] to our network graph. We then use relationships identified in the CAIDA AS Relationships Dataset for July 2012, overwriting any relationships previously identified through Gao's algorithm as necessary [10]. Finally, we use a set of sibling relationships heuristically identified from similarities in RIPE WHOIS records to correct misclassified sibling relationships. This approach results in relationship assignments for 88% of the links in our dataset; those links without relationships come primarily from the CAIDA IPv4 Routed /24 AS Links dataset, to which Gao's algorithm cannot be applied. We exclude links with missing relationships from our path inference algorithm, which we describe next.

5.2.1 Autonomous System Path Inference

When considering autonomous systems as adversaries, those with the capability to deanonymize Tor traffic are those which exist upon the AS path between the client and guard *as well as* between the exit and destination. For each simulated client stream, we compute the AS path from client to guard and exit to destination using the algorithm proposed by Qiu which extends known AS paths drawn from BGP tables to all ASes using a shortest path variant [33]. We use these computed paths in our network adversary analysis in Section 6.2.

5.2.2 Internet Exchange Point Map

In addition to autonomous systems, we are interested in the prevalence of Internet exchange points as another network administrative domain which could compromise Tor circuits.

The IXP Mapping Project [4] gathers data about IXPs across the Internet, and seeks to identify the ASes which peer at each IXP. We use the IXP peerings dataset they provide to identify locations along inferred AS paths where traffic transits through an IXP. The dataset contains 58524 AS peers which connect through 199 distinct IXPs. These peers represent 19.1% of the links in our network map. In cases where multiple IXPs exist as peering locations between ASes, we include both IXPs. While this may slightly overstate the ability of IXPs to compromise streams, selecting one at random for each path may understate their ability. Our analysis in Section 6.2 will focus on the potentially stronger adversary.

6. SECURITY ANALYSIS OF TOR

We evaluate the security of the Tor network against a range of plausible adversaries and with respect to several metrics, with the goal of yielding concrete numbers that are highly informative and relevant to end users.

We consider two general types of adversaries. The first is an adversary that has the resources to run relays in the Tor network. Specifically, we take bandwidth – both upload and download – to be the limiting resource and consider an adversary that allocates that bandwidth to Tor relays in order to deanonymize Tor users. The second adversary is a network operator able to observe some portion of the underlying network over which Tor traffic is transported.

6.1 Relay Adversary

Adversaries who run relays represent the most plausible and well understood threat to Tor users. Tor relays are run by volunteers and the Tor Project applies no restrictions on operators. Clients select relays for circuits roughly in proportion to relay bandwidth, and thus the amount of traffic that an adversary is in a position to deanonymize is essentially only limited by the adversary's bandwidth. Bandwidth comes at a cost, however, and the Tor network is large enough that overwhelming the Tor network could be expen-

Rank	Bandwidth (MiB/s)	Largest family member
1	260.5	herngaard
2	115.7	chaoscomputerclub19
3	107.8	ndnr1
4	95.3	GoldDragon
5	80.5	Paint

Table 3: Top Tor families, 3/31/03 23:00. Bandwidth is minimum of average and observed.

sive. Thus we seek to establish an adversary with significant but reasonable bandwidth at its disposal.

We suppose that the adversary is able to contribute 100MiBps to the Tor network. Table 3 shows the top five families listed in the last consensus in March 2013, ordered by the smaller of their average and observed bandwidths (self-reported in server descriptors) and represented by the relay with the largest consensus bandwidth. We can see that several organizations already contribute on the order of 100MiB/s to Tor. Bandwidth need not be provided by a single relay, so an adversary could supply that bandwidth by controlling a large botnet or by pooling the resources of a malicious collective. Furthermore, as consumer broadband speeds continue to increase [31], the cost for an adversary to pose a serious threat to the Tor network will continue to decrease.

Tor has a non-trivial process for assigning selection weights in the consensus that involves independently measuring node performance and then applying a proportional integral derivative (PID) feedback controller to minimize selection weight oscillation. Rather than simulate this process, we use the fact that the "observed" bandwidth numbers that relays report in their descriptors are correlated with their consensus weights. We use linear regressions on the relays in consensuses during the simulation period to convert the bandwidths of the adversary's relays to consensus weights. We use separate regressions for guard relays and exit relays, which result in correlations of determination of $r^2 = .71$ and $r^2 = .69$, respectively.

Adversary Resource Allocation. The adversary must determine how best to allocate his bandwidth to maximize the chance of compromising streams. Because the same relay cannot be chosen twice on a circuit, he must run at least two relays in order to perform a correlation attack. We therefore suppose that the adversary targets one as a guard and one as an exit. We assume the malicious guard relay provides enough uptime to obtain the GUARD flag. We assume that the malicious exit relay is not allowed to obtain the GUARD flag and is given an exit policy that allows exit to all addresses and ports. Both relays will have sufficient bandwidth to obtain the FAST flag.

To determine a good bandwidth allocation between the guard and exit relay, we ran five experiments using TorPS that varied the allocation of 100MiB/s of bandwidth between the guard and exit relays. We tested guard-to-exit bandwidth ratios of 1:1, 2:1, 5:1, 10:1, and 50:1. Clients used the Typical user model over a simulated six-month period from October 2012 through March 2013. The results, displayed in Figure 1, show that the expected rate of exit compromise decreases as more bandwidth is allocated to the guard. Thus an adversary must trade off between the likelihood of obtaining a guard position and the volume of exit traffic seen. A 5:1 guard-to-exit ratio maximized the probability of compromising both sides of at least one stream during the simulation period, so we adopt this ratio for the remainder of our experiments, as would a strategic adversary.

Allocating more bandwidth to guards makes sense for the adversary because, in the consensuses we use, exit-only relays are given

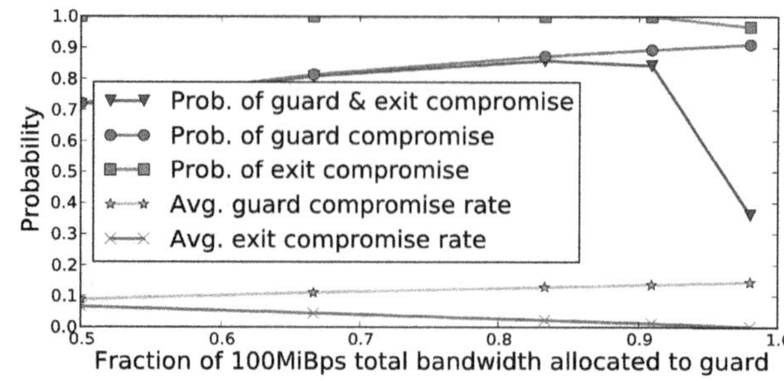

Figure 1: Probability to compromise at least one stream and rate of compromise, varying bandwidth allocation between guard and exit, 10/2012 – 3/2013.

a higher weight for use as an exit than guard-only relays are given for use as a guard. In addition, obtaining a guard is far more important for compromising the stream of a given user, as clients choose new guards much less frequently than new exits.

6.1.1 *Analysis*

We consider how different user behavior can have different security implications. For instance, sending many streams over Tor induces higher rates of circuit creation, increasing the number of chances the adversary has to compromise one. Alternatively, the specific destination addresses and ports that users connect to affect the probability a malicious exit is chosen because allowed exit policies differ from relay to relay.

We use TorPS to conduct simulations using each of the user models (described in Section 5.1.2) over a period from October 2012 to March 2013. We use several metrics to evaluate the security of those users against an adversary who runs one guard relay and one exit relay with 83.3 MiB/s and 16.7 MiB/s of bandwidth respectively. The results are shown in Figure 2.

Overall, we can see (Figure 2a) that in all user models there is more than an 80% chance of deanonymization within 6 months by a malicious guard and exit. The median time to full compromise is always less than 70 days. We also see that risk rises steadily over time. By looking separately at the times at which a guard or exit is compromised (Figures 2b and 2c), we see that the time it takes to choose a malicious guard, with a median of 50–60 days, dominates the time to choose a malicious exit, with a median of fewer than 2.5 days. This supports the suggestion of Elahi *et al.* [16] that the main impediment to full deanonymization by the adversary is being chosen as a guard by a given user. This implies that an adversary that observes the user's connection to the guard, such as an ISP, deanonymizes the destination much quicker than an adversary observing exit traffic, such as a malicious destination, deanonymizes the source.

That an adversary compromises some streams is significant, but how many he compromises is just as important. Figure 2d shows median rates of full compromise between 0.25% and 1.5%, depending on user behavior. Rates of full compromise are roughly the product of the rates of exit and guard compromise, and thus are an order of magnitude lower. Guard compromise rates are generally the same for all users, as we would expect given that the destination address and port are not considered when selecting guards. The guard compromise rates show some bimodality, which corresponds to the event that the malicious guard is chosen again after expiring. Exits are chosen independently for each new circuit, and thus the exit compromise-rate distribution is roughly normal with a mean of the fraction of exit bandwidth provided by the adversary.

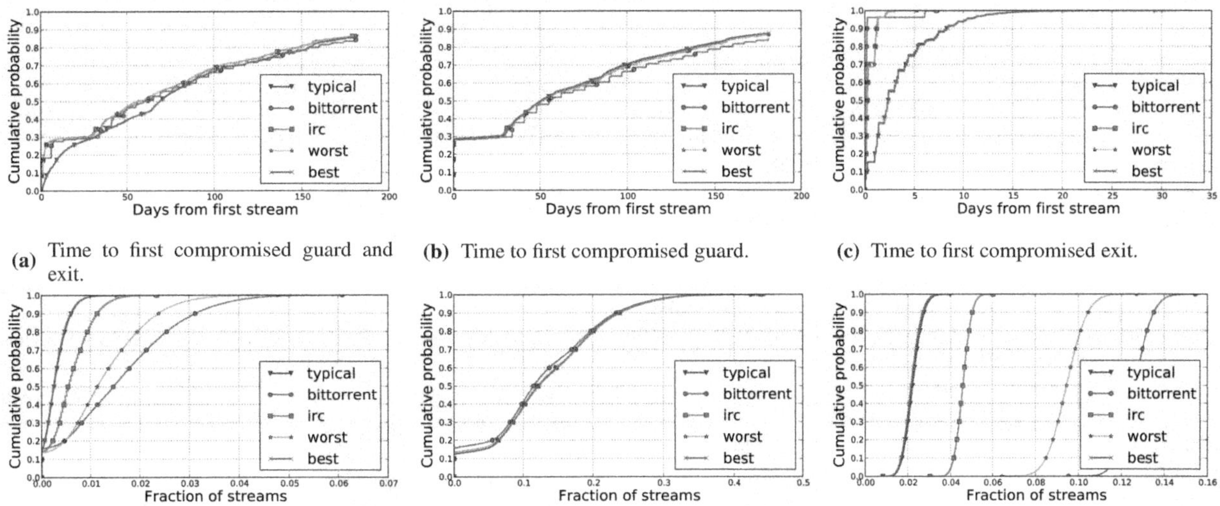

(a) Time to first compromised guard and exit.

(b) Time to first compromised guard.

(c) Time to first compromised exit.

(d) Fraction of streams with compromised guard and exit.

(e) Fraction of streams with compromised guard.

(f) Fraction of streams with compromised exit.

Figure 2: Empirical distribution of security metrics, 10/2012 – 3/2013, 83.3 MiB/s malicious guard and 16.7 MiB/s malicious exit.

This rate is roughly the compromise rate achieved by the adversary when chosen as the user's guards.

The differences in security between user models is due primarily to two factors: (*i*) the amount of user activity and (*ii*) the destination addresses and ports. Creating many streams increases the number of opportunities to choose malicious relays, and thus the speed at which that occurs, while connecting to destinations that are disallowed by many exits increases the chance that a selected exit relay will be malicious.

As described in Section 5, the BitTorrent model creates over 2.5 times as many streams as the Typical model and over 50 times as many as the IRC model. In addition, among the 171 different ports used are included several ports (6881, 6924, 6910, and 6966) that are rejected in the default Tor exit policy precisely because they are used by BitTorrent. Relatively few exits allow these ports, enabling the malicious exit to provide a larger fraction of that bandwidth. Thus we can see in Figure 2f that the BitTorrent model experiences exit compromise at a median time of less than 6 hours and median rate of over 12%, which is much quicker and more frequently than the Typical model. This translates to reduced security against full compromise as well. The IRC and WorstPort models see similarly bad security relative to the Typical user, as they both connect to ports that comparatively few exits support. Finally, we observe that the BestPort model has nearly identical compromise rates to the Typical model, which is not surprising as the Typical model only connects to port 80 in addition to 443, and nearly all exits that support 443 also support 80.

Finally, we consider the effect of changing how much bandwidth the adversary has and when he starts using it. Figure 3 shows the distribution of the time to full compromise of a Typical user as the adversary's bandwidth varies between 10MiB/s and 200MiB/s. Doubling the adversary's bandwidth roughly halves the time to first compromise, with the result that at 200MiB/s the adversary fully compromises a user within 30 days with probability 50%. On the other hand, an adversary that is limited to 10MiB/s (still more than a typical consumer-grade connection) has a less than 10% chance to compromise a user at all.

In addition, we show the time to full compromise when the adversary doesn't have a guard or exit relay until 12/1/2012, two

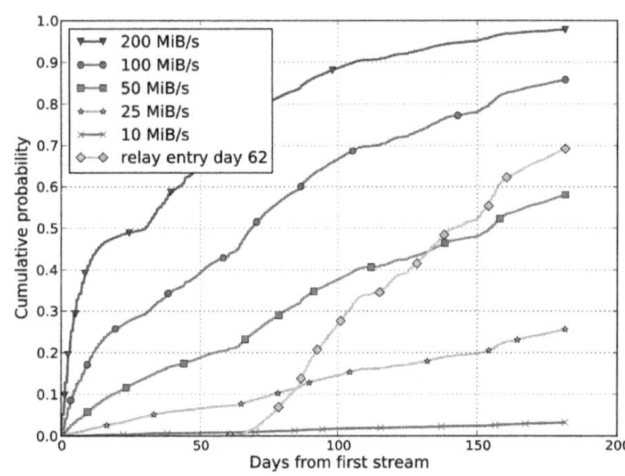

Figure 3: Time to first circuit with guard and exit compromised, varying total adversary bandwidth and date of malicious relay entry, 10/2012 – 3/2013

months into the simulation. At this point the user has already chosen guards after rotating them at least once. We can see that within the four remaining months of the simulation the adversary fully compromises the user with a probability of nearly 70%, which is nearly the probability of compromise after four months of running a relay from the outset.

6.2 Network Adversary

Unlike the relay adversary, a network adversary does not run relays in the hope that a client will choose one of those malicious relays at the guard and exit positions in its path. Instead, a network adversary leverages their position as a carrier of network traffic to correlate Tor traffic streams that cross their network *at some point* between the client and guard and exit and destination pairs.

We begin our discussion of how Tor clients are exposed to network adversaries by considering the placement of clients within the network and their behavior. We then consider the threat posed to those clients from three varieties of network adversaries: ASes, IXPs, and organizations which administer multiple IXPs.

6.2.1 Client Behavior and Location

We consider three types of clients in our analysis of a network-level adversary: Typical, BitTorrent, and IRC.

We do not consider the *WorstPort* and *BestPort* behavior patterns, as these are highly dependent upon exit policy diversity and do not directly affect a network adversary. Note, however, that an equivalently dangerous behavior pattern exists in the case of a network adversary: a client whose communication originates and terminates within the same autonomous system can be deanonymized by that autonomous system. All traffic will pass through the adversary on the path from client to guard and again on the path from exit to destination. We consider this an uninteresting case; for the remainder of this section, we *omit* ASes which contain clients, or destinations for a given client and activity, from the set of adversaries.

For each behavior, we use TorPS to conduct 50000 Monte Carlo simulations of three months of client activity spanning the period from January 2013 to March 2013. We use the output of these simulations to model multiple clients.

Client Location. TorPS simulated output paths are client agnostic; Tor currently makes no changes to path selection behavior based on client attributes (doing so could unintentionally decrease the safety of its users). However, since the path between client and guard is required to analyze exposure to network-level adversaries, we must place the clients somewhere within the network. We assign clients to the five most popular[3] client ASes (AS3320, AS3209, AS3269, AS13184, and AS6805) as identified by Edman and Syverson in 2009 [15], noting that similar techniques have been used recently by papers investigating Tor network security [44]. The five ASes include four from Germany and one from Italy. We then analyze the client-to-guard path five times for each sample stream from our Monte Carlo simulations, once for each of the client origins.

6.2.2 Network Adversaries

We consider three types of network adversaries: autonomous systems, Internet exchange points, and Internet exchange point organizations. A network connection often transits multiple ASes as it moves from source to destination; a network operator interested in deanonymizing Tor traffic need only have the traffic transit through its domain of control once on each side of the path.

IXPs represent points where ASes interconnect; traffic between multiple ASes may flow through a single IXP. In this position, IXPs may have significant ability to deanonymize Tor users.

As an extension of our IXP analysis, we also consider the situation in which a single organization may control multiple IXPs. Manually comparing IXP descriptions from the IXP Mapping Project and company websites for IXPs, we identify 19 IXP organizations which collectively administer 90 distinct IXPs. To identify the organizations which are able to compromise client streams we perform the same procedure as for individual IXPs, replacing IXP identifiers with organization identifiers where possible. We include IXPs for which we have no identified organization as standalone organizations.

6.2.3 Analysis

We begin our analysis by identifying a set of specific *adversarial entities* for each combination of client behavior and client origin. Previous work has often considered the ability of network adversaries to compromise Tor circuits independently, reporting that a large percentage of circuits can be deanonymized by *some* AS. While this is a useful metric for system operators who are concerned with the security of Tor in the aggregate, it is not credible to consider the set of all independent ASes as potential adversaries from the user perspective. We identify distinct *adversarial entities* specific to each simulated user origin and behavior. By focusing our analysis on the ability of these entities to compromise user streams, we are able to produce security metrics which are more relevant to an end user of Tor.

[3]We exclude Chinese ASes, since Tor has subsequently been blocked in China.

Adv. Type	ID	Description	Comp. %
AS	3356	Level 3 Communications	0.5%
AS	1299	TeliaNet Global	0.5%
AS	6939	Hurricane Electric	0.4%
IXP	286	DE-CIX Frankfurt	0.1%
IXP Org.	DE-CIX	DE-CIX	0.1%

Table 4: Identified Adversarial Entities for clients originating in AS3320 using BitTorrent. Comp. % gives the probability that that entity will compromise any given stream.

To identify candidate entities, we aggregate all streams over all client samples originating from a given client location. We then compute the client-side and destination-side paths, and count the number of streams in which a given adversarial entity (AS, IXP, or IXP organization) exists on both sides. We then select the entity which compromises the largest number of streams to understand the extent to which a strong adversary affects user security. Table 4 shows a sampling of the identified adversarial entities for BitTorrent users originating from AS3320.

Our simulation results show that there is significant variation in the ability of network adversaries to compromise Tor users depending on where the user is located, but that on the whole network adversaries present a significant potential threat. While we run experiments for all selected client origins (as described in Section 6.2.1), we display only the best and worst cases in our results for readability. We measure *best* and *worst* as the client origin with the smallest and largest area under the curve, respectively, in their CDF of time to compromise.

Against an AS-level adversary (Figure 4a), our results show compromise is highly likely in the worst case scenario regardless of user behavior. 45.9%, 64.9%, and 76.4% of Typical, IRC, and BitTorrent samples use a compromised stream within one day. At least one stream is compromised within the three month period for over 98% of samples. The best case client origins fare significantly better, but retain significant exposure to AS adversaries: IRC users are exposed within 44 days at the median. Although more than 50% of BitTorrent and Typical users evade compromise for the entire 90 day period, a significant proportion of them, 38% and 44% respectively, still use compromised streams.

IXPs (Figure 4b) and IXP organizations (Figure 4c) appear similar to the AS adversary in the worst case, but significantly less of a threat in the best case. Fewer than 20% of clients use a stream that could be compromised within three months. This difference is not terribly surprising: while IXPs represent high-degree connection points through the network, 80% of the network links do not traverse IXPs. Thus, the worst case likely indicates a situation in which the client's outbound path to a guard transits through an IXP while the best case traverses non-IXP links.

While IXPs and IXP organizations are generally similar, it is clear from the Typical user model that those concerned about the ability of IXPs to compromise Tor streams should consider organizations rather than individual IXP locations: in the best case standalone IXPs are able to compromise just 3.7% of samples within 30 days, while organizations compromise 12.4% in the same period.

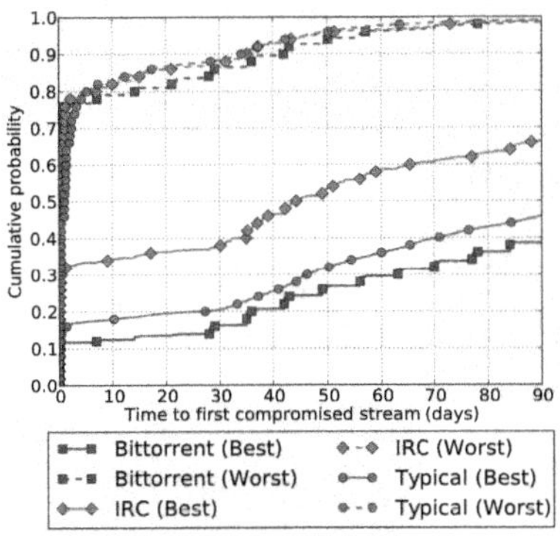

(a) Time to first stream compromised by AS adversary.

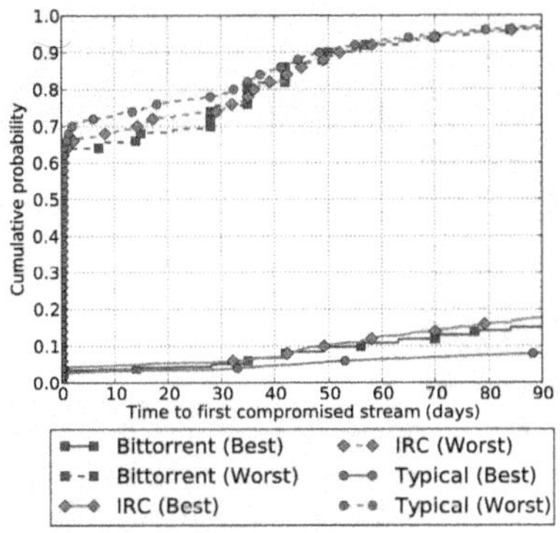

(b) Time to first stream compromised by IXP adversary.

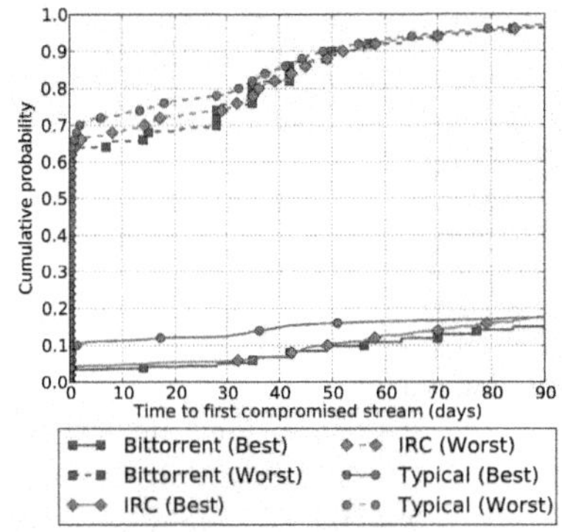

(c) Time to first stream compromised by IXP Org. adversary.

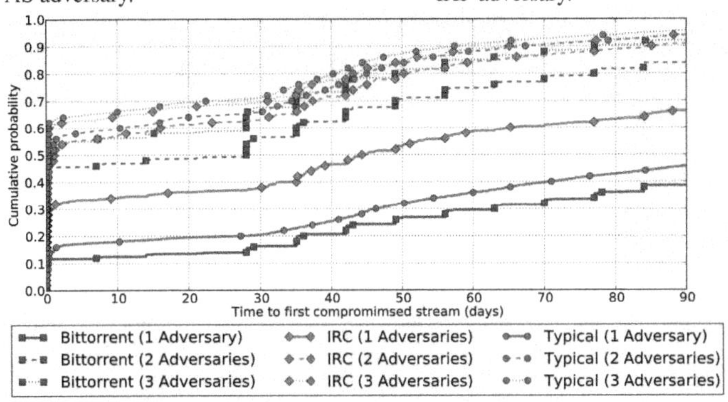

(d) Varying time to first compromise as an AS adversary controls more entities.

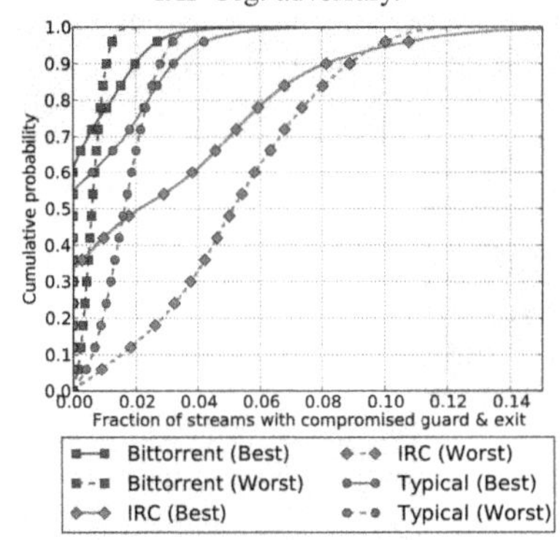

(e) Fraction of streams compromised by AS adversary.

Figure 4: Network adversary analysis. "best" and "worst" indicate the client origin from the top five ASes from [15] with the smallest and largest area under the curve, respectively. "N Adversaries" indicates an adversary that controls the top N AS entities.

We additionally consider how adversary strength affects the likelihood of stream compromise. We consider adversaries of varying strength by adjusting the number of *entities* they control from one to three. Thus, our weakest adversary controls the top *adversarial entity* of that type and the strongest controls the top three *adversarial entities*. Figure 4d shows how the time to first compromised stream drops as an adversary controls more of the top adversarial AS entities for each behavior model. Here we consider *only the best case* since just one AS entity is already able to compromise a significant fraction of samples in the worst case. The addition of even one more AS entity causes the number of samples compromised within 30 days to jump 156%, 65.8%, and 122% for BitTorrent, IRC, and Typical users. The amount of "ground" that two ASes can cover is significantly higher than the amount that one can cover.

In addition to the speed of compromise, we are equally interested in the probability that the adversary compromises any given stream. Figure 4e shows the fraction of streams that an AS adversary controlling the top entity compromises given a particular user activity. The probability of compromising each stream is quite low even in the worst case: 0.6%, 5.1% and 1.6% at the median for BitTorrent, IRC and Typical users respectively. As with the relay adversary, however, the compromises happen in higher-rate bursts during the period in which traffic to a guard is observable.

Discussion. At a high level, the network adversary analysis shows that – in contrast to the relay model – client behavior which results in low diversity of client destinations is most likely to result in a compromise. For example, a single AS adversary can compromise 50% of clients using IRC within 44 days, even under the most optimistic client placement. By contrast, fewer than half of Typical clients are compromised within the entire period, and BitTorrent users have even lower compromise rates. This effect is attributable to simple probability: as the set of destinations which the adversary must cover narrows it becomes more likely that the user picked at the same time a destination and guard that the adversary is near. An implication is that to the extent that Tor clients seek to evade a network adversary that can optimally position himself, they should go to a diverse set of destinations and should use as many different paths as possible.

It is also notable that a large number of clients encounter compromised streams very quickly followed by a steep decline in the rate. Figure 4e shows that the overall per-stream compromise rate is relatively low, so this phenomenon is somewhat surprising. Just as in the case of a relay adversary, this result is partly attributable to how guard selection interacts with relay selection. Given the initial set of guards, the path between the client and entry guard is relatively fixed. If the adversarial entity exists on the guard side of the path, then it need only wait until it appears on the exit side. However, if the entity does not exist on any of the paths from a client to it chosen guards, it will not compromise any streams until new guards are selected. This results in a relative plateau after initial compromises (disturbed only by minor guard as churn nodes leave the network or hibernate) until 30 days have passed and new guards begin to be selected.

Finally, while IXPs have a distinctly lower likelihood of compromising client traffic, it should be noted that the complexity of performing traffic correlation at an IXP is likely to be significantly lower than at an AS. ASes may span large regions and traffic may not pass through the same routers on the forward and return path, while IXPs by their very nature are geographically concentrated.

This may make it easier for a single rogue agent at an IXP to perform traffic analysis than it is to organize a concerted AS-wide effort. Tor users evaluating the ability of network adversaries to compromise their communications should consider this factor; IXPs may represent a lower overall threat profile, but have fewer obstacles to effecting a coordinated traffic analysis attack.

7. ALTERNATIVE PATH SELECTION

This paper has thus far focused on Tor's path selection protocol and has outlined severe security implications. Unsurprisingly, path selection algorithms also have a large impact on Tor's performance because they directly affect how client load is balanced among the available relay resources and therefore how congested relays become. Researchers have investigated and proposed several improvements to Tor's current path selection algorithm. This section explores the security implications of the most effective of these proposals to both inform the adoption of these changes by The Tor Project and to show how future work can apply our methods to provide accurate security assessments of new proposals.

7.1 Congestion Awareness

Based on the results of Wacek *et al.* [44], the most effective proposed improvements to path selection is the "instant response" mode of Congestion-Aware Tor (CAT) by Wang *et al.* [45]. The main idea in CAT is that clients create a local view of circuit congestion through opportunistic and active measurements of circuit round trip times (RTTs). Circuits that are or become too congested are ignored or dropped, respectively. To accomplish this, CAT collects five RTT measurements at circuit construction time before the circuit is used. When a pre-built circuit is needed, the client chooses the circuit with the lowest average circuit congestion, where circuit congestion for each of the RTT measurements is computed by subtracting the minimum RTT ever measured on that circuit. While using the circuit, the client continues to opportunistically measure circuit RTTs using existing Tor protocol cells. If the mean of the last 5 congestion measurements is greater than 0.5 seconds, the client stops using that circuit for new streams.[4]

7.2 Methodology

As CAT only slightly modifies Tor's original path selection algorithm, our methodology for evaluating CAT's security is largely the same as described in Section 5. However, we made several changes to TorPS to incorporate the new selection algorithm. In addition to implementing the instant response mode of CAT, we also needed a source for relay congestion over our analysis period. Although TorPS uses historical data collected from The Tor Project in order to build paths, data about relay congestion has not been collected historically.

Without available data about relay congestion in the live Tor network, we created relay-specific congestion models as follows. We created a virtual Tor network using Shadow [25] following a standard Tor network modeling approach [26]. As Shadow runs the real Tor software, we maximize fidelity to Tor protocols. We then implemented the CAT extensions in Tor[5] and instrumented Shadow to collect fine-grained timing information for packets as they travel between the virtual nodes and through the circuit. This timing information allows us to precisely isolate congestion due to network, kernel, or application latency, giving us a unique view of congestion at each relay over time.

[4]Although unspecified by Wang et al. [45], we assume the circuit is marked dirty and destroyed only when exiting streams are finished.

[5]Our CAT implementation is based on Tor stable version 0.2.3.25.

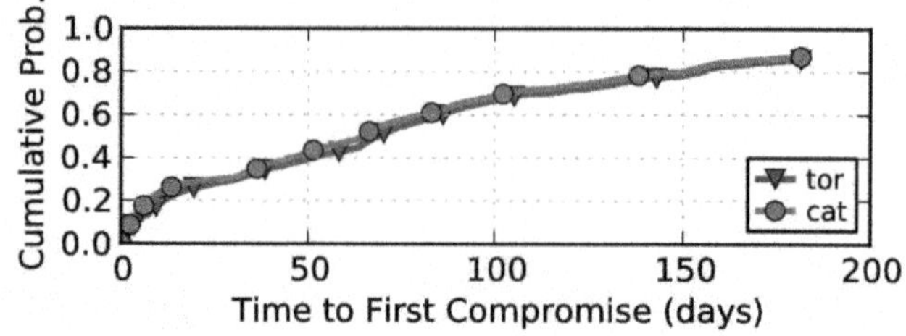

(a) Time to first compromised guard and exit.

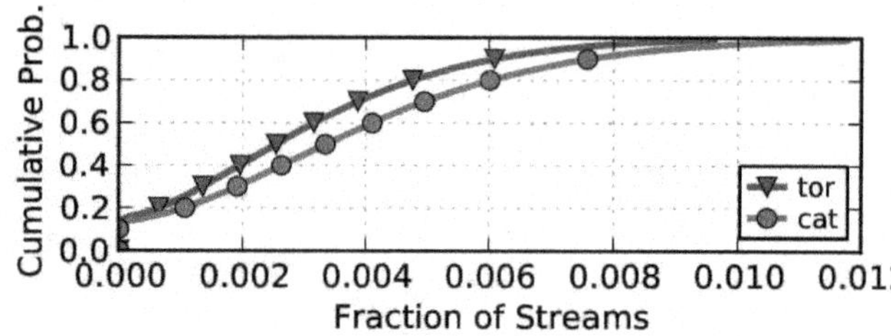

(b) Fraction of streams with compromised guard and exit.

Figure 5: Empirical distribution of security metrics, 10/2012 – 3/2013, 83.3 MiB/s malicious guard and 16.7 MiB/s malicious exit, Tor vs Congestion-aware Tor (CAT) path selection, "typical" user model.

Running thousands of Tor nodes simultaneously is time consuming, and therefore it is not feasible to gather congestion data for the 6-month analysis period that we require. Instead, we ran several short identical pairs of experiments with different seeds, and use the Kolmogorov-Smirnov (K-S) test statistic as a distance metric between each resulting pair of relay-specific congestion traces. We lengthen and repeat the experiment to increase our sample size until the median K-S distance of all relay trace pairs is below five percent, increasing our confidence in the consistency of congestion produced in our virtual network.

We create congestion *profiles* by smoothing each relay congestion trace by binning the values. We assign each simulated relay the profile with the closest consensus bandwidth weight to its own. When running the CAT path simulation, each relay's profile is queried whenever a congestion value would have been measured for that relay.

7.3 Analysis

Figure 5 shows the results of our CAT simulations with the relay adversary compared to Tor, under the typical user model. Figure 5a indicates that CAT reduces the time to first compromise, but that the difference is quite minor. This is expected: while congestion awareness affects which circuits get used, it does not affect selection of entry guards (recall that guards provide the largest influence on time to first compromise). However, congestion awareness does affect which circuits get used over time, which in turn directly affects the total fraction of streams that get compromised. Figure 5b indeed shows a more drastic increase in the total amount of streams that are compromised. This is likely caused by less congested adversarial relays biasing the client's circuit choices to those the adversary compromised. This behavior presents a new vector for attack: an adversary can bias the circuits that get used by the client to those it has compromised by increasing circuit response time for those circuits of which it is a member but has not compromised. This is an active attack similar to selective denial of service (but much harder to detect), and therefore it falls outside the scope of our adversary model. Note that we came to similar conclusions with the results from the BitTorrent and IRC user models.

8. CONCLUSION

We present in this paper a realistic and comprehensive analysis of the security of Tor against traffic correlation. Our approach carefully defines adversaries and uses them to define security metrics that capture user security over time. We propose adversaries that control one or more fixed ASes or IXPs. We present new, practical security metrics that show for the first time how long a user can stay anonymous and how often an adversary can deanonymize. We developed several tools and techniques to allow us to evaluate our security metrics on the live Tor network. These include models of user activity online, an up-to-date and comprehensive Internet map with BGP routes, and a model of relay congestion based on full-network simulations with Shadow.

The results show that Tor faces even greater risks from traffic correlation than previous studies suggested. An adversary that provides no more bandwidth than some volunteers do today can deanonymize any given user within three months of regular Tor use with over 50% probability and within six months with over 80% probability. We observe that use of BitTorrent is particularly unsafe, and we show that long-lived ports bear a large security cost for their performance needs. We also observe that the Congestion-Aware Tor proposal exacerbates these vulnerabilities.

Some of our results against an adversary controlling ASs or IXPs are similarly alarming. Some users experience over 95% chance of compromise within three months against a single AS or IXP. We see that users' security varies significantly with their location. However, an adversary with additional ASes or IXPs has much higher compromise speed, notably against even those users in "safer" locations. Such an adversary is highly relevant in today's setting in which many large organizations control multiple ASes or IXPs. Surprisingly, we observe that high diversity in destinations may actually result in improved security against a network adversary.

These results are somewhat gloomy for the current security of the Tor network. However, they do suggest several ways in which security could be significantly improved. The results against the relay adversary show that choosing multiple guards amplifies the probability that the adversary's guard is chosen. Reducing the default number of guards by some factor would immediately cut compromise rates by the same factor. Those same results show that guard expiration, which starts after 30 days, noticeably speeds up the time to first compromise. Increasing the time to expiration would significantly increase the time to compromise (in fact, the minimum guard expiration time was increased to 60 days in Tor version 0.2.4.12-alpha for exactly this reason). Elahi et al. [16] report some results on how making such changes in guard selection improves security. It seems more difficult to improve security against the network adversary, but several proposals have been given [15, 19, 28]. We suggest evaluating these defenses using the methodology we have presented as well as designing new solutions with our adversary models and security metrics in mind.

Our results do suggest that current users of Tor should carefully consider if it meets their security needs. In particular, users facing persistant adversaries who might run relays or monitor network traffic should be aware of the threat of traffic correlation. While improved defenses are still being developed, such users may be able to take defensive measures on their own. For example, they can choose to limit which relays their client will select using manual configuration options (EntryNodes, ExitNodes, ExcludeNodes, etc.). While this does break the uniformity of path selection among clients, that may be a worthwhile risk tradeoff for these users. Johnson et al. [27] suggest an approach along these lines that balances choosing relays using per-client trust with blending in with other clients.

A goal of our analysis is that it inform safer use of Tor and inspire more secure designs. Despite our pessimistic results, Tor has provided real and valuable privacy to thousands of users. We are optimistic that it can continue and improve this service.

Acknowledgments

We thank Leiah Stevermer for assistance with the user models. Work by Jansen, Johnson, and Syverson supported by ONR and DARPA. For work by Sherr and Wacek: This material is based upon work supported by the Defense Advanced Research Project Agency (DARPA) and Space and Naval Warfare Systems Center Pacific under Contract No. N66001-11-C-4020. Any opinions, findings and conclusions or recommendations expressed in this material are those of the author(s) and do not necessarily reflect the views of the Defense Advanced Research Project Agency and Space and Naval Warfare Systems Center Pacific. This work is partially supported by NSF CAREER CNS-1149832 and NSF grants CNS-1064986, CNS-1204347, and CNS-1223825.

References

[1] 0x539 Dev Group. Gobby: A Collaborative Text Editor. http://gobby.0x539.de, 2013.

[2] T. G. Abbott, K. J. Lai, M. R. Lieberman, and E. C. Price. Browser-Based Attacks on Tor. In *Privacy Enhancing Technologies Symposium (PETS)*, 2007.

[3] M. Akhoondi, C. Yu, and H. V. Madhyastha. LASTor: A Low-Latency AS-Aware Tor Client. In *IEEE Symposium on Security and Privacy (Oakland)*, 2012.

[4] B. Augustin, B. Krishnamurthy, and W. Willinger. IXPs: Mapped? In *ACM SIGCOMM Conference on Internet Measurement (IMC)*, November 2009.

[5] S. L. Blond, P. Manils, A. Chaabane, M. A. Kaafar, A. Legout, C. Castellucia, and W. Dabbous. De-anonymizing BitTorrent Users on Tor (poster). In *USENIX Symposium on Networked Systems Design and Implementation (NSDI)*, 2010.

[6] N. Borisov, G. Danezis, P. Mittal, and P. Tabriz. Denial of Service or Denial of Security? How Attacks on Reliability can Compromise Anonymity. In *ACM Conference on Computer and Communications Security (CCS)*, 2007.

[7] X. Cai, J. Heidemann, B. Krishnamurthy, and W. Willinger. Towards an AS-to-organization Map. In *Internet Measurement Conference*, 2010.

[8] X. Cai, X. C. Zhang, B. Joshi, and R. Johnson. Touching from a Distance: Website Fingerprinting Attacks and Defenses. In *ACM Conference on Computer and Communications Security (CCS)*, 2012.

[9] CAIDA. IPv4 Routed /24 Topology Dataset. http://www.caida.org/data/active/ipv4_routed_24_topology_dataset.xml, December 2012.

[10] CAIDA. The CAIDA AS Relationships Dataset. http://www.caida.org/data/active/as-relationships/, June 2012.

[11] D. L. Chaum. Untraceable Electronic Mail, Return Addresses, and Digital Pseudonyms. *Communications of the ACM*, 24(2):84–90, 1981.

[12] C. Díaz, S. Seys, J. Claessens, and B. Preneel. Towards Measuring Anonymity. In *Privacy Enhancing Technologies (PET)*, 2003.

[13] R. Dingledine, N. Mathewson, and P. Syverson. Tor: The Second-Generation Onion Router. In *USENIX Security Symposium (USENIX)*, 2004.

[14] P. Eckersley. How Unique is Your Browser? In *Privacy Enhancing Technologies Symposium (PETS)*, 2010.

[15] M. Edman and P. Syverson. AS-Awareness in Tor Path Selection. In *ACM Conference on Computer and Communications Security (CCS)*, 2009.

[16] T. Elahi, K. Bauer, M. AlSabah, R. Dingledine, and I. Goldberg. Changing of the Guards: A Framework for Understanding and Improving Entry Guard Selection in Tor. In *ACM Workshop on Privacy in the Electronic Society (WPES)*, 2012.

[17] Equinix. Equinix Internet Exchange Enables Efficient Interconnection between Hundreds of Networks. http://www.equinix.com/solutions/by-services/interconnection/exchanges/equinix-internet-exchange/.

[18] N. S. Evans, R. Dingledine, and C. Grothoff. A Practical Congestion Attack on Tor using Long Paths. In *USENIX Security Symposium (USENIX)*, 2009.

[19] N. Feamster and R. Dingledine. Location Diversity in Anonymity Networks. In *ACM Workshop on Privacy in the Electronic Society (WPES)*, 2004.

[20] J. Feigenbaum, A. Johnson, and P. Syverson. Probabilistic Analysis of Onion Routing in a Black-box Model. *ACM Transactions on Information and System Security (TISSEC)*, 15(3):14:1–14:28, 2012.

[21] L. Gao. On Inferring Autonomous System Relationships in the Internet. In *IEEE/ACM Transactions on Networking*, volume 9, pages 733–745, December 2001.

[22] S. Hahn and K. Loesing. Privacy-preserving Ways to Estimate the Number of Tor Users, November 2010. Available at https://metrics.torproject.org/papers/countingusers-2010-11-30.pdf.

[23] A. Hamel, J.-C. Grégoire, and I. Goldberg. The Misentropists: New Approaches to Measures in Tor. Technical Report 2011-18, Cheriton School of Computer Science, University of Waterloo, 2011.

[24] N. Hopper, E. Y. Vasserman, and E. Chan-Tin. How Much Anonymity Does Network Latency Leak? *ACM Transactions on Information and System Security (TISSEC)*, 13(2): 13, 2010.

[25] R. Jansen and N. Hopper. Shadow: Running Tor in a Box for Accurate and Efficient Experimentation. In *Network and Distributed System Security Symposium (NDSS)*, 2012.

[26] R. Jansen, K. Bauer, N. Hopper, and R. Dingledine. Methodically modeling the tor network. In *USENIX Workshop on Cyber Security Experimentation and Test (CSET)*, August 2012.

[27] A. Johnson, P. Syverson, R. Dingledine, and N. Mathewson. Trust-based anonymous communication: Adversary models and routing algorithms. In *Proceedings of the 18th ACM Conference on Computer and Communications Security (CCS 2011)*, pages 175–186. ACM, 2011.

[28] J. P. J. Juen. Protecting Anonymity in the Presence of Autonomous System and Internet Exchange Level Adversaries. Master's thesis, University of Illinois, 2012.

[29] S. J. Murdoch and G. Danezis. Low-Cost Traffic Analysis of Tor. In *IEEE Symposium on Security and Privacy (Oakland)*, 2005.

[30] S. J. Murdoch and P. Zieliński. Sampled Traffic Analysis by Internet-Exchange-Level Adversaries. In *Privacy Enhancing Technologies (PET)*, 2007.

[31] Office of Engineering and Technology and Consumer and Governmental Affairs Bureau. A Report on Consumer Wireline Broadband Performance in the U.S. Technical report, Federal Communications Commission, February 2013.

[32] L. Øverlier and P. Syverson. Locating Hidden Servers. In *IEEE Symposium on Security and Privacy (Oakland)*, 2006.

[33] J. Qiu and L. Gao. AS Path Inference by Exploiting Known AS Paths. In *Global Telecommunications Conference*, 2006.

[34] A. Serjantov and G. Danezis. Towards an Information Theoretic Metric for Anonymity. In *Privacy Enhancing Technologies (PET)*, 2003.

[35] M. Sherr, M. Blaze, and B. T. Loo. Scalable Link-Based Relay Selection for Anonymous Routing. In *Privacy Enhancing Technologies Symposium (PETS)*, August 2009.

[36] R. Smits, D. Jain, S. Pidcock, I. Goldberg, and U. Hengartner. BridgeSPA: Improving Tor Bridges with Single Packet Authorization. In *ACM Workshop on Privacy in the Electronic Society (WPES)*, 2011.

[37] P. Syverson. Why I'm not an Entropist. In *International Workshop on Security Protocols*, 2009.

[38] P. Syverson, G. Tsudik, M. Reed, and C. Landwehr. Towards an Analysis of Onion Routing Security. In *Designing Privacy Enhancing Technologies*, 2000.

[39] The Tor Project. Changelog Tor 0.2.4.12-alpha. https://gitweb.torproject.org/tor.git?a=blob_plain;hb=HEAD;f=ChangeLog.

[40] Tor Project, Inc. Tor Metrics Portal. https://metrics.torproject.org/, 2013.

[41] Tor Project, Inc. The Tor Project. https://www.torproject.org/, 2013.

[42] TorPS. TorPS: The Tor Path Simulator. http://torps.github.io, 2013.

[43] University of Oregon. RouteViews Project. http://www.routeviews.org/, 2013.

[44] C. Wacek, H. Tan, K. Bauer, and M. Sherr. An Empirical Evaluation of Relay Selection in Tor. In *Network and Distributed System Security Symposium (NDSS)*, 2013.

[45] T. Wang, K. Bauer, C. Forero, and I. Goldberg. Congestion-aware Path Selection for Tor. In *Financial Cryptography and Data Security (FC)*, 2012.

[46] L. Wasserman. *All of Nonparametric Statistics (Springer Texts in Statistics)*. Springer-Verlag New York, Inc., Secaucus, NJ, USA, 2006.

[47] M. Wright, M. Adler, B. N. Levine, and C. Shields. The Predecessor Attack: An Analysis of a Threat to Anonymous Communications Systems. *ACM Transactions on Information and System Security (TISSEC)*, 4(7):489–522, November 2004.

PCTCP: Per-Circuit TCP-over-IPsec Transport for Anonymous Communication Overlay Networks

Mashael AlSabah*
Qatar Computing Research Institute
Department of Computer Science and Engineering, Qatar University
malsabah@qu.edu.qa

Ian Goldberg
Cheriton School of Computer Science
University of Waterloo
iang@cs.uwaterloo.ca

ABSTRACT

Recently, there have been several research efforts to design a transport layer that meets the security requirements of anonymous communications while maximizing the network performance experienced by users. In this work, we argue that existing proposals suffer from several performance and deployment issues and we introduce PCTCP, a novel anonymous communication transport design for overlay networks that addresses the shortcomings of the previous proposals. In PCTCP, every overlay path, or *circuit*, is assigned a separate kernel-level TCP connection that is protected by IPsec, the standard security layer for IP.

To evaluate our work, we focus on the Tor network, the most popular low-latency anonymity network, which is notorious for its performance problems that can potentially deter its wider adoption and thereby impact its anonymity. Previous research showed that the current transport layer design of Tor, in which several circuits are multiplexed in a single TCP connection between any pair of routers, is a key contributor to Tor's performance issues.

We implemented, experimentally evaluated, and confirmed the potential gains provided by PCTCP in an isolated testbed and on the live Tor network. We ascertained that significant performance benefits can be obtained using our approach for web clients, while maintaining the same level of anonymity provided by the network today. Our realistic large-scale experimental evaluation of PCTCP shows improvements of more than 60% for response times and approximately 30% for download times compared to Tor. Finally, PCTCP only requires minimal changes to Tor and is easily deployable, as it does not require all routers on a circuit to upgrade.

Categories and Subject Descriptors

C.2.0 [**Computer-Communication Networks**]: General— *Data communications*; C.2.1 [**Computer-Communication Networks**]: Network Architecture and Design; C.4 [**Computer Systems Organization**]: Performance of Systems; K.4.1 [**Computers and Society**]: Public Policy Issues—*Privacy*

*Work done while at the University of Waterloo

CCS'13, November 4–8, 2013, Berlin, Germany.

ACM 978-1-4503-2477-9/13/11 ...$15.00.
http://dx.doi.org/10.1145/2508859.2516715.

General Terms

Measurement, Performance, Security

Keywords

Tor, transport design, performance improvement

1. INTRODUCTION

While advances to the Internet have enabled users to easily interact and exchange information online, they have also created several opportunities for adversaries to prey on users' private information. Whether the motivation for data collection is commercial, where service providers sell data for marketers, or political, where a government censors, blocks and tracks its people, or even personal, for cyberstalking purposes, there is no doubt that the consequences of personal information leaks can be severe.

Consequently, several solutions emerged, a key example of which is Tor [14]. Tor is the most widely used privacy-preserving network that empowers people with low-latency anonymous online access. That is, people can surf the Internet without the fear of revealing their identity or location. Since its introduction in 2003, Tor has successfully evolved to support hundreds of thousands of users using approximately 3000 volunteer-operated routers run all around the world. Incidents of sudden increases in Tor's usage, coinciding with global political events, confirm the importance of the Tor network for Internet users today [13].

Despite Tor's increasing popularity, the bitter reality is that it offers anonymity at the expense of intolerable performance costs. Not only do performance problems hinder Tor's wider adoption, but they can have an immense impact on its anonymity. If users are discouraged from Tor's below-mediocre service, the anonymity set of all users would eventually shrink, which in turn reduces the anonymity guarantees obtained from the network today.

For this reason, the Tor research community has been intensively investigating the sources of the performance problems in Tor, as well as proposing remedies to enhance the usability of Tor. First, one major problem in Tor is traffic congestion, which has a number of causes. One cause for congestion is the high client-to-relay ratio which is approximately 165:1. To help reduce the client-to-relay ratio, incentive-based schemes have been introduced to encourage users to donate bandwidth to the network to reduce the traffic pressure on the routers [20, 27, 29].

Congestion is also magnified because a small fraction of users use greedy file-sharing applications that can consume up to 40% of the bandwidth [24]. What adds to the problem is Tor's lack of congestion control and awareness, as Tor only implements an end-to-end window-based flow-control algorithm that does not react to congestion. To address these problems, some congestion control and avoidance techniques have been proposed to reduce congestion [6, 43]. To reduce the effects that greedy applications impose on the network, static and dynamic throttling approaches have been proposed for clients' connections [21, 27].

Regardless of all these intensive efforts, performance problems will continue to persist in Tor, even if the above proposals are employed. A major culprit is Tor's poor transport design, which has been shown to add unnecessary latency [15, 31]. Tor multiplexes circuits (overlay paths established through the Tor network) from different users over the same TCP connection. Reardon and Goldberg [31] observed that since heavy circuits are often multiplexed with light circuits in the same TCP connection, and since heavy circuits have higher loss rates, they result in unfair application of the TCP congestion control of the shared connection on all circuits. As a design solution, Reardon and Goldberg proposed TCP-over-DTLS, where every circuit gets a separate user-level TCP connection, and DTLS is used for encrypting and securing the communication between routers. Unfortunately, TCP-over-DTLS faces the following design drawbacks:

- **Performance:** User-level implementations of TCP provide significantly lower performance than their kernel-level counterparts in terms of throughput and consume substantially more CPU cycles [10, 16], a scarce resource in Tor. Such heavy costs might render any performance benefits moot if a user-level TCP scheme is deployed at a wide scale.
- **Deployability:** First, the unavailability of a reliable user-level TCP stack with a license that is compatible with Tor is a major obstacle facing TCP-over-DTLS.[1] Second, for any pair of routers to use TCP-over-DTLS, both routers need to upgrade their transport design.

Our Approach. In this work, we seek to enhance the performance and usability of the Tor network for interactive application users. We tackle the performance problem in Tor at its roots, and focus on fixing the weaknesses in Tor's transport design. This work is not concerned with the lack of bandwidth resources, as there have been several proposals that address this problem, as we described above. We propose PCTCP, a new transport design for Tor in which a separate kernel-level TCP connection is dedicated to every circuit. To protect and secure communication between routers, we use IPsec, the standard security layer for IP. Our design significantly improves the performance of Tor while maintaining its threat model. Additionally, PCTCP requires only minimal changes to the software. Our design combines the advantages of the previous TCP-over-DTLS proposal, while avoiding its deployment and performance shortcomings, inherent from using a user-level TCP stack. Furthermore, PCTCP does not require all routers on the circuit to upgrade, except for enabling IPsec communication for a pair of routers that wish to use PCTCP. Our design has a significantly easier road to deployment.

Contributions. This is the first work that implements a new transport design, for anonymous communication systems in general and for the Tor anonymity network in particular, and evaluates it with realistic large-scale experiments, as well as live network experiments. In designing and implementing PCTCP, we offer the following contributions:

- We propose and implement PCTCP, a novel transport design for anonymous communication systems in general and for Tor in particular that avoids the deployability and performance drawbacks of previous designs.

[1] Reardon and Goldberg used the Daytona TCP stack for their implementation and measurements. Unfortunately, Daytona cannot be used for the Tor network due to its unavailability for open-source projects.

- We carry out small-scale experiments on the live Tor network to evaluate our design. Our results show significant reductions in delays observed. At the 75th percentile, our response times are improved by more than 47% and our download times are improved by 27%.
- We further evaluate our design by performing a series of large-scale experiments on a network emulator with a topology that closely approximates the performance of the live Tor network. Our results show significant performance benefits for the download and response times of web clients.
- Our simple, yet effective, approach is incrementally deployable, as our changes, except for enabling IPsec communication between any pair of routers using PCTCP, are local to individual routers and do not affect their operation with other routers.

The rest of the paper is structured as follows. We provide the reader with the necessary background on Tor and IPsec in section 2 and compare our work to previous work in section 3. Then, we elaborate on our design in section 4 and evaluate it in section 5. Finally, we discuss some open issues regarding our design and experiments in section 6 and conclude in section 7.

2. BACKGROUND

In this section, we start by providing an overview of the Tor network and its current transport design. Then, we introduce and explain the basic functionality of IPsec.

2.1 Tor

Tor is a low-latency anonymization network that is based on the concept of onion routing. The network consists of approximately 3000 volunteer-operated relays [39], known as *Onion Routers* (ORs). Each OR creates a *router descriptor* that contains its contact information, such as its IP address, ports, public keys, and its bandwidth capabilities, and sends the descriptor to *directory authorities*. Tor clients, nicknamed *Onion Proxies* (OPs), download the router descriptors from directories to build paths, referred to as *circuits*, through the network before they can communicate with their Internet destinations. Each circuit usually consists of three ORs, which are referred to as the *entry guard*, *middle*, and *exit* OR, according to their position in the circuit. ORs in a circuit are connected by TCP connections and TLS [12] is used to provide hop-by-hop authenticity, data integrity and confidentiality.

Circuit Construction. For performance reasons, an OP preemptively creates a number of spare circuits for its user applications. When the OP receives a new TCP stream from a user application, it attaches it to an appropriate pre-established circuit. If no such circuit exists, the OP builds a new circuit by first selecting three routers, X_i, according to Tor's bandwidth-weighted router selection algorithm. Next, to start establishing the circuit, the OP sends a *create_fast* command to X_1, which responds with a *created_fast* reply. To extend the Diffie-Hellman (DH) channel, the OP sends an *extend* command to X_1, containing in its payload a *create* command and the first half of the DH handshake for router X_2 encrypted to X_2's public key. Router X_1 forwards this *create* command to router X_2, and when it receives a *created* cell back from router X_2, it forwards its payload in an *extended* cell to the OP to finish the client's DH handshake with router X_2. The same procedure is carried out for each subsequent OR added to the circuit.

The OP acts as a SOCKS proxy to communicate with user applications. The OP divides the user's data into 512-byte fixed-sized

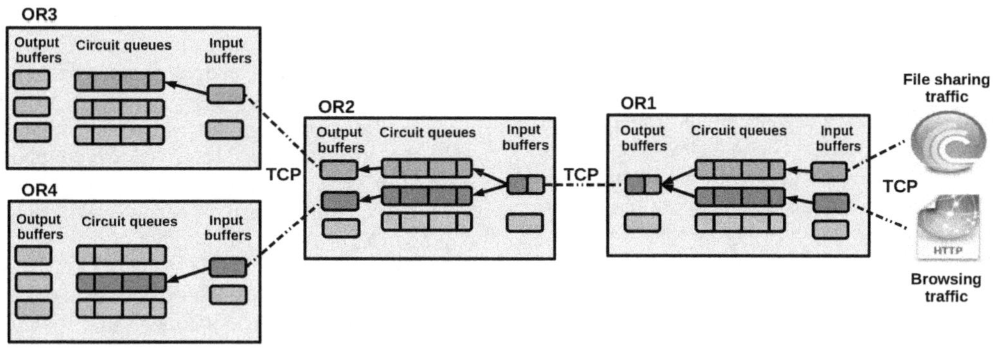

Figure 1: The cross-circuit interference problem: the figure demonstrates the cross-circuit interference problem when a single TCP connection is shared between a loud and a quiet circuit. OR1, acting as an exit for both circuits, receives file-sharing data and web browsing data on two different connection input buffers. The cells then are pushed to their circuit queues. Since the next hop for each circuit is OR2, both circuits share the same connection output buffer. Since the file-sharing circuit is expected to drop more data on the connection between OR1 and OR2, the web browsing circuit experiences more delays due to the unfair application of the TCP congestion control on the shared connection.

cells, adds a layer of encryption for every node on the forward path, and then cells are source-routed through the established circuits. Every hop, on receiving a relay cell, looks up the corresponding circuit, decrypts the relay header and payload with the session key for that circuit, replaces the circuit ID of the header, and forwards the decrypted cell to the next OR. When the exit OR receives the cell, it removes the last layer of the encryption, and establishes the connection on behalf of the user to the intended destination.

Threat Model. Anonymity is maintained for Tor's users because only the entry OR receives a direct connection from a user, and only the exit OR forms a direct connection to the destination. Therefore, no single entity can link users to their destinations. The threat model in Tor assumes a local active adversary that can watch part of the network. The anonymity of a Tor circuit is compromised if the adversary can watch the two ends, the entry and exit, of the circuit.

Cross-Circuit Interference Problem. Tor's OPs and ORs communicate with each other using TCP connections. Every OR-to-OR TCP connection multiplexes circuits from several users. Reardon [31] pointed out that this design can potentially hinder the performance of interactive circuits. This problem is illustrated in Figure 1. The connection between OR1 and OR2 in the figure depicts a scenario where a noisy circuit, carrying BitTorrent traffic for example, is multiplexed with a circuit carrying interactive web browsing traffic. In this case, TCP congestion control would be unfairly applied on both circuits whenever the noisy circuit triggers congestion, due to lost or dropped packets, on the shared TCP connection. Since the amount of data transmitted by file sharing applications is significantly larger than that by interactive applications, it is expected that bulk application circuits trigger congestion control more often than interactive circuits. However, TCP congestion control would apply on all circuits equally and would result in extended queueing times for data cells in TCP output buffers and thereby, longer delays observed by clients.

Tor's Queuing Architecture Tor uses a tiered buffer architecture to manage cells traveling through circuits, as also shown in Figure 1. When an OR receives a cell from an external server or from another OR or OP, the cell is passed from the kernel TCP receive buffer to a corresponding 32 KiB connection-level input buffer in Tor. After the cell is encrypted or decrypted, it is placed on the appropriate FIFO circuit queue. Since several circuits share the same connection output buffer, a scheduler is used to retrieve cells from the circuit queues to be placed on a 32 KiB output buffer. Finally, the cells are sent to the kernel TCP send buffer which flushes them to the next OR or OP.

2.2 IPsec

IP security (IPsec) [22] is a collection of standards that provides security at the network (IP) layer. It defines several protocols that enable authenticating and/or encrypting IP data packets. It consists of mainly two sub-protocols: *Authentication Header* (AH) and *Encapsulating Security Payload* (ESP). We next briefly describe each sub-protocol and their modes of operation.

The AH protocol allows two communicating points to authenticate, and protect the integrity of the data they exchange. Although the AH protocol guards against spoofing and replay attacks, it does not encrypt the data traveling between the two ends, so an eavesdropper can view the contents of the data packets.

The ESP protocol, on the other hand, enables both authentication and encryption, which provides confidentiality of the transferred data. The two communicating ends need to have secret keys to decrypt the packets. IPsec provides a variety of key-exchange and authentication algorithms.

For both protocols, there are two modes of IPsec operation: either the *transport* or the *tunnel* mode. Transport mode is used to secure the connection, consisting of the traffic from different applications, between two hosts. The payload of the IP packet, which typically contains TCP or UDP data, is encrypted or authenticated and an ESP or an AH header is added to the packet. The original IP header also remains in the packet.

Tunnel mode, on the other hand, secures not only host-to-host communication, but it also can be used to protect communication between subnets to subnets or hosts to subnets. In this mode, the whole IP packet is encrypted or authenticated and a new IP header is added to the encrypted packet in addition to the AH or ESP header. Using ESP in tunnel mode provides the strongest security for communication at the expense of a few extra bytes per packet as an overhead. However, when only host-to-host communication is required, ESP protocol in transport mode suffices.

In the next section, we present previous work on anonymous communication transport design for Tor. After that, we introduce our proposed anonymous communication transport for Tor and how we use IPsec to secure communication between Tor ORs.

3. RELATED WORK

Since Tor was introduced around a decade ago, it has received a great amount of attention. Several aspects of Tor's design have been intensively investigated including Tor's routing [4,33,35], scalability [25,26] and enhancing its awareness and handling of congestion [6,17,21,37,43]. There are also several proposals that aim to increase the total number of ORs using incentive schemes [20,27, 29].

New transport designs for Tor have also been investigated and considered by several previous proposals [31,40,42]; Murdoch [28] provides a summary and compares all these previous possible transport designs. He categorizes the available designs into three different architectures: hop-by-hop reliability, initiator-to-exit reliability or initiator-to-server reliability. Although Murdoch does not experimentally evaluate these design choices, he expects that a hop-by-hop reliability approach will be the most promising approach. Next, we summarize the first two design categories and contrast them with our design. For more details on the initiator-to-server design architecture, we refer the reader to Freedom [9] and Murdoch's summary [28].

TCP-over-DTLS is an example of the hop-by-hop reliability design, which is also the same design approach we adopt in PCTCP. The TCP-over-DTLS proposal advocates for using a user-level TCP connection to manage every user circuit over DTLS—the datagram alternative to TLS—to provide confidentiality and authenticity of Tor's traffic. Since every circuit is managed by its own TCP connection, every circuit is guaranteed reliability and in-order delivery of cells. Furthermore, congestion control is performed at the circuit level, which solves the cross-circuit interference problem. Several differences separate PCTCP from TCP-over-DTLS. First, PCTCP uses mature IPsec protocols to hide TCP/IP header information, whereas TCP-over-DTLS uses the relatively rare DTLS for the same purpose. Also, TCP-over-DTLS introduces deployment and performance issues that hinder its adoption (as highlighted in Section 1). PCTCP avoids these problems by using the kernel-level TCP stack, and by having an easier path to deployment. Second, while initial experiments performed on a localhost private Tor network showed slightly less degraded latency results, as compared to Tor, when packet drop rates increased, there is still a need for further realistic large-scale experiments in order to obtain conclusive results of the potential benefits.[2]

UDP-OR [42] is an example of an initiator-to-exit reliability design. In this design, an OP and the exit OR of the circuit maintain a TCP connection, while intermediate ORs communicate using UDP, an unreliable transport protocol. While this design significantly simplifies the operations of the intermediate routers, it still suffers from several problems. The first problem is that since hop-by-hop communication is unreliable, there will be a need to change the cryptographic protocols that are implemented in Tor as the current circuit encryption scheme depends on in-order delivery of cells. Another problem is that this design uses the OP's host TCP stack, rather than a user-level one, which opens the door for OS fingerprinting attacks [23] in which the exit node can learn information about the client. Second, since a circuit's round trip time is large, it would take the TCP endpoints a significant amount of time before congestion is triggered. Also, with the high variability of circuit performance in Tor, a non-trivial amount of tuning for TCP parameters, including congestion timers, thresholds and windows, may be required for the TCP endpoints; see section 4 for more details.

Torchestra [17] was recently proposed to enhance the performance of interactive application users of Tor. In that proposal, two TCP connections are used for OR-to-OR communication. One TCP connection is dedicated for light circuits and another is dedicated for heavy circuits. An Exponentially Weighted Moving Average (EWMA) algorithm of the number of cells sent on a circuit, originally proposed by Tang and Goldberg [37], is used to classify circuits into light and heavy categories. Previous work [5] suggested that this metric alone is not enough to distinguish circuits.[3] Also, Torchestra has not been examined using large-scale experimentations to understand the system-level effects of utilizing it. Finally, to benefit from Torchestra, all ORs on the circuits need to upgrade, as two TCP connections, as well as a new command cell type, are needed between every pair of ORs in a circuit.

Tschorsch *et al.* [40] consider the impact of several proposed transport designs for Tor on throughput, packet loss, delay and fairness. For their analysis, the authors use a TCP performance model proposed by Padhye *et al.* [30]. They examine the performance of several proposed transport designs for Tor using a discrete-event simulator, and conclude that they expect that a joint congestion control that detects loss rates and congestion for all circuits traversing an overlay node would be a good direction. The authors ruled out the use of parallel TCP connections, such as in PCTCP, as a design option, as more connections traversing a bottleneck may result in higher packet losses, which reduces throughput. We argue that packet losses mainly occur for the connections carrying bulk traffic, as they send significantly more data than connections carrying interactive applications. We also demonstrate through comprehensive emulation and live-network experiments that our approach is effective.

4. PROPOSED TRANSPORT

Before embarking on the description of PCTCP, we first ask ourselves, why not adopt and implement an end-to-end TCP approach, which has been proposed as a possible transport design for Tor. We start by explaining why we avoided such an approach, and then we elaborate on our design.

4.1 Why not end-to-end TCP?

One transport design that has received some positive speculation in the Tor research community is the end-to-end TCP design. This design is inspired by many previous proposals [9,11,42]. The basic idea of this design is that a TCP connection is maintained by the two ends of the circuit. In the context of Tor, one end is the client and the other end can be the exit OR or the destination server. Communication between intermediate ORs is carried out using a datagram protocol, such as UDP. We next point out some weaknesses in this design choice.

Tuning Parameters TCP is a reliable transport. If a packet gets dropped or lost due to congestion or routing problems in the underlying IP network, TCP's congestion control algorithm is triggered and the sender retransmits the lost packet. Also, TCP ensures that the Tor process, residing at the application layer, receives data in the order they were sent. This functionality significantly simplifies the task of data processing for Tor. By contrast, a datagram protocol like UDP, or its secure DTLS alternative, do not implement reliability or in-order delivery.

[2] One difficulty is that TCP-over-DTLS is implemented in a 5-year-old version of Tor (0.2.0.25). Since Tor's data structures, queuing and networking have changed over time, a direct comparison between PCTCP and TCP-over-DTLS is meaningless. Also, Reardon *et al.* reported that they found many bugs in both Daytona and OpenSSL's DTLS implementation, which affected their results.

[3] Unfortunately, the classification accuracy was not discussed in Torchestra [17].

In the end-to-end TCP design for Tor, it is assumed that reliable in-order delivery is maintained only by the end points. There are several shortcomings with this design that might worsen the experience of Tor users. The biggest challenge is how to best tune the TCP parameters to yield a reasonable performance for Tor. TCP relies on duplicate acknowledgement packets sent by the receiver to detect congestion which signals that several out of order packets have been received at the destination. Moreover, TCP also relies on retransmission timers at the sender to detect loss of packets.

Typically, retransmission timers should be equal to the round-trip-time (RTT) between a source and a destination. In a network like Tor, where the RTT of circuits can be several seconds long, it can be easily seen that a client would detect congestion very late. Of course, the client can set a smaller retransmission timer to detect congestion faster; however, one should be careful not to send redundant packets too quickly, as this might cause even further congestion. Striking a good balance between how fast we want to detect congestion and how careful we should be before we decide we are experiencing congestion is a very difficult problem. Also, considering the timing characteristics of Tor circuits, which are notorious for their highly variable performance, one soon realizes that an end-to-end TCP solution for Tor is unwise.

Interoperability and Anonymity. An important aspect of any new transport design for Tor is to ensure that it can be smoothly integrated to work with the existing Tor network infrastructure without disrupting the operation of the network and its users. Recall that Tor today currently has thousands of ORs and hundreds of thousands of users. The network has not experienced significant downtime since its deployment in 2003. Using a drastically different transport design such as end-to-end TCP would require the network to pause its operation while ORs and users update. As a workaround, it might be possible for ORs upgraded with end-to-end TCP to coexist with unmodified ORs; however, this might open the door for fingerprinting or partitioning attacks. For example, an upgraded malicious exit can reduce the anonymity set of the entry guard used on a circuit from the set of all entry guards in the network to the smaller set of upgraded entry guards. Therefore, one shortcoming of upgrading to an end-to-end TCP design is possibly hindering the anonymity provided by the network.

Cryptographic Protocols. An inherent consequence of allowing an unreliable transport is for the Tor process to expect lost packets. Since Tor uses the Advanced Encryption Standard (AES) in counter mode for encrypting and decrypting cells at ORs, lost or dropped cells will cause subsequent cells to be unrecognized. Therefore, adopting an end-to-end TCP approach requires changing the cryptographic protocols that are currently used in Tor; this is another obstacle facing such a design.

4.2 PCTCP

The aim of this work is to address the shortcomings of the transport design in Tor. In particular, our goal is to reduce the impact of the cross-circuit interference problem which hinders the experience of interactive application users. Based on our discussion in section 4.1, we believe that reliability should be maintained on a per-hop basis for Tor circuits. Therefore, in this work, we advocate for maintaining TCP connections between each adjacent pair of ORs that comprise a circuit. In particular, we propose two key design changes to Tor's transport.

4.2.1 *Kernel-mode per-circuit TCP*

We propose using a separate kernel-mode TCP connection for each circuit for Tor. Our design is similar to the TCP-over-DTLS design that was introduced by Reardon and Goldberg in the sense that reliable in-order delivery of data is implemented between every two communicating ORs. Also, both designs ensure that congestion control is performed at the circuit granularity. The elimination of connection-sharing among circuits ensures that we isolate the effects of loud circuits on the quiet ones; a cell dropped or lost from one circuit will only affect that particular circuit.

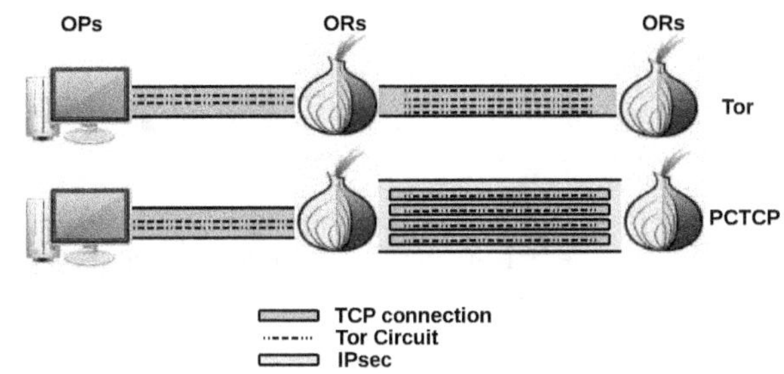

Figure 2: Design comparison between Tor and PCTCP.

However, one key difference between PCTCP and TCP-over-DTLS is that for circuit management, PCTCP uses kernel-mode TCP connections for every circuit, while TCP-over-DTLS uses a user-space TCP implementation. The lack of availability of a reliable open-source user-level TCP stack whose license is compatible with that of Tor hinders the deployability of the TCP-over-DTLS solution. Furthermore, PCTCP uses IPsec to protect the communication between ORs whereas TCP-over-DTLS uses DTLS. One issue that is inherent from using DTLS is that it is rarely used today on the Internet. IPsec, on the other hand, is increasingly common, as it is utilized in many implementations of Virtual Private Network (VPNs) [34]. Consequently, the rarity of DTLS makes it easier to be blocked by censors without fearing side effects. Blocking IPsec would be more problematic, as blocking it may interrupt the operation of legitimate businesses and organizations.

We next describe how we modify the behaviour of Tor to support PCTCP. Recall that during the circuit construction process, every time an OP attempts to extend the circuit by one more hop, it sends an *extend* command cell to the current last OR on the partially constructed circuit. When an OR X_i receives an *extend* cell to another OR X_j, X_i checks if it has a current TCP connection with X_j. If a connection exists, X_i uses that connection to send the *create* cell; otherwise, it creates a new TCP connection to X_j before a *create* cell is sent.

In PCTCP, when an OR X_i receives an *extend* command cell to X_j, PCTCP always establishes a new TCP connection from X_i to X_j. In PCTCP, we maintain the same queueing architecture of Tor, except that our design eliminates the contention that occurs among circuits when they share the same connection output buffer, as each circuit queue is mapped to a single output and a single input connection buffer. When a circuit is torn down, its corresponding TCP connections are closed.

Figure 2 visualizes a design comparison between Tor and PCTCP. As the figure shows, between an OP and an OR, PCTCP, like Tor, maintains a single TCP connection, which can multiplex several circuits from the same user. However, PCTCP dedicates a separate TCP connection for each circuit between any two ORs.

This design has the advantage that it does not require clients to upgrade, as each client in our design continues to maintain a single TCP connection with each of its entry guards. Moreover, the modifications proposed in PCTCP are only local to each OR. This means that not all ORs in the circuit need to upgrade to benefit from PCTCP. For example, if the middle and exit ORs are the only

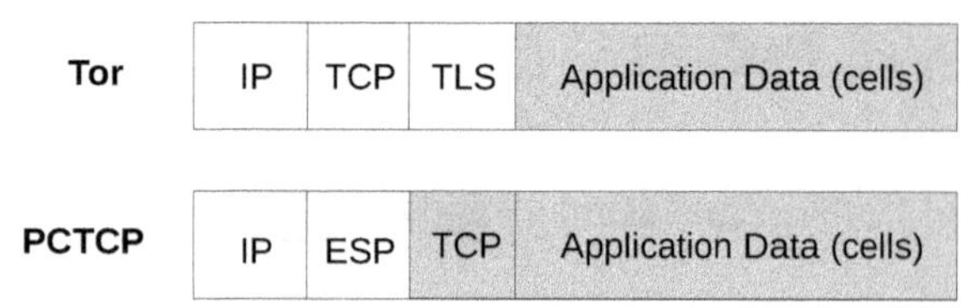

Figure 3: Packet headers for current Tor and for PCTCP. The grey shaded area depicts the encrypted part of the packet. The upper figure shows the design of the Tor packets at the network (IP) layer. TLS is used to encrypt the TCP payload, but not the TCP header. The lower figure depicts the packet format when PCTCP is used. The whole IP payload, which contains the TCP segment, is encrypted. An ESP header is added between the encrypted data and the IP header.

ORs upgraded with PCTCP on a circuit, that pair of ORs will use PCTCP for their communication even if the entry guard is not upgraded. Nevertheless, more performance gains should be obtained when more ORs on the circuit upgrade.

4.2.2 Replace TLS with IPsec

One issue that arises with our design so far is that it allows an adversary monitoring a relay to easily count the total number of circuits that are currently serviced by the monitored relay. Furthermore, the adversary can perform traffic analysis to infer the activity of each circuit [5]. While it is not clear how this extra information can be beneficial for a non-global adversary,[4] there is no doubt that such a design reduces the overall anonymity of the system and its users. To alleviate this problem, we propose using the ESP protocol of IPsec in transport mode to encrypt and protect the traffic between the ORs using PCTCP. Since IPsec can encrypt the IP packet payload, TCP connection ports will be encrypted and hidden from an eavesdropper. This makes it more difficult for an adversary to perform traffic analysis on TCP connections between routers. Figure 3 compares the format of PCTCP and Tor data packet headers.

Using ESP makes the TLS encryption redundant for PCTCP for OR-to-OR communication, as ESP can provide the hop-by-hop authenticity and data confidentiality that is currently provided by TLS in Tor. Furthermore, like TLS, ESP provides perfect forward secrecy for the data on connections, and prevents an attacker from modifying data. For two ORs to authenticate each other, they can use a certificate-based authentication method that is provided by IPsec. Since ORs issue a long-term identity key that they use to sign their descriptors, they can use the same identity key to sign their IPsec certificates.

Alternatively, ORs can use a public-key authentication approach. An OR could publish its IPsec public key with its signed descriptor to the directory authorities. Then, when other ORs download the descriptors, they can find each other's public keys and use them to start the IPsec connections. Communication between ORs and directory authorities or OPs can continue to use the traditional TLS connections that are used in Tor today.

Ideally, a user-mode IPsec implementation integrated with Tor would be the best option. First, OR operators would not have to deal with the details of setting up IPsec. Second, for user-mode IPsec to operate, superuser privileges are not needed. However, with the lack of an available user-space IPsec implementation, we default to the kernel-mode IPsec option. Luckily, installing IPsec is a one-time operation which typically should not require periodic maintenance. To facilitate this operation for non-expert OR operators, Tor should ship with scripts for IPsec configurations.

[4] The threat model of Tor assumes an active local adversary.

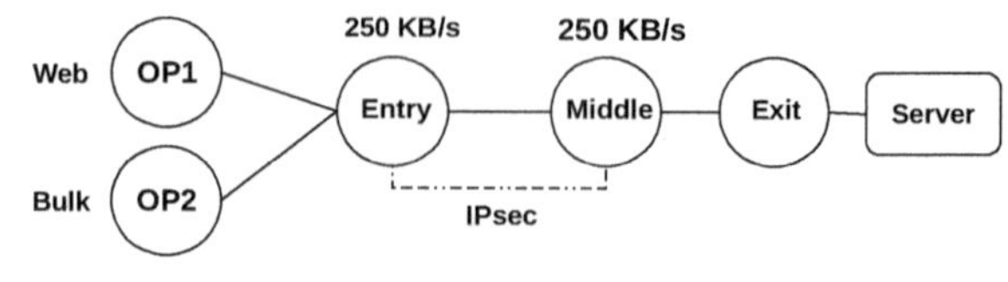

Figure 4: Network setup for the live experiment

5. EXPERIMENTS

To evaluate the performance benefits possible with PCTCP, we have implemented our proposed transport in a stable release of the Tor source code (0.2.2.39). Our implementation, which changes fewer than 20 lines of code in the Tor OR application, can be easily turned on or off using a configuration option for any OR. We first performed small-scale experiments on the live Tor network. We also performed a series of large-scale experiments on an isolated testbed using different traffic loads. As evaluation metrics, we use the *download time*, the time needed for a client to finish downloading a file over a Tor circuit after issuing a request, and the *time-to-first-byte*, which is the time it takes the client to receive the first chunk of the file data after issuing a download request.

5.1 Live Experiments

To test our new proposed design, we first conducted some experiments on the live Tor network in October and November 2012. We next describe our experimental setup and then present our results.

Experimental Setup. Our setup is shown in Figure 4. We configured an IPsec connection, using OpenSwan [3], between our two ORs, entry and middle, which we deployed on the live Tor network. Our entry implements PCTCP which can be enabled as a configuration option only for our clients, so as not to affect other users of the network. Our middle OR runs an unmodified Tor process, but, as above, has an IPsec connection configured. For gathering Tor measurements, we simply turned off the option to enable PCTCP from the configuration of the entry and disabled the IPsec connection. Both ORs have been configured with a bandwidth rate of 250 KB/s. Our ORs obtained the FAST flag by the authority directories, which allows them to be selected by the network clients for their circuits.[5] To protect the privacy of other users, we configure both ORs to belong to the same *Tor family*, which prevents other users' unmodified Tor clients from choosing them both on one circuit. Also, we do not disable TLS in order to avoid risking other users' privacy in case of an accidental misconfiguration. We next describe our two experiments and present our results.

In our live experiment, we run two clients. One client acts as the bulk traffic generator by continuously downloading a 5 MB file without pausing between downloads. The second client is an interactive web browsing client that downloads a 300 KB file and pauses randomly for 3 to 30 seconds between downloads. We have also

[5] Our ORs did not achieve the STABLE flag because they were not running continuously between our experiments. Note that the STABLE status is mainly used for services that need long lived connections (such as SSH on port 22), whereas a FAST status, which our ORs obtained, is requird for most services like web browsing, which comprises the majority of the network traffic.

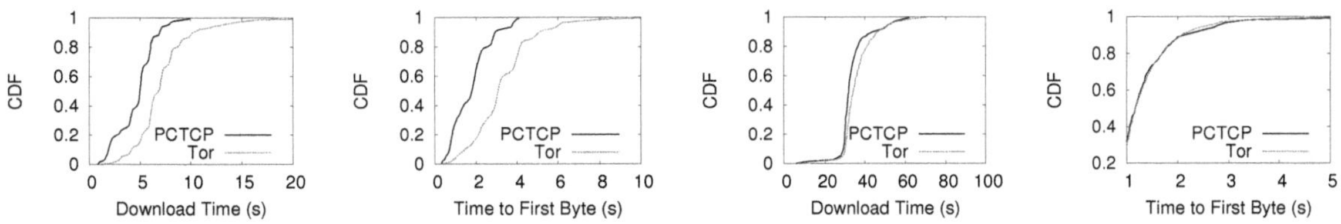

(a) Web client (b) Web client (c) Bulk client (d) Bulk client

Figure 5: Performance of the web and bulk clients in the live experiment

implemented the *MeasureMe* [5] cell. Briefly, this is a new command cell type that is sent by our clients to any OR on a circuit they create to inform the OR to gather statistics only for the respective circuit.

Results. Figure 5(a) depicts the download time performance for Tor and PCTCP for the web client.[6] With PCTCP, it takes 4.9 seconds to finish downloading, while Tor takes 6.8 seconds at the median. The improvements become more visible for the 4th quartile, as download times show a 26% improvement when PCTCP is used. Figure 5(b) shows the time-to-first-byte results for PCTCP and Tor. Again, the results consistently show strong improvements that are magnified at the third and 4th quartiles. For instance, at the 75th percentile, the time-to-first-byte for Tor clients is approximately 4 seconds, whereas for PCTCP clients, it is only 2.1 seconds, which is a more than 47% improvement.

Finally, Figure 5(c) demonstrates that the PCTCP bulk client exhibited slightly better performance than the Tor bulk client. Note that in this experiment, the introduction of the bulk downloader consumes the majority of the available bandwidth between entry and middle. Nevertheless, PCTCP still maintains the performance advantage for web clients compared to Tor. In Figure 5(d), both PCTCP and Tor produced very similar fast time-to-first-byte results as the light web traffic did not introduce congestion to the bulk client.

5.2 Large-scale experiments

Emulation Tools. In order to understand the system-level effects of our proposed transport, we use ExperimenTor [8], a Tor network emulation-based testbed that is based on the Modelnet network emulation platform [41]. Modelnet offers the ability to evaluate large-scale distributed networked systems using commodity hardware and OSes. Briefly, our Modelnet setup consists of two machines, an emulator node and a virtual node. The virtual node runs the Tor network, which consists of directory authorities, ORs and OPs. The virtual node also runs the destination servers. Communication among the different nodes on the Tor network and the destination servers is routed through the emulation node, which provides the underlying IP network emulation. Several network parameters such as the bandwidth, propagation delay and drop rate can by configured on the network topology deployed on the emulator node to provide a realistic underlying network emulation. In our experiments, we use the network and Tor topology models that were recently proposed by Jansen *et al.* [18] in order to accurately produce a scaled-down Tor network that that closely approximates the performance of the live network.

Configuring IPsec. One challenging task in our experiments is to enable an IPsec connection between any two ORs in the network. We found that the IPsec implementation we used (Linux Openswan U2.6.23/K2.6.38 (klips)) does not start the IPsec tunnel between two virtual interfaces that reside in the same machine. To overcome this problem, we introduced an intermediary node between our virtual and emulator nodes.

We set up an IPsec tunnel between the virtual node and the intermediary, whose only purpose is to receive packets on the IPsec tunnel and forward them to the emulator. The emulator performs the network emulation and then forwards the packets back to their destinations in the virtual node. That way, a packet between any two ORs is forced to go through an IPsec connection. For stock Tor performance experiments, we disabled the IPsec tunnel between the virtual and the intermediary nodes.

Underlying Network Topology. We use the network topology that was produced and published[7] by Jansen *et al.* in an effort to methodically model the Tor network for ExperimenTor and Shadow [19]. Briefly, the authors form a complete network graph consisting of vertices that correspond to different locations (countries, American states and Canadian provinces) with upstream, downstream and packet loss properties that they obtained from the Ookla Net Index dataset [2]. All vertices are connected by edges with approximated latency,[8] jitter, and packet loss properties.

Overlay Tor Topology. We follow the footsteps of Jansen *et al.* and create a scaled-down topology that consists of 500 Tor clients (OPs), 50 Tor ORs, and 50 HTTP servers. Of the 50 ORs, 5 work as directory authorities. Our ORs are assigned bandwidth values that are sampled from the bandwidth distribution of the live Tor network ORs. We create two client types: web clients and bulk clients. Our client model is based on a previous study of the exit Tor traffic by McCoy *et al.* [24]. The study found that 93% of connections that exited the Tor network are HTTP connections which consumed approximately 60% of traffic volume. They also found that file sharing applications consumed approximately 40% of the bandwidth in Tor. During our experiments, our web clients continuously fetch fixed-sized 320 KiB files, and pause randomly for 1 to 30 seconds between fetches. Our bulk clients continuously download 5 MiB files without pausing. Finally, we first use a web-to-bulk client ratio of 19:1, as recommended by Jansen *et al.*(Figures 7(a)–7(d)). In addition, we also repeated our experiments on the same network topology where we lower the web-to-bulk client ratio to 9:1 in order to test PCTCP with different traffic loads and with increased congestion (Figures 7(e)–7(h)).

Model Accuracy. Before we present our results, we first compare the performance of our stock Tor bulk and web clients, which we obtained from our testbed, to the performance of the live Tor network published by the Tor metrics portal [38]. This comparison step was also carried out by Jansen *et al.* The purpose of this step is to confirm that our testbed measurements can indeed approxi-

[6] Note that the stair-step pattern is a consequence of Tor's token bucket algorithm which flushes data once per second. This pattern becomes more visible with increased congestion. In versions of Tor more recent than the stable version we used, this flushing has been increased to ten times per second.

[7] The model files are available for download from the authors' websites (http://www.mit.edu/~ke23793/misc/tormodel_exptor.tar.gz).

[8] The authors use iPlane [1] RTTs to approximate latency.

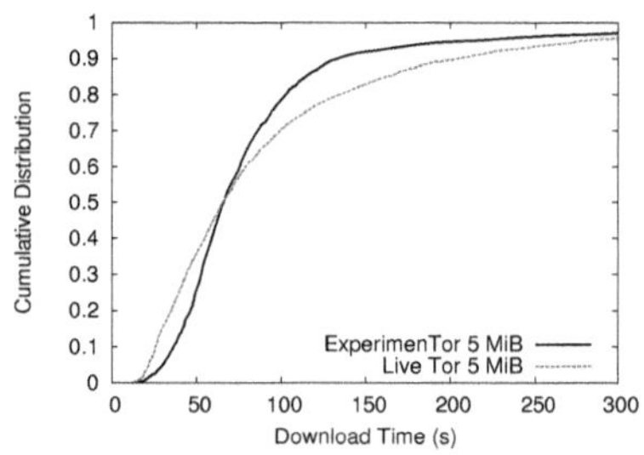

(a) Large files

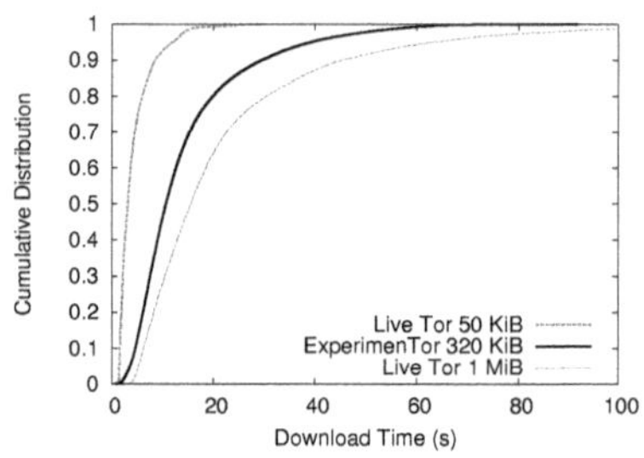

(b) Small files

Figure 6: Comparison between the performance of torperf (Live Tor), and our scaled-down testbed Tor network (ExperimenTor)

mate the measurements taken from the live network, even though our network is significantly scaled down.

Figure 6(a) compares the distribution of the download times of our testbed bulk downloaders and those measured by torperf, a tool that measures download performance on the live Tor network. The two distributions display comparable performance and they indeed intersect at the median. That is, 50% of the 5 MiB downloads take 65 seconds or less on the live network, and the same is true on our testbed. Figure 6(b) compares the results of our 320 KiB downloads and torperf's 50 KiB, and 1 MiB downloads.[9] As expected, the distribution of download times for our web clients fits between the distributions of download times between torperf's 1 MiB and 50 KiB file downloads.

Results. Now that we have verified that our Tor model closely approximates the performance of the Tor network, we next shift attention to our results.[10] Figure 7(a) compares the download time observed by web clients when stock Tor and PCTCP are used. The figure shows significant improvement for the slowest 50% of the downloads, especially for the 4th quartile of the download times. For example, the download times for Tor range from 17–90 seconds, whereas for PCTCP, the download times range from 14–56 seconds.

In Figure 7(b), significant time-to-first-byte improvements can be observed when PCTCP is used, as compared to Tor. At the median, it takes Tor clients 3.6 seconds before the browser starts changing for them, whereas PCTCP clients only wait for 1.6 seconds, which is a 55% improvement. For the 75th percentile response times, the time-to-first-byte is only 2 seconds for PCTCP users, whereas Tor clients experience delays of up to 6 seconds. This increases the observed improvements to 66%.

[9] Torperf only maintains the results of 5 MiB, 1 MiB and 50 KiB file downloads.

[10] For simplicity, we have not disabled TLS in PCTCP experiments even though it is not needed in our design due to the use of IPsec.

We observe in Figure 7(c) that download times for bulk clients are slightly improved when PCTCP is used. The improvement is roughly 20% for 80% of the requests. For example, the median download time for stock Tor is 65 seconds, whereas for PCTCP, the median download time is approximately 51 seconds. Also, the time-to-first-byte results are significantly improved for the bulk downloaders, as can be seen in Figure 7(d). This suggests that congestion is vastly reduced in the network.

Under heavier traffic loads, the amount of available bandwidth in the network decreases, which affects the benefits we observe for the download time. The download time comparison between PCTCP and Tor for web and bulk clients when the ratio of web-to-bulk clients is 9:1, depicted in Figures 7(e) and 7(g), shows that PCTCP improves the long tail of the distribution for the web clients by approximately 20%. The reason for the improvement is that, despite the lack of spare bandwidth, PCTCP allows each circuit at the transport layer to get its fair share of the bandwidth and forces the bulk downloads present in the system to back off whenever they attempt to get more than their allocated bandwidth, as evidenced by the degradation of the bulk client performance shown in Figure 7(g). With PCTCP, heavy circuits might observe more delays because such circuits are expected to drop more cells, and their respective TCP connections would back off more frequently as a result of the separate TCP congestion control. However, performance improvements can be observed even for bulk clients if more bandwidth was available. For example, we have observed significant improvements for both web and bulk clients in the higher-bandwidth experiments we report in Appendix A.

Figures 7(f) and 7(h) show the significant time-to-first-byte improvements for both the web clients and the bulk downloaders. The improvements at the 75th percentile are more than 60% for both the web and bulk clients.

Summary of results. Based on our observations, we conclude that PCTCP produces significant performance benefits that can certainly be perceived by clients. The download time improvements depend on the amount of available bandwidth in the network. If the network has spare bandwidth to offer, PCTCP will improve the experience of all users in the system. When the network operates at its capacity, web clients will notice download time enhancements, while bulk clients will observe degraded performance. However, in all experimental scenarios, PCTCP significantly improves the response times in the network for all clients.

To maximize the benefits of using PCTCP, it should be used in combination with previous proposals that aim to increase the amount of available bandwidth in the network, such as traffic classification [5], throttling approaches [21,27] or approaches aimed to incentivize clients to run ORs [20,29].

6. DISCUSSION

We next discuss a variety of open issues regarding PCTCP.

6.1 Anonymity Implications

Since our transport proposal is designed for Tor, an anonymity network, it is essential to consider the anonymity implications of our design. In particular, it is important to ensure that our new design does not add new vulnerabilities to the Tor network. Recall that the anonymity of a circuit is compromised in Tor if its two ends, the entry and exit, are compromised. Therefore, one issue to consider is whether using PCTCP can reduce the anonymity set of the ORs used in a circuit. For example, can an exit OR reduce

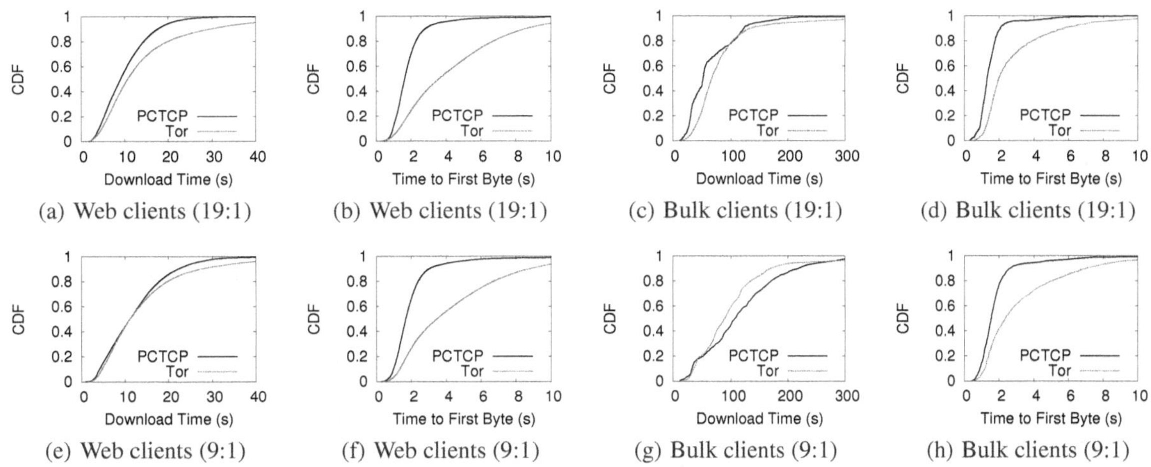

(a) Web clients (19:1) (b) Web clients (19:1) (c) Bulk clients (19:1) (d) Bulk clients (19:1)

(e) Web clients (9:1) (f) Web clients (9:1) (g) Bulk clients (9:1) (h) Bulk clients (9:1)

Figure 7: Performance of all clients in the large-scale experiment under different traffic loads. Figures 7(a)–7(d) show the performance of all clients when the web-to-bulk client ratio is 19:1, whereas Figures 7(e)–7(h) show the performance when we increase congestion by setting the web-to-bulk client ratio to 9:1.

the anonymity set of the entry OR used on a circuit because of PCTCP?[11]

First, with exception of the IPsec connections, the changes that are imposed by PCTCP on any OR are local. That is, our design does not introduce a new cell type or require other ORs on the circuit to upgrade. If an entry OR uses PCTCP, then only the middle OR will notice because the middle has to agree to establish the IPsec connection with entry and because it receives more than one TCP connection from the upgraded entry. Those changes do not affect the exit OR in the circuit; therefore, the exit would not be able to know if entry belongs to the set of upgraded ORs or not. Even if the exit learns from router descriptors that middle is an upgraded OR, the exit would still not be able to know if entry is upgraded or not.

Furthermore, one might wonder if dedicating separate TCP connections might open the door to timing attacks. First, a connection between the OP and the OR is very similar for Tor and PCTCP. Second, because the communication between ORs is protected using IPsec, it would be difficult for the adversary to extract specific circuit information even though each circuit uses a separate TCP connection. Therefore, PCTCP does not introduce any new threats to the Tor network.

6.2 Incremental Deployment

One advantage of PCTCP is that it is incrementally deployable in two steps. The first step towards deployment is enabling IPsec communication among ORs. Basically, ORs need to advertise in their descriptors that they are willing to accept IPsec connections. Then, IPsec-enabled ORs can try to establish IPsec connections proactively among each other. When OR1 wishes to use PCTCP with OR2, it can check if it has an existing IPsec connection with OR2,[12] in which case OR1 can proceed with using PCTCP. If OR1 detects no IPsec connection with OR2, it uses the default Tor TLS connection with OR2 and multiplexes the circuits in the same connection.

[11] It is important to prevent the two ends of the circuit from learning about each other to prevent active or legal attacks.

[12] For Openswan, the visibility of IPsec for an application can be established using the libwhack API.

6.3 Experimental Limitations

To be able to faithfully test and evaluate our new transport proposal, we ran a series of testbed experiments on different network topologies using different traffic models and loads. Regardless of our efforts, we recognize that our large-scale experiments were conducted on an isolated experimental testbed. We were unable to experiment with larger topologies because we are limited by our CPU, bandwidth and memory resources.

However, to ensure that we report accurate results, we followed the methodology of Jansen *et al.* [18] to produce an accurate model of the Tor network. We also used their published topology files in order to avoid biased results that might be obtained using a different experimental setup. Finally, we carried out additional experiments on the live Tor network to confirm our results.

6.4 IPsec through NATs

One challenge that IPsec faced in the past is its inability to connect to hosts behind NATs. As a result, NAT-Traversal [36] (NAT-T) has evolved to address this problem. NAT-T can be used when two hosts detect that if they are behind a NAT. In the context of Tor, this problem is currently irrelevant as most Tor ORs are publicly reachable; however, there are some efforts to enable the operation of ORs from behind NATs [7]. In this case, IPsec can still benefit from NAT-T.

6.5 File Descriptor and Memory Usage

One issue to consider is how this work affects the very busy routers on the live network. Since Tor uses a weighted-bandwidth OR selection algorithm where ORs are selected in proportion to their bandwidth, some high-bandwidth ORs service thousands of circuits at the same time. This means that, with PCTCP, such routers are expected to maintain thousands of file descriptors at the same time. One might wonder if such a requirement might raise memory usage concerns due to the TCP buffer space allocated in the kernel for each file descriptor.

To get an idea of how many file descriptors would be needed when PCTCP is used, we examined a fast exit OR on the live network configured with a bandwidth of 100 Mb/s, which puts it among the fastest 6% of the network routers. This fast exit OR used roughly 10,000 file descriptors for its communication with other

ORs and with destination servers. Since an exit OR uses one file descriptor for each *stream* within a circuit, the number of circuits it is handling is certainly less than the number of file descriptors it is using. Note that intermediate routers are currently expected to use a number of file descriptors that is equal to the number of ORs in the network, which is approximately 3000. We therefore expect that other intermediate ORs, such as middles or entries that have the same bandwidth capabilities as the fast exit, to use between 3000 and 10,000 file descriptors if they use PCTCP. In short, file descriptor and memory usage should not be a problem with PCTCP, as even the busiest entry and middle ORs running PCTCP should consume fewer of these resources than the existing Tor network requires exit ORs to support today.

However, one possible way to reduce the number of file descriptors is to use a threshold algorithm. For instance, every OR can use PCTCP up to a certain threshold of the number of circuits being serviced, which can be configured by the relay operator. If the number of circuits serviced exceeds the threshold, the OR can multiplex new incoming circuits in existing connections in a round-robin manner. Even better, an OR can use a classification approach similar to Torchestra [17], where the OR avoids multiplexing loud circuits with the quiet ones. In short, we do not believe memory management issues are detrimental to PCTCP, as several solutions exist to address them.

6.6 Future Work

One important area for future investigation is to implement other transport proposals such as TCP-over-DTLS and UDP-OR, in order to compare their performance to that of PCTCP in large-scale network emulation. Tor's forthcoming transport abstraction layer [32] should greatly facilitate this task.

Another area for future work is to consider an alternative queueing design for Tor that reduces the number of times cells are copied. Indeed, our design eliminates the need for circuit queues as every input buffer corresponds to single output buffer, which means that data can be copied immediately from the input buffer to the output buffer after being encrypted or decrypted.

7. CONCLUSION

In this work, we recognize the importance of the Tor network as a privacy-preserving tool online and seek to enhance its performance for interactive application users. To this end, we propose PCTCP, a new anonymous communication transport design for Tor which allows every circuit to use a separate kernel-level TCP connection protected by IPsec. Our design is easily deployable and requires minimal changes to routers. PCTCP avoids the deployability and performance problems that were introduced by TCP-over-DTLS due to the use of a user-level TCP stack. Furthermore, experimental evaluation of PCTCP shows vast improvement gains, while maintaining the threat model of the Tor network. Our realistic large-scale experiments show that it is possible to obtain improvements of more than 60% for response times and approximately 30% for download times when PCTCP is used, as compared to Tor.

Acknowledgements.

We thank the anonymous reviewers for their helpful comments and suggestions. We thank NSERC, ORF, and The Tor Project, Inc. for funding this research.

8. REFERENCES

[1] iPlane: Data. http://iplane.cs.washington.edu/data/data.html. Accessed Feb. 2013.

[2] Net Index Dataset. http://www.netindex.com/source-data/. Accessed Feb. 2013.

[3] OpenSwan. https://www.openswan.org/projects/openswan/. Accessed Feb. 2013.

[4] M. Akhoondi, C. Yu, and H. V. Madhyastha. LASTor: A Low-Latency AS-Aware Tor Client. In *Proceedings of the 2012 IEEE Symposium on Security and Privacy*, SP '12, pages 476–490, Washington, DC, USA, 2012. IEEE Computer Society.

[5] M. AlSabah, K. Bauer, and I. Goldberg. Enhancing Tor's performance using real-time traffic classification. In *Proceedings of the 2012 ACM conference on Computer and communications security*, CCS '12, pages 73–84. ACM, 2012.

[6] M. AlSabah, K. Bauer, I. Goldberg, D. Grunwald, D. McCoy, S. Savage, and G. M. Voelker. DefenestraTor: Throwing out Windows in Tor. In *11th Privacy Enhancing Technologies Symposium*, pages 134–154, July 2011.

[7] J. Appelbaum. Tor and NAT devices increasing bridge & relay reachability or enabling the use of NATâĂŞPMP and UPnP by defaults. https://trac.torproject.org/projects/tor/attachment/ticket/4960/tor-nat-plan.pdf, August 2012. Accessed Feb. 2013.

[8] K. Bauer, M. Sherr, D. McCoy, and D. Grunwald. ExperimenTor: A Testbed for Safe and Realistic Tor Experimentation. In *Proceedings of the 4th USENIX Workshop on Cyber Security Experimentation and Test (CSET)*, pages 51–59, August 2011.

[9] P. Boucher, A. Shostack, and I. Goldberg. Freedom Systems 2.0 Architecture. White paper, Zero Knowledge Systems, Inc., December 2000.

[10] T. Braun, C. Diot, A. Hoglander, and V. Roca. An Experimental User Level Implementation of TCP. Technical Report RR-2650, INRIA, Sept. 1995.

[11] Z. Brown. Pragmatic IP Anonymity. http://www.cypherspace.org/cebolla/cebolla.pdf, June 2002. Accessed Feb. 2013.

[12] T. Dierks and E. Rescorla. RFC 5246âĂŤThe Transport Layer Security (TLS) Protocol Version 1.2. http://www.ietf.org/rfc/rfc5246.txt, August 2008.

[13] R. Dingledine. Tor and Circumvention: Lessons Learned. In *Proceedings of the 31st Annual Conference on Advances in Cryptology (CRYPTO)*, pages 485–486, August 2011.

[14] R. Dingledine, N. Mathewson, and P. Syverson. Tor: The Second-Generation Onion Router. In *Proceedings of the 13th USENIX Security Symposium*, pages 303–320, August 2004.

[15] R. Dingledine and S. Murdoch. Performance Improvements on Tor or, Why Tor is Slow and What We're Going to Do about It. http://www.torproject.org/press/presskit/2009-03-11-performance.pdf, March 2009.

[16] A. Edwards and S. Muir. Experiences implementing a high performance TCP in user-space. In *Proceedings of the conference on Applications, technologies, architectures, and protocols for computer communication*, SIGCOMM '95, pages 196–205. ACM, 1995.

[17] D. Gopal and N. Heninger. Torchestra: Reducing Interactive Traffic Delays over Tor. In *Proceedings of the 2012 ACM*

Workshop on Privacy in the Electronic Society (WPES 2012), pages 31–42. ACM, 2012.

[18] R. Jansen, K. Bauer, N. Hopper, and R. Dingledine. Methodically Modeling the Tor Network. In *Proceedings of the USENIX Workshop on Cyber Security Experimentation and Test (CSET 2012)*, August 2012.

[19] R. Jansen and N. Hopper. Shadow: Running Tor in a Box for Accurate and Efficient Experimentation. In *Proceedings of the 19th Network and Distributed Security Symposium*, February 2012.

[20] R. Jansen, N. Hopper, and Y. Kim. Recruiting New Tor Relays with BRAIDS. In *Proceedings of the 17th ACM Conference on Computer and Communications Security*, CCS '10, pages 319–328. ACM, 2010.

[21] R. Jansen, P. Syverson, and N. Hopper. Throttling Tor Bandwidth Parasites. In *21st USENIX Security Symposium*, August 2012.

[22] S. Kent and R. Atkinson. RFC 2401âĂŤSecurity Architecture for the Internet Protocol. `http://www.ietf.org/rfcs/rfc2401.txt`, November 1998.

[23] T. Kohno, A. Broido, and K. C. Claffy. Remote Physical Device Fingerprinting. *IEEE Trans. Dependable Secur. Comput.*, 2(2):93–108, Apr. 2005.

[24] D. McCoy, K. Bauer, D. Grunwald, T. Kohno, and D. Sicker. Shining Light in Dark Places: Understanding the Tor Network. In *Proceedings of the 8th Privacy Enhancing Technologies Symposium*, pages 63–76, July 2008.

[25] J. McLachlan, A. Tran, N. Hopper, and Y. Kim. Scalable Onion Routing with Torsk. In *Proceedings of the 16th ACM conference on Computer and Communications Security*, CCS '09, pages 590–599. ACM, 2009.

[26] P. Mittal, F. Olumofin, C. Troncoso, N. Borisov, and I. Goldberg. PIR-Tor: Scalable Anonymous Communication Using Private Information Retrieval. In *Proceedings of the 20th USENIX Security Symposium*, August 2011.

[27] W. B. Moore, C. Wacek, and M. Sherr. Exploring the Potential Benefits of Expanded Rate Limiting in Tor: Slow and Steady Wins the Race with Tortoise. In *Proceedings of the 27th Annual Computer Security Applications Conference (ACSAC)*, pages 207–216, December 2011.

[28] S. J. Murdoch. Comparison of Tor Datagram Designs. *Tor Project Technical Report*, November 2011.

[29] T.-W. J. Ngan, R. Dingledine, and D. S. Wallach. Building Incentives into Tor. In *Proceedings of Financial Cryptography*, pages 238–256, January 2010.

[30] J. Padhye, V. Firoiu, D. Towsley, and J. Kurose. Modeling TCP throughput: a simple model and its empirical validation. In *Proceedings of the ACM SIGCOMM '98 conference on Applications, technologies, architectures, and protocols for computer communication*, SIGCOMM '98, pages 303–314. ACM, 1998.

[31] J. Reardon and I. Goldberg. Improving Tor Using a TCP-over-DTLS Tunnel. In *Proceedings of the 18th USENIX Security Symposium*, August 2009.

[32] A. Shepard. Build abstraction layer around TLS. `https://trac.torproject.org/projects/tor/ticket/6465`. Accessed Feb. 2013.

[33] M. Sherr, M. Blaze, and B. T. Loo. Scalable Link-Based Relay Selection for Anonymous Routing. In *PETS '09: Proceedings of the 9th International Symposium on Privacy Enhancing Technologies*, pages 73–93, Berlin, Heidelberg, 2009. Springer-Verlag.

[34] C. Shue, Y. Shin, M. Gupta, and J. Y. Choi. Analysis of IPSec overheads for VPN servers. In *Proceedings of the First international conference on Secure network protocols*, NPSEC'05, pages 25–30, Washington, DC, USA, 2005. IEEE Computer Society.

[35] R. Snader and N. Borisov. A Tune-up for Tor: Improving Security and Performance in the Tor Network. In *Proceedings of the Network and Distributed Security Symposium (NDSS)*, February 2008.

[36] A. H. T. Kivinen, B. Swander and V. Volpe. RFC 3947—Negotiation of NAT-Traversal in the IKE. `http://www.ietf.org/rfc/rfc3947.txt`, January 2005.

[37] C. Tang and I. Goldberg. An Improved Algorithm for Tor Circuit Scheduling. In *Proceedings of the 17th ACM Conference on Computer and Communications Security (CCS)*, pages 329–339, October 2010.

[38] The Tor Project. Tor Metrics Portal: Data. `https://metrics.torproject.org/data.html#performance`. Accessed Feb. 2013.

[39] The Tor Project. Tor Metrics Portal: Network. `http://metrics.torproject.org/network.html`. Accessed Feb. 2013.

[40] F. Tschorsch and B. Scheurmann. How (not) to Build a Transport Layer for Anonymity Overlays. In *Proceedings of the ACM Sigmetrics/Performance Workshop on Privacy and Anonymity for the Digital Economy*, June 2012.

[41] A. Vahdat, K. Yocum, K. Walsh, P. Mahadevan, D. Kostić, J. Chase, and D. Becker. Scalability and Accuracy in a Large-scale Network Emulator. *SIGOPS Oper. Syst. Rev.*, 36(SI):271–284, Dec. 2002.

[42] C. Viecco. UDP-OR: A Fair Onion Transport Design. `http://www.petsymposium.org/2008/hotpets/udp-tor.pdf`, 2008. Accessed Feb. 2013.

[43] T. Wang, K. Bauer, C. Forero, and I. Goldberg. Congestion-aware Path Selection for Tor. In *Proceedings of Financial Cryptography and Data Security (FC'12)*, February 2012.

APPENDIX

A. LARGE-SCALE EXPERIMENTS USING A HIGHER-BANDWIDTH TOPOLOGY

To observe the effect of PCTCP in a potential future Tor network with more available bandwidth, we construct an experiment on ExperimenTor using a higher-bandwidth underlying Modelnet network topology. Our overlay Tor network is a scaled-down network in which we run 400 clients and 20 Tor routers. The ORs are assigned bandwidth capabilities that are sampled from the bandwidth distribution of the live Tor network ORs. We test the performance of PCTCP in this topology using a light traffic load of 39:1 web-to-bulk client ratio, and using a high traffic load of 9:1 web-to-bulk client ratio.

We also experiment with PCTCP on ExperimenTor using a higher-bandwidth underlying Modelnet network topology. Our overlay Tor network is a scaled-down network in which we run 400 clients and 20 Tor routers. The ORs are assigned bandwidth capabilities that are sampled from the bandwidth distribution of the live Tor network ORs. We test the performance of PCTCP in this topology

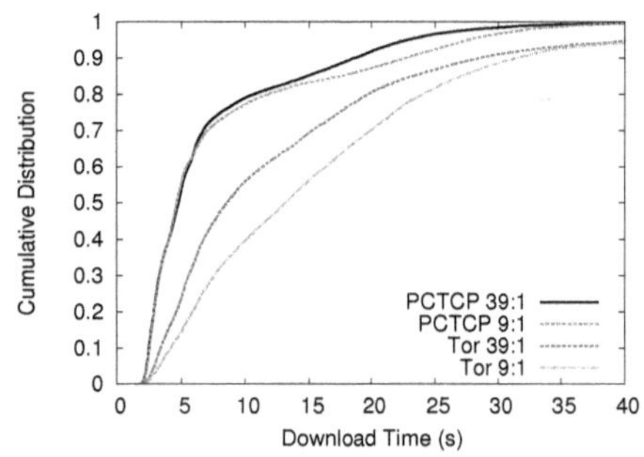

(a) Web clients

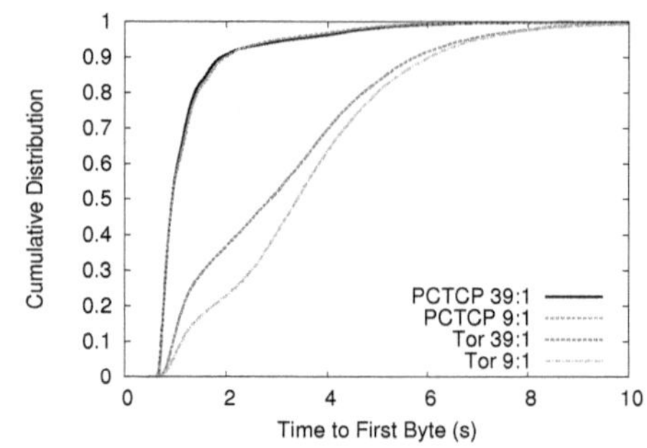

(b) Web clients

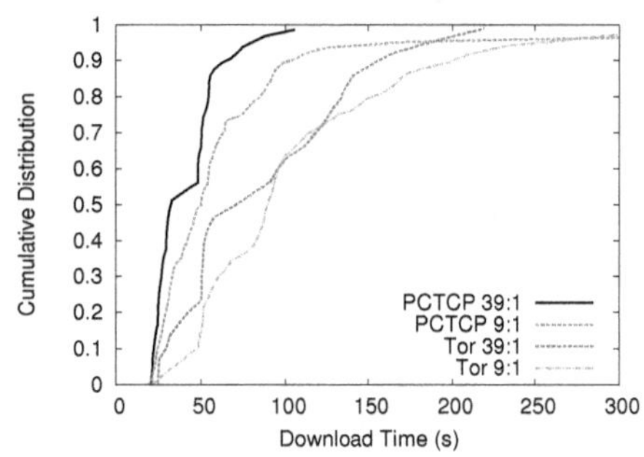

(c) Bulk clients

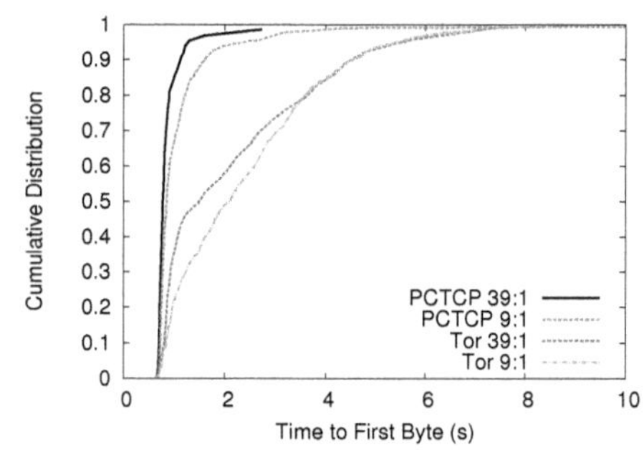

(d) Bulk clients

Figure 8: Performance of the web clients in a high-bandwidth network of 400 clients and 20 routers. Compare to Figure 7.

using a light traffic load of 39:1 web-to-bulk client ratio, and using a high traffic load of 9:1 web-to-bulk client ratio.

Figure 8 shows the download time and time-to-first-byte comparisons for Tor and PCTCP using the different traffic loads for the web and bulk clients. The figures show that for Tor clients, the performance degrades faster, compared to PCTCP clients, as we increase the traffic load in the network by decreasing the web-to-bulk client ratio. For example, for the web client, the median time-to-first-byte remains 0.9 seconds for PCTCP under the low and high traffic loads, whereas the corresponding value in Tor degrades by approximately 20%. This is also true for the download time distribution. The median download time for PCTCP remains the same as we increase the load (though the 4th quartile is slightly degraded), whereas the median download time for Tor clients degrades by more than 30%.

Cover Your ACKs: Pitfalls of Covert Channel Censorship Circumvention

John Geddes
University of Minnesota
Minneapolis, MN 55404
geddes@cs.umn.edu

Max Schuchard
University of Minnesota
Minneapolis, MN 55404
schuch@cs.umn.edu

Nicholas Hopper
University of Minnesota
Minneapolis, MN 55404
hopper@cs.umn.edu

ABSTRACT

In response to increasingly sophisticated methods of blocking access to censorship circumvention schemes such as Tor, recently proposed systems such as Skypemorph, FreeWave, and CensorSpoofer have used voice and video conferencing protocols as "cover channels" to hide proxy connections. We demonstrate that even with perfect emulation of the cover channel, these systems can be vulnerable to attacks that detect or disrupt the covert communications while having no effect on legitimate cover traffic. Our attacks stem from differences in the channel requirements for the cover protocols, which are peer-to-peer and loss tolerant, and the covert traffic, which is client-proxy and loss intolerant. These differences represent significant limitations and suggest that such protocols are a poor choice of cover channel for general censorship circumvention schemes.

Categories and Subject Descriptors

C.2.0 [**Computer-Communication Networks**]: Security and Protection

General Terms

Security

Keywords

Censorship;Anonymity;CensorSpoofer;FreeWave;SkypeMorph

1. INTRODUCTION

Internet censorship has become a widespread issue as ISPs, often under control of repressive governments, filter their users' access to the Internet. In response, users have employed proxy-based circumvention schemes, where clients connect to proxies (or chains of proxies) that relay requests to the rest of the Internet, hiding the clients' true destinations. Censors have responded by employing increasingly sophisticated techniques, including protocol fingerprinting, deep packet inspection, and active probing, to identify and block access to circumvention systems as well.

CCS'13, November 4–8, 2013, Berlin, Germany.
Copyright 2013 ACM 978-1-4503-2477-9/13/11 ...$15.00.
http://dx.doi.org/10.1145/2508859.2516742.

Recently, several circumvention systems have emerged that attempt to use popular communication systems already in place as a *cover-protocol* for anonymous communication. This allows for encrypted communication under the guise of legitimate traffic, making detection, enumeration, and blocking difficult for potential censors. In this paper we examine three such systems with different approaches. SkypeMorph [18] mimics Skype communication in an effort to hide connections to Tor bridges, FreeWave [11] uses a modem to tunnel IP traffic through a voice over IP (VoIP) session, and CensorSpoofer [22] uses IP spoofing and asynchronous communication while mimicking VoIP.

Recently, Houmansadr, Brubaker and Shmatikov [9] have shown that accurately mimicking a modern cover protocol can be challenging, listing several methods a censor could use to distinguish CensorSpoofer and SkypeMorph traffic from legitimate traffic. It is not hard to imagine improved versions of these systems that interact directly with the cover-protocol system, replacing only encrypted contents with covert data, or using an approach similar to FreeWave.

In this paper we demonstrate that even in this case, inherent problems can arise when using covert channels for censorship circumvention. These issues arise due to mismatches between the cover protocol and the proxy protocol, and can violate both the *unobservability* and *unblockability* principles of anonymity systems, crucial for censorship-resistant communication. We highlight three types of mismatches:

- *Architectural mismatches* occur when the cover protocol and the circumvention scheme have different communication architectures, as when a peer-to-peer VoIP protocol is used as a cover for a client-proxy architecture. These mismatches can allow easy identification of proxies and connections, leading to dynamic blocking rules. An example is the FreeWave system, which uses Skype supernodes as relays in an attempt to hide the location of proxies; however, Skype clients use supernodes only as a last resort, *after* attempting direct contact with the destination of a call; thus attempting to contact a FreeWave proxy node will reveal the IP address. We document similar problems with SkypeMorph and CensorSpoofer in section 5.

- *Channel mismatches* occur when the cover protocol and the circumvention scheme have different requirements on the reliability of transmissions. For example, many VoIP and streaming video protocols use UDP and are designed to tolerate packet losses and duplication, whereas proxied TCP connections require reliable transmission. This can lead to attacks that allow a censor to drop or duplicate traffic at a level that is tolerable to the legitimate cover protocol but renders the covert channel useless. As an example, we show

how an adversary can indefinitely stall a Skypemorph transfer while having no effect on the quality of voice calls by dropping a handful of packets and delivering duplicate packets at a 5% rate, through *targeted dropping* of SkypeMorph acknowledgement (ACK) packets. Similar problems in CensorSpoofer and FreeWave are documented in section 4.

- *Content Mismatches* occur when significant differences between the content embedded in a covert channel and the expected contents cause noticeable differences in traffic patterns, even though the cover protocol is perfectly emulated. For example, in section 6 we show that the audio signal of a modem is sufficiently divergent from the audio signals of human speech that a VoIP protocol (such as Skype) using variable bit rate (VBR) encoding will generate easily distinguishable distributions on packet lengths for the two cases: FreeWave over Skype generates length sequences with a dramatically lower variance than spoken language.

The rest of the paper is organized as follows. In Section 2 we review previous anonymity systems and the issues surrounding them, followed by a more complete discussion of SkypeMorph, FreeWave, and CensorSpoofer. Section 3 covers our experimental setup for evaluating these schemes. In Section 4 we cover issues that all three systems have in dealing with using an error tolerant channel for reliable transmission. Following that Section 5 discusses the pitfalls of using a peer to peer cover-protocol system for anonymous communication that is inherently built around a client-proxy model. Section 6 focuses on FreeWave and problems that the system has with cross-content delivery of IP traffic over VoIP. Finally we wrap up with discussion and conclusions in Section 7.

2. BACKGROUND AND RELATED WORK

Censorship circumvention systems attempt to provide users unrestricted access to the Internet while staying hidden from a censoring ISP. The main goals of these censorship-resilient systems is to provide *unobservability*, whereby a censor is unable to tell whether or not a client is participating in the system, and *unblockability* meaning a censor cannot block access to the system without also blocking access to the entire Internet or a popular service. One common approach is to use encrypted tunnels through one or more proxies in an attempt to hide the actual destination from censors, as exemplified by Tor [8], Anonymizer [3], and JAP [1]. These systems are vulnerable to attacks that enumerate and block the proxy nodes, preventing users from accessing the system. To combat this Tor introduced private bridge relays [7] whose information is unlisted, and tightly access-controlled. Even under this restricted access, it has been shown that bridges are vulnerable to enumeration [17], and while methods were developed to prevent these techniques [21], there is documented evidence of nations such as China and Iran performing deep packet inspection on outgoing TLS connections and successfully identifying Tor bridges [2].

Another class of censorship circumvention systems is decoy routing [12] schemes, such as Telex [27] and Cirripede [10]. Instead of using proxies in an end-to-end manner, these systems use an end-to-middle approach using decoy routers along the path of routers forwarding packets to an unblocked end host. By using steganographic cryptography, a client can notify one of the intermediate decoy routers to deflect a TLS connection to a covert destination, providing an encrypted connection to the covert host unbeknownst to the censor. In principle, these schemes make enumeration more difficult, since censors that identify a proxied connection can only identify *paths* that contain decoy routers, and censors do not directly control the path a connection travels once it exits the censored ISP. However, as shown in [20], without extensive deployment, even small nations have enough resources to enumerate participating routers via path intersection, and are able to successfully route around and avoid decoy routers while cutting off a negligible amount of the overall Internet. Furthermore there exist several mechanisms that allow a censor to detect clients using these systems, and even in some circumstances identify the actual covert destination.

A third class of censorship-resilient systems attempt to use cover-protocols to hide anonymous communication. Using popular cover-protocols that censors would be hesitant to block gives these systems an avenue for embedding anonymous communication in apparently legitimate cover traffic. The remainder of this section will cover the details of the three systems, SkypeMorph, FreeWave, and CensorSpoofer, that are the focus of the remainder of this paper.

2.1 SkypeMorph

SkypeMorph [18] attempts to address the *unobservability* problem with Tor bridges, where large censors are able to utilize deep packet inspection to fingerprint TLS connections made to bridges [2]. In order to connect to a bridge running SkypeMorph, a client obtains the Skype ID of the bridge through some out of band channel. Once the identity is known, the SkypeMorph client uses the Skype infrastructure to locate proxies and conduct the session setup, utilizing chat functionality inside Skype to conduct key exchange and negotiate a unique port at which to contact the SkypeMorph bridge. Once this step has concluded, the client initiates a video call directly to the SkypeMorph node, which reveals the bridge's IP address to the user. The SkypeMorph node detects the incoming call, ignores it, and begins listening on the negotiated port for data traffic from the user. At this point the user ceases to use the actual Skype client, and simply attempts to mimic one by sending encrypted data through a traffic shaper to make packet sizes and sending times similar to traffic from a Skype video call.

2.2 FreeWave

FreeWave [11] is a standalone censorship circumvention system addressing both *unobservability* and *unblockability*. While similar in concept to SkypeMoprh, FreeWave takes the mimicry of VoIP calls a step further by actually sending IP traffic over voice using a virtual modem. In FreeWave, the user places a VoIP call to the proxy server using Skype, a popular VoIP client. FreeWave users call a publicly known Skype ID, relying on Skype's native encryption to hide which ID they are calling. Proxy nodes are configured to ignore direct incoming calls, forcing Skype to bridge the connection with the help of a super-node. From the censor's perspective, the user is either making a call to a random Skype node, or using the random Skype node to bridge a call. Blocking the proxies will not prevent the user from connecting to them, since they always connect via a random intermediary. Data sent to and from the proxy is modulated into sounds via a software modem, which in turn pipes those sounds to a virtual sound card, which transmits them to the proxy server via the Skype call.

2.3 CensorSpoofer

CensorSpoofer [22], proposed by Wang et al., attempts to avoid detection by mimicking VoIP calls placed over the Session Initiation Protocol (SIP) [19]. The key observation of CensorSpoofer is that traffic generated by web browsing is highly asymmetrical. A small amount of traffic, the HTTP request, is sent by the user and a large volume of traffic, the actual content, in turn flows from the server to the client. Thus in the CensorSpoofer architecture, the client uses a possibly low bandwidth channel, an email message for example, to send a request to the proxy; the proxy then fetches the content on behalf of the user. Meanwhile the user initiates a VoIP call to a unique SIP ID which has been registered by the proxy for that user only.

SIP IDs include both a user and a domain. In order to locate the IP address which maps to a given SIP ID the user contacts the SIP server in charge of the given domain. The server in turn contacts the host running the given ID, which can respond with an IP address it would like to be contacted at. In CensorSpoofer the proxy does *not* respond with its own IP address, rather it selects a random host, referred to as the dummy host, on the Internet which `nmap` [16] does not show to be either off-line or have a closed SIP port. Since VoIP data and SIP messages are commonly sent via UDP, the proxy can spoof the IP address of the dummy host when sending subsequent SIP messages along with "call data" which will be delivered to the client. Since the user never discovers the IP address of the proxy, the censor cannot enumerate and block proxies by posing as a user. The proxy then sends the the content it fetched on behalf of the user by making it appear like encrypted VoIP data coming from the dummy user by spoofing IP and UDP headers accordingly. The client also sends junk data to the dummy host to complete the illusion of a VoIP call between the user and the dummy host. The dummy host ignores this junk data as it does not actually have a VoIP call between itself and the user.

2.4 Mimicry Issues

As described in [18, 22], SkypeMorph and CensorSpoofer only use the cover-protocol system for initialization, after which the client and proxy communicate directly, outside the cover-protocol. Houmansadr *et al.* [9] examined these schemes, along with StegoTorus [23], and found numerous inconsistencies and issues where they did not properly mimic some part of the cover-protocol correctly, leading to easy detection by a censor, violating the goal of *unobservability*. Common problems include failure to mimic side protocols such as control channels, not correctly reacting to errors like malformed or missing packets, and producing predictable patterns not reflective of actual cover-protocol traffic. Houmansadr *et al.* thus argue that mimicry of this form is fundamentally flawed, since there are too many interdependent protocols and subsystems to accurately mimic outside the cover-protocol system.

We argue that even if these flaws are overcome by re-engineering the systems to actively participate and embed data directly in the cover protocol, as FreeWave does, the resulting schemes would still be significantly flawed due to their use of cover protocols that do not support the requirements of generic client-proxy interaction. These flaws lead directly to attacks violating both *unobservability* and *unblockability*, as we describe in the remainder of this paper.

3. EXPERIMENTAL SETUP

This section briefly covers the experimental setup for SkypeMorph, FreeWave, and CensorSpoofer along with some of the metrics we're interested in.

3.1 SkypeMorph

For the SkypeMoprh experiments, we extracted the code for the packetizer module from SkypeMorph [1] and created a stand alone client and server that utilized this module. Included in the client and server were modules allowing fine grained control over network conditions that the censor might want to control, such as latency, jitter, packet loss, and packet replay. The client and server ran on separate machines running Ubuntu 12.10 over a 100 Mbps LAN.

3.2 FreeWave

Due to patent issues there is limited access to the modem specified in [11], so we rebuilt the modulator based on the specifications using a square root raised cosine filter pulse function to map symbols to the waveform which was then passed through a passband filter with center frequency f_C. The demodulator only consisted of shifting the received audio signal by the center frequency f_C and then running it through another square root raised cosine filter in order to extract the symbols. Since our experiments were only concerned with the transmission of symbols, the remaining parts of the modem, including the channel encoder, bit interleaver and QAM mapper, were omitted. These were implemented in Matlab using the Communications System Toolbox.

We focused on two main aspects of the functionality of the modem. First is traffic generation related to packet lengths produced by sending modem traffic over Skype. To collect this data two Ubuntu 12.10 virtual machines were started running Skype version 4.1.0.20, one machine we'll designate the client and the other the server. Once a Skype call was initiated between the client and server, the client was configured with pavucontrol [2] to redirect audio from the soundcard to the microphone. Then an audio file was played while running `tcpdump` to collect packet lengths sent from the client to server during transmission. Along with the audio generated by the modem, we used samples of speech data from the Oregon Graduate Institute Center for Speech Learning and Understanding's "22 Language" telephone speech corpus [15]. Samples longer than 10 seconds were played over Skype while recording the packet lengths, resulting in a total of 44 samples across 5 languages.

The other metric we are interested in is distortion of the raw symbols being sent by the modem (not to be confused with the actual IP traffic sent) along with the quality of the underlying audio communiciation. For this we used the SILK SDK [3] which includes tools to encode and decode audio files while varying parameters and simulating certain network conditions, such as packet loss. Using the codec tools instead of sending the data over Skype gives FreeWave the best case scenario, removing other noise added by network conditions. In addition this allowed us to collect a much larger sample size while varying different parameters, producing more accurate results. Then, to measure the quality of actual audio instead of the modem, we used a matlab script [4] to measure the MOS of audio compared to the output from the SILK encoder.

3.3 CensorSpoofer

The main focus of CensorSpoofer were the asynchronous transmission mechanisms. For these experiments a simple client and server were built where the server would transmit directly to the client with various forward error correction possibilities. CensorSpoofer mimics VoIP clients that use constant bitrate (CBR) codecs which dictates the traffic patterns. We chose to mimic G.711 which sends packets of size 190 bytes every 20 milliseconds. In addition it would simulate various types of packet loss, including burst or random, along with modules allowing more specific and targeted packet loss strategies.

[1] `http://crysp.uwaterloo.ca/software/CodeTalkerTunnel.html`

[2] `http://freedesktop.org/software/pulseaudio/pavucontrol/`

[3] `http://cdn.dev.skype.com/upload/SILK_SDK_SRC_v1.0.9.zip`

[4] `http://www.mathworks.com/matlabcentral/fileexchange/33820-pesq-matlab-wrapper/`

4. DIFFERENTIAL ERROR TOLERANCE

Anonymous communication must guarantee reliable transmission across its censorship-resilient system. While previous systems rely on the underlying mechanisms of TCP to guarantee reliable transmission, SkypeMorph, FreeWave and CensorSpoofer all transmit data over UDP using cover-protocols that have some amount of error tolerance. This forces those systems to implement their own mechanisms for reliable transmission, which a censor can interfere with and effectively block the underlying anonymous communication while still leaving a usable medium for legitimate traffic.

4.1 Packet Loss Thresholds

The main way a censor can attempt to interfere with anonymous communication traffic being sent over error tolerant channels is by inducing some amount of packet loss in an effort to disrupt the anonymous communication while still allowing legitimate usage of the cover-protocol. The majority of voice and video communication systems have various ways of dealing with packet loss, such as forward error correction and lowering the bitrate of the information being sent. While what amount of reduced quality due to packet loss is "acceptable" is an inherently subjective question, here we'll cover some work looking at the trade-offs.

To score the quality of a VoIP call the mean opinion score (MOS), which is the average of a set of subjective rankings on a scale from 1 to 5, where 5 represents the best quality possible. Ding and Goubran [6] looked at the impact of packet loss rates on the quality of VoIP communication and how it affected MOS.

Codec	0%	5%	10%	15%	20%
G.729	4.31	3.76	3.45	3.11	2.79
G.723.1 r63	4.25	3.74	3.41	3.10	2.76
G.723.1 r53	4.22	3.71	3.37	2.99	2.74

Table 1: Mean opinion scores of different VoIP codecs with varying levels of packet loss rates.

Table 1 shows the results based on their model with MOS ranging between 2.74 - 3.11 when packet loss rates get in the range of 15-20%. In terms of impairment 2 represents "annoying" and 3 is "slightly annoying". We posit this represents an upper bound of packet loss a censor could impose on VoIP connections while still maintaining usability, particular with some of the newer codecs.

Zhang *et al.* conducted similar research on Skype video calls [28], looking at how various network conditions effected video rates and quality. They found that past 10% packet loss rates Skype switches from normal to conservative state. Both the sending rate and video rate plummet after this threshold, where their model shows a drop in MOS from 3.5 to effectively 0. Based on this research we can assume a hard upper bound of 10% packet loss available to a censor, anything higher would effectively block access to Skype video communication.

4.2 FreeWave Modem

In order to directly use the VoIP network, FreeWave modulates raw data through a modem which transmits data frames through the VoIP client and over the network to the FreeWave proxy. Each data frame sent by the modem begins with a known preamble block used for synchronization, ensuring the demodulator is able to find the starting place of the actual data symbols sent. After the demodulator filters and samples the audio waveform it receives, it scans through and finds the point of maximum correlation and declares that to be the starting point of the data frame. If the wrong starting point is identified the demodulator will be unable to correctly decode the rest of the data, giving a censor a potential avenue to interrupt data transfer over FreeWave.

There are several different parameters and modes of operation that, while not explicitly mentioned in [11], are inherent in the design of the modem and will effect a censor attempting to cause the modem to desynchronize. First there is the length of the preamble, where the longer preambles give the modem a higher probability of correctly finding the starting point. Next there is the data frame length and how many data blocks are transfered. The preamble and signal parameter blocks could only be sent at the very beginning when the FreeWave client initiates the connection with the FreeWave server and remains in constant communication with null data being transfered during inactivity. Similarly the modem could be in constant communication with null data, however each data frame would be a fixed size of N data blocks. Another option is that the modem directly handles the data being transfered and sends batches of data at a time in the frames.

We first examined the effects of varying packet loss rates on correctly synchronizing with different preamble lengths. Using the modem we recorded 10 seconds of transmission of random symbols and encoded the output with FEC enabled. Then for each packet loss rate, the output from the encoder was decoded 100 times with the randomized packet loss rate so we could determine the percent of transfers that would succeed. We next fixed a starting point for the preamble, and varying the preamble length would scan through the decoded symbols, calculating 16000 points of correlation, and marking the preamble as the point with the highest correlation score. If this point was the actual start of the preamble the transfer was marked as a success, otherwise it was labeled as failed, even if the actual preamble had the 2nd highest score.

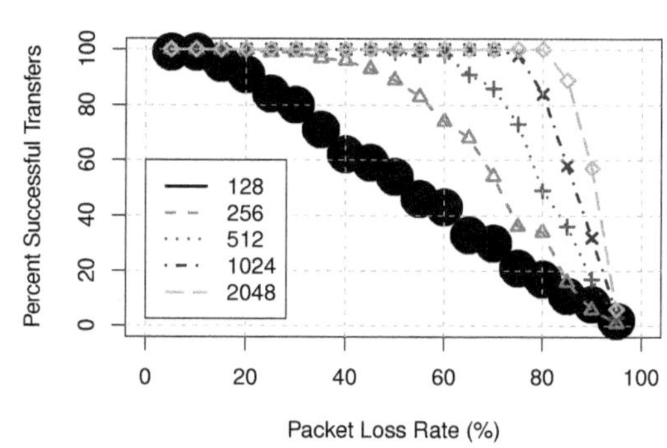

Figure 1: Percent of successfull transfers in FreeWave with different preamble lengths, while varying the packet loss rate.

Figure 1 shows the results of varying packet loss rates with respect to different preamble lengths. We see that even using fairly small lengths still results in a large percent of successful transfers with standard packet loss rates one would expect in a normal network. This is a combination of the fact that error correction in VoIP is able to compensate for small amounts of packet loss, and that correlation with random data produces very low scores, resulting in a fairly low threshold the preamble's score must be above. However we see that no matter how long the preamble, extremely high packet loss rates above 90% are able to prevent the modem from properly synchronizing, since with that high of packet loss the FEC codes are unable to recoup the loss data. While these packet loss rates would effectively kill all VoIP communication, the modem only embeds the preamble at the beginning of the connection. A preamble of length 2048 would take roughly 0.25 seconds to transmit, so a censor only needs to apply high packet loss rates for less

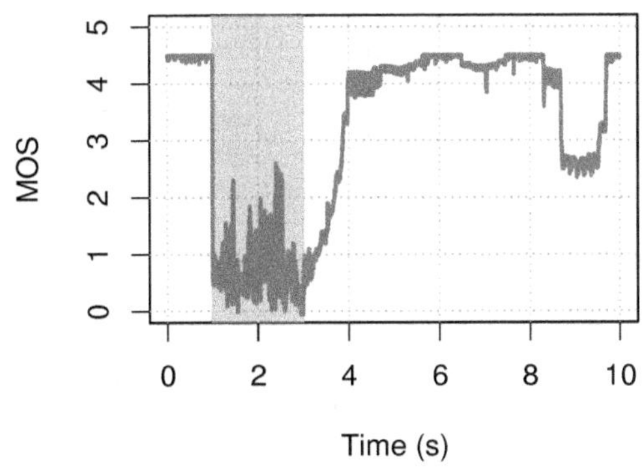

Figure 2: Targeted packet dropping to cause desynchronization in the shaded region with resulting effects on the Mean Opinion Score of the communication.

than a second to cause modem desynchronization while leaving the remainder of the connection untouched. Figure 2 shows a scenario where a censor applies 95% packet loss for a two second interval it believes contains the preamble, while leaving the remainder of the transmission in tact resulting in only a few seconds of incomprehensible communication.

In order to perform targeted packet dropping to prevent synchronization, a censor would need to know an approximation on when the preamble was sent in order to drop a large percentage of those packets. This is directly related to the different configurations of how data frames are composed and when they are sent. The first method mentioned where synchronization only occurs during the initial connection is easy to interrupt based on the evidence that high packet loss prevents synchronization with almost any preamble length. Even using a wide window for possible preamble packets, if a censor merely drops enough packets at the very beginning of the communication, it will prevent all the FreeWave modem from synchronizing while only being a minor inconvenience on actual VoIP communication. The logical extension from this protocol is to have fixed data frame sizes, allowing repeated chances at synchronization. Given predictable pattern of fixed data frame lengths and preamble positions, a censor can effectively target packets only containing preamble data. This allows a censor to completely desynchronize the modem with low packet rate loss, meaning any actual VoIP communication would be relatively unaffected allowing honest clients to still communicate. Another potential mode of operation is to have the modem send a data frame whenever it receives data either directly from the browser or off the network. In this case, the modem is only sending data frames when it actually has data to send and is quiet the rest of the time, only needing to synchronize over each frame. Since the preamble is always at the beginning of the data frame, a censor can just target the first burst of packets sent to drop in order to distort the preamble block.

4.3 SkypeMorph

In SkypeMorph the client and proxy directly communicate outside the cover-protocol system, so in order to handle data corruption and packet loss SkypeMorph implements its own retransmission mechanisms adapted from TCP to fit their traffic shaping model. The packetizer module in SkypeMorph has one thread for sending packets and one for receiving packets, both of which handle packet loss and retransmission. The sending thread ensures that packets get flagged as an ACK every 100 ms or so with the last sequence number seen. The receiving thread keeps track of the last ACK seen, and on seeing the same ACK 4 times in a row it resets the sending thread's head sequence number, causing the data starting from the new sequence number to all be retransmitted.

4.3.1 Tracking ACKs

A censor might want to target and interfere with packets containing acknowledgements in order to slow down or even halt the data transfer, so they need some way of accurately tracking ACK packets. Here we take advantage of the fairly deterministic way in which packets are flagged as ACK. The sending thread in the packetizer keeps track of the last time t_{ACK} an ACK packet was sent, and the first packet sent at time $t \geq t_{ACK} + 100$ms gets marked as an ACK packet. Therefore, the censor can keep track of the last time it knows an ACK packet was sent, and the first packet seen past the 100 ms window it knows is the next ACK packet. However, due to network jitter we cannot always assume the first packet seen after 100 ms is the ACK packet. In some cases either the actual ACK packet is received before the 100 ms interval and would be missed, or a non-ACK packet is delayed and appears to be the first packet after the 100 ms window, getting misclassified.

To accommodate this, the censor can keep track of different paths of probable ACK packets. First, we'll consider a *train* of packets as a group of packets in which the difference in the successive receive times for each packet is less than some ϵ [5], i.e. for any two consecutive packets received at times t_i, t_{i+1}, we have $t_{i+1} - t_i < \epsilon$. Then, when examining a window of probable ACK packets, consider the first packet in each packet train as possible ACK packets and branch a path off from there. We only consider the first packet because there is a higher probability of it being the ACK packet, and it also decreases any potential from skewing too far from the actual path (in that it is better to underestimate than overestimate).

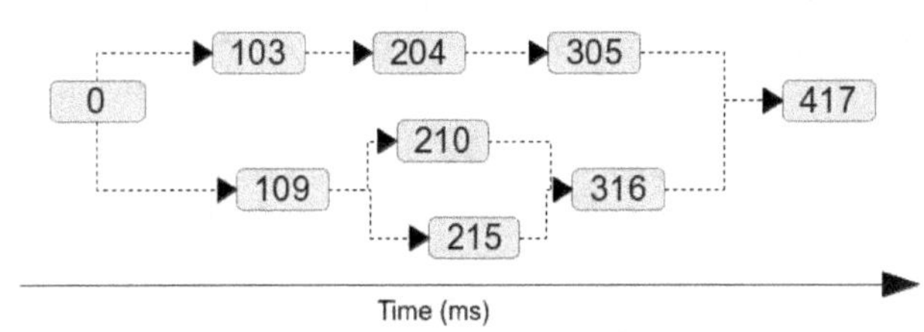

Figure 3: Example of a censor tracking paths of ACK packets in SkypeMorph, where the boxes correspond to potential ACKs flagged by the algorithm with the time they were recieved.

An example of this process can be seen in Figure 3, where multiple paths branch off from possible ACK packets. Note that it is entirely possible, and even likely, that paths will merge back to single possible ACK packets when there is only one possible packet train available in both windows. The problem with this technique is many times multiple packets could be potential ACK packets where a censor wants to select just one. To accomidate this, the censor computes a probability for each packet based on the probability distribution $p(x)$ of time differences between successive ACK packets. Since a packet may have multiple paths from some starting point, we first compute the probability of individual paths with times $\{t_1^i, t_2^i, \ldots, t_n^i\}$ as such:

$$P(path_i) = \frac{1}{n-1} \prod_{j=1}^{n-1} p(t_{j+1}^i - t_j^i)$$

[5] We used $\epsilon = 1$ ms in our experiments

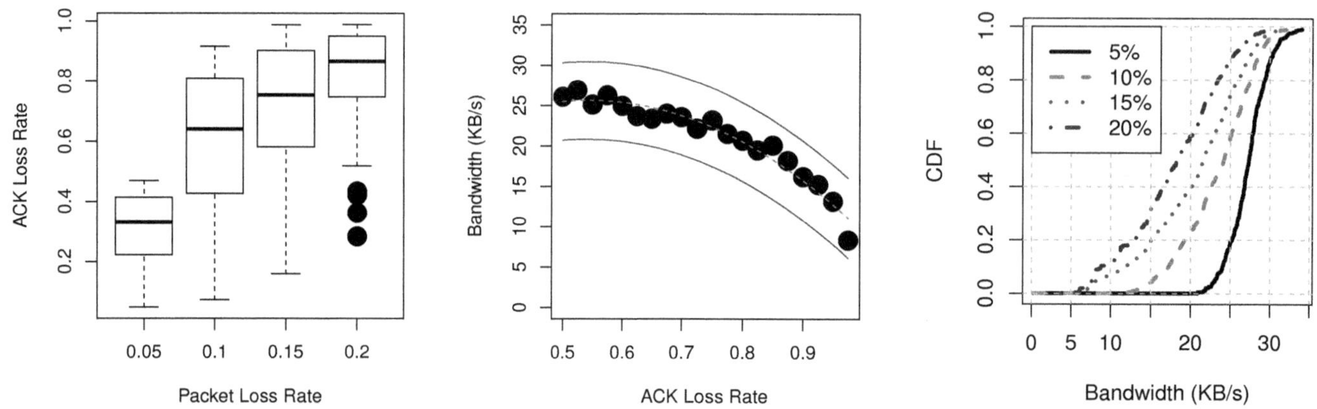

(a) Packet vs ACK Loss Rate (b) ACK Loss Rate vs Bandwidth (c) Packet Loss vs Bandwidth

Figure 4: While the censor is attempting to drop ACK packets in SkypeMorph, (a) shows percent of ACKs dropped with different caps on packet loss rate (b) looks at how varying ACK loss rates effect overall bandwidth and (c) shows CDF of available bandwidth based on packet loss rates.

Then the probability assigned to the actual packet is just the average of the probabilities computed over all paths belonging to that packet.

4.3.2 Dropping ACKs

One avenue for distrupting the data transfer is for the censor to drop as many ACK packets as possible, increasing the delay in responding to packet loss causing throughput to drop. First we explored the range of ACK loss rates that can be achieved for varying packet loss rates. The packet dropping algorithm described was implemented on the client side with overall packet loss capped at a set rate. For each packet loss rate 100 downloads were performed to get the distribution of ACK loss rates achieved. Figure 4a shows these distributions for packet loss rates of 5, 10, 15 and 20%. Note that out of all packet sent, a full 10% of them are marked as ACK packets. This places a hard upper bound on packet loss rate of 5%, where at most 50% of all ACK packets will be able to be dropped with perfect accuracy, which did have a maximum ACK loss rate of 47%. Interestingly, packet loss rates of 10% and 15% had a very large span of possible ACK loss rates. These wide discrepancies are caused by the fact that occasionally in the ACK packet tracking algorithm you will see two distinct paths emerge. Dropping packets in both paths would result in packet loss rates exceeding the cap, forcing the algorithm to choose the probabilistically higher paths, which it will ultimately stick with the remainder of the transfer unless they happen to merge later. When it happens to choose the wrong path to follow, you see the very low ACK drop rates in Figure 4a. The distribution narrows considerably for packet loss rate of 20%, due to the fact that it's able to drop packets in both paths and still stay under the packet loss cap, something which could not be done with packet loss rates of 10 and 15%.

Dropping ACK packets from the client to server causes the server to take longer in responding to packet loss and start resending lost data. The end result from this is that it will decrease the throughput and increase the time it takes the server to transmit data, which is what the censor is ultimately interested in. To determine the effects of various ACK loss rates, the client was configured to directly drop ACK packets at a capped rate. The experiment would vary the ACK loss rate, performing 100 downloads for each chosen rate, while the server had a static packet loss rate of 10%. This was kept static because varying it had little effect on the overall bandwidth. Since the server rewinds the entire buffer back to the first packet lost and then retransmits everything beyond that, it doesn't matter how many packets past that initial lost packet were dropped. The experiments showed an initial drop from 34 KB/s to 27 KB/s even with the smallest amounts of ACK packet droping, and then the bandwidth held stable until ACK loss rates went past 50%. The results for rates past this threshold are in Figure 4b, showing the regression of the median bandwidth value along with the 95th confidence interval. While there is a slow decrease in observed bandwidth, after 80% it accelerates downward reaching as low as 5-10 KB/s for ACK loss rates past 90%.

Given the large variation in both ACK loss rates and observed bandwidth, we want to see what the end result is when looking at packet loss rate from targeted packet dropping compared to the observed bandwidth, as these are the two parameters a censor is concerned about. Figure 4c shows a CDF of observed bandwidth for packet loss rates ranging from 5 to 20%. Since packet loss rate of 5% has an upper bound of a 50% ACK drop rate, it's not surprising that we don't see the bandwidth drop much below 25 KB/s as this was the constant rate seen for ACK loss rates ranging from 5 to 50%. For packet loss rates from 15-20%, considered to be a rough upper bound on the censor packet dropping capability, we see roughly about a quarter of transfers dropping below 15 KB/s bandwidth. While these rates may not seem like a large reduction compared to the initial 34 KB/s seen with SkypeMorph, the initial paper [18] noted that the normal bridge operated at 200 KB/s, implying that the combination means 90-95% reduction in available bandwidth.

4.3.3 Replaying ACKs

While the packet dropping techniques served more as a throttling mechanism than outright blocking, an active censor can also attempt to replay packets over the cover-protocol, while having little impact on legitimate traffic. SkypeMorph uses sequence numbers to keep track of what parts of the buffered data are being transfered, so upon receiving any overlapping or duplicate data, it's able to detect this and either drop the packet or discard the data.

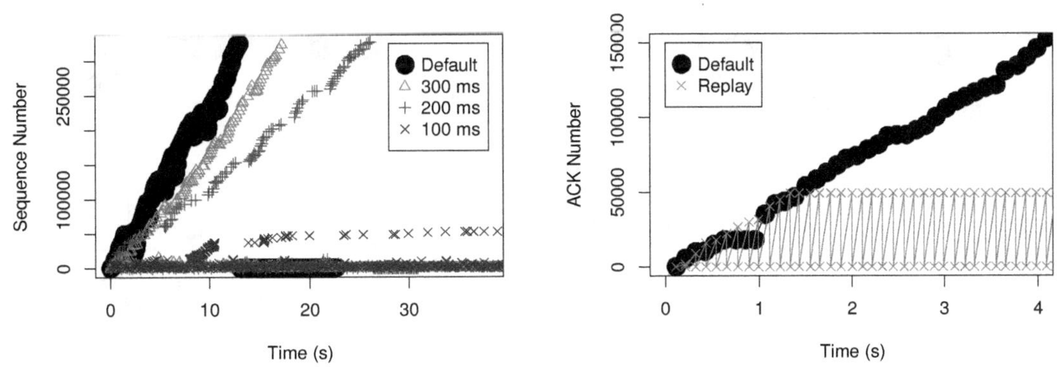

(a) Time to transfer data with varying ACK replay intervals

(b) ACK number sent by client with and without single ACK injection

Figure 5: SkypeMorph ACK replay attacks with (a) showing the progression of the sent sequence number when replaying 4 ACK packets at a time at different intervals and (b) shows the effects on the received ACK number when injecting a single ACK packet every 100ms.

Before the check for duplicate data happens, SkypeMorph first checks the packet flag to determine whether the packet is an ACK or not, and if so processes the ACK number before the data duplication check is performed. This is done because dummy packets not transferring any real data can be flagged as ACK, so the ACK check needs to be done before the data processing. This opens up a potential packet replay attack to the censor, where they have the capability of replay old ACK packets seen and have them legitimately processed by the SkypeMorph client, even if the data is discarded. The censor runs the same ACK tracking algorithm as discussed previously and waits until all paths merge into a single possible ACK, increasing the probability of correctly selecting an ACK packet. This ACK packet can be replayed to the server in bursts of 4 at a time, so they will be received simultaneously causing the server to reset its current sequence number and roll back the buffer.

For the experiment we configured the client to record the first packet that appeared alone in the possible ACK window, and replay it 4 times in a row at a fixed interval, while the server was configured with a static 10% packet loss rate. We ran an experiment in default mode with no ACK replays, and then replaying ACKs in intervals of 300 ms, 200 ms, and 100 ms. The results for this experiment are shown in Figure 5a. Replaying ACKs at intervals of 200 and 300 ms does significantly increase the amount of time it takes to transfer data, but it doesn't completely kill the transfer. This is because after the train of replays are sent, the next valid ACK that the server receives will reset the current ACK value and will roll forward the buffer to this position, as it assumes it has received everything before the ACK counter. For the interval of 100 ms, we see a very dramatic reduction in how much data is able to be sent, having it take around 40 seconds to send as much data normally sent in the first 5 seconds.

This result leads to a lower resource and more efficient replay attack. The server needs to receive 4 packets with the same ACK number before it rolls back and starts retransmitting data. Therefore, while inducing a small amount of packet loss from the server to the client, a censor can simply inject a recorded ACK packets once every 100 ms, continually causing the server to reset the current ACK value and preventing the ACK counter from ever reaching high enough to rewind the buffer. Figure 5b shows the ACK number received by the server under default operation and while performing the single ACK injection. We can see the received ACK number jumping between the legitimate ACK value and the replay ACK being injected. Once a packet is dropped from the server to the client, the client keeps sending the server the same ACK number in an attempt to notify of data loss, but since the injected packet keeps reseting the current ACK counter the server never resends the data, stalling out the transfer and completely killing the connection.

4.4 CensorSpoofer

CensorSpoofer uses asynchronous communication in order to hide the identify of the proxy, having data flow only from the proxy to the client. This means the client cannot notify the proxy of lost packets or missing data like SkypeMorph was able to do. So in order to reliably transmit data they suggest two methods of error correction, one using an XOR encoder/decoder to send redundant packets and the other to use forward error correction codes such as Reed-Solomon. We explore these methods and how they hold up to a censor attempting to disrupt communication between a CensorSpoofer client and server.

4.4.1 XOR Encoding

The XOR encoder/decoder has a redundant packet sent for every n packets transmitted, so given packets $(p_1, p_2, \cdots, p_n)$, the packet $r = p_1 \oplus p_2 \oplus \cdots \oplus p_n$ is constructed and sent after packet p_n. By including a simple packet counter at the beginning of each packet, the client will be able to detect if a packet was lost, and as long as $n-1$ of the remaining packets in the n packet window were received, the client will be able to reconstruct the missing packet simply by XORing the packets together. Assuming uniform packet loss, this type of system will be able to handle a rate of $\frac{1}{n+1}$ packet loss. There are, however, problems with making this assumption.

The first problem is that one of the common causes of packet loss is due to buffers filling up and having to drop packets, which in turn causes bursts of packets to be dropped [4]. This means that there will be a very high chance that packet loss will cause more than one packet to be dropped from the n packet window, meaning that the lost data will not be able to be recovered. The more troublesome problem is that an active censor could prevent any client from attempting to use CensorSpoofer by dropping a few consecutive packets, ensuring that data being transfered over CensorSpoofer is lost while barely effecting the usage of legitimate VoIP communication. As we can see in Figure 7, even using the smallest possible value of $n = 2$ a censor can still cause a large amount of data loss, ensuring all data transfers would fail when using XOR encoding.

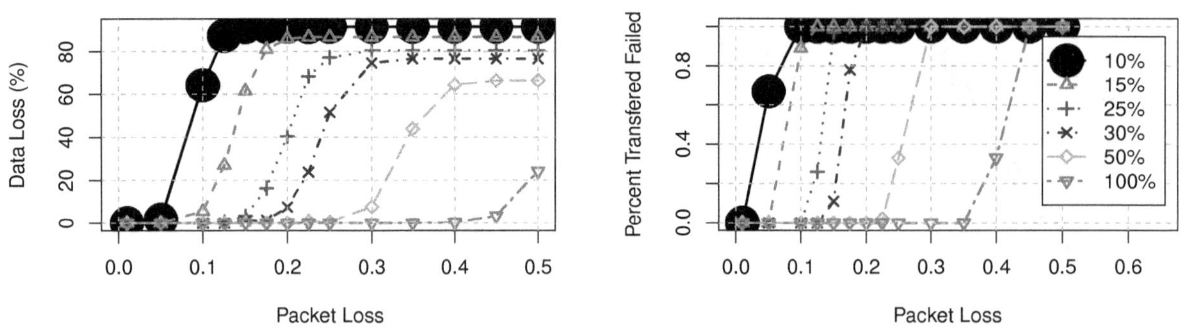

(a) Percent Data Loss (b) Percent Transfered Failed

Figure 6: Effects of packet loss in CensorSpoofer while producing varying overhead values based on Reed-Solomon parameters, looking at both (a) percent of data loss and (b) percent of failed transfers while using Reed-Solomon with different overhead.

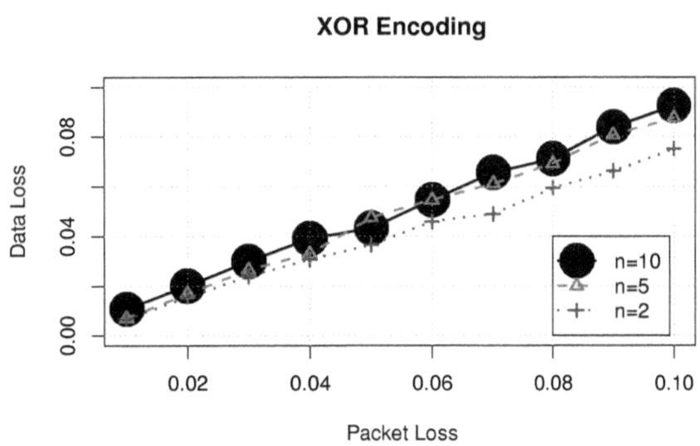

Figure 7: Percent of data loss in CensorSpoofer compared to packet loss rates when using XOR encoding with different n packet windows for redundant data.

4.4.2 Reed-Solomon

The other method mentioned that could be used by CensorSpoofer was a forward error correcting code such as Reed-Solomon, a popular code used in many error-prone mediums. Reed-Solomon codes are parameterized by encoding messages of k symbols, where each symbol is m-bits and the resulting encoded block is $n = 2^m - 1$ symbols. Such a code can correct up to $n - k$ errors if the location of the erroneous symbols are known, otherwise it can only correct up to $\frac{n-k}{2}$ errors. While this offers more reliable error correction in the presence of packet loss, we can still run into some of the same problems that we previously did. The naive way to perform the encoding is to split the data into blocks b_i of size k symbols, encode each block $b'_i = \texttt{Reed-Solomon}(b_i, n, k)$ resulting in n symbols, then transmit the encoded blocks $b'_1, b'_2, b'_3, \ldots$ to the client. Since reliable transmission means that *all* data encoded in the blocks must be recovered, a censor that can cause enough packet loss to corrupt a single block would cause the entire transmission to fail. For example, a common Reed-Solomon code has $m = 8$ bit symbols with $(n, k) = (255, 223)$ message and block lengths. So in order to send a 320 KB file, a server would need to transmit 1470 encoded blocks, only one of which needs to be corrupted in order to stop the transmission.

From examining both these schemes, we can identify the real problem is that for a server sending an averaged sized web file, a censor only has to drop a small amount of continuous packets to cause a portion of the data to be corrupted, thus disrupting the entire transmission. In order to fix this problem, we need to introduce a bit interleaver which causes a single block to be dispersed throughput multiple packets instead of being concentrated in a single packet. Using a random bit interleaver, we experimented with different Reed-Solomon parameters, fixing $n = 255$ and varying k while expressing the combination in terms of overhead of extra data transfered, equivalent to $\frac{n-k}{k}$. For each set of parameters we performed 100 downloads of a 320 KB file and recorded the average percent of data loss during the downloads and the percent of failed transfers. Figure 6 shows the packet loss thresholds for overhead values ranging from 10 to 50%. With the combination of a random bit interleaver and forward error correction, the server would still need to encode with 50% overhead to to avoid losing data below the 20% packet loss rate threshold.

5. PROXY MODEL IN P2P SYSTEMS

Many of these censorship circumvention systems attempt to apply a client-proxy system of anonymous communication to a dynamic peer-to-peer system outside their control. For example, SkypeMorph and FreeWave both use Skype or other peer-to-peer VoIP systems as their cover-protocol. This section explores some of the difficulties that arises when forcing a proxy model into a peer-to-peer system.

5.1 Tor Over Skype

The main problem SkypeMorph attempts to solve is the ability of censors to enumerate Tor bridges and blacklist them. By using Skype as the protocol to mimic, it makes it hard for censors to detect and enumerate these bridges, and outright blocking popular services like Skype is something many censors would like to avoid. However, attempting to use the Skype network to tunnel Tor connections through is problematic due to fundamental different use cases for Tor verses VoIP. The Skype system is peer to peer with sporadic short lived connections made between unique clients, while the client-proxy model in Tor sees long lived connections between many clients and a single proxy. These differing use cases open up potential avenues for a censor to fingerprint SkypeMorph.

Figure 8 shows the ratio of daily bridge users from Syria, Iran, and China compared to the total number of bridge relays in the Tor network. Syria and Iran peaked at around 8-12 times as many users as available bridges, and while China currently fluctuates below that, they at one point saw ratio as high as 120 users to bridges be-

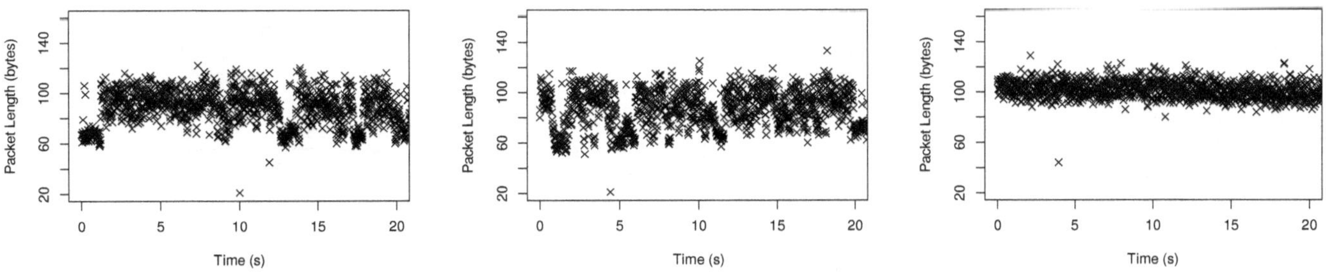

(a) English Packet Lengths (b) Portuguese Packet Lengths (c) Modem Packet Lengths

Figure 9: Skype packet lengths of English and Portuguese speech samples from the OPI corpus compared to modem audio sent over Skype.

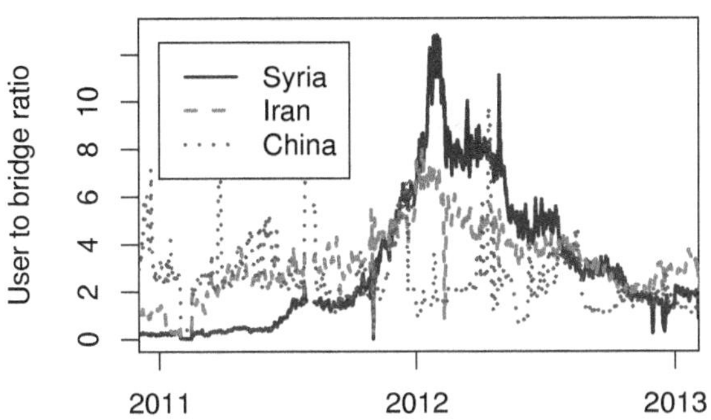

Figure 8: Ratio of daily Tor bridge users from Syria, Iran, and China compared to the overall number of available Tor bridges.

fore China started blocking access. Having so many unique clients connecting through each bridge daily is going to create traffic patterns quite different than one would expect from a normal Skype user. For example, long lived connections spanning many hours will be much longer than the most video calls where only 5% last longer than and hour [5], having multiple simultaneous connections overlapping at different time windows, and clients that seemingly communicate non-stop with a large number of unique clients around the clock. These characteristics do not even need to be able to definitively identify SkypeMorph connections, they can tolerate some small amount of false positives and only need to be able to exclude a large number of actual Skype connections. Once a connection is flagged a censor can attempt to create a SkypeMorph connection to the client under suspicion in order to verify that it's a SkypeMorph bridge.

This also points to a problem that would be faced when deploying SkypeMoprh bridges into the Tor network. A large number of Tor bridges are already blacklisted by censoring countries, only new bridges unknown by these countries deploying SkypeMorph would be able to be reached by the clients. This implies an even smaller base of reachable SkypeMoprh bridges available to these countries, which could be potentially swarmed as clients attempt to use them amplifying the statistics mentioned previously, making it even easier for the SkypeMorph bridges to be flagged.

5.2 FreeWave Proxies

FreeWave prevents this type of fingerprinting by using supernodes in the Skype network as proxies, which then forward the connection to the actual FreeWave server and off to the end destination. However, there are other issues for relying on an external system for proxying connections. At the end of the day, software developers building a product that runs on top of an existing system have to make assumptions about how that base system will behave. One of the largest problems with directly utilizing an existing VoIP client for censorship circumvention is that these assumptions, which security guarantees can depend on, do not always hold up over time. Changes made without announcement can result in failures of the system to uphold its security goals. An excellent example of this is FreeWave's assumptions about how and when Skype clients attempt to use supernodes as a proxy for VoIP connections. FreeWave assumes that by placing a Skype node behind a NAT box it will cause Skype to automatically use a supernode to bridge VoIP connections. This was shown by prior research [13] to be the case. However Skype is a constantly changing system and its behavior evolves over time, in many cases without announcement.

While at the time FreeWave was designed Skype might have been more willing to use supernodes, currently Skype clients attempt, no matter the details of the network they reside in, to directly connect to each other. A Skype client sitting behind a NAT box will send multiple packets to the client it is calling, even if that client also resides behind a NAT box. Only if those packets fail to reach their destination will the caller fall back to a supernode. Additionally, the callee will attempt to send packets in response directly to the caller, even if the caller is actively using a supernode to reach the callee. The issue for FreeWave users is that this allows the censor to flag connections that are using Skype to connect to FreeWave servers. The censor can easily enumerate the IP addresses of the FreeWave servers by placing calls to the FreeWave VoIP IDs and examining which IP addresses Skype attempts to directly connect to. The censor can then flag hosts that send UDP packets to, or receive UDP packets from, those IP addresses. This issue can, to some extent, be fixed by adding the FreeWave server to a firewall on the user's machine, and user's IP address to a firewall on the server side. However, it still serves as an excellent illustration of the issues with using an active system that is in constant flux. In order to not rely on the underlying architecture of Skype, FreeWave would have to resort to a framework similar to SkypeMorph, where proxy IDs are secret and distributed out of band. This would allow FreeWave clients to directly connect to proxies using the Skype ID. But then we are operating in the same environment presented in Section 5.1 with all the same problems of using a proxy model in a peer to peer system.

The peer to peer system used by many VoIP based systems present alternative methods for the censor to detect FreeWave users. Continuing to focus on Skype, using supernodes as proxies exposes the

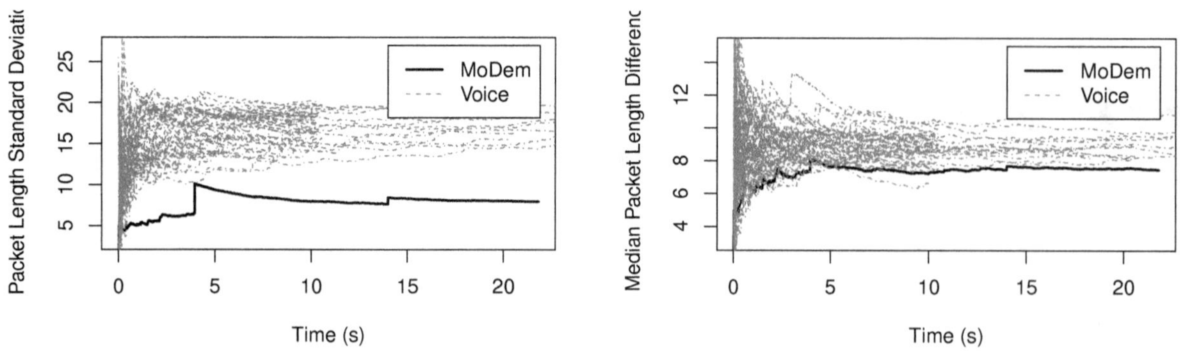

(a) Packet length standard deviation over time

(b) Average Packet Differences Over Time

Figure 10: While tracking connections over Skype, these show how the modem in FreeWave compares to actual voice data when comparing the (a) standard deviation of observed packet lengths and (b) the average difference between difference between packet lengths

user to identification should the censor observe the supernode. As shown previously, the censor can use Skype to enumerate the IP addresses of FreeWave servers. Since the supernode is a simple one hop proxy, the censor can then defeat the unobservability of FreeWave simply by observing traffic through supernodes. While many censors might find this out of their scope of capabilities, others would find the task trivial. For example, China currently forces users to run its own version of Skype called TomSkype [14]. This is currently done so Chinese censors can view instant messaging chat between users. It would be a simple change to force TomSkype to only select supernodes that reside inside China, making linkage between the two IP addresses carrying out a call possible.

6. CROSS-CONTENT DELIVERY

Extensive research has been done on information leakage in encrypted VoIP calls [26, 25, 24], showing how a censor can identify languages spoken, recognize key phrases, and even reconstruct parts of the conversation. This is possible due to the fact that when using variable bitrate (VBR) codecs, common in applications like Skype and Google Talk, there is a strong correlation between how much voice data there is to send and the packet length (in contrast to constant bitrate codecs which have fixed lengths). Previous methods that take advantage of this information leakage are generally fairly complex, relying on Hidden Markov Models or classifiers such as $k-$Nearest Neighbor or χ^2. While these techniques might work for analyzing a targeted VoIP call, implementing these methods on a large scale would be very computationally intensive and impractical or even impossible to perform across all calls. To this end, Houmansadr *et al.* demonstrate that FreeWave over Skype has similar traffic statistics to actual Skype communication, comparing minimum, maximum, and average packet sizes.

While the very basic traffic statistics are similar, there still might exist an intermediate test geared specifically towards FreeWave traffic that can still be performed with ease. The simplest model used for exploiting the information leakage was the χ^2 in [26] for language classification. In this case the model had to differentiate between 22 different possible languages, our task is considerably easier only needing a binary classification. Using the packet lengths generated by the samples from Oregon Graduate Institute corpus [15] mentioned in Section 3, we compared the distribution of packet lengths to those generated by the modem. Figure 11 shows the probability density functions of the minimum, maximum, and average packet lengths seen over the OGI sample set, with the corresponding value for the modem marked on each density.

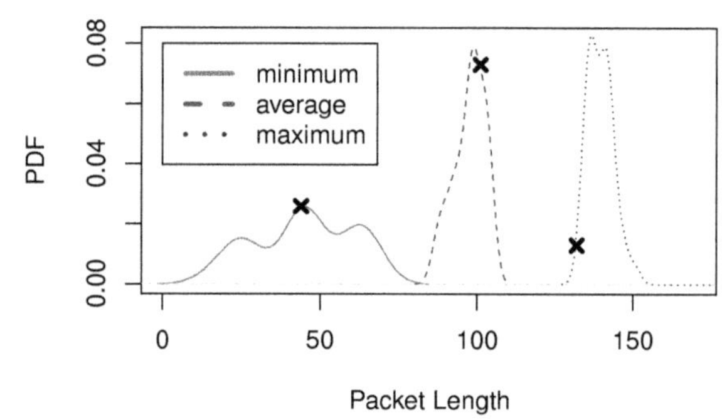

Figure 11: Distribution of minimum/average/maximum packet lengths of actual voice data, with **x** marking values computed for the FreeWave modem packet lengths

The minimum and average packet length for modem overlaps almost perfectly with the densities for actual speech, and while the maximum value is close to the left tail, it still overlaps implying that you cannot distinguish modem from potential legitimate VoIP traffic using only these metrics, confirming the original claim. However, as seen in Figure 10, there is still a very noticeable difference in stream of packet lengths seen with the modem compared to actual speech. Modem packet lengths seen in Figure 9c have a much tighter distribution then either the English or Portuguese samples.

Using this intuition, we can build computationally simplistic binary classifiers that can detect modem traffic from actual speech. Figure 10 shows the divergence of modem verses speech while tracking either standard deviation of the observed packet lengths over time, or simply keeping track of the average inter packet length difference. The average inter packet length difference starts to diverge for the modem connection after around 10 seconds, but while the average is lower than all but one of the samples, it's still fairly close to the other averages potentially making it harder to differentiate and lead to false positives. Tracking the standard deviation produces much better results, starting to significantly diverge after only 5 seconds. Furthermore, the standard deviation on packet length for the modem ends up being 2.0 - 2.5 times lower than all of the speech standard deviation, making it much easier to classify without the risk of false positives. Being able to use such a low resource classifier lets a censor conduct widespread monitoring of encrypted VoIP calls instead of being limited to targeting specific connections.

7. CONCLUSION

With the increase in technologies available to censoring regimes, achieving unobservability in censorship-resilient systems is becoming increasingly difficult. In response there have been a new wave of systems that attempt to use popular services such as VoIP as a cover-protocol for anonymous communication. While the use of mimicry has been shown to be a flawed approach, these systems can be improved to actively participate in the cover-protocol, removing their reliance on mimicry techniques. We show that even removing the dependence on mimicry is not enough to achieve unobservability alone, as there are significant problems in delivering anonymous communication over these cover protocols.

First, we show there are issues in differential error tolerance between the anonymous communication and legitimate cover-protocol traffic. By using an unreliable channel to tunnel data, these systems must implement their own mechanisms for ensuring reliable data transmission. Due to the fact that the cover-protocols are error tolerant and can still operate while incurring packet loss rates from 10-15%, a censor is able to interfere with the mechanisms attempting to ensure reliable transmission, limiting the use of anonymous communication while retaining usability of legitimate use of the cover-protocol. Next, we demonstrate the inherent problems in forcing a client-proxy model on to a peer-to-peer system. Diverging use cases for the different systems allow for noticeable traffic patterns that can be flagged by censors, easily breaking unobservability. Additionally, we explore the pitfalls of relying on a dynamic external network for proxies, as changes can quickly break censorship circumvention. Finally we look at issues in cross-content delivery, showing that even when fully participating in the cover-protocol system, issues arise in attempting to deliver content outside the normal scope of operation, leading to low cost methods of detection.

Acknowledgments We thank the anonymous reviewers for their valuable feedback and suggestions. This research was supported by NSF grants CNS-0917154, CNS-1223421, and CNS-1314637.

8. REFERENCES

[1] JAP: The JAP anonymity & privacy homepage. http://anon.inf.tu-dresden.de/.

[2] Knock Knock Knockin' on Bridges' Doors. https://blog.torproject.org/blog/knock-knock-knockin-bridges-doors.

[3] The Anonymizer. https://www.anonymizer.com/.

[4] BOLOT, J.-C. End-to-end packet delay and loss behavior in the internet. In *Conference proceedings on Communications architectures, protocols and applications* (New York, NY, USA, 1993), SIGCOMM '93, ACM, pp. 289–298.

[5] BONFIGLIO, D., MELLIA, M., MEO, M., AND ROSSI, D. Detailed analysis of skype traffic. *Multimedia, IEEE Transactions on 11*, 1 (2009).

[6] DING, L., AND GOUBRAN, R. A. Speech quality prediction in voip using the extended e-model. In *Global Telecommunications Conference, 2003. GLOBECOM'03. IEEE* (2003), vol. 7, IEEE, pp. 3974–3978.

[7] DINGLEDINE, R., AND MATHEWSON, N. Design of a blocking-resistant anonymity system. Tech. rep., Tor Project, November 2006.

[8] DINGLEDINE, R., MATHEWSON, N., AND SYVERSON, P. Tor: the second-generation onion router. In *Proceedings of the 13th conference on USENIX Security Symposium* (2004), USENIX Association.

[9] HOUMANSADR, A., BRUBAKER, C., AND SHMATIKOV, V. The parrot is dead: Observing unobservable network communications. In *Security and Privacy (SP), 2011 IEEE Symposium on* (2013), IEEE.

[10] HOUMANSADR, A., NGUYEN, G. T., CAESAR, M., AND BORISOV, N. Cirripede: circumvention infrastructure using router redirection with plausible deniability. In *Proceedings of the 18th ACM Conference on Computer and Communications Security (CCS)* (2011).

[11] HOUMANSADR, A., RIEDL, T., BORISOV, N., AND SINGER, A. I want my voice to be heard: Ip over voice-over-ip for unobservable censorship circumvention. NDSS.

[12] KARLIN, J., ELLARD, D., JACKSON, A. W., JONES, C. E., LAUER, G., MANKINS, D. P., AND STRAYER, W. T. Decoy routing: Toward unblockable internet communication. In *Proceedings of the USENIX Workshop on Free and Open Communications on the Internet (FOCI)* (2011).

[13] KHO, W., BASET, S. A., AND SCHULZRINNE, H. Skype relay calls: Measurements and experiments. In *INFOCOM Workshops 2008, IEEE* (2008), IEEE.

[14] KNOCKEL, J., CRANDALL, J. R., AND SAIA, J. Three researchers, five conjectures: An empirical analysis of tom-skype censorship and surveillance. In *USENIX Workshop Free and Open Communications on the Internet (FOCI)* (2011).

[15] LANDER, T., COLE, R. A., OSHIKA, B., AND NOEL, M. The ogi 22 language telephone speech corpus. In *Proc. Eurospeech* (1995), vol. 95.

[16] LYON, G. F. *Nmap Network Scanning: The Official Nmap Project Guide to Network Discovery and Security Scanning.* Insecure, 2009.

[17] MCLACHLAN, J., AND HOPPER, N. On the risks of serving whenever you surf: vulnerabilities in tor's blocking resistance design. In *Proceedings of the 8th ACM workshop on Privacy in the electronic society* (2009), ACM.

[18] MOHAJERI MOGHADDAM, H., LI, B., DERAKHSHANI, M., AND GOLDBERG, I. Skypemorph: protocol obfuscation for tor bridges. In *Proceedings of the 2012 ACM conference on Computer and communications security* (New York, NY, USA, 2012), CCS '12, ACM, pp. 97–108.

[19] ROSENBERG, J., SCHULZRINNE, H., CAMARILLO, G., JOHNSTON, A., PETERSON, J., SPARKS, R., HANDLEY, M., AND SCHOOLER, E. SIP: Session Initiation Protocol. RFC 3261 (Proposed Standard), June 2002. Updated by RFCs 3265, 3853, 4320, 4916, 5393, 5621, 5626, 5630, 5922, 5954, 6026, 6141.

[20] SCHUCHARD, M., GEDDES, J., THOMPSON, C., AND HOPPER, N. Routing around decoys. In *Proceedings of the 2012 ACM conference on Computer and communications security* (2012), ACM.

[21] SMITS, R., JAIN, D., PIDCOCK, S., GOLDBERG, I., AND HENGARTNER, U. Bridgespa: improving tor bridges with single packet authorization. In *Proceedings of the 10th annual ACM workshop on Privacy in the electronic society* (2011), ACM.

[22] WANG, Q., GONG, X., NGUYEN, G. T., HOUMANSADR, A., AND BORISOV, N. Censorspoofer: asymmetric communication using ip spoofing for censorship-resistant web browsing. In *Proceedings of the 2012 ACM conference on Computer and communications security* (New York, NY, USA, 2012), CCS '12, ACM, pp. 121–132.

[23] WEINBERG, Z., WANG, J., YEGNESWARAN, V., BRIESEMEISTER, L., CHEUNG, S., WANG, F., AND BONEH, D. Stegotorus: a camouflage proxy for the tor anonymity system. In *Proceedings of the 2012 ACM conference on Computer and communications security* (2012), ACM.

[24] WHITE, A. M., MATTHEWS, A. R., SNOW, K. Z., AND MONROSE, F. Phonotactic reconstruction of encrypted voip conversations: Hookt on fon-iks. In *Security and Privacy (SP), 2011 IEEE Symposium on* (2011), IEEE.

[25] Wright, C. V., Ballard, L., Coull, S. E., Monrose, F., and Masson, G. M. Spot me if you can: Uncovering spoken phrases in encrypted voip conversations. In *Security and Privacy, 2008. SP 2008. IEEE Symposium on* (2008), IEEE.

[26] Wright, C. V., Ballard, L., Monrose, F., and Masson, G. M. Language identification of encrypted voip traffic: Alejandra y roberto or alice and bob. In *Proceedings of the 16th USENIX Security Symposium* (2007).

[27] Wustrow, E., Wolchok, S., Goldberg, I., and Halderman, J. A. Telex: anticensorship in the network infrastructure. In *Proceedings of the 20th USENIX Conference on Security (SEC)* (2011).

[28] Zhang, X., Xu, Y., Hu, H., Liu, Y., Guo, Z., and Wang, Y. Profiling skype video calls: Rate control and video quality. In *INFOCOM, 2012 Proceedings IEEE* (2012), IEEE.

An Analysis of the EMV Channel Establishment Protocol

Christina Brzuska
School of Computer Science,
Tel Aviv University
brzuska@post.tau.ac.il

Nigel P. Smart
Department of Computer
Science, University of Bristol
nigel@cs.bris.ac.uk

Bogdan Warinschi
Department of Computer
Science, University of Bristol
bogdan@cs.bris.ac.uk

Gaven J. Watson
Department of Computer
Science, University of Bristol
gaven.watson@bristol.ac.uk

ABSTRACT

With over 1.6 billion debit and credit cards in use worldwide, the EMV system (a.k.a. "Chip-and-PIN") has become one of the most important deployed cryptographic protocol suites. Recently, the EMV consortium has decided to upgrade the existing RSA based system with a new system relying on Elliptic Curve Cryptography (ECC). One of the central components of the new system is a protocol that enables a card to establish a secure channel with a card reader. In this paper we provide a security analysis of the proposed protocol, we propose minor changes/clarifications to the "Request for Comments" issued in Nov 2012, and demonstrate that the resulting protocol meets the intended security goals.

The structure of the protocol is one commonly encountered in practice: first run a key-exchange to establish a shared key (which performs authentication and key confirmation), only then use the channel to exchange application messages. Although common in practice, this structure takes the protocol out of the reach of most standard security models for key-exchange. Unfortunately, the only models that can cope with the above structure suffer from some drawbacks that make them unsuitable for our analysis. Our second contribution is to provide new security models for channel establishment protocols. Our models have a more inclusive syntax, are quite general, deal with a realistic notion of authentication (one-sided authentication as required by EMV), and do not suffer from the drawbacks that we identify in prior models.

Categories and Subject Descriptors

C.2.0 [**Computer-Communication Networks**]: General—*security and protection*; K.6.5 [**Management of Computing and Information Systems**]: Security and Protection—*authentication*

Keywords

Key Exchange; Channel Establishment

CCS'13, November 4–8, 2013, Berlin, Germany.
ACM 978-1-4503-2477-9/13/11.
http://dx.doi.org/10.1145/2508859.2516748.

1. INTRODUCTION

The EMV chip-and-pin system is used to secure a vast number of the world's credit card and ATM transactions and protects electronic banking in many countries [15]. The USA is due to switch from magnetic stripe to EMV cards from October 2015; after this time if a terminal (or ATM) does not support EMV then the merchant (ATM owner) will be liable for any fraudulent transactions and not the card issuer. The current EMV system uses RSA public-key cryptography, combined with DES and AES based symmetric-key cryptography. In the system, bank or credit card customers receive a plastic card containing an embedded chip that holds several cryptographic keys and can perform various cryptographic operations. The card is used to communicate with a terminal (typically a point-of-sale terminal in a shop, but other terminals are possible). In addition the card can produce cryptographically secured data which is sent to the cardholder and merchant's banks for processing. Nonetheless, the cryptographic functionality provided by the card in its first generation incarnation is relatively limited.

As part of a major reworking of the system, the EMV consortium has decided to replace RSA with ECC based systems and to let the card provide additional cryptographic functionalities. In November 2012 EMVCo released a Request-For-Comments [16] on a draft specification for an important sub-protocol within the system; namely a protocol that allows a card to establish a channel with a terminal. Calling the security of these protocols "important" is a serious understatement: the total number of public keys and certificates (1.62 billion [15]) deployed in the EMV systems dwarfs the paltry 5.8 million TLS certificates found in [11].

The problem of establishing and implementing secure channels is central to practical uses of cryptography and a superficial look at existing literature would lead one to believe that this is a solved problem. What can be simpler than first running a secure key-exchange protocol and then using the resulting keys to encrypt and authenticate the messages to be sent?

Indeed, there is a plethora of works looking at key establishment [4, 5, 9] and a similar number of works treating secure channels based on shared keys [1, 6, 18]. Unfortunately, traditional key agreement models such as those following the schema set out by Bellare and Rogaway [4] have been shown to be less useful to analyze deployed protocols. In particular, they demand for session keys to be indistinguishable from a random string. However, whenever practical protocols implement explicit key confirmation, then key indistinguishability is violated.

Realizing that real-world protocols, such as TLS, are therefore outside the reach of the traditional models for key-exchange and channels, has triggered renewed interest in formal models for secure channels [17, 13, 7]. These approaches deal with what is essentially an overlap between the key-exchange part and the secure channel part of a channel-establishment protocol by either modifying the protocol, analyzing the overall protocol monolithically, or developing methods that allow for a modular analysis despite the overlapping phases.

The structure of the EMV protocol for establishing channels follows the recipe described above: during the key-exchange phase itself, the channel is already used before the deployed keys are accepted; and the messages that are sent over the channel are crucial for the security of the overall protocol. Our work can therefore be seen as a continuation of the recent thrust on research on models for channel establishment protocols. Below we describe the state-of-the art for such models, identify some of their weaknesses, and overview our results.

EXISTING MODELS FOR SECURE CHANNEL ESTABLISHMENT. When studying the combined properties of a key establishment and a secure channel protocol, one usually considers a security game where the execution model and the attack interface for key exchange and secure channels are "glued" together; and the adversary tries to break the secure channel using additional information that possibly leaked during the key-exchange phase. In particular, such a model also allows to analyze protocols that do not clearly separate the two components.

There are currently two approaches to prove the security in such a model. Very roughly, the first approach is to relax the security requirement on the keys by demanding that they are sufficiently strong to be used for the primitives that make-up the channel, and then show that the channel security relies only on these primitives. This *modular approach* is explored in [7], where a game-based composition theorem shows that a key-exchange protocol that is sufficiently strong for the primitives and a channel whose security reduces to these primitives automatically yield a secure protocol in the composed security model. The approach is shown to work for real-world protocols such as TLS.

In this paper, we prefer to avoid the machinery needed to work within this framework and instead concentrate on the approach of Jager et al. [13]. They propose to analyze channel establishment protocols, monolithically, with respect to a security model devised for this specific task. The models that they give are tailored for TLS and are not immediately applicable for EMV. Worse, both the original version of the model [13] and a more recent refined version [12] do not seem to appropriately capture the level of security that one would like. In brief, the former model is too strong, to the point that it actually rules as insecure protocols like TLS and the one that we analyze in this paper. The refined version, on the other hand seems to be too weak, as it takes away one of the adversary's abilities, an ability that reflects possible real-world powers.

A bit more in detail, the issue concerns the ability of an adversary to "reveal" a key, and its interaction with how "partnering" is defined. We explain these concepts next. Traditionally, reveal queries model the unintended leakage of session keys from a participant to assure that keys which leak from one session should not affect the security of other sessions. To distinguish between the same session and "other sessions", key exchange protocols match each session of a protocol with a single session of the intended partner via a partnering mechanism [3]. One of the first formulations of partnering relies on "matching" conversations [4] (the outgoing/incoming messages of one sessions are the same as the incoming/outgoing messages of its partner). The requirement is that if a session accepts, then it has had a matching conversation with "the right" partner. Unfortunately, in any protocol where some messages are sent encrypted with the key that is derived, the above requirement cannot hold. An attacker can proceed as follows. When an encrypted message goes on the network, block it, reveal the key that was used for encryption and then send to the recipient a different encryption of the same message, deploying fresh randomness. The two partners will not have a matching conversation, although the protocol will be executed successfully. In the full version of this paper [8] we describe an attack against entity authentication via matching conversations for TLS when an adversary is permitted to reveal keys as soon as they are derived. We stress that our attack uncovers subtleties in modelling and is not an actual attack on the TLS protocol. This attack demonstrates why neither version of ACCE is suitable for analysing these types of channel establishment protocol. The original ACCE model is too strong (the attack rules TLS insecure) and the revised too weak (the attack is no longer captured). Our model sits neatly in the middle, giving the adversary the capabilities of this attack but not treating it as an attack against the security of the protocol.

One approach to circumvent this attack is to preclude the adversary from performing such a reveal. This is the approach taken in [12] which only considers that keys can be revealed once the session in which they are derived had accepted. We find this restriction unsatisfactory. If reveals are considered possible, then they should be able to target a key as soon as that key has been derived. In particular, revealing a key that has just been used to perform an encryption should be allowed. A more in-depth discussion of weaknesses present in the existent models for channel-establishment protocols is given in the full version of this paper [8].

Our Contribution

In this paper we present a new definitional framework which addresses the problems identified in previous approaches. In particular we present a security model which is particularly tailored to the case of key-exchange followed by the creation of a secure channel. Our new framework is conceptually simpler than previous models and can be further extended to capture one-sided key agreement followed by composition with a secure channel. Providing a general model rather than one tailored specifically to EMV is important. A general framework can be used to analyse any channel establishment protocol and sets a clear goal that all such protocols should achieve. As a result, it is not only much easier to perform future analyses of such protocols but also facilitates comparison of different protocols which have now been proved secure with respect to the same notion of security. Below we highlight some of our contributions and techniques.

MODELS FOR CHANNEL-ESTABLISHMENT PROTOCOLS. For entity authentication, we deal with the realistic case of one-sided authentication. This is demanded by the protocol that we analyze: the card is authenticated, while the terminal is not. The EMV system is designed to authenticate the card holder. Intuitively, the only goal, a fraudulous terminal can pursue when interacting with a card, is to extract authentication data from the card in order to impersonate it later. As impersonation attacks are taken care of by secure one-sided authenticated key agreement protocols already, one-sided authentication is considered a sufficient security goal in light of the costs that a certification structure for terminals would induce. We remark that existing models for channel-establishment concentrate on mutual authentication, and the case of one-sided authentication had been considered only sporadically in the key-exchange literature.

We also resolve the issue of bad interaction between partnering and reveal queries. Here, we take a different route than [13, 12]. Instead of weakening the adversary, we relax the partnering requirement: we only demand that partners agree on a common session identifier. This approach originates in the work of Bellare, Pointcheval, and Rogaway [3], is standard in key-exchange literature, and reflects an intuitively appealing level of security.

Finally we model and analyze unlinkability properties of the proposed protocol from EMVCo. One of the new design criteria of the protocol is a mild form of unlinkability; an adversary that sees a message flow between a terminal and a card should not be able to link this card's current transaction with a previous transaction from the same card. The new protocol aims to ensure this by using the channel to secure *all* traffic coming from the card. Thus any card identifying information (most importantly the certificate) will never be sent to the terminal in the clear. However the proposed protocol also uses a performance optimization in that the card uses a small ephemeral private key. We establish that using a small ephemeral key in this way should be avoided.

PROTOCOL ANALYSIS & EMV RECOMMENDATIONS. The EMV channel establishment protocol consists of a key exchange phase and an application phase. The key exchange phase is an ECC-based Diffie-Hellman-like protocol with one-sided authentication. We analyze the EMV channel establishment protocol and identify the assumptions under which it can be proved secure with respect to the notion that we put forth. We end this introduction by pointing out a number of recommendations related to the EMV protocol which have been passed to the designers as a result of our analysis:

1. The resulting Diffie–Hellman key should be hashed down to obtain the used symmetric keys. The proposal in [16] says to use a hash function or the x-coordinate of the elliptic curve point as the key derivation function. The x-coordinate of an elliptic curve point is a high-entropy value only. That is, it is not a random string, as required by primitives such as the ciphers that are deployed in the secure channel. We thus strongly recommend to extract the entropy via hashing and not use the x-coordinate directly.

2. The resulting keys should be used in a uni-directional manner; thus two keys need to be obtained from the hashing process. This avoids a large number of potential replay attacks on the application layer. If this was not done, the application layer would need to be implemented extremely carefully to thwart these attacks. Having two keys, one for each direction, makes the design of a secure application layer less vulnerable.

3. The card ephemeral key a should *not* be selected from the set $\{0,1\}^{32}$. We suggest that it is not restricted in size and instead chosen at random from $\mathbb{F}_q$. If the value a is selected from the set $\{0,1\}^{32}$, then this has a significant effect on security. Not only does it reduce the scheme's ability to achieve unlinkablity. But in addition, when a is selected from a small set an adversary could establish two sessions of one card which share the same key with a single terminal.

SCOPE The EMV standard has a huge scope, and not all of the next generation sub-protocols are currently fully defined. The goal of this paper is to analyse the proposed key exchange protocol according to the stipulated security goals while assuming as little as possible about the other protocols. For the secure channel, we have implicitly assumed, as this is not stated in [16], that the resulting secure channel should be secure against adversaries both deleting messages and playing messages out of order; since this is the usual definition of a secure channel. We did not assume any further security guarantees of the channel or other protocols; these need to be defined and proven separately from this paper.

2. SCHEME

Our presentation follows that in [16], augmented with information obtained from public discussions with the authors of the protocol at several meetings. The basic underlying idea of the protocol is to use a Diffie–Hellman key exchange in which one side (the card) has a static public key. In order to achieve unlinkability the certificate of this public key is not passed in the clear; instead, the card's static Diffie–Hellman key share is randomized by an additional ephemeral secret. The resulting Diffie–Hellman key is then hashed using a cryptographic hash function; which we will model as a random oracle.

The protocol uses a Diffie–Hellman group defined over an elliptic curve $G = E(\mathbb{F}_p)$ having group order a prime q and also uses a base point $P \in G$. The prime q is a function of an implicit security parameter k, but in practice the group is fixed and so all our results are given in the concrete security setting.

After the protocol has established secret keys, it uses them in a secure channel protocol ($\mathsf{SendCh}, \mathsf{ReceiveCh}$). On input an application message m and state st_e, SendCh returns a channel message $\mathfrak{ch}$. On input a channel message $\mathfrak{ch}$ and state st_d, $\mathsf{ReceiveCh}$ returns an application message m. The secure channel protocol is based on a stateful authenticated-encryption (AE) scheme $\mathsf{AE} = \{\mathsf{enc}, \mathsf{dec}\}$. We assume that all plaintext headers used by the secure channel are unauthenticated, implying that no header is sent in clear as part of the AE scheme. The states st_e and st_d here model the fact that in practice sequence numbers are used to ensure that messages are delivered in order, thus the operations are stateful. We assume that the underlying AE scheme satisfies the properties of indistinguishability under chosen-ciphertext attack (IND-sfCCA) and integrity of plaintexts (INT-sfPTXT) for such stateful schemes, assuming the key-agreement scheme has generated a randomly distributed key. See Appendix A for formal definitions of these security notions.

We also assume that there is a public-key signature algorithm used to define certificates. In particular each card C has a long term public/private key pair (Q_C, d), where $d \in \mathbb{F}_q$ and $Q_C = dP \in G$. A certificate is a signature/message pair $\mathsf{cert}_C = (\mathsf{sig}_{\mathsf{sk}}(Q_C), Q_C)$ provided by an issuing authority with a key pair $(\mathsf{pk}, \mathsf{sk})$ for some (unspecified) public-key signature algorithm $(\mathsf{sig}, \mathsf{ver})$. All that we require of the signature algorithm is that it be existentially unforgeable under a chosen-message attack (EUF-CMA). To save space we reserve a precise definition for this standard notion to the full version of our paper [8].

We are now in a position to define the EMV key establishment and secure channel protocol in Figure 1. As well as the components above, the protocol makes use of a hash function H that takes elements in the group G and maps them onto a pair of keys for the AE scheme. The keys are used to secure the communication in both directions; we propose the use of two keys so that replay attacks are prevented at the level of the protocol as opposed to needing to be dealt with at the application layer.

As mentioned in the introduction the proposal by EMVCo [16] suggest that the ephemeral secret[1] a should be small, (less than 2^{32}). They state that this choice is "set to be fit for purpose for blinding a one-off session key". First note that the unlinkability property may be hard to achieve when a is small: Given two public keys Q_1 and Q_2 and the first message of a session aQ_i, there is an obvious square-root attack which determines Q_i when a is small, i.e. an attack which runs in time roughly 2^{16} operations.

More seriously, the security of entity authentication would also be at risk. An adversary can perform an attack which allows two sessions of a card to share the same key with a single terminal.

[1] In the EMV draft a is denoted r.

Card (C)		Terminal (T)
$a \xleftarrow{r} \mathbb{F}_q$	$\xrightarrow{A=aQ_C}$	
	$\xleftarrow{E=eP}$	$e \xleftarrow{r} \mathbb{F}_q$
$(\kappa_e^C, \kappa_d^C) = \mathsf{H}(daE)$		$(\kappa_d^T, \kappa_e^T) = \mathsf{H}(eA)$
$(\mathfrak{ch}, st_e^C) = \mathsf{SendCh}_{\kappa_e^C}(\mathrm{cert}_C \| a \| Q_C; st_e^C)$	$\xrightarrow{\mathfrak{ch}}$	$(\mathrm{cert}_C \| a \| Q_C, st_d^T) = \mathsf{ReceiveCh}_{\kappa_d^T}(\mathfrak{ch}; st_d^T)$
		Check $\mathsf{ver}_{\mathsf{pk}}(\mathrm{cert}_C, Q_C) \stackrel{?}{=}$ true
		Check $aQ_C \stackrel{?}{=} A$
$(\mathfrak{ch}_1, st_e^C) = \mathsf{SendCh}_{\kappa_e^C}(m_1; st_e^C)$	$\xrightarrow{\mathfrak{ch}_1}$	$(m_1, st_d^T) = \mathsf{ReceiveCh}_{\kappa_d^T}(\mathfrak{ch}_1; st_d^T)$
...		...
$(m_2, st_d^C) = \mathsf{ReceiveCh}_{\kappa_d^C}(\mathfrak{ch}_2; st_d^C)$	$\xleftarrow{\mathfrak{ch}_2}$	$(\mathfrak{ch}_2, st_e^T) = \mathsf{SendCh}_{\kappa_e^T}(m_2; st_e^T)$.

Figure 1: Combined Authenticated Key Agreement Scheme and Secure Channel Protocol. Note that $\kappa_e^C = \kappa_d^T$ and $\kappa_d^C = \kappa_e^T$.

Consider a card with public key $Q = dP$ and assume that the ephemeral blinding exponents a are small. In the first session the card chooses a_1 at random and sends a_1Q. The terminal will respond by choosing e at random and returning $E = eP$. Their established key for this session will then be $\kappa = a_1deP$. Next the card wants to establish a second session. It chooses at random a new ephemeral blind a_2 and sends a_2Q. When the ephemeral blinds (a_1 and a_2) are small then an adversary can easily find $a' = a_1/a_2$. The adversary can then calculate $a'E$ and return this to the card. This second card session now establishes the key $a_2d(a'E) = a_2d(a_1/a_2)eP = a_1deP = \kappa$; the same key as the first session. As a result of this (depending on the setting) the adversary may be able to perform a replay attack on the second card session.

There are other approaches which could prevent the latter attack (in cases where unlinkability is not an issue) but we believe increasing the size of a to be the simplest and to offer the least chance of implementation errors being introduced. In the rest of the paper we assume that a is chosen from $\mathbb{F}_q$ and therefore our security results apply only to this case.

3. NEW SECURITY MODELS

In this section we present our security models for the secure channel establishment and unlinkability. Most of the section is however devoted to the more complex case of modeling secure channel establishment.

PRELIMINARIES. Before giving our new definition we present some preliminary definitions. Let I be the set of participants. Each participant has a distinct ID i, long-term public key pk_i and corresponding secret key sk_i. The protocol description is defined by two efficiently computable stateful (sub)-protocols $P = \{\Pi, \mathcal{G}\}$. The protocol Π defines how honest parties behave and $\mathcal{G}$ is a public/private key pair generation algorithm. Each execution of this algorithm maintains the following state information:

- $st_k \in \{0,1\}^*$ is some state for the key exchange.
- $\delta \in \{\texttt{derived}, \texttt{accept}, \texttt{reject}, \bot\}$ is current state of the key exchange (initialised to $\bot$).
- $\rho \in \{\texttt{initiator}, \texttt{responder}\}$ is the role of the participant.
- sid a session identifier.
- pid a partner identifier
- $\kappa = (\kappa_e^\rho, \kappa_d^\rho) \in (\{0,1\}^* \cup \{\bot\})^2$. This is the agreed pair of keys. The order of these keys depends on the role $\rho \in \{\texttt{initiator}, \texttt{responder}\}$ and $\kappa = (\bot, \bot)$ unless $\delta = \texttt{derived}$.

A CLASS OF PROTOCOLS. In this paper we are concerned with the large class of protocols obtained by combining key-exchange with channel protocols, and where the two components cannot be easily disentangled. Existing models are either too specific [13] or do not consider the case of overlap between the components [7].

The syntax that we provide for such protocols naturally implies a classification of the different types of messages that may occur in an execution. The classification is a crucial ingredient of our security definitions. Specifically, we identify three different execution "modes" of protocols: establishing a key, sending, respectively receiving messages from the established channel. Formally, we define the honest operation of a participant by a triple $\Pi = (\mathsf{KeyExch}, \mathsf{SendCh}, \mathsf{ReceiveCh})$.

Some of the messages sent during the key-exchange may travel over the channel so, strictly speaking, KeyExch may make use of the latter algorithms. To facilitate the description of the resulting complex interaction we define the algorithm EstChannel which, essentially, is in charge of establishing the channel. This algorithm may make calls to the algorithms defining Π. As an example, for EMV, one can view EstChannel as everything above the line drawn in Figure 1, see Figure 4 in Section 4 for full details. At any point during its execution protocol Π takes as input a message m and a message type, $\texttt{type} \in \{\texttt{ap}, \texttt{ch}\}$ (indicating whether the message was received from the user's application or the channel, respectively), runs the appropriate algorithm, and returns the output of that algorithm.

We now detail the execution of Π which is summarised in Figure 2. Prior to the channel being established (i.e. prior to $\delta = \texttt{accept}$) whenever the input message m has type $\texttt{ch}$ then EstChannel will be called. This algorithm will make calls to KeyExch in order to establish the keys of the secure channel. The algorithm KeyExch takes as input a message m and a state st_k, and outputs a new message m' and updated state st_k (shared with EstChannel). The state st_k is used to manage the internal state of KeyExch and will contain the session identifier sid, partner identifier pid, the state of keys δ, the established keys κ_e, κ_d, the states of the secure channel st_e, st_d, and any additional information α. Before any keys have been derived ($\delta = \perp$), EstChannel forwards messages directly to KeyExch. Once keys have been derived ($\delta = \texttt{derived}$) then we enter the key confirmation stage. At this point EstChannel initialises the states st_e, st_d of the secure channel and makes appropriate[2] calls to SendCh and ReceiveCh before and after calling KeyExch. Finally, once KeyExch outputs $\delta = \texttt{accept}$ the secure channel has been successfully established.

After the channel has been established whenever the input message type is ch then ReceiveCh will be called. This models messages that are received from the channel (for decryption). It takes as input a message m and state st_d and outputs a message m' for output to the user's application.

When the message type is ap then SendCh will be called. This models application messages that are input to be sent (encrypted) on the channel. It takes as input a message m and state st_e and outputs a message m' for output to the channel. Note that if keys have not yet been established ($\delta \neq \texttt{accept}$) then such a call to SendCh will output $\perp$.

```
Protocol Π(m, type):
if type = ch ∧ δ ≠ accept then
    (m'; st_k) ← EstChannel(m; st_k)
else if type = ch then
    (m'; st_d) ← ReceiveCh_{κ_d}(m; st_d)
else (type = ap)
    (m'; st_e) ← SendCh_{κ_e}(m; st_e)
return m'
```

Figure 2: Honest Protocol Execution

EXECUTION MODEL. We consider the standard execution model for key exchange protocols where an adversary $\mathcal{A}$, is assumed to control all communication between participating parties i.e. the adversary can intercept all messages sent and inject any message that he wishes. Let Π_i^s denote the oracle modelling participant $i \in I$ engaged in session s of the protocol described above. Each oracle Π_i^s runs the program Π and maintains the states of that program instance. The adversary can make the following queries:

- $\mathsf{NewSession}(i, \rho)$: Create a session for user i with role ρ.
- $\mathsf{Send}(\Pi_i^s, m, \texttt{type})$: Sends a message m to Π_i^s with type, type. As a result Π_i^s will run Π on input $(m, \texttt{type})$.
- $\mathsf{Reveal}(\Pi_i^s)$: reveals the current session key κ of Π_i^s.
- $\mathsf{Corrupt}(i)$: reveals the long-term private key of i.

PARTNERING AND FRESHNESS. In order to define security for key-exchange protocols it is necessary to define the notion of partnering. Two participants should only establish a shared key if they have been successfully partnered. There are many approaches to defining such a notion. We begin by discussing the concept of *matching conversations*, introduced by Bellare and Rogaway [4] in the context of authenticated key exchange. A participant's conversation can be defined as a transcript of all the messages it receives and sends. As the name suggest, matching conversations defines two participants to be partnered if their transcripts *match*. It is this approach which is followed by Jager et al. [13] in their definition of ACCE. Unfortunately, when protocols use the session key to encrypt messages as part of a key-confirmation step, attacks may be possible which violate the requirements of matching conversations[3]. For further details see the full version of this paper [8]. Notice however that while such attacks violate the matching conversation property, they should perhaps not be considered attacks. The plaintext that was sent by one party still reached its intended recipient. We interpret this attack as a limitation of the model: it may rule out as insecure protocols with no obvious weaknesses.

Our formulation is routed in the definition of partnering based on session identifiers by Bellare et al. [3]. Informally, Bellare et al. declared two oracles partnered if they have already derived keys and i) they both share the same session identifier *sid*, ii) they derived the same key κ, and iii) one oracle is an initiator and the other a responder. Moreover, to ensure each oracle accepted with only a single partner we also ask that iv) there should exist no other oracle which has derived keys and holds the same session identifier. Bellare et al. make a distinction between an oracle accepting and terminating. Accepting defines the event that the session keys have been established but the key confirmation steps are still to follow. An oracle terminates after the key confirmation steps have completed. Once keys are accepted they may be revealed but the key-exchange protocol has yet to terminate. We argue that a key is not "accepted" until after the key confirmation step since this step may fail. As a result, we use the terms derived and accepted, where derived corresponds to Bellare et al.'s accepted and our accepted corresponds to their terminated.

The specific formulation we give is similar but a stronger notion than that of Rogaway and Stegers [20]. First we define a notion of partnering which informally states that two oracles which have derived keys are *partners* if they share the same session identifier. The definition makes use of the following predicate on two oracles Π_i^s and Π_j^t holding $(\kappa_i^s, sid_i^s, pid_i^s)$ and $(\kappa_j^t, sid_j^t, pid_j^t)$, respectively:

$$\mathsf{P}(\Pi_i^s, \Pi_j^t) = \begin{cases} \mathsf{true} & \text{if } sid_i^s = sid_j^t \ \wedge \ \delta_i^s, \delta_j^t \in \{\texttt{derived}, \texttt{accept}\} \\ \mathsf{false} & \text{otherwise} \end{cases}$$

Definition 1. (Partner) Two oracles Π_i^s and Π_j^t are said to be partnered if $\mathsf{P}(\Pi_i^s, \Pi_j^t) = \mathsf{true}$.

We follow this with three further definitions related to partnering which will be necessary when we give our main security definitions later. It shall be required that partnerings are valid, confirmed and unique. In short these three requirements ensure that any oracle that accepts, has a partner and that this partner is unique. More specifically, *Valid* means that partners will have corresponding partner identifiers (i.e. they both believe they are talking with each other), have different roles and share the same key. *Confirmed* partners ensures that for each oracle that accepts there exists *at least* one partner and for *unique* partners that there exists *at most* one.

Definition 2. (Valid Partners) A protocol $P = \{\Pi, \mathcal{G}\}$ ensures *valid partners* if the bad event notval does not occur, where notval is defined as follows:

$$\exists\, \Pi_i^s, \Pi_j^t \text{ such that: } \left(\mathsf{P}(\Pi_i^s, \Pi_j^t) = \mathsf{true}\right) \wedge \left(pid_i^s \neq j \ \vee \ pid_j^t \neq i \ \vee \ \rho_i^s = \rho_j^t \ \vee \ \kappa_i^s \neq \kappa_j^t\right).$$

Definition 3. (Confirmed Partners) A protocol $P = \{\Pi, \mathcal{G}\}$ ensures *confirmed partners* if the bad event notconf does not occur,

[2]Such calls will be dependent on the specific protocol construction.

[3]The adversary reveals the key and then uses this to re-encrypt the confirmation message with new randomness. The two transcripts now differ for this message.

where notconf is defined as follows:

$$\exists\, \Pi_i^s \text{ such that: } \delta_i^s = \texttt{accept}$$
$$\wedge\ i, pid_i^s \text{ not corrupt } \wedge \left(\mathsf{P}(\Pi_i^s, \Pi_j^t) = \mathsf{false}\ :\ \forall \Pi_j^t\right).$$

Definition 4. (Unique Partners) A protocol $P = \{\Pi, \mathcal{G}\}$ ensures *unique partners* if the bad event notuni does not occur, where notuni is defined as follows:

$$\exists \Pi_i^s, \Pi_j^t, \Pi_k^r \text{ such that: } (j,t) \neq (k,r)$$
$$\wedge\ \mathsf{P}(\Pi_i^s, \Pi_j^t) = \mathsf{true}\ \wedge\ \mathsf{P}(\Pi_i^s, \Pi_k^r) = \mathsf{true}.$$

A concept that plays a central role in defining security in two-party protocols is that of "freshness". Intuitively, an oracle is fresh if it has accepted and an adversary had not "tampered" with it in any way, i.e. the adversary has not revealed or corrupted the oracle or its partner. This can be viewed as being related to the bad event notconf with the extra requirement that the oracle has not been revealed. A notion of freshness is necessary when defining security since the security guarantees are only for such oracles. The next definition formalises the concept. As with partnering we first introduced a predicate, $\mathsf{F}(\Pi_i^s) = \mathsf{true}$, if and only if:

1. $\delta_i^s = \texttt{accept}$.
2. Oracle Π_i^s has not been revealed and user i is not corrupted.
3. No partner oracle of Π_i^s has been revealed and no parent of such a oracle has been corrupted.

Definition 5. (Fresh) An oracle Π_i^s is **fresh** if $\mathsf{F}(\Pi_i^s) = \mathsf{true}$.

3.1 Security Definitions: Two-Sided Authentication Setting

We formulate three levels of security: entity authentication, message authentication and message privacy. The later definitions rely on entity authentication and we start by defining that definition.

ENTITY AUTHENTICATION. We consider that an adversary violates entity authentication if he can get a session to accept even if there is no unique session of its intended partner that has derived the same key. More formally, we wish to verify that none of the bad events notval, notconf, notuni occurs (cf. Definitions 2, 3, 4).

First consider the entity authentication experiment entauth that generates public/private key pairs for each user $i \in I$ (by running $\mathcal{G}$) and returns the public keys to $\mathcal{A}_{\mathsf{ent}}$. The experiment then allows the adversary $\mathcal{A}_{\mathsf{ent}}$ to make the queries $\mathsf{NewSession}(i, \rho)$, $\mathsf{Reveal}(\Pi_i^s)$, $\mathsf{Corrupt}(i)$ as well as $\mathsf{Send}(\Pi_i^s, m, \texttt{type})$ with operations $\texttt{type} \in \{\texttt{ap}, \texttt{ch}\}$. We say that an adversary violates entity authentication (and hence "wins" this experiment) if one of the bad events (notval, notconf, notuni) occurs. The adversary's advantage is defined to be:

$$\mathbf{Adv}_{\Pi}^{\mathsf{entauth}}(\mathcal{A}_{\mathsf{ent}}) = \Pr[\mathsf{notval} \vee \mathsf{notconf} \vee \mathsf{notuni}].$$

Definition 6. (Entity Authentication (EA)) Protocol $P = \{\Pi, \mathcal{G}\}$ is a (t, ϵ_{EA})-**secure EA protocol** if for all adversaries $\mathcal{A}_{\mathsf{ent}}$ running in time at most t, $\mathbf{Adv}_{\Pi}^{\mathsf{entauth}}(\mathcal{A}_{\mathsf{ent}}) \leq \epsilon_{EA}$.

To define the security experiments for message authentication and privacy we shall make use of the following notation for lists maintained for each Π_i^s as follows:

- Application messages sent Ap-S_i^s, i.e. the list of all messages m *input* to $\mathsf{Send}(\Pi_i^s, m, \texttt{ap})$.
- Channel messages sent Ch-S_i^s, i.e. the list of all *outputs* from $\mathsf{Send}(\Pi_i^s, m, \texttt{ap})$.
- Channel messages received Ch-R_i^s, i.e. the list of all messages m *input* to $\mathsf{Send}(\Pi_i^s, m, \texttt{ch})$.
- Application messages received Ap-R_i^s, i.e. the list of all *outputs* from $\mathsf{Send}(\Pi_i^s, m, \texttt{ch})$.

As described at the beginning of this section during the execution of a protocol an oracle can receive two types of input, an application message (user input) or a channel message (received from the wire). Once a channel is established whenever an application message is input to Send, the protocol Π is run and a channel message will be output and sent on the channel. Similarly whenever a channel message is input to Send, the protocol Π is run and an application message will be output to the user. The above lists help us keep track of these messages and facilitate checks necessary in the following security models.

MESSAGE AUTHENTICATION. We now turn our attention to message authentication. Here we wish to ensure the integrity and authenticity of all messages sent over the channel. For any two partner oracles Π_i^s and Π_j^t, the oracle Π_i^s should only *successfully* receive messages which were output by Π_j^t and vice versa. In the definition which follows we formalise the intuition above by requiring that for any fresh oracle Π_i^s with unique partner Π_j^t, the following holds $\mathsf{Prefix}(\text{Ap-R}_i^s, \text{Ap-S}_j^t) = \mathsf{true}$, where $\mathsf{Prefix}(X, Y)$ is the function which outputs true if X is a prefix of Y (provided not empty) and false otherwise. If this does not hold then the adversary was successfully fooled Π_i^s into receiving an application message which was not output by the partnered oracle Π_j^t.

Consider the authentication experiment auth that generates public/private key pairs for each user $i \in I$ (by running $\mathcal{G}$) and returns the public keys to $\mathcal{A}$. The adversary is permitted to make the queries $\mathsf{NewSession}(i, \rho)$, $\mathsf{Reveal}(\Pi_i^s)$, $\mathsf{Corrupt}(i)$ as well as $\mathsf{Send}(\Pi_i^s, m, \texttt{type})$ with message $\texttt{type} \in \{\texttt{ap}, \texttt{ch}\}$. On query $\mathsf{Send}(\Pi_i^s, m, \texttt{type})$, the game behaves as in Figure 3(a).

For the session matching, we consider the notion of partnering as specified in Definition 1. The notion of freshness that we use in the following definition is according to Definition 5.

We define the following game $\mathbf{Exec}_{\Pi}^{\mathsf{auth}}(\mathcal{A})$ between an adversary $\mathcal{A}$ and challenger $\mathcal{C}$:

1. The challenger $\mathcal{C}$ generates public/private key pairs for each user $i \in I$ (by running $\mathcal{G}$) and returns the public keys to $\mathcal{A}$.[4]
2. $\mathcal{A}$ is allowed to make as many NewSession, Reveal, Corrupt, Send queries as it likes.
3. The adversary stops with no output.

We say that an adversary $\mathcal{A}$ wins the game if there exists Π_i^s with unique partner Π_j^t such that $\mathsf{F}(\Pi_i^s) = \mathsf{true}$ and the list Ap-R_i^s is not a prefix of Ap-S_j^t.

We define the adversary's advantage as:

$$\mathbf{Adv}_{\Pi}^{\mathsf{auth}}(\mathcal{A}) = \Pr[\exists \Pi_i^s, \Pi_j^t : \mathsf{F}(\Pi_i^s) = \mathsf{true} \wedge \mathsf{P}(\Pi_i^s, \Pi_j^t) = \mathsf{true}$$
$$\wedge\ \mathsf{Prefix}(\text{Ap-R}_i^s, \text{Ap-S}_j^t) = \mathsf{false}].$$

Definition 7. (Message Authentication (MA)) A protocol $P = \{\Pi, \mathcal{G}\}$ is a (t, ϵ_{MA})-**secure MA protocol** if for all adversaries $\mathcal{A}_{\mathsf{auth}}$ running in time at most t, $\mathbf{Adv}_{\Pi}^{\mathsf{auth}}(\mathcal{A}_{\mathsf{auth}}) \leq \epsilon_{MA}$.

MESSAGE PRIVACY. Next we consider the notion of message privacy. Our definition follows the standard indistinguishability

[4]Note that in the scheme considered in this paper, public keys of cards are not actually made public to $\mathcal{A}$ but are sent in encrypted form during the confirmation step.

$\mathsf{Send}(\Pi_i^s, m, \mathtt{type})$:
$m' \leftarrow \Pi_i^s(m, \mathtt{type})$
if $\delta = \mathtt{accept}$ and $\mathtt{type} = \mathtt{ap}$ **then**
  $\text{Ap-S}_i^s \leftarrow \text{Ap-S}_i^s \| m$
else if $\delta = \mathtt{accept}$ and $\mathtt{type} = \mathtt{ch}$ **then**
  if $m' \neq \perp$ **then** $\text{Ap-R}_i^s \leftarrow \text{Ap-R}_i^s \| m'$
return m'

(a) Send query for auth game.

$\mathsf{SendLR}(\Pi_i^s, m_0, m_1, \mathtt{type})$
if $\delta = \mathtt{accept}$ and $\mathtt{type} = \mathtt{ap}$ **then**
  $m' \leftarrow \Pi_i^s(m_{b_i^s}, \mathtt{ap})$
  $\text{Ch-S}_i^s \leftarrow \text{Ch-S}_i^s \| m'$
else if $m_0 \neq m_1$ **then** $m' := \perp$
else
  $m' \leftarrow \Pi_i^s(m_0, \mathtt{type})$
  if $\delta = \mathtt{accept}$ and $\mathtt{type} = \mathtt{ch}$ **then**
    if $m' \neq \perp$ and Π_i^s has a partner Π_j^t **then**
      $\text{Ch-R}_i^s \leftarrow \text{Ch-R}_i^s \| m_0$
      if $\mathsf{Prefix}(\text{Ch-R}_i^s, \text{Ch-S}_j^t) = \mathsf{true}$ **then** $m' := \emptyset$
return m'

(b) SendLR query for priv game.

Figure 3: The Send (resp. SendLR) query for the auth (resp. priv) games

paradigm. The adversary should not be able to determine which set of message $\{m_{01}, m_{02}, m_{03}, ...\}$ and $\{m_{11}, m_{12}, m_{13}, ...\}$ has been transmitted on the secure channel.

The message privacy experiment priv initializes the states as in the authentication experiment auth, except that each session now also holds a random secret bit b_i^s. As before, the adversary can make the queries $\mathsf{NewSession}(i, \rho)$, $\mathsf{Reveal}(\Pi_i^s)$, $\mathsf{Corrupt}(i)$. In addition, we introduce a left-right version of $\mathsf{Send}(\Pi_i^s, m, \mathtt{type})$ which we use to model message privacy. Specifically, the query $\mathsf{SendLR}(\Pi_i^s, m_0, m_1, \mathtt{type})$ takes as input two messages and returns $\mathsf{Send}(\Pi_i^s, m_{b_i^s}, \mathtt{type})$. When $\mathtt{type} \neq \mathtt{ap}$ we require that these two message are equal,

$$\mathsf{SendLR}(\Pi_i^s, m, m, \mathtt{type}) = \mathsf{Send}(\Pi_i^s, m, \mathtt{type}).$$

As before, two sessions are considered partners by Definition 1. On the $\mathsf{SendLR}(\Pi_i^s, m_0, m_1, \mathtt{type})$ query, the game behaves as in Figure 3(b). We note that once the channel is establish, whenever $\mathsf{SendLR}(\Pi_i^s, m, m, \mathtt{ch})$ is called (i.e. the input is a channel message), we allow the protocol to run as normal but check the lists CR_i^s and CS_j^t. If the message m was a channel output from Π_i^s's partner Π_j^t then SendLR will not return anything. This allows the adversary to progress the state of an oracle but prevents them from trivially winning the game. The formulation is closely related to IND-sfCCA which we give in Appendix refapp:defn.

We define the following game $\mathbf{Exec}_\Pi^{\mathsf{priv}}(\mathcal{A})$ between an adversary $\mathcal{A}$ and challenger $\mathcal{C}$:

1. The challenger $\mathcal{C}$, generates public/private key pairs for each user $i \in I$ (by running $\mathcal{G}$) and returns the public keys to $\mathcal{A}$.[5]
2. $\mathcal{A}$ is allowed to make as many NewSession, Reveal, Corrupt, SendLR queries as it likes.
3. Finally $\mathcal{A}$ outputs a tuple (i, s, b').

We say the adversary $\mathcal{A}$ wins if its output $b' = b_i^s$ and $\mathsf{F}(\Pi_i^s) = \mathsf{true}$ (and has a unique partner) and the output of $\mathbf{Exec}_\Pi^{\mathsf{priv}}(\mathcal{A})$ is set to 1. Otherwise the output is 0. Formally we define the advantage of $\mathcal{A}$ as

$$\mathbf{Adv}_\Pi^{\mathsf{priv}}(\mathcal{A}) = |\Pr[\mathbf{Exec}_\Pi^{\mathsf{priv}}(\mathcal{A}) = 1] - 1/2|.$$

Definition 8. (Message Privacy (MP)) A protocol $P = \{\Pi, \mathcal{G}\}$ is a (t, ϵ_{MP})**-secure MP protocol** if for all adversaries $\mathcal{A}_{\mathsf{priv}}$ running in time at most t, $\mathbf{Adv}_\Pi^{\mathsf{priv}}(\mathcal{A}_{\mathsf{priv}}) \leq \epsilon_{MP}$.

We call a channel establishment protocol secure if it satisfies all of the three notions above. We call the resulting notion EAMAP for obvious reasons.

Definition 9. (EAMAP) Protocol $P = \{\Pi, \mathcal{G}\}$ is a (t, ϵ)**-secure EAMAP protocol** if it is a (t, ϵ)-secure EA protocol, a (t, ϵ)-secure MA protocol and a (t, ϵ)-secure MP protocol.

Remark 1. Our definitions are with respect to the specific type of protocol construction defined in Figure 2. We note however, that our notions can be extended to more general classes of protocols by simply placing fewer restrictions on the Send queries.

Remark 2. Our mechanism of defining message authentication by requiring that the list of messages received by a party is a prefix of the list of the messages sent by its partner is quite flexible. By appropriately modifying this requirement one can also capture more relaxed notions e.g. where packet dropping or reordering is allowed. Furthermore, we expect that with appropriate restrictions this mechanism can also be adapted to deal with fragmentation. This is a common feature of many secure/authenticated channels in practice and has been formally studied by Boldyreva et al. [6], but is not relevant for EMV.

3.2 Security Definitions: One-Sided Authentication Setting

The above security definitions enforce mutual authentication, yet in many scenarios of practical concern only one party needs to be authenticated. For example, the protocol we consider requires authentication of the credit card but does not authenticate the communicating terminal. To model this situation we split our set of participants I in two. Let C be the set of authenticated participants (the cards) and let T by the set of unauthenticated participants (the terminals), where unauthenticated participants do not hold a long-term private/public key pair. This formalisation is the same as that of registered and unregistered users in [17]. We say authenticated participants are always initiators and unauthenticated are always responders. As a result of this change we must alter our previous security definitions for entity authentication, message authentication, message privacy and their combination (EAMAP) to consider a one-sided protocol.

ONE-SIDED ENTITY AUTHENTICATION. In the one-sided setting a terminal $j \in T$ wishes to authenticate a card $i \in C$ and establish a key (additionally a secure channel) with this card. Since all $j \in T$ have no long-term secret then it would always be possible for an adversary to impersonate an unauthenticated participant and establish a session with a real card. We need only aim to ensure that a genuine card session is authenticated to an unauthenticated terminal.

We first describe informally the changes we must make to the original two-sided definitions. Recall the definition of partnering (cf. Definition 1 and the associated Definitions 2, 3 and 4). We are now only concerned with the case where a terminal is partnered correctly, i.e. for every terminal that accepts there exists a card session and this card session is unique. As a result this means we must

[5]Note that in the scheme considered in this paper, public keys of cards are not actually made public to $\mathcal{A}$ but are sent in encrypted form during the confirmation step.

give new one-sided versions of the definitions for valid partners and confirmed partners. These new definitions now specifically focus on the terminal, ensuring that it believes it is talking to the correct card and it is a responder (in the case of valid), and its partner is not corrupt (in the case of confirmed). Note that we do not adjust the uniqueness definition since we still wish to ensure that both a single card session cannot be partnered with two terminal sessions and a single terminal session cannot be partnered with two card sessions.

Definition 10. (One-Sided Valid Partners) Protocol $P = \{\Pi, \mathcal{G}\}$ ensures *valid partners* if the bad event os-notval does not occur, where os-notval is defined as follows:

$$\exists\, \Pi_i^s, \Pi_j^t \text{ such that: } i \in T \ \wedge\ j \in C \ \wedge \left(\mathsf{P}(\Pi_i^s, \Pi_j^t) = \mathsf{true}\right) \wedge \left(pid_i^s \neq j \ \vee\ \rho_i^s \neq \texttt{responder} = \rho_j^t \ \vee\ \kappa_i^s \neq \kappa_j^t\right).$$

Definition 11. (One-Sided Confirmed Partners) Protocol $P = \{\Pi, \mathcal{G}\}$ ensures *one-sided confirmed partners* if os-notconf does not occur, where os-notconf is defined as follows:

$$\exists\, \Pi_i^s \text{ such that: } i \in T \ \wedge\ \delta_i^s = \texttt{accept} \wedge\ pid_i^s \text{ not corrupt} \wedge \left(\mathsf{P}(\Pi_i^s, \Pi_j^t) = \mathsf{false}\ :\ \forall \Pi_j^t\right).$$

We consider an adversary that violates one-sided entity authentication if he can get a terminal session to accept if there is no unique card session that has derived the same key. More formally, we define the os-entauth experiment in a similar fashion to before but now say that an adversary violates one-sided entity authentication (and hence "wins" this experiment) if one of the bad events (os-notval, os-notconf, notuni) occurs. The adversary's advantage is defined to be:

$$\mathbf{Adv}_{\Pi}^{\text{os-entauth}}(\mathcal{A}_{\text{ent}}) = \Pr[\text{os-notval} \vee \text{os-notconf} \vee \text{notuni}].$$

Definition 12. (One-Sided EA (OS-EA)) A protocol $P = \{\Pi, \mathcal{G}\}$ is a (t, ϵ_{EA})**-secure OS-EA protocol** if for all adversaries $\mathcal{A}_{\text{ent}}$ running in time at most t, $\mathbf{Adv}_{\Pi}^{\text{os-entauth}}(\mathcal{A}_{\text{ent}}) \leq \epsilon_{EA}$.

ONE-SIDED MESSAGE AUTHENTICATION AND PRIVACY. In order to adapt the definitions of message authenticity and privacy we must consider a one-sided version of freshness. The reason behind this again being that we wish to discount the trivial attack when the adversary impersonates an unauthenticated terminal $j \in T$. A card oracle is defined to be OS-fresh if it has accepted, has not been revealed or corrupted and it is partnered with a genuine terminal oracle. A terminal oracle is defined to be OS-fresh if it has accepted, has not been revealed and it is partnered with a card oracle that has not been revealed or corrupted. We formalise one-sided freshness as follows. As before we define a predicate, $\mathsf{OSF}(\Pi_i^s) = \mathsf{true}$, if and only if:

1. $\delta_i^s = \texttt{accept}$.
2. Oracle Π_i^s has not been revealed.
3. If $i \in C$ then it is uncorrupted and has a partner Π_j^t, where $j \in T$.
4. If $i \in T$ then Π_i^s has a partner Π_j^t, where $j \in C$.
5. No oracle Π_j^t, such that $\mathsf{P}(\Pi_i^s, \Pi_j^t) = \mathsf{true}$, has been revealed and if $j \in C$ then it is uncorrupted.

Definition 13. (One-Sided Fresh) An oracle Π_i^s, is **OS-fresh** if $\mathsf{OSF}(\Pi_i^s) = \mathsf{true}$.

Using the above we can alter our previous experiments of auth and priv by requiring that the winning oracle is OS-fresh. We therefore obtain one-sided versions os-auth and os-priv, respectively.

Definition 14. (OS-MA/OS-MP) A protocol $P = \{\Pi, \mathcal{G}\}$ is a (t, ϵ)**-secure OS-MA protocol** (or OS-MP resp.) if for all adversaries $\mathcal{A}$ running in time at most t, $\mathbf{Adv}_{\Pi}^{\text{os-auth}}(\mathcal{A}) \leq \epsilon$ (or $\mathbf{Adv}_{\Pi}^{\text{os-priv}}(\mathcal{A}) \leq \epsilon$ resp.).

We call a channel establishment protocol with one-sided authentication secure if it satisfies all three of the notions above.

Definition 15. (OS-EAMAP) A protocol $P = \{\Pi, \mathcal{G}\}$ is a (t, ϵ)**-secure OS-EAMAP protocol** if it is a (t, ϵ)-secure OS-EA protocol, a (t, ϵ)-secure OS-MA protocol and a (t, ϵ)-secure OS-MP protocol.

3.3 Security Definitions: Unlinkability

A further property that the EMVCo protocol aims to achieve is unlinkability. This means that it should be hard for an adversary to determine when two particular sessions involve the same card. Goldberg et al. [10] define a related notion of anonymity and unlinkability. They aim to prove a scheme secure if an authenticated party remains anonymous to its unauthenticated partner and hence call this *internal anonymity*. Here we are concerned with eavesdroppers external to the execution and hence define a new notion for *external unlinkability*.

We define this security property in terms of a game between adversary $\mathcal{A}$ and challenger $\mathcal{C}$, $\mathbf{Exec}_{\Pi}^{\text{unlink}}(\mathcal{A})$. Informally, the adversary is able to interact with the card and terminal much as in the key agreement game. At some point the adversary halts the first part of his game, and outputs two card identities on which it wishes to be challenged. The challenger then picks one of these two identities and passes to the adversary new oracles (i.e. card/terminal session) with respect to the chosen identity. The adversary can then make additional queries, bar Reveal or Corrupt queries on the two test oracles. At the end of the experiment the adversary needs to output which identity the challenger selected. More formally the game is defined as follows:

1. The challenger $\mathcal{C}$, generates public/private key pairs for each user $i \in C$ (by running $\mathcal{G}$) and returns the public keys to $\mathcal{A}$[6].
2. $\mathcal{A}$ is allowed to make as many NewSession, Reveal, Corrupt, Send queries as it likes.
3. At some point $\mathcal{A}$ outputs two identities $i_0 \in C$ and $i_1 \in C$.
4. The challenger then chooses a bit $b \xleftarrow{r} \{0,1\}$ and creates new oracles $\mathcal{O}_C = \Pi_{i_b}^s$ and $\mathcal{O}_T = \Pi_{j}^t$, (for some $j \in T$), by calling NewSession.
5. $\mathcal{A}$ continues making queries NewSession, Reveal, Corrupt, Send. However, $\mathcal{A}$ is allowed to query oracles $\mathcal{O}_C$ and $\mathcal{O}_T$ only with the Send query.
6. Eventually $\mathcal{A}$ stops and outputs a bit b'.

We say the adversary $\mathcal{A}$ wins if its output $b' = b$ and $\mathsf{P}(\mathcal{O}_C, \mathcal{O}_T) = \mathsf{true}$. In this case the output of $\mathbf{Exec}_{\Pi}^{\text{unlink}}(\mathcal{A})$ is set to one, otherwise the output is zero. We define the advantage of $\mathcal{A}$ to be

$$\mathbf{Adv}_{\Pi}^{\text{unlink}}(\mathcal{A}) = |\Pr[\mathbf{Exec}_{\Pi}^{\text{unlink}}(\mathcal{A}) = 1] - 1/2|.$$

Definition 16. (Unlinkability) A protocol $(\Pi, \mathcal{G})$ is $(t, \epsilon_{\text{unlink}})$-unlinkable, if for all $\mathcal{A}$ running in time t, $\mathbf{Adv}_{\Pi}^{\text{unlink}}(\mathcal{A}) \leq \epsilon_{\text{unlink}}$.

[6] Note that in the scheme considered in this paper, public keys of cards are not actually made public to $\mathcal{A}$ but are sent in encrypted form during the confirmation step.

4. SECURITY ANALYSIS

In this section we state our main security results, and in particular clarify the assumptions under which the proposed EMV channel-establishment protocol is secure, namely the security of the signature scheme that is used to produce the certificates and, the Gap-DH and CDH assumptions in the group that underlies the scheme. We provide formal definitions of these assumptions later in this section.

Before stating our main security results we first give a formal description of the EMV protocol $P = \{\Pi, \mathcal{G}\}$. Here $\mathcal{G}$ is the key-generation algorithm of the underlying signature scheme. As described at the start of Section 3, we define Π in terms of a key-exchange protocol KeyExch and two algorithms which define the secure channel SendCh, ReceiveCh. In order to define channel establishment we utilise an additional algorithm EstChannel which makes calls to the underlying key exchange protocol KeyExch and secure channel algorithms SendCh, ReceiveCh. For simplicity we do not give a separate description of KeyExch but instead define EstChannel directly. We require three further algorithms which are used during the execution, loadkey, keyid, initial. An execution of a card oracle will involve a call to loadkey which will retrieve the public key Q, secret key d and certificate cert associated to an identity i. Recall that $Q = dP$ and cert $= (\mathsf{sig}_{\mathsf{sk}}(Q), Q)$. An execution of a terminal oracle will involve a call to keyid which will retrieve the identity j associated to a public key Q. The algorithm initial will initialise the states of the secure channel st_e, st_d.

In Figure 4 we define the execution of EstChannel for a session s of a party i with state $st_k = (\alpha, \delta, \rho, st_e, st_d, \kappa_e, \kappa_d, pid, sid)$ where each variable is initiated as $\perp$, the value α is used to store a and A for the card and the terminal respectively.

We now state our main security result.

THEOREM 1. *If the Gap-DH problem is hard, the CDH problem is hard,* AE = (enc, dec) *is an ind-sfcca secure and int-sfptxt secure AE scheme, and the signature scheme* (sig, ver) *used to produce card certificates is EUF-CMA, then the EMV protocol* $P = \{\Pi, \mathcal{G}\}$ *in Figures 1 and 4 is secure in the sense of OS-EAMAP. In particular we have*

- *If there exists an adversary $\mathcal{A}$ running in time at most t against the entity authentication property of OS-EAMAP security then there are adversaries $\mathcal{B}, \mathcal{C}, \mathcal{D}, \mathcal{E}$, such that*

$$\begin{aligned}\mathbf{Adv}_{\Pi}^{\text{os-entauth}}(\mathcal{A}) \leq\ & \mathbf{Adv}_{(\text{sig},\text{ver})}^{\text{eufcma}}(\mathcal{B}) \\ & + n_C \cdot (1 - 1/|h|) \cdot \mathbf{Adv}_{E(\mathbb{F}_p)}^{\text{Gap-DH}}(\mathcal{C}) \\ & + n_S \cdot n_C \cdot \mathbf{Adv}_{\text{AE}}^{\text{int-0}}(\mathcal{D}) \\ & + n_C^2 \cdot \mathbf{Adv}_{E(\mathbb{F}_p)}^{\text{CDH}}(\mathcal{E}),\end{aligned}$$

where $\mathcal{B}, \mathcal{C}, \mathcal{D}, \mathcal{E}$ each run in time $t + O(\mu)$ where μ is total number of bits queried.

- *If there exists an adversary $\mathcal{A}$ running in time at most t against the message authentication property of OS-EAMAP security then there are adversaries $\mathcal{B}$, $\mathcal{C}$ and $\mathcal{D}$, such that*

$$\begin{aligned}\mathbf{Adv}_{\Pi}^{\text{os-auth}}(\mathcal{A}) \leq\ & n_S \cdot (n_C + n_T) \cdot \mathbf{Adv}_{\text{AE}}^{\text{intsfptxt}}(\mathcal{D}) \\ & + n_C \cdot (1 - 1/|h|) \cdot \mathbf{Adv}_{E(\mathbb{F}_p)}^{\text{Gap-DH}}(\mathcal{C}) \\ & + \mathbf{Adv}_{\Pi}^{\text{os-entauth}}(\mathcal{B}),\end{aligned}$$

where $\mathcal{B}$ runs in time t and, $\mathcal{C}$ and $\mathcal{D}$ each run in time $t + O(\mu)$ where μ is total number of bits queried.

- *If there exists an adversary $\mathcal{A}$ against the message privacy property of OS-EAMAP security then there are adversaries $\mathcal{B}$, $\mathcal{C}$ and $\mathcal{D}$, such that*

$$\begin{aligned}\mathbf{Adv}_{\Pi}^{\text{os-priv}}(\mathcal{A}) \leq\ & n_S \cdot (n_C + n_T) \cdot \mathbf{Adv}_{\text{AE}}^{\text{indsfcca}}(\mathcal{D}) \\ & + n_C \cdot (1 - 1/|h|) \cdot \mathbf{Adv}_{E(\mathbb{F}_p)}^{\text{Gap-DH}}(\mathcal{C}) \\ & + \mathbf{Adv}_{\Pi}^{\text{os-entauth}}(\mathcal{B}),\end{aligned}$$

where $\mathcal{B}$ runs in time t and, $\mathcal{C}$ and $\mathcal{D}$ each run in time $t + O(\mu)$ where μ is total number of bits queried.

where n_C is the number of cards in the system, n_T the number of terminals, n_S the number of sessions and $|h|$ is the output size of the hash function.

```
EstChannel(i, m; st_k):
case i ∈ C
  (Q, d, cert) ← loadkey(i)
  case ρ
    =⊥: (ch, st_k) ← HelloCard(Q, st_k)
    = initiator: (ch, st_k) ← ConfirmCard(m, Q, d, cert, st_k)
case i ∈ T
  case δ
    =⊥: (ch, st_k) ← HelloTerminal(m, st_k)
    = derived: (ch, st_k) ← ConfirmTerminal(m, st_k)
return (ch, st_k)

HelloCard(Q, st_k):
Parse st_k as (⊥, ⊥, ⊥, ⊥, ⊥, ⊥, ⊥, ⊥)
a ←r F_q; A ← aQ
α := a; ρ := initiator
st_k := (α, ⊥, ρ, ⊥, ⊥, ⊥, ⊥, ⊥)
return (A, st_k)

HelloTerminal(A, st_k):
Parse st_k as (⊥, ⊥, ⊥, ⊥, ⊥, ⊥, ⊥, ⊥)
ρ := responder; α := A
e ←r F_q; E ← eP
κ_d||κ_e ← H(eA); sid := κ_d||κ_e
δ := derived
(st_e, st_d) ← initial(st_k)
st_k := (α, δ, ρ, st_e, st_d, κ_e, κ_d, ⊥, sid)
return (E, st_k)

ConfirmCard(E, Q, d, cert, st_k):
Parse st_k as (a, ⊥, ρ, ⊥, ⊥, ⊥, ⊥, ⊥, ⊥)
δ := accept
κ_e||κ_d ← H(daE); sid := κ_e||κ_d
(st_e, st_d) ← initial(st_k)
(ch, st_e) ← SendCh_{κ_e}(cert||a||Q; st_e)
st_k := (a, δ, ρ, st_e, st_d, κ_e, κ_d, ⊥, sid)
return (ch, st_k)

ConfirmTerminal(ch, st_k):
Parse st_k as (A, δ, ρ, st_e, st_d, κ_e, κ_d, ⊥, sid)
(cert||a||Q, st_d) ← ReceiveCh_{κ_d}(ch; st_d)
if ver_pk(cert, Q) = true ∧ aQ = A then
    δ := accept; pid ← keyid(Q)
else δ := reject
st_k := (A, δ, ρ, st_e, st_d, κ_e, κ_d, pid, sid)
return (δ, st_k)
```

Figure 4: Channel Establishment Protocol EstChannel **for EMV.**

Note that int-0 defines security for an adversary against intsfptxt (or intsfctxt) that is permitted no encryption oracle queries.

We now prove each of the entity authentication, message authentication and message privacy properties in turn.

Before proceeding with the main proof we first examine a related concept of Key Secrecy for a simpler protocol, π, described in Figure 5. To analyse this protocol we are only interested in whether the secret key remains secret, and so we introduce a new security game to model this fact. The security definition for Weak Key Secrecy can in found in Appendix B.

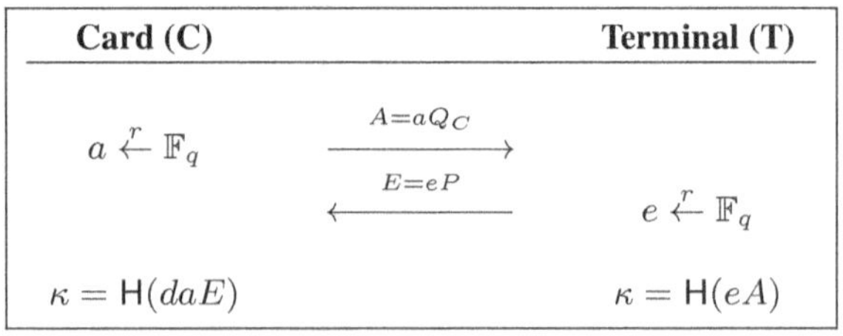

Figure 5: Unauthenticated Key-Agreement Scheme

Given this definition we can now analyse the protocol in Figure 5. The proof relies on the following problem being hard.

Definition 17. (Gap Diffie–Hellman) Let $\mathcal{O}_{\mathsf{DDH}}$ be an oracle that solves the DDH problem in G, i.e. takes as input $rP, sP, tP \in G$, and outputs one if $tP = rsP$ and zero otherwise.
The Gap Diffie–Hellman problem then asks that given $aP, bP \in G$ where $a, b \xleftarrow{r} \mathbb{F}_q$, and access to $\mathcal{O}_{\mathsf{DDH}}$, compute abP (i.e. solve CDH). The advantage of an adversary $\mathcal{A}$ against the Gap Diffie–Hellman problem is defined by

$$\mathbf{Adv}_G^{\mathsf{Gap\text{-}DH}}(\mathcal{A}) = \Pr[a, b \xleftarrow{r} \mathbb{F}_q : \mathcal{A}^{\mathcal{O}_{\mathsf{DDH}}}(aP, bP) = abP].$$

LEMMA 1. *The weak key secrecy of the reduced protocol π is reducible to the Gap Diffie–Hellman assumption, i.e. we have for all adversaries $\mathcal{A}$ there exists an adversary $\mathcal{B}$ such that*

$$\mathbf{Adv}_\pi^{\mathsf{wKSec}}(\mathcal{A}) \leq n_C \cdot (1 - 1/|h|) \cdot \mathbf{Adv}_{E(\mathbb{F}_p)}^{\mathsf{Gap\text{-}DH}}(\mathcal{B}),$$

where n_C is the number of cards in the system and $|h|$ is the output length of the hash function.

The proof of this lemma uses a technique first presented by Kudla and Paterson [14] for analysing a hashed Diffie–Hellman based key agreement protocol. Our proof can be found in the full version of this paper [8].

4.1 One-sided Entity Authentication

We now turn to proving the different properties in our main theorem, starting with one-sided entity authentication. We make use of the following definition.

Definition 18. (Computational Diffie–Hellman) The CDH problem then asks that given $rP, sP \in G$, where $r, s \xleftarrow{r} \mathbb{F}_q$, compute rsP. The advantage of an adversary $\mathcal{A}$ against the CDH problem is defined by

$$\mathbf{Adv}_G^{\mathsf{CDH}}(\mathcal{A}) = \Pr[r, s \xleftarrow{r} \mathbb{F}_q : \mathcal{A}(rP, sP) = rsP].$$

LEMMA 2. *If the gap-DH and CDH problems are hard,* $\mathsf{AE} = (\mathsf{enc}, \mathsf{dec})$ *is an int-0 secure AE scheme, and the signature scheme* $(\mathsf{sig}, \mathsf{ver})$ *used to produce card certificates is EUF-CMA, then the EMV protocol $P = \{\Pi, \mathcal{G}\}$ is secure in the sense of OS-EA. In particular, if there exists an adversary $\mathcal{A}$ against $P = \{\Pi, \mathcal{G}\}$ in the sense of* os-entauth *then there are adversaries $\mathcal{B}$, $\mathcal{C}$, $\mathcal{D}$ and $\mathcal{E}$ such that*

$$\begin{aligned}\mathbf{Adv}_\Pi^{\mathsf{os\text{-}entauth}}(\mathcal{A}) \leq\ & \mathbf{Adv}_{(\mathsf{sig},\mathsf{ver})}^{\mathsf{eufcma}}(\mathcal{B}) \\ & + n_C \cdot (1 - 1/|h|) \cdot \mathbf{Adv}_{E(\mathbb{F}_p)}^{\mathsf{Gap\text{-}DH}}(\mathcal{C}) \\ & + n_S \cdot n_C \cdot \mathbf{Adv}_{\mathsf{AE}}^{\mathsf{int\text{-}0}}(\mathcal{D}) \\ & + n_C^2 \cdot \mathbf{Adv}_{E(\mathbb{F}_p)}^{\mathsf{CDH}}(\mathcal{E}),\end{aligned}$$

where n_C is the number of cards in the system, n_S the number of sessions and $|h|$ is the output size of the hash function.

PROOF. Let $\mathcal{A}$ be an adversary that wins the os-entauth experiment, that is the adversary succeeds in getting one of the bad events os-notval, os-notconf, notuni to occur. Then using the inequality $\Pr[A \vee B] \leq \Pr[A] + \Pr[B|\neg A]$, we obtain:

$$\begin{aligned}& \mathbf{Adv}_\Pi^{\mathsf{os\text{-}entauth}}(\mathcal{A}) \\ & = \Pr[\mathsf{os\text{-}notval} \vee \mathsf{os\text{-}notconf} \vee \mathsf{notuni}] \\ & \leq \Pr[\mathsf{os\text{-}notconf}] + \Pr[\mathsf{os\text{-}notval} \vee \mathsf{notuni}|\neg\mathsf{os\text{-}notconf}] \\ & \leq \Pr[\mathsf{os\text{-}notconf}] + \Pr[\mathsf{notuni}] \\ & \qquad + \Pr[\mathsf{os\text{-}notval}|\neg\mathsf{os\text{-}notconf} \wedge \neg\mathsf{notuni}].\end{aligned}$$

In the full version of the paper [8] we prove the following bounds:

$$\begin{aligned}\Pr[\mathsf{os\text{-}notconf}] \leq\ & \mathbf{Adv}_{(\mathsf{sig},\mathsf{ver})}^{\mathsf{eufcma}}(\mathcal{B}) \\ & + n_C \cdot (1 - 1/|h|) \cdot \mathbf{Adv}_{E(\mathbb{F}_p)}^{\mathsf{Gap\text{-}DH}}(\mathcal{C}) \\ & + n_S \cdot n_C \cdot \mathbf{Adv}_{\mathsf{AE}}^{\mathsf{int\text{-}0}}(\mathcal{D}).\end{aligned}$$

$$\Pr[\mathsf{notuni}] \leq n_C^2 \cdot \mathbf{Adv}_{E(\mathbb{F}_p)}^{\mathsf{CDH}}(\mathcal{E}).$$

$$\Pr[\mathsf{os\text{-}notval}|\neg\mathsf{os\text{-}notconf} \wedge \neg\mathsf{notuni}] = 0.$$

□

4.2 One-sided Message Authentication

We now turn to the message authentication property:

LEMMA 3. *If the Gap-DH problem is hard in $E(\mathbb{F}_p)$,* $\mathsf{AE} = (\mathsf{enc}, \mathsf{dec})$ *is an int-sfptxt secure AE scheme and $P = \{\Pi, \mathcal{G}\}$ is secure in the sense of* os-entauth, *then $P = \{\Pi, \mathcal{G}\}$ is secure in the sense of* os-auth. *In particular if there is an adversary $\mathcal{A}$ against the* os-auth *property then there are adversaries $\mathcal{B}, \mathcal{C}$ and $\mathcal{D}$ such that*

$$\begin{aligned}\mathbf{Adv}_\Pi^{\mathsf{os\text{-}auth}}(\mathcal{A}) \leq\ & n_S \cdot (n_C + n_T) \cdot \mathbf{Adv}_{\mathsf{AE}}^{\mathsf{intsfptxt}}(\mathcal{D}) \\ & + n_C \cdot (1 - 1/|h|) \cdot \mathbf{Adv}_{E(\mathbb{F}_p)}^{\mathsf{Gap\text{-}DH}}(\mathcal{C}) \\ & + \mathbf{Adv}_\Pi^{\mathsf{os\text{-}entauth}}(\mathcal{B}),\end{aligned}$$

where n_C is the number of cards in the system, n_T the number of terminals, n_S the number of sessions and $|h|$ is the output size of the hash function.

PROOF. We shall prove this result via a sequence of games. Let $\mathcal{A}$ be an adversary attacking Π in the sense of auth.
Game 0: This game is identical to $\mathbf{Exec}_\Pi^{\mathsf{os\text{-}auth}}(\mathcal{A})$.

$$\Pr[\mathsf{Game0} \Rightarrow 1] = \mathbf{Adv}_\Pi^{\mathsf{os\text{-}auth}}(\mathcal{A}).$$

Game 1: This proceeds identically to the previous game but aborts if a terminal ($i \in T$) oracle Π_i^s accepts but has no unique partner oracle which establishes the same key. It is easy to see that if this event occurs then one of the events os-notval, os-notconf, notuni has occurred. Therefore,

$$\Pr[\mathsf{Game0} \Rightarrow 1] \leq \Pr[\mathsf{Game1} \Rightarrow 1] + \mathbf{Adv}_\Pi^{\mathsf{os\text{-}entauth}}(\mathcal{B}).$$

Game 2: This proceeds identically to the previous game but aborts if $\mathcal{A}$ makes a query to H which reveals the key for an oracle Π_i^s. Again it is easy to see that

$$\Pr[\mathsf{Game1} \Rightarrow 1] \leq \Pr[\mathsf{Game2} \Rightarrow 1] + \mathbf{Adv}_\pi^{\mathsf{wKSec}}(\mathcal{C}').$$

Game 3: The challenger now selects at random an oracle $\Pi_{i^*}^{s^*}$. The game aborts if $\mathsf{Prefix}(\text{Ap-R}_i^s, \text{Ap-S}_j^t) = \mathsf{false}$ for $(i, s) \neq (i^*, s^*)$. Since i^* is chosen at random from $I = C \cup T$ we have:

$$\Pr[\mathsf{Game2} \Rightarrow 1] \leq n_S \cdot (n_C + n_T) \cdot \Pr[\mathsf{Game3} \Rightarrow 1].$$

It remains to study the probability that $\mathcal{A}$ wins ($\mathsf{Game3} \Rightarrow 1$). We shall use $\mathcal{A}$ in $\mathsf{Game3}$ to construct a new adversary $\mathcal{D}$ against the INT-sfPTXT security of AE. What we effectively do is set the output of the random oracle H for the key corresponding to $\Pi_{i^*}^{s^*}$ to be the key chosen at random for the INT-sfPTXT experiment. The adversary $\mathcal{D}$ will use its enc and dec oracles to provide simulations of $\mathcal{A}$'s Send queries with $\Pi_{i^*}^{s^*}$ or $\Pi_{j^*}^{t^*}$ (where $\mathsf{P}(\Pi_{i^*}^{s^*}, \Pi_{j^*}^{t^*}) = \mathsf{true}$) as the input session. All other queries NewSession, Reveal, Corrupt and all other Send queries will be simulated internally by $\mathcal{D}$. We further explain how Send queries for $\Pi_{i^*}^{s^*}$ or $\Pi_{j^*}^{t^*}$ are simulated. When $\mathcal{A}$ makes a Send query for $\Pi_{i^*}^{s^*}$ or $\Pi_{j^*}^{t^*}$ before $\delta = \texttt{derived}$, $\mathcal{D}$ performs the key exchange himself by using appropriate randomness. Once $\delta = \texttt{derived}$, $\mathcal{D}$ must make calls to enc and dec in order to perform the key confirmation. Since the confirmation message received/sent by $\Pi_{i^*}^{s^*}$ should be equal to that sent/received by the partnered card/terminal session respectively, when $\mathcal{D}$ calls dec he will not be given the plaintext due to restrictions on decryption queries in the INT-sfPTXT model. If this happens then he accepts the card session and sets $\delta = \texttt{accept}$, otherwise he sets $\delta = \texttt{reject}$. After $\delta = \texttt{accept}$ whenever $\mathcal{A}$ makes a Send query where $\texttt{type} = \mathsf{ap}$ or ch, $\mathcal{D}$ calls his enc or dec oracle, respectively. Since $\mathcal{A}$ does not make any reveal queries or hash queries corresponding to the key of $\Pi_{i^*}^{s^*}$ the simulation remains perfect. If $\mathcal{A}$ wins the auth game then $\mathsf{Prefix}(\text{Ap-R}_{i^*}^{s^*}, \text{Ap-S}_{j^*}^{t^*}) = \mathsf{false}$ and thus $\mathcal{A}$ has output a ciphertext forgery which allows $\mathcal{D}$ to win the INT-sfPTXT game.

$$\Pr[\mathsf{Game3} \Rightarrow 1] \leq \mathbf{Adv}_{\mathsf{AE}}^{\mathsf{intsfptxt}}(\mathcal{D}).$$

Combining all of the above we obtain

$$\begin{aligned}
&\mathbf{Adv}_{\Pi}^{\mathsf{os\text{-}auth}}(\mathcal{A}) \\
&= \Pr[\mathsf{Game0} \Rightarrow 1] \\
&\leq \Pr[\mathsf{Game1} \Rightarrow 1] + \mathbf{Adv}_{\Pi}^{\mathsf{os\text{-}entauth}}(\mathcal{B}) \\
&\leq \Pr[\mathsf{Game2} \Rightarrow 1] + \mathbf{Adv}_{\pi}^{\mathsf{wKSec}}(\mathcal{C}') + \mathbf{Adv}_{\Pi}^{\mathsf{os\text{-}entauth}}(\mathcal{B}) \\
&\leq n_S \cdot (n_C + n_T) \cdot \Pr[\mathsf{Game3} \Rightarrow 1] + \mathbf{Adv}_{\pi}^{\mathsf{wKSec}}(\mathcal{C}') \\
&\qquad + \mathbf{Adv}_{\Pi}^{\mathsf{os\text{-}entauth}}(\mathcal{B}) \\
&\leq n_S \cdot (n_C + n_T) \cdot \mathbf{Adv}_{\mathsf{AE}}^{\mathsf{intsfptxt}}(\mathcal{D}) + \mathbf{Adv}_{\pi}^{\mathsf{wKSec}}(\mathcal{C}') \\
&\qquad + \mathbf{Adv}_{\Pi}^{\mathsf{os\text{-}entauth}}(\mathcal{B})
\end{aligned}$$

With the final result following from applying Lemmas 1 and 2. □

4.3 One-sided Message Privacy

We now turn to the message privacy property:

LEMMA 4. *If the Gap-DH problem is hard in $E(\mathbb{F}_p)$,* $\mathsf{AE} = (\mathsf{enc}, \mathsf{dec})$ *is an ind-sfcca secure AE scheme and $P = \{\Pi, \mathcal{G}\}$ is secure in the sense of* os-entauth. *Then $P = \{\Pi, \mathcal{G}\}$ is secure in the sense of* os-priv, *i.e. any adversary $\mathcal{A}$ against the* os-priv *property can be turned into adversaries $\mathcal{B}$, $\mathcal{C}$ and $\mathcal{D}$ such that*

$$\begin{aligned}
\mathbf{Adv}_{\Pi}^{\mathsf{os\text{-}priv}}(\mathcal{A}) \leq\ & n_S \cdot (n_C + n_T) \cdot \mathbf{Adv}_{\mathsf{AE}}^{\mathsf{indsfcca}}(\mathcal{D}) \\
&+ n_C \cdot (1 - 1/|h|) \cdot \mathbf{Adv}_{E(\mathbb{F}_p)}^{\mathsf{Gap\text{-}DH}}(\mathcal{C}) \\
&+ \mathbf{Adv}_{\Pi}^{\mathsf{os\text{-}entauth}}(\mathcal{B}),
\end{aligned}$$

The proof of this is similar to Lemma 3; details can be found in the full version of this paper [8]. We again use game hopping with almost identical hops to the previous proof. The final step is to argue that security in Game 3 is reducible to IND-sfCCA security.

4.4 Unlinkability

Finally, we present our theorem for unlinkability:

THEOREM 2. *If gap-DH is hard and* $\mathsf{AE} = (\mathsf{enc}, \mathsf{dec})$ *is an ind-sfcca secure AE scheme, then $P = \{\Pi, \mathcal{G}\}$ is secure in the sense of* unlink*; in particular we have*

$$\begin{aligned}
&\mathbf{Adv}_{\Pi}^{\mathsf{unlink}}(\mathcal{A}) \\
&\leq n_C^2 \cdot \left(\mathbf{Adv}_{\mathsf{AE}}^{\mathsf{indsfcca}}(\mathcal{C}) + n_C \cdot (1 - 1/|h|) \cdot \mathbf{Adv}_{E(\mathbb{F}_p)}^{\mathsf{Gap\text{-}DH}}(\mathcal{B})\right)
\end{aligned}$$

where, again, n_C is the number of cards in the system and $|h|$ is the output size of the hash function.

Note that if a were instead chosen to be of size 2^{32} (as suggested by the RFC) our security analysis would show only 16 bits of security. We refer the reader to the proof in Appendix C for further details.

5. ACKNOWLEDGEMENTS

This work was support in part by ERC Advanced Grant ERC-2010-AdG-267188-CRIPTO. The second author was also partially supported by a Royal Society Wolfson Merit Award. The first author was supported by the Israel Science Foundation (grant 1076/11 and 1155/11), the Israel Ministry of Science and Technology (grant 3-9094), and the German-Israeli Foundation for Scientific Research and Development (grant 1152/2011).

6. REFERENCES

[1] Mihir Bellare, Tadayoshi Kohno, and Chanathip Namprempre. Breaking and provably repairing the SSH authenticated encryption scheme: A case study of the encode-then-encrypt-and-mac paradigm. *ACM Trans. Inf. Syst. Secur.*, 7(2):206–241, 2004.

[2] Mihir Bellare and Chanathip Namprempre. Authenticated encryption: Relations among notions and analysis of the generic composition paradigm. In Tatsuaki Okamoto, editor, *ASIACRYPT*, volume 1976 of *Lecture Notes in Computer Science*, pages 531–545. Springer, 2000.

[3] Mihir Bellare, David Pointcheval, and Phillip Rogaway. Authenticated key exchange secure against dictionary attacks. In Bart Preneel, editor, *EUROCRYPT*, volume 1807 of *Lecture Notes in Computer Science*, pages 139–155. Springer, 2000.

[4] Mihir Bellare and Phillip Rogaway. Entity authentication and key distribution. In Douglas R. Stinson, editor, *CRYPTO*, volume 773 of *Lecture Notes in Computer Science*, pages 232–249. Springer, 1993.

[5] Simon Blake-Wilson, Don Johnson, and Alfred Menezes. Key agreement protocols and their security analysis. In Michael Darnell, editor, *IMA Int. Conf.*, volume 1355 of *Lecture Notes in Computer Science*, pages 30–45. Springer, 1997.

[6] Alexandra Boldyreva, Jean Paul Degabriele, Kenneth G. Paterson, and Martijn Stam. Security of symmetric encryption in the presence of ciphertext fragmentation. In David Pointcheval and Thomas Johansson, editors, *EUROCRYPT*, volume 7237 of *Lecture Notes in Computer Science*, pages 682–699. Springer, 2012.

[7] Christina Brzuska, Marc Fischlin, Nigel P. Smart, Bogdan Warinschi, and Stephen C. Williams. Less is more: Relaxed yet composable security notions for key exchange. *IACR Cryptology ePrint Archive*, 2012:242, 2012.

[8] Christina Brzuska, Nigel P. Smart, Bogdan Warinschi, and Gaven J. Watson. An analysis of the EMV channel establishment protocol. *IACR Cryptology ePrint Archive*, 2013:31, 2013.

[9] Ran Canetti and Hugo Krawczyk. Analysis of key-exchange protocols and their use for building secure channels. In Birgit Pfitzmann, editor, *EUROCRYPT*, volume 2045 of *Lecture Notes in Computer Science*, pages 453–474. Springer, 2001.

[10] Ian Goldberg, Douglas Stebila, and Berkant Ustaoglu. Anonymity and one-way authentication in key exchange protocols. *Designs, Codes and Cryptography*, 2012. Online first; print version to appear.

[11] Nadia Heninger, Zakir Durumeric, Eric Wustrow, and J.Alex Halderman. Mining your Ps and Qs: Detection of widespread weak keys in network devices. In *USENIX Security Symposium – 2012*, pages 205–220, 2012.

[12] Tibor Jager, Florian Kohlar, Sven Schäge, and Jörg Schwenk. On the security of TLS-DHE in the standard model. *IACR Cryptology ePrint Archive*, 2011:219, 2011.

[13] Tibor Jager, Florian Kohlar, Sven Schäge, and Jörg Schwenk. On the security of TLS-DHE in the standard model. In Reihaneh Safavi-Naini and Ran Canetti, editors, *CRYPTO*, volume 7417 of *Lecture Notes in Computer Science*, pages 273–293. Springer, 2012.

[14] Caroline Kudla and Kenneth G. Paterson. Modular security proofs for key agreement protocols. In Bimal K. Roy, editor, *ASIACRYPT*, volume 3788 of *Lecture Notes in Computer Science*, pages 549–565. Springer, 2005.

[15] EMVCo LLC. EMV deployment statistics. *http://www.emvco.com/about_emvco.aspx?id=202*, 2012.

[16] EMVCo LLC. EMV ECC key establishment protocols. *http://www.emvco.com/specifications.aspx?id=243*, 2012.

[17] Paul Morrissey, Nigel P. Smart, and Bogdan Warinschi. The TLS handshake protocol: A modular analysis. *J. Cryptology*, 23(2):187–223, 2010.

[18] Kenneth G. Paterson, Thomas Ristenpart, and Thomas Shrimpton. Tag size does matter: Attacks and proofs for the tls record protocol. In Dong Hoon Lee and Xiaoyun Wang, editors, *ASIACRYPT*, volume 7073 of *Lecture Notes in Computer Science*, pages 372–389. Springer, 2011.

[19] John Pollard. Monte Carlo methods for index computation mod p. *Mathematics of Computation*, 32:918–924, 1978.

[20] Phillip Rogaway and Till Stegers. Authentication without elision: Partially specified protocols, associated data, and cryptographic models described by code. In *CSF*, pages 26–39. IEEE Computer Society, 2009.

APPENDIX

A. BASIC SECURITY DEFINITIONS

The underlying AE scheme we assume satisfies the following two properties which are variants of the stateful security models of Bellare et al. [1] and Paterson et al. [18].

An adversary against a stateful encryption scheme needs to be given the capability to progress the scheme's state without trivially winning the security experiment. It is for this reason that there is a subtle difference between the standard notions of Indistinguishability under Chosen-Ciphertext Attack (IND-CCA) and Integrity of Plaintexts (INT-PTXT)[2], and their stateful versions IND-sfCCA and INT-sfPTXT. An adversary against IND-sfCCA and INT-sfPTXT security is permitted to query the decryption oracle with an output from the encryption oracle in order to progress the state but the output of this query should *not* be returned to the adversary (to avoid the trivial attack).

In order to match with our security definitions of auth and priv we alter previous IND-sfCCA of Bellare et al. [1] and introduce a new notion for INT-sfPTXT (which is analogous to the definition of INT-sfCTXT given by Bellare at al.) to now compare the lists M-E and C-E with M-D and C-D respectively. In the case of IND-sfCCA, C-E is the list of all ciphertexts output by the encryption oracle and C-D is the list of all ciphertexts *successfully* decrypted by the decryption oracle. For INT-sfPTXT the lists M-E, M-D correspond to plaintext messages input to and output from the encryption and decryption oracle, respectively. In order to prevent an adversary trivially winning he is not permitted to see the output of the decryption oracle if C-D (M-D resp.) is a prefix of C-E (M-E resp.), i.e. if all ciphertexts (plaintexts resp.) decrypted so far were output by the encryption oracle in the case of IND-sfCCA or if all plaintexts output so far were inputs to the encryption oracle in the case of INT-sfPTXT.

Definition 19. (IND-sfCCA) Consider the scheme $\mathsf{AE} = \{\mathsf{enc}_\kappa, \mathsf{dec}_\kappa\}$. Let $\mathcal{A}$ be an adversary with access to a left-or-right encryption oracle $\mathsf{enc}_\kappa(h, \mathsf{LR}_b(m_0, m_1); st_e)$ and a decryption oracle $\mathsf{dec}_\kappa(h, c; st_d)$. It is mandated that any two messages queried to $\mathsf{enc}_\kappa(h, \mathsf{LR}_b(m_0, m_1); st_e)$ have equal length. We define an experiment as follows:

$\mathbf{Exec}_{\mathsf{AE}}^{\mathsf{indsfcca}\text{-}b}(\mathcal{A})$
$\kappa \xleftarrow{r} \{0,1\}^k$, $\text{C-E} := \emptyset$, $\text{C-D} := \emptyset$, $st_e := \emptyset$ and $st_d := \emptyset$
Run $\mathcal{A}^{\mathsf{enc}_\kappa, \mathsf{dec}_\kappa}$
  Reply to $\mathsf{enc}_\kappa(h, \mathsf{LR}_b(m_0, m_1); st_e)$ as follows:
    $(c, st_e) \xleftarrow{r} \mathsf{enc}_\kappa(h, m_b; st_e)$
    $\text{C-E} \leftarrow \text{C-E} \cup c$; $\mathcal{A} \Leftarrow c$
  Reply to $\mathsf{dec}_\kappa(h, c; st_d)$ as follows:
    $(m, st_d) \xleftarrow{r} \mathsf{dec}_\kappa(h, c; st_d)$
    if $m \neq \perp$ **then**
      $\text{C-D} \leftarrow \text{C-D} \cup c$
      if $\mathsf{Prefix}(\text{C-D}, \text{C-E}) = \mathsf{false}$ **then** $\mathcal{A} \Leftarrow m$
Until $\mathcal{A}$ returns a bit b'
return b'

The attacker wins when $b' = b$, and his advantage is defined as

$$\mathbf{Adv}_{\mathsf{AE}}^{\mathsf{indsfcca}}(\mathcal{A}) = 2\Pr[\mathbf{Exec}_{\mathsf{AE}}^{\mathsf{indsfcca}\text{-}b}(\mathcal{A}) = b] - 1.$$

Definition 20. (INT-sfPXT) Consider the scheme $\mathsf{AE} = \{\mathsf{enc}_\kappa, \mathsf{dec}_\kappa\}$. Let $\mathcal{A}$ be an adversary with oracle access to $\mathsf{enc}_\kappa(h, m; st_e)$ and $\mathsf{dec}_\kappa(h, c; st_d)$. We define an experiment as follows:

$\mathbf{Exec}_{\mathsf{AE}}^{\mathsf{intsfptxt}}(\mathcal{A})$
$\kappa \xleftarrow{r} \{0,1\}^k$, $d := 0$
M-E $:= \emptyset$, M-D $:= \emptyset$, $st_e := \emptyset$ and $st_d := \emptyset$
Run $\mathcal{A}^{\mathsf{enc}_\kappa, \mathsf{dec}_\kappa}$
  Reply to $\mathsf{enc}_\kappa(h, m; st_e)$ as follows:
    $(c, st_e) \xleftarrow{r} \mathsf{enc}_\kappa(h, m; st_e)$
    M-E $\leftarrow$ M-E $\cup\, m$; $\mathcal{A} \Leftarrow c$
  Reply to $\mathsf{dec}_\kappa(h, c; st_d)$ as follows:
    $(m, st_d) \xleftarrow{r} \mathsf{dec}_\kappa(h, c; st_d)$
    if $m \neq \perp$ **then**
      M-D $\leftarrow$ M-D $\cup\, m$; $\mathcal{A} \Leftarrow 1$
      if Prefix(M-D, M-E) $=$ false **then** $d := 1$
    else $\mathcal{A} \Leftarrow 0$
Until $\mathcal{A}$ halts
return d

The advantage $\mathbf{Adv}_{\mathsf{AE}}^{\mathsf{intsfptxt}}(\mathcal{A})$ of an adversary is defined as

$$\mathbf{Adv}_{\mathsf{AE}}^{\mathsf{intsfptxt}}(\mathcal{A}) = \Pr[\mathbf{Exec}_{\mathsf{AE}}^{\mathsf{intsfptxt}}(\mathcal{A}) = 1].$$

In addition we define the related notion int-0 which considers an adversary $\mathcal{A}$ against intsfptxt (or in fact intsfctxt) that is permitted no encryption oracle queries.

B. KEY SECRECY

We define the following game $\mathbf{Exec}_{\Pi}^{\mathsf{KSec}}(\mathcal{A})$ between an adversary $\mathcal{A}$ and challenger $\mathcal{C}$:

1. The challenger $\mathcal{C}$, generates public/secret key pairs for each user $i \in I$ (by running $\mathcal{G}$) and returns the public keys to $\mathcal{A}$.
2. Adversary $\mathcal{A}$ is allowed to make as many NewSession, Send, Reveal, Corrupt queries as it likes.
3. Finally $\mathcal{A}$ outputs a pair Π^* and κ^*.

We say the adversary $\mathcal{A}$ wins if $\mathsf{F}(\Pi^*) =$ true and κ^* is the key agreed by Π^*. In this case the output of $\mathbf{Exec}_{\Pi}^{\mathsf{KSec}}(\mathcal{A})$ is set to 1. Otherwise the output is 0. We define the advantage of $\mathcal{A}$ to be

$$\mathbf{Adv}_{\Pi}^{\mathsf{KSec}}(\mathcal{A}) = |\Pr[\mathbf{Exec}_{\Pi}^{\mathsf{KSec}}(\mathcal{A}) = 1]|.$$

Definition 21. (Key Secrecy) $P = \{\Pi, \mathcal{G}\}$ is a $(t, \epsilon_{\mathsf{KSec}})$-**key secret AK protocol** if for all adversaries $\mathcal{A}$ running in time t the following holds:

1. In the presence of a benign adversary on Π_i^s and Π_j^t both oracles accept holding the same session identifier *sid*, the same session key κ, and this key is distributed uniformly at random on $\{0,1\}^k$.
2. $\mathcal{A}$'s advantage is bounded by $\mathbf{Adv}_{\Pi}^{\mathsf{KSec}}(\mathcal{A}) \leq \epsilon_{\mathsf{KSec}}$.

We can also define a weaker version of this model for one-sided authentication by running the experiment in the same way as before but changing the winning condition slightly. We say the adversary $\mathcal{A}$ wins the wKSec experiment if $\mathsf{OSF}(\Pi^*) =$ true and κ^* is the key agreed by Π^*.

Definition 22. (Weak Key Secrecy) $P = \{\Pi, \mathcal{G}\}$ is a $(t, \epsilon_{\mathsf{wKSec}})$-**weak Key-secure AK protocol** if for all adversaries $\mathcal{A}$ running in time t the following holds:

1. In the presence of a benign adversary on Π_i^s and Π_j^t both oracles accept holding the same session identifier *sid*, the same session key κ and this key is distributed uniformly at random on $\{0,1\}^k$.
2. $\mathcal{A}$'s advantage is bounded by $\mathbf{Adv}_{\Pi}^{\mathsf{wKSec}}(\mathcal{A}) \leq \epsilon_{\mathsf{wKSec}}$.

C. PROOF OF THEOREM 2

PROOF. We shall prove this result via a sequence of games. Let $\mathcal{A}$ be an adversary attacking Π in the sense of unlink.
Game 0: This game is identical to $\mathbf{Exec}_{\Pi}^{\mathsf{unlink}}(\mathcal{A})$.

$$\Pr[\mathsf{Game0} \Rightarrow 1] - \frac{1}{2} = \mathbf{Adv}_{\Pi}^{\mathsf{unlink}}(\mathcal{A}).$$

Game 1: The challenger now selects at random i_0^* and i_1^*. The game aborts and returns random b' if $\mathcal{A}$ does not output $i_0 = i_0^*$ and $i_1 = i_1^*$. We obtain

$$\Pr[\mathsf{Game0} \Rightarrow 1] - \frac{1}{2} \leq n_C^2 \cdot \left(\Pr[\mathsf{Game1} \Rightarrow 1] - \frac{1}{2}\right).$$

Game 2: This proceeds identically to the previous game but aborts if $\mathcal{A}$ makes a query to H which reveals the key for the oracle $\mathcal{O}$. We obtain

$$\Pr[\mathsf{Game1} \Rightarrow 1] \leq \Pr[\mathsf{Game2} \Rightarrow 1] + \mathbf{Adv}_{\pi}^{\mathsf{wKSec}}(\mathcal{B}').$$

Game 3: This proceeds identically to the previous game except that whenever Send is called with $\mathcal{O}_C$ and $\mathtt{type} = \mathtt{ap}$ then the challenger replaces m with a random message which it then encrypts. Again it is easy to see that we obtain

$$\Pr[\mathsf{Game2} \Rightarrow 1] \leq \Pr[\mathsf{Game3} \Rightarrow 1] + \mathbf{Adv}_{\mathsf{AE}}^{\mathsf{indsfcca}}(\mathcal{C}).$$

It remains to study the probability that $\mathcal{A}$ wins ($\mathsf{Game2} \Rightarrow 1$). Since ciphertexts are now distributed uniformly at random the only useful information that $\mathcal{A}$ can determine are the public keys $Q_{i_0^*}$, $Q_{i_1^*}$, and the blinded challenge value $aQ_{i_b^*}$. Since a is chosen at random from $\mathbb{F}_q$, then the distributions $(Q_{i_0^*}, Q_{i_1^*}, aQ_{i_0^*})$ and $(Q_{i_0^*}, Q_{i_1^*}, aQ_{i_1^*})$ are identical, i.e. the advantage is zero even if the adversary is computationally unbounded. We therefore have:

$$\Pr[\mathsf{Game3} \Rightarrow 1] - \frac{1}{2} = 0.$$

Combining all of the above:

$$\begin{aligned}
&\mathbf{Adv}_{\Pi}^{\mathsf{unlink}}(\mathcal{A})\\
&= \Pr[\mathsf{Game0} \Rightarrow 1] - \frac{1}{2}\\
&\leq n_C^2 \cdot \left(\Pr[\mathsf{Game1} \Rightarrow 1] - \frac{1}{2}\right)\\
&\leq n_C^2 \cdot \left(\Pr[\mathsf{Game2} \Rightarrow 1] - \frac{1}{2} + \mathbf{Adv}_{\pi}^{\mathsf{wKSec}}(\mathcal{B}')\right)\\
&\leq n_C^2 \cdot \left(\mathbf{Adv}_{\mathsf{AE}}^{\mathsf{indsfcca}}(\mathcal{C}) + \mathbf{Adv}_{\pi}^{\mathsf{wKSec}}(\mathcal{B}')\right)\\
&\leq n_C^2 \cdot \left(\mathbf{Adv}_{\mathsf{AE}}^{\mathsf{indsfcca}}(\mathcal{C}) + n_C \cdot (1 - 1/|h|) \cdot \mathbf{Adv}_{E(\mathbb{F}_p)}^{\mathsf{Gap\text{-}DH}}(\mathcal{B})\right).
\end{aligned}$$

□

We note that if we were permitted to have a small (as would be the case in the original EMV proposal) distinguishing the two distributions $(Q_{i_0^*}, Q_{i_1^*}, aQ_{i_0^*})$ and $(Q_{i_0^*}, Q_{i_1^*}, aQ_{i_1^*})$ may no longer be hard. Let l denote the maximum bit length of a. The real question of interest would then be how small can l be before the above problem becomes easy for computationally bounded adversaries. It is clear that the best attack against the problem for $2^l \ll q$ will be Pollard Lambda method [19], which runs in time $O(2^{l/2})$. This implies that a 32-bit randomizer a only gives 16 bits of security and an 80-bit randomizer only gives 40 bits of security.

On the Security of TLS Renegotiation

Florian Giesen
Horst Görtz Institut
Ruhr-Universität Bochum, Germany
florian.giesen@rub.de

Florian Kohlar
Horst Görtz Institut
Ruhr-Universität Bochum, Germany
florian.kohlar@rub.de

Douglas Stebila
Queensland University of Technology
Brisbane, Australia
stebila@qut.edu.au

ABSTRACT

The Transport Layer Security (TLS) protocol is the most widely used security protocol on the Internet. It supports negotiation of a wide variety of cryptographic primitives through different cipher suites, various modes of client authentication, and additional features such as renegotiation. Despite its widespread use, only recently has the full TLS protocol been proven secure, and only the core cryptographic protocol with no additional features. These additional features have been the cause of several practical attacks on TLS. In 2009, Ray and Dispensa demonstrated how TLS renegotiation allows an attacker to splice together its own session with that of a victim, resulting in a man-in-the-middle attack on TLS-reliant applications such as HTTP. TLS was subsequently patched with two defence mechanisms for protection against this attack.

We present the first formal treatment of renegotiation in secure channel establishment protocols. We add optional renegotiation to the authenticated and confidential channel establishment model of Jager et al., an adaptation of the Bellare–Rogaway authenticated key exchange model. We describe the attack of Ray and Dispensa on TLS within our model. We show generically that the proposed fixes for TLS offer good protection against renegotiation attacks, and give a simple new countermeasure that provides renegotiation security for TLS even in the face of stronger adversaries.

Categories and Subject Descriptors

C.2.0 [**Computer–Communication Networks**]: General —*security and protection*

Keywords

Transport Layer Security (TLS); renegotiation; security models; key exchange

CCS'13, November 4–8, 2013, Berlin, Germany.

ACM 978-1-4503-2477-9/13/11 ... $15.00.
http://dx.doi.org/10.1145/2508859.2516694.

1. INTRODUCTION

The Transport Layer Security (TLS) protocol, the successor of the Secure Sockets Layer (SSL) protocol, provides secure channel establishment on the Internet. It is commonly used to protect information sent via the Hypertext Transfer Protocol (HTTP) on the web, and many other application layer protocols such as email and file transfer. TLS consists of a *handshake* protocol, used to agree on security parameters, establish a secret key, and authenticate the parties; and a *record layer* protocol, used to send encrypted data.

Despite the importance of TLS, progress on formally modelling the security of TLS has been slow. A technicality of TLS prevents it from being proven secure in standard authenticated key exchange (AKE) models: in AKE, the session key must be indistinguishable from a random key of the same length. However, the final handshake message of the TLS protocol is encrypted under the session key, so an adversary can distinguish the session key from a random key by trying to verify the final handshake message. Some analyses [17, 22] have shown that a truncated form of the TLS handshake is AKE-secure. Others [12] deal with a substantially weaker security requirement, namely unauthenticated key agreement. Krawczyk [19] analyzed a variant of the TLS record layer.

Only very recently have analyses of unmodified TLS functionality appeared. Paterson *et al.* [23] showed that TLS's MAC-then-encode-then-encrypt record layer when used with CBC encryption (with certain length restrictions) satisfies *length-hiding authenticated encryption (LHAE)*. Jager *et al.* [16] gave the first full proof of the security of (one ciphersuite of) unmodified TLS in a strong security model. Jager *et al.* introduced a variant of the Bellare–Rogaway authenticated key exchange model, called *authenticated and confidential channel establishment (ACCE)*. They proved that the TLS 1.2 protocol using the `TLS_DHE_DSS_WITH_3DES_EDE_CBC_SHA` ciphersuite (which we shorten to `TLS_DHE_DSS_`) is a secure ACCE protocol, under standard assumptions on the cryptographic components. Ciphersuites based on RSA key transport and static Diffie–Hellman have since been shown ACCE-secure by both Kohlar *et al.* [18] and Krawczyk *et al.* [20]. (An alternative modular approach to proving the full security of TLS was given by Brzuska *et al.* [5].)

But TLS is not just a basic secure channel: it consists of hundreds of variants with many optional complex functionalities. Alert messages report various error conditions. Previous sessions can be resumed with a shortened handshake. As of August 2013, over 300 ciphersuites—combinations of cryptographic primitives—have been standardized. Client authentication is optional, and can be certificate-based or password-based. Various additional options can be specified via extensions and optional fields. Record layer communication can be compressed. And most importantly for this paper, after a TLS handshake has been completed and transmission on the record layer has started, parties can renegotiate the handshake. There have been many attacks on TLS over the years, such Bleichenbacher's attack [4] and others involving padding, and Ray and Dispensa's renegotiation attack [24], all of which exploit flaws outside the core cryptographic primitives of TLS.

In this paper, we focus on renegotiation, which allows two parties to either (a) obtain a fresh session key, (b) change cryptographic parameters, or (c) change authentication credentials. For example, if a client needs to authenticate using a client certificate but wishes to not reveal her identity over a public channel, she could first authenticate anonymously (or with pseudonymous credentials), then renegotiate using her real certificate; since the renegotiation messages are transmitted within the existing record layer, the transmission of her certificate is encrypted, and thus she obtains privacy for her identity. We will examine TLS renegotiation in detail, especially in light of previously identified practical attacks related to TLS renegotiation.

Despite the utility of renegotiation in real-world protocols—beyond TLS, renegotiation, rekeying, or reauthentication is also used in the Secure Shell (SSH) protocol, Internet Key Exchange version 2, the Tor anonymity protocol, and others—there has been almost no research in the literature on the security of protocols involving renegotiation, with the exception of a brief note on the TLS renegotiation attack by Farrell [10] and the recent thesis of Gelashvili [13], which uses the Scyther tool to automatically identify the TLS renegotiation attack. Bhargavan *et al.* [2] implement TLS supporting a variety of ciphersuites and define an application programming interface for TLS which differentiates between renegotiated phases; using typechecking, the implementation is shown secure according to a formal specification, albeit with a restricted adversary who cannot corrupt session keys.

1.1 The TLS Renegotiation Issue

All versions of TLS [7, 8, 9], and SSL v3 [11] before it, support optional renegotiation. After the initial handshake is completed and secure communication begins in the record layer, either party can request renegotiation. The client can request renegotiation by sending a new `ClientHello` message in the current record layer (i.e., encrypted under the current session key); the server can request renegotiation by sending a `HelloRequest` message in the record layer, which triggers the client to send a new `ClientHello` message.

In November 2009, Ray and Dispensa [24] described a man-in-the-middle attack that exploits how certain TLS-reliant applications—such as HTTP over TLS [25]—process data across renegotiations. The attack is shown in Figure 1. The attacker Eve observes Alice attempting to establish a TLS session with Bob. Eve delays Alice's initial `ClientHello` and instead establishes her own TLS session with Bob and transmits a message m_0 over that record layer. Then Eve passes Alice's initial `ClientHello` to Bob over the Eve–Bob record layer. Bob views this as a valid renegotiation and responds accordingly; Eve relays the handshake messages between Alice and Bob, who eventually establish a new record layer to which Eve has no access. Alice then transmits a message m_1 over the Alice–Bob record layer.

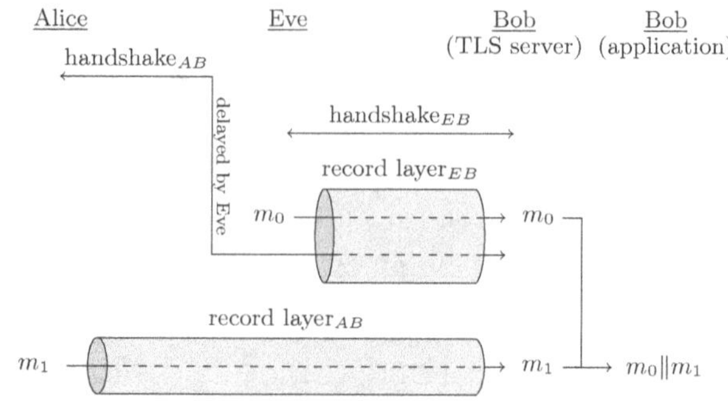

Figure 1: Ray and Dispensa's man-in-the-middle renegotiation attack on TLS-reliant applications

This is not strictly speaking an attack on TLS but on how some applications process TLS-protected data. It results from some applications, including HTTPS [24] and SMTPS [28], concatenating m_0 and m_1 and treating them as coming from the same party in the same context. For example, if Eve sends the HTTP request m_0 and Alice sends the HTTP request m_1, where

m_0 = "`GET /orderPizza?deliverTo=123-Fake-St` ↩
`X-Ignore-This: `"
m_1 = "`GET /orderPizza?deliverTo=456-Real-St` ↩
`Cookie: Account=111A2B`"

(where ↩ denotes new-line character), then the concatenated request (across multiple lines for readability) is

$m_0\|m_1$ = "`GET /orderPizza?deliverTo=123-Fake-St` ↩
`X-Ignore-This: GET /orderPizza`
`?deliverTo=456-Real-St` ↩
`Cookie: Account=111A2B`"

The "`X-Ignore-This:`" prefix is an invalid HTTP header, and since this header, without a new line character, is concatenated with the first line of Alice's request, so this line is ignored. However, the following line, Alice's account cookie, is still processed. Eve is able to have the pizza delivered to herself but paid for by Alice.

It should be noted that Ray and Dispensa's attack works for both server-only authentication and mutual authentication modes of TLS: the use of client certificates in general does not prevent the attack [24, 28].

1.2 Countermeasures Added to TLS

The immediate recommendation due to this attack was to disable renegotiation except in cases where it was essential. Subsequently, the Internet Engineering Task Force (IETF) TLS working group developed RFC 5746 [26] to provide countermeasures to this attack, with the goal of applicability to SSLv3.0 and TLS versions 1.0–1.2. Two countermeasures were standardized: the *Signalling Ciphersuite Value (SCSV)* and the *Renegotiation Information Extension (RIE)*. In RIE, the parties include the key confirmation value from the previous handshake in a `ClientHello`/`ServerHello` extension [3], demonstrating they have the same view of the previous handshake, or a distinguished null value if not renegotiation. SCSV is a slight modification that is more compatible with buggy implementations. A diagram showing the message flow for a generic TLS ciphersuite with SCSV/RIE countermeasures appears in Figure 2 in Appendix B. According to one survey [27], as of July 2013, 82% of TLS-enabled websites support SCSV/RIE, with 9% still supporting insecure renegotiation and 9% not supporting renegotiation.

1.3 Contributions

Security model for renegotiable channel establishment protocols. In Section 2, we present a new security model for renegotiable protocols. Since our goal is to analyze the security of TLS, we start from the ACCE model, rather than AKE security models. The primary difference in our model for renegotiable protocols is that each party's oracle (session) can have multiple *phases*; each new phase corresponds to a renegotiation in that session, and can involve the same or different long-term keys.[1] This is qualitatively different than simply having multiple sessions, since short-term values from one phase of a session may be used in the renegotiation for the next phase, whereas multiple sessions only share long-term values. Each oracle maintains state and encryption/MAC keys for each phase. Like in TLS, our formalism allows control messages to be sent on the encrypted channel. Our extension to the ACCE model also models server-only authentication in addition to mutual authentication.

The basic goals of a *secure renegotiable ACCE protocol* are that (a) the adversary should not be able to read or inject messages on the encrypted channel, and (b) whenever parties successfully renegotiate, they should have exactly the same view of all previous negotiations and all encrypted messages sent in all previous phases of that session, even when values from previous phases have been compromised.

Analysis of TLS without and with SCSV/RIE countermeasures. Based on the TLS renegotiation attack of Ray and Dispensa, we see in Section 3 that TLS without countermeasures is not secure in our model for renegotiation. We subsequently show in Section 4 that, generically, TLS with the SCSV/RIE countermeasures of RFC 5746 [26] is a *weakly secure renegotiable ACCE protocol.* In this slightly weaker—but still quite reasonable—model, the adversary is slightly restricted in the previous secrets she is allowed to reveal.

Our approach for proving the renegotiable security of TLS with SCSV/RIE countermeasures is modular. We *cannot* generically prove that an ACCE-secure TLS ciphersuite is, with SCSV/RIE, a weakly secure renegotiable ACCE, because the protocol itself is modified by including SCSV/RIE and hence a black-box approach does not work. Instead, we consider *tagged TLS* where an arbitrary tag can be provided as an extension. Via a chain of results and models, we show that if a tagged TLS ciphersuite is secure in an ACCE variant where **Finished** messages are revealed, then that TLS ciphersuite with SCSV/RIE is a weakly secure renegotiable ACCE protocol. This provides a generic justification for the security of SCSV/RIE. Proving that TLS ciphersuite secure in this tagged variant model seems to be almost no harder than a proof that it is ACCE-secure; we only needed to change a few lines from the ACCE security proof of **TLS_DHE_DSS_** [16].

New countermeasure for TLS. TLS with SCSV/RIE cannot meet our strongest notion of renegotiable security, only the weaker notion described above. In the strong definition, even if the adversary learns the session key of one phase, parties who later renegotiate still should detect any earlier

[1]Note that TLS standards use different words. We say a single *session* can have multiple *phases*; the TLS standards refer to a single *connection* having multiple *sessions.*

	Secure multi-phase ACCE (Defn. 3)	**Weakly secure renegotiable ACCE** (Defn. 5)	**Secure renegotiable ACCE** (Defn. 4)
Secure against Ray–Dispensa-type attacks	×	✓	✓[1]
TLS w/o countermeasures	—	× (§3)	× (§3)
with SCSV/RIE (if tagged-ACCE-fin-secure)	—	✓ (Thm. 1)	× (§4.1)
with new countermeasure (if tagged-ACCE-fin-secure)	✓ (Thm. 4)	✓ (Thm. 4)	✓ (Thm. 4)

[1] For secure renegotiable ACCE, security holds even if session keys from one phase are revealed while that phase is active.

Table 1: Summary of security notions and results on TLS

message injections by the adversary. Though the ability to learn session keys of phases while the protocol is still running makes the adversary quite powerful, this may be realistic in scenarios with long-lived session keys, for example with session resumption. We present in Section 5 a simple adjustment to the renegotiation information extension—adding a fingerprint of the transcript of the previous phase's record layer—so TLS can achieve this stronger security notion. This countermeasure can be seen as providing *record layer recognition,* confirming that both parties have the same view of all communicated messages, rather than just *handshake recognition* as in the SCSV/RIE countermeasure.

Table 1 summarizes our results on TLS and renegotiation countermeasures. While our theorems are specific to TLS, our definitional framework is suitable for any channel establishment protocol that involves renegotiation, and could for example be used to check if renegotiation in the Secure Shell (SSH) protocol really is secure [21].

On composability and the choice of ACCE. It would be desirable to prove the security of the TLS renegotiation countermeasures via some kind of composability framework, such as universal composability or the game-based composability framework of Brzuska *et al.* [5]. Unfortunately, this is not possible with existing security definitions for TLS. The TLS renegotiation countermeasures are not achieved by *composing* in a black-box manner one protocol or primitive with another. Instead, the SCSV/RIE countermeasure looks inside the protocol and changes it in a white-box way: it *modifies* the messages sent by the protocol, and *re-uses* an internal value. Thus we cannot make use of existing security results in a black-box compositional way. Our approach is the "next best thing": we modify an existing security definition (ACCE) in what seems to be a minimal way, adding just enough "hooks" to get at the internal values needed to modify and re-use the required values for the SCSV/RIE countermeasure. We are then able to prove in a fully generic way that any TLS protocol that satisfies this slightly modified ACCE notion with hooks is, when using the SCSV/RIE countermeasure, secure against renegotiation attacks. Since the hooks added are quite small, it is not much work to change a proof that a TLS ciphersuite is ACCE secure to show that it satisfies this slightly modified ACCE notion as well.

Of the two existing definitional approaches for proving the full security of the TLS protocol [16, 5], we chose the ACCE approach over the game-based composability approach because renegotiation in TLS makes extensive use of the interplay between the handshake and record layer.

Moreover, the modifications we make to the execution environment to enable analysis of renegotiable ACCE protocols can be adapted to capture renegotiation and rekeying in other types of protocols such as authenticated key exchange.

2. SECURITY DEFINITIONS FOR MULTI-PHASE AND RENEGOTIABLE ACCE

In this section we describe what a multi-phase authenticated and confidential channel establishment (ACCE) protocol is and our various renegotiation security notions. Essentially, a multi-phase protocol can have many key exchanges—each called a *phase*—linked to a single session. Our definition builds on the ACCE definition of Jager *et al.* [16], which combined the Bellare–Rogaway model for authenticated key exchange [1] with a Jager *et al.*'s stateful variant of Paterson *et al.*'s length-hiding authenticated encryption [23].

Notation. If S is a set, $x \xleftarrow{\$} S$ denotes sampling a value x uniformly at random from S. $x \xleftarrow{\$} \mathcal{A}(y)$ denotes the output x of the probabilistic algorithm $\mathcal{A}$ when run on input y and randomly chosen coins. $\mathcal{A}^{\mathcal{O}(\cdot)}$ means $\mathcal{A}$ is run with access to oracle $\mathcal{O}(\cdot)$. The notation $[1, n]$ denotes the set $\{1, 2, \ldots, n\}$; $\texttt{phases}[\ell]$ denotes the ℓth entry in the 1-indexed array $\texttt{phases}$ and $|\texttt{phases}|$ denotes the number of entries in the array. $\pi_A^s.x$ denotes variable x stored in oracle instance π_A^s.

2.1 Overview

The first security notion, a *secure multi-phase ACCE protocol*, is a straightforward extension of the ACCE model to allow multiple, independent phases per session; notably, we require essentially no link between phases:

- An adversary breaks *(multi-phase) authentication* if a party accepts in a phase with uncorrupted long-term keys, but no matching phase exists at the peer.
- An adversary breaks *confidentiality/integrity* if it can guess the bit b involved in a confidentiality/integrity experiment similar to stateful length-hiding authenticated encryption.

Our main security definition is a *secure renegotiable ACCE protocol*, which strengthens the authentication notion: parties should successfully renegotiate only when they have exact same view of everything that happened before.

- An adversary breaks *renegotiation authentication* if a party accepts in a phase where long-term keys have not been corrupted, but either no matching phase exists at the peer *or some previous handshake or record layer transcript does not match.*

However, it is not possible to prove that TLS with the SCSV/RIE countermeasures is a secure renegotiable ACCE protocol: as we will see in Section 3, the strong definition requires that the views of parties match when successfully renegotiating, even when previous sessions' long-term secret keys or session keys were revealed. TLS's SCSV/RIE countermeasures do not fully protect against the case when these secret values are revealed.

As a result, we introduce the weaker, though still quite reasonable, notion of a *weakly secure renegotiable ACCE protocol*, and prove in Section 3 that the SCSV/RIE countermeasure for TLS generically provides it:

- An adversary breaks *weak renegotiation authentication* if a party accepts in a phase with uncorrupted long-term keys *and session keys for each earlier phase were not revealed while that phase was active*, but either no matching phase exists at the peer or some previous handshake or record layer transcript does not match.

We proceed by describing the execution environment for adversaries interacting with multi-phase ACCE protocols, then define the various security notions described above.

2.2 Execution Environment

Parties. The environment consists of n_{pa} parties, $\{P_1, \ldots, P_{n_{\text{pa}}}\}$. Each party P_A is a potential protocol participant, and has a list of n_{ke} long-term key pairs $(pk_{A,1}, sk_{A,1}), \ldots, (pk_{A,n_{\text{ke}}}, sk_{A,n_{\text{ke}}})$. We assume that each party P_A is uniquely identified by any one of its public keys $pk_{A,*}$. In practice, there may be other identities that are bound to these public keys, e.g. by using certificates, but this is out of scope of this paper. It is common in AKE security models to assume ideal distribution of long-term public keys for simplicity [1, 6, 16].

Sessions. Each party P_A can participate in up to n_{se} sessions, which are independent executions of the protocol and can be concurrent or subsequent; all of a party's sessions have access to the same list of its long-term key pairs, as well as a trusted list of all parties' public keys. Each session $s \in [1, n_{\text{se}}]$ is presented to the environment as an oracle π_A^s. Each oracle π_A^s records in a variable $\pi_A^s.d$ the oracle corresponding to the intended communication partner, e.g.$\pi_A^s.d = \pi_B^t$. As well, the variable $\rho \in \{\mathsf{Client}, \mathsf{Server}\}$ records the role of the oracle. Parties can play the role of the client in some sessions and of the server in other sessions, but their role is fixed across all phases within a session.

Phases. Each session can consist of up to n_{ph} phases. Each phase consists of two stages: a *pre-accept*, or "handshake", stage, which is effectively an AKE protocol that establishes a session key and performs mutual or server-only authentication; and a *post-accept*, or "record layer", stage, which provides a stateful communication channel with confidentiality and integrity. A list $\pi_A^s.\texttt{phases}$ of different phase states is maintained; we sometimes use the notation $\pi_A^{s,\ell}$ for $\pi_A^s.\texttt{phases}[\ell]$. There can be at most n_{ph} phases per oracle. The last entry of $\pi_A^s.\texttt{phases}$ contains the state of the current phase, which may still be in progress. Each entry $\pi_A^s.\texttt{phases}[\ell]$ in the log contains:

- pk, the public key used by π_A^s in that phase,
- pk', the public key that π_A^s observed as being used for its peer in that phase[2],
- $\omega \in \{0, 1\}$, denoting the authentication mode used, where 0 indicates that server-only authentication is used in that phase and 1 indicates mutual authentication,
- Δ, a counter used to keep track of the current status of the protocol execution,
- α, either $\texttt{accept}$, $\texttt{reject}$, or $\emptyset$ (for in-progress),
- k, the encryption and/or MAC key(s) established by π_A^s in that phase,
- T, the transcript of all (plaintext) messages sent and received by π_A^s during the pre-accept stage of that phase,

[2]One of the public keys may remain empty, if no client authentication is requested.

- RT_s and RT_r, the transcripts of all ciphertexts sent and received (respectively) in the post-accept phase by π_A^s encrypted under the key established in that phase,
- b, a random bit sampled by the oracle at the beginning of the phase, and
- st, some additional temporary state (which may, for instance, be used to store ephemeral Diffie–Hellman exponents for the handshake, or state for the sLHAE scheme for the record layer).

Once a phase of a protocol accepts (that is, an encryption key has been negotiated and authentication is believed to hold), then α is set to `accept`. If the protocol rejects and the oracle wishes to discontinue operation, the counter Δ can be set to the special symbol `reject`. Whenever a new handshake initialization message is received, the oracle adds a new entry to its `phases` list. The variable ω is set at some point during (or before) the protocol execution, depending on the protocol specification (e.g.in case of TLS, the server can send the message `CertificateRequest` to request client, i.e. mutual, authentication, otherwise server-only authentication is used). Application data messages sent and received encrypted under a newly established encryption key (e.g. messages sent in the TLS record layer) will be appended to variables RT_s and RT_r in the latest entry of the log. If handshake messages for the renegotiation of a new phase are encrypted under the previous phase's session key (as they are in TLS), the plaintext messages are appended to variable T in the new entry of the phase log, and ciphertexts are appended to RT in the previous phase.

REMARK 1. *The introduction of multiple* `phases` *is the main difference compared to previous AKE and ACCE models. We need to allow multiple authentications and key exchanges within one oracle to capture the functionality of renegotiation. When limited to a single phase and when each party has only one long-term key pair, our execution environment/security experiment is equivalent to the original ACCE model of Jager* et al. *[16].*

Adversarial interaction. The adversary interacts with oracles by issuing the following queries, which allow her to control (forward/alter/create/drop) all communication on the public channel (Send), learn parties' long-term secret keys (Corrupt), learn session keys (Reveal), and control sending and receiving of arbitrary messages on the encrypted record layer (Encrypt/Decrypt) using a stateful symmetric encryption scheme StE [23].

- Send(π_A^s, m): The adversary can use this query to send any (plaintext) message m of its choosing to (the current phase of) oracle π_A^s. The oracle will respond according to the protocol specification, depending on its internal state. Some distinguished control messages have special behaviour:
  - $m = (\texttt{newphase}, pk, \omega)$ triggers an oracle to initiate renegotiation of a new phase (or new session if first phase). Note that the action here may vary based on the role of the party: for example, when renegotiating in TLS, a client would prepare a new `ClientHello` message, encrypt it by calling the Encrypt oracle below, and then return the ciphertext to the adversary for delivery; a server would correspondingly prepare an encrypted `ServerHelloRequest` message.
  - $m = (\texttt{ready}, pk, \omega)$ activates a (server) oracle to use the public key pk in its next phase.

  For the above control messages, pk indicates the long-term public key pk the oracle should use in the phase and ω indicates the authentication mode to use; the oracle returns $\perp$ if it does not hold the secret key for pk. Since the control messages do not specify the identity of the peer, this is instead learned during the run of the protocol: we are using a post-specified peer model [6]. Delivery of encrypted messages in the post-accept stage are handled by the Decrypt query below. For protocols such as TLS that perform renegotiation within the encrypted channel, the oracle may reply with an error symbol $\perp$ if it has at least one entry in `phases` and $m \neq (\texttt{newphase}, \cdot)$ or $(\texttt{ready}, \cdot)$.
- Corrupt(P_A, pk): Oracle π_A^1 responds with the long-term secret key $sk_{A,i}$ corresponding to public key $pk = pk_{A,i}$ of party P_A, or $\perp$ if there is no i such that $pk = pk_{A,i}$. This is the *weak corruption model*, meaning we do not allow the adversary to obtain the party's internal state nor register rogue keys.
- Reveal(π_A^s, ℓ): Oracle π_A^s responds with the key(s) π_A^s.`phases`$[\ell].k$ used in phase ℓ, or $\emptyset$ if no such value exists. Since the TLS record layer is unidirectional, there are both encryption and decryption keys, and for most ciphersuites also MAC keys, so all 4 keys ($K_{\mathsf{enc}}^{C\to S}, K_{\mathsf{enc}}^{S\to C}, K_{\mathsf{mac}}^{C\to S}, K_{\mathsf{mac}}^{S\to C}$) would be revealed, though one could refine if desired.
- Encrypt($\pi_A^s, ctype, m_0, m_1, len, hd$): This query takes as input a content type $ctype$, messages m_0 and m_1, a length len, and header data hd. Content type `control` is used for handshake messages. The adversary cannot query this oracle with $ctype = \texttt{control}$. Through an abuse of notation, we allow the party itself to call this oracle with `control` to encrypt protocol messages that must be sent encrypted; this abuse of notation allows the party to construct encrypted protocol messages while all aspects of the security experiment remain synchronized. Content type `data` is used for record layer messages; in this case, one of the two messages (chosen based on bit b) is encrypted for the adversary to distinguish. Encrypt depends on the random bit b sampled by π_A^s at the beginning of the current phase. It maintains a counter u initialized to 0 and an encryption state st_e, and proceeds as follows:
  1. $u_A^s \leftarrow u_A^s + 1$
  2. If ($ctype = \texttt{control}$) AND caller is not π_A^s, then return $\perp$
  3. $(C^{(0)}, st_e^{(0)}) \xleftarrow{\$} \mathsf{StE.Enc}(k, len, hd, ctype\|m_0, st_e)$
  4. $(C^{(1)}, st_e^{(1)}) \xleftarrow{\$} \mathsf{StE.Enc}(k, len, hd, ctype\|m_1, st_e)$
  5. If $(C^{(0)} = \perp)$ OR $(C^{(1)} = \perp)$, then return $\perp$
  6. $(C_A^s[u_A^s], st_e) \leftarrow (C^{(b_s^A)}, st_e^{(b_s^A)})$
  7. Return $C_A^s[u_A^s]$
- Decrypt(π_A^s, C, hd): This query takes as input a ciphertext C and header data hd. If π_A^s has not accepted in the current phase, then it returns $\perp$. Decrypt maintains a counter v and a switch `diverge`, both initialized to 0, and a decryption state st_d, and proceeds as described below. If the decryption of C contains a `control` message, then the oracle processes the message according to the protocol specification, which may include updating the state of the oracle and/or creating a new

phase, and returns any protocol response message to the adversary, which may or may not be encrypted by calling Encrypt according to the protocol specification. Technically it proceeds as follows:

1. $(B,t) \leftarrow \pi_A^s.d$, $v_A^s \leftarrow v_A^s + 1$, $m' \leftarrow \emptyset$
2. $(ctype \| m, st_d) = \mathsf{StE.Dec}(k, hd, C, st_d)$
3. If $(v_A^s > u_B^t)$ OR $(C \neq C_B^t[v_A^s])$, then $\mathsf{diverge} \leftarrow 1$
4. If $(b_A^s = 1)$ AND $(\mathsf{diverge} = 1)$, then $m' \leftarrow m$
5. If $ctype = \texttt{control}$, then $r' \leftarrow$ protocol response for m
6. Else $r' \leftarrow \perp$
7. Return (m', r')

REMARK 2. *Note that k may be a 'multi-part' key with different parts for encryption, decryption, and MAC; we assume* StE.Enc *and* StE.Dec *know which parts to use. Also note that the 'protocol response for m'' may be encrypted by the party internally making an* Encrypt *call.*

The behaviour of the Decrypt oracle in this combined definition for confidentiality and integrity can be somewhat difficult to understand. It extends that of stateful length-hiding authenticated encryption as originally defined by Paterson *et al.* [23].

2.3 Security Definitions

In the original security definition for ACCE protocols, security is defined by requiring that (i) the protocol is a secure authentication protocol, thus any party π_A^s reaches the post-accept state only if there exists another party π_B^t such that π_A^s has a matching conversation (in the sense of [16]) to π_B^t, and (ii) data transmitted in the post-accept stage over a secure channel is secure (in a sense similar to sLHAE).

We extend this notion to include security when a session has multiple phases that can be renegotiated. We will give several security definitions with different levels of security against renegotiation attacks, as described in the introduction to Section 2.

Each security notion is formally defined as a game played between an adversary $\mathcal{A}$ and a challenger $\mathcal{C}$, with the same overall setup but different winning conditions. In each game, the challenger implements the collection of oracles $\{\pi_A^s : A \in [1, n_{\text{pa}}], s \in [1, n_{\text{se}}]\}$. At the beginning of the game, the challenger generates n_{ke} long-term key pairs $(pk_{A,1}, sk_{A,1}), \ldots, (pk_{A,n_{\text{ke}}}, sk_{A,n_{\text{ke}}})$ for each party P_A; we assume that, within a party, all public key pairs are distinct. (That distinct parties have distinct key pairs comes as a consequence of the protocol being secure.) The adversary receives all parties' public keys as input. The adversary may issue Send, Corrupt, Reveal, Encrypt, and Decrypt queries to the oracles and eventually terminates.

DEFINITION 1 (CORRECT MULTI-PHASE ACCE). *We say Π is a* correct multi-phase ACCE protocol *if, for all oracles π_A^s with destination address $\pi_A^s.d = \pi_B^t$, and for all $\ell, \ell' \in [1, n_{\text{ph}}]$ for which $\pi_A^s.\mathtt{phases}[\ell].T$ and $\pi_B^t.\mathtt{phases}[\ell'].T$ are matching conversations, it holds that $\pi_A^s.\mathtt{phases}[\ell].\alpha = \pi_B^t.\mathtt{phases}[\ell'].\alpha = \mathtt{accept}$, $\pi_A^s.\mathtt{phases}[\ell].\omega = \pi_B^t.\mathtt{phases}[\ell].\omega$ and $\pi_A^s.\mathtt{phases}[\ell].k = \pi_B^t.\mathtt{phases}[\ell'].k$.*

2.3.1 Confidentiality.

All of our notions for secure ACCE protocols will require confidentiality/integrity of the post-accept stage record layer in each uncorrupted phase. Intuitively, an adversary should not be able to guess the bit b used in the Encrypt/Decrypt oracles in a phase where she has not impersonated the parties (i.e., corrupted the long-term secret keys before the phase accepted) or revealed the session key of the party or its peer. As with the ACCE notion of Jager *et al.* [16], this notion ensures forward security: corrupting long-term secret keys after completion of a session should not impact confidentiality/integrity of messages.

DEFINITION 2 (CONFIDENTIALITY/INTEGRITY). *Suppose an algorithm $\mathcal{A}$ with running time τ interacts with a multi-phase ACCE protocol Π in the above execution environment and returns a tuple (A, s, ℓ, b'). If*

C1. *$\pi_A^s.\mathtt{phases}[\ell].\alpha = \mathtt{accept}$; and*
C2. *$\mathcal{A}$ did not query* $\mathsf{Corrupt}(P_A, \pi_A^s.\mathtt{phases}[\ell].pk)$ *before π_A^s accepted in phase ℓ; and*
C3. *$\mathcal{A}$ did not query* $\mathsf{Corrupt}(P_B, \pi_A^s.\mathtt{phases}[\ell].pk')$ *before π_A^s accepted in phase ℓ, where $\pi_A^s.d = \pi_B^t$; and*
C4. *$\mathcal{A}$ did not query* $\mathsf{Reveal}(\pi_A^s, \ell)$*; and*
C5. *$\mathcal{A}$ did not query* $\mathsf{Reveal}(\pi_B^t, \ell')$*, where $\pi_B^t = \pi_A^s.d$ is π_A^s's intended communication partner, and ℓ' is any phase for which $\pi_B^t.\mathtt{phases}[\ell'].T$ is a matching conversation to $\pi_A^s.\mathtt{phases}[\ell].T$; and*
C6. $|\Pr[\pi_A^s.\mathtt{phases}[\ell].b = b'] - 1/2| \geq \epsilon$,

*then we say $\mathcal{A}$ (τ, ϵ)-*breaks confidentiality/integrity of Π.

2.3.2 Secure multi-phase ACCE.

First we state a straightforward extension of the ACCE model to protocols with multiple phases, but with essentially no security condition relating one phase to another. This definition captures the properties of TLS without any renegotiation countermeasures, and will be used as a stepping stone in our generic result in Section 4. For this simplest notion of authentication, an adversary should not be able to cause a phase to accept unless there exists a phase at the peer with a matching pre-accept handshake transcript, provided she has not impersonated the parties (i.e., corrupted long-term secret keys before the phase accepted).

DEFINITION 3 (SECURE MULTI-PHASE ACCE). *Suppose an algorithm $\mathcal{A}$ with running time τ interacts with a multi-phase ACCE protocol Π in the above execution environment and terminates. If, with probability at least ϵ, there exists an oracle π_A^s with $\pi_A^s.d = \pi_B^t$ and a phase ℓ such that*

A1. *$\pi_A^s.\mathtt{phases}[\ell].\alpha = \mathtt{accept}$; and*
A2. *$\mathcal{A}$ did not query* $\mathsf{Corrupt}(P_A, \pi_A^s.\mathtt{phases}[\ell].pk)$ *before π_A^s accepted in phase ℓ; and*
A3. *$\mathcal{A}$ did not query* $\mathsf{Corrupt}(P_B, \pi_A^s.\mathtt{phases}[\ell].pk')$ *before π_A^s accepted in phase ℓ; and*
A4. *if $\pi_A^s.\mathtt{phases}[\ell].\omega = 0$ then $\pi_A^s.\rho =$* Client*; and*
A5. *$\mathcal{A}$ did not query* $\mathsf{Reveal}(\pi_B^t, \ell')$ *before π_A^s accepted in phase ℓ for any ℓ' such that $\pi_B^t.\mathtt{phases}[\ell'].T$ is a matching conversation to $\pi_A^s.\mathtt{phases}[\ell].T$; and*
M. *there is no ℓ' such that $\pi_B^t.\mathtt{phases}[\ell'].T$ is a matching conversation to $\pi_A^s.\mathtt{phases}[\ell].T$*

*then we say that $\mathcal{A}$ (τ, ϵ)-*breaks authentication of Π.

*A protocol Π is a (τ, ϵ)-*secure multi-phase ACCE protocol *if there exists no algorithm $\mathcal{A}$ that (τ, ϵ)-breaks confidentiality/integrity (Def. 2) or authentication (as above) of Π.*

In **A1** and **M** we redefine the $\mathtt{NoMatch}$-condition from [1]. In **A2** we exclude leaking of the secret long-term keys of the accepting party (necessary for example to counter key compromise impersonation attacks). In **A3** we exclude corruptions of the peer. In **A4** (only for server-only authentication), we ensure that the adversary only wins by making a client-oracle maliciously accept. In **A5** we exclude trivial attacks that exist for protocols with explicit key confirmation and probabilistic computations under the negotiated key.

The secure multi-phase ACCE definition when limited to a phase per session and a single key pair per party ($n_{\text{ph}} = n_{\text{ke}} = 1$) collapses to an extension of the original ACCE definition, the extension being support for server-only authentication.

2.3.3 Secure renegotiable ACCE.

We next strengthen the authentication notion to include renegotiation. Intuitively, an adversary should not be able to cause a phase to accept unless there exists a phase at the peer with a matching pre-accept handshake transcript and all previous phases' handshake and record layer transcripts match, provided she has not impersonated the parties in the current phase. We will show in Section 5 that TLS with our proposed countermeasure satisfies this definition.

DEFINITION 4 (SECURE RENEGOTIABLE ACCE). *Suppose an algorithm $\mathcal{A}$ with running time τ interacts with a multi-phase ACCE protocol Π in the above execution environment and terminates. If, with probability at least ϵ, there exists an oracle π_A^s with $\pi_A^s.d = \pi_B^t$ and a phase ℓ^* such that*
A1–A5 *as in Definition 3 with ℓ^*, and either*
M′(a) *π_B^t.*$\mathtt{phases}[\ell^*].T$ *is not a matching conversation to π_A^s.*$\mathtt{phases}[\ell^*].T$ *or*
M′(b) *for some $\ell < \ell^*$, π_A^s.*$\mathtt{phases}[\ell].T \| RT_s \| RT_r \neq \pi_B^t.\mathtt{phases}[\ell].T \| RT_r \| RT_s$;
we say $\mathcal{A}$ (τ, ϵ)-breaks renegotiation authentication of Π.

A protocol Π *is a* (τ, ϵ)-secure renegotiable ACCE protocol *if there exists no algorithm $\mathcal{A}$ that* (τ, ϵ)*-breaks confidentiality/integrity (Def. 2) or renegotiation authentication (as defined above) of* Π.

2.3.4 Weakly secure renegotiable ACCE.

Unfortunately, TLS with SCSV/RIE does not meet Def. 4 because, as we will see in Section 4.1, revealing session keys in earlier phases allows the adversary to change the messages on the record layer in earlier phases, but SCSV/RIE will not detect this.

Of course, revealing earlier phases' session keys while that phase is active and still expecting detection when renegotiating later is a strong security property, and the lack of this property does not imply an attack in most scenarios. Our desire to characterize the renegotiable security of the SCSV/RIE countermeasure motivates a slightly weaker renegotiation notion: when previous phases' session keys are not revealed while that phase is active and the current phase's long-term secret keys are not corrupted, no adversary should be able to cause a phase to accept unless there exists a phase at the peer with a matching pre-accept handshake transcript and all previous phases' handshake and record layer transcripts match.

DEFINITION 5 (WEAKLY SECURE RENEGOTIABLE ACCE). *Suppose an algorithm $\mathcal{A}$ with running time τ interacts with a multi-phase ACCE protocol Π in the above execution environment and terminates. If, with probability at least ϵ, there exists an oracle π_A^s with $\pi_A^s.d = \pi_B^t$ and a phase ℓ^* such that all conditions from Def. 4, as well as the following additional conditions are satisfied:*
A6. *$\mathcal{A}$ did not issue a* $\mathsf{Reveal}(\pi_A^s, \ell)$ *query before π_A^s accepted in phase $\ell + 1$, for every $\ell < \ell^*$, and*
A7. *$\mathcal{A}$ did not issue a* $\mathsf{Reveal}(\pi_B^t, \ell)$ *query before π_A^s accepted in phase $\ell + 1$, for every $\ell < \ell^*$;*
then we say that $\mathcal{A}$ (τ, ϵ)-breaks weak renegotiation authentication of Π.

A protocol Π *is a* (τ, ϵ)-weakly secure renegotiable ACCE protocol *if there exists no algorithm $\mathcal{A}$ that* (τ, ϵ) *breaks confidentiality/integrity (Def. 2) or weak renegotiation authentication (as defined above) of* Π.

REMARK 3. *While conditions **A6** and **A7** prohibit the adversary from revealing encryption keys of previous phases while active* for the purposes of breaking authentication, *the confidentiality/integrity aspect of Def. 5 still places no such restriction on previous encryption keys being revealed.*

REMARK 4. *The chain of implications between Defns. 3–5 is as follows: secure renegotiable ACCE protocol (Defn. 4) $\Longrightarrow$ weakly secure renegotiable ACCE (Defn. 5) $\Longrightarrow$ secure multi-phase ACCE (Defn. 3) $\Longrightarrow$ ACCE protocol [16]. The separations are strict, as seen in Table 1.*

3. TLS RENEGOTIATION (IN)SECURITY

We now discuss how the original TLS protocol, without SCSV/RIE countermeasures, fits into our model, and show how the attack of Ray and Dispensa is captured in the model.

Jager *et al.* [16] in their full version described how to map TLS into the ACCE model. We highlight a few components of that mapping, and the alterations needed for renegotiation.

Oracles generally respond to Send, Encrypt, and Decrypt queries as specified by the TLS handshake and record layer protocols. The Send control message $m = (\mathtt{newphase}, pk)$ when sent to a client causes the client to send a new `ClientHello` message, and when sent to a server causes the server to send a new `HelloRequest` message. For the Encrypt and Decrypt queries, we use a content type field *ctype* that corresponds to the `ContentType` field of the `TLSPlaintext` data type in the TLS record layer specification [9, §6.2.1]:

Packets with `ContentType=change_cipher_spec (20)` or `handshake (22)` are considered in our model to have *ctype* = `control` and packets with `ContentType=application_data (23)` are considered in our model to have *ctype* = `data`. We do not explicitly handle `ContentType=alert (21)` messages. The Reveal query reveals the encryption and MAC keys derived from the master secret key, *not* the master secret key itself.

3.1 TLS without countermeasures is not a (weakly) secure renegotiable ACCE

Recall the TLS renegotiation attack by Ray and Dispensa [24], as described previously in Figure 1 on page . The attacker Eve observes Alice attempting to establish a TLS session with Bob. Eve delays Alice's initial `ClientHello` and instead establishes her own TLS session with Bob and transmits a message m_0 over that record layer. Then Eve passes Alice's initial `ClientHello` to Bob over the Eve–Bob record layer. Bob views this as a valid renegotiation and responds accordingly; Eve relays the handshake messages between Alice and Bob, who will eventually establish a new record layer to which Eve has no access. Alice then transmits a message m_1 over the Alice–Bob record layer. Intuitively, this is a valid attack: Alice believes this is the initial handshake, but Bob believes this is a renegotiated handshake.

Formally, this attack is captured in our weakly secure renegotiable ACCE model of Definition 5 as follows. Assume Alice and Bob each have a single oracle instance, and Eve has carried out the above attack. Then for Bob's oracle π^1_{Bob}, the value of ℓ^* is 2: the last entry in **phases** where Bob has a matching handshake transcript to some handshake transcript in Alice's oracle π^1_{Alice} is the second (and last) **phases** entry. The attacker has broken renegotiation authentication at both Alice and Bob's instances. At Alice by satisfying condition $\mathbf{M'(a)}$ (Alice's first handshake transcript does not match Bob's first handshake transcript), and at Bob by satisfying both $\mathbf{M'(a)}$ (Bob's second handshake transcript does not match Alice's second handshake transcript) and $\mathbf{M'(b)}$ (for every $\ell < 2$, Bob's ℓth handshakes/record layer transcripts do not match Alice's). Thus TLS without countermeasures is not a weakly secure or secure renegotiable ACCE.

4. RENEGOTIATION SECURITY OF TLS WITH SCSV/RIE COUNTERMEASURE

In this section we analyze the security of TLS with the SCSV/RIE countermeasures proposed in RFC 5746 [26]. We first see, in Section 4.1, that the SCSV/RIE countermeasures are not enough to prove that TLS satisfies our strongest notion, a secure renegotiable ACCE (Defn. 4).

Our goal will be to show that TLS with the SCSV/RIE countermeasures is a weakly secure renegotiable ACCE. Ideally, we would do so generically, with a result saying something like "If a TLS ciphersuite is a secure ACCE, then that TLS ciphersuite with SCSV/RIE is a weakly secure renegotiable ACCE." As noted in the introduction, we do so generically since the protocol is *modified* to include the countermeasure values in the **ClientHello** and **ServerHello** messages, and thus we cannot make use of the ACCE security of the particular TLS ciphersuite in a black-box way. Moreover, we must ensure that revealing the **Finished** values from the previous handshake does not impact its security. Although these barriers prevent a generic black-box result, a white-box examination of the proof details of **TLS_DHE_DSS_** [16] finds that only small changes are needed in the proof.

We will provide a sequence of definitions and results that justifies the security of the SCSV/RIE countermeasure.

1. Define a modified ACCE security model, called *tagged-ACCE-fin*, specific to TLS, in which the adversary can reveal **Finished** messages after the handshake completes and supply tags to be used in extensions.
2. Define *tagged TLS* as a modification of a standard ciphersuite in which arbitrary opaque data can be placed in an extension field in the **ClientHello** and **ServerHello** messages.
3. Explain how the existing proof of that **TLS_DHE_DSS_** is ACCE secure can be modified in a very minor way to show that tagged **TLS_DHE_DSS_** is tagged-ACCE-fin-secure.
4. Show that, if a TLS ciphersuite is tagged-ACCE-fin secure, then that TLS ciphersuite with SCSV/RIE is a secure multi-phase ACCE.
5. Show that, if a TLS ciphersuite with SCSV/RIE is a secure multi-phase ACCE, then it is also a weakly secure renegotiable ACCE.

Combined, these results yield (a) a general result justifying the security of the SCSV/RIE countermeasure, and (b) that **TLS_DHE_DSS_** with SCSV/RIE countermeasures is a weakly secure renegotiable ACCE.

4.1 TLS with SCSV/RIE is not a secure renegotiable ACCE

Definition 4 requires that, even when the adversary can reveal previous phases' session keys, the parties will not successfully renegotiate if the attacker has manipulated the record layer. The SCSV/RIE countermeasures do not protect against this type of adversary. They only provide assurance that handshake transcripts from previous phases match exactly. TLS itself of course provides integrity protection for record layer transcripts via the message authentication codes, but Definition 4 allows the adversary to reveal the encryption and MAC keys of previous phases. Thus, an adversary who reveals the current encryption and MAC keys can modify record layer messages but Alice and Bob will still successfully renegotiate a new phase (although the adversary must not alter the number of messages sent, as the *number* of record layer messages sent in the previous phase happens to be protected by SCSV and RIE countermeasures).

We emphasize that while this demonstrates a theoretical weakness in TLS renegotiation countermeasures compared to our very strong security model, it does not translate into an attack on TLS renegotiation countermeasures when intermediate phases' encryption and MAC keys are not revealed. SCSV/RIE meets its original goal of authenticating the previous handshake.

4.2 Tagged-ACCE model and tagged TLS

In this section we introduce a variant of the ACCE model from which we can prove a generic result on the renegotiable security of TLS with countermeasures. In our models, the tag can be an arbitrary string. For our purpose of analyzing TLS with SCSV/RIE countermeasures, the tag will be the previous phase's **Finished** messages.

4.2.1 Tagged-ACCE security model

The *tagged-ACCE* security model is an extension of the ACCE security model to allow arbitrary tags as follows. Since the original ACCE definition of Jager *et al.* [16] does not support server-only authentication, while our definition allows both authentication modes, we extend the ACCE definition implied by limiting multi-phase ACCE (Definition 3) to a single phase ($n_{\text{ph}} = 1$) and at most one public key per party ($n_{\text{ke}} = 1$).

The phases log **phases** is extended with an additional per-phase variable *tag*.

- $\mathsf{Send}(\pi^s_A, m)$. The adversary can specify an arbitrary tag during session initialization.
  - If $m = (\mathbf{newphase}, \omega, tag)$, the party sets its internal variable $\rho \leftarrow \mathsf{Client}$, sets authentication mode ω, stores tag, and responds with the first protocol message.
  - If $m = (\mathbf{ready}, \omega, tag)$, the party sets $\rho \leftarrow \mathsf{Server}$, authentication mode ω, stores tag, and responds with the next protocol message, if any.

The freshness and winning conditions of tagged-ACCE are unchanged from ACCE.

4.2.2 Tagged-ACCE-fin security model

We will work with a further variant, *tagged-ACCE-fin*, which is not a fully general security model but instead is tied specifically to generic TLS protocols of the form given in Figure 2. It adds the following query:

- $\mathsf{RevealFin}(\pi_A^s)$: If $\alpha = \texttt{accept}$, then return the fin_C and fin_S values sent/received by the queried oracle. Return $\emptyset$ otherwise.

The following queries are modified:

- $\mathsf{Encrypt}(\pi_A^s, ctype, m_0, m_1, len, hd)$: The adversary is not prevented from querying with $ctype = \texttt{control}$.
- $\mathsf{Decrypt}(\pi_A^s, C, hd)$: No semantic meaning is associated with $ctype = \texttt{control}$ messages. In other words, line 5 of Decrypt is removed.

We extend the Encrypt- and Decrypt-queries to allow the adversary to send and receive messages on the encrypted channel with content type `control`. The freshness and winning conditions of tagged-ACCE-fin are as in ACCE.

REMARK 5. *Revealing the **Finished** messages is very specific to the TLS protocol family and is not necessarily relevant for other protocols. Imagine, for example, a variant of the SCSV/RIE countermeasure where a separate hash of the complete transcript as it was sent over the channel is used as an authenticator. Since this value can be computed by any passive adversary, leaking this value could not affect security.*

4.2.3 Tagged TLS

Figure 2 shows a generic TLS ciphersuite, along with the SCSV/RIE extensions denoted in green with a dagger. By *tagged TLS*, we mean the generic TLS ciphersuite from Figure 2, without any of the SCSV/RIE extensions shown in green, but where an arbitrary string can be placed in the ext_C and ext_S fields. In other words, it is a normal TLS ciphersuite, but with an arbitrary extension field that just carries strings that are not being interpreted as having any particular meaning.

As noted in the beginning of this section, we cannot generically prove that, if a TLS ciphersuite is ACCE-secure, then the tagged version of that ciphersuite is tagged-ACCE- or tagged-ACCE-fin-secure, as we have made white-box modifications to the TLS protocol in introducing the SCSV/RIE countermeasure. Thus we cannot use its security results in a black-box manner. However, in most cases, a white-box approach, where the actual security proof is modified or extended, should be possible, and even very easy. This was indeed the case when we examined tagged **TLS_DHE_DSS_**.

THEOREM 1 (INFORMAL). *Under the same assumptions on the cryptographic building blocks as in Jager* et al. *[16],* **TLS_DHE_DSS_** *is a secure tagged-ACCE-fin protocol.*

The formal theorem statement and proof are omitted due to the space limitation and appear in the full version [14]. The proof follows almost exactly the proof by Jager *et al.* [16] that **TLS_DHE_DSS_** is a secure ACCE protocol. Leaking the **Finished** messages does not affect security due to a game hop where, due pseudorandomness of the PRF, the **Finished** messages are replaced with uniformly random values independent of any information exchanged during the handshake. Including arbitrary extra data in the handshake messages does not impact security.

4.3 TLS with SCSV/RIE is multi-phase-secure

We begin by showing that including the SCSV/RIE countermeasure does not *weaken* security: putting the **Finished** messages in the **ClientHello** and **ServerHello** does not introduce any vulnerabilities. Having done so, in the next subsection we will show how including the SCSV/RIE countermeasure yields a weakly secure renegotiable ACCE.

THEOREM 2. *Let Π be a generic tagged TLS ciphersuite as described in Section 4.2. Assume that Π is $(\tau, \epsilon_{\mathsf{tagged}})$-tagged-ACCE-fin-secure. Let Π' denote Π with SCSV/RIE countermeasures as described in Figure 2. For any adversary that $(\tau', \epsilon_{\mathsf{mp}})$-breaks the multi-phase ACCE security of Π' with $\tau \approx \tau'$, it holds that $\epsilon_{\mathsf{mp}} \leq 2\epsilon'$, where ϵ' is obtained from ϵ by replacing all instances of n_{pa} in ϵ with $n_{\mathsf{pa}} \cdot n_{\mathsf{ke}}$ and replacing all instances of n_{se} in ϵ with $n_{\mathsf{se}} \cdot n_{\mathsf{ph}}$. (Recall that $n_{\mathsf{pa}}, n_{\mathsf{se}}, n_{\mathsf{ph}}$, and n_{ke} are the maximum number of parties, sessions per party, phases per session, and keypairs per party, respectively.)*

Due to the page limitation we only give the proof strategy here and refer to the anonymous full version [14] for the details.

Proof idea: We will construct a multi-phase ACCE simulator $\mathcal{S}$ for Π' that makes use of a tagged-ACCE-fin challenger $\mathcal{C}$ for Π. $\mathcal{S}$ will simulate every (party, public-key) pair and every (session, phase) pair with distinct parties and sessions in $\mathcal{C}$. For the most part, $\mathcal{S}$ will relay queries down to $\mathcal{C}$ and return the result. However, for queries that relate to renegotiation (Send, Decrypt), $\mathcal{S}$ carefully manages the handshake messages to transition one session in $\mathcal{C}$ to another. □

REMARK 6. *A simulation similar to the one in the proof allows us to prove that TLS with SCSV/RIE countermeasures is a multi-phase ACCE protocol, even when different ciphersuites are used in different phases. The simulator interacts with a different tagged-ACCE-fin challenger for each ciphersuite; when a renegotiation inside one ciphersuite will result in a new ciphersuite, the simulator uses the* Encrypt/Decrypt *queries in the old ciphersuite to encrypt the* Send *messages from the handshake of the new ciphersuite. Unfortunately, for this multi-ciphersuite simulation to work, it is essential that public keys not be shared across ciphersuites: this technique could show that switching between an RSA-based ciphersuite and an ECDSA-based ciphersuite is safe. However, to analyze using the same RSA public key in two different ciphersuites, one would have to take an alternative approach, as it may not be possible to generically prove that re-using the same public key in two ACCE protocols is safe.*

4.4 TLS with SCSV/RIE is a weakly secure renegotiable ACCE

We are now in a position to show that the use of the SCSV/RIE countermeasure in TLS results in a weakly secure renegotiable ACCE. We will do so generically, starting from the consequence of the previous theorem: that TLS with SCSV/RIE is a secure multi-phase ACCE.

THEOREM 3. *Let Π be a TLS ciphersuite with SCSV/RIE countermeasures, as described in Figure 2. If Π is a $(\tau, \epsilon_{\mathsf{mp}})$-secure multi-phase ACCE protocol, and* PRF *is a $(\tau, \epsilon_{\mathsf{prf}})$-secure pseudorandom function, then Π is a (τ, ϵ)-weakly secure renegotiable ACCE, with $\epsilon = \epsilon_{\mathsf{mp}} + \epsilon_{\mathsf{prf}}$.*

The full proof of the theorem appears in Appendix A.

Intuitively, the use of the RIE countermeasure guarantees that each party who renegotiates has the same view of (a) whether they are renegotiating, and (b) which handshake is the "previous" handshake. We can chain these together to obtain the property of a secure renegotiable ACCE: parties who renegotiate have the same view of all previous handshakes. If this is violated, either the non-renegotiable aspects of TLS have been broken, or a collision has been found in the computation of the renegotiation indication extension.

We can combine Theorems 2 and 3 to obtain the central results of the paper, justifying the security of the SCSV/RIE countermeasure:

COROLLARY 1. *If a tagged TLS ciphersuite* Π *as described in Section 4.2 is a secure tagged-ACCE-fin protocol and* PRF *is a secure pseudorandom function, then that TLS ciphersuite* Π *with SCSV/RIE countermeasures as described in Figure 2 is a weakly secure renegotiable ACCE.* □

COROLLARY 2. *Under the same assumptions as in Theorem 1,* `TLS_DHE_DSS_` *with SCSV/RIE countermeasures is a weakly secure renegotiable ACCE protocol.* □

5. RENEGOTIATION SECURITY OF TLS WITH A NEW COUNTERMEASURE

We now present a new TLS renegotiation countermeasure that provides integrity protection for the record layer transcript upon renegotiation (even when previous phases' session keys are leaked while the phase is still active), thereby achieving the full security of Definition 4. This countermeasure is quite straightforward: by including a hash of all record layer messages in the renegotiation information extension, parties can confirm that they share the same view of their previous record layers.

The renegotiation information extension already contains a fingerprint of the previous phrase's handshake transcript via the `client_verify_data` ($fin_C^{(-1)}$) and `server_verify_data` ($fin_S^{(-1)}$) values. We modify the renegotiation information extension to include an additional value, the fingerprint of the encrypted messages sent over the previous phase's record layer. In particular, if negotiating:

$$ext_C \leftarrow fin_C^{(-1)} \parallel \mathsf{PRF}(ms^{(-1)}, label_5 \| H(RT_s^{(-1)} \| RT_r^{(-1)})) \quad (1)$$

where $ms^{(-1)}$ is the previous phase's master secret, H is a collision-resistant hash function, and $RT_s^{(-1)} \| RT_r^{(-1)}$ is the client's view of the previous phase's record layer transcript; the server uses $RT_r^{(-1)} \| RT_s^{(-1)}$ instead. Appropriate checks are performed by the server. With this additional information, the two parties will now not complete renegotiation unless they have matching views of the record layer transcripts from the previous phase.

In practice, it is not difficult to, on an incremental basis, compute hashes of the ciphertexts sent and received over the record layer in that phase. In particular, it is not necessary to store all record layer messages to input to the hash function all at once, as common programming APIs for hash functions allow the hash value to be provided incrementally. However, the cost of the MAC computation can dominate the cryptographic cost of record layer computations [15]. The new countermeasure is only suitable for TLS communications over a reliable channel and could not be used with DTLS communications over an unreliable channel.

Alternatively, if the sLHAE scheme for the record layer is implemented as encrypt-then-MAC or MAC-then-encrypt, it should be possible to use MAC contained in the last encrypted message of the sLHAE scheme instead of the hash value computed above; this would result in no additional performance impact and would be easier to implement.

THEOREM 4. *Let* Π *be a TLS ciphersuite with the original RIE countermeasures as in Figure 2 but using* ext_C *as in equation (1). If* Π *is a* $(\tau, \epsilon_{\mathsf{mp}})$*-secure multi-phase ACCE protocol,* H *is a* $(\tau, \epsilon_{\mathsf{h}})$*-collision-resistant hash function, and* PRF *is a* $(\tau, \epsilon_{\mathsf{prf}})$*-secure pseudorandom function, then* Π *is a* (τ, ϵ)*-secure renegotiable ACCE, where* $\epsilon = \epsilon_{\mathsf{mp}} + \epsilon_{\mathsf{h}} + \epsilon_{\mathsf{prf}}$.

The proof proceeds similarly to that of Theorem 3. The main difference is that, in one case, the removal of restrictions **A6** and **A7** means we can no longer reduce down to a violation of confidentiality/integrity in the multi-phase security of Π, and instead have to rely on the new countermeasure to detect non-matching record layer transcripts and reduce to the security of the PRF and hash function.

We refer to the full version [14] for the full proof.

6. CONCLUSION

Although two-party protocols for establishing secure communication have been extensively studied in the literature and are widely used in practice, this is the first work to consider the important practical issue of renegotiation, in which parties update one or more aspects of their connection — authentication credentials, cryptographic parameters, or simply refresh their session key. The importance of correctly implementing renegotiation was highlighted by the 2009 attack of Ray and Dispensa on how certain applications process data from renegotiable TLS connections.

We have developed a formal model for describing the security of renegotiable cryptographic protocols, focussing on authenticated and confidential channel establishment (ACCE) protocols. We have specifically analyzed renegotiation in the TLS protocol, identifying the original attack of Ray and Dispensa in our model. We have provide a generic proof that the SCSV/RIE countermeasure offers good protection against renegotiation attacks, and give a new countermeasure that provides renegotiation security even in the face of slightly stronger adversaries. In practice, the SCSV/RIE countermeasure may be good enough.

Renegotiation, reauthentication, and rekeying are important features of many other applied cryptographic protocols. Future applied work includes examining the security of rekeying in protocols such as SSH or IKEv2 in our model. Open theoretical questions include how to adapt our approach for defining secure renegotiation to other primitives, in particular authenticated key exchange protocols. The overall security of TLS still has many important open questions, including the security of other TLS ciphersuites and the formal analysis of other complex functionality such as alerts and error messages. TLS session resumption [9, §F.1.4] is another important functionality of TLS, and it appears that our multi-phase ACCE model may be the right model in which to analyze its security, another interesting open problem. Given that attacks continue to be found outside the core key agreement component of TLS, further research into modelling the security of TLS in increasingly realistic scenarios is well-motivated.

Acknowledgements

The authors gratefully acknowledge discussions with Colin Boyd, Cas Cremers, Kenny Paterson, Jörg Schwenk, and the authors of the SCSV/RIE countermeasure [26], and the advice of anonymous reviewers. The research was supported by an Australian Technology Network–German Academic Exchange Service (ATN-DAAD) joint research cooperation scheme grant. D.S. was supported by an Australian Research Council (ARC) Discovery Project.

7. REFERENCES

[1] M. Bellare and P. Rogaway. Entity authentication and key distribution. In *Proc. CRYPTO'93*, vol. 773 of *LNCS*, pp. 232–249.

[2] K. Bhargavan, C. Fournet, M. Kohlweiss, A. Pironti, and P.-Y. Strub. Implementing tls with verified cryptographic security. In *IEEE Symposium on Security & Privacy*, 2013. `http://mitls.rocq.inria.fr/`.

[3] S. Blake-Wilson, M. Nystroem, D. Hopwood, J. Mikkelsen, and T. Wright. Transport Layer Security (TLS) extensions, June 2003. RFC 3546.

[4] D. Bleichenbacher. Chosen ciphertext attacks against protocols based on the RSA encryption standard PKCS #1. In *Proc. CRYPTO'98*, vol. 1462 of *LNCS*, pp. 1–12.

[5] C. Brzuska, M. Fischlin, N. P. Smart, B. Warinschi, and S. C. Williams. Less is more: Relaxed yet composable security notions for key exchange. *Int. J. Information Security*, 12(4):267–297.

[6] R. Canetti and H. Krawczyk. Security analysis of IKE's signature-based key-exchange protocol. In *Proc. CRYPTO 2002*, vol. 2442 of *LNCS*, pp. 143–161.

[7] T. Dierks and C. Allen. The TLS protocol version 1.0, January 1999. RFC 2246.

[8] T. Dierks and E. Rescorla. The Transport Layer Security (TLS) protocol version 1.1, April 2006. RFC 4346.

[9] T. Dierks and E. Rescorla. The Transport Layer Security (TLS) protocol version 1.2, August 2008. RFC 5246.

[10] S. Farrell. Why didn't we spot that? *IEEE Internet Computing*, 14(1):84–87, Jan.–Feb. 2010.

[11] A. O. Freier, P. Karlton, and P. C. Kocher. The Secure Sockets Layer (SSL) protocol version 3.0, August 2011. RFC 6101; republication of original SSL 3.0 specification by Netscape of November 18, 1996.

[12] S. Gajek, M. Manulis, O. Pereira, A.-R. Sadeghi, and J. Schwenk. Universally composable security analysis of TLS. In *Proc. ProvSec 2008*, vol. 5324 of *LNCS*, pp. 313–327.

[13] R. Gelashvili. Attacks on re-keying and renegotiation in key exchange protocols, April 2012. Bachelor's thesis, ETH Zurich.

[14] F. Giesen, F. Kohlar, and D. Stebila. On the security of TLS renegotiation (full version), 2013. `http://eprint.iacr.org/2012/630`.

[15] V. Gupta, D. Stebila, S. Fung, S. C. Shantz, N. Gura, and H. Eberle. Speeding up secure web transactions using elliptic curve cryptography. In *Proc. NDSS 2004*. The Internet Society, Feb. 2004.

[16] T. Jager, F. Kohlar, S. Schäge, and J. Schwenk. On the security of TLS-DHE in the standard model. In *Proc. CRYPTO 2012*, vol. 7417 of *LNCS*, pp. 273–293. Full version: `http://eprint.iacr.org/2011/219`.

[17] J. Jonsson and B. S. Kaliski Jr. On the security of RSA encryption in TLS. In *Proc. CRYPTO 2002*, vol. 2442 of *LNCS*, pp. 127–142.

[18] F. Kohlar, S. Schäge, and J. Schwenk. On the security of TLS-DH and TLS-RSA in the standard model, 2013. `http://eprint.iacr.org/2013/367`.

[19] H. Krawczyk. The order of encryption and authentication for protecting communications (or: How secure is SSL?). In *Proc. CRYPTO 2001*, vol. 2139 of *LNCS*, pp. 310–331.

[20] H. Krawczyk, K. G. Paterson, and H. Wee. On the security of the TLS protocol: A systematic analysis. In *Proc. CRYPTO 2013*, vol. 8042 of *LNCS*, pp. 429–448.

[21] D. Miller. SSL vulnerability and SSH, November 2009. `http://lists.mindrot.org/pipermail/openssh-unix-dev/2009-November/028003.html`.

[22] P. Morrissey, N. P. Smart, and B. Warinschi. A modular security analysis of the TLS handshake protocol. In *Proc. ASIACRYPT 2008*, vol. 5350 of *LNCS*, pp. 55–73.

[23] K. G. Paterson, T. Ristenpart, and T. Shrimpton. Tag size does matter: Attacks and proofs for the TLS record protocol. In *Proc. ASIACRYPT 2011*, vol. 7073 of *LNCS*, pp. 372–389.

[24] M. Ray and S. Dispensa. Renegotiating TLS, November 2009.

[25] E. Rescorla. HTTP over TLS, May 2000. RFC 2818.

[26] E. Rescorla, M. Ray, S. Dispensa, and N. Oskov. Transport Layer Security (TLS) renegotiation indication extension, February 2010. RFC 5746.

[27] Trustworthy Internet Movement. SSL Pulse, July 2013. `https://www.trustworthyinternet.org/ssl-pulse/`.

[28] T. Zoller. TLS & SSLv3 renegotiation vulnerability. Technical report, G-SEC, 2009. `http://www.g-sec.lu/practicaltls.pdf`.

APPENDIX

A. PROOF OF THEOREM 3

PROOF. Suppose $\mathcal{A}$ breaks the weak renegotiable ACCE security of the protocol Π. We will show that either $\mathcal{A}$ breaks the multi-phase ACCE security of Π or $\mathcal{A}$ can be used to construct another algorithm that breaks either the security of the PRF or the multi-phase ACCE security of Π.

We approach the proof in three cases: either $\mathcal{A}$ has broken the confidentiality/integrity of the weakly secure renegotiable ACCE, or $\mathcal{A}$ has broken the weak renegotiation authentication of the weakly secure renegotiable ACCE, the latter by meeting either condition $\mathbf{M}'(\mathbf{a})$ or $\mathbf{M}'(\mathbf{b})$.

Confidentiality/integrity. Since the winning conditions for the confidentiality/integrity part of the security game are the same for both definitions, every adversary who breaks confidentiality/integrity in the weakly secure renegotiable ACCE security game for Π breaks confidentiality/integrity in the multi-phase ACCE security game for Π.

Authentication — $\mathbf{M}'(\mathbf{a})$. Suppose $\mathcal{A}$ wins the weak renegotiable ACCE security experiment for Π using condition $\mathbf{M}'(\mathbf{a})$. Either there is no ℓ at all such that $\pi_B^t.\mathsf{phases}[\ell].T$ matches $\pi_A^s.\mathsf{phases}[\ell^*].T$, or there is such an ℓ but $\ell \neq \ell^*$.

First consider the case where there is no ℓ at all such that π_B^t.phases$[\ell].T$ matches π_A^s.phases$[\ell^*].T$. That meets condition **M** of Definition 3 for Π.

Now consider the case where there is an ℓ such that π_B^t.phases$[\ell].T$ matches π_A^s.phases$[\ell^*].T$ but $\ell \neq \ell^*$. Assume without loss of generality $\ell < \ell^*$ (otherwise we could swap the oracles).

There must exist some value $j \in [1, \ell - 1]$ such that π_A^s.phases$[\ell^* - j].T \neq \pi_B^t$.phases$[\ell - j].T$. In particular, $j \leq \ell - 1$, since in π_B^t's first phase its outgoing message m_1 contains $ext_C =$ empty but π_A^s received a message m_1 with $ext_c \neq$ empty. Let j be minimal. Then π_B^t.phases$[\ell - j + 1].T$ matches π_A^s.phases$[\ell^* - j + 1].T$. In particular, messages m_1 of those two transcripts are equal, and so are messages m_2 of those two transcripts. Since RIE is being used, m_1 and m_2 contain $fin_C^{(-1)}$ and $fin_S^{(-1)}$, and since π_A^{s,ℓ^*-j+1} accepted, both π_A^{s,ℓ^*-j+1} and $\pi_B^{t,\ell-j+1}$ used the same $fin_C^{(-1)}$ and $fin_S^{(-1)}$ values. But at each party, $fin_C^{(-1)}$ and $fin_S^{(-1)}$ are the hash (using a PRF) of the handshake transcripts from phases π_A^{s,ℓ^*-j} and $\pi_B^{t,\ell-j}$, and we know that these handshake transcripts are not equal. This means a collision has occurred in PRF, which happens with negligible probability.

Assuming PRF is secure and Π is a secure multi-phase ACCE, no $\mathcal{A}$ can achieve conditions **M′(a)** and **A1**–**A7**.

Authentication — **M′(b)**. Now suppose $\mathcal{A}$ wins the weak renegotiable ACCE security experiment for Π using condition **M′(b)** but not **M′(a)**. In particular, for every $\ell' < \ell^*$, π_A^s.phases$[\ell'].T = \pi_B^t$.phases$[\ell'].T$ *but* there is some $\ell < \ell^*$ such that π_A^s.phases$[\ell].RT_s \| RT_r \neq \pi_B^t$.phases$[\ell].RT_r \| RT_s$. Choose ℓ minimal. Let v be the smallest index such that the vth ciphertext C_v of π_A^s.phases$[\ell].RT_s \| RT_r$ is not equal to the vth ciphertext of π_B^t.phases$[\ell].RT_r \| RT_s$.

Assume without loss of generality that C_v was received by π_A^s as the vth ciphertext but was not sent by π_B^t as the vth ciphertext. (The alternative is that C_v was *sent* by π_A^s as the vth ciphertext but was not received by π_B^t as the vth ciphertext. However, we could then focus on everything from π_B^t's perspective and apply the same argument.)

This means that when $\mathcal{A}$ called Decrypt(π_A^s, C_v, hd), if $b = 0$ then Decrypt returned $(\perp, \cdot)$, whereas if $b = 1$ then Decrypt returned $(m', \cdot)$ where $m' \neq \perp$. Our simulator can thus output (A, s, ℓ, b') for its guess of b' as above, and this will equal b with probability at least ϵ, making condition **C6** hold in Definition 3. We need to show that conditions **C1**–**C5** also hold for (A, s, ℓ).

Since $\mathcal{A}$ wins the weak renegotiable ACCE experiment using condition **M′(b)**, we have that **A1**–**A7** all hold. We want to show that, at the time that π_A^s accepted in phase $\ell + 1$, conditions **C1**–**C5** also hold for (A, s, ℓ).

- **C1**: **A1** implies **C1**, since if π_A^s has rejected in any phase prior to ℓ^* then it would not have a phase ℓ^*.
- **C2** and **C3**: Conditions **A2** and **A3** of Definition 5 do not imply that $\mathcal{A}$ did not ask Corrupt queries prohibited by **C2** and **C3**. However, we do have that π_A^s.phases$[\ell].T = \pi_B^t$.phases$[\ell].T$; in other words, $\mathcal{A}$ was not *active* in the handshake for phase ℓ. Thus, $\mathcal{A}$ is *equivalent* to an adversary who did not ask any Corrupt queries for public keys used in phase ℓ until after π_A^s accepts in phase ℓ.
- **C4**: **A6** implies **C4**, at the time that π_A^s accepted.
- **C5**: Since π_A^s chooses nonce r_C (if a client) or r_S (if a server) randomly, except with negligible probability there is no $\ell' < \ell$ such that π_A^s.phases$[\ell'].T = \pi_A^s$.phases$[\ell].T$. By **A7**, $\mathcal{A}$ did not issue Reveal(π_B^t, ℓ) before π_A^s accepted in phase $\ell + 1$. Thus at the time that π_A^s accepted, $\mathcal{A}$ did not issue Reveal(π_B^t, ℓ') to any phase with π_B^t.phases$[\ell'].T = \pi_A^s$.phases$[\ell].T$, satisfying condition **C5**.

Thus, assuming Π is a secure multi-phase ACCE no $\mathcal{A}$ can achieve conditions **M′(b)** and **A1**–**A7**. □

B. GENERIC TLS PROTOCOL WITH SCSV/RIE COUNTERMEASURE

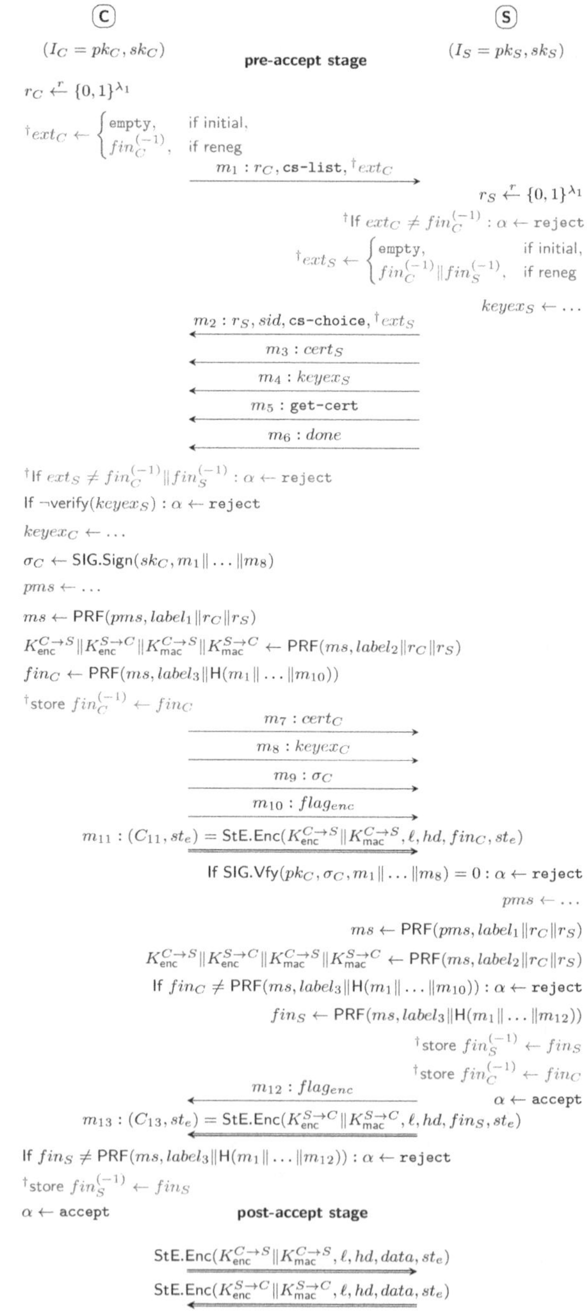

Figure 2: Generic TLS handshake protocol with †SCSV/RIE renegotiation countermeasures

Using SMT Solvers to Automate Design Tasks for Encryption and Signature Schemes

Joseph A. Akinyele*
Johns Hopkins University
Baltimore, MD, USA
akinyelj@cs.jhu.edu

Matthew Green†
Johns Hopkins University
Baltimore, MD, USA
mgreen@cs.jhu.edu

Susan Hohenberger‡
Johns Hopkins University
Baltimore, MD, USA
susan@cs.jhu.edu

ABSTRACT

Cryptographic design tasks are primarily performed by hand today. Shifting more of this burden to computers could make the design process faster, more accurate and less expensive. In this work, we investigate tools for programmatically altering existing cryptographic constructions to reflect particular design goals. Our techniques enhance both security and efficiency with the assistance of advanced tools including Satisfiability Modulo Theories (SMT) solvers.

Specifically, we propose two complementary tools, AutoGroup and AutoStrong. AutoGroup converts a pairing-based encryption or signature scheme written in (simple) symmetric group notation into a specific instantiation in the more efficient, asymmetric setting. Some existing symmetric schemes have hundreds of possible asymmetric translations, and this tool allows the user to optimize the construction according to a variety of metrics, such as ciphertext size, key size or computation time. The AutoStrong tool focuses on the security of digital signature schemes by automatically converting an existentially unforgeable signature scheme into a *strongly* unforgeable one. The main technical challenge here is to automate the "partitioned" check, which allows a highly-efficient transformation.

These tools integrate with and complement the AutoBatch tool (ACM CCS 2012), but also push forward on the complexity of the automation tasks by harnessing the power of SMT solvers. Our experiments demonstrate that the two design tasks studied can be performed automatically in a matter of seconds.

*Joseph A. Akinyele's work was supported in part by National Science Foundation (NSF) grant CNS-1154035.

†Matthew Green's work was supported in part by the Defense Advanced Research Projects Agency (DARPA) and the Air Force Research Laboratory (AFRL) under contract FA8750-11-2-0211 and the Office of Naval Research (ONR) contract N00014-11-1-0470.

‡Susan Hohenberger's work was supported in part by NSF CNS-1154035 and CNS-1228443; the DARPA and the AFRL under contract FA8750-11-2-0211, DARPA N11AP20006, the ONR under contract N00014-11-1-0470, and a Microsoft Faculty Fellowship. Applying to all authors, the views expressed are those of the author(s) and do not reflect the official policy or position of the Department of Defense, the NSF, or the U.S. Government.

CCS'13, November 4–8, 2013, Berlin, Gernany.

http://dx.doi.org/10.1145/2508859.2516718.

Categories and Subject Descriptors

D.4.6 [**Security and Protection**]: Cryptographic controls, Authentication, Access controls, Verification

Keywords

Digital Signatures, Public-Key Encryption, Pairing-Based Cryptography, Automation, Cryptographic Compilers

1. INTRODUCTION

Cryptographic design is challenging, time consuming and mostly performed by hand. A natural question to ask is: to what extent can computers ease this burden? Which common design tasks can computers execute faster, more accurately or less expensively?

In particular, this work investigates tools for programmatically altering existing cryptographic constructions in order to enhance efficiency or security design goals. For instance, digital signatures, which are critical for authenticating data in a variety of settings, ranging from sensor networks to software updates, come in many possible variations based on efficiency, functionality or security. Unfortunately, it is often infeasible or tedious for humans to document each possible optimal variation for each application. It would be enormously valuable if there could be a small number of simple ways to present a scheme – as simple as possible to avoid human-error in the design and/or verification process – and then computers could securely provide any variation that may be required by practitioners.

A simple, motivating example (which we explore in this work) is the design of pairing-based signature schemes, which are often presented in a simple "symmetric" group setting that aids in exposition, but does not map to the specific pairing-based groups that maximize efficiency. Addressing this disconnect is ripe for an automated tool.

Summary of Our Contributions In this work, we explore two novel types of design problems for pairing-based cryptographic schemes. The first tool (AutoGroup) deals with efficiency, while the second (AutoStrong) deals with security. We illustrate how they interact in Figure 1. The tools take a Scheme Description Language (SDL) representation of a scheme (and optionally some user optimization

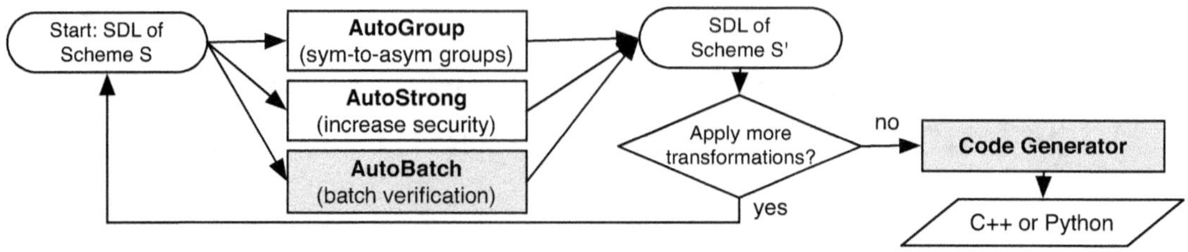

Figure 1: A high-level presentation of the new automated tools, AutoGroup and AutoStrong. They take as input a Scheme Description Language (SDL) representation of a cryptographic scheme and output an SDL representation of a transformation of the scheme, which can possibly be further transformed by another tool. These tools are compatible with the existing AutoBatch tool and Code Generator (shaded). An SDL input to the Code Generator produces a software implementation of the scheme in either C++ or Python.

constraints) and output an SDL representation of the altered scheme. This SDL output can be run through another tool or a Code Generator to produce C++ or Python software.

A contribution of this work is that we integrated our tools with the publicly-available source code for AutoBatch [3,4] of Akinyele et al. (ACM CCS 2012), a tool that automatically identifies a batch verification algorithm for a given signature scheme, therein weaving together a larger automation system. For instance, a practitioner could take any symmetric-pairing signature scheme from the literature, use AutoGroup to reduce its bandwidth in the asymmetric setting, use AutoBatch to reduce its verification time, and then automatically obtain a C++ implementation of the optimized construction. Our work appears unique in that we apply advanced tools, such as SMT solvers and Mathematica, to perform complex design tasks related to pairing-based schemes.

Automated Task 1: Optimize Efficiency of an Encryption or Signature Scheme via User Constraints. Pairings are often studied because they can realize new functionalities, e.g., [17, 19], or offer low-bandwidth solutions, e.g., [17, 21]. Pairing (a.k.a., bilinear) groups consist of three groups $\mathbb{G}_1, \mathbb{G}_2, \mathbb{G}_T$ with an efficient bilinear map $e : \mathbb{G}_1 \times \mathbb{G}_2 \rightarrow \mathbb{G}_T$. Many protocols are presented in a *symmetric* setting where $\mathbb{G}_1 = \mathbb{G}_2$ (or equivalently, there exists an efficient isomorphism from $\mathbb{G}_1$ to $\mathbb{G}_2$ or vice versa).

While symmetric groups simplify the description of new cryptographic schemes, the corresponding groups are rarely the most efficient setting for implementation [32]. The state of the art is to use *asymmetric* groups where $\mathbb{G}_1 \neq \mathbb{G}_2$ and no efficient isomorphism exists between the two. See for instance the work of Ramanna, Chatterjee and Sarkar [50] (PKC 2012) which translates the dual system encryption scheme of Waters [57] from the symmetric to a handful of asymmetric settings.

Such conversions currently require manual analysis (of all steps) – made difficult by the fact that certain operations such as group hash functions only operate in a single group. Moreover, in some cases, there are hundreds of possible symmetric to asymmetric translations, making it tedious to identify the optimal translation for a particular application.

We propose a tool called AutoGroup that automatically provides a "basic" translation from symmetric to asymmetric groups.[1] It employs an SMT solver to identify valid group assignments for all group elements and also accepts user constraints to optimize the efficiency of the scheme according to a variety of metrics, including signature/ciphertext size, signing/encryption time, and public parameter size. The tool is able to enumerate the full set of possible solutions (which may run to the hundreds), and can rapidly identify the most efficient solution.

Automated Task 2: Strengthen the Security of a Digital Signature Scheme. Most signature schemes are presented under the classic, existential unforgeability definition [35], wherein an adversary cannot produce a signature on a "new" message. However, *strong* unforgeability guarantees more – that the adversary cannot produce a "new" signature even on a previously signed message. Strongly-unforgeable signatures are often used as a building block in signcryption [6], chosen-ciphertext secure encryption [25,28] and group signatures [7,18].

There are a number of general transformations from classic to strong security [14, 15, 37, 53–55], but also a highly-efficient transformation due to Boneh, Shen and Waters [22] that only applies to "partitioned" schemes. We propose a tool called AutoStrong that automatically decides whether a scheme is "partitioned" and then applies BSW if it is and a general transformation otherwise. The partitioned test is non-trivial, and our tool harnesses the power of both an SMT solver and Mathematica to make this determination. We are careful to err only on false negatives (which impact efficiency), but not false positives (which could compromise security.) Earlier works [14,15] claimed that there were "very few" examples of partitioned schemes; however, our tool proved this was not the case by identifying valid partitions for most schemes we tested.

1.1 Related Work

Many exciting works have studied how to automate various cryptographic tasks. Automation has been introduced into the design process for various security protocols [38, 40, 49, 52], optimizations to software implementations involving elliptic-curves [10] and bilinear-map functions [48], the batch verification of digital signature schemes [4], secure two-party computation [36,41,42], and zero-knowledge proofs [5,8,9,23,43].

[1]By "basic", we mean that it translates the scheme as written into the asymmetric setting, with minor optimizations performed, but does not attempt a re-imagining of the construction based on a stronger asymmetric complexity assumption. While the latter is sometimes possible, e.g., [50], it may not be required in some applications and the novel security analysis required places it beyond the current ability of our automation tools. See Section 3.3 for more.

Our current work is most closely related to the AutoBatch tool of Akinyele et al. [4]. We borrow our tool-naming system from their paper and designed our tools so that they can integrate with the publicly-available source code of AutoBatch [3] to form a larger, more comprehensive solution. This work is different from AutoBatch in that it attacks new, more complicated design tasks and integrates external SMT solvers and Mathematica to find its solutions.

Prior work on automating the writing and verification of cryptographic proofs, such as the EasyCrypt work of Barthe et al. [13], are complimentary to but distinct from our effort. Their goal was automating the construction and verification of (game-based) cryptographic *proofs*. Our goal is automating the construction of cryptographic *schemes*. A system that combines both to automate the design of a scheme and then automate its security analysis would be optimal.

2. TOOLS USED

Our automations make use of three external tools. First, Z3 [26, 46] is a freely-available, state-of-the-art and highly efficient Satisfiability Modulo Theories (SMT) solver produced by Microsoft Research. SMT is a generalization of boolean satisfiability (SAT) solving, which determines whether assignments exist for boolean variables in a given logical formula that evaluates the formula to *true*. SMT solvers builds on SAT to support many rich first-order theories such as equality reasoning, arithmetic, and arrays. In practice, SMT solvers have been used to solve a number of constraint-satisfaction problems and are receiving increased attention in applications such as software verification, program analysis, and testing. Z3 in particular has been used as a core building block in API design tools such as Spec#/Boogie [11, 27] and in verifying C compilers such as VCC.

We leverage Z3 v4.3.1 to perform reasoning over statements involving arithmetic, quantifiers, and uninterpreted functions. We use Z3's theories for equality reasoning combined with the decision procedures for linear arithmetic expressions and elimination of universal quantifiers (*e.g.*, $\forall x$) over linear arithmetic. Z3 includes support for uninterpreted (or *free*) functions which allow any interpretation consistent with the constraints over free functions and variables.

Second, we utilize the development platform provided by Wolfram Research's Mathematica [59] (version 9), which allows us to simplify equations for several of our analytical techniques. We leverage Mathematica in our automation to validate that given cryptographic algorithms have certain mathematical properties. Finally, we utilize some of the publicly-available source code of the AutoBatch tool [3], including its Scheme Description Language (SDL) parser and its Code Generator, which translates an SDL representation to C++ or Python.

3. AUTOGROUP

In this section, we present and evaluate a tool, called AutoGroup, for automatically altering a cryptographic scheme's algebraic setting to optimize for efficiency.

3.1 Background on Pairing Groups

Let $\mathbb{G}_1, \mathbb{G}_2, \mathbb{G}_T$ be algebraic groups of prime order p.[2] We say that $e : \mathbb{G}_1 \times \mathbb{G}_2 \rightarrow \mathbb{G}_T$ is a pairing (a.k.a., bilinear map) if it is: efficiently-computable, (*bilinear*) for all $g \in \mathbb{G}_1$, $h \in \mathbb{G}_2$ and $a, b \leftarrow \mathbb{Z}_p$, $e(g^a, h^b) = e(g,h)^{ab}$; and (*non-degenerate*) if g generates $\mathbb{G}_1$ and h generates $\mathbb{G}_2$, then $e(g,h) \neq 1$. This is called the *asymmetric* setting. A specialized case is the *symmetric* setting, where $\mathbb{G}_1 = \mathbb{G}_2$.[3]

In practice, all efficient candidate constructions for pairing groups are constructed such that $\mathbb{G}_1$ and $\mathbb{G}_2$ are groups of points on some elliptic curve E, and $\mathbb{G}_T$ is a subgroup of a multiplicative group over a related finite field. The group of points on E defined over $\mathbb{F}_p$ is written as $E(\mathbb{F}_p)$. Usually $\mathbb{G}_1$ is a subgroup of $E(\mathbb{F}_p)$, $\mathbb{G}_2$ is a subgroup of $E(\mathbb{F}_{p^k})$ where k is the embedding degree, and $\mathbb{G}_T$ is a subgroup of $\mathbb{F}^*_{p^k}$. In the symmetric case $\mathbb{G}_1 = \mathbb{G}_2$ is usually a subgroup of $E(\mathbb{F}_p)$.

The challenge in selecting pairing groups is to identify parameters such that the size of $\mathbb{G}_T$ provides acceptable security against the MOV attack [44]. Hence the size of p^k must be comparable to that of an RSA modulus to provide the same level of security – hence elements of $\mathbb{F}_{p^k}$ must be of size approximately 3,072 bits to provide security at the 128-bit symmetric equivalent level. The group order q must also be large enough to resist the Pollard-ρ attack on discrete logarithms, which means in this example $q \geq 256$.

Two common candidates for implementing pairing-based constructions are supersingular curves [31, 47] in which the embedding degree k is ≤ 6 and typically smaller (an example is $|p| = 1536$ for the 128-bit security level at $k = 2$), or ordinary curves such as MNT or Barreto-Naehrig (BN) [12]. In BN curves in particular, the embedding degree $k = 12$, thus $|p| = |q|$ can be as small as 256 bits at the 128-bit security level, with a corresponding speedup in field operations.

A challenge is that the recommended BN subgroups do not possess an efficiently-computable isomorphism from $\mathbb{G}_1$ to $\mathbb{G}_2$ or vice versa, which necessitates re-design of some symmetric cryptographic protocols. A related issue is that BN curves permit efficient hashing only into the group $\mathbb{G}_1$. This places restrictions on the set of valid group assignments we can use.

3.2 How AutoGroup Works

AutoGroup is a new tool for automatically translating a pairing-based encryption or signature scheme from the symmetric-pairing setting to the asymmetric-pairing setting. At a high-level, AutoGroup takes as input a representation of a cryptographic protocol (*e.g.*, signature or encryption scheme) written in a Domain-Specific Language called Scheme Description Language (SDL), along with a description of the optimizations desired by the user. These optimizations may describe a variety of factors, e.g., requests to minimize computational cost, key size, or ciphertext / signature size. The tool outputs a new SDL representation of the scheme, one that comprises the optimal assignment of groups for the given constraints. The assignment of groups is non-trivial, as many schemes are additionally constrained by features of common asymmetric bilinear groups settings, most notably, restrictions on which groups admit efficient hashing. At a high level, AutoGroup works by reducing this constrained group assignment problem to a boolean satisfiability problem, applying an SMT solver, and processing the results. We next describe the steps of AutoGroup, as illustrated in Figure 2.

[2]Pairing groups may also have composite order, but we will be focusing on the more efficient prime order setting here.

[3]An alternative instantiation of the symmetric setting has $\mathbb{G}_1 \neq \mathbb{G}_2$ but admits an efficiently-computable isomorphism between the groups.

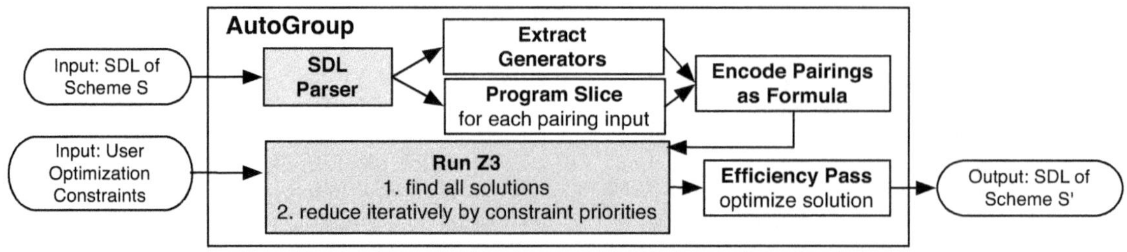

Figure 2: A high-level presentation of the AutoGroup tool, which uses external tools Z3 and SDL Parser.

1. Extract Generator Representation. The first stage of the AutoGroup process involves parsing SDL to identify all base generators of $\mathbb{G}$ that are used in the scheme. For each generator $g \in \mathbb{G}$, AutoGroup creates a pair of generators $g_1 \in \mathbb{G}_1$ and $g_2 \in \mathbb{G}_2$. This causes an increase in the parameter size of the scheme, something that we must address in later steps.

We assume the Parser knows the basic structure of the scheme, and can identify the algorithm responsible for parameter generation. This allows us to parse the algorithm to observe which generators that are created. When AutoGroup detects the first generator, it marks this as the "base" generator of $\mathbb{G}$ and splits g into a pair $g_1 \in \mathbb{G}_1$ and $g_2 \in \mathbb{G}_2$. Every subsequent group element sampled by the scheme is defined in terms of the base generators. For example, if the setup algorithm next calls for "choosing a random generator h in $\mathbb{G}$", then AutoGroup will select a random $t' \in \mathbb{Z}_p$ and compute new elements $h_1 = g_1^{t'}$ and $h_2 = g_2^{t'}$.

2. Traceback Inputs to the Pairing Function. Recall that the pairing function $e(A, B)$ takes two inputs. We extract all the pairings required in the scheme; these might come from the setup algorithm, encryption/signing, or decryption/verification. Prior to tracing the pairing inputs, we split pairings of the form $e(g, A \cdot B)$ as $e(g, A) \cdot e(g, B)$ to prepare for encoding pairings as logical formulas in the SMT solver. In the final step of AutoGroup we recombine the pairings to preserve efficiency. We reuse techniques introduced in [4, 29] to split and combine pairings in AutoGroup.

After splitting applicable pairings, we obtain a program slice for each variable input to determine which (symmetric) generators were involved in computing it. This also helps us later track which variables are affected when an assignment for a given variable is made in $\mathbb{G}_1$ or $\mathbb{G}_2$. Consider the example $A = X \cdot Y$. Clearly, the group assignment of A affects variables X and Y, and capturing the slice for each pairing input variable is crucial for AutoGroup to perform correct re-assignment for the subset of affected variables.

3. Convert Pairings to Logical Formulas. Asymmetric pairings require that one input to the function be in $\mathbb{G}_1$, and the other be in $\mathbb{G}_2$. Conversion from a symmetric to an asymmetric pairing can be reduced to a constraint satisfiability problem; we model the asymmetric pairing as an inequality operator over binary variables. This is analogous because an inequality constraint enforces that the binary variables either have a 0 or 1 value, but not both for the equation to be satisfiable. Therefore, we express symmetric pairings as a logical formula of inequality operators over binary variables separated by conjunctive connectors (*e.g.*, $A \neq B \wedge C \neq D$). We then employ an SMT solver to find a satisfiable solution and apply the solver's solution to produce an equivalent scheme in the asymmetric setting.

4. Convert Pairing Limitations into Constraints. When translating from the symmetric to the asymmetric pairing setting, we encounter several limitations that must be incorporated into our model. Chief among these are limitations on hashing: in some asymmetric groups, hashing to $\mathbb{G}_2$ is not possible. In other groups, there is no such isomorphism, but it is possible to hash into $\mathbb{G}_1$. Depending on the groups that the user selects, we must identify an asymmetric solution that respects these constraints. Fortunately these constraints can easily be expressed in our formulae, by simply assigning the output of hash functions to a specific group, e.g., $\mathbb{G}_1$.

5. Execute SMT Solver. We run the logical formula plus constraints through an SMT solver to identify a satisfying assignment of variables. The solver checks for a satisfiable solution and produces a model of 0 (or $\mathbb{G}_1$) and 1 (or $\mathbb{G}_2$) values for the pairing input variables that satisfies the specified constraints. We can go one step further and enumerate all the unique solutions (or models) found by the solver for a given formula and constraints. After obtaining all the possible models, we utilize the solver to evaluate each model and determine the solutions that satisfies the user's application-specific requirements.

6. Satisfy Application-specific Requirements. To facilitate optimizations in the asymmetric setting that suit user applications, we allow users to specify additional constraints on the chosen solution. There are two possible ways of tuning AutoGroup: one set of options focus on reducing the size of certain scheme outputs. For public key encryption, the user can choose to minimize the representation of the secret keys, ciphertext or both. Similarly, for signatures schemes, the user can optimize for minimal-sized public keys, signatures or both. The second set of options focus on reducing algorithm execution times. This is possible due to the fact that for many candidate asymmetric groups, group operations in $\mathbb{G}_1$ are dramatically more efficient than those that take place in $\mathbb{G}_2$. Users may also combine various operations, in order to find an optimal solution based on a combination of size and operation time.

We find application-specific solutions by minimizing an objective function over all the possible models obtained from the solver. Our objective function is straightforward and calculated as follows:

$$F(A, C, w_1, w_2) = \sum_{i=1}^{n}((1 - a_i) \cdot w_1 + a_i \cdot w_2) \cdot c_i$$

where $A = a_i, \ldots, a_n$ and represents the pairing input variables, w_1 and w_2 denote *weights* over groups $\mathbb{G}_1$ and $\mathbb{G}_2$, respectively, $C = c_i, \ldots, c_n$ and each c_i corresponds to the *cost* for each a_i. Each input variable a_i can have a value of $0 = \mathbb{G}_1$ or $1 = \mathbb{G}_2$. We now describe how the above options are converted into parameters of F and discuss how the SMT solver is used to obtain a minimal solution.

For each parameter that we intend to optimize, we define a *weight function* that evaluates each candidate solution according to some metric. For each assigned variable, the weight function calculates the total "cost" of the construction as a function of some cost value for the specific variable, as well as an overall cost for an assignment of $\mathbb{G}_1$ and $\mathbb{G}_2$. In the case of ciphertext size we assign the cost value to 1 for each group element that appears in the ciphertext, and 0 for all others. For encryption time, we assign a cost that corresponds to the number of group operations applied to this variable during the encryption operation. The overall cost value then determines the cost of placing a value in one of the two groups – for size-related calculations, this roughly corresponds to the length of a group element's representation, and for operation time it corresponds to the cost of a single group operation. By assigning these costs correctly, we are able to create a series of different weight functions that represent all of the different values that we would like to minimize (e.g., ciphertext size, parameter size, time).

If the user chooses to optimize for multiple criteria simultaneously, we must find a model that balances between all of these at the same time. This is not always possible. For example, some schemes admit solutions that favor a minimized secret key size or ciphertext size, but not both. In this case, we allow the user to determine which constraint to relax and thereby select the next best solution that satisfies their requirements.

7. Evaluate and Process the Solution. Once the application-specific solution is obtained from the solver, the next step is to apply the solution to produce an asymmetric scheme. As indicated earlier, we interpret the solution for each variable as $0 = \mathbb{G}_1$ and $1 = \mathbb{G}_2$. To apply the solution, we first pre-process each algorithm in SDL to determine how the pairing inputs are affected by each assignment. Consider a simplistic example: $e(A, B)$ where $A = g^a$ and $B = h^b$. Let us assume that the satisfying solution is that $A \in \mathbb{G}_1$ and $B \in \mathbb{G}_2$. Therefore, we would rewrite these two variables as $A = g_1^a$ and $B = h_2^b$ where $g_1 \in \mathbb{G}_1$ and $h_2 \in \mathbb{G}_2$. The program slice recorded for each pairing input in step (2) provides the necessary information to correctly rewrite the scheme in the asymmetric setting.

In addition to rewriting the scheme, AutoGroup performs several final optimizations. First, it removes any unused parameter values in the public and secret keys. For signature schemes, we try to optimize further by reducing the public parameters used per algorithm. In particular, we trace which variables in the public key are actually used during signing and verification. For elements that appear only in the signing (resp. decryption) algorithms, we split the public key into two: one is kept just for computing signatures (resp. decryption), and the other is given out for use in encryption/verification. Second, AutoGroup performs an additional efficiency check and attempts to optimize pairing product equations to use as few pairings as possible. This is due to the decoupling of pairings in earlier phases of translating the scheme to the asymmetric setting or perhaps, just a loose design by the original SDL designer. In either case, we apply pairing optimization techniques from previous work [4, 29] to provide this automatic efficiency check. Finally, AutoGroup outputs a new SDL of the modified scheme.

We do not offer the efficiency check of AutoGroup as a standalone tool for symmetric groups at present, because our experience inclines us to believe that most practitioners concerned with efficiency will want to work in asymmetric groups. However, our results herein also demonstrate that a simple tool of this sort is efficient and feasible.

3.3 Security Analysis of AutoGroup

Whether a scheme is translated by hand (as is done today [50]) or automatically (as in this work), a completely separate question applying to both is: is the resulting asymmetric scheme secure? The answer is not immediately clear. Unlike the signature transformation that we automate in Section 4 that already has an established security proofs showing that the transformations preserve security, the theoretical underpinnings of symmetric-to-asymmetric translations are less explored. Here are some things we can say.

First, the original proof of security is under a symmetric pairing assumption, and thus can no longer immediately apply since the construction and assumption are changing their algebraic settings. This would seem to require the identification of a new complexity assumption together with a new proof of security. In many examples, e.g., [21], the new assumption and proof are only minor deviations from the original ones, e.g., where the CDH assumption in $\mathbb{G}$ (given $[g, g^a, g^b]$, compute g^{ab}) is converted in a straight-forward manner to the co-CDH assumption in $(\mathbb{G}_1, \mathbb{G}_2)$ (given $[g_1, g_2, g_2^a]$, compute g_1^a). However, there could be cases where a major change is required to the proof of security. For instance, in some asymmetric groups it is not possible to hash into $\mathbb{G}_2$, but in these groups there exists an isomorphism from $\mathbb{G}_2$ to $\mathbb{G}_1$. In other groups there is no such isomorphism, but it is possible to hash into $\mathbb{G}_2$. So if a scheme requires both for the security proof, that scheme may not be realizable in the asymmetric setting (see [32] for more).

In best practices today, a human first devises the new construction (based on their desired optimizations) and then the human works to identify the new assumption and proof. Our current work automates the first step in this process, and hopefully gives the human more time to spend on the second step. In this sense, our automation is arguably faster, and no less secure than what is done by hand today.

However, a more satisfactory solution requires a deeper theoretical study of symmetric-to-asymmetric pairing translations, which we feel is an important open problem, but which falls outside the scope of the current work. What can one prove about the preservation of security in symmetric-to-asymmetric translations? Is it necessary to dig into the proof of security? Or could one prove security of the asymmetric scheme solely on the assumption of security of the symmetric one? Will this work the same for encryption, signatures and other protocols? Do the rules by which translations are done (by hand or AutoGroup) need to change based on these findings? These questions remain open.

3.4 Experimental Evaluation of AutoGroup

To determine the effectiveness of our automation, we evaluate several encryption and signature schemes on a variety of optimization combinations supported by our tool. We sum-

Encryption	Time			Approx. Size		Num.
	Keygen•	Encrypt•	Decrypt•	Secret Key	Ciphertext	Solutions
ID-Based Enc.						
BB04 [16, §4] Symmetric (SS1536)	59.9 ms	64.8 ms	125.4 ms	3072 bits	6144 bits	
Asymmetric (BN256) [Min. CT]	4.8 ms	7.8 ms	27.6 ms	2048 bits	3584 bits	4
Gentry06 [33, §3.1] Symmetric (SS1536)	39.9 ms	176.2 ms	67.8 ms	3072 bits	7680 bits	
Asymmetric (BN256) [Min. SK]	1.4 ms	41.0 ms	19.1 ms	512 bits	7168 bits	4
WATERS09 [57, §3.1] Symmetric (SS1536)	294.6 ms	286.8 ms	612.8 ms	13824 bits	18432 bits	
Asymmetric (BN256) [Min. SK/CT/Exp]	12.6 ms	19.2 ms	128.0 ms	5376 bits	8704 bits	256
Broadcast Encryption						
BGW05 [20, §3.1] Symmetric (SS1536) ($n = 100$)	1992.2 ms	119.6 ms	136.9 ms	19200 bytes	6144 bits	
Asymmetric (BN256) [Min. SK]	70.4 ms	25.7 ms	28.5 ms	3200 bytes	5120 bits	4

•Average time measured over 100 test runs and the standard deviation in all test runs were within ±1% of the average.

Figure 3: AutoGroup on encryption schemes under various optimization options. We show running times and sizes for several schemes generated in C++ and compare symmetric to automatically generated asymmetric implementations at the same security levels (roughly equivalent with 3072 bit RSA). For IBE schemes, we measured with the identity string length at 100 bytes. For BGW, n denotes the number of users in the system.

marize the results of our experiments on encryption schemes in Figure 3 and signature schemes in Figure 5.

System Configuration. All of our benchmarks were executed on a 2.66GHz 6-core Intel Xeon Mac Pro with 10GB RAM running Mac OS X 10.8.3 using only a single core of the Intel processor. Our implementation utilizes the MIRACL library (v5.5.4), Charm v0.43 [2] in C++ due to the efficiency gains over Python code, and Z3 SMT solver (v4.3.1). We based our implementations on the MIRACL library to fully compare each scheme's performance using symmetric and asymmetric curves at equivalent security levels.

Results. To demonstrate the soundness of AutoGroup on encryption and signature schemes, we compare algorithm running times, key and ciphertext/signature sizes between symmetric and asymmetric solutions. We tested AutoGroup on a variety of optimization combinations to extract different asymmetric solutions. In each test case, AutoGroup reports all the unique solutions, obtains the best solution for given user-specified constraints, and generates the executable code of the solution in a reasonable amount of time. AutoGroup execution time on each test case is reported in Figure 6, but does not include time for generating the C++ of the SDL output.

4. AUTOSTRONG

In this section, we present and evaluate a tool, called AutoStrong, for automatically generating a strongly-unforgeable signature from an unforgeable signature scheme.

4.1 Background on Digital Signatures

A digital signature scheme is comprised of three algorithms: key generation, signing and verification. The classic (or "regular") security definition for signatures, as formulated by Goldwasser, Micali and Rivest [35], is called *existential unforgeability with respect to chosen message attacks*, wherein any p.p.t. adversary, given a public key and the ability to adaptively ask for a signature on any message of its choosing, should not be able to output a signature/message pair that passes the verification equation and yet where the message is "new" (was not queried for a signature), with non-negligible probability.

An, Dodis and Rabin [6] formulated *strong unforgeability* where the adversary should not only be unable to generate a signature on a "new" message, but also be unable to generate a different signature for an already signed message. Strongly-unforgeable signatures have many applications including building signcryption [6], chosen-ciphertext secure encryption systems [25, 28] and group signatures [7, 18].

Partitioned Signatures In 2006, Boneh, Shen and Waters [22] connected these two security notions, by providing a general transformation that converts any *partitioned* (defined below) existentially unforgeable signature into a strongly unforgeable one.

Definition 4.1 (Partitioned Signature [22]). *A signature scheme is* partitioned *if it satisfies two properties for all key pairs* (pk, sk)*:*

- **Property 1:** *The signing algorithm can be broken into two deterministic algorithms F_1 and F_2 so that a signature on a message m using secret key sk is computed as follows:*
  1. *Select a random r from a suitable randomness space.*
  2. *Set $\sigma_1 = F_1(m, r, sk)$ and $\sigma_2 = F_2(r, sk)$.*
  3. *Output the signature (σ_1, σ_2).*
- **Property 2:** *Given m and σ_2, there is at most one σ_1 such that (σ_1, σ_2) verifies as a valid signature on m under pk.*

As one example of a partitioned scheme, Boneh et al. partition DSS [45] as follows, where x is the secret key:

$$F_1(m, r, x) = r^{-1}(m + xF_2(r, x)) \mod q$$
$$F_2(r, x) = (g^r \mod p) \mod q$$

Our empirical evidence shows that many discrete-log and pairing-based signatures in the literature are partitioned. Interestingly, some prominent prior works [14, 15] claimed that there were "few" examples of partitioned schemes "beyond Waters [56]", even though our automation discovered several examples existing prior to the publication of these works. We conjecture that it is not always easy for a human to detect a partition.

Chameleon Hashes The BSW transform uses a *chameleon hash* [39] function, which is characterized by the nonstandard property of being collision-resistant for the signer but collision tractable for the recipient. The chameleon hash

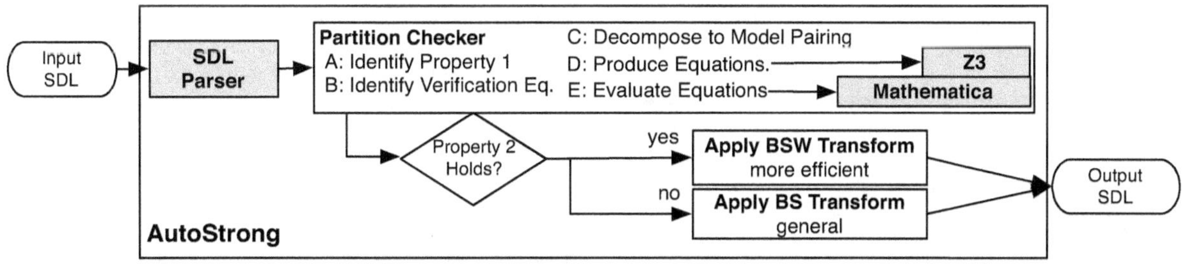

Figure 4: A high-level presentation of the AutoStrong tool, which uses external tools Z3, Mathematica and SDL Parser.

is created by establishing public parameters and a secret trapdoor. The hash itself takes as input a message m and an auxiliary value s. There is an efficient algorithm that on input the trapdoor, any pair (m_1, s_1) and any additional message m_2, finds a value s_2 such that $\text{ChamHash}(m_1, s_1) = \text{ChamHash}(m_2, s_2)$.

Boneh et al. [22] employ a specific hash function based on the hardness of finding discrete logarithms.[4] Since pairing groups also require the DL problem to be hard, this chameleon hash does not add any new complexity assumptions. It works as follows in $\mathbb{G}$, where g generates $\mathbb{G}$ of order p. To setup, choose a random trapdoor $t \in \mathbb{Z}_p{}^*$ and compute $h = g^t$. The public parameters include the description of $\mathbb{G}$ together with g and h. The trapdoor t is kept secret. To hash on input $(m, s) \in \mathbb{Z}_p{}^2$, compute

$$\text{ChamHash}(m, s) = g^m h^s.$$

Later, given any pair m, s and any message m', anyone with the trapdoor can compute a consistent value $s' \in \mathbb{Z}_p$ as

$$s' = (m - m')/t + s$$

such that $\text{ChamHash}(m, s) = \text{ChamHash}(m', s')$.

The BSW Transformation The transformation [22] is efficient and works as follows. Let $\Pi_p = (\mathsf{Gen}_p, \mathsf{Sign}_p, \mathsf{Verify}_p)$ be a partitioned signature, where the signing algorithm is partitioned using functions F_1 and F_2. Suppose the randomness for Sign_p is picked from some set R. Let $||$ denote concatenation. BSW constructs a new scheme Π as:

$\mathsf{Gen}(1^\lambda)$: Select a group $\mathbb{G}$ with generator g of prime order p (with λ bits). Select a random $t \in \mathbb{Z}_p$ and compute $h = g^t$. Select a collision-resistant hash function $H_{cr} : \{0,1\}^* \to \mathbb{Z}_p$. Run $\mathsf{Gen}_p(1^\lambda)$ to obtain a key pair (pk_p, sk_p). Set the keys for the new system as $pk = (pk_p, H_{cr}, \mathbb{G}, g, h, p)$ and $sk = (pk, sk_p, t)$.

$\mathsf{Sign}(sk, m)$: A signature on m is generated as follows:

1. Select a random $s \in \mathbb{Z}_p$ and a random $r \in R$.
2. Set $\sigma_2 = F_2(r, sk_p)$.
3. Compute $v = H_{cr}(m||\sigma_2)$.
4. Compute the chameleon hash $m' = g^v h^s$.
5. Compute $\sigma_1 = F_1(m', r, sk_p)$ and output the signature $\sigma = (\sigma_1, \sigma_2, s)$.

[4]Indeed, we observe that substituting an arbitrary chameleon hash could break the transformation. Suppose $H(m, s)$ ignores the last bit of s (it is easy to construct such a hash assuming chameleon hashes exist.) Then the BSW transformation using this hash would result in a signature of the form (σ_1, σ_2, s), which is clearly not strongly unforgeable, since the last bit can be flipped.

$\mathsf{Verify}(pk, m, \sigma)$: A signature $\sigma = (\sigma_1, \sigma_2, s)$ on a message m is verified as follows:

1. Compute $v = H_{cr}(m||\sigma_2)$.
2. Compute the chameleon hash $m' = g^v h^s$.
3. Output the result of $\mathsf{Verify}_p(pk_p, m', (\sigma_1, \sigma_2))$.

THEOREM 4.2 (SECURITY OF BSW TRANSFORM [22]). *The signature scheme* $\Pi = (\mathsf{Gen}, \mathsf{Sign}, \mathsf{Verify})$ *is strongly existentially unforgeable assuming the underlying scheme* $\Pi_p = (\mathsf{Gen}_p, \mathsf{Sign}_p, \mathsf{Verify}_p)$ *is existentially unforgeable,* H_{cr} *is a collision-resistant hash function and the discrete logarithm assumption holds in* $\mathbb{G}$.

The Bellare-Shoup Transformation The BSW transformation [22], which only works for partitioned signatures, sparked significant research interest into finding a general transformation for *any* existentially unforgeable signature scheme. Various solutions were presented in [14, 15, 37, 53–55], as well as an observation in [14] that an *inefficient* transformation was implicit in [34].

We follow the work of Bellare and Shoup [14, 15], which is less efficient than BSW and, for our case, requires a stronger complexity assumption, but works on any signature. Their approach uses *two-tier* signatures, which are "weaker" than regular signatures as hybrids of regular and one-time schemes. In a two-tier scheme, a signer has a primary key pair and, each time it wants to sign, it generates a fresh secondary key pair and produces a signature as a function of the both secret keys and the message. Both public keys are required to verify the signature. Bellare and Shoup transform any regular signature scheme by signing the signature from this scheme with a strongly unforgeable two-tier scheme. They also show how to realize a strongly unforgeable two-tier signature scheme by applying the Fiat-Shamir [30] transformation to the Schnorr identification protocol [51], which requires a one-more discrete logarithm-type assumption.

The BS transformation works as follows. Let $\Pi_r = (\mathsf{Gen}_r, \mathsf{Sign}_r, \mathsf{Verify}_r)$ be a regular signature scheme and let $\Pi_t = (\mathsf{PGen}_t, \mathsf{SGen}_t, \mathsf{Sign}_t, \mathsf{Verify}_t)$ be a two-tiered strongly unforgeable scheme. A new signature scheme Π is constructed as:

$\mathsf{Gen}(1^\lambda)$: Run $\mathsf{Gen}_r(1^\lambda) \to (pk_r, sk_r)$ and $\mathsf{PGen}_t(1^\lambda) \to (ppk, psk)$. Output the pair $\text{PK} = (pk_r, ppk)$ and $\text{SK} = (sk_r, psk)$.

$\mathsf{Sign}(\text{SK}, m)$: A signature on m is generated as follows:

1. Parse SK as (sk_r, psk).
2. Run $\mathsf{SGen}_t(1^\lambda) \to (spk, ssk)$.
3. Sign the message and secondary key as $\sigma_1 \leftarrow \mathsf{Sign}_r(sk_r, (spk||m))$.

4. Sign the first signature as $\sigma_2 \leftarrow \mathsf{Sign}_t(psk, ssk, \sigma_1)$.
5. Output the signature $\sigma = (\sigma_1, \sigma_2, spk)$.

$\mathsf{Verify}(\mathrm{PK}, m, \sigma)$**:** A signature $\sigma = (\sigma_1, \sigma_2, spk)$ on a message m is verified as follows:

1. Parse PK as (pk_r, ppk).
2. If $\mathsf{Verify}_r(pk_r, (spk||m), \sigma_1) = 0$, then return 0.
3. If $\mathsf{Verify}_t(ppk, spk, \sigma_1, \sigma_2)$, then return 0.
4. Otherwise, return 1.

THEOREM 4.3 (SECURITY OF BS TRANSFORMATION [15]). *If the input scheme is existentially unforgeable, then the output signature is strongly existentially unforgeable assuming the strong unforgeability of the two-tier scheme.*

The Transformation used in AutoStrong For our purposes, we employ the following hybrid transformation combining BSW and Bellare-Shoup. On input a signature scheme, we automate the following procedure:

1. Identify a natural partition satisfying property 1 and test if it has property 2. (We allow false negatives, but not false positives. See Section 4.3.)
2. If a valid partition is found, apply the BSW transformation [22] (using SHA-256 and the DL-based chameleon hash above).
3. If a valid partition is not found, apply the Bellare-Shoup transformation [14,15] (using the Schnorr Fiat-Shamir based two-tier scheme suggested in [15].)
4. Output the result.

The security of this transformation follows directly from the results of [15,22] as stated in Theorems 4.2 and 4.3. *The most challenging technical part is step one: determining if a scheme is partitioned.*

4.2 How AutoStrong Works

AutoStrong takes as input the SDL description of a digital signature scheme along with some metadata.[5] At a high-level, it runs the transformation described at the end of the last section, where the most challenging step is testing whether a scheme is *partitioned* according to Definition 4.1.

We now describe each step involved in testing that Properties 1 and 2 are satisfied and how we utilize Z3 and Mathematica to prove such properties, as illustrated in Figure 4.

Identify Property 1. The first goal is to identify the variables in the signature that should be mapped to σ_1 or σ_2 according to Definition 4.1. We assume that the input signature scheme is existentially unforgeable.[6] Given this assumption, our objective is to identify the portions of the signature that are computed based on the message and designate that component as σ_1. All other variables in the signature that do not meet this criteria are designated as σ_2. We determine that we have designated the correct variables for property 1 if and only if the variable mapping satisfy property 2. We test only the most "natural" division for property 1, which could result in a false negative, but this won't impact the security, so our system allows it.

To illustrate each step, we will show how our tool identifies the partition in the CL signature scheme [24].

CL signatures [24]: Key generation consists of selecting a generator, $g \in \mathbb{G}$, then randomly sampling $x \in \mathbb{Z}_q$ and $y \in \mathbb{Z}_q$. It sets $sk = (x, y)$ and $pk = (g, X = g^x, Y = g^y)$. To sign a message $m \in \mathbb{Z}_q$, the signer samples a uniformly from $\mathbb{G}$ and computes the signature as:

$$\sigma = (a, b = a^y, c = a^{x+m\cdot x\cdot y}).$$

The verifier can check σ by ensuring that $e(a, Y) = e(g, b)$ and $e(X, a) \cdot e(X, b)^m = e(g, c)$.

Intuitively, our logic would identify that c is dependent on the message, therefore, identifying that $\sigma_1 = c$ and $\sigma_2 = (a, b)$ which satisfies the definition of property 1. The next challenge is to determine whether property 2 holds given our identified mapping for σ_1 and σ_2.

Prove Property 2. Proving that a scheme satisfies this property requires the ability to abstractly evaluate the verification equations on the input variables. We require this ability to automatically prove that there exists at most one σ_1 which verifies under a fixed σ_2, m and pk for all possible inputs. To this end, the partition checker determines whether a σ_1' exists such that $\sigma_1' \neq \sigma_1$ and is a valid signature over the fixed variables. Finding such a σ_1' means the signature is not partitioned. The checker determines whether it can find a solution or if it can determine that *no* such solution exists. If no solutions exist, then the signature is indeed partitioned. Stated more precisely, does there exist a $\sigma_1' \neq \sigma_1$ such that the following condition holds:

$$\mathsf{Verify}(pk, m, (\sigma_1, \sigma_2)) = 1 \wedge \mathsf{Verify}(pk, m, (\sigma_1', \sigma_2)) = 1$$

At a high-level, our goal is to evaluate the pairing-based verification algorithms in a way that allows us to find a contradiction to the aforementioned condition. Recall that the bilinearity property of pairings states that $e(g^a, g^b) = e(g, g)^{ab}$ holds for all $a, b \in \mathbb{Z}_q$ where $g \in \mathbb{G}$. We observe that pairings can be modeled as an abstract function that performs multiplication in the exponent. Because the rules of multiplication and addition hold in the exponent, we can abstractly reduce pairings to basic integer arithmetic.

To accomplish this, we leverage Z3 to model the bilinearity of pairings so that it is possible to automatically evaluate them. Our partition checker relies on Z3's uninterpreted functions and universal quantifiers to reduce pairing product equations to simpler equations over the exponents. However, this reduction alone is not sufficient to completely evaluate the verification equations as required for detecting a partitioned signature. To satisfy the property 2 condition, we also need a way to evaluate these equations on all possible inputs. Z3 was less suited for this task and instead, we employ the Mathematica scripting framework to evaluate such equations. Our solution consists of five steps:

Step 1: Decompose Verification Equations. To model pairings using an SMT solver, we encode the verification equations into a form that the solver can interpret. The first phase extracts the verification equations in SDL, then decomposes the equations in terms of the generators and exponents used. We leverage recent term rewriting extensions introduced in the SDL Parser by Akinyele et al. [4].

[5]The user must specify the variables that denote message, signature, key material in a configuration file.

[6]We remark that we tested the partition checker for AutoStrong on schemes that are not existentially unforgeable to fully vet the checker (see Figure 5), but the resulting output in these cases may not be strongly unforgeable.

Signature	Security	Time Sign•	Time Verify•	Approx. Size Public Key*	Approx. Size Signature	Num. Solutions
CL04 [24, §3.1] Symmetric (SS1536)	EU-CMA	169.8 ms	316.6 ms	3072 bits	4608 bits	
Symmetric (SS1536)	SU-CMA	192.0 ms	387.8 ms	4608 bits	6144 bits	
Asymmetric (BN256) [Min. SIG]	SU-CMA	3.4 ms	56.8 ms	2048 bits	1024 bits	2
BB Short [17, §3] Symmetric (SS1536)	EU-CMA	21.5 ms	102.1 ms	7680 bits	3072 bits	
Symmetric (SS1536)	SU-CMA	62.8 ms	142.8 ms	9216 bits	4608 bits	
Asymmetric (BN256) [Min. PK]	SU-CMA	5.0 ms	18.3 ms	3840 bits	1536 bits	2
WATERS05 [56, §4] Symmetric (SS1536)	EU-CMA	47.9 ms	195.2 ms	4608 bits†	3072 bits	
Symmetric (SS1536)	SU-CMA	88.7 ms	236.4 ms	6144 bits†	4608 bits	
Asymmetric (BN256) [Min. SIG]	SU-CMA	6.5 ms	62.9 ms	2560 bits†	768 bits	8
WATERS09 [58, §6.1] Symmetric (SS1536)	WU-CMA	258.5 ms	896.8 ms	23040 bits	13824 bits	
Asymmetric (BN256) [Min. PK/SIG]	WU-CMA	13.6 ms	129.2 ms	12544 bits	5376 bits	256
ACDKNO12 [1, §5.3] Symmetric (SS1536)	RMA	346.4 ms	1307 ms	23040 bits	12288 bits	
Asymmetric (BN256) [Min. PK/SIG/Exp]	RMA	23.3 ms	279.9 ms	3840 bits	8192 bits	1024

•Average time measured over 100 test runs and the standard deviation in all test runs were within ±1% of the average.

*Refers to the approximate size of public parameters used in verification.

†Estimates do not include the public parameters for the Water's hash.

Figure 5: We show the result of AutoGroup and AutoStrong on signature schemes. For CL, BB, and Waters (with length of identities, $\ell = 128$), we first apply AutoStrong to determine that the signature scheme is partitioned, then apply the BSW transform to obtain a strongly unforgeable signature in the symmetric setting. We then feed this as input to AutoGroup to realize an asymmetric variant under a given optimization. We also tested AutoStrong on the DSE signature and ACDK structure-preserving signature, even though these are not known to be existentially unforgeable. A partition was found for ACDK, but not DSE.

Their techniques allow us to keep track of how variables are computed in terms of the generators and exponents. With knowledge of how each variable is computed, we are able to fully decompose each equation in an automated fashion.

Our technique for modeling pairings in Z3 requires that decomposition of verification equations be guided by a few rules. First, generators must be rewritten in terms of some base generator, g, if the scheme is specified in the symmetric setting.[7] For example, the random generator $a \in \mathbb{G}$ chosen in CL would be represented as $g^{a'}$ for $a' \in \mathbb{Z}_q$. Second, hashing statements of the form $v = H(m)$ where $v \in \mathbb{G}$ are rewritten as $g^{v'}$ for some $v' \in \mathbb{Z}_q$.[8] Third, we do not decompose any variable designated as σ_1 for the purposes of determining whether a signature is partitioned. The intuition is that since σ_1' variables are adversarially controlled we also treat σ_1 as a black box. Finally, whenever we encounter signatures that compute a product over a list of elements – as in the case of the Waters hash, for example [56] – we require the user to provide an upper bound on the number of elements in this list (if known) so that we can "unroll" the product calculation and further apply our rules. When all the above reduction rules are automatically applied to the CL signature, we obtain the following equations:

$$e(a, Y) = e(g, b) \text{ becomes } e(g^{a'}, g^y) = e(g, (g^{a'})^y)$$

$$e(X, a) \cdot e(X, b)^m = e(g, c) \text{ becomes } e(g^x, g^{a'}) \cdot e(g^x, (g^{a'})^y)^m = e(g, g^{c'})$$

Note that c' denotes the σ_1 for CL and is a free variable. All other variables that comprise m, pk, and σ_2 are fixed.

Step 2: Encode Rules for Evaluating Pairings. Once we have decomposed the verification equation as shown above, the next step is to encode the equations in terms that Z3 can understand. After the pairing equations are rewritten entirely using the base generator, we can model the behavior of pairings by simply focusing on the exponents. To capture the bilinearity of pairings, we rely on two features in Z3: uninterpreted functions and universal quantifiers. As mentioned earlier, uninterpreted functions enable one to abstractly model a function's behavior. Our model of a pairing is an uninterpreted function, E, that takes two integer variables and has a few mathematical properties. First, we define the multiplication rule as $\forall s, t : E(s, t) = s \cdot t$. Second, we define the addition rule as $\forall s, t, u : E(s+t, u) = s \cdot u + t \cdot u$.[9] Third, we adhere to the multiplicative notation in SDL and convert pairing products defined in terms of multiplication to addition and division to subtraction.

These rules are straightforward and sufficient for evaluating pairings. Moreover, by defining exponents in terms of integers, Z3 can apply all the built-in simplification rules for multiplication and addition. As a result, the solver uses these rules to reduce any pairing-based verification equation into a simpler integer equation.

To automatically encode the equations, we first simplify the decomposed pairing equation as much as possible using previous techniques [4]. Then, we convert each pairing to the modeled pairing function, E and remove the base generators. Upon simplifying and encoding the decomposed CL equations, we obtain the following:

$$e(g^{a'}, g^y) = e(g, (g^{a'})^y) \text{ becomes } E(a', y) = E(1, a' \cdot y)$$

$$e(g^x, g^{a'}) \cdot e(g^x, (g^{a'})^y)^m = e(g, g^{c'}) \text{ becomes } E(x, a') + E(x \cdot m, a' \cdot y) = E(1, c')$$

Step 3: Execute SMT Solver. After encoding the pairing functions in terms of E, the next step is to employ the solver to evaluate it. We first specify our rules in the SMT solver then evaluate these rules on each input equation. The result is a simplified integer equation representation of the verification algorithm. For the above CL formulas, the solver determines that the first equation is *true* for all possible in-

[7]The same would apply for asymmetric pairings except that we would specify $\mathbb{G}_1$ generators in terms of a base generator g_1 and $\mathbb{G}_2$ in terms of g_2.

[8]Note that this term re-writing is used only to determine whether a solution exists. The actual variables a' and v' would not (necessarily) be known in the real protocol.

[9]Similarly, $E(s, t+u) = s \cdot t + s \cdot u$

puts because a' and y are fixed variables. For the second equation, the solver produces: $a' \cdot x + a' \cdot x \cdot m \cdot y = c'$.

Step 4: Evaluate equations. At this point, we have obtained the integer equation version of the verification equation; we can now concretely express the conditions for property 2. That is,

$$c' \neq c'' \wedge a' \cdot x + a' \cdot x \cdot m \cdot y = c' \wedge a' \cdot x + a' \cdot x \cdot m \cdot y = c''$$

We use Mathematica to prove that no such c'' exists assuming the verification condition is correct via the Mathematica Script API. In particular, we utilize the *FindInstance* function to mathematically find proof over non-zero real numbers then subsequently try finding a solution over integers. If *no* such solution exists, the *FindInstance* will return such a statement and the result is interpreted as an indicator that the signature is partitionable. Otherwise, the signature may not be partitionable.

During this step, we make an explicit assumption that the verification condition is mathematically correct. Suppose that this was not the case. In this scenario, our technique would also determine that it is not possible to find a σ_1' such that $\sigma_1' \neq \sigma_1$ and verifies over fixed variables. In reality, however, no σ_1 and σ_2 pair can produce a valid signature because the verification equation does not hold for *any* input. To limit the possibility of such scenarios, our partition checker offers a sanity check on the correctness of the input verification equations.

By relaxing the rule for decomposing the variables that are designated as σ_1 in Step 1, we can evaluate the verification equation over all inputs using Mathematica. For the CL signature, a full decomposition would produce the following equation in the exponent:

$$a' \cdot x + a' \cdot x \cdot m \cdot y = a' \cdot (x + x \cdot m \cdot y)$$

It is sufficient to leverage the *Simplify* function within Mathematica to evaluate that this holds for all possible inputs. Since Mathematica has built-in techniques for solving equations of this sort, it becomes trivial to show that the above equation is correct in all cases (due to the law of distribution). We subsequently inform the user on the output of this sanity check, which is useful for determining the correctness of SDL signature descriptions.

Step 5: Apply Transformation. Once the partition checker determines whether the signature is partitioned or not, we apply the efficient BSW transform if deemed partitioned or the less-efficient BS transform if not as described in Section 4.1. We elaborate further in the full version.

4.3 Security Analysis of AutoStrong

The theoretical security of the unforgeable-to-strongly-unforgeable transformations that we use in AutoStrong were previously established in [14, 15, 22], as discussed in Section 4.1.[10] The security of the BSW transform only holds, however, if the input scheme is partitioned. Our partition test allows false negatives, but not false positives. That is, our algorithm may fail to identify a scheme as partitioned even though it is, which results in a less efficient final scheme, but it will not falsely identify a scheme as partitioned when it is not, which would result in a security failure. To see why this claim holds, consider that the partition tester guesses a partition, Z3 interprets the verification equation as a system of equations, and then Mathematica fixes the variables on one partition side and asks how many solutions there are for the free variables on the other side. If 0 or 1 are found, then the scheme meets the partitioned definition. If more than 1 is found, then it is not partitioned. If there is no answer (program crash or times out), then we consider it not partitioned. Thus, false negatives can occur, but not false positives (in theory). Proving that there are no software or hardware errors in AutoStrong, Z3, Mathematica or the underlying software and hardware on which they run is outside the scope of this work. We did experimentally verify AutoStrong's outputs and no errors were found.

[10] Perfect correctness is assumed in these transformations. All schemes tested have perfect correctness, except the Waters DSE signatures [57]. With a negligible probability, the verification algorithm of this scheme will reject an honestly-generated signature. After applying the BS transformation to the DSE scheme, this negligible error probability is carried over in the verification of the strongly-secure scheme.

4.4 Experimental Evaluation of AutoStrong

In 2008 [15], Bellare and Shoup remarked that "unfortunately, there seem to be hardly any [partitioned signature] schemes". Interestingly, our experimental results show that there are in fact many partitioned schemes, including a substantial number invented prior to 2008. We evaluated AutoStrong by testing it on a collection of signatures, including Camenisch-Lysyanskaya [24], short Boneh-Boyen [17], Waters 2005 [56], Waters Dual-System (DSE) signature [57], and a structure-preserving scheme of Abe *et al.* [1].

Of the above signatures, all but one – the Waters DSE signature – were successfully partitioned. We do not know whether the Waters DSE signature can be partitioned, although we suspect that the "randomness freedom" in the dual-system structure may inherently be at odds with the uniqueness property of the partitioned test. Although the Abe *et al.* scheme is partitioned, applying either the BSW or BS transformations destroys its structure-preserving property. An interesting open problem would be to refine the BSW or BS transformations to preserve the structured property. Figure 6 shows the time that it took our tool to identify the partitioning and output the revised signature equations. Figure 5 illustrates the performance and size of the resulting signatures, when evaluated on two different types of curve (using AutoGroup to calculate the group assignments).

5. CONCLUSION

We explored two new tasks in cryptographic automation. First, we presented a tool, AutoGroup, for automatically translating a symmetric pairing scheme into an asymmetric pairing scheme. The tool allows the user to choose from a variety of different optimization options. Second, we presented a tool, AutoStrong, for automatically altering a digital signature scheme to achieve *strong unforgeability* [6]. The tool automatically tests whether a scheme is "partitioned" according to a notion of Boneh et al. [22] and then applies a highly-efficient transformation if it is partitioned or a more general transformation otherwise. To perform some of these complex tasks, we integrated Microsoft's Z3 SMT Solver and Mathematica into our tools. Our performance measurements indicated that these standard cryptographic design tasks can be quickly, accurately and cost-effectively performed in an automated fashion. We leave open the ques-

Process	BB-IBE	Gentry	Waters09-Enc	BGW	CL	BB Short Sig	Waters05	Waters09-Sig	ACDKNO
AutoGroup	0.33s	0.34s	4.30s	0.55s	0.34s	0.31s	0.54s	4.16s	17.65s
AutoStrong	-	-	-	-	0.28s	0.27s	0.37s	3.99s	1.23s

Figure 6: Running time required by the AutoGroup and AutoStrong routines to process the schemes discussed in this work (averaged over 10 test runs). The running time for AutoGroup includes the execution time of the Z3 SMT solver. The running time for AutoStrong also includes Z3 and Mathematica and the application of the BSW transformation. In all cases, the standard deviation in the results were within ±3% of the average. For AutoGroup, running times are correlated with the number of unique solutions found and the minimization of the weighted function using Z3. AutoStrong running times are highly correlated with the complexity of the verification equations.

tion of which other design tasks are well suited for SMT solvers.

Acknowledgments

The authors thank Brent Waters for technical discussions involving the BSW transformation and the Waters DSE signatures. The authors are also grateful to Avi Rubin and Matthew Pagano for helpful discussions.

6. REFERENCES

[1] Masayuki Abe, Melissa Chase, Bernardo David, Markulf Kohlweiss, Ryo Nishimaki, and Miyako Ohkubo. Constant-size structure-preserving signatures: Generic constructions and simple assumptions. Cryptology ePrint Archive, Report 2012/285, 2012. http://eprint.iacr.org/.

[2] Joseph A. Akinyele, Christina Garman, Ian Miers, Matthew W. Pagano, Michael Rushanan, Matthew Green, and Aviel D. Rubin. Charm: a framework for rapidly prototyping cryptosystems. *Journal of Cryptographic Engineering*, 3(2):111–128, 2013.

[3] Joseph A. Akinyele, Matthew Green, Susan Hohenberger, and Matthew W. Pagano. AutoBatch Toolkit. https://github.com/jhuisi/auto-tools.

[4] Joseph A. Akinyele, Matthew Green, Susan Hohenberger, and Matthew W. Pagano. Machine-generated algorithms, proofs and software for the batch verification of digital signature schemes. In *ACM CCS*, pages 474–487, 2012.

[5] José Bacelar Almeida, Endre Bangerter, Manuel Barbosa, Stephan Krenn, Ahmad-Reza Sadeghi, and Thomas Schneider. A certifying compiler for zero-knowledge proofs of knowledge based on σ-protocols. In *ESORICS'10*, pages 151–167, 2010.

[6] Jee Hea An, Yevgeniy Dodis, and Tal Rabin. On the security of joint signature and encryption. In *EUROCRYPT*, volume 2332, pages 83–107, 2002.

[7] Giuseppe Ateniese, Jan Camenisch, Marc Joye, and Gene Tsudik. A practical and provably secure coalition-resistant group signature scheme. In *CRYPTO '00*, volume 1880, pages 255–270, 2000.

[8] Michael Backes, Matteo Maffei, and Dominique Unruh. Zero-knowledge in the applied pi-calculus and automated verification of the direct anonymous attestation protocol. In *IEEE Symposium on Security and Privacy*, pages 202–215, 2008.

[9] Endre Bangerter, Thomas Briner, Wilko Henecka, Stephan Krenn, Ahmad-Reza Sadeghi, and Thomas Schneider. Automatic generation of sigma-protocols. In *EuroPKI'09*, pages 67–82, 2009.

[10] M. Barbosa, A. Moss, and D. Page. Compiler assisted elliptic curve cryptography. In *OTM Conferences (2)*, pages 1785–1802, 2007.

[11] Mike Barnett, K. Rustan M. Leino, and Wolfram Schulte. The spec# programming system: An overview. pages 49–69. Springer, 2004.

[12] Paulo S. L. M. Barreto and Michael Naehrig. Pairing-friendly elliptic curves of prime order. In *SAC*, volume 3897, pages 319–331, 2006. http://cryptojedi.org/papers/\#pfcpo.

[13] Gilles Barthe, Benjamin Grégoire, Sylvain Heraud, and Santiago Zanella Béguelin. Computer-aided security proofs for the working cryptographer. In *CRYPTO*, pages 71–90, 2011.

[14] Mihir Bellare and Sarah Shoup. Two-tier signatures, strongly unforgeable signatures, and fiat-shamir without random oracles. In *PKC*, pages 201–216, 2007.

[15] Mihir Bellare and Sarah Shoup. Two-tier signatures from the fiat-shamir transform, with applications to strongly unforgeable and one-time signatures. *IET Information Security*, 2(2):47–63, 2008.

[16] Dan Boneh and Xavier Boyen. Efficient selective-id secure identity-based encryption without random oracles. In Christian Cachin and JanL. Camenisch, editors, *Advances in Cryptology - EUROCRYPT 2004*, volume 3027 of *Lecture Notes in Computer Science*, pages 223–238. Springer Berlin Heidelberg, 2004.

[17] Dan Boneh and Xavier Boyen. Short signatures without random oracles. In *EUROCRYPT*, volume 3027, pages 382–400, 2004.

[18] Dan Boneh, Xavier Boyen, and Hovav Shacham. Short group signatures. In *CRYPTO '04*, volume 3152 of LNCS, pages 45–55, 2004.

[19] Dan Boneh and Matthew K. Franklin. Identity-based encryption from the Weil pairing. In *CRYPTO*, pages 213–229, 2001.

[20] Dan Boneh, Craig Gentry, and Brent Waters. Collusion resistant broadcast encryption with short ciphertexts and private keys. In *CRYPTO'05*, pages 258–275, 2005.

[21] Dan Boneh, Ben Lynn, and Hovav Shacham. Short signatures from the Weil pairing. In *ASIACRYPT*, volume 2248 of LNCS, pages 514–532, 2001.

[22] Dan Boneh, Emily Shen, and Brent Waters. Strongly unforgeable signatures based on computational Diffie-Hellman. In *PKC*, pages 229–240, 2006.

[23] J. Camenisch, M. Rohe, and A.R. Sadeghi. Sokrates - a compiler framework for zero- knowledge protocols. In *the Western European Workshop on Research in Cryptology*, WEWoRC, 2005.

[24] Jan Camenisch and Anna Lysyanskaya. Signature schemes and anonymous credentials from bilinear maps. In *CRYPTO*, volume 3152, pages 56–72, 2004.

[25] Ran Canetti, Shai Halevi, and Jonathan Katz. Chosen-ciphertext security from identity-based encryption. In *EUROCRYPT*, pages 207–222, 2004.

[26] Leonardo De Moura and Nikolaj Bjørner. Z3: an efficient smt solver. In *Proceedings of the Theory and practice of Software*, TACAS'08/ETAPS'08, pages 337–340, 2008.

[27] Robert DeLine, K. Rustan, and M. Leino. Boogie pl: A typed procedural language for checking object-oriented programs. Technical Report MSR-TR-2005-70.

[28] Danny Dolev, Cynthia Dwork, and Moni Naor. Nonmalleable cryptography. *SIAM J. Comput.*, 30(2):391–437, 2000.

[29] Anna Lisa Ferrara, Matthew Green, Susan Hohenberger, and Michael Østergaard Pedersen. Practical short signature batch verification. In *CT-RSA*, volume 5473 of LNCS, pages 309–324, 2009.

[30] Amos Fiat and Adi Shamir. How to prove yourself: Practical solutions to identification and signature problems. In *CRYPTO*, pages 186–194, 1986.

[31] Steven D. Galbraith. Supersingular curves in cryptography. In *ASIACRYPT*, pages 495–513, 2001.

[32] Steven D. Galbraith, Kenneth G. Paterson, and Nigel P. Smart. Pairings for cryptographers, 2006. Cryptology ePrint Archive: Report 2006/165.

[33] Craig Gentry. Practical identity-based encryption without random oracles. In *EUROCRYPT*, pages 445–464, 2006.

[34] Oded Goldreich. *The Foundations of Cryptography - Volume 2, Basic Applications.* Cambridge University Press, 2004.

[35] S. Goldwasser, S. Micali, and R. Rivest. A digital signature scheme secure against adaptive chosen-message attacks. *SIAM J. Comp.*, 17(2), 1988.

[36] Wilko Henecka, Stefan Kögl, Ahmad-Reza Sadeghi, Thomas Schneider, and Immo Wehrenberg. Tasty: tool for automating secure two-party computations. In *ACM CCS*, pages 451–462, 2010.

[37] Qiong Huang, Duncan S. Wong, and Yiming Zhao. Generic transformation to strongly unforgeable signatures. In *ACNS*, pages 1–17, 2007.

[38] Shinsaku Kiyomoto, Haruki Ota, and Toshiaki Tanaka. A security protocol compiler generating C source codes. In *ISA'08*, pages 20–25, 2008.

[39] Hugo Krawczyk and Tal Rabin. Chameleon signatures. In *NDSS*, 2000.

[40] Stefan Lucks, Nico Schmoigl, and Emin Islam Tatli. Issues on designing a cryptographic compiler. In *WEWoRC*, pages 109–122, 2005.

[41] Philip MacKenzie, Alina Oprea, and Michael K. Reiter. Automatic generation of two-party computations. In *ACM CCS*, pages 210–219, 2003.

[42] Dahlia Malkhi, Noam Nisan, Benny Pinkas, and Yaron Sella. Fairplay – a secure two-party computation system. In *USENIX Security'04*, pages 287–302, 2004.

[43] Sarah Meiklejohn, C. Chris Erway, Alptekin Küpçü, Theodora Hinkle, and Anna Lysyanskaya. ZKPDL: a language-based system for efficient zero-knowledge proofs and electronic cash. In *USENIX Security'10*, pages 193–206, 2010.

[44] A. Menezes, S. Vanstone, and T. Okamoto. Reducing elliptic curve logarithms to logarithms in a finite field. In *STOC*, pages 80–89, 1991.

[45] Alfred Menezes, Paul C. van Oorschot, and Scott A. Vanstone. *Handbook of Applied Cryptography.* CRC Press, 1996.

[46] Leonardo Moura and Grant Olney Passmore. The strategy challenge in SMT solving. In *Automated Reasoning and Mathematics*, volume 7788, pages 15–44. 2013.

[47] Dan Page, Nigel Smart, and Fre Vercauteren. A comparison of MNT curves and supersingular curves. *Applicable Algebra in Eng,Com and Comp*, 17(5):379–392, 2006.

[48] Luis J. Dominguez Perez and Michael Scott. Designing a code generator for pairing based cryptographic functions. In *Pairing'10*, pages 207–224, 2010.

[49] Davide Pozza, Riccardo Sisto, and Luca Durante. Spi2java: Automatic cryptographic protocol java code generation from spi calculus. In *Advanced Information Networking and Applications*, pages 400–, 2004.

[50] Somindu C. Ramanna, Sanjit Chatterjee, and Palash Sarkar. Variants of Waters' dual system primitives using asymmetric pairings - (extended abstract). In *PKC '12*, pages 298–315, 2012.

[51] Claus-Peter Schnorr. Efficient signature generation by smart cards. *J. Cryptology*, 4(3):161–174, 1991.

[52] Dawn Xiaodong Song, Adrian Perrig, and Doantam Phan. Agvi - automatic generation, verification, and implementation of security protocols. In *Computer Aided Verification*, pages 241–245, 2001.

[53] Ron Steinfeld, Josef Pieprzyk, and Huaxiong Wang. How to strengthen any weakly unforgeable signature into a strongly unforgeable signature. In *CT-RSA*, pages 357–371, 2007.

[54] Isamu Teranishi, Takuro Oyama, and Wakaha Ogata. General conversion for obtaining strongly existentially unforgeable signatures. In *INDOCRYPT*, pages 191–205, 2006.

[55] Isamu Teranishi, Takuro Oyama, and Wakaha Ogata. General conversion for obtaining strongly existentially unforgeable signatures. *IEICE Transactions*, 91-A(1):94–106, 2008.

[56] Brent Waters. Efficient identity-based encryption without random oracles. In *EUROCRYPT '05*, volume 3494 of LNCS, pages 320–329. Springer, 2005.

[57] Brent Waters. Dual system encryption: Realizing fully secure ibe and hibe under simple assumptions. In *CRYPTO*, pages 619–636, 2009.

[58] Brent Waters. Dual system encryption: Realizing fully secure ibe and hibe under simple assumptions. Cryptology ePrint Archive, Report 2009/385, 2009. `http://eprint.iacr.org/`.

[59] Wolfram. Mathematica, version 9. `http://www.wolfram.com/mathematica/`.

The Science, Engineering and Business of Cyber Security

Ravi Sandhu
Institute for Cyber Security and
Department of Computer Science
University of Texas at San Antonio
San Antonio, Texas
ravi.sandhu@utsa.edu

ABSTRACT

I will use the rare opportunity of this keynote talk to give my perspective on the general state and future prospects for cyber security, and the consequences of this perspective with respect to cyber security research and education. The ambiguous status of computer science in modern academia has persisted through the thirty plus years of my career. Does it belong in the College of Science or the College of Engineering? How about the College of Business? Is it worthy of a separate College of its own? I believe this ambiguity is a manifestation of the fundamental difference between computer science relative to traditional sciences and engineering disciplines. The forces of science, engineering and business come together and reconcile in a particularly unique way in computer science, and within computer science cyber security brings additional peculiarities to this reconciliation.

My outlook on cyber security is generally optimistic. I believe at the consumer level market and social forces will drive developed societies to a relatively low assurance of security and privacy analogous to the current state of internet security. The large-scale adoption of internet services across diverse global populations is one indicator that the average consumer is reasonably comfortable with the collateral risks. But nothing is automatic, so social organization will be required to compensate for the intrusions of big government and big business which may turn out to be the much bigger problem than big crime. At the same time I share the concern of many senior national security officials and thought leaders on the increasingly grave threat of cyberwar and cyberterrorism. The US Department of Defense has publicly recognized cyberspace as a man-made domain on par with land, sea, air and space within which wars will be conducted and facilitated. Many other nations and militaries are preparing offensive and defensive cyber capabilities.

My talk will elaborate on these notions and seek to glean some lessons for cyber security researchers.

CCS'13, November 4-8, 2013, Berlin, Germany.
ACM 978-1-4503-2477-9/13/11.
http://dx.doi.org/10.1145/2508859.2516755.

Categories and Subject Descriptors

K.6.5 [**Management of Computing and Information Systems**]: Security and Protection

Keywords

Science, Engineering, Business

BIOGRAPHY

Ravi Sandhu is Executive Director of the Institute for Cyber Security at the University of Texas at San Antonio, where he holds the Lutcher Brown Endowed Chair in Cyber Security in the Department of Computer Science. Previously he was on the faculty at George Mason University (1989-2007) and Ohio State University (1982-1989). He holds BTech and MTech degrees from IIT Bombay and Delhi respectively, and MS and PhD degrees from Rutgers University. He is a Fellow of IEEE, ACM and AAAS, and has received awards from IEEE, ACM, NSA and NIST. A prolific and highly cited author, his research has been funded by NSF, NSA, NIST, DARPA, AFOSR, ONR, AFRL and private industry. His papers have accumulated over 25,000 Google Scholar citations including over 6,000 citations for his seminal role-based access control paper. He has authored over 235 papers with over 100 co-authors. He is ranked as the number one non-cryptographer and number five overall at Microsoft Academic Search for Security and Privacy. His papers on role-based access control established it as the dominant form of access control in practical systems. His numerous other models and mechanisms have also had considerable influence. He is Editor-in-Chief of the IEEE Transactions on Dependable and Secure Computing, and founding General Chair of the ACM Conference on Data and Application Security and Privacy. He previously served as founding Editor-in-Chief of ACM Transactions on Information and System Security and on the editorial board for IEEE Internet Computing. He was Chairman of ACM SIGSAC, and founded the ACM Conference on Computer and Communications Security and the ACM Symposium on Access Control Models and Technologies and chaired their Steering Committees for many years. He has served as General Chair, Program Chair and Committee Member for numerous security conferences. He has consulted for leading industry and government organizations, and has lectured all over the world. He was a co-founder of TriCipher, a Silicon Valley security start-up acquired by VMware. He is an inventor on 29 security technology patents. His web site is at www.profsandhu.com.

AVANT-GUARD: Scalable and Vigilant Switch Flow Management in Software-Defined Networks

Seungwon Shin† Vinod Yegneswaran‡ Phillip Porras‡ Guofei Gu†
†Texas A&M University ‡SRI International
{swshin,guofei}@cse.tamu.edu {vinod, porras}@csl.sri.com

ABSTRACT

Among the leading reference implementations of the Software Defined Networking (SDN) paradigm is the OpenFlow framework, which decouples the control plane into a centralized application. In this paper, we consider two aspects of OpenFlow that pose security challenges, and we propose two solutions that could address these concerns. The first challenge is the inherent communication bottleneck that arises between the data plane and the control plane, which an adversary could exploit by mounting a *control plane saturation attack* that disrupts network operations. Indeed, even well-mined adversarial models, such as scanning or denial-of-service (DoS) activity, can produce more potent impacts on OpenFlow networks than traditional networks. To address this challenge, we introduce an extension to the OpenFlow data plane called *connection migration*, which dramatically reduces the amount of data-to-control-plane interactions that arise during such attacks. The second challenge is that of enabling the control plane to expedite both detection of, and responses to, the changing flow dynamics within the data plane. For this, we introduce *actuating triggers* over the data plane's existing statistics collection services. These triggers are inserted by control layer applications to both register for asynchronous call backs, and insert conditional flow rules that are only activated when a trigger condition is detected within the data plane's statistics module. We present AVANT-GUARD, an implementation of our two data plane extensions, evaluate the performance impact, and examine its use for developing more scalable and resilient SDN security services.

Categories and Subject Descriptors

C.2.0 [**Computer-Communication Networks**]: Security and Protection

Keywords

Software-defined network (SDN); OpenFlow; control plane saturation attack; security and resilience

CCS'13, November 4–8, 2013, Berlin, Germany.

http://dx.doi.org/10.1145/2508859.2516684 .

1. INTRODUCTION

As enterprise networks and data centers expand in size and complexity, they pose greater administrative challenges and demand enhanced automation in orchestrating their computer and network resources. The network research community postulates that one approach to meeting these challenges lies within the tenet of software-defined networking (SDN) [19]. By decoupling the control logic from the closed and proprietary implementations of traditional network devices, SDN enables researchers and practitioners to design new innovative network functions and protocols in a much easier, flexible, and more powerful way. The OpenFlow framework [20] is an embodiment of the SDN concept. In recent years, *OpenFlow* (OF) has steadily matured from a research idea explored in academic milieus [8, 4, 5] to the current SDN standard-bearing reference implementation with considerable momentum in industry.

We believe that OpenFlow provides new research opportunities for the network security community [26, 3, 10]. For example, OF could offer a dramatic simplification in the design and integration of complex network security applications into large networks. Unfortunately, the potential for OpenFlow to provide meaningful advancements to the state of network defense must be tempered by the recognition that OpenFlow itself introduces serious security challenges. In this paper, we explore potential solutions to two such security challenges. First, OpenFlow networks lack *scalability* between the data and control planes. This enables targeted attacks by an external entity who crafts an inbound stream of flow requests to inundate communications between the controller and switch in an adversary model that we refer to as the *control plane saturation attack*. Second, OpenFlow offers very limited support for network monitoring applications that seek a fine-grained tracking of operations at the data plane, thus making difficult the support of many security applications that require *expeditious* access to critical changes in network-traffic patterns.

Scalability Challenge. The root cause of the first challenge, scalability, lies in the operation of the OpenFlow "southbound" protocol, which separates the control plane from the data plane to enable centralized and fine-grained control of network flows. When an OpenFlow switch receives a packet belonging to a new flow for which it has no matching handling rules, it forwards the packet to its OpenFlow controller. The controller responds with one or more *flow rules* that indicate how the switch should process this flow and future flows that satisfy the rule's match criteria. Here, the centralized controller, designed to mediate these flow requests, quickly becomes a scaling bottleneck, i.e., a potential *Achilles heel* of the network during anomalous traffic bursts such as flash crowds and denial-of-service attacks. Even worse, because an external input stream ultimately drives the data-to-control plane interactions, an adversary can produce a series of unique flow requests (e.g., using a set of distributed botclients) to quickly saturate the control plane with new flow requests. At the same time, the data plane also suffers from saturation attacks because switches have limited resources to buffer (TCP/UDP) flow-initiation until the controller issues a flow rule that states how the flow shall be handled. Hence, control plane saturation also has direct implications for the data plane's operational ability. Adversary models such as DDoS and network scanning, which have been thoroughly dealt with by the security community, pose potential *new threats* to the scalability of the centralized control layer model of OpenFlow (and more broadly to the general SDN paradigm).

Responsiveness Challenge. The second challenge (i.e., responsiveness) stems from the need for expeditious access to critical data plane activity patterns. Network-monitoring applications often need to collect network statistics for tasks such as tracking flow- and network-wide packet statistics or to measure the activity of various entities communicating through the switch (e.g., to identify DoS attacks, which impact the data plane). Current SDN technologies such as OpenFlow only allow applications to explicitly *pull/poll* such information from each switch. Unfortunately, such interfaces are not sufficient for monitoring applications that require the data plane statistics in order to track and respond to malicious or degenerate operating conditions. Aggressive polling degrades data plane performance and may still not provide the latency reduction desired by security services to react to detected attacks. In addition, though security applications often require an inspection of packet contents that match some criteria, OpenFlow offers no mechanism to facilitate such policies.

We investigate the viability of our security specific extensions to OpenFlow in the context of a new system framework that we call AVANT-GUARD (AG). There are several critical issues that we address through the development of this framework. The first issue is determining the type of intelligence to be added to the data plane, i.e., what sort of statistics should we capture at the switch layer? Second, we need to develop effective techniques to report network statistics to the control plane. Third, we need to develop new mechanisms that quickly react to identified attacks. Finally, our implementation should strive to minimize changes to the OpenFlow protocol and have negligible performance impact. In essence, we recognize the design objective to keep the OpenFlow data plane as simple as possible, but the current tradeoff imposed by this design is a serious adversary model in which remote entities can halt operations of the entire network with relatively minimal traffic flows.

To this end, this paper makes the following contributions:

- We propose a strategic and focused extension to the data plane called *connection migration* that we argue yields the significant benefit of halting the threats of the saturation attack. To the best of our knowledge, *connection migration* is the first attempt in this direction to be embedded into an SDN network.
- We propose a new technique called an *actuating trigger* that addresses the responsiveness challenge by providing condition-triggered push capability in SDN devices.
- We design and implement AVANT-GUARD to integrate both *connection migration* and *actuating triggers* in a reference SDN (OpenFlow) software switch. We implement several exemplar OpenFlow security applications that demonstrate how AVANT-GUARD enhances the flexibility and robustness with which these applications can be implemented. Our performance evaluation also indicates that AVANT-GUARD incurs a very small overhead.

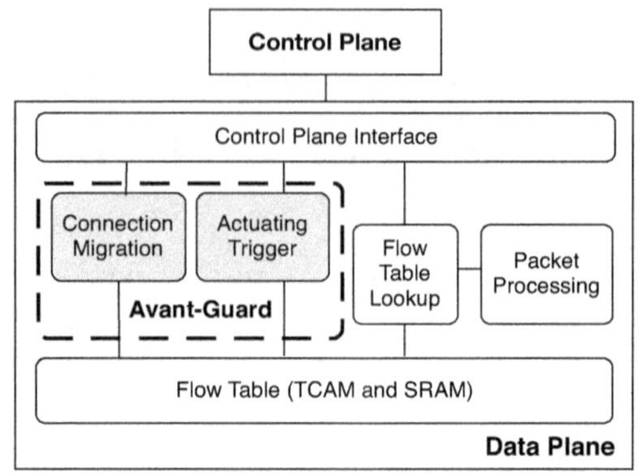

Figure 1: Conceptual architecture of AVANT-GUARD

2. PROBLEM STATEMENT

In this paper, we plan to investigate and answer the following research questions:

- Can we add (hopefully minimal) intelligence to the data plane to increase the resilience of the data-plane-to-control-plane interaction to anomalous control-plane floods?
- Is there an alternative to the existing polling strategy that may enable the control plane to acquire lower-latency knowledge of the traffic dynamics flowing through the data plane?
- Can OpenFlow applications leverage this information to detect and react more efficiently to anomalous traffic patterns?

Specifically, the key design objectives of our AVANT-GUARD (AG) framework include the following:

- Scalability and Resilience: AG must improve resilience of the OF network with minimal impact on overall scalability.
- Transparency: AG must require no changes to software running on end hosts.
- Incremental Deployment: AG must minimize changes to the OpenFlow network and enable incremental deployment. Though AG switches would require an AG-aware controller, both should be able to interoperate with other OF switches in the network.
- Minimal Collateral Impact: AG should introduce minimal additional delay to legitimate connections on the network.

3. SYSTEM DESIGN

To address the problems discussed in the previous section, we present AVANT-GUARD as a security extension to the OpenFlow data plane. In this section, we present the AVANT-GUARD design.

3.1 Overall Architecture

AVANT-GUARD extends the existing OpenFlow data plane with the addition of two new modules: 1) a *connection migration module* and 2) an *actuating trigger module*. AVANT-GUARD also slightly modifies existing data plane modules to support our target features. The conceptual diagram for AVANT-GUARD in the data plane is shown in Figure 1.

Inspired by the SYN proxy, which handles TCP connections in a middle box, we propose *connection migration* to sift failed TCP sessions at the data plane prior to any notification to the control plane. It collaborates with an *access table* and maintains TCP session information at the data plane to provide session details to the control plane. The *actuating trigger* enables collection of network status information and packet payload information more efficiently than existing data planes. Additionally, it offers *conditional flow rule activation*, i.e., the ability to activate flow rules (or actions) when some events happen.

3.2 Connection Migration

The objective of connection migration is to add intelligence to the data plane to differentiate those sources that will complete TCP connections from sources that will not. To do this, we extend the data plane to proxy the TCP handshake, and we only expose those flow requests to the control plane that complete the handshake. We present the operation of connection migrations in a stage diagram consisting of four stages: (i) classification, (ii) report, (iii) migration, and (iv) relay. Each stage and transitions between them are shown in Figure 2. When a source initiates a connection, the connection migration (CM) module engages the source in the stateless TCP handshake using SYN cookies [2]. The connection is assigned the classification stage. On handshake completion, CM notifies the control plane of the flow request, transitioning the connection to the report stage. If the control plane allows migration, CM initiates the real target host with the TCP handshake, which transitions the connection to the migration stage. Then, if the target accepts the handshake, CM notifies the control plane, and the connection enters the report stage. Finally, if the control plane allows the data plane to relay packets, CM completes the connection between the source and target, and the connection is migrated to the relay stage. Next, we examine the details of each stage.

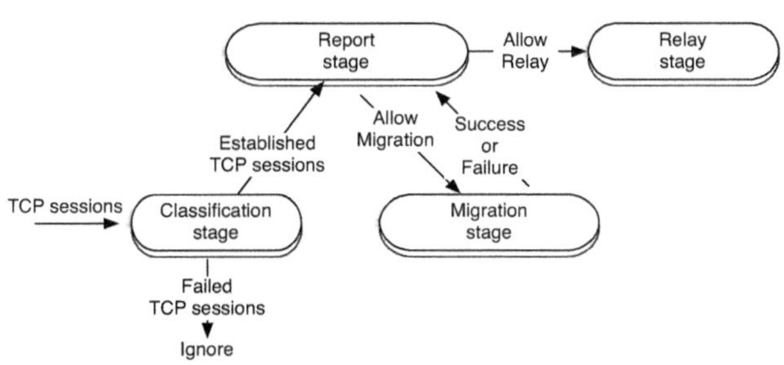

Figure 2: Stage diagram of connection migration

Classification Stage: In this stage, connection migration classifies useful TCP sessions (i.e., established TCP sessions) from connections that would result in client-side timeout (i.e., failed TCP sessions). Inspired by the SYN cookie algorithm, connection migration shields the control plan from client-side failed connection floods (e.g., which arise from DoS and reconnaissance activities), as shown in Figure 3 and 4. When the data plane receives a TCP SYN/RST/FIN packet (Figure 3), the data plane first checks if a matched flow rule exists in a flow table. If so, the data plane immediately forwards the packet. Otherwise, the data plane first updates the access table that contains information on all TCP connection attempts, by increasing the connection attempt counter for an IP address (i.e., the access table collects TCP session information). The data plane then checks whether this packet is a TCP SYN packet, and if so generates a sequence number for this packet with a hash function[1] (i.e., SYN cookie) and returns a TCP SYN/ACK packet to a peer who sends the TCP SYN packet with the generated sequence number. If the packet is not a TCP SYN packet (i.e., TCP FIN or TCP RST), it is rejected and the data plane can optionally return a TCP RST package or simply ignore the source.

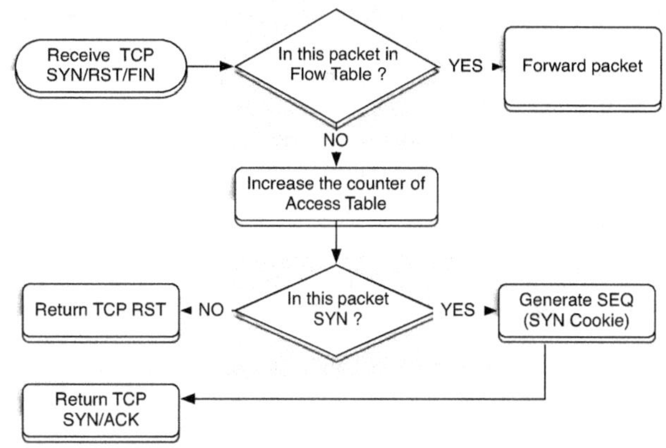

Figure 3: Flowchart for handling TCP SYN/RST/FIN packets

If the peer sends a TCP ACK packet to the data plane (Figure 4), the data plane follows the handling method shown in Figure 3. In this case, the data plane first checks the flow table to determine whether there exists a matched flow corresponding to the ACK packet. If so, the device forwards the packet. Otherwise, it validates the SYN cookie to determine whether this packet completes a TCP session or was sent unsolicited. If this ACK packet contains an appropriate SYN cookie, the TCP handshake is established. Upon completion of the handshake, the data plane reports the flow request to the control plane (i.e., step 4 in Figure 5). Otherwise, the connection request is considered an incomplete probe; a RST is sent, and the access table counters are adjusted.

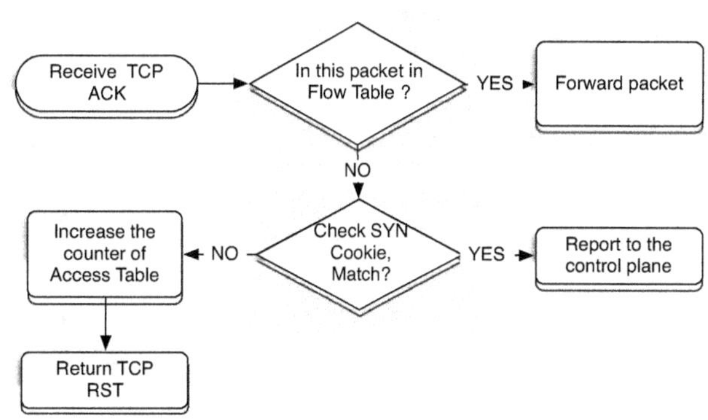

Figure 4: Flowchart for handling TCP ACK packets

Report Stage: For each connection validated by the classification stage, the report stage first determines if there is an existing flow rule to handle the session. If not, the data plane reports this flow request to the control plane. The data plane extracts the header information of a flow representing the TCP session, and sends this

[1]We use 4-tuple information as inputs for this hash function.

information to the control plane with a specific command. The control plane then decides whether to allow migration of this session. If so, the connection is transitioned to the migration stage.

Migration Stage: During the migration stage, the CM module initiates a TCP connection handshake with the connection's destination host. If the host responds with a TCP SYN/ACK packet, the data plane finalizes this session by sending a TCP ACK packet to the host. The data plane also reports this information (i.e., establishment of a TCP session with a real target host) to the control plane. If the data plane fails to establish the TCP session with destination hosts (due to an unavailable host or closed port), this result will also be reported to the control plane.

Relay Stage: After the data plane successfully establishes a TCP session with a real target host, it enters the relay stage where it relays all TCP data packets between a connection source and destination as occurs during normal TCP sessions.

Example Connection Migration Scenario: To illustrate connection migration, consider the interaction shown in Figure 5. If the data plane receives a TCP SYN packet from the host A (1) and this packet does not match an existing flow rule in the device, it automatically responds with a TCP SYN/ACK packet to host A (2). Then, if host A sends a TCP ACK packet to complete this TCP session (3), the switch knows that a TCP session is successfully established, and it reports this event to the control plane. Then, the control plane decides whether to allow the connection to migrate on to the real destination host (i.e., host B). Assuming the connection is allowed, the control plane activates a flow rule with what we propose as the *Migrate* action. When a migrate action rule is received by the data plane it initiates a TCP connection to host B (6) and completes the connection (7, 8). If the migration is successful, the device notifies the control plane of this event (9). Finally, the control plane inserts a *Relay* action into the data plane, causing it to relay all packets between host A and B. At this time, the device need not add a new rule; rather, it only needs to change the action field of the existing flow rule. Hence, the rule will be changed from (A-1) to (A-2). Operations 1-3 represent the classification stage; 4-5 and 9-10 denote the reporting stages, 6-8 refer to the migration stage, and 11-12 refer to the relay stage.

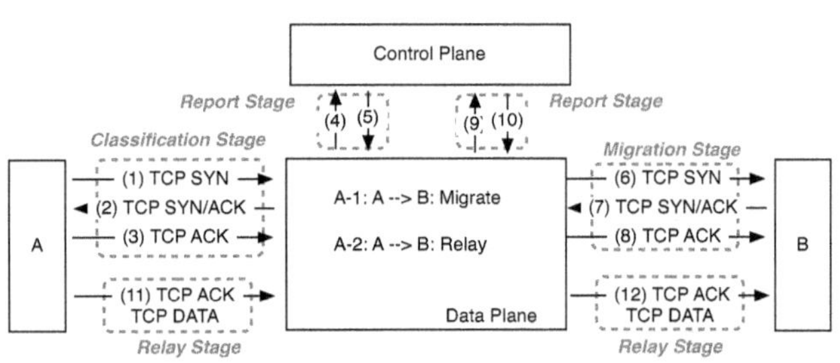

Figure 5: Example connection migration scenario

Impact on Control Plane Saturation: Connection migration offers an immediate benefit for maintaining control operations in the presence of well-known adversarial models that engage in both spoofed and non-spoofed attacks against an OpenFlow network. In the context of spoofed flooding attacks (e.g., spoofed TCP SYN floods that may saturate the control plane with bogus connection requests), all such flow requests are nullified at the classification stage. For non-spoofed connection floods (e.g., those that may arise from an aggressive scanner), connection migration converts the OpenFlow network into a *whitehole* network [9]. From the source's perspective, all probes to the ports and IP address ranges of the OpenFlow network appear to produce a TCP handshake response, hindering the source from knowing which IP and port combinations are actually alive.

In the case of the flow-rule-flooding problem in the data plane, connection migration addresses this concern through its adoption of stateless TCP handshaking with SYN cookies. Because the SYN cookie algorithm does not require any state management, a device does not need to store any flow rules for failed or malicious TCP connection attempts. It can reduce the effect of flow-rule-flooding problem. Because of this, connection migration enhances an OpenFlow network's *resilience* and *scalability* to network flooding attacks.

Collecting TCP Session Information: Based on information from access tables in the data plane, the control plane acquires two important attributes from each source that contacts the network: (i) the number of all connection attempts, captured in the access table (defined as A_1) and (ii) the number of established connections recorded within the connection migration report (defined as A_2). Analysis of the ratio of failed TCP connections of a peer (A_1 - A_2) and the number of established TCP connections (A_2) can often be used to detect various flooding and probing behavior.

3.2.1 Delayed Connection Migration

Knowledgeable adversaries may infer the use of connection migration and attempt to produce flooding packets by establishing many real TCP sessions. They can use multiple processes, threads, or many zombie PCs to generate fake TCP connections. However, for some protocols, such as HTTP, in which the client is expected to send the first data packet, we can extend connection migration to incorporate *delayed connection migration*. Here, we operate a variant of connection migration in which the key difference is that the classifying stage will delay the transition to the reporting stage until it receives the client's TCP data packet. This scenario is shown in Figure 6. As shown in Figure 6, the data plane delays the reporting time (5) until it receives more evidence (i.e., data packet) from a TCP session initiator (4).

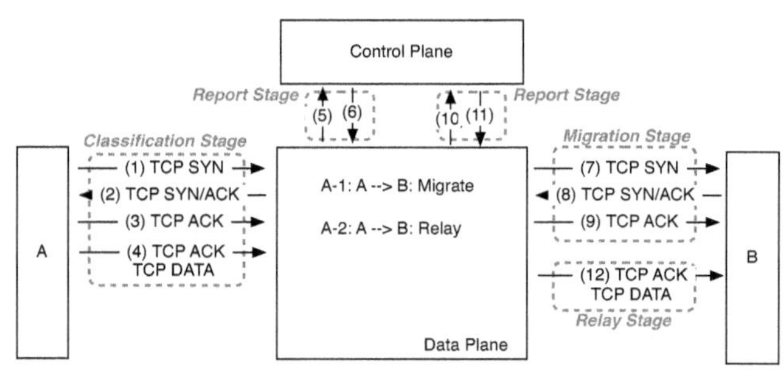

Figure 6: Example delayed connection migration scenario

3.3 Actuating Triggers

We propose to extend OpenFlow with *actuating triggers* which enable the data plane to asynchronously report network status and payload information to the control plane. In addition, actuating triggers can be used to activate a flow rule under some predefined conditions to help the control plane manage network flows without delays. The actuating trigger consists of four main operations. First, the control plane needs to define a traffic statistic condition under which notification is warranted. Second, the control plane registers this condition to the data plane. Third, the data plane checks the condition against its current locally collected packet and flow statistics to determine if the condition is satisfied. Fourth, when the data plane determines that the condition is satisfied by its current statistics, it may 1) trigger a call-back event to the control plane to indicate that the condition is met, or 2) insert a flow rule into a specified flow table.

Next, we discuss this operation in detail. The conceptual diagram of event triggering and its operation sequence are shown in Figure 7.

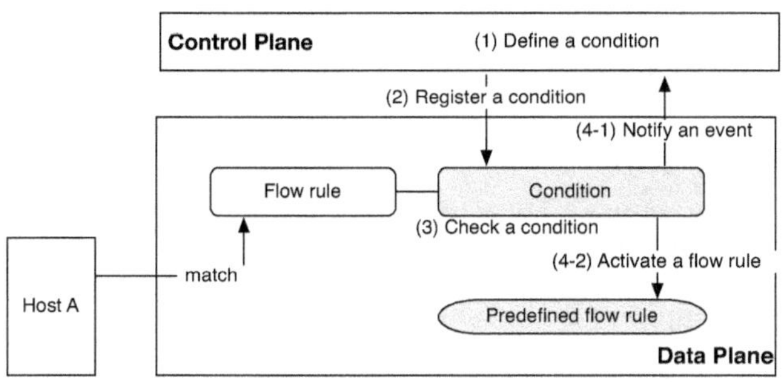

Figure 7: Example event triggering scenario

Defining a Condition: AVANT-GUARD supports three types of actuating trigger conditions: *(i)* payload-based, *(ii)* traffic-rate-based, and *(iii)* rule-activation. Conditions can be extended in the future. To define each type of condition, the control plane uses the following format.

```
{type: condition: pointer}
```

The type field is a 2-bit data structure representing three condition types: 00 = payload, 01 = traffic rate, and 10 = rule activation. The condition field varies for each type. For payload, the condition field is a 1-bit Boolean, indicating 1 for payload investigation required and 0 for no investigation required. For both traffic-rate and rule-activation conditions, the control plane uses a 22-bit data structure, which consists of a 2-bit, 4-bit, and 16-bit field. The 2-bit field specifies whether the control plane wishes to register for time-related metrics (e.g., packets per second (PPS) and bytes per seconds (BPS)), where 10 represents PPS, and 01 represents the BPS. 00 indicates the control plane has registered for raw counts. 8. The 4-bit data structure represents comparator options and covers five different cases. The first three are simple: *(i)* 0001 for *equal*, *(ii)* 0010 for *greater than*, and *(iii)* 0100 for *less than*. If the control plane wants to define compound comparators, it can simply combine *(i)* and *(ii)* (i.e., 0011) for *greater than or equal to*, and *(i)* and *(iii)* for *less than or equal to*. If the control plane sets the highest bit as 1 (i.e., 1000), the data plane needs to check PPS or BPS. The latter 16-bit structure represents the trigger value to be matched by the current statistics and enables the control plane to employ trigger ranges from 0 and 65,535.

The pointer part is used when the control plane wants to activate a predefined flow rule in which the pointer indicates where the flow rule is stored. If the data plane finds that a condition defined by the control plane is satisfied and there is a pointer attached to the condition, the data plane follows the pointer and activates the flow rule into the flow table. We extend the data plane to support a function that installs the predefined flow rules, which we can implement via an extension to the `dpctl` command.

To clarify this idea, we provide an example scenario. We assume that the control plane wants to define a conditional flow-rule insertion that will activate when a flow exceeds 32 bytes per second. To do this, the type field is set to 10 to indicate this is a network-status-based trigger. The 22-bit condition field is set as follows: the 2-bit field is set to 10 to indicate a time metric, the 4-bit comparator field is 0010 (for equality), and the 16-bit trigger value field is 32.

Condition Registration: When the control plane creates a conditional flow rule, it will be delivered to the data plane through an existing communication channel (e.g., the OpenFlow network interface). When the data plane receives this condition, it gets installed into its flow table.

Traffic Rate Monitoring: Whenever the data plane receives a packet, it updates statistical information for related fields (e.g., packet count of a flow rule). This is standard functionality in the implementation of existing OpenFlow switches which we utilized for our trigger implementation. We augment the data plane logic by adding a trigger-evaluation function which incorporates its own counter management logic within the data plane. This counter is mainly used for our network-status trigger evaluation.

In addition, we add a 16-bit data structure to store time information, which we use in our PPS and BPS calculations. These triggers are particularly useful in security applications for monitoring traffic and flow rate anomalies. PPS, BPS, and counts, can be computed on packet arrival or calculated independently based on the internal clock. The advantage of a clocked-based calculation strategy is that one can define *less-than*-based trigger evaluates (e.g., trigger when a rate falls below 10 packets per second). Packet-based calculations support *equality* and *greater-than* triggers and are computed when a trigger interval has been exceeded. For AVANT-GUARD we have implemented traffic-based rate computation.

Event Notification: When the data plane detects a signal satisfying a pre-defined condition, it notifies the control plane using a new "trigger" message extension that we added to OpenFlow.

Selective Packet Payload Delivery to the Control Plane: Packet delivery to the control plane is controlled by a flag bit (i.e., 1 bit) in the flow table of the data plane. A set flag bit implies that the control plane wants to receive packet payloads that match this flow rule condition.

The running scenario for this function is described in Figure 8. In this scenario, we assume that the control plane wants to investigate packet payloads being delivered from a host at 10.0.0.1. First, the control plane simply asks the data plane to deliver packet payloads when the source IP address of packets is 10.0.0.1 (1). Second, the data plane sets the condition field for payload of a matched flow rule (i.e., flow rule whose source IP address field is 10.0.0.1) (2). If the data plane receives a packet from a host whose IP address is 10.0.0.1 (3), it forwards the packet (with payload) to the control plane (4). In this case, we just need to add a 1-bit flag to each flow rule entry in the data plane.

Conditional Flow Rule Activation: In addition to asynchronous event notifications, we also employ triggers to introduce conditional flow rule activation. This is a powerful feature that enables a security application to predefine a course of action strategy for handling flows when the network encounters certain operating conditions that can be expressed through switch statistics. For example, when a DDoS targets a server, the control plane can find this based on the event delivered by the data plane. Then, the data plane will enforce a flow rule to stop the attack. However, this process will delay the reaction to the attack because it requires a transaction

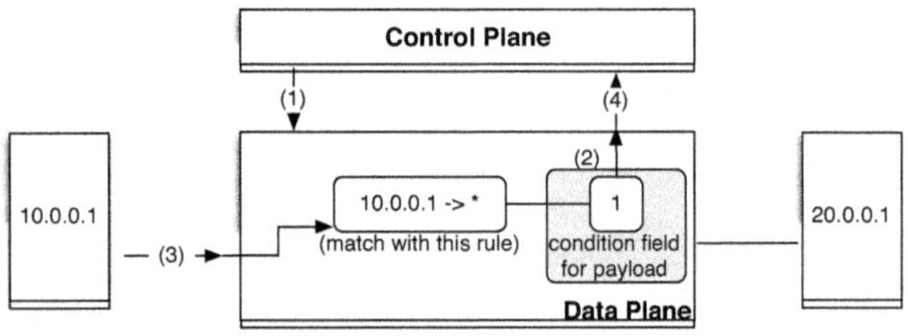

Figure 8: Scenario illustrating packet payload delivery to the control plane

between the data plane and the control plane. If the control plane already installed a flow rule for stopping this attack, the data plane need not notify the control plane to get a flow rule; instead it simply activates the installed rule.

To efficiently implement this function, we add new entries to store flow rules into the data plane. The format of these new entries is the same as a normal flow-rule entry in the data plane. The only difference is that the rules stored in these entries can only be activated by the condition field for the flow rule. The condition for activating a flow rule is the same as the condition field for status, which we explain below.

This idea is realized by adding two components to the data plane: (i) memory to store flow rules, and (ii) pointers to find installed flow rules. The pointer is an 8-bit data structure attached to a condition (i.e., the data plane manages up to 256 predefined flow rules).

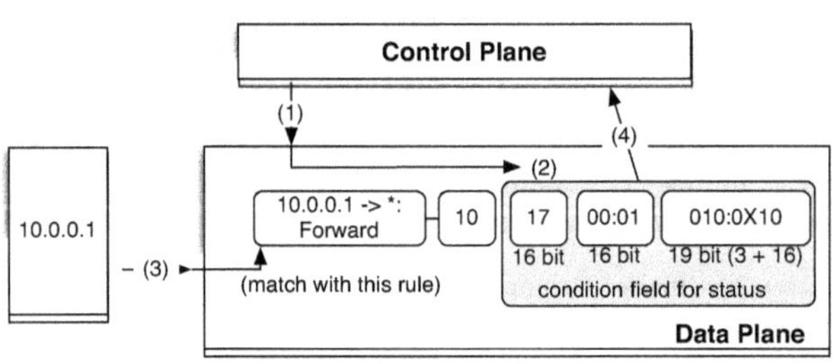

Figure 9: Scenario illustrating trigger-based notification to the control-plane

To illustrate how a flow rule is activated, we show an operational scenario in Figure 10. The condition in this Figure is the same as the condition presented in Figure 9. In this scenario, we assume that the control plane wants to block a flow if the flow generates more than 16 packets per second. In this case, the control plane can define this condition as we do above (1-3), and request that the data plane notify the control plane of this event (4). In addition, it will install a predefined flow rule (5) to BLOCK this traffic.

4. SYSTEM IMPLEMENTATION

We implemented AVANT-GUARD into the software-based OpenFlow reference switch (we call this the software OF switch) [21]. This reference implementation covers OpenFlow specification 1.0.0 [20], and it functions as the data plane. We modified the source code of this implementation to support connection migration and actuating triggers.

Specifically, we modified the packet_receive routine in the software OF switch to respond to new connection attempts with SYN/ACKs. The SYN cookie algorithm generates the SEQ number of this packet.

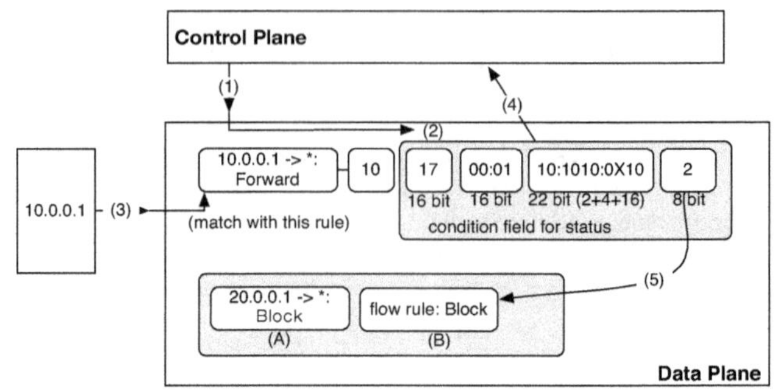

Figure 10: Scenario illustrating trigger-based activation of flow rules

If the packet-receiving routine subsequently receives a TCP ACK (i.e., matching the previously generated SYN cookie), it requests permission from the control plane to migrate the connection. Upon receiving permission, the modified OF switch will initiate a TCP connection to the real target host. To relay subsequent TCP packets through a migrated channel, we also add functions to carefully modify the corresponding ACK or SEQ numbers of each TCP packet.

We added three new data structures into the software OF switch to support actuating triggers. We modified the switch to check whenever it updates the counter for each flow (or other variables). If a counter value satisfies a condition that is defined by the control plane, the switch generates a signal back to the control plane. To implement flow rule activations, we created a data structure that can hold predefined flow rules. The data structure's format is the same as the existing flow-rule data structure (i.e., hash table and linked list) in the software OF switch.

Although most of the implementation involves extensions to the data plane (i.e., the software OF switch), minimal modification is also required to the control plane to support the aforementioned new features. Hence, we extended the source code of the POX controller [23] to support these capabilities. To support the novel functionality of AVANT-GUARD, we have added ten new OpenFlow commands as listed in Table 1. These commands are implemented in both the software OF switch and the POX controller.

4.1 Hardware Implementation Strategies

Below, we consider how our proposed OpenFlow switch extensions can be realized in a hardware-based implementation.

Traditional SDN Data Plane: First, we review the traditional SDN data plane architecture, which is illustrated in Figure 11 (A). This architecture is based on the NetFPGA implementation of the OpenFlow switch by the OpenFlow inventors [18]. Our focus here is the ASIC implementation used to conduct packet handling operations inside the switch. This implementation consists of six main modules: (i) the input arbiter, which forwards a packet to following logic; (ii) header parse, which parses a packet header; (iii) exact match lookup, which finds a flow rule (w/o wildcards) for a packet; (iv) wildcard lookup, which finds a flow rule (with wildcard) for a packet; (v) the arbiter, which decides operations of a packet (forward or drop); and (vi) the packet editor, which forwards or modifies a packet. In addition, flow rules are stored in a TCAM or SRAM (outside of the ASIC), and a counter storing statistical values for each flow rule is attached to the TCAM or SRAM.

We illustrate the operation of this hardware switch implementation using the following scenario. First, if the data plane receives

Command	*Direction*	*Explanation*
OFPFC_MIGRATE	C → D	allow connection migration
OFPFC_RELAY	C → D	allow data relay
OFPFC_REG_PAYLOAD	C → D	register payload condition
OFPFC_REG_STATUS	C → D	register network status condition
OFPFC_REG_RULE	C → D	register a new flow rule
OFPR_NEWFLOW	D → C	report a new flow
OFPR_MIGRATE_SUCCESS	D → C	report a migration result (SUCCESS)
OFPR_MIGRATE_FAIL	D → C	report a migration result (FAIL)
OFPR_PAYLOAD	D → C	deliver payload
OFPR_STATUS	D → C	report a detected event

Table 1: New OpenFlow commands implemented by AVANT-GUARD **(*C* denotes control plane, and *D* denotes data plane)**

a packet, the lookup component checks the TCAM or SRAM to see if a flow rule handling this packet exists. If so, it forwards the packet to the arbiter. Otherwise, it asks the control plane through an interface running on the CPU.

Implementation of Connection Migration: To implement connection migration in hardware, we need to modify three components in the data plane and add two new data structures into the data plane. The new data-plane architecture with connection migration is presented in Figure 11(B). The header parser is modified to extract TCP flags, and the arbiter is modified to force the packet editor to initiate connection migration or to reply with a TCP SYN/ACK packet. We add a connection-handler module to the packet editor. This module can initiate connection migration or answer a connection request by sending the SYN/ACK.

We also add two new data structures to support the relay stage of connection migration. Because our data plane needs to manage two TCP connections as a single connection, it should change the ACK or SEQ number of each packet. We only need to track the difference between the SEQ number of SYN packets (SYN from a connection initiator to the data plane) and the inside connection (SYN from the data plane to the destination of our migration). This difference value will be stored in an ACK/SEQ delta structure, and the number of this value is the same as the number of migrated connections.

TCP connections also come with certain TCP options, such as timestamp, and our data plane should handle this value as we do for ACK or SEQ change. To support this, we have added an optional structure into the data plane to track the TCP timestamps between external and internal connections. However, this is optional, because the data plane could also simply discard such options during TCP negotiation.

Implementation of Actuating Triggers: To implement our actuating trigger in hardware, we add two data structures for storage into the data plane. This architecture is shown in Figure 11(B). All condition fields for the actuating trigger are collectively labeled as Condition in this Figure, and they are attached to counters in the data plane. Also, predefined flow rules can be implemented by adding the same components for flow rules (TCAM and SRAM). For implementations that are cost sensitive, we may share existing TCAM or SRAM storage for these flow rules (not denoted in the Figure).

Off-ASIC Implementation of AVANT-GUARD**:** The architecture described above involves adding new components to the ASIC in the data plane which is both costly and complex. Here, we are inspired by Mogul's research [11], which suggests we may move some components out of the ASIC, and could potentially leverage the switch CPU and DRAM to implement certain functionality. In this case, we cannot avoid modifying existing components (i.e., modified header parser), but we can offload some storage requirements from the ASIC by moving data structures into DRAM. This architecture is presented in Figure 11(C). As shown in this figure, we place all storage into DRAM. Logic that resides in the ASIC could access DRAM content through the CPU (e.g., via a PCI interface). This approach trades off some performance for simplified development cost.

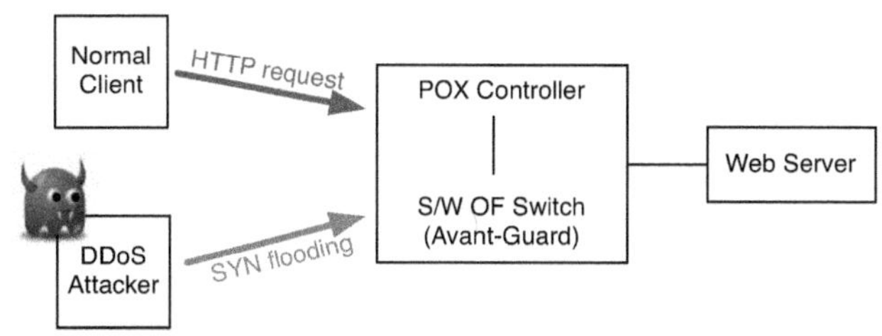

Figure 12: Environment for network saturation attack scenario

5. EVALUATION

In this section, we present how SDN security researchers and practitioners can leverage the benefit of AVANT-GUARD to develop simpler and stronger network security applications.

5.1 AVANT-GUARD Use Cases

We first describe an example use case for a security application and then compare two scenarios: (*i*) implementing the security application with existing OpenFlow technology and (*ii*) implementing the same function with AVANT-GUARD. We select three common network threats for comparison: (*i*) network saturation attack, (*ii*) network scanning attack, and (*iii*) network intrusion attack. For each case, we employ the software OF reference switch implementation [21] for our data plane, and AVANT-GUARD has been implemented into this reference implementation. We turn on or off the functions of AVANT-GUARD to compare the functions of each case. For the control plane, we use a modified POX controller [23] for both switches. The host running this S/W OF switch (w AVANT-GUARD or w/o AVANT-GUARD) was configured with an Intel Core-i5 CPU and 8 GB of memory.

5.1.1 Network Saturation Attack

Example Scenario: The test environment for this experiment is shown in Figure 12. It includes an OpenFlow switch (i.e., the data plane) in which AVANT-GUARD has been implemented; a POX network controller; a server that hosts a web service; a normal client that contacts the server with HTTP requests; and an attacker who performs a TCP SYN flood attack.

In this scenario, we measure the response time (i.e., the time it takes a normal client to fetch a page of data from the remote

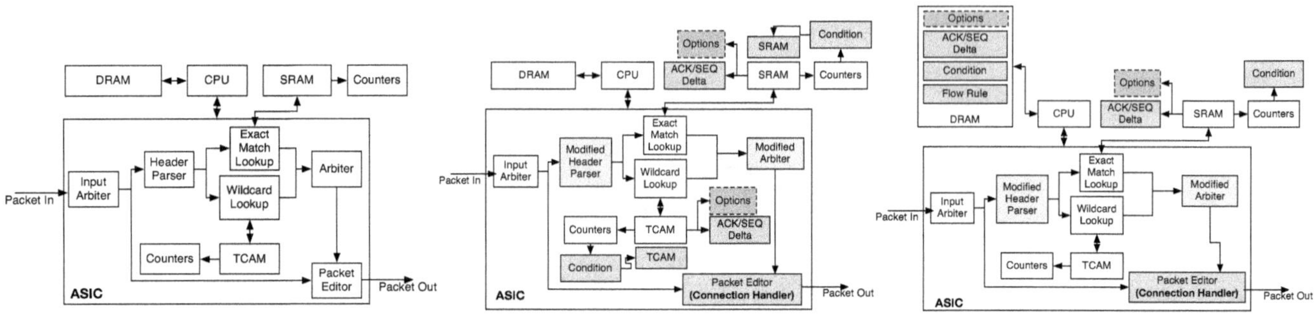

(A) Traditional SDN switch | **(B) AVANT-GUARD SDN switch** | **(C) Off-ASIC implementation**

Figure 11: Hardware architectural designs of (A) Traditional SDN switch (B) SDN switch with connection migration and actuating triggers and (C) SDN switch with connection migration and actuating triggers off-ASIC

Item	*Case*	*Response Time*	*Overhead*
Original	w/o DDoS	0.3917 s	-
	w/ DDoS	∞	∞
AVANT-GUARD	w/o DDoS	0.3990 s	1.86 %
	w/ DDoS	0.4001 s	2.1 %

Table 2: Average response time of each test case (Overhead means the percentage of additional response time compared with the Original - w/o DDoS case)

server under two situations: with and without background TCP SYN floods in this OpenFlow network). The attacker generates 1,000 connection attempts per second to the server, and we repeat this over 500 seconds to measure the average response time.

The test result showing the average response time is summarized in Table 2. The normal client can retrieve the web page in 0.4 seconds, but it does not get any response during a background TCP SYN flood attack due to the effect of control/data plane saturation mentioned earlier. However, AVANT-GUARD can effectively defend the network from this attack, enabling the normal client to retrieve the webpage without any problem, because our data plane automatically and transparently classifies and removes the malicious TCP connection attempts. Our system introduces only a negligible delay overhead (around 2.1%) for the normal client, even during severe saturation attacks.

We also measure the overhead of connection migration on normal TCP connections during normal network operations (i.e., without attacks) using the same experimental setup shown in Figure 12. From Table 2, we can see that the overhead caused by connection migration on normal TCP connections is minimal (1.86 %).

To further show the effect of saturation attacks on normal traffic in detail, we vary the packet-sending rate of the network saturation attack from 0 to 800 per second, and we send the requests from 10 benign clients to a target web server at the same time. The test results are shown in Figure 13, and we can easily observe that requests from benign clients are hardly delivered to the web server when the network saturation attack happens using the unmodified OpenFlow switch (nearly 0% when the flooding attack sends more than 100 packets per second). However, with AVANT-GUARD, all requests from benign clients are delivered to the web server, even while the network is under a severe network saturation attack.

Implementation Comparison: To detect TCP SYN flood attacks with an OpenFlow application, the application typically must be aware of the TCP session information (e.g., whether or not a TCP connection is successful). However, this session management will cause control flow saturation issues that we discussed earlier.

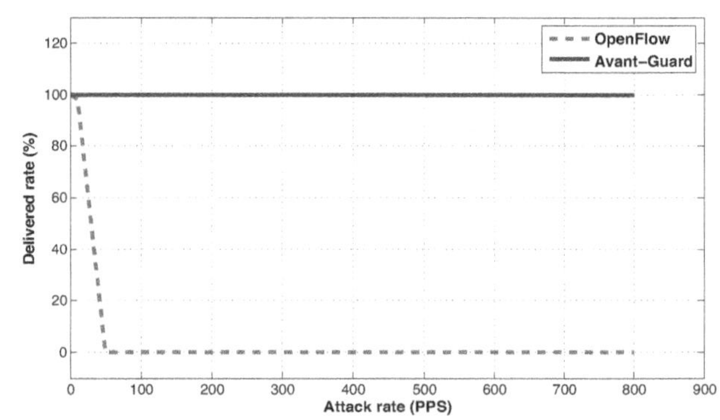

Figure 13: Percentage of successfully delivered packets to the web server from benign clients

That is the data plane will receive many TCP SYN packets that it will report to the control plane, which also receives the same number of requests from the attack. Currently, OpenFlow does not provide any way to reduce this effect.

With an AVANT-GUARD application, because the data plane automatically responds to all TCP SYN packets without high overhead, the data plane need not handle (i.e., forward or drop packets) all attack packets. In addition, the control plane only receives the requests for a successfully established TCP connection. Thus, the control plane does not suffer from network saturation attacks, and the application can easily detect such attacks. In this case, AVANT-GUARD makes the control plane and the SDN network more resilient and scalable.

5.1.2 Network Scanning Attack

Example Scenario: We test how our system defends a network from a network scan attack, and the test environment is shown in Figure 14. In this test, we use Nmap [24] to vertically scans all network ports of a file server (10.0.0.2) that only opens network port 10000.

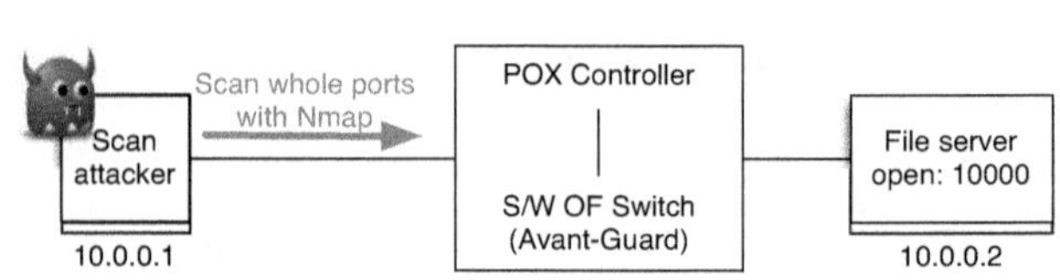

Figure 14: Environment for network scan attack scenario

If we employ AVANT-GUARD, the data plane automatically maintains the information on the TCP connection attempts in the access table and reports session information to the control plane, which can easily detect scan attempts by applying a simple threshold-based scan-detection algorithm. Here, we write a simple security application for detection of a network scan attack that regards a remote host as a scanner if it initiates five failed TCP connection attempts. This application only needs to ask the data plane to report the information on the TCP connection attempts; it does not itself need to maintain TCP sessions. The detection result is marked with a red rectangle in Figure 15.

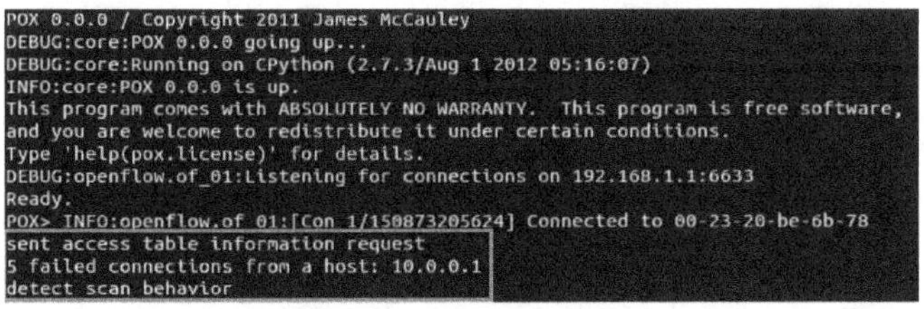

Figure 15: Network scan-detection result

Implementation Comparison: To detect a TCP scanning attack with an OpenFlow application, we need to check whether each TCP session is successful at the application layer. However, this check requires that the application manages each TCP flow making it vulnerable to control flow saturation attacks. If we implement the same application with AVANT-GUARD, it only needs to periodically read the access table to collect TCP session information.

In addition to this, we can implement the whitehole function with AVANT-GUARD easily. The whitehole function provided by our system can be easily observed by looking at Nmap scan results. In the absence of our approach, Nmap can successfully scan the file server, and finds that network port 10000 is open, as shown in Figure 16. Figure 17 shows the scan results of Nmap when applying our system (the network environment is the same as in Figure 14). Although the file server only opens port 10000, Nmap thinks that *all* network ports are open.

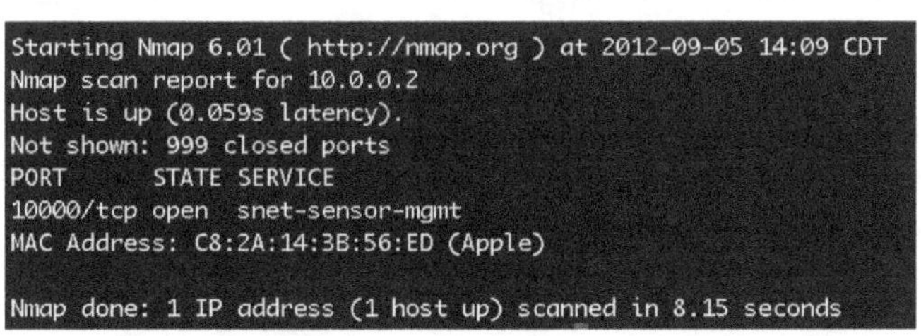

Figure 16: Nmap scan result without AVANT-GUARD

5.1.3 *Network Intrusion Attack*

Example Scenario: We set up an attack scenario as shown in Figure 18, and in this case, an attacker (10.0.0.1) sends an RPC buffer overflow attack to another host in the network (10.0.0.2). Here we assume two things: (i) the control plane already requested the data plane to deliver packet payloads delivered to 10.0.0.2 and (ii) a security application has a signature for the attack. In this test scenario, the application uses snort rules to detect malicious payloads. The result is shown in Figure 19, where we find that the security application accurately detects the attack (red rectangle in Figure).

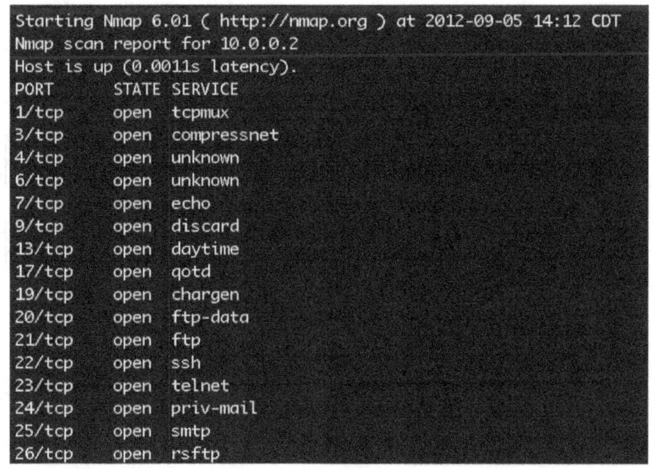

Figure 17: Nmap scan result with AVANT-GUARD - Whitehole

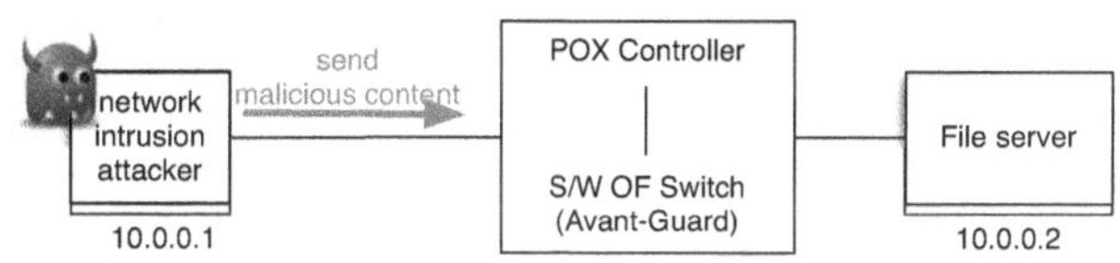

Figure 18: Network intrusion attack scenario

Implementation Comparison: An attacker can send malicious contents (e.g., exploits) to infect a target victim. To date, many approaches for detecting network intrusions have been proposed, and most of them rely on deep packet inspection to identify known attack patterns. However, an OpenFlow control plane (and applications) cannot see all network packet payloads. This is because OpenFlow was originally designed to handle mostly layer 2/3 network traffic. The data plane only reports network header information to the control plane, and if there is a matching flow rule in the flow table, the data plane does not even report header information to the control plane.

The actuating trigger module of AVANT-GUARD provides a new capability that can deliver a packet payload to the control plane (i.e., condition for packet payload). In this case, the AVANT-GUARD application simply defines a condition involving header fields (e.g., source or destination IP) that it wants to investigate and then forwards these criteria to the switch. The switch will report every packet payload that matches the condition to the application.

5.2 Overhead Measurement

When we measure the performance overhead of AVANT-GUARD, we use the same test environment as in Figure 12.

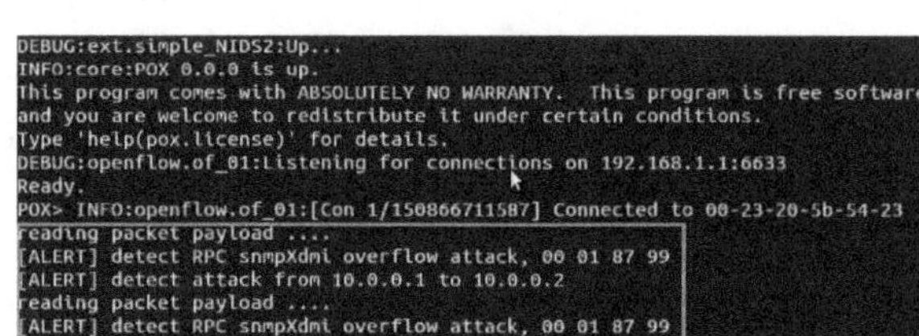

Figure 19: Network intrusion detection based on simple payload inspection

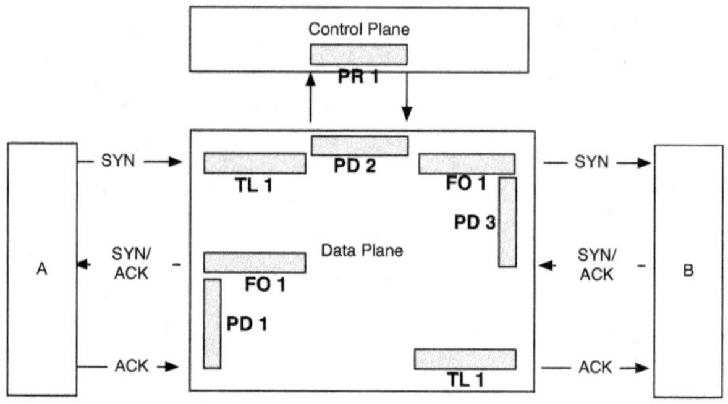

Figure 20: Breakdown of connection establishment delays in OpenFlow

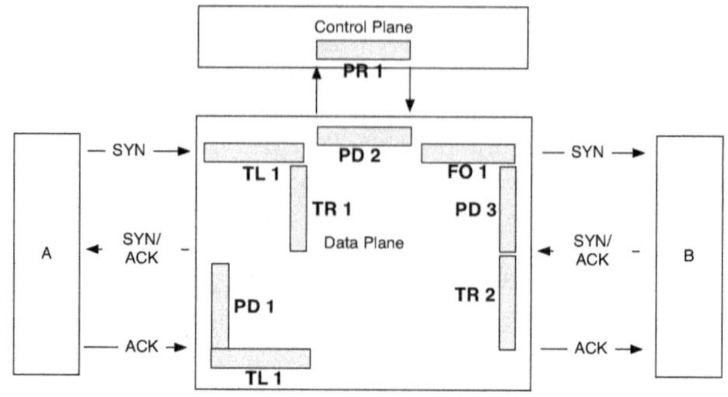

Figure 21: Breakdown of connection establishment delays in AVANT-GUARD

5.2.1 *Connection Migration*

To understand the overhead of connection migration at the micro level, we analyze the internal operations for establishing a TCP session in two cases: (i) using the software OF switch reference implementation and (ii) using the AVANT-GUARD extension. Figures 20 and 21 illustrate the breakdown of connection-establishment delays in the two systems, respectively.

In the case of a typical OF switch, the delay in establishing a new TCP session for which there is no flow rule can be broken down into seven components that start with the switch receiving a TCP SYN packets and end with the transmission of the ACK packet to the target server: (i) lookup a flow table and forward (TL1); (ii) ask the control plane for a flow rule and receive the rule (PD2) - (processing time in the control plane (PR1) is not included); (iii) insert a flow rule and forward (FO1); (iv) receive a SYN/ACK packet (PD3); (v) forward a packet based on the flow rule (FO1); (vi) receive an ACK packet (PD1); and (vii) lookup a table and forward (TL1).

In the case of AVANT-GUARD, the breakdown is a little different because the data plane automatically responds with SYN/ACK packet. With AVANT-GUARD the eight operations include: (i) lookup a flow table and forward (TL1); (ii) generate a SYN/ACK packet (TR1); (iii) receive an ACK packet (PD1); (iv) lookup the flow table (TL1); (v) ask the control plane to get a permission for migration and receive the rule for migration (PD2) - (processing time in the control plane (PR1) is not included); (vi) forward a SYN packet to a target host (FO1); (vii) receive a SYN/ACK packet (PD3); and $(viii)$ generate an ACK packet and send it (TR2).

We summarize the delay breakdown in the two cases as follows:

- OpenFlow case = TL1 + PD2 + FO1 + PD3 + FO1 + PD1 + TL1
- AVANT-GUARD case = TL1 + TR1 + PD1 + TL1 + PD2 + FO1 + PD3 + TR2

We instrumented the software switch to measure the respective delay of each component and illustrate them in Figures 22 and 23. To get these results, we initiated many TCP connection attempts to a switch and then used the average values from our measurements. The average connection establishment delay in the OF software switch case is 1608.6 us; for AVANT-GUARD the average is 1618.74 us. Thus, the overhead of connection migration is 0.626%, which is very small.

However, the delays here are dominated by the propagation delay. If we remove PD1, PD2, and PD3 from the above measurements, the original S/W OF switch incurs a composite delay of 32.4 us, and AVANT-GUARD incurs a delay of 42.54 us. In this case, the overhead is 23.84%, which is somewhat more substantial, but still not prohibitive.

5.2.2 *Actuating Triggers*

To estimate the overhead of actuating triggers, we measure the time to check each condition (e.g., traffic-rate based condition) and to activate a flow rule. Our results are summarized in Table 3. For the traffic-rate based condition, we simply define a condition that checks if the PPS of a flow is greater than 100. We see that the overhead for each condition is relatively small (even nearly 0 in the case of payload-based condition). In comparison with the elapsed time for connection migration, condition checks only involve around 1.6% of overhead.

Item	*time*
Traffic-rate based condition	0.322 us
Payload-based condition	≈ 0 us
Rule activation	1.697 us

Table 3: Time for checking each condition

The time for activating a flow rule based on a condition includes the time for checking the traffic-rate based condition and the time for looking up a flow table. In our measurement, it is 1.697 us. This time is significantly less than typical propagation delay between the data plane and the control plane (i.e., PD2). In our setup, the time for PD2 is 459.81 us, and the time for activating a flow rule is just 0.36% of PD2. Thus, we can say that our approach significantly reduces the time for threat reaction/mitigation. For example, if a network is subject to SYN flood attacks at a rate of 1,000,000 per second (1 packet per us), then this network will receive at least 460 packets before stopping the attack. However, with AVANT-GUARD, only two additional packets would be received after the data plane reacts to the attack.

6. RELATED WORK

Our work is inspired by several parallel studies that explore security threats in SDNs [1, 14, 28] and attempt to deliver innovative security applications with SDN technology. Mehdi et al. developed SDN applications for detecting network scan attacks [17]. Jafarian et al. suggested a random host mutation approach to protecting a network from scanning attacks[10]. Popa et al. designed a new security application for a cloud network [22]. Braga et al. created a DDoS detection application using SDN [3]. Shin et al. proposed a new security-monitoring-as-a-service framework for a cloud network [25]. Unlike our approach which fundamentally alters flow management at SDN switch level, these studies focus on creating specific high-level SDN applications to provide improved security services. We believe that all these applications can benefit

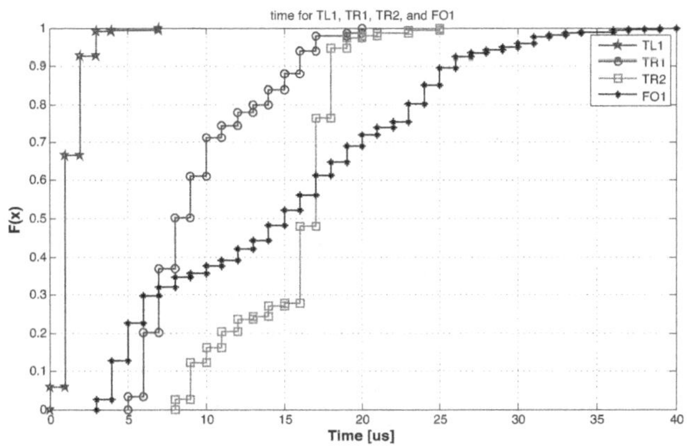

Figure 22: CDF of measured component delays (part 1)

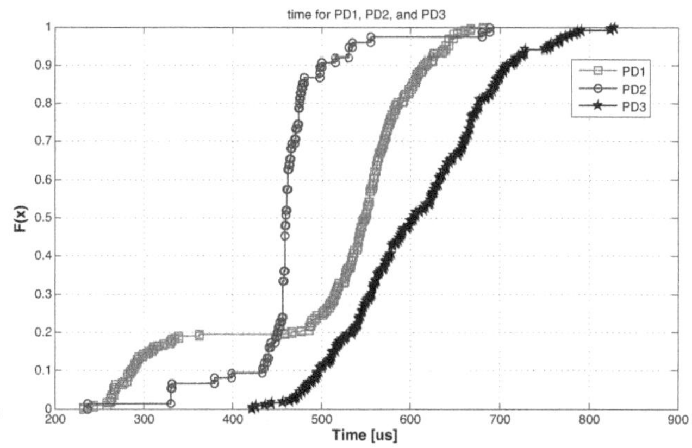

Figure 23: CDF of measured component delays (part 2)

from AVANT-GUARD. For example, the applications for detecting scan attacks in [17, 10] no longer need to manage TCP session by themselves because they can simply leverage AVANT-GUARD. FRESCO [26] is a a new framework designed to help accelerate the development of SDN security applications. We believe such frameworks can benefit from the resilience and trigger capabilities provided by AVANT-GUARD.

AVANT-GUARD's connection migration function is inspired by the SYN cookie, and there are many commercial products employing the SYN cookie idea to defeat TCP SYN flooding attacks (e.g., Cisco Guard [6] and Juniper Junos [12]). In addition, Mahimka et al. proposed a middle-box solution that can defeat network flooding attacks [16]. To our knowledge, we are the first to apply SYN cookies and connection migration in an SDN network.

Researchers have also proposed new architectures to improve SDN performance by reducing the communication between the switch and controller. Onix [13], Maestro [30], and Hyperflow [27] attempt to build more scalable SDN networks using distributed control planes. While we share a common goal in improving the scalability of SDN networks, we differ in the specific techniques that we propose to achieve this goal and in our emphasis on security. Mogul et al. proposed a new data plane architecture to reduce memory space by moving counters to the control plane [11]. Lu et al. [15] devised a new SDN architecture that handles a part of packet processing in the CPU. DIFANE [29] proposed a new solution that seeks to reduce switch-to-controller traffic by keeping all traffic in the data plane and selectively directing packets through intermediate switches that store the necessary rules. DevoFlow [7] seeks to improve the visibility and statistics gathering capabilities of OpenFlow and suggests a new data plane architecture to manage flow rules efficiently. However, the goals and approach of these studies are very different from our work in that these systems are focused on improving performance under normal network conditions while AVANT-GUARD introduces new techniques to improve network resilience under attacks. The concept of *actuating triggers* is similar to event-triggers described in DevoFlow, with the key difference that our triggers result in the dynamic insertion of a flow rule. In contrast, DevoFlow event-triggers simply result in a call back to the controller.

7. LIMITATIONS AND DISCUSSION

We now discuss some limitations in our work. First, the connection migration component of AVANT-GUARD primarily improves resilience against TCP SYN flood and network scanning attacks. Thus, it might not help application developers who want to defend against application layer DoS attacks or attacks based on UDP or ICMP protocols. However, delayed connection migration and actuating triggers could be selectively used to mitigate the impact of such attacks. Further, most well-known network services are based on TCP and most common network attacks are against TCP-based services. Thus, AVANT-GUARD would benefit the majority of network systems and applications. Extending AVANT-GUARD to better support more sophisticated attacks and non-TCP flows is future work.

Second, the use of connection migration imposes a small but measurable delay to normal network connections. This represents a very reasonable trade-off between security and performance. To reduce unnecessary overhead, we envision that certain networks may turn off connection migration by default and initiate it only under duress. This policy could be expressed as an actuating trigger. In addition, it could be combined with whitelists or dynamic reputation schemes to improve the quality of service to legitimate users during attacks. In our future work, we hope to more thoroughly investigate such trade-offs that occur when using connection migration and design better guidelines for different scenarios.

8. CONCLUSIONS AND FUTURE WORK

In this paper, we propose AVANT-GUARD, a new framework to advance the security and resilience of OpenFlow networks with greater involvement from the data-plane layer. The goal of AVANT-GUARD is to make SDN security applications more scalable and responsive to dynamic network threats. A key challenge, which we address, is the inherent bottleneck introduced by the interface between the control plane and the data plane that knowledgeable adversaries can exploit. Connection migration enables the data plane to shield the control plane from such saturation attacks. The second challenge is the issue of responsiveness. SDN security applications need expeditious access to network statistics from the data plane as a method for quickly responding to network threats. To address this, we introduce actuating triggers that automatically insert flow rules when the network is under duress. We present a software implementation of AVANT-GUARD, and demonstrate that the overhead imposed by the AVANT-GUARD security extensions is minimal, with connection delay increases of much less than a 1% overhead, while providing resilience to an important adversarial model that may hinder SDN adoption.

Acknowledgements. This material is based upon work supported by the Defense Advanced Research Projects Agency (DARPA) and the United States Air Force under Contract No. FA8750-11-C-0249 and by the National Science Foundation (NSF) under Grant no. CNS-0954096. All opinions, findings and conclusions or recommendations expressed herein are those of the author(s) and do not necessarily reflect the views of DARPA, the United States Air Force or NSF. It is approved for Public Release, Distribution Unlimited.

9. REFERENCES

[1] K. Benton, L. J. Camp, and C. Small. Openflow vulnerability assessment. In *Proceedings of the second ACM SIGCOMM workshop on Hot topics in software defined networking (HotSDN)*, 2013.

[2] D. J. Bernstein. SYN Cookies. http://cr.yp.to/syncookies.html.

[3] R. S. Braga, E. Mota, and A. Passito. Lightweight DDoS Flooding Attack Detection Using NOX/OpenFlow. In *Proceedings of the 35th Annual IEEE Conference on Local Computer Networks (LCN)*, 2010.

[4] M. Casado, M. J. Freedman, J. Pettit, J. Luo, N. McKeown, and S. Shenker. Ethane: Taking Control of the Enterprise. In *Proceedings of ACM SIGCOMM*, 2007.

[5] M. Casado, T. Garfinkel, M. Freedman, A. Akella, D. Boneh, N. McKeowon, and S. Shenker. SANE: A Protection Architecture for Enterprise Networks. In *Proceedings of the Usenix Security Symposium*, August 2006.

[6] Cisco. Cisco Guard Anomaly Detector. http://www.cisco.com/en/US/prod/collateral/modules/ps2706/ps6235/produc%t_data_sheet0900aecd80220a7c.html.

[7] A. Curtis, J. Mogul, J. Tourrilhes, P. Yalagandula, P. Sharma, and S. Banerjee. DevoFlow: Scaling Flow Management for High-Performance Networks. In *Proceedings of ACM SIGCOMM*, 2011.

[8] A. Greenberg, G. Hjalmtysson, D. A. Maltz, A. Myers, J. Rexford, G. Xie, H. Yan, J. Zhan, and H. Zhang. A Clean Slate 4D Approach to Network Control and Management. In *Proceedings of ACM Computer Communications Review*, 2005.

[9] G. Gu, Z. Chen, P. Porras, and W. Lee. Misleading and Defeating Importance-Scanning Malware Propagation. In *Proceedings of International Conference on Security and Privacy in Communication Networks (SecureComm)*, 2007.

[10] J. H. Jafarian, E. Al-Shaer, and Q. Duan. Openflow Random Host Mutation: Transparent Moving Target Defense using Software Defined Networking. In *Proceedings of the 1st ACM Workshop on Hot Topics in Software Defined Networks (HotSDN)*, 2012.

[11] P. C. Jeffrey C. Mogul. Hey, You Darned Counters! Get Off My ASIC! In *Proceedings of the 1st ACM Workshop on Hot Topics in Software Defined Networks (HotSDN)*, 2012.

[12] Juniper. Junos Security Configuration. http://www.juniper.net/us/en/products-services/nos/junos/.

[13] T. Koponen, M. Casado, N. Gude, J. Stribling, L. Poutievski, M. Zhu, R. Ramanathan, Y. Iwata, H. Inoue, T. Hama, and S. Shenker. Onix: A Distributed Control Platform for Large-scale Production Networks. In *Proceedings of the Symposium on Operating Systems Design and Implementation (OSDI)*, 2010.

[14] D. Kreutz, F. M. Ramos, and P. Verissimo. Towards Secure and Dependable Software-Defined Networks. In *Proceedings of the second ACM SIGCOMM workshop on Hot Topics in Software Defined Networking (HotSDN)*, 2013.

[15] G. Lu, R. Miao, Y. Xiong, and C. Guo. Using CPU as a Traffic Co-processing Unit in Commodity Switches. In *Proceedings of the 1st ACM Workshop on Hot Topics in Software Defined Networks (HotSDN)*, 2012.

[16] A. Mahimka, J. Dange, V. Shmatikov, H. Vin, and Y. Zhang. dFence: Transparent Network-based Denial of Service Mitigation. In *Proceedings of the Symposium on Networked Systems Design and Implementation (NSDI)*, 2007.

[17] S. Mehdi, J. Khalid, and S. Khayam. Revisiting Traffic Anomaly Detection Using Software Defined Networking. In *Recent Advances in Intrusion Detection (RAID)*, 2011.

[18] J. Naous, D. Erickson, G. A. Covington, G. Appenzeller, and N. McKeown. Implementing an OpenFlow switch on the NetFPGA Platform. In *Proceedings of the 4th ACM/IEEE Symposium on Architectures for Networking and Communications Systems (ANCS)*, 2008.

[19] Open Networking Foundation. Software-Defined Networking: The New Norm for Networks. Technical report, 2012. https://www.opennetworking.org/images/stories/downloads/white-papers/wp%-sdn-newnorm.pdf.

[20] OpenFlow. OpenFlow Switch Specification version 1.0.0. Technical report, 2010. http://www.openflow.org/documents/openflow-spec-v1.0.0.pdf.

[21] OpenFlow.org. OpenFlow Switching Reference System. http://www.openflow.org/wp/downloads/.

[22] L. Popa, M. Yu, S. Y. Ko, I. Stoica, and S. Ratnasamy. CloudPolice: Taking Access Control out of the Network. In *Proceedings of the 9th ACM Workshop on Hot Topics in Networks (HotNets)*, 2010.

[23] POX. Python Network Controller. http://www.noxrepo.org/pox/about-pox/.

[24] N. Security. http://nmap.org/.

[25] S. Shin and G. Gu. CloudWatcher: Network Security Monitoring Using OpenFlow in Dynamic Cloud Networks (or: How to Provide Security Monitoring as a Service in Clouds?). In *Proceedings of the 7th Workshop on NPSec*, 2012.

[26] S. Shin, P. Porras, V. Yegneswaran, M. Fong, G. Gu, and M. Tyson. FRESCO: Modular Composable Security Services for Software-Defined Networks. In *Proceedings of the 20th Annual Network and Distributed System Security Symposium (NDSS)*, 2013.

[27] A. Tootoonchian and Y. Ganjali. HyperFlow: A Distributed Control Plane for OpenFlow. In *Proceedings of the Internet Network Management Workshop/Workshop on Research on Enterprise Networking (INM/WREN)*, 2010.

[28] X. Wen, Y. Chen, C. Hu, C. Shi, and Y. Wang. Towards a secure controller platform for openflow applications. In *Proceedings of the second ACM SIGCOMM workshop on Hot topics in software defined networking (HotSDN)*, 2013.

[29] M. Yu, J. Rexford, M. J. Freedman, and J. Wang. Scalable Flow-based Networking with DIFANE. In *Proceedings of ACM SIGCOMM*, 2010.

[30] T. S. E. N. Zheng Cai, Alan L. Cox. Maestro: Balancing Fairness, Latency and Throughput in the OpenFlow Control Plane. *Rice University Technical Report TR11-07.*

MinimaLT: Minimal-latency Networking Through Better Security

W. Michael Petullo
United States Military Academy
West Point, New York USA
mike@flyn.org

Xu Zhang
University of Illinois at Chicago
Chicago, Illinois USA
xzhang@cs.uic.edu

Jon A. Solworth
University of Illinois at Chicago
Chicago, Illinois USA
solworth@ethos-os.org

Daniel J. Bernstein
University of Illinois at Chicago TU Eindhoven
Chicago, Illinois USA Eindhoven, Netherlands
djb@cr.yp.to

Tanja Lange
TU Eindhoven
Eindhoven, Netherlands
tanja@hyperelliptic.org

ABSTRACT

Minimal Latency Tunneling (MinimaLT) is a new network protocol that provides ubiquitous encryption for maximal confidentiality, including protecting packet headers. MinimaLT provides server and user authentication, extensive Denial-of-Service protections, privacy-preserving IP mobility, and fast key erasure. We describe the protocol, demonstrate its performance relative to TLS and unencrypted TCP/IP, and analyze its protections, including its resilience against DoS attacks. By exploiting the properties of its cryptographic protections, MinimaLT is able to eliminate three-way handshakes and thus create connections faster than unencrypted TCP/IP.

Categories and Subject Descriptors

C.2.2 [**Network Protocols**]: Protocol architecture

Keywords

Network security; protocol; encryption; authentication

1 Introduction

Our goal is to protect *all* networking against eavesdropping, modification, and, to the extent possible, Denial of Service (DoS). To achieve this goal, networking must protect privacy, provide strong (i.e., cryptographic) authentication of both servers and users, be easy to configure, and perform well. These needs are not met by existing protocols.

Hardware and software improvements have eliminated historical cryptographic performance bottlenecks. Now, strong symmetric encryption can be performed on a single CPU core at Gb/s rates [40], even on resource-constrained mobile devices [8]. Public-key cryptography, once so agonizingly slow that systems would try to simulate it with symmetric key cryptography [36], is now performed at tens of thousands of operations per second on commodity CPUs. Due to these advances, along with the threats found on the Internet, researchers are increasingly calling for the protection of all network traffic [10, 51, 20, 13].

However, one performance metric is a fundamental limitation—network latency [28]. Latency is critical for users [55]. For example, Google found that a latency increase of 500ms resulted in a 25% dropoff in page searches, and studies have shown that user experience degrades at latencies as low as 100ms [12]. In response, there have been several efforts to reduce latency for both TCP and encrypted networking [14, 41, 37, 10, 48, 56].

We describe here MinimaLT, a secure network protocol which delivers protected data on the first packet of a typical client-server connection. MinimaLT provides cryptographic authentication of servers and users; encryption of communication; simplicity of protocol, implementation, and configuration; clean IP-address mobility; and DoS protections.

MinimaLT's design intentionally crosses network layers for two reasons. First, security problems often occur in the seams between layers. For example, Transport Layer Security (TLS) is vulnerable to attacks on TCP/IP headers due to its layering; connection-reset (RST) and sequence-number attacks interrupt TLS connections in a way that is difficult to correct or even detect [18, 3, 59]. Second, multi-layer design enables MinimaLT to improve performance.

Particularly challenging has been to provide key erasure ("forward secrecy") at low latency. **Key erasure** means that even an attacker who captures network traffic and later obtains all long-term private keys cannot decrypt past packets or identify the parties involved in communication. Traditionally, key erasure is implemented with Diffie-Hellman key exchange (DH) in a way that imposes a round trip before sending any sensitive data. MinimaLT eliminates this round trip, instead obtaining the server's ephemeral key during a directory service lookup (§3.4 and §5.2). Furthermore, MinimaLT inverts the normal mandatory start-of-connection handshake, instead ensuring connection liveness using a server-initiated handshake only when a host's resources become low (§5.7). Eliminating these round trips makes MinimaLT *faster than unencrypted TCP/IP at establishing connections.*

A second challenge is to make connections portable across IP addresses to better support mobile computing. MinimaLT allows the user to start a connection from home, travel to work, and continue to use that connection. This avoids application recovery overhead and lost work for operations which would otherwise be interrupted by a move. MinimaLT IP mobility does not require intermediary hosts or redirects, enabling it to integrate cleanly into protocol processing (§5.6). To provide better privacy, MinimaLT blinds third parties to IP-address portability, preventing them from linking a connection across different IP addresses.

Public domain. This work was supported by the US National Science Foundation under grants CNS-0964575 and 1018836, the European Commission under Contract ICT-2007-216676 ECRYPT II and INFSO-ICT-284833 PUFFIN, and by the Netherlands Organisation for Scientific Research (NWO) under grant 639.073.005. Permanent ID of this document: 4613afc97aa0c7b8c45bc08f46c2e120. Date: September 15, 2013.
CCS'13, November 4–8, 2013, Berlin, Germany.
ACM 978-1-4503-2477-9/13/11. http://dx.doi.org/10.1145/2508859.2516737.

A third challenge is DoS prevention. A single host cannot thwart an attacker with overwhelming resources [30], but MINIMALT protects against attackers with fewer resources. In particular, MINIMALT dynamically increases the ratio of client (i.e., attacker) to server resources needed for a successful attack. MINIMALT employs a variety of defenses to protect against DoS attacks (§7.6).

A fourth challenge is authentication and authorization. Experience indicates that network-based password authentication is fraught with security problems [29, 54, 42, 11], and thus cryptographic authentication is needed. Our authentication framework supports both identified and non-identified (pseudonym) users (§3.1). We designed MINIMALT to integrate into systems with strong authorization controls.

To meet these challenges, we have produced a clean-slate design, starting from User Datagram Protocol (UDP), by concurrently considering multiple network layers. We found an unexpected synergy between speed and security. The reason that the Internet uses higher-latency protocols is that, historically, low-latency protocols such as T/TCP have allowed such severe attacks [14] as to make them undeployable. It turns out that providing strong authentication elsewhere in the protocol stops all such attacks without adding latency.

MINIMALT was designed for, and implemented in, Ethos, an experimental Operating System (OS) [52]. Ethos's primary goal is to make it easier to write robust applications, i.e., applications able to withstand attacks. MINIMALT serves as Ethos' native network protocol; it is part of Ethos' authentication suite which includes a Public Key Infrastructure (PKI) named sayI [53] and a networking API [47, 46]. We have also ported MINIMALT to Linux.

MINIMALT provides the features of TCP/IP (reliability, flow control, and congestion control), and adds encryption, authentication, clean IP mobility, and DoS protections, all while providing key erasure and reducing latency.

§2 summarizes the threats for which MINIMALT provides countermeasures. The next four sections explain how MINIMALT works and how fast it is: §3 describes the central objects, §4 describes the message format, §5 describes the protocol dynamics, and §6 provides a performance evaluation. §7 explains why MINIMALT was designed the way it was, and §8 compares MINIMALT to related work.

2 Threat model

We are concerned with an attacker that will attempt to violate the confidentiality and integrity of network traffic. Our attacker can observe and modify arbitrary packets, might be a Man-in-the-Middle (MitM), might provide fraudulent services which attempt to masquerade as legitimate services, or might attempt to fraudulently assume the identity of a legitimate user. An attacker who gains complete control over clients and servers, through physical access or otherwise, might be able to decrypt or identify the parties communicating with very recent and future packets. However, he should be unable to do so with older packets.

In addition, we want to weaken attacks on availability. DoS attacks from *known* users are expected to be addressed through de-authorizing abusive users or non-technical means. An *anonymous* attacker might try to affect availability, through transmission-, computation-, and memory-based DoS. An attacker with enough resources (or control over the network) can always affect availability, so

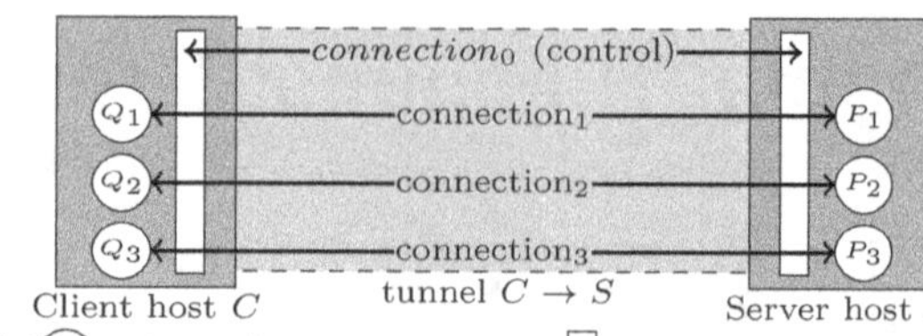

Figure 1: A tunnel encapsulates all of the connections between a given pair of hosts; connections are user-process-to-service and the server cryptographically authenticates each client user (the control connection does not involve application programs)

we attempt to drive up his costs by making his attack at least as expensive as the cost to defend against it. Here the ability to spoof the source IP address of a packet *and* capture a reply should not allow much easier attacks.

We are also want to make it difficult for an attacker to link a user's connection across different IP addresses. For example, if a user suspends his laptop at home and wakes it up at a wireless café, a network eavesdropper should not be able to infer from the protocol that these belong to the same user. We do not address the linking of flows associated with the same IP address, as this type of protection is better afforded by techniques such as onion routing [16].

3 MinimaLT objects

This section introduces the central objects that interact in the MINIMALT architecture. MINIMALT uses public keys to identify servers and users; creates encrypted tunnels between hosts, through which authenticated user-to-service connections are multiplexed; and publishes ephemeral server keys in a directory service to reduce latency by eliminating setup handshakes. To provide a complete picture for a MINIMALT deployment, this section concludes by describing how to integrate MINIMALT's directory service with DNS and the X.509 PKI (used by web browsers). This is not part of the protocol; it is merely one possible way to combine a directory service with the existing Internet infrastructure.

3.1 Public keys

MINIMALT is decidedly public-key-based. Both servers and users are identified by their public keys; such keys serve as a Universally Unique ID (UUID) [61, 50, 35]. Users prove their identity to servers by providing ciphertext which depends on both their and the server's keys (§5.8). A user may be known—i.e., the underlying system is aware of a real-world identity associated with the user's public key—or he may be a **stranger**—a user whose real world identity is unknown. We consider a stranger who produces a new identity for each request **anonymous**. Whether strangers or anonymous users are allowed is left to the underlying system's authorization policy.

3.2 Tunnels

A MINIMALT **tunnel** is a point-to-point entity that encapsulates the set of connections between a client and an authenticated server, as we depict in Figure 1. MINIMALT creates a tunnel on demand to service a local application's outgoing connection request or in response to the first packet received from a host (both are subject to the underlying system's authorization controls). In Figure 1, let Q_1 be the first program on client C to request a connection to server S. C first establishes a tunnel endpoint, and then sends a mes-

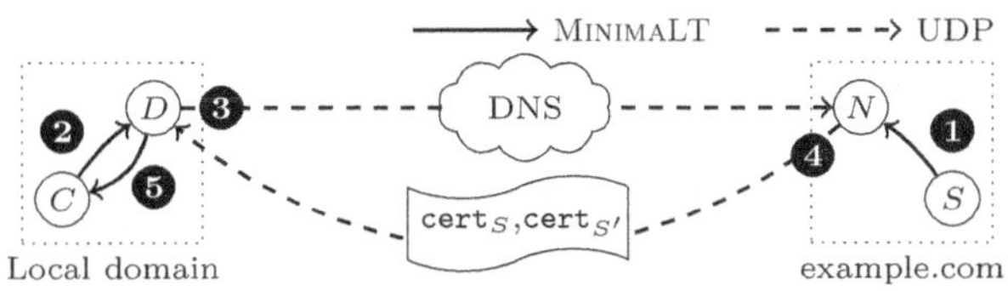

Figure 2: An external directory service query

sage to S; S receives this message and then completes the tunnel. (We describe this more completely in §5.) Tunnels provide server authentication, encryption, congestion control, and reliability; unlike with TLS/TCP, these services do not repeat for each individual connection.

3.3 Connections

A MinimaLT tunnel contains a set of **connections**, that is, a single tunnel between two hosts encapsulates an arbitrary number of connections. Each connection is user-authenticated and provides two-way communication between a client application and a service. In addition to multiplexing any number of standard application-to-service connections, each MinimaLT tunnel has a single **control connection**, along which administrative requests flow (§4.1).

3.4 Directory and Name service

Central to MinimaLT are its directory and name services. These services provide certificates called **service records**, which contain the information that a client needs to authenticate and communicate with a server. A **directory service** receives client queries containing a server hostname, and responds with the server's service record. Servers register their own service record using a **name service**. Thus the hosts involved in the authentication of a server are the client C, server S, directory service D, and name service N.

Contents of a service record A service record is made up of two certificates: a long-term certificate $\texttt{cert}_S$ and an ephemeral certificate $\texttt{ecert}_S$. The long-term certificate binds S's long-term public key with S's hostname. The ephemeral certificate is signed by S's long-term key and contains S's IP address, UDP port, protocol version number (now 0), minimum first packet size (padding), long-term key, ephemeral key, and the ephemeral key's lifetime. Thus this certificate includes the information which is traditionally returned by DNS, plus cryptographic parameters which in other protocols are negotiated during a handshake. The protocol version number allows algorithm upgrades; protocol changes always involve changing the version number.

Hosts Within an organization, an administrator maintains clients and servers, as well as one directory and one name service. Each server S periodically uploads S's service record to its local N. Before communicating with S, the client C requests S's service record from its local D. Once a client has S's service record, it can form a tunnel to S.

We note that *only* the interactions C–S, C–D, and S–N are part of MinimaLT. The communication D–N is not part of the MinimaLT protocol. We describe, for completeness, an implementation that uses DNS. The implementation is very simple: D does a DNS lookup on the hostname which returns S's service record. No changes are needed to DNS software: MinimaLT only adds service records as DNS TXT records.

Establishing a connection We depict an external lookup in Figure 2. The full sequence is as follows:

(1) S sends its service record to its local N;
(2) C requests S's service record from its local D (if D has cached S's service record, then skip to step 5);
(3) D makes a DNS query for S to N;
(4) N replies to D with S's service record; and
(5) D replies to C with S's service record.

Finally, after verifying the signatures on S's service record, C establishes a tunnel with S.

In successive sections, we will ignore steps (3) and (4) which are not part of the MinimaLT protocol. Further information on communication between C and D is given in §5.2 and between S and N is given in §5.4.

Discussion The directory service is designed for easy deployability on the Internet today while guaranteeing at least as much security as is currently obtained from the X.509 PKI used in TLS. In particular, a client C checks an X.509 certificate chain leading to the long-term public key for server S, in the same way that web browsers today check such chains. This chain is transmitted over DNS, obtaining three benefits compared to transmitting the chain later in the protocol: (1) The chain automatically takes advantage of DNS caching. (2) Even when not cached, the latency of transmitting the chain is usually overlapped with existing latency for DNS queries. (3) Any security added to DNS automatically creates an extra obstacle for the attacker, forcing the attacker to break *both* DNS security and X.509 security.

For comparison, if a client obtains merely an IP address from DNS and then requests an X.509 certificate chain from that IP address (the normal use of TLS today), then the attacker wins by breaking X.509 security alone. If a client instead obtains the S public key from DNS as a replacement for X.509 certificate chains then the attacker wins by breaking DNS security alone.

The integration of MinimaLT's directory services with DNS affects DNS configurations in two ways. First, the DNS record's time to live must be set to less than or equal to the key-erasure interval of the host it describes. We expect this to have a small impact, because most Internet traffic is to organizations that already use short times to live (e.g., 300 seconds for `www.yahoo.com` and `www.google.com`, and 60 seconds for `www.amazon.com`). Second, DNS replies will grow due to the presence of additional fields. The largest impact is the long-term certificate, which as mentioned above is encoded today as an X.509 certificate.

We do not claim that DNS and X.509 are satisfactory from a performance perspective or from a security perspective, but improved systems and replacement systems will integrate trivially with MinimaLT. We are planning a sayI implementation [53] which will have a stronger trust model and better performance.

4 MinimaLT packet format

Here we describe the MinimaLT packet format which we will build on in §5 to describe MinimaLT's packet flow. MinimaLT's simple packet format spans three protocol layers: the connection, tunnel, and delivery layers. We depict this format in Figure 3 and Table 1.

The plaintext portion of the packet contains the Ethernet, IP, and UDP headers; the Tunnel ID (TID); a number-used-once (nonce); and two optional fields that can be used during tunnel initiation—an ephemeral public key and a puzzle. A client provides the public key only on the first packet for

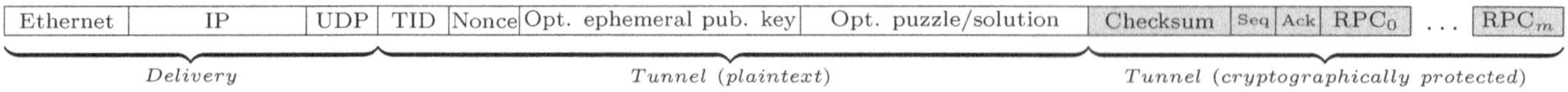

Figure 3: Packet format with plaintext in white and cryptographically protected portion in gray

	Field	Size (bytes) First	Size (bytes) Successive
Deliv.	Ethernet Header	14	14
	IP	20	20
	UDP	8	8
Rel. & Crypto.	Tunnel ID	8	8
	Nonce	8	8
	Ephemeral public key	32	n/a
	Puzzle/solution	148	n/a
	Checksum	16	16
	Sequence Num.	4	4
	Acknowledgment	4	4
Con.	Connection ID	4	4
	RPC	variable	
	Total (except RPC)	282	86

Table 1: Tunnel's first/successive packets

a tunnel, and a server requires puzzles opportunistically to prevent memory and computation attacks.

The packet's cryptographically protected portion contains ciphertext and the ciphertext's cryptographic checksum. The ciphertext contains a sequence number, acknowledgment number, and series of Remote Procedure Calls (RPCs).

4.1 RPCs

Each MinimaLT connection communicates a series of RPCs. An RPC is of the form $f_c(a_0, a_1, \ldots)$, where f is the name of the remote function, c is the connection on which the RPC is sent, and $a_0, a_1, \ldots$ are its arguments. On the wire this is encoded as $c, f, a_0, a_1, \ldots$ A single packet can contain multiple RPCs from one connection or from multiple connections within the same tunnel.

One connection is distinguished: connection 0 is the control connection, which hosts all management operations. These include creating, closing, accepting, and refusing connections; providing service records (§5.4); rekeying (§5.5) and IP address changes (§5.6); puzzles (§5.7); and flow control (§5.9). We reference the following RPCs:

RPC	Description
$\mathsf{create}_0(c, y)$	create anonymous connection c of type y
$\mathsf{createAuth}_0(c, y, U, x)$	create an authenticated connection for the user with long-term public key U, who generates authenticator x
$\mathsf{close}_0(c)$	close connection c
$\mathsf{ack}_0(c)$	creation of c successful
$\mathsf{refuse}_0(c)$	connection c refused
$\mathsf{requestCert}_0(S)$	get host S's service record
$\mathsf{giveCert}_0(\mathtt{cert}_S, \mathtt{ecert}_S)$	provide the service record for server S (contents described in §3.4)
$\mathsf{ok}_0()$	last request was OK
$\mathsf{nextTid}_0(t, C')$	advertise future TID to prepare for a rekey or IP address change (§5.5)
$\mathsf{rekeyNow}_0()$	server request for rekey
$\mathsf{puzz}_0(q, H(r), w, n')$	pose a puzzle (§5.7)
$\mathsf{puzzSoln}_0(r, n')$	provide a puzzle solution r
$\mathsf{windowSize}_0(c, n)$	adjust conn. receive window (§5.9)

All data on connections other than the control connection are sent unchanged to their corresponding applications.

In general, each service provided by a host supports a set of service-specific RPCs on standard connections. Our illustrations use the following sample RPC:

$\mathsf{serviceRequest}_c(\ldots)$	a request for some type of service on connection c

4.2 Authenticated encryption

MinimaLT is built on top of a high-level cryptographic abstraction, public-key authenticated encryption, to protect both confidentiality and integrity of messages sent from one public key to another. It is well known (see, e.g., [6, 7, 32, 25]) how to build public-key authenticated encryption on top of lower-level primitives: use static DH to assign a shared secret to the two public keys; use keys derived from the shared secret to encrypt each message and to authenticate each ciphertext. Note that low-level cryptographic message authentication should not be confused with user authentication and host authentication.

The input to public-key authenticated encryption is a plaintext to encrypt, the sender's secret key, the receiver's public key, and a nonce (a message number used only once for this pair of keys). The output is an authenticated ciphertext which is longer than the plaintext because it includes an authenticator (a cryptographic checksum). The inverse operation produces the original plaintext given an authenticated ciphertext, the same nonce, the receiver's secret key, and the sender's public key.

Each MinimaLT packet contains one authenticated ciphertext, together with the nonce used to create the ciphertext. The corresponding plaintext consists of reliability information (a sequence number and an acknowledgment number) and the concatenation of the RPCs sent in this packet.

MinimaLT chooses monotonically increasing nonces within each tunnel; our implementation uses time-based nonces. Once used, a nonce is never repeated for the same tunnel. The client uses odd nonces, and the server uses even nonces, so there is no risk of the two sides generating the same nonce. Clients enforce key uniqueness by randomly generating a new ephemeral public key for each new tunnel; this is a low-cost operation. For a host which operates as both client and server, its client ephemeral key is in addition to (and different from) its server ephemeral key.

MinimaLT uses the public-key authenticated encryption mechanism from NaCl [6], with 32-byte public keys, 16-byte authenticators, and 8-byte nonces. Except for these sizes and the performance reported in §6 our description of MinimaLT is orthogonal to this choice of encryption mechanism.

4.3 Tunnel IDs and ephemeral public keys

The tunnel establishment packet (the first packet sent between two hosts) contains a TID and the sending host's ephemeral public DH key. The TID is pseudo-randomly generated by the initiator. The public key is ephemeral to avoid identifying the client host to a third party.

Subsequent packets use the TID to identify the tunnel and thus do not repeat the DH key. The recipient uses the TID to look up the tunnel's shared secret used to verify and decrypt the authenticated ciphertext inside the packet. The TID is 64 bits—1/4 the size of a public key—with one bit indicating the presence of a public key in the packet, one bit indicating the presence of a puzzle/solution (see §5.7), and 62 bits identifying a tunnel.

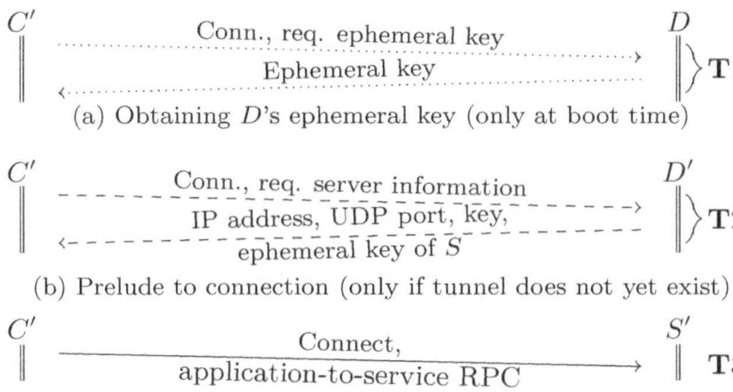

(a) Obtaining D's ephemeral key (only at boot time)

(b) Prelude to connection (only if tunnel does not yet exist)

(c) Connection establishment

Figure 4: MINIMALT protocol trace

4.4 Delivery

MINIMALT concatenates tunnel information with the authenticated ciphertext and places the result into a UDP packet for delivery across existing network infrastructure. A MINIMALT packet on the wire thus contains standard Ethernet, IP, and UDP headers. The UDP header allows packets to traverse NATed networks [19] and enables user-space implementations of MINIMALT. Aside from the UDP length field, the delivery fields (including UDP port numbers) are ignored by MINIMALT. The MINIMALT protocol details are orthogonal to the structure of IPv4/v6 addresses.

5 MinimaLT packet flow

This section explains how a MINIMALT client C forms a tunnel and connects to a server S. All application data, as well as client and user identity, is encrypted under ephemeral keys that will soon be discarded. (IP addresses by necessity are visible.) Once a tunnel is formed, successive connections are created using RPCs within the existing tunnel.

We show a complete three-step connection in Figure 4: **T1** facilitates the request by C for D's ephemeral key (only required if this is C's first lookup since booting); **T2** protects the connection between C' and D' (used to request S's ephemeral key, the analogue of a DNS lookup); and **T3** protects communication between C' and S'. This section also covers more advanced issues such as rekeying and IP-address mobility; DoS protections; user authenticators; and congestion control.

We do not usually distinguish between a host (or user), their long-term public key, and their long-term private key, instead relying on context to disambiguate them. Figure 5 describes the notation we will use during the course of our description.

We show packets on a single line such as

$$t, n, C', \boxed{s, a, \ldots}\ {}^{C' \to S'}_{n}$$

which indicates a tunnel establishment packet (visible by the presence of the plaintext C', as described in §4.3) from C to S using keys C' and S' to box (encrypt and authenticate) the message '$s, a, \ldots$' under nonce n. Each packet has a new nonce but for conciseness we simply write n rather than n_1, n_2, etc. The same comment applies for sequence numbers (s) and acknowledgments (a).

5.1 Initial communication of C with D (T1)

After booting, C establishes a tunnel with D (Figure 4a, tunnel T1). (C's static configuration contains its directory service's IP address, UDP port, and long-term public key D.) C generates a single-use public key C' and uses it to create a bootstrap tunnel with the directory service.

$$t, n, C', \boxed{s, a, \mathsf{requestCert}_0(D)}\ {}^{C' \to D}_{n}$$

$$t, n, \boxed{s, a, \mathsf{giveCert}_0(\mathtt{cert}_D, \mathtt{ecert}_D)}\ {}^{D \to C'}_{n}$$

D responds with a service record ($\mathtt{cert}_D$,$\mathtt{ecert}_D$) containing its own ephemeral key, D'. C does not make further use of tunnel T1.

t	A tunnel ID (described in §4)
n	A nonce (described in §4)
s	A sequence number
a	An acknowledgment number
0 or c	A connection ID (0 for the control connection)
p	A puzzle
r	A puzzle solution (i.e., response)
C, D, N, S	The client, directory, name, and server long-term public/private key
C', D', N', S'	An ephemeral client, directory, name, and server public/private key
U	A user's public/private key
x	A user authenticator (described in §5.8)
$C \to S$	A message from the client to the server, using keys C and S
$H(m)$	The cryptographic hash of message m
$\boxed{m}\ {}^{k}_{n}$	Encrypt and authenticate message m using symmetric key k and nonce n
$\boxed{m}\ {}^{S \to P}_{n}$	Encrypt and authenticate message m using a symmetric key derived from private key S and public key P; n is a nonce

Figure 5: Notation

5.2 Subsequent communication of C with D (T2)

C uses D' to establish another tunnel with D (Figure 4b, tunnel T2) to request S's service record. This tunnel uses a fresh C', is key-erasure-protected, and is established by:

$$t, n, C', \boxed{s, a, \mathsf{requestCert}_0(S)}\ {}^{C' \to D'}_{n}$$

$$t, n, \boxed{s, a, \mathsf{giveCert}_0(\mathtt{cert}_S, \mathtt{ecert}_S)}\ {}^{D' \to C'}_{n}$$

Successive connections to the same server S skip both T1 and T2. T2 remains open for C to look up other servers.

5.3 Communication of C with S (T3)

After receiving $\mathtt{cert}_S$ and $\mathtt{ecert}_S$, C is ready to negotiate a tunnel with the end server (Figure 4, tunnel T3). C encrypts packets to the server using S' (from $\mathtt{ecert}_S$) and a fresh C'. Because C places its ephemeral public key in the first packet, both C and S can immediately generate a shared symmetric key using DH without compromising key erasure. Thus C can include application-to-service data in the first packet to S. That is,

$$t, n, C', \boxed{\begin{array}{l} s,\ a,\ \mathsf{nextTid}_0(t, C'), \\ \mathsf{createAuth}_0(1, \text{serviceName}, U, x), \\ \mathsf{serviceRequest}_1(\ldots) \end{array}}\ {}^{C' \to S'}_{n}$$

Upon receiving $\mathsf{createAuth}_0$, S verifies the authenticator x (§5.8) and decides if the client user U is authorized to connect. If so, S creates the new connection, here with ID 1. The server ensures no two tunnels share the same C'. Once this tunnel is established, C erases the secret key belonging to C'; the tunnel continues to use the shared secret of C' and S'. (We describe the purpose of $\mathsf{nextTid}_0$ in §5.5.) The server can then immediately process the service-specific $\mathsf{serviceRequest}_1$ on this new connection.

5.4 Communication of S with N

Before a client may connect, S must register its own IP address, UDP port, public key S, certificate on S, and current ephemeral public key S' with an ephemeral-key name service

N. This is done using the $\mathsf{giveCert_O}$ RPC:

$$t, n, \boxed{s, a, \mathsf{giveCert_O}(\mathtt{cert}_S, \mathtt{ecert}_S)}\ {}^{S' \to N'}_{n}$$

$$t, n, \boxed{s, a, \mathsf{ok_O}()}\ {}^{N' \to S'}_{n}$$

(Here we assume S already has a tunnel to N.) In the local case N may be the same as D, but in general information must be pushed or pulled from N to D (§3.4).

5.5 Rekeying and key erasure

MinimaLT implements a property called **fast key erasure** which means that key erasure can take place at any time, without interrupting existing connections. A client uses a $\mathsf{nextTid_O}$ RPC to indicate the new TID t that will prompt a rekey; this RPC also includes a C' for reasons we describe in §7.4. Servers invoke $\mathsf{rekeyNow_O}$ when their key-erasure interval expires. In any case, each host erases the previous key after beginning to use the next. Clients invoke $\mathsf{nextTid_O}$ within each tunnel initiation packet (§5.3).

A client causes a rekey when its key-erasure interval expires or when it receives a $\mathsf{rekeyNow_O}$ RPC from the server. To cause such a rekey, the client (1) computes a new symmetric key by cryptographically hashing the tunnel's existing symmetric key; (2) computes a new $\overline{C'}$ indistinguishable from a legitimate public key; and (3) issues a tunnel initiation packet using t and $\overline{C'}$ which is encrypted with the new symmetric key and contains a successive $\mathsf{nextTid_O}$ RPC. The server (1) notices that the tunnel initiation packet contains the t from the previous $\mathsf{nextTid_O}$; (2) computes the new symmetric key and unboxes the packet; and (3) verifies that the current $\mathsf{nextTid_O}$'s $\overline{C'}$ parameter matches the plaintext public key on the tunnel initiation packet. If each verification succeeds, then the server transitions to the new tunnel parameters; otherwise it behaves as with a failed tunnel initialization.

5.6 IP-address mobility

Because MinimaLT identifies tunnels by their TID, a tunnel's IP and UDP port can change without affecting communication. After changing its IP address or UDP port, a client simply does a rekey.

5.7 Puzzles

A MinimaLT server under load that receives a tunnel establishment packet from a stranger client for an authorized service does not immediately create the tunnel. Instead, it produces a puzzle that must be solved by the client before the server will proceed. First, the server computes the solution (i.e., response) to a puzzle:

$$r = \boxed{C', S'}\ {}^{k}_{n'}$$

where k is a secret used only for puzzles. It then selects a value w that determines the difficulty of the puzzle, and calculates q by zeroing r's rightmost w bits. The server sends the puzzle of the form $[q, H(r), w, n']$ to the client in the following packet:

$$t, n, [q, H(r), w, n']$$

(Note that the square brackets do not affect the packet; they merely make our notation more readable.) The server next forgets about the client's request.

The client must solve the puzzle, i.e., reconstruct r from q and $H(r)$, and provide its solution r along with n' in a new tunnel establishment packet boxed using the same C' and S'. To find this solution, the client brute forces the rightmost w bits of q, checking each resulting candidate d to see if $H(d) = H(r)$. If this equivalence holds, the client has found $d = r$. (This brute force work imposes a high load on C without affecting S.) The client then responds to the server with:

$$t, n, C', [r, n'], \boxed{s, a, \ldots}\ {}^{C' \to S'}_{n}$$

To confirm a solution, the server decrypts r using k and n', confirms that the plaintext contains C' and S', and ensures that n' is within an acceptable window. Although the server had forgotten r, these protections ensure that r cannot be reused for other tunnel establishment attempts.

MinimaLT also provides a puzzle RPC that can be used inside a tunnel for liveness testing. The puzzle format used by this RPC is the same as that which is used in the tunnel header.

5.8 User authenticators

Every user serviced by MinimaLT is identified by his public key. The $\mathsf{createAuth_O}$ authenticator is the server's long-term public key encrypted and authenticated using the server's long-term public key, the user's long-term private key U, and a fresh nonce n never reused for U:

$$n, \boxed{S}\ {}^{U \to S}_{n}$$

The effect of user authenticators is determined by the server's local authorization policy.

5.9 Congestion and flow control

MinimaLT's tunnel headers contain the fields necessary to implement congestion control, namely sequence number and acknowledgment fields. We presently use a variation of TCP's standard algorithms [22].

MinimaLT hosts adjust per-connection flow control using the $\mathsf{windowSize_O}$ RPC. MinimaLT subjects individual connections to flow control, so $\mathsf{windowSize_O}$ takes as parameters both a connection ID and size. MinimaLT currently implements TCP-style flow control.

As with TCP [27], efficient congestion control is an area of open research [23], and we could substitute an emerging algorithm with better performance. MinimaLT does have one considerable effect on congestion control: controls are aggregated for all connections in a tunnel, rather than on individual connections. Since a single packet can contain data for several connections, the server no longer needs to allocate separate storage for tracking the reliability of each connection. This also means that MinimaLT need not repeat the discovery of the appropriate transmission rate for each new connection, and a host has more information (i.e., multiple connections) from which to derive an appropriate rate. The disadvantage is that a lost packet can affect all connections in aggregate.

6 Performance evaluation

In this section we evaluate MinimaLT's performance, specifically packet overhead, latency and throughput. For performance under DoS, see §7.6. We focus on server performance, because even resource-constrained smartphones can adequately handle their own load. While servers have faster CPUs, they are relatively slow compared to their network capacity and the number of clients they serve. Furthermore, a server DoS is much more damaging than a client DoS.

6.1 Packet header overhead

MinimaLT's network bandwidth overhead is modest. The overhead is due to the cryptography, and includes the nonce, TID, and checksum (the public key/puzzle fields are rarely present and are thus insignificant overall). MINIMALT requires 32 bytes more for its headers than TCP/IP; this represents 6% of the minimum Internet MTU of 576 bytes, and 2% of 1518-byte Ethernet packets.

6.2 Latency and throughput

We experimentally evaluate MINIMALT's performance in three areas: (1) the serial rate at which MINIMALT establishes tunnels/connections, primarily to study the effect of latency on the protocol; (2) the rate at which MINIMALT establishes tunnels/connections when servicing many clients in parallel; and (3) the throughput achieved by MINIMALT.

We benchmarked MINIMALT on Ethos. All of our performance tests were run on two identical computers with a 4.3 GHz AMD FX-4170 quad-core processor, 16GB of memory, and a Gb/s Ethernet adapter. We benchmarked in 64-bit mode and on only one core to simplify cross-platform comparisons.

Serial tunnel/connection establishment latency In each of our serial connection benchmarks, a client sequentially connects to a server, sends a 28-byte application-layer request, and receives a 58-byte response. We measure the number of such operations completed in 30 seconds; the connections do not perform a DNS/directory service lookup. We performed this experiment under a variety of network latencies using Linux's netem interface.

We compare against OpenSSL 1.0.0j using its s_server and s_time utilities, running on version 3.3.4 of the Linux kernel. We configured OpenSSL to use 2,048-bit RSA as recommended by NIST [4] (although 2,048-bit RSA provides 112-bit security, less than that of MINIMALT's 128-bit security), along with 128-bit AES, ephemeral DH, and client-side certificates (i.e., cipher suite DHE-RSA-AES128-SHA). In order to ensure disk performance did not skew our results, we modified s_server to provide responses from memory instead of from the filesystem. We also wrote a plaintext benchmark which behaves similarly, but makes direct use of the POSIX socket API without cryptographic protections.

To produce results analogous to OpenSSL, we simulated both (1) many abbreviated connection requests for high reuse by clients and (2) many full connection requests for no reuse by clients, we tested both (1) the vanilla MINIMALT stack and (2) a MINIMALT stack we modified to artificially avoid tunnel reuse.

Figure 6a shows full connection performance ratios between MINIMALT vs. TCP and MINIMALT vs. OpenSSL. For each connection, MINIMALT creates a new tunnel and authenticates the client user; TCP performs a three-way handshake; and OpenSSL performs full TCP and TLS handshakes. After this initial setup, our benchmark completes an application-data round trip. Most surprisingly, MINIMALT creates connections faster than unencrypted TCP, beginning before native LAN latencies+1/2 ms (LAN+1/2 ms). MINIMALT is about twice as fast as unencrypted TCP at latencies above LAN+4 ms, and MINIMALT is four to six times faster than OpenSSL.

Figure 6b shows abbreviated connections. Here MINIMALT reuses an existing tunnel and OpenSSL takes advantage of its session ID to execute an abbreviated connection. Both protocols avoid computing a shared secret using DH, except in the case of the first connection. Abbreviated MINIMALT connections surpass the performance of unencrypted TCP at LAN+1/4 ms latencies. At higher latencies, MINIMALT is two times the performance of TCP and three times the performance of OpenSSL.

At high latencies, the protocol performance ratios approach the numbers predicted by counting the round trips inherent in each protocol. We attribute our results to MINIMALT's efficient tunnel/connection establishment (especially at high latencies) and to the speed of the NaCl library (especially at low latencies).

Figure 6c revisits the measurements described for Figure 6a, this time plotting the actual time each connection took in log scale. At LAN+1/16 ms, a MINIMALT, TCP, and OpenSSL connection took 1.32ms, 0.68ms, and 7.63ms, respectively. At LAN+256ms, the times were 0.53s, 1s, and 2.13s, respectively.

Figure 6d displays abbreviated connection time. At LAN+1/16 ms, a MINIMALT and OpenSSL connection took 1.03ms and 1.67ms, respectively. At LAN+256ms, the times were 0.52s and 1.60s, respectively. (TCP times are the same as in Figure 6c.)

Tunnels per run	User Auth.	Connections per second	DH per conn.
One		18,453	0
One	✓	8,576	1
Many		7,827	1
Many	✓	4,967	2

Table 2: Connection establishment with many clients

Tunnel establishment throughput with many clients We created a second connection benchmark to estimate the CPU load on a MINIMALT server servicing many clients. To do this, we ran two client OS instances, each forking several processes that connected to the server repeatedly as new clients; here each virtual machine instance was running on a distinct processor core within a single computer. Because this experiment concerns CPU use and not latency, these clients do not write any application-layer data, they only connect. Using xenoprof and xentop, we determined that the server was crypto-bound (i.e., 63% of CPU use was in cryptography-related functions—primarily public key—and the server CPU load was nearly 100%). We measured the number of full connections per second achieved under this load, and varied our configuration from accepting fully-anonymous users (no authenticators), to verifying a new user authenticator for each connection request. Our MINIMALT server established 4,967–7,827 tunnels per second, as shown in Table 2 (rows 3–4).

Given the minimal tunnel request size of 1,024 bytes, our hosts can (on a single core) service 61.15Mb/s of tunnel requests from anonymous users and at least 38.80Mb/s of tunnel requests from authenticated users. We note that the latter is the worst case for authenticated users; in general, we would cache the result of the DH computations necessary to validate user authenticators, as authenticators use long-term keys. Thus in practice we expect the authenticated user case to approach that of anonymous users.

Connection establishment throughput with many clients We repeated the previous experiment, but this time avoided DH computations by repeatedly creating connections using a single tunnel between each client and the server. Table 2 (rows 1–2) shows that our rates ranged from 8,576–18,453 per second, depending on the presence of user authenticators. The connection rate over a single tunnel is important for applications which require many connections

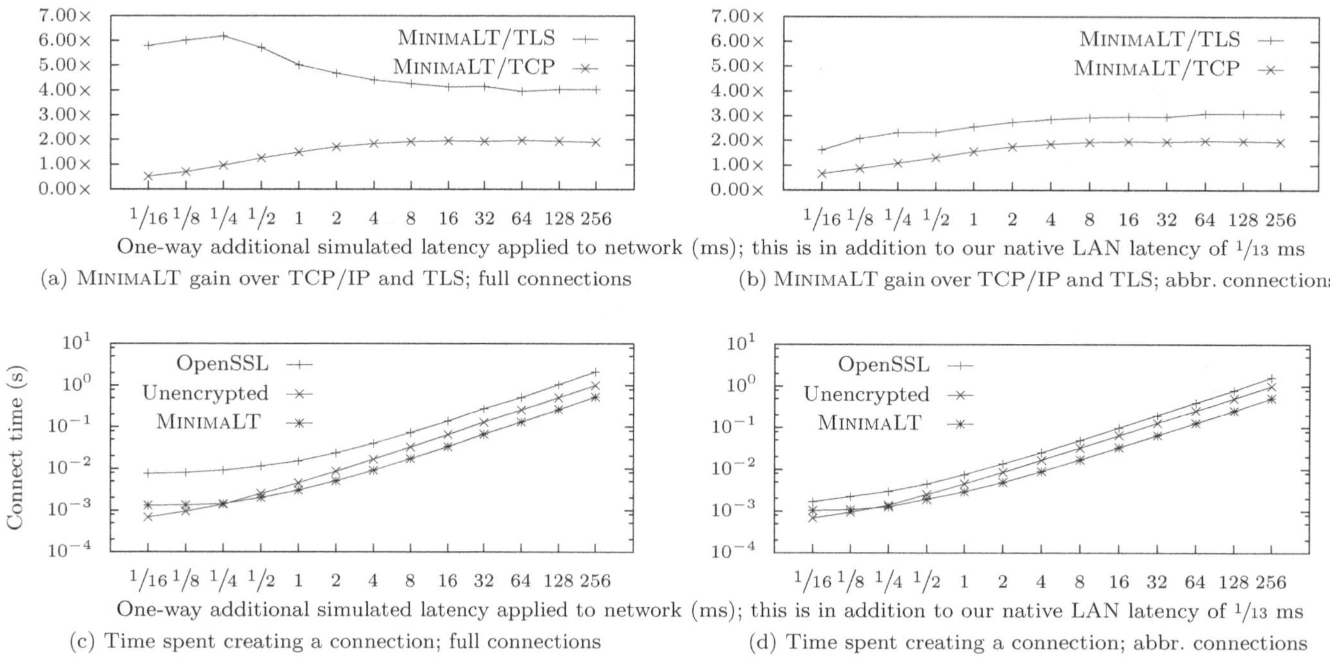

(a) MinimaLT gain over TCP/IP and TLS; full connections

(b) MinimaLT gain over TCP/IP and TLS; abbr. connections

(c) Time spent creating a connection; full connections

(d) Time spent creating a connection; abbr. connections

Figure 6: Serial tunnel/connection establishment latency

and when using many applications to communicate with the same server. Our comments about cached DH results in the preceding experiment apply here as well; we would expect in practice the rate of the authenticated case will approach the anonymous case.

A theoretical throughput limit We used SUPERCOP [5] to measure the time it takes our hardware to compute a shared secret using DH, approximately 293,000 cycles or 14,000 shared-secret computations per second. MinimaLT's tunnel establishment rate approaches 56% of this limit, with the remaining time including symmetric key cryptography, scheduling, and network stack processing.

System	Bytes per second
Line speed	125,000,000
Unencrypted	117,817,528
MinimaLT	113,945,258
OpenSSL	111,448,656

Table 3: Data throughput (ignoring protocol overhead)

Single-connection data throughput Table 3 describes our throughput results, observed when running programs that continuously transmitted data on a single connection for thirty seconds. MinimaLT approaches the throughput achieved by unencrypted networking and runs at 91% of line speed (Gb/s). Indeed, MinimaLT's cryptography runs at line speed; header size differences are the primary reason the unencrypted benchmark outperforms MinimaLT.

7 Design rationale

7.1 Cryptographic security

Tunnel IDs and nonces are visible on the network, and follow a clear pattern for each client-server pair. Essentially the same information is available through a simple log of IP addresses of packets sent. Mobile clients automatically switch to new tunnel IDs when they change IP addresses, as we described in §5.6. Ephemeral client public keys are visible when each tunnel is established, but are not reused and are not connected to any other client information.

Other information is boxed (encrypted and authenticated) between public keys at the ends of the tunnel. These boxes can be created and understood using either of the two corresponding private keys, but such keys are maintained locally inside MinimaLT hosts. The attacker can try to violate confidentiality by breaking the encryption, or violate integrity by breaking the authentication, but MinimaLT uses modern cryptographic primitives that are designed to make these attacks very difficult. The attacker can also try to substitute his public key for a legitimate public key, fooling the client or server into encrypting data to the attacker or accepting data actually from the attacker, but this requires violating integrity of previous packets: for example, before the client encrypts data to D', the client obtains D' from a boxed packet between D and C'. MinimaLT's reliability and connection headers are part of the ciphertext, so they are also protected against tampering and eavesdropping.

7.2 The benefits of RPCs

In contrast to byte-oriented protocols, we use RPCs within MinimaLT's connection layer as they result in a clean design and implementation; they are also general and fast (§6). RPCs have a long history dating to the mid-1970s [60, 9].

The tunnel, and the RPCs within it, are totally sequenced; thus RPCs are executed in order (as opposed to separately implemented connections—as in TLS—where ordering between connections is not fixed). This enables a clean separation of the control connection from other connections, and we have found that this simplifies both the protocol and its implementation. Furthermore, placing multiple RPCs in one packet amortizes the overhead due to MinimaLT's delivery and tunnel fields across multiple connections.

7.3 The benefits of tunnels

Tunnels make it more difficult for an attacker to use traffic analysis to infer information about communicating parties. Of course, traffic analysis countermeasures have limits [43]; for obvious cost reasons we did not include extreme protections against traffic analysis, such as using white noise to maintain a constant transmission rate. MinimaLT also reduces packet overhead by using TIDs rather than repeating the public key in every packet.

Tunnels are independent of the IP address of C; this means that C can resume a tunnel after moving to a new location (typically prompting the use of the next ephemeral key as described below), avoiding tunnel-establishment latency and application-level recovery due to a failed connection. This reduced latency is useful for mobile applications, in which IP-address assignments may be short-lived, and thus overhead may prevent any useful work from being done before an address is lost.

MINIMALT reduces an attacker's ability to link tunnels across IP address changes because its TID changes when its IP address changes. What remains is temporal analysis, where an attacker notices that communication on one IP address stops at the same time that communication on another starts. However, the attacker cannot differentiate for sure between IP mobility and an unrelated tunnel establishment. Blinding information below the network layer—for example, the Ethernet MAC—is left to other techniques.

7.4 Rekeying

Rekeying is critical for allowing key erasure during a long connection: it allows clients and servers to periodically forget old encryption keys, protecting those keys against an attacker who later compromises clients and servers. Rekeying also supports IP-address mobility without explicitly linking the old address to the new address.

Creating the new key by hashing is more efficient than creating it by a new DH, avoiding both public-key operations and superfluous round trips.

The client creates a new public key, so that there is no packet-format distinction between a rekeying tunnel-initiation packet and a completely new tunnel-initiation packet. Rather than generating a key pair and using only the public key, a public key can directly and more efficiently be generated as a random point on an elliptic curve.

There are two copies of C' in a rekeying packet, one in the clear and one inside the boxed part, verified by the server to be identical. Without this verification, an active attacker could modify the public key sent in the clear, observe that the server still accepts this packet, and confidently conclude that this is a rekey rather than a completely new tunnel.

A client-side administrator sets his host's key-erasure interval as a matter of policy. The server's policy is slightly more sensitive, because the server must maintain its ephemeral key pairs as long as they are advertised through the directory service. An attacker who seizes a server could combine the ephemeral keys with captured packets to regenerate any symmetric key within the ephemeral key window. Thus even if the client causes a rekey, the server's ephemeral key window dominates on the server side.

If a user believes a server's ephemeral key lifetime is long enough to put his communications at risk, then he could choose not to communicate with the server. Except for the case of a malicious server which does not destroy expired ephemeral keys (and ought not to be trusted in the first place), MINIMALT's directory service provides the lifetime information needed to make these decisions, whether directly by a human or by automated tools.

7.5 User authenticators

Because authenticators are transmitted inside boxes (as ciphertext), they are protected from eavesdropping, and because the authenticator is tied to the server's (certified) public key, the server cannot use it to masquerade as the user to a third-party MINIMALT host. Of course, any server could choose to ignore the authenticator or perform operations the client did not request, but that is unavoidable. If third-party auditability is desired then users can choose to interact only with servers that take requests in the form of certificates.

7.6 Denial of service

DoS protections in MINIMALT are intended to maintain availability against much more severe attacks than are handled by current Internet protocols. Of course, an exceptionally powerful attacker will be able to overwhelm a MINIMALT server, but DoS protections are useful even in such extreme situations as a way to consume the attacker's resources and limit the number of DoS victims. Of particular concern are DoS attacks which consume memory or computational resources; the protocol cannot directly defend against network exhaustion attacks, although it avoids contributing to such attacks by preventing amplification.

We introduced anonymous and stranger-authorized services in §3.1. Anonymous services (i.e., permit create_0) perform a DH computation to compute a shared secret and maintain tunnel data structures that consume just under 5KB each (this is configurable; most memory use is due to incoming and outgoing packet buffers). Stranger-authorized services (i.e, require $\mathsf{createAuth}_0$, but permit strangers) additionally perform a public-key decryption to validate each new user authenticator encountered. MINIMALT puzzles serve as a countermeasure to DoS attacks on these services [33], and we now describe how they are applied at key points of the MINIMALT protocol. (Recall that administrators can additionally address DoS attacks from *known* users through de-authorization or non-technical means.)

Before establishing a tunnel In the case of anonymous services, a single attacker could generate a large number of ephemeral public keys to create many tunnels, with each tunnel consuming the resources described above. Furthermore, the attacker's host might avoid creating a tunnel data structure or performing any cryptographic operations, thus making the attack affect the server disproportionately.

MINIMALT addresses these attacks using puzzles present in its tunnel headers. Servicing tunnel requests in excess of the limits discussed in §6.2 would cause a server to require these puzzles, and because they take $O(2^{w-1})$ operations for a client to solve, the server can require clients to pay a wide range of computational costs to connect, here w is a 32-bit value. On the other hand, puzzles are of little burden on the server; our test hardware can generate and verify 386,935 puzzles per second. Since a puzzle interrogation and padded solution packet are 206 and 1,024 bytes, respectively, a single CPU core can verify puzzles at 394% of Gb/s line speed.

Clients overloaded by puzzles (possibly forged by a MitM attacker) can choose how to allocate CPU time, for example prioritizing connections that succeed without puzzles.

Amplification attacks against third parties At tunnel establishment, an anonymous or stranger-authorized MINIMALT service might respond to packets from clients which spoof another host's IP address. This is always possible with the directory service, which initially must react to a request from an unknown party before transitioning to key-erasure-protected authentication. A MitM could spoof the source of packets and even complete a successive puzzle interrogation. A weaker attacker could elicit a response to the first packet sent to a server. Given this, MinimaLT is designed to minimize amplification attacks, in which a request is smaller than its reply (to a spoofed source address). A connection request causes a connection acknowledgment or puzzle interrogation; both responses are smaller than the request. Flow-control acknowledgments are randomized so that blind clients cannot request further packets.

After establishing a tunnel Given a tunnel, an attacker can easily forge a packet with garbage in place of ciphertext and send it to a service. This forces MinimaLT to decrypt the packet and verify its checksum, wasting processor time. However, MinimaLT's symmetric cryptography on established tunnels operates at line speed on commodity hardware (§6.2), so DoS would be equivalent to the attacker exhausting the network.

MinimaLT can send puzzle RPCs arbitrarily, so a server can use low cost (i.e., small w) puzzles to check whether clients remain available, and then garbage collect idle connections. Additionally, a server can increase the value of w to make clients pay a computational cost to keep a connection alive. We use cryptographically protected RPCs to pose and solve these puzzles to prevent an attacker from attempting RST-style mischief [18].

Creation of fictitious strangers Stranger services are vulnerable to further CPU attacks—attackers could generate false user identities that would fail authentication, but only after the server performed a public-key decryption. A server will apply the puzzle RPCs when connection rates exceed the limits discussed in §6.2.

An attacker could also generate verifiable authenticators and connect to a stranger-authorized service many times as different stranger users. This would cause a system to generate accounts for each stranger identity. However, this is no different from any other creation of pseudo-anonymous accounts; it is up to the system to decide how to allocate account resources to strangers. Perhaps the rate is faster, but unlike many contemporary pseudo-anonymous services, a MinimaLT system can prune stranger accounts as necessary; the stranger's long-term resources (e.g., files on disk) will remain isolated and become available if the account is later regenerated because public keys remain temporally unique [50]. Of course, applications could impose additional requirements (e.g., a Captcha) before allowing a stranger to consume persistent resources like disk space.

8 Comparison to previous work

Table 4 compares MinimaLT to several earlier Internet protocols. MinimaLT is unique in that it provides encryption and authentication with fast key erasure while allowing a client to include data in the first packet sent to a server (often forgoing pre-transmission round trips entirely). MinimaLT also contains robust DoS protections.

We have omitted one very recent protocol from Table 4: Google's QUIC, which was developed independently of and concurrently with MinimaLT. Our preliminary assessment of the QUIC protocol documentation (released in late June 2013) is that QUIC uses some of the same latency-reducing techniques as MinimaLT, but does not overlap DNS/directory service lookups with tunnel establishment. QUIC also appears to have lower security goals than MinimaLT: for example, allowing earlier data in long-term connections to be retroactively decrypted.

8.1 Security advantages over TLS

TLS [15] is widely deployed as the primary mechanism for securing Internet communication across administrative domains, and in particular as the primary network security layer in web browsers. The importance of TLS warrants a multifaceted comparison of TLS with MinimaLT. We already showed in §6 that MinimaLT is more efficient than TLS, but we also claim that MinimaLT has several important security advantages over TLS, as discussed below.

8.1.1 Cryptographic abstractions TLS builds on separate cryptographic primitives for public-key cryptography, secret-key encryption, etc. Unfortunately, composing these low-level primitives turns out to be complicated and error-prone. For example, the BEAST attack [17] and the very recent Lucky 13 attack [2] recovered TLS-encrypted cookies by exploiting the fragility of the "authenticate-pad-encrypt" mechanism used by TLS to combine secret-key encryption with secret-key authentication. TLS implementations have worked around these particular attacks by (1) sending extra packets to hide the "IV" used by BEAST and (2) modifying implementations to hide the timing leaks used by Lucky 13; however, further attacks would be unsurprising.

The modern trend is for cryptographers to take responsibility for providing secure higher-level primitives. For example, cryptographers have defined robust high-performance "AEAD" primitives that handle authentication and encryption all at once using a shared secret key [45], taking care of many important details such as padding and key derivation. This simplifies protocol design, eliminating the error-prone step of having each protocol combine separate mechanisms for authentication and encryption. TLS 1.2 (not yet widely deployed) supports AEAD primitives.

MinimaLT is built on top of an even higher-level primitive, *public-key* authenticated encryption, as mentioned in §4.2. This further simplifies protocol design.

8.1.2 Verifiability One might think that existing protocol-analysis tools are already powerful enough to formally verify the confidentiality and integrity properties of a clean high-level protocol such as MinimaLT, assuming that the underlying cryptographic primitives are secure. However, the security properties of authenticated encryption using non-interactive DH were only very recently formalized (see [25]), and more work is required to develop a higher-level security calculus on top of these properties; note that replacing authenticated encryption with *unauthenticated* encryption would eliminate the security of typical protocols that use authenticated encryption. Thus, we do not claim that MinimaLT is formally verified.

However, we do claim that MinimaLT will be far easier to verify than TLS, and that there are far fewer opportunities for mistakes in MinimaLT than in TLS. Attempts to verify the security of TLS (such as [32]) have so far covered only limited portions of TLS, and have not prevented a seemingly never-ending string of announcements of TLS security failures, such as the BEAST and Lucky 13 attacks cited above. The unverified portions of TLS are more complex than the entire MinimaLT protocol.

8.1.3 Security goals TLS is normally implemented as a user-space library that adds cryptographic network protections to an insecure transport layer, TCP. This structure prevents TLS from providing strong protection against DoS: packets that deny service at the TCP layer are not even seen by TLS.

TLS can provide some key erasure through the use of ephemeral DH. Here the server generates a new DH key pair for each TLS session, and it uses this key pair to negotiate the session key with the client [38]. This means that past session keys remain secret even if a server's long-term key is compromised. On the other hand, a TLS session itself might remain in use for a long time, and session keys are obviously vulnerable to physical compromise as long as they are in use. This effect is compounded when servers support abbreviated connections [39]. In contrast, MinimaLT implements its key erasure using periodic rekeys, as we described in §5.5. Placing a time limit on keys simplifies security analysis because it removes the effect of variable session lifetimes.

8.1.4 Robustness Many Internet applications avoid the use of TLS or use weak TLS options [58]. Even well-meaning developers routinely misuse complex TLS APIs, resulting in security holes [26, 21]. Optionally, TLS can provide user-level authentication using client-side certificates, but authorization is left to application logic. MinimaLT forgoes backwards compatibility to provide a simpler, less mistake-prone platform, and it subsumes much of the work traditionally left to application programmers.

Another benefit of MinimaLT's clean-slate design is a simpler code base. OpenSSL contains 252,000 C Lines of Code (LoC). Much of this code might not be used, depending on how a service is configured or because it also implements utilities and benchmarks, but our study found 74,000 LoC associated with the DHE-RSA-AES128-SHA cipher suite. Additionally, there is code in the OS to support TCP/IP. In contrast, MinimaLT's design results in a protocol code base of 12,000 LoC along with NaCl, where our choice of ciphers uses another 6,920 LoC.

8.2 Advantages over other protocols

TCP's three-way handshake establishes a random Initial Sequence Number (ISN). This is necessary for two reasons: (1) the ISN serves as a weak authenticator (and liveness check) because a non-MitM attacker must predict it to produce counterfeit packets, and (2) the ISN reduces the likelihood that a late packet will be delivered to the wrong application.

MinimaLT encrypts the sequence number, provides cryptographic authentication, and checks liveness using puzzles, addressing (1). MinimaLT uses TIDs, connection IDs, and nonces to detect late packets, addressing (2). Thus MinimaLT can include application data in a connection's first packet, as discussed above, eliminating the need for a transport-layer three-way handshake. Extra round trips are necessary only if the tunnel does not exist; and then only when the client does not have S's service record or is presented with a puzzle. If the server provides a puzzle, it means that the server is under heavy load so that additional latency is unavoidable.

TCP Fast Open (TFO) [48] clients can request a TFO cookie that allows them to forgo TCP's three-way handshake on future connections. However, since any client may request a TFO cookie, a client may spoof its sending IP address to mount a DoS attack against a server; under this condition, the server must again require a three-way handshake. To benefit from TFO, a server application must be idempotent, a requirement that MinimaLT avoids.

Structured Stream Transport (SST) [24] allows applications to associate lightweight network streams with an existing stream, reducing the number of three-way handshakes incurred by applications and providing semantics useful for applications that use both data and control connections. MinimaLT eliminates the handshake on even the first connection, and MinimaLT's tunnels do not require a programmer's explicit use of a lightweight stream API.

Internet Protocol Security (IPsec) provides very broad confidentiality and integrity protections because it is generally implemented in the OS kernel. For example, IPsec can be configured such that *all* communication between node A and node B is protected. This universality simplifies assurance. IPsec also provides fast key erasure at the expense of a DH computation [34]. Many key management protocols have been proposed for IPsec; we were particularly inspired by Just Fast Keying due to its simplicity, focus on forward secrecy, and DoS resilience [1]. IPsec's major shortcoming is that its protections stop at the host; it focuses on network isolation and host authentication/authorization. For example, IPsec does not authenticate or authorize users.

Labeled IPsec [31] combines IPsec and Security-Enhanced Linux (SELinux) [44] to provide more comprehensive network protections. Using a domain-wide authorization policy, the system (1) associates SELinux labels with IPsec security associations, (2) limits a process's security associations (connections) using a kernel authorization policy, and (3) employs a modified inetd that executes worker processes in a security domain corresponding to the label associated with an incoming request. In this manner, labeled IPsec can solve many of the authentication deficiencies in plain IPsec. However, labeled IPsec builds upon the Linux kernel, SELinux, and IPsec, each of which are very complex. Furthermore, IPsec security association granularity limits the granularity of controls in labeled IPsec. In contrast, MinimaLT is designed from scratch, significantly simplifying policy specification, implementation, and use.

Many researchers have attempted to reduce the latency inherent in TLS and TCP. False Start (no longer used), Snap Start, and certificate pre-fetching have accelerated establishing a TLS session [41, 37, 56]. Datagram Transport Layer Security (DTLS) [49] provides TLS protections on top of UDP, which is useful when reliability is unnecessary. However, DTLS shares TLS' initial handshake latency.

Like MinimaLT, tcpcrypt [10] investigated ubiquitous encryption, but it maintains backwards compatibility with TCP. Tcpcrypt provides hooks that applications may use to provide authentication services and determine whether a channel is encrypted. MinimaLT's approach is different; it is clean-slate and eases host assurance by moving authentication and encryption services to the system layer.

Stream Control Transmission Protocol (SCTP) provides reliable delivery and congestion control [57], but it differs from TCP in that it can bundle messages from multiple applications (i.e., *chunks*) into a single packet. MinimaLT borrows this technique.

9 Conclusion

MinimaLT provides network confidentiality, integrity, privacy, server authentication, user authentication, and DoS protections with a simple protocol and implementation.

	TCP	TCP Fast Open	SST	IPsec	Labeled IPsec	TLS	False Start	Snap Start	Tcpcrypt	MinimaLT
Encrypt			✓	✓	✓	✓	✓	✓	✓	✓
Key erasure after session				✓	✓	✓	✓	✓	✓	✓
User authentication					✓	✓	✓	✓	✓	✓
Fast (time-based) key erasure				✓	✓					✓
Robust DoS protections										✓
Round trips before client sends data*	2	2	2	≥4	≥4	4	3	2	3	1
... if server is already known	1	1	1	≥3	≥3	3	2	1	2	0
... in abbreviated case†	1	0	0	1	1	2	2	1	1	0

*Includes one round trip for DNS/directory service lookup of unknown server
†Assumes protocol-specific information cached from previous connection to same server

Table 4: Comparison of MinimaLT with other network protocols

A particular concern for protected networking is latency, as research has shown users are very sensitive to delay. MinimaLT combines directory services and tunnel establishment in a new way to minimize latency—even outperforming unencrypted TCP. MinimaLT's first round trip is performed only once, at system boot time. The second is a protected analogue of a DNS lookup and is required under the same circumstances as DNS. Thus in the typical case, MinimaLT clients transmit encrypted data to an end server in the first packet sent.

MinimaLT establishes a tunnel which can be long-lived. Of course, the tunnel can be terminated at any time, but absent resource constraints MinimaLT is intended to maintain tunnels even across system suspends and network migration. This makes for a more reliable system as recovery code needs to be run less often.

Future work will focus on increasing tunnel establishment rates by offloading public key operations to other CPU cores. We expect a roughly N-fold improvement in cryptography from using N cores, and thus expect Gb/s-speed tunnel establishment with 16 cores. (When not under attack, MinimaLT would use far fewer cores.) We also plan to build proxies which will enable MinimaLT to talk to legacy applications. We expect to soon release Ethos and our Linux MinimaLT implementation as open source software.

10 Acknowledgments

This material is based upon work supported by the US National Science Foundation under grants CNS-0964575 and 1018836, the European Commission under Contract ICT-2007-216676 ECRYPT II and INFSO-ICT-284833 PUFFIN, and by the Netherlands Organisation for Scientific Research (NWO) under grant 639.073.005. Volker Roth, our shepherd, provided extensive feedback, especially to improve the paper's organization. We also thank Wenyuan Fei, Yaohua Li, and Siming Chen for their reviews of initial drafts, our anonymous referees for comments on subsequent drafts, and the United States Military Academy and Army Cyber Center for their support.

11 References

[1] W. Aiello, S. M. Bellovin, M. Blaze, R. Canetti, J. Ioannidis, A. D. Keromytis, and O. Reingold. Just Fast Keying: Key agreement in a hostile Internet. *ACM Trans. Inf. Syst. Secur.*, 7(2):242–273, May 2004.

[2] N. AlFardan and K. Paterson. Lucky thirteen: Breaking the TLS and DTLS record protocols. In *Proceedings of the 2013 IEEE Symposium on Security and Privacy*, pages 526–540, Washington, DC, USA, May 2013. IEEE Computer Society Press.

[3] K. J. Argyraki, P. Maniatis, O. Irzak, S. Ashish, and S. Shenker. Loss and delay accountability for the internet. In *Proceedings of the 2007 International Conference on Network Protocols*, pages 194–205, Washington, DC, USA, 2007. IEEE Computer Society Press.

[4] E. Barker, W. Barker, W. Burr, W. Polk, and M. Smid. Recommendation for key management—Part 1: General (revised). US National Institute of Standards and Technology, Mar. 2007. `http://csrc.nist.gov/publications/nistpubs/800-57/sp800-57-Part1-revised2_Mar08-2007.pdf` (accessed Aug 26, 2013).

[5] D. J. Bernstein and T. Lange. eBACS: ECRYPT Benchmarking of Cryptographic Systems. `http://bench.cr.yp.to/` (accessed Aug 26, 2013).

[6] D. J. Bernstein, T. Lange, and P. Schwabe. NaCl: Networking and cryptography library. `http://nacl.cr.yp.to/` (accessed Aug 26, 2013).

[7] D. J. Bernstein, T. Lange, and P. Schwabe. The security impact of a new cryptographic library. In *International Conference on Cryptology and Information Security in Latin America*, volume 7533, pages 159–176. Springer, 2012.

[8] D. J. Bernstein and P. Schwabe. NEON crypto. In *Workshop on Cryptographic Hardware and Embedded Systems*, volume 7428, pages 320–339. Springer, 2012.

[9] A. Birrell and B. J. Nelson. Implementing remote procedure calls. *ACM Transactions on Computer Systems*, 2(1):39–59, Feb. 1984.

[10] A. Bittau, M. Hamburg, M. Handley, D. Mazières, and D. Boneh. The case for ubiquitous transport-level encryption. In *Proceedings of the the 19th USENIX Security Symposium*, Berkeley, CA, USA, Aug. 2010. USENIX Association.

[11] J. Bonneau, C. Herley, P. C. van Oorschot, and F. Stajano. The quest to replace passwords: A framework for comparative evaluation of web authentication schemes. In *Proceedings of the 2012 IEEE Symposium on Security and Privacy*, pages 553–567, Washington, DC, USA, May 2012. IEEE Computer Society Press.

[12] S. K. Card, G. G. Robertson, and J. D. Mackinlay. The information visualizer, an information workspace. In *Proceedings of the 1991 Conference on Human Factors in Computing Systems*, pages 181–188, New York, NY, USA, Apr. 1991. ACM.

[13] L. Constantin. Facebook to roll out HTTPS by default to all users, Nov. 2012. `http://www.computerworld.com/s/article/9233897/Facebook_to_roll_out_HTTPS_by_default_to_all_users` (accessed Aug 26, 2013).

[14] M. de Vivo, G. O. de Vivo, R. Koeneke, and G. Isern. Internet vulnerabilities related to TCP/IP and T/TCP. *SIGCOMM Comput. Commun. Rev.*, 29(1):81–85, Jan. 1999.

[15] T. Dierks and C. Allen. RFC 2246: The TLS protocol version 1, Jan. 1999. Status: PROPOSED STANDARD.

[16] R. Dingledine, N. Mathewson, and P. F. Syverson. Tor: The second-generation onion router. In *Proceedings of the 13th USENIX Security Symposium*, pages 303–320, Berkeley, CA, USA, Aug. 2004. USENIX Association.

[17] T. Duong and J. Rizzo. Here come the ⊕ ninjas. In *Ekoparty Security Conference*, 2011.

[18] P. Eckersley, F. von Lohmann, and S. Schoen. Packet forgery by ISPs: A report on the Comcast affair. Electronic Frontier Foundation, Nov. 2007.

https://www.eff.org/files/eff_comcast_report.pdf (accessed Aug 26, 2013).

[19] K. Egevang and P. Francis. RFC 1631: The IP network address translator (NAT), May 1994. Status: INFORMATIONAL.

[20] Electronic Frontier Foundation. HTTPS everywhere. https://www.eff.org/https-everywhere (accessed Aug 26, 2013).

[21] S. Fahl, M. Harbach, T. Muders, M. Smith, L. Baumgärtner, and B. Freisleben. Why Eve and Mallory love Android: an analysis of Android SSL (in)security. In *Proceedings of the 19th ACM Conference on Computer and Communications Security*, pages 50–61, New York, NY, USA, 2012. ACM.

[22] S. Floyd. RFC 2914: Congestion control principles, Sept. 2000. Status: INFORMATIONAL.

[23] B. Ford. Directions in Internet transport evolution. *IETF Journal*, 3(3):29–32, Dec. 2007.

[24] B. Ford. Structured streams: a new transport abstraction. In *Proceedings of the 2007 conference on Applications, technologies, architectures, and protocols for computer communications*, pages 361–372, New York, NY, USA, 2007. ACM.

[25] E. S. Freire, D. Hofheinz, E. Kiltz, and K. G. Paterson. Non-interactive key exchange. In *PKC 2013*, volume 7778, pages 254–271. Springer, 2013.

[26] M. Georgiev, S. Iyengar, S. Jana, R. Anubhai, D. Boneh, and V. Shmatikov. The most dangerous code in the world: validating SSL certificates in non-browser software. In *Proceedings of the 19th ACM Conference on Computer and Communications Security*, pages 38–49, New York, NY, USA, 2012. ACM.

[27] J. Gettys and K. Nichols. Bufferbloat: dark buffers in the internet. *Commun. ACM*, 55(1):57–65, Jan. 2012.

[28] P. K. Gummadi, S. Saroiu, and S. D. Gribble. King: estimating latency between arbitrary Internet end hosts. In *Proceedings of the 2nd Workshop on Internet Measurement*, pages 5–18, New York, NY, USA, 2002. ACM.

[29] A. Hiltgen, T. Kramp, and T. Weigold. Secure Internet banking authentication. *IEEE Security Privacy*, 4(2):21–29, March–April 2006.

[30] J. Ioannidis and S. M. Bellovin. Implementing pushback: Router-based defense against DDoS attacks. In *Proceedings of the 9th Network and Distributed System Security Symposium*, Reston, VA, USA, Feb. 2002. The Internet Society.

[31] T. Jaeger, K. Butler, D. H. King, S. Hallyn, J. Latten, and X. Zhang. Leveraging IPsec for mandatory access control across systems. In *Proceedings of the 2nd ACM conference on Computer and Communications Security*, New York, NY, USA, Aug. 2006. ACM.

[32] T. Jager, F. Kohlar, S. Schäge, and J. Schwenk. On the security of TLS-DHE in the standard model. In *Crypto 2012*, volume 7417, pages 273–293. Springer, 2012.

[33] A. Juels and J. G. Brainard. Client puzzles: A cryptographic countermeasure against connection depletion attacks. In *Proceedings of the 6th Network and Distributed System Security Symposium*, Reston, VA, USA, Feb. 1999. The Internet Society.

[34] C. Kaufman. RFC 4306: Internet key exchange (IKEv2) protocol, Dec. 2005. Status: PROPOSED STANDARD.

[35] A. D. Keromytis, S. Ioannidis, M. B. Greenwald, and J. M. Smith. The STRONGMAN architecture. In *Proceedings of the 3rd DARPA Information Survivability Conference and Exposition*, volume 1, pages 178–188, 2003.

[36] B. Lampson, M. Abadi, M. Burrows, and E. Wobber. Authentication in distributed systems: Theory and practice. *ACM Transactions on Computing Systems*, 10(4):265–310, Nov. 1992.

[37] A. Langley. Transport Layer Security (TLS) Snap Start. Internet Engineering Task Force, June 2010. http://tools.ietf.org/html/draft-agl-tls-snapstart-00 (accessed Aug 26, 2013).

[38] A. Langley. Forward secrecy for Google HTTPS, Nov. 2011. https://www.imperialviolet.org/2011/11/22/forwardsecret.html (accessed Aug 26, 2013).

[39] A. Langley. How to botch TLS forward secrecy, June 2013. https://www.imperialviolet.org/2013/06/27/botchingpfs.html (accessed Aug 26, 2013).

[40] A. Langley, N. Modadugu, and W.-T. Chang. Overclocking SSL. In *Velocity: Web Performance and Operations Conference*, Santa Clara, CA, June 2010. http://www.imperialviolet.org/2010/06/25/overclocking-ssl.html (accessed Aug 26, 2013).

[41] A. Langley, N. Modadugu, and B. Moeller. Transport Layer Security (TLS) False Start. Internet Engineering Task Force, June 2010. http://tools.ietf.org/html/draft-bmoeller-tls-falsestart-00 (accessed Aug 26, 2013).

[42] E. Le Malécot, Y. Hori, and K. Sakurai. Preliminary insight into distributed SSH brute force attacks. *Proceedings of the IEICE General Conference*, page 2, Mar. 2008.

[43] M. Liberatore and B. N. Levine. Inferring the source of encrypted HTTP connections. In *Proceedings of the 13th ACM Conference on Computer and Communications Security*, pages 255–263, New York, NY, USA, Oct. 2006. ACM.

[44] P. Loscocco and S. Smalley. Integrating flexible support for security policies into the Linux operating system. In *Proceedings of the FREENIX Track: 2001 USENIX Annual Technical Conference*, pages 29–42, Berkeley, CA, June 2001. The USENIX Association.

[45] D. McGrew. RFC 5116: An interface and algorithms for authenticated encryption, 2008. Status: PROPOSED STANDARD.

[46] W. M. Petullo and J. A. Solworth. Authentication in Ethos. https://www.ethos-os.org/papers/, June 2013.

[47] W. M. Petullo and J. A. Solworth. Simple-to-use, secure-by-design networking in Ethos. In *Proceedings of the Sixth European Workshop on System Security*, New York, NY, USA, Apr. 2013. ACM. https://www.ethos-os.org/papers/.

[48] S. Radhakrishnan, Y. Cheng, J. Chu, A. Jain, and B. Raghavan. TCP fast open. In *Proceedings of the 7th International Conference on Emerging Networking Experiments and Technologies*, New York, NY, USA, 2011. ACM.

[49] E. Rescorla and N. Modadugu. RFC 6347: Datagram transport layer security version 1.2, 2012. Status: PROPOSED STANDARD.

[50] R. L. Rivest and B. Lampson. SDSI — a simple distributed security infrastucture. Technical report, MIT, Apr. 1996.

[51] S. Schillace. Default HTTPS access for Gmail, Jan. 2010. http://gmailblog.blogspot.com/2010/01/default-https-access-for-gmail.html (accessed Aug 26, 2013).

[52] J. A. Solworth. The Ethos operating system. http://www.ethos-os.org.

[53] J. A. Solworth and W. Fei. sayI: Trusted user authentication at Internet scale. https://www.ethos-os.org/papers/, Aug. 2013.

[54] D. X. Song, D. Wagner, and X. Tian. Timing analysis of keystrokes and timing attacks on SSH. In *Proceedings of the 10th USENIX Security Symposium*, Berkeley, CA, USA, Aug. 2001. USENIX Association.

[55] S. Souders. Velocity and the bottom line. O'Reilly Media, July 2009. http://programming.oreilly.com/2009/07/velocity-making-your-site-fast.html (accessed Aug 26, 2013).

[56] E. Stark, L.-S. Huang, D. Israni, C. Jackson, and D. Boneh. The case for prefetching and prevalidating TLS server certificates. In *Proceedings of the 19th Network and Distributed System Security Symposium*, Reston, VA, USA, 2012. The Internet Society.

[57] R. Stewart. RFC 4960: Stream Control Transmission Protocol, Sept. 2007. Status: PROPOSED STANDARD.

[58] N. Vratonjic, J. Freudiger, V. Bindschaedler, and J.-P. Hubaux. The inconvenient truth about web certificates. In *Proceedings of the 10th Workshop on the Economics of Information Security*, June 2011.

[59] N. Weaver, R. Sommer, and V. Paxson. Detecting forged TCP reset packets. In *Proceedings of the 16th Network and Distributed Systems Security Symposium*, Reston, VA, USA, Feb. 2009. The Internet Society.

[60] J. E. White. A high-level framework for network-based resource sharing. In *Proceedings of the 1976 National Computer Conference and Exposition*, pages 561–570, New York, NY, USA, 1976. ACM.

[61] E. Wobber, M. Abadi, M. Burrows, and B. Lampson. Authentication in the Taos operating system. In *Proceedings of the 14th Symposium on Operating System Principles*, pages 256–269, New York, NY, USA, 1993. ACM.

Impact of Integrity Attacks on Real-Time Pricing in Smart Grids

Rui Tan[1] Varun Badrinath Krishna[1] David K. Y. Yau[1,2] Zbigniew Kalbarczyk[3]
[1]Advanced Digital Sciences Center, Illinois at Singapore
[2]Singapore University of Technology and Design, Singapore
[3]University of Illinois at Urbana-Champaign, Urbana, IL, USA
{tanrui, varun.bk, david.yau}@adsc.com.sg, kalbarcz@illinois.edu

ABSTRACT

Modern information and communication technologies used by smart grids are subject to cybersecurity threats. This paper studies the impact of integrity attacks on real-time pricing (RTP), a key feature of smart grids that uses such technologies to improve system efficiency. Recent studies have shown that RTP creates a closed loop formed by the mutually dependent real-time price signals and price-taking demand. Such a closed loop can be exploited by an adversary whose objective is to destabilize the pricing system. Specifically, small malicious modifications to the price signals can be iteratively amplified by the closed loop, causing inefficiency and even severe failures such as blackouts. This paper adopts a control-theoretic approach to deriving the fundamental conditions of RTP stability under two broad classes of integrity attacks, namely, the *scaling* and *delay* attacks. We show that the RTP system is at risk of being destabilized only if the adversary can compromise the price signals advertised to smart meters by reducing their values in the scaling attack, or by providing old prices to over half of all consumers in the delay attack. The results provide useful guidelines for system operators to analyze the impact of various attack parameters on system stability, so that they may take adequate measures to secure RTP systems.

Categories and Subject Descriptors

B.8.2 [**Performance and Reliability**]: Performance Analysis and Design Aids; K.6.5 [**Management of Computing and Information Systems**]: Security and Protection

Keywords

Smart grid; real-time pricing; stability; cyber security

1. INTRODUCTION

A smart grid is an enhanced electrical grid that uses modern information and communication technologies to improve system reliability and efficiency. However, these computerized and networking technologies are subject to security threats that range from personal breaches [22] to sophisticated cyber attacks launched by hostile organizations to cause widespread outages [31]. As a sophisticated cyber-physical system, a smart grid features complex closed-loop feedback controls in various physical [18] and economic components [7], which maintain desirable system performance in the presence of dynamics and uncertainties. However, the impacts of cyber attacks against these closed loops on smart grids have received limited research attention. Without a systematic understanding of these impacts, system designers and operators will not be able to truly assess how these attacks may undermine the system's ability to provide mission-critical services, and hence take appropriate defensive measures against the possible threats. This paper makes a step in this direction by quantifying, through both analysis and simulations, the impact of cyber attacks on real-time pricing (RTP) in smart grids, which involves closed-loop controls to stabilize the electricity market.

Dynamic pricing [10] is a widely adopted means to balance electricity generation and consumption. The electricity price in the wholesale market is updated periodically (e.g., every hour) to match generation with dynamic demand. In contrast, many current retail markets adopt static pricing schemes such as fixed and time-of-use tariffs, under which the consumers have limited incentives to adapt their electricity consumption to market conditions. This lack of incentives results in high peak demands that strain infrastructure capacities and unnecessarily increase operational costs. By relaying the real-time wholesale prices to end users, RTP has been considered a key feature of smart grids, which can reduce over-provisioning and improve system efficiency. Unfortunately, as analyzed in [25], there exists a fundamental *information asymmetry* between the system operators and consumers under RTP. Specifically, a system operator needs to determine the price, which is supposed to clear the market, prior to the consumption decisions made by consumers. As the system operator typically has limited knowledge about the consumers, its best practice is to determine the price based on historical demand. As a result, RTP creates a closed loop formed by the mutually dependent real-time prices and price-taking demand [25]. Such a closed loop can increase the system's sensitivity to dynamics and lower its robustness against situational uncertainties. As such, it can be exploited by an adversary whose objective is to destabilize the RTP system. Specifically, small modifications to the signals in the closed loop made by the adversary can

CCS'13, November 4–8, 2013, Berlin, Gernany.

http://dx.doi.org/10.1145/2508859.2516705.

be iteratively amplified by the feedback, causing inefficiency and significantly fluctuating demand, and possibly leading to severe failures such as blackouts.

In smart grids, the real-time price signals are exposed to different security threats at the source, during network transmissions, and at the consumer-level smart meters. In particular, recent studies [22, 26] have shown that many smart meters lack basic security measures to ensure the integrity and authenticity of their input/output data. In light of these infrastructure vulnerabilities, imperative questions regarding RTP security include, "Can the malicious compromise of real-time price signals destabilize the system and cause severe failures such as outages? If so, to what extent do the price signals need to be compromised?" A main challenge in answering these questions stems from the complex coupling between the attacker actions and the closed-loop RTP system. For instance, an attack against a few smart meters can cause monetary losses to individual victims, but it will not be able to destabilize the whole system. But if the adversary is able to compromise a sufficiently large number of consumers, the real-time price control mechanisms, which are designed to stabilize the system, may fail to mitigate the attack's impact. This impact may then pervade the whole system due to the iterative feedback. However, it is challenging to quantify these critical stability boundaries accurately, in order to characterize the impact of the attacks.

In this paper, we adopt a control-theoretic approach, which captures the closed-loop nature of the RTP, to deriving fundamental stability conditions under credible integrity attacks. Based on the linearization of general abstract models of supply and demand, the RTP problem is formulated as a classical control problem for a linear time-invariant (LTI) system. We develop a basic pricing algorithm that sets the price adjustment proportional to the observed error between supply and demand. It ensures stability and captures the essence of stability-ensuring RTP systems. Therefore, the security analysis based on this algorithm provides a baseline understanding of the security of these systems. We adopt a control-theoretic metric, namely, the *region of stability*, to characterize the security of the closed-loop RTP system with respect to important and practical adversary models. Specifically, we consider two common and broad classes of integrity attacks, which we call the *scaling* and *delay* attacks, where the prices advertised to smart meters are compromised by a scaling factor (so that the meters will use the wrong prices) and by corrupted timing information (so that the meters will use old prices), respectively. In addition to directly tampering with traffic sent to the smart meters, these attacks can be accomplished by indirect techniques that are less effort intensive. For instance, the delay attack can be realized by compromising the time synchronization of deployed smart meters. Note that current commercial smart meters [28] synchronize their clocks by either built-in GPS receivers or a network time protocol (NTP) supported by time servers [28]. Both approaches have been shown to be vulnerable to realistic attack methods [4,23]. As both attacks can be modeled as LTI transfer functions, the security analysis can be conducted under a LTI setting.

Based on our analytical framework, we derive the region of stability for both the scaling and delay attacks. In particular, we show that the RTP system will remain stable if (i) the compromised prices are amplified versions of the true prices under the scaling attack (i.e., the scaling factor exceeds one), or (ii) less than half of the consumers in the pricing system are compromised in the delay attack. On the other hand, if the adversary can break either of these two conditions, the system may experience severely fluctuating demand arising from the system instability. We report GridLAB-D [2] simulation results for a distribution system consisting of 1405 consumers to verify our analysis and demonstrate possible system emergencies (e.g., line and transformer overload events) caused by the integrity attacks. Our results provide insights for securing RTP in smart grids. For instance, for the adversary to achieve the goal of compromising the price signals to at least half of the consumers, she may focus her efforts on shared support infrastructures such as the NTP time servers. This highlights the importance of securing these servers.

The rest of this paper is organized as follows. Section 2 reviews related work. Section 3 presents the market model. Section 4 defines the RTP stability problem, and develops a control-theoretic formulation of the problem. Section 5 analyzes the impact of the scaling and delay attacks on the RTP system. Section 6 discusses extensions of the analysis framework to address a broader class of attacks that are combinations of multiple scaling and delay attacks. Section 7 presents simulation results. Section 8 concludes.

2. RELATED WORK

The security of smart grids is attracting increasing research attention. In particular, false data injection attacks against the state estimation of electrical grids have been extensively studied. In [21], Liu et al. systematically examine the conditions for bypassing a bad data detection mechanism of state estimation under various adversary capability models. Later studies [16, 17, 20, 32, 33] show that the false data injection attacks can lead to increased system operation costs due to inordinate generation dispatch [33] or energy routing [20], as well as economic losses due to misconduct of electricity markets [16, 17, 32]. In particular, the studies in [16, 17, 32] focus on false data injection attacks on real-time wholesale markets. They primarily emphasize attacks on critical measurements, which are often well protected by system operators. Moreover, they ignore demand response of end users to prices. In contrast, our work considers integrity attacks that target distributed smart meters that are much more vulnerable, and also accounts for demand response involving the end users. All these related studies [16,17,20,21,32,33] analyze attacks on systems using constrained optimization formulations such as power flow dispatch. The closed loop characterizing the RTP system in our work imposes specific challenges in the security analysis due to its iterative nature.

The security of a broader class of cyber-physical systems that feature complex closed loops has been studied recently. In [12], Cárdenas et al. identify challenges in the security analysis of these systems. In [11], the authors use simulations to study the impacts of integrity and denial-of-service attacks on a chemical reactor with multiple sensors and control loops. In [8], the authors perform security threat assessment of supervisory control and data acquisition systems for water supply. These studies focus on demonstrating the possibility of pushing the system to a certain state (e.g., unsafe pressure in a chemical reactor) by tampering with the sensor and/or control signals. They fall short of characterizing fully the fundamental critical stability conditions.

Table 1: Summary of Notation*

Symbol	Definition	Unit
T	pricing period	hour
k	index of current pricing period	n/a
λ_k	true price signal, $\lambda_k \in [\lambda_{\min}, \lambda_{\max}]$	\$/MWh
λ'_k	compromised price signal	\$/MWh
λ^*_k	clearing price	\$/MWh
b_k	total baseline demand	MW
$w(\lambda_k)$	total price-responsive demand	MW
$d(k, \lambda_k)$	total demand	MW
D	a constant in the CEO model	MW
ϵ	price elasticity of demand	n/a
$s(\lambda_k)$	scheduled total generation	MW
$\widehat{s}(\lambda_k)$	realized total generation	MW
p	slope of linear supply model	MW/(\$/MWh)
q	intercept of linear supply model	MW
e_k	generation scheduling error	MW
η	price stabilization gain, $\eta \in (0, 1)$	n/a
λ_o	price stabilization operating point	\$/MWh
C	the set of all consumers	n/a
C'	the set of consumers under attack	n/a
ρ	$\simeq \lvert C'\rvert / \lvert C\rvert$	n/a
γ	amplification of scaling attack	n/a
τ	time delay of delay attack	T
h	marginal demand-supply ratio	n/a

* The unit of a quantity is omitted in the paper if it is specified here.

3. PRELIMINARIES

This section presents the market model adopted in this paper, which comprises an *independent system operator* (ISO) (Section 3.1), a set of consumers (Section 3.2), and a set of suppliers (Section 3.3). For both consumers and suppliers, we first describe general abstract models, and then discuss concrete empirical models commonly used in literature. The analytical results in this paper (i.e., Propositions 1 to 5) are based on the abstract models, while the empirical models (i.e., a constant elasticity of own-price demand model and a linear supply model) are used for the numerical examples and simulations. The notation used in this paper is summarized in Table 1. We also use the following mathematical notation: $\dot{f}(x)$ denotes the first derivative of function $f(x)$; $f^{-1}(x)$ denotes the inverse of function $f(x)$; $\mathbb{R}^+/\mathbb{R}^-$ denotes the set of positive/negative real numbers; $\mathbb{Z}^+$ denotes the set of positive integers.

3.1 ISO Model and RTP Schemes

The ISO is a profit-neutral agent, which aims to clear the market, i.e., match supply and demand. It determines a clearing price every T hours and announces it to the suppliers and end consumers. Specifically, the price for the kth pricing period $[k \cdot T, (k+1) \cdot T]$, denoted by λ_k, is announced at time instant $(k - k_0) \cdot T$, where k_0 is a non-negative integer. Hence, this scheme corresponds to ex-ante pricing. We assume that the price must be within a range, i.e., $\lambda_k \in [\lambda_{\min}, \lambda_{\max}]$, where $\lambda_{\max} > \lambda_{\min} \in \mathbb{R}^+$. Note that in many electricity markets, suppliers sell electricity to utilities in wholesale markets, and utilities sell electricity to end consumers in retail markets. The market model adopted in this paper directly relays real-time wholesale prices to end consumers, which preserves the principles of RTP and simplifies the analysis. This model has been employed in previous studies (e.g., [25] and references therein) and is consistent with the essence of several experimental RTP programs [10] provided by utilities, which include Board of Public Utilities in New Jersey, Baltimore Gas and Electric Company in Maryland, and Duquesne Light in Pennsylvania. In these programs, the hourly wholesale prices published by PJM Interconnection LLC[1] are used directly as retail prices, where $T = 1$ and $k_0 = 0$. A few other experimental RTP programs give customers advance notice of hourly prices. For instance, $k_0 = 1$ for the RTP-HA-2 program of Georgia Power [6]. To simplify the discussion, we focus on RTP schemes without advance notice, i.e., $k_0 = 0$. However, our analysis can be easily extended to encompass advance notice. In reality, locational prices can be applied to address location-dependent transmission costs. In many areas, as generation cost dominates transmission cost, variations of locational prices are often small. For instance, the relative standard deviation of the locational prices for 219 locations published by PJM is often around 5% only [5]. As this paper focuses on the impact of integrity attacks on RTP systems, we ignore the small variations in the locational prices. Thus, we assume that all the suppliers and consumers are subject to the same real-time price λ_k.

3.2 Consumers

Abstract demand model: Let C denote the set of consumers in the system. For consumer $j \in C$, let $b_{k,j}$ denote the *baseline demand* in the kth pricing period, which is exogenous, bounded, dependent on time, but independent of λ_k. For instance, for a household, the baseline demand can characterize the minimum necessary power usage, such as cooking and a minimum level of illumination. Let $v_j(x - b_{k,j})$ denote the additional value (unit: \$/hour) derived from consuming a total of x units of power in the kth pricing period, where $x \geq b_{k,j}$. We assume that $v_j(\cdot)$ is a strictly increasing and strictly concave function. Let $d_j(k, \lambda_k)$ denote the demand of consumer j in the kth pricing period given price λ_k. We denote $w_j(\lambda_k) = \dot{v}_j^{-1}(\lambda_k)$, where $\dot{v}_j^{-1}(\cdot)$ represents the inverse function of $\dot{v}_j(\cdot)$. The demand is given by

$$d_j(k, \lambda_k) = \arg\max_x \left(v_j(x - b_{k,j}) - \lambda_k \cdot x\right) = b_{k,j} + w_j(\lambda_k).$$

In the above equation, $v_j(x - b_{k,j}) - \lambda_k \cdot x$ is the additional utility beyond the baseline by consuming totally x units of power. The $w_j(\lambda_k)$ is referred to as *price-responsive demand*. It is easy to verify that $w_j(\lambda_k)$ is a decreasing function of λ_k. By denoting $b_k = \sum_{j \in C} b_{k,j}$ and $w(\lambda_k) = \sum_{j \in C} w_j(\lambda_k)$, the total demand, denoted by $d(k, \lambda_k)$, is given by

$$d(k, \lambda_k) = \sum\nolimits_{j \in C} d_j(k, \lambda_k) = b_k + w(\lambda_k). \qquad (1)$$

As there are a large number of consumers, we assume that $b_{k,j}$ and $v_j(\cdot)$ are unknown to the ISO. However, the ISO knows the historical total demand $\{d(h, \lambda_h) | h \in [0, k-1]\}$. The above derivations, which are based on the basic concept of *utility* in economics, explain the consumer's demand response to price. Human-induced demand response has been observed in previous studies [29]. With the increasing adoption of smart appliances and home automation systems, this demand response will become more automated.

Empirical demand model: The constant elasticity of own-price (CEO) model [14] is a simple model that can be used to characterize the total price-responsive demand, which is defined by $w(\lambda_k) = D \cdot \lambda_k^{\epsilon}$, where D and ϵ are positive and negative constants, respectively. The ϵ is referred to as the *price elasticity of demand*, which is typically within $(-1, 0)$ [13, 19].

[1]PJM is a Regional Transmission Organization (RTO). This paper does not distinguish between ISO and RTO.

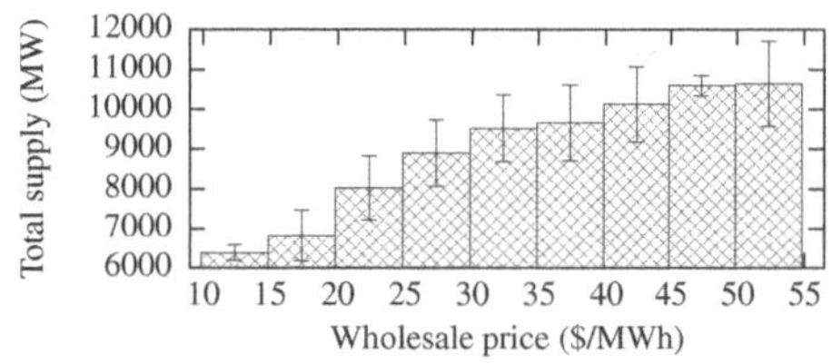

Figure 1: Total supply vs. wholesale price [1].

3.3 Suppliers

Abstract supply model: Each supplier aims to maximize its profit. Let S denote the set of suppliers in the system. For any supplier $i \in S$, let the function $c_i(x)$ represent the cost (unit: \$/hour [15, p. 534]) of producing and transmitting x units of power. We assume that $c_i(x)$ is a strictly convex and non-negative function over the support $x \geq 0$. Moreover, we assume that $c_i(x)$ is an asymptotically increasing function, i.e., $\exists x_0 \geq 0$, $\dot{c}_i(x) > 0$ if $x > x_0$. Let $s_i(\lambda_k)$ denote the quantity of power that supplier i schedules to generate in the kth pricing period given price λ_k, which is given by $s_i(\lambda_k) = \arg\max_x (\lambda_k \cdot x - c_i(x)) = \dot{c}_i^{-1}(\lambda_k)$. Note that $\lambda_k \cdot x - c_i(x)$ is the profit from generating x units of power. It is easy to verify that $s_i(\lambda_k)$ is an increasing function of λ_k. We assume that the generation capacity of the supplier i is at least $s_i(\lambda_{\max})$. In this paper, we consider centralized bulk generation rather than distributed generation. Therefore, an ISO can estimate $\{c_i(\cdot)|\forall i \in S\}$ as there are typically a limited number of suppliers. Let $s(\lambda_k)$ denote the *scheduled* total supply in the kth pricing period, i.e., $s(\lambda_k) = \sum_{i\in S} s_i(\lambda_k)$. We note that, in current electricity wholesale markets, the supply and price are often determined through a bidding process [14], which is generally governed by the costs of generation and transmission. In a competitive bidding-based wholesale market, the resultant supply and price will well reflect the supply model derived from the cost model. We assume that the *realized* total generation in the kth pricing period, denoted by $\widehat{s}(\lambda_k)$, is always equal to the total demand $d(k, \lambda_k)$. This is consistent with the current technologies in power grids. For instance, when the demand exceeds the scheduled generation, the system operators will observe a dropping voltage and frequency, and generation can be increased to meet demand and maintain the voltage and frequency at their nominal values.

Empirical supply model: Quadratic cost functions have been widely adopted in the analyses of power generation systems [15], i.e., $c_i(x) = \alpha_i x^2 + \beta_i x + \delta_i$, where $\alpha_i > 0$. To make $c_i(x)$ non-negative over $x \geq 0$, we have a few additional conditions: $\delta_i \geq 0$ if $\beta_i \geq 0$, or $\delta_i \geq \frac{\beta_i^2}{4\alpha_i}$ if $\beta_i < 0$. Therefore, if $\lambda_k \geq \beta_i$, $s_i(\lambda_k) = \frac{1}{2\alpha_i}(\lambda_k - \beta_i)$; otherwise, $s_i(\lambda_k) = 0$. To simplify the evaluation based on this empirical supply model, we assume that $\beta_i < 0$ and $\delta_i \geq \frac{\beta_i^2}{4\alpha_i}$, such that the total supply can be simplified as $s(\lambda_k) = p \cdot \lambda_k + q$, where $p = \sum_{i\in S} \frac{1}{2\alpha_i} > 0$ and $q = \sum_{i\in S} -\frac{\beta_i}{2\alpha_i} > 0$. We now empirically verify this linear supply model using the half-hourly total supply data of New South Wales (NSW), Australia, provided by the Australian Energy Market Operator (AEMO) [1]. Fig. 1 shows the histogram of total supply versus the wholesale price in January, 2012. We can see that the relationship between the average supply and price is nearly linear. A linear fitting of the total supply shown in Fig. 1 yields $p = 152$ and $q = 4503$. Such a linear relationship can also be seen in the investigation of the electricity market of California [29, p. 112], where the demand does not exceed the generation capacity.

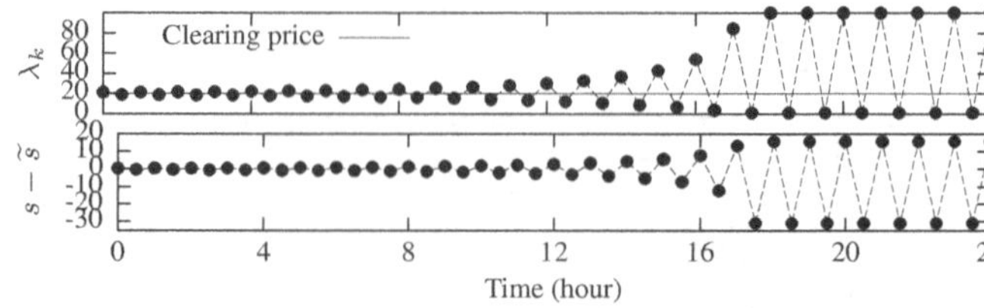

Figure 2: An example of unstable solution [25] under the linear supply and CEO demand models. Top figure: Evolution of price. Bottom figure: Generation scheduling error in GW. (p=152, q=4503, $\epsilon = -0.6$, b_k=2000, λ_k^*=20, λ_0=21, $\lambda_{\min}$=1, $\lambda_{\max}$=100)

4. THE RTP PROBLEM AND SOLUTIONS

This section formally states the RTP problem, examines an existing solution, and proposes a new basic control-theoretic solution with provable *bounded-input bounded-output stability* (referred to as *stability* for short in this paper). Based on our solution, the security analysis in Section 5 lays the foundation for understanding the impact of attacks on feedback-based RTP systems.

4.1 The RTP Problem and Solution Stability

At time instant $k \cdot T$, the ISO aims to find the *clearing price* for the period $[k \cdot T, (k+1) \cdot T]$, denoted by λ_k^*, such that the scheduled supply matches demand, i.e., $s(\lambda_k^*) = d(k, \lambda_k^*)$. However, as $d(k, \lambda_k)$ is unknown, in practice, the ISO sets the price to match the scheduled supply and *predicted* demand (denoted by $\widetilde{d}(k, \lambda_k)$). Formally, we define

RTP Problem: Find λ_k such that $s(\lambda_k) = \widetilde{d}(k, \lambda_k)$.

Straightforward solutions to this problem may lead to significantly fluctuating prices. For instance, a direct feedback approach [25], which uses $d(k-1, \lambda_{k-1})$ as the predicted demand $\widetilde{d}(k, \lambda_k)$, can yield oscillating prices as shown in Fig. 2. The root cause of the oscillation is the unstable closed-loop system formed by the direct feedback. When the system is unstable, the price set by the ISO will oscillate or diverge, even if the initial price is very close to the true clearing price. The oscillations may lead to severe consequences. When the diverging prices reach low values, the increased demand may cause overload of the transmission and distribution networks. Moreover, as shown in Fig. 2, the unstable system may experience significant *generation scheduling errors* (i.e., $s(\lambda_k) - \widehat{s}(\lambda_k)$). Although reserve generating capacity can help compensate for the errors, their use may increase the cost of operating the system.

To study the impact of integrity attacks on the RTP systems, we should start with RTP schemes that are stable in the absence of attacks. In Section 4.2, we examine the stability of an existing RTP scheme [25] in the absence of attacks. Its poor stability properties motivate us to design a basic control-theoretic RTP scheme with provable stability in the absence of attacks. This is the subject of Section 4.3.

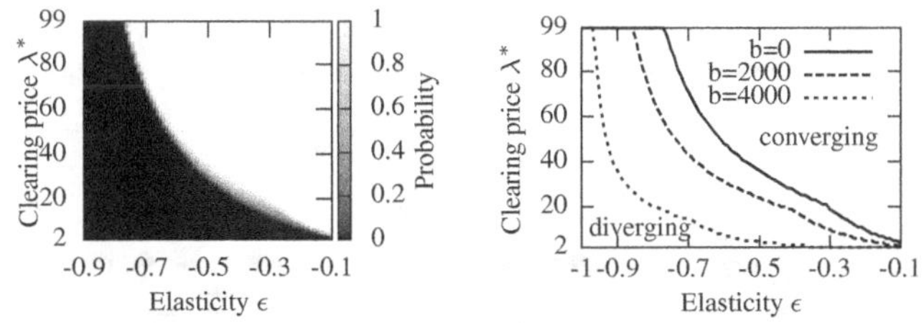

(a) Map of convergence probability ($b = 0$).
(b) Stability boundary under various settings of b.

Figure 3: Stability of direct feedback approach under the linear supply and CEO demand models.

4.2 Direct Feedback Approach

A direct feedback approach to the RTP problem has been studied in [25]. The conditions for global stability[2] of the approach, i.e., the properties of $s(\cdot)$ and $d(\cdot,\cdot)$ that ensure global stability, have also been analyzed in [25]. The approach is briefly reviewed as follows. It predicts $d(k, \lambda_k)$ by the most recent demands based on an autoregression model, and determines the price λ_k accordingly. For instance, the simplest autoregression model uses $d(k-1, \lambda_{k-1})$ as $\widetilde{d}(k, \lambda_k)$ and the closed-loop system is expressed as $s(\lambda_k) = d(k-1, \lambda_{k-1})$. It is also referred to as the *persistence model.* Thus, the price is determined as $\lambda_k = s^{-1}(d(k-1, \lambda_{k-1}))$. If direct feedback based on the persistence model is not globally stable, it is difficult to stabilize those systems globally with an autoregression-based direct feedback approach [25]. Hence, global stability under the persistence model is particularly important. By applying Corollary 3 in [25], our analysis [30] shows that under the linear supply and CEO demand models, where $\epsilon \in (-1, 0)$ and b_k is a non-negative constant b, the system $\lambda_k = s^{-1}(d(k-1, \lambda_{k-1}))$ is not globally stable.

As the direct feedback approach is not globally stable, its convergence highly depends on the system state. If b_k is time-varying, it can push the system to a state that eventually leads to divergence. A few realistic constraints may affect the system stability. For instance, even if the system is not globally stable, the system may converge when the initial price is within the allowed range $[\lambda_{\min}, \lambda_{\max}]$. Moreover, if a tentative price is out of the range $[\lambda_{\min}, \lambda_{\max}]$, it will be rounded to $\lambda_{\min}$ or $\lambda_{\max}$. Hence, we conduct numerical experiments that account for these realistic constraints for better understanding. The settings of the supply model are $p = 152$ and $q = 4503$, which are obtained in Fig. 1. Given a clearing price $\lambda^* \in [\lambda_{\min}, \lambda_{\max}]$, the coefficient D is set by solving $s(\lambda^*) = d(\lambda^*)$, i.e., $D = \frac{p\lambda^* + q - b}{\lambda^{*\epsilon}}$, where $b \in [0, p\lambda_{\min} + q)$ to ensure $D > 0$ for any valid λ^*. Fig. 3(a) shows a map of the probability that the system is converging when $b = 0$. To calculate the probability, the initial price sweeps the range $[\lambda_{\min}, \lambda_{\max}]$ and the probability is calculated as the fraction of the initial prices that lead to system convergence. Fig. 3(a) shows that the probability is mostly either 0 or 1 and the transition region with the probability within $(0, 1)$ is sharp. Fig. 3(b) plots the boundaries between the converging and diverging regions under various settings of b, where its valid range is $[0, 4503)$. For instance, when $b = 4000$, the system can be diverging if $\epsilon = -0.8$ and $\lambda^* < 20$. For the data shown in Fig. 1, about 20% of the prices are lower than 20. Therefore, the direct feedback approach can be unstable with significant probabilities.

[2]The system is *globally stable* if the price converges to the clearing price given any positive initial price.

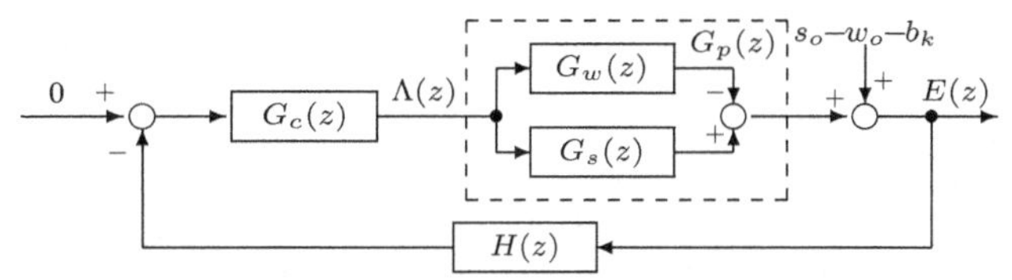

Figure 4: The control-theoretic price stabilization. $\Lambda(z)$ and $E(z)$ are the z-transforms of λ_k and e_k.

4.3 Control-Theoretic Price Stabilization

The results in Section 4.2 show the necessity of control laws for stabilizing the RTP systems. This section develops a basic control-theoretic price stabilization algorithm with provable stability. The main objective of this paper is to identify the fundamental impacts of integrity attacks against the vulnerable real-time price signals on the stability of the RTP systems with well designed control laws. More sophisticated price stabilization algorithms could be developed. However, our security analysis in Section 5, which is based on our basic control-theoretic algorithm, provides fundamental baselines for understanding the security properties of RTP systems running such sophisticated algorithms.

The objective of price stabilization is to minimize the generation scheduling error and adapt to the time-varying baseline load. We reformulate the RTP problem as a classical discrete-time feedback control problem. Under this formulation, the ISO observes the generation scheduling error in the previous pricing period, and then uses it to guide the setting of the price in the next pricing period. Specifically, let e_k denote the generation scheduling error, i.e., $e_k = s(\lambda_k) - d(k, \lambda_k)$. The objective is to maintain the *controlled variable* e_k close to its *reference*, which is zero. The *manipulated variable* is λ_k, and $s(\lambda_k) - d(k, \lambda_k)$ is the *controlled system.* The block diagram of the feedback control loop is shown in Fig. 4. We let $G_c(z)$, $G_p(z)$, and $H(z)$ denote the transfer functions of the price stabilization algorithm, the controlled system, and the observation system, which are expressed in the z-transform domain. The z-transform [24] provides a compact representation for discrete-time functions, where z represents a time shift operation. As b_k is bounded and independent of λ_k, it can be modelled as a *disturbance* to the system [24].

We now derive the expressions of $G_p(z)$ and $H(z)$. To preserve generality, our design is based on the abstract supply and demand models $s(\lambda)$ and $w(\lambda)$, which can be non-linear as in the CEO model. In controller design, a common approach to dealing with non-linear systems is to adopt local linearization [24]. Specifically, $s(\lambda) \simeq s(\lambda_o) + \dot{s}(\lambda_o) \cdot (\lambda - \lambda_o)$ and $w(\lambda) \simeq w(\lambda_o) + \dot{w}(\lambda_o) \cdot (\lambda - \lambda_o)$, where λ_o is a *fixed operating point.* By denoting $s_p(\lambda) = \dot{s}(\lambda_o)\lambda$, $s_o = s(\lambda_o) - \dot{s}(\lambda_o)\lambda_o$, $w_p(\lambda) = \dot{w}(\lambda_o)\lambda$, and $w_o = w(\lambda_o) - \dot{w}(\lambda_o)\lambda_o$, we have $s(\lambda) \simeq s_p(\lambda) + s_o$ and $w(\lambda) \simeq w_p(\lambda) + w_o$. As s_o and w_o are independent of λ, as shown in Fig. 4, we can collect them with the price-independent b_k. The transfer functions of the proportional models $s_p(\lambda)$ and $w_p(\lambda)$ are $G_s(z) = \dot{s}(\lambda_o)$ and $G_w(z) = \dot{w}(\lambda_o)$, respectively. Therefore, $G_p(z) = G_s(z) - G_w(z) = \dot{s}(\lambda_o) - \dot{w}(\lambda_o)$. As the price stabilization algorithm uses the observed generation scheduling error in the previous pricing period to adjust the price for the current pricing period, $H(z) = z^{-1}$, which represents the delay of one pricing period. Based on the above modeling, we have the following proposition, which can be proved by examining whether the poles of the system are located within a unit circle centered at the origin of the z-plane. The details of the proof are omitted due to space constraints and can be found in [30].

PROPOSITION 1. *For the linearized system $G_p(z) = \dot{s}(\lambda_o) - \dot{w}(\lambda_o)$ with λ_o fixed and the observation system $H(z) = z^{-1}$, the following price stabilization algorithm ensures stability: $\lambda_k = \lambda_{k-1} - \frac{2\eta}{\dot{s}(\lambda_o)-\dot{w}(\lambda_o)} \cdot e_{k-1}$, where $\eta \in (0,1)$.*

The transfer function of the above algorithm is $G_c(z) = \frac{2\eta}{(\dot{s}(\lambda_o)-\dot{w}(\lambda_o))(1-z^{-1})}$. From control theory, when b_k is a constant, the system converges the fastest when $\eta = 0.5$, as the system's pole is at the origin [24]. The convergence speed is particularly important for adapting to fast time-varying baseline load so that the convergence is achieved before a significant change of baseline load. However, our analysis in Section 5 shows that we generally need to set a smaller η to reduce the impact of attacks. In other words, we have to sacrifice convergence speed for resilience to attacks.

As discussed in Section 3.2, $w(\cdot)$ is unknown to the ISO. In practice, the ISO can estimate $\dot{w}(\lambda_o)$ based on the history of price-demand pairs. Our analysis in Section 6.1 shows that, if the relative error in estimating $\dot{w}(\lambda_o)$ is less than $100\times(1-\eta)\%$, the algorithm given by Proposition 1 remains stable. For instance, if $\eta = 0.5$, the relative error bound is 50%, which is a tractable requirement for most estimation algorithms. Moreover, for a smaller η that is set to increase resilience to attacks, the error bound will be larger. As the focus of this paper is to analyze the fundamental impact of integrity attacks on system stability under the control law in Proposition 1, we do not elaborate on the estimation algorithm, and the analysis in Section 5 assumes that the ISO can accurately estimate $\dot{w}(\lambda_o)$. Section 6.1 also discusses the impact of inaccurate $\dot{w}(\lambda_o)$ on the security analysis.

The price stabilization algorithm in Proposition 1 assumes a fixed operating point λ_o. However, intuitively, if the operating point λ_o adapts to the current price, the linear approximations to $s(\lambda)$ and $w(\lambda)$ can be more accurate. Specifically, by setting $\lambda_o = \lambda_{k-1}$, we have the following algorithm:

$$\lambda_k = \lambda_{k-1} - \frac{2\eta}{\dot{s}(\lambda_{k-1}) - \dot{w}(\lambda_{k-1})} \cdot e_{k-1}. \quad (2)$$

Although there is a lack of rigorous theory to support the technique of adapting λ_o to the current price, our numerical experiments show that the algorithm in Eq. (2) is always stable under all the settings shown in Fig. 3. The numerical examples and simulations conducted in the rest of this paper employ the algorithm in Eq. (2). Fig. 5(a) shows the evolution of price with fixed baseline load. When $\eta = 0.5$, λ_k converges to λ^* after two pricing periods. When $\eta = 0.2$, the system has a longer settling time. When $\eta = 0.8$, the price oscillates but converges. The oscillation is caused by a negative pole [24]. Fig. 5 will also be used as a running example in Section 5 to illustrate the impact of attacks.

5. INTEGRITY ATTACKS TO RTP

This section studies the impact of two integrity attacks on RTP systems under the RTP scheme given by Proposition 1.

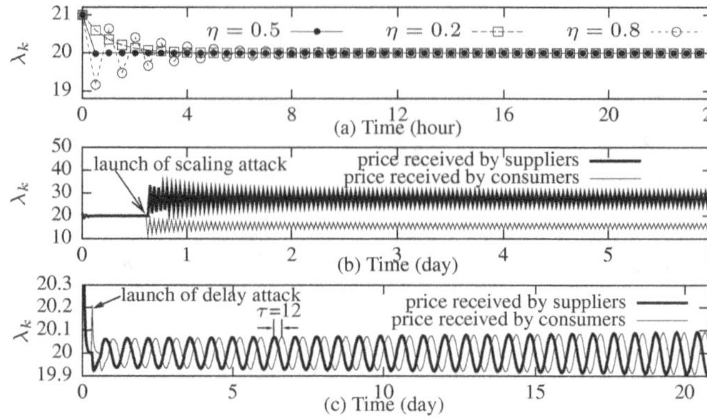

Figure 5: A running example under the linear supply and CEO demand models ($T = 0.5$, $\epsilon = -0.8$, $b_k = 2000$, $\lambda^* = 20$, $\lambda_0 = 21$). (a) Price stabilization; (b) Scaling attack ($\eta = 0.8$, $\rho = 1$, $\gamma = 0.57$); (c) Delay attack ($\eta = 0.2$, $\rho = 1$, $\tau = 12$).

5.1 Attack Models and Impact Metrics

We consider integrity attacks on the price signals received by a subset of consumers. If the price signal received by a consumer is subject to attack, the price signal applied for the current pricing period (denoted by λ'_k) is different from the true price λ_k. The integrity attacks on the price signals can be launched in different ways. For instance, once the adversary has compromised the intermediate nodes in the communication network of the smart grid (e.g., routers) and obtained the decryption/encryption keys held by the ISO and/or smart meters, the adversary can intercept and forge price data packets. Moreover, recent reverse engineering and penetration tests [22, 26] have shown that many smart meters lack basic security measures to ensure integrity and authenticity of the input/output data. These security vulnerabilities can be exploited to maliciously change the price signals. We would like to point out that the integrity attacks do pose strong requirements for the adversary. They require that the adversary is able to modify the price information, either at the source, during transmissions, or at the smart meters. However, these attacks in a cyber environment are certainly feasible and credible, and it would be wrongfully complacent to ignore their possibility. In this paper, as the price signals sent to the centralized suppliers are often well protected, we assume that they are not subject to attacks. However, our analysis framework can be easily extended to account for possible attacks on the suppliers.

5.1.1 Attack Models

As the number of consumers in a smart grid is often large, the number of compromised consumers is an important metric for the adversary's capability and resource availability. Let C' denote the set of consumers whose price signals are compromised, where $C' \subseteq C$, and $w'(\lambda_k)$ denote the total price-responsive demand in the presence of an attack. Thus, $w'(\lambda_k) = \sum_{j\in C'} w_j(\lambda'_k) + \sum_{j\in C\setminus C'} w_j(\lambda_k)$. We define

$$\rho = \frac{\sum_{j\in C'} w_j(\lambda'_k)}{\sum_{j\in C} w_j(\lambda'_k)} = \frac{\sum_{j\in C'} w_j(\lambda'_k)}{w(\lambda'_k)}, \quad (3)$$

which characterizes the fraction of consumers receiving the compromised price signals. If the consumers are *homoge-*

neous (i.e., $w_j(\cdot)$ is same for all j), ρ is a constant, i.e., $\rho = |C'|/|C|$. If they are heterogeneous, ρ is a function of λ'_k. The extensive numerical evaluation in [30] shows that, if the heterogeneous consumers follow the CEO model, $\rho \simeq |C'|/|C|$ with a variation of less than 0.003 and hence can be practically treated as a constant. Moreover, we make the following approximation:

$$\sum\nolimits_{j\in C\setminus C'} w_j(\lambda_k) \simeq (1-\rho)\sum\nolimits_{j\in C'} w_j(\lambda_k) = (1-\rho)w(\lambda_k). \quad (4)$$

The numerical evaluation in [30] shows that relative approximation error of Eq. (4) is less than 1%. Therefore, in the presence of integrity attacks, we have

$$w'(\lambda_k) \simeq \rho w(\lambda'_k) + (1-\rho)w(\lambda_k). \quad (5)$$

If the price signals can be arbitrarily modified, the capability requirements of an adversary would be high. In this paper, we consider "constrained" integrity attacks, where the malicious modifications follow certain rules and can be realized with lower capability and resource requirements. Note that the adversary must be able to cause more severe damage to the system if she is assumed to be able to modify the price signals arbitrarily. An attack can be characterized by the parameters for the rule, which is denoted by $\mathcal{A}$. We consider two kinds of integrity attacks:

Scaling attack $\mathcal{A} = (\rho, \gamma)$: The compromised price is a scaled version of the true price, i.e., $\lambda'_k = \gamma\lambda_k$, $\gamma \in \mathbb{R}^+$.

Delay attack $\mathcal{A} = (\rho, \tau)$: The compromised price is an old price, i.e., $\lambda'_k = \lambda_{k-\tau}$, $\tau \in \mathbb{Z}^+$.

These two attacks can be launched in various ways. The price values or time stamps in data packets sent to the smart meters can be maliciously modified during transmissions in vulnerable communication networks. Moreover, they can be launched in indirect ways. For instance, the delay attack can be launched by modifying the smart meters' internal clocks. Smart meters typically assign a memory buffer to store received prices. If a smart meter's clock has a lag, it will store newly received prices in the buffer and apply an old price for the present. Furthermore, attacks on the clocks can be realized by compromising vulnerable time synchronization protocols or the time servers that provide timing information to the smart meters. A few smart meter products [28] synchronize their clocks via a built-in GPS receiver, which is vulnerable and subject to remote attacks that are effective across large geographic areas [23].

In this paper, we assume that at most one kind of attack is in effect. Moreover, we assume that the attack parameters are the same for all the compromised consumers. For instance, if a delay attack with $\tau = 2$ is launched, all the compromised consumers experience the same delay of two pricing periods. These simplifications allow us to better understand the impact of each attack on the RTP system, which is the basis for understanding more complex scenarios such as heterogeneous attack parameters and combinations of attack types. In Section 6.2, we will briefly discuss how to extend our analysis to address these more complex cases.

5.1.2 Attack Impact Metrics

This section defines two metrics for the impact of the integrity attacks on system stability. We first define the *marginal demand-supply ratio*, which is a quantity that can significantly affect the system stability under attacks.

DEFINITION 1. *Marginal demand-supply ratio is* $h = \left|\frac{\dot{w}(\lambda_o)}{\dot{s}(\lambda_o)}\right|$.

From Definition 1, h depends on the operating point λ_o. As discussed in Section 4.3, the gain coefficient η of the price stabilization algorithm affects the system stability in a major way. Therefore, we define the following metric:

DEFINITION 2. *Given attack $\mathcal{A}$, the* region of operating point stability *under attack, denoted by* $\text{ROS}_{\lambda_o}(\mathcal{A})$, *is*

$\text{ROS}_{\lambda_o}(\mathcal{A}) = \{(h,\eta)|\textit{The system is stable under attack } \mathcal{A}\}$.

The above metric depends on λ_o. We define a second metric that is independent of λ_o:

DEFINITION 3. *Given attack $\mathcal{A}$, the* region of stability *under attack, denoted by* $\text{ROS}(\mathcal{A})$, *is*

$\text{ROS}(\mathcal{A}) = \{\eta|\textit{The system is stable under attack } \mathcal{A}, \forall h > 0\}$.

The above two metrics are important for understanding the impact of integrity attacks on the stability of the RTP system under the price stabilization algorithm in Proposition 1. In particular, the $\text{ROS}(\mathcal{A})$ specifies the range of η that ensures system stability under attack $\mathcal{A}$. Hence, the ROS allows us to compare the impacts of different integrity attacks. For two attacks $\mathcal{A}_1$ and $\mathcal{A}_2$, if $\text{ROS}(\mathcal{A}_1) \subset \text{ROS}(\mathcal{A}_2)$, the ISO has more flexibility in setting η under $\mathcal{A}_2$ than $\mathcal{A}_1$, to achieve faster convergence. Thus, the system is more resilient to $\mathcal{A}_2$ than $\mathcal{A}_1$. From the adversary's perspective, $\mathcal{A}_1$ is more effective than $\mathcal{A}_2$. Note that, when the RTP system with $\eta \in \text{ROS}(\mathcal{A})$ is stable under attack $\mathcal{A}$, the compromised consumers may still experience monetary losses and the system may run at low efficiency. However, this paper focuses on the impact of attacks on the system stability, which is a fundamental system requirement. In Sections 5.2 and 5.3, we will derive the ROS_{λ_o} and ROS for the scaling and delay attacks.

5.2 Impact of Scaling Attack

The local linearization of Eq. (5) with $\lambda'_k = \gamma\lambda_k$ is

$$\begin{aligned} w'(\lambda_k) \simeq & \rho \cdot (w(\gamma\lambda_o) + \dot{w}(\gamma\lambda_o)\cdot(\gamma\lambda_k - \gamma\lambda_o)) \\ & + (1-\rho)\cdot(w(\lambda_o) + \dot{w}(\lambda_o)\cdot(\lambda_k - \lambda_o)). \end{aligned}$$

By collecting the price-independent terms with b_k, the transfer function of the price-dependent component is $G_w(z) = \rho\gamma\dot{w}(\gamma\lambda_o) + (1-\rho)\dot{w}(\lambda_o)$. To make the analysis tractable, for the scaling attack, we only focus on a class of price-responsive demand models that satisfy $\dot{w}(\gamma\lambda) = \dot{w}(\lambda)\cdot\mu(\gamma|\Theta)$, where Θ is the set of model parameters of $w(\cdot)$ and the function $\mu(\gamma|\Theta)$ is independent of λ and always positive. Such a $\dot{w}(\cdot)$ is said to be *decomposable.* For instance, under the CEO model, $\Theta = \{D, \epsilon\}$, and $\mu(\gamma|\Theta) = \gamma^{\epsilon-1}$. For simplicity of exposition, we denote $\mu(\gamma|\Theta)$ as μ in the rest of this paper. Therefore, $G_w(z) = \rho\gamma\mu\dot{w}(\lambda_o) + (1-\rho)\dot{w}(\lambda_o)$, and $G_p(z) = G_s(z) - G_w(z) = \dot{s}(\lambda_o) - \rho\gamma\mu\dot{w}(\lambda_o) - (1-\rho)\dot{w}(\lambda_o)$. The closed-loop transfer function [24] under the attack is

$$T_c(z) = \frac{G_c(z)G_p(z)}{1+G_c(z)G_p(z)H(z)} = \frac{2\eta(1+\rho\gamma\mu h+h-\rho h)z}{P(z)},$$

where the *system characteristic function* $P(z) = (h+1)(z-1) + 2\eta(1+\rho\gamma\mu h + h - \rho h)$. Note that $G_p(z)$, $H(z)$, and $G_c(z)$ have been obtained in Section 4.3.

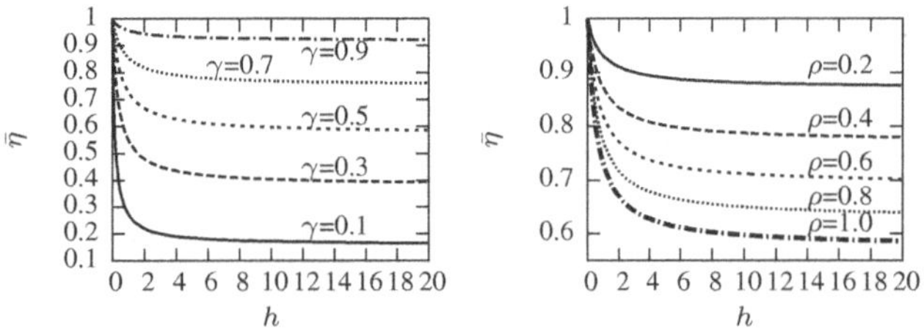

(a) $\rho = 1$ (b) $\gamma = 0.5$

Figure 6: Stability boundaries under scaling attack, abstract supply model, and CEO demand model ($\epsilon = -0.8$, ROS_{λ_o} are the regions below the boundaries).

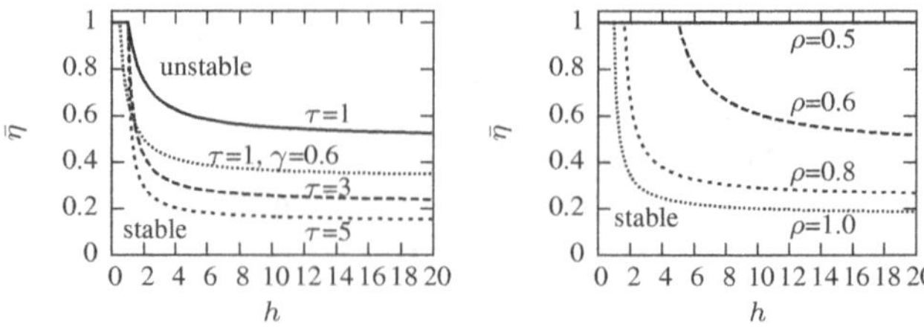

(a) $\rho = 1$ (b) $\tau = 4$

Figure 7: Stability boundaries under delay attack and abstract supply/demand models. (In the left figure, the curve with $\tau = 1$ and $\gamma = 0.6$ is for combined attack discussed in Section 6.2.)

5.2.1 Region of Operating Point Stability

PROPOSITION 2. *For the linearized system based on a fixed operating point λ_o and a decomposable $\dot{w}(\cdot)$, $\text{ROS}_{\lambda_o}(\rho, \gamma) = \{(h, \eta) | 0 < \eta < \min\{1, \bar{\eta}\}, \forall h > 0\}$, where*

$$\bar{\eta} = \frac{h+1}{h+1+\rho h(\gamma\mu - 1)}. \tag{6}$$

PROOF. If all the poles of $T_c(z)$ (i.e., roots of $P(z)$) are within the unit circle centered at the origin of z-plane, the system is stable [24]. If $\eta < \bar{\eta}$, the pole is within the circle. As $\eta \in (0, 1)$, η takes the minimum of 1 and $\bar{\eta}$. □

Remark 1. Under the CEO demand model, by replacing $\mu = \gamma^{\epsilon-1}$ in Eq. (6), we have $\bar{\eta} = \frac{h+1}{h+1+\rho h(\gamma^{\epsilon}-1)}$. Fig. 6 plots the stability boundaries when $\epsilon = -0.8$, where the ROS_{λ_o} are the regions below the boundaries. We can see that the ROS_{λ_o} shrinks with increased ρ and decreased γ. This can be easily proved by the monotonicity of $\bar{\eta}$. Moreover, it is consistent with the intuitions that (i) the system becomes more unstable when more consumers are compromised, and (ii) the increased demand due to a decreased γ poses more challenges to the system.

We now use the numerical example in Fig. 5(b) to verify our analysis. Fig. 5(b) shows the price signals received by the suppliers and consumers, respectively, when $\gamma = 0.57$. We can see that the price does not converge. The average value of h is 0.850, which falls in the unstable region ($h > 0.786$) according to the analytical ROS_{λ_o}. Note that when $\gamma = 0.59$, the price converges and the average value of h is 0.862, which falls in the stable region ($h < 0.908$) according to the analytical ROS_{λ_o}. Therefore, Proposition 2 successfully characterizes the critical stability boundary. Note that, as the settings for Fig. 5(b) are close to the stability boundary, the price oscillates in a small range. For smaller γ, the price can severely oscillate, as shown in Section 7.

5.2.2 Region of Stability

PROPOSITION 3. *For the linearized system based on a decomposable $\dot{w}(\cdot)$, when $\gamma\mu \in (0, 1]$, $\text{ROS}(\rho, \gamma) = \{\eta | 0 < \eta < 1\}$; when $\gamma\mu > 1$, $\text{ROS}(\rho, \gamma) = \{\eta | 0 < \eta < \inf_{h>0} \bar{\eta}\}$, where $\inf_{h>0} \bar{\eta} = \frac{1}{1+\rho(\gamma\mu-1)}$.*

PROOF. When $\gamma\mu \in (0, 1]$, $\bar{\eta} \geq 1$. From Proposition 2, if $0 < \eta < 1$, the system is stable regardless of h. When $\gamma\mu > 1$, $\bar{\eta}$ is a bounded decreasing function of h. Its infimum $\inf_{h>0} \bar{\eta} = \lim_{h\to+\infty} \bar{\eta} = \frac{1}{1+\rho(\gamma\mu-1)}$. Therefore, if $0 < \eta < \inf_{h>0} \bar{\eta}$, the system is stable regardless of h. □

Remark 2. Under the CEO demand model, replacing $\mu = \gamma^{\epsilon-1}$ in Proposition 3 yields the following result. When $\gamma \geq 1$, $\text{ROS}(\rho, \gamma) = \{\eta | 0 < \eta < 1\}$; when $\gamma \in (0, 1)$, $\text{ROS}(\rho, \gamma) = \{\eta | 0 < \eta < \inf_{h>0} \bar{\eta}\}$, where $\inf_{h>0} \bar{\eta} = \frac{1}{1+\rho(\gamma^{\epsilon}-1)}$. Therefore, under the CEO model, if the adversary amplifies the price, the system remains stable. This result is consistent with the intuition that decreased demand due to the amplified price poses no challenges to the system. Fig. 8(a) plots $\inf_{h>0} \bar{\eta}$ when $\epsilon = -0.8$. We can see that ROS shrinks with increased ρ and decreased γ. This can be easily proved by the monotonicity of $\inf_{h>0} \bar{\eta}$.

5.3 Impact of Delay Attack

The local linearization of Eq. (5) with $\lambda'_k = \lambda_{k-\tau}$ is

$$\begin{aligned} w'(\lambda_k) \simeq & \rho \cdot (w(\lambda_o) + \dot{w}(\lambda_o) \cdot (\lambda_{k-\tau} - \lambda_o)) \\ & + (1-\rho) \cdot (w(\lambda_o) + \dot{w}(\lambda_o) \cdot (\lambda_k - \lambda_o)). \end{aligned}$$

By collecting the price-independent terms with b_k, the transfer function of the price-dependent component is $G_w(z) = z^{-\tau}\rho\dot{w}(\lambda_o) - (1-\rho)\dot{w}(\lambda_o)$, where $z^{-\tau}$ represent a delay of τ pricing periods. Therefore, $G_p(z) = G_s(z) - G_w(z) = \dot{s}(\lambda_o) - z^{-\tau}\rho\dot{w}(\lambda_o) - (1-\rho)\dot{w}(\lambda_o)$. The closed-loop transfer function under the attack is

$$T_c(z) = \frac{G_c(z)G_p(z)}{1+G_c(z)G_p(z)H(z)} = \frac{2\eta(1+(1-\rho)h)z^{\tau+1} + 2\rho\eta hz}{P(z)},$$

where the system characteristic function is

$$P(z) = (h+1)z^{\tau+1} + (2\eta + 2\eta(1-\rho)h - h - 1)\, z^{\tau} + 2\eta\rho h.$$

5.3.1 Region of Operating Point Stability

As $P(z)$ is a $(\tau+1)$-order polynomial, it is extremely difficult to derive the closed-form formulas for the poles of $T_c(z)$. Various methods have been developed to test the stability without explicitly solving for the poles [24]. Among them, the Jury test [24, p. 185] is preferred because the coefficients of $P(z)$ are real numbers. The Jury test constructs a table based on the coefficients of $P(z)$ and derives the stability conditions from the table. Given ρ, we can derive the closed-form ROS_{λ_o} for different τ from the Jury test. However, the expressions become more complicated for larger τ. We numerically compute the ROS_{λ_o} based on the Jury test for various settings of τ and ρ. Fig. 7 plots the stability boundaries, where the ROS_{λ_o} are the regions below the boundaries. From Fig. 7, the ROS_{λ_o} shrinks with τ and ρ, which is consistent with intuition. We have the following proposition. The proof is based on the Jury test, which is omitted due to space constraints and can be found in [30].

Algorithm 1 Compute $\mathrm{ROS}(\rho, \tau)$ when $\rho \in (0.5, 1]$

```
Input: ρ and τ
Output: lim_{h→+∞} η̄(h|ρ, τ)
 1: if τ = 1 then
 2:     return 1/(2·ρ)
 3: end if
 4: X = 1, Y = 2ηρ, Z = 2ηρ(1 − 2η(1 − ρ))
 5: for i = 1 to τ do
 6:     U = X·X − Y·Y,  V = Z,  W = (X·Z·Z)/Y
 7:     X = U,  Y = V,  Z = W
 8: end for
 9: Q(η|ρ) = X·X − Y·Y − Z
10: return minimum root of Q(η|ρ) = 0 over η ∈ (0, 1)
```

Note: Line 4 to Line 9 are symbolic calculation, where the bold capitals are symbolic expressions of η and ρ.

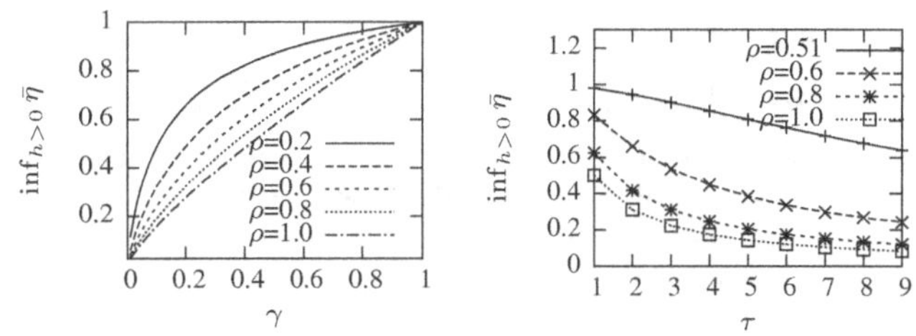

(a) Scaling attack (abstract supply model and CEO demand model with ϵ=-0.8)

(b) Delay attack (abstract supply and demand models)

Figure 8: Upper bound of ROS.

PROPOSITION 4. *For the linearized system with a fixed operating point* λ_o, $\mathrm{ROS}_{\lambda_o}(\rho, \tau+1) \subseteq \mathrm{ROS}_{\lambda_o}(\rho, \tau)$.

We now use the numerical example in Fig. 5 to verify our analysis. Fig. 5(c) shows the price signals received by the suppliers and consumers, respectively, when $\eta = 0.2$, $\rho = 1$, $\tau = 12$. We can see that the price diverges. The average value of h is 1.455390, which falls in the unstable region ($h > 1.447$) according to the Jury test. Note that when $\tau = 11$, the price does converge and the average value of h is 1.455335, which falls in the stable region ($h < 1.522$) according to the Jury test. Therefore, the Jury test successfully characterizes the critical stability boundary. As the settings for Fig. 5(c) are close to the stability boundary, the price diverges slowly. For larger τ, the price can diverge quickly.

5.3.2 Region of Stability

We observe from Fig. 7(b) that, when $\rho = 0.5$, the system is stable for $\eta \in (0, 1)$. We have the following proposition.

PROPOSITION 5. *For the linearized system, if* $\rho \in (0, 0.5]$, $\forall \tau \in \mathbb{Z}^+$, $\mathrm{ROS}(\rho, \tau) = \{\eta | 0 < \eta < 1\}$.

The proof can be found in the appendix, where we prove that if $\rho \in (0, 0.5]$, all roots of $P(z)$ are within the unit circle centered at the origin in the z-plane and hence the system is stable [24]. From Proposition 5, to launch a successful delay attack that destabilizes the system, the adversary has to compromise no less than a half of the consumers. The intuition behind this result is that the compromised price-responsive load must predominate to affect the operation of the system. This result poses strong requirements for the adversary. However, she could accomplish the goal by targeting shared infrastructures such as the time servers that provide timing information to all the smart meters. On the other hand, the need for the adversary to compromise a large fraction of the meters in order to be effective is indicative of the resilience of the price stabilization algorithm given by Proposition 1 to delay attacks.

We now discuss the ROS when $\rho \in (0.5, 1]$. From Fig. 7, the stability boundary curves are non-increasing and converge to limits when $h \to +\infty$. Let $\bar{\eta}(h|\rho, \tau)$ denote the stability boundary curve for particular ρ and τ. Therefore,

$$\mathrm{ROS}(\rho, \tau) = \{\eta | 0 < \eta < \lim_{h \to +\infty} \bar{\eta}(h|\rho, \tau)\}.$$

When $\tau = 1$, the limit is simply $\frac{1}{2\rho}$. However, for larger τ, it is extremely difficult to derive the closed-form formula for the limit, primarily because of the iterative nature of the Jury test. Instead, we use an algorithm to define $\mathrm{ROS}(\rho, \tau)$, which is shown in Algorithm 1. This algorithm is developed based on key observations from the Jury test procedure. Fig. 8(b) plots $\lim_{h \to +\infty} \bar{\eta}(h|\rho, \tau)$, which is computed by Algorithm 1, versus τ under various settings of ρ. We also use the Jury test to compute $\bar{\eta}(h|\rho, \tau)$ with a large setting for h (specifically, $h = 10^{10}$). The results are the same as in Fig. 8(b). From the figure, we can see that the ROS shrinks with ρ and τ, which is consistent with intuition.

6. DISCUSSIONS

In this section, we discuss the impact of inaccuracy in estimating $\dot{w}(\lambda_o)$ on the analysis in the previous sections. We also discuss how to extend our analysis to address more complicated attack models.

6.1 Impact of Inaccuracy in Estimating $\dot{w}(\lambda_o)$

As the price-dependent demand model $w(\cdot)$ is unknown to the ISO, we derive an upper bound for the error in estimating $\dot{w}(\lambda_o)$, to ensure the stability of the algorithm in Proposition 1. Let $\widetilde{\dot{w}(\lambda_o)}$ denote the estimated $\dot{w}(\lambda_o)$, and $E_w = \frac{\dot{w}(\lambda_o) - \widetilde{\dot{w}(\lambda_o)}}{\dot{w}(\lambda_o)}$ denote the relative estimation error. The stability condition $0 < \eta < 1$ can be rewritten as $0 < \frac{2\eta}{\dot{s}(\lambda_o) - \dot{w}(\lambda_o)} < \frac{2}{\dot{s}(\lambda_o) - \dot{w}(\lambda_o)}$. As long as $0 < \frac{2\eta}{\dot{s}(\lambda_o) - \widetilde{\dot{w}(\lambda_o)}} < \frac{2}{\dot{s}(\lambda_o) - \dot{w}(\lambda_o)}$, the system is stable. This condition can be derived as $E_w < (1-\eta)\left(1 - \frac{\dot{s}(\lambda_o)}{\dot{w}(\lambda_o)}\right)$. As $1 - \frac{\dot{s}(\lambda_o)}{\dot{w}(\lambda_o)} > 1$, $E_w < (1-\eta)$ is a sufficient condition for stability.

We now discuss the impact of inaccurate $\widetilde{\dot{w}(\lambda_o)}$ on the security analysis results in Section 5. From the definition of E_w, we have $\widetilde{\dot{w}(\lambda_o)} = (1 - E_w)\dot{w}(\lambda_o)$. Note that $E_w < 1$ since $\widetilde{\dot{w}(\lambda_o)} > 0$. By replacing h with $|1 - E_w| \cdot h$ in Proposition 2, we have a new result in the presence of the estimation error E_w. From the proofs of Propositions 3, 4, and 5, they are independent of h. Therefore, these propositions still hold in the presence of estimation errors.

6.2 Superimposed and Heterogeneous Attacks

In this section, we discuss how to extend our analysis framework to address a class of integrity attacks that are the superimposition of scaling and delay attacks. We also discuss how to adapt our analysis to scenarios in which the attack models/parameters are different for different compromised consumers.

From discrete-time control theory [24], our analysis framework can be applied to derive the ROS_{λ_o} and ROS under any integrity attack that can be modeled as a linear time-invariant (LTI) system with the transfer function $\frac{\Lambda'(z)}{\Lambda(z)} = \frac{\sum_{i=0}^{n} a_i z^{-i}}{\sum_{j=0}^{m} b_j z^{-j}}$, where the $\Lambda(z)$ and $\Lambda'(z)$ are the z-transforms of λ_k and λ'_k. In the time domain, λ'_k is given by the linear combination of λ_{k-i} and λ'_{k-j}, where $0 \le i \le n$ and $1 \le j \le m$. The scaling and delay attacks studied in Section 5 are special cases of this general attack model. For instance, under the delay attack, $b_0 = 1$, $b_j = 0$ for $j \ge 1$, $a_\tau = 1$, $a_i = 0$ for $i \ne \tau$. This general attack model can also be regarded as the superimposition of scaling and delay attacks. We now illustrate the enhanced impact of attack superimposition using a simple example: $\lambda'_k = \gamma \cdot \lambda_{k-\tau}$. Under this attack superimposition, the closed-loop system characteristic function of Eq. (5) is

$$P(z) = (h+1)z^{\tau+1} + (2\eta + 2\eta(1-\rho)h - h - 1)z^{\tau} + 2\eta\rho h\gamma\mu,$$

where μ is defined in Section 5.2. We can still apply the Jury test to derive the $\mathrm{ROS}_{\lambda_o}(\rho, \gamma, \tau)$ and $\mathrm{ROS}(\rho, \gamma, \tau)$. Fig. 7(a) shows the stability boundary for this attack superimposition with $\rho = 1$, $\gamma = 0.6$, and $\tau = 1$. The ROS_{λ_o} of this attack superimposition is smaller than the delay attack with $\rho = 1$ and $\tau = 1$, which means stronger attack impact.

If two subsets of consumers are subject to two different attacks that happen simultaneously in the grid, Eq. (5) can be rewritten as $w'(\lambda_k) = \rho_1 w(\lambda'_k) + \rho_2 w(\lambda''_k) + (1-\rho_1-\rho_2)w(\lambda_k)$, where ρ_1 and ρ_2 are the fractions of consumers subject to the two attacks, and λ'_k and λ''_k are the corresponding compromised prices. Our analysis framework still applies once the models of λ'_k and λ''_k are specified. The attack with different parameters (e.g., consumers are subject to different delays) can be treated as simultaneous attacks.

7. TRACE-DRIVEN SIMULATIONS

We use GridLAB-D [2], an electric power distribution system simulator, to evaluate the impact of integrity attacks. GridLAB-D captures many physical characteristics such as power line capacities and impedances. Hence, we can validate our analysis under the realism provided by GridLAB-D. Moreover, it can record emergency events that occur when the current ratings of lines and power ratings of transformers are exceeded. Such events could cause sustained service interruptions to consumers. These events are of particular interest to us, because they help us understand the physical consequences caused by the integrity attacks.

7.1 Simulation Methodology and Settings

We use a distribution feeder specification [27], which covers a moderately populated urban area and comprises 1405 houses, 2134 buses, 3314 triplex buses, 1944 transformers, 1543 overhead lines, 335 underground lines, and 1631 triplex lines. For this small-scale distribution feeder, locational prices are usually not applicable and hence all the houses are subject to the same price as discussed in Section 3.1. By leveraging the extensibility of GridLAB-D, we develop new modules that implement the CEO model for each single house, the price stabilization algorithm in Eq. (2), and the attack strategies. We measure the instantaneous power of the entire feeder at the root node. Its peak value over the previous pricing period is used as $d(\lambda_{k-1})$ in Eq. (2). As we focus on evaluating the physical consequences of attacks, we do not simulate the logistics of the attacks and assume that the adversary can gain access to the meters of his choosing. Specifically, if a house is not subject to attacks, it directly reads the real-time price from the *ISO module*; otherwise, it reads the price from an *adversary module* that modifies the price according to the attack models. All the attacks are launched after the system has converged.

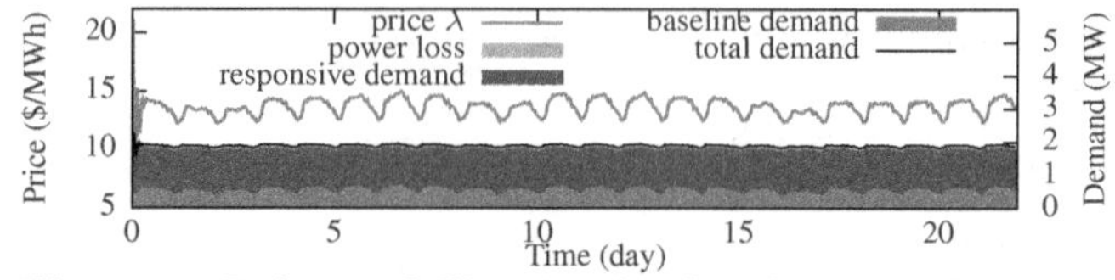

Figure 9: Price stabilization in the absence of attack.

We adopt the CEO demand model for each single house, where the parameters are drawn from normal distributions: $D_i \sim \mathcal{N}(7, 3.5^2)$ (unit: kW) and $\epsilon_i \sim \mathcal{N}(-0.8, 0.1^2)$. Under this setting, if the price is within $[10, 20]$, the per-house price-responsive demand is within $[0.65, 1.1]$ kW. To improve the realism of the simulations, we use the half-hourly total demand trace from March 1st to 22nd, 2013, of NSW, Australia, provided by AEMO [1] as the baseline load. The baseline load of a single house is set to be a scaled version of the real data trace. The resultant range of the per-house baseline load is $[0.276, 0.488]$ kW. Hence, when the price is within $[10, 20]$, the demand of a household is within $[0.9, 1.6]$ kW, which is consistent with the average demand of a household in reality [3]. In our simulations, the price is updated every half an hour, to be consistent with the setting of the demand data traces [1]. In each pricing period, the simulated demand remains constant. For the supply model, the settings obtained in Fig. 1 (i.e., $p = 152$ and $q = 4503$) are for the whole NSW region. They must be scaled down to fit the simulated feeder with 1405 houses. From the facts that there are 2.8 million households in NSW [3] and 57% of AEMO's supply is for residential demand [9, p. 15], the two parameters are scaled as follows: $p = \frac{57\% \times 152}{2800000/1405} = 43.638 \times 10^{-3}$ and $q = \frac{57\% \times 4503}{2800000/1405} = 1.287$. Other default settings include: $T = 0.5$, $\lambda_{\min} = 1$, $\lambda_{\max} = 200$, and $\eta = 0.5$.

7.2 Simulation Results

Price stabilization: The first set of simulations evaluate the effectiveness of the direct feedback approach [25] and our control-theoretic price stabilization algorithm in Eq. (2). In the simulations, the direct feedback approach is unstable, where the price oscillates between $\lambda_{\min}$ and $\lambda_{\max}$. The total demand reaches 10 MW a few hours after the start of the simulation, and GridLAB-D reports that four distribution lines are overloaded. Fig. 9 plots the price and resultant demands under our price stabilization approach in Eq. (2). We can see that the price fluctuates slightly for a few hours after the start of the simulation, due to an inappropriate initial price. After the system converges, it can well adapt to the time-varying baseline load. The generation scheduling error is close to zero, which means that the clearing price is achieved. We also evaluate the impact of an inaccurate consumer model $w(\lambda) = \widetilde{D}\lambda^{\widetilde{\epsilon}}$ on the system performance. The evaluation results are consistent with our analysis in Section 6.1. For instance, when $\eta = 0.5$, the system keeps stable if i) $(D - \widetilde{D})/D < 0.67$ and $\widetilde{\epsilon} = \epsilon$, or ii) $0.05\epsilon < \widetilde{\epsilon} < 2.15\epsilon$ and $\widetilde{D} = D$. Therefore, the price stabilization algorithm is resilient to inaccuracies of the estimated consumer model.

Scaling attack: Fig. 10 plots the true and compromised prices, as well as the breakdown of demand under the scal-

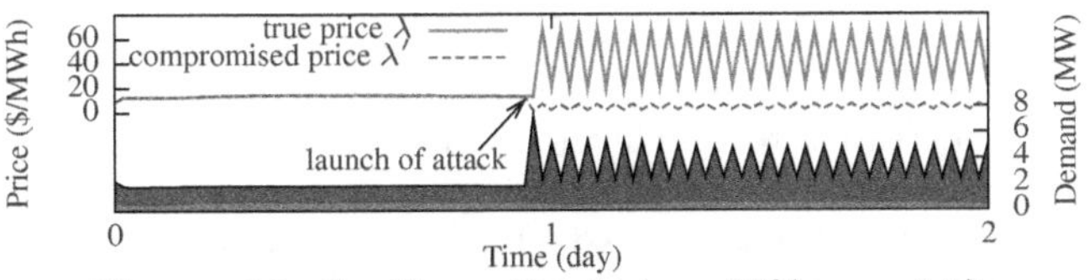

Figure 10: Scaling attack ($\rho = 65\%$, $\gamma = 0.1$).

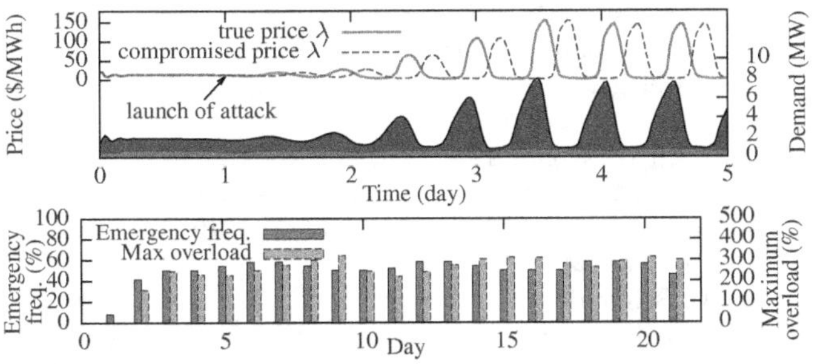

Figure 11: Impact of delay attack ($\rho = 100\%$, $\tau = 9$). (a) Prices and demands; (b) emergencies.

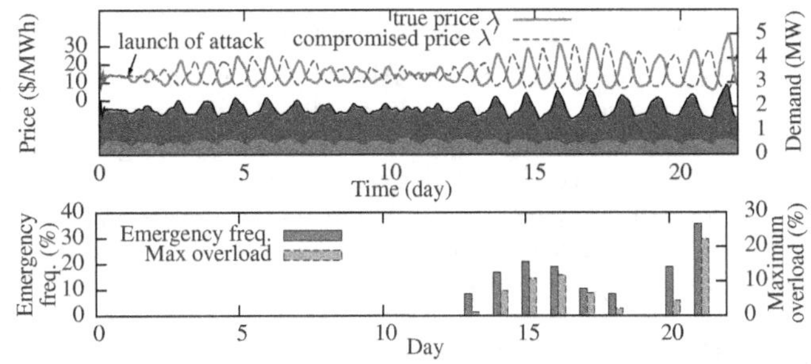

Figure 12: Impact of delay attack ($\rho = 65\%$, $\tau = 24$). (a) Prices and demands; (b) emergencies.

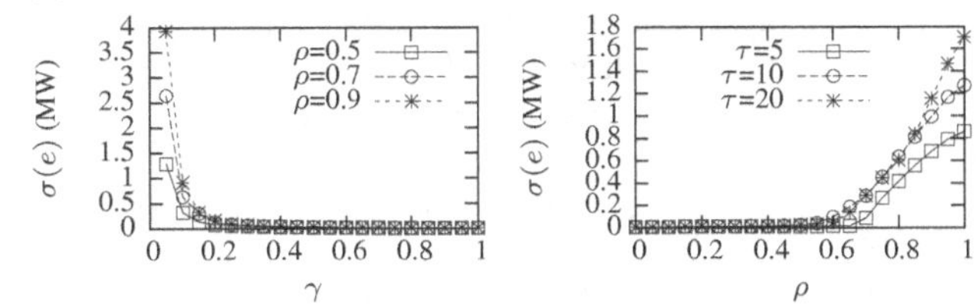

(a) Scaling attack (b) Delay attack

Figure 13: System volatility under attacks.

ing attack. We can see that the price as well as the demand fluctuates severely. GridLAB-D reports excessive distribution line overload events after the launch of the attack. We also extensively evaluate the impact of the scaling attack with different settings of ρ and γ. We use the standard deviation of the generation scheduling error after the launch of the attack, denoted by $\sigma(e)$, as the system volatility metric. A near-zero $\sigma(e)$ means convergence, while a considerably large $\sigma(e)$ means oscillation or divergence. Fig. 13(a) plots $\sigma(e)$ versus γ under various settings of ρ. We can see that the system volatility increases with ρ and decreases with γ.

Delay attack: Fig. 11(a) and Fig. 12(a) show the evolution of price and the breakdown of demand under the delay attacks with different parameters. We also investigate the emergency events reported by GridLAB-D. The *overload* of a distribution line or a transformer is defined as the percentage of the exceeded current/power with respect to the rated value. Fig. 11(b) and Fig. 12(b) plot the *emergency frequency* and maximum overload in each day. The emergency frequency is defined as the ratio of the number of pricing periods with reported emergency events to the number of pricing periods per day (i.e., 48). In Fig. 11, a small generation scheduling error caused by the time-varying baseline load will be amplified iteratively along the control loops, after the launch of the attack. The overload can be up to 350%. In practice, such a high overload will cause circuit breakers to open and hence regional blackouts. In Fig. 12, the system appears to diverge and then converge again without causing any emergencies. However, it diverges again from the 12th day due to the changing baseline load, causing excessive emergencies. This illustrates the stealthiness of the delay attack that causes marginal system stability. Lastly, we evaluate the impact of the delay attack with different settings of ρ and τ. The results are shown in Fig. 13(b). We can clearly see that when $\rho < 0.5$, the system remains stable, which is consistent with Proposition 5.

8. CONCLUSION

This paper systematically investigates the impact of scaling and delay attacks on the stability of RTP systems. We characterize the impact using a control-theoretic metric, *region of stability*. We show that, to destabilize the RTP system, it is necessary for the adversary to reduce the price in a scaling attack or compromise more than half of the smart meters in a delay attack. We conduct trace-driven simulations to validate our analysis. The results of this paper improve our understanding of the security of RTP systems so that suitable defensive measures can be taken.

8.1 Limitations and Future Work

In this paper, we have made a few simplifying assumptions and have pointed them out. Care is thus required when applying our results to general real-world settings, e.g., large-scale smart grids, where locational prices are important. Particularly, Propositions 1 to 5 are based on the linearized abstract supply and demand models at a fixed operating point.[3] The security analysis in Propositions 2 to 5 is based on the approximate aggregate demand model in Eq. (5). These simplifications enable us to study the RTP susceptibility to malicious attacks under LTI settings. However, for systems that involve non-linear, time-variant, or stochastic components and complex market structures, the LTI assumptions may not hold and our analysis may lead to inaccuracies in characterizing such systems.

It is interesting for further research to address the following issues not considered in this paper. First, our analysis framework can be extended to address attacks that cannot be modeled as LTI systems. Second, for large-scale systems where locational prices are important, the system behavior may deviate from our analysis when the power network is congested due to price oscillations. Locational prices can be considered by integrating economic dispatch into the analysis. Third, this paper considers simplified system models while preserving the principles of RTP. Extensions are possible that consider various practical factors such as suppliers' ramp constraints, energy storage, load shifting, bidding markets, and ex-ante RTP with ex-post adjustments.

[3]The numerical results and simulations use the algorithm in Eq. (2), which uses the current price as the operating point.

9. ACKNOWLEDGEMENTS

We thank our shepherd Dr. Alvaro A. Cárdenas and the anonymous reviewers for providing valuable feedback on this work. This work was supported in part by Singapore's Agency for Science, Technology and Research (A⋆STAR) under the Human Sixth Sense Programme, and in part by U.S. National Science Foundation under grant numbers CNS-0963715 and CNS-0964086.

10. REFERENCES

[1] Austrilian energy market operator. `www.aemo.com.au`.

[2] GridLAB-D. `www.gridlabd.org`.

[3] How energy is used in the home. `www.bit.ly/h9YHzV`.

[4] Multiple vulnerabilities in NTP. `www.bit.ly/GzDJ5a`.

[5] PJM operational data. `www.bit.ly/diyZ9t`.

[6] RTP-HA-2 program. `www.georgiapower.com`.

[7] F. Alvarado. The stability of power system markets. *IEEE Trans. Power Syst.*, 14(2):505–511, 1999.

[8] S. Amin, X. Litrico, S. Sastry, and A. M. Bayen. Cyber security of water SCADA systems-Part I: Analysis and experimentation of stealthy deception attacks. *IEEE Trans. Control Syst. Technol.*, 2012.

[9] Australian Energy market operator. 2011 national electricity forecasting. `www.bit.ly/ZQzkOs`.

[10] G. Barbose, C. Goldman, R. Bharvirkar, N. Hopper, M. Ting, and B. Neenan. Real time pricing as a default or optional service for C&I customers: A comparative analysis of eight case studies. Technical report, Lawrence Berkeley National Laborary, 2005.

[11] A. A. Cárdenas, S. Amin, Z.-S. Lin, Y.-L. Huang, C.-Y. Huang, and S. Sastry. Attacks against process control systems: risk assessment, detection, and response. In *ASIACCS*, 2011.

[12] A. A. Cárdenas, S. Amin, and S. Sastry. Secure control: Towards survivable cyber-physical systems. In *1st Intl. Workshop on Cyber-Physical Systems*, 2008.

[13] M. Filippini. Short-and long-run time-of-use price elasticities in Swiss residential electricity demand. *Energy Policy*, 39(10):5811–5817, 2011.

[14] S. Fleten and E. Pettersen. Constructing bidding curves for a price-taking retailer in the norwegian electricity market. *IEEE Trans. Power Syst.*, 20(2):701–708, 2005.

[15] J. Grainger and W. Stevenson. *Power system analysis.* McGraw-Hill, 1994.

[16] L. Jia, R. J. Thomas, and L. Tong. Impacts of malicious data on real-time price of electricity market operations. In *Intl. Conf. System Sciences*, 2012.

[17] O. Kosut, L. Jia, R. J. Thomas, and L. Tong. Malicious data attacks on the smart grid. *IEEE Trans. Smart Grid*, 2(4):645–658, 2011.

[18] P. Kundur. *Power system stability and control.* Tata McGraw-Hill Education, 1994.

[19] M. G. Lijesen. The real-time price elasticity of electricity. *Energy economics*, 29(2):249–258, 2007.

[20] J. Lin, W. Yu, X. Yang, G. Xu, and W. Zhao. On false data injection attacks against distributed energy routing in smart grid. In *ICCPS*, 2012.

[21] Y. Liu, P. Ning, and M. K. Reiter. False data injection attacks against state estimation in electric power grids. In *CCS*, 2009.

[22] S. McLaughlin, D. Podkuiko, S. Miadzvezhanka, A. Delozier, and P. McDaniel. Multi-vendor penetration testing in the advanced metering infrastructure. In *ACSAC*, 2010.

[23] T. Nighswander, B. Ledvina, J. Diamond, R. Brumley, and D. Brumley. GPS software attacks. In *CCS*, 2012.

[24] K. Ogata. *Discrete-time control systems.* Prentice-Hall Englewood Cliffs, NJ, 2 edition, 1995.

[25] M. Roozbehani, M. Dahleh, and S. Mitter. Volatility of power grids under real-time pricing. *IEEE Trans. Power Syst.*, 27(4):1926–1940, 2012.

[26] I. Rouf, H. Mustafa, M. Xu, W. Xu, R. Miller, and M. Gruteser. Neighborhood watch: security and privacy analysis of automatic meter reading systems. In *CCS*, 2012.

[27] K. P. Schneider, Y. Chen, D. P. Chassin, R. Pratt, D. Engel, and S. Thompson. Modern grid initiative distribution taxonomy final report. Technical report, Pacific Northwest National Laborary, 2008.

[28] Schneider Electric. Technical note of ION smart meter. `www.bit.ly/15W9GR4`.

[29] J. Sweeny. *The California electricity crisis.* Hoover Institution Press, 2002.

[30] R. Tan, V. Badrinath Krishna, D. K. Y. Yau, and Z. Kalbarczyk. Impact of integrity attacks on real-time pricing in smart grids. Technical report, Advanced Digital Sciences Center, 2013. `http://publish.illinois.edu/cps-security/files/2013/08/stability.pdf`.

[31] The Wall Street Journal. Spies penetrate U.S. electric grid. `http://on.wsj.com/fhGdG`.

[32] L. Xie, Y. Mo, and B. Sinopoli. Integrity data attacks in power market operations. *IEEE Trans. Smart Grid*, 2(4):659–666, 2011.

[33] Y. Yuan, Z. Li, and K. Ren. Modeling load redistribution attacks in power systems. *IEEE Trans. Smart Grid*, 2(2):382–390, 2011.

APPENDIX: PROOF FOR PROPOSITION 5

Denote $u_1 = h+1$, $u_2 = 2\eta + 2\eta(1-\rho)h - h - 1$, $u_3 = 2\eta\rho h$, and $P(z) = u_1 z^{\tau+1} + u_2 z^{\tau} + u_3$, where $u_1 > 0$ and $u_3 > 0$. Express any system pole (i.e., root of $P(z) = 0$) in polar coordinates: $z = A(\cos\theta + i\sin\theta)$, where $A > 0$. $P(z) = 0$ can be rewritten as two equations: $A^{\tau}(u_1 A\cos(\tau+1)\theta + u_2\cos\tau\theta) = -u_3$ and $A^{\tau}(u_1 A\sin(\tau+1)\theta + u_2\sin\tau\theta) = 0$. Adding the squares of the two equations yields $g(A) = 0$, where $g(A) = u_1^2 A^{2\tau+2} + 2u_1u_2\cos\theta A^{2\tau+1} + u_2^2 A^{2\tau} - u_3^2$. Thus, any pole satisfies $g(A) = 0$. We can verify that $g(1) > 0$ when $\rho \in (0, 0.5]$. Moreover, $\dot{g}(A) = A^{2\tau} m(A)$, where $m(A) = u_1^2(2\tau+2)A + 2u_1u_2(2\tau+1)\cos\theta + \frac{2\tau u_2^2}{A}$ is a convex function with its minimum at $A^* = \left|\frac{u_2}{u_1}\right|\sqrt{\frac{\tau}{\tau+1}}$. We can verify that $\left|\frac{u_2}{u_1}\right| < 1$ if $\rho \in (0, 0.5]$. Thus, $A^* < 1$ and the minimum of $m(A)$ for $A \geq 1$ is $m(1)$, which satisfies $m(1) \geq u_1^2(2\tau+2) - 2u_1|u_2|(2\tau+1) + 2\tau u_2^2 = 2(u_1 - |u_2|)(\tau(u_1 - |u_2|) + u_1)$. If $u_2 < 0$, $u_1 - |u_2| = 2\eta + 2\eta(1-\rho)h > 0$; if $u_2 \geq 0$, $u_1 - |u_2| = 2(1-\eta) + 2h(1 - \eta(1-\rho)) > 0$. Hence, $m(A) > 0$ and $\dot{g}(A) > 0$ for $A \geq 1$. Recalling $g(1) > 0$, we have $g(A) > 0$ for $A \geq 1$. Hence, $A < 1$ for all poles and the system is stable.

Configuration-based IDS for Advanced Metering Infrastructure

Muhammad Qasim Ali and Ehab Al-Shaer
Department of Software and Information Systems
University of North Carolina Charlotte
mali12@uncc.edu, ealshaer@uncc.edu

ABSTRACT

Smart grid deployment initiatives have been witnessed in the past recent years. Smart grids provide bi-directional communication between meters and headend system through Advanced Metering Infrastructure (AMI). Recent studies highlight the threats targeting AMI. Despite the need of tailored Intrusion Detection Systems (IDS) for the smart grid [6], very limited progress has been made in this area. Unlike traditional networks, smart grid has its own unique challenges, such as limited computational power devices and potentially high deployment cost, that restrict the deployment options of intrusion detectors. We show that smart grid exhibits deterministic and predictable behavior that can be accurately modeled to develop intrusion detection system. In this paper, we show that AMI behavior can be modeled using event logs collected at smart collectors, which in turn can be verified using the specifications invariant generated from the configurations of the AMI devices. Event logs are modeled using fourth order Markov Chain and specifications are written in Linear Temporal Logic (LTL). The approach provides robustness against evasion and mimicry attacks, however, we discuss that it still can be evaded to a certain extent. We validate our approach on a real-world dataset of thousands of meters collected at the AMI of a leading utility provider.

Categories and Subject Descriptors

C.2.0 [**Computer-Communication Networks**]: General—*Security and Protection*

Keywords

Intrusion Detection Systems; Advanced Metering Infrastructure; Smart Grid

1. INTRODUCTION

The paradigm for energy infrastructures is being shifted to a new era. Legacy infrastructures are being replaced with the state-of-the-art smart grids. In the last few years, leading utility providers have taken the initiative of shifting to smart grid in order to efficiently manage the power while providing useful features [21]. The basic premise of moving to smart grid infrastructure is to manage it efficiently while providing uninterrupted low cost energy. The new smart infrastructure supports numerous cyber and physical devices that exhibit a high level dependency. Thus, smart grid is a highly complex and critical cyber-physical system that requires very rigid security considerations.

An important core network in a smart grid is Advanced Metering Infrastructure (AMI). AMI provides bi-directional communication for monitoring and demand-response functions between end devices at customers' premise like smart meters and headend at utility provider's office. Bi-directional communication in an AMI makes it possible for an end user to use the energy efficiently at low cost. Moreover, headend system can remotely configure, upgrade, and request meter reading etc. using the AMI. This inherent criticality and availability of the AMI makes it a high potential target for the large-scale attacks that can potentially cause major regional blackout.

Despite these facts, limited progress has been made so far in order to detect malicious behavior. Recent studies including those by the federal government have shown that AMI is facing immense potential threats [6, 12, 17, 24, 25], which could affect the deployment and growth of smart grid. These outline existing vulnerabilities and exploitations, even though secure communication protocols were used. These vulnerabilities were exploited to penetrate in the AMI to gain control of a number of nodes for nefarious purposes. To countermeasure, some efforts have been made to prevent these threats [4, 5, 8].

Figure 1 presents a typical example of the AMI. This figure shows that the meters communicate with the smart collectors using various mediums and smart collectors communicate with the headend system (and vice versa) using public networks. Unlike traditional networks, AMI has its own requirements which pose significant challenges for monitoring and intrusion detection since it may require capturing network traffic. First, sensor deployment in the meters is practically infeasible due to the limited computational power and space resources at the node [22]. Second, although some researchers have suggested the meter-based sensors [4, 8, 27], smart grid providers as well as vendors firmly avoid this option due to the prohibitive cost increase associated with the large number of meter deployments. Therefore, most IDS proposals for the AMI lack practical feasibility.

CCS'13, November 4–8, 2013, Berlin, Germany.
Copyright 2013 ACM 978-1-4503-2477-9/13/11 ...$15.00.
http://dx.doi.org/10.1145/2508859.2516745.

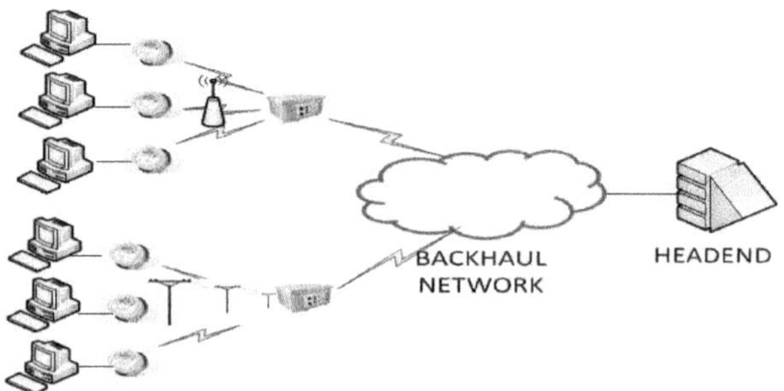

Figure 1: Basic AMI network

Deploying detection module at the smart collector provides the benefit of monitoring both the meter-collector and collector-headend communication. Moreover, AMI communication activity is by default logged at the smart collector thus it does not pose any extra burden. Although device configuration and log's integrity is protected using headend-collector key-pairing, this AMI feature was never exploited for monitoring and characterizing the AMI behavior. AMI is a special purpose network and its traffic dynamics are often very low since it supports a limited number of protocols and it is configuration-driven. Moreover, similar devices from limited vendors are usually deployed. To exploit the limited behavior, simple specification-based intrusion detection techniques are proposed in the recent literature [4] instead of traditional anomaly-based intrusion detectors.

In this paper, we present a novel device configuration based stochastic model checking intrusion detection technique. It is designed to fit the requirements and log characteristics of the AMI. We model the AMI infrastructure behavior using the logs generated at the smart collector. Stochastic model based on 4-th order markov chain is used, since it exhibits a low conditional entropy, in order to represent the AMI probabilistic behavior. Probabilistic behavior is observed as a result of its configuration and nature of the network. Specifications written in Linear Temporal Logic (LTL) are automatically generated from the a-priori known configurations of the AMI devices (smart meters and collectors), which in turn are then probabilistically verified using the stochastic model generated from the smart collector's logs. The proposed technique exhibits high accuracy and it can be easily deployed in the existing AMI of a smart grid. Moreover, the approach provides robustness against evasion and mimicry attacks, however, we discuss that it can be still evaded to a certain extent. For experimentation and evaluation we use a real-world dataset of more than two thousand meters obtained as a result of our collaboration with a leading smart grid based utility provider. Our experimental evaluation shows promising results for the proposed model i.e., accuracy rate of more than 95% with negligible false alarms of 0.2%.

The rest of the paper is organized as follows. Section 2 discusses the related work followed by the dataset described in Section 3. Section 4 discusses the statistical analysis of the logs collected at the smart collectors. Based on the analysis, a stochastic model is proposed in Section 5. Properties are specified using LTL language which is described in Section 6. Attack model and evaluation of the proposed approach is shown in Section 7 along-with the discussion on robustness against evasion, scalability and limitations. Section 8 concludes the work followed by the background of AMI in the Appendix.

2. RELATED WORK

Intrusion detection has gained tremendous attention and many anomaly-based IDS techniques have been proposed for the cyber systems [9, 10, 13]. For example, n-gram based intrusion detection and markov chain based approaches have been proposed in the past [26]. n-gram can be seen as prediction using n-1 markov model. However, a markov chain moves from one state to the next using a weighted list of possible future states. n-gram can calculate the likelihood for next state, however, it only gives the statistical distribution and cannot maintain the temporal order. Since AMI supports limited protocols and configurations, temporal specifications can be defined for markov chain model to devise specification-based intrusion detector. Though n-gram can be used to design anomaly detection system based on statistical distribution, we believe specification-based approach is better suited for intrusion detection in AMI due to its nature.

The novelty of our approach lies in characterizing AMI configuration as a baseline for developing a reliable IDS (high detection and low false positive rate), while considering the practical computation and operational constrains of AMI. To the best of our knowledge, no approach exists yet which uses configurations for deriving the LTL properties for markov model.

Recently proposed techniques have reduced the false positive rate for traditional networks [19]. However, we focus our attention to the smart grid since these techniques require learning and are computationally extensive. Therefore, they do not fit the application requirements of a smart grid.

In [23], an anomaly detection technique for smart grid has been proposed. It considers the temporal anomalies and rank potential intrusion events based on the credibility impact on power system. It also considers the scenario where simultaneous cyber intrusions are launched over multiple substations. The work focuses on the cyber security of substations in a smart grid. A survey on supervisory control and data acquisition system (SCADA) specific intrusion detection and prevention is presented in [28]. However, these techniques do not cater for the intrusions on an AMI.

In addition to intrusion detection, few studies have been conducted to highlight the cyber security issues in an AMI of a smart grid [3,6]. A distributed intrusion detection technique in a multi-layer architecture of smart grid is proposed in [27]. It proposes a three layer architecture for home area network, neighborhood area network and wide area network. It uses trained support vector machines (SVM) for attack classification at each layer. In [5], the requirements and architectural directions are discussed for intrusion detection in an AMI. Based on the requirements and architectural directions highlighted in [5], a specification-based intrusion detection technique has been proposed in [4]. This approach defines a formal model for C12.22 standard protocol which is used by different meters in the AMI for communication purposes. It verifies the specification at the application layer in order to identify anomalous behavior. The proposed approach is protocol specific. However, not all the deployed smart grids are using this protocol for communication. Therefore, it cannot be applied to those AMI infrastructures. Moreover, there is no standard implementation of the protocol available and many vendors keep the implementation proprietary. An intrusion detection architecture for the AMI has been proposed in [8]. It uses data mining

Table 1: Sample meter configuration after anonymization

Meter	Vendor	Memory (MB)	Usage Sample Schedule (secs)	Reporting Time (mins)
meter1	vendor1	512MB	20	1
meter2	vendor1	512MB	40	1
meter3	vendor2	784MB	15	2
meter4	vendor3	784MB	30	1

Table 2: Sample smart collector configuration after anonymization

Smart Collector	Vendor	Neighboring Meters	Link Type	Reporting Time (Mins)	Buffer Size (GB)
SC1	vendor1	meter1, meter2	Link1	1	4
SC2	vendor1	meter3	Link2	2	4
SC3	vendor1	meter4, meter5	Link3	2	6
SC4	vendor2	meter6	Link4	1	6

based intrusion detection technique for the AMI. It requires deployment at smart meter, smart collector and headend system.

All of the proposed approaches for intrusion detection in the AMI assume a computationally expensive intrusion detection module deployment at the meter level. However, this may not be practically feasible since meters do not have enough computation power [22]. If the detection modules are to be deployed as a stand alone unit next to the meter, it requires significantly higher cost. We argue that due to this higher deployment cost, industrial deployments of the intrusion detector for the AMI have not been witnessed yet. In this work, we propose a solution which is cost effective and practical since it can be deployed either in the headend system or in the AMI.

3. DATASET

In AMI, the real-world dataset is important since all of the contemporary work uses simulation which may not necessarily reflect the true behavior of the system under consideration. Therefore, it is very important to analyze a real-world dataset in order to reveal its true behavior. To this end, we use real-world dataset collected at an AMI of a leading smart grid based utility provider. A smart grid testbed is also established by the utility provider at our institute in order to conduct experiments locally in a controlled environment. It includes a monitoring/management node which is capable of monitoring and configuring the nodes in an AMI, also referred as Network Management System (NMS). The testbed also includes the multiple smart meters and smart collectors, both of which are capable of bi-directional communication.

Since it is not practically feasible to capture network traffic, we work with the event logs generated at the smart collector. Since event logging is an inherent capability of a smart collector, it does not impose any extra burden on the smart collector. These logs are saved at smart collector for sometime and then deleted in a cyclic manner. We conduct offline analysis of the logs in order to avoid any service disruption. We collected logs of multiple smart collectors for a total period of two weeks in two sessions of one week each denoted by Log-1 and Log-2. Approximately more than two thousand meters were communicating with the smart collectors. The AMI infrastructure used devices from multiple vendors. Sample and anonymized basic configuration of the meters is shown in Table 1. In the AMI under consideration, reporting mode for the meters was 'push' i.e., the meter will send scheduled readings by itself at the interval specified in the 'Reporting Time'. 'Usage Sampling' tells

Table 3: Sample log observed at smart collector

Time (Relative)	Source	Destination	Size (KB)	Type (Communication)
388.3709	meter1	SC1	28	0
602.6901	SC1	meter1	2	0
633.5265	meter2	SC1	5	3
388.3709	SC1	meter2	38	2

the number of seconds after which a sample is taken. Similarly, Table 2 shows the configuration of the smart collectors. It can be observed that the smart collector is aware of its neighboring meters and the link through which they are connected. In our case study, meters were communicating with the smart collectors using both the power line and wireless media. However, the analysis and technique discussed in this work is generic and should hold across other communication models as well.

Sample log entries of a smart collector are shown in Table 3. These entries are simplified and anonymized to show only the information required in this work. Each log entry has the event time stamp. Here we show the relative time stamp with respect to the start of the logging event. However, it is absolute in practice. Time stamp is followed by the source and destination ID of the nodes involved in the communication event. Size of the communication is also logged in kilo bytes (KB). Lastly, the type of event is also logged. For example, 0 represents that it was a meter reading report. $1, 2$ and 3 represents disconnect/reconnect, upgrade and load management communication, respectively. We show the statistical analysis of the logs collected in the next section which forms the basis of our model.

4. STATISTICAL ANALYSIS

We analyzed a number of statistical properties of the log entries. One relevant property that provided us with interesting insights was the analysis of their temporal dependence. It can be intuitively argued that, as long as the log entries are produced by benign events, the log entries observed should exhibit a certain level of temporal dependence. In case of malicious behavior, perturbations in this dependence structure are flagged as anomalous. Therefore, the level of temporal dependence can serve as an important metric for modeling the log entries.

Autocorrelation measures the on-average temporal dependence between the random variables in a stochastic process at different points in time. For a given lag k, the autocorrelation function of a stochastic process X_n (where n is the time index) is defined as:

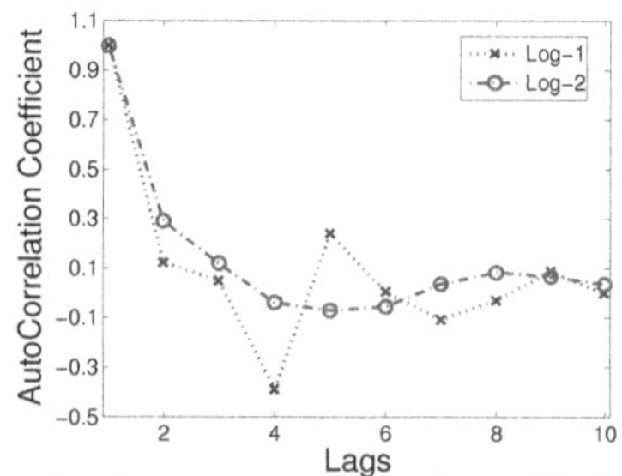

Figure 2: Autocorrelation coefficient trend

$$\rho[k] = \frac{E\{X_0 X_k\} - E\{X_0\}E\{X_k\}}{\sigma_{X_0}\sigma_{X_k}}, \quad (1)$$

where $E\{.\}$ represents the expectation operation, σ_{X_k} is the standard deviation of the random variable at time lag k and the stochastic process X realizes the log entries, thus X_n is the log entry at index n. The value of the autocorrelation function lies in the range $[-1, 1]$, where $\rho[k] = 1$ means perfect correlation at lag k (which is obviously true for $k = 0$) and $\rho[k] = 0$ means no correlation at lag k.

Figure 2 shows the autocorrelation function plotted against the log entries represented by lags. For both the logs, a certain level of temporal dependence can be easily observed at small lags. This correlation decays in time and eventually drops down to a negligible value. Temporal dependence is present for two reasons. First, meters respond to the smart collector requests in a short period of time. Second, regular requests and reports are seen thus justifying the homogeneity.

Since log entries are correlated at small lags, they can be modeled using markov chains. Moreover, it is well-known that a decaying temporal dependence structure can be accurately modeled using markov chains [18]. Therefore, the concern here is to identify the order of markov chain model that should be used to accurately model the log entries. To determine the markovian order, we conduct analysis on different markov chain orders. The order can be identified by noting the probabilities at different markov chain orders. If the probability is low at a given order, the next log entry can be predicted with high accuracy. First, we investigate the probability distribution of log entries at different markov chain orders and then use the conditional entropy based measure proposed in [18].

Let the log entry tuple at discrete time instance n represents the realization of a random variable derived from a stochastic process X_n. This process is a markov chain if it satisfies the markov property, which is defined as:

$$\begin{aligned} &\Pr\{\mathrm{X}_n = j\,|\mathrm{X}_{n-1} = i, \mathrm{X}_{n-2} = i_{n-2}, \ldots, \mathrm{X}_0 = i_0\} \\ &\quad = \Pr\{\mathrm{X}_n = j\,|\mathrm{X}_{n-1} = i\} = p_{j|i}. \end{aligned} \quad (2)$$

In other words, the probability of choosing a next state is only dependent on the current state of the markov chain.

In the present context, we can define a markov chain model X_n for an entry by treating each unique log entry tuple individually and assigning them to non-overlapping bins. Here we assign each unique tuple to each bin. Therefore, the number of bins will be dependent on the number of unique log entry tuples. Each bin then represents a state of the markov chain, while the set of all bin indices ψ is its state space. Based on this state representation, we can define a 1-st order markov chain, $X_n^{(1)}$, in which each bin represents a state of the random process. Probability of each state i can be calculated by counting the number of times state i occurred and dividing it by the total occurrences of all the states in the markov chain model X_n. Similarly, an l-th order markov chain, $X_n^{(l)}$, can be defined in which each state is an l-tuple $\langle i_0, i_1, \ldots, i_{l-1}\rangle$ representing the values taken by the random process in the last l time instances i.e., l log entries in our case. In this case the occurrences of l-tuple together will be counted. This will increase the size of state space ψ since different combinations of l-tuple are possible.

Figure 3 shows the state probabilities calculated for log entries for different markov chain orders. We calculated it for up to 4-th order markov chain as shown in Figure 3. It can be clearly observed that as the order of markov chain increases, i.e., first order to fourth order, total number of states ψ increases, which is the *x-axis* in Figure 3(a) to (d). However, it gives us an interesting insight that as the order increases, very few states have higher probability of occurrence and rest of the states' probabilities drop to a negligible value. Therefore, using a higher order markov chain, we can actually identify the most likely states which will be observed in the logs. Thus it increases the predictability and likeliness of those states. Here, selection of appropriate markov chain order is important since a higher order yields higher number of possible states and requires more memory. To explore it further, we use the conditional entropy based measure [18] for the log entries for different markov chain orders. This measure will tell us that at what order of markov chain we have most of the information about the next time instance i.e., log entry.

Conditional entropy, $H(B|A)$, of two discrete random variables A and B characterizes the information remaining in B when A is already known. Phrased differently, conditional entropy is 'information about B *not* given by A'. If A and B are highly correlated, most of the information about B is communicated through A and $H(B|A)$ is small. On the other hand, if p_A and p_B (which respectively represent the probability mass functions of A and B) are quite different then $H(B|A)$ assumes a high value, which means that most of the information about B is not given by A. In the limiting cases, $H(B|A) = 0$ when $A = B$, while $H(B|A) = H(B)$ when A and B are independent.

The transition probability matrix of the 1-st order markov chain $P^{(1)}$ can be computed by counting the number of times the state i is followed by state j. The resulting $|\psi^{(1)}|$ histograms can be normalized to obtain the state-wise transition probability mass functions as the rows of $P^{(1)}$.

We can find the conditional probability of the 1-st order markov chain as:

$$H^{(1)} = -\sum_{i\in\psi^{(1)}} \pi_i^{(1)} \sum_{j\in\psi^{(1)}} p_{j|i}^{(1)} \log_2\left(p_{j|i}^{(1)}\right), \quad (3)$$

where $\pi_i^{(1)}$ is the average probability of being in state i which is computed by counting the total number of times each state is visited and then normalizing the frequency histogram.

The measure $H^{(1)}$ defines how much average information is remaining in log entry X_n when it is calculated using log entry X_{n-1}. If the entry is not highly correlated with entries before X_{n-1}, $H^{(1)}$ will be relatively large implying that information about X_n *not* provided by X_{n-1} is high. In such a

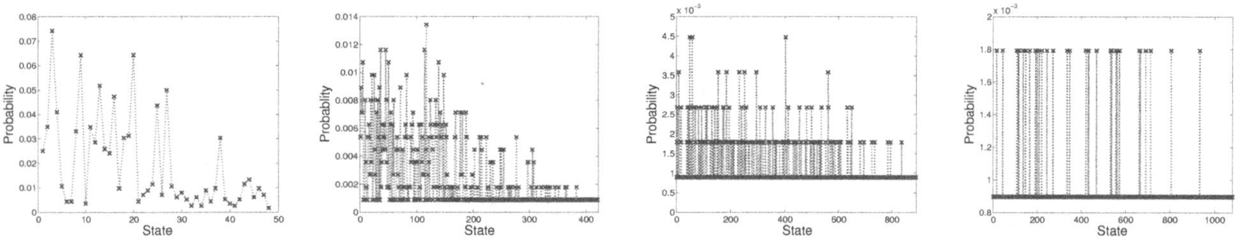

(a) First Order (b) Second Order (c) Third Order (d) Fourth Order

Figure 3: State Probabilities for Higher Order Markov Chain

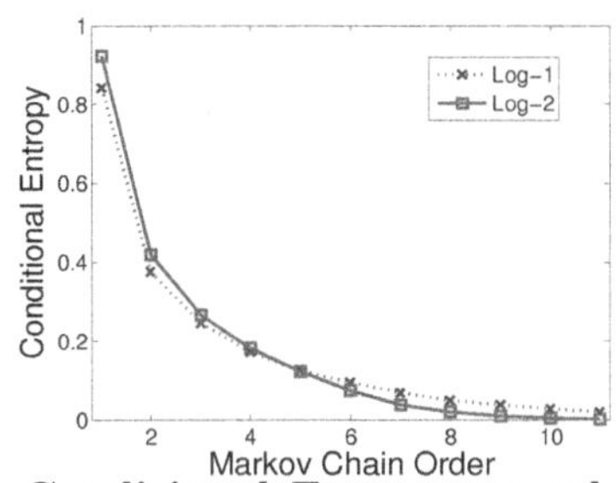

Figure 4: Conditional Entropy trend over Markov Chain orders

case, we use higher l-th order markov chain, $X_n^{(l)}$ as defined previously, in which each state is an l-tuple $\langle i_0, i_1, \ldots, i_{l-1}\rangle$ representing the values taken by the random process in the last l time instances. Aggregating multiple time instances in a single state allows us to satisfy the markov property, and hence a transition probability matrix $P^{(l)}$ can be computed by counting the number of times $\langle i_0, i_1, \ldots, i_{l-1}\rangle$ is followed by state $\langle i_1, \ldots, i_{l-1}, i_l\rangle$. The conditional entropy of $X_n^{(l)}$ defined on $\psi^{(l)}$ can then be computed using the same method as (3). It is easy to observe that $H^{(1)} \geq H^{(2)} \geq \ldots \geq H^{(l)}$, as each older entry can either be independent of, or provide some information about the present entry. The number of previous entries required to accurately predict the next entry can then be determined by plotting $H^{(l)}$ as the function of the markov chain order, $l = 1, 2, \ldots$. The order at which the conditional entropy saturates defines the total number of previous entries which have conveyed as much information of the present entry as possible. It can be clearly seen in Figure 4 that log entries exhibit a decaying trend over higher order markov chain. It can be seen that it exhibits an exponential decay trend until the 4-th order, which was expected since very few states had higher probability in Figure 3(d) at the same order. It is clear that most of the information about the next instance is already given at the fourth order since conditional entropy drops to a negligible value i.e., ≤ 0.2. Therefore, we model using the fourth order since it gives enough information and increases predictability. However, we also show the results for third order markov chain which exhibits a little low accuracy but improves scalability since it exhibits less number of states. In later section, we show that higher order markov chain exhibits better accuracy but it increases the number of states as compared to the lower order. Therefore, the choice of markov chain order is a trade-off between scalability (number of states) and accuracy. This is discussed in detail in the later sections, however, we build a model using the fourth order markov chain.

5. MODEL

Since our model is built on the logs of smart collectors, we first look at the format of a log entry. It can be represented as:

$$t, s_{id}, d_{id}, sz, ty$$

where t represents the time stamp at which the event was observed for which the entry is logged. s_{id} and d_{id} refers to the source and destination, respectively, of the communication observed. It can either be the meter or smart collector. Size of the communication is denoted by sz. The type of communication is defined by ty. Therefore, in this model we use the above information. We can encode the state of the network with the following characteristic function:

$$\sigma : s_{id} \wedge d_{id} \wedge sz \wedge ty \rightarrow \{true, false\} \quad (4)$$

The function σ encodes the state of the network by evaluating to *true* whenever the parameters used as input to the function correspond to the log entry in the smart collector. If the AMI observes 5 different log entries, then exactly 5 different assignments to σ function will result to *true*. Since each smart collector is independent, we learn the markov model for each smart collector separately.

A Labeled Markov Chain (LMC) is a tuple $M = \{Q, \Sigma, \pi, \tau, L\}$, where Q is a finite set of states, π is an initial probability distribution τ is the transition probability function and L is a labeling function. Atomic propositions AP are assigned to states by a labeling function using $\Sigma = 2^{AP}$. Each state was assigned a unique label derived from σ, which is used to define the state. A probability distribution for sequence of states can then be defined using markov chain. LMC M with alphabet Σ induces the probability distribution P_M^{π} over Σ^w through labeling of the states.

Set of states Q is strongly connected if for each state pair (q_i, q_j) there exist a path $q_0, q_1, \ldots, q_n$ such that $q_h \in Q$ for $0 \leq h \leq n$, $\tau(q_h, q_{h+1}) > 0, q_0 = q_i$, and $q_n = q_h$. Therefore, if Q is strongly connected, then M is said to be strongly connected. A distribution π_M^s is a stationary distribution for M if it satisfies

$$\pi^s_{(q)} = \sum_{\acute{q} \in Q} \pi^s(\acute{q})\tau(\acute{q}, q)$$

Since we are interested in keeping the history of previously visited states, we focus on the probability suffix automata (PSA). A PSA is an extended LMC with a labeling function $H : Q \rightarrow \Sigma^{\leq N}$, which represents the history of previously visited, at most N, states. However, if the history is fixed to N, i.e., $\Sigma^{=N}$, the LMC will be called $(N+1)th$ order markov chain since it includes the current state too. Therefore, each state q_i will be associated with a string s_i such that $s_i = H(q_i)L(q_i)$.

Algorithm 1: Learn Markov Model

Data: Sequence S
Result: Finite state machine based on 4-th order Markov Model

```
Initialize empty Graph;
S = {σ_i | ∀σ_i ∈ Σ} ;
∀σ_i Pr(σ_i) > 0 ;
while S ≠ φ do
    Slide window by one σ at instance i ;
    Pick s_i ∈ S ;
    if s_i ∈ Graph then
        Make directed edge from s_{i-1} to s_i ;
    end
    else
        Create node s_i in Graph ;
        Make directed edge from s_{i-1} to s_i ;
    end
end
```

Since the AMI system under consideration is a real-time system and can not be restarted with different initial states, we argue that the model learning technique should be able to start observing data from the system at any given time and can work with a single long sequence of observations. Suppose we have sequence $S = \sigma_1, \sigma_2, \ldots, \sigma_n$, $\sigma_i \in Q$, where σ represents a state as shown in Equation 4. Since our statistical analysis showed that conditional entropy is negligible at 4-th order, therefore, we use 4-th order markov chain. A finite state machine having directed graph can be learned from the given sequence S. Each state in the graph at time i will be represented by a tuple of 4 i.e., $\langle \sigma_{i-3}, \sigma_{i-2}, \ldots, \sigma_i \rangle$, where σ_i is the $L(q_i)$ and the rest are $H(q_i)$. Therefore, it can be realized as s_i in the finite state machine.

Algorithm 1 explains the learning of a markov model from the given sequence of log entries. It initializes an empty graph and then starts observing the sequence S. It utilizes a sliding window approach where window slides at instance i by one entry i.e., σ. However, the size of window to observe $s_i \in S$ is kept to 4 which is the order of model. If s_i already exists in graph then a directed edge from s_{i-1} to s_i is created, if the directed edge does not exist already. However, if s_i does not exist in graph, then a node is also created for s_i. This process keeps repeating until S is empty. Once the state machine is created, it is easy to calculate the transition probability matrix for that. For each state s_i in graph, $\sum_{\forall \sigma_i \in \Sigma} \tau(s_i, \sigma_i) = 1$.

Since a log entry σ is a conjunction of different variables, total possible combinations can exceed and may require a lot of processing power. However, it can be calculated for each network under consideration. In our case study, 10 bits were assigned to s_{id} and d_{id}, 8 bits for sz and 3 bits for type ty of communication. Therefore, the possible number of σ are $2^{10} \times 2^{10} \times 2^8 \times 2^3$ which is a relatively large number. Since the model treats each smart collector's log separately, either source or destination of each log entry will be fixed to the id of that particular smart collector. Moreover, a smart collector can only be connected to its neighboring nodes/meters. In our case study, the smart collector was connected to 8 other devices. Therefore, the number of σ reduces to $1 \times 8 \times 2^8 \times 2^3$, which is relatively smaller. Since 4-th order markov model is being used, possible combinations of four σ can yield to a lot of states. To this end, the proposed algorithm only takes the combinations which are observed in the sequence S and only keeps the edges which are observed since all the combinations are not possible due to configuration, thus reducing the size of transition probability matrix.

6. PROPERTIES SPECIFICATION FOR MODEL CHECKING

Since the proposed model is based on markov chain and exhibits a temporal dependence, we define properties in Linear time Temporal Logic (LTL) [2]. Unlike traditional model checking, stochastic model checking allows you to check that with what probability the property is satisfied by the model. These probabilities can be thresholded in order to accommodate the unseen behavior up to a certain extent. LTL over the alphabets Σ is defined by the syntax:

$$\varphi ::= true \mid \sigma \mid \varphi_1 \wedge \varphi_2 \mid \neg\varphi \mid \bigcirc\varphi \mid \varphi_1 \cup \varphi_2 \quad (\sigma \in \Sigma)$$

The derived additional operators $\Box$ (always) and $\diamond$ (eventually) are also used in the LTL.

Let φ be the LTL formula over Σ. An LTL formula can be satisfied for a sequence of alphabets s which is a state definition in our case having $s = \sigma_1, \sigma_2, \ldots, \sigma_n$ where $\sigma_i \in \Sigma$. Therefore, the probabilistic LTL can be defined as:

$$\phi ::= P_{\bowtie p}(\varphi), \quad \bowtie \;\in \{\geq, >, \leq, <, =\}; \quad p \in [0,1]; \; \varphi \in \text{LTL}$$

Since the system under consideration is an online system and can not be restarted with a specific initial state, we use the stationary distributions for satisfiability. LTL properties can be verified with the markov chain model built in the earlier section. For example, if a configuration parameter defines the sampling rate and report size, a property can be written that whenever a report request is received the reply should have this particular size. Temporally it can be stated that given the system is in 'request' state, the next expected state is 'reply_with_size_h'. In the PRISM model checker tool [20], the 'next' state operator is defined using 'X'. For the given state, you can 'filter' the state space to 'current' state only. We wrote a small parser which reads the configuration and generates the properties in LTL format for the tool.

The properties can be derived from the configurations and the security control guidelines such as NISTIR 7628 by NIST. Since the configurations shown are related to reading report, below we show some examples of the properties derived from the configuration. Let γ be the number of meters associated with a smart collector. One basic example is that whenever a report reading request is generated, a meter should respond with a report. It can be formulated as:

$$\phi ::= P_{\geq d_1}(rrep_i | rreq_i), \quad 1 \leq i \leq \gamma \tag{5}$$

where $rreq_i$ and $rrep_i$ represents the reading request and reading report, respectively, for meter i. However, d_1 is used as a probability threshold that this property should be satisfied with the probability greater than or equal to d_1. The property defined here is in conditional probability syntax, however, it can be represented in LTL as:

$$P_{\geq d_1}(\Box(rreq_i \rightarrow \bigcirc rrep_i)) \tag{6}$$

This is a strict property since it says that the *next* state has to be the $rrep_i$. However, a relaxed property can be defined as:

$$P_{\geq d_1}(\Box(rreq_i \rightarrow \diamond rrep_i)) \tag{7}$$

which says that eventually $rrep_i$ will be seen once $rreq_i$ is observed. However, we use the strict property (Equation 6) in our experiments. Similarly, it can also be defined that the report generated should have a size with in the limits defined since sampling rate is fixed. It can be formulated as:

$$\phi ::= P_{\geq d_2}(rsz_i | rrep_i), \quad 1 \leq i \leq \gamma \tag{8}$$

where rsz_i denotes the report size for meter i. However, $rsz_i \in sz_i$ which is a valid report size set for meter i. Moreover, Equation 5 and 8 can be combined to show the temporal behavior i.e., whenever a reading request is generated, it is followed by the reading reply which has a valid size.

Moreover, a meter should not send the reading report twice in the next T_1 consecutive time periods. It can be formulated as:

$$\phi ::= P_{\leq d_3}(rrep_i | rrep_i), \quad 1 \leq i \leq \gamma \tag{9}$$

where d_3 is thresholded with $\leq$ that the probability of seeing such a behavior should be less than d_3. Suppose t_1 is a counter which observe values in the range $\{1, 2, \ldots, T_1\}$. Equation 9 can be represented in LTL as:

$$P_{\leq d_3}(\Box\ rrep_i \rightarrow (\neg rrep_i \cup t_1 \geq T_1)) \tag{10}$$

To avoid flooding the smart collector with reports from multiple meters at the same time, the associated meters were configured to have different reporting intervals. Therefore, smart collector will not receive consecutive reports from multiple meters in consecutive T_2 time periods. It can be formulated as:

$$\phi ::= P_{\leq d_4}(rrep_j | rrep_i), \quad i \neq j, \quad 1 \leq (i, j) \leq \gamma \tag{11}$$

this prevents the multiple meters from sending the reports after each other for consecutive T_2 time periods. It can be represented in LTL as:

$$P_{\leq d_4}(\Box\ rrep_i \rightarrow \neg rrep_j \cup t_2 \geq T_2), \forall_{j=1}^{\gamma} \tag{12}$$

Moreover, the thresholds d_x are learnt from the model built using the benign logs collected under normal condition i.e., without any attack. However, they can also be manually configured based on the requirements of the network under consideration. We show the examples of reading reports property specification, however, other types of configurations are also specified the same way using LTL. These properties are dependent on the configuration of the network under consideration.

7. EXPERIMENTATION & EVALUATION

Before discussing the experimentation and evaluation, we first discuss the attack model.

7.1 Attack Model

Since we work with the logs collected at a smart collector, attacks which do not involve any communication with the smart collector or do not create a log entry would not be detected. This has been highlighted in the limitations of our work. However, affect of such attacks would be limited to a particular area. In short, our focus is on the large scale attacks which include compromising a large number of meters to cause a major blackout in the area. These attacks are, but not limited to, spoofing, denial of service, distributed denial of service, scanning, penetration, evasion, mimicry etc. For example, a denial of service attack on the smart collectors or its associated meters will cause the service disruption in the area. Similarly, distributed denial of service attack on the large number of meters or smart collectors can cause a major blackout in the wider area. Since the infrastructure exhibits a deterministic behavior and is homogenous in nature; spoofing, mimicry and evasion techniques can inject similar traffic without being detected thus resulting in the destabilization of the infrastructure. Mimicry attacks can compromise a number of meters and operate as they are legitimate thus bypassing detection. This work is not focused on the energy theft by individual users. Intrusion detectors specially designed for detecting individual user's energy theft have been proposed recently [15,16].

Traditional attacks like denial of service will be detected by the property 10 since it will create multiple entries in a time windows shorter than $T1$. Similarly, distributed denial of service will cause the property 12 to be invalid since it will cause multiple sources to create log entries in a time window shorter than $T2$. If a penetration attack is launched against the AMI, it will be detected depending on the attack graph. If the penetration is supposed to go through the smart collector or it tampers with the meter (by changing the configuration), it will be detected since the meter will not behave according to the a-priori known configurations. Similarly, malware which tampers with the meter configuration will be detected as well.

Data injection attacks which only tamper with the usage information will not be detected. Same holds true for the mimicry attacks and evasion techniques. To countermeasure this, we propose a simple randomization module which introduces a notion of randomness in the meter behavior while staying deterministic for the smart collector. It is discussed in the subsequent section.

To evaluate the proposed scheme, we generate attacks in a controlled environment in the smart grid testbed. We use different attack scenarios which include not only different attack types but also different attack locations. Since the home area network has access to the smart meter, we consider two scenarios for this location i.e., 1) try to compromise the meter and tamper with its configuration, 2) using the smart meter as entry point to an AMI, we launch scanning, DoS, evasion, mimicry and data injection traffic. For scanning and DoS, we generate low rate attacks i.e., 0.1pkts/sec to 1pkts/sec. Both the above mentioned scenarios were implemented for these attacks. For evasion, mimicry and spoofing, we placed a switch in between the meters and collector; and attached an attack machine to it. We wrote a simple program which uses the same configuration as that of a meter and generate similar reading reports in the same format. In order to be evasive, less than 5% of the total generated traffic by the machine was injected traffic and 95% was the mimic traffic. For mimicry and spoofing attacks, all the traffic was mimic traffic without any injected traffic. Injected traffic includes malicious commands like random file uploads, requesting reports at irregular intervals (requesting report itself is not an attack), administrative commands without proper authorization and failed authorization attempts. These logs were collected from the smart collectors and were labeled as malicious. Malicious logs were mixed into the real-world logs collected at an AMI of the utility provider for the purpose of the accuracy evaluation. It was made sure that the volume of malicious logs do not exceed 10% in the mixed log (benign and malicious).

7.2 Robustness against Evasion and Mimicry Attacks

Since evasion and mimicry attacks leverage the known behavior of the network, they tend to stay below the radar to go undetected. To this end, we propose a simple yet effective module for the smart meters. Due to the homogenous and deterministic nature of the network, it is not difficult for an attacker to learn the behavior. Therefore, we randomize one of the configuration parameter which makes it difficult for the attacker to guess. However, other parameters can be randomized too using the same semantics. We randomize the reporting interval parameter in the configuration. Let int_i denote the set containing all the possible valid configuration values for the report interval for meter i, where int_i^t is the randomly selected configuration value at time t for the meter i. To introduce a certain level of randomization, a meter should have enough possible valid configuration values to pick from. It can be formulated as:

$$|int_i| \geq \theta \qquad (13)$$

The greater the θ, the higher the randomization. To select a value randomly from the given set, we use a simple hash function since it is effective and computationally inexpensive too.

$$int(t+1) = H(k_i, t, int_i^t) mod\ l\ +\ 1 \qquad (14)$$

where k_i denotes the pre-shared key between the meter i and the smart collector, t represents the time and l is the size of possible values that is used to keep the value in the given range. The hash function takes the key and the previously selected reporting interval to introduce unpredictability for the attacker and predictability for the smart collector. Reporting interval will be chosen every time before sending the report. Smart collector will do the same computation in order to verify if the report was expected at the given time or not. Calculated time interval will be used in property 10 to identify any non-compliance behavior. In our experiment, we implemented this simple module on the NMS machine which was capable of remotely configuring the meters. The module was written in C language using the NMS API to configure the time interval for each report. Similarly, for model checking the module calculates the time interval and provides it to the property for the respective log entry validation.

Robustness of the presented approach against evasion depends on two factors: (1) the probability threshold used in the verification properties, and (2) the configuration parameter randomization. Since the reporting interval is verified by a property which is thresholded, in case of a low threshold evasion is possible to a certain extent because significant deviation can be allowed. For example, if the property threshold is 0.9, it means that 90% of the reports should be in the correct time and 10% can be deviated to accommodate any unexpected network behavior as learnt from the log training. Thus, attackers can leverage this 10% to launch mimicry and evasion attacks. If we assume that the key is not known to attackers, but other configuration parameters can be known, an attacker has to accurately guess the reporting time from a range of values such that success ratio will be above the property threshold in order to evade detection. However, this accuracy (evasion) is highly dependent on the parameter randomization range. For example, if the range defined as 10 minutes in discrete intervals of one second each, then the probability that the attacker can guess the correct time interval (attack probability) is as low as 0.0017. In order to evade the detection, the attack probability must be greater than or equal to the property threshold. However, this case is extremely unlikely unless randomization range is poorly selected and/or the property threshold has been immaturely determined based on improper training data set (e.g., unclean or very few samples).

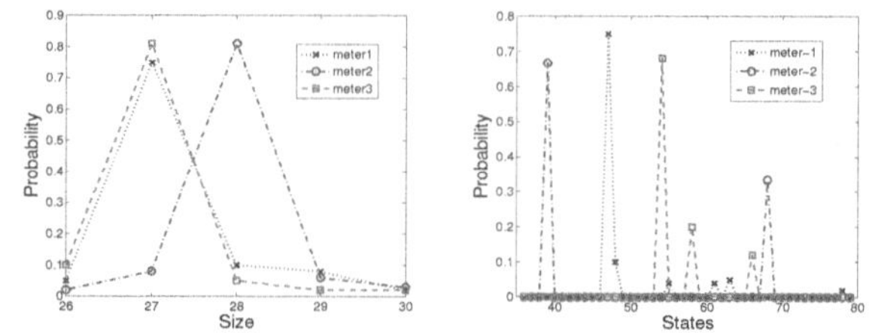

(a) Response for Reading Request (b) Response for Load Management Request

Figure 5: Response Probabilities when a request was generated for Reading and Load Management

7.3 Accuracy Evaluation

The basic premise of our work is to develop a model using the logs of smart collector and verify the configuration properties written in LTL. If a property is verified against the model with probability $p > d$, where d is set as a threshold, we say that it is normal, otherwise, it is anomalous. Threshold d was learnt separately for each property by noting the property verification probability using the benign logs model (without attack).

Logs were collected from the smart collectors which were connected to the multiple meters. Moreover, meters had different configurations which make the dataset diverse. Therefore, the model is not limited to a specific type of configuration and can actually model different configuration sets due to its markovian nature. Before discussing the accuracy evaluation, we first show the basic behavior of the three randomly selected meters. These three meters use different configurations for the report size. It gives us interesting insight about the temporally deterministic behavior. Then we analyze that how well the model represents the system behavior. Please note that this temporal behavioral analysis was done without the randomization module and attack traffic. The model checking was conducted using a probabilistic symbolic model checker tool PRISM [20].

7.3.1 *Temporal Behavior of the Model*

Since the model preserves the temporal behavior, the properties can be seen as the conditional probability i.e., $P(A|B)$, where state B has already been observed (given). Therefore, it can be stated as 'what is the probability of seeing state A given state B?'. It can be easily written in the LTL using the 'next' or 'eventually' operator for the state A by filtering all the states except the current/given state i.e., B as discussed in an earlier section.

Figure 5 shows the conditional probabilities given that the request was made for a particular meter for the usage reading and load management as shown in Figure 5(a) and 5(b), respectively. We provide the results for three meters only. However, similar results were observed for the other meters as well. Figure 5(a) shows the probability of response size, given that the system was currently in the reading request

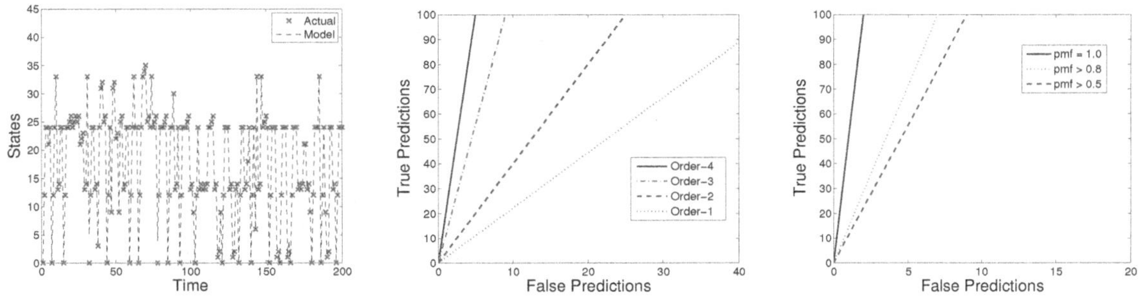

(a) Model Prediction (b) Different Markov Chain order (c) Varying pmf on fourth order model

Figure 6: Prediction accuracy for different markov chain order and pmf for fourth order model

state i.e., a usage/reading request was sent to a meter. It can be seen that all the three meters generated response within the range of 26 to 30KB with different probabilities. Two meters generated response of size 27KB with higher probability and the third meter generated response of size 28KB. These responses belong to different states in the model since size was used as a variable in the tuple (σ) used for the state definition. However, none of the meter generated a response of size more than 30 or less than 26KB which was set as a variance boundary. The reading response size depends on the sampling rate of the meter. Since the response size of the reading request was within the range, the property 'whenever a reading request is generated, the next observed state is reading response with the size modeled' (combining equation 6 and 8) was verified with the probability 1. Here the probability 1 can be realized as the sum of all the probabilities of the states having size within the range of 26 to 30KB. Please note that the system can be in one state at a given time i.e., either request sent to meter 1 or meter 2. These conditional probabilities were calculated separately for the next state given that the system was in the request state.

Similarly, Figure 5(b) shows the next state transition probabilities given that the system was in a load management request state. It can be seen that all the three meters probabilistically responded to the request. Meter 2 (green line with circular marker) showed the two transition probabilities. Response of size 9KB with probability close to 0.65 and size 6KB with probability close to 0.35. Similarly, meter-1 responded with 6 different sizes. All of these sizes were within the range of 5 to 10KB. Lastly, meter-3 responded with the three different sizes where one size was most likely and the other two were less likely. It can be observed that whenever the system was in a load management request state, the response state was observed next with the probability of 1. However, response also had multiple states depending on the size of the response which was used as a variable in defining the state s consisting of multiple σ. Therefore, it can be concluded that the model exhibits a temporally deterministic behavior for the system under consideration. It is clear that the temporal probabilities for the properties can be learnt from the model built using the benign logs. Now we analyze whether the model truly represents the system or in other words how well the model represents the logs.

7.3.2 *Model Accuracy*

In order to determine whether the model actually represents the logs or not, we conduct a model accuracy experiment as shown in Figure 6. It does not include the attack traffic or property verification. We divide the benign logs into two halves. The first half was used to build a model using Algorithm 1. Second half was used as the test dataset and the model was applied on it for the prediction. For each step, the current state was learned and based on the current state, the next state was predicted using the model i.e., states having higher probabilities in probability mass function (pmf) were predicted. Figure 6(a) shows the prediction using the fourth order model. The red cross marker denotes the actual states observed in the test log. However, blue dashed line represents the prediction of the model. It can be observed that the model predicts the future states with high accuracy though few false predictions (less than 2%) were encountered as well. These false predictions were observed as a result of the unseen behavior since the benign log was divided into two halves. As a result, few lower probability states were not observed after a certain state s (i.e., tuple history of order four) present in the first half, thus yielding to false prediction. To check the model confidence, we did the prediction using one hour learning to one week learning. In all the cases, the false predictions observed were below 2%.

We used different criterion and show the results in Figure 6(b) and (c). We count the total number of predictions and classify whether they were true or not. In Figure 6(b), we used different markov chain orders i.e., the current state was defined using one tuple or multiple tuple history. It can be observed in Figure 6(b) that the fourth order markov chain provides the best prediction accuracy as compared to the lower order markov chains. In another experiment, we change the pmf bound used for the prediction. For example, pmf of 0.5 means minimum number of next transition states having probabilities sum of 0.5. If there are three possible next states based on the current state having probabilities 0.6, 0.2 and 0.2, only state having 0.6 probability will be selected as the 'predicted' state since it has the probability greater than or equal to 0.5. However, if none of the states has probability higher than 0.5, minimum number of multiple states will be selected whose sum reaches 0.5. Figure 6(c) shows the prediction accuracy for the different pmf. It can be seen that pmf of 1 i.e., based on the current state all the next possible states in the model are predicted, provides the best accuracy with a very low false prediction rate. It can be intuitively argued that this false prediction rate will be the bound for the false positive for the attack detection accuracy, since this shows how well the model represents the data. Therefore, it can be concluded that the fourth order

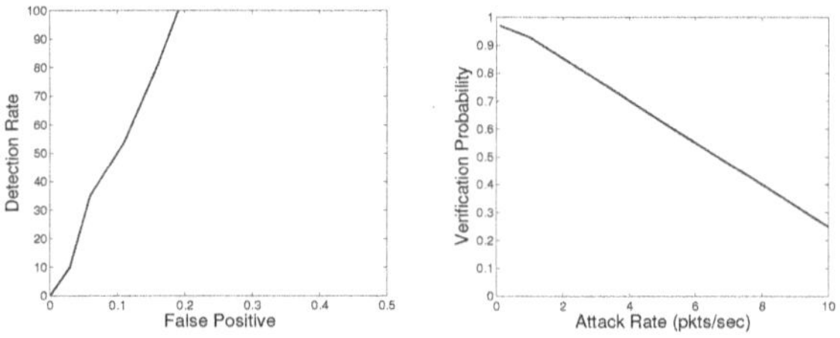

(a) Detection Accuracy (b) Probability vs Attack rate

Figure 7: Detection Accuracy and Verification Probability vs Attack rate

markov chain can accurately model the underlying network with minimal loss, hence we use the fourth order for the model checking.

7.3.3 Detection Accuracy

Mixed data was used to calculate the detection accuracy which had attack and benign logs both. Since the attack logs were generated separately in a controlled environment, the time stamps of the attack logs were adjusted by a fixed constant to have the same time window as of normal/benign logs. Allowed communication type ty values were used for the attack logs since other communication types do not exist in the model and can be detected easily. For attack detection, model learning was done in a continuous online learning fashion using a sliding window approach. The size of the sliding window was kept to one hour and the sliding window interval was set to one minute. Model was learnt separately for each smart collector in the dataset and detection results were averaged. Figure 7(a) shows the detection accuracy achieved by the presented model. It can be seen that high detection rate of more than 95% was achieved with a negligible false alarm rate of approximately 0.2%. Logs were collected from smart collectors for approximately 2000 meters. Average false alarm rate varies from 0.75 to 1.008 false alarms per meter per week, depending upon the threshold used for detection rates $> 70\%$. Please note that these rates are on the entire dataset collected. The utility provider we worked with has hundreds of thousand smart meters in a state. This might increase to millions of meters in a state for large-scale providers. These could be managed by one or multiple headend systems. Receiver Operating Characteristics (ROC) curve is generated by changing the verification probability (threshold) of configuration-based LTL properties which were verified against the model built using the mixed data logs. It is intuitive that the attack activity does not follow the state transitions as allowed in the temporal properties. Therefore, the higher volume of attack activity as compared to the benign activity can be easily detected even with the loose probability verification threshold. On the other hand, the lower volume of attack activity will be detected by the strict probability verification threshold. Figure 7(b) shows the effect of verification probability for multiple degree of DoS attacks. It can be observed that the higher attack rate is detectable with a loose verification probability threshold.

Complexity of the probabilistic model checker (PRISM) for a markov chain model and LTL property verification is doubly exponential in the size of LTL formula and polynomial in the size of state space [14]. Algorithm 1 was implemented in Java on a dual core machine to learn the model from the logs. The run-time complexity is in hundreds of milliseconds ($\approx$ 300ms) and the memory size of the model for each collector was few kilobytes ($\approx$ 20KB). The complexity was measured using HPROF [11] tool. Model was then verified against the LTL properties using PRISM. The run-time complexity of the properties verification is approximately 1.5 secs.

The presented model can be used in two fashions: 1) use a centralized approach and build a single giant model for the entire AMI, defining smart collector in either source or destination, the model can reduce the state space to possible states only for that particular smart collector, in this case offline model checking can be done in the headend by pulling the logs, 2) if the giant state machine exceeds the scalability limit of the model checker, each smart collector can be modeled separately. In case of modeling each smart collector separately, the model checking can be done online or offline, depending on the computational power available. Therefore, the proposed approach is flexible.

7.4 Scalability

In this section we discuss the scalability of the approach. PRISM is shown to be scalable up to 10^{10} states [20]. We also investigate the maximum number of meters that can be handled with various markov chain orders as shown in Figure 8. We show this for multiple markov chain orders i.e., 1 to 4 in Figure 8. For the first order markov chain, it can be observed from Figure 8(a) that the number of states increase linearly with the number of meters. In this case, it can accommodate up to 25000 meters per collector, although we show it up to 1000 meters in the graph in order to show the linear trend.

Similarly, the second order markov chain can handle up to 5000 meters as shown in Figure 8(b). It can be observed that the trend tends to be exponential. Scalability for third and fourth order markov chain is shown in Figure 8(c) and (d), respectively. It can be clearly observed that both the markovian orders increase the state space exponentially with the increase in number of meters. More specifically, the third and fourth order markov chains can work up to 108 and 16 meters, respectively.

Since many vendors (including our smart grid provider collaborator) use $8-16$ smart meters per collector, we found that using the fourth order markov chain is the optimal choice to maximize accuracy. We also found that many major vendors use similar limited number of meters per collector due to limited bandwidth or coverage, in power line communication and WiFi, respectively [1, 7]. However, vendors might support different models of the AMI technologies that offer different capacity of handling meters. For example, some smart grid providers/vendors plan to use other technologies that can support hundreds of meters per collector [7].

For this reason, we discuss two approaches that offer much more scalable solution but with reasonable accuracy sacrificing. First, third order markov chain can be used since it also incurs a low conditional entropy as shown in Figure 2(b). Moreover, it shows acceptable prediction accuracy, with slightly more false predictions as compared to fourth order as shown in Figure 6(b). Second, we alternatively extend the fourth order markov chain approach to handle more meters by state compression. Moreover, logs can also be divided based on the group of meters (16 in each) to conduct the analysis.

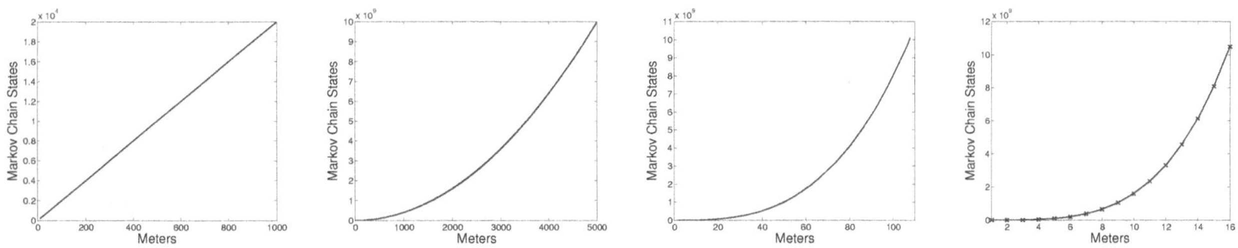

(a) First Order (b) Second Order (c) Third Order (d) Fourth Order

Figure 8: Meters vs Number of States

It can be seen from Figure 3(d) that very few (only tens of) states are highly likely (high probability) out of 1000. Thus, eventually less than 10% states are seen more frequently than others. Therefore, once the graph is made using Algorithm 1, we run a compression algorithm to remove the nodes having lower probability. We run the detection accuracy using the compressed model and note that it incurs an increase in the false positive rate i.e., from 0.2% to 0.3% while maintaining the same detection accuracy. However, the compressed state model can easily scale to more than 1000 meters per collector. Choosing the appropriate alternative approach depends on the AMI network technology under consideration.

7.5 Limitations

In this section we discuss the limitations of the proposed approach

- The original fourth order markov chain based approach only scales up to 16 meters per collector. In actual, a smart collector may have higher number of meters associated with it. To combat this, we discussed an alternative in the scalability section which supports upto 1000 meters per collector while incurring a slight increase in false alarm rate. Moreover, the original approach can also be used by dividing a smart collector's log into multiple chunks based on the groups of smart meters. Each chunk may have up to 16 meters grouped into it. This can easily be done by filtering the log based on the meter id.

- Attacks which do not involve communication with a smart collector will not be detected. However, we believe that the effect of such attacks would be limited to a particular area i.e., not large scale.

- Evasion robustness relies on the key used for interval randomization. We assume that the key is secured and attacker can not access it. However, if the key is compromised, attacker can evade the detection algorithm by generating traffic at the expected time intervals (calculated by key) using the configurations known to the attacker.

- Since AMI uses static configurations with limited protocols and applications, communication patterns do not change. Therefore, re-training is not required. However, if the re-training data, for any reason such as concept-drifting, includes malicious activities, attackers may evade the proposed technique. We see this is unlikely to happen if the retraining is performed on large number of smart collectors.

- The technique provides robustness against evasion, however, an attacker that has full access to and complete knowledge of the AMI may still be able to evade it.

8. CONCLUSION

In this work, we present a fourth order markov chain based model for intrusion detection since it incurs lower conditional entropy and higher prediction accuracy. Moreover, it fits the state space requirement of the AMI network under consideration. The novelty of the model lies in the configuration-based stochastic modeling of the AMI using the logs collected at smart collector and device configuration. Moreover, considering the challenges of AMI network, the proposed approach is practical since it does not require high computation power and memory in the field. However, it can also work offline in the substation by pulling the smart collector logs from the area. Therefore, it is flexible and incurs low cost. However, if smart collectors provide enough computation and memory, it can be deployed in parallel. It also does not need to be trained, unlike traditional intrusion detectors. The model provides acceptable detection accuracy of more than 95% with false alarm rate close to 0.2%. The model can be easily extended and customized based on the AMI network under consideration using other information in the logs and configurations. Therefore, the scope is not limited to what is presented here.

Acknowledgments

This work is a result of joint collaborative effort with a leading smart grid based utility provider. The work was done as part of the urban city project initiated by the utility provider which monitors several buildings for data analysis. We appreciate their expertise, effort in creating an AMI testbed in our university for testing, and sharing the data.

9. REFERENCES

[1] Ambient communication nodes. `http://www.ambientcorp.com/prod-nodes/`.

[2] Baier, C., and Katoen, J. P. *Principles of Model Checking*. The MIT Press, 2008.

[3] Baumeister, T. Literature review on smart grid cyber security. Tech. rep., Department of Information and Computer Sciences, University of Hawaii, 2010.

[4] Berthier, R., and Sanders, W. Specification-based intrusion detection for advanced metering infrastructures. In *IEEE 17th Pacific Rim International Symposium on Dependable Computing (PRDC)* (2011).

[5] Berthier, R., Sanders, W., and Khurana, H. Intrusion detection for advanced metering infrastructures: Requirements and architectural directions. In *First IEEE International Conference on Smart Grid Communications (SmartGridComm)* (2010).

[6] Cleveland, F. M. Cyber security issues for advanced metering infrasttructure (AMI). In *IEEE Power and Energy Society General Meeting - Conversion and Delivery of Electrical Energy in the 21st Century* (2008).

[7] Echelon data concentrator. `http://www.echelon.com/products/controllers/meter-data-concentrator/default.htm`.

[8] Faisal, M. A., Aung, Z., Williams, J., and Sanchez, A. Securing advanced metering infrastructure using intrusion detection system with data stream mining. In *Proceedings of Pacific Asia Workshop on Intelligence and Security Informatics (PAISI)* (2012).

[9] Garcia-Teodoro, P., Díaz-Verdejo, J. E., Maciá-Fernández, G., and Vázquez, E. Anomaly-based network intrusion detection: Techniques, systems and challenges. *Computers & Security* (2009).

[10] Gu, Y., McCullum, A., and Towsley, D. Detecting anomalies in network traffic using maximum entropy estimation. In *Proceedings of the ACM SIGCOMM Conference on Internet Measurement (IMC)* (2005).

[11] HPROF: A heap/CPU profiling tool. `http://docs.oracle.com/javase/7/docs/technotes/samples/hprof.html`.

[12] Idaho National Laboratory (INL). NSTB assessments summary report: Common industrial control system cyber security weaknesses, May 2010.

[13] Jung, J., Paxson, V., Berger, A. W., and Balakrishnan, H. Fast portscan detection using sequential hypothesis testing. In *Proceedings of the IEEE Symposium on Security and Privacy* (2004).

[14] Kwiatkowska, M., and Parker, D. Advances in probabilistic model checking. In *Proceedings 2011 Marktoberdorf Summer School: Tools for Analysis and Verification of Software Safety and Security* (2012).

[15] Mashima, D., and Cárdenas, A. A. Evaluating electricity theft detectors in smart grid networks. In *Research in Attacks, Intrusions, and Defenses* (2012).

[16] McLaughlin, S., Podkuiko, D., and McDaniel, P. Energy theft in the advanced metering infrastructure. *Critical Information Infrastructures Security* (2010).

[17] McLaughlin, S., Podkuiko, D., Miadzvezhanka, S., Delozier, A., and McDaniel, P. Multi-vendor penetration testing in the advanced metering infrastructure. In *Proceedings of the 26th Annual Computer Security Applications Conference, (ACSAC)* (2010).

[18] Merhav, M., Gutman, M., and Ziv, J. On the estimation of the order of a markov chain and universal data compression. *IEEE Transactions on Information Theory* (1989).

[19] Perdisci, R., Ariu, D., Fogla, P., Giacinto, G., and Lee, W. McPAD: A multiple classifier system for accurate payload-based anomaly detection. *Computer Networks* (2009).

[20] Probabilistic symbolic model checker PRISM. `http://www.prismmodelchecker.org/`.

[21] Smart grid news. `http://www.smartgridnews.com`.

[22] Smart meter - ARM. `http://www.arm.com/markets/embedded/smart-meter.php`.

[23] Ten, C., Hong, J., and Liu, C. Anomaly detection for cybersecurity of the substations. *IEEE Transactions on Smart Grid* (2011).

[24] The White House. Homeland Security Presidential Directive 7: Critical infrastructure identification, prioritization and protection, December 2003.

[25] U.S. Government Accountability office (GAO). information security: TVA needs to address weaknesses in control systems and networks, 2008.

[26] Wang, K., and Stolfo, S. J. Anomalous payload-based network intrusion detection. In *Recent Advances in Intrusion Detection (RAID)* (2004).

[27] Zhang, Y., Wang, L., Sun, W., Green, R., and Alam, M. Distributed intrusion detection system in a multi-layer network architecture of smart grids. *IEEE Transactions on Smart Grid* (2011).

[28] Zhu, B., and Sastry, S. SCADA-specific intrusion detection/prevention systems: A survey and taxonomy. In *First Workshop on Secure Control Systems (SCS)* (2010).

APPENDIX

A. BACKGROUND

Smart grids have two major networks i.e., power distribution and communication network. Power distribution network is intuitively the same as the legacy power network which is responsible for power generation, transmission and distribution to the consumers. However, communication network is responsible for monitoring different devices in the smart grid, thus providing the ease of management and efficient energy consumption. AMI is a core component of a smart grid responsible for the bi-directional communication between the headend and the meter. Basic architecture of an AMI is shown in Figure 1. AMI has three main components i.e., Home Area Network (HAN), Neighborhood Area Network (NAN), and Wide Area Network (WAN). HAN can be realized as the customer home network which is connected with the smart meter. Therefore, the smart meter acts as an interface for a HAN as it connects AMI and HAN in the bi-directional communication mode. NAN is responsible for the communication between the smart collectors and the smart meters. NAN scales from hundreds to thousands of nodes including the smart meters and the smart collectors. Lastly, WAN is mainly responsible for the backhaul connectivity of the NAN to the headend system.

Different communication channels can be used by the AMI for different components. For example, NAN may use wireless or power line communication in order to interact among nodes. Moreover, WAN uses the high range and bandwidth technologies for the purpose of connecting NAN to the headend. It can use cellular technologies or other dedicated communication medium. Usually utility providers utilize the existing network from a third party in order to connect the NAN to the headend.

Practical Constructions and New Proof Methods for Large Universe Attribute-Based Encryption

Yannis Rouselakis
The University of Texas at Austin
jrous@cs.utexas.edu

Brent Waters*
The University of Texas at Austin
bwaters@cs.utexas.edu

ABSTRACT

We propose two large universe Attribute-Based Encryption constructions. In a large universe ABE system any string can be used as an attribute and attributes need not be enumerated at system setup. Our first construction establishes a novel large universe Ciphertext-Policy ABE scheme on prime order bilinear groups, while the second achieves a significant efficiency improvement over the large universe Key-Policy ABE system of Lewko-Waters and Lewko. Both schemes are selectively secure in the standard model under two "q-type" assumptions similar to ones used in prior works. Our work brings back "program and cancel" techniques to this problem and aims in providing practical large universe ABE implementations.

To showcase the efficiency improvements over prior constructions, we provide implementations and benchmarks of our schemes in Charm; a programming environment for rapid prototyping of cryptographic primitives. We compare them to implementations of the only three published constructions that offer unbounded ABE in the standard model.

Categories and Subject Descriptors

E.3 [**Data**]: Data Encryption—*Public key cryptosystems*

General Terms

Security; Theory

*Supported by NSF CNS-0915361 and CNS-0952692, CNS-1228599 DARPA through the U.S. Office of Naval Research under Contract N00014-11-1-0382, DARPA N11AP20006, Google Faculty Research award, the Alfred P. Sloan Fellowship, Microsoft Faculty Fellowship, and Packard Foundation Fellowship. Any opinions, findings, and conclusions or recommendations expressed in this material are those of the author(s) and do not necessarily reflect the views of the Department of Defense or the U.S. Government.

CCS'13, November 4–8, 2013, Berlin, Germany.

ACM 978-1-4503-2477-9/13/11 ...$15.00.
http://dx.doi.org/10.1145/2508859.2516672.

Keywords

attribute-based encryption; large universe; unbounded; q-type assumptions; ciphertext-policy; key-policy; Charm

1. INTRODUCTION

Traditionally, public key encryption schemes provided any user with the ability to share data with another specific user in a private manner. However, in many applications we would like to have the additional capability to encrypt data for a set of users according to a specific policy on their credentials. For example, one might want to store data in a public server such that only parties with credentials of specific forms are able to decrypt. Instead of encrypting the data once for each party it would be beneficial to be able to encrypt only once for all desired parties. This encryption notion, called *Attribute-Based Encryption* (ABE), was introduced by Sahai and Waters [36]. In this setting, each user possesses a set of attributes/credentials and a secret key that corresponds to these credentials. The encrypting party can define any Boolean formula on the possible attributes and a user can decrypt if and only if his attribute set satisfies the Boolean formula.

Several attribute-based constructions have been presented since then (see related work below). A common classification property is whether a system is a "small universe" or "large universe" constructions. In "small universe" constructions the size of the attribute space is polynomially bounded in the security parameter and the attributes were fixed at setup. Moreover, the size of the public parameters grew linearly with the number of attributes. In "large universe" constructions, on the other hand, the size of the attribute universe can be exponentially large, which is a desirable feature.

Achieving the large universe property can be challenging. Different works either imposed restrictions on the expressiveness of the policies or were proved secure in the random oracle model. For example, in [20] a bound n was fixed at setup on the number of attributes that could be used while encrypting a message. For constructions that had no bounds on the expressiveness of policies and constant sized public parameters, the random oracle security model was used.

The above restrictions place undesirable burdens on the deployment of ABE schemes. If the designer of the system desires the benefits of avoiding the random oracle heuristic, he has to pick a specific bound for the expressiveness of the system at the setup time; either the size of the attribute universe or the bound on the policies. If the bound is too small, the system might exhaust its functionality and will have to be completely rebuilt. For example, consider the design of a framework that allows Attribute-Based Encryption in a huge multinational company and suppose that, as this company expands, a large number of new attributes have to be added to the system. If this number exceeds the bound set during the initial deployment of the system, then the company would have to re-deploy the (expanded) system and possibly re-encrypt all its data spending a huge amount of expenses. On the other hand, if the bound chosen is too big, the increased size of the public parameters will impose an unnecessary efficiency burden on all operations.

The first large-universe constructions in the standard model were presented in the recent work of Lewko and Waters [25]. They presented the first large universe KP-ABE construction, secure in the standard model. The system was proved *selectively* secure under static assumptions. The authors of [25] refer to their construction as an "unbounded" scheme, in the sense that the public parameters do not impose additional limitations on the functionality of the systems. Their scheme is indeed large universe, since the size of the attribute universe is exponentially large in the security parameter.

The authors utilized the *dual system* framework on composite order groups to prove security. While this framework is highly useful for the proofs, the actual constructions require use of bilinear groups of large composite order. As a result, these schemes sustain a significant efficiency overhead in comparison to prime order ABE constructions. In a recent result [22] building on [30, 32, 23, 17], one can actually "emulate" the effects of the composite order groups by creating special subspaces of vectors, called *dual vector spaces* introduced by Okamoto and Takashima, and construct a large universe KP-ABE system on prime order groups. This improves the efficiency of the original construction, but there is still a significant performance penalty due to the required size of the vectors.

In a subsequent work by Okamoto and Takashima [33], another unbounded KP-ABE scheme and the first unbounded CP-ABE scheme are presented. Both of them are the first *fully* secure unbounded ABE schemes in the standard model and utilize the *dual vector spaces* framework. Their systems are unbounded, since the size of the public parameters is constant and does not impose any limitations on the size of the attribute universe. However, the traditional notion of "large"-"small" universe is not applicable, since each "attribute" can take one or more different values from an *exponential-sized* space, instead of "present"/"not present". The total number of these sub-universes should be *polynomial* in the security parameter and the maximum number of times each sub-universe can be used in a policy is a parameter fixed at the setup of the system. As this bound is increased, the overall efficiency of the system is impaired. In our benchmarks, we implement the most efficient "basic version" of their constructions where this parameter is equal to 1, i.e. each sub-universe can be present only once in each policy.

Goals and Contributions We present new constructions and proof techniques for Large Universe ABE in the standard model. Departing from the above recent trends, our constructions are proved *selectively* secure using what is know as partitioning style techniques.

We believe that this is an interesting avenue to explore for two reasons. First, by considering selective model of security we are able to get more efficient and more practical constructions. While full security is the strongest notion of security, we believe selective is still a meaningful notion and can be a reasonable trade off for performance in some circumstances. In addition, new partitioning proofs can give different and new insights into the security or the style of a construction.

Second, Lewko and Waters [26] recently showed a surprising connection between Dual System Encryption and older selective proofs. Prior fully secure ABE systems [23] required an additional (relative to selective schemes) limit t on the number of times an attribute could be used in a formula. The public parameters and ciphertext size for KP-ABE (key size for CP-ABE) grew proportionally to the bound t. Lewko and Waters showed that through a new "delayed parameter" variant of Dual System Encryption this limit could be done away with. An integral part of their proof was that it leveraged older "program and cancel" style techniques. Given this recent work, a reasonable conclusion is that developing selectively secure proofs might typically become a first step to developing full security. (We note that the large universe construction of [25] was only proved selectively secure.)

We aim to get practical large-universe ABE schemes by adapting and expanding the system from [25] into the prime order setting. In proving security we go back to more traditional "program and cancel" techniques instead of the dual system framework. We present two practical large universe ABE constructions (one CP-ABE and one KP-ABE) in prime order bilinear groups both selectively secure in the standard model under two different q-type assumptions. Our three main objectives in this work were *large universe constructions*, *efficiency*, and *security in the standard model.* Both schemes support a "large universe" attribute space and their public parameters consist of a constant number of group elements. No bounds or other restrictions are imposed on the monotonic Boolean formulas or the attribute sets used by the algorithms of the schemes; thus eliminating the need for design decisions at setup. The efficiency objective refrained us from using composite order groups or dual pairing vector spaces, while to achieve security in the standard model we relied on non static (q-type) assumptions and selective notions. These assumptions are non static in the sense that a polynomial number of terms is given to the adversary and therefore they are intuitively stronger than the static ones. However, the polynomial number of terms gives the ability to the simulator of the proof to embed the additional entropy in the constant number of public parameters. We showcase different techniques for harnessing the power of these assumptions to achieve our large universe constructions. Finally, we demonstrate the efficiency of our constructions by implementing our schemes. We compare performance results to other ABE schemes in prime order groups.

Our Techniques The techniques used to achieve our goals and prove the security of our schemes fall in the category of *partitioning* methodologies. In this setting the simulator of the reduction sets up the public parameters of the systems in such a way that the set of the possible policies (for KP-ABE) or the powerset of the attribute universe (for CP-ABE) is partitioned in two disjoint sets. One for which he can create the secret keys and answer the attackers' queries, and one for which this is not possible, where the challenge query should belong. Since we are dealing with selective security notions, the simulator knows in advance the required challenge set and therefore the suitable partition. However due to the fact that we are aiming for large universe ABE, which implies constant size public parameters, the simulator has to embed a polynomial amount of "challenge information" in them. This is achieved by utilizing the non static power of our assumptions. Namely, the assumptions' "size" depends on the size of the declared challenge query. The additional terms available to the simulator allow him to create all the necessary terms for the reduction.

Both our schemes work in a "layered" fashion in order to encrypt information securely and being able to decrypt. In the KP-ABE construction, which is simpler and directly inspired by the composite order construction of [25], two "layers" are employed: the "secret sharing" layer and the "attribute layer". The first layer is responsible for the sharing of the master secret key during the key generation algorithm and the storing of the blinding factor randomness during the encryption algorithm. The "attribute layer" holds information about the attributes used in both key generation and encryption phases. A "binder term" is utilized to connect the two layers in a secure way. In the CP-ABE construction the situation is slightly more complicated due to the fact that the policies are applied on the ciphertext side. As a result, the "sharing" is applied to the blinding factor randomness and not on the master secret key. Therefore, an additional "binder term" in the public parameters is being used to allow correct decryption using the master secret key. As we will see, the assumptions and the corresponding reductions follow closely this "layer" intuition.

Finally, we mention that both constructions use the "individual randomness" technique from [25] in the "attribute layer" to achieve the large universe functionality. The component for each attribute is masked by a different randomness and as a result no restrictions are imposed on the policies or the attributes, since each component is individually randomized.

1.1 Related Work

Attribute-Based Encryption was introduced by Sahai and Waters [36]. The refinement of the two notions was given in [20] and many CP-ABE and KP-ABE selectively secure constructions followed [6, 15, 19, 34, 35, 43]. Most of them work for monotonic access structures with the exception of the schemes by Ostrovsky, Sahai, and Waters [34], who showed how to realize negation by incorporating specific revocation schemes into the GPSW construction. Fully secure constructions in the standard model were first provided by Okamoto and Takashima [32] and Lewko, Okamoto, Sahai, Takashima, and Waters [23]. The first large universe KP-ABE construction in the standard model was given in [25] (composite order groups) and the first fully secure unbounded constructions were given in [33]. Okamoto and Takashima initiated the dual pairing vector space framework in various works [30, 31, 32], which lead to the first large universe KP-ABE construction in prime order group groups by Lewko [22]. Parameterized (non static) assumptions were introduced in [7] and used in several subsequent works [18, 43]. The problem of an environment with multiple central authorities in ABE was considered in [13, 14, 24], while several authors have presented schemes that do not address the problem of collusion resistance [40, 28, 11, 2, 3, 4].

We note that several techniques in ABE schemes have roots in Identity-Based Encryption [37, 8, 16, 7, 42, 18, 9]. Finally, we mention here the related concept of Predicate Encryption introduced by Katz, Sahai, and Waters [21] and further refined in [39, 38, 31, 23, 32, 10].

1.2 Organization

In Sec. 2 we introduce some notation, background information about access structures and linear secret-sharing schemes, and the complexity assumption for our CP-ABE scheme. Section 3 contains the algorithms and the selective security definition for CP-ABE schemes. Our CP-ABE construction and the security proof are in Sec. 4. Finally, implementations and efficiency results are presented in Sec. 5. The assumption for our KP-ABE construction is in App. A. In App. B and App. C we present the KP-ABE algorithms with the security definition, and our KP-ABE construction with the security proof, respectively.

2. PRELIMINARIES

2.1 Notation

For $n \in \mathbb{N}$, we define $[n] \stackrel{\text{def.}}{=} \{1, 2, \ldots, n\}$. Also, for $n_1, n_2, \ldots, n_k \in \mathbb{N}$: $[n_1, n_2, \ldots, n_k] \stackrel{\text{def.}}{=} [n_1] \times [n_2] \times \ldots \times [n_m]$. When $\mathcal{S}$ is a set, we denote by $s \stackrel{\$}{\leftarrow} \mathcal{S}$ the fact that the variable s is picked uniformly at random from $\mathcal{S}$. We write $s_1, s_2, \ldots, s_n \stackrel{\$}{\leftarrow} \mathcal{S}$ as shorthand for $s_1 \stackrel{\$}{\leftarrow} \mathcal{S}, s_2 \stackrel{\$}{\leftarrow} \mathcal{S}, \ldots, s_n \stackrel{\$}{\leftarrow} \mathcal{S}$. By $\mathsf{negl}(n)$ we denote a negligible function in n and by PPT probabilistic polynomial-time.

The set of matrices of size $m \times n$ with elements in $\mathbb{Z}_p$ is denoted by $\mathbb{Z}_p^{m \times n}$. Special subsets are the set of row vectors of length n: $\mathbb{Z}_p^{1 \times n}$, and column vectors of length n: $\mathbb{Z}_p^{n \times 1}$. When $\vec{v}$ is a vector (of any type), we will denote by v_i the i-th element and by $\langle \vec{v}, \vec{w} \rangle$ the inner product of vectors $\vec{v}$ and $\vec{w}$.

2.2 Access Structures and Linear Secret-Sharing Schemes

In this section, we present the formal definitions of access structures and linear secret-sharing schemes introduced in [5], adapted to match our setting.

Definition 2.1 (Access Structures [5]). *Let $\mathcal{U}$ be the attribute universe. An* access structure *on $\mathcal{U}$ is a collection $\mathbb{A}$ of non-empty sets of attributes, i.e. $\mathbb{A} \subseteq 2^{\mathcal{U}} \setminus \{\ \}$. The sets in $\mathbb{A}$ are called the* authorized sets *and the sets not in $\mathbb{A}$ are called the* unauthorized sets.

Additionally, an access structure is called monotone *if $\forall B, C \in \mathbb{A}$: if $B \in \mathbb{A}$ and $B \subseteq C$, then $C \in \mathbb{A}$.*

In our constructions, we only consider monotone access structures, which means that as a user (CP-ABE setting) acquires more attributes, he will not lose his possible decryption privileges. General access structures in large universe ABE can be realized by splitting the attribute universe in half and treating the attributes of one half as the negated versions of the attributes in the other half [20]. We note that if the access structure is encoded as a monotonic Boolean formula over attributes[1], there is a generic algorithm that

[1]A monotonic Boolean formula consists of only AND, OR, and threshold gates, for example $A_1 \wedge (A_2 \vee A_3)$. This means

generates the corresponding access policy in polynomial time [5, 24].

Definition 2.2 (Linear Secret-Sharing Schemes (LSSS) [5]). *Let p be a prime and $\mathcal{U}$ the attribute universe. A secret-sharing scheme Π with domain of secrets $\mathbb{Z}_p$ realizing access structures on $\mathcal{U}$ is* linear over $\mathbb{Z}_p$ *if*

1. *The shares of a secret $s \in \mathbb{Z}_p$ for each attribute form a vector over $\mathbb{Z}_p$.*
2. *For each access structure $\mathbb{A}$ on $\mathcal{U}$, there exists a matrix $M \in \mathbb{Z}_p^{\ell \times n}$, called the share-generating matrix, and a function ρ, that labels the rows of M with attributes from $\mathcal{U}$, i.e. $\rho : [\ell] \to \mathcal{U}$, which satisfy the following:*

   During the generation of the shares, we consider the column vector $\vec{v} = (s, r_2, \ldots, r_n)^\top$, where $r_2, \ldots, r_n \xleftarrow{\$} \mathbb{Z}_p$. Then the vector of ℓ shares of the secret s according to Π is equal to $M\vec{v} \in \mathbb{Z}_p^{\ell \times 1}$. The share $(M\vec{v})_j$ where $j \in [\ell]$ "belongs" to attribute $\rho(j)$.

   We will be referring to the pair (M, ρ) as the policy of the access structure $\mathbb{A}$.

According to [5], each secret-sharing scheme (not only the linear ones) should satisfy the *reconstruction requirement* (each authorized set can reconstruct the secret) and the *security requirement* (any unauthorized set cannot reveal any partial information about the secret).

In our setting, let $\mathcal{S}$ denote an authorized set for the access structure $\mathbb{A}$ encoded by the policy (M, ρ). Then let I be the set of rows whose labels are in $\mathcal{S}$, i.e. $I = \{i | i \in [\ell] \wedge \rho(i) \in \mathcal{S}\}$. The reconstruction requirement asserts that the vector $(1, 0, \ldots, 0)$ is in the span of rows of M indexed by I. This means that there exist constants $\{\omega_i\}_{i \in I}$ in $\mathbb{Z}_p$ such that for any valid shares $\{\lambda_i = (M\vec{v})_i\}_{i \in I}$ of a secret s according to Π, it is true that: $\sum_{i \in I} \omega_i \lambda_i = s$. Additionally, it has been proved in [5] that the constants $\{\omega_i\}_{i \in I}$ can be found in time polynomial in the size of the share-generating matrix M.

On the other hand, for unauthorized sets $\mathcal{S}'$ no such constants $\{\omega_i\}$ exist. Moreover, in this case it is also true that if $I' = \{i | i \in [\ell] \wedge \rho(i) \in \mathcal{S}'\}$, there exists a vector $\vec{w} \in \mathbb{Z}_p^{1 \times n}$, such that its first component w_1 is any non zero element in $\mathbb{Z}_p$ and $\langle \vec{M_i}, \vec{w} \rangle = 0$ for all $i \in I'$, where $\vec{M_i} = (M_{i,1}, M_{i,2}, \ldots, M_{i,n})$; the i-th row of M.

2.3 Assumption 1

For our CP-ABE construction we will use a q-type assumption on prime order bilinear groups, denoted by q-1, which is similar to the Decisional Parallel Bilinear Diffie-Hellman Exponent Assumption [43]. It is parameterized by a security parameter $\lambda \in \mathbb{N}$ and an integer q, polynomial in λ. We assume that there exists a group generator algorithm $\mathcal{G}(1^\lambda) \to (p, \mathbb{G}, \mathbb{G}_T, e)$ that outputs the description of the (symmetric) bilinear group of order $p = \Theta(2^\lambda)$. This assumption can be proved secure in the generic group model, but the proof is omitted due to space constraints. It is defined via the following game between a challenger and an attacker:

Initially the challenger calls the group generation algorithm with input the security parameter, picks a random group element $g \xleftarrow{\$} \mathbb{G}$, and $q+2$ random exponents $a, s, b_1, b_2, \ldots, b_q \xleftarrow{\$} \mathbb{Z}_p$. Then he sends to the attacker the group description $(p, \mathbb{G}, \mathbb{G}_T, e)$ and all of the following terms:

$$
\begin{array}{ll}
g, g^s & \\
g^{a^i}, g^{b_j}, g^{sb_j}, g^{a^i b_j}, g^{a^i / b_j^2} & \forall (i,j) \in [q,q] \\
g^{a^i b_j / b_{j'}^2} & \forall (i,j,j') \in [2q,q,q] \text{ with } j \neq j' \\
g^{a^i / b_j} & \forall (i,j) \in [2q,q] \text{ with } i \neq q+1 \\
g^{s a^i b_j / b_{j'}}, g^{s a^i b_j / b_{j'}^2} & \forall (i,j,j') \in [q,q,q] \text{ with } j \neq j'
\end{array}
$$

The challenger also flips a random coin $b \xleftarrow{\$} \{0,1\}$ and if $b = 0$, it gives to the attacker the term $e(g,g)^{sa^{q+1}}$. Otherwise it gives a random term $R \xleftarrow{\$} \mathbb{G}_T$. Finally the attacker outputs a guess $b' \in \{0,1\}$.

Definition 2.3. *We say that the q-1 assumption holds if all PPT attackers have at most a negligible advantage in λ in the above security game, where the advantage is defined as* $\mathsf{Adv} = \Pr[b' = b] - 1/2$.

Remark: Notice the absence of the term g^{a^{q+1}/b_j} in the fourth line of the assumption. If this term were given to the attacker, then he could break the assumption trivially by pairing it with the corresponding g^{sb_j} term. On the other hand, the term $g^{a^{q+1} b_j / b_{j'}^2}$ is given, and this poses no problems in the generic group model since $j \neq j'$ and by possible pairing the adversary cannot get rid of the b_j's.

3. CIPHERTEXT - POLICY ATTRIBUTE - BASED ENCRYPTION

3.1 Algorithms

A Ciphertext-Policy Attribute-Based Encryption scheme consists of the following four PPT algorithms:

- $\mathsf{Setup}(1^\lambda) \to (pp, msk)$: The Setup algorithm takes the security parameter $\lambda \in \mathbb{N}$ encoded in unary and outputs the public parameters pp and the master secret key msk. We assume that the public parameters contain a description of the attribute universe $\mathcal{U}$. [2]
- $\mathsf{KeyGen}(1^\lambda, pp, msk, \mathcal{S}) \to sk$: The key generation algorithm takes as inputs the public parameters pp, the master secret key msk and a set of attributes $\mathcal{S} \subseteq \mathcal{U}$. The security parameter is included in the inputs to ensure that it is polynomial time in λ. The algorithm generates a secret key corresponding to $\mathcal{S}$.
- $\mathsf{Encrypt}(1^\lambda, pp, m, \mathbb{A}) \to ct$: The encryption algorithm takes as inputs the public parameters pp, a plaintext message m, and an access structure $\mathbb{A}$ on $\mathcal{U}$. It outputs the ciphertext ct.
- $\mathsf{Decrypt}(1^\lambda, pp, sk, ct) \to m$: The decryption algorithm takes as inputs the public parameters pp, a secret key sk, and a ciphertext ct. It outputs the plaintext m.

Correctness: We require that a CP-ABE scheme is correct, i.e the decryption algorithm correctly decrypts a ciphertext of an access structure $\mathbb{A}$ with a secret key on $\mathcal{S}$, when $\mathcal{S}$ is an authorized set of $\mathbb{A}$. Formally:

that as a key (in CP-ABE) or a ciphertext (in KP-ABE) acquires more attributes it will not lose the decryption capabilities.

[2]In previous CP-ABE constructions the attribute universe $\mathcal{U}$ (or its size) was one of the arguments of the Setup algorithm. In our constructions, the attribute universe depends only on the size of the underlying group $\mathbb{G}$, which depends on the security parameter λ and the group generation algorithm.

Definition 3.1. *A CP-ABE scheme is* correct *when for all messages m, and all attribute sets $\mathcal{S}$ and access structures $\mathbb{A}$ with $\mathcal{S} \in \mathbb{A}$ (i.e. for $\mathcal{S}$ authorized), any pair (pp, msk) output from $\mathsf{Setup}(1^\lambda)$, any secret key sk output from $\mathsf{KeyGen}(1^\lambda, pp, msk, \mathcal{S})$, and any ciphertext ct output by $\mathsf{Encrypt}(1^\lambda, pp, m, \mathbb{A})$, it is true that: $\mathsf{Decrypt}(1^\lambda, pp, sk, ct) = m$.*

3.2 CP-ABE Selective Security

In this section we present the definition of selective security for CP-ABE schemes. This is described by a game between a challenger and an attacker and is parameterized by the security parameter $\lambda \in \mathbb{N}$. The phases of the game are the following:

- **Initialization:** In this phase the attacker declares the challenge access structure $\mathbb{A}^*$, which he will try to attack, and sends it to the challenger.
- **Setup:** Here the challenger calls the $\mathsf{Setup}(1^\lambda)$ algorithm and sends the public parameters pp to the attacker.
- **Query Phase 1:** In this phase the attacker can adaptively ask for secret keys for the sets of attributes $\mathcal{S}_1$, $\mathcal{S}_2$, ..., $\mathcal{S}_{Q_1}$. For each $\mathcal{S}_i$ the challenger calls $\mathsf{KeyGen}(msk, \mathcal{S}_i) \to sk_i$ and sends sk_i to the attacker. The restriction that has to be satisfied for each query is that none of the queried sets satisfies the challenge access structure, i.e. $\forall i \in [Q_1] : \mathcal{S}_i \notin \mathbb{A}^*$.
- **Challenge:** The attacker declares two equal-length plaintexts m_0 and m_1 and sends them to the challenger. He flips a random coin $b \in \{0,1\}$ and calls $\mathsf{Encrypt}(m_b, \mathbb{A}^*) \to ct$. He sends ct to the attacker.
- **Query Phase 2:** This the same as query phase 1. The attacker asks for the secret key for the sets $\mathcal{S}_{Q_1+1}$, $\mathcal{S}_{Q_1+2}$, ..., $\mathcal{S}_Q$, for which the same restriction holds: $\forall i \in [Q] : \mathcal{S}_i \notin \mathbb{A}^*$.
- **Guess:** The attacker outputs his guess $b' \in \{0,1\}$ for b.

Definition 3.2. *A CP-ABE scheme is* selectively secure *if all PPT attackers have at most a negligible advantage in λ in the above security game, where the advantage of an attacker is defined as $\mathsf{Adv} = \Pr[b' = b] - 1/2$.*

4. OUR LARGE UNIVERSE CP-ABE

In this section we present our large universe CP-ABE construction. The public parameters consist of the six group elements $(g, u, h, w, v, e(g,g)^\alpha)$, which intuitively are utilized in two separate "layers" to achieve secure large universe CP-ABE. In the "attribute layer", the u, h terms provide a Boneh-Boyen-style [7] hash function $(u^A h)$, while in the "secret sharing layer" the w term holds the secret randomness r during key generation and the shares of the secret randomness s during encryption. The v term is used to "bind" the two layers together. The g and $e(g,g)^\alpha$ terms are used to introduce the master secret key functionality and allow correct decryption.

4.1 Construction

Our scheme consists of the following four algorithms:

- $\mathsf{Setup}(1^\lambda) \to (pp, msk)$: The setup algorithm calls the group generator algorithm $\mathcal{G}(1^\lambda)$ and gets the descriptions of the groups and the bilinear mapping $D = (p, \mathbb{G}, \mathbb{G}_T, e)$, where p is the prime order of the groups $\mathbb{G}$ and $\mathbb{G}_T$. The attribute universe is $\mathcal{U} = \mathbb{Z}_p$.

Then the algorithm picks the random terms $g, u, h, w, v \xleftarrow{\$} \mathbb{G}$ and $\alpha \xleftarrow{\$} \mathbb{Z}_p$. It outputs

$$pp = (D, g, u, h, w, v, e(g,g)^\alpha) \qquad msk = (\alpha)$$

- $\mathsf{KeyGen}(msk, \mathcal{S} = \{A_1, A_2, \ldots, A_k\} \subseteq \mathbb{Z}_p) \to sk$: Initially, the key generation algorithm picks $k+1$ random exponents $r, r_1, r_2, \ldots, r_k \xleftarrow{\$} \mathbb{Z}_p$. Then it computes $K_0 = g^\alpha w^r$, $K_1 = g^r$, and for every $\tau \in [k]$

$$K_{\tau,2} = g^{r_\tau} \text{ and } K_{\tau,3} = (u^{A_\tau} h)^{r_\tau} v^{-r}$$

The secret key output is $sk = (\mathcal{S}, K_0, K_1, \{K_{\tau,2}, K_{\tau,3}\}_{\tau \in [k]})$.

- $\mathsf{Encrypt}(m \in \mathbb{G}_T, (M, \rho)) \to ct$: The encryption algorithm takes the plaintext message m and the access structure encoded in an LSSS policy, with $M \in \mathbb{Z}_p^{\ell \times n}$ and $\rho : [\ell] \to \mathbb{Z}_p$. First, it picks $\vec{y} = (s, y_2, \ldots, y_n)^\top \xleftarrow{\$} \mathbb{Z}_p^{n \times 1}$. In the terminology of Sec. 2.2, s is the random secret to be shared among the shares. The vector of the shares is $\vec{\lambda} = (\lambda_1, \lambda_2, \ldots, \lambda_\ell)^\top = M\vec{y}$.

It then picks ℓ random exponents $t_1, t_2, \ldots, t_\ell \xleftarrow{\$} \mathbb{Z}_p$ and calculates $C = m \cdot e(g,g)^{\alpha s}$, $C_0 = g^s$, and for every $\tau \in [\ell]$

$$C_{\tau,1} = w^{\lambda_\tau} v^{t_\tau}, \quad C_{\tau,2} = (u^{\rho(\tau)} h)^{-t_\tau} \text{ and } C_{\tau,3} = g^{t_\tau}$$

The ciphertext output is

$$ct = ((M, \rho), C, C_0, \{C_{\tau,1}, C_{\tau,2}, C_{\tau,3}\}_{\tau \in [\ell]})$$

- $\mathsf{Decrypt}(sk, ct) \to m$: Firstly, the decryption algorithm calculates the set of rows in M that provide a share to attributes in $\mathcal{S}$, i.e. $I = \{i : \rho(i) \in \mathcal{S}\}$. Then it computes the constants $\{\omega_i \in \mathbb{Z}_p\}_{i \in I}$ such that $\sum_{i \in I} \omega_i \vec{M}_i = (1, 0, \ldots, 0)$, where $\vec{M}_i$ is the i-th row of the matrix M. These constants exist if the set $\mathcal{S}$ is an authorized set of the policy (c.f. Sec. 2.2).

Then it calculates

$$B = \frac{e(C_0, K_0)}{\prod_{i \in I} (e(C_{i,1}, K_1) e(C_{i,2}, K_{\tau,2}) e(C_{i,3}, K_{\tau,3}))^{\omega_i}}$$

where τ is the index of the attribute $\rho(i)$ in $\mathcal{S}$ (it depends on i). The algorithm outputs $m = C/B$.

Correctness: If the attribute set $\mathcal{S}$ of the secret key is authorized, we have that $\sum_{i \in I} \omega_i \lambda_i = s$. Therefore:

$$B = \frac{e(g,g)^{\alpha s} e(g,w)^{rs}}{\prod_{i \in I} e(g,w)^{r\omega_i \lambda_i} e(g,v)^{r t_i \omega_i} e(g, u^{\rho(i)} h)^{-r_\tau t_i \omega_i}} \cdot \frac{1}{\prod_{i \in I} e(g, u^{\rho(i)} h)^{r_\tau t_i \omega_i} e(g,v)^{-r t_i \omega_i}}$$
$$= \frac{e(g,g)^{\alpha s} e(g,w)^{rs}}{e(g,w)^{r \sum_{i \in I} \omega_i \lambda_i}} = e(g,g)^{\alpha s}$$

4.2 Proof of Selective Security

We will prove the following theorem regarding the selective security of our CP-ABE scheme:

Theorem 4.1. *If the q-1 assumption holds then all PPT adversaries with a challenge matrix of size $\ell \times n$, where $\ell, n \leq q$, have a negligible advantage in selectively breaking our scheme.*

Proof. To prove the theorem we will assume that there exists a PPT attacker $\mathcal{A}$ with a challenge matrix that satisfies the restriction, which has a non negligible advantage $\mathsf{Adv}_{\mathcal{A}}$ in selectively breaking our scheme. Using this attacker we will build a PPT simulator $\mathcal{B}$ that attacks the q-1 assumption with a non negligible advantage.

Initialization: $\mathcal{B}$ receives the given terms from the assumption and a challenge policy (M^*, ρ^*) from $\mathcal{A}$. We have that M^* is an $\ell \times n$ matrix, where $\ell, n \leq q$, and $\rho^* : [\ell] \to \mathbb{Z}_p$.

Setup: The simulator $\mathcal{B}$ has to provide $\mathcal{A}$ the public parameters of the system. In order to do that it implicitly sets the master secret key of the scheme to be $\alpha = a^{q+1} + \tilde{\alpha}$, where a, q are set in the assumption and $\tilde{\alpha} \xleftarrow{\$} \mathbb{Z}_p$ is a known to $\mathcal{B}$ random exponent. Notice that this way α is correctly distributed and a is information-theoretically hidden from $\mathcal{A}$. Then $\mathcal{B}$ picks the random exponents $\tilde{v}, \tilde{u}, \tilde{h} \xleftarrow{\$} \mathbb{Z}_p$ and using the assumption gives to $\mathcal{A}$ the following public parameters:

$$\begin{aligned}
g &= g \\
u &= g^{\tilde{u}} \cdot \textstyle\prod_{(j,k)\in[\ell,n]} \left(g^{a^k/b_j^2}\right)^{M^*_{j,k}} \\
h &= g^{\tilde{h}} \cdot \textstyle\prod_{(j,k)\in[\ell,n]} \left(g^{a^k/b_j^2}\right)^{-\rho^*(j) M^*_{j,k}} \\
w &= g^a \\
v &= g^{\tilde{v}} \cdot \textstyle\prod_{(j,k)\in[\ell,n]} \left(g^{a^k/b_j}\right)^{M^*_{j,k}} \\
e(g,g)^\alpha &= e(g^a, g^{a^q}) \cdot e(g,g)^{\tilde{\alpha}}
\end{aligned}$$

The term w is properly distributed in $\mathcal{A}$'s view because the term $e(g,g)^\alpha$ hides the exponent a information-theoretically. The terms v, u, h are also properly distributed due to $\tilde{v}, \tilde{u}, \tilde{h}$, respectively. Notice that all terms can be calculated by the simulator using suitable terms from the assumption and the challenge policy given by $\mathcal{A}$.

As one can see, the "attribute layer", which consists of the terms u, h, is made up of terms whose exponents have b_i^2 in the denominator, the "binder term" v has b_i, and the "secret sharing layer" w has only one power of a. This scaling of the powers of b_i will allow our simulator to properly simulate all terms.

Query phases 1 and 2: Now the simulator has to produce secret keys for non authorized sets of attributes requested by $\mathcal{A}$. In both phases the treatment is the same. We describe here the way $\mathcal{B}$ works in order to create a key for an attribute set $\mathcal{S} = \{A_1, A_2, \ldots, A_{|\mathcal{S}|}\}$ received by $\mathcal{A}$.

Since $\mathcal{S}$ is non authorized for (M^*, ρ^*), there exists a vector $\vec{w} = (w_1, w_2, \ldots, w_n)^\top \in \mathbb{Z}_p^n$ such that $w_1 = -1$ and $\langle \vec{M}_i^*, \vec{w} \rangle = 0$ for all $i \in I = \{i | i \in [\ell] \wedge \rho^*(i) \in \mathcal{S}\}$ (c.f. Sec. 2.2). The simulator calculates $\vec{w}$ using linear algebra. Then it picks $\tilde{r} \xleftarrow{\$} \mathbb{Z}_p$ and implicitly sets

$$r = \tilde{r} + w_1 a^q + w_2 a^{q-1} + \ldots + w_n a^{q+1-n} = \tilde{r} + \sum_{i\in[n]} w_i a^{q+1-i}$$

This is properly distributed due to $\tilde{r}$. Then using the suitable terms from the assumption it calculates:

$$\begin{aligned}
K_0 = g^\alpha w^r &= g^{a^{q+1}} g^{\tilde{\alpha}} g^{a\tilde{r}} \prod_{i\in[n]} g^{w_i a^{q+2-i}} \\
&= g^{\tilde{\alpha}} (g^a)^{\tilde{r}} \prod_{i=2}^{n} \left(g^{a^{q+2-i}}\right)^{w_i} \\
K_1 = g^r &= g^{\tilde{r}} \prod_{i\in[n]} \left(g^{a^{q+1-i}}\right)^{w_i}
\end{aligned}$$

Additionally, for all $\tau \in [|\mathcal{S}|]$ it has to compute the terms $K_{\tau,2} = g^{r_\tau}$ and $K_{\tau,3} = (u^{A_\tau} h)^{r_\tau} v^{-r}$. The common part v^{-r} for these terms is the following:

$$\begin{aligned}
& v^{-\tilde{r}} \left(g^{\tilde{v}} \prod_{(j,k)\in[\ell,n]} g^{a^k M^*_{j,k}/b_j} \right)^{-\sum_{i\in[n]} w_i a^{q+1-i}} \\
&= v^{-\tilde{r}} \prod_{i\in[n]} \left(g^{a^{q+1-i}}\right)^{-\tilde{v} w_i} \cdot \prod_{\substack{(i,j,k)\in \\ [n,\ell,n]}} g^{-w_i M^*_{j,k} a^{q+1+k-i}/b_j} \\
&= \underbrace{v^{-\tilde{r}} \prod_{i\in[n]} \left(g^{a^{q+1-i}}\right)^{-\tilde{v} w_i} \cdot \prod_{\substack{(i,j,k)\in \\ [n,\ell,n], i\neq k}} \left(g^{\frac{a^{q+1+k-i}}{b_j}}\right)^{-w_i M^*_{j,k}}}_{\Phi} \\
&\quad \cdot \prod_{(i,j)\in[n,\ell]} g^{-w_i M^*_{j,i} a^{q+1}/b_j} \\
&= \Phi \cdot \prod_{j\in[\ell]} g^{-\langle \vec{w}, \vec{M}^*_j \rangle a^{q+1}/b_j} = \Phi \cdot \prod_{\substack{j\in[\ell] \\ \rho^*(j)\notin S}} g^{-\langle \vec{w}, \vec{M}^*_j \rangle a^{q+1}/b_j}
\end{aligned}$$

The Φ part can be calculated by the simulator using the assumption, while the second part has to be canceled by the $(u^{A_\tau} h)^{r_\tau}$ part. So for every attribute $A_\tau \in S$ the simulator sets implicitly

$$\begin{aligned}
r_\tau &= \tilde{r}_\tau + r \cdot \sum_{\substack{i'\in[\ell] \\ \rho^*(i')\notin S}} \frac{b_{i'}}{A_\tau - \rho^*(i')} \\
&= \tilde{r}_\tau + \tilde{r} \cdot \sum_{\substack{i'\in[\ell] \\ \rho^*(i')\notin S}} \frac{b_{i'}}{A_\tau - \rho^*(i')} + \sum_{\substack{(i,i')\in[n,\ell] \\ \rho^*(i')\notin S}} \frac{w_i b_{i'} a^{q+1-i}}{A_\tau - \rho^*(i')}
\end{aligned}$$

where $\tilde{r}_\tau \xleftarrow{\$} \mathbb{Z}_p$ and therefore r_τ is properly distributed. The use of the b_i's in the numerators of the fractions is explained by the "layer" intuition presented before. Namely, these b_i will cancel with the b_i^2 denominators in the "attribute layer" and provide a cancellation for the unknown part of v^{-r}.

Also, notice that r_τ is well-defined only for attributes in the specific unauthorized set $\mathcal{S}$ or unrelated attributes (outside the policy), since the sum is over the i' such that $\rho^*(i') \notin \mathcal{S}$. Therefore, for all $A_\tau \in \mathcal{S}$ or $A_\tau \notin \rho^*([\ell])$, the denominators $A_\tau - \rho^*(i')$ are non zero. If the simulator tries to include more attributes of the policy in the key (and possibly make a key for an authorized set), he would have to divide by zero (see Figure 1). Namely, the set of secret keys is partitioned in two sets: the unauthorized, which the simulator can create using the above method, and the authorized, which the simulator cannot create.

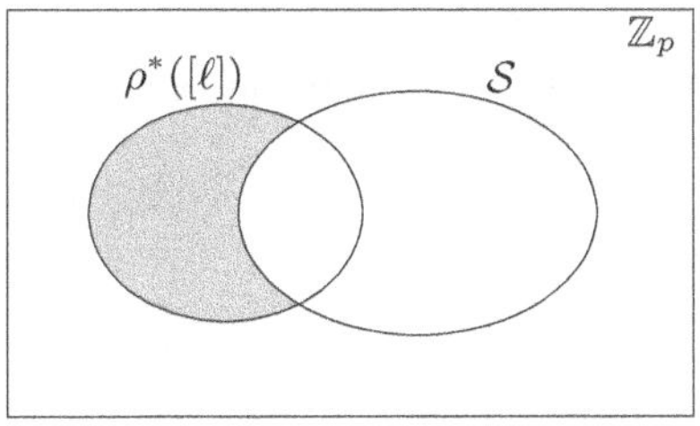

Figure 1: The simulator can not create the components for attributes in the gray area.

After some algebraic manipulations, the $(u^{A_\tau} h)^{r_\tau}$ part of $K_{\tau,3}$ is computed as:

$$
\begin{aligned}
&(u^{A_\tau} h)^{\tilde{r}_\tau} \cdot (K_{\tau,2}/g^{\tilde{r}_\tau})^{\tilde{u}A_\tau+\tilde{h}} \\
&\cdot \prod_{\substack{(i',j,k)\in[\ell,\ell,n]\\ \rho^*(i')\notin S}} g^{\tilde{r}(A_\tau-\rho^*(j))M^*_{j,k}b_{i'}a^k/(A_\tau-\rho^*(i'))b_j^2} \\
&\cdot \prod_{\substack{(i,i',j,k)\in[n,\ell,\ell,n]\\ \rho^*(i')\notin S}} g^{(A_\tau-\rho^*(j))w_i M^*_{j,k}b_{i'}a^{q+1+k-i}/(A_\tau-\rho^*(i'))b_j^2} \\
&= \Psi \cdot \prod_{\substack{(i,j)\in[n,\ell]\\ \rho^*(j)\notin S}} g^{(A_\tau-\rho^*(j))w_i M^*_{j,i}b_j a^{q+1+i-i}/(A_\tau-\rho^*(j))b_j^2} \\
&= \Psi \cdot \prod_{\substack{j\in[\ell]\\ \rho^*(j)\notin S}} g^{\langle \vec{w}, \vec{M}^*_j\rangle a^{q+1}/b_j}
\end{aligned}
$$

where Ψ includes the remaining terms of the product. The Ψ and $K_{\tau,2}$ terms can be calculated using the suitable terms of our assumption. The second part of $(u^{A_\tau} h)^{r_\tau}$ cancels exactly with the problematic part of v^{-r}. Therefore the simulator can calculate $K_{\tau,2}$ and $K_{\tau,3}$ for all $A_\tau \in \mathcal{S}$ and hand over the secret key $sk = (\mathcal{S}, K_0, K_1, \{K_{\tau,2}, K_{\tau,3}\}_{\tau\in[|\mathcal{S}|]})$ to the attacker $\mathcal{A}$.

Challenge: The attacker will output a pair of messages (m_0, m_1) of the same length. In this phase the simulator flips a random coin $b \xleftarrow{\$} \{0,1\}$ and constructs

$$C = m_b \cdot T \cdot e(g, g^s)^{\tilde{\alpha}} \qquad \text{and} \qquad C_0 = g^s$$

where T is the challenge term and g^s the corresponding term of the assumption.

The simulator sets implicitly $\vec{y} = (s,\ sa + \tilde{y}_2,\ sa^2 + \tilde{y}_3,\ \ldots,\ sa^{n-1} + \tilde{y}_n)^\top$, where $\tilde{y}_2, \tilde{y}_3, \ldots, \tilde{y}_n \xleftarrow{\$} \mathbb{Z}_p$. We see that the secret s and the vector $\vec{y}$ are properly distributed, since s was information theoretically hidden from $\mathcal{A}$ and the $\tilde{y}_i$'s are picked uniformly at random. As a result, since $\vec{\lambda} = M^*\vec{y}$ we have that

$$\lambda_\tau = \sum_{i\in[n]} M^*_{\tau,i} s a^{i-1} + \sum_{i=2}^{n} M^*_{\tau,i}\tilde{y}_i = \sum_{i\in[n]} M^*_{\tau,i} s a^{i-1} + \tilde{\lambda}_\tau$$

for each row $\tau \in [\ell]$.

Notice that the terms $\tilde{\lambda}_\tau = \sum_{i=2}^{n} M^*_{\tau,i}\tilde{y}_i$ are known to the simulator. For each row the simulator $\mathcal{B}$ sets implicitly $t_\tau = -sb_\tau$. This is properly distributed as well, because the b_i's are information theoretically hidden from the attacker. Using the above, $\mathcal{B}$ calculates:

$$
\begin{aligned}
C_{\tau,1} &= w^{\lambda_\tau} v^{t_\tau} = w^{\tilde{\lambda}_\tau} \cdot \prod_{i\in[n]} g^{M^*_{\tau,i} s a^i} \cdot \left(g^{sb_\tau}\right)^{-\tilde{v}} \\
&\cdot\cdot \prod_{(j,k)\in[\ell,n]} g^{-M^*_{j,k}a^k sb_\tau/b_j} \\
&= w^{\tilde{\lambda}_\tau} \cdot \left(g^{sb_\tau}\right)^{-\tilde{v}} \cdot \prod_{i\in[n]} g^{M^*_{\tau,i} s a^i} \cdot \prod_{k\in[n]} g^{-M^*_{\tau,k}a^k sb_\tau/b_\tau} \\
&\cdot \prod_{\substack{(j,k)\in[\ell,n]\\ j\neq\tau}} g^{-M^*_{j,k}a^k sb_\tau/b_j} = \\
&= w^{\tilde{\lambda}_\tau} \cdot \left(g^{sb_\tau}\right)^{-\tilde{v}} \cdot \prod_{\substack{(j,k)\in[\ell,n]\\ j\neq\tau}} \left(g^{sa^k b_\tau/b_j}\right)^{-M^*_{j,k}} \\
C_{\tau,2} &= \left(u^{\rho^*(\tau)} h\right)^{-t_\tau} = \left(g^{sb_\tau}\right)^{-(\tilde{u}\rho^*(\tau)+\tilde{h})} \\
&\cdot \left(\prod_{(j,k)\in[\ell,n]} g^{(\rho^*(\tau)-\rho^*(j))M^*_{j,k}a^k/b_j^2}\right)^{-sb_\tau} \\
&= \left(g^{sb_\tau}\right)^{-(\tilde{u}\rho^*(\tau)+\tilde{h})} \\
&\cdot \prod_{\substack{(j,k)\in[\ell,n]\\ j\neq\tau}} \left(g^{sa^k b_\tau/b_j^2}\right)^{-(\rho^*(\tau)-\rho^*(j))M^*_{j,k}} \\
C_{\tau,3} &= g^{t_\tau} = \left(g^{sb_\tau}\right)^{-1}
\end{aligned}
$$

Notice that by using $t_\tau = -sb_\tau$ we "raised" the exponents of the "binder" term v so that they cancel with the unknown powers of w^{λ_τ}. Therefore, the simulator hands over the ciphertext $ct = ((M^*, \rho^*),\ C,\ C_0,\ \{C_{\tau,1}, C_{\tau,2}, C_{\tau,3}\}_{\tau\in[\ell]})$ to the attacker $\mathcal{A}$.

Guess: After the query phase 2, where the simulator creates the secret keys as described above, the attacker outputs a guess b' for the challenge bit. If $b' = b$ the simulator outputs 0, i.e. it claims that the challenge term is $T = e(g,g)^{sa^{q+1}}$. Otherwise, it outputs 1.

If $T = e(g,g)^{sa^{q+1}}$ then $\mathcal{A}$ played the proper security game, because $C = m_b \cdot T \cdot e(g, g^s)^{\tilde{\alpha}} = m_b \cdot e(g,g)^{\alpha s}$. On the other hand, if T is a random term of $\mathbb{G}_T$ then all information about the message m_b is lost in the challenge ciphertext. Therefore the advantage of $\mathcal{A}$ is exactly 0. As a result, if $\mathcal{A}$ breaks the security game with a non negligible advantage, $\mathcal{B}$ has a non negligible advantage in breaking the q-1 assumption. □

5. IMPLEMENTATION AND EVALUATION

Implementation Details We implemented our schemes in Charm [1]; a framework developed to facilitate the rapid prototyping of cryptographic schemes and protocols. It is based on the Python language which allows the programmer to write code similar to the theoretical implementations. However, the routines that implement the dominant group operations use the PBC library [27] (written natively in C) and the time overhead imposed by the use of Python is usually less than 1%. Charm also provides routines for applying and using LSSS schemes needed for Attribute-Based systems.

All Charm routines use formally asymmetric groups (although the underlining groups might be symmetric) and therefore we translated our schemes to the asymmetric setting. Namely, we have three groups $\mathbb{G}_1, \mathbb{G}_2$ and $\mathbb{G}_T$ and the pairing e is a function from $\mathbb{G}_1 \times \mathbb{G}_2$ to $\mathbb{G}_T$. The assumptions and the security proofs can be translated to the asymmetric setting in a generic way. We notice here that we tried to implement our algorithms so that more operations are executed in the $\mathbb{G}_1$ group than in the $\mathbb{G}_2$ and that encryption consists mainly of operations in $\mathbb{G}_1$, compared to key generation. The reason is that the time taken to execute them in the $\mathbb{G}_1$ group is considerably smaller than $\mathbb{G}_2$ in specific asymmetric groups such as the "MNT224" elliptic curve group. We tested the schemes on all ECC groups provided by Charm, i.e. three super-singular symmetric groups and two MNT asymmetric groups [29].

For more information on Charm we refer the reader to [12, 1]. The source code of our implementations can be found in [41]. All our benchmarks were executed on a dual core Intel® Xeon® CPU W3503@2.40GHz with 2.0GB RAM running Ubuntu R10.04 and Python3.2.3.

We implemented our two ABE schemes (of Sec. 4 and App. C), the prime order KP-ABE construction from [22], and the two basic[3] constructions from [33]. Actually, in [22] a large universe prime order HIBE is provided, but the transformation to KP-ABE is straightforward by substituting in the key generation algorithm the additive shares of the secrets with the LSSS shares and the identities with the attributes $\rho(\tau)$. This modified construction is the one we used for comparison to our KP-ABE scheme.

Time Benchmarks In Table 1 we present time benchmarks in different elliptic curve groups for some sample policies ($\approx$ size 4 attributes).

Regarding the comparison between our schemes and prior works, we notice the big gap between the timings of our constructions and prior ones. This is due to the fact that dual vector spaces of high dimension ($\approx$ 10 - 14) are utilized, which increase the number of group operations by big factors. We remind the reader that the OT schemes are fully secure, while our scchemes and the LW schemes are selectively secure.

Regarding the practicality, in general, of both our schemes we notice that the KeyGen, Encrypt, and Decrypt times of our algorithms are relatively small. They are all under 100ms, with the exception of the super singular 1024-bit curve. Even for this curve the times for each algorithm are under the 700 msec mark. Although one would expect that as the policies and the attributes sets grow bigger these times will increase, the additional overhead will grow only linearly. Thus we believe that the two constructions constitute the most practical implementations of large universe ABE, secure in the standard model.

6. REFERENCES

[1] Joseph A. Akinyele, Matthew Green, and Avi Rubin. Charm: A framework for rapidly prototyping cryptosystems. Cryptology ePrint Archive, Report 2011/617, 2011. http://eprint.iacr.org/.

[2] Sattam S. Al-Riyami, John Malone-Lee, and Nigel P. Smart. Escrow-free encryption supporting cryptographic workflow. *Int. J. Inf. Sec.*, 5(4):217–229, 2006.

[3] Walid Bagga, Refik Molva, and Stefano Crosta. Policy-based encryption schemes from bilinear pairings. In *ASIACCS*, page 368, 2006.

[4] Manuel Barbosa and Pooya Farshim. Secure cryptographic workflow in the standard model. In *INDOCRYPT*, pages 379–393, 2006.

[5] Amos Beimel. *Secure Schemes for Secret Sharing and Key Distribution*. PhD thesis, Dept. of Computer Science, Technion, 1996.

[6] John Bethencourt, Amit Sahai, and Brent Waters. Ciphertext-policy attribute-based encryption. In *IEEE Symposium on Security and Privacy*, pages 321–334, 2007.

[7] Dan Boneh and Xavier Boyen. Efficient selective-id secure identity-based encryption without random oracles. In *EUROCRYPT*, pages 223–238, 2004.

[8] Dan Boneh and Matthew K. Franklin. Identity-based encryption from the Weil pairing. In *CRYPTO*, pages 213–229, 2001.

[9] Dan Boneh, Craig Gentry, and Michael Hamburg. Space-efficient identity based encryption without pairings. In *FOCS*, pages 647–657, 2007.

[10] Dan Boneh, Amit Sahai, and Brent Waters. Functional encryption: Definitions and challenges. In *TCC*, pages 253–273, 2011.

[11] Robert W. Bradshaw, Jason E. Holt, and Kent E. Seamons. Concealing complex policies with hidden credentials. In *ACM Conference on Computer and Communications Security*, pages 146–157, 2004.

[12] Charm. http://www.charm-crypto.com.

[13] Melissa Chase. Multi-authority attribute based encryption. In *TCC*, pages 515–534, 2007.

[14] Melissa Chase and Sherman S. M. Chow. Improving privacy and security in multi-authority attribute-based encryption. In *ACM Conference on Computer and Communications Security*, pages 121–130, 2009.

[15] Ling Cheung and Calvin C. Newport. Provably secure ciphertext policy ABE. In *ACM Conference on Computer and Communications Security*, pages 456–465, 2007.

[16] Clifford Cocks. An identity based encryption scheme based on quadratic residues. In *IMA Int. Conf.*, pages 360–363, 2001.

[17] David Mandell Freeman. Converting pairing-based cryptosystems from composite-order groups to prime-order groups. In *EUROCRYPT*, pages 44–61, 2010.

[18] Craig Gentry. Practical identity-based encryption without random oracles. In *EUROCRYPT*, pages 445–464, 2006.

[19] Vipul Goyal, Abhishek Jain, Omkant Pandey, and Amit Sahai. Bounded ciphertext policy attribute based encryption. In *ICALP (2)*, pages 579–591, 2008.

[20] Vipul Goyal, Omkant Pandey, Amit Sahai, and Brent Waters. Attribute-based encryption for fine-grained

[3]Where each sub-universe can appear at most once in the policy.

Curve	Type	Scheme	Setup	KeyGen	Encrypt	Decrypt
"SS512"	KP-ABE	[App.C]	19.1	49.1	30.7	14.7
		LW [22]	447.2	642.3	483.4	44.7
		OT [33]	673.7	924.4	933.5	65.6
	CP-ABE	[Sec.4]	25.0	32.9	52.0	16.6
		OT [33]	678.0	922.9	938.5	66.0
"SS1024"	KP-ABE	[App.C]	71.5	626.3	396.8	325.3
		LW [22]	5553.3	9283.8	6978.3	1098.8
		OT [33]	7904.3	13389.3	13582.0	1735.7
	CP-ABE	[Sec.4]	110.8	431.0	669.3	374.4
		OT [33]	7898.9	13393.2	13598.7	1740.4
"MNT159"	KP-ABE	[App.C]	21.1	48.1	44.3	36.4
		LW [22]	692.2	1666.3	168.9	125.2
		OT [33]	930.7	2435.1	320.6	178.4
	CP-ABE	[Sec.4]	23.5	43.8	53.5	41.5
		OT [33]	929.9	2396.2	326.7	183.5
"MNT201"	KP-ABE	[App.C]	28.4	59.2	60.2	49.7
		LW [22]	929.8	2301.1	237.8	173.6
		OT [33]	1237.1	3338.3	453.3	251.5
	CP-ABE	[Sec.4]	31.3	58.7	71.9	57.4
		OT [33]	1235.1	3328.7	463.3	251.8
"MNT224"	KP-ABE	[App.C]	34.2	73.4	74.2	60.9
		LW [22]	1150.9	2896.0	302.1	215.6
		OT [33]	1514.9	4156.3	572.4	309.8
	CP-ABE	[Sec.4]	37.9	73.2	88.2	74.4
		OT [33]	1511.7	4140.0	584.5	310.7

Table 1: Typical running times in milliseconds of each scheme. KeyGen and Encrypt **are called with attribute sets and policies of size 4, while** Decrypt **with common attribute sets of size 2. "MNT" are the Miyaji, Nakabayashi, Takano curves (asymmetric pairing groups), while "SS" are super singular curves (symmetric pairing groups). The number after the type of the curve denotes the size of the base field in bits.**

access control of encrypted data. In *ACM Conference on Computer and Communications Security*, pages 89–98, 2006.

[21] Jonathan Katz, Amit Sahai, and Brent Waters. Predicate encryption supporting disjunctions, polynomial equations, and inner products. In *EUROCRYPT*, pages 146–162, 2008.

[22] Allison B. Lewko. Tools for simulating features of composite order bilinear groups in the prime order setting. In *EUROCRYPT*, pages 318–335, 2012.

[23] Allison B. Lewko, Tatsuaki Okamoto, Amit Sahai, Katsuyuki Takashima, and Brent Waters. Fully secure functional encryption: Attribute-based encryption and (hierarchical) inner product encryption. In *EUROCRYPT*, pages 62–91, 2010.

[24] Allison B. Lewko and Brent Waters. Decentralizing attribute-based encryption. In *EUROCRYPT*, pages 568–588, 2011.

[25] Allison B. Lewko and Brent Waters. Unbounded HIBE and attribute-based encryption. In *EUROCRYPT*, pages 547–567, 2011.

[26] Allison B. Lewko and Brent Waters. New proof methods for attribute-based encryption: Achieving full security through selective techniques. In *CRYPTO*, pages 180–198, 2012.

[27] Ben Lynn. The Stanford pairing based crypto library. `http://crypto.stanford.edu/pbc`.

[28] Gerome Miklau and Dan Suciu. Controlling access to published data using cryptography. In *VLDB*, pages 898–909, 2003.

[29] Atsuko Miyaji, Masaki Nakabayashi, and Shunzo Takano. Characterization of elliptic curve traces under fr-reduction. In *ICISC*, pages 90–108, 2000.

[30] Tatsuaki Okamoto and Katsuyuki Takashima. Homomorphic encryption and signatures from vector decomposition. In *Pairing*, pages 57–74, 2008.

[31] Tatsuaki Okamoto and Katsuyuki Takashima. Hierarchical predicate encryption for inner-products. In *ASIACRYPT*, pages 214–231, 2009.

[32] Tatsuaki Okamoto and Katsuyuki Takashima. Fully secure functional encryption with general relations from the decisional linear assumption. In *CRYPTO*, pages 191–208, 2010.

[33] Tatsuaki Okamoto and Katsuyuki Takashima. Fully secure unbounded inner-product and attribute-based encryption. In *ASIACRYPT*, pages 349–366, 2012.

[34] Rafail Ostrovsky, Amit Sahai, and Brent Waters. Attribute-based encryption with non-monotonic access structures. In *ACM Conference on Computer and Communications Security*, pages 195–203, 2007.

[35] Matthew Pirretti, Patrick Traynor, Patrick McDaniel, and Brent Waters. Secure attribute-based systems. In *ACM Conference on Computer and Communications Security*, pages 99–112, 2006.

[36] Amit Sahai and Brent Waters. Fuzzy identity-based encryption. In *EUROCRYPT*, pages 457–473, 2005.

[37] Adi Shamir. Identity-based cryptosystems and signature schemes. In *CRYPTO*, pages 47–53, 1984.

[38] Emily Shen, Elaine Shi, and Brent Waters. Predicate privacy in encryption systems. In *TCC*, pages 457–473, 2009.

[39] Elaine Shi and Brent Waters. Delegating capabilities in predicate encryption systems. In *ICALP (2)*, pages 560–578, 2008.

[40] Nigel P. Smart. Access control using pairing based cryptography. In *CT-RSA*, pages 111–121, 2003.

[41] Source code of our constructions. `www.cs.utexas.edu/~jrous/`.

[42] Brent Waters. Efficient identity-based encryption without random oracles. In *EUROCRYPT*, pages 114–127, 2005.

[43] Brent Waters. Ciphertext-policy attribute-based encryption: An expressive, efficient, and provably secure realization. In *Public Key Cryptography*, pages 53–70, 2011.

APPENDIX

A. ASSUMPTION 2

For our KP-ABE construction we will use a q-type assumption on prime order bilinear groups, denoted by q-2, which is similar to the Decisional Bilinear Diffie-Hellman Assumption augmented with q parameters b_i. It is parameterized by a security parameter $\lambda \in \mathbb{N}$ and an integer q, polynomial in λ. We assume that there exists a group generator algorithm $\mathcal{G}(1^\lambda) \to (p, \mathbb{G}, \mathbb{G}_T, e)$ that outputs the description of the (symmetric) bilinear group of order $p = \Theta(2^\lambda)$. This assumption can be proved secure in the generic group model, but the proof is omitted due to space constraints. It is defined via the following game between a challenger and an attacker:

Initially the challenger calls the group generation algorithm with input the security parameter, picks a random group element $g \xleftarrow{\$} \mathbb{G}$, and $q+3$ random exponents x, y, z, $b_1, b_2, \ldots, b_q \xleftarrow{\$} \mathbb{Z}_p$. Then he sends to the attacker the group description $(p, \mathbb{G}, \mathbb{G}_T, e)$ and all of the following terms:

$$
\begin{array}{ll}
g, g^x, g^y, g^z, g^{(xz)^2} & \\
g^{b_i}, g^{xzb_i}, g^{xz/b_i}, g^{x^2zb_i}, g^{y/b_i^2}, g^{y^2/b_i^2} & \forall i \in [q] \\
g^{xzb_i/b_j}, g^{yb_i/b_j^2}, g^{xyzb_i/b_j}, g^{(xz)^2 b_i/b_j} & \forall i, j \in [q], i \neq j
\end{array}
$$

The challenger also flips a random coin $b \xleftarrow{\$} \{0,1\}$ and if $b = 0$ it gives to the attacker the term $e(g,g)^{xyz}$. Otherwise it gives a random term $R \xleftarrow{\$} \mathbb{G}_T$. Finally the attacker outputs a guess $b' \in \{0,1\}$.

Definition A.1. *We say that the q-2 assumption holds if all PPT attackers have at most a negligible advantage in λ in the above security game, where the advantage is defined as* $\mathsf{Adv} = \Pr[b' = b] - 1/2$.

B. KEY-POLICY ATTRIBUTE-BASED ENCRYPTION

B.1 Algorithms

A Key-Policy Attribute-Based Encryption scheme consists of the following four PPT algorithms:

• $\mathsf{Setup}(1^\lambda) \to (pp, msk)$: The Setup algorithm takes the security parameter $\lambda \in \mathbb{N}$ encoded in unary and outputs the public parameters pp and the master secret key msk. We assume that the public parameters contain a description of the attribute universe $\mathcal{U}$.

• $\mathsf{KeyGen}(1^\lambda, pp, msk, \mathbb{A}) \to sk$: The key generation algorithm takes as inputs the public parameters pp, the master secret key msk and an access structure $\mathbb{A}$ on $\mathcal{U}$. The algorithm generates a secret key corresponding to $\mathbb{A}$.

• $\mathsf{Encrypt}(1^\lambda, pp, m, \mathcal{S}) \to ct$: The encryption algorithm takes as inputs the public parameters pp, a plaintext message m, and a set of attributes $\mathcal{S} \subseteq \mathcal{U}$. It outputs the ciphertext ct.

• $\mathsf{Decrypt}(1^\lambda, pp, sk, ct) \to m$: The decryption algorithm takes as inputs the public parameters pp, a secret key sk, and a ciphertext ct. It outputs the plaintext m.

Correctness: We require that a KP-ABE scheme is correct, i.e the decryption algorithm correctly decrypts a ciphertext on $\mathcal{S}$ with a secret key of an access structure $\mathbb{A}$ when $\mathcal{S}$ is an authorized set of $\mathbb{A}$. Formally:

Definition B.1. *A KP-ABE scheme is* correct *when for all messages m, and all attribute sets $\mathcal{S}$ and access structures $\mathbb{A}$ with $\mathcal{S} \in \mathbb{A}$ (i.e. for $\mathcal{S}$ authorized), any pair (pp, msk) output from* $\mathsf{Setup}(1^\lambda)$*, any secret key sk output from* $\mathsf{KeyGen}(1^\lambda, pp, msk, \mathbb{A})$*, and any ciphertext ct output by* $\mathsf{Encrypt}(1^\lambda, pp, m, \mathcal{S})$*, it is true that:* $\mathsf{Decrypt}(1^\lambda, pp, sk, ct) = m$.

B.2 KP-ABE Selective Security

The selective security game for KP-ABE is described by a game between a challenger and an attacker and is parameterized by the security parameter $\lambda \in \mathbb{N}$. The phases of the game are the following:

• **Initialization:** In this phase the attacker declares the challenge attribute set $\mathcal{S}^*$, which he will try to attack, and sends it to the challenger.

• **Setup:** Here the challenger calls the $\mathsf{Setup}(1^\lambda)$ algorithm and sends the public parameters pp to the attacker.

• **Query Phase 1:** In this phase the attacker can adaptively ask for secret keys for the access structures $\mathbb{A}_1, \mathbb{A}_2, \ldots, \mathbb{A}_{Q_1}$. For each $\mathbb{A}_i$ the challenger calls $\mathsf{KeyGen}(msk, \mathbb{A}_i) \to sk_i$ and sends sk_i to the attacker. The restriction that has to be satisfied for each query is that none of the queried policies is satisfied by the challenge attribute set, i.e. $\forall i \in [Q_1] : \mathcal{S}^* \notin \mathbb{A}_i$.

• **Challenge:** The attacker declares two equal-length plaintexts m_0 and m_1 and sends them to the challenger. He flips a random coin $b \in \{0,1\}$ and calls $\mathsf{Encrypt}(m_b, \mathcal{S}^*) \to ct$. He sends ct to the attacker.

• **Query Phase 2:** This the same as query phase 1. The attacker asks for the secret key for the access structures $\mathbb{A}_{Q_1+1}, \mathbb{A}_{Q_1+2}, \ldots, \mathbb{A}_Q$, for which the same restriction holds: $\forall i \in [Q] : \mathcal{S}^* \notin \mathbb{A}_i$.

• **Guess:** The attacker outputs his guess $b' \in \{0,1\}$ for b.

Definition B.2. *A KP-ABE scheme is* selectively secure *if all PPT attackers have at most a negligible advantage in λ in the above security game, where the advantage of an attacker is defined as* $\mathsf{Adv} = \Pr[b' = b] - 1/2$.

C. OUR LARGE UNIVERSE KP-ABE

In this section we present our large universe KP-ABE scheme. We mention here that it can be converted to an HIBE scheme using non repeating identities, "AND" policies and delegation capabilities (c.f. [25]). The intuition behind the functionality of this construction is simpler than the CP-ABE. In this setting the public parameters consist of the five terms $(g, u, h, w, e(g,g)^{\alpha})$. There is one term less due to the fact that now the master secret key α is the secret to be shared during all the key generation calls. As a result the "secret sharing layer" uses the g term only and the w term is used to "bind" this layer to the u, h "attribute layer".

C.1 Construction

Our scheme consists of the following four algorithms.

• $\mathsf{Setup}(1^{\lambda}) \to (pp, msk)$: The setup algorithm calls the group generator algorithm $\mathcal{G}(1^{\lambda})$ and gets the descriptions of the groups and the bilinear mapping $D = (p, \mathbb{G}, \mathbb{G}_T, e)$, where p is the prime order of the groups $\mathbb{G}$ and $\mathbb{G}_T$. The attribute universe is $\mathcal{U} = \mathbb{Z}_p$.

Then the algorithm picks the random terms $g, u, h, w \xleftarrow{\$} \mathbb{G}$ and $\alpha \xleftarrow{\$} \mathbb{Z}_p$. It outputs

$$pp = (D, g, u, h, w, e(g,g)^{\alpha}) \qquad msk = (\alpha)$$

• $\mathsf{KeyGen}(msk, (M, \rho)) \to sk$: Initially, the algorithm picks $\vec{y} = (\alpha, y_2, \ldots, y_n)^{\top}$ where $y_2, \ldots, y_n \xleftarrow{\$} \mathbb{Z}_p$. In the terminology of Sec. 2.2, the master secret key α is the secret to be shared among the shares. The vector of the shares is

$$\vec{\lambda} = (\lambda_1, \lambda_2, \ldots, \lambda_{\ell})^{\top} = M\vec{y}$$

It then picks ℓ random exponents $t_1, t_2, \ldots, t_{\ell} \xleftarrow{\$} \mathbb{Z}_p$ and for every $\tau \in [\ell]$ it computes

$$K_{\tau,0} = g^{\lambda_{\tau}} w^{t_{\tau}} \qquad K_{\tau,1} = \left(u^{\rho(\tau)} h\right)^{-t_{\tau}} \qquad K_{\tau,2} = g^{t_{\tau}}$$

The secret key is $sk = ((M, \rho), \{K_{\tau,0}, K_{\tau,1}, K_{\tau,2}\}_{\tau \in [\ell]})$.

• $\mathsf{Encrypt}(m, \mathcal{S} = \{A_1, A_2, \ldots, A_k\} \subseteq \mathbb{Z}_p) \to ct$: Initially, the algorithm picks $k+1$ random exponents $s, r_1, r_2, \ldots, r_k \xleftarrow{\$} \mathbb{Z}_p$. It computes $C = m \cdot e(g,g)^{\alpha s}$, $C_0 = g^s$, and for every $\tau \in [k]$ it computes

$$C_{\tau,1} = g^{r_{\tau}} \qquad C_{\tau,2} = (u^{A_{\tau}} h)^{r_{\tau}} w^{-s}$$

The ciphertext is $ct = (\mathcal{S}, C, C_0, \{C_{\tau,1}, C_{\tau,2}\}_{\tau \in [k]})$.

• $\mathsf{Decrypt}(sk, ct) \to m$: The algorithm finds the set of rows in M that provide a share to attributes in $\mathcal{S}$, i.e. $I = \{i : \rho(i) \in \mathcal{S}\}$. Then it calculates constants $\{\omega_i \in \mathbb{Z}_p\}_{i \in I}$ such that $\sum_{i \in I} \omega_i \vec{M}_i = (1, 0, \ldots, 0)$, where M_i is the i-th row of the matrix M. These constants exist if the set $\mathcal{S}$ is an authorized set of the policy (c.f. Sec. 2.2).

Then it calculates

$$B = \prod_{i \in I} \left(e(C_0, K_{i,0}) e(C_{\tau,1}, K_{i,1}) e(C_{\tau,2}, K_{i,2})\right)^{\omega_i}$$

where τ is the index of the attribute $\rho(i)$ in $\mathcal{S}$ (it depends on i). The algorithm outputs $m = C/B$.

Correctness: If the attribute set $\mathcal{S}$ of the ciphertext is authorized, we have that $\sum_{i \in I} \omega_i \lambda_i = \alpha$. Therefore:

$$\begin{aligned} B &= \prod_{i \in I} e(g,g)^{s\omega_i\lambda_i} e(g,w)^{st_i\omega_i} \\ &\cdot e(g, u^{\rho(i)}h)^{-r_{\tau}t_i\omega_i} e(g, u^{\rho(i)}h)^{r_{\tau}t_i\omega_i} e(g,w)^{-st_i\omega_i} \\ &= e(g,g)^{s\sum_{i \in I}\omega_i\lambda_i} = e(g,g)^{\alpha s} \end{aligned}$$

C.2 Proof of Selective Security

We will prove the following theorem regarding the selective security of our KP-ABE scheme:

Theorem C.1. *If the q-2 assumption holds, then all PPT adversaries with a challenge attribute set of size k, where $k \leq q$, have a negligible advantage in selectively breaking our scheme.*

Proof. To prove the theorem we will assume that there exists a PPT attacker $\mathcal{A}$ with a challenge attribute set that satisfies the restriction, which has a non negligible advantage $\mathsf{Adv}_{\mathcal{A}}$ in selectively breaking our scheme. Using this attacker we will build a PPT simulator $\mathcal{B}$ that attacks the q-2 assumption with a non negligible advantage.

Initialization: Initially, $\mathcal{B}$ receives the given terms from the assumption and an attribute set $\mathcal{S}^* = \{A_1^*, A_2^*, \ldots, A_k^*\} \subseteq \mathcal{U}$.

Setup: Now, the simulator $\mathcal{B}$ has to provide $\mathcal{A}$ the public parameters of the system. In order to do that it implicitly sets the master secret key of the scheme to be $\alpha = xy$, where x, y are set in the assumption. Notice that this way α is properly distributed. Then $\mathcal{B}$ picks the random exponents $\tilde{u}, \tilde{h} \xleftarrow{\$} \mathbb{Z}_p$ and gives to $\mathcal{A}$ the following terms:

$$\begin{aligned} &g = g \\ &u = g^{\tilde{u}} \cdot \textstyle\prod_{i \in [k]} g^{y/b_i^2} \\ &h = g^{\tilde{h}} \cdot \textstyle\prod_{i \in [k]} g^{xz/b_i} \cdot \prod_{i \in [k]} \left(g^{y/b_i^2}\right)^{-A_i^*} \\ &w = g^x \\ &e(g,g)^{\alpha} = e(g^x, g^y) \end{aligned}$$

Since x is information-theoretically hidden from $\mathcal{A}$, because it is multiplied by y in α, the term w is properly uniformly random in $\mathbb{G}$. The terms u, h are properly distributed due to $\tilde{u}, \tilde{h}$ respectively. Notice that all terms can be calculated by the simulator using suitable terms from the assumption and the challenge set $\mathcal{S}^*$ given by $\mathcal{A}$.

In the KP-ABE proof we see that the "binder term" of the CP-ABE reduction has been contained in the "attribute layer"; namely the g^{xz/b_i} of the h term. Since the master secret key α is shared in all key generation queries in KP-ABE, we don't need any more the extra functionality provided by the powers of a.

Query phases 1 and 2: The simulator has to produce secret keys for policies requested by $\mathcal{A}$, for which the set $\mathcal{S}^*$ is not authorized. In both phases the treatment is the same. We describe here the way $\mathcal{B}$ works in order to create a key for a policy (M, ρ) with $M \in \mathbb{Z}_p^{\ell \times n}$ and $\rho : [\ell] \to \mathbb{Z}_p$.

Since $\mathcal{S}^*$ is non authorized for (M, ρ), there exists a vector $\vec{w} = (w_1, w_2, \ldots, w_n)^{\top} \in \mathbb{Z}_p^n$ such that $w_1 = 1$ and $\langle \vec{M}_{\tau}, \vec{w} \rangle = 0$ for all $\tau \in [\ell]$ such that $\rho(\tau) \in \mathcal{S}^*$ (c.f. Sec. 2.2). The simulator calculates $\vec{w}$ using linear algebra. The vector $\vec{y}$ that will be shared is implicitly

$$\vec{y} = xy\vec{w} + (0, \tilde{y}_2, \tilde{y}_3, \ldots, \tilde{y}_n)^\top$$

where $\tilde{y}_2, \tilde{y}_3, \ldots, \tilde{y}_n \xleftarrow{\$} \mathbb{Z}_p$. This vector is properly distributed because its first component is $xy = \alpha$ and the remaining components are uniformly random in $\mathbb{Z}_p$. Therefore for each row $\tau \in [\ell]$ the share is

$$\begin{aligned}\lambda_\tau &= \langle \vec{M}_\tau, \vec{y} \rangle = xy\langle \vec{M}_\tau, \vec{w} \rangle + \langle \vec{M}_\tau, (0, \tilde{y}_2, \tilde{y}_3, \ldots, \tilde{y}_n)^\top \rangle \\ &= xy\langle \vec{M}_\tau, \vec{w} \rangle + \tilde{\lambda}_\tau\end{aligned}$$

As we mentioned above for each row τ for which $\rho(\tau) \in \mathcal{S}^*$ it is true that $\langle \vec{M}_\tau, \vec{w} \rangle = 0$. Therefore in this case $\lambda_\tau = \tilde{\lambda}_\tau = \langle \vec{M}_\tau, (0, \tilde{y}_2, \tilde{y}_3, \ldots, \tilde{y}_n)^\top \rangle$; hence its value is known to the simulator. In that case it picks $t_\tau \xleftarrow{\$} \mathbb{Z}_p$ and outputs the terms $K_{\tau,0}, K_{\tau,1}, K_{\tau,2}$ as in the KeyGen algorithm.

On the other hand, for each row τ for which $\rho(\tau) \notin \mathcal{S}^*$ it picks $\tilde{t}_\tau \xleftarrow{\$} \mathbb{Z}_p$ and sets implicitly

$$t_\tau = -y\langle \vec{M}_\tau, \vec{w} \rangle + \sum_{i \in [k]} \frac{xzb_i \langle \vec{M}_\tau, \vec{w} \rangle}{\rho(\tau) - A_i^*} + \tilde{t}_\tau$$

Since $\rho(\tau) \notin \mathcal{S}^*$ the above fractions are defined and t_τ is properly distributed due to $\tilde{t}_\tau$. The intuition behind this choice is that the y exponent "raises" the power of w to the secret $\alpha = xy$. However, this also results to xyz/b_i exponents from h. Thus, the cancellation is provided by the xzb_i exponents on the y/b_i^2 part. Now the simulator can compute the following terms using the assumption:

$$\begin{aligned}K_{\tau,0} &= g^{\lambda_\tau} w^{t_\tau} \\ &= g^{xy\langle \vec{M}_\tau, \vec{w} \rangle + \tilde{\lambda}_\tau} \cdot g^{-xy\langle \vec{M}_\tau, \vec{w} \rangle + \sum_{i \in [k]} \frac{x^2 z b_i \langle \vec{M}_\tau, \vec{w} \rangle}{\rho(\tau) - A_i^*}} \cdot w^{\tilde{t}_\tau} \\ &= g^{\tilde{\lambda}_\tau} \cdot \prod_{i \in [n]} \left(g^{x^2 z b_i}\right)^{\langle \vec{M}_\tau, \vec{w} \rangle / (\rho(\tau) - A_i^*)} \cdot w^{\tilde{t}_\tau}\end{aligned}$$

$$\begin{aligned}K_{\tau,1} &= (u^{\rho(\tau)} h)^{-t_\tau} = \\ &= g^{y\langle \vec{M}_\tau, \vec{w} \rangle (\rho(\tau)\tilde{u} + \tilde{h})} \prod_{i \in [k]} g^{-xzb_i(\rho(\tau)\tilde{u} + \tilde{h})\langle \vec{M}_\tau, \vec{w} \rangle / (\rho(\tau) - A_i^*)} \\ &\cdot \prod_{i \in [k]} g^{xyz\langle \vec{M}_\tau, \vec{w} \rangle / b_i} \prod_{(i,j) \in [k,k]} g^{-(xz)^2 b_j \langle \vec{M}_\tau, \vec{w} \rangle / b_i(\rho(\tau) - A_j^*)} \\ &\cdot \prod_{i \in [k]} g^{y^2 \langle \vec{M}_\tau, \vec{w} \rangle \left(\rho(\tau) - A_i^*\right) / b_i^2} \cdot (u^{\rho(\tau)} h)^{-\tilde{t}_\tau} \\ &\cdot \prod_{(i,j) \in [k,k]} g^{-xyz\langle \vec{M}_\tau, \vec{w} \rangle b_j \left(\rho(\tau) - A_i^*\right) / b_i^2 (\rho(\tau) - A_j^*)} \\ &= (g^y)^{\langle \vec{M}_\tau, \vec{w} \rangle (\rho(\tau)\tilde{u} + \tilde{h})} \prod_{i \in [k]} \left(g^{xzb_i}\right)^{-(\rho(\tau)\tilde{u} + \tilde{h})\langle \vec{M}_\tau, \vec{w} \rangle / (\rho(\tau) - A_i^*)} \\ &\cdot \prod_{(i,j) \in [k,k]} \left(g^{(xz)^2 b_j / b_i}\right)^{-\langle \vec{M}_\tau, \vec{w} \rangle / (\rho(\tau) - A_j^*)} \\ &\cdot \prod_{i \in [k]} \left(g^{y^2 / b_i^2}\right)^{\langle \vec{M}_\tau, \vec{w} \rangle \left(\rho(\tau) - A_i^*\right)} \cdot (u^{\rho(\tau)} h)^{-\tilde{t}_\tau} \\ &\cdot \prod_{\substack{(i,j) \in [k,k] \\ i \neq j}} \left(g^{xyzb_j / b_i^2}\right)^{-\langle \vec{M}_\tau, \vec{w} \rangle \left(\rho(\tau) - A_i^*\right) / (\rho(\tau) - A_j^*)}\end{aligned}$$

$$\begin{aligned}K_{\tau,2} &= g^{t_\tau} \\ &= (g^y)^{-\langle \vec{M}_\tau, \vec{w} \rangle} \cdot \prod_{i \in [k]} \left(g^{xzb_i}\right)^{\langle \vec{M}_\tau, \vec{w} \rangle / (\rho(\tau) - A_i^*)} \cdot g^{\tilde{t}_\tau}\end{aligned}$$

Therefore $\mathcal{B}$ can reply to $\mathcal{A}$'s query with the entire secret key $sk = \left((M, \rho), \{K_{\tau,0}, K_{\tau,1}, K_{\tau,2}\}_{\tau \in [\ell]}\right)$.

Challenge: The attacker will output a pair of messages (m_0, m_1) of the same length. In this phase the simulator flips a random coin $b \xleftarrow{\$} \{0,1\}$ and sets implicitly $s = z$ from the q-2 assumption. Also, it sets $r_\tau = b_\tau$ for every level $\tau \in [k]$. These parameters are properly distributed since $z, b_1, \ldots, b_q$ are information-theoretically hidden from the attacker's view. Now the simulator can compute the following terms using the assumption:

$$\begin{aligned}C &= m_b \cdot T \qquad C_0 = g^s = g^z \\ C_{\tau,1} &= g^{r_\tau} = g^{b_\tau} \\ C_{\tau,2} &= (u^{A_\tau^*} h)^{r_\tau} \cdot w^{-s} \\ &= g^{b_\tau(\tilde{u}A_\tau^* + \tilde{h})} \cdot \prod_{i \in [k]} g^{xzb_\tau / b_i} \prod_{i \in [k]} g^{yb_\tau\left(A_k^* - A_i^*\right)/b_i^2} \cdot g^{-xz} \\ &= \left(g^{b_\tau}\right)^{\tilde{u}A_\tau^* + \tilde{h}} \cdot \prod_{\substack{i \in [k] \\ i \neq \tau}} g^{xzb_\tau / b_i} \prod_{\substack{i \in [k] \\ i \neq \tau}} \left(g^{yb_\tau / b_i^2}\right)^{A_\tau^* - A_i^*}\end{aligned}$$

As one can see, the choice of $r_\tau = b_\tau$ "raises" one of the xz/b_i components to xz and achieves the cancellation with w^{-s}. The simulator hands over the ciphertext $ct = \left(\mathcal{S}^*, C, C_0, \{C_{\tau,1}, C_{\tau,2}\}_{\tau \in [k]}\right)$ to the attacker $\mathcal{A}$.

Guess: After the query phase 2, where the simulator creates the secret keys as described above, the attacker outputs a guess b' for the challenge bit. If $b' = b$ the simulator outputs 0, i.e. it claims that the challenge term is $T = e(g,g)^{xyz}$. Otherwise, it outputs 1.

If $T = e(g,g)^{xyz}$ then $\mathcal{A}$ played the proper security game, because $C = m_b \cdot T = m_b \cdot e(g,g)^{\alpha s}$. On the other hand, if T is a random term of $\mathbb{G}_T$ then all information about the message m_b is lost in the challenge ciphertext. Therefore the advantage of $\mathcal{A}$ is exactly 0. As a result, if $\mathcal{A}$ breaks the security game with a non negligible advantage, $\mathcal{B}$ has a non negligible advantage in breaking the q-2 assumption. $\square$

Blackbox Traceable CP-ABE: How to Catch People Leaking Their Keys by Selling Decryption Devices on eBay

Zhen Liu
Shanghai Jiao Tong University
Shanghai, China
City University of Hong Kong
Hong Kong SAR, China
zhenliu7@cityu.edu.hk

Zhenfu Cao
Shanghai Jiao Tong University
Shanghai, China
zfcao@cs.sjtu.edu.cn

Duncan S. Wong
City University of Hong Kong
Hong Kong SAR, China
duncan@cityu.edu.hk

ABSTRACT

In the context of Ciphertext-Policy Attribute-Based Encryption (CP-ABE), if a decryption device associated with an attribute set $S_{\mathcal{D}}$ appears on eBay, and is alleged to be able to decrypt any ciphertexts with policies satisfied by $S_{\mathcal{D}}$, no one including the CP-ABE authorities can identify the malicious user(s) who build such a decryption device using their key(s). This has been known as a major practicality concern in CP-ABE applications, for example, providing fine-grained access control on encrypted data. Due to the nature of CP-ABE, users get decryption keys from authorities associated with attribute sets. If there exists two or more users with attribute sets being the supersets of $S_{\mathcal{D}}$, existing CP-ABE schemes cannot distinguish which user is the malicious one who builds and sells such a decryption device. In this paper, we extend the notion of CP-ABE to support *Blackbox Traceability* and propose a concrete scheme which is able to identify a user whose key has been used in building a decryption device from multiple users whose keys associated with the attribute sets which are all the supersets of $S_{\mathcal{D}}$. The scheme is efficient with sub-linear overhead and when compared with the very recent (non-traceable) CP-ABE scheme due to Lewko and Waters in Crypto 2012, we can consider this new scheme as an extension with the property of *fully collusion-resistant blackbox traceability* added, i.e. an adversary can access an arbitrary number of keys when building a decryption device while the new tracing algorithm can still identify at least one particular key which must have been used for building the underlying decryption device. We show that this new scheme is secure against adaptive adversaries in the standard model, and is highly expressive by supporting any monotonic access structures. Its additional traceability property is also proven against adaptive adversaries in the standard model.

As of independent interest, in this paper, we also consider another scenario which we call it "*found-in-the-wild*". In this scenario, a decryption device is found, for example, from a black market, and reported to an authority (e.g. a law enforcement agency). The decryption device is found to be able to decrypt ciphertexts with certain policy, say $\mathbb{A}$, while the associated attribute set $S_{\mathcal{D}}$ is **missing**. In this found-in-the-wild scenario, we show that the Blackbox Traceable CP-ABE scheme proposed in this paper can still be able to find the malicious users whose keys have been used for building the decryption device, and our scheme can achieve *selective* traceability in the standard model under this scenario.

Categories and Subject Descriptors

E.3 [**Data Encryption**]: Public key cryptosystems

Keywords

Attribute-Based Encryption; Blackbox Traceability

1. INTRODUCTION

Ciphertext-Policy Attribute-Based Encryption (CP-ABE), introduced by Goyal et al. [11], is a versatile one-to-many encryption mechanism which enables fine-grained access control over encrypted data. Suppose Alice wants to encrypt a message for all PhD students and alumni in the Department of Mathematics, but she does not know or is not possible to find out the identities of all the eligible receivers, and the set of eligible receivers could also be dynamic. Intuitively, Alice, in this example, is to encrypt a message under "(Mathematics AND (PhD Student OR Alumni))", which is an *access policy* defined over descriptive *attributes*, so that only those receivers who have their decryption keys associated with the attributes which satisfy this policy can decrypt.

Traditional public key encryption and identity-based encryption [23, 3] are inefficient to realize the requirement in the example above as they are for one-to-one encryption. Broadcast Encryption (BE) [8] may not be suitable either as the encryptor in BE has to know and specify the exact identities/indices of the receivers. In CP-ABE, an authority issues different decryption keys to each user based on the attributes the user possesses. During encryption, an encryptor specifies an access policy for the resulting ciphertext. If and only if a receiver's attributes satisfy the access policy of the ciphertext can the receiver decrypt the ciphertext.

Among the CP-ABE schemes recently proposed [2, 7, 10, 24, 15, 20, 12, 16], progress has been made on the schemes' security, access policy expressivity, and efficiency. In [16], Lewko and Waters proposed a new proofing technique and

CCS'13, November 4–8, 2013, Berlin, Germany.
Copyright 2013 ACM 978-1-4503-2477-9/13/11 ...$15.00.
http://dx.doi.org/10.1145/2508859.2516683.

obtained a CP-ABE which is fully secure (i.e. provably secure against adaptive adversaries in the standard model), highly expressive (i.e. supporting any monotonic access structures) and efficient, and additionally eliminates the one-use restriction that previous schemes [15, 20] have. Specifically, the security proof in [15, 20] relies on the *one-use restriction* that a single attribute can only be used once in a policy, and directly extending the schemes in [15, 20] to allow attribute reuse would incur significant tradeoffs in efficiency.

One of the major practicality issues of CP-ABE to date is the lacking of effective solutions to identify malicious users which intentionally expose their secret decryption keys, for example, for financial gain. Due to the nature of CP-ABE, access policies associated with the ciphertexts do not have to contain the exact identities of the eligible receivers. Instead, access policies are role-based and the attributes are generally *shared* by multiple users. For example, both Bob (with attributes {Bob, Alumni, Mathematics}) and Tom (with attributes {Tom, Alumni, Mathematics}) could share a decryption key corresponding to attributes {Alumni, Mathematics} and be able to decrypt the ciphertext in the example above, while the key has no identity information. As a result, a malicious user, with his attributes shared with multiple other users, might have an intention to leak the corresponding decryption key or some *decryption privilege* in the form of a decryption blackbox/device in which the decryption key is embedded, for example, for financial gain or for some other incentives, as there is little risk of getting caught.

This is an interesting problem in practice as leaking a decryption key or a more advanced decryption device/blackbox may entail financial gain and even better, the malicious user has very little risk of getting caught. To address this problem, we require a CP-ABE system to support *traceability*. There are two levels of traceability. Level one is *Whitebox Traceability*, by which given a well-formed decryption key as input, a *tracing algorithm* can find out the user which owns the key. This also includes a scenario that a malicious user sells a new well-formed decryption key for financial gain, and the new decryption key is created from his own key.

Level two is *Blackbox Traceability*, by which given a *decryption blackbox/device*, while the decryption key and even the decryption algorithm could be hidden, the tracing algorithm, which treats the decryption blackbox as an oracle, can still find out the malicious user whose key must have been used in constructing the decryption blackbox.

The problem of building a secure CP-ABE supporting traceability has recently been studied in [18, 17, 19]. However, as we will review that an *expressive Blackbox* Traceable CP-ABE is yet to be built: (1) the ciphertext access policies in [18, 17] only support a single AND gate with wildcard; (2) the traceable CP-ABE in [19] is as fully secure, highly expressive and efficient as a conventional CP-ABE such as the one in [15], but it only supports level one Whitebox Traceability, i.e., it deters malicious users from leaking or selling well-formed decryption keys, but it cannot deter them from selling decryption blackboxes/devices. Below is an example on the importance of achieving Blackbox Traceability.

Key-like Decryption Blackbox for Sale. Using his decryption key (or the decryption keys from multiple colluded malicious users), a malicious user builds a decryption blackbox/device (i.e. a CP-ABE Decryption Blackbox) and sells it on eBay for financial gain. To invalidate the possible whitebox tracing algorithms, the seller keeps the embedded decryption keys and (possibly complicated) algorithms hidden and the device works as a decryption blackbox. Then, to attract potential buyers, the seller describes and advertises that the decryption blackbox functions like a decryption key associated with an attribute set $S_{\mathcal{D}}$, i.e., if a ciphertext access policy can be satisfied by $S_{\mathcal{D}}$, the device can decrypt the ciphertext. For simplicity, we call such a decryption blackbox as a ***key-like decryption blackbox***. In practice, such a key-like decryption blackbox could be quite useful and deemed to be very attractive to potential buyers, and the resulting financial gain could be a big incentive for malicious users to build and sell such a blackbox.

1.1 Our Results

In this paper, we propose a new CP-ABE which is fully secure (i.e. provably secure against adaptive adversaries in the standard model), highly expressive (i.e. supporting any monotonic access structures), and blackbox traceable. Furthermore, this new CP-ABE achieves *fully collusion-resistant* blackbox traceability, that is, the tracing algorithm can find out at least one of the malicious users even if there are an arbitrary number of malicious users colluding by pulling all of their decryption keys together when building a key-like decryption blackbox. Note that collusion-resistant traceability is orthogonal to collusion-resistant security, which is the primary requirement of CP-ABE. *In this paper, traceability is regarded as an additional feature besides the traditional CP-ABE full security, high expressivity and efficiency.*

In addition, the traceability of the scheme is public, that is, anyone can run the tracing algorithm with no additional secret needed. When compared with the most efficient conventional (non-traceable) highly expressive CP-ABE currently available, this new scheme *adds* the public and fully collusion-resistant blackbox traceability with the price of adding only $O(\sqrt{\mathcal{K}})$ elements in the ciphertext and public key, rather than expanding the sizes linearly with $\mathcal{K}$, where $\mathcal{K}$ is the number of users in the system, while the private key size and decryption efficiency mainly remain comparable and are independent of the value of $\mathcal{K}$.

To the best of our knowledge, this is the first CP-ABE that simultaneously supports public and fully collusion-resistant blackbox traceability, full security, high expressivity, and without the one-use restriction, and for a system with fully collusion-resistant blackbox traceability, sub-linear overhead is the most efficient one to date. Table 1.1 compares our scheme with that in [15, 16, 19] in terms of performance and features (i.e. traceability and one-use restriction), as all the four schemes are fully secure and highly expressive.

In Sec. 2, following the standard definition of conventional CP-ABE, we give a 'functional' definition of CP-ABE, in which we specify a unique index $k \in \{1, \ldots, \mathcal{K}\}$ to each decryption key, that later will enable us to define a tracing algorithm Trace which supports fully collusion-resistant blackbox traceability against key-like decryption blackbox. We call the resulting scheme a Blackbox Traceable CP-ABE (or BT-CP-ABE for short).

On the construction of BT-CP-ABE, instead of building one directly, we first define a simpler primitive called Augmented CP-ABE (or AugCP-ABE for short), then we extend it to BT-CP-ABE. In Sec. 3.1, we define AugCP-ABE as $(\mathsf{Setup_A}, \mathsf{KeyGen_A}, \mathsf{Encrypt_A}, \mathsf{Decrypt_A})$, which is similar to BT-CP-ABE, except that the encryption algorithm

	Ciphertext Size	Private Key Size	Public Key Size	Pairing Computation in Decryption	Traceability	Without One-Use Restriction
[15]	$2l+2$	$\|S\|+2$	$\|\mathcal{U}\|+3$	$2\|I\|+1$	No	×
[16]	$2l+3$	$\|S\|+3$	$\|\mathcal{U}\|+4$	$2\|I\|+2$	No	√
[19]	$2l+3$	$\|S\|+4$	$\|\mathcal{U}\|+4$	$2\|I\|+1$	whitebox	×
this work	$2l$ $+17\sqrt{\mathcal{K}}$	$\|S\|+4$	$\|\mathcal{U}\|+3$ $+4\sqrt{\mathcal{K}}$	$2\|I\|+10$	public, blackbox, fully collusion-resistant	√

[1] All the four schemes are fully secure and highly expressive (i.e. supporting any monotonic access structures).
[2] Let l be the size of an access policy, $|S|$ the size of the attribute set of a private key, $|\mathcal{U}|$ the size of the attribute universe, and $|I|$ the number of attributes in a decryption key that satisfies a ciphertext's access policy.

Table 1: Comparison with the conventional CP-ABE in [15, 16] and the traceable CP-ABE in [19]

$\mathsf{Encrypt_A}(\mathsf{PP}, M, \mathbb{A}, \bar{k})$ takes one more parameter $\bar{k} \in \{1, \ldots, \mathcal{K}+1\}$, and the encrypted message M can be recovered using a decryption key $\mathsf{SK}_{k,S}$, which is identified by $k \in \{1, \ldots, \mathcal{K}\}$ and described by an attribute set S, provided that $(k \geq \bar{k}) \wedge (S$ satisfies $\mathbb{A})$, where $\mathbb{A}$ is an access policy. Also, we define the security of AugCP-ABE using message-hiding and (encryption) index-hiding games. In Sec. 3.2, we show how to transform an AugCP-ABE scheme with message-hiding and index-hiding properties to a fully secure BT-CP-ABE scheme. In Sec. 4, we propose an efficient and highly expressive AugCP-ABE scheme, and show that it is message-hiding and index-hiding against adaptively adversaries in the standard model. Combining it with the result in Sec. 3.2, we obtain an efficient, fully secure and highly expressive BT-CP-ABE scheme.

In Sec. 5, we consider the blackbox traceability for another type of decryption blackboxes, which we refer to as ***policy-specific decryption blackbox***. A policy-specific decryption blackbox is a decryption blackbox that is able to decrypt ciphertexts with some specific access policy, say $\mathbb{A}_\mathcal{D}$. In other words, unlike a key-like decryption blackbox which has an attribute set, for example, $S_\mathcal{D}$ attached as the alleged decryption capability as the blackbox advertised by the seller, a policy-specific decryption blackbox is only known to be able to decrypt ciphertexts with some specific policy $\mathbb{A}_\mathcal{D}$. The policy-specific decryption blackbox reflects a different (and possibly more sophisticated) attacking scenario which we call it *"found-in-the-wild."* In this scenario, a decryption blackbox is found, for example, from a black market, and reported to an authority which could be a law enforcement agency. The decryption blackbox's associated attribute set $S_\mathcal{D}$ is missing as it is "found-in-the-wild" while after some testing, it is found that the blackbox can decrypt ciphertexts with certain access policy, say $\mathbb{A}_\mathcal{D}$. Interestingly, we show that our BT-CP-ABE scheme is also traceable (where the traceability definition needs to be modified accordingly, the modification is minor) against this policy-specific decryption blackbox, although the traceability can only be proven against selective adversaries.

2. DEFINITIONS

We first review the definition of CP-ABE which is based on the work of [15, 16] with the exception that in our 'functional' definition, we explicitly assign and identify users using unique indices, and let $\mathcal{K}$ be the number of users in a CP-ABE system. Then we introduce the traceability definition against key-like decryption blackbox. Predefining the number of users is indeed a weakness as well as a necessary cost for achieving blackbox traceability, but we stress that in practice, this should not incur much concern, and all the existing blackbox traceable systems (e.g. [14, 5, 6, 9]) have the same setting. Also being consistent with the conventional definition of CP-ABE [15, 16], the user indices are not used in normal encryption (i.e. the encryptors do not need to know the indices of any users in order to encrypt) and different users (with different indices) may have the same attribute set.

2.1 CP-ABE and Security Models

A Ciphertext-Policy Attribute-Based Encryption (CP-ABE) system consists of four algorithms:

$\mathsf{Setup}(\lambda, \mathcal{U}, \mathcal{K}) \to (\mathsf{PP}, \mathsf{MSK})$. The algorithm takes as input a security parameter λ, the attribute universe $\mathcal{U}$, and the number of users $\mathcal{K}$ in the system, then runs in polynomial time in λ, and outputs the public parameter PP and a master secret key MSK.

$\mathsf{KeyGen}(\mathsf{PP}, \mathsf{MSK}, S) \to \mathsf{SK}_{k,S}$. The algorithm takes as input the public parameter PP, the master secret key MSK, and an attribute set S, and outputs a private decryption key $\mathsf{SK}_{k,S}$, which is assigned and identified by a unique index $k \in \{1, \ldots, \mathcal{K}\}$.

$\mathsf{Encrypt}(\mathsf{PP}, M, \mathbb{A}) \to CT$. The algorithm takes as input the public parameter PP, a message M, and an access policy $\mathbb{A}$ over $\mathcal{U}$, and outputs a ciphertext CT such that only users whose attributes satisfy $\mathbb{A}$ can recover M. $\mathbb{A}$ is implicitly included in CT.

$\mathsf{Decrypt}(\mathsf{PP}, CT, \mathsf{SK}_{k,S}) \to M$ or $\perp$. The algorithm takes as input the public parameter PP, a ciphertext CT, and a private key $\mathsf{SK}_{k,S}$. If S satisfies CT's access policy, the algorithm outputs a message M, otherwise it outputs $\perp$ indicating the failure of decryption.

Now we define the security of a CP-ABE system using a message-hiding game, which is a typical semantic security game and is based on that for conventional CP-ABE [15, 16] security against adaptive adversaries, except that each key is identified by a unique index. Although the index of each user is assigned by the KeyGen algorithm, to capture the security that an attacker can adaptively choose keys to corrupt, we allow the adversary to specify the index when he makes a key query, i.e., to query a private decryption key for an attribute set S, the adversary submits (k, S) to the challenger, where k is the index to be assigned to the corresponding decryption key.

It is worth noticing that: (1) for clarity, for $i = 1$ to q, the adversary submits (index, attribute set) pair (k_i, S_{k_i}) to query a private key for attribute set S_{k_i}, where $q \leq \mathcal{K}$, $k_i \in \{1, \ldots, \mathcal{K}\}$, and $k_i \neq k_j$ $\forall 1 \leq i \neq j \leq q$ (this is to guarantee that each user/key can be *uniquely* identified by an index); and (2) for $k_i \neq k_j$ we do not require $S_{k_i} \neq S_{k_j}$, i.e., different users/keys may have the same attribute set. We remark that these two points apply to the rest of the paper.

$\mathsf{Game}_{\mathsf{MH}}$. The Message-hiding game is defined between a challenger and an adversary $\mathcal{A}$ as follows:

Setup. The challenger runs $\mathsf{Setup}(\lambda, \mathcal{U}, \mathcal{K})$ and gives the public parameter PP to $\mathcal{A}$.

Phase 1. For $i = 1$ to q_1, $\mathcal{A}$ adaptively submits (k_i, S_{k_i}), and the challenger responds with $\mathsf{SK}_{k_i, S_{k_i}}$.

Challenge. $\mathcal{A}$ submits two equal-length messages M_0, M_1 and an access policy $\mathbb{A}^*$. The challenger flips a random coin $b \in \{0, 1\}$, and gives $\mathcal{A}$ an encryption of M_b under $\mathbb{A}^*$.

Phase 2. For $i = q_1{+}1$ to q, $\mathcal{A}$ adaptively submits (k_i, S_{k_i}), and the challenger responds with $\mathsf{SK}_{k_i, S_{k_i}}$.

Guess. $\mathcal{A}$ outputs a guess $b' \in \{0, 1\}$ for b.

$\mathcal{A}$ wins the game if $b' = b$ under the **restriction** that $\mathbb{A}^*$ cannot be satisfied by any of the queried attribute sets $S_{k_1}, \ldots, S_{k_q}$. The advantage of $\mathcal{A}$ is defined as $\mathsf{MHAdv}_{\mathcal{A}} = |\Pr[b' = b] - \frac{1}{2}|$.

DEFINITION 1. *A $\mathcal{K}$-user CP-ABE system is secure if for all polynomial-time adversaries $\mathcal{A}$ the advantage* $\mathsf{MHAdv}_{\mathcal{A}}$ *is negligible in λ.*

It is clear that a secure CP-ABE system defined as above has all the appealing properties that a conventional CP-ABE system [15, 16] has, that is, fully collusion-resistant security, fine-grained access control on encrypted data, and efficient one-to-many encryption.

2.2 BT-CP-ABE: Traceability

Now we define the traceability against key-like decryption blackbox, and call the new system a Blackbox Traceable CP-ABE (or BT-CP-ABE for short). Our definition is loosely related to the traitor tracing feature in broadcast encryption [6, 9]. A key-like decryption blackbox $\mathcal{D}$ in our setting is viewed as a probabilistic circuit that takes as input a ciphertext CT and outputs a message M or $\perp$, and such a decryption blackbox does not need to be perfect, namely, we only require it to be able to decrypt with non-negligible success probability. *In particular, the adversary (i.e. seller) describes a key-like decryption blackbox $\mathcal{D}$ with a non-empty attribute set $S_{\mathcal{D}}$ and a non-negligible probability value ϵ (i.e. $0 < \epsilon \leq 1$ is polynomially related to λ), and advertises that for any access policy $\mathbb{A}$, if it can be satisfied by $S_{\mathcal{D}}$, this blackbox $\mathcal{D}$ can decrypt the corresponding ciphertext associated with $\mathbb{A}$ with probability at least ϵ.* Note that ϵ is the lower-bound of $\mathcal{D}$'s decryption ability, e.g., suppose $\mathbb{A}_1$ is a ciphertext's access policy satisfied by $S_{\mathcal{D}}$ and $\mathcal{D}$ can decrypt the ciphertext with probability 0.1, even if $\mathcal{D}$ can decrypt ciphertexts under other valid access policies (satisfied by $\mathcal{D}$) with probability 1, the seller can only declare an $\epsilon \leq 0.1$. Obviously for some attribute set $S_{\mathcal{D}}$, ϵ is closer to 1, which implies that the decryption ability of $\mathcal{D}$ is closer to that of a private key with attribute set $S_{\mathcal{D}}$, and hence $\mathcal{D}$ is more attractive to potential buyers who are interested in decrypting ciphertexts with access policies which can be satisfied by $S_{\mathcal{D}}$. We now define a tracing algorithm as follows.

$\mathsf{Trace}^{\mathcal{D}}(\mathsf{PP}, S_{\mathcal{D}}, \epsilon) \to \mathbb{K}_T \subseteq \{1, \ldots, \mathcal{K}\}$. *This is an oracle algorithm that interacts with a key-like decryption blackbox $\mathcal{D}$. By given the public parameter* PP, *a non-empty attribute set $S_{\mathcal{D}}$, and a probability value (lower-bound) ϵ, the algorithm runs in time polynomial in λ and $1/\epsilon$, and outputs an index set $\mathbb{K}_T \subseteq \{1, \ldots, \mathcal{K}\}$ which identifies the set of malicious users. Note that ϵ has to be polynomially related to λ.*

The following Tracing Game captures the notion of **fully collusion-resistant traceability**. In the game, the adversary targets to build a decryption blackbox $\mathcal{D}$ that functions as a private decryption key with attribute set $S_{\mathcal{D}}$ (as the name of key-like decryption blackbox implies). The tracing algorithm, on the other side, is designed to extract the index of at least one of the malicious users whose decryption keys have been used for constructing $\mathcal{D}$.

$\mathsf{Game}_{\mathsf{TR}}$. The Tracing Game is defined between a challenger and an adversary $\mathcal{A}$ as follows:

Setup. The challenger runs $\mathsf{Setup}(\lambda, \mathcal{U}, \mathcal{K})$ and gives the public parameter PP to $\mathcal{A}$.

Key Query. For $i = 1$ to q, $\mathcal{A}$ adaptively submits (k_i, S_{k_i}), and the challenger responds with $\mathsf{SK}_{k_i, S_{k_i}}$.

(Key-like) Decryption Blackbox Generation. $\mathcal{A}$ outputs a decryption blackbox $\mathcal{D}$ associated with a non-empty attribute set $S_{\mathcal{D}} \subseteq \mathcal{U}$ and a non-negligible probability (lower-bound) value ϵ.

Tracing. The challenger runs $\mathsf{Trace}^{\mathcal{D}}(\mathsf{PP}, S_{\mathcal{D}}, \epsilon)$ to obtain an index set $\mathbb{K}_T \subseteq \{1, \ldots, \mathcal{K}\}$.

Let $\mathbb{K}_{\mathcal{D}} = \{k_i | 1 \leq i \leq q\}$ be the index set of keys corrupted by the adversary. We say that the adversary $\mathcal{A}$ wins the game if the following conditions hold:

1. For any access policy $\mathbb{A}$ that is satisfied by $S_{\mathcal{D}}$, we have
$$\Pr[\mathcal{D}(\mathsf{Encrypt}(\mathsf{PP}, M, \mathbb{A})) = M] \geq \epsilon,$$
where the probability is taken over the random choices of message M and the random coins of $\mathcal{D}$. A decryption blackbox satisfying this condition is said to be a *useful key-like decryption blackbox*.
2. $\mathbb{K}_T = \emptyset$, or $\mathbb{K}_T \not\subseteq \mathbb{K}_{\mathcal{D}}$, or ($S_{\mathcal{D}} \not\subseteq S_{k_t}$ $\forall k_t \in \mathbb{K}_T$).

We denote by $\mathsf{TRAdv}_{\mathcal{A}}$ the probability that adversary $\mathcal{A}$ wins this game.

DEFINITION 2. *A $\mathcal{K}$-user Blackbox Traceable CP-ABE system is traceable if for all polynomial-time adversaries $\mathcal{A}$ the advantage* $\mathsf{TRAdv}_{\mathcal{A}}$ *is negligible in λ.*

Remark: For a useful key-like decryption blackbox $\mathcal{D}$, the traced $\mathbb{K}_T$ must satisfy $(\mathbb{K}_T \neq \emptyset) \wedge (\mathbb{K}_T \subseteq \mathbb{K}_{\mathcal{D}}) \wedge (\exists k_t \in \mathbb{K}_T$ *s.t.* $S_{k_t} \supseteq S_{\mathcal{D}})$ for traceabililty. (1) $(\mathbb{K}_T \neq \emptyset) \wedge (\mathbb{K}_T \subseteq \mathbb{K}_{\mathcal{D}})$ captures the preliminary traceability that the tracing algorithm can extract at least one malicious user and the coalition of malicious users cannot frame any innocent user. Note that such a preliminary traceability is a *weak traceability* that may not be useful enough in practice. Specifically, consider a key-like decryption blackbox $\mathcal{D}$ built from the private decryption keys of users k_1 and k_2 who were authorized high-value attribute set S_{k_1} and low-value attribute set S_{k_2}, respectively, and assume that $S_{k_2} \not\supseteq S_{k_1}$ and the decryption ability of $\mathcal{D}$ is described by $S_{\mathcal{D}} = S_{k_1}$, e.g., $S_{\mathcal{D}} = S_{k_1} = \{\text{Senior Manager}\}$, and $S_{k_2} = \{\text{Intern}\}$. A scheme is considered to be weak traceable if its Trace algorithm only extracts k_2 from $\mathcal{D}$ as the malicious user. This may not be satisfactory in practice as $\mathcal{D}$ having the decryption ability of attribute set {Senior Manager} implies that there must be some user having attribute "Senior Manager" participated in building $\mathcal{D}$ yet the algorithm was only able to trace $\mathcal{D}$ to an "Intern", who has less to lose. (2) ($\exists k_t \in \mathbb{K}_T$ *s.t.* $S_{k_t} \supseteq S_{\mathcal{D}}$) captures *strong traceability* that the Trace algorithm can extract at least one malicious user whose private key enables $\mathcal{D}$ to have the decryption ability corresponding to $S_{\mathcal{D}}$, i.e., whose attribute set is a superset of $S_{\mathcal{D}}$. As a related work, comparable weak and strong traceability notions in the setting of predicate encryption were considered in [14]. In this paper we focus on the strong traceability of CP-ABE, and unless stated otherwise, by the *traceability* we mean the *strong traceability*.

Note that the tracing game above does not limit the number of colluded users. Also note that, as of [5, 6, 9, 14], we are modeling a stateless (resettable) decryption blackbox – the decryption blackbox is just an oracle and maintains no state between activations.

3. AUGMENTED CP-ABE

Following the routes of [5, 6, 9], instead of constructing a BT-CP-ABE directly, we define a simpler primitive called Augmented CP-ABE (or AugCP-ABE for short) and its security notions first, then we show that a secure AugCP-ABE can be transformed to a secure and traceable BT-CP-ABE scheme. In Sec. 4, we propose a concrete construction of AugCP-ABE.

3.1 Def nitions

An AugCP-ABE system consists of the following four algorithms, in particular, different from a conventional CP-ABE, the encryption algorithm takes one more parameter $\bar{k} \in \{1, \ldots, \mathcal{K}+1\}$.

$\mathsf{Setup_A}(\lambda, \mathcal{U}, \mathcal{K}) \rightarrow (\mathsf{PP}, \mathsf{MSK})$. The algorithm takes as input a security parameter λ, the attribute universe $\mathcal{U}$, and the number of users $\mathcal{K}$ in the system, then runs in polynomial time in λ, and outputs the public parameter PP and a master secret key MSK.

$\mathsf{KeyGen_A}(\mathsf{PP}, \mathsf{MSK}, S) \rightarrow \mathsf{SK}_{k,S}$. The algorithm takes as input PP, the master secret key MSK, and an attribute set S, and outputs a private key $\mathsf{SK}_{k,S}$, which is assigned and identified by a unique index $k \in \{1, \ldots, \mathcal{K}\}$.

$\mathsf{Encrypt_A}(\mathsf{PP}, M, \mathbb{A}, \bar{k}) \rightarrow CT$. The algorithm takes as input PP, a message M, an access policy $\mathbb{A}$ over $\mathcal{U}$, and an index $\bar{k} \in \{1, \ldots, \mathcal{K}+1\}$, and outputs a ciphertext CT. **$\mathbb{A}$ is included in CT, but the value of $\bar{k}$ is not.**

$\mathsf{Decrypt_A}(\mathsf{PP}, CT, \mathsf{SK}_{k,S}) \rightarrow M$ or $\perp$. The algorithm takes as input PP, a ciphertext CT, and a private key $\mathsf{SK}_{k,S}$. If S satisfies CT's access policy, the algorithm outputs a message M, otherwise it outputs $\perp$ indicating the failure of decryption.

Correctness. For any attribute set $S \subseteq \mathcal{U}$, $k \in \{1, \ldots, \mathcal{K}\}$, access policy $\mathbb{A}$ over $\mathcal{U}$, $\bar{k} \in \{1, \ldots, \mathcal{K}+1\}$, and message M, suppose $(\mathsf{PP}, \mathsf{MSK}) \leftarrow \mathsf{Setup_A}(\lambda, \mathcal{U}, \mathcal{K})$, $\mathsf{SK}_{k,S} \leftarrow \mathsf{KeyGen_A}(\mathsf{PP}, \mathsf{MSK}, S)$, $CT \leftarrow \mathsf{Encrypt_A}(\mathsf{PP}, M, \mathbb{A}, \bar{k})$. If ($S$ satisfies $\mathbb{A}$) $\wedge (k \geq \bar{k})$ then $\mathsf{Decrypt_A}(\mathsf{PP}, CT, \mathsf{SK}_{k,S}) = M$.

It is worth noticing that during decryption if the attribute set S of a private decryption key satisfies the access policy $\mathbb{A}$ of a ciphertext, the decryption works, regardless of the value of key index k or encryption index $\bar{k}$, but whether the output message is equal to the encrypted message is determined by the values of k and $\bar{k}$. i.e., if and only if (S satisfies $\mathbb{A}$) $\wedge$ $(k \geq \bar{k})$, can $\mathsf{SK}_{k,S}$ correctly decrypt a ciphertext encrypted using $(\mathbb{A}, \bar{k})$. Note that if we always set $\bar{k} = 1$, then the functions of AugCP-ABE are identical to that of BT-CP-ABE. Actually, the idea behind converting an AugCP-ABE scheme to a BT-CP-ABE scheme is to construct an AugCP-ABE scheme with (encryption) index-hiding property, and then always set $\bar{k} = 1$ in normal encryption, while use $\bar{k} \in \{1, \ldots, \mathcal{K}+1\}$ in generating ciphertexts for tracing.

Security. We define the security of AugCP-ABE in the following three games, where the first two are for message-hiding, and the third one is for the index-hiding property. In the first two **message-hiding games** between a challenger and an adversary $\mathcal{A}$, $\bar{k} = 1$ (the first game, $\mathsf{Game^A_{MH_1}}$) and $\bar{k} = \mathcal{K}+1$ (the second game, $\mathsf{Game^A_{MH_{\mathcal{K}+1}}}$).

Setup. The challenger runs $\mathsf{Setup_A}(\lambda, \mathcal{U}, \mathcal{K})$ and gives the public parameter PP to $\mathcal{A}$.

Phase 1. For $i = 1$ to q_1, $\mathcal{A}$ adaptively submits (k_i, S_{k_i}), and the challenger responds with $\mathsf{SK}_{k_i, S_{k_i}}$.

Challenge. $\mathcal{A}$ submits two equal-length messages M_0, M_1 and an access policy $\mathbb{A}^*$. The challenger flips a random coin $b \in \{0, 1\}$, and sends $CT \leftarrow \mathsf{Encrypt_A}(\mathsf{PP}, M_b, \mathbb{A}^*, \bar{k})$ to $\mathcal{A}$.

Phase 2. For $i = q_1 + 1$ to q, $\mathcal{A}$ adaptively submits (k_i, S_{k_i}), and the challenger responds with $\mathsf{SK}_{k_i, S_{k_i}}$.

Guess. $\mathcal{A}$ outputs a guess $b' \in \{0, 1\}$ for b.

$\mathsf{Game^A_{MH_1}}$. In the Challenge phase the challenger sends $CT \leftarrow \mathsf{Encrypt_A}(\mathsf{PP}, M_b, \mathbb{A}^*, 1)$ to $\mathcal{A}$. $\mathcal{A}$ wins the game if $b' = b$ under the **restriction** that $\mathbb{A}^*$ cannot be satisfied by any of the queried attribute sets $S_{k_1}, \ldots, S_{k_q}$. The advantage of $\mathcal{A}$ is defined as $\mathsf{MH^A_1Adv}_{\mathcal{A}} = |\Pr[b' = b] - \frac{1}{2}|$.

$\mathsf{Game^A_{MH_{\mathcal{K}+1}}}$. In the Challenge phase the challenger sends $CT \leftarrow \mathsf{Encrypt_A}(\mathsf{PP}, M_b, \mathbb{A}^*, \mathcal{K}+1)$ to $\mathcal{A}$. $\mathcal{A}$ wins the game if $b' = b$. The advantage of $\mathcal{A}$ is defined as $\mathsf{MH^A_{\mathcal{K}+1}Adv}_{\mathcal{A}} = |\Pr[b' = b] - \frac{1}{2}|$.

DEFINITION 3. *A $\mathcal{K}$-user Augmented CP-ABE system is message-hiding if for all polynomial-time adversaries $\mathcal{A}$ the advantages $\mathsf{MH^A_1Adv}_{\mathcal{A}}$ and $\mathsf{MH^A_{\mathcal{K}+1}Adv}_{\mathcal{A}}$ are negligible in λ.*

$\mathsf{Game^A_{IH}}$. In the third game, **index-hiding game**, for any non-empty attribute set $S^* \subseteq \mathcal{U}$, we define **the strictest access policy** as $\mathbb{A}_{S^*} = \bigwedge_{x \in S^*} x$, and require that an adversary cannot distinguish between an encryption using $(\mathbb{A}_{S^*}, \bar{k})$ and $(\mathbb{A}_{S^*}, \bar{k}+1)$ without a private decryption key $\mathsf{SK}_{\bar{k}, S_{\bar{k}}}$ where $S_{\bar{k}} \supseteq S^*$. The game takes as input a parameter $\bar{k} \in \{1, \ldots, \mathcal{K}\}$ which is given to both the challenger and the adversary $\mathcal{A}$. The game proceeds as follows:

Setup. The challenger runs $\mathsf{Setup_A}(\lambda, \mathcal{U}, \mathcal{K})$ and gives the public parameter PP to $\mathcal{A}$.

Key Query. For $i = 1$ to q, $\mathcal{A}$ adaptively submits (k_i, S_{k_i}), and the challenger responds with $\mathsf{SK}_{k_i, S_{k_i}}$.

Challenge. $\mathcal{A}$ submits a message M and a non-empty attribute set S^*. The challenger flips a random coin $b \in \{0,1\}$, and sends $CT \leftarrow \mathsf{Encrypt_A}(\mathsf{PP}, M, \mathbb{A}_{S^*}, \bar{k}+b)$ to $\mathcal{A}$.

Guess. $\mathcal{A}$ outputs a guess $b' \in \{0,1\}$ for b.

$\mathcal{A}$ wins the game if $b' = b$ under the **restriction** that none of the queried pairs $\{(k_i, S_{k_i})\}_{1 \le i \le q}$ can satisfy $(k_i = \bar{k}) \wedge (S_{k_i}$ satisfies $\mathbb{A}_{S^*})$, i.e. $(k_i = \bar{k}) \wedge (S_{k_i} \supseteq S^*)$. The advantage of $\mathcal{A}$ is defined as $\mathsf{IH^AAdv}_{\mathcal{A}}[\bar{k}] = |\Pr[b' = b] - \frac{1}{2}|$.

DEFINITION 4. *A $\mathcal{K}$-user Augmented CP-ABE system is index-hiding if for all polynomial-time adversaries $\mathcal{A}$ the advantages $\mathsf{IH^AAdv}_{\mathcal{A}}[\bar{k}]$ for $\bar{k} = 1, \ldots, \mathcal{K}$ are negligible in λ.*

3.2 Reducing BT-CP-ABE to AugCP-ABE

We now show that an AugCP-ABE with message-hiding and index-hiding implies a secure and traceable BT-CP-ABE. Let $\Sigma_{\mathsf{A}} = (\mathsf{Setup_A}, \mathsf{KeyGen_A}, \mathsf{Encrypt_A}, \mathsf{Decrypt_A})$ be an AugCP-ABE with message-hiding and index-hiding, define $\mathsf{Encrypt}(\mathsf{PP}, M, \mathbb{A}) = \mathsf{Encrypt_A}(\mathsf{PP}, M, \mathbb{A}, 1)$, then $\Sigma = (\mathsf{Setup_A}, \mathsf{KeyGen_A}, \mathsf{Encrypt}, \mathsf{Decrypt_A})$ is a BT-CP-ABE derived from Σ_{A}, and the tracing algorithm is defined as

$\mathsf{Trace}^{\mathcal{D}}(\mathsf{PP}, S_{\mathcal{D}}, \epsilon) \rightarrow \mathbb{K}_T \subseteq \{1, \ldots, \mathcal{K}\}$: Given a key-like decryption blackbox $\mathcal{D}$ associated with a non-empty attribute set $S_{\mathcal{D}}$ and probability $\epsilon > 0$, the tracing algorithm works as follows: [1]

1. For $k = 1$ to $\mathcal{K}+1$, do the following:
   (a) The algorithm repeats the following $8\lambda(\mathcal{K}/\epsilon)^2$ times:
      i. Sample M from the message space at random.
      ii. Let $CT \leftarrow \mathsf{Encrypt_A}(\mathsf{PP}, M, \mathbb{A}_{S_{\mathcal{D}}}, k)$, where $\mathbb{A}_{S_{\mathcal{D}}}$ is the strictest access policy of $S_{\mathcal{D}}$.
      iii. Query oracle $\mathcal{D}$ on input CT which contains $\mathbb{A}_{S_{\mathcal{D}}}$, and compare the output of $\mathcal{D}$ with M.
   (b) Let $\hat{p}_k$ be the fraction of times that $\mathcal{D}$ decrypted the ciphertexts correctly.
2. Let $\mathbb{K}_T$ be the set of all $k \in \{1, \ldots, \mathcal{K}\}$ for which $\hat{p}_k - \hat{p}_{k+1} \geq \epsilon/(4\mathcal{K})$. Then output $\mathbb{K}_T$ as the index set of the private decryption keys of malicious users.

Remark: Note that the *strictest access policy* used in the index-hiding game $\mathsf{Game^A_{IH}}$ and the tracing algorithm Trace does not impose any limitation to traceable CP-ABE. Instead, it is an efficient way to ensure that the traced malicious users are the reasonable suspects. As a key-like decryption blackbox $\mathcal{D}$ is advertised that it functions like a private decryption key with attribute set $S_{\mathcal{D}}$, a ciphertext associated with the strictest access policy $\mathbb{A}_{S_{\mathcal{D}}}$ will be decrypted by $\mathcal{D}$ accordingly. Although it might look more appealing to have the index-hiding property for any access policy, the following Theorem 1 shows that the strictest access policy is sufficient for ensuring the traceability against key-like decryption blackbox for the derived BT-CP-ABE scheme.

THEOREM 1. *If Σ_{A} is an AugCP-ABE with message-hiding and index-hiding properties, then Σ is a secure and traceable BT-CP-ABE.*

[1] The tracing algorithm uses a technique based on that in broadcast encryption by [5, 6, 9].

PROOF. Note that Σ is a special case of Σ_{A} where the encryption algorithm always sets $\bar{k} = 1$. Hence, $\mathsf{Game_{MH}}$ for Σ is identical to $\mathsf{Game^A_{MH_1}}$ for Σ_{A}, which implies that $\mathsf{MHAdv}_{\mathcal{A}}$ for Σ in $\mathsf{Game_{MH}}$ is equal to $\mathsf{MH^A_1Adv}_{\mathcal{A}}$ for Σ_{A} in $\mathsf{Game^A_{MH_1}}$, i.e., if Σ_{A} is message-hiding (in $\mathsf{Game^A_{MH_1}}$), then Σ is secure.

Now we show that if Σ_{A} is message-hiding (in $\mathsf{Game^A_{MH_{\mathcal{K}+1}}}$) and index-hiding, Σ is traceable. In the proof sketch below, which is based on that of [5, 6, 9], we show that if the key-like decryption blackbox output by the adversary is a useful one then the traced $\mathbb{K}_T$ will satisfy $(\mathbb{K}_T \neq \emptyset) \wedge (\mathbb{K}_T \subseteq \mathbb{K}_{\mathcal{D}}) \wedge (\exists k_t \in \mathbb{K}_T \ s.t. \ S_{k_t} \supseteq S_{\mathcal{D}})$ with overwhelming probability, which implies that the adversary can win the game $\mathsf{Game_{TR}}$ only with negligible probability, i.e., $\mathsf{TRAdv}_{\mathcal{A}}$ is negligible.

Let $\mathcal{D}$ be the key-like decryption blackbox output by the adversary, and $S_{\mathcal{D}}$ be the attribute set describing $\mathcal{D}$. Define

$$p_{\bar{k}} = \Pr[\mathcal{D}(\mathsf{Encrypt_A}(\mathsf{PP}, M, \mathbb{A}_{S_{\mathcal{D}}}, \bar{k})) = M],$$

where the probability is taken over the random choice of message M and the random coins of $\mathcal{D}$. We have that $p_1 \geq \epsilon$ and $p_{\mathcal{K}+1}$ is negligible. The former follows the fact that $\mathcal{D}$ is a useful key-like decryption blackbox, and the later follows that Σ_{A} is message-hiding (in $\mathsf{Game^A_{MH_{\mathcal{K}+1}}}$). Then there must exist some $k \in \{1, \ldots, \mathcal{K}\}$ such that $p_k - p_{k+1} \geq \epsilon/(2\mathcal{K})$. By the Chernoff bound it follows that with overwhelming probability, $\hat{p}_k - \hat{p}_{k+1} \geq \epsilon/(4\mathcal{K})$. Hence, we have $\mathbb{K}_T \neq \emptyset$.

For any $k \in \mathbb{K}_T$ (i.e., $\hat{p}_k - \hat{p}_{k+1} \geq \frac{\epsilon}{4\mathcal{K}}$), we know, by Chernoff, that with overwhelming probability $p_k - p_{k+1} \geq \epsilon/(8\mathcal{K})$. Clearly $(k \in \mathbb{K}_{\mathcal{D}}) \wedge (S_k \supseteq S_{\mathcal{D}})$ since otherwise, $\mathcal{D}$ can be directly used to win the index-hiding game for Σ_A. Hence, we have $(\mathbb{K}_T \subseteq \mathbb{K}_{\mathcal{D}}) \wedge (S_{\mathcal{D}} \subseteq S_k \ \forall k \in \mathbb{K}_T)$. □

4. AN EFFICIENT AUGMENTED CP-ABE

Now we construct an AugCP-ABE scheme that is as secure and expressive as the CP-ABE scheme in [16]. To obtain traceability in the derived BT-CP-ABE scheme we will use the standard tracing techniques which were used by [5, 6, 9] in the setting of broadcast encryption. The challenge is to apply the tracing techniques to the setting of CP-ABE *securely and efficiently.*

4.1 Preliminaries

Before proposing a concrete construction for AugCP-ABE, we first review some preliminaries.

Linear Secret-Sharing Schemes. As of previous work, we use linear secret-sharing schemes (LSSS) to realize monotonic access structures which specify the access policies associated with ciphertexts. The formal definitions of access structures and LSSS can be found in [24, 15, 16]. Informally, an LSSS is a share-generating matrix A whose rows $\{A_i\}$ are labeled by attributes through a function ρ. When we consider the column vector $\vec{v} = (s, r_2, \ldots, r_n)$, where $s \in \mathbb{Z}_p$ is the secret to be shared and $r_2, \ldots, r_n \in \mathbb{Z}_p$ are randomly chosen, $A\vec{v}$ is the vector of l shares of the secret s, and the share $\lambda_i = (A\vec{v})_i$, i.e. the inner product $A_i \cdot \vec{v}$, belongs to attribute $\rho(i)$. A user's attribute set S satisfies the LSSS access matrix if the rows labeled by the attributes in S have the *linear reconstruction* property, which means that there exist constants $\{\omega_i\}$ such that, for any valid shares $\{\lambda_i\}$ of a secret s according to the LSSS matrix, we have $\sum_i \omega_i \lambda_i = s$. Essentially, a user will be able to decrypt a ciphertext with access matrix A if and only if the rows of A labeled by the user's attributes include the vector $(1, 0, \ldots, 0)$ in their span.

Composite Order Bilinear Groups. Let $\mathcal{G}$ be a group generator, which takes a security parameter λ and outputs $(p_1, p_2, p_3, \mathbb{G}, \mathbb{G}_T, e)$ where p_1, p_2, p_3 are distinct primes, $\mathbb{G}$ and $\mathbb{G}_T$ are cyclic groups of order $N = p_1p_2p_3$, and $e : \mathbb{G} \times \mathbb{G} \to \mathbb{G}_T$ a map such that: (1) (Bilinear) $\forall g, h \in \mathbb{G}, a, b \in \mathbb{Z}_N, e(g^a, h^b) = e(g, h)^{ab}$, (2) (Non-Degenerate) $\exists g \in \mathbb{G}$ such that $e(g, g)$ has order N in $\mathbb{G}_T$. Assume that group operations in $\mathbb{G}$ and $\mathbb{G}_T$ as well as the bilinear map e are computable in polynomial time with respect to λ. Let $\mathbb{G}_{p_1}$, $\mathbb{G}_{p_2}$ and $\mathbb{G}_{p_3}$ be the subgroups of order p_1, p_2 and p_3 in $\mathbb{G}$, respectively. These subgroups are "orthogonal" to each other under the bilinear map e: if $h_i \in \mathbb{G}_{p_i}$ and $h_j \in \mathbb{G}_{p_j}$ for $i \neq j$, then $e(h_i, h_j) = 1$ (the identity element in $\mathbb{G}_T$). More details can be found in [15, 16].

Complexity Assumptions. The message-hiding property of our AugCP-ABE scheme will rely on four assumptions (the Assumption 1 in [16], the General Subgroup Decision Assumption, the 3-Party Diffie-Hellman Assumption in a Subgroup, and the Source Group q-Parallel BDHE Assumption in a Subgroup), which are used in [16] to achieve full security of their CP-ABE scheme while eliminating the one-use restriction. The index-hiding property will rely on two assumptions (3-Party Diffie-Hellman Assumption and Decisional Linear Assumption) that are used in [6] to achieve traceability in the setting of broadcast encryption. We refer to [16, 6] for the details of these assumptions.

Notations. Suppose the number of users $\mathcal{K}$ in the system equals m^2 for some m [2]. We arrange the users in an $m \times m$ matrix and uniquely assign a tuple (i, j) where $1 \leq i, j \leq m$, to each user. A user at position (i, j) of the matrix has index $k = (i-1) * m + j$. For simplicity, we directly use (i, j) as the index where $(i, j) \geq (\bar{i}, \bar{j})$ means that $((i > \bar{i}) \vee (i = \bar{i} \wedge j \geq \bar{j}))$. The use of pairwise notation (i, j) is purely a notational convenience, as $k = (i-1) * m + j$ defines a bijection between $\{(i, j) | 1 \leq i, j \leq m\}$ and $\{1, \ldots, \mathcal{K}\}$. For a positive integer, say m, by $[m]$ we mean the set $\{1, 2, \ldots, m\}$. For a given vector $\vec{v} = (v_1, \ldots, v_d)$, by $g^{\vec{v}}$ we mean the vector $(g^{v_1}, \ldots, g^{v_d})$. Furthermore, for $g^{\vec{v}} = (g^{v_1}, \ldots, g^{v_d})$ and $g^{\vec{w}} = (g^{w_1}, \ldots, g^{w_d})$, by $g^{\vec{v}} \cdot g^{\vec{w}}$ we mean the vector $(g^{v_1+w_1}, \ldots, g^{v_d+w_d})$, i.e. $g^{\vec{v}} \cdot g^{\vec{w}} = g^{\vec{v}+\vec{w}}$, and by $e_d(g^{\vec{v}}, g^{\vec{w}})$ we mean $\prod_{k=1}^{d} e(g^{v_k}, g^{w_k})$, i.e. $e_d(g^{\vec{v}}, g^{\vec{w}}) = \prod_{k=1}^{d} e(g^{v_k}, g^{w_k}) = e(g, g)^{(\vec{v} \cdot \vec{w})}$ where $(\vec{v} \cdot \vec{w})$ is the inner product of $\vec{v}$ and $\vec{w}$. Given a bilinear group order N, one can randomly choose $r_x, r_y, r_z \in \mathbb{Z}_N$, and set $\vec{\chi}_1 = (r_x, 0, r_z)$, $\vec{\chi}_2 = (0, r_y, r_z)$, $\vec{\chi}_3 = \vec{\chi}_1 \times \vec{\chi}_2 = (-r_yr_z, -r_xr_z, r_xr_y)$. Let $span\{\vec{\chi}_1, \vec{\chi}_2\}$ be the subspace spanned by $\vec{\chi}_1$ and $\vec{\chi}_2$, i.e. $span\{\vec{\chi}_1, \vec{\chi}_2\} = \{\nu_1\vec{\chi}_1 + \nu_2\vec{\chi}_2 | \nu_1, \nu_2 \in \mathbb{Z}_N\}$. We can see that $\vec{\chi}_3$ is orthogonal to the subspace $span\{\vec{\chi}_1, \vec{\chi}_2\}$ and $\mathbb{Z}_N^3 = span\{\vec{\chi}_1, \vec{\chi}_2, \vec{\chi}_3\} = \{\nu_1\vec{\chi}_1 + \nu_2\vec{\chi}_2 + \nu_3\vec{\chi}_3 | \nu_1, \nu_2, \nu_3 \in \mathbb{Z}_N\}$. For any $\vec{v} \in span\{\vec{\chi}_1, \vec{\chi}_2\}$, we have $(\vec{\chi}_3 \cdot \vec{v}) = 0$, and for random $\vec{v} \in \mathbb{Z}_N^3$, $(\vec{\chi}_3 \cdot \vec{v}) \neq 0$ occurs with overwhelming probability.

4.2 Our Approach

Note that the Traitor Tracing schemes in broadcast encryption [5, 6, 9] achieved fully collusion-resistant blackbox traceability at the cost of sub-linear overhead, which is the most efficient level to date. It will be tempting to try in a straightforward way to combine such a Traitor Tracing system and a CP-ABE for obtaining a BT-CP-ABE. However, the resulting system cannot achieve the desired security (i.e. *strong* traceability). Consider the following (misguided) approach. Suppose that we created both a CP-ABE and a Traitor Tracing system each for $\mathcal{K}$ users, where each user has the same index in both systems. To encrypt a message M, an algorithm splits the message randomly into two pieces M_P and M_I such that $M_P \cdot M_I = M$, then encrypts M_P under CP-ABE and M_I under the Traitor Tracing system. To decrypt, we need to decrypt under both systems. However, such an approach can only provide weak traceability[3]. In particular, if two users, Alice with attribute set S_A in CP-ABE and index k_A in both systems, and Bob with attribute set S_B in CP-ABE and index k_B in both systems, collude to make a decryption blackbox $\mathcal{D}$ with attribute set $S_{\mathcal{D}} \subseteq S_A$, while $S_B \cap S_A = \emptyset$. The blackbox uses Alice's key (the part corresponding to S_A) to decrypt the ciphertext from the CP-ABE system and Bob's key (the part corresponding to k_B) to decrypt the ciphertext from the Traitor Tracing system. The tracing algorithm would identify Bob as a malicious user, but S_B is uncorrelated to $S_{\mathcal{D}}$.

The idea behind the techniques of achieving **strong** traceability is to set a user's private decryption key such that it must be *simultaneously* used in both CP-ABE and the Tracing part in a BT-CP-ABE. Boneh and Waters [6] handled a similar situation where they intertwined a broadcast encryption scheme [4] and a Traitor Tracing scheme [5] to build an Augmented Broadcast Encryption (AugBE) scheme. Inspired by their approach, we tried to intertwin a CP-ABE [16] and a Traitor Tracing system [9] to build an AugCP-ABE scheme. The obstacle comes from the setting that in CP-ABE the decryption privilege of a user is determined by his attributes rather than by his index as in broadcast encryption. In particular, in AugBE [6, 9], the indices of users are simultaneously used to determine users' decryption privilege (for broadcast encryption part) and to identify users (for Tracing), and the construction and the proof of index-hiding of AugBE [6, 9] are based on this fact. In contrast, in BT-CP-ABE, the attributes are used to determine users' decryption privilege (for CP-ABE part) while the indices are used to identify users (for Tracing part), and to intertwine the two essentially uncorrelated parts, we need new ideas and techniques.

A straightforward combination will result in schemes that are either not provable or inefficient with ciphertext of size $O(\sqrt{\mathcal{K}} \cdot |\mathbb{A}|)$ where $|\mathbb{A}|$ is the size of an access policy. In the following, based on the CP-ABE in [16] with our particular designs and contructions, we propose a *secure* AugCP-ABE which is also *efficient* with ciphertext of size $O(\sqrt{\mathcal{K}} + |\mathbb{A}|)$.

4.3 AugCP-ABE Construction

$\mathsf{Setup_A}(\lambda, \mathcal{U}, \mathcal{K} = m^2) \to (\mathsf{PP}, \mathsf{MSK})$. Let $\mathbb{G}$ be a bilinear group of order $N = p_1p_2p_3$ (3 distinct primes, whose size is determined by λ), $\mathbb{G}_{p_i}$ the subgroup of order p_i in $\mathbb{G}$ (for $i = 1, 2, 3$), and $g, f, h \in \mathbb{G}_{p_1}$, $g_3 \in \mathbb{G}_{p_3}$ the generators of corresponding subgroups. The algorithm randomly chooses exponents

$$\{\alpha_i,\ r_i,\ z_i \in \mathbb{Z}_N\}_{i \in [m]},\ \{c_j \in \mathbb{Z}_N\}_{j \in [m]},\ \{a_x \in \mathbb{Z}_N\}_{x \in \mathcal{U}}.$$

[2]If the number of users is not a square, we add some "dummy" users to pad to the next square.

[3]A similar approach was used in [14] to introduce weak traceability to predicate encryption.

The public parameter PP includes the description of the group and the following elements:

$$\Big(g,\ f,\ h,\ \ \{E_i = e(g,g)^{\alpha_i}, G_i = g^{r_i},\ Z_i = g^{z_i}\}_{i\in[m]},\ \ \{H_j = g^{c_j}\}_{j\in[m]},\ \ \{U_x = g^{a_x}\}_{x\in\mathcal{U}} \Big).$$

The master secret key is set to

$$\mathsf{MSK} = (\ \alpha_1,\ldots,\alpha_m,\ \ r_1,\ldots,r_m,\ \ c_1,\ldots,c_m,\ \ g_3\ ).$$

A counter $ctr = 0$ is implicitly included in MSK.

$\mathsf{KeyGen_A}(\mathsf{PP},\mathsf{MSK},S) \to \mathsf{SK}_{(i,j),S}$. The algorithm first sets $ctr = ctr + 1$ and computes the corresponding index in the form of (i,j) where $1 \le i,j \le m$ and $(i-1)*m+j = ctr$. Then it randomly chooses $\sigma_{i,j}, \delta_{i,j} \in \mathbb{Z}_N$ and $R, R', R'', R''', R_x (x \in S) \in \mathbb{G}_{p_3}$, and outputs a private key $\mathsf{SK}_{(i,j),S} =$

$$\Big(\ K_{i,j} = g^{\alpha_i} g^{r_i c_j} f^{\sigma_{i,j}} h^{\delta_{i,j}} R,\ \ K'_{i,j} = g^{\sigma_{i,j}} R',\ K''_{i,j} = g^{\delta_{i,j}} R'',\ K'''_{i,j} = Z_i^{\sigma_{i,j}} R''',\ \ \{K_{i,j,x} = U_x^{\sigma_{i,j}} R_x\}_{x\in S}\ \Big).$$

The value of (i,j) is implicitly contained in $\mathsf{SK}_{(i,j),S}$.

$\mathsf{Encrypt_A}(\mathsf{PP}, M, \mathbb{A} = (A,\rho), (\bar{i},\bar{j})) \to CT$. A is an $l \times n$ LSSS matrix and ρ maps each row A_k of A to an attribute $\rho(k) \in \mathcal{U}$. The algorithm randomly chooses

$$\kappa,\ \tau,\ s_1,\ldots,s_m,\ t_1,\ldots,t_m \in \mathbb{Z}_N,\quad \vec{v}_c,\ \vec{w}_1,\ldots,\vec{w}_m \in \mathbb{Z}_N^3,\quad \xi_1,\ldots,\xi_l \in \mathbb{Z}_N,\quad \vec{u} = (\pi, u_2,\ldots,u_n) \in \mathbb{Z}_N^n.$$

In addition, it randomly chooses $r_x, r_y, r_z \in \mathbb{Z}_N$, and sets $\vec{\chi}_1 = (r_x, 0, r_z)$, $\vec{\chi}_2 = (0, r_y, r_z)$, $\vec{\chi}_3 = \vec{\chi}_1 \times \vec{\chi}_2 = (-r_y r_z, -r_x r_z, r_x r_y)$. Then it randomly chooses

$$\vec{v}_i \in \mathbb{Z}_N^3\ \forall i \in \{1,\ldots,\bar{i}\},\qquad \vec{v}_i \in span\{\vec{\chi}_1,\vec{\chi}_2\}\ \forall i \in \{\bar{i}+1,\ldots,m\},$$

and creates the ciphertext $\langle (A,\rho),\ (\vec{R}_i, \vec{R}'_i, Q_i, Q'_i, Q''_i, Q'''_i, T_i)_{i=1}^m, (\vec{C}_j, \vec{C}'_j)_{j=1}^m,\ (P_k, P'_k)_{k=1}^l \rangle$ as follows:

1. For each row $i \in [m]$:
   - if $i < \bar{i}$: randomly chooses $\hat{s}_i \in \mathbb{Z}_N$, and sets
   $$\vec{R}_i = g^{\vec{v}_i},\ \vec{R}'_i = g^{\kappa \vec{v}_i},\ \ Q_i = g^{s_i},\ Q'_i = f^{s_i} Z_i^{t_i} f^{\pi},\ Q''_i = h^{s_i},\ Q'''_i = g^{t_i},\ \ T_i = E_i^{\hat{s}_i}.$$
   - if $i \ge \bar{i}$: sets
   $$\vec{R}_i = G_i^{s_i \vec{v}_i},\ \ \vec{R}'_i = G_i^{\kappa s_i \vec{v}_i},\ \ Q_i = g^{\tau s_i (\vec{v}_i\cdot\vec{v}_c)},\ \ Q'_i = f^{\tau s_i(\vec{v}_i\cdot\vec{v}_c)} Z_i^{t_i} f^{\pi},\ \ Q''_i = h^{\tau s_i(\vec{v}_i\cdot\vec{v}_c)},\ \ Q'''_i = g^{t_i},\ \ T_i = M \cdot E_i^{\tau s_i(\vec{v}_i\cdot\vec{v}_c)}.$$
2. For each column $j \in [m]$:
   - if $j < \bar{j}$: randomly chooses $\mu_j \in \mathbb{Z}_N$, and sets $\vec{C}_j = H_j^{\tau(\vec{v}_c + \mu_j \vec{\chi}_3)} \cdot g^{\kappa \vec{w}_j}$, $\vec{C}'_j = g^{\vec{w}_j}$.
   - if $j \ge \bar{j}$: sets $\vec{C}_j = H_j^{\tau \vec{v}_c} \cdot g^{\kappa \vec{w}_j}$, $\vec{C}'_j = g^{\vec{w}_j}$.
3. For each $k \in [l]$: sets $P_k = f^{A_k\cdot\vec{u}} U_{\rho(k)}^{-\xi_k}$, $P'_k = g^{\xi_k}$.

$\mathsf{Decrypt_A}(\mathsf{PP}, CT, \mathsf{SK}_{(i,j),S}) \to M$ or $\perp$. The algorithm parses CT to $CT = \langle (A,\rho), (\vec{R}_i, \vec{R}'_i, Q_i, Q'_i, Q''_i, Q'''_i, T_i)_{i=1}^m, (\vec{C}_j, \vec{C}'_j)_{j=1}^m, (P_k, P'_k)_{k=1}^l \rangle$. If S does not satisfy (A,ρ), the algorithm outputs $\perp$, otherwise it

1. Computes constants $\{\omega_k \in \mathbb{Z}_N\}$ such that $\sum_{\rho(k)\in S} \omega_k A_k = (1,0,\ldots,0)$, then computes
$$D_P = \prod_{\rho(k)\in S} \big(e(K'_{i,j}, P_k) e(K_{i,j,\rho(k)}, P'_k)\big)^{\omega_k} = \prod_{\rho(k)\in S} \big(e(g^{\sigma_{i,j}}, f^{A_k\cdot\vec{u}})\big)^{\omega_k} = e(g^{\sigma_{i,j}}, f)^{\pi}.$$
2. Computes $D_I = \frac{e(K_{i,j}, Q_i)\cdot e(K'''_{i,j}, Q'''_i)}{e(K'_{i,j}, Q'_i)\cdot e(K''_{i,j}, Q''_i)} \cdot \frac{e_3(\vec{R}'_i, \vec{C}'_j)}{e_3(\vec{R}_i, \vec{C}_j)}$.
3. Computes $M' = T_i/(D_P \cdot D_I)$ as the output message. Assume the encrypted message is M and the encryption index is $(\bar{i},\bar{j})$, it can be verified that only when $(i > \bar{i})$ or $(i = \bar{i} \wedge j \ge \bar{j})$, $M' = M$ will hold. This follows from the facts that for $i > \bar{i}$, we have $(\vec{v}_i \cdot \vec{\chi}_3) = 0$ (since $\vec{v}_i \in span\{\vec{\chi}_1, \vec{\chi}_2\}$), and for $i = \bar{i}$, we have that $(\vec{v}_i \cdot \vec{\chi}_3) \ne 0$ happens with overwhelming probability (since $\vec{v}_i$ is randomly chosen from $\mathbb{Z}_N^3$).

Remark: In $\mathsf{Encrypt_A}$, π is the secret shared according to the LSSS (A,ρ), and is for generating ciphertext components $(P_k, P'_k)_{k=1}^l$, so that only users with eligible attribute sets can recover $D_P = e(g,f)^{\pi\sigma_{i,j}}$. To intertwine the CP-ABE part and Tracing part, f^{π} is embedded in Q'_i, i.e., in Tracing ciphertext components, although $(\vec{R}_i, \vec{R}'_i, Q_i, T_i, \vec{C}_j, \vec{C}'_j)$ are the same as that of [9], Q'_i is different and Q''_i and Q'''_i are new components we introduced. We stress that $Z_i^{t_i}$ (in Q'_i) is the crucial component that intertwines the Tracing part (i.e. $f^{\tau s_i(\vec{v}_i\cdot\vec{v}_c)}$ for $i \ge \bar{i}$ and f^{s_i} for $i < \bar{i}$) and the CP-ABE part (i.e. f^{π}) *securely and efficiently.* In a straightforward combination without $Z_i^{t_i}$ (i.e. $Q'_i = f^{\tau s_i(\vec{v}_i\cdot\vec{v}_c)} f^{\pi}$ for $i \ge \bar{i}$ and $Q'_i = f^{s_i} f^{\pi}$ for $i < \bar{i}$), the index-hiding property will be hard to prove, and to obtain provable index-hiding, different π_i has to be used for different i (i.e. $Q'_i = f^{\tau s_i(\vec{v}_i\cdot\vec{v}_c)} f^{\pi_i}$ for $i \ge \bar{i}$ and $Q'_i = f^{s_i} f^{\pi_i}$ for $i < \bar{i}$), but this will make the CP-ABE part have ciphertext size of $O(\sqrt{\mathcal{K}}\cdot l)$, rather than $O(l)$ as above. The using of $Z_i^{t_i}$ (and the introduction of Q'_i, Q''_i and Q'''_i) enables us to prove the index-hiding property while achieving (efficient) ciphertext size of $O(\sqrt{\mathcal{K}} + l)$. In particular, when reducing the index-hiding property to the 3-Party Diffie-Hellman assumption, $f^{\tau s_i(\vec{v}_i\cdot\vec{v}_c)}$ and f^{π} will contain terms of g^{bc} and g^{ac} respectively, where the simulator cannot compute, and only with the help of $Z_i^{t_i}$ the simulator can cancel them and form the challenge ciphertext, i.e., let Z_i contain the term g^c and t_i contain the terms b and a, so that the terms g^{bc} and g^{ac} in $f^{\tau s_i(\vec{v}_i\cdot\vec{v}_c)}$ and f^{π} can be canceled out by those in $Z_i^{t_i}$, while $Q'''_i = g^{t_i}$ can be formed using terms $A = g^a$ and $B = g^b$. Details are given in Appendix A.1, i.e. the proof of Lemma 1.

4.4 AugCP-ABE Security

The following Theorem 2 and 3 prove that our AugCP-ABE scheme is message-hiding, and Theorem 4 prove that our AugCP-ABE scheme is index-hiding.

THEOREM 2. *Under the Assumption 1, the General Subgroup Decision Assumption, the 3-Party Diffie-Hellman Assumption in a Subgroup, and the Source Group q-Parallel BDHE Assumption in a Subgroup, no polynomial time adversary can win* $\mathsf{Game}^{\mathsf{A}}_{\mathsf{MH}_1}$ *with non-negligible advantage.*

PROOF. Note that the structures of CP-ABE part of our AugCP-ABE scheme are similar to that of the CP-ABE scheme in [16], the proof of Theorem 2 is also similar to that of [16]. For simplicity, here we prove the theorem by reducing the message-hiding property of our AugCP-ABE scheme in $\mathsf{Game}^{\mathsf{A}}_{\mathsf{MH}_1}$ to the security of CP-ABE scheme in [16]. Complete proof will be given in the full paper. □

THEOREM 3. *No polynomial time adversary can win the game* $\mathsf{Game}^{\mathsf{A}}_{\mathsf{MH}_{\mathcal{K}+1}}$ *with non-negligible advantage.*

PROOF. The argument for message-hiding in $\mathsf{Game}^{\mathsf{A}}_{\mathsf{MH}_{\mathcal{K}+1}}$ is very straightforward since an encryption to index $\mathcal{K}+1 = (m+1,1)$ contains no information about the message. The simulator simply runs actual $\mathsf{Setup}_{\mathsf{A}}$ and $\mathsf{KeyGen}_{\mathsf{A}}$ algorithms and encrypts the message M_b by the challenge access policy $\mathbb{A}^*$ and index $(m+1,1)$. Since for all $i=1$ to m, the values of $T_i = E_i^{\hat{s}_i}$ contains no information about the message, the bit b is perfectly hidden and $\mathsf{MH}^{\mathsf{A}}_{\mathcal{K}+1}\mathsf{Adv}_{\mathcal{A}} = 0$. □

THEOREM 4. *Suppose that the 3-Party Diffie-Hellman Assumption in a Subgroup (defined in [16]), the 3-Party Diffie-Hellman Assumption (defined in [9]) and the Decisional Linear Assumption hold. Then no polynomial time adversary can win* $\mathsf{Game}^{\mathsf{A}}_{\mathsf{IH}}$ *with non-negligible advantage.*

PROOF. Theorem 4 follows from the following Lemma 1 and Lemma 2 immediately. □

LEMMA 1. *Suppose that the 3-Party Diffie-Hellman Assumption in a Subgroup holds. Then no polynomial time adversary can distinguish between an encryption to* $(\bar{i},\bar{j})$ *and* $(\bar{i},\bar{j}+1)$ *in* $\mathsf{Game}^{\mathsf{A}}_{\mathsf{IH}}$ *with non-negligible advantage.*

PROOF. In $\mathsf{Game}^{\mathsf{A}}_{\mathsf{IH}}$, the adversary $\mathcal{A}$ will eventually behave in one of two different ways:

- **Case I:** In Key Query phase, $\mathcal{A}$ will not submit $((\bar{i},\bar{j}), S_{(\bar{i},\bar{j})})$ for some attribute set $S_{(\bar{i},\bar{j})}$ to query the corresponding private key. In Challenge phase, $\mathcal{A}$ submits a message M and a non-empty attribute set S^*. There is not any restriction on S^*.
- **Case II:** In Key Query phase, $\mathcal{A}$ will submit $((\bar{i},\bar{j}), S_{(\bar{i},\bar{j})})$ for some attribute set $S_{(\bar{i},\bar{j})}$ to query the corresponding private key. In Challenge phase, $\mathcal{A}$ submits a message M and a non-empty attribute set S^* with the restriction that $S_{(\bar{i},\bar{j})}$ does not satisfy the corresponding strictest access policy $\mathbb{A}_{S^*}$ (i.e. $S^* \setminus S_{(\bar{i},\bar{j})} \neq \emptyset$).

The **Case I** is easy to handle using the similar proof ideas in [9] as the adversary will not query a private key with the challenge index $(\bar{i},\bar{j})$. The **Case II** captures the index-hiding requirement for CP-ABE in that even if a user has a key with index $(\bar{i},\bar{j})$ he cannot distinguish between an encryption to $(\mathbb{A}_{S^*},(\bar{i},\bar{j}))$ and $(\mathbb{A}_{S^*},(\bar{i},\bar{j}+1))$ if the corresponding attribute set $S_{(\bar{i},\bar{j})}$ does not satisfies $\mathbb{A}_{S^*}$. This is the most challenging part of achieving the strong traceability in CP-ABE securely and efficiently, and our particular construction (of the crucial components $Z_i^{t_i}$ (in Q_i') and $Q_i''' = g^{t_i}$ in the ciphertext) is driven by and serves this aim. These ciphertext components are crucial for the proof to use the underlying assumption to simulate the real attack game when $\mathcal{A}$ behaves in **Case II**. The proof details of Lemma 1 can be found in Appendix A.1. □

LEMMA 2. *Suppose that the 3-Party Diffie-Hellman Assumption in a Subgroup (defined in [16]), the 3-Party Diffie-Hellman Assumption (defined in [9]) and the Decisional Linear Assumption hold. Then no polynomial time adversary can distinguish between an encryption to* $(\bar{i},m)$ *and* $(\bar{i}+1,1)$ *in* $\mathsf{Game}^{\mathsf{A}}_{\mathsf{IH}}$ *with non-negligible advantage.*

PROOF. Similar to the proof of Lemma 6.3 in [9], to prove this lemma we define the following hybrid experiments: H_1: Encrypt to $(\bar{i},\bar{j}=m)$; H_2: Encrypt to $(\bar{i},\bar{j}=m+1)$; and H_3: Encrypt to $(\bar{i}+1,1)$. Lemma 2 follows from the following Claim 1 and Claim 2. □

CLAIM 1. *Suppose that the 3-Party Diffie-Hellman Assumption in a Subgroup holds. Then no polynomial time adversary can distinguish between experiments* H_1 *and* H_2 *with non-negligible advantage.*

PROOF. The proof is identical to that of Lemma 1. □

CLAIM 2. *Suppose that the 3-Party Diffie-Hellman Assumption and the Decisional Linear Assumption hold. Then no polynomial time adversary can distinguish between experiments* H_2 *and* H_3 *with non-negligible advantage.*

PROOF. The indistinguishability of H_2 and H_3 can be proven using a proof similar to that of Lemma 6.3 in [9], which was used to prove the indistinguishability of similar hybrid experiments for their Augmented Broadcast Encryption (AugBE) scheme. For simplicity, we will prove Claim 2 by a reduction from our AugCP-ABE scheme to the AugBE scheme in [9]. Complete proof will be given in the full paper. □

5. POLICY-SPECIFIC DECRYPTION BLACKBOX

In previous sections, we considered the traceability against key-like decryption blackboxes, which allow a seller (on eBay) to advertise the alleged decryption privilege of a blackbox $\mathcal{D}$ by an attribute set $S_{\mathcal{D}}$. The seller can claim that $\mathcal{D}$ can decrypt a ciphertext (with at least a non-negligible probability) if the ciphertext access policy $\mathbb{A}$ is satisfied by $S_{\mathcal{D}}$. Note that $\mathbb{A}$ can be any arbitrary access policy as long as it can be satisfied by $S_{\mathcal{D}}$. This type of decryption blackboxes are very powerful and therefore, could also be one of the most crucial issues to solve in practice using a blackbox tracing algorithm. In this section, we focus our attention on another interesting scenario which requires us to deal with another type of decryption blackboxes, which we call it a *policy-specific decryption blackbox.*

Policy-Specific Decryption Blackbox on Sale. Attempting to invalidate the possible tracing algorithm (such as the one we proposed above), a malicious user may build and sell a decryption blackbox which decrypts ciphertexts with a specific access policy only. Such a decryption blackbox, which we call it a *policy-specific decryption blackbox,* has weaker decryption ability than that of the previous key-like decryption blackbox, as it decrypts ciphertexts with a specific access policy only rather than any arbitrary access policy as long as it is satisfied by a specific attribute set. In practice, a seller or a malicious user may set the price lower for such a policy-specific decryption blackbox, and advertises that it can decrypt any ciphertexts associated with access policy $\mathbb{A}_{\mathcal{D}}$. Below is another scenario, which we call it "found-in-the-wild", where policy-specific decryption blackboxes may be concerned.

A law enforcement agency gets a warrant to search a suspect's computer and finds a decryption blackbox. As the suspect might try to destroy evidence, the explicit description of the blackbox's (decryption) ability might be gone, while the law enforcement agency only has certain clue on the certain access policy associated to the ciphertexts that the blackbox can decrypt.

Though the corresponding attribute set is not available and only a specific access policy $\mathbb{A}_{\mathcal{D}}$ is known that the associated ciphertexts can be decrypted by a policy-specific decryption blackbox, interesting, we notice that the AugCP-ABE scheme in Sec. 4 also implies a fully secure BT-CP-ABE scheme with (selective) traceability against this policy-specific decryption blackbox. On its formal definition, it is similar to that of key-like decryption blackbox, with the following differences:

1. Trace algorithm: The tracing algorithm takes an access policy $\mathbb{A}_D$ as input, i.e. $\mathsf{Trace}^{\mathcal{D}}(\mathsf{PP}, \mathbb{A}_{\mathcal{D}}, \epsilon)$ and the rest is the same as before.
2. $\mathsf{Game}_{\mathsf{TR}}$: In the (Policy-specific) Decryption Blackbox Generation phase, the adversary $\mathcal{A}$ outputs a decryption blackbox $\mathcal{D}$ associated with an access policy $\mathbb{A}_{\mathcal{D}}$ and a non-negligible probability ϵ. $\mathcal{A}$ wins $\mathsf{Game}_{\mathsf{TR}}$ if
   (a) $\Pr[\mathcal{D}(\mathsf{Encrypt}(\mathsf{PP}, M, \mathbb{A}_{\mathcal{D}})) = M] \geq \epsilon$, where the probability is taken over the random choices of message M and the random coins of $\mathcal{D}$.
   (b) $\mathbb{K}_T = \emptyset$, or $\mathbb{K}_T \not\subseteq \mathbb{K}_{\mathcal{D}}$, or $(\forall k_t \in \mathbb{K}_T, S_{k_t}$ *does not satisfy* $\mathbb{A}_{\mathcal{D}}$).
3. $\mathsf{Game}_{\mathsf{IH}}$: We do not need the concept of strictest access policy here, i.e., in the $\mathsf{Challenge}$ phase, $\mathcal{A}$ submits a message M and an access policy $\mathbb{A}^*$, and the challenger sends $CT \leftarrow \mathsf{Encrypt}_{\mathsf{A}}(\mathsf{PP}, M, \mathbb{A}^*, \bar{k} + b)$ to $\mathcal{A}$. Here we have to define a weaker model of $\mathsf{Game}_{\mathsf{IH}}$, where $\mathcal{A}$ is required to declare $\mathbb{A}^*$ before seeing the public parameter, and the defined index-hiding property is referred to as *selective* index-hiding.
4. Similar to Theorem 1, we can show that an AugCP-ABE with message-hiding and (selective) index-hiding properties implies a secure and (selectively) traceable BT-CP-ABE against policy-specific decryption blackbox.

To prove the message-hiding and index-hiding properties of the AugCP-ABE scheme under the definition above for policy-specific decryption blackbox, we only need to modify a few proofing details of Lemma 1, and the proof idea is similar to the current one for key-like decryption blackbox. In the proof of Lemma 1 for key-like decryption blackbox, as the challenge ciphertext is generated using the strictest access policy of the challenge attribute set S^*, we can have a guess on a particular attribute $\bar{x}$ and consequently prove the index-hiding against adaptive adversaries. However, in the case of policy-specific decryption blackbox, the challenge ciphertext is generated using the challenge access policy $\mathbb{A}^*$, where it is hard to have a successful guess unless we consider only the selective adversaries. In summary, the resulting BT-CP-ABE scheme is fully secure and selectively traceable against policy-specific decryption blackbox.

6. RELATED WORK

Sahai and Waters [22] introduced Attribute-Based Encryption (ABE) for addressing the fuzzy identity matching problem in IBE. Goyal et al. [11] later formalized the notions of CP-ABE and Key-Policy ABE (KP-ABE). KP-ABE systems available in the literature include [21, 15, 20, 1], however, these systems do not address the traceability problem.

Katz and Schröder [14] introduced the notion of traceability in the context of predicate encryption [13], where they proposed a generic construction that adds traceability to any inner-product predicate encryption (IPE) scheme with the price of adding overhead linear in $\mathcal{K}$ (the number of users) to the original scheme. Note that although IPE (e.g., the most expressive schemes to date in [13]) implies IBE, BE and KP-ABE, it cannot efficiently implement the functions of expressive CP-ABE. The advances of our work is making are twofold in the sense that we add traceability (1) to an existing expressive CP-ABE scheme (2) at the expense of sub-linear (i.e. $\sqrt{\mathcal{K}}$) overhead, although our result is specific rather than generic as [14] is.

7. CONCLUSION

In this paper, we proposed a new CP-ABE scheme that simultaneously supports fully collusion-resistant (and public) blackbox traceability and high expressivity (i.e., supporting any monotonic access structures), as well as without the one-use restriction. The scheme is proved secure against adaptive adversaries in the standard model. For the traceability against key-like decryption blackbox, the scheme is proved traceable against adaptive adversaries in the standard model, and for the traceability against policy-specific decryption blackbox, the scheme can be proved traceable against selective adversaries in the standard model. Compared with the most efficient conventional (non-traceable) CP-ABE schemes currently available with high expressivity and full security in the standard model, the new CP-ABE adds fully collusion-resistant (and public) blackbox traceability with the price of adding only $O(\sqrt{\mathcal{K}})$ elements in the ciphertext and public key.

8. ACKNOWLEDGMENTS

The work was supported by the National Natural Science Foundation of China (No. 61033014 and No. 61161140320) and a grant from the RGC of the HKSAR, China (Project No. CityU 123511).

9. REFERENCES

[1] N. Attrapadung, B. Libert, and E. de Panafieu. Expressive key-policy attribute-based encryption with constant-size ciphertexts. In *Public Key Cryptography*, pages 90–108, 2011.

[2] J. Bethencourt, A. Sahai, and B. Waters. Ciphertext-policy attribute-based encryption. In *IEEE Symposium on Security and Privacy*, pages 321–334. IEEE Computer Society, 2007.

[3] D. Boneh and M. K. Franklin. Identity-based encryption from the weil pairing. In *CRYPTO*, pages 213–229, 2001.

[4] D. Boneh, C. Gentry, and B. Waters. Collusion resistant broadcast encryption with short ciphertexts and private keys. In *CRYPTO*, pages 258–275, 2005.

[5] D. Boneh, A. Sahai, and B. Waters. Fully collusion resistant traitor tracing with short ciphertexts and private keys. In *EUROCRYPT*, pages 573–592, 2006.

[6] D. Boneh and B. Waters. A fully collusion resistant broadcast, trace, and revoke system. In *ACM Conference on Computer and Communications Security*, pages 211–220, 2006.

[7] L. Cheung and C. C. Newport. Provably secure ciphertext policy abe. In *ACM Conference on Computer and Communications Security*, pages 456–465, 2007.

[8] A. Fiat and M. Naor. Broadcast encryption. In *CRYPTO*, pages 480–491, 1993.

[9] S. Garg, A. Kumarasubramanian, A. Sahai, and B. Waters. Building efficient fully collusion-resilient traitor tracing and revocation schemes. In *ACM Conference on Computer and Communications Security*, pages 121–130, 2010.

[10] V. Goyal, A. Jain, O. Pandey, and A. Sahai. Bounded ciphertext policy attribute based encryption. In *ICALP (2)*, pages 579–591, 2008.

[11] V. Goyal, O. Pandey, A. Sahai, and B. Waters. Attribute-based encryption for fine-grained access control of encrypted data. In *ACM Conference on Computer and Communications Security*, pages 89–98, 2006.

[12] J. Herranz, F. Laguillaumie, and C. Ràfols. Constant size ciphertexts in threshold attribute-based encryption. In *Public Key Cryptography*, pages 19–34, 2010.

[13] J. Katz, A. Sahai, and B. Waters. Predicate encryption supporting disjunctions, polynomial equations, and inner products. In *EUROCRYPT*, pages 146–162, 2008.

[14] J. Katz and D. Schröder. Tracing insider attacks in the context of predicate encryption schemes. In *ACITA*, 2011.

[15] A. B. Lewko, T. Okamoto, A. Sahai, K. Takashima, and B. Waters. Fully secure functional encryption: Attribute-based encryption and (hierarchical) inner product encryption. In *EUROCRYPT*, pages 62–91, 2010.

[16] A. B. Lewko and B. Waters. New proof methods for attribute-based encryption: Achieving full security through selective techniques. In *CRYPTO*, pages 180–198, 2012.

[17] J. Li, Q. Huang, X. Chen, S. S. M. Chow, D. S. Wong, and D. Xie. Multi-authority ciphertext-policy attribute-based encryption with accountability. In *ASIACCS*, pages 386–390, 2011.

[18] J. Li, K. Ren, and K. Kim. A2be: Accountable attribute-based encryption for abuse free access control. *IACR Cryptology ePrint Archive*, 2009:118, 2009.

[19] Z. Liu, Z. Cao, and D. S. Wong. White-box traceable ciphertext-policy attribute-based encryption supporting any monotone access structures. *IEEE Transactions on Information Forensics and Security*, 8(1):76–88, 2013.

[20] T. Okamoto and K. Takashima. Fully secure functional encryption with general relations from the decisional linear assumption. In *CRYPTO*, pages 191–208, 2010.

[21] R. Ostrovsky, A. Sahai, and B. Waters. Attribute-based encryption with non-monotonic access structures. In *ACM Conference on Computer and Communications Security*, pages 195–203, 2007.

[22] A. Sahai and B. Waters. Fuzzy identity-based encryption. In *EUROCRYPT*, pages 457–473, 2005.

[23] A. Shamir. Identity-based cryptosystems and signature schemes. In *CRYPTO*, pages 47–53, 1984.

[24] B. Waters. Ciphertext-policy attribute-based encryption: An expressive, efficient, and provably secure realization. In *Public Key Cryptography*, pages 53–70, 2011.

APPENDIX

A. PROOFS

A.1 Proof of Lemma 1

PROOF. Suppose there exists a polynomial time adversary $\mathcal{A}$ that breaks the index-hiding game with advantage ϵ. We build a PPT algorithm $\mathcal{B}$ to solve a 3-Party Diffie-Hellman problem instance in a subgroup as follows.

$\mathcal{B}$ receives the 3-Party Diffie-Hellman challenge in a subgroup from the challenger as $(N, \mathbb{G}, \mathbb{G}_T, e,\ g, g_2, g_3,\ A = g^a, B = g^b, C = g^c, T)$, where $\mathbb{G}$ is a bilinear group of order $N = p_1 p_2 p_3$, $\mathbb{G}_{p_i}$ is the subgroup of order p_i in $\mathbb{G}$ $(i = 1, 2, 3)$, g, g_2 and g_3 are generators of $\mathbb{G}_{p_1}$, $\mathbb{G}_{p_2}$ and $\mathbb{G}_{p_3}$ respectively, and a, b, c are randomly chosen from $\mathbb{Z}_N$. $\mathcal{B}$'s goal is to determine $T = g^{abc}$ or T is a random element from $\mathbb{G}_{p_1}$.

Setup. Firstly, $\mathcal{B}$ randomly chooses an attribute $\bar{x} \in \mathcal{U}$ to guess that $\bar{x}$ will be in the challenge attribute S^* (regardless of whether $\mathcal{A}$ behaves in **Case I** or **Case II**) and will not be in $S_{(\bar{i},\bar{j})}$ if $\mathcal{A}$ behaves in **Case II**. Then $\mathcal{B}$ randomly chooses

$$\{\alpha_i \in \mathbb{Z}_N\}_{i\in[m]},\ \{r_i,\ z'_i \in \mathbb{Z}_N\}_{i\in[m]\setminus\{\bar{i}\}},\ \{c_j \in \mathbb{Z}_N\}_{j\in[m]\setminus\{\bar{j}\}},$$
$$\{a_x \in \mathbb{Z}_N\}_{x\in\mathcal{U}\setminus\{\bar{x}\}},\ \ r'_{\bar{i}},\ z_{\bar{i}},\ c'_{\bar{j}},\ a'_{\bar{x}} \in \mathbb{Z}_N,$$

and $\eta, \theta \in \mathbb{Z}_N$. $\mathcal{B}$ gives $\mathcal{A}$ the public parameter PP:

$$\Big(\ g,\ f = C^{\eta},\ h = g^{\theta},\ \ \{E_i = e(g,g)^{\alpha_i}\}_{i\in[m]},$$
$$\{G_i = g^{r_i},\ Z_i = C^{z'_i}\}_{i\in[m]\setminus\{\bar{i}\}},\ G_{\bar{i}} = B^{r'_{\bar{i}}},\ Z_{\bar{i}} = g^{z_{\bar{i}}}$$
$$\{H_j = g^{c_j}\}_{j\in[m]\setminus\{\bar{j}\}},\ H_{\bar{j}} = C^{c'_{\bar{j}}},$$
$$\{U_x = g^{a_x}\}_{x\in\mathcal{U}\setminus\{\bar{x}\}},\ U_{\bar{x}} = C^{a'_{\bar{x}}}\ \Big).$$

Note that $\mathcal{B}$ implicitly chooses $r_{\bar{i}}, c_{\bar{j}}, a_{\bar{x}} \in \mathbb{Z}_N$ and $\{z_i \in \mathbb{Z}_N\}_{i\in[m]\setminus\{\bar{i}\}}$ such that

$$br'_{\bar{i}} \equiv r_{\bar{i}} \bmod p_1,\ \ cc'_{\bar{j}} \equiv c_{\bar{j}} \bmod p_1,\ \ ca'_{\bar{x}} \equiv a_{\bar{x}} \bmod p_1,$$
$$cz'_i \equiv z_i \bmod p_1\ \forall i \in [m] \setminus \{\bar{i}\}.$$

Key Query. To respond to $\mathcal{A}$'s query for $((i,j), S_{(i,j)})$,

- if $(i,j) \neq (\bar{i},\bar{j})$: $\mathcal{B}$ randomly chooses $\sigma_{i,j}, \delta_{i,j} \in \mathbb{Z}_N$ and $R, R', R'', R''', R_x (x \in S_{(i,j)}) \in \mathbb{G}_{p_3}$, then creates the private key $\mathsf{SK}_{(i,j),S_{(i,j)}} = \big(K_{i,j},\ K'_{i,j},\ K''_{i,j},$

$K'''_{i,j},\ \{K_{i,j,x}\}_{x\in S_{(i,j)}})$ as

$$K_{i,j}=\begin{cases}g^{\alpha_i}g^{r_ic_j}f^{\sigma_{i,j}}h^{\delta_{i,j}}R, & : i\neq\bar{i}, j\neq\bar{j}\\ g^{\alpha_i}B^{r'_ic_j}f^{\sigma_{i,j}}h^{\delta_{i,j}}R, & : i=\bar{i}, j\neq\bar{j}\\ g^{\alpha_i}C^{r_ic'_j}f^{\sigma_{i,j}}h^{\delta_{i,j}}R, & : i\neq\bar{i}, j=\bar{j}\end{cases}$$

$$K'_{i,j}=g^{\sigma_{i,j}}R',\ K''_{i,j}=g^{\delta_{i,j}}R'',\ K'''_{i,j}=Z_i^{\sigma_{i,j}}R''',$$

$$K_{i,j,x}=U_x^{\sigma_{i,j}}R_x\ \forall x\in S_{(i,j)}.$$

- if $(i,j)=(\bar{i},\bar{j})$: it means that $\mathcal{A}$ behaves in **Case II**. If $\bar{x}\in S_{(i,j)}$, then $\mathcal{B}$ aborts and outputs a random $b'\in\{0,1\}$ to the challenger. Otherwise, $\mathcal{B}$ randomly chooses $\sigma'_{\bar{i},\bar{j}}\in\mathbb{Z}_N$ and sets the value of $\sigma_{\bar{i},\bar{j}}$ by implicitly setting $\sigma'_{\bar{i},\bar{j}}-br'_{\bar{i}}c'_{\bar{j}}/\eta\equiv\sigma_{\bar{i},\bar{j}} \bmod p_1$. In addition $\mathcal{B}$ randomly chooses $\delta_{\bar{i},\bar{j}}\in\mathbb{Z}_N$ and $R,R',R'',R''',R_x(x\in S_{(i,j)})\in\mathbb{G}_{p_3}$. $\mathcal{B}$ creates the private key $\mathsf{SK}_{(\bar{i},\bar{j}),S_{(\bar{i},\bar{j})}}=(K_{\bar{i},\bar{j}},\ K'_{\bar{i},\bar{j}},\ K''_{\bar{i},\bar{j}},\ K'''_{\bar{i},\bar{j}},\ \{K_{\bar{i},\bar{j},x}\}_{x\in S_{(\bar{i},\bar{j})}})$ as

$$K_{\bar{i},\bar{j}}=g^{\alpha_{\bar{i}}}f^{\sigma'_{\bar{i},\bar{j}}}h^{\delta_{\bar{i},\bar{j}}}R,\ \ K'_{\bar{i},\bar{j}}=g^{\sigma'_{\bar{i},\bar{j}}}B^{-r'_{\bar{i}}c'_{\bar{j}}/\eta}R',$$

$$K''_{\bar{i},\bar{j}}=g^{\delta_{\bar{i},\bar{j}}}R'',\ \ K'''_{\bar{i},\bar{j}}=(g^{\sigma'_{\bar{i},\bar{j}}}B^{-r'_{\bar{i}}c'_{\bar{j}}/\eta})^{z_{\bar{i}}}R''',$$

$$K_{\bar{i},\bar{j},x}=(g^{\sigma'_{\bar{i},\bar{j}}}B^{-r'_{\bar{i}}c'_{\bar{j}}/\eta})^{a_x}R_x\ \forall x\in S_{(i,j)}.$$

Challenge. $\mathcal{A}$ submits a message M and an attribute set S^*. If $\bar{x}\notin S^*$ then $\mathcal{B}$ aborts and outputs a random $b'\in\{0,1\}$ to the challenger. Otherwise, $\mathcal{B}$ constructs the LSSS matrix (A^*,ρ) for $\mathbb{A}_{S^*}$. Let $l\times n$ be the size of (A^*,ρ). Note that $S^*\setminus\{\bar{x}\}$ does not satisfy $\mathbb{A}_{S^*}$, $\mathcal{B}$ first computes a vector $\vec{u}\in\mathbb{Z}_N^n$ that has first entry equal to 1 and is orthogonal to all of the rows A_k^* of A^* such that $\rho(k)\in S^*\setminus\{\bar{x}\}$ (such a vector must exist since $S^*\setminus\{\bar{x}\}$ fails to satisfy (A^*,ρ), and it is efficiently computable). $\mathcal{B}$ randomly chooses

$$\tau',\ s_1,\ldots,s_{\bar{i}-1},s'_{\bar{i}},s_{\bar{i}+1},\ldots,s_m\ \in\mathbb{Z}_N,$$
$$t'_1,\ldots,t'_{\bar{i}-1},t_{\bar{i}},t'_{\bar{i}+1},\ldots,t'_m\ \in\mathbb{Z}_N,$$
$$\vec{w}_1,\ldots,\vec{w}_{\bar{j}-1},\vec{w}'_{\bar{j}},\ldots,\vec{w}'_m\ \in\mathbb{Z}_N^3,$$
$$\{\xi'_k\in\mathbb{Z}_N\}_{\forall k\in[l]\ s.t.\ \rho(k)=\bar{x}},\ \ \{\xi_k\in\mathbb{Z}_N\}_{\forall k\in[l]\ s.t.\ \rho(k)\neq\bar{x}},$$
$$\pi'\in\mathbb{Z}_N,\ \ \vec{u}'\ \in\mathbb{Z}_N^n,$$

with the first entry of $\vec{u}'$ equal to zero. It also randomly chooses $r_x,r_y,r_z\in\mathbb{Z}_N$, and sets $\vec{\chi}_1=(r_x,0,r_z)$, $\vec{\chi}_2=(0,r_y,r_z)$, $\vec{\chi}_3=\vec{\chi}_1\times\vec{\chi}_2=(-r_yr_z,-r_xr_z,r_xr_y)$.

$\mathcal{B}$ randomly chooses $(\nu_{c,1},\nu_{c,2},\nu_{c,3})\in\mathbb{Z}_N^3$. Let $\vec{v}_c^p=\nu_{c,1}\vec{\chi}_1+\nu_{c,2}\vec{\chi}_2$ and $\vec{v}_c^q=\nu_{c,3}\vec{\chi}_3$, implicitly setting $\vec{v}_c=a^{-1}\vec{v}_c^p+\vec{v}_c^q$, $\mathcal{B}$ creates the ciphertext $\langle(A,\rho),\ (\vec{R}_i,\vec{R}'_i,Q_i,Q'_i,Q''_i,Q'''_i,T_i)_{i=1}^m,\ (\vec{C}_j,\vec{C}'_j)_{j=1}^m,\ (P_k,P'_k)_{k=1}^l\rangle$ as follows:

1. For each row $i\in[m]$:
   - if $i<\bar{i}$: it randomly chooses $\vec{v}_i\in\mathbb{Z}_N^3$ and $\hat{s}_i\in\mathbb{Z}_N$, then sets
   $$\vec{R}_i=g^{\vec{v}_i},\ \vec{R}'_i=B^{\vec{v}_i},\ Q_i=g^{s_i},\ Q'_i=f^{s_i}Z_i^{t'_i}f^{\pi'},$$
   $$Q''_i=h^{s_i},\ Q'''_i=g^{t'_i}A^{\eta\tau's'_{\bar{i}}(\vec{v}_{\bar{i}}\cdot\vec{v}_c^q)/z'_i},\ \ T_i=E_i^{\hat{s}_i}.$$
   - if $i=\bar{i}$: it randomly chooses $\vec{v}_{\bar{i}}\in\mathbb{Z}_N^3$, then sets
   $$\vec{R}_i=g^{r'_{\bar{i}}s'_{\bar{i}}\vec{v}_{\bar{i}}},\ \ \vec{R}'_i=B^{r'_{\bar{i}}s'_{\bar{i}}\vec{v}_{\bar{i}}},$$
   $$Q_i=g^{\tau's'_{\bar{i}}(\vec{v}_{\bar{i}}\cdot\vec{v}_c^p)}A^{\tau's'_{\bar{i}}(\vec{v}_{\bar{i}}\cdot\vec{v}_c^q)},$$
   $$Q'_i=C^{\eta\tau's'_{\bar{i}}(\vec{v}_{\bar{i}}\cdot\vec{v}_c^p)}Z_i^{t_{\bar{i}}}f^{\pi'},\ \ Q''_i=Q_i^{\theta},\ \ Q'''_i=g^{t_{\bar{i}}},$$
   $$T_i=M\cdot e(g^{\alpha_i},Q_i).$$
   - if $i>\bar{i}$: it randomly chooses $\vec{v}_i\in span\{\vec{\chi}_1,\vec{\chi}_2\}$, then sets
   $$\vec{R}_i=g^{r_is_i\vec{v}_i},\ \ \vec{R}'_i=B^{r_is_i\vec{v}_i},$$
   $$Q_i=B^{\tau's_i(\vec{v}_i\cdot\vec{v}_c^p)},\ Q'_i=Z_i^{t'_i}f^{\pi'},\ Q''_i=Q_i^{\theta},$$
   $$Q'''_i=g^{t'_i}B^{\frac{-\eta\tau's'_i(\vec{v}_i\cdot\vec{v}_c^p)}{z'_i}}A^{\frac{\eta\tau's'_{\bar{i}}(\vec{v}_{\bar{i}}\cdot\vec{v}_c^q)}{z'_i}},$$
   $$T_i=M\cdot e(g^{\alpha_i},Q_i).$$
2. For each $j\in[m]$:
   - if $j<\bar{j}$: it randomly chooses $\mu'_j\in\mathbb{Z}_N$ and implicitly sets the value of μ_j such that $(ab)^{-1}\mu'_j\nu_{c,3}-\nu_{c,3}\equiv\mu_j \bmod N$, then sets
   $$\vec{C}_j=B^{c_j\tau'\vec{v}_c^p}\cdot g^{c_j\tau'\mu'_j\vec{v}_c^q}\cdot B^{\vec{w}_j},\ \ \vec{C}'_j=g^{\vec{w}_j}.$$
   - if $j=\bar{j}$: $\vec{C}_j=T^{c'_{\bar{j}}\tau'\vec{v}_c^q}\cdot B^{\vec{w}'_j},\ \ \vec{C}'_j=g^{\vec{w}'_j}\cdot C^{-c'_{\bar{j}}\tau'\vec{v}_c^p}$.
   - if $j>\bar{j}$: $\vec{C}_j=B^{c_j\tau'\vec{v}_c^p}\cdot B^{\vec{w}'_j},\ \ \vec{C}'_j=g^{\vec{w}'_j}\cdot A^{-c_j\tau'\vec{v}_c^q}$.
3. For each $k\in[l]$:
   - if $\rho(k)\neq\bar{x}$: it sets $P_k=f^{A_k^*\cdot\vec{u}'}U_{\rho(k)}^{-\xi_k},\ \ P'_k=g^{\xi_k}$.
   - if $\rho(k)=\bar{x}$: it sets
   $$P_k=f^{\pi'A_k^*\cdot\vec{u}}f^{A_k^*\cdot\vec{u}'}C^{-a_{\bar{x}}\xi'_k},$$
   $$P'_k=g^{\xi'_k}A^{-\eta\tau's'_{\bar{i}}(\vec{v}_{\bar{i}}\cdot\vec{v}_c^q)(A_k^*\cdot\vec{u})/a_{\bar{x}}}.$$

Note that $\mathcal{B}$ implicitly chooses $\kappa,\tau,\ s_{\bar{i}},\ t_i(i\in[m]\setminus\{\bar{i}\})\in\mathbb{Z}_N$, $\vec{w}_j\in\mathbb{Z}_N^3(j\in\{\bar{j},\ldots,m\})$, $\pi\in\mathbb{Z}_N$, $\vec{u}\in\mathbb{Z}_N^n$, and $\{\xi_k\in\mathbb{Z}_N\}_{k\in[l]\ s.t.\ \rho(k)=\bar{x}}$ such that

$$b\equiv\kappa \bmod p_1,\ \ ab\tau'\equiv\tau \bmod p_1,\ \ s'_{\bar{i}}/b\equiv s_{\bar{i}} \bmod p_1,$$
$$\forall i\in\{1,\ldots,\bar{i}-1\}:\quad t'_i+\eta a\tau's'_{\bar{i}}(\vec{v}_{\bar{i}}\cdot\vec{v}_c^q)/z'_i\equiv t_i \bmod p_1,$$
$$\forall i\in\{\bar{i}+1,\ldots,m\}:$$
$$t'_i-\eta b\tau's'_i(\vec{v}_i\cdot\vec{v}_c^p)/z'_i+\eta a\tau's'_{\bar{i}}(\vec{v}_{\bar{i}}\cdot\vec{v}_c^q)/z'_i\equiv t_i \bmod p_1,$$
$$\vec{w}'_{\bar{j}}-cc'_{\bar{j}}\tau'\vec{v}_c^p\equiv\vec{w}_{\bar{j}} \bmod p_1,$$
$$\forall j\in\{\bar{j}+1,\ldots,m\}:\quad \vec{w}'_j-ac_j\tau'\vec{v}_c^q\equiv\vec{w}_j \bmod p_1,$$
$$\pi'-a\tau's'_{\bar{i}}(\vec{v}_{\bar{i}}\cdot\vec{v}_c)\equiv\pi \bmod p_1,\ \ \vec{u}=\pi\vec{u}+\vec{u}',$$
$$\forall k\in[l]\ s.t.\ \rho(k)=\bar{x}:$$
$$\xi'_k-\eta a\tau's'_{\bar{i}}(\vec{v}_{\bar{i}}\cdot\vec{v}_c^q)(A_k^*\cdot\vec{u})/a_{\bar{x}}\equiv\xi_k \bmod p_1.$$

If $T=g^{abc}$, then the ciphertext is a well-formed encryption to the index $(\bar{i},\bar{j})$. If T is randomly chosen, say $T=g^r$ for some random $r\in\mathbb{Z}_N$, the ciphertext is a well-formed encryption to the index $(\bar{i},\bar{j}+1)$ with implicitly setting $\mu_{\bar{j}}$ such that $(\frac{r}{abc}-1)\nu_{c,3}\equiv\mu_{\bar{j}} \bmod p_1$.

Guess. $\mathcal{A}$ outputs a guess $b'\in\{0,1\}$ to $\mathcal{B}$, then $\mathcal{B}$ outputs this b' to the challenger.

Note that when $\mathcal{B}$ does not abort, the distributions of the public parameter, private keys and challenge ciphertext are same as the real scheme. As $S^*\neq\emptyset$ and if $\mathcal{A}$ behaves in **Case II** then the attribute set $S_{(\bar{i},\bar{j})}$ must satisfy $S^*\setminus S_{(\bar{i},\bar{j})}\neq\emptyset$, the event that $\mathcal{B}$ does not abort will happen with probability at least $1/|\mathcal{U}|$. Thus, $\mathcal{B}$'s advantage in the 3-Party Diffie-Hellman game will be at least $\epsilon/|\mathcal{U}|$. As of the fully secure CP-ABE schemes in [15, 20, 16], the size of attribute universe (i.e. $|\mathcal{U}|$) in our scheme is also polynomial in the security parameter λ. Thus a degradation of $O(1/|\mathcal{U}|)$ in the security reduction is acceptable. □

Obfuscation Resilient Binary Code Reuse through Trace-oriented Programming

Junyuan Zeng[1], Yangchun Fu[1], Kenneth A. Miller[1], Zhiqiang Lin[1], Xiangyu Zhang[2], Dongyan Xu[2]
[1]Dept. of Computer Science, The University of Texas at Dallas, 800 W. Campbell Rd, Richardson, TX 75080
[2]Dept. of Computer Science and CERIAS, Purdue University, 305 N. University St, West Lafayette, IN 47907
[1]{jxz101120, yxf104020, kam103020, zxl111930}@utdallas.edu
[2]{xyzhang, dxu}@cs.purdue.edu

ABSTRACT

With the wide existence of binary code, it is desirable to reuse it in many security applications, such as malware analysis and software patching. While prior approaches have shown that binary code can be extracted and reused, they are often based on static analysis and face challenges when coping with obfuscated binaries. This paper introduces trace-oriented programming (TOP), a general framework for generating new software from existing binary code by elevating the low-level binary code to C code with templates and inlined assembly. Different from existing work, TOP gains benefits from dynamic analysis such as resilience against obfuscation and avoidance of points-to analysis. Thus, TOP can be used for malware analysis, especially for malware function analysis and identification. We have implemented a proof-of-concept of TOP and our evaluation results with a range of benign and malicious software indicate that TOP is able to reconstruct source code from binary execution traces in malware analysis and identification, and binary function transplanting.

Categories and Subject Descriptors

D.2.7 [**Software Engineering**]: Distribution, Maintenance, and Enhancement—*Restructuring, reverse engineering, and re-engineering*; D.2.m [**Software Engineering**]: Miscellaneous—*Reusable Software*; D.4.6 [**Operating Systems**]: Security and Protection—*Invasive software*

General Terms

Security

Keywords

Binary code reuse, trace-oriented programming, taint analysis, dynamic decompilation

1. INTRODUCTION

Binary code reuse involves extracting selected pieces of code from an application binary, recompiling and linking them with other components, and producing a new software program. Binary code reuse is desirable in many security applications such as malware code inspection and classification, legacy binary program retrofitting, security function transplanting, and source code recovery.

While decompilation [16, 17] has long been adopted for source code recovery and hence binary code reuse, it is based on static analysis and has limitations. For example, a state-of-the-art decompilation tool, Hex-Rays [2] is able to generate C code that is semantically equivalent to the original binary code in terms of execution effects. It was used to recover the Stuxnet source code in 2011 [19]. However, the source code generated by Hex-Rays may be unsafe. More specifically, it does not fully recover non-trivial indirect jump targets or function pointers, due to its static analysis nature; nor does it deal with binaries with *obfuscation*, such as instruction aliasing [3] or encrypted binary code case (e.g., those obfuscated by packers). While there are recent advances for improving static decompilation, such as semantic-preserving structural analysis [51], some challenges still remain. Moreover, the recovered source code very often may not be directly compilable.

Recent efforts – notably BCR [9] and Inspector Gadget [38] – can extract part of a malware binary for reuse or inspection. However, they are also not safe as they rely on incomplete dynamic analysis without a reliable mechanism to remedy the partial information acquired from the dynamic execution. Virtuoso [24] is a technique that extracts execution traces and translates them to executable python programs that could run outside the platform. In addition to similar limitations, it requires special runtime support – a python interpreter – to execute and often incurs high performance overhead (up to hundreds of times of slowdown). VMST [29] addresses Virtuoso's limitations but it only supports kernel functions and requires a heavy-weight dual-VM architecture [30].

This paper presents a new binary code reuse framework called *trace-oriented programming* (TOP) which is built on dynamic binary analysis. The basic idea of TOP is that, given a binary (possibly obfuscated), through dynamic analysis of its execution, we collect instruction traces and translate the executed instructions into a high level program representation using C with templates and inlined assembly (for better performance). Such a program representation can be directly compiled and linked with other code to produce new software. Unlike static analysis-based decompilation, TOP is based on dynamic analysis. Therefore, it has better resilience against obfuscation [18] and it does not require any binary points-to [8, 39, 48] or alias analysis [22, 7].

A by-product of TOP is the ability to instrument the newly generated code with additional guards, thereby gaining the ability to mitigate the incompleteness caused by dynamic analysis. In particular, since TOP targets binary code reuse, where the recovered code needs to run independently or be linked with other programs, it

CCS'13, November 4–8, 2013, Berlin, Germany.
Copyright 2013 ACM 978-1-4503-2477-9/13/11 ...$15.00.
http://dx.doi.org/10.1145/2508859.2516664.

must ensure that the newly generated reusing code (i.e., the reusable software component) reproduces the same behavior with the traces and flag exceptions if the behavior is not consistent with the traces. In other words, there is no gray area in the newly generated code, with its behavior well-defined by the traces. By instrumenting the code while reconstructing its source code, TOP is able to achieve such behavior consistencies.

We have implemented a TOP prototype and evaluated it with a range of benign and obfuscated binary programs. Our evaluation results show that we can directly compile the reconstructed source code into new binaries, and run them correctly with the functionality we have traced. Using TOP, we demonstrate two compelling applications: (1) malicious code inspection and identification, and (2) security function transplanting.

In summary, this paper makes the following contributions:

- We present trace-oriented programming (TOP), a new framework to reconstruct program source code from execution traces. Unlike decompilation that statically transforms a piece of binary code, TOP dynamically translates it with more runtime information and directly generates reusable software components.
- We devise a number of enabling techniques for TOP such as program control structure recovery, address symbolization, safety instrumentation, and instruction-to-C translation. These techniques work together to recover the source code from dynamic execution of a binary, and ensure that the recovered code has well-defined behavior consistent with the execution traces.
- We propose a systematic technique to symbolize the function pointers that are initialized and in global memory regions. To the best of our knowledge, this has not been proposed in any existing static decompilation technique including Hex-Rays.
- We have built our prototype systems for Windows and Linux platforms, and tested them with over one hundred pieces of benign and obfuscated binary code. In addition, we apply TOP to two security applications: malware analysis (e.g., unpacking) and identification, and security function transplanting.

The rest of the paper is structured as follows. In §2, we motivate TOP, and give an overview of our key techniques. The detailed design of TOP is presented in §3, followed by the evaluation in §4. Then in §5, we demonstrate the application of TOP in four usage scenarios. We discuss limitations and future work in §6, and review and compare with related work in §7. Finally, §8 concludes this paper.

2. BACKGROUND AND OVERVIEW

2.1 Goals and Properties

Targeting binary code reuse, TOP differs from the traditional static analysis-based decompilation techniques in that it performs *dynamic decompilation of program traces*. The salient properties of TOP are as follows:

- **Resilient against Obfuscation.** For intellectual property protection or anti-malware analysis purpose, many binary programs are obfuscated. Obfuscation techniques [18] range from instruction aliasing, garbage code insertion, register reassignment, instruction substitution, to binary code encryption and packing [35], and even virtualization-based obfuscation [53]. However, no matter how complicated the obfuscation technique is, the obfuscated program has to be executable. From its execution traces, we can recover the program's source code, although it may not be exactly the same as the original code (e.g., those obfuscated with virtualization), and reuse it in new programs.
- **Free from Point-to and Alias Analysis.** It is challenging to perform point-to or alias analysis [8, 39, 48, 22, 7] statically. However, since TOP is based on dynamic execution, the point-to relations are exercised directly, hence there is no need to perform complicated point-to analysis to figure out pointers' targets.
- **Concrete Instead of Abstract Values.** Similar to concolic testing [33, 52] (a mix of symbolic and concrete execution), concrete values are sometimes preferred in some reuse scenarios. By using TOP, values of the variables accessed during the program's execution can be observed. When generating the new source code, some arguments can be replaced with concrete values to avoid certain complicated tasks, such as environment setup and pre-condition computation; and a function pointer can be replaced with a concrete function call if the pointer always points to a specific function in the trace.

2.2 Challenges

It is a well-established approach to translate machine code back to human readable disassembled code (which is called disassemble). However, from disassembled code to high-level code (i.e., decompilation [16, 17, 46]), there is no standard approach and no significant breakthrough in the past few years for native code (although decompilation is more successful for other low-level code such as Java-bytecode [43]).

TOP is built atop dynamic binary instrumentation (DBI) which can be used to generate execution traces. However, the traces from DBI-tools (e.g., PIN [41] and QEMU [4]) cannot be reused directly, and we must solve the following challenges:

- **Control Structure Identification.** Normally a trace is a sequence of instructions executed by the CPU, and there is no explicit control structure inside. For example, the loop is unrolled, and callers and callees become sequential in the trace. Therefore, we have to identify the program control structures such as loops and function calls for the C code being generated.
- **Type Classification of Literal Values.** The literal value (i.e., the immediate value) in an instruction can be associated with different types, such as a global or read-only data address, a function pointer or a constant. If the literal value refers to a memory access or a function pointer, it has to be converted to the address which is associated with the generated C code instead of the original binary code. Therefore, we have to develop techniques to precisely differentiate the types of the literal values and symbolize them.
- **Safe Reuse.** Based on dynamic analysis, TOP faces the code coverage challenge. However, our goal is to make the non-exhaustively executed code reusable and ensure that the recovered code is safe and consistent with the traces. For example, as shown in Fig. 2, if we do not have any safety check in the partially executed code, the original semantics of the program may get violated. Thus, we have to develop techniques to ensure the safety of the recovered source code.

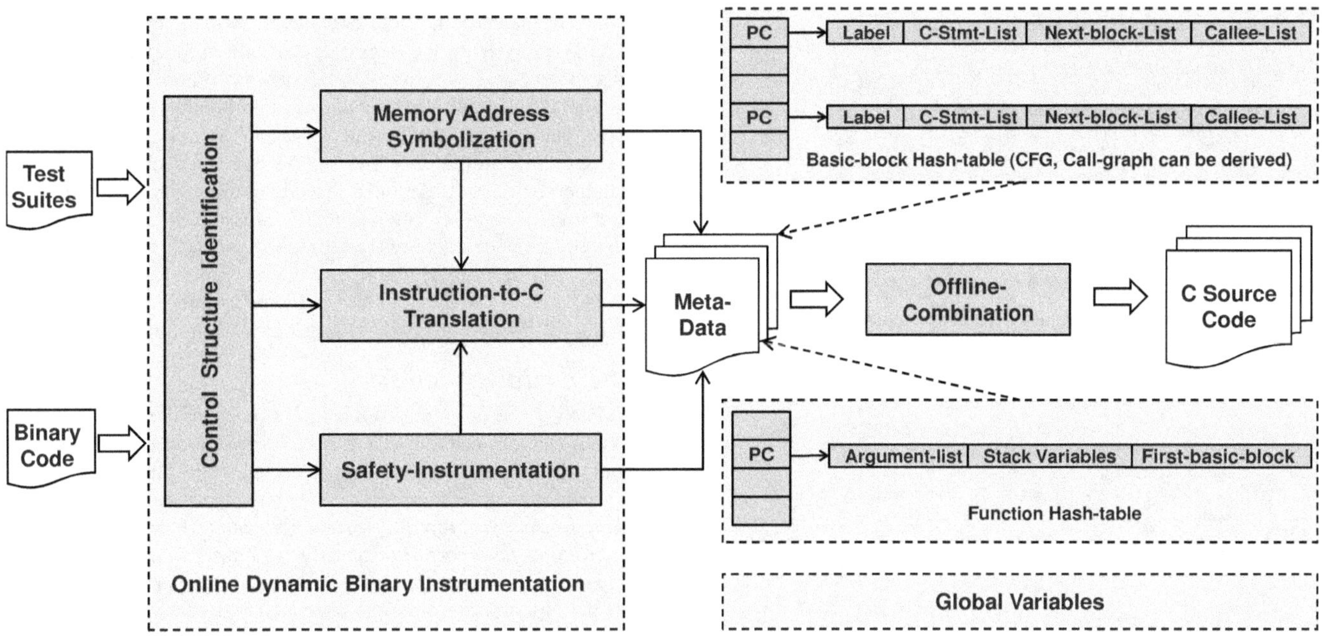

Figure 1: Overview of TOP Framework.

```
1 if (year_of_service > 10) {
2     if (salary < 100000.0)
3         salary = 100000.0;
4     else
5         salary = salary*1.02;
6 }
```

(a) Original Source Code

```
1 if (year_of_service > 10) {
2     if (salary < 100000.0)
3         salary = 100000.0;
6 }
```

(b) Naively Recovered Source Code from Trace

Figure 2: Partial code recovery issue faced by TOP. Assume the provided input is `year_of_service = 15` and `salary = 80,000`. An unsafe code recovered includes lines 1, 2, 3, and 6 of the original program.

2.3 Overview

An overview of TOP is presented in Fig. 1. The input to TOP is the application binary code and a test suite; and the output is the executed, modularized, and reusable components with C source code representation, which can then be directly compiled and linked to generate new programs.

There are five key components in TOP, four of which are designed using online DBI. More specifically, through dynamically monitoring executed instructions, we will identify the control structure of the code (§3.1) such as function calls, loops, and branches; discover the literal value types and relocate them with symbols (if necessary) such that they can be recompiled (§3.2); collect the control flow graph (CFG) for safety instrumentation (§3.3); and translate instructions using inline assembly for C code (§3.4). Finally, we will have all the meta-data necessary to reconstruct the C code. The offline-combination component (§3.5) will combine multiple runs if necessary and emit the final C code.

3. DETAILED DESIGN

3.1 Control Structure Identification

The typical control structures in binary code include sequence, selection or conditional branch (`jcc`, namely jump if condition is met; there are 77 such instructions in x86 [1]), and repetition (i.e., loop). However, loop is essentially a special case of conditional branch which has a backward edge in the control flow graph (CFG). In other words, at the binary level, we only see instructions being executed either sequentially, or with a control flow transfer (including explicit ones such as `jcc/jmp/ret/call` and implicit ones such as `push/ret`).

Our goal is to translate binary code (more precisely the dynamically disassembled code) into C code that can be recompiled. In fact, control structures are already encoded in the binary, especially in the program's CFG, where each node represents a basic block (BB) in which instructions are executed sequentially; and a directed edge represents the control flow transfer (such as `jcc/jmp`).

CFG is not only crucial to *control structure identification*, but also important for our *safety instrumentation* technique (§3.3) with the goal of tolerating incomplete execution (i.e., only one of the two branches of a conditional gets executed and dynamically decompiled). Therefore, the first step of TOP is to dynamically build a program's CFG based on executed instructions.

Dynamic CFG Construction. Since we target programs that may be obfuscated or metamorphic, we cannot rely on static analysis (e.g., static disassembler). Hence, our key idea for CFG construction is to leverage the exercised instruction addresses to safely connect the BBs (with their successors and predecessors) during the program's execution. In particular, we focus on handling metamorphism that may cause instructions being dynamically modified or replaced (e.g., those obfuscated by packers). The procedure for dynamic CFG construction is presented in Algorithm 1.

For a given executing instruction with address PC, if the instruction is `jcc/jmp/call` (line 4 -11), we will first get the PC of the next instruction (line 5) and retrieve its current layer. The reason to introduce a layer (an unsigned integer) for each PC is to track the version of the newly generated code, and use $\langle PC, layer\rangle$ as the unique index to access a basic block hash table (BBHT). Without layers, we cannot have a one-to-one mapping because the same address can be overwritten and one PC can be mapped to different

```
1: Input: PC, the current executing instruction address; Shadow: the shadow
   memory of the accessed program address space, which stores the current memory
   overwriting layers.
2: Output: Partial CFG stored in the basic block hash table (BBHT)
3: DynamicBinaryInstrumentation (PC, BB) {
4:     if (Inst(PC) ∈ {jcc, jmp, call})
5:         next_pc ← Next({jcc, jmp, call})
6:         layer ← GetShadowLayer(Shadow, next_pc)
7:         N ← GetBB(next_pc, layer);
8:         T ← Set of exercised successor of PC;
9:             if (N ∉ T)
10:                Insert N to BB's successor in BBHT;
11:                Insert BB as N's predecessor in BBHT;
12:    else if (Inst(PC) ∈ {ret})
13:        next_pc ← Stack(ESP),
14:        layer ← GetShadowLayer(Shadow, next_pc)
15:        N ← GetBB(next_pc, layer);
16:        T ← Set of exercised successor of PC;
17:            if (N ∉ T)
18:                Insert N to BB's successor in BBHT;
19:                Insert BB as N's predecessor in BBHT;
20:    else if (Inst(PC) ∈ {Memory Write})
21:        Increase the layer by one in the shadow memory.
22:    Append PC to BB if this PC has not been visited;
23: }
```

Algorithm 1: *Dynamic CFG Construction*

instructions at different times (e.g., in different unpacking phases if the program is packed by multiple packers). Next, we will retrieve the next BB (i.e., N) of $\langle next\_pc, layer\rangle$ (line 7); if N does not exist, `GetBB` will create one. After that, it retrieves all the successors of current PC, and updates the successor and predecessor of the current BB (line 10-11). Handling of `ret` is similar, except that we have to fetch its next PC from the stack (line 13). Also, for memory write instructions, since we need to track the layer of a memory address, we retrieve the current layer for the overwritten address and increase it by one. Then whenever an instruction is fetched from the memory, we can retrieve its layer from the shadow memory. At the end of the execution of the current instruction, we will append the PC to the current BB if it is visited for the first time (line 22). Note that our BBHT contains all the control flow transfer information of the executed instructions, all of our following components will leverage the information collected in BBHT as illustrated in Fig. 1.

3.2 Memory Address Symbolization

During program execution, many instruction and memory data addresses become concrete. For instance, the target of a control flow transfer instruction is a concrete instruction address, and the target of a memory access operation is also a concrete address. However, in the recovered code, we often cannot directly use these concrete addresses. Instead, we have to symbolize and relocate them. We call this procedure *Memory Address Symbolization.*

In general, we have to perform (1) instruction operand symbolization and (2) global data symbolization. We do not need to symbolize heap or stack memory addresses because they are dynamically allocated and intrinsically relocatable. For instruction operand symbolization, we need to rewrite a concrete address or literal value with a symbolized address (such as a label). For instance, as shown in the first example in Table 1, we need to rewrite the target address of direct `call` with the address of `func_dest_addr`; and the destination address of `je` with label `L_dest_addr`. For global data symbolization (the third and fourth examples in Table 1), we need to rewrite the instructions that use concrete addresses of the global variables. Also, we need to rewrite the initial value stored in a global variable if the value itself is an address of a global variable or a function pointer.

Unfortunately, memory address symbolization is challenging. This is because literal values are widely used in many instructions. Many of them are not addresses even though some of them look like so. Only from the later data use of a value, we can infer if it is a memory address, a pointer (with its content being a memory address), or a double pointer (from a two-layer pointer dereference). Also, there could be indirect `call/jmp` or even `ret` (as shown in the second example in Table 1). We have to back track to decide whether their target operand is directly or indirectly derived from any literal value representing a global address. To this end, we adopt a data dependence tracking (i.e., taint analysis [15, 47, 20]) algorithm to resolve the instructions whose operands need rewriting, and the global memory addresses that need to be updated with new symbols. In the following, we present the detailed design of our algorithm.

3.2.1 *Taint Sources*

The goal of our algorithm is to (1) pinpoint the instructions that have a memory operand that needs to be symbolized and (2) pinpoint every global data location that stores an initial function pointer or a global data pointer which need to be symbolized. Therefore, *our taint source contains the instruction address (PC) whenever an instruction involves a literal value operand, or a data value that appears to be a global pointer or a function pointer.* For either case, we are able to determine the operand or the data value is indeed a global/function pointer by observing that it gets dereferenced at a later point. We replace the origin of the operand, which is indexed by the taint source using its PC, with a symbol; or the origin of the memory data indexed by the taint source using its value with a symbol. We will use the examples in Table 1 to illustrate how our analysis works.

Consider the third example in Table 1 (line 8-11 in the third column). When line 8 gets executed, we will assign the shadow record for `eax` as S[`eax`]=8 (PC) because "`mov eax, 0x424a38`" has a literal value. Instruction address 8 will be used later to update the source operand 0x424a38 at location 8 if the taint sink point (discussed below) indicates that `eax` stores a memory address. When line 9 "`mov ecx, DWORD PTR [eax]`" is executed, it is a taint sink point as it dereferences the value stored in `eax`. We hence know that `eax` stores a global memory address. We then update the operand at address 8, and generate an address-symbolized instruction "`mov eax, OFFSET global_data+0x8`" as shown in line 8 in the last column in Table 1. Also, this instruction denotes a new taint source as the value stored in `eax`=0x424a38 is 0x424a34 that appears to be a pointer pointing to the global area. Hence, the memory address of the source operand is assigned to the shadow record of `eax`, S[`ecx`]=0x424a38.

3.2.2 *Taint Propagations*

Much like all other taint analysis, the taint record gets propagated along with data movement instructions, and data arithmetic (because of pointer value computation) instructions. For instance, along with data movement instruction at line 10 "`mov edi, ecx`", S[`ecx`]=0x424a38 will be propagated to `edi` (i.e., S[`edi`]=0x424a38).

3.2.3 *Taint Sinks*

A taint sink is an instruction point that can reveal the type of the operand: whether a literal value is a global memory address or relative address for `call/jmp` target; or whether the involved memory operand is a pointer. Therefore, nearly all instructions are possible taint sinks. When a taint sink instruction is executed, we will update the assembly code depending on whether it involves instruction operand symbolization or global data symbolization.

Case I: Instruction Operand Symbolization. There are many instructions that take literal values. For some instructions we can

Examples		Original Assembly Code	Address Symbolized Code

Instruction Operand Symbolization	Direct Symbolization	`1: je 0x401175`
		`2: call 0x401028`
		`3: mov DWORD PTR 0x424a30, 0x1`
			`1: je L_0x401175`
			`2: call func_0x401028`
			`3: mov DWORD PTR [global_data+0x0], 0x1`

	Indirect Symbolization	`4: push 0x401058`
		`5: ret`
		
		`6: mov eax, 0x409200`
		`7: call eax`
			`4: push OFFSET L_0x401058`
			`5: ret`
			
			`6: mov eax, OFFSET func_0x409200`
			`7: call eax`

Global Data Symbolization	Implicitly Initialized Global Data	`8: mov eax, 0x424a38`
		`9: mov ecx, DWORD PTR [eax]`
		`10: mov edi, ecx`
		`11: mov ebx, DWORD PTR [edi]`
		
		`12: call DWORD PTR 0x424a3c`
			`8: mov eax, OFFSET global_data+0x8`
			`9: *(int*)(global_data+0x8) = global_data+0x4`
			`10: mov ecx, DWORD PTR [eax]`
			`11: mov edi, ecx`
			`12: mov ebx, DWORD PTR[edi]`
			
			`13: *(int*)(global_data+0xc) = func_0x40102d`
			`14: call DWORD PTR [global_data+0xc]`

	Explicitly Initialized Global Data	`13: mov DWORD PTR 0x424a38, 0x424a30`
		`14: mov ecx, DWORD PTR 0x424a38`
		`15: mov DWORD PTR [ecx],0x4`
		
		`16: mov DWORD PTR 0x424a3c, 0x401032`
		`17: call DWORD PTR 0x424a3c`
			`15: mov DWORD PTR [global_data+0x8],OFFSET global_data+0x0`
			`16: mov ecx, DWORD PTR [global_data+0x8]`
			`17: mov DWORD PTR [ecx],0x4`
			
			`18: mov DWORD PTR [global_data+0xc],func_0x401032`
			`19: call DWORD PTR [global_data+0xc]`

Table 1: Examples of Memory Address Symbolization.

immediately infer that the operand is a memory address (we call it direct symbolization). For the others we must infer based on later data use (we call it indirect symbolization). Therefore, we have the following two strategies:

- **Direct Symbolization.** Direct symbolization applies to the direct control flow-related instructions (i.e., `call`/`jmp`/`jcc`). In particular, if the operand of such an instruction is a literal value, we will directly symbolize it. For instance, as shown in line 1-2 of the first example in Table 1, we will directly symbolize `0x401175` with a label `L_0x401175` for the `je` instruction; and `0x401028` with `fun_0x401028` for the `call` instruction. Direct symbolization is critical for unpacking. Usually the last step when finishing unpacking is through a control flow transfer instruction (`jmp`/`call`/`ret`). If we do not symbolize the target address of the last instruction, TOP would only capture the code for unpacking and the new code's semantics will not be consistent with our traces.
- **Indirect Symbolization.** At the data use point, after we determine the literal value to be a symbol address, we will look for the target instruction based on the PC in the taint record and rewrite the symbol. For instance, as shown in the second example in Table 1, at line 7 when "`call eax`" gets executed, we can infer that the value stored in `eax` is actually a function entry address. Since the taint record of `eax` is S[`eax`]=6, we will then rewrite the operand of the instruction at PC=6 and symbolize the literal value as `fun_0x409200`. For the return instruction, we will also check the taint record of the operand that is from the top of the stack. If it is tainted, we will update the target instruction as well. For instance, because line 4 "`push 0x401058`" and line 5 directly return, fetching value 0x401058 from the stack (this instruction is actually a case of control flow obfuscation), we will rewrite the operand of the `push` instruction as `L_0x401058`. Note that for a normal `call` instruction, unlike in this case, we will not taint its return address on the stack.

Case II: Global Data Symbolization. Compared with instruction operand symbolization, global data symbolization is more complicated and it requires not only translating the concrete global address into symbolic address, but also translating the *pointed* data stored in the global variable as symbolic. There are also two cases for global data symbolization depending on whether the global data accessed is implicitly initialized or explicitly initialized (or redefined).

- **Implicitly Initialized Global Data.** A global pointer (either data pointer or function pointer) could be initialized by a compiler, often with no more update during program execution. In this case, we need to symbolize the stored pointer value explicitly (with an assignment statement to be inserted at the beginning of the recovered code); otherwise the translated program will crash.

  Take the instruction at line 11: "`mov ebx, DWORD PTR [edi]`" as an example (the third row in Table 1). When this instruction is executed, we can infer that `edi` stores a pointer. At this moment, S[`edi`]=0x424a38, which indicates that we are dereferencing a memory address pointed to by the value stored in 0x424a38. In other words, we know that 0x424a38 actually stores a pointer and this pointer is implicitly initialized (because there is no other instruction to define this memory address). Therefore, we have to explicitly translate the content stored in 0x424a38. In this case, it happens to be 0x424a34. That is why we add an explicit assignment statement at line A in the last column (the address of this instruction depends on the final recovered code but it needs to inserted at the beginning of the recovered code).

  This example also indicates that *we need to track data-def and data-use of the memory cell* (details are elided since it is a standard algorithm). If there is no data-def for a particular memory cell, it will be a case of implicit data initialization. Similarly, for line 12 "`call DWORD PTR 0x424a3c`", we will add a function pointer initialization statement at line B in the last column, and that function pointer happens to point to a function at address 0x40102d. Similar to the statement in line A, this assignment statement should be placed at the beginning of the recovered code.

- **Explicitly Initialized Global Data.** If a global function pointer is explicitly redefined (e.g., memory `0x424a38` in line 13), its handling will be simpler. We only need to symbolize the address of the global variable, without adding any explicit assignment statement (e.g., lines A and B in Table 1) for the global pointer variable. Instead, we will use the original program's code to dereference the memory. For instance, in the fourth example in Table 1, we only need to symbolize the operand at line 13 for memory addresses 0x424a38 and 0x424a30, and similarly at line 14 for memory address 0x424a38.

Again, we do not need to symbolize program heap and stack addresses. The main reason is that those addresses are dynamic hence the program code itself will initialize them and dereference them correspondingly. It is also important to note that *Memory Address Symbolization* is new in TOP; and none of the existing decompilation techniques, including Hex-Rays, has solved this problem, especially for global initialized pointer data.

3.3 Safety Instrumentation

TOP features the assurance of safety while leveraging the precise but incomplete dynamic analysis. To achieve this goal, we need to ensure that *the recovered code either behaves the same way as the original binary, or must throw predefined runtime safety exceptions.* We call this property *reuse safety*.

There are two root causes for safety violation: (1) A conditional jump (i.e., `jcc`) may not have both branches covered (as shown in Fig. 2) and (2) an indirect `jmp/call` may not have all its targets covered.

- **Handling Missing Conditional Branches.** If only one of the branches is executed in a `jcc` instruction, TOP will generate a piece of exception handling code that will print a warning message and exit the program if the control flow of the recovered code falls through the missing branch. This warning message will be used to debug and refine the extracted code. In particular, we can leverage the input that induces the warning as an additional input to increase code coverage.

- **Handling Indirect Jumps.** Similar to conditional branches, indirect jumps/calls can lead to safety issues due to incomplete path coverage. Two types of indirect jump/call – `jmp/call` register and `jmp/call` memory – are considered. TOP translates an indirect jump/call into a list of conditional jumps with the possible values of the symbolized indirect jump/call operands as conditions. To guarantee safety, an assertion is added to the beginning of the conditional jump list to check if the target is among the symbolized addresses. In other words, our code creates a white list of the symbolized target addresses; any unknown (new) target will be captured and thrown out.

With the safety instrumentations above, we ensure that, when the recovered code is executed again, it will follow the original program's semantics or throw exceptions. Any attempt to execute a control flow path not executed before will be warned.

3.4 Instruction-to-C Translation

After we collect the program's CFG (§3.1), relocate concrete memory addresses to symbols (§3.2), and instrument the extracted program to ensure safety (§3.3), the next step is to translate the low-level instructions into C code. Since our targeted usage scenario is binary code reuse, users may not be interested in the implementation details of the extracted components but only their functionality – for example, a user may not care how a cipher function is implemented. Therefore, in the generated C code, we largely use the inlined assembly and their operands will be updated with symbolized addresses if any.

Also, since our goal is to recover the extracted code in the form of source code, we could generate the source code for instructions at various levels, including user level, library level, and even kernel level (if we use virtual machine-based dynamic instrumentation). However, we are most interested in the user-level code (because library code already exists). As such, the recovery process needs to stop when encountering a well-defined API. We also need to dump the code from the beginning of the execution by default, or from the entry to the exit points specified by the user.

API Resolution. The goal of API resolution is to instruct our analysis to stop further tracing when entering the body of a library function and, at the same time, to use the well-defined interface and the API symbols to generate the function call (e.g., `malloc`, `printf`, `recv`). While there might be API-obfuscation in the binary code (e.g., to hide malware behavior from static analysis), our dynamic analysis can discover such obfuscation.

At a high level, our API resolution technique turns off address space randomization (which can be done by TOP users because they control the execution), and identifies the starting address for each library call. At runtime, we check whether the PC of an instruction matches any pre-defined API's PC. For Linux, we extract all the APIs in `glibc` and other dependent libraries if any, and resolve each API's symbol, arguments, and the starting PC.

For Windows binary, if DLLs are loaded at the virtual addresses specified as the image base address in a DLL's PE header[1], we will create a lookup hash table that contains all the virtual addresses of each exported API function from all known DLLs. If the calling target address can be found in the lookup table, we will retrieve the API calling context (i.e., name and arguments). If the DLLs are loaded to a nonstandard base address by system calls to explicitly map them to a different address space, we will look for specific calls to `NtOpenSection` which identifies the DLL name, and calls to `NtMapViewOfSection` which provides the DLL's base address. We then use the base address of this DLL to add those API addresses inside it.

Instruction Translation. Since TOP cares about code functionality more than code readability, we use a straightforward but effective inlined assembly rewriting approach to generate the corresponding C code. In particular, we traverse the BBHT (§3.1), starting from a user-specified address or a default address. For each executed instruction, if an absolute address is used, we will replace it with our symbolic address. If there is a missing branch that is not executed, we will instrument it with a safety check. If there is a global data access, we will associate it with an index (global variables are mapped to a big array) and initialize it with value in the memory. A control flow target will be rewritten as a specific symbolic label. If we encounter the end instruction, we will dump the C source code. Note that the C code is not just inlined assembly because we do recover information that is lacking in assemblies, such as variable types and function interfaces.

3.5 Offline Combination

To enable the *combination of multiple runs* of a binary, we also design a feature that serializes our in-memory meta-data to disk files, and then use the *offline-combination* component to combine the multiple runs for larger coverage. For offline combination, all

[1] Since the bases of standard Windows DLLs do not conflict with each other, the loader and linker can load all DLLs at their specified base virtual addresses.

Benchmark Programs			Online Phase of TOP			Offline Combination		Recovered	Consis-
Category	Binary Programs	Assembly Code (LOC)	*#Symbolized* Addresses	*#Safety* Checks	Time (sec)	Test Cases	KLEE/TOP Coverage(%)	Source Size (KLOC)	tent w/ Traces?
Hash	sha512sum	25331	133	39	0.25	35	59.53	15.4	✓
	sha384sum	25331	133	39	0.25	45	59.74	15.4	✓
	sha256sum	9129	122	36	0.09	36	60.70	5.5	✓
File	vdir	18676	788	196	0.71	65	26.93	4.8	✓
	dir	18676	507	116	0.19	70	25.67	4.8	✓
	ls	18676	501	116	0.19	68	25.81	4.8	✓
Privilege	chown	10099	216	88	0.05	58	39.53	4.1	✓
	chmod	9811	208	81	0.02	54	29.77	2.9	✓
	chgrp	9436	196	80	0.04	50	31.08	2.9	✓
Disk	du	14887	487	173	0.06	66	38.43	5.7	✓
	df	9100	290	74	0.11	58	32.92	2.9	✓
	sync	4221	45	9	0.21	18	39.26	1.6	✓
Process	sleep	4541	85	25	0.08	58	42.05	1.9	✓
	kill	4935	83	31	0.04	37	38.71	1.9	✓
	nice	4680	43	11	0.05	47	41.17	1.9	✓
Environ-ment	who	6097	363	147	0.20	27	36.34	2.2	✓
	env	4292	53	13	0.09	22	33.01	1.4	✓
	printenv	4290	50	9	0.09	12	24.08	1.0	✓
Utility	od	10172	245	61	0.09	119	53.42	5.5	✓
	pr	7611	480	130	1.01	79	40.03	3.0	✓
	wc	5959	210	45	0.24	45	44.47	2.7	✓

Table 2: Evaluation results with top-3 binary programs in 7 categories (in terms of recovered source code size).

the serialized meta-data are loaded into memory, and the CFG in the multiple meta-data is traversed. Whenever there is a path that is executed in one run but not in another, we will eliminate the safety instrumentation code and combine the two runs. After the combination, given the starting PC of a target function to reuse, TOP will traverse the BBHT, translate the instructions, and dump the source code reachable from the target function.

4. EVALUATION

We have implemented a proof-of-concept prototype of TOP. To handle obfuscated Windows binary code, we choose QEMU-1.0.1 [4] as the underlying dynamic binary instrumentation engine. We perform virtual machine introspection (VMI) [31] to inspect the target process and thread, intercept all executed instructions, collect context information, and resolve and store the information in the BBHT. To show the effectiveness and generality of TOP, we have implemented process/thread introspection and API resolution for both Windows and Linux. It is important to note that the five key components of TOP are *generic*, hence there is no need to customize for Windows and Linux.

More specifically, TOP needs to trace binary execution at thread level. To identify thread-level context, our introspection will use both process ID (by traversing the corresponding kernel data structure) and kernel stack pointer (with the lower 12 bits masked). This is because each thread will have a unique kernel stack (besides user level stack). Also, many programs create new processes. TOP tracks process creation by inspecting relevant system calls, and performs binary code translation and isolation for all child processes.

In this section, we present the results of evaluating TOP with a large number of legacy Linux binary programs (§4.1) and obfuscated Windows binaries (§4.2). The evaluation is performed on a machine with Intel Core i-7 CPU with 8GB physical Memory. The host Linux platform runs kernel-2.6.38; and the guest OS is Ubuntu-11.04 or Windows XP SP3.

4.1 Evaluation with Legacy Linux Binaries

Unlike the large pool of obfuscated binaries on Windows, much fewer obfuscated binaries exist on Linux. Hence our evaluation of TOP for normal, un-obfuscated binaries is mainly performed on Linux. We use the coreutils-6.11 package as our benchmark suite. Our goal is to use TOP to generate C code from execution traces, and further recompile them to generate customized binaries. We compare the functionality of the new binaries with the original ones for effectiveness evaluation.

Effectiveness. There are in total 100 programs in coreutils-6.11. Most of them are single process except three multi-threaded programs, `sort`, `mkdir` and `ginstall`. TOP can detect the thread-level control flow correctly. In our experiment, we compile them with "`gcc -O2`", strip out their symbols, and run each of them to generate the corresponding source code from the trace.

When running these programs, we do not provide explicit command line option (e.g., we just type `ls`), unless we have to provide one such as for `cat`. For those that require files as input, we provide files with a size of 1KB. Next, we run the the recompiled binaries with the same option for tracing, and compare the output to test whether we retain the correct semantics of the original binary with the given inputs.

As expected, all 100 benchmark programs run successfully, and consistently generate the same result as their original counterparts for the same input. If we enter any other command line options, the new programs will generate exceptions and exit gracefully. Note that in such a case, the user can choose to further generate a more complete version of the recovered program using the exception-inducing input. For space constraint, we classify these 100 programs into seven categories and rank the source code size (in terms of LOC) generated for each program, as shown in the first column of Table 2. For each category, we report the top 3 programs in the 2nd column of Table 2 for detailed presentation of our results. The 4th column reports the number of symbolized memory addresses, and the 5th reports the number of safety checks TOP added. These results reveal more details about the internal operations of TOP as well as the program-specific characteristics in these aspects. We observe that all programs require hundreds of symoblized addresses. For safety checks, the number varies across programs.

Performance Overhead. There are two kinds of performance overhead: (1) overhead of TOP tracing binary execution and generating

Obfuscated Samples	#bytes	Obfuscation Techniques	Anti-Disas.	Anti-Debug	Anti-VM	#Symbolized	#Safety	#LOC	Coverage	Consistent?
garbage_bytes.exe	1536	Adding garbage bytes	✓			3	1	38	71.4%	✓
program_control_flow.exe	1536	CFG Obfuscation (push/jmp)	✓			3	0	30	100%	✓
pushret.exe	1536	CFG Obfuscation (push/ret)	✓			3	0	40	100%	✓
call_trick.exe	1536	CFG Obfuscation (call/push/ret)	✓			8	0	71	100%	✓
middle_instruction.exe	1536	Instruction Aliasing	✓			10	1	78	100%	✓
Win32.Bamital.exe	22016	Encryption Packer	✓			303	37	1264	-	✓
Virus.Win32.Adson.exe	5632	Compression Packer	✓			60	6	739	-	✓
hardware_bp.exe	1536	Hardware Breakpoint		✓		12	4	78	70.8%	✓
heapflags.exe	1536	Heap Flags Detection		✓		9	1	59	81.8%	✓
instr_counting.exe	1536	Instruction Counting		✓		12	3	136	65.6%	✓
ntglobal.exe	1536	PEB NtGlobalFlag		✓		9	1	71	81.8%	✓
peb.exe	1536	IsDebuggerPresent		✓		9	1	59	81.8%	✓
rdtsc.exe	1536	RDTSC Instruction Timing		✓		8	1	75	90.0%	✓
softice.exe	1536	Softice Interrupt		✓		8	1	75	83.3%	✓
software_bp.exe	1536	Soft Breakpoint Detection		✓		10	1	77	91.7%	✓
ss_register.exe	1536	SS Register		✓		9	1	83	88.2%	✓
anti-vm_in_instruction.exe	1536	Anti-Vmware IN Instruction			✓	7	0	59	100%	✓

Table 3: Evaluation results with 17 obfuscated binary programs.

new source code and (2) overhead of new software generated compared with the original software.

For the 100 programs, TOP on average runs about 0.2 second to generate the new program from a single trace. To further study performance overhead, we present the TOP runtime (incurred by its four online components) in the 6th column in Table 2. For each program, it takes less than one second for TOP to finish, except utility `pr` that takes 1.01 seconds. For each new program generated, we recompile and run it using the same arguments as those used for tracing. Since the translated code is almost identical to the original assembly code, the new program incurs negligible performance overhead, thanks to the use of inlined assembly.

Coverage. Recall that TOP supports combining multiple traces into one program (§3.5). To evaluate this feature, we use KLEE [12] to generate test cases as inputs for program tracing by TOP. To simplify the experiment, we use the same KLEE command for coreutils programs[2]. The 7th and 8th columns of Table 2 show the number of test cases and the coverage for each program (use `klee-stats` command), respectively. The final source code size of these programs is reported in the 9th column of Table 2. Meanwhile, the average offline combination time (not shown in Table 2) is 0.18 second.

4.2 Evaluation with Obfuscated Windows Binaries

Obfuscated binaries, especially those of malware, abound on Windows. The goal of binary code obfuscation is to disrupt analysis of the code and deter reverse engineering efforts. In general, there are three types of widely used binary analysis platforms: disassembler, debugger, and virtual machine (VM). Consequently, obfuscation techniques can be categorized into anti-disassembler, anti-debugger, and anti-VM. For each category, there exist a variety of techniques. For example in the anti-dissembler category, there exist the techniques of garbage code insertion, control flow obfuscation, instruction aliasing, binary code compression, and encryption.

To evaluate the resilience of TOP against these obfuscation techniques, we select 15 representative obfuscated samples from [5] (shown in Table 3), which cover the state-of-the-art obfuscation techniques. The samples and their source code, plus two additional binary-only, packed samples, are from *offensivecomputing.net*. Note that a reason for selecting the 15 samples is that they allow us to verify the recovered code's correctness. For the two packed malware samples, we have no knowledge about their implementation, except that they are packed.

Effectiveness. Interestingly, many of these binary samples have only 1536 bytes as shown in the 2nd column of Table 3. The reason is that their source code is very small, each containing only a few lines of code for simple demonstration of an obfuscation technique. That also explains why the recovered source code is also small (shown in the 9th column). For all the obfuscated samples, TOP successfully recovers their source code from traces. We have run the recovered and recompiled programs and verified that they have consistent semantics with the original binaries (last column).

To better illustrate the strength of TOP, consider the two pieces of assembly code in Table 4, one from the sample `middle_instruction.exe` for instruction aliasing, and the other from `garbage_bytes.exe` for adding garbage code. For instruction aliasing, we see that the original code's execution at line 3 will jump to the middle of the instruction at line 1 as the condition for `jz` is always true (by `xor` in line 2). Then `eb 05` in line 1 would be disassembled as a direct `jmp` which goes to line 5. In other words, the garbage byte in line 4 will never be executed. However, IDA Pro cannot disassemble this obfuscated code because it would disassemble `db` as opcode `call` at line 5 in the second column. Due to incorrect alignment of instructions, the subsequent disassembling would be incorrect. In contrast, TOP dynamically generates the correct results as shown in the third column. Note that in line 6, TOP adds a safety guard (`jmp`) to handle partial coverage issue. For the second example, since a garbage byte `0x6a` in line 3 is introduced, IDA Pro fails to perform static disassembling. In both cases, we can compile the code generated by TOP.

Performance overhead. With the small size of the majority of these samples, TOP quickly recovers their source code within several milliseconds. For `Win32.Bamital.exe` and `Virus.Win32.Adson.exe` which are real-world malware, it takes TOP about 14 seconds to perform online tracing. The reason for the much

[2] http://ccadar.github.io/klee/CoreutilsExperiments.html

Original Assembly Code	Disassembly from IDA Pro	Disassembly from TOP

`66 b8 eb 05  mov  ax,0x05eb`
`31 c0  xor  eax, eax`
`74 fa  jz  $-4`
`e8  db 0xe8 ;garbage byte`
`58  pop  eax`
`(middle_instruction.exe)`
	`loc_401006:`
	`mov  ax, 5EBh`
	`xor  eax, eax`
	`jz  loc_401008`
	`call  near ptr 6A98686Bh`
		`mov  ax, 0x5eb`
		`xor  eax, eax`
		`jz  loc_0x401008`
		`jmp  loc_ERROR`
		`loc_0x401008:`
		`jmp  loc_0x40100f`
		`loc_0x40100f:`
		`pop  eax`

`31 c0  xor  eax, eax`
`74 01  jz  .destination`
`6a  db 0x6a ;garbage byte`
`.destination:`
`58  pop  eax`
`(garbage_bytes.exe)`
	`xor  eax, eax`
	`jz  loc_401007+1`
	`loc_401007:`
	`push  58h`
		`xor  eax, eax`
		`jz  loc_0x401008`
		`jmp  loc_ERROR`
		`loc_0x401008:`
		`pop  eax`

Table 4: Disassembling results from IDA Pro and TOP for obfuscated programs.

longer time is that both malware binaries involve many iterations for decryption and decompression.

Coverage. Unlike the Linux samples, we do not have KLEE to generate test cases for the obfuscated binaries to improve coverage. Instead, we perform a manual check on the coverage for the obfuscated samples with source code, as reported in the 10nd column. The TOP-generated code has high coverage, with 5 of them having 100% coverage. For the two malware samples, we do not estimate their coverage due to lack of ground truth.

5. APPLICATIONS

With the capability of translating binary execution traces into C code, TOP enables a variety of security applications. In this section, we demonstrate two such applications: malware unpacking and identification, and security function transplanting.

5.1 Malware Unpacking and Identification

Many malware programs today are heavily armored with anti-analysis mechanisms to make analysis of them difficult. Binary code packing is the most common anti-reverse engineering technique. According to a recent report, 34.79% of the malwares is packed [49]. An earlier research paper [35] reports that over 80% of malware is packed. Dynamic analysis has been shown a promising approach to unpacking malware [50, 42, 36, 35, 54].

Unpacking. Based on dynamic analysis, TOP naturally possesses the capability of unpacking malware. To this end, we design an unpacking plugin based on TOP. As we trace the entire execution of a binary (using layers), we are able to detect the unpacking code and the real program code. The real program code is the one that is finally settled in the memory and executed. It might happen that a packer could alternatingly execute the unpacking code and the real code (though we have not seen such a case in the wild). In that case, we might not be able to identify the real code based on full lifetime tracing. Still TOP will output all the traced code, which can be further analyzed to identify the unpacking code.

To test TOP's unpacking capability, we use 10 publicly available packers often used by malware authors and by researchers of many related efforts [50, 42, 36, 35, 54]). For the "testing goat" program, we use Windows `tasklist.exe`, a command console program with a binary of 77824 bytes, to generate packed samples. The samples are created using the default configuration for all the packers. To test multi-layer packing, we deliberately create two samples that are packed by two packers. Finally we have 12 samples: 10 are packed once and two are packed twice. We run all these samples without any command line option.

The evaluation results are reported in Table 5. The first column shows the size of packed `tasklist.exe`, and the second column shows the packer used for packing. We report the numbers of symbolized addresses, safety checks, traced functions, and lines of code, of the generated source code. The TOP unpacking plugin can successfully detect the unpacking routine and the real `tasklist.exe` code, even if the sample binary is packed by two packers. Interestingly, as shown in the last 4 columns of Table 5, the real `tasklist.exe` programs generated by tracing the 12 samples (under the same configuration) have identical results across the samples. Next, we recompile the generated source code of `tasklist.exe` and execute it with the same command line option of the original program. We confirm that the outputs are the same as that generated by the original `tasklist.exe`.

Identification. Having been able to unpack malware, TOP can be further applied to malware identification. As shown in Table 5, each packer has its own distinctive features; and the code that follows the unpacking code belongs to the real program code. As such, we can identify the prefix of the recovered code to identify packers, and eliminate the unpacking code to expose the real program code. In particular, we could perform source code diff-ing (text-based) to identify the unpacking prefix; or we could build and normalize the program control structures (e.g., CFGs) to identify the prefix.

To perform malware identification, we first generate a suite of (un)packer signatures. Given an unknown binary, we run it using TOP. By comparing the output with the signatures, we eliminate the unpacking code. Then, we can apply various techniques to identify/classify the real malware code (e.g., source code diff-ing and control structure comparison). In our experiment, for simplicity, we use source text diff-ing, which indicates that the recovered programs from the samples are actually the same piece of malware. This is also confirmed by the last four columns of Table 5.

5.2 Security Function Transplanting

Binary code reuse is meaningful for both goodware and malware. To extract the binary code of interest, a user only needs to designate the entry point and exit point, and TOP will automatically translate the executed instructions into C code. This code includes all the functions called and the symbolized global data accessed.

Goodware Function Reuse. We take an MD5 hash algorithm implementation as an example. Program `md5sum` (from coreutils) is a widely used cryptographic hash tool whose implementation contains an important function `digest_file` (instruction address: 0x8049f70 in our experiment) which computes the MD5 digest of a given file.

Binary Size (KB)	Packer	Unpacking Code				Recovered tasklist.exe Code			
		#Fun	#LOC	#Symbolized	#Safety	#Fun	#LOC	#Symbolized	#Safety
34.00	UPX	1	169	34	1	144	5748	1171	271
39.50	ASPack	14	913	140	16	144	5748	1171	271
363.50	ASProtect	19	504	86	3	144	5748	1171	271
46.46	RlPack	30	734	145	22	144	5748	1171	271
34.00	MPress	9	941	126	20	144	5748	1171	271
32.16	Mew	11	616	114	0	144	5748	1171	271
34.04	XComp	9	282	84	2	144	5748	1171	271
33.66	XPack	9	262	80	2	144	5748	1171	271
29.98	WinUnPakc	17	390	49	2	144	5748	1171	271
35.50	PEcompact	6	171	31	0	144	5748	1171	271
42.50	ASPack	14	864	130	16	144	5748	1771	271
	ASPack	14	913	140	16				
39.50	ASPack	14	797	113	16	144	5748	1771	271
	XPack	9	262	80	2				

Table 5: Evaluation results with 10 publicly available packers using `tasklist.exe` as a testing goat program.

To avoid the effort of re-implementation, a programmer can run `md5sum` binary on TOP with tracing/translation entry point being 0x8049f70 and exit point being 0x804a07e (the `ret` instruction of function `digest_file`). TOP automatically generates the source code of all the executed functions during tracing, including `fun_0x8049f70` and 11 other sub-routines, symbolizes 151 addresses, and adds 32 checks. Next, the generated function can be reused as a normal C function in developing new software. We have successfully developed a file comparison program that performs MD5 hash check for two input files by reusing function `fun_0x8049f70` and its subroutines.

Malware Function Reuse. For demonstration purpose, we target three functions – two for environment detection and one for stream cipher – in malware code and show how to reuse them. The environment detection functions are from the two samples `anti-vm_in_instruction.exe` and `hardware_bp.exe` we have tested earlier. Our purpose is to extract the functions for VM and debugger detection and reuse them in new programs. We have successfully extracted these two functions and linked them with other software components.

We have also extracted an `RC4` stream cipher function from `Worm:Win32/Sality.AU`. Since the malware is packed, we run TOP to get the trace of the whole program, from which we identify the `RC4` cipher function. Our manual analysis reveals that the entry address of the `RC4` function is 0x401212 and the exit address is 0x402723. We then run the malware on TOP again, symbolizing 86 memory addresses and adding 24 checks for this function and its 5 callees. Now we can write a new program to reuse the cipher function and confirm the correctness of its functionality.

6. DISCUSSIONS AND FUTURE WORK

The main limitation of TOP is the incomplete coverage that arises from its dynamic analysis approach. The recovered code only reflects the traced behavior and rejects the behavior that is not exercised. As demonstrated in our evaluation, path coverage can be improved by advanced program testing techniques (e.g., symbolic execution [12, 14]). Part of our future work is to better integrate these techniques into TOP.

The current focus of TOP is its source code reconstruction and reuse capability. Hence we have not attempted to make the recovered code more readable or optimized. Our future work will address the readability issue by introducing a richer set of structures (e.g., `do-while` and `for` structures for loops) and leveraging advanced decompilation techniques (e.g., Hex-Rays [2], Boomerage [27], and Phoenix [51], which tend to achieve better readability). We also plan to optimize the recovered code (e.g., by eliminating unnecessary safety guards). Consider the `middle_instruction.exe` example in Table 4. We could have removed the `jmp loc_ERROR` guard because `xor eax, eax` will clear the zero flag.

TOP is currently platform and environment dependent. More particularly, it requires the same kernel and library support to compile and execute the reconstructed code. It also relies on the presence of the same needed external resources as the original executions, such as configuration files.

TOP currently has an effective scheme to ensure control flow safety, which is the challenge we have encountered in the programs we consider. It is possible that more complicated and subtle safety conditions may arise when TOP is applied to more complex programs. Also, the offline trace merging process simply merges control flow paths, which may not be sufficient when more extremal situations are encountered (e.g., when executions are non-deterministic). We plan to further investigate these issues.

TOP may not be able to recover the source code of all binaries. For example, a malware program may involve virtualization-based obfuscation [53]. Even though TOP can generate its source code from traces, the virtualization code will be recovered as well. Moreover, TOP cannot handle hypervisor-level malware such as the red pill, due to the lack of hypervisor-level tracing capability. This limitation will be addressed by our future work.

It is well known that broken dependences caused by control flows pose an issue for taint analysis in general. However, that is *not* an issue for TOP because we use taint analysis in a very restricted context. Specifically, to handle indirect control transfers, we use it to back track from an indirect invocation to the original instruction that loads the indirect target and replace the target with a symbol to ensure that the corresponding function becomes relocatable. The propagation from the original load of the target and the invocation must be via data dependence. It is possible that the invocation is relevant to other instructions through control dependences, yet it is unnecessary to symbolize those relevant instructions. While it is possible that aggressive obfuscation may cause problems for TOP in the future, we have not encountered such a case in our experiments.

7. RELATED WORK

Decompilation. Decompilation is the process of reconstructing program source code from code in lower-level languages (e.g., assembly or machine code) [16, 6]. Tools like HexRay [2], Boomerage [27], and Phoenix [51] offer a variety of techniques to elevate low-level assembly instructions to higher-level source code. While these techniques are all based on static analysis, TOP is based on dynamic analysis, one of the first decompilation techniques to do so.

Binary Code Extraction and Reuse. Our work is closely related to BCR [9], Inspector Gadget [38], Virtuoso [24], and VMST [29]. While the discussion of these systems can be found in §1, we note again that TOP is a novel technique that translates all executed instructions into C code, with automatic addition of safety checking code. Moreover, the recovered code is readily reusable and incurs negligible performance overhead compared with the original binary (§4). Moreover, TOP does not focus on identification of functional components for reuse.

Most recently, in a parallel effort of TOP we proposed Bistro [23], which is a binary manipulation, rewriting and instrumentation infrastructure that allows *binary-to-binary* functional component extraction (from one binary) and implanting (in another binary). Different from TOP, Bistro operates directly and statically on binaries.

Dynamic Data Dependency Tracking. TOP leverages dynamic data dependence tracking (i.e., taint analysis) to symbolize memory addresses. Data dependence tracking has been widely applied to many security applications, such as data lifetime tracking [15], exploit detection [20], vulnerability discovery [44, 28, 13, 34, 32], protocol and data structure reverse engineering (e.g., [11, 21, 56, 10, 40, 55], and malware analysis [25]). TOP does not make any new advances in taint analysis per se but demonstrates its new application – memory address symbolization.

Malware Analysis and Unpacking. Unpacking aims at uncovering the original malicious code which had been packed by a variety of (binary) transformations. Unpacking techniques exist, such as PolyUnpack [50], OmniUnpack [42], Renovo [36], Justin [35], and Eureka [54]. There also exist a wide range of malware analysis techniques [45, 26, 37, 38]. TOP complements these efforts and enables useful malware analysis capabilities such as malware identification and function extraction.

8. CONCLUSION

We have presented trace-oriented programming (TOP), a new framework to enable the reuse of legacy binary code from execution traces. Through dynamic execution of a binary, TOP collects necessary information such as control structures, memory addresses and accesses, and safety information; and then translates each executed instruction into a predefined template or inlined assembly according to its semantics. While TOP shares the same goal with existing decompilation techniques, it enjoys unique benefits from dynamic analysis, such as being obfuscation resilient and free from point-to analysis. We have implemented a proof-of-concept TOP prototype. Our evaluation results with over 100 legacy binaries (including malware binaries) indicate the effectiveness, efficiency, and safety of TOP and demonstrate the application of TOP to malware analysis and security function reuse.

Acknowledgement

We thank the anonymous reviewers for their insightful comments. Kenneth A. Miller is supported by a DoD scholorship under contract H98230-12-1-0452. This research is funded by DARPA under contract 12011593. Any opinions, findings, and conclusions in this paper are those of the authors only and do not necessarily reflect the views of the funding agencies.

9. REFERENCES

[1] Intel-64 and IA-32 Architectures Software Developer's Manual Combined Volumes 3A, 3B, and 3C.

[2] Hex-rays decompiler SDK. http://www.hex-rays.com/.

[3] Making a disassembler: Instruction aliasing. http://trusted-disassembler.blogspot.com/2012/12/instruction-aliasing.html.

[4] QEMU: an open source processor emulator. http://www.qemu.org/.

[5] BRANCO, R. R. Scientific but not academical overview of malware anti-debugging, anti-disassembly and anti-vm technologies. In *Black Hat Technical Security Conf.* (Las Vegas, Nevada, July 2012).

[6] BREUER, P. T., AND BOWEN, J. P. Decompilation: The enumeration of types and grammars. *ACM Trans. Program. Lang. Syst. 16*, 5 (1994), 1613–1647.

[7] BRUMLEY, D., AND NEWSOME, J. Alias analysis for assembly. Tech. Rep. CMU-CS-06-180, Carnegie Mellon University School of Computer Science, 2006.

[8] BURKE, M. G., CARINI, P. R., CHOI, J.-D., AND HIND, M. Flow-insensitive interprocedural alias analysis in the presence of pointers. In *Proceedings of the 7th International Workshop on Languages and Compilers for Parallel Computing* (London, UK, 1995), Springer-Verlag, pp. 234–250.

[9] CABALLERO, J., JOHNSON, N. M., MCCAMANT, S., AND SONG, D. Binary code extraction and interface identification for security applications. In *Proceedings of the 17th Annual Network and Distributed System Security Symposium (NDSS'10)* (San Diego, CA, February 2010).

[10] CABALLERO, J., POOSANKAM, P., KREIBICH, C., AND SONG, D. Dispatcher: Enabling active botnet infiltration using automatic protocol reverse-engineering. In *Proceedings of the 16th ACM Conference on Computer and and Communications Security (CCS'09)* (Chicago, Illinois, USA, 2009), pp. 621–634.

[11] CABALLERO, J., AND SONG, D. Polyglot: Automatic extraction of protocol format using dynamic binary analysis. In *Proceedings of the 14th ACM Conference on Computer and and Communications Security (CCS'07)* (Alexandria, Virginia, USA, 2007), pp. 317–329.

[12] CADAR, C., DUNBAR, D., AND ENGLER, D. Klee: Unassisted and automatic generation of high-coverage tests for complex systems programs. In *USENIX Symposium on Operating Systems Design and Implementation (OSDI'08)* (San Diego, CA, 2008).

[13] CADAR, C., GANESH, V., PAWLOWSKI, P. M., DILL, D. L., AND ENGLER, D. R. Exe: Automatically generating inputs of death. In *Proceedings of the 13th ACM Conference on Computer and Communications Security (CCS'06)* (Alexandria, Virginia, USA, 2006), ACM, pp. 322–335.

[14] CHIPOUNOV, V., KUZNETSOV, V., AND CANDEA, G. S2e: a platform for in-vivo multi-path analysis of software systems. In *Proceedings of the sixteenth international conference on Architectural support for programming languages and operating systems* (Newport Beach, California, USA, 2011), ASPLOS '11, pp. 265–278.

[15] CHOW, J., PFAFF, B., CHRISTOPHER, K., AND ROSENBLUM, M. Understanding data lifetime via whole-system simulation. In *Proceedings of the 13th USENIX Security Symposium* (2004).

[16] CIFUENTES, C. Reverse Compilation Techniques. *PhD thesis, Queensland University of Technology* (1994).

[17] CIFUENTES, C., AND GOUGH, K. J. Decompilation of binary programs. *Softw. Pract. Exper. 25*, 7 (July 1995), 811–829.

[18] COLLBERG, C., THOMBORSON, C., AND LOW, D. A taxonomy of obfuscating transformations. *Technical Report 148, Department of Computer Science, University of Auckland* (1997).

[19] CONSTANTIN, L. Decompiled stuxnet code published online, 2011. http://news.softpedia.com/news/Anonymous-Publishes-Decompiled-Stuxnet-Code-184448.shtml.

[20] CRANDALL, J. R., WU, S. F., AND CHONG, F. T. Minos: Architectural support for protecting control data. *ACM Trans. Archit. Code Optim. 3*, 4 (2006), 359–389.

[21] CUI, W., PEINADO, M., CHEN, K., WANG, H. J., AND IRUN-BRIZ, L. Tupni: Automatic reverse engineering of input formats. In *Proceedings of the 15th ACM Conference on Computer and Communications Security (CCS'08)* (Alexandria, Virginia, USA, October 2008), pp. 391–402.

[22] DEBRAY, S. K., MUTH, R., AND WEIPPERT, M. Alias analysis of executable code. In *Symposium on Principles of Programming Languages (POPL'98)* (1998), pp. 12–24.

[23] DENG, Z., ZHANG, X., AND XU, D. Bistro: Binary component extraction and embedding for software security applications. In *Proceedings of 18th European Symposium on Research in Computer Security (ESORICS'13)* (Egham, UK, September 2013), LNCS.

[24] DOLAN-GAVITT, B., LEEK, T., ZHIVICH, M., GIFFIN, J., AND LEE, W. Virtuoso: Narrowing the semantic gap in virtual machine introspection. In *Proceedings of the* 32nd *IEEE Symposium on Security and Privacy* (Oakland, CA, USA, 2011), pp. 297–312.

[25] EGELE, M., KRUEGEL, C., KIRDA, E., YIN, H., , AND SONG, D. Dynamic spyware analysis. In *Proceedings of the 2007 USENIX Annual Technical Conference (Usenix'07)* (June 2007).

[26] EGELE, M., KRUEGEL, C., KIRDA, E., YIN, H., AND SONG, D. Dynamic spyware analysis. In *ATC'07: 2007 USENIX Annual Technical Conference on Proceedings of the USENIX Annual Technical Conference* (Santa Clara, CA, 2007), USENIX Association, pp. 1–14.

[27] EMMERIK, M. V., AND WADDINGTON, T. Using a decompiler for real-world source recovery. In *Proceedings of the 11th Working Conference on Reverse Engineering* (2004), pp. 27–36.

[28] FORRESTER, J. E., AND MILLER, B. P. An empirical study of the robustness of Windows NT applications using random testing. In *Proceedings of the 4th Conference on USENIX Windows Systems Symposium* (Seattle, Washington, 2000), USENIX Association, pp. 1–10.

[29] FU, Y., AND LIN, Z. Space traveling across vm: Automatically bridging the semantic gap in virtual machine introspection via online kernel data redirection. In *Proceedings of* 33rd *IEEE Symposium on Security and Privacy* (May 2012).

[30] FU, Y., AND LIN, Z. Exterior: Using a dual-vm based external shell for guest-os introspection, configuration, and recovery. In *Proceedings of the Ninth Annual International Conference on Virtual Execution Environments* (Houston, TX, March 2013).

[31] GARFINKEL, T., AND ROSENBLUM, M. A virtual machine introspection based architecture for intrusion detection. In *Proceedings Network and Distributed Systems Security Symposium (NDSS'03)* (February 2003).

[32] GODEFROID, P., KIEZUN, A., AND LEVIN, M. Y. Grammar-based whitebox fuzzing. In *Proceedings of the ACM SIGPLAN Conference on Programming Language Design and Implementation (PLDI'08)* (Tucson, AZ, USA, 2008), ACM, pp. 206–215.

[33] GODEFROID, P., KLARLUND, N., AND SEN, K. Dart: Directed automated random testing. In *Proceedings of the 2005 ACM SIGPLAN Conference on Programming Language Design and Implementation (PLDI'05)* (Chicago, IL, USA, 2005), ACM, pp. 213–223.

[34] GODEFROID, P., LEVIN, M., AND MOLNAR, D. Automated whitebox fuzz testing. In *Proceedings of the 15th Annual Network and Distributed System Security Symposium (NDSS'08)* (San Diego, CA, February 2008).

[35] GUO, F., FERRIE, P., AND CKER CHIUEH, T. A study of the packer problem and its solutions. In *Proceedings of the 11th International Symposium on Recent Advances in Intrusion Detection (RAID 2008)* (Boston, USA, September 2008).

[36] KANG, M. G., POOSANKAM, P., AND YIN, H. Renovo: a hidden code extractor for packed executables. In *Proceedings of the 2007 ACM Workshop on Recurring malcode* (Alexandria, Virginia, USA, 2007), ACM, pp. 46–53.

[37] KOLBITSCH, C., COMPARETTI, P. M., KRUEGEL, C., KIRDA, E., ZHOU, X., AND WANG, X. Effective and efficient malware detection at the end host. In *Proceedings of the 18th conference on USENIX security symposium* (Montreal, Canada, 2009), pp. 351–366.

[38] KOLBITSCH, C., HOLZ, T., KRUEGEL, C., AND KIRDA, E. Inspector gadget: Automated extraction of proprietary gadgets from malware binaries. In *Proceedings of 2010 IEEE Security and Privacy* (Oakland, CA, May 2010).

[39] LIANG, D., AND HARROLD, M. J. Efficient points-to analysis for whole-program analysis. In *Proceedings of the 7th European Software Engineering Conference held jointly with the 7th ACM SIGSOFT International Symposium on Foundations of Software Engineering (ESEC/FSE-7)* (Toulouse, France, 1999), Springer-Verlag, pp. 199–215.

[40] LIN, Z., ZHANG, X., AND XU, D. Automatic reverse engineering of data structures from binary execution. In *Proceedings of the 17th Annual Network and Distributed System Security Symposium (NDSS'10)* (San Diego, CA, February 2010).

[41] LUK, C.-K., COHN, R., MUTH, R., PATIL, H., KLAUSER, A., LOWNEY, G., WALLACE, S., REDDI, V. J., AND HAZELWOOD, K. Pin: Building customized program analysis tools with dynamic instrumentation. In *Proceedings of ACM SIGPLAN Conference on Programming Language Design and Implementation (PLDI'05)* (Chicago, IL, USA, 2005), pp. 190–200.

[42] MARTIGNONI, L., CHRISTODORESCU, M., AND JHA, S. Omniunpack: Fast, generic, and safe unpacking of malware. In *Proceedings of the 23rd Annual Computer Security Applications Conference (ACSAC'07)* (2007), pp. 431–441.

[43] MIECZNIKOWSKI, J., AND HENDREN, L. J. Decompiling java bytecode: Problems, traps and pitfalls. In *Proceedings of the 11th International Conference on Compiler Construction* (London, UK, UK, 2002), CC '02, Springer-Verlag, pp. 111–127.

[44] MILLER, B. P., FREDRIKSEN, L., AND SO, B. An empirical study of the reliability of UNIX utilities. In *Proceedings of the Workshop of Parallel and Distributed Debugging* (1990), Academic Medicine, pp. 9–19,.

[45] MOSER, A., KRUEGEL, C., AND KIRDA, E. Exploring multiple execution paths for malware analysis. In *Proceedings of the 2007 IEEE Symposium on Security and Privacy* (Washington, DC, USA, 2007), IEEE Computer Society, pp. 231–245.

[46] MYCROFT, A. Type-based decompilation (or program reconstruction via type reconstruction). In *Proceedings of the 8th European Symposium on Programming Languages and Systems (ESOP'99)* (London, UK, 1999), Springer-Verlag, pp. 208–223.

[47] NEWSOME, J., AND SONG, D. Dynamic taint analysis for automatic detection, analysis, and signature generation of exploits on commodity software. In *Proceedings of the 14th Annual Network and Distributed System Security Symposium (NDSS'05)* (San Diego, CA, February 2005).

[48] PEARCE, D. J., KELLY, P. H., AND HANKIN, C. Efficient field-sensitive pointer analysis of c. *ACM Trans. Program. Lang. Syst. 30*, 1 (2007), 4.

[49] RODRIGO RUBIRA BRANCO, G. N. B., AND NETO, P. D. Scientific but not academical overview of malware anti-debugging, anti-disassembly and antivm technologies. Tech. rep., "NOSPAM" qualys.com, Qualys-Vulnerability and Malware Research Labs.

[50] ROYAL, P., HALPIN, M., DAGON, D., EDMONDS, R., AND LEE, W. Polyunpack: Automating the hidden-code extraction of unpack-executing malware. In *Proceedings of the 22nd Annual Computer Security Applications Conference (ACSAC'06)* (Washington, DC, USA, 2006), IEEE Computer Society, pp. 289–300.

[51] SCHWARTZ, E. J., LEE, J., WOO, M., AND BRUMLEY, D. Native x86 decompilation using semantics-preserving structural analysis and iterative control-flow structuring. In *Proceedings of the 22nd USENIX Security Symposium* (Washington DC, USA, 2013), USENIX Association.

[52] SEN, K., MARINOV, D., AND AGHA, G. Cute: A concolic unit testing engine for c. In *Proceedings of the 10th European Software Engineering Conference held jointly with 13th ACM SIGSOFT International Symposium on Foundations of Software Engineering (ESEC/FSE-13)* (Lisbon, Portugal, 2005), ACM, pp. 263–272.

[53] SHARIF, M., LANZI, A., GIFFIN, J., AND LEE, W. Automatic reverse engineering of malware emulators. In *Proceedings of the 2009 30th IEEE Symposium on Security and Privacy* (2009), SP '09, pp. 94–109.

[54] SHARIF, M., YEGNESWARAN, V., SAIDI, H., AND PORRAS, P. Eureka: A framework for enabling static analysis on malware. In *Proceedings of the 13th European Symposium on Research in Computer Security* (Malaga, Spain, October 2008), LNCS.

[55] SLOWINSKA, A., STANCESCU, T., AND BOS, H. Howard: A dynamic excavator for reverse engineering data structures. In *Proceedings of the 18th Annual Network and Distributed System Security Symposium (NDSS'11)* (San Diego, CA, February 2011).

[56] WONDRACEK, G., MILANI, P., KRUEGEL, C., AND KIRDA, E. Automatic network protocol analysis. In *Proceedings of the 15th Annual Network and Distributed System Security Symposium (NDSS'08)* (San Diego, CA, February 2008).

Chucky: Exposing Missing Checks in Source Code for Vulnerability Discovery

Fabian Yamaguchi
University of Göttingen
Göttingen, Germany

Christian Wressnegger
idalab GmbH
Berlin, Germany

Hugo Gascon
University of Göttingen
Göttingen, Germany

Konrad Rieck
University of Göttingen
Göttingen, Germany

Abstract

Uncovering security vulnerabilities in software is a key for operating secure systems. Unfortunately, only some security flaws can be detected automatically and the vast majority of vulnerabilities is still identified by tedious auditing of source code. In this paper, we strive to improve this situation by accelerating the process of manual auditing. We introduce CHUCKY, a method to expose missing checks in source code. Many vulnerabilities result from insufficient input validation and thus omitted or false checks provide valuable clues for finding security flaws. Our method proceeds by statically tainting source code and identifying anomalous or missing conditions linked to security-critical objects. In an empirical evaluation with five popular open-source projects, CHUCKY is able to accurately identify artificial and real missing checks, which ultimately enables us to uncover 12 previously unknown vulnerabilities in two of the projects (Pidgin and LibTIFF).

Categories and Subject Descriptors

D.2.4 [**Software Engineering**]: Software/Program Verification; K.6.5 [**Management of Computing and Information Systems**]: Security and Protection

Keywords

Vulnerabilities; Static Analysis; Anomaly Detection

1. INTRODUCTION

Detecting and eliminating vulnerabilities in software is a key for operating secure computer systems. The slightest flaw in the design or implementation of software can severely undermine its security and make it an easy victim for attackers. Several security incidents of the last years are actually the result of critical vulnerabilities in software, for example, the attacks conducted by Stuxnet [8], the drive-by download attacks exploiting Java flaws [24] and the recently discovered UPNP flaws in millions of home routers [21].

Finding vulnerabilities in software is a classic problem of computer security. Unfortunately, an automatic approach for finding arbitrary vulnerabilities cannot exist. According to Rice's theorem, checking whether a program contains vulnerable code using another program is undecidable in the general case [12].

As a result of this limitation, security research has focused on discovering specific types of vulnerabilities. For example, the usage of potentially dangerous functions, such as `strcpy` and `strcat`, can be easily detected by scanning for these functions [e.g., 3, 36, 39]. Similarly, analysis techniques such as fuzzing [e.g., 22, 33] and taint analysis [e.g., 23, 26] can help in spotting insecure flows of data in software. Sophisticated methods using symbolic execution can even discover flaws in unusual code branches [e.g., 1, 9, 37]. Many of these approaches, however, are hard to operate effectively in practice and opaque to a security analyst [see 11, 14]. Consequently, the vast majority of security flaws is still discovered by tedious and time-consuming manual analysis.

In this paper, we strive to improve this situation by accelerating the process of manual auditing. To this end, we introduce CHUCKY, a method for automatically identifying missing checks in source code. Many types of vulnerabilities result from insufficient validation of input and thus omitted checks provide valuable clues for finding security flaws. For example, if the length of data copied to a buffer is checked in 9 out of 10 functions in a program, it is evident that the function missing the check is a prime candidate for security auditing. To identify such functions, CHUCKY statically taints the source code and detects anomalous or missing conditions linked to security-critical objects, such as memory buffers. By comparing regular checks with missing ones, CHUCKY is able to suggest correct conditions and potential fixes to the analyst.

Our method operates independent of external information and additional annotations, as for example used by the static security checker *Splint* [7]. Instead we build on the assumption that missing or faulty checks are rare events and the majority of conditions imposed on security-critical objects in a software project are correct. While this assumption is satisfied for mature software projects, it does not hold true in all cases. We discuss limitations of our approach in Section 5 specifically.

CCS'13, November 4–8, 2013, Berlin, Germany.

ACM 978-1-4503-2477-9/13/11 ...$15.00.
http://dx.doi.org/10.1145/2508859.2516665.

We demonstrate the efficacy of our approach in a qualitative and quantitative evaluation, where we analyze missing checks in the code of the following popular open-source projects: Firefox, Linux, LibPNG, LibTIFF and Pidgin. For all projects, CHUCKY is able to identify artificial and real missing checks accurately with few false positives. This accuracy ultimately enables us to identify 12 different previously unknown vulnerabilities in two of the projects, namely Pidgin and LibTIFF.

In summary, we make the following contributions:

- **Identification of missing checks.** We introduce a novel method for static analysis of source code that is able to automatically identify missing checks for vulnerability discovery.
- **Anomaly detection on conditions.** Our method embeds functions in a vector space, such that missing and unusual expressions in their conditions can be identified automatically.
- **Top-down and bottom-up analysis.** Taint analysis enables us to spot missing checks on untrusted input sources (top-down) as well as when accessing security-critical sinks (bottom-up).
- **Suggestion of corrections.** During auditing our method is able to suggest potential fixes to an analyst by highlighting differences between a missing check and regular ones.

The rest of this paper is structured as follows: we review missing-check vulnerabilities in Section 2 and introduce CHUCKY in Section 3 along with technical details. We evaluate its ability to expose missing checks on real source code in Section 4. Limitations and related work are discussed in Section 5 and 6, respectively. Section 7 concludes the paper.

2. MISSING-CHECK VULNERABILITIES

Many critical classes of vulnerabilities in software are a direct consequence of missing checks. This includes flaws in access control, such as missing checks of user permissions, as well as purely technical defects, such as buffer and integer overflows resulting from missing range checks. The consequences of these classes of vulnerabilities can be dramatic. For example, in January 2013 a vulnerability in the Java 7 runtime caused by a missing check in an access control component allowed attackers to install malware on millions of hosts (CVE-2013-0422). Thus, finding missing checks is crucial for securing software and computer systems.

Throughout this paper, we adopt the terminology established in the field of taint analysis for discussing missing checks [see 29]. In taint analysis, data entering a program via a *source* is monitored as it propagates to a *sink*, possibly undergoing validation in the process. Using this terminology we can discriminate two types of security checks in source code, both of which CHUCKY is designed to analyze.

- **Checks implementing security logic.** Programs implementing access control, such as Web applications or operating system kernels, perform security checks to restrict access to resources. Methods to detect specific types of these flaws have been proposed for Web applications [31] as well as Linux kernel code [34]. In this setting, parameters or global variables act as input sources, which need to be validated. As an example, consider the first check in Figure 1, where the parameter `user` is validated before allowing the remaining code of the function to be executed.

```
1  int foo(char *user, char *str, size_t n)
2  {
3    char buf[BUF_SIZE], *ar;
4    size_t len = strlen(str);
5
6    if(!is_privileged(user))
7      return ERROR;
8
9    if(len >= BUF_SIZE) return ERROR;
10   memcpy(buf, str, len);
11
12   ar = malloc(n);
13   if(!ar) return ERROR;
14
15   return process(ar, buf, len);
16 }
```

Figure 1: Exemplary security checks in a C function: a check implementing security logic (line 6) and two checks ensuring secure API usage (line 9 and 13).

- **Checks ensuring secure API usage.** Regardless of security logic, checks to ensure secure operation of internal and external APIs are required. As an example, consider the last two checks shown in Figure 1. To protect from buffer overflows, the first check validates the variable `len` derived from the source `strlen` before it is propagated to the sink `memcpy`. Moreover, the second check validates the return value of the source `malloc` to ensure that subsequent code does not cause a denial of service condition by dereferencing a NULL-pointer.

CHUCKY is based on the key observation that sources and sinks are usually employed many times within a code base, each time requiring similar security checks to be implemented. As a consequence, there often exist typical patterns for checking data retrieved from sources or propagated to sinks. If such patterns can be automatically inferred from the code, it is possible to detect deviations from these patterns and thereby spot potential vulnerabilities.

3. IDENTIFYING MISSING CHECKS

Exposing missing checks in source code poses two main challenges: First, typical checks must be determined automatically by leveraging information scattered throughout the code base. Second, any deviations from these checks need to be detected and presented to the analyst while browsing the code. Moreover, the analyst must be able to easily comprehend how the method arrives at its results.

To address these problems, our method implements a five-step procedure, which can be executed for each source and sink referenced by a selected function. This procedure combines techniques from static analysis and machine learning to determine missing checks and provide supporting evidence. The five steps are illustrated in Figure 2 and outlined in the following:

1. **Robust Parsing.** Conditions, assignments and API symbols are first extracted from a function's source code using a robust parser [20]. In particular, the

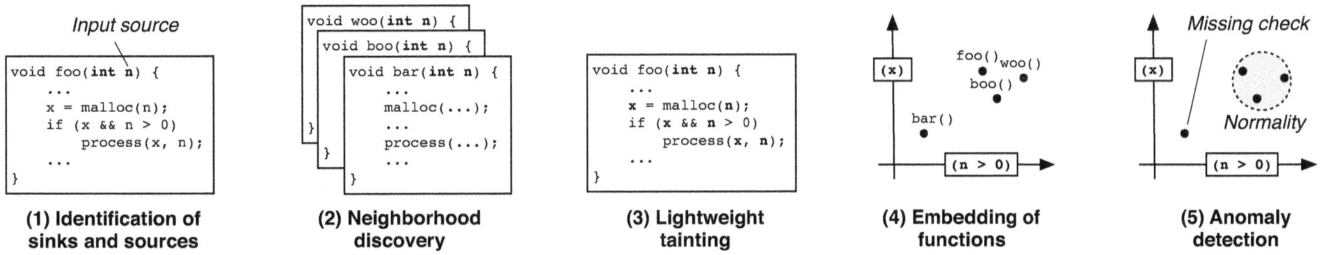

Figure 2: Overview of Chucky: (1) sources and sinks are identified, (2) functions with similar context are grouped, (3) variables depending on the sources/sinks are tainted, (4) functions are embedded in a vector space using tainted conditions, and (5) functions with anomalous or missing conditions are detected.

sources and sinks used in each of the functions are determined. The remaining four steps are then executed for each source or sink independently.

2. **Neighborhood discovery.** The necessity of a check highly depends on the context code operates in. Our method thus identifies functions in the code base operating in a similar context to that of the selected function using techniques inspired by natural language processing (Section 3.2).

3. **Lightweight tainting.** To determine only those checks associated with a given source or sink, lightweight tainting is performed for the function under examination and all its neighbors in top-down and bottom-up direction (Section 3.3).

4. **Embedding of functions.** The selected function and its neighbors are then embedded in a vector space using the tainted conditions such that they can be analyzed using machine learning techniques (Section 3.4).

5. **Anomaly Detection.** The embedding of functions enables us to geometrically search for missing checks. In particular, we compute a model of normality over the functions, such that anomalous checks can be identified by large distances from this model (Section 3.5).

In the following sections, we describe these steps in more detail and provide the necessary technical as well as theoretical background.

3.1 Robust Parsing

Reasoning about missing checks requires a deep understanding of program syntax. CHUCKY therefore begins by parsing code using a robust parser for C/C++ developed during our research. The parser is based on an island grammar [see 20] for the parser generator ANTLR [25] and provides abstract syntax trees (ASTs) for all functions of a code base even when declarations can only be resolved partially. This allows CHUCKY to be directly employed without requiring code to be compiled or a build environment to be configured. To encourage more research in the area, we have made our parser available as open-source software[1]. CHUCKY employs this parser to extract the following information from each function.

[1]https://github.com/fabsx00/joern

- **Sources and sinks.** All function parameters, function calls as well as global and local variables are potential sources or sinks of information, each of which may be tied to a unique set of conditions required for secure operation. CHUCKY therefore begins by extracting all sources and sinks from each function. The granularity of the analysis is further increased by taking fields of structures into account. As an example, consider Figure 3 where all sources and sinks of the function `foo` are marked.
- **API symbols**. Additionally, we extract API symbols as a prerequisite for neighborhood discovery (see Section 3.2). All types used in parameter and local variable declarations as well as the names of all functions called are considered as API symbols.
- **Assignments.** Assignments describe the flow of information between variables, which we exploit to determine conditions related to a sink by performing lightweight tainting (see Section 3.3). For each assignment, we store the subtree of the AST referring to the left- and right-value of the assignment.
- **Conditions.** Ultimately, functions are compared in terms of the conditions they impose when using a source or sink (see Sections 3.4 and 3.5). As conditions, we consider all expressions of control statements such as those introduced by the keywords `if`, `for` or `while` as well as those found in conditional expressions. To provide access to partial expressions, we store conditions as references to corresponding subtrees of the AST rather than as flat strings.

Upon completion of this step, patterns can be determined for each of the extracted sources and sinks and analyzed for missing checks, as explained in the following sections.

3.2 Neighborhood Discovery

Security checks are often highly context dependent. For example, omitting checks on string operations may be perfectly acceptable when parsing configuration files, while posing a serious threat when processing network data. CHUCKY accounts for this difference by only comparing the function under examination to functions sharing a similar context. This is achieved by identifying the *neighborhood* of the function, that is, related functions using similar API symbols. The rationale behind this choice is that the combination of interfaces used by a function is characteristic for the subsystem it operates in as well as the functionality it implements.

```
1  int foo(char *user, char *str, size_t n)
2  {
3    char buf[BUF_SIZE], *ar;
4    size_t len = strlen(str);
5
6    if(!is_privileged(user))
7      return ERROR;
8
9    if(len >= BUF_SIZE) return ERROR;
10   memcpy(buf, str, len);
11
12   ar = malloc(n);
13   if(!ar) return ERROR;
14
15   return process(ar, buf, len);
16 }
```

Figure 3: C function with sources and sinks: All parameters (line 1), global and local variables (lines 3,4 and 9) and function calls (line 4, 6, 10, 12 and 15) are marked for analysis.

For discovering these neighboring functions, we adapt the classic *bag-of-words model* from natural language processing that is commonly used to compare text documents [28]. Similar to the words in these documents, we represent each function in the code base by the API symbols it contains. We then map the functions to a vector space, whose dimensions are associated with the frequencies of these symbols [see 41]. Functions using a similar API lie close to each other in this vector space, whereas functions with different context are separated by large distances.

Formally, we define a mapping ϕ from the set of all functions $X = \{x_1, \ldots, x_m\}$ to $\mathbb{R}^{|A|}$ where A is the set of all API symbols contained in X. This mapping is given by

$$\phi : X \to \mathbb{R}^{|A|}, \quad \phi(x) \mapsto \big(I(x,a) \cdot \mathrm{TFIDF}(x,a,X)\big)_{a \in A}$$

where I is an indicator function defined as

$$I(x,a) = \begin{cases} 1 & \text{if } x \text{ contains API symbol } a \\ 0 & \text{otherwise} \end{cases}$$

and $\mathrm{TFIDF}(x,a,X)$ a standard weighting term from information retrieval [28]. The rationale behind the use of this term is to lower the impact of very frequently used API symbols on the similarity of functions.

This geometric representation enables us to identify the k-nearest neighbors $\mathcal{N} \subset X$ of the selected function x with respect to the source or sink s. We determine this set $\mathcal{N}$ by first extracting all functions of the code base that reference s. We then calculate the cosine distance of their corresponding vectors to $\phi(x)$ and finally select those k functions with the smallest distance.

Note, that Chucky is not very sensitive to the choice of the parameter k, as we demonstrate in Section 4, where values between 10 and 30 provide good performance. As a result of the neighborhood discovery, only the function under examination and its neighbors need to be processed in the following steps of the analysis.

3.3 Lightweight Tainting

Among the many checks present in a regular function, only a subset is relevant for a chosen source or sink. Analyzing the function in terms of its use of a specific source or sink therefore requires unrelated checks to be discarded automatically. However, this selection of relevant checks is not trivial, as it requires the flow of data between variables to be taken into account.

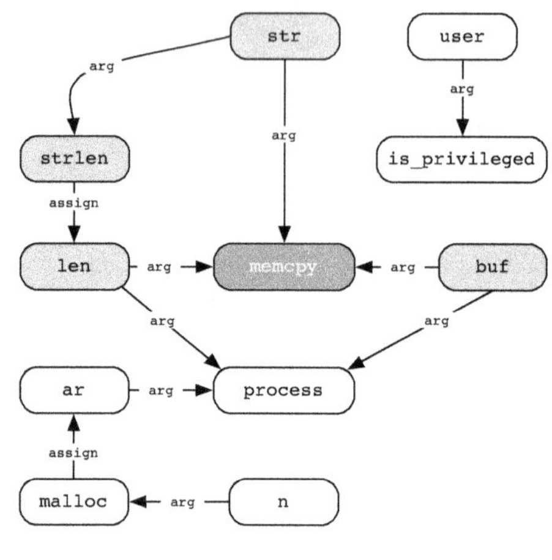

Figure 4: Dependency graph for function `foo`. Nodes reachable from `memcpy` are shaded, where the taint propagation stops at function boundaries. Isolated nodes are omitted.

To address this problem, Chucky performs lightweight tainting of the code of the target function and all its neighbors for each source or sink in two stages:

1. **Dependency modelling.** A directed graph is created to model the dependencies between variables. The nodes of the graph correspond to the identifiers used in the function (i.e., sources and sinks), while the edges reflect assignments between identifiers. Edges are also added if identifiers are parameters of functions.

2. **Taint propagation.** Starting from the identifier corresponding to a selected source or sink, the graph is traversed in top-down as well as bottom-up direction to discover all related identifiers. The propagation stops at function boundaries, that is, edges from parameters to functions are not followed.

An example of a dependency graph for the function `foo` from Figure 3 is shown in Figure 4. The identifier `memcpy` has been picked as source/sink for the analysis. Three identifiers are tainted (gray shading) including directly connected nodes, such as `len` and `buf`, as well as indirectly linked nodes, such as `strlen`.

Once the tainted identifiers for a function are known, we examine its conditions (see Section 3.1) and remove a condition if it does not reference at least one of the tainted identifiers. We thus restrict the conditions analyzed in subsequent steps only to those conditions related to the source or sink under examination.

3.4 Embedding of Functions

In the last two steps, we leverage the information distributed across the function neighborhood to determine typical checks and deviations thereof using anomaly detection. Similar to the technique for neighborhood discovery (Section 3.2), this method for anomaly detection operates on numerical vectors and thus the functions need to be again embedded in a suitable vector space. We implement this embedding as follows.

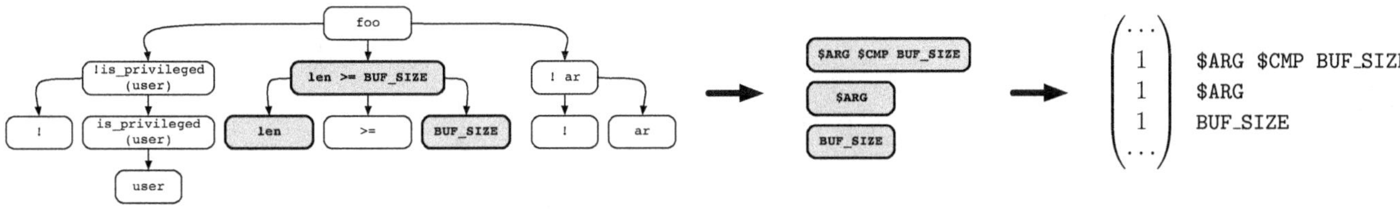

Figure 5: Schematic depiction of embedding. Conditions related to the specified source/sink are extracted from the abstract syntax tree and mapped to a vector space using their expressions.

Upon completion of the previous step, conditions related to the source or sink s are known for each function. We proceed to extract all expressions (including sub-expressions) contained in each of these conditions. The expressions then undergo a simple normalization to account for small syntactical differences in the formulation of checks. In detail, the normalization consists of two transformations.

1. **Removal of negations.** Since CHUCKY does not account for the actions taken upon evaluation of an expression, negations are removed as the first step of normalization. For the same reason, relational operators are replaced by the symbol `$CMP`. Furthermore, numbers are replaced by `$NUM` since for example, the expression `x < 10` is equivalent to `x < 1 + 9`.

2. **Normalization of arguments and return values** If the source or sink of interest is a function, its return value is renamed to `$RET` while any variables directly influencing its arguments are renamed to `$ARG`. This allows return values and arguments of functions to be compared regardless of the names of variables chosen.

Finally, the functions can be embedded in a vector space by applying a mapping φ, which transforms functions into numerical vectors. To represent each function by all normalized expressions contained in its conditions, we define E to be the set of all normalized expressions and φ as

$$\varphi : X \to \mathbb{R}^{|E|}, \quad \varphi(x) \mapsto \big(I(x,e)\big)_{e \in E}$$

where I is an indicator function defined as

$$I(x,e) = \begin{cases} 1 & \text{if } x \text{ contains } e \text{ in a condition} \\ 0 & \text{otherwise.} \end{cases}$$

Note that while the total number of expressions contained in the code base may be very large, the vast majority of functions contains only few of these expressions. In practice, this allows for memory efficient implementations using hash maps or sorted arrays [27].

Figure 5 illustrates this process for the function `foo` from Figure 1. The single condition related to the sink `memcpy` is first determined and all sub-expressions are extracted and normalized. Finally, the vectorial representation is obtained by applying the mapping φ.

3.5 Anomaly Detection

Based on the embedding of functions, we are finally able to determine missing checks geometrically. To this end, a model of normality quantifying the importance of each expression contained in a check is derived from the embedded neighbors. Measuring the distance to this model allows us to determine checks that are present in most neighbors but are missing in the examined function. This enables CHUCKY to pinpoint the exact missing check and report its absence to the analyst. Moreover, an anomaly score can be calculated, allowing particularly interesting code to be returned to the analyst for immediate inspection. Mathematically, this process is implemented as follows.

For each source or sink s used in a function x under consideration, a model of normality is calculated based on its neighbors $\mathcal{N}$. Recalling that in the previous step, each neighbor is mapped to a vector in the space spanned by the expressions contained in its conditions, a natural choice for this model is the center of mass of all embedded neighbor vectors. The model $\mu \in \mathbb{R}^{|E|}$ is thus computed over all k embedded neighbour functions as

$$\mu = \frac{1}{|\mathcal{N}|} \sum_{n \in \mathcal{N}} \varphi(n)$$

Each coordinate of μ represents the fraction of the neighbors, that contain a particular Boolean expression in its conditions as a number between 0 and 1. For example, a score of 0.9 in the coordinate associated with the expression `$RET $CMP $NUM` indicates that 90% the function's neighbors check the return value against a literal number while only 10% do not.

Identifying missing checks is now easy as it merely requires assessing the difference between the embedded function vector $\varphi(x)$ and the model of normality μ. To this end, we calculate the distance vector $d \in \mathbb{R}^{|E|}$ given by

$$d = \mu - \varphi(x).$$

Each coordinate of the vector d is a value between -1 and +1. Positive numbers denote Boolean expressions that are checked by a fraction of neighbors but missing in the function under consideration x, i.e., *missing checks*. In contrast, negative numbers denote expressions checked in x but not present in any of its neighbors.

Finally, from the distance vector we compute an anomaly score suitable to rank functions according to the likelihood that it is omitting a check. We define this anomaly score for a function x as

$$f(x) = ||\mu - \varphi(x)||_\infty = \max_{e \in E} \big(\mu_e - I(x,e)\big)$$

that is, the anomaly score is given by the largest coefficient of the vector d. Recalling that positive numbers denote missing expressions, the rationale behind this choice is to rank functions high if many neighbors contain an expression, which is not present in the function of interest. Furthermore, the maximum norm is chosen, because functions deviating from its neighbors in a single concrete expression—while containing all other expressions—are usually more interesting than functions differing from their neighbors entirely.

4. EMPIRICAL EVALUATION

We proceed to evaluate our method on the source code of five popular software projects: Firefox, Linux, LibPNG, LibTIFF and Pidgin. In particular, we are interested in CHUCKY's detection performance when tasked to identify missing checks as well as its practical value in real source code audits. We begin by conducting a controlled experiment (Section 4.1) involving artificial as well as real missing checks leading to vulnerabilities discovered in the past. Finally, we study our method's ability to assist in the discovery of previously unknown vulnerabilities by providing case studies (Section 4.2).

4.1 Missing Check Detection

To evaluate the detection performance of CHUCKY, the security history of each of the five projects is reviewed. In each code base, we uncover cases where a security check is present in many functions but omitted in others, thus causing vulnerabilities.

In all but one case, these vulnerabilities are critical, allowing an attacker to fully compromise the software. Additionally, we take care to choose samples involving different cases of vulnerabilities, e.g., missing checks for security logic, function arguments, function return values. In the following we provide a detailed description of our dataset. Table 1 summarizes this information.

- **Firefox.** The JavaScript engine of the popular Web browser Firefox (version 4.0) contains 5,649 functions and 372,450 lines of code. A failure to check the number of arguments passed to native code implementations of JavaScript functions (i.e., the parameter `argc`) leads to a use-after-free vulnerability (CVE-2010-3183). Ten utility functions implementing array operations perform the same security check to avoid this.

- **Linux.** The filesystem code of the Linux operating system kernel (version 2.6.34.13) contains 19,178 functions and 955,943 lines of code. A missing check before setting an ACL allows to bypass file system permissions (CVE-2010-2071). The check involves the parameter `dentry` and its structure field `dentry->d_inode`. Eight functions of different filesystems implement a corresponding security check correctly.

- **LibPNG.** The image processing library LibPNG (version 1.2.44) contains 437 functions and 40,255 lines of code. A missing check of the PNG chunk's size (i.e., the parameter `length`) results in a memory corruption (CVE-2011-2692). Nineteen functions processing PNG chunks perform the same critical check to avoid this.

- **LibTIFF.** The image processing library LibTIFF (version 3.9.4) contains 609 functions and 33,335 lines of code. Missing checks of the length field of TIFF directory entries (i.e., the parameter `dir` and its field `dir->tdir_count`) lead to two independent stack-based buffer-overflows (CVE-2006-3459 and CVE-2010-2067). Nine functions processing TIFF directory entries perform a security check to avoid this problem.

- **Pidgin.** The instant messaging library of the popular instant messenger Pidgin (version 2.7.3) contains 7,390 functions and 332,762 lines of code. A missing check of the return value of the internal base64-decoding routine `purple_base64_decode` leads to a denial-of-service vulnerability (CVE-2010-3711). Eighteen functions parsing network data in Pidgin perform a corresponding security check correctly to avoid this.

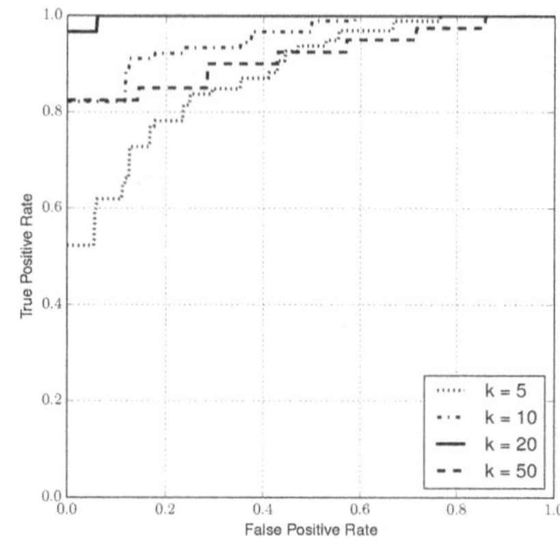

(a) Averaged ROC curve

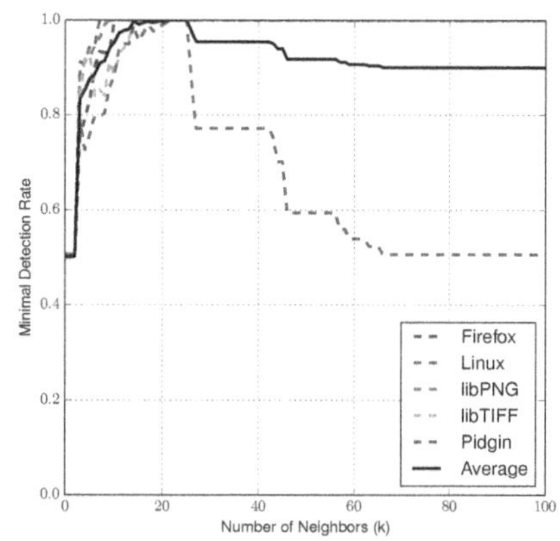

(b) AUC (Minimal Detection Rate)

Figure 6: Detection performance for the five projects with neighborhoods of different size.

For each code base we begin our evaluation by patching the known vulnerabilities. We then proceed to create several experiments in a round-robin fashion for each security check, where we remove the check from one function while leaving all other functions untouched. Vulnerabilities are thus deliberately introduced in order to allow us to measure our methods ability to identify them.

CHUCKY is then employed to rank functions by analyzing their use of the source or sink requiring validation. Note that while only those functions known to be vulnerable or non-vulnerable are included in the ranking, the entire code base is considered for neighborhood selection. The experiment thus reflects the situation encountered in practice and performs no simplifications.

These experiments allow us to assess our method's ability to rediscover those vulnerabilities reported to the projects in the past but go one step further by exploring CHUCKY's capability to discover artificially introduced vulnerabilities. In total, the dataset allows us to perform 64 experiments independently (see last column of Table 1).

Project	Component	Vulnerability	LOC	# functions	# with check
Firefox 4.0	JavaScript engine	CVE-2010-3183	372450	5649	10
Linux 2.6.34.13	Filesystem code	CVE-2010-2071	955943	19178	8
LibPNG 1.2.44	Entire library	CVE-2011-2692	40255	473	19
LibTIFF 3.9.4	Entire library	CVE-2010-2067	33335	609	9
Pidgin 2.7.3	Messaging	CVE-2010-3711	332762	7390	18

Table 1: Overview of our dataset. For each project the missing-check vulnerability, the lines of code (LOC), the number of functions and the number of functions involving the check is listed.

Figure 6(a) shows the ROC curves of our method averaged over all projects for neigborhoods of different size k, where the detection rate is plotted against the false-positive rate for different thresholds. For low values of k, such as $k = 5$, already 50% of the missing checks can be detected with few false positives. With increasing k, CHUCKY is able to identify more missing conditions, where finally almost all missing checks in the five code bases are detected with $k = 20$ at a detection rate of 96%.

We further investigate the effect of the number of neighbors on the detection performance by generating individual ROC curves for values of k between 1 and 100 using the *Area Under Curve* (AUC) as a performance measure [2]. Figure 6(b) shows the results of this experiment. For $k = 25$ we attain *perfect results* across all code bases allowing all vulnerabilities to be detected with no false positives. While we do not assume that an optimal choice of k exists for arbitrary code bases, for the projects under consideration, the average number of functions operating in a similar context thus seems to be around 25. For all further evaluations we thus fix k to 25.

Moreover, we can observe that for those code bases where APIs have been insecurely used (Firefox, LibPNG, LibTIFF and Pidgin), the maximum performance is achieved when k is chosen above a certain threshold. This confirms that in these cases, the majority of functions employing the source or sink perform the security check, thus making neighborhood discovery rather dispensable. In the case of Linux, where missing checks in security logic need to be identified, the performance drops when k becomes too large. We examine this case in detail and find that the source `dentry` is used many times across the code base while a security check is only required in few cases. Neighborhood discovery thus becomes essential in order to create a model of normality only from functions that operate in a similar context.

This quantitative evaluation demonstrates the potential of CHUCKY. All of the considered vulnerabilities are successfully identified by our method and would have been spotted if CHUCKY had been applied to the respective software projects in the past.

4.2 Discovery of Vulnerabilities

First and foremost, CHUCKY is designed to assist an analyst in day-to-day auditing. In the following, we therefore study our method's ability to assist in the discovery of previously unknown vulnerabilities in practice. In particular, we describe how 7 previously unknown vulnerabilities have been discovered by applying CHUCKY on two real-world projects, namely, LibTIFF and Pidgin. We have conducted further studies uncovering 5 more unknown vulnerabilities. For the sake of brevity however, we omit these and details of the vulnerabilities here.

To ensure that all vulnerabilities found by CHUCKY are previously unknown, we update the code of both software projects to the most recent version. At the time of writing, these are version 4.0.3 for LibTIFF and 2.10.6 for Pidgin.

4.2.1 LibTIFF Case Study

In the first case study, we employ CHUCKY to uncover vulnerabilities in LibTIFF, an image processing library and suite of tools for the Tagged Image File Format (TIFF). Image processing libraries are a popular target for attackers as parsing images securely is a challenging task. In particular, integer overflow vulnerabilities when dealing with image dimensions (i.e., image width and height) are a common problem. We therefore use CHUCKY to rank all functions of the code base according to anomalous use of any parameters or local variables named `width`, `height`, `w` or `h`.

```
1  static int
2  tiffcvt(TIFF* in, TIFF* out)
3  {
4    uint32 width, height; /* image width & height */
5    uint16 shortv;
6    float floatv;
7    char *stringv;
8    uint32 longv;
9    uint16 v[1];
10
11   TIFFGetField(in, TIFFTAG_IMAGEWIDTH, &width);
12   TIFFGetField(in, TIFFTAG_IMAGELENGTH, &height);
13
14   CopyField(TIFFTAG_SUBFILETYPE, longv);
15   [...]
16   if( process_by_block && TIFFIsTiled( in ) )
17     return( cvt_by_tile( in, out ) );
18   else if( process_by_block )
19     return( cvt_by_strip( in, out ) );
20   else
21     return( cvt_whole_image( in, out ) );
22 }
```

Figure 7: Missing checks of the variables width and height in the function `tiffcvt`.

From the 74 functions dealing with these variables, CHUCKY reports only a single function with an anomaly score of 100%. We examine the reported function `tiffcvt` (Figure 7) to find that the `width` and `height` fields are obtained directly from the image file at lines 11 and 12 and are not checked. CHUCKY reports that all neighbors of the function perform a check on the variable `height` while 79% additionally perform a check on the variable `width`.

Indeed, this missing check leads to an integer overflow when calling the function `cvt_by_strip` shown in Figure 8, for which 50% of its neighbors suggest an additional check for the `width` field. Triggering this overflow, a buffer smaller than expected can be allocated at line 11, resulting in a heap-based buffer overflow when calling `TIFFReadRGBAStrip`

Score	Source File	Function Name
0.92	tools/thumbnail.c	initScale
0.88,	tools/rgb2ycbcr.c	cvtRaster
0.88	tools/rgb2ycbcr.c	setupLuma
0.88	tools/ycbcr.c	setupLuma
0.84	tools/pal2rgb.c	main
0.84	tools/tiff2bw.c	main
0.80	libtiff/tif_print.c	TIFFPrintDirectory
0.80	tools/raw2tiff.c	guessSize
0.76	tools/sgisv.c	svRGBContig
0.76	tools/sgisv.c	svRGBSeparate

Table 2: Top ten functions returned for the sink *_TIFFmalloc*. All 10 functions fail to check the return value of the sink. Vulnerabilities are indicated by dark shading.

```
1  static int
2  cvt_by_strip( TIFF *in, TIFF *out )
3
4  {
5    uint32* raster; /* retrieve RGBA image */
6    uint32  width, height; /* image width & height */
7    [...]
8    TIFFGetField(in, TIFFTAG_IMAGEWIDTH, &width);
9    TIFFGetField(in, TIFFTAG_IMAGELENGTH, &height);
10   /* Allocate strip buffer */
11   raster = (uint32*)
12    _TIFFmalloc(width*rowsperstrip*sizeof (uint32));
13   if (raster == 0) {
14     TIFFError(TIFFFileName(in),
15               "No space for raster buffer");
16     return (0);
17   } [...]
18   for(row=0;ok&&row<height;row+=rowsperstrip )
19     { [...]
20       /* Read the strip into an RGBA array */
21       if (!TIFFReadRGBAStrip(in,row,raster)) {
22         [...]
23       } [...]
24     }
25   _TIFFfree( raster ); [...]
26   return ok;
27 }
```

Figure 8: Integer overflow in the function `cvt_by_strip` caused by the missing check in the caller `tiffcvt`. In effect, a buffer overflow results when calling `TIFFReadRGBAStrip`.

on line 21.CHUCKY thus leads us almost directly to a possibly exploitable memory corruption vulnerability.

In a second example, our method is used to uncover NULL pointer dereferenciations. To this end, all functions of the code base are analyzed for missing or unusual checks for `_TIFFMalloc`, a simple wrapper around `malloc`.

In total 237 functions call `_TIFFMalloc`. Table 2 shows the top ten of these functions ranked by our method according to anomalous use of `_TIFFMalloc`. In each of the ten cases, CHUCKY reports that a check for the return value (expression `$RET`) is performed by the vast majority of neighbors, while it is missing in the identified functions. Note, that at no point, the checks required for the use of `_TIFFMalloc` have been specified explicitly; instead CHUCKY leverages the information distributed across the code base to determine these security checks automatically. We confirm the missing checks in all ten cases. In four of these, the omitted check allows attackers to cause a denial-of-service condition by providing specifically crafted input, whereas in other cases, only a software defect is identified.

```
1  cvtRaster(TIFF* tif, uint32* raster,
2            uint32 width, uint32 height)
3  {
4    uint32 y;
5    tstrip_t strip = 0;
6    tsize_t cc, acc;
7    unsigned char* buf;
8    uint32 rwidth = roundup(width, horizSubSampling);
9    uint32 rheight = roundup(height, vertSubSampling);
10   uint32 nrows = (rowsperstrip > rheight ?
11                   rheight : rowsperstrip);
12   uint32 rnrows = roundup(nrows,vertSubSampling);
13
14   cc = rnrows*rwidth + 2*((rnrows*rwidth) /
15      (horizSubSampling*vertSubSampling));
16   buf = (unsigned char*)_TIFFmalloc(cc);
17   // FIXME unchecked malloc
18   for (y = height; (int32) y > 0; y -= nrows){
19     uint32 nr = (y > nrows ? nrows : y);
20     cvtStrip(buf, raster + (y-1)*width, nr, width);
21     nr = roundup(nr, vertSubSampling);
22     acc = nr*rwidth + 2*((nr*rwidth)/
23      (horizSubSampling*vertSubSampling));
24     if(!TIFFWriteEncodedStrip(tif,strip++,
25                               buf,acc)){
26       _TIFFfree(buf); return (0);
27     }
28   }
29   _TIFFfree(buf); return (1);
30 }
```

Figure 9: A missing check detected in the function `cvtRaster` of the library LibTIFF.

As an example, let us consider the function `cvtRaster` shown in Figure 9. This function provides an illustrative example because the programmer confirms that the return value of `_TIFFMalloc` requires validation in the comment on line 17. In this particular case, the method reports that 85% of the function's neighbors validate the return value and 40% compare it to the constant *NULL*. No other Boolean expression is found to consistently occur across all neighbors in more than 30% of the cases. Furthermore, from all symbols used in the function, the deviation in its use of `_TIFFMalloc` is most pronounced. The function is thus among the top 15% in the global ranking and thus CHUCKY points the analyst to vulnerability even if an interest in `_TIFFMalloc` is not expressed explicitly.

4.2.2 Pidgin Case Study

In the second case study, we employ CHUCKY to uncover two denial-of-service vulnerabilities in Pidgin's implementation of the Microsoft Instant Messaging Protocol. In particular, we find that a vulnerability exists allowing users to remotely crash the instant messengers without requiring cooperation from the victims side. As starting point for our analysis, we review the C standard library for commonly used functions, which crash upon reception of a NULL pointer as an argument. As an example, the sinks `atoi` and `strchr` are chosen and CHUCKY is employed to rank all functions according to missing or faulty checks for these sinks.

Table 3 shows all functions with an anomaly score of over 50%, that is, cases where more than half of the neighbors suggest a check to be introduced. Furthermore, in all cases, CHUCKY indicates that the arguments passed to the sinks need to be checked. With this information, we are able to

Score	Source File	Function Name
0.84	msn.c	msn_normalize
0.76	oim.c	msn_oim_report_to_user
0.72	oim.c	msn_parse_oim_xml
0.72	msnutils.c	msn_import_html
0.64	switchboard.c	msn_switchboard_add_user
0.64	slpcall.c	msn_slp_sip_recv
0.60	msnutils.c	msn_parse_socket
0.60	contact.c	msn_parse_addr..._contacts
0.60	contact.c	msn_parse_each_member
0.60	command.c	msn_command_from_string
0.56	msg.c	msn_message_parse_payload

Table 3: Top ten functions returned for the sinks `atoi` and `strchr` in Pidgin's implementation of the Microsoft Instant Messenger Protocol. Vulnerabilities are indicated by dark shading.

discover two cases among the top ten missing checks allowing attackers to remotely crash Pidgin.

First Example.

For the function `msn_parse_oim_xml` shown in Figure 10, CHUCKY reports that 72% of its neighbors validate arguments passed to `atoi` while this function does not. Indeed, this is the case on line 19 where the variable `unread` is passed to `atoi` unchecked. Moreover, CHUCKY reports that 75% of the function neighbors check the return value of `xmlnode_get_data` while this function does not. Combined, these two missing checks allow Pidgin to be crashed by sending an XML-message with an empty "E/UI" node. This causes `xmlnode_get_data` to return a NULL pointer on line 13, which is then propagated to `atoi` resulting in a crash.

```
1  static void
2  msn_parse_oim_xml(MsnOim *oim, xmlnode *node)
3  {
4    xmlnode *mNode;
5    xmlnode *iu_node;
6    MsnSession *session = oim->session;
7    [...]
8    iu_node = xmlnode_get_child(node, "E/IU");
9
10   if(iu_node != NULL &&
11    purple_account_get_check_mail(session->account))
12    {
13      char *unread = xmlnode_get_data(iu_node);
14      const char *passports[2] =
15        { msn_user_get_passport(session->user) };
16      const char *urls[2] =
17        { session->passport_info.mail_url };
18
19      int count = atoi(unread);
20
21      /* XXX/khc: pretty sure this is wrong */
22      if (count > 0)
23        purple_notify_emails(session->account->gc,
24                             count, FALSE, NULL,
25                             NULL, passports,
26                             urls, NULL, NULL);
27      g_free(unread);
28    }
29   [...]
30 }
```

Figure 10: Missing check in the function `msn_parse_oim_xml` of the instant messenger Pidgin.

Second Example.

For the function `msn_message_parse_payload` shown in Figure 11, CHUCKY reports a failure to check the argument passed to `strchr` with an anomaly score of 56%. The vulnerable call can be seen on line 15 and can be triggered by sending a message containing the string "Content-Type" immediately followed by two successive carriage return line feed sequences. This causes the variable `value` to be set to NULL on line 10. This value propagates to `strchr` on line 15 causing the crash of Pidgin. This vulnerability is particularly interesting as it can be triggered by other users of the MSN service.

```
1  void
2  msn_message_parse_payload(MsnMessage *msg, [...])
3  {
4    [...]
5    for (cur = elems; *cur != NULL; cur++)
6      {
7        const char *key, *value; [...]
8        tokens = g_strsplit(*cur, ": ", 2);
9        key = tokens[0];
10       value = tokens[1];
11       [...]
12       if (!strcmp(key, "Content-Type"))
13         {
14           char *charset, *c;
15           if ((c = strchr(value, ';')) != NULL)
16             {
17               [...]
18             }
19           msn_message_set_content_type(msg, value);
20         }
21       else
22         {
23           msn_message_set_attr(msg, key, value);
24         }
25       g_strfreev(tokens);
26     }
27   g_strfreev(elems);
28   /* Proceed to the end of the "\r\n\r\n" */
29   tmp = end + strlen(body_dem);
30   [...]
31   g_free(tmp_base);
32 }
```

Figure 11: Missing check in the function `msn_message_parse_payload` of the instant messenger Pidgin.

5. LIMITATIONS

Similar to other methods for the discovery of security flaws, CHUCKY cannot overcome the inherent limitations of vulnerability identification. While our method is able to expose missing security checks effectively, it cannot verify whether these truly lead to vulnerabilities in practice. This limitation, however, can be alleviated by the analyst, as he can guide the search for vulnerabilities by only inspecting security-critical sources and sinks, such as common memory, network and parsing functions. As our experiments demonstrate, this often enables CHUCKY to pinpoint missing checks related to vulnerabilities with little manual effort.

In contrast to other methods, CHUCKY does not require external information or code annotations to identify missing checks. The method is capable of operating on the code base of a software project alone. This advantage comes at price: our approach is based on the assumption that the majority of checks in a code base are correct and missing checks are rare. While this assumption holds true for mature software projects, it is not necessary satisfied by software at an early stage of development. Consequently, CHUCKY is better suited for finding vulnerabilities in stable code.

It is also important to note that CHUCKY makes no attempts to evaluate expressions. Semantically equivalent checks thus cannot be detected, which may lead to false positives in practice. Moreover, our method is only able to detect checks if they are missing entirely and cannot detect checks performed too late. Combining our method with existing techniques from data flow analysis and symbolic execution therefore seems to be an interesting direction for future work.

Finally, there exist many types of vulnerabilities that have no relation to missing checks and thus cannot be exposed by CHUCKY. Nonetheless, it is a common practice of developers to add checks before potential vulnerabilities and security-critical code, for example for protecting buffers, limiting access to resources or changing the program flow. All these checks can be exposed by CHUCKY and hence our method addresses a wide range of possible security flaws.

6. RELATED WORK

The theory and practice of finding vulnerabilities in software is a classic field of computer security. Due to their generic nature, missing-check vulnerabilities border on a wide range of previous research. In the following, we point out relations to this work and related approaches.

Static Code Analysis.

In practice, checking tools such as *Microsoft PREfast* [15] or *PScan* [5] are used to statically find vulnerabilities in source code. These tools possess built-in information about correct API usage and common programming mistakes, which severely limits the kind of vulnerabilities these tools can detect. An alternative route is taken by scanners such as *Splint* [7], which allow code annotations to be supplied by analysts. However, creating these annotations and rules regarding API usage is both time consuming and challenging as it requires an intimate understanding of both internal and external APIs of a target program.

Several approaches seize the idea of inspecting the temporal properties of API usage [e.g., 6, 16, 38] and attempt to provide this information across projects [e.g., 10, 43]. Such properties would, for instance, indicate that a *lock* function call usually is followed by a call to the *unlock* function. Software defects can thus be detected by identifying anomalies, which do not comply with the derived set of rules. Conditions, however, are not analyzed and therefore, these approaches are not suited for finding missing checks.

Tan et al. [34] analyze API call sequences to identify necessary security checks whereas the mapping between a specific check and the event that is required to be checked is specified in advance. Similarly, Livshits et al. [18] focus on inferring information flow specifications by modelling propagation graphs. In contrast, CHUCKY attempts to find missing checks in a more general scope and without additional specification of the sensitive code regions or functions.

Other work goes one step further and makes use of additional auxiliary information like software revision histories [19, 40] or different API implementations [32]. Similar to CHUCKY, Son et al. [31] intend not to make use of annotations or any external specifications. Instead they rely on software engineering patterns commonly used in web applications and SQL queries that alter the database as security-sensitive events. Therefore, this approach is tightly bound to web applications while CHUCKY can be applied in any programming environment if a suitable parser is available.

In many approaches, infrequent but correct patterns might cause false positives due to a biased notion of normality. Thummalapenta and Xie [35] address this by introducing *alternative patterns*. We discussed this limitation with respect to CHUCKY in Section 5. Another more general method coined as vulnerability extrapolation [41, 42] learns from known security flaws and finds locations that might exhibit a similar vulnerability. We build on this method for the neighborhood discovery described in Section 3.2.

Taint Analysis and Symbolic Execution.

Taint analysis or taint tracking is a method for performing information flow analysis. Data of interest is "tainted" and tracked from a source through the system to a specified sink. In principle one differentiates between static and dynamic taint analysis. Dynamic taint tracking has been used for the discovery of vulnerabilities [e.g., 23, 37]. However, since CHUCKY is strictly operating on source code, we do not discuss dynamic approaches at this point. Static taint tracking has been effectively used for detecting vulnerabilities such as format string vulnerabilities in C programs [30] or SQL injections and cross-site scripting [13, 17].

Nevertheless, taint analysis implies some limitations that come down to its passive view on the data flow. Symbolic execution can overcome these by actively exploring the code's state space and execution paths [1, 4, 9, 37]. Due to this state exploration, symbolic execution becomes intractable without heuristics to reduce the number of branches that need to be analyzed. As a result it hardly can be used for code auditing in practice [11].

7. CONCLUSIONS

Vulnerabilities in software are a persistent problem and one of the root causes of many security incidents. Discovering security flaws is a challenging and often daunting task, as automatic approaches are inherently limited in spotting vulnerable code. As a remedy, we introduce CHUCKY in this paper, a method that can automatically detect missing checks in software and thereby help to accelerate the manual auditing of source code. Instead of struggling with the limits of automatic approaches, our method aims at assisting a human analyst by providing information about missing security checks and potential fixes. Our evaluation demonstrates the potential of this approach, since we are able to uncover 12 previously unknown vulnerabilities in popular software projects among the first missing checks.

Finally, CHUCKY can interface with many other techniques for finding vulnerabilities. For example, exposed missing checks might be further analyzed using techniques for fuzzing or symbolic execution. These techniques could allow to narrow down the actual consequences of a missing check and might help to rank detected flaws according to their severity. Moreover, we currently plan to integrate CHUCKY in a visual development environment and analyze its capabilities to expose missing security checks directly during the development of software.

Acknowledgments

The authors acknowledge funding from *BMBF* under the project PROSEC (FKZ 01BY1145).

References

[1] T. Avgerinos, S. K. Cha, B. L. T. Hao, and D. Brumley. AEG: Automatic Exploit Generation. In *Proc. of Network and Distributed System Security Symposium (NDSS)*, 2011.

[2] A. Bradley. The use of the area under the ROC curve in the evaluation of machine learning algorithms. *Pattern Recognition*, 30(7):1145–1159, 1997.

[3] B. Chess and M. Gerschefske. Rough auditing tool for security. Google Code, `http://code.google.com/p/rough-auditing-tool-for-security/`, visited February, 2013.

[4] M. Cova, V. Felmetsger, G. Banks, and G. Vigna. Static detection of vulnerabilities in x86 executables. In *Proc. of Annual Computer Security Applications Conference (ACSAC)*, pages 269–278, 2006.

[5] A. DeKok. Pscan: A limited problem scanner for c source files. `http://deployingradius.com/pscan/`, visited February, 2013.

[6] D. Engler, D. Y. Chen, S. Hallem, A. Chou, and B. Chelf. Bugs as deviant behavior: A general approach to inferring errors in systems code. In *Proc. of ACM Symposium on Operating Systems Principles (SOSP)*, pages 57–72, 2001.

[7] D. Evans and D. Larochelle. Improving security using extensible lightweight static analysis. *IEEE Software*, 19(1):42–51, 2002.

[8] N. Falliere, L. O. Murchu, , and E. Chien. W32.stuxnet dossier. Symantec Corporation, 2011.

[9] P. Godefroid, M. Y. Levin, and D. Molnar. SAGE: whitebox fuzzing for security testing. *Communications of the ACM*, 55(3):40–44, 2012.

[10] N. Gruska, A. Wasylkowski, and A. Zeller. Learning from 6,000 projects: lightweight cross-project anomaly detection. In *Proc. of the International Symposium on Software Testing and Analysis (ISSTA)*, pages 119–130, 2010.

[11] S. Heelan. Vulnerability detection systems: Think cyborg, not robot. *IEEE Security & Privacy*, 9(3):74–77, 2011.

[12] J. Hopcroft and J. Motwani, R. Ullmann. *Introduction to Automata Theory, Languages, and Computation*. Addison-Wesley, 2 edition, 2001.

[13] N. Jovanovic, C. Kruegel, and E. Kirda. Pixy: A static analysis tool for detecting web application vulnerabilities. In *Proc. of IEEE Symposium on Security and Privacy*, pages 6–263, 2006.

[14] J. A. Kupsch and B. P. Miller. Manual vs. automated vulnerability assessment: A case study. In *Proc. of Workshop on Managing Insider Security Threats (MIST)*, pages 83–97, 2009.

[15] J. R. Larus, T. Ball, M. Das, R. DeLine, M. Fähndrich, J. Pincus, S. K. Rajamani, and R. Venkatapathy. Righting software. *IEEE Software*, 21(3):92–100, 2004.

[16] Z. Li and Y. Zhou. PR-Miner: automatically extracting implicit programming rules and detecting violations in large software code. In *Proc. of European Software Engineering Conference (ESEC)*, pages 306–315, 2005.

[17] B. Livshits and M. S. Lam. Finding security vulnerabilities in java applications with static analysis. In *Proc. of USENIX Security Symposium*, 2005.

[18] B. Livshits, A. V. Nori, S. K. Rajamani, and A. Banerjee. Merlin: specification inference for explicit information flow problems. In *Proc. of ACM SIGPLAN International Conference on Programming Languages Design and Implementation (PLDI)*, 2009.

[19] B. Livshits and T. Zimmermann. Dynamine: finding common error patterns by mining software revision histories. In *Proc. of European Software Engineering Conference (ESEC)*, pages 296–305, 2005.

[20] L. Moonen. Generating robust parsers using island grammars. In *Proc. of Working Conference on Reverse Engineering (WCRE)*, pages 13–22, 2001.

[21] H. Moore. Security flaws in universal plug and play: Unplug. don't play. Technical report, Rapid 7, 2013.

[22] C. Mulliner, N. Golde, and J.-P. Seifert. Sms of death: From analyzing to attacking mobile phones on a large scale. In *Proc. of USENIX Security Symposium*, 2011.

[23] J. Newsome and D. Song. Dynamic taint analysis for automatic detection, analysis, and signature generation of exploits on commodity software. In *Proc. of Network and Distributed System Security Symposium (NDSS)*, 2005.

[24] J. W. Oh. Recent Java exploitation trends and malware. Presentation at Black Hat Las Vegas, 2012.

[25] T. Parr and R. Quong. ANTLR: A predicated-LL(k) parser generator. *Software Practice and Experience*, 25:789–810, 1995.

[26] G. Portokalidis, A. Slowinska, and H. Bos. Argos: an emulator for fingerprinting zero-day attacks for advertised honeypots with automatic signature generation. *ACM SIGOPS Operating Systems Review*, 40(4):15–27, Apr. 2006.

[27] K. Rieck and P. Laskov. Linear-time computation of similarity measures for sequential data. *Journal of Machine Learning Research (JMLR)*, 9(Jan):23–48, Jan. 2008.

[28] G. Salton and M. J. McGill. *Introduction to Modern Information Retrieval*. McGraw-Hill, 1986.

[29] E. Schwartz, T. Avgerinos, and D. Brumley. All you ever wanted to know about dynamic taint analysis and forward symbolic execution (but might have been afraid to ask). In *Proc. of IEEE Symposium on Security and Privacy*, pages 317–331, 2010.

[30] U. Shankar, K. Talwar, J. S. Foster, and D. Wagner. Detecting format string vulnerabilities with type qualifiers. In *Proc. of USENIX Security Symposium*, pages 201–218, 2001.

[31] S. Son, K. S. McKinley, and V. Shmatikov. Rolecast: finding missing security checks when you do not know what checks are. In *Proc. of ACM International Conference on Object Oriented Programming Systems Languages and Applications (SPLASH)*, 2011.

[32] V. Srivastava, M. D. Bond, K. S. Mckinley, and V. Shmatikov. A security policy oracle: Detecting security holes using multiple API implementations. In *Proc. of ACM SIGPLAN International Conference on Programming Languages Design and Implementation (PLDI)*, 2011.

[33] M. Sutton, A. Greene, and P. Amini. *Fuzzing: Brute Force Vulnerability Discovery*. Addison-Wesley Professional, 2007.

[34] L. Tan, X. Zhang, X. Ma, W. Xiong, and Y. Zhou. Autoises: automatically inferring security specifications and detecting violations. In *Proc. of USENIX Security Symposium*, 2008.

[35] S. Thummalapenta and T. Xie. Alattin: Mining alternative patterns for detecting neglected conditions. In *Proc. of the International Conference on Automated Software Engineering (ASE)*, pages 283–294, 2009.

[36] J. Viega, J. Bloch, Y. Kohno, and G. McGraw. ITS4: A static vulnerability scanner for C and C++ code. In *Proc. of Annual Computer Security Applications Conference (ACSAC)*, pages 257–267, 2000.

[37] T. Wang, T. Wei, Z. Lin, and W. Zou. IntScope: Automatically detecting integer overflow vulnerability in x86 binary using symbolic execution. In *Proc. of Network and Distributed System Security Symposium (NDSS)*, 2009.

[38] A. Wasylkowski, A. Zeller, and C. Lindig. Detecting object usage anomalies. In *Proc. of European Software Engineering Conference (ESEC)*, pages 35–44, 2007.

[39] D. A. Wheeler. Flawfinder. `http://www.dwheeler.com/flawfinder/`, visited February, 2013.

[40] C. C. Williams and J. K. Hollingsworth. Automatic mining of source code repositories to improve bug finding techniques. *IEEE Transactions on Software Engineering*, 31:466–480, 2005.

[41] F. Yamaguchi, F. Lindner, and K. Rieck. Vulnerability extrapolation: Assisted discovery of vulnerabilities using machine learning. In *Proc. of 5th USENIX Workshop on Offensive Technologies (WOOT)*, pages 118–127, Aug. 2011.

[42] F. Yamaguchi, M. Lottmann, and K. Rieck. Generalized vulnerability extrapolation using abstract syntax trees. In *Proc. of 28th Annual Computer Security Applications Conference (ACSAC)*, pages 359–368, Dec. 2012.

[43] H. Zhong, T. Xie, L. Zhang, J. Pei, and H. Mei. Mapo: Mining and recommending API usage patterns. In *Proc. of the European Conference on Object-Oriented Programming(ECOOP)*, pages 318–343, 2009.

Scheduling Black-box Mutational Fuzzing

Maverick Woo   Sang Kil Cha   Samantha Gottlieb   David Brumley
Carnegie Mellon University
{pooh,sangkilc,sgottlie,dbrumley}@cmu.edu

ABSTRACT

Black-box mutational fuzzing is a simple yet effective technique to find bugs in software. Given a set of program-seed pairs, we ask how to schedule the fuzzings of these pairs in order to maximize the number of unique bugs found at any point in time. We develop an analytic framework using a mathematical model of black-box mutational fuzzing and use it to evaluate 26 existing and new randomized online scheduling algorithms. Our experiments show that one of our new scheduling algorithms outperforms the multi-armed bandit algorithm in the current version of the CERT Basic Fuzzing Framework (BFF) by finding 1.5× more unique bugs in the same amount of time.

Categories and Subject Descriptors

D.2.5 [**Software Engineering**]: Testing and Debugging—*Testing Tools*

General Terms

Security

Keywords

Software Security; Fuzz Configuration Scheduling

1 Introduction

A General (or professor) walks into a cramped cubicle, telling the lone security analyst (or graduate student) that she has one week to find a zero-day exploit against a certain popular OS distribution, all the while making it sound as if this task is as easy as catching the next bus. Although our analyst has access to several program analysis tools for finding bugs [8, 10, 11, 21] and generating exploits [4, 9], she still faces a harsh reality: the target OS distribution contains thousands of programs, each with potentially tens or even hundreds of yet undiscovered bugs. What tools should she use for this mission? Which programs should she analyze, and in what order? How much time should she dedicate to a given program? Above all, how can she maximize her likelihood of success within the given time budget?

CCS'13, November 4–8, 2013, Berlin, Germany.

http://dx.doi.org/10.1145/2508859.2516736.

In this paper, we focus on the setting where our analyst has chosen to find bugs via *black-box mutational fuzzing.* At a high level, this technique takes as input a program p and a seed s that is usually assumed to be a well-formed input for p. Then, a program known as a black-box mutational *fuzzer* is used to *fuzz* the program p with the seed s, i.e., execute p on a potentially malformed input x obtained by randomly mutating s in a precise manner to be described in §2. Through repeated fuzzings, we may discover a number of inputs that crash p. These crashing inputs are then passed to downstream analyses to triage each crash into a corresponding bug, test each newly-discovered bug for exploitability, and generate exploits when possible.

Intuitively, our analyst may try to improve her chances by finding the greatest number of *unique* bugs among the programs to be analyzed within the given time budget. To model this, let us introduce the notion of a *fuzz campaign.* We assume our analyst has already obtained a list of program-seed pairs (p_i, s_i) to be fuzzed through prior manual and/or automatic analysis. A fuzz campaign takes this list as input and reports each new (previously unseen) bug when it is discovered. As a simplification, we also assume that the fuzz campaign is orchestrated in *epochs.* At the beginning of each epoch we select one program-seed pair based only on information obtained during the campaign, and we fuzz that pair for the entire epoch. This latter assumption has two subtle but important implications. First, though it does not limit us to fuzzing with only one computer, it does require that every computer in the campaign fuzz the same program-seed pair during an epoch. Second, while our definition of a *fuzz configuration* in §2 is more general than a program-seed pair, we also explain our decision to equate these two concepts in our present work. As such, what we need to select for each epoch is really a fuzz configuration, which gives rise to our naming of the *Fuzz Configuration Scheduling* (FCS) problem.

To find the greatest number of unique bugs given the above problem setting, our analyst must allocate her time wisely. Since initially she has no information on which configuration will yield more new bugs, she should explore the configurations and reduce her risk by fuzzing each configuration for an adequate amount of time. As she starts to identify some configurations that she believes may yield more new bugs in the future, she should also exploit this information by increasing the time allocated to fuzz these configurations. Of course, any increase in exploitation reduces exploration, which may cause our analyst to under-explore and miss configurations that are capable of yielding more new bugs. This is the classic "exploration vs. exploitation" trade-off, which signifies that we are dealing with a Multi-Armed Bandit (MAB) problem [5].

Unfortunately, merely recognizing the MAB nature of our problem is not sufficient to give us an easy solution. As we explain in §3, even though there are many existing MAB algorithms and some even come with excellent theoretical guarantees, we are not aware of any MAB algorithm that is designed to cater to the specifics of finding *unique* bugs using black-box mutational fuzzing. For example, suppose we have just found a crash by fuzzing a program-seed pair and the crash gets triaged to a new bug. Should an MAB algorithm consider this as a high reward, thus steering itself to fuzz this pair more frequently in the future? Exactly what does this information tell us about the probability of finding another new bug from this pair in future fuzzes? What if the bug was instead a duplicate, i.e., one that has already been discovered in a previous fuzz run? Does that mean we should assign a zero reward since this bug does not contribute to the number of unique bugs found?

As a first step to answer these questions and design more suitable MAB algorithms for our problem, we discover that the memoryless property of black-box mutational fuzzing allows us to formally model the repeated fuzzings of a configuration as a bug arrival process. Our insight is that this process is a *weighted* variant of the Coupon Collector's Problem (CCP) where each coupon type has its own fixed but initially *unknown* arrival probability. We explain in §4.1 how to view each fuzz run as the arrival of a coupon and each unique bug as a coupon type. Using this analogy, it is easy to understand the need to use the weighted variant of the CCP (WCCP) and the challenge in estimating the arrival probabilities.

The WCCP connection has proven to be more powerful than simply affording us clean and formal notation—not only does it explain why our problem is impossible to optimize in its most general setting due to the No Free Lunch Theorem, but it also pinpoints how we can circumvent this impossibility result if we are willing to make certain assumptions about the arrival probabilities in the WCCP (§4.2). Of course, we also understand that our analyst may not be comfortable in making any such assumptions. This is why we have also investigated how she can use the statistical concept of *confidence intervals* to estimate an upperbound on the sum of the arrival probabilities of the unique bugs that remain to be discovered in a fuzz configuration. We argue in §4.3 why this upperbound offers a pragmatic way to cope with the above impossibility result.

Having developed these analytical tools, we explore the design space of online algorithms for our problem in §4.4. We investigate two epoch types, five belief functions that estimate future bug arrival using past observations, two MAB algorithms that use such belief functions and three that do not. By combining these dimensions, we obtain 26 online algorithms for our problem. While some of these algorithms have appeared in prior work, the majority of them are new. In addition, we also present offline algorithms for our problem in §4.5. In the case where the sets of unique bugs from each configuration are disjoint, we obtain an efficient algorithm that computes the offline *optimal*, i.e., the maximum number of unique bugs that can be found by any algorithm in any given time budget. In the other case where these sets may overlap, we also propose an efficient heuristic that lowerbounds the offline optimal.

To evaluate our online algorithms, we built FUZZSIM, a novel replay-based fuzz simulation system that we present in §5. FUZZSIM is capable of simulating any online algorithm using pre-recorded fuzzing data. We used it to implement numerous algorithms, including the 26 presented in this paper. We also collected two extensive sets of fuzzing data based on the most recent stable release of the Debian Linux distribution up to the time of our data collection. To this end, we first assembled 100 program-seed pairs comprising FFMpeg with 100 different seeds and another 100 pairs comprising 100 different Linux file conversion utilities, each with an input seed that has been manually verified to be valid. Then, we fuzzed *each* of these 200 program-seed pairs for 10 days, which amounts to 48,000 CPU hours of fuzzing in total. The performance of our online algorithms on these two datasets is presented in §6. In addition, we are also releasing FUZZSIM as well as our datasets in support of open science. Besides replicating our experiments, this will also enable fellow researchers to evaluate other algorithms. For details, please visit `http://security.ece.cmu.edu/fuzzsim/`.

2 Problem Setting and Notation

Let us start by setting out the definitions and assumptions needed to mathematically model black-box mutational fuzzing. Our model is motivated by and consistent with real-world fuzzers such as **zzuf** [16]. We then present our problem statement and discuss several algorithmic considerations. For the rest of this paper, the terms "fuzzer" and "fuzzing" refer to the black-box mutational variant unless otherwise stated.

2.1 Black-box Mutational Fuzzing

Black-box mutational fuzzing is a dynamic bug-finding technique. It endeavors to find bugs in a given program p by running it on a sequence of inputs generated by randomly mutating a given seed input s. The program that generates these inputs and executes p on them is known as a black-box mutational fuzzer. In principle, there is no restriction on s other than it being a string with a finite length; however, in practice, s is often chosen to be a well-formed input for p in the interest of finding bugs in p more effectively. With each execution, p either crashes or properly terminates. Multiple crashes, however, may be due to the same underlying bug. Thus there needs to be a bug-triage process to map each crash into its corresponding bug. Understanding the effects of these multiplicities is key to analyzing black-box mutational fuzzing.

To formally define black-box mutational fuzzing, we need a notion of "random mutations" for bit strings. In what follows, let $|s|$ denote the bit-length of s.

DEFINITION 2.1. *A* random mutation of a bit b *is the exclusive-or*[1] *of the bit b and a uniformly-chosen bit. With respect to a given* mutation ratio $r \in [0, 1]$, *a* random mutation of a string s *is generated by first selecting $d = r \cdot |s|$ different bit-positions uniformly at random among the $\binom{|s|}{d}$ possible combinations and then randomly mutating those d bits in s.*

[1]Mutations in the form of unconditionally setting or unsetting the bit are possible, but they are both harder to analyze mathematically and less frequently used in practice. To justify the latter, we note that **zzuf** defaults to exclusive-or.

Definition 2.2. *A black-box mutational fuzzer is a randomized algorithm that takes as input a fuzz configuration, which comprises (i) a program p, (ii) a seed input s, and (iii) a mutation ratio $r \in [0, 1]$. In a* fuzz run, *the fuzzer generates an input x by randomly mutating s with the mutation ratio r and then runs p on x. The* outcome *of this fuzz run is a crash or a proper termination of p.*

At this point, it is convenient to set up one additional notation to complement Definition 2.1. Let $H_d(s)$ denote the set of all strings obtained by randomly-mutating s with the mutation ratio $r = d/|s|$. This notation highlights the equivalence between the set of all obtainable inputs and the set of all $|s|$-bit strings within a Hamming distance of d from s. In this notation, the input string x in Definition 2.1 is simply a string chosen uniformly at random from $H_d(s)$. As we explain below, in this paper we use a globally-fixed mutation ratio and therefore d is fixed once s is given. This is why we simply write $H(s)$ instead of $H_d(s)$.

We now state and justify several assumptions of our mathematical model, all of which are satisfied by typical fuzzers in practice.

Assumption 1. *Each seed input has* finite *length.*

This assumption is always satisfied when fuzzing file inputs. In practice, some fuzzers can also perform stream fuzzing, which randomly mutates each bit in an input stream with a user-configurable probability. Notice that while the expected number of randomly-mutated bits is fixed, the actual number is *not*. We do not model stream fuzzing.

Assumption 2. *An execution of the program exhibits* exactly *one of the following two possible outcomes—it either crashes or properly terminates.*

In essence, this assumption means we focus exclusively on finding bugs that lead to crashes. Finding logical bugs that do not lead to crashes would typically require a correctness specification of the program under test. At present, such specifications are rare in practice and therefore this assumption does not impose a severe restriction.

Assumption 3. *The outcome of an execution of the program depends* solely *on the input x generated by the fuzzer.*

This assumption ensures we are not finding bugs caused by input channels not under the fuzzer's control. Since the generated input alone determines whether the program crashes or terminates properly, all bugs found during fuzzing are deterministically reproducible. In practice, inputs that do not cause a crash in downstream analyses are discarded.

Mutation Ratio. We include the mutation ratio as a third parameter in our definition of fuzz configurations given in Definition 2.2. Our choice reflects the importance of this parameter in practice since different seeds may need to be fuzzed at different mutation ratios to be effective in finding bugs. However, in order to evaluate a large number of scheduling algorithms, our work is based on a replay simulation as detailed in §5. Gathering the ground-truth fuzzing data for such simulations is resource-intensive, prohibitively so if we examine multiple mutation ratios. As such, our current project globally fixes the mutation ratio at 0.0004, the default value used in `zzuf`. Accordingly, we suppress the third parameter of a fuzz configuration in this paper, effectively equating program-seed pairs with fuzz configurations. For further discussion related to the mutation ratio, see §6.6.

2.2 Problem Statement

Given a list of K fuzz configurations $\{(p_1, s_1), \cdots, (p_K, s_K)\}$ and a time budget T, the *Fuzz Configuration Scheduling* problem seeks to maximize the number of *unique* bugs discovered in a fuzz campaign that runs for a duration of length T. A *fuzz campaign* is divided into *epochs*, starting with epoch 1. We consider two *epoch types*: fixed-run and fixed-time. In a fixed-run campaign, each epoch corresponds to a constant number of fuzz runs; since the time required for individual fuzz runs may vary, fixed-run epochs may take variable amounts of time. On the other hand, in a fixed-time campaign, each epoch corresponds to a constant amount of time. Thus, the number of fuzz runs completed may vary across fixed-time epochs.

An online algorithm $\mathcal{A}$ for the Fuzz Configuration Scheduling problem operates before each epoch starts. When the campaign starts, $\mathcal{A}$ receives the number K. Suppose the campaign has completed ℓ epochs so far. Before epoch $(\ell + 1)$ begins, $\mathcal{A}$ should select a number $i \in [1, K]$ based on the information it has received from the campaign. Then the entire epoch $(\ell + 1)$ is devoted to fuzzing (p_i, s_i). When the epoch ends, $\mathcal{A}$ receives a sequence of IDs representing the outcomes of the fuzz runs completed during the epoch. If an outcome is a crash, then the returned ID is the bug ID computed by the bug triage process, which we assume is non-zero. Otherwise, the outcome is a proper termination, and the returned ID is 0. Also, any ID that has never been encountered by the campaign prior to epoch $(\ell + 1)$ is marked as new. Notice that a new ID can signify either the first proper termination in the campaign or a new bug discovered during epoch $(\ell + 1)$. Besides the list of IDs, $\mathcal{A}$ also receives statistical information about the epoch. In a fixed-run campaign, it receives the time spent in the epoch; in a fixed-time campaign, it receives the number of fuzz runs that ended inside the epoch.

Algorithmic Considerations. We now turn to a few technical issues that we withheld from the above problem statement. First, we allow $\mathcal{A}$ to be either deterministic or randomized. This admits the use of various existing MAB algorithms, many of which are indeed randomized.

Second, notice that $\mathcal{A}$ receives only the number of configurations K but not the actual configurations. This formulation is to prevent $\mathcal{A}$ from analyzing the content of any p_i's or s_i's. Similarly, we prevent $\mathcal{A}$ from analyzing bugs by sending it only the bug IDs but not any concrete representation.

Third, $\mathcal{A}$ also does not receive the time budget T. This forces $\mathcal{A}$ to make its decisions without knowing how much time is left. Therefore, $\mathcal{A}$ has to attempt to discover new bugs as early as possible. While this rules out any algorithm that adjusts its degree of exploration based on the time left, we argue that this not a severe restriction from the perspective of algorithm design. For example, one of the algorithms we use is the EXP3.S.1 algorithm [2]. It copes with the unknown time horizon by partitioning time into exponentially longer periods and picking new parameters at the beginning of each period, which has a known length.

Fourth, our analysis assumes that the K fuzz configurations are chosen such that they yield disjoint sets of bugs. This assumption is needed so that we can consider the bug arrival process of fuzzing each configuration independently. While this assumption may be valid when every configuration involves a different program, as in one of our two datasets, satisfying it when one program can appear in multiple configurations is non-trivial. In practice, it is achieved by selecting seeds that exercise different code regions. For example, in our other data set, we use seeds of various file formats to fuzz the different file parsers in a media player.

Finally, at present we do not account for the time spent in bug triage, though this process requires considerable time. In practice, triaging a crash takes approximately the same amount of time as the fuzz run that initially found the crash. Therefore, bug triage can potentially account for over half of the time spent in an epoch if crashes are extremely frequent. We plan to incorporate this consideration into our project at a future time.

3 Multi-Armed Bandits

As explained in §1, the Fuzz Configuration Scheduling problem is an instance of the classic Multi-Armed Bandit (MAB) problem. This has already been observed by previous researchers. For example, the CERT Basic Fuzzing Framework (BFF) [14], which supports fuzzing a single program with a collection of seeds and a set of mutation ratios, uses an MAB algorithm to select among the seed-ratio pairs during a fuzz campaign. However, we must stress that recognizing the MAB nature of our problem is merely a first step. In particular, we should not expect an MAB algorithm with provably "good" performance, such as one from the UCB [3] or the EXP3 [2] families, to yield good results in our problem setting. There are at least two reasons for this.

First, although many of these algorithms are proven to have optimal *regret* in various forms, the most common form of regret does not actually give good guarantees in our problem setting. In particular, this form of regret measures the difference between the expected reward of an algorithm and the reward obtained by consistently fuzzing the single best configuration that yields the greatest number of unique bugs. However, we are interested in evaluating performance relative to the total number of unique bugs from *all* K configurations, which may be much greater than the number from one *fixed* configuration. Thus, the low-regret guarantee of many MAB algorithms is in fact measuring against a target that is likely to be much lower than what we desire. In other words, given our problem setting, these algorithms are not guaranteed to be competitive at all!

Second, while there exist algorithms with provably low regret in a form suited to our problem setting, the actual regret bounds of these algorithms often do not give meaningful values in practice. For example, one of the MAB algorithms we use is the EXP3.S.1 algorithm [2], proven to have an expected *worst-case regret* of $\frac{S+2e}{\sqrt{2}-1}\sqrt{2K\ell\ln(K\ell)}$, where S is a certain hardness measure of the problem instance as defined in [2, §8] and ℓ is the number of epochs in our problem setting. Even assuming the easiest case where S equals to 1 and picking K to be a modest value of 10, the value of this bound when $\ell = 4$ is already slightly above 266. However, as we see in §6, the number of bugs we found in our two datasets are 200 and 223 respectively. What this means is that this regret bound is very likely to dwarf the number of bugs that can be found in real-world software after a very small number of epochs. In other words, even though we have the right kind of guarantee from EXP3.S.1, the guarantee quickly becomes meaningless in practical terms.

Having said the above, we remark that this simply means such optimal regret guarantees may not be useful in *ensuring* good results. As we will see in §6, EXP3.S.1 can still obtain reasonably good results in the right setting.

4 Algorithms for the FCS Problem

Our goal in this section is to investigate how to design online algorithms for the Fuzz Configuration Scheduling problem. We largely focus on developing the design space (§4.4), making heavy use of the mathematical foundation we lay out in §4.1 and §4.3. Additionally, we present two impossibility results in §4.2, one of which requires a precise condition that greatly informs our algorithm design effort. We also present two offline algorithms for our problem. While such algorithms may not be applicable in practice, a unique aspect of our project allows us to use them as benchmarks which we measure our online algorithms against. We explain this along with the offline algorithms in §4.5.

4.1 Fuzzing as a Weighted CCP

Let us start by mathematically modeling the process of repeatedly fuzzing a configuration. As we explained in §2, the output of this process is a stream of crashes intermixed with proper terminations, which is then transformed into a stream of IDs by a bug triage process. Since we want to maximize the number of unique bugs found, we are naturally interested in when a new bug arrives in this process. This insight quickly leads us to the Coupon Collector's Problem (CCP), a classical arrival process in probability theory.

The CCP concerns a consumer who obtains one coupon with each purchase of a box of breakfast cereal. Suppose there are M different coupon types in circulation. One basic question about the CCP is: what is the expected number of purchases required before the consumer amasses k ($\leq M$) *unique* coupons? In its most elementary formulation, each coupon is chosen uniformly at random among the M coupon types. In this setting, many questions related to the CCP—including the one above—are relatively easy to answer.

Viewing Fuzzing as WCCP with Unknown Weights. Unfortunately, our problem setting actually demands a weighted variant of the CCP which we dub the WCCP. Intuitively, this is because the probabilities of the different outcomes from a fuzz run are not necessarily (and unlikely to be) uniform. This observation has also been made by Arcuri et al. [1].

Let $(M-1)$ be the actual number of unique bugs discoverable by fuzzing a certain configuration. Then including proper termination of a fuzz run as an outcome gives us exactly M distinct outcome types. We thus relate the process of repeatedly fuzzing a configuration to the WCCP by viewing fuzz run outcomes as coupons and their associated IDs as coupon types.

However, unlike usual formulations of the WCCP where the distribution of outcomes across type is given, in our problem setting this distribution is unknown *a priori*. In particular, there is no way to know the true value of M for a configuration without exhaustively fuzzing all possible mutations. As such, we utilize statistical estimations of these distributions rather than the ground-truth in our algorithm design. An important question to consider is whether accurate estimations are feasible.

We now explain why we prefer the sets of bugs from different configurations used in a campaign to be disjoint. Observe that our model of a campaign is a combination of multiple independent WCCP processes. If a bug that is new to one process has already been discovered in another, then this bug cannot contribute to the total number of unique bugs. This means that overlap in the sets of bugs diminishes the fidelity of our model, so that any algorithm relying on its predictions may suffer in performance.

WCCP Notation. Before we go on, let us set up some additional notation related to the WCCP. In an effort to avoid excessive indices, our notation implicitly assumes a fixed configuration (p_i, s_i) that is made apparent by context. For example, M, the number of possible outcomes when fuzzing a given configuration as defined above, follows this convention.

(i) Consider the fixed sequence σ of outcomes we obtain in the course of fuzzing (p_i, s_i) during a campaign. We label an outcome as type k if it belongs to the kth distinct type of outcome in σ. Let $\mathcal{P}_k$ denote the probability of encountering a type-k outcome in σ, i.e.,

$$\mathcal{P}_k = \frac{|\{x \in H(s_i) : x \text{ triggers an outcome of type } k\}|}{|H(s_i)|}. \quad (1)$$

(ii) Although both the number and frequency of outcome types obtainable by fuzzing (p_i, s_i) are unknown a priori, during a campaign we do have empirical observations for these quantities up to any point in σ. Let $\hat{M}(\ell)$ be the number of distinct outcomes observed from epoch 1 through epoch ℓ. Let $n_k(\ell)$ be the number of inputs triggering outcomes of type k observed throughout these ℓ epochs. Notice that over the course of a campaign, the sequence σ is segmented into subsequences, each of which corresponds to an epoch in which (p_i, s_i) is chosen. Thus, the values of $\hat{M}(\cdot)$ and $n_k(\cdot)$ will not change if (p_i, s_i) is not chosen for the current epoch. With this notation, we can also express the empirical probability of detecting a type-k outcome following epoch ℓ as

$$\hat{\mathcal{P}}_k(\ell) = \frac{n_k(\ell)}{\sum_{k'=1}^{\hat{M}(\ell)} n_{k'}(\ell)}.$$

4.2 Impossibility Results

No Free Lunch. The absence of any assumption on the distribution of outcome types in the WCCP quickly leads us to our first impossibility result. In particular, *no* algorithm can consistently outperform other algorithms for the FCS problem. This follows from a well-known impossibility result in optimization theory, namely the "No Free Lunch" theorem by Wolpert and Macready [22]. Quoting Wolpert and Macready, their theorem implies that "any two optimization algorithms are equivalent when their performance is averaged across all possible problems." In our problem setting, maximizing the number of bugs found in epoch $(\ell + 1)$ amounts to, for each configuration, estimating its $\mathcal{P}_{\hat{M}(\ell)+1}$ in equation (1) using only past observations from that configuration. Intuitively, by averaging across all possible outcome type distributions, any estimation will be incorrect *sufficiently often* and thus lead to suboptimal behavior that cancels any advantage of one algorithm over another.

While we may consider this result to be easy to obtain once we have properly set up our problem using §2 and §4.1, we consider it to be an important intellectual contribution for the pragmatic practitioners who remain confident that they *can* design algorithms that outperform others. In particular, the statement of the No Free Lunch theorem itself reveals precisely how we can circumvent its conclusion—our estimation procedure must *assume* the outcome type distributions have particular characteristics. Our motto is thus "there is no free lunch—please bring your own prior!"

Tight K-Competitiveness. Our second impossibility result shows that there are problem instances in which the time spent by any deterministic online algorithm to find a given number of unique bugs in a fixed-time campaign is at least K times larger than the time spent by an optimal offline algorithm. Using the terminology of competitive analysis, this shows that the competitive ratio of any deterministic online algorithm for this problem is at least K.

To show this, we fix a deterministic algorithm A and construct a contrived problem instance in which there is only *one* bug among all the configurations in a campaign. Since A is deterministic, there exists a unique pair (p_i^*, s_i^*) that gets chosen *last*. In other words, the other $(K-1)$ pairs have all been fuzzed for at least one epoch when (p_i^*, s_i^*) is fuzzed for the first time. If the lone bug is only triggered by fuzzing (p_i^*, s_i^*), then A will have to fuzz for at least K epochs to find it.

For an optimal offline algorithm, handling this contrived scenario is trivial. Since it is offline, it has full knowledge of the outcome distributions, enabling it to hone in on the special pair (p_i^*, s_i^*) and find the bug in the first epoch. This establishes that K is a lowerbound for the competitive ratio of any deterministic algorithm.

Finally, we observe that Round-Robin is a deterministic online algorithm that achieves the competitive ratio K in *every* problem instance. It follows immediately that K is tight.

4.3 Upperbounding the Probability of Seeing a New Outcome During Fuzzing

Having seen such strong impossibility results, let us consider what a pragmatist might do before bringing in any prior on the outcome type distribution. In other words, if we do not want to make any assumptions on this distribution, is there a justifiable approach to designing online algorithms for the FCS problem?

We argue that the answer is yes. Consider two program-seed pairs (p_1, s_1) and (p_2, s_2) for which we have *upperbounds* on the probability of finding a new outcome if we fuzz them once more. Assume that the upperbound for (p_1, s_1) is the higher of the two.

We stress that what we know are merely upperbounds—it is still possible that the true probability of yielding a new outcome from fuzzing (p_1, s_1) is lower than that of (p_2, s_2). Nonetheless, with no information beyond the ordering of these upperbounds, fuzzing (p_1, s_1) first is arguably the more prudent choice. This is because to do otherwise would indicate a belief that the actual probability of finding a new outcome by fuzzing (p_1, s_1) in the next fuzz run is lower than the upperbound for (p_2, s_2).

Accepting this argument, how might we obtain such upperbounds? We introduce the Rule of Three for this purpose.

Rule of Three. Consider an experiment of independent Bernoulli trials with identical success and failure probabilities p and $q = (1-p)$. Suppose we have carried out $N \geq 1$ trials so far and every trial has been a success. What can we say about q other than the fact that it must be (i) at least 0 to be a valid probability and (ii) strictly less than 1 since p is evidently positive? In particular, can we place a lower upperbound on q?

Unfortunately, the answer is a resounding *no*: even with q arbitrarily close to 1, we still have $(p^N > 0)$. This means our observation really *could* have happened even if it is extremely unlikely.

Fortunately, if we are willing to rule out the possibility of encountering extremely unlikely events, then we may compute a lower upperbound for q by means of a confidence interval. For example, a 95% confidence interval on q outputs an interval that includes the true value of q of the underlying experiment with 95% certainty. In other words, if the outputted interval does not contain the true value of q for the experiment, then the observed event must have a likelihood of at most 5%.

For the above situation, there is particularly neat technique to compute a 95% confidence interval on q. Known as the "Rule of Three", this method simply outputs 0 and $3/N$ for the lowerbound and upperbound, respectively. The lowerbound is trivial, and the upperbound has been shown to be a good approximation for $N > 30$. See [15] for more information on this technique, including the relationship between 95% confidence and the constant 3.

How We Use Rule of Three. In order to apply the Rule of Three, we must adapt our fuzzing experiments with any $M > 1$ possible outcome types to fit the mold of Bernoulli trials.

We make use of a small trick. Suppose we have just finished epoch ℓ and consider a particular configuration (p_i, s_i). Using our notation, we have observed $\hat{M}(\ell)$ different outcomes so far and for $1 \le k \le \hat{M}(\ell)$, we have observed $n_k(\ell)$ counts of outcome of type k. Let $N(\ell) = \sum_{k=1}^{\hat{M}(\ell)} n_k(\ell)$ denote the total number of fuzz runs for this pair through epoch ℓ. The trick is to define a "success" to be finding an outcome of type 1 through type $\hat{M}(\ell)$. Then, in hindsight, it *is* the case that our experiment has only yielded success so far.

With this observation, we may now apply the Rule of Three to conclude that $[0, 3/N(\ell)]$ is a 95% confidence interval on the "failure" probability—the probability that fuzzing this configuration will result in an outcome type that we have *not* seen before, i.e., a new outcome. Then, as desired, we have an easy-to-compute upperbound on the probability of finding a new outcome for each configuration.

We introduce one more piece of notation before proceeding: define the Remaining Probability Mass (RPM) of (p_i, s_i) at the end of epoch ℓ, denoted $\text{RPM}(\ell)$, to be the probability of finding a new outcome if we fuzz (p_i, s_i) once more. Note that the pair in $\text{RPM}(\ell)$ is implicit, and that this value is upperbounded by $3/N(\ell)$ if we accept a 95% confidence interval.

4.4 Design Space

In this section, we explore the design space that a pragmatist may attempt when designing online algorithms for the Fuzz Configuration Scheduling problem. A depiction of the design space, along with our experimental results, is given in Table 2 in §6. Our focus here is to explain our motivation for choosing the three dimensions we explore and the particular choices we include in each dimension. By combining these dimensions, we obtain 26 online algorithms for our problem. We implemented these algorithms inside a simulator, FuzzSim, the detail of which is presented in §5.

Epoch Type. We consider two possible definitions of an epoch in a fuzz campaign. The first is the more traditional choice and is used in the current version of CERT BFF v2.6 [14]; the second is our proposal.

Fixed-Run. Each epoch executes a constant number of fuzz runs. In FuzzSim, a fixed-run epoch consists of 200 runs. Note that any differential in fuzzing speed across configurations translates into variation in the time spent in fixed-run epochs.

Fixed-Time. Each epoch is allocated a fixed amount of time. In FuzzSim, a fixed-time epoch lasts for 10 seconds. Our motivation to investigate this epoch type is to see how heavily epoch time variation affects the results obtained by systems with fixed-run epochs.

Belief Metrics. Two of the MAB algorithms we present below make use of a belief metric that is associated with each configuration and is updated after each epoch. Intuitively, the metrics are designed such that fuzzing a configuration with a higher metric *should* yield more bugs in expectation. The first two beliefs below use the concept of RPM to achieve this without invoking any prior; the remaining three embrace a "bug prior". For now, suppose epoch ℓ has just finished and we are in the process of updating the belief for the configuration (p_i, s_i).

RPM. We use the upperbound in the 95% confidence interval given by the Rule of Three to approximate $\text{RPM}(\ell)$. The belief is simply $3/N(\ell)$.

Expected Waiting Time Until Next New Outcome (EWT). Since RPM does not take into account of the speed of each fuzz run, we also investigate a speed-normalized variant of RPM. Let $\text{Time}(\ell)$ be the cumulative time spent fuzzing this configuration from epoch 1 to epoch ℓ. Let $\text{avgTime}(\ell)$ be the average time of a fuzz run, i.e., $\frac{\text{Time}(\ell)}{N(\ell)}$. Let W be a random variable denoting the waiting time until the next new outcome. Recall that $\text{RPM}(\ell)$ is the probability of finding a new outcome in the next fuzz run and assume it is independent of $\text{avgTime}(\ell)$. To compute $E[W]$, observe that either we find a new outcome in the next fuzz run, or we do not and we have to wait again. Therefore,

$$\begin{aligned} E[W] &= \text{RPM}(\ell) \times \text{avgTime}(\ell) \\ &\quad + (1 - \text{RPM}(\ell)) \times (\text{avgTime}(\ell) + E[W]). \end{aligned}$$

(Notice that RPM does not change even in the second case; what changes is our upperbound on RPM.) Solving for $E[W]$ yields $\frac{\text{avgTime}(\ell)}{\text{RPM}(\ell)}$, and we substitute in the upperbound of the 95% confidence interval for $\text{RPM}(\ell)$ to obtain $E[W] \ge \frac{\text{avgTime}(\ell)}{3/N(\ell)} = \frac{\text{Time}(\ell)}{3}$. Since a larger waiting time is less desirable, the belief used is its reciprocal, $3/\text{Time}(\ell)$.

Rich Gets Richer (RGR). This metric is grounded in what we call the "bug prior", which captures our empirical observation that code tends to be either robust or bug-ridden. Programs written by programmers of different skill levels or past testing of a program might explain this real-world phenomenon. Accordingly, demonstrated bugginess of a program serves as a strong indicator that more bugs will be found in that program and thus the belief is $\hat{M}(\ell)$.

Density. This is a runs-normalized variant of RGR and is also the belief used in CERT BFF v2.6 [14]. The belief function is $\hat{M}(\ell)/N(\ell)$. Observe that this is the belief function of RPM scaled by $\hat{M}(\ell)/3$. In other words, Density can be seen as RPM adapted with the bug prior.

Rate. This is a time-normalized variant of RGR. The belief function is $\hat{M}(\ell)/\textsc{Time}(\ell)$. Similar to Density, Rate can be seen as EWT adapted with the bug prior.

Bandit Algorithms. Since the FCS problem is an instance of an MAB problem, naturally we explore a number of MAB algorithms.

Round-Robin. This simply loops through the configurations in a fixed order, dedicating one epoch to each configuration. Note that Round-Robin is a non-adaptive, deterministic algorithm.

Uniform-Random. This algorithm selects uniformly at random from the set of configurations for each epoch. Like Round-Robin, this algorithm is non-adaptive; however, it is randomized.

Weighted-Random. Configurations are selected at random in this algorithm, with the probability associated with each configuration is linked to the belief metric in use. The weight of a well-performing configuration is adjusted upward via the belief metric, thereby increasingly the likelihood of selecting that configuration in future epochs. This mechanism functions in reverse for configurations yielding few or no bugs.

ϵ-Greedy. The ϵ-Greedy algorithm takes an intuitive approach to the exploration vs. exploitation trade-off inherent to MAB problems. With probability ϵ, the algorithm selects a configuration uniformly at random for exploration.With probability $(1-\epsilon)$, it chooses the configuration with the highest current belief, allowing it to exploit its current knowledge for gains. The constant ϵ serves as a parameter balancing the two competing goals, with higher ϵ values corresponding to a greater emphasis on exploration.

EXP3.S.1. This is an advanced MAB algorithm by Auer et al. [2] for the non-stochastic MAB problem. We picked this algorithm for three reasons. First, it is from the venerable EXP3 family, and so likely to be picked up by practitioners. Second, this is one of the EXP3 algorithms that is not parameterized by any constants and thus no parameter tuning is needed. Third, this algorithm is designed to have an optimal worst-case regret, which is a form of regret that suits our problem setting. Note that at its core EXP3.S.1 is a weighted-random algorithm. However, since we do not have a belief metric that corresponds to the one used in EXP3.S.1, we did not put it inside the Weighted-Random group.

4.5 Offline Algorithms

Early on in our research design, we recognized the importance of evaluating a large number of algorithms. Out of budgetary constraints, we have taken a simulation approach so that we can replay the events from previous fuzzings to try out new algorithms. Since we have recorded all the events that may happen during any fuzz campaign of the same input configurations, we can even attempt to compute what an optimal offline algorithm would do and compare the results of our algorithms against it. In the case when the configurations do not yield duplicated bugs, such as in our Inter-Program dataset (§6), we devise a pseudo-polynomial time algorithm that computes the offline optimal. In the other case where duplicated bugs are possible, we propose a heuristic to post-process the solution from the above algorithm to obtain a lowerbound on the offline optimal.

No Duplicates. Assuming that the sets of unique bugs from different configurations are disjoint, our algorithm is a small variation on the dynamic programming solution to the Bounded Knapsack problem. Let K be the number of configurations and B be the total number of unique bugs from all K configurations. Let $t(i,b)$ be the minimum amount of time it takes for configuration i to produce b unique bugs. Note that $t(i,b)$ is assumed to be ∞ when configuration i never produces b unique bugs in our dataset. We claim that $t(i,b)$ can be pre-computed for all $i \in [1,K]$ and $b \in [0,B]$, where each entry takes amortized $O(1)$ time given how events are recorded in our system.

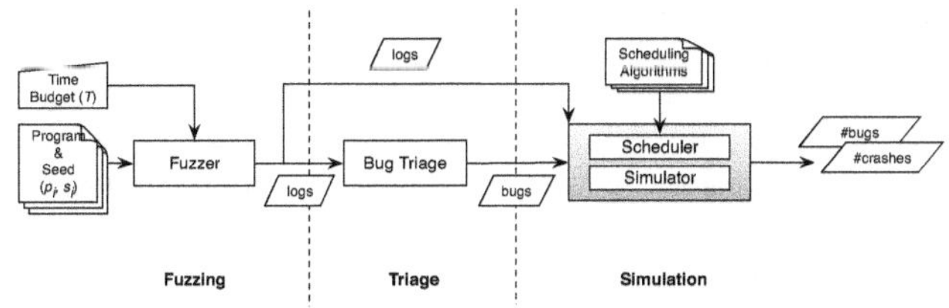

Figure 1: FuzzSim architecture.

Let $m(i,b)$ be the minimum amount of time it takes for configurations 1 through i to produce b unique bugs. We want to compute $m(K,b)$ for $b \in [0,B]$. By definition, $m(1,b) = t(1,b)$ for $b \in [0,B]$. For $i > 1$, observe that $m(i,b) = \min_{c\in[0,B]}\{t(i,c) + m(i-1,b-c)\}$. This models partitioning the b unique bugs into c unique bugs from configuration i and $(b-c)$ unique bugs from configurations 1 through $(i-1)$. Computing each $m(i,b)$ entry takes $O(B)$ time. Since there are $O(K \times B)$ entries, the total running time is $O(K \times B^2)$.

Discounting Duplicates. The above algorithm is incorrect when the sets of unique bugs from different configurations are not disjoint. This is because the recurrence formula of $m(i,b)$ assumes that the c unique bugs from configuration i are different from the $(b-c)$ unique bugs from configurations 1 through $(i-1)$. In this case, we propose a heuristic to compute a lowerbound on the offline optimal.

After obtaining the $m(i,b)$ table from the above, we post-process bug counts by the following discount heuristic. First, we compute the maximum number of bugs that can be found at each time by the above algorithm by examining the K-th row of the table. Then, by scanning forward from time 0, whenever the bug count goes up by one due to a duplicated bug (which must have been found using another configuration), we discount the increment. Since the optimal offline algorithm can also pick up exactly the same bugs in the same order as the dynamic programming algorithm, our heuristic is a valid lowerbound on the maximum number of bugs that an optimal offline algorithm would find.

5 Design & Implementation

This section presents FuzzSim, our replay-based fuzz simulation system built for this project. We describe the three steps in FuzzSim and explain the benefit of its design, which is then followed by its implementation detail. Of special note is that we are releasing our source code and our datasets in support of open science at the URL found in §5.2.

5.1 Overview

FuzzSim is a simulation system for black-box mutational fuzzing that is designed to run different configuration scheduling algorithms using logs from previous fuzzings. Figure 1 summarizes the design of FuzzSim, which employs a three-step approach: (1) fuzzing, (2) triage, and (3) simulation.

Fuzzing. The first step is fuzzing and collecting run logs from a fuzzer. FuzzSim takes in a list of program-seed pairs (p_i, s_i) and a time budget T. It runs a fuzzer on each configuration for the full length of the time budget T and writes to the log each time a crash occurs. Log entries are recorded as 5-tuples of the form (p_i, s_i, time stamp, #runs, mutation identifier).

In our implementation, we fuzz with **zzuf**, one of the most popular open-source fuzzers. **zzuf** generates a random input from a seed file as described in §2.1. The randomization in **zzuf** can be reproduced given the mutation identifier, thus enabling us to reproduce a crashing input from its seed file and the log entry associated with the crash. For example, an output tuple of (**FFMpeg**, a.avi, 100, 42, 1234) specifies that the program **FFMpeg** crashed at the 100-th second with an input file obtained from "a.avi" according to the mutation identifier 1234. Interested readers may refer to **zzuf** [16] for details on mutation identifiers and the actual implementation.

The deterministic nature of **zzuf** allows FuzzSim to triage bugs after completing all fuzz runs first. In other words, FuzzSim does not compute bug identifiers during fuzzing and instead re-derives them using the log. This does not affect any of our algorithms since none of them relies on the actual IDs. In our experiments, we have turned off address space layout randomization (ASLR) in both the fuzzing and the triage steps in order to reproduce the same crashes.

Triage. The second step of FuzzSim maps crashing inputs found during fuzzings into bugs. At a high level, the triage phase takes in the list of 5-tuples (p_i, s_i, time-stamp, #runs, mutation identifier) logged during the fuzzing step and outputs a new list of 5-tuples of the form (p_i, s_i, time-stamp, #runs, bug identifier). More specifically, FuzzSim replays each recorded crash under a debugger to collect stack traces. If FuzzSim does not detect a crash during a particular replay, then we classify that test case to be a non-deterministic bug and discard it.

We then use the collected stack traces to produce bug identifiers, essentially hashes of the stack traces. In particular, we use the fuzzy stack hash algorithm [19], which identifies bugs by hashing the normalized line numbers from a stack trace. With this algorithm, the number of stack frames to hash has a significant influence on the accuracy of bug triage. For example, taking the full stack trace often leads to misclassifying a single bug into multiple bugs, whereas taking only the top frame can easily lead to two different bugs being mis-classified as one. To match the state of the art, FuzzSim uses the top 3 frames as suggested in [19]. We stress that even though inaccurate bug triage may still occur with this choice of parameter, perfecting bug triage techniques is beyond the scope of this paper.

Simulation. The last step simulates a fuzz campaign on the collected ground-truth data from the previous steps using a user-specified scheduling algorithm. More formally, the simulation step takes in a scheduling algorithm and a list of 5-tuples of the form (p_i, s_i, timestamp, #runs, bug identifier) and outputs a list of 2-tuples (timestamp, #bugs) that represent the accumulated time before the corresponding number of unique bugs are observed under the given scheduling algorithm.

Since FuzzSim can simulate any scheduling algorithm in an offline fashion using the pre-recorded ground-truth data, it enables us to efficiently compare numerous scheduling algorithms without actually running a large number of fuzz campaigns. During replay, FuzzSim outputs a timestamp whenever it finds a new bug. Therefore, we can easily plot and compare different scheduling algorithms by comparing the number of bugs produced under the same time budget.

We summarize FuzzSim's three-step algorithm below.

`Fuzzing`: $(\{(p_i, s_i)\}, T)$
  $\to$ {p_i, s_i, timestamp, #runs, mutation id}

`Triage`: {(p_i, s_i, timestamp, #runs, mutation id)}
  $\to$ {(p_i, s_i, timestamp, #runs, bug id)}

`Simulation`: {(p_i, s_i, timestamp, #runs, bug id)}
  $\to$ {(timestamp, #bugs)}

Algorithm 1: FuzzSim algorithms.

5.2 Implementation & Open Science

We have implemented our data collection and bug triage modules in approximately 1,000 lines of OCaml. This includes the capability to run and collect crash logs from Amazon EC2. We used **zzuf** version 0.13. Our scheduling engine is also implemented in OCaml and spans about 1,600 lines. This covers the 26 online and the 2 offline algorithms presented in this paper.

We invite our fellow researchers to become involved in this line of research. In support of open science, we release both our datasets and the source code of our simulator at `http://security.ece.cmu.edu/fuzzsim/`.

6 Evaluation

To evaluate the performance of the 26 algorithms presented in §4, we focus on the following questions:

1. Which scheduling algorithm works best for our datasets?
2. Why does one algorithm outperform the others?
3. Which of the two epoch types—fixed-run or fixed-time—works better, and why?

6.1 Experimental Setup

Our experiments were performed on Amazon EC2 instances that have been configured with a single Intel 2GHz Xeon CPU core and 4GB RAM each. We used the most recent Debian Linux distribution at the time of our experiment (April 2013) and downloaded all programs from the then-latest Debian Squeeze repository. Specifically, the version of FFMpeg we used is SVN-r0.5.10-4:0.5.10-1, which is based on a June 2012 FFMpeg release with Debian-specific patches.

6.2 Fuzzing Data Collection

Our evaluation makes use of two datasets: (1) FFMpeg with 100 different input seeds, and (2) 100 different Linux applications, each with a corresponding input seed. We refer to these as the "intra-program" and the "inter-program" datasets respectively.

For the intra-program dataset, we downloaded 10,000 video/image sample files from the MPlayer website at `http://samples.mplayerhq.hu/`. From these samples, we selected 100 files uniformly at random and took them as our input

Dataset	#runs	#crashes	#bugs
Intra-program	636,998,978	906,577	200
Inter-program	4,868,416,447	415,699	223

Table 1: Statistics from fuzzing the two datasets.

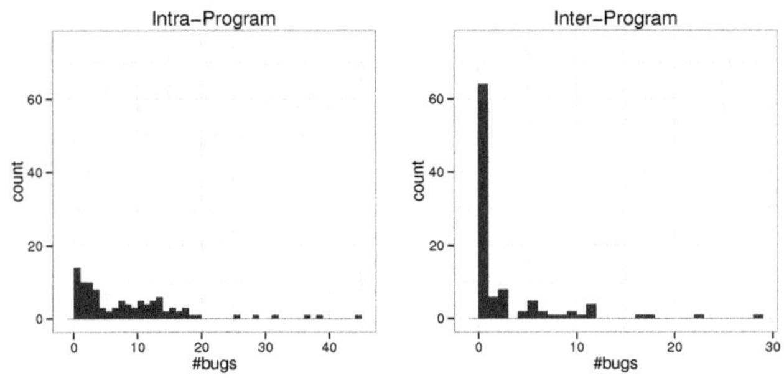

Figure 2: Distribution of the number of bugs per configuration in each dataset.

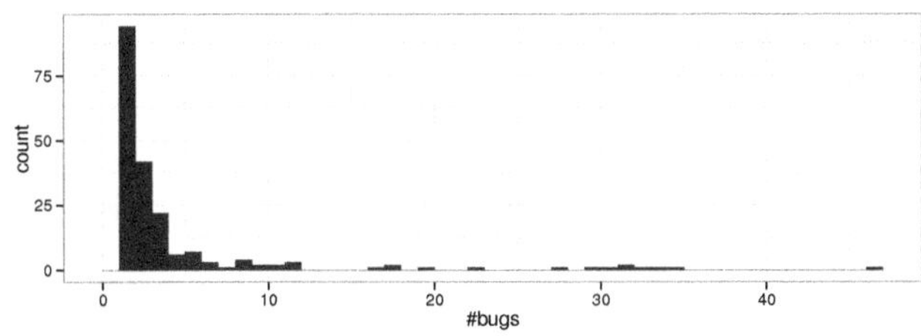

Figure 3: Distribution of bug overlaps across multiple seeds for the intra-program dataset.

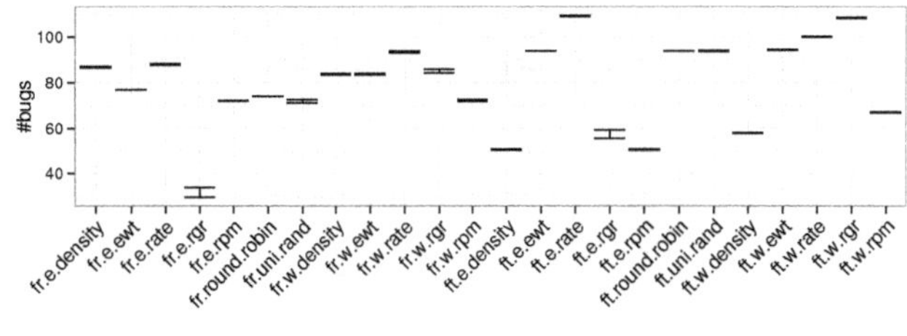

(a) Intra-program.

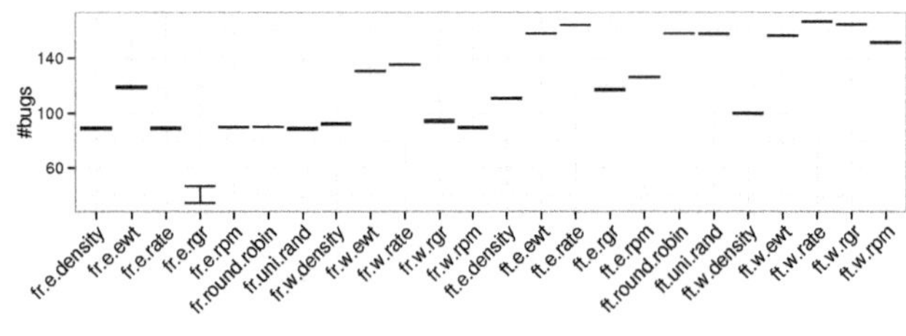

(b) Inter-program.

Figure 4: The average number of bugs over 100 runs for each scheduling algorithm with error bars showing a 99% confidence interval. "ft" represents fixed-time epoch; "fr" represents fixed-run epoch; "e" represents ϵ-Greedy; "w" represents Weighted-Random.

seeds. The collected seeds include various audio and video formats such as ASF, QuickTime, MPEG, FLAC, etc. We then used `zzuf` to fuzz FFMpeg with each seed for 10 days.

For the inter-program dataset, we downloaded 100 different file conversion utilities in Debian. To select these 100 programs, we first enumerated all file conversion packages tagged as "use::converting" in the Debian package tags interface (debtags). From this list of packages, we manually identified 100 applications that take a file name as a command line argument. Then we manually constructed a valid seed for each program and the actual command line to run it with the seed. After choosing these 100 program-seed pairs, we fuzzed each for 10 days as well. In total, we have spent 48,000 CPU hours fuzzing these 200 configurations.

To perform bug triage, we identified and re-ran every crashing input from the log under a debugger to obtain stack traces for hashing. After triaging with the fuzzy stack hash algorithm described in §5.1, we found 200 bugs from the intra-program dataset and 223 bugs from the inter-program dataset. Table 1 summarizes the data collected from our experiments. The average fuzzing throughput was 8 runs per second for the intra-program dataset and 63 runs per second for the inter-program dataset. This difference is due to the higher complexity of FFMpeg when compared to the programs in the inter-program dataset.

6.3 Data Analysis

What does the collected fuzzing data look like? We studied our data from fuzzing and triage to answer two questions: (1) How many bugs does a configuration trigger? (2) How many bugs are triggered by multiple seeds in the intra-program dataset?

We first analyzed the distribution of the number of bugs in the two datasets. On average, the intra- and the inter-program datasets yielded 8.2 and 2.4 bugs per configuration respectively. Figure 2 shows two histograms, each depicting the number of occurrences of bug counts. There is a marked difference in the distributions from the two datasets: 64% of configurations in the inter-program dataset produce no bugs, whereas the corresponding number in the intra-program dataset is 15%. We study the bias of the bug count distribution in §6.4.

Second, we measured how many bugs are shared across seeds in the intra-program dataset. As an extreme case, we found a bug that was triggered by 46 seeds. The average number of seeds leading to a given bug is 4. Out of the 200 bugs, 97 were discovered from multiple seeds. Figure 3 illustrates the distribution of bug overlaps. Our results suggest that there is a small overlap in the code exercised by different seed files even though they have been chosen to be of different types. Although this shows that our bug disjointness assumption in the WCCP model does not always hold in practice, the low average number of seeds leading to a given bug in our dataset means that the performance of our algorithms should not have been severely affected.

6.4 Simulation

We now compare the 26 scheduling algorithms based on the 10-day fuzzing logs collected for the intra- and inter-program datasets. To compare the performance of scheduling algorithms, we use the total number of unique bugs reported by the bug triage process. Recall from §4.4 that these algorithms vary across three dimensions: (1) epoch types, (2) belief metrics, and (3) MAB algorithms. For each valid combination (see Table 2), we ran our simulator 100 times and averaged the results to study the effect of randomness on each scheduling algorithm. In our experiments, we allocated 10 seconds to each epoch for fixed-time campaigns and 200 runs for fixed-run campaigns. For the ϵ-Greedy algorithm, we chose ϵ to be 0.1.

Table 2 summarizes our results. Each entry in the table represents the average number of bugs found by 100 sim-

Dataset	Epoch	MAB algorithm	#bugs found for each belief				
			RPM	EWT	Density	Rate	RGR
Intra-Program	Fixed-Run	ϵ-Greedy	72	77	87	88	32
		Weighted-Random	72	84	84	**93**	85
		Uniform-Random			72		
		EXP3.S.1			58		
		Round-Robin			74		
	Fixed-Time	ϵ-Greedy	51	94	51	**109**	58
		Weighted-Random	67	94	58	100	108
		Uniform-Random			94		
		EXP3.S.1			95		
		Round-Robin			94		
Inter-Program	Fixed-Run	ϵ-Greedy	90	119	89	89	41
		Weighted-Random	90	131	92	**135**	94
		Uniform-Random			89		
		EXP3.S.1			72		
		Round-Robin			90		
	Fixed-Time	ϵ-Greedy	126	158	111	164	117
		Weighted-Random	152	157	100	**167**	165
		Uniform-Random			158		
		EXP3.S.1			161		
		Round-Robin			158		

Table 2: Comparison between scheduling algorithms.

ulations of a 10-day campaign. We present ϵ-Greedy and Weighted-Random at the top of each epoch-type row group, each showing five entries that correspond to the belief metric used. For the other three MAB algorithms, we only show a single entry in the center because these algorithms do not use our belief metrics. Figure 4 describes the variability of our data using error bars showing a 99% confidence interval. Notice that 94% of our scheduling algorithms have a confidence interval that is less than 2 (bugs). RGR gives the most volatile algorithms. This is not surprising because RGR tends to under-explore by focusing too much on bug-yielding configurations that it encounters early on in a campaign. In the remainder of this section, we highlight several important aspects of our results.

Fixed-time algorithms prevail over fixed-run algorithms. In the majority of Table 2, except for RPM and Density in the intra-program dataset, fixed-time algorithms always produced more bugs than their fixed-run counterparts. Intuitively, different inputs to a program may take different amounts of time to execute, leading to different fuzzing throughputs. A fixed-time algorithm can exploit this fact and pick configurations that give higher throughputs, ultimately testing a larger fraction of the input space and potentially finding more bugs. To investigate the above exceptions, we have also performed further analysis on the intra-program dataset. We found that the performance of the fixed-time variants of RPM and Density greatly improves in longer simulations. In particular, *all* fixed-time algorithms outperform their fixed-run counterparts after day 11.

Along the same line, we observe that fixed-time algorithms yield 1.6× more bugs on average when compared to their fixed-run counterparts in the inter-program dataset. In contrast, the improvement is only 1.1× in the intra-program dataset. As we have explained above, fixed-time algorithms tend to perform more fuzz runs and potentially finding more bugs by taking advantage of faster configurations. Thus, if the runtime distribution of fuzz runs is more biased, as in the case of the inter-program dataset, then fixed-time algorithms tend to gain over their fixed-run counterparts.

Time-normalization outperforms runs-normalization. In our results, EWT always outperforms RPM and Rate always outperforms Density. We believe that this is because EWT and Density do not spend more time on slower programs and slower programs are not necessarily buggier. The latter hypothesis seems highly plausible to us; if true, it would imply that time-normalized belief metrics are more desirable than runs-normalized metrics.

Fixed-time Rate works best. In both datasets, the best-performing algorithms use fixed-time epochs and Rate as belief (entries shown in boldface in Table 2). Since Rate can be seen as a time-normalized variant of RGR, this gives further evidence of the superiority of time normalization. In addition, it also supports the plausibility of the bug prior.

6.5 Speed of Bug Finding

Besides the number of bugs found at the end of a fuzz campaign, the speed at which bugs are discovered is also an important metric for evaluating scheduling algorithms. We address two questions in this section. First, is there a scheduling algorithm that prevails throughout an entire fuzz campaign? Second, how effective are the algorithms with respect to our offline algorithm in §4.5? To answer the questions, we first show the speed of each algorithm in Figure 5 and Figure 6 by computing the number of bugs found over time. For brevity and readability, we picked for each belief metric the algorithm that produced the greatest average number of unique bugs at the end of the 10-day simulations.

Speed. We observe that Rate and RGR are in the lead for the majority of the time during our 10-day simulations. In other words, not only do they find more unique bugs at the end of the simulations, but they also outperform other algorithms at almost any given time. This lends further credibility to the bug prior.

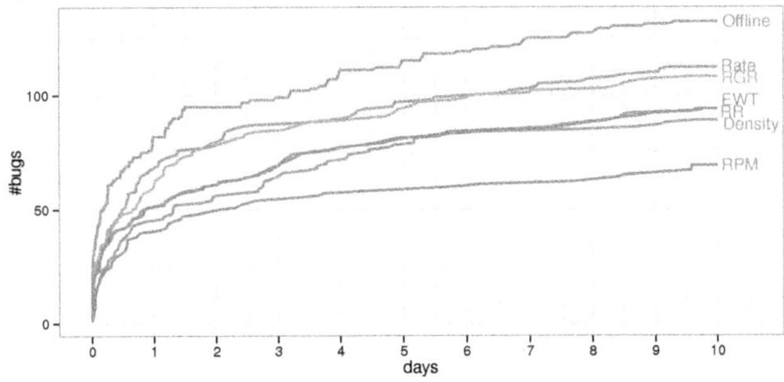

Figure 5: Bug finding speed of different belief-based algorithms for the intra-program dataset.

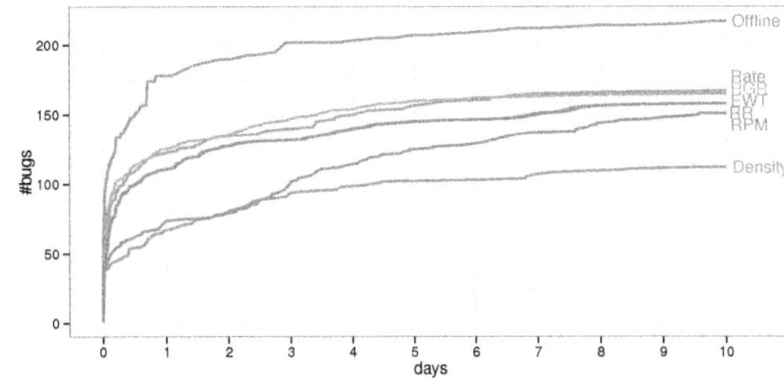

Figure 6: Bug finding speed of different belief-based algorithms for the inter-program dataset.

Effectiveness. We also compare the effectiveness of each algorithm by observing how it compares against our offline algorithm. We have implemented the offline algorithm discussed in §4.5 including the post-processing step that discounts duplicated bugs and computed the solution for each dataset. The numbers of bugs found by the offline algorithm for the intra- and the inter-program datasets are 132 and 217 respectively. (Notice that due to bug overlaps and the discount heuristic, these are lowerbounds on the offline optimal.) As a comparison, Rate found 83% and 77% of bugs in the intra- and inter-program datasets, respectively. Based on these numbers, we conclude that Rate-based algorithms are effective.

6.6 Comparison with CERT BFF

At present, the CERT Basic Fuzzing Framework (BFF) [14] is the closest system that makes use of scheduling algorithms for fuzz campaigns. In this section, we evaluate the effectiveness of BFF's scheduling algorithm using our simulator.

Based on our study of the source code of BFF v2.6 (the latest version as of this writing), it uses a fixed-run weighted-random algorithm with Density ($\frac{\#\text{bugs}}{\#\text{runs}}$) as its belief metric. However, a key feature of BFF prevented us from completely implementing its algorithm in our simulation framework. In particular, while BFF focuses on fuzzing a single program, it considers not only a collection of seeds but also a set of predetermined mutation ratios. In other words, instead of choosing program-seed pairs as in our experiments, BFF chooses seed-ratio pairs with respect to a single program. Since our simulator does not take mutation ratio into account, it can only emulate BFF's algorithm in configuration selection using a fixed mutation ratio. We note that adding the capability to vary the mutation ratio is prohibitively expensive for us: FuzzSim is an offline simulator, and therefore we need to collect ground-truth data for all possible configurations. Adding a new dimension into our current system would directly multiply our data collection cost.

Going back to our evaluation, let us focus on the Weighted-Random rows in Table 2. Density with fixed-run epochs (BFF) yields 84 and 92 bugs in the two datasets. The corresponding numbers for Rate with fixed-time epochs (our recommendation) are 100 and 167, with respective improvements of 1.19× and 1.82× (average 1.5×). Based on these numbers, we believe future versions of BFF may benefit from switching over to Rate with fixed-time epochs.

7 Related Work

Since its introduction in 1990 by Miller et al. [18], fuzzing in its various forms has become the most widely-deployed technique for finding bugs. There has been extensive work to improve upon their ground-breaking work. A major thrust of this research concerns the generation of test inputs for the target program and the two main paradigms in use are mutational and generational fuzzing [17].

More recently, sophisticated techniques for dynamic test generation have been applied in fuzzing [8, 11]. White-box fuzzing [7] is grounded in the idea of "data-driven improvement," which uses feedback from previous fuzz runs to "focus limited resources on further research and improve future runs." The feedback data used in determining inputs is obtained via symbolic execution and constraint solving; other work in feedback-driven input generation relies on taint analysis and control flow graphs [13, 20]. Our works bears some similarity to feedback-driven or evolutionary fuzzing in that we also use data from previous fuzz runs to improve fuzzing effectiveness. However, the black-box nature of our approach implies that feedback is limited to observing crashes. Likewise, our focus on mutating inputs means that we do not construct brand new inputs and instead rely on selecting among existing configurations. Thus, our work can be cast as dynamic scheduling of fuzz configurations.

Despite its prominence, we know of no previous work that has systematically investigated the effectiveness of different scheduling algorithms in fuzzing. Our approach focuses on allocating resources for black-box mutational fuzzing in order to maximize the number of unique bugs found in any period of time. The closest related work is the CERT Basic Fuzzing Framework (BFF) [14], which considers parameter selection for `zzuf`. Like BFF, we borrow techniques from Multi-Armed Bandits (MAB) algorithms. However, unlike BFF, which considers repeated fuzz runs as independent Bernoulli trials, we model this process as a Weighted Coupon Collector's Problem (WCCP) with unknown weights to capture the decrease in the probability of finding a new bug over the course a fuzz campaign.

In constructing our model, we draw heavily on research in software reliability as well as random testing. The key insight of viewing random testing as coupon collecting was recently made in [1]. A key difference between our work and [1] is that their focus is on the formalization of random testing, whereas our goal is to maximize the number of bugs found in a fuzz campaign. Software reliability refers to the probability of failure-free operation for a specified time period and execution environment [6]. As a measure of software quality, software reliability is used within the software engineering community to "plan and control resources during the development process" [12], which is similar to the motivation behind our work.

8 Conclusion and Future Work

In this paper we studied how to find the greatest number of unique bugs in a fuzz campaign. We modeled black-box mutational fuzzing as a WCCP process with unknown weights and used the condition in the No Free Lunch theorem to guide us in designing better online algorithms for our problem. In our evaluation of the 26 algorithms presented in this paper, we found that the fixed-time weighted-random algorithm with the Rate belief metric shows an average of 1.5× improvement over its fixed-run Density-based counterpart, which is currently used by the CERT Basic Fuzzing Framework (BFF). Since our current project does not investigate the effect of varying the mutation ratio, a natural follow-up work would be to investigate how to add this capability to our system in an affordable manner.

Acknowledgment

The authors thank Will Dormann, Jonathan Foote, and Allen Householder of CERT for encouragement and fruitful discussions. This material is based upon work funded and supported by the Department of Defense under Contract No. FA8721-05-C-0003 with Carnegie Mellon University for the operation of the Software Engineering Institute, a federally funded research and development center. This material has been approved for public release and unlimited distribution.

References

[1] A. Arcuri, M. Z. Iqbal, and L. Briand. Formal Analysis of the Effectiveness and Predictability of Random Testing. In *International Symposium on Software Testing and Analysis*, pages 219–229, 2010.

[2] P. Auer, N. Cesa-Bianchi, Y. Freund, and R. E. Schapire. The Nonstochastic Multiarmed Bandit Problem. *Journal on Computing*, 32(1):48–77, 2002.

[3] P. Auer, N. Cesa-Bianchi, and F. Paul. Finite-time Analysis of the Multiarmed Bandit Problem. *Machine Learning*, 47(2-3):235–256, 2002.

[4] T. Avgerinos, S. K. Cha, B. T. H. Lim, and D. Brumley. AEG: Automatic Exploit Generation. In *Proceedings of the Network and Distributed Systems Security Symposium*, 2011.

[5] D. A. Berry and B. Fristedt. *Bandit Problems: Sequential Allocation of Experiments.* Chapman and Hall, 1985.

[6] A. Bertolino. Software testing research: Achievements, challenges, dreams. In *Future of Software Engineering*, pages 85–103, 2007.

[7] E. Bounimova, P. Godefroid, and D. Molnar. Billions and Billions of Constraints: Whitebox Fuzz Testing in Production. In *Proceedings of the International Conference on Software Engineering*, pages 122–131, 2013.

[8] C. Cadar, D. Dunbar, and D. Engler. KLEE: Unassisted and Automatic Generation of High-coverage Tests for Complex Systems Programs. In *Proceedings of the USENIX Symposium on Operating System Design and Implementation*, pages 209–224, 2008.

[9] S. K. Cha, T. Avgerinos, A. Rebert, and D. Brumley. Unleashing Mayhem on Binary Code. In *Proceedings of the IEEE Symposium on Security and Privacy*, pages 380–394, 2012.

[10] D. Engler, D. Chen, S. Hallem, A. Chou, and B. Chelf. Bugs as Deviant Behavior: A General Approach to Inferring Errors in Systems Code. In *Proceedings of the ACM Symposium on Operating System Principles*, pages 57–72, 2001.

[11] P. Godefroid, M. Y. Levin, and D. Molnar. SAGE: Whitebox Fuzzing for Security. *Communications of the ACM*, 55(3):40–44, 2012.

[12] A. L. Goel. Software Reliability Models: Assumptions, Limitations, and Applicability. *IEEE Transactions on Software Engineering*, 11(12):1411–1423, 1985.

[13] N. Gupta, A. P. Mathur, and M. L. Soffa. Automated Test Data Generation Using An Iterative Relaxation Method. In *Proceedings of the ACM SIGSOFT International Symposium on Foundations of Software Engineering*, pages 231–244, 1998.

[14] A. D. Householder and J. M. Foote. Probability-Based Parameter Selection for Black-Box Fuzz Testing. Technical Report August, CERT, 2012.

[15] B. D. Jovanovic and P. S. Levy. A Look at the Rule of Three. *The American Statistician*, 51(2):137–139, 1997.

[16] C. Labs. zzuf: multi-purpose fuzzer. `http://caca.zoy.org/wiki/zzuf`.

[17] R. McNally, K. Yiu, D. Grove, and D. Gerhardy. Fuzzing: The State of the Art. Technical Report DSTO–TN–1043, Defence Science and Technology Organisation, 2012.

[18] B. P. Miller, L. Fredriksen, and B. So. An Empirical Study of the Reliability of UNIX Utilities. *Communications of the ACM*, 33(12):32–44, 1990.

[19] D. Molnar, X. Li, and D. Wagner. Dynamic Test Generation To Find Integer Bugs in x86 Binary Linux Programs. In *Proceedings of the USENIX Security Symposium*, pages 67–82, 2009.

[20] C. Pacheco, S. K. Lahiri, M. D. Ernst, and T. Ball. Feedback-Directed Random Test Generation. In *Proceedings of the International Conference on Software Engineering*, pages 75–84, 2007.

[21] D. Wagner, J. S. Foster, E. A. Brewer, and A. Aiken. A First Step towards Automated Detection of Buffer Overrun Vulnerabilities. In *Proceedings of the Network and Distributed Systems Security Symposium*, pages 3–17, 2000.

[22] D. Wolpert and W. Macready. No free lunch theorems for optimization. *IEEE Transactions on Evolutionary Computation*, 1(1):67–82, 1997.

Fast Two-Party Secure Computation with Minimal Assumptions

[Extended Abstract]*

abhi shelat
University of Virginia
85 Engineer's Way
Charlottesville, Virginia, U.S.A.
abhi@virginia.edu

Chih-hao Shen
University of Virginia
85 Engineer's Way
Charlottesville, Virginia, U.S.A.
shench@virginia.edu

ABSTRACT

Almost all existing protocols for secure two-party computation require a specific hardness assumption, such as DDH, discrete logarithm, or a random oracle, even after assuming oracle access to the oblivious transfer functionality for their correctness and/or efficiency. We propose and implement a Yao-based protocol that is secure against malicious adversaries and enjoys the following benefits:

1. it requires the minimal hardness assumption, i.e., OTs;
2. it uses 10 rounds of communication plus OT rounds;
3. it has the optimal overhead complexity (for an approach that uses the circuit-level cut-and-choose technique); and
4. it is embarrassingly parallelizable in the sense that each circuit can be processed in a pipelined manner, and all circuits can be processed in parallel.

To achieve these properties, we describe novel solutions for the three main obstacles for achieving security against malicious adversaries in a cut-and-choose garbled-circuit protocol. We propose an efficient proof to establish the *generator's output authenticity*; we suggest the use of an auxiliary circuit that computes a hash to ensure *the generator's input consistency*; and we advance the performance of Pinkas and Lindell's state-of-the-art approach for handling *the selective failure attack*.

Not only does our protocol require weaker cryptographic assumptions, but our implementation of this protocol also demonstrates a several factor improvement over the best prior work which relies on specific number-theoretic assumptions. Thus, we show that performance does not require specific algebraic assumptions.

*A full version is at `http://eprint.iacr.org/2013/196`.

CCS'13, November 4–8, 2013, Berlin, Germany.

ACM 978-1-4503-2477-9/13/11 ...$15.00.
http://dx.doi.org/10.1145/2508859.2516698.

Categories and Subject Descriptors

F.0 [**Theory of Computation**]: General

Keywords

The Yao protocol, Malicious Model, Cut-and-Choose

1. INTRODUCTION

Secure Two-Party Computation (2PC) aims to allow two parties to collaborate in a way that achieves maximal privacy of their inputs with simultaneous guarantees of correctness of outputs. The correctness property guarantees that when both parties follow the protocol honestly, the protocol output is indeed the output of the objective function. The privacy property ensures that during the protocol execution, neither party can learn more than that derivable from her own input and output.

The first generic solution for Secure 2PC in the *honest-but-curious* model was proposed by Yao [26]. In this protocol, both parties agree on an objective function and its boolean circuit format (called the *objective circuit*) in advance[1]. One party (denoted by GEN) constructs a garbled version of this objective circuit, and the other party (denoted by EVAL) obliviously evaluates this garbled circuit to compute an output. By oblivious evaluation we mean that EVAL does not learn any intermediate value of the computation. This protocol satisfies the two security properties if both participants follow the protocol instructions honestly.

This basic protocol must be hardened to handle the situation in which either party arbitrarily deviates from the given instructions, e.g. by constructing a faulty circuit that purposely reveals EVAL's private input.

The *circuit-level cut-and-choose* technique is one of the most efficient methods that enforce honest circuit garbling [11, 15, 16, 19, 23]. This technique instructs GEN to prepare multiple copies of the garbled circuit, each with independent randomness, and instructs EVAL then to randomly pick a fraction of the circuits whose randomness is later revealed. If any of the chosen circuits (called the *check circuits*) is not consistent with the revealed randomness, EVAL aborts and GEN is caught cheating; otherwise, EVAL starts to evaluate the remaining circuits (called the *evaluation circuits*) as instructed in the Yao protocol. Finally, EVAL takes the majority of the evaluation outputs as the final output. As

[1]The equivalence between the objective function and the objective circuit is out of the scope of this paper.

a result, a malicious GEN constructs either too many faulty circuits and gets caught, or only a few and does not influence the final output at all. This approach is efficient because it can naturally be run in parallel.

Besides the threat of faulty circuits, there remain three other subtle but equally critical security issues that need to be addressed when dealing with malicious adversaries. The first two in fact result from the use of multiple garbled circuits (as instructed by the circuit-level cut-and-choose technique): *two-output function handling* and GEN*'s input consistency*. The third issue is also known as the *selective failure attack*. Prior solution to these three concerns either requires specific hardness assumptions or introduces large overheads in communication and computation.

1.1 Contributions

Our main contribution is to construct an *optimal* protocol in the circuit-level cut-and-choose-based category such that (1) it requires minimal hardness assumptions, namely, an oblivious transfer (OT) secure in the presence of malicious adversaries; (2) it introduces little computational and communicational overhead to solve the above three security issues. In particular, its complexity is linear (in terms of the security parameter) in the original Yao protocol, which is the best a circuit-level cut-and-choose-based solution could ever achieve. In other words, we show that *malicious security comes almost for free* both in terms of required hardness assumptions and various protocol performance metrics. Let n denote the input/output size, k denote the security parameter, and σ denote the number of garbled circuits needed[2]. The contributions of this work are as follows:

1. We propose a novel witness-indistinguishable proof to ensure GEN's output authenticity. This proof requires only standard primitives (a symmetric encryption scheme and commitment scheme to be precise) and incurs about the same amount of overhead as garbling and evaluating GEN's output gates. In other words, it requires only $O(\sigma n)$ symmetric operations; prior approaches require $O(\sigma^2 n)$ symmetric operations [15, 22] or $O(\sigma n)$ symmetric operations plus $O(\sigma)$ algebraic operations [11].

2. We suggest the use of an auxiliary circuit to achieve GEN's input consistency. This auxiliary circuit computes the (universal) hash of GEN's input. By utilizing an XOR-homomorphic hash, we are able to evaluate the auxiliary circuit almost for free. Our solution is much more efficient than the prior works which need $O(\sigma^2 n)$ symmetric operations [15, 18] or $O(\sigma n)$ algebraic operations [23].

3. Most importantly, the above two techniques allow us to handle issues of two-output functions and GEN's input consistency while entirely avoiding algebraic operations, except for those needed by OTs. Lindell and Pinkas' [15] and Woodruff's [25] approaches are the only prior works, to the best of our knowledge, that enjoy this property. Nevertheless, our approach works in a more efficient manner as shown in Table 1.

4. Lindell and Pinkas suggested the use of a k-probe-resistant matrix (cf. Definition 5) to defend against the selective failure attack [15]. This solution has little overhead while combining with the free-XOR technique. However, it increases the number of OTs needed at the same time. While XOR gates can be computed almost for free, the OTs can not. While there exist extension techniques for OTs, not all variants of OTs can be efficiently extended. We therefore design a probabilistic algorithm based on Reed-Solomon code such that the number of OTs needed can be as low as 25% of that in the original Lindell and Pinkas' solution.

5. We propose an optimization technique that can save communication overhead by up to 60% (when 60% of all the garbled circuits are check circuits) with the price of a slight increase of computation overhead. We stress that our technique compares favorably with the Random Seed Checking technique [14]. In particular, our approach is compatible with the pipelining technique [8].

6. Based on an open-source system [14], we experimentally verify our theories by developing some of the above techniques. The integrated system can process 650,000+ gates per second on Stampede [24]. This is the fastest maliciously secure 2PC system reported.

[2]Typically, the number of garbled circuits needed is linear to the security parameter, that is, $\sigma = O(k)$.

1.2 Related Work

Prior work on converting the Yao protocol into a maliciously secure one based on the cut-and-choose technique [11, 14–16, 18, 22, 23, 25] reports several completely different approaches. Jarecki and Shmatikov suggested an approach that needs only a single copy of the garbled circuit, but this approach requires expensive zero-knowledge proof of correctness for every single gate [10] that also rely on specific RSA-based hardness assumptions. Nielson et al. reported a solution that uses efficient OTs to generate a pool of authenticated primitives [21]. With these primitives, both parties are able to securely evaluate a boolean circuit based on the generic Goldreich, Micali, and Wigderson protocol [5]. However, this protocol requires interactive communication for every AND gate, and therefore the number of rounds of communication depends on the circuit. While suitable for small circuits, large complicated circuits will require thousands of back-and-forth messages. Damgård et al. proposed a solution that uses somewhat homomorphic encryption to precompute a bunch of triples that are later used to securely compute an arithmetic circuit [1].

Among other approaches in the cut-and-choose-based category, our approach demonstrates superior performance in terms of the number of symmetric or algebraic operations needed, as shown in Table 1. Note that by "in the cut-and-choose-based category," we mean that the number of the garbled circuits needed is linear to the security parameter. So there is a hidden cost of $O(kC)$ of symmetric cryptographic operations in all these approaches, where C is circuit size. More details about Table 1 will be given in Section 3.

Our approach is also as competitive as any other in terms of computation complexity, round complexity, and the computation assumptions needed, as shown in Table 2. While Jarecki and Shmatikov's approach requires hundreds of expensive algebraic operations per gate, ours does not need any (given oracle access to OTs) [10]. Although Neilson et al.'s approach favorably compares to our approach in terms of computation complexity, ours requires constant communication rounds while theirs needs rounds linear to the circuit depth [21]. At last, since Damgård et al.'s approach works

	Gen. Input Consist.		Gen. Output Auth.		Assumptions
	Symm. Op.	Alge. Op.	Symm. Op.	Alge. Op.	(besides OT)
[15]	$O(k^2n)$		$O(k^2n)$		OWF
[11]	$O(k^2n)$		$O(kn)$	$O(k)$	Discrete Log.
[16]	$O(kn)$	$O(kn)$	not mentioned		Decisional Diffie-Hellman
[23]	$O(kn)$	$O(kn)$	$O(kn)$	$O(kn)$	Discrete Log.
[14]	$O(kn)$	$O(kn)$	$O(kn)$	$O(k)$	Discrete Log.
This Work	$O(kn)$		$O(kn)$		OWF

Table 1: Complexity of various circuit-level cut-and-choose-based approaches in terms of symmetric (or algebraic) operations.

with arithmetic circuits, it is incomparable to our work and thus omitted in the table [1]

	Symm. Op.	Alge. Op.	Rounds	Assumptions
[10]	$O(C)$	$O(C)$	$O(1)$	DCR + RSA
[20]	$O(\frac{k}{\lg C}C)$	$O(\frac{k}{\lg C}C)$	$O(1)$	Discrete Log
[21]	$O(\frac{k}{\lg C}C)$		$O(D_f)$	Random Oracle
[2]	$O(\frac{k}{\lg C}C)$		$O(1)$	Random Oracle
This work	$O(kC)$		$O(1)$	OWF

Table 2: Overall complexity comparison with prior works, where C is the circuit size and D_f is the circuit depth.

We recently noticed an independent work by Mohassel and Riva that also proposes an optimal Yao-based protocol [19]. Their protocol indeed shares the same asymptotic complexity as ours and also relies on minimal assumptions. The protocols for ensuring GEN's output authenticity in both works are essentially the same. Both protocols capture the idea that EVAL provides a unique random key corresponding to each of GEN's output wires as the proof of authenticity.

However, our approach favorably compares to theirs for two reasons:

First, for each of GEN's output wires in each of the garbled circuits, Mahassel and Riva's protocol requires two possible random keys, which correspond to 0 or 1, to be encrypted and exchanged, whereas our protocol only needs the one that corresponds to GEN's output value to be encrypted and exchanged. In other words, although both solutions need $O(\sigma n)$ symmetric cryptographic operations, ours has a smaller constant factor.

Second, their approach for checking GEN's input consistency uses a different instance of circuit garbling, in which GEN's and EVAL's roles are reversed. Hence, their solution requires $O(n)$ extra instances of OTs *in which the roles are reversed*, which is arguably more expensive than the extra $O(nk)$ cryptographic symmetric operations in our solution.

Paper Organization: We give background and notations in Section 2, show how the three attacks are handled by cryptographic primitives in Section 3, and provide a detailed description of our main protocol in Section 4. Finally, experimental results are reported in Section 5.

2. PRELIMINARIES

We denote by $f(x, y) \mapsto (f_1(x, y), f_2(x, y))$ a two-output objective function, where GEN with input x gets output $f_1(x, y)$ and EVAL with input y gets output $f_2(x, y)$. For simplicity, $f_1(x, y)$ and $f_2(x, y)$ are often noted as f_1 and f_2, respectively. We use $f_1 = \perp$ or $f_2 = \perp$ to indicate that either GEN or EVAL gets no output. We denote by $\mathsf{com}(x; r)$ the commitment to message x with randomness r. The randomness may be omitted for simplicity. We denote by $\mathsf{enc}_e(x)$ the encryption of message x under encryption key e and by $\mathsf{dec}_d(c)$ the decryption of ciphertext c under decryption key d. Additionally, we denote by $x \| y$ or sometimes (x, y) the concatenation of x and y, and by $[n]$ the set $\{1, 2, \ldots, n\}$ for some $n \in \mathbb{N}$. We also use the notation that $x^{(j)}$'s superscript implies that this variable is related to the j-th circuit.

For the rest of this paper, we denote by k the security parameter, by σ the number of copies of the garbled circuit needed (also known as the statistical security parameter), and by n the size of a participant's input and output.

3. MALICIOUS SECURITY

Our protocols achieve security against malicious adversaries according to the standard ideal-real paradigm for defining security. In the full version of this paper, we present the standard definition of ideal-real security and prove that our protocols achieve this notion using proof techniques already highlighted in [15] and [23]. In this abstract, we focus on a high-level discussion of our contributions—namely, how we solve the three security issues faced by the protocol that transforms the Yao protocol into one that is secure in the malicious model via the cut-and-choose technique.

3.1 Two-Output Function Handling

For many real-world applications, both parties want to learn an output from the secure computation. Since EVAL always learns its output, the challenge is for GEN to learn hers securely. In particular, a solution needs to achieve GEN's *output privacy* and *output authenticity*. The former requires that EVAL does not learn GEN's output, and the latter requires that GEN gets either an authentic output or no output at all, in which case EVAL is caught cheating. We stress that the two-output protocols we consider are not *fair*, that is, EVAL may learn its own output but refuse to send GEN's back—but if so, EVAL is caught cheating.

Goldreich suggested the use of an auxiliary circuit that encrypts GEN's output and computes the digital signature of the resulting ciphertext so that a malicious EVAL could neither learn GEN's output from the ciphertext nor forge an arbitrary signature [4]. Later, Lindell and Pinkas proposed an approach that uses one-time-pad encryption and one-time MAC circuits instead, which incurs $O(kn)$ extra gates per circuit [15]. Kiraz presented a two-party protocol in which a zero-knowledge proof of size $O(\sigma)$ is executed at the end [11]. shelat and Shen reported a signature-based solution that adds $O(n)$ gates to each circuit, and requires a WI proof of size $O(\sigma + n)$ [23] under specific complexity assumptions.

Our approach solves GEN's output privacy problem with a one-time-pad encryption circuit, which requires only $O(n)$ extra XOR-gates per circuit. The novel part of our approach is that we tackle the output authenticity problem in a way that uses only $O(n)$ symmetric operations per circuit and no algebraic operations at all (hence no number-theoretic intractability assumption is needed). Our idea comes from the following three observations.

We first observe that the random keys retrieved from evaluating GEN's output gates can in fact serve as "message authentication codes" sufficient for EVAL to prove GEN's output authenticity [3]. Recall that the Yao protocol ensures that EVAL learns exactly one of the two random keys assigned to each wire. So the knowledge of the retrieved random key corresponding to GEN's output wire is more than enough for EVAL to show the output authenticity. What remains is how EVAL demonstrates this knowledge without revealing the index of the garbled circuit from which EVAL retrieves the random key. This index has been shown to be exploitable in breaching EVAL's input privacy [11].

The second observation we have, which is also pointed out in shelat and Shen's work [23], is that a WI proof suffices the purposes here. Let us consider the case in which GEN (plays as the verifier) has private input $U = \{u^{(j)}\}_{j\in[s]}$ for some $s \in \mathbb{N}$, and EVAL (plays as the prover) knows $u^{(m)}$ for some $m \in [s]$. In the honest-but-curious model, a simple WI proof of EVAL's knowledge $u^{(m)}$ can be done as follows:

1. GEN picks random nonce r, and sends EVAL $\{\mathsf{enc}_u(r)\}_{u\in U}$.

2. EVAL receives $C = \{c^{(j)}\}_{j\in[s]}$ and returns $\mathsf{dec}_{u^{(m)}}(c^{(m)})$.

3. GEN receives r' and accepts if $r' = r$, or aborts otherwise.

This proof is sound because an EVAL with no knowledge of any $u^{(m)} \in U$ can only guess r with negligible probability. However, this proof is not WI in the malicious model. In fact, a malicious GEN may pick distinct $r^{(j)}$s and send EVAL

$$(\mathsf{enc}_{u^{(1)}}(r^{(1)}), \mathsf{enc}_{u^{(2)}}(r^{(2)}), \ldots, \mathsf{enc}_{u^{(s)}}(r^{(s)}))$$

so that $u^{(m)}$ can later be deduced by locating r' in $\{r^{(j)}\}_{j\in[s]}$.

To force GEN to behave honestly in Step 1, we suggest that GEN discloses (U, r) after receiving r' so that EVAL could check if C is constructed correctly. Our third observation is that this disclosure does not compromise GEN's input privacy. Indeed, EVAL should have already learned the majority of U from the circuit evaluation, and r is a random nonce that has no information about GEN's input at all. So GEN's input is not leaked through (U, r). Moreover, this disclosure does not compromise the soundness of the protocol since after GEN receives r', EVAL has already delivered its proof of authenticity so that learning (U, r) afterwards will not change the proof retroactively. Nonetheless, we stress that GEN should not learn r' *before* EVAL finishes the check, and nor should EVAL be able to change r' after the check. This property suggests the use of a commitment scheme. Our idea is that EVAL commits to $\mathsf{dec}_{u^{(m)}}(c^{(m)})$ instead of giving it away in clear. After GEN reveals (U, r), EVAL checks if C is indeed correctly generated. If the check fails, EVAL aborts; otherwise, EVAL decommits to r'. Then GEN checks if $r' = r$ and responds as in the honest-but-curious protocol.

One more issue is that a malicious GEN could learn EVAL's private input $u^{(m)}$ with non-negligible probability by faking its private inputs from the beginning. More specifically, a malicious GEN could guess $u^{(m)}$ with probability $1/s$ and then pretend that its private input is

$$\bar{U} = (\bar{u}^{(1)}, \ldots, \bar{u}^{(m-1)}, u^{(m)}, \bar{u}^{(m+1)}, \ldots, \bar{u}^{(s)})$$

instead of U, where $\bar{u}^{(j)}$ is randomly picked. With this attack, a malicious GEN is capable of providing checkable ciphertexts C when EVAL's private input is indeed $u^{(m)}$. In particular, the fact that EVAL can provide the correct nonce r confirms that its private input is indeed $u^{(m)}$. A straightforward way to get around this issue is for the two parties to share the commitments to GEN's private inputs in the first place. By the binding property of the commitment scheme, a malicious GEN cannot change its private inputs at will. The correctness of these commitments will be guaranteed by the circuit-level cut-and-choose technique.

The complete description of our GEN's output authenticity protocol is presented in Figure 1, and the security of this protocol is stated in Lemma 1.

Common Input: security parameter 1^k, statistical security parameter 1^s, commitments to GEN's private input $\{(\mathsf{com}(u_0^{(j)}), \mathsf{com}(u_1^{(j)}))\}_{j\in[s]}$, and bit b.

Private Input: GEN has $\{(u_0^{(j)}, u_1^{(j)})\}_{j\in[s]}$ and EVAL has random key v corresponding to GEN's output wire of value b in the m-th garbled circuit for some $m \in [s]$.

1. GEN picks random nounce $r \in \{0,1\}^k$ and sends EVAL $\{\mathsf{enc}_u(r)\}_{u\in U}$, where $U = \{u_b^{(j)}\}_{j\in[s]}$.
2. EVAL gets $\{c^{(j)}\}_{j\in[s]}$ and sends GEN $\mathsf{com}(\mathsf{dec}_v(c^{(m)}))$.
3. After getting $\mathsf{com}(r')$, GEN decommits to U.
4. EVAL checks the decommitted values $\{u^{(j)}\}_{j\in[s]}$ that
   (a) if $\mathsf{com}(u_b^{(j)})$ is correctly opened to $u^{(j)}$ for all j?
   (b) if $\mathsf{dec}_{u^{(j)}}(c^{(j)}) \stackrel{?}{=} \mathsf{dec}_{u^{(s)}}(c^{(s)})$ for all $j \in [s-1]$?

   EVAL aborts if any of the checks fails; otherwise, it decommits to r'.
5. GEN accepts the proof if $\mathsf{com}(r')$ is correctly opened and $r' = r$; otherwise, it rejects.

Figure 1: A WI proof for GEN's output authenticity with malicious security (where EVAL plays the role of the prover)

LEMMA 1. *Let $\{(u_0^{(j)}, u_1^{(j)})\}_{j\in[s]}$ be GEN's private input, and let commitments $\{(com(u_0^{(j)}), com(u_1^{(j)}))\}_{j\in[s]}$ and bit b be the common inputs. If all $u_b^{(j)}$s are uniformly distributed over $\{0,1\}^k$, then the protocol presented in Figure 1 satisfies the following properties:*

1. ***(Completeness)** If* EVAL *knows $u_b^{(j)}$ for some $j \in [s]$,* GEN *always accepts.*

2. ***(Soundness)** If* EVAL *does not know any of $u_b^{(j)}$s,* GEN *rejects with probability at least $1 - 2^{-k}$.*

3. ***(Witness-indistinguishability)*** *Let* VIEW_v *denote the view of* GEN *from running the protocol with* EVAL *using input* v. *If* EVAL *knows any* V *of* $\{u_b^{(j)}\}_{j\in[s]}$, *then for any* $v_1, v_2 \in V$, $\{\text{VIEW}_{v_1}\}_{k\in\mathbb{N}}$ *and* $\{\text{VIEW}_{v_2}\}_{k\in\mathbb{N}}$ *are computationally indistinguishable.*

3.2 Generator's Input Consistency

In the cut-and-choose technique, multiple copies of the garbled circuit are constructed and then either checked or evaluated. It is conceivable that a malicious GEN may provide inconsistent inputs to different evaluation circuits. Lindell and Pinkas showed that for some functions, it is not difficult for a malicious GEN to use inconsistent inputs to extract information of EVAL's input [15]. For instance, suppose both parties agree upon the objective function

$$f((a_1, a_2, a_3), (b_1, b_2, b_3)) \mapsto (a_1 b_1 \oplus a_2 b_2 \oplus a_3 b_3, \perp),$$

where a_i and b_i is GEN's and EVAL's i-th input bit, respectively. Instead of providing (a_1, a_2, a_3) consistently, a malicious GEN may send $(1,0,0)$, $(0,1,0)$, and $(0,0,1)$ to different evaluation circuits. In the end, GEN learns the majority bit of EVAL's input, which is the extra information that EVAL did not agree to reveal.

Several approaches have been proposed to defend this attack. Mohassel and Franklin proposed the equality-checker technique, which requires $O(\sigma^2 n)$ commitments to be computed and exchanged [18]. Lindell and Pinkas developed an approach that also requires $O(\sigma^2 n)$ commitments [15]. Later, they realized that $O(\sigma^2 n)$ commitments are too much of the communication overhead, and then further suggested a pseudo-random synthesizer that relies on efficient zero-knowledge proofs under specific hardness assumptions and requires $O(\sigma n)$ algebraic operations [16]. shelat and Shen proposed the use of malleable claw-free collections, which also uses $O(\sigma n)$ algebraic operations, but they showed that the witness-indistinguishability is sufficient [23]. Our approach gets the best of the both worlds, i.e., it requires only $O(\sigma n)$ symmetric cryptographic operations.

We tackle this issue with an auxiliary circuit, in addition to the objective circuit, that computes a function of GEN's input. At a high level, the circuit-level cut-and-choose technique ensures the correctness of this auxiliary circuit, and its output is used to ensure GEN's input consistency. In particular, for this idea to work, we need to endow the output of this auxiliary circuit with *collision-free* and *hiding* properties. The former ensures that the consistency of the auxiliary outputs implies the consistency of GEN's inputs, and the latter ensures that the auxiliary outputs do not reveal any information about GEN's inputs.

A natural candidate for this auxiliary circuit is a commitment circuit. The binding and hiding properties of a commitment scheme satisfy the two security properties needed here. This is a conceptually much simpler solution. We, however, failed to find a commitment circuit that introduces less overhead than the previous state-of-the-art solution does. Fortunately, we figured that a universal hash circuit is a sufficient and much more efficient alternative. We next give the definition of universal hash functions, and then we discuss how we achieve both collision-free and hiding properties with a universal hash circuit. Finally, we present an efficient instantiation with proper parameters.

DEFINITION 2 (UNIVERSAL HASH). *A collection of hash functions* $\mathcal{H} = \{h | h : A \to B\}$ *is called* universal *if for any distinct* $x, y \in A$, *the probability that a uniformly chosen* $h \in \mathcal{H}$ *satisfies that* $h(x) = h(y)$ *is at most* $1/|B|$.

3.2.1 Collision-Free Property

This property comes naturally with universal hash functions. Indeed, Definition 2 shows that for any distinct x, y, if they are *fixed* before h is *uniformly* chosen, their hashes are unlikely to collide. This suggests that the collision-free property can be achieved by letting GEN commit to (fix) its inputs before a hash function is jointly (uniformly) picked. Later, the consistency of GEN's inputs can be verified by checking the consistency of the auxiliary outputs (the hashes). Since both the objective circuit and the auxiliary circuit share the same input from GEN, GEN's input consistency to the auxiliary circuits implies the same to the objective circuits. Our protocol is outlined as follows:

1. GEN commits to its inputs $x^{(1)}, x^{(2)}, \ldots, x^{(\sigma)}$, where $x^{(j)}$ denotes its input to the j-th garbled circuit.

2. GEN and EVAL jointly and uniformly pick $h \in \mathcal{H}$.

3. GEN constructs σ copies of the garbled circuit. Each circuit contains two parts: the objective circuit and the auxiliary circuit. While the first part computes the objective function, the j-th auxiliary circuit uses the input wires of the objective circuit to compute $h(x^{(j)})$.

4. EVAL asks to check the correctness of a random fraction of the garbled circuits. If the check fails, EVAL aborts; otherwise, EVAL asks GEN to decommit to its inputs for the remaining (unchecked) circuits.

5. EVAL first evaluates the remaining auxiliary circuits. If the evaluation outputs (the hashes) are not consistent, EVAL aborts; otherwise, EVAL proceeds to evaluating the remaining objective circuits.

Since the cut-and-choose technique employs a majority operation at the end, the final evaluation output will not be influenced by a few inconsistent inputs introduced by a malicious GEN. We next argue, at a high level, that with high probability, the protocol outlined above enjoys the desired security property that GEN*'s inputs to the majority of the remaining circuits are consistent.* Indeed, if a malicious GEN is able to pass the hash consistency check and provide inconsistent inputs to the majority of the remaining objective circuits, there are only three possibilities:

1. *The (auxiliary) circuits are faulty:* The cut-and-choose technique ensures that with high probability, this only happens to a minority of the remaining circuits.

2. GEN *is really lucky to have found a collision:* By Definition 2, this happens with probability at most $1/|B|$, which becomes negligible if B is properly chosen.

3. GEN *is able to break the binding property of the commitments:* Since universal hash functions do not even provide pre-image resistance, given h and $h(x^{(i)})$, it can be easy to find $x^{(j)}$ such that $h(x^{(i)}) = h(x^{(j)})$. So if GEN is able to open the commitment from Step 1 to some value computed after h is chosen in Step 2, it breaks the desired security property. However, this would imply that GEN is able to break the commitment scheme's binding property, which happens with negligible probability too.

REMARK 3.1. *Since the above protocol is not the final version of our solution, we only provide the intuitions for now. A simpler and more elaborate protocol will be given in Figure 2, but the same outline and security argument will apply.*

3.2.2 Hiding Property

A deterministic universal hash $h : A \to B$ provides the collision-free property we need, yet it is insufficient for the purposes here due to the lack of the hiding property. Indeed, if the size of domain A is small, EVAL could exhaustively compute the hash of all possibilities in A and then deduce $x^{(j)} \in A$ from $h(x^{(j)})$. If the hashes are pseudo-random, they reveal little information about the input, which is the hiding property we desire. In particular, the celebrated left-over-hash lemma [9] (LHL) states that the output of a uniformly picked universal hash function h is pseudo-random (even if h is made public) as long as the input has enough (min-)entropy. Consequently, we suggest that function $f(x, y) \mapsto (f_1, f_2)$ is converted to $g(x||r, y) \mapsto (f_1, h(x||r)||f_2)$, where r is randomness properly picked by GEN at the beginning and h is a universal hash function uniformly picked *after* GEN commits to its new input $x||r$.

We argue that our approach does provide the hiding property even when h is public. Indeed, given $h(x||r)$ and h, if r is long enough (has enough entropy), for any x', there must exist r' such that $h(x||r) = h(x'||r')$. This shows that giving away hash $h(x||r)$ does not rule out any possibilities of x.

3.2.3 Efficient Instantiation

We suggest the use of the matrix universal hash family

$$\mathcal{M}_{k,m} = \{h_M | \; h_M(x) = M \cdot x \text{ for some } M \in \{0,1\}^{k \times m}\},$$

for some $m \in \mathbb{N}$. A nice property of this hash family is that it is $\oplus$-homomorphic, that is, for any $x, y \in \{0,1\}^m$ and $h_M \in \mathcal{M}_{k,m}$, it holds that $h_M(x \oplus y) = h_M(x) \oplus h_M(y)$.

This homomorphism allows an efficient instantiation of the protocol outlined above. The main idea is to let EVAL learn GEN's input hash $h_M(x)$ not by circuit evaluation but by first giving away $h_M(\pi)$ and then revealing $x \oplus \pi$, where π is a randomly chosen one-time pad. The $\oplus$-homomorphism of h_M then allows EVAL to compute $h_M(x) = h_M(\pi) \oplus h_M(x \oplus \pi)$ without learning x. We stress that although using this technique allows hashes to be computed locally, we still have to maintain the main structure of the above protocol outline, that is, letting GEN commit to its inputs before h_M is jointly picked and letting EVAL learn the hash of the input to the evaluation circuits. The complete protocol of our GEN's input consistency check is presented in Figure 2, and its security is stated in Lemma 3.

LEMMA 3. *Let $k, \sigma \in \mathbb{N}$ be common inputs such that $\sigma = O(k)$. Suppose* GEN *has private inputs $\{x^{(1)}, x^{(2)}, \ldots, x^{(\sigma)}\}$, and* EVAL *has private input $S \subset [\sigma]$. If $|S| = c \cdot \sigma$ for some $1 > c > 0$ and* EVAL *accepts the proof presented in Figure 2, the probability that no $x^{(j)}$ appears more than $|S|/2$ times in multiset $\{x^{(j)}\}_{j \in S}$ is negligible in k.*

REMARK 3.2. *We stress that* GEN*'s private input $x^{(j)}$ in Figure 2 refers to the concatenation of its actual input and a random input as previously discussed. It is also worth-mentioning that k in Lemma 3 is also the security parameter for the commitment scheme used in Figure 2.*

Common Input: security parameter 1^k, statistical security parameter 1^σ, perfectly-hiding commitment scheme com, and matrix hash function family $\mathcal{M}_{k,m}$ for some $m \in \mathbb{N}$.

Private Input: GEN has $x^{(1)}, x^{(2)}, \ldots, x^{(\sigma)} \in \{0,1\}^m$, and EVAL has subset $S \subset [\sigma]$.

1. GEN randomly picks $\pi^{(1)}, \pi^{(2)}, \ldots, \pi^{(\sigma)} \in \{0,1\}^m$.
2. For all $j \in [\sigma]$, GEN commits to $x^{(j)}$ by sending $\mathsf{com}(\pi^{(j)})$ and $\mathsf{com}(x^{(j)} \oplus \pi^{(j)})$ to EVAL.
3. GEN and EVAL jointly pick a random $h_M \in \mathcal{M}_{k,m}$.
4. GEN sends $h_M(\pi^{(1)}), h_M(\pi^{(2)}), \ldots, h_M(\pi^{(\sigma)})$ to EVAL.
5. EVAL receives $h_\pi^{(1)}, h_\pi^{(2)}, \ldots, h_\pi^{(\sigma)}$. Next,
   - if $j \in [s] \backslash S$, GEN decommits $\mathsf{com}(\pi^{(j)})$ to $\pi'^{(j)}$, and EVAL checks if $h_\pi^{(j)} = h_M(\pi'^{(j)})$;
   - if $j \in S$, GEN decommits $\mathsf{com}(x^{(j)} \oplus \pi^{(j)})$ to $y^{(j)}$, and EVAL computes $h_x^{(j)} = h_M(y^{(j)}) \oplus h_\pi^{(j)}$.

   EVAL rejects if any of the commitments fails to open, any of the checks fails, or for any distinct $a, b \in S$, $h_x^{(a)} \neq h_x^{(b)}$; otherwise, EVAL accepts.

Figure 2: A proof for GEN's input consistency

REMARK 3.3. *We allow* EVAL *to select S, the set of circuits to evaluate. This saves the effort of jointly picking set S, but still guarantees that whatever S that* EVAL *picks will not compromise* GEN*'s privacy. Lemma 3 holds as long as S is a constant fraction of $[\sigma]$. The use of perfectly-hiding commitment schemes avoids the problems with the well-known* Selective Decommitment Attack.

Finally, we suggest the parameters for security level 2^{-k}. By Definition 2, GEN cannot find a collision with probability better than $1/|B|$. So $|B|$ needs to be at least 2^k. As to the size of random input r, the LHL lemma shows that if the min-entropy of $x||r$ is at least $k + 2k = 3k$ and the output hash is k-bits long, then the output is indistinguishable from a truly random k-bit string with probability at least $1 - 2^{-k}$. Since we make no assumptions about the input distribution of x, a simple approach is to uniformly pick r such that $|r| = 3k$. We can do better by exploiting specific properties of $\mathcal{M}_{k,m}$ and reach the same goal with $|r| = 2k + \lg(k)$ as shown in Lemma 4.

LEMMA 4. *Let X_n denote $\{0,1\}^n$ for some $n \in \mathbb{N}$ and $\mathcal{M}_{k,m}$ be defined as above. For any $x \in X_n$ and any $t \geq 2k + \lg(k)$, distributions $\{(h, h(x||r))\}$ and $\{(h, y)\}$ are statistically indistinguishable with probability at least $1 - 2^{-k}$, where h, r, and y are uniformly chosen from $\mathcal{M}_{k,n+t}, X_t$, and X_k, respectively.*

3.3 Selective Failure Attack

The *Selective Failure Attack* possible in the presence of malicious adversaries has been pointed out by Mohassel and Franklin [18] and by Kiraz and Schoenmakers [12]. This attack occurs when a malicious GEN assigns (K_0, K_1) to an EVAL's input wire in the garbled circuit while using (K_0, K_1^*) instead in the corresponding OT such that $K_1 \neq K_1^*$. Consequently, if EVAL has input 1, it learns K_1^*, gets stuck during the evaluation, and GEN eventually learns EVAL's input.

Lindell and Pinkas [15] suggested that EVAL picks matrix $M \in \{0,1\}^{n\times m}$ for some $m \in \mathbb{N}$ and computes its new input $\bar{y} \in \{0,1\}^m$ such that $M \cdot \bar{y} = y$. An auxiliary circuit will later convert $\bar{y}$ back to y to use as input to the original circuit. The insight is that although selective failures allow GEN to probe some partial information of $\bar{y}$, it is possible that this partial information does not reveal any information about EVAL's actual input y. For this approach to work, the security property needed is formulated as follows:

DEFINITION 5. *For some $m, n, k \in \mathbb{N}$, $M \in \{0,1\}^{n\times m}$ is called* k-probe-resistant *if for any non-empty $L \subset [n]$, the Hamming distance of $\bigoplus_{i\in L} M_i$ is at least k, where M_i denotes the i-th row of matrix M.*

As long as M is k-probe-resistant, a malicious GEN will have to successfully probe k bits of $\bar{y}$ in order to gain any partial information of y, the probability of which is negligible. [15] shows that when M is uniformly chosen from $\{0,1\}^{n\times m}$ where $m = \max(4n, 8k)$, the probability that M fails to be k-probe-resistant will be negligible. We stress that matrix M can even be made public so that the auxiliary circuit could consist of only XOR-gates, which requires no communication overhead and can be computed efficiently when combining with the free-XOR trick [13]. In short, not only does this approach elegantly reduce the selective failure attack problem to the classic error correcting code construction, it also has the potential to incur only little overhead.

Our idea to construct a k-probe-resistant matrix is to use a maximum distance separable code such as Reed-Solomon codes.[3] We will work on the Reed-Solomon code over $\mathbb{F}_{2^t}$ for some $t \in \mathbb{N}$ with codeword size N and message size K.

By optimizing parameters, we prove the following in the full version of this paper:

LEMMA 6. *Let $P_1, P_2, \ldots, P_n$ be distinct, non-zero polynomials with degree at least $K-1$ uniformly picked from $F_{2^t}[x]$, where integer $K \geq (\lg(n)+n+k)/t$. The probability that there exist some $i \in [n]$ and some $L \subset [n]\backslash\{i\}$ such that $P_i = \sum_{j\in L} P_j$ is at most 2^{-k}.*

Finally, we describe and *implement* an algorithm to find a k-probe-resistant M with high probability and prove the correctness of this algorithm as follows:

THEOREM 7. *With probability at least $1-2^{-k}$, the algorithm presented in Figure 5 outputs a k-probe-resistant matrix $M \in \{0,1\}^{n\times m}$ such that $m \in \mathbb{N}$ and $m \leq \lg(n)+n+k+k\cdot\max(\lg(4n),\lg(4k))$.*

4. THE MAIN PROTOCOL

We now give the full description of our main protocol that is based on the Yao protocol presented in Appendix B.[4]

[3]This direction has indeed been mentioned by Lindell and Pinkas: "an explicit construction can be achieved using any explicit linear code. [15]" Here, we develop their idea further by describing an explicit solution that enjoys the optimal performance—optimal asymptotic complexity with a constant factor of one is worth reporting.

[4]We stress that although the Yao protocol is a well-known work, readers are encouraged to get familiarized with our notations and presentation, which serve as a steppingstone to better understanding our main protocol.

Common Input: security parameter 1^k, statistical security parameter 1^σ, symmetric cipher (enc, dec) with semantic security, perfectly-hiding commitment scheme com, and objective function $f : (x, y) \mapsto (f_1, f_2)$.

Private Input: GEN has input x and EVAL has input y.

Private Output: GEN receives f_1, EVAL receives f_2.

1. **(New Inputs)** GEN uniformly picks $r \in \{0,1\}^{2k+\lg(k)}$ and $e \in \{0,1\}^{|f_1|}$, while EVAL samples k-probe-resistant matrix M and computes $\bar{y}$ such that $M \cdot \bar{y} = y$. From now on, GEN's input refers to $\bar{x} = x||e||r = \bar{x}_1\bar{x}_2\ldots\bar{x}_{m_1}$ and EVAL's input refers to $\bar{y} = \bar{y}_1\bar{y}_2\ldots\bar{y}_{m_2}$, where $\bar{x}_i$ and $\bar{y}_i$ denote the i-th bit of $\bar{x}$ and $\bar{y}$, respectively.

   REMARK 4.1. *r is GEN's random input used to achieve the hiding property of the hash of GEN's input and protect GEN's input privacy, and e is the one-time pad used to encrypt f_1 and protect GEN's output privacy.*

   REMARK 4.2. *By definition, k-probe-resistant matrix M has to have full (row) rank. So for any y, there must exist some $\bar{y}$ such that $M \cdot \bar{y} = y$. Also, given y and M, $\bar{y}$ can be efficiently computed by Gaussian elimination.*

2. **(Pick the Randomness)** For all $j \in [\sigma]$, GEN picks randomness $\rho^{(j)}$ for the j-th garbled circuit and uses $\rho^{(j)}$ to compute $(K_{i,0}^{(j)}, K_{i,1}^{(j)}, \pi_i^{(j)}) \in \{0,1\}^{2k+1}$ for all wires. Let $W_{i,b}^{(j)}$ denote key-locator pair $(K_{i,b}^{(j)}, b \oplus \pi_i^{(j)})$. From now on, $W_{i,b}^{(j)}$ is called the *label* that corresponds to wire w_i of value b in the j-th garbled circuit.

   REMARK 4.3. *Randomness $\rho^{(j)}$ can be considered as either a pool of truly random bits or a truly random seed to a pseudo-random number generator. It has internal states that keep track of used and fresh random bits, and it always returns fresh random bits when it is used. When later requested, GEN needs to reveal $\rho^{(j)}$'s initial state so that EVAL will be able to regenerate the random bits that GEN used to construct the j-th garbled circuit.*

3. **(Commit to Input Label Pairs)** Let $\{w_i\}_{i\in[m_1]}$ be the wires corresponding to GEN's input and $\{w_{m_1+i}\}_{i\in[m_2]}$ be those corresponding to EVAL's input. For each $j \in [\sigma]$, GEN uses randomness $\rho^{(j)}$ to commit to the label pairs assigned to $\{w_i\}_{i\in[m_1+m_2]}$ by sending commitments $\Theta^{(j)}$ and $\Omega^{(j)}$ to EVAL, where

$$\Theta^{(j)} = \{\mathsf{com}(W^{(j)}_{i,0\oplus\pi_i^{(j)}}; \theta_i^{(j)}), \mathsf{com}(W^{(j)}_{i,1\oplus\pi_i^{(j)}}; \theta_i^{(j)})\}_{i\in[m_1]},$$

$$\Omega^{(j)} = \{\mathsf{com}(W^{(j)}_{m_1+i,0}), \mathsf{com}(W^{(j)}_{m_1+i,1})\}_{i\in[m_2]}.$$

   REMARK 4.4. *The statement "GEN uses randomness ρ to commit to something" means that the randomness, such as $\theta_i^{(j)}$ here, needed in the commitment is computed from ρ in a standard, verifiable way. Also, recall that some commitment may have its randomness omitted for presentation simplicity, for example, $\Omega^{(j)}$.*

   REMARK 4.5. *GEN commits to the label pairs assigned to GEN's and EVAL's input wires so that when EVAL later receives proper decommitments, it will know that the decommitted labels are valid. Moreover, the commitment pairs assigned to* GEN*'s input wires need to be randomly swapped so that each label's semantics is independent of its location. In other words, the location of a successfully decommitted label will not disclose* GEN*'s input to* EVAL. *This random swap is done by reusing the permutation bit* $\pi_i^{(j)}$ *that is assigned to each wire and used to permute entries in garbled truth tables. In contrast, the commitment pairs corresponding to* EVAL*'s input wires need to follow a known order so that* EVAL *can know the semantics of its input labels and can verify that the successfully decommitted labels actually match its input. As a result, the commitment pairs in* $\Theta^{(j)}$ *are randomly swapped so that the commitment to b-label of the i-th wire is the* $(2\cdot i+b\oplus\pi_i^{(j)})$*-th entry, whereas in* $\Omega^{(j)}$*, the commitment to b-label of the i-th wire is the* $(2\cdot i+b)$*-th entry.*

4. **(Fix Gen's Input)** For each $i \in [m_1]$ and $j \in [\sigma]$, GEN commits to its input by sending commitments $\{\Gamma^{(j)}\}_{j\in[\sigma]}$ to EVAL, where $\Gamma^{(j)} = \{\mathsf{com}(W_{i,\bar{x}_i}^{(j)}; \gamma_i^{(j)})\}_{i\in[m_1]}$.

REMARK 4.6. *It is crucial that commitments* $\Gamma^{(j)}$ *cannot use the randomness from* $\rho^{(j)}$ *like commitments* $\Theta^{(j)}$ *do. If so,* EVAL *will learn* GEN*'s inputs to check circuits.*

REMARK 4.7. *Commitments* $\Theta^{(j)}$ *in the previous step along with commitments* $\Gamma^{(j)}$ *in this step play the role of Step 2 of our* GEN*'s input consistency check shown in Figure 2. In particular,* $\Theta^{(j)}$ *here is equivalent to* $\mathsf{com}(\pi^{(j)})$ *there since the swapping pattern in* $\Theta^{(j)}$ *is exactly* $\pi^{(j)}$*, and* $\Gamma^{(j)}$ *here is equivalent to* $\mathsf{com}(x^{(j)}\oplus\pi^{(j)})$ *there since the committed label* $W_{i,\bar{x}_i}^{(j)} = (K_{i,\bar{x}_i}^{(j)}, \bar{x}_i \oplus \pi_i^{(j)})$.

5. **(Determine the Objective Circuit)** EVAL first reveals M, and then both parties jointly run a coin flipping protocol to uniformly pick $H \in \{0,1\}^{k\times m_1}$. Both parties now have determined the objective circuit C that computes $g : (\bar{x},\bar{y}) \mapsto (\perp,(c,g_2))$, where $\bar{x} = x||e||r$, $y = M\cdot\bar{y}$, $g_1 = f_1(x,y)$, $c = g_1 \oplus e$, and $g_2 = f_2(x,y)$.

REMARK 4.8. *Choosing* H *plays the role of Step 3 of our* GEN*'s input consistency check presented in Figure 2. The coin-flipping protocol should guarantee unbiased output even in the presence of one malicious party; thus a three-round protocol suffices.*

6. **(Commit to Output Label Pairs)** Let $\{w_i\}_{i\in O}$ be the wires corresponding to EVAL's output and $O = O_1 \cup O_2$, where O_1 contains all the wire indices corresponding to output c and O_2 has those corresponding to output g_2. For each $j\in[\sigma]$, GEN uses randomness $\rho^{(j)}$ to commit to the label pairs assigned to $\{w_i\}_{i\in O_1}$ by sending commitments $\Phi^{(j)} = \{\mathsf{com}(W_{i,0}^{(j)}),\mathsf{com}(W_{i,1}^{(j)})\}_{i\in O_1}$ to EVAL.

REMARK 4.9. *Commitments* $\{\Phi^{(j)}\}_{j\in[\sigma]}$ *are part of the common input for our* GEN*'s output authenticity proof.*

7. **(Eval's Input OTs)** For each $i \in [m_2]$, both parties run a $\binom{2}{1}$-OT in which GEN's input equals

$$\left(\{(W_{m_1+i,0}^{(j)}\}_{j\in[\sigma]}, \{(W_{m_1+i,1}^{(j)})\}_{j\in[\sigma]}\right)$$

and EVAL's input equals $\bar{y}_i$. Let $Y^{(j)}$ denote the set of decommitments EVAL received for the j-th garbled circuit, that is, $Y^{(j)} = \{(W_{m_1+i,\bar{y}_i}^{(j)})\}_{i\in[m_2]}$.

REMARK 4.10. *There are* $\sigma\cdot m_2$ *decommitments needed for* EVAL *to retrieve its input labels from* $\sigma\cdot m_2$ *commitment pairs* $\{\Omega^{(j)}\}_{j\in[\sigma]}$*, which* EVAL *received in Step 3. These decommitments are grouped according to* EVAL*'s input index i as* GEN*'s input to the OTs and grouped according to circuit index j as decommitments* $Y^{(j)}$.

8. **(Circuit OTs)** EVAL randomly picks $S \subset [\sigma]$ such that $|S| = 2\sigma/5$. Let $s\in\{0,1\}^\sigma$ such that $s_j = 1$ if $j\in S$; or $s_j = 0$ otherwise. If $s_j = 0$, EVAL will learn the randomness and check the j-th circuit; otherwise, EVAL will retrieve GEN's input labels and evaluate the j-th circuit. More specifically, for each $j\in[\sigma]$, both parties run a $\binom{2}{1}$-OT in which EVAL's input equals s_j and GEN's input equals $(\rho^{(j)},(X_1^{(j)},X_2^{(j)},h_\pi^{(j)}))$, where

$$X_1^{(j)} = \{(W_{i,\bar{x}_i}^{(j)},\gamma_i^{(j)})\}_{i\in[m_1]}, X_2^{(j)} = \{(W_{i,\bar{x}_i}^{(j)},\theta_i^{(j)})\}_{i\in[m_1]},$$

and $h_\pi^{(j)} = H\cdot(\pi_1^{(j)}||\pi_2^{(j)}||\cdots||\pi_{m_1}^{(j)})$.

REMARK 4.11. *The above* $\binom{2}{1}$*-OTs could run in parallel if they provide security for parallel execution.*

REMARK 4.12. *Decommitments* $X_1^{(j)}$ *and* $X_2^{(j)}$ *are used for* EVAL *to retrieve* GEN*'s input labels from commitments* $\Gamma^{(j)}$ *received in Step 4 and* $\Theta^{(j)}$ *received in Step 3, respectively. In particular, each decommitment in* $X_2^{(j)}$ *opens one of a pair of commitments in* $\Theta^{(j)}$.

REMARK 4.13. *Revealing* $h_\pi^{(j)}$*s plays the role of Step 4 of our* GEN*'s input consistency check shown in Figure 2.*

9. **(Garble the Circuit)** For each gate $g : \{0,1\}\times\{0,1\}\mapsto\{0,1\}$ with input wires w_a and w_b and output wire w_c, GEN computes its garbled truth table

$$\begin{aligned}G(g)^{(j)} =(&\langle\pi_a^{(j)},\pi_b^{(j)}\rangle,\langle\pi_a^{(j)},1\oplus\pi_b^{(j)}\rangle,\\ &\langle 1\oplus\pi_a^{(j)},\pi_b^{(j)}\rangle,\langle 1\oplus\pi_a^{(j)},1\oplus\pi_b^{(j)}\rangle),\end{aligned}$$

where $\langle b_1,b_2\rangle = \mathsf{enc}_{K_{a,b_1}^{(j)}}(\mathsf{enc}_{K_{b,b_2}^{(j)}}(W_{c,g(b_1,b_2)}^{(j)}))$.

REMARK 4.14. *Once* $(K_{i,0}^{(j)},K_{i,1}^{(j)},\pi_i^{(j)})$*s are chosen for all wires, no more randomness is needed for generating the j-th garbled circuit. So* $\rho^{(j)}$ *is not needed here.*

10. **(Check the Circuit)** Let $\{w_i\}_{i\in O}$ be the circuit-output wires. GEN then sends $\{G(C)^{(j)}\}_{j\in[\sigma]}$ to EVAL, where

$$G(C)^{(j)} = \left(\{G(g)^{(j)}\}_{g\in C},\{\pi_i^{(j)}\}_{i\in O}\right).$$

- **(Check Circuits)** For each $j\in[\sigma]\backslash S$, EVAL checks:
  (a) if randomness $\rho^{(j)}$ received in Step 8 can regenerate commitments $\{\Theta^{(j)},\Omega^{(j)},\Phi^{(j)}\}$ received in Step 3 and Step 6 and reconstruct garbled circuit $G(C)^{(j)}$?
  (b) if hash $h_\pi^{(j)}$ received in Step 8 (via circuit-OT) is indeed equal to $H\cdot(\pi_1^{(j)}||\pi_2^{(j)}||\cdots||\pi_{m_1}^{(j)})$, in which permutation bit $\pi_i^{(j)}$ is computed from randomness $\rho^{(j)}$?
- **(Evaluation Circuits)** For each $j\in S$, EVAL checks:
  (a) if $X_1^{(j)}$ and $X_2^{(j)}$ received in Step 8 successfully opens $\Gamma^{(j)}$ and half of $\Theta^{(j)}$ received in Step 4, respectively? and if the decommitted labels match? Namely,

i. if the i-th entry of $X_1^{(j)}$ successfully opens the i-th entry of $\Gamma^{(j)}$?

ii. if the i-th entry of $X_2^{(j)}$ successfully opens the $(2 \cdot i + \bar{x}_i \oplus \pi_i^{(j)})$-th entry of $\Theta^{(j)}$?

iii. if the i-th decommitted labels from the above two steps coincide?

(b) if $Y^{(j)}$ received in Step 7 successfully opens half of the commitments in $\Omega^{(j)}$? Namely, if the i-th entry of $Y^{(j)}$ successfully opens the $(2 \cdot i + \bar{y}_i)$-th entry of $\Omega^{(j)}$?

EVAL aborts immediately if a failure occurs.

REMARK 4.15. *For evaluation circuits, the fact that decommitments $X_2^{(j)}$ (resp. $Y^{(j)}$) successfully open $\Theta^{(j)}$ (resp. $\Omega^{(j)}$) shows that the majority of the decommitted labels corresponding to* GEN*'s (resp.* EVAL*'s) input are valid. Furthermore, the fact that the decommitted labels from commitments $\Gamma^{(j)}$ coincide with those from commitments $\Theta^{(j)}$ shows that* GEN *indeed commits to its inputs before H is chosen, which is the necessary condition for our 2-universal hash idea to work.*

11. **(Evaluate the Circuit)** For each $j \in S$, EVAL has obtained garbled circuit $G(C)^{(j)}$ and $(m_1 + m_2)$ labels corresponding to the $(m_1 + m_2)$ circuit-input wires of C. EVAL then evaluates the circuit as follows:

(a) For each gate g with retrieved labels $W_a^{(j)} = (K_a^{(j)}, \delta_a^{(j)})$ and $W_b^{(j)} = (K_b^{(j)}, \delta_b^{(j)})$ corresponding to the gate-input wires, EVAL picks the $(2 \cdot \delta_a^{(j)} + \delta_b^{(j)})$-th entry E in $G(g)^{(j)}$ and computes label $W_c^{(j)} = \mathsf{dec}_{K_b^{(j)}}(\mathsf{dec}_{K_a^{(j)}}(E))$ corresponding to the gate-output wire.

(b) For each circuit-output wire with retrieved label $W_i^{(j)} = (K_i^{(j)}, \delta_i^{(j)})$, EVAL computes wire value $b_i^{(j)} = \delta_i^{(j)} \oplus \pi_i^{(j)}$.

EVAL interprets $\{b_i^{(j)}\}_{i \in O}$ as $(c^{(j)}, g_2^{(j)})$. Let $Z^{(j)}$ denote the labels that came with $c^{(j)}$.

12. **(Gen's Input Consistency Check)** For all $i \in [m_1]$ and $j \in S$, let $W_i^{(j)} = (K_i^{(j)}, \delta_i^{(j)})$ be the decommitted label corresponding to the i-th bit of GEN's input to the j-th garbled circuit. EVAL computes $h_{\bar{x}}^{(j)} = h_{\pi}^{(j)} \oplus H \cdot (\delta_1^{(j)} || \delta_2^{(j)} || \cdots || \delta_{m_1}^{(j)})$ for all $j \in S$, and then verifies GEN's input consistency by checking if for all $a, b \in S$, $h_{\bar{x}}^{(a)} = h_{\bar{x}}^{(b)}$. EVAL aborts if any of the checks fails.

REMARK 4.16. *Checking the correctness of $h_{\pi}^{(j)}$s received in Step 10 and the checks here play the role of Step 5 of our* GEN*'s input consistency check in Figure 2.*

13. **(Majority Operation)** Let (c, g_2) be the most common tuple in $\Pi = \{(c^{(j)}, g_2^{(j)})\}_{j \in S}$. EVAL aborts if (c, g_2) is not the majority in Π, that is, (c, g_2) does not appear more than $\frac{|\Pi|}{2} = \frac{\sigma}{5}$ times in Π; otherwise, EVAL outputs g_2.

14. **(Gen's Output Authenticity Proof)** The two parties conduct the protocol presented in Figure 1. In particular, the common inputs include security parameter 1^k, statistical security parameter $1^{|S|}$, commitments to label pairs assigned to GEN's output wires $\{\Phi^{(j)}\}_{j \in S}$, and GEN's alleged output c. Also, GEN's input equals $\{W_{i,0}^{(j)}, W_{i,1}^{(j)}\}_{i \in O, j \in S}$ and EVAL's input equals $Z^{(j)}$ for some $j \in S$ such that $c^{(j)} = c$. If the proof fails, GEN aborts; otherwise, GEN outputs $c \oplus e$.

THEOREM 8. *Assume that the $\binom{2}{1}$-OT protocol is secure in the presence of malicious adversaries, and there exist a perfectly-hidng commitment scheme, a family of pseudo-random functions, the main protocol* (GEN, EVAL) *presented above securely computes $f : (x, y) \mapsto (f_1, f_2)$ in the presence of malicious adversaries.*

The proof sketch is provided in Appendix C.

5. EXPERIMENTAL RESULTS

In this section, we report empirical evidence of our performance advantages over prior work. We implemented our work on top of the open-source project—KSS [14]. We ran our experiments on the grid Stampede hosted in Texas Advanced Computing Center. Each instance of the experiments invokes 32 computing nodes; each node has 32GB memory and two 2 Intel Xeon E5-2680 2.7G processors; and each processor has 8 cores.

5.1 Performance of our Proposed Technique

We show the performance of our GEN's input consistency check and k-probe-resistant matrix generating algorithm compared with the prior state-of-the-art in Figure 3.

We first compare the performance of the KSS system with that of the KSS system integrated with our GEN's input consistency check. This experiment is conducted by using both systems to evaluate circuits of various input sizes. These circuits compute 2^n blocks of AES128 encryption, where $n = 1, 2, \ldots, 10$ in which GEN provides inputs for 2^n blocks of AES128 (and thus has a 2^{n+7}-bit input), EVAL provides a 128-bit encryption key, and EVAL receives the 2^{n+7}-bit ciphertext. Figure 3a shows that when the input size increases only to a moderate level (2^{17}), the performance gap due to GEN's input consistency check has almost dominated the whole protocol execution. Specifically, the wall-clock running of the improved protocol is 48.8 seconds versus 92.1 seconds for KSS (which was the fastest published protocol whose results we could replicate on our setup).

Next, we show in Figure 3b that as GEN's input size increases, the ratio between the width and height of the k-probe-resistant matrices generated by our algorithm indeed approximates 1, while the ratio of those generated by Lindell and Pinkas's approach remains constant 4. This comparison suggests that for a circuit that has OTs as the dominant component, the overall protocol execution time could be reduced to 25% simply by replacing the k-probe-resistant matrix generated by the original work with the one generated by our algorithm.

5.2 Performance of the Main Protocol

We show in Figure 4 the overall execution time of our system securely evaluating circuits EDT-4095[5], RSA-256[6], and 1024-AES128. Overall, our system is able to handle 650,000+ (or ~ 200,000 non-XOR) gates per second. We

[5]This circuit computes the edit distance of two 4,095-bit inputs.

[6]This circuit computes a 256-bit modular exponentiation.

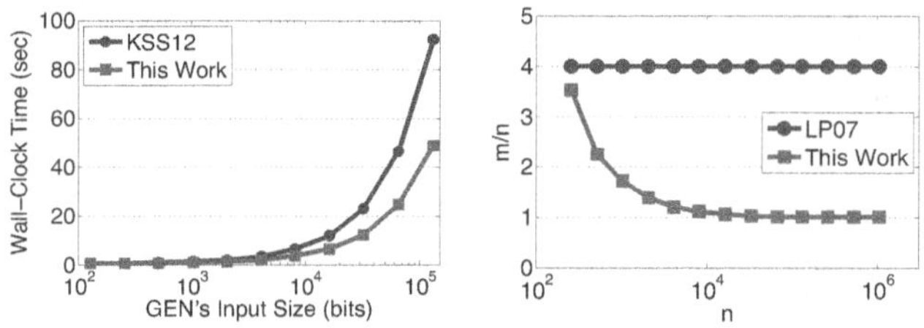

(a) (b)

Figure 3: Performance comparison with prior works

		Gen (sec)	Eval (sec)	Comm (MB)
OT	comp	0.4±0.09%	–	6
	comm	0.1± 1%	0.3±0.6%	
cut-& chk	comp	–	–	9
	comm	–	–	
Inp. Chk	comp	0.8± 1%	0.3±0.2%	2,008
	comm	0.3± 1%	0.9± 1%	
Evl.	comp	11.4± 0.6%	28.0±0.4%	72,271
	comm	9.2± 1%	30.3±0.8%	
Total	comp	12.6± 0.3%	28.0±0.2%	74,294
	comm	9.6± 1%	31.5±0.4%	

Table 3: The 95% two-sided confidence intervals of the computation andcommunication time for each stage in the 1024-AES128 experiment $(x, y) \mapsto (\perp, 1024\text{-AES128}_y(x))$.

also observe that for all three circuits that we evaluated, more than 60% of the execution time is spent on communicating the huge amount of data, the garbled circuits. If we consider only the circuit garbling, the rate that our system actually achieves could be as high as 1,600,000+ (or 500,000+ non-XOR) gates per second, with the help of various optimization techniques, including SSE2 and AESNI instruction sets, and the free-XOR technique.

circuit	gates	(non-XOR)	time (sec)	comm.
EDT-4095	5.9B	(2.4B)	9,042	18 TB
RSA-256	0.93B	(0.33B)	1,437	3 TB
1024-AES128	32M	(9.3M)	49	74 GB

Figure 4: The performance of our main protocol with $k = 80$ and $\sigma = 256$. All numbers in "time" column come from an average of 30 data points and have the 95% confidence interval $< 1\%$.

6. ACKNOWLEDGEMENTS

We thank Benny Pinkas and Ben Riva for their graciousness in correcting an earlier draft of this manuscript and the anonymous reviewers for their insightful comments.

This work is supported by the Defense Advanced Research Projects Agency (DARPA) and the Air Force Research Laboratory (AFRL) under contract FA8750-11-2-0211. The views and conclusions contained in this document are those of the authors and should not be interpreted as representing the official policies, either expressed or implied, of the Defense Advanced Research Projects Agency or the US government.

7. REFERENCES

[1] I. Damgård, V. Pastro, N. Smart, and S. Zakarias. Multiparty Computation from Somewhat Homomorphic Encryption. CRYPTO '12. `http://eprint.iacr.org/2011/535`.

[2] T. K. Frederiksen, T. P. Jakobsen, J. B. Nielsen, P. S. Nordholt, and C. Orlandi. MiniLEGO: Efficient Secure Two-Party Computation From General Assumptions. EUROCRYPT '13. `http://eprint.iacr.org/2013/155`.

[3] R. Gennaro, C. Gentry, and B. Parno. Non-Interactive Verifiable Computing: Outsourcing Computation to Untrusted Workers. CRYPTO'10, pages 465–482.

[4] O. Goldreich. *Foundations of Cryptography: Volume 2, Basic Applications*. Cambridge University Press, 2004.

[5] O. Goldreich, S. Micali, and A. Wigderson. How to Play any Mental Game. STOC '87, pp. 218–229.

[6] V. Goyal, P. Mohassel, and A. Smith. Efficient Two-Party and Multiparty Computation against Covert Adversaries. EUROCRYPT'08, pp. 289–306.

[7] D. Hofheinz. Possibility and Impossibility Results for Selective Decommitments. *J. Cryptol.*, 24(3):470–516, 2011.

[8] Y. Huang, D. Evans, J. Katz, and L. Malka. Faster Secure Two-Party Computation using Garbled Circuits. USENIX SEC'11, pp. 35–35.

[9] R. Impagliazzo and D. Zuckerman. How to Recycle Random Bits. SFCS '89.

[10] S. Jarecki and V. Shmatikov. Efficient Two-Party Secure Computation on Committed Inputs. EUROCRYPT '07, pp. 97–114.

[11] M. Kiraz. *Secure and Fair Two-Party Computation*. PhD thesis, Technische Universiteit Eindhoven, 2008.

[12] M. Kiraz and B. Schoenmakers. A Protocol Issue for The Malicious Case of Yao's Garbled Circuit Construction. In *27th Symposium on Information Theory in the Benelux*, 2006.

[13] V. Kolesnikov and T. Schneider. Improved Garbled Circuit: Free XOR Gates and Applications. ICALP '08, pp. 486–498.

[14] B. Kreuter, a. shelat, and C. Shen. Billion-Gate Secure Computation with Malicious Adversaries. USENIX SEC'12, 2012.

[15] Y. Lindell and B. Pinkas. An Efficient Protocol for Secure Two-Party Computation in the Presence of Malicious Adversaries. EUROCRYPT '07.

[16] Y. Lindell and B. Pinkas. Secure Two-Party Computation via Cut-and-Choose Oblivious Transfer. TCC'11, pp. 329–346.

[17] D. Malkhi, N. Nisan, B. Pinkas, and Y. Sella. Fairplay: A Secure Two-Party Computation System. USENIX SEC'04, volume 13, pp. 287–302.

[18] P. Mohassel and M. Franklin. Efficiency Tradeoffs for Malicious Two-Party Computation. PKC'06, pp. 458–473.

[19] P. Mohassel and B. Riva. Garbled Circuits Checking Garbled Circuits: More Efficient and Secure Two-Party Computation, 2013. `http://eprint.iacr.org/2013/051`.

[20] J. Nielsen and C. Orlandi. LEGO for Two-Party Secure Computation. TCC'09, volume 5444 of *LNCS*, pages 368–386.

[21] J. B. Nielsen, P. S. Nordholt, C. Orlandi, and S. S. Burra. A New Approach to Practical Active-Secure Two-Party Computation. CRYPTO '12, 2012.

[22] B. Pinkas, T. Schneider, N. P. Smart, and S. C. Williams. Secure Two-Party Computation is Practical. ASIACRYPT '09, pp. 250–267.

[23] a. shelat and C.-H. Shen. Two-Output Secure Computation with Malicious Adversaries. EUROCRYPT'11, pp 386–405.

[24] Stampede. Tacc stampede. `http://www.tacc.utexas.edu/resources/hpc/stampede`.

[25] D. Woodruff. Revisiting the Efficiency of Malicious Two-Party Computation. EUROCRYPT'07, volume 4515 of *LNCS*, pp. 79–96.

[26] A. C. Yao. Protocols for Secure Computations. SFCS '82, pp. 160–164.

APPENDIX

A. ALGORITHM

Input: EVAL's input size n and a security parameter 1^k
Output: A k-probe-resistant $M \in \{0,1\}^{n\times m}$ for some $m \in \mathbb{N}$

1 **begin**
2 $\quad t \leftarrow \lceil \max(\lg(4n), \lg(4k)) \rceil$
3 $\quad$ **while** $2^{t-1} > k + (\lg(n) + n + k)/(t-1)$ **do**
4 $\quad\quad t \leftarrow t - 1$;
5 $\quad$ **end**
6 $\quad K \leftarrow \lceil (\lg(n) + n + k)/t \rceil$;
7 $\quad N \leftarrow K + k - 1$;
8 $\quad$ **for** $i \leftarrow 1$ ***to*** n **do**
9 $\quad\quad$ Pick $P(x) = \sum_{i=0}^{K-1} a_i x^i$, where $a_i \leftarrow_R \mathbb{F}_{2^t}$;
10 $\quad\quad M_i \leftarrow [P(1)_2 || P(2)_2 || \ldots || P(N)_2]$
11 $\quad$ **end**
12 $\quad$ **return** M; // $M \in \{0,1\}^{n\times m}$, where $m = Nt$
13 **end**

Figure 5: A probabilistic algorithm to generate a k-probe-resistant matrix $M \in \{0,1\}^{n\times m}$ for some $m \in \mathbb{N}$. Line 2-5 is to find the minimum t such that $2^t \geq k + (\lg(n) + n + k)/t$, and $P(i)_2$ denotes a $t \times 1$ row vector over $\{0,1\}$.

B. THE YAO PROTOCOL

Our presentation uses the permuted garbled truth table technique [17] (also known as the *point-and-permute* technique in the literature). Briefly, this technique suggests to assign each wire w_i an extra random permutation bit π_i. The circuit garbling and evaluating is then slightly modified: for GEN, each garbled truth table is constructed in the way that its entries are permuted according to its input wires' permutation bits; and for EVAL, each random key now comes with a *locator* that helps EVAL identify the right entry in the garbled truth table to decrypt.

For each wire, EVAL learns exactly one key-locator pair out of the two assigned to that wire from the circuit evaluation, and the learned locator is in fact the evaluation result of that wire one-time padded with the permutation bit. This property ensures that EVAL is oblivious to the intermediate result of the circuit evaluation and allows EVAL to learn the output by revealing the permutation bits assigned to circuit-output wires.

Common Input: security parameter 1^k, boolean circuit C that computes $f(x,y)$, and symmetric encryption scheme $(\mathsf{enc}, \mathsf{dec})$ with semantic security.

Private Input: GEN has private input $x = x_1 x_2 \cdots x_{m_1}$ and EVAL has private input $y = y_1 y_2 \cdots y_{m_2}$, where x_i and y_i denote the i-th bit of x and y, respectively.

Output: Both GEN and EVAL receive $f(x,y)$ at the end.

1. **(Pick the Randomness)** GEN picks $(K_{i,0}, K_{i,1}, \pi_i) \in \{0,1\}^{2k+1}$ at random for each wire w_i. Let $W_{i,b}$ denote the key-locator pair $(K_{i,b}, b \oplus \pi_i)$. $W_{i,b}$ is called the *label* corresponding to wire w_i of value b hereafter.
2. **(Retrieve Input Labels)** Let $\{w_i\}_{i\in[m_1]}$ be the wires corresponding to GEN's input, and let $\{w_{m_1+i}\}_{i\in[m_2]}$ be those corresponding to EVAL's input.

(a) **(Gen's Input Labels)** GEN sends EVAL the labels corresponding to its input $\{W_{i,x_i}\}_{i\in[m_1]}$.

(b) **(Eval's Input Labels)** For each $i \in [m_2]$, GEN and EVAL execute a $\binom{2}{1}$-OT in which GEN's input equals $(W_{m_1+i,0}, W_{m_1+i,1})$ and EVAL's input equals y_i.

3. **(Garble the Circuit)** For each gate $g : \{0,1\}\times\{0,1\} \to \{0,1\}$ with input wires w_a and w_b and output wire w_c, GEN computes its garbled truth table

$$G(g) = (\langle \pi_a, \pi_b \rangle, \langle \pi_a, 1 \oplus \pi_b \rangle, \langle 1 \oplus \pi_a, \pi_b \rangle, \langle 1 \oplus \pi_a, 1 \oplus \pi_b \rangle),$$

where $\langle b_1, b_2 \rangle = \mathsf{enc}_{K_{a,b_1}}(\mathsf{enc}_{K_{b,b_2}}(W_{c,g(b_1,b_2)}))$.

Let $\{w_i\}_{i\in O}$ be the circuit-output wires. GEN sends EVAL

$$G(C) = (\{G(g)\}_{g\in C}, \{\pi_i\}_{i\in O}).$$

4. **(Evaluate the Circuit)** EVAL has obtained circuit $G(C)$ and $(m_1 + m_2)$ labels corresponding to the $(m_1 + m_2)$ circuit-input wires. EVAL evaluates the circuit as follows:

(a) For each gate g with retrieved input labels $W_a = (K_a, \delta_a)$ and $W_b = (K_b, \delta_b)$, EVAL picks the $(2\cdot\delta_a + \delta_b)$-th entry E in $G(g)$ and computes the output label $W_c = (K_c, \delta_c) = \mathsf{dec}_{K_b}(\mathsf{dec}_{K_a}(E))$.

(b) For each circuit-output wire w_i with corresponding label $W_i = (K_i, \delta_i)$, EVAL computes the wire value $b_i = \delta_i \oplus \pi_i$. Recall that π_i for wire w_i comes with $G(C)$.

Finally, EVAL interprets $\{b_i\}_{i\in O}$ as $f(x,y)$ and sends it to GEN. Both parties output $f(x,y)$.

C. MAIN THEOREM PROOF SKETCH

We sketch the construction of simulators S_1 and S_2 such that any malicious GEN* (resp. EVAL*) cannot tell whether it is working with S_1 (resp. S_2) in the ideal model or with honest EVAL (resp. GEN) in the real model.

Malicious Gen*

Simulator S_1 acts as an honext EVAL in the main protocol all the way until the step of OTs except that S_1 uses a fake input $\bar{y}'$. In particular, S_1 first fake input y' and then finds a pre-image $\bar{y}'$ such that $M \cdot \bar{y}' = y'$, where M is the k-probe-resitant matrix sampled at the beginning.

This fake input $\bar{y}'$ is used as input to EVAL's input OTs. The OT's receiver security ensures that GEN* (as the OT sender) cannot distinguish the OT receiver's input being $\bar{y}'$ provided by S_1 in the ideal model from being $\bar{y}$ provided by EVAL in the real model.

Next, for the circuit OTs, S_1 invokes the OT's simulator (the existence of which is guaranteed by OT's security) to extract both inputs from GEN*, including randomness $\rho^{(j)}$, decommitments $(X_1^{(j)}, X_2^{(j)})$ to GEN's input labels, and hash $h_\pi^{(j)}$. A garbled circuit is *bad* if the retrieved randomness cannot be used to regenerate the provided commitments and garbled circuit. S_1 aborts if more than $\sigma/5$ of the garbled circuits are bad. This step is indistinguishable from the real model due to the cut-and-choose technique. In particular, if more than $\sigma/5$ circuits are bad, EVAL in the real model would abort with high probability too since the probability that none of the bad circuits is checked is negligible.

If S_1 does not abort, it learns the randomness of at least $4\sigma/5$ good garbled circuits. Note that after GEN* passes the circuit checking, S_1 also learns decommitments $(X_1^{(j)}, X_2^{(j)})$ for the $2\sigma/5$ evaluation circuits. In other words, S_1 learns the randomness of at least $\sigma/5$ evaluation circuits, which are good circuits too. The binding property of the commitments ensures that S_1 learns the private inputs that GEN* provided to those good evaluation circuits. S_1 aborts if these private inputs are inconsistent. This step is indistinguishable from the real model due to GEN's input consistency check because the check ensures that the probability of good evaluation circuits having inconsistent inputs is negligible.

Let GEN*'s private input extracted from above be $\bar{x}' = x'||r'||e'$. S_1 sends x' to the external trusted party and gets $f_1(x', y)$ in return, where $y = M \cdot \bar{y}$. If S_1 in the ideal model (resp. EVAL in the real model) has come to this far, with high probability, GEN* must have provided majority good evaluation circuits with valid input labels corresponding to GEN*'s input $\bar{x}'$ and S_2's input $\bar{y}'$ (resp. EVAL's input $\bar{y}$). So the majority of EVAL's evaluation outputs are exactly $f_1(x', y) \oplus e'$. This implies that GEN* cannot distinguish S_1 on input $\bar{y}'$ but providing $f_1(x', y) \oplus e'$ (from the external party) versus EVAL on input $\bar{y}$ and provding the evaluation output $f_1(x', y) \oplus e'$. Furthermore, the k-probe-resistant matrix ensures that the difference between the probability that S_1 on fake input y' aborts (due to selective failure) and the probability that EVAL on real input y aborts is negligible.

Finally, since S_1 knows the randomness of many circuits, it also knows the random keys corresponding to GEN*'s encrypted output $f_1(x', y) \oplus e'$. S_1 is able to complete the GEN's Output Authenticity Proof as EVAL does.

Malicious Eval*

Simulator S_2 honestly follows the main protocol all the way until the step of OTs except that S_2 picks a random $\bar{x}' \in \{0,1\}^{m_1}$ at the beginning and uses this fake input as input. In particular, S_2 commits to fake input $\bar{x}'$ in Step 4 by committing to the corresponding labels. The commitments are denoted by $\{\Gamma^{(j)}\}_{j\in[\sigma]}$. Then S_2 invokes OT's simulator S_2^{OT} (whose existence is guaranteed by OT's security) to extract EVAL*'s input to OTs, that is, its private input $\bar{y}'$ to EVAL's Input OTs and the choice string s' to Circuit OTs. Recall that s' determines the check circuits and evaluation circuits. Next, S_2 externally invokes the trusted third party with input $y' = M \cdot \bar{y}'$ and gets $f_2(x, y')$ in return. Note that M is the k-probe-resistant matrix received from EVAL* before OTs. After this, if $s'_j = 0$, the j-th garbled circuit is a check circuit and needs to be honestly constructed according to objective circuit C; otherwise, the j-th garbled circuit is an evaluation circuit and is constructed in a way that it always outputs $(h', c', f_2(x, y'))$, where h' and c' are randomly picked by S_2. From now on, S_2 follows the Main protocol faithfully. Finally, if S_2 accepts in the step of GEN's Output Authenticity Proof, it sends 1 to the external oracle so that S_1 gets $f_1(x, y')$; otherwise, S_2 sends 0 to the external oracle so that S_1 gets $\perp$.

Here we argue at a high level that EVAL* cannot distinguish S_2 using fake input $\bar{x}'$ in the ideal model versus GEN using real input $\bar{x}$ in the real model.

For check circuits, the only difference between S_2 in the ideal model and GEN in the real model is the committed message in $\Gamma^{(j)}$. Note that this commitment is never opened for check circuits. Therefore, if EVAL* is able to distinguish S_2 committing to fake input $\bar{x}'$ from GEN committing to real input $\bar{x}$ in any check circuit, EVAL* is able to break the hiding property of the commitment scheme.

For evaluation circuits, the information EVAL* learned related the other party's input is the location of the decommitted labels within each pair of commitments and the evaluation output:

1. Recall that the pairs of commitments to the labels assigned to GEN's input wires are randomly swapped by permutation bits $\{\pi_i^{(j)}\}_{i\in[m_1], j\in[\sigma]}$. This random swapping implies that the location learned in the ideal model is $\bar{x}' \oplus \pi'^{(j)}$, where $\pi'^{(j)} = \pi'^{(j)}_1||\pi'^{(j)}_2||\ldots||\pi'^{(j)}_{m_1}$, while that learned in the real model is $\bar{x} \oplus \pi^{(j)}$, where $\pi^{(j)} = \pi_1^{(j)}||\pi_2^{(j)}||\ldots\pi_{m_1}^{(j)}$. Since $\pi'^{(j)}$ and $\pi^{(j)}$ are independently chosen from the uniform distribution, the location information is statistically indistinguishable.
2. The other message that might give S_2 away is the evaluation output. First, we claim that EVAL* always gets consistent output among different garbled circuits. Indeed, in the real model, since GEN is assumed to be honest, the outputs from the evaluation circuits are identical, and similarly, in the ideal model, S_2 also generates evaluation circuits that have a fixed output. So it remains to argue that (h, c, f_2) in the real model is indistinguishable from (h', c', f_2') in the ideal model. Intuitively, h and h' are indistinguishable due to the hiding property of our 2-universal hash scheme, c and c' are indistinguishable due to the perfect secrecy of the one-time pad encryption, and f_2 and f_2' are indistinguishable due to the simulation security of OTs.

More Efficient Oblivious Transfer and Extensions for Faster Secure Computation

Gilad Asharov, Yehuda Lindell
Cryptography Research Group
Bar-Ilan University, Israel
asharog@cs.biu.ac.il, lindell@biu.ac.il

Thomas Schneider, Michael Zohner
Engineering Cryptographic Protocols Group
TU Darmstadt, Germany
thomas.schneider@ec-spride.de,
michael.zohner@ec-spride.de

ABSTRACT

Protocols for secure computation enable parties to compute a joint function on their private inputs without revealing anything but the result. A foundation for secure computation is oblivious transfer (OT), which traditionally requires expensive public key cryptography. A more efficient way to perform many OTs is to extend a small number of base OTs using OT extensions based on symmetric cryptography.
In this work we present optimizations and efficient implementations of OT and OT extensions in the semi-honest model. We propose a novel OT protocol with security in the standard model and improve OT extensions with respect to communication complexity, computation complexity, and scalability. We also provide specific optimizations of OT extensions that are tailored to the secure computation protocols of Yao and Goldreich-Micali-Wigderson and reduce the communication complexity even further. We experimentally verify the efficiency gains of our protocols and optimizations. By applying our implementation to current secure computation frameworks, we can securely compute a Levenshtein distance circuit with 1.29 billion AND gates at a rate of 1.2 million AND gates per second. Moreover, we demonstrate the importance of correctly implementing OT within secure computation protocols by presenting an attack on the FastGC framework.

Categories and Subject Descriptors

F.1.2 [**Modes of computation**]: Interactive and reactive computation—*cryptographic protocols*

Keywords

Secure computation; oblivious transfer extensions; semi-honest adversaries

CCS'13, November 4–8, 2013, Berlin, Germany.
Copyright 2013 ACM 978-1-4503-2477-9/13/11 ...$15.00.
http://dx.doi.org/10.1145/2508859.2516738.

1. INTRODUCTION

1.1 Background

In the setting of secure two-party computation, two parties P_0 and P_1 with respective inputs x and y wish to compute a joint function f on their inputs without revealing anything but the output $f(x, y)$. This captures a large variety of tasks, including privacy-preserving data mining, anonymous transactions, private database search, and many more. In this paper, we consider semi-honest adversaries who follow the protocol, but may attempt to learn more than allowed via the protocol communication. We focus on semi-honest security as this allows construction of highly efficient protocols for many application scenarios. This model is justified e.g., for computations between hospitals or companies that trust each other but need to run a secure protocol because of legal restrictions and/or in order to prevent inadvertent leakage (since only the output is revealed from the communication). Semi-honest security also protects against potential misuse by some insiders and future break-ins, and can be enforced with software attestation. Moreover, understanding the cost of semi-honest security is an important stepping stone to efficient malicious security. We remark that also in a large IARPA funded project on secure computation on big data, IARPA stated that the semi-honest adversary model is suitable for their applications [27].

Practical secure computation. Secure computation has been studied since the mid 1980s, when powerful feasibility results demonstrated that any efficient function can be computed securely [15, 51]. However, until recently, the bulk of research on secure computation was theoretical in nature. Indeed, many held the opinion that secure computation will never be practical since carrying out cryptographic operations for every gate in a circuit computing the function (which is the way many protocols work) will never be fast enough to be of use. Due to many works that pushed secure computation further towards practical applications, e.g., [4, 5, 8, 11, 13, 21, 24, 30, 35–37, 44, 50], this conjecture has proven to be wrong and it is possible to carry out secure computation of complex functions at speeds that five years ago would have been unconceivable. For example, in FastGC [24] it was shown that AES can be securely computed with 0.2 seconds of preprocessing time and just 0.008 seconds of online computation. This has applications to private database search and also to mitigating server breaches in the cloud by sharing the decryption key for sensitive data between two servers and never revealing it (thereby forcing an attacker to compromise the security of two servers instead of one). In addition, [24] carried out a secure computation of a circuit of size *1.29 billion AND gates*, which until recently would have been thought impossible. Their computation took 223 minutes, which is arguably too long for most applications. However, it demonstrated that large-scale secure computation can be achieved. The FastGC framework was a breakthrough result regarding the practicality of secure computation and has been used in many subsequent works, e.g., [22, 23, 25, 26, 44]. However, it is possible to still do much better. The secure computation framework of [49] improved the results of FastGC [24] by a factor of 6-80, depending on the network latency. Jumping ahead, we obtain additional speedups for both secure computation frameworks [24] and [49]. Most notably, when applying our improved OT implementation to the framework of [49], we are able to evaluate the 1.29 billion AND gate circuit in just 18 minutes. We conclude that significant efficiency improvements can still be made, considerably broadening the tasks that can be solved using secure computation in practice.

Oblivious transfer and extensions. In an *oblivious transfer (OT)* [48], a sender with a pair of input strings (x_0, x_1) interacts with a receiver who inputs a choice bit σ. The result is that the receiver learns x_σ without learning anything about $x_{1-\sigma}$, while the sender learns nothing about σ. Oblivious transfer is an extremely powerful tool and the foundation for almost all efficient protocols for secure computation. Notably, Yao's garbled-circuit protocol [51] (e.g., implemented in FastGC [24]) requires OT for every input bit of one party, and the GMW protocol [15] (e.g., implemented in [8, 49]) requires OT for every AND gate of the circuit. Accordingly, the efficient instantiation of OT is of crucial importance as is evident in many recent works that focus on efficiency, e.g., [8,16,19,22–24,26,34,37,43,49]. In the semi-honest case, the best known OT protocol is that of [40], which has a cost of approximately 3 exponentiations per 1-out-of-2 OT. However, if thousands, millions or even billions of oblivious transfers need to be carried out, this will become prohibitively expensive. In order to solve this problem, *OT extensions* [2, 28] can be used. An OT extension protocol works by running a small number of OTs (say, 80 or 128) that are used as a base for obtaining many OTs via the use of cheap symmetric cryptographic operations only. This is conceptually similar to public-key encryption where instead of encrypting a large message using RSA, which would be too expensive, a hybrid encryption scheme is used such that only a single RSA computation is carried out to encrypt a symmetric key and then the long message is encrypted using symmetric operations only. Such an OT extension can actually be achieved with extraordinary efficiency; specifically, the protocol of [28] requires only three hash function computations on a single block per oblivious transfer (beyond the initial base OTs).

Related Work. There is independent work on the efficiency of OT extension with security against stronger malicious adversaries [17, 42, 43]. In the semi-honest model, [20] improved the implementation of the OT extension protocol of [28] in FastGC [24]. They reduce the memory footprint by splitting the OT extension protocol sequentially into multiple rounds and obtain speedups by instantiating the pseudorandom generator with AES instead of SHA-1. Their implementation evaluates 400,000 OTs (of 80-bit strings without precomputations) per second over WiFi; we propose additional optimizations and our fastest implementation evaluates more than 700,000 OTs per second over WiFi, cf. Tab. 4.

1.2 Our Contributions and Outline

In this paper, we present more efficient protocols for OT extensions. This is somewhat surprising since the protocol of [28] sounds optimal given that only three hash function computations are needed per transfer. Interestingly, our protocols do not lower the number of hash function operations. However, we observe that significant cost is incurred due to other factors than the hash function operations. We propose several algorithmic (§4) and protocol (§5) optimizations and obtain an OT extension protocol (General OT, G-OT §5.3) that has lower communication, faster computation, and can be parallelized. Additionally, we propose two OT extension protocols that are specifically designed to be used in secure computation protocols and which reduce the communication and computation even further. The first of these protocols (Correlated OT, C-OT §5.4) is suitable for secure computation protocols that require correlated inputs, such as Yao's garbled circuits protocol with the free-XOR technique [32, 51]. The second protocol (Random OT, R-OT §5.4) can be used in secure computation protocols where the inputs can be random, such as GMW with multiplication triples [1, 15] (cf. §5.1). We apply our optimizations to the OT extension implementation of [49] (which is based on [8]) and demonstrate the improvements by extensive experiments (§6).[1] A summary of the time complexity for 1-out-of-2 OTs on 80-bit strings is given in Fig. 1. While the original protocol of [28] as implemented in [49] evaluates 2^{23} OTs in 18.0 s with one thread and in 14.5 s with two threads, our improved R-OT protocol requires only 8.4 s with one thread and 4.2 s with two threads, which demonstrates the scalability of our approach.

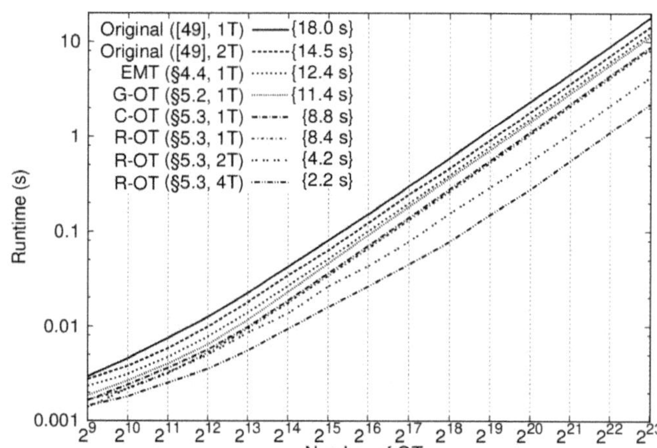

Figure 1: Runtime for 1-out-of-2 OT extension optimizations on 80-bit strings. The reference and number of threads is given in (); the time for 2^{23} OTs is given in {}.

Secure random number generation. In §3 we emphasize that when OT protocols are used as building block in a secure computation protocol, it is very important that random values are generated with a cryptographically strong

[1]Our implementation is available online at `http://encrypto.de/code/OTExtension`.

random number generator. In fact, we show an attack on the latest version of the FastGC [24] implementation (version v0.1.1) of Yao's protocol which uses a weak random number generator. Our attack allows the full recovery of the inputs of both parties. To protect against our attack, a cryptographically strong random number generator needs to be used (which results in an increased runtime).

Faster semi-honest base OT without random oracle. In the semi-honest model, the OT of [40] is the fastest known with $2+n$ exponentiations for the sender and $2n$ fixed-base exponentiations for the receiver, for n OTs. However, it is proven secure only in the random oracle model, which is why the authors of [40] also provide a slower semi-honest OT that relies on the DDH assumption, which has complexity $4n$ fixed-base + $2n$ double exponentiations for the sender and $1+3n$ fixed-base + n exponentiations for the receiver. In §5.2 we construct a protocol secure under the Decisional Diffie-Hellmann (DDH) assumption that is much faster when many transfers are run (as in the case of OT extensions where 80 base OTs are needed) and is only slightly slower than the fastest OT in the random oracle model (§6.1).

Faster OT extensions. In §5.3 we present an improved version of the original OT extension protocol of [28] with reduced communication and computation complexity. Furthermore, we demonstrate how the OT extension protocol can be processed in independent blocks, allowing OT extension to be parallelized and yielding a much faster runtime (§4.1). In addition, we show how to implement the matrix transpose operation using a cache-efficient algorithm that operates on multiple entries at once (§4.2); this has a significant effect on the runtime of the protocol. Finally, we show how to reduce the communication by approximately one quarter (depending on the bit-length of the inputs). This is of great importance since local computations of the OT extension protocol are so fast that the communication is often the bottleneck, especially when running the protocol over the Internet or even wireless networks.

Extended OT functionality. Our improved protocol can be used in any setting that regular OT can be used. However, with a mind on the application of secure computation, we further optimize the protocol by taking into account its use in the protocols of Yao [51] and GMW [15] in §5.4. For Yao's garbled circuits protocol, we observe that the OT extension protocol can choose the first value randomly and output it to the sender while the second value is computed as a function of the first value. For the GMW protocol. we observe that the OT extension protocol can choose both values randomly and output them to the sender. In both cases, the communication is reduced to a *half* (or even less) of the original protocol of [28].

Experimental evaluation and applications. In §6 we experimentally verify the performance improvements of our proposed optimizations for OT and OT extension. In §7 we demonstrate their efficiency gains for faster secure computation, by giving performance benchmarks for various application scenarios. For the Yao's garbled circuits framework FastGC [24], we achieve an improvement up to factor 9 for circuits with many inputs for the receiver, whereas we improve the runtime of the GMW implementation of [49] by factor 2, e.g., a Levenshtein distance circuit with 1.29 billion AND gates can now be evaluated at a rate of 1.2 million AND gates per second.

2. PRELIMINARIES

In the following, we summarize the security parameters used in our paper (§2.1) and describe the OT extension protocol of [28] (§2.2), Yao's garbled circuits protocol (§2.3), and the GMW protocol (§2.4) in more detail. Standard definitions of security are given in Appendix A.

2.1 Security Parameters

Throughout the paper, we denote the symmetric security parameter by κ. Tab. 1 lists usage times (time frames) for different values of the symmetric security parameter κ (SYM) and corresponding field sizes for finite field cryptography (FFC) and elliptic curve cryptography (ECC) as recommended by NIST [45]. For FCC we use a subgroup of order $q = 2\kappa$. For ECC we use Koblitz curves which had the best performance in our experiments.

Security (Time Frames)	SYM	FFC	ECC
Short (legacy)	80	1024	K-163
Medium (< 2030)	112	2048	K-243
Long (> 2030)	128	3072	K-283

Table 1: Security parameters and recommended key sizes.

2.2 Oblivious Transfer and OT Extension

The m-times 1-out-of-2 OT functionality for ℓ-bit strings, denoted $m \times OT_\ell$, is defined as follows: The sender S inputs m pairs of strings $\mathbf{x}_i^0, \mathbf{x}_i^1 \in \{0,1\}^\ell$ ($1 \le i \le m$), the receiver R inputs a string $\mathbf{r} = (r_1, \ldots, r_m)$ of length m, and R obtains $\mathbf{x}_j^{r_j}$ ($1 \le j \le m$) as output. OT ensures that S learns nothing about $\mathbf{r}$ and R learns nothing about $\mathbf{x}_j^{1-r_j}$. An *OT extension protocol* implements the $m \times OT_\ell$ functionality using a small number of actual OTs, referred to as base OTs, and cheap symmetric cryptographic operations. In [28] it is shown how to implement the $m \times OT_\ell$ functionality using a single call to $\kappa \times OT_m$, and $3m$ hash function computations. Note that $\kappa \times OT_m$ can be implemented via a single call to $\kappa \times OT_\kappa$ in order to obliviously transfer symmetric keys, and then using a pseudo-random generator G to obliviously transfer the actual inputs of length m (cf. [26,28]). In the first step of [28], S chooses a random string $\mathbf{s} \in_R \{0,1\}^\kappa$, and R chooses a random $m \times \kappa$ bit matrix $T = [\mathbf{t}^1 \mid \ldots \mid \mathbf{t}^\kappa]$, where $\mathbf{t}^i \in \{0,1\}^m$ denotes the i-th column of T. The parties then invoke the $\kappa \times OT_m$ functionality, where R plays the sender with inputs $(\mathbf{t}^i, \mathbf{t}^i \oplus \mathbf{r})$ and S plays the receiver with input $\mathbf{s}$. Let $Q = [\mathbf{q}^1 \mid \ldots \mid \mathbf{q}^\kappa]$ denote the $m \times \kappa$ matrix received by S. Note that $\mathbf{q}^i = (s_i \cdot \mathbf{r}) \oplus \mathbf{t}^i$ and $\mathbf{q}_j = (r_j \cdot \mathbf{s}) \oplus \mathbf{t}_j$ (where $\mathbf{t}_j$, $\mathbf{q}_j$ are the j-th rows of T and Q, respectively). S sends (y_j^0, y_j^1) where $y_j^0 = x_j^0 \oplus H(\mathbf{q}_j)$ and $y_j^1 = x_j^1 \oplus H(\mathbf{q}_j \oplus \mathbf{s})$, for $1 \le j \le m$. R finally outputs $z_j = y_j^{r_j} \oplus H(\mathbf{t}_j)$ for every j. The protocol is secure assuming that $H : \{0,1\}^m \mapsto \{0,1\}^\ell$ is a random oracle, or a correlation robust function as in Definition A.2; see [28] for more details.

2.3 Yao's Garbled Circuits Protocol

Yao's garbled circuits protocol [51] allows two parties to securely compute an arbitrary function that is represented as Boolean circuit. The sender S encrypts the Boolean gates of the circuit using symmetric keys and sends the encrypted function together with the keys that correspond to his input bits to the receiver R. R then uses a 1-out-of-2 OT to obliviously obtain the keys that correspond to his inputs and evaluates the encrypted function by decrypting it gate by gate. To obtain the output, R sends the resulting keys to S or S provides a mapping from keys to output bits. We emphasize that Yao's garbled circuits protocol requires a 1-out-of-2 OT on κ-bit strings for *each input bit of R*. For our experiments we use the Yao's garbled circuits framework FastGC [24].

2.4 The GMW Protocol

The protocol of Goldreich, Micali, and Wigderson (GMW) [15] also represents the function to be computed as a Boolean circuit. Both parties secret-share their inputs using the XOR operation and evaluate the Boolean circuit as follows. An XOR gate is computed by locally XORing the shares while an AND gate is evaluated interactively with the help of a multiplication triple [1,49] which can be precomputed by two random 1-out-of-2 OTs on bits (cf. §5.1). To reconstruct the outputs, the parties exchange their output shares. The performance of GMW depends on the number of OTs and on the depth of the evaluated circuit, since the evaluation of AND gates requires interaction. For our experiments we use the GMW framework of [49], which is an optimization of the framework of [8] for the two party case.

3. RANDOM NUMBER GENERATION

The correct instantiation of primitives in implementations of cryptographic protocols is a challenging task, since various security properties have to be met. For instance, an important security property of a pseudo-random generator (PRG) is its unpredictability, i.e., given a sequence of pseudo-random bits $x_1...x_n$, the next bit x_{n+1} should not be predictable. If the security property of the primitive is not met, the security of the overall scheme can be compromised. We found that this was the case for the FastGC framework in version 0.1.1 [24] that uses the standard Java Random class in order to generate random values used in the base OTs, the random choices of vector $\mathbf{s}$ and matrix T in the OT extension, and the input keys of the garbled circuit. Overall, this enables an attack that allows each party to recover the inputs of the respective other party, as we will describe now.

3.1 The Java Random Class

The Java Random class implements a so-called *truncated linear congruential generator (T-LCG)* with secret seed $\psi \in \{0,1\}^{48}$. Random numbers can be generated by invoking the `next` method of an object of the Java Random class which takes as input the requested number of random bits b (for $1 \leq b \leq 32$), updates the seed $\psi' = (\alpha\psi + \beta)$ *mod* m, and returns the topmost b bits of ψ, where α = 0x5DEECE66D, β = 0xB, and $m = 2^{48}$ are public constants. If more than 32 random bits are needed, `next` is called repeatedly until a sufficient number of bits has been generated.

The security of T-LCGs was widely studied and they were shown to be predictable [18], even if the generated sequence is not directly output [3]. In case of the Java Random class, each iteration reveals b bits of the seed, leaving a remaining entropy of $48 - b$ bits. Furthermore, consecutive values can be used to build linear equations.

For our analysis, we assume that the generated random value has at least length 64 bits, i.e., it was generated by two consecutive calls to the `next` method with $b = 32$. This holds for the FastGC framework [24] which uses a Java Random object to generate symmetric keys and the columns of the T matrix (we use the first 64 bits only). To predict the output of the Java Random object, we recover its secret seed $\psi = \psi_1...\psi_{48}$ using the 64 bit output $d = d_1...d_{64}$. Since the topmost 32 bits are directly used as output, we have $\psi_{17}...\psi_{48} = d_1...d_{32}$. In addition, we have $\psi'_{17}...\psi'_{48} = d_{33}...d_{64}$. Now, the remaining lower 16 bits $\psi_1...\psi_{16}$ can be recovered using the linear equation $\psi' = (\alpha\psi + \beta) \bmod m$. Specifically, for each of the 2^{16} possible values of ψ we compute $(\alpha\psi+\beta) \bmod m - (\psi'_{17}...\psi'_{48}) \cdot 2^{16}$. Now, for the correct value of ψ the result will be zero in the 32 most-significant bits and so will be smaller than 2^{16}, whereas for all other values it will be larger (with high probability). In practice, this suffices for finding the entire seed ψ in 2^{16} steps, which takes under a second. The recovered secret seed ψ can then be used to predict the output of the Java Random object.

3.2 Exploiting the Weak PRG in FastGC [24]

We demonstrate how the usage of the Java Random class in version v0.1.1 of the FastGC [24] framework can be exploited such that the sender can recover the input bits of the receiver using the T matrix generated in the OT extension protocol (cf. §2.2), and the receiver can recover the input bits of the sender using the sender's input keys to the garbled circuit. We implemented and verified both attacks on FastGC, which both run in less than a second. Note that both attacks are carried out on the honestly generated transcript, as required for the setting of semi-honest adversaries.

Recovering the Receiver's Inputs. The sender can recover the receiver's input bits using the T matrix, which is chosen randomly by the receiver in the OT extension (cf. §2.2). Upon receiving the matrix $Q = [\mathbf{q}^1 \mid \ldots \mid \mathbf{q}^\kappa]$, the sender knows that $\mathbf{q}^i = \mathbf{t}^i$, if $s_i = 0$, and $\mathbf{q}^i = \mathbf{t}^i \oplus \mathbf{r}$, if $s_i = 1$. Hence, whenever the receiver has $s_i = 0$, the sender obtains $\mathbf{q}^i = \mathbf{t}^i$ and can recover an intermediate seed ψ of the Java Random object that was used to generate this column of T. Afterwards, the sender computes for $j > i$ consecutive random outputs $\mathbf{t}^j$ until he obtains a column $\mathbf{q}^j \neq t^j$ where $s_j = 1$ which occurs with overwhelming probability $1 - \frac{\kappa+1}{2^\kappa}$. Now, the sender can recover the receiver's input bits $\mathbf{r}$ by computing $\mathbf{q}^j \oplus \mathbf{t}^j = \mathbf{t}^j \oplus \mathbf{r} \oplus \mathbf{t}^j = \mathbf{r}$.

Recovering the Sender's Inputs. The receiver can recover the sender's input bits using the sender's input keys to the garbled circuit. In FastGC, the sender generates random symmetric keys $k_i \in \{0,1\}^\kappa$ for each of his ℓ input bits $b_i \in \{0,1\}$ using the same Random object. If $b_i = 0$, he sends $K_i = k_i$ to the receiver, else he sends $K_i = k_i \oplus (\Delta||0)$, where $\Delta \in \{0,1\}^{\kappa-1}$ is a constant global value [32]. In order to recover the sender's input bits, the receiver iteratively computes a candidate for the seed with which K_i was generated, computes the next $\ell - i$ keys k'_j $(i < j \leq \ell)$ and checks whether the candidate seed generates a consistent view for the observed values K'_j. If $b_i = 0$, then $K_i = k_i$ and the receiver knows that he has recovered the correct seed by finding either $k'_{i+1} \oplus k'_{i+2} = K_{i+1} \oplus K_{i+2}$ if there are at least two more input bits $b_{i+1} = b_{i+2} = 1$ or $k'_j = K_j$ if another input bit is $b_j = 0$. Once the receiver has found such a $b_i = 0$, he can recover all subsequent input bits by checking whether $k'_j = K_j$ $(\Rightarrow b_j = 0)$ or not $(\Rightarrow b_j = 1)$. If $b_i = 1$, then $K_i = k_i \oplus (\Delta||0)$ and the receiver recovers the wrong seed such that neither $K'_j = K_j$ nor $K'_{i+1} \oplus K'_{i+2} = K_{i+1} \oplus K_{i+2}$ hold with very high probability. Thus, the receiver knows that $b_i = 1$ and repeats the attack for $i+1$. Note that this attack fails if the sender has less than three input bits or all except the last two input bits of the sender are set to 1. In this case, however, the receiver can recover the input bits with high probability by using the remaining $\kappa - 64$ bits of the key to check if the candidate seed is correct.

Securing FastGC [24]. Securing the FastGC framework is relatively easy, since Java also provides a cryptographically strong random number generator, called SecureRandom, which by default is implemented based on SHA-1.[2] Replacing all usage of the Random class by SecureRandom increased the runtime of our experiments in §7 by around $0.5 - 4\%$, depending on the application. A complementary method to reduce the overhead in runtime is to use our correlated input OT extension of §5.4 which eliminates the need of generating a random T matrix s.t. our attack for reconstructing the receiver's inputs no longer works. Nevertheless, all randomness that is needed (even for our method) must be generated using SecureRandom.

4. ALGORITHMIC OPTIMIZATIONS

In the following we describe algorithmic optimizations that improve the scalability and computational complexity of OT extension protocols. We identified computational bottlenecks in OT extension by micro-benchmarking the 1-out-of-2 OT extension implementation of [49].[3] We found that the combined computation time of S and R was mostly spent on three operations: the matrix transposition (43%), the evaluation of H, implemented with SHA-1 (33%), and the evaluation of G, implemented with AES (14%). To speed up OT extension, we propose to use parallelization (§4.1) and an efficient algorithm for bit-matrix transposition (§4.2). Note that these implementation optimizations are of general nature and can be applied to our, but also to other OT extension protocols with security against stronger active/malicious adversaries, e.g., [28, 43]. As we will show later in our experiments in §6.2, both algorithmic improvements result in substantially faster runtimes, but only in settings where the computation is the bottleneck, i.e., over a fast network such as a LAN.

4.1 Blockwise Parallelized OT Extension

Previous OT extension implementations [8, 49] improved the performance of OT extension by using a *vertical* pipelining approach, i.e., one thread is associated to each step of the protocol: the first thread evaluates the pseudorandom generator G and the second thread evaluates the correlation robust function H (cf. §2.2). However, as evaluation of G is faster than evaluation of H, the workload between the two threads is distributed unequally, causing idle time for the first thread. Additionally, this method for pipelining is designed to run exactly two threads and thus cannot easily be scaled to a larger number of threads.

As observed in [20], a large number of OT extensions can be performed by *sequentially* running the OT extension protocol on blocks of fixed size. This reduces the total memory consumption at the expense of more communication rounds. We propose to use a *horizontal* pipelining approach that splits the matrices processed in the OT extension protocol into *independent* blocks that can be processed in parallel using multiple threads with equal workload, i.e., each of the N threads evaluates the OT extension protocol for $\frac{m}{N}$ inputs in parallel. Each thread uses a separate socket to communicate with its counterpart on the other party, s.t. network scheduling is done by the operating system.

4.2 Efficient Bit-Matrix Transposition

The computational complexity of cryptographic protocols is often measured by counting the number of invocations of cryptographic primitives, since their evaluation often dominates the runtime. However, non-cryptographic operations can also have a high impact on the overall run time of executions although they might seem insignificant in the protocol description. Matrix transposition is an example for such an operation. It is required during the OT extension protocol to transpose the $m \times \kappa$ bit-matrix T (cf. §2.2), which is created column-wise but hashed row-wise. Although transposition is a trivial operation, it has to be performed individually for each entry in T, making it a very costly operation.

We propose to efficiently implement the matrix transposition using Eklundh's algorithm [10], which uses a divide-and-conquer approach to recursively swap elements of adjacent rows (cf. Fig. 2). This decreases the number of swap operations for transposing a $n \times n$ matrix from $\mathcal{O}(n^2)$ to $\mathcal{O}(n \log_2 n)$. Additionally, since we process a bit-matrix, we can perform multiple swap operations in parallel by loading multiple bits into one register. Thereby, we again reduce the number of swap operations from $\mathcal{O}(n \log_2 n)$ to $\mathcal{O}(\lceil \frac{n}{r} \rceil \log_2 n)$, where r is the register size of the CPU ($r = 64$ for the machines used in our experiments). Jumping ahead to the evaluation in §6, this reduced the total time for the matrix transposition by approximately a factor of 9 from 7.1 s to 0.76 s per party.

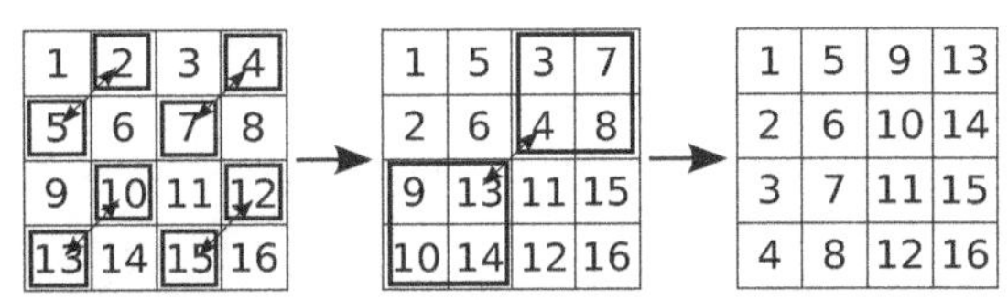

Figure 2: Efficient matrix transposition of a 4×4 matrix using Eklundh's algorithm.

5. PROTOCOL OPTIMIZATIONS

In this section, we show how to efficiently base the GMW protocol on random 1-out-of-2 OTs (§5.1), introduce a new OT protocol (§5.2), outline an optimized OT extension protocol (§5.3), and optimize OT extension for usage in secure computation protocols (§5.4).

5.1 GMW with Random 1-out-of-2 OTs

An AND gate in the GMW protocol can be computed efficiently using the multiplication triple functionality [1]: the parties hold no input, and the functionality chooses random bits $a_0, a_1, b_0, b_1, c_0, c_1$ under the constraint that $c_0 \oplus c_1 = (a_0 \oplus a_1)(b_0 \oplus b_1)$. Each P_i receives the shares labeled with i. To precompute the multiplication triples, previous works suggest to use 1-out-of-4 bit OT [8, 49].

---

[2]In response to our findings, the usage of Random has been replaced with SecureRandom in version 0.1.2 of FastGC.

[3]Note that the implementation in [49] performs 1-out-of-4 OT, but we adapted their implementation since our protocol optimizations in §5 target 1-out-of-2 OT extension.

In the following, we present a different approach for generating multiplication triples using two random 1-out-of-2 OTs on bits (R-OT). The R-OT functionality is exactly the same as OT, except that the sender gets two random messages as *outputs*. Later in §5.4, we will show that R-OT can be instantiated more efficiently than OT. In comparison to 1-out-of-4 bit OTs, using two R-OTs only slightly increases the computation complexity (one additional evaluation of G and H and two additional matrix transpositions), but improves the communication complexity by a factor of 2.

In order to generate a multiplication triple, we first introduce the f^{ab} functionality that is implemented in Algorithm 1 using R-OT. In the f^{ab} functionality, the parties hold no input and receive random bits $((a,u),(b,v))$, under the constraint that $ab = u \oplus v$. Now, note that for a multiplication triple $c_0 \oplus c_1 = (a_0 \oplus a_1)(b_0 \oplus b_1) = a_0b_0 \oplus a_0b_1 \oplus a_1b_0 \oplus a_1b_1$. The parties can generate a multiplication triple by invoking the f^{ab} functionality twice: in the first invocation P_0 acts as R to obtain (a_0, u_0) and P_1 acts as S to obtain (b_1, v_1) with $a_0b_1 = u_0 \oplus v_1$; in the second invocation P_1 acts as R to obtain (a_1, u_1) and P_0 acts as S to obtain (b_0, v_0) with $a_1b_0 = u_1 \oplus v_0$. Finally, each P_i sets $c_i = a_ib_i \oplus u_i \oplus v_i$. For correctness, observe that $c_0 \oplus c_1 = (a_0b_0 \oplus u_0 \oplus v_0) \oplus (a_1b_1 \oplus u_1 \oplus v_1) = a_0b_0 \oplus (u_0 \oplus v_1) \oplus (u_1 \oplus v_0) \oplus a_1b_1 = a_0b_0 \oplus a_0b_1 \oplus a_1b_0 \oplus a_1b_1 = (a_0 \oplus a_1)(b_0 \oplus b_1)$, as required. A proof sketch for security is given in Appendix B.

Algorithm 1 Random $(a,u),(b,v)$ with $ab = u \oplus v$

1: R chooses $a \in_R \{0,1\}$.
2: S and R perform a R-OT with a as input of R. S obtains bits x_0, x_1 and R obtains bit x_a as output.
3: R sets $u = x_a$; S sets $b = x_0 \oplus x_1$ and $v = x_0$. [Note that $ab = u \oplus v$ as $ab = a(x_0 \oplus x_1) = (a(x_0 \oplus x_1) \oplus x_0) \oplus x_0 = x_a \oplus x_0 = u \oplus v$.]
4: R outputs (a,u) and S outputs (b,v).

5.2 Optimized Oblivious Transfer

The best known protocols for oblivious transfer with security in the presence of semi-honest adversaries are those of Naor-Pinkas [40]. They present two protocols; a more efficient protocol that is secure in the random oracle model and a less efficient protocol that is secure in the standard model and under standard assumptions. In this section, we describe a new semi-honest OT protocol that is secure in the standard model and is essentially an optimized instantiation of the OT protocol of [12]. When implemented over elliptic curves, our protocol is about three times faster than the standard model OT of [40] and only two times slower than the random oracle OT of [40] (see §6.1 for a comparison of the protocol runtimes). Hence, our protocol is a good alternative for those preferring to not rely on random oracles.

Our $n \times OT_\ell$ protocol is based on the DDH assumption and uses a key derivation function (KDF); see Definition A.1. We also assume that it is possible to sample a random element of the group, and the DDH assumption will remain hard even when the coins used to sample the element are given to the distinguisher (i.e., (g,h,g^a,h^a) is indistinguishable from (g,h,g^a,g^b) for random a,b, even given the coins used to sample h). This holds for all known groups in which the DDH problem is assumed to be hard and can be implemented as described next. For finite fields, one can sample a random element $h \in \mathbb{Z}_p$ of order q by choosing a random $x \in_R \mathbb{Z}_p$ and computing $h = x^{(p-1)/q}$ until $h \neq 1$. For elliptic curves, one chooses a random x-coordinate, obtains a quadratic equation for the y-coordinate and randomly chooses one of the solutions as h (if no solution exists, start from the beginning).

The computational complexity of our protocol for $n \times OT_\ell$ is $2n$ exponentiations for the sender $S$and $2n$ *fixed-base* exponentiations for the receiver R (in fixed-base exponentiations, the same "base" g is raised to the power of many different exponents; more efficient exponentiation algorithms exist for this case [38, Sec. 14.6.3]). In addition, S computes the KDF function $2n$ times, and R computes it n times. R samples n random group elements according to the above definition. See Protocol 5.1 for a detailed description of the protocol.

PROTOCOL 5.1 (**Optimized $n \times OT_\ell$ Protocol**).

Inputs: S holds n pairs (x_i^0, x_i^1) of ℓ-bit strings, for every $1 \leq i \leq n$. R holds the selection bits $\boldsymbol{\sigma} = (\sigma_1, \ldots, \sigma_n)$. The parties agree on a group $\langle \mathbb{G}, q, g \rangle$ for which the DDH is hard, and a key derivation function KDF.

First Round (Receiver): Choose random exponents $\alpha_i \in_R \mathbb{Z}_q$ and random group elements $h_i \in_R \mathbb{G}$ for every $1 \leq i \leq n$. Then, for every i, set (h_i^0, h_i^1) as follows:

$$(h_i^0, h_i^1) \stackrel{\text{def}}{=} \begin{cases} (g^{\alpha_i},\ h_i) & \text{if } \sigma_i = 0 \\ (h_i,\ g^{\alpha_i}) & \text{if } \sigma_i = 1 \end{cases}$$

Send the pairs (h_i^0, h_i^1) to S.

Second Round (Sender): Choose a random element $r \in_R \mathbb{Z}_q$ and compute $u = g^r$. Then, for each pair (h_i^0, h_i^1) compute the keys: $(k_i^0, k_i^1) = ((h_i^0)^r, (h_i^1)^r)$ and compute the pair of ciphertexts:

$$v_i^0 = x_i^0 \oplus \mathsf{KDF}(k_i^0) \quad \text{and} \quad v_i^1 = x_i^1 \oplus \mathsf{KDF}(k_i^1).$$

Send u together with the n pairs (v_i^0, v_i^1) to R.

Output Computation (Receiver): For every $1 \leq i \leq n$, set $k_i^{\sigma_i} = u^{\alpha_i}$ and $x_i^{\sigma_i} = v_i^{\sigma_i} \oplus \mathsf{KDF}(k_i^{\sigma_i})$. R outputs $(x_1^{\sigma_1}, \ldots, x_n^{\sigma_n})$; S has no output.

The protocol is secure in the presence of a semi-honest adversary (see Definition A.3). The view of a corrupted sender consists of the pairs $\{(h_i^0, h_i^1)\}_{i=1}^n$ which are completely independent of the receiver's inputs, and therefore can be simulated perfectly. For the corrupted receiver, we need to show the existence of a simulator $\mathcal{S}_1$ that produces a computationally-indistinguishable view, given the inputs and outputs of the receiver, i.e., $\boldsymbol{\sigma}$ and $(x_1^{\sigma_1}, \ldots, x_n^{\sigma_n})$, without knowing the other sender values $(x_1^{1-\sigma_1}, \ldots, x_n^{1-\sigma_n})$. $\mathcal{S}_1$ works by running an execution of the protocol playing an honest S using inputs $x_1^{\sigma_1}, \ldots, x_n^{\sigma_n}$ and using $x_i^{1-\sigma_i} = 0$ for all $1 \leq i \leq n$. The only difference between the view of the receiver generated by the simulator and in a real execution is regarding the values $\{v_i^{1-\sigma_i}\}_{i=1}^n$, which equal $x_i^{1-\sigma_i} \oplus \mathsf{KDF}(k_i^{1-\sigma_i})$ in a real execution and just $\mathsf{KDF}(k_i^{1-\sigma_i})$ in the simulation. From the security of the KDF with respect to DDH (see Definition A.1), and using a standard hybrid argument, the values $(\mathsf{KDF}(k_1^{1-\sigma_1}), \ldots, \mathsf{KDF}(k_n^{1-\sigma_n})) = (\mathsf{KDF}(h_1^r), \ldots, \mathsf{KDF}(h_n^r))$ are indistinguishable from n uniform strings $z_1, \ldots, z_n$ each of size ℓ (even when the distinguisher sees $\langle \mathbb{G}, q, g, u = g^r \rangle$). This implies that the values $\{v_i^{1-\sigma_i}\}_{i=1}^n$ in the real execution are computationally indistinguishable from those in the simulation.

An additional optimization for random OT. When constructing OT extensions (see §2.2) the parties first run $\kappa \times OT_\kappa$ on random inputs (this holds for our optimized

OT extension protocol, and also for the original protocol of [28] if $\kappa \times OT_m$ is implemented via $\kappa \times OT_\kappa$ as described in §2.2). Observe that in this case, the sender only needs to send $u = g^r$ to the receiver R; the parties can then derive the values locally (S by computing $x_i^0 = \mathsf{KDF}((h_i^0)^r)$ and $x_i^1 = \mathsf{KDF}((h_i^1)^r)$, and R by computing $x_i^{\sigma_i} = \mathsf{KDF}(u^{\alpha_i})$). This reduces the *communication* since the elements v_i^0 and v_i^1 do not have to be sent. In addition, this means that the messages sent by S and R are actually independent of each other, and so the protocol consists of a *single round* of communication. (As pointed out in [43], this optimization can also be carried out on the protocols of Naor-Pinkas [40]. However, those protocols still require two rounds of communication which can be a drawback in high latency networks.) The timings that appear in §7 are for an implementation that uses this additional optimization.[4]

5.3 Optimized General OT Extension

In the following, we optimize the $m \times OT_\ell$ extension protocol of [28], described in §2.2. Recall, that in the first step of the protocol in [28], R chooses a huge $m \times \kappa$ matrix $T = [\mathbf{t}^1|\dots|\mathbf{t}^\kappa]$ while S waits idly. The parties then engage in a $\kappa \times OT_m$ protocol, where the inputs of the receiver are $(\mathbf{t}^i, \mathbf{t}^i \oplus \mathbf{r})$ where $\mathbf{r}$ is its input in the outer $m \times OT_\ell$ protocol (m selection bits). After the OT, S holds $\mathbf{t}^i \oplus (s_i \cdot \mathbf{r})$ for every $1 \le i \le \kappa$. As described in the appendices of [26,28], the protocol can be modified such that R only needs to choose two small $\kappa \times \kappa$ matrices $K_0 = [\mathbf{k}_1^0|\dots|\mathbf{k}_\kappa^0]$ and $K_1 = [\mathbf{k}_1^1|\dots|\mathbf{k}_\kappa^1]$ of seeds. These seeds are used as input to $\kappa \times OT_\kappa$; specifically R's input as sender in the i-th OT is $(\mathbf{k}_i^0, \mathbf{k}_i^1)$ and, as in [28], the input of S is s_i. To transfer the m-bit tuple $(\mathbf{t}^i, \mathbf{t}^i \oplus \mathbf{r})$ in the i-th OT, R expands $\mathbf{k}_i^0$ and $\mathbf{k}_i^1$ using a pseudo-random generator G, sends $(\mathbf{v}_i^0, \mathbf{v}_i^1) = (G(\mathbf{k}_i^0) \oplus \mathbf{t}^i, G(\mathbf{k}_i^1) \oplus \mathbf{t}^i \oplus \mathbf{r})$, and S recovers $G(\mathbf{k}_i^{s_i}) \oplus \mathbf{v}_i^{s_i}$.

Our main observation is that, instead of choosing $\mathbf{t}^i$ randomly, we can set $\mathbf{t}^i = G(\mathbf{k}_i^0)$. Now, R needs to send only one m-bit element $\mathbf{u}^i = G(\mathbf{k}_i^0) \oplus G(\mathbf{k}_i^1) \oplus \mathbf{r}$ to S (whereas in previous protocols of [26, 28] two m-bit elements were sent). Observe that if S had input $s_i = 0$ in the i-th OT, then it can just define its output $\mathbf{q}^i$ to be $G(\mathbf{k}_i^0) = G(\mathbf{k}_i^{s_i})$. In contrast, if S had input $s_i = 1$ in the i-th OT, then it can define its output $\mathbf{q}^i$ to be $G(\mathbf{k}_i^1) \oplus \mathbf{u}^i = G(\mathbf{k}_i^{s_i}) \oplus \mathbf{u}^i$. Since $\mathbf{u}^i = G(\mathbf{k}_i^0) \oplus G(\mathbf{k}_i^1) \oplus \mathbf{r}$, we have that $G(\mathbf{k}_i^1) \oplus \mathbf{u}^i = G(\mathbf{k}_i^0) \oplus \mathbf{r} = \mathbf{t}^i \oplus \mathbf{r}$, as required. The full description of our protocol is given in Protocol 5.2. This optimization is significant in applications of $m \times OT_\ell$ extension where m is very large and ℓ is short, such as in GMW. In typical use-cases for GMW (cf. §7), m is in the size of several millions to a billion, while ℓ is one. Thereby, the communication complexity of GMW is almost reduced by half.

In addition, as in [26], observe that unlike [28] the initial OT phase in Protocol 5.2 is completely independent of the actual inputs of the parties. Thus, the parties can perform the initial OT phase before their inputs are determined. Finally, another problem that arises in the original protocol of [28] is that the entire $m \times \kappa$ matrix is transmitted together and processed. This means that the number of OTs to be obtained must be predetermined and, if m is very large, this results in considerable latency as well as memory management issues. As in [20], our optimization enables us to process small blocks of the matrix at a time, reducing latency, computation time, and memory management problems. In addition, it is possible to continually extend OTs, with no a priori bound on m. This is very useful in a secure computation setting, where parties may interact many times together with no a priori bound.

[4]We remark that, in order to prove the security of this optimization in the standard model (without a random oracle), we need to change the ideal functionality for the random OT such that for every i, the output of the sender is $(\beta_i^0, x_i^0 = \mathsf{KDF}(g^{\beta_i^0}))$ and $(\beta_i^1, x_i^1 = \mathsf{KDF}(g^{\beta_i^1}))$, and the output of the receiver is $(\sigma_i, \beta_i^{\sigma_i}, \mathsf{KDF}(g^{\beta_i^{\sigma_i}}))$. That is, in addition to receiving their input and output from the random OT functionality, the parties receive the "discrete log" of the pertinent values. This additional information is of no consequence in *our* applications of random OT.

PROTOCOL 5.2 **(General OT extension protocol).**

Inputs: S holds m pairs (x_j^0, x_j^1) of ℓ-bit strings, for every $1 \le j \le m$. R holds m selection bits $\mathbf{r} = (r_1, \dots, r_m)$.

Initial OT Phase (base OTs):

1. S choose a random string $\mathbf{s} = (s_1, \dots, s_\kappa)$ and R chooses κ pairs of κ-bits seeds $\{(\mathbf{k}_i^0, \mathbf{k}_i^1)\}_{i=1}^{\kappa}$.
2. The parties invoke the $\kappa \times OT_\kappa$-functionality, where S plays the *receiver* with input $\mathbf{s}$ and R plays the *sender* with inputs $(\mathbf{k}_i^0, \mathbf{k}_i^1)$ for every $1 \le i \le \kappa$.
3. For every $1 \le i \le \kappa$, let $\mathbf{t}^i = G(\mathbf{k}_i^0)$. Let $T = [\mathbf{t}^1|\dots|\mathbf{t}^\kappa]$ denote the $m \times \kappa$ bit matrix where the i-th column is $\mathbf{t}^i$, and let $\mathbf{t}_j$ denote the j-th row of T, for $1 \le j \le m$.

OT extension Phase[a]**:**

1. R computes $\mathbf{t}^i = G(\mathbf{k}_i^0)$ and $\mathbf{u}^i = \mathbf{t}^i \oplus G(\mathbf{k}_i^1) \oplus \mathbf{r}$, and sends $\mathbf{u}^i$ to S for every $1 \le i \le \kappa$.
2. For every $1 \le i \le \kappa$, S defines $\mathbf{q}^i = (s_i \cdot \mathbf{u}^i) \oplus G(\mathbf{k}_i^{s_i})$. (Note that $\mathbf{q}^i = (s_i \cdot \mathbf{r}) \oplus \mathbf{t}^i$.)
3. Let $Q = [\mathbf{q}^1|\dots|\mathbf{q}^\kappa]$ denote the $m \times \kappa$ bit matrix where the i-th column is $\mathbf{q}^i$. Let $\mathbf{q}_j$ denote the j-th row of the matrix Q. (Note that $\mathbf{q}_j = (r_j \cdot \mathbf{s}) \oplus \mathbf{t}_j$.)
4. S sends (y_j^0, y_j^1) for every $1 \le j \le m$, where:
$$y_j^0 = x_j^0 \oplus H(j, \mathbf{q}_j) \quad \text{and} \quad y_j^1 = x_j^1 \oplus H(j, \mathbf{q}_j \oplus \mathbf{s})$$
5. For $1 \le j \le m$, R computes $x_j^{r_j} = y_j^{r_j} \oplus H(j, \mathbf{t}_j)$.

Output: R outputs $(x_1^{r_1}, \dots, x_n^{r_n})$; S has no output.

[a]This phase can be iterated. Specifically, R can compute the next κ bits of $\mathbf{t}^i$ and $\mathbf{u}^i$ (by applying G to get the next κ bits from the PRG for each of the seeds and using the next κ bits of its input in $\mathbf{r}$) and send the block of $\kappa \times \kappa$ bits to S (κ bits from each of $\mathbf{u}^1, \dots, \mathbf{u}^\kappa$).

THEOREM 5.3. *Assuming that G is a pseudorandom generator and H is a correlation-robust function (as in Definition A.2), Protocol 5.2 privately-computes the $m \times OT_\ell$-functionality in the presence of semi-honest adversaries, in the $\kappa \times OT_\kappa$-hybrid model.*

Proof: We first show that the protocol indeed implements the $m \times OT_\ell$-functionality. Then, we prove that the protocol is secure where the sender is corrupted, and finally that it is secure when the receiver is corrupted.

Correctness. We show that the output of the receiver is $(x_1^{r_1}, \dots, x_m^{r_m})$ in an execution of the protocol where the inputs of the sender are $((x_1^0, x_1^1), \dots, (x_m^0, x_m^1))$ and the input of the receiver is $\mathbf{r} = (r_1, \dots, r_m)$. Let $1 \le j \le m$, we show that $z_j = x_j^{r_j}$. We have two cases:

1. $\boldsymbol{r_j} = \mathbf{0}$: Recall that $\mathbf{q}_j = (r_j \cdot \mathbf{s}) \oplus \mathbf{t}_j$, and so $\mathbf{q}_j = \mathbf{t}_j$.

Thus:

$$z_j = y_j^0 \oplus H(\mathbf{t}_j) = x_j^0 \oplus H(\mathbf{q}_j) \oplus H(\mathbf{t}_j)$$
$$= x_j^0 \oplus H(\mathbf{t}_j) \oplus H(\mathbf{t}_j) = x_j^0$$

2. $\boldsymbol{r_j = 1}$: In this case $\mathbf{q}_j = \mathbf{s} \oplus \mathbf{t}_j$, and so:

$$z_j = y_j^1 \oplus H(\mathbf{t}_j) = x_j^1 \oplus H(\mathbf{q}_j \oplus \mathbf{s}) \oplus H(\mathbf{t}_j)$$
$$= x_j^1 \oplus H(\mathbf{t}_j) \oplus H(\mathbf{t}_j) = x_j^1$$

Corrupted Sender. The view of the sender during the protocol contains the output from the $\kappa{\times}OT_\kappa$ invocation and the messages $\mathbf{u}^1, \ldots, \mathbf{u}^\kappa$. The simulator $\mathcal{S}_0$ simply outputs a uniform string $\mathbf{s} \in \{0,1\}^\kappa$ (which is the only randomness that S chooses in the protocol, and therefore w.l.o.g. can be interpreted as the random tape of the adversary), κ random seeds $\mathbf{k}_1^{s_1}, \ldots, \mathbf{k}_\kappa^{s_\kappa}$, which are chosen uniformly from $\{0,1\}^\kappa$, and κ random strings $\mathbf{u}^1, \ldots, \mathbf{u}^\kappa$, chosen uniformly from $\{0,1\}^m$. In the real execution, $(\mathbf{s}, \mathbf{k}_1^{s_1}, \ldots, \mathbf{k}_\kappa^{s_\kappa})$ are chosen in exactly the same way. Each value $\mathbf{u}^i$ for $1 \le i \le \kappa$ is defined as $G(\mathbf{k}_i^0) \oplus G(\mathbf{k}_i^1) \oplus \mathbf{r}$. Since $\mathbf{k}_i^{1-s_i}$ is unknown to S (by the security of the $\kappa{\times}OT_\kappa$ functionality), we have that $G(\mathbf{k}_i^{1-s_i})$ is indistinguishable from uniform, and so each $\mathbf{u}^i$ is indistinguishable from uniform. Therefore, the view of the corrupted sender in the simulation is indistinguishable from its view in a real execution.

Corrupted Receiver. The view of the corrupted receiver consists of its random tape and the messages $((y_1^0, y_1^1), \ldots, (y_m^0, y_m^1))$ only. The simulator $\mathcal{S}_1$ is invoked with the inputs and outputs of the receiver, i.e., $\mathbf{r} = (r_1, \ldots, r_m)$ and $(x_1^{r_1}, \ldots, x_m^{r_m})$. $\mathcal{S}_1$ then chooses a random tape ρ for the adversary (which determines the $\mathbf{k}_i^0, \mathbf{k}_i^1$ values), defines the matrix T, and computes $y_j^{r_j} = x_j^{r_j} \oplus H(\mathbf{t}_j)$ for $1 \le j \le m$. Then, it chooses each $y_j^{1-r_j}$ uniformly and independently at random from $\{0,1\}^\ell$. Finally, it outputs $(\rho, (y_1^0, y_1^1), \ldots, (y_m^0, y_m^1))$ as the view of the corrupted receiver.
We now show that the output of the simulator is indistinguishable from the view of the receiver in a real execution. If $r_j = 0$, then $\mathbf{q}_j = \mathbf{t}_j$ and thus $(y_j^0, y_j^1) = (x_j^0 \oplus H(\mathbf{t}_j), x_j^1 \oplus H(\mathbf{t}_j \oplus \mathbf{s}))$. If $r_j = 1$, $\mathbf{q}_j = \mathbf{t}_j \oplus \mathbf{s}$ and therefore $(y_j^0, y_j^1) = (x_j^0 \oplus H(\mathbf{t}_j \oplus \mathbf{s}), x_j^1 \oplus H(\mathbf{t}_j))$. In the simulation, the values $y_j^{r_j}$ are computed as $x_j^{r_j} \oplus H(\mathbf{t}_j)$ and therefore are identical to the real execution. It therefore remains to show that the values $(y_1^{1-r_1}, \ldots, y_m^{1-r_m})$ as computed in the real execution are indistinguishable from random strings as output in the simulation. As we have seen, in the real execution each $y_j^{1-r_j}$ is computed as $x_j^{1-r_j} \oplus H(\mathbf{t}_j \oplus \mathbf{s})$. Since H is a correlation robust function, it holds that:

$$\{\mathbf{t}_1, \ldots, \mathbf{t}_m, H(\mathbf{t}_1 \oplus \mathbf{s}), \ldots, H(\mathbf{t}_m \oplus \mathbf{s})\} \stackrel{c}{\equiv} \{U_{m\cdot\kappa+m\cdot\ell}\}$$

for random $\mathbf{s}, \mathbf{t}_1, \ldots, \mathbf{t}_m \in \{0,1\}^\kappa$, where U_a defines the uniform distribution over $\{0,1\}^a$ (see Definition A.2). In the protocol we derive the values $\mathbf{t}_1, \ldots, \mathbf{t}_m$ by applying a pseudorandom generator G to the seeds $\mathbf{k}_1^0, \ldots, \mathbf{k}_\kappa^0$ and transposing the resulting matrix. We need to show that the values $H(\mathbf{t}_1 \oplus \mathbf{s}), \ldots, H(\mathbf{t}_m \oplus \mathbf{s})$ are still indistinguishable from uniform in this case. However, this follows from a straightforward hybrid argument (namely, that replacing truly random $\mathbf{t}^i$ values in the input to H with pseudorandom values preserves the correlation robustness of H). We conclude that the ideal and real distributions are computationally indistinguishable. ■

5.4 Optimized OT Extension in Yao & GMW

The protocol described in §5.3 implements the $m \times OT_\ell$ functionality. In the following, we present further optimizations that are specifically tailored to the use of OT extensions in the secure computation protocols of Yao and GMW.

Correlated OT (C-OT) for Yao. Before proceeding to the optimization, let us focus for a moment on Yao's protocol [51] with the free-XOR [32] and point-and-permute [37] techniques.[5] Using this techniques, the sender does not choose all keys for all wires independently. Rather, it chooses a global random value $\delta \in_R \{0,1\}^{\kappa-1}$, sets $\Delta = \delta||1$, and for every wire w it chooses a random key $k_w^0 \in_R \{0,1\}^\kappa$ and sets $k_w^1 = k_w^0 \oplus \Delta$. Later in the protocol, the parties invoke OT extension to let the receiver obliviously obtain the keys associated with its inputs. This effectively means that, instead of having to obliviously transfer two fixed independent bit strings, the sender needs to transfer two random bit strings with a fixed correlation. We can utilize this constraint on the inputs in order to save additional bandwidth in the OT extension protocol. Recall that in the last step of Protocol 5.2 for OT extension, S computes and sends the messages $y_j^0 = x_j^0 \oplus H(\mathbf{q}_j)$ and $y_j^1 = x_j^1 \oplus H(\mathbf{q}_j \oplus \mathbf{s})$. In the case of Yao, we have that $x_j^0 = k_w^0$ and $x_j^1 = k_w^1 = k_w^0 \oplus \Delta$. Since k_w^0 is just a random value, S can set $k_w^0 = H(\mathbf{q}_j)$ and can send the *single* value $y_j = \Delta \oplus H(\mathbf{q}_j) \oplus H(\mathbf{q}_j \oplus s)$. R defines its output as $H(\mathbf{t}_j)$ if $r_j = 0$ or as $y_j \oplus H(\mathbf{t}_j)$ if $r_j = 1$. Observe that if $r_j = 0$, then $\mathbf{t}_j = \mathbf{q}_j$ and R outputs $H(\mathbf{q}_j) = x_j^0 = k_w^0$, as required. In contrast, when $r_j = 1$, it holds that $\mathbf{t}_j = \mathbf{q}_j \oplus \mathbf{s}$ and thus $y_j \oplus H(\mathbf{q}_j \oplus \mathbf{s}) = \Delta \oplus H(\mathbf{q}_j) = \Delta \oplus k_w^0 = k_w^1$, as required. Thus, in the setting of Yao's protocol when using the free-XOR technique, it is possible to save bandwidth. As the keys k_w^0, k_w^1 used in Yao are also of length κ, the bandwidth is reduced from 3κ bits that are transmitted in every iteration of the extension phase to 2κ bits, effectively reducing the bandwidth by one third. Proving the security of this optimization requires assuming that H is a random oracle, in order to "program" the output to be as derived from the OT extension. In addition, we define a different OT functionality, called *correlated OT (C-OT)*, that receives Δ and chooses the sender's inputs uniformly under the constraint that their XOR equals Δ. Since Yao's protocol uses random keys under the same constraint, the security of Yao's protocol remains unchanged when using this optimized OT extension. Note that by using the correlated input OT extension protocol, the server needs to garble the circuit *after* performing the OT extension; this order is also needed for the pipelining approach used in many implementations, e.g., [24, 34, 36]. We remark that this optimization can be used in the more general case where in each pair one of the inputs is chosen uniformly at random and the other input is computed as a function of the first. Specifically, the sender has different functions f_j for every $1 \le j \le m$, and receives random values x_j^0 as output from the extension protocol, which defines $x_j^1 = f_j(x_j^0)$. E.g., for Yao's garbled circuits protocol, we have $x_j^1 = f_j(x_j^0) = \Delta \oplus x_j^0$.

Random-OT (R-OT) for GMW. When using OT extensions for implementing the GMW protocol, the efficiency can be improved even further. In this case, the inputs for S in every OT are *independent random* bits b^0 and b^1 (see §5.1 for how to evaluate AND gates using two random OTs).

[5] Our optimization is also compatible with the garbled row reduction technique of [47].

Thus, the sender can allow the random OT extension protocol (functionality) R-OT to determine *both* of its inputs randomly. This is achieved in the OT extension protocol by having S define $b^0 = H(\mathbf{q}_j)$ and $b^1 = H(\mathbf{q}_j \oplus s)$. Then, R computes b^{r_j} just as $H(\mathbf{t}_j)$. The receiver's output is correct because $\mathbf{q}_j = (r_j \cdot \mathbf{s}) \oplus \mathbf{t}_j$, and thus $H(\mathbf{t}_j) = H(\mathbf{q}_j)$ when $r_j = 0$, and $H(\mathbf{t}_j) = H(\mathbf{q}_j \oplus \mathbf{s})$ when $r_j = 1$. With this optimization, we obtain that the entire communication in the OT extension protocol consists only of the initial base OTs, together with the messages $\mathbf{u}^1, \ldots, \mathbf{u}^\kappa$, and there are *no* y_j messages. This is a dramatic improvement of bandwidth. As above, proving the security of this optimization requires assuming that H is a random oracle, in order to "program" the output to be as derived from the OT extension. In addition, the OT functionality is changed such that the sender receives both of its inputs from the functionality, and the receiver just inputs $\mathbf{r}$ (see [43, Fig. 26]).

Summary. The original OT extension protocol of [28] and our proposed improvements for $m \times OT_\ell$ are summarized in Tab. 2. We compare the communication complexity of R and S for m parallel 1-out-of-2 OT extensions of ℓ-bit strings, with security parameter κ (we omit the cost of the initial $\kappa \times OT_\kappa$). We also compare the assumption on the function H needed in each protocol, where CR denotes Correlation-Robustness and RO denotes Random Oracle.

Protocol	Applicability	R → S	S → R	H
Original [28]	All applications	$2m\kappa$	$2m\ell$	CR
G-OT §5.3	All applications	$m\kappa$	$2m\ell$	CR
C-OT §5.4	only x_j^0 random	$m\kappa$	$m\ell$	RO
R-OT §5.4	x_j^0, x_j^1 random	$m\kappa$	0	RO

Table 2: Sent bits for sender S and receiver R for m 1-out-of-2 OT extensions of ℓ-bit strings and security parameter κ.

6. EXPERIMENTAL EVALUATION

In the following, we evaluate the performance of our proposed optimizations. In §6.1 we compare our base OT protocol (§5.2) to the protocols of [40] and in §6.2 we evalute the performance of our algorithmic (§4) and protocol optimizations (§5.3 and §5.4) for OT extension.

Benchmarking Environment. We build upon the C++ OT extension implementation of [49] which implements the OT extension protocol of [28] and is based on the implementation of [8]. We use SHA-1 to instantiate the random oracle and the correlation robust function and AES-128 in counter mode to instantiate the pseudo-random generator and the key derivation function. Our benchmarking environment consists of two 2.5 GHz Intel Core2Quad CPU (Q8300) Desktop PCs with 4 GB RAM, running Ubuntu 10.10 and OpenJDK 6, connected by a Gigabit LAN.

6.1 Base OTs

In the following, we compare the performance of the OT protocols of Naor and Pinkas [40] in the random oracle (RO) and standard (STD) model to our STD model OT protocol of §5.2 for different libraries. We either use finite field cryptography (FFC) (based on the GNU-Multiprecision library v.5.0.5) or elliptic curve cryptography (ECC) (based on the Miracl library v.5.6.1). We measure the time for performing κ 1-out-of-2 base OTs on κ-bit strings, for symmetric security parameter κ, using the key sizes from Tab. 1. The runtimes are shown in Tab. 3.

For the short term security parameter, FFC using GMP outperforms ECC using Miracl by factor 2 for all protocols. However, starting from a medium term security parameter, ECC becomes increasingly more efficient and outperforms FCC by more than factor 2 for the long term security parameter. For ECC, we can observe that [40]-RO is about 5-6 times faster than [40]-STD but only 2 times faster than our §5.2-STD protocol. For FFC, our §5.2-STD protocol becomes more inefficient with increasing security parameter, since the random sampling requires nearly full-range exponentiations as opposed to the subgroup exponentiations in [40]-RO and [40]-STD.

Security	**[40]-RO**	**[40]-STD**	**§5.2-STD**
GMP (FFC)			
Short [ms]	18 (±0.9)	99 (±0.6)	41 (±3.3)
Medium [ms]	107 (±3.4)	629 (±3.3)	352 (±18)
Long [ms]	288 (±7.9)	1,681 (±4.7)	1,217 (±47)
Miracl (ECC)			
Short [ms]	39 (±1.6)	178 (±0.3)	61 (±2.5)
Medium [ms]	82 (±2.9)	418 (±0.6)	137 (±5.0)
Long [ms]	138 (±5.0)	763 (±0.8)	239 (±7.5)

Table 3: Performance results and standard deviations for base OTs.

6.2 OT Extension

To evaluate the performance of OT extension, we measure the time for generating the random inputs for the OT extension protocol and the overall OT extension protocol execution on 10,000,000 1-out-of-2 OTs on 80-bit strings for the short-term security setting, excluding the times for the base OTs. Tab. 4 summarizes the resulting runtimes for the original version without (Orig [49] (1 T)) and with pipelining (Orig [49] (2 T)), the efficient matrix transposition (EMT §4.2), the general protocol optimization (G-OT §5.3), the correlated OT extension protocol (C-OT §5.4), the random OT extension protocol (R-OT §5.4), as well as a two and four threaded version of R-OT (2 T and 4 T, cf. §4.1). The line (x T) denotes the number of threads, running on each party. Since our optimizations target both, the runtime as well as the amount of data that is transferred, we assume two different bandwidth scenarios: LAN (Gigabit Ethernet with 1 GBit bandwidth) and WiFi (simulated by limiting the available bandwidth to 54 MBit and the latency to 2 ms). As our experiments in Tab. 4 show, the LAN setting benefits from computation optimizations (as computation is the bottleneck), whereas the WiFi setting benefits from communication optimizations (as the network is the bottleneck). All timings are the average of 100 executions with one party acting as sender and the other as receiver. Note that each version includes all prior listed optimizations.

LAN setting. The original OT extension implementation of [49] has a runtime of 20.61 s without pipelining, which is reduced to only 80% (16.57 s) when using pipelining. Implementing the efficient matrix transposition of §4.2 decreases the runtime to 70% of the one-threaded original version (14.43 s) and already outperforms the pipelined version even though only one thread is used. The general improved OT extension protocol of §5.3 removes the need to

Network	Orig [49] (1 T)	Orig [49] (2 T)	EMT §4.2 (1 T)	G-OT §5.3 (1 T)	C-OT §5.4 (1 T)	R-OT §5.4 (1 T)	R-OT §5.4 (2 T, §4.1)	R-OT §5.4 (4 T, §4.1)
LAN [s]	20.61 (±0.07)	16.57 (±0.33)	14.43 (±0.05)	13.92 (±0.07)	10.60 (±0.03)	10.00 (±0.02)	5.03 (±0.08)	2.62 (±0.05)
WiFi [s]	30.69 (±0.18)	30.42 (±0.20)	30.45 (±0.24)	29.36 (±0.26)	14.39 (±0.14)	14.22 (±0.12)	14.23 (±0.18)	14.23 (±0.22)

Table 4: Performance results and standard deviations for 10,000,000 1-out-of-2 OTs on 80-bit strings using our optimizations in §4 and §5.

generate the random matrix T, which reduces the runtime to 13.92 s. The C-OT extension of §5.4 decreases the runtime to 10.60 s, since the protocol generates the random input values for the sender. The R-OT extension of §5.4 further decreases the runtime to 10.00 s, since the last communication step is eliminated. Finally, the parallelized OT extension of §4.1 results in a nearly linear decrease in runtime to 50% (5.03 s) for two threads and to 26% (2.62 s) for four threads. Overall, using two threads, we decreased the runtime in the LAN setting by a factor of 3 compared to the two-threaded original implementation.

WiFi setting. In the WiFi setting, we observe that the one and two threaded original implementation is already slower compared to the LAN setting. Moreover, all optimizations that purely target the runtime have little effect, since the network has become the bottleneck. We therefore focus on the optimizations for the communication complexity. The G-OT optimization of §5.3 only slightly decreases the runtime since both parties have the same up and download bandwidth and the channel from sender to receiver becomes the bottleneck (cf. Tab. 2).[6] The C-OT extension of §5.4 reduces the runtime by a factor of 2, corresponding to the reduced communication from sender to receiver which is now equal to the communication in the opposite direction. The R-OT extension of §5.4 only slightly decreases the runtime, since now the channel from receiver to sender has become the bottleneck. Finally, the multi-threading optimization of §4.1 does not reduce the runtime as the network is the bottleneck.

7. APPLICATION SCENARIOS

OT extension is the foundation for efficient implementations of many secure computation protocols, including Yao's garbled circuits implemented in the FastGC framework [24] and GMW implemented in the framework of [8, 49]. To demonstrate how both protocols benefit from our improved OT extensions, we apply our implementations to both frameworks and consider the following secure computation use-cases: Hamming distance (§7.1), set-intersection (§7.2), minimum (§7.3), and Levenshtein distance (§7.4). The overall performance results are summarized in Tab. 5 and discussed in §7.5. All experiments were performed under the same conditions as in §6 (LAN setting) using the random-oracle protocol of [40] as base OT. We extended the FastGC framework [24] to call our C++ OT implementation using the Java Native Interface (JNI). We stress that the goal of our performance measurements is to highlight the efficiency gains of our improved OT protocols, but not to provide a comparison between Yao's garbled circuits and the GMW protocol.

[6]For shorter strings or if the channel would have a higher bandwidth from sender to receiver (e.g., a DSL link), the runtime would decrease already for the G-OT optimization.

7.1 Hamming Distance

The Hamming distance between two ℓ-bit strings is the number of positions that both strings differ in. Applications of secure Hamming distance computation include privacy-preserving face recognition [46] and private matching for cardinality threshold [29]. As shown in [24,49], using a circuit-based approach is a very efficient way to securely compute the face recognition algorithm of [46] which uses $\ell = 900$. We use the compact Hamming distance circuit of [6] with size $\ell - HW(\ell)$ AND gates and ℓ input bits for the client, where $HW(\ell)$ is the Hamming weight of ℓ.

7.2 Set-Intersection

Privacy-preserving set-intersection allows two parties, each holding a set of σ-bit elements, to learn the elements they have in common. Applications include governmental law enforcement [9], sharing location data [41], and botnet detection [39]. Several Boolean circuits for computing the set-intersection were described and evaluated in [23]. The authors of [23] state that for small σ (up to $\sigma = 20$ in their experiments), the bitwise AND (BWA) circuit achieves the best performance. This circuit treats each element $e \in \{0,1\}^\sigma$ as an index to a bit-sequence $\{0,1\}^{2^\sigma}$ and denotes the presence of e by setting the respective bit to 1. The parties then compute the set-intersection as the bitwise AND of their bit-sequences. We build the BWA circuit for $\sigma = 20$, resulting in a circuit with $2^\sigma = 1{,}048{,}576$ AND gates and input bits for the client. To reduce the memory footprint of the FastGC framework [24], we split the overall circuit and the OTs on the input bits into blocks of size $2^{16} = 65{,}536$.

7.3 Secure Minimum

Securely computing the minimum of a set of values is a common building block in privacy-preserving protocols and is used to find best matches, e.g., for face recognition [11] or online marketplaces [8]. We use the scenario considered in [36] that securely computes the minimum of $N = 1{,}000{,}000$ $\ell = 20$-bit values, where each party holds 500,000 values. Using the minimum circuit construction of [31], our circuit has $2\ell N - 2\ell \approx 40{,}000{,}000$ AND gates and the client has $\frac{N}{2}\ell = 10{,}000{,}000$ input bits. We note that the performance of the garbled circuit implementation of [36] is about the same as that of FastGC [24] – their circuit has twice the size and takes about twice as long to evaluate. For the FastGC framework we again evaluate the overall circuit by iteratively computing the minimum of at most 2,048 values.

7.4 Levenshtein Distance

The Levenshtein distance denotes the number of operations that are needed to transform a string a into another string b using an alphabet of bit-size σ. It can be

Implementation	Base-OTs	Hamming §7.1	Set-Intersect. §7.2	Minimum §7.3	Levenshtein §7.4
FastGC [24]	470 ms	149 ms (86.8 ms)	249 s (227 s)	1094 s (552 s)	265 min (148 ms)
FastGC [24] fixed with CPRG	482 ms	155 ms (87.6 ms)	253 s (227 s)	1106 s (554 s)	266 min (157 ms)
FastGC [24] with C-OT (4 T)	69 ms	85 ms (4.4 ms)	27 s (0.96 s)	593 s (15 s)	266 min (15 ms)
GMW [49]	142 ms	79 ms (46.5 ms)	1.91 s (1.34 s)	44 s (41 s)	—
GMW [49] with R-OT (4 T)	28 ms	30 ms (11.3 ms)	0.93 s (0.51 s)	21 s (19 s)	18 min (11 min)
AND gates	-	896	1,048,576	39,999,960	1,290,653,042
Client input bits	-	900	1,048,576	10,000,000	2,000

Table 5: Performance results for the frameworks of [24] and [49] with and without our optimized OT implementation. The time spent in the OT extensions is given in ().

used for privacy-preserving matching of DNA and protein-sequences [24]. We use the same circuit and setting as [24] with $\sigma = 2$ to compare strings a and b of size $|a| = 2{,}000$ and $|b| = 10{,}000$. The resulting circuit has 1.29 billion AND gates and $\sigma|a| = 4{,}000$ input bits for the client. The GMW framework of [49] was not able to evaluate the Levenshtein circuit since their OT extension implementation tries to process all OTs at once and their framework tries to store the whole circuit in memory, thereby exceeding the available memory of our benchmarking environment. Hence, we changed their underlying circuit structure to support large-scale circuits by deleting gates that were used and building the circuit iteratively.

7.5 Discussion

We discuss the results of our experiments in Tab. 5 next. For the FastGC framework [24], our improved OT extension implementation written in C++ and using 4 threads is more than one order of magnitude faster than the corresponding single-threaded Java routine of the original implementation. The improvements on total time depend on the ratio between the number of client inputs and the circuit size: for circuits with many client inputs (§7.1, §7.2, §7.3), we obtain a speedup by factor 2 to 9, whereas for large circuits with few inputs (§7.4) the improvement for OTs has a negligible effect on the total runtime. To further improve the runtime of large circuits, a faster engine for circuit garbling, e.g., [4], could be combined with our improved OT implementation. For the GMW framework [49], the total runtime is dominated by the time for performing OT extension, which we reduce by factor 2.

Acknowledgements. We thank David Evans and the anonymous reviewers of ACM CCS for their helpful comments on our paper. The first two authors were funded by the European Research Council under the European Union's Seventh Framework Programme (FP/2007-2013) / ERC Grant Agreement n. 239868. The third and fourth author were supported by the German Federal Ministry of Education and Research (BMBF) within EC SPRIDE and by the Hessian LOEWE excellence initiative within CASED.

8. REFERENCES

[1] D. Beaver. Efficient multiparty protocols using circuit randomization. In *Advances in Cryptology – CRYPTO'91*, volume 576 of *LNCS*, pages 420–432. Springer, 1991.

[2] D. Beaver. Correlated pseudorandomness and the complexity of private computations. In *Symposium on Theory of Computing (STOC'96)*, pages 479–488. ACM, 1996.

[3] M. Bellare, S. Goldwasser, and D. Micciancio. "pseudo-random" number generation within cryptographic algorithms: The DDS case. In *Advances in Cryptology – CRYPTO'97*, volume 1294 of *LNCS*, pages 277–291. Springer, 1997.

[4] M. Bellare, V. Hoang, S. Keelveedhi, and P. Rogaway. Efficient garbling from a fixed-key blockcipher. In *Symposium on Security and Privacy*, pages 478–492. IEEE, 2013.

[5] A. Ben-David, N. Nisan, and B. Pinkas. FairplayMP: a system for secure multi-party computation. In *Computer and Communications Security (CCS'08)*, pages 257–266. ACM, 2008.

[6] J. Boyar and R. Peralta. The exact multiplicative complexity of the Hamming weight function. *Electronic Colloquium on Computational Complexity (ECCC'05)*, (049), 2005.

[7] R. Canetti. Security and composition of multiparty cryptographic protocols. *J. Cryptology*, 13(1):143–202, 2000.

[8] S. G. Choi, K.-W. Hwang, J. Katz, T. Malkin, and D. Rubenstein. Secure multi-party computation of Boolean circuits with applications to privacy in on-line marketplaces. In *Cryptographers' Track at the RSA Conference (CT-RSA'12)*, volume 7178 of *LNCS*, pages 416–432. Springer, 2012.

[9] E. De Cristofaro and G. Tsudik. Practical private set intersection protocols with linear complexity. In *Financial Cryptography and Data Security (FC'10)*, volume 6052 of *LNCS*, pages 143–159. Springer, 2010.

[10] J. O. Eklundh. A fast computer method for matrix transposing. *IEEE Transactions on Computers*, C-21(7):801–803, 1972.

[11] Z. Erkin, M. Franz, J. Guajardo, S. Katzenbeisser, I. Lagendijk, and T. Toft. Privacy-preserving face recognition. In *Privacy Enhancing Technologies Symposium (PETS'09)*, volume 5672 of *LNCS*, pages 235–253. Springer, 2009.

[12] S. Even, O. Goldreich, and A. Lempel. A randomized protocol for signing contracts. *Communmunications of the ACM*, 28(6):637–647, 1985.

[13] K. Frikken, M. Atallah, and C. Zhang. Privacy-preserving credit checking. In *Electronic Commerce (EC'05)*, pages 147–154. ACM, 2005.

[14] O. Goldreich. *Foundations of Cryptography*, volume 2: Basic Applications. Cambridge University Press, 2004.

[15] O. Goldreich, S. Micali, and A. Wigderson. How to play any mental game or a completeness theorem for protocols with honest majority. In *Symposium on Theory of Computing (STOC'87)*, pages 218–229. ACM, 1987.

[16] S. D. Gordon, J. Katz, V. Kolesnikov, F. Krell, T. Malkin, M. Raykova, and Y. Vahlis. Secure two-party computation in sublinear (amortized) time. In *Computer and Communications Security (CCS'12)*, pages 513–524. ACM, 2012.

[17] D. Harnik, Y. Ishai, E. Kushilevitz, and J. B. Nielsen. OT-combiners via secure computation. In *Theory of Cryptography (TCC'08)*, volume 4948 of *LNCS*, pages 393–411. Springer, 2008.

[18] J. Håstad and A. Shamir. The cryptographic security of truncated linearly related variables. In *Symposium on Theory of Computing (STOC'85)*, pages 356–362. ACM, 1985.

[19] W. Henecka, S. Kögl, A.-R. Sadeghi, T. Schneider, and I. Wehrenberg. TASTY: Tool for Automating Secure Two-partY computations. In *Computer and Communications Security (CCS'10)*, pages 451–462. ACM, 2010.

[20] W. Henecka and T. Schneider. Faster secure two-party computation with less memory. In *ACM Symposium on Information, Computer and Communications Security (ASIACCS'13)*, pages 437–446. ACM, 2013.

[21] A. Holzer, M. Franz, S. Katzenbeisser, and H. Veith. Secure two-party computations in ANSI C. In *Computer and Communications Security (CCS'12)*, pages 772–783. ACM, 2012.

[22] Y. Huang, P. Chapman, and D. Evans. Privacy-preserving applications on smartphones. In *Hot topics in security (HotSec'11)*. USENIX, 2011.

[23] Y. Huang, D. Evans, and J. Katz. Private set intersection: Are garbled circuits better than custom protocols? In *Network and Distributed Security Symposium (NDSS'12)*. The Internet Society, 2012.

[24] Y. Huang, D. Evans, J. Katz, and L. Malka. Faster secure two-party computation using garbled circuits. In *Security Symposium*. USENIX, 2011.

[25] Y. Huang, J. Katz, and D. Evans. Quid-pro-quo-tocols: Strengthening semi-honest protocols with dual execution. In *Symposium on Security and Privacy*, pages 272–284. IEEE, 2012.

[26] Y. Huang, L. Malka, D. Evans, and J. Katz. Efficient privacy-preserving biometric identification. In *Network and Distributed Security Symposium (NDSS'11)*. The Internet Society, 2011.

[27] Intelligence Advanced Research Projects Activity (IARPA). Security and Privacy Assurance Research (SPAR) Program, 2010.

[28] Y. Ishai, J. Kilian, K. Nissim, and E. Petrank. Extending oblivious transfers efficiently. In *Advances in Cryptology – CRYPTO'03*, volume 2729 of *LNCS*, pages 145–161. Springer, 2003.

[29] A. Jarrous and B. Pinkas. Secure hamming distance based computation and its applications. In *Applied Cryptography and Network Security (ACNS'09)*, volume 5536 of *LNCS*, pages 107–124. Springer, 2009.

[30] F. Kerschbaum. Automatically optimizing secure computation. In *Computer and Communications Security (CCS'11)*, pages 703–714. ACM, 2011.

[31] V. Kolesnikov, A.-R. Sadeghi, and T. Schneider. Improved garbled circuit building blocks and applications to auctions and computing minima. In *Cryptology And Network Security (CANS'09)*, volume 5888 of *LNCS*, pages 1–20. Springer, 2009.

[32] V. Kolesnikov and T. Schneider. Improved garbled circuit: Free XOR gates and applications. In *International Colloquium on Automata, Languages and Programming (ICALP'08)*, volume 5126 of *LNCS*, pages 486–498. Springer, 2008.

[33] H. Krawczyk. Cryptographic extraction and key derivation: The HKDF scheme. In *Advances in Cryptology – CRYPTO'10*, volume 6223 of *LNCS*, pages 631–648. Springer, 2010.

[34] B. Kreuter, A. Shelat, and C.-H. Shen. Billion-gate secure computation with malicious adversaries. In *Security Symposium*. USENIX, 2012.

[35] P. MacKenzie, A. Oprea, and M. K. Reiter. Automatic generation of two-party computations. In *Computer and Communications Security (CCS'03)*, pages 210–219. ACM, 2003.

[36] L. Malka. VMCrypt - modular software architecture for scalable secure computation. In *Computer and Communications Security (CCS'11)*, pages 715–724. ACM, 2011.

[37] D. Malkhi, N. Nisan, B. Pinkas, and Y. Sella. Fairplay — a secure two-party computation system. In *Security Symposium*, pages 287–302. USENIX, 2004.

[38] A. Menezes, P. C. van Oorschot, and S. A. Vanstone. *Handbook of Applied Cryptography*. CRC Press, 1996.

[39] S. Nagaraja, P. Mittal, C.-Y. Hong, M. Caesar, and N. Borisov. Botgrep: Finding P2P bots with structured graph analysis. In *Security Symposium*, pages 95–110. USENIX, 2010.

[40] M. Naor and B. Pinkas. Efficient oblivious transfer protocols. In *ACM-SIAM Symposium On Discrete Algorithms*, SODA '01, pages 448–457. Society for Industrial and Applied Mathematics, 2001.

[41] A. Narayanan, N. Thiagarajan, M. Lakhani, M. Hamburg, and D. Boneh. Location privacy via private proximity testing. In *Network and Distributed Security Symposium (NDSS'11)*. The Internet Society, 2011.

[42] J. B. Nielsen. Extending oblivious transfers efficiently - how to get robustness almost for free. Cryptology ePrint Archive, Report 2007/215, 2007.

[43] J. B. Nielsen, P. S. Nordholt, C. Orlandi, and S. S. Burra. A new approach to practical active-secure two-party computation. In *Advances in Cryptology – CRYPTO'12*, volume 7417 of *LNCS*, pages 681–700. Springer, 2012.

[44] V. Nikolaenko, U. Weinsberg, S. Ioannidis, M. Joye, D. Boneh, and N. Taft. Privacy-preserving ridge regression on hundreds of millions of records. In *Symposium on Security and Privacy*, pages 334–348. IEEE, 2013.

[45] NIST. NIST Special Publication 800-57, Recommendation for Key Management Part 1: General (Rev. 3). Technical report, 2012.

[46] M. Osadchy, B. Pinkas, A. Jarrous, and B. Moskovich. SCiFI - a system for secure face identification. In *Symposium on Security and Privacy*, pages 239–254. IEEE, 2010.

[47] B. Pinkas, T. Schneider, N. P. Smart, and S. C. Williams. Secure two-party computation is practical. In *Advances in Cryptology – ASIACRYPT'09*, volume 5912 of *LNCS*, pages 250–267. Springer, 2009.

[48] M. O. Rabin. *How to exchange secrets with oblivious transfer*, TR-81 edition, 1981. Aiken Computation Lab, Harvard University.

[49] T. Schneider and M. Zohner. GMW vs. Yao? Efficient secure two-party computation with low depth circuits. In *Financial Cryptography and Data Security (FC'13)*, LNCS. Springer, 2013.

[50] A. Schröpfer and F. Kerschbaum. Demo: secure computation in JavaScript. In *Computer and Communications Security (CCS'11)*, pages 849–852. ACM, 2011.

[51] A. C. Yao. How to generate and exchange secrets. In *Foundations of Computer Science (FOCS'86)*, pages 162–167. IEEE, 1986.

APPENDIX

A. DEFINITIONS

We let κ denote the security parameter. A function $\mu(\cdot)$ is negligible if for every positive polynomial $p(\cdot)$ and all sufficiently large n it holds that $\mu(n) < 1/p(n)$. A distribution ensemble $X = \{X(a,n)\}_{a\in\mathcal{D}_n, n\in\mathbb{N}}$ is an infinite sequence of random variables indexed by $a \in \mathcal{D}_n$ and $n \in \mathbb{N}$. Two distribution ensembles X, Y are *computationally indistinguishable*, denoted $X \stackrel{c}{\equiv} Y$ if for every non-uniform polynomial time algorithm D there exists a negligible function $\mu(\cdot)$ such that for every n, and every $a \in \mathcal{D}_n$:

$$|\Pr[D(X(a,n),a,n)=1] - \Pr[D(Y(a,n),a,n]| \leq \mu(n).$$

Key Derivation Function. The following definition is an adaptation of the general definition of [33] for the case of the DDH problem. Intuitively, the adversary should not be able to distinguish between an output of the KDF function and a uniform string. Let $\mathsf{Gen}(1^\kappa)$ be a function that produces a group $(\mathbb{G}, q, g)$ for which the DDH problem is believed to be hard. We define:

DEFINITION A.1 (KEY-DERIVATION FUNCTION). *A key derivation function* KDF *with ℓ-bit output is said to be* secure with respect to DDH *if for any* PPT *attacker $\mathcal{A}$ there exists a negligible function $\mu(\cdot)$ such that:*

$$|\Pr[\mathcal{A}(\mathbb{G},q,g,g^r,h,\mathsf{KDF}(h^r))=1] - \Pr[\mathcal{A}(\mathbb{G},q,g,g^r,h,z)=1]| \leq \mu(\kappa)$$

where $(\mathbb{G},q,g) = \mathsf{Gen}(1^\kappa)$, r is distributed uniformly in $\mathbb{Z}_q$ and z is distributed uniformly in $\{0,1\}^\ell$.

Correlation Robust Function. We present a definition for correlation robust function. The definition is based on the definition in [28].

DEFINITION A.2. *[Correlation Robustness] An efficiently computable function $H : \{0,1\}^\kappa \to \{0,1\}^\ell$ is said to be* correlation robust *if it holds that:*

$$\{\mathbf{t}_1,\ldots,\mathbf{t}_m, H(\mathbf{t}_1\oplus\mathbf{s}),\ldots,H(\mathbf{t}_m\oplus\mathbf{s})\} \stackrel{c}{\equiv} \{U_{m\cdot\kappa+m\cdot\ell}\}$$

where $\mathbf{t}_1,\ldots,\mathbf{t}_m,\mathbf{s}$ are chosen uniformly and independently at random from $\{0,1\}^\kappa$, and $U_{m\cdot\kappa+m\cdot\ell}$ is the uniform distribution over $\{0,1\}^{m\cdot\kappa+m\cdot\ell}$.

Secure Two-Party Computation. We give a formal definition for security of a two party protocol in the presence of a semi-honest adversary. The definition is the standard definition, see [7,14].The view of the party P_0 during an execution of a protocol π on inputs (x,y), denoted $\text{VIEW}_i^\pi(x,y)$, is defined to be $(x,r;\vec{m})$ where x is P_0's private input, r its internal coin tosses, and $\vec{m}$ are the messages it has received in the execution. The view of P_1 is defined analogously. Let $\text{OUTPUT}^\pi(x,y)$ denote the output pair of both parties in a real execution of the protocol. We are now ready to security definition:

DEFINITION A.3. *Let $f : (\{0,1\}^*)^2 \to (\{0,1\}^*)^2$ be a (possible randomized) two-party functionality, and let $f_i(x,y)$ denotes the ith element of $f(x,y)$. Let π be a protocol. We say that π* privately–computes *f if for every $(x,y) \in (\{0,1\}^*)^2$: $\text{OUTPUT}^\pi(x,y) = f(x,y)$ and there exists a pair of probabilistic polynomial-time* PPT *algorithms $\mathcal{S}_0, \mathcal{S}_1$:*

$$\{\mathcal{S}_0(x, f_0(x,y)), f(x,y)\}_z \stackrel{c}{\equiv} \{\text{VIEW}_0^\Pi(x,y), \text{OUTPUT}^\pi(x,y)\}_z$$
$$\{\mathcal{S}_1(y, f_1(x,y)), f(x,y)\}_z \stackrel{c}{\equiv} \{\text{VIEW}_1^\Pi(x,y), \text{OUTPUT}^\pi(x,y)\}_z$$

where $z = (x,y) \in (\{0,1\}^*)^2$.

In case the function f is *deterministic* (like in the OT functionality), there is no need to consider the joint distribution of the outputs and the view, and it is enough to show that the output of the simulator $\mathcal{S}_i$ is indistinguishable from the view of the party P_i.

B. MULTIPLICATION TRIPLE PROTOCOL

In this section, we show that the protocol presented in §5.1 privately computes the multiplication triple functionality.

First, we consider the f^{ab} functionality. The protocol implements the functionality since any random $(b,v),(a,u)$, for which $ab = u\oplus v$, can be written as $(b,v) = (x_0\oplus x_1, x_0)$ and $(a,u) = (a, ab\oplus v) = (a, x_a)$, since it holds that: $ab\oplus v = ab\oplus x_0 = a(x_0\oplus x_1)\oplus x_0 = x_a$. The inputs and outputs of each party fully determine its view, and therefore simulators are trivial and just re–arrange their inputs. Consistency of the generated view with the output of the parties holds trivially.

We turn to the multiplication triple functionality. It is easy to verify that the protocol implements the functionality. Regarding simulation, a simulator $\mathcal{S}_0$ is given (a_0,b_0,c_0), chooses random u_0 and defines: $v_0 = c_0\oplus a_0b_0\oplus u_0$. Since u_0, v_0 are random and hidden from the distinguisher, the view is consistent with (a_1,b_1,c_1). A simulator for $\mathcal{S}_1$ works the same, and security holds from the same reasoning (i.e., $v_1 = a_0b_1\oplus u_0$ is random since u_0 is hidden from the distinguisher, and v_1 is fully determined from c_1,a_1,b_1,u_1).

An Architecture for Practical Actively Secure MPC with Dishonest Majority

Marcel Keller
Department of Computer Science, University of Bristol
m.keller@bristol.ac.uk

Peter Scholl
Department of Computer Science, University of Bristol
Peter.Scholl@bristol.ac.uk

Nigel P. Smart
Department of Computer Science, University of Bristol
nigel@cs.bris.ac.uk

ABSTRACT

We present a runtime environment for executing secure programs via a multi-party computation protocol in the preprocessing model. The runtime environment is general and allows arbitrary reactive computations to be performed. A particularly novel aspect is that it automatically determines the minimum number of rounds needed for a computation, given a specific instruction sequence, and it then uses this to minimize the overall cost of the computation. Various experiments are reported on, on various non-trivial functionalities. We show how, by utilizing the ability of modern processors to execute multiple threads at a time, one can obtain various tradeoffs between latency and throughput.

Categories and Subject Descriptors

C.2.0 [**Computer-Communication Networks**]: General—*security and protection*; D.4.6 [**Operating Systems**]: Security and Protection—*cryptographic controls*

Keywords

Multi-Party Computation

1. INTRODUCTION

Recent years have seen great advances in practical variants of protocols for secure Multi Party Computation (MPC). Initially these practical instantiations came in the restricted security model of dealing with passive (semi-honest) adversaries [3, 6, 25, 32, 9]. However, more recent work has focused on the case of full active security [5, 11, 15, 26, 27], or sometimes covert security [13].

MPC protocols come in two flavours: one flavour based on Yao circuits and one flavour based on secret sharing. In those based on Yao circuits (which are predominantly focused on the two party case) a function to be evaluated is expressed first as a boolean circuit. The boolean circuit is then "encrypted" by one party in a process known as garbling. The encryptor then passes the encrypted circuit over to the other player, who then evaluates the circuit on their own input. The input of the evaluating player is obtained from the encryptor via an oblivious transfer protocol.

CCS'13, November 4–8, 2013, Berlin, Germany.
ACM 978-1-4503-2477-9/13/11.
http://dx.doi.org/10.1145/2508859.2516744.

The first implementation of the Yao approach in the semi-honest setting was the FairPlay system [25], which was followed by an implementation in the active security case [24]. Following the work in [28] it has been common to benchmark such Yao based implementations against evaluating the AES circuit, see for example [16, 17, 23, 31]. The state-of-the-art in terms of Yao based computation would currently appear to be the system in [20].

In the secret sharing based approach initial practical work focused mainly on the case of three parties with only one allowed semi-honest adversary [6, 32]. Systems such as [11, 32] could cope with larger numbers of players, and more powerful adversaries, but only with a significant degradation in performance. Recent practical MPC work in the secret sharing tradition has focused on full active security against a dishonest majority, utilizing a form of "shared MAC" to provide security [5, 13, 15, 26]. It is in this area that our work is focused. Whilst secret sharing based approaches are not as well tailored to evaluate functions such as AES, the AES functionality is still used as an important benchmark in this area [12, 13, 21, 22].

Another aspect of modern practical work on secret sharing based MPC protocols is the fact that they are often presented in a "preprocessing model". In this model one is allowed to perform in an "offline phase" the generation of random data, which will be consumed in the "online phase". The key aspect is that the data produced in the offline phase must be generic and not depend on the inputs to the function (which are unknown until the online phase), nor too tied to the specific function being evaluated (which again may not be known until the online phase commences).

The final consideration is whether the protocol supports fully reactive computation. By this we mean that, after a function result has been determined, one can execute another function; with the precise choice of the new function depending on the output of the first computation. A fully reactive computation allows this process to be continued ad infinitum, including possibly executing the offline phase again if the preprocessed data runs out.

Previous implementation work, in the secret sharing setting, has mainly focused on the underlying MPC protocol and how to perform specific pre-defined functionalities; for example, the AES circuit above. The traditional approach is to express the function to be evaluated is described as an arithmetic circuit and then this circuit is evaluated by executing a sequence of addition and multiplication "gates". This is a throw back to the origins of MPC in the theoretical community; where functions are always represented as arithmetic circuits.

In this work we focus on modern secret sharing based MPC protocols in the pre-processing model whose online phase is actively secure, for example the SPDZ protocol [13, 14, 15] or the Tiny-OT protocol [26], or even the earlier information theoretic based protocols such as VIFF [11]. In practice such protocols *do not* execute arithmetic circuits; they can evaluate far more elaborate basic operations since they have the ability to selectively "open" secret data. In fact if the pre-processed data is so called "Beaver Multiplication Triples", then a multiplication gate is actually implemented as a sequence of local additions and selective openings; and of course consuming some pre-processed data.

Shifting ones viewpoint to treating the three operations of local additions, "open" and consuming pre-processed data as the basic operations enables far more expressive operations. This viewpoint is indeed implicit in the work of [10] which examines protocols for comparison, bit-extraction and exponentiation amongst others. The key ability utilized, in its most basic form, is to enable a secret value to be masked, and then the masked value to be opened. Whilst this might seem a small additional functionality, it turns out in practice that such an operation allows one to perform highly complex tasks without needing to resort to their description as an arithmetic circuit.

Shifting ones view point in this way is also important from a practical perspective as the main bottleneck in implementations is the scheduling of the open instructions. By focusing on "open", as opposed to multiplication, as the key operation to optimize one can achieve significant performance improvements.

In this work we present the design of an efficient runtime execution environment for the protocols in the SPDZ family [13, 14, 15], much of our work will extend to other protocols such as Tiny-OT [26]. This protocol family supports fully malicious (active) or covert security, is in the preprocessing model and can (using the techniques of [14]) support fully reactive computation. Unlike prior work we concentrate only on the online phase and show how to design efficient compilers and a runtime environment to enable high level operations. Prior implementation work on the SPDZ family has either concentrated on the specific functionalities over small finite fields, such as evaluating AES [13], or has focused on the more mathematically complex offline phase [14, 15].

Our focus is on more general purpose computation, and in particular how to enable a general purpose high level function description, which is then translated into low level operations, which are then executed by an MPC runtime engine. In particular we present experimental results for an actively secure online phase for various high level functionalities such as integer multiplication and comparison, fixed point and floating point operations as well as runtimes for AES. Our AES runtimes are significantly better than prior runtimes for AES using other actively secure MPC implementations.

Our prime motivation is to understand how to engineer the overall runtime environment, rather than the design of specific protocols. We therefore utilize prior work of others for our higher level functions, i.e. for integer comparison we use [7], for fixed point numbers we use [8], for floating point numbers we use [1], for AES we use the techniques of [13]. Whilst much of our design is biased towards the SPDZ protocol, many aspects can be directly extended to other MPC protocols that only involve broadcasting shares to all parties for communication. This is true for all protocols based on Beaver's technique [2]. However, the basic idea of automatically optimizing the communication pattern is also applicable to protocols based on Shamir secret sharing such as [4]. Other work, e.g. [19, 29], on optimization for MPC compilers has focused on issues related to what information is leaked when values are revealed to enable branching; this is an orthogonal question to those that we consider.

We present our experimental results in the following way. We show how one can trade, for the different high level functionalities, latency for throughput. In many previous works on MPC the focus has been on throughput or latency alone. This however is not realistic; in a given application scenario one is likely to have a specific latency and a specific throughput one has to meet for the MPC solution to be applicable. We show how, by batching different numbers of operations together, and by running in different numbers of threads, one is able to trade throughput for latency. This allows one to reach a specific *sweet spot* for a given application.

In summary, existing MPC implementations do not provide active security against a dishonest majority, do not scale (efficiently) to any number of parties, require knowledge of (and manual optimizations for) the underlying MPC protocol, or are generally not very efficient. To our knowledge, we present the first MPC implementation that achieves the highest level of security in the online phase, efficiently scales to at least five parties, provides a high-level language that does not require a detailed understanding of MPC, and is competitive with previous implementations achieving the same level of security. To accomplish this, we use the SPDZ protocol for the desired security and scalability, and we have implemented a compiler for a Python-like language that optimizes the communication pattern of the program. The compiler outputs a bytecode that can be interpreted by a virtual machine. For efficiency, this virtual machine is implemented in C++ and kept relatively simple. We believe that our approach optimally combines usability with the efficiency gains of using machine code and avoiding idle time caused by the multi-round nature of MPC based on arithmetic circuits.

2. OVERVIEW OF THE SPDZ PROTOCOL

At the core of our work is a multiparty computation protocol in the preprocessing model, with specific properties. In particular we assume the preprocessing produces so-called Beaver Multiplication Triples. These are triples of secret shared random values, such that the third random value is the product of the first two. In addition we assume the ability to produce other forms of pre-processed data. For more details see below.

There are a number of modern protocols in this family, and we will focus on those in the SPDZ ("Speedz") family, [14, 15]. This family is an extension of a protocol first introduced by by Bendlin *et al.* [5]. The advantage of this approach is that expensive, public-key machinery can be offloaded into the preprocessing phase. The online phase uses (essentially) only cheap, information-theoretically secure primitives and can therefore be extremely efficient. Moreover, the technique comes with extremely strong security guarantees: the online phase is actively secure against a dishonest majority of corrupted players, irrespective of the security of the offline phase. Thus we obtain a protocol which is actively (resp. covertly) secure if we combine our online phase with an offline phase which is actively (resp. covertly) secure as in [15] (resp. [14]). In addition our online phase can evaluate reactive functionalities (i.e. multiple sequential programs) and not just execute secure function evaluation.

Throughout this exposition we assume a number of players n and a finite field $\mathbb{F}_q$ over which computations will be performed have been fixed. The basic data type used is a secret sharing scheme over the field $\mathbb{F}_q$. Each party in the protocol P_i has a uniform share $\alpha_i \in \mathbb{F}_q$ of a secret value $\alpha = \alpha_1 + \cdots + \alpha_n$, thought of as a fixed MAC key. We say that a data item $a \in \mathbb{F}_p$ is $\langle\cdot\rangle$-shared if P_i holds a tuple $(a_i, \gamma(a)_i)$, where a_i is an additive secret sharing of a, i.e. $a = a_1 + \cdots + a_n$, and $\gamma(a)_i$ is an additive secret sharing of $\gamma(a) := \alpha \cdot a$, i.e.

$$\gamma(a) = \gamma(a)_1 + \cdots + \gamma(a)_n.$$

2.1 Offline Phase

In this section we summarize the data produced during the offline phase of the SPDZ protocol that is required by our runtime. The main purpose of the preprocessing phase is to generate multiplication triples, namely shares of random values $\langle a \rangle, \langle b \rangle, \langle c \rangle$ satisfying $a \cdot b = c$, which are used to multiply secret shared values during the online phase using a technique of Beaver [2].

Whilst multiplication triples are the only data theoretically needed for the online phase, we can also use the offline phase from [14, 15] to create additional raw data that improves the efficiency of certain operations. In Table 1 we detail all data that is used during the online phase in our various higher level functions. The input data is used to enable parties to input values into the computation, see [15], we shall not discuss this further in this paper. The square data is used to perform squaring of shared values more efficiently than general multiplications; this is useful in general computation but does not feature in our specific examples later in the paper. The inv tuples are used for constant round protocols for integer comparison; we shall see later that the logarithmic round protocols are actually more efficient in practice for the data types we are interested in.

Command	Outputs	Properties
triple	$\langle a \rangle, \langle b \rangle, \langle c \rangle$	$a, b \xleftarrow{\$} F_p, c = a \cdot b$
square	$\langle a \rangle, \langle b \rangle$	$a \xleftarrow{\$} F_p, b = a^2$
bit	$\langle b \rangle$	$b \xleftarrow{\$} \{0, 1\}$
input	$\langle r \rangle$	$r \xleftarrow{\$} F_p$
inv	$\langle a \rangle, \langle a' \rangle$	$a \xleftarrow{\$} F_p, a' = a^{-1}$

Table 1: Data Prepared During the Offline Phase

The offline phase is assumed to produce five files of pre-processed data for each player. Each file containing the relevant shares of the above data. Exactly how much of each type of data one needs to compute in the offline phase is of course unknown until the exact function one is computing is known. However, one can make a heuristic over estimate of this number. In addition as soon as data produced in the offline phase has been exhausted one can return to the offline phase to compute some more (note this option is only available if one is using the MAC checking strategy described in [14]).

2.2 Online phase

During the online phase the parties compute on open values (i.e. values which are not secret shared) and secret values (i.e. values which are secret shared). All standard arithmetic ($+$, $\times$, $/$, $\%$) and bitwise boolean ($\vee$, $\wedge$, $\oplus$) operations can be performed on open values; where for the latter boolean operations we assume a fixed binary representation of values within the finite field $\mathbb{F}_q$. The arithmetic operations can also be applied to one value which is shared and one value which is opened, resulting in a new value which is shared. Finally, in terms of arithmetic operations, two shared values can be added together to result in a shared value. Another set of operations deal with loading data from the files precomputed in the offline phase. These are all shared random values, subject to the constraints given in Table 1.

All of the prior operations are "local", i.e. they do not require any interaction between the parties. As these local operations which produce shared values are performed, the parties can locally update the value of their shares of the associated MAC value. The power of the online phase comes from the ability to interactively "open" shared values so as to produce opened values. In such an operation a shared value $\langle a \rangle$ is opened to reveal a to all parties, but the associated shared MAC values, $a \cdot \alpha$, are kept secret.

To protect the parties against malicious parties the shared MACs of all such opened values need to be checked for correctness, and this must be done in a way so that neither the MAC key nor the MAC value itself is revealed. This is done using the protocol described in [14]. We execute this protocol so that batches of MAC values are checked all at once; in particular we batch up to 100,000 such MAC values to be checked into one operation. Thus the MAC checking protocol is executed after every 100,000 such openings, and once at the end of the computation to check any remaining values.

In [15] the following $O(n)$ protocol is suggested for performing the opening operation on the shared value $\langle a \rangle$.

- The players pick an arbitrary "nominated player", say P_1.
- Players P_i for $i = 2, \cdots, n$ send P_1 the value a_i.
- P_1 computes $a = a_1 + \cdots + a_n$ and sends a to all other players.

It is readily seen that the communication complexity of the above protocol is that each player (on average) sends a total of three field elements per opening. However, in practice we have found the following naive protocol to be more efficient.

- P_i sends a_i to all other players.
- Each player locally computes $a = a_1 + \cdots + a_n$.

Here the parties need to each send $n-1$ field elements per opening, which will be worse than the prior method as soon as $n > 3$. However, in practice we found that the naive method performs better than the $O(n)$ method for $n \leq 5$. This is because it is a one round protocol as opposed to a two round protocol. This dependence of efficiency on rounds will be a feature of our work and we will take a great deal of trouble in later sections in minimizing the round complexity of the entire computation in an automatic manner. Clearly to minimize rounds across a computation many different values to be opened can be opened at once in either of the methods above.

From the above description of the basic functionalities of the online phase it is not clear whether such a runtime is universal, i.e. can compute any arbitrary function. Since every function can be expressed as an arithmetic circuit over $\mathbb{F}_q$ and addition of shared values is a local operation, all that remains to show universality is to demonstrate that multiplication can be performed. Given two shared values $\langle x \rangle, \langle y \rangle$, to multiply them we take a precomputed multiplication triple $\{\langle a \rangle, \langle b \rangle, \langle c \rangle\}$ and then the parties open the values $\alpha = x + a$ and $\beta = y + b$. The shared value $\langle x \cdot y \rangle$ can then be computed from the local operation

$$\langle x \cdot y \rangle = (\alpha - \langle a \rangle) \cdot (\beta - \langle b \rangle) = \alpha \cdot \beta - \beta \cdot \langle a \rangle - \alpha \cdot \langle b \rangle + \langle c \rangle .$$

Thus multiplication is itself composed of our three primitive operations of local additions, open and consuming pre-processed data.

3. VIRTUAL MACHINE

To implement the online protocol we took a 'ground up' approach to architecture, starting with a very simple register-based virtual machine that can be run on an ordinary desktop computer by each party. By focussing initially on the low level design details we have obtained a high performance implementation with minimal overhead, leaving decisions for optimization and compilation to a higher level. Our virtual machine could be used to run code from a variety of language descriptions, given a cross-compiler to output the appropriate bytecode. To demonstrate this we use a simple language based on Python for all our programs. Details of the compilation process and special-purpose optimizations that we developed to reduce communication costs are given in Section 4.

Programs to be run by the virtual machine must be encoded into bytecode as assembly-like instructions (generally produced by a higher level compiler), which are then parsed and executed. To make the most of modern multi-core processors, we allow a number of such precomputed bytecode files to run simultaneously, each in a separate thread of the runtime virtual machine. This then leads to an additional level of complication in relation to how the bytecode files consume data from the offline phase, how the bytecode files are scheduled across a large computation and communicate with each other, and how branching and looping are to be performed. In this section we describe the low level design decisions which we have made to solve these problems. To ease exposition we shall refer to a single sequence of bytecode instructions as a *tape* in the following presentation.

The virtual machine consists of a memory holding a fixed number of clear and secret shared values. This memory is long term, and as the virtual machine starts up/shuts down the memory is read from/written to the player's local disk. In addition the virtual machine runs a series of $t+1$ threads; one thread acts as a control thread while the other t threads have the task of executing (or not) a tape of bytecode. The t tape-running threads open pairwise point-to-point communication channels with the associated threads in the other players' runtime environments. There is no limit to the number of concurrent tapes, t, but in practice one will be restricted by the number of cores. For our test machines with eight cores, we found best performance when t is limited to seven or fewer.

The control thread executes the main program, or *schedule*. This is a program which specifies exactly which tape should be run at which point. The schedule also specifies which, and how many, tapes are executed in parallel; with up to t such tapes may be executed in parallel. The control thread takes the tapes to be executed at a given step in the program, passes them to the execution threads, and then waits for the threads to finish their execution, at which point the control thread processes the next stage of the program. Communication between tapes is done via reading and writing to the virtual machine's long term memory. To avoid unnecessary stalls there is no locking mechanism provided to this memory. So if two simultaneously running threads execute a read and a write, or two writes, to the same memory location then the result is undefined since it is unspecified as to which order the associated instructions will be performed in. Thus in this respect we have traded speed for safety at the lowest level; it is the task of the compiler or programmer to ensure the safe behaviour of concurrently running bytecode.

We now turn to discussing the execution threads and the associated bytecode instructions within each tape. Each execution thread has its own local shared and clear memory. To avoid confusion with the long term memory we shall call this local memory a *register file*, referring to the values as shared or clear *registers*. The values of a register are not assumed to be maintained between an execution thread running one tape and the next tape, so all passing of values between two sequential tape executions must be done by reading and writing to the main virtual machine memory. Again, whilst this may seem like a very primitive approach to take, we are ensuring that there is no unnecessary overhead and bloat in the virtual machine, leaving more complex elements to the next level up.

The bytecode instructions within a tape are influenced by the RISC design strategy, coming in only three basic types; corresponding to the operations described in Section 2.2. The first of these most closely resembles traditional assembly code instructions, consisting of load and store operations for moving registers to and from the long term memory, and instructions for executing *local* arithmetic and bitwise logical operations described in Section 2.2, that can be performed without interaction. All of this class of bytecode instructions are of the simple one output, one or two input variety found in modern processors, where the inputs may be registers or immediate values and the output register type depends on the input types as specified earlier. The other two types of instructions are data access instructions, which serve to load data from the preprocessing phase, and a special instruction to open shared register values into clear registers. Note that this last instruction is the only one requiring interaction between players. We now turn to discussing each of these special MPC instruction types in turn.

The instructions for loading data from the preprocessing phase are denoted `triple`, `square`, `bit`, `input` and `inv`, and they take as argument three, two, one, one and two shared registers respectively. The associated data is loaded from the precomputed data and loaded into the registers given as arguments. This leads to the problem that multiple concurrent tapes could read the same data from the precomputed global store. Thus the control thread on passing a tape to an execution thread for execution first calculates a (reasonable) upper bound on the amount of pre-processing data it will consume before it is executed. This can be easily done in the case of programs with no loops by simply counting the number of such instructions in the tape. Then the control thread allocates a specific portion of the unused precomputed data to the thread for use within this tape. This solution avoids complexity in the offline phase (by not requiring it to produce separate data for each thread) or added complexity to the online phase (by not requiring a locking mechanism to access the precomputed data), both of which would negatively affect program complexity and/or performance. The cost for this simple solution comes when executing tapes containing branching instructions, an issue we return to in Appendix A.

The process of opening secret values is covered by two instructions. The `startopen` instruction takes as input a set of m shared registers, and `stopopen` an associated set of m clear registers, where m can be an arbitrary integer. They then execute the protocol from Section 2.2 to open the shared registers and place the results into the designated clear registers. The fact that we can perform m of these operations in parallel is vital in improving the throughput and latency of applications run on the virtual machine. Furthermore, splitting the process in two steps allows one to execute local instructions while the runtime is waiting for data from other parties to arrive.

4. THE COMPILATION PROCESS

To produce the bytecode tapes required by our virtual machine, we developed a compiler for a simple high-level language derived from Python. The compiler takes a Python-like program description, extracts individual threads from this and breaks each thread down into basic blocks. The individual basic blocks are then optimized and each thread used to produce a bytecode tape for the virtual machine. Our optimization guarantees that, within a basic block, the program will be compiled with the *minimum possible* number of rounds of communication. This, coupled with the familiarity to many of the Python programming language, ensures that the workload of implementing complex MPC functionalities is eased considerably.

Instead of the traditional approach of using parsing and lexing tools for compilation, we chose to implement the core language features as a Python library, so that programs can be executed by

Python itself, which then produces the relevant bytecode. This allows for (compile-time) access to many of Python's powerful features such as list comprehensions, classes and functions with relatively little effort. The library consists of a set of functions for creating, storing and loading clear and secret shared data types; loading preprocessed data and more complex features such as threading and branching. We then use operator overloading to provide transparent support for arithmetic functions on our data types.

Upon execution, the Python code creates bytecode instructions from our library functions and the overloaded arithmetic operators, whilst keeping track of the appropriate threading and basic block information. Complex functions such as secret multiplication and comparison are expanded into sequences of the basic RISC-like instructions described in Section 3. Note that at this stage the open instructions will only have one shared and one clear register as arguments.

So despite our RISC instructions not supporting complex operations such as the multiplication of two shared values in $\mathbb{F}_q$, we can easily implement this using the compiler. This abstraction is key to our approach; we do not at the low level execute a program corresponding to an arithmetic circuit over $\mathbb{F}_q$ as in other approaches. We instead execute only a sequence of operations which are linear operations on the shared values, open instructions, or load precomputed data. All high level operations can be built up from these instructions; and indeed more efficient high level operations can be built which do not involve reduction to arithmetic circuits.

Using the above ideas we arrive at a point where we have produced a set of bytecode tapes in static single assignment (SSA) form, with an unbounded number of clear and shared registers, and standard compiler optimizations such as common subexpression elimination can be performed if required. We then optimize the communication complexity of each tape by reordering and merging the open instructions, as follows:

- Calculate the *program dependency graph* $G = (V, E)$, whose vertices correspond to instructions in the bytecode, and directed edges represent dependencies between instructions.

- Let $T \subseteq V$ denote the set of **startopen** vertices and let S be the subset of T with no preceding nodes in T.

- Since all nodes in S are independent of each other, we now merge them together into a single source node (and instruction) s, and do the same with associated **stopopens**.

- To compute the remaining merges that can be done, assign weights to edges as follows:

$$w_{i,j} = \begin{cases} -1 & \text{if } v_j \in T \setminus S \\ 0 & \text{otherwise} \end{cases}$$

  This ensures that the length of a path between any two nodes is exactly -1 times the number of **startopen** nodes lying on the path, excluding the first node and any source **startopen** nodes.

- For each vertex v, compute dist_v, the shortest distance from the merged source s to v. Since G is a DAG, this can be done in linear time with a standard shortest paths algorithm using dynamic programming.

- Merge all **startopens** (and their associated **stopopens**) that are the same distance from s (by the shortest path property, these must all be independent).

After this step, all independent **startopen** and **stopopen** instructions in the original program have been merged together. We can now compute a topological ordering of G to produce a program with the minimal number of rounds of communication for the given instruction sequence.

To illustrate the benefit of this, we implemented a standard polynomial approximation for the floating point $\sin(x)$ function. If this is compiled without merging open instructions (bar those merges which are automatically encoded in the lower level constituent operations) one would obtain a round complexity of 5874. On application of our optimizer the number of rounds reduces to 759.

When computing the topological ordering, we calculate which round of openings each instruction depends on and which round of openings depends on the instruction. This can be done similarly to the shortest paths method above, traversing G in reverse order. Instructions that do not have a dependency in both directions, like memory operations, are placed close to the remaining dependency or close to the beginning if there is no dependency at all. This reduces the memory usage of the virtual machine because it reduces the lifetime of registers.

Finally, there are instructions that have dependencies in both ways, i.e. those that depend on some opening round i, while at the same time opening round $i+1$ depends on them, clearly have to be placed between the two rounds. However, instructions that only depend on rounds up to i and are independent of round $i+1$ can be placed between the **startopen** and **stopopen** of round $i+1$. This utilizes the time used for waiting for data from other parties for performing local computations.

To complete compilation, the compiler allocates registers. Since all programs are in SSA form at this point, the allocation is straightforward. The compiler processes the program backwards, allocates a register whenever a register is read for the last time, and deallocates it whenever a register is written to. This ensures that a minimal numbers of registers are used, which minimizes memory usage of the virtual machine.

```
x = a * b + c * d
y = a * x
z = reveal(e)
```

Figure 1: A sample program.

For way of illustration, Figure 1 shows a possible high-level program, and Figure 2 shows the corresponding output of the compiler. The semantics are as follows: Registers starting with `s` hold secret values, registers starting with `c` clear values. `adds`, `addm`, `subs`, `mulc`, and `mulm` denote addition, subtraction, and multiplication, respectively. The result is assigned to the first register, with the last letter of the instruction denoting the type of the inputs: `s` for secret, `c` for clear, and `m` for mixed. The instruction `triple` loads a multiplication triple into the given registers. Finally, `startopen` opens any number of secret registers, and `stopopen` assigns the results of the last `startopen` to the clear registers. The compiler mapped `a`-`e` to `s0`-`s4`, `x` to `s5`, `y` to `s6`, and `z` to `c0`. Note that the openings required for the multiplications `a*b` and `c*d` and the opening of `e` are all merged together in the first `startopen`/`stopopen` pair. Furthermore, the triple needed for the multiplication `a*x` is loaded only after that. This allows for the registers `s6`-`s8` to be used for something else prior to that, thus reducing the register usage.

Vector operations.

The virtual machine also supports vector instructions like adding two vectors of registers and storing the result in a vector of regis-

```
triple s13, s10, s14
triple s11, s12, s5
subs s9, s3, s10
subs s7, s2, s13
subs s6, s1, s12
subs s8, s0, s11
startopen s8, s6, s7, s9, s4
stopopen c1, c3, c4, c5, c0
triple s7, s8, s6
subs s9, s0, s7
mulc c2, c4, c5
mulm s13, s13, c5
mulm s10, s10, c4
adds s10, s14, s10
adds s10, s10, s13
addm s10, s10, c2
mulc c2, c1, c3
mulm s11, s11, c3
mulm s12, s12, c1
adds s5, s5, s12
adds s5, s5, s11
addm s5, s5, c2
adds s5, s5, s10
subs s10, s5, s8
startopen s9, s10
stopopen c1, c2
mulm s8, s8, c1
adds s6, s6, s8
mulm s7, s7, c2
adds s6, s6, s7
mulc c1, c1, c2
addm s6, s6, c1
```

Figure 2: Compiled sample program.

ters. This does not significantly improve the performance of the runtime (in that one could obtain the same effect using multiple copies of the non-vectorized instructions), but vectorized instructions reduces memory and time needed for the compilation. Vector instructions are based on the basic instructions and take the size of the vector as an additional parameter. The further parameters have the same format as for basic instruction. Register and memory addresses are interpreted as the base address of the vector, and constants as constants. Furthermore, the high-level language allows to declare vectors of secret and clear values. Operations on those are compiled into vector instructions.

The key reason for enabling such vector instructions is to enable SIMD processing of multiple programs in the same thread. By introducing vectorized processing we can obtain high SIMD parallelism without compromising the speed of the compiler. We shall see later that the SIMD execution of higher level operations, such as floating point operations and AES evaluations, allow one to obtain a higher throughput without sacrificing latency too much. Thus the vectorized instructions give us a another way of obtaining higher throughput via parallelism, in addition to the execution of multiple tapes in multiple threads.

5. RUN TIME ARITHMETIC

The runtime comes in two variants. One for working with finite fields $\mathbb{F}_q$ where q is a "large" prime, say $q \approx 2^{128}$. This runtime variant is more suited to general purpose computations; it supports integer operations and working on fixed and floating point numbers as we shall describe later. Here we assume a statistical security parameter of 40, i.e. we allow deviations in the statistical distributions of the various shared value output of 2^{-40}. The second runtime is for working with functionalities more related to binary circuit descriptions, and it works in the finite field $\mathbb{F}_{2^{40}}$. The choice of this specific finite field is to obtain a probability of an active adversary cheating of 2^{-40}, as well as to enable the efficient evaluation of the AES functionality using the field embedding technique described in [13]. We now discuss each variant in turn:

5.1 The Large Prime Variant

Here we represent a signed t-bit integer value, where $t < 128$, by its value modulo the 128-bit prime q. Using the basic embedding of the range $[-2^{t-1}, 2^{t-1} - 1]$ into $[0, q-1]$, we can then provide standard integer operations such as addition, multiplication and comparison. Note however that "wrap around" will only occur in the range $[0, q-1]$ and not in $[-2^{t-1}, 2^{t-1} - 1]$ unless special code is produced to do so.

For some computations, we may wish to decompose a secret shared integer into bits and then perform bitwise operations on the resulting shared bits. This can be done using fairly standard bit decomposition techniques [7], but we achieve further efficiency gains through use of shared bits from the preprocessing. In particular the following bit decomposition technique is used in the floating point addition protocol of [1] which we use. We pause to overview how a bit decomposition is performed using the precomputed shared random bits: Given a shared value $\langle x \rangle$ which is known to represent an integer which is $m < 128 - 40 = 88$ bits long, we use a set of $m + 40$ shared bits $\{\langle b_i \rangle\}_{i=0}^{m+39}$ (loaded via the bit operation) to obtain t sharings of the t least significant bits of x. The shared masking value $\langle y \rangle = \sum_{i=0}^{m+39} 2^i \langle b_i \rangle$ is first computed, and applied to $\langle x \rangle$ to obtain $\langle c \rangle = 2^{m+40} + 2^m + \langle x \rangle - \langle y \rangle$. The value $\langle c \rangle$ is then opened and the result taken modulo 2^m to obtain $r = x - y \mod 2^m$. We then take the m least significant bits of r, and the shared bits $\{\langle b_i \rangle\}_{i=0}^{m-1}$, and execute the circuit for binary addition on these to compute the result. Since $\langle x \rangle$ is known to be m bits long, the length of $\langle y \rangle$ provides 40 bits of statistical security when revealing $x - y$.

This last step requires us to efficiently evaluate binary circuits for shared bit values over a large finite field. The usual approach is to execute a squaring for every XOR operation, since $a \oplus b = (a-b)^2$ over the integers for binary a and b. This is relatively expensive; so we instead adopt one of two different approaches.

- For the bitwise addition circuit used in bit decomposition above, we use the technique from [30]. In this circuit for every XOR of two bit values we also need to compute their AND. If $a, b \in \{0, 1\}$ then computing $a \wedge b$ is the same as computing their integer product; and compute $a \oplus b$ is the the integer calculation $a + b - 2 \cdot a \cdot b$, and so comes at no additional cost (since $a \wedge b$ is also needed).

- For more general binary circuits, the overhead of multiplying at every XOR gate can be costly, so we propose an alternative method for avoiding this. We simply execute an addition operation instead of XOR, and keep track of the maximum size of the resulting shared integer. When the result may exceed 2^{128-40}, or we need to return the final bit value, we can reduce the integer modulo two by applying the bit decomposition procedure (with $m = 1$) to output the least significant bit. This allows us to emulate binary circuits of reasonable depth at very little extra cost, bar the unavoidable overhead of arithmetic modulo q.

Fixed and floating point arithmetic: In addition to integer types, our compiler supports fixed and floating point arithmetic. Our fixed point arithmetic type consists of a secret shared integer of size up to 64 bits, with the point fixed at 32 binary places. Our secure floating point representation is based on the IEEE single precision format, where the significand has 24 bits of precision and the exponent 8 bits. This allows both significands and exponents to be stored as 128-bit field elements, leaving plenty of room for expansion after addition and multiplication with a 40-bit statistical security parameter.

The results of floating point operations are compliant to the IEEE standard, except we do not currently handle errors for overflow or invalid operations. Clearly any error handling performed must be secret to preserve privacy; we could use secret shared bits to handle error flags (as described in [1]) but chose to omit this for simplicity.

Note that we always use deterministic truncation in our protocols, and not the probabilistic rounding method of [8]. Whilst more efficient, the probabilistic method leads to lower accuracy and more complex analysis of errors, and is impractical for operations like comparison, where a deterministic result is required.

5.2 The $\mathbb{F}_{2^{40}}$ Variant

We also present results for a runtime based on secret sharing over the field $\mathbb{F}_{2^{40}}$. This field size is chosen to enable us to upper bound the probability of an active adversary going undetected by of 2^{-40}, which is a common value in previous work on actively secure MPC protocols. In addition the field $\mathbb{F}_{2^{40}}$ enables us to efficiently embed a copy of $\mathbb{F}_{2^8}$ within it; this was shown to be useful in [13] in evaluating an AES functionality. In a similar way we embed the binary field $\mathbb{F}_2$ into $\mathbb{F}_{2^{40}}$ thus enabling the evaluation of binary circuits.

Unlike the case of the large prime characteristic field, for the characteristic two fields, our offline phase only produces triples, bits and input sharings. We shall see in Section 6.2 that our runtime is able to evaluate the AES functionality rather efficiently. In particular one can obtain a factor of 100 improvement in either latency of throughput on the previous best runtimes for AES evaluation with active security [13]. In addition in trading throughput for latency one can always obtain a factor of 10 improvement in either of these values (and a factor of 100 improvement in the other) over the results in [13]. However, we shall see that the runtime is less efficient at evaluating complex general binary circuits.

6. EXPERIMENTAL RESULTS

Our basic experimental setup was as follows. We used two machines with Intel i7-2600S CPU's running at 2.8 GHz with 4GB of RAM, connected by a local area network. Each machine represents a party to the computation. Our experimental setup could have been performed with more than two parties with only a marginal decrease in performance.

Each program was written using our system and then compiled to bytecode tapes. Each tape was run ℓ times (with ℓ at least 50, the precise value depending on the experiment being carried out) sequentially in a single thread, and then the experiment repeated using tapes which had been vectorized with our SIMD instructions. For the SIMD experiments, a tape executed n versions of the algorithm in parallel with all of the communication batched together, for values of n in $\{1, 2, 3, 4, 5, 10, 16, 32, 64, 128\}$. Finally the same set of experiments were carried out running in t threads instead of one, for $t \in \{1, 4, 7\}$. The upper bound of seven was chosen since our processors had eight cores and one thread was acting as the controller thread.

For all experiments we measured performance using *throughput* and *latency*. Latency is simply the average execution time for $n \cdot t$ operations (obtained by dividing the total runtime by ℓ), whilst throughput is the number of operations executed per second. We plot these measures against other in the graphs that follow, showing tradeoffs that are possible depending on the application. Reading the graphs from left-to-right, the number n of operations in parallel is increased; note that the first data point always corresponds to $n = 1$, for purely sequential operations. Higher values of n result is higher latency as more data needs to be passed across the network in each communication. However, we can also see for most functionalities that at a certain point increasing n no longer buys us any extra throughput, and indeed it can decrease the throughput in some cases.

The reason for focusing on the trade-off between throughput and latency is as follows. Whilst many previous works on MPC focus on throughput only (i.e. number of AES operations per second), they often hide the high latency needed to achieve such high throughputs. In a real application one will have a specific latency one is trying to achieve, with throughput often being a secondary consideration. By presenting graphs which show the trade-off between throughput and latency, one can more accurately see the kind of performance characteristics a real world application would enjoy.

6.1 Arithmetic Circuits in Large Characteristic

In this section we detail the performance of our runtime when working in $\mathbb{F}_q$, for q a 128-bit prime. The most basic operation interactive operation is multiplication of secret shared values, for which we give timings below. We then discuss integer comparison, where we assume the input values are guaranteed to be 32 bit or 64 bit signed integers. Integer comparison is, unlike for standard processors, more expensive than multiplication. Having integer comparison allows us to implement sorting of lists with sorting networks. From comparison we move onto computing on approximations to real number computations using fixed point and floating point arithmetic. Table 6.1 summarizes the various costs and complexities of the algorithms discussed in this section.

6.1.1 Integer Multiplication

The basic non-local operation performed by the run time is executing an integer multiplication in the field $\mathbb{F}_q$. This requires a single round of communication, with each player needing to send two elements in $\mathbb{F}_q$ to each other player. In Figure 3 we present the how the latency and throughput varies depending on how many threads are used, and how many multiplications per thread are executed in a SIMD like manner per thread.

6.1.2 Integer Comparison

Comparison of secret shared integers is a fundamental operation in secure computation, used extensively throughout our fixed and floating point arithmetic below. The protocols we use all subtract one input from the other and compare the result to zero by extracting the most significant bit without doing bitwise decomposition.

For the comparison operation we implemented two protocols described by Catrina and de Hoogh [7], one with logarithmic round complexity and one in constant rounds but with slightly higher communication costs. The logarithmic rounds solution evaluates a binary circuit for computing the carry bit from binary addition, using this to obtain the comparison result. The constant rounds variant takes a different approach, using an efficient prefix multiplication protocol to compute the prefix products $p_i = \prod_{j=i}^{k}(d_j + 1) = 2^{\sum_{j=i}^{k} d_j}$, where $d_i = a_i \oplus b_i$, from which the comparison bit can be derived. The prefix multiplication by Damgård *et al.* [10] works as follows: Given non-zero inputs $x_0, x_1, x_2, \ldots$ opening the masked values $x_0 a_0^{-1}, a_0 x_1 a_1^{-1}, a_1 x_1 a_2^{-1}, \ldots$ for random non-zero $a_0, a_1, \ldots$ allows to compute $a_0 a_1, a_0 a_1 a_2, \ldots$ in a con-

Protocol	Rounds	Triples	Bits	Inverses
Multiplication	1	1	0	0
32-Bit Comparison (Constant Rounds)	4	61	143	31
32-Bit Comparison (Logarithmic Rounds)	5	52	72	0
64-Bit Comparison (Constant Rounds)	4	125	207	63
64-Bit Comparison (Logarithmic Rounds)	6	114	104	0
Fixed Point Mult.	7	63	168	0
Floating Point Mult.	15	95	218	0
Floating Point Add	47	483	2185	32
Fixed Point Comp.	10	73	159	0
Floating Point Comp.	7	124	104	0

Table 2: Round and communication complexities of the large prime field protocols.

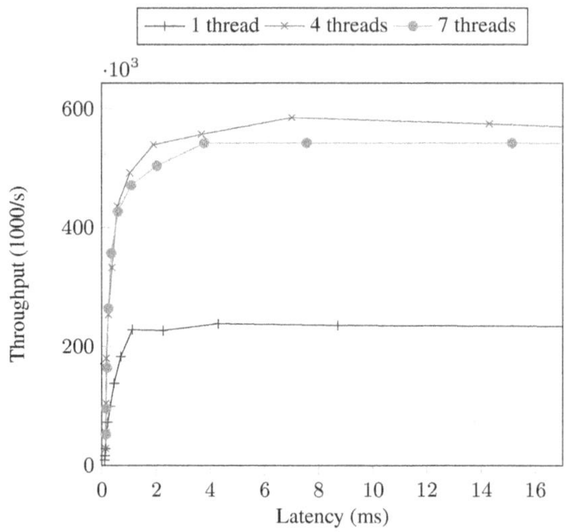

Figure 3: Integer multiplication

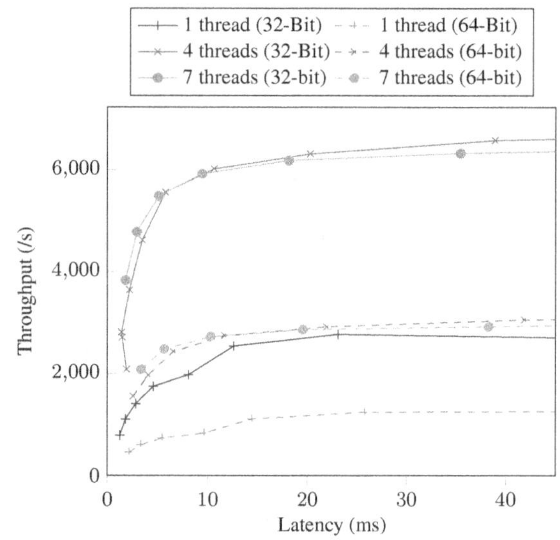

Figure 4: Integer comparison (logarithmic rounds protocol).

stant number of rounds. Catrina and de Hoogh also gave a second constant rounds protocol with better communication complexity, however this exploits properties of Shamir secret sharing which we cannot use.

For 32-bit comparison (resp. 64-bit comparison) operations with a 40-bit statistical security parameter, the logarithmic rounds solution requires six (resp. seven) rounds of communication, compared with four for the constant rounds protocol. However, the amount of data transmitted is 20% smaller; 121 (resp. 249) required openings for the logarithmic round version as opposed to 155 (resp. 315) for the constant round version (32-bit). Our experiments indicate that the saving of one round in the constant variant is dominated by the communication cost of sending more data in each round. The resulting performance is around 20% slower for the constant round method compared to the logarithmic round method. Therefore we used the logarithmic rounds protocol for all comparison and higher-level operations. Note that our implementations have slightly differing round and communication complexities to those stated in [7], firstly because we can generate shared bits without interaction using our preprocessing, and also as their constant rounds solution uses a special public output multiplication protocol, which cannot be applied to our setting.

6.1.3 Sorting

Based on integer comparison, we implemented odd-even merge sorting networks similarly to Jónsson et al. [18]. Our results are shown in Figure 5. For the implemented sizes they are similar to the results by Jónsson *et al.* Note that the figures are based on only one sequential sorting operation, using one thread for shorter lists and seven threads for longer lists. The latter improves the performance because sorting networks are highly parallelizable by design.

Sorting networks are the most efficient known method for fully private sorting because the most sorting algorithms rely on branching, which is not possible in multi-party computation if the condition is supposed to stay secret. Sorting networks only use compare-and-swap operations, which guarantee that the first output is the minimum of the two inputs. It is straightforward to implement this operation using comparison. Odd-even merge sorting networks have complexity $O(n \cdot \log^2 n)$. While this is not optimal, there is no known sorting network with complexity $O(n \cdot \log n)$ that is efficient for practical parameters.

6.1.4 Fixed and Floating Point Arithmetic

As explained earlier fixed point arithmetic is implemented using a secret shared integer of size up to 64 bits, with the point fixed at 32 binary places. Here addition is simply a local operation (as with integer arithmetic) and multiplication consists of multiplying

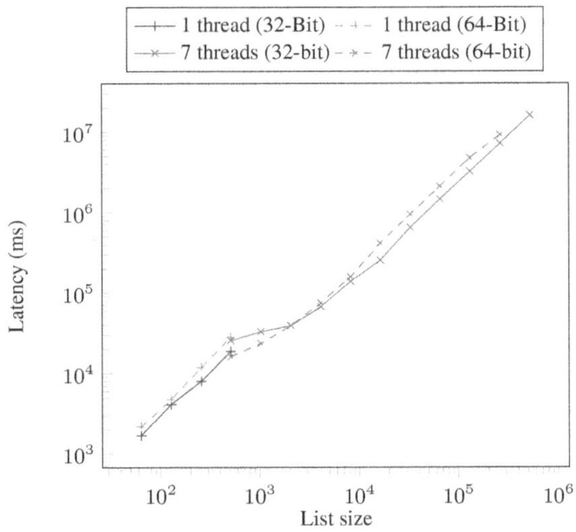

Figure 5: Sorting.

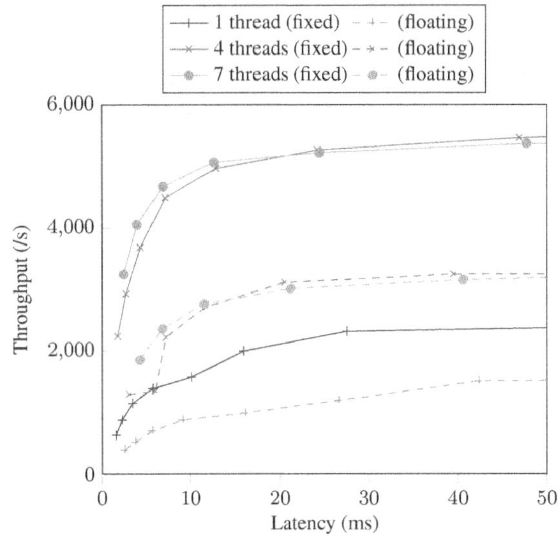

Figure 7: Fixed and floating point multiplication

the two integers and truncating the result by 32 bits. This is essentially the same cost as a 32-bit comparison operation. The relevant performance is presented in Figures 7 and 8.

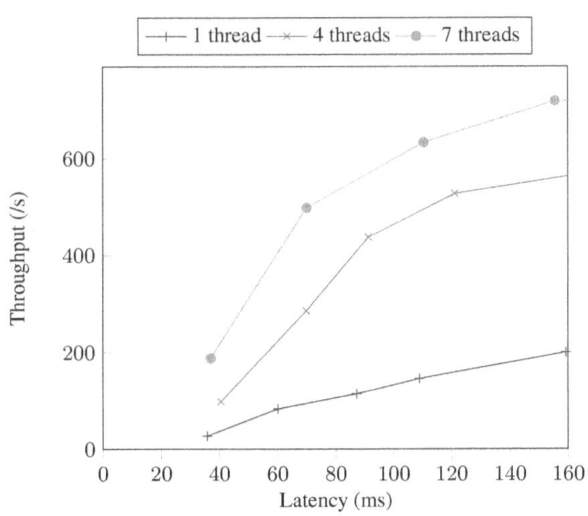

Figure 6: Floating point addition

We use the floating point protocols from [1] for addition, multiplication and comparison (see Figures 6, 7, 8). From these operations other more complex floating computations can be built up. As was also the case with integer comparison earlier, the complexities of our protocols improve upon those stated in [1] due to the preprocessing we use. Floating point protocols make extensive use of comparison and bitwise addition protocols, for which using precomputed shared bits improves performance considerably. Recall that our floating point operations are almost compliant to the IEEE standard for single precision floating point numbers; the only deviation being how we handle errors for overflow and invalid operations.

As can be seen in Figure 7, the difference in performance between fixed and floating point multiplication is not huge; floating point is only a factor of two slower. It is in addition, however, where floating point operations really suffer. This is due to the need to obliviously align the exponents of both inputs, whereas fixed point addition is a simple local operation (as with integers). With the comparison operation, floating point is slightly faster due to the smaller lengths of integers involved, despite the protocol being more complex.

Our throughput results compare favourably with those for a passively secure, three-party protocol based on Shamir secret sharing from [1]. They had a similar setup to ours, also running on a local network, and our operations are roughly an order of magnitude faster when maximum parallelism is used, probably due to our sophisticated implementation techniques described earlier.

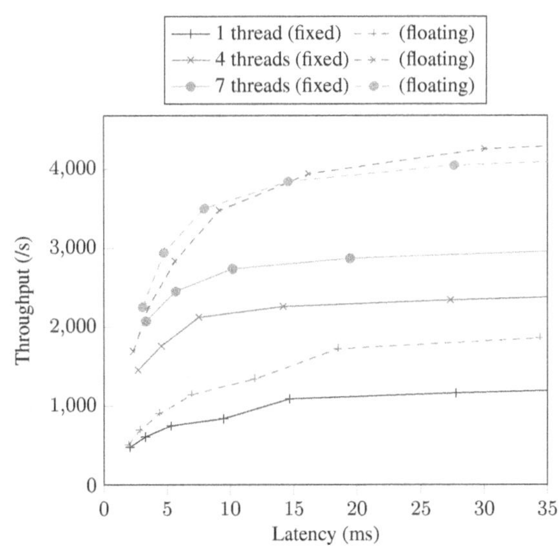

Figure 8: Fixed and floating point comparison operation (less than)

6.2 Circuits in Characteristic Two

For our experiments in characteristic two we settled on the following six functionalities as exemplars: AES (with and without the key schedule included), DES (again with and without the key schedule included), MD5, SHA-1 and SHA-256. The reason for selecting these was firstly, as has already been mentioned, AES is the standard example in the field and secondly, the circuits for DES, MD5, SHA-1 and SHA-256 are readily available. In addition if one is using AES as a prototypical PRF in an application it is interesting to compare just how much more efficient it is compared to other PRF's used in various cryptographic operations.

In Table 6.2 we present various statistics associated with these functionalities; how many multiplication triples they consume, how many bits, and how many rounds of communication are required, all for a single invocation of the functionality. Note, this latter figure is determined automatically by our compilation strategy to be the minimum necessary given the algorithm used to compute the function. The DES, MD5, SHA-1 and SHA-256 functionalities were computed via their standard binary circuit description whereas the AES functionality made use of arithmetic description over $\mathbb{F}_{2^8}$ and the efficient bit-decomposition method to compute the S-Box from [12, 13].

6.2.1 AES

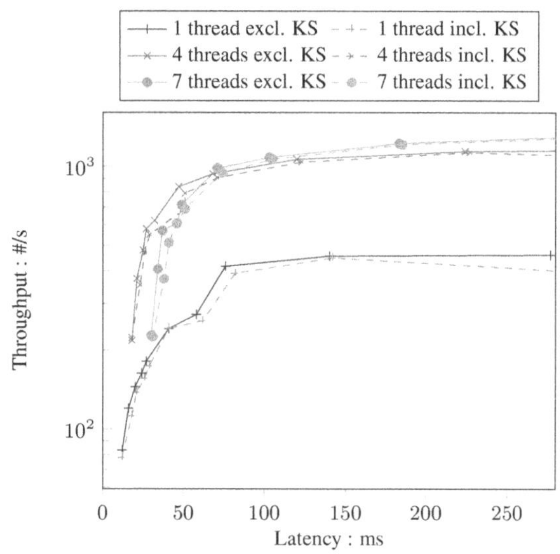

Figure 9: AES runtimes

In this functionality we assume a single AES secret key k, which has been shared between the parties. The goal of the functionality is to evaluate the AES function on a single block of public data, producing a shared output ciphertext block. From Figure 9 we can see that having a pre-expanded secret key shared between the parties makes very little difference in the execution times. We also see that with either four or seven threads a throughput of roughly 1000 blocks per second is easily obtainable; with a latency of around 100ms. The smallest latency comes when using a single thread and only batching up a single AES execution at a time; here we obtain a latency of around 12ms, but only a throughput of 83 blocks per second. Note, that the performance we obtain with our runtime is at least an order of magnitude better than that obtained in [13], without introducing any algorithmic improvements. Our improvement is purely down to a deeper understanding of how to schedule and execute MPC instructions.

6.2.2 DES

In Figure 10 we present a similar experiment for the DES cipher. Notice, just as for AES there is little difference between evaluating the cipher with a pre-expanded key and having to evaluate the key

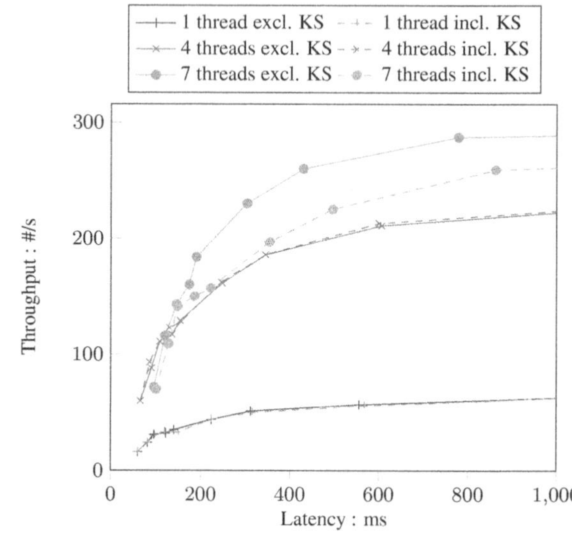

Figure 10: DES runtimes

schedule using MPC. Except in the case of running seven threads, in which case having to execute the key schedule significantly reduces the throughput. The latency and throughput are about ten times worse than what was obtained from AES. This however is not (directly) because we are evaluating a binary circuit over $\mathbb{F}_2$ as opposed to working with bytes in $\mathbb{F}_{2^8}$, it is more a function of the number of rounds of communication needed and the amount of data communicated in those rounds.

6.2.3 MD5, SHA-1 and SHA-256

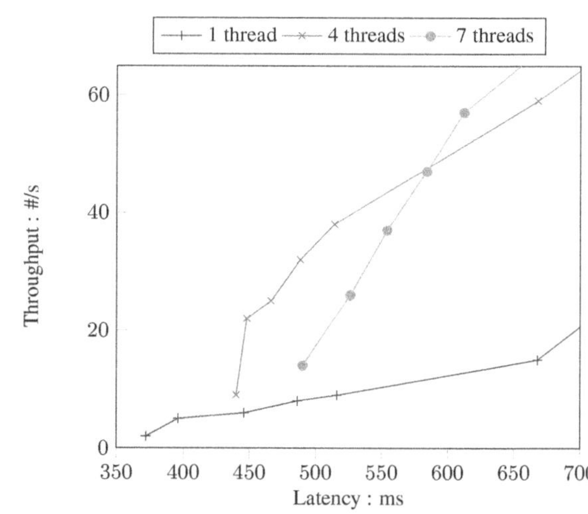

Figure 11: MD5 runtimes

When applying the runtime to the MD5, SHA-1 and SHA-256 circuits one sees that the number of multiplications/rounds has an even more dramatic effect. The latency increases and the throughput decreases as the number of rounds increases, and the number of triples consumed increases. See Figures 11, 12 and 13 for details.

7. ACKNOWLEDGEMENTS

The third author was supported in part by a Royal Society Wolfson Merit Award. This work has been supported in part by ERC

Functionality	Rounds	Triples	Bits
AES (incl. Key Schedule)	50	1200	3200
AES (excl. Key Schedule)	50	960	2560
DES (incl. Key Schedule)	263	18124	0
DES (excl. Key Schedule)	261	18175	0
MD5	2972	29084	0
SHA-1	5503	37300	0
SHA-256	3976	90825	0

Table 3: Round and required pre-processed data for the various functionalities in characteristic two.

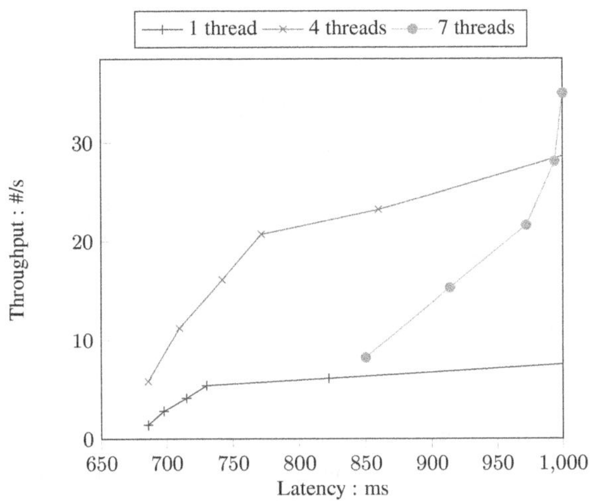

Figure 12: SHA-1 runtimes

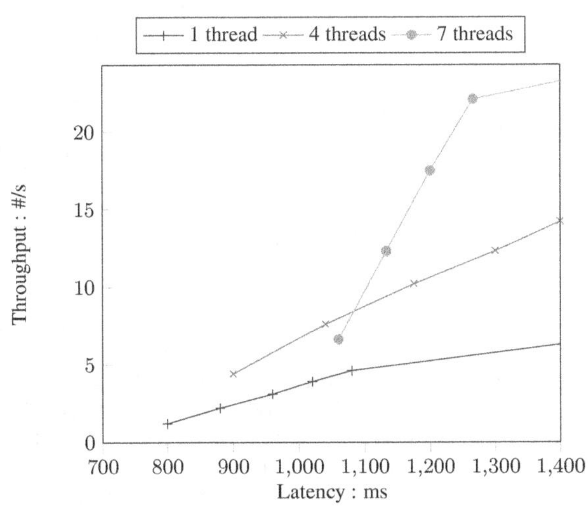

Figure 13: SHA-256 runtimes

Advanced Grant ERC-2010-AdG-267188-CRIPTO and by EPSRC via grant EP/I03126X.

8. REFERENCES

[1] M. Aliasgari, M. Blanton, Y. Zhang, and A. Steele. Secure computation on floating point numbers. In *Network and Distributed System Security Symposium – NDSS 2013*, 2013.

[2] D. Beaver. Efficient multiparty protocols using circuit randomization. In J. Feigenbaum, editor, *CRYPTO*, volume 576 of *Lecture Notes in Computer Science*, pages 420–432. Springer, 1991.

[3] A. Ben-David, N. Nisan, and B. Pinkas. FairplayMP: a system for secure multi-party computation. In P. Ning, P. F. Syverson, and S. Jha, editors, *ACM Conference on Computer and Communications Security*, pages 257–266. ACM, 2008.

[4] M. Ben-Or, S. Goldwasser, and A. Wigderson. Completeness theorems for non-cryptographic fault-tolerant distributed computation (extended abstract). In J. Simon, editor, *STOC*, pages 1–10. ACM, 1988.

[5] R. Bendlin, I. Damgård, C. Orlandi, and S. Zakarias. Semi-homomorphic encryption and multiparty computation. In *EUROCRYPT*, volume 6632 of *Lecture Notes in Computer Science*, pages 169–188, 2011.

[6] D. Bogdanov, S. Laur, and J. Willemson. Sharemind: A framework for fast privacy-preserving computations. In *ESORICS*, volume 5283 of *Lecture Notes in Computer Science*, pages 192–206. Springer, 2008.

[7] O. Catrina and S. de Hoogh. Improved primitives for secure multiparty integer computation. In J. A. Garay and R. D. Prisco, editors, *SCN*, volume 6280 of *Lecture Notes in Computer Science*, pages 182–199. Springer, 2010.

[8] O. Catrina and A. Saxena. Secure computation with fixed-point numbers. In *Financial Cryptography*, volume 6052 of *Lecture Notes in Computer Science*, pages 35–50. Springer, 2010.

[9] S. G. Choi, K.-W. Hwang, J. Katz, T. Malkin, and D. Rubenstein. Secure multi-party computation of boolean circuits with applications to privacy in on-line marketplaces. In O. Dunkelman, editor, *CT-RSA*, volume 7178 of *Lecture Notes in Computer Science*, pages 416–432. Springer, 2012.

[10] I. Damgård, M. Fitzi, E. Kiltz, J. B. Nielsen, and T. Toft. Unconditionally secure constant-rounds multi-party computation for equality, comparison, bits and exponentiation. In S. Halevi and T. Rabin, editors, *Theory of Cryptography – TCC 2006*, volume 3876 of *Lecture Notes in Computer Science*, pages 285–304. Springer, 2006.

[11] I. Damgård, M. Geisler, M. Krøigaard, and J. B. Nielsen. Asynchronous multiparty computation: Theory and implementation. In S. Jarecki and G. Tsudik, editors, *Public Key Cryptography – PKC 2009*, volume 5443 of *Lecture Notes in Computer Science*, pages 160–179. Springer, 2009.

[12] I. Damgård and M. Keller. Secure multiparty AES. In R. Sion, editor, *Financial Cryptography*, volume 6052 of *Lecture Notes in Computer Science*, pages 367–374. Springer, 2010.

[13] I. Damgård, M. Keller, E. Larraia, C. Miles, and N. P. Smart. Implementing AES via an actively/covertly secure dishonest-majority MPC protocol. In *SCN*, volume 7485 of

Lecture Notes in Computer Science, pages 241–263. Springer, 2012.

[14] I. Damgard, M. Keller, E. Larraia, V. Pastro, P. Scholl, and N. P. Smart. Practical Covertly Secure MPC for Dishonest Majority – or: Breaking the SPDZ Limits. In *To appear - ESORICS*. Springer, 2013.

[15] I. Damgård, V. Pastro, N. P. Smart, and S. Zakarias. Multiparty computation from somewhat homomorphic encryption. In *CRYPTO*, volume 7417 of *Lecture Notes in Computer Science*, pages 643–662. Springer, 2012.

[16] W. Henecka, S. Kögl, A.-R. Sadeghi, T. Schneider, and I. Wehrenberg. Tasty: tool for automating secure two-party computations. In E. Al-Shaer, A. D. Keromytis, and V. Shmatikov, editors, *ACM Conference on Computer and Communications Security*, pages 451–462. ACM, 2010.

[17] Y. Huang, D. Evans, J. Katz, and L. Malka. Faster secure two-party computation using garbled circuits. In *USENIX Security Symposium*. USENIX Association, 2011.

[18] K. V. Jónsson, G. Kreitz, and M. Uddin. Secure multi-party sorting and applications. *IACR Cryptology ePrint Archive*, 2011:122, 2011.

[19] F. Kerschbaum. Automatically optimizing secure computation. In Y. Chen, G. Danezis, and V. Shmatikov, editors, *ACM Conference on Computer and Communications Security*, pages 703–714. ACM, 2011.

[20] B. Kreuter, A. Shelat, and C.-H. Shen. Towards billion-gate secure computation with malicious adversaries. In *USENIX Security Symposium – 2012*, pages 285–300, 2012.

[21] J. Launchbury, I. S. Diatchki, T. DuBuisson, and A. Adams-Moran. Efficient lookup-table protocol in secure multiparty computation. In P. Thiemann and R. B. Findler, editors, *ICFP*, pages 189–200. ACM, 2012.

[22] S. Laur, R. Talviste, and J. Willemson. Aes block cipher implementation and secure database join on the sharemind secure multi-party computation framework, 2012.

[23] Y. Lindell, E. Oxman, and B. Pinkas. The IPS compiler: Optimizations, variants and concrete efficiency. In P. Rogaway, editor, *CRYPTO*, volume 6841 of *Lecture Notes in Computer Science*, pages 259–276. Springer, 2011.

[24] Y. Lindell, B. Pinkas, and N. P. Smart. Implementing two-party computation efficiently with security against malicious adversaries. In R. Ostrovsky, R. D. Prisco, and I. Visconti, editors, *Security and Cryptography for Networks – SCN 2008*, volume 5229 of *Lecture Notes in Computer Science*, pages 2–20. Springer, 2008.

[25] D. Malkhi, N. Nisan, B. Pinkas, and Y. Sella. Fairplay - Secure two-party computation system. In *USENIX Security Symposium – 2004*, pages 287–302, 2004.

[26] J. B. Nielsen, P. S. Nordholt, C. Orlandi, and S. S. Burra. A new approach to practical active-secure two-party computation. In *CRYPTO*, volume 7417 of *Lecture Notes in Computer Science*, pages 681–700. Springer, 2012.

[27] J. B. Nielsen and C. Orlandi. LEGO for two-party secure computation. In *TCC*, volume 5444 of *Lecture Notes in Computer Science*, pages 368–386. Springer, 2009.

[28] B. Pinkas, T. Schneider, N. P. Smart, and S. C. Williams. Secure two-party computation is practical. In M. Matsui, editor, *Advances in Cryptology – ASIACRYPT 2009*, volume 5912 of *Lecture Notes in Computer Science*, pages 250–267. Springer, 2009.

[29] A. Rastogi, P. Mardziel, M. Hicks, and M. A. Hammer. Knowledge inference for optimizing secure multi-party computation. Manuscript, 2013.

[30] SecureSCM Project:. Cryptographic aspects - security analysis, 2010. secureSCM deliverable D9.2.

[31] A. Shelat and C.-H. Shen. Two-output secure computation with malicious adversaries. In K. G. Paterson, editor, *EUROCRYPT*, volume 6632 of *Lecture Notes in Computer Science*, pages 386–405. Springer, 2011.

[32] SIMAP Project. SIMAP: Secure information management and processing. `http://alexandra.dk/uk/Projects/Pages/SIMAP.aspx`.

APPENDIX

A. BRANCHING/LOOPING

Due to the way the precomputed data is processed the runtime needs to know before executing a specific bytecode tape within a thread how much precomputed data will be consumed. This produces a particular issue in relation to branching and looping. We distinguish three cases:

- Loops where the number of iterations are known at compile time.
- Conditional branches forwards (as in `if-then-else` constructions).
- Conditional branches backwards (as in `do-while` loops).

We note that conditional branching can only be executed on opened values; we do not allow branching on shared values. We now discuss each of the above three cases in turn.

For loops where the number of iterations is known at compile time, we can determine the amount of precomputed data used within the loop by simply counting each instruction which loads data by the requisite number of times the loop is executed; with a suitable modification for nested loops. Forward conditional branches essentially allow one to conditionally skip code portions; thus by simply counting the total number of instructions which load precomputed data we will obtain an upper bound on the amount of precomputed data; this will be enough for the runtime to allocate different portions of the precomputed data to each bytecode tape within each thread.

The main issue occurs with conditional branches backwards; these arise for loop constructions where the number of iterations cannot be determined at compile time. Here a design decision has to be made, either we install logic to cope with this case (which would incur a large performance penalty) or we restrict the use of such constructs in some way. We decided to come up with the following constraint, after considering various use-cases. The main problem arises from not being able to allocate portions of the existing pool of precomputed data to each thread. Thus we impose a constraint on the main control thread in that it cannot execute any bytecode tape containing a conditional backward branch with any other thread at the same time. This means that tapes which could in theory be executed concurrently will be executed serially. Then the actual amount of precomputed data consumed during the execution can be determined; rather than estimated ahead of time. We found this compromise provided a suitable balance between efficiency and applicability; we can process the single tape very fast, at the expense of not being able to execute multiple tapes in parallel for such situations.

Belief Semantics of Authorization Logic

Andrew K. Hirsch
Department of Computer Science
George Washington University
Washington, D.C., United States
akhirsch@gwu.edu

Michael R. Clarkson
Department of Computer Science
George Washington University
Washington, D.C., United States
clarkson@gwu.edu

ABSTRACT

A formal belief semantics for authorization logics is given. The belief semantics is proved to subsume a standard Kripke semantics. The belief semantics yields a direct representation of principals' beliefs, without resorting to the technical machinery used in Kripke semantics. A proof system is given for the logic; that system is proved sound with respect to the belief and Kripke semantics. The soundness proofs are mechanized in Coq.

Categories and Subject Descriptors

D.4.6 [**Operating Systems**]: Security and Protection—*Access controls*; F.4.1 [**Mathematical Logic and Formal Languages**]: Mathematical Logic—*modal logic, model theory, proof theory, mechanical theorem proving*

Keywords

Authorization logic; NAL; CDD

1. INTRODUCTION

Authorization logics are used in computer security to reason about whether *principals*—computer or human agents—are permitted to take actions in computer systems. The distinguishing feature of authorization logics is their use of a says connective: intuitively, if principal p believes that formula ϕ holds, then formula p says ϕ holds. Access control decisions can then be made by reasoning about (i) the beliefs of principals, (ii) how those beliefs can be combined to derive logical consequences, and (iii) whether those consequences entail *guard formulas*, which must hold for actions to be permitted.

Many systems that employ authorization logics have been proposed (see [1, 10] for surveys; see also [5–9, 11, 12, 17, 23, 28, 29, 32–35, 40, 42, 45, 52]), but few authorization logics have been given a formal semantics [4, 18, 19, 22, 26]. Though semantics might not be immediately necessary to deploy authorization logics in real systems, semantics yield insight into the meaning of formulas, and semantics enable proof systems to be proved sound—which might require proof rules and axioms to be corrected, if there are any lurking errors in the proof system.

For the sake of security, it is worthwhile to carry out such soundness proofs. Given only a proof system, we must trust that the proof system is correct. But given a proof system and a soundness proof, which shows that any provable formula is semantically valid, we now have evidence that the proof system is correct, hence trustworthy. The soundness proof thus relocates trust from the proof system to the proof itself—as well as to the semantics, which ideally offers more intuition about formulas than the proof system itself.

Semantics of authorization logics are usually based on *possible worlds*, as used by Kripke [31]. *Kripke semantics* posit an indexed *accessibility relation* on possible worlds. If at world w, principal p considers world w' to be possible, then (w, w') is in p's accessibility relation. We denote this as $w \leq_p w'$. Authorization logics use Kripke semantics to give meaning to the says connective: semantically, p says ϕ holds in a world w iff for all worlds w' such that $w \leq_p w'$, formula ϕ holds in world w'. Hence a principal says ϕ iff ϕ holds in all worlds the principal considers possible.[1]

The use of Kripke semantics in authorization logic thus requires installation of possible worlds and accessibility relations into the semantics, solely to give meaning to says. That's useful for studying properties of logics and for building decision procedures. But, unfortunately, it doesn't seem to correspond to how principals reason in real-world systems. Rather than explicitly considering possible worlds and relations between them, principals typically begin with some set of base formulas they believe to hold—perhaps because they have received digitally signed messages encoding those formulas, or perhaps because they invoke system calls that return information—then proceed to reason from those formulas. So could we instead stipulate that each principal p have a set of beliefs $\omega(p)$, called the *worldview* of p, such that p says ϕ holds iff $\phi \in \omega(p)$? That is, a principal says ϕ iff ϕ is in the worldview[2] of the principal?

This paper answers that question in the affirmative. We give two semantics for an authorization logic: a Kripke semantics (§3), and a new *belief semantics* (§2), which employs

CCS'13, November 4–8, 2013, Berlin, Germany.

http://dx.doi.org/10.1145/2508859.2516667.

[1] The says connective is, therefore, closely related to the modal necessity operator $\Box$ [27] and the epistemic knowledge operator K [15].

[2] Worldviews were first employed by NAL [43], which pioneered an informal semantics based on them.

worldviews to interpret says.[3] We show (§4) that belief semantics subsume Kripke semantics, in the sense that a belief model can be constructed from any Kripke model. A formula is valid in the Kripke model iff it is valid in the constructed belief model. As a result, the technical machinery of Kripke semantics can be replaced by belief semantics. This potentially increases the trustworthiness of an authorization system, because the semantics is closer to how principals reason in real systems.

The particular logical system we introduce in this paper is FOCAL, First-Order Constructive Authorization Logic. FOCAL extends a well-known authorization logic, cut-down dependency core calculus (CDD) [2], from a propositional language to a language with first-order functions and relations on system state. Functions and relations are essential for reasoning about authorization in a real operating system—as exemplified in Nexus Authorization Logic (NAL) [43], of which FOCAL and CDD are both fragments.

Having given two semantics for FOCAL, we then turn to the problem of proving soundness. It turns out that the NAL proof system is unsound with respect to the semantics presented here: NAL allows derivation of a well-known formula (cf. §5.2) that our semantics deems invalid. A priori, the fault could lie with our semantics or with NAL's proof system. However, if the logic is to be used in a distributed setting without globally-agreed upon state, then the proof system should not allow the formula to be derived. So if NAL is to be used in such settings, its proof system needs to be corrected. CDD is also unsound with respect to our semantics. However, CDD has been proved sound with respect to a different semantics [19]. This seeming discrepancy—sound vs. unsound—illuminates a previously unexplored difference (§5.2) between how NAL and CDD interpret says.

To achieve soundness for FOCAL, we develop a revised proof system; the key technical change is using localized hypotheses in the proof rules. In §5, we prove the soundness of our proof system with respect to both our belief and Kripke semantics. This result yields the first soundness proof with respect to belief semantics for an authorization logic.

Having relocated trust into the soundness proof, we then seek a means to increase the trustworthiness of that proof. We formalize the syntax, proof system, belief semantics, and Kripke semantics in the Coq proof assistant,[4] and we mechanize the proofs of soundness for both the belief semantics and the Kripke semantics. That mechanization relocates trust from our soundness proof to Coq, which is well-studied and is the basis of many other formalizations. Our Coq formalization contains about 2,400 lines of code.[5]

This paper thus advances the theory of computer security with the following novel contributions:

- the first formal belief semantics for authorization logic,
- a proof that Kripke semantics can be transformed into belief semantics,
- a proof system that is sound with respect to belief and Kripke semantics, and
- the first machine-checked proof of soundness for an authorization-logic proof system.

[3]Our belief models are an instance of the *syntactic* approach to modeling knowledge [13, 15, 30, 37].

[4]`http://coq.inria.fr`

[5]Our implementation is available from `http://faculty.cs.gwu.edu/~clarkson/projects/focal/`.

$$\begin{aligned}\tau &::= x \mid f(\tau,\ldots,\tau)\\ \phi &::= \mathsf{true} \mid \mathsf{false} \mid r(\tau,\ldots,\tau) \mid \tau_1 = \tau_2\\ &\mid \phi_1 \wedge \phi_2 \mid \phi_1 \vee \phi_2 \mid \phi_1 \Rightarrow \phi_2 \mid \neg\phi\\ &\mid (\forall x : \phi) \mid (\exists x : \phi)\\ &\mid \tau \;\mathsf{says}\; \phi \mid \tau_1 \;\mathsf{speaksfor}\; \tau_2\end{aligned}$$

Figure 1: Syntax of FOCAL

We proceed as follows. §2 presents FOCAL's belief semantics; and §3, the Kripke semantics. §4 relates the belief semantics to the Kripke semantics. §5 gives a proof system and proves its soundness with respect to both semantics. §6 discusses related work, and §7 concludes. All proofs appear in the appendix.

2. BELIEF SEMANTICS

FOCAL is a constructive, first-order, multimodal logic. The key features that distinguish it as an authorization logic are the says and speaksfor connectives, invented by Lampson et al. [32]. These are used to reason about authorization—for example, access control in a distributed system can be modeled in the following standard way:

Example 1. *A* guard *implements access control for a printer p. To permit printing to p, the guard must be convinced that guard formula PrintServer* says *printTo(p) holds, where PrintServer is the principal representing the server process. That formula means PrintServer believes printTo(p) holds. To grant printer access to user u, the print server can issue the statement u* speaksfor *PrintServer. That formula means anything u says, the PrintServer must also say. So if u* says *printTo(p), then PrintServer* says *printTo(p), which satisfies the guard formula hence affords the user access.*

Figure 1 gives the formal syntax of FOCAL. There are two syntactic classes, terms τ and formulas ϕ. Metavariable x ranges over first-order variables, f over first-order functions, and r over first-order relations.

Formulas of FOCAL do not permit monadic second-order universal quantification, unlike CDD and NAL. In NAL, that quantifier was used only to define false and speaksfor as syntactic sugar. FOCAL instead adds these as primitive connectives to the logic. FOCAL also defines $\neg\phi$ as a primitive connective, but it could equivalently be defined as syntactic sugar for $\phi \Rightarrow \mathsf{false}$.

Syntactically, FOCAL is thus CDD without second-order quantification, but with first-order terms and quantification and a primitive speaksfor connective. Likewise, FOCAL is NAL without second-order quantification, subprincipals, group principals, and restricted delegation, but with a primitive speaksfor connective.

2.1 Semantic models

The belief semantics of FOCAL combines first-order constructive models with worldviews, which are used to interpret says and speaksfor. To our knowledge, this semantics is new in the study of authorization logics. Our presentation mostly follows the semantics of intuitionistic predicate calculus given by Troelstra and van Dalen [48].

First-order models. A *first-order model with equality* is a tuple $(D, =, R, F)$. The purpose of a first-order model is to interpret the first-order fragment of the logic, specifically first-order quantification, functions, and relations. D is a set, the *domain* of individuals. Semantically, quantification in the logic ranges over these individuals. R is a set $\{r_i \mid i \in I\}$ of relations on D, indexed by set I. Likewise, F is a set $\{f_j \mid j \in J\}$ of functions on D, indexed by set J. There is a distinguished equality relation $=$, which is an equivalence relation on D, such that equal individuals are indistinguishable by relations and functions.

To interpret first-order variables, the semantics employs *valuation* functions, which map variables to individuals. We write $v(x)$ to denote the individual that variable x represents in valuation v. And we write $v[d/x]$ to denote the valuation that is the same as v except that $v(x) = d$.

Constructive models. A *constructive model* is a tuple $(W, \leq, s)$. The purpose of constructive models is to extend first-order models to interpret the constructive fragment of the logic, specifically implication and universal quantification. W is a set, the possible worlds. We denote an individual world as w. Intuitively, a world w represents the state of knowledge of a constructive reasoner. *Constructive accessibility relation* $\leq$ is a partial order on W. If $w \leq w'$, then the constructive reasoner's state of knowledge could grow from w to w'. But unlike in classical logic, the reasoner need not commit to a formula ϕ being either true or false at a world. Suppose that at world w', where $w \leq w'$, the reasoner concludes that ϕ holds. And at world w'', where $w \leq w''$, the reasoner concludes that $\neg\phi$ holds. But at world w, the reasoner has not yet concluded that either ϕ or $\neg\phi$ holds. Then Excluded Middle $(\phi \vee \neg\phi)$ doesn't hold at w.

Function s is the *first-order interpretation function.* It assigns a first-order model $(D_w, =_w, R_w, F_w)$ to each world w. Let the individual elements of R_w be denoted as $r_{i,w}$, and the elements of F_w as $f_{j,w}$. Thus, s enables a potentially different first-order interpretation at each world. But to help ensure that the constructive reasoner's state of knowledge only grows—hence never invalidates a previously admitted construction—we require s to be monotonic w.r.t. $\leq$. That is, if $w \leq w'$ then (i) $D_w \subseteq D_{w'}$, (ii) $d =_w d'$ implies $d =_{w'} d'$, (iii) $r_{i,w} \subseteq r_{i,w'}$, and (iv) for all tuples $\vec{d}$ of individuals in D_w, it holds that $f_{j,w}(\vec{d}) =_w f_{j,w'}(\vec{d})$.

It's natural to wonder why we chose to introduce possible worlds into the semantics here after arguing against them in §1. Note, though, that the worlds in the constructive model are being used to model only the constructive reasoner—which we might think of as the guard, who exists outside the logic and attempts to ascertain the truth of formulas—not any of the principals reasoned about inside the logic. Moreover, we have not introduced any accessibility relations for principals, but only a single accessibility relation for the constructive reasoner. So the arguments in §1 don't apply. It would be possible to eliminate our usage of possible worlds by employing a *Heyting algebra semantics* [49] of constructive logic. But possible worlds blend better with the Kripke semantics in §3.

It's also natural to wonder why FOCAL is constructive rather than classical. Schneider et al. [43] write that constructivism preserves evidence: "Constructive logics are well suited for reasoning about authorization... because constructive proofs include all of the evidence used for reaching a conclusion and, therefore, information about accountability is not lost. Classical logics allow proofs that omit evidence." They argue that Excluded Middle, used as an axiom in a proof, would omit evidence by failing to indicate whether access was granted on the basis of ϕ holding or $\neg\phi$ holding. Garg and Pfenning [20] also champion the notion of evidence in authorization logics, writing that "[constructive logics] keep evidence contained in proofs as direct as possible." Regardless, we believe that a classical version of FOCAL could be created without difficulty.

Belief models. A *belief model* is a tuple $(W, \leq, s, P, \omega)$. The purpose of belief models is to extend constructive models to interpret says and speaksfor. The first part of a belief model, $(W, \leq, s)$, must itself be a constructive model. The next part, P, is the set of principals. Although individuals can vary from world to world in a model, the set of principals is fixed across the entire model. Assuming a fixed set of principals is consistent with other authorization logics [18, 19, 22], with constructive multimodal logics [44, 51] (which have a fixed set of modalities), and with classical multimodal epistemic logics [15] (which have an indexed set modalities, typically denoted K_i, where the index set is fixed)—even though constructivist philosophy might deem it more sensible to allow P to grow with $\leq$.

Because we make no syntactic distinction between individuals and principals, all principals must also be individuals: P must be a subset of D_w for every w. First-order quantification can therefore range over individuals as well as principals. For example, to quantify over all principals, we can write $(\forall x : \mathit{IsPrin}(x) \Rightarrow \phi)$, where IsPrin is a relation that holds for all $x \in P$. Nonetheless, this does not constitute truly intuitionistic quantification, because the domain of principals is constant. Quantification over a non-constant domain of principals is theoretically of interest, but we know of no authorization logic that has used it.

We define an equality relation $\doteq$ on principals, such that principals are equal iff they are equal at all worlds. Formally, $p \doteq p'$ iff, for all w, it holds that $p =_w p'$.

The final part of a belief model, worldview function ω, yields the beliefs of a principal p: the set of formulas that p believes to hold in world w under first-order valuation v is $\omega(w, p, v)$. For sake of simplicity, §1 used notation $\omega(p)$ when first presenting the idea of worldviews. Now that we're being precise, we also include w and v as arguments. To ensure that the constructive reasoner's knowledge grows monotonically, worldviews must be monotonic w.r.t. $\leq$:

> **Worldview Monotonicity:** If $w \leq w'$ then $\omega(w, p, v) \subseteq \omega(w', p, v)$.

To ensure that whenever principals are equal they have the same worldview, we require the following:

> **Worldview Equality:** If $p \doteq p'$, then, for all w and v, it holds that $\omega(w, p, v) = \omega(w, p', v)$.

And we also require the following conditions to ensure that valuations cannot cause worldviews to distinguish alpha-equivalent formulas:

Worldview Valuations:

1. If $x \notin FV(\phi)$ then $\phi \in \omega(w, p, v)$ iff, for all $d \in D_w$, it holds that $\phi \in \omega(w, p, v[d/x])$.

2. If $x \in FV(\phi)$ and $y \notin FV(\phi)$ then, for all $d \in D_w$, it holds that $\phi \in \omega(w, p, v[d/x])$ iff $\phi[y/x] \in \omega(w, p, v[d/y])$, where $\phi[y/x]$ denotes the capture-avoiding substitution of y for x in formula ϕ.

Condition (1) ensures that if x is irrelevant to ϕ, then the value of x is also irrelevant to whether p believes ϕ. Condition (2) ensures that if x is relevant to ϕ, then only its value—not its name—is relevant to whether p believes ϕ.

2.2 Semantic validity

Figure 2 gives a belief semantics of FOCAL. The validity judgment is written $B, w, v \models \phi$ where B is a belief model and w is a world in that model. As is standard, $B \models \phi$ holds iff, for all w and v, it holds that $B, w, v \models \phi$; whenever $B \models \phi$, then ϕ is a *necessary* formula in model B. And $B, v \models \phi$ holds iff for all w, it holds that $B, w, v \models \phi$; whenever $B, v \models \phi$, then ϕ is a *valuation-necessary* formula. Likewise, $\models \phi$ holds iff, for all B, it holds that $B \models \phi$; and whenever $\models \phi$, then ϕ is a *validity*. Let $B, w, v \models \Gamma$, where Γ is a set of formulas, denote that for all $\psi \in \Gamma$, it holds that $B, w, v \models \psi$. Finally, $\Gamma \models \phi$ holds iff, for all B, w, and v, it holds that $B, w, v \models \Gamma$ implies $B, w, v \models \phi$; whenever $\Gamma \models \phi$, then ϕ is a *logical consequence* of Γ.

The semantics relies on an auxiliary *interpretation* function μ that maps syntactic terms τ to semantic individuals:

$$\mu(x) = v(x)$$
$$\mu(f_j(\vec{\tau})) = f_{j,w}(\mu(\vec{\tau}))$$

Implicitly, μ is parameterized on belief model B, world w, and valuation v, but for notational simplicity we omit writing these as arguments to μ unless necessary for disambiguation. Variables x are interpreted by looking up their value in v; functions f_j are interpreted by applying their first-order interpretation $f_{j,w}$ at world w to the interpretation of their arguments. Notation $\vec{\tau}$ represents a list $\tau_1, \tau_2, \ldots, \tau_n$ of terms. And $\mu(\vec{\tau})$ denotes the pointwise application of μ to each element of that list, producing $\mu(\tau_1), \ldots, \mu(\tau_n)$.

The first-order, constructive fragment of the semantics is routine. The semantics of says is the intuitive semantics we wished for in §1: A principal $\mu(\tau)$ says ϕ exactly when ϕ is in that principal's worldview $\omega(w, \mu(\tau), v)$. And a principal $\mu(\tau_1)$ speaks for another principal $\mu(\tau_2)$ exactly when, in all constructively accessible worlds, everything $\mu(\tau_1)$ says, $\mu(\tau_2)$ also says.

Note that some syntactic terms may represent individuals that are not principals. For example, the integer 42 is presumably not a principal in P, but it could be an individual in some domain D_w. An alternative would be to make FOCAL a two-sorted logic, with one sort for individuals and another sort for principals. Instead, we allow individuals who aren't principals to have beliefs, because it simplifies the definition of the logic. The worldviews of non-principal individuals contain all formulas. Formally, for any individual d such that $d \notin P$, and for any world w, valuation v, and formula ϕ, it holds that $\phi \in \omega(w, d, v)$.

We impose a few *well-formedness* conditions on worldviews in this semantics, in addition to Worldview Monotonicity and Worldview Equality. Worldviews must be *closed under logical consequence*—that is, principals must believe all the formulas that are a consequence of their beliefs.

Worldview Closure: If $\Gamma \subseteq \omega(w, p, v)$ and $\Gamma \models \phi$, then $\phi \in \omega(w, p, v)$.

Worldview Closure means that principals are *fully logically omniscient* [15]. With its known benefits and flaws [39, 47], this has been a standard assumption in authorization logics since their inception [32].

The remaining well-formedness conditions are optional, in the sense that they are necessary only to achieve soundness of particular proof rules in §5. Eliminate those rules, and the following conditions would be eliminated.

Worldviews must ensure that says is a *transparent* modality. That is, for any principal p, it holds that p says ϕ exactly when p says (p says ϕ):

Says Transparency: $\phi \in \omega(w, \mu(\tau), v)$ iff τ says $\phi \in \omega(w, \mu(\tau), v)$.

So says supports *positive introspection*: if p believes that ϕ holds, then p is aware of that belief, therefore p believes that p believes that ϕ holds. The converse of that holds as well. Recent authorization logics include transparency [3, 43], and it is well known (though sometimes vigorously debated) in epistemic logic [25, 27]. Says Transparency corresponds to rules SAYS-LI and SAYS-RI in figure 5.

Worldviews must enable principals to delegate, or *hand-off*, to other principals: if a principal q believes that p $\mathsf{speaksfor}$ q, it should hold that p does speak for q. Hand-off, as the following axiom, existed in the earliest authorization logic [32]:

$$(q \ \mathsf{says}\ (p \ \mathsf{speaksfor}\ q)) \Rightarrow (p \ \mathsf{speaksfor}\ q) \quad (1)$$

To support it, we adopt a condition that ensures whenever q believes p speaks for q, then it really does:

Belief Hand-off: If (p $\mathsf{speaksfor}$ q) $\in \omega(w, q, v)$ then $\omega(w, p, v) \subseteq \omega(w, q, v)$.

Belief Hand-off corresponds to rule SF-I in figure 5.

3. KRIPKE SEMANTICS

The Kripke semantics of FOCAL combines first-order constructive models with modal (Kripke) models [15, 27, 44]. Similar semantic models have been explored before (see, e.g., [18, 22, 51]). Indeed, the only non-standard part of our semantics is the treatment of $\mathsf{speaksfor}$, and that part turns out to be a generalization of previous classical semantics. Nonetheless, we are not aware of any authorization logic semantics that is equivalent to or subsumes our semantics. First-order and constructive models were already presented in §2, so we begin here with modal models.

3.1 Modal models

A *modal model* is a tuple $(W, \leq, s, P, A)$. The purpose of modal models is to extend constructive models to interpret says and $\mathsf{speaksfor}$. The first part of a modal model, $(W, \leq, s)$, must itself be a constructive model. The next part, P, is the set of principals. As with belief models, all principals must be individuals, so P must be a subset of D_w for every w. Principal equality relation $\doteq$ is defined just as in belief models. The final part of a modal model, A, is a set $\{\leq_p \mid p \in P\}$ of binary relations on W, called the *principal accessibility relations*.[6] If $w \leq_p w'$, then at world w, principal p considers world w' possible. To ensure that equal principals have the same beliefs, we require

[6] In our notation, an unsubscripted $\leq$ always denotes the constructive relation, and a subscripted $\leq$ always denotes a principal relation.

$$
\begin{array}{lll}
B,w,v \models \mathsf{true} & & \text{always} \\
B,w,v \models \mathsf{false} & & \text{never} \\
B,w,v \models r_i(\vec{\tau}) & \text{iff} & \mu(\vec{\tau}) \in r_{i,w} \\
B,w,v \models \tau_1 = \tau_2 & \text{iff} & \mu(\tau_1) =_w \mu(\tau_2) \\
B,w,v \models \phi_1 \wedge \phi_2 & \text{iff} & B,w,v \models \phi_1 \text{ and } B,w,v \models \phi_2 \\
B,w,v \models \phi_1 \vee \phi_2 & \text{iff} & B,w,v \models \phi_1 \text{ or } B,w,v \models \phi_2 \\
B,w,v \models \phi_1 \Rightarrow \phi_2 & \text{iff} & \text{for all } w' \geq w : B,w',v \models \phi_1 \text{ implies } B,w',v \models \phi_2 \\
B,w,v \models \neg\phi & \text{iff} & \text{for all } w' \geq w : B,w',v \not\models \phi \\
B,w,v \models (\forall x : \phi) & \text{iff} & \text{for all } w' \geq w, d \in D_{w'} : B,w',v[d/x] \models \phi \\
B,w,v \models (\exists x : \phi) & \text{iff} & \text{there exists } d \in D_w : B,w,v[d/x] \models \phi \\
B,w,v \models \tau \mathsf{\ says\ } \phi & \text{iff} & \phi \in \omega(w,\mu(\tau),v) \\
B,w,v \models \tau_1 \mathsf{\ speaksfor\ } \tau_2 & \text{iff} & \text{for all } w' \geq w : \omega(w',\mu(\tau_1),v) \subseteq \omega(w',\mu(\tau_2),v)
\end{array}
$$

Figure 2: FOCAL validity judgment for belief semantics

$$
\begin{array}{lll}
K,w,v \models \tau \mathsf{\ says\ } \phi & \text{iff} & \text{for all } w', w'' : w \leq w' \leq_{\mu(w',\tau)} w'' \text{ implies } K,w'',v \models \phi \\
K,w,v \models \tau_1 \mathsf{\ speaksfor\ } \tau_2 & \text{iff} & \leq^w_{\mu(\tau_1)} \supseteq \leq^w_{\mu(\tau_2)} \\
K,w,v \models \ldots & \text{iff} & \textit{same as figure 2, but substituting } K \textit{ for } B
\end{array}
$$

Figure 3: FOCAL validity judgment for Kripke semantics

Accessibility Equality: If $p \doteq p'$, then $\leq_p = \leq_{p'}$.

Like $\leq$ in a constructive model, we require s to be monotonic w.r.t. each $\leq_p$. This requirement enforces a kind of constructivity on each principal p, such that from a world in which individual d is constructed, p cannot consider possible any world in which d has not been constructed. Unlike $\leq$, none of the $\leq_p$ are required to be partial orders: they are not required to satisfy reflexivity, anti-symmetry, or transitivity.

That non-requirement raises an important question. In epistemic logics, the properties of what we call the "principal accessibility relations" determine what kind of knowledge is modeled [15]. If, for example, these relations must be reflexive, then the logic models *veridical* knowledge: if p says ϕ, then ϕ indeed holds. But that is not the kind of knowledge we seek to model with FOCAL, because principals may say things that in fact do not hold. So what are the right properties, or *frame conditions*, to require of our principal accessibility relations? We briefly delay presenting them, so that we can present the Kripke semantics.

3.2 Semantic validity

Figure 3 gives a Kripke semantics of FOCAL. The validity judgment is written $K,w,v \models \phi$ where K is a modal model and w is a world in that model. Only the judgments for the says and speaksfor connectives are given in figure 3. For the remaining connectives, the Kripke semantics is the same as the belief semantics in figure 2. Interpretation function μ remains unchanged from §2, except that it is now implicitly parameterized on K instead of B.

To understand the semantics of says, first observe the following. Suppose that, for all worlds w', it holds that $w \leq w'$ implies $w = w'$.[7] Then the semantics of says simplifies to the standard semantics of $\Box$ in classical modal logic [27]:

$$
K,w,v \models \tau \mathsf{\ says\ } \phi \quad \text{iff} \quad \text{for all } w'' : w \leq_{\mu(\tau)} w'' \text{ implies } K,w,v \models \phi.
$$

That is, a principal believes a formula holds whenever that formula holds in all accessible worlds. The purpose of the quantification over w', where $w \leq w'$, in the unsimplified semantics of says is to achieve *monotonicity* of the constructive reasoner:

Proposition 1. *If $K,w,v \models \phi$ and $w \leq w'$ then $K,w',v \models \phi$.*

That is, whenever ϕ holds at a world w, if the constructive reasoner is able to reach an extended state of knowledge at world w', then ϕ should continue to hold at w'. Without the quantification over w' in the semantics of says, monotonicity is not guaranteed to hold. Constructive modal logics have, unsurprisingly, also used this semantics for $\Box$ [44,51], and a similar semantics has been used in authorization logic [18].

Note that, if there do not exist any worlds w' and w'' such that $w \leq w' \leq_{\mu(\tau)} w''$, then at w, principal τ will say any formula ϕ, including false. When a principal says false at world w, we deem that principal *compromised* at w.

As for the semantics of speaksfor, it might be tempting to try defining it as syntactic sugar:

$$
\tau_1 \mathsf{\ speaksfor\ } \tau_2 \quad \equiv \quad \forall \phi : \tau_1 \mathsf{\ says\ } \phi \Rightarrow \tau_2 \mathsf{\ says\ } \phi
$$

However, the formula on the right-hand side is not a well-formed formula of FOCAL, because it quantifies over syntactic formulas. So the semantics of speaksfor cannot interpret it directly in terms of says.[8]

Instead, the FOCAL semantics of speaksfor generalizes the classical Kripke semantics of speaksfor [4,26]. Classically,

$$
K,w,v \models \tau_1 \mathsf{\ speaksfor\ } \tau_2 \quad \text{iff} \quad \leq_{\mu(\tau_1)} \supseteq \leq_{\mu(\tau_2)}. \tag{2}
$$

[7]This condition corresponds to the axiom of excluded middle. So it makes sense that adding the frame condition would result in the classical semantics of $\Box$.

[8]It is possible [19,43] to instead use second-order quantifiers to achieve a direct interpretation. That solution would unnecessarily complicate our semantics by introducing second-order quantifiers solely for the sake of defining speaksfor.

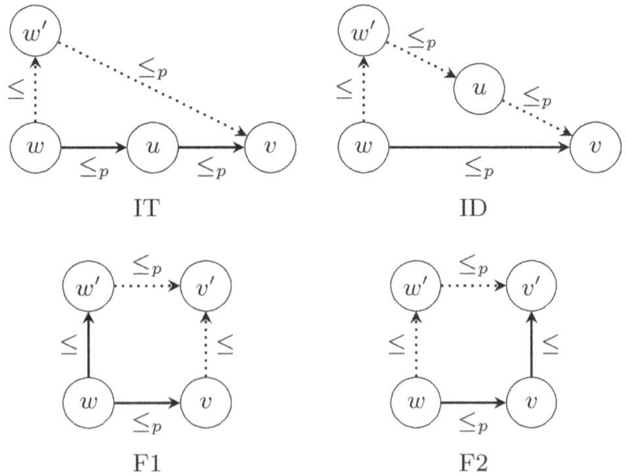

Figure 4: Frame conditions for Kripke semantics

That is, the accessibility relation of τ_1 must be a superset of the accessibility relation of τ_2. However, that definition does not account for constructive accessibility, and it even turns out to interact badly with hand-off.

We therefore relax the classical semantics of speaksfor:

$$K, w, v \models \tau_1 \text{ speaksfor } \tau_2 \quad \text{iff} \quad \leq^w_{\mu(\tau_1)} \supseteq \leq^w_{\mu(\tau_2)} \qquad (3)$$

where $\leq^w_{\mu(p)}$ is defined to be $\leq_p |_{[w]_p}$,[9] and $[w]_p$ is defined to be the set of worlds w' such that w' is reachable from w, or vice-versa, by relation $(\leq \cup \leq_p)^*$. Note that whenever $[w]_p$ equals W (as it would in classical logic[10]), it holds that $\leq^w_{\mu(p)}$ equals $\leq_p$.

The validity judgment for FOCAL is therefore quite standard, except for speaksfor, where it generalizes classical logic. Although we would prefer to adopt a well-known constructive semantics of speaksfor, neither of the two we're aware of seems to work for FOCAL: ICL [19] would impose an axiom called Unit that we do not want to include (cf. §5.2), and BL_{sf} [22] does not include hand-off (1), which we want to optionally support (cf. §2.2 and §3.3).

3.3 Frame conditions

We now return to the discussion begun in §3.1 of the frame conditions for FOCAL. The first two frame conditions we impose help to ensure Says Transparency:

> **IT:** If $w \leq_p u \leq_p v$, then there exists a w' such that $w \leq w' \leq_p v$.

> **ID:** If $w \leq_p v$, then there exists a w' and u such that $w \leq w' \leq_p u \leq_p v$.

Figure 4 depicts these conditions; dotted lines indicate existentially quantified edges. IT helps to guarantee if p says ϕ then p says (p says ϕ); ID does the converse.[11]

[9] If R is a binary relation on set A, then $R|_X$ is the *restriction* of R to A, where $X \subseteq A$. That is, $R|_X = \{(x, x') \mid (x, x') \in R \text{ and } x \in X \text{ and } x' \in X\}$.

[10] When frame condition $\leq \, = W \times W$ is imposed, constructive logic collapses to classical. Under that condition, every world w' would be reachable from w, hence $[w]_p = W$.

[11] IT and ID are abbreviations for intuitionistic transitivity and intuitionistic density.

Note how, if $w = w'$, the conditions reduce to the classical definitions of transitivity and density. Those classical conditions are exactly what guarantee transparency in classical modal logic.

IT and ID are not quite sufficient to yield transparency. By also imposing the following frame condition, we do achieve transparency:[12]

> **F2:** If $w \leq_p v \leq v'$, then there exists a w' such that $w \leq w' \leq_p v'$.

F2 is depicted in figure 4. It is difficult to motivate F2 solely in terms of authorization logic, though it has been proposed in several Kripke semantics for constructive modal logics [14, 16, 41, 44]. But there are two reasons why F2 is desirable for FOCAL:

- Assuming F2 holds, IT and ID are not only sufficient but also necessary conditions for transparency—a result that follows from work by Plotkin and Stirling [41]. So in the presence of F2, transparency in FOCAL is precisely characterized by IT and ID.

- Suppose FOCAL were to be extended with a $\Diamond$ modality. It could be written τ suspects ϕ, with semantics $K, w, v \models \tau$ suspects ϕ iff there exists w' such that $w \leq_{\mu(\tau)} w'$ and $K, w', v \models \phi$. We would want says and suspects to interact smoothly. For example, it would be reasonable to expect that $\neg(\tau$ suspects $\phi)$ implies τ says $\neg\phi$. For if τ does not suspect ϕ holds anywhere, then τ should believe $\neg\phi$ holds. Condition F2 guarantees that implication [41]. So F2 prepares FOCAL for future extension with a suspects modality.[13]

To ensure the validity of hand-off, we impose the following frame condition:

> **H:** For all principals p and worlds w, if there do not exist any worlds w' and w'' such that $w \leq w' \leq_p w''$, then, for all p', it must hold that $\leq^w_{\mu(p)} \subseteq \leq^w_{\mu(p')}$.

This condition guarantees that if a principal p becomes compromised at world w, then the reachable component of its accessibility relation will be a subset of all other principals'. By the FOCAL semantics of speaksfor, all other principals therefore speak for p at w.

Each frame condition above was imposed, not for ad hoc purposes, but because of a specific need in the proof of the soundness result of §5. So with appropriate deletion of rules from the proof system, each of the above frame conditions could be eliminated. IT and ID should be removed if rules SAYS-LI and SAYS-RI (from figure 5) are removed; F2 should be removed if rule SAYS-LRI is removed; and H should be removed if rule SF-I is removed.

Finally, we impose one additional condition to achieve the equivalence results (theorem 1 and proposition 2) of §4:

[12] F2 is the name given this condition by Simpson [44].

[13] Were suspects to be added to FOCAL, it would also be desirable to impose a fourth frame condition: if $w \leq w'$ and $w \leq_p v$, then there exists a v' such that $v \leq v'$ and $w' \leq_p v'$. This condition, named F1 by Simpson [44], guarantees [41] that τ suspects ϕ implies $\neg(\tau$ says $\neg\phi)$. It also guarantees monotonicity (cf. proposition 1) for suspects. Figure 4 depicts F1. Simpson [44, p. 51] argues that F1 and F2 could be seen as fundamental, not artificial, frame conditions for constructive modal logics.

WSF: $K, w, v \models \tau$ speaksfor τ' iff, for all ϕ, if $K, w, v \models \tau$ says ϕ then $K, w, v \models \tau'$ says ϕ.

This condition restricts the class of Kripke models to those where speaksfor is the *weak speaksfor* connective [4, 26]. In fact, we'd prefer to use WSF directly as the semantics of speaksfor in figure 3.[14] But it wouldn't be a well-founded definition of $\models$, because ϕ could itself be τ speaksfor τ', leading to a circularity in the semantic definition. So we instead impose WSF as a separate axiom.

4. SEMANTIC TRANSFORMATION

We have now given two semantics for FOCAL, a belief semantics (§2) and a Kripke semantics (§3). How are these two semantics related? It turns out that a Kripke model can be transformed into a belief model, but the converse does not hold—as we now explain.

Given a modal model K, there is a natural way to construct a belief model from it: assign each principal a worldview containing exactly the formulas that the principal says in K. Call this construction *k2b*, and let *k2b*(K) denote the resulting belief model.

To give a precise definition of *k2b*, we need to introduce a new notation. Given a principal $p \in P$, formula p says ϕ is not necessarily well-formed, because p is not necessarily a syntactic term. So let $K, w, v \models \hat{p}$ says ϕ be defined as follows: for all w' and w'' such that $w \leq w' \leq_p w''$, it holds that $K, w'', v \models \phi$. This definition simply unrolls the semantics of says to produce something well-formed.[15]

The precise definition of *k2b* is as follows: if $K = (W, \leq, s, P, A)$, then *k2b*(K) is belief model $(W, \leq, s, P, \omega)$, where $\omega(w, p, v)$ is defined to be $\{\phi \mid K, w, v \models \hat{p}$ says $\phi\}$.

Our first concern is whether *k2b*(K) produces a belief model that is equivalent to K. In particular, a formula should be valid in K iff it is valid in *k2b*(K). Construction *k2b* does produce equivalent models:

Theorem 1. *For all K, w, v, and ϕ, $K, w, v \models \phi$ iff k2b$(K), w, v \models \phi$.*

Our second concern is whether *k2b*(K) satisfies all the conditions required by §2: Worldview Monotonicity, Worldview Equality, Worldview Closure, Says Transparency, and Belief Hand-off. If a belief model B does satisfy these conditions, then B is *well-formed*. And modal model K is well-formed if it satisfies all the conditions required by §3: Accessibility Equality, IT, ID, F2, H, and WSF. Construction *k2b* does, indeed, produce well-formed belief models:

Proposition 2. *For all well-formed modal models K, belief model k2b(K) is well-formed.*

We might wonder whether there is a construction that can soundly transform belief models into Kripke models. Consider trying to transform the following belief model B into a Kripke model:

> B has a single world w and a proposition (i.e., a nullary relation) X, such that, for all v, it holds that $B, w, v \not\models X$. Suppose that principal p's worldview contains X—i.e., for all v, it holds that $X \in \omega(w, p, v)$—and that p's worldview does not contain false. By the semantics of says, it holds that $B, w, v \models p$ says X.

When transforming B to a Kripke model K, what edges could we put in $\leq_p$? There are only two choices: $\leq_p$ could be empty, or $\leq_p$ could contain the single edge (w, w). If $\leq_p$ is empty, then p is compromised, hence p says false. That contradicts our assumption that false is not in p's worldview. If $w \leq_p w$, then for w' and w'' such that $w \leq w' \leq_p w''$, it does not hold that $K, w'', v \models X$, because w and w'' can only be instantiated as w, and because $B, w, v \not\models X$. Hence p does not say X. That contradicts our assumption that X is in p's worldview. So we cannot construct an accessibility relation $\leq_p$ that causes the resulting Kripke semantics to preserve validity of formulas from the belief semantics.

There is, therefore, no construction that can soundly transform belief models into Kripke models—unless, perhaps, the set of worlds is permitted to change. We conjecture that it is possible to synthesize a new set of possible worlds, and equivalence relations on them, yielding a Kripke model that preserves validity of formulas from the belief model.

5. PROOF SYSTEM

FOCAL's derivability judgment is written $\Gamma \vdash \phi$ where Γ is a set of formulas called the *context*.[16] As is standard, we write $\vdash \phi$ when Γ is the empty set. In that case, ϕ is a *theorem*. We write Γ, ϕ to denote $\Gamma \cup \{\phi\}$.

Figure 5 presents the proof system. In it, $\phi[\tau/x]$ denotes capture-avoiding substitution of τ for x in ϕ. The first-order fragment of the proof system is routine (e.g., [38, 46, 50]).[17] Because of IMP-I, the deduction theorem holds for FOCAL [24]. SAYS-LRI, SAYS-LI, and SAYS-RI use notation τ says Γ, which means that τ says all the formulas in set Γ. Formally, τ says Γ is defined as $\{\tau$ says $\phi \mid \phi \in \Gamma\}$.

The usual sequent calculus structural rules of contraction and exchange are admissible. But weakening (our rule WEAK) is not admissible: it must be directly included in the proof system, because the conclusions of SAYS-{LRI,LI,RI} capture their entire context Γ inside says.

SAYS-LRI corresponds [27] to standard axiom K along with rule N from epistemic logic; SAYS-RI, to standard axiom 4; and SAYS-LI, to the converse $C4$ [3] of 4:

$$
\begin{aligned}
K:&\quad \vdash (p \text{ says } (\phi \Rightarrow \psi)) \Rightarrow (p \text{ says } \phi) \Rightarrow (p \text{ says } \psi),\\
N:&\quad \text{From} \vdash \phi \text{ infer} \vdash p \text{ says } \phi,\\
4:&\quad \vdash (p \text{ says } \phi) \Rightarrow (p \text{ says } (p \text{ says } \phi)),\\
C4:&\quad \vdash (p \text{ says } (p \text{ says } \phi)) \Rightarrow (p \text{ says } \phi).
\end{aligned}
$$

K and SAYS-LRI mean that *modus ponens* applies inside says. They correspond to Worldview Closure. $C4$ and 4, along with SAYS-LI and SAYS-RI, mean that p says (p says ϕ) is equivalent to p says ϕ; they correspond to Says Transparency

[14] If FOCAL included second-order quantification as a logical connective, speaksfor could be defined as syntactic sugar [2], avoiding the awkwardness of WSF.

[15] Another solution would be to stipulate that every principal p can be named by a term $\hat{p}$ in the syntax.

[16] These formulas are *localized hypotheses*, which the proof system uses instead of the hypothetical judgments found in natural deduction systems. Similar to the left-hand side Γ of a sequent $\Gamma \Longrightarrow \Delta$, the localized hypotheses are assumptions being used to derive right-hand side Δ. Unlike a sequent, Γ is a set, not a sequence.

[17] Under the usual constructive definition of $\neg\phi$ as $\phi \Rightarrow$ false, rules NOT-I and NOT-E are admissible and could be eliminated from the proof system.

$$\frac{}{\Gamma, \phi \vdash \phi}\ \textsc{hyp} \qquad \frac{\Gamma \vdash \phi}{\Gamma, \psi \vdash \phi}\ \textsc{weak} \qquad \frac{}{\Gamma \vdash \mathsf{true}}\ \textsc{true-i} \qquad \frac{\Gamma \vdash \mathsf{false}}{\Gamma \vdash \phi}\ \textsc{false-e} \qquad \frac{\Gamma \vdash \phi \quad \Gamma \vdash \psi}{\Gamma \vdash \phi \wedge \psi}\ \textsc{and-i} \qquad \frac{\Gamma \vdash \phi \wedge \psi}{\Gamma \vdash \phi}\ \textsc{and-le}$$

$$\frac{\Gamma \vdash \phi \wedge \psi}{\Gamma \vdash \psi}\ \textsc{and-re} \qquad \frac{\Gamma \vdash \phi_1}{\Gamma \vdash \phi_1 \vee \phi_2}\ \textsc{or-li} \qquad \frac{\Gamma \vdash \phi_2}{\Gamma \vdash \phi_1 \vee \phi_2}\ \textsc{or-ri} \qquad \frac{\Gamma \vdash \phi_1 \vee \phi_2 \quad \Gamma, \phi_1 \vdash \psi \quad \Gamma, \phi_2 \vdash \psi}{\Gamma \vdash \psi}\ \textsc{or-e} \qquad \frac{\Gamma, \phi \vdash \psi}{\Gamma \vdash \phi \Rightarrow \psi}\ \textsc{imp-i}$$

$$\frac{\Gamma \vdash \phi \quad \Gamma \vdash \phi \Rightarrow \psi}{\Gamma \vdash \psi}\ \textsc{imp-e} \qquad \frac{\Gamma, \phi \vdash \mathsf{false}}{\Gamma \vdash \neg\phi}\ \textsc{not-i} \qquad \frac{\Gamma \vdash \phi \quad \Gamma \vdash \neg\phi}{\Gamma \vdash \mathsf{false}}\ \textsc{not-e} \qquad \frac{\Gamma \vdash \phi \quad x \notin FV(\Gamma)}{\Gamma \vdash (\forall x : \phi)}\ \textsc{forall-i} \qquad \frac{\Gamma \vdash (\forall x : \phi)}{\Gamma \vdash \phi[\tau/x]}\ \textsc{forall-e}$$

$$\frac{\Gamma \vdash \phi[\tau/x]}{\Gamma \vdash (\exists x : \phi)}\ \textsc{exists-i} \qquad \frac{\Gamma \vdash (\exists x : \phi) \quad \Gamma, \phi \vdash \psi \quad x \notin FV(\Gamma, \psi)}{\Gamma \vdash \psi}\ \textsc{exists-e} \qquad \frac{}{\Gamma \vdash \tau = \tau}\ \textsc{eq-r} \qquad \frac{\Gamma \vdash \tau_1 = \tau_2}{\Gamma \vdash \tau_2 = \tau_1}\ \textsc{eq-s}$$

$$\frac{\Gamma \vdash \tau_1 = \tau_2 \quad \Gamma \vdash \tau_2 = \tau_3}{\Gamma \vdash \tau_1 = \tau_3}\ \textsc{eq-t} \qquad \frac{\Gamma \vdash \tau_i = \tau_i'}{\Gamma \vdash f(\tau_1, \ldots, \tau_n) = f(\tau_1', \ldots, \tau_n')}\ \textsc{eq-fun} \qquad \frac{\Gamma \vdash r(\tau_1, \ldots, \tau_n) \quad \Gamma \vdash \tau_i = \tau_i'}{\Gamma \vdash r(\tau_1', \ldots, \tau_n')}\ \textsc{eq-rel}$$

$$\frac{\Gamma \vdash \phi}{\tau\ \mathsf{says}\ \Gamma \vdash \tau\ \mathsf{says}\ \phi}\ \textsc{says-lri} \qquad \frac{\Gamma \vdash \tau\ \mathsf{says}\ \phi}{\tau\ \mathsf{says}\ \Gamma \vdash \tau\ \mathsf{says}\ \phi}\ \textsc{says-li} \qquad \frac{\tau\ \mathsf{says}\ \Gamma \vdash \phi}{\tau\ \mathsf{says}\ \Gamma \vdash \tau\ \mathsf{says}\ \phi}\ \textsc{says-ri} \qquad \frac{\Gamma \vdash \tau_2\ \mathsf{says}\ (\tau_1\ \mathsf{speaksfor}\ \tau_2)}{\Gamma \vdash \tau_1\ \mathsf{speaksfor}\ \tau_2}\ \textsc{sf-i}$$

$$\frac{\Gamma \vdash \tau_1\ \mathsf{speaksfor}\ \tau_2 \quad \Gamma \vdash \tau_1\ \mathsf{says}\ \phi}{\Gamma \vdash \tau_2\ \mathsf{says}\ \phi}\ \textsc{sf-e} \qquad \frac{}{\Gamma \vdash \tau\ \mathsf{speaksfor}\ \tau}\ \textsc{sf-r} \qquad \frac{\Gamma \vdash \tau_1\ \mathsf{speaksfor}\ \tau_2 \quad \Gamma \vdash \tau_2\ \mathsf{speaksfor}\ \tau_3}{\Gamma \vdash \tau_1\ \mathsf{speaksfor}\ \tau_3}\ \textsc{sf-t}$$

Figure 5: FOCAL derivability judgment

in the belief semantics. In the Kripke semantics, SAYS-RI corresponds to IT; and SAYS-LI, to ID. (Note, we do not argue that 4 and $C4$ are necessary in authorization logics; we simply show how to support them.)

SF-I corresponds to hand-off (1). SF-E uses speaksfor to deduce beliefs. SF-R and SF-T state that speaksfor is reflexive and transitive.

5.1 Soundness

Our first soundness theorem for FOCAL states that if ϕ is provable from assumptions Γ, and that if a belief model validates all the formulas in Γ, then that model must also validate ϕ. Therefore, any provable formula is valid in the belief semantics:

Theorem 2. *If $\Gamma \vdash \phi$ and $B, w, v \models \Gamma$, then $B, w, v \models \phi$.*

The result is, to our knowledge, the first proof of soundness for an authorization logic w.r.t. a belief semantics. The proof of theorem 2 relies on the following proposition, which states monotonicity of validity w.r.t. $\leq$:

Proposition 3. *If $B, w, v \models \phi$ and $w \leq w'$ then $B, w', v \models \phi$.*

Our second soundness theorem for FOCAL states that any provable formula is valid in the Kripke semantics:

Theorem 3. *If $\Gamma \vdash \phi$ and $K, w, v \models \Gamma$, then $K, w, v \models \phi$.*

The proof of that theorem relies on proposition 1 (monotonicity of the Kripke semantics). We have mechanized the proofs of theorems 2 and 3 and propositions 1 and 3 in Coq.

5.2 State in distributed systems

FOCAL was derived from CDD [2] and NAL [43]. But we deliberately designed the FOCAL proof system such that its theory differs in one important way from theirs. We discuss our motivation for this change, next.

There are two standard ways of "importing" beliefs into a principal's worldview. The first is rule N from §5, also known as the rule of Necessitation: from $\vdash \phi$, infer $\vdash p$ says ϕ. The second is an axiom known as Unit: $\vdash \phi \Rightarrow (p\ \mathsf{says}\ \phi)$. Though superficially similar, it is well-known that Necessitation and Unit lead to different theories. Abadi [3] explores some of the proof-theoretic differences, particularly some of the surprising consequences of Unit in classical authorization logic. In the example below, we focus on one difference that does not seem to have been explored in constructive authorization logic:

Example 2. *Machines M_1 and M_2 execute processes P_1 and P_2, respectively. M_1 has a register R. Let Z be a proposition representing "register R is currently set to zero." According to Unit, $\vdash Z \Rightarrow (P_1\ \mathsf{says}\ Z)$ and $\vdash Z \Rightarrow (P_2\ \mathsf{says}\ Z)$. The former means that a process on a machine knows the current contents of a register on that machine; the latter means that a process on a different machine must also know the current contents of the register. But according to Necessitation, if $\vdash Z$ then $\vdash P_1$ says Z and $\vdash P_2$ says Z. Only if R is guaranteed to be constant—i.e., it can never at any time be anything other than zero—must the two processes say so.*

Unit, therefore, is appropriate when propositions (or relations or functions) represent global state upon which all principals are guaranteed to agree. But when propositions represent local state that could be unknown to some principals, Unit would arguably be an invalid axiom. A countermodel demonstrating Unit's invalidity is easy to construct—for example, stipulate a world w at which Z holds, and let P_1's worldview contain Z but P_2's worldview not contain Z. That countermodel doesn't apply to Necessitation, because Z is not a theorem in it, therefore the principals may disagree on Z's validity.

Prior work has objected to Unit for other reasons (cf. §6), but not for this difference between local and global state. We are unaware of any authorization logic that rejects Necessitation, which is widely accepted along with axiom K (cf. §5) in *normal modal logic* [27].

FOCAL is designed for reasoning about state in distributed systems, where principals (such as machines) may have local state, and where global state does not necessarily exist—the reading at a clock, for example, is not agreed upon by all principals. So Unit would be invalid for FOCAL principals; Necessitation is the appropriate choice. We therefore include Necessitation in FOCAL in the form of rule SAYS-LRI. Having that rule in our proof system is equivalent to having both Necessitation and K in a natural-deduction proof system [27, p. 214, where SAYS-LRI is called LR]. Unit, on the other hand, is invalid in FOCAL's semantics, and FOCAL's proof system is sound w.r.t. its semantics, so it's impossible to derive Unit in FOCAL.

Similarly, NAL principals do not necessarily agree upon global state. NAL does include Necessitation as an inference rule and does not include Unit as an axiom. However, NAL permits Unit to be derived as a theorem:[18]

$$\dfrac{\dfrac{[\phi]^1}{p \textsf{ says } \phi}\ \text{NAL-SAYS-I}}{\phi \Rightarrow p \textsf{ says } \phi}\ \text{NAL-IMP-I}_1$$

NAL's proof system is, therefore, arguably unsound w.r.t. our belief semantics: there is a formula (Unit) that is a theorem of the system but that is not semantically valid.

NAL extends CDD's proof system, so we might suspect that CDD is also unsound w.r.t. our semantics. And it is. However, CDD has been proved sound w.r.t. a *lax logic* semantics [19]. That semantics employs a different intuition about says than NAL. CDD understands p says ϕ to mean "when combining the [statement ϕ] that the [guard] believes with those that [p] contributes, the [guard] can conclude ϕ... the [guard's] participation is left implicit" [2, p. 13]. In other words, the guard's beliefs are imported into p's beliefs at each world. That results in a different meaning of says than FOCAL or NAL employs.

Since Abadi's invention of CDD [2], the says connective is frequently assumed to satisfy the *monad* [36] laws, which include Unit. But FOCAL rejects Unit, so FOCAL's says connective is not a monad. The monad laws also include an axiom named Bind, which turns out to be invalid in FOCAL's semantics.[19] We don't know whether rejecting the monad laws will have any practical impact on FOCAL. But the seminal authorization logic, ABLP [4], didn't adopt the monad laws. Likewise, Garg and Pfenning [21] reject Unit in their authorization logic BL_0; they demonstrate that Unit leads to counterintuitive interpretations of some formulas involving delegation. And Abadi [1] notes that Unit "should be used with caution (if at all)," suggesting that it be replaced with the weaker axiom $(p \textsf{ says } \phi) \Rightarrow (q \textsf{ says } p \textsf{ says } \phi)$. Genovese et al. [22] carry out that suggestion. So in rejecting the monad laws, FOCAL is at least in good company.

[18]Rules NAL-IMP-I and NAL-SAYS-I are given by Schneider et al. [43]. The brackets around ϕ at the top of the proof tree indicate that it is used as a hypothesis [50]. The appearance of "1" as a super- and subscript indicate where the hypothesis is introduced and cancelled.

[19]The terms "monad," "lax logic," and the combination of axioms Unit and Bind all three convey the same mathematical structure, so it's not surprising that FOCAL differs from all of them.

6. RELATED WORK

FOCAL has the first formal belief semantics of any authorization logic. Belief semantics have been used in only one other authorization logic, NAL [43], which has only an informal semantics based on worldviews.

But many of the pieces of FOCAL, including its semantics and proof system, are naturally derived from previous work. We summarize here what we borrowed vs. what we invented; the main body of the paper contains detailed citations. FOCAL's belief semantics is a standard first-order constructive semantics, but the addition of worldviews to interpret says and speaksfor is novel (with the exception of NAL, which used worldviews informally). FOCAL's Kripke semantics for everything except speaksfor is likewise standard, and its frame conditions (except H and WSF) are already well-known in constructive modal logic, but the application of IT and ID to authorization logic seems to be novel. FOCAL's proof system, excluding says and speaksfor, is a straightforward first-order constructive proof system. The fragment for says is our own adaptation of natural-deduction rules for the $\Box$ connective. The fragment for speaksfor corresponds to standard definitions used in many authorization logics.

Semantic structures similar to our belief models have been investigated in the context of epistemic logic [13, 15, 37]. Konolige [30] proves an equivalence result for classical propositional logic similar to our theorem 1.

Garg and Abadi [19] give a Kripke semantics for a logic they call ICL, which could be regarded as a propositional fragment of FOCAL. The ICL semantics of says, however, uses *invisible* worlds to permit principals to be oblivious to the truth of formulas at some worlds. That makes Unit (§5.2) valid in ICL, whereas Unit is invalid in FOCAL.

Garg [18] studies the proof theory of a logic called DTL_0, and gives a Kripke semantics that uses both invisible worlds and *fallible* worlds, at which false is permitted to be valid. Instead of Unit, it uses the axiom $p \textsf{ says } ((p \textsf{ says } \phi) \Rightarrow \phi)$. That axiom is unsound in FOCAL. DTL_0 does not have a speaksfor connective.

Genovese et al. [22] study several uses for Kripke semantics with an authorization logic they call BL_{sf}, which also could be regarded as a propositional fragment of FOCAL. They show how to generate evidence for why an access should be denied, how to find all logical consequences of an authorization policy, and how to determine which additional credentials would allow an access. However, the Kripke semantics of BL_{sf} differs from FOCAL's in its interpretation of both says and speaksfor, so the results of Genovese et al. are not immediately applicable to FOCAL.

Garg and Pfenning [20] prove *non-interference* properties for a first-order constructive authorization logic. Such properties mean that one principal's beliefs cannot interfere with another principal's beliefs unless there is some trust relationship between those principals. Abadi [2] also proves such a property for dependency core calculus (DCC), which is the basis of authorization logic CDD. We conjecture that similar properties could be proved for FOCAL.

7. CONCLUDING REMARKS

This work began with the idea of giving a Kripke semantics to NAL. Proving soundness—at first on paper, not in Coq—turned out to be surprising, because Unit is semantically invalid but derivable in NAL (§5.2). The complexity of the resulting Kripke semantics motivated us to seek a simpler semantics. We were inspired by the informal world-view semantics of the NAL rationale [43] and elaborated that into our belief semantics (§2). In future work, we plan to upgrade FOCAL to handle NAL's advanced features, including *intensional group principals*.

Mechanizing the proofs of soundness in Coq was frequently rewarding. It exposed several bugs (in either our proof system or our semantics) and gave us high confidence in the correctness of the result. We expect further benefits, too. Other researchers can now use our formalization as a basis for mechanizing results about authorization logics. And from the formalization of the FOCAL proof system in Coq, we could next extract a *verified theorem checker*. It would input a proof of a FOCAL formula, expressed in the FOCAL proof system, and output whether the proof is correct. Coq would verify that the checker correctly implements the FOCAL proof system. After FOCAL is upgraded to handle all of NAL's features, the resulting theorem checker could replace the current Nexus [45] theorem checker, which is implemented in C. A verified theorem checker would arguably be more trustworthy than the C implementation, thus increasing the trustworthiness of the operating system.

Our goal was to increase the trustworthiness of authorization logics, hence our concentration on soundness results. Another worthwhile goal would to be increase the utility of authorization logics, and toward that end we could investigate the *completeness* of FOCAL: are all valid formulas provable? A few authorization logics—ICL [19], DTL_0 [18], and BL_{sf} [22]—do have completeness results for Kripke semantics; however, none of those is immediately applicable to FOCAL.[20] We leave adaptation of them as future work.

Acknowledgments

Fred B. Schneider consulted on the design of the proof system and the Kripke semantics, and he suggested the idea of proving an equivalence between belief and Kripke semantics. We thank him, Martín Abadi, Deepak Garg, Joe Halpern, Dexter Kozen, Colin Stirling, and Kevin Walsh for discussions related to this work. We also thank Adam Chlipala, Kristopher Micinski, and the coq-club mailing list for assistance with Coq. The anonymous reviewers of CSF 2013 and CCS 2013 provided invaluable feedback. The Kripke semantics of FOCAL was created while Clarkson was a postdoctoral researcher at Cornell. This work was supported in part by AFOSR grants F9550-06-0019, FA9550-11-1-0137, and FA9550-12-1-0334, NSF grants 0430161, 0964409, and CCF-0424422 (TRUST), ONR grants N00014-01-1-0968 and N00014-09-1-0652, and a grant from Microsoft.

8. REFERENCES

[1] M. Abadi. Logic in access control. In *Proc. IEEE Symposium on Logic in Computer Science (LICS)*, pages 228–233, 2003.

[2] M. Abadi. Access control in a core calculus of dependency. *Electronic Notes in Theoretical Computer Science*, 172:5–31, Apr. 2007.

[20] ICL uses a lax logic semantics that is incompatible with FOCAL's definition of says. DTL_0 uses a Kripke semantics with *invisible* and *fallible* worlds, and it omits the speaksfor connective. And BL_{sf} encodes speaksfor as a first-order relation, rather than defining it with accessibility relations, and it does not provide a weak speaksfor semantics.

[3] M. Abadi. Variations in access control logic. In *Proc. Conference on Deontic Logic in Computer Science (DEON)*, pages 96–109, 2008.

[4] M. Abadi, M. Burrows, B. Lampson, and G. Plotkin. A calculus for access control in distributed systems. *ACM Transactions on Programming Languages and Systems*, 15(4):706–734, Sept. 1993.

[5] A. W. Appel and E. W. Felten. Proof-carrying authentication. In *Proc. ACM Conference on Computer and Communications Security (CCS)*, pages 52–62, 1999.

[6] L. Bauer, S. Garriss, J. M. McCune, M. K. Reiter, J. Rouse, and P. Rutenbar. Device-enabled authorization in the Grey system. In *Proc. Information Security Conference (ISC)*, pages 431–445, 2005.

[7] M. Y. Becker, C. Fournet, and A. D. Gordon. SecPAL: Design and semantics of a decentralized authorization language. *Journal of Computer Security*, 18(4):619–665, 2010.

[8] M. Y. Becker and P. Sewell. Cassandra: Distributed access control policies with tunable expressiveness. In *Proc. IEEE Workshop on Policies for Distributed Systems and Networks (POLICY)*, pages 159–168, 2004.

[9] J. G. Cederquist, R. Corin, M. A. C. Dekker, S. Etalle, J. I. den Hartog, and G. Lenzini. Audit-based compliance control. *Int'l Journal of Information Security*, 6(2–3):133–151, 2007.

[10] P. Chapin, C. Skalka, and X. S. Wang. Authorization in trust management: Features and foundations. *ACM Computing Surveys*, 40(3):1–48, 2008.

[11] A. Cirillo, R. Jagadeesan, C. Pitcher, and J. Riely. Do As I SaY! Programmatic access control with explicit identities. In *Proc. IEEE Computer Security Foundations Symposium (CSF)*, pages 16–30, 2007.

[12] J. DeTreville. Binder, a logic-based security language. In *IEEE Symposium on Security and Privacy*, pages 105–113, 2002.

[13] R. A. Eberle. A logic of believing, knowing and inferring. *Synthese*, 26:356–382, 1974.

[14] W. B. Ewald. Intuitionistic tense and modal logic. *Journal of Symbolic Logic*, 51(1):166–179, 1986.

[15] R. Fagin, J. Y. Halpern, Y. Moses, and M. Y. Vardi. *Reasoning About Knowledge*. MIT Press, Cambridge, Massachusetts, 1995.

[16] G. Fischer Servi. Semantics for a class of intuitionistic modal calculi. In M. L. D. Chiara, editor, *Italian Studies in the Philosophy of Science*, pages 59–72. D. Riedel Publishing Company, Dordrecht, Holland, 1981.

[17] C. Fournet, A. D. Gordon, and S. Maffeis. A type discipline for authorization policies. In *Proc. European Symposium on Programming (ESOP)*, pages 141–156, 2005.

[18] D. Garg. Principal-centric reasoning in constructive authorization logic. In *Workshop on Intuitionistic Modal Logic and Applications (IMLA)*, 2008.

[19] D. Garg and M. Abadi. A modal deconstruction of access control logics. In *Proc. Conference on Foundations of Software Science and Computational Structures (FOSSACS)*, pages 216–230, 2008.

[20] D. Garg and F. Pfenning. Non-interference in constructive authorization logic. In *Proc. IEEE Computer Security Foundations Workshop (CSFW)*, pages 283–296, 2006.

[21] D. Garg and F. Pfenning. Stateful authorization logic: Proof theory and a case study. In *Proc. Conference on Security and Trust Management (STM)*, pages 210–225, 2010.

[22] V. Genovese, D. Garg, and D. Rispoli. Labeled sequent calculi for access control logics: Countermodels, saturation and abduction. In *Proc. IEEE Computer Security Foundations Symposium (CSF)*, pages 139–153, 2012.

[23] Y. Gurevich and I. Neeman. DKAL: Distributed-knowledge authorization language. In *Proc. IEEE Computer Security Foundations Symposium (CSF)*, pages 149–162, 2008.

[24] R. Hakli and S. Negri. Does the deduction theorem fail for modal logic? *Synthese*, 187(3):849–867, 2012.

[25] J. Hintikka. *Knowledge and Belief*. Cornell University Press, Ithaca, New York, 1962.

[26] J. Howell. *Naming and Sharing Resources across Administrative Domains*. PhD thesis, Dartmouth College, 2000.

[27] G. E. Hughes and M. J. Cresswell. *A New Introduction to Modal Logic*. Routledge, London, 1996.

[28] L. Jia, J. A. Vaughan, K. Mazurak, J. Zhao, L. Zarko, J. Schorr, and S. Zdancewic. AURA: A programming language for authorization and audit. In *Proc. ACM Int'l Conference on Functional Programming (ICFP)*, pages 27–38, 2008.

[29] T. Jim. SD3: A trust management system with certified evaluation. In *IEEE Symposium on Security and Privacy*, pages 106–115, 2001.

[30] K. Konolige. *A Deduction Model of Belief*. Morgan Kaufmann, Los Altos, California, 1986.

[31] S. Kripke. A semantical analysis of modal logic I: Normal modal propositional calculi. *Zeitschrift für Mathematische Logik und Grundlagen der Mathematik*, 9:67–96, 1963. Announced in *Journal of Symbolic Logic*, 24:323, 1959.

[32] B. Lampson, M. Abadi, M. Burrows, and E. Wobber. Authentication in distributed systems: Theory and practice. *ACM Transactions on Computer Systems*, 10(4):265–310, Nov. 1992.

[33] C. Lesniewski-Laas, B. Ford, J. Strauss, R. Morris, and M. F. Kaashoek. Alpaca: extensible authorization for distributed services. In *Proc. ACM Conference on Computer and Communications Security (CCS)*, pages 432–444, 2007.

[34] N. Li, B. N. Grosof, and J. Feigenbaum. A practically implementable and tractable delegation logic. In *IEEE Symposium on Security and Privacy*, pages 27–42, 2000.

[35] N. Li, J. C. Mitchell, and W. H. Winsborough. Design of a role-based trust-management framework. In *IEEE Symposium on Security and Privacy*, pages 114–130, 2002.

[36] E. Moggi. Notions of computation and monads. *Journal of Information and Computation*, 93(1):55–92, July 1991.

[37] R. Moore and G. Hendrix. Computational models of beliefs and the semantics of belief structures. Technical Note 187, SRI International, 1979.

[38] S. Negri and J. von Plato. Sequent calculus in natural deduction style. *Journal of Symbolic Logic*, 66:1803–1816, 2001.

[39] R. Parikh. Knowledge and the problem of logical omniscience. In *Proc. Int'l Symposium on Methodologies for Intelligent Systems (ISMIS)*, pages 432–439, 1987.

[40] A. Pimlott and O. Kiselyov. Soutei, a logic-based trust-management system. In *Proc. Functional and Logic Programming Symposium (FLOPS)*, pages 130–145, 2006.

[41] G. Plotkin and C. Stirling. A framework for intuitionistic modal logics. In *Proc. Conference on Theoretical Aspects of Reasoning about Knowledge (TARK)*, pages 399–406, 1986.

[42] J. Polakow and C. Skalka. Specifying distributed trust management in LolliMon. In *ACM Workshop on Programming Languages and Analysis for Security (PLAS)*, 2006.

[43] F. B. Schneider, K. Walsh, and E. G. Sirer. Nexus authorization logic (NAL): Design rationale and applications. *ACM Transactions on Information and System Security*, 14(1):8:1–28, June 2011.

[44] A. K. Simpson. *The Proof Theory and Semantics of Intuitionistic Modal Logic*. PhD thesis, University of Edinburgh, 1994.

[45] E. G. Sirer, W. de Bruijn, P. Reynolds, A. Shieh, K. Walsh, D. Williams, and F. B. Schneider. Logical attestation: An authorization architecture for trustworthy computing. In *Proc. ACM Symposium on Operating Systems Principles (SOSP)*, pages 249–264, 2011.

[46] M. H. Sørensen and P. Urzyczyn. *Lectures on the Curry-Howard Isomorphism*, volume 149 of *Studies in Logic and the Foundations of Mathematics*. Elsevier, Amsterdam, 2006.

[47] R. Stalnaker. The problem of logical omniscience, I. *Synthese*, 89:425–440, 1991.

[48] A. S. Troelstra and D. van Dalen. *Constructivism in Mathematics: Volume I*, volume 121 of *Studies in Logic and the Foundations of Mathematics*. Elsevier, Amsterdam, 1988.

[49] A. S. Troelstra and D. van Dalen. *Constructivism in Mathematics: Volume II*, volume 123 of *Studies in Logic and the Foundations of Mathematics*. Elsevier, Amsterdam, 1988.

[50] D. van Dalen. *Logic and Structure*. Springer, Berlin, fourth edition, 2004.

[51] D. Wijesekera. Constructive modal logics I. *Annals of Pure and Applied Logic*, 50(3):271–301, Dec. 1990.

[52] E. Wobber, M. Abadi, M. Burrows, and B. Lampson. Authentication in the Taos operating system. *ACM Transactions on Computer Systems*, 12(1):3–32, Feb. 1994.

APPENDIX: PROOFS

Proposition 1.

If $K, w, v \models \phi$ and $w \leq w'$ then $K, w', v \models \phi$.

Proof. By structural induction on ϕ. This proof has been mechanized in Coq. □

Theorem 1.

For all K, w, v, and ϕ, it holds that $K, w, v \models \phi$ iff $k2b(K), w, v \models \phi$.

Proof. First, we show the forward direction: $K, w, v \models \phi$ implies $k2b(K), w, v \models \phi$. All of the cases except says and $\mathsf{speaksfor}$ are straightforward, because those are the only two cases where the interpretation of formulas differs in the two semantics.

- Case $\phi = \tau \text{ says } \psi$. Suppose $K, w, v \models \tau \text{ says } \psi$. By the definition of $k2b$, formula $\psi \in \omega(w, \mu(\tau), v)$. By the belief semantics of says, it must hold that $k2b(K), w, v \models \tau \text{ says } \psi$.
- Case $\phi = \tau \text{ speaksfor } \tau'$. Assume $K, w, v \models \tau \text{ speaksfor } \tau'$. We need to show that, for all $w' \geq w$, it holds that $\omega(w', \mu(\tau), v) \subseteq \omega(w', \mu(\tau'), v)$. So let w' and ψ be arbitrary such that $w' \geq w$ and $\psi \in \omega(w', \mu(\tau), v)$, and we'll show that $\psi \in \omega(w', \mu(\tau'), v)$. By the definition of $k2b$, it holds that $K, w', v \models \tau \text{ says } \psi$. Note that, by proposition 1 and our original assumption, we have that $K, w', v \models \tau \text{ speaksfor } \tau'$. From those last two facts, and from the Kripke semantics of says and speaksfor, it follows that $K, w', v \models \tau' \text{ says } \psi$. By the definition of $k2b$, it therefore holds that $\psi \in \omega(w', \mu(\tau'), v)$.

Second, we show the backward direction: $K, w, v \models \phi$ is implied by $k2b(K), w, v \models \phi$. Again, all of the cases except says and speaksfor are straightforward, because those are the only two cases where the interpretation of formulas differs in the two semantics.

- Case $\phi = \tau \text{ says } \psi$. Suppose $k2b(K), w, v \models \tau \text{ says } \psi$. By the belief semantics of says, we have that $\psi \in \omega(w, \mu(\tau), v)$. By the definition of $k2b$, it holds that $K, w, v \models \tau \text{ says } \psi$.
- Case $\phi = \tau \text{ speaksfor } \tau'$. Assume $k2b(K), w, v \models \tau \text{ speaksfor } \tau'$. By the belief semantics of speaksfor, we have that, for all $w' \geq w$, it holds that $\omega(w', \mu(\tau), v) \subseteq \omega(w', \mu(\tau'), v)$. Let w' be w. Then $\omega(w, \mu(\tau), v) \subseteq \omega(w, \mu(\tau'), v)$. By the definitions of $k2b$ and subset, it follows that, for all ϕ, if $K, w, v \models \tau \text{ says } \phi$ then $K, w, v \models \tau' \text{ says } \phi$. By WSF, we therefore have that $K, w, v \models \tau \text{ speaksfor } \tau'$. □

Proposition 2.

For all well-formed modal models K, belief model $k2b(K)$ is well-formed.

Proof. Let $B = k2b(K)$. For B to be well-formed it must satisfy several conditions, which were defined in §2. We now show that these hold for any such B constructed by $k2b$.

1. Worldview Monotonicity. Assume $w \leq w'$ and $\phi \in \omega(w, p, v)$. By the latter assumption and the definition of $k2b$, we have that $K, w, v \models \hat{p} \text{ says } \phi$. From proposition 1, it follows that $K, w', v \models \hat{p} \text{ says } \phi$. By the definition of $k2b$, it then holds that $\phi \in \omega(w', p, v)$. Therefore $\omega(w, p, v) \subseteq \omega(w', p, v)$.
2. Worldview Equality. Assume $p \doteq p'$. Then by Accessibility Equality, $\leq_p$ equals $\leq_{p'}$. By the Kripke semantics of says, it follows that $K, w, v \models p \text{ says } \phi$ iff $K, w, v \models p' \text{ says } \phi$. By the definition of $k2b$, therefore, $\omega(w, p, v) = \omega(w, p', v)$.
3. Worldview Closure. Assume $\Gamma \subseteq \omega(w, p, v)$ and $\Gamma \models \phi$, that is, ϕ is a logical consequence of Γ in belief structure B. By the definition of $k2b$, we have $\omega(w, p, v) = \{\phi \mid K, w, v \models \hat{p} \text{ says } \phi\}$. So for all $\psi \in \Gamma$, it holds that $K, w, v \models \hat{p} \text{ says } \psi$. By the Kripke semantics of says, it follows that for all w' and w'' such that $w \leq w' \leq_p w''$, it holds that $K, w'', v \models \psi$. Thus $K, w'', v \models \Gamma$. So $k2b(K), w'', v \models \Gamma$ by theorem 1. By our initial assumption that $\Gamma \models \phi$, it follows that $k2b(K), w'', v \models \phi$. Again applying theorem 1, we have that $K, w'', v \models \phi$. By the Kripke semantics of says, it follows that $K, w, v \models \hat{p} \text{ says } \phi$. Therefore, by the definition of $k2b$, we have $\phi \in \omega(w, p, v)$.
4. Says Transparency. We prove the "iff" by proving both directions independently.

   ($\Rightarrow$) Assume $\phi \in \omega(w, p, v)$. By the definition of $k2b$, it holds that $K, w, v \models \hat{p} \text{ says } \phi$. From IT and F2, it follows that $K, w, v \models \hat{p} \text{ says } (\hat{p} \text{ says } \phi)$. By the definition of $k2b$, therefore, $(\hat{p} \text{ says } \phi) \in \omega(w, p, v)$.

   ($\Leftarrow$) Assume $(\hat{p} \text{ says } \phi) \in \omega(w, p, v)$. By the definition of $k2b$, it holds that $K, w, v \models \hat{p} \text{ says } (\hat{p} \text{ says } \phi)$. From ID, it follows that $K, w, v \models \hat{p} \text{ says } \phi$. By the definition of $k2b$, therefore, $\phi \in \omega(w, p, v)$.
5. Belief Hand-off. We actually prove a stronger result—an "iff" rather than just an "if". By the definitions of subset and $k2b$, we have that $\omega(w, p, v) \subseteq \omega(w, q, v)$ holds iff for all ϕ, if $K, w, v \models \hat{p} \text{ says } \phi$ then $K, w, v \models \hat{q} \text{ says } \phi$. By WSF, that holds iff $K, w, v \models \hat{p} \text{ speaksfor } \hat{q}$. By the fact below, that holds iff $K, w, v \models \hat{q} \text{ says } (\hat{p} \text{ speaksfor } \hat{q})$. By the definition of $k2b$, that holds iff $\hat{q} \text{ speaksfor } \hat{p} \in \omega(w, q, v)$.

   Fact: in the Kripke semantics, $\models \hat{q} \text{ says } (\hat{p} \text{ speaksfor } \hat{q}) \iff \hat{p} \text{ speaksfor } \hat{q}$. The proof of that fact has been mechanized in Coq. □

Theorem 2.

If $\Gamma \vdash \phi$ and $B, w, v \models \Gamma$, then $B, w, v \models \phi$.

Proof. By induction on the derivation of $\Gamma \vdash \phi$. This proof has been mechanized in Coq. □

Theorem 3.

If $\Gamma \vdash \phi$ and $K, w, v \models \Gamma$, then $K, w, v \models \phi$.

Proof. By induction on the derivation of $\Gamma \vdash \phi$. This proof has been mechanized in Coq. □

Proposition 3.

If $B, w, v \models \phi$ and $w \leq w'$ then $B, w', v \models \phi$.

Proof. By structural induction on ϕ. This proof has been mechanized in Coq. □

Automatic Verification of Protocols with Lists of Unbounded Length

Bruno Blanchet
INRIA Paris-Rocquencourt, France
Bruno.Blanchet@inria.fr

Miriam Paiola
INRIA Paris-Rocquencourt, France
Miriam.Paiola@inria.fr

ABSTRACT

We present a novel automatic technique for proving secrecy and authentication properties for security protocols that manipulate lists of unbounded length, for an unbounded number of sessions. This result is achieved by extending the Horn clause approach of the automatic protocol verifier ProVerif. We extend the Horn clauses to be able to represent lists of unbounded length. We adapt the resolution algorithm to handle the new class of Horn clauses, and prove the soundness of this new algorithm. We have implemented our algorithm and successfully tested it on several protocol examples, including XML protocols coming from web services.

Categories and Subject Descriptors

C.2.2 [**Computer-communication networks**]: Network Protocols—*Protocol verification*

Keywords

Security protocols; verification; lists; web services; Horn clauses; resolution.

1. INTRODUCTION

Security protocols are protocols that rely on cryptographic primitives such as encryption and signatures for securing communication between several parties. They aim at ensuring security properties such as secrecy or authentication. However, attacks are often found against protocols that were thought correct. Furthermore, security flaws cannot be detected by testing since they appear only in the presence of an attacker. The confidence in these protocols can then be increased by a formal analysis that proves the desired security properties. To ease formal verification, one often uses the symbolic, so-called Dolev-Yao model [13], which abstracts from the details of cryptographic primitives and considers messages as terms. In this work, we also rely on this model.

The formal verification of security protocols with fixed-size data structures has been extensively studied. However, some protocols, for instance XML protocols of web services, use more complex data structures, such as lists. The verification of protocols that manipulate such data structures has been less studied and presents additional difficulties: these complex data structures add another cause of undecidability.

In this work, we extend the verifier ProVerif [7] to protocols with lists of unbounded length. ProVerif is an automatic verifier that takes as input a protocol, translates it into a representation in first-order logic clauses, and uses a resolution algorithm to determine whether a fact is derivable from the clauses. One can then infer security properties of the protocol. For instance, ProVerif uses a fact $\text{att}(M)$ to mean that the attacker may have the message M. If $\text{att}(s)$ is not derivable from the clauses, then s is secret. The main goal of this approach is to prove security properties of protocols without bounding the number of sessions of the protocol.

Like other protocol verifiers, ProVerif can analyze protocols with lists if we fix the lengths of the lists a priori. However, if the protocol is verified only for some lengths, attacks may exist for other lengths. If there is an attack against a protocol, then there is a bound such that this attack appears with lists shorter than the bound, but this bound depends on the protocol and is not easy to compute. So our goal is to extend ProVerif to the verification of protocols with lists of any length without bounding the length (and still not bounding the number of sessions). To obtain this result, we extend the language of Horn clauses, introducing a new kind of clauses, generalized Horn clauses, to be able to represent lists of any length. We adapt the resolution algorithm to deal with these new clauses, and prove the soundness of the new algorithm. The obtained algorithm can prove secrecy and authentication properties. (More precisely, the authentication property that we consider is non-injective agreement [17]: if some participant B terminates the protocol with some parameters, then A started the protocol with the same parameters.) This algorithm performs approximations, so it may fail to prove security properties that actually hold, and it does not always terminate. This is unavoidable because the problem of verifying protocols with an unbounded number of sessions is undecidable. However, the algorithm works well in practice: we have implemented it and successfully tested it on several protocol examples (see Section 6). Applications of our results include in particular the treatment of XML protocols such as web services, XML documents being modeled using possibly nested lists. In this paper, we focus mainly on these protocols. We illustrate our work on the SOAP extension [9] to XML signatures [4]. XML signatures allow one to sign several parts of an XML

CCS'13, November 4–8, 2013, Berlin, Germany.

http://dx.doi.org/10.1145/2508859.2516679.

document, recorded in a SignedInfo element, which can be modeled as a list of references to the signed parts of the document. A known attack [18] may occur when the document contains several Body elements, and the signed Body is not the one that is used for subsequent treatments. Our tool detects this attack, and proves that a corrected version is secure. Another possible application is the verification of some group protocols that manipulate lists that contain one element for each group member, with an unbounded number of group members.

1.1 Related Work

The first approach considered for proving protocols with recursive data structures was interactive theorem proving: a recursive authentication protocol was studied for an unbounded number of participants, using Isabelle/HOL [20], and using rank functions and PVS [10]. However, this approach requires considerable human effort.

Truderung [22] showed a decidability result (in NEXPTIME) for secrecy in recursive protocols, which include transformations of lists, for a bounded number of sessions. This result was extended to a class of recursive protocols with XOR [16] in 3-NEXPTIME. Chridi et al [11, 12] present an extension of the constraint-based approach in symbolic protocol verification to handle a class of protocols (Well-Tagged protocols with Autonomous keys) with unbounded lists in messages. They prove that the insecurity problem for Well-Tagged protocols with Autonomous keys is decidable for a bounded number of sessions.

Several approaches were considered for verifying XML protocols [6, 21, 15, 3], by translating them to the input format of a standard protocol verifier: the tool TulaFale [6] uses ProVerif as back-end; Kleiner and Roscoe [21, 15] translate WS-Security protocols to FDR; Backes et al [3] use AVISPA. All these approaches have little or no support for lists of unbounded length. For instance, TulaFale has support for list membership with unbounded lists, but does not go further.

Recently, Paiola and Blanchet [19] showed that, for a certain class of Horn clauses, if secrecy is proved by ProVerif for lists of length one, then secrecy also holds for lists of unbounded length. Their target applications are group protocols and XML protocols. However, this work is limited to secrecy, and the class of protocols that they handle is limited to protocols that treat all elements of lists uniformly. When their reduction result does not apply, a different approach is needed. We propose such an approach in this paper. We provide a practical algorithm that can prove both secrecy and authentication properties of protocols that manipulate different list elements in different ways.

1.2 Outline

The next section recalls the technique used by ProVerif. In Section 3, we introduce our running example and motivate the introduction of a new type of clauses, the generalized Horn clauses, that we will use to model group protocols. In Section 4, we formally define generalized Horn clauses, and their semantics by giving their translation into Horn clauses. In Section 5, we adapt the resolution algorithm to generalized Horn clauses and prove its soundness. Section 6 summarizes our experimental results. Because of space constraints, the proofs of all our results and additional details on our algorithm can be found in the long version of the paper, available at [8], together with our implementation.

2. A REMINDER ON PROVERIF

ProVerif translates the initial protocol into a set of Horn clauses. The syntax of these clauses is defined in Figure 1.

$p ::=$	patterns
$\quad x, y, z, v, w$	variable
$\quad a[p_1, \dots, p_n]$	name
$\quad f(p_1, \dots, p_n)$	constructor application
$F ::= pred(p)$	facts
$R ::= F_1 \wedge \dots \wedge F_n \Rightarrow F$	Horn clause

Figure 1: Syntax of Horn clauses

The patterns represent messages that are exchanged between participants of the protocol. A variable can represent any pattern. Names represent atomic values, such as keys and nonces. Each participant can create new names. Instead of creating a fresh name at each run of the protocol, the created names are considered as functions represented by the pattern $a[p_1, \dots, p_n]$. These functions take as arguments the messages previously received by the principal that creates the name as well as session identifiers, which are variables that take a different value at each run of the protocol, to distinguish names created in different runs. As shown in, e.g., [7], this representation of names is a sound approximation. When a name has no arguments, we write a instead of $a[\,]$. We use a for a generic name and identifiers in sans serif font (e.g., sk) for fixed names.

The fact att(p) means that the attacker may have the pattern (message) p. ProVerif models authentication as correspondence assertions, such as "if event $e(x)$ has been executed, then event $e'(x)$ has been executed". It uses the fact m-event(p) to represent that the event p must have been executed, and the fact event(p) to represent that the event p may have been executed.

A clause $F_1 \wedge \dots \wedge F_n \Rightarrow F$ means that, if all facts F_i are true, then the conclusion F is also true. We use R for a clause, H for its hypothesis, and C for its conclusion. The hypothesis of a clause is considered as a multiset of facts. A clause with no hypothesis $\Rightarrow F$ is written simply F.

Cryptographic primitives are represented by functions. There are two kinds of functions: constructors and destructors. A constructor f is a function that explicitly appears in the patterns that represent messages and builds new patterns of the form $f(p_1, \dots, p_n)$. Destructors manipulate patterns. A destructor g is defined by a set $def(g)$ of rewrite rules of the form $g(p_1, \dots, p_n) \rightarrow p$ where $p_1, \dots, p_n, p$ are patterns with only variables and constructors and the variables of p appear in $p_1, \dots, p_n$. Using constructors and destructors, one can represent data structures and cryptographic operations. For instance, $senc(m, k)$ is the constructor that represents the symmetric key encryption of the message m under the key k. The corresponding destructor $sdec(m', k)$ returns the decryption of m' if m' is a message encrypted under k. The rewrite rule that defines $sdec$ is

$$sdec(senc(m, k), k) \rightarrow m.$$

A protocol is represented by three sets of Horn clauses:

- initial knowledge of the attacker: we have a fact att(p) for each p initially known by the attacker.
- abilities of the attacker:
  att$(\mathsf{a}[x])$

for each constructor f of arity n:
$\text{att}(x_1) \wedge \cdots \wedge \text{att}(x_n) \Rightarrow \text{att}(f(x_1, \ldots x_n))$
for each destructor g,
for each rule $g(p_1, \ldots, p_n) \rightarrow p$ in $def(g)$:
$\text{att}(p_1) \wedge \cdots \wedge \text{att}(p_n) \Rightarrow \text{att}(p)$
The first clause represents the ability of the attacker to create fresh names: all fresh names that the attacker may create are represented by the names $\mathsf{a}[x]$ for any x. The other clauses mean that if the attacker has some messages, then he can apply constructors and destructors to them.

- the protocol itself: for each message p of the protocol sent by agent A, we have the clause $\text{att}(p_1) \wedge \cdots \wedge \text{att}(p_n) \wedge \text{m-event}(p'_1) \wedge \ldots \wedge \text{m-event}(p'_{n'}) \Rightarrow \text{att}(p)$, where A receives messages $p_1, \ldots, p_n$ and executes events $p'_1, \ldots, p'_{n'}$ before sending message p. Indeed, if the attacker has $p_1, \ldots, p_n$, then he can send them to A and intercept A's reply p; the events $p'_1, \ldots, p'_{n'}$ are executed by A during this operation.

  Similarly, for each event p executed by A, we have the clause $\text{att}(p_1) \wedge \cdots \wedge \text{att}(p_n) \wedge \text{m-event}(p'_1) \wedge \ldots \wedge \text{m-event}(p'_{n'}) \Rightarrow \text{event}(p)$, where A receives messages $p_1, \ldots, p_n$ and executes events $p'_1, \ldots, p'_{n'}$ before executing event p.

Let $\mathcal{R}_1$ be the set of these clauses. This representation of protocols by Horn clauses is approximate, mainly because Horn clauses that represent the protocol can be applied any number of times instead of only once per session. However, it is sound: if the attacker knows p after the events $p_1, \ldots, p_n$ have been executed, then $\text{att}(p)$ is derivable from $\mathcal{R}_1$ and the facts $\text{m-event}(p_1), \ldots, \text{m-event}(p_n)$. In particular, if $\text{att}(p)$ is not derivable from $\mathcal{R}_1$ and any facts $\text{m-event}(p')$, then the protocol preserves the secrecy of p. If the event p is executed after the events $p_1, \ldots, p_n$, then $\text{event}(p)$ is derivable from $\mathcal{R}_1$ and the facts $\text{m-event}(p_1), \ldots, \text{m-event}(p_n)$. (This is proved by Theorem 1 in [7] when the clauses are generated from a pi calculus model of the protocol.)

ProVerif determines whether a fact is derivable from the clauses using resolution with free selection [2]: it combines pairs of clauses by resolution; the literals upon which we resolve are chosen by a selection function. Next, we detail this algorithm.

We say that R_1 subsumes R_2 when R_2 can be obtained by adding hypotheses to an instance of R_1. In this case, all facts derivable using R_2 can also be derived by R_1, so R_2 can be eliminated. Formally, subsumption is defined by:

Definition 1 (Subsumption). *We say that $R_1 = H_1 \Rightarrow C_1$ subsumes $R_2 = H_2 \Rightarrow C_2$, and we write $R_1 \sqsupseteq R_2$, if and only if there exists a substitution σ such that $\sigma C_1 = C_2$ and $\sigma H_1 \subseteq H_2$ (multiset inclusion).*

When the conclusion of a clause R unifies with a hypothesis of a clause R', resolution creates a new clause that corresponds to applying R and R' one after the other.

Definition 2 (Resolution). *Let R and R' be two clauses, $R = H \Rightarrow C$ and $R' = H' \Rightarrow C'$. Assume that there exists $F_0 \in H'$ such that C and F_0 are unifiable and σ is their most general unifier. In this case, we define $R \circ_{F_0} R' = \sigma(H \cup (H' \setminus \{F_0\})) \Rightarrow \sigma C'$. The clause $R \circ_{F_0} R'$ is the result of resolving R' with R upon F_0.*

$\text{SATUR}(\mathcal{R}_0) =$

1. $\mathcal{R} \leftarrow \text{ELIM}(\mathcal{R}_0)$.
2. Repeat until a fixpoint is reached
   for each $R \in \mathcal{R}$ such that $sel(R) = \emptyset$,
   for each $R' \in \mathcal{R}$, for each $F_0 \in sel(R')$ such that $R \circ_{F_0} R'$ is defined,
   $\mathcal{R} \leftarrow \text{ELIM}(\{R \circ_{F_0} R'\} \cup \mathcal{R})$.
3. Return $\{R \in \mathcal{R} \mid sel(R) = \emptyset\}$.

Figure 2: ProVerif's Algorithm

The facts upon which we resolve are selected through a selection function:

Definition 3 (Selection function). *A selection function is a function from clauses to sets of facts, such that $sel(H \Rightarrow C) \subseteq H$. If $F \in sel(R)$, we say that F is selected in R. If $sel(R) = \emptyset$, we say that no hypothesis is selected in R, or that the conclusion of R is selected.*

The algorithm is correct with any selection function that never selects facts of the form $\text{m-event}(p)$, but the choice of the selection function can change the behavior of the algorithm. Facts $\text{att}(x)$ where x is a variable can be unified with all facts $\text{att}(M)$, so we should avoid selecting $\text{att}(x)$ to reduce the number of possible resolution steps. Hence a good selection function satisfies the following formula:

$$sel(H \Rightarrow C) = \begin{cases} \{F_0\} & \text{where } F_0 \in H, \\ & \text{for all variables } x, F_0 \neq \text{att}(x), \text{ and} \\ & \text{for all patterns } p, F_0 \neq \text{m-event}(p) \\ \emptyset & \text{if there exists no such } F_0 \end{cases}$$

The resolution algorithm is shown in Figure 2. It transforms the initial set of clauses into a new one that derives the same facts. The algorithm $\text{SATUR}(\mathcal{R}_0)$ has 3 steps:

- The first step inserts in $\mathcal{R}$ the clauses in $\mathcal{R}_0$ after elimination of subsumed clauses by ELIM: when $R' \sqsupseteq R$ and both R and R' are in $\mathcal{R}$, R is removed by $\text{ELIM}(\mathcal{R})$.
- The second step is a fixpoint iteration that adds the clauses created by resolution: if the conclusion of a clause R such that $sel(R) = \emptyset$ unifies with $F_0 \in sel(R')$, then the resolution $R \circ_{F_0} R'$ is added to $\mathcal{R}$. Then, subsumed clauses are eliminated by ELIM.
- Finally, the algorithm returns the clauses in $\mathcal{R}$ with no selected hypothesis.

Let $\mathcal{F}_{\text{me}}$ be any set of facts of the form $\text{m-event}(p)$.

Theorem 1 (Lemma 2 in [7]). *Let F be a closed fact and $\mathcal{R}_0$ a set of clauses. F is derivable from $\mathcal{R}_0 \cup \mathcal{F}_{\text{me}}$ if and only if it is derivable from $\text{SATUR}(\mathcal{R}_0) \cup \mathcal{F}_{\text{me}}$.*

To prove that a closed fact $\text{att}(p)$ is not derivable from $\mathcal{R}_0 \cup \mathcal{F}_{\text{me}}$, we use the following result, where att' is a new predicate:

Corollary 1. *If $\text{SATUR}(\mathcal{R}_1 \cup \{\text{att}(p) \Rightarrow \text{att}'(p)\})$ contains no clause of the form $H \Rightarrow \text{att}'(p')$, then $\text{att}(p)$ is not derivable from $\mathcal{R}_1 \cup \mathcal{F}_{\text{me}}$ for any $\mathcal{F}_{\text{me}}$. So, by soundness of the clauses, the protocol preserves the secrecy of p.*

Indeed, if $\text{SATUR}(\mathcal{R}_1 \cup \{\text{att}(p) \Rightarrow \text{att}'(p)\})$ contains no clause of the form $H \Rightarrow \text{att}'(p')$, then $\text{att}'(p)$ is not derivable from $\text{SATUR}(\mathcal{R}_1 \cup \{\text{att}(p) \Rightarrow \text{att}'(p)\}) \cup \mathcal{F}_{\text{me}}$, so by Theorem 1, $\text{att}'(p)$ is not derivable from $\mathcal{R}_1 \cup \{\text{att}(p) \Rightarrow \text{att}'(p)\} \cup \mathcal{F}_{\text{me}}$, so $\text{att}(p)$ is not derivable from $\mathcal{R}_1 \cup \mathcal{F}_{\text{me}}$. Similarly, we also have:

COROLLARY 2 (COROLLARY 2 IN [7]). *Suppose that all clauses of* $\text{SATUR}(\mathcal{R}_1)$ *that conclude* $\text{event}(e(p))$ *for some* p *are of the form* $\text{m-event}(e'(p')) \wedge H \Rightarrow \text{event}(e(p'))$ *for some* H *and* p'. *Then, for all* $\mathcal{F}_{\text{me}}$, *for all* p, *if* $\text{event}(e(p))$ *is derivable from* $\mathcal{R}_1 \cup \mathcal{F}_{\text{me}}$, *then* $\text{m-event}(e'(p)) \in \mathcal{F}_{\text{me}}$. *So by soundness of the clauses, the protocol satisfies the correspondence "if* $e(x)$ *has been executed, then* $e'(x)$ *has been executed".*

3. MOTIVATION

This section motivates this work, explaining the introduction of a new type of clauses through a running example.

3.1 Running Example

As a running example, we use a version of the SOAP extension to XML signatures [9]. SOAP envelopes are XML documents with a mandatory Body containing a request, response or a fault message together with an optional Header element containing application-specific information about the message (for example security information). In particular, the SOAP header can carry digital signature information within a SOAP envelope, as follows:

```
<Envelope>
  <Header>
    <Signature>
      <SignedInfo>
        <Reference URI="#theBody">
          <DigestValue> hash of the body </DigestValue>
        </Reference>
        <Reference URI="#x1">
          <DigestValue> hash of the content of x1
          </DigestValue>
        </Reference>
        ...
      </SignedInfo>
      <SignatureValue>
        signature of SignedInfo with key sk
      </SignatureValue>
    </Signature>
  </Header>
  <Body Id="#theBody"> request </Body>
</Envelope>
```

The Signature header contains two components. The first component is a SignedInfo element, which is basically a list of references to the elements of the message that are signed, designated by their identifier and accompanied by a DigestValue, a hash of their content. The hash may be computed with the hash function SHA-1. The second component of the Signature header is the signature of the SignedInfo element using a secret key sk.

We consider a simple protocol in which a client sends such a message to a server. The server processes the document and checks the signature before authorizing the request given in the Body: if the SignedInfo contains a Reference to an element with tag Body, then he will authorize the request. This protocol should guarantee that the server authorizes only requests signed by legitimate clients.

This protocol is subject to a known wrapping attack [18]: an attacker can intercept an envelope and create a new envelope wrapping the Body in the Header and adding a new body with a different id and a different request. The server will verify the signature and authorize the fake request made by the attacker. This attack is possible because the server does not check that the signed Body is the one he authorizes.

3.2 Need for Generalizing Horn Clauses

In order to model the previous example, we suppose that the XML parser parses the SOAP envelope as a pair, containing as first component a list of triplets (tag, id, corresponding content) and as second component the content of the mandatory body. The list in the first component is helpful so that one can retrieve the content of an element from its id by looking up the list. The content of the Signature header is modeled as a pair (*SignedInfo*, *SignatureValue*); *SignedInfo* is a list of pairs containing an id and the hash of the content corresponding to the id; *SignatureValue* is the signature of *SignedInfo* with a secret key sk. We use such a simple model for illustrative purposes.

A given XML document can then be represented using lists of fixed length (and other standard functions). We denote by $\langle p_1, \ldots, p_h \rangle$ a list of fixed length h; such lists are modeled as a family of constructors, one for each length.

However, the receiver of the SOAP envelope accepts messages containing any number of headers, and the SignedInfo element may also contain references to any number of elements in the message. Therefore, we need lists of variable length in order to model the expected message. So we introduce the construct $\mathit{list}(i \leq M, p_i)$ which stands for $\langle p_1, \ldots, p_M \rangle$, for an unknown M (inspired by [12, 19]).

Thanks to this new construct, we can model the SOAP envelope from the point of view of the server: $(\mathit{list}(i \leq M, (\mathit{tag}_i, \mathit{id}_i, \mathit{cont}_i)), r)$, where tag_i, id_i, and cont_i are variables representing tags, identifiers, and contents respectively and r is the variable for the request. The server has to check the signature, that is, he has to verify that the list contains a tag tag_j equal to Signature and that cont_j contains a correct signature. These checks can be represented by the following equations: $\mathit{tag}_j \doteq \mathsf{Signature}$, $\mathit{cont}_j \doteq (\mathit{sinfo}, \mathit{sign}(\mathit{sinfo}, \mathsf{sk}))$, $\mathit{sinfo} \doteq \mathit{list}(k \leq N, (\mathit{id}_{\phi(k)}, \mathit{sha1}(\mathit{cont}_{\phi(k)})))$, where the function ϕ is a mapping from the index k of each element in the sinfo list to its index $\phi(k)$ in the list that represents the whole message. Furthermore, one of the signed elements must have tag Body, that is, $\phi(m) \doteq d$, $\mathit{tag}_d \doteq \mathsf{Body}$. We cannot directly replace the variables tag_i, id_i, and cont_i with their values given by these equations, because in the list $\mathit{list}(i \leq M, (\mathit{tag}_i, \mathit{id}_i, \mathit{cont}_i))$, all elements tag_i, id_i and cont_i need to have the same form, while the equations give different forms to different elements. So we keep the equations in the clause for future use. The equations allow us to handle protocols that treat elements of lists non-uniformly.

We can represent that the adversary has a SOAP envelope by $\text{att}((\mathit{list}(i \leq M, (\mathit{tag}_i, \mathit{id}_i, \mathit{cont}_i)), r))$. The adversary can build such a SOAP envelope from its components, so we need to express that the adversary has $(\mathit{tag}_i, \mathit{id}_i, \mathit{cont}_i)$ for all $i \leq M$. We use a conjunction $\bigwedge_{i \in [1,M]} \text{att}((\mathit{tag}_i, \mathit{id}_i, \mathit{cont}_i))$ for this purpose. More generally, $\bigwedge_{(i_1, \ldots i_h) \in I} F$ represents the conjunction of facts F for all indices $(i_1, \ldots, i_h) \in I$.

After modeling the clauses, we need to perform resolution on these generalized clauses. Let $[1, M] = \{1, \ldots, M\}$ and suppose that we resolve $R_2 = \bigwedge_{i \in [1,M]} \text{att}(\mathit{sha1}(\mathit{cont}_{\phi(i)})) \Rightarrow$

event($e(r)$) with the clause $R_1 = \text{att}(x) \Rightarrow \text{att}(\textit{sha1}(x))$, that is, we use R_1 to derive one hypothesis of R_2, say the one of index $i = k_1 \in [1, M]$. So we unify $\text{att}(\textit{sha1}(x))$ with $\text{att}(\textit{sha1}(\textit{cont}_{\phi(k_1)}))$, yielding the equality $x \doteq \textit{cont}_{\phi(k_1)}$. The obtained clause would then be:

$$\text{att}(x_1) \wedge \bigwedge_{i\in[1,M]\smallsetminus\{k_1\}} \text{att}(\textit{sha1}(\textit{cont}_{\phi(i)})) \wedge \{x_1 \doteq \textit{cont}_{\phi(k_1)}\} \Rightarrow \text{event}(e(r))$$

The variable x is renamed into x_1 to distinguish it from the variable x in R_1. The obtained clause can then again be resolved with R_1 for some $i = k_2 \in [1, M] \smallsetminus \{k_1\}$, yielding

$$\text{att}(x_1) \wedge \text{att}(x_2) \wedge \bigwedge_{i\in[1,M]\smallsetminus\{k_1,k_2\}} \text{att}(\textit{sha1}(\textit{cont}_{\phi(i)})) \wedge \{x_1 \doteq \textit{cont}_{\phi(k_1)}, x_2 \doteq \textit{cont}_{\phi(k_2)}\} \Rightarrow \text{event}(e(r))$$

which can again be resolved with R_1, and so on. Since M is not bounded, such resolution steps yield an infinite loop. To avoid this loop, we define a resolution step that simultaneously resolves R with several instances of R' for i in any non-empty subset $I \subseteq [1, M]$. We name such a step *hyperresolution* by analogy with the hyperresolution rule that allows one to resolve one clause with several clauses [14]. To perform hyperresolution, we first transform R_1 into a clause R_1' corresponding to the combination of several instances of R_1, one for each $i \in I$. This step is named *immersion* and yields $R_1' = \bigwedge_{i\in I} \text{att}(x_i) \Rightarrow \text{att}(\textit{sha1}(x_i))$. We can then perform hyperresolution with R_2 and obtain:

$$\bigwedge_{i\in I} \text{att}(x_i) \wedge \bigwedge_{i\in[1,M]\smallsetminus I} \text{att}(\textit{sha1}(\textit{cont}_{\phi(i)})) \wedge \{\bigwedge_{i\in I} x_i \doteq \textit{cont}_{\phi(i)}\} \Rightarrow \text{event}(e(r)).$$

When $I = [1, M]$, the second hypothesis is removed and the substitution of $\textit{cont}_{\phi(i)}$ for x_i is performed for all i, so we obtain

$$\bigwedge_{i\in[1,M]} \text{att}(\textit{cont}_{\phi(i)}) \Rightarrow \text{event}(e(r)).$$

When $I \neq [1, M]$, to have a more symmetric notation and to simplify the language of sets used in conjunctions, we introduce a symbol I' for $[1, M] \smallsetminus I$, and keep the constraint that $I \uplus I' = [1, M]$: I and I' are disjoint and their union is $[1, M]$. The clause is then denoted by

$$I \uplus I' = [1, M], \bigwedge_{i\in I} \text{att}(\textit{cont}_{\phi(i)}) \wedge \bigwedge_{i\in I'} \text{att}(\textit{sha1}(\textit{cont}_{\phi(i)})) \Rightarrow \text{event}(e(r)).$$

where I and I' represent non-empty subsets of $[1, M]$.

4. GENERALIZED HORN CLAUSES

This section formally defines the syntax and semantics of *generalized Horn Clauses*, which were motivated informally in the previous section.

4.1 Syntax

The syntax of these new clauses is defined in Figure 3. The patterns p^G that represent messages are enriched with several new constructs. The variables may have indices $x_{\iota_1,\dots,\iota_h}$. The pattern for function application $f(p_1^G, \dots, p_l^G)$ includes not only constructor application but also names $a[p_1^G, \dots, p_l^G]$ where a is a name without index. We consider tuples $(p_1, \dots, p_l^G)$ and lists of fixed length $\langle p_1^G, \dots, p_l^G\rangle$ as particular constructors. We suppose that the implementation of the protocol uses distinct encodings for tuples and for lists, so that they cannot be confused with each other. The

$\iota ::=$	index term
$\quad i$	index variable
$\quad \phi(\iota_1, \dots, \iota_h)$	function application
$p^G, p'^G ::=$	patterns
$\quad x_{\iota_1,\dots,\iota_h}$	variable ($h \geq 0$)
$\quad f(p_1^G, \dots, p_l^G)$	function application
$\quad a_\iota^M[p_1^G, \dots, p_l^G]$	indexed names
$\quad \textit{list}(i \leq M, p^G)$	list constructor
$J ::=$	set computation
$\quad I$	set symbol
$\quad \{()\}$	singleton
$\quad J \times [1, M]$	product
$\mathcal{C} ::= \bigwedge_{(i_1,\dots i_h)\in J}$	conjunction
$F^G ::= \mathcal{C}\, \textit{pred}(p^G)$	fact
$E ::= \mathcal{C}\, p^G \doteq p'^G$	equation over patterns
$E' ::= \mathcal{C}\, \iota \doteq \iota'$	equation over indices
$\mathcal{E} ::= \{E_1, \dots, E_n, E_1', \dots, E_{n'}'\}$	set of equations
$\mathcal{I} ::= I_1 \uplus \dots \uplus I_h = J$	constraint over sets
$\textit{Cts} ::= \{\mathcal{I}_1, \dots, \mathcal{I}_n\}$	set of constraints
$R^G ::= \textit{Cts}, F_1^G \wedge \dots \wedge F_n^G \wedge \mathcal{E} \Rightarrow \textit{pred}(p^G)$	generalized Horn clause

Figure 3: Syntax of generalized Horn clauses

construct $a_\iota^M[p_1^G, \dots, p_l^G]$ represents a fresh name a indexed by ι in $[1, M]$. For instance, in the context of group protocols, it may represent a name created by the group member number ι, inside a group of size M. We use the construct $\textit{list}(i \leq M, p^G)$ to represent lists of length M.

We extend facts to model the possibility of having a conjunction of facts depending on indices, so that the facts become $\bigwedge_{(i_1,\dots,i_h)\in J} \textit{pred}(p^G)$. The set J can be a product of a set symbol I or a singleton $\{()\}$ and of different sets $[1, M]$, depending on different bounds M. The symbol $[1, M]$ represents the set $\{1, \dots, M\}$. The symbol $[1, M]$ allows us to keep the information that an index ranges over the full set of indices of bound M, while other set symbols I represent an unknown, non-empty set of indices. We write $[1, M]$ instead of $\{()\} \times [1, M]$. For example, intuitively, $\bigwedge_{i\in[1,N]} \textit{pred}(p^G)$ represents $\textit{pred}(p^G\{i \mapsto 1\}) \wedge \dots \wedge \textit{pred}(p^G\{i \mapsto N\})$, where $p^G\{i \mapsto i'\}$ denotes p^G in which i has been replaced with i'. The conjunction $\mathcal{C} = \bigwedge_{(i_1,\dots,i_h)\in J}$ with $J = \{()\}$ and $h = 0$ is omitted: the fact $\mathcal{C}\, \textit{pred}(p^G)$ is then simply $\textit{pred}(p^G)$.

In the generalized Horn clause $\textit{Cts}, F_1^G \wedge \dots \wedge F_n^G \wedge \mathcal{E} \Rightarrow \textit{pred}(p^G)$, there are two new members: a *set of constraints* $\textit{Cts}$ and a *set of equations* $\mathcal{E}$. The first one is a set of constraints on sets used in conjunctions: the constraint $I_1 \uplus \dots \uplus I_h = J$ means that $I_1, \dots, I_h$ are pairwise disjoint and their union is J. The second one is a set of equations that represent the substitutions that cannot be done because the equations hold for some but not all values of the indices. These equations can be equations over patterns E and equations over indices E'. The clause $\textit{Cts}, F_1^G \wedge \dots \wedge F_n^G \wedge \mathcal{E} \Rightarrow \textit{pred}(p^G)$ means that, if the constraints in $\textit{Cts}$ are satisfied, and the facts $F_1^G, \ldots, F_n^G$ and the equations in $\mathcal{E}$ hold, then the fact $pred(p^G)$ also holds. The conclusion of a clause does not contain a conjunction $\mathcal{C}$: we can simply leave the indices of $pred(p^G)$ free to mean that $pred(p^G)$ can be concluded for any value of these indices.

The clauses are required to satisfy the following invariants:

1. In a conjunction $\bigwedge_{(i_1,\ldots,i_h)\in J}$, the indices $i_1, \ldots, i_h$ are pairwise distinct.

2. Each set symbol I occurs at most once in each constraint in Cts.

3. Each set symbol I occurs in at most one left-hand side of a constraint in Cts.

4. If a set symbol I occurs in a conjunction or in the right-hand side of a constraint in Cts, then it occurs in exactly one left-hand side of a constraint in Cts.

We use H^G for hypothesis and C^G for conclusions. When Cts or $\mathcal{E}$ are empty, we omit them in the clause.

4.2 Representation of the Protocol

The representation of the abilities of the attacker includes the clauses given in Section 2. For our running example, $\mathsf{att}(pk(\mathsf{sk}))$, $\mathsf{att}(\mathsf{Signature})$, $\mathsf{att}(\mathsf{Body})$ represent that the attacker initially knows the public key $pk(\mathsf{sk})$ and the constants Signature and Body, and the clauses

$$\begin{array}{ll}
\mathsf{att}(\mathsf{a}[x]) & \\
\mathsf{att}(x) \wedge \mathsf{att}(y) \Rightarrow \mathsf{att}(sign(x,y)) & \mathsf{att}((x,y)) \Rightarrow \mathsf{att}(x) \\
\mathsf{att}(x) \Rightarrow \mathsf{att}(pk(x)) & \mathsf{att}((x,y)) \Rightarrow \mathsf{att}(y) \\
\mathsf{att}(x) \Rightarrow \mathsf{att}(sha1(x)) & \mathsf{att}(x) \Rightarrow \mathsf{att}(\langle x\rangle) \\
\mathsf{att}(x) \wedge \mathsf{att}(y) \Rightarrow \mathsf{att}((x,y)) & \mathsf{att}(\langle x\rangle) \Rightarrow \mathsf{att}(x)
\end{array}$$

represent that the attacker can create fresh names, sign messages, create its own public keys, apply hash functions, compose and decompose pairs and lists of length one. We have similar clauses for triples and lists of length two. (These arities are the only ones used in our example.)

In addition, we have clauses for $list$, which generalize clauses for tuples and lists of fixed length:

$$\bigwedge_{i\in[1,M]} \mathsf{att}(x_i) \Rightarrow \mathsf{att}(list(j \le M, x_j)) \tag{1}$$

$$\mathsf{att}(list(j \le M, x_j)) \Rightarrow \mathsf{att}(x_i) \tag{2}$$

Let us now give clauses that represent the protocol itself. To model the authentication, we use two events b and e. The event $b(r)$ means that the client sends the request r; the event $e(r)$ means that the server authorizes the request r. Our goal is to prove that, if $e(r)$ is executed, then $b(r)$ has been executed. We suppose that the only element signed by the client is the Body. Hence the document can be represented as follows: $(\langle(\mathsf{Signature}, \mathsf{ids}, (\langle(\mathsf{idb}, sha1(\mathsf{Req}))\rangle, sign((\langle(\mathsf{idb}, sha1(\mathsf{Req}))\rangle, \mathsf{sk})))), (\mathsf{Body}, \mathsf{idb}, \mathsf{Req})\rangle, \mathsf{Req})$, where ids is the identifier of the Signature and idb the one of the Body. The client executes the event $b(\mathsf{Req})$, then sends the SOAP envelope on the network and the attacker intercepts it, so we have the clause:

$$\begin{array}{l}\mathsf{m\text{-}event}(b(\mathsf{Req})) \Rightarrow \mathsf{att}((\langle(\mathsf{Signature}, \mathsf{ids}, (\langle(\mathsf{idb}, sha1(\mathsf{Req}))\rangle, \\ \quad sign((\langle(\mathsf{idb}, sha1(\mathsf{Req}))\rangle, \mathsf{sk})))), (\mathsf{Body}, \mathsf{idb}, \mathsf{Req})\rangle, \mathsf{Req})).\end{array} \tag{3}$$

The server expects a document $(list(i \le M, (tag_i, id_i, cont_i)), r)$; he checks the signature, and if the check succeeds, he executes the event $e(r)$:

$$\begin{array}{l}
\mathsf{att}((list(i \le M, (tag_i, id_i, cont_i)), r)) \wedge \\
\{tag_j \doteq \mathsf{Signature}, cont_j \doteq (sinfo, sign(sinfo, \mathsf{sk})), \\
\quad sinfo \doteq list(k \le N, (id_{\phi(k)}, sha1(cont_{\phi(k)}))), \\
\quad \phi(m) \doteq d, tag_d \doteq \mathsf{Body}\} \Rightarrow \\
\qquad \mathsf{event}(e(r))
\end{array} \tag{4}$$

This clause uses the equations explained in Section 3.2.

As already mentioned in Section 3.1, this protocol has a wrapping attack. The corrected version of this protocol additionally requires that the signed body is the one that the server authorizes. This additional check can be modeled by adding the equation $cont_d \doteq r$ in the clause (4).

4.3 Type System

In this section, we define a simple type system for generalized Horn clauses, to guarantee that the indices of all variables vary in the appropriate interval.

DEFINITION 4. *An index i is bound if:*

- *it appears as an index of a conjunction defining a fact, so, for instance, in the fact $\bigwedge_{(i_1,\ldots,i_h)\in J} pred(p^G)$, $i_1, \ldots, i_h$ are bound in $pred(p^G)$.*

- *it appears as an index for a list constructor, that is, in the pattern $list(i \le M, p^G)$, i is bound in p^G.*

We identity facts, equations, and clauses up to renaming of bound indices. For simplicity, we suppose that the bound indices of clauses have been renamed so that they have pairwise distinct names, and names distinct from the names of free indices. The set of free indices of a fact F^G, of a clause R^G, or of an hypothesis H^G is denoted by $fi(F^G)$, $fi(R^G)$, $fi(H^G)$ respectively.

In the type system, the type environment Γ is a list of type declarations:

- $i : [1, M]$ means that i is of type $[1, M]$, that is, intuitively, the value of index i can vary between 1 and the value of the bound M;

- $\phi : [1, M_1] \times \cdots \times [1, M_h] \to [1, M]$ means that the function ϕ expects as input h indices of types $[1, M_j]$, for $j = 1, \ldots, h$ and computes an index of type $[1, M]$;

- $x\_ : [1, M_1] \times \cdots \times [1, M_h]$ means that the variable x expects indices of types $[1, M_1], \ldots, [1, M_h]$;

- $I : [1, M_1] \times \cdots \times [1, M_h]$ means that the elements of set I are tuples of h indices, each of type $[1, M_j]$ for $j = 1, \ldots, h$.

The type system defines the judgments:

- $\Gamma \vdash \iota : [1, M]$, which means that ι has type $[1, M]$ in the type environment Γ;

- $\Gamma \vdash J : [1, M_1] \times \cdots \times [1, M_h]$, which means that the elements of set J are tuples of h indices, each of type $[1, M_j]$ for $j = 1, \ldots, h$ in the type environment Γ;

- $\Gamma \vdash p^G$, $\Gamma \vdash F^G$, $\Gamma \vdash E$, $\Gamma \vdash E'$, $\Gamma \vdash \mathcal{I}$, $\Gamma \vdash R^G$, which mean that p^G, F^G, E, E', $\mathcal{I}$, R^G, respectively, are well-typed in the type environment Γ.

The typing rules are straightforward and are given in the long version of the paper [8]. They basically guarantee that all indices have their expected type.

We suppose that all clauses are well-typed, and we consider that each clause R^G comes with its type environment Γ such that $\Gamma \vdash R^G$. It is easy to verify that the clauses of our running example are all well-typed.

4.4 Translation from Generalized Horn Clauses to Horn Clauses

A generalized Horn clause represents several Horn clauses: for each value of the bounds M, set symbols I, functions ϕ, and free indices i that occur in a generalized Horn clause R^G, R^G corresponds to a certain Horn clause. This section formally defines this correspondence.

DEFINITION 5. *Given a well-typed generalized Horn clause $\Gamma \vdash R^G$, an environment T for $\Gamma \vdash R^G$ is a function that associates:*

- *to each bound M that appears in R^G or Γ an integer M^T;*
- *to each index i such that $i : [1, M] \in \Gamma$, an index $i^T \in \{1, \dots, M^T\}$;*
- *to each index function ϕ such that $\phi : [1, M_1] \times \dots \times [1, M_h] \to [1, M] \in \Gamma$, a function $\phi^T : \{1, \dots, M_1^T\} \times \dots \times \{1, \dots, M_h^T\} \to \{1, \dots, M^T\}$.*
- *to each set symbol I such that $\mathcal{I} : [1, M_1] \times \dots \times [1, M_h] \in \Gamma$, a set I^T such that $\emptyset \subset I^T \subseteq \{1, \dots, M_1^T\} \times \dots \times \{1, \dots, M_h^T\}$;*

Given an environment T and values $v_1, \dots, v_h$, we write $T[i_1 \mapsto v_1, \dots, i_h \mapsto v_h]$ for the environment that associates to indices $i_1, \dots, i_h$ the values $v_1, \dots, v_h$ respectively and that maps all other values like T.

Given an environment T for $\Gamma \vdash R^G$, the generalized Horn clause R^G is translated into the standard Horn clause R^{GT} defined as follows. We denote respectively $p^{GT}, E^T, \dots$ the translation of $p^G, E, \dots$ using the environment T.

The translation of an index term ι such that $\Gamma \vdash \iota : [1, M]$ is an integer $\iota^T \in \{1, \dots, M^T\}$ defined as follows:

$$\iota^T = \begin{cases} i^T & \text{if } \iota = i \\ \phi^T(\iota_1^T, \dots, \iota_h^T) & \text{if } \iota = \phi(\iota_1, \dots, \iota_h) \end{cases}$$

The translation of a pattern p^G is defined as follows:

$$\begin{aligned} (x_{\iota_1, \dots, \iota_h})^T &= x_{\iota_1^T, \dots, \iota_h^T} \\ f(p_1^G, \dots, p_l^G)^T &= f(p_1^{GT}, \dots, p_l^{GT}) \\ a_\iota^M[p_1^G, \dots, p_l^G]^T &= a_{\iota^T}^{M^T}[p_1^{GT}, \dots, p_l^{GT}] \\ list(i \le M, p^G)^T &= \langle p^{GT[i \mapsto 1]}, \dots, p^{GT[i \mapsto M^T]} \rangle \end{aligned}$$

The translation of $list(i \le M, p^G)$ is a list of length M^T.

The translation of a set computation J is a set of tuples defined by:

$$J^T = \begin{cases} I^T & \text{if } J = I \\ \{()\} & \text{if } J = \{()\} \\ J'^T \times \{1, \dots, M^T\} & \text{if } J = J' \times [1, M] \end{cases}$$

In this definition, the cross product $\times$ decomposes tuples before building the whole tuple, so that $J'^T \times \{1, \dots, M^T\} = \{(v_1, \dots, v_h, v) \mid (v_1, \dots, v_h) \in J'^T, v \in \{1, \dots, M^T\}\}$.

Given a conjunction $\mathcal{C} = \bigwedge_{(i_1, \dots, i_h) \in J}$ and an environment T, we define the set of environments $T^{\mathcal{C}} = \{T[i_1 \mapsto v_1, \dots, i_h \mapsto v_h] \mid (v_1, \dots, v_h) \in J^T\}$: these environments map the indices $i_1, \dots, i_h$ of the conjunction to all their possible values in J^T and map all other values like T.

The translation of a fact $F = \mathcal{C}\, pred(p^G)$ is

$$(\mathcal{C}\, pred(p^G))^T = pred(p_1) \wedge \dots \wedge pred(p_k)$$

where $\{p_1, \dots, p_k\} = \{p^{GT'} \mid T' \in T^{\mathcal{C}}\}$, and $(F_1 \wedge \dots \wedge F_n)^T = F_1^T \wedge \dots \wedge F_n^T$.

The translation of a set of equations $\mathcal{E}$ is the set $\mathcal{E}^T$ obtained by translating the equations E, E' as follows:

- $(\mathcal{C}\, \iota \doteq \iota')^T = \begin{cases} true & \text{if for all } T' \in T^{\mathcal{C}}, \iota^{T'} = \iota'^{T'} \\ false & \text{otherwise.} \end{cases}$
- $(\mathcal{C}\, p^G \doteq p'^G)^T = \{p^{GT'} = p'^{GT'} \mid T' \in T^{\mathcal{C}}\}$.
- If $\forall E' \in \mathcal{E}, E'^T = true$, then $\mathcal{E}^T = \bigcup_{E \in \mathcal{E}} E^T$; otherwise, $\mathcal{E}^T$ is undefined.

The equations over indices can be evaluated to *true* or *false* knowing the environment T. The equations over generalized patterns are translated into equations over patterns. A set of equations $\mathcal{E}$ is translated into a set of equations over patterns if all equations over indices are true. Otherwise, the translation of $\mathcal{E}$ is undefined.

Given a set of constraints *Cts* and an environment T, we say that T satisfies *Cts* when, for all equations $I_1 \uplus \dots \uplus I_m = J$ in *Cts*, we have that $I_1^T \uplus \dots \uplus I_m^T = J^T$, that is, $I_1^T, \dots, I_m^T$ are pairwise disjoint and their union is J^T.

Given a set of equations $\{p_1 = p_1', \dots, p_n = p_n'\}$ over standard patterns, we define as usual its most general unifier $\text{MGU}(\{p_1 = p_1', \dots, p_n = p_n'\})$ as the most general substitution σ such that $\sigma p_i = \sigma p_i'$ for all $i \in \{1, \dots, n\}$, $dom(\sigma) \cup fv(im(\sigma)) \subseteq fv(p_1, p_1', \dots, p_n, p_n')$, and $dom(\sigma) \cap fv(im(\sigma)) = \emptyset$, where $fv(p)$ designates the (free) variables of p, $dom(\sigma)$ is the domain of σ: $dom(\sigma) = \{x \mid \sigma x \neq x\}$, and $im(\sigma)$ is the image of σ: $im(\sigma) = \{\sigma x \mid \sigma x \neq x\}$. We denote by $\{x_1 \mapsto p_1, \dots, x_n \mapsto p_n\}$ the substitution that maps x_i to p_i for all $i = 1, \dots, n$.

Finally, we define the translation of the generalized Horn clause $R^G = Cts, H^G \wedge \mathcal{E} \Rightarrow pred(p^G)$ as follows. If T does not satisfy *Cts*, $\mathcal{E}^T$ is undefined, or the unification of $\mathcal{E}^T$ fails, then R^{GT} is undefined. Otherwise, $R^{GT} = \text{MGU}(\mathcal{E}^T)H^{GT} \Rightarrow \text{MGU}(\mathcal{E}^T)pred(p^{GT})$.

When $\mathcal{R}^G$ is a set of well-typed generalized Horn clauses (i.e., a set of pairs of a type environment Γ and a clause R^G such that $\Gamma \vdash R^G$), we define $\mathcal{R}^{GT} = \{R^{GT} \mid \Gamma \vdash R^G \in \mathcal{R}^G$, T is an environment for $\Gamma \vdash R^G$ and R^{GT} is defined$\}$. In terms of abstract interpretation, the sets of generalized Horn clauses ordered by inclusion constitute the abstract domain, the sets of Horn clauses ordered by inclusion the concrete domain, and $\mathcal{R}^{GT}$ is the concretization of $\mathcal{R}^G$.

5. RESOLUTION FOR GENERALIZED HORN CLAUSES

In this section, we adapt ProVerif's resolution algorithm to generalized Horn clauses: we first define adapted algorithms for subsumption, resolution, and unification, and then use these components to build the new resolution algorithm.

5.1 Subsumption

To adapt the subsumption test to generalized Horn clauses, we first define adapted notions of substitutions, then define subsumption and prove its soundness.

DEFINITION 6 (SUBSTITUTIONS). *We denote by ρ a substitution that maps:*

- *bounds to bounds $\rho(M) = N$;*
- *index variables to index terms: $\rho(i) = \iota$;*
- *set symbols to set symbols: $\rho(I) = I'$;*
- *function symbols ϕ to function symbols: $\rho(\phi) = \phi'$.*

We denote by σ^G a substitution that maps variables to patterns: $\sigma^G(x_{i_1,\dots,i_h}) = p^G$ where $fi(p^G) \subseteq \{i_1, \dots, i_h\}$.

As usual, substitutions are extended from variables to index terms, patterns, facts, equations, constraints, and clauses as homomorphisms: for instance, $\rho(\phi(\iota_1, \dots, \iota_k)) = (\rho(\phi))(\rho(\iota_1), \dots, \rho(\iota_k))$. However, since the grammar of generalized Horn clauses is richer than usual, we need to notice two points:

- Substitutions avoid the capture of bound indices: if $i \notin dom(\rho)$ and $i \notin fi(im(\rho))$, $\rho(list(i \leq M, p^G)) = list(i \leq \rho(M), \rho(p^G))$, which can be guaranteed by renaming i if necessary. We have similar formulas for indices bound by conjunctions as well as for substitutions σ^G.
- The substitutions σ^G are extended from variables $x_{i_1,\dots,i_h}$ with indices $i_1, \dots, i_h$ to variables $x_{\iota_1,\dots,\iota_h}$ with terms $\iota_1, \dots, \iota_h$ as indices: if $\sigma^G(x_{i_1,\dots,i_h}) = p^G$, then $\sigma^G(x_{\iota_1,\dots,\iota_h}) = \rho p^G$ where $\rho = \{i_1 \mapsto \iota_1, \dots, i_h \mapsto \iota_h\}$.

We need a notion of subsumption between type environments, which is intuitively $\rho\Gamma_1 \subseteq \Gamma_2$. However, we cannot use exactly $\rho\Gamma_1 \subseteq \Gamma_2$ because ρ maps indices to index terms and not to indices, so we define $\Gamma_1 \leq_\rho \Gamma_2$ by:

- for each $i : [1, M] \in \Gamma_1$, we have $\Gamma_2 \vdash \rho i : [1, \rho M]$;
- for each $\phi : [1, M_1] \times \cdots \times [1, M_h] \to [1, M] \in \Gamma_1$, we have $\rho\phi : [1, \rho M_1] \times \cdots \times [1, \rho M_h] \to [1, \rho M] \in \Gamma_2$;
- for each $I : [1, M_1] \times \cdots \times [1, M_h] \in \Gamma_1$, we have $\rho I : [1, \rho M_1] \times \cdots \times [1, \rho M_h] \in \Gamma_2$;
- for each $x\_ : [1, M_1] \times \cdots \times [1, M_h] \in \Gamma_1$, we have $x\_ : [1, \rho M_1] \times \cdots \times [1, \rho M_h] \in \Gamma_2$.

DEFINITION 7 (SUBSUMPTION). *Given two well-typed generalized Horn clauses, $\Gamma_1 \vdash R_1^G$ and $\Gamma_2 \vdash R_2^G$, with $R_1^G = Cts_1, H_1^G \wedge \mathcal{E}_1 \Rightarrow C_1^G$ and $R_2^G = Cts_2, H_2^G \wedge \mathcal{E}_2 \Rightarrow C_2^G$, we say that $\Gamma_1 \vdash R_1^G$ subsumes $\Gamma_2 \vdash R_2^G$, and we write $\Gamma_1 \vdash R_1^G \sqsupseteq \Gamma_2 \vdash R_2^G$, if there exist substitutions ρ and σ^G such that $\sigma^G \rho C_1^G = C_2^G$, $\sigma^G \rho H_1^G \subseteq H_2^G$ (multiset inclusion), $\sigma^G \rho \mathcal{E}_1 \subseteq \mathcal{E}_2$ (modulo commutativity of $\doteq$), $\rho Cts_1 \subseteq Cts_2$ (modulo associativity and commutativity of $\uplus$), and $\Gamma_1 \leq_\rho \Gamma_2$.*

This definition is similar to subsumption for standard clauses but uses the richer substitutions introduced above.

Example 1. The clause

$$R_1^G = \{I \uplus I_1 = [1, M]\}, \textstyle\bigwedge_{i \in I} \mathsf{att}(sign(x_i, \mathsf{sk}^L_{\phi(l)})) \wedge \{\textstyle\bigwedge_{m \in I_1} y_m \doteq \mathsf{c}^M_m\} \Rightarrow \mathsf{att}(y_l)$$

typed by the type environment $\Gamma_1 = \{I : [1, M], I_1 : [1, M], x\_ : [1, M], \phi : [1, M] \to [1, L], y\_ [1, M], l : [1, M]\}$, subsumes the clause

$$R_2^G = \{I' \uplus I_1' = [1, N]\}, \textstyle\bigwedge_{j \in I'} \mathsf{att}(sign((\mathsf{r}^N_{\psi(j)}, \mathsf{s}^N_{\psi(j)}), \mathsf{sk}^O_{\varphi(\psi(k))})) \wedge \{\textstyle\bigwedge_{n \in I_1'} z_n \doteq \mathsf{c}^N_n\} \Rightarrow \mathsf{att}(z_{\psi(k)}).$$

typed by the environment $\Gamma_2 = \{I' : [1, N], I_1' = [1, N], \psi : [1, N] \to [1, N], \varphi : [1, N] \to [1, O], k : [1, N], z\_ : [1, N], k : [1, N]\}$ With $\rho = \{M \mapsto N, L \mapsto O, I \mapsto I', I_1 \mapsto I_1', \phi \mapsto \varphi, l \mapsto \psi(k)\}$ and renaming the bound indices i into j and m into n, we obtain:

$$\rho R_1^G = \{I' \uplus I_1' = [1, N]\}, \textstyle\bigwedge_{j \in I'} \mathsf{att}(sign(x_j, \mathsf{sk}^O_{\varphi(\psi(k))})) \wedge \{\textstyle\bigwedge_{n \in I_1'} y_n \doteq \mathsf{c}^N_n\} \Rightarrow \mathsf{att}(y_{\psi(k)})$$

and conclude that R_1^G subsumes R_2^G using the substitution

$$\sigma^G = \{x_i \mapsto (\mathsf{r}^N_{\psi(i)}, \mathsf{s}^N_{\psi(i)}), y_i \mapsto z_i\}.$$

The following theorem shows the soundness of subsumption for generalized Horn clauses.

THEOREM 2 (SUBSUMPTION). *Let $\Gamma_1 \vdash R_1^G$ and $\Gamma_2 \vdash R_2^G$ be two well-typed clauses. If $\Gamma_1 \vdash R_1^G \sqsupseteq \Gamma_2 \vdash R_2^G$ then, for all environments T_2 for $\Gamma_2 \vdash R_2^G$ such that $R_2^{GT_2}$ is defined, there exists an environment T_1 for $\Gamma_1 \vdash R_1^G$ such that $R_1^{GT_1}$ is defined and $R_1^{GT_1} \sqsupseteq R_2^{GT_2}$.*

As for standard clauses, our resolution algorithm for generalized Horn clauses will eliminate subsumed clauses. This theorem shows that, if R_2^G is eliminated in the algorithm for generalized Horn clauses because it is subsumed by R_1^G, then all corresponding clauses $R_2^{GT_2}$ would be eliminated in the algorithm for standard clauses: $R_2^{GT_2}$ is subsumed by some $R_1^{GT_1}$.

The subsumption test is approximate, because clauses that have the same meaning may sometimes be written in different forms. For instance, one can compose two functions ϕ and ψ, always writing $\phi(\psi(i, j))$ instead of a single function $\psi(i, j)$. These two formulas yield the same translation into standard Horn clauses, but are considered different by the subsumption test. This approximation does not contradict the soundness of subsumption, and the subsumption test is precise enough for the proof to succeed on our examples.

Because of the presence of indices, the algorithm for computing the substitutions ρ and σ^G required in Definition 7 is more complex than for standard clauses. We detail it in the long version of the paper [8].

5.2 Resolution and Hyperresolution

As introduced in Section 3.2, resolution becomes hyperresolution for generalized clauses. We first give the formal definition of hyperresolution, then explain it.

DEFINITION 8 (HYPERRESOLUTION). *Let* $R_1^G = Cts_1, H_1^G \wedge \mathcal{E}_1 \Rightarrow C_1^G$ *and* $R_2^G = Cts_2, F_0^G \wedge H_2^G \wedge \mathcal{E}_2 \Rightarrow C_2^G$ *be two clauses. We rename* R_1^G *and* R_2^G *so that they do not use common names for bounds* M*, variables* x*, indices* i*, functions on indices* ϕ*, and set symbols* I*.*

First case: $F_0^G = \bigwedge_{(i_1,\dots,i_h)\in J} pred_2(p_2^G)$ $(h \neq 0)$*. Let* $\Gamma_1 \vdash R_1^G$ *and* J *such that* $\Gamma_2 \vdash J : [1, M_1] \times \dots \times [1, M_h]$*. The immersion of* R_1^G *into* $(i_1, \dots, i_h) \in J$ *is the clause* $imm(R_1^G, (i_1, \dots, i_h) \in J)$ *obtained by replacing:*

1. *all free indices* i *of* R_1^G *with* $\phi'(i_1, \dots, i_h)$*, where a new function symbol* ϕ' *is associated to each free index* i *of* R_1^G*;*
2. *all index terms* $\phi(\iota_1, \dots, \iota_k)$ *with* $\phi'(i_1, \dots, i_h, \iota_1, \dots, \iota_k)$*, where a new function symbol* ϕ' *is associated to each function symbol* ϕ *in* R_1^G*;*
3. *all variables* $x_{\iota_1,\dots,\iota_k}$ *in* R_1^G *with* $x_{i_1,\dots,i_h,\iota_1,\dots,\iota_k}$*;*
4. *all conjunctions* $\bigwedge_{(j_1,\dots,j_k)\in[1,M'_1]\times\dots\times[1,M'_k]}$ *in* H_1^G *and* $\mathcal{E}_1$ *with* $\bigwedge_{(i_1,\dots,i_h,j_1,\dots,j_k)\in J\times[1,M'_1]\times\dots\times[1,M'_k]}$*;*
5. *all conjunctions* $\bigwedge_{(j_1,\dots,j_k)\in I\times[1,M'_1]\times\dots\times[1,M'_l]}$ *in* H_1^G *and* $\mathcal{E}_1$ *with* $\bigwedge_{(i_1,\dots,i_h,j_1,\dots,j_k)\in I'\times[1,M'_1]\times\dots\times[1,M'_l]}$*, where a new set symbol* I' *is associated to each set symbol* I *in* R_1^G*;*
6. *all constraints* $I_1 \uplus \dots \uplus I_n = [1, M'_1] \times \dots \times [1, M'_k]$ *in* Cts_1 *with* $I'_1 \uplus \dots \uplus I'_n = J \times [1, M'_1] \times \dots \times [1, M'_k]$ *and all constraints* $I_1 \uplus \dots \uplus I_n = I \times [1, M'_1] \times \dots \times [1, M'_k]$ *in* Cts_1 *with* $I'_1 \uplus \dots \uplus I'_n = I' \times [1, M'_1] \times \dots \times [1, M'_k]$*.*

Let $imm(R_1^G, (i_1, \dots, i_h) \in J) = Cts_J, H_J^G \wedge \mathcal{E}_J \Rightarrow pred_1(p_1^G)$*. If* $pred_1 = pred_2$*, we define:*

$$R_1^G \circ^{\text{Full}}_{F_0^G} R_2^G = Cts_J \cup Cts_2, H_J^G \wedge H_2^G \wedge (\{\textstyle\bigwedge_{(i_1,\dots,i_h)\in J} p_1^G \doteq p_2^G\} \cup \mathcal{E}_J \cup \mathcal{E}_2) \Rightarrow C_2^G$$

Let I' *and* I'' *be fresh set symbols. Let* $imm(R_1^G, (i_1, \dots, i_h) \in I') = Cts_{I'}, H_{I'}^G \wedge \mathcal{E}_{I'} \Rightarrow pred_1(p_1^G)$*. If* $pred_1 = pred_2$*, we define:*

$$R_1^G \circ^{\text{Part}}_{F_0^G} R_2^G = Cts_{I'} \cup Cts_2 \cup \{I' \uplus I'' = J\}, (H_{I'}^G \wedge \textstyle\bigwedge_{(i_1,\dots,i_h)\in I''} pred_2(p_2^G) \wedge H_2^G) \wedge (\{\textstyle\bigwedge_{(i_1,\dots,i_h)\in I'} p_1^G \doteq p_2^G\} \cup \mathcal{E}_{I'} \cup \mathcal{E}_2) \Rightarrow C_2^G.$$

Second case: $F_0^G = pred_2(p_2^G)$ *(ordinary resolution). If* $pred_1 = pred_2$*, we define* $R_1^G \circ^{\text{Full}}_{F_0^G} R_2^G = Cts_1 \cup Cts_2, H_1^G \wedge H_2^G \wedge (\{p_1^G \doteq p_2^G\} \cup \mathcal{E}_1 \cup \mathcal{E}_2) \Rightarrow C_2^G$*.* $R_1^G \circ^{\text{Part}}_{F_0^G} R_2^G$ *is undefined.*

Intuitively, the immersion of $R^G = H^G \Rightarrow C^G$ into $(i_1, \dots, i_h) \in J$ corresponds to $\bigwedge_{(i_1,\dots,i_h)\in J} H^G(i_1, \dots, i_h) \Rightarrow C^G(i_1, \dots, i_h)$, which represents the combination of a distinct instance of R^G for each $(i_1, \dots, i_h) \in J$, as outlined in Section 3.2. To represent distinct instances of R^G, the free indices i, variables x, and functions ϕ use $(i_1, \dots, i_h)$ as additional indices or arguments. Sets I should also become functions of the indices $(i_1, \dots, i_h)$; however, to simplify the syntax of generalized Horn clauses, we avoid sets that depend on indices: when $\bigwedge_{(j_1,\dots,j_k)\in I\times[1,M_1]\times\dots\times[1,M_l]} pred(p^G) \in H^G$, instead of writing

$$\textstyle\bigwedge_{(i_1,\dots,i_h)\in J} \bigwedge_{(j_1,\dots,j_k)\in I(i_1,\dots,i_h)\times[1,M_1]\times\dots\times[1,M_l]} pred(p^G)$$

we write $\bigwedge_{(i_1,\dots,i_h,j_1,\dots,j_k)\in I'\times[1,M_1]\times\dots\times[1,M_l]} pred(p^G)$ where the symbol I' stands for $\{(i_1, \dots, i_h, j_1, \dots, j_{k-l}) \mid (i_1, \dots, i_h) \in J, (j_1, \dots, j_{k-l}) \in I(i_1, \dots, i_h)\}$. This leads to point 5 of the definition of immersion, and the corresponding transformation of constraints in point 6. This transformation introduces a minor approximation, since the obtained clause does not keep the information on how the set I' is built.

In order to resolve $R_2^G = Cts_2, F_0^G \wedge H_2^G \wedge \mathcal{E}_2 \Rightarrow C_2^G$ with R_1^G upon $F_0^G = \bigwedge_{(i_1,\dots,i_h)\in J} pred_2(p_2^G)$, we perform the resolution on any non-empty subset I' of J. We distinguish two cases: either I' is the full set J, and we produce the full hyperresolution $R_1^G \circ^{\text{Full}}_{F_0^G} R_2^G$, or I' is a strict subset of J, and we produce the partial hyperresolution $R_1^G \circ^{\text{Part}}_{F_0^G} R_2^G$. In the latter case, using the set I'' such that $I' \uplus I'' = J$, R_2^G can also be written $R_2^G = Cts_2 \cup \{I' \uplus I'' = J\}, \bigwedge_{(i_1,\dots,i_h)\in I'} pred_2(p_2^G) \wedge \bigwedge_{(i_1,\dots,i_h)\in I''} pred_2(p_2^G) \wedge H_2^G \wedge \mathcal{E}_2 \Rightarrow C_2^G$. We can then perform resolution upon $F_{I'}^G = \bigwedge_{(i_1,\dots,i_h)\in I'} pred_2(p_2^G)$ for the full set I'. We use the immersion to compute a clause $R_{I'}^G$ that corresponds to instances of R_1^G for all $(i_1, \dots, i_h) \in I'$, and then perform a fairly standard resolution step: we require that the conclusion of $R_{I'}^G$ equals the hypothesis $F_{I'}^G$ of R_2^G and generate the combined clause. (The unification of the conclusion of $R_{I'}^G$ with the hypothesis $F_{I'}^G$ of R_2^G is delayed until the simplification of clauses, described in Section 5.3.)

When $h = 0$ and $J = \{()\}$, $F_0^G = pred_2(p_2^G)$ and J is a singleton, so $R_1^G \circ^{\text{Part}}_{F_0^G} R_2^G$ does not exist, and we perform an ordinary resolution step. (Immersion is not necessary.)

THEOREM 3 (RESOLUTION). *Let* $\Gamma_1 \vdash R_1^G$ *and* $\Gamma_2 \vdash R_2^G$ *be two well-typed clauses, such that* $R_2^G = Cts_2, F_0^G \wedge H_2^G \wedge \mathcal{E}_2 \Rightarrow C_2^G$*. We have* $\Gamma_{\text{Full}} \vdash R_1^G \circ^{\text{Full}}_{F_0^G} R_2^G$ *and* $\Gamma_{\text{Part}} \vdash R_1^G \circ^{\text{Part}}_{F_0^G} R_2^G$ *for some type environments* Γ_{Full} *and* Γ_{Part} *(when these clauses are defined).*

Let T_i *be an environment for* $\Gamma_i \vdash R_i^G$ *such that* $R_i^{GT_i}$ *is defined, for* $i = 1, 2$*. Let* $F_0 \in \text{MGU}(\mathcal{E}_2^{T_2})F_0^{GT_2}$ *be a fact in the hypothesis of* $R_2^{GT_2}$ *that comes from the translation* F_0^G*. Suppose that* $R_1^{GT_1}$ *and* $R_2^{GT_2}$ *can be resolved upon* F_0 *into the clause* R*. Then* R *is equal to* $(R_1^G \circ^{\text{Full}}_{F_0^G} R_2^G)^T$ *or* $(R_1^G \circ^{\text{Part}}_{F_0^G} R_2^G)^T$ *up to renaming of variables, for some environment* T *for* $\Gamma_{\text{Full}} \vdash R_1^G \circ^{\text{Full}}_{F_0^G} R_2^G$ *(resp.* $\Gamma_{\text{Part}} \vdash R_1^G \circ^{\text{Part}}_{F_0^G} R_2^G$*).*

Example 2. Let us consider the following two clauses:

$$R_1^G = \text{att}(x) \Rightarrow \text{att}(\mathit{sha1}(x)) \tag{5}$$

$$R_2^G = \textstyle\bigwedge_{i\in[1,L]} \text{att}(\mathit{sha1}(\mathit{cont}_{\phi(i)})) \wedge \text{att}(\mathit{sign}(\mathit{list}(i \le L, \mathit{sha1}(\mathit{cont}_{\phi(i)})), \mathsf{sk})) \Rightarrow \text{event}(e(r)) \tag{6}$$

To compute the partial hyperresolution of (6) with (5) for a set I, we compute the immersion of (5) into $i \in I$: we add to x the index i and we add a conjunction $\bigwedge_{i\in I}$ in the hypothesis (replacing the omitted empty conjunction $\bigwedge_{()\in\{()\}}$):

$$\textstyle\bigwedge_{i\in I} \text{att}(x_i) \Rightarrow \text{att}(\mathit{sha1}(x_i)) \tag{7}$$

Partial hyperresolution yields

$$R_1^G \circ^{\text{Part}}_{F_0} R_2^G = \{I \uplus I' = [1, L]\}, \textstyle\bigwedge_{i\in I} \text{att}(x_i) \wedge \bigwedge_{i\in I'} \text{att}(\mathit{sha1}(\mathit{cont}_{\phi(i)})) \wedge \text{att}(\mathit{sign}(\mathit{list}(i \le L, \mathit{sha1}(\mathit{cont}_{\phi(i)})), \mathsf{sk})) \wedge \{\bigwedge_{i\in I} \mathit{sha1}(x_i) \doteq \mathit{sha1}(\mathit{cont}_{\phi(i)})\} \Rightarrow \text{event}(e(r)) \tag{8}$$

This clause will be further simplified by the transformations given in Section 5.3.

5.3 Simplification of Clauses

We use several additional transformations in order to simplify clauses. Some of these transformations are easily adapted from similar transformations already used in ProVerif. We summarize here the new transformations and refer the reader to the long version of the paper [8] for details on all these transformations.

5.3.1 Unification

Instead of performing unification as part of resolution, we simplify equations a posteriori. The main simplifications are as follows. (The others are detailed in the long version of the paper [8].)

- We decompose equations. We replace the equation $\mathcal{C}\, f(p_1^G, \dots, p_k^G) \doteq f(p_1'^G, \dots, p_k'^G)$ with $\mathcal{C}\, p_1^G \doteq p_1'^G$, ..., $\mathcal{C}\, p_k^G \doteq p_k'^G$. We replace the equation $\mathcal{C}\, a_\iota^M[p_1^G, \dots, p_k^G] \doteq a_{\iota'}^{M'}[p_1'^G, \dots, p_k'^G]$ with $\mathcal{C}\, p_1^G \doteq p_1'^G$, ..., $\mathcal{C}\, p_k^G \doteq p_k'^G$, $\mathcal{C}\, \iota \doteq \iota'$ and replace every occurrence of M' in the clause with M. We replace the equation $\bigwedge_{(i_1,\dots,i_h)\in J} \mathit{list}(i \le M, p^G) \doteq \mathit{list}(i \le M', p'^G)$ with $\bigwedge_{(i_1,\dots,i_h,i)\in J\times[1,M]} p^G \doteq p'^G$ and replace every occurrence of M' in the clause with M.

  The equation $\bigwedge_{(i_1,\dots,i_{h'})\in J} \mathit{list}(i \le M, p^G) \doteq \langle p_1^G, \dots, p_h^G\rangle$ can be handled in two ways. The preferred solution is to instantiate M into the integer h. In this instantiation, variables x that have an index of type $[1, M]$ become h variables x_1, ..., x_h, and functions ϕ that have an argument of type $[1, M]$ become h functions ϕ_1, ..., ϕ_h. After instantiation, we apply unification again on the obtained clause(s). This solution is applied when the clause contains no function ϕ with a result of type $[1, M]$, no set symbol I with a type that contains $[1, M]$, and no name with an index of type $[1, M]$. (Otherwise, the instantiated clause may not fit in our language of clauses.) When this instantiation cannot be applied, we replace the equation with

  $$\bigwedge_{(i_1,\dots,i_{h'},i)\in J\times[1,M]} x_{i_1,\dots,i_{h'},i} \doteq p^G,$$
  $$\bigwedge_{(i_1,\dots,i_{h'},i)\in I_1} x_{i_1,\dots,i_{h'},i} \doteq p_1^G, \dots,$$
  $$\bigwedge_{(i_1,\dots,i_{h'},i)\in I_h} x_{i_1,\dots,i_{h'},i} \doteq p_h^G$$

  and add the constraint $I_1 \uplus \dots \uplus I_h = J \times [1, M]$, where x is a fresh variable and $I_1, \dots, I_h$ are fresh set symbols. Intuitively, the variable $x_{i_1,\dots,i_{h'},i}$ contains the i-th element of the list. This solution introduces an approximation: we remember that the elements of the list are p_1^G, ..., p_h^G but we forget their order and their number of repetitions.

  The clause is removed when the two sides of the equation have different root function symbols. The equation is removed when its two sides are identical.

- When there is an equation $\bigwedge_{(i_1,\dots,i_h)\in J} x_{\iota_1,\dots,\iota_k} \doteq p^G$, we replace $x\_$ with its value (provided the indices of x match, and no occurrence of x in p'^G can be replaced; the latter condition serves to avoid loops).

- When there is an equation $i \doteq \iota$ and i does not occur in ι, we replace i with ι and delete the equation.

- When one of the two sides of an equation is a variable that does not occur anywhere else in the clause, we remove that equation.

Example 3. Applying these transformations, the clause (8) becomes

$$R_1^G \circ_{F_0}^{\text{Part}} R_2^G = \{I \uplus I' = [1, L]\}, \bigwedge_{i\in I} \mathsf{att}(\mathit{cont}_{\phi(i)}) \wedge$$
$$\bigwedge_{i\in I'} \mathsf{att}(\mathit{sha1}(\mathit{cont}_{\phi(i)})) \wedge \quad (9)$$
$$\mathsf{att}(\mathit{sign}(\mathit{list}(i \le L, \mathit{sha1}(\mathit{cont}_{\phi(i)})), \mathsf{sk})) \Rightarrow \mathsf{event}(e(r))$$

Indeed, the equation $\bigwedge_{i\in I} \mathit{sha1}(x_i) \doteq \mathit{sha1}(\mathit{cont}_{\phi(i)})$ first becomes $\bigwedge_{i\in I} x_i \doteq \mathit{cont}_{\phi(i)}$, then $\mathit{cont}_{\phi(i)}$ is substituted for x_i, and the equation is removed.

The unication algorithm is not complete, in that for some complex equations, it may be unable to use the equations to simplify the clause or to remove it, even though that would be sound. This limitation may be lead to false attacks. In practice, the algorithm is still precise enough to be able the prove all desired properties of our case studies (Section 6).

5.3.2 Merging of Sets

When a clause uses two disjoint sets I and I' in the same facts and equations (up to renaming), we merge these two sets into a single set I''. This transformation is key to obtain termination of the algorithm: when a clause R^G is obtained by partial hyperresolution of two clauses R_1^G and R_2^G, it can be resolved again with R_1^G into R'^G, and so on, which would yield an infinite loop. However, by merging sets in R'^G, we can build a clause that is subsumed by R^G, and so removed, which stops the loop. We illustrate this point on an example. The clause (9) can be resolved again by partial hyperresolution with the clause (6). We obtain:

$$\{I \uplus I' = [1, L], I_1 \uplus I_1' = I'\}, \bigwedge_{i\in I} \mathsf{att}(\mathit{cont}_{\phi(i)}) \wedge$$
$$\bigwedge_{i\in I_1} \mathsf{att}(\mathit{cont}_{\phi(i)}) \wedge$$
$$\bigwedge_{i\in I_1'} \mathsf{att}(\mathit{sha1}(\mathit{cont}_{\phi(i)})) \wedge$$
$$\mathsf{att}(\mathit{sign}(\mathit{list}(i \le L, \mathit{sha1}(\mathit{cont}_{\phi(i)})), \mathsf{sk})) \Rightarrow \mathsf{event}(e(r))$$

which could be resolved again with (6). However, after replacing the two constraints with $I \uplus I_1 \uplus I_1' = [1, L]$, we merge I and I_1 together into the set I_2:

$$\{I_2 \uplus I_1' = [1, L]\}, \bigwedge_{i\in I_2} \mathsf{att}(\mathit{cont}_{\phi(i)}) \wedge$$
$$\bigwedge_{i\in I_1'} \mathsf{att}(\mathit{sha1}(\mathit{cont}_{\phi(i)})) \wedge$$
$$\mathsf{att}(\mathit{sign}(\mathit{list}(i \le L, \mathit{sha1}(\mathit{cont}_{\phi(i)})), \mathsf{sk})) \Rightarrow \mathsf{event}(e(r))$$

This clause will be removed by the algorithm of Section 5.4, because it is subsumed by (9), so the loop is avoided.

The merging of sets is not always able to avoid loops that come from partial hyperresolution, in particular when a fresh bound M is created at each partial hyperresolution step. This limitation is the main new cause of non-termination, but its impact is limited in practice since the selection function is tuned to avoid partial hyperresolution when possible.

5.3.3 Soundness of Simplification

Let $\textsc{simp}(\Gamma \vdash R^G)$ be the set of well-typed generalized Horn clauses obtained by simplifying R^G as described above. This function is naturally extended to sets of clauses. The following theorem shows the soundness of SIMP.

$\text{SATUR}^G(\mathcal{R}_0^G) =$

1. $\mathcal{R}^G \leftarrow \text{ELIM}^G(\text{SIMP}(\mathcal{R}_0^G))$.
2. Repeat until a fixpoint is reached:
   for each $\Gamma \vdash R^G \in \mathcal{R}^G$ such that $sel^G(R^G) = \emptyset$,
   for each $\Gamma' \vdash R'^G \in \mathcal{R}^G$, for each $F_0^G \in sel^G(R'^G)$,
   $\mathcal{R}^G \leftarrow \text{ELIM}^G(\text{SIMP}(\{\Gamma_{\text{Full}} \vdash R^G \circ_{F_0^G}^{\text{Full}} R'^G,$
   $\Gamma_{\text{Part}} \vdash R^G \circ_{F_0^G}^{\text{Part}} R'^G\}) \cup \mathcal{R}^G)$.
3. Return $\{\Gamma \vdash R^G \in \mathcal{R}^G \mid sel^G(R^G) = \emptyset\}$.

Figure 4: New Resolution Algorithm

THEOREM 4. *Let $\Gamma \vdash R^G$ be a well-typed generalized Horn clause. For all environments T for $\Gamma \vdash R^G$, if R^{GT} is defined, then there exist a clause $\Gamma' \vdash R'^G \in \text{SIMP}(\Gamma \vdash R^G)$ and an environment T' for $\Gamma' \vdash R'^G$ such that $R'^{GT'} \sqsupseteq R^{GT}$.*

5.4 Extension of the Resolution Algorithm

The resolution algorithm for generalized Horn clauses simulates the one for standard Horn clauses. We need to define a generalized selection function sel^G.

DEFINITION 9 (GENERALIZED SELECTION FUNCTION). *A generalized selection function is a function from generalized Horn clauses to sets of facts, such that $sel^G(Cts,\ H^G \wedge \mathcal{E} \Rightarrow C^G) \subseteq H^G$.*

Similarly to the case of standard Horn clauses, a good generalized selection function does not select $\text{m-event}(p^G)$ nor $\text{att}(x_{\iota_1,\dots,\iota_h})$. Furthermore, resolution is much simpler for facts $\text{att}(p^G)$ without conjunction than for facts with conjunction, so we select a fact without conjunction when possible. Hence, we use the following selection function:

$$sel^G(Cts,\ H^G \wedge \mathcal{E} \Rightarrow C^G) = \begin{cases} \{\text{att}(p^G)\} & \text{if } \text{att}(p^G) \in H^G \text{ for some non-variable } p^G \\ \emptyset & \text{if the first case does not apply and} \\ & C^G = \text{att}(p^G) \text{ for some non-variable } p^G \\ \{\mathcal{C}\,\text{att}(p^G)\} & \text{if the previous cases do not apply and} \\ & \mathcal{C}\,\text{att}(p^G) \in H^G \text{ for some non-variable } p^G \\ \emptyset & \text{otherwise} \end{cases}$$

The resolution algorithm is shown in Figure 4. It mimics the algorithm of Figure 2: $\text{SATUR}^G(\mathcal{R}_0^G)$ first inserts in $\mathcal{R}^G$ the clauses in $\mathcal{R}_0^G$ after elimination of subsumed clauses by ELIM^G: when $\Gamma' \vdash R'^G$ subsumes $\Gamma \vdash R^G$ and both $\Gamma \vdash R^G$ and $\Gamma' \vdash R'^G$ are in $\mathcal{R}^G$, $\Gamma \vdash R^G$ is removed by $\text{ELIM}^G(\mathcal{R}^G)$. Next, the resolution algorithm performs hyperresolution until a fixpoint is reached. Finally, it returns the clauses in $\mathcal{R}^G$ with no selected hypothesis.

Let $\mathcal{F}_{\text{me}}$ be any set of facts of the form $\text{m-event}(p)$.

THEOREM 5. *Let F be a well-typed closed fact and $\mathcal{R}_0^G$ a set of well-typed generalized Horn clauses. If F is derivable from $\mathcal{R}_0^{G\mathcal{T}} \cup \mathcal{F}_{\text{me}}$, then F is derivable from*

$$(\text{SATUR}^G(\mathcal{R}_0^G))^{\mathcal{T}} \cup \mathcal{F}_{\text{me}}.$$

This result shows the soundness of our algorithm. Its proof is adapted from the proof of SATUR (Theorem 1) and uses the soundness theorems for resolution, simplification, and subsumption.

To prove that a closed fact $\text{att}(p^{GT})$ is not derivable from $\mathcal{R}_1^{G\mathcal{T}} \cup \mathcal{F}_{\text{me}}$, we use the following result, where att' is a new predicate:

COROLLARY 3. *If $\text{SATUR}^G(\mathcal{R}_1^G \cup \{\text{att}(p^G) \Rightarrow \text{att}'(p^G)\})$ contains no clause of the form $\Gamma \vdash Cts, H^G \wedge \mathcal{E} \Rightarrow \text{att}'(p'^G)$, then, for all environments T, $\text{att}(p^{GT})$ is not derivable from $\mathcal{R}_1^{G\mathcal{T}} \cup \mathcal{F}_{\text{me}}$.*

This corollary is proved like Corollary 1, and makes it possible to prove that the protocol preserves the secrecy of p, for lists of any length.

COROLLARY 4. *Suppose that all clauses of $\text{SATUR}^G(\mathcal{R}_1^G)$ that conclude $\text{event}(e(p^G))$ for some p^G are of the form $\Gamma \vdash Cts, \bigwedge_{(i_1,\dots,i_h)\in[1,M_1]\times\dots\times[1,M_h]} \text{m-event}(e'(p'^G)) \wedge H^G \wedge \mathcal{E} \Rightarrow \text{event}(e(\rho p'^G))$ for some Γ, Cts, $i_1,\dots,i_h$, $M_1,\dots,M_h$, H^G, $\mathcal{E}$, p'^G, and some substitution ρ that maps indices $i_1,\dots,i_h$ to index terms. Then, for all $\mathcal{F}_{\text{me}}$, for all p, if $\text{event}(e(p))$ is derivable from $\mathcal{R}_1^{G\mathcal{T}} \cup \mathcal{F}_{\text{me}}$, then $\text{m-event}(e'(p)) \in \mathcal{F}_{\text{me}}$.*

This corollary makes it possible to prove that the protocol satisfies the correspondence "if $e(x)$ has been executed, then $e'(x)$ has been executed".

6. EXPERIMENTAL RESULTS

Our algorithm cannot prove authentication for our running example. Indeed, the result of SATUR^G contains a clause of the form

$$\text{att}(r) \wedge \text{m-event}(b(\mathsf{Req})) \wedge \mathcal{E} \Rightarrow \text{event}(e(r))$$

where r does not occur in $\mathcal{E}$. This clause does not satisfy Corollary 4: the event $e(r)$ may be executed for any r that the adversary has, even though only $b(\mathsf{Req})$ has been executed. This clause corresponds to the wrapping attack described in Section 3.1.

In contrast, our algorithm proves authentication for the corrected version of our running example. The only clause in the result of SATUR^G that concludes $\text{event}(e(p^G))$ is of the form

$$\text{m-event}(e(\mathsf{Req})) \wedge \mathcal{E} \Rightarrow \text{event}(e(\mathsf{Req}))$$

Hence, using Corollary 4, we can conclude that, if event $e(r)$ has been executed, then event $b(r)$ has been executed as well. (In our case, the only possible value of r is the request Req of the client.)

In addition to this protocol, we tested our tool on the XML protocols studied in [5]: password digest, password-based signature, X.509 signature, and firewall-based authentication. These are web services security protocols, whose goal is to authenticate a client to a web service. The first two protocols depend on password-based authentication: a password is shared between the user and the server. In the first protocol, a digest of the password, a nonce, and a timestamp is sent by the client to the server. In the second protocol, the client signs its request using a signature key generated from the password. The X.509 signature protocol uses public-key signatures based on X.509 certificates. Finally, the firewall-based authentication protocol uses a SOAP-level firewall in addition to the server and the client. The client uses a password-based signature; the firewall verifies this signature, and when this authentication succeeds, adds a new `firewall` header, signed using its X.509 certificate, indicating that it has authenticated the client. For all these protocols, we automatically proved the authentication property proved manually in [5].

Finally, we also modeled the Asokan-Ginzboorg group protocol [1], and proved the secrecy of the session key. This property was already proved in [19], but on a model less precise than ours. For all these examples, our tool terminates in less than 0.5 s on a MacBook Air 1.4 Ghz. The input files for all these case studies can be found at [8].

7. CONCLUSION AND FUTURE WORK

We have proposed a new type of clauses, generalized Horn clauses, useful to represent protocols that manipulate lists of unbounded length. We have adapted the definitions previously introduced for Horn clauses to these new clauses. We have thus obtained a new algorithm for verifying secrecy and authentication properties for protocols with lists, which we have proved correct and implemented. We have successfully tested our tool on several XML protocols.

ProVerif supports a variant of the applied pi calculus for modeling protocols. However, in this paper, we need to model protocols with generalized Horn clauses. We plan to extend the input language of ProVerif to model protocols with lists of unbounded length, and to translate it automatically to generalized Horn clauses. We also plan to provide an input format with messages in XML, in the style of the tool TulaFale [6], with an extension to unbounded lists.

8. ACKNOWLEDGMENTS

This work was partly supported by the ANR project ProSe (decision number ANR-2010-VERS-004-01). It was partly done while the authors were at École Normale Supérieure, Paris.

9. REFERENCES

[1] N. Asokan and P. Ginzboorg. Key agreement in ad hoc networks. *Computer Communications*, 23(17):1627–1637, 2000.

[2] L. Bachmair and H. Ganzinger. Resolution theorem proving. In A. Robinson and A. Voronkov, editors, *Handbook of Automated Reasoning*, volume 1, chapter 2, pages 19–100. North Holland, 2001.

[3] M. Backes, S. Mödersheim, B. Pfitzmann, and L. Viganò. Symbolic and cryptographic analysis of the secure WS-ReliableMessaging scenario. In *FoSSaCS'06*, volume 3921 of *LNCS*, pages 428–445. Springer, 2006.

[4] M. Bartel, J. Boyer, B. Fox, B. LaMacchia, and E. Simon. XML signature syntax and processing (second edition). Available at `http://www.w3.org/TR/xmldsig-core/`.

[5] K. Bhargavan, C. Fournet, and A. D. Gordon. A semantics for web services authentication. In *POPL'04*, pages 198–209. ACM, 2004.

[6] K. Bhargavan, C. Fournet, A. D. Gordon, and R. Pucella. Tulafale: A security tool for web services. In *FMCO'03*, volume 3188 of *LNCS*, pages 197–222. Springer, 2004.

[7] B. Blanchet. Automatic verification of correspondences for security protocols. *Journal of Computer Security*, 17(4):363–434, July 2009.

[8] B. Blanchet and M. Paiola. Automatic verification of protocols with lists of unbounded length. Long version, files available at `http://prosecco.gforge.inria.fr/personal/bblanche/publications/BlanchetPaiolaCCS13.html`, 2013.

[9] A. Brown, B. Fox, S. Hada, B. LaMacchia, and H. Maruyama. SOAP security extensions: Digital signature. Available at `http://www.w3.org/TR/SOAP-dsig/`.

[10] J. Bryans and S. Schneider. CSP, PVS and recursive authentication protocol. In *DIMACS Workshop on Formal Verification of Security Protocols*, Sept. 1997.

[11] N. Chridi, M. Turuani, and M. Rusinowitch. Constraints-based Verification of Parameterized Cryptographic Protocols. Research Report RR-6712, INRIA, 2008.

[12] N. Chridi, M. Turuani, and M. Rusinowitch. Decidable analysis for a class of cryptographic group protocols with unbounded lists. In *CSF'09*, pages 277–289. IEEE Computer Society, 2009.

[13] D. Dolev and A. C. Yao. On the security of public key protocols. *IEEE Transactions on Information Theory*, IT-29(12):198–208, Mar. 1983.

[14] L. Georgieva, U. Hustadt, and R. A. Schmidt. A new clausal class decidable by hyperresolution. In *CADE-18*, volume 2392 of *LNCS*, pages 260–274. Springer, 2002.

[15] E. Kleiner and A. W. Roscoe. On the relationship between web services security and traditional protocols. In *MFPS 21*, volume 155 of *Electronic Notes in Theoretical Computer Science*, pages 583–603, 2006.

[16] R. Küsters and T. Truderung. On the automatic analysis of recursive security protocols with XOR. In W. Thomas and P. Weil, editors, *STACS'07*, volume 4393 of *LNCS*, pages 646–657. Springer, 2007.

[17] G. Lowe. A hierarchy of authentication specifications. In *CSFW'97*, pages 31–43. IEEE Computer Society, June 1997.

[18] M. Mcintosh and P. Austel. XML signature element wrapping attacks and countermeasures. In *SWS'05*, pages 20–27. ACM, 2005.

[19] M. Paiola and B. Blanchet. Verification of security protocols with lists: from length one to unbounded length. In *POST'12*, volume 7215 of *LNCS*, pages 69–88. Springer, 2012.

[20] L. C. Paulson. Mechanized proofs for a recursive authentication protocol. In *CSFW'97*, pages 84–95. IEEE Computer Society Press, 1997.

[21] A. W. Roscoe and E. Kleiner. Web Services Security: a preliminary study using Casper and FDR. In *Automated Reasoning for Security Protocol Analysis (ARSPA'04)*, 2004.

[22] T. Truderung. Selecting theories and recursive protocols. In *CONCUR 2005*, volume 3653 of *LNCS*, pages 217–232. Springer, 2005.

Relational Abstraction in Community-Based Secure Collaboration

Philip W. L. Fong and Pooya Mehregan
University of Calgary
{ pwlfong, pmehrega }@ucalgary.ca

Ram Krishnan
University of Texas at San Antonio
ram.krishnan@utsa.edu

ABSTRACT

Users of an online community are willing to share resources because they can expect reasonable behaviour from other members of the community. Such expectations are known as social contracts. In this work, we study the specification and enforcement of social contracts in a computer mediated collaboration environment. Specifically, we examine social contracts that contain both relationship- and history-based elements. A series of policy languages, all based on modal and temporal logics, with increasing expressiveness, have been proposed to express social contracts. Reference monitors are designed to correctly and efficiently enforce the specified policies. A technique called "relational abstraction" is employed to reduce the reference monitor into a purely relationship-based protection system, that is, what is commonly known as a social network system.

Categories and Subject Descriptors

D.4.6 [**Security and Protection**]: Access Controls

Keywords

Online community; Social contract; Relationship-based access control; History-based access control; Policy language; Reference monitor; Temporal logic; Hybrid logic

1. INTRODUCTION

Online communities are increasingly organized around social computing platforms or other collaborative software. Examples include collaborative authoring through Wiki and Google Docs, internet forums, online calendar sharing, or open-source development platforms like Source Forge. Proprietary collaboration software tools, such as IBM LotusLive and Microsoft Office 365, are also representative examples.

Individuals are willing to get together as a community, in which they feel safe to share their resources, because they can expect reasonable behaviour from other members of the community. Such behavioural expectations that form the foundation of a community is called a ***social contract*** [27].

Social contracts must be carefully articulated as well as enforced in order for them to be effective in binding individuals into a community. This work is about supporting the effective articulation and enforcement of social contracts in online communities. We use the term ***Community-based Secure Collaboration (CSC)*** to refer to the kind of online collaboration that is mediated by a globally specified and enforced social contract.

From an access control perspective, social contracts determine what accesses are acceptable, and what are not. For example, a seller who has never missed a delivery shall be granted a preferred seller status, which in turn allows her to access privileged advertisement channels. As another example, a volunteer programmer who has contributed code to a certain module of an open source software shall not be a tester for that module. Social contracts typically contain access policies that are not only about who the requestor is (identity), what quality he has (attribute) or the kind of job functions he assumes (role). In the era of social computing, it is typical for social contracts to have policies of the following kinds:

- ***Relationship-based.*** Some policies base authorization decisions on how users are related to one another.
- ***History-based.*** Other policies determine accessibility by considering how users interacted with one another in the past, or how they were related to one another in the past.

Previous works in access control have addressed isolated requirements of social contract articulation and enforcement, but none provides a generic framework for specifying and enforcing policies that are simultaneously relationship based and history based. Krukow *et al.* [25, 26] proposed a history-based framework for specifying the interaction protocol between a pair of users using Pure Past Linear Temporal Logic (PPLTL), and designed an execution monitor architecture for enforcing such policies. Yet, the scheme cannot support interaction protocols (aka social contracts) that span the joint behaviour of a community of individuals. Fong [16] proposed a formal model for Relationship-based Access Control (ReBAC), in which the protection state is a social network of users, authorization decisions are based on how users are related to one another, and policies are expressed in a modal logic, with subsequent extension to employ hybrid logic as a policy language [6]. That line of work, however, does not take into account the historical interactions and

CCS'13, November 4–8, 2013, Berlin, Germany.
Copyright 2013 ACM 978-1-4503-2477-9/13/11 ...$15.00.
http://dx.doi.org/10.1145/2508859.2516720.

relationships among users. Krishnan *et al.* [24, 22] studied a specific type of social contract that is built on the protection abstraction of groups, and employed First-Order Linear Temporal Logic (FOLTL) to specify interaction protocols. The intended application is secure information sharing. They also studied the correspondence between the formal specification and its implementation via reference monitors [23]. While their work has a history-based flavour, it applies only to a specific kind of social contract, and access control constraints are phrased in terms of the concerned user and object in a group rather than generic relationships among them or among groups.

Building on the three lines of research above, this work makes the following contributions.

1. We devised an access control model for supporting CSC (§ 5). The protection system tracks the history of the community's state, which takes the form of generalized social networks. Social contracts are expressed as policies that guard the interaction events of users.

2. Extending the modal logic of Fong [16], we designed a policy language that incorporates both modal and temporal operators for expressing intermingled relationship-based and history-based policy elements (§ 6).

3. We proposed a reference monitor architecture for enforcing social contracts specified in our policy language (§ 7). To reduce the space usage of the monitor, we employed a technique that we call ***relational abstraction***, in which historical dealings between two parties are documented as binary relationships between them. A pleasantly surprising consequence is that the resulting reference monitor tracks a single generalized social network rather than a history of social networks. Thus we obtain the core thesis of this work: *although the CSC model offers specification convenience in terms of mixing history- and relationship-based policy elements, the underlying enforcement mechanism can be optimized into a ReBAC system!*

4. Recognizing the need for further expressiveness, we proposed a hybridized extension of our policy language (§ 8). By employing relational abstraction once again, we obtained a novel fragment of the hybridized policy language that is amenable to efficient enforcement, thereby recovering the core thesis that the reference monitor is essentially a ReBAC system.

Consult [17] for proofs of theorems.

2. RELATED WORK

Relationship-Based Access Control.

With the advent of social network systems, Gates [20] and Carminati and Ferrari [10] independently coined the term Relationship-Based Access Control to refer the access control models in which inter-personal relationships form the basis of authorization decisions. Fong formalized this type of access control in a ReBAC model [16], and showed that classical access control approaches, such as RBAC, do not offer the right abstractions for expressing policies commonly found in social computing and electronic health record systems. By adopting relationship-based access control (ReBAC), one avoids tedious role parameterization and achieves delegation in an elegant manner. A modal logic [5] with a single propositional symbol has been adopted for specifying ReBAC policies. Subsequent works study the expressiveness of ReBAC policy languages [18], and extend the modal language by way of hybridization [6] (i.e., incorporating constructs from hybrid logic [1]).

Cheng *et al.* proposed a ReBAC model with a regular expression-based policy language [12]. They subsequently extended their model to capture not only user-to-user relationships, but also user-to-resource and resource-to-resource relationships [11].

None of the above works take into account the history of interactions and relationships in policy specification and enforcement. Support for temporal reasoning is necessary for expressing interaction protocols in social contracts. A contribution of this work is to demonstrate that such a history-based extension of ReBAC is a non-trivial research undertake, involving complex algorithm design issues and shift of representation (via relational abstraction) to achieve space-efficient enforcement. This present work is also capable of expressing user-to-resource and resource-to-resource relationships.

Other Protection Models for Social Computing.

Carminati *et al.* proposed an access control model for social network systems that is based on a trust metric [9]. A subsequent work explored the use of established semantic web technologies for encoding policies and relationships [7, 8]. ACON is an access control model designed specifically for social computing [30, 29]. It controls user activities by considering, e.g., user and resource attributes as well as user-to-user relationships.

History-Based Access Control.

History-based access control tracks past access events and uses access history as the basis for authorization. Previous work includes both system implementation techniques [14] as well as theoretical study of enforceability [31, 15, 21, 28]. Of particular relevance to this work is the work of Krukow *et al.* [25, 26]. They used a PPLTL as a policy language for specifying the interaction protocol between two parties, and proposed a reference monitor framework for enforcing the policies. Their work does not capture community-wide policies.

Our reference monitor framework employs two related techniques for optimizing space usage: (1) using LTL expansion laws [2, Chapter 5] to reduce dependencies on history, and (2) augmenting the generalized social network with additional edges to record historical dealings between parties. Similar techniques have been employed in previous works: (1) in [3, 25, 26] and (2) in [13, 4]. Our novelty has been in applying these techniques in (a) demonstrating that a ReBAC system is all that one requires to enforce CSC policies specified in our policy languages, and (b) devising an appropriate fragment of our hybridized policy language that is amenable to such optimization techniques.

Group-centric Secure Information Sharing.

Krishnan *et al.* proposed a formal specification of group-centric secure information sharing (g-SIS) [24, 22]. LTL is employed to specify the various properties of groups, as well as accessibility conditions. In this sense, g-SIS authorization is history-based. Yet g-SIS is only a specific form of community, and the specification approach does not support notions of accessibility that depends on relationships among users or groups. Subsequent work also applies formal methods to establish the correspondence between a stateless specification and a stateful implementation (i.e., reference monitor) of g-SIS [23]. In our work, the policy specification is guaranteed to be faithfully enforced by the reference monitor architecture. Manual application of formal methods is not required.

3. USE CASES

This section outlines use cases that are representative of the applications targeted by our CSC protection model.

EXAMPLE 1 (ONLINE SOCIAL NETWORKS (OSNS)). *OSNs such as Facebook have recently been used for purposes other than staying in touch with friends. Specifically, people in many countries coordinated and planned their political gatherings and demonstrations using Facebook. This drew the attention of totalitarian governments, resulting in surveillance of such OSNs. It is therefore desirable for users to be able to set up fine-grained access control policies.*

Sarah, a member of an OSN, is a supporter for a minority party called Fighting Citizens (FC). FC has been banned from further activities by the majority party, which has risen to power recently. In the past, Sarah has posted contents in favour of FC in an OSN group of FC supporters. She as well as other members of that group wish to prevent certain users from joining that group. Specifically, OSN users who previously joined OSN groups associated with the governing party are not allowed to join the FC-supporter group.

EXAMPLE 2 (ONLINE COAUTHORING COMMUNITIES). *Some online communities, such as Wikipedia, provide users with an environment for coauthoring contents and collective editing. Since deviant users may not conform to the social contract that defines a community, such communities need to be equipped with means for formal articulation of social contracts as well as mechanisms for enforcing these contracts. The following are sample components of such social contracts.*

1. *A user who has been reported for using inappropriate language for two times is suspended for further editing.*
2. *A user who has already created two distinct objects that have since remained untouched by any member of the community (including herself) is not allowed to further create new objects.*

4. NOTATIONS

Sets and Functions.

Let $\mathbb{N}$ be the set of natural numbers $\{0, 1, 2, \ldots\}$, and $\mathbb{B}$ be the set of boolean values $\{0, 1\}$.

Given a function $f : A \to B$, we write $\mathsf{dom}(f)$ for the domain of f (i.e., the set A), and $\mathsf{ran}(f)$ for the range of f (i.e., the set $\{f(x) \mid x \in A\}$). We write $f : A' \rightharpoonup B$ if $\mathsf{dom}(f) \subseteq A'$ and $\mathsf{ran}(f) \subseteq B$. Suppose $f : A \rightharpoonup B$, $a \in A$, and $b \in B$. We then write $f[a \mapsto b]$ to denote the function $g : A \rightharpoonup B$ such that $g(a) = b$, and $g(x) = f(x)$ for $x \neq a$. Given $a_1, a_2, \ldots, a_n \in A$ and $b_1, b_2, \ldots, b_n \in B$, where $a_1, a_2, \ldots, a_n$ are pairwise distinct, we write $\{a_1 \mapsto b_1, a_2 \mapsto b_2, \ldots, a_n \mapsto b_n\}$ to denote the function $g : A \rightharpoonup B$ such that $g(a_1) = b_1$, $g(a_2) = b_2$, ..., $g(a_n) = b_n$.

Relational Structures.

Intuitively, a ***relational structure*** (or simply a ***graph***) is an edge-labelled directed graph. Formally, a relational structure is a pair $G = \langle V, \{R_l\}_{l \in \mathcal{L}}\rangle$. The component V is a *finite* set of vertices. The component $\{R_l\}_{l \in \mathcal{L}}$ is an indexed family of binary relations. The set $\mathcal{L}$ is a *finite* set of edge labels. For each label $l \in \mathcal{L}$, $R_l \subseteq V \times V$ is a binary relation defined over V. We also write $V(G)$, $E(G)$ and $R_l(G)$ to represent V, $\{R_l\}_{l \in \mathcal{L}}$ and R_l respectively.

Given a *countably infinite* set $\mathcal{V}$ and a *finite* set $\mathcal{L}$, we denote by $\mathcal{G}[\mathcal{V}, \mathcal{L}]$ the set of all relational structures $\langle V, \{R_l\}_{l \in \mathcal{L}}\rangle$ for which $V \subseteq \mathcal{V}$. Note that $\mathcal{L}$ is *common* across every $G \in \mathcal{G}[\mathcal{V}, \mathcal{L}]$, and $V(G)$ is always finite by definition.

Given $G \in \mathcal{G}[\mathcal{V}, \mathcal{L}]$, $u, v \in \mathcal{V}$, and e may or may not be a member of $\mathcal{L}$, then $G + e(u, v)$ denotes the graph $\langle V'$, $\{R'_l\}_{l \in \mathcal{L} \cup \{e\}}\rangle$, where $V' = V(G) \cup \{u, v\}$, $R'_e = R_e \cup \{(u, v)\}$ if $e \in \mathcal{L}$, $R'_e = \{(u, v)\}$ if $l \notin \mathcal{L}$, and $R'_l = R_l$ if $l \neq e$.

5. ACCESS CONTROL MODEL

This section defines a formal model for Community-based Secure Collaboration. The model consists of two parts: (a) a behaviour model for the community (§ 5.1), and (b) a protection system that constrains the behaviour of that community based on explicitly specified policies (§ 5.2).

5.1 Community

A community is modeled as a state transition system. At any point of time, the community is in a ***social state*** (§ 5.1.1). A ***communication event*** (§ 5.1.2) that occurs within a state triggers a ***state transition*** (§ 5.1.3), bringing the community to a new social state. Formally, a community is specified as a ***community schema***, which is a 4-tuple $\langle \mathcal{V}, \mathcal{R}, \mathcal{E}, \rightarrow\rangle$. We explain the four components below.

5.1.1 Social States

A community evolves over time. At any point of time the community is in a certain social state. In this work we are interested in basing authorization decisions on the history of this evolving social state. We see the social state of a community to be relational in nature: the social state is characterized by, for example, interpersonal relationships that are either persistant or transient, past dealings with one another, and their reputational assessment of one another. There are also times when users and their relationships are not sufficient for modelling the community's state. For example, there may be non-user entities including resources (e.g., files, photos, user profiles, etc) and social constructions (e.g., groups, departments, etc), as well as their relationships with one another and with users, that may inform authorization decisions. We use the generic term ***entities*** to refer to either user or non-user entities.

We model the social state of a community as a relational structure. Recall that a relational structure is an edge-labelled directed graph. The vertices of the graph represent entities (i.e., either users or non-user entities). A directed edge models a relationship between two entities, and the label of the edge indicates the type of relationship represented by that edge. Note that the social network of the users in the community is a subgraph of this relational structure.

In a community schema $\langle \mathcal{V}, \mathcal{R}, \mathcal{E}, \rightarrow\rangle$, the component $\mathcal{V}$ is a countably infinite set of ***entity identifiers***. The social state of the community is made up of a finite subset of $\mathcal{V}$. The component $\mathcal{R}$ is a finite set of ***relation identifiers***.

The set $\mathcal{R}$ specifies the set of relationship types among entities. Therefore, the space of social states is the set $\mathcal{G}[\mathcal{V}, \mathcal{R}]$.

5.1.2 Communication Events

As a community evolves over time, its social state changes. We assume that a community evolves only because of user activities, and model an activity as a ***communication event*** (or simply an ***event***). In essence, the model does not account for any spontaneous change in social state that is not accompanied by an event explicitly tracked by the protection system[1]. In short, an event is the sole trigger for a community to transition from one social state to another.

The objective of the protection system is to control the triggering of communication events. While a communication event may involve many participants, we assume that only two of them are significant for the purpose of authorization. More specifically, the request to trigger a communication event presents to the reference monitor an ***event signature*** of the form $e(u, v)$, where:

- e is an ***event identifier***, the type of this event,
- u is the ***initiator***, the entity to initiate this event, and
- v is the ***target***, the entity to which this event is directed.

For example, the event signature send(john, mary) represents the event of John sending Mary a message. From the perspective of the protection system, only the event signature (but not the event) is visible. Hereafter we use the terms event and event signature interchangeably. We also write $\mathcal{ES}[\mathcal{E}, \mathcal{V}]$ for the set of all event signatures $e(u, v)$ for which $e \in \mathcal{E}$ and $u, v \in \mathcal{V}$.

The component $\mathcal{E}$ in a community schema $\langle \mathcal{V}, \mathcal{R}, \mathcal{E}, \rightarrow \rangle$ is a *finite, non-empty* set of event identifiers for that community.

5.1.3 State Transition

Given a community schema $\langle \mathcal{V}, \mathcal{R}, \mathcal{E}, \rightarrow \rangle$, the last component $\cdot \xrightarrow{\cdot} \cdot \subseteq \mathcal{G}[\mathcal{V}, \mathcal{R}] \times \mathcal{ES}[\mathcal{E}, \mathcal{V}] \times \mathcal{G}[\mathcal{V}, \mathcal{R}]$ is a transition relation. That is, $G \xrightarrow{e(u,v)} H$ when the occurrence of event $e(u, v)$ in state G transitions the community into state H.

Furthermore, the transition relation must be ***well-formed***: if $G \xrightarrow{e(u,v)} H$, then $V(G) = V(H)$ and $u, v \in V(G)$. Intuitively, a well-formed transition does not alter the vertex set of the graph, and the initiator and target are both members of the vertex set. That is, entity creation is modeled as dormant entities becoming active over time[2].

5.2 Protection System

If a community schema specifies the possible behaviour of a community, then a protection system specifies a mechanism that constrains such behaviour (§ 5.2.3). Specifically, such a protection system is a reference monitor. When a communication event is to be triggered, the signature of that event is first presented to the protection system for authorization (§ 5.2.4). Unless the system grants the event, the latter will be suppressed. The reference monitor is stateful: it tracks the historical evolution of social state of the community, as well as events that occurred in the past (§ 5.2.1). The reference monitor applies an access control policy to the reference monitor state when an authorization decision is to be made (§ 5.2.2).

5.2.1 Traces

We model the history of the community in a ***trace***, which is a sequence of relational structures. More specifically, a sequence of transitions

$$G_0 \xrightarrow{e_1(u_1,v_1)} G_1 \xrightarrow{e_2(u_2,v_2)} G_2 \cdots \xrightarrow{e_n(u_n,v_n)} G_n$$

can be encoded as the sequence of relational structures

$$G_0 \cdot (G_1 + e_1(u_1, v_1)) \cdot (G_2 + e_2(u_2, v_2)) \cdots (G_n + e_n(u_n, v_n))$$

That is, the first element of the sequence, G_0, is the oldest snapshot in the history, and, for each time point $0 < i \leq n$, the relational structure $G_i + e_i(u_i, v_i)$ contains both the social state G_i as well as an edge that records the communication event that produced G_i (i.e., the event $e_i(u_i, v_i)$). In summary, the history of a community is modeled as a sequence from $\mathcal{G}[\mathcal{V}, \mathcal{L}]^+$, where $\mathcal{L} = \mathcal{R} \uplus \mathcal{E}$. An edge with a label in $\mathcal{R}$ is a ***relation edge***, and an edge with a label in $\mathcal{E}$ is an ***event edge***. Such a sequence is what we call a trace.

Suppose we fix $\mathcal{V}$ and $\mathcal{L} = \mathcal{R} \uplus \mathcal{E}$. A trace $\gamma = G_0 G_1 \cdots G_n$ is ***well formed*** if both of the following hold:

- $G_0 \in \mathcal{G}[\mathcal{V}, \mathcal{R}]$, and
- for $1 \leq i \leq n$, $G_i = G'_i + e_i(u, v)$ for some $G'_i \in \mathcal{G}[\mathcal{V}, \mathcal{R}]$ and $e \in \mathcal{E}$.

We denote by $\mathcal{T}[\mathcal{V}, \mathcal{R}, \mathcal{E}]$ the set of all well-formed traces.

5.2.2 Access Control Policies

A protection system controls the authorization of communication events in a community. In such a system, one needs to impose policies for access control. A ***policy predicate*** (or simply a ***policy***) P is a function of the following signature.

$$\mathcal{T}[\mathcal{V}, \mathcal{R}, \mathcal{E}] \times \mathcal{V} \times \mathcal{V} \rightarrow \mathbb{B} \tag{1}$$

That is, a policy $P(\gamma, u, v)$ takes as input a well-formed trace γ, an initiator vertex u and a recipient vertex v, and returns a boolean authorization decision. We write $\mathcal{P}[\mathcal{V}, \mathcal{R}, \mathcal{E}]$ for the set of all policies with the signature on line (1).

5.2.3 Protection System

Given a community schema $\mathcal{C} = \langle \mathcal{V}, \mathcal{R}, \mathcal{E}, \rightarrow \rangle$, a ***protection system*** for $\mathcal{C}$ is a pair $\langle \mathcal{C}, policy \rangle$, where the function $policy : \mathcal{E} \rightarrow \mathcal{P}[\mathcal{V}, \mathcal{R}, \mathcal{E}]$ assigns a policy predicate to each event identifier. That is, policy predicate $policy(e)$ mediates the triggering of events of type e.

5.2.4 Authorization

A ***protection state*** (i.e., a state of the protection system) contains the information by which authorization decisions are made. In our case, a protection state is simply a well-formed trace γ. Note that this identification of protection states to well-formed traces is conceptual, meaning that the

[1]Examples of such spontaneous events may include time out, change of environmental conditions, or feedback events generated by the system itself. One way to accommodate such events into our model, is to introduce a special entity into the relational structure, for representing the community itself. An event in which both the initiator and target are this special entity represents a spontaneous event.

[2]This requirement is imposed to reduce the complexity of presentation. The subtlety of entity creation can be easily incorporated into the model, at the cost of unnecessary complexities that do not inspire.

actual implementation of the protection system may choose to encode the protection state in some space-efficient representations, which is exactly what we will do in § 7. For now, we focus on the conceptual description of the model.

Let $\gamma = G_0 \cdot (G_1 + e_1(u_1, v_1)) \cdot (G_2 + e_2(u_2, v_2)) \cdots (G_n + e_n(u_n, v_n))$ be a well-formed trace (i.e., a protection state), where $n \geq 0$, $G_i \in \mathcal{G}[\mathcal{V}, \mathcal{R}]$ for $0 \leq i \leq n$, and $e_i \in \mathcal{E}$ for $1 \leq i \leq n$. Then we write $\mathsf{head}(\gamma)$ for the graph G_n.

We model *both* the transition of protection states and authorization with the binary relation $\Longrightarrow \subseteq \mathcal{T}[\mathcal{V}, \mathcal{R}, \mathcal{E}] \times \mathcal{T}[\mathcal{V}, \mathcal{R}, \mathcal{E}]$. Intuitively, the relation $\Longrightarrow$ transitions one protection state (which is a well-formed trace) to another protection state (which is also a well-formed trace) of length one more than the first. Formally, the transition below holds

$$\gamma \Longrightarrow \gamma \cdot (G + e(u, v))$$

whenever both of the following conditions are met:

1. $\mathsf{head}(\gamma) \xrightarrow{e(u,v)} G$. That is, G is the next social state according to the social state transition relation.

2. $policy(e)(\gamma, u, v) = 1$. That is, the policy predicate assigned to event e authorizes the transition.

Example 3 (Online Social Networks). *We model Example 1 using our protection model. We begin by describing the community $\mathcal{C} = \langle \mathcal{V}, \mathcal{R}, \mathcal{E}, \rightarrow \rangle$. The entity set is $\mathcal{V} = \mathcal{U} \uplus \mathcal{G}$, which is partitioned into the set $\mathcal{U}$ of users and the set $\mathcal{G}$ of user groups. We assume that groups may "black-list" one another. For example, the FC group black-lists all the groups associated with the majority party. To support that, the relation identifier set is set up to be $\mathcal{R} = \{\,\mathsf{bl}\,\}$, such that if there is a* bl *edge from group g_1 to group g_2, it means g_1 has black-listed g_2. We assume that the* bl *edges are static, and they do not change over time. At run time, users may join groups. We model that by setting the event identifier set to be $\mathcal{E} = \{\,\mathsf{join}\,\}$, such that the event signature $\mathsf{join}(u, g)$ signifies the event of user u joining group g. Now the transition relation models group joining activities. Specifically, $G \xrightarrow{\mathsf{join}(u,g)} G$. That is, the relational structure that represents the social state of the community does not change over time, as the social state contains only* bl *edges. However, the graphs in a trace will contain* join *edges that record group joining events.*

The protection system $\langle \mathcal{C}, policy \rangle$ specifies a policy predicate $policy(\mathsf{join})$ for guarding group joining events. Specifically, $policy(\mathsf{join})(\gamma, u, g)$ will check if u has previously joined a group g' that is black-listed by g.

Example 4 (Online Coauthoring Communities). *Consider $\mathcal{C} = \langle \mathcal{V}, \mathcal{R}, \mathcal{E}, \rightarrow \rangle$, the community of Example 2. There are two kinds of entities. $\mathcal{S}$ is the set of subjects, $\mathcal{O}$ is the set of objects, and we set $\mathcal{V} = \mathcal{S} \uplus \mathcal{O}$. There is only one relation identifier: $\mathcal{R} = \{\,\mathsf{own}\,\}$. An* own *edge from subject s to object o signifies that s is the creator of o. We assume that objects that have not yet been created are already in the relational structure. "Uncreated" objects are not joined to any* own *edge.*

We model three event identifiers: $\mathcal{E} = \{\mathsf{create}, \mathsf{edit}, \mathsf{report}\}$. The event $\mathsf{create}(s, o)$ signifies that s is creating a new object o. The event $\mathsf{edit}(s, o)$ signifies that s is editing an existing object o. The event $\mathsf{report}(s_1, s_2)$ indicates that s_1 reports the use of inappropriate language by s_2.

The transition "$G \xrightarrow{\mathsf{create}(s,o)} G + \mathsf{own}(s, o)$" adds an own *edge from the initiator s to the target o. The transition "$G \xrightarrow{\mathsf{edit}(s,o)} G$" does not alter the social state, and the same is true for "$G \xrightarrow{\mathsf{report}(s_1,s_2)} G$".*

The protection system $\langle \mathcal{C}, policy \rangle$ defines the policy predicates $policy(\mathsf{create})$, $policy(\mathsf{edit})$ and $policy(\mathsf{report})$ for guarding the three kinds of events.

5.3 Discussion

A limitation in the scope of this work is that our protection model handles only communication events with a binary signature. While many interaction patterns are binary or reducible to binary signatures, some other lose semantics if we force a binary representation. Group messaging is an example of events that can be represented as a binary event. The idea is to model the group by an entity, and members are related to the group entity by membership edges. The initiator of the communication event is the message sender, and the target is the group entity. While the effect of the event may involve updating a subgraph that contains the member vertices, the *event signature* itself involves only the message sender (initiator) and the group vertex (target). An example of a high-arity event is a real-estate transaction, involving a buyer, a seller, and their agents. This time the event signature has to capture all the four parties, since it is necessary to ensure that the agents are indeed representing the buyer and the seller, and that there is no issue of dual agency. When the access control policy for an event needs to verify a relationship among three or more parties, a binary event signature is not sufficient. Although we are fully aware there are event signatures with an arity higher than two, this work illustrates that even by considering only binary events, the technical challenges are already daunting, necessitating careful design of enforcement mechanisms (§7 and §8.2). Further extension to handle events of higher arity is a future work.

6. POLICY LANGUAGE

One of the goals of this work is to provide configurability to online communities founded on social contracts. As social contract evolves, it should not necessitate recompiling the system source code. Rather, the community administrator shall be equipped with declarative policy languages that let him or her revise the social contract without rebuilding the system. This section describes such a declarative policy language. The targeted users of our policy languages are not end users in the community, but rather community administrators. The situation is analogous to, say, configuring a system with technically-oriented policy languages such as XACML. Our design goal is therefore the balancing of expressiveness and enforceability.

Recall that authorization decisions are reached by consulting policy predicates, each of which takes as input the community's history, the initiator and the target, and returns a boolean authorization decision. The policy language in this section is designed for expressing such a predicate. This language forms the basis of a more expressive language to be described in § 8. For now we examine this basic policy language to facilitate the development of our core thesis in § 7.

Our policy language is an extension of the modal language proposed in [16]. That modal language offers a means to specify binary relations between a pair of vertices in a relational structure. Inspired by [22], we extend that language by incorporating the pure-past temporal operators of Linear Temporal Logic (LTL). The result is a language that allows us to articulate binary relations of a pair of vertices in the backdrop of an evolving relational structure. We name this language $\mathcal{TR}$ (for temporal-relational).

6.1 Syntax

Policies are expressed as ***formulas*** in $\mathcal{TR}$. The abstract syntax of formulas is given below:

$$\phi ::= \top \mid \mathsf{target} \mid \neg\phi \mid \phi \vee \phi \mid \langle l\rangle\phi \mid \langle -l\rangle\phi \mid \mathcal{Y}\,\phi \mid \phi\,\mathcal{S}\,\phi$$

where $l \in \mathcal{L}$, with $\mathcal{L}$ being the edge label set (i.e., $\mathcal{R} \uplus \mathcal{E}$). We write $\mathsf{Form}_{\mathcal{TR}}(\mathcal{L})$ to denote the set of all formulas generated by the above grammar.

A formula ϕ essentially specifies a search to be performed by an agent that "crawls around" a given trace $\gamma = G_0G_1\cdots G_n$, and determines along the way if the initiator and the target forms a certain binary relation. As the search unfolds, at any point of time, the agent is standing at a certain coordinate (i, u) within the trace γ, where i is a time point, and u is a vertex of the relational structure G_i. The agent may do three things: (1) Check the current location of the agent (via target or $\top$); (2) Move about in the relational structure of the current time point (via $\langle l\rangle\phi$ or $\langle -l\rangle\phi$); (3) Move back in time (via $\mathcal{Y}\,\phi$ or $\phi_1\,\mathcal{S}\,\phi_2$). The above checks can be composed using basic boolean connectives such as negation ($\neg$) and disjunction ($\vee$). We formalize the above intuitive description in the following.

6.2 Semantics

The semantics of $\mathcal{TR}$ is defined in terms of the satisfaction relation $\models$. Given a trace $\gamma = G_0G_1\cdots G_n$ for which $n \geq 0$, an index i such that $0 \leq i \leq n$, and vertices $u, v \in V(G_n)$, the satisfaction relation $\gamma, i, u, v \models \phi$ is defined as follows:

- $\gamma, i, u, v \models \top$ always holds.
- $\gamma, i, u, v \models \mathsf{target}$ iff $u = v$.
- $\gamma, i, u, v \models \neg\phi$ iff it is not the case that $\gamma, i, u, v \models \phi$.
- $\gamma, i, u, v \models \phi_1 \vee \phi_2$ iff $\gamma, i, u, v \models \phi_1$ or $\gamma, i, u, v \models \phi_2$.
- $\gamma, i, u, v \models \langle l\rangle\phi$ iff there exists $u' \in V(G_i)$ such that $(u, u') \in R_l(G_i)$ and $\gamma, i, u', v \models \phi$.
- $\gamma, i, u, v \models \langle -l\rangle\phi$ iff there exists $u' \in V(G_i)$ such that $(u', u) \in R_l(G_i)$ and $\gamma, i, u', v \models \phi$.
- $\gamma, i, u, v \models \mathcal{Y}\,\phi$ iff $i > 0$ and $\gamma, i-1, u, v \models \phi$.
- $\gamma, i, u, v \models \phi_1\,\mathcal{S}\,\phi_2$ iff there exists j, $0 \leq j \leq i$, such that both (a) $\gamma, j, u, v \models \phi_2$, and (b) for all k, $j < k \leq i$, we have $\gamma, k, u, v \models \phi_1$.

Note that, in the inductive definition of $\models$, the pair (i, u) is the "coordinate" of the agent, and γ and v remains constant as the structural induction unfolds. In particular v gives the meaning of the propositional symbol target, which records the target entity's location.

Lastly, we also write the shorthand $\gamma, u, v \models \phi$ to mean $\gamma, n, u, v \models \phi$. (Recall that $n = |\gamma| - 1$.) That is, we begin traversal at the most recent time point. Essentially, this shorthand checks if a certain binary relationship exists between u and v within the history γ. The binary relation in question is specified as ϕ, with the propositional symbol target representing v, and the agent begins evaluation at u.

6.3 Derived forms

Standard derived forms can be defined as follows:

$$\bot = \neg\top \qquad \phi_1 \wedge \phi_2 = \neg(\neg\phi_1 \vee \neg\phi_2) \qquad \mathcal{O}\,\phi = \top\,\mathcal{S}\,\phi$$
$$[l]\phi = \neg\langle l\rangle\neg\phi \qquad [-l]\phi = \neg\langle -l\rangle\neg\phi \qquad \mathcal{H}\,\phi = \neg\,\mathcal{O}\,\neg\phi$$

The box operator $[l]$ is the dual of $\langle l\rangle$. Specifically, the formula $[l]\phi$ holds at coordinate (i, u) if every l-neighbor of u satisfies ϕ at time point i. The converse $[-l]$ can be understood similarly. The "once" operator $\mathcal{O}$ checks that there was at least one time point in the past for which the operand formula ϕ holds. The "historically" operator $\mathcal{H}$ checks that the operand formula ϕ holds in every past time point.

6.4 Policy predicate

Given a formula ϕ, we write $[\![\phi]\!]$ to denote the policy predicate induced by ϕ. Specifically, $[\![\phi]\!](\gamma, u, v)$ returns 1 whenever $\gamma, u, v \models \phi$.

Previously, a protection system is defined as a pair $\langle \mathcal{C}$, *policy*$\rangle$. The component *policy* is supposed to map event identifiers to *policy predicates*. As we will use our policy language to express policy predicates, we also allow *policy* to be a function of type $\mathcal{E} \rightarrow \mathsf{Form}_{\mathcal{TR}}(\mathcal{R} \cup \mathcal{E})$: that is, *policy* assigns a formula to each event identifier. We then take $[\![policy(e)]\!]$ to be the policy predicate guarding event identifier e. We adopt this convention uniformly in the following.

With the convention above, the range of the function *policy*, written $\mathsf{ran}(policy)$, is the set of all formulas that are used by the protection system for guarding event identifiers. This set will be of interest to us in the sequel.

6.5 Examples

EXAMPLE 5 (ONLINE SOCIAL NETWORKS). *Continuing with Example 3, we capture the policy of Example 1 as policy*(join). *Specifically, the formula below specifies the policy predicate that guards the event* $\mathsf{join}(u, g)$*:*

$$\neg\,\mathcal{O}\langle\mathsf{join}\rangle\langle-\mathsf{bl}\rangle\mathsf{target}$$

The formula exploits the fact that the social state does not change over time.

EXAMPLE 6 (ONLINE COAUTHORING COMMUNITIES). *Continuing with Example 4, we capture Policy 1 of Example 2 as policy*(create). *Specifically, the event* $\mathsf{create}(s, o)$ *is allowed only if the following holds.*

$$\neg\,\mathcal{O}\,((\langle-\mathsf{report}\rangle\top) \wedge (\mathcal{Y}\,\mathcal{O}\langle-\mathsf{report}\rangle\top)) \tag{2}$$

The formula detects violation of Policy 1 by looking for two distinct, historical occurrences of report *edges that point to the initiator.*

7. REFERENCE MONITOR

7.1 Motivation

The enforcement of policies can be achieved by a reference monitor, which is essentially an implementation of the protection system as described in § 5.2. To fix thoughts, let

G_0 be the initial social state of the community, and G_t be the social state of the community after the t'th transition ($t \geq 1$). Define also traces $\gamma_0 = G_0$, and $\gamma_t = \gamma_{t-1} \cdot G_t$ (for $t \geq 1$). That is, γ_t is the history of the community after the t'th transition. At time point t, if the reference monitor intercepts an event signature $e(u, v)$, it evaluates the policy predicate $policy(e)$ against γ_t, u and v. Therefore, a naively implemented reference monitor will have to track the entire history of the community (i.e., γ_t). In addition, if authorization is successful, then transition occurs, and the reference monitor will have to update its internal state to $\gamma_{t+1} = \gamma_t \cdot G_{t+1}$. This naive implementation strategy is obviously not practical for its unreasonable memory requirement. We explore in the following a space-efficient implementation strategy, in which the memory usage is comparable to tracking only one relational structure.

7.2 Implementation Strategy

The core insight is inspired by the work of Krukow *et al.* [26], who proposed a scheme for enforcing a safety property, specified as a pure-past LTL formula, using a reference monitor. Every authorization decision is made by a constant-time check against the current state of the reference monitor. The space requirement for their reference monitor is linear to the size of the formula but independent of the size of the history. Every system transition involves the execution of an "update algorithm," which changes the internal state of the reference monitor. Efficient memory usage is possible because of the extensive application of ***expansion laws*** in LTL [2, Chapter 5]. Applying their insights to our case, we observe the following:

$$\gamma_{t+1}, u, v \models \mathcal{Y}\phi \text{ iff } \gamma_t, u, v \models \phi \quad (3)$$

$$\gamma_{t+1}, u, v \models \phi_1 \mathcal{S} \phi_2 \text{ iff } (\gamma_{t+1}, u, v \models \phi_2) \text{ or } \Big((\gamma_t, u, v \models \phi_1 \mathcal{S} \phi_2) \text{ and } (\gamma_{t+1}, u, v \models \phi_1)\Big) \quad (4)$$

Note that, in the cases above, the evaluation of a formula at time point $t+1$ can be reduced to either (i) the evaluation of a subformula at time point t, or (ii) the evaluation of a *proper* subformula at time point $t+1$. This suggests the reference monitor only needs to track the evaluation results of all subformulas at a given time, and, when a transition occurs, the reference monitor updates the evaluation results by consulting the evaluation results of the previous state, and performs the updates from subformulas to superformulas.

7.3 Notation

We begin by defining a few supporting notations. We write $\mathsf{succ}^l_G(u)$ to denote the set $\{v \in V(G) \mid (u, v) \in R_l(G)\}$. That is, $\mathsf{succ}^l_G(u)$ is the set of all l-successors of vertex u in graph G. Similarly, the set of all l-predecessors of u in G, written $\mathsf{pred}^l_G(u)$, is the set $\{v \in V(G) \mid (v, u) \in R_l(G)\}$. Let $\mathsf{sub}(\phi)$ be the set of all subformulas of ϕ. Note that ϕ is also considered a subformula of ϕ itself. A subformula of ϕ that is not ϕ itself is called a ***proper subformula***. Given a set Φ of formulas, we also write $\mathsf{sub}(\Phi)$ for $\bigcup_{\phi \in \Phi} \mathsf{sub}(\phi)$. An enumeration of the formulas in a set Φ of formulas is in an ***admissible order*** if the enumeration is generated as follows:

AO-1 First, list the formulas for which the outermost operator is $\mathcal{Y}$. Among these formulas, list the superformulas before the subformulas.

Algorithm 1: *Update*(G, B)

in : $G \in \mathcal{G}[\mathcal{V}, \mathcal{R} \cup \mathcal{E}]$
in out: $B : \mathsf{sub}(\mathsf{ran}(policy)) \times V(G) \times V(G) \to \mathbb{B}$
for $\phi \in \mathsf{sub}(\mathsf{ran}(policy))$, *in an admissible order,* **do**
  for $u \in V(G)$ **do**
    for $v \in V(G)$ **do**
      switch ϕ **do**
        case $\top$
          $B[\phi][u][v] \leftarrow 1$;
        case target
          $B[\phi][u][v] \leftarrow (u = v)$;
        case $\neg\phi_1$
          $B[\phi][u][v] \leftarrow \neg B[\phi_1][u][v]$;
        case $\phi_1 \vee \phi_2$
          $B[\phi][u][v] \leftarrow B[\phi_1][u][v] \vee B[\phi_2][u][v]$;
        case $\langle l \rangle \phi_1$
          $B[\phi][u][v] \leftarrow \bigvee_{u' \in \mathsf{succ}^l_G(u)} B[\phi_1][u'][v]$;
        case $\langle -l \rangle \phi_1$
          $B[\phi][u][v] \leftarrow \bigvee_{u' \in \mathsf{pred}^l_G(u)} B[\phi_1][u'][v]$;
        case $\mathcal{Y}\phi_1$
          $B[\phi][u][v] \leftarrow B[\phi_1][u][v]$;
        case $\phi_1 \mathcal{S} \phi_2$
          $B[\phi][u][v] \leftarrow B[\phi_2][u][v] \vee (B[\phi][u][v] \wedge B[\phi_1][u][v])$;

AO-2 Second, list the remaining formulas, with subformulas listed before the superformulas.

For example, the following enumeration of the members of $\mathsf{sub}(\mathcal{Y}\mathcal{Y}\langle l \rangle\mathsf{target})$ is in an admissible order:

$$\mathcal{Y}\mathcal{Y}\langle l \rangle\mathsf{target} \qquad \mathcal{Y}\langle l \rangle\mathsf{target} \qquad \mathsf{target} \qquad \langle l \rangle\mathsf{target}$$

7.4 Reference Monitor State

The mutable state of the reference monitor is captured in a pair of data structures $\langle G, B \rangle$:

1. G is a relational structure, and
2. $B : \mathsf{sub}(\mathsf{ran}(policy)) \times V(G) \times V(G) \to \mathbb{B}$ is a three-dimensional boolean matrix. The first index is a subformula of a member of $\mathsf{ran}(policy)$, which is the set of formulas used by the protection system for guarding event identifiers. The last two indices are vertices of G. Each entry of the matrix holds a boolean value.

It is an invariant of the reference monitor that, after the t'th transition, the following conditions hold:

$$G = G_t \quad (5)$$

$$B[\phi][u][v] = 1 \text{ iff } \gamma_t, u, v \models \phi \quad (6)$$

7.5 Authorization and State Transition

At time point t, suppose an event signature $e(u, v)$ is intercepted, then the following steps will be performed by the reference monitor:

1. Look up formula $\phi = policy(e)$.
2. Look up $B[\phi][u][v]$. If the value is 0, reject the event signature. Otherwise, proceed with the following steps.
3. Update G to G_{t+1}.

4. Update B by invoking Algorithm 1. The algorithm takes two arguments: (a) the updated graph G, and (b) the matrix B. On return, B will be updated.

(It is assumed that system parameters such as $\mathcal{R}$, $\mathcal{E}$ and *policy* are global information known to the algorithm.) Steps 1 and 2 are responsible for making authorization decisions. Steps 3 and 4 are responsible for updating the internal state of the reference monitor. At the core of this procedure is the invocation of Algorithm 1 to update B.

We explain how Algorithm 1 works at the intuitive level. The algorithm essentially goes through the entries of the matrix B in a specific order, updating each entry it encounters by values of other entries. Lines 8, 10, 12, 14, 16 and 18 are direct encoding of the semantic definitions of $\top$, target, $\neg$, $\vee$, $\langle l \rangle$ and $\langle -l \rangle$. Line 20 is the encoding of (3), the expansion law for $\mathcal{Y}$. Line 22 is the encoding of (4), the expansion law for $\mathcal{S}$. The correctness of the algorithm hinges on the order in which the subformulas are enumerated on line 3.

THEOREM 7. *Suppose B satisfies invariant (6). If Algorithm 1 is invoked with G_{t+1} and B, then on return B satisfies the following condition:*

$$B[\phi][u][v] = 1 \textit{ iff } \gamma_{t+1}, u, v \models \phi$$

To establish invariants (5) and (6) in the first place, the reference monitor is to (i) set G to G_0, (ii) set all entries of B to 0, and then (iii) invoke Algorithm 1.

THEOREM 8. *Let $M = \sum_{\phi \in \mathsf{ran}(policy)} |\phi|$, $N = |V(G)|$, and $E = \sum_{l \in \mathcal{R} \cup \mathcal{E}} |R_l(G)|$. Algorithm 1 runs in time $O(MN(N+E))$. The space requirement for the reference monitor is the space for maintaining G plus $O(MN^2)$ bits overhead for matrix B.*

7.6 Reference Monitor as ReBAC System

The boolean matrix B could be seen as an array of adjacency matrices. Specifically, for each formula ϕ in $\mathsf{sub}(\mathsf{ran}(policy))$, the submatrix $B[\phi][\cdot][\cdot]$ characterizes a binary relation R_ϕ over $V(G)$, such that $(u, v) \in R_\phi$ iff $\gamma_t, u, v \models \phi$. Therefore, the internal state of the reference monitor, comprising of G and B, could be seen as a single relational structure $\langle V(G), \{R_l\}_{l \in \mathcal{L}} \rangle$ where $\mathcal{L} = \mathcal{R} \cup \mathcal{E} \cup \mathsf{sub}(\mathsf{ran}(policy))$. If we interpret the reference monitor state in this way, then the reference monitor essentially tracks a single relational structure, and makes authorization decisions by consulting the topology of this relational structure. *In short, the reference monitor is essentially a ReBAC system!* Specifically, if the entities of the community are all users, then the reference monitor is a social network system.

This result is surprising. Even though we have introduced a temporal dimension to policy predicates, it turns out that the enforcement of these policies requires only the tracking of a single relational structure, rather than a full history of relational structures, as long as we specify policy predicates using $\mathcal{TR}$. That is, space efficiency is predicated on restraining the expressiveness of our policy language.

What is even more interesting is the way history information is tracked. Specifically, history information is abstracted into binary relations between entities (i.e., the binary relations R_ϕ above). This is possible because the policy language can only express the past dealings between two parties (i.e., the initiator and the target). This is essentially a generalization of the core observation of [16]. It has been observed in [16] that a modal logic with exactly one propositional symbol can be used for representing a binary relation between two entities in a relational structure. In our policy language, this is generalized to include a temporal dimension: a modal-temporal language with exactly one propositional symbol can be used for representing the past dealings between two entities. We call this methodological technique ***relational abstraction***:

> *By constraining the policy language to express only past dealings between two entities, history information can be tracked by binary relations.*

8. A HYBRID POLICY LANGUAGE

While the policy language $\mathcal{TR}$ serves well in highlighting the core thesis of this work, it is limited in expressive power. In § 8.1, we extend $\mathcal{TR}$ by incorporating constructs from hybrid logic [1, 6]. Hybrid logic offers constructs that are normally found in first-order logic rather than modal logic: the ability to name an entity and later on refer to it. This is required for separating entities and to reposition search focus. Then in § 8.2, we look at the enforcement of policies under this extension, especially in how the core thesis of this work is played out in such an expressive language.

8.1 Hybridization

We introduce hybrid constructs into the policy language $\mathcal{TR}$, resulting in a policy language that we call $\mathcal{HTR}$.

8.1.1 Syntax

The syntax of $\mathcal{HTR}$ differs from $\mathcal{TR}$ in two ways: (1) the specialized propositional symbol target is now generalized to entity variables, and (2) new constructs are introduced for defining entity variables and repositioning the crawling agent. The grammar of a formula in $\mathcal{HTR}$ is shown below.

$$\begin{aligned}\phi ::= {} & \top \mid \neg\phi \mid \phi \vee \phi \mid \langle l \rangle \phi \mid \langle -l \rangle \phi \mid \mathcal{Y}\phi \mid \phi \mathcal{S} \phi \mid \\ & x \mid \downarrow x \,.\, \phi \mid @_x\, \phi \end{aligned} \tag{7}$$

where $l \in \mathcal{L}$, $\mathcal{L}$ is the edge label set, and $x \in \mathsf{Var}$ is an ***entity variable***. We assume that the set Var provides a countably infinite supply of entity variables, and that target is a distinguished member of Var.

On the first line of (7) are the constructs inherited from $\mathcal{TR}$ (with the omission of target). Hybridization introduces three new constructs on the second line. Common to the three constructs is the assumption that a formula is evaluated with respect to a ***variable assignment***. A variable assignment defines the values of some entity variables. In particular, each variable is bound to a single entity in the relational structure. The first new construct x, an entity variable, tests if the crawling agent is currently located at the entity referenced by x. This is a generalization of target, as target is but a member of Var. A second new construct is the ***binder*** ($\downarrow$). The formula $\downarrow x \,.\, \phi$ introduces a new variable definition, binding x to the current location of the crawling agent. The third new construct is the ***satisfaction operator*** ($@_x$). The formula $@_x\, \phi$ repositions the crawling agent to the entity referenced by x, and then evaluates ϕ from that location. The formal semantics is given below.

8.1.2 Semantics

The semantics of formulas is given by the relation $\gamma, i, g, u \Vdash \phi$. As before, ϕ is evaluated in the context of a trace $\gamma =$

$G_0 \ldots G_n$, recording the history of evolution of a relational structure. During evaluation, the crawling agent is situated a certain time index i where $0 \le i \le n$, and located at a certain entity $u \in V(G_i)$. In addition, the formula is evaluated against a variable assignment $g : \mathsf{Var} \rightharpoonup \mathcal{V}$, which assigns an entity to each of the variables in $\mathsf{dom}(g)$. Formally, the evaluation of formulas is defined as follows.

- $\gamma, i, g, u \Vdash \top$ always holds.
- $\gamma, i, g, u \Vdash \neg\phi$ iff it is not the case that $\gamma, i, g, u \Vdash \phi$.
- $\gamma, i, g, u \Vdash \phi_1 \vee \phi_2$ iff $\gamma, i, g, u \Vdash \phi_1$ or $\gamma, i, g, u \Vdash \phi_2$.
- $\gamma, i, g, u \Vdash \langle l \rangle \phi$ iff there exists $u' \in V(G_i)$ such that $(u, u') \in R_l(G_i)$ and $\gamma, i, g, u' \Vdash \phi$.
- $\gamma, i, g, u \Vdash \langle -l \rangle \phi$ iff there exists $u' \in V(G_i)$ such that $(u', u) \in R_l(G_i)$ and $\gamma, i, g, u' \Vdash \phi$.
- $\gamma, i, g, u \Vdash \mathcal{Y}\phi$ iff $i > 0$ and $\gamma, i-1, g, u \Vdash \phi$.
- $\gamma, i, g, u \Vdash \phi_1 \,\mathcal{S}\, \phi_2$ iff there exists j, $0 \le j \le i$, such that both (a) $\gamma, j, g, u \Vdash \phi_2$, and (b) for all k, $j < k \le i$, we have $\gamma, k, g, u \Vdash \phi_1$.
- $\gamma, i, g, u \Vdash x$ iff $u = g(x)$.
- $\gamma, i, g, u \Vdash \downarrow x \,.\, \phi$ iff $\gamma, i, g[x \mapsto u], u \Vdash \phi$.
- $\gamma, i, g, u \Vdash @_x \phi$ iff $\gamma, i, g, g(x) \Vdash \phi$.

All the semantic rules are familiar except for the last three. The construct x tests if the crawling agent is located at the entity referenced by x (i.e., $u = g(x)$). The construct $\downarrow x \,.\, \phi$ extends the current assignment into $g[x \mapsto u]$, in which x is bound to the current location u, and then the subformula ϕ is evaluated with this extended assignment. The construct $@_x \phi$ repositions the crawling agent at $g(x)$, that is, the entity referenced by variable x, before ϕ is evaluated.

We introduce two shorthands. First, we write $\gamma, u, v \Vdash_x \phi$ to assert $\gamma, n, \{x \mapsto v\}, u \Vdash \phi$, where $n = |\gamma| - 1$. This shorthand asserts that a certain binary relationship exists between u and v within the trace γ, and the binary relation is specified as formula ϕ, where the variable x is used in ϕ to denote the second end point of the relationship. Second, we write $\gamma, u, v \Vdash \phi$ to assert $\gamma, u, v \Vdash_{\mathsf{target}} \phi$.

8.1.3 Derived forms and other syntactic conventions

The same set of derived forms from § 6.3 can be defined for the extended language.

With the introduction of entity variables and the binder, the notion of ***free variables*** will play a crucial role in the following discussion. Intuitively, a free variable is one that is not within the scope of a binder that defines that variable. Given a formula ϕ, we write $\mathsf{fv}(\phi)$ for the set of free variables of ϕ. The formal definition of $\mathsf{fv}(\cdot)$ is given in [17].

A formula ϕ is ***regular*** iff it satisfies the following:

1. No two binders in ϕ bind the same variable. (That is, every binder defines a unique variable.)
2. For every subformula of ϕ that has the form $\downarrow x \,.\, \phi_1$, we have $x \in \mathsf{fv}(\phi_1)$. (That is, no binder is redundant.)

By renaming variables and eliminating redundant binders, every irregular formula can be rewritten into a semantically equivalent formula that is regular, without increase in formula size. From now on, we assume that all formulas are regular. We call this the ***regularity convention***.

8.1.4 Policy Predicate

Given a formula ϕ for which $\mathsf{fv}(\phi) \subseteq \{\mathsf{target}\}$, we write $[\![\phi]\!]$ to denote the policy predicate induced by ϕ, such that $[\![\phi]\!](\gamma, u, v)$ returns 1 iff $\gamma, u, v \Vdash \phi$. As before, we adopt the convention that the *policy* component of a protection system maps event identifiers to formulas.

8.1.5 Examples

We illustrate the utility of hybridization with two examples. The first illustrates the use of hybrid constructs to "reposition" the crawler.

The advanced example below illustrates the use of hybrid constructs to name entities in the present, and then go back in time to verify past relationships among named entities.

EXAMPLE 9 (ONLINE COAUTHORING COMMUNITIES). *Revisiting Example 6, we specify Policy 2 of Example 2 using $\mathcal{HTR}$. We begin by defining a utility formula ϕ_o.*

$$\phi_o = @_o \neg\, \mathcal{O}\langle -\mathsf{edit}\rangle \top \qquad (8)$$

Given an entity variable o, the formula ϕ_o checks that o has never been edited in the past. With this, the requirements of Policy 2 can be captured by the following formula.

$$\neg\Big(\downarrow s \,.\langle \mathsf{own}\rangle \downarrow o_1 \,.\, @_s\langle \mathsf{own}\rangle \downarrow o_2 \,.(\neg o_1 \wedge \phi_{o_1} \wedge \phi_{o_2})\Big) \qquad (9)$$

The formula above begins by defining two entity variables, o_1 and o_2, both are owned by the initiator s in the present ($\downarrow s \,.\langle \mathsf{own}\rangle \downarrow o_1 \,.\, @_s\langle \mathsf{own}\rangle \downarrow o_2 \ldots.$). It then checks that o_1 and o_2 are distinct ($\neg o_1$). The check ϕ_o is then applied to both o_1 and o_2, verifying that each of o_1 and o_2 has never been edited in the past. Finally, the above check corresponds to a violation of Policy 2, and thus the outermost negation ($\neg$) ensures absence of violations. To appropriate the above, we set policy(create) *to the conjunction of (2) and (9).*

8.2 Enforcement

The enforcement of $\mathcal{HTR}$ is non-trivial. With $\mathcal{TR}$, the evaluation of every subformula can be tracked by a binary relation in the internal state of the reference monitor. This is possible because there is only one propositional symbol. By hybridization, we introduce an arbitrary number of variables into subformulas. Specifically, a formula with k free variables represents a relation of arity $k+1$. Therefore, the space requirement of the reference monitor grows exponentially with the number of variables involved.

Fortunately, one can constrain the expressiveness of $\mathcal{HTR}$ slightly, to obtain a language fragment that still retains much of the advantages of the hybrid language, but yields a reference monitor with the same space requirement of $\mathcal{TR}$. The trick, again, is relational abstraction, now applied in a meticulous manner. We will demonstrate once again the core thesis of § 7.6, that the reference monitor of the resulting policy language is comparable to a ReBAC system.

8.2.1 Overview of Strategy

A ***temporal formula*** is one in which the outermost operator is a temporal operator (i.e., $\mathcal{Y}\phi$ or $\phi_1 \,\mathcal{S}\, \phi_2$). Note that the reference monitor needs to track additional state information (i.e., B) other than the current relational structure (i.e., G) because of the existence of temporal subformulas. If a formula contains no temporal operators, then a local model checking algorithm for hybrid logic, such as the one in [6], will suffice. It is when state transition occurs that the update algorithm needs to abstract the evaluation of temporal subformulas into binary relations. To apply this technique of relational abstraction, we impose syntactic restrictions on the hybrid policy language, such that every temporal subformula of a policy must have no more than one free variable. With this restriction, temporal subformulas again represent binary relations, which can be tracked by the reference monitor in a space-efficient manner. As before, this amounts to the reference monitor tracking a single relational structure, such that history information is recorded as edges.

The syntactic restriction still allows certain subformulas to express higher-arity relations, so long as they are not temporal formulas. Intuitively, the crawling agent is allowed to remember multiple locations through the use of variables so long as it is crawling within the relational structure of a single time point. When the agent moves through time, then it is only allowed to remember at most one variable. With these restrictions, the subformulas that represent binary relations are handled by a bottom-up update algorithm in the spirit of [26], and the higher-arity relations are handled by a top-down update algorithm [19], which trades time efficiency for space efficiency. Our novelty is in the careful scheduling of top-down and bottom-up processing by exploiting the the syntactic structure of the language fragment, as well as combining the techniques of [19] and [26].

8.2.2 A Language Fragment

A formula ϕ is ***proper*** iff both conditions below hold.

1. $|\mathsf{fv}(\phi')| \leq 1$ for every temporal subformula $\phi' \in \mathsf{sub}(\phi)$.

2. $\mathsf{fv}(\phi) \subseteq \{\mathsf{target}\}$.

Intuitively, a proper formula is such that every temporal subformula has at most one free variable, and the only free variable permitted in the formula itself is target. Let $\mathcal{HTR}^-$ be the fragment of $\mathcal{HTR}$ that contains only proper formulas.

Given a formula in $\mathcal{HTR}$, checking if it is proper (and thus belongs to $\mathcal{HTR}^-$) takes time linear to the size of the formula. This is achieved simply by calling $\mathsf{fv}(\cdot)$ once on the formula, annotating each subformula by its free variables, and checking that the two conditions above hold.

The following example illustrates that, despite requiring temporal subformulas to be proper, $\mathcal{HTR}^-$ is still expressive enough for specifying useful policies.

EXAMPLE 10. *Formulas (8) and (9) from Example 9 are both proper. See Example 11 for a justification.*

8.2.3 Preprocessing via Annotation

Our claim is that $\mathcal{HTR}^-$ permits a space-efficient implementation of the reference monitor, because temporal formulas represent binary relations rather than high-arity relations. To help the reference monitor recognize subformulas that correspond to binary relations, so that the reference monitor can switch to an appropriate model checking strategy for each kind of subformulas (i.e., bottom-up for binary relations, and top-down for higher-arity relations), we introduce an annotation scheme for formulas in $\mathcal{HTR}$. Specifically, we introduce an annotation construct $\lceil\cdot\rceil_x$ for $\mathcal{HTR}$ formulas and their subformulas.

The grammar for an ***annotated formula*** φ is given below.

$$\begin{aligned}\varphi &::= \rho \mid \lceil\rho\rceil_x\\ \rho &::= \top \mid \neg\varphi \mid \varphi \vee \varphi \mid \langle l\rangle\varphi \mid \langle -l\rangle\varphi \mid \mathcal{Y}\varphi \mid \varphi\,\mathcal{S}\,\varphi \mid\\ &\quad\ x \mid {\downarrow} x\,.\,\varphi \mid @_x\,\varphi\end{aligned}$$

An annotated formula is like an $\mathcal{HTR}$ formula, except that each subformula (including the formula itself) can be optionally decorated by an annotation construct. If an $\mathcal{HTR}$ formula ϕ is obtained from an annotated formula φ by removing all occurrences of the annotation construct, then ϕ is said to be the ***erasure*** of φ, and φ is said to be an ***annotation*** of ϕ.

The intended meaning of an annotated formula $\lceil\rho\rceil_x$ is that $\mathsf{fv}(\rho) \subseteq \{x\}$. Intuitively, $\lceil\cdot\rceil_x$ imposes an "upper bound" to the free variable set of ρ. We make this requirement formal as follows. First, we extend the definition of $\mathsf{fv}(\cdot)$ to account for annotated formulas:

$$\mathsf{fv}(\lceil\rho\rceil_x) = \mathsf{fv}(\rho) \cup \{x\}$$

Second, φ is ***well annotated*** if every subformula (including φ itself) of the form $\lceil\rho\rceil_x$ is such that $\mathsf{fv}(\rho) \subseteq \{x\}$. That is, a well annotated formula is one in which the annotation constructs mean what they are supposed to mean.

A well annotated formula φ is ***properly annotated*** (or simply ***proper***) iff both of the following conditions hold.

1. Every temporal subformula ρ is decorated by an annotation construct, as in $\lceil\rho\rceil_x$, for some variable x.

2. φ is of the form $\lceil\rho\rceil_{\mathsf{target}}$.

A properly annotated formula φ is ***completely annotated*** (or simply ***complete***) iff every subformula ρ that satisfies $|\mathsf{fv}(\rho)| \leq 1$ is decorated by an annotation construct $\lceil\cdot\rceil_x$ for some appropriately selected x. Intuitively, a complete annotation is one in which every subformula that can potentially be annotated without violating the well-annotation requirement is indeed annotated. That is, a complete annotation conveys maximal information to the model checker.

EXAMPLE 11 (ONLINE COAUTHORING COMMUNITIES). *A complete annotation of (8) in Example 9 is the following.*

$$\phi_o = \lceil @_o\lceil\neg\lceil\mathcal{O}\lceil\langle -\mathsf{edit}\rangle\lceil\top\rceil_o\rceil_o\rceil_o\rceil_o\rceil_o$$

A complete annotation of (9) in Example 9 is given below.

$$\begin{aligned}&\lceil\neg\lceil{\downarrow} s\,.\,\lceil\langle\mathsf{own}\rangle\lceil{\downarrow} o_1\,.\,@_s\lceil\langle\mathsf{own}\rangle\lceil{\downarrow} o_2\,.\\ &\qquad(\lceil\lceil\neg\lceil o_1\rceil_{o_1}\rceil_{o_1} \wedge \phi_{o_1}\rceil_{o_1}\wedge\\ &\qquad\qquad\phi_{o_2})\rceil_{o_1}\rceil_{o_1}\rceil_s\rceil_s\rceil_{\mathsf{target}}\rceil_{\mathsf{target}}\end{aligned}$$

The following proposition offers alternative characterizations of the $\mathcal{HTR}^-$ language.

PROPOSITION 12.

1. *An $\mathcal{HTR}$ formula ϕ is in $\mathcal{HTR}^-$ iff ϕ has a proper annotation.*

2. *The complete annotation of an $\mathcal{HTR}$ formula exists whenever the formula belongs to $\mathcal{HTR}^-$. When it exists, the complete annotation of an $\mathcal{HTR}$ formula is unique.*

3. *Given an $\mathcal{HTR}^-$ formula ϕ, constructing its complete annotation takes only time linear to the size of ϕ.*

Given a completely annotated formula φ, a subformula of the form $\lceil \rho \rceil_x$ is called an α subformula: i.e., α subformulas represent binary relations. A subformula that is not decorated in φ is called a β subformula: i.e., β subformulas represent higher-arity relations. See the Appendix for a formal treatment.

Hereafter we assume that the *policy* component of the protection system maps event identifiers to completely annotated formulas. That is, the inputs to the update algorithm of the reference monitor are completely annotated formulas.

8.2.4 Reference Monitor Implementation

The reference monitor for $\mathcal{HTR}^-$ has the same basic structure as the one in § 7. Specifically, its internal state is a pair $\langle G, B \rangle$, similar to the pair discussed in § 7.4, and this state is updated using the steps described in § 7.5. The main differences are two. First, the dimensions of B are slightly different from before. Second, in Step 4 of the update procedure, rather than invoking Algorithm 1 for updating B, a different algorithm is invoked.

The component B of the monitor state is a three-dimensional boolean matrix. There is an entry $B[\alpha][u][v]$ for every α subformula of members of $\mathsf{ran}(policy)$ and for every $u, v \in V(G)$. The difference is that, in the previous monitor state the first dimension ranges among the *subformulas* of $\mathsf{ran}(policy)$, whereas for the present monitor state the first dimension ranges among the α *subformulas* of $\mathsf{ran}(policy)$.

The invariant of the reference monitor is the conjunction of (5) and the following.

$$B[\lceil \rho \rceil_x][u][v] = 1 \text{ iff } \gamma_t, u, v \Vdash_x \mathit{erasure}(\rho) \qquad (10)$$

Here, $\mathit{erasure}(\rho)$ denotes the erasure of ρ. While the index v in (6) is the entity referenced by target, the index v in (10) is the entity referenced by the annotation variable x.

The updating of B is conducted by a pair of algorithms in the Appendix. The updating of entries $B[\varphi][\cdot][\cdot]$, for α subformulas φ, is handled by a bottom-up algorithm in the style of Algorithm 1. A top-down algorithm is invoked as a subroutine to process β subformulas.

8.2.5 Complexity

To articulate the time complexity of the update algorithms, we define the notion of ***local binder nesting degree (LBND)*** of an α formula. Specifically, the LBND of $\lceil \rho \rceil_x$ is the nesting degree of binders ($\downarrow$) that appear within the top-level decoration $\lceil \cdot \rceil_x$ but not in nested decorations. For example, the LBND of the following formula is 2.

$$\lceil (\downarrow x_2 \,.\, \downarrow x_3 \ldots. \lceil \downarrow x_5 \ldots. \rceil_{x_4}) \wedge (\downarrow x_6 \ldots.) \rceil_{x_1}$$

THEOREM 13. *Let $M = \sum_{\varphi \in \mathsf{ran}(policy)} |\varphi|$, $N = |V(G)|$, $E = \sum_{l \in \mathcal{R} \cup \mathcal{E}} |R_l(G)|$, and D be the maximum LBND among all members of $\mathsf{ran}(policy)$. The update algorithm in the Appendix runs in time $O(MN^{D+1}(N+E))$. The space usage is the size of G plus $O(MN^2)$ bits overhead for matrix B.*

So long as we limit D to a constant, the time complexity is polynomial. To put this into perspective, the formulas in Example 9 has a maximum LBND of 1 (see also Example 11).

9. CONCLUSION AND FUTURE WORK

We proposed an access control model for supporting collaborative communities that are founded on social contracts made up of both relationship- and history-based elements. Through the development of a series of policy languages and their reference monitors, we demonstrated the thesis that, although CSC offers the convenience of specification via both relationship- and history-based policy elements, the underlying enforcement mechanism can be rendered purely relationship based. This space efficiency is achieved by relational abstraction, in which the past dealings between two parties are abstracted into edges in a relational structure.

Future work includes the formal characterization of expressiveness: What policies can be enforced via relational abstraction? Another direction is to explore the optimization of the update algorithm for the reference monitor: If the transition relation only makes local changes to the social state, then can we bound the updates made to the reference monitor state? A third direction is the development of technologies for facilitating policy engineering. This includes the devising of graphical formalisms for editing policies, capturing reusable social contract patterns at a higher level of abstraction, and designing policy composition frameworks for combining canned policy modules.

10. ACKNOWLEDGMENTS

We thank the anonymous reviewers for their helpful comments. This research was supported in part by an NSERC Discovery Grant and a Canada Research Chair.

11. REFERENCES

[1] Carlos Areces and Balder ten Cate. Hybrid logics. In Patrick Blackburn, Johan van Benthem, and Frank Wolter, editors, *Handbook of Modal Logic*, chapter 14, pages 821–868. Elsevier, 2007.

[2] C. Baier and J.-P. Katoen. *Principles of Model Checking*. MIT, 2008.

[3] H. Barringer, A. Goldberg, K. Havelund, and K. Sen. Rule-based runtime verification. In *Proc. of VMCAI'04*, volume 2937 of *LNCS*, 2004.

[4] D. Basin, F. Klaedtke, and S. Müller. Policy monitoring in first-order temporal logic. In *Proc. of CAV'10*, volume 6174 of *LNCS*, 2010.

[5] P. Blackburn, M. de Rijke, and Y. Venema. *Modal Logic*. Cambridge, 2001.

[6] G. Bruns, P. W. L. Fong, I. Siahaan, and M. Huth. Relationship-based access control: Its expression and enforcement through hybrid logic. In *Proc. of CODASPY'12*, San Antonio, TX, USA, Feb. 2012.

[7] B. Carminati, E. Ferrari, R. Heatherly, M. Kantarcioglu, and B. Thuraisingham. A semantic web based framework for social network access control. In *Proc. of SACMAT'09*, Stresa, Italy, June 2009.

[8] B. Carminati, E. Ferrari, R. Heatherly, M. Kantarcioglu, and B. Thuraisinghaim. Semantic web-based social network access control. *Computers and Security*, 30(2–3):108–115, 2011.

[9] B. Carminati, E. Ferrari, and A. Perego. Enforcing access control in Web-based social networks. *ACM TISSEC*, 13(1), 2009.

[10] Barbara Carminati and Elena Ferrari. Enforcing relationships privacy through collaborative access

control in web-based social networks. In *Proceedings of CollaborateCom'09*, November 2009.

[11] Y. Cheng, J. Park, and R. Sandhu. Relationship-based access control for online social networks: Beyond user-to-user relationships. In *Proc. of the 4th IEEE Int. Conf. on Information Privacy, Security, Risk & Trust (PASSAT'12)*, Amsterdam, Netherlands, September 2012.

[12] Y. Cheng, J. Park, and R. Sandhu. A user-to-user relationship-based access control model for online social networks. In *Proceedings of DBSec'12*, 2012.

[13] Jan Chomicki. Efficient checking of temporal integrity constraints using bounded history encoding. *ACM TODS*, 20(2), 1995.

[14] Úlfar Erlingsson and Fred B. Schneider. IRM enforcement of Java stack inspection. In *Proc. of the 2000 IEEE Symp. on Security and Privacy (S&P'00)*, pages 246–255, Berkeley, CA, USA, May 2000.

[15] Philip W. L. Fong. Access control by tracking shallow execution history. In *Proceedings of the 2004 IEEE Symposium on Security and Privacy (S&P'04)*, pages 43–55, Berkeley, CA, USA, May 2004.

[16] Philip W. L. Fong. Relationship-based access control: Protection model and policy language. In *Proc. of CODASPY'11*, San Antonio, TX, USA, Feb. 2011.

[17] Philip W. L. Fong, Pooya Mehregan, and Ram Krishnan. Relational abstraction in community-based secure collaboration. Technical Report 2013-1045-12, Department of Computer Science, University of Calgary, August 2013.

[18] Philip W. L. Fong and Ida Siahaan. Relationship-based access control policies and their policy languages. In *Proc. of SACMAT'11*, Innsbruck, Austria, June 2011.

[19] M. Franceschet and M. de Rijke. Model checking hybrid logics. *J. Applied Logic*, pages 279–304, 2006.

[20] Carrie E. Gates. Access Control Requirements for Web 2.0 Security and Privacy. In *IEEE W2SP'07*, Oakland, CA, USA, 2007.

[21] K. W. Hamlen, G. Morrisett, and F. B. Schneider. Computability classes for enforcement mechanisms. *ACM TOPLAS*, 28(1), 2006.

[22] R. Krishnan, J. Niu, R. Sandhu, and W. H. Winsborough. Group-centric secure information sharing models for isolated groups. *ACM TISSEC*, 14(3), 2011.

[23] R. Krishnan and R. Sandhu. Authorization policy specification and enforcement for group-centric secure information sharing. In *Proc. of the 7th Int. Conf. on Info. Sys. Security (ICISS'11)*, volume 7093 of *LNCS*. Springer, 2011.

[24] Ram Krishnan, Ravi Sandhu, Jianwei Niu, and William Winsborough. Foundations for group-centric secure information sharing models. In *Proceedings of SACMAT'09*, Stresa, Italy, June 2009.

[25] K. Krukow, M. Nielsen, and V. Sassone. A framework for concrete reputation-systems with applications to history-based access control. In *Proceedings of CCS'05*, Alexandria, VA, USA, November 2005.

[26] K. Krukow, M. Nielsen, and V. Sassone. A logical framework for history-based access control and reputation systems. *J. Computer Security*, 16(1):63–101, 2008.

[27] M. H. Lessnoff. *Social Contract*. Macmillan, 1986.

[28] J. Ligatti, L. Bauer, and D. Walker. Run-time enforcement of non-safety policies. *ACM TISSEC*, 12(3), 2009.

[29] J. Park, R. Sandhu, and Y. Cheng. ACON: Activity-centric access control for social computing. In *Proc. of the 5th Int. Conf. on Availability, Reliability & Security (ARES'11)*, Vienna, Austria, August 2011.

[30] J. Park, R. Sandhu, and Y. Cheng. A user-activity-centric framework for access control in online social networks. *IEEE Internet Computing*, 15(5), 2011.

[31] F. B. Schneider. Enforceable security policies. *ACM TISSEC*, 3(1), 2000.

APPENDIX

A. PRELIMINARIES

Completely annotated formulas have certain structures.

OBSERVATION 14. *The complete annotation φ of an $\mathcal{HTR}^-$ formula satisfies the following grammar:*

$$\varphi ::= \alpha \qquad\qquad \psi ::= \alpha \mid \beta$$
$$\alpha ::= \lceil \top \rceil_x \mid \lceil \neg\alpha \rceil_x \mid \lceil \alpha \vee \alpha \rceil_x \mid \lceil \langle l \rangle \alpha \rceil_x \mid \lceil \langle -l \rangle \alpha \rceil_x \mid$$
$$\lceil \mathcal{Y}\, \alpha \rceil_x \mid \lceil \alpha\, \mathcal{S}\, \alpha \rceil_x \mid \lceil x \rceil_x \mid \lceil \downarrow x \,.\, \psi \rceil_x \mid \lceil @_x\, \alpha \rceil_x$$
$$\beta ::= \neg\psi \mid \psi \vee \psi \mid \langle l \rangle \psi \mid \langle -l \rangle \psi \mid \downarrow x \,.\, \psi \mid @_x\, \psi$$

If we construct the abstract syntax tree (AST) of a completed annotated formula φ according to the grammar above, then we call an AST node that corresponds to the non-terminal α an α subformula, and one that corresponds to the non-terminal β a β subformula.

The syntactic structure of a complete annotation φ provides the recursive structure of the model checker. As we shall see, the α subformulas are processed bottom-up, while the β subformulas are processed top-down.

Let $\mathsf{sub}_\alpha(\varphi)$ and $\mathsf{sub}_\beta(\varphi)$ denote respectively the set of α subformulas and the set of β subformulas of a completely annotated formula φ. We write $\mathsf{sub}_\psi(\varphi)$ for $\mathsf{sub}_\alpha(\varphi) \cup \mathsf{sub}_\beta(\varphi)$. As before, we overload $\mathsf{sub}_\alpha(\cdot)$, $\mathsf{sub}_\beta(\cdot)$ and $\mathsf{sub}_\psi(\cdot)$ to take a *set* of completely annotated formulas as an argument: i.e., if Φ is a set of completely annotated formulas, then $\mathsf{sub}_\alpha(\Phi) = \cup_{\varphi\in\Phi} \mathsf{sub}_\alpha(\varphi)$.

Given a set Φ of α formulas, an enumeration of Φ's members is in an ***admissible order*** if the enumeration is generated in accordance to the following.

α-AO-1 First, list the α formulas of the form $\lceil \mathcal{Y}\, \alpha \rceil_x$. Among them, list superformulas before subformulas.

α-AO-2 Second, list the remaining α formulas, with subformulas listed before superformulas.

B. UPDATING ALGORITHMS

In Step 4 of the update procedure, Algorithm 2 is invoked to update B. Algorithm 2 in turn invokes Algorithm 3.

Algorithm 2, *Update*$^\Uparrow$, is a bottom-up model checking algorithm for α subformulas. Algorithm 3, *Update*$^\Downarrow$, is a top-down model checking algorithm invoked by *Update*$^\Uparrow$ to evaluate β subformulas. The recursion pattern of the two algorithms closely follow the grammar in Observation 14.

Algorithm 2: $\mathit{Update}^{\Uparrow}(G, B)$

```
1  in      : $G \in \mathcal{G}[\mathcal{V}, \mathcal{R} \cup \mathcal{E}]$
2  in out: $B : \mathsf{sub}_\alpha(\mathsf{ran}(\mathit{policy})) \times V(G) \times V(G) \to \mathbb{B}$
3  local  : $C : \mathsf{sub}_\psi(\mathsf{ran}(\mathit{policy})) \times V(G) \to \mathbb{B}$
4  for $\alpha \in \mathsf{sub}_\alpha(\mathsf{ran}(\mathit{policy}))$, in an admissible order, do
5    for $u \in V(G)$ do
6      for $v \in V(G)$ do
7        switch $\alpha$ do
8          case $\lceil \top \rceil_x$
9            $B[\alpha][u][v] \leftarrow 1$;
10         case $\lceil \neg \alpha_1 \rceil_x$
11           $B[\alpha][u][v] \leftarrow \neg B[\alpha_1][u][v]$;
12         case $\lceil \alpha_1 \vee \alpha_2 \rceil_x$
13           $B[\alpha][u][v] \leftarrow B[\alpha_1][u][v] \vee B[\alpha_2][u][v]$;
14         case $\lceil \langle l \rangle \alpha_1 \rceil_x$
15           $B[\alpha][u][v] \leftarrow \bigvee_{u' \in \mathsf{succ}^l_G(u)} B[\alpha_1][u'][v]$;
16         case $\lceil \langle -l \rangle \alpha_1 \rceil_x$
17           $B[\alpha][u][v] \leftarrow \bigvee_{u' \in \mathsf{pred}^l_G(u)} B[\alpha_1][u'][v]$;
18         case $\lceil \mathcal{Y} \alpha_1 \rceil_x$
19           $B[\alpha][u][v] \leftarrow B[\alpha_1][u][v]$;
20         case $\lceil \alpha_1 \,\mathcal{S}\, \alpha_2 \rceil_x$
21           $B[\alpha][u][v] \leftarrow B[\alpha_2][u][v] \vee (B[\alpha][u][v] \wedge B[\alpha_1][u][v])$;
22         case $\lceil x \rceil_x$
23           $B[\alpha][u][v] \leftarrow (u = v)$;
24         case $\lceil \downarrow x \,.\, \psi_1 \rceil_y$
25           $\mathit{Update}^{\Downarrow}(G, B, C, \psi_1, \{x \mapsto u, y \mapsto v\})$;
26           $B[\alpha][u][v] \leftarrow C[\psi_1][u]$;
27         case $\lceil @_x \, \alpha_1 \rceil_x$
28           $B[\alpha][u][v] \leftarrow B[\alpha_1][v][v]$;
```

Algorithm 2. The bottom-up model checker $\mathit{Update}^{\Uparrow}$ has a structure almost identical to that of *Update*. It enumerates α subformulas in some admissible order, as defined by α-**AO-1** and α-**AO-2** (line 4). For each subformula α, it updates the submatrix $B[\alpha][\cdot][\cdot]$. The updates of lines 9, 11, 13, 15, 17, 19 and 21 are identical to their counterparts in Algorithm 1. Line 23 functions in the same way as line 10 of Algorithm 1. Line 28 performs update in the case of $\lceil @_x \, \alpha_1 \rceil_x$. (Note that the x in $\lceil \cdot \rceil_x$ must be the same variable as the x in $@_x \, \alpha_1$.) Essentially the evaluation of $@_x \, \alpha_1$ at u is the same as the evaluation of α_1 at v, which is the entity referenced by x.

The genuinely complex case is that of $\lceil \downarrow x \,.\, \psi_1 \rceil_y$, the update of which begins on line 24. What is at stake is that B is only capable of differentiating the evaluations of an α formula $\lceil \rho \rceil_x$ at entity u for different bindings of x. The binder ($\downarrow$) now introduces an additional binding, causing B not to be able to capture the bindings of multiple variables. Consequently, the bottom-up model checking strategy no longer applies. The top-down updating algorithm (Algorithm 3) is thus invoked (line 25) to evaluate ψ_1 with an extended variable assignment (containing assignments for both x and y). The result of evaluation is deposited into the matrix C. Such results are then copied back into B (line 26).

Algorithm 3. The top-down algorithm $\mathit{Update}^{\Downarrow}$ evaluates a formula ψ in G at every $u \in V(G)$, with a variable assignment g that defines the free variables in ψ. On return, the evaluation results are stored in a boolean matrix C, such that $C[\psi][u]$ holds the evaluation of ψ at entity u.

Algorithm 3: $\mathit{Update}^{\Downarrow}(G, B, C, \psi, g)$

```
1  in      : $G \in \mathcal{G}[\mathcal{V}, \mathcal{R} \cup \mathcal{E}]$
2  in      : $B : \mathsf{sub}_\alpha(\mathsf{ran}(\mathit{policy})) \times V(G) \times V(G) \to \mathbb{B}$
3  in out: $C : \mathsf{sub}_\psi(\mathsf{ran}(\mathit{policy})) \times V(G) \to \mathbb{B}$
4  in      : $\psi \in \mathsf{sub}_\psi(\mathsf{ran}(\mathit{policy}))$
5  in      : $g : \mathsf{Var} \rightharpoonup V(G)$
6  switch $\psi$ do
7    case $\neg \psi_1$
8      $\mathit{Update}^{\Downarrow}(G, B, C, \psi_1, g)$;
9      for $u \in V(G)$ do
10       $C[\psi][u] \leftarrow \neg C[\psi_1][u]$;
11   case $\psi_1 \vee \psi_2$
12     $\mathit{Update}^{\Downarrow}(G, B, C, \psi_1, g)$;
13     $\mathit{Update}^{\Downarrow}(G, B, C, \psi_2, g)$;
14     for $u \in V(G)$ do
15       $C[\psi][u] \leftarrow C[\psi_1][u] \vee C[\psi_2][u]$;
16   case $\langle l \rangle \psi_1$
17     $\mathit{Update}^{\Downarrow}(G, B, C, \psi_1, g)$;
18     for $u \in V(G)$ do
19       $C[\psi][u] \leftarrow \bigvee_{u' \in \mathsf{succ}^l_G(u)} C[\psi_1][u']$;
20   case $\langle -l \rangle \psi_1$
21     $\mathit{Update}^{\Downarrow}(G, B, C, \psi_1, g)$;
22     for $u \in V(G)$ do
23       $C[\psi][u] \leftarrow \bigvee_{u' \in \mathsf{pred}^l_G(u)} C[\psi_1][u']$;
24   case $@_x \, \psi_1$
25     $\mathit{Update}^{\Downarrow}(G, B, C, \psi_1, g)$;
26     for $u \in V(G)$ do
27       $C[\psi][u] \leftarrow C[\psi_1][g(x)]$;
28   case $\downarrow x \,.\, \psi_1$
29     for $u \in V(G)$ do
30       $\mathit{Update}^{\Downarrow}(G, B, C, \psi_1, g[x \mapsto u])$;
31       $C[\psi][u] \leftarrow C[\psi_1][u]$;
32   case $\lceil \rho \rceil_x$
33     for $u \in V(G)$ do
34       $C[\psi][u] \leftarrow B[\psi][u][g(x)]$;
```

The storage for C is allocated entirely in Algorithm 2 (line 3), and C is then passed into Algorithm 3 [3]. The matrix B is passed as an *input* argument: i.e., it is not mutated.

The algorithm computes recursively. The base case is when ψ is an α formula. Admissible ordering guarantees that the evaluation of this α formula is already in B. Line 33 copies that evaluation from B to C. (Recall that, if ψ is of the form $\lceil \rho \rceil_x$, then $B[\psi][u][v]$ is the evaluation of ψ at u with the variable assignment $g = \{x \mapsto v\}$.) The inductive case is when ψ is a β formula. In this case, $\mathit{Update}^{\Downarrow}$ is called recursively to evaluate the subformulas of ψ, the results of which is used for evaluating ψ itself.

The cases of $\neg\psi_1$, $\psi_1 \vee \psi_2$, $\langle l \rangle \psi_1$, $\langle -l \rangle \psi_1$ and $@_x \, \psi_1$ are relatively straightforward. The case of $\downarrow x \,.\, \psi_1$, however, warrants further explanation. Specifically, when $\mathit{Update}^{\Downarrow}$ is recursively invoked to evaluate the subformula ψ_1 on line 29, the variable assignment is extended to $g[x \mapsto u]$, such that x points to u during the evaluation of ψ_1.

[3]One could have presented Algorithm 3 in such a way that the storage for C is allocated dynamically, on demand. Such a presentation reduces comprehensibility without saving anything in the asymptotic space complexity.

When Kids' Toys Breach Mobile Phone Security

Abdul Serwadda and Vir V. Phoha
Louisiana Tech University
Ruston, LA 71272,USA
{ase007,phoha}@latech.edu

ABSTRACT

Touch-based verification—the use of touch gestures (e.g., swiping, zooming, etc.) to authenticate users of touch screen devices— has recently been widely evaluated for its potential to serve as a second layer of defense to the PIN lock mechanism. In all performance evaluations of touch-based authentication systems however, researchers have assumed naïve (zero-effort) forgeries in which the attacker makes no effort to mimic a given gesture pattern.

In this paper we demonstrate that a simple "Lego" robot driven by input gleaned from general population swiping statistics can generate forgeries that achieve alarmingly high penetration rates against touch-based authentication systems. Using the best classification algorithms in touch-based authentication, we rigorously explore the effect of the attack, finding that it increases the Equal Error Rates of the classifiers by between 339% and 1004% depending on parameters such as the *failure-to-enroll* threshold and the type of touch stroke generated by the robot. The paper calls into question the zero-effort impostor testing approach used to benchmark the performance of touch-based authentication systems.

Categories and Subject Descriptors

K.6.5 [**Management of Computing and Information Systems**]: Security and Protection—authentication

General Terms

Security

Keywords

Biometrics, Touch Gestures, Authentication, Attack, Robot

1. INTRODUCTION

Recently, there has been considerable research on the application of touch gestures for continuous authentication on mobile phones (e.g., see [17][16][27]). The underlying philosophy behind this type of authentication is that if a mobile device could learn the owner's touch pattern during routine operations (such as swiping, zooming and clicking/tapping), an adversary who gets access to the phone can be thwarted based on the mismatch between touch patterns. While several studies (e.g., see [17][27][16]) have shown evidence that indicates that this type of authentication holds a lot of promise, the performance evaluation methodology used in all these studies revolves around a *zero-effort* [9] threat model in which the adversary is assumed to be unable to pull off a sophisticated forgery.

The zero-effort threat model, although well understood not to be representative of the state-of-the-art threats [9], is for several reasons fronted by researchers as being able to sufficiently capture the threat that a touch-based authentication system would face in practice. For instance, in one of the recent papers on touch biometrics, Frank et al. [17] make the following arguments to rule out the need for stringent penetration testing of their system:

> *.... we can hardly imagine someone learning the touch behavior of 30 features, such as pressure, distribution of acceleration, etc., just by looking over the shoulder* [17].

> *...A more successful but more involved attack would be to place a malware application on the user's device. This malware could learn and report the touch pattern if the details of how to compute the features are known to the attacker... However, we argue that a user with malware on the device has already lost the race against the attacker* [17].

These arguments—echoed in many other papers—are sound without doubt. Notably though, the notion that these two attacks (malware and a form of shoulder surfing) represent the full spectrum of threats that the system could face is for several reasons debatable. In particular, by assuming these two as the only threats, researchers in this area appear to disregard the following two attributes of a touch biometrics system: 1) Users' behavioral biometrics patterns exhibit a great deal of intra-user variability and overlap across a large population, implying that for certain types of users (see [30][23] for examples of biometric user categories), statistics extracted from a large population database could be used to create forgeries that significantly increase error rates (e.g., see [8][26]). Given access to population statistics, an adversary could learn a great deal of information about a given user's pattern without having to physically observe the victim's pattern or depend on a malware application to learn the pattern, 2) The three gestures on which touch-based

CCS'13, November 4–8, 2013, Berlin, Germany.
Copyright 2013 ACM 978-1-4503-2477-9/13/11 ...$15.00.
http://dx.doi.org/10.1145/2508859.2516659.

continuous authentication systems are built (i.e., clicking or tapping, swiping to move screen content vertically, and swiping to move screen content horizontally — see [17][16]) can very easily be implemented using elementary robotic devices available in many homes and grocery stores (see [5]). Given a touch gesture pattern that is to be executed on the phone, a simple robotic/mechanical device (as opposed to malware) would be a cheaper and much less sophisticated option for an adversary who seeks to retrieve a valuable resource from a stolen smart phone.

The two attributes cited above motivate the attack designed in this paper. We implement a robotic attack that achieves alarmingly high success rates against continuous touch-based authentication systems. Driven by input gleaned from general population (swiping) statistics, the attack uses a standard Lego Mindstorms NXT robotic kit [3] to control a "*finger*" that is designed to replicate the human finger properties sensed by the state-of-the-art touch based authentication systems. Using a large touch biometrics dataset, we demonstrate the lethality of the attack against the best verification algorithms in touch-based authentication.

The following attributes convince us that the attack could easily get embraced by adversaries if continuous touch-based authentication got widely deployed:

No specialized expertise (or experience) required: The algorithmic and mechanical design of the attack revolves around some of the most basic Lego robotic skills taught in middle school in the USA (e.g., see [20]) and many other parts of the world. While the attack could be designed based on exquisite programming of both the robot's sensors and the motors, the paper seeks to emphasize the simplicity of the attack—we implement a design that only requires the motors to be programmed.

Analog domain and sample-level attributes: The attack is launched in the analog domain, and thus cannot be easily stopped by conventional software solutions like would be the case for a malware attack. Additionally, the attack is sample-level meaning that the attacker needn't know about the internal implementation details of the verification algorithms or features used by the system. As long as the robot performs the swiping operation, the underlying classification system will extract the required features from the touch strokes.

No extra-ordinary access privileges required: The attack does not require template access; it is driven by general information on how the "*common user*" is likely to swipe on the phone. This kind of information can easily be retrieved from publicly accessible data sets (e.g., see [4]), and to some extent from research findings such as ours (e.g., see Section 4.2).

The main contribution of this paper is the demonstration that robotic devices pose a major threat to touch-based authentication. Because this threat has never been considered by researchers in this field, the paper has the potential to spark off a complete repackaging of touch-based authentication systems. The design of these systems (e.g., features, template-building approach, etc.), and the methodology used to test their resistance to impostors are examples of aspects of touch-based authentication that could see change as a result of our findings.

The rest of this paper is organized as follows: We discuss related work in Section 2, our data collection and preprocessing in Section 3 and the attack design in Section 4. We present the attack results in Section 5 and our conclusions in Section 6.

2. RELATED WORK

To put this paper into context with previous work, we examine two streams of past research: works which explored algorithmic (or non zero-effort) attacks against behavioral biometric systems, and works which studied the use of touch gestures for authentication. The latter category of research has two branches, namely, continuous authentication and "entry point" authentication. In continuous authentication (e.g., see [17][16][27]), users' touch gestures are monitored throughout a phone usage session. In "entry point" authentication on the other hand, users are authenticated based on how they execute a certain (possibly secret) gesture (e.g., see [24][25] [13]) at the entry point to an application or to the phone itself (i.e., login). Our attack is targeted against continuous authentication, so we delve deeper into past research which explored this type of authentication.

Using a dataset of 41 users, Frank et al. [17] obtained Equal Error Rates (EERs) of between 0 and 4% when a k-Nearest Neighbors (k-NN) classifier and a Support-Vector Machine (SVM) were used to continuously authenticate users based on their touch gestures. The study was based on 30 features extracted while users swiped/scrolled (to move screen content vertically or horizontally) as they read text and browsed images. In [27], a digital sensor glove was shown to enhance the performance of a touch gesture-based continuous authentication system. Using a Decision Tree, Random Forest and Bayes Net classifier, the authors showed that the glove reduced the error rates seen during authentication. For instance, for the Bayes Net classifier, a False Accept Rate (FAR) of 11.96% and a False Reject Rate (FRR) of 8.53% respectively reduced to 2.14% and 1.63% when the glove was used. Similar improvements were noted for the other two classifiers.

More recently, Li et al. [16] evaluated the performance of a live implementation of a touch-based authentication system on a mobile phone. Leveraging a "hack into the lower layer of an Android system [16]", the system monitored touch gestures across all applications installed on the phone. Based on a group of 75 users who were allowed to freely interact with the phones for days, the SVM-based authentication system was shown to attain classification accuracies as high as 95%.

All three papers cited above employ a zero-effort testing approach in which the system's resistance to attack is gauged based on simplistic attacks in which samples from a subset of the population are used to attack samples drawn from a given user. It is on this front that this paper advances the state-of-the-art, calling for more rigorous biometric testing methodologies that are at par with the sophisticated adversarial technologies being seen today. The works by Ballard et al. [9], Tey et al. [21] and Serwadda et al. [26] resonate with our research, demonstrating new breeds of impostor attacks against two biometric modalities that are very closely related to touch based authentication.

Ballard et al. showcase two attacks against handwriting biometrics: one launched by trained forgers, the other based on a generative algorithm. Tey et al. and Serwadda et al. on the other hand demonstrate two attacks against password-based keystroke authentication, with the former being based on trained forgers, and the latter being based on a generative algorithm which uses general population statistics as input. In all three papers, the attacks are shown to significantly degrade system performance relative to the standard zero-effort attacks.

Although this emerging breed of impostor attacks shares the same motivation as our work, our attack has several operational and technical attributes that put it apart from the other attacks. Notably, the very low level of expertise required to implement the attack, the low cost of equipment required and the fact that it is a hardware-based attack majorly distinguish it from the above cited attacks (attributes described in Section 1 portray these differences in more detail).

3. DATA AND FEATURES USED FOR OUR INVESTIGATIONS

3.1 Data Collection Process

We conducted two data collection experiments using two Android applications that captured the way in which users touched the mobile phone screen. The gestures that users typically perform on a touch screen include zooming (in and out), clicking (tapping), swiping to switch between screens (i.e., horizontal swiping) and swiping to move a page up and down (i.e, vertical swiping). The tap gesture does not hold enough information to strongly separate between a large group of users [17], while the zoom gesture does not occur frequently enough to guarantee that a continuous authentication application will always have enough data to make classification decisions [17]. For these reasons, a number of works on continuous touch-based authentication hinge around the two swipe gestures (e.g., see [17])[1]. We will focus on these two gestures in this paper.

For each of a set of points on a touch stroke registered on the screen during swiping, the applications recorded the: 1) x and y coordinates, 2) time at which the finger touched the point in question, 3) area occluded between the finger and the screen, 4) the pressure exerted on the screen and 5) the orientation of the phone (i.e., landscape or portrait). The two Android applications basically simulated how users read text and view images on the touch screen. Based on a short paragraph of text or an image, users had to answer several questions by selecting one of two to four alternative answers that we provided per question. On reading a question, each user would scroll/swipe back to the image or block of text containing clues to the solution, before scrolling/swiping towards the answers section where the user would select one of the choices provided.

Both applications were based on the same idea, although each application was based on a different set of questions/images. In the first phase of experiments (which we also refer to as *Session I*), users interacted with one application. They then returned on another day at their convenience to interact with the second application (i.e., during *Session II*). All participants used the same brand of phone—the Google Nexus S running Android version 4.0—so as to avoid bias in our findings that might be caused by differences in the way in which different phones extract information from touch gestures.

[1]Li et al. [16] used the tap gesture in conjunction with the two swipe gestures. However they found that it had very poor discriminability in comparison to the two swipe gestures.

3.2 Feature Extraction and Preprocessing

Before extracting features from the data, we performed an outlier filtering step to eliminate very short strokes since these likely originated from click events (or taps), as opposed to swiping (scrolling). Frank et al. [17] performed a similar step on users' strokes before proceeding with the classification process. Having removed outliers, we extracted 28 features from each stroke. There is currently no universal feature-set that researchers use to represent a distinct stroke. For example, Frank et al. [17] defined 30 features and discarded 3 of them after feature analysis, Li et al. [16] defined 13 features (or 14 features if the x and y coordinates of a point are considered as distinct features) and discarded 4 of them after feature analysis while Feng et al. [27] used 53 features. For this work we used 28 features that we believe best summarize the statistical attributes of a touch stroke. A description of how we computed these features follows:

Using the pressure and area readings at different points along a stroke, we respectively built a pressure vector, P, and an area vector, A, to represent the pressure and area associated with the stroke. We computed the velocity between every pair of consecutive points along a stroke, and used these values to generate the velocity vector, V. Finally, for every pair of points in V, we computed the acceleration, and generated an acceleration vector, A'.

For each of the four vectors A, P, V and A', we computed five measures to summarize a user's mean behavior, variability in behavior and extreme behavior along a stroke. These were: 1) lower quartile, 2) second quartile, 3) third quartile, 4) mean, and, 5) standard deviation. This gave a total of 20 (=4× 5) features per stroke. The last 8 features making up a vector representing a stroke were: the x and y coordinates of the starting points, the x and y coordinates of the end points, the distance between the end and starting points of a stroke, the time taken to complete the stroke, the tangent of the angle between the line joining the end-points of a stroke and the horizontal, and the sum of distances between every pair of adjacent points on a stroke.

4. ATTACK DESIGN

4.1 General Assumptions

The attacks launched in this paper assume an adversary who gets physical access to a phone for which touch-based continuous authentication is the only active layer of defence. In practice, this scenario may arise for an attacker who : 1) breaks the PIN lock mechanism (e.g., using methods such as those in [6][22]), or, 2) finds a phone in which the PIN lock has been disabled temporarily (e.g., a user who sets a very long timeout for the PIN lock), or, 3) finds a phone in which the PIN lock has been completely disabled by the owner [17]. To be able to determine the amount of extra security that touch-based continuous authentication adds to the standard PIN lock in the worst case, we believe that these assumptions must necessarily be made. See [7], for an investigation in which a similar assumption (i.e., that the adversary has access to the victim's password) was made in order to enable rigorous evaluation of the security of Randomized Biometric Templates (RBTs).

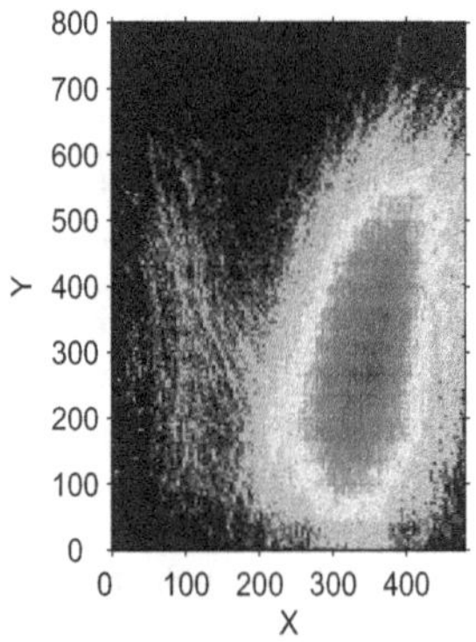

(a) Spatial distribution of swiping activity during vertical swiping.

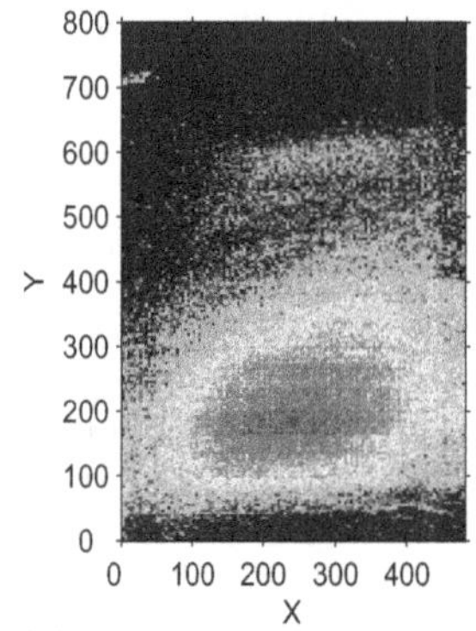

(b) Spatial distribution of swiping activity during horizontal swiping.

Figure 1: Color map showing the spatial distribution of touch strokes on the phone screen. A high intensity of blue corresponds to regions which saw very few strokes, while a high intensity of red implies a region which saw intense swiping activity. The phone was being used in portrait mode when the strokes were generated. Note that the coordinate system used on the figures is different from that used by the Android system.

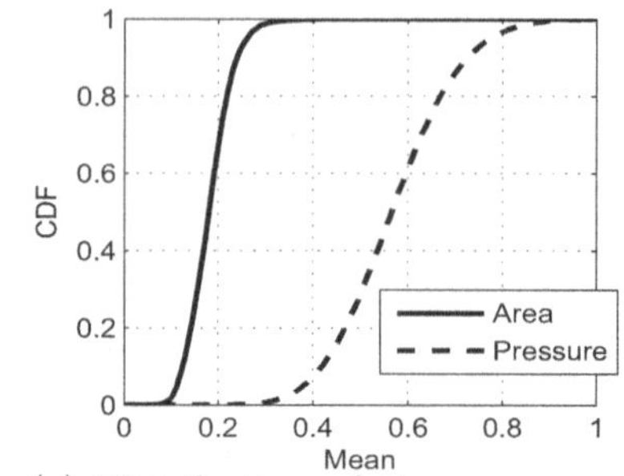

(a) Distribution of the mean pressure and mean area across touch strokes.

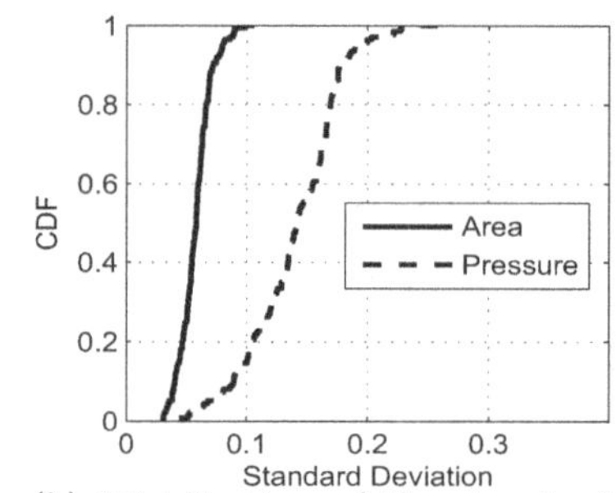

(b) Distribution of the standard deviation of the mean pressure and mean area across touch strokes.

Figure 2: CDFs expressing the mean and variability of area and pressure seen across the population.

In the attack itself, the attacker will seek to view private information on the phone (e.g., emails, pictures, etc.,) without triggering the anomaly detection mechanism. The attack thus basically proceeds by scrolling/swiping through documents on the phone. In practice we believe that the attacker could even assist the robot during certain operations (e.g., occasionally clicking at a challenging location), since the anomaly detector will most likely not be sensitive enough to detect a few anomalous clicks. Next we discuss the underlying statistical observations that drive the attack, and the details of the mechanical and algorithmic design of the robot.

4.2 How do People Swipe on the Phone?

To design the attacks, we first examine the way in which people swipe in general. How random is swiping behavior across a population? Are there certain distinct traits that manifest frequently across a large number of users? This section provides answers to these and related questions. Due to space limitations, we only present results on the pressure exerted on the screen, the area between the finger and the screen and the region of the phone at which most swiping is done. Other measures such as the time taken to complete a stroke, the velocity of the finger and the length of a stroke, to mention but a few, are left out here but will be used to guide the attack design.

4.2.1 Location of Swiping Activity

Figure 1 shows the density of touch strokes captured at different positions of the phone screen during the first phase of experiments. The dark blue color corresponds to regions which saw very little or no swiping/scrolling activity while a high intensity of red corresponds to regions which saw a lot of swiping. Observe (Figure 1(a)) that the vast majority of vertical strokes generated by our user population originated from points having X values in the neighborhood of 300 units, and terminated at a position with an X value of close to 400 units (and vice versa). Notably, this region of high activity comprises less than 50% of the screen display. The heart of the red region (which tends towards black) occupies an even much smaller portion of the screen. Similar traits (see Figure 1(b)) were seen with horizontal swiping.

Based on evidence provided through this plot, an adversary with access to general population statistics could potentially significantly narrow down the scope of features such as: 1) the x coordinate of the start point of a stroke, 2) the y coordinate of the start point of a stroke, 3) the x coordinate of the end point of a stroke, 3) the y coordinate of the end point of a stroke, 4) the duration of a stroke, 5) the summation of distances between consecutive points of a stroke, and 6) the direction of the end-to end line, among other features. These features represent a good proportion of the features used to characterize users' touch gestures in past research (e.g., see [17][16]), and will also be used in this study.

Regarding the cause of the clustering tendency, our conjecture is that the high density of strokes on the right side of the screen (i.e., taking the case of vertical swiping for instance) was likely because the majority of users are right handed, tending to hold the phone in the right hand and swiping with the thumb, or holding the phone in the left hand and swiping using one of the fingers on the right hand. In any of these two scenarios, a user is very likely to swipe in the manner reflected in the figure. We do not rule out the possibility that certain applications could depict variations

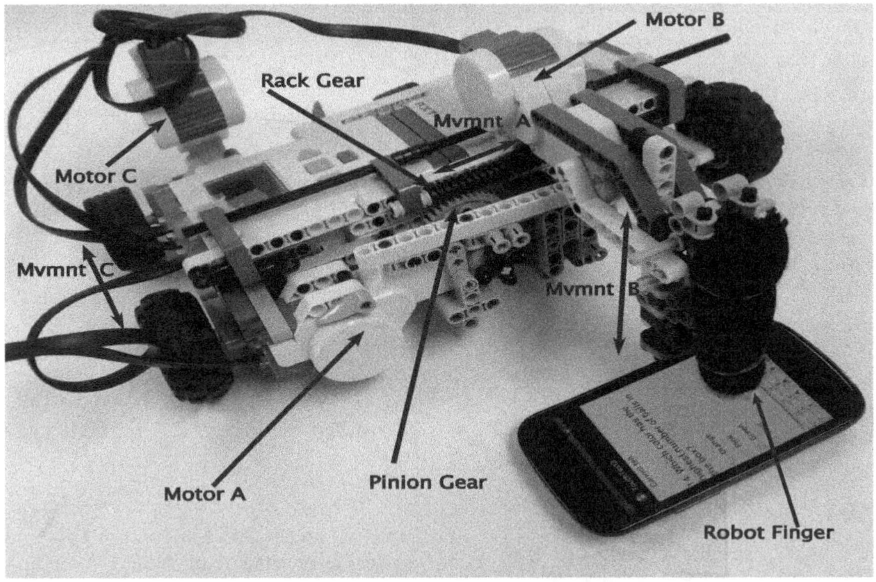

Figure 3: Mechanical design of the robot. The three motors (Motor A, Motor B and Motor C) are respectively responsible for moving the robot finger left and right (Mvmt A), up and down (Mvmt B) and back and forth (Mvmt C). Motor B contributes to the pressure exerted on the screen. Depending on the input parameters to the motors (see Algorithm 1), the superposition of the three primitive motor movements is able to produce touch strokes with different properties.

from the pattern shown in the figure. In this case we argue that a committed attacker who has interest in breaking into such applications can make research on the swiping traits associated with these applications.

4.2.2 Finger Area and Pressure on the Screen

Figure 2(a) shows the distribution of the mean area touched by the finger and the mean pressure exerted on the screen across a subset of our full user population. To plot the figures, we computed each user's mean area (and mean pressure) and plotted the results on the CDF. Observe that over 80% of the population had a mean area of between 0.1 and 0.25 and that about 50% of the population had mean pressure values of between 0.4 and 0.6. These user proportions already suggest that a large number of users could be clustered around a narrow band of values (for both pressure and area). To get a more concrete insight into the possible clustering of users' profiles, we studied the variability seen by users for each of these two variables.

Particularly, we computed the standard deviation of the mean area and mean pressure exhibited by each of the users represented in Figure 2(a), and then plotted these values on a CDF (Figure 2(b)). Taking the case of pressure for instance, the figure shows that about 40% of the users had a standard deviation of over 0.15. Assuming users' mean pressure values follow a Gaussian distribution, a user with a standard deviation of 0.15 could see her/his biometric pattern fall on a band having a width of up to 0.6 units (i.e., 2 standard deviations on either side of the mean). Given such a wide span, an input selected from the earlier mentioned clustered regions (Figure 2(a)) could have a good chance of falling within such a user's feature range.

Similar observations made for the other features (e.g., velocity, length of strokes, start point of stroke, etc.) further prompted us to hypothesize that generic information from the population could possibly enable us to implement a successful attack on a subset of the users.

4.3 Mechanical Design

4.3.1 Design of the Robot

Figure 3 depicts the robot design. The main components of the robot are: 2 NXT Intelligent bricks, 3 motors, 1 rack gear, 1 pinion gear, 4 wheels and the robotic arm stroking the screen. Throughout the rest of the paper we will refer to this robotic arm as the robot finger (or the finger). The two Intelligent bricks, one of which serving as the CPU of the system, are joined to form the chassis on which other components are built. Motor C, which propels the wheels, is responsible for moving the finger back and forth. Motor A on the other hand drives the pinion and rack gear system to move the finger left and right. Motor B moves the finger up and down, and thus helps control the pressure exerted by the finger on the screen. Depending on the way in which the three motors are configured (see Algorithm 1), the robot can create strokes having different properties (e.g., velocity, direction, pressure, etc.).

4.3.2 Fabrication of the Finger

We had three main design considerations regarding the object to be used to touch the screen. These were: 1) the object had to be able to register touch events on the capacitative screen, 2) it had to easily match the finger surface area as needed, 3) it had to be soft to avoid damaging the screen, and 4) it had to be made from cheap, domestically accessible materials. The fourth point rules out technologies such as prosthetics [10] that despite guaranteeing artificial fingers that could match many of the properties of a human finger, would make the attack implementation expensive, and likely defeat our aim of demonstrating how easily the attack can

ALGORITHM 1: Swiping Mechanism

```
Input: numOfSwipes//Number of Swipes;
Input: SLRight//Step length right;
Input: speedRight//Speed right;
Input: SLFwd//Step length forward;
Input: SLBkwd//Step length backward;
Input: speedFwd//Speed forward;
Input: speedBkwd//Speed backward;
Input: speedUpDown//Finger up-down speed;
Input: numOfSteps
//Number of steps needed to complete the swipe;
GenerateSwipingSteps()
for i←1 to numOfSwipes do
    rfs=GRandom(μ1,σ1); //Gaussian noise in speed
    FingerDown(speedUpDown);
    for j←1 to (p) //Steps upward-right
    do
        FingerForward(speedFwd,SLFwd);
        FingerRight(speedRight+rfs,SLRight);
    for k←1 to (NumOfSteps-p)//Steps downward-right
    do
        FingerBackward(speedBkwd,SLBkwd);
        FingerRight(speedRight+rfs,SLRight);
    FingerUp();
    FingerBack();
    Wait(swipeInterval);//Inter-swipe interval
```

be launched based on materials that are cheaply available off the shelf.

To address all four points we fabricated the finger surface from play-doh [28], a malleable compound that children use to model different kinds of play-objects. Although play-doh on its own was able to register touch points on the screen, we housed it inside a touch screen glove (see [2]) in order to have close control of the finger area touching the screen. In all experiments we set our finger area to be approximately 0.15 units, which was the mean value we observed across our user population. The area setting itself was manual—we iteratively molded the play-doh and tested it on the phone (during preliminary experiments) until the area value stabilized at around 0.15 units. When the motors pushed the play-doh against the touch screen during scrolling, the play-doh, owing to its softness, would see some amount of deformation. These small variations in play-doh touch surface area did not affect our attack that much, since human fingers also see variations in area along the path of a stroke.

Perhaps one interesting observation worth noting here is that when we connected a battery (AA type) to the play-doh during the attack, the area registered on the phone screen increased. A possible reason for this is that the effective area of contact between the screen and the phone is not only dependent on the physical area of contact between the two, but, it also depends on the extent of electrical contact between them. We leveraged this property to introduce changes in the finger area during the experiments.

4.4 Algorithmic Design of Robot Movements

4.4.1 Overview

We formulated an algorithm that can generate a wide variety of touch strokes depending on the parameters passed

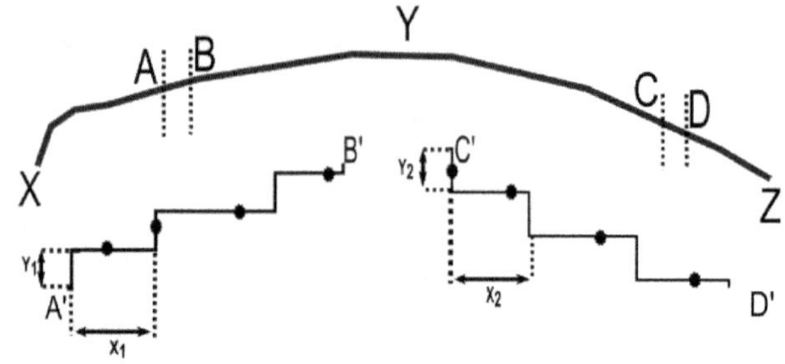

Figure 4: Demonstrating the steps taken by the robot during execution of a swipe gesture. The path seen by the Android system is just a collection of points (e.g., the black dots in the figure) sampled from the physical path traversed on the phone screen.

to it. The attack launched in this paper was just one special case of the algorithm (i.e., a specific set of inputs). We first describe the generic algorithm, and then narrow down to the specific case which we used for our attacks. Before delving into the details of the algorithm, we note that we used the Bricx Command Center IDE (BricxCC) [1] for the algorithm implementation. Unlike the standard Lego Mindstorms NXT IDE (see [3]) which uses a drag and drop graphical interface, BricxCC supports NXC, a high level programming language whose syntax is similar to that of the C language. With the NXC language, we were able to easily fine-tune our code without going through the tedious process of re-aligning and modifying the graphical components (as would be the case with the Mindstorms NXT IDE).

4.4.2 General Algorithm

We describe the mechanism of the attack (Algorithm 1) based on the touch stroke represented in Figure 4. We generalize an arbitrary touch stroke as comprising of either or both of an upward trajectory (e.g., XY) and a downward trajectory (e.g., YZ). To traverse the upward path between X and Y, the robot first moves the finger downwards onto the phone at speed specified by the parameter *speedUpDown* (see method *FingerDown*), before embarking on a series of very short vertical and horizontal steps having the *sawtooth-like* structure represented along A'B'. The short vertical step (i.e., Y_1) is executed using the method *FingerForward* (see (Algorithm 1)) while the short horizontal step (i.e., X_1) that immediately proceeds the vertical step is executed using the method *FingerRight*. The algorithm repeats (loops) this process until the peak position (i.e., Y) is reached (i.e., after, say, p iterations).

On the downward trajectory (YZ) the algorithm uses the same approach used for the upward trajectory, except that the vertical steps are now downwards (see the method *FingerBackward*), while the horizontal steps continue towards the right (i.e., using the method *FingerRight*). On reaching the point Z, the robot lifts the finger off the phone (see *FingerUp*), moves it back towards X (see *FingerBack*), and then swipes again after a random interval.

Each of the methods executing the short steps takes two parameters, one of which is a speed input (e.g., speedFwd), the other a distance input (e.g., SLFwd). These parameters enable us to control the speed and distance covered in each step. During each *swipe* (we interchangeably refer

Parameters / Values	Horizontal Swiping	Vertical Swiping
numOfSteps	4	4
SLRight	4	4
SLFwd	2	0
SLBkwd	0	2
speedRight	49	53
speedBkwd	0	20
speedFwd	20	0
speedUpDown	20	20
p	4	0
numOfSwipes	300	300
μ_1	2	2
σ_1	2	2

Table 1: Parameter settings used for the attack on the portrait strokes. According to the specifications of the LEGO system, the speed parameters (i.e., speedRight, speedBkwd, speedFwd) are in terms of the power of the robot motor, while the distance parameters (SLRight, SLFwd, SLBkwd) are expressed in terms of the angle of rotation.

to a full path, such as one from X to Z as a *swipe* or a *stroke*), we compute the random noise term, *rfs*, and use it to perturb the speed inputs to the *FingerRight* method. This perturbation, in addition to the noise arising from the mechanical dynamics of the robot, enabled us to simulate the randomness that humans exhibit during the execution of a stroke. We only add the noise factors to the inputs of the *FingerRight* method and not to those of the *FingerForward* or *FingerBackward* methods because the long distance along the horizontal direction (e.g., along the straight line from X to Z) gives more room for error than the very short span towards the direction perpendicular to the straight line XZ.

A critical difference between the arbitrary stroke shown in Figure 4 and the typical touch stroke produced by humans is that the strokes generated by humans deviate very slightly from a straight line. For this reason, to generate a stroke similar to XY (see Figure 4), our settings were such that the steps along the normal to the straight line XZ were shorter than those in the direction along XZ. This resulted into strokes that were much less crooked than the stroke shown in Figure 4. Given that the *actual stroke* registered by the Android system is just a combination of points sampled[2] from the physical stroke (e.g., see solid dots on zig-zag line in Figure 4), evidence of crookedness was further erased from our strokes, with the vast majority of strokes registered by the system depicting a smooth shape.

Table 1 summarizes the algorithm settings that we used for the attack for both the vertical and horizontal swipes in portrait mode. To generate a horizontal stroke, we positioned the phone such that the finger started around the point with coordinates (363, 541) and moved towards the point having the coordinates (145, 588). For the vertical strokes, the phone was positioned such that the start coordinates were approximately (320,613) and the direction of the finger being towards the point (352,400). As mentioned earlier, the randomization factor (and the randomness emerging out of the mechanical interactions between robot components) ensured that the different variables saw slight changes between strokes. We set the *speedUpDown* parameter (speed at which finger meets phone screen) to 20 units so as to get pressure outputs of between 0.4 and 0.6.

Depending on factors such as the area of the finger and the initial position of the finger relative to the phone, one may have to set a different value for the *speedUpDown* parameter in order to get pressure outputs in this range. Like in the case of the finger area (see Section 4.3.2.), we not only iteratively set the pressure during initial experiments, but also depended on a connected battery to increase the pressure to the required range. To ease the task of setting the various attack parameters, we enabled pointer locations (under developer options) so as to view the strokes and their associated raw feature outputs on the screen during the fine-tuning phase. All attack parameters were set based on an initial set of experiments in which we compared the robotic output with the mean behavior seen across a subset of the users who were not subjected to the attack.

[2]On our Google Nexus phones, we found that the system recorded touch points at an interval of 15 *ms* on average.

5. ATTACK PERFORMANCE EVALUATION

5.1 Verification Algorithms

We demonstrate the impact of the attack using a Support Vector Machine (SVM) [11] and the k-Nearest Neighbors (k-NN) classifier [12]. We select these two verification algorithms because they have recently been shown in [16] and [17] to perform very well for continuous touch-based authentication. We briefly describe the mechanisms of operation of the two algorithms below:

5.1.1 Support Vector Machine

An SVM is a binary classifier which uses a hyperplane to separate two data classes in such a way that the margin between the two classes is maximized. The margin is the distance between the hyperplane and the boundary observations which are also referred to as support vectors. For classes that are not linearly separable in a given feature space, it is sometimes necessary to map the original data points to a higher dimensional space with the aid of a kernel function. We used the Gaussian radial-basis function as our kernel, like was done in [17].

5.1.2 k-Nearest Neighbors

During training, this classifier does not have to extract any model from the data—it only stores the feature vectors from the different classes (in our case two classes). Given a new observation that is to be assigned a class label, the k-NN classifier assigns it to the class A if the majority of the k closest training vectors to the new observation belong to the class A. Different researchers use different measures to represent the distance between the training vectors and a test observation. Similarly to Frank et al. [17], we use the Euclidean distance metric.

For both the k-NN and SVM, we used WEKA [29] via its Java API to implement the classification system. We used k=9 for the k-NN classifier since this value gave us the best performance. For all other parameters across the two classifiers, we used the WEKA defaults.

5.2 Training and Testing Methodology

5.2.1 Training and Zero-effort Testing

Training was done based on data collected during *Session I* while zero-effort testing was done based on data collected during *Session II*. For each user, we distinguished between portrait and landscape strokes, and further distinguished between horizontal and vertical strokes for each of the two phone orientations. This way, each user had four reference templates. The reason for separating between these four types of strokes was because certain features change depending on the type of stroke and the way in which the phone is held when the stroke is executed. For example, for the typical user, a horizontal stroke executed in portrait mode will very likely have different start and end-points (among other features) from a horizontal stroke executed in landscape mode. Owing to the mismatch between features, a classification mechanism that does not distinguish between these two types of strokes will likely perform unreliably.

In practice we believe that a touch-based authentication application should use all four types of reference templates since users can switch between stroke types depending on the type and organization of content they read on the phone. Regardless of whether a user is biased towards a certain type of stroke, the system should be able to accurately perform classification during those times when the user executes the other kinds of strokes.

For each of the four categories of strokes, we only performed our analysis for those users who executed at least 80 strokes during *Session I*. For the portrait strokes we had 106 and 118 users who met this 80 strokes requirement for the horizontal and vertical strokes respectively. For the landscape strokes, we had 41 and 50 users who met the requirement for the horizontal and vertical strokes respectively. For training, we used 80 strokes executed by the user in question (i.e., genuine or positive class) and 5 strokes from each of the other users (i.e., the impostor or negative class) for each of the four categories of strokes.

To establish a baseline against which to measure the impact of the robotic attack, we carried out zero-effort testing for each user. In these tests, to launch an *impostor attack* against a given user's template, we used 10 strokes from each of the other users. To carry out a *genuine attack* against a given user's template, we used all the strokes captured from that particular user during *Session II*. Because a user will every now and then execute a stroke which is very distinct from the rest of her strokes, we used a block of strokes, rather than a single stroke to make authentication decisions.

Each legitimate or impostor authentication attempt was based on a single vector derived from 10 consecutive feature vectors (or strokes). The single authentication vector was computed such that its elements were the component-wise means of the 10 vectors contained in a sliding window. From the results obtained from these tests, we generated four Detection Error Tradeoff (DET) curves [18] for each user, one for each kind of swiping. From each of these curves, we determined the Equal Error Rate (EER), a performance measure that is widely used to evaluate the performance of biometrics systems (e.g., see [15][17][9]).

5.2.2 Robotic Testing

The robotic testing process was the same as that described in Section 5.2.1, except that the *impostor attack* was based on samples generated by the robot. We will refer to the impostor attack in this case as the *robotic impostor attack* or *robotic attack*. We used 600 strokes generated by the robot to carry out this attack against each user. Like we did in the zero-effort tests (Section 5.2.1), we again generated four DET curves for each user, and calculated the EER from each of the curves.

5.3 Robotic Attack Results

In this section we present the attack results. In order to make a thorough performance evaluation while avoiding duplication, we focus on the portrait strokes since the landscape strokes did not provide any major new insights. We present some performance highlights of the landscape strokes in Appendix 2.

5.3.1 Rationale Behind Failure to Enroll Policy

For behavioral biometric modalities, there are certain users whose biometric footprint is so inconsistent that even a zero-effort attack can attain very high penetration rates. To demonstrate the success of an algorithmic attack against such users is not as meaningful as, for instance, demonstrating it against the most consistent users on the system. For this reason, we employed a "*failure to enroll*" policy, in which we only enrolled users whose EERs were less than a certain EER threshold (α) for both classifiers. Our attack performance evaluation was done at values of α ranging from 0.2 to 0.08. We chose an upper bound of α=0.2 because we believe that a user with an EER higher than that would probably not use the technology anyway. For the lower bound we decided to use α=0.08 because the number of users able to enroll on the system became too small for values of α less than that.

5.3.2 Mean Impact of the Attack

For different values of α, we computed the mean EER and standard deviation of the EERs across the population before and after the robotic impostor attack. Figures 5 and 6 respectively summarize these results for the horizontal and vertical touch strokes. The bottom (horizontal) axis shows the different EER thresholds (α), while the top (horizontal) axis shows the number of users who were able to enroll onto the system at each value of α.

Before the robotic attack was launched we obtained EERs of between 0.13 and 0.035 (see plots on the left side of Figures 5 and 6)[3]. These EERs are higher than the EERs reported in [17], but comparable to those reported in [27] during the sub-set of experiments in which the users did not wear a digital sensor glove. With our baseline EERs (i.e., before attack) being comparable to the EERs reported in the literature, we proceeded to evaluate the impact of the robotic attack.

Observe (Figures 5(b), 5(d), 6(b), 6(d)) that for both the vertical and horizontal strokes, the attack drastically increased both the mean EERs and the standard deviation of the EERs. The high mean EERs indicate that users begin to see very high False Reject Rates (FRRs), while impostors see equally high False Acceptance Rates (FARs). Also, the high variance in EERs implies that system perfor-

[3]While our vertical scale for the left side plots makes it hard to view the EERs precisely, we decided to use it (this scale) because it eases comparison with the plots to the right (i.e.. the post-attack plots)

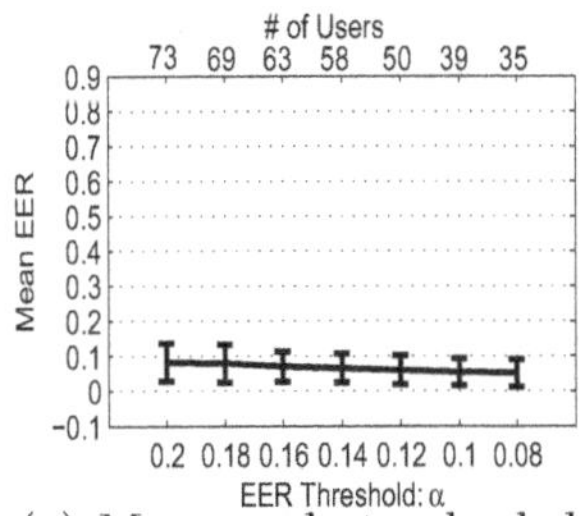

(a) Mean and standard deviation of EERs obtained for the SVM verifier before the robotic attack.

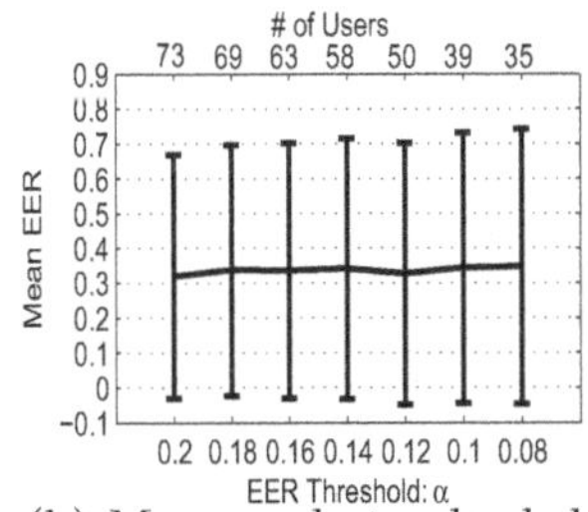

(b) Mean and standard deviation of EERs obtained for the SVM verifier after the robotic attack.

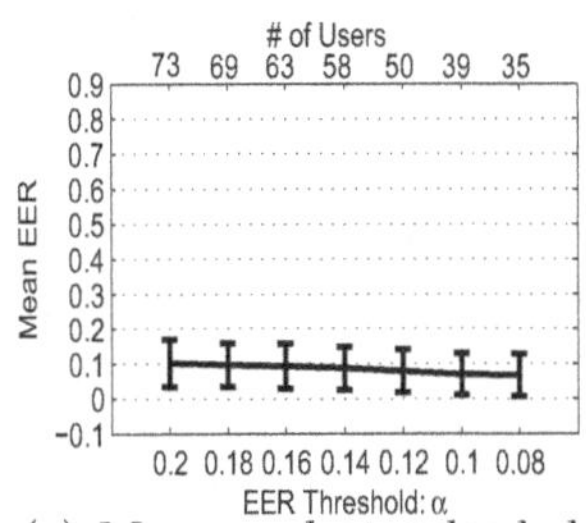

(c) Mean and standard deviation of EERs obtained for the k-NN verifier before the robotic attack.

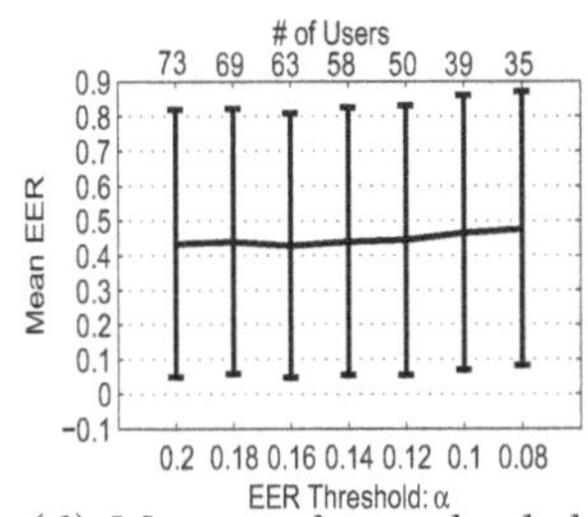

(d) Mean and standard deviation of EERs obtained for the k-NN verifier after the robotic attack.

Figure 5: Impact of the robotic attack on the horizontal strokes generated in portrait mode. The error bars indicate one standard deviation from the mean EER. The bottom axis shows the *failure to enroll* thresholds, α, while the top axis shows the number of users who are able to enroll for each value of α.

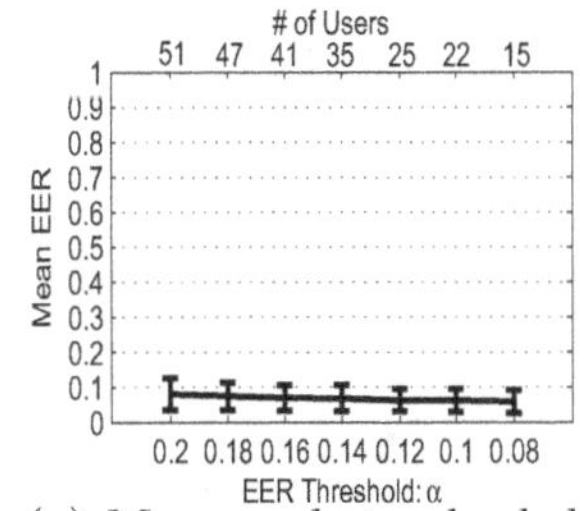

(a) Mean and standard deviation of EERs obtained for the SVM verifier before the robotic attack.

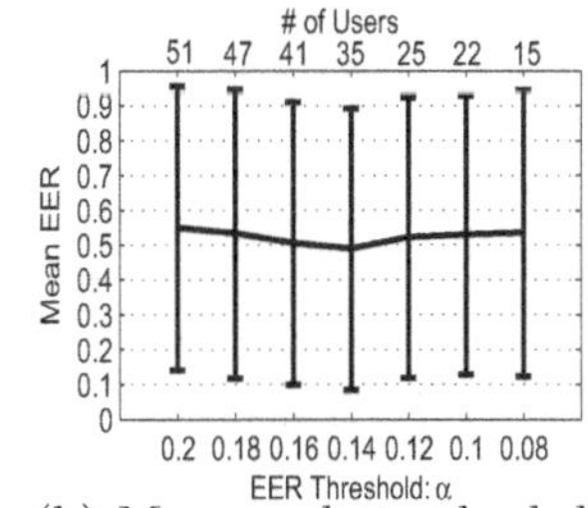

(b) Mean and standard deviation of EERs obtained for the SVM verifier after the robotic attack.

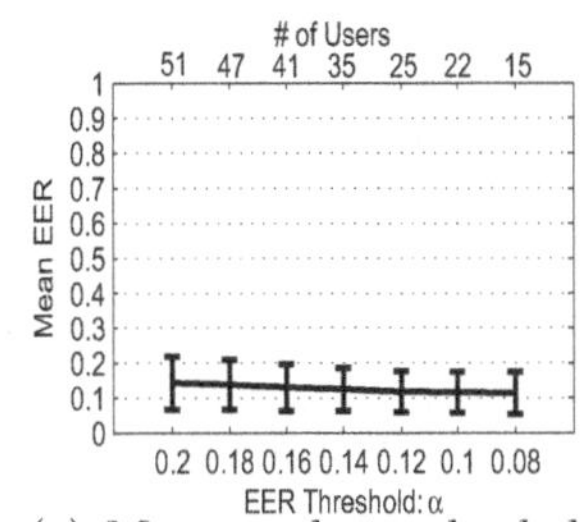

(c) Mean and standard deviation of EERs obtained for the k-NN verifier before the robotic attack.

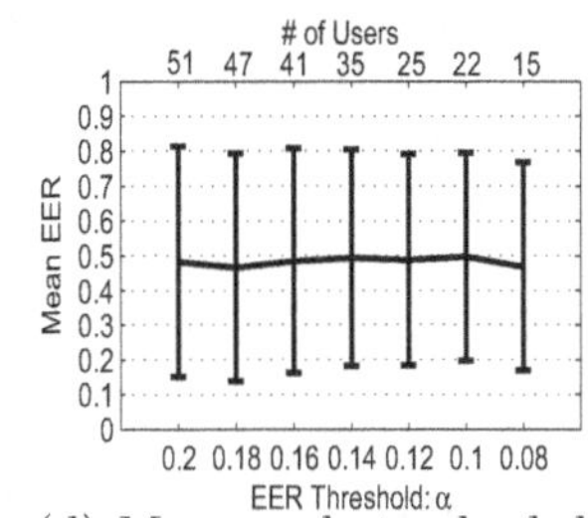

(d) Mean and standard deviation of EERs obtained for the k-NN verifier after the robotic attack.

Figure 6: Impact of the robotic attack on the vertical strokes generated in portrait mode. The error bars indicate one standard deviation from the mean EER. The bottom axis shows the *failure to enroll* thresholds, α, while the top axis shows the number of users who are able to enroll for each value of α.

mance becomes very unreliable/unpredictable as a result of the attack. It is noteworthy that the heightened EERs and standard deviations persist for both verification algorithms even when the system is used only by the best performing users (i.e., α=0.08). This implies that a defence mechanism centered around barring the poor users from enrolling onto the system would not thwart the attack.

Table 2 gives a more precise view of the impact of the attack on the mean EERs. The table shows the percentage change in mean system EER seen by each verification algorithm as a result of the attack. Regardless of the verification algorithm or *failure to enroll* threshold, the percentage change in mean EER is beyond 200% in all cases, and over 900% in the most extreme case. These results confirm why the robotic attack would significantly degrade the performance of a touch-based authentication system.

5.3.3 Impact of the Attack on each User

To better explain the dynamics of the mean EER and EER variability seen in Figures 5 and 6, we studied the impact of the attack on each user. For this analysis we only present results for α=0.2 and α=0.08 since the other values of α did not give us any new insights. Figure 7 summarizes these results for both verification algorithms. The plot reveals two salient features:

1. There was a proportion of between 20% to 40% of the population whose EER changes were negative (Figures 7(a), 7(c) and 7(d)). For these kinds of users, the robotic attack actually performed worse (i.e., caused lower EERs) than the zero-effort attack. Since our attack was designed based on data gleaned from the population, this trend suggests that about 20-40% of the users had a touch gesture biometric footprint that was very distinct from that of the majority of the users.

2. There was a proportion of users who had EER changes that were extremely high (close to 1). These types of users likely had their touch biometric patterns very similar to the mean behavior exhibited across the population.

These two features to some extent explain the high variance seen in Figures 5(b), 5(d), 6(b) and 6(d), since a combination of users seeing decrements in EER and others seeing very drastic increments in EER must have resulted into a population having very high variability in EER overall.

Despite the results presented up to this point already showing evidence for a highly successful attack, rigorous performance evaluation calls for statistical significance testing to rule out the impact of random effects. We used the Wilcoxon signed-rank test [14] to determine whether the effect of the attack was statistically significant. For instance, for the enrollment threshold α, let V_{knn_1} denote the vector of EERs obtained across the population for the k-NN verifier (i.e., for horizontal strokes in portrait mode) before the robotic attack, and V_{knn_2} denote the corresponding vector obtained after the robotic attack. The two vectors are such

α	SVM		k-NN	
	Horizontal	Vertical	Horizontal	Vertical
0.2	392%	686%	430%	339%
0.18	428%	721%	460%	339%
0.16	486%	726%	465%	373%
0.14	520%	722%	511%	398%
0.12	546%	848%	567%	416%
0.1	636%	861%	668%	430%
0.08	675%	921%	714%	411%

Table 2: Percentage increment in mean EER due to the robotic impostor attack on the portrait strokes. For each stroke type and enrollment threshold α, the increment in mean EER is expressed as a percentage of the mean EER obtained during the zero-effort attack.

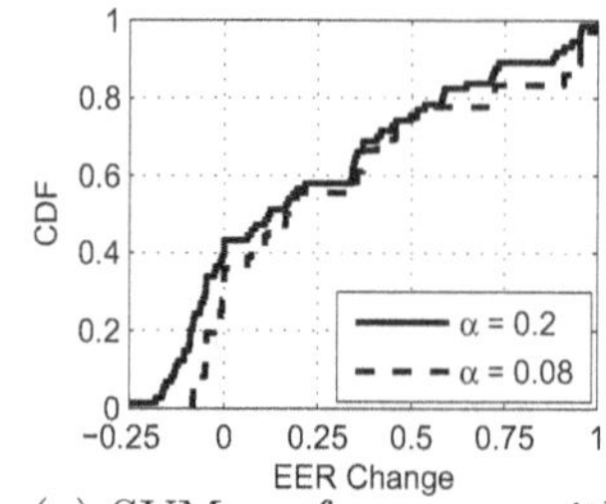

(a) SVM performance with the horizontal strokes.

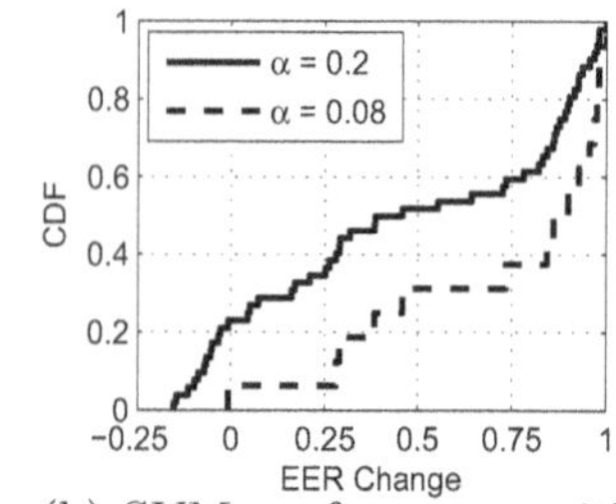

(b) SVM performance with the vertical strokes.

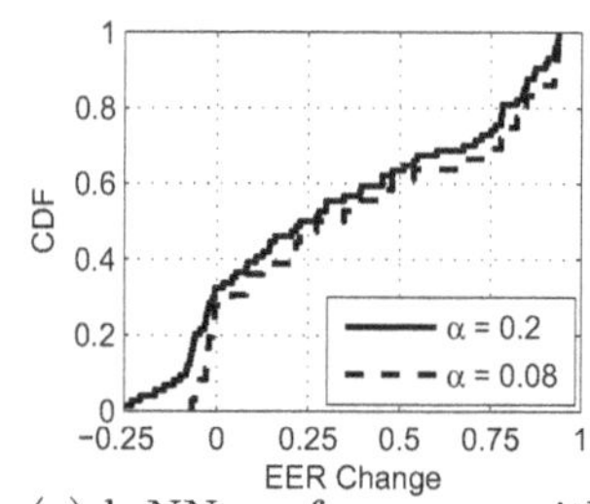

(c) k-NN performance with the horizontal strokes.

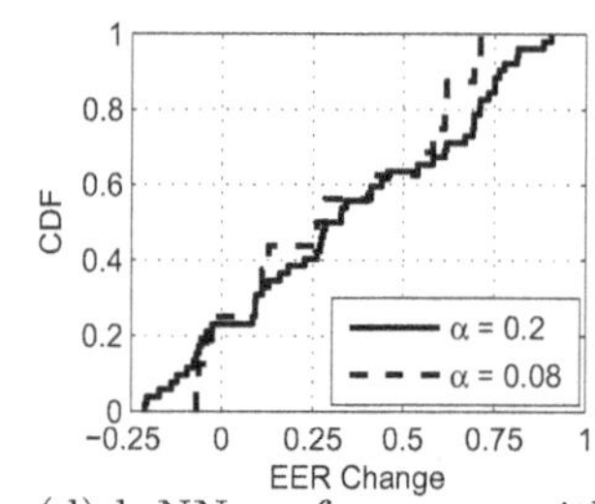

(d) k-NN performance with the vertical strokes.

Figure 7: Impact of the attack on each user's portrait strokes. For each user, we subtracted the EER seen under the zero-effort attack from that seen under the robotic attack and then plotted the CDFs of these changes in EER for each of the two extreme failure-to-enroll thresholds.

that if the EER located in position j for the vector V_{knn_1} belongs to the user j, then the EER located in position j for the vector V_{knn_2} also belongs to user j. We run the Wilcoxon signed-rank test on the differences vector V_{knn_1}-V_{knn_2} to determine whether the attack significantly affected the k-NN verifier's classification performance. For both verifiers and all stroke types and enrollment thresholds, we undertook a similar process. As was done in [26][15], we zeroed on this test after finding that the differences vectors in all the scenarios evaluated were far from Gaussian (based on observations of Q-Q plots and results of Kolmogorov Smirnov (K-S) normality tests [19]).

Formally, the null hypothesis was that the difference in EER before and after the robotic attack was insignificant. The alternative hypothesis was that the EERs under the robotic attack were higher. For all verifiers, enrollment thresholds and stroke types, we rejected the null hypothesis at the 5% significance level (see highlight of P values in Table 4—Appendix 3). Based on these results, we concluded that the attack significantly degraded the performance of the two classification algorithms.

6. CONCLUSIONS

In this paper we have evaluated the impact of a robotic attack against touch-based authentication. Using the best verification algorithms in the domain, we have shown the attack to significantly degrade classification performance. There are several aspects of our attack that might need further research. First, like most past studies in this area (e.g., see [17], [27]), our data collection was based on a group of users who used a small number of specialized applications (two applications in our case). In practice, people use a wide range of applications, some of which are designed for tasks which could prompt "touch signatures" (e.g., with regard to regions of the phone that people touch) that are very distinct from those seen with the *common* applications. It would be interesting to determine how the attack scales to a large number of applications.

Another area worthy of investigation is whether a touch stroke could be decomposed into a set of features that are more resilient to this kind of attack than our features. Because touch-based authentication does not yet have a standard set of features universally used by all researchers, we defined a set of 28 features that captured the key statistical attributes exhibited along a stroke. The underlying philosophy behind our feature definitions is not so different from that of the features used in past work (e.g., see [17][16]), however, this does not guarantee that all feature-sets will succumb to the attack in exactly the same way. It is thus interesting to determine how much less or how much more the other features are affected by the attack.

The above factors notwithstanding, our attack highlights a previously unknown threat to touch-based authentication. Given the low cost of the robots and the simplicity of the attack, we believe that the attack would realistically be launched by adversaries if touch-based authentication got widely deployed in its current form. For sophisticated adversaries who may use more advanced robots (or advanced designs of the same robot) in conjunction with information gleaned about the intended victim, the effect of the attack could even get much worse. Our findings do not only call for more stringent performance evaluation of touch-based authentication systems, but should also motivate research into technologies which could defend against the larger family of robotic attacks, one instance of which has been demonstrated in this paper.

7. ACKNOWLEDGEMENTS

We are immeasurably indebted to Diksha Shukla, Rajesh Kumar and Zibo Wang for their help during the design, implementation and performance evaluation of the robotic attack. We also thank Krystal Corbett and David Irakiza for pointing us to play-doh as finger material. This work was supported in part by the Louisiana Board of Regents under P-KSFI Grant LEQSF(2007-12)- ENHPKSFI-PRS-03.

8. REFERENCES

[1] Bricx command center 3.3. http://bricxcc.sourceforge.net/. Last accessed in April, 2013.

[2] A gloves. original touch screen gloves. http://www.amazon.com/Agloves-Original-Touchscreen-Gloves-Texting/dp/B005GXMM5W. Last accessed in April, 2013.

[3] Lego mindstorms. http://mindstorms.lego.com/en-us/default.aspx. Last accessed in April, 2013.

[4] Touchalytics. http://www.mariofrank.net/touchalytics/. Last accessed in April, 2013.

[5] Walmart. http://www.walmart.com/ip/LEGO-Mindstorms-NXT-2.0/11081183. Last accessed in April, 2013.

[6] A. J. Aviv, K. Gibson, E. Mossop, M. Blaze, and J. M. Smith. Smudge attacks on smartphone touch screens. In *Proceedings of the 4th USENIX conference on Offensive technologies*, WOOT'10, pages 1–7, Berkeley, CA, USA, 2010. USENIX Association.

[7] L. Ballard, S. Kamara, F. Monrose, and M. K. Reiter. Towards practical biometric key generation with randomized biometric templates. In *Proceedings of the 15th ACM conference on Computer and communications security*, CCS '08, pages 235–244, New York, NY, USA, 2008. ACM.

[8] L. Ballard, D. Lopresti, and F. Monrose. Evaluating the security of handwriting biometrics. In *The 10 th International Workshop on the Foundations of Handwriting Recognition*, pages 461–466, 2006.

[9] L. Ballard, D. Lopresti, and F. Monrose. Forgery quality and its implications for behavioral biometric security. *Transactions on Systems Man and Cybernetics Part B*, 37(5):1107–1118, Oct. 2007.

[10] J.-J. Cabibihan. Patient-specific prosthetic fingers by remote collaboration - a case study. *CoRR*, abs/1105.1028, 2011.

[11] C. Cortes and V. Vapnik. Support-vector networks. *Machine Learning*, 20(3):273–297, Sept. 1995.

[12] T. Cover and P. Hart. Nearest neighbor pattern classification. *IEEE Transactions on Information Theory*, 13(1):21–27, Sept. 2006.

[13] A. De Luca, A. Hang, F. Brudy, C. Lindner, and H. Hussmann. Touch me once and i know it's you!: implicit authentication based on touch screen patterns. In *Proceedings of the 2012 ACM annual conference on Human Factors in Computing Systems*, CHI '12, pages 987–996, New York, NY, USA, 2012. ACM.

[14] R. D. Gibbons. *Nonparametric Statistical Inference.* M. Dekker, 2nd edition, 1985.

[15] K. S. Killourhy and R. A. Maxion. Comparing anomaly-detection algorithms for keystroke dynamics. In *DSN*, pages 125–134, 2009.

[16] L. Li, X. Zhao, and G. Xue. Unobservable reauthentication for smart phones. In *Proceedings of the 20th Network and Distributed System Security Symposium*, NDSS'13. Internet Society, 2013.

[17] F. Mario, B. Ralf, M. Eugene, M. Ivan, and S. Dawn. Touchalytics: On the applicability of touchscreen input as a behavioral biometric for continuous authentication. *IEEE Transactions on Information Forensics and Security*, 8(1):136–148, 2013.

[18] A. F. Martin, G. R. Doddington, T. Kamm, M. Ordowski, and M. A. Przybocki. The det curve in assessment of detection task performance. In *Fifth European Conference on Speech Communication and Technology*, EUROSPEECH '97. ISCA, 1997.

[19] F. J. Massey. The Kolmogorov-Smirnov test for goodness of fit. *Journal of the American Statistical Association*, 46(253):68–78, 1951.

[20] E. Mauch. Using technological innovation to improve the problem-solving skills of middle school students: Educators' experiences with the lego mindstorms robotic invention system. *Clearing House*, 74(4):211–214, April 2001.

[21] T. C. Meng, P. Gupta, and D. Gao. I can be you: Questioning the use of keystroke dynamics as a biometric. In *NDSS,2013*, Feb 2013.

[22] E. Owusu, J. Han, S. Das, A. Perrig, and J. Zhang. Accessory: password inference using accelerometers on smartphones. In *Proceedings of the Twelfth Workshop on Mobile Computing Systems and Applications*, HotMobile '12, pages 9:1–9:6, New York, NY, USA, 2012. ACM.

[23] A. Ross, A. Rattani, and M. Tistarelli. Exploiting the "doddington zoo" effect in biometric fusion. In *Proceedings of the 3rd IEEE international conference on Biometrics: Theory, applications and systems*, BTAS'09, pages 264–270, Piscataway, NJ, USA, 2009. IEEE Press.

[24] N. Sae-Bae, K. Ahmed, K. Isbister, and N. Memon. Biometric-rich gestures: a novel approach to authentication on multi-touch devices. In *Proceedings of the 2012 ACM annual conference on Human Factors in Computing Systems*, CHI '12, pages 977–986, New York, NY, USA, 2012. ACM.

[25] N. Sae-Bae, N. Memon, and K. Isbister. Investigating multi-touch gestures as a novel biometric modality. In *Biometrics: Theory, Applications and Systems (BTAS), 2012 IEEE Fifth International Conference on*, pages 156–161, 2012.

[26] A. Serwadda and V. V. Phoha. Examining a large keystroke biometrics dataset for statistical-attack openings. *ACM Transactions on Information and System Security*, 16(2):(in press), 2013.

[27] F. Tao, L. Ziyi, C. Bogdan, B. Daining, and S. Weidong. Continuous mobile authentication using touchscreen gestures. In *Proceedings of the 12th IEEE Conference on Technologies for Homeland Security*, HST'12, 2012.

[28] T. Walsh. *Timeless Toys: Classic Toys and the Playmakers Who Created Them.* McMeel Publishing, 2005.

[29] I. H. Witten and E. Frank. *Data Mining: Practical Machine Learning Tools and Techniques.* Morgan Kaufmann, San Francisco, 2nd edition, 2005.

[30] N. Yager and T. Dunstone. The biometric menagerie. *IEEE Transactions on Pattern Analysis and Machine Intelligence*, 32(2):220–30, 2010.

Appendix 1: Some Robot Design Considerations

Pinion and Rack Gear: For the pinion and rack gear to remain engaged throughout the attack, the finger and its attached mechanism must be able to exert enough weight on the gears. This weight however must not be too much, but rather should be adequate to enable smooth movement of the gears.

Play-doh Fingers: In the state in which it is purchased from the grocery store, play-doh is too soft to make a firm finger. We exposed the play-doh to fresh air for a few days to enable it to harden a bit. Care must however be taken to ensure that it does not become too hard.

Appendix 2: Performance Highlights of the Robotic Attack on the Landscape Strokes

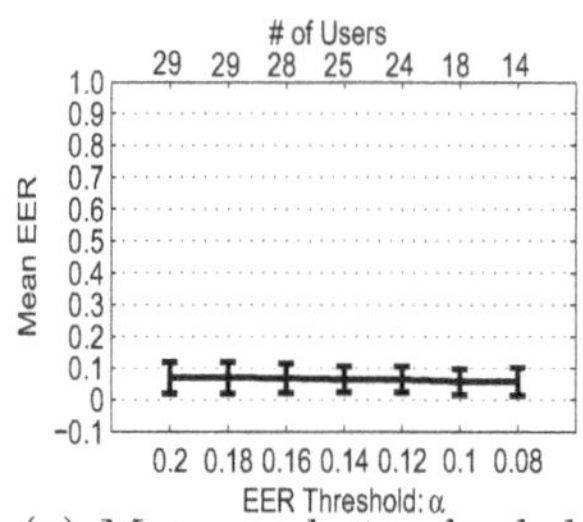

(a) Mean and standard deviation of EERs obtained for the SVM verifier <u>*before*</u> the robotic attack.

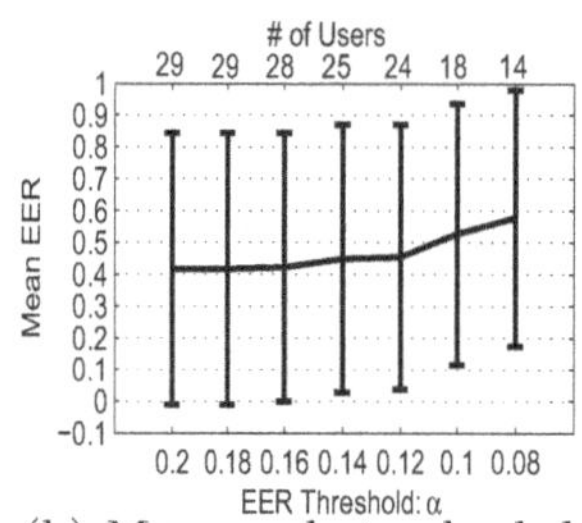

(b) Mean and standard deviation of EERs obtained for the SVM verifier <u>*after*</u> the robotic attack.

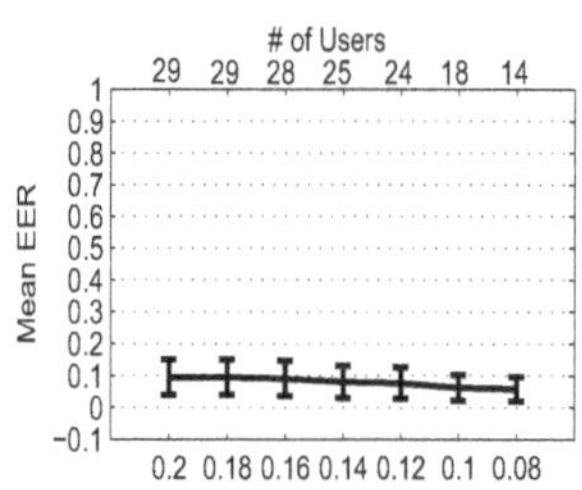

(c) Mean and standard deviation of EERs obtained for the k-NN verifier <u>*before*</u> the robotic attack.

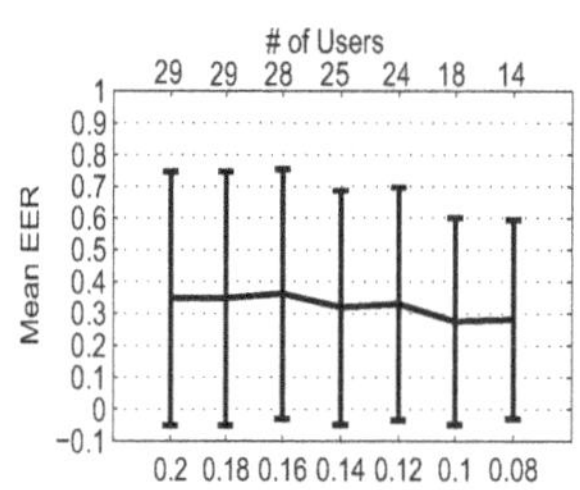

(d) Mean and standard deviation of EERs obtained for the k-NN verifier <u>*after*</u> the robotic attack.

Figure 8: Impact of the robotic attack on the classification of the <u>*horizontal*</u> strokes generated in landscape mode. The error bars indicate one standard deviation from the mean EER. The bottom axis shows the *failure to enroll* thresholds, α, while the top axis shows the number of users who are able to enroll for each value of α.

α	SVM		k-NN	
	Horizontal	Vertical	Horizontal	Vertical
0.2	592%	494%	366%	395%
0.18	592%	489%	366%	372%
0.16	616%	523%	399%	382%
0.14	696%	540%	395%	404%
0.12	703%	550%	431%	421%
0.1	929%	546%	440%	408%
0.08	1004%	546%	495%	408%

Table 3: Percentage increment in mean EER due to the robotic impostor attack on the landscape strokes. For each stroke type and enrollment threshold α, the increment in mean EER is expressed as a percentage of the mean EER obtained during the zero-effort attack.

Appendix 3: Statistical Significance Tests on the Performance of the Attack

α	SVM		kNN	
	Horizontal	Vertical	Horizontal	Vertical
0.2	1.40E-05	8.14E-08	1.04E-07	1.81E-07
0.18	7.50E-06	1.99E-07	2.57E-08	6.90E-07
0.16	7.27E-06	4.53E-07	8.48E-08	6.69E-07
0.14	6.46E-06	4.16E-06	7.38E-08	1.21E-06
0.12	1.20E-04	1.67E-05	9.03E-07	5.10E-05
0.1	1.48E-04	4.02E-05	1.60E-05	9.90E-05
0.08	7.57E-05	5.30E-04	1.56E-05	2.71E-03

Table 4: P values returned by the Wilcoxon signed-rank test on the impact of the robotic attack on the performance of the k-NN and SVM verification algorithms for the portrait strokes.

Vetting Undesirable Behaviors in Android Apps with Permission Use Analysis

Yuan Zhang[1] Min Yang[1] Bingquan Xu[1] Zhemin Yang[1]
Guofei Gu[2] Peng Ning[3] X. Sean Wang[1] Binyu Zang[1]

[1]School of Computer Science, Fudan University, China
{yuanxzhang, m_yang, xubingquan, yangzhemin, xywangCS, byzang}@fudan.edu.cn
[2]SUCCESS Lab, Texas A&M University, USA, guofei@cse.tamu.edu
[3]Department of Computer Science, North Carolina State University, USA, pning@ncsu.edu

Abstract

Android platform adopts permissions to protect sensitive resources from untrusted apps. However, after permissions are granted by users at install time, apps could use these permissions (sensitive resources) with no further restrictions. Thus, recent years have witnessed the explosion of undesirable behaviors in Android apps. An important part in the defense is the accurate analysis of Android apps. However, traditional syscall-based analysis techniques are not well-suited for Android, because they could not capture critical interactions between the application and the Android system.

This paper presents *VetDroid*, a dynamic analysis platform for reconstructing sensitive behaviors in Android apps from a novel permission use perspective. *VetDroid* features a systematic framework to effectively construct permission use behaviors, i.e., how applications use permissions to access (sensitive) system resources, and how these acquired permission-sensitive resources are further utilized by the application. With permission use behaviors, security analysts can easily examine the internal sensitive behaviors of an app. Using real-world Android malware, we show that *VetDroid* can clearly reconstruct fine-grained malicious behaviors to ease malware analysis. We further apply *VetDroid* to 1,249 top free apps in Google Play. *VetDroid* can assist in finding more information leaks than TaintDroid [24], a state-of-the-art technique. In addition, we show how we can use *VetDroid* to analyze fine-grained causes of information leaks that TaintDroid cannot reveal. Finally, we show that *VetDroid* can help identify subtle vulnerabilities in some (top free) applications otherwise hard to detect.

Categories and Subject Descriptors

D.4.6 [**Operating Systems**]: Security and Protection; D.2.1 [**Software Engineering**]: Requirements/Specifications

Keywords

Android security; permission use analysis; vetting undesirable behaviors; Android behavior representation

CCS'13, November 4–8, 2013, Berlin, Germany.
Copyright 2013 ACM 978-1-4503-2477-9/13/11 ...$15.00.
1 http://dx.doi.org/10.1145/2508859.2516689.

1. INTRODUCTION

Smartphone platforms are becoming more and more popular these days [5]. To protect sensitive resources in the smartphones, permission-based isolation mechanism [13] is used by modern smartphone systems to prevent untrusted apps from unauthorized accesses. In Android, an app needs to explicitly request a set of permissions when it is installed. However, after permissions are granted to an app, there is no way to inspect and restrict how these permissions are used by the app to utilize sensitive resources. Unsurprisingly, Android has attracted a huge number of attacks. According to McAfee threat report of Q3 2012 [6], Android remains the largest target for mobile malware and the number almost doubled in Q4 2012. While these malware apps are clear examples containing undesirable behaviors, unfortunately even in supposedly benign apps, there could also be many hidden undesirable behaviors such as privacy invasion.

An important part in the fight against these undesirable behaviors is the analysis of sensitive behaviors in Android apps. Traditional analysis techniques reconstruct program behaviors from collected program execution traces. A rich literature exists (see, e.g., [14, 16, 21, 22, 33, 40, 49]) that focuses on solutions to construct effective behavior representations. All these research efforts have mostly used system calls to depict software behaviors because system calls capture the intrinsic characteristics of the interactions between an application and the underlying system. Previous studies differ from each other only in how to structure the set of system calls made by the applications [17]. However, previous work is not readily applicable due to the following unique features of Android:

Android Framework Managed Resources. Android is an application framework on top of Linux kernel [51] where applications do not directly use system calls to access system resources. Instead, most system resources in Android are managed and protected by the Android framework, and the application-system interactions occur at a higher semantic level (such as accessing contacts, call history) than system calls at the Linux Kernel level. Indeed, Android provides specific APIs for applications to access system resources and regulates the access rules. Using system calls to learn the interaction behaviors between applications and Android will lose a semantic view of accesses to Android resources, degrading the quality and precision of the reconstructed behaviors.

Binder Inter-Process Communication (IPC). In Android, system services are provided in separated processes, with a convenient IPC mechanism (Binder) to facilitate the communication among system services and applications. Binder IPC is heavily used in Android and recommended in the design of applications. The wide use of IPC also brings problems to traditional syscall-level behavior reconstruction. First, traditional solutions would only intercept a lot of system calls used to interact with the Binder driver, hiding the real actions performed by the application. Second, the use of IPC in Android apps breaks the execution flow of an app into chains among multiple processes, making the evasion of traditional syscall-based behavior monitoring easier [42].

Event Triggers. Android employs an event trigger mechanism to notify interested applications when certain (hardware) events occur. In this model, for example, if an application wants to be notified when the phone's location changes, it just needs to register a callback for such an event. When Android sniffs a location change event from the location sensors, it notifies all the interested applications of the latest location by invoking their registered callbacks. This asynchronous resource access model via system delivery is quite different from the synchronous application-request access model. A key observation is that application registered callbacks are application code, so they could evade system call interception. As a result, traditional behavior reconstruction methods will lose such important application behaviors.

The above analysis indicates that a general method to reconstruct sensitive behaviors of Android apps is highly desired. Since Android does not use system calls as the main mechanism to isolate applications, system calls do not appear to be a good vehicle for representing behaviors. Considering the unique permission-based isolation mechanism in Android, we propose to reconstruct sensitive behaviors for Android apps from a novel *permission use* perspective, i.e., how applications use permissions to interact with the Android system and sensitive resources. We define a new concept, *permission use behavior*, which captures what and how permissions are used to access system resources, as well as how these resources are further utilized by the application internally. Accordingly, we define two kinds of permission use points: *Explicit permission use points (E-PUP)* denote those callsites of Android APIs in applications that explicitly request the permission-sensitive resources; *Implicit permission use points (I-PUP)* denote the use points of the acquired sensitive resources that are requested with permissions. For example, assume an application requests both `ACCESS_FINE_LOCATION` and `INTERNET` permissions during the installation time. Its permission use behavior should track the explicit points where these two permissions are requested and also all the implicit points where the location and network resources are used inside the application. In this case, any point where two permissions are intertwined is of particular interest because it might indicate possible location leakage to the network.

In this paper, we design a dynamic analysis system called *VetDroid* to automatically construct permission use behaviors for Android apps. *VetDroid* features a systematic permission use analysis to identify a *complete* set of *E-PUP*s and *I-PUP*s with *accurate* permission use information during the runtime. Our proposed permission use analysis is composed of two components: *E-PUP Identifer* which intercepts all invocations to Android APIs and sniffs accurate permission check information from Android's permission enforcement system to identifies all the *E-PUP*s with accurate permission use information, and *I-PUP Tracker* which takes the asynchronous resource delivery model into account to recognize the exact delivery point in the application for each resource requested at a *E-PUP* and locates all the *I-PUP*s of these resources by permission-based tainting analysis. *VetDroid* also features a driver to enlarge the scope of the dynamic analysis to cover more application behaviors and a behavior profiler to generate behavior graphs with highlighted sensitive behaviors for analysts to examine.

To evaluate the effectiveness of permission use behavior and *VetDroid*, we first use *VetDroid* to analyze real-world Android malware. The results show that the permission use behaviors reconstructed by *VetDroid* can significantly ease the malware analysis. We further apply *VetDroid* to more than one thousand top free apps in Google Play Store. *VetDroid* finds more information leaks than the state-of-the-art leak detection system TaintDroid [24], and shows its capability to analyze the fine-grained incentives of information leaks among the apps. Furthermore, *VetDroid* even detects subtle *Account Hijack Vulnerability* in a top free Android app. The analysis overhead caused by *VetDroid* is reasonably low for an offline analysis tool.

This paper makes the following major contributions:

- We analyze the limitations of existing syscall-based behavior analysis methods when applied to Android platform and propose permission use behavior as a new perspective to analyze Android apps.
- We present a systematic framework to reconstruct permission use behaviors. Our automated solution is able to completely identify all possible permission use points with accurate permission information.
- We implement a prototype system, *VetDroid*, and evaluate its effectiveness in analyzing real-world Android apps. *VetDroid* not only greatly eases the analysis of malware behaviors, but also assists in identifying fine-grained causes for information leakages and even subtle vulnerabilities in benign Android apps otherwise hard to detect.

The rest of this paper is organized as follows. §2 introduces some background information about Android and defines the permission use behavior. §3 describes our overall behavior reconstruction approach. After that, we present our evaluation results in §4 and discuss possible limitations & further improvements in §5. Finally, we discuss related work in §6 and conclude our paper in §7.

2. PROBLEM STATEMENT

2.1 Android Background

Android is the most popular mobile operating system today. It is built on top of more than 100 open source projects including Linux kernel. To enhance the security, Android is designed to be a privilege-separated operating system, in which each application runs with a distinct system identity (Linux UID and GID). The system components are also isolated into distinct identities. With the help of the identity isolation mechanism in Linux, applications in Android are isolated from each other and from the system.

Android employs a quite efficient and convenient IPC mechanism, Binder, which is extensively used for interaction between applications as well as for application-OS interfaces. Binder is implemented as a kernel driver and user-level applications could just interact with it through standard system calls, e.g., open(), ioctl(). Binder is the key infrastructure of Android system and aggressively used to connect various parts of the system together.

To facilitate resource accessing from isolated applications and data sharing among applications and the system, Android designs a permission-based security mechanism [26]. Each application needs permissions to access system resources. These permissions are granted from users at install time. At runtime, each application is checked by Android before accessing sensitive resources. Any access to resources without granted permissions will be denied. The permission mechanism in Android is fine-grained [30] which is different from iOS [11]. In Android 4.2, there are 130 items of sensitive resources that are protected with permissions [1].

The Android application framework forces a component-based application model [26] to increase the code reusability. It does not have a main() function or any single entry point for execution. Instead, Android apps must be developed in terms of components. There are four types of components defined in Android's programming model: *Activity* component has a user interface and handles the interactions with user, *Service* component performs background processing, *ContentProvider* component stores and shares data such as a relational database, and *BroadcastReceiver* component handles messages from other components, including the system. The primary mechanism for component interactions is through an *Intent*, which is simply a message object encapsulating the information of interest to the component that receives the intent such as the action to be taken and the data to act on, and some meta data managed by Android system. A component can be protected by permissions and only those applications with granted permissions can interact with the privileged component.

2.2 Motivation

Existing work [14, 21, 33, 40, 49] on behavior analysis has mostly used system calls to depict application's internal behaviors. However, previous work has problems when applied to Android platform due to Android's new security model. As explained in §1, these problems make traditional solutions not well-suited for monitoring fine-grained Android behaviors such as accesses to Android managed resources, interactions with system services through Binder IPC, and responses to privileged system events.

TaintDroid [24] alerts information leaks inside an Android app via dynamic taint tracking. AppIntent [57] redefines the privacy leakage as user-unintended sensitive data transmission and designs a new technique, event-space constraint symbolic execution, to distinguish intended and unintended transmission. However the two tools could neither analyze other kinds of undesirable behaviors such as stealthily sending SMS, nor examine the internal logic of sensitive behaviors. ProfileDroid [53] is a behavior profiling system for Android apps which is also not suitable for analyzing internal behavior logic. DroidScope [56] is an analysis platform designed for Android that extends traditional techniques to cover Java semantics. However, the problem of analyzing Android apps is not simple as how to capture behaviors from different language implementations. It is hard to conduct effective analysis without considering Android's specific security mechanism. Permission Event Graph [20], which represents the temporal order between Android events and permission requests, is proposed to characterize unintended sensitive behaviors. However, this technique could not capture the internal logic of permission usage, especially when multiple permissions are intertwined.

From the above short analysis of existing work, we find that they do not take full consideration of permission-based isolation mechanism in Android [13], which we believe to be important to understand behaviors of these applications. Thus, in this paper we propose to reconstruct permission use behaviors as a new and complementary aspect in analyzing Android apps.

2.3 Definition of Permission Use Behavior

Permission use behaviors aim to capture apps' internal sensitive behaviors on utilizing system resources that are protected by some permissions. According to the lifecycle of utilizing system resources inside an app, we define different kinds of permission use points (PUP). First, an app needs to invoke some Android APIs to request system resources, which we call *resource request stage*. If the requested resources are protected by some permissions, Android's permission enforcement system will check whether this app has been granted the corresponding permissions at install time. Because permission checks explicitly occur during *resource request stage*, we denote the callsites in the app that invoke Android APIs to request protected system resources as *explicit permission use points (E-PUP)*.

After the *resource request stage*, system resources may be delivered to the app synchronously or asynchronously, depending on the API used to request resources. The *resource delivery point* is the starting point to learn the behaviors of utilizing sensitive resources inside an app, and thus is very important for reconstructing permission use behaviors.

Finally, when the requested resources have been delivered to the app, they may be processed by application-specific logic, which reflects the internal behaviors of utilizing sensitive resources. For example, the location resource may be used by an app to suggest the restaurants nearby, or may be used by a malicious entity to track the victim. Although the further processing of acquired resources in an app does not cause additional permission checks against the app, it is still important to track the further use of these resources. In this paper, these internal use points of the protected resources are denoted as *implicit permission use points (I-PUP)*. *I-PUP*s make the critical behaviors stand out from other irrelevant application-specific actions to ease the analysis of the app.

Permission Use Behavior. As described above, *E-PUP*s capture what and where permissions are used by the application, while *I-PUP*s capture how the application uses permissions to implement their specific logic. However, a single permission use point only represents a sensitive action performed by the application, and does not necessarily capture a meaningful behavior for analyzing applications. Based on the *E-PUP*s and *I-PUP*s, we now formally define permission use behaviors.

DEFINITION 1. *A Permission Use Behavior is a function call graph $G = (V, E, \alpha)$ over a set of permissions P where:*

- *the set of vertices $V = V_{E-PUP} \cup V_{I-PUP}$, and it consists of all E-PUPs and I-PUPs,*
- *the set of edges $E \sqsubseteq V \times V$, and each edge connects nodes that use the same permission,*
- *the labeling function $\alpha : V \rightarrow P$, and it associates each node with permission(s) it uses.*

With permission use behaviors, the interactions between applications and the Android system are effectively abstracted because it describes how applications request system resources and internally use the acquired system resources. However, the two kinds of permission use points are hard to identify due to some unique features of Android and application-specific logic. We thus design an analysis platform called *VetDroid* to automatically reconstruct permission use behaviors from Android apps.

3. VETDROID DESIGN

The overview of *VetDroid* design is shown in Figure 1. Sample applications are first loaded into *Application Driver*, which automatically executes the application in our sandbox (details described in §3.3). During the execution, *Permission Use Analysis* module identifies all the *E-PUP*s, *I-PUP*s and their relationships. These behaviors are recorded by *Log Tracer* with runtime information into a log file. The log file is offline processed by *Behavior Profiler* to automatically construct behavior representations (details described in §3.4).

The key challenge in our approach is on the effectiveness of *permission use analysis*, i.e., how to *completely* identify all the permission use points with *accurate* permission information

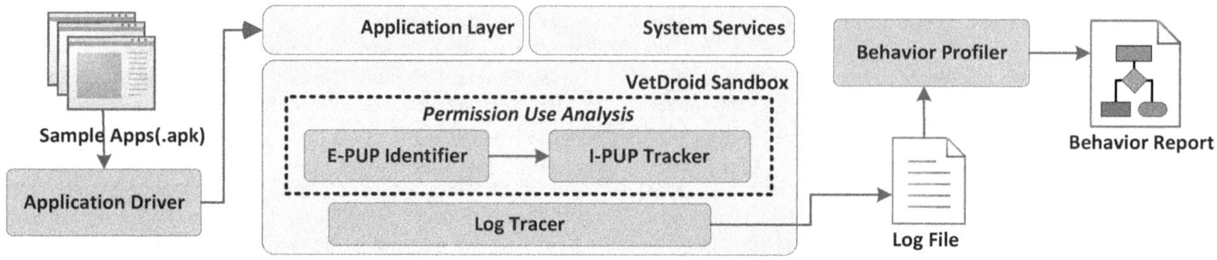

Figure 1: Overview of *VetDroid* to reconstruct permission use behaviors for Android apps.

and *precisely* track their relationships. To correctly capture the behaviors of using permissions inside an app, we analyze the execution flow of the application with regards to Android's special permission mechanism and programming model. Our systematic permission use analysis contains two main components: *E-PUP Identifier*, which identifies all *E-PUPs* with accurate permission information (details described in §3.1); and *I-PUP Tracker*, which keeps tracking of the resources requested at each *E-PUP* to trace all *I-PUPs* (details described in §3.2).

3.1 E-PUP Identifier

During the execution, applications may request system resources that are protected by some permissions. *E-PUPs* represent such behaviors in the application. The key feature of an *E-PUP* is that it's a callsite that invokes an Android API, and a permission check occurs during the execution of this API. To reconstruct effective permission use behaviors, the *E-PUP Identifier* should have two properties. First, it should completely identify all the callsites that invoke privileged Android APIs. Second, it should catch accurate information about the permission checked by Android during the execution of an API; otherwise the correctness and preciseness of the reconstructed behaviors cannot be guaranteed.

Existing work [12,27] has built privileged API lists with required permissions. It seems that our *E-PUP Identifier* could leverage such API-permission lists to identify *E-PUPs* by intercepting all APIs during the execution, and then looking up the permissions that would be checked in an API-permission list by matching API signatures. Unfortunately, existing API-permission lists are either incomplete [27] or inaccurate [12]. Stowaway [27] uses Java reflection to execute Android APIs and monitors what permissions are checked by the system. To create appropriate arguments for each API, Stowaway uses API fuzzing to automatically generate test cases. Although Stowaway's API-permission list is accurate, it is quite incomplete due to the fuzzer's inability to generate complete inputs for all Android APIs. To achieve a good coverage, PScout [12] adopts static analysis to extract API-permission lists from Android source code. Although PScout's API-permission list is relatively complete, it is not accurate enough, because an Android API could use different permissions at runtime according to its arguments, which is also acknowledged by its authors [12]. To implement a *both* complete and accurate *E-PUP Identifier*, we need to design a new technique, as described below.

3.1.1 E-PUP Identification Strategy

Based on our definition of *E-PUP*, we propose a straightforward identification strategy. First, our technique identifies the *application-system interface*, which is a code boundary between application code and system code. Based on the *application-system interface*, *E-PUP Identifier* could intercept all calls to Android APIs. Then, by monitoring permission check events in Android's

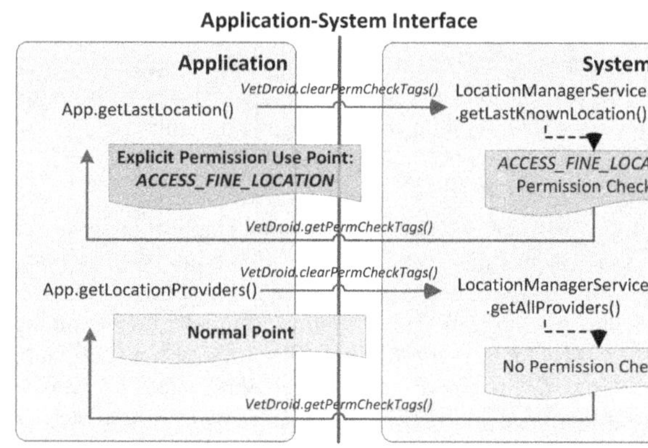

Figure 2: An example of identifying *E-PUPs*.

permission enforcement system during the execution of an API and propagating the exact permission check information to the application side, *E-PUP Identifier* could *completely* identify all the *E-PUPs* with *accurate* permission use information, including those invoked through Java reflection or Java Native Interface.

Figure 2 shows an example of identifying *E-PUPs* at the application side. In this example, *App.getLastLocation()* invokes *getLastKnownLocation()* API of *LocationManagerService* to get the last known location. Before invoking this API, *VetDroid* clears the permission check information in the thread-local storage using *VetDroid.clearPermCheckTags()*. During the execution of this API, Android's permission enforcement system performs a permission check on `ACCESS_FINE_LOCATION` permission. At last, after the execution of *getLastKnownLocation()* API, *VetDroid* invokes *VetDroid.getPermCheckTags()* to propagate the permission check information from the enforcement system to the application side. With the propagated permission check information, this callsite in *App.getLastLocation()* is identified as an *E-PUP* of `ACCESS_FINE_LOCATION` permission.

The *application-system interface* is recognized at every function call site by checking whether the caller is application code and the callee is system code. As Android apps are mostly developed in the Java language and run on the Dalvik virtual machine, we instrument Dalvik to monitor all function calls. The algorithm to perform code origin checks should be very efficient, otherwise a huge performance penalty would be introduced. Fortunately, we find an efficient way to differentiate application code from system code by checking their class loader, because system code is loaded by a distinct class loader in Dalvik to ensure the VM integrity.

3.1.2 Acquire Permission Check Information

The complete identification of permission checks is the key to identify *E-PUPs*. With the permission check information, it's easy

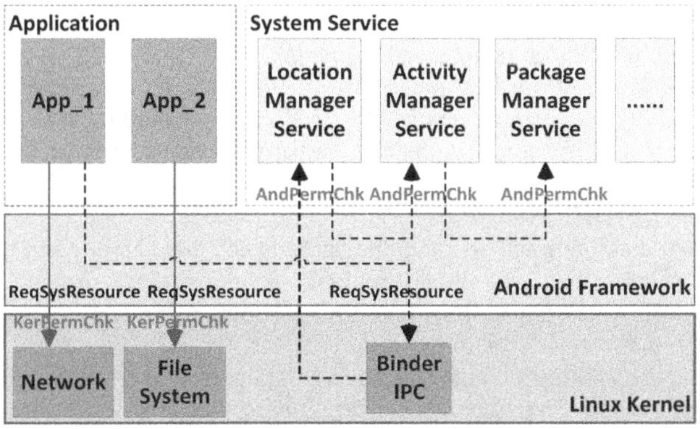

Figure 3: Two kinds of permission checks in Android's permission enforcement system.

to judge whether an application-system interface is an *E-PUP* or a normal call site (see *App.getLocationProviders()* in Figure 2).

Android's permission system is enforced by two modules: Android system services and Linux kernel. According to the different permission enforcing techniques, we differentiate two kinds of permission checks in Android's permission enforcement system: *Android permission check* and *Kernel permission check*. Figure 3 illustrates these two kinds of permission checks:

Android Permission Check (AndPermChk). When an app tries to access system resources that are protected by Android system services such as contacts and locations, *AndPermChks* occurred. Figure 3 gives an example of *AndPermChk*. *App_1* tries to acquire the current location by invoking an interface of *LocationManagerService* via Binder. *LocationManagerService* first checks whether *App_1* has been granted `ACCESS_FINE_LOCATION` permission by invoking the general permission check interface of *ActivityManagerService*. The *AndPermChk* requests are finally redirected to *PackageManagerService* except the permission requests from the system itself are granted immediately. *PackageManagerService* handles the permission check request by looking up a table that records all the granted permissions for each application when it is installed. According to the permission check result, *LocationManagerService* judges whether to accept or deny the request from *App_1*.

Kernel Permission Check (KerPermChk). The permissions to protect file system and network are enforced by the Linux kernel. As Figure 3 shows, the accesses to these resources should pass *KerPermChks*. In Android, a unique GID is assigned to each kernel-enforced permission. An app is checked to verify whether it has the corresponding GID before accessing the protected resource.

Our identification of permission checks is implemented in Android's permission enforcement system, while *E-PUP Identifier* needs to acquire permission check information at the application side to judge whether a callsite is an *E-PUP* and what permission is used by an *E-PUP*. For the two types of permission checks, the permission check information is propagated differently:

Propagate AndPermChk Information. As Figure 3 shows, *AndPermChk* is performed in a separate Android process. The application side has no idea about what permission is checked by what system service. It is difficult to automatically propagate the permission check information from a separate service process to the application. Since Android apps employ Binder to invoke remote interfaces of a service process and the result is also returned via Binder, we choose to extend the Binder driver and its communication protocol to propagate the permission check information during the IPC procedure. As all *AndPermChks* are finally handled by *ActivityManagerService*, we instrument its permission check logic to convey the permission check information to the Binder driver. With the extended Binder driver, this permission check information can be propagated back to the application side.

Propagate KerPermChk Information. With a unique GID assigned to every kernel-enforced permission, *KerPermChk* is enforced by the GID isolation mechanism. We instrument the GID isolation logic to record the checked GID into a kernel thread-local storage. The checked permission can be recognized by mapping the checked GID to the corresponding permission reversely. To acquire the permission check information from the kernel at the *application-system interface*, two system calls are added to access and clear the checked GID in the kernel thread-local storage.

Thus, with permission check information propagated to the application side, *E-PUP Identifier* could identify all *E-PUPs* with accurate permission use information.

3.2 I-PUP Tracker

While *E-PUPs* represent the behaviors of how an application use permissions to request sensitive resources, *I-PUPs* capture the internal behaviors of how the application manipulates these protected resources. To track the resources use points inside an app, *I-PUP Tracker* first needs to recognize the delivery point for each requested resource in the application.

3.2.1 Recognize Resource Delivery Point

Android's programming model complicates the identification of resource delivery points in the application. Callbacks are heavily used in Android to monitor privileged system events, such as location change events and phone state change events. There are three types of callbacks in Android that can be registered to deliver system resources: *BroadcastReceiver*, *PendingIntent*, and *Listener*. *BroadcastReceiver* is one of the four types of components defined in the Android application model, as described in §2. *PendingIntent* [7] is a special Intent that can be sent back from a separate process on behalf of its creator. According to the ways of instantiating, a *PendingIntent* can be sent to an Activity, a Service or a BroadcastReceiver. *Listener* is a specialized class to handle callbacks that can be triggered remotely.

For most cases, *BroadcastReceivers* are declared in the app's manifest file and registered to the system when the app is installed. Android also provides APIs to register *BroadcastReceivers* at runtime. *PendingIntents* and *Listeners* are registered via specific Android APIs. Since callbacks are used by a small number of Android APIs, we choose to recognize the resource delivery point by monitoring those APIs that may register callbacks.

Although PScout's privileged API list [12] is not accurate enough for *E-PUP Identifier*, it provides a complete list for picking out APIs that register callbacks. However, there are more than 10,000 distinct APIs in PScout's API list for every Android version, so it is hard to manually check every API. Thus, we use an automatic method to filter out most APIs that definitely cannot register callbacks, and manually check a small number of remaining APIs.

Since only one specific API can register *BroadcastReceivers* at runtime, our automatic filtering method mainly selects APIs that register *PendingIntents* or *Listeners*. Our selection strategy is to find all potential APIs whose arguments may contain a *PendingIntent* or a *Listener*. We observe that *Listeners* can be invoked from a separate/remote process, so they are Binder objects. Our selection algorithm first finds all the subclasses that extend *android.os.Binder*. As an API may declare an interface as the argument type, our algorithm further collects a list for the interfaces that each Binder subclass implements. At last, our filtering method looks up PScout's API list to select those APIs with an argument type contained in the subclass list or the interface list. For Android 2.3, our filtering method finds 232 APIs that may register *Listeners*. *PendingIntent* is easy to handle, because it is defined as a final class in Android. After a search on PScout's API list, our method finds 58 APIs whose arguments contain a *PendingIntent*. Then we manually verify the total 286 APIs (4 APIs register both *PendingIntents* and *Listeners*), and eventually we confirm 89 APIs register *PendingIntents* or *Listeners* to acquire protected system resources. In this procedure, our automatic API filtering method greatly reduces the manual efforts.

For our selected APIs that register callbacks, the resource delivery point is the registered callback. While for other APIs, the *E-PUP* is also the resource delivery point. Since *BroadcastReceiver* can be registered by the manifest file, we parse the manifest file of each analyzed app to collect declared *BroadcastReceivers* and mark their *onReceive()* functions as the resource delivery points. After the resource delivery points are recognized, the *I-PUPs* can be tracked by following the resource usage inside the app.

3.2.2 Permission-based Taint Analysis

After the resource is delivered to the application, it can be used in different ways with application-specific logic that makes the identification of *I-PUPs* quite difficult. To solve this problem, we use dynamic taint tracking to capture the resource usage inside the application. However, traditional taint analysis cannot be applied directly. The key challenge is to automatically taint related data for each delivered resource with permission information. Our permission-based taint analysis works in the following steps.

Tag Allocation. A taint tag is allocated at each *E-PUP* to mark the requested resource with corresponding permission check information. The taint tag is represented as a 32-bit integer. Each bit of the tag corresponds to a unique *E-PUP*. Our tag allocation is context-sensitive, which means the same tag will be assigned to *E-PUPs* with the same calling context. The reason for this strategy is to prevent the explosion of tag bits while different *E-PUPs* are still distinguishable.

Automatic Data Tainting. After a taint bit is allocated for an *E-PUP*, the corresponding acquired system resource needs to be automatically tainted with the tag. The automatic data tainting occurs at the resource delivery point for each *E-PUP*. For APIs that register callbacks, a wrapper is added around each registered callback to taint the delivered protected data according to the concrete type of the callback so that the related data gets tainted only when the callback is triggered. For other APIs, two kinds of data are automatically tainted according to the signature of the API: 1) The return value of the API at each *E-PUP* should be tainted with the corresponding tag. 2) As Java is an object-oriented language, the state of an object may be modified by instance methods. For instance APIs, we also taint the invoked object with the tag allocated at the *E-PUP*.

Identify I-PUPs. Dynamic taint tracking is employed to follow the propagation of tainted resource data. *I-PUP* is identified by recognizing the use point of tainted data. The granularity of the identification is quite important to the quality and efficiency of the *I-PUP Tracker*. It could be performed at the instruction-level, but a single instruction is too fine-grained to depict a meaningful action. Thus, we choose to identify *I-PUP* at the function-level. We intercept all function invocations in the Dalvik virtual machine and compute a taint tag for each function. The tag for a function is calculated by a bitwise OR operation on the taint tags of its parameter values. If the tag is non-zero, the function is an *I-PUP* for the permission represented by the tag.

After identifying resource delivery points and performing the permission-based taint analysis, *I-PUP Tracker* could trace all the use points of resources with accurate permission information.

3.3 Application Driver

Unlike traditional applications, there is no single entry point for an Android app. It brings problems to automatically executing Android apps. Our *Application Driver* adopts a component-based testing strategy. It automatically extracts *Activities* and *Services* from the application and runs each component in the sandbox for a while (the time depends on the concrete hardware platform). Additionally, *Monkey* [9] is used to exercise the user interface for each *Activity*.

Furthermore, some behaviors of Android apps are triggered by events. Our *Application Driver* also injects fake events (such as the arrival of new SMS, location change) during the monitoring when certain callbacks are registered. With the runtime injected events, *Permission Use Analysis* module could reconstruct more permission use behaviors from the application.

It is worth noting that our *Application Driver* could not guarantee a complete coverage over all possible behaviors. In fact, this is generally a difficult problem for all dynamic analysis work. This paper tries to design a better behavior approximation for analyzing Android apps, and leaves the coverage problem as our future work (as discussed in §5).

3.4 Behavior Profiler

During the execution of the application in *VetDroid* sandbox, *Log Tracer* collects the behaviors reported by *Permission Use Analysis* module with runtime information to a log file. *Behavior Profiler* analyzes the log file offline to automatically generate permission use graphs for further analysis.

Behavior Profiler first identifies all the *E-PUPs* from the log file. For each *E-PUP*, *Behavior Profiler* further collects all *I-PUPs* for the requested permission by tracking the same tag bit. By connecting these permission use points according to the execution orders, *Behavior Profiler* could draw a permission use graph for each permission.

As Android adopts a fine-grained permission model [30] to protect system resources, our insight is that applications usually need to use multiple permissions together to accomplish a meaningful behavior. Based on this observation, *Behavior Profiler* searches all the permission use graphs to connect those graphs with an overlapped node (which uses at least two permissions) to form a new permission use graph. The permission use graph with multiple permissions captures interesting behaviors for analysis, as will be demonstrated later in the evaluation. *Behavior Profiler* automatically discards permission use graphs that use only a single (less interesting) permission with the exception of those graphs using a high-risk permission such as `SEND_SMS`, `CALL_PHONE`. The profiled permission use graphs capture the behaviors of using permissions inside an application, especially when multiple permissions are intertwined. With such permission use graphs, experts could inspect the internal logic of Android apps to analyze suspicious behaviors, verify programming logic, etc.

4. PROTOTYPE & EVALUATION

A prototype of *VetDroid* is implemented based on Gingerbread (Android 2.3).[1] This prototype currently supports running on

[1]Note that our techniques are not limited to this specific version.

Samsung Nexus S phones and emulators. The *Application Driver* and *Behavior Profiler* are implemented in Python. *E-PUP Identifier* instruments the Dalvik virtual machine to intercept all API invocations, and enhances the Linux kernel as well as the Binder driver to acquire accurate permission use information at the application side. *I-PUP Tracker* modifies the Android framework to monitor registrations and invocations of application callbacks, and extends the taint tracking logic in TaintDroid [24] to implement the permission-based taint analysis (as described before). In all, *VetDroid* modifies and enhances several main components in Android including the Linux kernel, the Binder driver, the Dalvik virtual machine, to implement a systematic permission use analysis framework.

We evaluate *VetDroid* from three aspects. We first apply *VetDroid* to real-world Android malware and analyze their internal malicious behaviors with permission use graphs. Next, we report our findings on vetting more than one thousand top free apps in Google Play with *VetDroid*. Finally, we measure the runtime overhead of *VetDroid*.

4.1 Real-World Malware Study

We have used *VetDroid* to analyze 600 Android malware samples that we have collected from Malware Genome Project [59]. To efficiently construct permission use behaviors, *Application Driver* runs these samples in 10 emulators and each component is executed for 120 seconds. Our hardware platform is an AMD server with 4*4 cores (2GHz) and 16GB memory. In all, 5,990 components are executed, which last totally about 22 hours (i.e., 2.2 minutes per sample). The reconstructed behaviors are automatically classified by their *E-PUP*s and further manually confirmed and categorized.

Table 1 lists six example categories of interesting malicious behaviors [59] captured by *VetDroid*. We can find that these malware either steals users' sensitive data or incurs financial charge. We also compare the analysis results with those reported by Malware Genome Project [59]. Unfortunately, the Command and Control (C&C) servers [58] used by some samples were not available during the analysis and some malicious behaviors are only triggered under certain contexts, so some behaviors reported in [59] were not observed. In all, *VetDroid* successfully analyzed 21 malware families and more importantly reconstructed their detailed behaviors, demonstrating its effectiveness in aiding malware analysis. More interestingly, *VetDroid* captured some previously unreported behaviors in dissected malware samples. For example, we found 38 BaseBridge samples exhibit *SMS Stealing* behavior and 1 Zitmo sample has *SMS Blocking* behavior, which have not been reported by Malware Genome Project yet. This further illustrates the advantages of our new analysis technique to help reveal undesirable behaviors.

Due to space limit, we can only present some interesting case studies analyzed by *VetDroid* with permission use graphs: *GGTracker*, *SMSReplicator*, *TapSnake*. The permission use graphs capture the complete execution flow related to the malicious behaviors.[2] The nodes with filled colors represent *E-PUP*s, while other nodes represent *I-PUP*s. The edges in the graph depict the flow among permission use points.

1) Analysis of GGTracker.

GGTracker is known for its intent to automatically sign up infected users to premium services. Due to the second-confirmation policy required in some countries, *GGTracker* needs to stealthily reply to an acknowledge SMS message sent from the service provider to sign up a premium-rate service. This behavior is critical to understand the internal logic of this malware.

[2]In this paper we only present partial permission use graphs.

Behaviors	#	Malware Families
Steal SMS	46	BaseBridge, SMSReplicator, Zitmo, Gone60
Steal Phone Number	38	ADRD, YZHC, GoldDream, Pjapps, GGTracker GingerMaster, DroidDream, DroidKungFu[1-4]
Steal Contact	8	Zitmo, Gone60, Walkinwat
Track Loc.	9	TapSnake, DroidDream, DroidKungFu1 Bgserv, DroidKungFu2, DroidKungFu4
Send SMS	43	Pjapps, Zsone, Walkinwat, RogueSPPush GGTracker, FakePlayer, SMSReplicator
Block SMS	22	Zitmo, RogueSPPush, GGTracker, Zsone

Table 1: Example behaviors analyzed by *VetDroid*

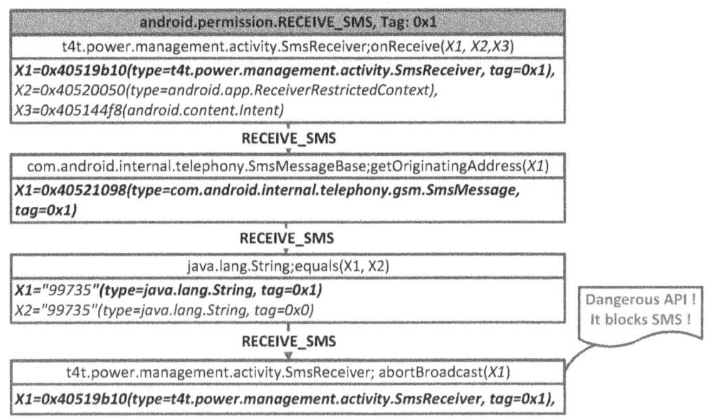

Figure 4: *SMS Blocking* behavior in *GGTracker*.

We observe two kinds of behaviors in *GGTracker* with *VetDroid*. Figure 4 shows the *SMS blocking* behavior. When a new SMS arrives, *t4t.power.management.activity.SmsReceiver* is triggered. Then *getOriginatingAddress* is invoked to get the sender's number of this message. The permission use graph clearly expresses the constraints on the sender's number in this malware. If this SMS is sent from "99735", this message is blocked by invoking *abortBroadcast()*. This function suppresses the broadcasting of the event about the arrival of a new SMS. Since *GGTracker* registers its BroadcastReceiver with the highest priority, this SMS is hidden from the user. By checking the constraints on the sender's number from the graph, we can direct the *Application Driver* to inject faked SMS from other numbers (this can be easily implemented with an emulator [8]) to cover more interested behaviors. At last, we confirm *GGTracker* also blocks SMS from "46621", "96512", "33335", "36397", etc.

Besides, we also observe *SMS Auto Reply* behavior by iteratively changing the sender's number of the faked SMS. From Figure 5, we could find that when the malware intercepts a SMS from "41001", it automatically replies an SMS to "41001" with the content "YES" using the *sendTextMessage* API. The *SMS Auto Reply* behavior is critical in this kind of malware that stealthily signs up infected users to premium services. With *VetDroid*, this behavior is clearly revealed, enabling the detection and prevention of such attacks.

System Call Trace. To have a brief comparison with syscall-based analysis, we use *strace* to collect system call trace during the execution of *SMS Auto Reply* behavior, as showed in Table 2. From the collected 33 system calls, it's hard to recognize them as *SMS Auto Reply* behavior due to the loss of fine-grained semantic and context information, while *VetDroid* can clearly reconstruct such behavior with the analysis of permission use points and behaviors.

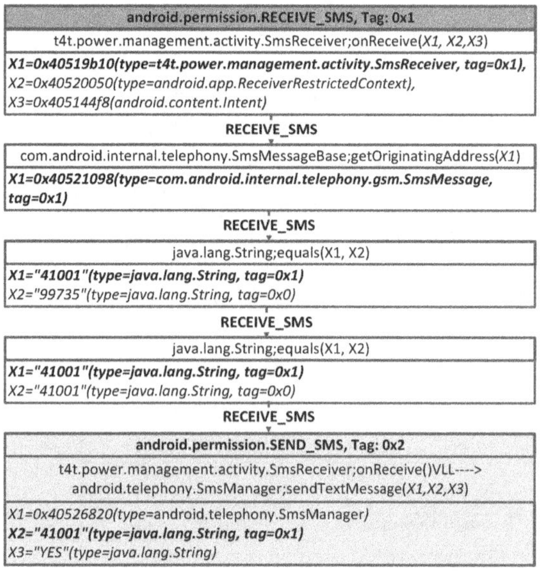

Figure 5: ***SMS Auto Reply*** **behavior in** ***GGTracker*****.**

syscall	#	Comments
ioctl	8	Binder communication
stat64,access	9	app's resource file
getpid,gettid	8	process information
clock_gettime	7	time information
writev	1	log operation

Table 2: System call trace for ***SMS Auto Reply*** **behavior.**

2) Analysis of SMSReplicator.

SMSReplicator [3] is a spyware app targeting infected users' incoming short messages. This malware protects itself by hiding its icon. *SMSReplicator* not only leaks SMS messages, but also incurs additional financial charge. As Figure 6 shows, all the incoming SMS messages are intercepted by this malware using a *BroadcastReceiver* (*com.dlp.SMSReplicatorSecret.SMSReceiver*). The SMS is instantiated using *createFromPdu()* function of *SmsMessage*. *SMSReplicator* further queries the contacts to find the sender of the intercepted message. The name of the sender and the message body is concatenated to send to a number specified by the attacker via SMS. This graph clearly shows the permission use points of three critical permissions (`RECEIVE_SMS, READ_CONTACTS, SEND_SMS`). It is relatively easy to recognize this behavior as *SMS Forwarding*. We can find that *SMS Auto Reply* behavior and *SMS Forwarding* behavior are similar in intercepting and sending SMS. However, with the reconstructed permission use behaviors which track the internal application logic (Figure 5 and Figure 6), their divergent malicious intents get clearly differentiated.

3) Analysis of TapSnake.

TapSnake [2] tracks the infected user by sending the latest location to a remote server. To hide its malicious intent, this malware disguises itself as the classic "snake" video game. During the installation, this malware asks users to grant `ACCESS_FINE_LOCATION` and `INTERNET` permissions. Considering these permissions are required by most legitimate advertising libraries [37], most users choose to grant these permissions without any idea about how these permissions will be used.

As showed in Figure 7, *TapSnake* first registers a callback (*net.maxicom.android.snake.LocationListener*) for the location change

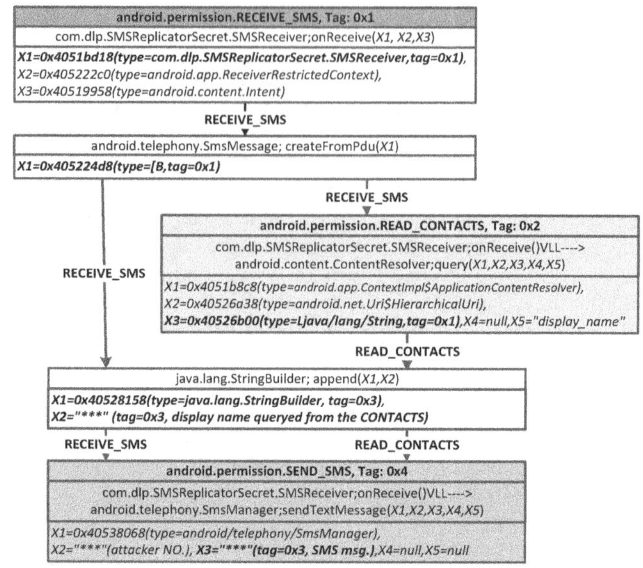

Figure 6: ***SMS Forwarding*** **behavior in** ***SMSReplicator*****.**

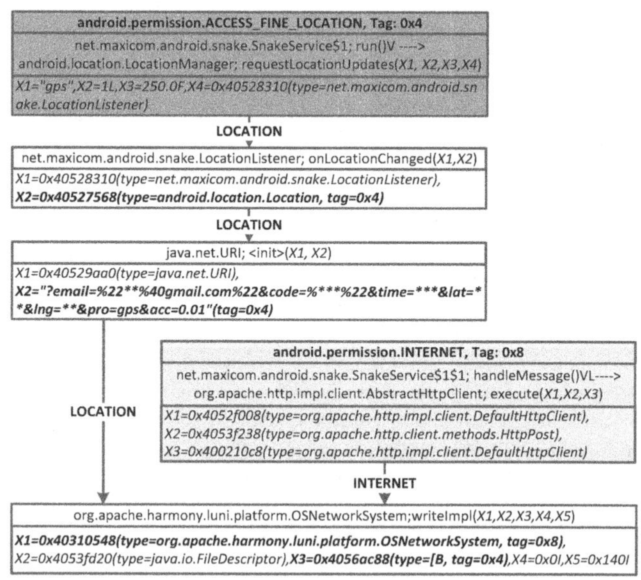

Figure 7: ***Location Track*** **behavior in** ***TapSnake*****.**

event. When location changes, the *onLocationChanged* function is invoked asynchronously by Android to deliver the latest location. *TapSnake* further performs some string operations on the location object to encode the location into a URL. The encoded URL is passed to the *execute()* function of *AbstractHttpClient*. The latest location that is encoded in the URL is eventually exfiltrated to the server *http://gpsdatapoints.appspot.com*.

4.2 Vetting Market Apps

Next, we use *VetDroid* to vet 1,249 top (benign) apps crawled from Google Play official store. These apps are top free apps crawled from 32 different categories such as games, education, entertainment, finance, social, sports, tools. We also use multiple emulators to parallelize the process of reconstructing permission use behaviors for these apps. There are several interesting findings.

Leak Resource	TaintDroid	VetDroid
IMEI	135	135
Phone Number	7	7
Location	17	24
Network State	0	28

Table 3: Information leakage results.

Finding 1: *VetDroid* can assist in finding more information leaks than TaintDroid. Based on the reconstructed permission use behaviors, we implement a simple permission-based filter that selects permission use graphs with at least one permission to read system resource and one permission to exfiltrate data to a remote party. The selected graphs are further classified with regard to *E-PUPs*. We manually check these classified behaviors and confirm four kinds of information leaks, as listed in Table 3.

We also use TaintDroid [24] to run these apps with the exact same inputs to the *Application Driver*. The results are also presented in Table 3. We can see that *VetDroid* detects 7 more location leaks than TaintDroid. After a further investigation on these cases, we find that the cell location (acquired through *TelephonyManager.getCellLocation()* API) is leaked in these cases while TaintDroid does not treat this kind of location as sensitive data. Since an app needs to use `ACCESS_COARSE_LOCATION` permission to get the cell location, *VetDroid* could automatically tracks the behaviors of leaking such kind of sensitive resource by following the permission usage. *VetDroid* also detects 28 cases that leak the device's network state to a remote party while TaintDroid's current implementation does not support detecting leaks of such sensitive resource. It is worth noting that TaintDroid could be improved to detect these leaks if we *proactively* and *manually* add ad-hoc logic to taint these sources. However, different from TaintDroid, *VetDroid* can *automatically* track such resources as long as they are in permission use behaviors. This experiment clearly demonstrates that using permissions to automatically and systematically capture application behaviors is superior to traditional simple taint analysis without permission in consideration.

Finding 2: *VetDroid* can inspect the fine-grained causes of information leakage. Our permission use behavior captures the internal logic of permission usages inside an app, thus enables us to analyze the fine-grained procedure of information leakage. We manually analyze the permission use behaviors of several information leaks reported by *VetDroid* to investigate the contexts of reading and leaking sensitive information. In this experiment, we mainly focus on *Phone Number* and *Location* leakage cases because they are relatively interesting.

Based on the context of information leakage, we find that many such information leaks are actually not caused by the app itself. Table 4 shows our analysis results. From this table, we could find that 15 out of 24 location leaks are actually caused by mobiles ads and payments. There is also one case that sends the phone number to a mobile promotion and publishing company (Mobile Public). Cell locations that are not tracked by TaintDroid are also used by Vserv and Handmark for better advertising.

Compared with TaintDroid that could only alert information leaks, the results show that *VetDroid* is capable of inspecting the fine-grained causes of sensitive information leakage by tracing the context of permission usage.

Finding 3: *VetDroid* can help detect subtle application vulnerabilities. Since SMS service is unique and quite important for smartphones, we analyze 33 apps that request both `RECEIVE_SMS` and `SEND_SMS` permissions by running these apps in *VetDroid*. By

Leak Resource	#	Leak Cause
Location	12	Inner-Active Ads Wetter Ads Flurry Ads Google Ads InMobi Ads Fortumo Payments
CellLocation	3	Vserv Ads Handmark
Phone Number	1	Mobile Public

Table 4: Information leak analysis results.

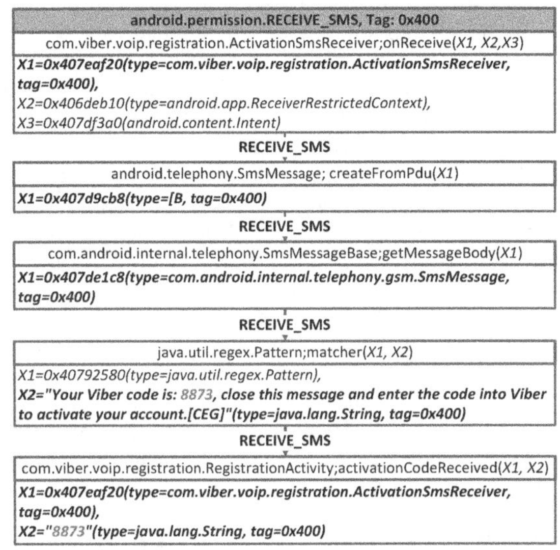

Figure 8: *SMS Activation* behavior in Viber.

carefully examining the permission use behaviors, we find that the Viber application is vulnerable to *Account Hijack attack*.

According to the website of Google Play, Viber is a free VoIP app that has been downloaded nearly 100 million times in recent 30 days worldwide. Viber provides users with free calls and messages to other Viber users. It also requests its user to bind his/her phone number which is used as his/her identity. When a call/message arrives, Viber will look up the sender's profile in the contact with the sender's phone number for a friendly notification.

To prevent a user from binding others' phone numbers, Viber server sends an activation SMS to the phone number. By verifying the activation code in the SMS, Viber can confirm whether the user owns the phone number or not. The activation phase is quite important for a popular communication app such as Viber. Otherwise, an attacker could bind a victim's phone number and send fake messages/calls to the victim's friends on behalf of the victim. This kind of *Account Hijack attack* could cause the same damage as *Facebook Account Hijack* [4].

We use *VetDroid* to reconstruct the permission use behavior of the activation process, as shown in Figure 8. As this figure shows, Viber intercepts incoming SMS messages in *ActivationSmsReceiver*, and extracts the activation code from the message body using a regular expression. Once an activation code is matched, the activation process is proceeded in the *RegistrationActivity.activationCodeReceived()* function.

By carefully examining the permission use behavior in Figure 8, it is easy to find that Viber does not check the origin of an activation SMS. Thus, an attacker could pass the activation by

	E-PUP	I-PUP	Log	ALL
Time	18.124%	10.385%	3.785%	32.294%
Mem.	0.100%	13.573%	0.637%	14.110%

Table 5: Results of execution time and memory footprint overhead on CaffeineMark benchmark.

intercepting the activation SMS from the victim and sending it to the attacker's Viber client, causing the victim's account hijacked. It is not hard to steal an SMS from a victim, especially when the *Account Hijack attack* on the victim could lead to a reasonable profit. SMS stealing could be possibly implemented by malware such as *SMSReplicator* [3], *Zitmo* [10] or social engineering. To further confirm this vulnerability, we perform an experiment to hijack the Viber account of a volunteer in our group. By stealthily replacing an app in his smartphone into our repackaged version (which has the similar *SMS Blocking and Stealing* behavior as *Zitmo*), the activation SMS from Viber server is forwarded by our repackaged app to the attacker's device. After binding the volunteer's phone number to the attacker's device, free calls and messages are successfully initiated to his friends on behalf of his identity. Interestingly, in a security study [52] that performed network traffic analysis of nine popular VoIP apps, Viber was considered to be immune from *Account Hijack attacks*, because the activation code was generated in the Viber server and thus cannot be hijacked by a man-in-the-middle attack. However, our internal permission use behavior analysis on Viber reveals that the missing check on the origin of activation SMS actually makes Viber vulnerable to *Account Hijack attack*.

4.3 Performance Overhead Evaluation

Due to the inline instrumentation on Android, our analysis tool incurs some extra runtime overhead. We perform experiments on our Nexus S to measure the overhead from two aspects: execution speed and memory footprint. Table 5 shows the results on CaffeineMark, a standard performance benchmark. Compared with the original Android system, *VetDroid* slows down the entire execution of the application by 32.294%, while increases the memory footprint by 14.110%. The main overhead of *I-PUP Tracker* is caused by our permission-based taint analysis which inherits the overhead of TaintDroid [24]. We believe this is a very reasonable and acceptable overhead for an offline analysis tool.

To measure the performance penalty in the worst case, we also write a benchmark app that invokes a privileged Android API 10,000 times and opens a socket 10,000 times. This case is used to measure the pure overhead caused by our permission check identification module. By measuring the execution time, we find the identification of *AndPermChk*s and *KerPermChk*s incurs an overhead of 80.108% and 238.870%, respectively. As the execution time of privileged calls represent only a small portion of the whole execution, *VetDroid* is quite efficient, especially as an offline analysis tool.

5. DISCUSSION

In this paper we focus on providing a new perspective for analyzing Android apps. To enlarge the analysis scope, our *Application Driver* utilizes several key features of Android, such as component-based programming model, event triggers. However, our technique alone could not guarantee all possible behaviors are captured within the short time an app is executed. The *Application Driver* could be enhanced with an automatic input generation system such as AppsPlayground [48], AppInspector [34], Dynodroid [43], or guided analysis technique such as multi-path exploration [44], forced/informed execution [54, 55].

Our *I-PUP Tracker* is built upon TaintDroid, thus inheriting similar limitations of TaintDroid such as incapable of tracking native code and implicit flows, which we leave as our future work. One possible way to solve the native code problem is to build a taint analysis system that seamlessly tracks Java code and native code. In addition, implicit flows can also be accurately tracked by selectively propagating tainted control dependencies as in DTA++ [38]. Furthermore, our *E-PUP Identifier* relies on the Android permission system for permission check identification. Thus our current implementation could not catch those behaviors that do not cause permission checks [35].

As our evaluation shows, *VetDroid* is not limited to analyze malicious apps, but also capable of analyzing benign apps. A key advantage of our approach is that it captures the application's sensitive behaviors with permission use graphs, which can significantly reduce irrelevant/uninteresting actions and let analysts focus on the critical behaviors when inspecting an app's internal logic. In practice, analysts can use *VetDroid* to automatically analyze a batch of apps and write simple scripts to select interested cases for further analysis (as demonstrated in our evaluation).

Compared with existing work, *Permission Use Behavior* provides a better approximation of sensitive behaviors inside an Android app. Thus, we believe *VetDroid* could be integrated with existing behavior-based malware detection techniques [14, 39] to extract effective malware signatures for clustering and detection.

6. RELATED WORK

Malware Analysis. As mentioned before, syscall-based solutions (e.g., syscall vector [16], syscall sequence with arguments [49], temporal pattern of syscalls [14], resource access model [40], syscall dependency graph [21, 22, 33]) are not well-suited for the Android platform due to the inability of monitoring Android-specific behaviors. DroidScope [56] seems to notice these problems by seamlessly reconstructing the semantics from system calls and Java. However, it only refines existing work, leaving the root problems of Android's special permission mechanism and programming model untouched. A survey on current Android malware characteristics was presented in [59] and [29]. DroidRanger [60] and RiskRanker [36] were two Android malware detectors that relied on existing knowledge about malicious symptoms. Although they were reported to detect known and unknown malware samples, they do not analyze the fine-grained internal behaviors of malware samples, which is the focus of *VetDroid*.

To analyze apps at market-scale, Chakradeo et al. [18] proposed app triage to efficiently allocate malware analysis resources. *VetDroid* can be combined with this technique into a practical market-scale application analysis solution.

Permission Analysis. Felt et al. [30] studied the effectiveness of the time-of-use and install-time permission grant mechanism. This work was extended in [28] to provide guidelines for platform designers in determining the most appropriate permission-granting mechanism for a given permission. Permission-based security rules were used by Kirin [25] to design a lightweight certification framework that could mitigate malware at install time. Apex [45] and Saint [46] were two extensions to the Android's permission system by introducing runtime constraints on the granted permissions.

To help end users understand application behaviors at install time, AppProfiler [50] devised a two-step translation technique which maps API calls to high-level behavior profiles. While *VetDroid* also tries to provide better behavior understanding, it is a tool provided for different users (security analysts) and it uses a different new technique/perspective (permission use behavior) to precisely capture application-system interactions and sensitive behaviors inside an app.

Barrera et al. [13] performed an empirical analysis on the expressiveness of Android's permission sets and discussed some potential improvements for Android's permission model. Felt et al. [27] proposed the first solution to systematically detect overprivileged permissions in Android apps and one-third of the applications in this study were found to be overprivileged. Probabilistic models of permission request patterns [32] or permission request sets [47] were also used to indicate the risk of new applications. To extract permission specifications for Android, Stowaway [27] used API fuzz testing while PScout [12] adopted static analysis on Android source code. However, these two permission specifications were limited in either completeness or preciseness, making them not well-suited for implementing *E-PUP Identifier*.

Permission re-delegation attack in Android was first introduced in [23,31]. Grace et al. [35] empirically evaluated the re-delegated permission leaks in pre-installed apps of stock Android smartphones. CHEX [41] and DroidChecker [19] were two tools that could detect such kind of capability leaks. Bugiel et al. [15] proposed system-centric and policy-driven runtime monitoring of communication channels between applications at both Android-level and kernel-level, which could prevent not only re-delegation attacks but also collusion attacks. Chen et al. [20] adopted static analysis to extract permission event graphs and examined the constraint conditions on events for each privileged API using model checking. However, it could not capture the internal logic of using permissions, especially when multiple permissions are intertwined.

Our *VetDroid* differs from all existing work in that it provides the first systematic framework to analyze permission use behaviors.

7. CONCLUSION

This paper presents *VetDroid*, the first approach to perform accurate permission use analysis to vet undesirable behaviors. To construct permission use behaviors, this paper proposes a systematic framework that completely identifies explicit and implicit permission use points with accurate permission information. *VetDroid* is shown to be able to clearly reconstruct malicious behaviors of real-world apps to ease malware analysis. It can also assist in finding information leaks, analyzing fine-grained causes of information leaks, and detecting subtle vulnerabilities in regular apps. In all, *VetDroid* provides a better vehicle for analyzing and examining Android apps, which brings benefits to malware analysis/detection, vulnerability analysis, and other related fields.

8. ACKNOWLEDGEMENTS

We would like to thank the anonymous reviewers for their insightful comments and feedback. This work is funded by National Natural Science Foundation of China (NO. 61103078, 61300027), Science and Technology Commission of Shanghai Municipality (NO. 11DZ2281500, 11511504404, 13511504402 and 13JC1400800), a joint program between China Ministry of Education and Intel numbered MOE-INTEL201202, Fundamental Research Funds for the Central Universities in China and Shanghai Leading Academic Discipline Project numbered B114. This work is also partially supported by the National Science Foundation under Grant no. CNS-0954096.

9. REFERENCES

[1] Android permissions. http://developer.android.com/reference/android/Manifest.permission.html.

[2] Androidos.tapsnake: Watching your every move. http://www.symantec.com/connect/blogs/androidostapsnake-watching-your-every-move.

[3] Android.smsreplicator. http://www.symantec.com/security_response/writeup.jsp?docid=2010-110214-1252-99.

[4] Facebook security phishing attack in the wild. http://www.securelist.com/en/blog/208193325/Facebook_Security_Phishing_Attack_In_The_Wild.

[5] Idc: Android market share reached 75% worldwide in q3 2012. http://techcrunch.com/2012/11/02/idc-android-market-share-reached-75-worldwide-in-q3-2012/.

[6] Mcafee threats report: Third quarter 2012. http://www.mcafee.com/ca/resources/reports/rp-quarterly-threat-q3-2012.pdf.

[7] Pendingintent. http://developer.android.com/reference/android/app/PendingIntent.html.

[8] Sms emulation using the android emulator. http://developer.android.com/tools/devices/emulator.html#sms.

[9] Ui/application exerciser monkey. http://developer.android.com/tools/help/monkey.html.

[10] Zeus-in-the-mobile - facts and theories. http://www.securelist.com/en/analysis/204792194/ZeuS_in_the_Mobile_Facts_and_Theories.

[11] Apple: ios 4. http://www.apple.com/iphone, 2011.

[12] K. W. Y. Au, Y. F. Zhou, Z. Huang, and D. Lie. Pscout: analyzing the android permission specification. In *Proc. of ACM CCS'12*, 2012.

[13] D. Barrera, H. G. Kayacik, P. C. van Oorschot, and A. Somayaji. A methodology for empirical analysis of permission-based security models and its application to android. In *Proc. of ACM CCS'10*, 2010.

[14] A. Bose, X. Hu, K. G. Shin, and T. Park. Behavioral detection of malware on mobile handsets. In *Proc. of MobiSys'08*, 2008.

[15] S. Bugiel, L. Davi, A. Dmitrienko, T. Fischer, A.-R. Sadeghi, and B. Shastry. Towards taming privilege-escalation attacks on Android. In *Proc. of NDSS'12*, Feb. 2012.

[16] I. Burguera, U. Zurutuza, and S. Nadjm-Tehrani. Crowdroid: behavior-based malware detection system for android. In *Proc. of SPSM'11*, 2011.

[17] D. Canali, A. Lanzi, D. Balzarotti, C. Kruegel, M. Christodorescu, and E. Kirda. A quantitative study of accuracy in system call-based malware detection. In *Proc. of ISSTA'12*, 2012.

[18] S. Chakradeo, B. Reaves, P. Traynor, and W. Enck. Mast: triage for market-scale mobile malware analysis. In *Proc. of WiSec'13*, 2013.

[19] P. P. Chan, L. C. Hui, and S. M. Yiu. Droidchecker: analyzing android applications for capability leak. In *Proc. of WiSec'12*, 2012.

[20] K. Z. Chen, N. Johnson, V. D'Silva, S. Dai, K. MacNamara, T. Magrino, E. X. Wu, M. Rinard, and D. Song. Contextual policy enforcement in android applications with permission event graphs. In *Proc. of NDSS'13*, February 2013.

[21] M. Christodorescu, S. Jha, and C. Kruegel. Mining specifications of malicious behavior. In *Proc. of ESEC-FSE'07*, 2007.

[22] P. M. Comparetti, G. Salvaneschi, E. Kirda, C. Kolbitsch, C. Kruegel, and S. Zanero. Identifying dormant functionality in malware programs. In *Proc. of IEEE S&P'10*, 2010.

[23] M. Dietz, S. Shekhar, Y. Pisetsky, A. Shu, and D. S. Wallach. Quire: lightweight provenance for smart phone operating systems. In *Proc. of USENIX Security'11*, 2011.

[24] W. Enck, P. Gilbert, B.-G. Chun, L. P. Cox, J. Jung, P. McDaniel, and A. N. Sheth. Taintdroid: an information-flow tracking system for realtime privacy monitoring on smartphones. In *Proc. of OSDI'10*, 2010.

[25] W. Enck, M. Ongtang, and P. McDaniel. On lightweight mobile phone application certification. In *Proc. of ACM CCS'09*, 2009.

[26] W. Enck, M. Ongtang, and P. McDaniel. Understanding android security. *IEEE Security and Privacy*, 7(1):50–57, Jan. 2009.

[27] A. P. Felt, E. Chin, S. Hanna, D. Song, and D. Wagner. Android permissions demystified. In *Proc. of ACM CCS'11*, 2011.

[28] A. P. Felt, S. Egelman, M. Finifter, D. Akhawe, and D. Wagner. How to ask for permission. In *Proc. of HotSec'12*, 2012.

[29] A. P. Felt, M. Finifter, E. Chin, S. Hanna, and D. Wagner. A survey of mobile malware in the wild. In *Proc. of SPSM'11*, 2011.

[30] A. P. Felt, K. Greenwood, and D. Wagner. The effectiveness of application permissions. In *Proc. of WebApps'11*, 2011.

[31] A. P. Felt, H. J. Wang, A. Moshchuk, S. Hanna, and E. Chin. Permission re-delegation: attacks and defenses. In *Proc. of USENIX Security'11*, 2011.

[32] M. Frank, B. Dong, A. P. Felt, and D. Song. Mining permission request patterns from android and facebook applications. In *Proc. of ICDM'12*, 2012.

[33] M. Fredrikson, S. Jha, M. Christodorescu, R. Sailer, and X. Yan. Synthesizing near-optimal malware specifications from suspicious behaviors. In *Proc. of IEEE S&P'10*, 2010.

[34] P. Gilbert, B.-G. Chun, L. P. Cox, and J. Jung. Vision: automated security validation of mobile apps at app markets. In *Proc. of 2nd international workshop on Mobile cloud computing and services (MCS'11)*, 2011.

[35] M. Grace, Y. Zhou, Z. Wang, and X. Jiang. Systematic detection of capability leaks in stock android smartphones. In *Proc. of NDSS'12*, 2012.

[36] M. Grace, Y. Zhou, Q. Zhang, S. Zou, and X. Jiang. Riskranker: scalable and accurate zero-day android malware detection. In *Proc. of MobiSys'12*, 2012.

[37] M. C. Grace, W. Zhou, X. Jiang, and A.-R. Sadeghi. Unsafe exposure analysis of mobile in-app advertisements. In *Proc. of WiSec'12*, 2012.

[38] M. G. Kang, S. McCamant, P. Poosankam, and D. Song. DTA++: Dynamic taint analysis with targeted control-flow propagation. In *Proc. of NDSS'11*, Feb. 2011.

[39] C. Kolbitsch, P. M. Comparetti, C. Kruegel, E. Kirda, X. Zhou, and X. Wang. Effective and efficient malware detection at the end host. In *Proc. of USENIX Security'09*, 2009.

[40] A. Lanzi, D. Balzarotti, C. Kruegel, M. Christodorescu, and E. Kirda. Accessminer: using system-centric models for malware protection. In *Proc. of ACM CCS'10*, 2010.

[41] L. Lu, Z. Li, Z. Wu, W. Lee, and G. Jiang. Chex: statically vetting android apps for component hijacking vulnerabilities. In *Prof. of ACM CCS'12*, 2012.

[42] W. Ma, P. Duan, S. Liu, G. Gu, and J.-C. Liu. Shadow attacks: Automatically evading system-call-behavior based malware detection. *Springer Journal in Computer Virology*, 2012.

[43] A. MacHiry, R. Tahiliani, and M. Naik. Dynodroid: An input generation system for android apps. Technical report, Program Analysis Group, Georgia Tech, 2012.

[44] A. Moser, C. Kruegel, and E. Kirda. Exploring multiple execution paths for malware analysis. In *Proc. of IEEE S&P'07*, 2007.

[45] M. Nauman, S. Khan, and X. Zhang. Apex: extending android permission model and enforcement with user-defined runtime constraints. In *Proc. of AsiaCCS'10*, 2010.

[46] M. Ongtang, S. McLaughlin, W. Enck, and P. McDaniel. Semantically rich application-centric security in android. In *Proc. of ACSAC'09*, 2009.

[47] H. Peng, C. Gates, B. Sarma, N. Li, Y. Qi, R. Potharaju, C. Nita-Rotaru, and I. Molloy. Using probabilistic generative models for ranking risks of android apps. In *Proc. of ACM CCS'12*, 2012.

[48] V. Rastogi, Y. Chen, and W. Enck. Appsplayground: Automatic security analysis of smartphone applications. In *Proc. of CODASPY'13*, 2013.

[49] K. Rieck, T. Holz, C. Willems, P. Düssel, and P. Laskov. Learning and classification of malware behavior. In *Proc. of DIMVA'08*, 2008.

[50] S. Rosen, Z. Qian, and Z. M. Mao. Appprofiler: a flexible method of exposing privacy-related behavior in android applications to end users. In *Proc. of CODASPY'13*, 2013.

[51] H.-G. Schmidt, K. Raddatz, A.-D. Schmidt, A. Camtepe, and S. Albayrak. Google android: A comprehensive introduction. Technical report, DAI-Labor, TU Berlin, 2009.

[52] S. Schrittwieser, P. Fruehwirt, P. Kieseberg, M. Leithner, M. Mulazzani, M. Huber, and E. R. Weippl. Guess who is texting you? evaluating the security of smartphone messaging applications. In *Prof. of NDSS'12*, Feb 2012.

[53] X. Wei, L. Gomez, I. Neamtiu, and M. Faloutsos. Profiledroid: multi-layer profiling of android applications. In *Proc. of Mobicom'12*, 2012.

[54] J. Wilhelm and T.-c. Chiueh. A forced sampled execution approach to kernel rootkit identification. In *Proc. of RAID'07*, 2007.

[55] Z. Xu, L. Chen, G. Gu, and C. Kruegel. Peerpress: utilizing enemies' p2p strength against them. In *Proc. of ACM CCS'12*, 2012.

[56] L. K. Yan and H. Yin. Droidscope: seamlessly reconstructing the os and dalvik semantic views for dynamic android malware analysis. In *Proc. of USENIX Security'12*, 2012.

[57] Z. Yang, M. Yang, Y. Zhang, G. Gu, P. Ning, and X. S. Wang. Appintent: Analyzing sensitive data transmission in android for privacy leakage detection. In *Proc. of ACM CCS'13*, 2013.

[58] H. R. Zeidanloo and A. A. Manaf. Botnet command and control mechanisms. In *Proc. of ICCEE'09*, 2009.

[59] Y. Zhou and X. Jiang. Dissecting android malware: Characterization and evolution. In *Proc. of IEEE S&P'12*, 2012.

[60] Y. Zhou, Z. Wang, W. Zhou, and X. Jiang. Hey, you, get off of my market: Detecting malicious apps in official and alternative Android markets. In *Proc. of NDSS'12*, 2012.

The Impact of Vendor Customizations on Android Security

Lei Wu, Michael Grace, Yajin Zhou, Chiachih Wu, Xuxian Jiang
Department of Computer Science
North Carolina State University
{lwu4, mcgrace, yajin_zhou, cwu10}@ncsu.edu, jiang@cs.ncsu.edu

ABSTRACT

The smartphone market has grown explosively in recent years, as more and more consumers are attracted to the sensor-studded multipurpose devices. Android is particularly ascendant; as an open platform, smartphone manufacturers are free to extend and modify it, allowing them to differentiate themselves from their competitors. However, vendor customizations will inherently impact overall Android security and such impact is still largely unknown.

In this paper, we analyze ten representative stock Android images from five popular smartphone vendors (with two models from each vendor). Our goal is to assess the extent of security issues that may be introduced from vendor customizations and further determine how the situation is evolving over time. In particular, we take a three-stage process: First, given a smartphone's stock image, we perform *provenance analysis* to classify each app in the image into three categories: apps originating from the AOSP, apps customized or written by the vendor, and third-party apps that are simply bundled into the stock image. Such provenance analysis allows for proper attribution of detected security issues in the examined Android images. Second, we analyze *permission usages* of pre-loaded apps to identify overprivileged ones that unnecessarily request more Android permissions than they actually use. Finally, in *vulnerability analysis*, we detect buggy pre-loaded apps that can be exploited to mount permission re-delegation attacks or leak private information.

Our evaluation results are worrisome: vendor customizations are significant on stock Android devices and on the whole responsible for the bulk of the security problems we detected in each device. Specifically, our results show that on average 85.78% of all pre-loaded apps in examined stock images are overprivileged with a majority of them directly from vendor customizations. In addition, 64.71% to 85.00% of vulnerabilities we detected in examined images from every vendor (except for Sony) arose from vendor customizations. In general, this pattern held over time – newer smartphones, we found, are not necessarily more secure than older ones.

CCS'13, November 4–8, 2013, Berlin, Germany.

ACM 978-1-4503-2477-9/13/11 ...$15.00.
http://dx.doi.org/10.1145/2508859.2516728.

Categories and Subject Descriptors

D.4.6 [**Security and Protection**]: Information flow controls; D.2.5 [**Software Engineering**]: Testing and Debugging—*Code inspections and walk-throughs*

Keywords

Android; Provenance; Customization; Static Analysis

1. INTRODUCTION

The smartphone market has grown explosively in recent years, as more and more consumers are attracted to the sensor-studded multipurpose devices. According to IDC [30], smartphone vendors shipped a total of 482.5 million mobile phones in the fourth quarter of 2012 – levels nearly equal to those of feature phones. Meanwhile, among smartphones, Google's Android captured almost 70% of the global smartphone market share last year [31], compared to about 50% the year before [20].

Android's popularity is due in part to it being an open platform. Google produces a baseline version of Android, then makes it freely available in the form of the Android Open Source Project (AOSP). Manufacturers and carriers are free to build upon this baseline, adding custom features in a bid to differentiate their products from their competitors. These customizations have grown increasingly sophisticated over time, as the hardware has grown more capable and the vendors more adept at working with the Android framework. Flagship devices today often offer a substantially different look and feel, along with a plethora of pre-loaded third-party apps.

From another perspective, vendor customizations will inherently impact overall Android security. Past work [24] has anecdotally shown that Android devices had security flaws shipped in their pre-loaded apps. Note that stock images include code from potentially many sources: the AOSP itself, the vendor, and any third-party apps that are bundled by the vendor or carrier. It is therefore important to attribute each particular security issue back to its source for possible bug-fixes or improvements.

In this paper, we aim to study vendor customizations on stock Android devices and assess the impact on overall Android security. Especially, we intend to determine the source of the security issues that trouble Android smartphone images, then further determine how the situation is evolving over time. To that end, we develop a three-stage process to evaluate a given smartphone's stock firmware image. First, we perform *provenance analysis*, aiming to classify each pre-loaded app into three categories: apps originating from the AOSP, apps customized or written by the vendor, and third-party apps that are simply bundled into the stock image. We then analyze, in two different ways, the security implications of each app: (1) *Permission usage analysis* compares the permissions requested by the app with those that it actually uses, looking for apps that request more permissions than they use. This situation is known as permission overprivilege, and it indicates a poor understanding of the Android security model; (2) *Vulnerability analysis*, in comparison, looks for two general types of actual security vulnerabilities: *permission re-delegation attacks* and *content leaks*. Permission re-delegation attacks allow unprivileged apps to act as though they have certain sensitive permissions, while content leaks allow such apps to gain (unauthorized) access to private data.

To facilitate our analysis, we implement a Security Evaluation Framework for Android called SEFA to evaluate stock smartphone images. Given a particular phone firmware image, SEFA first preprocesses it and imports into a local database a variety of information about the image, including the number of apps and numerous information about each app, such as the list of requested permissions, declared components, and the set of used Android APIs. Then SEFA compares each pre-loaded app with various ones in the original AOSP to determine its source and further performs a system-wide data-flow analysis to detect possible vulnerabilities. In our study, we have applied SEFA to ten flagship phone models from five popular vendors: Google, Samsung, HTC, LG, and Sony. For each vendor, we selected two phones: one from the current crop of Android 4.x phones, and one from the previous generation of 2.x devices. This slate of devices allows us to do two comparative analyses: *horizontal* differential analysis compares the various manufacturers' offerings for a given generation, while *vertical* differential analysis studies the evolution of any given vendor's security practices chronologically.

Our evaluation results show that more than 81.78% of pre-loaded apps (or 76.34% of LOC) on stock Android devices are due to vendor customizations. It is worrisome to notice that vendor customizations were, on the whole, responsible for the bulk of the security problems suffered by each device. On average, 85.78% of all pre-loaded apps in examined stock images are overprivileged with a majority of them directly from vendor customizations. And vendor apps consistently exhibited permission overprivilege, regardless of generation. Our results also show that vendor customizations are responsible for a large proportion of the vulnerabilities in each phone. For the Samsung, HTC, and LG phones, between 64.71% and 85.00% of the vulnerabilities were due to vendor customizations. This pattern was largely stable over time, with the notable exception of HTC, whose current offering is markedly more secure than the last-generation model we evaluated.

The rest of this paper is organized as follows. We present our methodology and system framework in Section 2, and describe implementation and evaluation results with case studies in Section 3. We then discuss for possible improvements in Section 4. Finally, we compare with related work and conclude this paper in Section 5 and Section 6 respectively.

2. DESIGN

The goal of this work is to study vendor customizations on stock Android devices and assess corresponding security impact. Note that the software stack running in these devices are complex, and their firmware is essentially a collaborative effort, rather than the work of a single vendor. Therefore, we need to categorize the code contained in a stock image based on its authorship and audit it for possible security issues. After that, we can attribute the findings of the security analyses to the responsible party, allowing us to better understand the state of smartphone security practices in the industry and spot any evident trends over time.

In Figure 1, we summarize the overall architecture of the proposed SEFA system. Our system takes a stock phone image as its input, preprocessing each app and importing the results into a database. This database, initially populated with a rich set of information about pre-loaded apps (including information from their manifest files, signing certificates, as well as their code, etc.), is then used by a set of subsequent analyses. Each analysis reads from the database, performs its analysis, and stores its findings in the database.

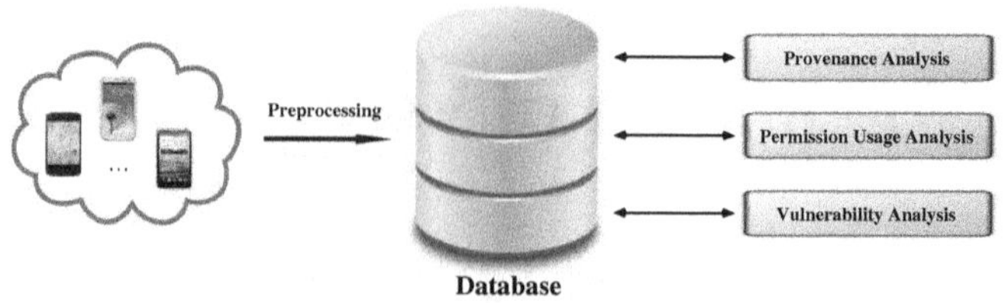

Figure 1: The overall architecture of SEFA

To study the impact of vendor customizations on the security of stock Android smartphones, we have developed three such analyses. First, to classify each app based on its presumed authorship, we perform *provenance analysis* (Section 2.1). This analysis is helpful to measure how much of the baseline AOSP is still retained and how much customizations have been made to include vendor-specific features or third-party apps. To further get a sense of the security and privacy problems posed by each app, we use two different analyses: *permission usage analysis* (Section 2.2) assesses whether an app requests more permissions than it uses, while *vulnerability analysis* (Section 2.3) scans the entire image for concrete security vulnerabilities that could compromise the device and cause damage to the user. Ultimately, by correlating the results of the security analyses with the provenance information we collected, we can effectively measure the impact of vendor customizations.

2.1 Provenance Analysis

The main purpose of provenance analysis is to study the distribution of pre-loaded apps and better understand the customization level by vendors on stock devices. Specifically, we classify pre-loaded apps into three categories:

- *AOSP app*: the first category contains apps that exist in the AOSP and may (or may not) be customized by the vendor.
- *vendor app*: the second category contains apps that do not exist in the AOSP and were developed by the vendor.
- *third-party app*: the last category contains apps that do not exist in the AOSP and were *not* developed by the vendor.

The idea to classify pre-loaded apps into the above three categories is as follows. First we collect AOSP app candidates by searching the AOSP, then we exclude these AOSP apps from the pre-loaded ones. After that, we can classify the remaining apps by examining their signatures (i.e., information in their certificate files) based on a basic assumption: third-party apps shall be private and will not be modified by vendors. Therefore, they will not share the same signing certificates with vendor apps.

In practice, this process is however not trivial. Since AOSP apps may well be customized by vendors, their signatures are likely to be changed as well. Although in many cases, the app names, package names or component names are unchanged, there do exist exceptions. For example, Sony's *Conversations* app, with package name `com.sonyericsson.conversations`, is actually a customized version of the AOSP *Mms* app named `com.android.mms`. In order to solve this problem, we perform a call graph similarity analysis, which has been demonstrated to be an effective technique even to assist malware clustering and provenance identification [29].

To generate the call graph required by any such analysis, we add all method calls that can be reached starting from any *entrypoint* method accessible to other apps or the framework itself. However, we are hesitant to use graph isomorphism techniques to compare these call graphs, as they are complex and have undesirable performance characteristics. Instead, we notice that later analysis (Section 2.3) will use *paths*, sequences of methods that start at an entrypoint and flow into a *sink* (i.e., API or field which may require sensitive permissions, lead to dangerous operations or meet other special needs). Therefore, we choose to preprocess each app, extract and compare the resulting paths, a much more straightforward process that still compare the parts of each app that we are most concerned with.

From our prototype, we observe that such a path-based similarity analysis is implementation-friendly and effective. Particularly, we use the return type and parameters (number, position and type) of each node (method) in the path as its signature. If the similarity between two paths exceeds a certain threshold, we consider these two paths are matching. And the similarity between two apps is largely measured based on the number of matched paths. In our prototype, to determine which apps belong to the AOSP, we accordingly take the approach: (1) by matching app names and package names; (2) by matching component names in the manifest file; (3) and then by calculating the similarity between paths and apps. We point out that a final manual verification is always performed to guarantee the correctness of the classification, which can also confirm the effectiveness of our heuristics.

During this stage, we also collect one more piece of information: the code size of pre-loaded apps measured by their lines of code (LOC). Although it is impossible for us to get all the source code of the pre-loaded apps, we can still roughly estimate their size based on their decompiled `.smali` code.[1] Therefore, we can draw a rough estimate of vendor customization from provenance analysis because the number and code size of apps are important indicators. In addition, we also collect firmware release dates and update cycles as supplementary information for our later evaluation (Section 3.1).

2.2 Permission Usage Analysis

Our next analysis stage is designed to detect instances of permission overprivilege, where an app requests more permissions than it uses. SEFA applies permission usage analysis to measure the adoption of the principle of least privilege in app development. Note that here it is only possible to get the usage of permissions defined in the standard AOSP framework. The usage of vendor-specific permissions cannot be counted because of the lack of related information.

There are four types of permissions in Android: *normal*, *dangerous*, *system* and *systemOrSignature*. The latter three are sensitive, because normal permissions are not supposed to be privileged enough to cause damage to the user. Specifically, we define permissions declared by element `uses-permission` in the manifest file as *requested permissions*, and permissions which are actually used (e.g., by using related APIs) as *used permissions* respectively. An *overdeclared permission* is a permission which is requested but not used. *Overprivileged apps* contain at least one overdeclared permission.

Algorithm 1 outlines our process for permission usage analysis. From the database, we have the initial requested permission set of apps (as it is in the manifest information), and our goal is to find the

Algorithm 1: Permission Usage Analysis

Input: initial info. in our database about pre-loaded apps
Output: overdeclared permission set of apps

$apps$ = all apps in one image;
$mappings$ = all permission mappings;
A = API invocation set;
I = intent usage set;
C = content provider usage set;
S = shared user id set;
R = requested-permission set;
$U = \emptyset$; `// used permission set`
$O = \emptyset$; `// overdeclared permission set`

foreach $s \in S$ **do**
    $tmp = \emptyset$;
    foreach $app \in s$ **do**
        $tmp = tmp \cup R[app]$;
    foreach $app \in s$ **do**
        $R[app] = tmp$;

foreach $app \in apps$ **do**
    foreach $a \in A[app]$ **do**
        $U[app]$.add($mappings[a]$);
    foreach $i \in I[app]$ **do**
        $U[app]$.add($mappings[i]$);
    foreach $c \in C[app]$ **do**
        $U[app]$.add($mappings[c]$);

foreach $app \in apps$ **do**
    $O[app] = R[app] - U[app]$;
return O

overdeclared permission set. Despite the initial requested permission set, we find it still needs to be augmented. Especially, there is a special manifest file attribute, `sharedUserId`, which causes multiple apps signed by the same developer certificate to share a user identifier, thus sharing their requested permission sets. (As permissions are technically assigned to a user identifier, not an app, all such apps will be granted the union of all the permissions requested by each app. Accordingly, apps with the same `sharedUserId` require extra handling to get the complete requested permission set.) Next, we leverage the known permission mapping built by earlier work [2] to determine which permissions are actually used.[2] Having built both the requested permission set and the used permission set, we can then calculate the overdeclared permission set.

Our approach to calculate the overdeclared permission set is conservative. Notice that some permissions declared in the manifest file may be deprecated in the corresponding standard Android framework. An example is the permission `READ_OWNER_DATA`[3] that was removed after API level 8 (i.e., Android version 2.2), but still declared by one app in the Nexus 4 (API level 17, or Android 4.2). We do not consider them as overdeclared permissions, because the vendor may retain deprecated permissions in the customized framework for its own usage.

[1] We use the *baksmali* [42] tool to translate the Android app's `.dex` code into the `.smali` format.

[2] Early studies including PScout [2] concern themselves only with those permissions that are available to third-party apps. In our study, we need to cover additional permissions defined at *system* and *systemOrSignature* levels, which may not be well documented.

[3] Without specification, the prefix of standard Android permission name `android.permission.` is omitted in this paper.

After obtaining the overdeclared permission set, we then analyze the overall permission usage of each device, and classify results by provenance. The distributions of overprivileged apps as well as overdeclared permissions can then both be studied. Further, we also perform horizontal and vertical analysis, i.e., cross-vendor, same-generation, vs. cross-generation, same-vendor comparisons.

2.3 Vulnerability Analysis

While our permission usage analysis aims to measure the software development practices used in the creation of each pre-loaded app, vulnerability analysis is concerned with finding real, actionable exploits within those apps. Specifically, we look for two representative types of vulnerabilities in the Android platform which stem from misunderstanding or misusing Android's permission system. First, we identify *permission re-delegation attacks* [18], which are a form of the classic confused deputy attack [27]. Such an attack exists if an app can gain access to an Android permission without actually requesting it. A typical example is an app which is able to send Short Message Service (SMS) messages without acquiring the (supposedly required) `SEND_SMS` permission. For the second kind of vulnerability, we consider *content leaks*, which essentially combines the two types of content provider vulnerabilities reported by Zhou and Jiang [52]: *passive content leaks* and *content pollution*. An unprotected content provider (i.e., one that takes no sensitive permission to protect its access) is considered to have a passive content leak if it is world-readable, and to have content pollution if it is world-writable. We extend this definition to cover both open and protected content providers. The protected ones are also interesting as there may also exist unauthorized accesses to them through the other three types of components which could serve as springboards for exploitation. For ease of presentation, we call these vulnerabilities *content leaks*.

As our main goal is to accurately locate possible vulnerabilities, we in this study consider the following adversary model: a malicious app, which is compatible with the phone, may be installed on the phone by the user. We do not expect the malicious app will request any sensitive permissions during installation, which means it will only rely on vulnerable apps to accomplish its goals: either steal money from the user, gather confidential data, or maliciously destroy data. In other words, we limit the attacker to only unprivileged third-party apps to launch their attacks.

Keeping this adversary model in mind, we focus our analysis on security-critical permissions – the ones that protect the functions that our adversary would most like to gain access to. Specifically, for permission re-delegation attacks, we focus on permissions that are able to perform dangerous actions, such as `SEND_SMS` and `MASTER_CLEAR`, because they may lead to serious damage to the user, either financially or in terms of data loss. As for content leaks, we ignore those whose exposures are likely to be intentional[4]. Note that some apps may be vulnerable to low-severity content leaks; for example, publicly-available information about a network TV schedule is not as sensitive as the user's banking credentials. In other words, we primarily consider serious content leaks whose exposures are likely to cause critical damages to the user.

To actually find these vulnerabilities, we rely on a few key techniques. An essential one is reachability analysis, which is used to determine all feasible paths from the entrypoint set of all Android components, regardless of whether we consider them to be protected by a sensitive permission (Section 2.3.1). To better facilitate vulnerability analysis, we define two varieties of sinks:

- *sensitive-sinks*: sensitive Android APIs which are related to sensitive permissions (e.g., `MASTER_CLEAR`) of our concern
- *bridge-sinks*: invocations that are able to indirectly trigger another (vulnerable) component, e.g., `sendBroadcast`

Note that any path reachable from an open entrypoint or component can be examined directly to see if it has a sensitive-sink. Meanwhile, we also determine whether it could reach any bridge-link that will trigger other protected components (or paths). The remaining paths, whose entrypoints are protected, are correlated with paths that contain bridge-sinks to form the complete vulnerable path, which is likely cross-component or even cross different apps. This is essentially a reflection-based attack and we will describe it in Section 2.3.2 in greater detail. All calculated (vulnerable) paths will subject to manual verification.

We stress that unlike some previous works (e.g., [24]) which mainly focus on discovery of vulnerabilities, this analysis stage primarily involves a more contextual evaluation of vulnerabilities, including distribution, evolution and the impact of customization. Especially, we use the distribution of vulnerable apps as a metric to assess possible security impact from vendor customizations. Note the detected vulnerabilities are classified into different categories by their provenance and leveraged to understand the corresponding impact of customization. As mentioned earlier, both horizontal and vertical impact analyses are performed.

2.3.1 Reachability Analysis

Our reachability analysis is performed in two steps. The first step is intra-procedural reachability analysis, which involves building related call graphs and resolving it by conventional *def-use* analysis [11]. The resolution starts from the initial state (pre-computed when the database is initially populated) and then gradually seeks a fixed point of state changes with iteration (due to various transfer functions). However, as the state space might be huge (due to combinatorial explosion), the convergence progress could be slow or even unavailable. In practice, we have to impose additional conditional constraints to control the state-changing iteration procedure. We call the result of intra-procedural analysis, i.e., the states of variables and fields, a *summary*.

The second step is inter-procedural reachability analysis that is used to propagate states between different methods. After each propagation, method summaries might be changed. In such cases, intra-procedural reachability analysis is performed again on each affected method to generate a new summary. Inter-procedural reachability analysis is also an iterative process, but takes longer and requires more space to converge; therefore, we use some heuristics to reduce the computational and space overhead. For instance, if a variable or field we are concerned with has already reached a sink, there is no need to wait for convergence. A more formal description of our reachability analysis is listed in Algorithm 3 (see Appendix A).

Paths of apps from different vendors but with similar functionality may share something in common, especially for those apps inherited from the standard AOSP framework. Here "common" does not mean that their source code is exactly the same, but is similar from the perspective of structure and functionality. Many devices reuse the code from the AOSP directly, without many modifications. If we have already performed reachability analysis on such a common path, there is no need to do it on its similar counterparts. We believe this improves system performance since reachability analysis is time consuming (especially when the state space is huge). Therefore, we also perform a similarity analysis as a part of the reachability analysis to avoid repetitive efforts.

[4]Some content providers are exported explicitly, such as `TelephonyProvider` in the app of the same name.

2.3.2 *Reflection Analysis*

To facilitate our analysis, we classify vulnerable paths into the following three types:

- *in-component*: a vulnerable path that starts from an unprotected component to a sink that is located in the same component.
- *cross-component*: a vulnerable path that starts from an unprotected component, goes through into other components within the same app, and then reaches a sink.
- *cross-app*: a vulnerable path that starts from an unprotected component of one app, goes through into another app's components, and eventually reaches a sink.

The in-component vulnerable paths are relatively common and have been the subject of recent studies [24, 34]. However, the latter two, especially the cross-app ones, have not been well studied yet, which is thus the main focus of our reflection analysis. Note that a reflection-based attack typically involves with multiple components that may not reside in the same app. A concrete example that is detected by our tool will be shown in Figure 6 (Section 3.3.1).

Traditional reachability analysis has been effective in detecting in-component vulnerable paths. However, it is rather limited for other cross-component or cross-app vulnerable paths. (A cross-app execution path will pass through a chain of related apps to ultimately launch an attack.) In order to identify them, a comprehensive analysis of possible "connection" between apps is necessary. To achieve that, our approach identifies not only possible reachable paths within each component, but also the invocation relationship for all components. The invocation relationship is essentially indicated by sending an *intent* [21] from one component to another, explicitly or implicitly. An explicit intent specifies the target component to receive it and is straightforward to handle. An implicit intent, on the other hand, may be sent anonymously without specifying the receiving component, thus requiring extra handling (i.e., *intent resolution* in Android) to determine the best one from the available components. In our system, SEFA essentially mimics the Android intent resolution mechanism by matching an intent against all possible `<intent-filter>` manifest declarations in the installed apps. However, due to the offline nature of our system, we have limited available information about how the framework behaves at run-time. Therefore, we develop the following two heuristics:

- A component from the same app is preferable to components from other apps.
- A component from a different app which shares the same sharedUserId is preferable to components from other apps.

If multiple component candidates still exist for a particular intent, we simply iterate each one to report possible vulnerable path and then manually verify it in a real phone setting. In Algorithm 2, we summarize the overall procedure. The basic idea here is to maintain a visited component list. For a particular component, the algorithm returns $\emptyset$ if it has been visited; otherwise we add it into the list, and check all possible components that are able to start up that component recursively.

3. IMPLEMENTATION AND EVALUATION

We have implemented a SEFA prototype as a mix of Java code and Python scripts with $11,447$ and $4,876$ lines of code (LOC) respectively. In our evaluation, we examined ten representative phones (Table 1) released between the end of 2010 and the end of 2012 by five popular vendors: Google, Samsung, HTC, LG, and Sony. The selected phone model either has great impact and is representative, or has huge market share. For example, Google's phones are designed to be reference models for their whole generation; Samsung is the market leader which occupies 39.6% of smartphone market share in 2012 [30]. To analyze these phone images, our system requires on average 70 minutes to process each image (i.e., around 30 seconds per app) and reports about 300 vulnerable paths for us to manually verify. Considering the off-line nature of our tool, we consider this acceptable, even though our tool could be optimized further to speed up our analysis.

[5]This category contains apps that exist in the AOSP and may (or may not) be customized by the vendor – Section 2.1. This definition also applies to Tables 3, 4 and 5.

Algorithm 2: Reflection Analysis

```
Input: current component, visited component list
Output: vulnerable path set
/* find vulnerable paths recursively from
   backward for current component                  */
c = current component;
VC = visited component list;
CC = components which are able to start up c;
V = ∅; // vulnerable path set
if c ∈ VC then
  | return V
else
  | VC.append(c);
foreach cc ∈ CC do
  | tmp = VC.clone();
  | V.add(Reflection Analysis(cc, tmp));
return V
```

3.1 Provenance Analysis

As mentioned earlier, the provenance analysis collects a wide variety of information about each device and classifies pre-loaded apps into three different categories. In Table 1, we summarize our results. Overall, these ten devices had 1,548 pre-loaded apps, totalling 114,427,232 lines of code (in terms of decompiled `.smali` code). A further break-down of these apps show that, among these devices, there are on average 28.2 (18.22%), 99.7 (64.41%), and 26.9 (17.38%) apps from the categories of AOSP, vendor and third-party, respectively. Note that the apps in the AOSP category may also be customized or extended by vendors (Section 2.1). As a result, the figures in the AOSP column of Table 1 should be considered an upper bound for the proportion of code drawn from the AOSP. Accordingly, on average, vendor customizations account for more than 81.78% of apps (or 76.34% of LOC) on these devices.

In our study, we selected two phone models for each vendor, one from the current crop of Android 4.x phones, and one from the previous generation of 2.x devices. Table 2 shows the initial release date of each phone model, as reported by GSM Arena [26]. As it turns out, these devices can be readily classified by their release dates: the past generation of devices all were initially released before 2012, while the current generation's products were released in 2012 or later. Therefore, we break them down into *pre-2012* and *post-2012* devices. Such classification is helpful to lead to certain conclusions. For example, as one might expect, the complexity of these devices is clearly increasing over time. In all cases, the post-2012 products from any given manufacturer contain more apps and LOC than their pre-2012 counterparts. Specifically, the HTC Wildfire S has 147 apps with 9,643,448 LOC, and the HTC One X has

Table 1: Provenance analysis of representative devices

			Total		AOSP app [5]		vendor app		third-party app	
Vendor	**Device**	**Version & Build #**	**# Apps**	**# LOC**	**# Apps (%)**	**# LOC (%)**	**# Apps**	**# LOC**	**# Apps**	**# LOC**
Samsung	Galaxy S2	2.3.4; I9100XWKI4	172	10,052,891	26 (15.12%)	2,419,155 (24.06%)	114	3,519,955	32	4,113,781
Samsung	Galaxy S3	4.0.4; I9300UBALF5	185	17,339,442	30 (16.22%)	6,344,721 (36.59%)	119	5,660,569	36	5,334,152
HTC	Wildfire S	2.3.5; CL362953	147	9,643,448	24 (16.33%)	2,759,415 (28.61%)	94	3,514,921	29	3,369,112
HTC	One X	4.0.4; CL100532	280	19,623,805	29 (10.36%)	4,718,633 (24.05%)	190	7,354,468	61	7,550,704
LG	Optimus P350	2.2; FRG83	100	6,160,168	27 (27.00%)	1,152,885 (18.72%)	40	604,197	33	4,403,086
LG	Optimus P880	4.0.3; IML74K	115	12,129,841	28 (24.35%)	3,170,950 (26.14%)	63	3,269,936	24	5,688,955
Sony	Xperia Arc S	2.3.4; 4.0.2.A.0.62	176	7,689,131	28 (15.91%)	1,164,691 (15.15%)	123	2,666,397	25	3,858,043
Sony	Xperia SL	4.0.4; 6.1.A.2.45	209	10,704,797	28 (13.40%)	1,800,690 (16.82%)	156	4,127,343	25	4,776,764
Google	Nexus S	2.3.6; GRK39F	73	5,234,802	31 (42.47%)	1,036,858 (19.81%)	41	2,821,874	1	1,376,070
Google	Nexus 4	4.2; JOP40C	91	15,848,907	31 (34.07%)	2,506,778 (15.82%)	57	12,156,673	3	1,185,456
Total			1548	114,427,232	282 (18.22%)	27,074,776 (23.66%)	997	45,696,333	269	41,656,123

Table 2: Release dates of examined Android devices

Device	Release Date[1]	Update Date [2] & Version
Nexus S	Dec 2010	4.0.4, Mar 2012; 4.1.2, Oct 2012
Nexus 4	Nov 2012	N/A
Wildfire S	May 2011	N/A
One X	May 2012	4.1.1, Nov 2012; 4.1.2, Mar 2013
Optimus P350	Feb 2011	N/A
Optimus P880	Jun 2012	4.1.2, Mar 2013
Galaxy S2	Apr 2011	2.3.6, Dec 2011; 4.0.3 Jul 2012; 4.1.1, Jan 2013; 4.1.2, Apr 2013
Galaxy S3	May 2012	4.1.1, Nov 2012; 4.1.2, Mar 2013
Xperia Arc S	Sep 2011	4.0.4, Aug 2012
Xperia SL	Sep 2012	4.1.2, May 2013

[1] The release dates may vary by area and carrier, but the difference is not that significant (e.g., around one month).

[2] The update dates collected here are mainly for markets in United States.

280 apps with 19,623,805 LOC. The number of apps and LOC increase 90.47% and 103.49%, respectively.

Our analysis also shows that, though the baseline AOSP is indeed getting more complicated over time – but vendor customizations are at least keeping pace with the AOSP. This trend is not difficult to understand, as vendors have every incentive to add more functionality to their newer products, especially in light of their competitors doing the same.

The Google-branded phones are particularly interesting. Both have relatively few apps, as they are designed to be reference designs with only minor alterations to the core AOSP. However, the Nexus 4 has over three times as many lines of code as were included in the Nexus S, despite adding only 18 apps. The Nexus S was the simplest phone we studied, while the Nexus 4 is the third most complex – only the HTC One X and Samsung Galaxy S3, which are well known for their extensive customization, have more LOC. We attribute this to the fact that the Nexus 4 includes newer versions of vendor-specific apps (e.g., Gmail) that have more functionality with larger code size.

Meanwhile, we also observe these devices experience slow update cycles: the *average interval* between two updates for a phone model is about half a year! Also, it is interesting to note that the updates in the United States tend to lag behind some other areas. For instance, users of the Samsung Galaxy S3 in the United Kingdom received updates to Android 4.1.1 (which was released in July 2012) in September 2012, while the updates were not available for users in the United States until January 2013. If we compare the update dates in Table 1 with the corresponding dates of Android releases [22], it often takes half a year for vendors to provide an official update (excepting Google's reference phones) for users in the United States, though in many cases carriers may share the blame. Overall, official updates can hardly be called timely, which thereby seriously affects the security of these devices.

3.2 Permission Usage Analysis

After determining the provenance of each pre-loaded app, our next analysis captures the instances of permission overprivilege, where an app requests more permissions than it uses. The results are summarized in Table 3. On average, there is an alarming fact that across the ten devices, 85.78% of apps are overprivileged. Even Google's reference devices do not necessarily perform better than the others; the Nexus S has the second most overprivileged apps of all the pre-2012 devices. Note that the situation appears to be getting slightly better as time goes on. The average percentage of overprivileged apps in the post-2012 devices has decreased to 83.61%, compared to 87.96% of all apps on pre-2012 devices. But this situation is still hardly reassuring. Interestingly, our results show that the proportion of overprivileged pre-loaded apps are more than the corresponding result of third-party apps (reported by [2, 17]). We believe there are two main reasons: 1) pre-loaded apps are more privileged than third-party apps, as they can request certain permissions not available to third-party ones; 2) pre-loaded apps are more frequent in specifying the sharedUserId property, thereby gaining many (possibly unnecessary) permissions.

Specifically, if we take into account the provenance of each app, a different story emerges. Looking over the breakdowns in Table 3, the modest gains over time appear to be primarily attributable to a reduction in app overprivilege among AOSP apps; vendors appear to be responsible for roughly the same amount of overprivileged apps in each image (51.29% of all pre-2012 apps, vs. 52.71% of post-2012 apps). In this sense the vendors themselves do not appear to care significantly more about the least privilege principle than third-party app developers do, despite being, on average, much larger corporate entities.

In Figure 2, we summarize the distributions of overprivileged apps among pre-2012 devices and post-2012 devices respectively. The majority of overprivileged apps have no more than 10 overdeclared permissions. Note that pre-loaded apps have access to certain permissions that are not available to third-party apps. Therefore, these overdeclared permissions, if exploited, can lead to greater damage. For example, our results demonstrate that both `REBOOT` and `MASTER_CLEAR` are among overdeclared permissions that can allow for changing (important) device status or destroying user data without notification.

3.3 Vulnerability Analysis

Our vulnerability analysis led to several interesting results, especially once combined with our efforts to determine the provenance of each app. In particular, if we consider the distribution of vulnerable apps across each phone image (Table 4), the percentage of vulnerable apps of these devices varies from 1.79% to 14.97%. Applying our horizontal analysis to each generation of devices, it appears that the HTC Wildfire S and LG Optimus P880 have the

Table 3: Permission usage analysis of representative devices

Device	% of overprivileged apps among all pre-loaded apps (Pre-2012 devices)				Device	% of overprivileged apps among all pre-loaded apps (Post-2012 devices)			
	Total	AOSP app [5]	vendor app	third-party app		Total	AOSP app [5]	vendor app	third-party app
Nexus S	90.41%	38.36%	50.68%	1.37%	Nexus 4	79.12%	30.77%	48.35%	0.00%
Wildfire S	92.52%	15.65%	57.82%	19.05%	One X	78.21%	10.00%	50.71%	17.50%
Optimus P350	85.00%	23.00%	33.00%	29.00%	Optimus P880	91.30%	20.87%	50.43%	20.00%
Galaxy S2	88.37%	13.95%	58.14%	16.28%	Galaxy S3	87.57%	15.14%	55.68%	16.76%
Xperia Arc S	83.52%	14.20%	56.82%	12.50%	Xperia SL	81.82%	11.96%	58.37%	11.48%
Average	**87.96%**	**21.03%**	**51.29%**	**15.64%**	**Average**	**83.61%**	**17.75%**	**52.71%**	**13.15%**
Overall Average: 85.78%									

Table 4: Vulnerability analysis of representative devices (I)

Device	% of vulnerable apps among all apps (Pre-2012 devices)				Device	% of vulnerable apps among all apps (Post-2012 devices)			
	Total	AOSP app [5]	vendor app	third-party app		Total	AOSP app [5]	vendor app	third-party app
Nexus S	5.48%	2.74%	2.74%	0.00%	Nexus 4	2.20%	1.10%	1.10%	0.00%
Wildfire S	14.97%	4.76%	8.84%	1.36%	One X	1.79%	0.71%	0.71%	0.36%
Optimus P350	11.00%	4.00%	1.00%	6.00%	Optimus P880	10.43%	5.22%	5.22%	0.00%
Galaxy S2	12.21%	3.49%	6.98%	1.74%	Galaxy S3	6.49%	2.70%	3.24%	0.54%
Xperia Arc S	2.27%	1.14%	0.00%	1.14%	Xperia SL	1.91%	0.96%	0.48%	0.48%
Average	**8.99%**	**3.23%**	**3.91%**	**1.85%**	**Average**	**4.56%**	**2.14%**	**2.15%**	**0.28%**
Overall Average: 6.77%									

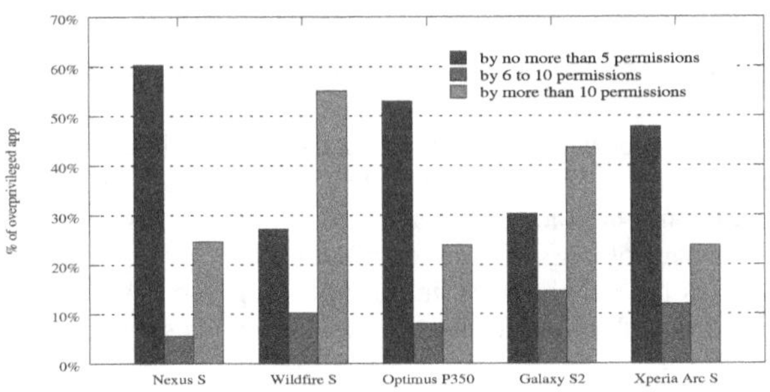

(a) Pre-2012 devices

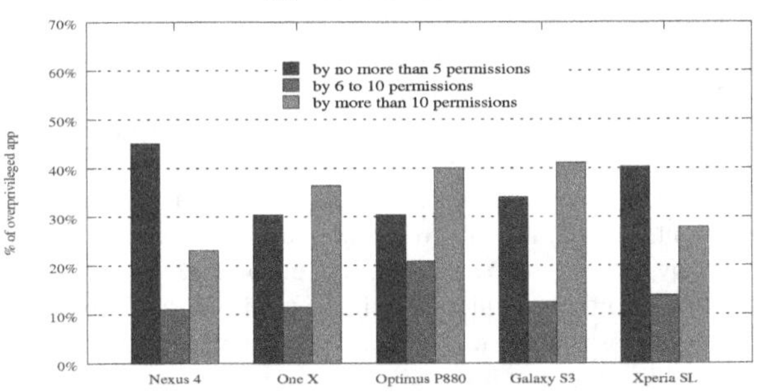

(b) Post-2012 devices

Figure 2: Distributions of overprivileged apps

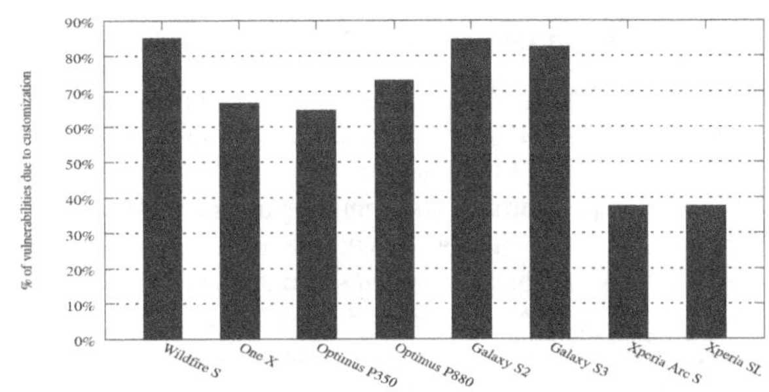

Figure 3: Vulnerabilities due to vendor customizations

most vulnerable apps in each generation. Inversely, the Sony Xperia Arc S and – interestingly – the HTC One X have the least vulnerable apps by proportion. As one may expect, Google's reference phones (especially the Nexus 4) both perform well compared to their contemporaries, as their images are designed to be a reference baseline. Our vertical analysis has an even more impressive result – the percentage of vulnerable apps across each generation dropped from an average of 8.99% last generation to 4.56% this generation. Even incorporating provenance information in the vertical analysis, there is a dramatic improvement for all three categories of app.

However, the percentage of vulnerable apps is not necessarily a good metric to measure the security of such devices. The complexity metrics we collected as part of our provenance analysis (see Table 1) show that the devices contain ever-increasing amounts of code. Therefore, while fewer vulnerabilities – as a percentage – may be introduced in newer phones, the sheer scale of their stock images works to counteract any gains. Furthermore, some vulnerable apps may contain more vulnerabilities than others. As a result, there is value in counting the absolute number of critical vulnerabilities as well as the proportion of vulnerable apps.

To this end, we summarize our results in that format in Table 5. When we use this table for vertical differential analysis, it tells quite a different story. While, indeed, the number of vulnerabilities in each generation of devices generally decreased, the reduction is nowhere near so dramatic. Furthermore, when considered in horizontal differential analysis, different devices take the crown for most and least secure devices in each generation. The HTC Wildfire S is still the least secure pre-2012 device, but only by a hair – the Samsung Galaxy S2 has only one fewer vulnerability. The Sony Xperia Arc S is tied with the Google Nexus S for the most secure pre-2012 device. Meanwhile, there is a complete shake-up among the post-2012 devices: the Samsung Galaxy S3 has 40 vulnerabilities to the LG Optimus P880's 26, while the HTC One X (at 15 vulnerabilities) falls to mid-pack, behind the Nexus 4 (at 3) and the Sony Xperia SL (at 8).

Table 5 still does not tell the complete story. Looking at the table's provenance analysis results, it appears that most of the vulnerabilities stem from the AOSP. However, recall that our provenance analysis concerns the original provenance of each *app*, not each *vulnerability*. To gather information about the provenance of each vulnerability, we manually examine each of the reported vulnerable paths. Our results are shown in Figure 3 (note that Google's phones are not included here because the AOSP is led by Google, making the distinction difficult). For the Samsung, HTC, and LG phones, the majority of vulnerabilities – between 64.71% and 85.00% – did *not* originate from the AOSP. However, for both of Sony's products,

Table 5: Vulnerability analysis of representative devices (II)

Pre-2012 devices					Post-2012 devices				
Device	# of vulnerabilities				Device	# of vulnerabilities			
	Total	AOSP app [1]	vendor app	third-party app		Total	AOSP app [1]	vendor app	third-party app
Nexus S	8	6	2	0	Nexus 4	3	2	1	0
Wildfire S	**40**	23	15	2	One X	15	12	2	1
Optimus P350	17	11	1	5	Optimus P880	26	17	9	0
Galaxy S2	**39**	18	18	3	Galaxy S3	**40**	20	12	8
Xperia Arc S	8	6	0	2	Xperia SL	8	6	1	1

[1]This category contains apps that exist in the AOSP and may (or may not) be customized by the vendor – Section 2.1.

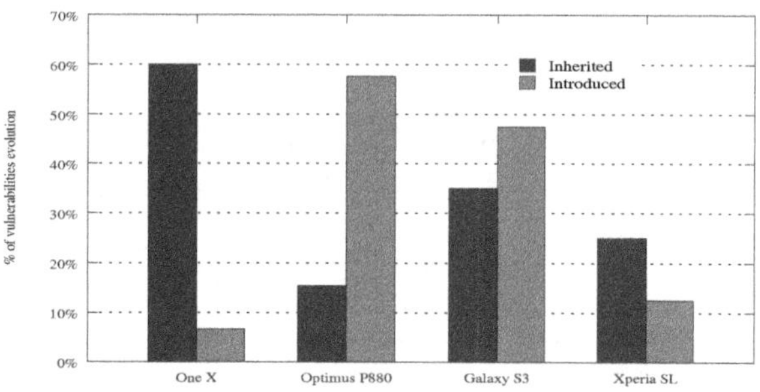

Figure 4: Vendor-specific vulnerability evolution

only 37.50% of vulnerabilities were caused by vendor customizations. In fact, one of Sony's modifications to the AOSP actually mitigated a pre-existing bug in it.

We can also apply vertical differential analysis to this data, and therefore look at the evolution of vulnerabilities over time. The post-2012 devices may have *inherited* some vulnerabilities that were never caught during the lifetime of the pre-2012 devices, as they often have code in common with earlier devices by the same manufacturer[6]; alternatively, they may have *introduced* new vulnerabilities in their new and altered features. Figure 4 depicts this evolutionary information, which varies wildly in proportion between different vendors. For example, for the HTC One X, about 60.00% of its vulnerabilities were inherited from the previous device, while the Samsung Galaxy S3 has more introduced vulnerabilities than inherited ones (47.50% vs. 35.00%).

Table 6: Classification of detected vulnerabilities

Name	Description
CALL_PRIVILEGED	Initiate a phone call (including emergency number) without requiring confirmation
MASTER_CLEAR	Wipe out user data and factory reset
REBOOT	Reboot the device
RECORD_AUDIO	Allows an application to record audio.
SEND_SMS	Allows an application to send SMS messages.
SHUTDOWN	Power off the device
WRITE_SMS	Allows an application to write SMS messages
OTHER	All the other dangerous/critical operations

No treatment of this topic would be complete without discussing the distribution of vulnerabilities that we found. Table 6 lists the vulnerabilities we focus on. We use the names of permission to represent the most common (i.e., shared by devices of different vendors) vulnerabilities for permission re-delegation attacks with explicit permission names, and use `OTHER` to represent all other vulnerabilities (including both types of studied vulnerabilities). Note that vulnerabilities belong to `OTHER` do not mean they are not critical, and the only reason is that they are more vendor- and model-specific. Table 7 lists the distribution of these vulnerabilities.

With these detected vulnerabilities, we have attempted to contact the corresponding vendors. While some of them have already been confirmed, other vendors have still not spoken with us even after several months. Among the detected vulnerabilities, we believe cross-app ones are the most challenging to detect. Figure 5 gives the percentage of cross-app vulnerabilities. On average, 8.90% vulnerabilities are of this type. In the following, we describe some specific vulnerabilities introduced due to vendor customizations.

[6]The relationship between each pair of devices may be not direct (i.e., predecessor and successor), but we can still regard these vulnerabilities as an inheritance because they are vendor-specific.

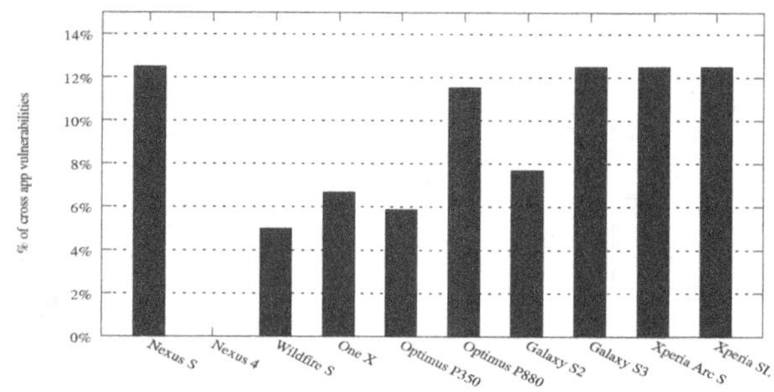

Figure 5: Distribution of cross-app vulnerabilities

3.3.1 Case Study: Samsung Galaxy S3

In the Samsung Galaxy S3, there is a pre-loaded app named *Keystring_misc*. This particular app has a protected component `PhoneUtilReceiver` that leads to a dangerous path for performing a factory reset, thus erasing all user data on the device. This path ends in the `phoneReset` method, which will broadcast an intent `android.intent.action.MASTER_CLEAR` to perform the operation. At first sight, this path seems to be *safe* because this component is protected by the `com.sec.android.app.phoneutil.permission.-KEYSTRING` permission, which is defined with the restrictive *systemOrSignature* protection level (i.e., only other firmware apps, or apps from Samsung, can invoke it).

Unfortunately, there exists another app named *FactoryTest* that contains a feasible path which is able to start up this very component in the *Keystring_misc* app. This arrangement is an example of a cross-app vulnerable path, which can be used to launch a reflection attack (Figure 6). Specifically, this app exports a service called `FtClient` without any protection. After being launched, the service will start a thread and then try to build connections with two hard-coded local socket addresses: `FactoryClientRecv` and `FactoryClientSend`. The established connections can be exploited to send commands through the first socket. Our manual investigation shows that there are many dangerous operations that can be triggered by this exploit, including `MASTER_CLEAR`, `REBOOT`, `SHUTDOWN` and `SEND_SMS`.

In our study, we also discover a number of other vulnerabilities. For example, there are four content providers in the *sCloudBackupProvider* app (with the package name of `com.sec.android.sCloud BackupProvider`). They expose access interfaces to specific databases, including `calllogs.db`, `sms.db`, `mms.db` and `settings.db`. Each of them is protected by two permissions, but with normal (non-sensitive) protection levels. Apparently, they are accessible to any

Table 7: Distribution of vulnerabilities among examined devices

Name	# of vulnerabilities									
	Google		HTC		LG		Samsung		Sony	
	Nexus S	Nexus 4	Wildfire S	One X	P350	P880	Galaxy S2	Galaxy S3	Xperia Arc S	Xperia SL
CALL_PRIVILEGED	1	0	2	1	1	3	2	4	1	1
MASTER_CLEAR	0	0	1	0	0	0	3	2	0	0
REBOOT	0	0	0	0	0	1	4	4	0	0
RECORD_AUDIO	0	0	1	0	0	1	1	1	0	0
SEND_SMS	3	2	6	3	4	4	7	7	3	3
SHUTDOWN	0	0	0	0	0	0	0	1	0	0
WRITE_SMS	2	0	5	6	3	3	4	4	2	2
OTHER	2	1	25	5	9	14	18	17	2	2
Total	8	3	40	15	17	26	39	40	8	8

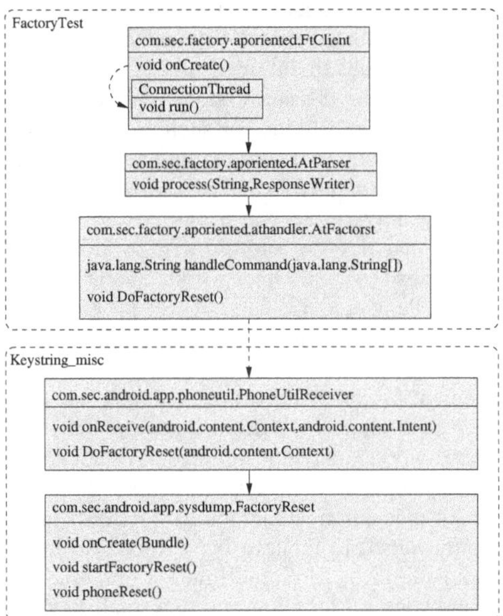

Figure 6: An example path of reflection attack

third-party app. Also, notice that this app exports four receivers without any protection, and it is able to craft specific intents that trigger corresponding backup actions to save various private information into these databases (e.g., standard SMS messages stored in `mmssms.db` will be copied into `sms.db`). After that, any app can simply retrieve these sensitive information (e.g., SMS messages and contacts information) through the corresponding four content providers without acquiring any sensitive permission.

3.3.2 *Case Study: LG Optimus P880*

The LG Optimus P880 has a number of vulnerabilities; here, we will detail two of them, leading to a permission re-delegation attack and a content leak respectively. However, unlike the Samsung vulnerabilities, neither of the ones we will describe are reflection attacks, making them easier to detect, describe, and exploit.

The first one is related to `REBOOT`, a permission reserved for system or pre-loaded apps. In the LG Optimus P880, there is an app named *LGSettings*, which is a customized version of the AOSP *Settings* app. This particular app exports an activity `com.android.settings.Reboot` (completely without permission protection). This activity will be triggered if an `android.intent.action.MAIN` intent is received, and its invocation will simply reboot the device directly. Note that the AOSP does not have the corresponding vulnerable component.

The second one is a rather direct content leak vulnerability. The `com.lge.providers.lgemail` content provider in the *LGEmail* app is not protected, and therefore exposes access to the *EMAIL.db*, a database that contains three tables named *EAccount*, *EMessageBox* and *EMessage*. These tables are very sensitive, as through them, all account and message related information (including message contents) can be exposed. Note that this app is customized from the AOSP *Email* app; however, in the AOSP, the corresponding content provider is protected by a permission named `com.android.email.permission.ACCESS_PROVIDER` with the *systemOrSignature* protection level. Therefore, LG's customization here adds a vulnerability to an otherwise-secure AOSP app.

4. DISCUSSION

While collecting the data for our evaluation, we saw some indirect evidence of software development policies in place at the various vendors. This evidence may be anecdotal, but we feel it is interesting enough to warrant mention. For example, Sony's standout performance does not appear to be accidental; in both their devices that we studied, the `eventstream` content provider (which was implemented as an SQLite database, as many are) actually had explicit checks for SQL injection attacks. Furthermore, Sony's customized version of the AOSP *Mms* app actually mitigated problems found in the unaltered problem. Similarly, as we remarked in Section 2.3, HTC made considerable progress between the release of the HTC Wildfire S and the One X, possibly due to early exposure of a large proportion of security vulnerabilities in earlier HTC's devices [39] and the efforts made by the corporation to take security to heart ever since. The One X makes extensive use of custom permissions to prevent further vulnerabilities from creeping into its firmware – a relatively straightforward approach to take, yet an effective one, as shown by our vulnerability analysis.

We also note that there are not very strong correlations between a number of superficial metrics and the number of vulnerabilities present in a stock firmware image. Code size does not strongly correlate: the Nexus 4 has the third-largest number of LOC, but the lowest number of vulnerabilities in the whole study. The number of apps does not correlate: both Sony devices perform very well, despite having a very large number of apps, while the LG devices do poorly on security even though they have the fewest apps of any non-reference device. Finally, even popularity does not appear to correlate with security: Samsung's Galaxy S3 was the most popular smartphone of 2012, having shipped in excess of 50 million units as of March 2013 [45], and yet it had the most vulnerabilities of any phone in its generation studied in this paper.

Lastly, we would like to acknowledge some of the limitations of our work. We do not cover the customization of system level code, which can be an interesting topic for future research. Our current prototype also has several constraints. First of all, our static analysis produces a relatively high false positive rate. On average, our analysis produces less than 300 paths per device. While it does not make too much effort to manually verify each path, it would be better if we could use a light-weight dynamic analyzer to reduce the manual workload. Secondly, we generate the call graph recursively. In order to avoid very deep (potentially infinite) recursion, we constrain our analysis in two ways: only acyclic graphs are allowed, and/or the maximum length of a path (or the maximum exploration time) is set as an upper boundary for safety. These constraints may prevent us from discovering certain vulnerabilities if there exists heavy code obfuscation that either extends the length of vulnerable path or modifies the sinks we use to define such paths. Fortunately, it is our experience that most pre-loaded apps (other than bundled third-party apps) are not extensively obfuscated. As a result, these constraints were primarily triggered by infinite recursion, not by overly long, yet valid, call chains.

5. RELATED WORK

Provenance Analysis In our system, provenance provides important context which we use when evaluating the results of our other analyses. However, determining the provenance of an app or a piece of code is a difficult problem, which has attracted much research. For example, traditional similarity measurement has been widely used in malware (e.g., virus and worm) clustering and investigation. Kruegel et al. [32] propose an approach to detect polymorphic worms by identifying structural similarities between control flow graphs. SMIT [29], a malware database management system based on malware's function-call graphs, is able to perform large scale malware indexing and queries. Note these approaches are mainly developed for PC malware and have considerably more sophistication – and complexity – than our own. In the same spirit, we use chains of method signatures to determine whether a pre-loaded app is, in fact, an altered version of a core AOSP app. Previous insights however should be able to further guide us in improving accuracy and completeness of our approach.

In the Android platform, one line of inquiry concerns detecting repackaged apps – apps that have been altered and re-uploaded by some party other than the original author. DroidMOSS [50], DNADroid [9] and PiggyApp [49] all focus on detecting repackaged apps in Android app markets, while AppInk [46] pays attention to deterring repackaging behavior with watermarking techniques. These efforts all must establish the ancestry of any given app, which mirrors our efforts to understand, longitudinally, the evolution of firmware images using vertical differential analysis. However, we are not as concerned with the arrow of time – it is obvious the relationship between the original AOSP image and the vendor's customizations, for legal reasons more than technical ones.

Lastly, mobile advertisement libraries have attracted a lot of attention, as they live within other apps and share their permissions. They have been demonstrated to be another important source of privacy leaks [23]; furthermore, Book et al.'s longitudinal study [5] shows that negative behaviors may be growing more common in such libraries over time. As a result, several mitigation measures have been proposed. Some add new APIs and permissions [36] to attempt to isolate such alien code; AdSplit [41], in contrast, moves advertisement code into another process to allow the core Android framework to issue it different permissions, and thus enforce a different policy. Our work has a strange kinship with these works, in that we similarly are interested in poorly-tagged vendor customizations mixed in with code from other sources. While we operate on a different scale to evaluate whole phone images instead of individual third-party apps, many of the same concepts apply. Furthermore, there similarly exists a disconnection between the trust a user may afford the open-source, heavily vetted AOSP and the vendor's customizations of it – attempting to mitigate the flaws introduced by the vendor would be an interesting topic for future work.

Permission Usage Analysis Our permission usage analysis is built upon the accumulated insight of a number of other works in this area. For example, Stowaway [17], Vidas et al. [44] and PScout [2] all study the problem of overprivileged third party apps and provide permission mappings in different ways. Barrera et al. [3] study the permission usage patterns of third party apps by applying self-organizing maps. None of these works analyze the problem of permission overprivilege in pre-loaded firmware apps, which is one key focus of our work.

Others have attempted to infer certain security-related properties about apps based solely on their requested permissions. Kirin [16], for example, looks for hard-coded dangerous combinations of permissions to warn the user about potential malware. Sarma et al. [40], Peng et al. [37] and Chakradeo et al. [7], on the other hand, use machine learning techniques to automatically classify apps as potentially malicious based on the permissions they seek. In this initial study, we do not attempt to look for such emergent effects in the permissions requested by a pre-loaded app as the examined stock images are released by reputable and trustworthy entities.

Vulnerability Analysis Several works have attempted to survey the landscape of malware on Android (e.g., MalGenome [51]) as well as general apps [15, 38]. Other works, like DroidRanger [53], RiskRanker [25], Peng et al. [37] and MAST [7] all have been concerned with finding malicious apps in app markets that contain a large number of benign apps. DroidScope [48] uses virtualization to perform semantic view reconstruction, much like a number of desktop systems, to analyze Android malware. The insights developed in these works are useful in informing our own about the potential dangers of third-party malicious apps.

Permission re-delegation vulnerabilities, a form of the classic confused-deputy attack [27], have been known to be a problem on the Android platform for some time. ComDroid [8], Woodpecker [24], and CHEX [34] all apply static analysis techniques to find vulnerabilities in either third party or pre-loaded apps. SEFA is most similar to the latter two systems. But our system also performs provenance analysis, allowing us to determine the impact of vendor customizations on security. While ComDroid and Woodpecker only could detect in-component vulnerabilities, CHEX could additionally detect cross-component ones. Our work is the most comprehensive yet, as it can find in-component, cross-component, and cross-app vulnerabilities. Specifically, cross-app vulnerabilities account for 8.90% of the vulnerabilities that we found, a significant proportion that also leads to similar, if not greater, security risks.

Several systems [6, 12, 18] aim to mitigate the permission re-delegation problem by either checking IPC call chains or by monitoring the run-time communication between apps. Other works try to protect security in a different manner. For example, virtualization techniques are leveraged by Cells [1] and L4Android [33]. MoCFI [10] implements a control-flow integrity enforcement framework for apps on iOS platform. These works are all complementary to our own, as similar techniques may be able to be applied to mitigate the impact of the flaws that we have detected.

Several systems, including TaintDroid [14], PiOS [13], Apex [35], MockDroid [4], TISSA [54], AppFence [28], Aurasium [47], SORBET [19] and CleanOS [43] aim to study privacy leak issues. They all try to protect (or mitigate) the privacy leak problem by modifying the underlying framework. There has been considerably less work related to content leaks. ContentScope [52] tries to identify vulnerabilities related to third-party, unprotected content providers. Our own work uses a similar concept, but is concerned with content providers in firmware. Note these content providers are only ever found in that context and we have to additionally cover protected content providers (that have not been addressed by earlier work).

6. CONCLUSION

In this paper, we evaluate the security impact of vendor customizations on Android devices by designing and implementing the SEFA analysis framework. This tool performs several analyses to study the provenance, permission usage and vulnerability distribution of the pre-loaded apps that make up a device's firmware image. We evaluated ten devices from five different vendors: two models from each vendor, representing two different generations. We then compare the various vendors' offerings for a given generation, as well as the evolution of any given vendor's security practices over time. Our results show that due to heavy vendor customizations, on average, over half of the apps in each image are overprivileged vendor apps, and more than 60% of the vulnerabilities we identified stemmed from the vendors' modifications to the firmware. Furthermore, for most of the manufacturers in our study, these patterns were stable over time, highlighting the need for heightened focus on security by the smartphone industry.

7. ACKNOWLEDGEMENTS

We would like to thank the anonymous reviewers for their comments that greatly helped improve the presentation of this paper. We also want to thank Kunal Patel, Wu Zhou and Minh Q. Tran for the helpful discussion. This work was supported in part by the US National Science Foundation (NSF) under Grants 0855297, 0855036, 0910767, and 0952640. Any opinions, findings, and conclusions or recommendations expressed in this material are those of the authors and do not necessarily reflect the views of the NSF.

8. REFERENCES

[1] J. Andrus, C. Dall, A. Van't Hof, O. Laadan, and J. Nieh. Cells: A Virtual Mobile Smartphone Architecture. In *Proceedings of the 23rd ACM Symposium on Operating Systems Principles*, SOSP '11, 2011.

[2] K. W. Y. Au, Y. F. Zhou, Z. Huang, and D. Lie. PScout: Analyzing the Android Permission Specification. In *Proceedings of the 19th ACM Conference on Computer and Communications Security*, CCS '12, 2012.

[3] D. Barrera, H. G. Kayacik, P. C. van Oorschot, and A. Somayaji. A Methodology for Empirical Analysis of Permission-Based Security Models and its Application to Android. In *Proceedings of the 17th ACM Conference on Computer and Communications Security*, CCS '10, 2010.

[4] A. R. Beresford, A. Rice, N. Skehin, and R. Sohan. MockDroid: Trading Privacy for Application Functionality on Smartphones. In *Proceedings of the 12th International Workshop on Mobile Computing Systems and Applications*, HotMobile '11, 2011.

[5] T. Book, A. Pridgen, and D. S. Wallach. Longitudinal Analysis of Android Ad Library Permissions. In *IEEE Mobile Security Technologies*, MoST '13, 2013.

[6] S. Bugiel, L. Davi, A. Dmitrienko, T. Fischer, A.-R. Sadeghi, and B. Shastry. Towards Taming Privilege-Escalation Attacks on Android. In *Proceedings of the 19th Annual Symposium on Network and Distributed System Security*, NDSS '12, 2012.

[7] S. Chakradeo, B. Reaves, P. Traynor, and W. Enck. MAST: Triage for Market-scale Mobile Malware Analysis. In *Proceedings of the 6th ACM Conference on Security and Privacy in Wireless and Mobile Networks*, WiSec '13, 2013.

[8] E. Chin, A. P. Felt, K. Greenwood, and D. Wagner. Analyzing Inter-Application Communication in Android. In *Proceedings of the 9th Annual International Conference on Mobile Systems, Applications, and Services*, MobiSys '11, 2011.

[9] J. Crussell, C. Gibler, and H. Chen. Attack of the Clones: Detecting Cloned Applications on Android Markets. In *Proceedings of 17th European Symposium on Research in Computer Security*, ESORICS '12, 2012.

[10] L. Davi, A. Dmitrienko, M. Egele, T. Fischer, T. Holz, R. Hund, S. Nurnberger, and A.-R. Sadeghi. MoCFI: A Framework to Mitigate Control-Flow Attacks on Smartphones. In *Proceedings of the 19th Annual Symposium on Network and Distributed System Security*, NDSS '12, 2012.

[11] Defuse. Use-define chain. `http://en.wikipedia.org/wiki/Use-define_chain`.

[12] M. Dietz, S. Shekhar, Y. Pisetsky, A. Shu, and D. S. Wallach. QUIRE: Lightweight Provenance for Smart Phone Operating Systems. In *Proceedings of the 20th USENIX Security Symposium*, USENIX Security '11, 2011.

[13] M. Egele, C. Kruegel, E. Kirda, and G. Vigna. PiOS: Detecting Privacy Leaks in iOS Applications. In *Proceedings of the 18th Annual Symposium on Network and Distributed System Security*, NDSS '11, 2011.

[14] W. Enck, P. Gilbert, B.-G. Chun, L. P. Cox, J. Jung, P. McDaniel, and A. N. Sheth. TaintDroid: An Information-Flow Tracking System for Realtime Privacy Monitoring on Smartphones. In *Proceedings of the 9th USENIX Symposium on Operating Systems Design and Implementation*, USENIX OSDI '10, 2010.

[15] W. Enck, D. Octeau, P. McDaniel, and S. Chaudhuri. A Study of Android Application Security. In *Proceedings of the 20th USENIX Security Symposium*, USENIX Security '11, 2011.

[16] W. Enck, M. Ongtang, and P. McDaniel. On lightweight mobile phone application certification. In *Proceedings of the 16th ACM Conference on Computer and Communications Security*, CCS '09, 2009.

[17] A. P. Felt, E. Chin, S. Hanna, D. Song, and D. Wagner. Android Permissions Demystified. In *Proceedings of the 18th ACM Conference on Computer and Communications Security*, CCS '11, 2011.

[18] A. P. Felt, H. Wang, A. Moshchuk, S. Hanna, and E. Chin. Permission Re-Delegation: Attacks and Defenses. In *Proceedings of the 20th USENIX Security Symposium*, USENIX Security '11, 2011.

[19] E. Fragkaki, L. Bauer, L. Jia, and D. Swasey. Modeling and Enhancing Android's Permission System. In *Proceedings of 17th European Symposium on Research in Computer Security*, ESORICS '12, 2012.

[20] Gartner. Gartner Says Worldwide Smartphone Sales Soared in Fourth Quarter of 2011 With 47 Percent Growth. `http://www.gartner.com/it/page.jsp?id=1924314`.

[21] Google. Intent. `http://developer.android.com/reference/android/content/Intent.html`.

[22] Google. Platform Versions. `http://developer.android.com/about/dashboards/index.html`.

[23] M. Grace, W. Zhou, X. Jiang, and A.-R. Sadeghi. Unsafe Exposure Analysis of Mobile In-App Advertisements. In *Proceedings of the 5th ACM Conference on Security and Privacy in Wireless and Mobile Networks*, WiSec '12, 2012.

[24] M. Grace, Y. Zhou, Z. Wang, and X. Jiang. Systematic Detection of Capability Leaks in Stock Android Smartphones. In *Proceedings of the 19th Annual Symposium on Network and Distributed System Security*, NDSS '12, 2012.

[25] M. Grace, Y. Zhou, Q. Zhang, S. Zou, and X. Jiang. RiskRanker: Scalable and Accurate Zero-day Android Malware Detection. In *Proceedings of the 10th International Conference on Mobile Systems, Applications and Services*, MobiSys '12, 2012.

[26] Gsmarena. `http://www.gsmarena.com/`.

[27] N. Hardy. The Confused Deputy: (or why capabilities might have been invented). *ACM SIGOPS Operating Systems Review*, 22, October 1988.

[28] P. Hornyack, S. Han, J. Jung, S. Schechter, and D. Wetherall. These Aren't the Droids You're Looking For: Retrofitting Android to Protect Data from Imperious Applications. In *Proceedings of the 18th ACM Conference on Computer and Communications Security*, CCS '11, 2011.

[29] X. Hu, T.-c. Chiueh, and K. G. Shin. Large-Scale Malware Indexing Using Function-Call Graphs. In *Proceedings of the 16th ACM Conference on Computer and Communications Security*, CCS '09, 2009.

[30] IDC. Strong Demand for Smartphones and Heated Vendor Competition Characterize the Worldwide Mobile Phone Market at the End of 2012, IDC Says. `https://www.idc.com/getdoc.jsp?containerId=prUS23916413#.UQIPbh0qaSp`.

[31] J. Koetsier. Android captured almost 70% global smartphone market share in 2012, Apple just under 20%. http://venturebeat.com/2013/01/28/android-captured-almost-70-global-smartphone-market-share-in-2012-apple-just-under-20/.

[32] C. Kruegel, E. Kirda, D. Mutz, W. Robertson, and G. Vigna. Polymorphic worm detection using structural information of executables. In *Proceedings of 8th International Symposium on Recent Advances in Intrusion Detection*, RAID '05, 2005.

[33] M. Lange, S. Liebergeld, A. Lackorzynski, A. Warg, and M. Peter. L4Android: A Generic Operating System Framework for Secure Smartphones. In *Proceedings of the 1st Workshop on Security and Privacy in Smartphones and Mobile Devices*, CCS-SPSM '11, 2011.

[34] L. Lu, Z. Li, Z. Wu, W. Lee, and G. Jiang. Chex: Statically vetting android apps for component hijacking vulnerabilities. In *Proceedings of the 19th ACM Conference on Computer and Communications Security*, CCS '12, 2012.

[35] M. Nauman, S. Khan, and X. Zhang. Apex: Extending Android Permission Model and Enforcement with User-Defined Runtime Constraints. In *Proceedings of the 5th ACM Symposium on Information, Computer and Communications Security*, ASIACCS '10, 2010.

[36] P. Pearce, A. P. Felt, G. Nunez, and D. Wagner. AdDroid: Privilege Separation for Applications and Advertisers in Android. In *Proceedings of the 7th ACM Symposium on Information, Computer and Communications Security*, ASIACCS '12, 2012.

[37] H. Peng, C. Gates, B. Sarma, N. Li, Y. Qi, R. Potharaju, C. Nita-Rotaru, and I. Molloy. Using probabilistic generative models for ranking risks of android apps. In *Proceedings of the 19th ACM Conference on Computer and Communications Security*, CCS '12, 2012.

[38] S. Rosen, Z. Qian, and Z. M. Mao. AppProïňĄler: A Flexible Method of Exposing Privacy-Related Behavior in Android Applications to End Users. In *Proceedings of the 3nd ACM Conference on Data and Application Security and Privacy*, CODASPY '13, 2013.

[39] A. Russakovskii. http://www.androidpolice.com/2011/10/01/massive-security-vulnerability-in-htc-android-devices-evo-3d-4g-thunderbolt-others-exposes-phone-numbers-gps-sms-emails-addresses-much-more/.

[40] B. Sarma, C. Gates, N. Li, R. Potharaju, C. Nita-Rotaru, and I. Molloy. Android Permissions: A Perspective Combining Risks and Benefits. In *Proceedings of the 17th ACM Symposium on Access Control Models and Technologies*, SACMAT '12, 2012.

[41] S. Shekhar, M. Dietz, and D. S. Wallach. AdSplit: Separating smartphone advertising from applications. In *Proceedings of the 21th USENIX Security Symposium*, USENIX Security '12, 2012.

[42] Smali. An assembler/disassembler for Android's dex format. http://code.google.com/p/smali/.

[43] Y. Tang, P. Ames, S. Bhamidipati, A. Bijlani, R. Geambasu, and N. Sarda. CleanOS: Limiting Mobile Data Exposure With Idle Eviction. In *Proceedings of the 11th USENIX Symposium on Operating Systems Design and Implementation*, USENIX OSDI '12, 2012.

[44] T. Vidas, N. Christin, and L. F. Cranor. Curbing Android permission creep. In *Proceedings of the 2011 Web 2.0 Security and Privacy Workshop*, W2SP '11, 2011.

[45] Wiki. Samsung Galaxy S3. http://en.wikipedia.org/wiki/Samsung_Galaxy_S_III.

[46] Z. Wu, X. Zhang, and X. Jiang. AppInk: Watermarking Android Apps for Repackaging Deterrence. In *Proceedings of the 8th ACM Symposium on Information, Computer and Communications Security*, ASIACCS '13, 2013.

[47] R. Xu, H. Saidi, and R. Anderson. Aurasium: Practical Policy Enforcement for Android Applications. In *Proceedings of the 21th USENIX Security Symposium*, USENIX Security '12, 2012.

[48] L. K. Yan and H. Yin. DroidScope: Seamlessly Reconstructing the OS and Dalvik Semantic Views for Dynamic Android Malware Analysis. In *Proceedings of the 21th USENIX Security Symposium*, USENIX Security '12, 2012.

[49] W. Zhou, Y. Zhou, M. Grace, X. Jiang, and S. Zou. Fast, Scalable Detection of 'Piggybacked' Mobile Applications. In *Proceedings of the 3nd ACM Conference on Data and Application Security and Privacy*, CODASPY '13, 2013.

[50] W. Zhou, Y. Zhou, X. Jiang, and P. Ning. DroidMOSS: Detecting Repackaged Smartphone Applications in Third-Party Android Marketplaces. In *Proceedings of the 2nd ACM Conference on Data and Application Security and Privacy*, CODASPY '12, 2012.

[51] Y. Zhou and X. Jiang. Dissecting Android Malware: Characterization and Evolution. In *Proceedings of the 33rd IEEE Symposium on Security and Privacy*, IEEE Oakland '12, 2012.

[52] Y. Zhou and X. Jiang. Detecting Passive Content Leaks and Pollution in Android Applications. In *Proceedings of the 20th Annual Symposium on Network and Distributed System Security*, NDSS '13, 2013.

[53] Y. Zhou, Z. Wang, W. Zhou, and X. Jiang. Hey, You, Get off of My Market: Detecting Malicious Apps in Official and Alternative Android Markets. In *Proceedings of the 19th Annual Symposium on Network and Distributed System Security*, NDSS '12, 2012.

[54] Y. Zhou, X. Zhang, X. Jiang, and V. W. Freeh. Taming Information-Stealing Smartphone Applications (on Android). In *Proceedings of the 4th International Conference on Trust and Trustworthy Computing*, TRUST '11, 2011.

APPENDIX

A. REACHABILITY ANALYSIS

Algorithm 3: Reachability Analysis

Input: path from entrypoint to sink
Output: path is reachable or not

$ret = false$;
intra_analysis(all nodes in path) ;
$nodes$ = nodes in the path;
$edges$ = edges in the path;

while *constraint does not meet* **do**
    $flag = false$;
    foreach $n \in nodes$ **do**
        $callee$ = callee set of n;
        if $callee = \emptyset$ **then**
            break;
        foreach $c \in callee$ **do**
            if $(n, c) \in edges$ **then**
                $flag = flag \cup$ c.summarize(n);
    if $flag$ **then**
        inter_analysis(c);
        if *constraint meets* **then**
            break;
    else
        break;

ret = reachability_check($path$ with summary information);
return ret

Unauthorized Origin Crossing on Mobile Platforms: Threats and Mitigation

Rui Wang
Microsoft Research
ruiwan@microsoft.com

Luyi Xing
Indiana University
luyixing@indiana.edu

XiaoFeng Wang
Indiana University
xw7@indiana.edu

Shuo Chen
Microsoft Research
shuochen@microsoft.com

ABSTRACT

With the progress in mobile computing, web services are increasingly delivered to their users through mobile apps, instead of web browsers. However, unlike the browser, which enforces origin-based security policies to mediate the interactions between the web content from different sources, today's mobile OSes do not have a comparable security mechanism to control the cross-origin communications between apps, as well as those between an app and the web. As a result, a mobile user's sensitive web resources could be exposed to the harms from a malicious origin.

In this paper, we report the first systematic study on this mobile cross-origin risk. Our study inspects the main cross-origin channels on Android and iOS, including intent, scheme and web-accessing utility classes, and further analyzes the ways popular web services (e.g., Facebook, Dropbox, etc.) and their apps utilize those channels to serve other apps. The research shows that lack of origin-based protection opens the door to a wide spectrum of cross-origin attacks. These attacks are unique to mobile platforms, and their consequences are serious: for example, using carefully designed techniques for mobile cross-site scripting and request forgery, an unauthorized party can obtain a mobile user's Facebook/Dropbox authentication credentials and record her text input. We report our findings to related software vendors, who all acknowledged their importance. To address this threat, we designed an origin-based protection mechanism, called *Morbs*, for mobile OSes. Morbs labels every message with its origin information, lets developers easily specify security policies, and enforce the policies on the mobile channels based on origins. Our evaluation demonstrates the effectiveness of our new technique in defeating unauthorized origin crossing, its efficiency and the convenience for the developers to use such protection.

Categories and Subject Descriptors

D.4.6 [**Operating Systems**]: Security and Protection – *access controls, invasive software*

Keywords: Android, iOS, same-origin policy, mobile platform.

1. INTRODUCTION

The popularity of smartphones, tablets and other mobile devices has brought in a plethora of software applications designed for running on these devices. Such applications, commonly known as *apps*, are typically used to deliver web services (data storage, social networking, web mails, etc.) through their compact user interfaces and simple program logic, which are tailored to mobile platforms. Moreover, other than interactions with their own web services, many of those apps are also built to work with other apps and services, leveraging the third-party's resources to enrich their functionalities. This is a trend that echoes web-API integrations extensively utilized in developing traditional, browser-based web applications. Examples include the apps that support social login and data sharing through the services offered by Facebook, Twitter, Google Plus, etc.

Mobile origin-crossing hazard. Those mobile apps essentially play the same role as traditional web browsers at the client side. However, different from conventional web applications, which enjoy browse-level protection for their sensitive data and critical resources (e.g., cookies), apps are hosted directly on mobile operating systems (e.g., Android, iOS), whose security mechanisms (such as Android's permission and sandbox model) are mainly designed to safeguard those devices' local resources (GPS locations, phone contacts, etc.). This naturally calls into question whether the apps' web resources are also sufficiently protected under those OSes. More specifically, web browsers enforce the *same origin policy* (SOP), which prevents the dynamic web content (e.g., scripts) of one domain from directly accessing the resources from a different domain. When the domain boundary has to be crossed, a designated channel needs to go through to ensure proper mediation. An example is the *postMessage* channel [5], which a domain uses to send a message to another domain by explicitly specifying the recipient's origin, and the browser mediates to ensure that only the content from that origin gets the message and the recipient is also well informed of the sender's origin. Such origin-based protection has become a de facto security standard for a modern browser. However, it is not present on any channels provided by mobile OSes for apps to communicate with each other or the web. As a result, the web content or apps from an untrusted domain may gain unauthorized access to the web resources of other apps/websites through those channels, causing serious security consequences.

As an example, consider the *scheme* mechanism [25][26] supported by Android and iOS, through which an app on phone/tablet can be invoked by a URL once it registers the URL's scheme (e.g., the "youtube" part of "youtube://watch?token=xxx", with "xxx" as the input parameter for the app). What an adversary can do is to post on Facebook a link that points to a malicious script hosted on his website. Once this link is clicked by the victim through the Facebook app on her iOS device, the script starts to run within the app's *WebView* instance, which is then redirected to a dynamically generated URL with the scheme of another app that the adversary wants to run on the victim's device and the parameters he chooses. As a result, the target app will be

CCS'13, November 4–8, 2013, Berlin, Germany.
Copyright © 2013 ACM 978-1-4503-2477-9/13/11…$15.00.
http://dx.doi.org/10.1145/2508859.2516727

invoked to blindly act on the adversary's command, such as logging into his Dropbox account to record the victim's inputs (Section 3.3.2), since the app is given no clue the origin (the adversary's site) of the request. In another case, the Android mobile browser processing a URL with the "fbconnect://" scheme from the Facebook server will deliver the secret token on the URL to an app from an arbitrary origin, as long as it claims to be able to handle that scheme (Section 3.3.1).

Such unauthorized origin crossing is related to the *confused deputy* problem [24] on mobile devices. Prior research on this subject, however, focuses on *permission redelegation* [10], which happens when an app with a permission requires sensitive system resources (e.g., a phone's GPS location) on behalf of another app without that permission. The interactions between the two apps go through an Inter-Process Call (IPC) that delivers a message called *intent* from one app to invoke the other app's *Activity* for services such as getting GPS coordinates. This *intent channel* can also be used to cross origins: for example, it allows an app from one origin to send intents to another app when the latter's related Activity is accidentally made public, a mobile *cross-site request forgery* (CSRF) attack [27]. However, given that those prior studies primarily aim at protecting mobile devices' local resources, the general problem has not been dug deeper: for example, it is not clear whether an app's *private* Activity can still be invoked by the intent message from an unauthorized origin, not to mention the security implications of other channels (such as the URL scheme) that can also be used for crossing domains.

Our findings. To better understand this critical security issue, we conducted the first systematic study on unauthorized origin-crossing over mobile OSes, including Android and iOS. In our study, we investigated all known channels that allow apps to cross domains, such as intent, scheme and utility classes for web communications, by dissecting popular apps like Facebook, Dropbox, Google Plus, Yelp, and their SDKs, to understand how they utilize these channels to serve other apps on different mobile OSes. Our study found 5 generic cross-origin weaknesses in those high-profile apps and SDKs, which can be exploited through CSRF, login CSRF and cross-site scripting (XSS). Many of those problems affect multiple apps and web services. They are unique to the communication channels on mobile OSes, which are fundamentally different from those within the browsers. The root cause of the vulnerabilities is the absence of origin-based protection. More specifically, due to missing origin information, an app or a mobile web service is often left with little clue about the true origin of an incoming message, nor does it have any control on where its outgoing message will be delivered to.

The consequences of these cross-origin attacks are dire. They allow a malicious app to steal the mobile device owner's Facebook, Dropbox authentication credentials, or even directly perform arbitrary operations on her Dropbox account (sharing, deleting, etc.) on Android. On iOS, a remote adversary without direct access to any app on the victim's device can stealthily log the phone into the adversary's Dropbox account through Google Plus, Facebook apps. As a result, the victim's text input on iPhone and iPad, her contacts and other confidential information are all exposed to the adversary once she uses popular editing and backup apps (e.g., PlainText, TopNotes, Nocs, Contacts Backup, etc.) that integrate Dropbox iOS SDK. We reported those problems to related parties, who all acknowledged the importance of our discoveries. We received over $7000 bounty for these findings, most of which were donated to charity. The details of such recognition together with demos of our attacks are posted online [31].

Origin-based defense. Without any OS-level support, not only does app development become highly error-prone, but software manufacturers can also have hard time fixing the problems after they are discovered. As examples, both Dropbox and Facebook need to spend a significant amount of effort to fix the security problems we discovered, which involves changing software architecture (Section 3.2.1) or deprecating some core features within their apps and SDKs (Section 3.3.1). To address these issues and facilitate convenient development of securer apps, we present in this paper the design of the first mobile origin-based defense mechanism, called *Morbs*. Our approach mediates all the cross-origin channels on Android and iOS, including intent, scheme and the utility classes for web communications, and enables a developer to specify to the OS authorized origins her app/website can receive requests from and/or send responses to.

We implemented Morbs on Android in a way that fully preserves its compatibility with existing apps. Moreover, we show that through our mechanism, the developers can easily gain controls on all cross-origin events, avoiding the ordeal experienced by Facebook, Dropbox, and other companies. Our evaluation on the implementation also shows that it is both effective, stopping all the exploits we found, and efficient, incurring only a negligible impact on performance (< 1% overhead).

The source code of Morbs is publicly available on GitHub [40].

Contributions. We summarize the paper's contributions here:

- *New problem.* Up to our knowledge, the research reported here is the first attempt to systematically understand unauthorized origin crossing on mobile OSes. The discovery made by our study brings to light the presence of such vulnerabilities in high-profile apps and more importantly, the seriousness and pervasiveness of the problem.
- *New techniques.* We developed new origin-based protection for existing mobile OSes, which works with apps/websites to oversee the communication channels on these systems.
- *Implementation and evaluation.* We implemented our design on Android, and evaluated its effectiveness, efficiency, compatibility, and usability to the app developer.

Roadmap. The rest of the paper is organized as follows: Section 2 describes the mobile channels used for apps to communicate with each other or the web; Section 3 elaborates our study on mobile cross-origin problems and our findings; Section 4 presents our defense mechanism Morbs, Section 5 reports the evaluation of our techniques; Section 6 compares our work with other related research; Section 7 concludes the paper and discusses the future research.

2. MOBILE CHANNELS

Today's mobile OSes (including Android and iOS) provide various channels for apps to communicate with each other or the web. Those channels include *intent*, *scheme*, and *web-accessing utility classes* (which we elaborate later in the section). As shown in , an app communicates with other apps through the intent or scheme channel. It can also invoke the browser to load a webpage using an intent and be triggered by the web content rendered in the browser through a URL scheme. Moreover, the app can simply acquire and display any web content through the WebView class, which embeds a browser-like widget within the app, and directly talks to a web server using the methods provided by the HttpClient classes. Note that the intent channel is Android-specific, while others are also available on iOS. Unlike the domain-crossing mechanisms within a browser (e.g., postMessage), these mobile channels are not under the origin-based protection: messages exchanged do not carry any origin information that the sender/receiver can inspect, and are completely unmediated with regard to where they come from.

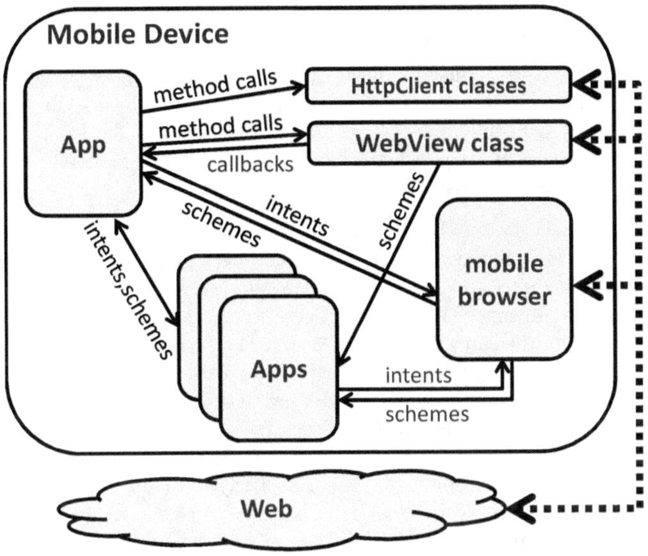

Figure 1 Mobile communication channels

Here we elaborate how those channels work:

- *Intent*. An intent is an inter-process message delivered through an IPC. It is a channel only supported by Android. Through intent messaging, one app on Android can activate the background Services, Activities (application components with user interfaces) or Broadcast-Receivers of another app, as well as the Activities/Services of its own. Intent invocation is conducted through APIs such as *startActivity*, *startActivityForResult*, and *startService*. An app developer can specify a set of intents the app can receive from other apps in its manifest file. However, the intent channel never labels the origin of each message (i.e., who created it). This causes the problem we elaborate in Section 3.2.1.

- *URL scheme*. As discussed before, scheme is supported by both Android and iOS, which allows an app or website to use a URL to invoke another app (on iOS) or its Activity/Service components (on Android) that claim the scheme of that URL. For example, the URL "youtube://watch?token=xxx" can be used to start the YouTube app to play the video "xxx". When such a URL is loaded in the mobile browser or a WebView instance, the OS will launch the target app with this URL as input. In addition, an app can also invoke other apps through the schemes they registered. On Android, scheme invocation is implemented through the intent channel: a scheme URL is wrapped in an intent instance, and invoked by an app through the same set of APIs that also serve intent messages, such as *startActivity*. On iOS, this is done through *openURL* API. Again, the OSes do not mediate the scheme-based invocations using origins.

- *Web-accessing utility classes*. Mobile platforms provide several utility classes for apps to communicate with the web. We call them *web-accessing utility classes*. For example, both Android and iOS support the WebView class (called UIWebView on iOS), which an app can embed for displaying webpages. An app can interact with its WebView instance through a set of method calls or callbacks. For example, it can call *loadURL* on Android (*loadRequest* on iOS) with a URL to load a page into the instance; it can also register events, like URL loading, to inspect every URL its WebView instance processes through a callback *shouldStartLoadWithRequest* (iOS) or *shouldOverrideUrlLoading* (Android). In addition, the mobile platforms provide utility classes for an app to directly talk to a web server without loading its web content. HttpClient [36] or HttpURLConnection [37] (Android) and NSURLConnection [38] [39] (iOS) are such examples. We call those classes (for direct communication with web servers) *HttpClient classes*. Origin-based protection is not in the picture here: e.g., a WebView/HttpClient instance never labels which app is the origin of an HTTP request.

3. ATTACKS

In this section, we elaborate our study on unauthorized origin crossing on mobile OSes. What we want to understand here are whether the ways real-world apps utilize those channels for cross-origin communications indeed expose them to attackers, and whether those apps have proper means to mitigate such a threat and safeguard their operations over those channels. For this purpose, we systematically analyzed high-profile apps on both Android and iOS, including the official apps of Facebook and Dropbox and their SDKs, and the official Google Plus and Yelp app. Note that these SDKs are very popular. They have been integrated into many real-world apps. Problems discovered there may have a broad impact. In our research, we looked into how those apps use the aforementioned cross-origin channels to interact with other apps, or the web. The study reveals the pervasive presence of subtle yet serious cross-origin vulnerabilities, allowing an unauthorized party to activate an app remotely with arbitrary input parameters, call its internal Activities, steal user's authentication credentials and even directly manipulate its operations.

Such discoveries were made through an in-depth analysis on the code and operations of those apps. Specifically, for Android apps, we decompiled the binary code of their latest versions using apktool [33] and AndroChef Java Decompiler [34] in order to analyze their program logic related to the mobile channels. When it comes to iOS apps, decompiling their executables is often hard. Therefore, we resorted to a black-box traffic analysis to understand those apps' interactions with other parties (apps, web services, etc.). We also studied the SDKs provided by Facebook and Dropbox, whose source code is publically available. In the rest of the section, we report our findings. The demos of our exploits on those apps and other supplementary materials are posted on the web [31].

3.1 Adversary Model

Our adversary model describes practical threats to different mobile platforms. On Android, we consider an adversary who can trick a user into installing a malicious app on her device. That app, however, may not have any permission considered to be dangerous by Android. Also, threats to Android can come directly from the web, when the victim uses her mobile app or browser to view malicious web content posted by the adversary on a website. On iOS, we only consider this remote threat (from a malicious website), not the malicious app, given the fact that Apple's vetting process on iOS apps is more restrictive than that of Android apps, and few malicious apps have been reported so far. Note that we treated Android and iOS differently to respect the realistic threats those systems face: we could have found more issues had we assumed the presence of malicious apps on iOS. Finally, we do not consider an adversary with OS-level controls.

3.2 Exploiting the Intent Channel

The security implication of the intent channel on Android has been studied in prior research [10][27]. All existing work, however, focuses on how such a channel can be leveraged by a malicious app to invoke a legitimate app's Activities that are accidentally made public by the app's developer. In our research, we found that even the private Activities not exposed to the public, which is meant to be called only by the app itself, can be triggered by an app from an unauthorized origin. This problem has a serious consequence, letting the malicious app gain great control of the victim app. We discovered this vulnerability on both the Facebook app and the Dropbox app. Here we use the Dropbox app as an example to explain where the problem is.

3.2.1 Next Intent (Android)

An Android app can have two types of Activities, private or public. By default, an Activity is private, meaning that only the code inside the app can invoke it. When the app developer sets the "exported" property of the Activity to true, or she declares at least one intent for the Activity in the manifest of the app, the Activity becomes public, in which case other apps can invoke the Activity with an intent instance as an argument.

Our analysis on the Dropbox app reveals that the app exposes a few Activities, such as login, which is meant to be public. An interesting observation is that when any of its public Activities are invoked by an intent instance, the Activity first needs to check whether the user is in a logged-in status. If not, it redirects him to the login Activity before proceeding with its own task. Specifically, the Activity creates a new intent instance, in which the current intent, the one it receives from another app, is saved under the key "com.dropbox.activity.extra.NEXT_INTENT" (called "NEXT_INTENT" here). The new intent instance is then issued by the app itself to invoke LoginOrNewAcctActivity (the login Activity). Once the user completes her login, the login Activity retrieves the original intent instance from "NEXT_INTENT", and uses it to invoke the unfinished public Activity to fulfill its task.

The cross-origin exploit. It turns out that this next-intent feature can be exploited by a malicious app to cross origins and invoke the Dropbox app's private Activity. Since the login Activity is public, a malicious app can trigger it with an intent instance, in which the attacker puts another intent instance under the "NEXT_INTENT" key. The second instance points to a private Activity of the Dropbox app. This login intent will not be noticed by the user if she is already in the logged-in status, and cause little suspicion if she is not, simply because it is the authentic Dropbox app that asks the user to log in. Either way, once the login is done, LoginOrNewAcctActivity retrieves the intent content under the "NEXT_INTENT" key and use it to call the startActivity API. Since startActivity is now invoked by the Dropbox app itself, all of its Activities, including those private ones, can be executed, even though the next-intent actually comes from a different origin, the malicious app. The root cause of this problem is that the startActivity API never checks (and also has no means to check) the provenance of the intent under the "NEXT_INTENT" key, due to the lack of origin-based protection on the mobile OS. In the absence of the origin information (here, the app creating the intent), even an app's private Activity can be exposed to unauthorized parties.

The problem goes beyond a single app. In the Facebook app, we discovered the same problem in a public Activity called UriAuthHandler. The Facebook app also checks the login status, and directs the user to the login Activity, and uses "CALLING_INTENT" (equivalent to "NEXT_INTENT") as a key to store the current intent instance. This channel is equally vulnerable and can be abused in the same way, as found in our study. We suspect that other apps with this type of next-intent feature are also subject to the same exploit.

Attacks and consequences. Once the origin is crossed illegitimately, the door is open to all kinds of abuses. In our research, we implemented two attacks (one against the Dropbox app, another one against the Facebook app) to demonstrate the serious security consequences of the problem.

Our attack on the Facebook app leverages a private Activity LoggedOutWebViewActivity. The Activity takes a URL as an input parameter and loads the content pointed by the URL into a WebView instance. What can happen here is that a malicious app running on the same device can drop a Javascript file onto its SD card (Secure Digital memory card) and exploit the next-intent feature to run LoggedOutWebViewActivity with the URL pointing to that Javascript file. Since the SD card is viewed as a local storage by Android, the script is allowed to access contents from all Internet domains [32]. Specifically in our attack, the script injected can make arbitrary AJAX requests to facebook.com and read the contents of the responses. Given that all such requests carry the user's Facebook cookie, this cross-origin scripting ends up allowing the adversary to perform arbitrary operations on the user's account, and obtain all private data.

For the Dropbox app, we exploited a private Activity VideoPlayerActivity, which has an input parameter "EXTRA_METADATA_URL" that specifies a URL from which to fetch the metadata for a video file. In a normal situation, this URL points to a file kept by dropbox.com. However, our next-intent exploit enables a malicious app to set the URL to arbitrary web domain, such as "http://attacker.com". When the Dropbox app makes a request with that URL, it always assumes the recipient to be dropbox.com and attaches to the request an authentication header, as opposed to applying the conventional origin-based cookie policy. Since right now, EXTRA_METADATA_URL points to "http://attacker.com", the adversary gets the header and can use it to gain a full access to the user's Dropbox account.

Vendor responses. Fixing this problem turns out to be much more complicated than it appears to be. Specifically, the Dropbox security team told us they were "*working on changing the architecture in our Android app to make that API secure*", but the next-intent feature is "*unfortunately also very useful for us*". Facebook also said that this problem "will take some time to fix". As an acknowledgement to the importance of our work, Facebook awarded us $5000 bounty for finding this vulnerability, which we donated to charity. Dropbox also awarded us 100GB free storage for each author, and included our names on their special thanks page. The details of those software vendors' responses can be found here [31]. From our communications with the vendors, it can be seen that addressing this next-intent problem from the developer side alone can be hard. In Section 4, we show how a well-thought-out OS-level support can make this type of flaws more convenient to fix.

3.3 Abusing the Scheme Channel

As discussed in Section 2, scheme is an important cross-origin channel supported by both Android and iOS. Through this channel, an app on those OSes can be invoked by a URL (with the scheme the app claims) from another app or from a webpage in a WebView instance or a browser (see in Section 2). In our research, we found that this channel can be easily abused for unauthorized origin crossing, enabling a malicious app to acquire a user's authentication token with Facebook or perform a login CSRF on iOS, as described below.

3.3.1 Fbconnect (Android)

Facebook provides a *Dialog mechanism* [35] through its apps and SDKs for both Android and iOS. Using the mechanism, an app can send through the Facebook official app a Dialog request to query the Facebook server for sensitive user data (e.g., access token) or operate on the user's account (e.g., sharing a post). Among all the arguments carried by the Dialog request are *client_id*, the ID assigned to the sender app by Facebook, and *redirect_uri*, which is set to "fbconnect://success". In the case that the user's access token is requested, the Facebook server displays a dialog within Facebook app's WebView instance to ask for the user's consent, and upon receiving it, the server redirects the WebView instance to "fbconnect://success#...", where the secret token is attached to the "…" part of the message. This token is then extracted by the Facebook app, which later dispatches it to the target app (i.e., the sender of the Dialog request) associated with the *client_id*.

The URL "fbconnect://success#..." is just used for delivering data from the Facebook server to its official app. However, if this URL is loaded in the mobile browser, a serious attack can happen. More specifically, a malicious app on the device first registers this fbconnect:// scheme, and then invokes the browser to load a Dialog URL, in an attempt to request the sensitive data of another app (e.g., the TexasHoldem app) from the Facebook server. This can be easily done by setting *client_id* in the URL to that of TexasHoldem because an app's client_id is public. Also, within the browser, the dialog may not even show up to alert the user, if it is already in the logged-in status. As a result, Facebook will redirect the browser to "fbconnect://success#...". Unlike the Facebook app, the browser treats this URL as a scheme invocation, and therefore will trigger the scheme's handler (i.e., the malicious app) with the URL as an argument. This exposes to the malicious app the victim's Facebook secret token for the TexasHoldem app. We tested the attack on an Android device (Galaxy Tab 2) and confirmed that the malicious app can get the user's access token, authorization code and other secrets. In this case, we can see that although the Facebook server is the sender of the scheme message, it cannot control which app to receive the message through the mobile browser. This is different from what happens within a web browser: for example, if a script from a.com sends a message to b.com through the postMessage API, it can specify the recipient domain and the browser then guarantees that only b.com gets the message. On today's mobile OS, however, there is no way that the Facebook server can specify the authorized receiver of its scheme URL, not to mention any mechanism to enforce this security policy.

Also note that the fbconnect problem here is present on both Android and iOS. However, given that iOS malware is rare, the risk it poses is mainly to Android (see our adversary model).

Vendor response. Without the OS support, this problem turns out to be even harder to fix than the next-intent issue. We reported it to Facebook on Sept. 11, 2012. On Jan. 22, 2013, Facebook security team told us that they took steps to "ensure that popular app stores block apps that attempt to register this URI schema". Moreover, they were "crafting a formal deprecation plan for the fbconnect schema", but this plan needs a "several month deprecation period" because "all of our embedded SDKs currently depend upon this functionality". On March 20, 2013, Facebook informed us that they "crafted a plan for the deprecation of the fbconnect schema in the next major release". They expect to "see this disappear entirely as users continue to upgrade". They awarded us a bounty of $1500 for this finding, which we donated to charity.

3.3.2 Invoking Apps from the Web (Android and iOS)

In this section, we elaborate a new security threat that comes from a malicious website the user visits with a mobile device. The root cause of the problem has been confirmed to exist on both Android and iOS. For the simplicity of presentation, here we just use iOS as an example to explain the problem.

Mobile apps typically use their WebView instances to render web content. Such content could come from less trustworthy web sources, such as public posts on Facebook and restaurant reviews from the strangers on Yelp. In our research, we found that during such rendering of web content, whenever the WebView instance of an app is directed by the content to a URL with a scheme registered by another app on the same device, the latter will be automatically invoked, without being noticed by the user, and act on the parameters given by the URL. This is dangerous because the app receiving the scheme message which carries the URL cannot distinguish whether this message comes from the sender app itself or from the web content within the app's WebView instance, which causes the confusion about the message's true origin. Here we use two examples to show the consequences of this confusion.

Login CSRF attacks on Dropbox iOS SDK. We studied the latest version (v.1.3.3) of Dropbox iOS SDK, which enables a 3rd-party app on iOS to link to the device owner's Dropbox account, using Dropbox as the app's storage. Here, we use PlainText [41], a popular text-editing app, as an example to explain what can go wrong, though apps using Dropbox iOS SDK are all vulnerable. Specifically, after the mobile user authorizes this account linking, the Dropbox app delivers to the PlainText app a scheme URL, which is in the following format: db-<APP_ID>://1/connect?oauth_token&oauth_token_secret&uid.

The URL includes 3 arguments, *oauth_token*, *oauth_token_secret*, and *uid*, which the PlainText app uses to communicate with the Dropbox server to complete the account linking. However, we found that the linking process can be exploited to launch a serious login CSRF attack, *without* any malicious app running on the user's device. Specifically, in our attack, the adversary uses the 3 URL arguments collected from his own device to build a URL: db-<APP_ID>://1/connect?oauth_token'&oauth_token_ secret' & uid', where *oauth_token'*, *oauth_token _secret'*, and *uid'* are the adversary's Dropbox credentials, and APP_ID identifies the PlainText app. The attacker shares a malicious web URL (e.g. pointing to attacker.com) on his Google Plus status updates or comments. Once the victim user clicks it within the Google Plus app on her device, attacker.com is loaded in the app's WebView instance, and redirects the WebView to the scheme URL. As a result, the PlainText app is invoked with the URL as input. The app treats the URL as part of the scheme message from the Google Plus app, without knowing that it actually comes from the web content of attacker.com rendered in the Google Plus app's WebView. It is then unknowingly linked to the attacker's Dropbox account. When this happens, the app automatically sends the user's text input to the attacker's account. A demo of this attack is posted online [31]. We also checked a few other popular iPad apps using Dropbox SDK, including TopNotes, Nocs, and Contacts Backup to Dropbox. They are all found vulnerable.

Bypassing Facebook's app authentication mechanism. Many apps using Facebook iOS SDK, such as Yelp and TripAdvisor, may also render untrusted web contents within their WebView instances. Below we show that an attacker who posts a malicious link on Yelp can bypass an important mechanism Facebook uses to authenticate 3rd-party iOS apps. Specifically, when app A invokes the Facebook app through schemes such as "fbauth://", the Facebook app sends the app ID specified by app A and its bundle ID retrieved from the OS to the Facebook server for authentication. This prevents app A from impersonating another app to communicate with the Facebook server because it cannot manipulate the bundle ID. However, this protection does not work when a malicious page is loaded to the WebView instance of the Yelp app because the Facebook app cannot distinguish whether an incoming scheme message is from the Yelp app or a webpage in its WebView (the bundle ID from the OS always points to the Yelp app). Therefore, whoever posts a comment on Yelp acquires the same privilege as Yelp has on the victim's Facebook account.

Vendor response. We reported these problems to Dropbox, Google, and Facebook. For the first problem (login CSRF through Dropbox SDK), Dropbox started its investigation immediately after receiving our report. They have implemented a fix that needs to change both the SDKs and the Dropbox official apps on all platforms (including Android and iOS). Facebook mitigated the threat by deploying a whitelist inside the WebView instance of its official app, which only allows http, https, and ftp schemes. Google has not taken any actions so far [31]. Facebook awarded us $1000 for this finding. We also reported to Facebook the second case (bypassing its app authentication mechanism on iOS), which is still under investigation.

3.4 Attacks on Web-Accessing Utility Classes

As shown in , besides intent and scheme, origins can also be crossed on a mobile OS when an app directly calls the methods of the WebView/HttpClient classes or registers their callback events. Here we show how this channel can be abused.

3.4.1 Exploiting Callbacks (iOS)

On iOS, we studied a WebView callback method the Facebook app registers, *shouldStartLoadWithRequest*, which is triggered each time the app's WebView instance is navigated to a link. If this link is in the form "fbrpc://appID=xyz&foo=123", the callback method (provided by Facebook) creates a new URL "fbxyz://foo=123" to invoke an app with the appID "xyz" and set its input argument to "123". Note that this operation is different from the scheme-based invocation (from a web domain) described in Section 3.3.2, as in that case, a website directly runs a URL to invoke the target app on the mobile device (the sender of the scheme message is the website), while here such a URL is actually created by the callback method, which is implemented by the Facebook app (the sender is the Facebook app).

This mechanism can be exploited when a malicious link such as attacker.com is clicked by the user through her Facebook app. When this happens, the malicious content loaded to the WebView instance redirects to the fbrpc URL. Then the callback of the Facebook app generates a new scheme URL to launch any app the adversary wants to run on the victim's device with any argument value he sets. For example, we found that in this way, a popular app *Pinterest* can be activated by the adversary to sign onto the adversary's account on the victim's device, so as to dump the user's data with Pinterest into the adversary's account.

3.4.2 Exploiting Header-attachment (Android)

We also studied the HttpClient class, which is used by Android apps for direct HTTP communications with web servers. HttpClient allows a developer to specify the URL of a request and an HTTP header. The header is attached to the request. In the absence of origin-based protection, any header, including the one used for authentication, can be attached to a request sent to any website. A prominent example is the attack case described in Section 3.2.1: the adversary invokes the Dropbox app's Activity VideoPlayerActivity, which utilizes an HttpClient instance to load metadata from a URL with the user's authentication header attached. Since the URL is manipulated by the adversary to point to attacker.com, without origin checks, the authentication header goes to the adversary.

Note that this header-attachment issue by itself is a security flaw, as admitted by the Dropbox security team ("*Attaching the Authorization header to non-Dropbox URLs was definitely a serious security bug*" [31]). Actually the attack on a phone user's Dropbox account as described in Section 3.2.1 is built upon two security flaws, i.e., the next-intent and header-attachment issue.

4. ORIGIN-BASED DEFENSE

As described in the prior section, unlike web browsers, today's mobile OSes (i.e., Android and iOS) do not offer origin protection to the channels used by apps to communicate with each other or the web. As a result, cross-origin interactions on those systems can be easily abused to undermine the user's security and privacy, which even happens to highly popular apps built by security-savvy developers. Moreover, even after the problems were reported, the developers still had hard time in fixing them. This makes us believe that a generic solution to the problem should be built into mobile OSes, which have the observations of messages' origins, and the means to mediate the communication over those channels. In this section, we elaborate the first design for such protection, called *Morbs* (mobile origin based security), and its implementation on Android. We released the source code of the Android implementation on GitHub [40].

4.1 Design

Overview. Morbs is generic to iOS and Android. It is designed to achieve browser-like origin protection: 1) it exposes to the developers the true origins of the messages their apps/websites receive, enabling them to build protections based on such information; 2) it allows the developers to specify their intentions, in the form of whitelists of origins their apps/websites can get messages from and send messages to, and enforces policies transparently within the OS.

More specifically, an app or a web service that asks for origin protection first communicates its intended sender/recipient origins (the whitelists) to the OS. These policies are enforced by a reference monitor that mediates different mobile channels. The reference monitor is triggered by the messages delivered through these channels. Once invoked, it identifies the origins of the messages, which are either apps or web domains, and checks their policy compliance against the whitelists. Those running against the policies are blocked by Morbs.

A unique feature of Morbs is its capability to connect web activities (within WebView instances or the mobile browser) to the events that happen within the OS. For example, it exposes the true origin of a message to a recipient app when confusion arises on whether the message comes from another app or the web domain visited by that app's WebView instance. It also helps a web server specify to a mobile device a designate app on the device that can receive the server's scheme message. This capability is crucial for defeating unauthorized origin crossing on mobile devices. Following we elaborate our design.

Defining mobile origin. For web content, an origin is defined as a combination of scheme, host name, and port number [4]. However, this definition is insufficient for the origin protection on mobile platforms: here we need to consider not only web origins but also app identities and other local origins. To maintain the consistency with the web origins, we adopted a URL-like representation for those new origins, such as "app://<appID>", where <appID> is an app's package name (Android) or bundle ID (iOS), for example, "app://com.facebook.katana" for the Facebook app on Android and "app://com.getdropbox.Dropbox" for the Dropbox app on iOS. Likewise, messages from trusted sources like the OS are given a local origin "local://". For web domains, we adhere to the traditional origin definition [4].

Exposing origins. When a message is created by an app/website, Morbs sets the *origin* attribute (added by our approach) of the message to its creator (i.e., an app, a web domain, or local). This attribute always goes with the message within the OS, until it gets to its recipient app/website, where we remove the attribute. To help developers build their own protection, our design exposes the origin of a message through existing and new APIs. For example, on iOS, we can enhance the API for retrieving the bundle ID of the sender of a scheme message by returning the true origin of the message, which could be the domain of the web content within that app's WebView instance. In this way, Facebook will be able to find out that the scheme message it gets from the Yelp app actually comes from a webpage Yelp displays, not the app itself. Therefore, the exploit described in Section 3.3.2 will be defeated.

Default policy. It is well known that the browser by default enforces the SOP to the web content it hosts, but the same policy cannot be applied to all the apps on mobile platforms as it may disrupt their legitimate cross-origin communications. Our strategy is to implement the SOP only on the totally unexpected and insecure channel. An example is the next-intent communication described in Section 3.2.1, which is unexpected, since the private Activity of an app should only be invoked by the app's own intent when calling the startActivity API. Therefore, in this scenario, the SOP is always enforced.

Setting policies. Morbs allows a policy to be specified on a channel between an app and a web domain (*web policy*), as well as between two apps (*app policy*). An app policy defines legitimate inter-app communication, which goes through intent or scheme. A web policy is about app-web interactions, through scheme or web-accessing utility classes. An app or a website sets a policy on a specific channel to notify Morbs the list of senders authorized to send messages to it, and the list of recipients allowed to receive the messages it sends.

Setting a policy can be done through a new API *setOriginPolicy*, which an app can directly call. Here is its specification:

```
void setOriginPolicy(type, senderOrRecipient, channelID, origins)
```

Here, *type* identifies the type of the channel (intent, scheme, or utility class), *senderOrRecipient* specifies sender or recipient, *channelID* indicates the channel ID, and *origins* is the whitelist. Once invoked, setOriginPolicy first identifies a channel by *type*, and *channelID*, which is an OS-wide unique string. For example, the ID for the intent channel that triggers LoginActivity within the Facebook app is "com.facebook.katana.LoginActivity", in which "com.facebook.katana" is the Facebook app's package name. For a scheme, its channel ID is the corresponding scheme field on a URL. For web-accessing utility classes, they are identified by their class instances within an app. After a channel is identified, the API then extracts the whitelist that regulates the sender or the recipient (specified in *senderOrRecipient*) through this channel from the *origins* parameter.

Although *setOriginPolicy* offers a generic interface for policy specification, it cannot be directly invoked by a website to set its policies. To address this problem, Morbs provides mechanisms for indirectly accessing this API, including a JavaScript API *setMobileAllowedOrigins*, through which the dynamic content from a website can set policies within the mobile browser or a WebView instance, and a header *mobile-allowed-origins* in HTTP responses that inform the browser or a WebView instance of the parties on the device allowed to get the message. The app developer can also leverage other indirect mechanisms to define her policies whenever she is building the app's functionality over a mobile channel. Specifically, Morbs allows the developer to set her policies regarding a scheme/intent her app claims within the app's manifest file (for Android) or .plist (for iOS), under a new property *allowedOrigins*. In this way, she can turn on our origin protection for her app without changing its code. Other ways for policy setting include a new argument *allowedOrigins* for the API that delivers scheme/intent messages, and a new API *setAllowedOrigins* used to define policies for utility classes such as WebView and HttpClient. An advantage of using these indirect ways is that they only require one argument (i.e., *origins*) from the developer because other arguments are set by default.

Enforcing policies. Morbs runs a reference monitor to enforce security policies on different channels. Whenever a message is delivered over a channel, the reference monitor is triggered to identify its origin and calls a function *checkOriginPolicy* to check its policy compliance. The function's specification is as follows:

```
bool checkOriginPolicy(type, senderOrRecipient, channelID, from, to)
```

Intuitively, the function searches Morbs policy base to find out whether the current sender (specified in the *from* argument) is allowed to deliver the message to the recipient (*to*) through the specific channel (*type and channelID*). Note that *checkOriginPolicy* needs to be called twice (one for checking the sender origin against the recipient's policy and the other for checking the recipient origin against the sender's policy). The message is allowed to go through only if both checks succeed.

Both *setOriginPolicy* and *checkOriginPolicy* operate on the Morbs policy base that keeps all policies. *setOriginPolicy* inserts a policy into the database and *checkOriginPolicy* searches the database for an applicable policy, checking whether a sender/recipient origin is on the whitelist included in the policy. The performance of this compliance check is critical because it needs to be invoked for every message going through these channels. To make it efficient, Morbs leverages the hash-table search to quickly locate a target within the database.

4.2 Implementation

We implemented our design on Android (Figure 2). At the center of our system are the *setOriginPolicy* API and the ReferenceMonitor class, in which the most important function is *checkOriginPolicy*. They were built into the Thread class of the Dalvik Virtual Machine. The *setOriginPolicy* API is open to all apps, while ReferenceMonitor is kept for the OS, which is only accessible to the code running inside the Android OS kernel.

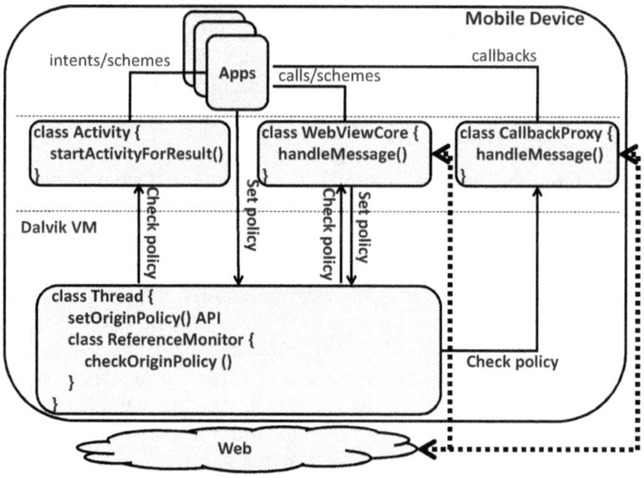

Figure 2 The framework of Morbs on Android

In the presence of the centralized policy compliance check (*checkOriginPolicy*), the task of ReferenceMonitor (i.e., policy enforcement) becomes trivial: all we need to do here is pulling the arguments, invoking *checkOriginPolicy* and raising an exception to drop a message when the check fails. In our implementation, the ReferenceMonitor class is used in the OS components related to these channels to conduct mediation. Specifically, for intent and scheme, the enforcement code was placed within the API *startActivityForResult*, which needs to be called by *startActivity*, when a message delivered through those channels attempts to start an Activity. Note that we chose not to do the security checks within the IPC mechanism: Android does not recommend inspecting intent data in IPC because the intent instances are serialized for high performance data transport [29]. For mediating web-app communications, we changed the *handleMessage* method within both the WebViewCore class and the CallbackProxy class. The two methods are the focal point of mobile browsers and WebView instances: all method invocations and callback handling from apps need to go through them. In addition, the *execute* method of HttpClient class was used to mediate apps' direct communication with web servers.

Challenge I: origin identification. Morbs attaches an *origin* attribute to every message exchanged through the mobile channels. On Android, both intent and scheme channels utilize the intent messages (Section 2). The constructor for generating an intent instance is hooked in our implementation to label an intent message with its app origin. Specifically, we added an *origin* property to the intent class. When the constructor is creating a new intent instance, it retrieves the package name of the app initiating the intent and fills in the *origin* property with the package name. For example, when the initiator is the Facebook app, the *origin* property should be marked as "app://com.facebook.katana", in which "com.facebook.katana" is the package name of Facebook app. However, this origin is not easy to identify in practice, since there is no API to help us find out the initiator directly. A simple solution is to get the whole call stack from the OS through *getStackTrace* API, and then inspect it to find out the caller. This approach turns out to be very expensive: in our test, extracting the call stack takes 1.35 ms in average. Our solution is to add an *origin* property to each thread that hosts an app. When the thread is created, the app's origin is attached to the property. Once an intent is initiated, the constructor then copies the origin information from the thread to the intent instance.

Challenge II: response inspection. To enable a web server to set its policies to a mobile device, Morbs needs to inspect the HTTP response to find the header *mobile-allowed-origins*. The response is processed by Android's native C++ libraries. Morbs (written in Java) cannot directly access it. In our implementation, we managed to get access to the header using Java Native Interface (JNI) [30]. JNI provides an API called *onReceivedData* through which C++ code can send messages to Java code. To inform Morbs of the content of the header, we modified the C++ code to identify the header *mobile-allowed-origins* within HTTP responses, and then call *onReceivedData* to deliver all policies described there to WebViewCore, where Morbs uses *setOriginPolicy* to complete this policy setting process.

5. EVALUATION

We evaluated the general design of Morbs and its implementation on Android to understand its effectiveness, performance, compatibility and utility to the app developers.

5.1 Effectiveness

We ran our implementation against the aforementioned cross-origin attacks (Section 3). Specifically, our experiment was conducted on Android 4.3 with Morbs running within an emulator. We installed both the vulnerable apps discovered in our research and the attacker apps. In the experiments, we first ran the attacker apps, and then checked whether the exploits were blocked by Morbs or not. Note that in some situations, we also need the developers to explicitly specify their whitelists of origins within their apps, in addition to the default policies. In the absence of those apps' source code, we had to directly enter those app-specific policies (whitelists) into the OS.

Preventing the exploits on intent. As described in Section 3.2.1, a malicious app can use the next-intent trick to invoke any private Activities of the victim app (the Dropbox app and the Facebook app). The content saved under the NEXT-INTENT key is essentially an intent, which needs to be first created by the malicious app before it is embedded into another intent (the one delivered to Dropbox app's login Activity). Under Morbs, the intent constructor sets the origins of both intents to the malicious app, which cannot be changed by the app. As a result, when *startActivity* is called to start the target private Activity, our reference monitor immediately finds that the origin of the next-intent is not the victim app itself, and stops this invocation according to the default policy (the SOP). Our tests confirmed that the vulnerabilities in both Dropbox app and Facebook app are fixed in this manner, without changing the apps' code.

Defeating the attacks on scheme. For the fbconnect problem described in Section 3.3.1, what Facebook wants to do is to return the data (e.g., secret tokens) from its server to the app associated with the *client_id* parameter within the Dialog request, not anyone that claims the fbconnect:// scheme. This intention is communicated by the Facebook server to the mobile OS through a list of legitimate recipient origins specified using its HTTP response header or the JavaScript API provided by Morbs. Specifically in our experiment, we inserted the header "mobile-allowed-origins: app://com.facebook.katana" into the HTTP response from the Facebook server, indicating that only the Facebook app can receive the data, and observed that the scheme invocation was stopped when the app that registered the fbconnect:// scheme was not the Facebook app. A video demo about this case can be found at [31].

When it comes to the apps using Dropbox iOS SDK (the first vulnerability described in Section 3.3.2), it is clear that their schemes associated with Dropbox are only supposed to be invoked by the Dropbox app. Using Morbs, the Dropbox SDK embedded in the apps specifies "app://com.getdropbox.Dropbox" (i.e., the Dropbox app) as the only legitimate sender origin for these schemes. As a result, our reference monitor ensures that any invocation of the schemes comes only from the Dropbox app, which defeats the attacks from a malicious webpage (through Facebook app or the Google Plus app). In the case of the attack using the Yelp app (second vulnerability described in Section 3.3.2), the problem comes from that the recipient of the scheme message, the Facebook app, cannot tell whether the origin of the message is indeed Yelp or a malicious website visited by the Yelp app's WebView instance. In the presence of Morbs, the true origin of the message is revealed as the website's domain, which enables Facebook to thwart the attack. Note that we did not actually run those fixes as the problems were found on iOS.

Mediating issues in web-accessing utility classes. For the case of the WebView callback within the Facebook app (Section 3.4.1), this callback should only respond to the event (i.e., processing the fbrpc URL) when this URL comes from the domains under Facebook's control. Let's assume Facebook app specifies "https://*.facebook.com" as the whitelist associated with the callback class UIWebViewDelegate, an operation that can be easily done using Morbs. As a result, the event initiated from "attacker.com" is ignored by the WebView, without triggering the callback *shouldStartLoadWithRequest*, while those from facebook.com continue to be handled. We further evaluated our implementation against the exploit on the HttpClient class (Section 3.4.2). This time, we set "https://*.dropbox.com" as the legitimate origin on the whitelist for the instance of the HttpClient class used in the Dropbox app. After that, we found that even after the adversary crossed the origins through the next-intent channel, he still cannot steal the Dropbox authentication header by sending requests to a non-dropbox.com URL, because it was blocked by our reference monitor according to the whitelist.

5.2 Performance

We evaluated the performance of our implementation on a Nexus 4 development phone. We compared the overhead of Morbs with the overall delay the user experiences in the absence of Morbs, to understand the performance impact that our approach can have on cross-origin communications. In the experiments, we call a Java API *nanoTime* to collect timing measurements at a precision of 1 nanosecond (i.e., 10^{-9} s). To measure the performance of a Morbs operation, we repeated it 10 times to get its average execution time. The operations we studied include setting policies and checking policy compliance. Among them, the compliance check is the focus of our evaluations, as the policy setting is just a one-time task. More specifically, we measured the delays for sending messages through intent, scheme, and utility classes in the absence of Morbs, and then compared them with the time spent on a policy compliance check. In all the cases, the impact of Morbs was found to be negligible (below 1%).

Performance of Morbs operations. On the Android OS with our Morbs implementation, we ran a test app to invoke the *setOriginPolicy* API, and measured the time for setting a policy. On average, this operation took 0.354 ms, which involves storing the content of the policy to a policy database maintained by the OS. To check the compliance with the policies, Morbs needs to search the database to find out whether the origin of the current sender or recipient is whitelisted. As described in Section 4.1, we leverage the hash-table search to quickly locate the policies. To understand the performance of this operation, we utilized a test app to invoke another test app through an intent message, which triggered the *checkOriginPolicy* function. We found that the whole compliance check process took 0.219 ms on average. Note that policy enforcement over other channels all utilizes the same ReferenceMonitor class, which is expected to bring in similar average delay.

Impacts on mobile communications. As described above, the performance impact of setting policies should be minimum, since it just incurs a one-time cost. Also for the policies declared within a manifest file, they are set when the app is installed, which does not affect its operations. Therefore, our focus was policy compliance check.

In the study, we measured the overall delays for sending a message through intent, scheme, and web-accessing utility classes without the policy compliance check. Table 1 shows the average delays for such communication, and their comparison with the overhead for a compliance check (0.219 ms). This gives a pretty good picture about the impact the check can have on such channels. Specifically, for the intent channel, we measured the time interval between the invocation of *startActivity* and the execution of *performCreate* (the first API the target Activity needs to call). After repeating the operation for 10 times, we observed an average delay of 42.142 ms when the sender and recipient were the same app, and 46.267 ms when they were not (see Table 1). On the other hand, the compliance check took only an average 0.219 ms. Therefore, the impact of this mediation on the intent communication was around 0.5%. For the scheme message delivered between two apps, it goes through the same intent mechanism. The mediation impact of Morbs on this communication was found to be 0.3% on average. We further measured the time a webpage takes to invoke an app through scheme, between the event when the method *handleMessage* in WebViewCore class is triggered to process the scheme URL, and when the *performCreate* API for the target test app is called. We found that this whole process took 115.301 ms and the impact of the policy checking there was 0.2%.

When we take into account the delays incurred by web-related operations, particularly those performed by the methods and callbacks of WebView and HttpClient class, the extra time spent on the policy compliance check can be comfortably ignored. Specifically, we measured the waiting time for loading a URL (specifically, google.com) through HttpClient, and WebView. For HttpClient, we measured the time interval between the creation of a class instance and the point when the instance receives the HTTP response, which took 225.035 ms on average. For WebView, we measured the interval between the start of page loading (*onPageStarted* is called) and its completion (*onPageFinished* is called), which took 692.955 ms. By comparison, the time Morbs spends on the compliance check (0.219 ms) become unnoticeable.

Table 1 Impact of policy compliance check

Channel	Type of Communication	Communication Delay w/o Morbs (ms)	Impact of Morbs policy checking
intent	in-app	42.142	0.52%
	cross-app	46.267	0.47%
scheme	app-app	64.077	0.34%
	web-app	115.301	0.19%
utility classes	HttpClient	225.035	0.10%
	WebView	692.955	0.03%

5.3 Compatibility and Developer's Effort

An important goal of Morbs is to maintain compatibility when possible and minimize the developer's effort to use its protection. Following we elaborate our study on these two issues.

Compatibility. To see whether our implementation can work with existing apps, we loaded Android with Morbs into a Nexus 4 development phone and evaluated the operations of top 20 free apps downloaded from Google Play market. Those apps were first analyzed: we disassembled their binary code and found that all of them use intent, 12 claim various schemes and all need to use the web through WebView and HttpClient classes. We then analyzed their functionalities in the presence or absence of Morbs mediation, by clicking on all buttons and using all of the services we could find. During the test, we did not observed any deviation of those apps' behaviors with and without our mechanism.

Developer's effort. As discussed before, to use Morbs, the developer only need to specify her whitelists through the interfaces (e.g., the *setOriginPolicy* API) we provide, which is straightforward for them to act on. This is compared to the case-by-case fixes that app developers are currently doing in response to our vulnerability reports. In Table 1, we give a comparison with regard to the vulnerabilities described in Section 3. The ways they are fixed (or to be fixed) ("Fix w/o Morbs") come from our conversations with corresponding software vendors. Here, how to fix the problem 4 (the exploit through Yelp app) and 5 (the callback loophole) is still unknown.

As we can see from the table, these vulnerabilities are much easier to fix with the support of Morbs. Specifically, for the next-intent problem (Section 3.2.1), both Dropbox and Facebook informed us that an effective fix takes time to build. Particularly, Dropbox explained that they need to "change the architecture" of their app, which involves non-trivial effort. In the presence of our origin-based protection, however, this next-intent cross-origin loophole is fixed without requiring any modification to the apps. As another example, for the fbconnect issue described in Section 3.3.1, Facebook chose to deprecate the use of fbconnect, which is a core feature in all of its native SDKs and official apps. This effort needs "a several month deprecation period", according to Facebook. Using Morbs, however, Facebook could easily fix the problem without touching any of its SDKs and apps, by simply adding an extra header, including the origins of the apps supposed to receive its message, to the HTTP response its server sends to mobile devices. Overall, as shown in the table, the current fixes to these problems are all case by case, while our solution is consistent in the way to set origin-based security policies (whitelist of authorized origins) and enforce the policies.

Table 2 Comparison of current fixes and the fixes with Morbs

Problems	Fix w/o Morbs	Fix w. Morbs
next-intent (Section 3.2.1)	Change architecture of the Dropbox app and the Facebook app	No modification
fbconnect (Section 3.3.1)	Deprecate this feature (affecting all apps with Facebook SDKs, and taking several months)	Facebook server specifies recipient whitelist by setting a header in HTTP response "mobile- allowed-origins: app://com.facebook.katana"
Dropbox iOS SDK (Section 3.3.2)	Change both the Dropbox apps and SDKs	Dropbox SDK specifies sender whitelist by adding an entry "allowedOrigins: app://com.getdropbox.Dropbox" under "URL scheme" in .plist file.
Yelp issue (Section 3.3.2)	Unknown	No modification
callback exploit (Section 3.4.1)	Unknown	Facebook app specifies sender whitelist by calling WebViewClient:setAllowedOrigins("https://*.facebook.com")
HTTPClient exploit (Section 3.4.2)	Change to the Dropbox app, adding code for checking whether a URL is from dropbox. com when attaching authorization header	Dropbox app specifies recipient whitelist by calling HTTPClient.setAllowedOrigins("https://*.dropbox.com").

6. RELATED WORK

Origin-based protection in web browsers. Origin-based protection is a cornerstone for browser security. All modern web browsers enforce the same-origin policy (SOP) [4] to protect the web content from one origin against unauthorized access from a different origin. Always at the center of browser security is the attacks that circumvent this protection, such as XSS, CSRF, login CSRF, and the defense that reinforces the browser and makes the protection hard to bypass [1][2][3]. Our research shows that serious cross-origin attacks can also happen on mobile platforms and therefore the origin-based protection is equally important to mobile security.

Under the SOP, cross-origin communication needs to go through designated channels with proper mediation. A prominent example is the *postMessage* channel [5], through which the web content of one origin can send messages to another domain, and the browser ensures that the recipient knows the true origin of the sender. However, the web developer of the recipient domain still needs to come up with her own policy enforcement logic, which could be error-prone. Alternatively, the browser can act on whitelisted origins specified by the developer. An example is the Cross-Origin Resource Sharing mechanism [6], through which the content from a.com can request resources from b.com server using XMLHttpRequest [7]. The server authorizes this cross-origin activity to the browser by attaching to its HTTP response a header "Access-Control-Allow-Origin: a.com", a whitelist for the requestor a.com. The browser then enforces this policy, sending the message only to a.com webpages.

The design of Morbs is pretty much in line with those browser-based security mechanisms. We bring in this origin-based protection to mobile platforms, making the true origin of each message observable to app/web developers and also helping them enforce their policies at the OS level.

Security on mobile platforms. The security framework of Android is built on i) the sandbox model [8], which separates an app's data and code execution from that of the rest of the system, and 2) the permission model [9], which grants each app different level of privileges to access system resources under the user's consent. Prior studies mainly focus on circumventing such protection to obtain private user data (e.g., GPS location, phone contacts) or perform privileged operations (e.g., sending SMS messages) without proper consents from the user [10][11][12][13][14][27]. Most related to our work here is permission re-delegation [10], in which an unprivileged app sends an intent to another app with a proper permission to act on its behalf, operating on the resources (e.g., GPS, user contacts, etc.) it is not supposed to touch. However, this problem has been studied mainly for understanding the threat to mobile devices' *local* resources. What we investigated is the protection of an app's *web* resources, which has not been explicitly included in Android's security models. Luo et al. conducted two studies specifically about security issues related to WebView: in [42], they categorized existing issues raised by other researchers and a number of issues discovered by them. Many of these issues were shown to affect Android applications that use the open-source package DroidGap; in [43], they proposed a type of attack called "touchjacking", which targets the weaknesses of WebView's handling of touch events.

To address those problems, numerous defense mechanisms have been proposed [17][18][19][20]. Particularly, information-flow techniques, such as TaintDroid [15] and Vision [16], are used to track the propagation of sensitive user data across a suspicious app at the instruction level. Different from those existing techniques, our protection mechanism is designed to keep track of the origin of the message exchanged between the initiator and the recipients for origin-based mediation. For this purpose, we only need to work on the API level (given that the OS is trusted), which is much more efficient. A related technique called Quire [21] enables Android to trace and sign the whole IPC chain observed by the OS during intent messaging, so that the recipient of an intent can find out its initiator. However, this approach is not designed to determine a request's *web* origin: for example, when an app is activated through a scheme URL generated by a malicious webpage displayed in the WebView instance of the Facebook app, looking at the IPC chain does not tell the recipient app that it is actually originated from the malicious domain.

Similar call-sequence analyses have been done on iOS to detect information leaks through iOS apps [22][23]. The focus of these analyses is on malicious apps, while our focus is on protecting benign apps.

7. CONCLUSION AND FUTURE WORK

Unlike traditional web applications, which enjoy browser-level origin-based protection, apps are hosted on mobile OSes, whose security models (e.g., sandbox and permission models) are not designed to safeguard resources based their web origins. Our research shows that in the absence of such protection, the mobile channels can be easily abused to gain unauthorized access to a user's sensitive web resources. We found 5 cross-origin issues in popular SDKs and high-profile apps such as Facebook and Dropbox, which can be exploited to steal their users' authentication credentials and other confidential information such as text input. Moreover, without the OS support for origin-based protection, not only is app development shown to be prone to such cross-origin flaws, but the developer may also have trouble fixing the flaws even after they are discovered. This points to the urgent need of building origin-based protection into mobile platforms. In our research, we designed and implemented the first such protection mechanism, *Morbs*, for mediating cross-origin communications at the OS level. Our evaluation shows that the new technique effectively and efficiently controls the risks that come with the communications, and can also be conveniently utilized by the app and web developers.

Our current implementation is for Android. Building this new protection on iOS is equally important. Also interesting is the effort to automatically analyze existing apps, to identify their cross-origin vulnerabilities and defend them using the origin protection we provided. More generally, given the trend that web services are increasingly delivered through apps, further investigations are needed to understand how to better protect users' web resources on mobile OSes, which were originally designed to safeguard a device's local resources.

8. ACKNOWLEDGEMENTS

We thank Seungyeop Han, Ravi Bhoraskar, and Jaeyeon Jung for their help on monitoring HTTPS traffic of Android emulator. Authors from Indiana University are supported in part by National Science Foundation CNS-1117106 and CNS-1223477.

9. REFERENCES

[1] Fogie, S., Grossman, J., Hansen, R., Rager, A., & Petkov, P. D. (2007). *XSS Attacks: Cross Site Scripting Exploits and Defense*. Syngress Publishing.

[2] Auger, R. (2008). The cross-site request forgery (csrf/xsrf) faq. *CGISecurity. com. Apr, 17.*

[3] Barth, A., Jackson, C., & Mitchell, J. C. (2008, October). Robust defenses for cross-site request forgery. In *Proceedings of the 15th ACM conference on Computer and communications security* (pp. 75-88). ACM.

[4] Barth, A. (2011). The web origin concept.

[5] Cross-document messaging – HTML standard. http://www.whatwg.org/specs/web-apps/current-work/multipage/web-messaging.html#web-messaging

[6] van Kesteren, A. (2010). Cross-origin resource sharing. *W3C Working Draft WD-cors-20100727.*

[7] Garrett, J. J. (2005). Ajax: A new approach to web applications.

[8] Android Developers: Security Tips. http://developer.android.com/training/articles/security-tips.html

[9] Android Developers: Permissions. http://developer.android.com/guide/topics/security/permissions.html

[10] Felt, A. P., Wang, H. J., Moshchuk, A., Hanna, S., & Chin, E. (2011, August). Permission re-delegation: Attacks and defenses. In *Proceedings of the 20th USENIX Security Symposium* (Vol. 18, pp. 19-31).

[11] Davi, L., Dmitrienko, A., Sadeghi, A. R., & Winandy, M. (2011). Privilege escalation attacks on android. In *Information Security* (pp. 346-360). Springer Berlin Heidelberg.

[12] Grace, M., Zhou, Y., Wang, Z., & Jiang, X. (2012, February). Systematic detection of capability leaks in stock Android smartphones. In *Proceedings of the 19th Annual Symposium on Network and Distributed System Security.*

[13] Schlegel, R., Zhang, K., Zhou, X., Intwala, M., Kapadia, A., & Wang, X. (2011, February). Soundcomber: A stealthy and context-aware sound trojan for smartphones. In *Proceedings*

of the 18th Annual Network and Distributed System Security Symposium (NDSS) (pp. 17-33).

[14] Schrittwieser, S., Frühwirt, P., Kieseberg, P., Leithner, M., Mulazzani, M., Huber, M., & Weippl, E. (2012, February). Guess Who's Texting You? Evaluating the Security of Smartphone Messaging Applications. In *Proceedings of the 19th Annual Symposium on Network and Distributed System Security*.

[15] Enck, W., Gilbert, P., Chun, B. G., Cox, L. P., Jung, J., McDaniel, P., & Sheth, A. N. (2010, October). TaintDroid: an information-flow tracking system for realtime privacy monitoring on smartphones. In *Proceedings of the 9th USENIX conference on Operating systems design and implementation* (pp. 1-6).

[16] Gilbert, P., Chun, B. G., Cox, L. P., & Jung, J. (2011, June). Vision: automated security validation of mobile apps at app markets. In *Proceedings of the second international workshop on Mobile cloud computing and services* (pp. 21-26). ACM.

[17] Bugiel, S., Davi, L., Dmitrienko, A., Fischer, T., Sadeghi, A. R., & Shastry, B. (2012, February). Towards taming privilege-escalation attacks on Android. In *19th Annual Network & Distributed System Security Symposium (NDSS)* (Vol. 17, pp. 18-25).

[18] Shekhar, S., Dietz, M., & Wallach, D. S. (2012). Adsplit: Separating smartphone advertising from applications. *CoRR, abs/1202.4030.*

[19] Fragkaki, E., Bauer, L., Jia, L., & Swasey, D. (2012). Modeling and enhancing Android's permission system. In *Computer Security–ESORICS 2012* (pp. 1-18). Springer Berlin Heidelberg.

[20] Davi, L., Dmitrienko, A., Egele, M., Fischer, T., Holz, T., Hund, R., ... & Sadeghi, A. R. (2012, February). MoCFI: A framework to mitigate control-flow attacks on smartphones. In *Proceedings of the 19th Annual Symposium on Network and Distributed System Security*.

[21] Dietz, M., Shekhar, S., Pisetsky, Y., Shu, A., & Wallach, D. S. (2011, August). Quire: Lightweight provenance for smart phone operating systems. In *Proceedings of the 20th USENIX Security Symposium*.

[22] Egele, M., Kruegel, C., Kirda, E., & Vigna, G. (2011, February). PiOS: Detecting privacy leaks in iOS applications. In *Proceedings of the Network and Distributed System Security Symposium*.

[23] Werthmann, T., Hund, R., Davi, L., Sadeghi, A. R., & Holz, T. (2013). PSiOS: Bring Your Own Privacy & Security to iOS Devices.

[24] Hardy, N. (1988). The Confused Deputy:(or why capabilities might have been invented). *ACM SIGOPS Operating Systems Review*, *22*(4), 36-38.

[25] Hermandroid. "Launching an Android application from a URL". http://androidsmith.com/2011/07/launching-an-android-application-from-a-url/

[26] Apple URL Scheme Reference. http://developer.apple.com/library/ios/#featuredarticles/iPhoneURLScheme_Reference/Introduction/Introduction.html

[27] Chin, E., Felt, A. P., Greenwood, K., & Wagner, D. (2011, June). Analyzing inter-application communication in Android. In *Proceedings of the 9th international conference on Mobile systems, applications, and services* (pp. 239-252). ACM.

[28] Android Developers: WebView.addJavaScriptInterface. http://developer.android.com/reference/android/webkit/WebView.html#addJavascriptInterface%28java.lang.Object,%20java.lang.String%29

[29] Android Developers: Parcel. http://developer.android.com/reference/android/os/Parcel.html

[30] Android Developers: Java Native Interface. http://developer.android.com/training/articles/perf-jni.html

[31] Supporting materials for this work. http://research.microsoft.com/en-us/um/people/ruiwan/mobile-origin/index.html

[32] A local file loaded from SD card to webview on Android can cross-domain. http://lists.grok.org.uk/pipermail/full-disclosure/2012-February/085619.html

[33] Android-apktool – A tool for reverse engineering Android apk files. http://code.google.com/p/android-apktool/

[34] AndroChef Java Decompiler. http://www.neshkov.com/ac_decompiler.html

[35] Facebook Developers – Dialogs Overview. https://developers.facebook.com/docs/reference/dialogs/

[36] Android Developers – HttpClient. http://developer.android.com/reference/org/apache/http/client/HttpClient.html

[37] Android Developers – HttpURLConnection. http://developer.android.com/reference/java/net/HttpURLConnection.html

[38] iOS Developer Library – NSURLConnection Class Reference. http://developer.apple.com/library/ios/#documentation/Cocoa/Reference/Foundation/Classes/NSURLConnection_Class/Reference/Reference.html#//apple_ref/occ/cl/NSURLConnection

[39] iOS Developer Library – Making HTTP and HTTPS Requests. http://developer.apple.com/library/ios/#documentation/NetworkingInternetWeb/Conceptual/NetworkingOverview/WorkingWithHTTPAndHTTPSRequests/WorkingWithHTTPAndHTTPSRequests.html

[40] The implementation of the mobile origin-based security mechanism (Morbs) on Android is published on GitHub. https://github.com/mobile-security/Morbs

[41] PlainText – Dropbox text editing for iPhone, iPod touch, and iPad. https://itunes.apple.com/us/app/plaintext-dropbox-text-editing/id391254385?mt=8

[42] Luo, T., Hao, H., Du, W., Wang, Y., & Yin, H. (2011, December). Attacks on WebView in the Android system. In *Proceedings of the 27th Annual Computer Security Applications Conference* (pp. 343-352).

[43] Luo, T., Jin, X., Ajai, A., & Du, W. Touchjacking attacks on web in android, ios, and windows phone. In *Proceedings of 5TH International Symposium on Foundations & Practice of Security (FPS 2012).*

Security Analysis of Pseudo-Random Number Generators with Input: /dev/random is not Robust *

Yevgeniy Dodis
Dept. of Computer Science
New York University

David Pointcheval
DI/ENS
ENS-CNRS-INRIA

Sylvain Ruhault
DI/ENS
ENS-CNRS-INRIA
and Oppida, France

Damien Vergnaud
DI/ENS
ENS-CNRS-INRIA

Daniel Wichs
Dept. of Computer Science
Northeastern University

ABSTRACT

A pseudo-random number generator (PRNG) is a deterministic algorithm that produces numbers whose distribution is indistinguishable from uniform. A formal security model for PRNGs with input was proposed in 2005 by Barak and Halevi (BH). This model involves an internal state that is refreshed with a (potentially biased) external random source, and a cryptographic function that outputs random numbers from the continually internal state. In this work we extend the BH model to also include a new security property capturing how it should accumulate the entropy of the input data into the internal state after state compromise. This property states that a good PRNG should be able to eventually recover from compromise even if the entropy is injected into the system at a very slow pace, and expresses the real-life expected behavior of existing PRNG designs.

Unfortunately, we show that neither the model nor the specific PRNG construction proposed by BH meet this new property, despite meeting a weaker robustness notion introduced by BH. From a practical side, we give a precise assessment of the Linux PRNGs, `/dev/random` and `/dev/urandom`. In particular, we show attacks proving that these PRNGs are not robust according to our definition, due to vulnerabilities in their entropy estimator and their internal mixing function. Finally, we propose a simple PRNG construction that is provably robust in our new and stronger adversarial model and we show that it is more efficient than the Linux PRNGs. We therefore recommend to use this construction whenever a PRNG with input is used for cryptography.

Categories and Subject Descriptors

D.4.6 [**Operating Systems**]: Security and Protection—*Cryptographic controls*; G.3 [**Mathematics of Computing**]: Probability and Statistics—*Random number generation*

Keywords

Randomness; Entropy; Security models; /dev/random

*A full version of this paper is available at Cryptology ePrint Archive, Report 2013/338

CCS'13, November 4–8, 2013, Berlin, Germany.

ACM 978-1-4503-2477-9/13/11 ...$15.00.
http://dx.doi.org/10.1145/2508859.2516653.

1. INTRODUCTION

Generating random numbers is an essential task in cryptography. Random numbers are necessary not only for generating cryptographic keys, but are also needed in steps of cryptographic algorithms or protocols (*e.g.* initialization vectors for symmetric encryption, password generation, nonce generation, ...). Cryptography practitioners usually assume that parties have access to perfect randomness. However, quite often this assumption is not realizable in practice and random bits in protocols are generated by a *Pseudo-Random Number Generator* (PRNG). When this is done, the security of the scheme depends of course in a crucial way on the quality of the (pseudo-)randomness generated. If a user has access to a truly random bit-string, he can use a *deterministic* (or *cryptographic*) PRNG to expand this short *seed* into a longer sequence which distribution is indistinguishable from the uniform distribution to a computationally-bounded adversary (which does not know the seed). However, in many situations, it is unrealistic to assume that users have access to secret and perfect randomness. In a PRNG with input, one only assumes that users can store a secret internal state and have access to a (potentially biased) random source.

In spite of being widely deployed in practice, PRNGs with input were only formalized by Barak and Halevi in 2005 [1]. They proposed a security notion, called *robustness*, to capture the fact that the bits generated should look random to an observer with (partial) knowledge of the internal state and (partial) control of the entropy source. Combining theoretical and practical analysis of PRNGs with input, this paper presents an extension of the Barak-Halevi security model and analyses the Linux PRNGs `/dev/random` and `/dev/urandom`.

Randomness weaknesses in cryptography. The lack of insurance about the generated random numbers can cause serious damages in cryptographic protocols, and vulnerabilities can be exploited by attackers. One striking example is the recent failure in the Debian Linux distribution [4], where a commented code in the OpenSSL PRNG with input led to insufficient entropy gathering and then to concrete attacks on TLS and SSH protocols. More recently, Lenstra, Hughes, Augier, Bos, Kleinjung and Wachter [15] showed that a non-negligible percentage of RSA keys share prime factors. Heninger, Durumeric, Wustrow and Halderman [9] presented an analysis of the behavior of Linux PRNG that explains the generation of low entropy keys when these keys are generated at boot time. Moreover, cryptographic algorithms are highly vulnerable to weaknesses in the underlying random number generation process. For instance, several works demonstrated that if nonces for DSS signature algorithm are generated with a weak PRNG then the secret key can be quickly recovered after seeing a few signatures (see [16] and references therein). This illustrates the need for precise evaluation of PRNGs based on clear security requirements.

Security Models. Descriptions of PRNGs with input are given in various standards [12, 10, 7]. They identified the following core components: the *entropy source* which is the source of randomness used by the generator to update an *internal state* which consists of all the parameters, variables, and other stored values that the PRNG uses for its operations.

Several desirable security properties for PRNGs with input have been identified in [10, 12, 7, 2]. These standards consider adversaries with various means: those who have access to the output of the generator; those who can (partially or totally) control the source of the generator and those who can (partially or totally) control the internal state of the generator (and combination of them). Several security notions have been defined:

- *Resilience*: an adversary must not be able to predict future PRNG outputs even if he can influence the entropy source used to initialize or refresh the internal state of the PRNG;
- *Forward security (*resp. backward security*)*: an adversary must not be able to predict past (*resp.* future) outputs even if he can compromise the internal state of the PRNG.

Desai, Hevia and Yin [5] modelled a PRNG as an iterative algorithm and formalized the above security properties in this context. Barak and Halevi [1] model a PRNG with input as a pair of algorithms (refresh, next) and define a new security property called *robustness* that implies resilience, forward and backward security. This property actually assesses the behavior of a PRNG after compromise of its internal state and responds to the guidelines for developing PRNG given by Kelsey, Schneier, Wagner and Hall [11].

Linux PRNG. In Unix-like operating systems, a PRNG with input was implemented for the first time for Linux 1.3.30 in 1994. The entropy source comes from device drivers and other sources such as latencies between user-triggered events (keystroke, disk I/O, mouse clicks, ...). It is gathered into an internal state called the *entropy pool*. The internal state keeps an estimate of the number of bits of entropy in the internal state and (pseudo-)random bits are created from the special files `/dev/random` and `/dev/urandom`. Barak and Halevi [1] discussed briefly the PRNG `/dev/random` but its conformity with their robustness security definition is not formally analyzed.

The first security analysis of these PRNGs was given in 2006 by Gutterman, Pinkas and Reinman [8]. It was completed in 2012 by Lacharme, Röck, Strubel and Videau [14]. Gutterman *et al.* [8] presented an attack based on kernel version 2.6.10 for which a fix has been published in the following versions. Lacharme *et al.* [14] gives a detailed description of the operations of the PRNG and provides a result on the entropy preservation property of the mixing function used to refresh the internal state.

Our Contributions. From a theoretical side, we propose a new formal security model for PRNGs with input, which encompasses all previous security notions [1]. This new property captures how a PRNG with input should accumulate the entropy of the input data into the internal state. This property was not initially formalized in [1] but it actually expresses the real-life expected behavior of a PRNG after a state compromise, where it is expected that the PRNG quickly recovers enough entropy.

On a practical side, we give a precise assessment of the two Linux PRNGs, `/dev/random` and `/dev/urandom`. We prove that these PRNGs are not robust and do not accumulate entropy properly, due to the behavior of their entropy estimator and their internal mixing function. We also analyze the PRNG with input proposed by Barak and Halevi. This scheme was proven robust in [1] but we prove that it does not generically satisfy our expected property of entropy accumulation. On the positive side, we propose a PRNG construction that is robust in the standard model and in our new stronger adversarial model.

Finally, we perfome benchmarks between our construction and the Linux PRNGs and we show that it is far more efficient than the Linux PRNGs for both internal state recovery and key generation.

2. PRELIMINARIES

Probabilities. When X is a distribution, or a random variable following this distribution, we denote $x \xleftarrow{\$} X$ when x is sample according to X. We denote by $M(X)$ the distribution probability of the output of the Turing machine M, while running on the input x drawn according to X, and with its random coins (if any). The notation $X \leftarrow Y$ says that X is assigned with the value of the variable Y, and that X is a random variable with distribution equal to that of Y. For a variable X and a set S (e.g., $\{0,1\}^m$ for some integer m), the notation $X \xleftarrow{\$} S$ denotes both assigning X a value uniformly chosen from S and letting X be a uniform random variable over S. The uniform distribution over n bits is denoted $\mathcal{U}_n$.

Indistinguishability. Two distributions X and Y are said (t, ε)-*computationally indistinguishable*, ($\mathbf{CD}_t(X, Y) \leq \varepsilon$), if for any distinguisher $\mathcal{A}$ running within time t, $\Pr[\mathcal{A}(X) = 1] - \Pr[\mathcal{A}(Y) = 1] \leq \varepsilon$. When $t = \infty$, meaning $\mathcal{A}$ is unbounded, we say that X and Y are ε-*close*, and their *statistical distance* is at most ε: $\mathbf{SD}(X, Y) \leq \varepsilon$.
$\mathbf{SD}(X, Y|Z) \leq \varepsilon$ (resp. $\mathbf{CD}_t(X, Y|Z) \leq \varepsilon$) is a shorthand for $\mathbf{SD}((X, Z), (Y, Z)) \leq \varepsilon$ (resp. $\mathbf{CD}_t((X, Z), (Y, Z)) \leq \varepsilon$.

Entropy. For a discrete distribution X over a set S, we denote its *min-entropy* by

$$\mathbf{H}_\infty(X) = \min_{x \in \mathsf{Supp}(X)} \{-\log \Pr[X = x]\}$$

where $\mathrm{Supp}(X) \subseteq S$ is the support of the distribution X. A distribution X is called a k-*source* if $\mathbf{H}_\infty(X) \geq k$. We also define worst-case min-entropy of X conditioned on another random variable Z by:

$$\mathbf{H}_\infty(X|Z) = -\log\left(\left[\max_{\substack{x\in\text{Supp}(X),\\ z\in\text{Supp}(Z)}} \Pr[X = x|Z = z]\right]\right) \quad (1)$$

It is worth noting that conditional min-entropy is defined more conservatively than usual, so that it satisfies the following relations (the first of which, called the *chain rule*, is not true for the "average-case" variant of conditional min-entropy):

$$\begin{aligned}\mathbf{H}_\infty(X, Z) - \mathbf{H}_\infty(Z) &\geq \mathbf{H}_\infty(X|Z)\\ &\geq \mathbf{H}_\infty(X, Z) - |Z| \geq \mathbf{H}_\infty(X) - |Z|\end{aligned} \quad (2)$$

where $|Z|$ is the bit-length of Z. **Extractors.** Let $\mathcal{H} = \{h_X : \{0,1\}^n \to \{0,1\}^m\}_{X\in\{0,1\}^d}$ be a hash function family. We say that $\mathcal{H}$ is a (k, ε)*-extractor* if for any random variable I over $\{0,1\}^n$ with $\mathbf{H}_\infty(I) \geq k$, the distributions $(X, h_X(I))$ and (X, U) are ε-close where X is uniformly random over $\{0,1\}^d$ and U is uniformly random over $\{0,1\}^m$. We say that $\mathcal{H}$ is ρ-universal if for any inputs $I \neq I' \in \{0,1\}^n$ we have $\Pr_{X\in\{0,1\}^d}[h_X(I) \neq h_X(I')] \leq \rho$.

Lemma 1 (Leftover-Hash Lemma). *Assume that $\mathcal{H}$ is ρ-universal where $\rho = (1+\alpha)2^{-m}$ for some $\alpha > 0$. Then, for any $k > 0$, it is also a (k, ε)-extractor for $\varepsilon = \frac{1}{2}\sqrt{2^{m-k} + \alpha}$.*

See Theorem 8.37 in [19] for a nicely explained proof of the above lemma.

Pseudorandom Generators. We say that a function $\mathbf{G} : \{0,1\}^m \to \{0,1\}^n$ is a (deterministic) (t, ε)*-pseudorandom generator* (PRG) if $\mathbf{CD}_t(\mathbf{G}(\mathcal{U}_m), \mathcal{U}_n) \leq \varepsilon$.

Game Playing Framework. For our security definitions and proofs we use the code-based game playing framework of [3]. A game GAME has an initialize procedure, procedures to respond to adversary oracle queries, and a finalize procedure. A game GAME is executed with an adversary $\mathcal{A}$ as follows. First, initialize executes, and its outputs are the inputs to $\mathcal{A}$. Then $\mathcal{A}$ executes, its oracle queries being answered by the corresponding procedures of GAME. When $\mathcal{A}$ terminates, its output becomes the input to the finalize procedure. The output of the latter is called the output of the game, and we let $\mathsf{GAME}^{\mathcal{A}} \Rightarrow y$ denote the event that this game output takes value y. In the next section, for all $\mathsf{GAME} \in \{\mathsf{RES}, \mathsf{FWD}, \mathsf{BWD}, \mathsf{ROB}, \mathsf{SROB}\}$, $\mathcal{A}^{\mathsf{GAME}}$ denotes the output of the adversary. We let $\mathsf{Adv}_{\mathcal{A}}^{\mathsf{GAME}} = 2\times\Pr[\mathsf{GAME}^{\mathcal{A}} \Rightarrow 1] - 1$. Our convention is that Boolean flags are assumed initialized to false and that the running time of the adversary $\mathcal{A}$ is defined as the total running time of the game with the adversary in expectation, including the procedures of the game.

3. PRNG WITH INPUT: MODELING AND SECURITY

DEFINITION ***(PRNG with input)*** A PRNG with input is a triple of algorithms $\mathcal{G} = (\mathsf{setup}, \mathsf{refresh}, \mathsf{next})$ and a triple $(n, \ell, p) \in \mathbb{N}^3$ where:

- setup: it is a probabilistic algorithm that outputs some public parameters seed for the generator.
- refresh: it is a deterministic algorithm that, given seed, a state $S \in \{0,1\}^n$ and an input $I \in \{0,1\}^p$, outputs a new state $S' = \mathsf{refresh}(S, I) = \mathsf{refresh}(\mathsf{seed}, S, I) \in \{0,1\}^n$.
- next: it is a deterministic algorithm that, given seed and a state $S \in \{0,1\}^n$, outputs a pair $(S', R) = \mathsf{next}(S, I) = \mathsf{next}(\mathsf{seed}, S, I)$ where $S' \in \{0,1\}^n$ is the new state and $R \in \{0,1\}^\ell$ is the output.

The integer n is the *state length*, ℓ is the output length and p is the input length of $\mathcal{G}$.

Before moving to defining our security notions, we notice that there are two adversarial entities we need to worry about: the *adversary* $\mathcal{A}$ whose task is (intuitively) to distinguish the outputs of the PRNG from random, and the *distribution sampler* $\mathcal{D}$ whose task is to produce inputs $I_1, I_2, \ldots$, which have high entropy *collectively*, but somehow help $\mathcal{A}$ in breaking the security of the PRNG. In other words, the distribution sampler models potentially adversarial environment (or "nature") where our PRNG is forced to operate. Unlike prior work, we model the distribution sampler *explicitly*, and believe that such modeling is one of the important technical and conceptual contributions of our work.

3.1 Distribution Sampler

The distribution sampler $\mathcal{D}$ is a *stateful* and *probabilistic* algorithm which, given the current state σ, outputs a tuple (σ', I, γ, z) where: (a) σ' is the new state for $\mathcal{D}$; (b) $I \in \{0,1\}^p$ is the next input for the refresh algorithm; (c) γ is some *fresh entropy estimation* of I, as discussed below; and (d) z is the *leakage* about I given to the attacker $\mathcal{A}$.

We denote by $q_{\mathcal{D}}$ the upper bound on number of executions of $\mathcal{D}$ in our security games, and say that $\mathcal{D}$ is *legitimate* if:[1]

$$\begin{aligned}\mathbf{H}_\infty(I_j \mid I_1, \ldots, I_{j-1}, I_{j+1}, \ldots, I_{q_{\mathcal{D}}},\\ z_1, \ldots, z_{q_{\mathcal{D}}}, \gamma_1, \ldots, \gamma_{q_{\mathcal{D}}}) \geq \gamma_j\end{aligned} \quad (3)$$

for all $j \in \{1, \ldots, q_{\mathcal{D}}\}$ where $(\sigma_i, I_i, \gamma_i, z_i) = \mathcal{D}(\sigma_{i-1})$ for $i \in \{1, \ldots, q_{\mathcal{D}}\}$ and $\sigma_0 = 0$.

We now explain the reason for explicitly requiring $\mathcal{D}$ to output the entropy estimate γ_j used in (3). Most complex PRNGs, including the Linux PRNG, are worried about the situation where the system might enter a prolonged state where no new entropy is inserted in the system. Correspondingly, such PRNGs typically include some ad hoc *entropy estimation procedure* E whose goal is to block the PRNG from outputting output value R_j until the state has not accumulated enough entropy γ^* (for some entropy threshold γ^*). Unfortunately, it is well-known that even approximating the entropy of a given distribution is a computationally hard problem [18]. This means that if we require our PRNG $\mathcal{G}$ to explicitly come up with such a procedure E, we are bound to either place some significant restrictions (or assumptions) on $\mathcal{D}$, or rely on some hoc and non standard assumptions. Indeed, as part of these work we will demonstrate some attacks on the entropy estimation of the Linux PRNG, illustrating how hard (or, perhaps, impossible?) it is to design a sound entropy estimation procedure E. Finally, we observe that the design of E is anyway completely *independent* of the mathematics of the actual refresh and next procedures, meaning that the latter can and *should* be evaluated independently of the "accuracy" of E.

Motivated by these considerations, we do not insist on any "entropy estimation" procedure as a mandatory part

[1]Since conditional min-entropy is defined in the worst-case manner in (1), the value γ_j in the bound below should not be viewed as a random variable, but rather as an arbitrary fixing of this random variable.

of the PRNG design, allowing us to elegantly side-step the practical and theoretical impossibility of sound entropy estimation. Instead, we chose to place the burden of entropy estimations on $\mathcal{D}$ *itself*, which allows us to concentrate on the *provable* security of the refresh and next procedures. In particular, in our security definition we will not attempt to verify if $\mathcal{D}$'s claims are accurate (as we said, this appears hopeless without some kind of heuristics), but will only require security when $\mathcal{D}$ is *legitimate*, as defined in (3). Equivalently, we can think that the entropy estimations γ_j come from the entropy estimation procedure E (which is now "merged" with $\mathcal{D}$), but only provide security assuming that E is correct in this estimation (which we know is hard in practice, and motivates future work in this direction).

However, we stress that: (a) the entropy estimates γ_j will only be used in our security definitions, but not in any of the actual PRNG operations (which will only use the "input part" I returned by $\mathcal{D}$); (b) we do not insist that a legitimate $\mathcal{D}$ can perfectly estimate the fresh entropy of its next sample I_j, but only provide a *lower bound* γ_j that $\mathcal{D}$ is "comfortable" with. For example, $\mathcal{D}$ is free to set $\gamma_j = 0$ as many times as it wants and, in this case, can even choose to leak the entire I_j to $\mathcal{A}$ via the leakage z_j![2] More generally, we allow $\mathcal{D}$ to inject new entropy γ_j as slowly (and maliciously!) as it wants, but will only require security when the counter c keeping track of the current "fresh" entropy in the system[3] crosses some entropy threshold γ^* (since otherwise $\mathcal{D}$ gave us "no reason" to expect any security).

3.2 Security Notions

In the literature, four security notions for a PRNG with input have been proposed: *resilience* (RES), *forward security* (FWD), *backward security* (BWD) and *robustness* (ROB), with the latter being the strongest notion among them. We now define the analogs of this notions in our stronger adversarial model, later comparing our modeling with the prior modeling of [1]. Each of the games below is parametrized by some parameter γ^* which is part of the claimed PRNG security, and intuitively measures the minimal "fresh" entropy in the system when security should be expected. In particular, minimizing the value of γ^* corresponds to a stronger security guarantee.

All four security games (RES(γ^*), FWD(γ^*), BWD(γ^*), ROB(γ^*)) are described using the game playing framework discussed earlier, and share the same initialize and finalize procedures in Figure 1 below. As we mentioned, our overall adversary is modeled via a pair of adversaries $(\mathcal{A}, \mathcal{D})$, where $\mathcal{A}$ is the actual attacker and $\mathcal{D}$ is a stateful distribution sampler. We already discussed the distribution sampler $\mathcal{D}$, so we turn to the attacker $\mathcal{A}$, whose goal is to guess the correct value b picked in the initialize procedure, which also returns to $\mathcal{A}$ the public value seed, and initializes several important variables: corruption flag corrupt, "fresh entropy counter" c, state S and sampler's $\mathcal{D}$ initial state σ.[4] In each of the games (RES, FWD, BWD, ROB), $\mathcal{A}$ has access to several oracles depicted in depicted in Figure 2. We briefly discuss these oracles:

$\mathcal{D}$-refresh. This is the key procedure where the distribution sampler $\mathcal{D}$ is run, and where its output I is used to refreshed the current state S. Additionally, one adds the amount of fresh entropy γ to the entropy counter c, and resets the corrupt flag to false when c crosses the threshold γ^*. The values of γ and the leakage z are also returned to $\mathcal{A}$. We denote by $q_{\mathcal{D}}$ the number of times $\mathcal{A}$ calls $\mathcal{D}$-refresh (and, hence, $\mathcal{D}$), and notice that by our convention (of including oracle calls into run-time calculations) the total run-time of $\mathcal{D}$ is implicitly upper bounded by the run-time of $\mathcal{A}$.

next-ror/get-next. These procedures provide $\mathcal{A}$ with either the real-or-random challenge (provided corrupt = false) or the true PRNG output. As a small subtlety, a "premature" call to get-next before corrupt = false resets the counter c to 0, since then $\mathcal{A}$ might learn something non-trivial about the (low-entropy) state S in this case.[5] We denote by q_R the total number of calls to next-ror and get-next.

get-state/set-state. These procedures provide $\mathcal{A}$ with the ability to either learn the current state S, or set it to any value S^*. In either case c is reset to 0 and corrupt is set to true. We denote by q_S the total number of calls to get-state and set-state.

We can now define the corresponding security notions for PRNGs with input. For convenience, in the sequel we sometime denote the "resources" of $\mathcal{A}$ by $T = (t, q_{\mathcal{D}}, q_R, q_S)$.

DEFINITION (***Security of PRNG with input***) A pseudorandom number generator with input $\mathcal{G}$ = (setup, refresh, next) is called $(T = (t, q_{\mathcal{D}}, q_R, q_S), \gamma^*, \varepsilon)$*-robust (resp. resilient, forward-secure, backward-secure)*, if for any adversary $\mathcal{A}$ running in time at most t, making at most $q_{\mathcal{D}}$ calls to $\mathcal{D}$-refresh, q_R calls to next-ror/get-next and q_S calls to get-state/set-state, and any legitimate distribution sampler $\mathcal{D}$ inside the $\mathcal{D}$-refresh procedure, the advantage of $\mathcal{A}$ in game ROB(γ^*) (resp. RES(γ^*), FWD(γ^*), BWD(γ^*)) is at most ε, where:

- ROB(γ^*) is the unrestricted game where $\mathcal{A}$ is allowed to make the above calls.
- RES(γ^*) is the restricted game where $\mathcal{A}$ makes no calls to get-state/set-state (i.e., $q_S = 0$).
- FWD(γ^*) is the restricted game where $\mathcal{A}$ makes no calls to set-state and a single call to get-state (i.e., $q_S = 1$) which is the very last oracle call $\mathcal{A}$ is allowed to make.
- BWD(γ^*) is the restricted game where $\mathcal{A}$ makes no calls to get-state and a single call to set-state (i.e., q_S = 1) which is the very first oracle call $\mathcal{A}$ is allowed to make.

Intuitively, (a) resilience protects the security of the PRNG when not corrupted against arbitrary distribution samplers $\mathcal{D}$, (b) forward security protects past PRNG outputs in case the state S gets compromised, (c) backward security security ensures that the PRNG can successfully recover from state compromise, provided enough fresh entropy is injected into the system, (d) robustness ensures arbitrary combination of the above. Hence, robustness is the strongest and

[2]Jumping ahead, setting $\gamma_j = 0$ corresponds to the bad-refresh(I_j) oracle in the earlier modeling of [1], which is not explicitly provided in our model.

[3]Intuitively, "fresh" refers to the new entropy in the system since the last state compromise.

[4]With a slight loss of generality, we assume that when S is random it is safe to set the corruption flag corrupt to false.

[5]We could slightly strengthen our definition, by only reducing c by ℓ bits in this case, but chose to go for a more conservative notion.

```
proc. initialize
seed ←$ setup; σ ← 0; S ←$ {0,1}^n; c ← n; corrupt ← false; b ←$ {0,1}
OUTPUT seed

proc. finalize(b*)
IF b = b* RETURN 1
ELSE RETURN 0
```

Figure 1: Procedures initialize **and** finalize **for** $\mathcal{G} = $ (setup, refresh, next)

```
proc. D-refresh
(σ, I, γ, z) ←$ D(σ)
S ← refresh(S, I)
c ← c + γ
IF c ≥ γ*,
    corrupt ← false
OUTPUT (γ, z)

proc. next-ror
(S, R_0) ← next(S)
R_1 ←$ {0,1}^ℓ
IF corrupt = true,
    c ← 0
    RETURN R_0
ELSE OUTPUT R_b

proc. get-next
(S, R) ← next(S)
IF corrupt = true,
    c ← 0
OUTPUT R

proc. get-state
c ← 0, corrupt ← true
OUTPUT S

proc. set-state(S*)
c ← 0, corrupt ← true
S ← S*
```

Figure 2: Procedures in games RES(γ^*), FWD(γ^*), BWD(γ^*), ROB(γ^*) **for** $\mathcal{G} = $ (setup, refresh, next)

the resilience is the weakest of the above four notions. In particular, all our provable constructions will satisfy the robustness notion, but we will use the weaker notions to better pinpoint some of our attacks.

3.3 Comparison to Barak-Halevi Model

Barak-Halevi Construction. We briefly recall the elegant construction of PRNG with input due to Barak and Halevi [1], since it will help us illustrate the key new elements (and some of the definitional choices) of our new model. This construction (which we call BH) involves a randomness extraction function Extract : $\{0,1\}^p \longrightarrow \{0,1\}^n$ and a standard deterministic PRG $\mathbf{G} : \{0,1\}^n \longrightarrow \{0,1\}^{n+\ell}$. As we explain below, the modeling of [1] did not have an explicit setup algorithm, and the refresh and next algorithms are given below:

- refresh$(S, I) = \mathbf{G}'(S \oplus \text{Extract}(I))$
- next$(S) = \mathbf{G}(S)$

Above $\mathbf{G}'$ denotes the truncation of $\mathbf{G}$ to the first n output bits. However, as we explain later, we will also consider the "simplified BH" construction, where $\mathbf{G}'$ is simply the identity function (i.e., refresh$(S, I) = S \oplus \text{Extract}(I)$).

Entropy Accumulation. Barak and Halevi proved the robustness of this construction in a model very similar to ours (indeed, their model was the inspiration for this work), but with several important differences. The most crucial such difference involves the modeling of the inputs I_j which are fed to the refresh procedure. Unlike our modeling, where the choice of such inputs and *their "fresh entropies"* γ_j is completely left to the distribution sampler $\mathcal{D}$ (via the $\mathcal{D}$-refresh procedure), the BH modeling only considered the following two extremes of our model. The attacker could either call the good-refresh procedure, which must produce an input I of *fresh entropy* γ *higher than the entropy threshold* γ^*, or call the bad-refresh procedure with an arbitrary, maliciously specified input I^*. Informally, the call to bad-refresh should not compromise the PRNG security whenever the compromised flag corrupt = false, while the call to good-refresh should result in an immediate "recovery", and always resets corrupt = true.

Hence, our key conceptual strengthening of the work of [1] will require security even if the entropy is accumulated slowly (and maliciously!), as opposed to in "one shot" (or "delayed" by calls to bad-refresh). Namely, we insist that a good PRNG with input should be able to recover from compromise as long as the *total* amount of fresh entropy accumulated over some *potentially long* period time crosses the threshold γ^*, instead of insisting that there must be *one* very high-entropy sample to aid the recovery. We informally term this new required property of PRNGs with input (which is very closely related to our formal notion of backward security) *entropy accumulation*, and notice that practical PRNGs, such a the Linux PRNG, seem to place a lot of (heuristic) effort in trying to achieve this property.

Unfortunately, we will show that the *BH construction is not entropy accumulating*, in general. Hence, their construction does not necessarily meet our stronger notion of robustness (or even backward security). Before presenting our attack on the BH construction, though, we discuss some other less critical differences between our models, since they will also help to simplify our presentation of the attack.

Entropy Estimates. Related to the above, [1] did not require $\mathcal{D}$ to explicitly output the entropy estimate γ. As we mentioned, though, this was replaced by the implicit requirement that the call to good-refresh must produce an input I with fresh entropy $\gamma \geq \gamma^*$. In contrast, our explicit modeling (justified in detail in Section 3.1) allows us to meaningfully formalize the notion of "entropy accumulation", by keeping a well defined fresh entropy counter c, and resetting corrupt = false when $c \geq \gamma^*$.

Importance of setup. As we mentioned, the modeling of [1] did not have an explicit setup algorithm to initialize public parameters seed. Instead, they assumed that the required randomness extractor Extract in their construction is good enough to extract nearly ideal randomness from any high-entropy distribution I output by the good-refresh procedure. Ideally, we would like to make no other assumptions about I except its min-entropy. Unfortunately, it is well known that no deterministic extractor is capable to simultaneously extract good randomness from *all* efficiently samplable high-entropy distributions (e.g., consider nearly full entropy distribution I which is random, except the first bit of Extract(I) is 0). This leaves us with two options. The first option, which seemed to be the preferred choice by [1], is to restrict the family of permitted high-entropy distributions I. While following this option is theoretically possible in our model as well, we find it to be somewhat restrictive and cumbersome to define, since we would like to allow our distribution sampler to output "variable-length" high-entropy distributions, where entropy might be accumulated very slowly over time.

Instead, we chose to follow the second option, which is much more universally accepted in the randomness extractor literature [17]: to assume the existence of the setup procedure which will output some public parameters seed which could be used by the procedures next and refresh. Applied to the construction of [1], for example, this will allow one to consider a *seeded* extractor Extract inside their next procedure, which can now extract entropy from *all* high-entropy distributions (see the resulting definition of seeded (k, ε)-extractors in Section 2). As a warning, this nice extra generality comes at a price that the public parameter seed is not passed to the distribution sampler $\mathcal{D}$, since otherwise $\mathcal{D}$ can still produce high-entropy (but adversarial) samples I such that next(refresh($0^n, I$)) always starts with a 0 bit. Although slightly restrictive, this elegantly side-steps the impossibility result above, while accurately modeling many real-life situations, where it is unreasonable to assume that the "nature" $\mathcal{D}$ would somehow bias its samples I depending on some random parameter seed chosen inside the initialization procedure.

State Pseudorandomness. Barak and Halevi [1] also insisted that the state S is indistinguishable from random once corrupt = false. While true in their specific construction (analyzed in their weaker model), we think that demanding this property is simultaneously too restrictive and also not very well motivated. For example, imagine a PRNG where the state S includes a (never random) Boolean flag which keeps track if the last PRNG call was made to the next procedure. We see a potential efficiency benefit gained by keeping such a flag (e.g., to speed up the subsequent next procedure when the flag is true), but see no reason why storing such a harmless flag makes such this PRNG design "insecure". In fact, our main construction in Section 4 also will not satisfy this property the very moment corrupt = false, but will only make S pseudorandom when the first call to next is made (which is the only thing that matters at the end).

In particular, looking at the analysis of [1], the (truncated) PRG $\mathbf{G}'$ inside the refresh procedure is only needed to ensure the state pseudorandomness of their construction. In other words, if one drops (only the) state pseudorandomness from the BH model, *the "simplified BH" construction is already robust in their model.* Motivated by this, we first give a very strong attack on the simplified BH construction in our stronger model, for *any* extractor Extract and PRG $\mathbf{G}$. This already illustrates the main difference between our models in terms of entropy accumulation. Then we show a more artificial (but still valid) attack on the "full BH" construction.

Attack on Simplified BH. Consider the following very simply simple distribution sampler $\mathcal{D}$. At any time period, it simply sets $I = \alpha^p$ for a fresh and random bit α, and also sets entropy estimate $\gamma = 1$ and leakage $z = \emptyset$. Clearly, $\mathcal{D}$ is legitimate. Hence, for any entropy threshold γ^*, the simplified BH construction must regain security after γ^* calls to the $\mathcal{D}$-refresh procedure following a state compromise. Now consider the following simple attacker $\mathcal{A}$ attacking the backward security (and, thus, robustness) of the simplified BH construction. It calls set-state(0^n), and then makes γ^* calls to $\mathcal{D}$-refresh followed by many calls to next-ror. Let us denote the value of the state S after j calls to $\mathcal{D}$-refresh by S_j, and let $Y(0) = \text{Extract}(0^p)$, $Y(1) = \text{Extract}(1^p)$. Then, recalling that refresh$(S, I) = S \oplus \text{Extract}(I)$ and $S_0 = 0^n$, we see that $S_j = Y(\alpha_1) \oplus \ldots Y(\alpha_j)$, where $\alpha_1 \ldots \alpha_j$ are random and independent bits. In particular, at any point of time there are only two possible values for S_j: if j is even, then $S_j \in \{0^n, Y(0) \oplus Y(1)\}$, and, if j is odd, then $S_j \in \{Y(0), Y(1)\}$. In other words, despite receiving γ^* random and independent bits from $\mathcal{D}$, the refresh procedure failed to accumulate more than 1 bit of entropy in the final state $S^* = S_{\gamma^*}$. In particular, after γ^* calls to $\mathcal{D}$-refresh, $\mathcal{A}$ can simply try both possibilities for S^* and easily distinguish real from random outputs with advantage arbitrarily close to 1 (by making enough calls to next-ror).

This shows that the simplified BH construction is *never* backward secure, despite being robust (modulo state pseudorandomness) in the model of [1].

Attack on "Full" BH. The above attack does not immediately extend to the full BH construction, due to the presence of the truncated PRG $\mathbf{G}'$. Instead, we show a less general attack for some (rather than any) extractor Extract and PRG $\mathbf{G}$. For Extract, we simply take any good extractor (possibly seeded) where $\text{Extract}(0^p) = \text{Extract}(1^p) = 0^n$. Such an extractor exists, since we can take any other initial extractor Extract$'$, and simply modify it on inputs 0^p and 1^p, as above, without much affecting its extraction properties on *high-entropy* distributions I. By the same argument, we can take any good PRG $\mathbf{G}$ where $\mathbf{G}(0^n) = 0^{n+\ell}$, which means that $\mathbf{G}'(0^n) = 0^n$.

With these (valid but artificial) choices of Extract and $\mathbf{G}$, we can keep the same distribution sampler $\mathcal{D}$ and the attacker $\mathcal{A}$ as in the simplified BH example. Now, however, we observe that the state S always remains equal to 0^n, irrespective of whether is it updated with $I = 0^p$ or $I = 1^p$, since the new state $S' = \mathbf{G}'(S \oplus \text{Extract}(I)) = \mathbf{G}'(0^n \oplus 0^n) = 0^n = S$. In other words, we have not gained even a single bit of entropy into S, which clearly breaks backward security in this case as well!

One may wonder if we can have a less obvious attack for any Extract and $\mathbf{G}$, much like in the simplified BH case. This turns out to be an interesting and rather non-trivial question. Indeed, the value of the state S_j after j calls to $\mathcal{D}$-refresh with inputs $I_1 \ldots I_j$ is equal to the "CBC-MAC" computation, with input $\vec{Y} = (Y_1 \ldots Y_j)$ and the initial value S_0, where $Y_j = \text{Extract}(I_j)$:

$$S_j = \mathbf{G}'(Y_j \oplus \mathbf{G}'(Y_{j-1} \ldots \oplus \mathbf{G}'(Y_1 \oplus S_0) \ldots))$$

Moreover, we only care about the case when $\mathbf{H}_\infty(\vec{I}) \geq \gamma^*$, which, under appropriate assumptions on Extract, would translate to a high-entropy guarantee on $\vec{Y}$. In this case, it is tempting to use the work of [6], who showed that the CBC-MAC is a good randomness extractor on high-entropy inputs $\vec{Y}$, provided that the truncated PRG $\mathbf{G}'$ is modeled as a random *permutation.* This result gives us hope that the full BH construction might be secure in our model, possibly under strong enough assumptions on the PRG $\mathbf{G}$ and/or the extractor Extract. Unfortunately, aside from assuming that $\mathbf{G}'$ is (close to) a random permutation, we cannot directly use the results of [6], since the initial state S_0 could be set by $\mathcal{A}$ in a way correlated with the inputs Y_j, as well as the "block cipher" $\mathbf{G}'$ (which invalidates the analysis of [6]).

Instead of following this interesting, but rather speculative direction, below we give an almost equally simple construction which is *provably robust* in the standard model, without any idealized assumptions.

3.4 Simpler Notions of PRNG Security

We define two properties of a PRNG with input which are intuitively simpler to analyze than the full robustness security. We show that these two properties, taken together, imply robustness.

Recovering Security. We define a notion of *recovering security.* It considers an attacker that compromises the state to some arbitrary value S_0. Following that, sufficiently many $\mathcal{D}$-refresh calls with sufficient entropy are made so as to set the corrupt flag to false and resulting in some updated state S. Then the output $(S^*, R) \leftarrow \mathsf{next}(S)$ looks indistinguishable from uniform. The formal definition is slightly more complicated since the attacker also gets to adaptively choose *when* to start using $\mathcal{D}$-refresh calls to update the state. Formally, we consider the following security game with an attacker $\mathcal{A}$, a sampler $\mathcal{D}$, and bounds $q_\mathcal{D}, \gamma^*$.

- The challenge chooses a seed $\mathsf{seed} \xleftarrow{\$} \mathsf{setup}$, and a bit $b \xleftarrow{\$} \{0,1\}$ uniformly at random. It sets $\sigma_0 := 0$. For $k = 1, \ldots, q_\mathcal{D}$, the challenger computes
$$(\sigma_k, I_k, \gamma_k, z_k) \leftarrow \mathcal{D}(\sigma_{k-1}).$$
- The attacker $\mathcal{A}$ gets seed and $\gamma_1, \ldots, \gamma_{q_\mathcal{D}}, z_1, \ldots z_{q_\mathcal{D}}$. It gets access to an oracle get-refresh() which initially sets $k := 0$ on each invocation increments $k := k + 1$ and outputs I_k. At some point the attacker $\mathcal{A}$ outputs a value $S_0 \in \{0,1\}^n$ and an integer d such that $k + d \leq q_\mathcal{D}$ and $\sum_{j=k+1}^{k+d} \gamma_j \geq \gamma^*$.
- For $j = 1, \ldots, d$, the challenger computes
$$S_j := \mathsf{refresh}(S_{j-1}, I_{k+j}, \mathsf{seed}).$$
If $b = 0$ it sets $(S^*, R) \leftarrow \mathsf{next}(S_d)$ and if $b = 1$ is sets $(S^*, R) \leftarrow \{0,1\}^{n+\ell}$ uniformly at random. The challenger gives $I_{k+d+1}, \ldots, I_{q_\mathcal{D}}$, and (S^*, R) to $\mathcal{A}$.
- The attacker $\mathcal{A}$ outputs a bit b^*.

We define the advantage of the attacker $\mathcal{A}$ and sampler $\mathcal{D}$ in the above game as $|2\Pr[b^* = b] - 1|$.

DEFINITION (***Recovering Security***) A PRNG with input has $(t, q_\mathcal{D}, \gamma^*, \varepsilon)$-*recovering security* if for any attacker $\mathcal{A}$ and legitimate sampler $\mathcal{D}$, both running in time t, the advantage of the above game with parameters $q_\mathcal{D}, \gamma^*$ is at most ε.

Preserving Security. We define a simple notion of *preserving security.* Intuitively, it says that if the state S_0 starts uniformly random and uncompromised, and then is refreshed with arbitrary (adversarial) samples $I_1, \ldots, I_d$ resulting in some final state S_d, then the output $(S^*, R) \leftarrow \mathsf{next}(S_d)$ looks indistinguishable from uniform.

Formally, we consider the following security game with an attacker $\mathcal{A}$.

- The challenger chooses an initial state $S_0 \leftarrow \{0,1\}^n$, a seed $\mathsf{seed} \leftarrow \mathsf{setup}$, and a bit $b \leftarrow \{0,1\}$ uniformly at random.
- $\mathcal{A}$ gets seed and specifies arbitrarily long sequence of values $I_1, \ldots, I_d$ with $I_j \in \{0,1\}^n$ for all $j \in [d]$.
- The challenger sequentially computes
$$S_j = \mathsf{refresh}(S_{j-1}, I_j, \mathsf{seed})$$
for $j = 1, \ldots, d$. If $b = 0$, $\mathcal{A}$ is given $(S^*, R) = \mathsf{next}(S_d)$ and if $b = 1$, $\mathcal{A}$ is given $(S^*, R) \leftarrow \{0,1\}^{n+\ell}$.
- $\mathcal{A}$ outputs a bit b^*.

We define the advantage of the attacker $\mathcal{A}$ in the above game as $|2\Pr[b^* = b] - 1|$.

DEFINITION (***Preserving Security***) A PRNG with input has (t, ε)-*preserving security* if the advantage of any attacker $\mathcal{A}$ running in time t in the above game is at most ε.

We now show that, taken together, recovering and preserving security notions imply the full notion of strong robustness (see Appendix A for proof).

Theorem 2. *If a PRNG with input has both $(t, q_\mathcal{D}, \gamma^*, \varepsilon_r)$-recovering security and (t, ε_p)-preserving security, then it is $((t', q_\mathcal{D}, q_R, q_S), \gamma^*, q_R(\varepsilon_r + \varepsilon_p))$-robust where $t' \approx t$.*

4. PROVABLY SECURE CONSTRUCTION

Let $\mathbf{G} : \{0,1\}^m \to \{0,1\}^{n+\ell}$ be a (deterministic) pseudorandom generator where $m < n$. We use the notation $[y]_1^m$ to denote the first m bits of $y \in \{0,1\}^n$. Our construction of PRNG with input has parameters n (state length), ℓ (output length), and $p = n$ (sample length), and is defined as follows:

- setup(): Output $\mathsf{seed} = (X, X') \leftarrow \{0,1\}^{2n}$.
- $S' = \mathsf{refresh}(S, I)$: Given $\mathsf{seed} = (X, X')$, current state $S \in \{0,1\}^n$, and a sample $I \in \{0,1\}^n$, output: $S' := S \cdot X + I$, where all operations are over $\mathbb{F}_{2^n}$.
- $(S', R) = \mathsf{next}(S)$: Given $\mathsf{seed} = (X, X')$ and a state $S \in \{0,1\}^n$, first compute $U = [X' \cdot S]_1^m$. Then output $(S', R) = \mathbf{G}(U)$.

Notice that we are assuming each input I is in $\{0,1\}^n$. This is without loss of generality: we can take shorter inputs and pad them with 0s, or take longer inputs and break them up into n-bit chunks, calling the refresh procedure iteratively.

On-line Extractor. Let's look at what happens if we start in some state S and call the refresh procedure d-times with the samples $I_{d-1}, \ldots, I_0$ (it will be convenient to index these in reverse order). Then the new state at the end of this process will be
$$S' := S \cdot X^d + I_{d-1} \cdot X^{d-1} + \cdots + I_1 \cdot X + I_0.$$
Let $\bar{I} := (I_{d-1}, \ldots, I_0)$ be the concatenation of all d samples. In the analysis we rely on the fact that the *polynomial evaluation* hash function defined by $h_X(\bar{I}) := \sum_{j=0}^{d-1} I_j \cdot X^j$ is $(d/2^n)$-universal meaning that the probability of any two distinct inputs colliding is at most $d/2^n$ over the random choice of X. In particular, we can think of our refresh procedure as computing this hash function in an *on-line* manner, processing the inputs I_j one-by-one without knowing the total number of future samples d, and keeping only a short local state.[6] In particular, the updated state after the d refreshes is $S' = S \cdot X^d + h_X(\bar{I})$. Unfortunately, $h_X(\cdot)$ is not sufficiently universal to make it a good extractor, and therefore we cannot argue that S' itself is random as long as $\bar{I}$ has entropy. Therefore, we need to apply an additional hash function $h'_{X'}(Y) = [X' \cdot Y]_1^m$ which takes as input $Y \in \{0,1\}^n$ and outputs a value $h_{X'}(T) \in \{0,1\}^m$. We show that the composition function $h^*_{X,X'}(\bar{I}) = h'_{X'}(h_X(\bar{I}))$ is a good randomness extractor. Therefore, during the evaluation of $(S'', R) = \mathsf{next}(S')$, the value
$$U = [X' \cdot S']_1^m = [X' \cdot S \cdot X^d]_1^m + h^*_{X,X'}(\bar{I})$$

[6]The fact that polynomial evaluation can be computed in such on-line manner is called Horner's method. It has countless applications in algorithm design and many areas of computer science.

is uniformly random as long as the refreshes $\bar{I}$ jointly have sufficient entropy. This is the main idea behind our construction. We formalize this via the following lemma, which provides the key to proving our main theorem.

Lemma 3. *Let d, n, m be integers, let $X, X', Y \in \mathbb{F}_{2^n}$, $\bar{I} = (I_{d-1}, \ldots, I_0) \in \mathbb{F}_{2^n}^d$. Define the hash function families:*

$$h_X(\bar{I}) := \sum_{j=0}^{d-1} I_j \cdot X^j, \qquad h'_{X'}(Y) := [X' \cdot Y]_1^m.$$

$$h^*_{X,X'}(\bar{I}) := h'_{X'}(h_X(\bar{I})) = \left[X' \cdot \sum_{j=0}^{d-1} I_j \cdot X^j \right]_1^m.$$

Then the hash-family $\mathcal{H} = \{h^*_{X,X'}\}$ is $2^{-m}(1 + d \cdot 2^{m-n})$-universal. In particular it is a (k, ε)-extractor as long as: $k \geq m + 2\log(1/\varepsilon) + 1$ and $n \geq m + 2\log(1/\varepsilon) + \log(d) + 1$.

Proof. For the first part, fix any $\bar{I} = (I_{d-1}, \ldots, I_0) \neq \bar{I}' = (I'_{d-1}, \ldots, I'_0)$: $\Pr_{X,X'}[h^*_{X,X'}(\bar{I}) = h_{X,X'}(\bar{I}')]$ is less than

$$\Pr_X \left[\begin{array}{c} h_X(\bar{I}) \\ = h_X(\bar{I}') \end{array} \right] + \Pr_{X,X'} \left[\begin{array}{c|c} h_{X'}(Y) & Y \neq Y' \\ = h_{X'}(Y') & Y := h_X(\bar{I}), \\ & Y' := h_X(\bar{I}') \end{array} \right]$$

$$\leq \Pr_X \left[\textstyle\sum_{j=0}^{d-1} (I_j - I'_j) \cdot X^j = 0 \right] + 2^{-m}$$

$$\leq d/2^n + 2^{-m} = 2^{-m}(1 + d2^{m-n}).$$

For the second part, we use the fact that $h_{X,X'}$ is $2^{-m}(1+\alpha)$-universal for $\alpha = d \cdot 2^{m-n}$. Hence, it is also a (k, ε)-extractor where $\varepsilon \leq \sqrt{2^{m-k} + \alpha} = \sqrt{2^{m-k} + d2^{m-n}}$ (See Lemma 1). This is ensured by our parameter choice. □

Theorem 4. *Let $n > m, \ell, \gamma^*$ be integers. Assume that $\mathbf{G} : \{0,1\}^m \to \{0,1\}^{n+\ell}$ is a deterministic (t, ε_{prg})-pseudorandom generator. Let $\mathcal{G} = $ (setup, refresh, next) be defined as above. Then $\mathcal{G}$ is a $((t', q_\mathcal{D}, q_R, q_S), \gamma^*, \varepsilon)$-robust PRNG with input where $t' \approx t$, $\varepsilon = q_R(2\varepsilon_{prg} + q_\mathcal{D}^2 \varepsilon_{ext} + 2^{-n+1})$ as long as $\gamma^* \geq m + 2\log(1/\varepsilon_{ext}) + 1, n \geq m + 2\log(1/\varepsilon_{ext}) + \log(q_\mathcal{D}) + 1$.*

The proof is deferred to Appendix A.

Benchmarks. Benchmarks between our contruction and Linux PRNGs are detailled in the full version. They are based on an optimistic hypothesis for Linux PRNGs, and even with this hypothesis, our construction appears to be more efficient: a full internal state recovery is two times faster and a 2048-bits key generation is ten times faster.

5. ANALYSIS OF THE LINUX PRNGS

The Linux operating system contains two PRNGs with input, /dev/random and /dev/urandom. They are part of the kernel and used in the OS security services or some cryptographic libraries. We give a precise description[7] of them in our model as a triple LINUX = (setup, refresh, next) and we prove the following theorem:

Theorem 5. *The Linux PRNGs /dev/random and /dev/urandom are not robust.*

Since the actual generator LINUX does not define any seed (*i.e.* the algorithm setup always outputs $\varnothing$), as mentioned above, it cannot achieve the notion of robustness. However, in Sections 5.4 and 5.6, we additionally mount concrete attacks that would work even if LINUX had used a seed. The attacks exploit two independent weaknesses, in the entropy estimator and the mixing functions, which would need both to be fixed in order to expect the PRNGs to be secure.

[7]All descriptions were done by source code analysis. We refer to version 3.7.8 of the Linux kernel.

5.1 General Overview

Security Parameters. The LINUX PRNG uses parameters $n = 6144$, $\ell = 80$, $p = 96$. The parameter n can be modified (but requires kernel compilation), and the parameters ℓ (size of the output) and p (size of the input) are fixed. The PRNG outputs the requested random numbers by blocks of $\ell = 80$ bits and truncates the last block if needed.

Internal State. The internal state of LINUX PRNG is a triple $S = (S_i, S_u, S_r)$ where $|S_i| = 4096$ bits, $|S_u| = 1024$ bits and $|S_r| = 1024$ bits. New data is collected in S_i, which is named the *input pool*. Output is generated from S_u and S_r which are named the *output pools*. When a call to /dev/urandom is made, data is generated from the pool S_u and when a call to /dev/random is made, data is generated from the pool S_r.

Functions refresh and next. There are two refresh functions, $\mathsf{refresh}_i$ that initializes the internal state and $\mathsf{refresh}_c$ that updates it continuously. There are two next functions, next_u for /dev/urandom and next_r for /dev/random.

Mixing Function. The PRNG uses a *mixing function* M, described in Section 5.5, to mix new data in the input pool and to transfer data between the pools.

Entropy Estimator. The PRNG uses an *entropy estimator*, described in Section 5.3, that estimates the entropy of new inputs and the entropy of the pools. The PRNG uses these estimations to control the transfers between the pools and how new input is collected. This is illustrated in Figure 3 and described in details in Section 5.2. The estimations are named E_i (entropy estimation of S_i), E_u (of S_u), E_r (of S_r).

5.2 Detailled Description

As illustrated in Figure 3, functions refresh and next are controlled by E_i, E_u, E_r. All functions rely on the same built-in function extract_buf that calls the mixing function M, a hash function H (the SHA1 function) and a folding function F defined with $\mathsf{F}(w_0, \cdots, w_4) = (w_0 \oplus w_3, w_1 \oplus w_4, w_{2_{[0\cdots15]}} \oplus w_{2_{[16\cdots31]}})$.

Initial $\mathsf{refresh}_i$. $\mathsf{refresh}_i(0, I) = \mathsf{M}(0, I)$.

Continuous $\mathsf{refresh}_c$. For all I, if $E_i \geq 3584$ input I is ignored (except 1 byte over 4096). When I is used E_i is increased with the estimated entropy of I and $\mathsf{refresh}_c(S, I) = \mathsf{M}(S_i, I)$.

PRNG Output with next_r. If $E_r \geq 8t$, then the output is generated directly from S_r: LINUX first calculates a hash across S_r, then mixes this hash back with S_r, hashes again the output of the mixing function and folds the result in half, giving $R = \mathsf{F} \circ \mathsf{H} \circ \mathsf{M}(S_r, \mathsf{H}(S_r))$ and $S'_r = \mathsf{M}(S_r, \mathsf{H}(S_r))$. This decreases E_r by $8t$ and the new value is $E_r - 8t$. If $E_r < 8t$, then depending on E_i, data is transferred from S_i to S_r. Let $\alpha_r = \min(\min(\max(t, 8), 128), \lfloor E_i/8 \rfloor)$.

- If $\alpha_r \geq 8$, then α_r bytes are transferred between S_i and S_r (so at least 8 bytes and at most 128 bytes are transferred between S_i and S_r, and S_i can contain 0 entropy. The transfer is made in two steps: first LINUX generates from S_i an intermediate data $T_i = \mathsf{F} \circ \mathsf{H} \circ \mathsf{M}(S_i, \mathsf{H}(S_i))$ and then it mixes it with S_r, giving the intermediate states $S'_i = \mathsf{M}(S_i, \mathsf{H}(S_i))$ and $S^*_r = \mathsf{M}(S_r, T_i)$. This decreases E_i by $8\alpha_r$ and increases E_r by $8\alpha_r$. Finally LINUX outputs t bytes from

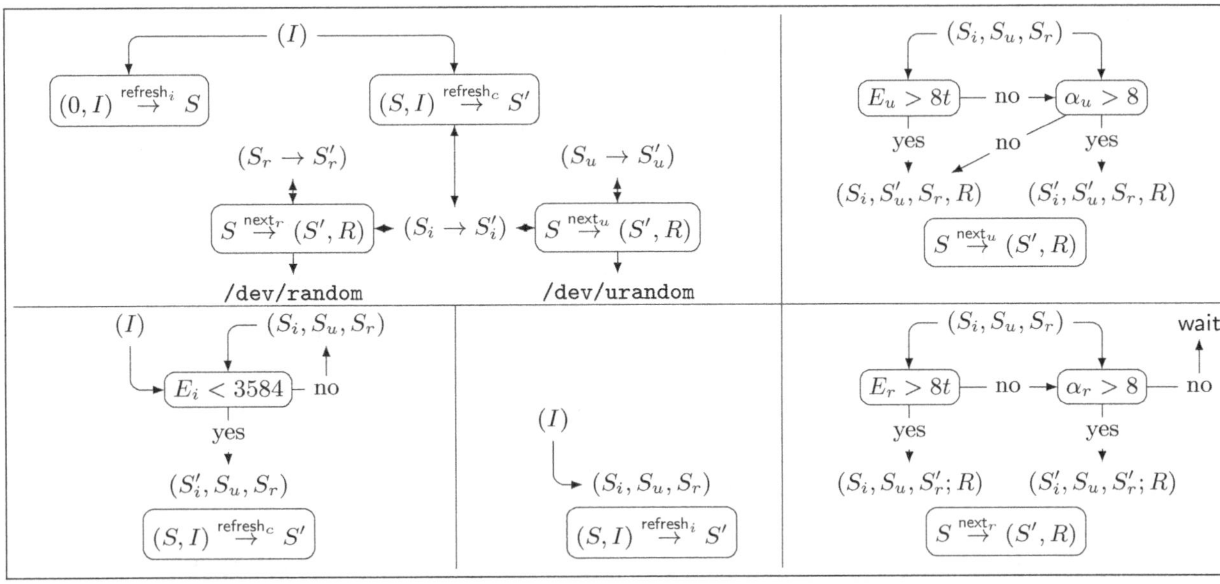

Figure 3: Relations between functions and pools for LINUX

S^*_r, this produces the final states $S'_r = \mathsf{M}(S^*_r, \mathsf{H}(S^*_r))$ and $R = \mathsf{F} \circ \mathsf{H} \circ \mathsf{M}(S^*_r, \mathsf{H}(S^*_r))$. This decreases E_r by $8t$.

- If $\alpha_r < 8$, then LINUX blocks and waits until S_i gets refreshed with I and until $\alpha_r \geq 8$.

PRNG Output with next$_u$. If $E_u \geq 8t$ then LINUX applies the same process as in the non-blocking case, outputs $R = \mathsf{F} \circ \mathsf{H} \circ \mathsf{M}(S_u, \mathsf{H}(S_u)))$ and sets $S'_u = \mathsf{M}(S_u, \mathsf{H}(S_u))$. If $E_u < 8t$ then LINUX behaves differently. Let $\alpha_u = \min(\min(\max(t, 8), 128), \lfloor E_i/8 \rfloor - 16)$:

- If $\alpha_u \geq 8$, the process is the same as in the non-blocking case, but with S_u, E_u and α_u instead of S_r, E_r and α_r.
- If $\alpha_u < 8$, then LINUX outputs the requested bytes from S_u without transferring data from S_i. Hence LINUX behaves as if $E_u \geq 8t$: $R = \mathsf{F} \circ \mathsf{H} \circ \mathsf{M}(S_u, \mathsf{H}(S_u))$, and $S'_u = \mathsf{M}(S_u, \mathsf{H}(S_u))$. This decreases E_u by $8t$ and the new value is 0.

This illustrates the difference between `/dev/urandom` and `/dev/random`: If the estimated entropy of the blocking pool S_r is less than $8t$ and no transfer is done, then `/dev/random` blocks, whereas `/dev/urandom` does never block and outputs the requested t bytes from the non-blocking pool S_u.

5.3 The Entropy Estimator

The entropy estimator is implemented in the built-in function add_timer_randomness which is used for refresh. Entropy is not estimated using input distribution but only using its timing. It calculates differences between timings associated with each event: $t_0, t_1, t_2, \ldots$ are the jiffies of events, $\delta_i = t_i - t_{i-1}$, $\delta^2_i = \delta_i - \delta_{i-1}$, $\delta^3_i = \delta^2_i - \delta^2_{i-1}$. Then, it calculates $\Delta_i = \min(|\delta_i|, |\delta^2_i|, |\delta^3_i|)$ and finally applies a logarithmic function to give the estimated entropy $H_i = 0$ if $\Delta_i < 2$, $H_i = 11$ if $\Delta_i > 2^{12}$, and $H_i = \lfloor \log_2(\Delta_i) \rfloor$ otherwise.

5.4 Attacks Based on the Entropy Estimator

As shown in Appendix B, it is possible to build a distribution $\mathcal{D}_0$ of null entropy for which the estimated entropy is high (*cf.* Lemma 6) and a distribution $\mathcal{D}_1$ of high entropy for which the estimated entropy is null (*cf.* Lemma 7). It is then possible to mount attacks on both `/dev/random` and `/dev/urandom`, which show that these two generators are not robust.

`/dev/random` is not robust. Let us consider an adversary $\mathcal{A}$ against the robustness of `/dev/random`, and thus in the game $\mathsf{ROB}(\gamma^*)$, that makes the following oracle queries: one get-state, several next-ror, several $\mathcal{D}$-refresh and one final next-ror. Then the state (S_i, S_r, S_u), the parameters E_i, E_u, E_r and the counter c defined in $\mathsf{ROB}(\gamma^*)$ evolve the following way:

- get-state: After a state compromise, $\mathcal{A}$ knows all parameters (but needs S_i, S_r, E_i, E_r) and $c = 0$.
- next-ror: After $\lfloor E_i/10 \rfloor + \lfloor E_r/10 \rfloor$ queries to next-ror, $E_i = E_r = 0$, $\mathcal{A}$ knows S_i and S_r and $c = 0$.
- $\mathcal{D}$-refresh: In a first stage, $\mathcal{A}$ refreshes LINUX with input from $\mathcal{D}_0$. After 300 queries, $E_i = 3584$ and $E_r = 0$. $\mathcal{A}$ knows S_i and S_r and $c = 0$.

  In a second stage, $\mathcal{A}$ refreshes LINUX with input $J \overset{\$}{\leftarrow} \mathcal{U}_{128}$. As $E_i = 3584$, these inputs are ignored as long as I contains less than 4096 bytes. After 30 queries, $\mathcal{A}$ knows S_i and S_r and $c = 3840$.
- next-ror: Since $E_r = 0$, a transfer is necessary between S_i and S_r before generating R. Since $E_i = 3584$, then $\alpha_b = 10$, such a transfer happens. But as $\mathcal{A}$ knows S_i and S_u, then $\mathcal{A}$ knows R.

Therefore, in the game $\mathsf{ROB}(\gamma^*)$ with $b = 0$, $\mathcal{A}$ obtains a 10-bytes string in the last next-ror-oracle that is predictable, whereas when $b = 1$, this event occurs only with probability 2^{-80}. It is therefore straightforward for $\mathcal{A}$ to distinguish the real and the ideal world.

`/dev/urandom` is not robust. Similarly, let us consider an adversary $\mathcal{A}$ against the robustness of `/dev/urandom` in the game $\mathsf{ROB}(\gamma^*)$ that makes the following oracle queries: one get-state that allows it to know S_i, S_u, E_i, E_u; $\lfloor E_i/10 \rfloor + \lfloor E_u/10 \rfloor$ next-ror, making $E_i = E_u = 0$; 100 $\mathcal{D}$-refresh with $\mathcal{D}_1$; and one next-ror, so that R will only rely on S_r as no transfer is done between S_i and S_u since $E_i = 0$. Then $\mathcal{A}$ is able to generate a predictable output R and to distinguish the real and the ideal worlds in $\mathsf{ROB}(\gamma^*)$.

5.5 The Mixing Function

The Mixing function M is the core of LINUX PRNG. It is implemented in the built-in function mix_pool_bytes. We give a complete description of M as it is used for refresh, its description for next differs only from internal parameters. It takes as input I of size one byte, the input pool S_i, considered as 128 32-bits words $S_0, \ldots, S_{127}$. It mixes I with 7 words of S_i (selected with an index k) and replaces one word of S_i with the result. Another index d defines a word rotation. In details:

- The byte I is converted into a 32-bit word, using standard C implicit cast, and rotated by d bits. At initialization, $d = 0$, and for each M call, if $k = 0 \bmod 128$ then $d = d + 14 \bmod 32$ else $d = d + 7 \bmod 32$.
- The obtained word is xor-ed with $S_{k+j \bmod 128}$ for $j \in \{0, 1, 25, 51, 76, 103\}$[8].
- The obtained word is mixed with a built-in *twist table* that is the binary representations of $\{0, \alpha^{32*j}\}, j = 1, \ldots 7$ in the field $(\mathbb{F}_2)/(Q)$, where $Q(x)$ is the CRC32 polynom[9] used for Ethernet protocol [13]. Denoting the primitive element α, this is described as $W \rightarrow W.\alpha^3 + \mathsf{R}(\mathsf{Q}(W, \alpha^{29}).\alpha^{32}, Q)$, where $\mathsf{Q}(A, B)$ is the quotient and $\mathsf{R}(A, B)$) the remainder in division A/B.
- Then S_k is replaced by the last word and $k = k + 1$.

5.6 Attack Based on the Mixing Function

In [14], a proof of state entropy preservation is given for one iteration of the mixing function M, assuming that the input and the internal state are independent: $\mathbf{H}_\infty(\mathsf{M}(S, I)) \geq \mathbf{H}_\infty(S)$ and $\mathbf{H}_\infty(\mathsf{M}(S, I)) \geq \mathbf{H}_\infty(I)$. Indeed, without independence and with more than one iteration of M, LINUX does not recover from state compromise. This contradicts the backward security and therefore the robustness.

LINUX is not backward secure. As shown in Appendix B, with Lemma 8, it is possible to build an input distribution $\mathcal{D}_2$ with arbitrary high entropy such that, after several $\mathcal{D}$-refresh, $\mathbf{H}_\infty(S) = 1$. Let us consider an adversary $\mathcal{A}$ that generates an input of distribution $\mathcal{D}_2$, and that makes the following oracle queries: set-refresh, γ^* calls to $\mathcal{D}$-refresh and many calls to next-ror. Then the state (S_i, S_r, S_u), the parameters E_i, E_u, E_r, k, d and the counter c of $\mathsf{BWD}(\gamma^*)$ evolve the following way:

- set-refresh: $\mathcal{A}$ sets $S_i = 0$, $S_r = S_u = 0$, $d = 0$, $k = 127$, and $c = 0$.
- $\mathcal{D}$-refresh: $\mathcal{A}$ refreshes LINUX with $\mathcal{D}_2$. After γ^* oracle queries, until $c \geq \gamma^*$, $\mathbf{H}_\infty(S) = 1$.
- next-ror: Since $\mathbf{H}_\infty(S) = 1$, $\mathbf{H}_\infty(R) = 1$.

Therefore, in the game $\mathsf{BWD}(\gamma^*)$ with $b = 0$, $\mathcal{A}$ always obtains an output in the last next-ror query with $\mathbf{H}_\infty(R) = 1$, whereas in $b = 1$, this event occurs only with negligible probability. It is therefore straightforward for $\mathcal{A}$ to distinguish the real and the ideal world.

6. CONCLUSION

We have proposed a new property for PRNG with input, that captures how it should accumulate entropy into the internal state. This property actually expresses the real expected behavior of a PRNG after a state compromise, where it is expected that the PRNG quickly recovers enough entropy. We gave a precise assessment of the Linux PRNGs `/dev/random` and `/dev/urandom`. We proved that these PRNGs do not achieve this property, due to the behavior of their *entropy estimator* and their *mixing function*. As pointed by Barak and Halevi [1], who advise against using run-time entropy estimation, our attacks are due to its use when data is transferred between pools in Linux PRNG. We therefore recommend that the functions of a PRNG do not rely on such an estimator.

Finally, we proposed a construction that meets our new property in the standard model and we showed that it is noticeably more efficient than the Linux PRNGs. Thus, from the perspective of speed and provable security, our construction appears vastly superior to Linux PRNGs. We therefore recommend to use this construction whenever a PRNG with input is used for cryptography.

[8]Similarly, the words chosen from S_r and S_u will be $S_{k+j \bmod 32}$ for $j \in \{0, 1, 7, 14, 20, 26\}$.

[9]$Q(x) = x^{32} + x^{26} + x^{23} + x^{22} + x^{16} + x^{12} + x^{11} + x^{10} + x^8 + x^7 + x^5 + x^4 + x^2 + x + 1$.

7. ACKNOWLEDGMENTS

Yevgeniy Dodis' research was partially supported by the gift from VMware Labs and NSF grants 1319051, 1314568, 1065288, 1017471. Damien Vergnaud's research was supported in part by the French ANR-12-JS02-0004 ROMAnTIC Project. Daniel Wichs's research was partially supported by NSF grant 1314722.

8. REFERENCES

[1] BARAK, B., AND HALEVI, S. A model and architecture for pseudo-random generation with applications to /dev/random. In *ACM CCS 05: 12th Conference on Computer and Communications Security* (Nov. 2005), V. Atluri, C. Meadows, and A. Juels, Eds., ACM Press, pp. 203–212.

[2] BARKER, E., AND KELSEY, J. Recommendation for random number generation using deterministic random bit generators. NIST Special Publication 800-90A, 2012.

[3] BELLARE, M., AND ROGAWAY, P. The security of triple encryption and a framework for code-based game-playing proofs. In *Advances in Cryptology – EUROCRYPT 2006* (May / June 2006), S. Vaudenay, Ed., vol. 4004 of *Lecture Notes in Computer Science*, Springer, pp. 409–426.

[4] CVE-2008-0166. Common Vulnerabilities and Exposures, 2008.

[5] DESAI, A., HEVIA, A., AND YIN, Y. L. A practice-oriented treatment of pseudorandom number generators. In *Advances in Cryptology – EUROCRYPT 2002* (Apr. / May 2002), L. R. Knudsen, Ed., vol. 2332 of *Lecture Notes in Computer Science*, Springer, pp. 368–383.

[6] DODIS, Y., GENNARO, R., HÅSTAD, J., KRAWCZYK, H., AND RABIN, T. Randomness extraction and key derivation using the CBC, cascade and HMAC modes. In *Advances in Cryptology – CRYPTO 2004* (Aug. 2004), M. Franklin, Ed., vol. 3152 of *Lecture Notes in Computer Science*, Springer, pp. 494–510.

[7] EASTLAKE, D., SCHILLER, J., AND CROCKER, S. *RFC 4086 - Randomness Requirements for Security*, June 2005.

[8] GUTTERMAN, Z., PINKAS, B., AND REINMAN, T. Analysis of the linux random number generator. In *2006 IEEE Symposium on Security and Privacy* (May 2006), IEEE Computer Society Press, pp. 371–385.

[9] HENINGER, N., DURUMERIC, Z., WUSTROW, E., AND HALDERMAN, J. A. Mining your Ps and Qs: Detection of widespread weak keys in network devices. In *Proceedings of the 21st USENIX Security Symposium* (Aug. 2012).

[10] Information technology - Security techniques - Random bit generation. ISO/IEC18031:2011, 2011.

[11] KELSEY, J., SCHNEIER, B., WAGNER, D., AND HALL, C. Cryptanalytic attacks on pseudorandom number generators. In *Fast Software Encryption – FSE'98* (Mar. 1998), S. Vaudenay, Ed., vol. 1372 of *Lecture Notes in Computer Science*, Springer, pp. 168–188.

[12] KILLMANN, W. AND SCHINDLER, W. A proposal for: Functionality classes for random number generators. AIS 20 / AIS31, 2011.

[13] KOOPMAN, P. 32-bit cyclic redundancy codes for internet applications. In *Proceedings of the 2002 International Conference on Dependable Systems and Networks* (Washington, DC, USA, 2002), DSN '02, IEEE Computer Society, pp. 459–472.

[14] LACHARME, P., ROCK, A., STRUBEL, V., AND VIDEAU, M. The linux pseudorandom number generator revisited. Cryptology ePrint Archive, Report 2012/251, 2012.

[15] LENSTRA, A. K., HUGHES, J. P., AUGIER, M., BOS, J. W., KLEINJUNG, T., AND WACHTER, C. Public keys. In *Advances in Cryptology – CRYPTO 2012* (Aug. 2012), R. Safavi-Naini and R. Canetti, Eds., vol. 7417 of *Lecture Notes in Computer Science*, Springer, pp. 626–642.

[16] NGUYEN, P. Q., AND SHPARLINSKI, I. The insecurity of the digital signature algorithm with partially known nonces. *Journal of Cryptology 15*, 3 (2002), 151–176.

[17] NISAN, N., AND ZUCKERMAN, D. Randomness is linear in space. *J. Comput. Syst. Sci. 52*, 1 (1996), 43–52.

[18] SAHAI, A., AND VADHAN, S. P. A complete problem for statistical zero knowledge. *J. ACM 50*, 2 (2003), 196–249.

[19] SHOUP, V. *A computational introduction to number theory and algebra.* Cambridge University Press, 2006.

APPENDIX

A. PROOFS FOR STANDARD-MODEL PRNG

A.1 Proof of Theorem 2

We will refer to the attacker's queries to either the get-next or next-ror oracle in the robustness game as "next queries". We assume that the attacker makes exactly q_R of them. We say that a next query is *uncompromised* if corrupt = false during the query, and we say it is *compromised* otherwise. Without loss of generality, we will assume that all compromised next queries that the attacker makes are to get-next and *not* next-ror (since next-ror does not do/output anything when corrupt = true).

We partition the uncompromised next queries into two subcategories: *preserving* and *recovering*. We say that an uncompromised next query is *preserving* if the corrupt flag remained set to false throughout the entire period between the previous next query (if there is one) and the current one. Otherwise, we say that an uncompromised next query is *recovering*. With any recovering next query, we can associate a corresponding *most recent entropy drain (mRED)* query which is the most recent query to either get-state, set-state, get-next that precedes the current next query. An mRED query must set the cumulative entropy estimate to $c = 0$. Moreover, with any recovering next query, we associate a corresponding sequence of *recovering samples* $\bar{I} = (I_j, \ldots, I_{j+d-1})$ which are output by all the calls to the $\mathcal{D}$-refresh oracle that precede the recovering next query, but follow the associated mRED query. It is easy to see that any such sequence of recovering samples $\bar{I}$ must satisfy the entropy requirements $\sum_{i=j}^{j+d-1} \gamma_i \geq \gamma^*$ where the ith call to $\mathcal{D}$-refresh oracle outputs (I_i, γ_i, z_i).

We define several hybrid games. Let **Game** 0 be the real-or-random security game as defined in Figure 2. Let **Game** i be a modification of this game where, for the first i next queries, if the query is *uncompromised*, then the challenger *always* chooses $(S, R) \leftarrow \{0,1\}^{\ell+n}$ uniformly at random during the query rather than using the next() function. As an intermediate, we also define a hybrid Game $(i + \frac{1}{2})$, which lies between **Game** i and **Game** $(i + 1)$. In particular, in **Game** $(i + \frac{1}{2})$, if the $(i+1)$st next query is *preserving* than the challenger acts as in **Game**$(i + 1)$ and chooses a random S, R, and otherwise it acts as in **Game** i and follows the original oracle specification. In all of these games, the output of the game is the output of the finalize oracle at the end, which is 1 if the attacker correctly guesses the challenge bit, and 0 otherwise.

We claim that for all $i \in \{0, \ldots, q_R - 1\}$, **Game** i is indistinguishable from **Game** $(i + \frac{1}{2})$, that in turn is indistinguishable from **Game** $(i + 1)$[10].

Claim 1. *Assuming that the PRNG has (t, ε_p)-preserving security, then for any attacker/distinguisher $\mathcal{A}, \mathcal{D}$ running in time $t' \approx t$, we have* $|\Pr[(\textbf{Game } i) = 1] - \Pr[(\textbf{Game } i + \frac{1}{2}) = 1]| \leq \varepsilon_p$.

Claim 2. *If the PRNG is $(t, q_{\mathcal{D}}, \gamma^*, \varepsilon_r)$-recovering secure, then for any attacker/distinguisher $\mathcal{A}, \mathcal{D}$ running in time $t' \approx t$, we have* $|\Pr[(\textbf{Game } i + \frac{1}{2}) = 1] - \Pr[(\textbf{Game } i + 1) = 1]| \leq \varepsilon_r$.

Combining the above two claims, and using the hybrid argument, we get:

$$|\Pr[(\textbf{Game } 0) = 1] - \Pr[(\textbf{Game } q_R) = 1]| \leq q_R(\varepsilon_r + \varepsilon_p).$$

Moreover **Game** q_R is completely independent of the challenger bit b. In particular, all next-ror queries return a random $R \xleftarrow{\$} \{0,1\}^\ell$ independent of the challenge bit b. Therefore, we have $\Pr[(\textbf{Game } q_R) = 1] = \frac{1}{2}$. Combining with the above, we see that the attacker's advantage in the original robustness game is $\left|\Pr[(\textbf{Game } 0) = 1] - \frac{1}{2}\right| \leq q_R(\varepsilon_r + \varepsilon_p)$.

A.2 Proof of Theorem 4

We show that $\mathcal{G}$ satisfies $(t', q_{\mathcal{D}}, \gamma^*, (\varepsilon_{prg} + q_{\mathcal{D}}^2 \varepsilon_{ext})$-recovering security and $(t', (\varepsilon_{prg} + 2^{-n+1}))$-preserving security. Theorem 4 then follows directly from Theorem 2.

[10]The proofs of these two claims are simple and we defer to them to the full version.

Claim 3. *The PRNG $\mathcal{G}$ has $(t', \varepsilon_{prg} + 2^{-n+1})$-preserving security*

Proof. Let **Game** 0 be the original preserving security game: the game outputs a bit which is set to 1 iff the attacker guesses the challenge bit $b^* = b$. If the initial state is $S_0 \xleftarrow{\$} \{0,1\}^n$, the seed is $\mathsf{seed} = (X, X')$, and the adversarial samples are $I_{d-1}, \ldots, I_0$ (indexed in reverse order where I_{d-1} is the earliest sample) then the refreshed state that incorporates these samples will be $S_d := S_0 \cdot X^d + \sum_{j=0}^{d-1} I_j \cdot X^j$. As long as $X \neq 0$, the value S_d is uniformly random (over the choice of S_0). We consider a modified **Game** 1, where the challenger simply chooses $S_d \xleftarrow{\$} \{0,1\}^n$ and we have

$$|\Pr[(\textbf{Game } 0) = 1] - \Pr[(\textbf{Game } 1) = 1]| \leq 2^{-n}.$$

Let $U = [S_d \cdot X']_1^m$ be the value computed by the challenger during the computation $(S, R) \leftarrow \mathsf{next}(S_d)$ when the challenge bit is $b = 0$. Then, as long as $X' \neq 0$, the value U is uniformly random (over the choice S_d). Therefore, we can define **Game** 2 where the challenger choose $U \xleftarrow{\$} \{0,1\}^n$ during this computation and we have:

$$|\Pr[(\textbf{Game } 1) = 1] - \Pr[(\textbf{Game } 2) = 1]| \leq 2^{-n}.$$

Finally $(S, R) = \mathsf{next}(S_d, \mathsf{seed}) = \mathbf{G}(U)$. Then (S, R) is (t, ε_{prg}) indistinguishable from uniform. Therefore we can consider a modified **Game** 3 where the challenger just choosing (S, R) at random even when the challenge bit is $b = 0$. Since the attacker runs in time $t' \approx t$, we have:

$$|\Pr[(\textbf{Game } 3) = 1] - \Pr[(\textbf{Game } 2) = 1]| \leq \varepsilon_{prg}.$$

Since **Game** 3 is independent of the challenge bit b, we have $\Pr[(\textbf{Game } 3) = 1] = \frac{1}{2}$ and therefore $|\Pr[(\textbf{Game } 0) = 1] - \frac{1}{2}| \leq \varepsilon_{prg} + 2^{-n+1}$. □

Claim 4. *The PRNG $\mathcal{G}$ has $(t', q_{\mathcal{D}}, \gamma^*, (\varepsilon_{prg} + q_{\mathcal{D}}^2 \varepsilon_{ext}))$-recovering security.*

Proof. Let **Game** 0 be the original recovering security game: the game outputs a bit which is set to 1 iff the attacker guesses the challenge bit $b^* = b$. We define **Game** 1 where, during the challenger's computation of $(S^*, R) \leftarrow \mathsf{next}(S_d)$ for the challenge bit $b = 0$, it chooses $U \xleftarrow{\$} \{0,1\}^m$ uniformly at random rather than setting $U := [X' \cdot S_d]_1^m$. We argue that

$$|\Pr[(\textbf{Game } 0) = 1] - \Pr[(\textbf{Game } 1) = 1]| \leq q_{\mathcal{D}}^2 \varepsilon_{ext}.$$

The loss of $q_{\mathcal{D}}^2$ comes from the fact that the attacker can choose the index k and the value d adaptively depending on the seed. In particular, assume that the above does not hold. Then there must exist some values $k^*, d^* \in [q_{\mathcal{D}}]$ such that the above distance is greater than ε_{ext} conditioned on the attacker making exactly k^* calls to $\mathsf{get\text{-}refresh}$ and choosing d^* refreshes in the game. We show that this leads to a contradiction. Fix the distribution on the subset of samples $\bar{I} = (I_{k^*+1}, \ldots, I_{k+d^*})$ output by $\mathcal{D}$ during the first step of the game, which must satisfy

$$\mathbf{H}_\infty(\bar{I} \mid \gamma_1, \ldots, \gamma_{q_{\mathcal{D}}}, z_1, \ldots, z_{q_{\mathcal{D}}}) \geq \gamma^*.$$

By Lemma 3, the function $h_{X,X'}(\bar{I})$ is a $(\gamma^*, \varepsilon_{ext})$-extractor, meaning that $(X, X', h_{X,X'}(\bar{I}))$ is ε_{ext}-close to (X, X', Z) where Z is random an independent of X, X'. Then, for any fixed choice of k^*, d^*, the way we compute U in **Game** 0:

$$U := [X' \cdot S_d]_1^m = [X' \cdot S_0 X^d]_1^m + h_{X,X'}(\bar{I})$$

is ε_{exst} close to a uniformly random U as chosen in **Game** 1. This leads to a contradiction, showing that the equation holds.

Finally, we define **Game** 2 where, during the challenger's computation of $(S^*, R) \leftarrow \mathsf{next}(S_d)$ for the challenge bit $b = 0$, it chooses (S^*, R) uniformly at random instead of $(S^*, R) \leftarrow \mathbf{G}(U)$ as in **Game** 1. Since the attacker runs in time $t' \approx t$, we have:

$$|\Pr[(\textbf{Game } 2) = 1] - \Pr[(\textbf{Game } 1) = 1]| \leq \varepsilon_{prg}.$$

Since **Game** 2 is independent of the challenge bit b, we have $\Pr[(\textbf{Game } 2) = 1] = \frac{1}{2}$ and therefore $|\Pr[(\textbf{Game } 0) = 1] - \frac{1}{2}| \leq \varepsilon_{prg}$. □

B. DISTRIBUTIONS USED FOR ATTACKS

B.1 Distributions Used in Attacks Based on the Entropy Estimator

Lemma 6. *There exists a stateful distribution $\mathcal{D}_0$ such that $\mathbf{H}_\infty(\mathcal{D}_0) = 0$, whose estimated entropy by* LINUX *is high.*

Proof. Let us define the 32-bits word distribution $\mathcal{D}_0$. On input a state i, $\mathcal{D}_0$ updates its state to $i+1$ and outputs a triple $(i+1, [W_1^i, W_2^i, W_3^i]) \xleftarrow{\$} \mathcal{D}_0(i)$, where $W_1^0 = 2^{12}, W_1^i = \lfloor \cos(i).2^{20} \rfloor + W_1^{i-1}$, $W_2^i = W_3^i = 0$. For each state, $\mathcal{D}_0$ outputs a 12-bytes input containing 0 bit of random data, we have $\mathbf{H}_\infty(\mathcal{D}_0) = 0$ conditioned on the previous and the future outputs (*i.e.* $\mathcal{D}_0$ is legitimate only with $\gamma_i = 0$ for all i). Then $\Delta_i > 2^{12}$ and $H_i = 11$. □

Lemma 7. *There exists a stateful distribution $\mathcal{D}_1$ such that $\mathbf{H}_\infty(\mathcal{D}_1) = 64$, whose estimated entropy by* LINUX *is null.*

Proof. Let us define the 32-bits word distribution $\mathcal{D}_1$. On input a state i, $\mathcal{D}_1$ updates its state to $i+1$ and outputs a triple: $(i+1, [W_1^i, W_2^i, W_3^i]) \xleftarrow{\$} \mathcal{D}_1(i)$, where $W_i = i, W_2 \xleftarrow{\$} \mathcal{U}_{32}$ and $W_3 \xleftarrow{\$} \mathcal{U}_{32}$. For each state, $\mathcal{D}_1$ outputs a 12-bytes input containing 8 bytes of random data, we have $\mathbf{H}_\infty(\mathcal{D}_1) = 64$ conditioned on the previous and the future outputs (*i.e.* $\mathcal{D}_1$ is legitimate with $\gamma_i = 64$ for all i). Then $\delta_i = 1$, $\delta_i^2 = 0$, $\delta_{i-1}^2 = 0$, $\delta_i^3 = 0$, $\Delta_i = 0$ and $H_i = 0$. □

B.2 Distribution Used in Attack Based on the Mixing Function

Lemma 8. *There exists a stateful distribution $\mathcal{D}_2$ such that $\mathbf{H}_\infty(\mathcal{D}_2) = 1$, for which $\mathbf{H}_\infty(S) = 1$ after t* refresh*, for arbitrary high t.*

Proof. Let us define the byte distributions $\mathcal{B}_{i,b}$ and $\mathcal{B}_{i,\$}$:

$$\mathcal{B}_{i,b} = \{(0, \cdots, b, \cdots, 0), b_i \leftarrow b, b_j = 0 \text{ if } i \neq j\}$$

$$\mathcal{B}_{i,\$} = \{(b_0, \cdots, b_7), b_i \xleftarrow{\$} \{0,1\}, b_j = 0 \text{ if } i \neq j\}$$

Let us define the 12 bytes distribution $\mathcal{D}_2$. On input a state i, $\mathcal{D}_2$ updates its state to $i+1$ and outputs 12 bytes:

$$(i+1, [B_0^i, \ldots, B_{11}^i]) \xleftarrow{\$} \mathcal{D}_2(i), \text{where } B_4^{10i} \leftarrow \mathcal{B}_{7,\$},$$
$$B_5^{10i} \leftarrow \mathcal{B}_{3,b}, B_4^{10i+2} \leftarrow \mathcal{B}_{2,b}, B_7^{10i+4} \leftarrow \mathcal{B}_{5,b},$$
$$B_6^{10i+6} \leftarrow \mathcal{B}_{1,b}, B_{10}^{10i+8} \leftarrow \mathcal{B}_{0,b}, \text{with } b = B_{4,7}^i$$

For each state i, $\mathcal{D}_2$ outputs a 12-bytes input containing 1 bit of random data (for $i = 0 \bmod 10$) or 0 bit of random data (for $i \neq 0 \bmod 10$). If $d = 0$, $k = 127$ and S is known, and noting $S^t = \mathsf{refresh}(S, \mathsf{refresh}(S^{t-1}, [B_0^{t-1}, \ldots, B_{11}^{t-1}]))$, $S^t = S_0^t, \ldots, S_{127}^t$, then S^t contains 1 random bit in word S_{127}^t, at position 10, for all t. □

Predictability of Android OpenSSL's Pseudo Random Number Generator

Soo Hyeon Kim*
The Attached Institute of ETRI
P.O. Box 1 Yuseong
Daejeon, South Korea
hyuni76@ensec.re.kr

Daewan Han
The Attached Institute of ETRI
P.O. Box 1 Yuseong
Daejeon, South Korea
dwh@ensec.re.kr

Dong Hoon Lee
Graduate School of
Information Security
Korea University, South Korea
donghlee@korea.ac.kr

ABSTRACT

OpenSSL is the most widely used library for SSL/TLS on the Android platform. The security of OpenSSL depends greatly on the unpredictability of its Pseudo Random Number Generator (PRNG). In this paper, we reveal the vulnerability of the OpenSSL PRNG on the Android. We first analyze the architecture of the OpenSSL specific to Android, and the overall operation process of the PRNG from initialization until the session key is generated. Owing to the nature of Android, the Dalvik Virtual Machine in Zygote initializes the states of OpenSSL PRNG early upon booting, and SSL applications copy the PRNG states of Zygote when they start. Therefore, the applications that use OpenSSL generate random data from the same initial states, which is a potential problem that may seriously affect the security of Android applications. Next, we investigate the possibility of recovering the initial states of the OpenSSL PRNG. To do so, we should predict the nine external entropy sources of the PRNG. However, we show that these sources can be obtained in practice if the device is fixed. For example, the complexity of the attack was $O(2^{32+t})$ in our smartphone, where t is the bit complexity for estimating the system boot time. In our experiments, we were able to restore the PRNG states in 74 out of 100 cases. Assuming that we knew the boot time, i.e., $t = 0$, the average time required to restore was 35 min on a PC with four cores (eight threads). Finally, we show that it is possible to recover the `PreMasterSecret` of the first SSL session with $O(2^{58})$ computations using the restored PRNG states, if the application is implemented by utilizing `org.webkit` package and a key exchange scheme is RSA. It shows that the vulnerability of OpenSSL PRNG can be a real threat to the security of Android.

Categories and Subject Descriptors

C.2.0 [**Computer-Communication Networks**]: General—*Security and protection*; C.2.2 [**Computer-Communication Networks**]: Network Protocols—*Applications*; E.3 [**Data**]: Data Encryption—*Standards*

Keywords

SSL/TLS; OpenSSL; Android; Pseudo Random Number Generator; Entropy

*This author is in the process of Korea University doctorate.

CCS'13, November 4–8, 2013, Berlin, Germany.
Copyright 2013 ACM 978-1-4503-2477-9/13/11 ...$15.00.
http://dx.doi.org/10.1145/2508859.2516706.

1. INTRODUCTION

With the great evolution of wireless Internet, smartphones and tablets have become popular communication devices. While various mobile operating systems are currently available, as of the second quarter of 2013, Android has dominated 79.3% of the smartphone market [5]. Because many Android applications transfer sensitive data over the Internet, their security is important which is an issue that has attracted significant attention.

SSL/TLS is one of the most important and well-known cryptographic protocols for secure communication. It is used by a variety of applications such as Web browsers, e-mail, and mobile commerce. The security of SSL depends greatly on the unpredictability of the Pseudo Random Number Generator (PRNG), because its outputs are used for generating session keys. Several SSL applications have been weakened owing to the lack of entropy of the PRNG [8, 17]. Therefore, it is important to investigate the security of PRNG in Android embedded devices. SSL is typically implemented using open libraries. In particular, OpenSSL [6] is widely used for Android. Our study therefore focuses on the OpenSSL PRNG on Android.

First, we studied the Android OpenSSL architecture and tracked the overall operation process of its PRNG from initialization up to the generation of session key. This study was conducted based on an analysis of the source codes, and an experiment using an Android test board. As a result, we found that the OpenSSL PRNG is initialized by the Zygote process upon the system boot, and that each application initializes its own OpenSSL PRNG state by copying the last state of Zygote. In other words, every SSL application generates random data from the same initial state. If an attacker can recover the state of the OpenSSL PRNG from any application, he can predict the important values, such as the encryption keys of the other applications.

Second, we intensively examined the entropy of external sources injected into the OpenSSL PRNG in order to estimate the complexity of recovering the initial states. The unpredictability of the OpenSSL PRNG is highly dependent on the data read from the Android kernel PRNG (`/dev/urandom`) at the system boot. However, we found that the

Android kernel PRNG cannot be supplied with sufficient external entropy until /dev/urandom is input into the OpenSSL PRNG. This vulnerability is regarded as the Android version of the boot-time entropy hole of the Linux PRNG [17]. We can therefore predict /dev/urandom upon booting without much complexity. The other sources can be predicted from `ClientHello` packets and the system information of the device. Roughly speaking, we claim that the initial states of an Android OpenSSL PRNG can be recovered practically. The exact attack complexity and strategy are described in Section 4.

To verify our discovery, we conducted experiments on Android smartphones following our attack strategy. We used two phones of the same model: one as a target and the other as a simulator. We acquired the information of the target phone needed for the attack in advance based on the analysis of the simulator phone. We then recovered the initial states of the target phone from the pre-acquired information and a `ClientHello` packet. The details of this method and its results are described in Section 5.

Finally, we analyzed that the vulnerability of the OpenSSL PRNG can affect the practical security of the Android device. When a PRNG generates random data for the `PreMasterSecret` (`PMS`), it uses the uninitialized memory values for another external entropy sources. In Section 6, we describe how these memory values can be predicted, and how the `PMS` can be obtained from SSL packets.

In summary, the contributions of this paper are as follows.

- We discovered that the OpenSSL PRNG of all Android applications generate random data from the same initial states and that these states can be restored in practice. For example, the complexity was $O(2^{32+t})$ in our phone, where t is the bit complexity for estimating the boot time of the phone. This vulnerability is caused by the Dalvik feature of the Android architecture, the boot-time entropy hole of the kernel PRNG, and the insufficient external entropy of the OpenSSL PRNG.
- We confirmed our discovery experimentally using smartphones. We were able to restore the initial OpenSSL PRNG states of applications in 74 out of 100 cases. Assuming that we knew the boot time, that is $t = 0$, the average time to restore the state was 35 min on a single PC with four cores (eight threads).
- We showed that it is possible to recover the `PMS` of the first SSL session with the restored OpenSSL PRNG states and $O(2^{58})$ computations, if SSL is implemented using the `org.webkit` package and the key exchange scheme is RSA. The representative application affected is the default Web browser.

Since the vulnerability we discovered is derived from the original structure of Android and the OpenSSL PRNG, it affects every Android application using OpenSSL. Further studies on methods for allocating memory addresses such as Address Space Layout Randomization (ASLR) may reduce the complexity or extend the affected applications in `PMS` recovery attacks. We therefore recommend that adequate countermeasures should be adopted immediately, and suggest some possible candidates in Section 7.

From this point, we refer to the Android kernel PRNG that originated from Linux PRNG as LPRNG, and the Android OpenSSL PRNG as APRNG.

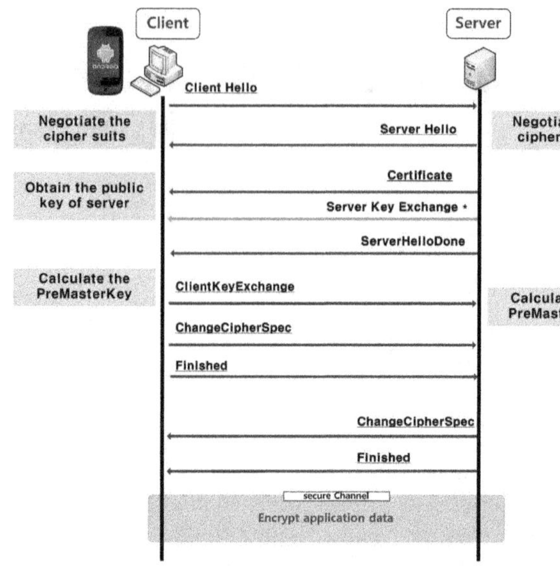

Figure 1: The SSL Handshake protocol

2. BACKGROUND

2.1 SSL/TLS

SSL/TLS is composed of two protocols: a handshake protocol and a record protocol. The handshake protocol negotiates security parameters, and authenticates the server and the client. The record protocol provides the compression and encryption of the application data. Herein, we briefly introduce the handshake protocol for further understanding of this paper. The steps involved in the protocol are shown in Figure 1.

1. The client sends a `ClientHello` message containing the following attributes: a list of supported ciphersuites, a session ID, and a 28-byte random nonce.
2. The server responds with a `ServerHello` message that includes a chosen ciphersuite and a nonce. Then, the server sends its identification in the form of a certificate list. Depending on the negotiated ciphersuite, a `ServerKeyExchange` message may also be sent, which contains the information to generate a `PMS`. Finally, the server sends a `ServerHelloDone` message that indicates the end of the negotiations.
3. The client uses a certificate to authenticate the server. If it secceeds, the client generates the `PMS` and sends a `ClientKeyExchange` message that contains the data needed by the server to calculate the `PMS`. Next, it sends a `ChangeCipherSpec` message in order to inform the server that future messages will be encrypted using the negotiated session key. Finally, it sends a `Finished` message containing the MAC of all previously exchanged messages in the handshake protocol.
4. In response, the server sends a `ChangeCipherSpec` message and its `Finished` message. Then, the Handshake protocol is finished and a secure communication channel is established.

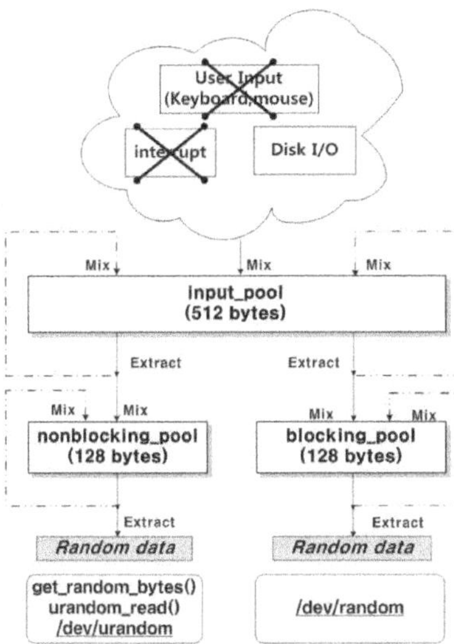

Figure 2: The structure of LPRNG

2.2 LPRNG

LPRNG is commonly used for generating random data needed in many secure services for a Linux kernel and applications. We briefly introduce the structure of the latest version of LPRNG according to [19].

It comprises three entropy pools: `input_pool`, `blocking_pool`, and `nonblocking_pool`. Figure 2 shows the overall structure of LPRNG. Each entropy pool has its own `entropy_counter`, which is decremented when its output is extracted from the pool, and incremented when new entropy is added. External entropy sources are mixed only in `input_pool`, which transfers its entropy to `blocking_pool` and `nonblocking_pool`. The external entropy is designed to be supplied from system interrupts, the disk I/O, and user inputs such as a keyboard or mouse, but some of them may not used depending on the platform. LPRNG provides `/dev/random` and `/dev/urandom`, which are device interfaces for reading random data. `/dev/random` reads from `blocking_pool`, and returns random bytes only when sufficient entropy has been collected. `/dev/urandom` reads from `nonblocking_pool`, and returns random bytes regardless of the amount of entropy generated.

2.3 Related Work

Ever since its introduction decades ago, many researchers have been scrutinizing the security of SSL/TLS. As a result, various weaknesses of the protocol have been revealed and fixed [10, 12, 13, 14, 18, 20, 21, 22]. Herein, we introduce a few results that are most closely related to our research.

In 2008, Bello [8] observed that the PRNG of Debian OpenSSL was predictable owing to an implementation bug. Yilek *et al.* [25] reported on the aftermath of this vulnerability. They predicted that the effect of the vulnerability on clients was limited because most of the popular Web browsers at the time did not use OpenSSL. Nowadays, mobile devices are becoming major tools for the Internet, and OpenSSL is mostly used on these devices. Thus, if any vulnerability exists in OpenSSL, the clients will be affected to the same extent as the servers. Our discovery described in this paper is an example of such vulnerability.

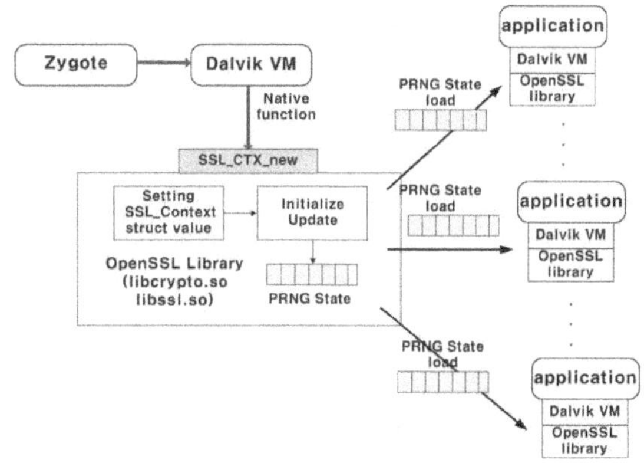

Figure 3: The architecture of Android OpenSSL

Heninger *et al.* [17] analyzed the vulnerability of weak public key pairs in network devices. They performed large-scale scans of TLS certificates and SSH host keys. After analyzing the scanned data, they discovered that there were many vulnerable RSA and DSA keys of network devices, and one of the reasons for this vulnerability was due to insufficient entropy of the LPRNG upon system booting. In our study, we show that this problem also applies to Android. Combined with the Zygote forking structure, this can be more serious for Android than for other embedded devices.

As mobile devices have become widely used, the studies on the use of SSL/TLS in Android have increased. Georgiev *et al.* [16] demonstrated that in many Android apps SSL/TLS implementations were insecure against MITM attacks. Fahl *et al.* [15] also reported that many applications contained the SSL/TLS code that was potentially vulnerable to MITM attacks. These vulnerabilities of Android SSL were due to implementation errors and developers' misunderstandings of the requirements for SSL security. In contrast, our discovery is related to the structural limitations of LRPNG and the Android architecture.

Ristenpart and Yilek [23] revealed that Virtual Machine (VM) resets could lead to randomness reuse and allow an attacker to compromise TLS sessions or expose a DSA signing key of server. They also suggested a general framework for hedging cryptographic operations against this type of randomness failure, and experimentally conformed that their framework can be applied to the OpenSSL library. The vulnerability of APRNG, which will be described in this paper, partly stems from the Dalvik Virtual Machine (DalvikVM) cloning architecture of Android. Our discovery is therefore another good example of the practical insecurities that arise owing to the reuses of VM states.

3. ANALYSIS OF ANDROID OPENSSL

In this section, we describe how the Android OpenSSL is implemented and how the APRNG is operated to generate the `ClientHello` nonce using the SDK class library.

3.1 Architecture of Android OpenSSL

SSL is implemented in the form of an open source library. The typical libraries include OpenSSL, GnuTLS, NSS, and so on. We focus on OpenSSL, because it is used by most Android applications. The Android OpenSSL provides

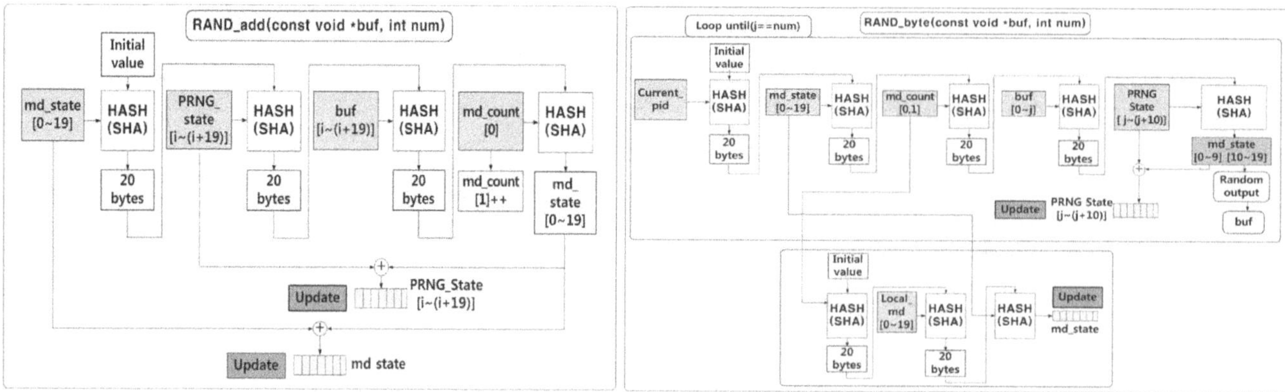

Figure 4: The process of RAND_add() and RAND_byte()

`libcrypto.so` for the cryptographic functions and `libssl.so` for SSL communications in the form of a system shared library.

Android is based on a customized Linux kernel with a Java program interface. Because system services and native or user applications run as Linux processes, each application is assigned to a unique `PID`. Since Android applications are based on Java programming, every application must run in its own instance of the DalvikVM. However, it takes a long time to initialize and operate the DalvikVM whenever a new application is launched. Therefore, Android uses a VM known as Zygote, which is the parent process of most Android applications.

Upon startup of Android, the Linux kernel starts the Zygote process by reading `init.rc`. It initializes a DalvikVM that pre-loads and pre-initializes the core library classes including the OpenSSL shared library. While the native function of DalvikVM sets `SSL_ConText(SSL_CTX)` for `SSLSOCKET`, the internal APRNG states are initialized and updated. Whenever Android applications that use OpenSSL are executed, their DalvikVMs copy and load the APRNG states of Zygote to their own APRNG states, as shown in Figure 3.

3.2 APRNG Operation Process

OpenSSL provides the user interfaces so that applications can select one of many random engines to generate random bytes. Android applications use the `SSLeay` random method. The APIs for the use of APRNG are as follows.

- `RAND_poll()`: initializes the PRNG states with the entropy sources.
- `RAND_add(void *`*buf*`, int `*n*`, double `*entropy*`)`: mixes *n* bytes of *buf* into PRNG states.
- `RAND_byte(void *`*buf*`, int `*n*`)`: generates *n* bytes of random data and puts into *buf*.

3.2.1 Initialization of the States

While an Android device is booting, Zygote creates a `SSL_CTX` for SSL communication. In the process of the `SSL_CTX` setting, Zygote executes `RAND_poll()` to initialize the APRNG states. `RAND_poll()` adds four entropy sources to the APRNG states by calling `RAND_add()`. These entropy sources will be described in detail in the next section.

3.2.2 Update of the States

The internal APRNG states comprise two entropy pools: 20 bytes of `md_state` and 1023 bytes of `PRNG_state`. The states are updated by using `RAND_add()` and `RAND_byte()`. PRNG has an unsigned integer array `md_count`, and `md_count[0]` is incremented by 1 whenever the `RAND_byte()` function is called. In addition, `md_count[1]` represents the total number of message blocks input to SHA-1 when the `RAND_add()` function is executed. The size of an input block for SHA-1 is 10 bytes.

In the `RAND_add()`, the data of *buf* are input into the APRNG states for updating. In the `RAND_byte()`, the existing (uninitialized) values of *buf* are input to SHA-1 as an external entropy source. The *buf* will contain newly generated random values after the execution of `RAND_byte()` is finished. The three internal variables `md_state`, `PRNG_state`, and `md_count` are also injected into SHA-1. The `PRNG_state` is updated by the output of SHA-1, which is xored with the previous `PRNG_state`. After finishing the update of the `PRNG_state`, the last hash output generated is xored with the previous `md_state`.

3.2.3 Extracting Random Bytes

`RAND_byte()` is used to extract random bytes. In this function, the application `PID` and three internal variables are mixed in SHA-1. The APRNG uses the bottom 10 bytes of the output of SHA-1 as random bytes. `PRNG_state` is updated by xoring the top 10 bytes of the hash output into the previous `PRNG_state`.

The operating processes of `RAND_add()` and `RAND_byte()` are depicted in Figure 4.

3.3 Generating ClientHello Nonce

Android applications use class interfaces to establish SSL connections. These classes are in the middle of the interface between the Java application and the OpenSSL library. Representative classes are the `org.webkit` and `javax.net.ssl` packages. The `org.webkit` package provides the `libchromium_net.so` library to establish an SSL connection using webkit socket. The `javax.net.ssl` package uses Java Secure Socket Extension (JSSE) and provides native functions so that applications can communicate using SSL.

As mentioned before, Android applications generate a `ClientHello` nonce from the states initialized by Zygote. The

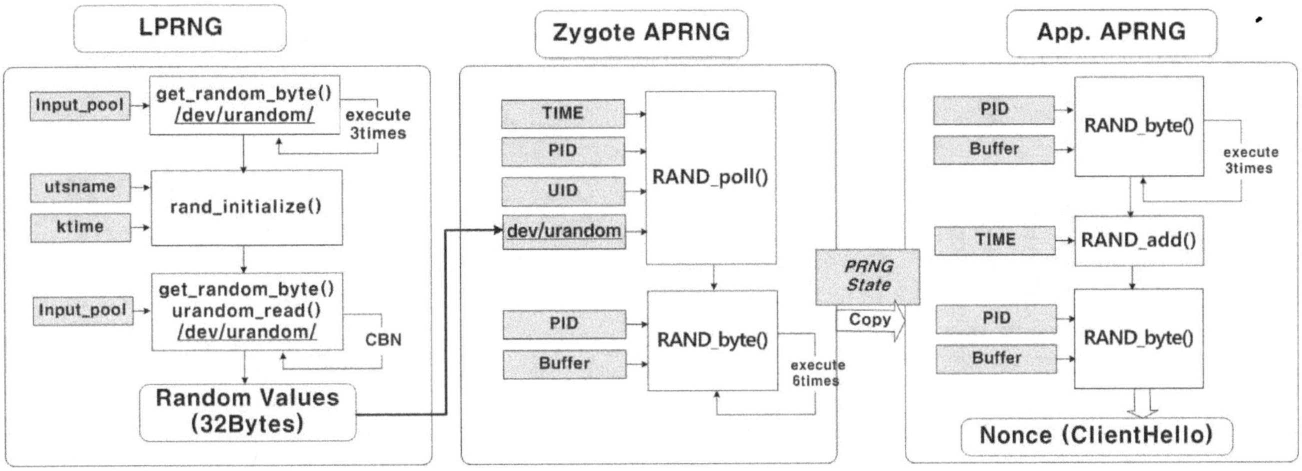

Figure 5: The procedure of generating ClientHello nonce in org.webkit package

generation process of this can be classified into two types depending on these packages. In this subsection, we explain in detail the case of `org.webkit`, and briefly describe the case of `javax.net.ssl`.

3.3.1 Generation of Random Values in /dev/urandom

As shown in Figure 5, Zygote reads the random values from `/dev/urandom` for initialization of the APRNG states. The user interface functions to read from `/dev/urandom` are `get_random_bytes()` and `urandom_read()`. The default size of an output block of LPRNG is 10 bytes. If the number of requested bytes is not a multiple of 10 bytes, the last block is truncated. If the `entropy_counter` of `input_pool` does not exceed the minimum needed (threshold), `/dev/urandom` outputs without mixing the output of `input_pool`. The threshold of `entropy_counter` is 192 bits in Android kernel 3.0.15.

Upon Android startup, all bytes of the LPRNG states are set to zero. In these states, the Linux kernel extracts 4 bytes of random data three times from `/dev/urandom` for the network setting, such as initializing `inet6` and computing `genid` for the `ipv4` address. The Linux Kernel then adds `ktime` and `utsname` to the `nonblocking_pool` as external entropy sources. The `ktime` is nano-second after the system boots, and `utsname` indicates name and information about current kernel.

While the initial process of the kernel starts the services registered in `init.rc`, the kernel and some of the applications extract random data from `/dev/urandom` for various purposes. For example, the kernel uses 6 bytes for assigning an Ethernet IP address, and 16 bytes whenever it loads the ELF format. Some Android processes request 4 bytes for `stack_chk_guard`, and applications using `SQLite` extract 256 bytes for initializing the states of their own PRNG. We note in advance that `stack_chk_guard` is importantly used in recovering the `PMS` of some SSL packets, as described in Section 6.

Because Zygote is also registered in `init.rc`, it is initialized upon system boot, and 32 random bytes from `/dev/urandom` are injected into APRNG during this process.

3.3.2 Operation of Zygote APRNG

While DalvikVM of Zygote creates `SSL_CTXs`, four entropy sources, i.e., `Time`, `PID`, `UID`, and `/dev/urandom`, are injected into the states during LPRNG initialization executed by `RAND_poll()`. The one read from `/dev/urandom` is 32 bytes, and the others are 4 bytes.

The APRNG executes `RAND_byte()` to generate 16 bytes of random data for setting the ticket key [7], which is used to resume a SSL session without requiring session-specific states at the server. The ticket key consists of three components, i.e., the key name, hmac key and AES key. Because DalvikVM of Zygote creates two `SSL_CTXs` for transferring and receiving, APRNG calls `RAND_byte()` six times in total. In `RAND_byte()`, APRNG uses the existing value of the output buffer as a small source of entropy. However, the value in the operation of Zygote is initialized to zero.

3.3.3 Operation of Application APRNG

When an application starts, it loads the initialized OpenSSL. To establish a session, it creates a new `SSL_CTX` by calling `SSL_CTX_new()`, which also calls `RAND_byte()` three times to set the ticket key. At this point, the application's `PID` and the output buffer value, which is initialized to zero, are mixed into the APRNG states. When OpenSSL performs the SSL handshake by invoking `SSL_connect()`, APRNG also adds the `Time` into the states. Next, the `ClientHello` nonce is generated and transferred to a server.

If the application uses the `javax.net.ssl` package for SSL, it has a little difference in the number of times to run `RAND_bytes()` for `SSL_CTX` and external input injected into the states. The APRNG generates 16 bytes of random values for `SSL_CTX_new()` six times and then adds the file information regarding `/dev/urandom`, 1024 bytes from `/dev/urandom`, and `Time` to its internal states before generating the `ClientHello` nonce.

4. PREDICTABILITY OF APRNG

The randomness of the APRNG depends on the unpredictability of the external entropy sources. The sources input into the APRNG are shown in the gray boxes in Figure 5. Among these, `/dev/urandom` is the most important in

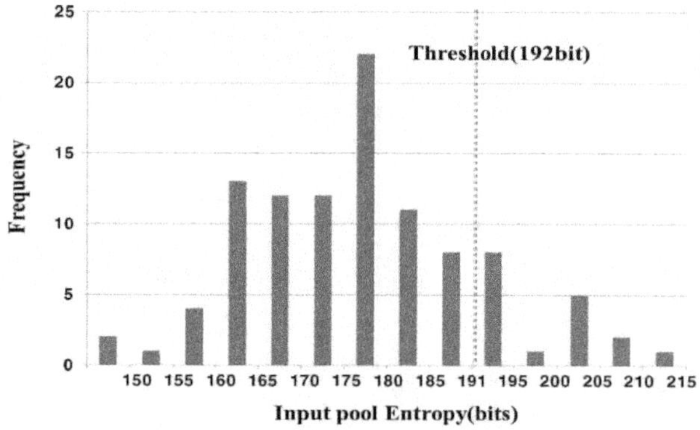

Figure 6: Input_pool entropy_counter at Zygote launch

terms of its size and complexity. LPRNG depends on external sources for randomness: `utsname`, `ktime`, and various device events, which are transferred by `input_pool`. However, an Android device has no user inputs such as a mouse or a keyboard, and has a few interrupts until Zygote is launched at the system boot. It is therefore possible that `input_pool` cannot transfer its entropy to `/dev/urandom` because of its low `entropy_counter` at boot time. If this actually occurs, and the complexities of the other entropy sources are low, we can predict the internal states of APRNG. In this section, we verify that these two hypotheses are true and demonstrate their effects on the vulnerability of the APRNG.

In the analysis, we conducted various experiments on an Android test board with the following configurations:

- Chip set: Exynos 4210
- CPU: Dual-core ARM Cortex-A9
- Memory: 1G Bytes
- OS: Android ICS 4.0.4 (kernel 3.0.15)

We used adb tool [2] and trace32 [9] to analyze the internal information of the board and applications.

4.1 Boot-time Entropy Hole of LPRNG

LPRNG is designed to be supplied with external entropy when system events such as a disk I/O operation, user input, and IRQ occur by calling the following functions: `add_disk_randomness()`, `add_input_randomness()`, and `add_interrupt_randomness()`. However, we found that `add_interrupt_randomness()` is not used in an Android device, which was already reported for other Linux platforms [11, 24]. The `add_input_randomness()` is rarely used, and is not used at boot time in an Android device. Thus, only disk I/O events are entropy sources for LPRNG before the Zygote launch. These events do not occur deterministically and are dependent on the devices, OS versions, and communication providers. We therefore need to conduct an experiment to determine how much entropy is fed into LPRNG from the disk events.

We measured the `entropy_counter` of `input_pool` when Zygote initialized OpenSSL. Figure 6 shows the frequency versus `entropy_counter` of `input_pool` for 100 test cases. The figure shows that the `entropy_counter` of the `input_pool` is less than the threshold (192 bit) at 83%. In these cases, `/dev/urandom` requested from the APRNG are generated using only two external sources: `utsname` and `ktime`.

Our experiment is highly limited, but we expect that this phenomenon will generally occur in Android. It was previously reported for other Linux platforms [17]. In addition to the above experiment on a test board, we also conducted another experiment on smartphones (Section 5), which convince us that our assertion will be true in practice.

4.2 Complexity of the Entropy Sources

Herein, we analyze the complexity of the entropy sources, which are fed into the state of APRNG until the `ClientHello` nonce is generated. The following elements should be checked:

- LPRNG: `utsname`, `ktime`, `CBN`
- Zygote APRNG: `UID`, `PID`, `Time`, `Buffer`
- Application APRNG: `PID`, `Time`, `Buffer`

4.2.1 utsname

Table 1: Example of utsname

`sysname`	Linux
`nodename`	(none)
`release`	3.0.15
`version`	#1 SMP PREEMPT Fri Feb 8 16:54:28 KST 2013
`machine`	armv7l
`domainname`	(none)

The `utsname` comprises six elements that contain information on the system and kernel. The `sysname`, `nodename`, and `domainname` have fixed values. The `machine` and `release` indicate the version of the chip and kernel, respectively, and `version` is the time when the kernel was compiled. Thus, they do not have many types of such elements, which will be same, if the devices are released by a manufacturer during the same period. Therefore, if an attacker fixes the target for an attack, he can see the device's `utsname` in advance. As an example, the `utsname` of our board is provided in Table 1.

4.2.2 ktime

The `ktime` is the time in nano-seconds when LPRNG calls `random_initialize()`. This function is usually executed within 2 seconds after a system boot. The complexity of `ktime` can therefore be roughly estimated as 31 bits. However, if we fix a device, we can reduce it to $25 \sim 28$ bits by more minutely analyzing the execution time of the function. For example, based on the analysis which we will present in Section 5, we can estimate the complexity of ktime as 26 bits in our phone.

4.2.3 CBN

We define the CBN (Computed Block Number) as the total number of random blocks (10 bytes) computed in `/dev/urandom` from the system boot to the start of the Zygote initialization. The CBN depends on the device model, OS version, and communication provider. It varies between 100 and 250. For example, in our experiment, it was 137 on the board and 210 on the phone. However, we observed that the `CBN`s of different devices are equal if the above properties of the devices are the same.

4.2.4 UID and PID

The size of the `UID` is 4 bytes in the source code, but is set to 0 in Android. The `PID` is assigned sequentially according to the order that the application is running. The PID has 15 bits of complexity in the source code. However, Android's initial processes and the manufacturer's built-in applications are executed in the order specified. Thus, the Zygote `PID` is less than 3000 and is nearly fixed in the the same model devices. The `PID`s of built-in applications, such as Web browsers, e-mail, and YouTube, do not significantly change. For example, the `PID` of the Web browser on our phone is on 2900~2950. We can therefore estimate the complexity of the Zygote `PID` on our phone as 0, and that of the application `PID` as 6.

4.2.5 Time

The `Time` refers to `gmt_unix_time`, the unit of which is in seconds. Since the application's `Time` is almost equal to the time shown in the `ClientHello` packet, we can predict it exactly. The Zygote module is launched upon system boot, and thus the Zygote `Time` can be approximated as the system boot time. Phones are usually rebooted more than once per week for battery changes or other reasons. Therefore, we estimate the complexity of the Zygote `Time` of a general phone as 20 bits. However, an attacker may obtain the approximate boot time of a targeted device through various methods. Possible situations and scenarios are described in the next subsection.

4.2.6 Buffer

The `Buffer` is the existing value of the RAM where the output of `RAND_byte()` will be stored. Its complexity therefore depends on how the buffer is defined and initialized in the function that calls `RAND_byte()`. The buffer used to generate the `ClientHello` nonce is initialized to all zeros, and we can therefore regard it as a fixed constant. However, this is not true for other cases such as `PMS` generation.

4.3 Vulnerability and Attack Strategy

So far, we have investigated the complexity of entropy sources for APRNG until the `ClientHello` nonce is generated for `org.webkit` based applications. Table 2 shows a summary of our analysis. In the second and third columns, we describe the bit complexity of the entropy sources in general devices and a fixed device, respectively. The bit complexities of our phone are given in the last column, where t is the bit complexity for estimating the boot time. As a conclusion, if we fix a device and acquire its information beforehand, they can be restored exactly except for `ktime`, application's `PID`, and Zygote `Time`.

The complexity of three unpredictable elements will be different according to chip speed, OS version, application, and system boot time. We can expect their sum to $50 \sim 55$ bits on a fixed device. However, Zygote `Time` is close to a system boot time. If we can find this value through 2^t trials, the states of APRNG can be recovered with $O(2^{35+t})$ computations. If t is 0, it can be accomplished in a few hours using a single PC, as demonstrated in the next section. We cannot say that it is impossible even if in the worst case where t is 20. It is well known that a brute force attack on DES with a key size of 56 bits can be accomplished within a day [4]. Therefore, we can state at a minimum that the APRNGs of applications based `org.webkit` are vulnerable.

Table 2: Entropy of APRNG (bit)

entropy sources	general devices	a fixed device	our phone
`utsname`	43	0	0
`ktime`	31	$25 \sim 28$	26
`CBN`	8	0	0
`UID`	0	0	0
Zygote `PID`	12	0	0
Zygote `Time`	20	20	t
Application `PID`	15	$5 \sim 7$	6
Application `Time`	0	0	0
`Buffer`	0	0	0
Total	129	$50 \sim 55$	$32 + t$

However, the problem does not end here. As we explained in Section 3, every SSL application starts with the same initial states of APRNG, which are updated by Zygote. Thus, if an attacker can restore the APRNG states of any specific application, he can obtain the states of all applications even those that are implemented by other packages and will run after the attack.

Now, we present a strategy for attacking APRNG of a device. An attacker fixes a target and obtains its information by conducting experiments on another device of the same model and OS version as the target.

If possible, the attacker obtains the time when the device was last booted up. It will reduce the attack time. Possible situations and scenarios can be considered are as follows: A man engaged in air travel is more likely to reboot his phone when arriving. There are many companies and organizations where the visitors need to leave their phone at a help desk according to the security policy. If the phone is not turned off, a staff member at the desk who wants to attack the phone can reboot it. In these cases, the attacker can guess the boot time of the phone.

Then, he collects `ClientHello` nonce packets of an `org.webkit` application such as the Web browser generated on the target. Finally, he computes a `ClientHello` nonce with unknown external sources as variables. By exhaustively searching for the variables within the ranges according to the the preacquired information, he compares the output with the real `ClientHello` nonce captured in the packet. If he finds variables with which two values are matched, he can restore the APRNG's initial states of all applications.

This result shows that the APRNG is vulnerable from a cryptographic perspective at least. More practical implications of this problem will be discussed in Section 6.

5. EXPERIMENT ON A PHONE

In this section, we present the results of experiments on restoring the initial state of APRNG in a smartphone using the attack strategy described in the previous section. We used two phones of the same model, one as a target and the other as a simulator, to obtain the information needed for an attack on the target.

5.1 Pre-acquisition of the Device Information

To obtain the information needed for our attack, we used the kernel log of the simulator phone by modifying the source

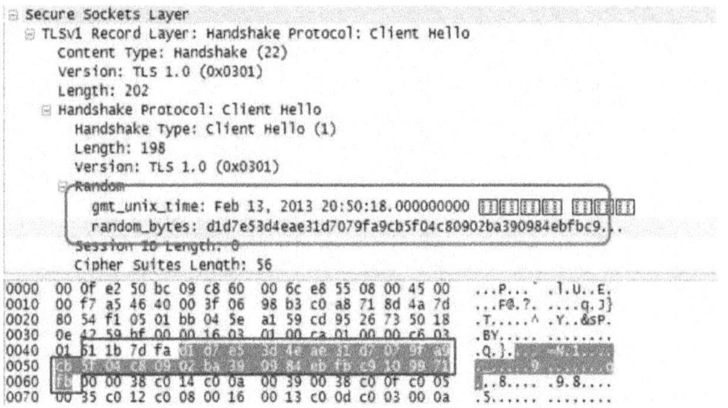

Figure 7: A captured SSL packet on the experiment

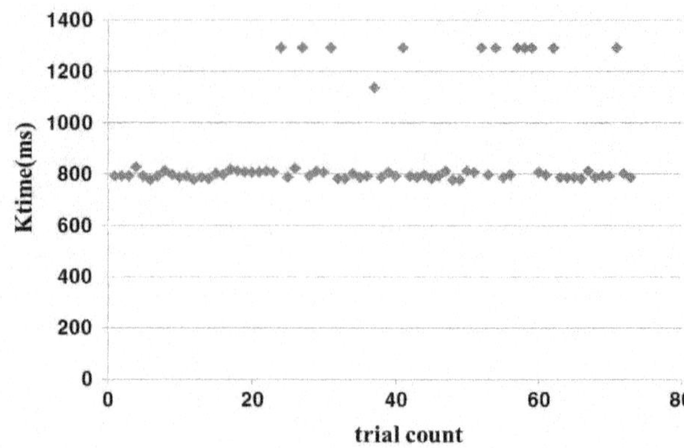

Figure 8: ktimes on the experiment

Table 3: Searching Range of Variables in the Attack

variable	searching range
`utsname`	same to that of Section 5.1
`ktime`	780∼830 ms, 1230∼1240 ms
`CBN`	210
Zygote `PID`	1845
Zygote `Time`	`0x511b7cce`∼`0x511b7ccf`
Application `PID`	2900∼2950
Application `Time`	`0x511b7dfa`

Table 4: Values found on the experiment

variable	value
`ktime` (ns)	790212920
Zygote `Time`	`0x511b7cce`
Application `PID`	2939
MD_state of SSL_CTX	c4 82 04 51 c6 e7 9a fe 3e 4a 85 f7 b6 e5 4f f7 67 17 b7 e9

code. We rebooted the phone 100 times and checked the variables.

The OS version used was Android 4.0.4 Ice Cream Sandwich. The `utsname` was same as that presented in Section 4.2, except the `release` is '3.0.15-1042229' and the `version` is '#3 SMP PREEMPT Fri Aug 17 20:49:17 KST 2012'. We could know the Zygote `PID` through the Android adb shell command, which was 1845. We could also see that, in most cases, the initialization of the LPRNG occurred at 770∼830 or 1298∼1230 ms after the system boot. This is the reason that we estimated the entropy of `ktime` as 26 bits in Section 4.2. Finally, we found that `CBN` was 210 for most cases.

5.2 Restoring the APRNG States

We rebooted the target phone and used the boot time to predict the Zygote `Time`, that is, we set t to 1. We then activated HTTPS using a Web browser a few minutes after system started. At the same time, we captured the `ClientHello` nonce of the SSL packets using Wireshark. We set the application `Time` equal to the packet time.

We constructed an SW program to execute the attack procedure described in Section 4.3. The variables are fixed or searched for within the range shown in Table 3, which are set by the acquired information. We executed this program on a PC configured with a Intel Core 3.60 GHz i7 CPU with four cores. Since it can be operated with eight threads, we parallelized the program by dividing the search range of `ktime` into eight parts.

As a result, we succeeded in finding unfixed variables. The captured `ClientHello` packet is shown in Figure 7, and the found values and restored `MD_state` are given in Table 4. We repeated the experiments 100 times on the same phone, and successfully found the unknowns 74 times. Figure 8 shows the distribution of `ktime`s of these cases.

6. EFFECT OF THE VULNERABILITY

As the main contribution of this paper, we showed that the initial state of APRNG can be restored practically with high probability. Then, how is the security of Android OpenSSL affected by this vulnerability? We analyze this subject in this section.

The main interest is whether the problem of APRNG poses a threat to the confidentiality of OpenSSL, such as a session key recovery. The session key is generated from the `PMS` and other known variables. As mentioned in Section 3.3, APRNG states cannot be restored in `javax.net.ssl` applications for extra unpredictable inputs, and thus the their `PMS`s cannot be recovered at this time. We therefore focus on `org.webkit` applications.

6.1 PMS Restoration

The generation of a `PMS` varies depending on the key exchange scheme of the negotiated ciphersuite. The 46 random bytes of `PMS` are generated directly by APRNG of client in RSA scheme. In the (EC)DH scheme, `PMS` is computed using the client's randomly generated private key and server's public key. It is notable that the random data related to the `PMS` are generated immediately after the `ClientHello` nonce is generated. Another `Time` value is added into the APRNG states, but it can be predicted because it is almost same as the time of the `ClientHello` packet. We can know the states of the APRNG after outputting the `ClientHello` nonce, and thus the remaining problem for recovering the `PMS` is to estimate the existing value of the output buffer.

The buffer is defined as a local variable in the RSA and as a dynamic variable in the EC(DH). It seems difficult to find the pattern of a dynamic variable. However, it is possible to track the values of a local variable, because such variables

Table 5: Comparison of buffer memory values

example	Memory value
case I	0063 00000000 6bdae5f2 0000000a 4e900379 403382cc 6bdae5f2 0000000a 4e900379 006257a0 6bdae5f2 0000000a
case II	00ed 00000000 869f1107 0000000a 4e9da379 403492cc 869f1107 0000000a 4e9da379 00529fc0 869f1107 0000000a
Pattern	WORD-1 WORD-2 WORD-3 WORD-4 WORD-5 WORD-6 WORD-3 WORD-4 WORD-5 WORD-7 WORD-3 WORD-4

are stored in the stack memory. We therefore analyzed the case of the RSA key exchange scheme.

Table 5 shows two examples of buffer values we should examine. These values are not totally random and have a certain pattern, which is abstracted in the last row of the table.

To the results of tracking the memory, we found that the 46 bytes of the buffer are written while `SSL_get_server_certificate()` function is executed. The use of each word is as follows, where `locking_callback()` is a function used to read the public key contained in the certificate.

- WORD-1: the address of a parameter of `SSL_get_server_certificate()`.
- WORD-2: the result when `verify_mode` of SSL is `SSL_VERIFY_NONE`, which is always `0x00000000`.
- WORD-3: the value of `stack_chk_guard` which is required by `locking_callback()`.
- WORD-4: the value of a variable used in `locking_callback()`, which is always `0x0000000a`.
- WORD-5: the starting address of `locking_callback()`.
- WORD-6: the address of a file in which `X509_pubkey_get()` is stored when the lock is set.
- WORD-7: the address of memory where sign algorithm are stored when the `X509_Certificate_type()` is executed.

WORD-2 and WORD-4 are fixed values. The other words vary at each time, but are not totally random as follows:

- WORD-1: the upper 7 bits are always 0.
- WORD-5: the upper 9 and lower 12 bits are fixed.
- WORD-6: the upper 12 and lower 12 bits are fixed.
- WORD-7: the upper 7 and lower 3 bits are fixed.

We can therefore estimate all of the variables, except for WORD-3, with $O(2^{50})$ complexity. WORD-3 (`stack_chk_guard`) is fully random data. However, it is read from `/dev/urandom` before the random data of `/dev/urandom` is input into Zygote APRNG. It can therefore be predicted from `ktime` and `utsname` found when we restore the APRNG states. The `CBN` is less than 250, and we can therefore predict WORD-3 at most $O(2^8)$ trials. The maximum complexity of restoring the `PMS` is thus $O(2^{58})$.

Note that the above complexity is not bitwise. To determine whether we estimated the unknowns exactly, we need to calculate a session key from the unknowns and decrypt the SSL packets. This requires dozens of hash computations and negotiated cipher operations such as RC4 or AES, which cannot be executed even 2^{50} times a year on a single PC. However, this may be accomplished practically if the attacker belongs to a well-funded enterprise or organizations.

Finally, we remark the possibility of improving the attack. The randomness of WORD-1, 5, 6, and 7 is due to the address ASLR provided beginning with Android 4.0 [1, 3]. If we can predict the ASLR operation more accurately on general devices, the `PMS` recovery attack may be improved. However, such a study is beyond the scope of this paper and will be the subject of future work.

6.2 Effect of Decrypting the First Session

Suppose that we obtain the first session of HTTPS requests from the recovered session key. The decrypted HTTPS request includes the request-line, the resource identified by the request, the HTTP header, and message bodies. Among them, the most important part is the HTTP header including a cookie. A cookie has information regarding the login and preferences when a user visits a Web site. If a user will visit the same site in the future, the data stored in the cookie can be used as an authentication token of the user.

An attackers can thereby impersonate a user request by stealing a full set of cookies from the recovered first session [14]. Then, other important information may be stolen, and other exploit attacks can be made based on this attack.

7. COUNTERMEASURE

The vulnerability of the APRNG described in this paper stems from the following independent causes: an application's direct use of SSL_CTX forked by Zygote, and the boot-time entropy hole of LPRNG, and the insufficient external entropy of APRNG.

The first is due to the fundamental operating structure of Android, which is related to Zygote forking, and therefore supplementing it will not be easy, and appears to be outside the scope of the information security community.

A well-known countermeasure for correcting the boot-time entropy hole of LPRNG is saving the status at shutdown, and writing it back to the pools at startup. This is recommended in general Linux systems, and can be achieved using a script activated during system startups and shutdowns. However, this countermeasure appears to be absent in Android. If possible, this method can be a simple and powerful countermeasure.

Adding more entropy sources to APRNG before generating ClinetHello nonce is another method to defeat our attack. Besides resistance to our attack, there is important reason to should consider this countermeasure. Since Zygote forking structure is hard to change in Android, the phenomenon that OpenSSL applications start with the same initial PRNG states cannot be easily remedied. However, this is much undesirable in the point of security. Therefore, Scattering the PRNG states randomly in each application's startup is needed. It is recommendable that Additional unpredictable entropy sources are mixed when each application starts.

8. CONCLUSION

In this paper, we revealed the vulnerability of the Android OpenSSL PRNG. After we investigated the operating process of Android OpenSSL, its concrete implementation, and the entropy sources of its PRNG, we claimed and verified that the initial states of APRNG can be recovered practically. We also showed that our discovery can be a real threat to Android by showing that the PMSs of some SSL sessions can be recovered practically.

To the best of our knowledge, most previously revealed Android SSL vulnerabilities are problems of individual applications, and can therefore be easily corrected at the application level from careful use and implementation. In contrast, the problem we identified is due to the structural limits of the Android architecture and LPRNG, and therefore affects every Android application that use OpenSSL. Further studies on the memory allocation and each device characteristic may reduce the complexity or extend the affected applications during practical attacks. We recommend that adequate countermeasures should be immediately adopted.

The security of Android is becoming increasingly important owing the widespread use of mobile devices. Our study serves as a reminder that more studies and supplements are needed to ensure the security of Android.

9. ACKNOWLEDGEMENTS

We would like to thank Peter Gutmann and the anonymous reviewers for their helpful comments and suggestions for enhancing the quality of this paper. Dong Hoon Lee is supported by Next-Generation Information Computing Development Program through the National Research Foundation of Korea (NRF) funded by the Ministry of Science, ICT & Future Planning (2010-0020726).

10. REFERENCES

[1] Address space layout randomization. http://en.wikipedia.org/wiki/Address_space_layout_randomization.

[2] Android debug bridge. http://developer.android.com/tools/.

[3] Android Security Overview. http://source.android.com/devices/tech/security/.

[4] Break DES in less than a single day. http://www.sciengines.com/company/news-a-events/74-des-in-1-day.html.

[5] IDC - Press Release. http://www.idc.com/getdoc.jsp?containerId=prUS24257413.

[6] OpenSSL. http://www.openssl.org/.

[7] RFC 4507: Transport Layer Security (TLS) Session Resumption without Server-Side State.

[8] The Debian Project. Openssl-Predictable Random Number Generator, DSA-1571-1. Available from http://www.debian.org/security/2008/dsa-1571.

[9] Trace32. http://www.lauterbach.com/.

[10] N. J. Alfardan and K. G. Paterson, Plaintext-Recovery Attacks Against Datagram TLS. In *Network and Distrubited System Security Symposium (NDSS 2012)*, 2012.

[11] T. Biege. Analysis of a Strong Pseudo Random Number Generator by anatomizing Linux' Random Number Device. Tech. rep., PhoneFactor, Inc., Nov. 2006.

[12] D. Brumley and D. Boneh. Remote Timing Attacks Are Practical. In *Proceedings of the 12th conference on USENIX Security Symposium - Volume 12* (Berkeley, CA, USA, 2003), USENIX Association, 2003.

[13] B. Canvel, A. Hiltgen, S. Vaudenay, and M. Vuagnoux. Password Interception in a SSL/TLS Channel. In *Proceedings of Advances in Cryptology - CRYPTO 2003*, Springer-Verlag, pp. 583–599, 2003.

[14] T. Duong and J. Rizzo. Here Come the Xor Ninjas. Tech. rep., May 2011.

[15] S. Fahl, M. Harbach, T. Muders, L. Baumgärtner, B. Freisleben, and M. Smith. Why Eve and Mallory Love Android: An Analysis of Android SSL (In)Security. In *Proceedings of the 2012 ACM conference on Computer and communications security*, pp. 50–61, 2012.

[16] M. Georgiev, S. Iyengar, S. Jana, R. Anubhai, D. Boneh, and V. Shmatikov. The Most Dangerous Code in the World: Validating SSL Certificates in Non-browser Software. In *Proceedings of the 2012 ACM conference on Computer and communications security*, pp. 38–49, 2012.

[17] N. Heninger, Z. Durumeric, E. Wustrow, and J. A. Halderman. Mining Your Ps and Qs: Detection of Widespread Weak Keys in Network Devices. In *Proceedings of the 21st USENIX Security Symposium*, pp. 205–220, 2012.

[18] V. Klima, O. Pokorny, and T. Rosa. Attacking RSA-Based Sessions in SSL/TLS. In *Proceedings of Cryptographic Hardware and Embedded Systems (CHES) 2003*, Springer, pp. 426–440, 2003.

[19] P. Lacharme. The Linux Pseudorandom Number Generator Revisited. IACR ePrint Arcive 2012/251. Available from http://eprint.iacr.org/2012/251.

[20] M. Marlinspike. More Tricks for Defeating SSL in Practice. In *Black Hat USA*, 2009.

[21] C. Meyer and J. Schwenk. Lessons Learned from Previous SSL/TLS Attacks: A Brief Chronology of Attacks and Weakness. IACR ePrint Arcive 2013/049. Available from http://eprint.iacr.org/2013/049.

[22] M. Ray and S. Dispensa. Renegotiating TLS. Technical Report, PhoneFactor, Inc., Nov. 2009.

[23] T. Ristenpart and S. Yilek. When Good Randomness Goes Bad: Virtual Machine Reset Vulnerabilities and Hedging Deployed Cryptography. In *Proceedings of the Network and Distributed System Security Symposium (NDSS) 2010*. Internet Society, 2010.

[24] T. Vuillemin, F. Goichon, C. Lauradoux, and G. Salagnac. Entropy Transfers in the Linux Random Number Generator. Research Report 8060, INRIA, Sept. 2012.

[25] S. Yilek, E. Rescorla, H. Shacham, B. Enright, and S. Savage. When Private Keys Are Public: Results From the 2008 Debian OpenSSL Vulnerability. In *Proceedings of IMC 2009*, pp. 15–27, 2009.

Delegatable Pseudorandom Functions and Applications

Aggelos Kiayias
Dept. of Informatics & Telecommunications
National and Kapodistrian U. of Athens, Greece
aggelos@di.uoa.gr

Stavros Papadopoulos
Dept. of Computer Science & Engineering
HKUST, Hong Kong
stavrosp@cse.ust.hk

Nikos Triandopoulos
RSA Laboratories
Cambridge MA, USA
nikolaos.triandopoulos@rsa.com

Thomas Zacharias
Dept. of Informatics & Telecommunications
National and Kapodistrian U. of Athens, Greece
thzacharias@di.uoa.gr

ABSTRACT

We put forth the problem of delegating the evaluation of a pseudorandom function (PRF) to an untrusted proxy and introduce a novel cryptographic primitive called *delegatable pseudorandom functions*, or DPRFs for short: A DPRF enables a proxy to evaluate a pseudorandom function on a strict subset of its domain using a trapdoor derived from the DPRF secret key. The trapdoor is constructed with respect to a certain *policy predicate* that determines the subset of input values on which the proxy is allowed to compute. The main challenge in constructing DPRFs is to achieve *bandwidth efficiency* (which mandates that the trapdoor is smaller than the precomputed sequence of the PRF values conforming to the predicate), while maintaining the pseudorandomness of unknown values against an attacker that adaptively controls the proxy. A DPRF may be optionally equipped with an additional property we call *policy privacy*, where any two delegation predicates remain indistinguishable in the view of a DPRF-querying proxy: achieving this raises new design challenges as policy privacy and bandwidth efficiency are seemingly conflicting goals.

For the important class of policy predicates described as (1-dimensional) *ranges*, we devise two DPRF constructions and rigorously prove their security. Built upon the well-known tree-based GGM PRF family [17], our constructions are generic and feature only logarithmic delegation size in the number of values conforming to the policy predicate. At only a constant-factor efficiency reduction, we show that our second construction is also policy private. Finally, we describe that their new security and efficiency properties render our DPRF schemes particularly useful in numerous security applications, including RFID, symmetric searchable encryption, and broadcast encryption.

CCS'13, November 4–8, 2013, Berlin, Germany.

http://dx.doi.org/10.1145/2508859.2516668.

Categories and Subject Descriptors

C.2.4 [**Communication Networks**]: Distributed Systems—*client/server, distributed applications*; E.3 [**Data Encryption**]; G.3 [**Probability and Statistics**]: random number generation; K.6.5 [**Management of Computing and Information Systems**]: Security and Protection—*authentication*

General Terms

Algorithms, Security, Theory

Keywords

delegation of computation; pseudorandom functions; RFIDs; searchable encryption; broadcast encryption; authentication

1. INTRODUCTION

Due to its practical importance, the problem of securely delegating computational tasks to untrusted third parties comprises a particularly active research area. Generally speaking, secure delegation involves the design of protocols that allow the controlled authorization for an—otherwise untrusted—party to compute a given function while achieving some target security property (e.g., the verifiability of results or privacy of inputs/outputs) and also preserving the efficiency of the protocols so that the delegation itself remains meaningful. Beyond protocols for the delegation of general functionalities (e.g., [18, 33]) a variety of specific cryptographic primitives have been considered in this context (see related work in Section 2).

Surprisingly enough, pseudorandom functions (PRFs), a fundamental primitive for emulating perfect randomness via keyed functions, thus, finding numerous applications in information security, have not been explicitly studied in the context of delegation of computations (of PRF values). We, hereby, initiate a study on this matter.

A new PRF concept. We introduce *delegatable pseudorandom functions*, or DPRFs for short, a novel cryptographic primitive which enables the delegation of the evaluation of a PRF to an untrusted proxy according to a given predicate that defines the inputs on which the proxy will evaluate the PRF.

Specifically, let $\mathcal{F}$ be a PRF family, and $\mathcal{P}$ a set of predicates, called the *delegation policy*, defined over the domain of $\mathcal{F}$. A DPRF is a triplet $(\mathcal{F}, T, C)$ constructed with respect to $\mathcal{P}$, which provides the elementary functionality shown in Figure 1: For any secret key k and a predicate $P \in \mathcal{P}$, the delegator computes a trapdoor τ via algorithm T, and τ is transmitted to the proxy. The latter then runs algorithm C on τ to derive exactly the set of PRF values $B_P = \{f_k(x)|P(x)\}$, where $f_k \in \mathcal{F}$, i.e., the PRF value on every input x satisfying predicate P, overall correctly enabling the evaluation of PRF f_k subject to predicate P *without* explicit knowledge of secret key k, or even the input values $A_P = \{x|P(x)\}$.

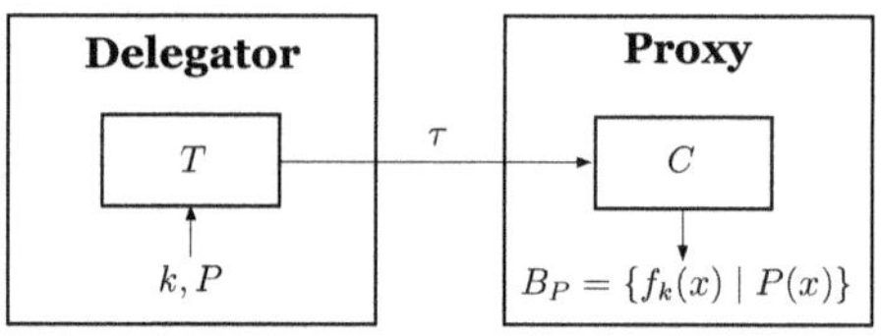

Figure 1: The DPRF functionality.

What motivates the above scheme is *bandwidth efficiency*: As long as the trapdoor τ is sublinear in the size $|B_P|$ of delegated PRF values, the delegation is meaningful as the delegator conserves resources (otherwise, the proxy could be provided directly with all the PRF values in B_P).

At the same time, the DPRF must retain the security properties of the underlying PRF, namely, (i) *pseudorandomness* for any value x conforming to the delegation predicate P, i.e., $P(x)$, and (ii) *unpredictability* for any nonconforming value x such that $\neg P(x)$. In addition, a DPRF can optionally satisfy a *policy-privacy* property which prevents the proxy from inferring information about P or the delegated (input) set A_P from the trapdoor τ.

Our definitional framework. We introduce a formal definitional framework for the new primitive of DPRFs, carefully capturing all the above technical requirements. We first rigorously define the *correctness* and *security* requirements that any DPRF should meet. Correctness captures the ability of the proxy to successfully evaluate the PRF on exactly those inputs (set A_P) specified by predicate P. Security captures the requirement that the delegation capabilities of the PRF do not compromise its core pseudorandomness property. But this condition goes beyond the standard security definition of PRFs, since the pseudorandomness attacker, in addition to the PRF oracle, may now adaptively query also a trapdoor oracle for delegation on predicates of its choice.

Equally important is also the *policy-privacy* property that a DPRF may optionally satisfy, intuitively capturing the inability of a malicious proxy to learn any (non-trivial) property about the delegated set A_P (that is not implied by B_P). Our security notion postulates that for any two predicates P, P' the corresponding trapdoors are indistinguishable, provided that $|A_P| = |A_{P'}|$ and the adversary issues no delegation queries that trivially separate B_P and $B_{P'}$.

GGM-based realization for range predicates. We devise two *bandwidth-efficient* and *provably secure* DPRF constructions for the case where the delegation policy contains predicates described by *1-dimensional ranges*. Range-based policies is an interesting use case, as many applications maintain an ordering over the PRF inputs, and delegation rights are defined with respect to ranges of such inputs.

Our first DPRF scheme is called *best range cover*, or BRC for short, and relies on the well-known GGM PRF family [17]. This family defines a PRF based on the hierarchical application of any length-doubling pseudorandom generator (PRG) according to the structure induced by a tree, where input values are uniquely mapped to root-to-leaf paths. By exploiting the above characteristics, our BRC scheme features logarithmic delegation size in the number $|A_P|$ of values conforming to the policy predicate, by having the trapdoor τ comprise a subset I_P of *internal* (or *partial*) PRF values that optimally cover the target range B_P of PRF values. We provide a formal security proof for the above scheme which, interestingly, does not trivially follow from the GGM security proof. The reason is that the adversary can now employ delegation queries to learn any internal PRF value in the tree, and not simply leaf PRF values as in the original security game in [17]. We note that, although similar "range-covering" GGM-based constructions appear in the literature, e.g., in [30], no formal security analysis has been given.

However, our BRC scheme does not satisfy policy privacy, as the structure of the PRF values in I_P leaks information about predicate P. This motivates our second construction, called *uniform range cover*, or URC for short. This scheme augments BRC in a way that renders all trapdoors corresponding to ranges of the same size indistinguishable. This is achieved by carefully having τ comprising a subset I'_P of PRF values that cover the target range B_P of PRF values less optimally: I'_P contains PRF values that are descendants of those values in I_P at a tree height that depends solely on $|B_P|$ (which by definition leaks to the adversary). More interestingly, by adopting the above change, URC retains both the asymptotic logarithmic bandwidth complexity of BRC and its DPRF security, but it crucially achieves a policy-privacy notion appropriately relaxed to our setting of range predicates. Inherently, as we argue, no efficient tree-based DPRF scheme can satisfy policy privacy, so we have to resort to a sufficient relaxation which we call *union policy privacy.*

Main applications. Finally, our DPRF schemes, equipped with bandwidth efficiency, security and policy privacy (URC only), lend themselves to new schemes that provide scalable solutions to a wide range of information security and applied cryptography settings that involve the controlled authorization of PRF-based computations. Generally, DPRFs are particularly useful in applications that rely on the evaluation of (secret) key-based cryptographic primitives on specific inputs (according to an underlying policy): Using a DPRF scheme then allows a cost-efficient, yet secure and private, key management for an untrusted proxy who is otherwise capable in executing a particular computational task.

We outline several such applications in which DPRFs are useful, including authentication and access control in RFIDs, efficient batch querying in searchable encryption, as well as broadcast encryption. Due to the underlying GGM building component, our DPRFs are extremely lightweight, as their practical implementation entails a few repeated applications of *any* efficient candidate instantiation of a PRG that is length doubling.

Summary of contributions. Our main contributions are:

- We initiate the study of policy-based delegation of the task of evaluating a pseudorandom function (PRF) on specific input values, and introduce the concept of *delegatable* PRFs (DPRFs).

- We develop a general and rigorous definitional framework for the new DPRF primitive, capturing properties such as *bandwidth efficiency*, *correctness*, *security* and *policy privacy*, and also offering a relaxed *union policy privacy* that is arguably necessary for tree-wise DPRF constructions.
- We present a framework for building DPRF schemes for the important case where the delegation policy is governed by range predicates over inputs; our framework augments the generic GGM construction framework of [17] to provide two concrete DPRF schemes, namely BRC and URC.
- We prove the security of our constructions in a modular way, thus also yielding the first security analysis of similar GGM-based key-delegation schemes, and the union-policy privacy of URC.
- We describe several key applications of DPRFs in the context of efficient key-delegation protocols for authentication, access control and encryption purposes.

Paper organization. Section 2 reviews related work. Section 3 formulates the DPRF primitive, Section 4 presents our two DPRF constructions for the case of range policies. Section 5 elaborates on the applicability of DPRFs. Finally, Section 6 concludes our paper with directions for future work. Selected proofs appear in the Appendix.

2. RELATED WORK

Secure delegation of computations. The notion of delegation of cryptographic operations is already mature: Starting from early work on proxy signatures [28] and proxy cryptography [5], basic primitives such as signatures (e.g., [6, 28]) and encryption (e.g.,[2, 19, 22]) have been studied in the context of an untrusted proxy who is authorized to operate on signatures or ciphertexts. Recently, there has also been an increased interest in verifiability and privacy of general outsourced computations (e.g., [1, 9, 10, 18, 33]) or specific crypto-related operations (e.g., [4, 15, 20]). To the best of our knowledge, however, no prior work explicitly and formally examines the delegation of PRFs.[1]

PRF extensions. Closer to our new DPRF primitive are the known extensions of PRFs, namely the *verifiable PRFs* (VPRFs) (e.g., [12, 27, 29]) and the *oblivious PRFs* (OPRFs) (e.g., [16, 23]). A VPRF provides a PRF value along with a non-interactive proof, which enables anyone to verify the correctness of the PRF value. Although such proofs can be useful in third-party settings, they are not related to the delegation of the PRF evaluation without the secret key. Similarly, an OPRF is a two-party protocol that securely implements functionality $(k, x) \to (\perp, f_k(x))$—that is, a party evaluates a PRF value without knowledge of the secret key. Yet, although the party that provides the key can be viewed to preserve resources, this setting does not match ours because there is no (i) input privacy (it is the second party who provides the input x), and (ii) bandwidth efficiency when applied over many values. Other related work includes *algebraic PRFs*, employed in [4] to achieve optimal private verification of outsourced computation.

[1]Delegating PRF evaluation in a similar vein as we consider here, was considered in [7, 8] after our work was submitted for publication.

GGM framework. This refers to the seminal work by Goldreich *et al.* [17], which shows how to generically construct a PRF given black-box access to a length-doubling PRG. The approach is based on a tree structure, over which hierarchical invocations of the PRG produce the PRF values at the leaves. Our constructions extend this framework in non-trivial ways: First, we support delegation of PRF evaluations; second, our security is proved in a much stronger adversarial setting where the adversary gets to adaptively learn also *internal* PRF values. The GGM framework, along with its tree-based key-derivation structure, have been widely used in the literature; also for special/limited delegation purposes in the context of access control [30], broadcast encryption [31] and forward security [21]. Yet, to the best of our knowledge, no such known key-derivation method has been analyzed fully in a security model like ours, which allows for adaptive PRF/delegation queries and addresses policy-privacy issues.

3. DEFINITIONS

A *pseudorandom function (PRF) family* $\mathcal{F}$ is a family of functions $\{f_k : A \to B \mid k \in \mathcal{K}\}$ so that $\mathcal{K}$ is efficiently samplable and all $\mathcal{F}, \mathcal{K}, A, B$ are indexed by a security parameter λ. The security property of a PRF is as follows: For any probabilistic polynomial-time (PPT) algorithm $\mathcal{A}$ running in time polynomial in λ it holds that

$$|\Pr[\mathcal{A}^{f_k(\cdot)} = 1] - \Pr[\mathcal{A}^{R(\cdot)} = 1]| = \mathsf{negl}(\lambda) ,$$

where negl denotes a negligible function and the probability above is taken over the coins of $\mathcal{A}$ and the random variables k and R which are uniformly distributed over the domains $\mathcal{K}$ and $(A \to B)$ respectively.

Delegatable PRFs. The notion of delegation for a PRF family $\mathcal{F}$ as above is defined with respect to a *delegation policy* $\mathcal{P}$, i.e., $\mathcal{P}$ is a set of predicates defined over A, also indexed by λ, where each predicate P has an efficient encoding. The set of elements in A that satisfy P is denoted as $A_P = \{x \in A \mid P(x)\}$.

Definition 1 (Delegatable PRF) *A triple* $(\mathcal{F}, T, C)$ *is a* delegatable PRF, *or* DPRF scheme, *for family* $\mathcal{F} = \{f_k : A \to B \mid k \in \mathcal{K}\}$ *with respect to policy* $\mathcal{P}$ *of predicates over* A, *provided it satisfies two properties,* correctness *and* security, *that are defined individually below.*

Correctness. We define T to be a PPT algorithm such that, given a description of $P \in \mathcal{P}$ and a key $k \in \mathcal{K}$, it outputs a "trapdoor" τ. The latter is intended to be used along with the deterministic PPT algorithm C for the PRF computation over every element of A that satisfies the predicate P. For fixed P, k, algorithm C can be viewed as a function

$$C : St_{P,k} \longrightarrow B \times St_{P,k} \ ,$$

where $St_{P,k}$ is a set of states, and for any $s \in St_{P,k}$ the output $C(s)$ is a pair that consists of a PRF value and a (new) state. We denote $C(s) = \langle C_L(s), C_R(s) \rangle$ and define recursively the set of *reachable* states from a subset S of $St_{P,k}$ as

$$\mathcal{R}(S) \triangleq S \cup \mathcal{R}(C_R(S)) \ .$$

The elements of the DPRF that are produced given an initial state s will be defined using the complete set of reachable states given s. For a singleton $S = \{s\}$, we will write $\mathcal{R}(s)$ instead of $\mathcal{R}(\{s\})$, and we will denote by $\mathcal{R}(s)$ the closure of s under $\mathcal{R}$, i.e., the fixpoint of the recursive equation for $\mathcal{R}$ that also contains s.

Definition 2 (Correctness) *The DPRF scheme $(\mathcal{F}, T, C)$ is* correct *for a policy $\mathcal{P}$ if for every $P \in \mathcal{P}$:*

1. $\{\tau \mid \tau \leftarrow T(P,k)\} \cup \{\bot\} \subseteq St_{P,k}$, *for any $k \in \mathcal{K}$* (initialization)*.*
2. $C_R(\bot) = \bot$ (termination condition)*.*
3. *There is a polynomial q such that for every $k \in \mathcal{K}$ and $\tau \leftarrow T(P,k)$:*
   (i) $\bot \in \mathcal{R}(\tau)$ (termination guarantee)*.*
   (ii) $|\mathcal{R}(\tau)| \leq q(\lambda)$ (feasibility)*.*
   (iii) $\{f_k(x) \mid P(x)\} = B_P = \{C_L(s) \mid s \in \mathcal{R}(\tau)\}$ (completeness)*.*

According to the above conditions, all possible trapdoors corresponding to a certain policy predicate P are valid initial inputs for C. Moreover, starting from an arbitrary trapdoor for P as initial input, the proxy can execute a number of steps of algorithm C, during which it successively computes the DPRF image of every argument x that satisfies P, and eventually terminate when it reaches the final state $\bot$, where no further useful information can be derived.

We note that condition 3.(ii) implies the restriction that the size of every policy predicate is polynomial. This stems from the fact that we consider the setting where the proxy wishes to eventually compute *all* the delegated PRF values. If this is not necessary (or desirable) for the DPRF application, the condition can be relaxed to any size of A_P (including super-polynomial sizes). In this case, the completeness condition (item 3.(iii) above) would be infeasible to meet, since the proxy cannot hope to be able to compute all the delegated PRF values. There are a number of ways to capture this by suitably modifying the way C works; for instance: (i) C may sample the uniform distribution over B_P, (ii) C may be given the value x as input, and return $f_k(x)$ if $x \in A_P$ and $\bot$ otherwise, (iii) C may be given the lexicographic rank of an element x within A_P and return $f_k(x)$ or $\bot$ otherwise.

Security. We consider the case where the proxy is malicious, and accordingly model DPRF security as an *oracle indistinguishability* game $\mathcal{G}^{\mathcal{A}}_{\mathsf{SEC}}$ carried out between an attacker $\mathcal{A}$ and a challenger $\mathcal{C}$ indexed by parameter λ. The game proceeds as shown in Figure 2. Note that due to the delegation capabilities of DPRFs, the security game $\mathcal{G}^{\mathcal{A}}_{\mathsf{SEC}}$ is more elaborate than the security game of a plain PRF: Indeed, in addition to issuing standard PRF queries, the pseudorandomness attacker may now adaptively query also a trapdoor oracle for delegation on predicates of its choice.

Definition 3 (Security) *A DPRF scheme $(\mathcal{F}, T, C)$ is* secure *for a policy $\mathcal{P}$ if for any PPT $\mathcal{A}$, it holds that*

$$\Pr[\mathcal{G}^{\mathcal{A}}_{\mathsf{SEC}}(1^\lambda) = 1] \leq \frac{1}{2} + \mathsf{negl}(\lambda) .$$

<u>*DPRF Security Game $\mathcal{G}^{\mathcal{A}}_{\mathsf{SEC}}(1^\lambda)$*</u>

1. The challenger $\mathcal{C}$ randomly selects k from $\mathcal{K}$.
2. The adversary $\mathcal{A}$ is allowed to interact with $\mathcal{C}$ and ask two types of queries:
   (a) *PRF queries* for a value $x \in A$; to those queries $\mathcal{C}$ responds with $f_k(x)$ and adds the value x to a set L_{que}.
   (b) *Delegation queries* for a policy predicate $P \in \mathcal{P}$; to those queries $\mathcal{C}$ responds with $\tau \leftarrow T(P,k)$ and adds P to a set L_{pol}.
3. The adversary $\mathcal{A}$ submits a challenge query x^* to which the challenger $\mathcal{C}$ responds as follows: It flips a coin b and if $b = 1$ it responds with $y^* = f_k(x^*)$, otherwise, it responds with a random value y^* from B.
4. The adversary $\mathcal{A}$ continues as in step 2.
5. The adversary $\mathcal{A}$ terminates by returning a single bit $\tilde{b}$. Subsequently the game returns a bit which is 1 if and only if the following holds true:
$$(b = \tilde{b}) \wedge (x^* \notin L_{\mathsf{que}}) \wedge \forall P \in L_{\mathsf{pol}} : \neg P(x^*) .$$

Figure 2: The DPRF security game.

We make the following observations about the definition. First, it is easy to see that a delegatable PRF is indeed a PRF. Specifically, any PRF attacker $\mathcal{A}$ against f_k can be turned into an attacker $\mathcal{A}'$ that wins the DPRF game $G^{\mathcal{A}}_{\mathsf{SEC}}(1^\lambda)$. We provide only a simple sketch of this which follows by a standard "walking" argument (the reader familiar with such arguments may skip to the next paragraph). Fix some PPT $\mathcal{A}$ and let α be its non-negligible distinguishing advantage. There will be some polynomial q so that, for any λ, $q(\lambda)$ is an upper bound on the number of queries submitted to $\mathcal{A}$'s oracle by $\mathcal{A}$. Given such q and for fixed λ, we define the *hybrid* oracle $(f_k/R)_j$ for any $j \in \{0, \ldots, q(\lambda)\}$ that operates as follows: $(f_k/R)_j$ responds as $f_k(\cdot)$ in the first j queries and as $R(\cdot)$ in the last $q(\lambda) - j$ queries. Taking such sequence of oracles into account, by triangular inequality, it follows that there exists some value $j \in \{0, \ldots, q(\lambda) - 1\}$ for which the distinguishing probability will be at least $\alpha/q(\lambda)$ for $\mathcal{A}$ to distinguish between two successive hybrid oracles $(f_k/R)_j$ and $(f_k/R)_{j+1}$ when R is a random function. This follows from the fact that $\mathcal{A}$ distinguishes the "extreme" hybrids $R(\cdot)$ and $f_k(\cdot)$ with probability α. We now construct $\mathcal{A}'$ as follows out of $\mathcal{A}$: $\mathcal{A}'$ plays the DPRF game and queries the DPRF function for the first j queries of $\mathcal{A}$. Then it submits the $(j+1)$-th query of $\mathcal{A}$ as the challenge. Finally, it completes the simulation of $\mathcal{A}$ by answering any remaining queries of $\mathcal{A}$ with random values drawn from B (w.l.o.g. the queries to the oracle are all distinct), and outputs what $\mathcal{A}$ does. It is easy to see that the distinguishing advantage of $\mathcal{A}'$ is $\alpha/2q(\lambda)$, i.e., non-negligible in λ.

Second, we observe that there is a trivial construction of a delegatable PRF from any PRF: Consider an ordering $\leq$ over A, e.g., the lexicographical order. For fixed P, k set $T(P,k) = \langle f_k(x_1), \ldots, f_k(x_{|A_P|}) \rangle = \tau$, where x_i is the i-th element of A_P according to $\leq$. Given τ, the set of states can be $St_{P,k} = \{\tau, (2,\tau), \ldots, (|A_P|, \tau), \bot\}$, and the reconstruction function C can be simply defined to be a table-lookup in τ. It is straightforward to show that $(\mathcal{F}, T, C)$ is a DPRF as long as the underlying family $\mathcal{F}$ is a PRF, since any delegation query can be interpreted as a series of polynomially many PRF queries.

The existence of a trivial DPRF construction with respect to arbitrary policies from any given PRF motivates our primitive: Interesting DPRF constructions will be those that are *bandwidth efficient*, i.e., they provide trapdoors with size that is *sublinear* in the number of elements that satisfy the corresponding policy predicate.

Policy privacy. We next introduce an additional privacy property that a DPRF scheme may optionally satisfy. This property goes beyond the standard (D)PRF security and is relevant in the context of PRF delegation for protecting the associated policy predicates over which the delegation is defined. We accordingly model this new privacy condition as a *predicate indistinguishability* game $\mathcal{G}^{\mathcal{A}}_{\mathsf{PP}}$ carried out between an attacker $\mathcal{A}$ and a challenger $\mathcal{C}$ indexed by a security parameter λ. The game proceeds as shown in Figure 3.

DPRF Policy Privacy Game $\mathcal{G}^{\mathcal{A}}_{\mathsf{PP}}(1^\lambda)$

1. The challenger $\mathcal{C}$ randomly selects k from $\mathcal{K}$.
2. The adversary $\mathcal{A}$ is allowed to interact with $\mathcal{C}$ and ask delegation queries on policy predicates $P \in \mathcal{P}$; to those queries $\mathcal{C}$ responds with $\tau \leftarrow T(P, k)$ and adds P to a set L_{pol}.
3. The adversary $\mathcal{A}$ submits two policy predicates P_0, P_1 to $\mathcal{C}$. The challenger flips a bit b and computes $\tau^* \leftarrow T(P_b, k)$. It returns τ^* to the adversary.
4. The adversary $\mathcal{A}$ continues as in step 2.
5. The adversary $\mathcal{A}$ terminates by returning a single bit $\tilde{b}$. Subsequently the game returns a bit that is 1 if and only if the following holds true:

$$(b = \tilde{b}) \wedge (|A_{P_0}| = |A_{P_1}|) \wedge (A_{P_0} \neq A_{P_1}) \wedge$$

$$\wedge \forall S \subseteq L_{\mathsf{pol}} : |(\bigcap_{P \in S} A_P) \cap A_{P_0}| = |(\bigcap_{P \in S} A_P) \cap A_{P_1}| \,.$$

Figure 3: The DPRF policy privacy game.

Definition 4 (Policy privacy) *A DPRF scheme* $(\mathcal{F}, T, C)$ *is* policy private *for a policy* $\mathcal{P}$ *if for any PPT* $\mathcal{A}$*, it holds that*

$$\Pr[\mathcal{G}^{\mathcal{A}}_{\mathsf{PP}}(1^\lambda) = 1] \leq \frac{1}{2} + \mathsf{negl}(\lambda) \,.$$

The above definition suggests that the trapdoor that corresponds to a certain policy predicate hides the predicate itself (i) at least among all (distinct) policy predicates that enable evaluations of the PRF on the same number of elements in its domain, and (ii) when the adversary does not make queries whose responses leak unequal parts of the PRF image of the two challenge predicates. Observe that all the restrictions stated are necessary: If $|A_{P_0}| \neq |A_{P_1}|$, then the adversary can distinguish P_0 from P_1 by counting the number $|\{C_L(s) \mid s \in \mathcal{R}(\tau^*)\}|$ of new PRF values it computes starting from state τ^* and ending in $\perp$. In addition, if the number of elements that satisfy simultaneously any set S of delegation queries and P_0 is different than the number of elements that satisfy S and P_1, then the adversary can distinguish the two predicates by counting the size of $\{C_L(s) \mid s \in \mathcal{R}(\tau^*)\} \cap (\bigcap_{P \in S} B_P)$.

We note that while the above formulation can capture a wide set of attacks against privacy, it can be strengthened further by allowing *multiple* challenge pairs of policy predicates. In this case, the policy-privacy game allows a multiple number of adversarial actions submitting pairs of policies (as in step 3 of the game) to be interleaved with delegation queries. The challenger always responds based on the same coin flip b. Interestingly, this *multiple-challenge policy privacy* formulation can be shown to be strictly stronger than the one corresponding to Definition 4.

On efficiently achieving policy privacy. We next argue that even though desirable, the above formulations of privacy conflict with our efficiency considerations (sublinear-size trapdoors) for a wide class of schemes. This will motivate relaxing the policy-privacy property as we will see in the end of the section; the reader unwilling to go over the details of the lower bound type of argument we sketch below may skip directly to the policy-privacy relaxation in the end of the section.

Assume that the policy predicates are ranges $[a, b]$ that lie in an interval $[0, 2^n - 1]$, where n is a positive integer. Then, no efficient and policy-private DPRF scheme exists, if the trapdoor-generation algorithm T is *deterministic*, and the delegated-computation algorithm C is *tree-wise*. This means that for each range, the trapdoor consists of a data structure of initial keys and meta-data that enable (by definition in a deterministic way) the calculation of the final set of PRF values through a tree-like derivation process, where the final underlying tree structure of this process depends only on the meta-data (and not on any of the initial keys). Indeed, if policy privacy is satisfied, then for every $0 < j \leq b - a$, the delegated computation of the PRF values in the intersection $[a+j, b]$ must be *indistinguishable* for $[a, b]$ and $[a+j, b+j]$. Otherwise, an adversary can make queries for all the PRF values in $[a + j, b]$ and, since it knows the way that each unique trapdoor of $[a, b]$ and $[a+j, b+j]$ computes the PRF values of the range $[a + j, b]$, can thus distinguish the two range predicates by making the corresponding equality tests. By induction, this implies that for any $j \in \{0, \ldots, b-a\}$, in the trapdoor of $[a, b]$ there exist distinct keys $d_0, \ldots, d_j$ that allow the computation of $f_k(a), \ldots, f_k(a + j)$, respectively. Thus, the size of the trapdoor of the range $[a, b]$ consists of at least $r = b - a + 1 = \#[a, b]$ keys which means that the DPRF cannot be efficient (i.e., enabling the delegation of the range with a trapdoor size less than the set of values being delegated).

The above argument suggests that, if policy privacy is to be attained, then we need trapdoors at least as long as the values we delegate. Note that the trivial construction for ranges mentioned above, i.e., when the trapdoor of $[a, b]$ is the sequence $\langle f_k(a), f_k(a + 1), \ldots, f_k(b)\rangle$, does not satisfy policy privacy. For instance, when delegating $[1, 3]$ and $[3, 5]$ the attacker can easily distinguish them by obtaining the value $f_k(3)$ (it belongs in the intersection hence the attacker is allowed to have it) and checking its location within the trapdoor vector. To achieve policy privacy for the trivial construction one needs to additionally permute the PRF values in the trapdoor in some fashion: It can be easily shown that a lexicographic ordering of these values suffices.

In our upcoming constructions, we obtain efficient DPRFs that use tree-wise derivations where the PRF values computed are at the leaves of a full binary tree, and the policy predicates are ranges of the form $[a, b]$, covered by one or more proper subtrees. In this case, even allowing a probabilistic trapdoor generator does not suffice to provide policy privacy for a very efficient scheme. To see this, let $[a, b]$ be a range of size r and τ be a trapdoor for $[a, b]$ of size $g(r) = O(\log^c r)$, i.e., $g(r)$ is polylogarithmic in r, hence also in λ. By the Pigeonhole principle, there exists a delegation key y in τ that computes all the values corresponding to a set $T \subseteq [a, b]$ of size at least $r/g(r)$, that is, a subtree T of depth at least $d \geq \log(r) - \log(g(r)) = \omega(1)$. The latter implies that there exists a value $x \in [a, b]$ with an *all-one suffix* of length d that is computed by this key y. (Here, a tree node contributes a 0 or 1 to root-to-leaves path labelings if it is a left or right child respectively). Since there are no more than $g(r)$ such possible values $x \in [a, b]$, an adversary has significant probability greater than $1/g(r)$ of guessing x. Then it can make a query x, receive $f_k(x)$ and submit as the challenge the two policies $P_0 = [a, b]$ and $P_1 = [x, b+(x-a)]$. After it receives the challenge trapdoor τ^*, it can locate all keys that correspond to subtrees of size $\geq d$ and check if there is a minimum leaf value (an all-zero path) in some of these subtrees that equals to $f_k(x)$. Then, the adversary can distinguish effectively P_0, P_1 since x cannot be covered by any subtree of size d in a trapdoor for $[x, b+(x-a)]$ (it must be covered by a leaf while $d > 1$). This argument can be extended to more general tree-like delegation schemes and for the case $g(r) = o(r)$, but we omit further details as it already demonstrates that efficient tree-like constructions require a somewhat more relaxed definition of policy privacy—which we introduce next.

Union policy privacy. We finally introduce the notion of *union policy privacy*, where the adversary is restricted from making queries in the *union* of the challenge policy predicates (but is allowed to query at arbitrary locations outside the targeted policy set). This privacy condition is a strict relaxation of the one corresponding to Definition 4, and we model it by a game $\mathcal{G}^{\mathcal{A}}_{\mathsf{UPP}}(1^\lambda)$ that proceeds *identically* as $\mathcal{G}^{\mathcal{A}}_{\mathsf{PP}}(1^\lambda)$, but terminates with 1 provided that the following (weaker set of) conditions are all met: (i) $b = \tilde{b}$, (ii) $|A_{P_0}| = |A_{P_1}|$, (iii) $A_{P_0} \neq A_{P_1}$ and (iv) $\forall P \in L_{\mathsf{pol}} : A_P \cap (A_{P_0} \cup A_{P_1}) = \emptyset$. To see the connection with Definition 4 observe that the latter condition is equivalent to

$$\forall S \subseteq L_{\mathsf{pol}} : |(\bigcap_{P \in S} A_P) \cap A_{P_0}| = |(\bigcap_{P \in S} A_P) \cap A_{P_1}| = 0 .$$

Note that for policies $\mathcal{P}$ consisting of disjoint predicates, the games $\mathcal{G}^{\mathcal{A}}_{\mathsf{PP}}(1^\lambda)$ and $\mathcal{G}^{\mathcal{A}}_{\mathsf{UPP}}(1^\lambda)$ are equivalent.

4. CONSTRUCTIONS

In this section we present DPRF schemes for *range* policy predicates. In Section 4.1 we describe a first construction, called *best range cover* (BRC), which satisfies the correctness and security properties of DPRFs, achieving trapdoors of logarithmic size in the range size. However, BRC lacks the policy-privacy property. In Section 4.2 we build upon BRC to obtain a DPRF scheme, called *uniform range cover* (URC), that is additionally (union) policy private, while retaining the trapdoor size complexity of BRC. In Section 4.3 we include the security proofs of the two schemes. In Section 4.4 we prove the union policy-privacy property of URC.

4.1 The BRC Construction

Let $G : \{0, 1\}^\lambda \rightarrow \{0, 1\}^{2\lambda}$ be a pseudorandom generator and $G_0(k), G_1(k)$ be the first and second half of the string $G(k)$, where the specification of G is public and k is a secret random seed (of bit length λ). The GGM pseudorandom function family [17] is defined as $\mathcal{F} = \{f_k : \{0, 1\}^n \rightarrow \{0, 1\}^\lambda\}_{k \in \{0,1\}^\lambda}$, such that

$$f_k(x_{n-1} \cdots x_0) = G_{x_0}(\cdots (G_{x_{n-1}}(k))) ,$$

where n is polynomial in λ and $x_{n-1} \cdots x_0$ is the input bitstring of size n.

The GGM construction defines a binary tree over the PRF domain. We illustrate this using Figure 4, which depicts a binary tree with 5 levels. The leaves are labeled with a decimal number from 0 to 15, sorted in ascending order. Every edge is labeled with 0 (resp. 1) if it connects a left (resp. right) child. We label every *internal* node with the binary string determined by the labels of the edges along the path from the root to this node. Suppose that the PRF domain is $\{0, 1\}^4$. Then, the PRF value of 0010 is $f_k(0010) = G_0(G_1(G_0(G_0(k))))$. Observe that the composition of G is performed according to the edge labels in the path from the root to leaf $2 = (0010)_2$, selecting the first (second) half of the output of G when the label of the visited edge is 0 (resp. 1) and using this half as the seed for the next application of G. Based on the above, the n-long binary representation of the leaf labels constitute the PRF domain, and every leaf is associated with the PRF value of its label—these values constitute the PRF range.

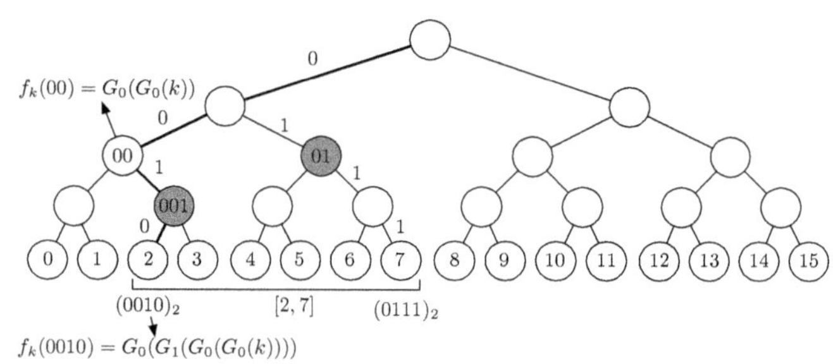

Figure 4: A GGM tree example.

Note that we can also associate every *internal* node of the GGM tree with a *partial* PRF value, by performing the composition of G as determined by the path from the root to that node. For example, node 00 in Figure 4 is associated with partial PRF $G_0(G_0(k))$. Henceforth, for simplicity, we denote by $f_k(x_{n-1} \cdots x_j)$ the partial PRF $G_{x_j}(\cdots (G_{x_{n-1}}(k)))$. Observe that if a party has the partial PRF $f_k(x_{n-1} \cdots x_j)$, then it can compute the PRF values of all 2^j inputs that have prefix $x_{n-1} \cdots x_j$, simply by following a DFS traversal in the subtree rooted at (the node labelled by) $x_{n-1} \cdots x_j$ and composing with seed $f_k(x_{n-1} \cdots x_j)$. In our running example, using the partial PRF value at node 00, we can derive the PRF values of the inputs in (decimal) range $[0, 3]$ as $f_k(0000) = G_0(G_0(f_k(00)))$, $f_k(0001) = G_1(G_0(f_k(00)))$, $f_k(0010) = G_0(G_1(f_k(00)))$, and $f_k(0011) = G_1(G_1(f_k(00)))$.

For any range $[a, b]$ of leaf labels, there is a (non-unique) set of subtrees in the GGM tree that *cover exactly* the corresponding leaves. For instance, $[2, 7]$ is covered by the subtrees rooted at nodes 001 and 01 (colored in grey). According to our discussion above, a party having the partial PRF values of these subtree roots and the subtree depths, it can derive all the PRF values of the leaves with labels in

$[a, b]$. In our example, having $(f_k(001), 1)$ and $(f_k(01), 2)$, it can derive the PRF values of the leaves with labels in $[2, 7]$. Our first construction is based on the above observations. In particular, given a range policy predicate $[a, b] \in \mathcal{P}$ with size $r = b - a + 1 = |A_P|$,[2] it finds the *minimum* number of subtrees that cover $[a, b]$. As such, we call this scheme as *best range cover* (BRC). A formal description follows.

The BRC DPRF construction is a triplet $(\mathcal{F}, T, C)$, where $\mathcal{F}$ is the GGM PRF family described above with tree depth n. The delegation policy is $\mathcal{P} = \{[a, b] \mid 0 \le a \le b \le a + \lambda^\gamma < 2^n\}$, where γ is a constant integer. Note that when $a = b$ the trapdoor sent to the proxy is (essentially) simply the PRF value $f_k(a)$. In the rest of the section, we focus on the non-trivial case where the range is not a singleton. When $a < b$, the trapdoor generation algorithm T of BRC, henceforth denoted by T_{BRC}, is given below.

The Trapdoor Generation Algorithm T_{BRC}

Input: $a, b : 0 \le a < b \le a + \lambda^\gamma \le 2^n - 1$ and $k \in \{0,1\}^\lambda$
Output: Trapdoor τ for computing $\{f_k(x) | x \in [a, b]\}$

1. $\tau \leftarrow \langle\rangle$
2. $t \leftarrow \max\{i \mid a_i \neq b_i\}$
3. **if** $(\forall i \le t:\ a_i = 0)$ **then**
4.   **if** $(\forall i \le t: b_i = 1)$ **then**
5.   **return** $(f_k(a_{n-1} \cdots a_{t+1}), t+1)$
6.   **else**
7.   Append $(f_k(a_{n-1} \cdots a_t), t)$ to τ
8. **else**
9. $\mu \leftarrow \min\{i \mid i < t \wedge a_i = 1\}$
10.   **for** $i = t - 1$ to $\mu + 1$
11.   **if** $a_i = 0$ **then**
12.   Append $(f_k(a_{n-1} \cdots a_{i+1}1), i)$ to τ
13.   Append $(f_k(a_{n-1} \cdots a_\mu), \mu)$ to τ
14. **if** $(\forall i \le t : b_i = 1)$ **then**
15.   Append $(f_k(b_{\nu-1} \cdots b_t), t)$ to τ
16. **else**
17. $\nu \leftarrow \min\{i \mid i < t \wedge b_i = 0\}$
18.   **for** $i = t - 1$ to $\nu + 1$
19.   **if** $b_i = 1$ **then**
20.   Append $(f_k(b_{n-1} \cdots b_{i+1}0), i)$ to τ
21.   Append $(f_k(b_{n-1} \cdots b_\nu), \nu)$ to τ
22. **return** τ

This algorithm takes as input a secret key k and a range predicate $[a, b] \in \mathcal{P}$. It outputs a delegation trapdoor τ that enables the computation of $f_k(x)$ for every x whose decimal representation is in $[a, b]$ (i.e., the PRF values of the leaves in the GGM tree with labels in $[a, b]$). Initially, T_{BRC} finds the first bit in which a and b differ (Line 2), which determines the common path from the root to leaves a and b. Suppose that this common path ends at node u. If $[a, b]$ is the set of labels that belong to the subtree with root u, then T_{BRC} outputs a single pair consisting of the partial PRF value that corresponds to u along with the depth of the subtree (Lines 3-5). Otherwise, T_{BRC} traverses the left and right subtree of u separately (Lines 7-13 and 14-21, respectively). We will describe only the left traversal (the right one is performed symmetrically). T_{BRC} considers the path $p_{v \to a}$ starting from the left child of u, denoted by v, to a. It checks whether a is the leftmost leaf of v's subtree. In this case the PRF value of v is included in τ along with the depth of v's subtree, and the traversal terminates (Lines 3,7). Otherwise, if $p_{v \to a}$ proceeds to the left child of v, it includes in the trapdoor the PRF value of the right child of v together with the depth of the subtree rooted at that child. In any case, it continues the traversal in the same fashion with the next node of $p_{v \to a}$ (Lines 8-13).

In the example of Figure 4, for input $[2, 7]$, algorithm T_{BRC} outputs trapdoor $\tau = \langle (f_k(001), 1), (f_k(01), 2) \rangle$. By construction, it is easy to see that T_{BRC} covers the input range with *maximal* subtrees, thus using a minimum number of them.

We next describe the reconstruction algorithm C of BRC. For fixed $P = [a, b]$ of size r and key k, we define the set of states as $St_{P,k} = \{\tau, (1, \tau), \ldots, (r-1, \tau), \bot\}$, where $\tau = \langle (y_1, d_1), \ldots, (y_m, d_m) \rangle$ is the trapdoor produced by algorithm T_{BRC}. Note that, every $y_i, i = 1, \ldots, m$ corresponds to a partial PRF value associated with the root of a GGM subtree. Therefore, there is a natural ordering of PRF values for a given τ, starting from the leftmost leaf of the subtree of y_1 to the rightmost leaf of the subtree of y_m. This order is not necessarily the same as the order of the leaves in the GGM tree.[3] Starting from the PRF value of the leftmost leaf of the y_1 subtree, C computes in every next step the PRF value of the next leaf in the ordering discussed above. Specifically, C starts with state τ and computes $C(\tau) = \langle G_0(\cdots(G_0(y_1))), (1, \tau) \rangle$, where the G_0 composition is performed d_1 times. Then, generally, given state (i, τ), C locates the unique subtree that covers the $(i+1)$-th leaf x in the ordering of τ. In particular, it finds the pair (y_t, d_t) in τ, where t is such that $\sum_{\rho=1}^{t-1} 2^{d_\rho} \le i < \sum_{\rho=1}^{t} 2^{d_\rho}$. Then, the suffix $x_{d_t - 1} \cdots x_0$ is the binary representation of $i - \sum_{\rho=1}^{t-1} 2^{d_\rho} \in [0, 2^{d_t} - 1]$. Given this suffix, C can compute $f_k(x) = G_{x_0}(\cdots(G_{x_{d_t-1}}(y_t)))$ and output $C((i, \tau)) = \langle G_{x_0}(\cdots(G_{x_{d_t-1}}(y_t))), (i+1, \tau) \rangle$. For the case where $d_t = 0$, C simply returns $f_k(x) = y_t$. Finally, for input state $(r-1, \tau)$, C outputs $\langle G_1(\cdots(G_1(y_m))), \bot \rangle$, where the G_1 composition is performed d_m times.

In the example of Figure 4, the trapdoor for range $[2, 14]$ is $\langle (f_k(01), 2), (f_k(001), 1), (f_k(10), 2), (f_k(110), 1), (f_k(1110), 0) \rangle$. Algorithm C computes the PRF values for leaves 4, 5, 6, 7, 2, 3, 8, 9, 10, 11, 12, 13, 14 in this order, i.e.,

$$C(\tau) = \langle G_0(G_0(f_k(01))), (1, \tau) \rangle = \langle f_k(0100), (1, \tau) \rangle \to$$
$$C((1, \tau)) = \langle G_1(G_0(f_k(01))), (2, \tau) \rangle = \langle f_k(0101), (2, \tau) \rangle \to$$
$$\vdots$$
$$C((12, \tau)) = \langle f_k(1110), \bot \rangle\ .$$

As described above, during the execution of C some partial PRF values in the GGM tree are computed *multiple* times; e.g., partial PRF value $f_k(011)$ is computed twice to derive $f_k(0110)$ and $f_k(0111)$. However, this can be easily avoided by employing a cache of size $O(r)$: Every PRF value is computed once, stored in the cache, and retrieved in a next step if necessary. In this manner, the computational cost of C can become $O(r)$, since we compute *one* PRF value for every node in the subtrees covering the range (of size r).

The correctness of BRC is stated in the following theorem.

Theorem 1 *The BRC DPRF construction $(\mathcal{F}, T, C)$ w.r.t. policy $\mathcal{P} = \{[a, b] \mid 0 \le a \le b \le a + \lambda^\gamma \le 2^n - 1\}$, where n is the depth of the underlying GGM tree, γ is a constant integer, and λ^γ is the maximum range size, is correct.*

[2]In the sequel, we use symbols r and $|A_P|$ interchangeably.

[3]This by-design feature of algorithm C comes at no efficiency cost in BRC, but it is crucial for policy privacy in URC.

PROOF. We show that all conditions of Definition 2 hold. Condition 1 can be easily seen to hold by the definition of the set of states $St_{P,k}$. Moreover, since $\mathcal{R}(\tau) = St_{P,k}$, conditions 2, 3.(i) and 3.(ii) are directly satisfied by the construction of algorithm C, and because the size of range r (which determines the number of values conforming to the range policy predicate) is upper bounded by λ^γ which is a polynomial.

Therefore, it remains to show that condition 3.(iii) holds. Note that, by construction, algorithm C computes exactly the PRF values of the leaves covered by the subtrees corresponding to the partial PRF values included in τ by algorithm T_{BRC}. Hence, it suffices to show that the labels of these leaves comprise *exactly* the set of values in $[a, b]$.

Let $t = \max\{i \mid a_i \neq b_i\}$ and V_1, V_2 be the sets of arguments of the PRF values that are computed in Lines 3-13 and 14-21 of T_{BRC}, respectively. If $V_2 = \emptyset$, then the input range is exactly covered by a single subtree (checks in lines 3 and 4 are true) and $V_1 = [a, b]$. Otherwise, it holds that

$$\begin{aligned} V_1 &= \{x \in [0, 2^n - 1] \mid x_{n-1} \cdots x_t = a_{n-1} \cdots a_t \wedge \\ &\quad \wedge (\exists i < t : [x_i = 1 \wedge a_i = 0] \vee x = a)\} \\ &= \{x \in [0, 2^n - 1] \mid a \leq x \leq a_{n-1} \cdots a_t 1 \cdots 1\} \\ &= [a, a_{n-1} \cdots a_t 1 \cdots 1] \, . \end{aligned}$$

Similarly, we get that $V_2 = [b_{n-1} \cdots b_t 0 \cdots 0, b]$. Observe that, by the definition of t, $a_t = 0$ and $b_t = 1$. Thus, it holds that $a_{n-1} \cdots a_t 1 \cdots 1 + 1 = b_{n-1} \cdots b_t 0 \cdots 0$. This means that $[a, b] = V_1 \cup V_2$, which concludes our proof. □

We next discuss the trapdoor size complexity in BRC. Let V_1, V_2 be defined as in the proof of Theorem 1. Then, $|V_1| + |V_2| = r$. We will analyze $|V_1|$ (the analysis for V_2 is similar). Observe that, in every step in Lines 3-13, the algorithm covers more than $\lfloor |V_1|/2 \rfloor$ values of V_1 with a *maximal* subtree of the sub-range defined by V_1. Iteratively, this means that the algorithm needs no more than $\log(r)$ maximal subtrees to cover the entire sub-range of V_1. Consequently, the total number of elements in τ is $O(\log(r))$.

We have explained the correctness of BRC and its efficient trapdoor size. We will also prove its security in Section 4.3. Nevertheless, BRC does not satisfy policy privacy, even for non-intersecting policy predicates. We illustrate this with an example using the tree of Figure 4. Consider the ranges $[2, 7]$ and $[9, 14]$, both with size 6, which generate trapdoors $\langle((f_k(001), 1), (f_k(01), 2)\rangle$ and $\langle(f_k(101), 1), (f_k(1001), 0), (f_k(110), 1), (f_k(1110), 0)\rangle$, respectively; these are trivially distinguishable due to their different sizes. This motivates our second DPRF construction presented next.

4.2 The URC Construction

Consider again the ranges $[2, 7]$ and $[9, 14]$ in the tree of Figure 4, for which BRC produces two distinguishable trapdoors, namely trapdoor $\langle(f_k(001), 1), (f_k(01), 2)\rangle$ and trapdoor $\langle(f_k(101), 1), (f_k(1001), 0), (f_k(110), 1), (f_k(1110), 0)\rangle$.

Now, instead of computing the trapdoor of $[2, 7]$ as above, assume that we generate an alternative trapdoor equal to $\langle(f_k(010), 1), (f_k(0010), 0), (f_k(011), 1), (f_k(0011), 0)\rangle$. Observe that this trapdoor appears to be indistinguishable to that of $[9, 14]$: Indeed, the two trapdoors have the same number of elements, the first parts of their elements are all partial PRFs, whereas their second parts (i.e., the depths) are pairwise equal. This suggests that, we could achieve policy privacy, if we could devise a trapdoor algorithm T such that, for *any* range predicate of a fixed size r it *always* generates a trapdoor with a *fixed* number of elements and a *fixed* sequence of depths. More simply stated, the algorithm should produce *uniform* trapdoors for ranges of the same size. The challenge is to design such an algorithm retaining the logarithmic trapdoor size of BRC. Next, we present our second DPRF construction, called *uniform range cover* (URC), which enjoys the efficiency of BRC and the union policy-privacy property.

URC builds upon BRC. In particular, it starts by producing a trapdoor as in BRC, and then modifies it to generate a uniform trapdoor for the given range r. Before embarking on its detailed description, we must investigate some interesting properties of the trapdoors of BRC, and provide some important definitions. Recall that a trapdoor in BRC is a sequence of elements, where the first part is a (full or partial) PRF value, and the second is a depth value.

Definition 5 *For an integer $r > 1$, a pair of non-negative integral sequences $D = ((k_1, \ldots, k_c), (l_1, \ldots, l_d))$ is called a* decomposition *of r, if the following hold:*

(i) $\sum_{i=1}^{c} 2^{k_i} + \sum_{j=1}^{d} 2^{l_j} = r$, and

(ii) $k_1 > \cdots > k_c$ and $l_1 > \cdots > l_d$.

A decomposition of r $D = ((k_1, \ldots, k_c), (l_1, \ldots, l_d))$ is a worst-case decomposition *(w.c.d.) of r if it is of maximum size, i.e., for every decomposition of r $D' = ((k'_1, \ldots, k'_{c'}), (l'_1, \ldots, l'_{d'}))$, we have that $c' + d' \leq c + d$. We define $M_D \triangleq \max\{k_1, l_1\}$ as the maximum integer that appears in D.*

By the description of algorithm T_{BRC} in BRC for fixed range size r, the depths in the trapdoor can be separated into two sequences that form a decomposition of r, unless the input range is exactly covered by a single subtree. Each sequence corresponds to a set of full binary subtrees of *decreasing* size that cover leaves in the range predicate. The usage of the worst case decomposition will become clear soon.

The next lemma shows that the maximum integer that appears in *any* decomposition of r (hence, the maximum depth of a subtree in a cover of a range of size r), can only take on one of two consecutive values that depend only on r.

Lemma 1 *Let $D = ((k_1, \ldots, k_c), (l_1, \ldots, l_d))$ be a decomposition of r. Define $B(r) \triangleq \lceil \log(r + 2) \rceil - 2$. Then $M_D \in \{B(r), B(r) + 1\}$. In addition, if $M_D = B(r) + 1$ then the second largest value is less than M_D.*

PROOF. By the two properties of D, we have that

$$\begin{aligned} r = \sum_{i=1}^{c} 2^{k_i} + \sum_{j=1}^{d} 2^{l_j} \leq 2^{k_1+1} + 2^{l_1+1} - 2 \leq \\ \leq 2^{M_D+2} - 2 \Leftrightarrow 2^{M_D+2} \geq r + 2 \Rightarrow M_D \geq B(r) \, . \end{aligned}$$

Since $2^{B(r)+2} \geq 2^{\log(r+2)} > r \geq 2^{k_1} + 2^{l_1}$, we have that the maximum value $M_D \in \{k_1, l_1\}$ is less than $B(r) + 2$ and k_1, l_1 cannot be both equal to $B(r) + 1$. □

By Lemma 1, the trapdoor that is generated by BRC for a range $P = [a, b]$ of size $|A_P| = r$, even if this trapdoor corresponds to a w.c.d. of r, consists of at most $|\{0, \ldots, B(r)\}| + |\{0, \ldots, B(r) + 1\}| = 2B(r) + 3$ pairs. Hence, the trapdoor size is $O(\log(r))$, which complies with the bound we described in Section 4.1. Moreover, since $|A_P| \leq \lambda^\gamma$, every trapdoor has no more than $2\lceil \log(\lambda^\gamma + 2)\rceil - 1$ pairs.

Observe that two trapdoors with depths that form the same decomposition appear indistinguishable. Moreover, we have proven that a trapdoor following a w.c.d. retains the logarithmic size in r. Therefore, our goal for the trapdoor algorithm T in URC, hereafter referred to as T_{URC}, is to construct a converter that takes as input a BRC trapdoor, and produces an alternative trapdoor that complies with a *fixed* worst-case decomposition. Before proceeding to the details of T_{URC}, we must prove the following vital theorem.

Theorem 2 *Let $D = ((k_1, \ldots, k_c), (l_1, \ldots, l_d))$ be a decomposition of r. Then all the elements in $\{0, \ldots, M_D\}$ appear in D iff D is a w.c.d. of r.*

PROOF. Assume that the implication does not hold and let x be the maximum integer in $\{0, \ldots, M_D\}$ that does not appear in D. Since $x < M_D$, $x+1$ is in $\{0, \ldots, M_D\}$. Assume w.l.o.g. that $l_j = x+1$. If $x > k_1$, then the decomposition of r, $((x, k_1, \ldots, k_c), (l_1, \ldots, l_{j-1}, x, l_{j+1}, \ldots, l_d))$, is of greater size than that of D. Similarly, if $i = \min\{i \mid x < k_i\}$, then the decomposition of r, $((k_1, \ldots, k_i, x, k_{i+1}, \ldots, k_c), (l_1, \ldots, l_{j-1}, x, l_{j+1}, \ldots, l_d))$, is of greater size than that of D. Both cases contradict the hypothesis, hence, x must appear in D.

For the converse, let $D' = ((k'_1, \ldots, k'_{c'}), (l'_1, \ldots, l'_{d'}))$ be a w.c.d. of r. Then, the integers $0, \ldots, M_{D'}$ appear in D'. By Lemma 1, all integers $0, \ldots, B(r)$ appear in D and D'. By removing the integers $0, \ldots, B(r)$ from D and D', the remaining integers are $y_1 \geq \ldots \geq y_s$ and $z_1 \geq \ldots \geq z_t$, respectively. Since an integer cannot appear more than twice in a decomposition of r and, by Lemma 1, the maximum possible value $B(r)+1$ cannot appear more than once, we have that $y_1, \ldots, y_s$ and $z_1, \ldots, z_t$ are sequences of distinct integers such that $\sum_{i=1}^{s} 2^{y_i} = \sum_{j=1}^{t} 2^{z_j}$. Assume that there exists a minimum index $\rho \leq s$ such that $y_\rho \neq z_\rho$ and that w.l.o.g. $y_\rho > z_\rho$. Then we have the contradiction

$$\sum_{i=1}^{s} 2^{y_i} \geq \sum_{i<\rho} 2^{y_i} + 2^{y_\rho} > \sum_{i<\rho} 2^{y_i} + 2^{z_\rho+1} - 1 \geq$$

$$\geq \sum_{i<\rho} 2^{z_i} + \sum_{i\geq\rho} 2^{z_i} = \sum_{j=1}^{t} 2^{z_j} = \sum_{i=1}^{s} 2^{y_i} .$$

Thus, $\{y_1, \ldots, y_s\}$ and $\{z_1, \ldots, z_t\}$ are equal, and therefore D is a w.c.d. of r. □

A consequence of Theorem 2 and Lemma 1 is that, for every integer $r > 1$, a w.c.d. of r is a proper re-arrangement of the integers that appear in the w.c.d. of r where the first sequence is $(B(r), \ldots, 0)$ and the second sequence is the remaining integers in the decomposition in decreasing order. We term this unique w.c.d. as the *uniform decomposition* of r. The main idea in URC is to always generate a trapdoor that complies with the uniform decomposition of r.

We are ready to describe algorithm T_{URC} in URC, whose pseudocode is provided below. The process starts with invoking the T_{BRC} algorithm of BRC to get an initial trapdoor τ (Line 1). If the input range is covered by a single subtree, then τ is reformed into two pairs that correspond to the child subtrees, so that the dephs in τ always form a decomposition (Lines 2-3). Let D be the decomposition implied by τ (Line 4). The loop in Lines 5-7 utilizes Theorem 2 and works as follows. It finds the highest depth x that does not exist in D, and "splits" the partial PRF value y_i in the rightmost pair in τ with depth $x+1$, producing two new partial PRF values with depth x, i.e., $y_i^0 = G_0(y_i)$ and $y_i^1 = G_1(y_i)$ (Line 6). Note that these values correspond to the two children of the subtree of y_i. Thus, if we substitute element $(y_i, x+1)$ by $(y_i^0, x), (y_i^1, x)$ in τ, then the trapdoor can still produce the same leaf PRF values as before. However, at all times we wish the sequence of depths in τ to form a decomposition. Hence, after removing $(y_i, x+1)$, we appropriately insert (y_i^0, x) in the left pair sequence and (y_i^1, x) in the right pair sequence of τ (Line 7). Upon termination of the loop, all the values in $\{0, \ldots, M_D\}$ appear in D and, thus, we have reached a w.c.d. according to Theorem 2. The process terminates, after properly re-arranging the elements of τ, such that they comply with the unique uniform decomposition of r (Lines 8-9). This is done deterministically, by simply filling the missing depths from $\{0, \ldots, B(r)\}$ in the left sequence with the unique appropriate pair that exists (by Theorem 2) in the right sequence.

The Trapdoor Generation Algorithm T_{URC}
Input: $a, b : 0 \leq a < b \leq a + \lambda^\gamma \leq 2^n - 1$ and $k \in \{0,1\}^\lambda$
Output: Trapdoor τ for computing $\{f_k(x) | x \in [a, b]\}$

1. Invoke $T_{\mathsf{BRC}}(a, b, k)$ and receive the output τ
2. **if** τ consists only of pair (y, d) **then**
3. $\quad \tau \leftarrow \langle (G_0(y), d-1), (G_1(y), d-1) \rangle$
4. Let $\tau = \langle (y_1, d_1), \ldots, (y_n, d_m) \rangle$ and $D = ((d_1, \ldots, d_c), (d_{c+1}, \ldots, d_m))$ be the corresponding decomposition of $r = b - a + 1$
5. **while** there is a maximum integer x in $\{0, \ldots, M_D\}$ that does not appear in D:
6. $\quad$ Find the rightmost pair $(y_i, x+1)$ and compute values $y_i^0 = G_0(y_i)$, $y_i^1 = G_1(y_i)$
7. $\quad$ Remove $(y_i, x+1)$ from τ, insert the pairs (y_i^0, x) and (y_i^1, x) in τ respecting the strictly decreasing order, and update D accordingly
8. **if** the leftmost sequence of D is not $(B(r), \ldots, 0)$ **then**
9. $\quad$ Fill leftmost sequence with values from rightmost sequence until it complies with the uniform decomposition of r
10. **return** τ

In our running example, for the range $[2, 7]$, the T_{URC} algorithm in URC converts the original token retrieved by the trapdoor algorithm of BRC, $\tau = \langle (f_k(001), 1), (f_k(01), 2) \rangle$, as follows (we underline a newly inserted element to the left sequence, and depict as bold a newly inserted element to the right sequence):

$$\langle (f_k(001), 1), (f_k(01), 2) \rangle$$
$$\downarrow$$
$$\langle \underline{(f_k(0010), 0)}, (f_k(01), 2), (\mathbf{f_k(0011), 0}) \rangle$$
$$\downarrow$$
$$\langle \underline{(f_k(010), 1)}, (f_k(0010), 0), (\mathbf{f_k(011), 1}), (f_k(0011), 0) \rangle .$$

The C algorithm of URC is identical to that of BRC, because the trapdoor in URC has exactly the format expected by this algorithm, i.e., pairs of PRF values corresponding to GGM subtrees along with their depths. Moreover, during the evolution of the initial BRC trapdoor into one of uniform decomposition in the T algorithm of URC, a partial PRF value y is substituted by two new PRF values that can generate the same leaf PRF values as y. As such, the correctness of the BRC scheme is inherited in URC. Finally, due to Lemma 1, the size of a w.c.d. (and, hence, also a uniform decomposition) of r is $O(\log(r))$, which means that the trapdoor size in URC is also $O(\log(r))$.

4.3 Security

In this section we prove the security of BRC and URC. Both proofs rely on the security of the pseudorandom generator of the underlying GGM construction. Note that the security proof does not follow straightforwardly from the GGM proof because contrary to the case of GGM where the adversary obtains only *leaf* PRFs, the adversary in a DPRF can obtain also *partial* PRF values in the GGM tree (via delegation queries). Note that the tree structure of a trapdoor (which is independent of k) for a range predicate P of size r is deterministic and public in both BRC and URC. Thus, when querying the oracle in the security game, the adversary can map the partial or full PRF values appearing in τ for a selected P to subtrees in the GGM tree. Based on this observation, we prove first the security of BRC against adversaries that query only *subtrees*, or equivalently *prefixes* for strings in $\{0,1\}^n$, where n is the depth of the GGM tree. We call this type of security *subtree security*. We conclude our proofs by showing that the subtree security of BRC implies the security of both schemes.

In order to prove the subtree security property of BRC, we insure and exploit the subtree security for two special cases. First, we consider the case that the adversary is non-adaptive, i.e., it poses all its queries in advance.

Lemma 2 *The BRC scheme with depth n and range size at most λ^γ is subtree secure against PPT adversaries that make all their queries, even the challenge query, non-adaptively.*

PROOF. Let $\mathcal{A}$ be a non-adaptive prefix-only PPT adversary against a BRC scheme with depth n and maximum range size λ^γ. Without loss of generality we assume that $\mathcal{A}$ always advances to step 3 (submits a challenge to the challenger).

We define recursively two sequences of PPT algorithms $\mathcal{A} = \mathcal{A}_n, \dots, \mathcal{A}_1$ and $\mathcal{S}_n, \dots, \mathcal{S}_1$ as follows.

For $i = n-1, \dots, 1$, $\mathcal{A}_i$ on input 1^λ, initially invokes $\mathcal{A}_{i+1}$ receiving all of its non-adaptive queries, and chooses a random value k' in $\{0,1\}^\lambda$. If a query $x_i \cdots x_t$ has the same most significant bit (MSB) as the challenge query, $\mathcal{A}_i$ makes the query $x_{i-1} \cdots x_t$, and responds with the received value y. Otherwise, it responds with the value $G_{x_t}(\cdots(G_{x_{i-1}}(k')))$. It returns $\mathcal{A}_{i+1}$'s output.

For $i = n, \dots, 1$, on input $(z_0, z_1) \in \{0,1\}^{2\lambda}$, $\mathcal{S}_i$ invokes $\mathcal{A}_i$ and receives all of its queries. For every query $x_{i-1} \cdots x_t$, it responds with $G_{x_t}(\cdots(G_{x_{i-2}}(z_{x_{i-1}})))$ (or z_{x_0} for $i = 1$). On the challenge phase, it flips a coin b and acts as the challenger in a DPRF security game with $\mathcal{A}_i$. It returns 1 iff $\mathcal{A}_i$ returns b.

Let q_i and p_i be the probabilities that $\mathcal{S}_i$ outputs 1 when it receives its input from the uniform distribution $U_{2\lambda}$ in $\{0,1\}^{2\lambda}$ and the pseudorandom distribution $G(U_\lambda)$, respectively. By the definition of $\mathcal{S}_i$, $p_n = \Pr[\mathcal{G}^{\mathcal{A}}_{\mathsf{SEC}}(1^\lambda) = 1]$ while $q_1 \le 1/2$, since it corresponds to a totally random game.

We next observe that $\mathcal{A}_{n-1}, \dots, \mathcal{A}_1$ behave like attackers against the subtree security of BRC schemes with respective depths $n-1, \dots, 1$. The behavior of A_i as an attacker is the same as A_{i+1}'s, when the latter interacts with a modified challenger that replaces the two possible partial PRF values for the MSB of a prefix, with two random values. Thus, following the previous notation, we have that $p_i = q_{i+1}$. Since $G(U_\lambda)$ and $U_{2\lambda}$ are indistinguishable, it holds that $|p_i - q_i| \le \epsilon_i(\lambda)$, where $\epsilon_i(\cdot)$ is a negligible function. Finally:

$$|p_n - q_1| = |\sum_{i=1}^{n}(p_i - q_i)| \le \sum_{i=1}^{n}|p_i - q_i| \le \sum_{i=1}^{n}\epsilon_i(\lambda) ,$$

hence $\Pr[\mathcal{G}^{\mathcal{A}}_{\mathsf{SEC}}(1^\lambda) = 1] = p_n \le q_1 + n \cdot \epsilon(\lambda) \le 1/2 + n \cdot \epsilon(\lambda)$, where $\epsilon(\lambda) = \max_i\{\epsilon_i(\lambda)\}$. $\square$

We use the above lemma to prove the security of a special category of BRC schemes, where the maximum range size is at least half of $A = [0, 2^n - 1]$, which represents the biggest interval where range predicates are defined. This will serve as a stepping stone for designing our final security proof.

Lemma 3 *The BRC scheme with depth n and maximum range size λ^γ is subtree secure if $2^{n-1} \le \lambda^\gamma < 2^n$.*

PROOF. Let $\mathcal{A}$ be a prefix-only adversary. We construct a non-adaptive prefix-only adversary $\mathcal{B}$ for the subtree security game that on input 1^λ chooses randomly a challenge x^* in $[0, 2^n - 1]$ and makes the n queries that cover all the possible values except from x^*. Namely, $\mathcal{B}$ makes queries $(x^*_{n-1} \oplus 1), \dots, (x^*_{n-1} \cdots x^*_i \oplus 1), \dots, (x^*_{n-1} \cdots x^*_0 \oplus 1)$ and submits challenge x^*. It receives responses $y_{n-1}, \dots, y_0$ respectively, along with y^* which is the response to x^*. Then, it invokes $\mathcal{A}$ and plays the security game with $\mathcal{A}$, as a challenger that can respond appropriately for every value that is not x^* or a range that does not contain x^*. If $\mathcal{A}$ sets x^* as a challenge, then $\mathcal{B}$ responds with y^*, and returns $\mathcal{A}$'s guess. Otherwise, $\mathcal{A}$ has either made a query which is a prefix of x^*, or it has submitted a challenge different than x^*, so $\mathcal{B}$ terminates the game it plays with $\mathcal{A}$ and returns a random bit, as its guess to its challenge.

Let E be the event that $\mathcal{B}$ guesses $\mathcal{A}$'s challenge, i.e. $\mathcal{A}$'s challenge is x^*. By the description of $\mathcal{B}$ we have that

$$\Pr[\mathcal{G}^{\mathcal{B}}_{\mathsf{SEC}}(1^\lambda) = 1 \wedge \neg E] = 1/2 \cdot (1 - 1/2^n) \quad \text{and}$$
$$\Pr[\mathcal{G}^{\mathcal{B}}_{\mathsf{SEC}}(1^\lambda) = 1 \wedge E] = 1/2^n \cdot \Pr[\mathcal{G}^{\mathcal{A}}_{\mathsf{SEC}}(1^\lambda) = 1] .$$

Since $\mathcal{B}$ is non-adaptive, by Lemma 2 we get that for some negligible function $\epsilon(\cdot)$, $\Pr[\mathcal{G}^{\mathcal{B}}_{\mathsf{SEC}}(1^\lambda) = 1] \le 1/2 + \epsilon(\lambda)$. By adding the above equations we have that

$$1/2^n \cdot (\Pr[\mathcal{G}^{\mathcal{A}}_{\mathsf{SEC}}(1^\lambda) = 1] - 1/2) + 1/2 \le 1/2 + \epsilon(\lambda) ,$$

so, $\Pr[\mathcal{G}^{\mathcal{A}}_{\mathsf{SEC}}(1^\lambda) = 1] \le 1/2 + 2^n \cdot \epsilon(\lambda) \le 1/2 + 2\lambda^\gamma \cdot \epsilon(\lambda)$. $\square$

We apply Lemma 3 to prove the subtree security of BRC.

Lemma 4 *The BRC scheme with depth n and maximum range size λ^γ is subtree secure.*

PROOF. See Appendix. $\square$

Finally, we prove that the subtree security of BRC implies the security of BRC and URC.

Theorem 3 *The BRC and URC schemes with depth n and maximum range size λ^γ are secure.*

PROOF. Let $\mathcal{A}$ be a PPT adversary that wins the DPRF security game of either BRC or URC with non-negligible advantage $\alpha(\cdot)$. As noted in the beginning of this section, any query $\mathcal{A}$ makes, can be represented as a sequence of $O(\log(\lambda^\gamma))$ subtrees, or equivalently of $O(\log(\lambda^\gamma))$ prefixes. Thus, we can construct a prefix-only adversary $\mathcal{A}'$ that invokes $\mathcal{A}$ and when it receives a query sequence $\langle x^1_{n-1} \cdots x^1_{t1},$

$\ldots, x^m_{n-1} \cdots x^m_{t^m}\rangle$ from $\mathcal{A}$, it makes all prefix queries separately, receives $y_1, \ldots, y_m$ and answers by $\langle y_1, \ldots, y_m\rangle$. $\mathcal{A}'$ also transfers $\mathcal{A}$'s challenge and outputs its guess. Therefore, it wins the DPRF security game with advantage $\alpha(\cdot)$, which contradicts Lemma 4. □

4.4 Policy Privacy

This section analyzes the policy privacy of URC. According to the lower bound argument we gave in Section 3, URC cannot be expected to satisfy the general policy-privacy property, because it is efficient. We illustrate this explicitly with a toy example. For challenge ranges $[2,5]$ and $[4,7]$, the trapdoors will contain PRF values corresponding to subtrees covering the ranges as $[2,3], \{4\}, \{5\}$ and $[4,5], \{6\}, \{7\}$, respectively. Therefore, the adversary can issue query for leaf 4 and receive a PRF value y. Having $\langle (y_1, 1), (y_2, 0), (y_3, 0)\rangle$ as challenge trapdoor, it can check whether $y_2 = y$, which happens only when $[2,5]$ was chosen by the challenger.

Nevertheless, in the theorem below we prove that URC achieves *union policy privacy*. The above attack is circumvented as in the union policy-privacy game, the adversary cannot obtain a PRF value for a leaf in the *intersection* of the challenge ranges, i.e., for 4 and 5.

Theorem 4 *The URC scheme with depth n and maximum range size λ^γ is a DPRF with union policy privacy.*

PROOF. See Appendix. □

5. APPLICATIONS

In this section we discuss interesting applications of the general DPRF primitive and our specialized constructions for range-based policies. We stress, though, that their applicability is not limited to these scenarios; we are confident that they can capture a much wider set of applications.

Authentication and access control in RFID. *Radio Frequency Identification* (RFID) is a popular technology that is expected to become ubiquitous in the near future. An RFID *tag* is a small chip with an antenna. It typically stores a unique ID along with other data, which can be transmitted to a *reading device* lying within a certain range from the tag. Suppose that a *trusted center* (TC) possesses a set of RFID tags (attached to books, clothes, etc.), and distributes RFID readers to specified locations (e.g., libraries, restaurants, etc.). Whenever a person or object carrying a tag lies in proximity with a reader, it transmits its data (e.g., the title of a book, the brand of a jacket, etc.). The TC can then retrieve these data from the RFID readers, and mine useful information (e.g., *hotlist* books and clothes, etc.).

Despite its merits, RFID technology is challenged by security and privacy issues. For example, due to the availability and low cost of the RFID tags, one can easily create tags with arbitrary information. As such, an adversary may *impersonate* other tags, and provide falsified data to legitimate readers. On the other hand, a reader can receive data from any tag in its vicinity. Therefore, sensitive information may be leaked to a reader controlled by an adversary. For example, the adversary may learn the ID and the title of a book stored in a tag, match it with public library records, and discover the identity and reading habits of an individual.

Motivated by the above, *authentication* and *access control* in RFID-based systems has been studied in the literature. A notable paradigm was introduced in [30], which can be directly benefited by DPRFs. At a high level, every tag is associated with a key, and the TC *delegates* to a reader a set of these keys (i.e., the reader is authorized to authenticate and access data from only a subset of the tags). The goal is for the TC to reduce certain costs, e.g., the size of the delegation information required to *derive* the tag keys while maintaining a high number of distinct keys in order to ensure that attacks can be compartmentalized.

Observe that a DPRF $(\mathcal{F}, T, C)$ is directly applicable to the above setting. $\mathcal{F}$ is defined on the domain of the tag IDs, and its range is the tag keys. Given a delegation predicate on the tag IDs, the TC generates a trapdoor via algorithm T, and sends it to the reader. The latter runs C on the trapdoor to retrieve the tag keys. In fact, for the special case where the access policy is a *range* of IDs, the delegation protocol suggested in [30] is identical to the non-private BRC scheme (we should stress though that [30] lacks rigorous definitions and proofs). Range-based policies are meaningful, since tag IDs may be sequenced according to some common theme (e.g., books on the same topic are assigned consecutive tag IDs). In this case, a range policy *concisely* describes a set of tags (e.g., books about a certain religion) and, hence, the system can enjoy the logarithmic delegation size of BRC. However, as explained in Section 4, BRC leaks the position of the IDs in the tree, which may further leak information about the tags. Although [30] addresses tag privacy, it provides no privacy formulation, and overlooks the above structural leakage. This can be mitigated by directly applying our policy-private URC construction for delegating tag keys to the readers. To sum up, DPRFs find excellent application in authentication and access control in RFIDs, enabling bandwidth-efficient tag key delegation from the TC to the reader. Moreover, policy-private DPRFs provide stronger protection for the tag IDs against the readers.

Batch queries in searchable symmetric encryption. Searchable symmetric encryption (SSE) (e.g., [11, 24]) enables processing queries directly on ciphertexts generated with symmetric encryption. Although SSE corresponds to a general paradigm, various works primarily support the special case of *keyword* queries. Here, we focus on the definitions and schemes of [11] that provide an acceptable level of provable security. The general framework underlying [11] is as follows. In an offline stage, a client encrypts his data with his secret key k, and uploads the ciphertexts $\mathbf{c}$ to an untrusted server. He also creates and sends a *secure index* I on the data for efficient keyword search, which is essentially an encrypted lookup table or inverted index. Given a keyword w, the client generates a query *token* τ_w using k, and forwards it to the server. It is important to stress that this "trapdoor" is merely comprised of one or more PRF values computed on w with k, which were used as keys to encrypt I. For simplicity and w.l.o.g., we assume that τ_w is a single PRF value. The server uses τ_w on I and retrieves the IDs of the ciphertexts associated with w. The results $c_1, \ldots, c_m$ are retrieved and transmitted back to the client, who eventually decrypts them with his key. The security goal is to protect *both* the data and the keyword from the server.

Suppose that the client wishes to search for a *batch* of N keywords $w_1, \ldots, w_N$. For instance, the client may ask for documents that contain *multiple* keywords of his choice (instead of just a single one). As another example, assume that the client's data are employee records, and each record contains a salary attribute that takes as values intervals of the form $[i\text{K}, (i+1)\text{K}]$ (i.e., instead of exact salaries). These intervals can serve as keywords in SSE search. Suppose that the client wishes to retrieve records with salaries in a *range* of intervals, e.g., [1K, 10K]. Observe that this cannot be processed with a single keyword query (no record is associated with [1K, 10K]). To overcome this while utilizing the SSE functionality, the client can ask 9 *distinct* queries with keywords "[1K, 2K]", "[2K, 3K]", ..., "[9K, 10K]", which cover the query range [1K, 10K]. Such scenarios are handled with "traditional" SSE as shown in Figure 5(a). Given a predicate P that describes the keywords $w_1, \ldots, w_N$ in the batch query, the client generates N trapdoors $\tau_{w_1}, \ldots, \tau_{w_N}$ using the standard SSE trapdoor algorithm. These trapdoors are sent to the server, which then searches I with every τ_{w_i} following the SSE protocol. Obviously, for large N, the client's computational and communication cost is greatly impacted.

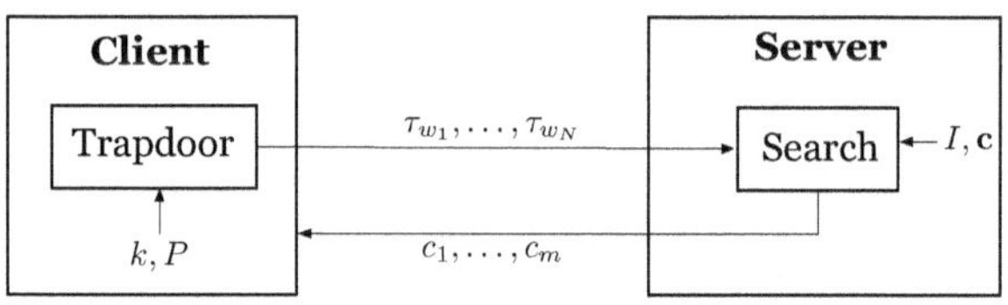

(a) "Traditional" SSE.

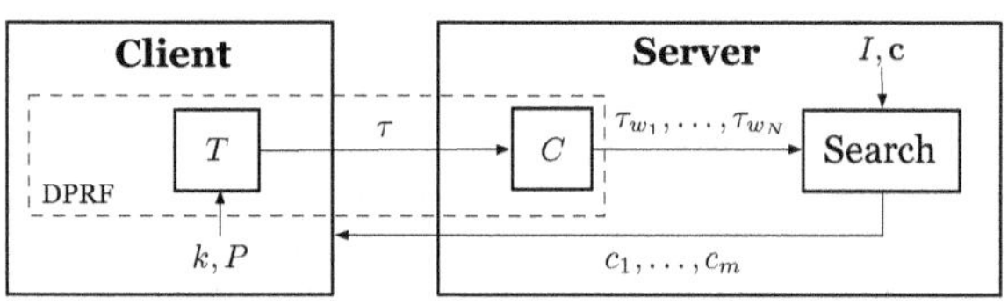

(b) SSE augmented with DPRFs.

Figure 5: Batch keyword query processing in SSE.

We can augment the discussed SSE framework with DPRF functionality, in order to support batch queries with *sublinear* (in N) processing and communication cost at the client, while providing provable security along the lines of [11]. Figure 5(b) illustrates our enhanced SSE architecture. Recall that τ_{w_i} is practically a PRF value, computed on w_i with key k. Therefore, instead of computing a PRF value for every w_i itself, the client *delegates* the computation of these PRF values to the server by employing a DPRF scheme $(\mathcal{F}, T, C)$, where $\mathcal{F}$ is defined over the domain of the keywords. Given predicate P and k, the client runs T and generates trapdoor τ, which is sent to the server. The latter executes C on τ to produce $\tau_{w_1}, \ldots, \tau_{w_N}$. Execution then proceeds in the same manner as in "traditional" SSE. Observe that, for the special case of ranges, if URC is used as the DPRF, the computational and communication cost at the client decreases from $O(N)$ to $O(\log(N))$. This transformation would work "out of the box" in combination to any SSE scheme that uses a PRF for creating tokens.

The above framework can be proven secure against *adaptive* adversaries along the lines of [11]. The most important alteration in the security game and proof is the formulation of the *information leakage* of the C algorithm of the DPRF. In particular, the level of keyword privacy that is provided by the construction is dictated by the level of policy privacy that is attained by the underlying DPRF. Specifically, given a DPRF with multi-instance policy privacy, it is easy to show that the same level of keyword privacy as in [11] can be achieved. Weaker notions of policy privacy (such as single-instance or union) result in correspondingly weaker notions of keyword privacy. For instance, recall that union policy privacy ensures indistinguishability of delegation queries not intersecting with previously asked queries. Thus, combining PRF-based SSE with our URC construction will provide this level of keyword privacy. Given the lower bound arguments for tree-wise constructions we sketched in Section 3, the privacy loss incurred by this tree-based design is the unavoidable cost for the exponential efficiency improvement in client-to-server communication. Efficient constructions attaining higher level of policy privacy might be feasible, but they will have to follow a non tree-base design paradigm.

Broadcast encryption. In a broadcast encryption scheme (e.g., [14, 31, 32]) a sender wishes to transmit data to a set of receivers so that at each transmission the set of receivers excluded from the recipient set can be chosen on the fly by the sender. In particular, this means that the sender has to be able to make an initial key assignment to the recipients, and then suitably use the key material so that only the specific set of users of its choosing can receive the message. In such schemes, it was early on observed that there is a natural tradeoff between receiver memory storage and ciphertext length (e.g., see lower bounds in [26]). The intuition behind this is that if the receivers have more keys, this gives to the sender more flexibility in the way it can encrypt a message to be transmitted.

In the above sense one can think of the key assignment step of a broadcast encryption scheme as a PRF defined over the set Φ which contains all distinct subsets that the broadcast encryption scheme assigns a distinct key. Given this configuration, the user u will have to obtain all the keys corresponding to subsets $S \in \Phi$ for which it holds that $u \in S$ (we denote those subsets by $S_u \subseteq \Phi$). In DPRF language this would correspond to a delegation policy for a PRF: users will need to store the trapdoor that enables the evaluation of any value in the delegated key set S_u.

Seen in this way, *any* DPRF is a key assignment mechanism for a broadcast encryption scheme that saves space on receiver storage. For example, our constructions for range-based policies give rise to the following broadcast encryption scheme: Receivers $[n] = \{1, \ldots, n\}$ are placed in sequence; each receiver $u \in [n]$ is initialized with the trapdoor for a range $[u - t, u + t]$ for some predetermined parameter $t \in \mathbb{Z}$. In this broadcast encryption scheme the sender can very efficiently enable any range of receivers that is positioned at distance at most t from a fixed location $v \in [n]$. This is done with a single ciphertext (encrypted with the key of location v). Any receiver of sufficient proximity t to location v can derive the corresponding decryption key from its trapdoor. Furthermore, given the efficiency of our construction, storage on receivers is only logarithmic on t. While the semantics of this scheme are more restricted than a full-fledged broadcast encryption scheme (which enables the sender to exclude any subset of users on demand), it succinctly illustrates the relation between broadcast encryption and DPRF; further investigation in the relation between the two primitives from a construction point of view will be motivated by our notion. Specifically, an efficient DPRF with domain Φ over a policy set $\mathcal{P} = \{S_u \mid u \in [n]\}$ will provide an efficient key assignment for a broadcast encryption scheme operating over Φ. Interestingly, the reverse is also true and a (suitably structured) broadcast encryption scheme will provide a DPRF with domain Φ and the policy set $\{S_u \mid u \in [n]\}$.

Regarding policy privacy, it is interesting to point out that this security property is yet unstudied in the domain of broadcast encryption. A different privacy notion has been considered in [3, 13, 25] that deals with the structure of ciphertexts in such schemes. Our policy privacy on the other hand deals with the privacy of memory contents from the receiver's point of view. Maintaining the indistinguishability of the storage contents is a useful security measure in broadcast encryption schemes, and our DPRF primitive will motivate the study of this security property in the context of broadcast encryption—note that none of the tree-like key-delegation methods used in broadcast encryption schemes prior to our work satisfies policy privacy.

6. CONCLUSION

We have introduced the concept of *delegatable pseudorandom functions* (DPRFs), a new cryptographic primitive that allows for policy-based computation at an untrusted proxy of PRF values, without knowledge of a secret or even the input values. We provided formal definitions of the core properties of DPRFs for (1) correctness, the ability of the proxy to compute PRF values only for inputs that satisfy a given predicate, (2) security, the standard pseudorandomness guarantee, but against a stronger adversary that also issues delegation queries, and (3) policy privacy, which prevents leakage of the secret preimages of the computed PRF values. Moreover, we presented two DPRF constructions for PRF delegation controlled by range-based policies, along with a comprehensive analysis in terms of their security and privacy guarantees and some inherent trade-offs with efficiency. Our proposed DPRF schemes are generic, yet practical, based on the well-understood and widely-adopted GGM design framework for PRFs and, as we showed, they find direct application in many key-delegation or key-derivation settings providing interesting new results.

Further exploration of DPRFs holds promise for many directions of interest. Open problems include: Designing DPRFs for other classes of predicates, establishing upper and lower bounds on the connection between efficiency and policy privacy, and studying applications in other settings.

Acknowledgments

We thank all anonymous reviewers for providing detailed comments and suggestions. The first and fourth authors were supported by projects CODAMODA of the European Research Council, Marie Curie RECUP, and respectively FINER of GSRT.

7. REFERENCES

[1] M. J. Atallah and K. B. Frikken. Securely outsourcing linear algebra computations. In *Proc. of the 5th Symposium on Information, Computer and Comm. Security (ASIACCS)*, pages 48–59. ACM, 2010.

[2] G. Ateniese, K. Fu, M. Green, and S. Hohenberger. Improved proxy re-encryption schemes with applications to secure distributed storage. *ACM Trans. Inf. Syst. Secur.*, 9(1):1–30, Feb. 2006.

[3] A. Barth, D. Boneh, and B. Waters. Privacy in encrypted content distribution using private broadcast encryption. In *Proc. of the 10th Int. Conf. on Financial Cryptography and Data Security*, pages 52–64. Springer, 2006.

[4] S. Benabbas, R. Gennaro, and Y. Vahlis. Verifiable delegation of computation over large datasets. In *Proc. of the 31st Annual Conf. on Advances in Cryptology (CRYPTO)*, pages 111–131. Springer, 2011.

[5] M. Blaze, G. Bleumer, and M. Strauss. Divertible protocols and atomic proxy cryptography. In *Proc. of the 17th Int. Conf. on the Theory and Application of Cryptographic Techniques (EUROCRYPT)*, pages 127–144. Springer, 1998.

[6] A. Boldyreva, A. Palacio, and B. Warinschi. Secure proxy signature schemes for delegation of signing rights. *Journal of Cryptology*, 25:57–115, 2012.

[7] D. Boneh and B. Waters. Constrained pseudorandom functions and their applications. In *Proc. of the 19th Int. Conf. on the Theory and Application of Cryptology and Information Security (ASIACRYPT)*, 2013. To appear; full version in *Cryptology ePrint Archive*, 2013:352.

[8] E. Boyle, S. Goldwasser, and I. Ivan. Functional signatures and pseudorandom functions. *IACR Cryptology ePrint Archive*, 2013:401, 2013.

[9] R. Canetti, B. Riva, and G. N. Rothblum. Practical delegation of computation using multiple servers. In *Proc. of the 18th Conf. on Computer and Comm. Security (CCS)*, pages 445–454. ACM, 2011.

[10] K.-M. Chung, Y. T. Kalai, and S. P. Vadhan. Improved delegation of computation using fully homomorphic encryption. In *Proc. of the 30th Annual Conf. on Advances in Cryptology (CRYPTO)*, pages 483–501. Springer, 2010.

[11] R. Curtmola, J. Garay, S. Kamara, and R. Ostrovsky. Searchable symmetric encryption: Improved definitions and efficient constructions. In *Proc. of the 13th Conf. on Computer and Comm. Security (CCS)*, pages 79–88. ACM, 2006.

[12] Y. Dodis and A. Yampolskiy. A verifiable random function with short proofs and keys. In *Proc. of the 8th Int. Workshop on Public Key Cryptography (PKC)*, pages 416–431. Springer, 2005.

[13] N. Fazio and I. M. Perera. Outsider-anonymous broadcast encryption with sublinear ciphertexts. In *Proc. of the 15th Int. Conf. on Public Key Cryptography (PKC)*, pages 225–242. Springer, 2012.

[14] A. Fiat and M. Naor. Broadcast encryption. In *Proc. of the 13st Annual Conf. on Advances in Cryptology (CRYPTO)*, pages 480–491. Springer, 1993.

[15] D. Fiore and R. Gennaro. Publicly verifiable delegation of large polynomials and matrix computations, with applications. In *Proc. of the 19th Conf. on Computer and Comm. Security (CCS)*, pages 501–512. ACM, 2012.

[16] M. J. Freedman, Y. Ishai, B. Pinkas, and O. Reingold. Keyword search and oblivious pseudorandom functions. In *Proc. of the 2nd Theory of Cryptography Conference (TCC)*, pages 303–324. Springer, 2005.

[17] O. Goldreich, S. Goldwasser, and S. Micali. How to construct random functions. *J. ACM*, 33(4):792–807, 1986.

[18] S. Goldwasser, Y. T. Kalai, and G. N. Rothblum. Delegating computation: interactive proofs for muggles. In *Proc. of the 40th Annual Symposium on Theory of Computing (STOC)*, pages 113–122. ACM, 2008.

[19] M. Green and G. Ateniese. Identity-based proxy re-encryption. In *Proc. of the 5th Int. Conf. on Applied Cryptography and Network Security (ACNS)*, pages 288–306. Springer, 2007.

[20] S. Hohenberger and A. Lysyanskaya. How to securely outsource cryptographic computations. In *Proc. of the 2nd Theory of Cryptography Conference (TCC)*, pages 264–282. Springer, 2005.

[21] G. Itkis. *Handbook of Information Security*, chapter Forward Security: Adaptive Cryptography—Time Evolution. John Wiley and Sons, 2006.

[22] A.-A. Ivan and Y. Dodis. Proxy cryptography revisited. In *Proc. of the 10th Network and Distributed System Security Symposium (NDSS)*. The Internet Society, 2003.

[23] S. Jarecki and X. Liu. Efficient oblivious pseudorandom function with applications to adaptive ot and secure computation of set intersection. In *Proc. of the 6th Theory of Cryptography Conference (TCC)*, pages 577–594. Springer-Verlag, 2009.

[24] S. Kamara, C. Papamanthou, and T. Roeder. Dynamic searchable symmetric encryption. In *Proc. of the 19th Conf. on Computer and Comm. Security (CCS)*, pages 965–976. ACM, 2012.

[25] B. Libert, K. G. Paterson, and E. A. Quaglia. Anonymous broadcast encryption: Adaptive security and efficient constructions in the standard model. In *Proc. of the 15th Int. Conf. on Public Key Cryptography (PKC)*, pages 206–224. Springer, 2012.

[26] M. Luby and J. Staddon. Combinatorial bounds for broadcast encryption. In *Proc. of the 17th Int. Conf. on the Theory and Application of Cryptographic Techniques (EUROCRYPT)*, pages 512–526. Springer, 1998.

[27] A. Lysyanskaya. Unique signatures and verifiable random functions from the DH-DDH separation. In *Proc. of the 22nd Annual Conf. on Advances in Cryptology (CRYPTO)*, pages 597–612. Springer, 2002.

[28] M. Mambo, K. Usuda, and E. Okamoto. Proxy signatures for delegating signing operation. In *Proc. of the 3rd Conf. on Computer and Comm. Security (CCS)*, pages 48–57. ACM, 1996.

[29] S. Micali, M. O. Rabin, and S. P. Vadhan. Verifiable random functions. In *Proc. of the 40th Annual Symposium on Foundations of Computer Science (FOCS)*, pages 120–130. IEEE, 1999.

[30] D. Molnar, A. Soppera, and D. Wagner. A scalable, delegatable pseudonym protocol enabling ownership transfer of RFID tags. In *Proc. of the 12th Int. Workshop on Selected Areas in Cryptography (SAC)*, pages 276–290. Springer, 2006.

[31] D. Naor, M. Naor, and J. Lotspiech. Revocation and tracing schemes for stateless receivers. In *Proc. of the 21st Annual Conf. on Advances in Cryptology (CRYPTO)*, pages 41–62. Springer, 2001.

[32] M. Naor and B. Pinkas. Efficient trace and revoke schemes. *Int. J. Inf. Sec.*, 9(6):411–424, 2010.

[33] B. Parno, M. Raykova, and V. Vaikuntanathan. How to delegate and verify in public: verifiable computation from attribute-based encryption. In *Proc. of the 9th Theory of Cryptography Conference (TCC)*, pages 422–439. Springer, 2012.

APPENDIX

Proof of Lemma 4

By Lemma 3, it suffices to focus on the case that $\lambda^\gamma < 2^{n-1}$. This is definitely the interesting case, since 2^n is normally superpolynomial in λ. Let $\mathcal{A}$ be a prefix-only adversary against BRC that makes at most $q(\lambda)$ queries (including the challenge) and d be the minimum integer that $\lambda^\gamma < 2^d$. We construct a PPT PRF distinguisher $\mathcal{B}$ that makes oracle queries of fixed size $n' = n - d \geq 1$. On input 1^λ, $\mathcal{B}$ flips a coin b, invokes $\mathcal{A}$ and initializes a security game, itself being the challenger. By the bound on the size of the ranges, all queries of $\mathcal{A}$ have length greater than n'. Thus, for every query $x_{n-1} \cdots x_t$, we have that $t < d$ and $\mathcal{B}$ responds by making a query $x_{n-1} \cdots x_d$, which is of length n', receiving a value y and answering to $\mathcal{A}$ as $G_{x_t}(\cdots(G_{x_{d-1}}(y)))$. When $\mathcal{A}$ submits a challenge, $\mathcal{B}$ acts as a normal challenger according to the coin flip b utilizing its oracle to determine the value up to level d as above. Finally, $\mathcal{B}$ returns 1 iff $\mathcal{A}$ returns b. Clearly, when $\mathcal{B}$'s oracle is a PRF f_k of length n', $\mathcal{B}$ returns 1 iff $\mathcal{A}$ wins, i.e $\Pr[\mathcal{G}^{\mathcal{A}}_{\mathsf{SEC}}(1^\lambda) = 1] = \Pr[\mathcal{B}^{f_k(\cdot)}(1^\lambda) = 1]$. Since f_k is a PRF, we have that for some negligible function $\epsilon(\cdot)$,

$$|\Pr[\mathcal{G}^{\mathcal{A}}_{\mathsf{SEC}}(1^\lambda) = 1] - \Pr[\mathcal{B}^{R(\cdot)}(1^\lambda) = 1]| \leq \epsilon(\lambda) . \quad (1)$$

Consequently, we can construct a prefix-only adversary $\tilde{\mathcal{A}}$ against a BRC with depth d and maximum range size λ^γ as follows: $\tilde{\mathcal{A}}$ invokes $\mathcal{A}$ and chooses a random index $j \in [q(\lambda)]$ and $q(\lambda) - 1$ random values $k_1, \ldots, k_{j-1}, k_{j+1}, \ldots, k_{q(\lambda)} \in \{0,1\}^\lambda$. Index j reflects $\tilde{\mathcal{A}}$'s attempt to guess which of all of possible different prefixes of length n' that will appear in $\mathcal{A}$'s queries will be the one that a prospective challenge query will have. Then $\tilde{\mathcal{A}}$ keeps count of the different prefixes of length n' that gradually appear and reacts to a query $x_{n-1} \cdots x_t$ according to the following checks:

(i) $x_{n-1} \cdots x_d$ is the i-th prefix and $i \neq j$: In this case, $\tilde{\mathcal{A}}$ responds with $G_{x_t}(\cdots(G_{x_{d-1}}(k_i)))$.

(ii) $x_{n-1} \cdots x_d$ is the j-th prefix: If all of the queries made by $\mathcal{A}$ that have the j-th prefix, along with $x_{n-1} \cdots x_t$, cover the whole subtree with root prefix $x_{n-1} \cdots x_d$, T_j, then $\tilde{\mathcal{A}}$ terminates the game with $\mathcal{A}$ and chooses a leaf $z_{d-1} \cdots z_0$ of T_j that has not been covered by $\mathcal{A}$'s previous queries. It submits $z_{d-1} \cdots z_0$ as its challenge and returns a random bit. Otherwise, $\tilde{\mathcal{A}}$ makes query $x_{d-1} \cdots x_t$ and responds with the received value y.

(iii) $t = 0$ and $x_{n-1} \cdots x_0$ is $\mathcal{A}$'s challenge: If $x_{n-1} \cdots x_d$ is not the j-th prefix, then $\tilde{\mathcal{A}}$ terminates the game with $\mathcal{A}$, chooses a leaf $z_{d-1} \cdots z_0$ of T_j not yet covered by $\mathcal{A}$'s queries, submits $z_{d-1} \cdots z_0$ as its challenge and returns a random bit. Otherwise, it submits challenge $x_{d-1} \cdots x_0$, receives value y^* and responds with y^*.

If $\tilde{\mathcal{A}}$ does not terminate the security game with $\mathcal{A}$, then it returns $\mathcal{A}$'s guess. By the choice of d, $2^{d-1} \leq \lambda^\gamma < 2^d$, hence Lemma 3 implies that $\tilde{\mathcal{A}}$ has negligible distinguishing advantage. Thus for some negligible function $\delta(\cdot)$,

$$\Pr[\mathcal{G}^{\tilde{\mathcal{A}}}_{\mathsf{SEC}}(1^\lambda) = 1] \leq 1/2 + \delta(\lambda) . \quad (2)$$

By the description of $\tilde{\mathcal{A}}$, the interaction between $\mathcal{A}$ and $\mathcal{B}$ in the case that $\mathcal{B}$'s oracle is random is fully simulated by $\tilde{\mathcal{A}}$ when the latter's guess for the prefix of $\mathcal{A}$'s challenge is correct. Formally, let E be the event that $\tilde{\mathcal{A}}$ guesses $\mathcal{A}$'s challenge. Then it holds that

$$\Pr[\mathcal{B}^{R(\cdot)}(1^\lambda) = 1] = \Pr[\mathcal{G}_{\mathsf{SEC}}^{\tilde{\mathcal{A}}}(1^\lambda) = 1 | E] \ . \quad (3)$$

By the description of $\tilde{\mathcal{A}}$ and (3), we have that

$$\Pr[\mathcal{G}_{\mathsf{SEC}}^{\tilde{\mathcal{A}}}(1^\lambda) = 1 \wedge \neg E] = 1/2 \cdot (1 - 1/q(\lambda)) \quad \text{and}$$
$$\Pr[\mathcal{G}_{\mathsf{SEC}}^{\tilde{\mathcal{A}}}(1^\lambda) = 1 \wedge E] = 1/q(\lambda) \cdot \Pr[\mathcal{B}^{R(\cdot)}(1^\lambda) = 1] \ ,$$

where we used that $\Pr[E] = 1/q(\lambda)$. Therefore,

$$\Pr[\mathcal{G}_{\mathsf{SEC}}^{\tilde{\mathcal{A}}}(1^\lambda) = 1] = 1/2 + 1/q(\lambda) \cdot (\Pr[\mathcal{B}^{R(\cdot)}(1^\lambda) = 1] - 1/2) \ ,$$

so by applying (2) we get

$$\Pr[\mathcal{B}^{R(\cdot)}(1^\lambda) = 1] \leq 1/2 + q(\lambda) \cdot \delta(\lambda) \ . \quad (4)$$

Finally, by (1) and (4) we conclude that

$$\Pr[\mathcal{G}_{\mathsf{SEC}}^{\mathcal{A}}(1^\lambda) = 1] \leq 1/2 + q(\lambda) \cdot \delta(\lambda) + \epsilon(\lambda) = \\ = 1/2 + \mathsf{negl}(\lambda) \ .$$

Proof of Theorem 4

Let $\mathcal{A}$ be a PPT adversary that wins the union policy privacy game with non-negligible distinguishing advantage $\alpha(\cdot)$. Let P_0, P_1 be the two challenge ranges and b the chosen random bit, hence $\mathcal{A}$ receives the challenge trapdoor τ_b for P_b. Denote each element of a decomposition D as (x, L) or (x, R), if it is integer x and belongs to the leftmost or rightmost sequence of D respectively. Define the ordering $<_D$ over the elements of D as follows: $(x, \mathrm{L}) <_D (y, \mathrm{R})$ or $(x, \mathrm{R}) <_D (y, \mathrm{L})$, if $x < y$ and $(x, \mathrm{L}) <_D (x, \mathrm{R})$. We define a sequence of hybrid games $\mathcal{G}_0^{\mathcal{A}}(1^\lambda), \ldots, \mathcal{G}_N^{\mathcal{A}}(1^\lambda)$, where N is the maximum size of a trapdoor output by T_{URC}. As shown in section 4.2, $N = 2\lceil \log(\lambda^\gamma + 2) \rceil - 1$. The game $\mathcal{G}_i$ is executed as the original game $\mathcal{G}_{\mathsf{UPP}}^{\mathcal{A}}(1^\lambda)$ during the pre-challenge and the post-challenge phase. Assume the pairs of the challenge trapdoor τ_b are arranged according to the ordering determined by the decomposition formed by the depths. The only modification in $\mathcal{G}_i^{\mathcal{A}}(1^\lambda)$ is that in the first i pairs of τ_b, the partial PRF values are the same as τ_b's, while all the other elements are replaced by random values in $\{0,1\}^\lambda$. In $\mathcal{G}_0^{\mathcal{A}}(1^\lambda)$, the challenge trapdoor consists of a number of pairs of random values attached to certain integers, independently of the choice of b. Therefore, $\Pr[\mathcal{G}_0^{\mathcal{A}}(1^\lambda) = 1] = 1/2$. Since $\mathcal{G}_N^{\mathcal{A}}(1^\lambda)$ is the union policy privacy game, it holds that

$$\Pr[\mathcal{G}_N^{\mathcal{A}}(1^\lambda) = 1] - \Pr[\mathcal{G}_0^{\mathcal{A}}(1^\lambda) = 1] \geq \alpha(\lambda) \ .$$

Let E_r be the event that the size of the challenge ranges $|A_{P_0}|, |A_{P_1}|$ that $\mathcal{A}$ submits is r. Then for some challenge bit $b \in \{0,1\}$ and $r \in [\lambda^\gamma]$:

$$\Pr[\mathcal{G}_N^{\mathcal{A}}(1^\lambda) = 1 \wedge b \wedge E_r] - \Pr[\mathcal{G}_0^{\mathcal{A}}(1^\lambda) = 1 \wedge b \wedge E_r] \geq \alpha(\lambda)/2\lambda^\gamma ,$$

which implies that there exists an $i \in [\lambda^\gamma]$ such that

$$\Pr[\mathcal{G}_i^{\mathcal{A}}(1^\lambda) = 1 \wedge b \wedge E_r] - \\ - \Pr[\mathcal{G}_{i-1}^{\mathcal{A}}(1^\lambda) = 1 \wedge b \wedge E_r] \geq \alpha(\lambda)/2N\lambda^\gamma \ . \quad (5)$$

We will show that for these fixed b, r, i, we can construct an adversary $\mathcal{A}_i$ for the security game of a BRC construction that has non-negligible winning advantage. The main idea is that $\mathcal{A}_i$ invokes $\mathcal{A}$ and simulates either $\mathcal{G}_i$ or $\mathcal{G}_{i-1}$ on selected challenge P_b of size r depending on the value of the challenge bit b_i for the security game $\mathcal{G}_{\mathsf{SEC}}^{\mathcal{A}_i}(1^\lambda)$.

On input 1^λ, $\mathcal{A}_i$ computes the uniform decomposition of r, U_r, and arranges its elements according to $<_{U_r}$. Let u_i be the integer that appears in the i-th element of U_r (trivially, when $r = 1$ then $u_i = u_1 = 0$). The BRC that $\mathcal{A}_i$ attacks has depth $n - u_i$. Specifically, $\mathcal{A}_i$ invokes $\mathcal{A}$ and answers all of its pre-challenge queries as follows: for each query $x_{n-1} \cdots x_t$, if $t \geq u_i$, it just transfers the query, receives value y, and responds with y. Otherwise, it makes query $x_{n-1} \cdots x_{u_i}$, receives value y, and responds with $G_{x_t}(\cdots (G_{x_{u_i - 1}}(y)))$. In the challenge phase, if $|A_{P_b}| \neq r$, then $\mathcal{A}_i$ terminates the game with $\mathcal{A}$, chooses a valid random challenge, and returns a random bit. Otherwise, it makes $i-1$ queries and computes the $<_{U_r}$-first $i-1$ partial delegation keys $y_1, \ldots, y_{i-1}$ of τ_b as in the pre-challenge phase, and sets the string $x^*_{n-1} \cdots x^*_{u_i}$ that corresponds to the i-th partial key as its challenge, receiving y^*. Note that since $\mathcal{A}$ is restricted from making queries within $A_{P_0} \cup A_{P_1}$, it makes no queries with prefix $x^*_{n-1} \cdots x^*_{u_i}$, thus $\mathcal{A}_i$'s challenge is valid. It arranges the values $y_1, \ldots, y_{i-1}, y^*$ according to the order that τ_b imposes and "fills" the $|U_r| - i$ remaining positions of an array like trapdoor τ_b with $|U_r| - i$ pairs consisting of random values from $\{0,1\}^\lambda$ along with the corresponding depths. It returns τ_b to $\mathcal{A}$ and answers to $\mathcal{A}$'s post-challenge queries as in the pre-challenge phase. If $\mathcal{A}$ returns b, then $\mathcal{A}_i$ returns 1, or else it returns a random bit.

The probability that $\mathcal{A}_i$ wins the security game is

$$\Pr[\mathcal{G}_{\mathsf{SEC}}^{\mathcal{A}_i}(1^\lambda) = 1] = \Pr[\mathcal{G}_{\mathsf{SEC}}^{\mathcal{A}_i}(1^\lambda) = 1 \wedge \neg E_r] + \\ + \Pr[\mathcal{G}_{\mathsf{SEC}}^{\mathcal{A}_i}(1^\lambda) = 1 \wedge E_r \wedge b_i = 1] + \\ + \Pr[\mathcal{G}_{\mathsf{SEC}}^{\mathcal{A}_i}(1^\lambda) = 1 \wedge E_r \wedge b_i = 0] \ . \quad (6)$$

It holds that $\Pr[\mathcal{G}_{\mathsf{SEC}}^{\mathcal{A}_i}(1^\lambda) = 1 \wedge \neg E_r] = 1/2 \cdot (1 - \Pr[E_r])$.

For the other two terms in the right part of (6), we observe that when $b_i = 1$, $\mathcal{A}_i$ simulates $\mathcal{G}_i$ when b and E_r occur, whereas when $b_i = 0$, $\mathcal{A}_i$ simulates $\mathcal{G}_{i-1}$ when b and E_r occur. Therefore, by the description of $\mathcal{A}_i$ we have that

$$\Pr[\mathcal{G}_{\mathsf{SEC}}^{\mathcal{A}_i}(1^\lambda) = 1 \wedge E_r \wedge b_i = 1] = \\ = 1 \cdot \Pr[\mathcal{G}_i^{\mathcal{A}}(1^\lambda) = 1 \wedge b \wedge E_r] + \\ + 1/2 \cdot \Pr[\mathcal{G}_i^{\mathcal{A}}(1^\lambda) \neq 1 \wedge b \wedge E_r] = \\ = 1/2 \cdot \Pr[b \wedge E_r] + 1/2 \cdot \Pr[\mathcal{G}_i^{\mathcal{A}}(1^\lambda) = 1 \wedge b \wedge E_r] \ ,$$

and

$$\Pr[\mathcal{G}_{\mathsf{SEC}}^{\mathcal{A}_i}(1^\lambda) = 1 \wedge E_r \wedge b_i = 0] = \\ = 0 \cdot \Pr[\mathcal{G}_{i-1}^{\mathcal{A}}(1^\lambda) = 1 \wedge b \wedge E_r] + \\ + 1/2 \cdot \Pr[\mathcal{G}_{i-1}^{\mathcal{A}}(1^\lambda) \neq 1 \wedge b \wedge E_r] = \\ = 1/2 \cdot \Pr[b \wedge E_r] - 1/2 \cdot \Pr[\mathcal{G}_{i-1}^{\mathcal{A}}(1^\lambda) = 1 \wedge b \wedge E_r].$$

By the independency of b and E_r, we have that $\Pr[b \wedge E_r] = 1/2 \cdot \Pr[E_r]$. Thus, we evaluate $\Pr[\mathcal{G}_{\mathsf{SEC}}^{\mathcal{A}_i}(1^\lambda) = 1]$ according to (6) as

$$\Pr[\mathcal{G}_{\mathsf{SEC}}^{\mathcal{A}_i}(1^\lambda) = 1] = 1/2 + 1/2 \cdot (\Pr[\mathcal{G}_i^{\mathcal{A}}(1^\lambda) = 1 \wedge b \wedge E_r] - \\ - \Pr[\mathcal{G}_{i-1}^{\mathcal{A}}(1^\lambda) = 1 \wedge b \wedge E_r]) \ .$$

Therefore by (5), $\Pr[\mathcal{G}_{\mathsf{SEC}}^{\mathcal{A}_i}(1^\lambda) = 1] \geq 1/2 + \alpha(\lambda)/4N\lambda^\gamma$, which contradicts Theorem 3.

Ensuring High-Quality Randomness in Cryptographic Key Generation

Henry Corrigan-Gibbs*
Stanford University
henrycg@stanford.edu

Wendy Mu
Stanford University
wmu@cs.stanford.edu

Dan Boneh
Stanford University
dabo@cs.stanford.edu

Bryan Ford
Yale University
bryan.ford@yale.edu

ABSTRACT

The security of any cryptosystem relies on the secrecy of the system's secret keys. Yet, recent experimental work demonstrates that tens of thousands of devices on the Internet use RSA and DSA secrets drawn from a small pool of candidate values. As a result, an adversary can derive the device's secret keys without breaking the underlying cryptosystem. We introduce a new threat model, under which there is a *systemic* solution to such randomness flaws. In our model, when a device generates a cryptographic key, it incorporates some random values from an *entropy authority* into its cryptographic secrets and then *proves* to the authority, using zero-knowledge-proof techniques, that it performed this operation correctly. By presenting an entropy-authority-signed public-key certificate to a third party (like a certificate authority or SSH client), the device can demonstrate that its public key incorporates randomness from the authority and is therefore drawn from a large pool of candidate values. Where possible, our protocol protects against eavesdroppers, entropy authority misbehavior, and devices attempting to discredit the entropy authority. To demonstrate the practicality of our protocol, we have implemented and evaluated its performance on a commodity wireless home router. When running on a home router, our protocol incurs a 1.7× slowdown over conventional RSA key generation and it incurs a 3.6× slowdown over conventional EC-DSA key generation.

Categories and Subject Descriptors

C.2.0 [**Computer-Communication Networks**]: General—*Security and protection*; C.2.2 [**Computer-Communication Networks**]: Network Protocols—*Applications*; E.3 [**Data Encryption**]: Public key cryptosystems

*Work conducted while author was a staff member at Yale University.

CCS'13, November 4–8, 2013, Berlin, Germany.

ACM 978-1-4503-2477-9/13/11 ...$15.00.
http://dx.doi.org/10.1145/2508859.2516680.

Keywords

entropy authority; cryptography; key generation; RSA; DSA; entropy; randomness

1. INTRODUCTION

A good source of randomness is crucial for a number of cryptographic operations. Public-key encryption schemes use randomness to achieve chosen-plaintext security, key-exchange algorithms use randomness to establish secret session keys, and commitment schemes use randomness to hide the committed value. The security of these schemes relies on the unpredictability of the random input values, so when the "random" inputs are not really random, dire security failures result [7, 8, 9, 10, 11, 12, 13, 14, 15, 16, 17, 18, 19, 20, 21, 26, 29, 32, 41].

Although the dangers of weak randomness have been part of the computer security folklore for years [26], entropy failures are still commonplace. In 2008, a single mistaken patch caused the OpenSSL distribution in all Debian-based operating systems to use only the process ID (plus a few other easy-to-guess values) as the seed for its pseudo-random number generator. This bug caused affected machines to select a 1024-bit RSA modulus from a pool of fewer than one million values, rather than the near-2^{1000} possible values [41]. By replaying the key generation process using each of the one million possible PRNG seeds, an adversary could recover the secret key corresponding to one of these weak public keys in a matter or hours or days.

Recent surveys [29, 32] of SSH and TLS public keys on the Internet demonstrate that hardware devices with poorly seeded random number generators have led to a proliferation of weak cryptographic keys. During the drafting of this paper, NetBSD maintainers discovered a bug caused by a "misplaced parenthesis" that could have caused NetBSD machines to generate cryptographic keys incorporating as few as 32 or 64 bits of entropy, instead of the 100+ expected bits [36]. Even more recently, a PRNG initialization bug in the Android operating system could have caused applications using the system to generate weak cryptographic keys [31].

Randomness failures continue to haunt cryptographic software for a number of reasons: the randomness "stack" in a modern operating system [39] is large and complex, there is no simple way to test whether a random number generator is really generating random numbers, and (at least in the context of cryptographic keys) there has never been a *systemic solution* to the randomness problem. The response to entropy failures has traditionally been *ad hoc*: each device manufacturer or software vendor patches RNG-related bugs in its own implementation (once discovered), without deploying techniques to prevent similar failures in the future. The quantity and severity of randomness failures suggests that this "fix the implementation" approach is grossly insufficient.

We offer the first systemic solution to the entropy problem in cryptographic key generation for public-key cryptosystems. In our protocol, a device generating a cryptographic keypair fetches random values from an *entropy authority* and incorporates these values into its cryptographic secrets. The device can later *prove* to third parties (e.g., a certificate authority or an SSH client) that the device's secrets incorporate the authority's random values, thus guaranteeing that the device's cryptographic keys are selected from a large enough pool of candidate values. Unlike certificate authorities in today's Internet, our entropy authorities are *not* trusted third parties: if the device has a strong entropy source, a malicious entropy authority learns no useful information about the device's secret key. We present versions of our protocol for RSA and DSA key generation and we offer proofs of security for each.

A subtlety of our solution is the threat model: under a traditional "global passive adversary" model, the adversary can completely simulate the view of a device that has a very weak entropy source. Thus, under the global passive adversary model, a device with a weak entropy source has no hope of generating strong keys. We propose an alternate threat model, in which the adversary can observe all communication *except for* one initial communication session between the device and the entropy authority. Under this more limited adversary model, which is realistic in many deployment scenarios, we can take advantage of an entropy authority to ensure the randomness of cryptographic keys.

The key generation protocols we present are useful both for devices with strong and weak entropy sources. In particular, if the device has a strong entropy source (the device can repeatedly sample from the uniform distribution over a large set of values), running the protocol *never weakens* the device's cryptographic keys. In contrast, if the device has a weak or biased entropy source, running the protocol can *dramatically strengthen* the device's keys by ensuring that its keys incorporate sufficient randomness. The device need not know whether it has a strong or weak entropy source: the same protocol is used in both cases.

A recent survey of public keys [29] suggests that embedded devices are responsible for generating the majority of weak cryptographic keys on the Internet. To demonstrate that our protocols are practical even on this type of computationally limited network device, we have evaluated the protocols on a $70 Linksys home router running the dd-wrt [22] operating system. Our RSA key generation protocol incurs less than a 2× slowdown on the Linksys router when generating a 2048-bit key, and our RSA and DSA protocols incur no more than 2 seconds of slowdown on a laptop and a workstation. The DSA version of our protocol is compatible with both elliptic-curve and finite-field groups. Our protocols generate standard RSA and DSA keys which are, for a given bit-length, as secure as their conventionally generated counterparts.

In prior work, Juels and Guajardo [30] present a protocol in which a possibly malicious device generates an RSA key in cooperation with a certificate authority. Their protocol prevents a device from generating an *ill-formed keypair* (e.g., an RSA modulus that is the product of more than two primes). We consider a different threat model. We ensure that a device samples its keys from a distribution with high min-entropy, but we do not prevent the device from generating malformed keys. Under this new threat model, we achieve roughly a 25× performance improvement over the protocol of Juels and Guajardo (as measured by the number of modular exponentiations that the device must compute). Section 7 compares the two protocols and discusses other related work.

After introducing our threat model in Section 2, we describe our key generation protocols in Section 3 and present security proofs in Section 4. Section 5 summarizes our evaluation results and Section 6 discusses issues related to integrating our protocols with existing systems.

1.1 Why Other Solutions Are Insufficient

Before describing our protocol in detail, we discuss a few other possible, but unsatisfactory, ways to prevent networked devices from using weak cryptographic keys.[1]

Possible Solution #1: Fix the implementation. One possible solution to the weak key problem is to simply make sure that cryptography libraries properly incorporate random values into the cryptographic secrets that they produce. Unfortunately, bugs and bad implementations are a fact of life in the world of software, and the subtleties of random number generation make randomness bugs particularly common. Implementations that seed their random number generators with public or guessable values (e.g., time, process ID, or MAC address) [8, 15, 16, 18, 18], implementations that use weak random number generators [10, 11, 12, 20, 21], and implementations without a good source of environmental entropy [29] are all vulnerable.

The complexity of generating cryptographically strong random numbers, the overwhelming number of randomness failures in deployed software, and the difficulty of detecting these failures during testing all indicate that "fix the implementation" is an insufficient solution to the weak key problem. Given that some implementations will be buggy, there should be a way to *assure* clients that their TLS and SSH servers are using strong keys, even if the client suspects that the servers do not have access to a good source of random values.

Possible Solution #2: Simple entropy server. A second possible solution would be to have devices fetch some random values from an "entropy sever" and incorporate these values (along with some random values that the device picks) into the device's cryptographic secrets. As long as the adversary cannot observe the device's communication with the server, the server would provide an effective source of environmental entropy.

One problem with this approach comes in attributing blame for failures. If a device using an entropy server produces

[1]By *weak keys* we mean keys sampled from a distribution with much less min-entropy than the user expects. For example, a 224-bit EC-DSA key sampled from a distribution with only 20 bits of min-entropy is weak.

weak keys, the device might *blame the entropy server* for providing it with weak random values. In turn, the entropy server could claim that it provided the device with strong random values but that the device failed to incorporate them into the device's cryptographic secrets. Without some additional protocol, a third party will not be able to definitively attribute the randomness failure to either the device or the entropy server.

Possible Solution #3: Key database. A third possible technique to prevent devices from using weak keys would be to deploy a "key database" that contains a copy of every public key on the Internet. A non-profit organization could run this database, much as the Electronic Frontier Foundation maintains the SSL Observatory [23], a static database of public keys on the Internet.

Whenever a device with a potentially weak entropy source generates a new keypair, the device would send its new public key to the key database. If the database already contains that key (or if the database contains an RSA modulus that shares a factor with the new key), the device would generate a fresh key and submit it to the database. The device would continue this generate-and-submit process until finding a unique key. At the end of the process, the device would be guaranteed to have a key that is unique, at least amongst the set of keys in the database.

Unfortunately, this proposed solution would *obscure* the entropy problem without fixing it. An attacker could replay the entire key generation process using the known initial state of a device with a weak entropy source to learn the secret keys of that device. By creating a centralized database of (possibly weak) keys, such a solution would make it easier for attackers to find and compromise weak keys.

2. SYSTEM OVERVIEW

Our proposed solution to the weak key problem, pictorially represented in Figure 1, takes place between a *device*, an *entropy authority*, a *certificate authority*[2] (optionally), and a *client*. We describe the roles of each of these participants before outlining our threat model and the security properties of the scheme.

2.1 Participants

Device. The *device* is the entity generating the RSA or DSA keypair that we want to ensure is sufficiently random, even if the device does not have access to a strong internal entropy source. The device might be an embedded device (e.g., a commodity wireless home router), or it might be a full-fledged server. The device could use the keypair it generates to secure HTTPS sessions and to authenticate itself in SSH sessions.

Entropy authority (EA). The *entropy authority* is the participant responsible for ensuring that a device's keypair is selected with enough randomness (is sampled independently from a distribution with high enough min-entropy). Just as a certificate authority verifies the identifying information (name, address, etc.) on a user's public key, the entropy authority verifies the *randomness* of a user's public key.

[2]IETF documents [5] use the term *certification authority* but we will follow common usage and use *certificate authority*.

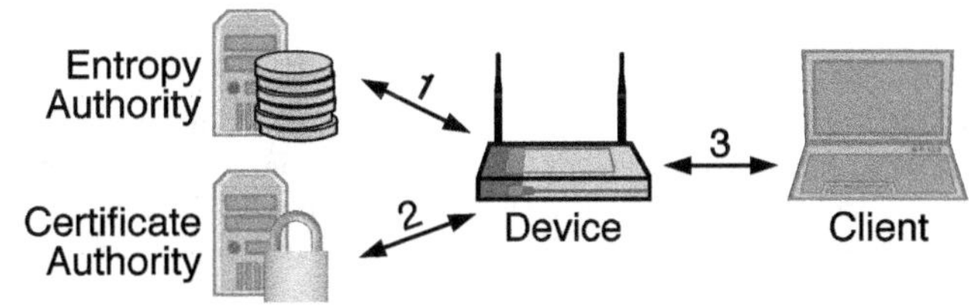

Figure 1: Overview of the protocol participants. (1) The device fetches random values from the entropy authority, proves to the authority that its key incorporates these values, and obtains a signature on the key from the EA. (2) The device submits its EA-signed public key to the certificate authority for signing. (3) The device presents an EA-signed key to a connecting client to prove that its keypair incorporates entropy from the authority.

As the device generates its cryptographic keypair, it fetches some random values from the entropy authority and then *proves* to the entropy authority that it has incorporated these values into its keypair. The entropy verifies this proof and then signs the device's public key. In practice, an entropy authority is just a public Web service with which the device interacts when the device first generates its a keypair. We assume that the entropy authority has a strong entropy source, but that the entropy authority might be malicious.

We imagine a future in which there are a large number of public entropy authorities on the Internet, run by corporate IT departments, certificate authorities, universities, and other large organizations. A device would select its entropy authority much as users select certificate authorities today: based on reputation and reliability. To defend against the failure (or maliciousness) of a single entropy authority, the device could interact with a number of entropy authorities to generate a single key, as we describe in Section 6.

Certificate authority (CA). The *certificate authority* plays the role of a conventional CA: the certificate authority confirms that the real-world identity of the device matches the identity listed in device's certificate, after which the CA signs the device's certificate. In our model, CAs will only sign certificates that have been signed first by an entropy authority. In this way, CAs are guaranteed to sign only public keys that are drawn from a distribution with high min-entropy. Since many certificates (particularly in embedded devices) are self-signed, the CA is an optional entity in our protocol.

Client. The *client* is anyone who connects to the device. In our model, the client can ensure that the device has a sufficiently random public key by verifying the entropy authority's signature on the key. Every client keeps a signature verification key for each entropy authority it trusts, just as today's Web browsers maintain a list of public keys for trusted root CAs.

2.2 Threat Model

Throughout the paper, we say that a device has a *strong entropy source* if it can repeatedly sample from the uniform distribution over some set (e.g., $\{0, 1\}$). We say that the device has a *weak entropy source* otherwise. A *strong key*, for our purposes, is a key independently sampled from a distribution over the set of possible keys that has at least

$k - \text{polylog}(k)$ bits of min-entropy, where k is the security parameter. In other words, a device generates strong keys if the probability that the device will generate a particular public key pk is at most $2^{-(k-\text{polylog}(k))}$ for all public keys pk. A *weak key* is any key that is not strong. We say that a participant is *honest* if it performs the protocol correctly and is *dishonest* otherwise.

The goal of our protocol is to have the device interact with the entropy authority in such a way that, after the interaction, the device holds a strong cryptographic key. This overall goal must be tempered a few realities. In particular, if a device has a no entropy source (or a very weak entropy source), then a *global* eavesdropper can always learn the device's secret key.

To see why this is so, consider that a device with no entropy source is just a deterministic process. Thus, the eavesdropper could always replay such a device's interaction with the entropy authority using the messages collected while eavesdropping. Thus, there is no hope for a completely deterministic device to generate keys that a global eavesdropper cannot guess.

To circumvent this fundamental problem, we consider instead a two-phase threat model:

1. *Set-up phase*: In the set-up phase, the device interacts with the entropy authority in a communication session that the adversary **cannot observe or modify**. In our key-generation protocols, this set-up communication session consists of two round-trip interactions between the device and the entropy authority.

2. *Long-term communication phase*: After the set-up stage ends, the adversary can observe and tamper with the traffic on all network links.

This threat model mimics SSH's implicit threat model: an SSH client gets one "free" interaction with the SSH server, in which the SSH server sends its public key to the client. As long as the adversary cannot tamper with this initial interaction, SSH protects against eavesdropping and man-in-the-middle attacks.

Under the adversary model outlined above, our key generation protocol provides the following security properties:

Protects device from a malicious EA. If the device has a strong entropy source, then the entropy authority learns no useful information about the device's secrets during a run of the protocol. We prove this property for the RSA protocol by demonstrating that the entropy authority can simulate its interaction with the device given only $O(\log k)$ bits of information about the RSA primes p and q. We prove this property for the DSA protocol by demonstrating that the entropy authority can perfectly simulate its interaction with the device given no extra information.

Protects device from CA and client. An honest device interacting with an honest entropy authority holds a strong key at the end of a protocol run, even if the device has a weak entropy source. When the device later interacts with a certificate authority (to obtain a public-key certificate) or with a client (to establish a TLS session), the device will send these parties a *strong* public key, even if the device has weak entropy source.

Protects EA from malicious device. If the entropy authority is honest, then the keys generated by this protocol will be strong, *even if* the device is dishonest. Intuitively, this property states that a faulty device cannot discard the random values that the entropy authority contributes to the key generation process.

A consequence of this security property is that a malicious device can never "discredit" an entropy authority by tricking the entropy authority into signing a key sampled from a low-entropy distribution. If a device does try to have the entropy authority sign a key sampled from a distribution with low min-entropy (a *weak key*), the authority will detect that the device misbehaved and will refuse to sign the key.

A nuance of this property is that the entropy authority *will accept public keys that are invalid*, as long as the keys are sampled independently from a distribution with high min-entropy. In essence, a faulty device in our protocol can create keys that are incorrect but random. For example, the device could pick an composite number as one of its RSA "primes," or it could use any number of other methods to "shoot itself in the foot" during the key generation process. Since the device can *always* compromise its own keypair (e.g., by publishing its secret key), we do not attempt to protect a completely malicious device from itself. Instead, we simply guarantee that any key that the entropy authority accepts will be drawn independently from a distribution with high min-entropy.

2.3 Non-threats

Our protocol addresses the threat posed by devices that use weak entropy sources to generate their cryptographic keys. We explicitly *do not* address these other broad vulnerability classes:

- **Adversarial devices.** If the device is completely adversarial, then the device can easily compromise its own security (e.g., by publishing its own secret key). Ensuring that such an adversarial device has high-entropy cryptographic keys is not useful, since *no* connection to such an adversarial device is secure.
- **Faulty cryptography library (or OS).** Our protocol does not attempt to protect against cryptographic software that is arbitrarily incorrect. Incorrect software can introduce any number of odd vulnerabilities (e.g., a timing channel that leaks the secret key), which we place out of scope.
- **Denial of service.** We do not address denial-of-service attacks by the entropy authority or certificate authority. In a real-world deployment, we expect that a device facing a denial-of-service attack by a CA or entropy authority could simply switch to using a new CA or EA.

3. PROTOCOL

This section describes a number of standard cryptographic primitives we require and then outlines our RSA and DSA key generation protocols.

3.1 Preliminaries

Our key generation protocols use the following cryptographic primitives.

Additively homomorphic commitments. We require an additively homomorphic and perfectly hiding commitment scheme. Given a commitment to x and a commitment to x', anyone should be able to construct a commitment to $x+x' \pmod{Q}$ without knowing the values x or x'. Our implementation uses Pedersen commitments [37]. Given public generators g, h of a group G with prime order Q, and a random value $r \in \mathbb{Z}_Q$, a Pedersen commitment to the value x is $\mathsf{Commit}(x; r) = g^x h^r$.[3] To ensure that the commitments are binding, participants must select the generators g and h in such a way that *no one* knows the discrete logarithm $\log_g h$.

The commitment scheme is additively homomorphic because the product of two commitments reveals a commitment to $x + x' \pmod{Q}$ with randomness $r + r' \pmod{Q}$:

$$\mathsf{Commit}(x + x'; r + r') = \mathsf{Commit}(x; r)\mathsf{Commit}(x'; r)$$

We abbreviate $\mathsf{Commit}(x; r)$ as $\mathsf{Commit}(x)$ when the randomness used in the commitment is not relevant to the exposition.

Of course, if the device has a weak entropy source the device will not be able to generate a strong random value r for use in the commitments. We use randomized commitments to hide a device's secrets *in case* the device does have a strong entropy source. Since a device does not necessarily know whether its randomness source is strong or weak, we must use the same constructions for devices with both strong and weak entropy sources.

Public-key signature scheme. We use a standard public-key signature scheme that is existentially unforgeable [27]. We denote the signing and verification algorithms by Sign and Verify.

Multiplication proof for committed values. We use a zero-knowledge proof-of-knowledge protocol that proves that the product of two committed values is equal to some third value. For example, given commitments C_x and C_y to values $x, y \in \mathbb{Z}_Q$, and a third product value $z \in \mathbb{Z}_Q$, the proof demonstrates that $z = xy \pmod{Q}$. We denote the prover and verifier algorithms by $\pi \leftarrow \mathsf{MulProve}(z, C_x, C_y)$ and $\mathsf{MulVer}(\pi, z, C_x, C_y)$.

We implement this proof using the method of Cramer and Damgård [6]. Written in Camenisch and Stadler's zero-knowledge proof notation [4], the multiplication proof proves the statement:

$$\mathsf{PoK}\{x, y, r_x, r_y, r_z : C_x = g^x h^{r_x} \wedge C_y = g^y h^{r_y} \wedge g^z h^{r_z} = (C_x)^y h^{r_z}\}$$

Application of the Fiat-Shamir heuristic [24] converts this interactive zero-knowledge proof protocol into a non-interactive proof in the random-oracle model [2]. When implemented using a hash function that outputs length-l binary strings, the non-interactive multiplication proof is $l + 3\lceil \log_2 Q \rceil$ bits long.

Common Public Keys. We assume that all participants hold a signature verification public-key for the entropy and certificate authorities.

3.2 RSA Key Generation

The RSA key generation protocol takes place between the device and the entropy authority. At the end of a successful run of the protocol, the device holds an RSA public modulus n that is independently sampled from a distribution over $\mathbb{Z}$ that has high min-entropy and the device also holds the entropy authority's signature σ on this modulus.

In Section 4.1 we prove that the RSA protocol satisfies the security properties defined in Section 2.2. In Section 6, we describe how a device could use this protocol to generate a self-signed X.509 certificate and how to integrate this protocol with today's certificate authority infrastructure.

Parameters. Before the protocol begins, the device and entropy authority must agree on a set of common system parameters. These parameters include the security parameter k, which determines the bit-length of the RSA primes p and q. For a given value of k, the participants must also agree on a prime-order group G used for the Pedersen commitments and zero-knowledge proofs. The prime order Q of the group G must be somewhat larger than the largest RSA modulus n generated by the protocol, so the participants should let $Q \approx 2^{2k+100}$. In addition, participants must agree on two generators g and h of the group G, such that *no one* knows the discrete logarithm $\log_g h$. In an implementation of the protocol, participants could generate g and h using a shared public hash function. Finally, they also agree on a small number Δ (e.g. $\Delta = 2^{16}$) discussed in Section 3.2.1 below.

Since the parameters contain only public values, all devices and entropy authorities could share one set of parameters (per key size).

Protocol Description. Figure 2 presents our RSA key generation protocol. To generate an RSA key, the device first selects k-bit integers x and y and sends randomized commitments to these values to the entropy authority. The entropy authority then selects k-bit integers x' and y' at random and returns these values to the device.

After confirming that x' and y' are of the correct length, the device searches for offsets δ_x and δ_y such that the sums $p = x + x' + \delta_x$ and $q = y + y' + \delta_y$ are suitable RSA primes. That is, p and q must be distinct primes such that $\gcd(p-1, e) = 1$ and $\gcd(q-1, e) = 1$, where e is the RSA encryption exponent. The device then sets $n \leftarrow pq$, generates commitments to p and q, and produces a non-interactive zero-knowledge proof of knowledge π that the product of the committed values is equal to n. The device sends n, δ_x, δ_y, and the the proof π to the entropy authority.

The validity of the proof π and the fact that the δ values are less than Δ convince the entropy authority that the device's RSA primes p and q incorporate the authority's random values x' and y'. At this point, the authority signs the modulus n and returns it to the device.

3.2.1 Finding Primes p and q

To maintain the security of the protocol, it is important that the δ values chosen in Step 3 are relatively small—if the device could pick an arbitrarily large δ_x value, for example, the device could set $\delta_x \leftarrow -x'$, which would make $p = x + x' - x' = x$, thereby cancelling out the effect of the random value x' contributed by the entropy authority. To prevent the device from "throwing away" the entropy authority's entropy in this way, we require that the δ values be less than some maximum value Δ, which depends on the security parameter k.

[3] We denote the group order with capital "Q" to distinguish it from the RSA prime q in $n = pq$ that we use later on.

Device		**Entropy Authority**
Step 1 choose $x, y \xleftarrow{R} [2^k, 2^{k+1})$ $C_x \leftarrow \mathsf{Commit}(x)$ $C_y \leftarrow \mathsf{Commit}(y)$		
	send C_x, C_y $\longrightarrow$	
		Step 2 choose $x', y' \xleftarrow{R} [2^k, 2^{k+1})$
	$\longleftarrow$ send x', y'	
Step 3 abort if $x', y' \notin [2^k, 2^{k+1})$ choose $0 \le \delta_x, \delta_y < \Delta$ s.t. $p \leftarrow x + x' + \delta_x$ $q \leftarrow y + y' + \delta_y$ are distinct primes, $\gcd(p-1, e) = 1$, and $\gcd(q-1, e) = 1$ abort if no such δ_x, δ_y exist let $n \leftarrow pq$ $C_p \leftarrow C_x g^{x'+\delta_x}$ $C_q \leftarrow C_y g^{y'+\delta_y}$ $\pi \leftarrow \mathsf{MulProve}(n, C_p, C_q)$		
	send $n, \delta_x, \delta_y, \pi$ $\longrightarrow$	
		Step 4 $C_p \leftarrow C_x g^{x'+\delta_x}$ $C_q \leftarrow C_y g^{y'+\delta_y}$ abort if $\delta_x, \delta_y \notin [0, \Delta)$ or $n \notin [2^{2k+2}, 2^{2k+4})$ or $\mathsf{MulVer}(\pi, n, C_p, C_q) \neq 1$ $\sigma \leftarrow \mathsf{Sign}_{\mathrm{EA}}(n)$
	$\longleftarrow$ send σ	
Step 5 abort if $\mathsf{Verify}_{\mathrm{EA}}(\sigma, n) \neq 1$ public key is (n, e, σ)		

Figure 2: RSA Key Generation Protocol

Picking the size of Δ requires some care: if Δ is too small, then there may be no suitable prime p in the range $[x+x', x+x'+\Delta)$, and the device will have to run the protocol many times before it finds suitable primes p and q. The value Δ should be large enough that the protocol will succeed with overwhelming probability, but not so large that the device can pick $n = pq$ arbitrarily.

Following Juels and Guajardo [30], if the density of primes is d_{prime} and the density of these special primes (with $\gcd(p-1, q-1, e) = 1$ is d_{special}, we conjecture that $d_{\text{special}}/d_{\text{prime}} = (e-1)/e$, where e is the RSA encryption exponent (a small odd prime constant). Under this conjecture and the Hardy-Littlewood [28] conjecture, Juels and Guajardo demonstrate that the probability that there is *no suitable prime* in the interval $[x+x', x+x'+\Delta)$ is at most $\exp(-\lambda)$ when $\Delta = \lambda \ln(x+x')(\frac{e}{e-1})$ as $(x+x') \to \infty$. To make this conjecture concrete: if we take $(x+x') \approx 2^{1024}$, the RSA encryption exponent $e = 65537$, and require a failure probability of at most 2^{-80}, then we should set $\Delta \approx 2^{16}$. In the very unlikely case that the device fails to find primes p and q in the right range, the device aborts and re-runs the protocol from the beginning.

3.2.2 *Eliminating Information Leakage*

The values δ_x and δ_y sent to the entropy authority in Step 3 of the protocol leak some information about p and q to the entropy authority. In particular, the authority learns that the prime gap before p (resp. q) has a width of at least δ_x (resp. δ_y). We argue in Section 4.1 the entropy authority cannot use this leakage to help it factor the modulus n.

Even so, it is possible to modify the protocol to completely eliminate this information leakage at some performance cost. One way to modify the protocol is to require that $\delta_x = \delta_y = 0$ in Step 3 of the protocol. If the values $x + x'$ and $y + y'$ are not prime, the device aborts the protocol and restarts it from the beginning. Since the probability that a random k-bit number is a suitable prime is near $1/k$ for large k, the device will have to run the protocol approximately k^2 times before it succeeds.

To reduce the number of communication rounds required for this revised protocol, the device could run the k^2 protocol iterations in parallel. The device would send k^2-length vectors of commitments to random values $\vec{x}, \vec{y}$ in Step 1 of the protocol and the entropy authority would return two vectors $\vec{x}', \vec{y}'$ in Step 2 of the protocol, with each vector having length k^2. The device would then iterate over the vectors until it finds an i such that $p \leftarrow x_i + x'_i$ and $q \leftarrow y_i + y'_i$ are distinct primes and $\gcd(p-1, q-1, e) = 1$. If the device fails to find such primes, it would abort and repeat the process.

3.3 DSA Key Generation

The DSA key generation protocol, which we present in Figure 3, takes place between a device and the entropy authority.

Parameters. We assume that, before the start of the protocol, participants have agreed upon an order-q group G used in the DSA signing process. If the device uses the elliptic-curve variant of DSA (EC-DSA), then the group G will be an elliptic curve group selected, for example, from one of the NIST standard curves [25]. Participants must also agree upon two public generators, g and h, of the group G such that *no one* knows the discrete logarithm $\log_g h$.

While we expect most new devices to primarily use EC-DSA keys, even new devices may also need to generate finite-field DSA keys for interoperability with legacy devices. When using the finite-field variant of DSA, the device may have to generate the parameters of the finite-field DSA group (a prime modulus p, a group order q, and a generator g) in addition to its keypair. To do this, the device and entropy authority could agree on a *domain parameter seed* using a coin-flipping protocol [3] and then use this shared seed to generate DSA parameters using the verifiable generation method specified in the Digital Signature standard [25, Appendix A].

Device		Entropy Authority
<u>Step 1</u> choose $x, r_x \xleftarrow{R} \mathbb{Z}_q$ $C_x \leftarrow \mathsf{Commit}(x; r_x)$		
	send C_x →	<u>Step 2</u> choose $x' \xleftarrow{R} \mathbb{Z}_q$
<u>Step 3</u> $a \leftarrow x + x' \bmod q$ $A \leftarrow g^a$	← send x'	
	send A, r_x →	<u>Step 4</u> abort if $Ah^{r_x} \neq C_x g^{x'}$ $\sigma \leftarrow \mathsf{Sign}_{\mathrm{EA}}(A)$
<u>Step 5</u> abort if $\mathsf{Verify}_{\mathrm{EA}}(\sigma, A) \neq 1$ public key is (A, σ)	← send σ	

Figure 3: DSA Key Generation Protocol

Protocol Description. To begin the key generation process depicted in Figure 3, the device picks a random value $x \in \mathbb{Z}_q$ and generates a randomized commitment to x. In the event that the device has a strong entropy source, the use of a randomized commitment prevents the entropy authority from learning the device's secret x. The device sends this commitment to the entropy authority.

Upon receiving the device's commitment, the entropy authority chooses a random value $x' \in \mathbb{Z}_q$ and returns this value to the device. The device sets its private key $a \leftarrow x+x' \bmod q$ and sets its public key to $A \leftarrow g^a$. The device then sends its public key A along with the randomness r_x used in the commitment to x to the entropy authority.

The entropy authority confirms that $Ah^{r_x} = C_x g^{x'}$, which convinces the entropy authority that A is equal to $g^{x+x'}$. The entropy authority then signs the device's public key A and returns it to the device.

4. SECURITY ANALYSIS

This section presents proofs that the RSA and DSA key generation protocols satisfy the security properties described in Section 2.

4.1 RSA Protocol

4.1.1 Protects Device from a Malicious EA

We first show that when the device has a strong entropy source a malicious EA learns no useful information about the device's resulting RSA secret key.

First, let us define a standalone RSA modulus generation algorithm which does not interact with an EA. The key generator takes as input a security parameter k and lower bounds $p_{\min}$ and $q_{\min}$ on the RSA primes p and q.

$\mathsf{PrimeGen}(k, p_{\min})$:
  choose a random x in $[2^k, 2^{k+1}]$
  find the smallest prime p s.t. $p \geq p_{\min} + x$
  output p

$\mathsf{RSAKeyGen}(k, p_{\min}, q_{\min})$:
  $p \leftarrow \mathsf{PrimeGen}(k, p_{\min})$, $q \leftarrow \mathsf{PrimeGen}(k, q_{\min})$
  output $n \leftarrow p \cdot q$

We say that a modulus generator outputs a *secure distribution of RSA moduli n* if the resulting family of RSA functions $x \to x^e \bmod n$ is a family of trapdoor one-way functions (where e is the RSA encryption exponent, a small prime constant). A secure modulus generator is sufficient for use in standard RSA encryption and RSA signature systems.

We use the following *RSA assumption* about algorithm RSAKeyGen above: algorithm $\mathsf{RSAKeyGen}(k, p_{\min}, q_{\min})$ outputs a secure distribution of RSA moduli for all $p_{\min}$ and $q_{\min}$ in the interval $[2^k, 2^{k+1})$.

The following theorem shows that even when interacting with a malicious EA, the RSA key generation protocol in Figure 2 outputs a secure distribution of RSA moduli. Furthermore, the protocol leaks at most $O(\log k)$ bits of information about the prime factors to the EA. This small leak does not harm security since if it were possible to invert the RSA function given the few leaked bits then it would also be possible to do it without, simply by trying all possible values for the leaked bits. Moreover, if desired this small leak can be eliminated at the cost of more computation, as explained in Section 3.2.2.

THEOREM 4.1. *Suppose the device has a strong entropy source (i.e., the device can repeatedly sample independent uniform bits in $\{0,1\}$). Then for all EA, the protocol in Figure 2 generates a secure distribution of RSA moduli assuming the RSA assumption above. Furthermore, EA's view of the protocol can be simulated with at most $O(\log k)$ advice bits with high probability.*

PROOF. Let $\mathcal{A}$ be a malicious EA that, given random commitments C_x, C_y, outputs $(x', y') \leftarrow \mathcal{A}(C_x, C_y)$. Then, since Pedersen commitments are information theoretically hiding, the protocol in Figure 2 outputs a modulus n sampled from the following distribution:

  choose random $C_x, C_y \xleftarrow{R} \mathbb{Z}_Q$
  $(p_{\min}, q_{\min}) \leftarrow \mathcal{A}(C_x, C_y)$
  output $\mathsf{RSAKeyGen}(k, p_{\min}, q_{\min})$

Therefore, by the RSA assumption about algorithm RSAKeyGen the protocol generates secure distribution of RSA moduli.

Next, to argue that the protocol leaks at most $O(\log k)$ bits of information about the prime factors with high probability, we construct a simulator S that simulates the transcript of a successful run of the protocol with $\mathcal{A}$ given only n and an additional $O(\log k)$ bits of information. This will prove that given n, the protocol leaks only $O(\log k)$ additional bits. The protocol transcript consists of

$$(C_x, C_y, x', y', n, \delta_x, \delta_y, \pi, \sigma)$$

where $n = pq$ and $p = x + x' + \delta_x$, $q = y + y' + \delta_y$ for some x, y. For a prime p let $\mathsf{pre}(p)$ be the prime immediately preceding p. The simulator S takes three arguments as input: the modulus $n = pq$ produced by a successful run of the protocol and the quantities

$$\Delta_p = \min(p - \mathsf{pre}(p),\ \Delta) \quad ; \quad \Delta_q = \min(q - \mathsf{pre}(q),\ \Delta)$$

The simulator works as follows:

$S(n, \Delta_p, \Delta_q)$:
  repeat:
    choose random $C_x, C_y \xleftarrow{R} \mathbb{Z}_Q$
    generate $(x', y') \leftarrow \mathcal{A}(C_x, C_y)$
  until $n \in \big[(x' + 2^k)(y' + 2^k),\ (x' + 2^{k+1})(y' + 2^{k+1})\ \big)$
  choose random δ_x in $[0, \Delta_p)$
  choose random δ_y in $[0, \Delta_q)$
  use the ZK simulator for Pedersen products to
    simulate a proof π that $n = (x + x' + \delta_x)(y + y' + \delta_y)$
    where x and y are the values committed in C_x, C_y.
  run $\mathcal{A}$ giving it $n, \delta_x, \delta_y, \pi$ and obtain σ
  output the simulated transcript:
    $(C_x, C_y, x', y', n, \delta_x, \delta_y, \pi, \sigma)$

The simulator S properly simulates the Pedersen commitments C_x, C_y and the quantities x', y', given that the protocol generated the modulus n. Similarly, given that $n = pq$ was the output we know that the random variable $x + x'$ is uniformly distributed in the interval $(\mathsf{pre}(p), p]$ whenever $p - \text{pre}(p) < \Delta$ and is uniform in $(p - \Delta, p]$ otherwise. Either way, the value of δ_x is uniform in $[0, \Delta_p)$. Hence S properly simulates δ_x and similarly δ_y. Finally, π is properly simulated using the ZK knowledge simulator for a proof of Pedersen products.

We explained in Section 3.2 that Δ_p and Δ_q are $O(k)$ in size with high probability, and therefore the protocol leaks at most $O(\log k)$ bits of information □

4.1.2 Protects Device from the CA and Client

Having established that the protocol protects a high-entropy device from the entropy authority, we demonstrate that an honest device interacting with an honest entropy authority holds a strong key at the end of a protocol run, even if the device has a weak entropy source.

THEOREM 4.2. *When interacting with an honest EA, the RSA protocol in Figure 2 generates a secure distribution of RSA moduli assuming the RSA assumption about algorithm* $\mathsf{RSAKeyGen}$.

PROOF. Let $\mathcal{A}$ be a device honestly following the protocol, but one that may have a weak entropy source. We let $\mathcal{A}()$ denote the x, y chosen by the device in Step 1. Given an honest EA, the protocol in Figure 2 outputs a modulus n sampled from the following distribution:

  $(p_{\min}, q_{\min}) \leftarrow \mathcal{A}()$
  output $\mathsf{RSAKeyGen}(k, p_{\min}, q_{\min})$

By the RSA assumption about algorithm $\mathsf{RSAKeyGen}$ the protocol generates secure RSA moduli. □

4.1.3 Protects EA from a Malicious Device

Suppose the device is *dishonest* and its goal is to discredit the entropy authority. The device may try to cause the EA to sign a modulus n in Step 4 of the protocol where n is sampled from a low entropy distribution. For example, the two prime factors of $n = pq$ may look non-random (e.g. their binary representation may end in many 1's) or n may have a non-trivial GCD with another public RSA modulus. The EA's signature would then serve as incriminating evidence that the "random" values x' and y' the EA contributed to the protocol in Step 2 were not sampled from the uniform distribution over $[2^k, 2^{k+1})$.

Note, however, that if the modulus n output by the device is an ill-formed RSA modulus—say n is not a product of two primes—then clearly the EA is not at fault since the device did not properly generate n. Therefore the EA need not worry about invalid moduli. It only cares about not signing low-entropy moduli.

The following theorem shows that an honest EA will never sign a low-entropy modulus.

THEOREM 4.3. *Consider an honest entropy authority interacting with a malicious polynomial-time device. Suppose that the RSA modulus n signed by an honest entropy authority in Step 4 is a product of two distinct primes $n = pq$ each in the range $[2^{k+1}, 2^{k+2})$. Then each of the primes is sampled from a distribution with at least $k - 2 - d\log(k)$ bits of min-entropy for some absolute constant d, even when conditioned on the other prime.*

PROOF SKETCH. We first show that n must be sampled from a distribution with sufficiently high min-entropy. In Step 4 of the protocol, the proof π convinces the EA that

$$n = (x + x' + \delta_x)(y + y' + \delta_y) \pmod{Q}$$

for some (unknown) x and y, where Q is the group order used for the Pedersen commitments. Recall that $Q > 2^{100}2^{2k}$. Since the device must commit to x before seeing x' we know that $x+x'$ is sampled independently from a distribution over $\mathbb{Z}_Q$ with min-entropy at least k (in the worst case, $x + x'$ is sampled uniformly from the integers in an interval of width 2^k). Since the device controls δ_x and $0 \le \delta_x < \Delta < c \cdot k$ for some absolute constant c, it follows that the min-entropy of $p_0 \leftarrow x + x' + \delta_x$ is at least $k - \log ck$. Similarly the min-entropy of $q_0 \leftarrow y + y' + \delta_y$ conditioned on p_0 is at least $k - \log ck$. Consequently, since n is a product of two primes, it can be shown for the distributions in question here that the min-entropy of $n = p_0 q_0 \bmod Q$ is at least $2k - d\log k$ for some constant d.

If n is the product of two primes $n = pq$ each in the range $[2^{k+1}, 2^{k+2})$ then each prime must be chosen from a distribution with min-entropy at least $k - 2 - d\log k$ (otherwise n cannot have min-entropy at least $2k - d\log k$). The theorem now follows. □

4.2 DSA Protocol

In this section, we prove that the DSA key generation protocol satisfies the security properties outlined in Section 2.

4.2.1 Protects Device from a Malicious EA

We first prove that a device with a strong entropy source leaks no information about its secret key to the entropy authority during a run of the protocol.

THEOREM 4.4. *If the device has a strong entropy source (i.e., the device can sample from the uniform distribution over a set), then the entropy authority can simulate its interaction with the device.*

PROOF. We construct a simulator S that, given a DSA public key $A = g^a$, outputs the transcript $(C_x, x', r_x, A, \sigma)$ of a protocol run between an honest device and a malicious entropy authority $\mathcal{A}$. The simulator S constructs the transcript as follows:

$S(A)$: choose random $r_x \xleftarrow{R} \mathbb{Z}_q$
set $C_x \leftarrow Ah^{r_x}$
generate $x' \leftarrow \mathcal{A}(C_x)$
run $\mathcal{A}$ on (A, r_x) to get a signature σ
output the simulated transcript: $(C_x, x', r_x, A, \sigma)$

The simulator's transcript is statistically indistinguishable from the transcript of a real protocol run between an honest device with a strong entropy source and the entropy authority $\mathcal{A}$. If the device has a strong entropy source, then the randomness r_x used in the commitment is sampled independently from the uniform distribution. The values C_x, x' and σ are constructed exactly as they would be in a real run of the protocol. □

4.2.2 *Protects Device from the CA and Client*

Having established that a device with a strong entropy source leaks no secret information to the entropy authority, we now demonstrate that the key produced by the protocol is sampled from the uniform distribution over the set of possible keys.

THEOREM 4.5. *If an honest entropy authority does not abort the key generation protocol, and if* either *the device* or *the entropy authority has a strong entropy source, then the public keys produced by the protocol in Figure 3 will be sampled independently from the uniform distribution over G.*

PROOF. If the entropy authority does not abort the key generation protocol, then the equality $Ah^{r_x} = C_x g^{x'}$ is satisfied in the Step 4 of the protocol. Rearranging these terms to compute the public key A: $A = C_x g^{x'}/h^{r_x} = g^{x+x'}$. To demonstrate that the public key $g^{x+x'}$ is uniformly distributed over the set of possible public keys, it suffices to show that *either* x or x' is selected uniformly at random from $\mathbb{Z}_q$ and that x and x' are independent.

If the device has a strong entropy source, then the device's secret value x will be selected uniformly from $\mathbb{Z}_q$. To show that x' is independent of x, we rely on the "perfect hiding" property of the Pedersen commitment scheme. The commitment C_x that the entropy authority sees before selecting its value x' is simply a value $g^x h^{r_x}$ selected at random from G. If x is independent of x' and x is uniformly distributed over $\mathbb{Z}_q$ then $g^{x+x'}$ is uniformly distributed over G.

If the entropy authority has a strong entropy source, then the entropy authority's value x' will be selected uniformly from $\mathbb{Z}_q$. Since the device must commit to x *before* it sees x', the only way that the device's value x can depend on x' is if the device is able to open its commitment C_x to a value x that depends on x'. The "computationally binding" property of the Pedersen commitment scheme prevents the device from opening C_x to a value that depends on x'. If the device could open the commitment to a value of its choice, the device would be able to compute discrete logarithms in G. If x is independent of x' and x' is sampled from the uniform distribution over $\mathbb{Z}_q$ then $g^{x+x'}$ is sampled from the uniform distribution over G. □

4.2.3 *Protects EA from a Malicious Device*

Theorem 4.2.2 holds *even if* the device is malicious, so a key produced from an interaction between a malicious device and an honest entropy authority will be strong.

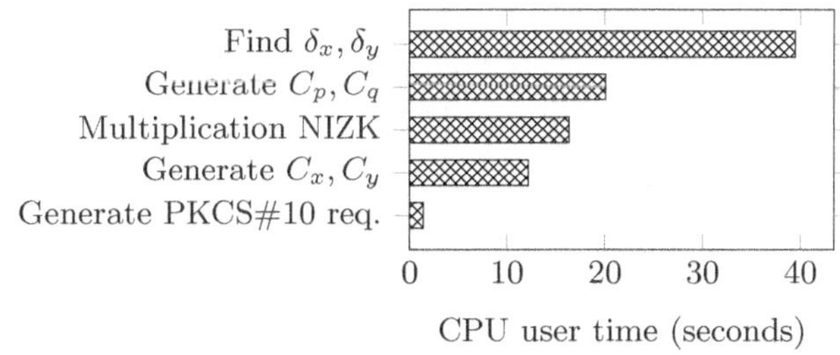

Figure 4: Operations taking longer than 0.05s during a run of the RSA protocol on the home router.

5. EVALUATION

To demonstrate the practicality of our RSA and DSA key generation protocols, we implemented the protocols in C using the OpenSSL cryptography library. We evaluated the performance of the protocols on three different devices: a Linux workstation with two 3.2 GHz Intel W3656 processors, a MacBook Pro laptop with a single 2.5 GHz dual-core processor, and a Linksys E2500-NP home router with a 300 MHz Broadcom BCM5357r2 processor. The entropy authority in all experiments was a modern Linux server and the DSA protocol experiments use the NIST P-224 elliptic curve as the elliptic curve DSA (EC-DSA) group [25].

Embedded devices, like the Linksys router we used in our evaluations, lack the keyboard, mouse, hard drive, and other peripherals used as entropy sources on full-fledged machines. As a result, these device are particularly susceptible to generating weak keys. By evaluating our key generation protocols on a $70 Linksys router, we demonstrate that the protocols are practical even on low-power, low-cost (and often low-entropy) embedded devices. For the purposes of evaluation, we installed the Linux-based dd-wrt [22] operating system on the Linksys router and ran our key generation protocol in a user-space Linux process.

Table 1 presents the wall-clock time required to generate a 2048-bit RSA key and a 224-bit EC-DSA key on each machine, averaged over eight trial runs. When running on the laptop and workstation, which have relatively fast CPUs, the bulk of the protocol overhead (roughly 90%) comes from the network latency in communicating with the entropy authority. On the CPU-limited home router, the protocol causes a near-2× slowdown, even without the network latency. Even so, running the EC-DSA protocol takes fewer than two seconds on all three of the devices.

The standard RSA keypair generation algorithm requires much more computation than the EC-DSA algorithm, so the cost of interacting with the entropy authority is amortized over a longer total computation in the RSA protocol. As a result, the slowdown factors on each of the three devices is smaller for the RSA protocol than for the DSA variant. The protocol incurs less than a 2× slowdown when running on the home router—generating a standard 2048-bit RSA keypair takes nearly 60 seconds and generating a keypair with the protocol takes just over 100 seconds. On the laptop and workstation, around 50% of the slowdown is due to network latency. On these faster devices, generating an RSA keypair using the protocol takes less than three seconds.

Figure 4 presents a graphical break-down of the CPU user time required to perform the most expensive operations in the RSA key generation protocol on the home router. Nearly half of the CPU time consumed during the protocol is spent

	EC-DSA (224-bit prime)				RSA (2048-bit)			
	No proto	Proto	Proto+Net	*Slowdown*	No proto	Proto	Proto+Net	*Slowdown*
Linksys Router	0.45	0.84	1.61	3.6×	59.16	96.93	101.57	1.7×
Laptop	0.03	0.08	0.72	28×	0.52	1.26	2.01	3.9×
Workstation	0.004	0.05	0.68	160×	0.16	0.65	1.41	8.7×

Table 1: Time (in seconds) to generate a keypair without our protocol, with a local EA, and with an EA via the Internet with ≈ 80 ms of round-trip latency. The Slowdown column indicates the slowdown factor of our protocol running over the Internet relative to the standard key generation algorithm.

in finding the δ_x and δ_y offset values to make the RSA factors p and q prime. Finding these offsets requires running the Miller-Rabin [38] primality test on a number of candidate primes. This expensive search for primes p and q is also required to generate an RSA modulus *without* our key generation protocol, so this search does not constitute protocol overhead.

The other expensive operations are computing the Pedersen commitments (each of which requires big-integer modular exponentiations) and generating the non-interactive zero-knowledge proof that n is the product of the values contained in the commitments C_p and C_q. The final expensive operation is generating the PKCS#10 certificate request, which the device signs with its newly generated RSA key.

Our implementation does not use fast multi-exponentiation algorithms [34] (e.g., for computing Pedersen commitments $g^a h^r$ quickly) or exploit parallelism to increase performance on multi-core machines. An aggressively optimized production-ready implementation could use these techniques to improve the performance of the protocol.

As shown in Figure 5, our protocol imposes a near-uniform 4× computation overhead (measured in CPU user time) on EC-DSA key generation. This slowdown arises because our EC-DSA protocol requires three elliptic curve point multiplications and a single signature verification, compared with the single elliptic curve point multiplication required in traditional EC-DSA key generation. At the smallest usable EC-DSA key size, 112 bits, the protocol set-up cost dominates the overall running time, so the protocol imposes a 5.6× overhead.

The computational overhead of generating RSA keys using our protocol decreases as the key size increases. The dominant *additional* cost of our RSA protocol is the cost of the modular exponentiations used in the commitment scheme and zero-knowledge proof generation. As k increases, the cost of finding the RSA primes grows faster than the additional cost of our protocol, so the computational overhead of our protocol tends to 1.

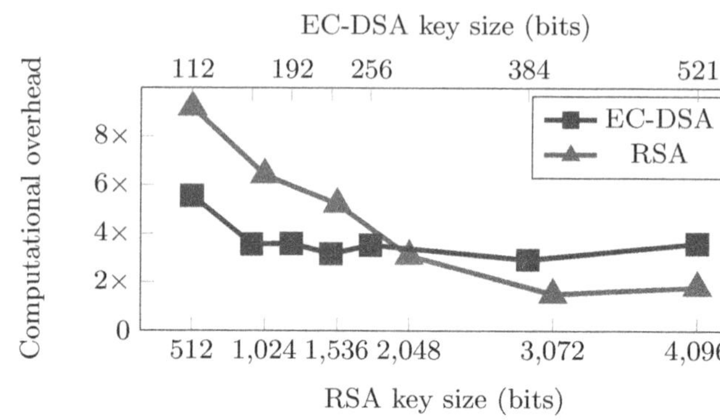

Figure 5: Computational overhead (in CPU user time) imposed when a laptop uses our key generation protocols to generate keypairs of various sizes.

6. IMPLEMENTATION CONCERNS

This section discusses a handful of practical implementation issues that a real-world deployment of our key generation protocols would have to address.

Integration with the CA infrastructure. Integrating our key generation protocols with the existing CA infrastructure would require only modest modifications to today's infrastructure. In a deployment of our key generation protocol, the device could interact with the entropy authority using an HTTP API. After the device obtains the entropy authority's signature on its public key, the device would embed the EA signature in an extension field in the PKCS#10 certificate signing request that the device sends to the certificate authority. Each certificate authority would maintain a list of public keys of approved entropy authorities (in the way that browsers and SSL libraries today maintain a list of root CA public keys). When a certificate authority receives a PKCS#10 request from a device, the CA would first check the validity of the EA's signature on the request. If the signature is valid and the CA is able to verify the identity of the requesting device, the CA would sign the certificate and return it to the device.

We expect that many commercial certificate authorities would be willing to serve as free public entropy authorities, since the computational cost of acting as an entropy authority is small (less than one CPU-second per protocol run). Organizations large enough to have their own IT departments might run their own internal entropy authorities as well.

Self-Signed Certificates and SSH. TLS servers often use self-signed certificates to provide link encryption without CA-certified identity. The analogue of a self-signed certificate in our setting is a certificate that is signed by the entropy authority but that is *not* signed by a certificate authority. This sort of certificate would convince a third party that the device's public key is sampled from a high-entropy distribution, without convincing a third party that the key corresponds to a particular real-world identity. As long as some EAs provide their services for free (which we expect), EA-signed certificates will be free, just as self-signed certificates are free today.

To generate such a certificate, the device would submit a PKCS#10 certificate signing request to the entropy authority at the end of Step 3 of the RSA protocol or Step 3 of the DSA protocol, along with other data it sends. The entropy authority would then sign the request and would return the EA-signed certificate to the device. TLS clients (e.g., Web browsers) would maintain a list of public keys of approved entropy authorities, just as today's client keep a list of approved root CAs. When a client connects to a device that uses an EA-signed certificate, the client would verify the EA's signature and would treat the certificate just as it treats self-signed certificates today.

SSH could similarly use EA-signed keys to use convince clients that a particular SSH host generated its public key using random values from an approved entropy authority. To accomplish this, the SSH server software would define a new public key algorithm type for EA-signed keys (e.g., `ssh-rsa-rand`). Keys of this type would contain the SSH host's normal public key, but they would also contain an EA's signature on the SSH host's public key (along with the fingerprint of the signing EA's key). SSH clients that support the `ssh-rsa-rand` key type would be able to verify the EA's signature on the host's key to confirm that that the host's key incorporates randomness from an approved entropy authority.

Other entropy issues. Our key generation protocol *only* ensures that a device's RSA or DSA keypair has sufficient randomness—it does not ensure randomness in other security-critical parts of the system (e.g., signing nonce generation, TLS session key selection, address space layout randomization). We focus on cryptographic key generation because attacks against weak public keys are especially easy to mount. Once a device publishes a weak public key, the device is likely to use the same public key for months or years. Thus, even if the device's entropy source strengthens over time (as the device gathers randomness from network interrupt timings, for example) the device's keys remains weak. Hedged public-key cryptography [1, 39], in conjunction with our key generation protocols, would help reduce the risk of bad randomness in signing and encryption, but solving all of these randomness problems is likely beyond the scope of any single system.

Distributing trust with many entropy authorities. As we note in Section 2, if the device has a weak entropy source then there is no way to protect the device against a eavesdropper that observes *all communication* between the device and the EA. Our threat model excludes the possibility of such an eavesdropper, but if the device is particularly concerned about eavesdroppers on its initial conversation with the EA, the device could run a modified version of the protocol with *many* entropy authorities instead of just one. With multiple EAs, an eavesdropper would have to observe the device's communication with *all* of the EAs to learn the device's secret key. We sketch the multi-authority DSA protocol here. A similar modification allows RSA key generation with multiple entropy authorities.

In the multi-authority DSA protocol, the device commits to its random value x and sends $C_x \leftarrow \mathsf{Commit}(x; r)$ to each of N entropy authorities. Each entropy authority responds with (x_i, r_i, σ_i), where x_i and r_i are random values in $\mathbb{Z}_q$ and $\sigma_i \leftarrow \mathsf{Sign}_{EA_i}(C_x, \mathsf{Commit}(x_i; r_i))$. The device's secret key is then $a = x + \Sigma_i x_i \bmod q$. The device can obtain a signature on its public key g^a from each entropy authority by presenting each authority with its public key, its commitment to x, the randomness r it used to commit to x, the set $\vec{r}$ of nonces used in the entropy authorities' commitments, the set $\vec{C}$ of commitments to each of the entropy authority's random values, and the set of entropy authority signatures $\vec{\sigma}$: $(g^a, C_x, r, \vec{r}, \vec{C}, \vec{\sigma})$. Each authority verifies each EA signature σ_i, confirms that $g^a h^{r+\Sigma_i r_i} = C_x(\Pi_i C_i)$, and signs the device's public key g^a.

	Single exp.	Double exp.
Juels-Guajardo protocol [30]	319	35
This paper	8	4

Figure 6: Approximate number of k-bit modular exponentiations the device must compute to generate a k-bit RSA modulus.

Default keys. Roughly 5% of TLS hosts on the Internet in 2012 used *default keys*, which are pre-loaded into the device's firmware by the manufacturer [29]. Typically, any two such devices of the same model and firmware version will ship with the same public and secret key. To recover a default secret key, an attacker can download the firmware for the device from the manufacturer's Web site or look up the default key in a database designed for that purpose [33].

Our protocol does not protect against a manufacturer who installs the same keypair in many devices. If a manufacturer wants all of her devices to ship with a default keypair signed by an entropy authority, the manufacturer could run our key generation protocol *once* in the factory, and then install this single EA-signed keypair in every device shipped.

Installing the same keypair in many devices is tantamount to publishing the device's secret key, which is an "attack" which we cannot hope to prevent. As a heuristic defense against default keys, a client connecting to a device could require that the device use a certificate that was generated after the manufacture of the device (as indicated, for example, by an EA-signed timestamp on the certificate).

7. RELATED WORK

Hedged public-key cryptography [1, 39] addresses the problem of weak randomness during message *signing* or *encryption*, whereas our work addresses the problem of randomness during *key generation*. Cryptographic hedging provides no protection against randomness failures when generating cryptographic keys but deployed systems could use hedging in conjunction with our key-generation protocols to defend against weak randomness after generating their cryptographic keys.

Intel's Ivy Bridge processor implements a hardware instruction that exploits physical uncertainty in a dedicated circuit to gather random numbers [40]. A hardware random number generator provides a new and potentially rich source of entropy to cryptographic applications. Devices without hardware random number generators could use a variety of other techniques to gather possibly unpredictable values early in the system boot process [35]. Even so, having a rich entropy source does not mean that software developers will properly incorporate the entropy into cryptographic secrets. Our protocol ensures that keys will have high entropy, even if the cryptographic software ignores or misuses hardware-supplied randomness.

Juels and Guajardo [30] offer a protocol for RSA key generation that is superficially similar to the one we present here. The Juels-Guajardo protocol protects against *kleptography* [42], in which a device's cryptography library is adversarial, and *repudiation*, in which a signer intentionally generates a weak cryptographic signing key so that the signer can disown signed messages in the future. To prevent against these very strong adversaries, their protocol requires a number of additional zero-knowledge proofs that are unnecessary in our model. Using the number of modular exponentiations as a proxy for protocol execution time, the Juels-Guajardo protocol would likely take over 40 minutes to execute on the home router we used in our experiments, while our protocol takes fewer than two minutes (see Figure 6). In addition, Juels and Guajardo do *not* address the issue of a device whose source of randomness is so weak that it cannot create blinding commitments or establish a secure SSL session.

8. CONCLUSION

This paper presents a systemic solution to the problem of low-entropy keys. We present a new threat model, in which a device generating cryptographic secrets may have one communication session with an *entropy authority* which an eavesdropper cannot observe. Under this threat model, we describe protocols for generating RSA and DSA keypairs that do not weaken keys for devices that have a strong entropy source, but that can considerably strengthen keys generated on low-entropy devices. Our key generation protocols incur tolerable slow-downs, even on a CPU-limited home router. The threat model and protocols presented herein offer a promising solution to the long-standing problem of weak cryptographic keys.

Acknowledgements

We thank David Wolinsky, Ewa Syta, and Zooko Wilcox-O'Hearn for their helpful comments. This material is based upon work supported by the Defense Advanced Research Agency (DARPA) and SPAWAR Systems Center Pacific, Contracts No. N66001-11-C-4018 and N66001-11-C-4022. This work was also supported by NSF and a Google faculty award.

9. REFERENCES

[1] M. Bellare, Z. Brakerski, M. Naor, T. Ristenpart, G. Segev, H. Shacham, and S. Yilek. Hedged public-key encryption: How to protect against bad randomness. In *ASIACRYPT*, pages 232–249. Springer, 2009.

[2] M. Bellare and P. Rogaway. Random oracles are practical: A paradigm for designing efficient protocols. In *CCS*, pages 62–73, 1993.

[3] M. Blum. Coin flipping by telephone: a protocol for solving impossible problems. *ACM SIGACT News*, 15(1):23–27, 1983.

[4] J. Camenisch and M. Stadler. Proof systems for general statements about discrete logarithms. Technical Report 260, Dept. of Computer Science, ETH Zurich, March 1997.

[5] S. Chokhani and W. Ford. Internet X.509 public key infrastructure certificate policy and certification practices framework, Mar. 1999. RFC 2527.

[6] R. Cramer and I. Damgård. Zero-knowledge proofs for finite field arithmetic, or: Can zero-knowledge be for free? In *CRYPTO*, pages 424–441. Springer, 1998.

[7] CVE-2001-0950: ValiCert Enterprise Validation Authority uses insufficiently random data, Jan. 2001.

[8] CVE-2001-1141: PRNG in SSLeay and OpenSSL could be used by attackers to predict future pseudo-random numbers, July 2001.

[9] CVE-2001-1467: mkpasswd, as used by Red Hat Linux, seeds its random number generator with its process ID, Apr. 2001.

[10] CVE-2003-1376: WinZip uses weak random number generation for password protected ZIP files, Dec. 2003.

[11] CVE-2005-3087: SecureW2 TLS implementation uses weak random number generators during generation of the pre-master secret, Sept. 2005.

[12] CVE-2006-1378: PasswordSafe uses a weak random number generator, Mar. 2006.

[13] CVE-2006-1833: Intel RNG Driver in NetBSD may always generate the same random number, Apr. 2006.

[14] CVE-2007-2453: Random number feature in Linux kernel does not properly seed pools when there is no entropy, June 2007.

[15] CVE-2008-0141: WebPortal CMS generates predictable passwords containing only the time of day, Jan. 2008.

[16] CVE-2008-0166: OpenSSL on Debian-based operating systems uses a random number generator that generates predictable numbers, Jan. 2008.

[17] CVE-2008-2108: GENERATE_SEED macro in php produces 24 bits of entropy and simplifies brute force attacks against the rand and mt_rand functions, May 2008.

[18] CVE-2008-5162: The arc4random function in FreeBSD does not have a proper entropy source for a short time period immediately after boot, Nov. 2008.

[19] CVE-2009-3238: Linux kernel produces insufficiently random numbers, Sept. 2009.

[20] CVE-2009-3278: QNAP uses rand library function to generate a certain recovery key, Sept. 2009.

[21] CVE-2011-3599: Crypt::DSA for Perl, when /dev/random is absent, uses the Data::Random module, Oct. 2011.

[22] dd-wrt. `http://dd-wrt.com/`.

[23] Electronic Frontier Foundation. The EFF SSL observatory. `https://www.eff.org/observatory`.

[24] A. Fiat and A. Shamir. How to prove yourself: practical solutions to identification and signature problems. In *CRYPTO*, pages 186–194, 1986.

[25] P. Gallagher and C. Furlani. FIPS 186-3: Digital signature standard, 2009.

[26] I. Goldberg and D. Wagner. Randomness and the Netscape browser. *Dr. Dobb's Journal–Software Tools for the Professional Programmer*, 21(1):66–71, 1996.

[27] S. Goldwasser, S. Micali, and R. L. Rivest. A digital signature scheme secure against adaptive chosen-message attacks. *SIAM Journal on Computing*, 17(2):281–308, 1988.

[28] G. H. Hardy and J. E. Littlewood. Some problems of *partitio numerorum*; III: On the expression of a number as a sum of primes. *Acta Mathematica*, 44(1):1–70, 1923.

[29] N. Heninger, Z. Durumeric, E. Wustrow, and J. A. Halderman. Mining your Ps and Qs: Detection of widespread weak keys in network devices. In *USENIX Security Symposium*, Aug. 2012.

[30] A. Juels and J. Guajardo. RSA key generation with verifiable randomness. In *PKC*, Feb. 2002.

[31] A. Klyubin. Some SecureRandom thoughts. `http://android-developers.blogspot.com/2013/08/some-securerandom-thoughts.html`, Aug. 2013.

[32] A. K. Lenstra, J. P. Hughes, M. Augier, J. W. Bos, T. Kleinjung, and C. Wachter. Ron was wrong, Whit is right. *IACR ePrint archive*, 64, 2012.

[33] littleblackbox: Database of private SSL/SSH keys for embedded devices. `https://code.google.com/p/littleblackbox/`.

[34] B. Möller. Algorithms for multi-exponentiation. In *Selected Areas in Cryptography*, pages 165–180, 2001.

[35] K. Mowery, M. Wei, D. Kohlbrenner, H. Shacham, and S. Swanson. Welcome to the Entropics: Boot-time entropy in embedded devices. In *IEEE Symposium on Security and Privacy*, 2013.

[36] NetBSD security advisory 2013-003: RNG bug may result in weak cryptographic keys. `ftp://ftp.netbsd.org/pub/NetBSD/security/advisories/NetBSD-SA2013-003.txt.asc`, Mar. 2013.

[37] T. P. Pedersen. Non-interactive and information-theoretic secure verifiable secret sharing. In *CRYPTO*, pages 129–140. Springer, 1992.

[38] M. O. Rabin. Probabilistic algorithm for testing primality. *Journal of Number Theory*, 12(1):128–138, 1980.

[39] T. Ristenpart and S. Yilek. When good randomness goes bad: Virtual machine reset vulnerabilities and hedging deployed cryptography. In *NDSS*, 2010.

[40] G. Taylor and G. Cox. Behind Intel's new random-number generator. *IEEE Spectrum*, Sept. 2011.

[41] S. Yilek, E. Rescorla, H. Shacham, B. Enright, and S. Savage. When private keys are public: Results from the 2008 Debian OpenSSL vulnerability. In *IMC*, pages 15–27, Nov. 2009.

[42] A. Young and M. Yung. Kleptography: Using cryptography against cryptography. In *EUROCRYPT*, pages 62–74, 1997.

FANCI: Identification of Stealthy Malicious Logic Using Boolean Functional Analysis

Adam Waksman Matthew Suozzo Simha Sethumadhavan

Computer Architecture and Security Technologies Lab
Department of Computer Science
Columbia University
New York, NY, USA
{waksman,simha}@cs.columbia.edu
{ms4249}@columbia.edu

ABSTRACT

Hardware design today bears similarities to software design. Often vendors buy and integrate code acquired from third-party organizations into their designs, especially in embedded/system-on-chip designs. Currently, there is no way to determine if third-party designs have built-in backdoors that can compromise security after deployment.

The key observation we use to approach this problem is that hardware backdoors incorporate logic that is nearly-unused, *i.e.* stealthy. The wires used in stealthy backdoor circuits almost never influence the outputs of those circuits. Typically, they do so only when triggered using external inputs from an attacker. In this paper, we present FANCI, a tool that flags suspicious wires, in a design, which have the potential to be malicious. FANCI uses scalable, approximate, boolean functional analysis to detect these wires.

Our examination of the TrustHub hardware backdoor benchmark suite shows that FANCI is able to flag all suspicious paths in the benchmarks that are associated with backdoors. Unlike prior work in the area, FANCI is not hindered by incomplete test suite coverage and thus is able to operate in practice without false negatives. Furthermore, FANCI reports low false positive rates: less than 1% of wires are reported as suspicious in most cases. All TrustHub designs were analyzed in a day or less. We also analyze a backdoor-free out-of-order microprocessor core to demonstrate applicability beyond benchmarks.

Categories and Subject Descriptors

B.6.2 [**Hardware**]: Logic Design—*Security and Trust*

Keywords

hardware; security; backdoors; functional analysis; intellectual property

CCS'13, November 4–8, 2013, Berlin, Germany.

1. INTRODUCTION

Malicious backdoors and intentional security flaws in hardware designs pose a significant threat to trusted computing [1, 2, 3]. This threat is growing in seriousness due to the ever-increasing complexity of hardware designs. A designer can hide a backdoor within a hardware design by writing one or a few lines of code in a way that slightly deviates from specification. For instance, a hardware backdoor, when triggered, might turn off the page protections for a certain range of addresses or weaken the cryptographic strength of a psuedo-random number generator. Such backdoors can be inserted either by third-party designers producing independent components or by malicious insiders working for an otherwise benign company. As a concrete example, King *et al.* designed a backdoor that triggers when a specific rare value appears on the memory bus [4].

In recent years, techniques have been proposed for protecting against hardware design backdoors, including unused circuit identification [5], validation of design properties at runtime [6], and methods for disabling backdoor triggers at runtime [7, 8]. Each of these solutions provides protection against some of the hardware backdoor attack space, and each of these techniques operates at least partially at runtime. Runtime techniques increase design complexity, due to the added effort of modifying designs to include runtime protections.

A key difference between our work and prior works is that our solution does not depend directly on validation and verification. This is extremely useful because validation and verification teams are often large (larger even than design teams) and hard to trust. Additionally, it can be hard in practice to verify third-party IP.

We propose a solution for discovering backdoors in hardware designs prior to fabrication using functional analysis. If backdoors can be detected statically, then the design can be fixed or rejected before it is taped-out and sent to market. The key insight behind our work – one that has been observed in prior works [5, 7] – is that backdoors are nearly always dormant (by design) and thus rely on *nearly-unused logic,* by which we mean logic that almost never determines the values of output wires. It is desirable to design backdoors with rare triggers to avoid unintentional exposure during design validation or other benign testing. In other words, triggers give stealth and control to the adversary. Our goal is to *statically* identify what we refer to as *weakly-affecting inputs*, which are input wires that have the capability to serve as backdoor triggers.

We propose a metric called *control value* to identify nearly-unused logic. This metric measures the degree of control that an input has on the operation and outputs of a digital circuit. The gist of our method is to approximate the truth table for each intermediate output in a design as a function of any wire that can determine that output. We then compute the influence of each input on the output. We show that control value computations can be approximated efficiently and accurately for real circuits and that control value is a useful measure for finding backdoors. We then present a tool called FANCI—Functional Analysis for Nearly-unused Circuit Identification. FANCI reads in a hardware design and flags a set of wires that appear suspicious. FANCI whitelists most of the design (usually more than 99%) and flags a few suspect wires to be code reviewed.

The intuition behind why FANCI works is that in a given design module, there are typically very few (or even zero) wires with low enough control values to be capable of serving as a backdoor trigger. Typically, a backdoor has more or less the following form: a good circuit and a malicious circuit exist. The outputs of both feed into something semantically equivalent to a multiplexer. The multiplexer is controlled by an input that selects the output of the malicious circuit when triggered. For this general arrangement to work, the control value for the control wire is made very low, and FANCI detects such wires.

While we are not theoretically guaranteed to find all backdoors, our empirical results support that the types of circuits designers create in the real world can be effectively analyzed using our tool. For the backdoored circuits in the TrustHub benchmark suite, we were able to detect all backdoors with low false positive rates. We were also able to analyze a backdoor-free, out-of-order microprocessor core without obtaining false positives, indicating that FANCI does not flag most commonly used circuits as backdoors. We argue that applying FANCI to designs statically prior to applying runtime protections can only bolster defenses and never weakens them. Lastly, our method has pseudo-randomness built in to defeat adversaries that may have knowledge of our tools.

The rest of the paper is organized as follows. We first present our threat model in Section 2. We then describe our analysis algorithm and the way FANCI works in Section 3. We further show that our algorithm solves a previously unsolved problem in backdoor detection in Section 4. The results of our experiments are presented in Section 5. Finally, we discuss related work in Section 6 and conclusions in Section 7.

2. THREAT MODEL

In our threat model, an independent hardware designer or third-party intellectual property (IP) provider supplies us with a hardware design. This design is soft IP, encoded as either hardware description language (HDL, also sometimes referred to as RTL) source code, a gatelist or a netlist. Gatelists are produced by logic synthesis, and netlists are produced by physical synthesis. In each case, the design is a soft product that has not yet been sent to foundries for physical manufacture. The provider is malicious and has included hidden, malicious functionality that they are able to turn on at an opportune time for them. The nature of the malicious payload of the attack is not restricted.

Our goal as security engineers is to use non-runtime, validation- and verification-independent, functional analysis to identify which wires in a digital design could potentially be carrying backdoor signals. We want to flag a small number of wires and be assured that the malicious functionality is dependent on a subset of those suspicious wires. In other words, we need to avoid false negatives (a false negative would mean a backdoor that we do not detect).

False positives are also relevant. We must flag a small enough set of wires that security engineers or code reviewers can evaluate all of the suspicious wires by inspecting code. In other words, we must whitelist most of the design. We consider a wire to be a true positive if it is part of combinational logic used in the triggering of the backdoor. In other words, a true positive wire is part of the circuit that produces malicious activity. Our goal in this paper is detection, not correction. By detecting a backdoor prior to fabrication and deployment, we at least know that our provider is malicious before we apply compromised IP to our designs. We can then blacklist that provider and get our IP from a different source. We do not attempt automatic correction.

3. THE FANCI ALGORITHM AND TOOL

Algorithm 1 Flag Suspicious Wires in a Design

```
for all modules m do
  for all gates g in m do
    for all output wires w of g do
      T ← TruthTable(FanInTree(w))
      V ← Empty vector of control values
      for all columns c in T do
        Compute control of c (Section 3.2)
        Add control(c) to vector V
      end for
      Compute heuristics for V (Section 3.3)
      Denote w as suspicious or not suspicious
    end for
  end for
end for
```

We begin with a high-level overview of the algorithmic steps in FANCI and then describe each step individually. Algorithm 1 describes how suspicious wires are flagged within an untrusted design. For each module and for each gate in the module, we examine the outputs. When we refer to outputs we mean any wire that is the output of any gate, not just the output pins of a chip or a module in the design. Since we are looking at all wires (including internal ones), we do not unnecessarily bias our search for backdoor activity.

For each output wire, we construct a functional truth table for the corresponding inputs (*i.e.* the cone of input wires that feed into the given intermediate output, also called the fan-in tree). We then iterate through each of the input columns of the truth table [1]. For each column, we hold all other columns fixed. For each possible row, we check to see if the value of the column in question determines the output.

Mathematically, there are two different logical functions, the function one gets from fixing the input to digital zero and the function one gets from fixing the input to digital one. We are computing the boolean difference between these two functions. As a result, for each input wire, we get a number between zero and one (inclusive) that represents the fraction of the rows that are influenced or controlled based on the input column. Once we have done this for each input, we have a vector of these numbers. We then apply heuristics (described in Section 3.3) to these vectors to decide if the output wire is suspicious.

All of our analysis is done on a per-module basis. While a hardware backdoor can affect security of operations that happen in multiple modules, *i.e.* the payload of the backdoor can be spread across different modules, the actual trigger computation usually happens in only one circuit within one module. The choice to analyze per-module is practical but not mathematically necessary. As an added benefit, each module can be analyzed independently of each other, which means in the future our tool could be parallelized for improved scalability.

[1]This is similar to what is called zero-delay combinational logic simulation in CAD tools

Table 1: A small example of an unaffecting input dependency. Input C has no influence over the output O.

Input A	Input B	**Input C**	Output O
1	1	1	0
1	1	0	0
1	0	1	1
1	0	0	1
0	1	1	1
0	1	0	1
0	0	1	0
0	0	0	0

Table 2: An example of an always-affecting input dependency. C influences the value of the output O in every row.

Input A	Input B	**Input C**	Output O
1	1	1	1
1	1	0	0
1	0	1	0
1	0	0	1
0	1	1	0
0	1	0	1
0	0	1	1
0	0	0	0

Before getting into the further details of the algorithm and implementation, we provide some background and relevant terminology regarding digital wires and circuits.

3.1 Terminology

FANCI operates at the level of wires and gates, which are the basic building blocks of digital hardware. In this section we define the notion of dependency, control values and other relevant concepts in terms of these building blocks for the understanding of the FANCI tool and underlying algorithm.

Our goal is to identify suspicious circuits, and a suspicious circuit is one that is nearly unused. In prior related work [5], suspicious circuitry was defined as circuits that are not used or otherwise activated during design verification tests. Our definition contrasts in two key ways. First, we do not care about verification tests. Second, we consider wires to be suspicious if they are activated rarely rather than never at all. In other words, we are not simply looking for unused logic. We are looking for logic that is used rarely or in situations that have a low probability of being exercised during regular testing.

Dependence: We distinguish between two distinct dependence relations that can exist between wires. These are *physical dependence* and *value dependence*. A wire w_2 is *physically dependent* on another wire w_1 if the signal in w_2 receives signal from the wire w_1. In other words, there is a path of combinational logic connecting w_1 to w_2. Thus, the value that w_2 carries comes from computation that makes use of the value carried by w_1. We can also think of w_2 as the output of a small circuit for which w_1 is an input. Outputs are dependent on inputs. When we say that w_2 is dependent on w_1, we refer to physical dependency. If w_2 is dependent on w_1, then we say w_1 is a dependency of w_2. Thus, dependent and dependency are dual notions. A is a dependent of B when B is a dependency of A.

Value dependence means that there is functional dependence. A wire w_2 is value dependent on w_1 if the digital value taken on by w_2 changes depending on the value of w_1. Given that w_2 is physically dependent on w_1, w_1 potentially determines the value of w_2, but it is not guaranteed. For example, in the case of a circuit that always outputs digital one, the input values do not affect the output at all.

We break down value dependence into three relevant types. These terms convey the notion of how much one wire affects or influences another. They are *unaffecting, always-affecting and weakly-affecting*.

Unaffecting Dependency: A dependency of a wire is unaffecting if it never determines the value of its dependent wire. An example of this is shown in Table 1. The truth table shown represents a small circuit with three inputs (A, B, C) and one output (O). There are eight possible cases, broken into four pairings. Within each pairing, the value of C can be zero or one. However, that choice does not matter, because the value of the output O is fixed with respect to C.

The truth table is equivalent to a circuit where O is equal to the logical XOR of A and B. Within each pair of rows, the set of values for O is either all ones or all zeros. Thus, we say that the input C is an unaffecting dependency of the dependent output wire O.

Always-Affecting Dependency: The opposite of unaffecting is always-affecting. A dependency of a wire is always-affecting if the value of that dependency always influences the value of its dependent wire. An example is shown in Table 2. The circuit being represented is similar to the one from Table 1. In this case, however, every pair of rows is affected by the value of the input C.

The truth table is equivalent to a circuit where the output O is computed as the logical XOR of all three of its inputs. In this case, no matter what the values of A and B are, the value of C determines the computed value of the output.

Weakly-Affecting Dependency: Weakly-affecting dependencies are the ones we care about the most in this paper. This is because malicious backdoor triggers rely on weakly-affecting input dependencies for the implementation of nearly useless logic.

A weakly-affecting dependency is a case where one input wire affects an output but only very rarely. One example of this could be a large comparator. Consider a circuit that compares a 64-bit array of wires against the value 0xcafebeefcafebeef. Consider one of those 64 input wires, say the least significant bit. The output wire takes on the value one only if all 64 input wires match the specified comparison value. This means that the least significant bit only matters if the 63 other bits already match. In that case, the least significant bit would make the difference between 0xcafebeefcafebeee and 0xcafebeefcafebeef and thus the difference between and output of zero or one. However, in the other $2^{63} - 1$ cases, that least significant bit is irrelevant. For example, it does not matter if the input is 0xaaaaaaaaaaaaaaaa or 0xaaaaaaaaaaaaaaab. Thus, out of the 2^{63} total input case pairs, there is only a single one in which that input bit matters. Thus, it is a weakly-affecting dependency for the output wire.

In general, a wire w_2 has a weakly-affecting dependency w_1 if in nearly all cases the value of w_1 does not determine the value of w_2. In other words, for some threshold value $\epsilon > 0$ such that $\epsilon \ll 1$, the control value of w_1 on w_2 is less than ϵ.

If we consider the example from Section 1, of a backdoor where a comparator on the memory bus fires for one unique large data value on the bus, all of the input wires to that comparator are clear examples of weakly-affecting dependencies for the output wire that serves as the backdoor trigger.

Algorithm 2 Compute Control Value

```
1: count ← 0
2: c ← Column(w_1)
3: T ← TruthTable(w_2)
4: for all Rows r in T do
5:     x_0 ← Value of w_2 for c = 0
6:     x_1 ← Value of w_2 for c = 1
7:     if x_0 ≠ x_1 then
8:         count++
9:     end if
10: end for
11: result ← count / size(T)
```

Algorithm 3 Compute Approximate Control Value

```
numSamples ← N (usually 2^15)
n ← number of inputs
rowFraction ← numSamples / 2^n
count ← 0
c ← Column(w_1)
T ← TruthTable(w_2)
for all Rows r in T do
    if rand() < rowFraction then
        x_0 ← Value of w_2 for c = 0
        x_1 ← Value of w_2 for c = 1
        if x_0 ≠ x_1 then
            count++
        end if
    end if
end for
result ← count / numSamples
```

3.2 Computing Control Values

In this section, we discuss how to compute control values for the dependencies of wires that are the outputs of circuits. The discussion thus far has motivated why weakly-affecting dependencies are stealthy wires of interest. They are necessary for the implementation of malicious backdoors. In other words, if the output of a circuit or gate is carrying a stealthy, malicious signal, then some or all of its inputs are weakly-affecting. We compute control value to quantify how weak or strong the degree of effect is.

Roughly speaking, the control value of an input w_1 on an output w_2 quantifies how much the truth table representing the computation of w_2 is influenced by the column corresponding to w_1. Specifically, the control value is a number between zero and one quantifying what fraction of the rows in the truth table for a circuit are directly influenced by w_1. Note that this is independent of particular tests inputs that might be supplied during validation. Even with high quality test suites, most tests fail to exercise all of the internal circuits because input coverage and code coverage are not equivalent to internal state or value coverage. This provides attackers with an obvious way to hide their backdoors. By operating statically and looking at the truth tables, we can observe the behaviors of every gate in the design.

The algorithm to compute the control value of w_1 on w_2 is presented as Algorithm 2. We note that in step 3, we do not actually construct the exponentially large truth table. We instead construct the corresponding function, which is equivalent to a BDD.

There is one further and necessary optimization we make. Since the sizes of truth tables grow exponentially (with respect to the number of input wires), computing control values deterministically is exponentially hard. Thus, in our evaluation we approximate control values by only evaluating a constant-sized subset of the rows in the truth table. We choose the subset of rows uniformly at random at runtime to make it impossible for attackers to know which rows we will choose. This algorithm is depicted in Algorithm 3.

To take a simple example, suppose we have a wire w_2 that is dependent on an input wire w_1. Let w_2 have n other dependencies. From the set of possible values for those n wires (2^n-many), we choose a constant number, let us say for instance 10,000. Then for those 10,000 cases, we set w_1 to zero and then to one. For each of the 10,000 cases, we see if changing w_1 changes the value of w_2. If w_2 changes m times, then the approximate control value of w_1 on w_2 is $\frac{m}{10,000}$.

The fact that we choose the inputs at random is important. Backdoors can be designed to evade known validation test suites. Only by choosing at random can we guarantee that the attacker will not know what part of the truth table is going to be explored. Our hypothesis, which is supported by our results in Section 5, is that choosing a constant, large number of inputs at random is sufficient for the weak law of large numbers to take effect, resulting in small statistical deviations and high quality approximations.

3.3 Heuristics for Identifying Backdoors from Control Values

When we are finished computing approximate control values for each input, we have a vector of values for each output of each gate in the design. In this section we describe the heuristics that we use for making final decisions about wires in designs. Given a vector of control values, these heuristics determine whether or not a wire is suspicious enough to be flagged for inspection. For example, having only one weakly-affecting wire or a wire that is only borderline weakly-affecting might not be sufficiently suspicious. This might be a wire that is in the same module as a backdoor but has no relation to it. Or it could simply be a benign but slightly inefficient circuit. This is why we need heuristics for taking into account all of the control values in the vector.

Going back to the example where w_2 is our output, w_2 has a vector of $n+1$ control values from its inputs (w_1 and the n others), each between zero and one. These $n+1$ numbers are the $n+1$ control values from the dependencies of w_2. In this section, we discuss options for processing these vectors to make a distinction between suspicious and non-suspicious output wires.

For a small but real example of what these vectors can look like, consider a standard, backdoor-free multiplexer with two selection bits that are used to select between four data inputs. This common circuit is depicted in Figure 1. The output M of the multiplexer is dependent on all four data inputs and both selection bits. Semantically, the selection bits choose which of the four data values is consumed.

We can see intuitively what the control values are for the six input wires (computation for one input is shown explicitly in Figure 1). The situation is symmetric for each of the four data wires (A, B, C and D). They directly control the output M in the cases when the selection bits are set appropriately. This occurs in one fourth of the cases, and each of these data inputs has control value 0.25. This can also be confirmed by writing out the truth table and counting the rows.

The two selection bits have higher control values. A given selection bit chooses between two of the data values. For example, if $S_1 = 1$ then S_2 chooses between B and D. In that case S_2 matters if and only if $B \neq D$, which occurs in half of the cases. So the control values for the two selection bits are 0.50. The full vector of

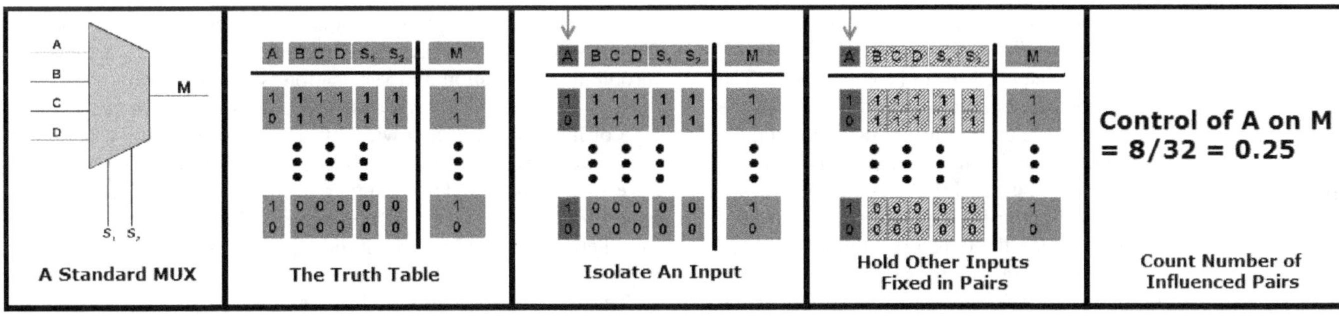

Figure 1: A standard 4-to-1 multiplexer. The output M takes on the value of one of the four data inputs (A, B, C, D) depending on the values of the two selection bits (S_1, S_2).

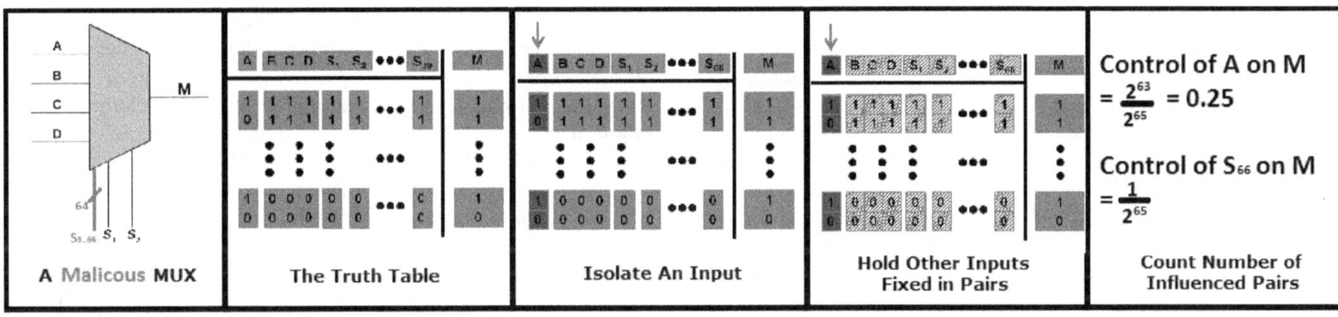

Figure 2: A malicious 4-to-1 multiplexer. The output M takes on the value of one of the four data inputs (A, B, C, D) depending on the values of the two selection bits (S_1, S_2). There are also 64 extra selection bits ($\{S_3, \cdots S_{66}\}$) that only change the output if they match a specific key.

control values for the output M contains six values, one for each of the six inputs. The values are:

$$[0.25, 0.25, 0.25, 0.25, 0.50, 0.50]$$

Intuitively, this is a benign circuit, as we would expect. All of the inputs are in the middle of the spectrum (not close to zero and not close to one) which is indicative of a common and efficient circuit.

Figure 2 depicts a malicious version of a multiplexer. There are 64 additional select bits. When those 64 bits match a specific 64-bit key, then the output of the multiplexer is changed to a malicious payload. In terms of the truth table, this affects only an exponentially small fraction of the output rows. The vector of control values we would get for the output M would include 64 additional values for those 64 extra input wires. Each of those control values would be on the order of 2^{-63}. Intuitively, this is an suspicious circuit, as it is a textbook backdoor. We next discuss heuristics for interpreting these vectors.

From a large circuit or large design, we get a variety of these control value vectors, one each per intermediate output within the circuit. The guarantee we have about the distribution of control values is at least one or a few of them will be zero or nearly zero for wires that belong to stealthy backdoor triggers. Thus, the vectors will contain at least some small values. The practical question is how to deal with these vectors and identify the output wires that are truly suspect from ones that are benign. Toward this end, we consider a few (but not all) different heuristics for evaluating these vectors. The general description is shown in Algorithm 4.

Median: The first option we consider is the median. In the case of backdoor triggers, the wires on the critical paths of the trigger generally have mostly unaffecting or very weakly-affecting dependencies, such as in the example displayed in Figure 1. Thus, the median is often close to zero. The median can be an imperfect metric when the data distribution is irregular, which does happen. Using only the median (as we confirm in our evaluation), can result in a few unnecessary false positives.

Algorithm 4 Compute a Heuristic for an Output Wire

$w \leftarrow$ output wire
$h \leftarrow$ heuristic function (*e.g.,* median)
$t \leftarrow$ threshold (between zero and one)
$v(w) \leftarrow$ vector of control values
$result(w) \leftarrow h(v(w))$
if $result(w) < t$ **then**
    return suspicious
else $\{result(w) \geq t\}$
    return not suspicious
end if

Mean: In addition to the median, we also consider the mean of the control values. The mean is slightly more sensitive to outliers. For example, if there are only a few dependencies, and one of them is unaffecting, that is likely to get noticed.

Both: Since there are potential limitations with both median and mean, we also consider the option of using both, *i.e.* flagging wires that have extreme values for both the mean and the median. We set a threshold for both the median and the mean, and we flag a wire as suspicious only if the median value is low and the mean value is also low. This helps in some cases to slightly diminish false positives. Details and comparisons are presented in Section 5.

Triviality: One last heuristic we consider in our implementation is one that we call *triviality*. In terms of control values, this is a weighted average of the values in the vector. We weight them by how often they are the only wire influencing the output to determine how much an output is influenced overall by its inputs. The purpose is to learn more about the output wire and less about the individual inputs. For instance, in a circuit that XORs many inputs, each input has a control value of 1.0, but it is never the case that one input completely controls the output, and the triviality of the output is only 0.5. Equivalently, this heuristic computes the fraction of the rows in the truth table in which the dependent output wire has the value zero (or symmetrically, the value one). In practice, we can compute triviality directly in this way by looking only at the output column, which often allows for faster runtime than the other heuristics.

The name 'triviality' refers to the fact that if the triviality value is zero or one then the circuit is completely trivial (always outputs zero or always outputs one). This metric quantifies how functionally trivial the sub-circuit computing a specific output wire is. Note that this metric is not a simple function of the control values, as it makes use of correlations, but we went with it because it worked well in practice. The exact value for triviality can vary from run to run depending on which rows are randomly selected, but it is probabilistically likely to vary by only a very small amount. Empirically, we did not see significant variance. Additionally, since triviality can be computed in this alternative way, it might be a good metric for unusually large modules or if computational runtime becomes relevant.

For each metric, it is necessary to have a cut-off threshold for what is suspicious and what is not. This value (between zero and one) can be chosen either *a priori* or after looking at the distrubtion of computed values. In practice, the latter often works better, as there are often natural breakpoints to choose as the threshold. Either way, the threshold is generally very small, *i.e.* $\ll .001$. Various other heuristics and/or thresholds could be considered in the future to attempt to gain improvements in terms of false positive rates.

4. RELATION TO STEALTHY, MALICIOUS CIRCUITS

Prior to our work, UCI [5] was the state-of-the-art in analyzing backdoors inserted during the design phase. The state-of-the-art in design backdoor attacks is a class of attacks known as *stealthy, malicious circuits* (SMCs) [9]. This class of attacks deterministically evades UCI and was a viable way to attack hardware designs prior to our work. As we will see, FANCI catches SMCs with high probability (approaching 1).

UCI is an analysis algorithm that looks at dataflow dependencies in hardware designs and looks for completely unused intermediate logic. It is a form of dynamic validation; in terms of our terminology, they identify dependencies that are always-affecting dependencies for a given test suite. Given the inputs in the test suite, if two wires always carry the same values as each other, there is an identity relationship, and the internal logic is unneeded. If the test suites were exhaustive, then UCI would have significantly fewer false positives. However, given the incompleteness of standard validation test suites, UCI has many false positives. For this reason, the Bluechip system was built to replace the removed logic with exception handlers that invoke runtime simulation software whenever false positives are encountered.

There are a few key differences between FANCI and UCI. The first is that FANCI does not require a validation test suite. This is valuable for two reasons. Today, third-party IP blocks often do not come with a validation test suite. Furthermore, if a validation suite is supplied, the malicious provider can change the validation test suite to help the compromised hardware evade UCI. A common problem in validation and verification is that achieving good code coverage and good interface coverage does not mean good coverage of internal states and wires. Certain rare states may never get tested at all, which can lead to bugs in commercial designs and also offers ways for backdoor designers to evade detection, such as misusing 'don't care' states. FANCI tests all logic equally, regardless of whether or not it is an input interface, and so it is impossible for a portion of the logic to go untested.

The second key difference between UCI and FANCI is that UCI is deterministic and discrete-valued in its approach. Given a test suite, a wire is only flagged if it is completely unused, regardless of its relations to other wires. In FANCI, we also catch nearly-unused wires, meaning wires that are not completely unused but which rarely alter output signals. For example, if a wire strongly affects the value of a nearby wire (and thus is not quiescent) but ultimately has only a small impact on an output wire a few hops away, we will notice that. A wire that is part of a backdoor trigger might also do useful work in a different part of the circuit, and we account for that. Another aspect of FANCI is that it takes into account the full vector of dependencies and uses heuristics to make a final decision. For example, if a wire affects two different outputs, one in a reasonable way and one only rarely, FANCI can notice that. In the designs we tested, there were many always-affecting dependency relationships that FANCI correctly did not flag. Those relationships could have been false positives in UCI.

To give a toy example, consider a double-inverter path, two inverters placed one after the other. This is a logical identify function, so it generates an always-affecting relationship that would be flagged by UCI. However, as long as the output of the double-inverter path is used, it would not be flagged by any of FANCI's current heuristics. This is a small example and could easily be hard-coded for in a practical implementation of UCI. However, it serves as a microcosm of the difference between the deterministic approach of UCI and the heuristic-based approach of FANCI.

Sturton *et al.* introduced stealthy, malicious circuits as a way to evade UCI. FANCI detects SMCs, and we explain the intuition behind why that is. The basic idea behind SMCs is to use logic that alters the values of intermediate wires but ultimately does not affect outputs. Using this backdoor class, Sturton et al. demonstrated basic circuit building blocks — such as AND and OR gates — that can be used to implement stealthy hardware backdoors. Thus, any small backdoor can be turned into an SMC and evade UCI. The truth table for one of the simplest SMCs is the following (reproduced from [9]):

t_1	t_0	i_1	i_0	h	f	Operation
0	0	0	0	0	0	Normal Operation
0	0	0	1	1	0	Normal Operation
0	0	1	0	0	0	Normal Operation
0	0	1	1	1	1	Normal Operation
0	1	0	0	0	0	Normal Operation
0	1	0	1	1	0	Normal Operation
0	1	1	0	0	0	Normal Operation
0	1	1	1	1	1	Normal Operation
1	0	0	0	0	0	Normal Operation
1	0	0	1	1	0	Normal Operation
1	0	1	0	0	0	Normal Operation
1	0	1	1	1	1	Normal Operation
1	1	0	0	1	1	Malicious Operation
1	1	0	1	1	0	Malicious Operation
1	1	1	0	1	1	Malicious Operation
1	1	1	1	1	1	Malicious Operation

There are two normal input bits i_1 and i_0 and two trigger bits t_1 and t_0. In terms of the output f, this is a classic backdoor trigger. Only when all of the trigger bits are set to one does the functionality change. In the other cases, the functionality is fixed, and the circuit looks like f is the AND of i_1 and i_0. The use of the intermediate variable h, which is distinct from f, makes it so that t_1 and t_0 are not truly quiescent. Thus, Sturton proved that UCI's defenses could be evaded.

Can FANCI detect stealthy, malicious circuits? Observe that the trigger wires – t_1 and t_0 – are weakly-affecting for the output f, *i.e.,* they only affect the value of f during malicious operation, which is a smaller fraction compared to normal operation. This fraction diminishes as the number of trigger bits increases. Thus, for the backdoors in this class of stealthy, malicious circuits, the trigger inputs will have low control values and will be caught by FANCI with high probability.

5. EVALUATION

For our implementation of FANCI, we developed a parser for gatelists that are compiled from the Verilog HDL, a popular language for hardware design. The concepts and algorithms we apply could be applied to VHDL or any other common HDL, as well as to hand-written gatelists. Though our analysis is language agnostic, we use Verilog for all evaluation purposes. We use benchmarks from the TrustHub suite, a popular benchmark suite for work on hardware backdoors [10]. TrustHub is a suite from an online community of hardware security researchers and includes a variety of different types of backdoors, intended to be both stealthy and effective. For some of these benchmarks, the gatelists were provided. For others, we acquired the gatelists from the Verilog source using the Synopsys logic synthesis tool, DC Compiler.

From a given gatelist, our goal is to construct a circuit representation that can be used to calculate different types of dependencies. We treat multiple-bit wires as sets of independent wires. Gates that represent multiple basic logic functions — such as an AND-OR-INVERTER (AOI) — are treated as functionally equivalent to their basic elements. We treat memory elements (*e.g.,* flip-flops) as their logical equivalents. For example, a D-flip-flop is treated as an identity function. We do this because exponential state-space exploration is infeasible, and as such treating state machines as stateful, rather than as their combinational counterparts, would be impractical. Since we track all internal wires (as opposed to only inputs and outputs), we catch sequential backdoors by catching the combinational logic used during internal state recognition.

5.1 Results for Detecting Backdoors

We evaluate the four heuristics presented in Section 3.3 on the TrustHub benchmarks. We perform one run on each design[2] with $2^{15} = 32,768$ input cases (truth table row pairs), with the row pairs chosen uniformly at random (without replacement).

The most important result is that we did not encounter false negatives. For each benchmark and each of the heuristics, we discovered at least one suspicious wire from each backdoor, which was enough for us to identify the functionality of the hidden backdoors. Different metrics can highlight different parts of the backdoor. The mean and median tend to highlight backdoor payload wires and are more similar to each other than to triviality. We hypothesize that this is because these payloads have triggers or resulting values from triggers as their inputs. Thus, several of the input wires have low control values. On the other hand, triviality focuses more on the output wire itself and as such tends to highlight backdoor trigger wires. Since these are wires that rarely toggle, their truth tables tend to score very low for triviality. Using multiple metrics in concert can help out in code review by flagging more of the wires associated with the backdoor and thus demarcating the boundary of the backdoor more clearly.

Figure 3 shows the results for the 18 TrustHub benchmarks we analyzed regarding false positives. For our results, we categorize the benchmarks into groups as they are categorized by TrustHub. These categories represent four different design types, containing a variety of backdoor triggering mechanisms. Each of the four groups contains a variety of backdoors manually included into a given design. The RS232 group contains eleven benchmarks, representing eleven different backdoors applied to a relatively small third-party UART controller. The S35932 and S38417 groups each contain three benchmarks, containing backdoors built into two gatelists whose source and description are not provided. The S15850 group contains only one benchmark. The S38417 group contains the largest designs in terms of area and number of gates, while the RS232 benchmarks, as the smallest, mostly contain sequential triggers. The s15850, s35932, and s38417 categories are qualitatively different from RS232 and more similar to each other. We experienced a decrease in false positive percentage for these larger designs, which we attribute to the fact that the total number of false positives did not vary significantly with respect to design size.

Additionally, the different benchmark categories achieve differing degrees of stealth (some are documented and others can be calculated manually). The stealth is imply the probability that a backdoor will accidentally reveal itself on a random test input. Most of the triggers in the RS232 category have a relatively high probability (*i.e.* low stealth) of going off randomly, as high as around one in a million. In the other categories, the probabilities are lower, ranging from one in several million to as low as around one in 2^{150}. The backdoors in the three low probability groups are the most realistic, since they are stealthy enough to evade detection by normal methods. The backdoors in the RS232 category go off with such high probability that validation testing would have a good chance of finding them. This is an aspect that made them more difficult to distinguish and resulted in slightly more false positives. From what we have empirically observed, the larger the design and the more well-hidden the backdoor, the better FANCI performs in terms of keeping false positive rates low.

Unsurprisingly (as shown in Figure 3), using the median by itself produced the most false positives on average. However, the difference is not large. The heuristic that produced the least false positives on average was triviality. All four metrics are effective enough for practical use. We also believe that other metrics could be considered in the future to achieve incremental improvements. A promising result we discovered was that the percentage of false positives diminished as we looked at larger designs (granted this is a small sample set). In other words, it appears that scaling up to larger designs does not greatly increase the total number of false positives (*i.e.* the effort of code review).

Figure 4 shows how many wires are flagged as suspicious on average for each of the benchmark groups by each of the different metrics. Each of the four metrics worked well, though the mean turned up the most suspicious wires on average (at the cost of slightly higher false positive rates). We see that all four metrics flag only a small number of critical wires, which means security engineers are given a small and targeted set to inspect. For most of the benchmarks, FANCI whitelists more than 99% of the designs, making code review and inspection a feasible task.

[2] If desirable, multiple runs could be performed to increase confidence. In practice, the same results tend to come up every time, but it cannot hurt.

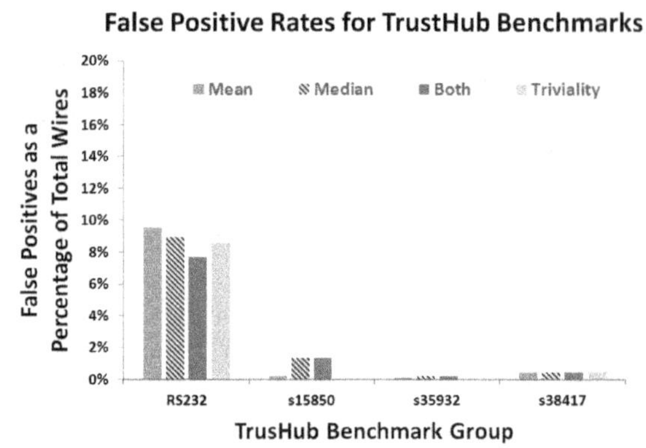

Figure 3: False positive rates for the four different metrics and for TrustHub benchmarks. The RS232 group — which is the smallest — has about 8% false positives. The others have much lower rates (less than 1%).

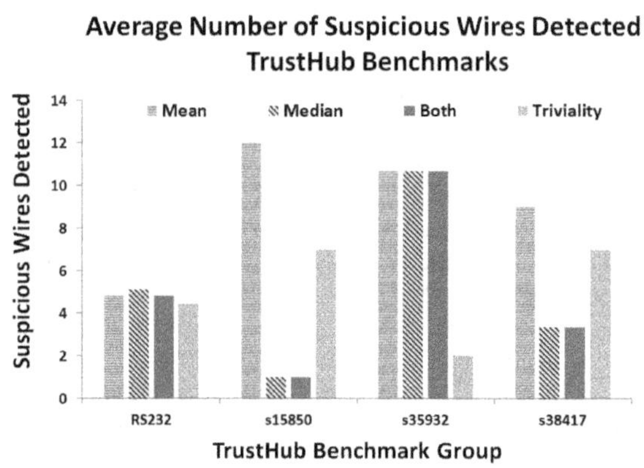

Figure 4: These are the total number of suspicious wires detected by each method for each type of backdoor design on average. For each design and each of the four methods we tried, we always found at least one suspicious wire. Thus, each of the four methods is empirically effective. However, some turned up larger portions of the trigger critical paths, proving to be more thorough for those cases.

We lastly test to see what happens as we increase and decrease the number of input rows we sample. The results are shown in Figure 5. We see that up to a certain point, the results improve. After that point, the results tend to converge and stay roughly the same. This is essentially the weak law of large numbers kicking in, and it allows FANCI to scale well. Note that due to randomness, sometimes we flag more values using less inputs. This ends up not affecting our results significantly, since the true positives tend to be clustered in the design, so adding or removing one wire does not make a large difference in code review. What we also learned from varying the number of inputs is that there are two sources of false positives. The first source is approximation. If we run only a few inputs, we get extra false positives, and if we run more inputs we get less false positives. The second source is from persistent positives, i.e. weakly-affecting signals that are in the design for legitimate reasons. The first type disappears quickly as the number of inputs gets large, which is why false positives due to approximation are not a major concern.

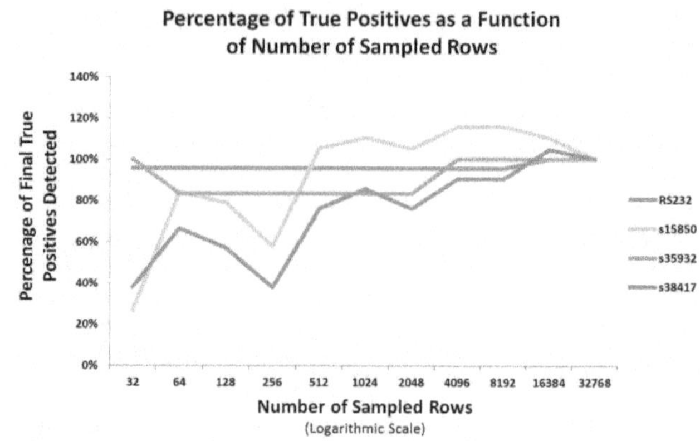

Figure 5: The trade-off between the number of inputs being used (*i.e.* running time) and the percentage of true positives caught, normalized to the results for 2^{15} inputs. Results are shown averaged over the four different metrics we used. The x-axis is on a logarithmic scale.

5.2 Runtime and Random Row Selection

The runtime for FANCI is roughly proportional to the size of the design under test in terms of number of total gates. In practice, the runtime for a normal module ranges from less than an hour to a couple of days using 2^{15} row pairs per approximate truth table. The runtime can be increased or decreased by changing the number of inputs tested. In practice we did not find it necessary to decrease this number. Given the sizes of third-party IP components on the market, the runtime for FANCI should not be a major problem for real-world scenarios. Our runtime in terms of number of gates scales similarly to many synthesis and analysis tools, since our tool and other tools require the parsing of every gate in the design.

To be precise, the asymptotic runtime for a deterministic algorithm would be in the set $\mathcal{O}(nd2^d)$ where n is the number of gates (or nodes) and d is the maximal degree of a node, *i.e.* the maximal number of inputs on which an intermediate wire can depend. Using approximate truth tables reduces the asymptotic runtime to the set $\mathcal{O}(nd)$. Making the (usually true) assumption that the degree is small and bounded, this reduces to the set $\mathcal{O}(n)$, which represents linear runtime. The algorithm is trivially parallelizable, since the algorithm is in essence a massive *for* loop. Our initial implementation is sequential, but in the future it could be made parallel if necessary.

Lastly, we do not do directed testing or targeting of specific rows in truth tables or specific inputs. We go with uniform randomness because any other method would be better for an attacker and worse for us as the security engineers (assuming the attacker knows our strategy).

5.3 Discussion of False Positives

One lesson learned from our experiments is that false positives tend to be consistent and are not greatly affected by the randomness of our sampling methods. We anticipate that the false positives we encounter in the future will bear similarities to each other, perhaps allowing for easier recognition. Some examples of potential false positives could be the most significant bit of a large counter or an input to an exception-recognition circuit. These circuits are semantically similar to backdoors, because they react to one specific rare case. For example, consider a floating point divider that throws a single exception, caused by a divide-by-zero error. Then for the data input representing the divisor, only the value zero invokes the exception-handling logic. The exception-handling logic is nearly-unused.

The existence of these circuits should not pose much of a problem, because counters and exceptions are easily recognizable in code review. Nevertheless, as an attacker, one could be motivated to include many such circuits to increase the false positive count. The problem from an attacker's point of view is that each of these false positives requires a costly circuit, and so building an entire design this way would be impractical. Additionally, these types of circuits tend to have obvious architectural purposes, and so adding thousands of them would be a dead giveaway in code review. For example, including a large number of exception handlers that serve no apparent purpose would be a source of concern during code inspection.

Our hypothesis was that in real designs (*i.e.* designs that one might buy as commercial IP), even malicious designers are forced to follow common design conventions and design reasonably efficient circuits. We believe that this is the reason we did not find a significant number of false positives in any of the designs we analyzed.

A related and important property of our approach is that it behaves well with respect to common, reusable structures. In modern designs, much of the circuitry is spent on reusable components, such as CAMs, RAMs, FIFOs, decoders, encoders, adders, registers, etc. For some simple designs, such as adders and multipliers, the results of FANCI have been mathematically verified. We have not had issues with false positives for these common types of structures. When identifying suspicious wires, we look for outliers. In these standard structures, there tend to be no outliers due to symmetry. Consider a CAM with 32-bit data entries. For each entry, there is a 32-bit data comparator, which includes some very low control value dependencies (on the order of $\frac{1}{2^{32}}$). However, each of the comparators is identical (or nearly identical), leaving no outliers to serve as false positives. Additionally, the nature of the structure should make it obvious in code review how many such wires should exist (often a power of two or otherwise documented number).

5.4 Out-of-Order Processor Case Study

In order to study FANCI on a larger and backdoor-free design, we use the FabScalar microprocessor core generation tool [11]. FabScalar is an HDL code generator that produces processor cores given a set of parameters. The core we choose to use is a moderately-sized, out-of-order core with four execution units and does not contain backdoors.

The core we analyze has a total of 56 modules. The modules contain about 1900 distinct wires on average, with the largest module containing slightly over 39,000 distinct wires. This largest one is abnormally large for a single module containing primarily combinational logic. However, as this is an auto-generated design, it is understandable. If it were being hand-written, it most likely would be broken into smaller, coherent pieces. While the overall design is larger than any of the modules from the TrustHub suite, and larger than typical third-party IP components, many of the individual modules are on average around the same size as modules in the TrustHub suite.

We were able to analyze each of the 56 modules in FabScalar using 2^{15} row pair samples per truth table, except for two of the abnormally large modules where we had to approximate more coarsely. The two largest modules are outliers and took several days to process, even using more coarse-grained approximation. These could more easily be analyzed in a commercial setting on a compute cluster. Additionally, many software optimizations (including parallelization) could be applied prior to commercialization.

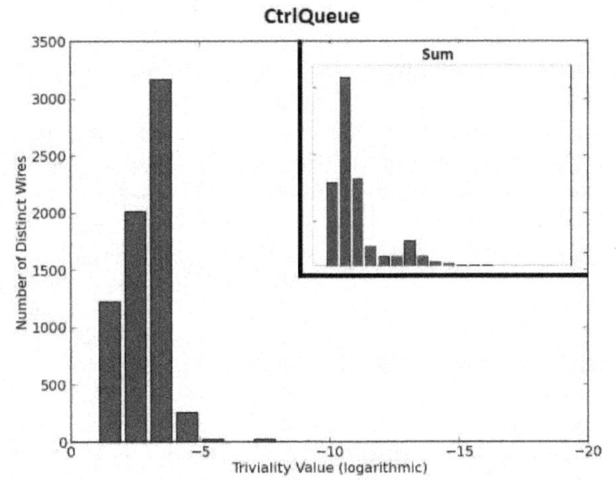

Figure 6: A histogram of the triviality values for wires in a typical FabScalar module called CtrlQueue. The biggest spikes occur at around $\frac{1}{2}$, $\frac{1}{4}$ and $\frac{1}{8}$, which is common. There are no major outliers. X-axis values are shown on a logarithmic scale, starting at one and getting smaller going to the right. Inlaid in the upper right is the sum of all 56 FabScalar modules.

As expected, we did not detect false positives in the benign FabScalar core. To garner further intuition for how our heuristics look for wires in benign hardware, we construct a histogram of a typical FabScalar module (shown in Figure 6). In this example, there are two major spikes at $\frac{1}{2}$, $\frac{1}{4}$ and $\frac{1}{8}$. The reason for the presence of spikes is that semantically similar wires tend to have similar values, as we saw in the example of a multiplexer. For this module, there are no suspicious outliers, with all of the values being more than 0.01 (and less than 0.99). We did not see any noticeable outliers, and our thresholds are typically less than 0.001. More data from FabScalar is included in the Appendix.

5.5 Security Discussion and Limitations

We briefly discuss some of the security properties discussed in this paper and the corresponding limitations.

• FANCI relies on the assumption that backdoors use weakly-affecting wires. This is valid in practice because they need to be stealthy. The more well-hidden the backdoor is, the more likely it is to be caught by FANCI because more well-hidden backdoors have lower control values. It is provable[3] that for a fixed-length combinational circuit path, achieving a given level of stealth requires a correspondingly low control value for one or more of the inputs. On the other hand, the less well-hidden it is, the more likely it is to evade FANCI but be caught during testing. We would call such an attack a ***Frequent-Action Backdoor***, where the idea is to put the backdoor in plain sight. Standard validation testing and FANCI are highly complementary.

• FANCI does not remove the need for standard code inspection/review practices. Consider as an example an attack where a malicious designer includes hundreds of backdoor-like circuits. Each of these circuits could turn on given a variety of rare triggers, with only one of them having a useful malicious payload. Thus, FANCI would flag all of them, mostly generating false positives. We would call this type of attack ***False Positive Flooding***. However, in addition to

[3]We leave out the full proof as it is out of scope for this venue.

the area bloat this would cause, it would be obvious in basic code inspection that this was not a reasonable design. FANCI specifically targets small, well-hidden backdoors, which are the type that are able to evade testing and code inspection.

• Functional analysis only applies to designs or discrete representations of designs. Functional analysis alone does not protect against backdoors inserted physically into a device by a malicious foundry, unless a functional representation can be reverse engineered from the device via decapping, which is not easy. We would call these types of attacks ***Physical or Parametric Backdoors.*** Functional analysis is one piece of hardware security and must exist as part of the larger security scope, which includes validation, code inspection and foundry-level techniques in addition to runtime methods

Our approach also works well against sequential backdoors but with limitations. Sequential backdoors are trigged not by one combinational input but by a stream of small inputs over time. In other words, they are triggered by the combination of an input and a specific internal state. Hypothetically, a sequential backdoor that makes use of an extremely large and contrivedly deep state machine might be able to evade detection or at least made detection more difficult. We would call an attack of this type a ***Pathological Pipeline Backdoor***. The idea is that by stretching out the backdoor trigger computation over a long stretch of logic, it makes the control value data more noisy and potentially more difficult to interpret. For example, if an input needs to determine an ultimate output with $\frac{1}{2^{32}}$ probability, this can be done with two sequential components, each with a probability of $\frac{1}{2^{16}}$ of turning on. The control value from beginning to end will still be $\frac{1}{2^{32}}$, but there will be many intermediate control values, and the overall metrics might not be as clean.

This scenario is one of the many cases where we find that FANCI is complementary to standard validation practices. While basic tests would be likely to catch an extremely large backdoor, FANCI is more likely to catch small, well-hidden backdoors. As we can see in Table 3, practical backdoors tend to have relatively small critical path lengths, and none of the backdoors we have encountered have used deep pipelining. In the table, we use path length (in number of gates) as a proxy for the depth and size of a backdoor trigger computation. These results could be interpreted as merely commentary on the specific types of backdoors that benchmark designers choose to build, or they could be interpreted as broadly representative of the way attackers build malicious circuits. Without a wider array of benchmarks, we cannot say for certain. However, it appears that the crucial part of a backdoor – even a relatively complex backdoor – tends to be composed of only a few gates, and this is good for security engineers.

Table 3: Average Length of Backdoor Critical Paths in TrustHub Benchmarks

TrustHub Benchmark Group	Average Backdoor Path Length
RS232	4.9
s15850	5.0
s35932	4.4
s38417	4.0

6. RELATED WORK

Hardware design backdoor detection, identification, categorization and protection are areas that have recently grown in interest. Hardware designs have been demonstrated to be highly vulnerable [1, 4]. Reese *et al.* evaluated how lightweight and stealthy one can make practical backdoors [12]. In recent years, there has been work both in design-time and in-the-field or runtime protection schemes.

Hicks *et al.* proposed a runtime method for averting backdoors [5]. This method has been shown to detect backdoors, thus raising the bar for the cleverness of hardware attacks. However, it is also vulnerable to sophisticated attacks, as demonstrated by Sturton *et al.* [9] and discussed in Section 4. The three key differences between our work and theirs: 1) our detection technique is exclusively design-time, 2) we do not rely on a validation suite to identify suspicious circuits, and 3) we provide a continuous measure of suspiciousness as opposed to a binary metric used by Hicks *et al.*

Also in the area of runtime techniques, Waksman and Sethumadhavan designed *TrustNet* [6], a methodology for integrating property checkers into hardware designs that can ensure that a wide array of properties are upheld at runtime. Waksman and Sethumadhavan also developed a technique for disabling digital hardware backdoors at runtime, which identifies possible trigger sources and prevents backdoor triggers from reaching malicious logic [7, 8]. Their work identifies the notion of a trigger as a rare signal that does not fire during validation testing. Our work with FANCI is complementary to that prior work, in part because it lessens the burden of trust on validation teams.

There has also been prior work in related areas of hardware supply-chain security, including the detection of physical backdoors added during fabrication [13, 14, 15, 16] and detecting actively running backdoors [17, 18]. This work generally assumes a trusted design, called a golden model, which we and others endeavor to make more of a reality.

The concept of influence of input variables over truth tables and boolean functions has been approached from a theoretical perspective at least as far back as 1988 [19]. As far as we know, we are the first to apply these concepts to hardware security. Our work does not rely on formal verification or require manual inspection or understanding of the inner-workings of designs.

7. CONCLUSIONS

The ability to identify and understand hardware backdoors at design time using static analysis mitigates the dangers of integrating third-party intellectual property components into hardware. We presented a concept called *control value*, which describes how wires within a design affect other wires. Using the idea of control value, we developed a methodology for identifying suspicious wires that have the capability to carry backdoor trigger signals. Specifically, we look at the influence wires have over intermediate outputs within a circuit and identify those wires that have an abnormally low degree of influence. Our method is scalable and approximate; to achieve our goals, we build truth tables of intermediate outputs in the circuit of interest and compute the control value by randomly sampling rows in the truth table. Using a tool we developed, called FANCI, we examined 18 TrustHub benchmarks. We were able to identify triggers in each of these benchmarks, obtaining low false positives rates (flagging less than 10 wires per design on average) in the process.

FANCI is the first tool for checking the security of third-party soft IP and regular hardware designs prior to fabrication. Similar to software static analysis tools, we envision FANCI being used as

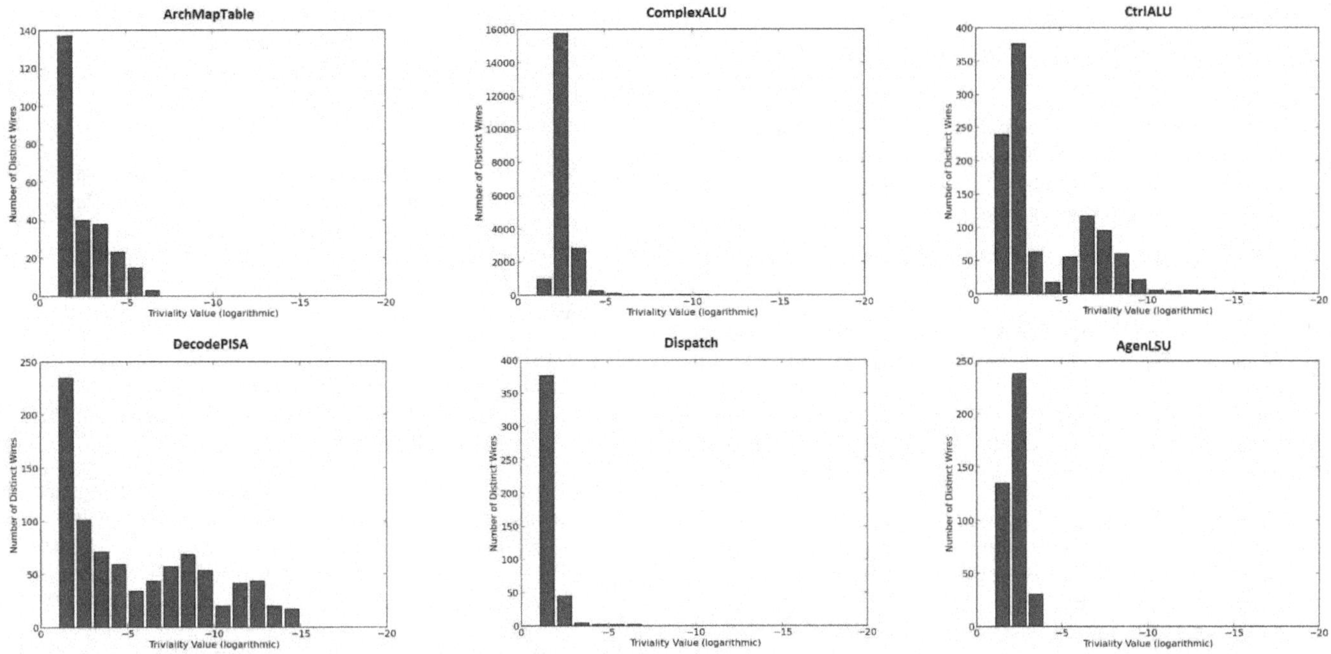

Figure 7: Histograms of the triviality values from three of the modules in the FabScalar core design we used. The y-axis shows the number of wires in each category, and the x-axis shows a logarithmic scale of the triviality values for the wires. Triviality scales from one to zero (going left to right), so the logarithmic values scale from zero to negative infinity.

a first line of defense for enhancing hardware security. It is complementary to runtime techniques for protecting against hardware attacks and also to standard testing practices. Additionally, it has fewer trust requirements as compared with previously existing runtime detection/protection techniques. While our tool is not theoretically guaranteed to find all backdoors, it is likely that backdoors that evade FANCI have to break the digital abstraction or have to be non-stealthy and thus detectable through normal means. Our experimental results support the claim that this methodology could be applied to real-world designs today. As designs get more complex and time to market shrinks, tools like FANCI that can target backdoors prior to fabrication are critical to the development of trustworthy systems.

ACKNOWLEDGEMENTS

We thank anonymous reviewers and members of the Computer Architecture and Security Technologies Lab (CASTL) at Columbia University for their feedback on this work. This work was supported by grants FA 99500910389 (AFOSR), FA 865011C7190 (DARPA), FA 87501020253 (DARPA), CCF/TC 1054844 (NSF) and gifts from Microsoft Research, WindRiver Corp, Xilinx and Synopsys Inc. This work is also supported through an Alfred P. Sloan Foundation Fellowship and the Department of Defense NDSEG Fellowship. Opinions, findings, conclusions and recommendations expressed in this material are those of the authors and do not necessarily reflect the views of the US Government or commercial entities.

APPENDIX

In Figure 7, we include some example histograms of the triviality values we found for wires in six of the modules from FabScalar, the benign microprocessor core that we tested with FANCI. In a normal design, most of the wires have values that are not extremely small, with values between $\frac{1}{8}$ and $\frac{1}{2}$ being very common. To make the results easier to read, we have combined the values between zero and $\frac{1}{2}$ with the values between $\frac{1}{2}$ and one. For example, 0.1 and 0.9 are plotted together, as are 0.7 and 0.3. Semantically, we care about the distance from $\frac{1}{2}$, so this is the easiest way to understand the data.

To take the example of the DecodePISA module, which experienced slightly lower triviality values than the other example modules, it turns out that most of the lower values belong to higher order bits of a 128-bit output packet called DecodedPacket0. Without knowing the intention of the original designer, it seems likely that these upper order bits are not always being used efficiently. However, the control values are not so low as to merit real suspicion. In addition to serving as a security method, these types of observations may also be useful for regular debugging and optimization by trusted designers.

As we can see in the histograms, the vast majority of wires are bunched up on the left side, having relatively normal values (closer to $\frac{1}{2}$ then to the extremes of zero or one). In FabScalar, we rarely see wires with values even less than 2^{-10}, which is still a relatively benign value (corresponding to roughly a one in one thousand chance of a certain behavior occurring). We can also see that while the values are mostly close to $2^{-1} = \frac{1}{2}$, the actual distributions vary from module to module. This is to be expected, as module designs are complex, and it is rare for two different modules to be exactly the same.

References

[1] Sally Adee. The Hunt for the Kill Switch. *IEEE Spectrum Magazine*, 45(5):34–39, 2008.

[2] Marianne Swanson, Nadya Bartol, and Rama Moorthy. Piloting Supply Chain Risk Management Practices for Federal Information Systems. In *National Institute of Standards and Technology*, page 1, 2010.

[3] United Stated Department of Defense. *High Performance Microchip Supply*, February 2005.

[4] Samuel T. King, Joseph Tucek, Anthony Cozzie, Chris Grier, Weihang Jiang, and Yuanyuan Zhou. Designing and Implementing Malicious Hardware. In *Proceedings of the 1st Usenix Workshop on Large-Scale Exploits and Emergent Threats*, pages 5:1–5:8, Berkeley, CA, USA, 2008. USENIX Association.

[5] Matthew Hicks, Samuel T. King, Milo M. K. Martin, and Jonathan M. Smith. Overcoming an Untrusted Computing Base: Detecting and Removing Malicious Hardware Automatically. In *Proceedings of the 31st IEEE Symposium on Security and Privacy*, pages 159–172, 2010.

[6] Adam Waksman and Simha Sethumadhavan. Tamper Evident Microprocessors. In *Proceedings of the 31st IEEE Symposium on Security and Privacy*, pages 173–188, Oakland, California, 2010.

[7] Adam Waksman and Simha Sethumadhavan. Silencing Hardware Backdoors. In *Proceedings of the 2011 IEEE Symposium on Security and Privacy*, pages 49–63, Oakland, California, 2011.

[8] Adam Waksman, Julianna Eum, and Simha Sethumadhavan. Practical, Lightweight Secure Inclusion of Third-Party Intellectual Property. In *Design and Test, IEEE*, pages 8–16, 2013.

[9] Cynthia Sturton, Matthew Hicks, David Wagner, and Samuel T. King. Defeating UCI: Building Stealthy and Malicious Hardware. In *Proceedings of the 2011 IEEE Symposium on Security and Privacy*, SP '11, pages 64–77, Washington, DC, USA, 2011. IEEE Computer Society.

[10] Mohammad Tehranipoor, Ramesh Karri, Farinaz Koushanfar, and Miodrag Potkonjak. TrustHub. http://trust-hub.org.

[11] Niket K. Choudhary, Salil V. Wadhavkar, Tanmay A. Shah, Hiran Mayukh, Jayneel Gandhi, Brandon H. Dwiel, Sandeep Navada, Hashem H. Najaf-abadi, and Eric Rotenberg. Fabscalar: Composing Synthesizable RTL Designs of Arbitrary Cores within a Canonical Superscalar Template. In *Computer Architecture (ISCA), 2011 38th Annual International Symposium on*, pages 11–22. IEEE, 2011.

[12] Trey Reece, Daniel Limbrick, Xiaowen Wang, Bradley Kiddie, and William Robinson. Stealth Assessment of Hardware Trojans in a Microcontroller. In *Proceedings of the 2012 International Conference on Computer Design*, pages 139–142, 2012.

[13] Sheng Wei, Kai Li, Farinaz Koushanfar, and Miodrag Potkonjak. Provably Complete Hardware Trojan Detection Using Test Point Insertion. In *Proceedings of the International Conference on Computer-Aided Design*, ICCAD '12, pages 569–576, New York, NY, USA, 2012. ACM.

[14] Dakshi Agrawal, Selçuk Baktir, Deniz Karakoyunlu, Pankaj Rohatgi, and Berk Sunar. Trojan Detection using IC Fingerprinting. In *IEEE Symposium on Security and Privacy*, pages 296–310, 2007.

[15] Mainak Banga, Maheshwar Chandrasekar, Lei Fang, and Michael S. Hsiao. Guided Test Generation for Isolation and Detection of Embedded Trojans in ICS. In *GLSVLSI '08: Proceedings of the 18th ACM Great Lakes symposium on VLSI*, pages 363–366, New York, NY, USA, 2008. ACM.

[16] Jie Li and J. Lach. At-Speed Delay Characterization for IC Authentication and Trojan Horse Detection. In *Hardware-Oriented Security and Trust, 2008. HOST 2008. IEEE International Workshop on*, pages 8–14, June 2008.

[17] Mainak Banga and Michael S. Hsiao. A Region Based Approach for the Identification of Hardware Trojans. In *Hardware-Oriented Security and Trust, 2008. HOST 2008. IEEE International Workshop on*, pages 40–47, June 2008.

[18] Hassan Salmani, Mohammad Tehranipoor, and Jim Plusquellic. New Design Strategy for Improving Hardware Trojan Detection and Reducing Trojan Activation Time. In *Hardware-Oriented Security and Trust, 2009. HOST '09. IEEE International Workshop on*, pages 66 –73, 2009.

[19] Jeff Kahn, Gil Kalai, and Nathan Linial. The Influence of Variables on Boolean Functions (Extended Abstract). pages 68–80, 1988.

Security Analysis of Integrated Circuit Camouflaging

Jeyavijayan Rajendran
ECE Department
Polytechnic Institute of NYU
Brooklyn, NY, USA, 1120
jv.ece@nyu.edu

Michael Sam
ECE Department
Polytechnic Institute of NYU
Brooklyn, NY, USA, 1120
msam01@students.poly.edu

Ozgur Sinanoglu
Faculty of Engineering
New York University - Abu Dhabi
Abu Dhabi, UAE, 129188
ozgursin@nyu.edu

Ramesh Karri
ECE Department
Polytechnic Institute of NYU
Brooklyn, NY, USA, 1120
rkarri@poly.edu

ABSTRACT

Camouflaging is a layout-level technique that hampers an attacker from reverse engineering by introducing, in one embodiment, dummy contacts into the layout. By using a mix of real and dummy contacts, one can camouflage a standard cell whose functionality can be one of many. If an attacker cannot resolve the functionality of a camouflaged gate, he/she will extract an incorrect netlist.

In this paper, we analyze the feasibility of identifying the functionality of camouflaged gates. We also propose techniques to make the dummy contact-based IC camouflaging technique resilient to reverse engineering. Furthermore, we judiciously select gates to camouflage by using techniques which ensure that the outputs of the extracted netlist are controllably corrupted. The techniques leverage IC testing principles such as justification and sensitization. The proposed techniques are evaluated using ISCAS benchmark circuits and OpenSparc T1 microprocessor controllers.

Categories and Subject Descriptors

B.2 [**Arithmetic and Logic Structures**]: Miscellaneous; B.6 [**Logic Design**]: Miscellaneous; B.7 [**Integrated Circuits**]: Miscellaneous

Keywords

IC reverse engineering; IC camouflaging; IP protection; IP piracy

1. INTRODUCTION

1.1 Reverse engineering of Integrated Circuits (ICs)

Reverse engineering of an IC is a process of identifying its structure, design and functionality. Traditionally, reverse engineering of IC's has been performed to collect competitive intelligence, to verify a design, and to check for commercial piracy and patent infringements. Reverse engineering can

- **identify the device technology** used in the IC. For instance, it was identified that Intel's Xeon processors use trigate transistors [1].
- **extract** the gate-level netlist[1] of the design. The gate-level netlist of a baseband processor from Texas Instruments was extracted in [2].
- **infer the functionality**. Reverse engineering on Apple's processor [3] revealed the type of graphic processing units used in iPhone 5.

Several techniques and tools have been developed to enable reverse engineering of an IC. [4] provides a tutorial on reverse engineering. Chipworks [5] and Degate [6] provide software products for reverse engineering. Shrinking device dimensions has not hampered reverse engineering. For instance, Intel's 22nm Xeon processor has been successfully reverse engineered [1].

While reverse engineering serves several benefits, an attacker can misuse it to steal and/or pirate a design. One can use the readily available tools and techniques for reverse engineering. On identifying a device technology, one can fabricate similar devices. One can extract a gate-level netlist and use it to design one's own IC or illegally sell it as an IP. Also, one can use the components extracted from competitor's products. This way one can reveal competitor's trade secrets. Because of these harmful effects, reverse engineering

[1]A gate-level netlist of a design consists of a set of interconnected logic gates such as NAND, NOR, AND, OR, XOR, XNOR, inverters, and memory elements such as flip-flops.

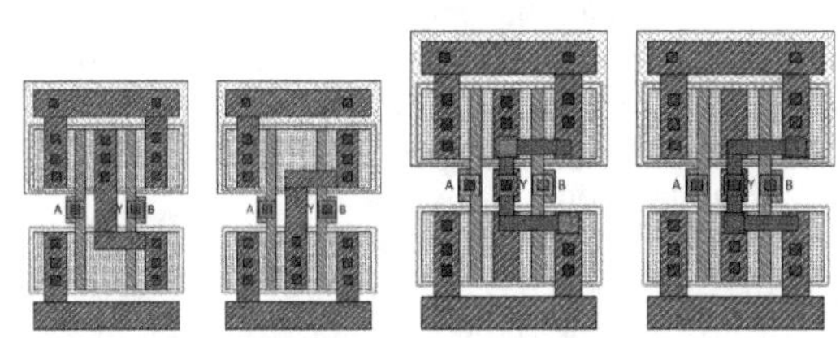

Figure 1: Standard cell layout of regular 2-input (a) NAND and (b) NOR gates. The metal layers are different and hence it is easy to differentiate them by just looking at the top metal layer. Camouflaged standard cell layouts of 2-input (c) NAND and (b) NOR gates. The metal layers are identical and hence it is difficult to differentiate them by just looking at the top metal layer.

CCS'13, November 4–8, 2013, Berlin, Germany.
Copyright 2013 ACM 978-1-4503-2477-9/13/11 ...$15.00.
http://dx.doi.org/10.1145/2508859.2516656.

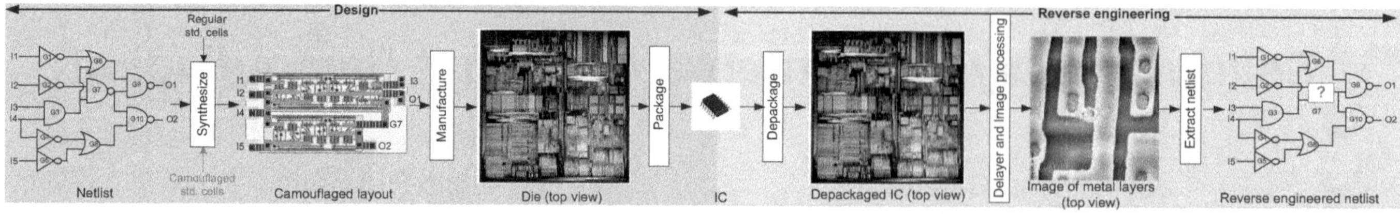

Figure 2: A design is synthesized into layout by using both regular standard cells and camouflaged standard cells. This layout is manufactured to obtain the IC. An attacker buys the camouflaged IC and depackages it. He/she delayers and images the metal layers and transistors. He/she then obtains the gate-level netlist by processing those images. However, the functionality of camouflaged cells cannot be resolved. For example, the functionality of G7 cannot be resolved.

was listed as one of the serious threats to semiconductor industry [7].

Detecting IP piracy by verifying competitor's IC requires that IP owners have access to that competitor's IC. Such a passive approach is bound to fail as potential adversaries can be anywhere across the globe. Proactive solutions that prevent, rather than detect, reverse engineering are preferable. For example, SypherMedia [8] provides IC camouflaging services for this purpose.

1.2 IC camouflaging to thwart reverse engineering

In one embodiment of IC camouflaging, the layouts of logic gates are designed to look identical, resulting in an incorrect extraction. For example, the layout of regular NAND cell (Figure 1(a)) and NOR ((Figure 1(b)) cell look different and are hence easy to reverse engineer. However, the layout of camouflaged NAND cell (Figure 1(c)) and NOR cell (Figure 1(d)) look identical and are difficult to differentiate [8–11]. When deceived into incorrectly interpreting the functionality of the camouflaged gate, the attacker may obtain a reverse engineered netlist that is different from the original. The netlist obtained by an attacker is the *deceiving netlist* where the functionality of the camouflaged gates are arbitrarily assigned.

Figure 2 shows how camouflaging protects an IC design against reverse engineering. A designer camouflages certain gates in the design[2]. For example, the NAND gate, G7, in Figure 2 is camouflaged. This design with camouflaged gates is then manufactured at a foundry. The manufactured IC is sold in the market. An attacker reverse engineers an IC by depackaging, delayering, imaging the layers, and extracting the netlist. However, in the extracted netlist, the functionality of the camouflaged gates are unknown. For example, in Figure 2, the functionality of G7 is unknown. An attacker assigns an arbitrary two-input function to it. Consequently, he may obtain an incorrect netlist.

To thwart reverse engineering of an IC, any camouflaging technique has to provide the following guarantees.

(1) **Resiliency to reverse engineering:** An attacker should not be able to identify the functionality of a camouflaged gate.

(2) **Corrupted outputs:** The outputs of the original and the deceiving netlists should be controllably different.

In this paper, we analyze the feasibility of identifying the functionality of the camouflaged gates. We propose an IC camouflaging technique that is resilient to reverse engineering. Furthermore, we judiciously select gates to camouflage by using techniques which ensure that the outputs of the deceiving netlist are controllably corrupted.

[2]A designer does not camouflage all the gates in the design because of the power, area, and delay overheads of the camouflaged gates. For example, the camouflaged NAND and NOR gates shown in Figure 1(c) and (d) are 1.5X bigger than their regular counterparts.

1.3 Contributions

The contributions[3] of this paper are:

- reverse engineering that can resolve the functionality of the camouflaged gates,
- a metric to measure the hardness of reverse engineering,
- a first technique to select the gates in a design to camouflage so that the functionality of the camouflaged gates can only be resolved by brute force,
- a second technique to select the gates to camouflage such that the deceiving netlist produces outputs which are controllably different from those of the original netlist, and
- evaluation of the proposed attack and defense techniques on OpenSparc T1 microprocessor [12].

The paper is organized as follows: Section 2 explains IC camouflaging and its security capabilities in detail. Section 3 describes the proposed techniques to reverse engineer a camouflaged IC. Section 4 details the proposed ways to select gates for camouflaging that is resilient to reverse engineering and can control the corruption at the outputs. Results of the proposed techniques on ISCAS benchmark circuits and controllers of OpenSparc processors are given in Section 5. Related work on IC reverse engineering and IP protection is summarized in Section 6. Section 7 concludes the paper.

2. IC CAMOUFLAGING

2.1 Steps in reverse engineering

IC reverse engineering involves the following steps [2].

- **Depackaging** the IC using corrosive chemicals.
- **Delayering** individual layers (metal, poly or diffusion) using corrosive chemicals.
- **Imaging** the top-view of each layer using an optical microscope or single electron microscope (SEM). The image may contain metal routing, contacts, vias and pins in that layer.
- **Annotation** aligns and stitches the images of different layers.
- **Extraction of gate-level netlist** from the annoted images. One can use the tools from Chipworks [5] and Degate [6] for this purpose.

[3]We are not proposing a new camouflaging technique. We are only improving the strength of existing techniques using principles from VLSI testing.

A reverse engineer may face the following difficulties.

Difficulty 1: Delayering the lower metal layers (M1 and M2) is difficult as compared to delayering higher metal layers (M3 and above) because lower metal layers are only a few tens of nanometers thick. Hence, a reverse engineer has to precisely control the strength of the chemicals used for delayering. Notwithstanding this difficulty, reverse engineers have successfully extracted information from the lower metal layers [2].

Difficulty 2: A reverse engineer can try to differentiate between a true and a dummy contact by slicing the die and imaging the side-view. However, there are hundreds of millions of contacts in an IC and an attacker has to slice the IC into million pieces to classify all of them. Hence, such reverse engineering will not be feasible.

Difficulty 3: A reverse engineer can use anisotropic techniques like reactive-ion etching to partially etch the layers. However, on using such techniques for top-down reverse engineering, by the time one reaches the bottom layers (where dummy contacts are placed), the dummy contacts are mostly eroded by the chemicals used to etch the upper layers. One may not know whether a broken/dummy contact is because of chemical erosion or camouflaging [13, 14].

2.2 Camouflaging using dummy contacts

The reverse engineer's inability to partially etch a layer is the basis for *dummy contacts*-based camouflaging [11]. Contacts are conducting materials that connect two adjacent metal layers or a metal layer 1 and poly. They pass through the dielectric that separates the two connecting layers. While the true contact has no gap, a dummy contact has a gap in the middle and fakes a connection between the layers.

Figure 3 shows the different layers of a logic gate with true and dummy contacts between M1 and poly. A true contact (Figure 3(a)) spans the entire dielectric and thus represents an electrical connection. However, a dummy contact (Figure 3(b)) has no electrical connection because of the gap. From the top view of the chip, both the true and dummy contacts appear identical under a microscope as shown in Figure 3.

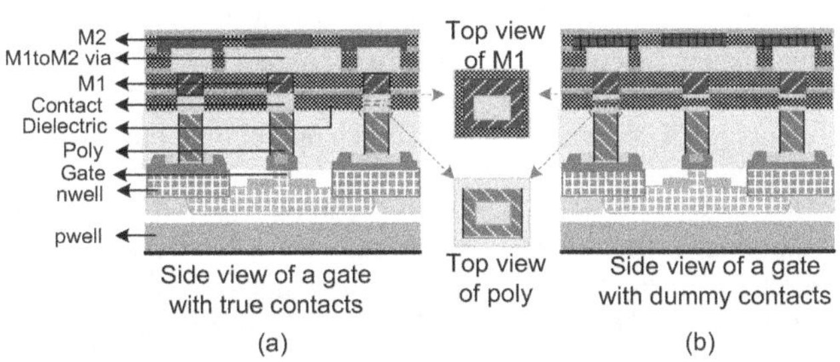

Figure 3: (a) A logic gate with true contacts and (b) a logic gate with dummy contacts. The top view, which is used by an attacker in reverse engineering, is identical for both the true and dummy contacts.

Table 1: List of true and dummy contacts to realize different functions using the camouflaged layout shown in Figure 4

Function	Contacts	
	True	Dummy
NAND	2, 4, 6, 8, 11, 12, 16, 17	1, 3, 5, 7, 9, 10, 13, 14, 15, 18, 19
NOR	2, 5, 6, 11, 12, 18, 19	1, 3, 4, 7, 8, 9, 10, 13, 14, 15, 16, 17
XOR	1, 3, 4, 7, 9, 10, 12, 13, 14, 15, 18, 19	2, 5, 6, 8, 11, 16, 17

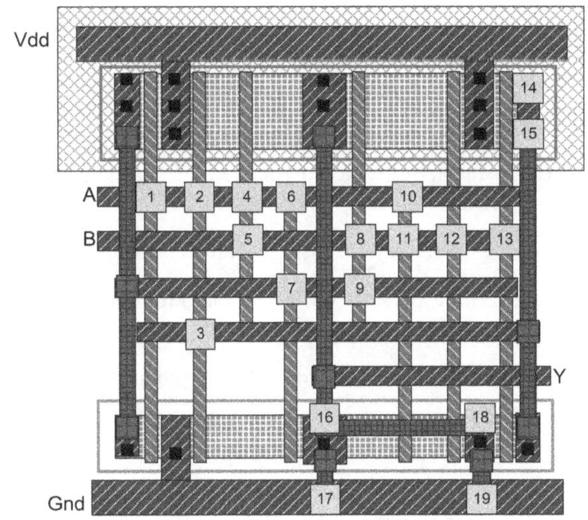

Figure 4: A generic camouflaged layout that can perform either as an XOR, NAND or NOR gate based on which contacts are true and dummy. The numbered boxes are the contacts.

2.3 Camouflaging standard cells

Standard cells perform a logic function and are used as building blocks in designing ICs. By using a mix of true and dummy contacts, one can design a standard cell whose functionality can be one of many. The true contacts dictate the functionality of a camouflaged gate. The use of optical and electrical microscopy will fail to identify the hidden functionality as they cannot differentiate between true and dummy contacts, complicating reverse engineering.

The more functionalities a camouflaged standard cell could implement, the more difficult the reverse engineering becomes. It is essential for a camouflaged standard cell to have a large number of transistors that can be connected in different ways to realize different logic functions. Of all the cells in the standard cell library, XOR and XNOR gates have the highest number of transistors (12). Hence, we choose to modify the layout of XOR and XNOR gates for camouflaging.

Figure 4 shows the layout of a camouflaged cell that can function as either 2-input XOR, NAND, or NOR. The sets of true and dummy contacts to implement different functions with the camouflaged gate are listed in Table 1. Similarly, one can design a camouflaged cell that can function as either 2-input XNOR, NAND or NOR.

3. REVERSE ENGINEERING A CAMOUFLAGED IC

3.1 Threat model

The attacker

1. has tools to reverse engineer an IC, i.e., the setup to delayer an IC, optical microscope or SEM to image the layers, and image processing software tools [5, 6].
2. can differentiate between a camouflaged standard cell and a regular standard cell from the images of different layers. This is possible because the images of regular and camouflaged standard cells are publicly available [8].
3. knows the list of functions that a camouflaged cell can implement. In our case, a camouflaged cell can implement one of {XOR, NAND, NOR} functions.

The objective of a reverse engineer is to determine the function implemented by every camouflaged gate. To reverse engineer a camouflaged IC, one performs the following steps.

1. Buys two copies of the target chip from the market.
2. Extracts the netlist with camouflaged gates from the first chip using the techniques listed in Section 2.1.
3. Computes input patterns using techniques from Section 3.2.
4. Applies these patterns on the second chip and obtains the outputs.
5. Resolves the functionality of camouflaged gates.

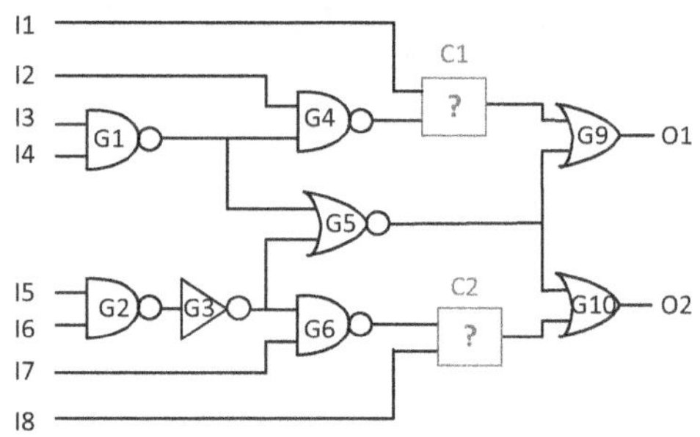

Figure 5: C1 and C2 are isolated camouflaged gates. An attacker can resolve the functionality C1 and C2 independent of each other.

3.2 Reverse engineering strategies

The critical step above is to generate the input patterns that help resolve the functionality of the camouflaged gates. The following two principles form the foundations in VLSI testing of manufacturing defects in ICs [15, 16].

Justification: The output of a gate can be justified to a known value by controlling one or more of its inputs. For example, an AND gate's output can be justified to '0' by setting one of its inputs to '0.'

Sensitization: A net can be sensitized to an output by setting all the side inputs of each gate in between to the non-controlling value of the gate. This way the value on the net is bijectively mapped to the value on the output.

3.2.1 Smart reverse engineering

Scenario: The attacker has completed the basic reverse engineering steps shown in Figure 2 and has the extracted netlist with regular and camouflaged gates. The critical step is to identify the functionality of the camouflaged gates. Each camouflaged gate could implement one of {XOR, NAND, NOR} functions. The attacker

1. justifies the inputs of the camouflaged gates to various two-input combinations, and
2. sensitizes their outputs to one of the primary outputs[4] to identify the response of the camouflaged gates to the two-input combinations.

[4]Primary outputs are output ports of the design which are accessible to an attacker.

Example 1: Consider the camouflaged gate C1 in Figure 5. The functionality of C1 can be resolved to be XOR by applying '010XXXX' at the inputs. This input pattern will justify the inputs of C1 to '00' and sensitizes the output of C1 to O1. If O1 is '0', then the functionality of C1 is resolved as XOR. Otherwise, the functionality of C1 can be resolved to be NOR by applying '110XXXX' at the inputs. This input pattern will justify the inputs of C1 to '10' and sensitize the output of C1 to O1. If O1 is '0', then the functionality of C1 is resolved as NOR. Otherwise, the functionality of C1 is resolved as NAND.

Camouflaged gates that do not have any circuit path interfering with other camouflaged gates are called *isolated* camouflaged gates. Example 1 illustrated how to attack isolated camouflaged gates. The attack gets complicated when the camouflaged gates interfere with each other. This is due to the complications arising from justification and sensitization in the presence of multiple camouflaged gates. We will illustrate this interference next.

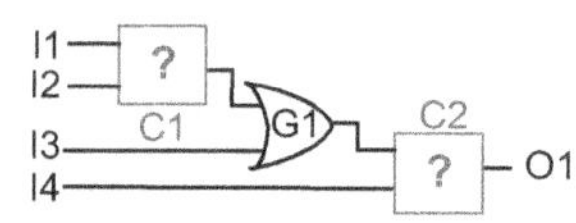

Figure 6: Interference between camouflaged gates, C1 and C2. An attacker targets C2 before targeting C1

3.2.2 Interference between camouflaged gates

Interferences between two camouflaged gates, C1 and C2, occur when C2 lies on a path between C1 and an output, and/or C1 and C2 converge at some other gate.

Smart reverse engineering: To identify the functionality of C2, an attacker has to find an input pattern that can justify the output of C1 to a known value and simultaneously resolve the functionality of C2 with the help of this known value.

Example 2: Consider the gates, C1 and C2, in Figure 6. The functionality of C1 can be one of {XOR, NAND, NOR}. Similarly, the functionality of C2 can be one of {XOR, NAND, NOR}. The functionality of C2 can be resolved to be an XOR by applying '1100' at the inputs. This pattern will justify the output of C1 to '0' irrespective of whether it functions as an XOR, NAND, or NOR, justify the inputs of C2 to '00,' and sensitize the output of C2 to O1. If O1 is 0, then the functionality of C2 is resolved as XOR.

Otherwise, the functionality of C2 can be resolved to be NOR by applying '1101' at the inputs. This pattern will justify the output of C1 to '0' irrespective of whether it functions as an XOR, NAND, or NOR, justify the inputs of C2 to '01,' and sensitize the output of C2 to O1. If O1 is 0, then the functionality of C2 is resolved as NOR. Otherwise, the functionality of C2 is resolved as NAND. After resolving the functionality of C2, C1 becomes an isolated camouflaged gate and its functionality can be resolved using the procedure specified for isolated camouflaged gates.

3.3 Limitations of smart reverse engineering

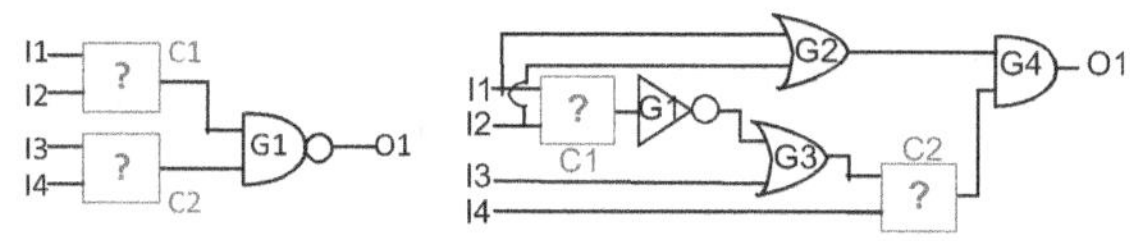

(a) (b)

Figure 7: (a) C1 and C2 are non-resolvable camouflaged gates, (b) C2 is a partially resolvable camouflaged gate.

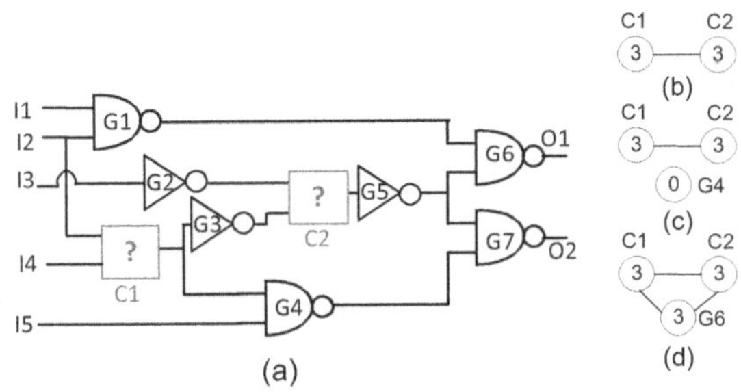

Figure 8: (a) A design camouflaged with 2 gates: C1 and C2, (b) Corresponding interference graph, (c) Interference graph with C1, C2, and G4 camouflaged, and (d) Interference graph with C1, C2, and G6 camouflaged. The number below the node label indicates the weight of a node.

While targeting a camouflaged gate, one cannot always generate an input pattern that can simultaneously justify the outputs of the other camouflaged gates to known values and resolve the functionality of the target gate. Consequently, an attacker cannot resolve the functionality of the camouflaged gates. Such gates are called non-resolvable camouflaged gates.

Example 3: Consider the camouflaged gates, C1 and C2, in Figure 7(a). If an attacker is trying to resolve C1, one needs to justify the output of C2 to '0', which is the only value that an XOR/NAND/NOR gate would produce for the input combination '11' non-ambiguously. However, setting C2's output to 0 will block C1's output from sensitizing to O1. Consequently, an attacker cannot resolve the functionality of C1. Similarly, an attacker cannot resolve the functionality of C2 in the presence of C1.

Sometimes an attacker can only partially resolve the functionality of a gate. Such gates are called partially resolvable camouflaged gates.

Example 4: Consider the camouflaged gates, C1 and C2, in Figure 7(b). If an attacker is trying to resolve that C2 is XOR, one needs to justify its inputs to '00' and justify C1's output to a known value ('0'). However, this is not possible as these two conditions are contradicting. On the contrary, if one is trying to resolve if C1 is NOR, one can use the input pattern 'X110'. This pattern will justify C2's inputs to '10', sensitize its output to O1, and justify C1's output to a known value ('0'). If O1's value is '1', C2 is resolved to be NOR. Otherwise, C2 functions as either NAND or XOR. However, an attacker cannot resolve the latter case. Thus, C2's functionality is only partially resolved.

3.4 Algorithm for attack

An attacker uses Algorithm 1 to resolve the functionality of the camouflaged gates. The attacker first identifies the isolated camouflaged gates and targets them. After that, one targets the resolvable interfering camouflaged gates. Only if one is able to generate an input pattern that simultaneously justifies the inputs of the target gate to the desired two-input combinations, justifies the output of other camouflaged gates to known values, and sensitizes the target gate's output to a primary output, the functionality of the target gate can be fully resolved. Finally, the functionality of non-resolvable and partially resolvable camouflaged gates are identified via brute force. As the functionality of a camouflaged gate is identified gradually in every iteration, it is replaced by the logic gate that performs the identified function. The overall computational effort depends on the amount of brute force applied.

Input : Camouflaged netlist, Functional IC
Output: Original netlist
Determine *Camouflaged gates*;
For each *remaining Camouflaged gate* **do**
  For each *Isolated camouflaged gate* **do**
    Compute and apply input pattern;
    Resolve *functionality* and update Netlist;
  end
  For each *Resolvable camouflaged gate* **do**
    if *there exists an input pattern* **then**
      Apply the input pattern;
      Resolve *functionality*, Update Netlist, Break;
    else
      ApplyBruteForce(), Break;
    end
  end
  For each *Partially resolvable camouflaged gate* **do**
    if *there exists an input pattern* **then**
      Apply the input pattern;
      Resolve partial *functionality*, Update Netlist, Break;
    else
      ApplyBruteForce(), Break;
    end
  end
  For each *Non-resolvable camouflaged gate* **do**
    ApplyBruteForce(), Break;
  end
end

ApplyBruteForce();
For each *possible combination of logic functions* **do**
  Generate random input patterns;
  Simulate the patterns and obtain the outputs OP_{sim};
  Apply the patterns on IC and obtain the outputs OP_{exe};
  if $OP_{sim} == OP_{exe}$ **then**
    Functionality of camouflaged gates = current combination of logic functions;
    Update netlist;
  end
end

Algorithm 1: Reverse engineering a camouflaged IC

4. REVERSE ENGINEERING RESILIENT IC CAMOUFLAGING

Strong IC camouflaging hinges on camouflaging gates with complex interferences among them. Next, using a graph-based notation, we relate the types of camouflaged gates to the degree of interference they introduce.

4.1 Interference graph

We introduce an *interference graph* to drive the selection of gates for camouflaging. In this graph, each node represents a camouflaged gate. An edge connects two nodes if the corresponding camouflaged gates interfere with each other. Each node has a weight based on its type. Isolated and fully resolvable camouflaged gates are represented as isolated nodes with zero weights. Partially resolvable camouflaged gates have a weight of two as an ambiguity between two different functions needs to be resolved. Non-resolvable camouflaged gates have a weight of three as an ambiguity between three different functions needs to be resolved.

The maximum weight of the clique in the interference graph determines the strength of camouflaging, as the clique weight dictates the amount of brute force required to identify the functionality of camouflaged gates. Hence, a defender prefers to camouflage gates such that the interference graph is fully connected with each node having a weight of three.

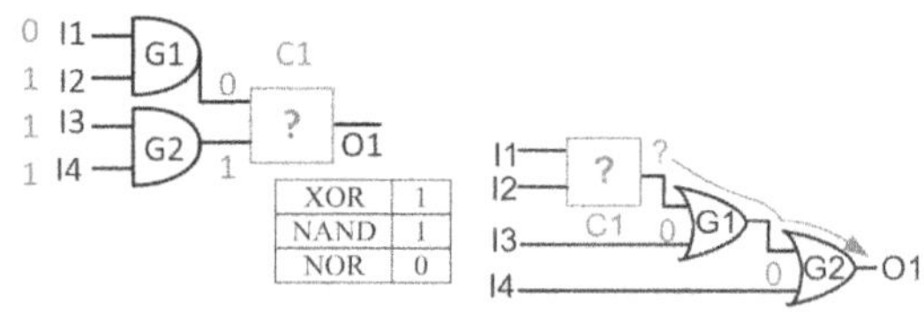

(a) (b)

Figure 9: (a) Activation of incorrect values at a camouflaged gate's output and (b) propagation of incorrect values from C1's output to O1.

Example 5: Consider the circuit shown in Figure 8(a). In this circuit, C1 and C2 are non-resolvable camouflaged gates and interfere with each other. Hence, their nodes have a weight of 3 and are connected by an edge as shown in Figure 8(b). If G4 is selected as the third gate to be camouflaged, then it creates an isolated node in the interference graph. This is because an attacker can use the patterns 'X1010' and 'X1011' to resolve the functionality of G4. However, if G6 is selected as the third gate to be camouflaged, then it creates a non-resolvable node in the interference graph. Furthermore, it will be connected to the nodes of C1 and C2. This will increase the maximum clique size from 6 to 9. Thus, it is better to camouflage G6 than G4.

4.2 Are non-resolvable nodes enough for camouflaging?

IC camouflaging based on non-resolvable nodes ensure that an attacker cannot resolve the functionality of camouflaged gates. But, it does not ensure that the *deceiving netlist*[5] produces incorrect outputs. If the deceiving netlist produces correct outputs for most of the inputs, then camouflaging is effectively weak and the attacker will benefit. For minimum correlation, 50% output bits should differ for every input pattern[6].

Corrupting the outputs involves two principles: activation and propagation.

Activation is the process of justifying multiple input lines such that the output of a misinterpreted camouflaged gate is different from that of the gate in the original netlist, introducing an ambiguity.

Example 6: Consider the circuit shown in Figure 9(a). This circuit produces incorrect outputs for 15 out of the 16 possible input patterns. Only when C1 receives '11', it fails to introduce an ambiguity as NAND, NOR, and XOR produce the same value ('0'). In all the other cases, ambiguity is activated at C1, which is desired for output corruption.

Propagation is sensitizing a value to as many outputs as possible. In case of IC camouflaging, one has to propagate the ambiguity from the output of a camouflaged gate to as many outputs as possible.

Example 7: Consider the circuit shown in Figure 9(b). This circuit propagates the incorrect value of C1 to O1 for only 4 out of the 16 possible input patterns. In 3 of these 4 cases, ambiguity is activated.

4.3 Output corruptibility

We need maximum corruption, and thus minimum correlation at the outputs. The camouflaged gates should thus be selected judiciously. The output corruptibility function can be defined as:

$$\text{Output corruptibility} = \sum_{\text{\# I/P patterns}} (\text{\# O/Ps with ambiguity activated and propagated}) \quad (1)$$

Camouflaging the gate with the highest output corruptibility is expected to reduce the usability of the reverse engineered netlist.

4.4 Algorithm for smart camouflaging

```
Input  : Original netlist, Number of gates to be camouflaged
Output: Camouflaged netlist
NumCamoGates = Number of gates to be camouflaged;
CamouflagedGates = { };
Calculate OutputCorruptibility for all gates;
SelectedGate = Gate with the highest OutputCorruptibility;
if SelectedGate ∉ NAND||NOR||XOR then
  | Synthesize SelectedGate using NAND||NOR||XOR;
end
Camouflage SelectedGate;
CamouflagedGates += SelectedGate;
Construct InterferenceGraph;
for i ← 2 to CamouflagedGates do
    NonResolvableGates = { };
    For each Gate_i in Netlist do
        if Gate_i ∉ CamouflagedGates then
            if Gate_i is Nonresolvable then
                | NonResolvableGates += Gate_i;
            end
        end
    end
    For each Gate_j in NonResolvableGates do
        | Compute OutputCorruptibility;
    end
    SelectedGate = NonResolvableGate with the highest
    OutputCorruptibility;
    if SelectedGate ∉ NAND||NOR||XOR then
        | Synthesize SelectedGate using NAND||NOR||XOR;
    end
    Camouflage SelectedGate;
    CamouflagedGates += SelectedGate;
    Update InterferenceGraph;
end
```

Algorithm 2: Reverse engineering-resilient IC camouflaging

A defender can use the interference graph and the output corruptibility metric to camouflage gates as illustrated in Algorithm 2. Every iteration of the algorithm selects a gate that (1) is non-resolvable, (2) increases the maximum clique size in the interference graph, and (3) increases the output corruptibility metric. The interference graph is updated in every iteration. When a selected gate is not one of {XOR, NAND, NOR}, it is synthesized into one of these gates, so that it can be camouflaged. The algorithm terminates when a desired number of gates are camouflaged.

5. RESULTS

5.1 Experimental Setup

We considered two types of camouflaged gates. The first type can implement one of {XOR, NAND,NOR} function. The second type can implement an {XNOR, NAND,NOR} function. We compared the effectiveness of four types of ways to select a gate for camouflaging (1) *random*, where randomly selected gates are cam-

[5]Deceiving netlist is the netlist where camouflaged gates are incorrectly reverse engineered.

[6]0% means all the output bits are correct and implies direct correlation, while 100% implies inverse correlation.

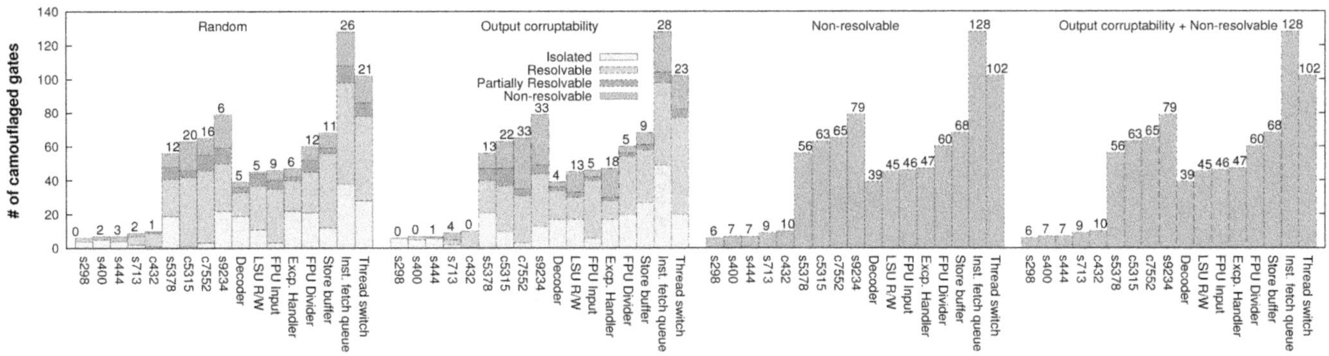

Figure 10: Types of camouflaged gates inserted by different ways of selecting gates to camouflage. Effective number of camouflaged gates for which an attacker will have to brute force are shown as numbers on top the bars. Note that *non-resolvable* and *output corruptibility + non-resolvable* selection techniques have same number of non-resolvable camouflaged gates (see discussion 1).

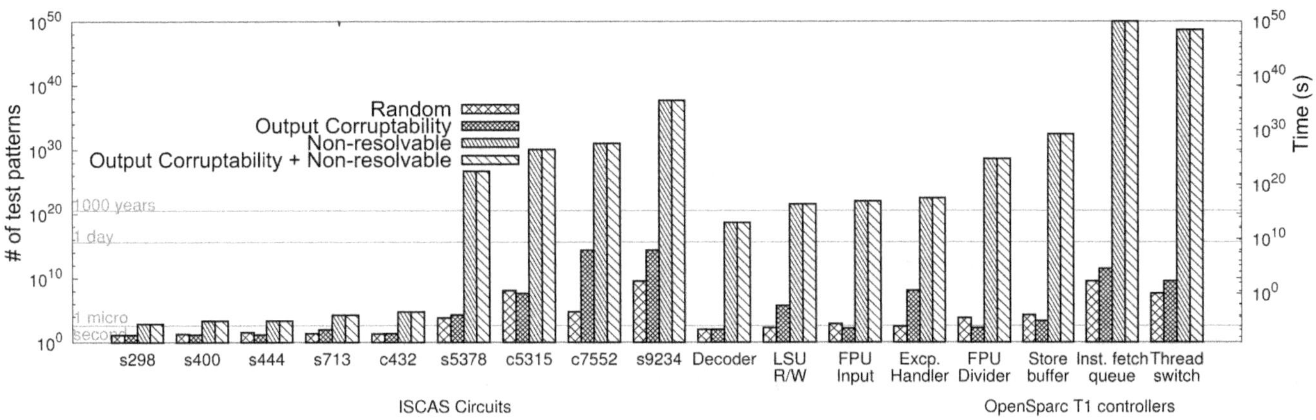

Figure 11: Number of possible test patterns that an attacker has to apply to resolve the functionality of camouflaged gates for different ways of selecting gates to camouflage.

ouflaged[7]; (2) *output corruptibility*, where the gates with high output corruptibility values are selected; (3) *non-resolvable*, where the gates are selected such that their functionality cannot be resolved; and (4) *output corruptibility + non-resolvable*, where the gates are selected using Algorithm 2.

These selection techniques are analyzed using ISCAS benchmark circuits [17] and OpenSparc T1 microprocessor controllers [12]. We used the HOPE fault simulation tool [18] to determine the input patterns for justification and sensitization for reverse engineering the functionality of a camouflaged gate. We used the HOPE tool to also calculate the output corruptibility by applying 1000 random input patterns. The Hamming distance between the outputs of the original netlist and the deceiving netlist was computed by applying 1000 random input patterns. To camouflage a circuit with a reasonable performance overhead, we camouflaged 5% of number of gates in that circuit. The area, power, and delay overheads are obtained using the Cadence RTL compiler [19].

5.2 Types of camouflaged gates and effective number of camouflaged gates

Figure 10 shows the number of each type of camouflaged gates for different ways in which gates to be camouflaged are selected. On *randomly* selecting gates, most of the gates are of isolated and resolvable types, benefiting the attacker. Only less than 20% of the camouflaged gates are either of partially resolvable or non-resolvable types, which require brute force. In *output corruptibility*-based selection, many of the gates are isolated to ensure corrupted outputs. An attacker can easily identify the functionality of camouflaged gates. In the *non-resolvable*- and *output corruptibility + non-resolvable*-based selections, all the camouflaged gates are non-resolvable, increasing the effort for an attacker.

Effective number of camouflaged gates: Since an attacker can always identify the functionality of isolated and fully resolvable gates, they do not cause any ambiguity to an attacker. In the case of partially resolvable camouflaged gates, the ambiguity is between two functions. In the case of non-resolvable camouflaged gates, the ambiguity is among three different functions. If there are 'N' partially resolvable and 'M' non-resolvable camouflaged gates, the total number of possible functions is $3^M \times 2^N$ for which an attacker has to brute force. The effective number of camouflaged gates is $log_3^{3^M \times 2^N} = M + Nlog_3^2$.

In Figure 10, the effective number of camouflaged gates are shown as numbers on top of the bars. The effective number of camouflaged gates of *random* and *output corruptibility* selections is less than that of *non-resolvable* and *output corruptibility + non-resolvable* selections. Therefore, the number of brute force attempts required to determine the functionality in *random* and *output corruptibility* selections is exponentially smaller than that of *non-resolvable* and *output corruptibility + non-resolvable* selections. In case of *random* and *output corruptibility* selections, the

[7] We chose random selection as the baseline as there is no publicly available algorithms to select gates to camouflage.

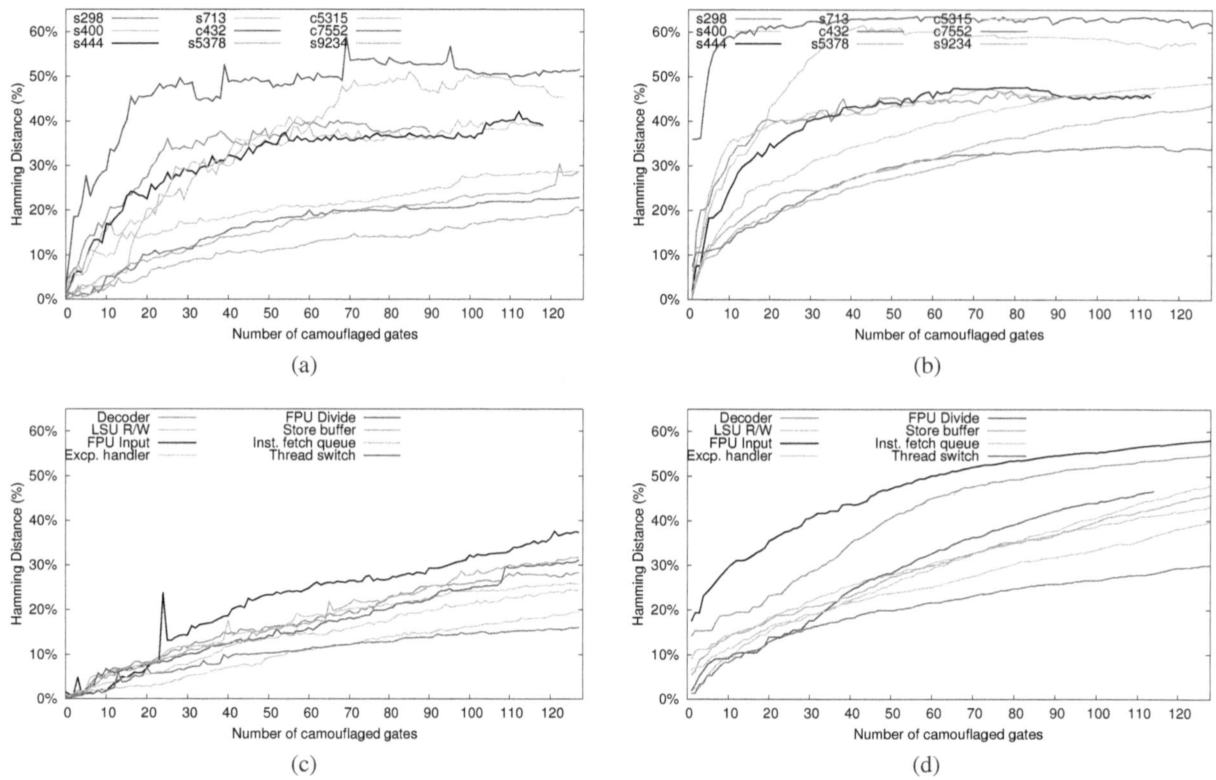

Figure 12: Hamming distance between the outputs of original and deceiving netlists. (a) Random camouflaging and (b) output corruptibility + non-resolvable selections on ISCAS circuits, (c) random camouflaging and (d) output corruptibility + non-resolvable selections on OpenSparc T1 controller modules.

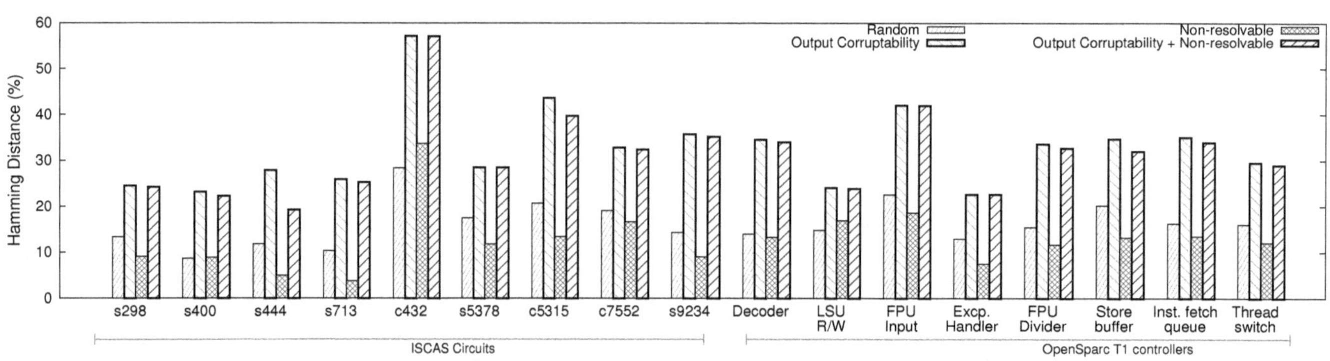

Figure 13: The best Hamming distance between the outputs of original and the deceiving netlists achieved when 5% of gates in the design are camouflaged for different ways of selecting gates to camouflage.

effective number of camouflaged gates is around one-fifth of the number of gates camouflaged. Thus for such selections, $4/5^{th}$ of the power, area, and delay budget spent on the camouflaged gates goes to waste.

5.3 Number of input patterns

Figure 11 shows the number of input patterns required to identify the functionality of camouflaged gates for different ways in which gates to be camouflaged are selected. The time scales are calculated assuming that an attacker can apply a billion patterns per second using a test equipment. *Non-resolvable-* and *output corruptibility + non-resolvable*-based selections require several thousands of years to break, even when only 40 gates are camouflaged.

5.4 Hamming distance analysis

Random selection is compared with *output corruptibility + non-resolvable*-based selection and the corresponding results are shown in Figure 12. When the gates are randomly selected, the Hamming distance between the outputs of original and deceiving netlists is less than that of *output corruptibility + non-resolvable*-based selection. Failure of activation and propagation is the main reason for this poor performance as discussed in Section 4.

The slope of the lines in Figure 12 indicate the performance of a selection technique. If the line is steeper, Hamming distance of desired level can be achieved with fewer camouflaged gates and hence, performance overhead will be smaller. As a result, *output corruptibility + non-resolvable*-based selection has smaller overhead than randomly camouflaging gates as it camouflages fewer gates to achieve a target Hamming distance.

Figure 13 compares the Hamming distance achieved upon camouflaging 5% of the gates in the design for different selection techniques. It can been seen that *output corruptibility*- and *output corruptibility + non-resolvable*-based selections almost achieve similar Hamming distance. However, *output corruptibility*-based selection has a slightly better Hamming distance than *output corruptibility + non-resolvable*-based selection because the latter has another objective to satisfy in addition. However, both of these selections perform better than *random* and *non-resolvable*-based selection.

5.5 Power, area, and delay overheads

Table 2: Power, area and delay overheads for implementing a function using a camouflaged standard cell instead of a regular standard cell.

Function	Camouflaged gate					
	XOR+NAND+NOR			XNOR+NAND+NOR		
	Power	Delay	Area	Power	Delay	Area
NAND	5.5X	1.6X	4X	5.1X	1.8X	4X
NOR	5.1X	1.1X	4X	4.8X	1.4X	4X
XOR	0.8X	0	1.2X	N/A		
XNOR	N/A			0.7X	0	1.2X

Table 2 shows the power, area and delay overheads for implementing a function using a camouflaged standard cell instead of a regular standard cell. The power overhead is more than 5X because of the power consumed by the unused transistors. For example, a regular NAND gate uses only 4 transistors, but a camouflaged NAND gate uses 12 transistors. Furthermore, these transistors are bigger than the ones used in regular gates. Thus, the camouflaged cells consume more leakage and switching power, occupy a larger area, and are slower than the regular cells.

Figure 14 shows the power, area, and delay overheads on camouflaging 5% of the gates using *output corruptibility + non-resolvable*-selection technique. The power overhead is around 105% on an average. However, this power consumption is negligible when compared to that of the power consumption of the OpenSparc processor because the power consumption of a camouflaged controller is a few microwatts whereas the power consumption of a processor is few tens of watts [20, 21]. Camouflaging the read/write controller of load store unit (LSU R/W) has the highest area overhead of 135%. However, this unit has only 4000 gates when compared to 34 million gates in OpenSparc T1 [21,22]. Thus, camouflaging has a negligible overhead in the context of large designs such as processors. Nevertheless, the *output corruptibility + non-resolvable*-based selection ensures the budget spent on power, delay and area overhead is effective by preventing an attacker from reverse engineering; other selection techniques do not ensure such protection. To control this overhead, one can pursue a power and delay constrained camouflaging.

5.6 Discussion

1. Why is *output corruptibility + non-resolvable*-based selection better than *output corruptibility* and *non-resolvable*-based selections?

As shown in Figure 13, *output corruptibility*-based selection achieves a better Hamming distance than *output corruptibility + non-resolvable*-based selection. However, as shown in Figure 10, *output corruptibility*-based selection results in mostly isolated and fully resolvable camouflaged gates. Thus, an attacker can easily identify the functionality of the camouflaged gates. In fact, *output corruptibility*-based selection has more isolated and fully resolvable camouflaged gates than *random* selection. *Output corruptibility + non-resolvable*-based selection results only in non-resolvable camouflaged gates. Thus, an attacker cannot identify the functionality of the camouflaged gates.

As shown in Figure 10, both *non-resolvable* and *output corruptibility + non-resolvable*-based selections result in non-resolvable camouflaged gates. However, *output corruptibility + non-resolvable*-based selection has a better Hamming distance than *non-resolvable*-based selection as shown in Figure 13. In fact, *random* selection has a better Hamming distance than *non-resolvable*-based selection. To summarize, *output corruptibility + non-resolvable*-based selection is better than *output corruptibility* and *non-resolvable*-based selection techniques.

2. Can one use simpler camouflaged cells (for example, the ones shown in Figure 1(c) and (d)) instead of a complex camouflaged cell (for example, the one shown in Figure 4)?

A designer may use simpler and less costly camouflaged gates, such as those that supports just NAND and NOR functions. The overhead of this simple camouflaged gate will be much smaller than the XOR-based camouflaged gate. For instance, the camouflaged NAND and NOR cells shown in Figure 1(c) and (d) have a power overhead of 1.3X, area overhead of 1.5X, and delay overhead of 1.2X on average over their regular counterparts. The overhead cost is much smaller when compared to the overheads of XOR-based camouflaged gates listed in Table 2. However, from security perspective these simple gates have the following disadvantages over an XOR-based camouflaged gate.

(1) two instead of three possible functions reduce the amount of ambiguity for an attacker.

(2) two two-input combinations ('00' and '11') can non-ambiguously justify the output to a known value, making it easier for an attacker; an XOR-based camouflaged gate has only one two-input combination ('11') for non-ambiguous justification, and

(3) only two two-input combinations ('01' and '10') activate the ambiguity which results in reduced output corruptibility; an XOR-based camouflaged gate activates ambiguity for three two-input combinations ('00', '01,' and '10').

Thus, a simple camouflaged gate will have less resiliency to reverse engineering than XOR-based camouflaged gate.

3. Can one camouflage the entire design?

Camouflaging the entire design can make it difficult to resolve the functionality. However, it will tremendously increase the power, area, and delay overheads. Thus, a designer has to limit the number of camouflaged gates to honor the design's power, area, and delay budget. Our technique ensures that such budget-constrained camouflaging gates cannot be reverse engineered.

4. Why should one camouflage the controllers?

A design can be broadly classified into two parts – controller and datapath units. A designer's secret IP is typically realized in the form of controllers. Thus, they have to be protected from reverse engineering. Furthermore, controllers are usually tiny (<1%) [21, 23]. For example, OpenSPARC has 11.6×10^6 gates; The considered controllers have 1.2×10^4 gates. Thus, at the design level, the overhead due to camouflaging the controllers is negligible. Datapath units are often repetition of smaller blocks. Thus, camouflage costs would also be repeating.

5. Is Hamming distance the right metric?

Strength of cryptographic algorithms are often evaluated not only using the Hamming distance but also using metrics such as strict avalanche criterion (SAC) and bit independence criterion (BIC) [24]. While in this paper, we considered Hamming distance as the metric to measure output corruptibility, one can also use SAC

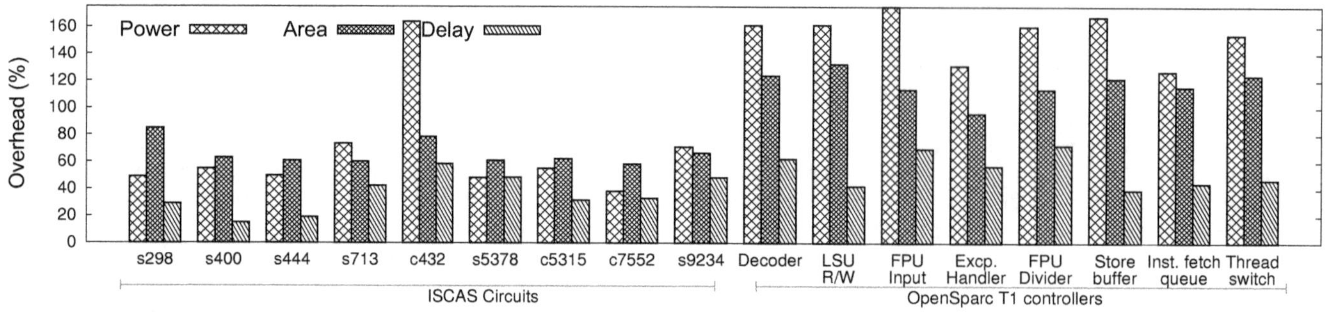

Figure 14: Power, area and delay overhead for camouflaging 5% of the gates using *output corruptibility + non-resolvable* selection.

and BIC for evaluation. However, calculating SAC and BIC becomes computationally infeasible for a design with a large number of inputs (>100). For example, the thread switch controller of OpenSparc T1 processor has 261 inputs. To calculate SAC and BIC, one has to apply 2^{261} input patterns. Hence, we choose the Hamming distance metric to analyze the effectiveness of our technique.

6. Can one use side-channel analysis to determine the functionality of camouflaged gates?
To prevent an attacker from resolving the functionality of a camouflaged gate using side-channel (power/delay) analysis, one can design a camouflaged gate that has similar power and delay characteristics independent of the functionality implemented by it.

6. RELATED WORK

6.1 Reverse engineering

IC reverse engineering techniques can be broadly classified into two types: extraction of gate-level netlist from layout, and extraction of functional specification from gate-level netlist. Reverse engineering of an IC to extract a gate-level netlist by performing the various steps shown in Figure 2 has been demostrated in [2,25]. An algorithm to extract a gate-level netlist from transistors has been presented in [26].

The DARPA IRIS program seeks to obtain the functional specification of a design by reverse engineering its gate-level netlist. Hansen et. al. exploited structural isomorphism to extract the functionality of datapath units [17]. Li et. al. reverse engineered the functionality of unknown units by performing behavioral matching against a library of components with known functionalities such as adders, counters, register files, and subtracters [27]. Subramanyan et. al. identified the functionality of unknown modules by performing Boolean satisfiability analysis with a library of components with known functionalities [28].

6.2 IC camouflaging

A design can be camouflaged by using lookalike standard cells [8]. These lookalike standard cells perform different logic functions while they have similar metal connections to deceive an attacker. Subtle changes are made in their layout to realize different logic functions. An attacker can look for these subtle changes in the layout to identify the functionality. The camouflaged gates considered in this paper look identical in all the metal layers but differ only in terms of true and dummy contacts, which cannot be distinguished by an attacker as discussed in Section 2.

An IC camouflaging technique can also leverage unused spaces in a chip and fill them with standard cells [13]. The outputs of these filler cells will not drive any active logic. One can also camouflage a design by using programmable standard cells [10]. Post-fabrication, these cells will be programmed using a control input. Similar to introducing dummy contacts, a designer can also create dummy channels, which will result in non-functional transistors [14]. Such non-functional transistors can be used to deceive an attacker. Using the techniques outlined in this paper, the security of all these camouflaging methods can be analyzed.

6.3 Hardware IP protection techniques

Logic obfuscation hides the functionality and implementation of a design by inserting additional components into it. Logic obfuscation techniques can be broadly classified into two types—sequential and combinational. In sequential logic obfuscation, additional logic (black) states are introduced in the finite state machine (FSM) of a design [23,29]. The FSM is modified in such a way that the design reaches a valid state only on applying the correct key. If the key is withdrawn, the design ends up in a black state. In combinational logic obfuscation, XOR/XNOR gates are introduced to conceal the functionality of a design [30]. The circuit will function correctly only on applying the correct value to these gates. An algorithm to insert XOR/XNOR gates for a stronger obfuscation has been proposed in [31]. An algorithm to ensure incorrect outputs on applying a wrong key has been proposed in [32]. Obfuscation is also performed by inserting memory elements [33]. The circuit will function correctly only when these elements are programmed correctly. These techniques require tamper-proof and non-volatile memories to store keys on-chip and safe exchange of keys between the IP designer and the user. However, IC camouflaging does not encounter such issues as it does not use keys. IC camouflaging is a complementary technique to logic obfuscation; IC camouflaging operates at layout-level while logic obfuscation techniques operate at gate- and register transfer levels.

Techniques such as watermarking and passive metering are also proposed to detect IC piracy. In watermarking techniques, a designer embodies his/her signature into the design [34]. During litigation, the designer can reveal the watermark and claim ownership of an IC/IP. Watermarks are constructed by adding additional states to the finite state machine of the design, adding secret constraints during high-level [35], logical, or physical synthesis [36]. In passive metering techniques, a unique device ID for every IC is created by leveraging process variations [23]. Physical unclonable functions are leveraged to produce such IDs [37,38]. If a user pirates an IC, he/she will be caught by tracking the device ID.

7. CONCLUSION

Although dummy contact-based IC camouflaging is an effective layout-level technique against reverse engineering, it is weak when the camouflaged gates are isolated and are fully resolvable. While a designer can camouflage all the gates, it incurs power, delay and area overheads. We show that camouflaging can be strengthened by judiciously selecting the gates in the design to camouflage, without incurring much overhead. The proposed techniques rely on resolvability and corruptibility metrics that deliver camouflaging solutions which are resilient to reverse engineering. This way the attacker is forced to do brute force.While we formulated these security requirements as constraints for automatic test pattern generation (ATPG) tools, one cause also use SAT based ATPG and equivalence-checking tools exist to guide selection of gates for IC camouflaging. Reverse engineering becomes complicated when other camouflaging techniques such as programmable cells [10] and dummy filler cells [14] are used in conjunction with dummy contacts. The proposed security metric can be used to evaluate the strength of these camouflaging techniques either individually or when combined.

8. ACKNOWLEDGMENTS

The authors thank Dr. Ron Cocchi from SypherMedia International for his valuable comments.

9. REFERENCES

[1] Chipworks, "Intel's 22-nm Tri-gate Transistors Exposed," http://www.chipworks.com/blog/technologyblog/2012/04/23/intels-22-nm-tri-gate-transistors-exposed/, 2012.

[2] R. Torrance and D. James, "The state-of-the-art in semiconductor reverse engineering," *in the Proc. of IEEE/ACM Design Automation Conference*, pp. 333–338, 2011.

[3] ExtremeTech, "iPhone 5 A6 SoC reverse engineered, reveals rare hand-made custom CPU, and tri-core GPU," http://www.extremetech.com/computing/136749-iphone-5-a6-soc-reverse-engineered-reveals-rare-hand-made-custom-cpu-and-a-tri-core-gpu.

[4] Silicon Zoo, "The layman's guide to ic reverse engineering," http://siliconzoo.org/tutorial.html.

[5] Chipworks, "Reverse engineering software," http://www.chipworks.com/en/technical-competitive-analysis/resources/reerse-engineering-software.

[6] Degate, http://www.degate.org/documentation/.

[7] SEMI, "Innovation is at risk as semiconductor equipment and materials industry loses up to $4 billion annually due to IP infringement," www.semi.org/en/Press/P043775, 2008.

[8] SypherMedia, "Syphermedia library circuit camouflage technology," http://www.smi.tv/solutions.htm.

[9] J. P. Baukus, L. W. Chow, R. P. Cocchi, and B. J. Wang, "Method and apparatus for camouflaging a standard cell based integrated circuit with micro circuits and post processing," *US Patent no. 20120139582*, 2012.

[10] J. P. Baukus, L. W. Chow, R. P. Cocchi, P. Ouyang, and B. J. Wang, "Building block for a secure cmos logic cell library," *US Patent no. 8111089*, 2012.

[11] J. P. Baukus, L. W. Chow, and W. Clark, "Integrated circuits protected against reverse engineering and method for fabricating the same using an apparent metal contact line terminating on field oxide," *US Patent no. 20020096776*, 2002.

[12] "Sun Microsystems, OpenSPARC T1 Processor," *http://www.opensparc.net/opensparc-t1/index.html*.

[13] J. P. Baukus, L. W. Chow, R. P. Cocchi, P. Ouyang, and B. J. Wang, "Camouflaging a standard cell based integrated circuit," *US Patent no. 8151235*, 2012.

[14] J. P. Baukus, L.-W. Chow, J. W. M. Clark, and G. J. Harbison, "Conductive channel pseudo block process and circuit to inhibit reverse engineering," *US Patent no. 8258583*, 2012.

[15] M. L. Bushnell and V. D. Agrawal, "Essentials of Electronic Testing for Digital, Memory, and Mixed-Signal VLSI Circuits," *Kluwer Academic Publishers, Boston*, 2000.

[16] M. Abramovici, M. A. Breuer, and A. D. Friedman, "Digital Systems Testing & Testable Design," *Wiley*, 1994.

[17] M. Hansen, H. Yalcin, and J. Hayes, "Unveiling the ISCAS-85 benchmarks: a case study in reverse engineering," *IEEE Design Test of Computers*, vol. 16, no. 3, pp. 72–80, 1999.

[18] H. Lee and D. S. Ha, "HOPE: An Efficient Parallel Fault Simulator for Synchronous Sequential Circuits," *IEEE Transactions on Computer-Aided Design of Integrated Circuits and Systems*, vol. 15, no. 9, pp. 1048–1058, 1996.

[19] Cadence, "RTL Compiler," www.cadence.com/products/ld/rtl_compiler.

[20] K. Constantinides, "Online low-cost defect tolerance solutions for microprocessor designs," web.eecs.umich.edu/ taustin/papers/Kypros_Thesis.pdf.

[21] A. Waksman, J. Eum, and S. Sethumadhavan, "Practical, lightweight secure inclusion of third-party intellectual property," *IEEE Design & Test*, no. 99, pp. 1–1, 2013.

[22] Oracle, "Opensparc internals," http://www.oracle.com/technetwork/systems/opensparc/opensparc-internals-book-1500271.pdf.

[23] Y. Alkabani and F. Koushanfar, "Active hardware metering for intellectual property protection and security," *in the Proc. of USENIX security*, pp. 291–306, 2007.

[24] H. Heys and S. Tavares, "Avalanche characteristics of substitution-permutation encryption networks," *IEEE Transactions on Computers*, vol. 44, no. 9, pp. 1131 –1139, 1995.

[25] R. Torrance and D. James, "The state-of-the-art in ic reverse engineering," *in the Proc. of Cryptographic Hardware and Embedded Systems*, pp. 363–381, 2009.

[26] W. M. V. Fleet and M. R. Dransfield, "Method of recovering a gate-level netlist from a transistor-level," *US Patent no. 6190433*, 1998.

[27] W. Li, Z. Wasson, and S. Seshia, "Reverse engineering circuits using behavioral pattern mining," *in the Proc. of IEEE International Symposium on Hardware-Oriented Security and Trust*, pp. 83–88, 2012.

[28] P. Subramanyan, N. Tsiskaridze, K. Pasricha, D. Reisman, A. Susnea, and S. Malik, "Reverse engineering digital circuits using functional analysis," *in the Proc. of IEEE/ACM Design Automation and Test in Europe*, 2013.

[29] R. Chakraborty and S. Bhunia, "HARPOON: An Obfuscation-Based SoC Design Methodology for Hardware Protection," *IEEE Transactions on Computer-Aided Design of Integrated Circuits and Systems*, vol. 28, no. 10, pp. 1493–1502, 2009.

[30] J. Roy, F. Koushanfar, and I. Markov, "EPIC: Ending Piracy of Integrated Circuits," *IEEE Computer*, vol. 43, no. 10, pp. 30–38, 2010.

[31] J. Rajendran, Y. Pino, O. Sinanoglu, and R. Karri, "Security analysis of logic obfuscation," *in the Proc. of IEEE/ACM Design Automation Conference*, pp. 83–89, 2012.

[32] ——, "Logic encryption: A fault analysis perspective," *IEEE Design, Automation Test in Europe*, pp. 953–958, 2012.

[33] A. Baumgarten, A. Tyagi, and J. Zambreno, "Preventing IC Piracy Using Reconfigurable Logic Barriers," *IEEE Design and Test of Computers*, vol. 27, no. 1, pp. 66–75, 2010.

[34] A. Kahng, J. Lach, W. Mangione-Smith, S. Mantik, I. Markov, M. Potkonjak, P. Tucker, H. Wang, and G. Wolfe, "Watermarking techniques for intellectual property protection," *in the Proc. of IEEE/ACM Design Automation Conference*, pp. 776–781, 1998.

[35] F. Koushanfar, I. Hong, and M. Potkonjak, "Behavioral synthesis techniques for intellectual property protection," *ACM Transactions on Design Automation of Electronic Systems*, vol. 10, no. 3, pp. 523–545, 2005.

[36] A. Kahng, S. Mantik, I. Markov, M. Potkonjak, P. Tucker, H. Wang, and G. Wolfe, "Robust IP watermarking methodologies for physical design," *in the Proc. of IEEE/ACM Design Automation Conference*, pp. 782–787, 1998.

[37] G. Suh and S. Devadas, "Physical Unclonable Functions for Device Authentication and Secret Key Generation," *in the Proc. of the IEEE/ACM Design Automation Conference*, pp. 9–14, 2007.

[38] J. Lee, D. Lim, B. Gassend, G. Suh, M. van Dijk, and S. Devadas, "A technique to build a secret key in integrated circuits for identification and authentication applications," *in the Proc. of IEEE Internationall Symposium on VLSI Circuits*, pp. 176–179, 2004.

[39] Cadence, "SoC Encounter," http://www.cadence.com/products/di/soc_encounter/ pages/default.aspx.

APPENDIX

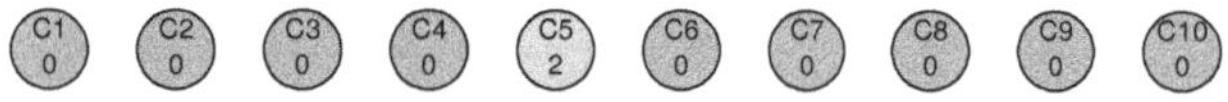

(a)

(b)

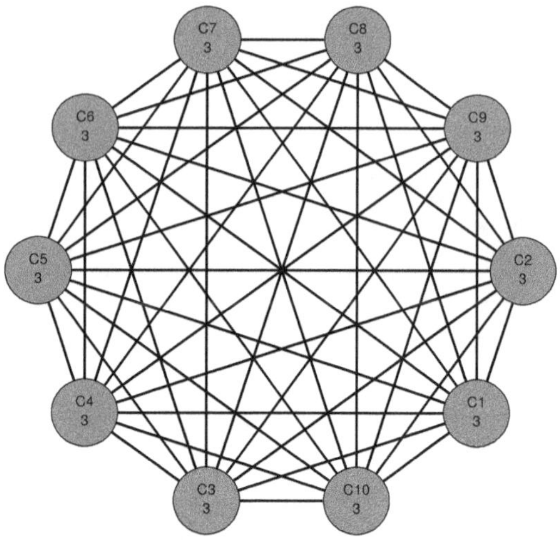

(c)

Figure 15: Interference graph for C432, one of the ISCAS benchmark circuits. This design has 36 inputs, 7 outputs, and 160 gates. 10 gates in this design are selected for camouflaging. The figure shows the interference graph when gates to camouflage are selected in three different ways. Nodes in green, yellow, blue, and red indicate isolated, fully resolvable, partially resolvable, and non-resolvable gates, respectively. The number below the node label indicates the weight of the node. (a) On *randomly* selecting gates, 9 gates are isolated and one gate is partially resolvable. In this interference graph, the number of brute force attempts required to resolve the functionality of camouflaged gates is 2. (b) When gates are selected using the*output corruptibility* metric, 9 gates are isolated and one gate is fully-resolvable. In this interference graph, the number of brute force attempts required to resolve the functionality of camouflaged gates is 0. (c) When gates are selected using the *output corruptibility + non-resolvability* metric, all the gates are non-resolvable. In this interference graph, the number of brute force attempts required to resolve the functionality of camouflaged gates is 3^{10}. When the gates are selected using the *non-resolvability* metric, the resultant interference graph is same the one in (c).

Controller	**Possible IP secret**	**# of gat**
Instruction queue	Cache line validation	2027
Instruction decoder	Decoding algorithm	771
Load Store unit read/write	Read/write priorities	899
Load store unit store buffer	Ordering of store operations	1360
Floating point input	Scheduling of FPU operations	916
Floating point divider	Division algorithm	1197
Exception handler	Supported exceptions	936
Trap logic unit	Interrupt handling & Machine states	2724

(a)

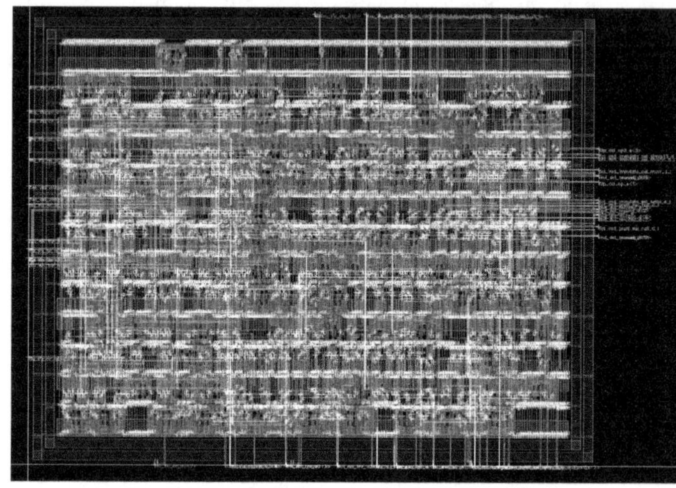

(b)

Figure 16: (a) Controllers of OpenSparc T1 microprocessor and their corresponding IP secret. (b) The layout with camouflaged gates for the controller unit of instruction decoder in OpenSparc T1 microprocessor. This design has 132 inputs, 89 outputs, 771 gates. 39 gates in this unit have been camouflaged. The design was synthesized for the library with camouflaged gates using Cadence RTL compiler [19]. The layout from the synthesized design was generated using Cadence SoC Encounter [39].

Low-Fat Pointers: Compact Encoding and Efficient Gate-Level Implementation of Fat Pointers for Spatial Safety and Capability-based Security

Albert Kwon
kwyoung@seas.upenn.edu
Department of ESE
200 S. 33rd Street
Philadelphia, PA 19104
United States

Udit Dhawan
udit@seas.upenn.edu
Department of ESE
200 S. 33rd Street
Philadelphia, PA 19104
United States

Jonathan M. Smith
jms@cis.upenn.edu
Department of CIS
3330 Walnut Street
Philadelphia, PA 19104
United States

Thomas F. Knight, Jr.
tk@ginkgobioworks.com
Gingko Bioworks
27 Drydock Ave.
Boston, MA 02210
United States

André DeHon
andre@acm.org
Department of ESE
200 S. 33rd Street
Philadelphia, PA 19104
United States

ABSTRACT

Referencing outside the bounds of an array or buffer is a common source of bugs and security vulnerabilities in today's software. We can enforce spatial safety and eliminate these violations by inseparably associating bounds with every pointer (*fat pointer*) and checking these bounds on every memory access. By further adding hardware-managed tags to the pointer, we make them unforgeable. This, in turn, allows the pointers to be used as *capabilities* to facilitate fine-grained access control and fast security domain crossing. Dedicated checking hardware runs in parallel with the processor's normal datapath so that the checks do not slow down processor operation (0% runtime overhead). To achieve the safety of fat pointers without increasing program state, we compactly encode approximate base and bound pointers along with exact address pointers for a 46b address space into one 64-bit word with a worst-case memory overhead of 3%. We develop gate-level implementations of the logic for updating and validating these compact fat pointers and show that the hardware requirements are low and the critical paths for common operations are smaller than processor ALU operations. Specifically, we show that the fat-pointer check and update operations can run in a 4 ns clock cycle on a Virtex 6 (40nm) implementation while only using 1100 6-LUTs or about the area of a double-precision, floating-point adder.

CCS'13, November 4–8, 2013, Berlin, Germany.

ACM 978-1-4503-2477-9/13/11 ...$15.00.
http://dx.doi.org/10.1145/2508859.2516713.

Categories and Subject Descriptors

B.8.0 [**Hardware**]: Performance and Reliability—*General*; C.1.3 [**Computer System Organization**]: Processor Architectures—*Capability Architectures*

Keywords

Processor; security; spatial confinement; fat pointer; capabilities; memory safety

1. INTRODUCTION

Computer systems security is a major and increasing concern, not least because of the increasing dependence on such systems for activities in daily life, such as communication, shopping and banking. Today's computers reflect biases in system design and organization that are often decades out of date—based on silicon budgets where orders of magnitude fewer transistors were available than today, and based on threat models where very few machines were networked and the data they held was of limited value. For example, today's systems only provide coarse-grained separation between processes using virtual memory contexts. Switching between virtual memory contexts is expensive, encouraging the use of coarse-grained contexts with no internal separation of privileges within the contexts. A virtual memory context typically holds a very large number of objects with no boundary to separate the access of one object from another, either intentionally or accidentally. The lack of fine-grained controls on object access enables unintended use or modification of data, such as buffer overflows. Despite long familiarity with their existence and exploitation [3], buffer overflow attacks remain a persistent source of security holes.

Leaving the burden of spatial safety enforcement to individual programmers no longer appears to be a viable approach to software security. If even a single programmer leaves a potential spatial safety violation in a program, that is an open attack vector for the program.

The alternative is to design our systems to automatically prevent spatial safety errors, protecting against silent corruption of the system or violations of program semantics. This can be done at the language level with bounds checked arrays (*e.g.* Java), at the compiler or runtime level by maintaining object base and bounds information, or at the hardware level. Many recent systems explore the use of *fat pointers* that extend the pointer representation with base and bounds information so that the runtime or hardware can prevent spatial safety violations (Sec. 2.1). Software level solutions typically come with high runtime overheads (50–120%) or weak protection guarantees limiting ubiquitous adoption.

Object capability systems [14, 17, 45, 34, 28, 40] are attractive for both their potential to enable programmer control of access rights and their support for least privilege. Using hardware supported tags [36, 18, 34, 23, 20] (Sec. 3.1), we can make fat pointers unforgeable so that they can serve as a basis for the *descriptors* used in hardware-based capability systems.

In this paper we assume that the safety benefits of fat pointers [27, 33, 31] and the security benefits of capabilities [29, 42] are well established from prior work, but that their costs have typically been considered too high for ubiquitous use in the past [19, 10]. To that end, we address how they might be efficiently implemented in hardware. Specifically, we explore (1) compact representations for fat pointers that limit their impact on memory footprint (3% worst case), (2) parallel hardware support for bounds checking that guarantees there is no runtime overhead for checking, and (3) hardware enforcement and management that allow the fat pointers to serve as object capabilities. That is, we spend hardware to eliminate the overheads of spatial safety checking. We evaluate the area and delay complexity of the hardware fat-pointer operations using an FPGA implementation.

Our novel contributions include:

- Design and evaluation of a new, compact fat-pointer encoding and implementation (BIMA) that has significantly lower gate depth (small cycle time) operations than previous work (*e.g.* [7]) while simultaneously retaining: (1) compact representation in memory, (2) low memory loss due to fragmentation (<3%), and (3) precise spatial bounds detection.
- Hardware that enforces the BIMA bounds checking and update, making the fat pointers unforgeable and non-bypassable. This allows the 64b pointer to serve as an object capability, achieving significant savings over schemes that required three full 64b words to encode a capability address, base, and bound (*e.g.* [43]).
- Pipeline organization that allows the BIMA encoding to run just as fast as the baseline processor without spatial safety checking.

2. BACKGROUND

2.1 Fat Pointer

Many modern systems have explored the maintenance and checking of explicit object base and bounds in order to maintain spatial safety. That is, rather than simply representing a pointer with its address, the system includes the base and bound address in the pointer representation, for a total of three words. Since this makes the pointer larger, it is often referred to as a *fat-pointer* scheme (*e.g.* [27], [33]). By checking against the base and bound during memory operations, the system can detect any spatial safety violations and prevent them from occurring:

```
if ((ptr.A >= ptr.base) && (ptr.A <= ptr.bound))
    perform load or store
else
    jump to error handler
```

The Secure Virtual Architecture (SVA) [11] lists fat pointers as a potential future direction for further performance improvement of OS kernel safety enforcement. Many schemes have introduced the pointers in the compiler when running on conventional hardware. These incur significant runtime and space overheads. Examples include: PAriCheck (9.5% average memory overhead and 49% runtime overhead on SPEC2000) [50], Baggy Bounds (worst-case 100% memory overhead; 15% average memory overhead and 60% runtime overhead on SPEC2000) [2], SoftBound (worst-case 200% memory overhead; 64% average memory overhead and 67% runtime overhead on SPEC and Olden benchmarks) [31], and CRED (26–130% runtime overhead) [39]. Other software schemes sacrifice guaranteed protection against all out-of-bound references in order to improve performance, such as Lightweight Bounds Checks (8.5% average memory overhead and 23% runtime overhead on SPEC2000) [21]. Furthermore, since these schemes depend on software maintenance and checking of guards, they are not suitable for use as capabilities since they only assist with voluntary confinement rather than providing mandatory access confinement.

HardBound is a hardware approach that attempts to maintain data structure layout compatibility by placing the bound information in a shadow space and reduces runtime overhead to 10–20% [15] but has a worst-case memory overhead of 200%. Moreover, the hardbound design is described only down to the micro-architectural level, providing no quantification of added gate count or necessary gate delay. Intel has recently announced a hardware-assisted approach for runtime memory bounds management [1] that appears very similar to HardBound.

Apart from the explicit fat-pointer approach for memory safety, some tagging mechanisms have been proposed that use metadata to perform spatial checks [12, 9]. The most lightweight version of these, uses a few extra bits per word to limit accidental spatial violations but not guarantee protection, while the more complete require over 100% area overhead and can have over 100% runtime overhead.

In contrast, our scheme has a worst-case 3% memory loss due to fragmentation (Sec. 4.5) and no runtime overhead (Sec. 5) while providing spatial safety semantics similar to HardBound and hardware enforcement that makes it suitable for supporting capabilities. Furthermore, we provide a gate-level design that allows us to quantify gate count and gate delays.

While most of the prior work was performed on x86 architectures, we will be using a RISC architecture as our baseline. As a crude estimate of the work performed by the fat-pointer checking with dedicated hardware, we identify the instruction sequences required to provide the same protection as our fat-pointer scheme in Tab. 1 and use instruction trace simulations for the SPEC2006 benchmarks (App. A) to calculate the impact on dynamic instruction count (Fig. 1). This is an overestimate in that a good compiler will optimize away some of these checks as redundant (*e.g.* [32]). Nonetheless, this illustrates the work performed by our fat-

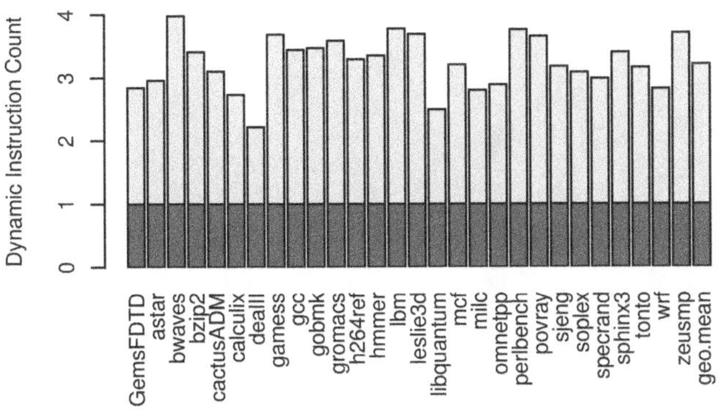

Figure 1: Dynamic instruction count for an ALPHA architecture performing spatial checks in software

pointer hardware and further motivates its need. In Fig. 1 we observe that there is an average of 220% overhead in the number of dynamic instructions executed for non-fat pointer hardware ISAs.

2.2 Object Capabilities

Typical isolation models for users of a shared computing resource include sharing disciplines for time (such as real-time or best-effort scheduling) and memory (such as read-write-execute access controls on objects in processor memory or secondary storage). Models for protection have included storage keys [25] associated with fixed size blocks of memory (*e.g.*, 2048 bytes on the System/360), programmer-defined contiguous regions of memory such as segments (*e.g.*, Burroughs descriptors [36]), and fixed-sized pages of memory comprising a protected virtual address space. Today, most virtual memory systems are implemented using several large "segments", *e.g.*, for a heap, stack and instructions, with an eye to both protection (*e.g.*, non-executable data segments) and sharing (*e.g.*, shared read-only segments). These segments are demand-paged, combining segmentation and paging in the style of Multics [35], primarily to exploit locality of reference [13]. Large segments and pages provide a coarse-grained form of hardware access control, but this coarse granularity (*e.g.*, for code, data and stack in UNIX) comes with security and performance consequences. First, there is no protection of individual objects contained within the segment, and second, the sizes of segments and pages are unrelated to the sizes of individual objects. Furthermore, switching security contexts is an expensive operation that discourages programmers from providing fine-grained separation.

Capability-based computer architectures provide hardware support for fine-grained access control. One example, the Cambridge CAP Computer [44], provided a set of "base-limit" registers that point to and delimit a segment of memory. These were augmented with bits indicating permitted accesses, *e.g.*, read, write and/or execute. A second example, HYDRA/C.mmp [46] implemented capabilities as a combination pointer and access rights, with access rights defined by a richer type system than that of the CAP Computer. A third and final example, the Intel 432 [37] provided a complex "Object Descriptor" with access rights and a structure incorporating a base address for the object and the lengths of both data and access parts. A data operand is a two-part value with an object selector (which can be interpreted as a base address) and a displacement. The displacement serves the role of a bound, giving a complex implementation of a base and bound. The basic protection mechanism for all three of these systems consists of a set of rights, and a base and bound pointer that is exercisable with appropriate rights. A major performance cost associated with these approaches is the multiple levels of indirection and table lookups for memory references; Colwell [10] provides considerable analysis of these overheads.

Other hardware systems have implemented similar constructs, *e.g.*, the 64-bit guarded pointers [8] of Carter, *et al.*, avoid translation tables by encoding permission bits and segment sizes in the pointer itself. This allows lightweight (cycle-by-cycle) context switches, allowing instructions from different threads with different security domains to be mixed in a processor pipeline and encouraging more fine-grained separation of privilege domains. Cambridge's CHERI [43] is a recent hardware capability architecture that has the goals of supporting a *hybrid capability model* as explored in Capsicum [42]. CHERI uses a 256b fat pointer as a capability including a full 64b address, 64b base, and 64b length. Our design improves on this greatly, and shows how the address, base, and bounds can be composed into a single 64b word for a 46b address space.

3. SIMPLIFIED SAFE PROCESSOR

We originally developed this fat-pointer scheme for the SAFE Processor [16]. Since the SAFE Processor includes a number of orthogonal safety innovations, we extract a reduced version of the SAFE processor, the *Simplified SAFE Processor* (`SAFElite`), to provide concrete context for the fat-pointer logic. Nonetheless, the fat-pointer implementation we describe, should be a useful component in a wide range of processor architectures.

The `SAFElite` is a simple 64b RISC processor with a four-stage pipeline as shown in Fig. 2. The `SAFElite` is a clean-slate ISA design that is not concerned with legacy binary compatibility. We use the `SAFElite` as a single-address space machine, with all applications and system services running in the same address space, exploiting the fat pointer object capabilities for privilege separation. Memory is structured into *segments*, a contiguous set of words addressable by a fat pointer. Memory in the `SAFElite` is garbage collected, thereby avoiding temporal safety hazards.

3.1 Hardware Types

The SAFE processor uses capabilities to constrain malicious activities at the hardware level. To support this, on top of a base RISC processor, we incorporate hardware mechanisms that allow us to enforce critical semantics to ensure a secured computation. First, we add a notion of native hardware types in the form of tags (*e.g.* [36, 44, 20]) to the words in the processor, such as *Integer* for integer words, *Instruction* for instructions, and *Pointers* for words that reference memory segments. These hardware types are added on top of the actual data payload. For the current discussion, let us assume that we have 8 bits allocated for the hardware types in `SAFElite` (making our memory and data path 72 bits wide). The hardware types could be larger or smaller depending on number of types desired, but even at 8 bits (256 types), `SAFElite` only incurs a total overhead of at most 16% ($\frac{72}{64} \times 1.03$; 3% worst-case memory fragmentation is explained in Sec. 4.5). Alternate implementations might prefer to avoid adding hardware type tag bits on top

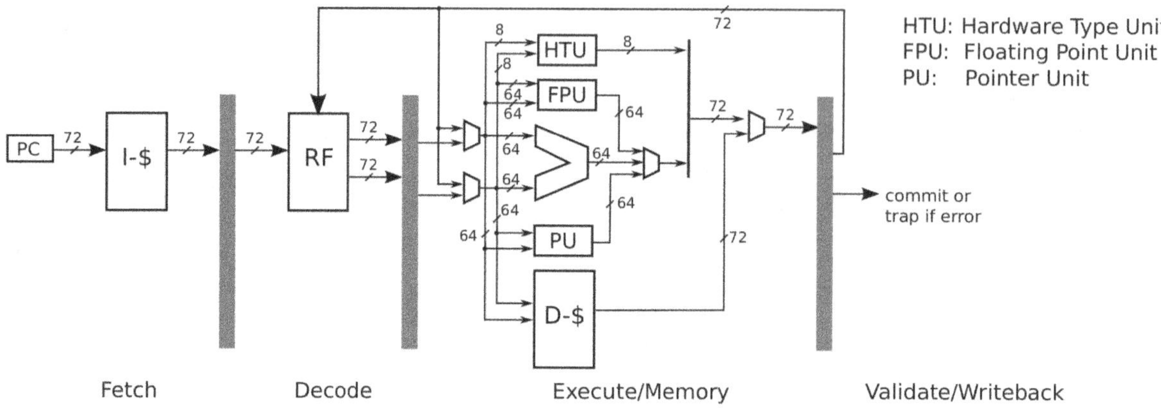

Figure 2: Simplified SAFE Processor Pipeline

of the 64b word. Some designs store metadata in a shadow space (*e.g.* [15]). Another alternative is to borrow bits from the base 64b word for hardware type.

Types limit how data can be used. Using these hardware types, the `SAFElite` avoids several attacks such as malicious code injection attacks that try to use input data that would be typed as an *Integer* as processor instructions. On `SAFElite` only a word with *Instruction* hardware type will be executed as an instruction. To support this, we add a *Hardware Type Unit* (HTU) to the `SAFElite` (see Fig. 2) to validate its entire operation with respect to the instruction and input operands (such as only an *Integer* can be added to an *Integer*). The Hardware Type Unit also assigns the hardware type to the result of a computation, if any.

Although 8b of hardware type allows up to 256 unique hardware types, for this paper we concentrate on the following hardware types:

- **Pointer:** hardware type on any word that is a well-formed and valid pointer to a segment of memory; pointers can be further subdivided by access, including Read-Only and Execute-Only Pointers.
- **Integer:** hardware type on a word that is used as a 64b bit vector
- **Out-of-Bounds-Pointer:** hardware type on a word that was previously a pointer, but has now preceded its base or exceeded its bound.
- **Out-of-Bounds-Memory-Location:** hardware type on the memory locations that seem to be referenced by a valid pointer but are not within bounds, as these lie beyond the precise bound of the segment (see Sec. 4.4)
- **Error:** SAFE and `SAFElite` allow us to invalidate an operation if it violates the intended semantics (*e.g.* [24]); in that case, we assign this hardware type on the operation's result. In general we may have more errors than the two Out-of-Bounds cases identified above, but we will not differentiate them further in this paper.
- **Other:** the set of hardware types on words that are not a pointer, integer, or error. We will not differentiate these further in this paper.

The hardware types allow the garbage collector to distinguish pointers from non-pointers, thereby facilitating garbage collection (GC). One hardware type is used to represent GC forwarding pointers.

In a conventional processor all the pointer arithmetic is achieved using regular arithmetic instructions. For example, the `addqi` instructions used in the ALPHA architecture for adding integers are also used to perform pointer arithmetic This poses a serious vulnerability that can be exploited to potentially create a memory reference to any location (*e.g.*, [38]). However, this is not possible in the `SAFElite` since the Hardware Type Unit does not allow typed pointer data to be offset by an integer using a regular `addm` (integer add modulo 2^{64}) instruction. Furthermore, the result of an `addm` instruction is an *Integer* that cannot be used as a *Pointer* for dereferencing memory. In order to perform pointer arithmetic in the `SAFElite`, we add a specialized instruction `addp` (add to pointer) for incrementing or decrementing a word with a pointer hardware type. Consequently, we add a new functional unit called the *Pointer Unit* (PU) as shown in Fig. 2 that is responsible for all the pointer-related arithmetic operations. Instructions used to access memory, namely `lw` (load word from memory) and `sw` (store word to memory), follow the same semantics as in a common processor, but instead require a pointer type argument (see Sec. 4.8).

3.2 Privileged Memory Management System

Control over creation and allocation is necessary to guarantee *unforgeability* of the pointers if they are to be used as capabilities [46]. We assume that the Memory Manager (MM) is a separate, privileged software subsystem that can create fat pointers. Only the MM has the privileges to create a new fat pointer. Ordinary code can call into the MM's allocation routine to obtain a new pointer. The full SAFE Processor supports calls into privileged domains (*gates*) that are as inexpensive as ordinary procedure calls [16].

3.3 Stack Protection

To get full advantage of the fat pointer protection, it would be valuable to use separate segments for each stack frame. For non-garbage-collected systems or hybrid systems where the compiler can stack-manage call frames, this can be supported with a special `pushframe` instruction[1] at the `SAFElite`-level to create subframes from a typed stack pointer and a special `popframe` instruction to return them. In hybrid cases, the garbage collector will need to distinguish these stack subframes and treat them differently. In

[1]This is similar to the `alloca` primitive in conventional systems that is used allocate memory space on the stack rather than the heap.

the full SAFE Processor, the call stack is not directly visible to user code and is used only for procedure control.

3.4 Compatibility

While our primary design is not concerned with legacy compatibility, our hardware could be added for capability support alongside legacy code as illustrated in the CHERI hybrid capability processor [43]. CHERI uses capabilities for fine-grained separation within a virtual-memory context. Capability-oblivious legacy code can call capability-aware subroutines, and capability-aware code can use capabilities to sandbox capability-oblivious software components. Types can effectively capture the operations allowed on a capability, so our hardware-typed pointer can provide the same functionality as the full 256b CHERI capability.

3.5 FPGA Implementation

To validate the operation and characterize the performance of the `SAFElite`, we prototyped the processor on an ML605 FPGA development board [47] from Xilinx with a Virtex 6 (xc6vlx240t-2 device) [48]. A 64-bit addition on this device takes close to 2 ns. However, with operations such as variable shifts, the Integer ALU can operate only at a latency of 4 ns. A moderate sized direct-mapped cache built using Block RAMs (discrete SRAM blocks on this FPGA device) can also be accessed with a delay under 2.5 ns. Therefore, it is necessary that all functional units, including the Pointer Unit, finish their operation within a 4 ns envelope in order to avoid increasing the processor cycle time.

4. COMPACT FAT POINTER ENCODING

In this section, we derive our compact fat-pointer encoding (Secs. 4.1–4.2), address issues with approximate sizing and out-of-bounds pointers (Secs. 4.3–4.4 and 4.7), and characterize the worst-case fragmentation effects (Sec. 4.5). We roundup the operations on the fat pointers (Sec. 4.8). Finally, we show the datapaths to support the fat-pointer operations and quantify their area and delay (Secs. 4.9–4.10).

4.1 Aligned Encoding

Keeping track of base and bound potentially requires three pointers. To get a more compact fat-pointer representation, let us first assume that the size of the segment the pointer is referencing is a power of two (i.e., 2^B for some B). Furthermore, assume that the pointer is aligned on the same power of two boundary. Then the base of the pointer can be determined by replacing B bits in the LSB with 0's:

$$\texttt{base} = \texttt{A} - (\texttt{A}\,\&\,((1 << \texttt{B}) - 1)) \tag{1}$$

Similarly, the bound can be represented by replacing the B LSBs with 1's. With the above assumptions, we can represent the pointer and its base and bound with an overhead of only $|B|$ bits, which is, at most, the log of the size of the address space. This is the scheme used for guarded pointers by Carter [8] and for the Baggy Bounds software scheme [2].

4.2 Floating-Point Size

This simple encoding could, however, result in large memory overhead through fragmentation: objects of size slightly larger than a power of two will waste nearly half of the allocated space. For example, for an object of size 33, we must allocate 64 words. To address this issue, instead of having the pointer as one large block, we can view it as a collection of several smaller blocks. If we used five bits for the number of blocks, we can allocate 17 blocks of size two for an object of size 33, forcing us to only allocate a segment one word larger than the desired allocation.

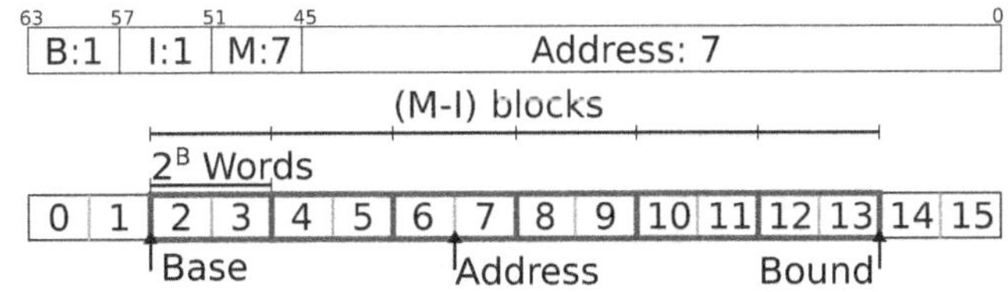

Figure 3: A typical pointer in the BIMA encoding scheme

The basic floating-point size approach was introduced by Aries [7] and is analogous to floating-point numbers. In both cases, we represent a range of values much larger than the number of bits used for encoding by separating precision (mantissa) from the exponent (B in our case). This results in an exact address representation, an exact base representation that has alignment restrictions, and an approximate bound representation that may force us to conservatively overestimate (round up) the segment size.

Given the alignment restrictions, we can reconstruct the base and bound pointers with just a few additional bits beyond the current pointer address. Furthermore, the reconstruction can be performed with simple logic that places these additional bits into the appropriate bit positions (deposits) on copies of the address. To encode both base and bounds, we use a minimum field, I, for the base, and maximum field, M, for the bound that specify the $|I| = |M|$ bits above the bottom B bits of the base and bound address. When we create a pointer, we deposit $|I|$ bits above the bottom B bits of the base to I, and do the same with the bound to M. We can almost recover the base and bound by simply shifting I and M by B and replacing the bottom $|I|+|B|$ bits in the address. We call this encoding scheme BIMA since its key fields are the block size exponent, B, the minimum bound, I, the maximum bound, M, and the address, A. Fig. 3 shows a typical pointer in the BIMA encoding scheme.

$$\begin{aligned}
\texttt{carry} &= 1 << (\texttt{B} + |\texttt{I}|) \\
\texttt{Atop} &= \left(\texttt{A}\,\&\,\overline{(\texttt{carry} - 1)}\right) \qquad (2) \\
\texttt{Mshift} &= \texttt{M} << \texttt{B} \\
\texttt{Ishift} &= \texttt{I} << \texttt{B} \\
\texttt{D}_{\texttt{under}} &= (\texttt{A} >> \texttt{B})[5:0] < \texttt{I}\ ? \\
&\quad (\texttt{carry} \mid \texttt{Atop}) - \texttt{Ishift} : \\
&\quad \texttt{Atop} - \texttt{Ishift} \qquad (3) \\
\texttt{D}_{\texttt{over}} &= (\texttt{A} >> \texttt{B})[5:0] > \texttt{M}\ ? \\
&\quad (\texttt{carry} \mid \texttt{Mshift}) - \texttt{Atop} : \\
&\quad \texttt{Mshift} - \texttt{Atop} \qquad (4)
\end{aligned}$$

It is not as simple as a deposit because the bits **above** the I or M bits in the word may need to be incremented. Nonetheless, this is easy to detect and accommodate. There are two possible cases for this scheme: the pointer has not incurred any carries in the A field beyond $|I| + B$ bits or it has. When there have been no carries beyond the bottom $|I| + B$ bits, the relevant bits that determined I and M have not changed. Therefore, the $|I|$ bits above the B bits will be greater than or equal to I and less than or equal to M. In this case we can compute the distance to underflow and overflow, D_{under} and D_{over}, by doing a $|I| + B$ subtraction using the bottom bits of A and the base and bound computed from simple shifts. When there is a carry, however, I could be larger than the corresponding bits in A and vice-versa for M. We can resolve this issue by adding one bit to the MSB of the smaller quantity (*i.e.*, add $2^{|I|+B}$). Eqs. 3 and 4 show the computation required.

To fit the encoding into one 64-bit word, we must use some of the bits to encode B, I, and M. For example, if we allocate 6 bits to each, that leaves us with 46b to specify the address. Since we use word addressing of 64b words, this is comparable (2^{49}=512TB) to the 40b byte addresses [26] (1TB) or 48b byte addresses (256TB) [4] currently supported by x86-64 architectures.

4.3 Out-of-Bounds

One consequence of the compact representation is that we cannot represent a pointer that points to an address that is not bounded by the base and bounds. Consequently, whenever a pointer is computed that violates its bounds, we represent it with a different hardware type, the Out-of-Bounds-Pointer. Producing an out-of-bounds pointer, itself, is not an error. It is common to increment a pointer until it exceeds the bound. The error only occurs when we attempt to use the Out-of-Bounds-Pointer as the address in a load or store operation. As a result, there is no bounds check at the time of the load, only a Hardware Type Unit check that the type of the word used as an address is still a valid, in-bounds pointer. This means that `addp` effectively both computes the new pointer and checks bounds. Note here that once a pointer goes out of bounds, it is permanently marked as an error. Any further updates on the pointer will not change the type back to Pointer.

4.4 Option to Enforce Exact Bounds

The floating-point size representation results in an approximate bound, meaning that there can be size mismatches between the pointer and the object. The segment thus will have some words that extend beyond the end of the object that will be unused and accessing these words will not be considered a violation on the basis of the compact fat-pointer bounds alone. Nonetheless, these extra words are not part of any other segment, so writes through pointers will never write into a different segment.

In systems, such as `SAFElite`, where type rules and forwarding pointers demand that we read every word before writing it, we can enforce exact bounds for all pointers by filling the extra words with type Out-of-Bounds-Memory-Location. When the processor performs a memory operation with a pointer within the fat-pointer bounds but reads an Out-of-Bounds-Memory-Location type, the hardware will flag the same error as an out-of-bounds pointer. In both of the cases of spatial violation, the processor will trap to a software handler that will resolve the error. This abstraction allows user-level applications to treat both kinds of out-of-bounds references in the same way.

4.5 Fragmentation

The BIMA encoding provides a better fit between the object and the segment than the exponential alignment and sizing (Sec. 4.1), but the approximate nature of the floating-point size representation also forces us to over-allocate memory to objects as noted above. Any object of size larger than $2^{|I|}$ may result in allocation of a segment larger than the object. Segments of odd size larger than $2^{|I|}$, for instance, will be collections of blocks of even size, and thus there would be at least one word that is wasted.

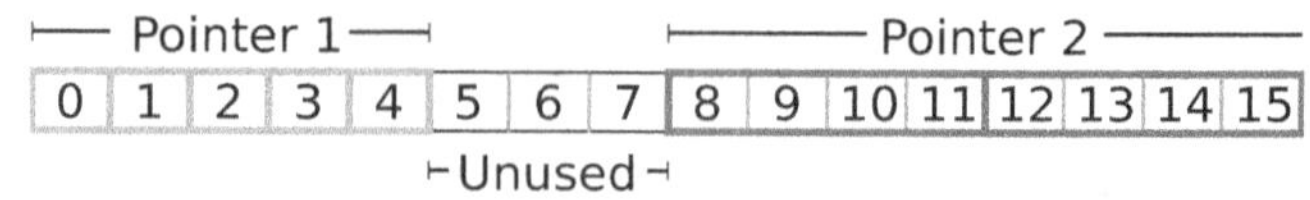

Figure 4: Example of external fragmentation

To compute the impact of the *internal fragmentation*, we note that maximizing $(M - I)$ and minimizing B will result in smaller internal fragmentation. The pointer will never be more than one 2^B block larger than the object. Thus, if we ensurethat the allocator will always use the largest $(M - I)$ and smallest B possible, the memory loss from *internal fragmentation* is less than $1/2^{|I|}$.

The encoding also specifies that blocks of size 2^B must be aligned, and the alignment could cause *external fragmentation*. In particular, with the simple allocation scheme that assigns blocks of memory in the order of the requests, we could have a large object following a small object. In this case, the smaller object could be using some words in the segment that would have been in the first block of the larger object. This forces the larger object to be aligned on the next boundary of 2^B, thus wasting nearly a whole block. For example, in Fig. 4, Pointer 1 is of size 5, and has $B = 0$. For the sake of illustration, assume $|I| = 2$. Pointer 2 is of size 8, and $B = 2$. Because Pointer 1 uses address 4, Pointer 2 must be aligned on the next 2^2 boundary, resulting in addresses 5, 6, and 7 being unused. Nevertheless, this can only waste at most one 2^B block. External fragmentation can therefore result in memory loss of at most $1/2^{|I|}$ of the allocated memory. Internal and external fragmentation together waste less than $1/2^{|I|-1}$ of memory. *If we choose $|I| = 6$, the maximum fraction of memory lost to fragmentation is 3%.* The external fragmentation could be reduced with a more sophisticated allocator that kept track of fragments and avoided placing small blocks on larger block alignment boundaries whenever possible. Nonetheless, the observation above shows that this is not absolutely necessary: such sophisticated alignment would *at most* eliminate worst-case external fragmentation and thereby only cut total fragmentation in half. Furthermore, note that the length of objects whose size is less than $2^{|I|}$ are always represented exactly; therefore, *for small objects there is* **no** *loss due to fragmentation.*

4.6 Decoded Bounds

The BIMA encoding demands that we decode the bounds in order to perform checks. We can avoid the delay associated with decoding bounds by storing decoded bounds (D_{under}, D_{over}) along with the pointer in the register file. Whenever the processor loads a pointer, the processor also computes the underflow and overflow distances in preparation for any necessary pointer computation. This does result in a larger register file from storing the distance values. However, as we will see in Sec. 4.9, it increases performance significantly with low overhead in area. Furthermore, since the decoded pointers are only stored in the register file, there is no overhead in the memory.

4.7 C Compatibility

For C compatibility, it is necessary to represent Out-of-Bounds pointers that are one element past the end of the array. In cases where the pointer size is larger than the allocated object, as discussed in Sec. 4.4, our scheme already accommodates the C-style Out-of-Bounds pointers. As long as no reference is made to the Out-of-Bounds-Memory-Location, no error is flagged. If the pointer is subsequently modified so that it comes back in bounds, it can be used. For cases where the pointer size is exact, our scheme as described would not allow the pointer to be advanced to one past the end of the array and then recovered as a pointer. The simplest way to support this feature would be to allocate a pointer that is at least one word longer and fill the memory location past the real end of the object with Out-of-Bounds-Memory-Location as described in the previous section. Note that this, retains the same worst-case 3% fragmentation overhead we establish in Sec. 4.5 beyond the object-size+1 allocation made.

A slight modification to the scheme would avoid paying for any extra memory locations. With our D_{under}, D_{over} scheme (Sec. 4.6) we could allow D_{over} to become negative and then check the sign of D_{over} on a memory operation. As long as the pointer is returned to in-bounds before a memory reference is made, no error is flagged. To handle the case of a one-element-over Out-of-Bounds being written to memory, we could add a distinguished C-Out-of-Bounds-by-One pointer type and convert to this pointer type at the point of writeback to memory. This feature is not included in the detailed evaluation that follows; we believe it would add area but not impact cycle time.

With suitable compiler and linker support, Nagarakatte reports that bounds can be applied to most legacy C programs without source code changes [30].

4.8 Operation

We now roundup the pointer-related operations that must be performed with the BIMA encoding.

4.8.1 newp

The MM subsystem uses a privileged instruction **`newp`** to create new fat pointers. Typically, these would be allocated out of an available block of memory (*e.g.* NewSpace or Copy-Space in a Garbage Collection scheme). **`newp`** can be used to decompose a large, unallocated segment into a collection of allocated segments.

4.8.2 offsetp

The **`offsetp`** instruction returns the offset of the pointer from its base. This is simply the D_{under} value in the register file, so requires no computation. Iterators can use the offset to identify the end of an array when the approximate bound (Sec. 4.2) makes the segment larger than the live data.

4.8.3 addp

Pointer arithmetic in **`SAFElite`** is done via an instruction called **`addp`**. The **`addp`** instruction is a three-operand (two sources, one destination) instruction where one source is the pointer we are changing, and the other is the offset. In BIMA, when we read the pointer to add the offset, we read the D_{under} and D_{over} associated with the pointer as well. We then add the offset to D_{under} to indicate that distance to underflow has changed by the offset. Similarly, we subtract the offset from D_{over}. The pointer is within bounds as long as both distances are non-negative since neither underflow or overflow has happened. If either distance is negative, we replace the hardware type of the pointer with Out-of-Bounds-Pointer.

4.8.4 sw

`SAFElite` has a two-operand store instruction, **`sw`**. Like many RISC architectures, there is a direct path from the register file to the memory. In the **`SAFElite`**, however, we check the type of the pointer in parallel with the memory access (see Fig. 2). As described before, if the address field is out of bounds, then the type of the pointer will be changed to an Out-of-Bounds-Pointer. Therefore if the word we are using as an address to store is an Out-of-Bounds-Pointer, we flag an out-of-bounds error. Otherwise, the operation is carried out as with any other processors.

When we are storing a pointer to memory, note the processor can just store the 64b BIMA pointer and ignore the decoded bounds D_{under} and D_{over}. They are redundant information and can be recomputed when loading the pointer back from the memory using the **`lw`** operation.

4.8.5 lw

`SAFElite` also has a load operation **`lw`** that is a one-source, one-destination instruction. On a **`lw`**, there are potentially two pointers that we need to check: the pointer we are using as the source, and the loaded value from memory that could be a pointer. The fat-pointer computation for the first pointer behaves the same as the store case: we check if the pointer is out of bounds, indicated by the Out-of-Bounds-Pointer type on the pointer.

The fat-pointer decode computation is unique to **`lw`**. The loaded value could be a pointer as well, and for future bounds checks from the loaded pointer, we need to determine its D_{under} and D_{over}. Therefore, we must decode the pointer before it is stored in the register file (See Fig. 6a).

4.8.6 Conventional Processor Equivalent

For the sake of comparison, Tab. 1 shows roughly the instructions required to simulate these operations on a RISC processor with no hardware support for fat pointers. Tab. 1 omits **`offsetp`** since it is not needed when using full 64b pointers to represent base and bound and **`newp`** since it is dominated by other instructions for allocation. Compiler analysis and support will often be able to remove some of the bounds checks and data movement (*e.g.* [32]).

4.9 Implementation

To evaluate the performance of the encoding scheme, we implemented a Pointer Unit (PU) for decoding and updating for both the BIMA and Aries fat pointers. The PU was designed[2] using Bluespec SystemVerilog [6] and implemented on a 40nm Xilinx Virtex 6 FPGA (xcv6vlx240t-2) [48].

4.9.1 Aries

While the BIMA scheme shares the basic strategy with Aries, our encoding is different in specific details that reduce the latency of the key operations. Instead of using a lower

[2] source code available at **`http://ic.ese.upenn.edu/distributions/fatptr_ccs2013`**

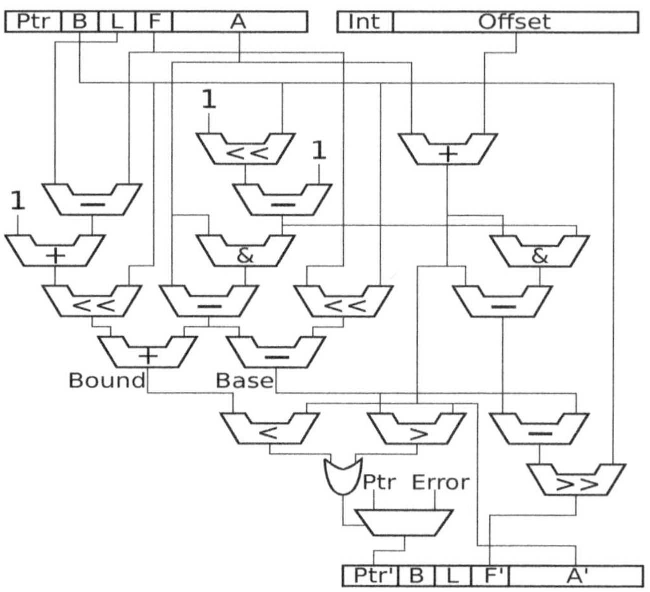

Figure 5: Data path for the Aries Encoding (`addp`)

(I) and upper (M) bound, Aries uses a length (L) and finger (F) field that effectively capture the same information. In both the BIMA and Aries cases the A field always points exactly to the current word. Since Aries does not have an I and M field, the Aries finger field records the offset of the current block form the base block in the record to allow bounds circuitry to calculate the base and bound. However, this has two problems: (1) it demands a more complicated decoding than BIMA, and (2) it demands that the finger field potentially be updated on every pointer increment. For reference, the data path for the Aries Pointer Unit is shown in Fig. 5.

4.9.2 BIMA Decode

The decode data path for the BIMA scheme is shown in Fig. 6a. Compared to the Aries encoding data path, the depth is smaller, and there are fewer variable shifts, resulting in significantly shorter delay. For $|B| = |L| = |I| = 6$, the delay is less than 4.8 ns up to 64b addresses. The delay comparison with Aries is shown in Fig. 9. This is over a 40% reduction in delay from Aries encoding on average. The delay and area of the BIMA decode is summarized in Figs. 7a and 8. Nonetheless, at 4.2 ns, the 46b decode is slightly longer than our target cycle time of 4 ns. The decoded bounds (Sec. 4.6) avoid the need to perform this decoding for any operation other than `lw`. In Sec. 5, we show that we can split the decode needed for `lw` across pipeline stages to prevent this operation from limiting the frequency of the processor or creating any new stall conditions.

4.9.3 BIMA Update

The update operation in the BIMA scheme is even simpler than the decode operation. As shown in Fig. 6b, the BIMA update data path consist only of additions, comparison, and a multiplexer. The delay of update is independent of size of I and B and is less than 4 ns for any number of address bits below 64 as shown in Fig. 7b, meaning the update operation will not degrade processor clock frequency. At $|A|=46$, BIMA update delay is less than half the Aries update delay (Fig. 9). Aries must check and update the F field on ever update operation. We note here that because decode and update are part of different instructions in BIMA, the delay of the two do not add; the delay of decode is relevant only for `lw`, while delay of update is only relevant for `addp`. Fig. 7b also summarizes the area for the update operation.

4.9.4 Area

The total area required by the BIMA scheme is the sum of the area of decode and update; for a 64b fat pointer with $|A|=46$, the pointer unit uses 1114 LUTs.[3] This is larger than the 956 LUTs required by the Aries encoding. Nonetheless, the total area is still comparable to the floating point adder used in `SAFElite`, which takes 940 LUTs [49].

4.9.5 Other Implementation Technologies

We include the FPGA delay and area comparison to provide a concrete point of comparison for the complexity of the key operations in the fat-pointer encoding schemes. Nonetheless, similar effects and benefits would occur in ASIC or custom implementation technology. Simply looking at Figs. 5, 6a, and 6b, we can see that the depth of operations is lower for the BIMA operations than the Aries implementation. This makes it clear the delay would be smaller in any implementation. Note that the slowest operation in each datapath is the variable shift. The Aries datapath requires two variable shifts while the BIMA decode requires only one and the BIMA update requires none. Furthermore, note that the slowest operation in the ALU is the variable shift. This alone is enough to explain (1) why the BIMA update, which requires no variable shifts, is faster than the ALU, (2) why the BIMA decode is only slightly slower than the ALU, and (3) why the Aries decode with two variable shifts is over twice the delay of the ALU. Consequently, these general timing relations will hold for custom implementations as well.

4.10 Decoded Bounds Implementation

In the baseline case where we do not add any hardware type metadata to the words, the register file width is 64b. Then, we can fit an entire 32-entry register file in two Virtex-6 BRAMs[4] organized as 512×64b, dual-ported memories. The base `SAFElite` uses two BRAMs to support one write and two read ports on 64b words. However, when we add an 8b hardware type metadata, the register file width is now 72b, and this forces us to use two BRAMs per read port or a total of 4 BRAMs, even though we are not using the entire width offered by two BRAMs. On top of this, when we add the decoded lower and upper bounds, we further increase the width of our register file by twice the width of our address size. Therefore, when the address size is 46b, the register file is $(72+2\times 46 =)$ 164b wide. The register file now requires 3 BRAMs per read port for a total of 6 BRAMs. If this were a full custom implementation, we would simply expand the 64b register file width to 164b, or a 156% overhead.

5. PIPELINING AND BYPASSING

The `SAFElite` has four pipeline stages as shown in Fig. 2. Without the fat-pointer computation, the processor runs at 4 ns clock cycle with full bypass of results to prevent stalls

[3]The Virtex 6 FPGA employs 6-input Look-Up Tables for logic. We refer to them simply as LUTs henceforth.
[4]BRAM=Block RAM, SRAM blocks in a Virtex-6 FPGA

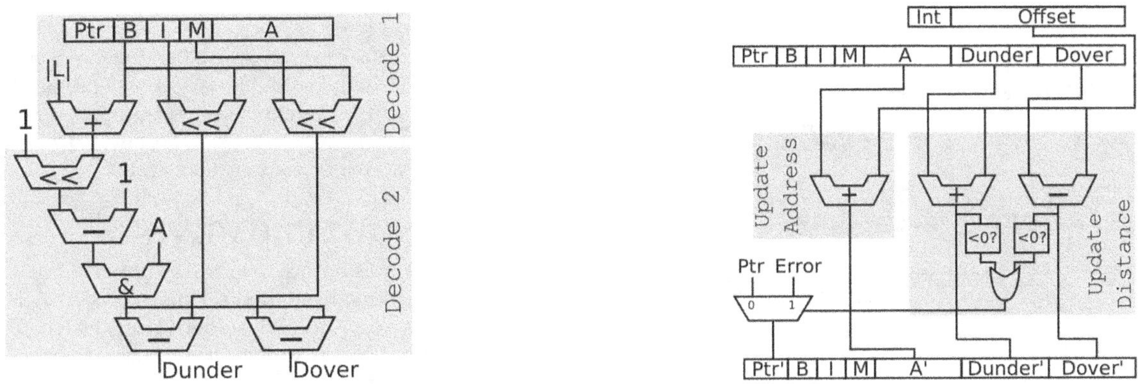

(a) BIMA Decode (`lw`) (b) BIMA Update (`addp`)

Figure 6: Data path for BIMA scheme

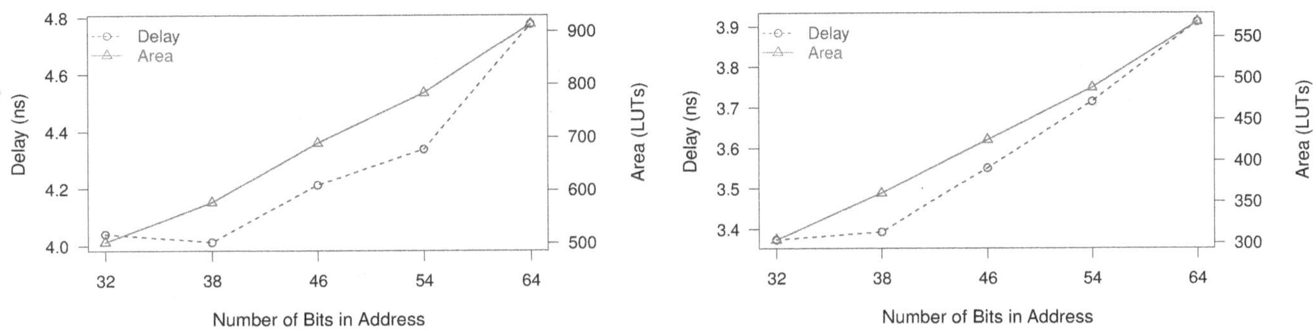

(a) BIMA Decode (`lw`) (b) BIMA Update (`addp`)

Figure 7: Area and Delay for BIMA scheme, $|B| = |I| = 6$

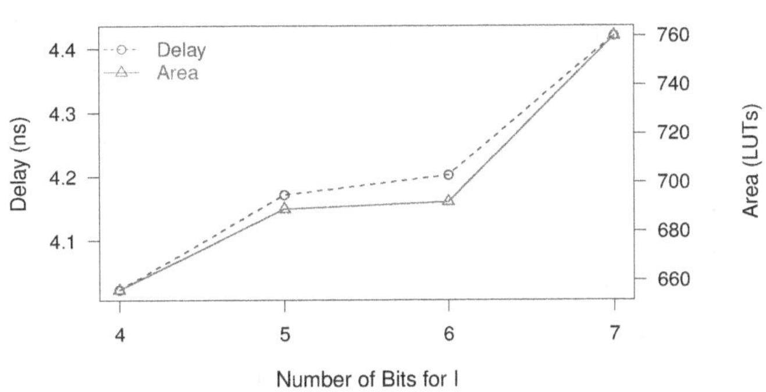

Figure 8: Area and delay for the BIMA decode (`lw`) for varying $|I|$ with $|B| = 6$, $|A| = 46$

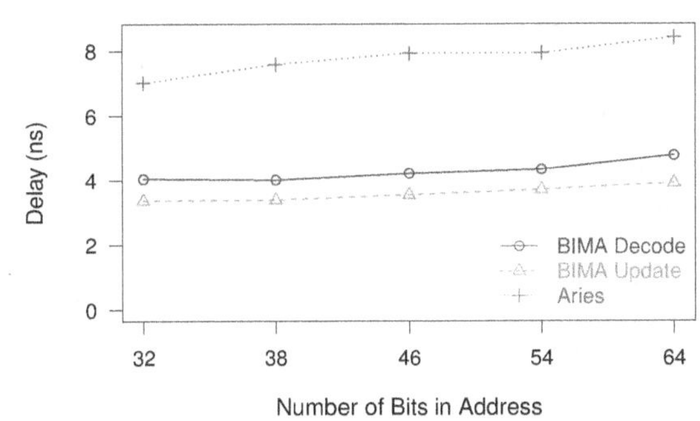

Figure 9: Delay comparison between Aries and BIMA encodings with $|I| = |L|$ with varying $|A|$

on `addp`, `lw`, and `sw` operations when the memory references hit in the L1 cache. Adding the 8 ns Aries `addp` operation to the pipeline could, however, dramatically degrade the processor's operating frequency.

The BIMA encoding also changes the pipeline due to the decoding of D_{under} and D_{over} after a load. The BIMA decode takes more than 4 ns for addresses using more than 46b, potentially increasing the cycle time. Also, if we decode the two distances in the last pipeline stage, then an `addp` operation whose argument is the pointer loaded from memory in an immediately preceding `lw` instruction (an `lw-addp` pair) requires a stall cycle: the D_{under} and D_{over} is needed for the `addp`, so we need to finish decoding the distances before `addp` can execute.

To mitigate this problem, we first split the decode data path into two stages—`Decode 1` and `Decode 2` in Fig. 6a. In our implementation, we can fetch from the data cache in less than 2.5 ns, so we use the remaining time in the Execute stage to execute the first part of decode (`Decode 1`). Then we finish the computation of D_{under} and D_{over} (`Decode 2`) in the Validate/Writeback stage. With this change, we avoid increasing the clock cycle. To remove the stall for `lw-addp`, we split the update (See Fig. 6b) into two stages as well: we keep the update address circuit (`Update Address`) in the

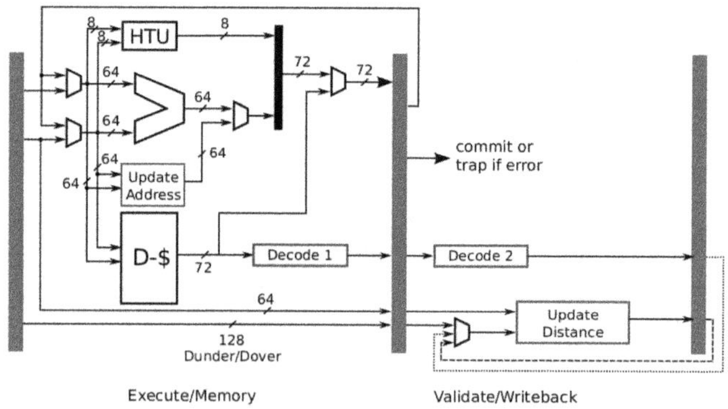

Figure 10: Last two stages of pipeline for BIMA encoding

Execute/Memory stage, and we move the update distance circuit (**Update Distance**) to the Validate/Writeback stage. Fig. 10 shows the resulting pipeline.

First we note that this change does not affect bypasses or stalls for any non-pointer computations. The number of pipeline stages stays the same, and any other unit remains unchanged. Let us now consider an `lw-addp` pair in this pipeline. The **addp** can happen immediately as the value (pointer) from memory can be bypassed in one cycle (dotted bypass in Fig. 10). While **addp** is computing the new address, **Decode 2** in the Validate/Writeback will have finished decoding the distances. Then the distances needed for **addp** will be available before the Validate/Writeback stage, and thus it will need no stall cycles. Similarly, an **addp-addp** pair does not cause any stalls either because we can bypass the D_{under} and D_{over} in the same fashion (dashed bypass in Fig. 10).

To avoid any stalls for an `addp-lw` pair, we use speculative execution. Since the target address is available by the end of the Execute stage, we bypass the updated address and load the value assuming the pointer is in bounds. When the **addp** distance update completes and the pointer used was determined to be out-of-bounds, we kill the load result, flush the pipeline, and trap to the error handler.

As a result, we maintain the same clock rate and stall conditions as the baseline processor without the Pointer Unit. That is, the BIMA encoding runs just as fast as the baseline processor without spatial safety checking (0% runtime overhead).

6. CONCLUSIONS

We have shown how it is possible to support fully mediated, fine-grained spatial safety without sacrificing performance. An appropriately low-fat pointer encoding keeps the memory impact small (64b pointers for a 46b address space) while simultaneously guaranteeing small and fast hardware decoding and small (<3%) memory fragmentation overhead. Even with an additional 8b tag on every word, the total memory overhead is under 16%. Suitable pipelining guarantees the extra work for decoding the low-fat pointer encoding does not create new stall cycles for the processor pipeline. Pointer updates are no more complex than additions, guaranteeing they do not degrade the processor clock cycle. Since software presents a large attack surface area (millions of lines of code in modern applications and kernels) with demonstrated high rates of vulnerability, there is an advantage to providing safety guarantees at the hardware level where the interface is narrower. Furthermore, as computers protect increasingly valuable assets, spending this modest number of relatively inexpensive transistors (comparable to a double-precision, floating-point adder) to increase safety and security seems a prudent investment.

7. ACKNOWLEDGMENTS

This material is based upon work supported by the DARPA CRASH program through the United States Air Force Research Laboratory (AFRL) under Contract No. FA8650-10-C-7090. The views expressed are those of the authors and do not reflect the official policy or position of the Department of Defense or the U.S. Government. Ben Karel, Cătălin Hriţcu, and Greg Morrisett provided valuable discussion and feedback on this paper.

8. REFERENCES

[1] Introduction to Intel Memory Protection extensions. `http://software.intel.com/en-us/articles/introduction-to-intel-memory-protection-extensions`. Accessed: 2013-08-01.

[2] P. Akritidis, M. Costa, M. Castro, and S. Hand. Baggy bounds checking: an efficient and backwards-compatible defense against out-of-bounds errors. In *Proceedings of the 18th Conference on USENIX Security Symposium*, pages 51–66, 2009.

[3] Aleph One. Smashing the Stack for Fun and Profit. *Phrack*, 7(49), November 1996.

[4] AMD Corporation. *AMD64 Architecture Programmer's Manual, Volume 2: System Programming*, revision 3.22 edition, September 2012.

[5] N. Binkert, B. Beckmann, G. Black, S. K. Reinhardt, A. Saidi, A. Basu, J. Hestness, D. R. Hower, T. Krishna, S. Sardashti, R. Sen, K. Sewell, M. Shoaib, N. Vaish, M. D. Hill, and D. A. Wood. The gem5 simulator. *SIGARCH Comput. Archit. News*, 39(2):1–7, Aug. 2011.

[6] Bluespec, Inc. Bluespec SystemVerilog.

[7] J. Brown, J. Grossman, A. Huang, and T. F. Knight, Jr. A capability representation with embedded address and nearly-exact object bounds. Technical Report 5, MIT AI Lab, April 2000. Aries Project.

[8] N. P. Carter, S. W. Keckler, and W. J. Dally. Hardware support for fast capability-based addressing. In *Proceedings of the international conference on Architectural support for programming languages and operating systems*, ASPLOS-VI, pages 319–327, 1994.

[9] S. Chen, B. Falsafi, P. B. Gibbons, M. Kozuch, T. C. Mowry, R. Teodorescu, A. Ailamaki, L. Fix, G. R. Ganger, B. Lin, and S. W. Schlosser. Log-based architectures for general-purpose monitoring of deployed code. In *1st Workshop on Architectural and System Support for Improving Software Dependability (ASID)*, pages 63–65. ACM, 2006.

[10] R. P. Colwell, E. F. Gehringer, and E. D. Jensen. Performance effects of architectural complexity in the Intel 432. *ACM Trans. Comput. Syst.*, 6:296–339, August 1988.

[11] J. Criswell, A. Lenharth, D. Dhurjati, and V. Adve. Secure virtual architecture: A safe execution

environment for commodity operating systems. In *Proceedings of the Symposium on Operating Systems Principles*, October 2007.

[12] D. Y. Deng and G. E. Suh. High-performance parallel accelerator for flexible and efficient run-time monitoring. In *IEEE/IFIP International Conference on Dependable Systems and Networks (DSN)*, pages 1–12. IEEE Computer Society, 2012.

[13] P. J. Denning and S. C. Schwartz. Properties of the working-set model. *Communications of the ACM*, 15(3):191–198, March 1972.

[14] J. B. Dennis and E. C. Van Horn. Programming semantics for multiprogrammed computations. *Communications of the ACM*, 9(3):143–155, March 1966.

[15] J. Devietti, C. Blundell, M. M. K. Martin, and S. Zdancewic. HardBound: Architectural support for spatial safety of the C programming language. In *Proceedings of the International Conference on Architectural Support for Programming Languages and Operating Systems*, pages 103–114, 2008.

[16] U. Dhawan, A. Kwon, E. Kadric, C. Hriţcu, B. C. Pierce, J. M. Smith, A. DeHon, G. Malecha, G. Morrisett, T. F. Knight, Jr., A. Sutherland, T. Hawkins, A. Zyxnfryx, D. Wittenberg, P. Trei, S. Ray, and G. Sullivan. Hardware support for safety interlocks and introspection. In *SASO Workshop on Adaptive Host and Network Security*, Sept. 2012.

[17] R. S. Fabry. Capability-based Addressing. *Communications of the ACM*, 17(7):403–412, July 1974.

[18] E. A. Feustel. On the advantages of tagged architecture. *IEEE Transactions on Computers*, C-22(7):644–656, July 1973.

[19] E. F. Gehringer and J. L. Keedy. Tagged architecture: How compelling are its advantages? In *Proceedings of the 12th International Symposium on Computer Architecture*, pages 162–170, 1985.

[20] R. Greenblatt, T. Knight, Jr., J. Holloway, D. Moon, and D. Weinreb. The LISP machine. In *Interactive Programming Environments*. McGraw-Hill, 1984.

[21] N. Hasabnis, A. Misra, and R. Sekar. Light-weight bounds checking. In *Proceedings of the Tenth International Symposium on Code Generation and Optimization*, pages 135–144, 2012.

[22] J. L. Henning. SPEC CPU2006 benchmark descriptions. *SIGARCH Comput. Archit. News*, 34(4):1–17, September 2006.

[23] M. E. Houdek, F. G. Soltis, and R. L. Hoffman. IBM System/38 Support for Capability-based Addressing. In *Proceedings of the Eighth Annual Symposium on Computer Architecture*, pages 341–348, 1981.

[24] C. Hriţcu, M. Greenberg, B. Karel, B. C. Pierce, and G. Morrisett. All your IFCException are belong to us. In *34th IEEE Symposium on Security and Privacy*, pages 3–17. IEEE Computer Society Press, May 2013.

[25] IBM. *IBM System/360 Principles of Operation*. 1968.

[26] Intel Corporation. *Intel64 and IA-32 Architectures Software Developer's Manual*, August 2012.

[27] T. Jim, J. G. Morrisett, D. Grossman, M. W. Hicks, J. Cheney, and Y. Wang. Cyclone: A safe dialect of C. In *ATEC '02: Proceedings of the General Track of the annual conference on USENIX Annual Technical Conference*, pages 275–288, 2002.

[28] D. Johnson. The Intel 432: A VLSI Architecture for Fault-Tolerant Computer Systems. *Computer*, 17:40–48, August 1984.

[29] H. M. Levy. *Capability Based Computer Systems*. Digital Press, 1984.

[30] S. Nagarakatte. *Practical Low-overhead Enforcement of Memory Safety for C Programs*. PhD thesis, University of Pennsylvania, 2012.

[31] S. Nagarakatte, J. Zhao, M. M. K. Martin, and S. Zdancewic. Softbound: Highly compatible and complete spatial memory safety for C. In *Proceedings of the ACM SIGPLAN Conference on Programming Language Design and Implementation*, pages 245–258, 2009.

[32] S. Nagarakatte, J. Zhao, M. M. K. Martin, and S. Zdancewic. CETS: Compiler enforced temporal safety for C. In *Proceedings of the International Symposium on Memory Management*, pages 31–40, 2010.

[33] G. C. Necula, J. Condit, M. Harren, S. McPeak, and W. Weimer. CCured: type-safe retrofitting of legacy software. *ACM Trans. Program. Lang. Syst.*, 27(3):477–526, May 2005.

[34] R. M. Needham and R. D. H. Walker. The Cambridge CAP computer and its protection system. In *Proceedings of the Symposium on Operating Systems Principles*, pages 1–10, Nov. 1977.

[35] E. I. Organick. *The MULTICS System: An Examination of Its Structure*. MIT Press, 1972.

[36] E. I. Organick. *Computer System Organization: The B5700/B6700 Series*. Academic Press, 1973.

[37] E. I. Organick. *A Programmer's View of the Intel 432 System*. McGraw-Hill, 1983.

[38] A. T. Phillips and J. S. Tan. Exploring security vulnerabilities by exploiting buffer overflow using the MIPS ISA. In *Proceedings of the SIGCSE technical symposium on Computer science education*, pages 172–176, New York, NY, USA, 2003. ACM.

[39] O. Ruwase and M. S. Lam. A practical dynamic buffer overflow detector. In *Proceedings of the 11th Annual Network and Distributed System Security Symposium*, pages 159–169, 2004.

[40] J. S. Shapiro, J. M. Smith, and D. J. Farber. Eros: a fast capability system. In *Proceedings of the Symposium on Operating Systems Principles*, pages 170–185. ACM, 1999.

[41] R. L. Sites. Alpha AXP Architecture. *Digital Technical Journal*, 4(4):1–17, 1992. Special Issue.

[42] R. N. M. Watson, J. Anderson, B. Laurie, and K. Kennaway. Capsicum: practical capabilities for UNIX. In *Proceedings of the 19th USENIX Security Symposium*, Washington, DC, August 2010.

[43] R. N. M. Watson, P. G. Neumann, J. Woodruff, J. Anderson, R. Anderson, N. Dave, B. Laurie, S. W. Moore, S. J. Murdoch, P. Paeps, M. Roe, and H. Saidi. CHERI: a research platform deconflating hardware virtualization and protection. In *Proc. RESoLVE*, March 2012.

[44] M. V. Wilkes and R. M. Needham. *The Cambridge CAP Computer and Its Operating System.* North Holland, 1979.

[45] W. Wulf, E. Cohen, W. Corwin, A. Jones, R. Levin, C. Pierson, and F. Pollack. Hydra: The kernel of a multiprocessor operating system. *Communications of the ACM*, 17(6):337–345, June 1974.

[46] W. A. Wulf, R. Levin, and S. P. Harbison. *HYDRA/C.mmp: An Experimental Computer System.* McGraw-Hill, 1981.

[47] Xilinx, Inc. Virtex-6 FPGA ML605 Evaluation Kit.

[48] Xilinx, Inc., 2100 Logic Drive, San Jose, CA 95124. *Virtex-6 FPGA Data Sheet: DC and Switching Characteristics*, September 2011. DS512.

[49] Xilinx, Inc., 2100 Logic Drive, San Jose, CA 95124. *LogiCORE IP Floating-Point Operator v6.0*, January 2012.

[50] Y. Younan, P. Philippaerts, L. Cavallaro, R. Sekar, F. Piessens, and W. Joosen. Paricheck: an efficient pointer arithmetic checker for C programs. In *Proceedings of the 5th ACM Symposium on Information, Computer and Communications Security*, pages 145–156, 2010.

APPENDIX

A. DYNAMIC INSTRUCTION IMPACT

Our main focus is to show the benefit of native hardware support to enforce spatial memory safety on every instruction. If we were to enforce the same level of checking using a conventional processor, we would need to replace a number of primitive operations with instruction sequences like those shown in Tab. 1 where in the second column we show the additional operations needed for spatial checking. In reality the compiler would add these extra instructions in the binary. However, we use instruction-trace based simulations to get a crude estimate of the impact on dynamic instruction count for such an enforcement without modifying any compiler. Our estimates illustrate how much work our investment in parallel checking hardware and compact encoding is effectively doing. These estimates are necessarily crude since the instruction sequences can be subverted below the level of the compiler, and do not account for optimizations a compiler could do to eliminate redundant checks. Also, we assume a single-issue in-order pipeline, whereas, on a superscalar processor, some of the extra instructions would fit in otherwise unused issue slots. For example, SoftBound reports only a 67% runtime overhead on 133% instruction count overhead [31].

A.1 Methodology

We evaluate the impact of the additional instructions for performing spatial checks on memory, on the programs from the SPEC2006 Benchmark Suite [22]. Instruction traces are produced using the `gem5` [5] environment simulating a 64-bit ALPHA ISA [41]. Since the ALPHA ISA used does not type pointers differently from integers, we must determine which values are actually pointers and require additional pointer operations. To do this, we first perform a pre-pass dataflow analysis that marks all registers used as addresses in load and store operations as pointers, then propagate that type information through the lifetime and use of those registers.

Table 1: Spatial Checking for Processors with no Fat Pointer Hardware Support

Primitive Operation	**ALPHA Operations**

pointer arithmetic
\$d←\$s+\$t
(Sec. 4.8.3)
	addq \$d.A, \$s.A, \$t
	cmpult \$q,\$d.A,\$s.base
	cmpult \$r,\$s.bound,\$d.A
	or \$q,\$q,\$r
	blbs \$q, bounds_error
	lda \$d.base,\$s.base,0
	lda \$d.bound,\$s.bound,0

store non-pointer mem[\$s]←\$t (Sec. 4.8.4)	cmpult \$q,\$s.A,\$s.base cmpult \$r,\$s.bound,\$s.A or \$q,\$q,\$r blbs \$q,bounds_error stq \$t,0(\$s)
store pointer mem[\$s]←\$t (Sec. 4.8.4)	cmpult \$q,\$s.A,\$s.base lda \$r,\$s.A,2 cmpult \$r,\$s.bound,\$r or \$q,\$q,\$r blbs \$q,bounds_error stq \$t.A,0(\$s.A) stq \$t.base,1(\$s.A) stq \$t.bound,2(\$s.A)
load non-pointer \$t←mem[\$s] (Sec 4.8.5)	cmpult \$q,\$s.A,\$s.base cmpult \$r,\$s.bound,\$s.A or \$q,\$q,\$r blbs \$q,bounds_error ldq \$t,0(\$s)

load pointer
\$t←mem[\$s]
(Sec. 4.8.5)
	cmpult \$q,\$s.A,\$s.base
	lda \$r,\$s.A,2
	cmpult \$r,\$s.bound,\$r
	or \$q,\$q,\$r
	blbs \$q,bounds_error
	ldq \$t.A,0(\$s.A)
	ldq \$t.base,1(\$s.A)
	ldq \$t.bound,2(\$s.A)

register target PC←\$s	cmpult \$q,\$s.A,\$s.base cmpult \$r,\$s.bound,\$s.A or \$q,\$q,\$r blbs \$q,bounds_error jr \$s.A

With all the registers annotated, we can then identify which operation must be an `addp` in our fat pointer architecture and which load and store operations are moving pointers to and from memory. Once identified, we perform a weighted sum of operations using the instruction counts from Tab. 1.

A.2 Overhead

Fig. 1 shows the estimated dynamic instructions in a non-fat pointer hardware ALPHA architecture performing spatial checks in software in comparison to our proposed architecture (see Sec. 3) with hardware support for fat pointers for a period of first 1 billion cycles. From the figure, we can observe that there is a maximum of 300% and on average, about 220% overhead in the number of dynamic instructions executed for performing spatial checks in software.

Breaking and Entering through the Silicon

Clemens Helfmeier,
Christian Boit
Berlin University of Technology
Department of Semiconductor Devices
Berlin, Germany
{clemens.helfmeier, christian.boit}
@tu-berlin.de

Dmitry Nedospasov,
Jan Krissler,
Jean-Pierre Seifert
Berlin University of Technology
Security in Telecommunications
Berlin, Germany
{dmitry, starbug, jpseifert}
@sec.t-labs.tu-berlin.de

Christopher Tarnovsky
IOActive
Vista, California
chris.tarnovsky@ioactive.com

ABSTRACT

As the surplus market of failure analysis equipment continues to grow, the cost of performing invasive IC analysis continues to diminish. Hardware vendors in high-security applications utilize security by obscurity to implement layers of protection on their devices. High-security applications must assume that the attacker is skillful, well-equipped and well-funded. Modern security ICs are designed to make readout of decrypted data and changes to security configuration of the device impossible. Countermeasures such as meshes and attack sensors thwart many state of the art attacks. Because of the perceived difficulty and lack of publicly known attacks, the IC backside has largely been ignored by the security community. However, the backside is currently the weakest link in modern ICs because no devices currently on the market are protected against fully-invasive attacks through the IC backside. Fully-invasive backside attacks circumvent all known countermeasures utilized by modern implementations. In this work, we demonstrate the first two practical fully-invasive attacks against the IC backside. Our first attack is fully-invasive backside microprobing. Using this attack we were able to capture decrypted data directly from the data bus of the target IC's CPU core. We also present a fully invasive backside circuit edit. With this attack we were able to set security and configuration fuses of the device to arbitrary values.

Keywords

Integrated Circuit Attack; Backside

Categories and Subject Descriptors

C.3 [**Special-Purpose and Application-Based Systems**]: Smartcards

CCS'13, November 4–8, 2013, Berlin, Germany.
ACM 978-1-4503-2477-9/13/11.
http://dx.doi.org/10.1145/2508859.2516717

1. INTRODUCTION

Smaller technology nodes in modern Integrated Circuits (ICs) have ushered in many innovations in IC manufacturing. In security ICs, the additional resources and complexities offered by modern manufacturing processes have allowed vendors to increase the security threshold of these devices. The available resources are utilized to implement additional sensors and countermeasures to thwart IC analysis. For example, all embedded memories are encrypted on modern security ICs [18]. Design rules applied to modern implementations ensure that security relevant signals are routed on the lower metal layers of a device making semi- and fully-invasive frontside analysis significantly more difficult to perform. One common countermeasure against such attacks are *meshes*, redundant layers of metallization on top of the device itself. Meshes are commonly categorized as *active* and *passive*. Passive meshes are simply additional layers of metallization designed to hamper semi-invasive attacks, such as laser fault injection [4].

For the fully-invasive attacker, passive meshes can be considered an additional deprocessing step, while active meshes are an actual preventative measure. Unlike passive meshes, active meshes are signal-bearing interconnects that are evaluated to verify the integrity of the device. Common invasive techniques, such as Microprobing and Focused Ion Beam (FIB) circuit edits, risk shorting the mesh to other signals on the device. Active meshes are commonly implemented over multiple layers of metallization, increasing the likelihood of a detectable fault. If the device is compromised and a fault is detected in the integrity of the mesh, the device can subsequently execute a mitigation routine that destroys any secret data stored on the device. Mesh complexities continue to become increasingly elaborate. In [7], the authors proposed stacking multiple IC dies to effectively integrate a high-density multi-metal-layer active mesh to fully encapsulate the device in the middle.

However, the additional cost as well as durability and manufacturability concerns will likely exclude their application in certain fields such as smartcards. Most devices for security applications remain single die solutions. Nevertheless, active meshes can be integrated onto single-die solutions as well. In [26], the first public attack against a modern multi-metal-layer active mesh was demonstrated. Here an Infineon SLE 66PE active mesh was circumvented. This particular mesh consists of two layers of signal bearing interconnects, with a passive mesh layer in between. To circumvent the mesh a tedious FIB circuit edit was employed to rewire the individual mesh traces, allowing for an opening large enough to interface with traces within the central processing unit's (CPU) core directly.

Current implementations lack sufficient protection of the IC backside. Hence, certain forms of semi-invasive analysis are completely unimpeded when implemented through the IC backside. Semi-invasive Photonic Emission Analysis (PEA), for example, can be utilized to recover the intrinsic emissions that occur when the transistor is switching [16, 22]. Such attacks are completely passive and cannot be detected by the device. However, they also require the integration of millions of traces and can easily be thwarted by limiting the amount of times an algorithm can be executed by the target device. Semi-invasive laser glitching has also been shown to be effective from the IC backside [28]. However, light sensors are commonly integrated into modern secure ICs and can also trigger attack mitigation routines upon detecting a laser spot.

In this work we present two successful fully-invasive backside attacks. Currently, no IC implementations protect the backside of the device against fully-invasive attacks. Two common goals of fully-invasive IC analysis is the exfiltration of decrypted data from the device's core and changes to the device configuration and security settings. We were able to successfully trench through a device's bulk silicon substrate and microprobe the data on the CPU core's databus. We succeeded in capturing decrypted data on the device as the data had already been deciphered by the hardware decryption function at this particular location within the circuit. We also successfully performed a backside circuit edit of the device's fuses by severing and connecting traces on the first metal layer of the device. The fuse bits are responsible for storing the device's security and configuration settings and could be set to arbitrary values by our attack. To the best of our knowledge this is the first work to demonstrate successful attacks that utilize fully-invasive backside microprobing and a successful backside FIB edit. Our attacks circumvent *all* countermeasures currently employed in security ICs. Countermeasures that protect against invasive attacks, such as active meshes, are currently only implemented on the frontside of the IC and do not protect against backside attacks.

The main contributions of this work are:

Backside Permanent Circuit Modification.
We successfully changed values stored within the device's configuration and security fuses. Fuses are commonly used to enable or disable certain functions on the IC, such as On-Chip-Debug (OCD) facilities. By utilizing such a circuit edit, security features such as copy protection can be circumvented.

Backside Data Exfiltration.
We were able to successfully microprobe the device's core databus. The location we chose ensured that the data had already been deciphered by the hardware decryption funciton. By setting the voltage at the output of our probing solution, or by tying the trace to a voltage rail on the device, the device can be prevented from executing branching instructions. If the clock of the device is slowed down significantly the control flow of the device's execution can be manipulated.

Mitigation techniques against such attacks.
We present several mitigation techniques that should be implemented in future generations of ICs to make such attacks significantly more difficult. A simple set of design rules can be applied to the device to make such attacks significantly less cost-effective for the attacker.

The rest of this work is structured as follows: In Section 2, we provide additional background information on the construction of modern ICs as well as their inherent vulnerabilities. Next, in Section 3, the details of our experimental setup are presented including the steps necessary for sample preparation. Our experimental results are presented and explained in Section 4. We discuss the impact on current generation and future IC implementations in Section 5. Finally we conclude the work in Section 6.

2. BACKGROUND

2.1 Terminology

The attacks introduced in this work penetrate all the layers of the device to various degrees. Hence, it benefits the reader to be familiar with the correct terminology. This section provides an overview of terms used in the rest of the paper and in Sections 3 and 4 in particular. This is by no means an exhaustive overview, as this section contains many generalizations. We encourage the reader to consult respected works on the topic of semiconductor manufacturing and IC failure analysis [19, 25].

Figure 1 depicts the construction of a modern IC as well as the result of modifications to the circuit. Transistors, consisting of drain and source diffused into the silicon (dark gray) and gate oxide and gate material deposited above the silicon (black), are formed adjacently. In Complementary Metal Oxide Semiconductor technology (CMOS) both types of transistors are required. P-type transistors are generally fabricated inside an n-doped well region, the n-well (medium gray). The n-wells are approximately one to two micrometers deep. By comparison, the drain and source diffusions are just two to three hundered nanometers in depth. The gate is formed between source and drain by depositing either poly-silicon or metal on top of the gate dielectric and silicon substrate. Transistors are separated from each other using various isolation technique. Older technologies used a process called Local Oxidation of Silicon (LOCOS) to create an isolation barrier, whereas modern technologies generally employ a process called Shallow Trench Isolation (STI). The STI (light gray), the n-wells and the drain and source diffusions are situated within the *silicon substrate* itself. The area consisting of the gate, the source and the drain is referred to as the *active area* of the transistor.

Individual transistors are connected with each other by *metal interconnects*, situated above the transistor level (dotted). These interconnects are often called *metalization* or simply *metal layers* as they are stacked on top of the transistors. In between two such metal layers, an *inter-level dielectric* (ILD) or *passivation* layer is fabricated, isolating the two metal layers electrically (light gray). To create electrical connections between two adjacent metal layers, vias are formed through the ILD. The connections between the first metal layer and the transistor devices are called *contacts*. The number of alternating interconnect layers and inter-level dielectric layers in ICs varies, depending on the process. Modern smartcards, for example, generally have 5-7 metal layers, including meshes. Devices of the same family requiring a lower security threshold, such as SIM cards, utilize only 3-5 metal layers. In security terminology the side of the device that contains the metallization is generally referred to as the IC *frontside*. The opposite side, which lacks any active devices and consists solely of the silicon substrate is referred to as the IC *backside*.

Modern ICs consist of many layers. Figure 1 illustrates a total of seven layers of metallization on top of the gate layer. Metallization is numbered from *metal 1* to *metal 7*. On modern security ICs such as the Infineon SLE 66PE, the metals 5, 6 and 7 form the meshes and shields. Meshes are designed to make attacks such as microprobing and circuit edits more difficult.

2.2 Sample Preparation

Invasive attacks are generally classified by the amount of sample preparation necessary to perform the attack. No sample preparation is required to perform *non-invasive* attacks. Partial or complete removal of the device package is necessary for *semi-invasive* attacks. In addition to depackaging *fully-invasive* attacks result in destructive modifications to the device [2].

In the past, invasive attacks were carried out through the frontside of the IC. Smaller feature sizes, additional metal layers and countermeasures, such as meshes and shields, have made such attacks substantially more difficult on modern security ICs. Additionally, design rules ensure that security-relevant traces are placed on lower layers of the device so that they cannot be probed as easily from the frontside. Hence, backside attacks become much more significant as they can circumvent these security measures directly.

ICs are usually concealed inside a package material that must first be removed so that invasive analysis can be performed. During frontside sample preparation, package materials, such as epoxy, are removed with wet-chemical etching to avoid destruction of the bond wires and topmost metalization layers. Depending on the materials used in the device package, different chemicals or a combination of mechanical and wet chemical etching may be necessary. Subsequently, an additional etching process is used to remove the passivation layers of the device. However, passivation layers can also be effectively removed using the FIB system directly. Nevertheless, certain types of devices, such as smartcards, must be rebonded as epoxy removal leaves them brittle. Moreover, frontside sample preparation is extremely difficult on devices that utilize flip-chip packages.

In contrast, backside preparation can be performed by mechanical milling or polishing of the device. With milling machines, such as the Ultratec ASAP-1, the package material and the silicon substrate are milled in a single automated process without the need for wet chemical etching. During this process the bond wires connecting the IC to the contacts remain intact as they are located on the frontside of the device. Moreover, the backside of the device can be accessed directly on most smartcard packages by simply removing the ground contact. After polishing the silicon substrate down to approximately 30 µm, the FIB is used to etch the remaining bulk silicon material, see Figure 1. Mechanical thinning of the silicon substrate speeds up the FIB circuit edit preparation significantly but can also be potentially omitted [20]. Changes in contrast of the FIB image indicate the doped silicon of the n-wells and are employed as endpoint detection during FIB thinning. This allows for access to every circuit node without significant degradation of overall device performance [6, 21].

2.3 Invasive IC Analysis

Invasive attacks are particularly powerful as they can directly alter the control flow of the program being executed by the device. Such attacks can also target specific locations of the device, for example, where the data has previously been decrypted by the hardware. Reverse-engineering techniques, such as automatic detection of gates, are employed to identify vulnerable logic [17]. After vulnerable logic has been identified, the inputs and outputs of the logic are targeted. Semi-invasive attacks, such as laser stimulation have been used to introduce momentary faults or adversely affect the leakage characteristics of the circuit so that data can be recovered non-invasively [23, 24]. Fully-invasive attacks commonly interface with the circuit directly. Such attacks are also capable of circumventing and disabling on-die countermeasures and directly manipulating data as it is processed by the IC. Two prevalent forms of fully-invasive IC analysis are microprobing and FIB circuit editing. Microprobing is generally used for data exfiltration, whereas FIB circuit edits are used to permanently modify the circuit.

Invasive microprobing allows for an attacker to interface directly with a target's data bus [2]. From the frontside, such attacks require an attacker to remove any layers of passivation covering the signals of interest. Once the data bus is contacted, the attacker can capture any data on the bus during execution. In practice, microprobing is limited by the amount of probing needles that can be simultaneously placed on an IC. However, fewer needles can be used if data is captured over multiple measurements [13].

One common microprobing technique is to use the needle to introduce static and dynamic transient faults to the circuit [4]. It is possible to set certain bus lines to an arbitrary value by grounding or driving them. By using multiple probing needles, an attacker can capture and manipulate data on the bus simultaneously. A common microprobing technique for readout of embedded memories is known as memory linearization [2]. In most instruction sets, the opcode encoding of branching instructions share a small set of bits. For example, for the Atmel AVR architecture used in both devices analyzed in this work, bit 15 is `1` for every branching instruction [3]. Hence, statically or dynamically setting bit 15 to `0`, i.e. grounding it with a probing needle, renders the device incapable of executing branching instructions during this period of time. Such techniques are used to selectively execute branches. Meanwhile, other parts of the processor architecture continue to function nominally. The program-counter continues to count up making it possible to sequentially readout all the memory addresses of the device [1].

FIB circuit edits are commonly performed in conjunction with other invasive attacks such as microprobing. FIBs are particularly useful when permanent modifications are necessary. FIBs are widely used to selectively remove passivation on an IC with a high degree of accuracy. A FIB circuit edit can connect nodes on the device as well as sever the connection between connected nodes. For example, code linearization can also be achieved with a FIB by tying bus

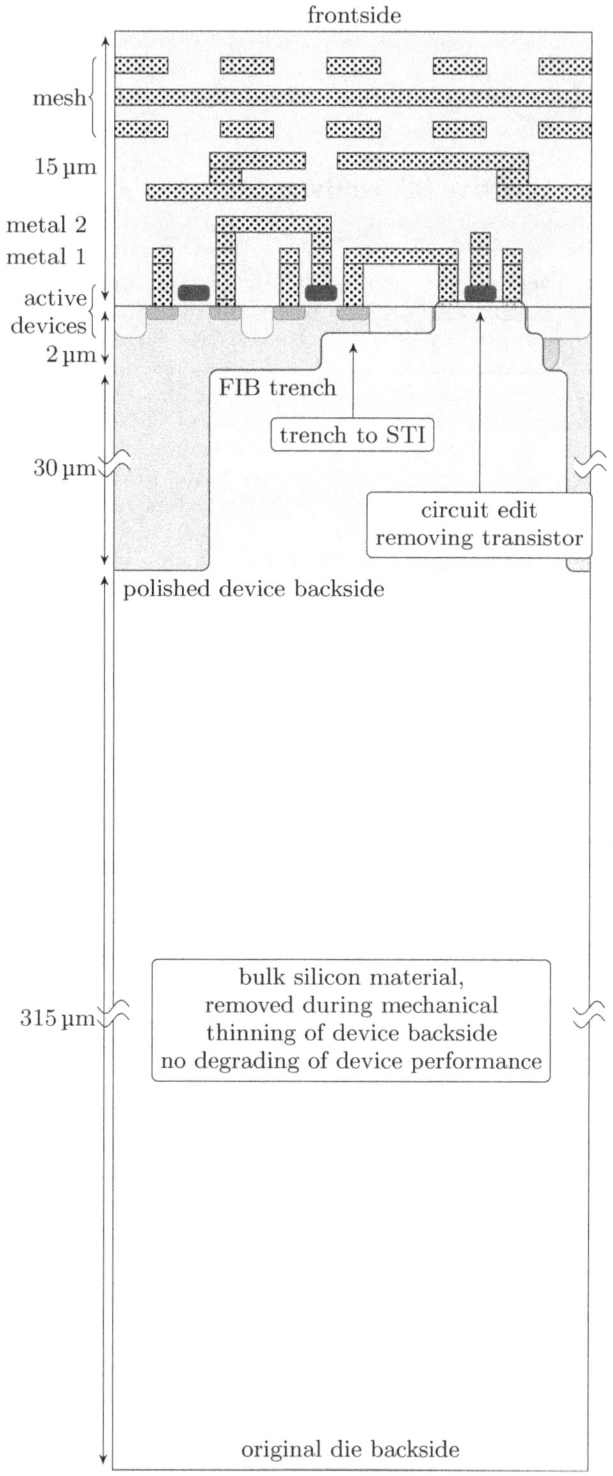

Figure 1: Cross section of a modern IC following backside preparation. After mechanically removing the bulk silicon material, the remaining device thickness is comparable to the thickness of the frontside. The device continues to operate nominally because the active transistors are unaffected. Such preparation techniques yield the attacker access to any signal on the device as they can expose every single node of the circuit.

lines to the ground and supply rails of the device. However, data must still be extracted by probing the data bus.

One particularly powerful application of the FIB is the manipulation of security sensors and circuits on the device. The output of a security sensor can be cut so that it cannot alert the CPU in case a fault is detected. FIBs are also widely employed to circumvent meshes [2]. They can be used to interface to layers of the IC that are otherwise buried under metallization. Using such techniques, even multi-signal active meshes can be rewired and an interconnect to a signal of interest can be created using FIB deposition [26].

Invasive IC analysis techniques are regarded state-of-the-art, yet they are only employed on the frontside of the device. By switching from frontside attacks to attacks through the silicon substrate, only the necessary sample preparation steps change. The attacks can otherwise be carried out in a similar fashion. In this work, we present the first successful micro-probing attack and the first permanent circuit modification performed through the backside of the device.

3. SETUP

This section outlines the failure analysis equipment employed to perform the attacks introduced in this work. Two different ICs were attacked in our experiments – the Atmel AT90SC3232C and the Atmel ATmega328P. The ATmega328P is a freely programmable microcontroller, whereas the AT90SC3232C is a security IC with the standard ISO7816 interface. Both ICs utilize the 8-bit AVR architecture.

3.1 Sample Preparation

All samples used in this work were mechanically backside thinned to approximately 30 µm of remaining bulk silicon thickness using the Ultratec ASAP-1 semi-automated polishing machine, see Figure 1. Both devices came in standard plastic surface-mount packages. The original packages were retained as the mechanical thinning of the substrate could be performed without depackaging the device.

The thinned devices were spin-coated with Ultratec's FIB friendly anti reflective coating (ARC) imaging fluid to enhance imaging contrast and protect the devices from aggressive chemicals during FIB processing. The devices were inversely soldered to a custom printed circuit board (PCB) that exposed the polished IC backside. The Hammamatsu PHEMOS-1000 was used to produce reflective laser scanning images of the ATMega328P. Points of interest were directly identified in the reflective laser image, see Figure 6. For the AT90SC3232 smartcard device, optical microscope images of metal layers one, two and three had been acquired prior to the experiments, see Figure 4.

3.2 Focused Ion Beam Preparation

The PCB carrying the respective device was then mounted in the FIB vacuum chamber of the DCG OptiFIB. This particular FIB system integrates a coaxial-optical path directly into the ion column allowing for optical microscope imaging simultaneously to FIB processing. Though the optical system simplifies navigation and increases process control capabilities during FIB editing, it is not mandatory for a successful attack. The FIB is equipped with gases for IC modification including xenon-di-flourine and iodine-based gases for etching. Insulator deposition gas and molybdenum-based conductor deposition gas were used for deposition. FIB navigation was performed using the coaxial optical column at

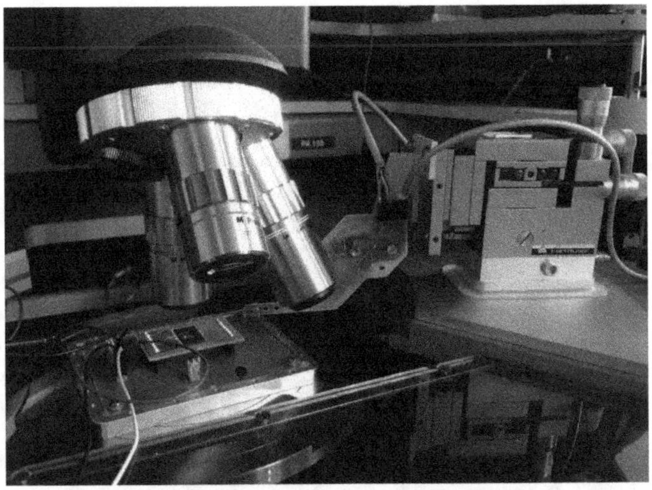

Figure 2: Probing station, custom probing buffer and the AT90SC3232C target device. The tungsten probing needle used for this work has a shaft diameter of 10 µm and an approximate point radius of 0.1 µm at its tip. As these dimensions are only a fraction of a human hair, the needle is not visible in the photograph.

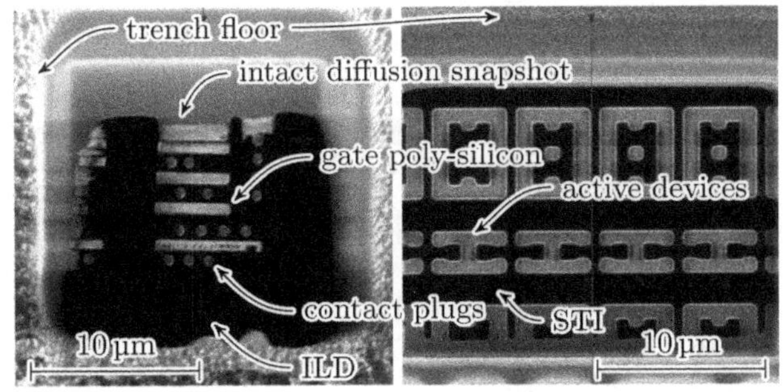

Figure 3: Endpoint images for the non-STI device (left) and the STI device (right). The endpoint for the milling process in both cases is the first visible material contrast. For non-STI devices the first material contrast is between the gate material and contact plugs. At this point the transistor has been severely damaged. For STI devices, the first material contrast is the STI layer. At this point, the devices retain full functionality with an active device thickness of approximately 300 nm.

a wavelength where the silicon substrate is transparent, i.e. 1000 nm.

After identifying and navigating to the area of interest, a FIB trench of 300 µm × 300 µm was milled down to the n-wells, leaving approximately 2 µm of active device thickness. The FIB trench surface was passivated by insulator deposition. At this stage, the device is fully-prepared for the FIB circuit edit. Additionally, the substrate is sufficiently thin such that the contrast images reveal the potential differences at the n-wells of the device, see Figure 7.

3.3 Backside Microprobing

Backside microprobing of the AT90SC3232C was carried out on a dedicated probing station, see Figure 2. A Karl Süss PA 150 probing station was used in conjunction with Karl Süss PH 150 micro-manipulators and GGB T-4-10 probing needles. To measure signals on the target device, the manipulators were equipped with a simple probing buffer circuit on a custom PCB. The probing buffer was designed to have a very low input capacitance, ensuring that slew-rates of on-chip signals did not degrade significantly. Moreover, such a setup makes it possible to probe even high speed signals. Signals were captured using the Rigol DS4030 digital storage oscilloscope.

4. RESULTS

The two devices used in this work differ significantly in technology. The ATmega328P is a relatively modern microcontroller that utilizes shallow trench isolation (STI) to separate individual transistors, see Figure 1 in Section 2. However, the AT90SC3232C is fabricated in an older process technology which utilized an isolation technique other than STI. In general, we will refer to the manufacturing process of the AT90SC3232C device as *non-STI*. Ironically, even though the feature sizes of this device are significantly larger, performing backside FIB edits on this device is more difficult. The lack of STI makes determining the endpoint of an etching process far more difficult and requires an experienced FIB operator, see Figure 3.

Finding the approximate position of the point of interest is possible using near-IR optical imaging. However, for the subsequent circuit edit, a more precise sample alignment is necessary. The differences in the fabrication of the two devices resulted in different alignment procedures for the respective backside FIB circuit edits. The milling process is continued in the vicinity of the point of interest. In case of the STI device, the STI layer provides the first material contrast in the secondary electron image and is clearly visible in Figure 3 as the dark area surrounding the active transistors. The STI contrast image allows for high precision alignment of the order of tens of nanometers without damaging the circuit.

Non-STI devices are damaged prior to reaching the first material contrast in the secondary electron image, see Figure 3. This is due to the fact that the depth of the isolation used in older devices is significantly less than in STI-devices. Hence, for a successful edit of non-STI devices a location must be carefully selected that contains no active devices, which would otherwise be damaged during milling. Subsequently the device is thinned down until a metal layer is exposed. The exposed metal can then be used for precise alignment of the sample.

After achieving high precision alignment, the FIB CE was carried out. Section 4.1 details the steps for contacting the decrypted bus lines of the AT90SC3232C. In section 4.2, the results of editing the fuse bits of the ATmega328P are presented.

4.1 Backside Data Exfiltration

For successful probing of non-STI processes, optical alignment must be used. From the optical image, the approximate position of the circuit edit location can be estimated.

Due to larger feature sizes of the non-STI processes, high precision is not necessarily required for success. After approximate optical navigation, metal interconnects on metal 2 can be exposed directly, see Figure 4. To verify the opening of the correct interconnect, the pattern is compared to the frontside optical microscope image acquired by delayering the device in a previous step. In our case, only a single interconnect needed to be contacted. To ensure that only the target metal interconnect is actually contacted, insulator is deposited over all of the metal interconnects. The target interconnect is then reopened and contacted using conductor deposition. Errors during this process can be corrected in a subsequent edit. Hence, such a circuit edit is near-foolproof. Figure 4 presents the circuit edit step-by-step. The lower right image shows the final result including the conductor deposition to increase the contact area for the microprobing needle. Note, the circuit continued to function nominally as microprobing has no adverse affects on system performance. Moreover if the attacker controls the system clock any performance degradation from the additional capacitance of the probing needle can be compensated for by reducing the system clock.

After modifying the device using the FIB, the device was placed in the probing station. The probing needle contacted the deposited conductor material, which in turn contacted the target metal interconnect. The device was stimulated by performing an ISO7816 cold reset of the device. The device's answer to reset was verified, and signal traces of the data on the bus line was captured, see Figure 5.

4.2 Backside Permanent Circuit Modification

Fuses are large single-bit non-volatile memory elements that can be empirically identified in the corresponding laser scanning reflective images, see Figure 6. All fuse bits had a similar structure and layout. Other than the large floating gate itself, each fuse consists of logic similar to the synthesized logic elsewhere on the device. Each fuse circuit also contained the analog circuitry necessary for programming, reading and storing the fuse bit information.

After milling the area of the fuse bits down to the n-wells, passive voltage contrast of the unpowered device was used for navigation. The fuse bits are visible as regular structures within the trench floor, see Figure 7. As the fuse bit information is stored in a floating gate transistor, the status will cause a minor alteration of the electrostatic field. This alternation can be detected by active or passive voltage contrast depending on the configuration, see Figure 7. For passive voltage contrast, the device is unpowered and thus incapable of preventing or detecting the operators actions. When the device is powered up, higher potential differences increase the contrast of the wells and the configuration of the floating gate, but also potentially risk detection by a circuit with adequate attack sensors. As this particular device is not equipped with backside sensitive FIB sensors, there is no penalty for powering the device while reading out the fuse configuration.

Fuse bits are based on floating gate transistors, similar to flash or EEPROM memory. The characteristic difference to other non-volatile memories is that fuse bits are generally not addressed or read-out like other memories. Instead the state of the fuse is used as enable signal for various circuitry on the device. Common situations are clock and boot configurations as well as security configurations to enable or disable the reading of the device memory. There are several possible approaches to set the fuses to arbitrary values. For

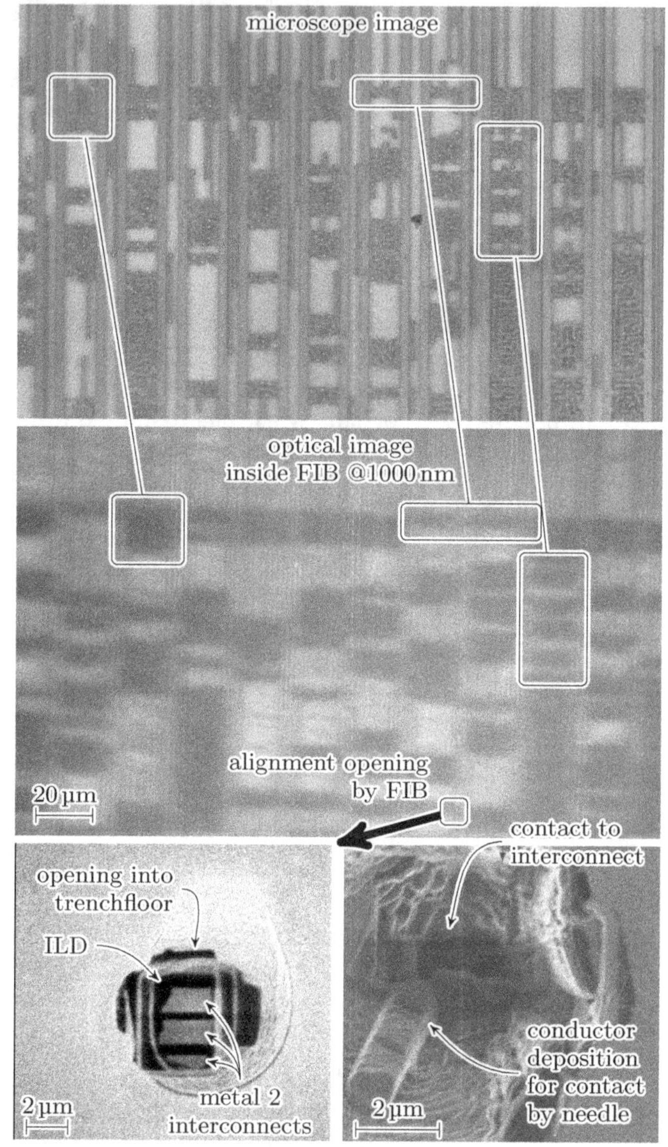

Figure 4: Backside navigation to the target site on the non-STI device. From frontside microscope images of the metal 1 layer (top image), active areas can be identified in optical near-IR image inside FIB chamber (middle image). The trench floor is then opened down to metal 2 (bottom left image), which then allows for precise alignment for final circuit edit (bottom right image). Note, on an STI device the STI layer would be used for alignment instead.

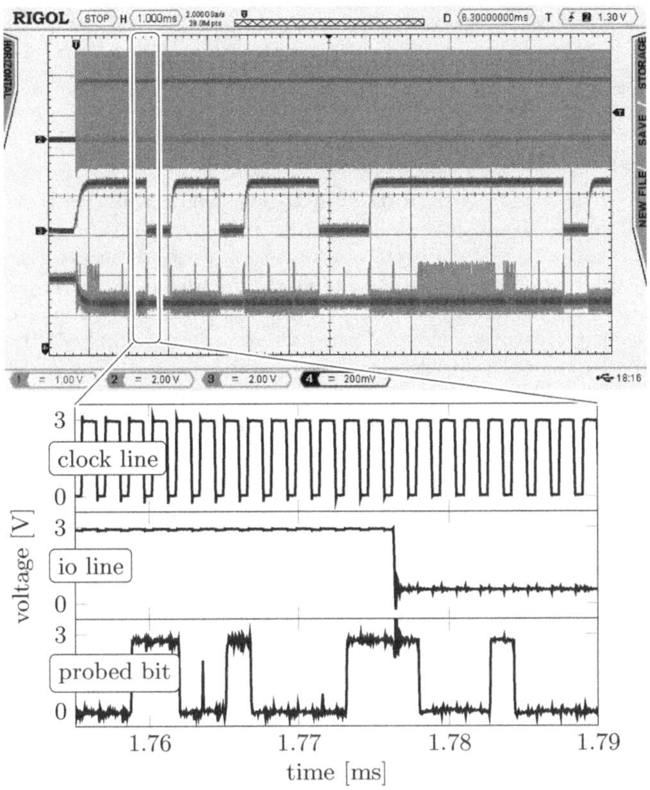

Figure 5: Captured trace and I/O interface status of the Atmel AT90S3232 security IC. The traces were captured on the backside prepared sample from the FIB circuit modification. A custom probing buffer circuit was used for conditioning the target signal.

example, the read amplifier or the digital output logic can be modified or driven. We chose to modify the floating gate structure as this structure is particularly large to facilitate high-voltage programming.

As the device is fabricated in an STI process, precise alignment can be achieved upon reaching the STI layer, see Figure 8. In order to set the fuse arbitrarily, the floating gate transistor is first removed, yielding a *programmed* fuse bit, according to the vendors terminology. Conversely, the fuse bit can be *erased* by depositing a conductive trace between the floating gate transistor's drain and source contact plugs, see Figure 9. These two circuit edit modifications can be performed multiple times on the same fuse bit, allowing for fuse states to be changed indefinitely. As the transistor is hard-wired to either on-state (conductor deposited) or off-state (transistor removed), the fuse bit can no longer be electrically programmed or erased. Thus, the specified function of the fuse bit is irreparably damaged by the circuit edit. However, since fuse bits are generally not modified during product life time, such an edit does not affect the overall functionality of the device. After altering the fuse bit state to either *programmed* or *erased* state, the device copy-protection mechanisms can be circumvented, yielding any secret information stored on the device.

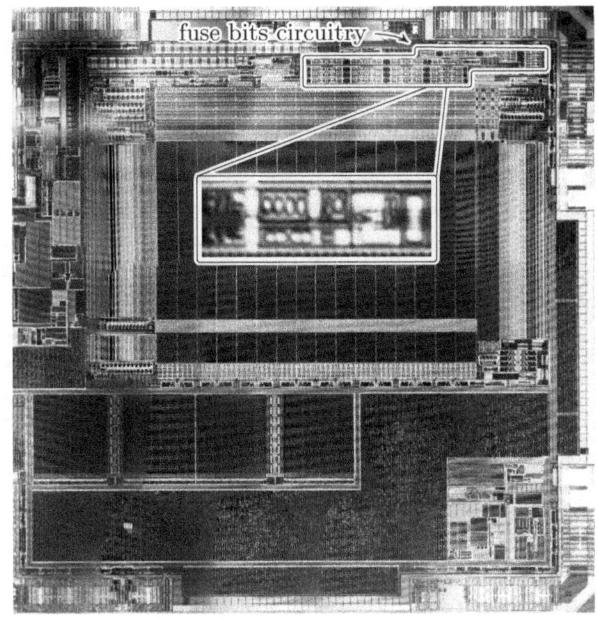

Figure 6: Laser scanning reflective image of the ATMega328P. The device contains a total of 40 fuse bits in the highlighted area. Each fuse bit consists of a non-volatile cell, programming circuitry and accompanying logic.

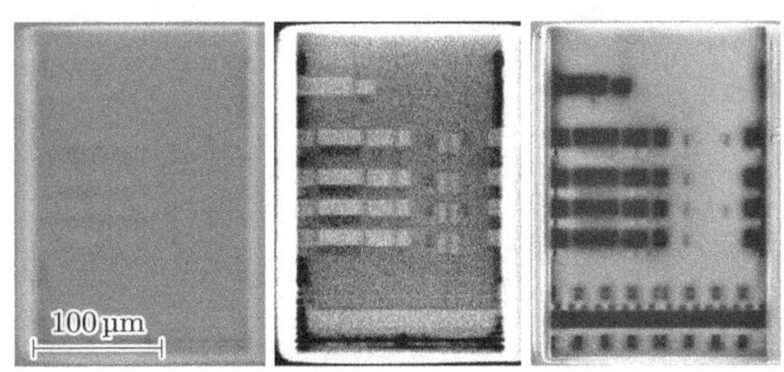

Figure 7: Secondary electron (SE) images of the trench floor containing eight fuse bit instances. The left-most image depicts the result after milling down to the n-wells. The middle image is the left-most image following after post-processing in an image editor. Note, that after post-processing the fuse status is clearly visible. The right most image shows the same location while the device is powered up. When powered there is sufficient contrast to read the fuse status without the need for image processing.

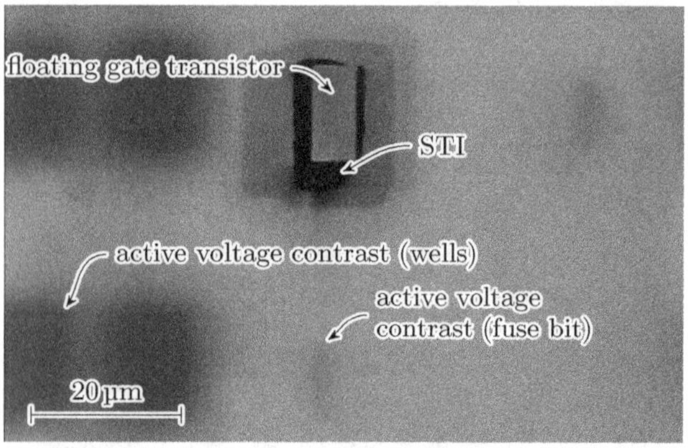

Figure 8: Secondary electron (SE) image of STI exposed floating gate transistor and surrounding fuse bit instances. The device was powered up during image acquisition. Hence, the fuse status is clearly visible in the active voltage contrast. The status of the adjacent fuse bits are visible as well.

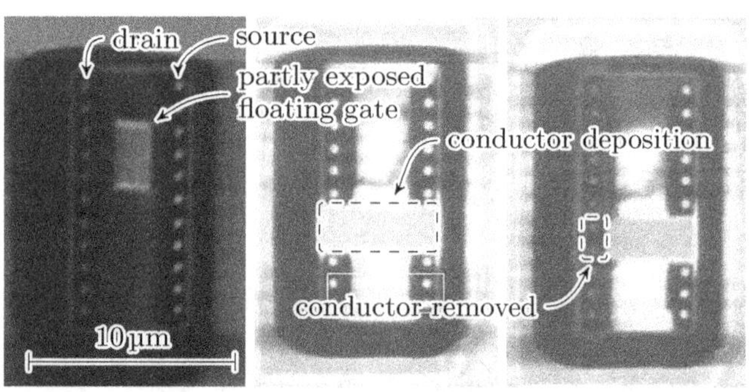

Figure 9: Secondary electron (SE) image of circuit edit on floating gate transistor. The three images show the removal of the floating gate transistor, exposure of the contact plugs and poly-silicon gate (left image), the shorting of source and drain by conductor deposition (middle image) and the subsequent removal of parts of the conductor deposition to again erase the fuse (right image). The device has been powered up for better visibility of the effect of the circuit edit: The left contact plug row shows up dark (no connection to right row) or light (electrical connection to right row), respectively.

5. DISCUSSION

In Section 4 we presented two fully-invasive attacks against modern ICs. In this section we consider the implications of these attacks.

5.1 Data Exfiltration

We successfully performed fully-invasive backside data exfiltration. To achieve this, the data bus signals on the metal 2 layer of the device were contacted. A probing needle connected to a simple probing buffer circuit was used to recover the data. The AT90SC3232C implements several modern security features. First of all, non-volatile memories of the device, i.e. the program memory, are encrypted. Hence, an attacker cannot decipher the program memory without first reverse engineering the encryption function and recovering the secret key. However, the data must also be deciphered in the core of the device as the CPU cannot execute encrypted data. Hence, our attack focused on a location within the CPU core where the data had already been deciphered by the hardware decryption function.

Our buffer-amplifier design included jumpers with which the probing needle could be grounded or set to the supply voltage of target. By setting the needle to a particular voltage, signals on the data bus of the target device can be overridden. For example, by grounding the signal, a logical `0` would subsequently be latched by the corresponding instruction register of the device. Since the AT90SC3232C utilizes the 8-bit AVR architecture, our attack targeted bit 15 of the data bus. This technique is widely used in memory linearization attacks where particular bus bits are overridden so that arbitrary instructions are latched [2]. The encoding of 8-bit AVR opcodes is such that all branching instructions are encoded with a `1` at bit 15. In the simplest memory linearization attack, the attacker simply grounds the line correspond to bit 15 ensuring that branching instructions are no longer decoded properly. The other bus lines remain unaffected. By dynamically driving the needle it is possible to selectively execute branches and alter the control flow of the program. With an additional FIB circuit edit memory linearization and microprobing of bit 15 can be performed simultaneously. The bus line can be severed from the output of the instruction register and tied to the ground rail so that a `0` will be statically latched by the core. Meanwhile, the valid output of the instruction register can be probed.

5.2 Permanent Circuit Modification

Many security countermeasures are implemented as hardware functions on modern security ICs. The fully-invasive backside circuit edit targeted the fuse bits of the Atmel ATMega328P. The ATMega328P utilizes the fuses to set certain device parameters such as clock configuration and startup delay. However these fuses also are responsible for storing security configuration parameters of the device, such as lock bits for controlling access to program memory. We successfully set the values stored in the fuses without utilizing the device's programming interface. Hence, our fully-invasive edit is capable of circumventing the copy protection implemented by the vendor. By setting fuse bits accordingly the contents of the device can be extracted over the serial programming interface even if it had previously been disabled. For this attack, the floating gate transistor was completely removed. Next, source and drain contacts of the device were either statically connected or disconnected, corresponding to the fuse bit being set or cleared. The same attack can be applied to other fuse technologies as well.

5.3 Countermeasures and Attack Mitigation

FIB circuit edits continue to be one of the biggest threats to IC security. To successfully perform such attacks the layout of the IC must first be reverse-engineered. Several approaches for reverse-engineering ICs have been proposed in previous works [14, 16, 17]. In reality, for most attacks it is sufficient to reverse-engineer just the datapath between non-volatile memory and the CPU core. Since the core cannot operate on encrypted data, the datapath by definition includes all the necessary decryption functions.

In [26], a frontside attack against a secure smart-card was demonstrated. The IC included both passive and active meshes as well as sensors to detect attacks. Security relevant signals were routed on the second metal layer. To attack the device, the security mechanisms first had to be circumvented, including rewiring the active mesh that covered the relevant area on the device. By contrast, the backside of the device lacked any protection mechanisms and many sensitive device nodes are directly exposed from the backside. Every single circuit node is directly accessible from the backside by contacting either the metallization or the transistor directly [6, 21]. As such, every signal on the device is susceptible to backside microprobing attacks.

Ironically, older generation ICs that lack STI are more difficult to attack from the backside. To microprobe the bus of the non-STI device, a site was isolated where the relevant signals were routed through an inactive area of the device. A relatively large FIB trench of several micrometers in size was then milled to expose the individual interconnect line. The size of the trench was sufficient to place the probing needle directly into the cavity. A much smaller trench could be milled if the trace was instead contacted with metal deposition. Nevertheless, finding a suitable location for the trench can be made significantly more difficult if the bus line serpentined over active areas of the device. Note, that this is only true for non-STI processes as the risk of misalignment makes contacting transistors directly impractical.

Modern ICs utilize STI. The STI layer offers an excellent reference for navigation without the risk of damaging the active devices. In an STI process, the transistors can be contacted directly, without the need to contact the metal interconnects. Hence, STI processes are at greater risk for successful microprobing.

Though, technically possible, practically contacting transistor nodes directly becomes more difficult for smaller process technologies. The success of the attack is largely determined by quality and generation of the equipment utilized by the attacker. In this work a ten year old FIB was used to successfully perform attacks on devices that were five to ten years old. Latest generation FIBs are entirely capable of performing circuit edits even on the latest technology nodes. Moreover, IC vendors regularly utilize FIBs for failure analysis applications on their latest generation ICs. These applications include circuit edits similar to those presented in this work.

However, the biggest threat posed to secure ICs are FIBs that are available on the worldwide surplus markets. Utilizing second-hand failure analysis equipment is significantly more cost-effective than purchasing new equipment. Such devices are generally at least one generation behind what is currently available on the market, but cost only a fraction of the price of new equipment.

Substantially less accuracy is necessary to contact the metallization. Moreover, only the inputs and outputs of a gate contain valid data. In standard cell design, input and outputs are generally routed on the first and second metal layer. These metal layers are substantially larger than the the minimal gate length in a given process technology and are directly exposed to attacks from the backside. Hence, even an older generation FIB is sufficient to contact the metal layers even of the most modern processes. For this reason, design rules should be applied to security relevant parts of the IC to make it more difficult to contact the target signals. To protect against frontside attacks, security relevant signals are buried in lower metal layers of the device. Hence, the attacker is first forced to remove and rewire any traces that cover the target signals. To protect against backside circuit edits, sensitive signals should be made as small as possible. One way to achieve this is to only use low-fanout gates, which are intrinsically smaller than other logic gates. Similarly, routing sensitive signals only locally reduces the attack surface for the signal. Furthermore, if sensitive nodes are only routed above active areas, a backside attack becomes extremely challenging as the attacker is forced to contact transistors directly.

Fully-invasive backside attacks also allow for permanent modification of the target circuit. Modern secure ICs implement a set of hardware countermeasures and defenses against fully-invasive attacks. Such defenses generally raise an exception to the CPU core or reset the device, potentially irreparably destroying any secret data stored on the device. However, since such security sensors are exposed from the backside, a skillful attacker can disable any sensors and subsequently probe the device without any penalty. In many cases for a successful backside circuit edit, it is sufficient to remove the hardware function entirely. For example, the circuit responsible for evaluating the integrity of an active mesh can be modified or completely removed and its outputs tied to static logic levels. Alternatively the state can be dynamically evaluated in software. However, because the attacker controls the data bus, any software countermeasures can be circumvented as well [26]. In this fashion active meshes as well as other device countermeasures can be completely disabled as even a compromised circuit will pass the integrity checks implemented on the IC.

Fuses are an example of such a hardware security function. In our experiments we succeeded in setting fuse bits to arbitrary values. Fuses are particularly relevant to security as fuses are often used to implement features such as copy-protection and permanently disabling On-Chip-Debug (OCD) facilities. Fuses are also commonly used as non-volatile memory for key storage as they can be programmed during device personalization. The fuses on most modern Atmel devices are protected by a passive mesh from the frontside of the IC. This is to prevent semi-invasive attacks such as laser fault injection and add additional steps to attacks from the frontside. From the backside, the fuses are completely exposed. We succeeded in reading out the values stored in the fuses without adversely affecting the circuit. Subsequently the fuses could be permanently modified by connecting and severing the floating gate transistor accordingly. Such an attack can also be directly applied to disable various security sensors on the device.

To protect against malicious backside circuit edits, backside integrity checks must be implemented [7]. Intrinsic properties and special coatings can be utilized to detect compromise of the IC backside [27]. However even these measures do not completely prevent invasive attacks. Such countermeasures can still be defeated by attacking the circuitry responsible integrity verification. From a theoretical point of view, for a truly secure device, the secret data must be intrinsically linked to a tamper evident property of the device. Any physical alternations to the device must render the device inoperable, for example by irreparably altering the key material. Physical Random Functions (PUF) are a promising field of research as the key material can be created from their response. However, PUFs have also been shown to be susceptible to semi- and fully-invasive attacks [9, 15]. Other information security approaches also provide potential solutions [5, 8, 10, 11, 12].

6. CONCLUSION

This work demonstrated the first practical fully-invasive backside attacks. Our first attack, backside microprobing, can be utilized for recovering data from the IC. Encryption implemented on modern devices can be circumvented by recovering unencrypted data from locations where the data has already been deciphered by the hardware. We succeeded in microprobing data deciphered by the hardware decryption function within the device's core. The second attack is a permanent backside circuit modification. Such circuit edits can be utilized for disabling hardware security functions and countermeasures. We succeeded in reading out and setting the device's configuration and security fuses to arbitrary values.

This work highlights the need for vendors to consider the threat of backside attacks as well. Currently, IC implementations lack protection of the IC backside. On high-security ICs countermeasures such as meshes make frontside invasive attacks difficult. One of the simplest solutions to make backside attacks significantly more difficult is to apply effective design rules on security relevant logic. By routing security relevant logic above active devices, the traces themselves are obstructed by the dense first layer of metallization as well as the gate materials. Another potential solution is to implement a mesh for the IC backside. One such solution was presented in [7], where a 3D mesh was introduced by stacking multiple dies. Though such a solution would be substantially more expensive than a single die solution it would essentially thwart any practical attacks known to date. It is technically possible to disconnect two individual dies or mill through multiple dies, however neither option is cost-effective for the attacker. Finally, by utilizing intrinsic properties of the device it is possible to implement schemes in which the device's unique secret key changes from the fully-invasive modifications performed by our attacks [27].

7. ACKNOWLEDGEMENTS

The authors would like to thank Andreas Eckert (TU-Berlin) for sample preparation as well as Olivier Thomas (Texplained S.A.R.L.) and Patrick Stewin (TU-Berlin) for their constructive criticism of the work. We would also like to sincerely thank the anonymous reviewers for their insightful comments that helped improve the paper significantly. This research was supported by the Helmholtz Research School on Security Technologies.

8. REFERENCES

[1] R. Anderson and M. Kuhn. Tamper resistance: a cautionary note. *Proceedings of the 2nd conference on Proceedings of the Second USENIX Workshop on Electronic Commerce-Volume 2*, 1996.

[2] R. J. Anderson. Security Engineering. In *A Guide to Building Dependable Distributed Systems*. Wiley, Nov. 2010.

[3] Atmel. AVR Instruction Set. `http://www.atmel.com/images/doc0856.pdf`, 2010.

[4] H. Bar-El, H. Choukri, D. Naccache, M. Tunstall, and C. Whelan. The Sorcerer's Apprentice Guide to Fault Attacks. In *Proceedings of the IEEE*, pages 370–382, 2006.

[5] N. Bitansky, R. Canetti, S. Goldwasser, S. Halevi, Y. T. Kalai, and G. N. Rothblum. Program obfuscation with leaky hardware. In *Advances in Cryptology - ASIACRYPT 2011*, pages 722–739. Springer, 2011.

[6] C. Boit, R. Schlangen, U. Kerst, and T. Lundquist. Physical techniques for chip-backside IC debug in nanotechnologies. *Design Test of Computers, IEEE*, 25(3):250–257, 2008.

[7] S. Briais, S. Caron, J.-M. Cioranesco, J.-L. Danger, S. Guilley, J.-H. Jourdan, A. Milchior, D. Naccache, and T. Porteboeuf. 3D hardware canaries. In *CHES'12: Proceedings of the 14th international conference on Cryptographic Hardware and Embedded Systems*. Springer-Verlag, Sept. 2012.

[8] D. Dachman-Soled and Y. T. Kalai. Securing circuits against constant-rate tampering. In *Advances in Cryptology - CRYPTO 2012*, pages 533–551. Springer, 2012.

[9] C. Helfmeier, D. Nedospasov, C. Boit, and J.-P. Seifert. Cloning Physically Unclonable Functions. *Hardware-Oriented Security and Trust (HOST), 2013 IEEE International Symposium on*, pages 1–6, 2013.

[10] Y. Ishai, M. Prabhakaran, A. Sahai, and D. Wagner. Private circuits II: Keeping secrets in tamperable circuits. In *Advances in Cryptology - EUROCRYPT 2006*, pages 308–327. Springer, 2006.

[11] Y. Ishai, A. Sahai, and D. Wagner. Private circuits: Securing hardware against probing attacks. In *Advances in Cryptology - CRYPTO 2003*, pages 463–481. Springer, 2003.

[12] Y. T. Kalai, B. Kanukurthi, and A. Sahai. Cryptography with tamperable and leaky memory. In *Advances in Cryptology - CRYPTO 2011*, pages 373–390. Springer, 2011.

[13] O. Kömmerling and M. Kuhn. Design Principles for Tamper-Resistant Security Processors. *USENIX Workshop on Smartcard Technology, Chicago, IL (10–11 May 1999) http://www. cl. cam. ac. uk/Research/Security/tamper*, 1999.

[14] W. Li, A. Gascon, P. Subramanyan, W. Y. Tan, A. Tiwari, S. Malik, N. Shankar, and S. A. Seshia. WordRev: Finding word-level structures in a sea of bit-level gates. *Hardware-Oriented Security and Trust (HOST), 2013 IEEE International Symposium on*, pages 67–74, 2013.

[15] D. Nedospasov, C. Helfmeier, J.-P. Seifert, and C. Boit. Invasive PUF Analysis. *Fault Tolerance in*

Cryptography – FDTC 2013, 2013.

[16] D. Nedospasov, A. Schlösser, J.-P. Seifert, and S. Orlic. Functional integrated circuit analysis. *Hardware-Oriented Security and Trust (HOST), 2012 IEEE International Symposium on*, pages 102–107, 2012.

[17] K. Nohl, D. Evans, Starbug, and H. Plötz. Reverse-engineering a cryptographic RFID tag. In *Proceedings of the 17th USENIX Security Symposium*. USENIX Association, July 2008.

[18] W. Rankl and W. Effing. *Smart Card Handbook*. Wiley Publishing, 4th edition, 2010.

[19] R. J. Ross, editor. *Microelectronic Failure Analysis: Desk Reference*. ASM International, 6 edition, 2011.

[20] C. Rue, S. Herschbein, and C. Scrudato. Backside Circuit Edit on Full-Thickness Silicon Devices. In *Conference Proceedings from the 34th International Symposium for Testing and Failure Analysis*, pages 141–150. ASM International, Nov. 2008.

[21] R. Schlangen, R. Leihkauf, U. Kerst, T. Lundquist, P. Egger, and C. Boit. Physical analysis, trimming and editing of nanoscale IC function with backside FIB processing. *Microelectronics Reliability*, 49(9–11):1158 – 1164, 2009. 20th European Symposium on the Reliability of Electron Devices, Failure Physics and Analysis.

[22] A. Schlösser, D. Nedospasov, J. Krämer, S. Orlic, and J. Seifert. Simple Photonic Emission Analysis of AES. *Cryptographic Hardware and Embedded Systems–CHES 2012*, pages 41–57, 2012.

[23] S. Skorobogatov. Optically Enhanced Position-Locked Power Analysis. *Cryptographic Hardware and Embedded Systems-CHES 2006*, pages 61–75, 2006.

[24] S. Skorobogatov and R. Anderson. Optical fault induction attacks. *Cryptographic Hardware and Embedded Systems, CHES 2002*, pages 31–48, 2003.

[25] S. M. Sze and K. K. Ng. *Physics of Semiconductor Devices*. Wiley-Interscience, Nov. 2006.

[26] C. Tarnovsky. Hacking the Smartcard Chip. In *Blackhat DC 2010*, Arlington, VA, Feb. 2010.

[27] P. Tuyls, G. J. Schrijen, B. Škorić, J. van Geloven, N. Verhaegh, and R. Wolters. Read-proof hardware from protective coatings. *Cryptographic Hardware and Embedded Systems-CHES 2006*, pages 369–383, 2006.

[28] J. van Woudenberg, M. Witteman, and F. Menarini. Practical Optical Fault Injection on Secure Microcontrollers. *Fault Diagnosis and Tolerance in Cryptography, FDTC 2011*, pages 91–99, 2011.

Author Index

www.ingramcontent.com/pod-product-compliance
Lightning Source LLC
LaVergne TN
LVHW080106011026
849160LV00013B/1041